The Merriam-Webster Dictionary

A Merriam-Webster®

MERRIAM-WEBSTER INC., *Publishers*

Springfield, Massachusetts, U.S.A.

A GENUINE MERRIAM-WEBSTER

The name *Webster* alone is no guarantee of excellence. It is used by a number of publishers and may serve mainly to mislead an unwary buyer.

A Merriam-Webster® is the registered trademark you should look for when you consider the purchase of dictionaries or other fine reference books. It carries the reputation of a company that has been publishing since 1831 and is your assurance of quality and authority.

Preface

THE NEW MERRIAM-WEBSTER DICTIONARY is the fourth in the line of Merriam-Webster paperback dictionaries which began in 1947. It is firmly based on previous editions, but it also draws much new information from Webster's Ninth New Collegiate Dictionary, which was published after the appearance of the last paperback edition. Every entry and every section has been reexamined so that this new paperback edition offers much that is new while preserving the best aspects of preceding editions. The core of the English vocabulary is to be found in the 60,000 entries included in this book, and every definition is based on examples of actual use found among the more than 13,500,000 citations in the Merriam-Webster files.

The heart of The New Merriam-Webster Dictionary is the A-Z vocabulary. It is followed by several sections that dictionary users have long found helpful: a list of foreign words and phrases that often occur in English texts but that have not yet become part of the English vocabulary; a list of nations of the world; a list of places in the United States having 16,500 or more inhabitants, with a summary by states; a similar list of places in Canada, with a summary by provinces and territories; and a section devoted to widely used signs and symbols. The A-Z vocabulary is preceded by an Explanatory Notes section that should be read carefully by every user of the dictionary. An understanding of the information contained in these notes will add markedly to the satisfaction and pleasure that come from looking into the pages of a dictionary.

The New Merriam-Webster Dictionary is the product of a company that has been publishing dictionaries for nearly 150 years. It has been edited by an experienced staff of professional lexicographers who believe it will serve well those who want a concise and handy record of the English vocabulary of today.

Editor in Chief
Frederick C. Mish

Manager of Editorial Operations and Planning
John M. Morse

Supervisor of Defining
E. Ward Gilman

Senior Editors
Robert D. Copeland • James G. Lowe
Roger W. Pease, Jr.

Associate Editors
Michael G. Belanger • Julie A. Collier
Kathleen M. Doherty • David B. Justice
Madeline L. Novak • Stephen J. Perrault

Assistant Editors
Paul F. Cappellano • Eileen M. Haraty
Peter D. Haraty • Daniel J. Hopkins

Editorial Staff

Editorial Assistant
Kelly L. Tierney

Librarian
Francine A. Roberts

Departmental Secretary
Helene Gingold

Head of Typing Room
Gloria J. Afflitto

Assistant Head of Typing Room
Ruth W. Gaines

Clerks and Typists
Georgette B. Boucher • Karin M. Henry
Florence A. Fowler • Patricia M. Jensen
Veronica P. McLymont • Barbara A. Winkler

Explanatory Notes

Entries

A boldface letter or a combination of such letters set flush with the left-hand margin of each column of type is a main entry. The main entry may consist of letters set solid, of letters joined by a hyphen, or of letters separated by one or more spaces:

> **hot** . . . *adj*
>
> **hot–blood·ed** . . . *adj*
>
> **hot dog** . . . *n*

The material in lightface type that follows each main entry on the same line and on succeeding indented lines presents information about the main entry.

The main entries follow one another in alphabetical order letter by letter: *bill of exchange* follows *billion*; *Day of Atonement* follows *daylight saving time*. Those containing an Arabic numeral are alphabetized as if the numeral were spelled out: *4-H* comes between *fourfold* and *Four Hundred*; *3-D* comes between *three* and *three-dimensional*. Those derived from proper names beginning with abbreviated forms of *Mac-* are alphabetized as if spelled *mac-*: *McCoy* comes after *Maccabees* and before *mace*.

A pair of guide words is printed at the top of each page. These indicate that the entries falling alphabetically between the words at the top of the outer column of each page are found on that page.

The guide words are usually the alphabetically first and the alphabetically last entries on the page:

adjacent • adopt

Occasionally the last printed entry is not the alphabetically last entry. On page 229, for example, *dot matrix* is the last main entry, but *dotting*, an inflected form at ²*dot*, is the alphabetically last entry and is therefore the second guide word. The alphabetically last entry is not used, however, if it follows alphabetically the first guide word on the succeeding page. Thus on page 287 *flatting* is not a guide word because it follows alphabetically the entry *flatboat* which is the first guide word on page 288.

Any boldface word—a main entry with definition, a variant, an inflected form, a defined or undefined run-on—may be used as a guide word.

When one main entry has exactly the same written form as another, the two are distinguished by superscript numerals preceding each word:

> ¹**egg** . . . *vb*   ¹**rash** . . . *adj*
>
> ²**egg** *n*   ²**rash** *n*

Words precede word elements made up of the same letters; solid compounds precede hyphenated compounds; hyphenated compounds precede open compounds; and lowercase entries precede those with an initial capital:

self . . . *n*	run-down . . . *n*	fed·er·al . . . *adj*
self- *comb form*	run--down . . . *adj*	Federal *n*
	run down . . . *vb*	

The centered dots within entry words indicate division points at which a hyphen may be put at the end of a line of print or writing. Thus the noun *res·er·va·tion* may be ended on one line and continued on the next in this manner:

                                        res-
ervation
                                        reser-
vation
                                        reserva-
tion

Centered dots are not shown after a single initial letter or before a single terminal letter because typesetters seldom cut off a single letter:

> evict . . . *vb*
>
> mighty . . . *adj*
>
> oleo . . . *n*

Nor are they usually shown at the second and succeeding homographs of a word:

> ¹pi·lot . . . *n*
>
> ²pilot *vb*
>
> ³pilot *adj*

There are acceptable alternative end-of-line divisions just as there are acceptable variant spellings and pronunciations, but no more than one division is shown for any entry in this dictionary.

A double hyphen at the end of a line in this dictionary (as in the definition at **dromedary**) stands for a hyphen that is retained when the word is written as a unit on one line. This kind of hyphen is represented in boldface words in this dictionary with an en dash, which appears whether or not it falls at the end of a line.

When a main entry is followed by the word *or* and another spelling, the two spellings are equal variants. Both are standard, and either one may be used according to personal inclination:

lou•ver or lou•vre

If two variants joined by *or* are out of alphabetical order, they remain equal variants. The one printed first is, however, slightly more common than the second:

coun•sel•or or coun•sel•lor

When another spelling is joined to the main entry by the word *also*, the spelling after *also* is a secondary variant and occurs less frequently than the first:

fo•gy also fo•gey

Secondary variants belong to standard usage and may be used according to personal inclination. If there are two secondary variants, the second is joined to the first by *or*. Once the word *also* is used to signal a secondary variant, all following variants are joined by *or*:

²wool•ly also wool•ie or wooly

Variants whose spelling puts them alphabetically more than a column away from the main entry are entered at their own alphabetical places and usually not at the main entry:

tsar . . . *var of* CZAR

Variants having a usage label appear only at their own alphabetical places:

la•bour *chiefly Brit var of* LABOR

To show all the stylings that are found for English compounds would require space that can be better used for other information. So this dictionary limits itself to a single styling for a compound:

book•sell•er

yes–man

home run

When a compound is widely used and one styling predominates, that styling is shown. When a compound is uncommon or when the evidence indicates that two or three stylings are approximately equal in frequency, the styling shown is based on the analogy of parallel compounds.

A main entry may be followed by one or more derivatives or by a homograph with a different functional label. These are run-on entries. Each is introduced by a lightface dash and each has a functional label. They are not defined, however, since their meanings are readily understood from the meaning of the root word:

healthy . . . *adj* . . . — health·i·ly . . . *adv* — health·i·ness . . . *n*

as·sent . . . *vb* . . . — assent *n*

A main entry may be followed by one or more phrases containing the entry word or an inflected form of it. These are also run-on entries. Each is introduced by a lightface dash but there is no functional label. They are, however, defined since their meanings are more than the sum of the meanings of their elements:

¹go . . . *vb* . . . — go to bat for : . . .

¹hand . . . *n* . . . — at hand : . . .

Defined phrases of this sort are run on at the entry constituting the first major element in the phrase. When there are variants, however, the run-on appears at the entry constituting the first major invariable element in the phrase:

¹seed . . . *n* . . . — go to seed *or* run to seed 1: . . .

Boldface words that appear within parentheses (as co·ca at co·caine and jet engine and jet propulsion at jet–propelled) are run-in entries.

Attention is called to the definition of *vocabulary entry* on page 814. The term *dictionary entry* includes all vocabulary entries as well as all boldface entries in the section headed "Foreign Words and Phrases."

Pronunciation

The matter between a pair of reversed virgules \ \ following the entry word indicates the pronunciation. The symbols used are explained in the chart printed inside the back cover.

A hyphen is used in the pronunciation to show syllabic division. These hyphens sometimes coincide with the centered dots in the entry word that indicate end-of-line division:

vol·ca·no \väl-ˈkā-nō\

Sometimes they do not:

grind·er \ˈgrīn-dər\

A high-set mark ˈ indicates major (primary) stress or accent; a low-set mark ˌ indicates minor (secondary) stress or accent:

cat·bird \ˈkat-ˌbərd\

The stress mark stands at the beginning of the syllable that receives the stress.

A syllable with neither a high-set mark nor a low-set mark is unstressed:

fig·ment \\'fig-mənt\\

The presence of variant pronunciations indicates that not all educated speakers pronounce words the same way. A second-place variant is not to be regarded as less acceptable than the pronunciation that is given first. It may, in fact, be used by as many educated speakers as the first variant, but the requirements of the printed page are such that one must precede the other:

eco·nom·ic \\ˌek-ə-'näm-ik, ˌē-kə-\\

flac·cid \\'flak-səd, 'flas-əd\\

Symbols enclosed by parentheses represent elements that are present in the pronunciation of some speakers but are absent from the pronunciation of other speakers, elements that are present in some but absent from other utterances of the same speaker, or elements whose presence or absence is uncertain:

fo·liage \\'fō-l(ē-)ij\\

duke \\'d(y)ük\\

Thus, the above parentheses indicate that some people say \\'fō-lē-ij\\ and others say \\'fō-lij\\; some \\'dük\\, others \\'dyük\\.

When a main entry has less than a full pronunciation, the missing part is to be supplied from a pronunciation in a preceding entry or within the same pair of reversed virgules:

out·er·most \\-ˌmōst\\

pa·la·ver \\pə-'lav-ər, -'läv-\\

The pronunciation of the first two syllables of *outermost* is found at the main entry *outer*. The hyphens before and after \\'läv\\ in the pronunciation of *palaver* indicate that both the first and the last parts of the pronunciation are to be taken from the immediately preceding pronunciation.

In general, no pronunciation is indicated for open compounds consisting of two or more English words that have own-place entry:

motor vehicle *n*

Only the first entry in a sequence of numbered homographs is given a pronunciation if their pronunciations are the same:

¹**mea·sure** \\'mezh-ər, 'māzh-\\ *n*

²**measure** *vb*

The pronunciation of unpronounced derivatives and compounds

run on at a main entry is a combination of the pronunciation at the main entry and the pronunciation of the other element as given at its alphabetical place in the vocabulary:

— nar·row·ness *n*

— at last

Thus, the pronunciation of *narrowness* is the sum of the pronunciations given at *narrow* and *-ness;* that of *at last,* the sum of the pronunciations of the two elements that make up the phrase.

Functional Labels

An italic label indicating a part of speech or some other functional classification follows the pronunciation or, if no pronunciation is given, the main entry. The eight traditional parts of speech are indicated as follows:

fa·ce·tious . . . *adj*	log·ger·head . . . *n*
al·to·geth·er . . . *adv*	in·to . . . *prep*
if . . . *conj*	we . . . *pron*
amen . . . *interj*	stul·ti·fy . . . *vb*

Other italicized labels used to indicate functional classifications that are not traditional parts of speech include:

blvd *abbr*	-hood . . . *n suffix*
self- *comb form*	-fy . . . *vb suffix*
super- . . . *prefix*	Na *symbol*
-ous . . . *adj suffix*	ought . . . *verbal auxiliary*
-al·ly . . . *adv suffix*	

Functional labels are sometimes combined:

can·ta·bi·le . . . *adv or adj*

Inflected Forms

Nouns

The plurals of nouns are shown in this dictionary when suffixation brings about a change of final *-y* to *-i-*, when the noun ends in a consonant plus *-o* or in *-ey*, when the noun ends in *-oo*, when the noun has an irregular plural or a zero plural or a foreign plural, when the noun is a compound that pluralizes any element but the last, when the noun has variant plurals, and when it is believed that the dictionary user might have reasonable doubts about the spelling of the plural or when the plural is spelled in a way contrary to what is expected:

dairy . . . *n, pl* dair·ies	deer . . . *n, pl* deer
po·ta·to . . . *n, pl* -toes	al·ga . . . *n, pl* al·gae
lack·ey . . . *n, pl* lackeys	broth·er–in–law . . . *n, pl* brothers–in–law
zoo . . . *n, pl* zoos	¹fish . . . *n, pl* fish *or* fish·es
tooth . . . *n, pl* teeth	²pi . . . *n, pl* pis

Cutback inflected forms are used when the noun has three or more syllables:

> atroc·i·ty . . . *n, pl* -ties

The plurals of nouns are usually not shown when the base word is unchanged by suffixation, when the noun is a compound whose second element is readily recognizable as a regular free form entered at its own place, or when the noun is unlikely to occur in the plural:

> car·rot . . . *n*
>
> horse·fly . . . *n*
>
> po·lyg·a·my . . . *n*

Nouns that are plural in form and that regularly occur in plural construction are labeled *n pl*:

> bifocals . . . *n pl*

Nouns that are plural in form but that are not always construed as plurals are appropriately labeled:

> taps . . . *n sing or pl*

Verbs

The principal parts of verbs are shown in this dictionary when suffixation brings about a doubling of a final consonant or an elision of a final -e or a change of final -y to -i-, when final -c changes to -ck- in suffixation, when the verb ends in -ey, when the inflection is irregular, when there are variant inflected forms, and when it is believed that the dictionary user might have reasonable doubts about the spelling of an inflected form or when the inflected form is spelled in a way contrary to what is expected:

beg . . . *vb* begged; beg·ging

equate . . . *vb* equat·ed; equat·ing

¹fry . . . *vb* fried; fry·ing

²panic *vb* pan·icked . . .; pan·ick·ing

obey . . . *vb* obeyed; obey·ing

¹break . . . *vb* broke . . .; bro·ken . . .; break·ing

¹trav·el . . . *vb* -eled *or* -elled; -el·ing *or* -el·ling

²visa *vb* vi·saed . . .; vi·sa·ing

²chagrin *vb* cha·grined . . .; cha·grin·ing

The principal parts of a regularly inflected verb are shown when it is desirable to indicate the pronunciation of one of the inflected forms:

²spell *vb* spelled \\'speld\\; spell·ing

²season *vb* sea·soned; sea·son·ing \\'sēz-(ᵊ-)niŋ\\

Cutback inflected forms are usually used when the verb has three or more syllables, when it is a two-syllable word that ends in *-l* and has variant spellings, and when it is a compound whose second element is readily recognized as an irregular verb:

mul·ti·ply . . . *vb* -plied; -ply·ing

cav·il . . . *vb* -iled *or* -illed; -il·ing *or* -il·ling

for·go *or* fore·go . . . *vb* -went . . .; -gone . . .; -go·ing

The principal parts of verbs are usually not shown when the base word is unchanged by suffixation or when the verb is a compound whose second element is readily recognizable as a regular free form entered at its own place:

²shield *vb*

¹out·reach . . . *vb*

Adjectives & Adverbs

The comparative and superlative forms of adjectives and adverbs are shown in this dictionary when suffixation brings about a doubling of a final consonant or an elision of a final *-e* or a change of final *-y* to *-i-*, when the word ends in *-ey*, when the inflection is irregular, and when there are variant inflected forms:

¹fat . . . *adj* fat·ter; fat·test

¹sure . . . *adj* sur·er; sur·est

¹dry . . . *adj* dri‧er . . .: dri‧est

hors‧ey *or* horsy . . . *adj* hors‧i‧er; -est

bad . . . *adj* worse . . .: worst

sly . . . *adj* sli‧er *also* sly‧er . . .: sli‧est *also* sly‧est

The superlative forms of adjectives and adverbs of two or more syllables are usually cut back:

scanty . . . *adj* scant‧i‧er: -est

¹ear‧ly . . . *adv* ear‧li‧er: -est

The comparative and superlative forms of regularly inflected adjectives and adverbs are shown when it is desirable to indicate the pronunciation of the inflected forms:

strong \ˈstrȯŋ\ *adj* stron‧ger \ˈstrȯŋ-gər\; stron‧gest \ˈstrȯŋ-gəst\

The inclusion of inflected forms in *-er* and *-est* at adjective and adverb entries means nothing more about the use of *more* and *most*
with these adjectives and adverbs than that their comparative and
superlative degrees may be expressed in either way: *kindlier or more
kindly; kindliest or most kindly*.

At a few adjective entries only the superlative form is shown:

²mere *adj* mer‧est

The absence of the comparative form indicates that there is no evidence of its use.

The comparative and superlative forms of adjectives and adverbs
are usually not shown when the base word is unchanged by suffixation or when the word is a compound whose second element is
readily recognizable as a regular free form entered at its own place:

²quiet *adj*

un‧hap‧py . . . *adj*

Inflected forms are not shown at undefined run-ons.

Capitalization

Most entries in this dictionary begin with a lowercase letter. A few
of these have an italicized label *often cap*, which indicates that the
word is as likely to be capitalized as not and that it is as acceptable
with an uppercase initial as it is with one in lowercase. Some entries
begin with an uppercase letter, which indicates that the word is usually capitalized. The absence of an initial capital or of an *often cap*
label indicates that the word is not ordinarily capitalized:

> spice . . . *n*
>
> ba·bel . . . *n, often cap*
>
> Quak·er . . . *n*

The capitalization of entries that are open or hyphenated compounds is similarly indicated by the form of the entry or by an italicized label:

> living room *n*
>
> in·dia ink . . . *n, often cap 1st I*
>
> all–Amer·i·can . . . *adj*
>
> German shepherd *n*
>
> lazy Su·san . . . *n*
>
> Jack Frost *n*

A word that is capitalized in some senses and lowercase in others shows variations from the form of the main entry by the use of italicized labels at the appropriate senses:

> Apoc·ry·pha . . . *n* 1 *not cap*
>
> [1]Pres·by·te·ri·an . . . *adj* 1 *often not cap*
>
> cath·o·lic . . . *adj* . . . 2 *cap*
>
> east·ern . . . *adj* 1 *often cap* . . . 2 *cap*

Etymology

This dictionary gives the etymologies for a number of the vocabulary entries. These etymologies are in boldface square brackets preceding the definition. Meanings given in roman type within these brackets are not definitions of the entry, but are meanings of the Middle English, Old English, or non-English words within the brackets.

The etymology gives the language from which words borrowed into English have come. It also gives the form of the word in that language or a representation of the word in our alphabet if the form in that language differs from that in English:

> ae·gis . . . [L, fr. Gk *aigis* goatskin]
>
> [1]sav·age . . . [ME *sauvage*, fr. MF, fr. ML *salvaticus*, fr. L
> *silvaticus* of the woods, wild . . .]

An etymology beginning with the name of a language (including ME or OE) and not giving the foreign (or Middle English or Old English) form indicates that this form is the same as the form of the entry word:

> ibi·dem . . . [L]
>
> na·dir . . . [ME, fr. MF . . .]

An etymology beginning with the name of a language (including ME or OE) and not giving the foreign (or Middle English or Old English) meaning indicates that this meaning is the same as the meaning expressed in the first definition in the entry:

> **tur·quoise** . . . [ME *turkeis, turcas,* fr. MF *turquoyse* . . .]

Small superscript figures following words or syllables in an etymology refer to the tone of the word or syllable they follow. They are used only with forms cited for languages in which tonal variations distinguish words of different meaning that would otherwise sound alike.

> **kow·tow** . . . [Chin *k'o*[1] *t'ou*[2]. fr. *k'o*[1] to bump + *t'ou*[2] head]

Usage

Three types of status labels are used in this dictionary—temporal, regional, and stylistic—to signal that a word or a sense of a word is not part of the standard vocabulary of English.

The temporal label *obs* for "obsolete" means that there is no evidence of use since 1755:

> [3]**post** *n* **1** *obs*

The label *obs* is a comment on the word being defined. When a thing, as distinguished from the word used to designate it, is obsolete, appropriate orientation is usually given in the definition:

> **far·thin·gale** . . . *n* . . . : a support (as of hoops) worn esp. in the 16th century to swell out a skirt

The temporal label *archaic* means that a word or sense once in common use is found today only sporadically or in special contexts:

> **com·mon·weal** . . . *n* . . . **1** *archaic*
>
> [1]**thou** . . . *pron, archaic*

A word or sense limited in use to a specific region of the U.S. has an appropriate label. The adverb *chiefly* precedes a label when the word has some currency outside the specified region, and a double label is used to indicate considerable currency in each of two specific regions:

> [2]**wash** *n* . . . **5** *West*
>
> **do·gie** . . . *n, chiefly West*

goo·ber . . . *n, South & Midland*

Words current in all regions of the U.S. have no label.

A word or sense limited in use to one of the other countries of the English-speaking world has an appropriate regional label:

> chem·ist . . . *n* . . . 2 *Brit*
>
> loch . . . *n, Scot*
>
> ²wireless *n* . . . 2 *chiefly Brit*

The label *dial* for "dialect" indicates that the pattern of use of a word or sense is too complex for summary labeling: it usually includes several regional varieties of American English or of American and British English:

> ¹boot . . . *n, chiefly dial*
>
> cal·a·boose . . . *n* . . . *dial*

The stylistic label *slang* is used with words or senses that are especially appropriate in contexts of extreme informality:

> ¹rap . . . *n* . . . 3 *slang*
>
> tick·er . . . *n* . . . 3 *slang*

There is no satisfactory objective test for slang, especially with reference to a word out of context. No word, in fact, is invariably slang, and many standard words can be given slang applications.

Definitions are sometimes followed by verbal illustrations that show a typical use of the word in context. These illustrations are enclosed in angle brackets, and the word being illustrated is usually replaced by a lightface swung dash. The swung dash stands for the boldface entry word, and it may be followed by an italicized suffix:

> ¹let·ter . . . *n* . . . 4 . . . ⟨the ~ of the law⟩
>
> deep–seated . . . *adj* . . . 2 . . . ⟨~ convictions⟩
>
> depth . . . *n* . . . 2 . . . ⟨the ~s of the woods⟩
>
> ¹fill . . . *vb* . . . 6 . . . ⟨laughter ~*ed* the room⟩

The swung dash is not used when the form of the boldface entry word is changed in suffixation, and it is not used for open compounds:

> en·gage . . . *vb* . . . 3 . . . ⟨*engaged* his friend's attention⟩
>
> drum up *vb* 1 . . . ⟨*drum up* business⟩

Definitions are sometimes followed by usage notes that give supplementary information about such matters as idiom, syntax, and semantic relationship. A usage note is introduced by a lightface dash:

fro . . . *adv* . . . — used in the phrase *to and fro*

²**gang** *vb* 1 . . . — usu. used with *up*

¹**jaw** . . . *n* . . . 2 . . . — usu. used in pl.

¹**ada·gio** . . . *adv or adj* . . . — used as a direction in music

blast off . . . *vb* . . . — used esp. of rocket-propelled devices

Sometimes a usage note is used in place of a definition. Some function words (as conjunctions and prepositions) have chiefly grammatical meaning and little or no lexical meaning; most interjections express feelings but are otherwise untranslatable into lexical meaning; and some other words (as honorific titles) are more amenable to comment than to definition:

or . . . *conj* — used as a function word to indicate an alternative

¹**in** . . . *prep* 1 — used to indicate physical surroundings

hal·le·lu·jah . . . *interj* . . . — used to express praise, joy, or thanks

ex·cel·len·cy . . . *n* . . . 2 — used as a title of honor

Sense Division

A boldface colon is used in this dictionary to introduce a definition:

found·ry . . . *n* . . . : a building or works where metal is cast

It is also used to separate two or more definitions of a single sense:

²**yellow** *n* 1 : a color between green and orange in the spectrum : the color of ripe lemons or sunflowers

Boldface Arabic numerals separate the senses of a word that has more than one sense:

idol . . . *n* 1 : an image worshiped as a god 2 : a false god 3 : an object of passionate devotion

A particular semantic relationship between senses is sometimes suggested by the use of one of the two italic sense dividers *esp* or *also*.

The sense divider *esp* (for *especially*) is used to introduce the most common meaning included in the more general preceding definition:

no·to·ri·ous . . . *adj* : generally known and talked of: *esp* : widely and unfavorably known

The sense divider *also* is used to introduce a meaning related to the preceding sense by an easily understood extension of that sense:

¹*flour* . . . *n* : finely ground and sifted meal of a grain (as wheat); *also* : a fine soft powder

The order of senses is historical: the sense known to have been first used in English is entered first. This is not to be taken to mean, however, that each sense of a multisense word developed from the immediately preceding sense. It is altogether possible that sense 1 of a word has given rise to sense 2 and sense 2 to sense 3, but frequently sense 2 and sense 3 may have developed independently of one another from sense 1.

When an italicized label follows a boldface numeral, the label applies only to that specific numbered sense. It does not apply to any other boldface numbered senses:

> **craft** . . . *n* . . . **3** *pl usu* **craft**
>
> ¹**fa·ther** . . . *n* . . . **2** *cap* . . . **5** *often cap*
>
> ²**preview** *n* . . . **2** *also* **pre·vue** \-₁vyü\
>
> **pub·li·can** . . . *n* . . . **2** *chiefly Brit*

At *craft* the *pl* label applies to sense **3** but to none of the other numbered senses At *father* the *cap* label applies only to sense **2** and the *often cap* label only to sense **5**. At *preview* the variant spelling and pronunciation apply only to sense **2**, as does the *chiefly Brit* label at *publican*.

Cross-Reference

Four different kinds of cross-references are used in this dictionary: directional, synonymous, cognate, and inflectional. In each instance the cross-reference is readily recognized by the lightface small capitals in which it is printed.

A cross-reference following a lightface dash and beginning with *see* is a directional cross-reference. It directs the dictionary user to look elsewhere for further information:

> ¹**yen** . . . *n* . . . — see MONEY table

A cross-reference following a boldface colon is a synonymous cross-reference. It may stand alone as the only definition for an entry or for a sense of an entry; it may follow an analytical definition; it may be one of two or more synonymous cross-references separated by commas:

> **maize** . . . *n* : INDIAN CORN
>
> **chap·let** . . . *n* . . . **2** : a string of beads : NECKLACE
>
> ²**dress** *n* . . . **2** : FROCK, GOWN
>
> **cheek** . . . *n* . . . **2** : IMPUDENCE, BOLDNESS, AUDACITY

A synonymous cross-reference indicates that a definition at the entry cross-referred to can be substituted as a definition for the entry or the sense in which the cross-reference appears.

A cross-reference following an italic *var of* ("variant of") is a cognate cross-reference:

Gipsy *var of* GYPSY

Occasionally a cognate cross-reference has a limiting label preceding *var of* as an indication that the variant is not standard English:

har·bour *chiefly Brit var of* HARBOR

A cross-reference following an italic label that identifies an entry as an inflected form (as of a noun or verb) is an inflectional cross-reference:

feet *pl of* FOOT

worn *past part of* WEAR

Inflectional cross-references appear only when the inflected form falls at least a column away from the entry cross-referred to.

Synonyms

A boldface **syn** near the end of an entry introduces words that are synonymous with the word being defined:

²**fear** . . . *n* . . . **syn** dread. fright. alarm. panic. terror. trepidation

Synonyms are not definitions although they may often be substituted for each other in context.

Combining Forms, Prefixes, & Suffixes

An entry that begins or ends with a hyphen is a word element that forms part of an English compound:

maxi- *comb form* 1 . . . (*maxi*-kilt)

ex- . . . *prefix* . . . (*ex*-president)

-ship . . . *n suffix* 1 . . . (friend*ship*)

Combining forms, prefixes, and suffixes are entered in this dictionary for two reasons: to make understandable the meaning of many undefined run-ons and to make recognizable the meaningful elements of words that are not entered in the dictionary.

Lists of Undefined Words

Lists of undefined words occur after the entries *anti-*, *in-*, *non-*, *over-*, *re-*, *self-*, *semi-*, *sub-*, *super-*, and *un-*. These words are undefined because they are self-explanatory: their meanings are simply the sum of a meaning of the prefix or combining form and a meaning of the second element.

Abbreviations & Symbols

Abbreviations and symbols for chemical elements are included as main entries in the vocabulary:

> **govt** *abbr* government
>
> **Fe** *symbol* . . . iron

Abbreviations have been normalized to one form. In practice, however, there is considerable variation in the use of periods and in capitalization (as *vhf*, *v.h.f.*, *VHF*, and *V.H.F.*), and stylings other than those given in this dictionary are often acceptable.

Symbols that are not capable of being alphabetized are included in a separate section of the back matter headed "Signs and Symbols."

Abbreviations Used in This Work

ab	about	*cap*	captial, capitalized
abbr	abbreviation	*cent*	century
abl	ablative	*Chin*	Chinese
acc	accusative	*comb*	combining
A.D.	anno Domini	*compar*	comparative
adj	adjective	*conj*	conjunction
adv	adverb	*Dan*	Danish
AF	Anglo-French	*dat*	dative
alter	alteration	*deriv*	derivative
Am	American	*dial*	dialect
AmerF	American French	*dim*	diminutive
AmerInd	American Indian	*E*	English
AmerSp	American Spanish	*Egypt*	Egyptian
Ar	Arabic	*Eng*	English
B.C.	before Christ	*Esk*	Eskimo
Brit	British	*esp*	especially
C	centigrade	*F*	Fahrenheit, French
Calif	California	*fem*	feminine
CanF	Canadian French	*Flem*	Flemish

fr	from	*OPer*	Old Persian
G	German	*orig*	originally
Gk	Greek	*part*	participle
Gmc	Germanic	*Per*	Persian
Heb	Hebrew	*perh*	perhaps
Hung	Hungarian	*Pg*	Portuguese
Icel	Icelandic	*pl*	plural
imit	imitative	*Pol*	Polish
imper	imperative	*pp*	past participle
interj	interjection	*prep*	preposition
IrGael	Irish Gaelic	*pres*	present
irreg	irregular	*prob*	probably
It	Italian	*pron*	pronoun, pronunci-
Jp	Japanese		ation
K	Kelvin	*prp*	present participle
L	Latin	*Russ*	Russian
LaF	Louisiana French	*Sc*	Scotch, Scots
LG	Low German	*ScGael*	Scottish Gaelic
LGk	Late Greek	*Scot*	Scottish
LHeb	Late Hebrew	*Serb*	Serbian
lit	literally	*sing*	singular
LL	Late Latin	*Skt*	Sanskrit
masc	masculine	*So*	South
ME	Middle English	*Sp*	Spanish
MexSp	Mexican Spanish	*St*	Saint
MF	Middle French	*superl*	superlative
MGk	Middle Greek	*Sw*	Swedish
ML	Medieval Latin	*syn*	synonym, synon-
modif	modification		ymy
MS	manuscript	*trans*	translation
n	noun	*Turk*	Turkish
neut	neuter	*US*	United States
NGk	New Greek	*USSR*	Union of Soviet
NHeb	New Hebrew		Socialist Repub-
NL	New Latin		lics
No	North	*usu*	usually
Norw	Norwegian	*var*	variant
n pl	noun plural	*vb*	verb
obs	obsolete	*vi*	verb intransitive
OE	Old English	*VL*	Vulgar Latin
OF	Old French	*vt*	verb transitive
OIt	Old Italian	*W*	Welsh
ON	Old Norse		

A

¹a \'ā\ *n, pl* a's *or as* \'āz\ *often cap* 1 : the 1st letter of the English alphabet 2 : a grade rating a student's work as superior

²a \ə, (')ā\ *indefinite article* : ONE, SOME — used to indicate an unspecified or unidentified individual ⟨there's ~ man outside⟩

³a *abbr, often cap* 1 absent 2 acre 3 alto 4 answer 5 area

AA *abbr* 1 Alcoholics Anonymous 2 antiaircraft 3 associate in arts

AAA *abbr* American Automobile Association

A and M *abbr* agricultural and mechanical

A and R *abbr* artists and repertory

aard·vark \'ärd-,värk\ *n* [obs. Afrikaans, fr. Afrikaans *aard* earth + *vark* pig] : a large burrowing African mammal that feeds on ants and termites with its sticky tongue

ab *abbr* about

AB *abbr* 1 able-bodied seaman 2 airman basic 3 [NL *artium baccalaureus*] bachelor of arts

ABA *abbr* American Bar Association

aback \ə-'bak\ *adv* : by surprise ⟨taken ~⟩

aba·cus \'ab-ə-kəs\ *n, pl* aba·ci \'ab-ə-,sī, -,kē\ *or* aba·cus·es : an instrument for making calculations by sliding counters along rods or grooves

¹abaft \ə-'baft\ *prep* : to the rear of

²abaft *adv* : toward or at the stern : AFT

ab·a·lo·ne \,ab-ə-'lō-nē\ *n* : a large edible sea mollusk with a flattened slightly spiral shell with holes along the edge

¹aban·don \ə-'ban-dən\ *vb* [ME *abandounen*, fr. MF *abandoner*, fr. *abandon*, n., surrender, fr. *a bandon* in one's power] : to give up completely : FORSAKE, DESERT — aban·don·ment *n*

²abandon *n* : a thorough yielding to natural impulses; *esp* : ENTHUSIASM, EXUBERANCE

aban·doned \ə-'ban-dənd\ *adj* : morally unrestrained syn profligate, dissolute, reprobate

abase \ə-'bās\ *vb* abased; abas·ing : HUMBLE, DEGRADE — abase·ment *n*

abash \ə-'bash\ *vb* : to destroy the composure of : EMBARRASS — abashment *n*

abate \ə-'bāt\ *vb* abat·ed; abat·ing 1 : to put an end to ⟨~ a nuisance⟩ 2 : to decrease in amount, number, or degree

abate·ment \ə-'bāt-mənt\ *n* 1 : DECREASE 2 : an amount abated; *esp* : a deduction from the full amount of a tax

ab·at·toir \'ab-ə-,twär\ *n* [F] : SLAUGHTERHOUSE

ab·ba·cy \'ab-ə-sē\ *n, pl* -cies : the office or term of office of an abbot or abbess

ab·bé \a-'bā, 'ab-,ā\ *n* : a member of the French secular clergy — used as a title

ab·bess \'ab-əs\ *n* : the superior of a convent for nuns

ab·bey \'ab-ē\ *n, pl* abbeys 1 : MONASTERY, CONVENT 2 : an abbey church

ab·bot \'ab-ət\ *n* [ME *abbod*, fr. OE, fr. LL *abbat-*, *abbas*, fr. LGk *abbas*, fr. Aramaic *abbā* father] : the superior of a monastery for men

abbr *abbr* abbreviation

ab·bre·vi·ate \ə-'brē-vē-,āt\ *vb* -at·ed; -at·ing : SHORTEN, CURTAIL; *esp* : to reduce to an abbreviation

ab·bre·vi·a·tion \ə-,brē-vē-'ā-shən\ *n* 1 : the act or result of abbreviating 2 : a shortened form of a word or phrase used for brevity esp. in writing

¹ABC \,ā-,bē-'sē\ *n, pl* ABC's *or* ABCs \-'sēz\ 1 : ALPHABET — usu. used in pl. 2 : RUDIMENTS

²ABC *abbr* American Broadcasting Company

Ab·di·as \ab-'dī-əs\ *n* — see BIBLE table

ab·di·cate \'ab-di-,kāt\ *vb* -cat·ed; -cat·ing : to give up (as a throne) formally — ab·di·ca·tion \,ab-di-'kā-shən\ *n*

ab·do·men \'ab-də-mən, ab-'dō-mən\ *n* 1 : the cavity in or area of the body between the chest and the pelvis 2 : the part of the body posterior to the thorax in an arthropod — ab·dom·i·nal \ab-'däm-ən-³l\ *adj* — ab·dom·i·nal·ly \-ē\ *adv*

ab·duct \ab-'dəkt\ *vb* : to take away (a person) by force : KIDNAP — ab·duc·tion \-'dək-shən\ *n* — ab·duc·tor \-tər\ *n*

abeam \ə-'bēm\ *adv or adj* : on a line at right angles to a ship's keel

abed \ə-'bed\ *adv or adj* : in bed

ab·er·ra·tion \,ab-ə-'rā-shən\ *n* 1 : deviation esp. from a moral standard or normal state 2 : unsoundness of mind : DERANGEMENT 3 : failure of a mirror or lens to produce exact point-to-point correspondence between an object and its image — ab·er·rant \a-'ber-ənt\ *adj*

abet \ə-'bet\ *vb* abet·ted; abet·ting [ME *abetten*, fr. MF *abeter*, fr. OF *beter* to bait] 1 : INCITE, ENCOURAGE 2 : to assist or support in the achievement of a purpose — abet·tor *or* abet·ter \-ər\ *n*

abey·ance \ə-'bā-əns\ *n* : a condition of suspended activity

ab·hor \ab-'hôr, ab-\ *vb* ab·horred; ab·hor·ring [ME *abhorren*, fr. L *abhorrēre*, fr. *ab-* + *horrēre* to shudder] : LOATHE, DETEST — ab·hor·rence \-əns\ *n*

ab·hor·rent \-ənt\ *adj* : LOATHSOME, DETESTABLE

abide \ə-ˈbīd\ vb **abode** \-ˈbōd\ or **abided; abid·ing 1** : BEAR, ENDURE **2** : DWELL, REMAIN, LAST

abil·i·ty \ə-ˈbil-ət-ē\ n, pl **-ties** : the quality of being able : POWER, SKILL

ab·ject \ˈab-ˌjekt, ab-ˈjekt\ adj : low in spirit or hope : CRINGING — **ab·jec·tion** \ab-ˈjek-shən\ n — **ab·ject·ly** \ˈab-ˌjekt-lē, ab-ˈjekt-\ adv — **ab·ject·ness** n

ab·jure \ab-ˈju̇r\ vb **ab·jured; ab·jur·ing 1** : to renounce solemnly : RECANT **2** : to abstain from — **ab·ju·ra·tion** \ˌab-jə-ˈrā-shən\ n

abl abbr ablative

ab·late \a-ˈblāt\ vb **ab·lat·ed; ab·lat·ing** : to remove or become removed by cutting, eating or wearing away, evaporating, or vaporizing

ab·la·tion \a-ˈblā-shən\ n **1** : surgical cutting and removal **2** : removal of a part (as the outside of a nose cone) by melting or vaporization

ab·la·tive \ˈab-lət-iv\ adj : of, relating to, or constituting a grammatical case (as in Latin) expressing typically the relation of separation and source — **ablative** n

ablaze \ə-ˈblāz\ adj or adv : being on fire : BLAZING

able \ˈā-bəl\ adj **abler** \-b(ə-)lər\; **ablest** \-b(ə-)ləst\ **1** : having sufficient power, skill, or resources to accomplish an object **2** : marked by skill or efficiency — **ably** \-blē\ adv

-able also **-ible** \ə-bəl\ adj suffix **1** : capable of, fit for, or worthy of (being so acted upon or toward) ⟨break*able*⟩ ⟨collect*ible*⟩ **2** : tending, given, or liable to ⟨knowledge*able*⟩ ⟨perish*able*⟩

able-bod·ied \ˌā-bəl-ˈbäd-ēd\ adj : having a sound strong body

abloom \ə-ˈblüm\ adj : BLOOMING

ab·lu·tion \ə-ˈblü-shən, a-ˈblü-\ n : the washing of one's body or part of it

ABM \ˌā-(ˌ)bē-ˈem\ n, pl **ABM's** or **ABMs** : ANTIBALLISTIC MISSILE

Ab·na·ki \ab-ˈnäk-ē\ n, pl **Abnaki** or **Abnakis** : a member of an American Indian people of Maine and southern Quebec

ab·ne·gate \ˈab-ni-ˌgāt\ vb **-gat·ed; -gat·ing 1** : SURRENDER, RELINQUISH **2** : DENY, RENOUNCE — **ab·ne·ga·tion** \ˌab-ni-ˈgā-shən\ n

ab·nor·mal \(ˌ)ab-ˈnȯr-məl\ adj : deviating from the normal or average — **ab·nor·mal·i·ty** \ˌab-nər-ˈmal-ət-ē, -(ˌ)nȯr-\ n — **ab·nor·mal·ly** \ab-ˈnȯr-mə-lē\ adv

¹aboard \ə-ˈbōrd\ adv **1** : ALONGSIDE **2** : on, onto, or within a car, ship, or aircraft **3** : in or into a group or association ⟨welcome new workers ∼⟩

²aboard prep : ON, ONTO, WITHIN

abode \ə-ˈbōd\ n **1** : STAY, SOJOURN **2** : HOME, RESIDENCE

abol·ish \ə-ˈbäl-ish\ vb : to do away with : ANNUL — **ab·o·li·tion** \ˌab-ə-ˈlish-ən\ n

ab·o·li·tion·ism \ˌab-ə-ˈlish-ə-ˌniz-əm\ n : advocacy of the abolition of slavery

— **ab·o·li·tion·ist** \-ˈlish-(ə-)nəst\ n or adj

A-bomb \ˈā-ˌbäm\ n : ATOM BOMB — **A-bomb** vb

abom·i·na·ble \ə-ˈbäm-(ə-)nə-bəl\ adj : ODIOUS, LOATHSOME, DETESTABLE

abominable snow·man \-ˈsnō-mən, -ˌman\ n, often cap A&S : a mysterious animal reported as existing in the high Himalayas and usu. thought to be a bear

abom·i·nate \ə-ˈbäm-ə-ˌnāt\ vb **-nat·ed; -nat·ing** [L abominari, lit., to deprecate as an ill omen, fr. ab- away + omen omen] : LOATHE, DETEST

abom·i·na·tion \ə-ˌbäm-ə-ˈnā-shən\ n **1** : something abominable **2** : DISGUST, LOATHING

ab·orig·i·nal \ˌab-ə-ˈrij-(ə-)nəl\ adj : ORIGINAL, INDIGENOUS, PRIMITIVE

ab·orig·i·ne \ˌab-ə-ˈrij-ə-nē\ n : a member of the original race of inhabitants of a region : NATIVE

aborn·ing \ə-ˈbȯr-niŋ\ adv : while being born or produced

¹abort \ə-ˈbȯrt\ vb **1** : to cause or undergo abortion **2** : to terminate prematurely ⟨∼ a spaceflight⟩ — **abor·tive** \-ˈbȯrt-iv\ adj

²abort n : the premature termination of a mission or of a procedure relating to an aircraft or spacecraft

abor·tion \ə-ˈbȯr-shən\ n : a premature birth occurring before the fetus can survive; also : an induced expulsion of a fetus after, accompanied by, or followed by its death

abor·tion·ist \-sh(ə-)nəst\ n : one who induces abortions

abound \ə-ˈbau̇nd\ vb **1** : to be plentiful : TEEM **2** : to be fully supplied

¹about \ə-ˈbau̇t\ adv **1** : on all sides **2** : AROUND **3** : NEARBY

²about prep **1** : on every side of **2** : near to **3** : on the verge of : GOING ⟨he was just ∼ to go⟩ **3** : CONCERNING

about-face \-ˈfās\ n : a reversal of direction or attitude — **about-face** vb

¹above \ə-ˈbəv\ adv **1** : in the sky; also : in or to heaven **2** : in or to a higher place; also : higher on the same page or on a preceding page

²above prep **1** : in or to a higher place than : OVER ⟨storm clouds ∼ the bay⟩ **2** : superior to ⟨he thought her far ∼ him⟩ **3** : more than : EXCEEDING

above·board \-ˌbōrd\ adv or adj : without concealment or deception : OPENLY

abp abbr archbishop

abr abbr abridged; abridgment

ab·ra·ca·dab·ra \ˌab-rə-kə-ˈdab-rə\ n **1** : a magical charm or incantation against calamity **2** : GIBBERISH

abrade \ə-ˈbrād\ vb **abrad·ed; abrad·ing 1** : to wear away by rubbing **2** : to wear down in spirit : IRRITATE — **abra·sion** \-ˈbrā-zhən\ n

¹abra·sive \ə-ˈbrā-siv\ n : a substance (as pumice) for grinding, smoothing, or polishing

²**abrasive** *adj* : tending to abrade : causing irritation ⟨∼ relationships⟩ — **abra·sive·ly** *adv* — **abra·sive·ness** *n*

abreast \ə-'brest\ *adv or adj* 1 : side by side 2 : up to a standard or level esp. of knowledge

abridge \ə-'brij\ *vb* **abridged; abridg·ing** [ME *abregen*, fr. MF *abregier*, fr. LL *abbreviare*, fr. L *ad* to + *brevis* short] : to lessen in length or extent — SHORTEN — **abridg·ment** *or* **abridge·ment** *n*

abroad \ə-'brȯd\ *adv or adj* 1 : over a wide area 2 : away from one's home 3 : outside one's country

ab·ro·gate \'ab-rə-ˌgāt\ *vb* **-gat·ed; -gat·ing** : ANNUL, REVOKE — **ab·ro·ga·tion** \ˌab-rə-'gā-shən\ *n*

abrupt \ə-'brəpt\ *adj* 1 : broken or as if broken of 2 : SUDDEN, HASTY 3 : so quick as to seem rude 4 : DISCONNECTED 5 : STEEP — **abrupt·ly** *adv*

abs *abbr* absolute

ab·scess \'ab-ˌses\ *n, pl* **ab·scess·es** [L *abscessus*, lit., act of going away, fr. *abscedere* to go away, fr. *abs-*, *ab-* away + *cedere* to go] : a collection of pus surrounded by inflamed tissue — **ab·scessed** \-ˌsest\ *adj*

ab·scis·sa \ab-'sis-ə\ *n, pl* **abscissas** *also* **ab·scis·sae** \-'sis-(ˌ)ē\ : the coordinate of a point in a plane coordinate system that is the distance of the point from the vertical axis found by measuring along the horizontal axis

ab·scis·sion \ab-'sizh-ən\ *n* 1 : the act or process of cutting off 2 : the natural separation of flowers, fruits, or leaves from plants — **ab·scise** \ab-'sīz\ *vb*

ab·scond \ab-'skänd\ *vb* : to depart secretly and hide oneself

ab·sence \'ab-səns\ *n* 1 : the state or time of being absent 2 : WANT, LACK 3 : INATTENTION

¹**ab·sent** \'ab-sənt\ *adj* 1 : not present 2 : LACKING 3 : INATTENTIVE

²**ab·sent** \ab-'sent\ *vb* : to keep (oneself) away

³**ab·sent** \'ab-sənt\ *prep* : in the absence of : WITHOUT

ab·sen·tee \ˌab-sən-'tē\ *n* : one that is absent or absents himself

absentee ballot *n* : a ballot submitted (as by mail) in advance of an election by a voter who is unable to be present at the polls

ab·sen·tee·ism \ˌab-sən-'tē-ˌiz-əm\ *n* : chronic absence (as from work or school)

ab·sent·mind·ed \ˌab-sənt-'mīn-dəd\ *adj* : unaware of one's surroundings or action : INATTENTIVE — **ab·sent·mind·ed·ly** *adv* — **ab·sent·mind·ed·ness** *n*

ab·sinthe *also* **ab·sinth** \'ab-ˌsinth\ *n* [F] : a liqueur flavored esp. with wormwood and anise

ab·so·lute \'ab-sə-ˌlüt, ˌab-sə-'lüt\ *adj* 1 : free from imperfection or mixture 2 : free from control, restriction, or qualification 3 : lacking grammatical connection with any other word in a sentence ⟨∼ construction⟩ 4 : POSITIVE ⟨∼ proof⟩ 5 : relating to the fundamental units of length, mass, and time 6 : relating to a temperature scale on which the zero point (absolute zero) corresponds to complete absence of heat equal to −273.15°C 7 : FUNDAMENTAL, ULTIMATE — **ab·so·lute·ly** *adv*

absolute pitch *n* 1 : the position of a tone in a standard scale independently determined by its rate of vibration 2 : the ability to sing or name a note asked for or heard

absolute value *n* : the numerical value of a real number that for a positive number or zero is equal to the number itself and for a negative number is equal to the positive number which when added to it is equal to zero

ab·so·lu·tion \ˌab-sə-'lü-shən\ *n* : the act of absolving : *esp* : a remission of sins pronounced by a priest in the sacrament of penance

ab·so·lut·ism \'ab-sə-ˌlüt-ˌiz-əm\ *n* 1 : the theory that a ruler or government should have unlimited power 2 : government by an absolute ruler or authority

ab·solve \əb-'zälv, -'sälv\ *vb* **absolved; ab·solv·ing** : to set free from an obligation or the consequences of guilt

ab·sorb \əb-'sȯrb, -'zȯrb\ *vb* 1 : ASSIMILATE, INCORPORATE 2 : to suck up or take in in the manner of a sponge 3 : to engage (one's attention) : ENGROSS 4 : to receive without recoil or echo ⟨a ceiling that ∼s sound⟩ 5 : to transform (radiant energy) into a different form usu. with a resulting rise in temperature — **ab·sorb·ing** *adj* — **ab·sorb·ing·ly** *adv*

ab·sor·bent *also* **ab·sor·bant** \əb-'sȯr-bənt, -'zȯr-\ *adj* : able to absorb ⟨∼ cotton⟩ — **ab·sor·ben·cy** \-bən-sē\ *n* — **absorbent** *also* **absorbant** *n*

ab·sorp·tion \əb-'sȯrp-shən, -'zȯrp-\ *n* 1 : a process of absorbing or being absorbed 2 : concentration of attention — **ab·sorp·tive** \-tiv\ *adj*

ab·stain \əb-'stān\ *vb* : to restrain oneself *syn* refrain, forbear — **ab·stain·er** *n* — **ab·sten·tion** \-'sten-chən\ *n*

ab·ste·mi·ous \ab-'stē-mē-əs\ *adj* [L *abstemius*, fr. *abs-* away + *temetum* mead] : sparing in use of food or drink : TEMPERATE — **ab·ste·mi·ous·ly** *adv*

ab·sti·nence \'ab-stə-nəns\ *n* : voluntary refraining esp. from eating certain foods or drinking liquor — **ab·sti·nent** \-nənt\ *adj*

abstr *abbr* abstract

¹**ab·stract** \ab-'strakt, 'ab-ˌstrakt\ *adj* 1 : considered apart from a particular instance 2 : expressing a quality apart from an object ⟨*whiteness* is an ∼ word⟩ 3 : having only intrinsic form with little or no pictorial representation ⟨∼ painting⟩ — **ab·stract·ly** *adv* — **ab·stract·ness** \-'strak(t)-nəs, -ˌstrak(t)-\ *n*

²**ab·stract** \\'ab-₁strakt; 2 also ab-'strakt\ n 1 : SUMMARY, EPITOME 2 : an abstract thing or state

³**ab·stract** \ab-'strakt, 'ab-₁strakt; 2 usu 'ab-₁strakt\ vb 1 : REMOVE, SEPARATE 2 : to make an abstract of : SUMMARIZE 3 : to draw away the attention of 4 : STEAL — **ab·stract·ed·ly** \ab-'strak-təd-lē, 'ab-₁strak-\ adv

abstract expressionism n : art that expresses the artist's attitudes and emotions through abstract forms — **abstract expressionist** n

ab·strac·tion \ab-'strak-shən\ n 1 : the act of abstracting : the state of being abstracted 2 : an abstract idea 3 : an abstract work of art

ab·struse \əb-'strüs, ab-\ adj : hard to understand : RECONDITE — **ab·struse·ly** adv — **ab·struse·ness** n

ab·surd \əb-'sərd, -'zərd\ adj [MF absurde, fr. L absurdus, fr. ab- from + surdus deaf, stupid] : RIDICULOUS, UNREASONABLE — **ab·sur·di·ty** \-ət-ē\ n — **ab·surd·ly** adv

abun·dant \ə-'bən-dənt\ adj [ME, fr. MF, fr. L abundant-, abundans, prp. of abundare to abound, fr. ab- from + unda wave] : more than enough : amply sufficient syn copious, plentiful, ample, bountiful — **abun·dance** \-dəns\ n — **abun·dant·ly** adv

¹**abuse** \ə-'byüs\ n 1 : a corrupt practice 2 : MISUSE 3 : coarse and insulting speech 4 : MISTREATMENT

²**abuse** \ə-'byüz\ vb **abused; abus·ing** 1 : to attack in words : REVILE 2 : to put to a wrong use : MISUSE 3 : MISTREAT — **abus·er** n — **abu·sive** \-'byü-siv\ adj — **abu·sive·ly** adv — **abu·sive·ness** n

abut \ə-'bət\ vb **abut·ted; abut·ting** : to touch along a border : border on

abut·ment \ə-'bət-mənt\ n : a structure that supports weight or withstands lateral pressure (as at the end of a bridge)

abysm \ə-'biz-əm\ n : ABYSS

abys·mal \ə-'biz-məl\ adj 1 : immeasurably deep : BOTTOMLESS 2 : absolutely wretched (~ living conditions of the poor) — **abys·mal·ly** adv

abyss \ə-'bis\ n 1 : the bottomless pit in old accounts of the universe 2 : an immeasurable depth

abys·sal \ə-'bis-əl\ adj : of or relating to the bottom waters of the ocean depths

ac abbr account

Ac symbol actinium

AC abbr 1 air-conditioning 2 alternating current 3 [L ante Christum] before Christ 4 [L ante cibum] before meals 5 area code

aca·cia \ə-'kā-shə\ n : any of numerous leguminous trees or shrubs with round white or yellow flower clusters and often fernlike leaves

acad abbr academic; academy

ac·a·deme \'ak-ə-₁dēm\ n : SCHOOL; also : academic environment

ac·a·dem·ic \₁ak-ə-'dem-ik\ adj 1 : of or relating to schools or colleges 2 : literary or general rather than technical 3 : theoretical rather than practical — **ac·a·dem·i·cal·ly** \-i-k(ə-)lē\ adv

ac·a·de·mi·cian \₁ak-əd-ə-'mish-ən, ə-₁kad-ə-\ n : a member of a society of scholars or artists

ac·a·dem·i·cism \₁ak-ə-'dem-ə-₁siz-əm\ also **acad·e·mism** \ə-'kad-ə-₁miz-əm\ n : manner, style, or content conforming to the traditions or rules of an academy or movement

acad·e·my \ə-'kad-ə-mē\ n, pl **-mies** [Gk Akadēmeia, school of philosophy founded by Plato, fr. Akadēmeia, gymnasium where Plato taught, fr. Akadēmos Greek mythological hero] 1 : a school above the elementary level; esp : a private high school 2 : a society of scholars or artists

acan·thus \ə-'kan-thəs\ n, pl **acan·thus·es** also **acan·thi** \-'kan-₁thī\ 1 : any of a genus of prickly herbs of the Mediterranean region 2 : an ornamentation (as on a column) representing the leaves of the acanthus

a cap·pel·la also **a ca·pel·la** \₁äk-ə-'pel-ə\ adv or adj [It a cappella in chapel style] : without instrumental accompaniment (the choir sang a cappella)

acc abbr accusative

ac·cede \ak-'sēd\ vb **ac·ced·ed; ac·ced·ing** 1 : to become a party to an agreement 2 : to express approval 3 : to enter upon an office syn agree, acquiesce, assent, consent, subscribe

ac·ce·le·ran·do \ä-₁chel-ə-'rän-dō\ adv or adj [It] : gradually faster — used as a direction in music

ac·cel·er·ate \ik-'sel-ə-₁rāt, ak-\ vb **-at·ed; -at·ing** 1 : to bring about earlier 2 : to speed up : QUICKEN — **ac·cel·er·a·tion** \-₁sel-ə-'rā-shən\ n

ac·cel·er·a·tor \ik-'sel-ə-₁rāt-ər, ak-\ n 1 : one that accelerates 2 : a pedal for controlling the speed of a motor-vehicle engine 3 : an apparatus for imparting high velocities to charged particles

ac·cel·er·om·e·ter \ik-₁sel-ə-'räm-ət-ər, ak-\ n : an instrument for measuring acceleration or vibrations

¹**ac·cent** \'ak-₁sent, ak-'sent\ vb : STRESS, EMPHASIZE

²**ac·cent** \'ak-₁sent\ n 1 : a distinctive manner of pronunciation (a foreign ~) 2 : prominence given to one syllable of a word esp. by stress 3 : a mark (as ´, `, ^) over a vowel in writing or printing used usu. to indicate a difference in pronunciation (as stress) from a vowel not so marked — **ac·cen·tu·al** \ak-'sench-(ə-)wəl\ adj

ac·cen·tu·ate \ak-'sen-chə-₁wāt\ vb **-at·ed; -at·ing** : ACCENT — **ac·cen·tu·a·tion** \-₁sen-chə-'wā-shən\ n

ac·cept \ik-'sept, ak-\ vb 1 : to receive willingly 2 : to agree to 3 : to assume an obligation to pay

ac·cept·able \ik-'sep-tə-bəl, ak-\ adj : capable or worthy of being accepted

— ac·cept·abil·i·ty \ik-ˌsep-tə-ˈbil-ət-ē, ak-\ n

ac·cep·tance \ik-ˈsep-təns, ak-\ n 1 : the act of accepting 2 : the state of being accepted or acceptable 3 : an accepted bill of exchange

ac·cep·ta·tion \ˌak-ˌsep-ˈtā-shən\ n : the generally understood meaning of a word

¹ac·cess \ˈak-ˌses\ n 1 : capacity to enter or approach 2 : a way of approach : ENTRANCE

²access vb : to get at : gain access to

ac·ces·si·ble \ik-ˈses-ə-bəl, ak-, ek-\ adj 1 : capable of being reached (~ by train) 2 : capable of being used, seen, or known : OBTAINABLE (~ information) — ac·ces·si·bil·i·ty \-ˌses-ə-ˈbil-ət-ē\ n

ac·ces·sion \ik-ˈsesh-ən, ak-\ n 1 : something added 2 : increase by something added 3 : the act of acceding to an office or position

ac·ces·so·ry also ac·ces·sa·ry \ik-ˈses-(ə-)rē, ak-\ n, pl -ries 1 : something helpful but not essential 2 : a person who though not present abets or assists in the commission of an offense syn appurtenance, adjunct, appendage, appendix — accessory adj

ac·ci·dence \ˈak-səd-əns\ n : a part of grammar that deals with inflections

ac·ci·dent \ˈak-səd-ənt\ n 1 : an event occurring by chance or unintentionally 2 : CHANCE (met by ~) 3 : a nonessential property

ac·ci·den·tal \ˌak-sə-ˈdent-ᵊl\ adj 1 : happening unexpectedly or by chance 2 : happening without intent or through carelessness syn casual, fortuitous, incidental, chance — ac·ci·den·tal·ly \-ˈdent-(ᵊ-)lē\ also ac·ci·dent·ly \-ˈdent-lē\ adv

ac·claim \ə-ˈklām\ vb 1 : APPLAUD, PRAISE 2 : to declare by acclamation syn extol, laud, commend, hail — acclaim n

ac·cla·ma·tion \ˌak-lə-ˈmā-shən\ n 1 : loud eager applause 2 : an overwhelming affirmative vote by shouting or applause rather than by ballot

ac·cli·mate \ˈak-lə-ˌmāt, ə-ˈklī-mət\ vb -mat·ed; -mat·ing : to accustom to a new climate or situation — ac·cli·ma·tion \ˌak-lə-ˈmā-shən, ˌak-ˌlī-\ n

ac·cli·ma·tize \ə-ˈklī-mə-ˌtīz\ vb -tized; -tiz·ing 1 : ACCLIMATE 2 : to become acclimated — ac·cli·ma·ti·za·tion \-ˌklī-mət-ə-ˈzā-shən\ n

ac·cliv·i·ty \ə-ˈkliv-ət-ē\ n, pl -ties : an ascending slope

ac·co·lade \ˈak-ə-ˌlād\ n [F, fr. accoler to embrace, fr. L ad- to + collum neck] : a recognition of merit : AWARD

ac·com·mo·date \ə-ˈkäm-ə-ˌdāt\ vb -dat·ed; -dat·ing 1 : to make fit or suitable : ADAPT, ADJUST 2 : HARMONIZE, RECONCILE 3 : to provide with something needed 4 : to hold without crowding 5 : to undergo visual accommodation

ac·com·mo·dat·ing adj : OBLIGING

ac·com·mo·da·tion \ə-ˌkäm-ə-ˈdā-shən\ n 1 : something supplied to satisfy a need; esp : LODGINGS — usu. used in pl. 2 : the act of accommodating : ADJUSTMENT 3 : the automatic adjustment of the eye for seeing at different distances

ac·com·pa·ni·ment \ə-ˈkəmp-(ə-)nē-mənt\ n : something that accompanies another; esp : subordinate music to support a principal voice or instrument

ac·com·pa·ny \ə-ˈkəmp-(ə-)nē\ vb -nied; -ny·ing 1 : to go or occur with : ATTEND 2 : to play an accompaniment for — ac·com·pa·nist \-(ə-)nəst\ n

ac·com·plice \ə-ˈkäm-pləs, -ˈkəm-\ n : an associate in crime

ac·com·plish \ə-ˈkäm-plish, -ˈkəm-\ vb : to bring to completion syn achieve, effect, execute, perform — ac·com·plish·er n

ac·com·plished \-plisht\ adj 1 : EXPERT, SKILLED 2 : established beyond doubt

ac·com·plish·ment \ə-ˈkäm-plish-mənt, -ˈkəm-\ n 1 : COMPLETION 2 : something completed or effected 3 : an acquired excellence or skill

¹ac·cord \ə-ˈkȯrd\ vb [ME accorden, fr. OF acorder, fr. L ad- to + cord-, cor heart] 1 : GRANT, CONCEDE 2 : AGREE, HARMONIZE — ac·cor·dant \-ˈkȯrd-ᵊnt\ adj

²accord n : AGREEMENT, HARMONY

ac·cor·dance \ə-ˈkȯrd-ᵊns\ n 1 : ACCORD 2 : the act of granting

ac·cord·ing·ly \ə-ˈkȯrd-iŋ-lē\ adv 1 : in accordance 2 : CONSEQUENTLY, SO

according to prep 1 : in conformity with (paid according to ability) 2 : as stated or attested by (according to her he wasn't home)

¹ac·cor·di·on \ə-ˈkȯrd-ē-ən\ n [G akkordion, fr. akkord chord] : a portable keyboard instrument with a bellows and reeds

²accordion adj : folding like the bellows of an accordion (~ pleats)

ac·cost \ə-ˈkȯst\ vb [MF accoster, deriv. of L ad- to + costa rib, side] : to approach and speak to esp. aggressively

¹ac·count \ə-ˈkaunt\ n 1 : a statement of business transactions 2 : an arrangement with a vendor to supply credit 3 : a statement of reasons, causes, or motives 4 : VALUE, IMPORTANCE (a person of no ~) 5 : a sum of money deposited in a bank and subject to withdrawal by the depositor — on account of : BECAUSE OF — on no account : under no circumstances — on one's own account : on one's own behalf

²account vb 1 : CONSIDER (I ~ him lucky) 2 : to give an explanation — used with for

ac·count·able \ə-ˈkaunt-ə-bəl\ adj 1 : ANSWERABLE, RESPONSIBLE 2 : EXPLICABLE — ac·count·abil·i·ty \-ˌkaunt-ə-ˈbil-ət-ē\ n

ac·coun·tant \ə-ˈkaunt-ᵊnt\ n : a person

skilled in accounting — **ac·coun·tan·cy** \-ᵊn-sē\ n

account executive n : a business executive (as in an advertising agency) in charge of a client's account

ac·count·ing \ə-ˈkau̇nt-iŋ\ n : the art or system of keeping and analyzing financial records

ac·cou·tre *or* **ac·cou·ter** \ə-ˈküt-ər\ vb **-cou·tred** *or* **-cou·tered**; **-cou·tring** *or* **-cou·ter·ing** \-ˈküt-ə-riŋ, ˈkü-triŋ\ : EQUIP, OUTFIT

ac·cou·tre·ment *or* **ac·cou·ter·ment** \ə-ˈküt-rə-mənt, -ˈküt-ər-mənt\ n [F] **1** : the act of equipping **2** : an accessory item — usu. used in pl. **3** : an identifying characteristic

ac·cred·it \ə-ˈkred-ət\ vb **1** : to endorse or approve officially **2** : CREDIT — **ac·cred·i·ta·tion** \-ˌkred-ə-ˈtā-shən\ n

ac·cre·tion \ə-ˈkrē-shən\ n **1** : growth or enlargement esp. by addition from without **2** : a product of accretion

ac·crue \ə-ˈkrü\ vb **-crued**; **ac·cru·ing** **1** : to come by way of increase **2** : to be added by periodic growth — **ac·cru·al** \-əl\ n

acct abbr account: accountant

ac·cul·tur·a·tion \ə-ˌkəl-chə-ˈrā-shən\ n : cultural modification of an individual or group by borrowing and adapting traits from another culture

ac·cu·mu·late \ə-ˈkyü-myə-ˌlāt\ vb **-lat·ed**; **-lat·ing** [L accumulare, fr. ad- + cumulare to heap up] : to heap or pile up syn amass, gather, collect, stockpile — **ac·cu·mu·la·tion** \-ˌkyü-myə-ˈlā-shən\ n — **ac·cu·mu·la·tor** \-ˈkyü-myə-ˌlāt-ər\ n

ac·cu·rate \ˈak-yə-rət\ adj : free from error : EXACT, PRECISE — **ac·cu·ra·cy** \-rə-sē\ n — **ac·cu·rate·ly** adv — **ac·cu·rate·ness** n

ac·cursed \ə-ˈkərst, -ˈkər-səd\ *or* **ac·curst** \ə-ˈkərst\ adj **1** : being under a curse **2** : DAMNABLE, EXECRABLE

ac·cus·al \ə-ˈkyü-zəl\ n : ACCUSATION

ac·cu·sa·tive \ə-ˈkyü-zət-iv\ adj : of, relating to, or being a grammatical case marking the direct object of a verb or the object of a preposition — **accusative** n

ac·cuse \ə-ˈkyüz\ vb **ac·cused**; **ac·cus·ing** : to charge with an offense : BLAME — **ac·cu·sa·tion** \ˌak-yə-ˈzā-shən\ n — **ac·cus·er** n

ac·cused \ə-ˈkyüzd\ n, pl **accused** : the defendant in a criminal case

ac·cus·tom \ə-ˈkəs-təm\ vb : to make familiar through use or experience

ac·cus·tomed \ə-ˈkəs-təmd\ adj : USUAL, CUSTOMARY

¹ace \ˈās\ n [ME as a die face marked with one spot, fr. OF, fr. L, unit, a copper coin] **1** : a playing card bearing a single large pip in its center **2** : a point (as in tennis) won by a single stroke **3** : a golf score of one stroke on a hole **4** : a combat pilot who has brought down five or more enemy planes **5** : one that excels

²ace vb **aced**; **ac·ing** **1** : to score an ace against (an opponent) **2** : to defeat decisively

³ace adj : of first rank or quality

ac·er·bate \ˈas-ər-ˌbāt\ vb **-bat·ed**; **-bat·ing** : IRRITATE, EXASPERATE

acer·bic \ə-ˈsər-bik, a-\ adj : acid in temper, mood, or tone

acer·bi·ty \ə-ˈsər-bət-ē\ n, pl **-ties** : SOURNESS, BITTERNESS

ace·tate \ˈas-ə-ˌtāt\ n **1** : a salt or ester of acetic acid **2** : a textile fiber made from cellulose and acetic acid; also : a fabric or plastic made of this fiber

ace·tic \ə-ˈsēt-ik\ adj : of, relating to, or producing acetic acid or vinegar

acetic acid n : a colorless pungent liquid acid that is the chief acid of vinegar and is used esp. in making chemical compounds

ace·tone \ˈas-ə-ˌtōn\ n : a volatile flammable fragrant liquid compound used in making other chemical compounds and as a solvent

ace·tyl·cho·line \ə-ˌsēt-ᵊl-ˈkō-ˌlēn\ n : a compound that is released at nerve endings of the autonomic nervous system and is active in the transmission of nerve impulses

acet·y·lene \ə-ˈset-ᵊl-ən, -ᵊl-ˌēn\ n : a colorless flammable gas used as a fuel (as in welding and soldering)

acet·yl·sal·i·cyl·ic acid \ə-ˌsēt-ᵊl-ˌsal-ə-ˌsil-ik-\ n : ASPIRIN 1

ache \ˈāk\ vb **ached**; **ach·ing** **1** : to suffer a usu. dull persistent pain **2** : LONG, YEARN — **ache** n

achieve \ə-ˈchēv\ vb **achieved**; **achiev·ing** [ME acheven, fr. MF achever to finish, fr. a- to (fr. L ad-) + chief end, head, fr. L caput] : to gain by work or effort syn accomplish, attain, realize — **achieve·ment** n — **achiev·er** n

Achil·les' heel \ə-ˌkil-ēz-\ n [fr. the story that the Gk. warrior Achilles was vulnerable only in the heel] : a vulnerable point

Achilles tendon \ə-ˌkil-ēz-\ n : the strong tendon joining the muscles in the calf of the leg to the bone of the heel

ach·ro·mat·ic \ˌak-rə-ˈmat-ik\ adj : giving an image almost free from extraneous colors (~ lens)

achy \ˈā-kē\ adj **ach·i·er**; **ach·i·est** : afflicted with aches — **ach·i·ness** n

¹ac·id \ˈas-əd\ adj **1** : sour or biting to the taste; also : sharp or sour in manner **2** : of or relating to an acid — **acid·i·ty** \ə-ˈsid-ət-ē\ n

²acid n **1** : a sour substance **2** : a usu. water-soluble chemical compound that has a sour taste, reacts with a base to form a salt, and reddens litmus **3** : LSD — **ac·id** \ˈas-id-ik\ adj

acid·i·fy \ə-ˈsid-ə-ˌfī\ vb **-fied**; **-fy·ing** **1** : to make or become acid **2** : to change into an acid — **acid·i·fi·ca·tion** \-ˌsid-ə-fə-ˈkā-shən\ n

ac·i·do·sis \ˌas-ə-ˈdō-səs\ n, pl **-do·ses** \-ˈdō-ˌsēz\ : an abnormal state of reduced alkalinity of the blood and body tissues

acid precipitation *n* : precipitation with above normal acidity that is caused esp. by atmospheric pollutants

acid rain *n* : acid precipitation in the form of rain

acid test *n* : a severe or crucial test

acid·u·lous \ə-ˈsij-ə-ləs\ *adj* : somewhat acid in taste or manner

ack *abbr* acknowledge; acknowledgment

ack–ack \ˈak-ˌak\ *n* [Brit. signalmen's telephone pron. of *AA*, abbr. of *antiaircraft*] : an antiaircraft gun; *also* : antiaircraft fire

ac·knowl·edge \ik-ˈnäl-ij, ak-\ *vb* **-edged; -edg·ing 1** : to recognize the rights or authority of **2** : to admit as true **3** : to express thanks for; *also* : to report receipt of **4** : to recognize as valid — **ac·knowl·edg·ment** *also* **ac·knowl·edge·ment** *n*

ACLU *abbr* American Civil Liberties Union

ac·me \ˈak-mē\ *n* [Gk *akmē*] : the highest point

ac·ne \ˈak-nē\ *n* [Gk *aknē*, MS var. of *akmē*, lit., point] : a skin disorder marked by inflammation of skin glands and hair follicles and by pimple formation esp. on the face

ac·o·lyte \ˈak-ə-ˌlīt\ *n* **1** : one who assists the clergyman in a liturgical service **2** : FOLLOWER

ac·o·nite \ˈak-ə-ˌnīt\ *n* **1** : MONKSHOOD **2** : a drug obtained from a common Old World monkshood

acorn \ˈā-ˌkȯrn, -kərn\ *n* : the nut of the oak

acorn squash *n* : an acorn-shaped dark green winter squash with a ridged surface and sweet yellow to orange flesh

acous·tic \ə-ˈkü-stik\ *or* **acous·ti·cal** \-sti-kəl\ *adj* **1** : of or relating to the sense or organs of hearing, to sound, or to the science of sounds **2** : deadening sound 〈~ tile〉 **3** : operated by or utilizing sound waves — **acous·ti·cal·ly** \-k(ə-)lē\ *adv*

acous·tics \ə-ˈkü-stiks\ *n sing or pl* **1** : the science of sound **2** : the qualities in a room that make it easy or hard for a person in it to hear distinctly

ac·quaint \ə-ˈkwānt\ *vb* [ME *acquainten*, deriv. of L *ad-* + *cognoscere* to know] **1** : to cause to know personally **2** : INFORM

ac·quain·tance \ə-ˈkwānt-ᵊns\ *n* **1** : personal knowledge **2** : a person with whom one is acquainted — **ac·quain·tance·ship** *n*

ac·qui·esce \ˌak-wē-ˈes\ *vb* **-esced; -esc·ing** : to accept or comply without open opposition **syn** consent, agree, assent, accede — **ac·qui·es·cence** \-ˈes-ᵊns\ *n* — **ac·qui·es·cent** \-ᵊnt\ *adj* — **ac·qui·es·cent·ly** *adv*

ac·quire \ə-ˈkwī(ə)r\ *vb* **ac·quired; ac·quir·ing** : to come into possession of : GET

ac·quired \ə-ˈkwī(ə)rd\ *adj* **1** : gained by or as a result of effort or experience **2** : caused by environmental forces and not passed from parent to offspring in the genes 〈~ characteristics〉

acquired immune deficiency syndrome *n* : AIDS

acquired immunodeficiency syndrome *n* : AIDS

ac·quire·ment \-mənt\ *n* **1** : ATTAINMENT, ACCOMPLISHMENT **2** : the act of acquiring

ac·qui·si·tion \ˌak-wə-ˈzish-ən\ *n* **1** : ACQUIREMENT **2** : something acquired

ac·quis·i·tive \ə-ˈkwiz-ət-iv\ *adj* : eager to acquire : GREEDY — **ac·quis·i·tive·ly** *adv* — **ac·quis·i·tive·ness** *n*

ac·quit \ə-ˈkwit\ *vb* **ac·quit·ted; ac·quit·ting 1** : to pronounce not guilty **2** : to conduct (oneself) usu. satisfactorily — **ac·quit·tal** \-ᵊl\ *n*

acre \ˈā-kər\ *n* **1** *pl* : LANDS, ESTATE **2** — see WEIGHT table

acre·age \ˈā-k(ə-)rij\ *n* : area in acres

ac·rid \ˈak-rəd\ *adj* **1** : sharp and biting in taste or odor **2** : bitterly irritating : CAUSTIC — **acrid·i·ty** \a-ˈkrid-ət-ē, ə-\ *n* — **ac·rid·ness** *n*

ac·ri·mo·ny \ˈak-rə-ˌmō-nē\ *n, pl* **-nies** : harsh or biting sharpness of language or feeling — **ac·ri·mo·ni·ous** \ˌak-rə-ˈmō-nē-əs\ *adj*

ac·ro·bat \ˈak-rə-ˌbat\ *n* [F *acrobate*, fr. Gk *akrobatēs*, fr. *akrobatos* walking up high, fr. *akros* topmost + *bainein* to go] : a performer of gymnastic feats — **ac·ro·bat·ic** \ˌak-rə-ˈbat-ik\ *adj*

ac·ro·bat·ics \ˌak-rə-ˈbat-iks\ *n sing or pl* : the performance of an acrobat

ac·ro·nym \ˈak-rə-ˌnim\ *n* : a word (as *radar*) formed from the initial letter or letters of each of the successive parts or major parts of a compound term

ac·ro·pho·bia \ˌak-rə-ˈfō-bē-ə\ *n* : abnormal dread of being at a great height

acrop·o·lis \ə-ˈkräp-ə-ləs\ *n* [Gk *akropolis*, fr. *akros* topmost + *polis* city] : the upper fortified part of an ancient Greek city

¹across \ə-ˈkrȯs\ *adv* **1** : to or on the opposite side **2** : so as to be understandable or acceptable : OVER 〈get the point ~〉

²across *prep* **1** : to or on the opposite side of 〈ran ~ the street〉 〈standing ~ the street〉 **2** : on at an angle 〈slapped him ~ the face〉 ; *esp* : on so as to cross 〈a log ~ the road〉

across–the–board *adj* **1** : placed to win if a competitor wins, places, or shows 〈an ~ bet〉 **2** : including all classes or categories 〈an ~ wage increase〉

acros·tic \ə-ˈkrȯs-tik\ *n* **1** : a composition usu. in verse in which the initial or final letters of the lines taken in order form a word or phrase **2** : a series of words of equal length arranged to read the same horizontally or vertically — **acrostic** *adj*

acryl·ic \ə-ˈkril-ik\ *n* **1** : ACRYLIC RESIN **2**

: a paint in which the vehicle is acrylic resin **3** : a quick-drying synthetic fiber used for woven and knitted cloth

acrylic resin *n* : a glassy thermoplastic used for cast and molded parts or as coatings and adhesives

¹act \ˈakt\ *n* **1** : a thing done : DEED **2** : STATUTE, DECREE **3** : a main division of a play; *also* : an item on a variety program **4** : an instance of insincere behavior : PRETENSE

²act *vb* **1** : to perform by action esp. on the stage; *also* : FEIGN, SIMULATE, PRETEND **2** : to conduct oneself : BEHAVE **3** : to perform a specified function **4** : to produce an effect

³act *abbr* **1** active **2** actual

ACT *abbr* Australian Capital Territory

actg *abbr* acting

ACTH \ˌā-ˌsē-(ˌ)tē-ˈāch\ *n* : a protein hormone of the pituitary gland that stimulates the adrenal cortex

act·ing \ˈak-tiŋ\ *adj* : doing duty temporarily or for another ⟨∼ president⟩

ac·tin·i·um \ak-ˈtin-ē-əm\ *n* : a radioactive metallic chemical element

ac·tion \ˈak-shən\ *n* **1** : a legal proceeding **2** : the manner or method of performing **3** : ACTIVITY **4** : ACT, DEED **5** : the accomplishment of a thing usu. over a period of time, in stages, or with the possibility of repetition **6** *pl* : CONDUCT **7** : COMBAT, BATTLE **8** : the events of a literary plot **9** : an operating mechanism ⟨the ∼ of a gun⟩; *also* : the way it operates ⟨stiff ∼⟩

ac·tion·able \ˈak-sh(ə)nə-bəl\ *adj* : affording ground for an action or suit at law

ac·ti·vate \ˈak-tə-ˌvāt\ *vb* **-vat·ed; -vat·ing 1** : to spur into action; *also* : to make active, reactive, or radioactive **2** : to treat (as carbon) so as to improve adsorptive properties **3** : to aerate (sewage) to favor the growth of organisms that cause decomposition **4** : to set up (a military unit) formally; *also* : to call to active duty — **ac·ti·va·tion** \ˌak-tə-ˈvā-shən\ *n*

ac·tive \ˈak-tiv\ *adj* **1** : causing action or change **2** : asserting that the grammatical subject performs the action represented by the verb ⟨∼ voice⟩ **3** : BRISK, LIVELY **4** : presently in operation or use **5** : tending to progress or to cause degeneration ⟨∼ tuberculosis⟩ — **active** *n* — **ac·tive·ly** *adv*

ac·tiv·ism \ˈak-ti-ˌviz-əm\ *n* : a doctrine or practice that emphasizes vigorous action for political ends — **ac·tiv·ist** \-vəst\ *n or adj*

ac·tiv·i·ty \ak-ˈtiv-ət-ē\ *n, pl* **-ties 1** : the quality or state of being active **2** : an occupation in which one is engaged

ac·tor \ˈak-tər\ *n* : one that acts in a play or motion picture

ac·tress \ˈak-trəs\ *n* : a woman who is an actor

Acts \ˈak(t)s\ *or* **Acts of the Apostles** — see BIBLE table

ac·tu·al \ˈak-ch(ə-w)əl\ *adj* : really existing : REAL — **ac·tu·al·i·ty** \ˌak-chə-ˈwal-ət-ē\ *n* — **ac·tu·al·iza·tion** \ˌak-ch(ə-w)ə-lə-ˈzā-shən\ *n* — **ac·tu·al·ize** \ˈak-ch(ə-w)ə-ˌlīz\ *vb*

ac·tu·al·ly \ˈak-ch(ə-w)ə-lē\ *adv* : in fact or in truth : REALLY

ac·tu·ary \ˈak-chə-ˌwer-ē\ *n, pl* **-ar·ies** : one who calculates insurance risks and premiums — **ac·tu·ar·i·al** \ˌak-chə-ˈwer-ē-əl\ *adj*

ac·tu·ate \ˈak-chə-ˌwāt\ *vb* **-at·ed; -at·ing 1** : to put into action **2** : to move to action — **ac·tu·a·tor** \-ˌwāt-ər\ *n*

act up *vb* **1** : MISBEHAVE **2** : to function improperly

acu·ity \ə-ˈkyü-ət-ē\ *n, pl* **-ities** : keenness of perception

acu·men \ə-ˈkyü-mən\ *n* : mental keenness and penetration **syn** discernment, insight, percipience, perspicacity

acu·pres·sure \ˈak-yü-ˌpresh-ər\ *n* : SHIATSU

acu·punc·ture \ˈak-yü-ˌpəŋk-chər\ *n* : an orig. Chinese practice of puncturing the body (as with needles) at specific points to cure disease or relieve pain — **acu·punc·tur·ist** \ˌak-yü-ˈpəŋk-chə-rəst\ *n*

acute \ə-ˈkyüt\ *adj* **acut·er; acut·est** [L *acutus,* pp. of *acuere* to sharpen, fr. *acus* needle] **1** : SHARP, POINTED **2** : containing less than 90 degrees ⟨an ∼ angle⟩ **3** : sharply perceptive; *esp* : mentally keen **4** : SEVERE ⟨∼ distress⟩; *also* : having a sudden onset, sharp rise, and short duration ⟨∼ inflammation⟩ **5** : of, marked by, or being an accent mark having the form ´ — **acute·ly** *adv* — **acute·ness** *n*

ad \ˈad\ *n* : ADVERTISEMENT

AD *abbr* **1** after date **2** [L *anno Domini*] in the year of our Lord — often printed in small capitals

ad·age \ˈad-ij\ *n* : an old familiar saying : PROVERB, MAXIM

¹ada·gio \ə-ˈdäj-(ē-ˌ)ō, -ˈdäzh-\ *adv or adj* [It] : in slow time — used as a direction in music

²adagio *n, pl* **-gios 1** : an adagio movement **2** : a ballet duet or trio displaying feats of lifting and balancing

¹ad·a·mant \ˈad-ə-mənt, -ˌmant\ *n* [ME, fr. OF, fr. L *adamant-, adamas* hardest metal, diamond, fr. Gk] : a stone believed to be impenetrably hard — **ad·a·man·tine** \ˌad-ə-ˈman-ˌtēn, -ˌtīn\ *adj*

²adamant *adj* : INFLEXIBLE, UNYIELDING — **ad·a·mant·ly** *adv*

Ad·am's apple \ˈad-əmz-\ *n* : the projection in front of the neck formed by the largest cartilage of the larynx

adapt \ə-ˈdapt\ *vb* : to make suitable or fit (as for a new use or for different conditions) **syn** adjust, accommodate, conform — **adapt·abil·i·ty** \ə-ˌdap-tə-ˈbil-ət-ē\ *n* — **adapt·able** *adj* — **ad·ap·ta·tion** \ˌad-ˌap-ˈtā-shən, -əp-\ *n* — **adap·tive** \ə-ˈdap-tiv\ *adj*

adapt·er *also* **adap·tor** \ə-ˈdap-tər\ *n* **1**

: one that adapts **2** : a device for connecting two dissimilar parts of an apparatus **3** : an attachment for adapting apparatus for uses not orig. intended

ADC *abbr* **1** aide-de-camp **2** Aid to Dependent Children

add \'ad\ *vb* **1** : to join to something else so as to increase in number or amount **2** : to combine (numbers) into one sum

ad·dend \'ad-ˌend\ *n* : a number to be added to another

ad·den·dum \ə-'den-dəm\ *n*, *pl* **-da** \-də\ [L] : something added; *esp* : a supplement to a book

¹ad·der \'ad-ər\ *n* **1** : a poisonous European viper or a related snake **2** : any of various harmless No. American snakes (as the hognose snake)

²add·er \'ad-ər\ *n* : one that adds; *esp* : a device that performs addition

¹ad·dict \ə-'dikt\ *vb* **1** : to devote or surrender (oneself) to something habitually or excessively **2** : to cause (a person) to become physiologically dependent upon a drug — **ad·dic·tive** \-'dik-tiv\ *adj*

²ad·dict \'ad-(ˌ)ikt\ *n* : one who is addicted (as to a drug)

ad·dic·tion \ə-'dik-shən\ *n* : the quality or state of being addicted; *esp* : compulsive need for habit-forming drugs

ad·di·tion \ə-'dish-ən\ *n* **1** : the act or process of adding; *also* : something added **2** : the operation of combining numbers to obtain their sum **syn** accretion, increment, accession, augmentation

ad·di·tion·al \ə-'dish-(ə-)nəl\ *adj* : coming by way of addition : ADDED, EXTRA — **ad·di·tion·al·ly** \-ē\ *adv*

¹ad·di·tive \'ad-ət-iv\ *adj* **1** : of, relating to, or characterized by addition **2** : produced by addition — **ad·di·tiv·i·ty** \ˌad-ə-'tiv-ət-ē\

²additive *n* : a substance added to another in small quantities to effect a desired change in properties ⟨food ∼s⟩

ad·dle \'ad-ᵊl\ *vb* **ad·dled; ad·dling** \'ad-(ə-)liŋ\ **1** : to throw into confusion : MUDDLE **2** : to become rotten ⟨addled eggs⟩

addn *abbr* addition

addnl *abbr* additional

add-on \'ad-ˌȯn, -ˌän\ *n* : something added as a supplement; *esp* : a component (as of a computer system) that increases capability

¹ad·dress \ə-'dres\ *vb* **1** : to direct the attention of (oneself) **2** : to direct one's remarks to : deliver an address to **3** : to mark directions for delivery on **4** : to identify (as a memory location) by an address

²ad·dress \ə-'dres, 'ad-ˌres\ *n* **1** : skillful management **2** : a formal speech : LECTURE **3** : the place where a person or organization may be communicated with **4** : the directions for delivery placed on mail **5** : a location (as in

a computer's memory) where particular data is stored

ad·dress·ee \ˌad-ˌres-'ē, ə-ˌdres-'ē\ *n* : one to whom something is addressed

ad·duce \ə-'d(y)üs\ *vb* **ad·duced; ad·duc·ing** : to offer as argument, reason, or proof **syn** advance, allege, cite, submit

-ade \'ād\ *n suffix* **1** : act : action ⟨blockade⟩ **2** : product; *esp* : sweet drink ⟨limeade⟩

ad·e·nine \'ad-ᵊn-ˌēn\ *n* : one of the purine bases that make up the genetic code of DNA and RNA

ad·e·noid \'ad-(ᵊ-)ˌnȯid\ *n* : an enlarged mass of tissue near the opening of the nose into the throat — usu. used in pl. — **adenoid** *or* **ad·e·noi·dal** \ˌad-(ᵊ-)'nȯid-ᵊl\ *adj*

aden·o·sine tri·phos·phate \ə-'den-ə-ˌsēn-trī-'fäs-ˌfāt\ *n* : ATP

ad·ept \'ad-ˌept\ *n* : EXPERT

adept \ə-'dept\ *adj* : highly skilled : EXPERT — **adept·ly** *adv* — **adept·ness** *n*

ad·e·quate \'ad-i-kwət\ *adj* : equal to or sufficient for a specific requirement — **ad·e·qua·cy** \-kwə-sē\ *n* — **ad·e·quate·ly** *adv*

ad·here \ad-'hiər, əd-\ *vb* **ad·hered; ad·her·ing** **1** : to give support : maintain loyalty **2** : to stick fast : CLING — **ad·her·ence** \-'hir-əns\ *n* — **ad·her·ent** \-ənt\ *adj or n*

ad·he·sion \ad-'hē-zhən, əd-\ *n* **1** : the act or state of adhering **2** : the union of bodily tissues abnormally grown together after inflammation; *also* : the newly formed uniting tissue **3** : the molecular attraction between the surfaces of bodies in contact

¹ad·he·sive \-'hē-siv, -ziv\ *adj* **1** : tending to adhere : STICKY **2** : prepared for adhering

²adhesive *n* : an adhesive substance

adhesive tape *n* : tape coated on one side with an adhesive mixture; *esp* : one used to secure bandages and cover wounds

¹ad hoc \'ad-'häk, -'hōk\ *adv* [L, for this] : for the case at hand apart from other applications

²ad hoc *adj* : concerned with or formed for a particular purpose ⟨an *ad hoc* committee⟩ ⟨*ad hoc* solutions⟩

adi·a·bat·ic \ˌad-ē-ə-'bat-ik\ *adj* : occurring without loss or gain of heat — **adi·a·bat·i·cal·ly** \-i-k(ə-)lē\ *adv*

adieu \ə-'d(y)ü\ *n, pl* **adieus** *or* **adieux** \ə-'d(y)üz\ : FAREWELL — often used interjectionally

ad in·fi·ni·tum \ˌad-ˌin-fə-'nīt-əm\ *adv or adj* : without end or limit

ad in·ter·im \ad-'in-tə-rəm, -ˌrim\ *adv* : for the intervening time — **ad interim** *adj*

adi·os \ˌad-ē-'ōs, ˌäd-\ *interj* [Sp *adiós*, lit., to God] — used to express farewell

ad·i·pose \'ad-ə-ˌpōs\ *adj* : of or relating to animal fat : FATTY

adj *abbr* **1** adjective **2** adjutant

ad·ja·cent \ə-ˈjās-ᵊnt\ *adj* : situated near or next syn adjoining, contiguous, abutting, juxtaposed, conterminous

ad·jec·tive \ˈaj-ik-tiv\ *n* : a word that typically serves as a modifier of a noun — **ad·jec·ti·val** \ˌaj-ik-ˈtī-vəl\ *adj* — **ad·jec·ti·val·ly** \-ē\ *adv*

ad·join \ə-ˈjóin\ *vb* : to be situated next to

ad·join·ing *adj* : touching or bounding at a point or line

ad·journ \ə-ˈjərn\ *vb* 1 : to suspend indefinitely or until a stated time 2 : to transfer to another place — **ad·journ·ment** *n*

ad·judge \ə-ˈjəj\ *vb* **ad·judged; ad·judg·ing** 1 : JUDGE, ADJUDICATE 2 : to hold or pronounce to be : DEEM 3 : to award by judicial decision

ad·ju·di·cate \ə-ˈjüd-i-ˌkāt\ *vb* **-cat·ed; -cat·ing** : to settle judicially — **ad·ju·di·ca·tion** \ə-ˌjüd-i-ˈkā-shən\ *n*

ad·junct \ˈaj-ˌəŋkt\ *n* : something joined or added to another but not essentially a part of it syn appendage, appurtenance, accessory, appendix

ad·jure \ə-ˈjùr\ *vb* **ad·jured; ad·jur·ing** : to command solemnly : urge earnestly syn beg, beseech, implore — **ad·ju·ra·tion** \ˌaj-ə-ˈrā-shən\ *n*

ad·just \ə-ˈjəst\ *vb* 1 : to bring to agreement : SETTLE 2 : to cause to conform : ADAPT, FIT 3 : REGULATE (∼ a watch) — **ad·just·able** *adj* — **ad·just·er** *also* **ad·jus·tor** \ə-ˈjəs-tər\ *n* — **ad·just·ment** \ə-ˈjəs(t)-mənt\ *n*

ad·ju·tant \ˈaj-ət-ənt\ *n* : one who assists; *esp* : an officer who assists a commanding officer by handling correspondence and keeping records

ad·ju·vant \ˈaj-ə-vənt\ *n* : one that helps or facilitates; *esp* : something that enhances the effectiveness of medical treatment — adjuvant *adj*

¹ad-lib \ˈad-ˈlib\ *vb* **ad-libbed; ad-lib·bing** : IMPROVISE — **ad-lib** *n*

²ad-lib *adj* : spoken, composed, or performed without preparation

ad lib \ˈad-ˈlib\ *adv* [NL *ad libitum*] 1 : at one's pleasure 2 : without limit

ad li·bi·tum \ad-ˈlib-ət-əm\ *adj* [NL, in accordance with desire] : omissible according to a performer's wishes — used as a direction in music

adm *abbr* administration: administrative

ADM *abbr* admiral

ad·man \ˈad-ˌman\ *n* : one who writes, solicits, or places advertisements

admin *abbr* administration

ad·min·is·ter \əd-ˈmin-ə-stər\ *vb* **-tered; -ter·ing** \-st(ə-)riŋ\ 1 : MANAGE, SUPERINTEND 2 : to mete out : DISPENSE 3 : to give ritually or remedially (∼ quinine for malaria) 4 : to perform the office of administrator — **ad·min·is·tra·ble** \-strə-bəl\ *adj* — **ad·min·is·trant** \-strənt\ *n*

ad·min·is·tra·tion \əd-ˌmin-ə-ˈstrā-shən, (ˌ)ad-\ *n* 1 : the act or process of administering 2 : MANAGEMENT 3 : the body of persons directing the government of a country 4 : the term of office of an administrative officer or body — **ad·min·is·tra·tive** \əd-ˈmin-ə-ˌstrāt-iv\ *adj* — **ad·min·is·tra·tive·ly** *adv*

ad·min·is·tra·tor \əd-ˈmin-ə-ˌstrāt-ər\ *n* : one that administers; *esp* : one who settles an intestate estate

ad·mi·ra·ble \ˈad-m(ə-)rə-bəl\ *adj* : worthy of admiration : EXCELLENT — **ad·mi·ra·bly** \-blē\ *adv*

ad·mi·ral \ˈad-m(ə-)rəl\ *n* [ME, fr. MF *amiral* admiral & ML *admiralis* emir, *admirallus* admiral, deriv. of Ar *amīr* commander] : a commissioned officer in the navy ranking next below a fleet admiral

ad·mi·ral·ty \ˈad-m(ə-)rəl-tē\ *n* 1 *cap* : a British government department formerly having authority over naval affairs 2 : the court having jurisdiction over maritime questions

ad·mire \əd-ˈmī(ə)r\ *vb* **ad·mired; ad·mir·ing** [MF *admirer*, fr. L *admirari*, fr. *ad-* to + *mirari* to wonder] : to regard with high esteem — **ad·mi·ra·tion** \ˌad-mə-ˈrā-shən\ *n* — **ad·mir·er** *n* — **ad·mir·ing·ly** \-ˈmī-riŋ-lē\ *adv*

ad·mis·si·ble \əd-ˈmis-ə-bəl\ *adj* : that can be or is worthy to be admitted or allowed : ALLOWABLE (∼ evidence) — **ad·mis·si·bil·i·ty** \-ˌmis-ə-ˈbil-ət-ē\ *n*

ad·mis·sion \əd-ˈmish-ən\ *n* 1 : the granting of an argument 2 : the acknowledgment of a fact 3 : the act of admitting 4 : the privilege of being admitted 5 : a fee paid for admission

ad·mit \əd-ˈmit\ *vb* **ad·mit·ted; ad·mit·ting** 1 : PERMIT, ALLOW 2 : to allow to enter 3 : to recognize as genuine or valid — **ad·mit·ted·ly** *adv*

ad·mit·tance \əd-ˈmit-ᵊns\ *n* : permission to enter

ad·mix \ad-ˈmiks\ *vb* : MINGLE, MIX

ad·mix·ture \ad-ˈmiks-chər\ *n* 1 : something added in mixing 2 : MIXTURE

ad·mon·ish \əd-ˈmän-ish\ *vb* : to warn gently : reprove with a warning syn chide, reproach, rebuke, reprimand, reprove — **ad·mon·i·tion** \ˌad-mə-ˈnish-ən\ *n* — **ad·mon·i·to·ry** \əd-ˈmän-ə-ˌtōr-ē\ *adj*

ad nau·se·am \ad-ˈnó-zē-əm\ *adv* [L] : to a sickening degree

ado \ə-ˈdü\ *n* 1 : bustling excitement : FUSS 2 : TROUBLE

adobe \ə-ˈdō-bē\ *n* [Sp, fr. Ar *aṭ-ṭūb*, fr. Coptic *tōbe*] 1 : sun-dried brick; *also* : clay for making such bricks 2 : a structure made of adobe bricks — adobe *adj*

ad·o·les·cence \ˌad-ᵊl-ˈes-ᵊns\ *n* : the process or period of growth between childhood and maturity — **ad·o·les·cent** \-ᵊnt\ *adj or n*

adopt \ə-ˈdäpt\ *vb* 1 : to take (a child of other parents) as one's own child 2 : to take up and practice as one's own

3 : to accept formally and put into effect — **adop·tion** \-'däp-shən\ *n*

adop·tive \ə-'däp-tiv\ *adj* : made or acquired by adoption (~ father) — **adop·tive·ly** *adv*

ador·able \ə-'dōr-ə-bəl\ *adj* **1** : worthy of adoration **2** : extremely charming — **ador·ably** \-blē\ *adv*

adore \ə-'dōr\ *vb* **adored; ador·ing** [MF *adorer*, fr. L *adorare*, fr. *ad-* to + *orare* to speak, pray] **1** : WORSHIP **2** : to regard with reverent admiration **3** : to be extremely fond of — **ad·o·ra·tion** \ˌad-ə-'rā-shən\ *n*

adorn \ə-'dōrn\ *vb* : to decorate with ornaments — **adorn·ment** *n*

ad·re·nal \ə-'drēn-ᵊl\ *adj* : of, relating to, or being a pair of endocrine organs (**adrenal glands**) that are located near the kidneys and produce several hormones and esp. epinephrine

adren·a·line \ə-'dren-ᵊl-ən\ *n* : EPINEPHRINE

adrift \ə-'drift\ *adv or adj* **1** : afloat without motive power or moorings **2** : without guidance or purpose

adroit \ə-'drȯit\ *adj* [F, fr. OF, fr. *a-* to + *droit* right] **1** : dexterous with one's hands **2** : SHREWD, RESOURCEFUL *syn* canny, clever, cunning, ingenious — **adroit·ly** *adv* — **adroit·ness** *n*

ad·sorb \ad-'sȯrb, -'zȯrb\ *vb* : to take up (as molecules of gases) and hold on the surface of a solid or liquid — **ad·sorp·tion** \-'sȯrp-shən, -'zȯrp-\ *n* — **ad·sorp·tive** \-'sȯrp-tiv, -'zȯrp-\ *adj*

ad·u·late \'aj-ə-ˌlāt\ *vb* **-lat·ed; -lat·ing** : to flatter or admire excessively — **ad·u·la·tion** \ˌaj-ə-'lā-shən\ *n*

¹adult \ə-'dəlt, 'ad-ˌəlt\ *adj* [L *adultus*, pp. of *adolescere* to grow up, fr. *ad-* to + *-olescere* (fr. *alescere* to grow)] : fully developed and mature — **adult·hood** *n*

²adult *n* : one that is adult; *esp* : a human being after an age (as 18) specified by law

adul·ter·ant \ə-'dəl-tə-rənt\ *n* : something used to adulterate another

adul·ter·ate \ə-'dəl-tə-ˌrāt\ *vb* **-at·ed; -at·ing** [L *adulterare*, fr. *ad-* to + *alter* other] : to make impure by mixing in a foreign or inferior substance — **adul·ter·a·tion** \-ˌdəl-tə-'rā-shən\ *n*

adul·tery \ə-'dəl-t(ə-)rē\ *n, pl* **-ter·ies** : sexual unfaithfulness of a married person — **adul·ter·er** \-tər-ər\ *n* — **adul·ter·ess** \-t(ə-)rəs\ *n* — **adul·ter·ous** \-t(ə-)rəs\ *adj*

ad·um·brate \'ad-əm-ˌbrāt\ *vb* **-brat·ed; -brat·ing** **1** : to foreshadow vaguely : INTIMATE **2** : to suggest or disclose partially : SHADE, OBSCURE — **ad·um·bra·tion** \ˌad-əm-'brā-shən\ *n*

adv *abbr* **1** adverb **2** advertisement

ad va·lor·em \ˌad-və-'lōr-əm\ *adj* [L, according to the value] : imposed at a percentage of the value (an *ad valorem* tax)

¹ad·vance \əd-'vans\ *vb* **ad·vanced; ad·vanc·ing** **1** : to bring or move forward **2** : to assist the progress of **3** : to promote in rank **4** : to make earlier in time **5** : LEND **6** : PROPOSE **7** : to raise in rate : INCREASE — **ad·vance·ment** *n*

²advance *n* **1** : a forward movement **2** : IMPROVEMENT **3** : a rise esp. in price or value **4** : OFFER — **in advance** : BEFOREHAND

³advance *adj* : made, sent, or furnished ahead of time

ad·van·tage \əd-'vant-ij\ *n* **1** : superiority of position **2** : BENEFIT, GAIN **3** : the 1st point won in tennis after deuce — **ad·van·ta·geous** \ˌad-ˌvan-'tā-jəs, -vən-\ *adj* — **ad·van·ta·geous·ly** *adv*

ad·vent \'ad-ˌvent\ *n* **1** *cap* : a penitential period beginning four Sundays before Christmas **2** : ARRIVAL; *esp, cap* : the coming of Christ

ad·ven·ti·tious \ˌad-vən-'tish-əs\ *adj* **1** : ACCIDENTAL, INCIDENTAL **2** : arising or occurring sporadically or in other than the usual location (~ buds) — **ad·ven·ti·tious·ly** *adv*

¹ad·ven·ture \əd-'ven-chər\ *n* **1** : a risky undertaking **2** : a remarkable or exciting experience — **ad·ven·tur·ous** \-'vench-(ə-)rəs\ *adj*

²adventure *vb* **-ven·tured; -ven·tur·ing** \-'vench-(ə-)riŋ\ : RISK, HAZARD

ad·ven·tur·er \əd-'vench-(ə-)rər\ *n* **1** : a person who engages in new and risky undertakings **2** : a person who follows a military career for adventure or profit **3** : a person who tries to gain wealth by questionable means

ad·ven·ture·some \əd-'ven-chər-səm\ *adj* : inclined to take risks

ad·ven·tur·ess \əd-'vench-(ə-)rəs\ *n* : a female adventurer

ad·verb \'ad-ˌvərb\ *n* : a word that typically serves as a modifier of a verb, an adjective, or another adverb — **ad·ver·bi·al** \ad-'vər-bē-əl\ *adj* — **ad·ver·bi·al·ly** \-ē\ *adv*

¹ad·ver·sary \'ad-və(r)-ˌser-ē\ *n, pl* **-sar·ies** : FOE

²adversary *adj* : involving antagonistic parties or interests

ad·verse \ad-'vərs, 'ad-ˌvərs\ *adj* **1** : acting against or in a contrary direction **2** : UNFAVORABLE — **ad·verse·ly** *adv*

ad·ver·si·ty \ad-'vər-sət-ē\ *n, pl* **-ties** : hard times : MISFORTUNE

ad·vert \ad-'vərt\ *vb* : REFER

ad·ver·tise \'ad-vər-ˌtīz\ *vb* **-tised; -tis·ing** **1** : INFORM, NOTIFY **2** : to call public attention to esp. in order to sell — **ad·ver·tis·er** *n*

ad·ver·tise·ment \ˌad-vər-'tīz-mənt; əd-'vərt-əs-mənt\ *n* **1** : the act of advertising **2** : a public notice intended to advertise something

ad·ver·tis·ing \'ad-vər-ˌtī-ziŋ\ *n* : the business of preparing advertisements

ad·vice \əd-'vīs\ *n* **1** : recommendation with regard to a course of action : COUNSEL **2** : INFORMATION, REPORT

ad·vis·able \əd-'vī-zə-bəl\ *adj* : proper

to be done : EXPEDIENT — **ad·vis·abil·i·ty** \-ˌvī-zə-ˈbil-ət-ē\ n

ad·vise \əd-ˈvīz\ vb **ad·vised; ad·vis·ing** 1 : to give advice to : COUNSEL 2 : INFORM, NOTIFY 3 : CONSULT, CONFER — **ad·vis·er** or **ad·vi·sor** \-ˈvī-zər\ n

ad·vised \əd-ˈvīzd\ adj : thought out : CONSIDERED ⟨well-*advised*⟩ — **ad·vis·ed·ly** \-ˈvī-zəd-lē\ adv

ad·vise·ment \əd-ˈvīz-mənt\ n : careful consideration

ad·vi·so·ry \əd-ˈvīz-(ə-)rē\ adj 1 : having or exercising power to advise 2 : containing advice

¹ad·vo·cate \ˈad-və-kət, -ˌkāt\ n [deriv. of L *advocare* to summon, fr. *ad-* + *vocare* to call] 1 : one who pleads another's cause 2 : one who argues or pleads for a cause or proposal — **ad·vo·ca·cy** \-və-kə-sē\ n

²ad·vo·cate \-ˌkāt\ vb **-cat·ed; -cat·ing** : to plead in favor of — **ad·vo·ca·tion** \ˌad-və-ˈkā-shən\ n

advt abbr advertisement

adz or **adze** \ˈadz\ n : a cutting tool that has a curved blade set at right angles to the handle and is used in shaping wood

AEC abbr Atomic Energy Commission

ae·gis \ˈē-jəs\ n [L, fr. Gk *aigis* goatskin] 1 : SHIELD, PROTECTION 2 : PATRONAGE, SPONSORSHIP

ae·o·li·an harp \ē-ˌō-lē-ən-\ n : a box with strings that produce musical sounds when wind blows on them

ae·on \ˈē-ən, ˈē-ˌän\ n : an indefinitely long time : AGE

aer·ate \ˈa(-ə)r-ˌāt\ vb **aer·at·ed; aer·at·ing** 1 : to supply (blood) with oxygen by respiration 2 : to supply or impregnate with air 3 : to combine or charge with gas — **aer·a·tion** \ˌa(-ə)r-ˈā-shən\ n — **aer·a·tor** \ˈa(-ə)r-ˌāt-ər\ n

¹ae·ri·al \ˈar-ē-əl, ā-ˈir-ē-əl\ adj 1 : inhabiting, occurring in, or done in the air 2 : AIRY 3 : of or relating to aircraft

²ae·ri·al \ˈar-ē-əl\ n : ANTENNA 2

ae·ri·al·ist \ˈar-ē-ə-ləst, ā-ˈir-\ n : a performer of feats above the ground esp. on a flying trapeze

ae·rie \ˈa(ə)r-ē, ˈi(ə)r-ē\ n : a highly placed nest (as of an eagle)

aer·o·bat·ics \ˌar-ə-ˈbat-iks\ n sing or pl : spectacular flying feats and maneuvers

aer·o·bic \ˌa(ə)r-ˈrō-bik\ adj : living or active only in the presence of oxygen ⟨~ bacteria⟩ — **aer·obe** \ˈa(-ə)r-ˌōb\ n — **aer·o·bi·cal·ly** \-bi-k(ə-)lē\ adv

aer·o·bics \-biks\ n sing or pl : a system of exercises designed to improve the body's ability to take in and use oxygen

aero·drome \ˈar-ə-ˌdrōm\ n, chiefly Brit : AIRFIELD, AIRPORT

aero·dy·nam·ics \ˌar-ō-dī-ˈnam-iks\ n : the science dealing with the forces acting on bodies in motion in a gas (as air) — **aero·dy·nam·ic** \-ik\ or **aero·dy·nam·i·cal** \-i-kəl\ adj — **aero·dy·nam·i·cal·ly** \-i-k(ə-)lē\ adv

aero·naut \ˈar-ə-ˌnȯt\ n : one who operates or travels in an airship or balloon

aero·nau·tics \ˌar-ə-ˈnȯt-iks\ n : the science of aircraft operation — **aero·nau·ti·cal** \-i-kəl\ or **aero·nau·tic** \-ik\ adj

aero·plane \ˈar-ə-ˌplān\ chiefly Brit var of AIRPLANE

aero·sol \ˈar-ə-ˌsäl, -ˌsȯl\ n 1 : a suspension of fine solid or liquid particles in a gas 2 : a substance (as an insecticide or cosmetic) dispensed from a pressurized container as an aerosol

aero·space \ˈar-ō-ˌspās\ n : the earth's atmosphere and the space beyond — **aerospace** adj

aery \ˈa(ə)r-ē\ adj **aer·i·er; -est** : having an aerial quality : ETHEREAL

aes·thete \ˈes-ˌthēt\ n : a person having or affecting sensitivity to beauty esp. in art

aes·thet·ic \es-ˈthet-ik\ adj 1 : of or relating to aesthetics : ARTISTIC 2 : appreciative of the beautiful — **aes·thet·i·cal·ly** \-i-k(ə-)lē\ adv

aes·thet·ics \-ˈthet-iks\ n : a branch of philosophy dealing with the nature, creation, and appreciation of beauty

aes·ti·vate var of ESTIVATE

AF abbr 1 air force 2 audio frequency

¹afar \ə-ˈfär\ adv : from, at, or to a great distance

²afar n : a great distance

AFB abbr air force base

AFC abbr 1 American Football Conference 2 automatic frequency control

AFDC abbr Aid to Families with Dependent Children

af·fa·ble \ˈaf-ə-bəl\ adj : courteous and agreeable in conversation — **af·fa·bil·i·ty** \ˌaf-ə-ˈbil-ət-ē\ n — **af·fa·bly** \ˈaf-ə-blē\ adv

af·fair \ə-ˈfaər\ n [ME *affaire*, fr. MF, fr. *a faire* to do] 1 : something that relates to or involves one : CONCERN 2 : a romantic or sexual attachment of limited duration

¹af·fect \ə-ˈfekt, a-\ vb 1 : to be fond of using or wearing 2 : SIMULATE, ASSUME, PRETEND

²affect vb : to produce an effect on : INFLUENCE, IMPRESS

af·fec·ta·tion \ˌaf-ˌek-ˈtā-shən\ n : an attitude or mode of behavior assumed by a person in an effort to impress others

af·fect·ed \ə-ˈfek-təd, a-\ adj 1 : pretending to some trait which is not natural 2 : artificially assumed to impress others — **af·fect·ed·ly** adv

af·fect·ing \ə-ˈfek-tiŋ, a-\ adj : arousing pity, sympathy, or sorrow ⟨an ~ story⟩ — **af·fect·ing·ly** adv

¹af·fec·tion \ə-ˈfek-shən\ n : tender attachment : LOVE — **af·fec·tion·ate** \-sh(ə-)nət\ adj — **af·fec·tion·ate·ly** adv

²affection n : DISEASE, DISORDER ⟨an ~ of the brain⟩

af·fer·ent \ˈaf-ə-rənt, -ˌer-ənt\ adj : bearing or conducting inward toward a more central part and esp. a nerve center (as the brain or spinal cord) ⟨~ nerves⟩

af·fi·ance \ə-'fī-əns\ *vb* **-anced; -anc·ing** : BETROTH, ENGAGE

af·fi·da·vit \ˌaf-ə-'dā-vət\ *n* [ML, he has made an oath] : a sworn statement in writing

¹af·fil·i·ate \ə-'fil-ē-ˌāt\ *vb* **-at·ed; -at·ing** : to associate as a member or branch — **af·fil·i·a·tion** \-ˌfil-ē-'ā-shən\ *n*

²af·fil·i·ate \-'fil-ē-ət\ *n* : an affiliated person or organization

af·fin·i·ty \ə-'fin-ət-ē\ *n, pl* **-ties** **1** : KINSHIP, RELATIONSHIP **2** : attractive force : ATTRACTION, SYMPATHY

af·firm \ə-'fərm\ *vb* **1** : CONFIRM, RATIFY **2** : to assert positively syn avow, avouch, declare, assert — **af·fir·ma·tion** \ˌaf-ər-'mā-shən\ *n*

¹af·fir·ma·tive \ə-'fər-mət-iv\ *adj* : asserting that the fact is so : POSITIVE

²affirmative *n* **1** : an expression of affirmation or assent **2** : the side that upholds the proposition stated in a debate

affirmative action *n* : an active effort to improve the employment or educational opportunities of members of minority groups and women

¹af·fix \ə-'fiks\ *vb* : ATTACH, ADD

²af·fix \'af-ˌiks\ *n* : one or more sounds or letters attached to the beginning or end of a word and serving to produce a derivative word or an inflectional form

af·fla·tus \ə-'flāt-əs\ *n* : divine inspiration

af·flict \ə-'flikt\ *vb* : to cause pain and distress to syn rack, try, torment, torture — **af·flic·tion** \-'flik-shən\ *n*

af·flic·tive \ə-'flik-tiv\ *adj* : causing affliction : DISTRESSING — **af·flic·tive·ly** *adv*

af·flu·ence \'af-ˌlü-ən(t)s; ə-'flü-, ə-\ *n* : abundant supply; *also* : WEALTH, RICHES — **af·flu·ent** \-ənt\ *adj*

af·ford \ə-'fōrd\ *vb* **1** : to manage to bear or bear the cost of without serious harm or loss **2** : PROVIDE, FURNISH

af·for·es·ta·tion \ə-ˌfōr-ə-'stā-shən\ *n* : the act or process of establishing forest cover — **af·for·est** \ə-'fōr-əst, -'fär-\ *vb*

af·fray \ə-'frā\ *n* : FIGHT, FRAY

af·fright \ə-'frīt\ *vb* : FRIGHTEN, ALARM — **affright** *n*

af·front \ə-'frənt\ *vb* **1** : INSULT : CONFRONT — **affront** *n*

af·ghan \'af-ˌgan\ *n* : a blanket or shawl of colored wool knitted or crocheted in sections

Af·ghan \'af-ˌgan\ *n* : a native or inhabitant of Afghanistan — **Afghan** *adj*

Afghan hound *n* : any of a breed of tall slim swift hunting dogs with a coat of silky thick hair and a long silky top knot

af·ghani \af-'gan-ē\ *n* — see MONEY table

afi·cio·na·do \ə-ˌfish(-ē)-ə-'näd-ō, -, fis-

ē-\ *n, pl* **-dos** [Sp, deriv. of *afición* affection] : DEVOTEE, FAN

afield \ə-'fēld\ *adv or adj* **1** : to, in, or on the field **2** : away from home **3** : out of the way : ASTRAY

afire \ə-'fī(ə)r\ *adj or adv* : being on fire : BURNING

AFL *abbr* American Football League

aflame \ə-'flām\ *adj or adv* : FLAMING

AFL-CIO *abbr* American Federation of Labor and Congress of Industrial Organizations

afloat \ə-'flōt\ *adj or adv* **1** : borne on or as if on the water **2** : being on board ship **3** : ADRIFT

aflut·ter \ə-'flət-ər\ *adj* **1** : FLUTTERING **2** : nervously excited

afoot \ə-'fut\ *adv or adj* **1** : on foot **2** : in action : in progress

afore·men·tioned \ə-'fōr-'men-chənd\ *adj* : mentioned previously

afore·said \-ˌsed\ *adj* : said or named before

afore·thought \-ˌthót\ *adj* : PREMEDITATED ⟨with malice ~⟩

a for·ti·o·ri \ˌä-ˌfōrt-ē-'ōr-ē\ *adv* [NL, lit., from the stronger (argument)] : with even greater reason

afoul of \ə-'faul-əv\ *prep* **1** : in or into collision or entanglement with **2** : in or into conflict with

Afr *abbr* Africa: African

afraid \ə-'frād, *South also* ə-'fre(ə)d\ *adj* : FRIGHTENED, FEARFUL

A–frame \'ā-ˌfrām\ *n* : a building having triangular front and rear walls with the roof reaching to the ground

afresh \ə-'fresh\ *adv* : ANEW, AGAIN

Af·ri·can \'af-ri-kən\ *n* **1** : a native or inhabitant of Africa **2** : NEGRO — **African** *adj*

African violet *n* : a tropical African plant widely grown indoors for its velvety fleshy leaves and showy purple, pink, or white flowers

Af·ri·kaans \ˌaf-ri-'käns\ *n* : a language developed from 17th century Dutch that is one of the official languages of the Republic of So. Africa

¹Af·ro \'af-rō\ *adj* : having the hair shaped into a round bushy mass

²Afro *n, pl* **Afros** : an Afro hairstyle

Af·ro-Amer·i·can \ˌaf-rō-ə-'mer-ə-kən\ *n* : an American of African and esp. of Negroid descent — **Afro-American** *adj*

aft \'aft\ *adv* : near, toward, or in the stern of a ship or the tail of an aircraft

AFT *abbr* American Federation of Teachers

¹af·ter \'af-tər\ *adv* : AFTERWARD, SUBSEQUENTLY

²after *prep* **1** : behind in place **2** : later than **3** : intent on the seizure, mastery, or achievement of ⟨he's ~ your job⟩

³after *conj* : following the time when

⁴after *adj* **1** : LATER **2** : located toward the rear

af·ter·birth \'af-tər-ˌbərth\ *n* : the placenta and membranes of the fetus that are expelled after childbirth

af·ter·burn·er \-,bər-nər\ *n* : a device incorporated in the tail pipe of a turbojet engine for injecting fuel into the hot exhaust gases and burning it to provide extra thrust

af·ter·care \-,keər\ *n* : the care, nursing, or treatment of a convalescent patient

af·ter·deck \-,dek\ *n* : the rear half of the deck of a ship

af·ter·ef·fect \'af-tə-rə-,fekt\ *n* : an effect that follows its cause after an interval

af·ter·glow \'af-tər-,glō\ *n* : a glow remaining where a light has disappeared

af·ter·im·age \'af-tə-,rim-ij\ *n* : a usu. visual sensation continuing after the stimulus causing it has ended

af·ter·life \'af-tər-,līf\ *n* : an existence after death

af·ter·math \-,math\ *n* 1 : a second-growth crop esp. of hay 2 : CONSEQUENCES, EFFECTS *syn* aftereffect, upshot, result, outcome

af·ter·noon \,af-tər-'nün\ *n* : the time between noon and evening

af·ter–shave \'af-tər-,shāv\ *n* : a usu. scented lotion for the face after shaving

af·ter·taste \-,tāst\ *n* : a sensation (as of flavor) continuing after the stimulus causing it has ended

af·ter–tax \'af-tər-,taks\ *adj* : remaining after payment of taxes and esp. of income tax (an ∼ profit)

af·ter·thought \-,thȯt\ *n* : a later thought; *also* : something thought of later

af·ter·ward \'af-tə(r)-wərd\ *or* **af·ter·wards** \-wərdz\ *adv* : at a later time

Ag *symbol* [L *argentum*] silver

AG *abbr* 1 adjutant general 2 attorney general

again \ə-'gen, -'gin\ *adv* 1 : once more : ANEW 2 : on the other hand 3 : in addition : BESIDES

against \ə-'genst\ *prep* 1 : directly opposite to : FACING 2 : in opposition to 3 : as defense from 4 : so as to touch or strike (threw him ∼ the wall); *also* : TOUCHING

¹**agape** \ə-'gāp\ *adj or adv* : having the mouth open in wonder or surprise : GAPING

²**aga·pe** \ä-'gä-pā, 'äg-ə-,pā\ *n* [Gk. lit., love] : self-giving loyal concern that freely accepts another and seeks his or her good

agar \'äg-,är\ *n* 1 : a jellylike substance extracted from a red alga and used esp. as a gelling and stabilizing agent in foods 2 : a culture medium containing agar

agar–agar \,äg-,är-'äg-,är\ *n* : AGAR

ag·ate \'ag-ət\ *n* 1 : a striped or clouded quartz 2 : a playing marble of agate or of glass

aga·ve \ə-'gäv-ē\ *n* : any of a genus of

spiny-leaved plants (as a century plant) related to the amaryllis

agcy *abbr* agency

¹**age** \'āj\ *n* 1 : the length of time during which a being or thing has lived or existed 2 : the time of life at which some particular qualification is achieved; *esp* : MAJORITY 3 : the latter part of life 4 : a long time 5 : a period in history

²**age** *vb* **aged; ag·ing** *or* **age·ing** 1 : to grow old or cause to grow old 2 : to become or cause to become mature or mellow

-age \ij\ *n suffix* 1 : aggregate : collection (track*age*) 2 : action : process (haul*age*) 3 : cumulative result of (break*age*) 4 : rate of (dos*age*) 5 : house or place of (orphan*age*) 6 : state : rank (vassal*age*) 7 : fee : charge (post*age*)

aged \'ā-jəd *for 1;* 'ājd *for 2*\ *adj* 1 : of advanced age 2 : having attained a specified age (a man ∼ 40 years)

age·less \'āj-ləs\ *adj* 1 : not growing old or showing the effects of age 2 : TIMELESS, ETERNAL (an ∼ story)

agen·cy \'ā-jən-sē\ *n, pl* **-cies** 1 : one through which something is accomplished : INSTRUMENTALITY 2 : the office or function of an agent 3 : an establishment doing business for another 4 : an administrative division (as of a government) *syn* means, medium, vehicle

agen·da \ə-'jen-də\ *n* : a list of things to be done : PROGRAM

agent \'ā-jənt\ *n* 1 : one that acts 2 : MEANS, INSTRUMENT 3 : a person acting or doing business for another *syn* attorney, deputy, proxy, delegate

Agent Orange *n* : an herbicide widely used in the Vietnam War that is composed of 2,4-D and 2,4,5-T and contains a toxic contaminant

agent pro·vo·ca·teur \,äzh-,äⁿ-prō-,väk-ə-'tər, 'ä-jənt-\ *n, pl* **agents provocateurs** \,äzh-,äⁿ-prō-,väk-ə-'tər, 'ä-jənts-prō-\ [F] : a person hired to infiltrate a group and incite its members to illegal action

age of consent : the age at which one is legally competent to give consent (as to marriage)

age–old \'āj-'ōld\ *adj* : having existed for ages : ANCIENT

ag·er·a·tum \,aj-ə-'rāt-əm\ *n, pl* **-tums** : any of a large genus of tropical American plants that are related to the daisies and have small showy heads of blue or white flowers

Ag·ge·us \a-'gē-əs\ *n* — see BIBLE table

¹**ag·glom·er·ate** \ə-'gläm-ə-,rāt\ *vb* **-at·ed; -at·ing** [L *agglomerare* to heap up, join, fr. *ad-* to + *glomer-, glomus* ball] : to gather into a mass : CLUSTER — **ag·glom·er·a·tion** \-,gläm-ə-'rā-shən\ *n*

²**ag·glom·er·ate** \-rət\ *n* : rock composed of volcanic fragments

ag·glu·ti·nate \ə-'glüt-ᵊn-,āt\ *vb* **-nat·ed;**

-nat·ing 1 : to cause to adhere : gather into a group or mass 2 : to cause (as red blood cells or bacteria) to collect into clumps — ag·glu·ti·na·tion \-ˌglüt-ᵊn-ˈā-shən\ n

ag·gran·dize \ə-ˈgran-ˌdīz, ˈag-rən-\ vb -dized; -diz·ing : to make great or greater — ag·gran·dize·ment \ə-ˈgran-dəz-mənt, -ˌdīz-; ˌag-rən-ˈdīz-\ n

ag·gra·vate \ˈag-rə-ˌvāt\ vb -vat·ed; -vat·ing 1 : to make more severe : IN-TENSIFY 2 : IRRITATE — ag·gra·va·tion \ˌag-rə-ˈvā-shən\ n

¹ag·gre·gate \ˈag-ri-gət\ adj : formed by the gathering of units into one mass

²ag·gre·gate \-ˌgāt\ vb -gat·ed; -gat·ing : to collect into one mass

³ag·gre·gate \-gət\ n : a mass or body of units or parts somewhat loosely associated with one another; also : the whole amount

ag·gre·ga·tion \ˌag-ri-ˈgā-shən\ n 1 : a group, body, or mass composed of many distinct parts 2 : the collecting of units or parts into a mass or whole

ag·gres·sion \ə-ˈgresh-ən\ n 1 : an unprovoked attack 2 : the practice of making attacks 3 : hostile, injurious, or destructive behavior or outlook esp. when caused by frustration — ag·gres·sor \-ˈgres-ər\ n

ag·gres·sive \ə-ˈgres-iv\ adj 1 : tending toward or exhibiting aggression; esp : marked by combative readiness 2 : marked by driving energy or initiative : ENTERPRISING — ag·gres·sive·ly adv — ag·gres·sive·ness n

ag·grieve \ə-ˈgrēv\ vb ag·grieved; ag·griev·ing 1 : to cause grief to 2 : to inflict injury on : WRONG

aghast \ə-ˈgast\ adj : struck with amazement or horror

ag·ile \ˈaj-əl\ adj : able to move quickly and easily — agil·i·ty \ə-ˈjil-ət-ē\ n

ag·i·tate \ˈaj-ə-ˌtāt\ vb -tat·ed; -tat·ing 1 : to move with an irregular rapid motion 2 : to stir up : EXCITE 3 : to discuss earnestly 4 : to attempt to arouse public feeling — ag·i·ta·tion \ˌaj-ə-ˈtā-shən\ n — ag·i·ta·tor \ˈaj-ə-ˌtāt-ər\ n

ag·it·prop \ˈaj-ət-ˌpräp\ n [Russ] : political propaganda promulgated esp. through the arts

agleam \ə-ˈglēm\ adj : GLEAMING

aglit·ter \ə-ˈglit-ər\ adj : GLITTERING

aglow \ə-ˈglō\ adj : GLOWING

ag·nos·tic \ag-ˈnäs-tik, əg-\ adj [Gk agnōstos unknown, unknowable, fr. a- un- + gnōstos known] : of or relating to the belief that the existence of any ultimate reality (as God) is unknown and prob. unknowable — agnostic n — ag·nos·ti·cism \-ˈnäs-tə-ˌsiz-əm\ n

ago \ə-ˈgō\ adj or adv : earlier than the present time

agog \ə-ˈgäg\ adj [MF en gogues in mirth] : full of excitement : EAGER

¹a-go-go \ä-ˈgō-ˌgō\ n [Whisky à Gogo, café and discotheque in Paris, France,

fr. F à gogo galore] : a nightclub for dancing to pop music : DISCOTHEQUE

²a-go-go adj : GO-GO

ag·o·nize \ˈag-ə-ˌnīz\ vb -nized; -niz·ing : to suffer or cause to suffer agony — ag·o·niz·ing·ly adv

ag·o·ny \ˈag-ə-nē\ n, pl -nies [ME agonie, fr. L agonia, fr. Gk agōnia struggle, anguish, fr. agōn gathering, contest for a prize] : extreme pain of mind or body syn suffering, distress, misery

agony column n : a newspaper column of personal advertisements relating esp. to missing relatives or friends

ago·ra \ˌäg-ə-ˈrä\ n, pl agó·rot \-ˈrōt\ — see shekel at MONEY table

ag·o·ra·pho·bia \ˌag-ə-rə-ˈfō-bē-ə\ n : abnormal fear of being in open spaces — ag·o·ra·pho·bic \-ˈfō-bik, -ˈfäb-ik\ adj or n

agr abbr agricultural; agriculture

agrar·i·an \ə-ˈgrer-ē-ən\ adj 1 : of or relating to land or its ownership (~ reforms) 2 : of or relating to farmers or farming interests — agrarian n — agrar·i·an·ism n

agree \ə-ˈgrē\ vb agreed; agree·ing 1 : ADMIT, CONCEDE 2 : to be similar : CORRESPOND 3 : to express agreement or approval 4 : to be in harmony 5 : to settle by common consent 6 : to be fitting or healthful : SUIT

agree·able \ə-ˈgrē-ə-bəl\ adj 1 : PLEASING, PLEASANT 2 : ready to consent 3 : being in harmony : CONSONANT — agree·able·ness n — agree·ably \-blē\ adv

agree·ment \ə-ˈgrē-mənt\ n 1 : harmony of opinion or action 2 : mutual understanding or arrangement; also : a document containing such an arrangement

agric abbr agricultural; agriculture

ag·ri·cul·ture \ˈag-ri-ˌkəl-chər\ n : FARMING, HUSBANDRY — ag·ri·cul·tur·al \ˌag-ri-ˈkəlch-(ə-)rəl\ adj — ag·ri·cul·tur·ist \-rəst\ or ag·ri·cul·tur·al·ist \-(-ə-)rə-ləst\ n

agron·o·my \ə-ˈgrän-ə-mē\ n : a branch of agriculture that deals with the raising of crops and the care of the soil — ag·ro·nom·ic \ˌag-rə-ˈnäm-ik\ adj — agron·o·mist \ə-ˈgrän-ə-məst\ n

aground \ə-ˈgraund\ adv or adj : on or onto the bottom or shore (ran ~)

agt abbr agent

ague \ˈā-gyü\ n : a fever (as malaria) with recurrent chills and sweating

ahead \ə-ˈhed\ adv or adj 1 : in or toward the front 2 : into or for the future (plan ~) 3 : in or toward a more advantageous position

ahead of prep 1 : in front or advance of 2 : in excess of : ABOVE

AHL abbr American Hockey League

ahoy \ə-ˈhȯi\ interj — used in hailing (ship ~)

AI abbr artificial intelligence

¹aid \ˈād\ vb : to provide with what is useful in achieving an end : ASSIST

²aid n 1 : ASSISTANCE 2 : ASSISTANT

AID *abbr* Agency for International Development

aide \'ād\ *n* : a person who acts as an assistant; *esp* : a military officer assisting a superior

aide-de-camp \,ād-di-'kamp, -'käm, *pl* **aides-de-camp** \,ädz-di-\ [F] : AIDE

aid·man \'ād-,man\ *n* : an army medical corpsman attached to a field unit

AIDS \'ādz\ *n* [*acquired immunodeficiency syndrome*] : a serious disease associated with infection of the cells of the immune system by a retrovirus, occurring esp. in homosexual and bisexual men and in intravenous drug abusers, and recognized clinically usu. by a life-threatening infection (as pneumonia) or Kaposi's sarcoma or both in addition to marked depression of the immune system

AIDS–related complex *n* : a collection of symptoms (as fever, weight loss, and lymphadenopathy) that is associated with the presence of antibodies to the AIDS virus and is followed by the development of AIDS in a certain proportion of cases

AIDS virus *n* : the retrovirus associated with AIDS and the AIDS-related complex

ai·grette \ā-'gret, 'ā-,gret\ *n* [F, plume, egret] : a plume or decorative tuft for the head

ail \'āl\ *vb* **1** : to be the matter with : TROUBLE **2** : to be unwell

ai·lan·thus \ā-'lan-thəs\ *n* : any of a genus of Asian trees or shrubs with pinnate leaves and ill-scented greenish flowers

ai·le·ron \'ā-lə-,rän\ *n* : a movable part of an airplane wing used in banking

ail·ment \'āl-mənt\ *n* : a bodily disorder

¹aim \'ām\ *vb* [ME *aimen*, fr. MF *aesmer* & *esmer*; MF *aesmer*, fr. OF, fr. *a-* to (fr. L *ad-*) + *esmer* to estimate, fr. L *aestimare*] **1** : to point a weapon at an object **2** : to direct one's efforts : ASPIRE **3** : to direct to or toward a specified object or goal

²aim *n* **1** : the direction of a weapon **2** : OBJECT, PURPOSE — **aim·less** \-ləs\ *adj* — **aim·less·ly** *adv* — **aim·less·ness** *n*

AIM *abbr* American Indian Movement

ain't \'ānt\ **1** : are not **2** : is not **3** : am not — though disapproved by many and more common in less educated speech, used orally in most parts of the U.S. by many educated speakers esp. in the phrase *ain't I*

Ai·nu \'ī-nü\ *n, pl* **Ainu** or **Ainus 1** : a member of an indigenous Caucasoid people of Japan **2** : the language of the Ainu people

¹air \'aər\ *n* **1** : the gaseous mixture surrounding the earth **2** : a light breeze **3** : COMPRESSED AIR (∼ sprayer) **4** : AIRCRAFT (∼ patrol) **5** : AVIATION (∼ safety) **6** : the medium of transmission of radio waves; *also* : RADIO, TELEVISION **7** : the outward appearance of a person or thing : MANNER **8** : an artificial manner **9** : MELODY, TUNE

²air *vb* **1** : to expose to the air **2** : to expose to public view

air bag *n* : a bag designed to fill automatically with gas to protect automobile passengers in case of accident

air·boat *n* : a shallow-draft boat driven by an airplane propeller

air·borne \'aər-,bōrn\ *adj* : supported or transported by air

air brake *n* **1** : a brake operated by a piston driven by compressed air **2** : a surface for lowering an airplane's speed

air·brush \-,brəsh\ *n* : a device for applying a fine spray (as of paint) by compressed air — **airbrush** *vb*

air–con·di·tion \,aər-kən-'dish-ən\ : to equip with an apparatus for filtering air and controlling its humidity and temperature — **air con·di·tion·er** \-'dish-(ə-)nər\ *n*

air·craft \'aər-,kraft\ *n, pl* **aircraft** : a vehicle for traveling through the air

aircraft carrier *n* : a warship with a deck on which airplanes can be launched and landed

air·drome \-,drōm\ *n* : AIRPORT

air·drop \-,dräp\ *n* : delivery of cargo or personnel by parachute from an airplane in flight — **air-drop** *vb*

Aire·dale terrier \'aər-,dāl-\ *n* : any of a breed of large terriers with a hard wiry coat

air·fare \-,faər\ *n* : fare for travel by airplane

air·field \'aər-,fēld\ *n* **1** : the landing field of an airport **2** : AIRPORT

air·flow \-,flō\ *n* : the motion of air relative to a body in it

air·foil \-,foil\ *n* : an airplane surface (as a wing or rudder) designed to produce reaction from the air

air force *n* : the military organization of a nation for air warfare

air·frame \-,frām\ *n* : the structure of an airplane or rocket without the power plant

air·freight \-'frāt\ *n* : freight transport by air in volume; *also* : the charge for this service

air gun *n* **1** : a gun operated by compressed air **2** : a hand tool that works by compressed air; *esp* : AIRBRUSH

air lane *n* : AIRWAY 1

air·lift \'aər-,lift\ *n* : transportation (as of supplies or passengers) by aircraft — **airlift** *vb*

air·line \-,līn\ *n* : a transportation system using airplanes

air·lin·er \'aər-,lī-nər\ *n* : a large passenger airplane operated by an airline

air lock *n* : an airtight chamber separating areas of different pressure

air·mail \'aər-,māl, -,māl\ *n* : the system of transporting mail by airplane; *also* : mail so transported — **airmail** *vb*

air·man \-mən\ *n* **1** : an enlisted man in

the air force in one of the three ranks below sergeant 2 : AVIATOR, PILOT

airman basic *n* : an enlisted man of the lowest rank in the air force

airman first class *n* : an enlisted person in the air force with a rank just below that of sergeant

air mass *n* : a large horizontally homogeneous body of air

air·mo·bile \'aər-ˌmō-bəl, -ˌbēl\ *adj* : of, relating to, or being a military unit whose members are transported to combat areas usu. by helicopter

air·plane \-ˌplān\ *n* : a fixed-wing aircraft heavier than air that is driven by a propeller or jet engine and supported by the reaction of the air against its wings

air·play \-ˌplā\ *n* : the playing of recorded material on the air by a radio station

air pocket *n* : a condition of the atmosphere that causes an airplane to drop suddenly

air police *n* : the military police of an air force

air·port \'aər-ˌpōrt\ *n* : a place maintained for the landing and takeoff of aircraft and for receiving and discharging passengers and cargo

air raid *n* : an attack by armed airplanes on a surface target

air·ship \'aər-ˌship\ *n* : a lighter-than-air aircraft having propulsion and steering systems

air·sick \-ˌsik\ *adj* : affected with motion sickness associated with flying — **air·sick·ness** *n*

air·space \-ˌspās\ *n* : the space above a nation and under its jurisdiction

air·speed \-ˌspēd\ *n* : the speed (as of an airplane) with relation to the air as distinguished from its speed relative to the earth

air·strip \-ˌstrip\ *n* : a runway without normal airport facilities

air·tight \'aər-ˌtīt\ *adj* 1 : so tightly sealed that no air can enter or escape 2 : leaving no opening for attack

air-to-air *adj* : launched from one airplane in flight at another; *also* : involving aircraft in flight

air·wave \'aər-ˌwāv\ *n* : AIR 6 — usu. used in pl.

air·way \-ˌwā\ *n* 1 : a regular route for airplanes 2 : AIRLINE

air·wor·thy \-ˌwər-thē\ *adj* : fit or safe for operation in the air (an ∼ plane) — **air·wor·thi·ness** *n*

airy \'a(ə)r-ē\ *adj* **air·i·er; -est** 1 : LOFTY 2 : lacking in reality : EMPTY 3 : DELICATE 4 : BREEZY

aisle \'īl\ *n* [ME *ile*, fr. MF *aile* wing, fr. L *ala*] 1 : the side of a church nave separated by piers from the nave proper 2 : a passage between sections of seats

ajar \ə-ˈjär\ *adj or adv* : partly open

AK *abbr* Alaska

aka *abbr* also known as

AKC *abbr* American Kennel Club

akim·bo \ə-ˈkim-bō\ *adj or adv* : having the hand on the hip and the elbow turned outward

akin \ə-ˈkin\ *adj* 1 : related by blood 2 : similar in kind

Al *symbol* aluminum

AL *abbr* 1 Alabama 2 American League 3 American Legion

¹**-al** \əl\ *adj suffix* : of, relating to, or characterized by ⟨direction*al*⟩

²**-al** *n suffix* : action : process ⟨rehears*al*⟩

Ala *abbr* Alabama

ALA *abbr* Automobile Legal Association

al·a·bas·ter \'al-ə-ˌbas-tər\ *n* 1 : a compact fine-textured usu. white and translucent gypsum mineral often carved into objects (as vases) 2 : a hard translucent calcite

à la carte \ˌal-ə-ˈkärt, ˌäl-ə-\ *adv or adj* [F] : with a separate price for each item on the menu

alac·ri·ty \ə-ˈlak-rət-ē\ *n* : cheerful readiness : BRISKNESS

à la mode \ˌal-ə-ˈmōd, ˌäl-ə-\ *adj* [F, according to the fashion] 1 : FASHIONABLE, STYLISH 2 : topped with ice cream

¹**alarm** \ə-ˈlärm\ *also* **ala·rum** \ə-ˈlär-əm, -ˈlar-\ *n* [ME *alarme*, fr. MF, fr. *all'arme*, lit., to the weapon] 1 : a warning signal 2 : the terror caused by sudden danger

²**alarm** *also* **alarum** *vb* 1 : to warn of danger 2 : to arouse to a sense of danger : FRIGHTEN

alarm·ist \ə-ˈlär-məst\ *n* : a person who alarms others esp. needlessly

alas \ə-ˈlas\ *interj* — used to express unhappiness, pity, or concern

al·ba·core \'al-bə-ˌkōr\ *n, pl* **-core** *or* **-cores** : any of several tunas

Al·ba·nian \al-ˈbā-nē-ən\ *n* : a native or inhabitant of Albania

al·ba·tross \'al-bə-ˌtrós, -ˌträs\ *n, pl* **-tross** *or* **-tross·es** : a large web-footed seabird related to the petrels

al·be·it \ól-ˈbē-ət, al-\ *conj* : even though : ALTHOUGH

al·bi·no \al-ˈbī-nō\ *n, pl* **-nos** : a person or lower animal lacking coloring matter in the skin, hair, and eyes — **al·bi·nism** \'al-bə-ˌniz-əm\ *n*

al·bum \'al-bəm\ *n* 1 : a book with blank pages used for making a collection (as of stamps) 2 : one or more phonograph records or tape recordings produced as a single unit

al·bu·men \al-ˈbyü-mən\ *n* 1 : the white of an egg 2 : ALBUMIN

al·bu·min \al-ˈbyü-mən\ *n* : any of numerous water-soluble proteins of blood, milk, egg white, and plant and animal tissues

al·bu·min·ous \al-ˈbyü-mə-nəs\ *adj* : containing or resembling albumen or albumin

alc *abbr* alcohol

al·cal·de \al-ˈkäl-dē\ *n* : the chief administrative and judicial officer of a Spanish or Spanish-American town

al·ca·zar \al-'käz-ər, -'kaz-\ n [Sp *alcázar*, fr. Ar *at-qaṣr* the castle] : a Spanish fortress or palace

al·che·my \'al-kə-mē\ n : medieval chemistry chiefly concerned with efforts to turn base metals into gold — **al·che·mist** \'al-kə-məst\ n

al·co·hol \'al-kə-ˌhȯl\ n [NL, fr. ML, powdered antimony, fr. Sp, fr. Ar *al-kuhul* the powdered antimony] 1 : a colorless flammable liquid that is the intoxicating element in fermented and distilled liquors 2 : any of various carbon compounds similar to alcohol 3 : beverages containing alcohol

¹**al·co·hol·ic** \ˌal-kə-'hȯl-ik, -'häl-\ adj 1 : of, relating to, caused by, or containing alcohol 2 : affected with alcoholism — **al·co·hol·i·cal·ly** \-i-k(ə-)lē\ adv

²**alcoholic** n : a person affected with alcoholism

al·co·hol·ism \'al-kə-ˌhȯl-ˌiz-əm\ n : continued excessive and usu. uncontrollable use of alcoholic drinks; *also* : the abnormal state associated with such use

al·cove \'al-ˌkōv\ n 1 : a nook or small recess opening off a larger room 2 : a niche or arched opening (as in a wall)

ald *abbr* alderman

al·der \'ȯl-dər\ n : a tree or shrub related to the birches and growing in wet areas

al·der·man \'ȯl-dər-mən\ n : a member of a city legislative body

ale \'āl\ n : an alcoholic beverage brewed from malt and hops that is usu. more bitter than beer

ale·a·tor·ic \ˌā-lē-ə-'tȯr-ik\ adj : improvised or random in character (∼ music)

ale·a·to·ry \'ā-lē-ə-ˌtōr-ē\ adj : ALEATORIC

alee \ə-'lē\ adv : on or toward the lee

ale·house \'āl-ˌhau̇s\ n : a place where ale is sold to be drunk on the premises

¹**alert** \ə-'lərt\ adj [It *all' erta*, lit., on the ascent] 1 : watchful against danger 2 : quick to perceive and act — **alert·ly** adv — **alert·ness** n

²**alert** n 1 : a signal given to warn of danger 2 : the period during which an alert is in effect

³**alert** vb 1 : WARN 2 : to make aware of

Aleut \ˌal-ē-'üt, ə-'lüt\ n 1 : a member of a people of the Aleutian and Shumagin islands and the western part of Alaska peninsula 2 : the language of the Aleuts

ale·wife \'āl-ˌwīf\ n : a food fish of the herring family abundant esp. on the Atlantic coast

Al·ex·an·dri·an \ˌal-ig-'zan-drē-ən\ adj 1 : of or relating to Alexander the Great 2 : HELLENISTIC

al·ex·an·drine \-'zan-drən\ n, *often cap* : a line of six iambic feet

al·fal·fa \al-'fal-fə\ n : a leguminous plant widely grown for hay and forage

al·fres·co \al-'fres-kō\ adj or adv [It] : taking place in the open air

alg *abbr* algebra

al·ga \'al-gə\ n, pl **al·gae** \'al-(ˌ)jē\ : any of a group of lower plants having chlorophyll but no vascular system and including seaweeds and related freshwater plants — **al·gal** \-gəl\ adj

al·ge·bra \'al-jə-brə\ n [ML, fr. Ar *al-jabr*] : a branch of mathematics using symbols (as letters) to explore the relationships between numbers and the operations used to work with them — **al·ge·bra·ic** \ˌal-jə-'brā-ik\ adj — **al·ge·bra·i·cal·ly** \-'brā-ə-k(ə-)lē\ adv

Al·ge·ri·an \al-'jir-ē-ən\ n : a native or inhabitant of Algeria — **Algerian** adj

AL·GOL or **Al·gol** \'al-ˌgäl, -ˌgȯl\ n [*algo*rithmic *l*anguage] : a language for programming a computer esp. to work scientific problems

Al·gon·qui·an \al-'gän-kwē-ən, -'gän-\ n : a member of an American Indian people of the Ottawa river valley

al·go·rithm \'al-gə-ˌrith-əm\ n : a procedure for solving a problem (as in mathematics)

¹**alias** \'ā-lē-əs, 'āl-yəs\ adv [L, otherwise, fr. *alius* other] : otherwise called

²**alias** n : an assumed or additional name

¹**al·i·bi** \'al-ə-ˌbī\ n [L, elsewhere, fr. *alius* other] 1 : a plea offered by an accused person of not having been at the scene of commission of an offense 2 : an excuse (as for failure)

²**alibi** vb -**bied**; -**bi·ing** 1 : to make an excuse for 2 : to offer an excuse

alien \'ā-lē-ən, 'āl-yən\ adj : FOREIGN

alien n : a foreign-born resident who has not been naturalized

alien·able \'āl-yə-nə-bəl, 'ā-lē-ə-nə-\ adj : transferable to the ownership of another (∼ property)

alien·ate \'ā-lē-ə-ˌnāt, 'āl-yə-\ vb -**at·ed**; -**at·ing** 1 : to transfer (property) to another 2 : to make hostile where previously friendship had existed : ESTRANGE — **alien·ation** \ˌā-lē-ə-'nā-shən, ˌāl-yə-\ n

alien·ist \-nəst\ n : PSYCHIATRIST; *esp* : one specializing in the legal aspects of psychology

¹**alight** \ə-'līt\ vb **alight·ed** also **alit** \ə-'lit\ **alight·ing** 1 : to get down (as from a vehicle) 2 : to come to rest from the air *syn* settle, land, perch

²**alight** adj : lighted up

align also **aline** \ə-'līn\ vb 1 : to bring into line 2 : to array on the side of or against a cause — **align·ment** also **aline·ment** n

¹**alike** \ə-'līk\ adj : LIKE *syn* akin, analogous, similar, comparable

²**alike** adv : EQUALLY

al·i·ment \'al-ə-mənt\ n : FOOD, NUTRIMENT

al·i·men·ta·ry \ˌal-ə-'men-t(ə-)rē\ adj : of, relating to, or functioning in nourishment or nutrition

alimentary canal n : a tube that extends

from the mouth to the anus and functions in the digestion and absorption of food and the elimination of residues

al·i·mo·ny \\'al-ə-ˌmō-nē\\ *n, pl* **-nies** [L *alimonia* sustenance, fr. *alere* to nourish] : an allowance made to one spouse by the other for support pending or after legal separation or divorce

A–line \\'ā-ˌlīn\\ *adj* : having a flared bottom and a close-fitting top ⟨an ∼ skirt⟩

alive \\ə-'līv\\ *adj* 1 : having life : LIVING 2 : being in force or operation 3 : SENSITIVE ⟨∼ to the danger⟩ 4 : ANIMATED ⟨streets ∼ with traffic⟩

al·iz·a·rin \\ə-'liz-ə-rən\\ *n* : an orange or red crystalline compound made synthetically and used as a red dye

alk *abbr* alkaline

al·ka·li \\'al-kə-ˌlī\\ *n, pl* **-lies** *or* **-lis** 1 : a substance (as a hydroxide) that has a bitter taste and neutralizes acids 2 : a mixture of salts in the soil of some dry regions in such amount as to make ordinary farming impossible — **al·ka·line** \\-kə-lən, -ˌlīn\\ *adj* — **al·ka·lin·i·ty** \\ˌal-kə-'lin-ət-ē\\ *n*

al·ka·loid \\'al-kə-ˌlȯid\\ *n* : any of various usu. basic and bitter organic compounds found esp. in seed plants

al·kane \\'al-ˌkān\\ *n* : a hydrocarbon in which each carbon atom is bonded to 4 other atoms

al·kyd \\'al-kəd\\ *n* : any of numerous thermoplastic synthetic resins used esp. for protective coatings

¹all \\'ȯl\\ *adj* 1 : the whole of 2 : the greatest possible 3 : every one of

²all *adv* 1 : WHOLLY 2 : so much ⟨∼ the better for it⟩ 3 : for each side ⟨the score is two ∼⟩

³all *pron* 1 : every one : the whole number, quantity, or amount ⟨∼ of you are welcome⟩ ⟨∼ of the money is gone⟩ 2 : EVERYTHING

Al·lah \\'al-ə, ä-'lä\\ *n* [Ar] : the supreme being of Islam

all–Amer·i·can \\ˌȯl-ə-'mer-ə-kən\\ *adj* 1 : composed wholly of American elements 2 : representative of the U.S. as a whole; *esp* : selected as the best in the U.S. — **all–American** *n*

all–around \\ˌȯl-ə-'raȯnd\\ *adj* : having ability in many fields : VERSATILE

al·lay \\ə-'lā\\ *vb* 1 : to reduce in severity 2 : to put at rest syn alleviate, lighten, relieve, ease, assuage

all clear *n* : a signal that a danger has passed

al·lege \\ə-'lej\\ *vb* **al·leged; al·leg·ing** 1 : to state as a fact without proof 2 : to bring forward as a reason or excuse — **al·le·ga·tion** \\ˌal-i-'gā-shən\\ *n* — **al·leg·ed·ly** \\ə-'lej-əd-lē\\ *adv*

al·le·giance \\ə-'lē-jəns\\ *n* 1 : loyalty owed by a citizen to his government 2 : loyalty to a person or cause

al·le·go·ry \\'al-ə-ˌgȯr-ē\\ *n, pl* **-ries** : the expression through symbolic figures and actions of truths or generalizations about human conduct or experi-

ence — **al·le·gor·i·cal** \\ˌal-ə-'gȯr-i-kəl\\ *adj*

¹al·le·gro \\ə-'leg-rō, -'lā-grō\\ *adv or adj* [It, merry] : in a brisk lively tempo — used as a direction in music

²allegro *n, pl* **-gros** : an allegro movement

al·le·lu·ia \\ˌal-ə-'lü-yə\\ *interj* : HALLELUJAH

al·ler·gen \\'al-ər-jən\\ *n* : something that causes allergy — **al·ler·gen·ic** \\ˌal-ər-'jen-ik\\ *adj*

al·ler·gist \\'al-ər-jəst\\ *n* : a specialist in allergies

al·ler·gy \\'al-ər-jē\\ *n, pl* **-gies** [G *allergie*, fr. Gk *allos* other + *ergon* work] : exaggerated or abnormal reaction (as by sneezing, itching, or rashes) to substances, situations, or physical states harmless to most people — **al·ler·gic** \\ə-'lər-jik\\ *adj*

al·le·vi·ate \\ə-'lē-vē-ˌāt\\ *vb* **-at·ed; -at·ing** : to make easier to be endured syn lighten, mitigate, relieve, allay — **al·le·vi·a·tion** \\ə-ˌlē-vē-'ā-shən\\ *n*

al·ley \\'al-ē\\ *n, pl* **alleys** 1 : a place for bowling; *esp* : a hardwood lane 2 : a narrow street or passageway esp. between buildings

al·ley·way \\'al-ē-ˌwā\\ *n* : ALLEY 2

All·hal·lows \\ȯl-'hal-ōz\\ *n, pl* **Allhallows** : ALL SAINTS' DAY

al·li·ance \\ə-'lī-əns\\ *n* : a union to promote common interests syn league, coalition, confederacy, federation

al·lied \\ə-'līd, 'al-ˌīd\\ *adj* : joined in alliance

al·li·ga·tor \\'al-ə-ˌgāt-ər\\ *n* [Sp *el lagarto* the lizard, fr. L *lacertus* lizard] : either of two large short-legged reptiles resembling crocodiles but having a shorter and broader snout

alligator pear *n* : AVOCADO

al·lit·er·ate \\ə-'lit-ə-ˌrāt\\ *vb* **-at·ed; -at·ing** 1 : to form an alliteration 2 : to arrange so as to make alliteration

al·lit·er·a·tion \\ə-ˌlit-ə-'rā-shən\\ *n* : the repetition of initial sounds in adjacent words or syllables — **al·lit·er·a·tive** \\-'lit-ə-ˌrāt-iv\\ *adj*

al·lo·cate \\'al-ə-ˌkāt\\ *vb* **-cat·ed; -cat·ing** : ALLOT, ASSIGN — **al·lo·ca·tion** \\ˌal-ə-'kā-shən\\ *n*

al·lot \\ə-'lät\\ *vb* **al·lot·ted; al·lot·ting** : to distribute as a share or portion syn assign, apportion, allocate — **al·lot·ment** *n*

all–out \\'ȯl-'aȯt\\ *adj* : using maximum energy or resources ⟨an ∼ offensive⟩

all over *adv* : EVERYWHERE

al·low \\ə-'laȯ\\ *vb* 1 : to assign as a share ⟨∼ time for rest⟩ 2 : to reckon as a deduction 3 : ADMIT, CONCEDE 4 : PERMIT 5 : to make allowance ⟨∼ for expansion⟩ — **al·low·able** *adj*

al·low·ance \\-əns\\ *n* 1 : an allotted share 2 : money given regularly for expenses 3 : the taking into account of mitigating circumstances

al·loy \\'al-ˌȯi, ə-'lȯi\\ *n* 1 : a substance composed of metals fused together 2

: an admixture of something that debases — **al·loy** \ə-ˈlȯi, ˈal-ˌȯi\ vb

all right adj **1** : beyond doubt : CERTAINLY **2** : SATISFACTORILY **3** : YES — **all right** adj

All Saints' Day n : a church feast observed November 1 in honor of all the saints

All Souls' Day n : a day of prayer observed November 2 for the souls of the faithful departed

all·spice \ˈȯl-ˌspīs\ n : the berry of a West Indian tree of the myrtle family; also : the mildly pungent and aromatic spice made from it

¹all-star \ˈȯl-ˌstär\ adj : composed wholly or chiefly of star performers

²all-star \ˈȯl-ˌstär\ n : a member of an all-star team

all told adv : with everything counted

al·lude \ə-ˈlüd\ vb **al·lud·ed; al·lud·ing** [L alludere, lit., to play with] : to refer indirectly or by suggestion — **al·lu·sion** \-ˈlü-zhən\ n — **al·lu·sive** \-ˈlü-siv\ adj — **al·lu·sive·ly** adv — **al·lu·sive·ness** n

al·lure \ə-ˈlu̇r\ vb **al·lured; al·lur·ing** : to entice by charm or attraction — **allure** n — **al·lure·ment** n

al·lu·vi·um \ə-ˈlü-vē-əm\ n, pl **-vi·ums** or **-via** \-vē-ə\ : soil material (as clay or gravel) deposited by running water — **al·lu·vi·al** \-vē-əl\ adj or n

¹al·ly \ə-ˈlī, ˈal-ˌī\ vb **al·lied; al·ly·ing** : to unite in alliance

²al·ly \ˈal-ˌī, ə-ˈlī\ n, pl **allies** : one united with another in an alliance

-al·ly \(ə-)lē\ adv suffix : ²-LY (terrifically)

al·ma ma·ter \ˌal-mə-ˈmät-ər\ n [L, fostering mother] **1** : a school, college, or university that one has attended **2** : the song or hymn of a school, college, or university

al·ma·nac \ˈȯl-mə-ˌnak, ˈal-\ n : a publication containing astronomical and meteorological data and often a miscellany of other information

al·man·dite \ˈal-mən-ˌdīt\ n : a deep red garnet containing iron and aluminum

al·mighty \ȯl-ˈmīt-ē\ adj **1** often cap : having absolute power over all ⟨Almighty God⟩ **2** : relatively unlimited in power

Almighty n : GOD 1

al·mond \ˈäm-ənd, ˈam-; ˈal-mənd\ n : a small tree related to the peach; also : the edible nutlike kernel of its fruit

al·mo·ner \ˈal-mə-nər, ˈäm-ə-\ n : a person who distributes alms

al·most \ˈȯl-ˌmōst, ȯl-ˈmōst\ adv : only a little less than : NEARLY

alms \ˈämz, ˈälmz\ n, pl **alms** [ME almesse, almes, fr. OE ælmesse, ælms, fr. L eleemosyna alms, fr. Gk eleēmosynē pity, alms, fr. eleēmōn merciful] : something given freely to relieve the poor

alms·house \-ˌhau̇s\ n, Brit : a privately financed home for the poor

al·oe \ˈal-ō\ n **1** : any of a large genus of

succulent chiefly southern African plants related to the lilies **2** pl : the dried juice of the leaves of an aloe used as a strong laxative and tonic

aloft \ə-ˈlȯft\ adv **1** : high in the air **2** : on or to the higher rigging of a ship

alo·ha \ä-ˈlō-ə, ä-ˈlō-hä\ interj [Hawaiian] — used to express greeting or farewell

alone \ə-ˈlōn\ adj **1** : separated from others **2** : not including anyone or anything else : ONLY syn lonely, lonesome, lone, solitary — **alone** adv

¹along \ə-ˈlȯŋ\ prep **1** : on or near in a lengthwise direction ⟨walk ~ the street⟩ ⟨sail ~ the coast⟩ **2** : at a point on or during ⟨stopped ~ the way⟩

²along adv **1** : FORWARD, ON **2** : as a companion or associate ⟨bring her ~⟩ **3** : all the time ⟨knew it all ~⟩

along·shore \ə-ˈlȯŋ-ˈshȯr\ adv or adj : along the shore or coast

¹along·side \-ˌsīd\ adv : along or by the side

²alongside prep : side by side with; specif : parallel to

alongside of prep : ALONGSIDE

aloof \ə-ˈlüf\ adj : removed or distant in interest or feeling : reserved — **aloof·ness** n

al·o·pe·cia \ˌal-ə-ˈpē-sh(ē-)ə\ n : BALDNESS

aloud \ə-ˈlau̇d\ adv : using the voice so as to be clearly heard

alp \ˈalp\ n : a high rugged mountain

al·paca \al-ˈpak-ə\ n : a So. American mammal related to the llama; also : its fine long woolly hair or cloth made from this

al·pha·bet \ˈal-fə-ˌbet, -bət\ n : the set of letters used in writing a language arranged in a conventional order

al·pha·bet·i·cal \ˌal-fə-ˈbet-i-kəl\ or **al·pha·bet·ic** \-ˈbet-ik\ adj **1** : arranged in the order of the letters of the alphabet **2** : of or employing an alphabet — **al·pha·bet·i·cal·ly** \-i-k(ə-)lē\ adv

al·pha·bet·ize \ˈal-fə-bə-ˌtīz\ vb **-ized; -iz·ing** : to arrange in alphabetical order — **al·pha·bet·iz·er** n

al·pha·nu·mer·ic \ˌal-fə-n(y)u̇-ˈmer-ik\ adj : consisting of letters and numbers and often other symbols ⟨an ~ code⟩ also : being a character in an alphanumeric system

al·pha particle \ˌal-fə-\ n : a positively charged particle identical with the nucleus of a helium atom that is ejected at high speed in certain radioactive transformations

alpha ray n : a stream of alpha particles

alpha rhythm n : ALPHA WAVE

alpha wave n : an electrical rhythm of the brain often associated with a state of wakeful relaxation

Al·pine \ˈal-ˌpīn\ adj **1** : relating to, located in, or resembling the Alps **2** mountains of south central Europe **2** often not cap : of, relating to, or growing on upland slopes above the highest elevation where trees grow

al·ready \ȯl-'red-ē\ *adv* : prior to a specified or implied time : PREVIOUSLY

al·right \ȯl-'rīt\ *adv* : ALL RIGHT

al·so \'ȯl-sō\ *adv* : in addition : TOO

al·so-ran \-ˌran\ *n* 1 : a horse or dog that finishes out of the money in a race 2 : a contestant that does not win

alt *abbr* 1 alternate 2 altitude

Alta *abbr* Alberta

al·tar \'ȯl-tər\ *n* 1 : a structure on which sacrifices are offered or incense is burned in worship 2 : a table used as a center of ritual

al·tar·piece \'ȯl-tər-ˌpēs\ *n* : a work of art that decorates the space above and behind the altar

¹**al·ter** \'ȯl-tər\ *vb* **al·tered; al·ter·ing** \-t(ə-)riŋ\ 1 : to make or become different 2 : CASTRATE, SPAY — **al·ter·a·tion** \ˌȯl-tə-'rā-shən\ *n*

²**alter** *abbr* alteration

al·ter·ca·tion \ˌȯl-tər-'kā-shən\ *n* : a noisy or angry dispute

al·ter ego \ˌȯl-tər-'ē-gō\ *n* [L, lit., second I] : a second self; *esp* : a trusted friend

¹**al·ter·nate** \'ȯl-tər-ˌnāt, 'al-\ *vb* **-nat·ed; -nat·ing** : to occur or cause to occur by turns — **al·ter·na·tion** \ˌȯl-tər-'nā-shən, ˌal-\ *n*

²**al·ter·nate** \-nət\ *adj* 1 : arranged or succeeding by turns 2 : every other 3 : being an alternative (an ~ route) — **al·ter·nate·ly** *adv*

³**alternate** *n* : SUBSTITUTE

alternating current *n* : an electric current that reverses its direction at regular intervals

al·ter·na·tive \ȯl-'tər-nət-iv, al-\ *adj* : that may be chosen in place of something else — **alternative** *n*

al·ter·na·tor \'ȯl-tər-ˌnāt-ər, 'al-\ *n* : an electric generator for producing alternating current

al·though *also* **al·tho** \ȯl-'thō\ *conj* : in spite of the fact that : even though

al·tim·e·ter \al-'tim-ət-ər, 'al-tə-ˌmēt-ər\ *n* : an instrument for measuring altitude

al·ti·tude \'al-tə-ˌt(y)üd\ *n* 1 : angular distance above the horizon 2 : vertical distance : HEIGHT 3 : the perpendicular distance in a geometric figure from the vertex to the base, from the vertex of an angle to the side opposite, or from the base to a parallel side or face

al·to \'al-tō\ *n, pl* **altos** [It, lit., high, fr. L *altus*] : the lowest female voice; *also* : a singer or instrument having the range of such a voice

al·to·geth·er \ˌȯl-tə-'geth-ər\ *adv* 1 : WHOLLY 2 : on the whole

al·tru·ism \'al-trü-ˌiz-əm\ *n* : unselfish interest in the welfare of others — **al·tru·ist** \-əst\ *n* — **al·tru·is·tic** \ˌal-trü-'is-tik\ *adj* — **al·tru·is·ti·cal·ly** \-ti-k(ə-)lē\ *adv*

al·um \'al-əm\ *n* 1 : either of two colorless crystalline aluminum-containing compounds having a sweetish-sour taste and used esp. as an emetic or as an astringent and styptic 2 : a colorless aluminum salt used in purifying water and in tanning and dyeing

alu·mi·na \ə-'lü-mə-nə\ *n* : the oxide of aluminum occurring in nature as corundum and in bauxite

al·u·min·i·um \ˌal-yə-'min-ē-əm\ *n, chiefly Brit* : ALUMINUM

alu·mi·nize \ə-'lü-mə-ˌnīz\ *vb* **-nized; -niz·ing** : to treat or coat with aluminum

alu·mi·num \ə-'lü-mə-nəm\ *n* : a silver-white malleable ductile light metallic element that is the most abundant metal in the earth's crust

alum·na \ə-'ləm-nə\ *n, pl* **-nae** \-(ˌ)nē\ : a woman graduate or former student of a college or school

alum·nus \ə-'ləm-nəs\ *n, pl* **-ni** \-ˌnī\ [L, foster son, pupil, fr. *alere* to nourish] : a graduate or former student of a college or school

al·ways \'ȯl-wēz, -wəz, -(ˌ)wāz\ *adv* 1 : at all times : INVARIABLY 2 : FOREVER

Alz·hei·mer's disease \'älts-ˌhī-mərz-, 'alz-\ *n* : a degenerative disease of the central nervous system characterized esp. by premature senile mental deterioration

am *pres 1st sing of* BE

¹**Am** *abbr* America; American

²**Am** *symbol* americium

¹**AM** \'ā-ˌem\ *n* : a broadcasting system using amplitude modulation; *also* : a radio receiver for broadcasts made by such a system — **AM** *adj*

²**AM** *abbr* 1 ante meridiem — often not cap. 2 [NL *artium magister*] master of arts

AMA *abbr* American Medical Association

amah \'äm-(ˌ)ä\ *n* : an Oriental female servant; *esp* : a Chinese nurse

amain \ə-'mān\ *adv, archaic* : with full force or speed

amal·gam \ə-'mal-gəm\ *n* 1 : an alloy of mercury with another metal used in making dental cements 2 : a mixture of different elements

amal·gam·ate \ə-'mal-gə-ˌmāt\ *vb* **-at·ed; -at·ing** : to unite into one body or organization — **amal·ga·ma·tion** \-ˌmal-gə-'mā-shən\ *n*

aman·u·en·sis \ə-ˌman-yə-'wen-səs\ *n, pl* **-en·ses** \-ˌsēz\ : one employed to write from dictation or to copy what another has written : SECRETARY

am·a·ranth \'am-ə-ˌranth\ *n* 1 : any of a large genus of coarse herbs sometimes grown for their showy flowers 2 : a flower that never fades

am·a·ran·thine \ˌam-ə-'ran-thən, -ˌthīn\ *adj* : relating to or resembling an amaranth : UNFADING, UNDYING

am·a·ryl·lis \ˌam-ə-'ril-əs\ *n* : any of various plants of a group related to the lilies; *esp* : any of several African herbs having bulbs and grown for their clusters of large showy flowers

amass \ə-'mas\ *vb* : ACCUMULATE

am·a·teur \'am-ə-ˌtər, -ət-ər, -ə-ˌt(y)ùr, -ə-ˌchùr, -ə-chər\ n [F, fr. L *amator* lover, fr. *amare* to love] 1 : a person who engages in a pursuit for pleasure and not as a profession 2 : a person who is not expert — **amateur** *adj*

am·a·teur·ish \ˌam-ə-'tər-ish, -'t(y)ùr-\ *adj* — **am·a·teur·ism** \'am-ə-ˌtər-ˌiz-əm, -ət-ə-ˌriz-, -ə-ˌt(y)ùr-ˌiz-, -ˌchùr-ˌiz-, -chə-ˌriz-\ *n*

am·a·tive \'am-ət-iv\ *adj* : disposed or disposing to love : AMOROUS — **am·a·tive·ly** *adv* — **am·a·tive·ness** *n*

am·a·tory \'am-ə-ˌtōr-ē\ *adj* : of or expressing sexual love

amaze \ə-'māz\ *vb* **amazed; amaz·ing** : to overwhelm with wonder : ASTOUND syn astonish, surprise, dumbfound — **amaze·ment** *n* — **amaz·ing·ly** *adv*

am·a·zon \'am-ə-ˌzän, -ə-zən\ *n* 1 *cap* : a member of a race of female warriors repeatedly warring with the ancient Greeks of mythology 2 : a tall strong masculine woman — **am·a·zo·ni·an** \ˌam-ə-'zō-nē-ən\ *adj, often cap*

amb *abbr* ambassador

am·bas·sa·dor \am-'bas-əd-ər\ *n* : a country's representative in a foreign land — **am·bas·sa·do·ri·al** \ˌbas-ə-'dōr-ē-əl\ *adj* — **am·bas·sa·dor·ship** *n*

am·ber \'am-bər\ *n* : a yellowish or brownish fossil resin used esp. for ornamental objects; *also* : the color of this resin

am·ber·gris \'am-bər-ˌgris, -ˌgrēs\ *n* : a waxy substance from the sperm whale used in making perfumes

am·bi·dex·trous \ˌam-bi-'dek-strəs\ *adj* : using both hands with equal ease — **am·bi·dex·trous·ly** *adv*

am·bi·ence *or* **am·bi·ance** \'am-bē-əns, äⁿ-byäⁿs\ *n* : a surrounding or pervading atmosphere

am·bi·ent \'am-bē-ənt\ *adj* : SURROUNDING

am·big·u·ous \am-'big-yə-wəs\ *adj* : capable of being understood in more than one way — **am·bi·gu·i·ty** \ˌam-bə-'gyü-ət-ē\ *n*

am·bi·tion \am-'bish-ən\ *n* [ME, fr. MF or L; MF, fr. L *ambition- ambitio,* lit., going around, fr. *ambitus*, pp. of *ambire,* fr. *ambi-* around + *ire* to go] : eager desire for success or power

am·bi·tious \am-'bish-əs\ *adj* : characterized by ambition — **am·bi·tious·ly** *adv*

am·biv·a·lence \am-'biv-ə-ləns\ *n* : simultaneous attraction toward and repulsion from a person, object, or action — **am·biv·a·lent** \-lənt\ *adj*

1am·ble \'am-bəl\ *vb* **am·bled; am·bling** \-b(ə-)liŋ\ : to go at an amble

2amble *n* : an easy gait esp. of a horse

am·bro·sia \am-'brō-zh(ē-)ə\ *n* : the food of the Greek and Roman gods — **am·bro·sial** \-zh(ē-)əl\ *adj*

am·bu·lance \'am-byə-ləns\ *n* : a vehicle equipped for carrying the injured or sick

am·bu·lant \'am-byə-lənt\ *adj* : moving about : AMBULATORY

1am·bu·la·to·ry \'am-byə-lə-ˌtōr-ē\ *adj* 1 : of, relating to, or adapted to walking 2 : able to walk about

2ambulatory *n, pl* **-ries** : a sheltered place (as in a cloister) for walking

am·bus·cade \'am-bə-ˌskād\ *n* : AMBUSH

am·bush \'am-ˌbùsh\ *n* : a trap by which concealed persons attack an enemy by surprise — **ambush** *vb*

amdt *abbr* amendment

ame·ba, ame·bic, ame·boid *var of* AMOEBA, AMOEBIC, AMOEBOID

ame·lio·rate \ə-'mēl-yə-ˌrāt\ *vb* **-rat·ed; -rat·ing** : to make or grow better : IMPROVE — **ame·lio·ra·tion** \-ˌmēl-yə-'rā-shən\ *n*

amen \(ˈ)ä-'men, (ˈ)ā-\ *interj* — used esp. at the end of prayers to express solemn ratification or approval

ame·na·ble \ə-'mē-nə-bəl, -'men-ə-\ *adj* 1 : ANSWERABLE 2 : easily managed : TRACTABLE

amend \ə-'mend\ *vb* 1 : to change for the better : IMPROVE 2 : to alter formally in phraseology

amend·ment \ə-'men(d)-mənt\ *n* 1 : correction of faults 2 : the process of amending a parliamentary motion or a constitution; *also* : the alteration so proposed or made

amends \ə-'men(d)z\ *n sing or pl* : compensation for injury or loss

ame·ni·ty \ə-'men-ət-ē, -'mē-nət-\ *n, pl* **-ties** 1 : AGREEABLENESS 2 : something serving to comfort or convenience 3 : a gesture observed in social relationships

Amer *abbr* America; American

amerce \ə-'mərs\ *vb* **amerced; amerc·ing** 1 : to penalize by a fine determined by the court 2 : PUNISH — **amerce·ment** *n*

Amer·i·can \ə-'mer-ə-kən\ *n* 1 : a native or inhabitant of No. or So. America 2 : a citizen of the U.S. — **American** *adj* — **Amer·i·can·ism** \-ə-kə-ˌniz-əm\ *n* — **Amer·i·can·iza·tion** \ə-ˌmer-ə-kə-nə-'zā-shən\ *n* — **Amer·i·can·ize** \ə-'mer-ə-kə-ˌnīz\ *vb*

Amer·i·ca·na \ə-ˌmer-ə-'kan-ə, -'kän-ə\ *n pl* : materials concerning or characteristic of America, its civilization, or its culture; *also* : a collection of these

American Indian *n* : a member of any of the aboriginal peoples of No. and So. America except the Eskimos

American plan *n* : a hotel plan whereby the daily rates cover the cost of room and meals

American Sign Language *n* : a sign language for the deaf in which meaning is conveyed by a system of hand gestures and placement

amer·i·ci·um \ˌam-ə-'ris(h)-ē-əm\ *n* : a radioactive metallic chemical element produced artificially from plutonium

AmerInd *abbr* American Indian

Am·er·in·di·an \ˌam-ə-'rin-dē-ən\ *adj*

: of or relating to American Indians or their culture — **Amerindian** *n*

am·e·thyst \'am-ə-thəst\ *n* [ME *amatiste*, fr. OF & L: OF, fr. L *amethystus*, fr. Gk *amethystos*, lit., remedy against drunkenness, fr. *a-* not + *methyein* to be drunk, fr. *methy* wine] : a gemstone consisting of clear purple or bluish violet quartz

ami·a·ble \'ā-mē-ə-bəl\ *adj* **1** : AGREEABLE **2** : having a friendly and sociable disposition — **ami·a·bil·i·ty** \,ā-mē-ə-'bil-ət-ē\ *n* — **ami·a·bly** \'ā-mē-ə-blē\ *adv*

am·i·ca·ble \'am-i-kə-bəl\ *adj* : FRIENDLY, PEACEABLE — **am·i·ca·bly** \-blē\ *adv*

amid \ə-'mid\ *or* **amidst** \-'midst\ *prep* : in or into the middle of : AMONG

amid·ships \ə-'mid-,ships\ *adv* : in or near the middle of a ship

ami·no acid \ə-,mē-nō-\ *n* : any of numerous nitrogen-containing acids that include some which are used by cells to build proteins

¹amiss \ə-'mis\ *adv* **1** : WRONGLY **2** : ASTRAY **3** : IMPERFECTLY

²amiss *adj* **1** : WRONG **2** : out of place

am·i·ty \'am-ət-ē\ *n, pl* **-ties** : FRIENDSHIP; *esp* : friendly relations between nations

am·me·ter \'am-,ēt-ər\ *n* : an instrument for measuring electric current in amperes

am·mo \'am-ō\ *n* : AMMUNITION

am·mo·nia \ə-'mō-nyə\ *n* [NL, fr. L *sal ammoniacus* sal ammoniac (ammonium chloride), lit., salt of Ammon, fr. Gk *ammōniakos* of Ammon, fr. *Ammōn* Ammon, Amen, an Egyptian god near one of whose temples it was prepared] **1** : a colorless gaseous compound of nitrogen and hydrogen used in refrigeration and in the making of fertilizers and explosives **2** : a solution (**ammonia water**) of ammonia in water

am·mo·ni·um \ə-'mō-nē-əm\ *n* : an ion or chemical group derived from ammonia by combination with hydrogen

ammonium chloride *n* : a white crystalline volatile salt used in batteries and as an expectorant

am·mu·ni·tion \,am-yə-'nish-ən\ *n* **1** : projectiles fired from guns **2** : explosive items used in war **3** : material for use in attack or defense

Amn *abbr* airman

am·ne·sia \am-'nē-zhə\ *n* : abnormal loss of memory — **am·ne·si·ac** \-z(h)ē-,ak\ *or* **am·ne·sic** \-zik, -sik\ *adj or n*

am·nes·ty \'am-nə-stē\ *n, pl* **-ties** : an act granting a pardon to a group of individuals — **amnesty** *vb*

am·nio·cen·te·sis \,am-nē-ō-,sen-'tē-səs\ *n, pl* **-te·ses** \-'tē-,sēz\ : the surgical insertion of a hollow needle through the abdominal wall and uterus of a pregnant female esp. to obtain fluid used to check for chromosomal abnormality and to determine sex

amoe·ba \ə-'mē-bə\ *n, pl* **-bas** *or* **-bae** \-(,)bē\ : any of various tiny one-celled protozoans that lack permanent cell organs and occur esp. in water and soil — **amoe·bic** \-bik\ *adj*

amoe·boid \-,bȯid\ *adj* : resembling an amoeba esp. in moving or readily changing shape

amok \ə-'mək, -'mäk\ *or* **amuck** \-'mək\ *adv* : in a violently excited state (run ~)

among \ə-'məŋ\ *also* **amongst** \-'məŋst\ *prep* **1** : in or through the midst of **2** : in the number or class of **3** : in shares to each of **4** : by common action of

amon·til·la·do \ə-,män-tə-'läd-ō\ *n, pl* **-dos** [Sp] : a medium dry sherry

amor·al \ā-'mȯr-əl\ *adj* : neither moral nor immoral; *esp* : being outside the sphere to which moral judgments apply — **amor·al·ly** *adv*

am·o·rous \'am-(ə-)rəs\ *adj* **1** : inclined to love **2** : being in love — **am·o·rous·ly** *adv* — **am·o·rous·ness** *n*

amor·phous \ə-'mȯr-fəs\ *adj* **1** : SHAPELESS, FORMLESS **2** : not crystallized

am·or·tize \'am-ər-,tīz, ə-'mȯr-\ *vb* **-tized; -tiz·ing** : to extinguish (as a mortgage) usu. by payment on the principal at the time of each periodic interest payment — **amor·ti·za·tion** \,am-ərt-ə-'zā-shən, ə-,mȯrt-\ *n*

Amos \'ā-məs\ — see BIBLE table

¹amount \ə-'maȯnt\ *vb* **1** : to reach as a total **2** : to be equivalent

²amount *n* **1** : the total number or quantity **2** : a principal sum plus the interest on it

amour \ə-'mȯr, ä-, a-\ *n* : a love affair esp. when illicit

amour pro·pre \,am-,ȯr-'prȯpr², ,äm-,ȯr-'prȯpr²\ *n* [F] : SELF-ESTEEM

¹amp \'amp\ *n* : AMPLIFIER; *also* : a unit consisting of an electronic amplifier and a loudspeaker

²amp *abbr* ampere

am·per·age \'am-p(ə-)rij\ *n* : the strength of a current of electricity expressed in amperes

am·pere \'am-,piər\ *n* : a unit of electric current equivalent to a steady current produced by one volt applied across a resistance of one ohm

am·per·sand \'am-pər-,sand\ *n* [fr. *and per se and*, spoken form of the phrase *& per se and*, lit., (the character) *&* by itself (stands for the word) *and*] : a character & used for the word *and*

am·phet·amine \am-'fet-ə-,mēn, -mən\ *n* : a compound or one of its derivatives used esp. as a stimulant of the nervous system

am·phib·i·an \am-'fib-ē-ən\ *n* **1** : an amphibious organism; *esp* : any of a class of animals (as frogs and newts) intermediate between fishes and reptiles **2** : a vehicle designed to operate on both land and water

am·phib·i·ous \am-ˈfib-ē-əs\ *adj* [Gk *amphibios*, lit., living a double life, fr. *amphi-* on both sides + *bios* mode of *life*] 1 : able to live both on land and in water 2 : adapted for both land and water 3 : made by joint action of land, sea, and air forces invading from the sea; *also* : trained for such action

am·phi·bole \ˈam-fə-ˌbōl\ *n* : any of a group of rock-forming minerals containing calcium, magnesium, iron, aluminum, and sodium combined with silica

am·phi·the·ater \ˈam-fə-ˌthē-ət-ər\ *n* : an oval or circular structure with rising tiers of seats around an arena

am·pho·ra \ˈam-fə-rə\ *n, pl* **-rae** \-ˌrē\ *or* **-ras** : an ancient Greek jar or vase with two handles that rise almost to the level of the mouth

am·ple \ˈam-pəl\ *adj* **am·pler** \-plər\ **am·plest** \-pləst\ 1 : LARGE, CAPACIOUS 2 : enough to satisfy : ABUNDANT — **am·ply** \-plē\ *adv*

am·pli·fy \ˈam-plə-ˌfī\ *vb* **-fied; -fy·ing** 1 : to expand by extended treatment 2 : to increase (voltage, current, or power) in magnitude or strength 3 : to make louder — **am·pli·fi·ca·tion** \ˌam-plə-fə-ˈkā-shən\ *n* — **am·pli·fi·er** \ˈam-plə-ˌfī(-ə)r\ *n*

am·pli·tude \-ˌt(y)üd\ *n* 1 : ample extent : FULLNESS 2 : the extent of a vibratory movement (as of a pendulum) or of an oscillation (as of an alternating current or a radio wave)

amplitude modulation *n* 1 : modulation of the amplitude of a radio carrier wave in accordance with the strength of the signal 2 : a broadcasting system using amplitude modulation

am·poule *or* **am·pule** *also* **am·pul** \ˈam-ˌpyül, -ˌpül\ *n* : a small sealed bulbous glass vessel used to hold a solution for hypodermic injection

am·pu·tate \ˈam-pyə-ˌtāt\ *vb* **-tat·ed; -tat·ing** : to cut off (~ a leg) — **am·pu·ta·tion** \ˌam-pyə-ˈtā-shən\ *n*

am·pu·tee \ˌam-pyə-ˈtē\ *n* : one who has had a limb amputated

amt *abbr* amount

amuck \ə-ˈmək\ *var of* AMOK

am·u·let \ˈam-yə-lət\ *n* : an ornament worn as a charm against evil

amuse \ə-ˈmyüz\ *vb* **amused; amus·ing** : to entertain in a light or playful manner : DIVERT — **amuse·ment** *n*

AMVETS \ˈam-ˌvets\ *abbr* American Veterans (of World War II)

am·y·lase \ˈam-ə-ˌlās, -ˌlāz\ *n* : any of several enzymes that accelerate the breakdown of starch and glycogen

an \ən, (ˈ)an\ *indefinite article* : A — used before words beginning with a vowel sound

¹**-an** \ən\ *or* **-ian** \(ē-)ən\ *also* **-ean** \(ē-)ən, ˈē-ən\ *n suffix* 1 : one that belongs to ⟨American⟩ ⟨Bostonian⟩ ⟨crustacean⟩ 2 : one skilled in or specializing in ⟨phonetician⟩

²**-an** *or* **-ian** *also* **-ean** *adj suffix* 1 : of or

belonging to ⟨American⟩ ⟨Floridian⟩ 2 : characteristic of : resembling ⟨Mozartean⟩

AN *abbr* airman (Navy)

an·a·bol·ic steroid \ˌan-ə-ˈbäl-ik-\ *n* : any of a group of synthetic hormones sometimes taken by athletes in training to increase temporarily the size of their muscles

anach·ro·nism \ə-ˈnak-rə-ˌniz-əm\ *n* 1 : the error of placing a person or thing in the wrong period 2 : one that is chronologically out of place — **anach·ro·nis·tic** \ə-ˌnak-rə-ˈnis-tik\ *adj*

an·a·con·da \ˌan-ə-ˈkän-də\ *n* : a large So. American snake that suffocates and kills its prey by constriction

an·a·dem \ˈan-ə-ˌdem\ *n, archaic* : GARLAND, CHAPLET

anae·mia, anae·mic *var of* ANEMIA, ANEMIC

an·aer·obe \ˈan-ə-ˌrōb\ *n* : an anaerobic organism

an·aer·o·bic \ˌan-ə-ˈrō-bik\ *adj* : living, active, or occurring in the absence of free oxygen

an·aes·the·sia, an·aes·thet·ic *var of* ANESTHESIA, ANESTHETIC

ana·gram \ˈan-ə-ˌgram\ *n* : a word or phrase made by transposing the letters of another word or phrase

¹**anal** \ˈān-ᵊl\ *adj* 1 : of, relating to, or situated near the anus 2 : of, relating to, or characterized by the stage of psychosexual development in psychoanalytic theory during which one is concerned esp. with feces 3 : of, relating to, or characterized by personality traits (as parsimony and ill humor) considered typical of fixation at the anal stage of development

²**anal** *abbr* 1 analogy 2 analysis; analytic

an·al·ge·sia \ˌan-ᵊl-ˈjē-zhə\ *n* : insensibility to pain — **an·al·ge·sic** \-ˈjē-zik, -sik\ *adj*

an·al·ge·sic \-ˈjē-zik, -sik\ *n* : an agent for producing analgesia

analog computer \ˌan-ᵊl-ˌóg-, -ˌäg-\ *n* : a computer that operates with numbers represented by directly measurable quantities (as voltages)

anal·o·gous \ə-ˈnal-ə-gəs\ *adj* : similar in one or more respects but not homologous

an·a·logue *or* **an·a·log** \ˈan-ᵊl-ˌóg, -ˌag\ *n* 1 : something that is analogous or similar to something else 2 : an organ similar in function to one of another animal or plant but different in structure or origin

anal·o·gy \ə-ˈnal-ə-jē\ *n, pl* **-gies** 1 : inference that if two or more things agree in some respects they will probably agree in others 2 : a likeness in one or more ways between things otherwise unlike — **an·a·log·i·cal** \ˌan-ᵊl-ˈäj-i-kəl\ *adj* — **an·a·log·i·cal·ly** \-i-k(ə-)lē\ *adv*

anal·y·sis \ə-ˈnal-ə-səs\ *n, pl* **-y·ses** \-ˌsēz\ [NL, fr. Gk, fr. *analyein* to break up, fr. *ana-* up + *lyein* to loosen] 1 : separation of a thing into the parts or elements of which it is composed 2 : an examination of a thing to determine its parts or elements; *also* : a statement showing the results of such an examination 3 : PSYCHOANALYSIS — **an·a·lyst** \'an-əl-əst\ *n* — **an·a·lyt·ic** \ˌan-əl-'it-ik\ *or* **an·a·lyt·i·cal** \-i-kəl\ *adj*

an·a·lyze \'an-əl-ˌīz\ *vb* **-lyzed; -lyz·ing** : to make an analysis of

an·a·pest \'an-ə-ˌpest\ *n* : a metrical foot of two unaccented syllables followed by one accented syllable — **an·a·pes·tic** \ˌan-ə-'pes-tik\ *adj or n*

an·ar·chism \'an-ər-ˌkiz-əm\ *n* : the theory that all government is undesirable — **an·ar·chist** \-kəst\ *n or adj* — **an·ar·chis·tic** \ˌan-ər-'kis-tik\ *adj*

an·ar·chy \'an-ər-kē\ *n* 1 : a social structure without government or law and order 2 : utter confusion — **an·ar·chic** \a-'när-kik\ *adj*

anas·to·mo·sis \ə-ˌnas-tə-'mō-səs\ *n, pl* **-mo·ses** \-ˌsēz\ 1 : the union of parts or branches (as of blood vessels) 2 : NETWORK

anat *abbr* anatomical; anatomy

anath·e·ma \ə-'nath-ə-mə\ *n* 1 : a solemn curse 2 : a person or thing accursed; *also* : one intensely disliked

anath·e·ma·tize \-ˌtīz\ *vb* **-tized; -tiz·ing** : to pronounce an anathema against : CURSE

anat·o·mize \ə-'nat-ə-ˌmīz\ *vb* **-mized; -miz·ing** : to dissect so as to examine the structure and parts; *also* : ANALYZE

anat·o·my \ə-'nat-ə-mē\ *n, pl* **-mies** [LL *anatomia* dissection, fr. Gk *anatomē*, fr. *anatemnein* to dissect, fr. *ana-* up + *temnein* to cut] 1 : a branch of science dealing with the structure of organisms 2 : structural makeup esp. of an organism or any of its parts 3 : a separating into parts for detailed study : ANALYSIS, ANATOMIZING — **an·a·tom·ic** \ˌan-ə-'täm-ik\ *or* **an·a·tom·i·cal** \-i-kəl\ *adj* — **an·a·tom·i·cal·ly** \-i-k(ə-)lē\ *adv* — **anat·o·mist** \ə-'nat-ə-məst\ *n*

anc *abbr* ancient

-ance \əns\ *n suffix* 1 : action or process (further*ance*) : instance of an action or process (perform*ance*) 2 : quality or state : instance of a quality or state (protuber*ance*) 3 : amount or degree (conduct*ance*)

an·ces·tor \'an-ˌses-tər\ *n* [ME *ancestre*, fr. OF, fr. L *antecessor* one that goes before, fr. *antecedere* to go before, fr. *ante-* before + *cedere* to go] : one from whom an individual is descended

an·ces·tress \'an-ˌses-trəs\ *n* : a female ancestor

an·ces·try \'an-ˌses-trē\ *n* 1 : line of descent : LINEAGE 2 : ANCESTORS — **an·ces·tral** \an-'ses-trəl\ *adj*

¹**an·chor** \'aŋ-kər\ *n* 1 : a heavy metal device attached to a ship that catches hold of the bottom and holds the ship in place 2 : ANCHORPERSON

²**anchor** *vb* **an·chored; an·chor·ing** \-k(ə-)riŋ\ : to hold or become held in place by or as if by an anchor

an·chor·age \'aŋ-k(ə-)rij\ *n* : a place suitable for ships to anchor

an·cho·rite \'aŋ-kə-ˌrīt\ *n* : HERMIT

an·chor·man \'aŋ-kər-ˌman\ *n* 1 : the member of a team who competes last 2 : an anchorperson who is a man

an·chor·per·son \-ˌpər-sən\ *n* : a broadcaster who reads the news and introduces the reports of other broadcasters

an·chor·wom·an \-ˌwùm-ən\ *n* 1 : a woman who competes last 2 : an anchorperson who is a woman

an·cho·vy \'an-ˌchō-vē, an-'chō-\ *n, pl* **-vies** *or* **-vy** : a small herringlike fish used esp. for sauces and relishes

an·cien ré·gime \äⁿs-yaⁿ-rā-zhēm\ *n* 1 : the political and social system of France before the Revolution of 1789 2 : a system no longer prevailing

¹**an·cient** \'ān-shənt\ *adj* 1 : having existed for many years 2 : belonging to times long past; *esp* : belonging to the period before the Middle Ages

²**ancient** *n* 1 : an aged person 2 *pl* : the peoples of ancient Greece and Rome

an·cil·lary \'an-sə-ˌler-ē\ *adj* 1 : SUBORDINATE, SUBSIDIARY 2 : AUXILIARY, SUPPLEMENTARY

-ancy \ən-sē\ *n suffix* : quality or state (flamboy*ancy*)

and \ən(d), (')and\ *conj* — used to indicate connection or addition esp. of items within the same class or type or to join words or phrases of the same grammatical rank or function

¹**an·dan·te** \än-'dän-ˌtā, -'dänt-ē\ *adv or adj* [It, lit., going, prp. of *andare* to go] : moderately slow — used as a direction in music

²**andante** *n* : an andante movement

and·iron \'an-ˌdī(-ə)rn\ *n* : one of a pair of metal supports for firewood in a fireplace

and/or \'an-'dòr\ *conj* — used to indicate that either *and* or *or* may apply ⟨men ~ women means men *and* women or men *or* women⟩

an·dro·gen \'an-drə-jən\ *n* : a male sex hormone

an·droid \'an-ˌdròid\ *n* : an automaton with human form

an·ec·dote \'an-ik-ˌdōt\ *n* [F, fr. Gk *anekdota* unpublished items, fr. *a-* not + *ekdidonai* to publish] : a brief story of an interesting usu. biographical incident — **an·ec·dot·al** \ˌan-ik-'dōt-ᵊl\ *adj*

ane·mia \ə-'nē-mē-ə\ *n* 1 : a condition in which blood is deficient in quantity, in red blood cells, or in hemoglobin and which is marked by pallor, weakness, and irregular heart action 2 : lack of vitality — **ane·mic** \ə-'nē-mik\ *adj*

an·e·mom·e·ter \ˌan-ə-'mäm-ət-ər\ *n*

: an instrument for measuring the force or speed of the wind

anem·o·ne \ə-'nem-ə-nē\ *n* : any of a large genus of herbs related to the buttercups that have showy flowers without petals but with conspicuous often colored sepals

anent \ə-'nent\ *prep* : ABOUT, CONCERNING

an·es·the·sia \‚an-əs-'thē-zhə\ *n* : loss of bodily sensation

an·es·the·si·ol·o·gy \-‚thē-zē-'äl-ə-jē\ *n* : a branch of medical science dealing with anesthesia and anesthetics — **an·es·the·si·ol·o·gist** \-jəst\ *n*

¹**an·es·thet·ic** \‚an-əs-'thet-ik\ *adj* : of, relating to, or capable of producing anesthesia

²**anesthetic** *n* : an agent that produces anesthesia — **anes·the·tist** \ə-'nes-thət-əst\ *n* — **anes·the·tize** \-thə-‚tīz\ *vb*

anew \ə-'n(y)ü\ *adv* : over again : from a new start

an·gel \'ān-jəl\ *n* [ME, fr. OF *angele*, fr. L *angelus*, fr. Gk *angelos*, lit., messenger] 1 : a spiritual being superior to man 2 : an attendant spirit (guardian ~) 3 : a winged figure of human form in art 4 : MESSENGER, HARBINGER 5 : a person held to resemble an angel 6 : a financial backer — **an·gel·ic** \an-'jel-ik\ *or* **an·gel·i·cal** \-i-kəl\ *adj* — **an·gel·i·cal·ly** \-i-k(ə-)lē\ *adv*

an·gel·fish \'ān-jəl-‚fish\ *n* : any of several bright-colored tropical fishes that are flattened from side to side

an·gel·i·ca \an-'jel-i-kə\ *n* : a biennial herb related to the carrot whose roots and fruit furnish a flavoring oil

an·ger \'aŋ-gər\ *n* [ME, affliction, anger, fr. ON *angr* grief] : a strong feeling of displeasure *syn* wrath, ire, rage, fury, indignation

²**anger** *vb* **an·gered; an·ger·ing** \-g(ə-)riŋ\ : to make angry

an·gi·na \an-'jī-nə\ *n* [L, quinsy] : a disorder (as of the heart) marked by attacks of intense pain; *esp* : ANGINA PECTORIS — **an·gi·nal** \an-'jīn-ᵊl\ *adj*

angina pec·to·ris \-'pek-t(ə-)rəs\ *n* : a heart disease marked by brief attacks of sharp chest pain caused by deficient oxygenation of heart muscles

an·gio·sperm \'an-jē-ə-‚spərm\ *n* : any of a class of vascular plants (as orchids or roses) having the seeds in a closed ovary

¹**an·gle** \'aŋ-gəl\ *n* 1 : a sharp projecting corner 2 : the figure formed by the meeting of two lines in a point 3 : a point of view 4 : a special technique or plan : GIMMICK

²**angle** *vb* **an·gled; an·gling** \-g(ə-)liŋ\ : to turn, move, or direct at an angle

³**angle** *vb* **an·gled; an·gling** \-g(ə-)liŋ\ : to fish with a hook and line — **an·gler** \-glər\ *n* — **an·gling** \-gliŋ\ *n*

an·gle·worm \'aŋ-gəl-‚wərm\ *n* : EARTHWORM

An·gli·can \'aŋ-gli-kən\ *adj* 1 : of or re-

lating to the established episcopal Church of England 2 : of or relating to England or the English nation — **Anglican** *n* — **An·gli·can·ism** \-kə-‚niz-əm\ *n*

an·gli·cize \'aŋ-glə-‚sīz\ *vb* **-cized; -cizing** *often cap* 1 : to make English (as in habits, speech, character, or outlook) 2 : to borrow (a foreign word or phrase) into English without changing form or spelling and sometimes without changing pronunciation — **an·gli·ci·za·tion** \‚aŋ-glə-sə-'zā-shən\ *n, often cap*

An·glo \'aŋ-glō\ *n, pl* **Anglos** : a non-Latin Caucasian inhabitant of the U.S.

An·glo-French \‚aŋ-glō-'french\ *n* : the French language used in medieval England

An·glo·phile \'aŋ-glə-‚fīl\ *also* **An·glo·phil** \-‚fil\ *n* : one who greatly admires England and things English

An·glo·phobe \'aŋ-glə-‚fōb\ *n* : one who is averse to England and things English

An·glo-Sax·on \‚aŋ-glō-'sak-sən\ *n* 1 : a member of any of the Germanic peoples who invaded England in the 5th century A.D. 2 : a member of the English people 3 : Old English — **Anglo-Saxon** *adj*

an·go·ra \aŋ-'gōr-ə, an-\ *n* 1 : yarn or cloth made from the hair of an Angora goat or rabbit 2 *cap* : any of a breed of cats, goats, or rabbits with a long silky coat

an·gry \'aŋ-grē\ *adj* **an·gri·er; -est** : feeling or showing anger *syn* enraged, wrathful, irate, indignant, mad — **an·gri·ly** \-grə-lē\ *adv*

angst \'äŋst\ *n* [G] : a feeling of anxiety

ang·strom \'aŋ-strəm\ *n* : a unit of length equal to one ten-billionth of a meter

an·guish \'aŋ-gwish\ *n* : extreme pain or distress esp. of mind — **an·guished** \-gwisht\ *adj*

an·gu·lar \'aŋ-gyə-lər\ *adj* 1 : having one or more angles 2 : sharp-cornered 3 : being thin and bony — **an·gu·lar·i·ty** \‚aŋ-gyə-'lar-ət-ē\ *n*

An·gus \'aŋ-gəs\ *n* : any of a breed of usu. black hornless beef cattle originating in Scotland

an·hy·drous \an-'hī-drəs\ *adj* : free from water

an·i·line \'an-ᵊl-ən\ *n* : an oily poisonous liquid used in making dyes, medicines, and explosives

an·i·mad·vert \‚an-ə-‚mad-'vərt\ *vb* : to remark critically : express censure — **an·i·mad·ver·sion** \-'vər-zhən\ *n*

¹**an·i·mal** \'an-ə-məl\ *n* 1 : any of a kingdom of living things typically differing from plants in capacity for active movement, in rapid response to stimulation, and in lack of cellulose cell walls 2 : a lower animal as distinguished from man; *also* : MAMMAL

²**animal** *adj* 1 : of, relating to, or derived

from animals **2** : of or relating to the physical as distinguished from the mental or spiritual *syn* carnal, fleshly, sensual

an·i·mal·cule \ˌan-ə-ˈmal-kyül\ *n* : a tiny animal usu. invisible to the naked eye

¹an·i·mate \ˈan-ə-mət\ *adj* : having life

²an·i·mate \ˌmāt\ *vb* **-mat·ed; -mat·ing 1** : to impart life to **2** : to give spirit and vigor to **3** : to make appear to move ⟨∼ a cartoon for motion pictures⟩ — **an·i·mat·ed** *adj*

an·i·ma·tion \ˌan-ə-ˈmā-shən\ *n* **1** : LIVELINESS, VIVACITY **2** : a motion picture made from a series of drawings simulating motions by means of slight progressive changes

an·i·mism \ˈan-ə-ˌmiz-əm\ *n* : attribution of conscious life to nature as a whole or to inanimate objects — **an·i·mist** \ˌməst\ *n* — **an·i·mis·tic** \ˌan-ə-ˈmis-tik\ *adj*

an·i·mos·i·ty \ˌan-ə-ˈmäs-ət-ē\ *n, pl* **-ties** : ILL WILL, RESENTMENT

an·i·mus \ˈan-ə-məs\ *n* : deep-seated resentment and hostility

an·ion \ˈan-ˌī-ən, -ˌī-ˌän\ *n* : a negatively charged ion

an·ise \ˈan-əs\ *n* : an herb related to the carrot with aromatic seeds (**aniseed** \ˌ(ə(s)-ˌsēd\) used in flavoring

an·is·ette \ˌan-ə-ˈset, -ˈzet\ *n* [F] : a usu. colorless sweet liqueur flavored with aniseed

ankh \ˈaŋk\ *n* : a cross having a loop for its upper vertical arm and serving esp. in ancient Egypt as an emblem of life

an·kle \ˈaŋ-kəl\ *n* : the joint or region between the foot and the leg

an·kle·bone \ˌan-kəl-ˈbōn, ˈaŋ-kəl-ˌbōn\ *n* : the bone that in human beings bears the weight of the body and with the tibia and fibula forms the ankle joint

an·klet \ˈaŋ-klət\ *n* **1** : something (as an ornament) worn around the ankle **2** : a short sock reaching slightly above the ankle

ann *abbr* **1** annals **2** annual

an·nals \ˈan-ᵊlz\ *n pl* **1** : a record of events in chronological order **2** : historical records — **an·nal·ist** \ᵊl-əst\ *n*

an·neal \ə-ˈnēl\ *vb* : to make (as glass or steel) less brittle by heating and then cooling

¹an·nex \ə-ˈneks, ˈan-ˌeks\ *vb* **1** : to attach as an addition **2** : to incorporate (as a territory) within a political domain — **an·nex·a·tion** \ˌan-ˌek-ˈsā-shən\ *n*

²an·nex \ˈan-ˌeks, -iks\ *n* : a subsidiary or supplementary structure

an·ni·hi·late \ə-ˈnī-ə-ˌlāt\ *vb* **-lat·ed; -lat·ing** : to destroy completely — **an·ni·hi·la·tion** \ˌnī-ə-ˈlā-shən\ *n*

an·ni·ver·sa·ry \ˌan-ə-ˈvərs-(ə-)rē\ *n, pl* **-ries** : the annual return of the date of some notable event and esp. a wedding

an·no Do·mi·ni \ˌan-ō-ˈdäm-ə-nē, -ˈdō-**

mə-, -ˌnī\ *adv, often cap A* [ML, in the year of the Lord] — used to indicate that a time division falls within the Christian era

an·no·tate \ˈan-ə-ˌtāt\ *vb* **-tat·ed; -tat·ing** : to furnish with notes — **an·no·ta·tion** \ˌan-ə-ˈtā-shən\ *n* — **an·no·ta·tor** \ˈan-ə-ˌtāt-ər\ *n*

an·nounce \ə-ˈnauns\ *vb* **-nounced; -nounc·ing 1** : to make known publicly **2** : to give notice of the arrival or presence of — **an·nounce·ment** *n*

an·nounc·er \ə-ˈnaun-sər\ *n* : a person who introduces radio or television programs, reads commercials and news summaries, and gives station identification

an·noy \ə-ˈnói\ *vb* : to disturb or irritate esp. by repeated acts : VEX *syn* irk, bother, pester, tease, harass — **an·noy·ing·ly** \-ˈnói-iŋ-lē\ *adv*

an·noy·ance \ə-ˈnói-əns\ *n* **1** : the act of annoying **2** : the state of being annoyed **3** : NUISANCE

¹an·nu·al \ˈan-yə(-wə)l\ *adj* **1** : covering the period of a year **2** : occurring once a year : YEARLY **3** : completing the life cycle in one growing season ⟨∼ plants⟩ — **an·nu·al·ly** \-ē\ *adv*

²annual *n* **1** : a publication appearing once a year **2** : an annual plant

annual ring *n* : the layer of wood produced by a single year's growth of a woody plant

an·nu·i·tant \ə-ˈn(y)ü-ət-ənt\ *n* : a beneficiary of an annuity

an·nu·i·ty \ə-ˈn(y)ü-ət-ē\ *n, pl* **-i·ties** : an amount payable annually; *also* : the right to receive such a payment

an·nul \ə-ˈnəl\ *vb* **an·nulled; an·nul·ling** : to make legally void — **an·nul·ment** *n*

an·nu·lar \ˈan-yə-lər\ *adj* : ring-shaped

annular eclipse *n* : an eclipse in which a thin outer ring of the sun's disk is not covered by the moon's disk

an·nun·ci·ate \ə-ˈnən-sē-ˌāt\ *vb* **-at·ed; -at·ing** : ANNOUNCE

an·nun·ci·a·tion \ə-ˌnən-sē-ˈā-shən\ *n* **1** : ANNOUNCEMENT **2** *cap* : March 25 observed as a church festival commemorating the announcement of the Incarnation

an·nun·ci·a·tor \ə-ˈnən-sē-ˌāt-ər\ *n* : one that annunciates; *specif* : a usu. electrically controlled signal board or indicator

an·ode \ˈan-ˌōd\ *n* **1** : the positive electrode of an electrolytic cell **2** : the negative terminal of a battery **3** : the electron-collecting electrode of an electron tube — **an·od·ic** \a-ˈnäd-ik\ *or* **an·od·al** \-ˈnōd-ᵊl\ *adj*

an·od·ize \ˈan-ə-ˌdīz\ *vb* **-ized; -iz·ing** : to subject (a metal) to electrolytic action as the anode of a cell in order to coat with a protective or decorative film

an·o·dyne \ˈan-ə-ˌdīn\ *n* : something that relieves pain : a soothing agent

anoint \ə-ˈnóint\ *vb* **1** : to apply oil to

esp. as a sacred rite 2 : CONSECRATE — **anoint·ment** n

anom·a·lous \ə-¹näm-ə-ləs\ adj : deviating from a general rule : ABNORMAL

anom·a·ly \ə-¹näm-ə-lē\ n, pl **-lies** : something anomalous : IRREGULARITY

¹**anon** \ə-¹nän\ adv, archaic : SOON

²**anon** abbr anonymous; anonymously

anon·y·mous \ə-¹nän-ə-məs\ adj : of unknown or undeclared origin or authorship — **an·o·nym·i·ty** \ʌan-ə-¹nim-ət-ē\ n — anon·y·mous·ly \ə-¹nän-ə-məs-lē\ adv

anoph·e·les \ə-¹näf-ə-ʌlēz\ n [NL, genus name, fr. Gk anōphelēs useless, fr. a- not + ophelos advantage, help] : any of a genus of mosquitoes that includes all mosquitoes which transmit malaria to human beings

an·o·rec·tic \ʌan-ə-¹rek-tik\ also **an·o·ret·ic** \-¹ret-ik\ adj : ANOREXIC — anorectic n

an·o·rex·ia \ʌan-ə-¹rek-sē-ə\ n : loss of appetite esp. when prolonged

an·orex·ia ner·vo·sa \-ʌnər-¹vō-sə\ n : a psychological and endocrine disorder primarily of young women marked esp. by faulty eating patterns, malnutrition, and usu. excessive weight loss

an·o·rex·ic \ʌan-ə-¹rek-sik\ adj 1 : lacking or causing loss of appetite 2 : affected with or as if with anorexia nervosa — anorexic n

¹**an·oth·er** \ə-¹nəth-ər\ adj 1 : some other 2 : being one in addition : one more

²**another** pron 1 : an additional one : one more 2 : one that is different from the first or present one

ans abbr answer

¹**an·swer** \¹an-sər\ n 1 : something spoken or written in reply to a question 2 : a solution of a problem

²**answer** vb an·swered; an·swer·ing \¹ans-(ə-)riŋ\ 1 : to speak or write in reply to 2 : to be responsible 3 : to be adequate — answer·er n

an·swer·able \¹ans-(ə-)rə-bəl\ adj 1 : subject to taking blame or responsibility 2 : capable of being refuted

answering service n : a commercial service that answers telephone calls for its clients

¹**ant** \¹ant\ n : any of a family of small social insects related to the bees and living in communities usu. in earth or wood

²**ant** abbr antonym

Ant abbr Antarctica

ant- — see ANTI-

¹**-ant** \ənt\ n suffix 1 : one that performs or promotes (a specified action) (coolant) 2 : thing that is acted upon (in a specified manner) (inhalant)

²**-ant** adj suffix 1 : performing (a specified action) or being (in a specified condition) (propellant) 2 : promoting (a specified action or process) (expectorant)

ant·ac·id \ʌant-¹as-əd\ n : an agent that counteracts acidity — **antacid** adj

an·tag·o·nism \an-¹tag-ə-ʌniz-əm\ n 1 : active opposition or hostility 2 : opposition in physiological action — **an·tag·o·nis·tic** \-ʌtag-ə-¹nis-tik\ adj

an·tag·o·nist \-nəst\ n : ADVERSARY, OPPONENT

an·tag·o·nize \an-¹tag-ə-ʌnīz\ vb **-nized; -niz·ing** : to provoke the hostility of

ant·arc·tic \ant-¹ärk-tik, -¹ärt-ik\ adj, often cap : of or relating to the south pole or the region near it

antarctic circle n, often cap A&C : the parallel of latitude that is approximately 66½ degrees south of the equator

¹**an·te** \¹ant-ē\ n : a poker stake put up by each player before he sees his hand; also : an amount paid : PRICE

²**ante** vb an·ted; an·te·ing 1 : to put up (an ante) 2 : PAY

ant·eat·er \¹ant-ʌēt-ər\ n : any of several mammals (as an aardvark) that feed on ants

an·te·bel·lum \ʌant-i-¹bel-əm\ adj : existing before a war; esp : existing before the U.S. Civil War of 1861-65

an·te·ced·ent \ʌant-ə-¹sēd-ᵊnt\ n 1 : a noun, pronoun, phrase, or clause referred to by a personal or relative pronoun 2 : a preceding event or cause 3 pl : the significant conditions of one's earlier life 4 pl : ANCESTORS — antecedent adj

an·te·cham·ber \¹ant-i-ʌchām-bər\ n : ANTEROOM

an·te·date \¹ant-i-ʌdāt\ vb 1 : to date (a paper) as of an earlier day than that on which the actual writing or signing is done 2 : to precede in time

an·te·di·lu·vi·an \ʌant-i-də-¹lü-vē-ən, -dī-\ adj 1 : of the period before the biblical flood 2 : ANTIQUATED, OBSOLETE

an·te·lope \¹ant-ᵊl-ʌōp\ n, pl **-lope** or **-lopes** [ME, fabulous heraldic beast, prob. fr. MF antelop savage animal with sawlike horns, fr. ML anthalopus, fr. LGk antholops] 1 : any of various Old World cud-chewing mammals related to the oxen but with smaller lighter bodies and horns that extend upward and backward 2 : PRONGHORN

an·te me·ri·di·em \¹ant-i-mə-¹rid-ē-əm\ adj [L] : being before noon

an·ten·na \an-¹ten-ə\ n, pl **-nae** \-(ʌ)ē\ or **-nas** [ML, fr. L, sail yard] 1 : one of the long slender paired segmented sensory organs on the head of an arthropod (as an insect or crab) 2 pl usu **-nas** : a metallic device (as a rod or wire) for sending out or receiving radio waves

an·te·pe·nult \ʌant-i-¹pē-ʌnəlt\ also **an·te·pen·ul·ti·ma** \-ʌpi-¹nəl-tə-mə\ n : the 3d syllable of a word counting from the end — **an·te·pen·ul·ti·mate** \-pi-¹nəl-tə-mət\ adj or n

an·te·ri·or \an-¹tir-ē-ər\ adj 1 : situated before or toward the front 2 : situated near or nearer to the head 3 : coming before in time syn preceding, previous, prior, antecedent

an·te·room \'ant-i-ˌrüm, -ˌru̇m\ *n* : a room forming the entrance to another and often used as a waiting room

an·them \'an-thəm\ *n* **1** : a sacred vocal composition **2** : a song or hymn of praise or gladness

an·ther \'an-thər\ *n* : the part of a stamen of a seed plant that contains pollen

ant·hill \'ant-ˌhil\ *n* : a mound thrown up by ants or termites in digging their nest

an·thol·o·gy \an-'thäl-ə-jē\ *n, pl* **-gies** [NL *anthologia* collection of epigrams, fr. MGk, fr. Gk. flower gathering, fr. *anthos* flower + *logia* collecting, fr. *legein* to gather] : a collection of literary selections — **an·thol·o·gist** \-jəst\ *n* — **an·thol·o·gize** \-ˌjīz\ *vb*

an·thra·cite \'an-thrə-ˌsīt\ *n* : a hard glossy coal that burns without much smoke

an·thrax \'an-ˌthraks\ *n* : an infectious and usu. fatal bacterial disease of warm-blooded animals (as cattle and sheep); *also* : a bacterium causing anthrax

an·thro·po·cen·tric \ˌan-thrə-pə-'sen-trik\ *adj* : interpreting or regarding the world in terms of human values and experiences

¹an·thro·poid \'an-thrə-ˌpȯid\ *n* : any of several large tailless apes (as a gorilla)

²anthropoid *adj* **1** : resembling a human being esp. in shape **2** : resembling an ape esp. in action

an·thro·pol·o·gy \ˌan-thrə-'päl-ə-jē\ *n* : the science of human beings and esp. of their physical characteristics, their origin and the distribution of races, their environment and social relations, and their culture — **an·thro·po·log·i·cal** \-pə-'läj-i-kəl\ *adj* — **an·thro·pol·o·gist** \-'päl-ə-jəst\ *n*

an·thro·po·mor·phism \ˌan-thrə-pə-'mȯr-ˌfiz-əm\ *n* : an interpretation of what is not human or personal in terms of human or personal characteristics : HUMANIZATION — **an·thro·po·mor·phic** \-fik\ *adj*

an·ti \'an-ˌtī, 'ant-ē\ *n, pl* **antis** : one who is opposed

anti- \ˌant-i, -ē; ˌan-ˌtī\ *or* **ant-** *or* **anth-** *prefix* **1** : opposite in kind, position, or action **2** : opposing : hostile toward **3** : counteractive **4** : preventive of : curative of

antiaircraft	anti-imperialism
anti-American	anti-imperialist
antibacterial	antilabor
anticapitalist	antimalarial
anti-Catholic	antimicrobial
anticlerical	antislavery
anticolonial	antispasmodic
anticommunism	antistatic
anticommunist	antisubmarine
antidemocractic	antitank
antiestablishment	antitrust
antifascist	antiviral

an·ti·abor·tion \ˌant-ē-ə-'bȯr-shən, ˌan-ˌtī-\ *adj* : opposed to abortion

an·ti·bal·lis·tic missile \ˌant-i-bə-ˌlis-tik-, ˌan-ˌtī-\ *n* : a missile for intercepting and destroying ballistic missiles

an·ti·bi·ot·ic \-bī-'ät-ik, -bē-\ *n* : a substance produced by or derived by chemical alteration of a substance produced by a microorganism (as a fungus or bacterium) that in dilute solution inhibits or kills another microorganism — **antibiotic** *adj*

an·ti·body \'ant-i-ˌbäd-ē\ *n* : any of the bodily substances produced in response to specific foreign substances or organisms (as a disease-producing microorganism) and counteracting their effects

¹an·tic \'ant-ik\ *n* : an often wildly playful or funny act or action

²antic *adj* [It *antico* ancient, fr. L *antiquus*] **1** *archaic* : GROTESQUE **2** : PLAYFUL

an·ti·can·cer \ˌant-i-'kan-sər, ˌan-ˌtī-\ *adj* : used or effective against cancer (~ drugs)

An·ti·christ \'ant-i-ˌkrīst\ *n* **1** : one who denies or opposes Christ **2** : a false Christ

an·tic·i·pate \an-'tis-ə-ˌpāt\ *vb* **-pat·ed; -pat·ing 1** : to foresee and provide for beforehand **2** : to look forward to — **an·tic·i·pa·tion** \-ˌtis-ə-'pā-shən\ *n* — **an·tic·i·pa·to·ry** \-'tis-ə-pə-ˌtōr-ē\ *adj*

an·ti·cli·max \ˌant-i-'klī-ˌmaks\ *n* : something closing a series that is strikingly less important than what has preceded it — **an·ti·cli·mac·tic** \-klī-'mak-tik\ *adj*

an·ti·cline \'ant-i-ˌklīn\ *n* : an arch of layers of rock in the earth's crust

an·ti·co·ag·u·lant \ˌant-i-kō-'ag-yə-lənt\ *n* : a substance that hinders the clotting of blood — **anticoagulant** *adj*

an·ti·cy·clone \ˌant-i-'sī-ˌklōn\ *n* : a system of winds that rotates about a center of high atmospheric pressure — **an·ti·cy·clon·ic** \-sī-'klän-ik\ *adj*

¹an·ti·de·pres·sant \ˌant-i-di-'pres-³nt, ˌan-ˌtī-\ *adj* : used or tending to relieve psychic depression (~ drugs)

²antidepressant *n* : an antidepressant drug

an·ti·dote \'ant-i-ˌdōt\ *n* : a remedy to counteract the effects of poison

an·ti·fer·til·i·ty \-fər-'til-ət-ē\ *adj* : tending to control excess or unwanted fertility : CONTRACEPTIVE (~ agents)

an·ti·freeze \'ant-i-ˌfrēz\ *n* : a substance that prevents a liquid from freezing

an·ti·gen \'ant-i-jən\ *n* : a usu. protein or carbohydrate substance (as a toxin or an enzyme) capable of stimulating an immune response — **an·ti·gen·ic** \ˌant-i-'jen-ik\ *adj* — **an·ti·ge·nic·i·ty** \-jə-'nis-ət-ē\ *n*

an·ti·grav·i·ty \ˌant-i-'grav-ət-ē, ˌan-ˌtī-\ *adj* : reducing or canceling the effect of gravity

an·ti·he·ro \'ant-i-ˌhē-rō, 'an-ˌtī-\ *n* : a

an·ti·his·ta·mine \ˌant-iˈhis-tə-ˌmēn, ˌan-ˌtī-, -mən\ n : any of various drugs used in treating allergies and colds

an·ti·hy·per·ten·sive \-ˌhī-pər-ˈten-siv\ n : a substance that is effective against high blood pressure — **antihypertensive** adj

an·ti-in·flam·ma·to·ry \-inˈflam-ə-ˌtōr-ē\ adj : counteracting inflammation — **anti-inflammatory** n

an·ti-in·tel·lec·tu·al \-ˌint-əlˈek-chə-wəl\ adj : opposing or hostile to intellectuals or to an intellectual view or approach

an·ti·knock \ˌant-iˈnäk\ n : a fuel additive to prevent knocking in an internal-combustion engine

an·ti·log·a·rithm \ˌant-iˈlog-ə-ˌrith-əm, ˌan-ˌtī-, -ˈläg-\ n : the number corresponding to a given logarithm

an·ti·ma·cas·sar \ˌant-i-məˈkas-ər\ n : a cover to protect the back or arms of furniture

an·ti·mag·net·ic \ˌant-i-magˈnet-ik, ˌan-ˌtī-\ adj : having a balance unit composed of alloys that will not remain magnetized (an ～ watch)

an·ti·mat·ter \ˈant-iˌmat-ər\ n : matter composed of the counterparts of ordinary matter

an·ti·mo·ny \ˈant-ə-ˌmō-nē\ n : a brittle silvery white metallic chemical element used in alloys

an·ti·neu·tron \-ˈn(y)ü-ˌträn\ n : the uncharged antiparticle of the neutron

an·ti·no·mi·an \ˌant-iˈnō-mē-ən\ n : one who denies the validity of moral laws

an·tin·o·my \anˈtin-ə-mē\ n, pl -mies : a contradiction between two seemingly true statements

an·ti·nov·el \ˈant-iˌnäv-əl, ˈan-ˌtī-\ n : a work of fiction that lacks all or most of the traditional features of the novel

an·ti·nu·cle·ar \ˌant-iˈn(y)ü-klē-ər\ adj : opposing the use or production of nuclear power plants

an·ti·ox·i·dant \ˌant-ēˈäk-səd-ənt, ˌan-ˌtī-\ n : a substance that inhibits oxidation — **antioxidant** adj

an·ti·par·ti·cle \ˈant-iˌpärt-i-kəl, ˈan-ˌtī-\ n : an elementary particle identical to another elementary particle in mass but opposite to it in electric and magnetic properties

an·ti·pas·to \ˌant-iˈpas-tō, ˌänt-iˈpäs-\ n, pl -ti : any of various typically Italian hors d'oeuvres

an·tip·a·thy \anˈtip-ə-thē\ n, pl -thies 1 : settled aversion or dislike 2 : an object of aversion — **an·ti·pa·thet·ic** \ˌant-i-pəˈthet-ik\ adj

an·ti·per·son·nel \ˌant-i-ˌpərs-ᵊnˈel, ˌan-ˌtī-\ adj : designed for use against military personnel (～ mine)

an·ti·per·spi·rant \-ˈpər-spə-rənt\ n : a cosmetic preparation used to check excessive perspiration

an·tiph·o·nal \anˈtif-ə-ᵊl\ adj : performed by two alternating groups — **an·tiph·o·nal·ly** \-ē\ adv

an·ti·pode \ˈant-ə-ˌpōd\ n, pl **an·tip·o·des** \anˈtip-ə-ˌdēz\ [ME antipodes, pl., persons dwelling at opposite points on the globe, fr. L, fr. Gk, fr. pl. of antipod-, antipous with feet opposite, fr. anti- against + pod-, pous foot] : the parts of the earth diametrically opposite — usu. used in pl. — **an·tip·o·dal** \anˈtip-əd-ᵊl\ adj — **an·tip·o·de·an** \(ˌ)an-ˌtip-ə-ˈdē-ən\ adj

an·ti·pol·lu·tion \ˌant-i-pəˈlü-shən\ adj : designed to prevent, reduce, or eliminate pollution (～ laws)

an·ti·pope \ˈant-i-ˌpōp\ n : one elected or claiming to be pope in opposition to the pope canonically chosen

an·ti·pov·er·ty \ˌant-iˈpäv-ərt-ē, ˌan-ˌtī-\ adj : of or relating to legislation designed to relieve poverty

an·ti·pro·ton \-ˈprō-ˌtän\ n : the antiparticle of the proton

an·ti·quar·i·an \ˌant-əˈkwer-ē-ən\ adj 1 : of or relating to antiquities 2 : dealing in old books — **antiquarian** n — **an·ti·quar·i·an·ism** n

an·ti·quary \ˈant-ə-ˌkwer-ē\ n, pl -quar·ies : a person who collects or studies antiquities

an·ti·quat·ed \ˈant-ə-ˌkwāt-əd\ adj : OUT-OF-DATE, OLD-FASHIONED

¹**an·tique** \anˈtēk\ n : an object made in a bygone period

²**antique** adj 1 : belonging to antiquity 2 : OLD-FASHIONED 3 : of a bygone style or period

³**antique** vb -tiqued; -tiqu·ing : to finish or refinish in antique style : give an appearance of age to

an·tiq·ui·ty \anˈtik-wət-ē\ n, pl -ties 1 : ancient times 2 : great age 3 pl : relics of ancient times 4 pl : matters relating to ancient culture

an·ti-Sem·i·tism \ˌant-iˈsem-ə-ˌtiz-əm, ˌan-ˌtī-\ n : hostility toward Jews as a religious or social minority — **anti-Se·mit·ic** \-səˈmit-ik\ adj

an·ti·sep·tic \ˌant-əˈsep-tik\ adj 1 : killing or checking the growth of germs that cause decay or infection 2 : scrupulously clean : ASEPTIC — **antiseptic** n — **an·ti·sep·ti·cal·ly** \-ti-k(ə-)lē\ adv

an·ti·se·rum \ˈant-i-ˌsir-əm, ˈan-ˌtī-\ n : a serum containing antibodies

an·ti·so·cial \-ˈsō-shəl\ adj 1 : disliking the society of others 2 : contrary or hostile to the well-being of society (crime is ～)

an·tith·e·sis \anˈtith-ə-səs\ n, pl -e·ses \-ˌsēz\ 1 : the opposition or contrast of ideas 2 : the direct opposite

an·ti·thet·i·cal \ˌant-əˈthet-i-kəl\ also **an·ti·thet·ic** \-ik\ adj : constituting or marked by antithesis — **an·ti·thet·i·cal·ly** \-i-k(ə-)lē\ adv

an·ti·tox·in \ˌant-iˈtäk-sən\ n : an antibody that is able to neutralize a particular toxin, is formed when the toxin is introduced into the body, and is produced in lower animals for use in treating human diseases (as diphtheria); *also* : a serum containing antitoxin

an·ti·tu·mor \,ant-i-'t(y)ü-mər, ,an-,tī-\ *adj* : ANTICANCER

an·ti·ven·in \-'ven-ən\ *n* : an antitoxin to a venom; *also* : a serum containing such antitoxin

ant·ler \'ant-lər\ *n* [ME *aunteler*, fr. MF *antoillier*, fr. L *anteocularis* located before the eye, fr. *ante-* before + *oculus* eye] : the solid usu. branched horn of a deer; *also* : a branch of this horn — **ant·lered** \-lərd\ *adj*

ant lion *n* : any of various insects having a long-jawed larva that digs a conical pit in which it lies in wait for insects (as ants) on which it feeds

ant·onym \'ant-ə-,nim\ *n* : a word of opposite meaning

anus \'ā-nəs\ *n* [L] : the lower or posterior opening of the alimentary canal

an·vil \'an-vəl\ *n* 1 : a heavy iron block on which metal is shaped 2 : INCUS

anx·i·ety \aŋ-'zī-ət-ē\ *n*, *pl* **-eties** 1 : painful uneasiness of mind usu. over an anticipated ill 2 : abnormal apprehension and fear often accompanied by physiological signs (as sweating and increased pulse), by doubt about the nature and reality of the threat itself, and by self-doubt

anx·ious \'aŋk-shəs\ *adj* 1 : uneasy in mind : WORRIED 2 : earnestly wishing : EAGER — **anx·ious·ly** *adv*

¹**any** \'en-ē\ *adj* 1 : one chosen at random 2 : of whatever number or quantity

²**any** *pron* 1 : any one or ones ⟨take ∼ of the books you like⟩ 2 : any amount ⟨∼ of the money not used is to be returned⟩

³**any** *adv* : to any extent or degree : AT ALL ⟨could not walk ∼ farther⟩

any·body \-,bäd-ē, -bəd-\ *pron* : ANYONE

any·how \-,hau̇\ *adv* 1 : in any way 2 : NEVERTHELESS; *also* : in any case

any·more \,en-ē-'mōr\ *adv* 1 : any longer 2 : at the present time

any·one \-(,)wən\ *pron* : any person

any·place \-,plās\ *adv* : ANYWHERE

any·thing \-,thiŋ\ *pron* : any thing whatever

any·time \'en-ē-,tīm\ *adv* : at any time whatever

any·way \-,wā\ *adv* : ANYHOW

any·where \-,hwear\ *adv* : in or to any place

any·wise \-,wīz\ *adv* : in any way whatever

A–OK \,ā-ō-'kā\ *adv or adj* : very definitely OK

A1 \'ā-'wən\ *adj* : of the finest quality

A/1C *abbr* airman first class

aor·ta \ā-'ȯrt-ə\ *n*, *pl* **-tas** *or* **-tae** \-ē\

: the main artery that carries blood from the heart — **aor·tic** \-'ȯrt-ik\ *adj*

ap *abbr* 1 apostle 2 apothecaries'

AP *abbr* 1 American plan 2 Associated Press

apace \ə-'pās\ *adv* : SWIFTLY

Apache \ə-'pach-ē *for 1*; ə-'pash *for 2*\ *n*, *pl* **Apache** *or* **Apach·es** \-'pach-ēz, -'pash(-əz)\ 1 : a member of an American Indian people of the southwestern U.S.; *also* : any of the languages of the Apache people 2 *not cap* : a member of a gang of criminals esp. in Paris

ap·a·nage *var of* APPANAGE

apart \ə-'pärt\ *adv* 1 : separately in place or time 2 : ASIDE 3 : in two or more parts : to pieces

apart·heid \ə-'pär-,tāt, -,tīt\ *n* [Afrikaans] : a policy of racial segregation practiced in the Republic of So. Africa

apart·ment \ə-'pärt-mənt\ *n* : a room or set of rooms occupied as a dwelling; *also* : a building divided into individual dwelling units

ap·a·thy \'ap-ə-thē\ *n* 1 : lack of emotion 2 : lack of interest : INDIFFERENCE — **ap·a·thet·ic** \,ap-ə-'thet-ik\ *adj* — **ap·a·thet·i·cal·ly** \-i-k(ə-)lē\ *adv*

ap·a·tite \'ap-ə-,tīt\ *n* : any of a group of minerals that are phosphates of calcium and are used as a source of phosphorus

APB *abbr* all points bulletin

¹**ape** \'āp\ *n* 1 : any of the larger tailless primates (as a baboon or gorilla); *also* : MONKEY 2 : MIMIC, IMITATOR; *also* : a large uncouth person

²**ape** *vb* **aped**; **ap·ing** : IMITATE, MIMIC

²**ape–man** \'āp-,man\ *n* : a primate intermediate in character between true man and the higher apes

aper·çu \ä-per-'sü, ,ap-ər-'sü\ *n*, *pl* **aper·çus** \-sü(z), -'süz\ : an immediate impression; *esp* : INSIGHT

aper·i·tif \,äp-,er-ə-'tēf\ *n* : an alcoholic drink taken as an appetizer

ap·er·ture \'ap-ə(r)-,chu̇r, -chər\ *n* : OPENING, HOLE

apex \'ā-,peks\ *n*, *pl* **apex·es** *or* **api·ces** \'ā-pə-,sēz, 'ap-ə-\ : the highest point : PEAK

apha·sia \ə-'fā-zh(ē-)ə\ *n* : loss or impairment of the power to use or comprehend words — **apha·sic** \-zik\ *adj or n*

aph·elion \a-'fēl-yən\ *n*, *pl* **-elia** \-yə\ [NL, fr. *apo-* away from + Gk *hēlios* sun] : the point in an object's orbit most distant from the sun

aphid \'ā-fəd, 'af-əd\ *n* : a small insect that sucks the juices of plants

aphis \'ā-fəs, 'af-əs\ *n*, *pl* **aphi·des** \'ā-fə-,dēz, 'af-ə-\ : APHID

aph·o·rism \'af-ə-,riz-əm\ *n* : a short saying stating a general truth : MAXIM — **aph·o·ris·tic** \,af-ə-'ris-tik\ *adj*

aph·ro·di·si·ac \,af-rə-'diz-ē-,ak, -'dē-zē-\ *adj* : exciting sexual desire — **aphrodisiac** *n*

api·ary \'ā-pē-,er-ē\ *n*, *pl* **-ar·ies** : a

place where bees are kept — **api·a·rist** \ˈā-pē-ə-rəst\ *n*

api·cal \ˈā-pi-kəl, ˈap-i-\ *adj* : of, relating to, or situated at an apex — **api·cal·ly** \-k(ə-)lē\ *adv*

apiece \ə-ˈpēs\ *adv* : for each one

aplomb \ə-ˈpläm, -ˈpləm\ *n* [F, lit., perpendicularity, fr. MF, fr. *a plomb*, lit., according to the plummet] : complete composure or self-assurance

APO *abbr* army post office

Apoc *abbr* 1 Apocalypse 2 Apocrypha

apoc·a·lypse \ə-ˈpäk-ə-ˌlips\ *n* 1 : a writing prophesying a cataclysm in which evil forces are destroyed 2 *cap* — see BIBLE table — **apoc·a·lyp·tic** \-ˌpäk-ə-ˈlip-tik\ *also* **apoc·a·lyp·ti·cal** \-ti-kəl\ *adj*

Apoc·ry·pha \ə-ˈpäk-rə-fə\ *n* 1 *not cap* : writings of dubious authenticity 2 : books included in the Septuagint and Vulgate but excluded from the Jewish and Protestant canons of the Old Testament — see BIBLE table 3 : early Christian writings not included in the New Testament

apoc·ry·phal \-fəl\ *adj* 1 *often cap* : of or resembling the Apocrypha 2 : not canonical : SPURIOUS — **apoc·ry·phal·ly** \-ē\ *adv*

apo·gee \ˈap-ə-(ˌ)jē\ *n* [F *apogée*, fr. NL *apogaeum*, fr. Gk *apogaion*, fr. *apo* away from + *gē* earth] : the point at which an orbiting object is farthest from the body being orbited

apo·lit·i·cal \ˌā-pə-ˈlit-i-kəl\ *adj* 1 : having an aversion for or no interest in political affairs 2 : having no political significance — **apo·lit·i·cal·ly** \-k(ə-)lē\ *adv*

apol·o·get·ic \ə-ˌpäl-ə-ˈjet-ik\ *adj* : expressing apology — **apol·o·get·i·cal·ly** \-i-k(ə-)lē\ *adv*

apo·lo·gia \ˌap-ə-ˈlō-j(ē-)ə\ *n* : APOLOGY; *esp* : an argument in support or justification

apol·o·gize \ə-ˈpäl-ə-ˌjīz\ *vb* **-gized; -giz·ing** : to make an apology : express regret — **apol·o·gist** \-jəst\ *n*

apol·o·gy \ə-ˈpäl-ə-jē\ *n, pl* **-gies** 1 : a formal justification : DEFENSE 2 : an expression of regret for a wrong

apo·lune \ˈap-ə-ˌlün\ *n* : the point in a lunar orbit farthest from the moon's surface

apo·plexy \ˈap-ə-ˌplek-sē\ *n* : STROKE 3 — **apo·plec·tic** \ˌap-ə-ˈplek-tik\ *adj*

aport \ə-ˈpōrt\ *adv* : on or toward the left side of a ship

apos·ta·sy \ə-ˈpäs-tə-sē\ *n, pl* **-sies** : a renunciation or abandonment of a former loyalty (as to a religion) — **apos·tate** \ə-ˈpäs-ˌtāt, -tət\ *adj or n*

a pos·te·ri·o·ri \ˌä-pō-ˌstir-ē-ˈōr-ē\ *adj* [L, lit., from the latter] : relating to or derived by reasoning from observed facts — **a posteriori** *adv*

apos·tle \ə-ˈpäs-əl\ *n* 1 : one of the group composed of Jesus' 12 original disciples and Paul 2 : the first prominent missionary to a region or group 3 : one who initiates or first advocates a great reform — **apos·tle·ship** *n*

ap·os·tol·ic \ˌap-ə-ˈstäl-ik\ *adj* 1 : of or relating to an apostle or to the New Testament apostles 2 : of or relating to a succession of spiritual authority from the apostles 3 : PAPAL

¹apos·tro·phe \ə-ˈpäs-trə-(ˌ)fē\ *n* : the rhetorical addressing of a usu. absent person or a usu. personified thing (as in "O grave, where is thy victory?")

²apostrophe *n* : a punctuation mark ' used esp. to indicate the possessive case or the omission of a letter or figure

apos·tro·phize \ə-ˈpäs-trə-ˌfīz\ *vb* **-phized; -phiz·ing** : to address as if present or capable of understanding

apothecaries' weight *n* : a system of weights based on the troy pound and ounce and used chiefly by pharmacists — see WEIGHT table

apoth·e·cary \ə-ˈpäth-ə-ˌker-ē\ *n, pl* **-car·ies** [ME *apothecarie*, fr. ML *apothecarius*, fr. LL, shopkeeper, fr. L *apotheca* storehouse, fr. Gk *apothēkē*, fr. *apotithenai* to put away] : DRUGGIST

ap·o·thegm \ˈap-ə-ˌthem\ *n* : APHORISM, MAXIM

apo·the·o·sis \ə-ˌpäth-ē-ˈō-səs, ˌap-ə-ˈthē-ə-səs\ *n, pl* **-oses** \-ˌsēz\ 1 : DEIFICATION 2 : the perfect example

app *abbr* 1 apparatus 2 appendix

ap·pall *also* **ap·pal** \ə-ˈpȯl\ *vb* **ap·palled; ap·pall·ing** : to overcome with horror : DISMAY

Ap·pa·loo·sa \ˌap-ə-ˈlü-sə\ *n* : any of a breed of saddle horses developed in northwestern No. America that have small dark spots or blotches on a white coat

ap·pa·nage \ˈap-ə-nij\ *n* 1 : provision (as a grant of land) made by a sovereign or legislative body for dependent members of the royal family 2 : a rightful adjunct

ap·pa·ra·tus \ˌap-ə-ˈrat-əs, -ˈrāt-\ *n, pl* **-tus·es** *or* **-tus** [L] 1 : a set of materials or equipment for a particular use 2 : a complex machine or device : MECHANISM 3 : the organization of a political party or underground movement

¹ap·par·el \ə-ˈpar-əl\ *vb* **-eled** *or* **-elled; -el·ing** *or* **-el·ling** 1 : CLOTHE, DRESS 2 : ADORN

²apparel *n* : CLOTHING, DRESS

ap·par·ent \ə-ˈpar-ənt\ *adj* 1 : open to view : VISIBLE 2 : EVIDENT, OBVIOUS 3 : appearing as real or true : SEEMING — **ap·par·ent·ly** *adv*

ap·pa·ri·tion \ˌap-ə-ˈrish-ən\ *n* : a supernatural appearance : GHOST

ap·peal \ə-ˈpēl\ *vb* 1 : to take steps to have (a case) reheard in a higher court 2 : to plead for help, corroboration, or decision 3 : to arouse a sympathetic response — **appeal** *n*

ap·pear \ə-ˈpiər\ *vb* 1 : to become visible 2 : to come formally before an au-

thority 3 : SEEM **4** : to become evident **5** : to come before the public

ap·pear·ance \ə-'pir-əns\ *n* **1** : the act of appearing **2** : outward aspect : LOOK **3** : PHENOMENON

ap·pease \ə-'pēz\ *vb* **ap·peased; ap·peas·ing 1** : to cause to subside : ALLAY **2** : PACIFY, CONCILIATE : *esp* : to buy off by concessions — **ap·pease·ment** *n*

ap·pel·lant \ə-'pel-ənt\ *n* : one who appeals esp. from a judicial decision

ap·pel·late \ə-'pel-ət\ *adj* : having power to review decisions of a lower court

ap·pel·la·tion \,ap-ə-'lā-shən\ *n* : NAME, DESIGNATION

ap·pel·lee \,ap-ə-'lē\ *n* : one against whom an appeal is taken

ap·pend \ə-'pend\ *vb* : to attach esp. as something additional : AFFIX

ap·pend·age \ə-'pen-dij\ *n* **1** : something appended to a principal or greater thing **2** : a projecting part of the body (as an antenna) esp. when paired with one on each side syn accessory, adjunct, appendix, appurtenance

ap·pen·dec·to·my \,ap-ən-'dek-tə-mē\ *n, pl* **-mies** : surgical removal of the intestinal appendix

ap·pen·di·ci·tis \ə-,pen-də-'sīt-əs\ *n* : inflammation of the intestinal appendix

ap·pen·dix \ə-'pen-diks\ *n, pl* **-dix·es** *or* **-di·ces** \-də-,sēz\ [L] **1** : supplementary matter added at the end of a book **2** : a narrow blind tube usu. about three or four inches long that extends from the cecum in the lower right-hand part of the abdomen

ap·per·tain \,ap-ər-'tān\ *vb* : to belong as a rightful part or privilege

ap·pe·tite \'ap-ə-,tīt\ *n* [ME *apetit*, fr. MF, fr. L *appetitus*, fr. *appetere* to strive after, fr. *ad-* to + *petere* to go to] **1** : natural desire for satisfying some want or need esp. for food **2** : TASTE, PREFERENCE

ap·pe·tiz·er \'ap-ə-,tī-zər\ *n* : a food or drink taken just before a meal to stimulate the appetite

ap·pe·tiz·ing \-zin\ *adj* : tempting to the appetite — **ap·pe·tiz·ing·ly** *adv*

appl *abbr* applied

ap·plaud \ə-'plȯd\ *vb* : to show approval esp. by clapping

ap·plause \ə-'plȯz\ *n* : approval publicly expressed (as by clapping)

ap·ple \'ap-əl\ *n* : a rounded fruit with firm white flesh and a seedy core; *also* : a tree that bears this fruit

ap·ple·jack \-,jak\ *n* : a liquor distilled from fermented cider

ap·pli·ance \ə-'plī-əns\ *n* **1** : INSTRUMENT, DEVICE **2** : a piece of household equipment (as a stove or toaster) operated by gas or electricity

ap·pli·ca·ble \'ap-li-kə-bəl, ə-'plik-ə-\ *adj* : capable of being applied : RELEVANT — **ap·pli·ca·bil·i·ty** \,ap-li-kə-'bil-ət-ē, ə-,plik-ə-\ *n*

ap·pli·cant \'ap-li-kənt\ *n* : one who applies

ap·pli·ca·tion \,ap-lə-'kā-shən\ *n* **1** : the act of applying **2** : assiduous attention **3** : REQUEST; *also* : a form used in making a request **4** : something placed or spread on a surface **5** : capacity for use

ap·pli·ca·tor \'ap-lə-,kāt-ər\ *n* : one that applies; *esp* : a device for applying a substance (as medicine or polish)

ap·plied \ə-'plīd\ *adj* : put to practical use

ap·pli·qué \,ap-lə-'kā\ *n* [F] : a fabric decoration cut out and fastened to a larger piece of material — **appliqué** *vb*

ap·ply \ə-'plī\ *vb* **ap·plied; ap·ply·ing 1** : to put to practical use **2** : to place in contact : put or spread on a surface **3** : to employ with close attention **4** : to submit a request **5** : to have reference or connection

ap·point \ə-'pȯint\ *vb* **1** : to fix or set officially (~ a day for trial) **2** : to name officially **3** : to fit out : EQUIP

ap·poin·tee \ə-,pȯin-'tē, ,a-\ *n* : a person appointed

ap·poin·tive \ə-'pȯint-iv\ *adj* : subject to appointment

ap·point·ment \ə-'pȯint-mənt\ *n* **1** : the act of appointing **2** : a nonelective office or position **3** : an arrangement for a meeting **4** *pl* : FURNISHINGS, EQUIPMENT

ap·por·tion \ə-'pōr-shən\ *vb* **-tioned; -tion·ing** \-sh(ə-)nin\ : to distribute proportionately : ALLOT — **ap·por·tion·ment** *n*

ap·po·site \'ap-ə-zət\ *adj* : APPROPRIATE, RELEVANT — **ap·po·site·ly** *adv* — **ap·po·site·ness** *n*

ap·po·si·tion \,ap-ə-'zish-ən\ *n* : a grammatical construction in which a noun or pronoun is followed by another that explains it (as *the poet* and *Burns* in "a biography of the poet Burns")

ap·pos·i·tive \ə-'päz-ət-iv, a-\ *adj* : of, relating to, or standing in grammatical apposition — **appositive** *n*

ap·praise \ə-'prāz\ *vb* **ap·praised; ap·prais·ing** : to set a value on — **ap·prais·al** \-'prā-zəl\ *n* — **ap·prais·er** *n*

ap·pre·cia·ble \ə-'prē-shə-bəl\ *adj* : large enough to be recognized and measured — **ap·pre·cia·bly** \-blē\ *adv*

ap·pre·ci·ate \ə-'prē-shē-,āt\ *vb* **-at·ed; -at·ing 1** : to value justly **2** : to be grateful for **3** : to increase in value — **ap·pre·ci·a·tion** \-,prē-shē-'ā-shən\ *n*

ap·pre·cia·tive \ə-'prē-shət-iv, -shē-,āt-\ *adj* : having or showing appreciation

ap·pre·hend \,ap-ri-'hend\ *vb* **1** : ARREST **2** : to become aware of **3** : to look forward to with dread **4** : UNDERSTAND — **ap·pre·hen·sion** \-'hen-chən\ *n*

ap·pre·hen·sive \-'hen-siv\ *adj* : viewing the future with anxiety — **ap·pre·hen·sive·ly** *adv* — **ap·pre·hen·sive·ness** *n*

¹**ap·pren·tice** \ə-'prent-əs\ n 1 : a person learning a craft under a skilled worker 2 : BEGINNER — **ap·pren·tice·ship** n

²**apprentice** vb -ticed; -tic·ing : to bind or set at work as an apprentice

ap·prise \ə-'prīz\ vb ap·prised; ap·pris·ing : INFORM

ap·proach \ə-'prōch\ vb 1 : to move nearer to 2 : to be almost the same as 3 : to make advances to esp. for the purpose of creating a desired result 4 : to take preliminary steps toward — **approach** n — **ap·proach·able** adj

ap·pro·ba·tion \ap-rə-'bā-shən\ n : AP·PROVAL

¹**ap·pro·pri·ate** \ə-'prō-prē-ˌāt\ vb -at·ed; -at·ing 1 : to take possession of 2 : to set apart for a particular use

²**ap·pro·pri·ate** \ə-'prō-prē-ət\ adj : fitted to a purpose or use : SUITABLE syn proper, fit, apt, befitting — **ap·pro·pri·ate·ly** adv — **ap·pro·pri·ate·ness** n

ap·pro·pri·a·tion \ə-ˌprō-prē-'ā-shən\ n : money set aside by formal action for a specific use

ap·prov·al \ə-'prü-vəl\ n : an act of approving — **on approval** : subject to a prospective buyer's acceptance or refusal

ap·prove \ə-'prüv\ vb ap·proved; ap·prov·ing 1 : to have or express a favorable opinion of 2 : to accept as satisfactory : RATIFY

approx abbr approximate; approximately

¹**ap·prox·i·mate** \ə-'präk-sə-mət\ adj : nearly correct or exact — **ap·prox·i·mate·ly** adv

²**ap·prox·i·mate** \-ˌmāt\ vb -mat·ed; -mat·ing : to come near : APPROACH — **ap·prox·i·ma·tion** \ə-ˌpräk-sə-'mā-shən\ n

appt abbr appoint; appointed; appointment

ap·pur·te·nance \ə-'pərt-(ə)nəns\ n : something that belongs to or goes with another thing syn accessory, adjunct, appendage, appendix — **ap·pur·te·nant** \-(ə)nənt\ adj

Apr abbr April

APR abbr annual percentage rate

apri·cot \'ap-rə-ˌkät, 'ā-prə-\ n [deriv. of Ar al-birqūq] : an oval orange-colored fruit resembling the related peach and plum in flavor; also : a tree bearing apricots

April \'ā-prəl\ n [ME, fr. OF & L; OF avrill, fr. L Aprilis] : the 4th month of the year having 30 days

a pri·o·ri \ˌä-prē-'ōr-ē\ adj [L, from the former] 1 : characterized by or derived by reasoning from self-evident propositions 2 : independent of experience — **a priori** adv

apron \'ā-prən, -pərn\ n [ME, alter. (resulting fr. incorrect division of a napron) of napron, fr. MF naperon, dim. of nape cloth, modif. of L mappa napkin] 1 : a garment tied over the front of the body to protect the clothes 2 : a

paved area for parking or handling airplanes

¹**ap·ro·pos** \ˌap-rə-'pō, 'ap-rə-ˌpō\ adv [F à propos, lit., to the purpose] 1 : OPPORTUNELY 2 : BY THE WAY

²**apropos** adj : being to the point

apropos of prep : with regard to

apse \'aps\ n : a projecting usu. semi-circular and vaulted part of a building (as a church)

¹**apt** \'apt\ adj 1 : well adapted : SUITABLE 2 : having an habitual tendency : LIKELY 3 : quick to learn — **apt·ly** adv — **apt·ness** \'ap(t)-nəs\ n

²**apt** abbr 1 apartment 2 aptitude

ap·ti·tude \'ap-tə-ˌt(y)üd\ n 1 : natural ability : TALENT 2 : capacity for learning 3 : APPROPRIATENESS

aqua \'ak-wə, 'äk-\ n : a light greenish blue color

aqua·cul·ture also **aqui·cul·ture** \'ak-wə-ˌkəl-chər, 'äk-\ n : the cultivation of aquatic plants or animals (as fish or shellfish) for human use

aqua·ma·rine \ˌak-wə-mə-'rēn, ˌäk-\ n 1 : a bluish green gem 2 : a pale blue to light greenish blue

aqua·naut \'ak-wə-ˌnot, 'äk-\ n : a person who lives in an underwater shelter for an extended period

aqua·plane \-ˌplān\ n : a board towed behind a motorboat and ridden by a person standing on it — **aquaplane** vb

aqua re·gia \ˌak-wə-'rē-j(ē-)ə\ n [NL, lit., royal water] : a mixture of nitric and hydrochloric acids that dissolves gold or platinum

aquar·i·um \ə-'kwar-ē-əm\ n, pl -i·ums or -ia \-ē-ə\ 1 : a container (as a glass tank) in which living aquatic animals and plants are kept 2 : a place where aquatic animals and plants are kept and shown

Aquar·i·us \ə-'kwar-ē-əs\ n [L, lit., water carrier] 1 : a zodiacal constellation between Capricorn and Pisces usu. pictured as a man pouring water 2 : the 11th sign of the zodiac in astrology; also : one born under this sign

¹**aquat·ic** \ə-'kwät-ik, -'kwat-\ adj 1 : growing or living in or frequenting water 2 : performed in or on water

²**aquatic** n : an aquatic animal or plant

aqua·vit \'äk-wə-ˌvēt\ n : a clear liquor flavored with caraway seeds

aqua vi·tae \ˌak-wə-'vīt-ē, ˌäk-\ n [ME, fr. ML, lit., water of life] : a strong alcoholic liquor (as brandy)

aq·ue·duct \'ak-wə-ˌdəkt\ n 1 : a conduit for carrying running water 2 : a structure carrying a canal over a river or hollow 3 : a passage in a bodily part

aque·ous \'ā-kwē-əs, 'ak-wē-\ adj 1 : WATERY 2 : made of, by, or with water

aqueous humor n : a clear fluid occupying the space between the lens and the cornea of the eye

aqui·fer \'ak-wə-fər, 'äk-\ n : a water-bearing stratum of permeable rock, sand, or gravel

aq·ui·line \'ak-wə-ˌlīn, -lən\ *adj* **1** : of or resembling an eagle **2** : hooked like an eagle's beak ⟨an ∼ nose⟩

ar *abbr* arrival; arrive

Ar *symbol* argon

AR *abbr* Arkansas

-ar \ər\ *adj suffix* : of or relating to ⟨molecul*ar*⟩ : being ⟨spectacul*ar*⟩ : resembling ⟨oracul*ar*⟩

Ar·ab \'ar-əb\ *n* **1** : a member of a Semitic people of the Arabian peninsula in southwestern Asia **2** : a member of an Arabic-speaking people — **Arab** *adj* — **Ara·bi·an** \ə-ˈrā-bē-ən\ *adj or n*

ar·a·besque \ˌar-ə-ˈbesk\ *n* : a design of interlacing lines forming figures of flowers, foliage, and sometimes animals

¹Ar·a·bic \'ar-ə-bik\ *n* : a Semitic language of southwestern Asia and north Africa

²Arabic *adj* **1** : of or relating to the Arabs, Arabic, or the Arabian peninsula in southwestern Asia **2** : expressed in or making use of Arabic numerals

Arabic numeral *n* : one of the number symbols 1, 2, 3, 4, 5, 6, 7, 8, 9, and 0

ar·a·ble \'ar-ə-bəl\ *adj* : fit for or cultivated by plowing : suitable for crops

arach·nid \ə-ˈrak-nəd\ *n* : any of a class of usu. 8-legged arthropods comprising the spiders, scorpions, mites, and ticks — **arachnid** *adj*

Ar·a·ma·ic \ˌar-ə-ˈmā-ik\ *n* : an ancient Semitic language

Arap·a·ho *or* **Arap·a·hoe** \ə-ˈrap-ə-ˌhō\ *n, pl* **Arapaho** *or* **Arapahos** *or* **Arapahoe** *or* **Arapahoes** : a member of an American Indian people of the western U.S.

ar·bi·ter \'är-bət-ər\ *n* : one having power to decide : JUDGE

ar·bi·trage \'är-bə-ˌträzh\ *n* [F, fr. MF, arbitration] : the purchase and sale of the same or equivalent security in different markets in order to profit from price discrepancies

ar·bi·tra·geur \ˌär-bə-(ˌ)trä-ˈzhər\ *or* **ar·bi·trag·er** \'är-bə-ˌträzh-ər\ *n* : one who practices arbitrage

ar·bit·ra·ment \är-ˈbit-rə-mənt\ *n* **1** : the act of deciding a dispute **2** : the judgment given by an arbitrator

ar·bi·trary \'är-bə-ˌtrer-ē\ *adj* **1** : AUTOCRATIC, DESPOTIC **2** : determined by will or caprice : selected at random — **ar·bi·trari·ly** \ˌär-bə-ˈtrer-ə-lē\ *adv* — **ar·bi·trari·ness** \'är-bə-ˌtrer-ē-nəs\ *n*

ar·bi·trate \'är-bə-ˌtrāt\ *vb* **-trat·ed; -trat·ing 1** : to act as arbitrator **2** : to act on as arbitrator **3** : to submit for decision to an arbitrator — **ar·bi·tra·tion** \ˌär-bə-ˈtrā-shən\ *n*

ar·bi·tra·tor \'är-bə-ˌtrāt-ər\ *n* : one chosen to settle differences between two parties in a controversy

ar·bor \'är-bər\ *n* [ME *erber* plot of grass, arbor, fr. OF *herbier* plot of grass, fr. *herbe* herb, grass] : a shelter formed of or covered with vines or branches

ar·bo·re·al \är-ˈbōr-ē-əl\ *adj* **1** : of, relating to, or resembling a tree **2** : living in trees ⟨∼ monkeys⟩

ar·bo·re·tum \ˌär-bə-ˈrēt-əm\ *n, pl* **-retums** *or* **-re·ta** \-ˈrēt-ə\ [L, place grown with trees, fr. *arbor* tree] : a place where trees and plants are grown for scientific and educational purposes

ar·bor·vi·tae \ˌär-bər-ˈvīt-ē\ *n* : any of various evergreen trees with scalelike leaves that are related to the pines

ar·bu·tus \är-ˈbyüt-əs\ *n* : TRAILING ARBUTUS

¹arc \'ärk\ *n* **1** : a sustained luminous discharge of electricity (as between two electrodes) **2** : a continuous portion of a curved line (as part of the circumference of a circle)

²arc *vb* : to form an electric arc

ARC *abbr* **1** American Red Cross **2** AIDS-related complex

ar·cade \är-ˈkād\ *n* **1** : an arched or covered passageway; *esp* : one lined with shops **2** : a row of arches with their supporting columns

ar·cane \är-ˈkān\ *adj* : SECRET, MYSTERIOUS

¹arch \'ärch\ *n* **1** : a curved structure spanning an opening (as a door or window) **2** : something resembling an arch **3** : ARCHWAY

²arch *vb* **1** : to cover with an arch **2** : to form or bend into an arch

³arch *adj* **1** : CHIEF, EMINENT **2** : ROGUISH, MISCHIEVOUS — **arch·ly** *adv* — **arch·ness** *n*

⁴arch *abbr* architect; architectural; architecture

ar·chae·ol·o·gy *or* **ar·che·ol·o·gy** \ˌär-kē-ˈäl-ə-jē\ *n* : the study of past human life as revealed by relics left by ancient peoples — **ar·chae·o·log·i·cal** \-kē-ə-ˈläj-i-kəl\ *adj* — **ar·chae·ol·o·gist** \-kē-ˈäl-ə-jəst\ *n*

ar·cha·ic \är-ˈkā-ik\ *adj* **1** : belonging to an earlier time : ANTIQUATED **2** : having the characteristics of the language of the past and surviving chiefly in specialized uses ⟨∼ words⟩ — **ar·cha·i·cal·ly** \-i-k(ə-)lē\ *adv*

arch·an·gel \'ärk-ˌān-jəl\ *n* : an angel of high rank

arch·bish·op \ärch-ˈbish-əp\ *n* : a bishop of high rank — **arch·bish·op·ric** \-ə-(ˌ)prik\ *n*

arch·dea·con \-ˈdē-kən\ *n* : a clergyman who assists a diocesan bishop in ceremonial or administrative functions

arch·di·o·cese \-ˈdī-ə-səs, -ˌsēz, -ˌsēs\ *n* : the diocese of an archbishop

arch·duke \-ˈd(y)ük\ *n* **1** : a sovereign prince **2** : a prince of the imperial family of Austria

arch·en·e·my \'ärch-ˈen-ə-mē\ *n, pl* **-mies** : a principal enemy

Ar·cheo·zo·ic \ˌär-kē-ə-ˈzō-ik\ *adj* : of, relating to, or being the earliest era of geologic history extending from the formation of the earth almost 4 billion years ago to about 1.4 billion years ago — **Archeozoic** *n*

ar·chery \'ärch-(ə-)rē\ *n* : the art or practice of shooting with bow and arrows — **ar·cher** \'är-chər\ *n*

ar·che·type \'är-ki-₁tīp\ *n* : the original pattern or model of all things of the same type

arch·fiend \'ärch-'fēnd\ *n* : a chief fiend; *esp* : SATAN

ar·chi·epis·co·pal \₁är-kē-ə-'pis-kə-pəl\ *adj* : of or relating to an archbishop

ar·chi·man·drite \₁är-kə-'man-₁drīt\ *n* : a dignitary in an Eastern church ranking below a bishop

ar·chi·pel·a·go \₁är-kə-'pel-ə-₁gō, ₁är-chə-\ *n, pl* **-goes** *or* **-gos** 1 : a sea dotted with islands 2 : a group of islands

ar·chi·tect \'är-kə-₁tekt\ *n* : a person who plans buildings and oversees their construction

ar·chi·tec·ture \'är-kə-₁tek-chər\ *n* 1 : the art or science of planning and building structures 2 : method or style of building — **ar·chi·tec·tur·al** \₁är-kə-'tek-chə-rəl, -'tek-shrəl\ *adj* — **ar·chi·tec·tur·al·ly** \-ē-\ *adv*

ar·chi·trave \'är-kə-₁trāv\ *n* : the supporting horizontal member just above the columns in a building in the classical style of architecture

ar·chive \'är-₁kīv\ *n* : a place for keeping public records; *also* : public records — often used in pl.

ar·chi·vist \'är-kə-vəst, -₁kī-\ *n* : a person in charge of archives

ar·chon \'är-₁kän, -kən\ *n* : a chief magistrate of ancient Athens

arch·way \'ärch-₁wā\ *n* : a passageway under an arch; *also* : an arch over a passage

arc lamp *n* : a gas-filled electric lamp that produces light when a current arcs between incandescent electrodes

¹**arc·tic** \'ärk-tik, 'ärt-ik\ *adj* [ME *artik*, fr. L *arcticus*, fr. Gk *arktikos*, fr. *arktos* bear, Ursa Major, north] 1 *often cap* : of or relating to the north pole or the region near it 2 : FRIGID

²**arc·tic** \'ärt-ik, 'ärk-tik\ *n* : a rubber overshoe that reaches to the ankle or above

arctic circle *n, often cap A&C* : the parallel of latitude that is approximately 66½ degrees north of the equator

-ard \ərd\ *also* **-art** \ərt\ *n suffix* : one that is characterized by performing some action, possessing some quality, or being associated with some thing esp. conspicuously or excessively (braggart) (dullard)

ar·dent \'ärd-ᵊnt\ *adj* 1 : characterized by warmth of feeling : PASSIONATE 2 : FIERY, HOT 3 : GLOWING — **ar·dent·ly** *adv*

ar·dor \'ärd-ər\ *n* 1 : warmth of feeling : ZEAL 2 : burning heat

ar·du·ous \'ärj-(ə-)wəs\ *adj* : DIFFICULT, LABORIOUS — **ar·du·ous·ly** *adv* — **ar·du·ous·ness** *n*

¹**are** *pres 2d sing or pres pl of* BE

²**are** \'a(ə)r\ *n* — see METRIC SYSTEM table

ar·ea \'ar-ē-ə\ *n* 1 : a flat surface or space 2 : the amount of surface included (as within the lines of a geometric figure) 3 : REGION 4 : range or extent of some thing or concept : FIELD

area code *n* : a 3-digit number that identifies each telephone service area in a country (as the U.S. or Canada)

area·way \-₁wā\ *n* : a sunken space for giving access, air, and light to a basement

are·na \ə-'rē-nə\ *n* [L *harena, arena* sand, sandy place] 1 : an enclosed area used for public entertainment 2 : a sphere of activity or competition

ar·gent \'är-jənt\ *adj* : of or resembling silver : SILVERY

Ar·gen·tine \'är-jən-₁tēn, -₁tīn\ *or* **Ar·gen·tin·ean** *or* **Ar·gen·tin·i·an** \₁är-jən-'tin-ē-ən\ *n* : a native or inhabitant of Argentina — **Argentine** *or* **Argentinean** *or* **Argentinian** *adj*

ar·gen·tite \'är-jən-₁tīt\ *n* : a dark gray mineral that is an important ore of silver

ar·gil·la·ceous \₁är-jə-'lā-shəs\ *adj* : CLAYEY

ar·gon \'är-₁gän\ *n* [Gk, neut. of *argos* idle, lazy, fr. a- not + *ergon* work; fr. its relative inertness] : a colorless odorless gaseous chemical element found in the air and used for filling electric bulbs

ar·go·sy \'är-gə-sē\ *n, pl* **-sies** 1 : a large merchant ship 2 : FLEET

ar·got \'är-gət, -₁gō\ *n* : the language of a particular group or class esp. of the underworld

ar·gu·able \'är-gyə-wə-bəl\ *adj* : open to argument, dispute, or question

ar·gue \'är-gyü\ *vb* **ar·gued; ar·gu·ing** 1 : to give reasons for or against something 2 : to contend in words : DISPUTE 3 : DEBATE 4 : to persuade by giving reasons

ar·gu·ment \'är-gyə-mənt\ *n* 1 : a reason offered in proof 2 : discourse intended to persuade 3 : QUARREL

ar·gu·men·ta·tion \₁är-gyə-mən-'tā-shən\ *n* : the art of formal discussion

ar·gu·men·ta·tive \₁är-gyə-'ment-ət-iv\ *adj* : inclined to argue

ar·gyle *also* **ar·gyll** \'är-₁gīl\ *n, often cap* : a geometric knitting pattern of varicolored diamonds on a single background color; *also* : a sock knit in this pattern

aria \'är-ē-ə\ *n* : an accompanied elaborate vocal solo forming part of a larger work

ar·id \'ar-əd\ *adj* 1 : DRY, BARREN 2 : having insufficient rainfall to support agriculture — **arid·i·ty** \ə-'rid-ət-ē\ *n*

Ar·ies \'ar-(ē-)₁ēz\ *n* [L, lit., ram] 1 : a zodiacal constellation between Pisces and Taurus usu. pictured as a ram 2

: the 1st sign of the zodiac in astrology; *also* : one born under this sign

aright \ə-ˈrīt\ *adv* : RIGHTLY, CORRECTLY

arise \ə-ˈrīz\ *vb* **arose** \-ˈrōz\ ; **aris·en** \-ˈriz-ᵊn\ ; **aris·ing** \-ˈrī-ziŋ\ **1** : to get up **2** : ORIGINATE **3** : ASCEND **syn** rise, derive, spring, issue

ar·is·toc·ra·cy \ˌar-ə-ˈstäk-rə-sē\ *n, pl* **-cies 1** : government by a noble or privileged class; *also* : a state so governed **2** : the governing class of an aristocracy **3** : UPPER CLASS — **aris·to·crat** \ə-ˈris-tə-ˌkrat\ *n* — **aris·to·crat·ic** \ə-ˌris-tə-ˈkrat-ik\ *adj*

arith *abbr* arithmetic; arithmetical

arith·me·tic \ə-ˈrith-mə-ˌtik\ *n* **1** : a branch of mathematics that deals with computations with numbers **2** : COMPUTATION, CALCULATION — **ar·ith·met·ic** \ˌar-ith-ˈmet-ik\ *or* **ar·ith·met·i·cal** \-i-kəl\ *adj* — **ar·ith·met·i·cal·ly** \-i-k(ə-)lē\ *adv* — **arith·me·ti·cian** \ə-ˌrith-mə-ˈtish-ən\ *n*

arithmetic mean *n* : the sum of a set of numbers divided by the number of numbers in the set

Ariz *abbr* Arizona

ark \ˈärk\ *n* **1** : a boat held to resemble that of Noah at the time of the Deluge **2** : the sacred chest in which the ancient Hebrews kept the tablets of the Law

Ark *abbr* Arkansas

¹**arm** \ˈärm\ *n* **1** : a human upper limb; *also* : a corresponding limb of a lower animal with a backbone **2** : something resembling an arm in shape or position (an ~ of a chair) **3** : POWER, MIGHT (the ~ of the law) — **armed** \ˈärmd\ *adj* — **arm·less** *adj*

²**arm** *vb* : to furnish with weapons

³**arm** *n* **1** : WEAPON **2** : a branch of the military forces **3** *pl* : the hereditary heraldic devices of a family

ar·ma·da \är-ˈmäd-ə, -ˈmad-\ *n* : a fleet of armed ships

ar·ma·dil·lo \ˌär-mə-ˈdil-ō\ *n, pl* **-los** : any of several small burrowing mammals with the head and body protected by an armor of bony plates

Ar·ma·ged·don \ˌär-mə-ˈged-ᵊn\ *n* : a final conclusive battle between the forces of good and evil; *also* : the site or time of this

ar·ma·ment \ˈär-mə-mənt\ *n* **1** : military strength **2** : arms and equipment (as of a tank or combat unit) **3** : the process of preparing for war

ar·ma·ture \ˈär-mə-ˌchùr, -chər\ *n* **1** : a protective covering or structure (as the spines of a cactus) **2** : the part including the conductors in an electric generator or motor in which the current is induced; *also* : the movable part in an electromagnetic device (as an electric bell or a loudspeaker)

arm·chair \ˈärm-ˌche(ə)r\ *n* : a chair with supports for the arms

armed forces *n pl* : the combined military, naval, and air forces of a nation

arm·ful \ˈärm-ˌfùl\ *n, pl* **armfuls** *or* **arms·ful** \ˈärmz-ˌfùl\ : as much as the arm can hold

arm·hole \ˈärm-ˌhōl\ *n* : an opening for the arm in a garment

ar·mi·stice \ˈär-mə-stəs\ *n* : temporary suspension of hostilities by mutual agreement : TRUCE

arm·let \ˈärm-lət\ *n* : a band worn around the upper arm

ar·mor \ˈär-mər\ *n* **1** : protective covering **2** : armored forces and vehicles — **ar·mored** \-mərd\ *adj*

ar·mor·er \ˈär-mər-ər\ *n* **1** : one that makes arms and armor **2** : one that services firearms

ar·mo·ri·al \är-ˈmōr-ē-əl\ *adj* : of or bearing heraldic arms

ar·mo·ry \ˈärm-(ə-)rē\ *n, pl* **ar·mor·ies 1** : a place where arms are stored **2** : a factory where arms are made

arm·pit \ˈärm-ˌpit\ *n* : the hollow under the junction of the arm and shoulder

arm·rest \-ˌrest\ *n* : a support for the arm

ar·my \ˈär-mē\ *n, pl* **armies 1** : a body of men organized for war **2** *often cap* : the complete military organization of a country for land warfare **3** : a great number **4** : a body of persons organized to advance a cause

army ant *n* : any of various nomadic social ants

ar·my·worm \ˈär-mē-ˌwərm\ *n* : any of numerous moths whose larvae move about destroying crops

ar·ni·ca \ˈär-ni-kə\ *n* **1** : any of several herbs related to the daisies **2** : a soothing preparation of dried arnica flowers used on bruises and sprains; *also* : dried arnica flowers

aro·ma \ə-ˈrō-mə\ *n* : a usu. pleasing odor : FRAGRANCE — **ar·o·mat·ic** \ˌar-ə-ˈmat-ik\ *adj*

arose *past of* ARISE

¹**around** \ə-ˈraùnd\ *adv* **1** : in or along a circuit **2** : on all sides **3** : NEARBY **4** : from one place to another **5** : in an opposite direction (turn ~)

²**around** *prep* **1** : SURROUNDING (trees ~ the house) **2** : to or on the other side of (~ the corner) **3** : NEAR (stayed right ~ home) **4** : along the circuit of (go ~ the world)

arouse \ə-ˈraùz\ *vb* **aroused; arous·ing 1** : to awaken from sleep **2** : to stir up — **arous·al** \-ˈraù-zəl\ *n*

ar·peg·gio \är-ˈpej-(ē-)ˌō\ *n, pl* **-gios** [It fr. *arpeggiare* to play on the harp, fr. *arpa* harp] : a chord whose notes are performed in succession and not simultaneously

arr *abbr* **1** arranged **2** arrival; arrive

ar·raign \ə-ˈrān\ *vb* **1** : to call before a court to answer to an indictment **2** : to accuse of wrong or imperfection — **ar·raign·ment** *n*

ar·range \ə-ˈrānj\ *vb* **ar·ranged; ar·rang·ing 1** : to put in order **2** : to come to an agreement about : SETTLE **3** : to adapt (a musical composition) to voices or instruments other than those for which it was orig. written — **ar·range·ment** *n* — **ar·rang·er** *n*

ar·rant \'ar-ənt\ *adj* : being notoriously without moderation : EXTREME

ar·ras \'ar-əs\ *n, pl* **arras** 1 : TAPESTRY 2 : a wall hanging or screen of tapestry

¹ar·ray \ə-'rā\ *vb* 1 : to arrange in order 2 : to dress esp. splendidly

²array *n* 1 : a regular arrangement 2 : rich apparel 3 : an imposing group

ar·rears \ə-'riərz\ *n pl* 1 : a state of being behind in the discharge of obligations (in ~ with the payments) 2 : overdue debts

¹ar·rest \ə-'rest\ *vb* 1 : STOP, CHECK 2 : to take into legal custody

²arrest *n* 1 : the act of stopping; *also* : the state of being stopped 2 : the act of taking into custody by legal authority

ar·riv·al \ə-'rī-vəl\ *n* 1 : the act of arriving 2 : one that arrives

ar·rive \ə-'rīv\ *vb* **ar·rived; ar·riv·ing** 1 : to reach a destination 2 : to be near or at hand (the time to go finally *arrived*) 3 : to attain success

ar·ro·gant \'ar-ə-gənt\ *adj* : offensively exaggerating one's own importance — **ar·ro·gance** \-gəns\ *n* — **ar·ro·gant·ly** *adv*

ar·ro·gate \-ˌgāt\ *vb* **-gat·ed; -gat·ing** : to claim or seize without justification as one's right

ar·row \'ar-ō\ *n* 1 : a missile shot from a bow and usu. having a slender shaft, a pointed head, and feathers at the butt 2 : a pointed mark used to indicate direction

ar·row·head \'ar-ō-ˌhed\ *n* : the pointed end of an arrow

ar·row·root \-ˌrüt, -ˌrut\ *n* : an edible starch from the roots of any of several tropical American plants; *also* : a plant yielding arrowroot

ar·royo \ə-'rȯi-ə, -ō\ *n, pl* **-royos** [Sp] 1 : a watercourse in a dry region 2 : a water-carved gully or channel

ar·se·nal \'ärs-nəl, -ᵊn-əl\ *n* [deriv. of Ar *dār ṣinā'ah* house of manufacture] 1 : a place for making and storing arms and military equipment 2 : STORE, REPERTORY

ar·se·nic \'ärs-nik, -ᵊn-ik\ *n* 1 : a solid brittle poisonous chemical element of grayish color and metallic luster 2 : a very poisonous oxygen compound of arsenic used in making glass and insecticides

ar·son \'ärs-ᵊn\ *n* : the malicious burning of property

¹art \'ärt\ *n* 1 : skill acquired by experience or study 2 : a branch of learning; *esp* : one of the humanities 3 : an occupation requiring knowledge or skill 4 : the use of skill and imagination in the production of things of beauty; *also* : works so produced 5 : ARTFULNESS

²art *abbr* 1 article 2 artificial 3 artillery

-art — see -ARD

ar·te·ri·al \är-'tir-ē-əl\ *adj* 1 : of or relating to an artery; *also* : relating to or being the bright red oxygenated blood found in most arteries 2 : of, relating to, or being a route for through traffic

ar·te·ri·ole \är-'tir-ē-ˌōl\ *n* : one of the small terminal twigs of an artery that ends in capillaries — **ar·te·ri·o·lar** \-ˌtir-ē-'ō-lər\ *adj*

ar·te·rio·scle·ro·sis \är-ˌtir-ē-ō-sklə-'rō-səs\ *n* : a chronic disease in which arterial walls are abnormally thickened and hardened — **ar·te·rio·scle·rot·ic** \-'rät-ik\ *adj or n*

ar·tery \'ärt-ə-rē\ *n, pl* **-ter·ies** 1 : one of the tubular vessels that carry the blood from the heart 2 : a main channel of transportation or communication; *esp* : a principal channel in a branching system

ar·te·sian well \är-ˌtē-zhən-\ *n* 1 : a bored well gushing water like a fountain 2 : a relatively deep-bored well

art·ful \'ärt-fəl\ *adj* 1 : INGENIOUS 2 : CRAFTY — **art·ful·ly** \-ē\ *adv* — **art·ful·ness** *n*

ar·thri·tis \är-'thrīt-əs\ *n, pl* **-thri·ti·des** \-'thrit-ə-ˌdēz\ : inflammation of the joints — **ar·thrit·ic** \-'thrit-ik\ *adj or n*

ar·thro·pod \'är-thrə-ˌpäd\ *n* : any of a phylum of invertebrate animals comprising those (as insects, spiders, or crabs) with segmented bodies and jointed limbs — **arthropod** *adj*

ar·thros·co·py \är-'thräs-kə-pē\ *n, pl* **-pies** : visual examination of the interior of a joint (as the knee) with a special surgical instrument — **ar·thro·scope** \'är-thrə-ˌskōp\ *n* — **ar·thro·scop·ic** \ˌär-thrə-'skäp-ik\ *adj*

ar·ti·choke \'ärt-ə-ˌchōk\ *n* [It dial. *articiocco*, fr. Ar *al-khurshūf*] : a tall herb related to the daisies; *also* : its edible flower head

ar·ti·cle \'ärt-i-kəl\ *n* [ME, fr. OF, fr. L *articulus* joint, division, dim. of *artus* joint] 1 : a distinct part of a written document 2 : a nonfictional prose composition forming an independent part of a publication 3 : a word (as *an, the*) used with a noun to limit or give definiteness to its application 4 : a member of a class of things: *esp* : COMMODITY

ar·tic·u·lar \är-'tik-yə-lər\ *adj* : of or relating to a joint

¹ar·tic·u·late \är-'tik-yə-lət\ *adj* 1 : divided into meaningful parts : INTELLIGIBLE 2 : able to speak; *also* : expressing oneself readily and effectively 3 : JOINTED — **ar·tic·u·late·ly** *adv* — **ar·tic·u·late·ness** *n*

²ar·tic·u·late \-ˌlāt\ *vb* **-lat·ed; -lat·ing** 1 : to utter distinctly 2 : to unite by or as if by joints — **ar·tic·u·la·tion** \-ˌtik-yə-'lā-shən\ *n*

ar·ti·fact \'ärt-ə-ˌfakt\ *n* : a usu. simple object (as a tool) showing human workmanship or modification

ar·ti·fice \'ärt-ə-fəs\ *n* 1 : TRICK; *also* : TRICKERY 2 : an ingenious device; *also* : INGENUITY

ar·ti·fi·cer \är-ˈtif-ə-sər, ˈärt-ə-fə-sər\ *n* : a skilled workman

ar·ti·fi·cial \ˌärt-ə-ˈfish-əl\ *adj* 1 : produced by art rather than nature; *also* : made by man to imitate nature 2 : not genuine : FEIGNED — **ar·ti·fi·ci·al·i·ty** \-ˌfish-ē-ˈal-ət-ē\ *n* — **ar·ti·fi·cial·ly** \-ˈfish(ə-)lē\ *adv* — **ar·ti·fi·cial·ness** \-ˈfish-əl-nəs\ *n*

artificial insemination *n* : introduction of semen into the uterus or oviduct by other than natural means

artificial intelligence *n* : the capability of a machine to imitate intelligent human behavior

artificial respiration *n* : the rhythmic forcing of air into and out of the lungs of a person whose breathing has stopped

ar·til·lery \är-ˈtil-(ə-)rē\ *n, pl* **-ler·ies** 1 : large-bore mounted firearms usu. operated by crews 2 : a branch of the army armed with artillery — **ar·til·ler·ist** \-ˈtil-ə-rəst\ *n*

ar·ti·san \ˈärt-ə-zən, -sən\ *n* : a skilled manual worker

art·ist \ˈärt-əst\ *n* 1 : one who practices an art; *esp* : one who creates objects of beauty 2 : ARTISTE

ar·tiste \är-ˈtēst\ *n* : a skilled public performer

ar·tis·tic \är-ˈtis-tik\ *adj* : showing taste and skill — **ar·tis·ti·cal·ly** \-ti-k(ə-)lē\ *adv*

art·ist·ry \ˈärt-ə-strē\ *n* : artistic quality or ability

art·less \ˈärt-ləs\ *adj* 1 : lacking art or skill 2 : free from artificiality : NATURAL 3 : free from guile : SINCERE — **art·less·ly** *adv* — **art·less·ness** *n*

art nou·veau \ˌär(t)-nü-ˈvō\ *n, often cap A & N* [F, lit., new art] : a late 19th century decorative style characterized by sinuous lines and leaf-shaped forms

arty \ˈärt-ē\ *adj* **art·i·er; -est** : showily or pretentiously artistic — **art·i·ly** \ˈärt-ᵊl-ē\ *adv* — **art·i·ness** \-ē-nəs\ *n*

ar·um \ˈar-əm\ *n* : any of a genus of plants (as the jack-in-the-pulpit or a skunk cabbage) with flowers in a fleshy enclosed spike

ARV *abbr* American Revised Version

¹-ary \ˌer-ē\ *n suffix* : thing or person belonging to or connected with ⟨functionary⟩

²-ary *adj suffix* : of, relating to, or connected with ⟨budgetary⟩

Ary·an \ˈar-ē-ən, ˈer-; ˈär-yən\ *adj* 1 : INDO-EUROPEAN 2 : NORDIC — **Aryan** *n*

¹as \əz, (ˌ)az\ *adv* 1 : to the same degree or amount : EQUALLY ⟨~ green as grass⟩ 2 : for instance ⟨various trees, ~ oak or pine⟩ 3 : when considered in a specified relation ⟨my opinion ~ distinguished from his⟩

²as *conj* 1 : in the same amount or degree in which ⟨green ~ grass⟩ 2 : in the same way that ⟨farmed ~ his father before him had farmed⟩ 3

: WHILE, WHEN ⟨spoke to me ~ I was leaving⟩ 4 : THOUGH ⟨improbable ~ it seems⟩ 5 : SINCE, BECAUSE ⟨~ I'm not wanted, I'll go⟩ 6 : that the result is ⟨so guilty ~ to leave no doubt⟩

³as *pron* 1 : THAT — used after *same* or *such* ⟨it's the same price ~ before⟩ 2 : a fact that ⟨he's rich, ~ you know⟩

⁴as *prep* : in the capacity or character of ⟨this will serve ~ a substitute⟩

As *symbol* arsenic

AS *abbr* 1 American Samoa 2 Anglo-Saxon

asa·fet·i·da *or* **asa·foe·ti·da** \ˌas-ə-ˈfit-əd-ē, -ˈfet-əd-ə\ *n* : an ill-smelling plant gum formerly used in medicine

ASAP *abbr* as soon as possible

as·bes·tos \as-ˈbes-təs, az-\ *n* : a noncombustible grayish mineral that occurs in fibrous form and is used as a fireproof material

as·cend \ə-ˈsend\ *vb* 1 : to move upward : MOUNT, CLIMB 2 : to succeed to : OCCUPY ⟨he ~ed the throne⟩

as·cen·dan·cy *also* **as·cen·den·cy** \ə-ˈsen-dən-sē\ *n* : controlling influence : DOMINATION

¹as·cen·dant *also* **as·cen·dent** \ə-ˈsen-dənt\ *n* : a dominant position

²ascendant *also* **ascendent** *adj* 1 : moving upward 2 : DOMINANT

as·cen·sion \ə-ˈsen-chən\ *n* : the act or process of ascending

Ascension Day *n* : the Thursday 40 days after Easter observed in commemoration of Christ's ascension into heaven

as·cent \ə-ˈsent\ *n* 1 : the act of mounting upward : CLIMB 2 : degree of upward slope

as·cer·tain \ˌas-ər-ˈtān\ *vb* : to learn by inquiry — **as·cer·tain·able** *adj*

as·cet·ic \ə-ˈset-ik\ *adj* : practicing self-denial esp. for religious reasons : AUSTERE — **ascetic** *n* — **as·cet·i·cism** \-ˈset-ə-ˌsiz-əm\ *n*

ASCII \ˈas-kē\ *n* [*A*merican *S*tandard *C*ode for *I*nformation *I*nterchange] : a computer code for representing alphanumeric information

ascor·bic acid \ə-ˌskȯr-bik-\ *n* : VITAMIN C

as·cot \ˈas-kət, -ˌkät\ *n* [*Ascot* Heath, racetrack near Ascot, England] : a broad neck scarf that is looped under the chin

as·cribe \ə-ˈskrīb\ *vb* **as·cribed; as·crib·ing** : to refer to a supposed cause, source, or author : ATTRIBUTE — **as·crib·able** *adj* — **as·crip·tion** \-ˈskrip-shən\ *n*

asep·tic \ā-ˈsep-tik\ *adj* : free or freed from disease-causing germs

asex·u·al \ā-ˈsek-sh(ə-w)əl\ *adj* 1 : lacking sex or functional sex organs 2 : occurring or formed without the production and union of two kinds of germ cells ⟨~ reproduction⟩ — **asex·u·al·ly** \(ˈ)ā-ˈseksh-(ə-)wə-lē\ *adv*

as for *prep* : with regard to : CONCERNING ⟨*as for* the others, they were late⟩

¹ash \ˈash\ *n* 1 : any of a genus of trees

related to the olive and having winged seeds and bark with grooves and ridges 2 : the tough elastic wood of an ash

²ash n 1 : the solid matter left when material is burned 2 : fine mineral particles from a volcano 3 pl : the remains of the dead human body

ashamed \ə-'shāmd\ adj 1 : feeling shame 2 : restrained by anticipation of shame (~ to say anything) — asham·ed·ly \-'shā-məd-lē\ adv

ash·en \'ash-ən\ adj : resembling ashes (as in color); esp : deadly pale

ash·lar \'ash-lər\ n : hewn or squared stone; also : masonry of such stone

ashore \ə-'shȯr\ adv : on or to the shore

as how conj : THAT (allowed as how she was glad to be here)

ash·ram \'äsh-rəm\ n : a religious retreat esp. of a Hindu sage

ash·tray \'ash-ˌtrā\ n : a receptacle for tobacco ashes

Ash Wednesday n : the 1st day of Lent

ashy \'ash-ē\ adj ash·i·er; -est : ASHEN

Asian \'ā-zhən, -shən\ adj : of, relating to, or characteristic of the continent of Asia or its people — Asian n

Asi·at·ic \ˌā-z(h)ē-'at-ik\ adj : ASIAN — sometimes taken to be offensive — Asiatic n

¹aside \ə-'sīd\ adv 1 : to or toward the side 2 : out of the way : AWAY

²aside n : an actor's words heard by the audience but supposedly not heard by other characters on stage

aside from prep 1 : BESIDES (aside from being pretty, she's intelligent) 2 : with the exception of (aside from one D his grades are excellent)

as if conj 1 : as it would be if (it's as if nothing had changed) 2 : as one would if (he acts as if he'd never been away) 3 : THAT (it seems as if nothing ever happens around here)

as·i·nine \'as-ᵊn-ˌīn\ adj [L asininus, fr. asinus ass] : STUPID, FOOLISH — as·i·nin·i·ty \ˌas-ᵊn-'in-ət-ē\ n

ask \'ask\ vb asked \'as(k)t\ ask·ing 1 : to call on for an answer 2 : UTTER (~ a question) 3 : to make a request of (~ him for help) 4 : to make a request for (~ help of her) 5 : to set as a price (~ed $800 for the car) 6 : INVITE

askance \ə-'skans\ adv 1 : with a side glance 2 : with distrust

askew \ə-'skyü\ adv or adj : out of line : AWRY

ASL abbr American Sign Language

¹aslant \ə-'slant\ adv or adj : in a slanting direction

²aslant prep : over or across in a slanting direction

asleep \ə-'slēp\ adv or adj 1 : in or into a state of sleep 2 : DEAD 3 : NUMB 4 : INACTIVE

as long as conj 1 : provided that (do as you like as long as you get home on time) 2 : INASMUCH AS, SINCE (as long as you're up, turn on the light)

as of prep : AT, DURING, FROM, ON (takes effect as of July 1)

asp \'asp\ n : a small poisonous African snake

as·par·a·gus \ə-'spar-ə-gəs\ n : a tall branching perennial herb related to the lilies; also : its edible young stalks

as·par·tame \as-'pär-ˌtām\ n : a crystalline low-calorie sweetener

as·pect \'as-ˌpekt\ n 1 : a position facing a particular direction 2 : APPEARANCE, LOOK 3 : PHASE

as·pen \'as-pən\ n : any of several poplars with leaves that flutter in the slightest breeze

as·per·i·ty \a-'sper-ət-ē, ə-\ n, pl -ties 1 : ROUGHNESS 2 : harshness of temper

as·per·sion \ə-'spər-zhən\ n : the act of calumniating; also : a calumnious remark

as·phalt \'as-ˌfȯlt\ or as·phal·tum \as-'fȯl-təm\ n : a dark solid or somewhat plastic substance that is found in natural beds or obtained as a residue in petroleum refining and is used in paving streets, in roofing houses, and in paints

asphalt jungle n : a big city or a specified part of a big city

as·pho·del \'as-fə-ˌdel\ n : any of several Old World herbs related to the lilies and bearing flowers in long erect spikes

as·phyx·ia \as-'fik-sē-ə\ n : a lack of oxygen or excess of carbon dioxide in the body usu. caused by interruption of breathing and causing unconsciousness

as·phyx·i·ate \-sē-ˌāt\ vb -at·ed; -at·ing : SUFFOCATE — as·phyx·i·a·tion \-ˌfik-sē-'ā-shən\ n

as·pic \'as-pik\ n [F, lit., asp] : a savory meat jelly

as·pi·rant \'as-p(ə-)rənt, ə-'spī-rənt\ n : one who aspires syn candidate, applicant, seeker

as·pi·rate \'as-p(ə-)rət\ n 1 : an independent sound \h\ or a character (as the letter h) representing it 2 : a consonant having aspiration as its final component

as·pi·ra·tion \ˌas-pə-'rā-shən\ n 1 : the pronunciation or addition of an aspirate; also : the aspirate or its symbol 2 : a drawing of something in, out, up, or through by or as if by suction 3 : a strong desire to achieve something noble; also : an object of this desire

as·pire \ə-'spī(ə)r\ vb as·pired; as·pir·ing 1 : to have a noble desire or ambition 2 : to rise aloft

as·pi·rin \'as-p(ə-)rən\ n, pl aspirin or aspirins 1 : a white crystalline drug used to relieve pain and fever 2 : a tablet of aspirin

as regards or as respects prep : in regard to : with respect to

ass \'as\ n 1 : any of several long-eared animals smaller than the related horses; esp : DONKEY 2 : a stupid person

as·sail \ə-ˈsāl\ vb : to attack violently — **as·sail·able** adj — **as·sail·ant** n

as·sas·sin \ə-ˈsas-ᵊn\ n [deriv. of Ar ḥashshāshīn, pl. of ḥashshāsh hashish-user, fr. ḥashīsh hashish] : a murderer esp. for hire or fanatical reasons

as·sas·si·nate \ə-ˈas-ᵊn-ˌāt\ vb **-nat·ed; -nat·ing** : to murder by sudden or secret attack — **as·sas·si·na·tion** \-ˌsas-ᵊn-ˈā-shən\ n

as·sault \ə-ˈsȯlt\ n 1 : a violent attack 2 : an unlawful attempt or threat to do harm to another — **assault** vb

¹as·say \ˈas-ˌā, a-ˈsā\ n : analysis to determine the quantity of one or more components present in a sample (as of an ore or drug)

²as·say \a-ˈsā, ˈas-ˌā\ vb 1 : TRY, ATTEMPT 2 : to subject (as an ore or drug) to an assay 3 : to make a critical estimate of

as·sem·blage \ə-ˈsem-blij, 3 & 4 also ˌas-ˌäm-ˈbläzh\ n 1 : a collection of persons or things : GATHERING 2 : the act of assembling 3 : an artistic composition made from scraps, junk, and odds and ends 4 : the art of making assemblages

as·sem·ble \ə-ˈsem-bəl\ vb **-bled; -bling** \-b(ə-)liŋ\ 1 : to collect into one place : CONGREGATE 2 : to fit together the parts of 3 : to meet together : CONVENE

as·sem·bly \ə-ˈsem-blē\ n, pl **-blies** 1 : a gathering of persons : MEETING 2 cap : a legislative body; esp : the lower house of a legislature 3 : a signal for troops to assemble 4 : the fitting together of parts (as of a machine)

assembly language n : a symbolic language for programming a computer that is a close approximation of machine language

assembly line n : an arrangement of machines, equipment, and workers in which work passes from operation to operation in a direct line

as·sem·bly·man \ə-ˈsem-blē-mən\ n : a member of a legislative assembly

as·sem·bly·wom·an \-ˌwùm-ən\ n : a woman who is a member of an assembly

as·sent \ə-ˈsent\ vb : AGREE, CONCUR — **assent** n

as·sert \ə-ˈsərt\ vb 1 : to state positively 2 : to demonstrate the existence of syn declare, affirm, protest, avow, claim — **as·ser·tive** \-ˈsərt-iv\ adj — **as·ser·tive·ness** n

as·ser·tion \ə-ˈsər-shən\ n : a positive statement

as·sess \ə-ˈses\ vb 1 : to fix the rate or amount of 2 : to impose (as a tax) at a specified rate 3 : to evaluate for taxation — **as·sess·ment** n — **as·ses·sor** \-ər\ n

as·set \ˈas-ˌet\ n 1 pl : the entire property of a person or company that may be used to pay debts 2 : ADVANTAGE, RESOURCE

as·sev·er·ate \ə-ˈsev-ə-ˌrāt\ vb **-at·ed; -at·ing** : to assert earnestly — **as·sev·er·a·tion** \-ˌsev-ə-ˈrā-shən\ n

as·sid·u·ous \ə-ˈsij-(ə-)wəs\ adj : steadily attentive : DILIGENT — **as·si·du·i·ty** \ˌas-ə-ˈd(y)ü-ət-ē\ n — **as·sid·u·ous·ly** adv — **as·sid·u·ous·ness** n

as·sign \ə-ˈsīn\ vb 1 : to transfer (property) to another 2 : to appoint to a duty 3 : PRESCRIBE ⟨~ a lesson⟩ 4 : FIX, SPECIFY ⟨~ a limit⟩ 5 : ASCRIBE ⟨~ a reason⟩ — **as·sign·able** adj

as·sig·na·tion \ˌas-ig-ˈnā-shən\ n : an appointment for a lovers' meeting; also : the resulting meeting

assigned risk n : a poor risk (as an accident-prone motorist) that an insurance company is forced to insure by state law

as·sign·ment \ə-ˈsīn-mənt\ n 1 : the act of assigning 2 : something assigned

as·sim·i·late \ə-ˈsim-ə-ˌlāt\ vb **-lat·ed; -lat·ing** 1 : to take up and absorb as nourishment; also : to absorb into a cultural tradition 2 : COMPREHEND 3 : to make or become similar — **as·sim·i·la·tion** \-ˌsim-ə-ˈlā-shən\ n

¹as·sist \ə-ˈsist\ vb : HELP, AID — **as·sis·tance** \-ˈsis-təns\ n

²assist n 1 : an act of assistance 2 : the act of a player who enables a teammate to make a putout (as in baseball) or score a goal (as in hockey)

as·sis·tant \ə-ˈsis-tənt\ n : one who assists : HELPER

as·size \ə-ˈsīz\ n 1 : a judicial inquest 2 pl : the former regular sessions of the superior courts in English counties

assn abbr association

assoc abbr associate; associated; association

¹as·so·ci·ate \ə-ˈsō-s(h)ē-ˌāt\ vb **-at·ed; -at·ing** 1 : to join in companionship or partnership 2 : to connect in thought

²as·so·ci·ate \-s(h)ē-ət, -shət\ n 1 : a fellow worker : PARTNER 2 : COMPANION 3 often cap : a degree conferred esp. by a junior college ⟨~ in arts⟩ — **associate** adj

as·so·ci·a·tion \ə-ˌsō-s(h)ē-ˈā-shən\ n 1 : the act of associating 2 : an organization of persons : SOCIETY

as·so·cia·tive \ə-ˈsō-s(h)ē-ˌāt-iv, -shət-iv\ adj : of, relating to, or involved in association and esp. mental association

as·so·nance \ˈas-ə-nəns\ n : repetition of vowels esp. as an alternative to rhyme in verse

as soon as conj : immediately at or just after the time that ⟨we'll start as soon as he comes⟩

as·sort \ə-ˈsȯrt\ vb 1 : to distribute into like groups 2 : HARMONIZE

as·sort·ed \-ˈsȯrt-əd\ adj : consisting of various kinds

as·sort·ment \-ˈsȯrt-mənt\ n : a collection of assorted things or persons

asst abbr assistant

as·suage \ə-ˈswāj\ vb **as·suaged; as·suag·ing** 1 : to make (as pain or grief) less

: EASE **2** : SATISFY syn alleviate, relieve, lighten, mitigate

as·sume \ə-'süm\ vb **as·sumed; as·suming 1** : to take upon oneself **2** : to pretend to have **3** : to take as granted though never proved

as·sump·tion \ə-'səmp-shən\ n **1** : the taking up of a person into heaven **2** cap : a church festival commemorating the Assumption of Mary and celebrated on August 15 **3** : a taking upon oneself **4** : PRETENSION **5** : SUPPOSITION

as·sur·ance \ə-'shùr-əns\ n **1** : PLEDGE **2** chiefly Brit : INSURANCE **3** : SECURITY **4** : SELF-CONFIDENCE; also : AUDACITY

as·sure \ə-'shùr\ vb **as·sured; as·sur·ing 1** : INSURE **2** : to give confidence to **3** : to state confidently to **4** : to make certain the attainment of

as·sured \ə-'shùrd\ n, pl assured or assureds : the beneficiary of an insurance policy

as·ta·tine \'as-tə-ˌtēn\ n : an unstable radioactive chemical element

as·ter \'as-tər\ n : any of various mostly fall-blooming leafy-stemmed herbs with daisylike purple, white, pink, or yellow flower heads

as·ter·isk \'as-tə-ˌrisk\ n [L asteriscus, fr. Gk asteriskos, lit., little star, dim. of astēr] : a character * used as a reference mark or as an indication of the omission of letters or words

astern \ə-'stərn\ adv or adj **1** : in, at, or toward the stern **2** : BACKWARD

as·ter·oid \'as-tə-ˌrȯid\ n : one of thousands of small planets between Mars and Jupiter with diameters under 500 miles (800 kilometers)

asth·ma \'az-mə\ n : an often allergic disorder marked by difficulty in breathing and a cough — **asth·mat·ic** \az-'mat-ik\ adj or n

as though conj : AS IF

astig·ma·tism \ə-'stig-mə-ˌtiz-əm\ n : a defect in a lens or an eye causing improper focusing — **as·tig·mat·ic** \ˌas-tig-'mat-ik\ adj

astir \ə-'stər\ adj : being in action : MOVING

as to prep **1** : ABOUT, CONCERNING ⟨uncertain as to what went on⟩ **2** : ACCORDING TO ⟨graded as to size⟩

as·ton·ish \ə-'stän-ish\ vb : to strike with sudden and usu. great wonder : AMAZE — **as·ton·ish·ing·ly** adv — **as·ton·ish·ment** n

as·tound \ə-'staùnd\ vb : to fill with bewilderment or wonder — **as·tound·ing·ly** adv

¹**astrad·dle** \ə-'strad-ᵊl\ adv : on or above and extending onto both sides

²**astraddle** prep : ASTRIDE

as·tra·khan \'as-trə-kən, -ˌkan\ n, often cap **1** : karakul of Russian origin **2** : a cloth with a usu. wool, curled, and looped pile resembling karakul

as·tral \'as-trəl\ adj : of or relating to the stars

astray \ə-'strā\ adv or adj **1** : off the right way or route **2** : into error

¹**astride** \ə-'strīd\ adv **1** : with one leg on each side **2** : with legs apart

²**astride** prep : with one leg on each side of

¹**as·trin·gent** \ə-'strin-jənt\ adj : able or tending to shrink body tissues — **as·trin·gen·cy** \-jən-sē\ n

²**astringent** n : an astringent agent or substance

astrol abbr astrologer; astrology

as·tro·labe \'as-trə-ˌlāb\ n : an instrument for observing the positions of celestial bodies

as·trol·o·gy \ə-'sträl-ə-jē\ n : divination based on the supposed influence of the stars upon human events — **as·trol·o·ger** \-ə-jər\ n — **as·tro·log·i·cal** \ˌas-trə-'läj-i-kəl\ adj

astron abbr astronomer; astronomy

as·tro·naut \'as-trə-ˌnȯt\ n : a traveler in a spacecraft

as·tro·nau·tics \ˌas-trə-'nȯt-iks\ n : the science of the construction and operation of spacecraft — **as·tro·nau·tic** \-ik\ or **as·tro·nau·ti·cal** \-i-kəl\ adj

as·tro·nom·i·cal \ˌas-trə-'näm-i-kəl\ also **as·tro·nom·ic** \-ik\ adj **1** : of or relating to astronomy **2** : extremely large ⟨an ∼ amount of money⟩

astronomical unit n : a unit of length used in astronomy equal to the mean distance of the earth from the sun or about 93 million miles (150 million kilometers)

as·tron·o·my \ə-'strän-ə-mē\ n, pl **-mies** : the science of the celestial bodies and of their magnitudes, motions, and constitution — **as·tron·o·mer** \-ə-mər\ n

as·tro·phys·ics \ˌas-trə-'fiz-iks\ n : astronomy dealing esp. with the physical properties and dynamic processes of celestial objects — **as·tro·phys·i·cal** \-i-kəl\ adj — **as·tro·phys·i·cist** \-'fiz-(ə-)səst\ n

as·tute \ə-'st(y)üt, a-\ adj [L astutus, fr. astus craft] : shrewdly discerning; also : WILY — **as·tute·ly** adv — **as·tute·ness** n

asun·der \ə-'sən-dər\ adv or adj **1** : into separate pieces ⟨torn ∼⟩ **2** : separated in position

ASV abbr American Standard Version

¹**as well as** conj : and in addition : and moreover ⟨brave as well as loyal⟩

²**as well as** prep : in addition to : BESIDES ⟨the coach, as well as the team, is ready⟩

asy·lum \ə-'sī-ləm\ n [ME, fr. L, fr. Gk asylon, neut. of asylos inviolable, fr. a- not + sylon right of seizure] **1** : a place of refuge **2** : protection given to esp. political fugitives **3** : an institution for the care of the needy or afflicted and esp. of the insane

asym·met·ri·cal \ˌā-sə-'me-tri-kəl\ or **asym·met·ric** \-trik\ adj : not symmetrical — **asym·me·try** \(')ā-'sim-ə-trē\ n

as·ymp·tote \'as-əm(p)-ˌtōt\ n : a straight line that is associated with a curve and tends to approximate it along an infinite branch — **as·ymp·tot·ic** \ˌas-əm(p)-ˈtät-ik\ *adj* — **as·ymp·tot·i·cal·ly** \-i-k(ə-)lē\ *adv*

¹at \ət, (ˈ)at\ *prep* **1** — used to indicate a point in time or space ⟨be here ∼ 3 o'clock⟩ ⟨he is ∼ the hotel⟩ **2** — used to indicate a goal ⟨swung ∼ the ball⟩ ⟨laugh ∼ him⟩ **3** — used to indicate position or condition ⟨∼ rest⟩ **4** — used to indicate means, cause, or manner ⟨sold ∼ auction⟩

²at \ˈät\ *n, pl* **at** — see *kip* at MONEY table

At *symbol* astatine

AT *abbr* automatic transmission

at all \ət-ˈol, ə-ˈtol, at-ˈol\ *adv* : in any way : in any circumstances ⟨not *at all* likely⟩

at·a·vism \ˈat-ə-ˌviz-əm\ *n* : appearance in an individual of a character typical of ancestors more remote than its parents; *also* : such an individual or character — **at·a·vis·tic** \ˌat-ə-ˈvis-tik\ *adj*

ate *past of* EAT

¹-ate \ət, ˌāt\ *n suffix* **1** : one acted upon (in a specified way) ⟨distill*ate*⟩ **2** : chemical compound or complex derived from a (specified) compound or element ⟨acet*ate*⟩

²-ate *n suffix* **1** : office : function : rank : group of persons holding a (specified) office or rank ⟨episcop*ate*⟩ **2** : state : dominion : jurisdiction ⟨emir*ate*⟩

³-ate *adj suffix* **1** : acted on (in a specified way) : being in a (specified) state ⟨temper*ate*⟩ ⟨degener*ate*⟩ **2** : marked by having ⟨vertebr*ate*⟩

⁴-ate \ˌāt\ *vb suffix* : cause to be modified or affected by ⟨pollin*ate*⟩ : cause to become ⟨activ*ate*⟩ : furnish with ⟨aer*ate*⟩

ate·lier \ˌat-əl-ˈyā\ *n* **1** : an artist's studio **2** : WORKSHOP

athe·ist \ˈā-thē-əst\ *n* : one who denies the existence of God — **athe·ism** \-ˌiz-əm\ *n* — **athe·is·tic** \ˌā-thē-ˈis-tik\ *adj*

athe·nae·um or **athe·ne·um** \ˌath-ə-ˈnē-əm\ *n* : LIBRARY 1

ath·ero·scle·ro·sis \ˌath-ə-rō-sklə-ˈrō-səs\ *n* : arteriosclerosis characterized by the deposition of fatty substances in and the hardening of the inner layer of the arteries — **ath·ero·scle·rot·ic** \-ˈrät-ik\ *adj*

athirst \ə-ˈthərst\ *adj* **1** *archaic* : THIRSTY **2** : EAGER, LONGING

ath·lete \ˈath-ˌlēt\ *n* [ME, fr. L *athleta*, fr. Gk *athlētēs*, fr. *athlein* to contend for a prize, fr. *athlon* prize, contest] : one trained to compete in athletics

athlete's foot *n* : ringworm of the feet

ath·let·ic \ath-ˈlet-ik\ *adj* **1** : of or relating to athletes or athletics **2** : VIGOROUS, ACTIVE **3** : STURDY, MUSCULAR

ath·let·ics \ath-ˈlet-iks\ *n sing or pl* : exercises and games requiring physical skill, strength, and endurance

athletic supporter *n* : an elastic pouch used to support the male genitals and worn esp. during athletic activity

¹athwart \ə-ˈthwórt\ *prep* **1** : ACROSS **2** : in opposition to

²athwart *adv* : obliquely across

atilt \ə-ˈtilt\ *adv or adj* **1** : in a tilted position **2** : with lance in hand

Atl *abbr* Atlantic

at·las \ˈat-ləs\ *n* : a book of maps

atm *abbr* atmosphere; atmospheric

at·mo·sphere \ˈat-mə-ˌsfiər\ *n* **1** : the mass of air surrounding the earth **2** : a surrounding influence **3** : a unit of pressure equal to the pressure of air at sea level or about 14.7 pounds per square inch (10 newtons per square centimeter) **4** : a dominant effect — **at·mo·spher·ic** \ˌat-mə-ˈsfir-ik, -ˈsfer-\ *adj* — **at·mo·spher·i·cal·ly** \-i-k(ə-)lē\ *adv*

at·mo·sphe·rics \ˌat-mə-ˈsfir-iks, -ˈsfer-\ *n pl* : disturbances produced in a radio receiver by atmospheric electrical phenomena

atoll \ˈa-ˌtól, -ˌtäl, ˈā-\ *n* : a coral island consisting of a reef surrounding a lagoon

at·om \ˈat-əm\ *n* [ME, fr. L *atomus*, fr. Gk *atomos*, fr. *atomos* indivisible, fr. *a-* not + *temnein* to cut] **1** : a tiny particle : BIT **2** : the smallest particle of a chemical element that can exist alone or in combination

atom bomb *n* : a very destructive bomb utilizing the energy released by splitting the atom

atom·ic \ə-ˈtäm-ik\ *adj* **1** : of or relating to atoms, atomic energy, or atom bombs **2** : extremely small

atomic clock *n* : a precision clock regulated by the natural vibration of atoms or molecules (as of cesium or ammonia)

atomic energy *n* : energy that can be liberated by changes (as by fission or fusion) in the nucleus of an atom

atomic number *n* : the number of protons in the nucleus of an element

at·om·ize \ˈat-ə-ˌmīz\ *vb* **-ized; -iz·ing** : to reduce to minute particles

at·om·iz·er \ˈat-ə-ˌmī-zər\ *n* : a device for reducing a liquid to a very fine spray (as for spraying the throat)

atom smasher *n* : ACCELERATOR 3

aton·al \ā-ˈtōn-ᵊl\ *adj* : marked by avoidance of traditional musical tonality — **ato·nal·i·ty** \ˌā-tō-ˈnal-ət-ē\ *n* — **aton·al·ly** \ā-ˈtōn-ᵊl-ē\ *adv*

atone \ə-ˈtōn\ *vb* **atoned; aton·ing 1** : to make amends **2** : EXPIATE

atone·ment \ə-ˈtōn-mənt\ *n* **1** : the reconciliation of God and man through the death of Jesus Christ **2** : reparation for an offense

atop \ə-ˈtäp\ *prep* : on top of

ATP \ˌā-ˌtē-ˈpē\ *n* [*adenosine triphosphate*] : a compound that occurs widely in living tissue and supplies energy for many cellular processes by undergoing enzymatic hydrolysis

atri·um \ˈā-trē-əm\ *n, pl* **atria** \-trē-ə\ *also* **atri·ums 1** : the central hall of a

Roman house 2 : an anatomical cavity or passage; *esp* : one of the chambers of the heart that receives blood from the veins — **atri·al** \-trē-əl\ *adj*

atro·cious \ə-'trō-shəs\ *adj* 1 : savagely brutal, cruel, or wicked 2 : very bad : ABOMINABLE — **atro·cious·ly** *adv* — **atro·cious·ness** *n*

atroc·i·ty \ə-'träs-ət-ē\ *n, pl* **-ties** 1 : ATROCIOUSNESS 2 : an atrocious act or object

¹**at·ro·phy** \'a-trə-fē\ *n, pl* **-phies** : decrease in size or wasting away of a bodily part or tissue

²**atrophy** *vb* **-phied; -phy·ing** : to cause or undergo atrophy

at·ro·pine \'a-trə-ˌpēn\ *n* : a drug from belladonna and related plants used esp. to relieve spasms and to dilate the pupil of the eye

att *abbr* 1 attached 2 attention 3 attorney

at·tach \ə-'tach\ *vb* 1 : to seize legally in order to force payment of a debt 2 : to bind by personal ties 3 : FASTEN, CONNECT 4 : to be fastened or connected

at·ta·ché \ˌat-ə-'shā, ˌa-ˌta-, ə-ˌta-\ *n* [F] : a technical expert on the diplomatic staff of an ambassador

at·ta·ché case \ˌtash-ā-, ˌat-ə-'shā-\ *n* : a small thin suitcase used esp. for carrying papers and documents

at·tach·ment \ə-'tach-mənt\ *n* 1 : legal seizure of property 2 : connection by ties of affection and regard 3 : a device attached to a machine or implement 4 : a connection by which one thing is attached to another

¹**at·tack** \ə-'tak\ *vb* 1 : to set upon with force or words : ASSAIL, ASSAULT 2 : to set to work on

²**attack** *n* 1 : an offensive action 2 : a fit of sickness

at·tain \ə-'tān\ *vb* 1 : ACHIEVE, ACCOMPLISH 2 : to arrive at : REACH — **at·tain·abil·i·ty** \ə-ˌtā-nə-'bil-ət-ē\ *n* — **at·tain·able** *adj*

at·tain·der \ə-'tān-dər\ *n* : extinction of the civil rights of a person upon sentence of death or outlawry

at·tain·ment \ə-'tān-mənt\ *n* 1 : the act of attaining 2 : ACCOMPLISHMENT

at·taint \ə-'tānt\ *vb* : to condemn to loss of civil rights

at·tar \'at-ər\ *n* [Per *'atir* perfumed, fr. Ar. fr. *'itr* perfume] : a fragrant floral oil

at·tempt \ə-'tempt\ *vb* : to make an effort toward : TRY — **attempt** *n*

at·tend \ə-'tend\ *vb* 1 : to look after : TEND 2 : to be present with : ACCOMPANY 3 : to be present at 4 : to apply oneself 5 : to pay attention 6 : to take charge (I'll ～ to that)

at·ten·dance \ə-'ten-dəns\ *n* 1 : the act or fact of attending 2 : the number of persons present

¹**at·ten·dant** \ə-'ten-dənt\ *n* : one that attends another to render a service

²**attendant** *adj* : ACCOMPANYING ⟨～ circumstances⟩

at·ten·tion \ə-'ten-chən\ *n* 1 : the act or state of applying the mind to an object 2 : CONSIDERATION 3 : an act of courtesy 4 : a position of readiness for further orders assumed on command by a soldier — **at·ten·tive** \-'tent-iv\ *adj* — **at·ten·tive·ly** *adv* — **at·ten·tive·ness** *n*

at·ten·u·ate \ə-'ten-yə-ˌwāt\ *vb* **-at·ed; -at·ing** 1 : to make or become thin 2 : WEAKEN — **at·ten·u·a·tion** \-ˌten-yə-ˈwā-shən\ *n*

at·test \ə-'test\ *vb* 1 : to certify as genuine by signing as a witness 2 : MANIFEST 3 : TESTIFY — **at·tes·ta·tion** \ˌa-ˌtes-'tā-shən\ *n*

at·tic \'at-ik\ *n* : the space or room in a building immediately below the roof

¹**at·tire** \ə-'tī(ə)r\ *vb* **at·tired; at·tir·ing** : DRESS, ARRAY

²**attire** *n* : DRESS, CLOTHES

at·ti·tude \'at-ə-ˌt(y)üd\ *n* 1 : the arrangement of the parts of a body : POSTURE 2 : a mental position or feeling with regard to a fact or state 3 : the position of something in relation to something else

at·ti·tu·di·nize \ˌat-ə-'t(y)üd-ᵊn-ˌīz\ *vb* **-nized; -niz·ing** : to assume an affected mental attitude : POSE

attn *abbr* attention

at·tor·ney \ə-'tər-nē\ *n, pl* **-neys** : a legal agent qualified to act for persons in legal proceedings

attorney general *n, pl* **attorneys general** *or* **attorney generals** : the chief legal representative and adviser of a nation or state

at·tract \ə-'trakt\ *vb* 1 : to draw to or toward oneself : cause to approach 2 : to draw by emotional or aesthetic appeal **syn** charm, fascinate, allure, captivate, enchant — **at·trac·tive** \-'trak-tiv\ *adj* — **at·trac·tive·ly** *adv* — **at·trac·tive·ness** *n*

at·trac·tant \ə-'trak-tənt\ *n* : a substance used to attract insects or other animals

at·trac·tion \ə-'trak-shən\ *n* 1 : the act or power of attracting; *esp* : personal charm 2 : an attractive quality, object, or feature 3 : a force tending to draw particles together

attrib *abbr* attributive; attributively

¹**at·tri·bute** \'a-trə-ˌbyüt\ *n* 1 : an inherent characteristic 2 : a word ascribing a quality; *esp* : ADJECTIVE

²**at·trib·ute** \ə-'trib-yət\ *vb* **-ut·ed; -ut·ing** 1 : to explain as to cause or origin ⟨～ the illness to fatigue⟩ 2 : to regard as a characteristic **syn** ascribe, credit, charge, impute — **at·trib·ut·able** *adj* — **at·tri·bu·tion** \ˌa-trə-'byü-shən\ *n*

at·trib·u·tive \ə-'trib-yət-iv\ *adj* : joined directly to a modified noun without a linking verb ⟨*red* in *red hair* is an ～ adjective⟩ — **attributive** *n*

at·tri·tion \ə-'trish-ən\ *n* 1 : the act of wearing away by or as if by rubbing 2

: a reduction (as in personnel) as a result of resignation, retirement, or death

at·tune \ə-ˈt(y)ün\ vb : to bring into harmony : TUNE

atty abbr attorney

atyp·i·cal \ā-ˈtip-i-kəl\ adj : not typical : IRREGULAR

Au symbol [L aurum] gold

au·burn \ˈȯ-bərn\ adj : reddish brown — **auburn** n

au cou·rant \ˌō-kù-ˈrä°\ adj [F, lit., in the current] : UP-TO-DATE

¹auc·tion \ˈȯk-shən\ n [L auction-, auctio, lit., increase, fr. auctus, pp. of augēre to increase] : public sale of property to the highest bidder

²auction vb **auc·tioned; auc·tion·ing** \-sh(ə-)niŋ\ : to sell at auction

auction bridge n : a bridge game in which tricks made in excess of the contract are scored toward game

auc·tion·eer \ˌȯk-shə-ˈniər\ n : an agent who conducts an auction

auc·to·ri·al \ȯk-ˈtōr-ē-əl\ adj : of or relating to an author

aud abbr audit; auditor

au·da·cious \ȯ-ˈdā-shəs\ adj 1 : DARING, BOLD 2 : INSOLENT — **au·da·cious·ly** adv — **au·da·cious·ness** n — **au·dac·i·ty** \ȯ-ˈdas-ət-ē\ n

¹au·di·ble \ˈȯd-ə-bəl\ adj : capable of being heard — **au·di·bil·i·ty** \ˌȯd-ə-ˈbil-ət-ē\ n — **au·di·bly** \ˈȯd-ə-blē\ adv

²audible n : AUTOMATIC 2

au·di·ence \ˈȯd-ē-əns\ n 1 : a formal interview 2 : an opportunity of being heard 3 : an assembly of listeners or spectators

¹au·dio \ˈȯd-ē-ˌō\ adj 1 : of or relating to frequencies (as of radio waves) corresponding to those of audible sound waves 2 : of or relating to sound or its reproduction and esp. high-fidelity sound reproduction 3 : relating to or used in the transmission or reception of sound

²audio n 1 : the transmission, reception, or reproduction of sound 2 : the section of television or motion-picture equipment that deals with sound

au·di·ol·o·gy \ˌȯd-ē-ˈäl-ə-jē\ n : a branch of science dealing with hearing and esp. with the treatment of individuals having trouble with hearing — **au·di·o·log·i·cal** \-ē-ə-ˈläj-i-kəl\ adj — **au·di·ol·o·gist** \-ē-ˈäl-ə-jəst\ n

au·dio·phile \ˈȯd-ē-ō-ˌfīl\ n : one who is enthusiastic about high-fidelity sound reproduction

au·dio·vi·su·al \ˌȯd-ē-ō-ˈvizh-(ə-w)əl\ adj : of, relating to, or making use of both hearing and sight

au·dio·vi·su·als \-wəlz\ n pl : audiovisual materials (as filmstrips)

¹au·dit \ˈȯd-ət\ n : a formal examination and verification of financial accounts

²audit vb 1 : to perform an audit on or for 2 : to attend (a course) without expecting formal credit

¹au·di·tion \ȯ-ˈdish-ən\ n : HEARING; esp

: a trial performance to appraise an entertainer's merits

²audition vb **-tioned; -tion·ing** \-ˈdish-(ə-)niŋ\ : to give an audition to; also : to give a trial performance

au·di·tor \ˈȯd-ət-ər\ n 1 : LISTENER 2 : a person who audits

au·di·to·ri·um \ˌȯd-ə-ˈtōr-ē-əm\ n 1 : the part of a public building where an audience sits 2 : a hall or building used for public gatherings

au·di·to·ry \ˈȯd-ə-ˌtōr-ē\ adj : of or relating to hearing or to the sense or organs of hearing

auf Wie·der·seh·en \auf-ˈvēd-ər-ˌzān\ interj [G] — used to express farewell

Aug abbr August

au·ger \ˈȯ-gər\ n : a boring tool

aught \ˈȯt, ˈät\ n : ZERO, CIPHER

aug·ment \ȯg-ˈment\ vb : to ENLARGE, INCREASE — **aug·men·ta·tion** \ˌȯg-mən-ˈtā-shən\ n

au gra·tin \ō-ˈgrat-ᵊn, ȯ-, -ˈgrät-\ adj [F, lit., with the burnt scrapings from the pan] : covered with bread crumbs or grated cheese and browned

¹au·gur \ˈȯ-gər\ n 1 : DIVINER, SOOTHSAYER

²augur vb 1 : to foretell esp. from omens 2 : to give promise of : PRESAGE

au·gu·ry \ˈȯ-g(y)ə-rē\ n, pl -ries 1 : divination from omens 2 : OMEN, PORTENT

au·gust \ȯ-ˈgəst\ adj : marked by majestic dignity or grandeur — **au·gust·ly** adv — **au·gust·ness** n

Au·gust \ˈȯ-gəst\ n [ME, fr. OE, fr. L Augustus, fr. Augustus Caesar] : the eighth month of the year having 31 days

au jus \ō-ˈzhü(s), -ˈjüs; ō-zhœ̄\ adj [F] : served in the juice obtained from roasting

auk \ˈȯk\ n : any of several stocky black-and-white diving seabirds that breed in colder parts of the northern hemisphere

auld \ˈȯl(d), ˈäl(d)\ adj, chiefly Scot : OLD

aunt \ˈant, ˈänt\ n 1 : the sister of one's father or mother 2 : the wife of one's uncle

au pair \ˈō-ˌpaər\ n [F, on even terms] : a foreign girl who does domestic work for a family in return for room and board and the opportunity to learn the family's language

au·ra \ˈȯr-ə\ n 1 : a distinctive atmosphere surrounding a given source 2 : a luminous radiation

au·ral \ˈȯr-əl\ adj : of or relating to the ear or to the sense of hearing

aurar pl of EYRIR

au·re·ate \ˈȯr-ē-ət\ adj 1 : of a golden color or brilliance 2 : RESPLENDENT, ORNATE

au·re·ole \ˈȯr-ē-ˌōl\ or **au·re·o·la** \ȯ-ˈrē-ə-lə\ n 1 : HALO, NIMBUS

au re·voir \ˌȯr-əv-ˈwär\ n [F, lit., till seeing again] : GOOD-BYE

au·ri·cle \ˈȯr-i-kəl\ n : an atrium of the heart

au·ric·u·lar \ȯ-ˈrik-yə-lər\ adj 1 : told

privately ⟨∼ confession⟩ 2 : known by the sense of hearing

au·ro·ra \ə-'rōr-ə\ n, pl auroras or au·ro·rae \-(.)ē\ : a luminous phenomenon of streamers or arches of light appearing in the upper atmosphere esp. of a planet's polar regions — au·ro·ral \-əl\ adj

aurora aus·tra·lis \ȯ-'strā-ləs\ n : an aurora that occurs in earth's southern hemisphere

aurora bo·re·al·is \-.bōr-ē-'al-əs\ n : an aurora that occurs in earth's northern hemisphere

AUS abbr Army of the United States

aus·pice \'ȯ-spəs\ n, pl aus·pic·es \-spə-səz, -.sēz\ [L auspicium, fr. auspic-, auspex diviner by birds, fr. avis bird + specere to look, look at] 1 : observation in augury 2 : a prophetic sign or omen 3 pl : kindly patronage and protection

aus·pi·cious \ȯ-'spish-əs\ adj 1 : promising success : FAVORABLE 2 : FORTUNATE, PROSPEROUS — aus·pi·cious·ly adv

aus·tere \ȯ-'stiər\ adj 1 : STERN, SEVERE, STRICT 2 : ABSTEMIOUS 3 : UNADORNED ⟨∼ style⟩ — aus·tere·ly adv — aus·ter·i·ty \ȯ-'ster-ət-ē\ n

¹aus·tral \'ȯs-trəl\ adj : SOUTHERN

²aus·tral \au̇-'sträl\ n, pl aus·tral·es \-'sträl-ās\ also australs — see MONEY table

Aus·tra·lian \ȯ-'sträl-yən\ n : a native or inhabitant of Australia — Australian adj

Aus·tri·an \'ȯ-strē-ən\ n : a native or inhabitant of Austria — Austrian adj

Aus·tro·ne·sian \.ȯs-trə-'nē-zhən\ adj : of, relating to, or constituting a family of languages spoken in the area extending from Madagascar eastward through the Malay peninsula to Hawaii and Easter Island

auth abbr 1 authentic 2 author 3 authorized

au·then·tic \ə-'thent-ik, ȯ-\ adj : GENUINE, REAL — au·then·ti·cal·ly \-i-k(ə-)lē\ adv — au·then·tic·i·ty \.ȯ-.then-'tis-ət-ē\ n

au·then·ti·cate \ə-'thent-i-.kāt, ȯ-\ vb -cat·ed; -cat·ing : to prove genuine — au·then·ti·ca·tion \-.thent-i-'kā-shən\ n

au·thor \'ȯ-thər\ n [ME auctour, deriv. of L auctor originator, author, fr. auctus, pp. of augēre to increase] 1 : one that writes or composes a literary work 2 : one that originates or creates

au·thor·ess \'ȯ-th(ə-)rəs\ n : a woman author

au·thor·i·tar·i·an \ȯ-.thär-ə-'ter-ē-ən, ə-, -.thȯr-\ adj 1 : characterized by or favoring the principle of blind obedience to authority 2 : characterized by or favoring concentration of political power in an authority not responsible to the people

au·thor·i·ta·tive \ə-'thär-ə-.tāt-iv, ȯ-, -'thȯr-\ adj : supported by, proceed-

ing from, or being an authority : TRUSTWORTHY — au·thor·i·ta·tive·ly adv

au·thor·i·ty \ə-'thär-ət-ē, ȯ-, -'thȯr-\ n, pl -ties 1 : a citation used in support of a statement or in defense of an action; also : the source of such a citation 2 : one appealed to as an expert 3 : power to influence thought or behavior 4 : freedom granted : RIGHT 5 : persons in command; esp : GOVERNMENT

au·tho·rize \'ȯ-thə-.rīz\ vb -rized; -riz·ing 1 : SANCTION 2 : to give legal power to — au·tho·ri·za·tion \.ȯ-th(ə-)rə-'zā-shən\ n

au·thor·ship \'ȯ-thər-.ship\ n 1 : the state of being an author 2 : the source of a piece of writing, music, or art

au·tism \'ȯ-.tiz-əm\ n : absorption in self-centered subjective mental activity (as daydreaming, fantasies, delusions, and hallucinations) esp. when accompanied by marked withdrawal from reality — au·tis·tic \ȯ-'tis-tik\ adj

au·to \'ȯt-ō\ n, pl autos : AUTOMOBILE

au·to·bahn \'ȯt-ō-.bän, 'au̇t-\ n : a German expressway

au·to·bi·og·ra·phy \.ȯt-ə-bī-'äg-rə-fē, -bē-\ n : the biography of a person narrated by himself — au·to·bi·og·ra·pher \-fər\ n — au·to·bi·o·graph·i·cal \-.bī-ə-'graf-i-kəl\ adj

au·toch·tho·nous \ȯ-'täk-thə-nəs\ adj : INDIGENOUS, NATIVE

au·toc·ra·cy \ȯ-'täk-rə-sē\ n, pl -cies : government by one person having unlimited power — au·to·crat \'ȯt-ə-.krat\ n — au·to·crat·ic \.ȯt-ə-'krat-ik\ adj — au·to·crat·i·cal·ly \-i-k(ə-)lē\ adv

¹au·to·graph \'ȯt-ə-.graf\ n 1 : an original manuscript 2 : a person's signature written by hand

²autograph vb : to write one's signature on

au·to·im·mune \.ȯt-ō-im-'yün\ adj : of, relating to, or caused by antibodies or lymphocytes that attack molecules, cells, or tissues of the organism producing them ⟨∼ diseases⟩ — au·to·im·mu·ni·ty \-im-'yün-ət-ē\ n

au·to·mate \'ȯt-ə-.māt\ vb -mat·ed; -mat·ing 1 : to operate by automation 2 : to convert to automatic operation

¹au·to·mat·ic \.ȯt-ə-'mat-ik\ adj 1 : INVOLUNTARY 2 : made so that certain parts act in a desired manner at the proper time : SELF-ACTING — au·to·mat·i·cal·ly \-i-k(ə-)lē\ adv

²automatic n 1 : an automatic device; esp : an automatic firearm 2 : a substitute play called by a football quarterback at the line of scrimmage

au·to·ma·tion \.ȯt-ə-'mā-shən\ n 1 : the technique of making an apparatus, a process, or a system operate automatically 2 : the state of being operated automatically 3 : automatic operation of an apparatus, process, or system by mechanical or electronic devices that replace human operators

au·tom·a·tize \ȯ-'täm-ə-ˌtīz\ *vb* -tized; -tiz·ing : to make automatic — **au·tom·a·ti·za·tion** \-ˌtäm-ət-ə-'zā-shən\ *n*

au·tom·a·ton \ȯ-'täm-ət-ən, -ə-ˌtän\ *n, pl* -atons *or* -a·ta \-ət-ə, -ə-ˌtä\ 1 : an automatic machine; *esp* : ROBOT 2 : an individual who acts mechanically

au·to·mo·bile \'ȯt-ə-mō-ˌbēl, ˌȯt-ə-mə-'bēl\ *n* : a usu. 4-wheeled automotive vehicle for passenger transportation on streets and roadways — **au·to·mo·bil·ist** \-ˌbē-ləst, -'bē-\ *n*

au·to·mo·tive \ˌȯt-ə-'mōt-iv\ *adj* 1 : of or relating to automobiles, trucks, or buses 2 : SELF-PROPELLED

au·to·nom·ic nervous system \ˌȯt-ə-'näm-ik-\ *n* : a part of the vertebrate nervous system that governs involuntary actions and that consists of the sympathetic nervous system and the parasympathetic nervous system

au·ton·o·mous \ȯ-'tän-ə-məs\ *adj* : having the right or power of self-government — **au·ton·o·mous·ly** *adv* — **au·ton·o·my** \-mē\ *n*

au·top·sy \'ȯ-ˌtäp-sē, 'ȯt-əp-\ *n, pl* -sies [Gk *autopsia* act of seeing with one's own eyes, fr. *autos* self + *opsis* sight] : examination of a dead body usu. with dissection sufficient to determine the cause of death or extent of change produced by disease — **autopsy** *vb*

au·tumn \'ȯt-əm\ *n* : the season between summer and winter — **au·tum·nal** \ȯ-'təm-nəl\ *adj*

aux *or* **auxil** *abbr* auxiliary

¹**aux·il·ia·ry** \ȯg-'zil-yə-rē, -'zil-(ə-)rē\ *adj* 1 : providing help 2 : functioning in a subsidiary capacity 3 : accompanying a verb form to express person, number, mood, or tense (~ verbs)

²**auxiliary** *n, pl* -ries 1 : an auxiliary person, group, or device 2 : an auxiliary verb

aux·in \'ȯk-sən\ *n* : a plant hormone that stimulates growth in length

av *abbr* 1 avenue 2 average 3 avoirdupois

AV *abbr* 1 ad valorem 2 audiovisual 3 Authorized Version

¹**avail** \ə-'vāl\ *vb* : to be of use or advantage : HELP, BENEFIT

²**avail** *n* : USE (effort was of no ~)

avail·able \ə-'vā-lə-bəl\ *adj* 1 : USABLE 2 : ACCESSIBLE — **avail·abil·i·ty** \-ˌvā-lə-'bil-ət-ē\ *n*

av·a·lanche \'av-ə-ˌlanch\ *n* : a mass of snow, ice, earth, or rock sliding down a mountainside

avant-garde \ˌäv-ˌän(t)-'gärd\ *n* [F, vanguard] : those esp. in the arts who create or apply new or experimental ideas and techniques — **avant-garde** *adj*

av·a·rice \'av-(ə-)rəs\ *n* : excessive desire for wealth : GREED — **av·a·ri·cious** \ˌav-ə-'rish-əs\ *adj*

avast \ə-'vast\ *vb imper* — a nautical command to stop or cease

av·a·tar \'av-ə-ˌtär\ *n* [Skt *avatāra* descent] : INCARNATION

avaunt \ə-'vȯnt\ *adv* : AWAY, HENCE

avdp *abbr* avoirdupois

ave *abbr* avenue

Ave Ma·ria \ˌäv-ˌä-mə-'rē-ə\ *n* : HAIL MARY

avenge \ə-'venj\ *vb* avenged; aveng·ing : to take vengeance for — **aveng·er** *n*

av·e·nue \'av-ə-ˌn(y)ü\ *n* 1 : a way or route to a place or goal : PATH 2 : a broad street esp. when bordered by trees

aver \ə-'vər\ *vb* averred; aver·ring : to declare positively

¹**av·er·age** \'av-(ə-)rij\ *n* [modif. of MF *avarie* damage to ship or cargo, fr. It *avaria*, fr. Ar *'awārīyah* damaged merchandise] 1 : ARITHMETIC MEAN 2 : a ratio (as a rate per thousand) of successful tries to total tries (batting ~ of .303)

²**average** *adj* 1 : equaling or approximating an arithmetic mean 2 : being about midway between extremes 3 : not out of the ordinary : COMMON

³**average** *vb* av·er·aged; av·er·ag·ing 1 : to be at or come to an average 2 : to be usually 3 : to find the average of

averse \ə-'vərs\ *adj* : having an active feeling of dislike or reluctance (~ to exercise)

aver·sion \ə-'vər-zhən\ *n* 1 : a feeling of repugnance for something with a desire to avoid it 2 : something decidedly disliked

avert \ə-'vərt\ *vb* 1 : to turn aside or away (~ the eyes) 2 : to ward off

avg *abbr* average

avi·an \'ā-vē-ən\ *adj* [L *avis* bird] : of, relating to, or derived from birds

avi·ary \'ā-vē-ˌer-ē\ *n, pl* -ar·ies : a place where live birds are kept usu. for exhibition

avi·a·tion \ˌā-vē-'ā-shən, ˌav-ē-\ *n* 1 : the operation of heavier-than-air aircraft 2 : aircraft manufacture, development, and design — **avi·a·tor** \'ā-vē-ˌāt-ər, 'av-ē-\ *n*

avi·a·trix \ˌā-vē-'ā-triks, ˌav-ē-\ *n, pl* -trix·es \-trik-səz\ *or* -tri·ces \-trə-ˌsēz\ : a woman airplane pilot

av·id \'av-əd\ *adj* 1 : craving eagerly : GREEDY 2 : enthusiastic in pursuit of an interest — **avid·i·ty** \ə-'vid-ət-ē, a-\ *n* — **av·id·ly** *adv*

avi·on·ics \ˌā-vē-'än-iks, ˌav-ē-\ *n* : electronics designed for use in aerospace vehicles — **avi·on·ic** \-ik\ *adj*

avi·ta·min·osis \ˌā-ˌvīt-ə-mə-'nō-səs\ *n, pl* -o·ses \-ˌsēz\ : disease resulting from vitamin deficiency

avo \'av-(ˌ)ü\ *n, pl* **avos** — see *pataca* at MONEY table

avo·ca·do \ˌav-ə-'käd-ō, ˌäv-\ *n, pl* -dos *also* -does [modif. of Sp *aguacate*, fr. Nahuatl *ahuacatl*, lit., : testicle] : a usu. green pear-shaped fruit with rich oily flesh that is produced by a tropical American tree; *also* : this tree

avo·ca·tion \ˌav-ə-'kā-shən\ *n* : a

subordinate occupation pursued esp. for pleasure : HOBBY

av·o·cet \'av-ə-ˌset\ *n* : any of several long-legged shorebirds with webbed feet and slender upward-curving bills

avoid \ə-'vȯid\ *vb* 1 : to keep away from : SHUN 2 : to prevent the occurrence of 3 : to refrain from — **avoid·able** *adj* — **avoid·ance** \-ᵊns\ *n*

avoir·du·pois \ˌav-ərd-ə-'pȯiz\ *n* [ME *avoir de pois* goods sold by weight, fr. OF, lit., goods of weight] 1 : AVOIRDUPOIS WEIGHT 2 : WEIGHT, HEAVINESS; *esp* : personal weight

avoirdupois weight *n* : a system of weights based on a pound of 16 ounces and an ounce of 16 drams — see WEIGHT table

avouch \ə-'vau̇ch\ *vb* 1 : to declare positively : AVER 2 : GUARANTEE

avow \ə-'vau̇\ *vb* : to declare openly — **avow·al** \-'vau̇(-ə)l\ *n*

avun·cu·lar \ə-'vəŋ-kyə-lər\ *adj* : of, relating to, or resembling an uncle

await \ə-'wāt\ *vb* : to wait for : EXPECT

¹**awake** \ə-'wāk\ *vb* awoke \-'wōk\ *also* awaked \-'wākt\; awaked *or* awo·ken \-'wō-kən\ *also* awoke; awak·ing : to bring back to consciousness after sleep : wake up

²**awake** *adj* : not asleep; *also* : ALERT

awak·en \ə-'wā-kən\ *vb* awak·ened; awak·en·ing \-'wāk-(ə-)niŋ\ : AWAKE

¹**award** \ə-'wȯrd\ *vb* 1 : to give by judicial decision (~ damages) 2 : to give in recognition of merit or achievement (~ a prize)

²**award** *n* 1 : a final decision : JUDGMENT 2 : something awarded : PRIZE

aware \ə-'waər\ *adj* : having perception or knowledge : CONSCIOUS, INFORMED — **aware·ness** *n*

awash \ə-'wȯsh, -'wäsh\ *adj* 1 : washed by waves or tide 2 : AFLOAT 3 : FLOODED

¹**away** \ə-'wā\ *adv* 1 : from this or that place (go ~) 2 : out of the way 3 : in another direction (turn ~) 4 : out of existence (fade ~) 5 : from one's possession (give ~) 6 : without interruption (chatter ~) 7 : at a distance in space or time (far ~) (~ back in 1910)

²**away** *adj* 1 : ABSENT 2 : distant in space or time (a lake 10 miles ~)

¹**awe** \'ȯ\ *n* 1 : profound and reverent dread of the supernatural 2 : respectful fear inspired by authority

²**awe** *vb* awed; aw·ing : to inspire with awe

aweigh \ə-'wā\ *adj* : just clear of the bottom and hanging perpendicularly (anchors ~)

awe·some \'ȯ-səm\ *adj* 1 : expressive of awe 2 : inspiring awe

awe·struck \-ˌstrək\ *also* **awe·strick·en** \-ˌstrik-ən\ *adj* : filled with awe

aw·ful \'ȯ-fəl\ *adj* 1 : inspiring awe 2 : extremely disagreeable 3 : very great — **aw·ful·ly** \-ē\ *adv*

awhile \ə-'hwīl\ *adv* : for a while

awhirl \ə-'hwərl\ *adj* : in a whirl : WHIRLING

awk·ward \'ȯ-kwərd\ *adj* 1 : CLUMSY 2 : UNGRACEFUL 3 : difficult to explain : EMBARRASSING 4 : difficult to deal with — **awk·ward·ly** *adv* — **awk·ward·ness** *n*

awl \'ȯl\ *n* : a pointed instrument for making small holes

aw·ning \'ȯn-iŋ\ *n* : a rooflike cover (as of canvas) extended over or in front of a place as a shelter

AWOL \'ā-ˌwȯl, ˌā-ˌdəb-əl-yü-ˌō-'el\ *n* : a person who is absent without leave — **AWOL** *adj or adv*

awry \ə-'rī\ *adv or adj* 1 : ASKEW 2 : out of the right course : AMISS

ax *or* **axe** \'aks\ *n* : a chopping or cutting tool with an edged head fitted parallel to a handle

ax·i·al \'ak-sē-əl\ *adj* 1 : of, relating to, or functioning as an axis 2 : situated around, in the direction of, on, or along an axis — **ax·i·al·ly** \'ak-sē-ə-lē\ *adv*

ax·i·om \'ak-sē-əm\ *n* [L *axioma*, fr. Gk *axioma*, lit., honor, fr. *axioun* to think worthy, fr. *axios* worth, worthy] 1 : a statement generally accepted as true : MAXIM 2 : a proposition regarded as a self-evident truth — **ax·i·om·at·ic** \ˌak-sē-ə-'mat-ik\ *adj* — **ax·i·om·at·i·cal·ly** \-i-k(ə-)lē\ *adv*

ax·is \'ak-səs\ *n, pl* **ax·es** \-ˌsēz\ 1 : a real or imaginary straight line passing through a body that actually or supposedly revolves upon it (the earth's ~) 2 : one of the reference lines of a system of coordinates 3 : a straight line with respect to which a body or figure is symmetrical 4 : a bodily structure around which parts are arranged in a symmetrical way; *esp* : the main stem of a plant from which leaves and branches arise 5 : an alliance between major powers

ax·le \'ak-səl\ *n* : a shaft on which a wheel revolves

ayah \'ī-ə\ *n* [Hindi *āyā*, fr. Pg *aia*, fr. L *avia* grandmother] : a native nurse or maid in India

aya·tol·lah \ˌī-ə-'tō-lə, -'täl-ə, -'təl-ə, 'ī-ə-ˌ; ˌī-ə-tō-'lä\ *n* [Per, lit., sign of God, fr. Ar *ayat* sign, miracle + *allāh* God] : an Islamic religious leader — used as a title of respect

¹**aye** *also* **ay** \'ā\ *adv* : ALWAYS, EVER

²**aye** *also* **ay** \'ī\ *adv* : YES

³**aye** *also* **ay** \'ī\ *n, pl* **ayes** : an affirmative vote

AZ *abbr* Arizona

aza·lea \ə-'zāl-yə\ *n* : any of numerous rhododendrons with funnel-shaped blossoms and usu. deciduous leaves

az·i·muth \'az-(ə)məth\ *n* : horizontal direction expressed as an angular distance

Az·tec \'az-ˌtek\ *n* : a member of an American Indian people that founded the Mexican empire and were con-

quered by Hernan Cortes in 1519 —
Az·tec·an *adj*

azure \\'azh-ər\\ *n* : the blue of the clear sky — **azure** *adj*

B

¹b \\'bē\\ *n, pl* **b's** *or* **bs** \\'bēz\\ *often cap* **1** : the 2d letter of the English alphabet **2** : a grade rating a student's work as good

²b *abbr, often cap* **1** bachelor **2** bass **3** bishop **4** book **5** born

B *symbol* boron

Ba *symbol* barium

BA *abbr* **1** bachelor of arts **2** batting average

bab·bitt metal \\'bab-ət-\\ *n* : an alloy used for lining bearings; *esp* : one containing tin, copper, and antimony

bab·ble \\'bab-əl\\ *vb* **bab·bled; bab·bling** \\-(ə-)liŋ\\ **1** : to utter meaningless sounds **2** : to talk foolishly or excessively — **babble** *n* — **bab·bler** \\-(ə-)lər\\ *n*

babe \\'bāb\\ *n* **1** : BABY **2** *slang* : GIRL, WOMAN

ba·bel \\'bā-bəl, 'bab-əl\\ *n, often cap* [fr. the Tower of *Babel*, Gen 11:4–9] : a place or scene of noise and confusion; *also* : a confused sound *syn* hubbub, racket, din, uproar, clamor

ba·boon \\ba-'bün\\ *n* [ME *babewin*, fr. MF *babouin*, fr. *baboue* grimace] : any of several large apes of Asia and Africa with doglike muzzles

ba·bush·ka \\bə-'büsh-kə, -'bush-\\ *n* [Russ, grandmother, dim. of *baba* old woman] : a kerchief for the head

¹ba·by \\'bā-bē\\ *n, pl* **babies 1** : a very young child : INFANT **2** : the youngest or smallest of a group **3** : a childish person — **baby** *adj* — **ba·by·hood** *n* — **ba·by·ish** *adj*

²baby *vb* **ba·bied; ba·by·ing** : to tend or treat often with excessive care

baby's breath *n* : any of a genus of herbs that are related to the pinks and have small delicate flowers

ba·by-sit \\'bā-bē-₁sit\\ *vb* **-sat** \\-₁sat\\; **-sit·ting** : to care for children usu. during a short absence of the parents — **ba·by-sit·ter** *n*

bac·ca·lau·re·ate \\₁bak-ə-'lór-ē-ət\\ *n* **1** : the degree of bachelor conferred by colleges and universities **2** : a sermon delivered to a graduating class

bac·ca·rat \\₁bäk-ə-'rä, ₁bak-\\ *n* : a card game played esp. in European casinos

bac·cha·nal \\'bak-ən-°l, ₁bak-ə-'nal, ₁bäk-ə-'näl\\ *n* **1** : REVELER **2** : drunken revelry : BACCHANALIA

bac·cha·na·lia \\₁bak-ə-'näl-yə\\ *n, pl* **bacchanalia** : a drunken orgy — **bac·cha·na·lian** \\-'näl-yən\\ *adj or n*

bach·e·lor \\'bach-(ə-)lər\\ *n* **1** : a person who has received the lowest degree conferred by a 4-year college **2** : a man who has not married — **bach·e·lor·hood** *n*

bach·e·lor·ette \\₁bach-(ə-)lə-'ret\\ *n* : a young unmarried woman

bachelor's button *n* : a European plant related to the daisies and having blue, pink, or white flower heads

ba·cil·lus \\bə-'sil-əs\\ *n, pl* **-li** \\-₁ī\\ [NL, fr. ML, small staff, dim. of L *baculus* staff] : any of numerous rod-shaped bacteria; *also* : a disease-producing bacterium — **bac·il·lary** \\'bas-ə-₁ler-ē\\ *adj*

¹back \\'bak\\ *n* **1** : the rear or dorsal part of the human body; *also* : the corresponding part of a lower animal **2** : the part or surface opposite the front **3** : a player in the backfield in football — **back·less** \\-ləs\\ *adj*

²back *adv* **1** : to, toward, or at the rear **2** : AGO **3** : so as to be restrained or retarded **4** : to, toward, or in a former place or state **5** : in return or reply

³back *adj* **1** : located at or in the back; *also* : REMOTE **2** : OVERDUE **3** : moving or operating backward **4** : not current *syn* posterior, hind, rear

⁴back *vb* **1** : SUPPORT, UPHOLD **2** : to go or cause to go backward or in reverse **3** : to furnish with a back : form the back of

back·ache \\'bak-₁āk\\ *n* : pain in the back; *esp* : a dull persistent pain in the lower back

back–bench·er \\-'ben-chər\\ *n* : a rank-and-file member of a British legislature

back·bite \\-₁bīt\\ *vb* **-bit** \\-₁bit\\; **-bit·ten** \\-₁bit-°n\\; **-bit·ing** \\-₁bīt-iŋ\\ : to say mean or spiteful things about someone who is absent — **back·bit·er** *n*

back·board \\-₁bórd\\ *n* : a board or construction placed at the back or serving as a back

back·bone \\-'bōn, -₁bōn\\ *n* **1** : the bony column in the back of a vertebrate that is the chief support of the trunk and consists of a jointed series of vertebrae enclosing and protecting the spinal cord **2** : firm resolute character

back·drop \\'bak-₁dräp\\ *n* : a painted cloth hung across the rear of a stage

back·er \\'bak-ər\\ *n* : one that supports *syn* upholder, guarantor, sponsor, patron

back·field \\-₁fēld\\ *n* : the football players whose positions are behind the line

¹back·fire \\-₁fī(ə)r\\ *n* : a loud noise caused by the improperly timed explosion of fuel in the cylinder of an internal-combustion engine

²backfire *vb* **1** : to make or undergo a backfire **2** : to have a result opposite to what was intended

back·gam·mon \\'bak-₁gam-ən\\ *n* : a

game played with pieces on a double board in which the moves are determined by throwing dice

back·ground \'bak-ˌgraůnd\ n 1 : the scenery behind something 2 : the setting within which something takes place; *also* : the sum of a person's experience, training, and understanding

back·hand \'bak-ˌhand\ n : a stroke (as in tennis) made with the back of the hand turned in the direction in which the hand is moving; *also* : the side on which such a stroke is made — **backhand** vb

back·hand·ed \'bak-ˌhan-dəd\ adj 1 : using or made with a backhand 2 : INDIRECT, DEVIOUS; *esp* : SARCASTIC

back·hoe \-ˌhō\ n : an excavating machine having a bucket that is drawn toward the machine in operation

back·ing \'bak-iŋ\ n 1 : something forming a back 2 : SUPPORT, AID; *also* : a body of supporters

back·lash \'bak-ˌlash\ n 1 : a sudden violent backward movement or reaction 2 : a strong adverse reaction

¹**back·log** \-ˌlȯg, -ˌläg\ n 1 : a large log at the back of a hearth fire 2 : an accumulation of tasks unperformed or materials not processed

²**backlog** vb : to accumulate in reserve

back of *prep* : BEHIND

back out vb : to withdraw esp. from a commitment or contest

¹**back·pack** \'bak-ˌpak\ n : a camping pack supported by an aluminum frame and carried on the back

²**backpack** vb : to hike with a backpack — **back·pack·er** n

back·ped·al \'bak-ˌped-³l\ vb : RETREAT

back·rest \-ˌrest\ n : a rest for the back

back·side \-ˌsīd\ n : BUTTOCKS

back·slap \-ˌslap\ vb : to display excessive cordiality — **back·slap·per** n

back·slide \-ˌslīd\ vb -slid \-ˌslid\; -slid *or* -slid·den \-ˌslid-³n\; -slid·ing \-ˌslīd-iŋ\ : to lapse morally or in religious practice — **back·slid·er** n

back·spin \-ˌspin\ n : a backward rotary motion of a ball

¹**back·stage** \'bak-ˌstāj\ adj 1 : relating to or occurring in the area behind a stage 2 : of or relating to the private lives of theater people 3 : of or relating to the inner working or operation

²**back·stage** \'bak-ˈstāj\ adv 1 : in or to a backstage area 2 : SECRETLY

back·stairs \-ˌsta(ə)rz\ adj : SECRET, FURTIVE; *also* : SORDID, SCANDALOUS

¹**back·stop** \-ˌstäp\ n : something serving as a stop behind something else; *esp* : a screen or fence to keep a ball from leaving the field of play

²**backstop** vb 1 : to serve as a backstop to 2 : SUPPORT

back·stretch \'bak-ˈstrech\ n : the side opposite the homestretch on a racecourse

back·stroke \-ˌstrōk\ n : a swimming stroke executed on the back

back talk n : an impudent, insolent, or argumentative reply

back·track \'bak-ˌtrak\ vb 1 : to retrace one's course 2 : to reverse a position or stand

back·up \-ˌəp\ n : one that serves as a substitute or alternative

¹**back·ward** \'bak-wərd\ *or* **back·wards** \-wərdz\ adv 1 : toward the back 2 : with the back foremost 3 : in a reverse or contrary direction or way 4 : toward the past; *also* : toward a worse state

²**backward** adj 1 : directed, turned, or done backward 2 : DIFFIDENT, SHY 3 : retarded in development — **backward·ness** n

back·wash \'bak-ˌwȯsh, -ˌwäsh\ n : backward movement (as of water or air) produced by a propelling force (as the motion of oars)

back·wa·ter \-ˌwȯt-ər, -ˌwät-\ n 1 : water held or turned back in its course 2 : an isolated or backward place or condition

back·woods \-ˈwůdz\ n pl 1 : wooded or partly cleared areas far from cities 2 : a remote or isolated place

ba·con \'bā-kən\ n : salted and smoked meat from the sides or back of a pig

bacteria pl of BACTERIUM

bac·te·ri·cid·al \bak-ˌtir-ə-ˈsīd-³l\ adj : destroying bacteria — **bac·te·ri·cide** \-ˈtir-ə-ˌsīd\ n

bac·te·ri·ol·o·gy \bak-ˌtir-ē-ˈäl-ə-jē\ n 1 : a science dealing with bacteria 2 : bacterial life and phenomena — **bac·te·ri·o·log·ic** \bak-ˌtir-ē-ə-ˈläj-ik\ *or* **bac·te·ri·o·log·i·cal** \-ˈläj-i-kəl\ adj — **bac·te·ri·ol·o·gist** \bak-ˌtir-ē-ˈäl-ə-jəst\ n

bac·te·rio·phage \bak-ˈtir-ē-ə-ˌfāj\ n : any of various viruses that attack specific bacteria

bac·te·ri·um \bak-ˈtir-ē-əm\ n, pl -ria \-ē-ə\ [NL, fr. Gk *baktērion* staff] : any of a class of microscopic plants including some that are disease producers and others that are valued esp. for their chemical effects (as fermentation) — **bac·te·ri·al** \-ē-əl\ adj

bad \'bad\ adj **worse** \'wərs\; **worst** \'wərst\ 1 : below standard : POOR; *also* : UNFAVORABLE (a ∼ report) 2 : SPOILED, DECAYED 3 : WICKED; *also* : not well-behaved : NAUGHTY 4 : DISAGREEABLE (a ∼ taste); *also* : HARMFUL 5 : DEFECTIVE, FAULTY (∼ wiring); *also* : not valid (a ∼ check) 6 : UNWELL, ILL 7 : SORRY, REGRETFUL syn evil, wrong, immoral, iniquitous, wicked — **bad·ly** adv — **bad·ness** n

bade *past and past part of* BID

badge \'baj\ n : a device or token usu. worn as a sign of status

¹**bad·ger** \'baj-ər\ n : any of several sturdy burrowing mammals with long claws on their forefeet

²**badger** vb **bad·gered**; **bad·ger·ing** \'baj-(ə-)riŋ\ : to harass or annoy persistently

ba·di·nage \ˌbad-ᵊn-ᵊäzh\ *n* [F] : playful talk back and forth : BANTER

bad·land \ˈbad-ˌland\ *n* : a region marked by intricate erosional sculpturing and scanty vegetation — usu. used in pl.

bad·min·ton \ˈbad-ˌmint-ᵊn\ *n* : a court game played with light rackets and a shuttlecock volleyed over a net

Bae·de·ker \ˈbäd-i-kər, ᵇbed-\ *n* : GUIDE-BOOK

¹baf·fle \ˈbaf-əl\ *vb* **baf·fled; baf·fling** \-(ə-)liŋ\ : FRUSTRATE, THWART, FOIL; *also* : PERPLEX

²baffle *n* : a device (as a wall or screen) to deflect, check, or regulate flow (as of liquid or sound)

¹bag \ˈbag\ *n* : a flexible usu. closable container (as for storing or carrying)

²bag *vb* **bagged; bag·ging 1** : DISTEND, BULGE **2** : to put in a bag **3** : to get possession of; *esp* : to take in hunting **syn** trap, snare, catch, capture, collar

ba·gasse \bə-ˈgas\ *n* [F] : plant residue (as of sugarcane) left after a product (as juice) has been extracted

bag·a·telle \ˌbag-ə-ˈtel\ *n* [F] : TRIFLE

ba·gel \ˈbā-gəl\ *n* [Yiddish *beygel*, deriv. of Old High German *boug* ring] : a hard glazed doughnut-shaped roll

bag·gage \ˈbag-ij\ *n* **1** : the traveling bags and personal belongings of a traveler : LUGGAGE **2** : a worthless or contemptible woman

bag·gy \ˈbag-ē\ *adj* **bag·gi·er; -est** : puffed out or hanging like a bag — **bag·gi·ly** \ˈbag-ə-lē\ *adv* — **bag·gi·ness** \-ē-nəs\ *n*

bag·man \-mən\ *n* : a person who collects or distributes illicitly gained money on behalf of another

ba·gnio \ˈban-yō\ *n, pl* **bagnios** [It *bagno*, lit., public baths] : BROTHEL

bag of waters : a double-walled fluid-filled sac that encloses and protects the fetus in the womb and that breaks releasing its fluid during the process of birth

bag·pipe \ˈbag-ˌpīp\ *n* : a musical wind instrument consisting of a bag, a tube with valves, and sounding pipes — often used in pl.

ba·guette \ba-ˈget\ *n* [F, lit., rod] : a gem having the shape of a long narrow rectangle; *also* : the shape itself

baht \ˈbät\ *n, pl* **baht** *also* **bahts** — see MONEY table

¹bail \ˈbāl\ *n* : a container for ladling water out of a boat

²bail *vb* : to dip and throw out water from a boat

³bail *n* : security given to guarantee a prisoner's appearance when legally required; *also* : one giving such security or the release secured

⁴bail *vb* : to release under bail; *also* : to procure the release of by giving bail — **bail·able** \ˈbā-lə-bəl\ *adj*

⁵bail *n* : the arched handle of a pail or kettle

bai·liff \ˈbā-ləf\ *n* **1** : an aide of a British sheriff who serves writs and makes arrests; *also* : a minor officer of a U.S. court **2** : an estate or farm manager esp. in Britain : STEWARD

bai·li·wick \ˈbā-li-ˌwik\ *n* : one's special province or domain syn territory, field, sphere, domain, province

bails·man \ˈbālz-mən\ *n* : one who gives bail for another

bairn \ˈbaərn\ *n, chiefly Scot* : CHILD

¹bait \ˈbāt\ *vb* **1** : to persecute by continued attacks **2** : to harass with dogs usu. for sport (〜 a bear) **3** : to furnish (as a hook) with bait **4** : ALLURE, ENTICE **5** : to give food and drink to (as an animal) **syn** badger, heckle, hound

²bait *n* **1** : a lure for catching animals (as fish) **2** : LURE, TEMPTATION **syn** snare, trap, decoy, come-on, enticement

bai·za \ˈbī-(ˌ)zä\ *n* — see *rial* at MONEY table

baize \ˈbāz\ *n* : a coarse feltlike fabric

¹bake \ˈbāk\ *vb* **baked; bak·ing 1** : to cook or become cooked in dry heat esp. in an oven **2** : to dry and harden by heat (〜 bricks) — **bak·er** *n*

²bake *n* : a social gathering featuring baked food

baker's dozen *n* : THIRTEEN

bak·ery \ˈbā-k(ə-)rē\ *n, pl* **-er·ies** : a place for baking or selling baked goods

bake·shop \ˈbāk-ˌshäp\ *n* : BAKERY

baking powder *n* : a powder that consists of a carbonate, an acid, and a starch and that makes the dough rise in baking cakes and biscuits

baking soda *n* : SODIUM BICARBONATE

bak·sheesh \ˈbak-ˌshēsh\ *n* : payment (as a tip or bribe) to expedite service

bal *abbr* balance

bal·a·lai·ka \ˌbal-ə-ˈlī-kə\ *n* : a triangular wooden instrument related to the guitar and used esp. in the U.S.S.R.

¹bal·ance \ˈbal-əns\ *n* [ME, fr. OF, fr. LL *bilanc-, bilanx* having two scalepans, fr. L *bi* two + *lanc-, lanx* plate] **1** : a weighing device : SCALE **2** : a weight, force, or influence counteracting the effect of another **3** : an oscillating wheel used to regulate a watch or clock **4** : a state of equilibrium **5** : REMAINDER, REST; *esp* : an amount in excess esp. on the credit side of an account — **bal·anced** \-ənst\ *adj*

²balance *vb* **bal·anced; bal·anc·ing 1** : to compute the balance of an account **2** : to arrange so that one set of elements equals another; *also* : to equal or equalize in weight, number, or proportions **3** : WEIGH **4** : to bring or come to a state or position of equipoise; *also* : to bring into harmony or proportion

balance wheel *n* : a wheel that regulates or stabilizes the motion of a mechanism

bal·boa \bal-ˈbō-ə\ *n* — see MONEY table

bal·brig·gan \bal-ˈbrig-ən\ *n* : a knitted cotton fabric used esp. for underwear

bal·co·ny \'bal-kə-nē\ *n, pl* **-nies** **1** : a platform projecting from the side of a building and enclosed by a railing **2** : a gallery inside a building

¹**bald** \'bȯld\ *adj* **1** : lacking a natural or usual covering (as of hair) **2** : UN-ADORNED, PLAIN *syn* bare, barren, naked, nude — **bald·ness** *n*

²**bald** *vb* : to become bald

bal·da·chin \'bȯl-də-kən, 'bal-\ *or* **bal·da·chi·no** \ˌbal-də-'kē-nō\ *n, pl* **baldachins** *or* **baldachinos** : a canopy-like structure over an altar

bald eagle *n* : an eagle of No. America that when mature has white head and neck feathers and a white tail

bal·der·dash \'bȯl-dər-ˌdash\ *n* : NON-SENSE

bal·dric \'bȯl-drik\ *n* : a belt worn over the shoulder to carry a sword or bugle

¹**bale** \'bāl\ *n* : a large bundle or closely packed package

²**bale** *vb* **baled; bal·ing** : to pack in a bale — **bal·er** *n*

ba·leen \bə-'lēn\ *n* : WHALEBONE

bale·ful \'bāl-fəl\ *adj* : DEADLY, HARM-FUL; *also* : OMINOUS *syn* sinister, malefic, maleficent, malign

¹**balk** \'bȯk\ *n* **1** : HINDRANCE, CHECK, SETBACK **2** : an illegal motion of the pitcher in baseball while in position

²**balk** *vb* **1** : BLOCK, THWART **2** : to stop short and refuse to go on **3** : to commit a balk in sports *syn* frustrate, baffle, foil, thwart

balky \'bȯ-kē\ *adj* **balk·i·er; -est** : likely to balk

¹**ball** \'bȯl\ *n* **1** : a rounded body or mass (as at the base of the thumb or for use as a missile or in a game) **2** : a game played with a ball **3** : a pitched baseball that misses the strike zone and is not swung at by the batter **4** : a ball or thrown ball in various games ⟨foul ∼⟩

²**ball** *vb* : to form into a ball

³**ball** *n* : a large formal dance

bal·lad \'bal-əd\ *n* **1** : a simple song : AIR **2** : a narrative poem of strongly marked rhythm suitable for singing **3** : a slow romantic dance song

bal·lad·eer \ˌbal-ə-'dier\ *n* : a singer of ballads

¹**bal·last** \'bal-əst\ *n* **1** : heavy material used to stabilize a ship or control a balloon's ascent **2** : crushed stone laid in a railroad bed or used in making concrete

²**ballast** *vb* : to provide with ballast *syn* balance, stabilize, steady

ball bearing *n* : a bearing in which the revolving part turns upon steel balls that roll easily in a groove; *also* : one of the balls in such a bearing

ball·car·ri·er \'bȯl-ˌkar-ē-ər\ *n* : the football player carrying the ball in an offensive play

bal·le·ri·na \ˌbal-ə-'rē-nə\ *n* : a female ballet dancer

bal·let \'ba-ˌlā, ba-'lā\ *n* **1** : dancing in which fixed poses and steps are combined with light flowing movements

often to convey a story; *also* : a theatrical art form using ballet dancing **2** : a company of ballet dancers

bal·let·o·mane \ba-'let-ə-ˌmān\ *n* : a devotee of ballet

bal·lis·tic missile \bə-'lis-tik-\ *n* : a self-propelled missile that is guided during ascent and that falls freely during descent

bal·lis·tics \-tiks\ *n sing or pl* **1** : the science of the motion of projectiles (as bullets) in flight **2** : the flight characteristics of a projectile — **ballistic** *adj*

ball of fire : an unusually energetic person

¹**bal·loon** \bə-'lün\ *n* **1** : a bag filled with gas or heated air so as to rise and float in the atmosphere **2** : a toy consisting of an inflatable rubber bag — **bal·loon·ist** *n*

²**balloon** *vb* **1** : to travel in a balloon **2** : to swell or puff out **3** : to increase rapidly

¹**bal·lot** \'bal-ət\ *n* [It *ballotta* small ball used in secret voting, fr. It dial., dim. of *balla* ball] **1** : a piece of paper used to cast a vote **2** : the action or a system of voting; *also* : the right to vote

²**ballot** *vb* : to decide by ballot : VOTE

¹**ball·park** \'bȯl-ˌpark\ *n* : a park in which ball games are played

²**ballpark** *adj* : approximately correct ⟨∼ estimate⟩

ball·point \'bȯl-ˌpȯint\ *n* : a pen whose writing point is a small rotating metal ball that inks itself from an inner container

ball·room \'bȯl-ˌrüm, -ˌru̇m\ *n* : a large room for dances

bal·ly·hoo \'bal-ē-ˌhü\ *n, pl* **-hoos** : extravagant statements and claims made for publicity — **ballyhoo** *vb*

balm \'bäm, 'bȯlm\ *n* **1** : a fragrant healing or soothing lotion or ointment **2** : any of several spicy fragrant herbs **3** : something that comforts or soothes

balmy \'bäm-ē, 'bȯl-mē\ *adj* **balm·i·er; -est** **1** : gently soothing : MILD **2** : FOOLISH, ABSURD *syn* soft, bland, mild, gentle — **balm·i·ness** *n*

ba·lo·ney \bə-'lō-nē\ *n* : NONSENSE

bal·sa \'bȯl-sə\ *n* : the extremely light strong wood of a tropical American tree; *also* : the tree

bal·sam \'bȯl-səm\ *n* **1** : a fragrant aromatic and usu. resinous substance oozing from various plants; *also* : a preparation containing or smelling like balsam **2** : a balsam-yielding tree (as balsam fir) **3** : a common garden ornamental plant

balsam fir *n* : a resinous American evergreen tree that is widely used for pulpwood and as a Christmas tree

Bal·ti·more oriole \ˌbȯl-tə-ˌmȯr-\ *n* : a common American oriole in which the male is brightly colored with orange, black, and white

bal·us·ter \'bal-ə-stər\ *n* [F *balustre*, fr.

It *balaustro,* fr. *balaustra* wild pomegranate flower, fr. L *balaustium;* fr. its shape] : an upright support of a rail (as of a staircase)

bal·us·trade \-ə-ˌsträd\ *n* : a row of balusters topped by a rail

bam·boo \bam-ˈbü\ *n, pl* **bamboos** : any of various woody mostly tall tropical grasses including some with strong hollow stems used for building, furniture, or utensils

bamboo curtain *n, often cap B&C* : a political, military, and ideological barrier in the Orient

bam·boo·zle \bam-ˈbü-zəl\ *vb* **-boo·zled; -boo·zling** \-ˈbüz-(ə-)liŋ\ : TRICK, HOODWINK

¹**ban** \ˈban\ *vb* **banned; ban·ning** : PROHIBIT, FORBID

²**ban** *n* 1 : CURSE 2 : a legal or formal prohibiting

³**ban** \ˈbän\ *n, pl* **ba·ni** \ˈbän-ē\ — see *leu* at MONEY table

ba·nal \bə-ˈnäl, -ˈnal; ˈbān-ᵊl\ *adj* [F] : COMMONPLACE, TRITE — **ba·nal·i·ty** \bā-ˈnal-ət-ē\ *n*

ba·nana \bə-ˈnan-ə\ *n* : a treelike tropical plant bearing thick clusters of yellow or reddish finger-shaped fruit; *also* : this fruit

¹**band** \ˈband\ *n* 1 : something that binds, ties, or goes around 2 : a strip or stripe that can be distinguished (as by color or texture) from nearby matter 3 : a range of wavelengths (as in radio) 4 : a group of grooves on a phonograph record containing recorded sound

²**band** *vb* 1 : to tie up, finish, or enclose with a band 2 : to gather or unite in a company or for some common end — **band·er** *n*

³**band** *n* : a group of persons, animals, or things; *esp* : a group of musicians organized for playing together

¹**ban·dage** \ˈban-dij\ *n* : a strip of material used esp. in dressing wounds

²**bandage** *vb* **band·aged; band·ag·ing** : to dress or cover with a bandage

ban·dan·na *or* **ban·dana** \ban-ˈdan-ə\ *n* : a large colored figured handkerchief

B and B *abbr* bed-and-breakfast

band·box \ˈband(d)-ˌbäks\ *n* : a usu. cylindrical box for carrying clothing

band·ed \ˈban-dəd\ *adj* : having or marked with bands

ban·de·role *or* **ban·de·rol** \ˈban-də-ˌrōl\ *n* : a long narrow forked flag or streamer

ban·dit \ˈban-dət\ *n* [It *bandito,* fr. *bandire* to banish] 1 *pl also* **ban·dit·ti** \ban-ˈdit-ē\ : an outlaw who lives by plunder; *esp* : a member of a band of marauders 2 : ROBBER — **ban·dit·ry** \ˈban-də-trē\ *n*

ban·do·lier *or* **ban·do·leer** \ˌban-də-ˈlior\ *n* : a belt slung over the shoulder esp. to carry ammunition

band saw *n* : a saw in the form of an endless steel belt running over pulleys

band·stand \ˈband(d)-ˌstand\ *n* : a usu. roofed platform on which a band or orchestra performs outdoors

b and w *abbr* black and white

band·wag·on \ˈband-ˌwag-ən\ *n* 1 : a wagon carrying musicians in a parade 2 : a movement that attracts support because it seems to be gaining popularity

¹**ban·dy** \ˈban-dē\ *vb* **ban·died; ban·dy·ing** 1 : to exchange (as blows or quips) esp. in rapid succession 2 : to use in a glib or offhand way

²**bandy** *adj* : curved outward (∼ legs)

bane \ˈbān\ *n* 1 : POISON 2 : WOE, HARM; *also* : a source of this — **bane·ful** *adj*

¹**bang** \ˈbaŋ\ *vb* 1 : BUMP (fell and ∼ed his knee) 2 : to strike, thrust, or move usu. with a loud noise

²**bang** *n* 1 : a resounding blow 2 : a sudden loud noise

³**bang** *adv* : DIRECTLY, RIGHT

⁴**bang** *n* : a fringe of hair cut short (as across the forehead) — usu. used in pl.

⁵**bang** *vb* : to cut a bang in

Ban·gla·deshi \ˌbäŋ-glə-ˈdesh-ē\ *n* : a native or inhabitant of Bangladesh — **Bangladeshi** *adj*

ban·gle \ˈbaŋ-gəl\ *n* : BRACELET; *also* : a loose-hanging ornament

bang-up \ˈbaŋ-ˌəp\ *adj* : FIRST-RATE, EXCELLENT (a ∼ job)

bani *pl of* ³BAN

ban·ish \ˈban-ish\ *vb* 1 : to require by authority to leave a country 2 : to drive out : EXPEL **syn** exile, ostracize, deport, expel, relegate — **ban·ish·ment** *n*

ban·is·ter \ˈban-ə-stər\ *n* 1 : one of the upright supports of a handrail along a staircase 2 : the handrail of a staircase

ban·jo \ˈban-ˌjō\ *n, pl* **banjos** *also* **banjoes** : a musical instrument with a long neck, a drumlike body, and usu. five strings — **ban·jo·ist** *n*

¹**bank** \ˈbaŋk\ *n* 1 : a piled-up mass (as of cloud or earth) 2 : an undersea elevation 3 : rising ground bordering a lake, river, or sea 4 : the sideways slope of a surface along a curve or of a vehicle as it rounds a curve

²**bank** *vb* 1 : to form a bank about 2 : to cover (as a fire) with fuel to keep inactive 3 : to build (a curve) with the roadbed or track inclined laterally upward from the inside edge 4 : to pile or heap in a bank; *also* : to arrange in a tier 5 : to incline (an airplane) laterally

³**bank** *n* [ME, fr. MF or It; MF *banque,* fr. It *banca,* lit., bench] 1 : an establishment concerned esp. with the custody, loan, exchange, or issue of money, the extension of credit, and the transmission of funds 2 : a stock of or a place for holding something in reserve (a blood ∼)

⁴**bank** *vb* 1 : to conduct the business of a bank 2 : to deposit money or have

an account in a bank — **bank·er** *n* — **bank·ing** *n*

⁵**bank** *n* : a group of objects arranged close together (as in a row or tier) ⟨a ~ of file drawers⟩

bank·book \'baŋk-ˌbu̇k\ *n* : the depositor's book in which a bank records deposits and withdrawals

bank·card \-ˌkärd\ *n* : a credit card issued by a bank

bank note *n* : a promissory note issued by a bank and circulating as money

bank·roll \'baŋk-ˌrōl\ *n* : supply of money : FUNDS

¹**bank·rupt** \'baŋk-(ˌ)rəpt\ *n* : an insolvent person; *esp* : one whose property is turned over by court action to a trustee to be handled for the benefit of his creditors — **bankrupt** *vb*

²**bankrupt** *adj* 1 : reduced to financial ruin; *esp* : legally declared a bankrupt 2 : wholly lacking in or deprived of some essential ⟨~ soils⟩ — **bank·rupt·cy** \'baŋk-(ˌ)rəp-(t)sē\ *n*

¹**ban·ner** \'ban-ər\ *n* 1 : a piece of cloth attached to a staff and used by a leader as his standard 2 : FLAG

²**banner** *adj* : distinguished from all others esp. in excellence ⟨a ~ year⟩

ban·nock \'ban-ək\ *n* : a flat oatmeal or barley cake usu. cooked on a griddle

banns \'banz\ *n pl* : public announcement esp. in church of a proposed marriage

ban·quet \'baŋ-kwət\ *n* [MF, fr. It *banchetto*, fr. dim. of *banca* bench, bank] : a ceremonial dinner — **banquet** *vb*

ban·quette \baŋ-'ket\ *n* : a long upholstered bench esp. along a wall

ban·shee \'ban-shē\ *n* [ScGael *bean-sīth*, fr. or akin to Old Irish *ben síde* woman of fairyland] : a female spirit in Gaelic folklore whose wailing warns a family that one of them will soon die

ban·tam \'bant-əm\ *n* 1 : any of numerous small domestic fowls that are often miniatures of standard breeds 2 : a small but pugnacious person

¹**ban·ter** \'bant-ər\ *vb* : to speak to in a witty and teasing manner

²**banter** *n* : good-natured witty joking

bant·ling \'bant-liŋ\ *n* : a young child

Ban·tu \'ban-ˌtü\ *n, pl* **Bantu** *or* **Bantus** 1 : a member of a family of Negroid peoples occupying equatorial and southern Africa 2 : a group of African languages spoken generally in equatorial and southern Africa

Ban·tu·stan \ˌban-tu̇-'stan, ˌbän-tu̇-'stän\ *n* : an all-black enclave in the Republic of So. Africa with a limited degree of self-government

ban·yan \'ban-yən\ *n* [earlier *banyan* Hindu merchant, fr. Hindi *baniyā*; fr. a merchant's pagoda erected under a tree of the species in Iran] : a large East Indian tree whose aerial roots grow downward to the ground and form new trunks

ban·zai \bän-'zī\ *n* : a Japanese cheer or cry of triumph

bao·bab \'bau̇-ˌbab, 'bā-ə-\ *n* : an Old World tropical tree with short swollen trunk and sour edible gourdlike fruits

bap·tism \'bap-ˌtiz-əm\ *n* 1 : a Christian sacrament signifying spiritual rebirth and symbolized by the ritual use of water 2 : an act of baptizing — **bap·tis·mal** \bap-'tiz-məl\ *adj*

baptismal name *n* : GIVEN NAME

Bap·tist \'bap-təst\ *n* : a member of any of several Protestant denominations emphasizing baptism by immersion

bap·tis·tery *or* **bap·tis·try** \'bap-tə-strē\ *n, pl* **-ter·ies** *or* **-tries** : a place esp. in a church used for baptism

bap·tize \bap-'tīz, 'bap-ˌtīz\ *vb* **bap·tized; bap·tiz·ing** [ME *baptizen*, fr. OF *baptiser*, fr. L *baptizare*, fr. Gk *baptizein* to dip, baptize, fr. *baptos* dipped, fr. *baptein* to dip] 1 : to administer baptism to; *also* : CHRISTEN 2 : to purify esp. by an ordeal

¹**bar** \'bär\ *n* 1 : a long narrow piece of material (as wood or metal) used esp. for a lever, fastening, or support 2 : BARRIER, OBSTACLE 3 : the railing in a law court at which prisoners are stationed; *also* : the legal profession or the whole body of lawyers 4 : a stripe, band, or line much longer than wide 5 : a counter at which food or esp. drink is served; *also* : BARROOM 6 : a vertical line across the musical staff

²**bar** *vb* **barred; bar·ring** 1 : to fasten, confine, or obstruct with or as if with a bar or bars 2 : to mark with bars : STRIPE 3 : to shut or keep out : EXCLUDE 4 : FORBID, PREVENT

³**bar** *prep* : EXCEPT

bar *abbr* barometer; barometric

Bar *abbr* Baruch

barb \'bärb\ *n* 1 : a sharp projection extending backward (as from the point of an arrow) 2 : a biting critical remark — **barbed** \'bärbd\ *adj*

bar·bar·ian \bär-'ber-ē-ən\ *adj* 1 : of, relating to, or being a land, culture, or people alien to and usu. believed to be inferior to one's own 2 : lacking refinement, learning, or artistic or literary culture — **barbarian** *n*

bar·bar·ic \bär-'bar-ik\ *adj* 1 : BARBARIAN 2 : marked by a lack of restraint : WILD 3 : PRIMITIVE, UNSOPHISTICATED

bar·ba·rism \'bär-bə-ˌriz-əm\ *n* 1 : the social condition of barbarians; *also* : the use or display of barbarian or barbarous acts, attitudes, or ideas 2 : a word or expression that offends standards of correctness or purity

bar·ba·rous \'bär-b(ə-)rəs\ *adj* 1 : lacking culture or refinement 2 : using linguistic barbarisms 3 : mercilessly harsh or cruel — **bar·bar·i·ty** \bär-'bar-ət-ē\ *n* — **bar·ba·rous·ly** *adv*

¹**bar·be·cue** \'bär-bi-ˌkyü\ *n* : a social gathering at which barbecued food is served

²**barbecue** *vb* **-cued; -cu·ing** 1 : to cook

over hot coals or on a revolving spit **2**
: to cook in a highly seasoned vinegar
sauce
bar·bell \'bär-ˌbel\ *n* : a bar with adjustable weights attached to each end
used for exercise and in weight-lifting
competition
bar·ber \'bär-bər\ *n* [ME, fr. MF *barbe-
or*, fr. *barbe* beard, fr. L *barba*] : one
whose business is cutting and dressing hair and shaving and trimming
beards
bar·ber·ry \'bär-ˌber-ē\ *n* : any of a
genus of spiny shrubs bearing yellow
flowers followed by oblong red berries
bar·bi·tal \'bär-bə-ˌtȯl\ *n* : a white crystalline addictive hypnotic often administered in the form of its soluble
sodium salt
bar·bi·tu·rate \bär-'bich-ə-rət\ *n* : any
of various compounds (as a salt or ester) formed from an organic acid
(**bar·bi·tu·ric acid** \ˌbär-bə-ˌt(y)ȯr-
ik-\); *esp* : one used as a sedative or
hypnotic
bar·ca·role *or* **bar·ca·rolle** \'bär-kə-ˌrōl\
n : a Venetian boat song character-
ized by a beat suggesting a rowing
rhythm; *also* : a piece of music imitating this
bar chart *n* : BAR GRAPH
bar code *n* : a set of printed and variously spaced bars and sometimes numerals that is designed to be scanned
to identify the object it labels
bard \'bärd\ *n* : POET
¹**bare** \'baər\ *adj* **bar·er; bar·est 1** : NA-
KED **2** : UNCONCEALED, EXPOSED **3**
: EMPTY **4** : leaving nothing to spare
: MERE **5** : PLAIN, UNADORNED **syn**
nude, bald, naked — **bare·ness** *n*
²**bare** *vb* **bared; bar·ing** : to make or lay
bare : UNCOVER
bare·back \-ˌbak\ *or* **bare·backed**
\-ˌbakt\ *adv or adj* : without a saddle
bare·faced \-'fāst\ *adj* **1** : having the
face uncovered; *esp* : BEARDLESS **2**
: not concealed : OPEN
bare·foot \-ˌfu̇t\ *or* **bare·foot·ed** \-ˌfu̇t-
əd\ *adv or adj* : with bare feet
bare·hand·ed \-'han-dəd\ *adv or adj* **1**
: without gloves **2** : without tools or
weapons
bare·head·ed \-'hed-əd\ *adv or adj*
: without a hat
bare·ly \'baər-lē\ *adv* **1** : PLAINLY, MEA-
GERLY **2** : by a narrow margin : only
just (~ enough money) **syn** hardly,
scarcely
bar·fly \'bär-ˌflī\ *n* : a drinker who frequents bars
¹**bar·gain** \'bär-gən\ *n* **1** : AGREEMENT **2**
: an advantageous purchase **3** : a
transaction, situation, or event regarded in the light of its results
²**bargain** *vb* **1** : to negotiate over the
terms of an agreement; *also* : to come
to terms **2** : BARTER
¹**barge** \'bärj\ *n* **1** : a broad flat-bottomed boat usu. moved by towing **2**

: a motorboat supplied to a flagship
(as for an admiral) **3** : a ceremonial
boat elegantly furnished — **barge·man**
\-mən\ *n*
²**barge** *vb* **barged; barg·ing 1** : to carry
by barge **2** : to move or thrust oneself
clumsily or rudely
bari·tone \'bar-ə-ˌtōn\ *n* [F *baryton* or
It *baritono*, fr. Gk *barytonos* deep
sounding, fr. *barys* heavy + *tonos*
tone] : a male voice between bass and
tenor; *also* : a man with such a voice
bar·i·um \'bar-ē-əm\ *n* : a silver-white
metallic chemical element that occurs
only in combination
¹**bark** \'bärk\ *vb* **1** : to make the short
loud cry of a dog **2** : to speak or utter
in a curt loud tone : SNAP
²**bark** *n* : the sound made by a barking
dog
³**bark** *n* : the tough corky outer covering
of a woody stem or root
⁴**bark** *vb* **1** : to strip the bark from **2** : to
rub the skin from : ABRADE
⁵**bark** *n* : a 3-masted ship with foremast
and mainmast square-rigged and mizzenmast fore-and-aft rigged
bar·keep \'bär-ˌkēp\ *or* **bar·keep·er**
\-ˌkē-pər\ *n* : BARTENDER
bark·er \'bär-kər\ *n* : a person who
stands at the entrance esp. to a show
and tries to attract customers to it
bar·ley \'bär-lē\ *n* : a cereal grass with
seeds used as food and in making malt
liquors; *also* : its seed
bar mitz·vah \bär-'mits-və\ *n, often cap*
B&M [Heb *bar miṣwāh*, lit., son of
the (divine) law] **1** : a Jewish boy who
at about 13 years of age assumes religious responsibilities **2** : the ceremony recognizing a boy as a bar mitzvah
barn \'bärn\ *n* [ME *bern*, fr. OE
bereærn, fr. *bere* barley + *ærn* place]
: a building used esp. for storing hay
and grain and for housing livestock or
farm equipment
bar·na·cle \'bär-ni-kəl\ *n* : any of numerous small marine crustaceans
free-swimming when young but fixed
(as to rocks, whales, or ships) when
adult
barn·storm \'bärn-ˌstȯrm\ *vb* : to travel
through the country making brief
stops to entertain (as with shows or
flying stunts) or to campaign for political office
barn·yard \-ˌyärd\ *n* : a usu. fenced
area adjoining a barn
baro·graph \'bar-ə-ˌgraf\ *n* : a recording barometer
ba·rom·e·ter \bə-'räm-ət-ər\ *n* : an instrument for measuring atmospheric
pressure — **baro·met·ric** \ˌbar-ə-
'me-trik\ *adj*
bar·on \'bar-ən\ *n* : a member of the
lowest grade of the British peerage —
ba·ro·ni·al \bə-'rō-nē-əl\ *adj* — **bar·
ony** \'bar-ə-nē\ *n*
bar·on·age \-ə-nij\ *n* : PEERAGE
bar·on·ess \-ə-nəs\ *n* **1** : the wife or wid-

ow of a baron **2** : a woman holding a baronial title in her own right

bar·on·et \'bar-ə-nət\ *n* : a man holding a rank of honor below a baron but above a knight — **bar·on·et·cy** \-sē\ *n*

ba·roque \bə-'rōk, -'räk\ *adj* : marked by elaborate and sometimes grotesque ornamentation and esp. by curved and plastic figures

ba·rouche \bə-'rüsh\ *n* [G *barutsche*, fr. It *biroccio*, deriv. of LL *birotus* two-wheeled, fr. L *bi* two + *rota* wheel] : a 4-wheeled carriage with a high driver's seat in front and a folding top

bar·racks \'bar-əks\ *n sing or pl* : a building or group of buildings for lodging soldiers

bar·ra·cu·da \ˌbar-ə-'küd-ə\ *n, pl* **-da** *or* **-das** : any of several large predaceous sea fishes including some used for food

bar·rage \bə-'räzh, -'räj\ *n* : a heavy concentration of fire (as of artillery)

bar·ra·try \'bar-ə-trē\ *n, pl* **-tries 1** : the purchase or sale of office or preferment in church or state **2** : a fraudulent breach of duty by the master or crew of a ship intended to harm the owner or cargo **3** : the practice of inciting lawsuits or quarrels

barred \'bärd\ *adj* : STRIPED

¹bar·rel \'bar-əl\ *n* **1** : a round bulging cask with flat ends of equal diameter **2** : the amount contained in a barrel **3** : a cylindrical or tubular part (gun ∼)

²barrel *vb* **-reled** *or* **-relled; -rel·ing** *or* **-rel·ling 1** : to pack in a barrel **2** : to travel at high speed

barrel roll *n* : an airplane maneuver in which a complete revolution about the longitudinal axis is made

¹bar·ren \'bar-ən\ *adj* **1** : STERILE, UNFRUITFUL **2** : unproductive of results (a ∼ scheme) **3** : lacking interest or charm **4** : DULL, STUPID — **bar·ren·ness** \-ən-nəs\ *n*

²barren *n* : a tract of barren land

bar·rette \bä-'ret, bə-\ *n* : a clasp or bar for holding the hair in place

¹bar·ri·cade \'bar-ə-ˌkād, ˌbar-ə-'kād\ *vb* **-cad·ed; -cad·ing** : to block, obstruct, or fortify with a barricade

²barricade *n* [F, fr. MF, fr. *barriquer* to barricade, fr. *barrique* barrel] **1** : a hastily thrown-up obstruction or fortification **2** : BARRIER, OBSTACLE

bar·ri·er \'bar-ē-ər\ *n* : something that separates, demarcates, or serves as a barricade (racial ∼s)

barrier reef *n* : a coral reef roughly parallel to a shore and separated from it by a lagoon

bar·ring \'bär-iŋ\ *prep* : excluding by exception : EXCEPTING

bar·rio \'bär-ē-ˌō, 'bar-\ *n, pl* **-ri·os 1** : a district of a city or town in a Spanish-speaking country **2** : a Spanish-speaking quarter in a U.S. city

bar·ris·ter \'bar-ə-stər\ *n* : a British

counselor admitted to plead in the higher courts

bar·room \'bär-ˌrüm, -ˌrùm\ *n* : a room or establishment whose main feature is a bar for the sale of liquor

¹bar·row \'bar-ō\ *n* : a large burial mound of earth and stones

²barrow *n* : a male hog castrated while young

³barrow *n* **1** : HANDBARROW **2** : WHEELBARROW **3** : a cart with a boxlike body and two shafts for pushing it

Bart *abbr* baronet

bar·tend·er \'bär-ˌten-dər\ *n* : one that serves liquor at a bar

bar·ter \'bärt-ər\ *vb* : to trade by exchange of goods — **barter** *n*

Ba·ruch \'bär-ük, bə-'rük\ *n* — see BIBLE table

bas·al \'bā-səl\ *adj* **1** : situated at or forming the base **2** : BASIC

basal metabolism *n* : the turnover of energy in a fasting and resting organism using energy solely to maintain vital cellular activity, respiration, and circulation as measured by the rate at which heat is given off

ba·salt \bə-'sòlt, 'bā-ˌsòlt\ *n* : a dark fine-grained igneous rock — **ba·sal·tic** \bə-'sòl-tik\ *adj*

¹base \'bās\ *n, pl* **bas·es** \'bā-səz\ **1** : BOTTOM, FOUNDATION **2** : a side or face on which a geometrical figure stands; *also* : the length of a base **3** : a main ingredient or fundamental part **4** : the point of beginning an act or operation **5** : a place on which a force depends for supplies **6** : the number of units in a given digit's place of a number system that is required to give the numeral 1 in the next higher place (the decimal system uses a ∼ of 10); *also* : such a system using an indicated base (convert from ∼ 10 to ∼ 2) **7** : any of the four stations at the corners of a baseball diamond **8** : a chemical compound (as lime or ammonia) that reacts with an acid to form a salt, has a salty taste, and turns litmus blue **syn** basis, ground, groundwork, footing, foundation

²base *vb* **based; bas·ing 1** : to form or serve as a base for **2** : ESTABLISH

³base *adj* **1** : of inferior quality : DEBASED, ALLOYED **2** : CONTEMPTIBLE, IGNOBLE **3** : MENIAL, DEGRADING **4** : of little value **syn** low, vile, despicable, wretched — **base·ly** *adv* — **base·ness** *n*

base·ball \'bās-ˌbȯl\ *n* : a game played with a bat and ball by two teams on a field with four bases arranged in a diamond; *also* : the ball used in this game

base·board \-ˌbȯrd\ *n* : a line of boards or molding covering the joint of a wall and the adjoining floor

base-born \-'bȯrn\ *adj* **1** : of humble birth **2** : of illegitimate birth **3** : MEAN, IGNOBLE

base exchange *n* : a post exchange at a naval or air force base

base hit *n* : a hit in baseball that enables

the batter to reach base safely with no
error made and no base runner forced
out

base·less \-ləs\ *adj* : having no base or
basis : GROUNDLESS

base·line \'bās-ˌlīn\ *n* 1 : a line serving
as a basis esp. to calculate or locate
something 2 : the area within which a
baseball player must keep when running between bases

base·ment \-mənt\ *n* 1 : the part of a
building that is wholly or partly below
ground level 2 : the lowest or fundamental part of something

base on balls : an advance to first base
given to a baseball player who receives four balls

base runner *n* : a baseball player who is
on base or is attempting to reach a
base

¹**bash** \'bash\ *vb* 1 : to strike violently
: BEAT 2 : to smash by a blow

²**bash** *n* 1 : a heavy blow 2 : a festive
social gathering : PARTY

bash·ful \'bash-fəl\ *adj* : inclined to
shrink from public attention — **bash-
ful·ness** *n*

ba·sic \'bā-sik\ *adj* 1 : of, relating to, or
forming the base or essence : FUNDA-
MENTAL 2 : of, relating to, or having
the character of a chemical base (a ~
substance) *syn* underlying, basal, fundamental, primary — **ba·si·cal·ly** \-si-
k(ə-)lē\ *adv* — **ba·sic·i·ty** \bā-'sis-ət-ē\
n

ba·sil \'baz-əl, 'bās-\ *n* : either of two
mints with fragrant leaves used in
cooking

ba·sil·i·ca \bə-'sil-i-kə, -'zil-\ *n* [L, fr.
Gk *basilikē*, fr. fem. of *basilikos* royal, fr. *basileus* king] 1 : an early
Christian church building consisting
of nave and aisles with clerestory and
apse 2 : a Roman Catholic church giv-
en ceremonial privileges

bas·i·lisk \'bas-ə-ˌlisk, 'baz-\ *n* [ME, fr.
L. *basiliscus*, fr. Gk *basiliskos*, fr.
dim. of *basileus* king] : a legendary
reptile with fatal breath and glance

ba·sin \'bās-ⁿn\ *n* 1 : an open usu. circular vessel with sloping sides for
holding liquid (as water) 2 : a hollow
or enclosed place containing water;
also : the region drained by a river

ba·sis \'bā-səs\ *n, pl* **ba·ses** \-ˌsēz\ 1
: FOUNDATION, BASE 2 : a fundamental
principle

bask \'bask\ *vb* 1 : to expose oneself to
comfortable heat 2 : to enjoy something warmly comforting ⟨~ing in his
friends' admiration⟩

bas·ket \'bas-kət\ *n* : a container made
of woven material (as twigs or
grasses); *also* : any of various lightweight usu. wood containers — **bas-
ket·ful** *n*

bas·ket·ball \-ˌbȯl\ *n* : a game played on
a court by two teams who try to throw
an inflated ball through a raised goal;
also : the ball used in this game

basket case *n* 1 : one who has all four

limbs amputated 2 : one that is totally
incapacitated or inoperative

basket weave *n* : a textile weave resembling the checkered pattern of a plaited basket

bas mitz·vah \bäs-'mits-və\ *n, often cap*
B&M [Heb *bath miṣwāh*, lit., daughter of the (divine) law] 1 : a Jewish girl
who at about 13 years of age assumes
religious responsibilities 2 : the ceremony recognizing a girl as a bas mitzvah

Basque \'bask\ *n* 1 : a member of a
people inhabiting a region bordering
on the Bay of Biscay in northern
Spain and southwestern France 2
: the language of the Basque people —
Basque *adj*

bas–re·lief \ˌbä-ri-'lēf\ *n* [F] : a sculpture in relief with the design raised
very slightly from the background

¹**bass** \'bas\ *n, pl* **bass** *or* **bass·es** : any of
numerous sport and food fishes (as a
striped bass)

²**bass** \'bās\ *adj* : of low pitch

³**bass** \'bās\ *n* 1 : a deep sound or tone 2
: the lower half of the musical pitch
range 3 : the lowest male singing
voice 4 : a singer or instrument having a bass voice or part

bas·set hound \'bas-ət-\ *n* : any of an
old French breed of short-legged dogs
with long ears and crooked front legs

bas·si·net \ˌbas-ə-'net\ *n* : a baby's bed
that resembles a basket and often has
a hood over one end

bas·so \'bas-ō\ *n, pl* **bassos** *or* **bas·si**
\'bäs-ˌē\ [It] : a bass singer

bas·soon \bə-'sün\ *n* : a musical wind
instrument lower in pitch than the
oboe

bass·wood \'bas-ˌwu̇d\ *n* : any of several New World lindens or their wood

bast \'bast\ *n* : BAST FIBER

¹**bas·tard** \'bas-tərd\ *n* 1 : an illegitimate
child 2 : an offensive or disagreeable
person

²**bastard** *adj* 1 : ILLEGITIMATE 2 : of an
inferior or nontypical kind, size, or
form; *also* : SPURIOUS — **bas·tardy** *n*

bas·tard·ize \'bas-tər-ˌdīz\ *vb* **-ized; -iz-
ing** : to reduce from a higher to a lower state : DEBASE

¹**baste** \'bāst\ *vb* **bast·ed; bast·ing** 1 : to
sew with long stitches so as to keep
temporarily in place

²**baste** *vb* **bast·ed; bast·ing** : to moisten
(as meat) at intervals with liquid while
cooking

bast fiber *n* : a strong woody plant fiber
obtained chiefly from phloem and
used esp. in making ropes

bas·ti·na·do \ˌbas-tə-'nād-ō, -'näd-\ *or*
bas·ti·nade \ˌbas-tə-'nād, -'näd\ *n, pl*
-na·does *or* **-nades** 1 : a blow or beating esp. with a stick 2 : a punishment
consisting of beating the soles of the
feet

bas·tion \'bas-chən\ *n* : a projecting
part of a fortification; *also* : a fortified
position — **bas·tioned** \-chənd\ *adj*

¹**bat** \'bat\ *n* **1** : a stout stick : CLUB **2** : a sharp blow **3** : an implement (as of wood) used to hit a ball (as in baseball) **4** : a turn at batting — usu. used with *at*

²**bat** *vb* **bat·ted; bat·ting** : to hit with or as if with a bat

³**bat** *n* : any of an order of night-flying mammals with forelimbs modified to form wings

⁴**bat** *vb* **bat·ted; bat·ting** : WINK, BLINK

batch \'bach\ *n* **1** : a quantity (as of bread) baked at one time **2** : a quantity of material for use at one time or produced at one operation

bate \'bāt\ *vb* **bat·ed; bat·ing** : MODERATE, REDUCE

bath \'bath, 'bàth\ *n, pl* **baths** \'bathz, 'baths, 'bàthz, 'bàths\ **1** : a washing of the body **2** : water for washing the body **3** : a liquid in which objects are immersed so that it can act on them **4** : BATHROOM

bathe \'bāth\ *vb* **bathed; bath·ing 1** : to wash in liquid and esp. water: *also* : to apply water or a medicated liquid to ⟨*bathed* her eyes⟩ **2** : to take a bath; *also* : to take a swim **3** : to wash along, over, or against so as to wet **4** : to suffuse with or as if with light — **bath·er** *n*

bath·house \'bath-,haùs, 'bàth-\ *n* **1** : a building equipped for bathing **2** : a building containing dressing rooms for bathers

bathing suit *n* : SWIMSUIT

batho·lith \'bath-ə-,lith\ *n* : a great mass of igneous rock that forced its way into or between other rocks and that stopped in its rise a considerable distance below the surface

ba·thos \'bā-,thäs\ *n* [Gk, lit., depth] **1** : the sudden appearance of the commonplace in otherwise elevated matter or style **2** : insincere or overdone pathos — **ba·thet·ic** \bə-'thet-ik\ *adj*

bath·robe \'bath-,rōb, 'bàth-\ *n* : a loose usu. absorbent robe worn before and after bathing or as a dressing gown

bath·room \-,rüm, -,rùm\ *n* : a room containing a bathtub or shower and usu. a washbowl and toilet

bath·tub \-,təb\ *n* : a usu. fixed tub for bathing

bathy·scaphe \'bath-i-,skaf, -,skàf\ *also* **bathy·scaph** \-,skaf\ *n* : a navigable undersea craft for deep-sea exploration

bathy·sphere \-,sfiər\ *n* : a steel diving sphere for deep-sea observation

bathy·ther·mo·graph \,bath-i-'thər-mə-,graf\ *n* : an instrument that records water temperature as a function of depth

ba·tik \bə-'tēk, 'bat-ik\ *n* [Malay] **1** : an Indonesian method of hand-printing textiles by coating with wax the parts not to be dyed; *also* : a design so executed **2** : a fabric printed by batik

ba·tiste \bə-'tēst\ *n* : a fine sheer fabric of plain weave

bat·man \'bat-mən\ *n* : an orderly of a British military officer

ba·ton \bə-'tän\ *n* : STAFF, ROD; *esp* : a stick with which the leader directs an orchestra or band

bats·man \'bats-mən\ *n* : a batter esp. in cricket

bat·tal·ion \bə-'tal-yən\ *n* **1** : a large body of troops organized to act together : ARMY **2** : a military unit composed of a headquarters and two or more units (as companies)

¹**bat·ten** \'bat-ᵊn\ *vb* **bat·tened; bat·ten·ing** \'bat-(ə-)niŋ\ **1** : to grow or make fat **2** : THRIVE

²**batten** *n* : a strip of wood used esp. to seal or strengthen a joint

³**batten** *vb* **bat·tened; bat·ten·ing** \'bat-(ə-)niŋ\ : to fasten with battens

¹**bat·ter** \'bat-ər\ *vb* : to beat or damage with repeated blows

²**batter** *n* : a soft mixture (as for cake) basically of flour and liquid

³**batter** *n* : one that bats; *esp* : the player whose turn it is to bat

battering ram *n* : an ancient military machine for battering down walls

bat·tery \'bat-(ə-)rē\ *n, pl* **-ter·ies 1** : BEATING; *esp* : unlawful beating or use of force on a person **2** : a grouping of artillery pieces for tactical purposes; *also* : the guns of a warship **3** : a group of electric cells for furnishing electric current; *also* : a single electric cell ⟨a flashlight ∼⟩ **4** : a number of similar items grouped or used as a unit ⟨a ∼ of tests⟩ **5** : the pitcher and catcher of a baseball team

bat·ting \'bat-iŋ\ *n* : layers or sheets of cotton or wool (as for lining quilts)

¹**bat·tle** \'bat-ᵊl\ *n* [ME *batel*, fr. OF *bataille* battle, fortifying tower, battalion, fr. LL *battalia* combat, alter. of *battualia* fencing exercises, fr. L *battuere* to beat] : a general military engagement; *also* : an extended contest or controversy

²**battle** *vb* **bat·tled; bat·tling** \'bat-(ə-)liŋ\ : to engage in battle : CONTEND, FIGHT

bat·tle–ax \'bat-ᵊl-,aks\ *n* **1** : a long-handled ax formerly used as a weapon **2** : a quarrelsome domineering woman

battle fatigue *n* : COMBAT FATIGUE

bat·tle·field \'bat-ᵊl-,fēld\ *n* : a place where a battle is fought

bat·tle·ment \-mənt\ *n* : a decorative or defensive parapet on top of a wall

bat·tle·ship \-,ship\ *n* : a warship of the most heavily armed and armored class

bat·tle·wag·on \-,wag-ən\ *n* : BATTLESHIP

bat·ty \'bat-ē\ *adj* **bat·ti·er; -est** : CRAZY, FOOLISH

bau·ble \'bò-bəl\ *n* : TRINKET

baux·ite \'bòk-,sīt\ *n* : a clayey substance that is the chief ore of aluminum

bawd \'bȯd\ *n* 1 : MADAM 2 2 : PROSTITUTE

bawdy \'bȯd-ē\ *adj* **bawd·i·er; -est** : OBSCENE, LEWD — **bawd·i·ly** \'bȯd-ᵊl-ē\ *adv* — **bawd·i·ness** \-ē-nəs\ *n*

¹**bawl** \'bȯl\ *vb* : to cry or cry out loudly; *also* : to scold harshly

²**bawl** *n* : a long loud cry : BELLOW

¹**bay** \'bā\ *adj* : reddish brown

²**bay** *n* 1 : a bay-colored animal 2 : a reddish brown

³**bay** *n* : the European laurel; *also* : a shrub or tree resembling this

⁴**bay** *n* 1 : a section or compartment of a building or vehicle 2 : a compartment projecting outward from the wall of a building and containing a window (bay **window**)

⁵**bay** *vb* : to bark with deep low tones

⁶**bay** *n* 1 : the position of one unable to escape and forced to face danger 2 : a baying of dogs

⁷**bay** *n* : an inlet of a body of water (as the sea) usu. smaller than a gulf

bay·ber·ry \'bā-ˌber-ē\ *n* : a hardy deciduous shrub of coastal eastern No. America bearing small hard berries coated with a white wax used for candles; *also* : its fruit

bay leaf *n* : the dried leaf of the European laurel used in cooking

¹**bay·o·net** \'bā-ə-nət, ˌbā-ə-'net\ *n* : a daggerlike weapon made to fit on the muzzle end of a rifle

²**bayonet** *vb* **-net·ed** *also* **-net·ted; -net·ing** *also* **-net·ting** : to use or stab with a bayonet

bay·ou \'bī-ō, -ü\ *n* [Louisiana French, fr. Choctaw *bayuk*] : a marshy or sluggish body of water

bay rum *n* : a fragrant liquid used esp. as a cologne or after-shave lotion

ba·zaar \bə-'zär\ *n* 1 : a group of shops : MARKETPLACE 2 : a fair for the sale of articles usu. for charity

ba·zoo·ka \bə-'zü-kə\ *n* [*bazooka* (a crude musical instrument made of pipes and a funnel)] : a weapon consisting of a tube and launching an explosive rocket able to pierce armor

¹**BB** \'bē-ˌbē\ *n* : a small round shot pellet

²**BB** *abbr* base on balls

BBB *abbr* Better Business Bureau

BBC *abbr* British Broadcasting Corporation

bbl *abbr* barrel; barrels

BC *abbr* 1 before Christ — often printed in small capitals 2 British Columbia

BCD \ˌbē-ˌsē-'dē\ *n* [*binary coded decimal*] : a computer code for representing alphanumeric information

B cell *n* [*bone-marrow-derived cell*] : any of the lymphocytes that secrete antibodies when mature

B complex *n* : VITAMIN B COMPLEX

bd *abbr* 1 board 2 bound

bdl *or* **bdle** *abbr* bundle

bdrm *abbr* bedroom

be \(')bē\ *vb*, *past 1st & 3d sing* **was** \(')wəz, 'wäz\; *2d sing* **were** \(')wər\; *pl* **were**; *past subjunctive* **were**; *past part* **been** \(')bin\; *pres part* **being** \'bē-iŋ\; *pres 1st sing* **am** \əm, (')am\; *2d sing* **are** \ər, (')är\; *3d sing* **is** \(')iz, əz\; *pl* **are**; *pres subjunctive* **be** 1 : to equal in meaning or symbolically (God *is* love); *also* : to have a specified qualification or relationship (leaves *are* green) (this fish *is* a trout) 2 : to have objective existence (there *was* once an old woman); *also* : to have or occupy a particular place (here *is* your pen) 3 : to take place : OCCUR (the meeting *is* tonight) 4 — used with the past participle of transitive verbs as a passive voice auxiliary (the door *was* opened) 5 — used as the auxiliary of the present participle in expressing continuous action (he *is* sleeping) 6 — used as an auxiliary with the past participle of some intransitive verbs to form archaic perfect tenses 7 — used as an auxiliary with *to* and the infinitive to express futurity, prearrangement, or obligation (he *is* to come when called)

Be *symbol* beryllium

¹**beach** \'bēch\ *n* : a sandy or gravelly part of the shore of an ocean or lake

²**beach** *vb* : to run or drive ashore

beach buggy *n* : DUNE BUGGY

beach·comb·er \'bēch-ˌkō-mər\ *n* : one who searches along a shore for useful or salable flotsam and refuse

beach·head \'bēch-ˌhed\ *n* : an area on an enemy-held shore occupied by an advance attacking force to protect the later landing of troops or supplies

bea·con \'bē-kən\ *n* 1 : a signal fire 2 : a guiding or warning signal (as a lighthouse) 3 : a radio transmitter emitting signals for guidance of aircraft

¹**bead** \'bēd\ *n* [ME *bede* prayer, prayer bead, fr. OE *bed, gebed* prayer] 1 *pl* : a series of prayers and meditations made with a rosary 2 : a small piece of material pierced for threading on a line (as in a rosary) 3 : a small globular body 4 : a narrow projecting rim or band — **bead·ing** *n* — **beady** *adj*

²**bead** *vb* : to form into a bead

bea·dle \'bēd-ᵊl\ *n* : a usu. English parish officer whose duties include keeping order in church

bea·gle \'bē-gəl\ *n* : a small short-legged smooth-coated hound

beak \'bēk\ *n* : the bill of a bird and esp. of a bird of prey; *also* : a pointed projecting part — **beaked** \'bēkt\ *adj*

bea·ker \'bē-kər\ *n* 1 : a large drinking cup with a wide mouth 2 : a thin-walled laboratory vessel with a wide mouth

¹**beam** \'bēm\ *n* 1 : a large long piece of timber or metal 2 : the bar of a balance from which the scales hang 3 : the breadth of a ship at its widest part 4 : a ray or shaft of light 5 : a collection of nearly parallel rays (as X rays) or particles (as electrons) 6 : a

constant radio signal transmitted for the guidance of pilots; *also* : the course indicated by this signal

²**beam** *vb* 1 : to send out light 2 : to aim (a broadcast) by directional antennas 3 : to smile with joy

¹**bean** \'bēn\ *n* : the edible seed borne in pods by some leguminous plants; *also* : a plant or a pod bearing these

²**bean** *vb* : to strike on the head with an object

bean·bag \'bēn-ˌbag\ *n* : a cloth bag partially filled typically with dried beans and used as a toy

bean·ball \'bēn-ˌbȯl\ *n* : a pitched baseball thrown at a batter's head

bean curd *n* : a food like soft cheese made from soybeans

bean·ie \'bē-nē\ *n* : a small round tight-fitting skullcap

beano \'bē-nō\ *n, pl* **beanos** : BINGO

¹**bear** \'baər\ *n, pl* **bears** 1 *or pl* **bear** : any of a family of large heavy mammals with shaggy hair and small tails 2 : a gruff or sullen person 3 : one who sells (as securities) in expectation of a price decline — **bear·ish** *adj*

²**bear** *vb* **bore** \'bōr\; **borne** \'bōrn\ *also* **born** \'bȯrn\; **bear·ing** 1 : CARRY 2 : to be equipped with 3 : to give as testimony ⟨~ witness to the facts of the case⟩ 4 : to give birth to; *also* : PRODUCE, YIELD ⟨a tree that ~s regularly⟩ 5 : ENDURE, SUSTAIN ⟨~ pain⟩ ⟨bore the weight on piles⟩; *also* : to exert pressure or influence 6 : to be or become directed ⟨~ to the right⟩ — **bear·able** *adj* — **bear·er** *n*

¹**beard** \'biərd\ *n* 1 : the hair that grows on the face of a man 2 : a growth of bristly hairs (as on rye or the chin of a goat) — **beard·ed** \-əd\ *adj* — **beard·less** *adj*

²**beard** *vb* : to confront boldly

bear·ing \'ba(ə)r-iŋ\ *n* 1 : manner of carrying oneself : COMPORTMENT 2 : a supporting object, purpose, or point 3 : a machine part in which another part (as an axle or pin) turns 4 : an emblem in a coat of arms 5 : the position or direction of one point with respect to another or to the compass; *also* : a determination of position 6 *pl* : comprehension of one's situation 7 : connection with or influence on something; *also* : SIGNIFICANCE

bear·skin \'baər-ˌskin\ *n* : an article made of the skin of a bear

beast \'bēst\ *n* 1 : ANIMAL 1; *esp* : a 4-footed mammal 2 : a contemptible person *syn* brute, animal, creature

¹**beast·ly** \'bēst-lē\ *adj* **beast·li·er; -est** 1 : of, relating to, or resembling a beast 2 : ABOMINABLE, DISAGREEABLE — **beast·li·ness** \-lē-nəs\ *n*

²**beastly** *adv* : VERY

¹**beat** \'bēt\ *vb* **beat; beat·en** \'bēt-ᵊn\ *or* **beat; beat·ing** 1 : to strike repeatedly 2 : TREAD 3 : to affect or alter by beating ⟨~ metal into sheets⟩ 4 : to sound (as an alarm) on a drum 5 : OVERCOME;

also : SURPASS 6 : to act or arrive before ⟨~ his brother home⟩ 7 : THROB — **beat·er** *n*

²**beat** *n* 1 : a single stroke or blow esp. of a series; *also* : PULSATION 2 : a rhythmic stress in poetry or music or the rhythmic effect of these 3 : a regularly traversed course

³**beat** *adj* 1 : EXHAUSTED 2 : of or relating to beatniks

⁴**beat** *n* : BEATNIK

be·a·tif·ic \ˌbē-ə-'tif-ik\ *adj* : giving or indicative of great joy or bliss

be·at·i·fy \bē-'at-ə-ˌfī\ *vb* **-fied; -fy·ing** 1 : to make supremely happy 2 : to declare to have attained the blessedness of heaven and authorize the title "Blessed" for — **be·at·i·fi·ca·tion** \-ˌat-ə-fə-'kā-shən\ *n*

be·at·i·tude \bē-'at-ə-ˌt(y)üd\ *n* 1 : a state of utmost bliss 2 : any of the declarations made in the Sermon on the Mount (Mt 5:3–12) beginning "Blessed are"

beat·nik \'bēt-nik\ *n* : a person who behaves and dresses unconventionally and is inclined to exotic philosophizing and extreme self-expression

beau \'bō\ *n, pl* **beaux** \'bōz\ *or* **beaus** [F, fr. *beau* beautiful, fr. L *bellus* pretty] 1 : a man of fashion : DANDY 2 : SUITOR, LOVER

beau geste \bō-'zhest\ *n, pl* **beaux gestes** *or* **beau gestes** \bō-'zhest\ : a graceful or magnanimous gesture

beau ide·al \ˌbō-ī-'dē(-ə)l\ *n, pl* **beau ideals** : the perfect type or model

Beau·jo·lais \ˌbō-zhō-'lā\ *n* : a French red wine

beau monde \bō-'mänd, -mōⁿd\ *n, pl* **beau mondes** \-'män(d)z\ *or* **beaux mondes** \bō-mōⁿd\ : the world of high society and fashion

beau·te·ous \'byüt-ē-əs\ *adj* : BEAUTIFUL — **beau·te·ous·ly** *adv*

beau·ti·cian \byü-'tish-ən\ *n* : COSMETOLOGIST

beau·ti·ful \'byüt-i-fəl\ *adj* : characterized by beauty : LOVELY *syn* pretty, fair, comely, lovely — **beau·ti·ful·ly** \-f(ə-)lē\ *adv*

beautiful people *n pl, often cap B&P* : people who are identified with international society

beau·ti·fy \'byüt-ə-ˌfī\ *vb* **-fied; -fy·ing** : to make more beautiful — **beau·ti·fi·ca·tion** \ˌbyüt-ə-fə-'kā-shən\ *n* — **beau·ti·fi·er** *n*

beau·ty \'byüt-ē\ *n, pl* **beauties** : qualities that give pleasure to the senses or exalt the mind : LOVELINESS; *also* : something having such qualities

beauty shop *n* : an establishment where hairdressing, facials, and manicures are done

beaux arts \bō-'zär\ *n pl* [F] : FINE ARTS

bea·ver \'bē-vər\ *n, pl* **beavers** : a large fur-bearing rodent that builds dams and underwater houses of mud and sticks; *also* : its fur

be·calm \bi-'käm, -'kälm\ *vb* : to keep

(as a ship) motionless by lack of wind

be·cause \bi-'kóz, -'kəz\ *conj* : for the reason that

because of *prep* : by reason of

beck \'bek\ *n* : a beckoning gesture; *also* : SUMMONS

beck·on \'bek-ən\ *vb* **beck·oned; beck·on·ing** \-(ə-)niŋ\ : to summon or signal esp. by a nod or gesture; *also* : ATTRACT

be·cloud \bi-'klaùd\ *vb* : OBSCURE

be·come \bi-'kəm\ *vb* **-came** \-'kām\ ; **-come; -com·ing** 1 : to come to be ⟨~ tired⟩ 2 : to suit or be suitable to ⟨her dress ~s her⟩

be·com·ing \-'kəm-iŋ\ *adj* : SUITABLE, FIT; *also* : ATTRACTIVE — **be·com·ing·ly** *adv*

¹**bed** \'bed\ *n* 1 : an article of furniture to sleep on 2 : a plot of ground prepared for plants 3 : FOUNDATION, BOTTOM (river ~) 4 : LAYER, STRATUM

²**bed** *vb* **bed·ded; bed·ding** 1 : to put or go to bed 2 : to fix in a foundation — EMBED 3 : to plant in beds 4 : to lay or lie flat or in layers

bed-and-breakfast *adj* : offering lodging and breakfast ⟨a ~ place⟩ — **bed-and-breakfast** *n*

be·daub \bi-'dób\ *vb* : SMEAR

be·daz·zle \bi-'daz-əl\ *vb* : to confuse by or as if by a strong light — **be·daz·zle·ment** *n*

bed·bug \'bed-,bəg\ *n* : a wingless bloodsucking bug infesting houses and esp. beds

bed·clothes \'bed-,klō(th)z\ *n pl* : BEDDING 1

bed·ding \'bed-iŋ\ *n* 1 : materials for making up a bed 2 : FOUNDATION

be·deck \bi-'dek\ *vb* : ADORN

be·dev·il \bi-'dev-əl\ *vb* 1 : HARASS, TORMENT 2 : CONFUSE, MUDDLE

be·dew \bi-'d(y)ü\ *vb* : to wet with or as if with dew

bed·fast \'bed-,fast\ *adj* : BEDRIDDEN

bed·fel·low \'bed-,fel-ō\ *n* 1 : one sharing the bed of another 2 : a close associate : ALLY

be·di·zen \bi-'dīz-ᵊn, -'diz-\ *vb* [*be- + dizen,* fr. earlier *disen* to dress a distaff with flax, fr. Dutch] : to dress or adorn with showy or vulgar finery

bed·lam \'bed-ləm\ *n* [*Bedlam,* popular name for the Hospital of St. Mary of Bethlehem, London, an insane asylum, fr. ME *Bedlem* Bethlehem] 1 : an insane asylum 2 : a scene of uproar and confusion

bed·ou·in or **bed·u·in** \'bed(-ə)-wən\ *n, pl* **bedouin** or **bedouins** or **beduin** or **beduins** *often cap* : a nomadic Arab of the Arabian, Syrian, or No. African deserts

bed·pan \'bed-,pan\ *n* : a shallow vessel used by a person in bed for urination or defecation

bed·post \-,pōst\ *n* : the post of a bed

be·drag·gled \bi-'drag-əld\ *adj* : soiled and disordered as if by being drenched

bed·rid·den \'bed-,rid-ᵊn\ *adj* : kept in bed by illness or weakness

bed·rock \-'räk\ *n* : the solid rock underlying surface materials (as soil) — **bedrock** *adj*

bed·roll \-,rōl\ *n* : bedding rolled up for carrying

bed·room \-,rüm, -,rüm\ *n* : a room containing a bed and used esp. for sleeping

bed·side \'bed-,sīd\ *n* : the place beside a bed esp. of a sick or dying person

bed·sore \-,sōr\ *n* : an ulceration of tissue deprived of nutrition by prolonged pressure

bed·spread \-,spred\ *n* : a usu. ornamental outer cover for a bed

bed·stead \-,sted, -,stid\ *n* : the framework of a bed

bed·time \-,tīm\ *n* : time for going to bed

bed-wet·ting \-,wet-iŋ\ *n* : involuntary discharge of urine esp. in bed during sleep — **bed-wet·ter** *n*

¹**bee** \'bē\ *n* : a social and colonial 4-winged insect often kept in hives for the honey it produces; *also* : any of various related insects

²**bee** *n* : a gathering of people for a specific purpose

beech \'bēch\ *n, pl* **beech·es** or **beech** : any of a genus of deciduous hardwood trees with smooth gray bark and small sweet triangular nuts; *also* : the wood of a beech — **beech·en** \'bē-chən\ *adj*

beech·nut \'bēch-,nət\ *n* : the nut of a beech

¹**beef** \'bēf\ *n, pl* **beefs** \'bēfs\ or **beeves** \'bēvz\ 1 : the flesh of a steer, cow, or bull; *also* : the dressed carcass of a beef animal 2 : a steer, cow, or bull esp. when fattened for food 3 : MUSCLE, BRAWN 4 *pl* **beefs** : COMPLAINT

²**beef** *vb* 1 : STRENGTHEN — usu. used with *up* 2 : COMPLAIN

beef·eat·er \-,ēt-ər\ *n* : a yeoman of the guard of an English monarch

beef·steak \'bēf-,stāk\ *n* : a slice of beef suitable for broiling or frying

beefy \'bē-fē\ *adj* **beef·i·er; -est** : THICKSET, BRAWNY

bee·hive \'bē-,hīv\ *n* : HIVE 1, 3

bee·keep·er \-,kē-pər\ *n* : a raiser of bees — **bee·keep·ing** *n*

bee·line \-,līn\ *n* : a straight direct course

been *past part of* BE

beep·er \'bē-pər\ *n* : a portable electronic device that alerts the person carrying it when it receives a special radio signal

beer \'biər\ *n* : an alcoholic beverage brewed from malt and hops — **beery** *adj*

bees·wax \'bēz-,waks\ *n* : WAX 1

beet \'bēt\ *n* : a garden plant with edible leaves and a thick sweet root used as a vegetable, as a source of sugar, or as forage; *also* : its root

¹**bee·tle** \'bēt-ᵊl\ *n* : any of an order of

insects having four wings of which the stiff outer pair covers the membranous inner pair when not in flight

²**beetle** \bee-tled; bee-tling : to jut out : PROJECT

be·fall \bi-ˈfȯl\ *vb* **-fell** \-ˈfel\; **-fall·en** \-ˈfȯ-lən\ : to happen to : OCCUR

be·fit \bi-ˈfit\ *vb* : to be suitable to

be·fog \bi-ˈfȯg, -ˈfäg\ *vb* : OBSCURE; *also* : CONFUSE

¹**be·fore** \bi-ˈfȯr\ *adv or adj* **1** : in front **2** : EARLIER

²**before** *prep* **1** : in front of (stood ~ him) **2** : earlier than (got there ~ me) **3** : in a more important category than (put quality ~ quantity)

³**before** *conj* **1** : earlier than the time when (he got here ~ I did) **2** : more willingly than (he'd starve ~ he'd steal)

be·fore·hand \bi-ˈfȯr-ˌhand\ *adv or adj* : in advance

be·foul \bi-ˈfau̇l\ *vb* : SOIL

be·friend \bi-ˈfrend\ *vb* : to act as friend to

be·fud·dle \bi-ˈfəd-ᵊl\ *vb* : MUDDLE, CONFUSE

beg \ˈbeg\ *vb* **begged; beg·ging 1** : to ask as a charity; *also* : ENTREAT **2** : EVADE; *also* : assume as established (~ the question)

be·get \bi-ˈget\ *vb* **-got** \-ˈgät\; **-got·ten** \-ˈgät-ᵊn\ *or* **-got; -get·ting** : to become the father of : SIRE

¹**beg·gar** \ˈbeg-ər\ *n* : one that begs esp. as a way of life

²**beggar** *vb* **beg·gared; beg·gar·ing** \ˈbeg-(ə-)riŋ\ : IMPOVERISH

beg·gar·ly \ˈbeg-ər-lē\ *adj* **1** : marked by unrelieved poverty (a ~ life) **2** : contemptibly mean or inadequate

beg·gary \ˈbeg-ə-rē\ *n* : extreme poverty

be·gin \bi-ˈgin\ *vb* **be·gan** \-ˈgan\; **be·gun** \-ˈgən\; **be·gin·ning 1** : to do the first part of an action; *also* : to undertake or undergo initial steps : COMMENCE **2** : to come into being : ARISE; *also* : FOUND **3** : ORIGINATE, INVENT — **be·gin·ner** *n*

be·gone \bi-ˈgȯn\ *vb* : to go away : DEPART — used esp. in the imperative

be·go·nia \bi-ˈgōn-yə\ *n* : any of a genus of tropical herbs widely grown for their showy leaves and waxy flowers

be·grime \bi-ˈgrīm\ *vb* **be·grimed; be·grim·ing** : to make dirty

be·grudge \bi-ˈgrəj\ *vb* **1** : to give or concede reluctantly **2** : to take little pleasure in : be annoyed by **3** : to envy the pleasure or enjoyment of

be·guile \-ˈgīl\ *vb* **be·guiled; be·guil·ing 1** : DECEIVE, CHEAT **2** : to while away **3** : to coax by wiles

be·guine \bi-ˈgēn\ *n* [AmerF *béguine*, fr. F *béguin* flirtation] : a vigorous popular dance of the islands of Saint Lucia and Martinique

be·gum \ˈbā-gəm, ˈbē-\ *n* : a Muslim woman of high rank

be·half \bi-ˈhaf, -ˈhȧf\ *n* : BENEFIT, SUPPORT, DEFENSE

be·have \bi-ˈhāv\ *vb* **be·haved; be·hav·ing 1** : to bear, comport, or conduct oneself in a particular and esp. a proper way **2** : to act, function, or react in a particular way

be·hav·ior \bi-ˈhā-vyər\ *n* : way of behaving; *esp* : personal conduct — **be·hav·ior·al** \-vyə-rəl\ *adj*

be·hav·ior·ism \bi-ˈhā-vyə-ˌriz-əm\ *n* : a school of psychology concerned with the objective evidence of behavior without reference to conscious experience

be·head \bi-ˈhed\ *vb* : to cut off the head of

be·he·moth \bi-ˈhē-məth, ˈbē-ə-ˌmäth\ *n* : a huge powerful animal described in Job 40:15–24 that is probably the hippopotamus; *also* : something of monstrous size or power

be·hest \bi-ˈhest\ *n* **1** : COMMAND **2** : an urgent prompting

¹**be·hind** \bi-ˈhīnd\ *adv or adj* **1** : BACK, BACKWARD **2** : LATE, SLOW

²**behind** *prep* **1** : in or to a place or situation in back of or to the rear of (look ~ you) (the staff stayed ~ the troops) **2** : inferior to (as in rank) : BELOW (three games ~ the first-place team) **3** : in support of : SUPPORTING (we're ~ you all the way)

be·hind·hand \bi-ˈhīnd-ˌhand\ *adj* **1** : being in arrears **2** : lagging behind the times **syn** tardy, late, overdue, belated

be·hold \bi-ˈhōld\ *vb* **-held** \-ˈheld\; **-hold·ing 1** : to have in sight : SEE **2** — used imperatively to direct the attention **syn** view, observe, notice, espy — **be·hold·er** *n*

be·hold·en \bi-ˈhōl-dən\ *adj* : OBLIGATED, INDEBTED

be·hoof \bi-ˈhüf\ *n* : ADVANTAGE, PROFIT

be·hoove \bi-ˈhüv\ *or* **be·hove** \-ˈhōv\ *vb* **be·hooved** *or* **be·hoved; be·hoov·ing** *or* **be·hov·ing** : to be necessary, proper, or advantageous for

beige \ˈbāzh\ *n* : a pale dull yellowish brown — **beige** *adj*

be·ing \ˈbē-iŋ\ *n* **1** : EXISTENCE; *also* : LIFE **2** : the qualities or constitution of an existent thing **3** : a living thing; *esp* : PERSON

be·la·bor \bi-ˈlā-bər\ *vb* **1** : to assail (as with words) tiresomely or at length **2** : to beat soundly

be·lat·ed \bi-ˈlāt-əd\ *adj* : DELAYED, LATE

be·lay \bi-ˈlā\ *vb* **1** : to wind (a rope) around a pin or cleat in order to hold secure **2** : QUIT, STOP — used in the imperative

belch \ˈbelch\ *vb* **1** : to expel (gas) from the stomach through the mouth **2** : to gush forth (a volcano ~ing lava) — **belch** *n*

bel·dam *or* **bel·dame** \ˈbel-dəm\ *n* [ME *beldam* grandmother, fr. MF *bel*

beautiful + ME *dam* lady, mother]
: an old woman; *esp* : HAG

be·lea·guer \bi-'lē-gər\ *vb* 1 : BESIEGE 2
: HARASS ⟨*~ed* parents⟩

bel·fry \'bel-frē\ *n, pl* **belfries** [ME *bel-frey*, alter. of *berfrey*, fr. MF *berfrei*, deriv. of Gk *pyrgos phorētos* movable war tower] : a tower for a bell (as on a church); *also* : the part of the tower in which the bell hangs

Belg *abbr* Belgian; Belgium

Bel·gian \'bel-jən\ *n* : a native or inhabitant of Belgium — **Belgian** *adj*

be·lie \bi-'lī\ *vb* **-lied; -ly·ing** 1 : MISREPRESENT 2 : to prove (something) false 3 : to run counter to

be·lief \bə-'lēf\ *n* 1 : CONFIDENCE, TRUST 2 : something (as a tenet or creed) believed *syn* conviction, opinion, persuasion, sentiment

be·lieve \bə-'lēv\ *vb* **be·lieved; be·liev·ing** 1 : to have religious convictions 2 : to have a firm conviction about something : accept as true 3 : to hold as an opinion : SUPPOSE — **be·liev·able** *adj* — **be·liev·er** *n*

be·like \bi-'līk\ *adv, archaic* : PROBABLY

be·lit·tle \bi-'lit-ᵊl\ *vb* **-lit·tled; -lit·tling** \-'lit-ᵊl-iŋ\ : to make seem little or less; *also* : DISPARAGE

¹**bell** \'bel\ *n* 1 : a hollow metallic device that makes a ringing sound when struck 2 : the sounding or stroke of a bell (as on shipboard to tell the time); *also* : time so indicated 3 : something with the flared form of a typical bell

²**bell** *vb* : to provide with a bell

bel·la·don·na \₁bel-ə-'dän-ə\ *n* [It, lit., beautiful lady; fr. its cosmetic use] : a drug or extract used esp. to relieve spasms and pain or to dilate the eye and obtained from a poisonous European herb related to the potato; *also* : this herb

bell–bot·toms \'bel-₁bät-əmz\ *n pl* : pants with wide flaring bottoms — **bell–bottom** *adj*

bell·boy \'bel-₁bȯi\ *n* : BELLHOP

belle \'bel\ *n* : an attractive and popular girl or woman

belles let·tres \bel-'letr⁰\ *n pl* [F] : literature that is an end in itself and not practical or purely informative — **bel·le·tris·tic** \₁bel-ə-'tris-tik\ *adj*

bell·hop \'bel-₁häp\ *n* : a hotel or club employee who takes guests to rooms, carries luggage, and runs errands

bel·li·cose \'bel-i-₁kōs\ *adj* : WARLIKE, PUGNACIOUS *syn* belligerent, quarrelsome, combative, contentious, pugnacious — **bel·li·cos·i·ty** \₁bel-i-'käs-ət-ē\ *n*

bel·lig·er·en·cy \bə-'lij-(ə-)rən-sē\ *n* 1 : the status of a nation engaged in war 2 : BELLIGERENCE, TRUCULENCE

bel·lig·er·ent \-rənt\ *adj* 1 : waging war 2 : TRUCULENT *syn* bellicose, pugnacious, combative, contentious, warlike — **bel·lig·er·ence** \-rəns\ *n* — **belligerent** *n*

bel·low \'bel-ō\ *vb* 1 : to make the deep

hollow sound characteristic of a bull 2 : to call or utter in a loud deep voice — **bellow** *n*

bel·lows \-ōz, -əz\ *n sing or pl* : a closed boxlike device with sides that can be spread apart and then pressed together to draw in air and expel it through a tube

bells \'belz\ *n pl* : BELL-BOTTOMS

bell·weth·er \'bel-'weth-ər, -₁weth-\ *n* : one that takes the lead or initiative

¹**bel·ly** \'bel-ē\ *n, pl* **bellies** [ME *bely* bellows, belly, fr. OE *belg* bag, skin] 1 : ABDOMEN; *also* : STOMACH 2 : the underpart of an animal's body

²**belly** *vb* **bel·lied; bel·ly·ing** : BULGE

¹**bel·ly·ache** \'bel-ē-₁āk\ *n* : pain in the abdomen

²**bellyache** *vb* : COMPLAIN

belly button *n* : NAVEL

belly dance *n* : a usu. solo dance emphasizing movement of the belly — **belly dance** *vb* — **belly dancer** *n*

belly laugh *n* : a deep hearty laugh

be·long \bi-'lȯŋ\ *vb* 1 : to be suitable or appropriate; *also* : to be properly situated ⟨shoes *~* in the closet⟩ 2 : to be the property ⟨this *~s* to me⟩; *also* : to be attached (as through birth or membership) ⟨*~* to a club⟩ 3 : to form an attribute or part ⟨this wheel *~s* to the cart⟩ 4 : to be classified ⟨whales *~* among the mammals⟩

be·long·ings \-'lȯŋ-iŋz\ *n pl* : GOODS, EFFECTS, POSSESSIONS

be·loved \bi-'ləv(-ə)d\ *adj* : dearly loved — **beloved** *n*

¹**be·low** \bi-'lō\ *adv* 1 : in or to a lower place or rank 2 : on earth 3 : in hell *syn* under, beneath, underneath

²**below** *prep* 1 : in or to a lower place than 2 : inferior to (as in rank)

¹**belt** \'belt\ *n* 1 : a strip (as of leather) worn about the waist 2 : an endless band passing around pulleys or cylinders to communicate motion or convey material 3 : a region marked by some distinctive feature; *esp* : one suited to a particular crop

²**belt** *vb* 1 : to encircle or secure with a belt 2 : to beat with or as if with a belt 3 : to mark with an encircling band

³**belt** *n* 1 : a jarring blow : WHACK 2 : DRINK ⟨a *~* of whiskey⟩

belt–tightening *n* : a reduction in spending

belt·way \'belt-₁wā\ *n* : a highway skirting an urban area

be·lu·ga \bə-'lü-gə\ *n* : a white sturgeon of the Black sea, Caspian sea, and their tributaries that is a source of caviar

bel·ve·dere \'bel-və-₁diər\ *n* [It, lit., beautiful view] : a structure (as a summerhouse) designed to command a view

be·mire \bi-'mī(ə)r\ *vb* : to cover or soil with or sink in mire

be·moan \bi-'mōn\ *vb* : LAMENT, DEPLORE *syn* bewail, grieve, moan, weep

be·muse \bi-'myüz\ *vb* : BEWILDER, CONFUSE

¹**bench** \'bench\ *n* **1** : a long seat for two or more persons **2** : the seat of a judge in court; *also* : the office or dignity of a judge **3** : COURT; *also* : JUDGES **4** : a table for holding work and tools (a carpenter's ~)

²**bench** \'bench\ *vb* **1** : to furnish with benches **2** : to seat on a bench **3** : to remove from or keep out of a game

bench mark *n* **1** : a mark on a permanent object serving as an elevation reference in topographical surveys **2** *usu* **bench·mark** : a point of reference for measurement; *also* : STANDARD

bench warrant *n* : a warrant issued by a presiding judge or by a court against a person guilty of contempt or indicted for a crime

¹**bend** \'bend\ *vb* **bent** \'bent\; **bend·ing** **1** : to draw (as a bow) taut **2** : to curve or cause a change of shape in ⟨~ a bar⟩ **3** : to turn in a certain direction ⟨*bent* his steps toward town⟩ **4** : to make fast : SECURE **5** : SUBDUE **6** : RESOLVE, DETERMINE ⟨*bent* on self-destruction⟩; *also* : APPLY ⟨*bent* themselves to the task⟩ **7** : DEFLECT **8** : to curve downward **9** : YIELD, SUBMIT

²**bend** *n* : a knot by which a rope is fastened (as to another rope)

³**bend** *n* **1** : an act or process of bending **2** : something bent; *esp* : CURVE **3** *pl* : a painful and dangerous disorder caused by release of gas bubbles in the tissues upon too rapid decrease in air pressure after a stay in a compressed atmosphere

bend·er \'ben-dər\ *n* : SPREE

¹**be·neath** \bi-'nēth\ *adv* : BELOW, UNDERNEATH **syn** under, underneath, below

²**beneath** *prep* **1** : BELOW, UNDER ⟨stood ~ a tree⟩ **2** : unworthy of ⟨considered such behavior ~ her⟩

bene·dic·tion \ben-ə-'dik-shən\ *n* : the invocation of a blessing esp. at the close of a public worship service

bene·fac·tion \-'fak-shən\ *n* : a charitable donation **syn** contribution, alms, beneficence, offering

bene·fac·tor \'ben-ə-ˌfak-tər\ *n* : one that confers a benefit and esp. a benefaction

bene·fac·tress \-ˌfak-trəs\ *n* : a woman who is a benefactor

bene·fice \'ben-ə-fəs\ *n* : an ecclesiastical office to which the revenue from an endowment is attached

be·nef·i·cence \bə-'nef-ə-səns\ *n* **1** : beneficent quality **2** : BENEFACTION

be·nef·i·cent \-sənt\ *adj* : doing or producing good (as by acts of kindness or charity); *also* : productive of benefit

ben·e·fi·cial \ben-ə-'fish-əl\ *adj* : being of benefit or help : HELPFUL **syn** advantageous, profitable, favorable, propitious — **ben·e·fi·cial·ly** \-ē\ *adv*

ben·e·fi·cia·ry \ben-ə-'fish-ē-ˌer-ē, -'fish-(ə-)rē\ *n*, *pl* **-ries** : one that receives a benefit (as the income of a trust or the proceeds of an insurance)

¹**ben·e·fit** \'ben-ə-ˌfit\ *n* **1** : ADVANTAGE ⟨the ~s of exercise⟩ **2** : useful aid : HELP; *also* : material aid provided or due (as in sickness or unemployment) as a right **3** : a performance or event to raise funds for some person or cause

²**benefit** *vb* **-fit·ed** \-ˌfit-əd\ *also* **-fit·ted**; **-fit·ing** *also* **-fit·ting 1** : to be useful or profitable to **2** : to receive benefit

be·nev·o·lence \bə-'nev-(ə-)ləns\ *n* **1** : charitable nature **2** : an act of kindness : CHARITY — **be·nev·o·lent** \-lənt\ *adj*

be·night·ed \bi-'nīt-əd\ *adj* **1** : overtaken by darkness or night **2** : living in ignorance

be·nign \bi-'nīn\ *adj* **1** : of a gentle disposition; *also* : showing kindness **2** : of a mild kind; *esp* : not malignant ⟨~ tumors⟩ **syn** benignant, kind, kindly, good-hearted — **be·nig·ni·ty** \-'nig-nət-ē\ *n*

be·nig·nant \-'nig-nənt\ *adj* : BENIGN 1 **syn** kind, kindly, good-hearted

ben·i·son \'ben-ə-sən, -zən\ *n* : BLESSING, BENEDICTION

bent \'bent\ *n* **1** : strong inclination or interest; *also* : TALENT **2** : power of endurance **syn** talent, aptitude, gift, flair, knack, genius

ben·thic \'ben-thik\ *adj* : of, relating to, or occurring at the bottom of a body of water

ben·thos \'ben-ˌthäs\ *n* : organisms that live on or in the bottom of bodies of water

ben·ton·ite \'bent-ˌ°n-ˌīt\ *n* : an absorptive clay used esp. as a filler (as in paper)

bent·wood \'bent-ˌwu̇d\ *adj* : made of wood bent into shape ⟨a ~ rocker⟩

be·numb \bi-'nəm\ *vb* **1** : DULL, DEADEN **2** : to make numb esp. by cold

ben·zene \'ben-ˌzēn\ *n* : a colorless volatile flammable liquid hydrocarbon used in organic synthesis and as a solvent

ben·zine \'ben-ˌzēn\ *n* : any of various flammable petroleum distillates used as solvents for fats or as motor fuels

ben·zo·ate \'ben-zə-ˌwāt\ *n* : a salt or ester of benzoic acid

ben·zo·ic acid \ben-ˌzō-ik-\ *n* : a white crystalline acid used as a preservative and antiseptic and in synthesizing chemicals

ben·zo·in \'ben-zə-wən, -ˌzȯin\ *n* : a balsamlike resin from trees of southern Asia used esp. in medicine and perfumes

be·queath \bi-'kwēth, -'kwēth\ *vb* [ME *bequethen*, fr. OE *becwethan*, fr. *be-* + *cwethan* to say] **1** : to leave by will **2** : to hand down

be·quest \bi-'kwest\ *n* **1** : the action of bequeathing **2** : something bequeathed : LEGACY

be·rate \-'rāt\ *vb* : to scold harshly

Ber·ber \'bər-bər\ *n* : a member of a Caucasoid people of northwestern Africa

ber·ceuse \ber-'sə(r)z\ *n, pl* **berceuses** \-'sə(r)z(-əz)\ [F, fr. *bercer* to rock] 1 : LULLABY 2 : a musical composition that resembles a lullaby

¹**be·reaved** \bi-'rēvd\ *adj* : suffering the death of a loved one — **be·reave·ment** *n*

²**bereaved** *n, pl* **bereaved** : one who is bereaved

be·reft \-'reft\ *adj* 1 : deprived of or lacking something — usu. used with *of* 2 : BEREAVED

be·ret \bə-'rā\ *n* : a round soft cap with no visor

berg \'bərg\ *n* : ICEBERG

beri·beri \,ber-ē-'ber-ē\ *n* : a deficiency disease marked by weakness, wasting, and nerve damage and caused by lack of thiamine

berke·li·um \'bər-klē-əm\ *n* : an artificially prepared radioactive chemical element

Ber·mu·das \bər-'myüd-əz\ *n pl* : BERMUDA SHORTS

Bermuda shorts *n pl* : knee-length walking shorts

ber·ry \'ber-ē\ *n, pl* **berries** 1 : a small pulpy fruit (as a strawberry) 2 : a simple fruit (as a grape, tomato, or banana) with the wall of the ripened ovary thick and pulpy 3 : the dry seed of some plants (as coffee)

ber·serk \bə(r)-'sərk, -'zərk\ *adj* [ON *berserkr* warrior frenzied in battle, fr. *björn* bear + *serkr* shirt] : FRENZIED, CRAZED — **berserk** *adv*

¹**berth** \'bərth\ *n* 1 : room enough for a ship to maneuver 2 : the place where a ship lies at anchor 3 : a place to sit or sleep esp. on a ship or vehicle 4 : JOB, POSITION *syn* post, situation, office, appointment

²**berth** *vb* 1 : to bring or come into a berth 2 : to allot a berth to

ber·yl \'ber-əl\ *n* : a hard silicate mineral occurring as green, yellow, pink, or white crystals

be·ryl·li·um \bə-'ril-ē-əm\ *n* : a light strong metallic chemical element used as a hardener in alloys

be·seech \bi-'sēch\ *vb* **-sought** \-'sot\ or **-seeched**; **-seech·ing** : to ask earnestly : ENTREAT *syn* implore, beg, plead, supplicate, importune

be·seem \bi-'sēm\ *vb, archaic* : to be seemly or fitting : BEFIT

be·set \-'set\ *vb* 1 : TROUBLE, HARASS 2 : ASSAIL; *also* : to hem in : SURROUND

be·set·ting *adj* : persistently present or assailing

¹**be·side** \bi-'sīd\ *adv, archaic* : BESIDES

²**beside** *prep* 1 : by the side of (sit ~ me) 2 : BESIDES 3 : not relevant to

¹**be·sides** \bi-'sīdz\ *prep* 1 : other than (there's nobody here ~ me) 2 : together with (~ being pretty, she's intelligent)

²**besides** *adv* 1 : in addition : ALSO 2 : MOREOVER

be·siege \bi-'sēj\ *vb* : to lay siege to: *also* : IMPORTUNE — **be·sieg·er** *n*

be·smear \-'smiər\ *vb* : SMEAR

be·smirch \-'smərch\ *vb* : SMIRCH, SOIL

be·som \'bē-zəm\ *n* : BROOM

be·sot \bi-'sät\ *vb* **be·sot·ted; be·sot·ting** : to make dull or stupid; *esp* : to muddle with drunkenness

be·spat·ter \-'spat-ər\ *vb* : SPATTER

be·speak \bi-'spēk\ *vb* **-spoke** \-'spōk\; **-spo·ken** \-'spō-kən\; **-speak·ing** 1 : to hire or arrange for beforehand 2 : INDICATE, SIGNIFY 3 : FORETELL

be·sprin·kle \-'spriŋ-kəl\ *vb* : SPRINKLE

¹**best** \'best\ *adj, superlative of* GOOD 1 : excelling all others 2 : most productive (as of good or satisfaction) 3 : LARGEST, MOST

²**best** *adv, superlative of* WELL 1 : in the best way 2 : MOST

³**best** *n* : something that is best

⁴**best** *vb* : to get the better of : OUTDO

bes·tial \'bes-chəl\ *adj* 1 : of or relating to beasts 2 : resembling a beast esp. in lack of intelligence or reason

bes·ti·al·i·ty \,bes-chē-'al-ət-ē\ *n, pl* **-ties** 1 : the condition or status of a lower animal 2 : display or gratification of bestial traits or impulses

bes·ti·ary \'bes-chē-,er-ē\ *n, pl* **-ar·ies** : a medieval allegorical or moralizing work on the appearance and habits of animals

be·stir \bi-'stər\ *vb* : to rouse to action

best man *n* : the principal groomsman at a wedding

be·stow \bi-'stō\ *vb* 1 : PUT, PLACE, STOW 2 : to present as a gift : CONFER — **be·stow·al** *n*

be·stride \bi-'strīd\ *vb* **-strode** \-'strōd\; **-strid·den** \-'strid-ᵊn\; **-strid·ing** \-'strīd-iŋ\ : to ride, sit, or stand astride

¹**bet** \'bet\ *n* 1 : something that is risked or pledged on the outcome of a contest 2 : an agreement requiring the person whose guess about a result proves wrong to give something to a person whose guess proves right: *also* : the making of such an agreement

²**bet** *vb* **bet** *also* **bet·ted; bet·ting** 1 : to stake on the outcome of an issue (*bet* $2 on the race) 2 : to make a bet with 3 : to lay a bet

³**bet** *abbr* between

be·take \bi-'tāk\ *vb* **-took** \-'tuk\; **-tak·en** \-'tā-kən\; **-tak·ing** : to cause (oneself) to go

be·ta particle \'bāt-ə-\ *n* : an electron or positron ejected from an atomic nucleus during radioactive transformation; *also* : a high-speed electron or positron

beta ray *n* 1 : BETA PARTICLE 2 : a stream of beta particles

be·ta·tron \'bāt-ə-,trän\ *n* : an electron accelerator

be·tel \'bēt-ᵊl\ *n* : a climbing pepper whose leaves are chewed together with lime and betel nut as a stimulant esp. by southern Asians

be·tel nut *n* : the astringent seed of an Asian palm that is chewed with betel leaves

bête noire \‚bet-nə-'wär, ‚bāt-\ *n, pl* **bêtes noires** \‚bet-nə-'wär(z), ‚bāt-\ [F, lit., black beast] : a person or thing strongly disliked or feared

beth·el \'beth-əl\ *n* [Heb *bēth'ēl* house of God] : a place of worship esp. for seamen

be·think \bi-'thiŋk\ *vb* **-thought** \-'thȯt\ : **-think·ing** : to cause (oneself) to call to mind or consider

be·tide \bi-'tīd\ *vb* : to happen to

be·times \bi-'tīmz\ *adv* : in good time : EARLY *syn* soon, seasonably, timely

be·to·ken \bi-'tō-kən\ *vb* **-kened; -to·ken·ing** \-'tōk-(ə-)niŋ\ **1** : to give evidence of **2** : PRESAGE *syn* indicate, attest, bespeak, testify

be·tray \bi-'trā\ *vb* **1** : to lead astray; *esp* : SEDUCE **2** : to deliver to an enemy by treachery **3** : to prove unfaithful to **4** : to reveal unintentionally; *also* : SHOW, INDICATE *syn* mislead, delude, deceive, beguile — **be·tray·al** *n* — **be·tray·er** *n*

be·troth \bi-'träth, -'troth, -'trȯth, *or with* th\ *vb* : to promise to marry : AFFIANCE — **be·troth·al** *n*

be·trothed *n* : the person to whom one is betrothed

¹bet·ter \'bet-ər\ *adj, comparative of* GOOD **1** : more than half **2** : improved in health **3** : more attractive, favorable, or commendable **4** : more advantageous or effective **5** : improved in accuracy or performance

²better *vb* **1** : to make or become better **2** : SURPASS, EXCEL

³better *adv, comparative of* WELL **1** : in a superior manner **2** : to a higher or greater degree; *also* : MORE

⁴better *n* **1** : something better; *also* : a superior esp. in merit or rank **2** : ADVANTAGE

bet·ter·ment \'bet-ər-mənt\ *n* : IMPROVEMENT

bet·tor *or* **bet·ter** \'bet-ər\ *n* : one that bets

¹be·tween \bi-'twēn\ *prep* **1** : by the common action of (earned $10,000 ~ the two of them) **2** : in the interval separating (an alley ~ two buildings) **3** : marking or constituting the interrelation or interaction of (hostility ~ nations) **4** : in point of comparison of (choose ~ two cars)

²between *adv* : in an intervening space or interval

be·twixt \bi-'twikst\ *adv or prep* : BETWEEN

¹bev·el \'bev-əl\ *n* **1** : a device for adjusting the slant of the surfaces of a piece of work **2** : the angle or slant that one surface or line makes with another when not at right angles

²bevel *vb* **-eled** *or* **-elled; -el·ing** *or* **-el·ling** \'bev-(ə-)liŋ\ **1** : to cut or shape (as an edge or surface) to a bevel **2** : INCLINE, SLANT

bev·er·age \'bev-(ə-)rij\ *n* : a drinkable liquid

bevy \'bev-ē\ *n, pl* **bev·ies 1** : a large group or collection **2** : a group of animals and esp. quail together

be·wail \bi-'wāl\ *vb* : LAMENT *syn* deplore, bemoan, grieve, moan, weep

be·ware \-'waər\ *vb* : to be on one's guard : be wary of

be·wil·der \bi-'wil-dər\ *vb* **-wil·dered; -wil·der·ing** \-d(ə-)riŋ\ : PERPLEX, CONFUSE *syn* mystify, distract, puzzle — **be·wil·der·ment** *n*

be·witch \-'wich\ *vb* **1** : to affect by witchcraft **2** : CHARM, FASCINATE *syn* enchant, attract, captivate — **be·witch·ment** *n*

bey \'bā\ *n* **1** : a former Turkish provincial governor **2** : the former native ruler of Tunis or Tunisia

¹be·yond \bē-'änd\ *adv* **1** : FARTHER **2** : BESIDES

²beyond *prep* **1** : on or to the farther side of **2** : out of the reach or sphere of **3** : BESIDES

be·zel \'bē-zəl, 'bez-əl\ *n* **1** : a sloping edge on a cutting tool **2** : the faceted part of a cut gem that rises above the setting **3** : a usu. grooved rim holding a transparent covering (as on a watch)

bf *abbr* boldface

BG *or* **B Gen** *abbr* brigadier general

bhang \'baŋ\ *n* : a narcotic and intoxicant product of the hemp plant

Bi *symbol* bismuth

BIA *abbr* Bureau of Indian Affairs

bi·an·nu·al \(')bī-'an-yə(-wə)l\ *adj* : occurring twice a year — **bi·an·nu·al·ly** \-ē-\ *adv*

¹bi·as \'bī-əs\ *n* **1** : a line diagonal to the grain of a fabric **2** : PREJUDICE, BENT

²bias *adv* : on the bias : DIAGONALLY

³bias *vb* **bi·ased** *or* **bi·assed; bi·as·ing** *or* **bi·as·sing** : PREJUDICE

bi·as-ply tire \'bī-əs-‚plī-\ *n* : a pneumatic tire having crossed layers of ply cord set diagonally to the center line of the tread

bi·ath·lon \bī-'ath-lən, -‚län\ *n* : a composite athletic contest consisting of cross-country skiing and target shooting with a rifle

¹bib \'bib\ *n* : a protective cover tied under a child's chin to protect the clothes

²bib *abbr* Bible; biblical

bi·be·lot \'bē-bə-‚lō\ *n, pl* **bibelots** \-‚lō(z)\ : a small household ornament or decorative object

Bi·ble \'bī-bəl\ *n* [ME, fr. OF, fr. ML *biblia*, fr. Gk. pl. of *biblion* book, fr. *byblos* papyrus, book, fr. *Byblos*, ancient Phoenician city from which papyrus was exported] **1** : the sacred scriptures of Christians comprising the Old and New Testaments **2** : the sacred scriptures of Judaism or of some other religion — **bib·li·cal** \'bib-li-kəl\ *adj*

BOOKS OF THE OLD TESTAMENT

ROMAN CATHOLIC CANON	PROTESTANT CANON	ROMAN CATHOLIC CANON	PROTESTANT CANON
Genesis	Genesis	Wisdom	
Exodus	Exodus	Ecclesiasticus	
Leviticus	Leviticus	Isaias	Isaiah
Numbers	Numbers	Jeremias	Jeremiah
Deuteronomy	Deuteronomy	Lamentations	Lamentations
Josue	Joshua	Baruch	
Judges	Judges	Ezechiel	Ezekiel
Ruth	Ruth	Daniel	Daniel
1 & 2 Kings	1 & 2 Samuel	Osee	Hosea
3 & 4 Kings	1 & 2 Kings	Joel	Joel
1 & 2 Paralipom- enon	1 & 2 Chronicles	Amos	Amos
		Abdias	Obadiah
1 Esdras	Ezra	Jonas	Jonah
2 Esdras	Nehemiah	Micheas	Micah
Tobias		Nahum	Nahum
Judith		Habacuc	Habakkuk
Esther	Esther	Sophonias	Zephaniah
Job	Job	Aggeus	Haggai
Psalms	Psalms	Zacharias	Zechariah
Proverbs	Proverbs	Malachias	Malachi
Ecclesiastes	Ecclesiastes	1 & 2 Machabees	
Canticle of Canticles	Song of Solomon		

JEWISH SCRIPTURE

Law	1 & 2 Kings	Nahum	Song of Songs
Genesis	Isaiah	Habakkuk	Ruth
Exodus	Jeremiah	Zephaniah	Lamentations
Leviticus	Ezekiel	Haggai	Ecclesiastes
Numbers	Hosea	Zechariah	Esther
Deuteronomy	Joel	Malachi	Daniel
Prophets	Amos	*Hagiographa*	Ezra
Joshua	Obadiah	Psalms	Nehemiah
Judges	Jonah	Proverbs	1 & 2 Chronicles
1 & 2 Samuel	Micah	Job	

PROTESTANT APOCRYPHA

1 & 2 Esdras	Wisdom of Solomon	Baruch	Susanna
Tobit	Ecclesiasticus	Prayer of Azariah and the Song	Bel and the Dragon
Judith	or the Wisdom	of the Three	The Prayer of
Additions to Esther	of Jesus Son of Sirach	Holy Children	Manasses
			1 & 2 Maccabees

BOOKS OF THE NEW TESTAMENT

Matthew	Romans	1 & 2 Thess- alonians	1 & 2 Peter
Mark	1 & 2 Corinthians		1, 2, 3 John
Luke	Galatians	1 & 2 Timothy	Jude
John	Ephesians	Titus	Revelation (Ro-
Acts of the	Philippians	Philemon	man Catholic
Apostles	Colossians	Hebrews	canon:
		James	Apocalypse)

---

bib·li·og·ra·phy \,bib-lē-'äg-rə-fē\ *n, pl* **-phies 1 :** the history or description of writings or publications **2 :** a list of writings (as on a subject or of an author) — **bib·li·og·ra·pher** \-fər\ *n* — **bib·li·o·graph·ic** \-lē-ə-'graf-ik\ *also* **bib·li·o·graph·i·cal** \-i-kəl\ *adj*

bib·lio·phile \'bib-lē-ə-,fīl\ *n* : a lover of books

bib·u·lous \'bib-yə-ləs\ *adj* **1 :** highly absorbent **2 :** fond of alcoholic beverages

bi·cam·er·al \'bī-'kam-(ə-)rəl\ *adj* : having or consisting of two legislative branches

bi·car·bon·ate \'bī-'kär-bə-,nāt, -nət\ : an acid carbonate

bicarbonate of soda : SODIUM BICARBONATE

bi·cen·te·na·ry \ˌbī-sen-ˈten-ə-rē, bī-ˈsent-ᵊn-ˌer-ē\ n : BICENTENNIAL — **bicentenary** adj

bi·cen·ten·ni·al \ˌbī-sen-ˈten-ē-əl\ n : a 200th anniversary or its celebration — **bicentennial** adj

bi·ceps \ˈbī-ˌseps\ n, pl **biceps** also **bicepses** [NL, fr. L, two-headed, fr. bi- two + caput head] : a muscle (as in the front of the upper arm) having two points of origin

bi·chlo·ride of mercury \bī-ˈklōr-ˌīd-\ : MERCURIC CHLORIDE

¹**bick·er** \ˈbik-ər\ n : QUARRELING, ALTERCATION

²**bicker** vb **bick·ered**; **bick·er·ing** \-(ə)riŋ\ : to contend in petty altercation : SQUABBLE

bi·con·cave \ˌbī-(ˌ)kän-ˈkāv, bī-ˈkän-ˌkāv\ adj : concave on both sides (red blood cells are ∼)

bi·con·vex \ˌbī-(ˌ)kän-ˈveks, ˈbī-ˈkän-ˌveks\ adj : convex on both sides

bi·cus·pid \ˈbī-ˈkəs-pəd\ n : PREMOLAR

¹**bi·cy·cle** \ˈbī-ˌsik-əl\ n : a light 2-wheeled vehicle with a steering handle, saddle, and pedals

²**bicycle** vb **-cy·cled**; **-cy·cling** \-ˌsik-(ə)liŋ, -ˌsik-\ : to ride a bicycle — **bi·cy·cler** \-lər\ **bi·cy·clist** \-ləst\ n

¹**bid** \ˈbid\ vb **bade** \ˈbad, ˈbād\ or **bid**; **bid·den** \ˈbid-ᵊn\ or **bid** also **bade**; **bid·ding** 1 : COMMAND, ORDER 2 : INVITE 3 : to give expression to 4 : to make a bid : OFFER — **bid·der** n

²**bid** n 1 : an act of bidding; also : a chance or turn to bid 2 : an offer (as at an auction) of what one will give for something; also : the thing or sum offered 3 : INVITATION 4 : an announcement by a player in a card game of what he or she proposes to accomplish; also : an attempt to win or gain

bid·da·ble \ˈbid-ə-bəl\ adj 1 : OBEDIENT, DOCILE 2 : capable of being bid

bid·dy \ˈbid-ē\ n, pl **biddies** : a hen or young chicken

bide \ˈbīd\ vb **bode** \ˈbōd\ or **bid·ed**; **bided**; **bid·ing** 1 : WAIT, TARRY 2 : DWELL 3 : to wait for

bi·det \bi-ˈdā\ n : a fixture about the height of a chair seat used esp. for bathing the external genitals and the posterior parts of the body

bi·di·rec·tion·al \ˌbī-də-ˈrek-sh(ə-)nəl\ adj : involving, moving, or taking place in two usu. opposite directions — **bi·di·rec·tion·al·ly** adv

bi·en·ni·al \bī-ˈen-ē-əl\ adj 1 : taking place once in two years 2 : lasting two years 3 : producing leaves the first year and fruiting and dying the second year — **biennial** n — **bi·en·ni·al·ly** \-ē\ adv

bi·en·ni·um \bī-ˈen-ē-əm\ n, pl **-niums** or **-nia** \-ē-ə\ [L, fr. bi- two + annus year] : a period of two years

bier \ˈbir\ n : a stand bearing a coffin or corpse

bi·fo·cal \bī-ˈfō-kəl\ adj : having two focal lengths

bifocals \bī-ˈfō-kəlz\ n pl : eyeglasses with lenses that have one part that corrects for near vision and one for distant vision

bi·fur·cate \ˈbī-fər-ˌkāt, bī-ˈfər-\ vb **-cat·ed**; **-cat·ing** : to divide into two branches or parts — **bi·fur·ca·tion** \ˌbī-fər-ˈkā-shən\ n

big \ˈbig\ adj **big·ger**; **big·gest** 1 : large in size, amount, or scope 2 : PREGNANT; also : SWELLING 3 : IMPORTANT, IMPOSING syn great, large, oversize — **big·ness** n

big·a·my \ˈbig-ə-mē\ n : the act of marrying one person while still legally married to another — **big·a·mist** \-məst\ n — **big·a·mous** \-məs\ adj

big bang theory n : a theory in astronomy: the universe originated from the explosion of a single mass of material so that the pieces are still flying apart

big brother n 1 : an older brother 2 : a man who befriends a delinquent or friendless boy 3 cap both Bs : the leader of an authoritarian state or movement

Big Dipper n : DIPPER 3

big·foot \ˈbig-ˌfut\ n : SASQUATCH

big·horn \ˈbig-ˌhörn\ n, pl **bighorn** or **bighorns** : a wild sheep of mountainous western No. America

bight \ˈbīt\ n 1 : a curve in a coast: also : the bay formed by such a curve 2 : a slack part in a rope

big-name \ˈbig-ˈnām\ adj : widely popular (a ∼ performer) — **big name** n

big·ot \ˈbig-ət\ n : one intolerantly devoted to his or her own church, party, or opinion syn fanatic, enthusiast, zealot — **big·ot·ed** \-ət-əd\ adj — **big·ot·ry** \-ə-trē\ n

big shot \ˈbig-ˌshät\ n : an important person

big time \-ˌtīm\ n 1 : a high-paying vaudeville circuit requiring only two performances a day 2 : the top rank of an activity or enterprise — **big-tim·er** \-ˌtī-mər\ n

big top n 1 : the main tent of a circus 2 : CIRCUS

big·wig \ˈbig-ˌwig\ n : BIG SHOT

bike \ˈbīk\ n 1 : BICYCLE 2 : MOTORCYCLE

bik·er n : MOTORCYCLIST; esp : one who is a member of an organized gang

bike·way \ˈbīk-ˌwā\ n : a thoroughfare for bicycles

bi·ki·ni \bə-ˈkē-nē\ n : a woman's brief 2-piece bathing suit

bi·lat·er·al \bī-ˈlat-(ə-)rəl\ adj 1 : having or involving two sides 2 : affecting reciprocally two sides or parties — **bi·lat·er·al·ly** \-ē\ adv

bile \ˈbīl\ n 1 : a bitter greenish fluid secreted by the liver that aids in the digestion of fats 2 : an ill-humored mood

bilge \ˈbilj\ n 1 : the part of a ship that lies between the bottom and the point

87

where the sides go straight up **2** : stale or worthless remarks or ideas

bi·lin·gual \bī-ˈliŋ-gwəl\ *adj* : expressed in, knowing, or using two languages

bil·ious \ˈbil-yəs\ *adj* **1** : marked by or suffering from disordered liver function **2** : IRRITABLE, CHOLERIC — **bil·ious·ness** *n*

bilk \ˈbilk\ *vb* : CHEAT, SWINDLE

¹bill \ˈbil\ *n* : the jaws of a bird together with their horny covering; *also* : a mouth structure (as of a turtle) resembling these

²bill *vb* : to caress fondly

³bill *n* **1** : a written document or note; *esp* : a draft of a law presented to a legislature for enactment **2** : a written statement of a legal wrong suffered or of some breach of law **3** : an itemized statement of particulars **4** : an itemized account of the separate cost of goods sold, services performed, or work done **5** : an advertisement (as a poster or handbill) displayed or distributed **6** : a piece of paper money

⁴bill *vb* **1** : to enter in or prepare a bill; *also* : to submit a bill or account to **2** : to advertise by bills or posters

bill·board \-ˌbōrd\ *n* : a flat surface on which advertising bills are posted

¹bil·let \ˈbil-ət\ *n* **1** : an order requiring a person to provide lodging for a soldier; *also* : quarters assigned by or as if by such an order **2** : POSITION, APPOINTMENT

²billet *vb* : to assign lodging to by billet

bil·let-doux \ˌbil-ā-ˈdü\ *n, pl* **billets-doux** \-ā-ˈdü(z)\ [F *billet doux*, lit., sweet letter] : a love letter

bill·fold \ˈbil-ˌfōld\ *n* : WALLET

bil·liards \ˈbil-yərdz\ *n* : any of several games played on a rectangular table by driving balls against each other or into pockets with a cue

bil·lings·gate \ˈbil-iŋz-ˌgāt, *Brit usu* -git\ *n* [*Billingsgate*, old gate and fish market, London, England] : coarsely abusive language

bil·lion \ˈbil-yən\ *n* **1** : a thousand millions **2** *Brit* : a million millions — **billion** *adj* — **bil·lionth** \-yənth\ *adj or n*

bill of exchange : a written order from one party to another to pay to a person named in the bill a specified sum of money

¹bil·low \ˈbil-ō\ *n* **1** : WAVE; *esp* : a great wave **2** : a rolling mass (as of fog or flame) like a great wave — **bil·lowy** \ˈbil-ə-wē\ *adj*

²billow *vb* : to rise and roll in waves; *also* : to swell out (*~ing* sails)

bil·ly \ˈbil-ē\ *n, pl* **billies** : BILLY CLUB

billy club *n* : a heavy usu. wooden club; *esp* : a policeman's club

bil·ly goat \ˈbil-ē-\ *n* : a male goat

bi·met·al \ˈbī-ˌmet-ᵊl\ *adj* : BIMETALLIC — **bimetal** *n*

bi·me·tal·lic \ˌbī-mə-ˈtal-ik\ *adj* : made of two different metals — often used

of devices having a bonded expansive part — **bimetallic** *n*

bi·met·al·lism \ˈbī-ˈmet-ᵊl-ˌiz-əm\ *n* : the policy of using two metals as standard ratios to form a standard of value for a monetary system

¹bi·month·ly \ˈbī-ˈmənth-lē\ *adj* **1** : occurring every two months **2** : occurring twice a month : SEMIMONTHLY — **bimonthly** *adv*

²bimonthly *n* : a bimonthly publication

bin \ˈbin\ *n* : a box, crib, or enclosure used for storage

bi·na·ry \ˈbī-nə-rē\ *adj* **1** : consisting of two things or parts : DOUBLE **2** : relating to, being, or belonging to a system of numbers having 2 as its base (the ~ digits 0 and 1) **3** : involving a choice between or condition of two alternatives only (as on-off, yes-no) — **binary** *n*

binary star *n* : a system of two stars revolving around each other

bin·au·ral \bī-ˈnȯr-əl\ *adj* : of or relating to sound reproduction involving the use of two separated microphones and two transmission channels to achieve a stereophonic effect

bind \ˈbīnd\ *vb* **bound** \ˈbaúnd\ ; **binding 1** : TIE; *also* : to restrain as if by tying **2** : to put under an obligation; *also* : to constrain with legal authority **3** : BANDAGE **4** : to unite into a mass **5** : to compel as if by a pledge **6** : to strengthen or decorate with a band **7** : to fasten together and enclose in a cover (~ books) **8** : to exert a tying, restraining, or compelling effect — **bind·er** *n*

bind·ing \ˈbīn-diŋ\ *n* : something (as a ski fastening, a cover, or an edging fabric) used to bind

binge \ˈbinj\ *n* : SPREE

bin·go \ˈbiŋ-gō\ *n, pl* **bingos** : a game of chance played with cards having numbered squares corresponding to numbered balls drawn at random and won by covering five squares in a row

bin·na·cle \ˈbin-i-kəl\ *n* [alter. of ME *bitakle*, fr. Sp or Sp; Pg *bitácola* & Sp *bitácula*, fr. L *habitaculum* dwelling place, fr. *habitare* to inhabit] : a container holding a ship's compass

¹bin·oc·u·lar \bī-ˈnäk-yə-lər, bə-\ *adj* : of, relating to, or adapted to the use of both eyes — **bin·oc·u·lar·ly** *adv*

²bin·oc·u·lar \bə-ˈnäk-yə-lər, bī-\ *n* **1** : a binocular optical instrument (as a microscope) **2** : a hand-held optical instrument composed of two telescopes and a focusing device — usu. used in pl.

bi·no·mi·al \bī-ˈnō-mē-əl\ *n* **1** : a mathematical expression consisting of two terms connected by the sign plus (+) or minus (−) **2** : a biological species name consisting of two terms — **binomial** *adj*

bio·chem·is·try \ˌbī-ō-ˈkem-ə-strē\ *n* : chemistry that deals with the chemical compounds and processes occurring in living things — **bio·chem·i·cal** \-i-kəl\ *adj or n* — **bio·chem·ist** \-əst\ *n*

bio·de·grad·able \-di-'grād-ə-bəl\ *adj* : capable of being broken down esp. into innocuous products by the actions of living things (as microorganisms) ⟨a ∼ detergent⟩ — **bio·de·grad·abil·i·ty** \-ˌgrād-ə-'bil-ət-ē\ *n* — **bio·deg·ra·da·tion** \-ˌdeg-rə-'dā-shən\ *n* — **bio·de·grade** \-di-'grād\ *vb*

bio·feed·back \-'fēd-ˌbak\ *n* : the technique of making unconscious or involuntary bodily processes (as heartbeat or brain waves) objectively perceptible to the senses (as by use of an oscilloscope) in order to manipulate them by conscious mental control

biog *abbr* biographer; biographical; biography

bio·ge·og·ra·phy \ˌbī-ō-jē-'äg-rə-fē\ *n* : a branch of biology that deals with the distribution of plants and animals — **bio·ge·og·ra·pher** \-fər\ *n*

bi·og·ra·phy \bī-'äg-rə-fē, bē-\ *n, pl* **-phies** : a written history of a person's life; *also* : such writings in general — **bi·og·ra·pher** \-fər\ *n* — **bio·graph·i·cal** \ˌbī-ə-'graf-i-kəl\ *also* **bio·graph·ic** \-ik\ *adj*

biol *abbr* biologic; biological; biologist; biology

biological clock *n* : an inherent timing mechanism inferred to exist in some living systems (as a cell) in order to explain various cyclical physiological and behavioral responses

biological warfare *n* : warfare in which living organisms (as bacteria) are used to harm the enemy or his livestock and crops

bi·ol·o·gy \bī-'äl-ə-jē\ *n* [G *biologie,* fr. Gk *bios* mode of life + *logos* word] 1 : a science that deals with living beings and life processes 2 : the life processes of an organism or group — **bio·log·i·cal** \ˌbī-ə-'läj-i-kəl\ *also* **bio·log·ic** \-ik\ *adj* — **bi·ol·o·gist** \bī-'äl-ə-jəst\ *n*

bio·med·i·cal \ˌbī-ō-'med-i-kəl\ *adj* : of, relating to, or involving biological, medical, and physical science

bi·on·ic \bī-'än-ik\ *adj* : having normal biological capability or performance enhanced by or as if by electronic or mechanical devices

bio·phys·ics \ˌbī-ō-'fiz-iks\ *n* : a branch of science concerned with the application of physical principles and methods to biological problems — **bio·phys·i·cal** \-i-kəl\ *adj* — **bio·phys·i·cist** \-'fiz-ə-səst\ *n*

bi·op·sy \'bī-ˌäp-sē\ *n, pl* **-sies** : the removal of tissue, cells, or fluids from the living body for examination

bio·rhythm \'bī-ō-ˌrith-əm\ *n* : an inherent rhythm that appears to control or initiate various biological processes

bio·sphere \'bī-ə-ˌsfiər\ *n* 1 : the part of the world in which life can exist 2

: living beings together with their environment

bi·ot·ic \bī-'ät-ik\ *adj* : of or relating to life; *esp* : caused by living beings

bi·o·tin \'bī-ə-tən\ *n* : a member of the vitamin B complex found esp. in yeast, liver, and egg yolk and active in growth promotion

bio·tite \'bī-ə-ˌtīt\ *n* : a dark mica containing iron, magnesium, potassium, and aluminum

bi·par·ti·san \bī-'pärt-ə-zən\ *adj* : representing or composed of members of two parties

bi·par·tite \-'pär-ˌtīt\ *adj* 1 : being in two parts 2 : shared by two ⟨∼ treaty⟩

bi·ped \'bī-ˌped\ *n* : a 2-footed animal

bi·plane \'bī-ˌplān\ *n* : an airplane with two wings placed one above the other

bi·po·lar \bī-'pō-lər\ *adj* : having or involving the use of two poles — **bi·po·lar·i·ty** \ˌbī-pō-'lar-ət-ē\ *n*

bi·ra·cial \bī-'rā-shəl\ *adj* : of, relating to, or involving members of two races

¹**birch** \'bərch\ *n* 1 : any of a genus of mostly short-lived deciduous shrubs and trees with membranous outer bark and pale close-grained wood; *also* : this wood 2 : a birch rod or bundle of twigs for flogging — **birch** *or* **birch·en** \'bər-chən\ *adj*

²**birch** *vb* : WHIP, FLOG

Birch·er \'bər-chər\ *n* : a member or adherent of the John Birch Society — **Birch·ism** \'bər-ˌchiz-əm\ *n* — **Birch·ist** \-chəst\ *or* **Birch·ite** \-ˌchīt\ *n*

bird \'bərd\ *n* : any of a class of warm-blooded egg-laying vertebrates having the body feathered and the forelimbs modified to form wings

bird·bath \'bərd-ˌbath, -ˌbȧth\ *n* : a usu. ornamental basin set up for birds to bathe in

bird·house \-ˌhȧus\ *n* : an artificial nesting place for birds; *also* : AVIARY

bird·ie \'bərd-ē\ *n* : a score of one under par on a hole in golf

bird·lime \-ˌlīm\ *n* : a sticky substance smeared on twigs to snare small birds

bird of paradise : any of numerous brilliantly colored plumed birds of the New Guinea area

bird of prey : a carnivorous bird that feeds wholly or chiefly on carrion or on meat taken by hunting

bird·seed \'bərd-ˌsēd\ *n* : a mixture of small seeds (as of hemp or millet) used for feeding birds

bird's-eye \'bərd-ˌzī\ *adj* 1 : seen from above as if by a flying bird ⟨∼ view⟩; *also* : CURSORY 2 : marked with spots resembling birds' eyes ⟨∼ maple⟩; *also* : made of bird's-eye wood

bi·ret·ta \bə-'ret-ə\ *n* : a square cap with three ridges on top worn esp. by Roman Catholic clergymen

birr \'bir, 'bər\ *n* — see MONEY table

birth \'bərth\ *n* 1 : the act or fact of being born or of bringing forth young 2 : LINEAGE, DESCENT 3 : ORIGIN, BEGINNING

birth control *n* : control of the number of children born esp. by preventing or lessening the frequency of conception

birth·day \'bərth-ˌdā\ *n* : the day or anniversary of one's birth

birth defect *n* : a physical or biochemical defect present at birth and inherited or environmentally induced

birth·mark \'bərth-ˌmärk\ *n* : an unusual mark or blemish on the skin at birth

birth·place \-ˌplās\ *n* : place of birth or origin

birth·rate \-ˌrāt\ *n* : the number of births for every 100 or every 1000 persons in a given area or group during a given time

birth·right \-ˌrīt\ *n* : a right, privilege, or possession to which one is entitled by birth *syn* legacy, patrimony, heritage, inheritance

birth·stone \-ˌstōn\ *n* : a gemstone associated symbolically with the month of one's birth

bis·cuit \'bis-kət\ *n* [ME *bisquite*, fr. MF *bescuit*, fr. (*pain*) *bescuit* twice-cooked bread] **1** : a crisp flat cake; *esp, Brit* : CRACKER **2 2** : a small quick bread made from dough that has been rolled and cut or dropped from a spoon

bi·sect \'bī-ˌsekt\ *vb* : to divide into two usu. equal parts; *also* : CROSS, INTERSECT — **bi·sec·tion** \'bī-ˌsek-shən\ *n* — **bi·sec·tor** \-tər\ *n*

bi·sex·u·al \bī-'sek-sh(ə-w)əl\ *adj* **1** : possessing characters of or having sexual desire for both sexes **2** : of, relating to, or involving two sexes — **bisexual** *n* — **bi·sex·u·al·i·ty** \ˌbī-ˌsek-shə-'wal-ət-ē\ *n*

bish·op \'bish-əp\ *n* [ME *bisshop*, fr. OE *bisceop*, fr. L *episcopus*, fr. Gk *episkopos*, lit., overseer, fr. *epi-* on, over + *skeptesthai* to look] **1** : a clergyman ranking above a priest and typically governing a diocese **2** : any of various Protestant church officials who superintend other clergy **3** : a chess piece that can move diagonally across any number of adjoining unoccupied squares

bish·op·ric \'bish-ə-prik\ *n* **1** : DIOCESE **2** : the office of bishop

bis·muth \'biz-məth\ *n* : a heavy brittle grayish white metallic chemical element used in alloys and medicine

bi·son \'bīs-ᵊn, 'bīz-\ *n, pl* **bison** : BUFFALO **2**

bisque \'bisk\ *n* : a thick cream soup

bis·tro \'bēs-trō, 'bis-\ *n, pl* **bistros** [F] **1** : a small or unpretentious European restaurant **2** : BAR; *also* : NIGHTCLUB

¹bit \'bit\ *n* **1** : the part of a bridle that is placed in a horse's mouth **2** : the biting or cutting edge or part of a tool

²bit *n* **1** : a morsel of food; *also* : a small piece or quantity of something **2** : a small coin; *also* : a unit of value equal to 12½ cents **3** : something small or

trivial; *also* : an indefinite usu. small degree or extent ⟨a ~ tired⟩

³bit *n* [*binary digit*] : a unit of computer information equivalent to the result of a choice between two alternatives; *also* : its physical representation

¹bitch \'bich\ *n* **1** : a female canine; *esp* : a female dog **2** : a malicious, spiteful, and domineering woman

²bitch *vb* : COMPLAIN

¹bite \'bīt\ *vb* **bit** \'bit\; **bit·ten** \'bit-ᵊn\ *also* **bit; bit·ing** \'bīt-iŋ\ **1** : to grip with teeth or jaws; *also* : to wound or sting with or as if with fangs **2** : to cut or pierce with or as if with a sharp-edged instrument **3** : to cause to smart or sting **4** : CORRODE **5** : to take bait

²bite *n* **1** : the act or manner of biting **2** : MORSEL, SNACK **3** : a wound made by biting; *also* : a biting sensation

bit·ing \'bīt-iŋ\ *adj* : SHARP, CUTTING

bit·ter \'bit-ər\ *adj* **1** : being or inducing the one of the basic taste sensations that is acrid, astringent, or disagreeable and is suggestive of hops **2** : marked by intensity or severity (as of distress or hatred) **3** : extremely harsh or cruel — **bit·ter·ly** *adv* — **bit·ter·ness** *n*

bit·tern \'bit-ərn\ *n* : any of various small or medium-sized herons with a booming cry

bit·ters \'bit-ərz\ *n sing or pl* : a usu. alcoholic solution of bitter and often aromatic plant products used in mixing drinks and as a mild tonic

bit·ter·sweet \'bit-ər-ˌswēt\ *n* **1** : a poisonous nightshade with purple flowers and orange-red berries **2** : a woody vine with yellow capsules that open when ripe and disclose scarlet seed coverings

²bittersweet *adj* : being at once both bitter and sweet

bi·tu·mi·nous coal \bə-'t(y)ü-mə-nəs-, bī-\ *n* : a coal that when heated yields considerable volatile waste matter

bi·valve \'bī-ˌvalv\ *n* : an animal (as a clam) with a shell composed of two separate parts that open and shut — **bivalve** *adj*

¹biv·ouac \'biv-(ə-)ˌwak\ *n* [F, fr. LG *biwake*, fr. *bi* at + *wake* guard] : a temporary encampment or shelter

²bivouac *vb* **-ouacked; -ouack·ing** : to form a bivouac : CAMP

¹bi·week·ly \'bī-'wē-klē\ *adj* **1** : occurring every two weeks : FORTNIGHTLY **2** : occurring twice a week — **biweekly** *adv*

²biweekly *n* : a biweekly publication

bi·year·ly \-'yiər-lē\ *adj* **1** : BIENNIAL **2** : BIANNUAL

bi·zarre \bə-'zär\ *adj* : ODD, ECCENTRIC, FANTASTIC — **bi·zarre·ly** *adv*

bk *abbr* **1** bank **2** book

Bk *symbol* berkelium

bkg *abbr* banking

bkgd *abbr* background

bks *abbr* barracks

bkt *abbr* **1** basket **2** bracket

bl *abbr* **1** bale **2** barrel **3** blue

blab \'blab\ *vb* **blabbed; blab·bing** : TATTLE, GOSSIP

¹**black** \'blak\ *adj* **1** : of the color black; *also* : very dark **2** : SWARTHY **3** : of or relating to a group of dark-haired dark-skinned people **4** : NEGRO; *also* : AFRO-AMERICAN **5** : SOILED, DIRTY **6** : lacking light (a ~ night) **7** : WICKED, EVIL (~ deeds) (~ magic) **8** : DISMAL, GLOOMY (a ~ outlook) **9** : SULLEN (a ~ mood) — **black·ish** *adj* — **black·ly** *adv* — **black·ness** *n*

²**black** *n* **1** : a black pigment or dye; *also* : something (as clothing) that is black **2** : the color characteristic of soot or coal **3** : a person of a dark-skinned race; *esp* : NEGRO

³**black** *vb* : BLACKEN

black·a·moor \'blak-ə-ˌmu̇r\ *n* : NEGRO

black–and–blue \ˌblak-ən-'blü\ *adj* : darkly discolored from blood effused by bruising

black art *n* : MAGIC, WITCHCRAFT

black·ball \'blak-ˌbȯl\ *n* : a black object used to cast a negative vote; *also* : such a vote — **black·ball** *vb*

black bass *n* : any of several freshwater sunfishes native to eastern and central No. America

¹**black belt** \'blak-ˌbelt\ *n, often cap both Bs* : an area densely populated by blacks

²**black belt** \-'belt\ *n* **1** : a rating of expert (as in judo or karate) **2** : one who holds a black belt

black·ber·ry \'blak-ˌber-ē\ *n* : the usu. black or purple juicy but seedy edible fruit of various brambles; *also* : a plant bearing this fruit

black·bird \'blak-ˌbərd\ *n* : any of various birds (as the red-winged blackbird) of which the male is largely or wholly black

black·board \-ˌbȯrd\ *n* : a dark smooth surface (as of slate) used for writing or drawing on usu. with chalk

black·body \'blak-'bäd-ē\ *n* : a body or surface that completely absorbs incident radiation

black box *n* : a usu. complicated electronic device whose components and workings are unknown or mysterious to the user

black death *n* : a form of bacterial plague that spread rapidly in Europe and Asia in the 14th century

black·en \'blak-ən\ *vb* **black·ened; black·en·ing** \-(ə-)niŋ\ **1** : to make or become black **2** : DEFAME, SULLY

black eye *n* : a discoloration of the skin around the eye from bruising

black–eyed Su·san \ˌblak-ˌīd-'süz-ᵊn\ *n* : either of two No. American plants that are related to the daisies and have deep yellow to orange flower heads with dark conical centers

Black·foot \'blak-ˌfu̇t\ *n, pl* **Black·feet** *or* **Blackfoot** : a member of an American Indian people of Montana, Alberta, and Saskatchewan

black·guard \'blag-ərd, -ˌärd\ *n* : SCOUNDREL, RASCAL

black·head \'blak-ˌhed\ *n* : a small oily mass plugging the outlet of a skin gland

black·ing \'blak-iŋ\ *n* : a substance applied to something to make it black

¹**black·jack** \-ˌjak\ *n* **1** : a leather-covered club with a flexible handle **2** : a card game in which the object is to be dealt cards having a higher count than the dealer but not exceeding 21

²**blackjack** *vb* : to hit with or as if with a blackjack

black light *n* : invisible ultraviolet or infrared radiation

black·list \'blak-ˌlist\ *n* : a list of persons who are disapproved of and are to be punished (as by refusal of jobs or a boycott) — **blacklist** *vb*

black·mail \'blak-ˌmāl\ *n* : extortion by threats esp. of public exposure; *also* : something so extorted — **blackmail** *vb* — **black·mail·er** *n*

black market *n* : illicit trade in goods; *also* : a place where such trade is carried on

Black Mass *n* : a travesty of the Christian mass ascribed to worshipers of Satan

Black Muslim *n* : a member of a chiefly black group that professes Islamic religious belief

black nationalist *n, often cap B&N* : a member of a group of militant blacks who advocate separatism from whites and the formation of self-governing black communities — **black nationalism** *n, often cap B&N*

black·out \'blak-ˌau̇t\ *n* **1** : a period of darkness due to electrical power failure **2** : a transitory loss or dulling of vision or consciousness **3** : the prohibition or restriction of the telecasting of sports events to ensure ticket sales — **black out** \-'au̇t\ *vb*

Black Panther *n* : a member of an organization of militant black Americans

black power *n* : the mobilization of the political and economic power of black Americans esp. to further racial equality

black sheep *n* : a discreditable member of an otherwise respectable group

black·smith \'blak-ˌsmith\ *n* : a worker who shapes heated iron by hammering it

black·thorn \-ˌthȯrn\ *n* : a European thorny plum

black·top \'blak-ˌtäp\ *n* : a very dark material containing mixtures of hydrocarbons (as asphalt) used esp. for surfacing roads — **blacktop** *vb*

black widow *n* : a venomous New World spider having the female black with an hourglass-shaped red mark on the underside of the abdomen

blad·der \'blad-ər\ *n* : a sac in which liquid or gas is stored; *esp* : one in a vertebrate into which urine passes from the kidneys

blade \'blād\ n 1 : a leaf of a plant and esp. of a grass; *also* : the flat part of a leaf as distinguished from its stalk 2 : something (as the flat part of an oar or an arm of a propeller) resembling the blade of a leaf 3 : the cutting part of an instrument or tool 4 : SWORD; *also* : SWORDSMAN 5 : a dashing fellow (a gay ∼) 6 : the runner of an ice skate

blain \'blān\ n : an inflammatory swelling or sore

¹**blame** \'blām\ vb blamed; blam·ing [ME blamen, fr. OF blamer, fr. L blasphemare to blaspheme, fr. Gk blasphēmein] 1 : to find fault with 2 : to hold responsible or responsible for syn censure, denounce, condemn, criticize — blam·able adj

²**blame** n 1 : CENSURE, REPROOF 2 : responsibility for fault or error syn guilt, fault, culpability, onus — blame·less adj — blame·less·ly adv

blame·wor·thy \-,wər-thē\ adj : deserving blame — blame·wor·thi·ness n

blanch \'blanch\ vb 1 : BLEACH 2 : to make or become white or pale

blanc·mange \blə-'mänj, -'mänzh\ n [ME blancmanger, fr. MF blanc manger, lit., white food] : a dessert made from gelatin or a starchy substance and milk usu. sweetened and flavored

bland \'bland\ adj 1 : smooth in manner : SUAVE 2 : gently soothing (a ∼ diet) ; *also* : INSIPID syn gentle, mild, soft, balmy — bland·ly adv — bland·ness n

blan·dish·ment \'blan-dish-mənt\ n : flattering or coaxing speech or action : CAJOLERY

¹**blank** \'blaŋk\ adj 1 : showing or causing an appearance of dazed dismay; *also* : EXPRESSIONLESS 2 : DULL, EMPTY (∼ moments) 3 : free from writing or marks; *also* : having spaces to be filled in 4 : ABSOLUTE, DOWNRIGHT (∼ refusal) 5 : not shaped in final form — blank·ly adv — blank·ness n

²**blank** n 1 : an empty space 2 : a form with spaces for the entry of data 3 : the center of a target 4 : an unfinished form (as of a key) 5 : a cartridge with propellant and a wad but no projectile

³**blank** vb 1 : to cover or close up : OBSCURE 2 : to keep from scoring

blank check n 1 : a signed check with the amount unspecified 2 : complete freedom of action

¹**blan·ket** \'blaŋ-kət\ n 1 : a heavy woven often woolen covering 2 : a covering layer (a ∼ of snow)

²**blanket** vb : to cover with a blanket

³**blanket** adj : covering a group or class (∼ insurance) ; *also* : applicable in all instances (∼ rules)

blank verse n : unrhymed iambic pentameter

blare \'blaər\ vb blared; blar·ing : to sound loud and harsh; *also* : to proclaim loudly — blare n

blar·ney \'blär-nē\ n [Blarney stone, a stone in Blarney Castle, near Cork, Ireland, held to bestow skill in flattery on those who kiss it] : skillful flattery : BLANDISHMENT

bla·sé \blä-'zā\ adj [F] : not responsive to pleasure or excitement as a result of excessive indulgence; *also* : SOPHISTICATED

blas·pheme \blas-'fēm\ vb blas·phemed; blas·phem·ing 1 : to speak of or address with irreverence 2 : to utter blasphemy

blas·phe·my \'blas-fə-mē\ n, pl -mies 1 : the act of expressing lack of reverence for God 2 : irreverence toward something considered sacred — blas·phe·mous \-məs\ adj

¹**blast** \'blast\ n 1 : a violent gust of wind; *also* : its effect 2 : sound made by a wind instrument 3 : a current of air forced at high pressure through a hole in a furnace (blast furnace) 4 : a sudden withering esp. of plants : BLIGHT 5 : EXPLOSION; *also* : the often destructive wave of increased air pressure that moves outward from an explosion

²**blast** vb 1 : BLIGHT 2 : to shatter by or as if by an explosive

blast off \(')blast-'óf\ vb : TAKE OFF 4 — used esp. of rocket-propelled devices — blast-off \'blast-,óf\ n

bla·tant \'blāt-ᵊnt\ adj : offensively obtrusive : vulgarly showy syn vociferous, boisterous, clamorous, obstreperous — bla·tan·cy \-ᵊn-sē\ n — bla·tant·ly adv

blath·er \'blath-ər\ vb blath·ered; blath·er·ing \-(ə-)riŋ\ : to talk foolishly — blather n

blath·er·skite \'blath-ər-,skīt\ n : a blustering talkative person

¹**blaze** \'blāz\ n 1 : FIRE 2 : intense direct light accompanied by heat 3 : something (as a dazzling display or sudden outburst) suggesting fire (a ∼ of autumn leaves) syn glare, glow, flame

²**blaze** vb blazed; blaz·ing 1 : to burn brightly; *also* : to flare up 2 : to be conspicuously bright : GLITTER

³**blaze** vb blazed; blaz·ing : to make public

⁴**blaze** n : a white mark on the face of an animal 2 : a mark made on a tree or other fixed object usu. to leave a trail

⁵**blaze** vb blazed; blaz·ing : to mark (as a tree or trail) with blazes

blaz·er \'blā-zər\ n : a sports jacket often with notched collar and pockets that are stitched on

¹**bla·zon** \'blāz-ᵊn\ n 1 : COAT OF ARMS 2 : ostentatious display

²**blazon** vb bla·zoned; bla·zon·ing \'blāz-(ə-)niŋ\ 1 : to publish widely : PROCLAIM 2 : DECK, ADORN

bldg abbr building

bldr abbr builder

¹**bleach** \'blēch\ vb : WHITEN, BLANCH

²**bleach** n : a preparation used in bleaching

bleach·ers \'blē-chərz\ n sing or pl : a usu. uncovered stand containing lower-priced tiered seats for spectators

bleak \'blēk\ adj 1 : desolately barren and windswept 2 : lacking warm or cheering qualities — **bleak·ish** adj — **bleak·ly** adv — **bleak·ness** n

blear \'blir\ adj : dim with water or tears (~ eyes)

bleary \'blir-ē\ adj 1 : dull or dimmed esp. from fatigue or sleep 2 : poorly outlined or defined

bleat \'blēt\ n : the cry of a sheep or goat or a sound like it — **bleat** vb

bleed \'blēd\ vb **bled** \'bled\ ; **bleed·ing** 1 : to lose or shed blood 2 : to be wounded; also : to feel pain or distress 3 : to flow or ooze from a wounded surface; also : to draw fluid from (~ a tire) 4 : to extort money from

bleed·er \'blēd-ər\ n : one that bleeds; esp : HEMOPHILIAC

bleeding heart n 1 : a garden plant related to the poppies that has deep pink drooping heart-shaped flowers 2 : one who shows extreme sympathy esp. for the object of alleged persecution

¹**blem·ish** \'blem-ish\ vb : to spoil by a flaw : MAR

²**blemish** n : a noticeable flaw

¹**blench** \'blench\ vb [ME blenchen to deceive, blench, fr. OE blencan to deceive] : FLINCH, QUAIL **syn** shrink, recoil, wince, start

²**blench** vb : to grow or make pale

¹**blend** \'blend\ vb **blend·ed**; **blend·ing** 1 : to mix thoroughly 2 : to prepare (as coffee) by mixing different varieties 3 : to combine into an integrated whole 4 : HARMONIZE **syn** fuse, merge, mingle, coalesce — **blend·er** n

²**blend** n : a product of blending **syn** compound, composite, alloy, mixture

bless \'bles\ vb **blessed** \'blest\ also **blest** \'blest\; **bless·ing** [ME blessen, fr. OE blētsian, fr. blōd blood; fr. the use of blood in consecration] 1 : to hallow or consecrate by religious rite or word 2 : to make the sign of the cross over 3 : to invoke divine care for 4 : PRAISE, GLORIFY 5 : to confer happiness upon

bless·ed \'bles-əd\ also **blest** \'blest\ adj 1 : HOLY 2 : BEATIFIED 3 : DELIGHTFUL — **bless·ed·ness** n

bless·ing \'bles-in\ n 1 : the act or words of one who blesses 2 : a thing conducive to happiness 3 : grace said at a meal

blew past of BLOW

¹**blight** \'blīt\ n 1 : a plant disease or injury marked by withering; also : an organism causing a blight 2 : an impairing or frustrating influence; also : an impaired or damaged condition

²**blight** vb : to affect with or suffer from blight

blimp \'blimp\ n : a nonrigid airship

¹**blind** \'blīnd\ adj 1 : lacking or grossly deficient in ability to see; also : intended for blind persons 2 : not based on reason, evidence, or knowledge (~ faith) 3 : not intelligently controlled or directed (~ chance) 4 : performed solely by the aid of instruments within an airplane (a ~ landing) 5 : hard to discern or make out : HIDDEN (a ~ seam) 6 : lacking an opening or outlet (a ~ alley) — **blind·ly** adv — **blind·ness** \'blīn(d)-nəs\ n

²**blind** vb 1 : to make blind 2 : DAZZLE 3 : DARKEN; also : HIDE

³**blind** n 1 : something (as a shutter) to hinder vision or keep out light 2 : a place of concealment 3 : SUBTERFUGE

blind date n : a date between persons who have not previously met; also : either of these persons

blind·er \'blīn-dər\ n : either of two flaps on a horse's bridle to prevent it from seeing to the side

blind·fold \'blīn(d)-ˌfōld\ vb : to cover the eyes of or as if with a bandage — **blindfold** n

¹**blink** \'blink\ vb 1 : WINK 2 : TWINKLE 3 : EVADE, IGNORE

²**blink** n 1 : GLIMMER, SPARKLE 2 : a usu. involuntary shutting and opening of the eye

blink·er \'blin-kər\ n : a blinking light used as a signal

blin·tze \'blint-sə\ or **blintz** \'blints\ n [Yiddish blintse] : a thin rolled pancake with a filling usu. of cream cheese

blip \'blip\ n 1 : an image on a radar screen 2 : ABERRATION 1

bliss \'blis\ n : complete happiness : JOY **syn** beatitude, blessedness — **bliss·ful** \-fəl\ adj — **bliss·ful·ly** \-fə-lē\ adv

¹**blis·ter** \'blis-tər\ n 1 : a raised area of skin containing watery fluid; also : an agent that causes blisters 2 : something (as a raised spot in paint) suggesting a blister 3 : a disease of plants marked by large swollen patches on the leaves

²**blister** vb **blis·tered**; **blis·ter·ing** \-t(ə-)rin\ : to develop a blister; also : to cause blisters

blithe \'blīth, 'blīth\ adj **blith·er**; **blith·est** : happily lighthearted **syn** merry, jovial, jolly, jocund — **blithe·ly** adv — **blithe·some** \-səm\ adj

blitz \'blits\ n 1 : an intensive series of air raids 2 : a fast intensive campaign 3 : a rush of the passer by the defensive linebackers in football — **blitz** vb

blitz·krieg \-ˌkrēg\ n [G, lit., lightning war, fr. blitz lightning + krieg war] : a sudden violent enemy attack

bliz·zard \'bliz-ərd\ n : a long severe snowstorm

blk abbr 1 black 2 block

bloat \'blōt\ vb : to swell by or as if by filling with water or air

bloat·er \'blōt-ər\ n : a fat herring or mackerel lightly salted and smoked

blob \'bläb\ n : a small lump or drop of a thick consistency

bloc \'bläk\ n [F, lit., block] : a combination of individuals or groups (as nations) working for a common purpose

¹**block** \'bläk\ n 1 : a solid piece of substantial material (as wood or stone) 2 : HINDRANCE, OBSTRUCTION; also : interruption of normal function of body or mind ⟨heart ∼⟩ 3 : a frame enclosing one or more pulleys and having a hook or strap by which it may be attached to objects 4 : a quantity of things considered as a unit ⟨a ∼ of seats⟩ 5 : a large building divided into separate units (as apartments or offices) 6 : a row of houses or shops 7 : a city square; also : the distance along one of the sides of such a square 8 : a piece of material with a hand-cut design on its surface from which copies are to be made

²**block** vb 1 : OBSTRUCT, CHECK 2 : to outline roughly ⟨∼ out a statue⟩ 3 : to provide or support with a block ⟨∼ up a wheel⟩ syn bar, impede, hinder, obstruct

¹**block·ade** \blä-'kād\ vb **block·ad·ed; block·ad·ing** : to subject to a blockade

²**blockade** n : the shutting off of a place usu. by troops or ships to prevent entrance or exit

block·bust·er \'bläk-,bəs-tər\ n : one that is very large, successful, or violent ⟨a ∼ of a movie⟩

block·head \'bläk-,hed\ n : DOLT, DUNCE

block·house \-,haus\ n : a small strong building used as a shelter (as from enemy fire) or observation post

¹**blond** or **blonde** \'bländ\ adj : fair in complexion; also : of a light or bleached color ⟨∼ mahogany⟩ — **blond·ish** \-ish\ adj

²**blond** or **blonde** n : a person having blond hair

blood \'bləd\ n 1 : the red liquid that circulates in the heart, arteries, and veins of animals 2 : LIFEBLOOD; also : LIFE 3 : LINEAGE, STOCK 4 : KINSHIP; also : KINDRED 5 : the taking of life 6 : TEMPER, PASSION 7 : DANDY — **blood·less** adj — **blood-stained** \-,stānd\ adj — **bloody** adj

blood bank n : a place where blood or plasma is stored

blood·bath \'bləd-,bath, -,bath\ n : MASSACRE

blood count n : the determination of the number of blood cells in a specific volume of blood; also : the number of cells so determined

blood·cur·dling \-,kərd-(ə)liŋ\ adj : causing great horror or fear : TERRIFYING

blood·ed \'bləd-əd\ adj 1 : entirely or largely purebred ⟨∼ horses⟩ 2 : having blood of a specified kind ⟨warm-*blooded* animals⟩

blood group n : one of the classes into which human beings can be separated by the presence or absence in their blood of specific antigens

blood·hound \'bləd-,haund\ n : a large powerful hound with long drooping ears, a wrinkled face, and keen sense of smell

blood·let·ting \-,let-iŋ\ n 1 : PHLEBOTOMY 2 : BLOODSHED

blood·line \-,līn\ n : a sequence of direct ancestors esp. in a pedigree

blood·mo·bile \-mō-,bēl\ n : a motor vehicle equipped for collecting blood from donors

blood poisoning n : invasion of the bloodstream by virulent microorganisms from a focus of infection accompanied esp. by chills, fever, and prostration

blood pressure n : pressure of the blood on the walls of blood vessels and esp. arteries

blood·root \'bləd-,rüt, -,rut\ n : a plant related to the poppy that has a red root and sap, a solitary leaf, and a white flower in early spring

blood·shed \-,shed\ n : wounding or taking of life : CARNAGE, SLAUGHTER

blood·shot \-,shät\ adj : inflamed to redness ⟨∼ eyes⟩

blood·stain \-,stān\ n : a discoloration caused by blood — **blood-stained** \-,stānd\ adj

blood·stone \-,stōn\ n : a green quartz sprinkled with red spots

blood·stream \-,strēm\ n : the flowing blood in a circulatory system

blood·suck·er \-,sək-ər\ n : an animal that sucks blood; esp : LEECH — **blood·suck·ing** \-iŋ\ adj

blood test n : a test of the blood; esp : one for syphilis

blood·thirsty \'bləd-,thər-stē\ adj : eager to shed blood — **blood·thirst·i·ly** \-,thər-stə-lē\ adv — **blood·thirst·i·ness** \-stē-nəs\ n

blood type n : BLOOD GROUP — **blood·typ·ing** \-,tī-piŋ\ n

blood vessel n : a vessel (as a vein or artery) in which blood circulates in an animal

Bloody Mary \-'me(ə)r-ē\ n, pl **Bloody Marys** : a drink made essentially of vodka and tomato juice

¹**bloom** \'blüm\ n 1 : FLOWER 1; also : flowers or amount of flowers (as of a plant) 2 : the period or state of flowering 3 : a state or time of beauty and vigor 4 : a powdery coating esp. on fruits and leaves 5 : rosy color; also : an appearance of freshness or health — **bloomy** adj

²**bloom** vb 1 : to produce or yield flowers 2 : to glow esp. with healthy color syn flower, blossom

bloom·ers \'blü-mərz\ n pl [Amelia *Bloomer* †1894 Am. pioneer in feminism] : a woman's garment of short loose trousers gathered at the knee

bloop·er \'blü-pər\ n 1 : an embarrassing blunder made in public **2** : a fly ball hit barely beyond a baseball infield

¹blos·som \'bläs-əm\ *n* : the flower of a plant : BLOOM

²blossom *vb* : FLOWER, BLOOM

¹blot \'blät\ *n* **1** : SPOT, STAIN ⟨ink ∼s⟩ **2** : BLEMISH **syn** stigma, brand, slur

²blot *vb* **blot·ted; blot·ting 1** : SPOT, STAIN **2** : OBSCURE, ECLIPSE ⟨∼ out the sun⟩ **3** *obs* : MAR; *esp* : DISGRACE **4** : to dry or remove with or as if with blotting paper **5** : to make a blot

blotch \'bläch\ *n* : a usu. large and irregular spot or mark (as of ink or color) — **blotch** *vb* — **blotchy** *adj*

blot·ter \'blät-ər\ *n* **1** : a piece of blotting paper **2** : a book for preliminary records (as of sales or arrests)

blot·ting paper *n* : a soft spongy paper used to absorb ink

blouse \'blaús, 'blaúz\ *n* **1** : a loose outer garment like a smock **2** : a usu. loose garment reaching from the neck to about the waist level

¹blow \'blō\ *vb* **blew** \'blü\; **blown** \'blōn\; **blow·ing 1** : to move forcibly (the wind *blew*) **2** : to send forth a current of gas (as air) **3** : to act on with a current of gas or vapor; *esp* : to drive with such a current **4** : to sound or cause to sound ⟨∼ a horn⟩ **5** : PANT, GASP; *also* : to expel moist air in breathing (the whale *blew*) **6** : BOAST; *also* : BLUSTER **7** : MELT — used of an electrical fuse **8** : to shape or form by blown or injected air ⟨∼ glass⟩ **9** : to shatter or destroy by or as if by explosion **10** : to make breathless by exertion **11** : to spend recklessly — **blow·er** *n*

²blow *n* **1** : a usu. strong blowing of air : GALE **2** : BOASTING, BRAG **3** : a blowing from the mouth or nose or through or from an instrument

³blow *vb* **blew** \'blü\; **blown** \'blōn\; **blow·ing** : FLOWER, BLOOM

⁴blow *n* **1** : a forcible stroke **2** : COMBAT ⟨come to ∼s⟩ **3** : a severe and usu. unexpected calamity

blow–by–blow \-ˌbī-, -bə-\ *adj* : minutely detailed ⟨∼ account⟩

blow·fly \'blō-ˌflī\ *n* : any of various two-winged flies (as a bluebottle) that deposit their eggs or maggots on meat or in wounds

blow·gun \-ˌgən\ *n* : a tube from which an arrow or a dart may be shot by the force of the breath

blow·out \'blō-ˌaút\ *n* : a bursting of something (as a tire) because of pressure of the contents (as air)

blow·pipe \'blō-ˌpīp\ *n* : a small tube for blowing gas (as air) into a flame so as to concentrate and increase the heat

blow·sy *also* **blow·zy** \'blaú-zē\ *adj* : DISHEVELED, SLOVENLY

blow·torch \'blō-ˌtórch\ *n* : a small portable burner whose flame is made hotter by a blast of air or oxygen

blow·up \'blō-ˌəp\ *n* **1** : EXPLOSION **2** : an outburst of temper **3** : a photographic enlargement

blowy \'blō-ē\ *adj* : WINDY

BLT \ˌbē-ˌel-ˈtē\ *n* : a bacon, lettuce, and tomato sandwich

¹blub·ber \'bləb-ər\ *vb* **blub·bered; blub·ber·ing** \'bləb-(ə-)riŋ\ : to cry noisily

²blubber *n* **1** : the fat of large sea mammals (as whales) **2** : a noisy crying

blud·geon \'bləj-ən\ *n* : a short often loaded club

²bludgeon *vb* : to strike with or as if with a bludgeon

¹blue \'blü\ *adj* **blu·er; blu·est 1** : of the color blue; *also* : BLUISH **2** : MELANCHOLY; *also* : DEPRESSING **3** : PURITANICAL **4** : INDECENT

²blue *n* **1** : a color between green and violet in the spectrum : the color of the clear daytime sky **2** : something (as clothing or the sky) that is blue

blue baby *n* : a baby with bluish skin due to faulty circulation caused by a heart defect

blue·bell \-ˌbel\ *n* : any of various plants with blue bell-shaped flowers

blue·ber·ry \'blü-ˌber-ē, -b(ə-)rē\ *n* : the edible blue or blackish berry of various shrubs of the heath family; *also* : one of these shrubs

blue·bird \-ˌbərd\ *n* : any of several small songbirds related to the robin but with blue above esp. in the male

blue–black \-ˈblak\ *adj* : being of a dark bluish hue

blue·bon·net \'blü-ˌbän-ət\ *n* : a low-growing annual lupine of Texas with silky foliage and blue flowers

blue·bot·tle \'blü-ˌbät-ᵊl\ *n* : any of several blowflies with iridescent blue bodies or abdomens

blue cheese *n* : cheese marked with veins of greenish blue mold

blue–col·lar \'blü-ˈkäl-ər\ *adj* : of, relating to, or being the class of workers whose duties call for work clothes

blue·fish \-ˌfish\ *n* : a marine sport and food fish bluish above and silvery below

blue·grass \-ˌgras\ *n* : KENTUCKY BLUEGRASS

blue jay \-ˌjā\ *n* : an American crested jay with upper parts bright blue that occurs east of the Rocky mountains

blue jeans *n pl* : pants usu. made of blue denim

blue·nose \'blü-ˌnōz\ *n* : one who advocates a rigorous moral code

blue·point \'blü-ˌpóint\ *n* : a small delicate oyster orig. from Long Island, New York

blue·print \-ˌprint\ *n* **1** : a photographic print in white on a blue ground used esp. for copying mechanical drawings and architects' plans **2** : a detailed plan of action — **blueprint** *vb*

blues \'blüz\ *n pl* **1** : MELANCHOLY **2** : music in a style marked by recurrent minor intervals and melancholy lyrics

blue·stock·ing \\'blü-ˌstäk-iŋ\\ *n* : a woman having intellectual interests

blu·et \\'blü-ət\\ *n* : a low American herb with dainty solitary bluish flowers

blue whale *n* : a very large whalebone whale that may reach a weight of 100 tons (90 metric tons) and a length of 100 feet (30 meters)

¹**bluff** \\'bləf\\ *adj* 1 : having a broad flattened front 2 : rising steeply with a broad flat front 3 : OUTSPOKEN, FRANK *syn* abrupt, blunt, brusque, curt, gruff

²**bluff** *n* : a high steep bank : CLIFF

³**bluff** *vb* : to frighten or deceive by pretense or a mere show of strength

⁴**bluff** *n* : an act or instance of bluffing; *also* : one who bluffs

blu·ing *or* **blue·ing** \\'blü-iŋ\\ *n* : a preparation of blue or violet dyes used in laundering to counteract yellowing of white fabrics

blu·ish \\'blü-ish\\ *adj* : somewhat blue

blun·der \\'blən-dər\\ *vb* **blun·dered; blun·der·ing** \\-d(ə-)riŋ\\ 1 : to move clumsily or unsteadily 2 : to make a stupid or needless mistake

²**blunder** *n* : an avoidable and usu. serious mistake

blun·der·buss \\'blən-dər-ˌbəs\\ *n* [fr. obs. Dutch *donderbus*, fr. Dutch *donder* thunder + obs. Dutch *bus* gun] : an obsolete short-barreled firearm with a flaring muzzle

¹**blunt** \\'blənt\\ *adj* 1 : not sharp : DULL 2 : lacking in tact : BLUFF *syn* brusque, curt, gruff, abrupt, crusty — **blunt·ly** *adv* — **blunt·ness** *n*

²**blunt** *vb* : to make or become dull

¹**blur** \\'blər\\ *n* 1 : a smear or stain that obscures 2 : something vaguely seen or perceived — **blur·ry** \\-ē\\ *adj*

²**blur** *vb* **blurred; blur·ring** : DIM, CLOUD, OBSCURE

blurb \\'blərb\\ *n* : a short publicity notice (as on a book jacket)

blurt \\'blərt\\ *vb* : to utter suddenly and impulsively

blush \\'bləsh\\ *n* : a reddening of the face (as from modesty or confusion) : FLUSH — **blush** *vb* — **blush·ful** *adj*

blus·ter \\'bləs-tər\\ *vb* **blus·tered; blus·ter·ing** \\-t(ə-)riŋ\\ 1 : to blow in stormy noisy gusts 2 : to talk or act with noisy swaggering threats — **bluster** *n* — **blus·tery** \\-t(ə-)rē\\ *adj*

blvd *abbr* boulevard

B lymphocyte *n* : B CELL

BM *abbr* 1 basal metabolism 2 bowel movement

BMR *abbr* basal metabolic rate

BO *abbr* 1 body odor 2 box office 3 branch office

boa \\'bō-ə\\ *n* 1 : a large snake (as the **boa con·stric·tor** \\ˌbō-ə-kən-ˈstrik-tər\\ or the related anaconda) that suffocates and kills its prey by constriction 2 : a fluffy scarf usu. of fur or feathers

boar \\'bōr\\ *n* : a male swine; *also* : WILD BOAR

¹**board** \\'bōrd\\ *n* 1 : the side of a ship 2 : a thin flat length of sawed lumber; *also* : material (as cardboard) or a piece of material formed as a thin flat firm sheet 3 *pl* : STAGE 1 4 : a table spread with a meal; *also* : daily meals esp. when furnished for pay 5 : a table at which a council or magistrates sit 6 : a group or association of persons organized for a special responsibility (as the management of a business or institution); *also* : an organized commercial exchange

²**board** *vb* 1 : to go aboard ⟨~ a boat⟩ 2 : to cover with boards 3 : to provide or be provided with meals and often lodging — **board·er** *n*

board·ing·house \\'bōrd-iŋ-ˌhaùs\\ *n* : a house at which persons are boarded

board·walk \\'bōrd-ˌwòk\\ *n* : a promenade (as of planking) along a beach

boast \\'bōst\\ *vb* 1 : to praise oneself 2 : to mention or assert with excessive pride 3 : to prize as a possession; *also* : HAVE ⟨the house ~s a fireplace⟩ — **boast** *n* — **boast·ful** \\-fəl\\ *adj* — **boast·ful·ly** \\-ē\\ *adv*

boat \\'bōt\\ *n* : a vessel (as a canoe or ship) for traveling through water

boat·er \\'bōt-ər\\ *n* 1 : one that travels in a boat 2 : a stiff straw hat

boat·man \\'bōt-mən\\ *n* : a man who manages, works on, or deals in boats

boat·swain \\'bōs-ᵊn\\ *n* : a subordinate officer of a ship in charge of the hull and related equipment

¹**bob** \\'bäb\\ *vb* **bobbed; bob·bing** 1 : to move up and down jerkily or repeatedly 2 : to emerge, arise, or appear suddenly or unexpectedly

²**bob** *n* : a bobbing movement

³**bob** *n* 1 : a knob, knot, twist, or curl esp. of ribbons, yarn, or hair 2 : a short haircut of a woman or child 3 : FLOAT 2 4 : a weight hanging from a line

⁴**bob** *vb* **bobbed; bob·bing** : to cut hair in a bob

⁵**bob** *n, pl* **bob** *slang Brit* : SHILLING

bob·bin \\'bäb-ən\\ *n* : a cylinder or spindle for holding or dispensing thread (as in a sewing machine)

bob·ble \\'bäb-əl\\ *vb* **bob·bled; bob·bling** \\-(ə-)liŋ\\ : FUMBLE — **bobble** *n*

bob·by \\'bäb-ē\\ *n, pl* **bobbies** [*Bobby*, nickname for *Robert*, after Sir *Robert Peel*, who organized the London police force] *Brit* : POLICEMAN

bob·by pin \\'bäb-ē-\\ *n* : a flat wire hairpin with prongs that press close together

bob·cat \\'bäb-ˌkat\\ *n* : a small usu. rusty-colored No. American lynx

bob·o·link \\'bäb-ə-ˌliŋk\\ *n* : an American migratory songbird related to the meadowlarks

bob·sled \\'bäb-ˌsled\\ *n* 1 : a short sled usu. used as one of a joined pair 2 : a racing sled with two pairs of runners, a steering wheel, and a hand brake — **bobsled** *vb*

bob·white \\(')bäb-ˈhwīt\\ *n* : any of a

genus of quail; *esp* : one of the eastern and central U.S.

boc·cie *or* **boc·ci** *or* **boc·ce** \'bäch-ē\ *n* : Italian lawn bowling played on a long narrow court

bock \'bäk\ *n* : a dark heavy beer usu. sold in early spring

bod \'bäd\ *n* : BODY

¹bode \'bōd\ *vb* **bod·ed; bod·ing** : to indicate by signs : PRESAGE

²bode *past of* BIDE

bo·de·ga \bō-'dā-gə\ *n* [Sp, fr. L *apotheca* storehouse] : a store specializing in Hispanic groceries

bod·ice \'bäd-əs\ *n* [alter. of *bodies*, pl. of *body*] : the usu. close-fitting part of a dress above the waist

bodi·less \'bäd-i-ləs, 'bäd-ᵊl-əs\ *adj* : lacking a body or material form

¹bodi·ly \'bäd-ᵊl-ē\ *adj* : of or relating to the body (~ welfare)

²bodily *adv* **1** : in the flesh **2** : as a whole (lifted the crate up ~)

bod·kin \'bäd-kən\ *n* **1** : DAGGER **2** : a pointed implement for punching holes in cloth **3** : a blunt needle for drawing tape or ribbon through a loop or hem

body \'bäd-ē\ *n, pl* **bod·ies 1** : the physical whole of a living or dead organism; *also* : the trunk or main mass of an organism as distinguished from its appendages **2** : a human being : PERSON **3** : the main part of something **4** : a mass of matter distinct from other masses **5** : GROUP **6** : VISCOSITY, FIRMNESS **7** : richness of flavor — used esp. of wines — **bod·ied** \'bäd-ēd\ *adj*

body English *n* : bodily motions made in a usu. unconscious effort to influence the movement of a propelled object (as a ball)

body·guard \'bäd-ē-ˌgärd\ *n* : a personal guard; *also* : RETINUE

body stocking *n* : a sheer close-fitting one-piece garment for the torso that often has sleeves and legs

body·work \'bäd-ē-ˌwərk\ *n* : the making or repairing of vehicle bodies

Boer \'bōr, 'bu̇r\ *n* [Dutch, lit., farmer] : a South African of Dutch or Huguenot descent

¹bog \'bäg, 'bȯg\ *n* : wet, spongy, poorly drained, and usu. acid ground — **bog·gy** *adj*

²bog *vb* **bogged; bog·ging** : to sink into or as if into a bog

bo·gey *also* **bo·gie** *or* **bo·gy** \'bu̇g-ē, 'bō-gē *for 1;* 'bō-gē *for 2* \ *n, pl* **bogeys** *also* **bogies 1** : SPECTER, HOBGOBLIN; *also* : a source of fear or annoyance **2** : a score of one over par on a hole in golf

bo·gey·man \'bu̇g-ē-ˌman, 'bō-gē-, 'bü-gē-\ *n* : an imaginary monster used in threatening children

bog·gle \'bäg-əl\ *vb* **bog·gled; bog·gling** \-(ə-)liŋ\ : to overwhelm or be overwhelmed with fright or amazement

bo·gus \'bō-gəs\ *adj* : SPURIOUS, SHAM

Bo·he·mi·an \bō-'hē-mē-ən\ *n* **1** : a native or inhabitant of Bohemia **2** *often not cap* : VAGABOND, WANDERER **3** *of-*

ten not cap : a person (as a writer or artist) living an unconventional life — **bohemian** *adj, often cap*

¹boil \'bȯil\ *n* : an inflamed swelling on the skin containing pus

²boil *vb* **1** : to heat or become heated to a temperature (**boiling point**) at which vapor is formed and rises in bubbles (water ~s and changes to steam) ; *also* : to act on or be acted on by a boiling liquid (~ eggs) **2** : to be in a state of seething agitation

³boil *n* : the act or state of boiling

boil·er \'bȯi-lər\ *n* **1** : a container in which something is boiled **2** : a strong vessel used in making steam **3** : a tank holding hot water

boil·er·mak·er \'bȯi-lər-ˌmā-kər\ *n* : whiskey with a beer chaser

bois·ter·ous \'bȯi-st(ə-)rəs\ *adj* : noisily turbulent or exuberant — **bois·ter·ous·ly** *adv*

bok choy \'bäk-'chȯi\ *n* : a Chinese vegetable related to the mustards that forms a loose head of green leaves with long thick white stalks

bo·la \'bō-lə\ *or* **bo·las** \-ləs\ *n, pl* **bolas** \-ləz\ *also* **bo·las·es** [AmerSp *bolas*, fr. Sp *bola* ball] : a cord with weights attached to the ends for hurling at and entangling an animal

bold \'bōld\ *adj* **1** : COURAGEOUS, INTREPID **2** : IMPUDENT **3** : STEEP **4** : ADVENTUROUS, FREE (a ~ thinker) **syn** dauntless, brave, valiant — **bold·ly** *adv* — **bold·ness** \'bōl(d)-nəs\ *n*

bold·face \'bōl(d)-ˌfās\ *n* : a heavy-faced type; *also* : printing in boldface — **bold-faced** \-'fāst\ *adj*

bole \'bōl\ *n* : the trunk of a tree

bo·le·ro \bə-'le(ə)r-ō\ *n, pl* **-ros 1** : a Spanish dance or its music **2** : a short loose jacket open at the front

bo·li·var \bə-'lē-ˌvär, 'bäl-ə-vər\ *n, pl* **-vars** *or* **-va·res** \ˌbäl-ə-'vär-ˌās, ˌbō-li-\ — see MONEY table

boll \'bōl\ *n* : a seed pod (as of cotton)

boll weevil *n* : a small grayish weevil that infests the cotton plant both as a larva and as an adult

boll·worm \'bōl-ˌwərm\ *n* : any of several moths and esp. the corn earworm whose larvae feed on cotton bolls

bo·lo \'bō-lō\ *n, pl* **bolos** : a long heavy single-edged knife of Philippine origin

bo·lo·gna \bə-'lō-nē\ *n* [short for *Bologna sausage*, fr. *Bologna*, Italy] : a large smoked sausage of beef, veal, and pork

Bol·she·vik \'bōl-shə-ˌvik\ *n, pl* **Bolsheviks** *also* **Bol·she·vi·ki** \ˌbōl-shə-'vik-ē\ [Russ *bol'shevik*, fr. *bol'she* larger] **1** : a member of the party that seized power in Russia in the revolution of November 1917 **2** : COMMUNIST — **Bolshevik** *adj*

bol·she·vism \'bōl-shə-ˌviz-əm\ *n, often cap* : the doctrine or program of the Bolsheviks advocating violent overthrow of capitalism

¹bol·ster \'bōl-stər\ *n* : a long pillow or

cushion extending from side to side of a bed

²**bol·ster** vb **bol·stered; bol·ster·ing** \-st(ə-)riŋ\ : to support with or as if with a bolster; also : REINFORCE

¹**bolt** \'bōlt\ n 1 : a missile (as an arrow) for a crossbow or catapult 2 : a flash of lightning : THUNDERBOLT 3 : a sliding bar used to fasten a door 4 : a roll of cloth or wallpaper of specified length 5 : a rod with a head at one end and a screw thread at the other used to hold objects in place 6 : a metal cylinder that drives the cartridge into the chamber of a firearm

²**bolt** vb 1 : to move suddenly (as in fright or hurry) : START, DASH 2 : to break away (as from association) ⟨~ a political convention⟩ 3 : to secure or fasten with a bolt 4 : to swallow hastily or without chewing

³**bolt** n : an act of bolting

⁴**bolt** vb : SIFT ⟨~ flour⟩

bo·lus \'bō-ləs\ n 1 : a large pill 2 : a soft mass of chewed food

¹**bomb** \'bäm\ n 1 : a fused explosive device designed to detonate under specified conditions (as impact) 2 : a container of material (as insecticide) under pressure for release in a fine spray 3 : a long pass in football

²**bomb** vb : to attack with bombs

bom·bard \bäm-'bärd, bəm-\ vb 1 : to attack esp. with artillery or bombers 2 : to assail persistently 3 : to subject to the impact of rapidly moving particles (as electrons) — **bom·bard·ment** n

bom·bar·dier \,bäm-bə(r)-'diər\ n : a bomber-crew member who releases the bombs

bom·bast \'bäm-,bast\ n [fr. bombast cotton padding, fr. MF bombace, fr. ML bombax cotton, alter. of L bombyx silkworm, silk, fr. Gk] : pretentious wordy speech or writing — **bom·bas·tic** \bäm-'bas-tik\ adj

bom·ba·zine \,bäm-bə-'zēn\ n 1 : a silk fabric in twill weave dyed black 2 : a twilled fabric with silk warp and worsted filling

bomb·er \'bäm-ər\ n : one that bombs; esp : an airplane for dropping bombs

bomb·proof \'bäm-,prüf\ adj : safe against the explosive force of bombs

bomb·shell \'bäm-,shel\ n 1 : BOMB 1 2 : one that stuns, amazes, or completely upsets

bona fide \'bō-nə-,fīd, 'bän-ə-; ,bō-nə-'fīd-ē, -'fīd-ə\ adj [L, in good faith] 1 : made in good faith ⟨a bona fide agreement⟩ 2 : GENUINE, REAL ⟨a bona fide bargain⟩ syn authentic

bo·nan·za \bə-'nan-zə\ n [Sp, lit., fair weather, fr. ML bonacia, alter. of L malacia calm at sea, fr. Gk malakia, lit., softness, fr. malakos soft] : something yielding a rich return

bon·bon \'bän-,bän\ n : a candy with a creamy center and a soft covering (as of chocolate)

¹**bond** \'bänd\ n 1 : FETTER 2 : a binding

or uniting force or tie ⟨~s of friendship⟩ 3 : an agreement or obligation often made binding by a pledge of money or goods 4 : a person who acts as surety for another 5 : an interest-bearing certificate of public or private indebtedness 6 : the state of goods subject to supervision pending payment of taxes or duties due (imports held in ~)

²**bond** vb 1 : to assure payment of duties or taxes on (goods) by giving a bond 2 : to insure against losses caused by the acts of ⟨~ a bank teller⟩ 3 : to make or become firmly united as if by bonds ⟨~ iron to copper⟩

bond·age \'bän-dij\ n : SLAVERY, SERVITUDE

bond·hold·er \'bänd-,hōl-dər\ n : one that owns a government or corporation bond

bond·ing n : the formation of a close personal relationship esp. through frequent or constant association ⟨~ of mother and child⟩

bond·man \'bän(d)-mən\ n : SLAVE, SERF

¹**bonds·man** \'bän(d)z-mən\ n : BONDMAN

²**bondsman** n : SURETY 3

bond·wom·an \'bänd-,wùm-ən\ n : a female slave or serf

¹**bone** \'bōn\ n 1 : a hard largely calcareous tissue forming most of the skeleton of a vertebrate animal; also : one of the pieces of bone making up a vertebrate skeleton 2 : a hard animal substance (as ivory or whalebone) similar to true bone 3 : something made of bone — **bone·less** adj — **bony** also **bon·ey** \'bō-nē\ adj

²**bone** vb **boned; bon·ing** : to free from bones ⟨~ a chicken⟩

bone black n : the black carbon residue from calcined bones used esp. as a pigment

bone meal n : fertilizer or feed made of crushed or ground bone

bon·er \'bō-nər\ n : a stupid and ridiculous blunder

bone up vb 1 : CRAM 3 2 : to refresh one's memory ⟨boned up on the speech before giving it⟩

bon·fire \'bän-,fī(ə)r\ n [ME bonefire a fire of bones, fr. bon bone + fire] : a large fire built in the open air

bon·go \'bäŋ-gō\ n, pl bongos also bongoes [AmerSp bongó] : one of a pair of small tuned drums played with the hands

bon·ho·mie \,bän-ə-'mē\ n [F bonhomie, fr. bonhomme good-natured man, fr. bon good + homme man] : good-natured easy friendliness

bo·ni·to \bə-'nēt-ō\ n, pl -tos or -to : any of several medium-sized tunas

bon mot \bōⁿ-'mō\ n, pl bons mots \bōⁿ-'mō(z)\ or bon mots \-'mō(z)\ [F, lit., good word] : a clever remark

bon·net \'bän-ət\ n : a covering (as a cap) for the head; esp : a hat for a woman or infant tied under the chin

bon·ny \'bän-ē\ *adj* **bon·ni·er; -est** *chiefly Brit* : ATTRACTIVE, FAIR; *also* : FINE, EXCELLENT

bon·sai \bōn-'sī\ *n, pl* **bonsai** [Jp] : a potted plant (as a tree) dwarfed by special methods of culture; *also* : the art of growing such a plant

bo·nus \'bō-nəs\ *n* : something in addition to what is expected

bon vi·vant \,bän-vē-'vänt, ,bōⁿ-vē-'väⁿ\ *n, pl* **bons vivants** \,bän-vē-'vänts, ,bōⁿ-vē-'väⁿ(z)\ *or* **bon vivants** *same*\ [F, lit., good liver] : a person having cultivated, refined, and sociable tastes esp. in food and drink

bon voy·age \,bōⁿv-,wī-'äzh, -,wä-'yäzh; ,bän-\ *n* : FAREWELL — often used as an interjection

bonze \'bänz\ *n* : a Buddhist monk

boo \'bü\ *n, pl* **boos** : a shout of disapproval or contempt — **boo** *vb*

boo·by \'bü-bē\ *n, pl* **boobies** : an awkward ineffective person syn DOPE

booby hatch *n* : an insane asylum

booby prize *n* : an award for the poorest performance in a contest

booby trap *n* : a trap for the unwary; *esp* : a concealed explosive device set to go off when some harmless-looking object is touched

boo·dle \'büd-ᵊl\ *n* 1 : bribe money 2 : a large amount of money

¹**book** \'bük\ *n* 1 : a set of sheets bound into a volume 2 : a long written or printed narrative or record 3 : a major division of a long literary work 4 *cap* : BIBLE

²**book** *vb* 1 : to engage, reserve, or schedule by or as if by writing in a book (~ seats on a plane) 2 : to enter charges against in a police register

book·case \-,kās\ *n* : a piece of furniture consisting of shelves to hold books

book·end \-,end\ *n* : a support to hold up a row of books

book·ie \'bük-ē\ *n* : BOOKMAKER

book·ish \'bük-ish\ *adj* 1 : fond of books and reading 2 : inclined to rely unduly on book knowledge

book·keep·er \'bük-,kē-pər\ *n* : one who records the accounts or transactions of a business — **book·keep·ing** \-piŋ\ *n*

book·let \'bük-lət\ *n* : PAMPHLET

book·mak·er \'bük-,mā-kər\ *n* : one who determines odds and receives and pays off bets — **book·mak·ing** \-kiŋ\ *n*

book·mark \-,märk\ *or* **book·mark·er** \-,mär-kər\ *n* : a marker for finding a place in a book

book·mo·bile \'bük-mō-,bēl\ *n* : a truck that serves as a traveling library

book·plate \'bük-,plāt\ *n* : a label pasted in a book to show who owns it

book·sell·er \'bük-,sel-ər\ *n* : one who sells books; *esp* : the proprietor of a bookstore

book·shelf \-,shelf\ *n* : a shelf for books

book·worm \'bük-,wərm\ *n* 1 : a person unusually devoted to reading and study 2 : an insect larva (as of a beetle) that feeds on the binding and paste of a book

¹**boom** \'büm\ *n* 1 : a long spar used to extend the bottom of a sail 2 : a beam projecting from the upright pole of a derrick to support or guide the object lifted 3 : a line of floating timbers used to obstruct passage or catch floating objects

²**boom** *vb* 1 : to make a deep hollow sound : RESOUND 2 : to grow or cause to grow rapidly esp. in value, esteem, or importance

³**boom** *n* 1 : a booming sound or cry 2 : a rapid expansion or increase esp. of economic activity

boo·mer·ang \'bü-mə-,raŋ\ *n* [native name in Australia] : a bent or angular club that can be so thrown as to return near the starting point

¹**boon** \'bün\ *n* [ME, fr. ON *bōn* petition] : BENEFIT, BLESSING syn favor, gift, largess, present

²**boon** *adj* [ME *bon*, fr. MF, good] : INTIMATE, CONGENIAL

boon·docks \'bün-,däks\ *n pl* [Tagalog (language of the Philippines) *bundok* mountain] 1 : rough country filled with dense brush 2 : a rural area

boon·dog·gle \'bün-,däg-əl, -,dȯg-\ *n* : a useless or wasteful project or activity

boor \'bu̇r\ *n* 1 : YOKEL 2 : a rude or insensitive person syn churl, lout, clown, clodhopper — **boor·ish** *adj*

boost \'büst\ *vb* 1 : to push up from below 2 : INCREASE, RAISE (~ prices) 3 : AID, PROMOTE (voted a bonus to ~ morale) — **boost** *n* — **boost·er** *n*

¹**boot** \'büt\ *n, chiefly dial* : something to equalize a trade — **to boot** : BESIDES

²**boot** *vb, archaic* : AVAIL, PROFIT

³**boot** *n* 1 : a covering for the foot and leg 2 : a protective sheath (as of a flower) 3 *Brit* : an automobile trunk 4 : KICK; *also* : a discharge from employment 5 : a navy or marine corps trainee

⁴**boot** *vb* 1 : KICK 2 : to eject or discharge summarily

boot·black \'büt-,blak\ *n* : a person who shines shoes

boo·tee *or* **boo·tie** \'büt-ē\ *n* : an infant's knitted or crocheted sock

booth \'büth\ *n, pl* **booths** \'büthz, 'büths\ 1 : a small enclosed stall (as at a fair) 2 : a small enclosure giving privacy for a person (voting ~) (telephone ~) 3 : a restaurant accommodation having a table between backed benches

boot·leg \'büt-,leg\ *vb* : to make, transport, or sell (as liquor) illegally — **boot·leg** *adj or n* — **boot·leg·ger** *n*

boot·less \'büt-ləs\ *adj* : USELESS syn futile, vain, abortive, fruitless — **boot·less·ly** *adv*

boo·ty \'büt-ē\ *n, pl* **booties** : PLUNDER, SPOIL

¹**booze** \'büz\ *vb* **boozed; booz·ing** : to drink liquor to excess — **booz·er** *n*

²**booze** n : intoxicating liquor — **boozy** adj

bop \'bäp\ vb **bopped; bop·ping** : HIT, SOCK — **bop** n

BOQ abbr bachelor officers' quarters

bor abbr borough

bo·rate \'bōr-ˌāt\ n : a salt or ester of boric acid

bo·rax \'bōr-ˌaks\ n : a crystalline borate of sodium that occurs as a mineral and is used as a flux and cleanser

bor·del·lo \bȯr-'del-ō\ n, pl **-los** [It] : BROTHEL

¹**bor·der** \'bȯrd-ər\ n 1 : EDGE, MARGIN 2 : BOUNDARY, FRONTIER syn rim, brim, brink, fringe, perimeter

²**border** vb **bor·dered; bor·der·ing** \'bȯrd-(ə-)riŋ\ 1 : to put a border on 2 : ADJOIN 3 : VERGE

bor·der·land \'bȯrd-ər-ˌland\ n 1 : territory at or near a border 2 : an outlying or intermediate region often not clearly defined

bor·der·line \-ˌlīn\ adj : being in an intermediate position or state; esp : not quite up to what is standard or expected (~ intelligence)

¹**bore** \'bōr\ vb **bored; bor·ing** 1 : to make a hole in with or as if with a drill 2 : to make (as a well) by boring or digging away material syn perforate, drill, prick, puncture — **bor·er** n

²**bore** n 1 : a hole made by or as if by boring 2 : a cylindrical cavity 3 : the diameter of a hole or tube; also : the interior diameter of a gun barrel or engine cylinder

³**bore** past of BEAR

⁴**bore** n : a tidal flood with a high abrupt front

⁵**bore** n : one that causes boredom

⁶**bore** vb **bored; bor·ing** : to weary with tedious dullness

bo·re·al \'bōr-ē-əl\ adj : of, relating to, or located in northern regions

bore·dom \'bōrd-əm\ n : the condition of being bored

bo·ric acid \'bōr-ik-\ n : a white crystalline weak acid that contains boron and is used as an antiseptic

born \'bȯrn\ adj 1 : brought into life by birth 2 : NATIVE (American-*born*) 3 : having special natural abilities or character from birth (a ~ leader)

born–again adj : having experienced a revival of a personal faith or conviction (~ believer) (~ liberal)

borne past part of BEAR

bo·ron \'bōr-ˌän\ n : a chemical element that occurs in nature only in combination (as in borax)

bor·ough \'bər-ō\ n 1 : a British town that sends one or more members to Parliament; also : an incorporated British urban area 2 : an incorporated town or village in some U.S. states; also : any of the five political divisions of New York City 3 : a civil division of the state of Alaska corresponding to a county in most other states

bor·row \'bär-ō\ vb 1 : to take or receive (something) temporarily and with intent to return 2 : to take into possession or use from another source : DERIVE, APPROPRIATE (~ a metaphor)

borscht or **borsch** \'bȯrsh(t)\ n [Russ borshch] : a soup made mainly from beets

bosh \'bäsh\ n [Turk boş empty] : foolish talk or action : NONSENSE

bosky \'bäs-kē\ adj : covered with trees or shrubs

¹**bo·som** \'büz-əm, 'büz-\ n 1 : the front of the human chest; esp : the female breasts 2 : the part of a garment covering the breast 3 : the seat of secret thoughts and feelings — **bo·somed** \-əmd\ adj

²**bosom** adj : CLOSE, INTIMATE

¹**boss** \'bäs, 'bȯs\ n : a knoblike ornament : STUD

²**boss** vb : to ornament with bosses

³**boss** \'bȯs\ n 1 : one (as a foreman or manager) exercising control or supervision 2 : a politician who controls votes or dictates policies — **bossy** adj

⁴**boss** \'bȯs\ vb : to act as a boss : SUPERVISE

bo·sun \'bōs-ᵊn\ var of BOATSWAIN

bot abbr botanical; botany

bot·a·ny \'bät-(ᵊ-)nē\ n, pl **-nies** 1 : a branch of biology dealing with plants and plant life 2 : plant life (as of a given region); also : the biology of a plant or plant group — **bo·tan·i·cal** \bə-'tan-i-kəl\ adj — **bot·a·nist** \'bät-(ᵊ-)nəst\ n — **bot·a·nize** \-ˌnīz\ vb

botch \'bäch\ vb : to foul up hopelessly : BUNGLE — **botch** n

¹**both** \'bōth\ adj : being the two : affected

²**both** pron : both ones : the one as well as the other

³**both** conj — used as a function word to indicate and stress the inclusion of each of two or more things specified by coordinated words, phrases, or clauses (~ New York and London)

both·er \'bäth-ər\ vb **-ered; -er·ing** \-(ə-)riŋ\ : WORRY, PESTER, TROUBLE syn vex, annoy, irk, provoke — **bother** n — **both·er·some** \-səm\ adj

¹**bot·tle** \'bät-ᵊl\ n 1 : a container (as of glass) with a narrow neck and usu. no handles 2 : the quantity held by a bottle 3 : intoxicating liquor

²**bottle** vb **bot·tled; bot·tling** \'bät-(ᵊ-)liŋ\ 1 : to confine as if in a bottle : RESTRAIN 2 : to put into a bottle

bot·tle·neck \'bät-ᵊl-ˌnek\ n 1 : a narrow passage or point of congestion 2 : something that obstructs or impedes

bot·tom \'bät-əm\ n 1 : an under or supporting surface; also : BUTTOCKS 2 : the surface on which a body of water lies 3 : the lowest part or place; also : an inferior position (start at the ~) 4 : low land along a river — **bottom** adj — **bot·tom·less** adj

bot·tom·land \'bät-əm-ˌland\ n : BOTTOM 4

bottom line n 1 : the essential point : CRUX 2 : the final result : OUTCOME

bottom out vb : to reach a low point before rebounding (a security market that *bottoms out*)

bot·u·lism \'bäch-ə-ˌliz-əm\ n : acute food poisoning caused by a bacterial toxin in food

bou·doir \'büd-ˌwär, 'bud-\ n [F, fr. *bouder* to pout] : a woman's private room

bouf·fant \bü-'fänt, 'bü-ˌfänt\ adj [F] : puffed out (~ hairdos)

bough \'baü\ n : a usu. large or main branch of a tree

bought past and past part of BUY

bouil·la·baisse \ˌbü-yə-'bäs\ n [F] : a highly seasoned fish stew made with at least two kinds of fish

bouil·lon \'bü-ˌyän; 'bul-ˌyän, -yən\ n : a clear soup made usu. from beef

boul·der \'bōl-dər\ n : a large detached rounded or worn mass of rock — **bouldered** \-dərd\ adj

bou·le·vard \'bul-ə-ˌvärd, 'bül-\ n [F, modif. of Middle Dutch *bolwerc* bulwark: so called because the first boulevards were laid out on the sites of razed city fortifications] : a broad often landscaped thoroughfare

bounce \'baüns\ vb **bounced; bounc·ing** 1 : to cause to rebound (~ a ball) 2 : to rebound after striking — **bounce** n

bounc·er \'baün-sər\ n : someone employed in a public place to remove disorderly persons

¹bound \'baünd\ adj : intending to go

²bound n : LIMIT, BOUNDARY — **boundless** adj — **bound·less·ness** n

³bound vb 1 : to set limits to 2 : to form the boundary of 3 : to name the boundaries of

⁴bound past and past part of BIND

⁵bound adj 1 : constrained by or as if by bonds : CONFINED, OBLIGED 2 : enclosed in a binding or cover 3 : RESOLVED, DETERMINED; also : SURE

⁶bound n 1 : LEAP, JUMP 2 : REBOUND, BOUNCE

⁷bound vb : to spring, bounce

bound·ary \'baün-d(ə-)rē\ n, pl **-aries** : something that marks or fixes a limit (as of territory) **syn** border, frontier, march

bound·en \'baün-dən\ adj : BINDING

boun·te·ous \'baünt-ē-əs\ adj 1 : GENEROUS 2 : ABUNDANT — **boun·te·ous·ly** adv

boun·ti·ful \'baünt-i-fəl\ adj 1 : giving freely 2 : PLENTIFUL — **boun·ti·ful·ly** adv

boun·ty \'baünt-ē\ n, pl **bounties** [ME *bounte* goodness, fr. OF *bonté*, fr. L *bonitas*, fr. *bonus* good] 1 : GENEROSITY 2 : something given liberally 3 : a reward, premium, or subsidy given usu. for doing something

bou·quet \bō-'kā, bü-\ n [F, fr. MF, thicket, fr. OF *bosc* forest] 1 : flowers picked and fastened together in a bunch 2 : a distinctive aroma (as of wine) **syn** scent, fragrance, perfume, redolence

bour·bon \'bər-bən\ n : a whiskey distilled from a corn mash

bour·geois \'bürzh-ˌwä, bürzh-'wä\ n, pl **bourgeois** \-ˌwä(z), -'wä(z)\ [MF, lit., citizen of a town, fr. *borc* town, borough, fr. L *burgus* fortified place, of Gmc origin] : a middle-class person — **bourgeois** adj

bour·geoi·sie \ˌbürzh-ˌwä-'zē\ n : a social order dominated by bourgeois

bourn or **bourne** \'bōrn, 'bürn\ n, archaic : BOUNDARY; also : DESTINATION

bourse \'bürs\ n : a European stock exchange

bout \'baüt\ n 1 : CONTEST, MATCH 2 : OUTBREAK, ATTACK (a ~ of measles) 3 : SESSION

bou·tique \bü-'tēk\ n : a fashionable specialty shop

bou·ton·niere \ˌbüt-ᵊn-'iər\ n : a flower or bouquet worn in a buttonhole

bo·vine \'bō-ˌvīn, -ˌvēn\ adj : of, relating to, or resembling the ox or cow — **bovine** n

¹bow \'baü\ vb 1 : SUBMIT, YIELD 2 : to bend the head or body (as in submission, courtesy, or assent)

²bow n : an act or posture of bowing

³bow \'bō\ n 1 : BEND, ARCH; esp : RAINBOW 2 : a weapon for shooting arrows; also : ARCHER 3 : a knot formed by doubling a line into two or more loops 4 : a wooden rod strung with horsehairs for playing an instrument of the violin family

⁴bow \'bō\ vb 1 : BEND, CURVE 2 : to play (an instrument) with a bow

⁵bow \'baü\ n : the forward part of a ship — **bow** adj

bowd·ler·ize \'bōd-lə-ˌrīz, 'baüd-\ vb **-ized; -iz·ing** : to expurgate by omitting parts considered vulgar

bow·el \'baü-(ə)l\ n 1 : INTESTINE — usu. used in pl. 2 : one of the divisions of the intestine 3 pl : the inmost parts (the ~s of the earth)

bow·er \'baü-(ə)r\ n : a shelter of boughs or vines : ARBOR

¹bowl \'bōl\ n 1 : a concave vessel used to hold liquids 2 : a drinking vessel 3 : a bowl-shaped part or structure — **bowl·ful** \-ˌfül\ n

²bowl n 1 : a ball for rolling on a level surface in bowling 2 : a cast of the ball in bowling

³bowl vb 1 : to play a game of bowling; also : to roll a ball in bowling 2 : to travel (as in a vehicle) rapidly and smoothly 3 : to strike or knock down with a moving object; also : to overwhelm with surprise

bowlder var of BOULDER

bow-legged \'bō-ˌleg-əd\ adj : having legs that bow outward at or below the knee — **bow·leg** \'bō-ˌleg\ n

¹bowl·er \'bō-lər\ n : one that bowls

²bowl·er \'bō-lər\ n : DERBY 3

bow·line \'bō-lən, -ˌlīn\ *n* : a knot used to form a loop that neither slips nor jams

bowl·ing \'bō-liŋ\ *n* : any of various games in which balls are rolled on a green or alley at an object or a group of objects; *esp* : TENPINS

bow·man \'bō-mən\ *n* : ARCHER

bow·sprit \'bau̇-ˌsprit\ *n* : a spar projecting forward from the prow of a ship

bow·string \'bō-ˌstriŋ\ *n* : the cord connecting the two ends of a bow

¹**box** \'bäks\ *n, pl* **box** *or* **box·es** : an evergreen shrub or small tree used esp. for hedges

²**box** *n* **1** : a rigid typically rectangular receptacle often with a cover; *also* : the quantity held by a box **2** : a small compartment (as for a group of theater patrons); *also* : a boxlike receptacle or division **3** : any of six spaces on a baseball diamond where the batter, pitcher, coaches, and catcher stand **4** : PREDICAMENT

³**box** *vb* : to furnish with or enclose in or as if in a box

⁴**box** *n* : a punch or slap esp. on the ear

⁵**box** *vb* **1** : to strike with the hand **2** : to engage in boxing with : fight with the fists *syn* SMACK, CUFF, STRIKE, SLAP

box·car \'bäks-ˌkär\ *n* : a roofed freight car usu. with sliding doors in the sides

¹**box·er** \'bäk-sər\ *n* : one that engages in boxing

²**boxer** *n* : a compact short-haired usu. fawn or brindled dog of a breed of German origin

box·ing \'bäk-siŋ\ *n* : the sport of fighting with the fists

box office *n* : an office (as in a theater) where admission tickets are sold

box·wood \'bäks-ˌwu̇d\ *n* : the tough hard wood of the box; *also* : a box tree or shrub

boy \'bȯi\ *n* **1** : a male child : YOUTH **2** : SON — **boy·hood** \-ˌhu̇d\ *n* — **boy·ish** *adj* — **boy·ish·ly** *adv* — **boy·ish·ness** *n*

boy·cott \'bȯi-ˌkät\ *vb* [Charles C. *Boycott* †1897 E land agent in Ireland who was ostracized for refusing to reduce rents] : to refrain from having any dealings with — **boycott** *n*

Boy Scout *n* : a member of the Boy Scouts of America

boy·sen·ber·ry \'bȯiz-ᵊn-ˌber-ē, 'bȯis-\ *n* : a large bramble fruit with a raspberry flavor; *also* : the hybrid plant bearing it developed by crossing blackberries and raspberries

bp *abbr* bishop

BP *abbr* **1** blood pressure **2** boiling point

bpl *abbr* birthplace

BPOE *abbr* Benevolent and Protective Order of Elks

br *abbr* **1** branch **2** brass **3** brown

¹**Br** *abbr* Britain; British

²**Br** *symbol* bromine

BR *abbr* bedroom

bra \'brä\ *n* : BRASSIERE

¹**brace** \'brās\ *vb* **braced; brac·ing 1** *archaic* : to make fast : BIND **2** : to tighten preparatory to use; *also* : to get ready for : prepare oneself **3** : INVIGORATE **4** : to furnish or support with a brace; *also* : STRENGTHEN **5** : to set firmly; *also* : to gain courage or confidence

²**brace** *n, pl* **brac·es 1** *or pl* **brace** : two of a kind (~ of dogs) **2** : a crank-shaped device for turning a bit **3** : something (as a tie, prop, or clamp) that distributes, directs, or resists pressure or weight **4** *pl* : SUSPENDERS **5** : an appliance for supporting a body part (as the shoulders) **6** *pl* : dental appliances used to exert pressure to straighten misaligned teeth {or} or ~ : used to connect words or items to be considered together

brace·let \'brā-slət\ *n* [ME, fr. MF, dim. of *bras* arm, fr. L *bracchium*, fr. Gk *brachiōn*] : an ornamental band or chain worn around the wrist

bra·ce·ro \brä-'ser-ō\ *n, pl* -**ros** : a Mexican laborer admitted to the U.S. esp. for seasonal farm work

brack·en \'brak-ən\ *n* : a large coarse fern; *also* : a growth of such ferns

¹**brack·et** \'brak-ət\ *n* **1** : a projecting framework or arm designed to support weight; *also* : a shelf on such framework **2** : one of a pair of punctuation marks [ ] used esp. to enclose interpolated matter **3** : a continuous section of a series; *esp* : one of a graded series of income groups

²**bracket** *vb* **1** : to furnish or fasten with brackets **2** : to place within brackets; *also* : to separate or group with or as if with brackets

brack·ish \'brak-ish\ *adj* : somewhat salty — **brack·ish·ness** *n*

bract \'brakt\ *n* : an often modified leaf on or at the base of a flower stalk

brad \'brad\ *n* : a slender nail with a small head

brae \'brā\ *n, chiefly Scot* : a hillside esp. along a river

brag \'brag\ *vb* **bragged; brag·ging** : to talk or assert boastfully — **brag** *n*

brag·ga·do·cio \ˌbrag-ə-'dō-s(h)ē-ˌō, -(ˌ)shō\ *n, pl* -**cios 1** : BRAGGART, BOASTER **2** : empty boasting **3** : arrogant pretension : COCKINESS

brag·gart \'brag-ərt\ *n* : one who brags

Brah·man *or* **Brah·min** \'bräm-ən *for 1;* 'bräm-, 'bräm-, 'bram- *for 2*\ *n* **1** : a Hindu of the highest caste traditionally assigned to the priesthood **2** *usu* **Brahmin** : any of a breed of large vigorous humped cattle developed in the southern U.S. from Indian stock **3** *usu* **Brahmin** : a person of high social standing and cultivated intellect and taste

Brah·man·ism \'bräm-ə-ˌniz-əm\ *n* : orthodox Hinduism

¹**braid** \'brād\ *vb* **1** : to form (strands) into a braid : PLAIT; *also* : to make by braiding **2** : to ornament with braid

²**braid** *n* **1** : a cord or ribbon of three or

more interwoven strands; *also* : a length of braided hair **2** : a narrow ornamental fabric of intertwined threads

braille \'brāl\ *n, often cap* : a system of writing for the blind that uses characters made up of raised dots

¹brain \'brān\ *n* **1** : the part of the vertebrate nervous system that is the organ of thought and nervous coordination, is made up of nerve cells and their fibers, and is enclosed in the skull; *also* : a centralized mass of nerve tissue in an invertebrate **2** : INTELLECT, INTELLIGENCE — often used in pl. — **brained** \'brānd\ *adj* — **brain·less** *adj* — **brainy** *adj*

²brain *vb* **1** : to kill by smashing the skull **2** : to hit on the head

brain·child \-ˌchīld\ *n* : a product of one's creative imagination

brain death *n* : final cessation of activity in the central nervous system esp. as indicated by a flat electroencephalogram

brain drain *n* : a migration of professional people (as scientists) from one country to another usu. for higher pay

brain·storm \-ˌstȯrm\ *n* : a sudden burst of inspiration

brain·wash·ing \'brān-ˌwȯsh-iŋ, -ˌwäsh-\ *n* **1** : a forcible attempt by indoctrination to induce someone to give up his basic political, social, or religious beliefs and attitudes and to accept contrasting regimented ideas **2** : persuasion by propaganda or salesmanship — **brain·wash** *vb*

brain wave *n* : rhythmic fluctuation of voltage between parts of the brain; *also* : a current produced by brain waves

braise \'brāz\ *vb* **braised; brais·ing** : to cook (meat) slowly in fat and little moisture in a closed pot

¹brake \'brāk\ *n* : any of a genus of tall coarse ferns with compound fronds

²brake *n* : a device for slowing or stopping motion esp. by friction — **brakeless** *adj*

³brake *vb* **braked; brak·ing 1** : to slow or stop by or as if by a brake **2** : to apply a brake

⁴brake *n* : rough or wet land heavily overgrown (as with thickets or reeds)

brake·man \'brāk-mən\ *n* : a train crew member who inspects the train and assists the conductor

bram·ble \'bram-bəl\ *n* : any of a large genus of prickly shrubs (as a blackberry) related to the roses; *also* : any rough prickly shrub or vine

bran \'bran\ *n* : broken husks of cereal grain sifted from flour or meal

¹branch \'branch\ *n* [ME, fr. OF *branche*, fr. L *branca* paw] **1** : a natural subdivision (as a bough or twig) of a plant stem **2** : a division (as of an antler or a river) related to a whole like a plant branch to its stem **3** : a discrete unit or element of a complex

system (as of knowledge, people, or business); *esp* : a division of a family descended from one ancestor — **branched** \'brancht\ *adj*

²branch *vb* **1** : to develop branches **2** : DIVERGE

¹brand \'brand\ *n* **1** : a piece of charred or burning wood **2** : a mark made (as by burning) usu. to identify; *also* : a mark of disgrace : STIGMA **3** : a class of goods identified as the product of a particular firm or producer **4** : a distinctive kind (his own ~ of humor)

²brand *vb* **1** : to mark with a brand **2** : STIGMATIZE

bran·dish \'bran-dish\ *vb* : to shake or wave menacingly *syn* flourish, flash, flaunt

brand-new \'bran-ˈn(y)ü\ *adj* : conspicuously new and unused

bran·dy \'bran-dē\ *n, pl* **brandies** [short for *brandywine*, fr. Dutch *brandewijn*, fr. Middle Dutch *brantwijn*, fr. *brant* distilled + *wijn* wine] : a liquor distilled from wine or fermented fruit juice — **brandy** *vb*

brash \'brash\ *adj* **1** : IMPETUOUS **2** : aggressively self-assertive

brass \'bras\ *n* **1** : an alloy of copper and zinc; *also* : an object of brass **2** : brazen self-assurance — **brassy** *adj*

bras·se·rie \ˌbras-(ə-)ˈrē\ *n* : an informal usu. French restaurant serving simple hearty food

brass hat *n* : a high-ranking military officer

bras·siere \brə-ˈziər\ *n* : a woman's close-fitting undergarment designed to support the breasts

brat \'brat\ *n* : an ill-behaved child — **brat·ty** *adj*

bra·va·do \brə-ˈväd-ō\ *n, pl* **-does** or **-dos 1** : blustering swaggering conduct **2** : a show of bravery

¹brave \'brāv\ *adj* **brav·er; brav·est** [MF, fr. It & Sp *bravo* courageous, wild, fr. L *barbarus* barbarous] **1** : showing courage **2** : EXCELLENT, SPLENDID *syn* bold, intrepid, courageous, valiant — **brave·ly** *adv*

²brave *vb* **braved; brav·ing** : to face or endure bravely

³brave *n* : an American Indian warrior

brav·ery \'brāv-(ə-)rē\ *n, pl* **-er·ies** : COURAGE

bra·vo \'bräv-ō\ *n, pl* **bravos** : a shout of approval — often used as an interjection in applauding

bra·vu·ra \brə-ˈv(y)ür-ə\ *n* **1** : a florid brilliant musical style **2** : self-assured brilliant performance

brawl \'brȯl\ *n* : a noisy quarrel *syn* fracas, row, rumpus, scrap, fray, melee — **brawl** *vb* — **brawl·er** *n*

brawn \'brȯn\ *n* : strong muscles; *also* : muscular strength — **brawny** *adj*

bray \'brā\ *n* : the characteristic harsh cry of a donkey — **bray** *vb*

braze \'brāz\ *vb* **brazed; braz·ing** : to solder with an alloy (as brass) that melts at a lower temperature than that of the metals being joined — **braz·er** *n*

bra·zen \'brāz-ᵊn\ *adj* 1 : made of brass 2 : sounding harsh and loud 3 : of the color of brass 4 : marked by contemptuous boldness — **bra·zen·ly** *adv* — **bra·zen·ness** \'brāz-ᵊn-(n)əs\ *n*

¹**bra·zier** \'brā-zhər\ *n* : a worker in brass

²**brazier** *n* 1 : a vessel holding burning coals (as for heating) 2 : a device on which food is grilled

Bra·zil·ian \brə-'zil-yən\ *n* : a native or inhabitant of Brazil — **Brazilian** *adj*

Bra·zil nut \brə-'zil-\ *n* : a triangular oily edible nut borne in large capsules by a tall So. American tree; *also* : the tree

¹**breach** \'brēch\ *n* 1 : a breaking of a law, obligation, tie (as of friendship), or standard (as of conduct) 2 : an interruption or opening made by or as if by breaking through *syn* violation, transgression, infringement, trespass

²**breach** *vb* : to make a breach in

¹**bread** \'bred\ *n* 1 : baked food made basically of flour or meal 2 : FOOD

²**bread** *vb* : to cover with bread crumbs before cooking

bread·bas·ket \'bred-ˌbas-kət\ *n* : a major cereal-producing region

bread·fruit \-ˌfrüt\ *n* : a round usu. seedless fruit resembling bread in color and texture when baked; *also* : a tall tropical tree related to the mulberry and bearing breadfruit

bread·stuff \-ˌstəf\ *n* : GRAIN, FLOUR

breadth \'bredth, 'bretth\ *n* 1 : WIDTH 2 : SPACIOUSNESS; *also* : liberality of taste or views

bread·win·ner \'bred-ˌwin-ər\ *n* : a member of a family whose wages supply its livelihood

¹**break** \'brāk\ *vb* **broke** \'brōk\; **bro·ken** \'brō-kən\; **break·ing** 1 : to separate into parts usu. suddenly or violently : come or force apart 2 : TRANSGRESS ⟨~ a law⟩ 3 : to force a way into, out of, or through 4 : to disrupt the order or unity of ⟨~ ranks⟩ ⟨~ up a gang⟩; *also* : to bring to submission or helplessness 5 : EXCEED, SURPASS ⟨~ a record⟩ 6 : RUIN 7 : to make known 8 : HALT, INTERRUPT; *also* : to act or change abruptly (as a course or activity) 9 : to come esp. suddenly into being or notice (as day ~s) 10 : to fail under stress 11 : HAPPEN, DEVELOP — **break·able** *adj or n*

²**break** *n* 1 : an act of breaking 2 : a result of breaking; *esp* : an interruption of continuity (coffee ~) (a ~ for the commercial) 3 : a stroke of good luck

break·age \'brā-kij\ *n* 1 : the action of breaking 2 : articles or amount broken 3 : loss due to things broken

break·down \'brāk-ˌdaún\ *n* 1 : functional failure; *esp* : a physical, mental, or nervous collapse 2 : DISINTEGRATION 3 : DECOMPOSITION 4

: ANALYSIS, CLASSIFICATION — **break down** \(')brāk-'daún\ *vb*

break·er \'brā-kər\ *n* 1 : one that breaks 2 : a wave that breaks into foam (as against the shore)

break·fast \'brek-fəst\ *n* : the first meal of the day — **breakfast** *vb*

break·front \'brāk-ˌfrənt\ *n* : a large cabinet whose center section projects beyond the flanking end sections

break in \(')brāk-'in\ *vb* 1 : to enter a building by force 2 : INTERRUPT; *also* : INTRUDE 3 : TRAIN

break out \(')brāk-'aút\ *vb* 1 : to develop or erupt suddenly and with force 2 : to develop a skin rash

break·through \'brāk-ˌthrü\ *n* 1 : an act or instance of breaking through an obstruction or defensive line 2 : a sudden advance in knowledge or technique

break·up \'brāk-ˌəp\ *n* 1 : DISSOLUTION 2 : a division into smaller units — **break up** *vb*

break·wa·ter \'brāk-ˌwót-ər, -ˌwät-\ *n* : a structure built to protect a harbor or beach from the force of waves

bream \'brim, 'brēm\ *n, pl* **bream** *or* **breams** : any of various small freshwater sunfishes

breast \'brest\ *n* 1 : either of two milk-producing glandular organs situated on the front of the chest esp. in the human female 2 : the front part of the body between the neck and the abdomen 3 : the seat of emotion and thought

breast·bone \'bres(t)-ˌbōn, -ˌbōn\ *n* : STERNUM

breast–feed \'brest-ˌfēd\ *vb* : to feed (a baby) from a mother's breast rather than from a bottle

breast·plate \'bres(t)-ˌplāt\ *n* : a metal plate of armor for protecting the breast

breast·stroke \-ˌstrōk\ *n* : a swimming stroke executed by extending the arms in front of the head while drawing the knees forward and outward and then sweeping the arms back with palms out while kicking backward and outward

breast·work \'brest-ˌwərk\ *n* : a temporary fortification

breath \'breth\ *n* 1 : the act or power of breathing 2 : a slight breeze 3 : air inhaled or exhaled in breathing 4 : spoken sound 5 : SPIRIT — **breathless** *adj* — **breath·less·ly** *adv*

breathe \'brēth\ *vb* **breathed**; **breath·ing** 1 : to inhale and exhale 2 : LIVE 3 : to halt for rest 4 : to utter softly or secretly

breath·tak·ing \'breth-ˌtā-kiŋ\ *adj* 1 : making one out of breath 2 : EXCITING, THRILLING ⟨~ beauty⟩

brec·cia \'brech-(ē-)ə\ *n* : a rock consisting of sharp fragments held in fine-grained material

breech \'brēch\ *n* 1 *pl* *usu* 'brich-əz\ : trousers ending near the knee; *also*

: PANTS **2** : BUTTOCKS, RUMP **3** : the part of a firearm at the rear of the barrel

¹**breed** \'brēd\ *vb* **bred** \'bred\ ; **breeding 1** : BEGET; *also* : ORIGINATE **2** : to propagate sexually; *also* : MATE **3** : BRING UP, NURTURE **4** : to produce (fissionable material) from material that is not fissionable **syn** generate, reproduce, procreate, propagate — **breed·er** *n*

²**breed** *n* **1** : a strain of similar and presumably related plants or animals usu. developed under the influence of man **2** : KIND, SORT, CLASS

breed·ing *n* **1** : ANCESTRY **2** : training in polite social interaction **3** : sexual propagation of plants or animals

¹**breeze** \'brēz\ *n* : a light wind — **breezy** *adj*

²**breeze** *vb* **breezed**; **breez·ing** : to progress quickly and easily

breeze·way \'brēz-ˌwā\ *n* : a roofed open passage connecting two buildings (as a house and garage)

breth·ren \'breth-(ə-)rən, -ərn\ *pl of* BROTHER — used esp. in formal or solemn address

Brethren *n pl* : members of one of several Protestant denominations originating chiefly in a German religious movement and stressing personal religious experience

bre·vet \bri-'vet\ *n* : a commission giving a military officer higher nominal rank than that for which he receives pay — **brevet** *vb*

bre·via·ry \'brē-vyə-rē, -vē-, er-ē\ *n, pl* **-ries** : a book of prayers, hymns, psalms, and readings used by Roman Catholic priests

brev·i·ty \'brev-ət-ē\ *n, pl* **-ties** : shortness of duration; *esp* : shortness or conciseness of expression

brew \'brü\ *vb* **1** : to prepare (as beer) by steeping, boiling, and fermenting **2** : to prepare (as tea) by soaking in hot water — **brew** *n* — **brew·er** *n* — **brew·ery** \'brü-ə-rē, 'brü(-ə)r-ē\ *n*

bri·ar \'brī(-ə)r\ *n* : a tobacco pipe made from the root of a brier

¹**bribe** \'brīb\ *n* [ME, something stolen, fr. MF, bread given to a beggar] : something (as money or a favor) given or promised to a person to influence conduct

²**bribe** *vb* **bribed**; **brib·ing** : to corrupt or influence by offering a bribe — **brib·ery** \'brīb-(ə-)rē\ *n*

bric-a-brac \'brik-ə-ˌbrak\ *n pl* [F] : small ornamental articles

¹**brick** \'brik\ *n* : a block molded from moist clay and hardened by heat used esp. for building

²**brick** *vb* : to close, cover, or pave with bricks

brick·bat \'brik-ˌbat\ *n* **1** : a piece of a broken brick esp. when thrown as a missile **2** : an uncomplimentary remark

brick·lay·er \'brik-ˌlā-ər\ *n* : a person who builds or paves with bricks — **brick·lay·ing** \-ˌlā-iŋ\ *n*

¹**brid·al** \'brīd-ᵊl\ *n* [ME *bridale*, fr. OE *brydealu*, fr. *bryd* bride + *ealu* ale] : MARRIAGE, WEDDING

²**bridal** *adj* : of or relating to a bride or a wedding

bride \'brīd\ *n* : a woman just married or about to be married

bride·groom \'brīd-ˌgrüm, -ˌgrum\ *n* : a man just married or about to be married

brides·maid \'brīdz-ˌmād\ *n* : a woman who attends a bride at her wedding

¹**bridge** \'brij\ *n* **1** : a structure built over a depression or obstacle for use as a passageway **2** : something (as the upper part of the nose) resembling a bridge in form or function; *esp* : a platform over the deck of a ship **3** : an artificial replacement for missing teeth

²**bridge** *vb* **bridged**; **bridg·ing** : to build a bridge over — **bridge·able** *adj*

³**bridge** *n* : a card game for four players developed from whist

bridge·head \-ˌhed\ *n* : an advanced position seized in enemy territory as a foothold

bridge·work \-ˌwərk\ *n* : dental bridges

¹**bri·dle** \'brīd-ᵊl\ *n* **1** : headgear with which a horse is controlled **2** : CURB, RESTRAINT

²**bridle** *vb* **bri·dled**; **bri·dling** \'brīd-(ᵊ-)liŋ\ **1** : to put a bridle on; *also* : to restrain with or as if with a bridle **2** : to show hostility or scorn usu. by tossing the head

¹**brief** \'brēf\ *adj* **1** : short in duration or extent **2** : CONCISE; *also* : CURT — **brief·ly** *adv* — **brief·ness** *n*

²**brief** *n* **1** : a concise statement or document; *esp* : one summarizing a law client's case or a legal argument **2** *pl* : short snug underpants

³**brief** *vb* : to give final instructions or essential information to

brief·case \'brēf-ˌkās\ *n* : a flat flexible case for carrying papers

¹**bri·er** *or* **bri·ar** \'brī(-ə)r\ *n* : a plant (as a bramble or rose) with a thorny or prickly woody stem; *also* : a group or mass of brier bushes — **bri·ery** \'brī(-ə)r-ē\ *adj*

²**brier** *or* **briar** *n* : a heath of southern Europe with a root used for making pipes

brig \'brig\ *n* : a 2-masted square-rigged sailing ship

²**brig** *n* : the place of confinement for offenders on a naval ship

³**brig** *abbr* **1** brigade **2** brigadier

bri·gade \brig-'ād\ *n* **1** : a military unit composed of a headquarters, one or more units of infantry or armored forces, and supporting units **2** : a group organized for a particular purpose (as fire-fighting)

brig·a·dier general \ˌbrig-ə-ˌdiər-\ *n* : a commissioned officer (as in the army) ranking next below a major general

brig·and \'brig-ənd\ *n* : BANDIT — **brig·and·age** \-ən-dij\ *n*

brig·an·tine \'brig-ən-,tēn\ *n* : a 2-masted square-rigged ship not carrying a square mainsail

Brig Gen *abbr* brigadier general

bright \'brīt\ *adj* **1** : SHINING, RADIANT **2** : ILLUSTRIOUS, GLORIOUS **3** : INTELLIGENT, CLEVER; *also* : LIVELY, CHEERFUL **syn** brilliant, lustrous, beaming, radiant — **bright·ly** *adv* — **bright·ness** *n*

bright·en \'brīt-ᵊn\ *vb* **bright·ened;** **bright·en·ing** \'brīt-ᵊn-iŋ\ : to make or become bright or brighter — **bright·en·er** \-(ᵊ-)nər\ *n*

¹**bril·liant** \'bril-yənt\ *adj* [F *brillant*, prp. of *briller* to shine, fr. It *brillare*, fr. *brillo* beryl, fr. L *beryllus*] **1** : very bright **2** : STRIKING, DISTINCTIVE **3** : very intelligent **syn** radiant, lustrous, beaming, lucid, bright, lambent — **bril·liance** \-yəns\ *or* **bril·lian·cy** \-yən-sē\ *n* — **bril·liant·ly** *adv*

²**brilliant** *n* : a gem cut in a particular form with many facets

bril·lian·tine \'bril-yən-,tēn\ *n* : a usu. oily dressing for the hair

brim \'brim\ *n* : EDGE, RIM **syn** brink, border, verge, fringe — **brim·less** *adj*

brim·ful \-'fùl\ *adj* : full to the brim

brim·stone \'brim-,stōn\ *n* : SULFUR

brin·dled \'brin-dᵊld\ *adj* : having dark streaks or flecks on a gray or tawny ground ⟨a ~ Great Dane⟩

brine \'brīn\ *n* **1** : water saturated with salt **2** : OCEAN — **brin·i·ness** \'brī-nē-nəs\ *n* — **briny** \'brī-nē\ *adj*

bring \'briŋ\ *vb* **brought** \'brot\; **bring·ing** \'briŋ-iŋ\ **1** : to cause to come with one **2** : INDUCE, PERSUADE, LEAD **3** : PRODUCE, EFFECT **4** : to sell for — **bring·er** *n*

bring about *vb* : to cause to take place : EFFECT

bring up *vb* **1** : to give a parent's fostering care to **2** : to come or bring to a sudden halt **3** : to call to notice **4** : VOMIT

brink \'briŋk\ *n* **1** : an edge at the top of a steep place **2** : the point of onset

brio \'brē-ō\ *n* : VIVACITY, SPIRIT

bri·oche \brē-'ōsh, -'òsh\ *n* [F] : a roll baked from light yeast dough rich with eggs and butter

bri·quette *or* **bri·quet** \brik-'et\ *n* : a compacted often brick-shaped mass of fine material ⟨a charcoal ~⟩

brisk \'brisk\ *adj* **1** : ALERT, LIVELY **2** : INVIGORATING **syn** agile, spry, nimble — **brisk·ly** *adv* — **brisk·ness** *n*

bris·ket \'bris-kət\ *n* : the breast or lower chest of a quadruped

bris·ling *or* **bris·tling** \'briz-liŋ, 'bris-\ *n* : a small sardinelike herring

¹**bris·tle** \'bris-əl\ *n* : a short stiff coarse hair — **bristly** \-(ə-)lē\ *adj*

²**bristle** *vb* **bris·tled; bris·tling** \'bris-(ə-)liŋ\ **1** : to stand stiffly erect **2** : to show angry defiance **3** : to appear as if covered with bristles

Brit *abbr* Britain; British

Bri·tan·nia metal \bri-,tan-yə-, -,tan-ē-ə-\ *n* : a silver-white alloy of tin, antimony, and copper similar to pewter

Bri·tan·nic \bri-'tan-ik\ *adj* : BRITISH

britch·es \'brich-əz\ *n pl* : BREECHES, TROUSERS

Brit·ish \'brit-ish\ *n pl* : the people of Great Britain or the Commonwealth — **British** *adj*

British thermal unit *n* : the quantity of heat needed to raise the temperature of one pound of water one degree Fahrenheit

Brit·on \'brit-ᵊn\ *n* **1** : a member of a people inhabiting Britain before the Anglo-Saxon invasion **2** : a native or inhabitant of Great Britain

brit·tle \'brit-ᵊl\ *adj* **brit·tler** \'brit-(ᵊ-)lər\; **brit·tlest** \-ləst, -ᵊl-əst\ : easily broken or snapped : FRAGILE **syn** crisp, crumbly, friable

bro *abbr* brother

¹**broach** \'brōch\ *n* : a pointed tool

²**broach** *vb* **1** : to pierce (as a cask) in order to draw the contents **2** : to introduce as a topic of conversation

¹**broad** \'brod\ *adj* **1** : WIDE **2** : SPACIOUS **3** : CLEAR, OPEN **4** : OBVIOUS **5** : COARSE, CRUDE ⟨~ stories⟩ **6** : liberal in outlook **7** : GENERAL **8** : dealing with essential points — **broad·ly** *adv* — **broad·ness** *n*

²**broad** *n, slang* : WOMAN

¹**broad·cast** \'brod-,kast\ *vb* **broadcast** *also* **broad·cast·ed; broad·cast·ing** **1** : to scatter or sow broadcast **2** : to make widely known **3** : to transmit a broadcast — **broad·cast·er** *n*

²**broadcast** *adv* : to or over a wide area

³**broadcast** *n* **1** : the transmission of sound or images by radio or television **2** : a single radio or television program

broad·cloth \-,klòth\ *n* **1** : a smooth dense woolen cloth **2** : a fine soft cloth of cotton, silk, or synthetic fiber

broad·en \'brod-ᵊn\ *vb* **broad·ened; broad·en·ing** \'brod-(ᵊ-)niŋ\ : WIDEN

broad·loom \-,lüm\ *adj* : woven on a wide loom esp. in a solid color ⟨a ~ carpet⟩

broad–mind·ed \-'mīn-dəd\ *adj* : free from prejudice — **broad–mind·ed·ly** *adv* — **broad–mind·ed·ness** *n*

broad·side \-,sīd\ *n* **1** : a sheet of paper printed usu. on one side (as an advertisement) **2** : the part of a ship's side above the waterline **3** : all of the guns on one side of a ship; *also* : their simultaneous firing **4** : a volley of abuse or denunciation

broad–spectrum *adj* : having a wide range esp. of effectiveness ⟨~ antibiotics⟩

broad·sword \'brod-,sōrd\ *n* : a broad-bladed sword

broad·tail \-,tāl\ *n* : a flat and wavy fur or skin of a very young or premature karakul lamb

bro·cade \brō-'kād\ *n* : a usu. silk fabric with a raised design

broc·co·li \\'bräk-(ə-)lē\ n [It, pl. of *broc-colo* flowering top of a cabbage, dim. of *brocco* small nail, sprout, fr. L *broccus* projecting] : an open branching cauliflower whose young flowering shoots are used as a vegetable

bro·chette \brō-'shet\ n : SKEWER

bro·chure \brō-'shùr\ n [F, fr. *brocher* to sew, fr. MF, to prick, fr. OF *brochier*, fr. *broche* pointed tool] : PAMPHLET, BOOKLET

bro·gan \'brō-gən, brō-'gan\ n : a heavy shoe; *esp* : a work shoe reaching to the ankle

brogue \'brōg\ n : a dialect or regional pronunciation; *esp* : an Irish accent

broi·der \'bròid-ər\ vb : EMBROIDER — **broi·dery** \'bròid-(ə-)rē\ n

broil \'bròil\ vb : to cook by exposure to radiant heat : GRILL — **broil** n

broil·er \'bròi-lər\ n 1 : a utensil for broiling 2 : a young chicken fit for broiling

¹**broke** \'brōk\ past of BREAK

²**broke** adj : PENNILESS

bro·ken \'brō-kən\ adj 1 : SHATTERED 2 : having gaps or breaks : INTERRUPTED, DISRUPTED 3 : SUBDUED, CRUSHED 4 : BANKRUPT 5 : imperfectly spoken — **bro·ken·ly** adv

bro·ken·heart·ed \,brō-kən-'härt-əd\ adj : overcome by grief or despair

bro·ker \'brō-kər\ n : an agent who negotiates contracts of purchase and sale

bro·ker·age \'brō-k(ə-)rij\ n 1 : the business of a broker 2 : the fee or commission charged by a broker

bro·mide \'brō-,mīd\ n 1 : a compound of bromine and another element or chemical group including some (as potassium bromide) used as sedatives 2 : a trite remark or notion

bro·mid·ic \brō-'mid-ik\ adj : DULL, TIRESOME (~ remarks)

bro·mine \'brō-,mēn\ n [F *brome* bromine, fr. Gk *brōmos* stink] : a deep red liquid corrosive chemical element that gives off an irritating vapor

bronc \'bräŋk\ n : BRONCO

bron·chi·al \'bräŋ-kē-əl\ adj : of, relating to, or affecting the bronchi or their branches

bron·chi·tis \brän-'kīt-əs, bräŋ-\ n : inflammation of the bronchi and their branches — **bron·chit·ic** \-'kit-ik\ adj

bron·chus \'bräŋ-kəs\ n, pl **bron·chi** \'bräŋ-,kī, -,kē\ : either of the main divisions of the windpipe each leading to a lung

bron·co \'bräŋ-kō\ n, pl **broncos** [MexSp, fr. Sp, rough, wild] : an unbroken or partly broken range horse of western No. America; *also* : MUSTANG

bron·to·sau·rus \,bränt-ə-'sòr-əs\ or **bron·to·saur** \'bränt-ə-,sòr\ n [deriv. of Gk *brontē* thunder + *sauros* lizard] : any of various large 4-footed and probably herbivorous dinosaurs

Bronx cheer \'bräŋks-\ n : RASPBERRY 2

¹**bronze** \'bränz\ vb **bronzed; bronz·ing** : to give the appearance of bronze to

²**bronze** n 1 : an alloy of copper and tin and sometimes other elements; *also* : something made of bronze 2 : a yellowish brown color — **bronzy** \'brän-zē\ adj

brooch \'brōch, 'brüch\ n : an ornamental clasp or pin

¹**brood** \'brüd\ n : a family of young animals or children and esp. of birds

²**brood** vb 1 : to sit on eggs to hatch them; *also* : to shelter (hatched young) with the wings 2 : to think anxiously or gloomily about something : PONDER

³**brood** adj : kept for breeding (a ~ mare)

brood·er \'brüd-ər\ n 1 : one that broods 2 : a heated structure for raising young birds

¹**brook** \'brük\ vb : TOLERATE, BEAR

²**brook** n : a small natural stream of water

brook·let \-lət\ n : a small brook

brook trout n : a common speckled cold-water char of eastern No. America

broom \'brüm, 'brùm\ n 1 : any of several shrubs of the legume family with long slender branches and usu. yellow flowers 2 : an implement for sweeping orig. made from twigs — **broom·stick** \-,stik\ n

bros abbr brothers

broth \'bròth\ n, pl **broths** \'bròths, 'bròthz\ 1 : liquid in which meat or sometimes vegetable food has been cooked 2 : a fluid culture medium

broth·el \'bräth-əl, 'bròth-\ n : an establishment where prostitutes are available

broth·er \'brəth-ər\ n, pl **brothers** also **breth·ren** \'breth-(ə-)rən, 'breth-ərn\ 1 : a male having one or both parents in common with another individual; *also* : KINSMAN 2 : a kindred human being 3 : a man who is a religious but not a priest — **broth·er·li·ness** \-lē-nəs\ n — **broth·er·ly** \-lē\ adj

broth·er·hood \'brəth-ər-,hùd\ n 1 : the state of being brothers or a brother 2 : ASSOCIATION, FRATERNITY 3 : the whole body of persons in a business or profession

broth·er-in-law \'brəth-(ə-)rən-,lò, 'brəth-ərn-,lò\ n, pl **brothers-in-law** \'brəth-ərz-ən-\ : the brother of one's spouse; *also* : the husband of one's sister or of one's spouse's sister

brough·am \'brü-(ə)m, 'brō-(ə)m\ n 1 : a light closed horse-drawn carriage with the driver outside in front 2 : COUPÉ 2 3 : a sedan having no roof over the driver's seat

brought past and past part of BRING

brou·ha·ha \'brü-,hä-,hä\ n : HUBBUB, UPROAR

brow \'braù\ n 1 : the eyebrow or the ridge on which it grows; *also* : FORE-

HEAD 2 : the projecting upper part of a steep place

brow·beat \'brau̇-ˌbēt\ *vb* **-beat; -beat-en** \-ˌbēt-ᵊn\ *or* **-beat; -beat·ing** : to intimidate by sternness or arrogance : BULLY **syn** intimidate, hector

¹brown \'brau̇n\ *adj* : of the color brown; *also* : of dark or tanned complexion

²brown *n* : a color like that of coffee or chocolate that is a blend of red and yellow darkened by black — **brown·ish** *adj*

³brown *vb* 1 : to make or become brown

brown bag·ging \-'bag-iŋ\ *n* : the practice of carrying one's lunch usu. in a brown bag — **brown bag·ger** \-'bag-ər\ *n*

brown·ie \'brau̇-nē\ *n* 1 : a legendary cheerful elf who performs good deeds at night 2 *cap* : a member of the Girl Scouts from 6 through 8 years of age

brown-out \'brau̇n-ˌau̇t\ *n* : a curtailment in electrical power; *also* : a period of reduced illumination due to such curtailment

brown rice *n* : hulled but unpolished rice that retains most of the bran layers

brown·stone \'brau̇n-ˌstōn\ *n* : a dwelling faced with reddish brown sandstone

¹browse \'brau̇z\ *vb* **browsed; brows·ing** 1 : to feed on browse; *also* : GRAZE 2 : to read bits at random in a book or collection of books

²browse *n* : tender shoots, twigs, and leaves fit for food for cattle

bru·in \'brü-ən\ *n* : BEAR

¹bruise \'brüz\ *vb* **bruised; bruis·ing** 1 : to inflict a bruise on; *also* : to become bruised 2 : to break down by pounding (~ garlic for a salad)

²bruise *n* : a surface injury to flesh : CONTUSION

bruis·er \'brü-zər\ *n* : a big husky man

bruit \'brüt\ *vb* : to noise abroad

brunch \'brənch\ *n* : a meal that combines a late breakfast and an early lunch

bru·net *or* **bru·nette** \brü-'net\ *adj* [F *brunet*, masc., *brunette*, fem., brownish, fr. OF, fr. *brun* brown] : of dark or relatively dark pigmentation; *esp* : having brown or black hair and eyes — **brunet** *or* **brunette** *n*

brunt \'brənt\ *n* : the main shock, force, or stress esp. of an attack

¹brush \'brəsh\ *n* 1 : BRUSHWOOD 2 : scrub vegetation or land covered with it

²brush *n* 1 : a device composed of bristles set in a handle and used esp. for cleaning or painting 2 : a bushy tail (as of a fox) 3 : an electrical conductor that makes contact between a stationary and a moving part of a generator or motor 4 : a light rubbing or touching

³brush *vb* 1 : to treat (as in cleaning or painting) with a brush 2 : to remove

with or as if with a brush; *also* : to dispose of in an offhand manner 3 : to touch gently in passing

⁴brush *n* : SKIRMISH **syn** encounter, run-in

brush-off \'brəsh-ˌȯf\ *n* : an abrupt or offhand dismissal

brush up *vb* : to renew one's skill

brush·wood \'brəsh-ˌwu̇d\ *n* 1 : small branches lopped from trees or shrubs 2 : a thicket of shrubs and small trees

brusque \'brəsk\ *adj* [F *brusque*, fr. It *brusco*, fr. ML *bruscus* a plant with stiff twigs used for brooms] : CURT, BLUNT, ABRUPT **syn** gruff, bluff, crusty, short — **brusque·ly** *adv*

brus·sels sprout \ˌbrəs-əl(z)-\ *n*, *often cap B* : one of the edible small heads borne on the stalk of a cabbagelike plant; *also*, *pl* : this plant

bru·tal \'brüt-ᵊl\ *adj* 1 : resembling or befitting a brute (as in coarseness or cruelty) 2 : HARSH, SEVERE (~ weather) — **bru·tal·i·ty** \brü-'tal-ət-ē\ *n* — **bru·tal·ly** \'brüt-ᵊl-ē\ *adv*

bru·tal·ize \'brüt-ᵊl-ˌīz\ *vb* **-ized; -iz·ing** 1 : to make brutal 2 : to treat brutally

¹brute \'brüt\ *adj* [ME, fr. MF *brut* rough, fr. L *brutus* stupid, lit., heavy] 1 : of, relating to, or typical of beasts 2 : BRUTAL 3 : UNREASONING; *also* : purely physical

²brute *n* 1 : BEAST 1 2 : a brutal person **syn** animal, creature

brut·ish \'brüt-ish\ *adj* 1 : BRUTE 1 2 : stupidly cruel or sensual; *also* : UNREASONING

BS *abbr* bachelor of science

BSA *abbr* Boy Scouts of America

BSc *abbr* bachelor of science

bskt *abbr* basket

Bt *abbr* baronet

btry *abbr* battery

Btu *abbr* British thermal unit

bu *abbr* bushel

¹bub·ble \'bəb-əl\ *n* 1 : a globule of gas in a liquid 2 : a thin film of liquid filled with gas 3 : something lacking firmness or solidity — **bub·bly** \-(ə-)lē\ *adj*

²bubble *vb* **bub·bled; bub·bling** \'bəb-(ə-)liŋ\ : to form, rise in, or give off bubbles

bu·bo \'b(y)ü-bō\ *n*, *pl* **buboes** : an inflammatory swelling of a lymph gland

bu·bon·ic plague \b(y)ü-ˌbän-ik-\ *n* : a plague caused by a bacterium transmitted to human beings by flea bites and by buboes usu. in the groin

buc·ca·neer \ˌbək-ə-'niər\ *n* : PIRATE

¹buck \'bək\ *n*, *pl* **bucks** 1 *or pl* **buck** : a male animal (as a deer or antelope) 2 : DANDY 3 : DOLLAR

²buck *vb* 1 : to spring with a quick plunging leap (a ~ing horse) 2 : to charge against something; *also* : to strive for advancement sometimes without regard to ethical behavior

buck·board \-ˌbȯrd\ *n* : a 4-wheeled vehicle with a floor of long springy boards

buck·et \'bək-ət\ *n* 1 : PAIL 2 : an object resembling a bucket in collecting, scooping, or carrying something — **buck·et·ful** *n*

bucket seat *n* : a low separate seat for one person (as in an automobile)

buck·eye \'bək-ˌī\ *n* : a tree related to the horse chestnut that occurs chiefly in the central U.S.; *also* : its large nut-like seed

buck fever *n* : nervous excitement of an inexperienced hunter at the sight of game

¹buck·le \'bək-əl\ *n* : a clasp (as on a belt) for two loose ends

²buckle *vb* **buck·led; buck·ling** \'bək-(ə-)liŋ\ 1 : to fasten with a buckle 2 : to apply oneself with vigor 3 : to crumple up : BEND, COLLAPSE

³buckle *n* : BEND, FOLD, KINK

buck·ler \'bək-lər\ *n* : SHIELD

buck·ram \'bək-rəm\ *n* : a coarse stiff cloth used esp. for binding books

buck·saw \'bək-ˌsȯ\ *n* : a saw set in a usu. H-shaped frame and used for sawing wood

buck·shot \'bək-ˌshät\ *n* : lead shot that is from .24 to .33 inch (about 6.1 to 8.4 millimeters) in diameter

buck·skin \-ˌskin\ *n* 1 : the skin of a buck 2 : a soft usu. suede-finished leather — **buckskin** *adj*

buck·tooth \-'tüth\ *n* : a large projecting front tooth — **buck-toothed** \-'tütht\ *adj*

buck·wheat \-ˌhwēt\ *n* : either of two plants grown for their triangular seeds which are used as a cereal grain; *also* : these seeds

bu·col·ic \byü-'käl-ik\ *adj* [L *bucolicus,* fr. Gk *boukolikos,* fr. *boukolos* one who tends cattle, fr. *bous* head of cattle + *-kolos* (akin to L *colere* to cultivate)] : RURAL, RUSTIC

¹bud \'bəd\ *n* 1 : an undeveloped plant shoot (as of a leaf or a flower); *also* : a partly opened flower 2 : an asexual reproductive structure 3 : something not yet mature

²bud *vb* **bud·ded; bud·ding** 1 : to form or put forth buds; *also* : to reproduce by asexual buds 2 : to be or develop like a bud 3 : to propagate a desired variety (as of peach) by inserting a bud in a plant of a different variety

Bud·dhism \'bü-ˌdiz-əm, 'bu̇d-ˌiz-\ *n* : a religion of eastern and central Asia growing out of the teachings of Gautama Buddha — **Bud·dhist** \'büd-əst, 'bu̇d-\ *n or adj*

bud·dy \'bəd-ē\ *n, pl* **buddies** : COMPANION; *esp* : a fellow soldier

budge \'bəj\ *vb* **budged; budg·ing** : MOVE, STIR, SHIFT

bud·ger·i·gar \'bəj-(ə-)rē-ˌgär, ˌbəj-ə-'rē-\ *n* : a small brightly colored Australian parrot often kept as a pet

¹bud·get \'bəj-ət\ *n* [ME *bowgette,* fr. MF *bougette,* dim. of *bouge* leather bag, fr. L *bulga*] 1 : STOCK, SUPPLY 2 : a financial report containing estimates of income and expenses; *also* : a plan for coordinating income and expenses

²budget *vb* 1 : to allow for in a budget 2 : to draw up a budget

³budget *adj* : INEXPENSIVE

bud·gie \'bəj-ē\ *n* : BUDGERIGAR

¹buff \'bəf\ *n* 1 : a dull yellow-orange color 2 : FAN, ENTHUSIAST

²buff *adj* : of the color buff

buff *vb* : POLISH, SHINE

buf·fa·lo \'bəf-ə-ˌlō\ *n, pl* **-lo** *or* **-loes** *also* **-los** 1 : WATER BUFFALO 2 : a large shaggy-maned No. American wild bovine mammal with short horns and heavy forequarters with a large muscular hump

buf·fer \'bəf-ər\ *n* : something that lessens shock (as from a physical or financial blow)

²buffer *n* : one that buffs

¹buf·fet \'bəf-ət\ *n* : BLOW, SLAP

²buffet *vb* 1 : to strike with the hand; *also* : to pound repeatedly 2 : to struggle against or on *syn* beat, batter, drub, pummel, thrash

³buf·fet \(ˌ)bə-'fā, bü-\ *n* 1 : SIDEBOARD 2 : a counter for refreshments; *also* : a meal at which people serve themselves (as from a buffet)

buff leather *n* : a strong supple oil-tanned leather

buf·foon \(ˌ)bə-'fün\ *n* [MF *bouffon,* fr. It *buffone,* fr. ML *bufon-, bufo,* fr. L *bufo* toad] : CLOWN 2 *syn* fool, jester — **buf·foon·ery** \-(ə-)rē\ *n*

¹bug \'bəg\ *n* 1 : an insect or other creeping or crawling invertebrate animal; *esp* : an insect pest (as a bedbug) 2 : any of an order of insects with sucking mouthparts and incomplete metamorphosis that includes many plant pests 3 : an unexpected mistake or imperfection (a ~ in a computer program) 4 : a disease-producing germ; *also* : a disease caused by it 5 : a concealed listening device

²bug *vb* **bugged; bug·ging** 1 : BOTHER, ANNOY 2 : to plant a concealed microphone in

bug·a·boo \'bəg-ə-ˌbü\ *n, pl* **-boos** : BOGEY 1

bug·bear \'bəg-ˌba͟ər\ *n* : BOGEY 1; *also* : a source of dread

bug·gy \'bəg-ē\ *n, pl* **buggies** : a light carriage

bu·gle \'byü-gəl\ *n* [ME, buffalo, instrument made of buffalo horn, bugle, fr. OF, fr. L *buculus,* dim. of *bos* head of cattle] : a valveless brass wind instrument resembling a trumpet and used esp. for military calls — **bu·gler** \-glər\ *n*

build \'bild\ *vb* **built** \'bilt\; **build·ing** 1 : to form or have formed by ordering and uniting materials (~ a house); *also* : to bring into being or develop 2 : to produce or create gradually (~ an argument on facts) 3 : INCREASE, ENLARGE; *also* : ENHANCE 4 : to engage in building — **build·er** *n*

²**build** *n* : form or mode of structure; *esp* : PHYSIQUE

build·ing \'bil-diŋ\ *n* **1** : a usu. roofed and walled structure (as a house) for permanent use **2** : the art or business of constructing buildings

build-up \'bild-,əp\ *n* : the act or process of building up; *also* : something produced by this

built-in \'bil-'tin\ *adj* **1** : forming an integral part of a structure **2** : INHERENT

bulb \'bəlb\ *n* **1** : an underground resting stage of a plant (as a lily or an onion) consisting of a short stem base bearing one or more buds enclosed in overlapping leaves; *also* : a fleshy plant structure (as a tuber) resembling a bulb **2** : a plant having or growing from a bulb **3** : a rounded more or less bulb-shaped object or part (as for an electric lamp) — **bul·bous** \'bəl-bəs\ *adj*

Bul·gar·i·an \,bəl-'gar-ē-ən, bùl-\ *n* : a native or inhabitant of Bulgaria — **Bulgarian** *adj*

¹**bulge** \'bəlj\ *vb* **bulged; bulg·ing** : to become or cause to become protuberant

²**bulge** *n* : a swelling projecting part

bu·li·mia \b(y)ü-'lim-ē-ə, -'lēm-\ *n* : an abnormal and constant craving for food — **bu·lim·ic** \-'lim-ik\ *adj or n*

¹**bulk** \'bəlk\ *n* **1** : MAGNITUDE, VOLUME **2** : material (as indigestible fibrous residues of food) that forms a mass in the intestine **3** : a large mass **4** : the major portion

²**bulk** *vb* **1** : to have a bulky appearance **2** : to appear as a factor : LOOM

bulk·head \'bəlk-,hed\ *n* **1** : a partition separating compartments **2** : a structure built to cover a shaft or a cellar stairway

bulky \'bəl-kē\ *adj* **bulk·i·er; -est** : having bulk; *esp* : being large and unwieldy

¹**bull** \'bùl\ *n* **1** : the adult male of a bovine animal; *also* : a usu. adult male of various other large animals (as the elephant or walrus) **2** : one who buys securities or commodities in expectation of a price increase — **bullish** *adj*

²**bull** *adj* **1** : MALE **2** : large of its kind **3** : RISING (a ~ market)

³**bull** *n* [ME *bulle*, fr. ML *bulla*, fr. L *bulla* bubble, amulet] : a papal letter

⁴**bull** *n, slang* : NONSENSE

⁵**bull** *abbr* bulletin

¹**bull·dog** \'bùl-,dóg\ *n* : any of a breed of compact muscular short-haired dogs of English origin

²**bulldog** *vb* : to throw (a steer) by seizing the horns and twisting the neck

bull·doze \-,dōz\ *vb* **1** : to move, clear, or level with a tractor-driven machine (**bull·doz·er**) having a broad blade for pushing **2** : to force as if by using a bulldozer

bul·let \'bùl-ət\ *n* [MF *boulette* small ball & *boulet* missile, dims. of *boule*

ball] : a missile to be shot from a firearm — **bul·let·proof** \,bùl-ət-'prüf\ *adj*

bul·le·tin \'bùl-ət-ʔn\ *n* **1** : a brief public report intended for immediate release on a matter of public interest **2** : a periodical publication (as of a college) — **bulletin** *vb*

bull·fight \'bùl-,fīt\ *n* : a spectacle in which people ceremonially fight with and usu. kill bulls in an arena — **bullfight·er** *n*

bull·frog \-,frȯg, -,fräg\ *n* : FROG; *esp* : a large deep-voiced frog

bull·head \-,hed\ *n* : any of several common freshwater catfishes of the U.S.

bull·head·ed \-'hed-əd\ *adj* : stupidly stubborn : HEADSTRONG

bul·lion \'bùl-yən\ *n* : gold or silver esp. in bars or ingots

bull·ock \'bùl-ək\ *n* : a young bull: *also* : STEER

bull pen *n* : a place on a baseball field where relief pitchers warm up; *also* : the relief pitchers of a baseball team

bull session *n* : an informal discussion

bull's-eye \'bùl-,zī\ *n, pl* **bull's-eyes** : the center of a target; *also* : a shot that hits the bull's-eye

¹**bul·ly** \'bùl-ē\ *n, pl* **bullies** : a person habitually cruel to others who are weaker

²**bully** *adj* : EXCELLENT, FIRST-RATE — often used interjectionally

³**bully** *vb* **bul·lied; bul·ly·ing** : to behave as a bully toward : DOMINEER **syn** browbeat, intimidate, hector

bul·rush \'bùl-,rəsh\ *n* : any of several large rushes or sedges of wetlands

bul·wark \'bùl-(,)wərk, -,wȯrk; 'bəl-(,)wərk\ *n* **1** : a wall-like defensive structure **2** : a strong support or protection in danger

¹**bum** \'bəm\ *adj* **1** : WORTHLESS (~ advice) **2** : DISABLED (a ~ knee)

²**bum** *vb* **bummed; bum·ming 1** : to wander as a tramp; *also* : LOAF **2** : to seek or gain by begging

³**bum** *n* : an idle worthless fellow : LOAFER

bum·ble·bee \'bəm-bəl-,bē\ *n* : any of numerous large hairy social bees

bum·mer \'bəm-ər\ *n* : an unpleasant experience

¹**bump** \'bəmp\ *n* **1** : a local bulge; *esp* : a swelling of tissue **2** : a sudden forceful blow or impact — **bumpy** *adj*

²**bump** *vb* **1** : to strike or knock forcibly; *also* : to move or alter by bumping **2** : to collide with

¹**bum·per** \'bəm-pər\ *n* **1** : a cup or glass filled to the brim **2** : something unusually large — **bumper** *adj*

²**bump·er** \'bəm-pər\ *n* : a device for absorbing shock or preventing damage; *esp* : a metal bar at either end of an automobile

bump·kin \'bəmp-kən\ *n* : an awkward and unsophisticated country person

bump·tious \'bəmp-shəs\ *adj* : obtusely and often noisily self-assertive

bun \'bən\ *n* : a sweet biscuit or roll

¹**bunch** \'bənch\ *n* **1** : SWELLING **2** : CLUSTER, GROUP — **bunchy** *adj*

²**bunch** *vb* : to form into a group or bunch

bun·co *or* **bun·ko** \'bəŋ-kō\ *n, pl* **buncos** *or* **bunkos** : a swindling scheme — **bunco** *vb*

¹**bun·dle** \'bən-d°l\ *n* **1** : several items bunched and fastened together; *also* : something wrapped for carrying **2** : a considerable amount : LOT **3** : a small group esp. of mostly parallel nerve or muscle fibers

²**bundle** *vb* **bun·dled; bun·dling** \'bənd-(ə-)liŋ\ : to gather or tie in a bundle

bun·dling \'bənd-(ə-)liŋ\ *n* : a former custom of a courting couple's occupying the same bed without undressing

bung \'bəŋ\ *n* : the stopper in the bunghole of a cask

bun·ga·low \'bəŋ-gə-ˌlō\ *n* : a one-storied house with a low-pitched roof

bung·hole \'bəŋ-ˌhōl\ *n* : a hole for emptying or filling a cask

bun·gle \'bəŋ-gəl\ *vb* **bun·gled; bun·gling** \-g(ə-)liŋ\ : to do badly : BOTCH — **bungle** *n* — **bun·gler** \-g(ə-)lər\ *n*

bun·ion \'bən-yən\ *n* : an inflamed swelling of the first joint of the big toe

¹**bunk** \'bəŋk\ *n* : BED; *esp* : a built-in bed that is often one of a tier

²**bunk** *n* : BUNKUM, NONSENSE

bun·ker \'bəŋ-kər\ *n* **1** : a bin or compartment for storage (as for coal on a ship) **2** : a protective embankment or dugout **3** : a sand trap or embankment constituting a hazard on a golf course

bun·kum *or* **bun·combe** \'bəŋ-kəm\ *n* [*Buncombe* County, N.C.; fr. the defense of a seemingly irrelevant speech made by its congressional representative that he was speaking to Buncombe] : insincere or foolish talk

bun·ny \'bən-ē\ *n, pl* **-nies** : RABBIT

Bun·sen burner \'bən-sən-\ *n* : a gas burner usu. consisting of a straight tube with air holes at the bottom

¹**bunt** \'bənt\ *vb* **1** : BUTT **2** : to push or tap a baseball lightly without swinging the bat

²**bunt** *n* : an act or instance of bunting; *also* : a bunted ball

¹**bun·ting** \'bənt-iŋ\ *n* : any of numerous small stout-billed finches

²**bunting** *n* : a thin fabric used esp. for flags; *also* : FLAGS

¹**buoy** \'bü-ē, 'boi\ *n* **1** : a floating object anchored in water to mark something (as a channel, shoal, or rock) **2** : a float consisting of a ring of buoyant material to support a person who has fallen into the water

²**buoy** *vb* **1** : to mark by a buoy **2** : to keep afloat **3** : to raise the spirits of

buoy·an·cy \'bȯi-ən-sē, 'bü-yən-\ *n* **1** : the tendency of a body to float or rise when submerged in a fluid **2** : the power of a fluid to exert an upward force on a body placed in it **3** : resilience of spirit — **buoy·ant** \-ənt, -yənt\ *adj*

¹**bur** \'bər\ *var of* BURR

²**bur** *abbr* bureau

¹**bur·den** \'bərd-³n\ *n* **1** : LOAD; *also* : CARE, RESPONSIBILITY **2** : something oppressive : ENCUMBRANCE **3** : CARGO; *also* : capacity for cargo

²**burden** *vb* **bur·dened; bur·den·ing** \'bərd-(ə-)niŋ\ : LOAD, OPPRESS — **bur·den·some** \-səm\ *adj*

³**burden** *n* **1** : REFRAIN, CHORUS **2** : a main theme or idea : GIST

bur·dock \'bər-ˌdäk\ *n* : any of a genus of coarse composite herbs with globe-shaped flower heads surrounded by prickly bracts

bu·reau \'byur-ō\ *n, pl* **bureaus** *also* **bu·reaux** \-ōz\ [F, desk, cloth covering for desks, fr. OF *burel* woolen cloth, fr. L *burra* shaggy cloth] **1** : a chest of drawers for bedroom use **2** : an administrative unit (as of a government department) **3** : a branch of a publication or wire service in an important news center

bu·reau·cra·cy \byu-'räk-rə-sē\ *n, pl* **-cies** **1** : a body of appointive government officials **2** : administration characterized by specialization of functions under fixed rules and a hierarchy of authority; *also* : an unwieldy administrative system deficient in initiative and flexibility — **bu·reau·crat** \'byur-ə-ˌkrat\ *n* — **bu·reau·crat·ic** \ˌbyur-ə-'krat-ik\ *adj*

bur·geon \'bər-jən\ *vb* : to put forth fresh growth (as from buds) : grow vigorously : FLOURISH

bur·gess \'bər-jəs\ *n* **1** : a citizen of a borough **2** : an official or representative usu. of a borough

burgh \'bər-ō\ *n* : a Scottish town

bur·gher \'bər-gər\ *n* **1** : TOWNSMAN **2** : a prosperous solid citizen

bur·glary \'bər-glə-rē\ *n, pl* **-glar·ies** : forcible entry into a building and esp. a dwelling with intent to steal — **bur·glar** \-glər\ *n* — **bur·glar·ize** \'bər-glə-ˌrīz\ *vb*

bur·gle \'bər-gəl\ *vb* **bur·gled; bur·gling** \-g(ə-)liŋ\ : to commit burglary on

bur·go·mas·ter \'bər-gə-ˌmas-tər\ *n* : the chief magistrate of a town in some European countries

Bur·gun·dy \'bər-gən-dē\ *n, pl* **-dies** : a red or white table wine

buri·al \'ber-ē-əl\ *n* : the act or process of burying

burl \'bərl\ *n* : a hard woody often flattened hemispherical outgrowth on a tree

bur·lap \'bər-ˌlap\ *n* : a coarse fabric usu. of jute or hemp used esp. for bags

¹**bur·lesque** \(ˌ)bər-'lesk\ *n* [*burlesque*, adj. (comic, droll), fr. F, fr. It *burlesco*, fr. *burla* joke, fr. Sp] **1** : a witty or derisive literary or dramatic imitation **2** : broadly humorous theatrical entertainment consisting of several items (as songs, skits, or dances)

²**burlesque** *vb* **bur·lesqued; bur·lesqu·ing**
: to make ludicrous by burlesque
: MOCK **syn** caricature, parody, travesty

bur·ly \'bər-lē\ *adj* **bur·li·er; -est**
: strongly and heavily built : HUSKY
syn muscular, brawny, beefy, hefty

Bur·mese \,bər-'mēz, -'mēs\ *n, pl*
Burmese : a native or inhabitant of
Burma — **Burmese** *adj*

¹**burn** \'bərn\ *vb* **burned** \'bərnd, 'bərnt\
or **burnt** \'bərnt\; **burn·ing** 1 : to be
on fire 2 : to feel or look as if on fire
3 : to alter or become altered by or as
if by the action of fire or heat 4 : to
use as fuel (~ coal) ; *also* : to destroy
by fire (~ trash) 5 : to cause or make
by fire (~ a hole) ; *also* : to affect as
if by heat

²**burn** *n* : an injury or effect produced by
or as if by burning

burn·er \'bər-nər\ *n* : the part of a
fuel-burning or heat-producing device
where the flame or heat is produced

bur·nish \'bər-nish\ *vb* : to make shiny
esp. by rubbing : POLISH — **bur·nish·er**
n — **bur·nish·ing** *adj or n*

bur·noose *or* **bur·nous** \(,)bər-'nüs\ *n*
: a hooded cloak worn esp. by Arabs

burn·out \'bər-,naut\ *n* 1 : the cessation of operation of a jet or rocket
engine 2 : exhaustion of one's physical or emotional strength

burp \'bərp\ *n* : an act of belching —
burp *vb*

burp gun *n* : a small submachine gun

burr \'bər\ *n* 1 *usu* **bur** : a rough or
prickly envelope of a fruit: *also* : a
plant that bears burs 2 : roughness
left in cutting or shaping metal 3
: WHIR — **bur·ry** *adj*

bur·ri·to \bə-'rēt-ō\ *n* [AmerSp. fr. Sp.
lit., little donkey, dim. of *burro*] : a
flour tortilla rolled around a filling and
baked

bur·ro \'bər-ō, 'bur-\ *n, pl* **burros** [Sp]
: a usu. small donkey

¹**bur·row** \'bər-ō\ *n* : a hole in the
ground made by an animal (as a rabbit)

²**burrow** *vb* 1 : to form by tunneling (~
a way through the snow) ; *also* : to
make a burrow 2 : to progress by or as
if by digging — **bur·row·er** *n*

bur·sar \'bər-sər\ *n* : a treasurer esp. of
a college

bur·si·tis \(,)bər-'sīt-əs\ *n* : inflamma-
tion of the serous sac (**bur·sa** \'bər-
sə\) of a joint (as the elbow or shoulder)

¹**burst** \'bərst\ *vb* **burst** *or* **burst·ed**;
burst·ing 1 : to fly apart or into pieces
2 : to show one's feelings suddenly;
also : PLUNGE (~ into song) 3 : to enter or emerge suddenly : SPRING 4 : to
be filled to the breaking point

²**burst** *n* 1 : a sudden outbreak or effort
: SPURT 2 : EXPLOSION 3 : an act or result of bursting

Bu·run·di·an \bü-'rün-dē-ən\ *n* : a native or inhabitant of Burundi

bury \'ber-ē\ *vb* **bur·ied; bury·ing** 1 : to
deposit in the earth; *also* : to inter
with funeral ceremonies 2 : CONCEAL,
HIDE

¹**bus** \'bəs\ *n, pl* **bus·es** *or* **bus·ses** [short
for *omnibus*, fr. F, fr. L, for all, dat.
pl. of *omnis* all] : a large motor-driven
passenger vehicle

²**bus** *vb* **bused** *or* **bussed; bus·ing** *or* **bus-
sing** 1 : to travel or transport by bus 2
: to work as a busboy

³**bus** *abbr* business

bus·boy \'bəs-,böi\ *n* : a waiter's helper

bus·by \'bəz-bē\ *n, pl* **busbies** : a military full-dress fur hat

bush \'bush\ *n* 1 : SHRUB 2 : rough un-
cleared country 3 : a thick tuft or mat
— **bushy** *adj*

bushed \'busht\ *adj* : TIRED, EXHAUSTED

bush·el \'bush-əl\ *n* — see WEIGHT table

bush·ing \'bush-iŋ\ *n* : a usu. removable cylindrical lining in an opening of
a mechanical part to limit the size of
the opening, resist wear (as in a bearing for an axle), or serve as a guide

bush·mas·ter \'bush-,mas-tər\ *n* : a
large venomous tropical American
snake

bush·whack \-,hwak\ *vb* 1 : to live or
hide out in the woods 2 : AMBUSH —
bush·whack·er *n*

busi·ly \'biz-ə-lē\ *adv* : in a busy manner

busi·ness \'biz-nəs, -nəz\ *n* 1 : OCCUPA-
TION, CALLING; *also* : TASK, MISSION 2
: a commercial or industrial enterprise; *also* : TRADE (~ is good) 3 : AF-
FAIR, MATTER 4 : personal concerns
syn commerce, industry, trade, traffic

busi·ness·man \-,man\ *n* : a man engaged in business esp. as an executive

busi·ness·per·son \-,pərs-²n\ *n* : a businessman or businesswoman

busi·ness·wom·an \-,wum-ən\ *n* : a
woman engaged in business esp. as an
executive

bus·kin \'bəs-kən\ *n* 1 : a laced boot
reaching halfway to the knee 2 : tragic drama

buss \'bəs\ *n* : KISS — **buss** *vb*

¹**bust** \'bəst\ *n* [F *buste*, fr. It *busto*, fr.
L *bustum* tomb] 1 : sculpture representing the upper part of the human
figure 2 : the part of the human torso
between the neck and the waist; *esp*
: the breasts of a woman

²**bust** *vb* **bust·ed** *also* **bust; bust·ing** 1
: BREAK, SMASH; *also* : BURST 2 : to
ruin financially 3 : DEMOTE 4 : TAME 5
slang : ARREST

³**bust** *n* 1 : a drinking session 2 : a complete failure : FLOP 3 : a business
depression 4 : PUNCH, SOCK 5 *slang* : a
police raid

¹**bus·tle** \'bəs-əl\ *vb* **bus·tled; bus·tling**
\'bəs-(ə-)liŋ\ : to move or work in a
brisk fussy way

²**bustle** *n* : briskly energetic activity

³**bustle** *n* : a pad or frame formerly worn
to swell out the fullness at the back of
a woman's skirt

¹**busy** \ˈbiz-ē\ *adj* **bus·i·er; -est 1** : engaged in action : not idle **2** : being in use ⟨∼ telephones⟩ **3** : full of activity ⟨∼ streets⟩ **4** : OFFICIOUS **syn** employed, engaged, occupied

²**busy** *vb* **bus·ied; busy·ing** : to make or keep busy : OCCUPY

busy·body \ˈbiz-ē-ˌbäd-ē\ *n* : MEDDLER

busy·work \-ˌwərk\ *n* : work that appears productive but only keeps one occupied

¹**but** \(ˈ)bət\ *conj* **1** : except for the fact ⟨would have protested ∼ that he was afraid⟩ **2** : as to the following, namely ⟨there's no doubt ∼ he's the guilty one⟩ **3** : without the concomitant that ⟨never rains ∼ it pours⟩ **4** : on the contrary ⟨not one, ∼ two job offers⟩ **5** : yet nevertheless ⟨would like to go, ∼ I can't⟩; *also* : while on the contrary ⟨would like to go ∼ he is busy⟩ **6** : yet also ⟨came home sadder ∼ wiser⟩ ⟨poor ∼ proud⟩

²**but** *prep* : other than : EXCEPT ⟨there's no one here ∼ me⟩

bu·tane \ˈbyü-ˌtān\ *n* : either of two gaseous hydrocarbons used as a fuel

¹**butch·er** \ˈbuċh-ər\ *n* [ME *bocher*, fr. OF *bouchier*, fr. *bouc* he-goat] **1** : one who slaughters animals or dresses their flesh; *also* : a dealer in meat **2** : one that kills brutally or needlessly — **butch·ery** \-(ə-)rē\ *n*

²**butcher** *vb* **butch·ered; butch·er·ing** \-(ə-)riŋ\ **1** : to slaughter and dress for meat ⟨∼ hogs⟩ **2** : to kill barbarously

but·ler \ˈbət-lər\ *n* [ME *buteler*, fr. OF *bouteillier* bottle bearer, fr. *bouteille* bottle] : the chief male servant of a household

¹**butt** \ˈbət\ *vb* : to strike with the head or horns

²**butt** *n* : a blow or thrust with the head or horns

³**butt** *n* : a large cask

⁴**butt** *n* **1** : TARGET **2** : an object of abuse or ridicule

⁵**butt** *n* : a large, thicker, or bottom end of something

⁶**butt** *vb* **1** : ABUT **2** : to place or join edge to edge without overlapping

butte \ˈbyüt\ *n* : an isolated steep-sided hill

¹**but·ter** \ˈbət-ər\ *n* [ME, fr. OE *butere*, fr. L *butyrum* butter, fr. Gk *boutyron*, fr. *bous* cow + *tyros* cheese] **1** : a solid edible emulsion of fat obtained from cream by churning **2** : a substance resembling butter — **but·tery** *adj*

²**butter** *vb* : to spread with butter

but·ter-and-eggs \ˌbət-ə-rə-ˈnegz\ *n sing or pl* : a common perennial herb related to the snapdragon that has showy yellow and orange flowers

but·ter·cup \ˈbət-ər-ˌkəp\ *n* : any of a genus of herbs usu. having yellow flowers with five petals and sepals

but·ter·fat \-ˌfat\ *n* : the natural fat of milk and chief constituent of butter

but·ter·fin·gered \-ˌfiŋ-gərd\ *adj* : likely to let things fall or slip through the fingers — **but·ter·fin·gers** \-gərz\ *n sing or pl*

but·ter·fly \-ˌflī\ *n* : any of a group of slender day-flying insects with four broad wings covered with bright-colored scales

but·ter·milk \-ˌmilk\ *n* : the liquid remaining after butter is churned

but·ter·nut \-ˌnət\ *n* : the edible oily nut of an American tree related to the walnut; *also* : this tree

but·ter·scotch \-ˌskäch\ *n* : a candy made from brown sugar, corn syrup, and water; *also* : the flavor of such candy

but·tock \ˈbət-ək\ *n* **1** : the back of a hip that forms one of the fleshy parts on which a person sits **2** *pl* : the seat of the body : RUMP

¹**but·ton** \ˈbət-ᵊn\ *n* **1** : a small knob secured to an article (as of clothing) and used as a fastener by passing it through a buttonhole or loop **2** : something that resembles a button **3** : PUSH BUTTON

²**button** *vb* **but·toned; but·ton·ing** \ˈbət-(ᵊ-)niŋ\ : to close or fasten with buttons

but·ton·hole \ˈbət-ᵊn-ˌhōl\ *n* : a slit or loop for a button to pass through

²**buttonhole** *vb* : to detain in conversation by or as if by holding on to the outer garments of

but·tress \ˈbət-rəs\ *n* **1** : a projecting structure to support a wall **2** : PROP, SUPPORT

²**buttress** *vb* : PROP, SUPPORT

bu·tut \bù-ˈtüt\ *n* — see *dalasi* at MONEY table

bux·om \ˈbək-səm\ *adj* : healthily plump; *esp* : full-bosomed

¹**buy** \ˈbī\ *vb* **bought** \ˈbȯt\; **buy·ing** : to obtain for a price : PURCHASE; *also* : BRIBE — **buy·er** *n*

²**buy** *n* **1** : PURCHASE 1, 2 **2** : an exceptional value

¹**buzz** \ˈbəz\ *vb* **1** : to make a buzz **2** : to fly low over in an airplane

²**buzz** *n* : a low humming sound (as of bees in flight)

buz·zard \ˈbəz-ərd\ *n* : any of various usu. large birds of prey and esp. the turkey vulture

buzz·er \ˈbəz-ər\ *n* : a device that signals with a buzzing sound

buzz saw *n* : CIRCULAR SAW

BV *abbr* Blessed Virgin

BWI *abbr* British West Indies

bx *abbr* box

BX *abbr* base exchange

¹**by** \(ˈ)bī, bə\ *prep* **1** : NEAR ⟨stood ∼ the window⟩ **2** : through or through the medium of : VIA ⟨left ∼ the door⟩ **3** : PAST ⟨drove ∼ the house⟩ **4** : DURING, AT ⟨studied ∼ night⟩ **5** : no later than ⟨get here ∼ 3 p.m.⟩ **6** : through the means or direct agency of ⟨got it ∼ fraud⟩ ⟨was seen ∼ the others⟩ **7** : in conformity with : ACCORDING TO ⟨did it ∼ the book⟩ **8** : with respect to ⟨an

electrician ∼ trade) **9** : to the amount or extent of ⟨won ∼ a nose⟩ ⟨overpaid ∼ $3⟩ **10** — used to express relationship in multiplication, in division, and in measurements ⟨divide *a* ∼ *b*⟩ ⟨multiply ∼ 6⟩ ⟨15 feet ∼ 20 feet⟩

²**by** \'bī\ *adv* **1** : near at hand; *also* : IN ⟨stopped ∼ to chat⟩ **2** : PAST **3** : ASIDE, APART

bye \'bī\ *n* : a position of a participant in a tournament who has no opponent after pairs are drawn and advances to the next round without playing

by-elec·tion *also* **bye-election** \'bī-ə-ˌlek-shən\ *n* : a special election held between regular elections in order to fill a vacancy

by·gone \'bī-ˌgȯn\ *adj* : gone by : PAST — **bygone** *n*

by-law *or* **bye-law** \'bī-ˌlȯ\ *n* : a rule adopted by an organization for managing its internal affairs

by-line \'bī-ˌlīn\ *n* : a line at the beginning of a newspaper story or magazine article giving the writer's name

BYO *abbr* bring your own

BYOB *abbr* bring your own booze; bring your own bottle

¹**by·pass** \'bī-ˌpas\ *n* : a passage to one side or around a blocked or congested area

²**bypass** *vb* : to avoid by means of a bypass

by·path \-ˌpath, -ˌpàth\ *n* : BYWAY

by·play \'bī-ˌplā\ *n* : action engaged in at the side of a stage while the main action proceeds

by-prod·uct \-ˌpräd-(ˌ)əkt\ *n* : a product or result produced in addition to the main product or result

by·stand·er \-ˌstan-dər\ *n* : one present but not participating **syn** onlooker, witness, spectator, eyewitness

byte \'bīt\ *n* : a group of bits that a computer processes as a unit ⟨an 8-bit ∼⟩

by the way *adv* : in passing : INCIDENTALLY

by·way \'bī-ˌwā\ *n* **1** : a little-traveled side road **2** : a secondary aspect

by·word \-ˌwərd\ *n* **1** : PROVERB **2** : an object of scorn

C

¹**c** \'sē\ *n, pl* **c's** *or* **cs** \'sēz\ *often cap* **1** : the 3d letter of the English alphabet **2** : a grade rating a student's work as fair

²**c** *abbr, often cap* **1** calorie **2** carat **3** Celsius **4** cent **5** centigrade **6** centimeter **7** century **8** chapter **9** circa **10** cocaine **11** copyright

C *symbol* carbon

ca *abbr* circa

Ca *symbol* calcium

CA *abbr* **1** California **2** chartered accountant **3** chief accountant **4** chronological age

cab \'kab\ *n* **1** : a light closed horse‑drawn carriage **2** : TAXICAB **3** : the covered compartment for the engineer and controls of a locomotive; *also* : a similar compartment (as on a truck)

CAB *abbr* Civil Aeronautics Board

ca·bal \kə-'bal\ *n* [F *cabale*, fr. ML *cabbala* cabala, fr. Heb *quabbālāh*, lit., received (lore)] : a secret group of plotters or political conspirators

ca·ba·la \'kab-ə-lə, kə-'bäl-ə\ *n, often cap* **1** : a medieval Jewish mysticism marked by belief in creation through emanation and a cipher method of interpreting scriptures **2** : esoteric doctrine or beliefs

ca·bana \kə-'ban-(y)ə\ *n* : a shelter at a beach or swimming pool

cab·a·ret \ˌkab-ə-'rā\ *n* : NIGHTCLUB

cab·bage \'kab-ij\ *n* [ME *caboche*, fr. OF head] : a vegetable related to the turnip with a dense head of leaves

cab·bie *or* **cab·by** \'kab-ē\ *n, pl* **cabbies** : a driver of a cab

cab·in \'kab-ən\ *n* **1** : a private room on

a ship; *also* : a compartment below deck on a small boat for passengers or crew **2** : an aircraft or spacecraft compartment for passengers, crew, or cargo **3** : a small simple one-story house

cabin boy *n* : a boy acting as servant on a ship

cabin class *n* : a class of accommodations on a passenger ship superior to tourist class and inferior to first class

cabin cruiser *n* : CRUISER 3

cab·i·net \'kab-(ə-)nət\ *n* **1** : a case or cupboard for holding or displaying articles (as jewels, specimens, or documents) **2** : an upright case housing a radio or television receiver **3** : the advisory council of a head of state (as a president or sovereign)

cab·i·net·mak·er \-ˌmā-kər\ *n* : a woodworker who makes fine furniture —

cab·i·net·mak·ing \-ˌmā-kiŋ\ *n*

cab·i·net·work \-ˌwərk\ *n* : the finished work of a cabinetmaker

¹**ca·ble** \'kā-bəl\ *n* **1** : a very strong rope, wire, or chain **2** : a bundle of insulated wires usu. twisted around a central core **3** : CABLEGRAM **4** : CABLE TELEVISION

²**cable** *vb* **ca·bled; ca·bling** \'kā-b(ə-)liŋ\ : to telegraph by cable

cable car *n* : a vehicle moved by an endless cable

ca·ble·gram \'kā-bəl-ˌgram\ *n* : a message sent by a submarine telegraph cable

cable television *n* : a system of television reception in which signals from distant stations are sent by cable to the receivers of paying subscribers

cab·o·chon \'kab-ə-ˌshän\ *n* : a gem or bead cut in convex form and highly polished but not given facets; *also* : this style of cutting — **cabochon** *adv*

ca·boose \kə-'büs\ *n* : a car usu. at the rear of a freight train for the use of the train crew and railroad workers

cab·ri·o·let \ˌkab-rē-ə-'lā\ *n* [F] **1** : a light 2-wheeled one-horse carriage **2** : a convertible coupe

cab·stand \'kab-ˌstand\ *n* : a place for cabs to park while waiting for passengers

ca·cao \kə-'kau̇, -'kā-ō\ *n, pl* **cacaos** [Sp] : a So. American tree whose seeds (**cacao beans**) are the source of cocoa and chocolate; *also* : its dried fatty seeds

cac·cia·to·re \ˌkäch-ə-'tȯr-ē\ *adj* [It] : cooked with tomatoes and herbs ⟨veal ∼⟩

¹cache \'kash\ *n* [F] : a hiding place esp. for preserving provisions; *also* : something hidden or stored in a cache

²cache *vb* **cached; cach·ing** : to place or store in a cache

ca·chet \ka-'shā\ *n* [F] **1** : a seal used esp. as a mark of official approval **2** : a feature or quality conferring prestige; *also* : PRESTIGE **3** : a usu. flour paste capsule containing medicine **4** : a design, inscription, or advertisement printed or stamped on mail

cack·le \'kak-əl\ *vb* **cack·led; cack·ling** \-(ə-)liŋ\ **1** : to make the sharp broken cry characteristic of a hen **2** : to laugh or chatter noisily — **cackle** *n* — **cack·ler** \-(ə-)lər\ *n*

ca·coph·o·ny \ka-'käf-ə-nē\ *n, pl* **-nies** : harsh or discordant sound — **ca·coph·o·nous** \-nəs\ *adj*

cac·tus \'kak-təs\ *n, pl* **cac·ti** \-ˌtī\ *also* **cac·tus·es** *or* **cactus** : any of a large family of drought-resistant flowering plants with fleshy usu. jointed stems and with leaves replaced by scales or prickles

cad \'kad\ *n* : a man who does not behave like a gentleman esp. toward women — **cad·dish** \-ish\ *adj* — **cad·dish·ly** *adv* — **cad·dish·ness** *n*

ca·dav·er \kə-'dav-ər\ *n* : a dead body : CORPSE

ca·dav·er·ous \kə-'dav-(ə-)rəs\ *adj* : suggesting a corpse esp. in gauntness or pallor **syn** wasted, emaciated, gaunt — **ca·dav·er·ous·ly** *adv*

cad·die *or* **cad·dy** \'kad-ē\ *n, pl* **caddies** [F *cadet* military cadet] : one that assists a golfer esp. by carrying his clubs — **caddie** *or* **caddy** *vb*

cad·dy \'kad-ē\ *n, pl* **caddies** [Malay *kati* a unit of weight] : a small box, can, or chest; *esp* : one to keep tea in

ca·dence \'kād-³ns\ *n* : the measure or beat of a rhythmical flow : RHYTHM — **ca·denced** \-³nst\ *adj*

ca·den·za \kə-'den-zə\ *n* [It] : a brilliant sometimes improvised passage usu. toward the close of a musical composition

ca·det \kə-'det\ *n* [F, fr. F dial. *capdet* chief, fr. L *capitellum*, fr. L *caput* head] **1** : a younger son or brother **2** : a student in a service academy

Ca·dette scout \kə-ˌdet-\ *n* : a Girl Scout between the ages of 12 and 14

cadge \'kaj\ *vb* **cadged; cadg·ing** : SPONGE, BEG — **cadg·er** *n*

cad·mi·um \'kad-mē-əm\ *n* : a bluish white metallic chemical element used in protective platings

cad·re \'kad-rē\ *n* [F] **1** : FRAMEWORK **2** : a nucleus esp. of trained personnel capable of assuming control and training others **3** : a group of indoctrinated leaders active in promoting the interests of a revolutionary party

ca·du·ceus \kə-'d(y)ü-sē-əs, -shəs\ *n, pl* **-cei** \-sē-ˌī\ [L] **1** : the staff of a herald; *esp* : a representation of a staff with two entwined snakes and two wings at the top **2** : an insignia bearing a caduceus and symbolizing a physician

cae·cum *var of* CECUM

Cae·sar \'sē-zər\ *n* **1** : any of the Roman emperors succeeding Augustus Caesar — used as a title **2** *often not cap* : a powerful ruler : AUTOCRAT, DICTATOR; *also* : the civil or temporal power

caesarean *or* **caesarian** *var of* CESAREAN

cae·su·ra \si-'z(h)u̇r-ə\ *n, pl* **-suras** *or* **-su·rae** \-'z(h)u̇r-(ˌ)ē\ : a break in the flow of sound usu. in the middle of a line of verse

ca·fé \ka-'fā, kə-\ *n* [F, lit., coffee] **1** : RESTAURANT **2** : BARROOM **3** : NIGHTCLUB

ca·fé au lait \(ˌ)ka-ˌfā-ō-'lā\ *n* : coffee with hot milk in about equal parts

caf·e·te·ria \ˌkaf-ə-'tir-ē-ə\ *n* [AmerSp *cafetería* retail coffee store, fr. Sp *café* coffee] : a restaurant in which the customers serve themselves or are served at a counter

caf·feine \ka-'fēn, 'ka-ˌfēn\ *n* : a stimulating alkaloid found esp. in coffee and tea

caf·tan \kaf-'tan, 'kaf-ˌtan\ *n* [Russ *kaftan*, fr. Turk, fr. Per *qaftān*] : an ankle-length garment with long sleeves worn in countries of the eastern Mediterranean

¹cage \'kāj\ *n* **1** : an openwork enclosure for confining an animal **2** : something resembling a cage

²cage *vb* **caged; cag·ing** : to put or keep in or as if in a cage

ca·gey *also* **ca·gy** \'kā-jē\ *adj* **ca·gi·er; -est** : wary of being trapped or deceived : SHREWD — **ca·gi·ly** \'kā-jə-lē\ *adv* — **ca·gi·ness** \-jē-nəs\ *n*

CAGS *abbr* Certificate of Advanced Graduate Study

ca·hoot \kə-'hüt\ *n* : PARTNERSHIP, LEAGUE — usu. used in pl. ⟨officials in ∼s with the underworld⟩

cai·man \kā-'man, kī-; 'kā-mən\ *n* : any

of several Central and So. American relatives of the crocodiles

cairn \'kaərn\ *n* : a heap of stones serving as a memorial or a landmark

cais·son \'kā-ˌsän, 'kās-ᵊn\ *n* 1 : a usu. 2-wheeled vehicle for artillery ammunition 2 : a watertight chamber used in underwater construction work or as a foundation

caisson disease *n* : ³BEND 3

cai·tiff \'kāt-əf\ *adj* [ME *caitif*, fr. OF, captive, vile, fr. L *captivus* captive] : being base, cowardly, or despicable — **caitiff** *n*

ca·jole \kə-'jōl\ *vb* **ca·joled; ca·jol·ing** [F *cajoler*] : to persuade or coax esp. with flattery or false promises : WHEEDLE — **ca·jole·ment** *n* — **ca·jol·ery** \-'jōl-(ə-)rē\ *n*

Ca·jun \'kā-jən\ *n* : a Louisianian descended from French-speaking immigrants from Acadia (Nova Scotia)

¹**cake** \'kāk\ *n* 1 : a food made from batter that may be fried or baked into a usu. small flat shape 2 : a sweet baked food made from batter or dough usu. containing a leaven (as baking powder) 3 : a substance hardened or molded into a solid mass (a ∼ of soap)

²**cake** *vb* **caked; cak·ing** 1 : ENCRUST 2 : to form or harden into a cake

cake·walk \'kāk-ˌwȯk\ *n* 1 : a stage dance typically involving a high prance with backward tilt 2 : a one-sided contest

cal *abbr* 1 calendar 2 caliber

Cal *abbr* 1 California 2 calorie

cal·a·bash \'kal-ə-ˌbash\ *n* : the fruit of a gourd; *also* : a utensil made from its shell

cal·a·boose \'kal-ə-ˌbüs\ *n* [Sp *calabozo* dungeon] *dial* : JAIL

ca·la·di·um \kə-'lād-ē-əm\ *n* : any of a genus of tropical American ornamental plants related to the arums

cal·a·mari \ˌkäl-ə-'mär-ē\ *n* [It] : squid used as food

cal·a·mine \'kal-ə-ˌmīn\ *n* : a lotion of oxides of zinc and iron

ca·lam·i·ty \kə-'lam-ət-ē\ *n, pl* **-ties** 1 : great distress or misfortune 2 : an event causing great harm or loss and affliction : DISASTER — **ca·lam·i·tous** \-ət-əs\ *adj* — **ca·lam·i·tous·ly** *adv* — **ca·lam·i·tous·ness** *n*

calc *abbr* calculate; calculated

cal·car·e·ous \kal-'kar-ē-əs\ *adj* : containing calcium or calcium carbonate; *also* : resembling calcium carbonate in hardness

cal·cif·er·ous \kal-'sif-(ə-)rəs\ *adj* : producing or containing calcium carbonate

cal·ci·fy \'kal-sə-ˌfī\ *vb* **-fied; -fy·ing** : to make or become calcareous — **cal·ci·fi·ca·tion** \ˌkal-sə-fə-'kā-shən\ *n*

cal·ci·mine \'kal-sə-ˌmīn\ *n* : a thin water paint used esp. on plastered surfaces — **calcimine** *vb*

cal·cine \kal-'sīn\ *vb* **cal·cined; cal·cin·ing** : to heat to a high temperature but

without fusing to drive off volatile matter and often to reduce to powder — **cal·ci·na·tion** \ˌkal-sə-'nā-shən\ *n*

cal·cite \'kal-ˌsīt\ *n* : a crystalline mineral consisting of calcium carbonate — **cal·cit·ic** \kal-'sit-ik\ *adj*

cal·ci·um \'kal-sē-əm\ *n* : a silver-white soft metallic chemical element occurring only in combination

calcium carbonate *n* : a substance found in nature as limestone and marble and in plant ashes, bones, and shells

cal·cu·late \'kal-kyə-ˌlāt\ *vb* **-lat·ed; -lat·ing** [L *calculare*, fr. *calculus* small stone, pebble used in reckoning] 1 : to determine by mathematical processes : COMPUTE 2 : to reckon by exercise of practical judgment : ESTIMATE 3 : to design or adapt for a purpose 4 : COUNT, RELY — **cal·cu·la·ble** \-lə-bəl\ *adj* — **cal·cu·la·tor** \-ˌlāt-ər\ *n*

cal·cu·lat·ed \-ˌlāt-əd\ *adj* : undertaken after estimating the probability of success or failure (a ∼ risk)

cal·cu·lat·ing \-ˌlāt-iŋ\ *adj* : marked by shrewd consideration esp. of self-interest — **cal·cu·lat·ing·ly** *adv*

cal·cu·la·tion \ˌkal-kyə-'lā-shən\ *n* 1 : the process or an act of calculating 2 : the result of an act of calculating 3 : studied care : CAUTION

cal·cu·lus \'kal-kyə-ləs\ *n, pl* **-li** \-ˌlī\ *also* **-lus·es** [L, pebble (used in reckoning)] 1 : a method of computation or calculation in a special notation (as of logic) 2 : a branch of higher mathematics concerned esp. with rates of change and the finding of lengths, areas, and volumes 3 : a concretion usu. of mineral salts esp. in hollow organs or ducts

cal·de·ra \kal-'der-ə, kȯl-, -'dir-\ *n* [Sp, lit., caldron] : a large crater usu. formed by the collapse of a volcanic cone

cal·dron \'kȯl-drən\ *n* : a large kettle

¹**cal·en·dar** \'kal-ən-dər\ *n* 1 : an arrangement of time into days, weeks, months, and years; *also* : a sheet or folder containing such an arrangement for a period 2 : an orderly list

²**calendar** *vb* **-dared; -dar·ing** \-d(ə-)riŋ\ : to enter in a calendar

¹**cal·en·der** \'kal-ən-dər\ *vb* : to press (as cloth or paper) between rollers or plates so as to make smooth or glossy or to thin into sheets

²**calender** *n* : a machine for calendering

ca·lends \'kal-əndz, 'kāl-\ *n sing or pl* : the first day of the ancient Roman month

ca·len·du·la \kə-'len-jə-lə\ *n* : any of a genus of yellow-flowered herbs related to the daisies

¹**calf** \'kaf, 'kȧf\ *n, pl* **calves** \'kavz, 'kȧvz\ 1 : the young of the domestic cow; *also* : the young of various other large mammals (as the elephant or whale) 2 : CALFSKIN

²**calf** *n, pl* **calves** \'kavz, 'kávz\ : the fleshy back of the leg below the knee

calf-skin \'kaf-ˌskin, 'kaf-\ *n* : leather made of the skin of a calf

cal·i·ber *or* **cal·i·bre** \'kal-ə-bər\ *n* [MF *calibre*, fr. It *calibro*, fr. Ar *qālib* shoemaker's last] **1** : the diameter of a projectile **2** : the diameter of the bore of a gun **3** : degree of excellence or importance

cal·i·brate \'kal-ə-ˌbrāt\ *vb* **-brat·ed; -brat·ing 1** : to measure the caliber of **2** : to determine, correct, or put the measuring marks on ⟨~ a thermometer⟩ — **cal·i·bra·tion** \ˌkal-ə-'brā-shən\ *n*

cal·i·co \'kal-i-ˌkō\ *n, pl* **-coes** *or* **-cos** : cotton cloth; *esp* : a cheap cotton printed fabric — **calico** *adj*

Calif *abbr* California

Cal·i·for·nia poppy \ˌkal-ə-'fȯr-nyə-\ *n* : a widely cultivated herb with pale yellow to red flowers that is related to the poppies

cal·i·for·ni·um \ˌkal-ə-'fȯr-nē-əm\ *n* : an artificially prepared radioactive chemical element

cal·i·per *or* **cal·li·per** \'kal-ə-pər\ *n* **1** : an instrument with two adjustable legs used to measure the thickness of objects or distances between surfaces — used in pl. (a pair of ~s) **2** : a device consisting of two plates lined with a frictional material that press against the sides of a rotating wheel or disk in certain brake systems

ca·liph *or* **ca·lif** \'kā-ləf, 'kal-əf\ *n* : a successor of Muhammad as head of Islam — used as a title — **ca·liph·ate** \-ˌāt, -ət\ *n*

cal·is·then·ics \ˌkal-əs-'then-iks\ *n sing or pl* [Gk *kalos* beautiful + *sthenos* strength] : bodily exercises without apparatus or with light hand apparatus — **cal·is·then·ic** *adj*

calk \'kȯk\ *var of* CAULK

¹**call** \'kȯl\ *vb* **1** : SHOUT, CRY; *also* : to utter a characteristic cry **2** : to utter in a loud clear voice **3** : to announce authoritatively **4** : SUMMON **5** : to make a request or demand ⟨~ for an investigation⟩ **6** : to get or try to get in communication by telephone **7** : to demand payment of (a loan); *also* : to demand surrender of (as a bond issue) for redemption **8** : to make a brief visit **9** : to speak of or address by name : give a name to **10** : to estimate or consider for practical purposes ⟨~ it ten miles⟩ **11** : to halt because of unsuitable conditions **12** : to temporarily transfer control of computer processing to (as a section of a computer program) — **call·er** *n*

²**call** *n* **1** : SHOUT **2** : the cry of an animal (as a bird) **3** : a request or a command to come or assemble : INVITATION, SUMMONS **4** : DEMAND, CLAIM; *also* : REQUEST **5** : a brief usu. formal visit **6** : an act of calling on the telephone **7** : a temporary transfer of control of

computer processing to a particular set of instructions

cal·la lily \'kal-ə-\ *n* : a plant whose flowers form a fleshy yellow spike surrounded by a lilylike usu. white leaf

call·back \'kȯl-ˌbak\ *n* : a recall by a manufacturer of a product to correct a defect

call-board \-ˌbōrd\ *n* : a board for posting notices (as of rehearsal calls)

call down *vb* : REPRIMAND

call girl *n* : a prostitute with whom appointments are made by phone

cal·lig·ra·phy \kə-'lig-rə-fē\ *n* : beautiful or elegant handwriting; *also* : the art of producing such writing — **cal·lig·ra·pher** \-fər\ *n*

call in *vb* **1** : to order to return or be returned **2** : to summon to one's aid **3** : to report by telephone

call·ing \'kȯ-liŋ\ *n* **1** : a strong inner impulse toward a particular course of action **2** : the activity in which one customarily engages as an occupation

cal·li·ope \kə-'lī-ə-(ˌ)pē, 'kal-ē-ˌōp\ *n* [fr. *Calliope*, chief of the Muses, fr. L, fr. Gk *Kalliopē*] : a musical instrument consisting of a series of whistles played by keys arranged as in an organ

call number *n* : a combination of characters assigned to a library book to indicate its place on a shelf

call off *vb* : CANCEL

cal·los·i·ty \ka-'läs-ət-ē, kə-\ *n, pl* **-ties 1** : the quality or state of being callous **2** : CALLUS 1

¹**cal·lous** \'kal-əs\ *adj* **1** : being thickened and usu. hardened ⟨~ skin⟩ **2** : hardened in feeling — **cal·lous·ly** *adv* — **cal·lous·ness** *n*

²**callous** *vb* : to make callous

cal·low \'kal-ō\ *adj* [ME *calu* bald, fr. OE] : lacking adult sophistication : IMMATURE — **cal·low·ness** *n*

call-up \'kȯl-ˌəp\ *n* : an order to report for active military service

call up \(ˈ)kȯl-'əp\ *vb* : to summon for active military duty

¹**cal·lus** \'kal-əs\ *n* **1** : a callous area on skin or bark **2** : tissue that is converted into bone in the healing of a bone fracture

²**callus** *vb* : to form a callus

¹**calm** \'käm, 'kälm\ *adj* : marked by calm : STILL, PLACID, SERENE — **calm·ly** *adv* — **calm·ness** *n*

²**calm** *vb* : to make or become calm

³**calm** *n* **1** : a period or a condition of freedom from storms, high winds, or rough water **2** : complete or almost complete absence of wind **3** : a state of tranquility

cal·o·mel \'kal-ə-məl, -ˌmel\ *n* : a chloride of mercury used esp. as a purgative and fungicide

ca·lor·ic \kə-'lȯr-ik\ *adj* **1** : of or relating to heat **2** : of or relating to calories

cal·o·rie *also* **cal·o·ry** \'kal-(ə-)rē\ *n, pl* **-ries** : a unit for measuring heat; *esp*

: one for measuring the value of foods for producing heat and energy in the human body equivalent to the amount of heat required to raise the temperature of one kilogram of water one degree Celsius

cal·o·rif·ic \ˌkal-ə-ˈrif-ik\ *adj* : CALORIC

cal·o·rim·e·ter \ˌkal-ə-ˈrim-ət-ər\ *n* : an apparatus for measuring quantities of heat — **cal·o·rim·e·try** \ˌkal-ə-ˈrim-ə-trē\ *n*

cal·u·met \ˈkal-yə-ˌmet, -mət\ *n* : an American Indian ceremonial pipe

ca·lum·ni·ate \kə-ˈləm-nē-ˌāt\ *vb* **-at·ed; -at·ing** : to accuse falsely and maliciously : SLANDER **syn** defame, malign, libel, slander, traduce — **ca·lum·ni·a·tion** \-ˌləm-nē-ˈā-shən\ *n* — **ca·lum·ni·a·tor** \-ˈləm-nē-ˌāt-ər\ *n*

cal·um·ny \ˈkal-əm-nē\ *n, pl* **-nies** : false and malicious accusation — **ca·lum·ni·ous** \kə-ˈləm-nē-əs\ *adj*

calve \ˈkav, ˈkàv\ *vb* **calved; calv·ing** : to give birth to a calf

calves *pl of* CALF

Cal·vin·ism \ˈkal-və-ˌniz-əm\ *n* : the theological system of John Calvin and his followers — **Cal·vin·ist** \-və-nəst\ *n or adj* — **Cal·vin·is·tic** \ˌkal-və-ˈnis-tik\ *adj*

ca·lyp·so \kə-ˈlip-sō\ *n, pl* **-sos** : a style of music originating in the British West Indies and having lyrics that usu. satirize local personalities and events

ca·lyx \ˈkā-liks, ˈkal-iks\ *n, pl* **ca·lyx·es** or **ca·ly·ces** \ˈkā-lə-ˌsēz, ˈkal-ə-\ : the outside usu. green or leaflike part of a flower consisting of sepals

cam \ˈkam\ *n* : a rotating or sliding projection (as on a wheel) in a mechanical linkage by which rotary motion is transformed into linear motion or vice versa

ca·ma·ra·de·rie \ˌkam-(ə-)ˈrad-ə-rē, ˌkäm-(ə-)ˈräd-\ *n* [F] : friendly feeling and goodwill among comrades

cam·bi·um \ˈkam-bē-əm\ *n, pl* **-bi·ums** or **-bia** \-bē-ə\ : a thin cellular layer between xylem and phloem of most higher plants from which new tissues develop — **cam·bi·al** \-bē-əl\ *adj*

Cam·bri·an *adj* : of, relating to, or being the earliest period of the Paleozoic era — **Cambrian** *n*

cam·bric \ˈkām-brik\ *n* : a fine thin white linen or cotton fabric

came *past of* COME

cam·el \ˈkam-əl\ *n* : either of two large hoofed cud-chewing mammals used esp. in desert regions of Asia and Africa for carrying burdens and for riding

camel hair *also* **camel's hair** *n* **1** : the hair of a camel or a substitute for it **2** : cloth made of camel hair or of camel hair and wool

ca·mel·lia \kə-ˈmēl-yə\ *n* : any of several shrubs or trees related to the tea plant and grown in warm regions and

greenhouses for their showy roselike flowers

Cam·em·bert \ˈkam-əm-ˌbeər\ *n* : a soft surface-ripened cheese with a grayish rind and yellow interior

cam·eo \ˈkam-ē-ˌō\ *n, pl* **-eos 1** : a gem carved in relief; *also* : a small medallion with a profiled head in relief **2** : a brief appearance by a well-known actor in a play or movie

cam·era \ˈkam-(ə-)rə\ *n* : a closed lightproof box with a lens through which the image of an object is recorded on a light-sensitive material; *also* : an electronic device that forms an image and converts it into an electrical signal (as for television broadcast) — **cam·era·man** \ˈkam-(ə-)rə-ˌman, -mən\ *n*

Cam·er·oo·ni·an \ˌkam-ə-ˈrü-nē-ən\ *n* : a native or inhabitant of the Republic of Cameroon or the Cameroons region — **Cameroonian** *adj*

cam·i·sole \ˈkam-ə-ˌsōl\ *n* : a short sleeveless undergarment for women

camomile *var of* CHAMOMILE

cam·ou·flage \ˈkam-ə-ˌfläzh, -ˌfläj\ *n* [F] **1** : the disguising of military equipment with paint, nets, or foliage; *also* : the disguise itself **2** : a deceptive expedient — **camouflage** *vb*

¹camp \ˈkamp\ *n* **1** : a place where tents or buildings are erected for usu. temporary shelter **2** : a collection of tents or other shelters **3** : a body of persons encamped — **camp·ground** \-ˌgraùnd\ *n* — **camp·site** \-ˌsīt\ *n*

²camp *vb* **1** : to make or occupy a camp **2** : to live in a camp or outdoors

³camp *n* **1** : exaggerated effeminate mannerisms **2** : something so outrageous or in such bad taste as to be considered amusing — **camp** *adj* — **camp·i·ly** \ˈkam-pə-lē\ *adv* — **camp·i·ness** \-pē-nəs\ *n* — **campy** \ˈkam-pē\ *adj*

⁴camp *vb* : to engage in camp : exhibit the qualities of camp

cam·paign \kam-ˈpān\ *n* **1** : a series of military operations forming one distinct stage in a war **2** : a series of activities designed to bring about a particular result ⟨advertising ∼⟩ — **campaign** *vb* — **cam·paign·er** *n*

cam·pa·ni·le \ˌkam-pə-ˈnē-lē\ *n, pl* **-niles** or **-ni·li** \-ˈnē-lē\ : a usu. freestanding bell tower

cam·pa·nol·o·gy \ˌkam-pə-ˈnäl-ə-jē\ *n* : the art of bell ringing — **cam·pa·nol·o·gist** \-jəst\ *n*

camp·er \ˈkam-pər\ *n* **1** : one that camps **2** : a portable dwelling (as a specially equipped vehicle) for use during casual travel and camping

Camp Fire Girl *n* : a member of a national organization of girls from 7 to 18

camp follower *n* **1** : a civilian (as a prostitute) who follows a military unit to attend or exploit its personnel **2** : a follower of a group who is not an adherent; *esp* : a politician who joins a movement solely for personal gain

cam·phor \ˈkam(p)-fər\ *n* : a gummy volatile fragrant compound obtained from an evergreen Asian tree (**camphor tree**) and used esp. in medicine

camp meeting *n* : a series of evangelistic meetings usu. held outdoors

camp·o·ree \ˌkam-pə-ˈrē\ *n* : a gathering of Boy Scouts or Girl Scouts from a given geographic area

cam·pus \ˈkam-pəs\ *n* [L, plain] : the grounds and buildings of a college or school; *also* : a central grassy part of the grounds

cam·shaft \ˈkam-ˌshaft\ *n* : a shaft to which a cam is fastened

¹**can** \kən, (ˈ)kan\ *vb, past* **could** \kəd, (ˈ)kùd\; *pres sing & pl* **can** 1 : be able to 2 : may perhaps (~ he still be alive) 3 : be permitted by conscience or feeling to (you ~ hardly blame him) 4 : have permission or liberty to (you ~ go now)

²**can** \ˈkan\ *n* 1 : a typically cylindrical metal container or receptacle (garbage ~) (coffee ~) 2 : JAIL

³**can** \ˈkan\ *vb* **canned; can·ning** 1 : to put in a can : preserve by sealing in airtight cans or jars 2 *slang* : to discharge from employment 3 *slang* : to put a stop or an end to 4 : to record on discs or tape — **can·ner** *n*

Can *or* **Canad** *abbr* Canada; Canadian

Can·a·da goose \ˈkan-əd-ə-\ *n* : a common wild goose of No. America

Ca·na·di·an \kə-ˈnād-ē-ən\ *n* : a native or inhabitant of Canada — **Canadian** *adj*

ca·naille \kə-ˈnī, -ˈnāl\ *n* [F, fr. It *canaglia*, fr. *cane* dog] : RABBLE, RIFFRAFF

ca·nal \kə-ˈnal\ *n* 1 : a tubular passage in the body : DUCT 2 : an artificial waterway (as for boats or irrigation)

can·a·lize \ˈkan-ᵊl-ˌīz\ *vb* **-ized; -iz·ing** 1 : to provide with a canal or make into or like a channel 2 : to provide with an outlet; *esp* : to direct into preferred channels — **ca·nal·iza·tion** \ˌkan-ᵊl-ə-ˈzā-shən\ *n*

ca·na·pé \ˈkan-ə-pē, -ˌpā\ *n* [F, lit., sofa, fr. ML *canopeum, canapeum* mosquito net] : a piece of bread or toast or a cracker topped with a savory food

ca·nard \kə-ˈnärd\ *n* : a false or unfounded report or story

ca·nary \kə-ˈner-ē\ *n, pl* **ca·nar·ies** [fr. the *Canary* islands] 1 : a usu. sweet wine similar to Madeira 2 : a usu. yellow or greenish finch often kept in a cage 3 : a bright yellow

ca·nas·ta \kə-ˈnas-tə\ *n* [Sp, lit., basket] : rummy played with two full decks of cards plus four jokers

canc *abbr* canceled

can·can \ˈkan-ˌkan\ *n* : a woman's dance of French origin characterized by high kicking

¹**can·cel** \ˈkan-səl\ *vb* **-celed** *or* **-celled;**

-cel·ing *or* **-cel·ling** \-s(ə-)liŋ\ [ME *cancellen*, fr. MF *canceller*, fr. L *cancellare* to make like a lattice, fr. *cancer* lattice] 1 : to destroy the force or validity of : ANNUL 2 : to match in force or effect : OFFSET 3 : to cross out : DELETE 4 : to remove (a common divisor) from a numerator and denominator; *also* : to remove (equivalents) on opposite sides of an equation or account 5 : to mark (a postage stamp or check) so that it cannot be reused 6 : to neutralize each other's strength or effect — **can·cel·la·tion** \ˌkan-sə-ˈlā-shən\ *n* — **can·cel·er** *or* **can·cel·ler** \ˈkan(t)-s(ə-)lər\ *n*

²**cancel** *n* 1 : CANCELLATION 2 : a deleted part

can·cer \ˈkan-sər\ *n* [L, lit., crab] 1 *cap* : a zodiacal constellation between Gemini and Leo usu. pictured as a crab 2 *cap* : the 4th sign of the zodiac in astrology; *also* : one born under this sign 3 : a malignant tumor that tends to spread in the body 4 : a malignant evil that corrodes slowly and fatally — **can·cer·ous** \ˈkans-(ə-)rəs\ *adj* — **can·cer·ous·ly** *adv*

can·de·la·bra \ˌkan-də-ˈläb-rə, -ˈlab-\ *n* : an ornamental branched candlestick or lamp with several lights

can·de·la·brum \-rəm\ *n, pl* **-bra** \-rə\ *also* **-brums** : CANDELABRA

can·des·cent \kan-ˈdes-ᵊnt\ *adj* : glowing or dazzling esp. from great heat — **can·des·cence** \-ᵊns\ *n*

can·did \ˈkan-dəd\ *adj* 1 : FRANK, STRAIGHTFORWARD 2 : relating to photography of subjects acting naturally or spontaneously without being posed — **can·did·ly** *adv* — **can·did·ness** *n*

can·di·da·cy \ˈkan-(d)əd-ə-sē\ *n, pl* **-cies** : the state of being a candidate

can·di·date \ˈkan-(d)ə-ˌdāt, -(d)əd-ət\ *n* [L *candidatus*, fr. *candidatus* clothed in white, fr. *candidus* white; fr. the white toga worn by candidates in ancient Rome] : one who seeks or is proposed for an office, honor, or membership

can·di·da·ture \ˈkan-(d)əd-ə-ˌchùr\ *n, chiefly Brit* : CANDIDACY

can·died \ˈkan-dēd\ *adj* : preserved in or encrusted with sugar

¹**can·dle** \ˈkan-dᵊl\ *n* : a usu. slender mass of tallow or wax molded around a wick and burned to give light

²**candle** *vb* **can·dled; can·dling** \ˈkan-(d)liŋ, -dᵊl-iŋ\ : to examine (as eggs) by holding between the eye and a light — **can·dler** \-d(ᵊ-)lər\ *n*

can·dle·light \ˈkan-dᵊl-ˌlīt\ *n* 1 : the light of a candle; *also* : any soft artificial light 2 : the time when candles are lit : TWILIGHT

Can·dle·mas \ˈkan-dᵊl-məs\ *n* : February 2 observed as a church festival in commemoration of the presentation of Christ in the temple

can·dle·pin \-ˌpin\ *n* : a slender bowling

pin tapering toward top and bottom used in a bowling game (**candlepins**) with a smaller ball than that used in tenpins

can·dle·stick \-ˌstik\ *n* : a holder with a socket for a candle

can·dle·wick \-ˌwik\ *n* : a soft cotton yarn; *also* : embroidery made with this yarn usu. in tufts

can·dor \'kan-dər\ *n* : FRANKNESS, OUTSPOKENNESS

C and W *abbr* country and western

¹can·dy \'kan-dē\ *n*, *pl* **candies** : a confection made from sugar often with flavoring and filling

²candy *vb* **can·died; can·dy·ing 1** : to encrust in sugar often by cooking in a syrup **2** : to make attractive : SWEETEN **3** : to crystallize or become crystallized into sugar

candy strip·er \-ˌstrī-pər\ *n* : a teenage volunteer nurse's aide

¹cane \'kān\ *n* **1** : a slender hollow or pithy stem (as of a reed or bramble) **2** : a tall woody grass or reed (as sugarcane) **3** : a walking stick; *also* : a rod for flogging

²cane *vb* **caned; can·ing 1** : to beat with a cane **2** : to weave or make with cane — **can·er** *n*

cane·brake \'kān-ˌbrāk\ *n* : a thicket of cane

¹ca·nine \'kā-ˌnīn\ *n* [L *caninus*, fr. *canis* dog] **1** : a pointed tooth between the outer incisor and the first premolar **2** : DOG

²canine *adj* : of or relating to dogs or to the family to which they belong

can·is·ter \'kan-ə-stər\ *n* **1** : a small box for holding a dry product (as tea) **2** : a perforated container containing material to absorb or filter a harmful substance in the air

can·ker \'kaŋ-kər\ *n* : a spreading sore that eats into tissue — **can·ker·ous** \'kaŋ-k(ə-)rəs\ *adj*

can·ker·worm \-ˌwərm\ *n* : either of two moths and esp. their larvae that are pests of forest and shade trees

can·na \'kan-ə\ *n* : any of a genus of tropical herbs with large leaves and racemes of bright-colored flowers

can·na·bis \'kan-ə-bəs\ *n* : any of the psychoactive preparations (as marijuana) or chemicals (as THC) derived from hemp; *also* : HEMP

canned \'kand\ *adj* : prepared in standardized form for general use or wide distribution

can·nery \'kan-(ə-)rē\ *n*, *pl* **-ner·ies** : a factory for the canning of foods

can·ni·bal \'kan-ə-bəl\ *n* [NL *Canibalis* a member of a Caribbean Indian people, fr. Sp *Caníbal*, fr. a native word *Caniba* or *Carib*] : one that eats the flesh of its own kind — **can·ni·bal·ism** \'kan-ə-bə-ˌliz-əm\ *n* — **can·ni·bal·is·tic** \ˌkan-ə-bə-'lis-tik\ *adj*

can·ni·bal·ize \'kan-ə-bə-ˌlīz\ *vb* **-ized; -iz·ing 1** : to take usable parts from (as an inoperative machine) to construct or repair another machine **2** : to practice cannibalism

can·non \'kan-ən\ *n*, *pl* **cannons** or **cannon** [MF *canon*, fr. It *cannone*. lit., large tube, fr. *canna* reed, tube, fr. L, cane, reed] **1** : an artillery piece supported on a carriage or mount **2** : a large-caliber automatic gun on an aircraft

can·non·ade \ˌkan-ə-'nād\ *n* : a heavy fire of artillery — **cannonade** *vb*

can·non·ball \'kan-ən-ˌbȯl\ *n* : a usu. round solid missile for firing from a cannon

can·non·eer \ˌkan-ə-'niər\ *n* : an artillery gunner

can·not \'kan-ˌät; kə-'nät\ : can not — **cannot but** : to be unable to do otherwise than

can·nu·la \'kan-yə-lə\ *n*, *pl* **-las** or **-lae** \-ˌlē\ : a small tube for insertion into a body cavity or into a duct or vessel

can·ny \'kan-ē\ *adj* **can·ni·er; -est** : PRUDENT, SHREWD — **can·ni·ly** \'kan-əl-ē\ *adv* — **can·ni·ness** \-ē-nəs\ *n*

ca·noe \kə-'nü\ *n* : a light narrow boat with sharp ends and curved sides that is usu. propelled by paddles — **canoe** *vb* — **ca·noe·ist** *n*

¹can·on \'kan-ən\ *n* **1** : a regulation decreed by a church council; *also* : a provision of canon law **2** : an official or authoritative list (as of the saints or the books of the Bible) **3** : an accepted principle (the ~s of good taste)

²canon *n* : a clergyman on the staff of a cathedral

ca·ñon \'kan-yən\ *var of* CANYON

ca·non·i·cal \kə-'nän-i-kəl\ *adj* **1** : of, relating to, or forming a canon **2** : conforming to a general rule or acceptable procedure : ORTHODOX **3** : of or relating to a clergyman who is a canon — **ca·non·i·cal·ly** \-k(ə-)lē\ *adv*

ca·non·i·cals \-kəlz\ *n pl* : the vestments prescribed by canon for an officiating clergyman

can·on·ize \'kan-ə-ˌnīz\ *vb* **can·on·ized** \-ˌnīzd\ ; **can·on·iz·ing 1** : to declare an officially recognized saint **2** : GLORIFY, EXALT — **can·on·iza·tion** \ˌkan-ə-nə-'zā-shən\ *n*

canon law *n* : the law governing a church

canon regular *n*, *pl* **canons regular** : a member of one of several Roman Catholic religious institutes of regular priests living in community

can·o·py \'kan-ə-pē\ *n*, *pl* **-pies** [ME *canope*, fr. ML *canopeum* mosquito net, fr. L *conopeum*, fr. Gk *kōnōpion*, fr. *kōnōps* mosquito] : an overhanging cover, shelter, or shade — **canopy** *vb*

¹cant \'kant\ *n* **1** : an oblique or slanting surface **2** : TILT, SLANT

²cant *vb* : to give a slant to

³cant *vb* **1** : to beg in a whining manner **2** : to talk hypocritically

⁴cant *n* **1** : the special idiom of a profession or trade : JARGON **2** : insincere speech; *esp* : insincerely pious words or statements

Cant *abbr* Canticle of Canticles

can·ta·bi·le \kän-ˈtäb-ə-ˌlā\ *adv or adj* [It] : in a singing manner — used as a direction in music

can·ta·loupe *also* **can·te·loupe** \ˈkant-ᵊl-ˌōp\ *n* : MUSKMELON; *esp* : one with orange flesh and rough skin

can·tan·ker·ous \kan-ˈtaŋ-k(ə-)rəs\ *adj* : ILL-NATURED, QUARRELSOME — **can·tan·ker·ous·ly** *adv* — **can·tan·ker·ous·ness** *n*

can·ta·ta \kən-ˈtät-ə\ *n* [It] : a choral composition usu. accompanied by organ, piano, or orchestra

can·teen \kan-ˈtēn\ *n* [F *cantine* bottle case, canteen (store), fr. It *cantina* wine cellar, fr. *canto* corner] **1** : a flask for carrying liquids **2** : a place of recreation and entertainment for military personnel **3** : a small cafeteria or counter at which snacks are available

can·ter \ˈkant-ər\ *n* : a horse's 3-beat gait resembling but smoother and slower than a gallop — **canter** *vb*

Can·ter·bury bell \ˌkant-ə(r)-ˌber-ē-\ *n* : any of several plants related to the bluebell that are cultivated for their showy flowers

can·ti·cle \ˈkant-i-kəl\ *n* : SONG; *esp* : any of several liturgical songs taken from the Bible

Canticle of Canticles *n* — see BIBLE table

¹can·ti·le·ver \ˈkant-ᵊl-ˌē-vər\ *n* : a projecting beam or structure supported only at one end; *also* : either of a pair of such structures projecting toward each other so that when joined they form a bridge

²cantilever *vb* **1** : to project as a cantilever **2** : to build as a cantilever **3** : to support by a cantilever ⟨a ~ed shelf⟩

can·tle \ˈkant-ᵊl\ *n* : the upwardly projecting rear part of a saddle

can·to \ˈkan-ˌtō\ *n, pl* **cantos** [It, fr. L *cantus* song] : one of the major divisions of a long poem

can·ton \ˈkant-ᵊn, ˈkan-ˌtän\ *n* : a small territorial division of a country; *esp* : one of the political divisions of Switzerland — **can·ton·al** \ˈkant-ᵊn-əl, kan-ˈtän-ᵊl\ *adj*

can·ton·ment \kan-ˈtōn-mənt, -ˈtän-\ *n* : usu. temporary quarters for troops

can·tor \ˈkant-ər\ *n* : a synagogue official who sings liturgical music and leads the congregation in prayer

can·vas *also* **can·vass** \ˈkan-vəs\ *n* **1** : a strong cloth formerly much used for making tents and sails **2** : a set of sails **3** : a group of tents **4** : a piece of cloth prepared as a surface to receive oil paint; *also* : an oil painting **5** : the canvas-covered floor of a boxing or wrestling ring

can·vas·back \ˈkan-vəs-ˌbak\ *n* : a No. American wild duck with red head and gray back

¹can·vass *also* **can·vas** \ˈkan-vəs\ *vb* : to

go through (a district) or to go to (persons) to solicit votes or orders for goods or to determine public opinion or sentiment — **can·vass·er** *n*

²canvass *n* : an act of canvassing (as the solicitation of votes or survey of public opinion)

can·yon \ˈkan-yən\ *n* : a deep narrow valley with high steep sides

caou·tchouc \ˈkaù-ˌchùk, -ˌchük\ *n* : RUBBER 3

¹cap \ˈkap\ *n* **1** : a covering for the head esp. with a visor and no brim; *also* : something resembling such a covering **2** : a container holding an explosive charge **3** : an upper limit (as on expenditures)

²cap *vb* **capped; cap·ping 1** : to provide or protect with a cap **2** : to form a cap over : CROWN **3** : OUTDO, SURPASS **4** : CLIMAX

³cap *abbr* **1** capacity **2** capital **3** capitalize; capitalized

CAP *abbr* Civil Air Patrol

ca·pa·ble \ˈkā-pə-bəl\ *adj* : having ability, capacity, or power to do something : ABLE, COMPETENT — **ca·pa·bil·i·ty** \ˌkā-pə-ˈbil-ət-ē\ *n* — **ca·pa·bly** \ˈkā-pə-blē\ *adv*

ca·pa·cious \kə-ˈpā-shəs\ *adj* : able to contain much — **ca·pa·cious·ly** *adv* — **ca·pa·cious·ness** *n*

ca·pac·i·tance \kə-ˈpas-ət-əns\ *n* : the property of an electric nonconductor that permits the storage of energy

ca·pac·i·tor \kə-ˈpas-ət-ər\ *n* : an electronic circuit device for temporary storage of electrical energy

¹ca·pac·i·ty \kə-ˈpas-ət-ē\ *n, pl* **-ties 1** : legal qualification or fitness **2** : the ability to contain, receive, or accommodate **3** : extent of space : VOLUME **4** : ABILITY **5** : position or character assigned or assumed

²capacity *adj* : equaling maximum capacity ⟨a ~ crowd⟩

cap-a-pie *or* **cap-à-pie** \ˌkap-ə-ˈpē\ *adv* [MF] : from head to foot : at all points

ca·par·i·son \kə-ˈpar-ə-sən\ *n* **1** : an ornamental covering for a horse **2** : TRAPPINGS, ADORNMENT — **caparison** *vb*

¹cape \ˈkāp\ *n* **1** : a point of land jutting out into water **2** *usu cap* : CAPE COD COTTAGE

²cape *n* : a sleeveless garment hanging from the neck over the shoulders

Cape Cod cottage \ˌkāp-ˈkäd-\ *n* : a compact rectangular dwelling of one or one-and-a-half stories usu. with a steep gable roof

¹ca·per \ˈkā-pər\ *n* : the flower bud or young berry of a Mediterranean shrub pickled for use as a relish; *also* : this shrub

²caper *vb* **ca·pered; ca·per·ing** \-p(ə-)riŋ\ : to leap about in a playful manner : PRANCE

³caper *n* **1** : a frolicsome leap **2** : a capricious escapade **3** : an illegal or questionable act

cape·skin \\'kāp-,skin\\ *n* : a light flexible leather made from sheepskins

Cape Verd·ian \\-'vərd-ē-ən\\ *n* : a native or inhabitant of the Republic of Cape Verde

cap·ful \\'kap-,fùl\\ *n* : as much as a cap will hold

cap·il·lar·i·ty \\,kap-ə-'lar-ət-ē\\ *n, pl* **-ties** : the action by which the surface of a liquid where it is in contact with a solid (as in a slender tube) is raised or lowered depending on the relative attraction of the molecules of the liquid for each other and for those of the solid

¹cap·il·lary \\'kap-ə-,ler-ē\\ *adj* **1** : resembling a hair **2** : having a very small bore ⟨~ tube⟩ **3** : of or relating to capillaries or to capillarity

²capillary *n, pl* **-lar·ies** : any of the tiny thin-walled blood vessels that carry blood between the smallest arteries and their corresponding veins

¹cap·i·tal \\'kap-ət-ᵊl\\ *adj* **1** : conforming to the series A, B, C rather than a, b, c ⟨~ letters⟩ ⟨~ G⟩ **2** : punishable by death ⟨a ~ crime⟩ **3** : most serious ⟨a ~ error⟩ **4** : first in importance or position : CHIEF; *also* : being the seat of government ⟨the ~ city⟩ **5** : of or relating to capital ⟨~ expenditures⟩; *esp* : relating to or being assets that add to the long-term net worth of a corporation **6** : FIRST-RATE, EXCELLENT

²capital *n* **1** : accumulated wealth esp. as used to produce more wealth **2** : the total face value of shares of stock issued by a company **3** : capitalists considered as a group **4** : ADVANTAGE, GAIN **5** : a letter larger than the ordinary small letter and often different in form **6** : the capital city of a state or country; *also* : a city preeminent in some activity ⟨the fashion ~ of the world⟩

³capital *n* : the top part or piece of an architectural column

capital gain *n* : the increase in value of an asset (as stock or real estate) between the time it is bought and the time it is sold

capital goods *n pl* : machinery, tools, factories, and commodities used in the production of goods

cap·i·tal·ism \\'kap-ət-ᵊl-,iz-əm\\ *n* : an economic system characterized by private or corporate ownership of capital goods and by prices, production, and distribution of goods that are determined mainly in a free market

¹cap·i·tal·ist \\-əst\\ *n* **1** : a person who has capital esp. invested in business **2** : a person of great wealth : PLUTOCRAT **3** : a believer in capitalism

²capitalist *or* **cap·i·tal·is·tic** \\,kap-ət-ᵊl-'is-tik\\ *adj* **1** : owning capital **2** : practicing or advocating capitalism **3** : marked by capitalism — **cap·i·tal·is·ti·cal·ly** \\-ti-k(ə-)lē\\ *adv*

cap·i·tal·iza·tion \\,kap-ət-ᵊl-ə-'zā-shən\\ *n* **1** : the act or process of capitalizing **2** : the total amount of money used as capital in a business

cap·i·tal·ize \\'kap-ət-ᵊl-,īz\\ *vb* **-ized; -iz·ing 1** : to write or print with an initial capital or in capitals **2** : to convert into or use as capital **3** : to supply capital for **4** : to gain by turning something to advantage : PROFIT

cap·i·tal·ly \\'kap-ət-ᵊl-ē\\ *adv* : ADMIRABLY, EXCELLENTLY

cap·i·ta·tion \\,kap-ə-'tā-shən\\ *n* : a direct uniform tax levied on each person

cap·i·tol \\'kap-ət-ᵊl\\ *n* : the building in which a legislature holds its sessions

ca·pit·u·late \\kə-'pich-ə-,lāt\\ *vb* **-lat·ed; -lat·ing 1** : to surrender esp. on conditions agreed upon **2** : to cease resisting : ACQUIESCE *syn* submit, yield, succumb, cave, defer — **ca·pit·u·la·tion** \\-,pich-ə-'lā-shən\\ *n*

ca·pon \\'kā-,pän, -pən\\ *n* : a castrated male chicken

cap·puc·ci·no \\,kap-ə-'chē-nō, ,käp-\\ *n* [It, lit., Capuchin; fr. the likeness of its color to that of a Capuchin's habit] : espresso mixed with foamy hot milk or cream and often flavored with cinnamon

ca·pric·cio \\kə-'prē-ch(ē-,)ō\\ *n, pl* **-cios** : an instrumental piece in free form usu. lively in tempo and brilliant in style

ca·price \\kə-'prēs\\ *n* [F, fr. It *capriccio*, lit., head with hair standing on end, shudder, fr. *capo* head + *riccio* hedgehog] **1** : a sudden whim or fancy **2** : an inclination to change one's mind impulsively **3** : CAPRICCIO — **ca·pri·cious** \\kə-'prish-əs\\ *adj* — **ca·pri·cious·ly** *adv* — **ca·pri·cious·ness** *n*

Cap·ri·corn \\'kap-ri-,körn\\ *n* **1** : a zodiacal constellation between Sagittarius and Aquarius usu. pictured as a goat **2** : the 10th sign of the zodiac in astrology; *also* : one born under this sign

cap·ri·ole \\'kap-rē-,ōl\\ *n* : ³CAPER 1; *esp* : an upward leap of a horse with a backward kick at the height of the leap — **capriole** *vb*

caps *abbr* **1** capitals **2** capsule

cap·si·cum \\'kap-si-kəm\\ *n* : PEPPER 2

cap·size \\'kap-,sīz, kap-'sīz\\ *vb* **capsized; cap·siz·ing** : UPSET, OVERTURN

cap·stan \\'kap-stən, -,stan\\ *n* **1** : a machine for moving or raising heavy weights that consists of a vertical drum which can be rotated and around which cable is turned **2** : a rotating shaft that drives recorder tape

cap·su·lar \\'kap-sə-lər\\ *adj* : of, relating to, or resembling a capsule

cap·su·lat·ed \\-,lāt-əd\\ *adj* : enclosed in a capsule

¹cap·sule \\'kap-səl, -sül\\ *n* **1** : an enveloping cover (as of a bodily joint) ⟨a spore ~⟩; *esp* : an edible shell enclosing medicine or vitamins to be swal-

lowed **2** : a dry fruit made of two or more united carpels that splits open when ripe **3** : a small pressurized compartment for a pilot or astronaut
²**capsule** *adj* **1** : very brief **2** : very compact

Capt *abbr* captain

¹**cap·tain** \'kap-tən\ *n* **1** : a commander of a body of troops **2** : a commissioned officer in the army, air force, or marine corps ranking next below a major **3** : an officer in charge of a ship: *esp* : a commissioned officer in the navy ranking next below a rear admiral or a commodore **4** : a leader of a side or team **5** : a dominant figure — **cap·tain·cy** *n*

²**captain** *vb* : to be captain of : LEAD

cap·tion \'kap-shən\ *n* **1** : a heading esp. of an article or document : TITLE **2** : the explanatory matter accompanying an illustration **3** : a motion-picture subtitle — **caption** *vb*

cap·tious \'kap-shəs\ *adj* : marked by an inclination to find fault — **captious·ly** *adv* — **cap·tious·ness** *n*

cap·ti·vate \'kap-tə-ˌvāt\ *vb* **-vat·ed; -vat·ing** : to attract and hold irresistibly by some special charm or art — **cap·ti·va·tion** \ˌkap-tə-ˈvā-shən\ *n* — **cap·ti·va·tor** \'kap-tə-ˌvāt-ər\ *n*

cap·tive \'kap-tiv\ *adj* **1** : made prisoner esp. in war **2** : kept within bounds : CONFINED **3** : held under control — **captive** *n* — **cap·tiv·i·ty** \kap-ˈtiv-ət-ē\ *n*

cap·tor \'kap-tər\ *n* : one that captures

¹**cap·ture** \'kap-chər\ *n* **1** : the act of capturing **2** : one that has been captured

²**capture** *vb* **cap·tured; cap·tur·ing** **1** : to take captive : WIN, GAIN **2** : to preserve in a relatively permanent form

Ca·pu·chin \'kap-yə-shən\ *n* : a member of an austere branch of the order of St. Francis of Assisi engaged in missionary work and preaching

car \'kär\ *n* **1** : a vehicle moving on wheels **2** : the compartment of an elevator **3** : the part of a balloon or airship that carries passengers or equipment

ca·ra·bao \ˌkar-ə-ˈbau\ *n, pl* **-bao** *or* **-baos** : a water buffalo esp. in the Philippines

car·a·bi·neer *or* **car·a·bi·nier** \ˌkar-ə-bə-ˈniər\ *n* : a soldier armed with a carbine

car·a·cole \'kar-ə-ˌkōl\ *n* : a half turn to right or left executed by a mounted horse — **caracole** *vb*

ca·rafe \kə-ˈraf, -ˈräf\ *n* : a bottle with a flaring lip used esp. to hold wine

car·a·mel \'kar-ə-məl, 'kär-məl\ *n* **1** : an amorphous substance obtained by heating sugar and used for flavoring and coloring **2** : a firm chewy candy

car·a·pace \'kar-ə-ˌpās\ *n* : a protective case or shell on the back of some animals (as turtles or crabs)

¹**carat** *var of* KARAT

²**car·at** \'kar-ət\ *n* : a unit of weight for precious stones equal to 200 milligrams

car·a·van \'kar-ə-ˌvan\ *n* **1** : a group of travelers journeying together through desert or hostile regions **2** : a group of vehicles traveling in a file

car·a·van·sa·ry \ˌkar-ə-ˈvan-sə-rē\ *or* **car·a·van·se·rai** \-sə-ˌrī\ *n, pl* **-ries** *or* **-rais** *or* **-rai** [Per *kārwānsarāī*, fr. *kārwān* caravan + *sarāī* palace, inn] **1** : an inn in eastern countries where caravans rest at night **2** : HOTEL, INN

car·a·vel \'kar-ə-ˌvel\ *n* : a small 15th and 16th century ship with a broad bow, high narrow poop, and usu. three masts

car·a·way \'kar-ə-ˌwā\ *n* : an aromatic herb related to the carrot with fruits (**caraway seed**) used in seasoning and medicine; *also* : its fruit

car·bide \'kär-ˌbīd\ *n* : a compound of carbon with another element

car·bine \'kär-ˌbēn, -ˌbīn\ *n* : a short-barreled lightweight rifle

car·bo·hy·drate \ˌkär-bō-ˈhī-ˌdrāt, -drət\ *n* : any of various compounds composed of carbon, hydrogen, and oxygen (as sugars and starches)

car·bol·ic acid \kär-ˌbäl-ik-\ *n* : PHENOL

car·bon \'kär-bən\ *n* **1** : a nonmetallic chemical element occurring in nature as diamond and graphite and as a constituent of coal, petroleum, and limestone **2** : a sheet of carbon paper; *also* : CARBON COPY 1

car·bo·na·ceous \ˌkär-bə-ˈnā-shəs\ *adj* : relating to, containing, or composed of carbon

¹**car·bon·ate** \'kär-bə-ˌnāt, -nət\ *n* : a salt or ester of carbonic acid

²**car·bon·ate** \-ˌnāt\ *vb* **-at·ed; -at·ing** : to impregnate with carbon dioxide (a *carbonated* beverage) — **car·bon·ation** \ˌkär-bə-ˈnā-shən\ *n*

carbon black *n* : any of various black substances consisting chiefly of carbon used esp. as pigments

carbon copy *n* **1** : a copy made by carbon paper **2** : DUPLICATE

carbon dating *n* : the determination of the age of old material (as an archaeological specimen) by means of the content of carbon 14

carbon dioxide *n* : a heavy colorless gas that does not support combustion and is formed in animal respiration and in the combustion and decomposition of organic substances

carbon 14 *n* : a heavy radioactive form of carbon used in dating archaeological and geological materials

car·bon·ic acid \kär-ˌbän-ik-\ *n* : a weak acid that decomposes readily into water and carbon dioxide

car·bon·if·er·ous \ˌkär-bə-ˈnif-(ə-)rəs\ *adj* **1** : producing or containing carbon or coal **2** *cap* : of, relating to, or being the period of the Paleozoic era between the Devonian and the Permian — **Carboniferous** *n*

carbon monoxide *n* : a colorless odorless very poisonous gas formed by the incomplete burning of carbon

carbon paper *n* : a thin paper coated with a pigment and used for making copies

carbon tet·ra·chlo·ride \-ˌte-trə-ˈklȯr-ˌīd\ *n* : a colorless nonflammable toxic liquid used esp. as a solvent

carbon 12 *n* : the most abundant isotope of carbon having a nucleus of 6 protons and 6 neutrons and used as a reference in the determination of other atomic masses

car·boy \ˈkär-ˌbȯi\ *n* [Per *qarāba*, fr. Ar *qarrābah* demijohn] : a large container for liquids

car·bun·cle \ˈkär-ˌbəŋ-kəl\ *n* : a painful inflammation of the skin and underlying tissue that discharges pus from several openings — **car·bun·cu·lar** \ˌkär-ˈbəŋ-kyə-lər\ *adj*

car·bu·re·tor \ˈkär-b(y)ə-ˌrāt-ər\ *n* : an apparatus for supplying an internal-combustion engine with an explosive mixture of vaporized fuel and air

car·cass \ˈkär-kəs\ *n* : a dead body; *esp* : one of an animal dressed for food

car·cin·o·gen \kär-ˈsin-ə-jən\ *n* : an agent causing or inciting cancer — **car·ci·no·gen·ic** \ˌkärs-ᵊn-ō-ˈjen-ik\ *adj* — **car·ci·no·ge·nic·i·ty** \-jə-ˈnis-ət-ē\ *n*

car·ci·no·ma \ˌkärs-ᵊn-ˈō-mə\ *n, pl* **-mas** *or* **-ma·ta** \-mət-ə\ : a malignant tumor of epithelial origin — **car·ci·no·ma·tous** \-ˈō-mət-əs\ *adj*

¹**card** \ˈkärd\ *vb* : to comb with a card : cleanse and untangle before spinning — **card·er** *n*

²**card** *n* : an instrument for combing fibers (as wool or cotton)

³**card** *n* **1** : PLAYING CARD **2** *pl* : a game played with playing cards; *also* : card playing **3** : a usu. clownishly amusing person : WAG **4** : a flat stiff usu. small piece of paper, cardboard, or plastic **5** : PROGRAM; *esp* : a sports program

⁴**card** *vb* **1** : to list or schedule on a card **2** : SCORE

⁵**card** *abbr* cardinal

car·da·mom \ˈkärd-ə-məm\ *n* : the aromatic capsular fruit of an East Indian herb related to the ginger whose seeds are used as a condiment and in medicine; *also* : this plant

card·board \ˈkärd-ˌbȯrd\ *n* : PAPERBOARD

card–car·ry·ing \ˈkärd-ˌkar-ē-iŋ\ *adj* : being a regularly enrolled member of an organized group and esp. of the Communist party and not merely a sympathizer with its ideals and programs

card catalog *n* : a catalog (as of books) in which the entries are arranged systematically on cards

car·di·ac \ˈkärd-ē-ˌak\ *adj* **1** : of, relating to, or located near the heart **2** : of,

relating to, or affected with heart disease

car·di·gan \ˈkärd-i-gən\ *n* : a sweater or jacket usu. without a collar and with a full-length opening in the front

¹**car·di·nal** \ˈkärd-(ᵊ)nəl\ *n* [ME, fr. OF, fr. LL *cardinalis*, fr. L *cardo* hinge] **1** : an ecclesiastical official of the Roman Catholic Church ranking next below the pope **2** : a crested No. American finch that is nearly completely red in the male

²**cardinal** *adj* : of basic importance : CHIEF, MAIN, PRIMARY — **car·di·nal·ly** \-ē\ *adv*

car·di·nal·ate \-ət, -ˌāt\ *n* : the office, rank, or dignity of a cardinal

cardinal flower *n* : a No. American plant that bears a spike of brilliant red flowers

cardinal number *n* : a number (as 1, 5, 82, 357) that is used in simple counting and answers the question "how many?"

cardinal point *n* : one of the four principal compass points north, south, east, and west

car·di·ol·o·gy \ˌkärd-ē-ˈäl-ə-jē\ *n* : the study of the heart and its action and diseases — **car·di·ol·o·gist** \-ˈäl-ə-jəst\ *n*

car·dio·pul·mo·nary resuscitation \ˈkärd-ē-ō-ˈpu̇l-mə-ˌner-ē-\ *n* : a procedure to restore normal breathing after cardiac arrest that includes the clearance of air passages to the lungs, heart massage by the exertion of pressure on the chest, and the use of drugs

car·dio·vas·cu·lar \ˌkärd-ē-ō-ˈvas-kyə-lər\ *adj* : of or relating to the heart and blood vessels

card·sharp·er \ˈkärd-ˌshär-pər\ *or* **card·sharp** \-ˌshärp\ *n* : a cheater at cards

¹**care** \ˈkeər\ *n* **1** : a heavy sense of responsibility : WORRY, ANXIETY **2** : watchful attention : HEED **3** : CHARGE, SUPERVISION **4** : a person or thing that is an object of anxiety or solicitude

²**care** *vb* **cared; car·ing 1** : to feel anxiety **2** : to feel interest **3** : to give care **4** : to have a liking, fondness, taste, or inclination **5** : to be concerned about (~ what happens)

CARE *abbr* Cooperative for American Relief to Everywhere

ca·reen \kə-ˈrēn\ *vb* **1** : to cause (a boat) to lean over on one side **2** : to sway from side to side

¹**ca·reer** \kə-ˈriər\ *n* [MF *carrière*, fr. Old Provençal *carriera* street, fr. ML *carraria* road for vehicles, fr. L *carrus* car] **1** : a course of action or events; *esp* : a person's progress in his or her chosen occupation **2** : an occupation or profession followed as a life's work

²**career** *vb* : to go at top speed esp. in a headlong manner

care–free \ˈkeər-ˌfrē\ *adj* : free from care or worry

care·ful \-fəl\ *adj* **care·ful·ler; care·ful·**

lest 1 : using or taking care : VIGILANT **2** : marked by solicitude, caution, or prudence — **care·ful·ly** \-ē\ *adv* — **care·ful·ness** *n*

care·less \-ləs\ *adj* **1** : free from care : UNTROUBLED **2** : UNCONCERNED, INDIFFERENT **3** : not taking care **4** : not showing or receiving care — **care·less·ly** *adv* — **care·less·ness** *n*

¹ca·ress \kə-ˈres\ *n* : a tender or loving touch or embrace

²caress *vb* : to touch or stroke tenderly or lovingly — **ca·ress·er** *n*

car·et \ˈkar-ət\ *n* [L, it is missing, fr. *carēre* to be lacking : a mark ∧ used to indicate the place where something is to be inserted

care·tak·er \ˈkeər-ˌtā-kər\ *n* **1** : one in charge usu. as occupant in place of an absent owner **2** : one temporarily fulfilling the functions of an office

care·worn \-ˌwȯorn\ *adj* : showing the effects of grief or anxiety

car·fare \ˈkär-ˌfaər\ *n* : passenger fare (as on a streetcar or bus)

car·go \ˈkär-gō\ *n, pl* **cargoes** *or* **cargos** : the goods carried in a ship, airplane, or vehicle : FREIGHT

car·hop \ˈkär-ˌhäp\ *n* : one who serves customers at a drive-in restaurant

Ca·rib·be·an \ˌkar-ə-ˈbē-ən, kə-ˈrib-ē-ən\ *adj* : of or relating to the eastern and southern West Indies or the Caribbean sea

car·i·bou \ˈkar-ə-ˌbü\ *n, pl* **caribou** *or* **caribous** : any of several large deer of northern No. America and Siberia with palmate antlers in both sexes that are grouped with the reindeer in one species

car·i·ca·ture \ˈkar-i-kə-ˌchür\ *n* **1** : distorted representation to produce a ridiculous effect **2** : a representation esp. in literature or art having the qualities of caricature — **caricature** *vb* — **car·i·ca·tur·ist** \-ˌchür-əst\ *n*

car·ies \ˈkar-ēz\ *n, pl* **caries** : tooth decay

car·il·lon \ˈkar-ə-ˌlän\ *n* : a set of tuned bells sounded by hammers controlled by a keyboard

car·il·lon·neur \ˌkar-ə-lə-ˈnər\ *n* [F] : a carillon player

car·i·ous \ˈkar-ē-əs\ *adj* : affected with caries

car·load \ˈkär-ˌlōd, -ˌlōd\ *n* : a load that fills a car

car·mi·na·tive \kär-ˈmin-ət-iv\ *adj* : expelling gas from the alimentary canal — **carminative** *n*

car·mine \ˈkär-mən, -ˌmīn\ *n* : a vivid red

car·nage \ˈkär-nij\ *n* : great destruction of life : SLAUGHTER

car·nal \ˈkärn-ᵊl\ *adj* **1** : of or relating to the body **2** : SENSUAL — **car·nal·i·ty** \kär-ˈnal-ət-ē\ *n* — **car·nal·ly** \ˈkärn-ᵊl-ē\ *adv*

car·na·tion \kär-ˈnā-shən\ *n* : a cultivated pink of any of numerous usu. double-flowered varieties derived from an Old World species

car·nau·ba wax \kär-ˈnȯ-bə-, ˌkär-nə-ˈü-bə-\ *n* : a brittle yellowish wax from a Brazilian palm that is used esp. in polishes

car·ne·lian \kär-ˈnēl-yən\ *n* : a hard tough reddish quartz used as a gem

car·ni·val \ˈkär-nə-vəl\ *n* [It *carnevale*, fr. *carnelevare*, lit., removal of meat] **1** : a season of merrymaking just before Lent **2** : a boisterous merrymaking **3** : a traveling enterprise offering amusements **4** : an organized program of entertainment

car·niv·o·ra \kär-ˈniv-ə-rə\ *n pl* : carnivorous mammals

car·ni·vore \ˈkär-nə-ˌvȯr\ *n* : a flesh-eating animal; *esp* : any of an order of mammals (as dogs, cats, bears, minks, and seals) feeding mostly on animal flesh

car·niv·o·rous \kär-ˈniv-(ə-)rəs\ *adj* **1** : feeding on animal tissues **2** : of or relating to the carnivores — **car·niv·o·rous·ly** *adv* — **car·niv·o·rous·ness** *n*

car·ny *or* **car·ney** *or* **car·nie** \ˈkär-nē\ *n, pl* **carnies** *or* **carneys 1** : CARNIVAL 3 **2** : one who works with a carnival

car·ol \ˈkar-əl\ *n* : a song of joy, praise, or devotion — **carol** *vb* — **car·ol·er** *or* **car·ol·ler** \-ə-lər\ *n*

car·om \ˈkar-əm\ *n* **1** : a shot in billiards in which the cue ball strikes two other balls **2** : a rebounding esp. at an angle — **carom** *vb*

car·o·tene \ˈkar-ə-ˌtēn\ *n* : any of several orange to red pigments formed esp. in plants and used as a source of vitamin A

ca·rot·id \kə-ˈrät-əd\ *adj* : of, relating to, or being the chief artery or pair of arteries that pass up the neck and supply the head — **carotid** *n*

ca·rous·al \kə-ˈrau̇-zəl\ *n* : CAROUSE

ca·rouse \kə-ˈrau̇z\ *n* [MF *carrousse*, fr. *carous*, adv., all out (in *boire carous* to empty the cup), fr. G *garaus*] : a drunken revel — **carouse** *vb* — **ca·rous·er** *n*

car·ou·sel \ˌkar-ə-ˈsel, ˈkar-ə-ˌsel\ *n* : MERRY-GO-ROUND

¹carp \ˈkärp\ *vb* : to find fault : CAVIL, COMPLAIN — **carp·er** *n*

²carp *n, pl* **carp** *or* **carps** : a long-lived freshwater fish of sluggish waters often raised for food

¹car·pal \ˈkär-pəl\ *adj* : relating to the wrist or the bones of the wrist

²carpal *n* : a carpal element or bone

car·pe di·em \ˌkär-pē-ˈdē-ˌem, -ˈdī-\ *n* [L, enjoy the day] : enjoyment of the present without concern for the future

car·pel \ˈkär-pəl\ *n* : one of the highly modified leaves that together form the ovary of a flower of a seed plant

car·pen·ter \ˈkär-pən-tər\ *n* : one who builds or repairs wooden structures — **carpenter** *vb* — **car·pen·try** \-trē\ *n*

car·pet \ˈkär-pət\ *n* : a heavy fabric

used esp. as a floor covering — **carpet** *vb*

car·pet·bag \-ˌbag\ *n* : a traveling bag common in the 19th century

car·pet·bag·ger \-ˌbag-ər\ *n* : a Northerner in the South after the American Civil War usu. seeking private gain under the reconstruction governments

car·pet·ing \ˌkär-pət-iŋ\ *n* : material for carpets; *also* : CARPETS

car pool *n* : an arrangement by a group of automobile drivers who take turns driving their own cars and carrying the others as passengers — **car·pool** \-ˌpül\ *vb*

car·port \ˈkär-ˌpōrt\ *n* : an open-sided automobile shelter

car·pus \ˈkär-pəs\ *n* : the wrist or its bones

car·ra·geen·an *or* **car·ra·geen·in** \ˌkar-ə-ˈgē-nən\ *n* : a colloid extracted esp. from a dark purple branching seaweed and used in foods esp. to stabilize and thicken them

car·rel \ˈkar-əl\ *n* : a table with bookshelves often partitioned or enclosed for individual study in a library

car·riage \ˈkar-ij\ *n* 1 : the act of carrying 2 : manner of holding the body 3 : a wheeled vehicle 4 *Brit* : a railway passenger coach 5 : a movable part of a machine for supporting some other moving part

carriage trade *n* : trade from well-to-do or upper-class people

car·ri·er \ˈkar-ē-ər\ *n* 1 : one that carries 2 : a person or organization in the transportation business 3 : one who carries germs of a disease in his or her system but is immune to the disease 4 : one who has a gene for a trait or condition that is not expressed in his or her system 5 : an electromagnetic wave whose amplitude or frequency is varied in order to convey a radio or television signal

carrier pigeon *n* : a pigeon used esp. to carry messages

car·ri·on \ˈkar-ē-ən\ *n* : dead and decaying flesh

car·rot \ˈkar-ət\ *n* : the elongated orange-red root of a common garden plant that is eaten as a vegetable; *also* : this plant

car·rou·sel *var of* CAROUSEL

¹**car·ry** \ˈkar-ē\ *vb* **car·ried; car·ry·ing** 1 : to move while supporting : TRANSPORT, CONVEY, TAKE 2 : to influence by mental or emotional appeal 3 : to get possession or control of : CAPTURE, WIN 4 : to transfer from one place (as a column) to another (~ a number in addition) 5 : to have or wear on one's person; *also* : to bear within one 6 : INVOLVE, IMPLY 7 : to hold or bear (oneself) in a specified way 8 : to keep in stock for sale 9 : to sustain the weight or burden of : SUPPORT 10 : to prolong in space, time, or degree 11 : to keep on one's books as a debtor

12 : to succeed in (an election) 13 : to win adoption (as in a legislature) 14 : PUBLISH, PRINT 15 : to reach or penetrate to a distance

²**carry** *n* 1 : an act or method of carrying (fireman's ~) 2 : PORTAGE 3 : the range of a gun or projectile or of a struck or thrown ball

car·ry·all \ˈkar-ē-ˌȯl\ *n* 1 : a light covered carriage for four or more persons 2 : a capacious bag or case

carry away *vb* : to arouse to a high and often excessive degree of emotion

carrying charge *n* : a charge added to the price of merchandise sold on the installment plan

car·ry·on \ˈkar-ē-ˌȯn, -ˌän\ *n* : a piece of luggage suitable for being carried aboard an airplane by a passenger — **car·ry·on** \ˈkar-ē-ˌȯn, -ˌän\ *adj*

carry on \ˌkar-ē-ˈȯn, -ˈän\ *vb* 1 : CONDUCT, MANAGE 2 : to behave in a foolish, excited, or improper manner 3 : to continue in spite of hindrance or discouragement

carry out *vb* 1 : to put into execution 2 : to bring to a successful conclusion

car·sick \ˈkär-ˌsik\ *adj* : affected with motion sickness esp. in an automobile — **car sickness** *n*

¹**cart** \ˈkärt\ *n* 1 : a heavy 2-wheeled wagon 2 : a small wheeled vehicle

²**cart** *vb* : to convey in or as if in a cart — **cart·er** *n*

cart·age \ˈkärt-ij\ *n* : the act of or rate charged for carting

carte blanche \ˈkärt-ˈblän̈sh\ *n, pl* **cartes blanches** \ˈkärt-ˈblän̈sh(-əz)\ [F, lit., blank document] : full discretionary power

car·tel \kär-ˈtel\ *n* : a combination of independent business enterprises designed to limit competition **syn** pool, syndicate, monopoly, trust

car·ti·lage \ˈkärt-ᵊl-ij\ *n* : an elastic tissue composing most of the skeleton of embryonic and very young vertebrates and later mostly turning into bone in higher vertebrates — **car·ti·lag·i·nous** \ˌkärt-ᵊl-ˈaj-ə-nəs\ *adj*

car·tog·ra·phy \kär-ˈtäg-rə-fē\ *n* : the making of maps — **car·tog·ra·pher** \-fər\ *n*

car·ton \ˈkärt-ᵊn\ *n* : a cardboard box or container

car·toon \kär-ˈtün\ *n* 1 : a preparatory sketch (as for a painting) 2 : a drawing intended as humor, caricature, or satire 3 : COMIC STRIP — **cartoon** *vb* — **car·toon·ist** *n*

car·tridge \ˈkär-trij\ *n* 1 : a tube containing a complete charge for a firearm 2 : a container of material for insertion into an apparatus 3 : a case containing photographic film 4 : a small case containing a needle and transducer that attaches to the tone arm of a phonograph 5 : a case containing a magnetic tape or disk 6 : a case for holding integrated circuits containing a computer program (a video-game ~)

cart·wheel \'kärt-ˌhwēl\ *n* **1** : a large coin (as a silver dollar) **2** : a lateral handspring with arms and legs extended

carve \'kärv\ *vb* **carved; carv·ing 1** : to cut with care or precision : shape by cutting **2** : to cut into pieces or slices **3** : to slice and serve meat at table — **carv·er** *n*

cary·at·id \ˌkar-ē-'at-əd\ *n, pl* **-ids** *or* **-i·des** \-ə-ˌdēz\ : a sculptured draped female figure used as an architectural column

ca·sa·ba \kə-'säb-ə\ *n* : any of several muskmelons with a yellow rind and sweet flesh

¹cas·cade \kas-'kād\ *n* **1** : a steep usu. small waterfall **2** : something arranged in a series or succession of stages so that each stage derives from or acts upon the product of the preceding

²cascade *vb* **cas·cad·ed; cas·cad·ing** : to fall, pass, or connect in or as if in a cascade

cas·cara \kas-'kar-ə\ *n* : the dried bark of a small Pacific coastal tree of the U.S. and southern Canada used as a laxative; *also* : this tree

¹case \'kās\ *n* **1** : a particular instance or situation **2** : an inflectional form of a noun, pronoun, or adjective indicating its grammatical relation to other words; *also* : such a relation whether indicated by inflection or not **3** : what actually exists or happens : FACT **4** : a suit or action in law : CAUSE **5** : a convincing argument **6** : an instance of disease or injury; *also* : PATIENT **7** : INSTANCE, EXAMPLE — **in case 1** : IF **2** : as a precaution **3** : as a precaution against the event that — **in case of** : in the event of

²case *n* **1** : a box or container for holding something; *also* : a box with its contents **2** : an outer covering **3** : a divided tray for holding printing type **4** : CASING **2**

³case *vb* **cased; cas·ing 1** : to enclose in or cover with a case **2** : to inspect esp. with intent to rob

ca·sein \kā-'sēn, 'kā-sē-ən\ *n* : any of several phosphorus-containing proteins occurring in or produced from milk

case·ment \'kās-mənt\ *n* : a window sash that opens like a door; *also* : a window having such a sash

case·work \-ˌwərk\ *n* : social work that involves the individual person or family — **case·work·er** *n*

¹cash \'kash\ *n* [MF *or* It: MF *casse* money box, fr. It *cassa*, fr. L *capsa* chest] **1** : ready money **2** : money or its equivalent paid at the time of purchase or delivery

²cash *vb* : to pay or obtain cash for

ca·shew \'kash-ü, kə-'shü\ *n* : an edible kidney-shaped nut of a tropical

American tree related to the sumacs; *also* : the tree

¹ca·shier \ka-'shiər\ *vb* : to dismiss from service; *esp* : to dismiss in disgrace

²cash·ier \ka-'shiər\ *n* **1** : a bank official responsible for moneys received and paid out **2** : one who receives and records payments

cashier's check *n* : a check drawn by a bank upon its own funds and signed by its cashier

cash in *vb* **1** : to convert into cash ⟨*cash in* bonds⟩ **2** : to settle accounts and withdraw from a gambling game or business deal **3** : to obtain financial profit or advantage

cash·mere \'kazh-ˌmiər, 'kash-\ *n* : fine wool from the undercoat of an Indian goat (**cashmere goat**) or a yarn spun of this; *also* : a soft twilled fabric orig. woven from this yarn

cash register *n* : a business machine that indicates each sale and often records the money received

cas·ing \'kā-siŋ\ *n* **1** : something that encases **2** : the frame of a door or window

ca·si·no \kə-'sē-nō\ *n, pl* **-nos** [It, fr. *casa* house] **1** : a building or room for social amusements; *esp* : one used for gambling **2** *also* **cas·si·no** : a card game in which players win cards by matching those on the table

cask \'kask\ *n* [MF *casque* helmet, fr. Sp *casco* potsherd, skull, helmet, fr. *cascar* to break] : a barrel-shaped container usu. for liquids; *also* : the quantity held by such a container

cas·ket \'kas-kət\ *n* **1** : a small box (as for jewels) **2** : COFFIN

casque \'kask\ *n* : HELMET

cas·sa·va \kə-'säv-ə\ *n* : any of several tropical spurges with rootstocks yielding a nutritious starch from which tapioca is prepared; *also* : the rootstock or its starch

cas·se·role \'kas-ə-ˌrōl, 'kaz-\ *n* **1** : a dish in which food may be baked and served **2** : a dish cooked and served in a casserole

cas·sette *also* **ca·sette** \kə-'set\ *n* **1** : a lightproof container for photographic plates or film **2** : a plastic case containing magnetic tape

cas·sia \'kash-ə\ *n* **1** : a coarse cinnamon bark **2** : any of various East Indian leguminous herbs, shrubs, and trees of which several yield senna

cas·sit·er·ite \kə-'sit-ə-ˌrīt\ *n* : a dark mineral that is the chief tin ore

cas·sock \'kas-ək\ *n* : an ankle-length garment worn esp. by Roman Catholic and Anglican clergy

cas·so·wary \'kas-ə-ˌwer-ē\ *n, pl* **-war·ies** : any of several large birds closely related to the emu

¹cast \'kast\ *vb* **cast; cast·ing 1** : THROW, FLING **2** : DIRECT ⟨~ a glance⟩ **3** : to deposit (a ballot) formally **4** : to throw off, out, or away : DISCARD, SHED **5** : COMPUTE; *esp* : to add up **6** : to assign the parts of (a play) to actors; *also* : to assign to a role or part **7** : to shape (a substance) by pouring in liquid or plastic form into a mold and letting harden without pressure **8** : to make (as a knot or stitch) by looping or catching up

²**cast** *n* **1** : THROW, FLING **2** : a throw of dice **3** : the group of actors to whom parts in a play are assigned **4** : something formed in or as if in a mold; *also* : a rigid surgical dressing (as for protecting and supporting a fractured bone) **5** : TINGE, HUE **6** : APPEARANCE, LOOK **7** : something thrown out or off, shed, or expelled (worm ~s)

cas·ta·net \ˌkas-tə-ˈnet\ *n* [Sp *castañeta*, fr. *castaña* chestnut, fr. L *castanea*] : a rhythm instrument consisting of two small wooden, ivory, or plastic shells held in the hand and clicked together

cast·away \ˈkas-tə-ˌwā\ *adj* **1** : thrown away : REJECTED **2** : cast adrift or ashore as a survivor of a shipwreck — **castaway** *n*

caste \ˈkast\ *n* [Port *casta*, lit., race, lineage, fr. fem. of *casto* pure, chaste, fr. L *castus*] **1** : one of the hereditary social classes in Hinduism **2** : a division of a society based on wealth, inherited rank, or occupation **3** : social position : PRESTIGE **4** : a system of rigid social stratification

cas·tel·lat·ed \ˈkas-tə-ˌlāt-əd\ *adj* : having battlements like a castle

cast·er \ˈkas-tər\ *n* **1** *or* **cas·tor** : a small container to hold salt or pepper at the table **2** : a small wheel that turns freely and is used to support and move furniture, trucks, and machines

cas·ti·gate \ˈkas-tə-ˌgāt\ *vb* **-gat·ed; -gat·ing** : to punish or criticize severely — **cas·ti·ga·tion** \ˌkas-tə-ˈgā-shən\ *n* — **cas·ti·ga·tor** \ˈkas-tə-ˌgāt-ər\ *n*

cast·ing \ˈkas-tiŋ\ *n* **1** : CAST 7 **2** : something cast in a mold

casting vote *n* : a deciding vote cast by a presiding officer to break a tie

cast iron *n* : a hard brittle alloy of iron, carbon, and silicon cast in a mold

cas·tle \ˈkas-əl\ *n* **1** : a large fortified building or set of buildings **2** : a large or imposing house **3** : ³ROOK

castle in the air : an impracticable project

cast·off \ˈkas-ˌtȯf\ *adj* : thrown away or aside : DISCARDED — **cast·off** *n*

cas·tor oil \ˌkas-tər-\ *n* : a thick yellowish oil extracted from the poisonous seeds of an herb (**castor–oil plant**) and used as a lubricant and cathartic

cas·trate \ˈkas-ˌtrāt\ *vb* **cas·trat·ed; cas·trat·ing** : to deprive of sex glands and esp. testes — **cas·trat·er** *or* **cas·tra·tor** \-ər\ *n* — **cas·tra·tion** \ka-ˈstrā-shən\ *n*

ca·su·al \ˈkazh-(ə-w)əl\ *adj* **1** : resulting from or occurring by chance **2** : OCCASIONAL, INCIDENTAL **3** : OFFHAND, NONCHALANT **4** : designed for informal use

(~ clothing) — **ca·su·al·ly** \-ē\ *adv* — **ca·su·al·ness** *n*

ca·su·al·ty \ˈkazh-(ə-w)əl-tē\ *n, pl* **-ties 1** : serious or fatal accident **2** : a military person lost through death, injury, sickness, or capture or through being missing in action **3** : a person or thing injured, lost, or destroyed

ca·su·ist·ry \ˈkazh-ə-wə-strē\ *n, pl* **-ries** : adroit and esp. false or misleading argument or reasoning usu. about morals — **ca·su·ist** \-wəst\ *n* — **ca·su·is·tic** \ˌkazh-ə-ˈwis-tik\ *or* **ca·su·is·ti·cal** \-ti-kəl\ *adj*

ca·sus bel·li \ˌkäs-əs-ˈbel-ē, ˌkä-səs-ˈbel-ˌī\ *n, pl* **ca·sus belli** \ˌkäs-üs-, ˌkä-süs-\ [NL, occasion of war] : a cause or pretext for a declaration of war

¹**cat** \ˈkat\ *n* **1** : a common domestic mammal long kept by human beings as a pet or for catching rats and mice **2** : any of various animals (as the lion, lynx, or leopard) of the same family as the domestic cat **3** : a spiteful woman **4** : CAT-O'-NINE-TAILS **5** *slang* : GUY

²**cat** *abbr* catalog

CAT *abbr* computerized axial tomography

ca·tab·o·lism \kə-ˈtab-ə-ˌliz-əm\ *n* : destructive metabolism involving the release of energy and resulting in the breakdown of complex materials — **cat·a·bol·ic** \ˌkat-ə-ˈbäl-ik\ *adj*

cat·a·clysm \ˈkat-ə-ˌkliz-əm\ *n* : a violent change or upheaval — **cat·a·clys·mal** \ˌkat-ə-ˈkliz-məl\ *or* **cat·a·clys·mic** \-ˈkliz-mik\ *adj*

cat·a·comb \ˈkat-ə-ˌkōm\ *n* : an underground burial place with galleries and recesses for tombs

cat·a·falque \ˈkat-ə-ˌfalk, -ˌfȯ(l)k\ *n* : an ornamental structure sometimes used in solemn funerals to hold the body

cat·a·lep·sy \ˈkat-əl-ˌep-sē\ *n, pl* **-sies** : a trancelike nervous condition characterized esp. by loss of voluntary motion — **cat·a·lep·tic** \ˌkat-əl-ˈep-tik\ *adj or n*

¹**cat·a·log** *or* **cat·a·logue** \ˈkat-əl-ˌȯg\ *n* **1** : LIST, REGISTER **2** : a systematic list of items with descriptive details; *also* : a book containing such a list

²**catalog** *or* **catalogue** *vb* **-loged** *or* **-logued; -log·ing** *or* **-logu·ing 1** : to make a catalog of **2** : to enter in a catalog — **cat·a·log·er** *or* **cat·a·logu·er** *n*

ca·tal·pa \kə-ˈtal-pə\ *n* : a broad-leaved tree with showy flowers and long slim pods

ca·tal·y·sis \kə-ˈtal-ə-səs\ *n, pl* **-y·ses** \-ˌsēz\ : the change and esp. increase in the rate of a chemical reaction brought about by a substance (**cat·a·lyst** \ˈkat-əl-əst\) that is itself unchanged at the end of the reaction — **cat·a·lyt·ic** \ˌkat-əl-ˈit-ik\ *adj* — **cat·a·lyt·i·cal·ly** \-i-k(ə-)lē\ *adv*

catalytic converter *n* : an automobile exhaust-system component in which a catalyst changes harmful gases into mostly harmless products

cat·a·lyze \'kat-ᵊl-₁īz\ vb **-lyzed; -lyz·ing** : to bring about the catalysis of (a chemical reaction)

cat·a·ma·ran \₁kat-ə-mə-'ran\ n [Tamil (a language of southern India) kaṭṭumaram, fr. kaṭṭu to tie + maram tree] : a boat with twin hulls

cat·a·mount \'kat-ə-₁maúnt\ n : COUGAR; also : LYNX

cat·a·pult \'kat-ə-₁pəlt, -₁púlt\ n 1 : an ancient military machine for hurling missiles (as stones and arrows) 2 : a device for launching an airplane (as from an aircraft carrier) — catapult vb

cat·a·ract \'kat-ə-₁rakt\ n 1 : a cloudiness of the lens of the eye obstructing vision 2 : a large waterfall; also : steep rapids in a river

ca·tarrh \kə-'tär\ n : inflammation of a mucous membrane esp. of the nose and throat — **ca·tarrh·al** \-əl\ adj

ca·tas·tro·phe \kə-'tas-trə-(₁)fē\ n [Gk katastrophē, fr. katastrephein to overturn, fr. kata- down + strephein to turn] 1 : a great disaster or misfortune 2 : utter failure — **cat·a·stroph·ic** \₁kat-ə-'sträf-ik\ adj — **cat·a·stroph·i·cal·ly** \-i-k(ə-)lē\ adv

cata·ton·ic \₁kat-ə-'tän-ik\ adj : of, relating to, or marked by schizophrenia characterized esp. by stupor, negativism, rigidity, purposeless excitement, and abnormal posturing — catatonic n

cat·bird \'kat-₁bərd\ n : an American songbird with a catlike mewing call

cat·boat \'kat-₁bōt\ n : a single-masted sailboat with a single large sail extended by a long boom

cat·call \-₁kȯl\ n : a sound like the cry of a cat; also : a noise made to express disapproval — catcall vb

¹**catch** \'kach, 'kech\ vb **caught** \'kȯt\ ; **catch·ing** 1 : to capture esp. after pursuit 2 : TRAP 3 : to discover esp. unexpectedly : SURPRISE, DETECT 4 : to become suddenly aware of 5 : to take hold of : SNATCH ⟨~ at a straw⟩ 6 : INTERCEPT 7 : to get entangled 8 : to become affected with or by ⟨~ fire⟩ ⟨~ cold⟩ 9 : to seize and hold firmly; also : FASTEN 10 : OVERTAKE 11 : to be in time for ⟨~ a train⟩ 12 : to take in and retain 13 : to look at or listen to

²**catch** n 1 : something caught 2 : the act of catching; also : a game consisting of throwing and catching a ball 3 : something that catches or checks or holds immovable ⟨a door ~⟩ 4 : one worth catching esp. as a mate 5 : FRAGMENT, SNATCH 6 : a concealed difficulty or complication

catch·all \-₁ȯl\ n : something to hold a variety of odds and ends

catch–as–catch–can \₁kach-əz-₁kach-'kan, ₁kech-əz-₁kech-\ adj : using any means available

catch·er \'kach-ər, 'kech-\ n : one that catches; esp : a player stationed behind home plate in baseball

catch·ing \-iŋ\ adj 1 : INFECTIOUS, CONTAGIOUS 2 : ALLURING, CATCHY

catch·ment \'kach-mənt, 'kech-\ n 1 : the action of catching water 2 : something that catches water

catch on vb 1 : UNDERSTAND 2 : to become popular

catch·pen·ny \-₁pen-ē\ adj : designed esp. to get small sums of money from the ignorant ⟨a ~ plan⟩

catch–22 \-₁twent-ē-'tü\ n, pl **catch–22's** or **catch–22s** often cap C [fr. Catch-22, a paradoxical rule found in the novel Catch-22 (1961) by Joseph Heller] : a problematic situation for which the only solution is denied by a circumstance inherent in the problem or by a rule; also : the circumstance or rule that denies a solution

catch·up \'kech-əp, 'kach-\ var of CATSUP

catch up vb : to travel or work fast enough to overtake or complete

catch·word \'kach-₁wərd, 'kech-\ n 1 : GUIDE WORD 2 : a word or expression representative of a party, school, or point of view

catchy \'kach-ē, 'kech-\ adj **catch·i·er; -est** 1 : likely to attract attention 2 : easily remembered ⟨~ music⟩ 3 : TRICKY

cat·e·chism \'kat-ə-₁kiz-əm\ n : a summary or test (as of religious doctrine) usu. in the form of questions and answers — **cat·e·chist** \-kist\ n — **cat·e·chize** \-₁kīz\ vb

cat·e·chu·men \₁kat-ə-'kyü-mən\ n : a religious convert receiving training before baptism

cat·e·gor·i·cal \₁kat-ə-'gȯr-i-kəl\ adj 1 : ABSOLUTE, UNQUALIFIED 2 : of, relating to, or constituting a category — **cat·e·gor·i·cal·ly** \-i-k(ə-)lē\ adv

cat·e·go·rize \'kat-i-gə-₁rīz\ vb **-rized; -riz·ing** : to put into a category : CLASSIFY — **cat·e·go·ri·za·tion** \₁kat-i-gə-rə-'zā-shən\ n

cat·e·go·ry \'kat-ə-₁gȯr-ē\ n, pl **-ries** : a division used in classification; also : CLASS, GROUP, KIND

ca·ter \'kāt-ər\ vb 1 : to provide a supply of food 2 : to supply what is wanted — **ca·ter·er** n

cater·cor·ner \₁kat-ē-'kȯr-nər, ₁kat-ə-, ₁kit-ē-\ or **cat·er·cor·nered** adv or adj [obs. cater (four-spot of cards or dice) + E corner] : in a diagonal or oblique position

cat·er·pil·lar \'kat-ə(r)-₁pil-ər\ n [ME catyrpel, fr. OF catepelose, lit., hairy cat] : a wormlike often hairy insect larva esp. of a butterfly or moth

cat·er·waul \'kat-ər-₁wȯl\ vb : to make a harsh cry — caterwaul n

cat·fish \'kat-₁fish\ n : any of several big-headed stout-bodied fishes with slender tactile processes around the mouth

cat·gut \-₁gət\ n : a tough cord made usu. from sheep intestines

ca·thar·sis \kə-'thär-səs\ n, pl **ca·thar-**

ses \-_sēz\ 1 : an act of purging or purification 2 : elimination of a psychological problem by bringing it to consciousness and affording it expression

ca·thar·tic \kə-ˈthärt-ik\ adj or n : PURGATIVE

ca·the·dral \kə-ˈthē-drəl\ n : the principal church of a diocese

cath·e·ter \ˈkath-ət-ər\ n : a tube for insertion into a bodily passage or cavity esp. for injecting or drawing off material

cath·ode \ˈkath-ˌōd\ n 1 : the negative electrode of an electrolytic cell 2 : the positive terminal of a battery 3 : the electron-emitting electrode of an electron tube — ca·thod·ic \ka-ˈthäd-ik\ or cath·od·al \ˈkath-ˌōd-ᵊl\

cathode–ray tube n : a vacuum tube in which a beam of electrons is projected on a fluorescent screen and produces a luminous spot

cath·o·lic \ˈkath-(ə-)lik\ adj 1 : GENERAL, UNIVERSAL 2 cap : of or relating to Catholics and esp. Roman Catholics

Cath·o·lic \ˈkath-(ə-)lik\ n : a member of a church claiming historical continuity from the ancient undivided Christian church; esp : a member of the Roman Catholic Church — Ca·thol·i·cism \kə-ˈthäl-ə-ˌsiz-əm\ n

cath·o·lic·i·ty \ˌkath-ə-ˈlis-ət-ē\ n, pl -ties 1 cap : the character of being in conformity with a Catholic church 2 : liberality of sentiments or views 3 : comprehensive range

cat·ion \ˈkat-ˌī-ən\ n : the ion in an electrolyte that migrates to the cathode; also : a positively charged ion

cat·kin \ˈkat-kən\ n : a long flower cluster (as of a willow) bearing crowded flowers and prominent bracts

cat·like \-ˌlīk\ adj : resembling a cat or its behavior; esp : STEALTHY

cat·nap \-ˌnap\ n : a very short light nap — catnap vb

cat·nip \-ˌnip\ n : an aromatic mint that is esp. attractive to cats

cat–o'–nine–tails \ˌkat-ə-ˈnīn-ˌtālz\ n, pl cat–o'–nine–tails : a whip made of usu. nine knotted cords with a handle

CAT scan \ˈkat-, ˈsē-ˈā-ˈtē-\ n [computerized axial tomography] : an image made by computed tomography

CAT scanner n : a medical instrument consisting of integrated X-ray and computing equipment that is used to make CAT scans

cat's cradle n : a game played with a string looped on the fingers in such a way as to resemble a small cradle

cat's–eye \ˈkats-ˌī\ n, pl cat's–eyes : any of various iridescent gems

cat's–paw \-ˌpȯ\ n, pl cat's–paws : a person used by another as a tool

cat·sup \ˈkech-əp, ˈkach-; ˈkat-səp\ n [Malay kĕchap spiced fish sauce] : a seasoned tomato puree

cat·tail \ˈkat-ˌtāl\ n : a tall reedlike marsh plant with furry brown spikes of tiny flowers

cat·tle \ˈkat-ᵊl\ n pl : LIVESTOCK; esp : domestic bovines (as cows, bulls, or calves) — cat·tle·man \-mən, -ˌman\ n

cat·ty \ˈkat-ē\ adj cat·ti·er; -est : slyly spiteful — cat·ti·ly \ˈkat-ᵊl-ē\ adv — cat·ti·ness \-ē-nəs\ n

cat·ty–cor·ner or cat·ty–cor·nered var of CATERCORNER

CATV abbr community antenna television

cat·walk \ˈkat-ˌwȯk\ n : a narrow walk (as along a bridge)

Cau·ca·sian \kȯ-ˈkā-zhən, -ˈkazh-ən\ adj : of or relating to the white race of mankind — Caucasian n — Cau·ca·soid \ˈkȯ-kə-ˌsȯid\ adj or n

cau·cus \ˈkȯ-kəs\ n : a meeting of a group of persons belonging to the same political party or faction usu. to decide upon policies and candidates — cau·cus vb

cau·dal \ˈkȯd-ᵊl\ adj : of, relating to, or located near the tail or the hind end of the body — cau·dal·ly \-ē\ adv

cau·di·llo \kau̇-ˈthē-(y)ō, -ˈthēl-yō\ n, pl -llos : a Spanish or Latin-American military dictator

caught \ˈkȯt\ past and past part of CATCH

caul \ˈkȯl\ n : the inner fetal membrane of higher vertebrates esp. when covering the head at birth

cauldron var of CALDRON

cau·li·flow·er \ˈkȯ-li-ˌflau̇(-ə)r\ n [It cavolfiore, fr. cavolo cabbage (fr. L caulis stem, cabbage) + fiore flower] : a garden plant closely related to cabbage and grown for its compact edible head of undeveloped flowers; also : this head

cauliflower ear n : an ear deformed from injury and excessive growth of scar tissue

¹caulk \ˈkȯk\ vb [ME caulken, fr. OF cauquer to trample, fr. L calcare, fr. calx heel] : to make the seams of (a boat) watertight by filling with waterproofing material; also : to make tight against leakage (~ a pipe joint) — caulk·er n

²caulk also caulk·ing \ˈkȯ-kiŋ\ n : material used to caulk

cau·ri \ˈkau̇-rē\ n, pl cauris — see syli at MONEY table

caus·al \ˈkȯ-zəl\ adj 1 : expressing or indicating cause 2 : relating to or acting as a cause — cau·sal·i·ty \kȯ-ˈzal-ət-ē\ n — caus·al·ly \ˈkȯ-zə-lē\ adv

cau·sa·tion \kȯ-ˈzā-shən\ n 1 : the act or process of causing 2 : the means by which an effect is produced

¹cause \ˈkȯz\ n 1 : REASON, MOTIVE 2 : something that brings about a result; esp : a person or thing that is the agent of bringing something about 3 : a suit or action in court : CASE 4 : a question or matter to be decided 5 : a principle or movement earnestly supported — cause·less adj

²**cause** vb **caused; caus·ing** : to be the cause or occasion of — **caus·ative** \'kȯ-zət-iv\ adj — **caus·er** n

cause cé·lè·bre \ˌkȯz-sā-'lebrᵊ, ˌkȯz-\ n, pl **causes célèbres** \same\ [F, lit., celebrated case] 1 : a legal case that excites widespread interest 2 : a notorious incident or episode

cau·se·rie \ˌkȯz-(ə-)'rē\ n [F] 1 : an informal conversation : CHAT 2 : a short informal composition

cause·way \'kȯz-ˌwā\ n : a raised way or road across wet ground or water

¹**caus·tic** \'kȯ-stik\ adj 1 : CORROSIVE 2 : SHARP, INCISIVE (~ wit)

²**caustic** n 1 : a substance that burns or destroys organic tissue by chemical action 2 : SODIUM HYDROXIDE

cau·ter·ize \'kȯt-ə-ˌrīz\ vb **-ized; iz·ing** : to burn or sear usu. to prevent infection or bleeding — **cau·ter·iza·tion** \ˌkȯt-ə-rə-'zā-shən\ n

¹**cau·tion** \'kȯ-shən\ n 1 : ADMONITION, WARNING 2 : prudent forethought to minimize risk : WARINESS 3 : one that arouses astonishment — **cau·tion·ary** \-shə-ˌner-ē\ adj

²**caution** vb **cau·tioned; cau·tion·ing** \'kȯ-sh(ə-)niŋ\ : to advise caution to : WARN

cau·tious \'kȯ-shəs\ adj : marked by or given to caution : CAREFUL — **cau·tious·ly** adv — **cau·tious·ness** n

cav abbr 1 cavalry 2 cavity

cav·al·cade \ˌkav-əl-'kād\ n 1 : a procession of riders or carriages; also : a procession of vehicles 2 : a dramatic sequence or procession

¹**cav·a·lier** \ˌkav-ə-'liər\ n [MF, fr. It cavaliere, fr. Old Provençal cavalier, fr. LL caballarius groom, fr. L caballus horse] 1 : a mounted soldier : KNIGHT 2 cap : an adherent of Charles I of England 3 : a debonair person

²**cavalier** adj 1 : gay and easy in manner : DEBONAIR 2 : DISDAINFUL, HAUGHTY — **cav·a·lier·ly** adv

cav·al·ry \'kav-əl-rē\ n, pl **-ries** : troops mounted on horseback or moving in motor vehicles — **cav·al·ry·man** \-mən, -ˌman\ n

¹**cave** \'kāv\ n : a natural underground chamber with an opening to the surface

²**cave** vb **caved; cav·ing** 1 : to collapse or cause to collapse 2 : to cease to resist : SUBMIT — usu. used with in

ca·ve·at \'kā-vē-ˌat, -ˌät; 'käv-ē-ˌät\ n [L, let him beware] : WARNING

caveat emp·tor \-'emp-tər, -ˌtȯr\ n [NL, let the buyer beware] : a warning principle in trading that buyers should be alert to see that they get the quantity and quality paid for

cave-in \'kā-ˌvin\ n 1 : the action of caving in 2 : a place where earth has caved in

cave·man \'kāv-ˌman\ n 1 : a cave dweller esp. of the Stone Age 2 : one

who acts with rough or violent directness esp. toward women

cav·ern \'kav-ərn\ n : a cave often of large or unknown size — **cav·ern·ous** adj — **cav·ern·ous·ly** adv

cav·i·ar or **cav·i·are** \'kav-ē-ˌär, 'käv-\ n : the salted roe of a large fish (as sturgeon) used as an appetizer

cav·il \'kav-əl\ vb **-iled** or **-illed; il·ing** or **il·ling** \-(ə-)liŋ\ : to find fault without good reason : make frivolous objections — **cavil** n — **cav·il·er** or **cav·il·ler** n

cav·ing \'kā-viŋ\ n : the sport of exploring caves : SPELUNKING

cav·i·ta·tion \ˌkav-ə-'tā-shən\ n : the formation of partial vacuums in a liquid by a swiftly moving solid body (as a propeller) or by high-frequency sound waves; also : a cavity so formed

cav·i·ty \'kav-ət-ē\ n, pl **-ties** 1 : an unfilled space within a mass : a hollow place 2 : an area of decay in a tooth

ca·vort \kə-'vȯrt\ vb : PRANCE, CAPER

ca·vy \'kā-vē\ n, pl **cavies** : GUINEA PIG

caw \'kȯ\ vb : to utter the harsh call of the crow or a similar cry — **caw** n

cay \'kē, 'kā\ n : ⁴KEY

cay·enne pepper \ˌkī-ˌen-, ˌkā-\ n : a condiment consisting of ground dried fruits or seeds of a hot pepper

cay·man var of CAIMAN

Ca·yu·ga \kā-'ü-gə, kī-\ n, pl **Cayuga** or **Cayugas** : a member of an American Indian people of New York

Cay·use \kī-'(y)üs, kī-'(y)üs\ n 1 pl **Cayuse** or **Cayuses** : a member of an American Indian people of Oregon and Washington 2 pl cayuses, not cap, West : a native range horse of the western U.S.

Cb symbol columbium

CB \'sē-'bē\ n : CITIZENS BAND

CBC abbr Canadian Broadcasting Corporation

CBD abbr cash before delivery

CBS abbr Columbia Broadcasting System

CBW abbr chemical and biological warfare

cc abbr cubic centimeter

CC abbr 1 carbon copy 2 community college 3 country club

CCC abbr Civilian Conservation Corps

CCD \'sē-ˌsē-'dē\ n : CHARGE-COUPLED DEVICE

CCTV abbr closed-circuit television

CCU abbr 1 cardiac care unit 2 coronary care unit 3 critical care unit

ccw abbr counterclockwise

cd abbr cord

Cd symbol cadmium

CD abbr 1 certificate of deposit 2 Civil Defense

CDR abbr commander

CDT abbr central daylight (saving) time

Ce symbol cerium

CE abbr 1 chemical engineer 2 civil engineer 3 Corps of Engineers

cease \'sēs\ vb **ceased; ceas·ing** : to come or bring to an end : STOP

cease–fire \'sēs-'fī(ə)r\ n : a suspension of active hostilities

cease·less \'sēs-ləs\ adj : being without pause or stop : CONTINUOUS — **cease·less·ly** adv — **cease·less·ness** n

ce·cum \'sē-kəm\ n, pl **ce·ca** \-kə\ : the blind pouch at the beginning of the large intestine into which the small intestine opens — **ce·cal** \-kəl\ adj

ce·dar \'sēd-ər\ n : any of a genus of trees related to the pines that are noted for their fragrant durable wood; also : this wood

cede \'sēd\ vb **ced·ed; ced·ing** 1 : to yield or give up esp. by treaty 2 : AS-SIGN, TRANSFER — **ced·er** n

ce·di \'sād-ē\ n — see MONEY table

ce·dil·la \si-'dil-ə\ n : a mark placed under the letter c (as ç) to show that the c is to be pronounced like s

ceil·ing \'sē-liŋ\ n 1 : the overhead inside lining of a room 2 : the height above the ground of the base of the lowest layer of clouds when over half of the sky is obscured 3 : the greatest height at which an airplane can operate efficiently 4 : a prescribed upper limit (price ~)

cel·an·dine \'sel-ən-ˌdīn, -ˌdēn\ n : a yellow-flowered herb related to the poppies

cel·e·brate \'sel-ə-ˌbrāt\ vb **-brat·ed; -brat·ing** 1 : to perform (as a sacrament) with appropriate rites 2 : to honor (as a holiday) by solemn ceremonies or by refraining from ordinary business 3 : to observe a notable occasion with festivities 4 : EXTOL — **cel·e·brant** \-brənt\ n — **cel·e·bra·tion** \ˌsel-ə-'brā-shən\ n — **cel·e·bra·tor** \'sel-ə-ˌbrāt-ər\ n

cel·e·brat·ed \-əd\ adj : widely known and often referred to syn distinguished, renowned, noted, famous, illustrious, notorious

ce·leb·ri·ty \sə-'leb-rət-ē\ n, pl **-ties** 1 : the state of being celebrated : RE-NOWN 2 : a celebrated person

ce·ler·i·ty \sə-'ler-ət-ē\ n : SPEED, RAPIDITY

cel·ery \'sel-(ə-)rē\ n, pl **-er·ies** : a European herb related to the carrot and widely grown for the crisp edible stems of its leaves

celery cabbage n : CHINESE CABBAGE

ce·les·ta \sə-'les-tə\ or **ce·leste** \sə-'lest\ n : a keyboard instrument with hammers that strike steel plates

ce·les·tial \sə-'les-chəl\ adj 1 : HEAVENLY, DIVINE 2 : of or relating to the sky — **ce·les·tial·ly** \-ē\ adv

celestial navigation n : navigation by observation of the positions of celestial bodies

celestial sphere n : an imaginary sphere of infinite radius against which the celestial bodies appear to be projected

cel·i·ba·cy \'sel-ə-bə-sē\ n 1 : the state of being unmarried; esp : abstention

by vow from marriage 2 : CHASTITY

cel·i·bate \'sel-ə-bət\ n : one who lives in celibacy — **celibate** adj

cell \'sel\ n 1 : a small room (as in a convent or prison) usu. for one person; also : a small compartment, cavity, or bounded space 2 : a tiny mass of protoplasm that contains a nucleus, is enclosed by a membrane, and forms the fundamental unit of living matter 3 : a container holding an electrolyte either for generating electricity or for use in electrolysis 4 : a single unit in a device for converting radiant energy into electrical energy

cel·lar \'sel-ər\ n 1 : BASEMENT 1 2 : the lowest position (as in an athletic league) 3 : a stock of wines

cel·lar·age \'sel-ə-rij\ n : cellar space esp. for storage

cel·lar·ette or **cel·lar·et** \ˌsel-ə-'ret\ n : a case or cabinet for a few bottles of wine or liquor

cel·lo \'chel-ō\ n, pl **cellos** : a bass member of the violin family tuned an octave below the viola — **cel·list** \-əst\ n

cel·lo·phane \'sel-ə-ˌfān\ n : a thin transparent material made from cellulose and used as a wrapping

cel·lu·lar \'sel-yə-lər\ adj : of, relating to, or consisting of cells

cel·lu·lite \'sel-yə-ˌlīt\ n : lumpy fat in the thighs, hips, and buttocks of some women

cel·lu·lose \-ˌlōs\ n : a complex carbohydrate of the cell walls of plants used esp. in making paper or rayon — **cel·lu·los·ic** \ˌsel-yə-'lō-sik\ adj or n

Cel·sius \'sel-sē-əs\ adj : relating to or having a scale for measuring temperature on which the interval between the triple point and the boiling point of water is divided into 99.99 degrees with 0.01° being the triple point and 100.00° the boiling point

Celt \'selt, 'kelt\ n : a member of any of a group of peoples (as the Irish or Welsh) of western Europe — **Celt·ic** adj

cem·ba·lo \'chem-bə-ˌlō\ n, pl **-ba·li** \-ˌlē\ or **-balos** [It] : HARPSICHORD

¹**ce·ment** \si-'ment\ n 1 : a powder that is produced from a burned mixture chiefly of clay and limestone and that is used in mortar and concrete; also : CONCRETE 2 : a binding element or agency 3 : CEMENTUM; also : a substance for filling cavities in teeth

²**cement** vb 1 : to unite by or as if by cement 2 : to cover with concrete — **ce·ment·er** n

ce·men·tum \si-'ment-əm\ n : a specialized external bony layer of the part of a tooth normally within the gum

cem·e·tery \'sem-ə-ˌter-ē\ n, pl **-ter·ies** [ME cimitery, fr. MF cimitere, fr. LL coemeterium, fr. Gk koimētērion sleeping chamber, burial place, fr. koiman to put to sleep] : a burial ground : GRAVEYARD

cen·o·bite \'sen-ə-ˌbīt\ n : a member of

a religious group living together in a monastic community — **cen·o·bit·ic** \ˌsen-ə-'bit-ik\ *adj*

ceno·taph \'sen-ə-ˌtaf\ *n* [F *cénotaphe*, fr. L *cenotaphium*, fr. Gk *kenotaphion*, fr. *kenos* empty + *taphos* tomb] : a tomb or a monument erected in honor of a person whose body is elsewhere

Ce·no·zo·ic \ˌsē-nə-'zō-ik, ˌsen-ə-\ *adj* [deriv. of Gk *kainos* new, recent] : of, relating to, or being the most recent of the five eras of geologic history extending from about 70 million years ago to the present — **Cenozoic** *n*

cen·ser \'sen-sər\ *n* : a vessel for burning incense (as in a religious ritual)

¹cen·sor \'sen-sər\ *n* 1 : one of two early Roman magistrates whose duties included taking the census 2 : an official who inspects printed matter or sometimes motion pictures with power to suppress anything objectionable — **cen·so·ri·al** \sen-'sōr-ē-əl\ *adj*

²censor *vb* : to subject to censorship

cen·so·ri·ous \sen-'sōr-ē-əs\ *adj* : marked by or given to censure : CRITICAL — **cen·so·ri·ous·ly** *adv* — **cen·so·ri·ous·ness** *n*

cen·sor·ship \'sen-sər-ˌship\ *n* 1 : the action of a censor esp. in stopping the transmission or publication of matter considered objectionable 2 : the office of a Roman censor

¹cen·sure \'sen-chər\ *n* 1 : the act of blaming or condemning sternly 2 : an official reprimand

²censure *vb* **cen·sured; cen·sur·ing** \'sench-(ə-)riŋ\ : to find fault with and criticize as blameworthy — **cen·sur·able** *adj*

cen·sus \'sen-səs\ *n* 1 : a periodic governmental count of population 2 : COUNT, TALLY

¹cent \'sent\ *n* [MF, hundred, fr. L *centum*] 1 : a monetary unit equal to ¹⁄₁₀₀ of a basic unit of value — see *birr, dollar, gulden, leone, lilangeni, rand, rupee, shilling* at MONEY table 2 : a coin, token, or note representing one cent

²cent *abbr* 1 centigrade 2 central 3 century

cen·taur \'sen-ˌtȯr\ *n* : any of a race of creatures in Greek mythology half man and half horse

¹cen·ta·vo \sen-'täv-(ˌ)ō\ *n, pl* **-vos** — see *colon, cordoba, lempira, peso, quetzal, sucre* at MONEY table

²cen·ta·vo \-'täv-(ˌ)ü, -(ˌ)ō\ *n, pl* **-vos** — see *dobra, escudo, metical* at MONEY table

cen·te·nar·i·an \ˌsent-ᵊn-'er-ē-ən\ *n* : a person who is 100 or more years old

cen·te·na·ry \sen-'ten-ə-rē, 'sent-ᵊn-ˌer-ē\ *n, pl* **-ries** : CENTENNIAL — **centenary** *adj*

cen·ten·ni·al \sen-'ten-ē-əl\ *n* : a 100th anniversary or its celebration — **centennial** *adj*

¹cen·ter \'sent-ər\ *n* 1 : the point that is

equally distant from all points on the circumference of a circle or surface of a sphere; *also* : MIDDLE 1 2 : the point about which an activity concentrates or from which something originates 3 : a region of concentrated population 4 : a middle part 5 *often cap* : political figures holding moderate views esp. between those of conservatives and liberals 6 : a player occupying a middle position (as in football or basketball)

²center *vb* 1 : to place or fix at or around a center or central area 2 : to gather to a center : CONCENTRATE 3 : to have a center : FOCUS

cen·ter·board \'sent-ər-ˌbȯrd\ *n* : a retractable keel used esp. in sailboats

cen·ter·piece \'sent-ər-ˌpēs\ *n* 1 : an object in a central position; *esp* : an adornment in the center of a table 2 : one that is of central importance or interest

cen·tes·i·mal \sen-'tes-ə-məl\ *adj* : marked by or relating to division into hundredths

¹cen·tes·i·mo \chen-'tez-ə-ˌmō\ *n, pl* **-mi** \-(ˌ)mē\ — see *lira* at MONEY table

²cen·tes·i·mo \sen-'tes-ə-ˌmō\ *n, pl* **-mos** — see *balboa, peso* at MONEY table

cen·ti·grade \'sent-ə-ˌgrād, 'sänt-\ *adj* : relating to, conforming to, or having a thermometer scale on which the interval between the freezing and boiling points of water is divided into 100 degrees with 0° representing the freezing point and 100° the boiling point (10° ~)

cen·ti·gram \-ˌgram\ *n* — see METRIC SYSTEM table

cen·ti·li·ter \'sent-i-ˌlēt-ər\ *n* — see METRIC SYSTEM table

cen·time \'sän-ˌtēm\ *n* — see *dinar, dirham, franc, gourde* at MONEY table

cen·ti·me·ter \'sent-ə-ˌmēt-ər, 'sänt-\ *n* — see METRIC SYSTEM table

centimeter–gram–second *adj* — see CGS

cen·ti·mo \'sent-ə-ˌmō\ *n, pl* **-mos** — see *bolivar, colon, ekuele, guarani, peseta* at MONEY table

cen·ti·pede \'sent-ə-ˌpēd\ *n* [L *centipeda*, fr. *centi-* hundred + *pes* foot] : any of a class of long flattened segmented arthropods with one pair of legs on each segment except the first which has a pair of poison fangs

¹cen·tral \'sen-trəl\ *adj* 1 : constituting a center 2 : ESSENTIAL, PRINCIPAL 3 : situated at, in, or near the center 4 : centrally placed and superseding separate units (~ heating) — **cen·tral·ly** \-ē\ *adv*

²central *n* 1 : a telephone exchange or an operator handling calls there 2 : a central controlling office

cen·tral·ize \'sen-trə-ˌlīz\ *vb* **-ized; -iz·ing** : to bring to a central point or under central control — **cen·tral·iza·tion** \ˌsen-trə-lə-'zā-shən\ *n* — **cen·tral·iz·er** \'sen-trə-ˌlī-zər\ *n*

central nervous system *n* : the part of

the nervous system which integrates nervous function and activity and which in vertebrates consists of the brain and spinal cord

cen·tre *chiefly Brit var of* CENTER

cen·trif·u·gal \sen-'trif-yə-gəl, -'trif-i-gəl\ *adj* [NL *centrifugus*, fr. *centr-* center + *fugere* to flee] 1 : proceeding or acting in a direction away from a center or axis 2 : using or acting by centrifugal force

centrifugal force *n* : the force that tends to impel a thing or parts of a thing outward from a center of rotation

cen·tri·fuge \'sen-trə-,fyüj\ *n* : a machine using centrifugal force (as for separating substances of different densities or for removing moisture)

cen·trip·e·tal \sen-'trip-ət-²l\ *adj* [NL *centripetus*, fr. *centr-* center + L *petere* seek] : proceeding or acting in a direction toward a center or axis

centripetal force *n* : the force needed to keep an object revolving about a point moving in a circular path

cen·trist \'sen-trəst\ *n* 1 *often cap* : a member of a center party 2 : one who holds moderate views

cen·tu·ri·on \sen-'t(y)ùr-ē-ən\ *n* : an officer commanding a Roman century

cen·tu·ry \'sench-(ə-)rē\ *n, pl* **-ries** 1 : a subdivision of a Roman legion 2 : a group or sequence of 100 like things 3 : a period of 100 years

century plant *n* : a Mexican agave maturing and flowering only once in many years and then dying

CEO *abbr* chief executive officer

ce·phal·ic \sə-'fal-ik\ *adj* 1 : of or relating to the head 2 : directed toward or situated on or in or near the head

ce·ram·ic \sə-'ram-ik\ *n* 1 *pl* : the art or process of making articles from a nonmetallic mineral (as clay) by firing 2 : a product produced by ceramics — **ceramic** *adj*

ce·ra·mist \sə-'ram-əst\ *or* **ce·ram·i·cist** \sə-'ram-ə-səst\ *n* : one who engages in ceramics

¹**ce·re·al** \'sir-ē-əl\ *adj* [L *cerealis*, fr. *Ceres*, the Roman goddess of agriculture] : relating to grain or to the plants that produce it; *also* : made of grain

²**cereal** *n* 1 : a grass (as wheat) yielding grain suitable for food; *also* : its grain 2 : grain of a cereal prepared for use as a breakfast food

cer·e·bel·lum \,ser-ə-'bel-əm\ *n, pl* **-bellums** *or* **-bel·la** \-'bel-ə\ [ML, fr. L, dim. of *cerebrum*] : a part of the brain that projects over the medulla and is concerned esp. with coordination of muscular action and with bodily balance — **cer·e·bel·lar** \-'bel-ər\ *adj*

ce·re·bral cortex \sə-,rē-brəl-, ,ser-ə-\ *n* : the surface layer of gray matter of the cerebrum that functions chiefly in coordination of higher nervous activity

cerebral palsy *n* : a disorder caused by brain damage usu. before or during birth and marked esp. by defective muscle control

cer·e·brate \'ser-ə-,brāt\ *vb* **-brat·ed; -brat·ing** : THINK — **cer·e·bra·tion** \,ser-ə-'brā-shən\ *n*

ce·re·brum \sə-'rē-brəm, 'ser-ə-\ *n, pl* **-brums** *or* **-bra** \-brə\ [L] : the enlarged front and upper part of the brain that contains the higher nervous centers — **ce·re·bral** \sə-'rē-brəl, 'ser-ə-\ *adj* — **ce·re·bral·ly** \-ē\ *adv*

cere·cloth \'siər-,klòth\ *n* : cloth treated with melted wax or gummy matter and formerly used esp. for wrapping a dead body

cere·ment \'ser-ə-mənt, 'siər-mənt\ *n* : a shroud for the dead

¹**cer·e·mo·ni·al** \,ser-ə-'mō-nē-əl\ *adj* : of, relating to, or forming a ceremony — **cer·e·mo·ni·al·ly** \-ē\ *adv*

²**ceremonial** *n* : a ceremonial act or system : RITUAL, FORM

cer·e·mo·ni·ous \,ser-ə-'mō-nē-əs\ *adj* 1 : devoted to forms and ceremony 2 : CEREMONIAL 3 : according to formal usage or procedure 4 : marked by ceremony — **cer·e·mo·ni·ous·ly** *adv* — **cer·e·mo·ni·ous·ness** *n*

cer·e·mo·ny \'ser-ə-,mō-nē\ *n, pl* **-nies** 1 : a formal act or series of acts prescribed by law, ritual, or convention 2 : a conventional act of politeness 3 : a mere outward form 4 : FORMALITY

ce·re·us \'sir-ē-əs\ *n* : any of various cacti of the western U.S. and tropical America

ce·rise \sə-'rēs\ *n* [F, lit., cherry] : a moderate red

ce·ri·um \'sir-ē-əm\ *n* : a malleable metallic chemical element used esp. in alloys

cer·met \'sər-,met\ *n* : a strong alloy of a heat-resistant compound and a metal used esp. for turbine blades

cert *abbr* certificate; certification; certified; certify

¹**cer·tain** \'sərt-²n\ *adj* 1 : FIXED, SETTLED 2 : proved to be true 3 : of a specific but unspecified character ⟨~ people in authority⟩ 4 : DEPENDABLE, RELIABLE 5 : INDISPUTABLE, UNDENIABLE 6 : assured in mind or action — **cer·tain·ly** *adv*

²**certain** *pron* : certain ones

cer·tain·ty \-tē\ *n, pl* **-ties** 1 : something that is certain 2 : the quality or state of being certain

cer·tif·i·cate \sər-'tif-i-kət\ *n* 1 : a document testifying to the truth of a fact 2 : a document testifying that one has fulfilled certain requirements (as of a course or school) 3 : a document evidencing ownership or debt

cer·ti·fi·ca·tion \,sərt-ə-fə-'kā-shən\ *n* 1 : the act of certifying : the state of being certified 2 : a certified statement

certified milk *n* : milk produced in dairies that operate under the rules and regulations of an authorized medical milk commission

certified public accountant *n* : an accountant who has met the requirements of a state law and has been granted a state certificate

cer·ti·fy \'sərt-ə-ˌfī\ *vb* **-fied; -fy·ing 1** : VERIFY, CONFIRM **2** : to endorse officially **3** : to guarantee (a bank check) as good by a statement to that effect stamped on its face **4** : to provide with a usu. professional certificate or license *syn* accredit, approve, sanction, endorse — **cer·ti·fi·able** \-ˌfī-ə-bəl\ *adj* — **cer·ti·fi·ably** \-blē\ *adv* — **cer·ti·fi·er** *n*

cer·ti·tude \'sərt-ə-ˌt(y)üd\ *n* : the state of being or feeling certain

ce·ru·le·an \sə-'rü-lē-ən\ *adj* : AZURE

ce·ru·men \sə-'rü-mən\ *n* : EARWAX

cer·vi·cal \'sər-vi-kəl\ *adj* : of or relating to a neck or cervix

cer·vix \'sər-viks\ *n*, *pl* **cer·vi·ces** \-və-ˌsēz\ *or* **cer·vix·es 1** : NECK; *esp* : the back part of the neck **2** : a constricted portion of an organ or part; *esp* : the narrow outer end of the uterus

ce·sar·e·an *also* **ce·sar·i·an** \si-'zar-ē-ən, -'zer-\ *n* : CESAREAN SECTION — **cesarean** *also* **cesarian** *adj*

cesarean section *also* **cesarian section** *n* [fr. the legend that Julius Caesar was born this way] : surgical incision of the walls of the abdomen and uterus for delivery of offspring

ce·si·um \'sē-zē-əm\ *n* : a silver-white soft ductile chemical element

ces·sa·tion \se-'sā-shən\ *n* : a temporary or final ceasing (as of action)

ces·sion \'sesh-ən\ *n* : a yielding (as of rights) to another

cess·pool \'ses-ˌpül\ *n* : an underground pit or tank for receiving household sewage

cf *abbr* [L *confer*] compare

Cf *symbol* californium

CF *abbr* cystic fibrosis

cg *or* **cgm** *abbr* centigram

CG *abbr* **1** coast guard **2** commanding general

cgs \'sē-ˌjē-'es\ *adj*, *often cap C&G&S* : of, relating to, or being a system of units based on the centimeter as the unit of length, the gram as the unit of weight, and the second as the unit of time

ch *abbr* **1** chain **2** champion **3** chapter **4** church

CH *abbr* **1** clearinghouse **2** courthouse **3** customhouse

Cha·blis \'shab-ˌlē; sha-'blē\ *n*, *pl* **Cha·blis** \-ˌlēz, -'blēz\ **1** : a dry sharp white Burgundy wine **2** : a white California wine that is a blend of several grapes

cha–cha \'chä-ˌchä\ *n* : a fast rhythmic ballroom dance of Latin American origin

Chad·ian \'chad-ē-ən\ *n* : a native or inhabitant of Chad — **Chadian** *adj*

chafe \'chāf\ *vb* **chafed; chaf·ing 1** : IRRITATE, VEX **2** : FRET **3** : to warm by

rubbing **4** : to rub so as to wear away; *also* : to make sore by rubbing

cha·fer \'chā-fər\ *n* : any of various large beetles

¹chaff \'chaf\ *n* **1** : debris (as husks) separated from grain in threshing **2** : something comparatively worthless — **chaffy** \-ē\ *adj*

²chaff *n* : light jesting talk : BANTER

³chaff *vb* : to tease in a good-natured manner

chaf·fer \'chaf-ər\ *vb* : BARGAIN, HAGGLE — **chaf·fer·er** *n*

chaf·finch \'chaf-ˌinch\ *n* : a European finch with a cheerful song

chafing dish \'chā-fiŋ-\ *n* : a utensil for cooking food at the table

cha·grin \shə-'grin\ *n* : mental uneasiness or annoyance caused by failure, disappointment, or humiliation

²chagrin *vb* **cha·grined** \-'grind\; **cha·grin·ing** \-'grin-iŋ\ : to cause to feel chagrin

¹chain \'chān\ *n* **1** : a flexible series of connected links **2** : a chainlike surveying instrument; *also* : a unit of length equal to 66 feet (about 20 meters) **3** : a series of things linked together *syn* train, string, sequence, succession, series

²chain *vb* : to fasten, bind, or connect with a chain; *also* : FETTER

chain gang *n* : a gang of convicts chained together

chain letter *n* : a letter sent to several persons with a request that each send copies to an equal number of persons

chain mail *n* : flexible armor of interlocking metal rings

chain reaction *n* **1** : a series of events in which each event initiates the succeeding one **2** : a chemical or nuclear reaction yielding products that cause further reactions of the same kind

chain saw *n* : a portable power saw that has teeth linked together to form an endless chain

chain–smoke \'chān-ˌsmōk\ *vb* : to smoke esp. cigarettes continuously

chain store *n* : any of numerous stores under the same ownership that sell the same lines of goods

¹chair \'cheər\ *n* **1** : a seat with a back for one person **2** : ELECTRIC CHAIR **3** : an official seat; *also* : an office or position of authority or dignity **4** : CHAIRMAN

²chair *vb* : to act as chairman of

chair lift *n* : a motor-driven conveyor for skiers consisting of seats hung from a moving cable

chair·man \'cheər-mən\ *n* : the presiding officer of a meeting or of a committee — **chair·man·ship** *n*

chair·wom·an \-ˌwùm-ən\ *n* : a woman who acts as chairman

chaise \'shāz\ *n* **1** : a 2-wheeled carriage with a folding top **2** : a light carriage or pleasure cart

chaise longue \'shāz-'lȯŋ\ *n*, *pl* **chaise longues** \-'lȯŋ(z)\ [F *chaise longue*, lit., long chair] : a long couch-like chair

chaise lounge \-'laûnj\ n : CHAISE LONGUE

chal·ced·o·ny \kal-'sed-ᵊn-ē\ n, pl **-nies** : a translucent pale blue or gray quartz

chal·co·py·rite \,kal-kə-'pī-,rīt\ n : a yellow mineral constituting an important ore of copper

cha·let \sha-'lā\ n 1 : a herdsman's cabin in the Swiss mountains 2 : a building in the style of a Swiss cottage with a wide roof overhang

chal·ice \'chal-əs\ n : a drinking cup; esp : the eucharistic cup

¹**chalk** \'chôk\ n 1 : a soft limestone 2 : chalk or chalky material esp. when used as a crayon — **chalky** adj

²**chalk** vb 1 : to rub or mark with chalk 2 : to record with or as if with chalk — usu. used with up

chalk·board \'chôk-,bôrd\ n : BLACKBOARD

chalk up vb 1 : ASCRIBE, CREDIT 2 : ATTAIN, ACHIEVE

¹**chal·lenge** \'chal-ənj\ vb **chal·lenged; chal·leng·ing** [ME chalengen to accuse, fr. OF chalengier, fr. L calumniari to accuse falsely, fr. calumnia calumny] 1 : to order to halt and prove identity 2 : to take exception to : DISPUTE 3 : to issue an invitation to compete against one esp. in single combat : DARE, DEFY — **chal·leng·er** n

²**challenge** n 1 : a summons to a duel 2 : an invitation to compete in a sport 3 : a calling into question 4 : an exception taken to a juror 5 : a sentry's command to halt and prove identity 6 : a stimulating or interesting task or problem

chal·lis \'shal-ē\ n, pl **chal·lises** \-ēz\ : a lightweight clothing fabric of wool, cotton, or synthetic yarns

cham \'kam\ var of KHAN

cham·ber \'chām-bər\ n 1 : ROOM; esp : BEDROOM 2 : an enclosed space or compartment 3 : a hall for meetings of a legislative body 4 : a judge's consultation room — usu. used in pl. 5 : a legislative or judicial body; also : a council for a business purpose 6 : the part of a firearm that holds the cartridge or powder charge during firing — **cham·bered** \-bərd\ adj

cham·ber·lain \'chām-bər-lən\ n 1 : a chief officer in the household of a king or nobleman 2 : TREASURER

cham·ber·maid \-,mād\ n : a maid who takes care of bedrooms

chamber music n : music intended for performance by a few musicians before a small audience

chamber of commerce : an association of businesspeople for promoting commercial and industrial interests in the community

cham·bray \'sham-,brā\ n : a lightweight clothing fabric of white and colored threads

cha·me·leon \kə-'mēl-yən\ n [ME camelion, fr. MF, fr. L chamaeleon, fr. Gk chamaileōn, fr. chamai on the ground + leōn lion] : a small lizard whose skin changes color esp. according to its surroundings

¹**cham·fer** \'cham-fər\ n : a beveled edge

²**chamfer** vb 1 : to cut a furrow in (as a column) : GROOVE 2 : to make a chamfer on : BEVEL

cham·ois \'sham-ē\ n, pl **cham·ois** \-ē(z)\ 1 : a small goatlike antelope of Europe and the Caucasus region of the U.S.S.R. 2 also **cham·my** \-ē\ : a soft leather made esp. from the skin of the sheep or goat 3 : a cotton fabric made in imitation of chamois leather

cham·o·mile \'kam-ə-,mīl, -,mēl\ n : any of a genus of strong-scented herbs related to the daisies and having flower heads that yield a bitter medicinal substance

¹**champ** \'champ, 'chämp\ vb 1 : to chew noisily 2 : to show impatience of delay or restraint

²**champ** \'champ\ n : CHAMPION

cham·pagne \sham-'pān\ n : a white effervescent wine

cham·paign \sham-'pān\ n : a stretch of flat open country

¹**cham·pi·on** \'cham-pē-ən\ n 1 : a militant advocate or defender 2 : one that wins first prize or place in a contest 3 : one that is acknowledged to be better than all others

²**champion** vb : to protect or fight for as a champion syn back, advocate, uphold, support

cham·pi·on·ship \-,ship\ n 1 : the position or title of a champion 2 : the act of championing : DEFENSE 3 : a contest held to determine a champion

¹**chance** \'chans\ n 1 : something that happens without apparent cause 2 : the unpredictable element in existence : LUCK, FORTUNE 3 : OPPORTUNITY 4 : the likelihood of a particular outcome in an uncertain situation : PROBABILITY 5 : RISK 6 : a raffle ticket — **chance** adj — **by chance** : in the haphazard course of events

²**chance** vb **chanced; chanc·ing** 1 : to take place by chance : HAPPEN 2 : to come casually and unexpectedly — used with upon 3 : to leave to chance 4 : to accept the risk of

chan·cel \'chan-səl\ n : the part of a church including the altar and choir

chan·cel·lery or **chan·cel·lory** \'chans-(ə-)lə-rē\ n, pl **-ler·ies** or **-lor·ies** 1 : the position or office of a chancellor 2 : the building or room where a chancellor works 3 : the office or staff of an embassy or consulate

chan·cel·lor \'chan-s(ə-)lər\ n 1 : a high state official in various countries 2 : the head of a university 3 : a judge in the equity court in various states of the U.S. 4 : the chief minister of state in some European countries — **chancel·lor·ship** n

chan·cery \\'chans-(ə-)rē\ *n, pl* **-cer·ies** 1 : any of various courts of equity in the U.S. and Britain 2 : a record office for public or diplomatic archives 3 : a chancellor's court or office 4 : the office of an embassy

chan·cre \\'shaŋ-kər\ *n* [F, fr. L *cancer*] : a primary sore or ulcer at the site of entry of an infective agent (as of syphilis)

chan·croid \\'chaŋ-ˌkroid\ *n* : a sexually transmitted disease caused by a bacterium and characterized by chancres that differ from those of syphilis in lacking hardened margins

chancy \\'chan-sē\ *adj* **chanc·i·er; -est** *Scot* 1 : AUSPICIOUS 2 : RISKY

chan·de·lier \ˌshan-də-'liər\ *n* : a branched lighting fixture suspended from a ceiling

chan·dler \\'chan-dlər\ *n* [ME *chandeler* a maker or seller of candles, fr. MF *chandelier*, fr. OF, fr. *chandelle* candle, fr. L *candela*] : a dealer in provisions and supplies of a specified kind (ship's ~) — **chan·dlery** *n*

¹**change** \\'chānj\ *vb* **changed; chang·ing** 1 : to make or become different : ALTER 2 : to replace with another 3 : EXCHANGE 4 : to give or receive an equivalent sum in notes or coins of usu. smaller denominations or of another currency 5 : to put fresh clothes or covering on (~ a bed) 6 : to put on different clothes — **change·able** *adj* — **chang·er** *n*

²**change** *n* 1 : the act, process, or result of changing 2 : a fresh set of clothes to replace those being worn 3 : money given in exchange for other money of higher denomination 4 : surplus money returned to a person who offers payment exceeding the sum due 5 : coins esp. of small denominations — **change·ful** *adj* — **change·less** *adj*

change·ling \\'chānj-liŋ\ *n* : a child secretly exchanged for another in infancy

change of life : MENOPAUSE

change·over \\'chānj-ˌō-vər\ *n* : CONVERSION, TRANSITION

change ringing *n* : the art or practice of ringing a set of tuned bells in continually varying order

¹**chan·nel** \\'chan-ᵊl\ *n* 1 : the bed of a stream 2 : the deeper part of a waterway 3 : STRAIT 4 : a means of passage or transmission 5 : a range of frequencies of sufficient width for a single radio or television transmission 6 : a usu. tubular enclosed passage : CONDUIT 7 : a long gutter, groove, or furrow

²**channel** *vb* **-neled** *or* **-nelled; -neling** *or* **-nel·ling** 1 : to make a channel in 2 : to direct into or through a channel

chan·nel·ize \\'chan-ᵊl-ˌīz\ *vb* **-ized; -iz·ing** : CHANNEL — **chan·nel·iza·tion** \ˌchan-ᵊl-ə-'zā-shən\ *n*

chan·son \shäⁿ-'sōⁿ\ *n, pl* **chan·sons** \-'sōⁿ(z)\ : SONG : a cabaret song

¹**chant** \\'chant\ *vb* 1 : SING; *esp* : to sing a chant 2 : to sing or speak in the manner of a chant 3 : to celebrate or praise in song — **chant·er** *n*

²**chant** *n* 1 : a repetitive melody in which several words are sung to one tone : SONG; *esp* : a liturgical melody 2 : a manner of singing or speaking in musical monotones

chan·teuse \shäⁿ-'tə(r)z, shan-'tüz\ *n, pl* **chan·teuses** \-'tə(r)z(-əz), -'tüz(-əz)\ [F] : a female concert or nightclub singer

chan·tey *or* **chan·ty** \\'shant-ē, 'chant-\ *n, pl* **chanteys** *or* **chanties** : a song sung by sailors in rhythm with their work

chan·ti·cleer \ˌchant-ə-'kliər, ˌshant-\ *n* : ROOSTER

Cha·nu·kah \\'kän-ə-kə, 'hän-\ *var of* HANUKKAH

cha·os \\'kā-ˌäs\ *n* 1 *often cap* : the confused unorganized state existing before the creation of distinct forms 2 : complete disorder **syn** confusion, jumble, snarl, muddle, disarray — **cha·ot·ic** \kā-'ät-ik\ *adj* — **cha·ot·i·cal·ly** \-i-k(ə-)lē\ *adv*

¹**chap** \\'chap\ *vb* **chapped; chap·ping** : to dry and crack open usu. from wind and cold ⟨*chapped* lips⟩

²**chap** *n* : a jaw with its fleshy covering — usu. used in pl.

³**chap** *n* : FELLOW

⁴**chap** *abbr* chapter

chap·ar·ral \ˌshap-ə-'ral\ *n* 1 : a dense impenetrable thicket of shrubs or dwarf trees 2 : an ecological community of southern California comprised of shrubby plants

chap·book \\'chap-ˌbuk\ *n* : a small book of ballads, tales, or tracts

cha·peau \sha-'pō\ *n, pl* **cha·peaus** \-'pōz\ *or* **cha·peaux** \-'pō(z)\ [MF] : HAT

cha·pel \\'chap-əl\ *n* [ME, fr. OF *chapele*, fr. ML *cappella*, fr. LL *cappa* cloak; fr. the cloak of St. Martin of Tours preserved as a sacred relic in a chapel built for that purpose] 1 : a private or subordinate place of worship 2 : an assembly at an educational institution usu. including devotional exercises 3 : a place of worship used by a Christian group other than the established church

¹**chap·er·on** *or* **chap·er·one** \\'shap-ə-ˌrōn\ *n* [F *chaperon*, lit., hood, fr. MF, head covering, fr. *chape*] 1 : a person (as a matron) who accompanies young unmarried women in public for propriety 2 : an older person who accompanies young people at a social gathering to ensure proper behavior

²**chaperon** *or* **chaperone** *vb* **-oned; -on·ing** 1 : ESCORT, GUIDE 2 : to act as a chaperon to or for — **chap·er·on·age** \-ˌrō-nij\ *n*

chap·fall·en \\'chap-ˌfȯ-lən, 'chäp-\ *adj* 1 : having the lower jaw hanging loosely 2 : DEJECTED, DEPRESSED

chap·lain \'chap-lən\ *n* **1** : a clergyman officially attached to a special group (as the army) **2** : a person chosen to conduct religious exercises (as for a club) — **chap·lain·cy** \-sē\ *n*

chap·let \'chap-lət\ *n* **1** : a wreath for the head **2** : a string of beads : NECKLACE

chap·man \'chap-mən\ *n, Brit* : an itinerant dealer : PEDDLER

chaps \'shaps, 'chaps\ *n pl* [fr. MexSp *chaparreras*] : leather leggings resembling trousers without a seat that are worn esp. by western ranch hands

chap·ter \'chap-tər\ *n* **1** : a main division of a book **2** : a body of canons (as of a cathedral) **3** : a local branch of a society or fraternity

¹**char** \'chär\ *n, pl* **char** *or* **chars** : any of a genus of trouts (as the common brook trout) with small scales

²**char** *vb* **charred; char·ring** **1** : to burn to charcoal **2** : SCORCH **3** : to burn to a cinder

³**char** *vb* **charred; char·ring** : to work as a cleaning woman

char·a·banc \'shar-ə-baŋ\ *n, Brit* : a sight-seeing motor coach

char·ac·ter \'kar-ik-tər\ *n* [ME *caracter*, fr. MF *caractère*, fr. L *character* mark, distinctive quality, fr. Gk *charaktēr*, fr. *charassein* to scratch, engrave] **1** : a graphic symbol (as a letter) used in writing or printing **2** : a symbol that represents information; *also* : a representation of such a character that may be accepted by a computer **3** : a distinguishing feature : ATTRIBUTE **4** : the complex of mental and ethical traits marking a person or a group **5** : a person marked by conspicuous often peculiar traits **6** : one of the persons in a novel or play **7** : REPUTATION **8** : moral excellence

¹**char·ac·ter·is·tic** \,kar-ik-tə-'ris-tik\ *n* : a distinguishing trait, quality, or property

²**characteristic** *adj* : serving to mark individual character **syn** individual, peculiar, distinctive — **char·ac·ter·is·ti·cal·ly** \-ti-k(ə-)lē\ *adv*

char·ac·ter·ize \'kar-ik-tə-,rīz\ *vb* **-ized; -iz·ing** **1** : to describe the character of **2** : to be a characteristic of — **char·ac·ter·iza·tion** \,kar-ik-t(ə-)rə-'zā-shən\ *n*

cha·rades \shə-'rādz\ *n sing or pl* : a guessing game in which contestants act out the syllables of a word to be guessed

char·coal \'chär-,kōl\ *n* **1** : a porous carbon prepared from vegetable or animal substances **2** : a piece of fine charcoal used in drawing; *also* : a drawing made with charcoal

chard \'chärd\ *n* : a beet lacking the enlarged root but having leaves and stalks often cooked as a vegetable

char·don·nay \,shard-ᵊn-'ā\ *n, often cap* [F] : a dry white wine of Chablis type

¹**charge** \'chärj\ *vb* **charged; charg·ing** **1** : to load or fill to capacity **2** : to give an electric charge to; *also* : to restore the activity of (a storage battery) by means of an electric current **3** : to impose a task or responsibility on **4** : COMMAND, ORDER **5** : ACCUSE **6** : to rush against : rush forward in assault **7** : to make liable for payment; *also* : to record a debt or liability against **8** : to fix as a price — **charge·able** *adj*

²**charge** *n* **1** : a quantity (as of fuel or ammunition) required to fill something to capacity **2** : a store or accumulation of force **3** : an excess or deficiency of electrons in a body **4** : THRILL, KICK **5** : a task or duty imposed **6** : CARE, RESPONSIBILITY **7** : one given into another's care **8** : instructions from a judge to a jury **9** : COST, EXPENSE, PRICE; *also* : a debit to an account **10** : ACCUSATION, INDICTMENT **11** : ATTACK, ASSAULT

charge-coupled device *n* : a semiconductor device used esp. as an optical sensor

char·gé d'af·faires \shär-,zhäd-ə-'faer\ *n, pl* **chargés d'affaires** \-,zhā(z)d-ə-\ [F] : a diplomat who substitutes for an ambassador or minister

¹**charg·er** \'chär-jər\ *n* : a large platter

²**charg·er** *n* **1** : a device or a workman that charges something **2** : WAR-HORSE

char·i·ot \'char-ē-ət\ *n* : a 2-wheeled vehicle of ancient times used in war and in races and processions — **char·i·o·teer** \,char-ē-ə-'tiər\ *n*

cha·ris·ma \kə-'riz-mə\ *also* **char·ism** \'kar-,iz-əm\ *n, pl* **cha·ris·ma·ta** \kə-'riz-mət-ə\ *also* **charisms** : a personal quality of leadership arousing popular loyalty or enthusiasm — **char·is·mat·ic** \,kar-əz-'mat-ik\ *adj*

char·i·ta·ble \'char-ət-ə-bəl\ *adj* **1** : liberal in giving to needy people **2** : merciful or lenient in judging others **syn** benevolent, philanthropic, altruistic, humanitarian — **char·i·ta·ble·ness** — **char·i·ta·bly** \-blē\ *adv*

char·i·ty \'char-ət-ē\ *n, pl* **-ties** **1** : goodwill toward or love of humanity **2** : an act or feeling of generosity **3** : the giving of aid to the poor; *also* : ALMS **4** : an institution engaged in relief of the poor **5** : leniency in judging others **syn** mercy, clemency, lenity

char·la·tan \'shär-lə-tən\ *n* : a person pretending to knowledge or ability that he lacks : QUACK

Charles·ton \'chärl-stən\ *n* : a lively ballroom dance in which the knees are twisted in and out and the heels are swung sharply outward on each step

char·ley horse \'chär-lē-,hórs\ *n* : pain and stiffness from muscular strain in an arm or leg

¹**charm** \'chärm\ *n* [ME *charme*, fr. OF, fr. L *carmen* song, fr. *canere* to sing] **1** : an act or expression believed to have magic power **2** : something worn about the person to ward off evil or bring good fortune : AMULET **3** : a trait

that fascinates or allures **4** : physical grace or attraction **5** : a small ornament worn on a bracelet or chain

²**charm** *vb* **1** : to affect by or as if by a magic spell **2** : to protect by or as if by charms **3** : FASCINATE, ENCHANT *syn* allure, captivate, bewitch, attract — **charm·er** \'chär-mər\ *n*

charm·ing \'chär-miŋ\ *adj* : extremely pleasing or delightful — **charm·ing·ly** *adv*

char·nel house \'chärn-ᵊl-\ *n* : a building or chamber in which bodies or bones are deposited

¹**chart** \'chärt\ *n* **1** : MAP **2** : a sheet giving information in the form of a table, list, or diagram; *also* : GRAPH

²**chart** *vb* **1** : to make a chart of **2** : PLAN

¹**char·ter** \'chärt-ər\ *n* **1** : an official document granting rights or privileges (as to a colony, town, or college) from a sovereign or a governing body **2** : CONSTITUTION **3** : a written instrument from a society creating a branch **4** : a mercantile lease of a bank

²**charter** *vb* **1** : to grant a charter to **2** *Brit* : CERTIFY ⟨~ed engineer⟩ **3** : to hire, rent, or lease for temporary use — **char·ter·er** *n*

charter member *n* : an original member of an organization

char·treuse \shär-'trüz, -'trüs\ *n* : a variable color averaging a brilliant yellow green

char·wom·an \'chär-,wum-ən\ *n* : a cleaning woman esp. in large buildings

chary \'char-ē\ *adj* **chari·er;** **-est** [ME, sorrowful, dear, fr. OE *cearig* sorrowful, fr. *caru* sorrow] **1** : CAUTIOUS, CIRCUMSPECT **2** : SPARING — **char·i·ly** \'char-ə-lē\ *adv*

¹**chase** \'chās\ *n* **1** : PURSUIT; *also* : HUNTING **2** : QUARRY **3** : a tract of unenclosed land used as a game preserve

²**chase** *vb* **chased; chas·ing** **1** : to follow rapidly : PURSUE **2** : HUNT **3** : to seek out (*chasing* down clues) **4** : to cause to depart or flee : drive away **5** : RUSH, HASTEN

³**chase** *vb* **chased; chas·ing** : to decorate (a metal surface) by embossing or engraving

⁴**chase** *n* : FURROW, GROOVE

chas·er \'chā-sər\ *n* **1** : one that chases **2** : a mild drink (as beer) taken after hard liquor

chasm \'kaz-əm\ *n* : GORGE 2

chas·sis \'shas-ē, 'chas-ē\ *n, pl* **chas·sis** \-ēz\ : a supporting framework (as for the body of an automobile or the parts of a radio set)

chaste \'chāst\ *adj* **chast·er; chast·est** **1** : innocent of unlawful sexual intercourse : VIRTUOUS, PURE **2** : CELIBATE **3** : pure in thought : MODEST **4** : severe or simple in design — **chaste·ly** *adv* — **chaste·ness** *n*

chas·ten \'chās-ᵊn\ *vb* **chas·tened; chas·ten·ing** \'chās-(ᵊ-)niŋ\ : to correct

through punishment or suffering : DISCIPLINE; *also* : PURIFY — **chas·ten·er** *n*

chas·tise \chas-'tīz\ *vb* **chas·tised; chas·tis·ing** [ME *chastisen,* alter. of *chasten*] **1** : to punish esp. bodily **2** : to censure severely : CASTIGATE — **chas·tise·ment** \-mənt, 'chas-təz-\ *n*

chas·ti·ty \'chas-tət-ē\ *n* : the quality or state of being chaste; *esp* : sexual purity

cha·su·ble \'chaz-ə-bəl, 'chas-\ *n* : the outer vestment of the celebrant at the Eucharist

chat \'chat\ *n* : light familiar informal talk — **chat** *vb*

châ·teau \sha-'tō\ *n, pl* **châ·teaus** \-'tōz\ *or* **châ·teaux** \-'tō(z)\ [F, fr. L *castellum* castle, dim. of *castra* camp] **1** : a feudal castle in France **2** : a large country house **3** : a French vineyard estate

chat·e·laine \'shat-ᵊl-,ān\ *n* **1** : the mistress of a chateau **2** : a clasp or hook for a watch, purse, or keys

chat·tel \'chat-ᵊl\ *n* **1** : an item of tangible property other than real estate **2** : SLAVE, BONDMAN

chat·ter \'chat-ər\ *vb* **1** : to utter speechlike but meaningless sounds **2** : to talk idly, incessantly, or fast **3** : to click repeatedly or uncontrollably — **chatter** *n* — **chat·ter·er** *n*

chat·ter·box \'chat-ər-,bäks\ *n* : one who talks incessantly

chat·ty \'chat-ē\ *adj* **chat·ti·er; -est** : TALKATIVE — **chat·ti·ly** \'chat-ᵊl-ē\ *adv* — **chat·ti·ness** \-ē-nəs\ *n*

¹**chauf·feur** \'shō-fər, shō-'fər\ *n* [F, lit., stoker, fr. *chauffer* to heat] : a person employed to drive an automobile

²**chauffeur** *vb* **chauf·feured; chauf·feur·ing** \'shō-f(ə-)riŋ, shō-'fər-iŋ\ **1** : to do the work of a chauffeur **2** : to transport in the manner of a chauffeur

chaunt \'chönt, 'chänt\ *var of* CHANT

chau·vin·ism \'shō-və-,niz-əm\ *n* [F *chauvinisme,* fr. Nicolas *Chauvin,* soldier of excessive patriotism and devotion to Napoleon] **1** : excessive or blind patriotism **2** : an attitude of superiority toward members of the opposite sex — **chau·vin·ist** \-və-nəst\ *n or adj* — **chau·vin·is·tic** \,shō-və-'nis-tik\ *adj* — **chau·vin·is·ti·cal·ly** \-ti-k(ə-)lē\ *adv*

cheap \'chēp\ *adj* **1** : INEXPENSIVE **2** : costing little effort to obtain **3** : worth little : SHODDY, TAWDRY **4** : worthy of scorn **5** : STINGY — **cheap** *adv* — **cheap·ly** *adv* — **cheap·ness** *n*

cheap·en \'chē-pən\ *vb* **cheap·ened; cheap·en·ing** \'chēp-(ə-)niŋ\ **1** : to make or become cheap or cheaper in price or value **2** : to make tawdry

cheap·skate \'chēp-,skāt\ *n* : a niggardly person; *esp* : one seeking to avoid his or her share of costs

¹**cheat** \'chēt\ *vb* **1** : to deprive of something through fraud or deceit **2** : to practice fraud or trickery **3** : to vio-

late rules (as of a game) dishonestly — **cheat·er** n

²cheat n **1** : the act of deceiving : FRAUD, DECEPTION **2** : one that cheats : a dishonest person

¹check \'chek\ n **1** : a sudden stoppage of progress **2** : a sudden pause or break **3** : something that stops or restrains **4** : a standard for testing or evaluation **5** : EXAMINATION, INVESTIGATION **6** : the act of testing or verifying **7** : a written order to a bank to pay money **8** : a ticket or token showing ownership or identity **9** : a slip indicating an amount due **10** : a pattern in squares; *also* : a fabric in such a pattern **11** : a mark typically ✓ placed beside an item to show that it has been noted **12** : CRACK, SPLIT

²check vb **1** : to slow down or stop : BRAKE **2** : to restrain the action or force of : CURB **3** : to compare with a source, original, or authority : VERIFY **4** : to inspect or test for satisfactory condition **5** : to mark with a check as examined **6** : to consign for shipment for one holding a passenger ticket **7** : to mark into squares **8** : to leave or accept for safekeeping in a checkroom **9** : to correspond point by point : TALLY **10** : CRACK, SPLIT

check·book \'chek-ˌbuk\ n : a book containing blank checks

¹check·er \'chek-ər\ n : a piece in the game of checkers

²checker vb **check·ered; check·er·ing** \'chek-(ə-)riŋ\ **1** : to variegate with different colors or shades **2** : to vary with contrasting elements ⟨a ~ed career⟩ **3** : to mark into squares

³checker n : one that checks; esp : one who checks out purchases in a supermarket

check·er·ber·ry \'chek-ə(r)-ˌber-ē\ n : WINTERGREEN 1; also : the spicy red fruit of this plant

check·er·board \-ə(r)-ˌbōrd\ n : a board of 64 squares of alternate colors used in various games

check·ers \'chek-ərz\ n : a game for two played on a checkerboard with each player having 12 pieces

check in vb : to report one's presence or arrival (as at a hotel)

check·list \'chek-ˌlist\ n : a list of items that may easily be referred to

check·mate \'chek-ˌmāt\ vb [ME *chekmaten*, fr. *chekmate*, interj. used to announce checkmate, fr. MF *eschec mat*, fr. Ar *shāh māt*, fr. Per, lit., the king is left unable to escape] **1** : to thwart completely : DEFEAT, FRUSTRATE **2** : to attack (an opponent's king) in chess so that escape is impossible — **checkmate** n

check·off \'chek-ˌȯf\ n : the deduction of union dues from a worker's paycheck by the employer

check·out \'chek-ˌaut\ n **1** : the action or an instance of checking out **2** : a counter at which checking out is done

3 : the process of examining and testing something as to readiness for intended use **4** : the process of familiarizing oneself with the operation of a mechanical thing (as an airplane)

check out \-ˈaut\ vb **1** : to settle one's account (as at a hotel) and leave **2** : to total or have totaled the cost of purchases in a store and to make or receive payment for them

check·point \'chek-ˌpȯint\ n : a point at which a check is performed

check·room \-ˌrüm, -ˌrum\ n : a room at which baggage, parcels, or clothing is checked

check·up \-ˌəp\ n : EXAMINATION; esp : a general physical examination

ched·dar \'ched-ər\ n, often cap : a hard mild to sharp white or yellow cheese of smooth texture

cheek \'chēk\ n **1** : the fleshy side part of the face **2** : IMPUDENCE, BOLDNESS, AUDACITY **3** : BUTTOCK 1

cheek·bone \-'bōn, -ˌbōn\ n : the bone or bony ridge below the eye

cheeky \'chē-kē\ adj **cheek·i·er; -est** : IMPUDENT, SAUCY — **cheek·i·ly** \'chē-kə-lē\ adv — **cheek·i·ness** \-kē-nəs\ n

cheep \'chēp\ vb : to utter faint shrill sounds : PEEP — **cheep** n

¹cheer \'chiər\ n [ME *chere* face, cheer, fr. OF, face] **1** : state of mind or heart : SPIRIT **2** : ANIMATION, GAIETY **3** : hospitable entertainment : WELCOME **4** : food and drink for a feast **5** : something that gladdens **6** : a shout of applause or encouragement

²cheer vb **1** : to give hope or courage to : COMFORT **2** : to make glad **3** : to urge on esp. by shouts **4** : to applaud with shouts **5** : to grow or be cheerful — usu. used with up — **cheer·er** n

cheer·ful \'chir-fəl\ adj **1** : having or showing good spirits **2** : conducive to good spirits : pleasant and bright — **cheer·ful·ly** \-ē\ adv — **cheer·ful·ness** n

cheer·lead·er \'chiər-ˌlēd-ər\ n : a person who directs organized cheering esp. at a sports event

cheer·less \'chiər-ləs\ adj : BLEAK, DISPIRITING — **cheer·less·ly** adv — **cheer·less·ness** n

cheery \'chi(ə)r-ē\ adj **cheer·i·er; -est** : LIVELY, BRIGHT, GAY — **cheer·i·ly** \'chir-ə-lē\ adv — **cheer·i·ness** \-ē-nəs\ n

cheese \'chēz\ n : the curd of milk usu. pressed into cakes and cured for use as food

cheese·burg·er \'chēz-ˌbər-gər\ n : a hamburger containing a slice of cheese

cheese·cake \-ˌkāk\ n **1** : a dessert consisting of a creamy filling usu. containing cheese baked in a shell **2** : photographs of attractive usu. scantily clad women

cheese·cloth \-ˌklȯth\ n : a lightweight coarse cotton gauze

cheese·par·ing \-ˌpa(ə)r-iŋ\ n : miserly

or petty economizing — **cheeseparing** *adj*

cheesy \'chē-zē\ *adj* **chees·i·er; -est 1** : resembling, suggesting, or containing cheese **2** *slang* : CHEAP 3

chee·tah \'chēt-ə\ *n* [Hindu *cītā*, fr. Skt *citrakāya* tiger, fr. *citra* bright + *kāya* body] : a large long-legged spotted swift-moving African and formerly Asian cat

chef \'shef\ *n* **1** : a cook who manages the kitchen (as of a restaurant) **2** : COOK

chef d'oeu·vre \shā-dœvrᵃ\ *n, pl* **chefs d'oeuvre** \-dœvrᵃ\ : MASTERPIECE

chem *abbr* chemical; chemist; chemistry

¹**chem·i·cal** \'kem-i-kəl\ *adj* **1** : of, relating to, used in, or produced by chemistry **2** : acting or operated or produced by chemicals — **chem·i·cal·ly** \-i-k(ə-)lē\ *adv*

²**chemical** *n* : a substance obtained by a chemical process or used for producing a chemical effect

chemical engineering *n* : engineering dealing with the industrial application of chemistry

chemical warfare *n* : warfare using incendiary mixtures, smokes, or irritant, burning, or asphyxiating gases

che·mise \shə-'mēz\ *n* **1** : a woman's one-piece undergarment **2** : a loose straight-hanging dress

chem·ist \'kem-əst\ *n* **1** : one trained in chemistry **2** *Brit* : PHARMACIST

chem·is·try \'kem-ə-strē\ *n, pl* **-tries 1** : the science that deals with the composition, structure, and properties of substances and of the changes they undergo **2** : chemical composition or properties (the ~ of gasoline) **3** : a strong mutual attraction

che·mo·ther·a·py \,kē-mō-'ther-ə-pē\ *n* : the use of chemicals in the treatment or control of disease — **che·mo·ther·a·peu·tic** \-,ther-ə-'pyüt-ik\ *adj*

che·nille \shə-'nēl\ *n* [F, lit., caterpillar, fr. L *canicula*, dim. of *canis* dog] : a fabric with a deep fuzzy pile often used for bedspreads and rugs

cheque \'chek\ *chiefly Brit var of* ¹CHECK 7

cher·ish \'cher-ish\ *vb* **1** : to hold dear : treat with care and affection **2** : to keep deeply in mind

Cher·o·kee \'cher-ə-(,)kē\ *n, pl* **Cherokee** *or* **Cherokees** : a member of an American Indian people orig. of Tennessee and No. Carolina; *also* : their language

che·root \shə-'rüt\ *n* : a cigar cut square at both ends

cher·ry \'cher-ē\ *n, pl* **cherries** [ME *chery*, fr. OF *cherise* (taken as a plural), fr. LL *ceresia*, fr. L *cerasus* cherry tree, fr. Gk *kerasos*] **1** : the small fleshy pale yellow to deep blackish red fruit of a tree related to the roses; *also* : the tree or its wood **2**

: a variable color averaging a moderate red

chert \'chərt, 'chat\ *n* : a rock resembling flint and consisting essentially of fine crystalline quartz or fibrous chalcedony — **cherty** \-ē\ *adj*

cher·ub \'cher-əb\ *n* **1** *pl* **cher·u·bim** \'cher-(y)ə-,bim\ : an angel of the 2d highest rank **2** *pl* **cherubs** : a chubby rosy person — **che·ru·bic** \chə-'rü-bik\ *adj*

chess \'ches\ *n* : a game for two played on a board of 64 squares of alternate colors with each player having 16 pieces — **chess·board** \-,bōrd\ *n* — **chess·man** \-,man, -mən\ *n*

chest \'chest\ *n* **1** : a box, case, or boxlike receptacle for storage or shipping **2** : the part of the body enclosed by the ribs and sternum

ches·ter·field \'ches-tər-,fēld\ *n* : an overcoat with a velvet collar

chest·nut \'ches-(,)nət\ *n* **1** : the edible nut of any of a genus of trees related to the beech and oaks; *also* : this tree **2** : a grayish to reddish brown **3** : an old joke or story

chet·rum \'chet-rəm\ *n, pl* **chetrums** *or* **chetrum** — see *ngultrum* at MONEY table

che·val glass \shə-'val-\ *n* : a full-length mirror that may be tilted in a frame

che·va·lier \,shev-ə-'liər, shə-'val-,yā\ *n* : a member of one of various orders of knighthood or of merit

chev·i·ot \'shev-ē-ət\ *n, often cap* **1** : a twilled fabric with a rough nap **2** : a sturdy soft-finished cotton fabric

chev·ron \'shev-rən\ *n* : a sleeve badge of one or more V-shaped or inverted V-shaped stripes worn to indicate rank or service (as in the armed forces)

¹**chew** \'chü\ *vb* : to crush or grind with the teeth — **chew·able** *adj* — **chew·er** *n*

²**chew** *n* **1** : an act of chewing **2** : something for chewing

chewy \'chü-ē\ *adj* : requiring chewing (~ candy)

Chey·enne \shī-'an, -'en\ *n, pl* **Cheyenne** *or* **Cheyennes** [CanF, fr. Dakota *Shaiyena*, fr. *shaia* to speak unintelligibly] : a member of an American Indian people of the western plains of the U.S.; *also* : their language

chg *abbr* **1** change **2** charge

Chi·an·ti \kē-'änt-ē, -'ant-\ *n* : a dry usu. red wine

chiao \'tyau\ *n, pl* **chiao** : a monetary unit of the People's Republic of China equal to 1/10 yuan

chiar·oscu·ro \kē-,är-ə-'sk(y)ūr-ō\ *n, pl* **-ros** [It, fr. *chiaro* clear, light + *oscuro* obscure, dark] **1** : pictorial representation in terms of light and shade without regard to color **2** : the arrangement or treatment of light and dark parts in a pictorial work of art

¹**chic** \'shēk\ *n* : STYLISHNESS

²**chic** *adj* : cleverly stylish : SMART; *also* : currently fashionable

chi·cane \shik-ˈān\ *n* : CHICANERY

chi·ca·nery \-ˈān-(ə-)rē\ *n, pl* **-ner·ies** : TRICKERY, DECEPTION

Chi·ca·no \chi-ˈkän-ō\ *n, pl* **-nos** : an American of Mexican descent — **Chicano** *adj*

chi·chi \ˈshē-(ˌ)shē, ˈchē-(ˌ)chē\ *adj* [F] **1** : SHOWY, FRILLY **2** : ARTY, PRECIOUS **3** : CHIC — **chichi** *n*

chick \ˈchik\ *n* **1** : a young chicken; *also* : a young bird **2** : a young woman

chick·a·dee \ˈchik-ə-(ˌ)dē\ *n* : any of several small grayish American birds with black or brown caps

Chick·a·saw \ˈchik-ə-ˌsò\ *n, pl* **Chickasaw** *or* **Chickasaws** : a member of an American Indian people of Mississippi and Alabama

¹**chick·en** \ˈchik-ən\ *n* **1** : a common domestic fowl esp. when young; *also* : its flesh used as food **2** : COWARD

²**chicken** *adj* **1** *slang* : COWARDLY **2** *slang* : insistent on petty esp. military discipline

chicken feed *n, slang* : an insignificant sum of money

chick·en·heart·ed \ˌchik-ən-ˈhärt-əd\ *adj* : TIMID, COWARDLY

chicken out *vb* : to lose one's courage

chicken pox *n* : an acute contagious virus disease esp. of children characterized by a low fever and vesicles

chick–pea \ˈchik-ˌpē\ *n* : an Asian leguminous herb cultivated for its short pods with one or two edible seeds; *also* : its seed

chick·weed \ˈchik-ˌwēd\ *n* : any of several low-growing small-leaved weeds related to the pinks

chi·cle \ˈchik-əl\ *n* : a gum from the latex of a tropical evergreen tree used as the chief ingredient of chewing gum

chic·o·ry \ˈchik-(ə-)rē\ *n, pl* **-ries** : a usu. blue-flowered herb related to the daisies and grown for its root and for use in salads; *also* : its dried ground root used for flavoring or adulterating coffee

chide \ˈchīd\ *vb* **chid** \ˈchid\ *or* **chid·ed** \ˈchīd-əd\; **chid** *or* **chid·den** \ˈchid-ᵊn\ *or* **chided**; **chid·ing** \ˈchīd-iŋ\ : to speak disapprovingly to syn reproach, reprove, reprimand, admonish, scold, rebuke

¹**chief** \ˈchēf\ *adj* **1** : highest in rank **2** : most eminent or important syn principal, main, leading, major — **chief·ly** *adv*

²**chief** *n* **1** : the leader of a body or organization : HEAD **2** : the principal or most valuable part — **chief·dom** *n*

chief master sergeant *n* : a noncommissioned officer of the highest rank in the air force

chief of staff 1 : the ranking officer of a staff in the armed forces **2** : the ranking office of the army or air force

chief of state : the formal head of a national state as distinguished from the head of the government

chief petty officer *n* : an enlisted man in the navy ranking next below a senior chief petty officer

chief·tain \ˈchēf-tən\ *n* : a chief esp. of a band, tribe, or clan — **chief·tain·cy** \-sē\ *n* — **chief·tain·ship** *n*

chief warrant officer *n* : a warrant officer of senior rank

chif·fon \shif-ˈän, ˈshif-ˌ\ *n* [F, lit., rag, fr. *chiffe* old rag] : a sheer fabric esp. of silk

chif·fo·nier \ˌshif-ə-ˈniər\ *n* : a high narrow chest of drawers

chig·ger \ˈchig-ər\ *n* : a bloodsucking larval mite that irritates the skin

chi·gnon \ˈshēn-ˌyän\ *n* [F] : a knot of hair worn at the back of the head

Chi·hua·hua \chə-ˈwä-ˌwä\ *n* : a very small large-eared dog of a breed that originated in Mexico

chil·blain \ˈchil-ˌblān\ *n* : a sore or inflamed swelling (as on the feet or hands) caused by exposure to cold

child \ˈchīld\ *n, pl* **chil·dren** \ˈchil-drən\ **1** : an unborn or recently born person **2** : a young person between the periods of infancy and youth **3** : a male or female offspring : SON, DAUGHTER **4** : one strongly influenced by another or by a place or state of affairs — **child·ish** *adj* — **child·ish·ly** *adv* — **child·ish·ness** *n* — **child·less** *adj* — **child·less·ness** *n* — **child·like** *adj*

child–bear·ing \ˈchīld-ˌbar-iŋ\ *n* : CHILDBIRTH — **childbearing** *adj*

child·birth \-ˌbərth\ *n* : the act or process of giving birth to offspring

child·hood \-ˌhüd\ *n* : the state or time of being a child

child·proof \-ˌprüf\ *adj* : made to prevent tampering by children

child's play *n* : a simple task or act

Chil·ean \ˈchil-ē-ən, chə-ˈlā-ən\ *n* : a native or inhabitant of Chile — **Chilean** *adj*

chili *or* **chile** *or* **chil·li** \ˈchil-ē\ *n, pl* **chil·ies** *or* **chil·es** *or* **chil·lies 1** : a pungent pepper related to the tomato **2** : a thick sauce of meat and chilies **3** : CHILI CON CARNE

chili con car·ne \ˌchil-ē-ˌkän-ˈkär-nē, -kən-\ *n* [Sp *chile con carne* chili with meat] : a spiced stew of ground beef and chilies or chili powder usu. with beans

chili powder *n* : a seasoning made of ground hot peppers and other spices

¹**chill** \ˈchil\ *n* **1** : a feeling of coldness accompanied by shivering **2** : moderate coldness **3** : a check to enthusiasm or warmth of feeling

²**chill** *adj* **1** : moderately cold **2** : COLD, RAW **3** : DISTANT, FORMAL (a ~ reception) **4** : DEPRESSING, DISPIRITING

³**chill** *vb* **1** : to make or become cold or chilly **2** : to make cool esp. without freezing **3** : to harden the surface of (as metal) by sudden cooling — **chill·er** *n*

chilly \'chil-ē\ *adj* **chill·i·er; -est 1** : noticeably cold **2** : unpleasantly affected by cold **3** : lacking warmth of feeling — **chill·i·ness** *n*

¹**chime** \'chīm\ *n* **1** : a set of bells musically tuned **2** : the sound of a set of bells — usu. used in pl. **3** : a musical sound suggesting bells

²**chime** *vb* **chimed; chim·ing 1** : to make bell-like sounds **2** : to indicate (as the time of day) by chiming **3** : to be or act in accord : be in harmony

chime in *vb* : to break into or join in a conversation

chi·me·ra *or* **chi·mae·ra** \kī-'mir-ə, kə-\ *n* [L *chimaera*, fr. Gk *chimaira* she-goat, chimera] **1** : an imaginary monster made up of incongruous parts **2** : a frightful or foolish fancy

chi·me·ri·cal \-'mer-i-kəl\ *also* **chi·me·ric** \-ik\ *adj* **1** : FANTASTIC, IMAGINARY **2** : inclined to fantastic schemes

chim·ney \'chim-nē\ *n, pl* **chimneys 1** : a vertical structure extending above the roof of a building for carrying off smoke **2** : a glass tube around a lamp flame

chimp \'chimp, 'shimp\ *n* : CHIMPANZEE

chim·pan·zee \ˌchim-ˌpan-'zē, ˌshim-, -pən-; chim-'pan-zē, shim-\ *n* : an African manlike ape

¹**chin** \'chin\ *n* : the part of the face below the lower lip including the prominence of the lower jaw — **chin·less** *adj*

²**chin** *vb* **chinned; chin·ning** : to raise (oneself) while hanging by the hands until the chin is level with the support

chi·na \'chī-nə\ *n* : porcelain ware; *also* : domestic pottery in general

Chi·na·town \-ˌtau̇n\ *n* : the Chinese quarter of a city

chinch bug \'chinch-\ *n* : a small black and white bug destructive to cereal grasses

chin·chil·la \chin-'chil-ə\ *n* **1** : a small So. American rodent with soft pearl-gray fur; *also* : its fur **2** : a heavy long-napped woolen cloth

chine \'chīn\ *n* **1** : BACKBONE, SPINE; *also* : a cut of meat including the backbone or part of it **2** : RIDGE, CREST

Chi·nese \chī-'nēz, -'nēs\ *n, pl* **Chinese 1** : a native or inhabitant of China **2** : any of a group of related languages of China — **Chinese** *adj*

Chinese cabbage *n* **1** : BOK CHOY **2** : a Chinese vegetable related to the cabbage that forms tight elongate cylindrical heads of pale green to cream-colored leaves

Chinese checkers *n* : a game in which each player in turn transfers a set of marbles from a home point to the opposite point of a pitted 6-pointed star

Chinese gooseberry *n* : a subtropical vine that bears kiwifruit; *also* : KIWIFRUIT

Chinese lantern *n* : a collapsible translucent cover for a light

¹**chink** \'chiŋk\ *n* : a small crack or fissure

²**chink** *vb* : to fill the chinks of : stop up

³**chink** *n* : a slight sharp metallic sound

⁴**chink** *vb* : to make a slight sharp metallic sound

chi·no \'chē-nō\ *n, pl* **chinos 1** : a usu. khaki cotton twill **2** *pl* : an article of clothing made of chino

Chi·nook \shə-'nu̇k, chə-, -'nük\ *n, pl* **Chinook** *or* **Chinooks** : a member of an American Indian people of Oregon

chintz \'chints\ *n* : a usu. glazed printed cotton cloth

chintzy \'chint-sē\ *adj* **chintz·i·er; -est 1** : decorated with or as if with chintz **2** : GAUDY, CHEAP

chin–up \'chin-ˌəp\ *n* : the act of chinning oneself

¹**chip** \'chip\ *n* **1** : a small usu. thin and flat piece (as of wood) cut or broken off **2** : a thin crisp morsel of food **3** : a counter used in games (as poker) **4** *pl, slang* : MONEY **5** : a flaw left after a chip is removed **6** : a very small slice of silicon containing electronic circuits

²**chip** *vb* **chipped; chip·ping 1** : to cut or break chips from **2** : to break off in small pieces at the edges **3** : to play a chip shot

chip in *vb* : CONTRIBUTE

chip·munk \'chip-ˌməŋk\ *n* : any of various ground-dwelling squirrels found in No. America into Mexico and in Asia

chipped beef \'chip(t)-\ *n* : smoked dried beef sliced thin

¹**chip·per** \'chip-ər\ *n* : one that chips

²**chipper** *adj* : LIVELY, CHEERFUL

Chip·pe·wa \'chip-ə-ˌwȯ, -ˌwä, -ˌwā, -wə\ *n, pl* **Chippewa** *or* **Chippewas** : OJIBWA

chip shot *n* : a short usu. low shot to the green in golf

chi·rog·ra·phy \kī-'räg-rə-fē\ *n* : HANDWRITING, PENMANSHIP — **chi·ro·graph·ic** \ˌkī-rə-'graf-ik\ *adj*

chi·rop·o·dy \kə-'räp-əd-ē, shə-\ *n* : PODIATRY — **chi·rop·o·dist** \-əd-əst\ *n*

chi·ro·prac·tic \'kī-rə-ˌprak-tik\ *n* : a system of therapy based esp. on manipulation of body structures — **chi·ro·prac·tor** \-tər\ *n*

chirp \'chərp\ *n* : a short sharp sound characteristic of a small bird or cricket — **chirp** *vb*

¹**chis·el** \'chiz-əl\ *n* : a metal tool with a cutting edge at the end of a blade used in chipping away and shaping wood, stone, or metal

²**chisel** *vb* **-eled** *or* **-elled; -el·ing** *or* **-el·ling** \'chiz-(ə-)liŋ\ **1** : to work with or as if with a chisel **2** : to obtain by shrewd often unfair methods; *also* : CHEAT — **chis·el·er** \-(ə-)lər\ *n*

¹**chit** \'chit\ *n* [ME *chitte* kitten, cub] **1** : CHILD **2** : a pert young woman

²**chit** *n* [Hindi *ciṭṭhī* letter, note] : a signed voucher for a small debt

chit·chat \'chit-ˌchat\ *n* : casual or trifling conversation

chi·tin \'kīt-ᵊn\ *n* : a sugar polymer that

forms part of the hard outer integument esp. of insects — **chi·tin·ous** *adj*

chit·ter·lings \'chit-lənz\ *or* **chit·lins** \'chit-lənz\ *n pl* : the intestines of hogs esp. prepared as food

chi·val·ric \shə-'val-rik\ *adj* : relating to chivalry : CHIVALROUS

chiv·al·rous \'shiv-əl-rəs\ *adj* 1 : of or relating to chivalry 2 : marked by honor, courtesy, and generosity 3 : marked by especial courtesy to women — **chiv·al·rous·ly** *adv* — **chiv·al·rous·ness** *n*

chiv·al·ry \'shiv-əl-rē\ *n, pl* **-ries** 1 : a body of knights 2 : the system or practices of knighthood 3 : the spirit or character of the ideal knight

chive \'chīv\ *n* : an herb related to the onion that has leaves used for flavoring

chlo·ral hydrate \,klȯr-əl-\ *n* : a white crystalline compound used as a hypnotic and sedative

chlor·dane \'klȯr-,dān\ *also* **chlor·dan** \-,dan\ *n* : a viscous liquid insecticide

chlo·ride \'klȯr-,īd\ *n* : a compound of chlorine with another element or group

chlo·ri·nate \'klȯr-ə-,nāt\ *vb* **-nat·ed; -nat·ing** : to treat or cause to combine with chlorine or a chlorine-containing compound — **chlo·ri·na·tion** \,klȯr-ə-'nā-shən\ *n* — **chlo·ri·na·tor** \'klȯr-ə-,nāt-ər\ *n*

chlo·rine \'klȯr-,ēn\ *n* : a nonmetallic chemical element that is found alone as a heavy strong-smelling greenish yellow irritating gas and is used as a bleach, oxidizing agent, and disinfectant

chlo·rite \'klȯr-,īt\ *n* : a usu. green mineral found with and resembling mica

chlo·ro·flu·o·ro·car·bon \,klȯr-ə-'flȯr-ə-,kär-bən, -'flu̇r-\ *n* : a gaseous compound that contains carbon, chlorine, fluorine, and sometimes hydrogen and is used esp. as a solvent, a refrigerant, and an aerosol propellant

¹chlo·ro·form \'klȯr-ə-,fȯrm\ *n* : a colorless heavy fluid with etherlike odor used as a solvent and anesthetic

²chloroform *vb* : to treat with chloroform to produce anesthesia or death

chlo·ro·phyll \-,fil\ *n* : the green coloring matter of plants that functions in photosynthesis

chm *abbr* chairman

chock \'chäk\ *n* : a wedge for steadying something or for blocking the movement of a wheel — **chock** *vb*

chock·a·block \'chäk-ə-,bläk\ *adj* : very full : CROWDED

chock-full \'chək-'fu̇l, 'chäk-\ *adj* : full to the limit : CROWDED

choc·o·late \'chäk-(ə-)lət, 'chȯk-\ *n* [Sp. fr. Nahuatl (an Indian language of southern Mexico) *xocoatl*] 1 : a food prepared from ground roasted cacao beans; *also* : a drink prepared from this 2 : a candy made of or with a

coating of chocolate 3 : a dark brown color

Choc·taw \'chäk-,tȯ\ *n, pl* **Choctaw** *or* **Choctaws** : a member of an American Indian people of Mississippi, Alabama, and Louisiana; *also* : their language

¹choice \'chȯis\ *n* 1 : the act of choosing : SELECTION 2 : the power or opportunity of choosing : OPTION 3 : the best part 4 : a person or thing selected 5 : a variety offered for selection

²choice *adj* **choic·er; choic·est** 1 : worthy of being chosen 2 : selected with care 3 : of high quality

choir \'kwī(-ə)r\ *n* 1 : an organized company of singers esp. in a church 2 : the part of a church occupied by the singers

choir·boy \'kwī(-ə)r-,bȯi\ *n* : a boy member of a church choir

choir·mas·ter \-,mas·tər\ *n* : the director of a choir (as in a church)

choke \'chōk\ *vb* **choked; chok·ing** 1 : to hinder breathing (as by obstructing the windpipe) : STRANGLE 2 : to check the growth or action of 3 : CLOG, OBSTRUCT 4 : to decrease or shut off the air intake of the carburetor of a gasoline engine to make the fuel mixture richer 5 : to perform badly in a critical situation

²choke *n* 1 : the act of choking 2 : a narrowing in size toward the muzzle in the bore of a gun 3 : a valve for choking a gasoline engine

chok·er \'chō-kər\ *n* : something (as a necklace) worn tightly around the neck

chol·er \'käl-ər, 'kō-lər\ *n* : a tendency toward anger : IRASCIBILITY

chol·era \'käl-ə-rə\ *n* : a disease marked by severe vomiting and dysentery; *esp* : an often fatal epidemic disease (Asiatic cholera) chiefly of southeastern Asia caused by a bacillus

chol·er·ic \'käl-ə-rik, kə-'ler-ik\ *adj* 1 : IRASCIBLE 2 : ANGRY, IRATE

cho·les·ter·ol \kə-'les-tə-,rȯl\ *n* : a physiologically important waxy substance found in animal tissues and implicated experimentally in arteriosclerosis

chomp \'chämp, 'chȯmp\ *vb* : to chew or bite on something heavily

choose \'chüz\ *vb* **chose** \'chōz\; **cho·sen** \'chōz-ᵊn\; **choos·ing** \'chü-ziŋ\ 1 : to select esp. after consideration 2 : DECIDE 3 : to think proper : see fit : PLEASE — **choos·er** *n*

choosy *or* **choos·ey** \'chü-zē\ *adj* **choos·i·er; -est** : very particular in making choices

¹chop \'chäp\ *vb* **chopped; chop·ping** 1 : to cut by repeated blows 2 : to cut into small pieces : MINCE 3 : to strike (a ball) with a short quick downward stroke

²chop *n* 1 : a sharp downward blow or stroke 2 : a small cut of meat often including part of a rib **3** : a short abrupt motion (as of a wave)

³**chop** *n* **1** : an official seal or stamp **2** : a mark on goods to indicate quality or kind; *also* : QUALITY, GRADE

chop·house \'chäp-ˌhaȯs\ *n* : RESTAURANT

chop·per \'chäp-ər\ *n* **1** : one that chops **2** : HELICOPTER

chop·pi·ness \'chäp-ē-nəs\ *n* : the quality or state of being choppy

¹**chop·py** \'chäp-ē\ *adj* **chop·pi·er; -est** : CHANGEABLE, VARIABLE (a ~ wind)

²**choppy** *adj* **chop·pi·er; -est 1** : rough with small waves **2** : JERKY, DISCONNECTED — **chop·pi·ly** \'chäp-ə-lē\ *adv*

chops \'chäps\ *n pl* : the fleshy covering of the jaws

chop·stick \'chäp-ˌstik\ *n* : one of a pair of sticks used chiefly in oriental countries for lifting food to the mouth

chop su·ey \chäp-'sü-ē\ *n, pl* **chop sueys** : a dish made typically of bean sprouts, bamboo shoots, celery, onions, mushrooms, and meat or fish and served with rice

cho·ral \'kōr-əl\ *adj* : of, relating to, or sung by a choir or chorus or in chorus — **cho·ral·ly** \-ē\ *adv*

cho·rale \kə-'ral, -'räl\ *n* **1** : a hymn or psalm sung in church; *also* : a hymn tune or a harmonization of a traditional melody **2** : CHORUS, CHOIR

¹**chord** \'kȯrd\ *n* [alter. of ME *cord*, short for *accord*] : three or more musical tones sounded simultaneously

²**chord** *n* **1** : CORD, STRING; *esp* : a cord-like anatomical structure **2** : a straight line joining two points on a curve

chore \'chȯr\ *n* **1** *pl* : the daily light work of a household or farm **2** : a routine task or job **3** : a difficult or disagreeable task

cho·rea \kə-'rē-ə\ *n* : a nervous disorder marked by spasmodic uncontrolled movements

cho·re·og·ra·phy \ˌkōr-ē-'äg-rə-fē\ *n, pl* **-phies** : the art of dancing or of arranging dances and esp. ballets — **cho·reograph** \'kōr-ē-ə-ˌgraf\ *vb* — **cho·re·og·ra·pher** \ˌkōr-ē-'äg-rə-fər\ *n* — **cho·reo·graph·ic** \ˌkōr-ē-ə-'graf-ik\ *adj* — **cho·reo·graph·i·cal·ly** \-i-k(ə-)lē\ *adv*

cho·ris·ter \'kōr-ə-stər\ *n* : a singer in a choir

chor·tle \'chȯrt-ᵊl\ *vb* **chor·tled; chor·tling** \'chȯrt-(ᵊ-)liŋ\ : to laugh or chuckle esp. in satisfaction or exultation — **chortle** *n*

¹**chorus** \'kōr-əs\ *n* **1** : an organized company of singers : CHOIR **2** : a group of dancers and usu. singers (as in a musical comedy) **3** : a part of a song repeated at intervals **4** : a composition to be sung by a chorus; *also* : group singing **5** : sounds uttered by a number of persons or animals together

²**chorus** *vb* : to sing or utter in chorus

chose *past of* CHOOSE

cho·sen \'chōz-ᵊn\ *adj* : selected or marked for special favor or privilege

¹**chow** \'chaȯ\ *n* : FOOD

²**chow** *n* : CHOW CHOW

chow-chow \'chaȯ-ˌchaȯ\ *n* : chopped mixed pickles in mustard sauce

chow chow \'chaȯ-ˌchaȯ\ *n* : any of a breed of thick-coated straight-legged muscular dogs with a blue-black tongue and a short tail curled close to the back

chow·der \'chaȯd-ər\ *n* : a soup or stew made from seafood or vegetables and containing milk or tomatoes

chow mein \'chaȯ-'mān\ *n* : a seasoned stew of shredded or diced meat, mushrooms, and vegetables that is usu. served with fried noodles

chrism \'kriz-əm\ *n* : consecrated oil used esp. in baptism and confirmation

Christ \'krīst\ *n* [L *Christus*, fr. Gk *Christos*, lit., anointed, trans. of Heb *māshīaḥ*] : Jesus esp. as the Messiah — **Christ·like** *adj* — **Christ·ly** *adj*

chris·ten \'kris-ᵊn\ *vb* **chris·tened; chris·ten·ing** \'kris-(ᵊ-)niŋ\ **1** : BAPTIZE **2** : to name at baptism **3** : to name or dedicate (as a ship) by a ceremony suggestive of baptism — **chris·ten·ing** *n*

Chris·ten·dom \'kris-ᵊn-dəm\ *n* **1** : the entire body of Christians **2** : the part of the world in which Christianity prevails

¹**Chris·tian** \'kris-chən\ *n* : an adherent of Christianity

²**Christian** *adj* **1** : of or relating to Christianity **2** : based on or conforming with Christianity **3** : of or relating to a Christian **4** : professing Christianity

chris·ti·an·ia \ˌkris-chē-'an-ē-ə, ˌkris-tē-\ *n* : CHRISTIE

Chris·ti·an·i·ty \ˌkris-chē-'an-ət-ē\ *n* : the religion derived from Jesus Christ, based on the Bible as sacred scripture, and professed by Christians

Chris·tian·ize \'kris-chə-ˌnīz\ *vb* **-ized; -iz·ing** : to make Christian

Christian name *n* : GIVEN NAME

Christian Science *n* : a religion and system of healing founded by Mary Baker Eddy and taught by the Church of Christ, Scientist — **Christian Scientist** *n*

chris·tie *or* **chris·ty** \'kris-tē\ *n, pl* **christies** : a skiing turn made by shifting body weight forward and skidding into a turn with parallel skis

Christ·mas \'kris-məs\ *n* : December 25 celebrated as a church festival in commemoration of the birth of Christ and observed as a legal holiday

Christmas club *n* : a savings account in which regular deposits are made to provide money for Christmas shopping

Christ·mas·tide \'kris-mə-ˌstīd\ *n* : the season of Christmas

chro·mat·ic \krō-'mat-ik\ *adj* **1** : of or relating to color **2** : proceeding by half steps of the musical scale — **chro·mat·i·cism** \-'mat-ə-ˌsiz-əm\ *n*

chro·ma·to·graph \krō-'mat-ə-ˌgraf\ *n* : an instrument used in chromatography

chro·ma·tog·ra·phy \ˌkrō-mə-'täg-rə-fē\ *n* : the separation of a complex mixture into its component compounds as a result of the different rates at which the compounds travel through or over a stationary substance due to differing affinities for the substance — **chro·mato·graph·ic** \ˌkrō-ˌmat-ə-'graf-ik\ *adj* — **chro·mato·graph·i·cal·ly** \-i-k(ə-)lē\ *adv*

chrome \'krōm\ *n* **1** : CHROMIUM **2** : a chromium pigment **3** : something plated with an alloy of chromium

chro·mi·um \'krō-mē-əm\ *n* : a bluish white metallic element used esp. in alloys and chrome plating

chro·mo·some \'krō-mə-ˌsōm, -ˌzōm\ *n* : one of the usu. elongated bodies in a cell nucleus that contains most or all of the DNA or RNA comprising the genes — **chro·mo·som·al** \ˌkrō-mə-'sō-məl, -'zō-\ *adj*

chro·mo·sphere \'krō-mə-ˌsfiər\ *n* : the lower atmosphere of a star (as the sun)

chron *abbr* **1** chronicle **2** chronological; chronology

Chron *abbr* Chronicles

chron·ic \'krän-ik\ *adj* : marked by long duration or frequent recurrence (a ~ disease); *also* : HABITUAL (a ~ grumbler) — **chron·i·cal·ly** \-i-k(ə-)lē\ *adv*

¹chron·i·cle \'krän-i-kəl\ *n* : HISTORY, NARRATIVE

²chronicle *vb* **-cled; -cling** \-k(ə-)liŋ\ : to record in or as if in a chronicle — **chron·i·cler** \-k(ə-)lər\ *n*

Chronicles *n* — see BIBLE table

chro·no·graph \'krän-ə-ˌgraf\ *n* : an instrument for measuring and recording time intervals with accuracy — **chro·no·graph·ic** \ˌkrän-ə-'graf-ik\ *adj* — **chro·nog·ra·phy** \krə-'näg-rə-fē\ *n*

chro·nol·o·gy \krə-'näl-ə-jē\ *n, pl* **-gies** : the science that deals with measuring time and dating events **2** : a chronological list or table **3** : arrangement of events in the order of their occurrence — **chron·o·log·i·cal** \ˌkrän-ə-'läj-i-kəl\ *adj* — **chron·o·log·i·cal·ly** \-i-k(ə-)lē\ *adv* — **chro·nol·o·gist** \krə-'näl-ə-jəst\ *n*

chro·nom·e·ter \krə-'näm-ət-ər\ *n* : a very accurate timepiece

chrys·a·lid \'kris-ə-ləd\ *n* : CHRYSALIS

chrys·a·lis \'kris-ə-ləs\ *n, pl* **chrys·al·i·des** \kris-'al-ə-ˌdēz\ *or* **chrys·a·lis·es** : an insect pupa in a firm case without a cocoon

chry·san·the·mum \kris-'an-thə-məm\ *n* [L, fr. Gk *chrysanthemon*, fr. *chrysos* gold + *anthemon* flower] : any of a genus of plants related to the daisies including some grown for their showy flowers or for medicinal products or insecticides; *also* : a flower of a chrysanthemum

chrys·o·lite \'kris-ə-ˌlīt\ *n* : OLIVINE

chub \'chəb\ *n, pl* **chub** *or* **chubs** : any of various small freshwater fishes related to the carp

chub·by \'chəb-ē\ *adj* **chub·bi·er; -est** : PLUMP — **chub·bi·ness** *n*

¹chuck \'chək\ *vb* **1** : to give a pat or tap **2** : to toss or throw with a short motion of the arms **3** : DISCARD; *also* : EJECT **4** : to have done with

²chuck *n* **1** : a light pat under the chin **2** : TOSS

³chuck *n* **1** : a cut of beef including most of the neck and the parts around the shoulder blade and the first three ribs **2** : a device for holding work or a tool in a machine (as a lathe)

chuck·hole \'chək-ˌhōl\ *n* : POTHOLE

chuck·le \'chək-əl\ *vb* **chuck·led; chuck·ling** \-(ə-)liŋ\ : to laugh in a quiet hardly audible manner — **chuckle** *n*

chuck wagon *n* : a wagon equipped with a stove and food supplies

¹chug \'chəg\ *n* : a dull explosive sound made by or as if by a laboring engine

²chug *vb* **chugged; chug·ging** : to move or go with chugs

chuk·ka \'chək-ə\ *n* : a short usu. ankle-length leather boot with two pairs of eyelets

chuk·ker *or* **chuk·kar** \'chək-ər\ *or* **chuk·ka** \-ə\ *n* : a playing period of a polo game

¹chum \'chəm\ *n* : an intimate friend

²chum *vb* **chummed; chum·ming 1** : to room together **2** : to be a close friend

chum·my \'chəm-ē\ *adj* **chum·mi·er; -est** : INTIMATE, SOCIABLE — **chum·mi·ly** \'chəm-ə-lē\ *adv* — **chum·mi·ness** \-ē-nəs\ *n*

chump \'chəmp\ *n* : FOOL, BLOCKHEAD

chunk \'chəŋk\ *n* **1** : a short thick piece **2** : a sizable amount

chunky \'chəŋ-kē\ *adj* **chunk·i·er; -est 1** : STOCKY **2** : containing chunks

church \'chərch\ *n* [OE *cirice*, fr. LGk *kyriakon*, short for *kyriakon dōma*, lit., the Lord's house, fr. Gk *Kyrios* Lord + *dōma* house] **1** : a building esp. for Christian public worship **2** : the whole body of Christians **3** : DENOMINATION **4** : CONGREGATION **5** : public divine worship

church·go·er \'chərch-ˌgō(-ə)r\ *n* : one who habitually attends church — **church·go·ing** \-ˌgō-iŋ\ *adj or n*

church·less \'chərch-ləs\ *adj* : not affiliated with a church

church·man \'chərch-mən\ *n* **1** : CLERGYMAN **2** : a member of a church

church·war·den \'chərch-ˌword-ⁿn\ *n* : WARDEN 5

church·yard \-ˌyärd\ *n* : a yard that belongs to a church and is often used as a burial ground

churl \'chərl\ *n* **1** : a medieval peasant **2** : RUSTIC **3** : a rude ill-bred person — **churl·ish** *adj* — **churl·ish·ly** *adv* — **churl·ish·ness** *n*

¹churn \'chərn\ *n* : a container in which milk or cream is violently stirred in making butter

²**churn** \ *vb* **1** : to stir in a churn; *also* : to make (butter) by such stirring **2** : to shake around violently

churn out *vb* : to produce mechanically and in large quantity

chute \ˈshüt\ *n* **1** : an inclined surface, trough, or passage down or through which something may pass ⟨a coal ∼⟩ ⟨a mail ∼⟩ **2** : PARACHUTE

chut·ney \ˈchət-nē\ *n, pl* **chutneys** : a condiment of acid fruits with raisins, dates, and onions

chutz·pah \ˈhût-spə, ˈkût-, -(ˌ)spä\ *n* : supreme self-confidence

CIA *abbr* Central Intelligence Agency

cía *abbr* [Sp *compañía*] company

ciao \ˈchaů\ *interj* [It, fr. It dial., alter. of *schiavo* (I am your) slave, fr. ML *sclavus*] — used to express greeting or farewell

ci·ca·da \sə-ˈkād-ə\ *n* : any of a family of stout-bodied insects related to the aphids and having wide blunt heads and large transparent wings

ci·ca·trix \ˈsik-ə-ˌtriks\ *n, pl* **ci·ca·tri·ces** \ˌsik-ə-ˈtrī-ˌsēz\ [L] : a scar resulting from formation and contraction of fibrous tissue in a flesh wound

ci·ce·ro·ne \ˌsis-ə-ˈrō-nē, ˌchē-chə-\ *n, pl* -**ni** -(ˌ)nē\ : a guide who conducts sightseers

CID *abbr* Criminal Investigation Department

ci·der \ˈsīd-ər\ *n* : juice pressed from fruit (as apples) and used as a beverage, vinegar, or flavoring

cie [F *compagnie*] company

ci·gar \sig-ˈär\ *n* : a roll of tobacco for smoking

cig·a·rette \ˌsig-ə-ˈret, ˈsig-ə-ˌret\ *n* [F, dim. of *cigare* cigar] : a slender roll of cut tobacco enclosed in paper for smoking

cig·a·ril·lo \ˌsig-ə-ˈril-ō, -ˈrē-ō\ *n, pl* -**los** [Sp] **1** : a very small cigar **2** : a cigarette wrapped in tobacco rather than paper

ci·lan·tro \si-ˈlän-trō, -ˈlan-\ *n* : leaves of coriander used as a flavoring or garnish

cil·i·ate \ˈsil-ē-ˌāt\ *n* : any of a group of protozoans characterized by cilia

cil·i·um \ˈsil-ē-əm\ *n, pl* -**ia** \-ē-ə\ **1** : a minute short hairlike process; *esp* : one of a cell **2** : EYELASH

C in C *abbr* commander in chief

cinch \ˈsinch\ *n* **1** : a girth for holding a saddle or a pack in place **2** : a sure or an easy thing — **cinch** *vb*

cin·cho·na \siŋ-ˈkō-nə\ *n* : any of a genus of So. American trees; *also* : the bitter quinine-containing bark of a cinchona

cinc·ture \ˈsiŋk-chər\ *n* : BELT, GIRDLE

cin·der \ˈsin-dər\ *n* **1** : SLAG **2** *pl* : ASHES **3** : a hot piece of partly burned wood or coal **4** : a fragment of lava from an erupting volcano — **cinder** *vb* — **cin·dery** *adj*

cinder block *n* : a building block made of cement and coal cinders

cin·e·ma \ˈsin-ə-mə\ *n* **1** : a motion-picture theater **2** : MOVIES — **cin·e·mat·ic** \ˌsin-ə-ˈmat-ik\ *adj*

cin·e·ma·theque \ˌsin-ə-mə-ˈtek\ *n* : a small movie house specializing in avant-garde films

cin·e·ma·tog·ra·phy \ˌsin-ə-mə-ˈtäg-rə-fē\ *n* : motion-picture photography — **cin·e·ma·tog·ra·pher** \-fər\ *n* — **cin·e·mat·o·graph·ic** \-ˌmat-ə-ˈgraf-ik\ *adj*

cin·er·ar·i·um \ˌsin-ə-ˈrer-ē-əm\ *n, pl* -**ia** \-ē-ə\ : a place to receive the ashes of the cremated dead — **cin·er·ary** \ˈsin-ə-ˌrer-ē\ *adj*

cin·na·bar \ˈsin-ə-ˌbär\ *n* : a red mineral that is the only important ore of mercury

cin·na·mon \ˈsin-ə-mən\ *n* : a spice consisting of the highly aromatic bark of any of several trees related to the true laurel; *also* : a tree that yields cinnamon

cinque·foil \ˈsiŋk-ˌfȯil, ˈsaŋk-\ *n* : any of a genus of plants related to the roses with leaves having five lobes

¹**ci·pher** \ˈsī-fər\ *n* [ME, fr. MF *cifre*, fr. ML *cifra*, fr. Ar *ṣifr* empty, zero] **1** : ZERO, NAUGHT **2** : a method of secret writing

²**cipher** *vb* **ci·phered; ci·pher·ing** \-f(ə-)riŋ\ : to compute arithmetically

cir *or* **circ** *abbr* circular

cir·ca \ˈsər-kə\ *prep* : ABOUT ⟨∼ 1600⟩

cir·ca·di·an \ˌsər-ˈkād-ē-ən, ˌsər-kə-ˈdī-ən\ *adj* : being, having, characterized by, or occurring in approximately 24-hour intervals (as of biological activity)

¹**cir·cle** \ˈsər-kəl\ *n* **1** : a closed curve every point of which is equally distant from a fixed point within it **2** : something in the form of a circle **3** : an area of action or influence **4** : CYCLE **5** : a group bound by a common tie

²**circle** *vb* **cir·cled; cir·cling** \-k(ə-)liŋ\ **1** : to enclose in a circle **2** : to move or revolve around; *also* : to move in a circle

cir·clet \ˈsər-klət\ *n* : a small circle; *esp* : a circular ornament

cir·cuit \ˈsər-kət\ *n* **1** : a boundary around an enclosed space **2** : a moving or revolving around (as in an orbit) **3** : a regular tour (as by a judge) around an assigned territory **4** : the complete path of an electric current **5** : LEAGUE; *also* : a chain of theaters — **cir·cuit·al** \-kət-ᵊl\ *adj*

circuit breaker *n* : a switch that automatically interrupts an electric circuit under an abnormal condition

circuit court *n* : a court that sits at two or more places within one judicial district

cir·cu·itous \ˌsər-ˈkyü-ət-əs\ *adj* **1** : not being forthright or direct in language or action **2** : having a circular or winding course

cir·cuit·ry \ˈsər-kə-trē\ *n, pl* -**ries** : the plan or the components of an electric circuit

cir·cu·ity \sər-'kyü-ət-ē\ n, pl **-ities** : INDIRECTION

¹**cir·cu·lar** \'sər-kyə-lər\ adj 1 : having the form of a circle : ROUND 2 : moving in or around a circle 3 : CIRCUITOUS 4 : sent around to a number of persons (a ~ letter) — **cir·cu·lar·i·ty** \ˌsər-kyə-'lar-ət-ē\ n

²**circular** n : a paper (as an advertising leaflet) intended for wide distribution

cir·cu·lar·ize \'sər-kyə-lə-ˌrīz\ vb **-ized; -iz·ing** 1 : to send circulars to 2 : to poll by questionnaire

circular saw n : a power saw with a round cutting blade

cir·cu·late \'sər-kyə-ˌlāt\ vb **-lat·ed; -lat·ing** 1 : to move or cause to move in a circle, circuit, or orbit 2 : to pass from place to place or from person to person — **cir·cu·la·tion** \ˌsər-kyə-'lā-shən\ n

cir·cu·la·to·ry \'sər-kyə-lə-ˌtōr-ē\ adj : of or relating to circulation or the circulatory system

circulatory system n : the system of blood, blood vessels, lymphatic vessels, and heart concerned with the circulation of the blood and lymph

cir·cum·am·bu·late \ˌsər-kəm-'am-byə-ˌlāt\ vb **-lat·ed; -lat·ing** : to circle on foot esp. ritualistically

cir·cum·cise \'sər-kəm-ˌsīz\ vb **-cised; -cis·ing** : to cut off the foreskin of — **cir·cum·ci·sion** \ˌsər-kəm-'sizh-ən\ n

cir·cum·fer·ence \sər-'kəm-f(ə-)rəns\ n 1 : the perimeter of a circle 2 : the external boundary or surface of a figure or object

cir·cum·flex \'sər-kəm-ˌfleks\ n : the mark ˆ over a vowel

cir·cum·lo·cu·tion \ˌsər-kəm-lō-'kyü-shən\ n : the use of unnecessary words in expressing an idea

cir·cum·lu·nar \-'lü-nər\ adj : revolving about or surrounding the moon

cir·cum·nav·i·gate \-'nav-ə-ˌgāt\ vb : to go completely around esp. by water — **cir·cum·nav·i·ga·tion** \-ˌnav-ə-'gā-shən\ n

cir·cum·po·lar \-'pō-lər\ adj 1 : continually visible above the horizon (a ~ star) 2 : surrounding or found near a terrestrial pole

cir·cum·scribe \'sər-kəm-ˌskrīb\ vb 1 : to limit narrowly the range or activity of 2 : to draw a line around — **cir·cum·scrip·tion** \ˌsər-kəm-'skrip-shən\ n

cir·cum·spect \'sər-kəm-ˌspekt\ adj : careful to consider all circumstances and consequences : PRUDENT — **cir·cum·spec·tion** \ˌsər-kəm-'spek-shən\ n

cir·cum·stance \'sər-kəm-ˌstans\ n 1 : a fact or event that must be considered along with another fact or event 2 : surrounding conditions 3 pl : situation with regard to wealth 4 : CEREMONY 5 : CHANCE, FATE

cir·cum·stan·tial \ˌsər-kəm-'stan-chəl\ adj 1 : consisting of or depending on circumstances 2 : INCIDENTAL 3 : containing full details — **cir·cum·stan·tial·ly** \-ē\ adv

cir·cum·vent \ˌsər-kəm-'vent\ vb : to check or defeat esp. by stratagem

cir·cus \'sər-kəs\ n 1 : a usu. traveling show that features feats of physical skill and daring, wild animal acts, and performances by clowns 2 : a circus performance; also : the equipment, livestock, and personnel of a circus

cirque \'sərk\ n : a deep steep-walled mountain basin shaped like half a bowl

cir·rho·sis \sə-'rō-səs\ n, pl **-rho·ses** \-ˌsēz\ [NL. fr. Gk kirrhos orange-colored] : fibrosis esp. of the liver — **cir·rhot·ic** \-'rät-ik\ adj or n

cir·rus \'sir-əs\ n, pl **cir·ri** \'sir-ˌī\ : a wispy white cloud usu. of minute ice crystals at high altitudes

cis·lu·nar \(')sis-'lü-nər\ adj : lying between the earth and the moon or the moon's orbit

cis·tern \'sis-tərn\ n : an often underground tank for storing water

cit abbr 1 citation; cited 2 citizen

cit·a·del \'sit-əd-ᵊl, -ə-ˌdel\ n 1 : a fortress commanding a city 2 : STRONGHOLD

ci·ta·tion \sī-'tā-shən\ n 1 : an official summons to appear (as before a court) 2 : QUOTATION 3 : a formal statement of the achievements of a person; also : a specific reference in a military dispatch to meritorious performance of duty

cite \'sīt\ vb **cit·ed; cit·ing** 1 : to summon to appear before a court 2 : QUOTE 3 : to refer to esp. in commendation or praise

citi·fied \'sit-i-ˌfīd\ adj : of, relating to, or characterized by an urban style of living

cit·i·zen \'sit-ə-zən\ n 1 : an inhabitant of a city or town 2 : a person who owes allegiance to a government and is entitled to government protection — **cit·i·zen·ship** n

cit·i·zen·ry \-rē\ n, pl **-ries** : a whole body of citizens

citizens band n : a range of radio frequencies set aside for private radio communications

cit·ric acid \ˌsit-rik-\ n : a sour organic acid obtained from lemon and lime juices or by fermentation of sugars and used as a flavoring

cit·ron \'sit-rən\ n 1 : the oval lemon-like fruit of an Asian citrus tree 2 : a small hard-fleshed watermelon used esp. in pickles and preserves

cit·ro·nel·la \ˌsit-rə-'nel-ə\ n : an oil obtained from a grass of southern Asia and used in perfumes and as an insect repellent

cit·rus \'sit-rəs\ n, pl **citrus** or **cit·rus·es** : any of a genus of often thorny evergreen trees or shrubs grown in warm regions for their fruits (as the orange, lemon, lime, and grapefruit)

city \'sit-ē\ *n, pl* **cit·ies** [ME *citie* large or small town, fr. OF *cité* capital city, fr. ML *civitas*, fr. L. citizenship, state, city of Rome, fr. *civis* citizen] **1** : an inhabited place larger or more important than a town **2** : a municipality in the U.S. governed under a charter granted by the state; *also* : an incorporated municipal unit of the highest class in Canada

city manager *n* : an official employed by an elected council to direct the administration of a city government

city–state \'sit-ē-¹stāt, -ˌstāt\ *n* : an autonomous state consisting of a city and surrounding territory

civ *abbr* civil; civilian

civ·et \'siv-ət\ *n* : a yellowish strong-smelling substance obtained from a catlike mammal (**civet cat**) of Africa or Asia and used in making perfumes

civ·ic \'siv-ik\ *adj* : of or relating to a city, citizenship, or civic affairs

civ·ics \-iks\ *n* : a social science dealing with the rights and duties of citizens

civ·il \'siv-əl\ *adj* **1** : of or relating to citizens or to the state as a political body **2** : COURTEOUS, POLITE **3** : of or relating to legal proceedings in connection with private rights and obligations (the ~ code) **4** : of or relating to the general population : not military or ecclesiastical

civil defense *n* : the protective measures and emergency relief activities conducted by civilians in case of hostile attack, sabotage, or natural disaster

civil disobedience *n* : refusal to obey governmental commands esp. as a nonviolent means of protest

civil engineer *n* : an engineer whose training or occupation is in the designing and construction chiefly of public works (as roads or harbors) — **civil engineering** *n*

ci·vil·ian \sə-¹vil-yən\ *n* : a person not on active duty in a military, police, or fire-fighting force

ci·vil·i·ty \sə-¹vil-ət-ē\ *n, pl* **-ties 1** : POLITENESS, COURTESY **2** : a polite act or expression

civ·i·li·za·tion \ˌsiv-ə-lə-¹zā-shən\ *n* **1** : a relatively high level of cultural and technological development **2** : the culture characteristic of a time or place

civ·i·lize \'siv-ə-ˌlīz\ *vb* **-lized; -liz·ing 1** : to raise from a primitive state to an advanced and ordered stage of cultural development **2** : REFINE — **civ·i·lized** *adj*

civil liberty *n* : freedom from arbitrary governmental interference specifically by denial of governmental power — usu. used in pl.

civ·il·ly \'siv-ə(l)-lē\ *adv* **1** : in terms of civil rights, matters, or law (~ dead) **2** : in a civil manner : POLITELY

civil rights *n pl* : the nonpolitical rights of a citizen; *esp* : those guaranteed by

the 13th and 14th amendments to the Constitution and by acts of Congress

civil servant *n* : a member of a civil service

civil service *n* : the administrative service of a government

civil war *n* : a war between opposing groups of citizens of the same country

civ·vies \'siv-ēz\ *n pl* : civilian clothes as distinguished from a military uniform

CJ *abbr* chief justice

ck *abbr* **1** cask **2** check

cl *abbr* class

Cl *symbol* chlorine

¹**clack** \'klak\ *vb* **1** : CHATTER, PRATTLE **2** : to make or cause to make a clatter

²**clack** *n* **1** : rapid continuous talk : CHATTER **2** : a sound of clacking (the ~ of a typewriter)

clad \'klad\ *adj* **1** : CLOTHED, COVERED **2** : being or consisting of coins made of outer layers of one metal bonded to a core of a different metal (~ coinage)

¹**claim** \'klām\ *vb* **1** : to ask for as one's own; *also* : to take as the rightful owner **2** : to call for : REQUIRE **3** : to state as a fact : MAINTAIN

²**claim** *n* **1** : a demand for something due **2** : a right to something usu. in another's possession **3** : an assertion open to challenge **4** : something claimed

claim·ant \'klā-mənt\ *n* : a person making a claim

clair·voy·ant \klar-¹vȯi-ənt\ *adj* [F, fr. *clair* clear + *voyant* seeing] **1** : unusually perceptive **2** : having the power of discerning objects not present to the senses — **clair·voy·ance** \-əns\ *n* — **clairvoyant** *n*

clam \'klam\ *n* **1** : any of numerous bivalve mollusks including many that are edible **2** : DOLLAR

clam·bake \-ˌbāk\ *n* : a party or gathering (as at the seashore) at which food is cooked usu. on heated rocks covered by seaweed

clam·ber \'klam-bər\ *vb* **clam·bered; clam·ber·ing** \'klam-b(ə-)riŋ, -(ə-)riŋ\ : to climb awkwardly (as by scrambling)

clam·my \'klam-ē\ *adj* **clam·mi·er; -est** : being damp, soft, sticky, and usu. cool — **clam·mi·ness** *n*

¹**clam·or** \'klam-ər\ *n* **1** : a noisy shouting **2** : a loud continuous noise **3** : vigorous protest or demand — **clam·or·ous** *adj*

²**clamor** *vb* **clam·ored; clam·or·ing** \'klam-(ə-)riŋ\ : to make a clamor

¹**clamp** \'klamp\ *n* : a device that holds or presses parts together firmly

²**clamp** *vb* : to fasten with or as if with a clamp

clamp down \(¹)klamp-¹daūn\ *vb* : to impose restrictions : become repressive — **clamp·down** \'klamp-ˌdaūn\ *n*

clam·shell \'klam-ˌshel\ *n* : a bucket or grapple (as on a dredge) having two hinged jaws

clam up *vb* : to become silent

clan \\'klan\ *n* [ME, fr. ScGael *clann* offspring, clan, fr. Old Irish *cland* plant, offspring, fr. L *planta* plant] : a group (as in the Scottish Highlands) made up of households whose heads claim descent from a common ancestor — **clan·nish** *adj* — **clan·nish·ness** *n*

clan·des·tine \klan-'des-tən\ *adj* : held in or conducted with secrecy

clang \'klaŋ\ *n* : a loud metallic ringing sound — **clang** *vb*

clan·gor \'klaŋ-(g)ər\ *n* : a resounding clang or medley of clangs

clank \'klaŋk\ *n* : a sharp brief metallic ringing sound — **clank** *vb*

¹clap \'klap\ *vb* **clapped; clap·ping** **1** : to strike noisily **2** : APPLAUD

²clap *n* **1** : a loud noisy crash **2** : the noise made by clapping the hands

³clap *n* : GONORRHEA

clap·board \'klab-ərd; 'kla(p)-,bōrd\ *n* : a narrow board thicker at one edge than the other used for siding — **clapboard** *vb*

clap·per \'klap-ər\ *n* : one that makes a clapping sound; *esp* : the tongue of a bell

clap·trap \'klap-,trap\ *n* : pretentious nonsense

claque \'klak\ *n* [F, fr. *claquer* to clap] **1** : a group hired to applaud at a performance **2** : a group of self-seeking flatterers

clar·et \'klar-ət\ *n* [ME, fr. MF (*vin*) *claret* clear wine] : a dry red wine

clar·i·fy \'klar-ə-,fī\ *vb* **-fied; -fy·ing** : to make or become clear — **clar·i·fi·ca·tion** \,klar-ə-fə-'kā-shən\ *n*

clar·i·net \,klar-ə-'net\ *n* : a single-reed woodwind instrument in the form of a cylindrical tube with moderately flaring end — **clar·i·net·ist** *or* **clar·i·net·tist** \- əst-\ *n*

clar·i·on \'klar-ē-ən\ *adj* : brilliantly clear ⟨a ~ call to action⟩

clar·i·ty \'klar-ət-ē\ *n* : CLEARNESS

¹clash \'klash\ *vb* **1** : to make or cause to make a clash **2** : CONFLICT, COLLIDE

²clash *n* **1** : a noisy usu. metallic sound of collision **2** : a hostile encounter; *also* : a conflict of opinion

¹clasp \'klasp\ *n* **1** : a device (as a hook) for holding objects or parts together **2** : EMBRACE, GRASP

²clasp *vb* **1** : to fasten with a clasp **2** : EMBRACE **3** : GRASP

¹class \'klas\ *n* **1** : a group of students meeting regularly in a course; *also* : a group graduating together **2** : a course of instruction; *also* : the period when such a course is taught **3** : social rank; *also* : high quality **4** : a group of the same economic status or nature; *esp* : a major category in biological classification that is above the order and below the phylum **5** : a division or rating based on grade or quality — **class·less** *adj*

²class *vb* : CLASSIFY

class action *n* : a legal action undertaken in behalf of the plaintiffs and all others having an identical interest in the alleged wrong

¹clas·sic \'klas-ik\ *adj* **1** : serving as a standard of excellence; *also* : TRADITIONAL **2** : CLASSICAL **2 3** : notable esp. as the best example **4** : AUTHENTIC

²classic *n* **1** : a work of enduring excellence and esp. of ancient Greece or Rome; *also* : its author **2** : a traditional event

clas·si·cal \'klas-i-kəl\ *adj* **1** : CLASSIC **2** : of or relating to the ancient Greek and Roman classics **3** : of or relating to a form or system of primary significance before modern times ⟨~ economics⟩ **4** : concerned with a general study of the arts and sciences — **clas·si·cal·ly** \-k(ə-)lē\ *adv*

clas·si·cism \'klas-ə-,siz-əm\ *n* **1** : the principles or style of the literature or art of ancient Greece and Rome **2** : adherence to traditional standards believed to be universally valid — **clas·si·cist** \-səst\ *n*

clas·si·fied \'klas-ə-,fīd\ *adj* : withheld from general circulation for reasons of national security

clas·si·fy \'klas-ə-,fī\ *vb* **-fied; -fy·ing** : to arrange in or assign to classes — **clas·si·fi·able** *adj* — **clas·si·fi·ca·tion** \,klas-ə-fə-'kā-shən\ *n*

class·mate \'klas-,māt\ *n* : a member of the same class (as in a college)

class·room \-,rüm-, -,rùm\ *n* : a room (as in a school) in which classes meet

classy \'klas-ē\ *adj* **class·i·er; -est** : ELEGANT, STYLISH

clat·ter \'klat-ər\ *n* : a rattling sound (the ~ of dishes) — **clatter** *vb*

clause \'klóz\ *n* **1** : a group of words having its own subject and predicate but forming only part of a compound or complex sentence **2** : a separate part of an article or document

claus·tro·pho·bia \,klò-strə-'fō-bē-ə\ *n* : abnormal dread of being in closed or narrow spaces — **claus·tro·pho·bic** \-bik\ *adj*

clav·i·chord \'klav-ə-,kórd\ *n* : an early keyboard instrument in use before the piano

clav·i·cle \'klav-i-kəl\ *n* [F *clavicule*, fr. NL *clavicula*, fr. L, dim. of L *clavis* key] : COLLARBONE

cla·vier \klə-'viər; 'klä-vē-ər\ *n* **1** : the keyboard of a musical instrument **2** : an early keyboard instrument

¹claw \'klò\ *n* **1** : a sharp usu. curved nail on the toe of an animal **2** : a sharp curved process (as on the foot of an insect); *also* : a pincerlike organ at the end of a limb of some arthropods (as a lobster) — **clawed** \'klòd\ *adj*

²claw *vb* : to rake, seize, or dig with or as if with claws

clay \'klā\ *n* **1** : an earthy material that is plastic when moist but hard when fired and is used in making pottery; *also* : finely divided soil consisting largely of such clay **2** : EARTH, MUD **3** : a plastic substance used for modeling 4 : the mortal human body — **clay•ey** \'klā-ē\ adj

clay•more \'klā-ˌmōr\ n : a large 2-edged sword formerly used by Scottish Highlanders

clay pigeon n : a saucer-shaped target thrown from a trap in trapshooting

¹**clean** \'klēn\ adj 1 : free from dirt or disease 2 : PURE; also : HONORABLE 3 : THOROUGH (made a ~ sweep) 4 : TRIM (a ship with ~ lines) ; also : EVEN 5 : habitually neat — **clean** adv — **clean•ly** \'klēn-lē\ adv — **clean•ness** \'klēn-nəs\ n

²**clean** vb : to make or become clean — **clean•er** n

clean–cut \'klēn-'kət\ adj 1 : cut so that the surface or edge is smooth and even 2 : sharply defined or outlined 3 : giving an effect of wholesomeness

clean•ly \'klen-lē\ adj **clean•li•er; -est** 1 : careful to keep clean 2 : habitually kept clean — **clean•li•ness** n

clean room \'klēn-ˌrüm, -ˌrüm\ n : an uncontaminated room maintained for the manufacture or assembly of objects (as precision parts)

cleanse \'klenz\ vb **cleansed; cleans•ing** : to make clean — **cleans•er** n

¹**clean-up** \'klēn-ˌəp\ n 1 : an act or instance of cleaning 2 : a very large profit

²**cleanup** adj : being 4th in the batting order of a baseball team

clean up \(ˈ)klēn-'əp\ vb : to make a spectacular business profit

¹**clear** \'kliər\ adj 1 : BRIGHT, LUMINOUS; also : UNTROUBLED, SERENE 2 : CLOUDLESS 3 : CLEAN, PURE; also : TRANSPARENT 4 : easily heard, seen, or understood 5 : capable of sharp discernment; also : free from doubt 6 : INNOCENT 7 : free from restriction, obstruction, or entanglement — **clear** adv — **clear•ly** adv — **clear•ness** n

²**clear** vb 1 : to make or become clear 2 : to go away : DISPERSE 3 : to free from accusation or blame; also : to certify as trustworthy 4 : EXPLAIN 5 : to get free from obstruction 6 : SETTLE 7 : NET 8 : to get rid of : REMOVE 9 : to jump or go by without touching; also : PASS

³**clear** n : a clear space or part

clear•ance \'klir-əns\ n 1 : an act or process of clearing 2 : the distance by which one object clears another

clear–cut \'kliər-'kət\ adj 1 : sharply outlined 2 : DEFINITE, UNEQUIVOCAL

clear–head•ed \-'hed-əd\ adj : having a clear understanding : PERCEPTIVE

clear•ing \'kli(ə)r-iŋ\ n 1 : a tract of land cleared of wood and brush 2 : the passage of checks and claims through a clearinghouse

clear•ing•house \-ˌhaus\ n : an institution maintained by banks for making an exchange of checks and claims held by each bank against other banks

cleat \'klēt\ n : a piece of wood or metal fastened on or projecting from something to give strength, provide a grip, or prevent slipping

cleav•age \'klē-vij\ n 1 : a splitting apart : SPLIT 2 : the depression between a woman's breasts esp. when exposed by a low-cut dress

¹**cleave** \'klēv\ vb **cleaved** \'klēvd\ or **clove** \'klōv\ ; **cleaved; cleav•ing** : ADHERE, CLING

²**cleave** vb **cleaved** \'klēvd\ also **cleft** \'kleft\ or **clove** \'klōv\ ; **cleaved** also **cleft** or **clo•ven** \'klō-vən\ ; **cleav•ing** 1 : to divide by force : split asunder 2 : DIVIDE

cleav•er \'klē-vər\ n : a heavy chopping knife for cutting meat

clef \'klef\ n : a sign placed on the staff in music to show what pitch is represented by each line and space

cleft \'kleft\ n : FISSURE, CRACK

cleft palate n : a split in the roof of the mouth that appears as a birth defect

clem•a•tis \'klem-ət-əs; kli-'mat-əs\ n : a vine related to the buttercups that has showy usu. white or purple flowers

clem•en•cy \'klem-ən-sē\ n, pl **-cies** 1 : disposition to be merciful 2 : mildness of weather

clem•ent \-ənt\ adj 1 : MERCIFUL, LENIENT 2 : TEMPERATE, MILD

clench \'klench\ vb 1 : CLINCH 1 2 : to hold fast 3 : to set or close tightly

clere•sto•ry \'kliər-ˌstōr-ē\ n : an outside wall of a room or building that rises above an adjoining roof and contains windows

cler•gy \'klər-jē\ n : a body of religious officials authorized to conduct services

cler•gy•man \-ji-mən\ n : a member of the clergy

cler•ic \'kler-ik\ n : CLERGYMAN

cler•i•cal \'kler-i-kəl\ adj 1 : of or relating to the clergy or a clergyman 2 : of or relating to a clerk

cler•i•cal•ism \'kler-i-kə-ˌliz-əm\ n : a policy of maintaining or increasing the power of a religious hierarchy

clerk \'klərk, Brit 'klärk\ n 1 : CLERIC 2 : an official responsible for correspondence, records, and accounts; also : a person employed to perform general office work 3 : a store salesman — **clerk** vb — **clerk•ship** n

clev•er \'klev-ər\ adj 1 : showing skill or resourcefulness 2 : marked by wit or ingenuity — **clev•er•ly** adv — **clev•er•ness** n

clev•is \'klev-əs\ n : a U-shaped shackle used for attaching or suspending parts

¹**clew** \'klü\ n 1 : CLUE 2 : a metal loop on a lower corner of a sail for holding ropes

²**clew** vb : to haul (a sail) up or down by ropes through the clews

cli•ché \klē-'shā\ n [F] : a trite phrase or expression — **cli•chéd** \-'shād\ adj

¹**click** \'klik\ vb 1 : to make or cause to

make a click **2** : to fit or work together smoothly

²click *n* : a slight sharp noise

cli·ent \\'klī-ənt\\ *n* **1** : DEPENDENT **2** : a person who engages the professional services of another; *also* : PATRON, CUSTOMER

cli·en·tele \\,klī-ən-'tel, ,klē-ən-\\ *n* : a body of clients and esp. customers

cliff \\'klif\\ *n* : a high steep face of rock

cliff–hang·er \\-,haŋ-ər\\ *n* **1** : an adventure serial or melodrama usu. presented in installments each of which ends in suspense **2** : a contest whose outcome is in doubt up to the very end

cli·mac·ter·ic \\klī-'mak-t(ə-)rik\\ *n* **1** : a major turning point or critical stage **2** : MENOPAUSE; *also* : a corresponding period in the male

cli·mate \\'klī-mət\\ *n* [ME *climat*, fr. MF, fr. LL *clima*, fr. Gk *klima* inclination, latitude, climate, fr. *klinein* to lean] **1** : a region having specific climatic conditions **2** : the average weather conditions at a place over a period of years **3** : the prevailing set of conditions (as temperature and humidity) indoors **4** : a prevailing atmosphere or environment (the ∼ of opinion) — **cli·mat·ic** \\klī-'mat-ik\\ *adj* — **cli·mat·i·cal·ly** \\-i-k(ə-)lē\\ *adv*

cli·ma·tol·o·gy \\,klī-mə-'täl-ə-jē\\ *n* : the science that deals with climates — **cli·ma·to·log·i·cal** \\,klī-mət-əl-'äj-i-kəl\\ *adj* — **cli·ma·to·log·i·cal·ly** \\-k(ə-)lē\\ *adv* — **cli·ma·tol·o·gist** \\-mə-'täl-ə-jəst\\ *n*

¹cli·max \\'klī-,maks\\ *n* [L, fr. Gk *klimax* ladder, fr. *klinein* to lean] **1** : a series of ideas or statements so arranged that they increase in force and power from the first to the last; *also* : the last member of such a series **2** : the highest point **3** : ORGASM — **cli·mac·tic** \\klī-'mak-tik\\ *adj*

²climax *vb* : to come or bring to a climax

¹climb \\'klīm\\ *vb* **1** : to rise to a higher point **2** : to go up or down esp. by use of hands and feet; *also* : to ascend in growing — **climb·er** *n*

²climb *n* **1** : a place where climbing is necessary **2** : the act of climbing : ascent by climbing

clime \\'klīm\\ *n* : CLIMATE

¹clinch \\'klinch\\ *vb* **1** : to turn over or flatten the end of something sticking out (∼ a nail) ; *also* : to fasten by clinching **2** : to make final : SETTLE **3** : to hold fast or firmly

²clinch *n* **1** : a fastening by means of a clinched nail, rivet, or bolt **2** : an act or instance of clinching in boxing

clinch·er \\'klin-chər\\ *n* : one that clinches; *esp* : a decisive fact, argument, act, or remark

cling \\'kliŋ\\ *vb* **clung** \\'kləŋ\\ ; **cling·ing** **1** : to adhere as if glued; *also* : to hold or hold on tightly **2** : to have a strong emotional attachment

cling·stone \\'kliŋ-,stōn\\ *n* : any of various

ous fruits (as some peaches) whose flesh adheres strongly to the pit

clin·ic \\'klin-ik\\ *n* **1** : medical instruction featuring the examination and discussion of actual cases **2** : a group meeting for teaching a certain skill and working on individual problems (a reading ∼) **3** : a facility (as of a hospital) for diagnosis and treatment of outpatients

clin·i·cal \\'klin-i-kəl\\ *adj* **1** : of, relating to, or typical of a clinic; *esp* : involving direct observation of the patient **2** : scientifically dispassionate — **clin·i·cal·ly** \\-k(ə-)lē\\ *adv*

cli·ni·cian \\klin-'ish-ən\\ *n* : one qualified in the clinical practice of medicine, psychiatry, or psychology as distinguished from one specializing in laboratory or research techniques

¹clink \\'kliŋk\\ *vb* : to make or cause to make a sharp short metallic sound

²clink *n* : a clinking sound

clin·ker \\'kliŋ-kər\\ *n* : stony matter fused by fire (as in a furnace from impurities in coal) : SLAG

¹clip \\'klip\\ *vb* **clipped; clip·ping** : to fasten with a clip

²clip *n* **1** : a device that grips, clasps, or hooks **2** : a cartridge holder for a rifle

³clip *vb* **clipped; clip·ping** **1** : to cut or cut off with shears **2** : CURTAIL, DIMINISH **3** : HIT, PUNCH **4** : to illegally block (an opponent) in football

⁴clip *n* **1** : a 2-bladed instrument for cutting esp. the nails **2** : a sharp blow **3** : a rapid pace

clip·board \\'klip-,bōrd\\ *n* : a small writing board with a spring clip at the top for holding papers

clip joint *n, slang* : an establishment (as a nightclub) that makes a practice of defrauding its customers

clip·per \\'klip-ər\\ *n* **1** : an implement for clipping esp. the hair or nails — usu. used in pl. **2** : a fast sailing ship

clip·ping \\'klip-iŋ\\ *n* : a piece clipped from something (as a newspaper)

clique \\'klēk, 'klik\\ *n* [F] : a small exclusive group of people : COTERIE — **cliqu·ey** \\'klēk-ē, 'klik-\\ *adj* — **cliqu·ish** \\-ish\\ *adj*

cli·to·ris \\'klit-ə-rəs\\ *n, pl* **cli·to·ri·des** \\kli-'tōr-ə-,dēz\\ : a small organ at the anterior or ventral part of the vulva homologous to the penis — **cli·to·ral** \\-rəl\\ *adj*

clk *abbr* clerk

clo *abbr* clothing

¹cloak \\'klōk\\ *n* **1** : a loose outer garment **2** : something that conceals

²cloak *vb* : to cover or hide with a cloak

cloak–and–dag·ger *adj* : involving or suggestive of espionage

clob·ber \\'kläb-ər\\ *vb* **clob·bered; clob·ber·ing** \\-(ə-)riŋ\\ **1** : to pound mercilessly; *also* : to hit with force : SMASH **2** : to defeat overwhelmingly

cloche \\'klōsh\\ *n* [F, lit., bell] : a woman's small hat that somewhat resembles a helmet

¹**clock** \'kläk\ *n* : a timepiece not intended to be carried on the person

²**clock** *vb* **1** : to time (a person or a performance) by a timing device **2** : to register (as speed) on a mechanical recording device — **clock·er** *n*

³**clock** *n* : an ornamental figure on a stocking or sock

clock·wise \'kläk-,wīz\ *adv* : in the direction in which the hands of a clock move — **clockwise** *adj*

clock·work \-,wərk\ *n* : machinery containing a set of small cogwheels

clod \'kläd\ *n* **1** : a lump esp. of earth or clay **2** : a dull or insensitive person

clod·hop·per \-,häp-ər\ *n* **1** : an uncouth rustic **2** : a large heavy shoe

¹**clog** \'kläg\ *n* **1** : a weight so attached as to impede motion **2** : a thick-soled shoe

²**clog** *vb* **clogged; clog·ging 1** : to impede with a clog : HINDER **2** : to obstruct passage through **3** : to become filled with extraneous matter

cloi·son·né \,klȯiz-ᵊn-ˈā\ *adj* : a colored decoration made of enamels poured into the divided areas in a design outlined with wire or metal strips

¹**clois·ter** \'klȯi-stər\ *n* [ME *cloistre*, fr. OF, fr. ML *claustrum*, fr. L, bar, bolt, fr. *claudere* to close] **1** : a monastic establishment **2** : a covered usu. colonnaded passage on the side of a court — **clois·tral** \-strəl\ *adj*

²**cloister** *vb* : to shut away from the world

clone \'klōn\ *n* [Gk *klōn* twig] **1** : the offspring produced asexually from an individual (as a plant increased by grafting) **2** : an individual grown from a single body cell of its parent and genetically identical to the parent **3** : one that appears to be a copy of an original form — **clon·al** \'klōn-ᵊl\ *adj* — **clone** *vb*

clop \'kläp\ *n* : a sound made by or as if by a hoof or wooden shoe against pavement — **clop** *vb*

¹**close** \'klōz\ *vb* **closed; clos·ing 1** : to bar passage through : SHUT **2** : to suspend the operations (as of a school) **3** : END, TERMINATE **4** : to bring together the parts or edges of; *also* : to fill up **5** : GRAPPLE (~ with the enemy) **6** : to enter into an agreement — **clos·able** *or* **close·able** *adj*

²**close** \'klōz\ *n* : CONCLUSION, END

³**close** \'klōs\ *adj* **clos·er; clos·est 1** : having no openings or restricted **2** : narrowly restricting or restricted **3** : limited to a privileged class **4** : SECLUDED; *also* : SECRETIVE **5** : RIGOROUS **6** : SULTRY, STUFFY **7** : STINGY **8** : having little space between items or units **9** : fitting tightly; *also* : SHORT (~ haircut) **10** : NEAR **11** : INTIMATE (~ friends) **12** : ACCURATE **13** : decided by a narrow margin (a ~ game) — **close** *adv* — **close·ly** *adv* — **close·ness** *n*

closed circuit *n* : television installation in which the signal is transmitted by wire to a limited number of receivers

closed shop *n* : an establishment having only members of a labor union on the payroll

close-fist·ed \'klōs-ˈfis-təd\ *adj* : STINGY

close–knit \-ˈnit\ *adj* : closely bound together by social, cultural, economic, or political ties

close-mouthed \-ˈmau̇thd, -ˈmau̇tht\ *adj* : cautious in speaking

close·out \'klōz-,au̇t\ *n* : a sale of a business's entire stock at low prices

close out \'klōz-ˈau̇t\ *vb* **1** : to dispose of by a closeout **2** : to dispose of a business : sell out

¹**clos·et** \'kläz-ət, 'klȯz-\ *n* **1** : a small room for privacy **2** : a small compartment for household utensils or clothing **3** : WATER CLOSET

²**closet** *vb* : to take into a private room for an interview

close–up \'klōs-,əp\ *n* **1** : a photograph or movie shot taken at close range **2** : an intimate view or examination of something

clo·sure \'klō-zhər\ *n* **1** : an act of closing : the condition of being closed **2** : something that closes **3** : CLOTURE

clot \'klät\ *n* : a mass formed by a portion of liquid (as blood or cream) thickening and sticking together — **clot** *vb*

cloth \'klȯth\ *n, pl* **cloths** \'klȯthz, 'klȯths\ **1** : a pliable fabric made usu. by weaving or knitting natural or synthetic fibers and filaments **2** : TABLECLOTH **3** : distinctive dress of the clergy; *also* : CLERGY

clothe \'klȯth\ *vb* **clothed** *or* **clad** \'klad\ ; **cloth·ing 1** : DRESS **2** : to express by suitably significant language

clothes \'klō(th)z\ *n pl* **1** : CLOTHING **2** : BEDCLOTHES

clothes·horse \-,hȯrs\ *n* **1** : a frame on which to hang clothes **2** : a conspicuously dressy person

clothes moth *n* : a small pale insect whose larvae eat wool, fur, and feathers

clothes·pin \'klō(th)z-,pin\ *n* : a device for fastening clothes on a line

clothes·press \-,pres\ *n* : a receptacle for clothes

cloth·ier \'klȯth-yər, 'klō-thē-ər\ *n* : a maker or seller of clothing

cloth·ing \'klō-thiŋ\ *n* : garments in general

clo·ture \'klō-chər\ *n* : the closing or limitation (as by calling for a vote) of debate in a legislative body

¹**cloud** \'klau̇d\ *n* [ME, rock, cloud, fr. OE *clūd* rock, hill] **1** : a visible mass of water or ice particles usu. high in the air **2** : a usu. visible mass of minute airborne particles; *also* : a mass of obscuring matter in interstellar space **3** : CROWD, SWARM (a ~ of mosquitoes) **4** : something having a dark or threatening aspect — **cloud·i·ness** \-ē-nəs\ *n* — **cloud·less** *adj* — **cloudy** *adj*

²**cloud** vb **1** : to darken or hide with or as if with a cloud **2** : OBSCURE **3** : TAINT, SULLY

cloud·burst \-ˌbərst\ n : a sudden heavy rainfall

cloud·let \-lət\ n : a small cloud

cloud nine n : a feeling of extreme well-being or elation — usu. used with *on*

¹**clout** \ˈklaüt\ n **1** : a blow esp. with the hand **2** : PULL, INFLUENCE

²**clout** vb : to hit forcefully

¹**clove** \ˈklōv\ n : one of the small bulbs that grows at the base of the scales of a large bulb ⟨a ~ of garlic⟩

²**clove** past of CLEAVE

³**clove** n [ME *clowe*, fr. OF *clou* (*de girofle*), lit., nail of clove, fr. L *clavus* nail] : the dried flower bud of an East Indian tree used esp. as a spice

clo·ven \ˈklō-vən\ past part of CLEAVE

cloven foot n : a foot (as of a sheep) with the front part divided into two parts — **cloven-foot·ed** \-ˈfüt-əd\ adj

cloven hoof n : CLOVEN FOOT — **cloven-hoofed** \-ˈhüft, -ˈhüvd\ adj

clo·ver \ˈklō-vər\ n : any of a genus of leguminous herbs with usu. 3-parted leaves and dense flower heads

clo·ver·leaf \-ˌlēf\ n, pl **cloverleafs** \-ˌlēfs\ or **clo·ver·leaves** \-ˌlēvz\ : a road plan passing one highway over another and routing turning traffic without left turns or direct crossings

¹**clown** \ˈklaün\ n **1** : BOOR **2** : a fool or comedian in an entertainment (as a circus) — **clown·ish** adj — **clown·ish·ly** adv — **clown·ish·ness** n

²**clown** vb : to act like a clown

cloy \ˈklȯi\ vb : to disgust or nauseate with excess of something orig. pleasing — **cloy·ing·ly** \-iŋ-lē\ adv

clr abbr clear

¹**club** \ˈkləb\ n **1** : a heavy wooden stick or staff used as a weapon; *also* : BAT **2** : any of a suit of playing cards marked with a black figure resembling a clover leaf **3** : a group of persons associated for a common purpose; *also* : the meeting place of such a group

²**club** vb **clubbed; club·bing 1** : to strike with a club **2** : to unite or combine for a common cause

club·foot \ˈkləb-ˈfüt\ n : a misshapen foot twisted out of position from birth — **club-foot·ed** \-ˈfüt-əd\ adj

club·house \ˈkləb-ˌhaüs\ n **1** : a house occupied by a club **2** : locker rooms used by an athletic team

club sandwich n : a sandwich of three slices of bread with two layers of meat and lettuce, tomato, and mayonnaise

club soda n : SODA WATER 1

club steak n : a small steak cut from the end of the short loin

cluck \ˈklək\ n : the call of a hen esp. to her chicks — **cluck** vb

¹**clue** \ˈklü\ n : something that guides through an intricate procedure or maze; *esp* : a piece of evidence leading to the solution of a problem

²**clue** vb **clued; clue·ing** or **clu·ing** : to provide with a clue; *also* : to give information to ⟨~ me in⟩

¹**clump** \ˈkləmp\ n **1** : a group of things clustered together **2** : a heavy tramping sound

²**clump** vb : to tread clumsily and noisily

clum·sy \ˈkləm-zē\ adj **clum·si·er; -est 1** : lacking dexterity, nimbleness, or grace **2** : not tactful or subtle — **clum·si·ly** \ˈkləm-zə-lē\ adv — **clum·si·ness** \-zē-nəs\ n

clung past and past part of CLING

¹**clus·ter** \ˈkləs-tər\ n : GROUP, BUNCH

²**cluster** vb **clus·tered; clus·ter·ing** \-t(ə-)riŋ\ : to grow or gather in a cluster

¹**clutch** \ˈkləch\ vb : to grasp with or as if with the hand

²**clutch** n **1** : the claws or a hand in the act of grasping; *also* : CONTROL, POWER **2** : a device for gripping an object **3** : a coupling used to connect and disconnect a driving and a driven part of a mechanism; *also* : a lever or pedal operating such a coupling **4** : a crucial situation

³**clutch** adj : made, done, or successful in a crucial situation

⁴**clutch** n **1** : a nest or batch of eggs; *also* : a brood of chicks **2** : GROUP, BUNCH

clut·ter \ˈklət-ər\ vb : to fill or cover with a disorderly scattering of things

²**clutter** n : a crowded mass

cm abbr centimeter

Cm symbol curium

CM abbr [Commonwealth of the Northern Mariana Islands] Northern Mariana Islands

cmdr abbr commander

cml abbr commercial

CMSgt abbr chief master sergeant

CNO abbr chief of naval operations

CNS abbr central nervous system

co abbr **1** company **2** county

Co symbol cobalt

CO abbr **1** Colorado **2** commanding officer **3** conscientious objector

c/o abbr care of

¹**coach** \ˈkōch\ n **1** : a large closed 4-wheeled carriage with an elevated outside front seat for the driver **2** : a railroad passenger car esp. for day travel **3** : BUS **4** : a private tutor; *also* : one who instructs or trains a team of performers

²**coach** vb **1** : to go in a horse-drawn coach **2** : to instruct, direct, or prompt as a coach — **coach·er** n

coach·man \-mən\ n : a man whose business is driving a coach or carriage

co·ad·ju·tor \ˌkō-ə-ˈjüt-ər, kō-ˈaj-ət-ər\ n : ASSISTANT; *esp* : an assistant bishop having the right of succession

co·ag·u·lant \kō-ˈag-yə-lənt\ n : something that produces coagulation

co·ag·u·late \kō-ˈag-yə-ˌlāt\ vb **-lat·ed; -lat·ing** : CLOT — **co·ag·u·la·tion** \kō-ˌag-yə-ˈlā-shən\ n

¹**coal** \ˈkōl\ n **1** : EMBER **2** : a black solid combustible mineral used as fuel

²**coal** *vb* **1** : to supply with coal **2** : to take in coal

co·alesce \ˌkō-ə-ˈles\ *vb* **co·alesced; co·alesc·ing** : to grow together; *also* : FUSE **syn** merge, blend, mingle, mix — **co·ales·cence** \-ˈles-ᵊns\ *n*

coal·field \ˈkōl-ˌfēld\ *n* : a region where deposits of coal occur

coal gas *n* : gas from coal; *esp* : gas distilled from bituminous coal and used for heating

co·ali·tion \ˌkō-ə-ˈlish-ən\ *n* : UNION; *esp* : a temporary union for a common purpose — **co·ali·tion·ist** *n*

coal oil *n* : KEROSENE

coal tar *n* : tar distilled from bituminous coal and used in dyes and drugs

co·an·chor \ˈkō-ˌaŋ-kər\ *n* : a newscaster who shares the duties of head broadcaster

coarse \ˈkōrs\ *adj* **coars·er; coars·est 1** : of ordinary or inferior quality **2** : composed of large parts or particles (~ sand) **3** : CRUDE (~ manners) **4** : ROUGH, HARSH — **coarse·ly** *adv* — **coarse·ness** *n*

coars·en \ˈkōrs-ᵊn\ *vb* **coars·ened; coars·en·ing** \ˈkōrs-(ə-)niŋ\ : to make or become coarse

¹**coast** \ˈkōst\ *n* [ME *cost*, fr. MF *coste*, fr. L *costa* rib, side] **1** : SEASHORE **2** : a slide down a slope — **coast·al** *adj*

²**coast** *vb* **1** : to sail along the shore **2** : to move (as downhill on a sled or as on a bicycle while not pedaling) without effort

coast·er *n* **1** : one that coasts **2** : a shallow container or a plate or mat to protect a surface

coaster brake *n* : a brake in the hub of the rear wheel of a bicycle

coast guard *n* : a military force employed in guarding or patrolling a coast — **coast·guards·man** \ˈkōst-ˌgärdz-mən\ *n*

coast·line \ˈkōst-ˌlīn\ *n* : the outline or shape of a coast

¹**coat** \ˈkōt\ *n* **1** : an outer garment for the upper part of the body **2** : an external growth (as of fur or feathers) on an animal **3** : a covering layer

²**coat** *vb* : to cover usu. with a finishing or protective coat

coat·ing \ˈkōt-iŋ\ *n* : COAT, COVERING

coat of arms : the heraldic bearings (as of a person) usu. depicted on an escutcheon

coat of mail : a garment of metal scales or rings worn as armor

co·au·thor \ˈkō-ˈô-thər\ *n* : a joint or associate author — **coauthor** *vb*

coax \ˈkōks\ *vb* : WHEEDLE; *also* : to gain by gentle urging or flattery

co·ax·i·al \ˈkō-ˈak-sē-əl\ *adj* : having coincident axes — **co·ax·i·al·ly** \-ē\ *adv*

coaxial cable *n* : a cable that consists of a tube of electrically conducting material surrounding a central conductor

cob \ˈkäb\ *n* **1** : a male swan **2**

: CORN-COB **3** : a short-legged stocky horse

co·balt \ˈkō-ˌbôlt\ *n* [G *kobalt*, alter. of *kobold*, lit., goblin, fr. its occurrence in silver ore, believed to be due to goblins] : a tough shiny silver-white magnetic metallic chemical element found with iron and nickel

cobalt chloride *n* : a chloride of cobalt; *esp* : one that is blue when dry, turns deep pink in the presence of moisture, and is used to indicate humidity

cob·ble \ˈkäb-əl\ *vb* **cob·bled; cob·bling** \-(ə-)liŋ\ : to make or put together roughly or hastily

cob·bler \ˈkäb-lər\ *n* **1** : a mender or maker of shoes **2** : a deep-dish fruit pie with a thick crust

cob·ble·stone \ˈkäb-əl-ˌstōn\ *n* : a naturally rounded stone larger than a pebble and smaller than a boulder

co·bra \ˈkō-brə\ *n* : any of several venomous snakes of Asia and Africa that when excited expand the skin of the neck into a broad hood

cob·web \ˈkäb-ˌweb\ *n* [ME *coppeweb*, fr. *coppe* spider, fr. OE *ātor*coppe] **1** : SPIDERWEB; *also* : a thread spun by a spider or insect larva **2** : something flimsy or entangling

co·caine \kō-ˈkān, ˈkō-ˌkān\ *n* : a drug that is obtained from the leaves of a So. American shrub (**co·ca** \ˈkō-kə\), can result in severe psychological dependence, and is sometimes used as a local anesthetic

coc·cus \ˈkäk-əs\ *n, pl* **coc·ci** \ˈkäk-ˌ(s)ī\ : a spherical bacterium

coc·cyx \ˈkäk-siks\ *n, pl* **coc·cy·ges** \ˈkäk-sə-ˌjēz\ *also* **coc·cyx·es** \ˈkäk-sik-səz\ : the end of the spinal column beyond the sacrum esp. in man

co·chi·neal \ˈkäch-ə-ˌnēl\ *n* : a red dye made from the dried bodies of females of a tropical American insect (**cochineal insect**)

co·chlea \ˈkō-klē-ə, ˈkäk-lē-\ *n, pl* **co·chle·as** *or* **co·chle·ae** \-(k)lē-ˌē, -ˌī\ : the usu. spiral part of the inner ear containing nerve endings which carry information about sound to the brain — **co·chle·ar** \-lē-ər\ *adj*

¹**cock** \ˈkäk\ *n* **1** : the adult male of a bird and esp. of the protective domestic chicken **2** : VALVE, FAUCET **3** : LEADER **4** : the hammer of a firearm; *also* : the position of the hammer when ready for firing

²**cock** *vb* **1** : to draw back the hammer of a firearm **2** : to set or draw back in readiness for some action (~ your arm to throw) **3** : to turn or tilt usu. to one side

³**cock** *n* : a small pile (as of hay)

cock·ade \kä-ˈkād\ *n* : an ornament worn on the hat as a badge

cock·a·tiel \ˌkäk-ə-ˈtēl\ *n* : a small crested parrot often kept as a cage bird

cock·a·too \ˈkäk-ə-ˌtü\ *n, pl* **-toos** [D *kaketoe*, fr. Malay *kakatua*] : a large crested brilliantly colored Australian parrot

cock·a·trice \'käk-ə-trəs, -ˌtrīs\ *n* : a legendary serpent with a deadly glance

cock·crow \'käk-ˌkrō\ *n* : DAWN

cocked hat \'käkt-\ *n* : a hat with the brim turned up on two or three sides

cock·er·el \'käk-(ə-)rəl\ *n* : a young male domestic chicken

cock·er spaniel \ˌkäk-ər-\ *n* [*cocking* (woodcock hunting)] : any of a breed of small spaniels with long ears, square muzzle, and silky coat

cock·eyed \'käk-ˈīd\ *adj* 1 : turned or tilted to one side 2 : slightly crazy : FOOLISH

cock·fight \-ˌfīt\ *n* : a contest of game-cocks usu. fitted with metal spurs

¹**cock·le** \'käk-əl\ *n* : any of several weedy plants related to the pinks

²**cockle** *n* : a bivalve mollusk with a heart-shaped shell

cock·le·shell \-ˌshel\ *n* 1 : the shell of a cockle 2 : a light flimsy boat

cock·ney \'käk-nē\ *n, pl* **cockneys** [ME *cokeney*, lit., cocks' egg, fr. *cok* cock + *ey* egg, fr. OE *ǣg*] : a native of London and esp. of the East End of London; *also* : the dialect of a cockney

cock·pit \'käk-ˌpit\ *n* 1 : a pit for cockfights 2 : an open space in the deck from which a small boat is steered 3 : a space in an aircraft fuselage for the pilot

cock·roach \'käk-ˌrōch\ *n* : any of an order of active nocturnal insects including some which infest houses and ships

cock·sure \'käk-ˈshur\ *adj* 1 : perfectly sure : CERTAIN 2 : COCKY

cock·tail \'käk-ˌtāl\ *n* 1 : an iced drink made of liquor and flavoring ingredients 2 : an appetizer (as tomato juice) served as a first course of a meal

cocky \'käk-ē\ *adj* **cock·i·er; -est** : marked by overconfidence : PERT, CONCEITED — **cock·i·ly** \'käk-ə-lē\ *adv* — **cock·i·ness** \-ē-nəs\ *n*

co·coa \'kō-kō\ *n* 1 : CACAO 2 : chocolate deprived of some of its fat and powdered; *also* : a drink made of this heated with water or milk

co·co·nut \'kō-kə-(ˌ)nət\ *n* : a large edible nut produced by a tall tropical palm (**coconut palm**)

co·coon \kə-ˈkün\ *n* : a case usu. of silk which an insect larva forms and in which it passes the pupal stage

cod \'käd\ *n, pl* **cod** *also* **cods** : a soft-finned large-mouthed food fish of the No. Atlantic

COD *abbr* 1 cash on delivery 2 collect on delivery

co·da \'kōd-ə\ *n* : a closing section in a musical composition that is formally distinct from the main structure

cod·dle \'käd-ᵊl\ *vb* **cod·dled; cod·dling** \'käd-(ə-)liŋ\ 1 : to cook slowly in water below the boiling point 2 : PAMPER

¹**code** \'kōd\ *n* 1 : a systematic statement of a body of law 2 : a system of principles or rules (moral ∼) 3 : a system of signals 4 : a system of symbols (as in secret communication) with special meanings 5 : GENETIC CODE

²**code** *vb* **cod·ed; cod·ing** : to put into the form or symbols of a code

co·deine \'kō-ˌdēn, 'kōd-ē-ən\ *n* : a narcotic drug obtained from opium and used esp. in cough remedies

co·dex \'kō-ˌdeks\ *n, pl* **co·di·ces** \'kōd-ə-ˌsēz, 'käd-\ : a manuscript book (as of the Scriptures or classics)

cod·fish \'käd-ˌfish\ *n* : COD

cod·ger \'käj-ər\ *n* : an odd or cranky fellow

cod·i·cil \'käd-ə-səl, -ˌsil\ *n* : a legal instrument modifying an earlier will

cod·i·fy \'käd-ə-ˌfī, 'kōd-\ *vb* **-fied; -fy·ing** : to arrange in a systematic form — **cod·i·fi·ca·tion** \ˌkäd-ə-fə-ˈkā-shən, ˌkōd-\ *n*

cod·ling \'käd-liŋ\ *n* 1 : a young cod 2 : HAKE

co·ed \'kō-ˌed\ *n* : a female student in a coeducational institution — **coed** *adj*

co·ed·u·ca·tion \ˌkō-ˌej-ə-ˈkā-shən\ *n* : the education of male and female students at the same institution — **co·ed·u·ca·tion·al** \-sh(ə-)nəl\ *adj* — **co·ed·u·ca·tion·al·ly** \-ē\ *adv*

co·ef·fi·cient \ˌkō-ə-ˈfish-ənt\ *n* 1 : a constant factor as distinguished from a variable in a mathematical term 2 : a number that serves as a measure of some property (as of a substance or device)

coel·en·ter·ate \si-ˈlent-ə-ˌrāt, -rət\ *n* : any of a phylum of radially symmetrical invertebrate animals including the corals, sea anemones, and jellyfishes

co·equal \kō-ˈē-kwəl\ *adj* : equal with another — **coequal** *n* — **co·equal·i·ty** \ˌkō-ē-ˈkwäl-ət-ē\ *n* — **co·equal·ly** \kō-ˈē-kwə-lē\ *adv*

co·erce \kō-ˈərs\ *vb* **co·erced; co·erc·ing** 1 : RESTRAIN, REPRESS 2 : COMPEL 3 : ENFORCE — **co·er·cion** \-ˈər-zhən, -shən\ *n* — **co·er·cive** \-ˈər-siv\ *adj*

co·eval \kō-ˈē-vəl\ *adj* : of the same age — **coeval** *n*

co·ex·ist \ˌkō-ig-ˈzist\ *vb* 1 : to exist together or at the same time 2 : to live in peace with each other — **co·ex·is·tence** \-ˈzis-təns\ *n*

co·ex·ten·sive \ˌkō-ik-ˈsten-siv\ *adj* : having the same scope or extent in space or time

C of C *abbr* Chamber of Commerce

cof·fee \'kó-fē\ *n* [It & Turk; It *caffè*, fr. Turk *kahve*, fr. Ar *qahwah*] : a drink made from the roasted and ground seeds of a fruit of a tropical shrub or tree; *also* : these seeds (**coffee beans**) or a plant producing them

cof·fee·house \-ˌhaus\ *n* : a place where refreshments (as coffee) are sold

coffee klatch \-ˌklach\ *n* : KAFFEE-KLATSCH

cof·fee·pot \-ˌpät\ n : a pot for brewing or serving coffee

coffee shop n : a small restaurant

coffee table n : a low table customarily placed in front of a sofa

cof·fer \ˈkȯ-fər\ n : a chest or box used esp. for valuables

cof·fer·dam \-ˌdam\ n : a watertight enclosure from which water is pumped to expose the bottom of a body of water and permit construction

cof·fin \ˈkȯ-fən\ n : a box or chest for a corpse to be buried in

C of S abbr chief of staff

¹**cog** \ˈkäg\ n : a tooth on the rim of a wheel or gear — **cogged** \ˈkägd\ adj

²**cog** abbr cognate

co·gen·er·a·tion \ˌkō-jen-ə-ˈrā-shən\ n : the simultaneous generation of electricity and heat from the same fuel

co·gent \ˈkō-jənt\ adj : having power to compel or constrain : CONVINCING — **co·gen·cy** \-jən-sē\ n

cog·i·tate \ˈkäj-ə-ˌtāt\ vb -tat·ed; -tat·ing : THINK, PONDER — **cog·i·ta·tion** \ˌkäj-ə-ˈtā-shən\ n — **cog·i·ta·tive** \ˈkäj-ə-ˌtāt-iv\ adj

co·gnac \ˈkōn-ˌyak\ n : a French brandy

cog·nate \ˈkäg-ˌnāt\ adj 1 : of the same or similar nature 2 : RELATED; esp : related by descent from the same ancestral language — **cognate** n

cog·ni·tive \ˈkäg-nət-iv\ adj : of, relating to, or being conscious mental activity (as thinking, remembering, or learning) — **cog·ni·tion** \käg-ˈnish-ən\ n

cog·ni·zance \ˈkäg-nə-zəns\ n 1 : apprehension by the mind : AWARENESS 2 : NOTICE, HEED — **cog·ni·zant** \ˈkäg-nə-zənt\ adj

cog·no·men \käg-ˈnō-mən, ˈkäg-nə-\ n, pl **cognomens** or **cog·no·mi·na** \käg-ˈnäm-ə-nə, -ˈnō-mə-\ : NAME; esp : NICKNAME

co·gno·scen·te \ˌkän-yə-ˈshent-ē\ n, pl **-scen·ti** \-ē\ [obs. It] : CONNOISSEUR

cog·wheel \ˈkäg-ˌhwēl\ n : a wheel with cogs or teeth

co·hab·it \kō-ˈhab-ət\ vb : to live together as husband and wife — **co·hab·i·ta·tion** \-ˌhab-ə-ˈtā-shən\ n

co·here \kō-ˈhiər\ vb **co·hered; co·her·ing** : to stick together

co·her·ent \kō-ˈhir-ənt\ adj 1 : having the quality of cohering 2 : logically consistent — **co·her·ence** \-əns\ n — **co·her·ent·ly** adv

co·he·sion \kō-ˈhē-zhən\ n 1 : a sticking together 2 : molecular attraction by which the particles of a body are united — **co·he·sive** \-siv\ adj — **co·he·sive·ly** adv — **co·he·sive·ness** n

co·ho \ˈkō-ˌhō\ n, pl **cohos** or **coho** : a rather small salmon with light-colored flesh

co·hort \ˈkō-ˌhȯrt\ n 1 : a group of warriors or followers 2 : COMPANION, ACCOMPLICE

coif \ˈkȯif; 2 usu ˈkwäf\ n 1 : a close-fitting hat 2 : COIFFURE

coif·feur \kwä-ˈfər\ n [F] : HAIRDRESSER

coif·feuse \kwä-ˈfə(r)z, -ˈf(y)üz\ n : a female hairdresser

coif·fure \kwä-ˈfyùr\ n : a manner of arranging the hair

¹**coil** \ˈkȯil\ vb : to wind in a spiral shape

²**coil** n : a series of rings or loops (as of coiled rope, wire, or pipe) : RING, LOOP

¹**coin** \ˈkȯin\ n [ME, fr. MF, wedge, corner, fr. L cuneus wedge] : a piece of metal issued by government authority as money

²**coin** vb 1 : to make (a coin) esp. by stamping : MINT 2 : CREATE, INVENT (~ a phrase) — **coin·er** n

coin·age \ˈkȯi-nij\ n 1 : the act or process of coining 2 : COINS

co·in·cide \ˌkō-ən-ˈsīd, ˈkō-ən-ˌsīd\ vb **-cid·ed; -cid·ing** 1 : to occupy the same place in space or time 2 : to correspond or agree exactly

co·in·ci·dence \kō-ˈin-səd-əns\ n 1 : exact agreement 2 : occurrence together apparently without reason; also : an event that so occurs

co·in·ci·dent \-səd-ənt\ adj 1 : of similar nature 2 : occupying the same space or time — **co·in·ci·den·tal** \kō-ˌin-sə-ˈdent-ᵊl\ adj

co·itus \ˈkō-ət-əs\ n [L, fr. pp. of coire to come together] : SEXUAL INTERCOURSE — **co·ital** \-ət-ᵊl\ adj

¹**coke** \ˈkōk\ n : a hard gray porous fuel made by heating soft coal to drive off most of its volatile material

²**coke** n : COCAINE

col abbr 1 colonial; colony 2 column

Col abbr 1 colonel 2 Colorado 3 Colossians

COL abbr 1 colonel 2 cost of living

co·la \ˈkō-lə\ n : a carbonated soft drink usu. containing sugar, caffeine, caramel, and special flavoring

col·an·der \ˈkəl-ən-dər, ˈkäl-\ n : a perforated utensil for draining food

¹**cold** \ˈkōld\ adj 1 : having a low or decidedly subnormal temperature 2 : lacking warmth of feeling 3 : suffering or uncomfortable from lack of warmth — **cold·ly** adv — **cold·ness** \ˈkōld(d)-nəs\ n — **in cold blood** : with premeditation : DELIBERATELY

²**cold** n 1 : a condition marked by low temperature; also : cold weather 2 : a chilly feeling 3 : a bodily disorder popularly associated with chilling; esp : COMMON COLD

³**cold** adv : TOTALLY, FINALLY

cold-blood·ed \ˈkōld-ˈbləd-əd\ adj 1 : lacking normal human feelings 2 : having a body temperature not internally regulated but close to that of the environment 3 : sensitive to cold

cold duck n : a blend of sparkling burgundy and champagne

cold feet n pl : doubt or fear that prevents action

cold shoulder *n* : cold or unsympathetic behavior — **cold–shoul·der** *vb*

cold sore *n* : a group of blisters appearing in or about the mouth in the oral form of herpes simplex

cold sweat *n* : concurrent perspiration and chill usu. associated with fear, pain, or shock

cold turkey *n* : abrupt complete cessation of the use of an addictive drug

cold war *n* : a conflict characterized by the use of means short of sustained overt military action

cole·slaw \'kōl-ˌslò\ *n* [D *koolsla,* fr. *kool* cabbage + *sla* salad] : a salad made of raw cabbage

col·ic \'käl-ik\ *n* : sharp sudden abdominal pain — **col·icky** \'käl-i-kē\ *adj*

col·i·se·um \ˌkäl-ə-sē-əm\ *n* : a large structure esp. for athletic contests

coil *abbr* college

col·lab·o·rate \kə-'lab-ə-ˌrāt\ *vb* **-rat·ed; -rat·ing 1** : to work jointly with others (as in writing a book) **2** : to cooperate with an enemy force occupying one's country — **col·lab·o·ra·tion** \-ˌlab-ə-'rā-shən\ *n* — **col·lab·o·ra·tor** \-'lab-ə-ˌrāt-ər\ *n*

col·lage \kə-'läzh\ *n* [F, gluing] : an artistic composition of fragments (as of printed matter) pasted on a picture surface

¹**col·lapse** \kə-'laps\ *vb* **col·lapsed; col·laps·ing 1** : to shrink together abruptly **2** : DISINTEGRATE; *also* : to fall in : give way **3** : to break down physically or mentally; *esp* : to fall helpless or unconscious **4** : to fold down compactly — **col·laps·ible** *adj*

²**collapse** *n* : BREAKDOWN

¹**col·lar** \'käl-ər\ *n* **1** : a band, strip, or chain worn around the neck or the neckline of a garment **2** : something resembling a collar — **col·lar·less** *adj*

²**collar** *vb* : to seize by the collar; *also* : CAPTURE, GRAB

col·lar·bone \-ˌbōn\ *n* : the bone of the shoulder that joins the breastbone and the shoulder blade

col·lard \'käl-ərd\ *n* : a stalked smooth-leaved kale — usu. used in pl.

col·late \kə-'lāt; 'käl-ˌāt, 'kōl-ˌ\ *vb* **col·lat·ed; col·lat·ing 1** : to compare (as two texts) carefully and critically **2** : to assemble in proper order

¹**col·lat·er·al** \kə-'lat-(ə-)rəl\ *adj* **1** : associated but of secondary importance **2** : descended from the same ancestors but not in the same line **3** : PARALLEL **4** : of, relating to, or being collateral used as security; *also* : secured by collateral

²**collateral** *n* : property (as stocks) used as security for the repayment of a loan

col·la·tion \kə-'lā-shən, kä-, kō-\ *n* **1** : a light meal **2** : the act, process, or result of collating

col·league \'käl-ˌēg\ *n* : an associate esp. in a profession

¹**col·lect** \'käl-ikt, -ˌekt\ *n* : a short prayer comprising an invocation, petition, and conclusion

²**col·lect** \kə-'lekt\ *vb* **1** : to bring or come together into one body or place : ASSEMBLE **2** : to gather from numerous sources (∼ stamps) **3** : to gain control of (∼ his thoughts) **4** : to receive payment of — **col·lect·ible** *or* **col·lect·able** *adj or n* — **col·lec·tion** \-'lek-shən\ *n* — **col·lec·tor** \-'lek-tər\ *n*

³**col·lect** \kə-'lekt\ *adv or adj* : to be paid for by the receiver

col·lect·ed \kə-'lek-təd\ *adj* : SELF-POSSESSED, CALM

¹**col·lec·tive** \kə-'lek-tiv\ *adj* **1** : of, relating to, or denoting a group of individuals considered as a whole **2** : formed by collecting **3** : involving all members of a group as distinct from its individuals **4** : shared or assumed by all members of the group — **col·lec·tive·ly** *adv*

²**collective** *n* **1** : GROUP **2** : a cooperative unit or organization

collective bargaining *n* : negotiation between an employer and union representatives

col·lec·tiv·ism \kə-'lek-ti-ˌviz-əm\ *n* : a political or economic theory advocating collective control esp. over production and distribution

col·lec·tiv·ize \-ˌvīz\ *vb* **-ized; -iz·ing** : to organize under collective control

col·leen \kä-'lēn, 'käl-ˌēn\ *n* : an Irish girl

col·lege \'käl-ij\ *n* [ME, fr. MF, fr. L *collegium* society, fr. *collega* colleague, fr. *com-* with + *legare* to appoint] **1** : a building used for an educational or religious purpose **2** : an institution of higher learning granting a bachelor's degree; *also* : an institution offering instruction esp. in a vocational or technical field (barber ∼) **3** : an organized body of persons having common interests or duties (∼ of cardinals) — **col·le·giate** \kə-'lē-jət\ *adj*

col·le·gi·al·i·ty \kə-ˌlē-jē-'al-ət-ē\ *n* : the relationship of colleagues

col·le·gian \kə-'lē-jən\ *n* : a college student

col·le·gi·um \kə-'leg-ē-əm, -'läg-\ *n, pl* **-gia** \-ē-ə\ *or* **-giums** : a governing group in which each member has approximately equal power

col·lide \kə-'līd\ *vb* **col·lid·ed; col·lid·ing 1** : to come together with solid impact **2** : to come into conflict : CLASH — **col·li·sion** \-'lizh-ən\ *n*

col·lie \'käl-ē\ *n* : a large dog of a breed with rough-coated and smooth-coated varieties developed in Scotland for herding sheep

col·lier \'käl-yər\ *n* **1** : a coal miner **2** : a ship for carrying coal

col·liery \'käl-yə-rē\ *n, pl* **-lier·ies** : a coal mine and its associated buildings

col·li·mate \'käl-ə-ˌmāt\ *vb* **-mat·ed; -mat·ing** : to make (as rays of light) parallel

col·lo·ca·tion \ˌkäl-ə-'kā-shən\ *n* **1** : a placing together or side by side; *also* : the result of such placing **2** : a noticeable arrangement or conjoining of linguistic elements (as words)

col·lo·di·on \kə-'lōd-ē-ən\ *n* : a sticky substance that hardens in the air and is used to cover wounds and coat photographic films

col·loid \'käl-ˌȯid\ *n* : a substance in the form of submicroscopic particles that when in solution or suspension do not settle out; *also* : such a substance together with the medium in which it is dispersed — **col·loi·dal** \kə-'lȯid-ᵊl\ *adj*

colloq *abbr* colloquial

col·lo·qui·al \kə-'lō-kwē-əl\ *adj* : of, relating to, or characteristic of conversation and esp. of familiar and informal conversation

col·lo·qui·al·ism \-'lō-kwē-ə-ˌliz-əm\ *n* : a colloquial expression

col·lo·qui·um \kə-'lō-kwē-əm\ *n, pl* **-qui·ums** *or* **-quia** \-kwē-ə\ : CONFERENCE, SEMINAR

col·lo·quy \'käl-ə-kwē\ *n, pl* **-quies** : a usu. formal conversation or conference

col·lu·sion \kə-'lü-zhən\ *n* : secret agreement or cooperation for an illegal or deceitful purpose — **col·lu·sive** \-'lü-siv\ *adj*

Colo *abbr* Colorado

co·logne \kə-'lōn\ *n [Cologne,* Germany] : a perfumed liquid consisting of alcohol and aromatic oils — **co·logned** \-'lōnd\ *adj*

¹co·lon \'kō-lən\ *n, pl* **colons** *or* **co·la** \-lə\ : the part of the large intestine extending from the cecum to the rectum — **co·lon·ic** \kō-'län-ik\ *adj*

²colon *n, pl* **colons** : a punctuation mark : used esp. to direct attention to following matter

³co·lon \kō-'lōn\ *n, pl* **co·lo·nes** \-'lō-ˌnäs\ — see MONEY table

col·o·nel \'kərn-ᵊl\ *n* [alter. of *coronel*, fr. MF, fr. It *colonnello* column of soldiers, colonel, fr. L *columna*] : a commissioned officer (as in the army) ranking next below a brigadier general

¹co·lo·nial \kə-'lō-nē-əl, -nyəl\ *adj* **1** : of, relating to, or characteristic of a colony; *also* : possessing or composed of colonies **2** *often cap* : of or relating to the original 13 colonies forming the U.S.

²colonial *n* : a member or inhabitant of a colony

co·lo·nial·ism \-ˌiz-əm\ *n* : control by one power over a dependent area or people; *also* : a policy advocating or based on such control — **co·lo·nial·ist** \-əst\ *n or adj*

col·o·nist \'käl-ə-nəst\ *n* **1** : COLONIAL 2 : one who takes part in founding a colony

col·o·nize \'käl-ə-ˌnīz\ *vb* **-nized; -niz·ing 1** : to establish a colony in or on **2** : to settle in a colony — **col·o·ni·za·tion** \ˌkäl-ə-nə-'zā-shən\ *n* — **col·o·niz·er** *n*

col·on·nade \ˌkäl-ə-'nād\ *n* : an evenly spaced row of columns usu. supporting the base of the roof structure

col·o·ny \'käl-ə-nē\ *n, pl* **-nies 1** : a body of people living in a new territory; *also* : the territory inhabited by these people **2** : a localized population of organisms ⟨a ~ of bees⟩ **3** : a group with common interests situated in close association ⟨a writers' ~⟩ ; *also* : the area occupied by such a group

col·o·phon \'käl-ə-fən, -ˌfän\ *n* **1** : an inscription placed at the end of a book with facts relative to its production **2** : a distinctive symbol used by a printer or publisher

¹col·or \'kəl-ər\ *n* **1** : a phenomenon of light (as red or blue) or visual perception that enables one to differentiate otherwise identical objects; *also* : a hue as contrasted with black, white, or gray **2** : APPEARANCE **3** : complexion tint **4** *pl* : FLAG; *also* : military service (a call to the ~s) **5** : VIVIDNESS, INTEREST — **col·or·ful** *adj* — **col·or·less** *adj*

²color *vb* **col·ored; col·or·ing** \'kəl-(ə-)riŋ\ **1** : to give color to; *also* : to change the color of **2** : BLUSH

Col·o·ra·do potato beetle \ˌkäl-ə-'rad-ō-, -'räd-\ *n* : a black-and-yellow striped beetle that feeds on the leaves of the potato

col·or·ation \ˌkəl-ə-'rā-shən\ *n* : use or arrangement of colors

col·or·a·tu·ra \ˌkəl-ə-rə-'t(y)ur-ə\ *n* **1** : elaborate ornamentation in vocal music **2** : a soprano specializing in coloratura

col·or-blind \'kəl-ər-ˌblīnd\ *adj* : partially or totally unable to distinguish one or more chromatic colors — **color blindness** *n*

¹col·ored \'kəl-ərd\ *adj* **1** : having color **2** : SLANTED, BIASED **3** : of a race other than the white; *esp* : NEGRO

²colored *n, pl* **colored** *or* **coloreds** *often cap* : a colored person

col·or·fast \'kəl-ər-ˌfast\ *adj* : having color that does not fade or run — **col·or·fast·ness** *n*

co·los·sal \kə-'läs-əl\ *adj* : of very great size or degree

Co·los·sians \kə-'läsh-ənz\ *n* — see BIBLE table

co·los·sus \kə-'läs-əs\ *n, pl* **co·los·sus·es** \-'läs-ə-səz\ *or* **co·los·si** \-'läs-ˌī\ [L] : a gigantic statue; *also* : something of great size or scope

col·por·teur \'käl-ˌpȯrt-ər\ *n* [F] : a peddler of religious books

colt \'kōlt\ *n* : FOAL; *also* : a young male horse, ass, or zebra — **colt·ish** *adj*

col·um·bine \'käl-əm-ˌbīn\ *n* [ME, fr. ML *columbina*, fr. L, fem. of *columbinus* dovelike, fr. *columba* dove] : any of a genus of plants with showy spurred flowers that are related to the buttercups

co·lum·bi·um \kə-'ləm-bē-əm\ *n* : NIOBIUM

Columbus Day \kə-'ləm-bəs-\ *n* : the 2d Monday in October or formerly October 12 observed as a legal holiday in many states in commemoration of the landing of Columbus

col·umn \'käl-əm\ *n* 1 : one of two or more vertical sections of a printed page; *also* : a special department (as in a newspaper) 2 : a supporting pillar; *also* : something resembling such a column (a ~ of water) 3 : a long row (as of soldiers) — **co·lum·nar** \kə-'ləm-nər\ *adj*

col·um·nist \'käl-əm-(n)əst\ *n* : one who writes a newspaper or magazine column

com *or* **comm** *abbr* 1 command; commander 2 commerce; commercial 3 commission; commissioner 4 committee 5 common 6 commonwealth

co·ma \'kō-mə\ *n* : a state of deep unconsciousness caused by disease, injury, or poison — **co·ma·tose** \'kō-mə-ˌtōs, 'käm-ə-\ *adj*

Co·man·che \kə-'man-chē\ *n, pl* **Comanche** *or* **Comanches** : a member of an American Indian people ranging from Wyoming and Nebraska south into New Mexico and Texas

¹**comb** \'kōm\ *n* 1 : a toothed instrument for arranging the hair or for separating and cleaning textile fibers 2 : a fleshy crest on the head of a fowl 3 : HONEYCOMB — **comb** *vb* — **combed** \'kōmd\ *adj*

²**comb** *abbr* combination; combining

com·bat \kəm-'bat, 'käm-ˌbat\ *vb* -**bat·ed** *or* -**bat·ted**; -**bat·ing** *or* -**bat·ting** 1 : FIGHT, CONTEND 2 : to struggle or work against : OPPOSE — **com·bat** \'käm-ˌbat\ *n* — **com·bat·ant** \kəm-'bat-ᵊnt, 'käm-bət-ᵊnt\ *n* — **com·bat·ive** \kəm-'bat-iv\ *adj*

combat fatigue *n* : a traumatic neurotic or psychotic reaction occurring under conditions (as wartime combat) that cause intense stress

comb·er \'kō-mər\ *n* 1 : one that combs 2 : a long curling wave of the sea

com·bi·na·tion \ˌkäm-bə-'nā-shən\ *n* 1 : a result or product of combining 2 : a sequence of letters or numbers chosen in setting a lock 3 : the act or process of combining; *also* : the quality or state of being combined

¹**com·bine** \kəm-'bīn\ *vb* **com·bined**; **com·bin·ing** : to become one : UNITE

²**com·bine** \'käm-ˌbīn\ *n* 1 : COMBINATION; *esp* : one made to secure business or political advantage 2 : a machine that harvests and threshes grain while moving over the field

comb·ings \'kō-miŋz\ *n pl* : loose hairs or fibers removed by a comb

combining form *n* : a linguistic form that occurs only in compounds or derivatives

com·bo \'käm-bō\ *n, pl* **combos** : a small jazz or dance band

com·bus·ti·ble \kəm-'bəs-tə-bəl\ *adj* : capable of being burned — **com·bus·ti·bil·i·ty** \-ˌbəs-tə-'bil-ət-ē\ *n* — **combustible** *n*

com·bus·tion \kəm-'bəs-chən\ *n* 1 : an act or instance of burning 2 : slow oxidation (as in the animal body)

comdg *abbr* commanding

comdr *abbr* commander

comdt *abbr* commandant

come \('')kəm\ *vb* **came** \'kām\ ; **come**; **com·ing** \'kəm-iŋ\ 1 : APPROACH 2 : ARRIVE 3 : to reach the point of being or becoming (~ to a boil) 4 : AMOUNT (the bill *came* to $10) 5 : to take place 6 : ORIGINATE, ARISE 7 : to be available 8 : REACH, EXTEND 9 : to experience orgasm — **come across** : to meet or find by chance — **come to pass** : HAPPEN — **come upon** : to come across

come·back \'kəm-ˌbak\ *n* 1 : RETORT 2 : RECOVERY — **come back** \(ˌ)kəm-'bak\ *vb*

co·me·di·an \kə-'mēd-ē-ən\ *n* 1 : an actor in comedy 2 : an amusing person 3 : an entertainer specializing in comedy

co·me·di·enne \-ˌmēd-ē-'en\ *n* : a woman who is a comedian

come·down \'kəm-ˌdaún\ *n* : a descent in rank or dignity

com·e·dy \'käm-əd-ē\ *n, pl* -**dies** [ME, fr. MF *comedie*, fr. L *comoedia*, fr. Gk *kōmōidia*, fr. *kōmos* revel + *aeidein* to sing] 1 : a light amusing play with a happy ending 2 : a literary work treating a comic theme or written in a comic style 3 : humorous entertainment

come·ly \'kəm-lē\ *adj* **come·li·er**; -**est** : good-looking : HANDSOME — **come·li·ness** *n*

come off *vb* : SUCCEED

come-on \'kəm-ˌón, -ˌän\ *n* : INDUCEMENT, LURE

come out *vb* 1 : to come into public view 2 : to declare oneself 3 : TURN OUT 5 (everything *came out* all right) — **come out with** : SAY 1

com·er \'kəm-ər\ *n* : a promising beginner

¹**co·mes·ti·ble** \kə-'mes-tə-bəl\ *adj* : EDIBLE

²**comestible** *n* : FOOD — usu. used in pl.

com·et \'käm-ət\ *n* [ME *comete*, fr. OE *cometa*, fr. L, fr. Gk *komētēs*, lit., long-haired, fr. *komē* hair] : a small bright celestial body that develops a cloudy tail when near the sun

come to *vb* : to regain consciousness

come·up·pance \kə-'məp-əns\ *n* : a deserved rebuke or penalty

com·fit \'kəm-fət\ *n* : a candied fruit or nut

¹**com·fort** \'kəm-fərt\ *n* 1 : CONSOLATION 2 : freedom from pain, trouble, or anxiety; *also* : something that gives such freedom — **com·fort·less** *adj*

²**comfort** *vb* 1 : to give strength and hope to 2 : CONSOLE

com·fort·able \'kəm(f)t-ə-bəl, 'kəm-

comfortably·commission

comfortably·commission

fərt-\ *adj* **1** : providing comfort **2** : more than adequate **3** : feeling at ease — **com·fort·ably** \-blē\ *adv*

com·fort·er \'kəm-fə(r)t-ər\ *n* **1** : one that comforts **2** : QUILT

com·fy \'kəm-fē\ *adj* : COMFORTABLE

¹**com·ic** \'käm-ik\ *adj* **1** : relating to comedy or comic strips **2** : provoking laughter or amusement *syn* laughable, funny, farcical — **com·i·cal** *adj*

²**comic** *n* **1** : COMEDIAN **2** : COMIC BOOK

comic book *n* : a magazine containing sequences of comic strips

comic strip *n* : a group of cartoons in narrative sequence

coming \'kəm-iŋ\ *adj* **1** : APPROACHING, NEXT **2** : gaining importance

co·mi·ty \'käm-ət-ē, 'kō-mət-\ *n, pl* **-ties** : friendly civility : COURTESY

coml *abbr* commercial

comm *abbr* — see COM

com·ma \'käm-ə\ *n* : a punctuation mark , used esp. as a mark of separation within the sentence

¹**com·mand** \kə-'mand\ *vb* **1** : to direct authoritatively : ORDER **2** : DOMINATE, CONTROL, GOVERN **3** : to overlook from a strategic position

²**command** *n* **1** : the act of commanding **2** : ability to control : MASTERY **3** : an order given **4** : an electrical signal that actuates a device (as a computer); *also* : the activation of a device by means of such a signal **5** : a body of troops under a commander; *also* : an area or position that one commands **6** : a position of highest authority

com·man·dant \'käm-ən-ˌdant, -ˌdänt\ *n* : an officer in command

com·man·deer \ˌkäm-ən-'diər\ *vb* : to take possession of by force

com·mand·er \kə-'man-dər\ *n* **1** : LEADER, CHIEF; *esp* : an officer commanding an army or subdivision of an army **2** : a commissioned officer in the navy ranking next below a captain

commander in chief : one who holds supreme command of the armed forces

com·mand·ment \kə-'man(d)-mənt\ *n* : COMMAND, ORDER; *esp* : any of the Ten Commandments

command module *n* : a space vehicle module designed to carry the crew and reentry equipment

com·man·do \kə-'man-dō\ *n, pl* **-dos** *or* **-does** [Afrikaans *kommando*, fr. Dutch *commando* command] : a member of a military unit trained for surprise raids

command sergeant major *n* : a noncommissioned officer in the army ranking above a first sergeant

com·mem·o·rate \kə-'mem-ə-ˌrāt\ *vb* **-rat·ed; -rat·ing 1** : to call or recall to mind **2** : to serve as a memorial of — **com·mem·o·ra·tion** \-ˌmem-ə-'rā-shən\ *n*

com·mem·o·ra·tive \kə-'mem-(ə-)rət-iv, -'mem-ə-ˌrāt-iv\ *adj* : intended to commemorate an event

com·mence \kə-'mens\ *vb* **com·menced; com·menc·ing** : BEGIN, START

com·mence·ment \-mənt\ *n* **1** : the act or time of a beginning **2** : the graduation exercises of a school or college

com·mend \kə-'mend\ *vb* **1** : to commit to one's care **2** : RECOMMEND **3** : PRAISE — **com·mend·able** \-'men-də-bəl\ *adj* — **com·mend·ably** \-blē\ *adv* — **com·men·da·tion** \ˌkäm-ən-'dā-shən, -ˌen-\ *n*

com·men·su·ra·ble \kə-'mens-(ə-)rə-bəl\ *adj* : having a common measure; *esp* : divisible by a common unit an integral number of times

com·men·su·rate \kə-'mens(-ə)-rət, -'mench(-ə)-\ *adj* : equal in measure or extent; *also* : PROPORTIONAL, CORRESPONDING (a job ~ with her abilities)

com·ment \'käm-ˌent\ *n* **1** : an expression of opinion **2** : an explanatory, illustrative, or critical note or observation : REMARK — **comment** *vb*

com·men·tary \'käm-ən-ˌter-ē\ *n, pl* **-tar·ies** : a systematic series of comments

com·men·ta·tor \-ˌtāt-ər\ *n* : one who comments; *esp* : one who gives talks on news events on radio or television

com·merce \'käm-(ˌ)ərs\ *n* : the buying and selling of commodities : TRADE

¹**com·mer·cial** \kə-'mər-shəl\ *adj* : having to do with commerce; *also* : designed for profit or for mass appeal — **com·mer·cial·ly** \-ē\ *adv*

²**commercial** *n* : an advertisement broadcast on radio or television

com·mer·cial·ism \kə-'mər-shə-ˌliz-əm\ *n* **1** : a spirit, method, or practice characteristic of business **2** : excessive emphasis on profit

com·mer·cial·ize \-ˌlīz\ *vb* **-ized; -iz·ing 1** : to manage on a business basis for profit **2** : to exploit for profit

com·mi·na·tion \ˌkäm-ə-'nā-shən\ *n* : DENUNCIATION — **com·mi·na·to·ry** \'käm-ə-nə-ˌtōr-ē\ *adj*

com·min·gle \kə-'miŋ-gəl\ *vb* : MINGLE, BLEND

com·mis·er·ate \kə-'miz-ə-ˌrāt\ *vb* **-at·ed; -at·ing** : to feel or express pity : SYMPATHIZE — **com·mis·er·a·tion** \-ˌmiz-ə-'rā-shən\ *n*

com·mis·sar \'käm-ə-ˌsär\ *n* [Russ] : a Communist party official assigned to a military unit to teach and enforce party principles and policy

com·mis·sar·i·at \ˌkäm-ə-'ser-ē-ət\ *n* **1** : a system for supplying troops with food **2** : a department headed by a commissar

com·mis·sary \'käm-ə-ˌser-ē\ *n, pl* **-sar·ies** : a store for equipment and provisions esp. for military personnel

¹**com·mis·sion** \kə-'mish-ən\ *n* **1** : a warrant granting certain powers and imposing certain duties **2** : a certificate conferring military rank and authority **3** : authority to act as agent for another; *also* : something to be done by an agent **4** : a body of persons charged

with performing a duty **5** : the doing of some act; *also* : the thing done **6** : the allowance made to an agent for transacting business for another

²**commission** *vb* **-sioned; -mis·sion·ing** \-'mish-(ə-)niŋ\ **1** : to give a commission to **2** : to order to be made **3** : to put (a ship) into a state of readiness for service

commissioned officer *n* : an officer of the armed forces holding rank by virtue of a commission from the president

com·mis·sion·er \kə-'mish-(ə-)nər\ *n* **1** : a member of a commission **2** : an official in charge of a department of public service **3** : the administrative head of a professional sport — **com·mis·sion·er·ship** *n*

com·mit \kə-'mit\ *vb* **com·mit·ted; com·mit·ting 1** : to put into charge or trust : ENTRUST **2** : to put in a prison or mental institution **3** : TRANSFER, CONSIGN **4** : PERPETRATE (∼ a crime) **5** : to pledge or assign to some particular course or use — **com·mit·ment** *n* — **com·mit·tal** *n*

com·mit·tee \kə-'mit-ē\ *n* : a body of persons selected to consider and act or report on some matter — **com·mit·tee·man** \-mən\ *n* — **com·mit·tee·wom·an** \-,wùm-ən\ *n*

commo *abbr* commodore

com·mode \kə-'mōd\ *n* [F, fr. *commode*, adj., suitable, convenient, fr. L *commodus*, fr. *com-* with + *modus* measure] **1** : a movable washstand with cupboard underneath **2** : TOILET **3**

com·mo·di·ous \kə-'mōd-ē-əs\ *adj* : comfortably spacious : ROOMY

com·mod·i·ty \kə-'mäd-ət-ē\ *n, pl* **-ties 1** : a product of agriculture or mining **2** : an article of commerce (wheat and soybeans are traded as *commodities*)

com·mo·dore \'käm-ə-,dōr\ *n* **1** : a commissioned officer in the navy ranking next below a rear admiral **2** : an officer commanding a group of merchant ships; *also* : the chief officer of a yacht club

¹**com·mon** \'käm-ən\ *adj* **1** : belonging to or serving the community : PUBLIC **2** : shared by a number in a group **3** : widely or generally known, found, or observed : FAMILIAR (∼ knowledge) **4** : VERNACULAR 3 (∼ names) **5** : not above the average esp. in social status **syn** universal, general, generic — **com·mon·ly** *adv*

²**common** *n* **1** *pl* : the common people **2** *pl* : a dining hall **3** *pl, cap* : the lower house of the British and Canadian parliaments **4** : a piece of land held in common by a community — **in common** : shared together

com·mon·al·ty \'käm-ən-əl-tē\ *n, pl* **-ties** : the common people

common cold *n* : a contagious respiratory disease caused by a virus and characterized by a sore, swollen, and inflamed nose and throat, usu. by much mucus, and by coughing and sneezing

common denominator *n* **1** : a common multiple of the denominators of a number of fractions **2** : a common trait or theme

common divisor *n* : a number or expression that divides two or more numbers or expressions without remainder

com·mon·er \'käm-ə-nər\ *n* : one of the common people : one having no rank of nobility

common fraction *n* : a fraction in which the numerator and denominator are both integers and are separated by a horizontal or slanted line

common law *n* : a group of legal practices and traditions based on judges' decisions and social customs and usu. having the same force as laws passed by legislative bodies

common logarithm *n* : a logarithm whose base is 10

common market *n* : an economic unit formed to remove trade barriers among members

common multiple *n* : a multiple of each of two or more numbers or expressions

¹**com·mon·place** \'käm-ən-,plās\ *n* : something that is ordinary or trite

²**commonplace** *adj* : ORDINARY

common sense *n* : ordinary good sense and judgment

com·mon·weal \'käm-ən-,wēl\ *n* **1** *archaic* : COMMONWEALTH **2** : the general welfare

com·mon·wealth \-,welth\ *n* **1** : the body of people politically organized into a state **2** : STATE; *also* : an association or federation of autonomous states

com·mo·tion \kə-'mō-shən\ *n* **1** : DISTURBANCE, UPRISING **2** : AGITATION

com·mu·nal \kə-'myün-ᵊl, 'käm-yən-ᵊl\ *adj* **1** : of or relating to a commune or community **2** : marked by collective ownership and use of property **3** : shared or used in common

¹**com·mune** \kə-'myün\ *vb* **communed; com·mun·ing** : to communicate intimately

²**com·mune** \'käm-,yün; kə-'myün\ *n* **1** : the smallest administrative district in some European countries **2** : a community organized on a communal basis

com·mu·ni·ca·ble \kə-'myü-ni-kə-bəl\ *adj* : capable of being communicated (∼ diseases) — **com·mu·ni·ca·bil·i·ty** \-,myü-ni-kə-'bil-ət-ē\ *n*

com·mu·ni·cant \-'myü-ni-kənt\ *n* **1** : a church member entitled to receive Communion **2** : one that communicates; *esp* : INFORMANT

com·mu·ni·cate \kə-'myü-nə-,kāt\ *vb* **-cat·ed; -cat·ing 1** : to make known **2** : TRANSMIT, IMPART **3** : to receive Communion **4** : to be in communication **5** : JOIN, CONNECT

com·mu·ni·ca·tion \kə-ˌmyü-nə-ˈkā-shən\ *n* **1** : an act of transmitting **2** : MESSAGE **3** : exchange of information or opinions **4** : a means of communicating — **com·mu·ni·ca·tive** \kə-ˈmyü-nə-ˌkāt-iv, -ni-kət-iv\ *adj*

com·mu·nion \kə-ˈmyü-nyən\ *n* **1** : a sharing of something with others **2** *cap* : a Christian sacrament in which bread and wine are partaken of as a commemoration of the death of Christ; *also* : the act of receiving the sacrament **3** : intimate fellowship or rapport **4** : a body of Christians having a common faith and discipline

com·mu·ni·qué \kə-ˈmyü-nə-ˌkā, -ˌmyü-nə-ˈkā\ *n* : BULLETIN 1

com·mu·nism \ˈkäm-yə-ˌniz-əm\ *n* **1** : social organization in which goods are held in common **2** : a theory of social organization advocating common ownership of means of production and a distribution of products of industry based on need **3** *cap* : a political doctrine based on revolutionary Marxian socialism that is the official ideology of the U.S.S.R. and some other countries; *also* : a system of government in which one party controls state-owned means of production — **com·mu·nist** \-nəst\ *n or adj, often cap* — **com·mu·nis·tic** \ˌkäm-yə-ˈnis-tik\ *adj, often cap*

com·mu·ni·ty \kə-ˈmyü-nət-ē\ *n, pl* **-ties** **1** : a body of people living in the same place under the same laws; *also* : a natural population of plants and animals that interact ecologically and live in one place (as a pond) **2** : society at large **3** : joint ownership **4** : SIMILARITY, LIKENESS

community college *n* : a nonresidential 2-year college that is usu. government-supported

community property *n* : property held jointly by husband and wife

com·mu·ta·tion \ˌkäm-yə-ˈtā-shən\ *n* : substitution of one form of payment or penalty for another

com·mu·ta·tive \ˈkäm-yə-ˌtāt-iv, kə-ˈmyüt- ət-\ *adj* : of, relating to, having, or being the property that a given mathematical operation and set have when the result obtained using any two numbers of the set with the operation does not differ with the order in which the numbers are used 〈addition of the real numbers is ∼〉 — **com·mu·ta·tiv·i·ty** \kə-ˌmyüt-ə-ˈtiv-ət-ē, ˌkäm-yə-tə-\ *n*

com·mu·ta·tor \ˈkäm-yə-ˌtāt-ər\ *n* : a device (as on a generator or motor) for changing the direction of electric current

¹com·mute \kə-ˈmyüt\ *vb* **com·mut·ed; com·mut·ing 1** : EXCHANGE **2** : to substitute a less severe penalty for (one more severe) **3** : to travel back and forth regularly — **com·mut·er** *n*

²commute *n* : a trip made in commuting

comp *abbr* **1** comparative **2** compiled;

compiler **3** composition **4** compound

¹com·pact \kəm-ˈpakt, (ˈ)käm-\ *adj* **1** : SOLID, DENSE **2** : BRIEF, SUCCINCT **3** : occupying a small volume by efficient use of space 〈∼ camera〉 — **com·pact·ly** *adv* — **com·pact·ness** *n*

²compact *vb* : to pack together

³com·pact \ˈkäm-ˌpakt\ *n* **1** : a small case for cosmetics **2** : a small automobile

⁴com·pact \ˈkäm-ˌpakt\ *n* : AGREEMENT, COVENANT

compact disc *n* : a small plastic optical disc usu. containing recorded music

¹com·pan·ion \kəm-ˈpan-yən\ *n* [OF *compagnon*, fr. LL *companion-, companio*, lit., one who shares bread, fr. L *com-* together + *panis* bread] **1** : an intimate friend or associate : COMRADE **2** : one that is closely connected with something similar — **com·pan·ion·able** *adj* — **com·pan·ion·ship** *n*

²companion *n* : COMPANIONWAY

com·pan·ion·way \-ˌwā\ *n* : a ship's stairway from one deck to another

com·pa·ny \ˈkəmp-(ə-)nē\ *n, pl* **-nies 1** : association with others : FELLOWSHIP; *also* : COMPANIONS **2** : GUESTS **3** : a group of persons or things **4** : an infantry unit consisting of two or more platoons and normally commanded by a captain **5** : a group of musical or dramatic performers **6** : the officers and crew of a ship **7** : an association of persons for carrying on a business **syn** party, band, troop, troupe, corps, outfit

com·pa·ra·ble \ˈkäm-p(ə-)rə-bəl\ *adj* : capable of being compared **syn** parallel, similar, like, alike, corresponding — **com·pa·ra·bil·i·ty** \ˌkäm-p(ə-)rə-ˈbil-ət-ē\ *n*

¹com·par·a·tive \kəm-ˈpar-ət-iv\ *adj* **1** : of, relating to, or constituting the degree of grammatical comparison that denotes increase in quality, quantity, or relation **2** : RELATIVE 〈a ∼ stranger〉 — **com·par·a·tive·ly** *adv*

²comparative *n* : the comparative degree or a comparative form in a language

¹com·pare \kəm-ˈpaər\ *vb* **com·pared; com·par·ing 1** : to represent as like something : LIKEN **2** : to examine for likenesses and differences **3** : to inflect or modify (an adjective or adverb) according to the degrees of comparison

²compare *n* : the possibility of comparing 〈beauty beyond ∼〉

com·par·i·son \-ˈpar-ə-sən\ *n* **1** : the act of comparing : relative estimate **2** : change in the form of an adjective or adverb to show different levels of quality, quantity, or relation

com·part·ment \kəm-ˈpärt-mənt\ *n* **1** : a separate division **2** : a section of an enclosed space : ROOM

com·part·men·tal·ize \kəm-ˌpärt-ˈment-ᵊl-ˌīz\ *vb* **-ized; -iz·ing** : to separate into compartments

¹com·pass \'kəm-pəs, 'käm-\ *vb* [ME *compassen*, fr. OF *compasser* to measure, fr. (assumed) VL *compassare* to pace off, fr. L *com-* + *passus* pace] 1 : CONTRIVE, PLOT 2 : to make a circuit of; *also* : SURROUND 3 : BRING ABOUT, ACHIEVE

²compass *n* 1 : BOUNDARY, CIRCUMFERENCE 2 : an enclosed space 3 : RANGE, SCOPE 4 : a device for determining direction by means of a magnetic needle swinging freely and pointing to the magnetic north; *also* : a nonmagnetic device that indicates direction 5 : an instrument for drawing circles or transferring measurements consisting of two legs joined by a pivot

com·pas·sion \kəm-'pash-ən\ *n* : sympathetic feeling : PITY, MERCY — **com·pas·sion·ate** \-(ə-)nət\ *adj*

com·pat·i·ble \kəm-'pat-ə-bəl\ *adj* : able to exist or act together harmoniously (∼ colors) (∼ drugs) *syn* consonant, congenial, sympathetic — **com·pat·i·bil·i·ty** \-,pat-ə-'bil-ət-ē\ *n*

com·pa·tri·ot \kəm-'pā-trē-ət, -,trē-,ät\ *n* : a fellow countryman

com·peer \'käm-,pir\ *n* : EQUAL, PEER

com·pel \kəm-'pel\ *vb* **com·pelled; com·pel·ling** : to drive or urge with force : CONSTRAIN

com·pen·di·um \kəm-'pen-dē-əm\ *n, pl* **-di·ums** *or* **-dia** \-dē-ə\ 1 : a brief summary of a larger work or of a field of knowledge 2 : COLLECTION

com·pen·sate \'käm-pən-,sāt\ *vb* **-sat·ed; -sat·ing** 1 : to be equivalent to in value or effect : make up for 2 : PAY, REMUNERATE *syn* balance, offset, counterbalance, counterpoise — **com·pen·sa·tion** \,käm-pən-'sā-shən\ *n* — **com·pen·sa·to·ry** \kəm-'pen-sə-,tōr-ē\ *adj*

com·pete \kəm-'pēt\ *vb* **com·pet·ed; com·pet·ing** : CONTEND, VIE

com·pe·tence \'käm-pət-əns\ *n* 1 : adequate means for subsistence 2 : FITNESS, ABILITY

com·pe·ten·cy \-pət-ən-sē\ *n, pl* **-cies** : COMPETENCE

com·pe·tent \-pət-ənt\ *adj* : CAPABLE, FIT, QUALIFIED

com·pe·ti·tion \,käm-pə-'tish-ən\ *n* 1 : the act of competing : RIVALRY 2 : CONTEST, MATCH; *also* : one's competitors — **com·pet·i·tive** \kəm-'pet-ət-iv\ *adj* — **com·pet·i·tive·ly** *adv* — **com·pet·i·tive·ness** *n*

com·pet·i·tor \kəm-'pet-ət-ər\ *n* : one that competes : RIVAL

com·pile \kəm-'pīl\ *vb* **com·piled; com·pil·ing** [ME *compilen*, fr. MF *compiler*, fr. L *compilare* to plunder] 1 : to collect and edit into a volume 2 : to compose out of materials from other documents 3 : to translate (a computer program) with a compiler 4 : to build up gradually (∼ a record of four wins and two losses) — **com·pi·la·tion** \,käm-pə-'lā-shən\ *n*

com·pil·er \kəm-'pī-lər\ *n* 1 : one that

compiles 2 : a computer program that translates another program written in a programming language into machine language

com·pla·cence \kəm-'plās-ᵊns\ *n* : SATISFACTION; *esp* : SELF-SATISFACTION — **com·pla·cent** \-ᵊnt\ *adj* — **com·pla·cent·ly** *adv*

com·pla·cen·cy \-ᵊn-sē\ *n, pl* **-cies** : COMPLACENCE

com·plain \kəm-'plān\ *vb* 1 : to express grief, pain, or discontent 2 : to make a formal accusation — **com·plain·ant** *n* — **com·plain·er** *n*

com·plaint \kəm-'plānt\ *n* 1 : expression of grief, pain, or dissatisfaction 2 : a bodily ailment or disease 3 : a formal accusation against a person

com·plai·sance \kəm-'plās-ᵊns, ,käm-plā-'zans\ *n* [F] : disposition to please — **com·plai·sant** \-ᵊnt, -'zant\ *adj*

com·pleat \kəm-'plēt\ *adj* : PROFICIENT

com·plect·ed \kəm-'plek-təd\ *adj* : having a specified facial complexion (dark-*complected*)

¹com·ple·ment \'käm-plə-mənt\ *n* 1 : quantity needed to make a thing complete 2 : full quantity, number, or amount 3 : an added word by which a predicate is made complete 4 : a substance in blood that combines with antibodies to destroy antigens — **com·ple·men·ta·ry** \,käm-plə-'men-t(ə-)rē\ *adj*

²com·ple·ment \-,ment\ *vb* : to be complementary to : fill out

¹com·plete \kəm-'plēt\ *adj* **com·plet·er; -est** 1 : having no part lacking 2 : brought to an end 3 : fully realized : THOROUGH — **com·plete·ly** *adv* — **com·plete·ness** *n* — **com·ple·tion** \-'plē-shən\ *n*

²complete *vb* **com·plet·ed; com·plet·ing** 1 : FINISH, CONCLUDE 2 : to make whole or perfect

¹com·plex \'käm-,pleks\ *n* : something made up of or involving an often intricate combination of elements; *esp* : a system of repressed desires, memories, and ideas that exert a dominant influence on the personality and behavior (a guilt ∼)

²com·plex \käm-'pleks, kəm-'pleks, 'käm-,pleks\ *adj* 1 : composed of two or more parts 2 : consisting of a main clause and one or more subordinate clauses (∼ sentence) 3 : COMPLICATED, INTRICATE — **com·plex·i·ty** \käm-'plek-sət-ē, käm-\ *n*

complex fraction *n* : a fraction with a fraction or mixed number in the numerator or denominator or both

com·plex·ion \kəm-'plek-shən\ *n* 1 : the hue or appearance of the skin esp. of the face 2 : general appearance — **com·plex·ioned** \-shənd\ *adj*

complex number *n* : a number (as 3 + 4√(−1)) formed by adding a real number to the product of a real number and the square root of minus one

com·pli·ance \kəm-'plī-əns\ *n* 1 : the act

of complying to a demand or proposal
2 : a disposition to yield — **com·pli·ant**
\-ənt\ *adj*

com·pli·cate \'käm-plə-ˌkāt\ *vb* **-cat·ed;
-cat·ing** : to make or become complex
or intricate — **com·pli·ca·tion** \ˌkäm-
plə-'kā-shən\ *n*

com·pli·cat·ed \'käm-plə-ˌkāt-əd\ *adj*
: consisting of parts intricately combined **2** : difficult to analyze, understand, or explain — **com·pli·cat·ed·ly**
adv

com·plic·i·ty \kəm-'plis-ət-ē\ *n, pl* **-ties**
: the state of being an accomplice

¹**com·pli·ment** \'käm-plə-mənt\ *n* **1** : an
expression of approval or courtesy;
esp : a flattering remark **2** *pl* : best
wishes : REGARDS

²**com·pli·ment** \-ˌment\ *vb* : to pay a
compliment

com·pli·men·ta·ry \ˌkäm-plə-'men-
t(ə-)rē\ *adj* **1** : containing or expressing a compliment **2** : given free as a
courtesy (~ ticket)

com·ply \kəm-'plī\ *vb* **com·plied; com-
ply·ing** : ACQUIESCE, YIELD

¹**com·po·nent** \kəm-'pō-nənt, 'käm-ˌpō-\
n : a component part *syn* ingredient,
element, factor, constituent

²**com·po·nent** *adj* : serving to form a part
of : CONSTITUENT

com·port \kəm-'pōrt\ *vb* **1** : AGREE, AC-
CORD **2** : CONDUCT *syn* behave, acquit,
deport

com·port·ment \-mənt\ *n* : BEHAVIOR,
BEARING

com·pose \kəm-'pōz\ *vb* **com·posed;
com·pos·ing 1** : to form by putting together : FASHION **2** : to produce (as
pages of type) by composition **3** : AD-
JUST, ARRANGE **4** : CALM, QUIET **5** : to
practice composition (~ music) —
com·posed \-'pōzd\ *adj* — **com·pos·er**
\-'pō-zər\ *n*

composing stick *n* : a hand-held com-
positor's tray with an adjustable slide
for setting type

¹**com·pos·ite** \käm-'päz-ət, kəm-\ *adj* **1**
: made up of distinct parts or elements
2 : of, relating to, or being a large family of flowering plants (as the daisy)
that bear many small flowers united
into compact heads resembling single
flowers

²**composite** *n* **1** : something composite **2**
: a plant of the composite family *syn*
blend, compound, mixture, amalga-
mation

com·po·si·tion \ˌkäm-pə-'zish-ən\ *n* **1**
: the act or process of composing; *esp*
: arrangement of elements in artistic
form **2** : the arrangement of type for
printing **3** : MAKEUP, CONSTITUTION **4**
: a product of mixing various elements
or ingredients **5** : a literary, musical, or
artistic product; *esp* : ESSAY

com·pos·i·tor \kəm-'päz-ət-ər\ *n* : one
who sets type

com·post \'käm-ˌpōst\ *n* : a fertilizing

material consisting largely of decayed
organic matter

com·po·sure \kəm-'pō-zhər\ *n* : CALM-
NESS, SELF-POSSESSION

com·pote \'käm-ˌpōt\ *n* **1** : fruits
cooked in syrup **2** : a bowl (as of
glass) usu. with a base and stem from
which compotes, fruits, nuts, or
sweets are served

¹**com·pound** \(')käm-ˌpaund, kəm-\ *vb*
[ME *componen*, fr. MF *compondre*,
fr. L *componere*, fr. *com-* together +
ponere to put] **1** : COMBINE **2** : to form
by combining parts (~ a medicine) **3**
: SETTLE (~ a dispute) **4** : to increase
(as interest) by an amount that itself
increases; *also* : to add to **5** : to forbear prosecution of (an offense) in return for some reward

²**com·pound** \'käm-ˌpaund\ *adj* **1** : made
up of two or more parts **2** : composed
of united similar parts esp. of a kind
usu. separate (a ~ plant ovary) **3**
: formed by the combination of two or
more otherwise independent elements
(~ sentence)

³**com·pound** \'käm-ˌpaund\ *n* **1** : a word
consisting of parts that are words **2**
: something formed from a union of
elements or parts; *esp* : a distinct substance formed by the union of two or
more chemical elements *syn* mixture,
composite, blend, admixture, alloy

⁴**com·pound** \'käm-ˌpaund\ *n* [by folk
etymology fr. Malay *kampong* group
of buildings, village] : an enclosure
containing buildings

compound interest *n* : interest computed on the sum of an original principal
and accrued interest

com·pre·hend \ˌkäm-pri-'hend\ *vb* **1**
: UNDERSTAND **2** : INCLUDE — **com·pre-
hen·si·ble** \-'hen-sə-bəl\ *adj* — **com·
pre·hen·sion** \-'hen-chən\ *n* — **com·
pre·hen·sive** \-siv\ *adj*

¹**com·press** \kəm-'pres\ *vb* : to squeeze
together : CONDENSE *syn* constrict,
contract, shrink — **com·pressed** *adj* —
com·pres·sion \-'presh-ən\ *n* — **com·
pres·sor** \-'pres-ər\ *n*

²**com·press** \'käm-ˌpres\ *n* : a soft often
wet or medicated pad used to press
upon an injured bodily part

compressed air *n* : air under pressure
greater than that of the atmosphere

com·prise \kəm-'prīz\ *vb* **com·prised;
com·pris·ing 1** : INCLUDE, CONTAIN **2**
: to be made up of **3** : COMPOSE, CON-
STITUTE

¹**com·pro·mise** \'käm-prə-ˌmīz\ *n* : a settlement of differences reached by mutual concessions; *also* : the agreement thus made

²**compromise** *vb* **-mised; -mis·ing 1** : to
settle by compromise **2** : to endanger
the reputation of

comp·trol·ler \kən-'trō-lər, 'kämp-
ˌtrō-\ *n* : an official who audits and
supervises expenditures and accounts

com·pul·sion \kəm-'pəl-shən\ *n* **1** : CO-
ERCION **2** : an irresistible impulse *syn*

constraint, force, violence, duress —
com·pul·sive \-siv\ *adj* — **com·pul·so·ry** \-'pəls-(ə-)rē\ *adj*

com·punc·tion \kəm-'pəŋk-shən\ *n* : anxiety arising from guilt : REMORSE

com·pute \kəm-'pyüt\ *vb* **com·put·ed; com·put·ing** : CALCULATE, RECKON — **com·pu·ta·tion** \,käm-pyù-'tā-shən\ *n* — **com·pu·ta·tion·al** *adj*

computed tomography *n* : radiography in which a three-dimensional image of a body structure is constructed by computer from a series of plane cross-sectional images made along an axis

com·put·er \kəm-'pyüt-ər\ *n* : a programmable electronic device that can store, retrieve, and process data

com·put·er·ize \kəm-'pyüt-ə-,rīz\ *vb* **-ized; -iz·ing** 1 : to carry out, control, or produce by means of a computer 2 : to provide with computers 3 : to store in a computer; *also* : put into a form that a computer can use — **com·put·er·iza·tion** \-,pyüt-ə-rə-'zā-shən\ *n*

computerized axial tomography *n* : COMPUTED TOMOGRAPHY

com·rade \'käm-,rad, -rəd\ *n* [MF *comarade* group sleeping in one room, roommate, companion, fr. Sp *comarada*, fr. *cámara* room, fr. LL *camera*] : COMPANION, ASSOCIATE — **com·rade·ly** *adj* — **com·rade·ship** *n*

¹**con** \'kän\ *vb* **conned; con·ning** 1 : MEMORIZE 2 : STUDY

²**con** *adv* : in opposition : AGAINST

³**con** *n* : an opposing argument, person, or position

⁴**con** *vb* **conned; con·ning** 1 : SWINDLE 2 : PERSUADE, CAJOLE

⁵**con** *n* : CONVICT

con brio \kän-'brē-ō, kōn-\ *adv* : with spirit : VIGOROUSLY — used as a direction in music

conc *abbr* concentrated

con·cat·e·na·tion \(,)kän-,kat-ə-'nā-shən\ *n* : a series connected like links in a chain — **con·cat·e·nate** \kän-'kat-ə-,nāt\ *vb*

con·cave \(')kän-'kāv\ *adj* : curved or rounded inward like the inside of a bowl — **con·cav·i·ty** \kän-'kav-ət-ē\ *n*

con·ceal \kən-'sēl\ *vb* : to place out of sight : HIDE — **con·ceal·ment** *n*

con·cede \kən-'sēd\ *vb* **con·ced·ed; con·ced·ing** 1 : to admit to be true 2 : GRANT, YIELD **syn** allow, acknowledge, admit, avow, confess

con·ceit \kən-'sēt\ *n* 1 : excessively high opinion of oneself, one's appearance, or ability : VANITY 2 : an elaborate or strained metaphor — **con·ceit·ed** \-əd\ *adj*

con·ceive \kən-'sēv\ *vb* **con·ceived; con·ceiv·ing** 1 : to become pregnant 2 : to form an idea of : THINK, IMAGINE — **con·ceiv·able** \-'sē-və-bəl\ *adj* — **con·ceiv·ably** \-blē\ *adv*

con·cel·e·brant \kən-'sel-ə-brənt\ *n* : one of two or more members of the

clergy celebrating the Eucharist or Mass together

¹**con·cen·trate** \'kän-sən-,trāt\ *vb* **-trat·ed; -trat·ing** 1 : to gather into one body, mass, or force 2 : to make less dilute 3 : to fix one's powers, efforts, or attentions on one thing

²**concentrate** *n* : something concentrated

con·cen·tra·tion \,kän-sən-'trā-shən\ *n* 1 : the act or process of concentrating : the state of being concentrated; *esp* : direction of attention on a single object 2 : the relative content of a component : STRENGTH

concentration camp *n* : a camp where persons (as prisoners of war or political prisoners) are confined

con·cen·tric \kən-'sen-trik\ *adj* 1 : having a common center (∼ circles) 2 : COAXIAL

con·cept \'kän-,sept\ *n* : THOUGHT, NOTION, IDEA — **con·cep·tu·al** \kän-'sep-chə(-wə)l\ *adj*

con·cep·tion \kən-'sep-shən\ *n* 1 : the act of conceiving or being conceived 2 : the power to form ideas or concepts 3 : IDEA, CONCEPT 4 : the originating of something

con·cep·tu·al·ize \-'sep-chə-(wə-)-,līz\ *vb* **-ized; -iz·ing** : to form a conception of

¹**con·cern** \kən-'sərn\ *vb* 1 : to relate to 2 : to be the business of : INVOLVE 3 : ENGAGE, OCCUPY

²**concern** *n* 1 : INTEREST, ANXIETY 2 : AFFAIR, MATTER 3 : a business organization **syn** care, worry, anxiety, disquiet, unease

con·cerned \-'sərnd\ *adj* : ANXIOUS, TROUBLED

con·cern·ing \-'sər-niŋ\ *prep* : relating to : REGARDING

con·cern·ment \kən-'sərn-mənt\ *n* 1 : something in which one is concerned 2 : IMPORTANCE, CONSEQUENCE

¹**con·cert** \'kän-(,)sərt\ *n* 1 : agreement in a plan or design 2 : a concerted action 3 : a public performance of several musical compositions

²**con·cert** \kən-'sərt\ *vb* : to plan together

con·cert·ed \kən-'sərt-əd\ *adj* : mutually agreed on; *also* : performed in unison

con·cer·ti·na \,kän-sər-'tē-nə\ *n* : an instrument of the accordion family

con·cert·mas·ter \'kän-sərt-,mas-tər\ *or* **con·cert·meis·ter** \-,mī-stər\ *n* : the leader of the first violins of an orchestra and assistant to the conductor

con·cer·to \kən-'chert-ō\ *n, pl* **-ti** \-(,)ē\ *or* **-tos** [It] : a piece for one or more solo instruments and orchestra in three movements

con·ces·sion \kən-'sesh-ən\ *n* 1 : an act of conceding or yielding 2 : something yielded 3 : a grant by a government of land or of a right to use it 4 : a grant of a portion of premises for some specific purpose — **con·ces·sion·ary** \-'sesh-ə-,ner-ē\ *adj*

con·ces·sion·aire \kən-,sesh-ə-'na(ə)r,

-ᵗne(ə)r\ *n* : one that owns or operates a concession

conch \ˈkäŋk, ˈkänch\ *n, pl* **conchs** \ˈkäŋks\ *or* **conch·es** \ˈkän-chəz\ : a large spiral-shelled marine gastropod mollusk; *also* : its shell

con·cierge \kōⁿ-ˈsyerzh\ *n, pl* **con·cierges** \-ˈsyerzh(-əz)\ [F, fr. L *conservus* fellow slave, fr. *com-* with + *servus* slave] 1 : a resident in an apartment building who performs services for the tenants 2 : a usu. multilingual hotel staff member

con·cil·i·ate \kən-ˈsil-ē-,āt\ *vb* **-at·ed; -at·ing** 1 : to bring into agreement : RECONCILE 2 : to gain the goodwill of — **con·cil·i·a·tion** \-,sil-ē-ˈā-shən\ *n* — **con·cil·ia·to·ry** \-ˈsil-yə-,tōr-ē, -ˈsil-ē-ə-\ *adj*

con·cise \kən-ˈsīs\ *adj* : expressing much in few words : TERSE, SUCCINCT — **con·cise·ly** *adv* — **con·cise·ness** *n*

con·clave \ˈkän-,klāv\ *n* [ML, fr. L, room that can be locked, fr. *com-* together + *clavis* key] : a private gathering; *also* : CONVENTION

con·clude \kən-ˈklüd\ *vb* **con·clud·ed; con·clud·ing** 1 : to bring to a close : END 2 : DECIDE, JUDGE 3 : to bring about as a result *syn* close, finish, terminate, complete, halt, end

con·clu·sion \kən-ˈklü-zhən\ *n* 1 : the logical consequence of a reasoning process 2 : TERMINATION, END 3 : OUTCOME, RESULT — **con·clu·sive** \-siv\ *adj* — **con·clu·sive·ly** *adv*

con·coct \kən-ˈkäkt, kän-\ *vb* 1 : to prepare by combining diverse ingredients 2 : DEVISE ⟨~ a scheme⟩ — **con·coc·tion** \-ˈkäk-shən\ *n*

con·com·i·tant \-ˈkäm-ət-ənt\ *adj* : ACCOMPANYING, ATTENDING — **concomitant** *n*

con·cord \ˈkän-,kȯrd, ˈkäŋ-\ *n* : AGREEMENT, HARMONY

con·cor·dance \kən-ˈkȯrd-ᵊns\ *n* 1 : an alphabetical index of words in a book or in an author's works with the passages in which they occur 2 : AGREEMENT

con·cor·dant \-ᵊnt\ *adj* : HARMONIOUS, AGREEING

con·cor·dat \kən-ˈkȯr-,dat\ *n* : AGREEMENT, COVENANT

con·course \ˈkän-,kȯrs\ *n* 1 : a flocking together of people : GATHERING 2 : an open space or hall (as in a bus terminal) where crowds gather

con·cres·cence \kən-ˈkres-ᵊns\ *n* : a growing together — **con·cres·cent** \-ᵊnt\ *adj*

¹**con·crete** \kän-ˈkrēt, ˈkän-,krēt\ *adj* 1 : naming a real thing or class of things : not abstract 2 : not theoretical : ACTUAL 3 : made of or relating to concrete

²**con·crete** \ˈkän-,krēt, kän-ˈkrēt\ *vb* **con·cret·ed; con·cret·ing** 1 : SOLIDIFY 2 : to cover with concrete

³**con·crete** \ˈkän-,krēt, kän-ˈkrēt\ *n* : a hard building material made by mixing cement, sand, and gravel with water

con·cre·tion \kän-ˈkrē-shən\ *n* : a hard mass esp. when formed abnormally in the body

con·cu·bine \ˈkäŋ-kyủ-,bīn\ *n* [ME, fr. MF, fr. L *concubina*, fr. *com-* with + *cubare* to lie] : a woman who is not legally a wife but lives with a man and has a recognized position in his household — **con·cu·bi·nage** \kän-ˈkyü-bə-nij\ *n*

con·cu·pis·cence \kän-ˈkyü-pə-səns\ *n* : ardent sexual desire : LUST

con·cur \kən-ˈkər\ *vb* **con·curred; con·cur·ring** 1 : to act together 2 : AGREE 3 : COINCIDE *syn* unite, combine, cooperate, band, join

con·cur·rence \-ˈkər-əns\ *n* 1 : agreement in action or opinion 2 : CONJUNCTION, COINCIDENCE

con·cur·rent \-ˈkər-ənt\ *adj* 1 : happening or operating at the same time 2 : joint and equal in authority

con·cus·sion \kən-ˈkəsh-ən\ *n* 1 : AGITATION, SHAKING 2 : a sharp sudden blow or collision; *also* : bodily injury (as to the brain) resulting from a sudden jar

con·demn \kən-ˈdem\ *vb* 1 : to declare to be wrong 2 : to convict of guilt 3 : to sentence judically 4 : to pronounce unfit for use ⟨~ a building⟩ 5 : to declare forfeited or taken for public use *syn* denounce, censure, blame, criticize, reprehend — **con·dem·na·tion** \,kän-,dem-ˈnā-shən\ *n* — **con·dem·na·to·ry** \kən-ˈdem-nə-,tōr-ē\ *adj*

con·den·sate \ˈkän-dən-,sāt, kən-ˈden-\ *n* : a product of condensation

con·dense \kən-ˈdens\ *vb* **con·densed; con·dens·ing** 1 : to make or become more compact or dense : CONCENTRATE 2 : to change from vapor to liquid *syn* contract, shrink, compress, constrict — **con·den·sa·tion** \,kän-,den-ˈsā-shən, -dən-\ *n*

con·dens·er \kən-ˈden-sər\ *n* 1 : one that condenses 2 : CAPACITOR

con·de·scend \,kän-di-ˈsend\ *vb* 1 : to assume an air of superiority *syn* stoop, deign — **con·de·scend·ing·ly** \-ˈsen-diŋ-lē\ *adv* — **con·de·scen·sion** \-ˈsen-chən\ *n*

con·dign \kən-ˈdīn, ˈkän-,dīn\ *adj* : DESERVED, APPROPRIATE ⟨~ punishment⟩

con·di·ment \ˈkän-də-mənt\ *n* : something used to make food savory; *esp* : a pungent seasoning (as pepper)

¹**con·di·tion** \kən-ˈdish-ən\ *n* 1 : something essential to the occurrence of some other thing 2 : state of being 3 : station in life : social rank 4 : state in respect to fitness (as for action or use); *esp* : state of health 5 *pl* : state of affairs : CIRCUMSTANCES

²**condition** *vb* **di·tioned; di·tion·ing** 1 : to put into proper condition for action or use 2 : to adapt, modify, or mold to respond in a particular way 3 : to modify so that an act or response previously associated with one stimu-

lus becomes associated with another

con·di·tion·al \kən-'dish-(ə-)nəl\ *adj* : containing, implying, or depending on a condition — **con·di·tion·al·ly** \-ē\ *adv*

con·di·tioned *adj* : determined or established by conditioning

con·dole \kən-'dōl\ *vb* **con·doled; con·dol·ing** : to express sympathetic sorrow — **con·do·lence** \kən-'dō-ləns, 'kän-də-\ *n*

con·dom \'kän-dəm, 'kən-\ *n* : a usu. membranous or rubber sheath worn over the penis to prevent pregnancy or the transmission of sexually transmitted disease during sexual intercourse

con·do·min·i·um \,kän-də-'min-ē-əm\ *n, pl* **-ums** 1 : joint sovereignty (as by two or more nations) 2 : a politically dependent territory under condominium 3 : individual ownership of a unit (as an apartment) in a multiunit structure; *also* : a unit so owned

con·done \kən-'dōn\ *vb* **con·doned; con·don·ing** : to overlook or forgive (an offense) by treating the offender as if he had done nothing wrong *syn* excuse, pardon, forgive, remit — **con·do·na·tion** \,kän-də-'nā-shən\ *n*

con·dor \'kän-dər, -,dȯr\ *n* [Sp *cóndor*, fr. Quechua (a So. American Indian language) *kúntur*] : a very large American vulture of the high Andes; *also* : a related nearly extinct vulture of southern California now resident only in captivity

con·duce \kən-'d(y)üs\ *vb* **con·duced; con·duc·ing** : to lead or contribute to a result — **con·du·cive** *adj*

¹con·duct \'kän-(,)dəkt\ *n* 1 : MANAGEMENT, DIRECTION 2 : BEHAVIOR

²con·duct \kən-'dəkt\ *vb* 1 : GUIDE, ESCORT 2 : MANAGE, DIRECT 3 : to act as a medium for conveying 4 : BEHAVE, BEAR — **con·duc·tion** \-'dək-shən\ *n*

con·duc·tance \kən-'dək-təns\ *n* : the readiness with which a conductor transmits an electric current

con·duc·tive \kən-'dək-tiv\ *adj* : having the power to conduct (as heat or electricity) — **con·duc·tiv·i·ty** \,kän-,dək-'tiv-ət-ē\ *n*

con·duc·tor \kən-'dək-tər\ *n* 1 : one that conducts 2 : a collector of fares in a public conveyance 3 : the leader of a musical ensemble

con·duit \'kän-,d(y)ü-ət, -d(w)ət\ *n* 1 : a channel for conveying fluid 2 : a tube or trough for protecting electric wires or cables 3 : a means of transmitting or distributing

con·dyle \'kän-,dīl, -dᵊl\ *n* : an articular prominence of a bone — **con·dy·lar** \-də-lər\ *adj*

cone \'kōn\ *n* 1 : the scaly fruit of trees of the pine family 2 : a solid figure formed by rotating a right triangle about one of its legs 3 : a solid figure that slopes evenly to a point from a

usu. circular base 4 : something shaped like a cone

Con·es·to·ga \,kän-ə-'stō-gə\ *n* : a broad-wheeled covered wagon formerly used for transporting freight across the prairies

co·ney \'kō-nē\ *n, pl* **coneys** 1 : a rabbit or its fur 2 : PIKA

conf *abbr* conference

con·fab \'kän-,fab, kən-'fab\ *n* : CONFABULATION

con·fab·u·la·tion \kən-,fab-yə-'lā-shən\ *n* : CHAT; *also* : CONFERENCE

con·fec·tion \kən-'fek-shən\ *n* : a fancy dish or sweet; *also* : CANDY

con·fec·tion·er \-sh(ə-)nər\ *n* : a maker of or dealer in confections (as candies)

con·fec·tion·ery \-shə-,ner-ē\ *n, pl* **-er·ies** 1 : sweet foods 2 : a confectioner's place of business

Confed *abbr* Confederate

con·fed·er·a·cy \kən-'fed-(ə-)rə-sē\ *n, pl* **-cies** 1 : LEAGUE, ALLIANCE 2 *cap* : the 11 southern states that seceded from the U.S. in 1860 and 1861

¹con·fed·er·ate \kən-'fed-(ə-)rət\ *adj* 1 : united in a league : ALLIED 2 *cap* : of or relating to the Confederacy

²confederate *n* 1 : ALLY, ACCOMPLICE 2 *cap* : an adherent of the Confederacy

³con·fed·er·ate \-'fed-ə-,rāt\ *vb* **-at·ed; -at·ing** : to unite in a confederacy or a conspiracy

con·fed·er·a·tion \kən-,fed-ə-'rā-shən\ *n* 1 : an act of confederating : ALLIANCE 2 : LEAGUE

con·fer \kən-'fər\ *vb* **con·ferred; con·fer·ring** 1 : GRANT, BESTOW 2 : to exchange views : CONSULT — **con·fer·ee** \,kän-fə-'rē\ *n*

con·fer·ence \'kän-f(ə-)rəns\ *n* : an interchange of views; *also* : a meeting for this purpose

con·fess \kən-'fes\ *vb* 1 : to acknowledge or disclose one's misdeed, fault, or sin 2 : to acknowledge one's sins to God or to a priest 3 : to receive the confession of (a penitent) *syn* admit, own, avow, concede, grant

con·fessed·ly \-'fes-əd-lē\ *adv* : by confession : ADMITTEDLY

con·fes·sion \-'fesh-ən\ *n* 1 : an act of confessing (as in the sacrament of penance) 2 : an acknowledgment of guilt 3 : a formal statement of religious beliefs 4 : a religious body having a common creed — **con·fes·sion·al** *adj*

con·fes·sion·al \-'fesh-(ə-)nəl\ *n* : a place where a priest hears confessions

con·fes·sor \kən-'fes-ər, 2 *also* \'kän-,fes-\ *n* 1 : one that confesses 2 : a priest who hears confessions

con·fet·ti \kən-'fet-ē\ *n* [It, pl. of *confetto* sweetmeat, fr. ML *confectum*, fr. L *conficere* to prepare] : bits of colored paper or ribbon for throwing about in celebration

con·fi·dant \'kän-fə-,dant, -,dänt\ *n* : one to whom secrets are confided

con·fide \kən-'fīd\ *vb* **con·fid·ed; con-**

·fid·ing **1** : to have or show faith
: TRUST ⟨~ in a friend⟩ **2** : to tell confi-
dentially ⟨~ a secret⟩ **3** : ENTRUST

¹con·fi·dence \'kän-fəd-əns\ *n* **1** : TRUST,
RELIANCE **2** : SELF-ASSURANCE, BOLD-
NESS **3** : a state of trust or intimacy —
con·fi·dent \-fəd-ənt\ *adj* — con·fi-
dent·ly *adv*

²confidence *adj* : of or relating to swindling by false promises

con·fi·den·tial \ˌkän-fə-'den-chəl\ *adj* **1**
: SECRET, PRIVATE **2** : entrusted or treated with confidence ⟨~ clerk⟩ — con·fi-
den·tial·ly \-ē\ *adv*

con·fig·u·ra·tion \kən-ˌfig-yə-'rā-shən\
n : structural arrangement of parts
: SHAPE

con·fine \kən-'fīn\ *vb* con·fined; con·fin-
ing **1** : to restrict to a particular place
or situation **2** : IMPRISON **3** : to keep
within limits : RESTRAIN — con·fine-
ment *n* — con·fin·er *n*

con·fines \'kän-ˌfīnz\ *n pl* : BOUNDS,
BORDERS

con·firm \kən-'fərm\ *vb* **1** : to make
firm or firmer **2** : RATIFY **3** : to administer the rite of confirmation to **4** :
VERIFY, CORROBORATE — con·fir·ma-
to·ry \-'fər-mə-ˌtōr-ē\ *adj* — confirmed *adj*

con·fir·ma·tion \ˌkän-fər-'mā-shən\ *n* **1**
: a religious ceremony admitting a
person to full membership in a church
or synagogue **2** : an act of ratifying or
corroborating; *also* : PROOF

con·fis·cate \'kän-fə-ˌskāt\ *vb* -cat·ed;
-cat·ing [L *confiscare*, fr. *com-* with +
fiscus treasury] : to take possession
of by or as if by public authority —
con·fis·ca·tion \ˌkän-fə-'skā-shən\ *n* —
con·fis·ca·to·ry \kən-'fis-kə-ˌtōr-ē\ *adj*

con·fla·gra·tion \ˌkän-flə-'grā-shən\ *n*
: FIRE; *esp* : a large disastrous fire

¹con·flict \'kän-ˌflikt\ *n* **1** : WAR **2** : a
clash between hostile or opposing elements or ideas

²con·flict \kən-'flikt\ *vb* : to show antagonism or irreconcilability : CLASH

con·flu·ence \'kän-ˌflü-əns, kən-'flü-\ *n*
1 : a coming together at one point **2**
: the meeting or place of meeting of
two or more streams — con·flu·ent
\-ənt\ *adj*

con·flux \'kän-ˌfləks\ *n* : CONFLUENCE

con·fo·cal \kän-'fō-kəl\ *adj* : having the
same foci — con·fo·cal·ly \-ē\ *adv*

con·form \kən-'fȯrm\ *vb* **1** : to make or
be like : AGREE **2** : to obey customs or
standards — con·form·able *adj*

con·for·mance \kən-'fȯr-məns\ *n* : CON-
FORMITY

con·for·ma·tion \ˌkän-fȯr-'mā-shən\ *n*
: arrangement and congruity of parts

con·for·mi·ty \kən-'fȯr-mət-ē\ *n, pl* -ties
1 : HARMONY, AGREEMENT **2** : COMPLI-
ANCE, OBEDIENCE

con·found \kən-'faùnd, kän-\ *vb* **1** : to
throw into disorder or confusion : DIS-
MAY **2** : to mix up : CONFUSE **syn** bewilder, puzzle, perplex, befog

con·fra·ter·ni·ty \ˌkän-frə-'tər-nət-ē\ *n*

: a society devoted to a religious or
charitable cause

con·frere \'kän-ˌfreər, 'kōⁿ-\ *n* : COL-
LEAGUE, COMRADE

con·front \kən-'frənt\ *vb* **1** : to face esp.
in challenge : OPPOSE **2** : to cause to
face or meet — con·fron·ta·tion \ˌkän-
frən-'tā-shən\ *n*

Con·fu·cian·ism \kən-'fyü-shən-ˌiz-əm\
n : a religion growing out of the teachings of the Chinese philosopher Con-
fucius — Con·fu·cian *n or adj*

con·fuse \kən-'fyüz\ *vb* con·fused; con-
fus·ing **1** : to make mentally unclear
or uncertain; *also* : to disturb the
composure of **2** : to mix up : JUMBLE
syn muddle, befuddle, addle, fluster
— con·fus·ed·ly \-'fyü-zəd-lē\ *adv*

con·fu·sion \-'fyü-zhən\ *n* **1** : DISORDER,
JUMBLE **2** : turmoil or uncertainty of
mind

con·fute \kən-'fyüt\ *vb* con·fut·ed; con-
fut·ing : to overwhelm by argument
: REFUTE — con·fu·ta·tion \ˌkän-fyü-
'tā-shən\ *n*

cong *abbr* congress; congressional

con·ga \'käŋ-gə\ *n* : a Cuban dance of
African origin performed by a group
usu. in single file

con·geal \kən-'jēl\ *vb* **1** : FREEZE **2** : to
make or become hard or thick

con·ge·ner \'kän-jə-nər\ *n* : one related
to another; *esp* : one of the same taxo-
nomic genus as another plant or animal — con·ge·ner·ic \ˌkän-jə-'ner-ik\
adj

con·ge·nial \kən-'jē-nyəl\ *adj* **1** : KIN-
DRED, SYMPATHETIC **2** : suited to one's
taste or nature : AGREEABLE — con·ge-
ni·al·i·ty \-ˌjē-nē-'al-ət-ē\ *n* — con·ge-
nial·ly \-'jē-nyə-lē\ *adv*

con·gen·i·tal \kən-'jen-ə-tᵊl\ *adj* : existing at or dating from birth but usu. not
hereditary **syn** inborn, innate, natural

con·ger eel \ˌkän-gər-\ *n* : a large edible
marine eel

con·ge·ries \'kän-jə-ˌ(ˌ)rēz\ *n, pl*
congeries *same*\ : AGGREGATION, COL-
LECTION

con·gest \kən-'jest\ *vb* **1** : to cause excessive fullness of the blood vessels of
(as a lung) **2** : to obstruct by over-
crowding — con·ges·tion \-'jes-chən\ *n*
— con·ges·tive \-'jes-tiv\ *adj*

¹con·glom·er·ate \kən-'gläm-(ə-)rət\ *adj*
[L *conglomerare* to roll together, fr.
com- together + *glomerare* to wind
into a ball, fr. *glomer-, glomus* ball]
: made up of parts from various
sources

²con·glom·er·ate \-ə-ˌrāt\ *vb* -at·ed; -at-
ing : to form into a ball or mass —
con·glom·er·a·tion \-ˌgläm-ə-'rā-shən\
n

³con·glom·er·ate \-(ə-)rət\ *n* **1** : a mass
formed of fragments from various
sources; *esp* : a rock composed of
fragments varying from pebbles to
boulders held together by a cementing
material **2** : a widely diversified corporation

con·grat·u·late \kən-'grach-ə-ˌlāt\ *vb* **-lat·ed; -lat·ing** : to express sympathetic pleasure to on account of success or good fortune : FELICITATE — **con·grat·u·la·tion** \-ˌgrach-ə-'lā-shən\ *n* — **con·grat·u·la·to·ry** \-'grach-ə-lə-ˌtōr-ē\ *adj*

con·gre·gate \'käŋ-gri-ˌgāt\ *vb* **-gat·ed; -gat·ing** [ME *congregaten,* fr. L *congregare,* fr. *com-* together + *greg-, grex* flock] : ASSEMBLE

con·gre·ga·tion \ˌkäŋ-gri-'gā-shən\ *n* **1** : an assembly of persons met esp. for worship; *also* : a group that habitually so meets **2** : a company or order of religious persons under a common rule **3** : the act or an instance of congregating

con·gre·ga·tion·al \-sh(ə-)nəl\ *adj* **1** : of or relating to a congregation **2** *cap* : observing the faith and practice of certain Protestant churches which recognize the independence of each congregation in church matters — **con·gre·ga·tion·al·ism** \-ˌiz-əm\ *n, often cap* — **con·gre·ga·tion·al·ist** \-əst\ *n, often cap*

con·gress \'käŋ-grəs\ *n* **1** : an assembly esp. of delegates for discussion and usu. action on some question **2** : the body of senators and representatives constituting a nation's legislature — **con·gres·sio·nal** \kən-'gresh-(ə-)nəl\ *adj*

con·gress·man \'käŋ-grəs-mən\ *n* : a member of a congress

con·gress·wom·an \-ˌwùm-ən\ *n* : a female member of a congress

con·gru·ence \kən-'grü-əns, 'käŋ-grə-wəns\ *n* : the quality of according or coinciding : CONGRUITY — **con·gru·ent** \kən-'grü-ənt, 'käŋ-grə-wənt\ *adj*

con·gru·en·cy \-ən-sē, -wən-\ *n, pl* **-cies** : CONGRUENCE

con·gru·ity \kən-'grü-ət-ē, kän-\ *n, pl* **-ities** : correspondence between things — **con·gru·ous** \'käŋ-grə-wəs\ *adj*

con·ic \'kän-ik\ *adj* **1** : of or relating to a cone **2** : CONICAL

con·i·cal \'kän-i-kəl\ *adj* : resembling a cone esp. in shape

co·ni·fer \'kän-ə-fər, 'kōn-\ *n* : any of an order of shrubs or trees (as the pines) that usu. are evergreen and bear cones — **co·nif·er·ous** \kō-'nif-(ə-)rəs\ *adj*

conj *abbr* conjunction

con·jec·ture \kən-'jek-chər\ *n* : GUESS, SURMISE — **con·jec·tur·al** \-chə-rəl\ *adj* — **conjecture** *vb*

con·join \kən-'jȯin\ *vb* : to join together — **con·joint** \-'jȯint\ *adj*

con·ju·gal \'kän-ji-gəl, kən-'jü-\ *adj* : of or relating to marriage : MATRIMONIAL

¹**con·ju·gate** \'kän-ji-gət, -jə-ˌgāt\ *adj* **1** : united esp. in pairs : COUPLED **2** : of kindred origin and meaning ⟨*sing* and *song* are ~⟩

²**con·ju·gate** \-jə-ˌgāt\ *vb* **-gat·ed; -gat·ing**

1 : INFLECT ⟨~ a verb⟩ **2** : to join together : COUPLE

con·ju·ga·tion \ˌkän-jə-'gā-shən\ *n* **1** : a schematic arrangement of the inflectional forms of a verb **2** : the act of conjugating : the state of being conjugated

con·junct \kən-'jəŋkt, kän-\ *adj* : JOINED, UNITED

con·junc·tion \kən-'jəŋk-shən\ *n* **1** : UNION, COMBINATION **2** : occurrence at the same time **3** : a word that joins together sentences, clauses, phrases, or words

con·junc·ti·va \ˌkän-ˌjəŋk-'tī-və\ *n, pl* **-vas** *or* **-vae** \-(ˌ)vē\ : the mucous membrane lining the inner surface of the eyelids and continuing over the forepart of the eyeball

con·junc·tive \kən-'jəŋk-tiv\ *adj* **1** : CONNECTIVE **2** : CONJUNCT **3** : being or functioning like a conjunction

con·junc·ti·vi·tis \kən-ˌjəŋk-ti-'vīt-əs\ *n* : inflammation of the conjunctiva

con·junc·ture \kən-'jəŋk-chər\ *n* **1** : CONJUNCTION, UNION **2** : a combination of circumstances or events esp. producing a crisis

con·jure \'kän-jər, 'kən-* for 1, 2*; kən-'jùr *for 3*\ *vb* **con·jured; con·jur·ing** \'känj-(ə-)riŋ, 'kənj-; kən-'jù(ə)r-iŋ\ **1** : to implore earnestly or solemnly **2** : to practice magic; *esp* : to summon (as a devil) by sorcery **3** : to practice sleight of hand — **con·ju·ra·tion** \ˌkän-jù-'rā-shən, ˌkən-\ *n* — **con·jur·er** *or* **con·ju·ror** \'kän-jər-ər, 'kən-\ *n*

conk \'käŋk\ *vb* : BREAK DOWN; *esp* : STALL ⟨the motor ~ed out⟩

Conn *abbr* Connecticut

con·nect \kə-'nekt\ *vb* **1** : JOIN, LINK **2** : to associate in one's mind — **con·nec·tor** *n*

con·nec·tion \kə-'nek-shən\ *n* **1** : JUNCTION, UNION **2** : logical relationship : COHERENCE; *esp* : relation of a word to other words in a sentence **3** : family relationship **4** : BOND, LINK **5** : a person related by blood or marriage **6** : relationship in social affairs or in business **7** : an association of persons; *esp* : a religious denomination

¹**con·nec·tive** \kə-'nek-tiv\ *adj* : connecting or functioning in connecting — **con·nec·tiv·i·ty** \ˌkä-ˌnek-'tiv-ət-ē\ *n*

²**connective** : a word (as a conjunction) that connects words or word groups

con·nip·tion \kə-'nip-shən\ *n* : a fit of rage, hysteria, or alarm

con·nive \kə-'nīv\ *vb* **con·nived; con·niv·ing** [F or L; F *conniver,* fr. L *conivēre* to close the eyes, connive] **1** : to pretend ignorance of something one ought to oppose as wrong **2** : to cooperate secretly : give secret aid — **con·niv·ance** *n*

con·nois·seur \ˌkän-ə-'sər\ *n* : a critical judge in matters of art or taste

con·no·ta·tion \ˌkän-ə-'tā-shən\ *n* : a meaning in addition to or apart from the thing explicitly named or described by a word

con·no·ta·tive \'kän-ə-ˌtāt-iv, kə-'nōt-ət-\ *adj* **1** : connoting or tending to connote **2** : relating to connotation

con·note \kə-'nōt\ *vb* **con·not·ed; con·not·ing** : to suggest or mean along with or in addition to the explicit meaning

con·nu·bi·al \kə-'n(y)ü-bē-əl\ *adj* : of or relating to marriage : CONJUGAL

con·quer \'käŋ-kər\ *vb* **con·quered; con·quer·ing** -k(ə-)riŋ\ **1** : to gain by force of arms : WIN **2** : to get the better of : OVERCOME **syn** defeat, subjugate, subdue, overthrow, vanquish — **con·quer·or** \-kər-ər\ *n*

con·quest \'kän-ˌkwest, 'käŋ-\ *n* **1** : an act of conquering : VICTORY **2** : something conquered

con·quis·ta·dor \kȯn-'kēs-tə-ˌdȯr, kän-'k(w)is-\ *n, pl* **con·quis·ta·do·res** \-ˌkēs-tə-'dȯr-ēz, -ˌk(w)is-\ *or* **con·quis·ta·dors** : CONQUEROR; *esp* : a leader in the Spanish conquest of America and esp. of Mexico and Peru in the 16th century

cons *abbr* consonant

con·san·guin·i·ty \ˌkän-ˌsan-'gwin-ət-ē, -ˌsaŋ-\ *n, pl* **-ties** : blood relationship — **con·san·guin·e·ous** \-'gwin-ē-əs\ *adj*

con·science \'kän-chəns\ *n* : consciousness of the moral right and wrong of one's own acts or motives — **con·science·less** *adj*

con·sci·en·tious \ˌkän-chē-'en-chəs\ *adj* : guided by one's own sense of right and wrong **syn** scrupulous, honorable, honest, upright, just — **con·sci·en·tious·ly** *adv*

conscientious objector *n* : one who refuses to serve in the armed forces or to bear arms on moral or religious grounds

con·scious \'kän-chəs\ *adj* **1** : AWARE **2** : known or felt by one's inner self **3** : mentally awake or alert : not asleep or unconscious **4** : INTENTIONAL — **con·scious·ly** *adv* — **con·scious·ness** *n*

con·script \kən-'skript\ *vb* : to enroll by compulsion for military or naval service — **con·script** \'kän-ˌskript\ *n* — **con·scrip·tion** \kən-'skrip-shən\ *n*

con·se·crate \'kän-sə-ˌkrāt\ *vb* **-crat·ed; -crat·ing** **1** : to induct (as a bishop) into an office with a religious rite **2** : to make or declare sacred (~ a church) **3** : to devote solemnly to a purpose — **con·se·cra·tion** \ˌkän-sə-'krā-shən\ *n*

con·sec·u·tive \kən-'sek-(y)ət-iv\ *adj* : following in regular order : SUCCESSIVE — **con·sec·u·tive·ly** *adv*

con·sen·su·al \kən-'sench-(ə-)wəl, -'sen-shəl\ *adj* : involving or based on mutual consent

con·sen·sus \kən-'sen-səs\ *n* **1** : agreement in opinion, testimony, or belief **2** : collective opinion

¹con·sent \kən-'sent\ *vb* : to give assent or approval

²consent *n* : approval or acceptance of something done or proposed by another

con·se·quence \'kän-sə-ˌkwens\ *n* **1** : RESULT **2** : IMPORTANCE **syn** effect, outcome, aftermath, upshot

con·se·quent \-kwənt, -ˌkwent\ *adj* : following as a result or effect

con·se·quen·tial \ˌkän-sə-'kwen-chəl\ *adj* **1** : having significant consequences **2** : showing self-importance

con·se·quent·ly \'kän-sə-ˌkwent-lē, -kwənt-\ *adv* : as a result : ACCORDINGLY

con·ser·van·cy \kən-'sər-vən-sē\ *n, pl* **-cies** : an organization or area designated to conserve and protect natural resources

con·ser·va·tion \ˌkän-sər-'vā-shən\ *n* : PRESERVATION; *esp* : planned management of natural resources

con·ser·va·tion·ist \-sh(ə-)nəst\ *n* : a person who advocates conservation esp. of natural resources

con·ser·va·tism \kən-'sər-və-ˌtiz-əm\ *n* : disposition to keep to established ways : opposition to change

¹con·ser·va·tive \kən-'sər-vət-iv\ *adj* **1** : PRESERVATIVE **2** : disposed to maintain existing views, conditions, or institutions **3** : MODERATE, CAUTIOUS — **con·ser·va·tive·ly** *adv*

²conservative *n* : a person who is conservative esp. in politics

con·ser·va·tor \kən-'sər-vət-ər, 'kän-sər-ˌvāt-\ *n* **1** : PROTECTOR, GUARDIAN **2** : one named by a court to protect the interests of an incompetent (as a child)

con·ser·va·to·ry \kən-'sər-və-ˌtōr-ē\ *n, pl* **-ries** **1** : GREENHOUSE **2** : a place of instruction in one of the fine arts (as music)

¹con·serve \kən-'sərv\ *vb* **con·served; con·serv·ing** : to keep from losing or wasting : PRESERVE

²con·serve \'kän-ˌsərv\ *n* **1** : CONFECTION; *esp* : a candied fruit **2** : PRESERVE; *esp* : one prepared from a mixture of fruits

con·sid·er \kən-'sid-ər\ *vb* **-ered; -er·ing** \-(ə-)riŋ\ [ME *consideren,* fr. MF *considerer,* fr. L *considerare,* lit., to observe the stars, fr. *sider-, sidus* star] **1** : THINK, PONDER **2** : HEED, REGARD **3** : JUDGE, BELIEVE — **con·sid·ered** *adj*

con·sid·er·able \-'sid-ər-(ə-)bəl, -'sid-rə-bəl\ *adj* **1** : IMPORTANT **2** : large in extent, amount, or degree — **con·sid·er·ably** \-blē\ *adv*

con·sid·er·ate \kən-'sid-(ə-)rət\ *adj* : observant of the rights and feelings of others **syn** thoughtful, attentive

con·sid·er·a·tion \kən-ˌsid-ə-'rā-shən\ *n* **1** : careful thought : DELIBERATION **2** : a matter taken into account **3** : thoughtful attention **4** : JUDGMENT, OPINION **5** : RECOMPENSE

con·sid·er·ing \-(ə-)riŋ\ *prep* : in view of : taking into account

con·sign \kən-'sīn\ *vb* **1** : ENTRUST, COM-

MIT **2** : to deliver formally **3** : to send (goods) to an agent for sale — **con·sign·ee** \ˌkän-sə-ˈnē, -ˌsī-; kən-ˌsī-\ n — **con·sign·or** \ˈkän-sə-ˈnòr, -ˌsī-; kən-ˌsī-(i)n

con·sign·ment \kən-ˈsīn-mənt\ n : something consigned esp. in a single shipment

con·sist \kən-ˈsist\ vb **1** : to be inherent : LIE — used with in **2** : to be composed or made up

con·sis·tence \kən-ˈsis-təns\ n : CONSISTENCY

con·sis·ten·cy \-tən-sē\ n, pl **-cies 1** : COHESIVENESS, FIRMNESS **2** : agreement or harmony in parts or of different things **3** : UNIFORMITY (⟨~ of behavior⟩ — **con·sis·tent** \-tənt\ adj — **con·sis·tent·ly** adv

con·sis·to·ry \kən-ˈsis-t(ə-)rē\ n, pl **-ries** : a solemn assembly (as of Roman Catholic cardinals)

consol abbr consolidated

¹con·sole \ˈkän-ˌsōl\ n **1** : the desk-like part of an organ at which the organist sits **2** : a panel or cabinet for the controls of an electronic or mechanical device **3** : a cabinet for a radio or television set resting directly on the floor **4** : a small storage cabinet between bucket seats in an automobile

²con·sole \kən-ˈsōl\ vb **con·soled; con·sol·ing** : to soothe the grief of : COMFORT, SOLACE — **con·so·la·tion** \ˌkän-sə-ˈlā-shən\ n — **con·so·la·to·ry** \kən-ˈsōl-ə-ˌtōr-ē, -ˈsäl-\ adj

con·sol·i·date \kən-ˈsäl-ə-ˌdāt\ vb **-dat·ed; -dat·ing 1** : to unite or become united into one whole : COMBINE **2** : to make firm or secure **3** : to form into a compact mass — **con·sol·i·da·tion** \-ˌsäl-ə-ˈdā-shən\ n

con·som·mé \ˌkän-sə-ˈmā\ n [F] : a clear soup made from well-seasoned meat broth

con·so·nance \ˈkän-s(ə-)nəns\ n **1** : AGREEMENT, HARMONY **2** : repetition of consonants esp. as an alternative to rhyme in verse

¹con·so·nant \-s(ə-)nənt\ adj : having consonance, harmony, or agreement syn consistent, compatible, congruous, congenial, sympathetic, agreeable

²consonant n **1** : a speech sound (as \p\, \g\, \n\, \l\, \s\, \r\) characterized by constriction or closure at one or more points in the breath channel **2** : a letter other than a, e, i, o, and u — **con·so·nan·tal** \ˌkän-sə-ˈnant-ᵊl\ adj

¹con·sort \ˈkän-ˌsòrt\ n **1** : a ship accompanying another **2** : SPOUSE, MATE

²con·sort \kən-ˈsòrt\ vb **1** : to keep company **2** : ACCORD, HARMONIZE

con·sor·tium \kən-ˈsòrt-ē-əm, -ˈsòr-sh(ē-)əm\ n, pl **-sor·tia** \-ˈsòrt-ē-ə, -ˈsòr-sh(ē-)ə\ [L, fellowship] : an international business or banking agreement or combination

con·spec·tus \kən-ˈspek-təs\ n **1** : a brief survey or summary **2** : OUTLINE, SYNOPSIS

con·spic·u·ous \kən-ˈspik-yə-wəs\ adj : attracting attention : PROMINENT, STRIKING syn noticeable, remarkable, outstanding — **con·spic·u·ous·ly** adv

con·spir·a·cy \kən-ˈspir-ə-sē\ n, pl **-cies** : an agreement among conspirators : PLOT

con·spire \kən-ˈspī(ə)r\ vb **conspired; con·spir·ing** : to plan secretly an unlawful act : PLOT — **con·spir·a·tor** \-ˈspir-ət-ər\ n

const abbr **1** constant **2** constitution; constitutional

con·sta·ble \ˈkän-stə-bəl, ˈkən-\ n [ME conestable, fr. OF, fr. LL comes stabuli, lit., officer of the stable] : a public officer responsible for keeping the peace

con·stab·u·lary \kən-ˈstab-yə-, ˌler-ē\ n, pl **-lar·ies 1** : the police of a particular district or country **2** : a police force organized like the military

con·stan·cy \ˈkän-stən-sē\ n, pl **-cies 1** : firmness of mind **2** : STABILITY

¹con·stant \-stənt\ adj **1** : STEADFAST, FAITHFUL **2** : FIXED, UNCHANGING **3** : continually recurring : REGULAR — **con·stant·ly** adv

²constant n : something unchanging

con·stel·la·tion \ˌkän-stə-ˈlā-shən\ n : any of 88 groups of stars forming patterns

con·ster·na·tion \ˌkän-stər-ˈnā-shən\ n : amazed dismay and confusion

con·sti·pa·tion \ˌkän-stə-ˈpā-shən\ n : abnormally difficult or infrequent bowel movements — **con·sti·pate** \ˈkän-stə-ˌpāt\ vb

con·stit·u·en·cy \kən-ˈstich-ə-wən-sē\ n, pl **-cies** : a body of constituents; also : an electoral district

¹con·stit·u·ent \-wənt\ n **1** : one entitled to vote for a representative for a district **2** : a component part

²constituent adj **1** : COMPONENT **2** : having power to create a government or frame or revise a constitution

con·sti·tute \ˈkän-stə-ˌt(y)üt\ vb **-tut·ed; -tut·ing 1** : to appoint to an office or duty **2** : SET UP, ESTABLISH (⟨~ a law⟩ **3** : MAKE UP, COMPOSE

con·sti·tu·tion \ˌkän-stə-ˈt(y)ü-shən\ n **1** : an established law or custom **2** : the physical makeup of the individual **3** : the structure, composition, or makeup of something (⟨~ of the sun⟩ **4** : the basic law in a politically organized body; also : a document containing such law

¹con·sti·tu·tion·al \-sh(ə-)nəl\ adj **1** : of or relating to the constitution of body or mind **2** : of or relating to the constitution of a state or society — **con·sti·tu·tion·al·ly** \-ē\ adv

²constitutional n : an exercise (as a walk) taken for one's health

con·sti·tu·tion·al·i·ty \-ˌt(y)ü-shə-ˈnal-ət-ē\ n : the condition of being in accordance with the constitution of a state or society

con·sti·tu·tive \\'kän-stə-ˌt(y)üt-iv, kən-'stich-ət-iv\\ *adj* : CONSTITUENT, ESSENTIAL

constr *abbr* construction

con·strain \\kən-'strān\\ *vb* 1 : COMPEL, FORCE 2 : CONFINE 3 : RESTRAIN

con·straint \\-'strānt\\ *n* 1 : COMPULSION; *also* : RESTRAINT 2 : unnaturalness of manner produced by a repression of one's natural feelings

con·strict \\kən-'strikt\\ *vb* : to draw together : SQUEEZE — **con·stric·tion** \\-'strik-shən\\ *n* — **con·stric·tive** \\-'strik-tiv\\ *adj*

con·stric·tor \\kən-'strikt-ər\\ *n* : a snake that suffocates its prey by crushing in its coils

con·struct \\kən-'strəkt\\ *vb* : BUILD, MAKE — **con·struc·tor** \\-'strək-tər\\ *n*

con·struc·tion \\kən-'strək-shən\\ *n* 1 : INTERPRETATION 2 : the art, process, or manner of building; *also* : something built : STRUCTURE 3 : syntactical arrangement of words in a sentence — **con·struc·tive** \\-tiv\\ *adj*

con·struc·tion·ist \\-sh(ə-)nəst\\ *n* : one who construes a legal document (as the U.S. Constitution) in a specific way ⟨a strict ∼⟩

con·strue \\kən-'strü\\ *vb* **con·strued;** **con·stru·ing** 1 : to explain the mutual relations of words in a sentence; *also* : TRANSLATE 2 : EXPLAIN, INTERPRET — **con·stru·able** *adj*

con·sub·stan·ti·a·tion \\ˌkän-səb-ˌstan-chē-'ā-shən\\ *n* : the actual substantial presence and combination of the body of Christ with the eucharistic bread and wine

con·sul \\'kän-səl\\ *n* 1 : a chief magistrate of the Roman republic 2 : an official appointed by a government to reside in a foreign country to care for the commercial interests of that government's citizens — **con·sul·ar** \\-sə-lər\\ *adj* — **con·sul·ate** \\-lət\\ *n* — **con·sul·ship** *n*

con·sult \\kən-'səlt\\ *vb* 1 : to ask the advice or opinion of 2 : CONFER — **con·sul·tant** \\-ʲnt\\ *n* — **con·sul·ta·tion** \\ˌkän-səl-'tā-shən\\ *n*

con·sume \\kən-'süm\\ *vb* **con·sumed;** **con·sum·ing** 1 : DESTROY ⟨consumed by fire⟩ 2 : to spend wastefully 3 : to eat up : DEVOUR 4 : to absorb the attention of : ENGROSS — **con·sum·able** *adj* — **con·sum·er** *n*

con·sum·er·ism \\kən-'sü-mə-ˌriz-əm\\ *n* : the promotion of consumers' interests (as against false advertising)

¹**con·sum·mate** \\kən-'səm-ət\\ *adj* : COMPLETE, PERFECT syn finished, accomplished

²**con·sum·mate** \\'kän-sə-ˌmāt\\ *vb* **mat·ed; -mat·ing** : to make complete : FINISH, ACHIEVE — **con·sum·ma·tion** \\ˌkän-sə-'mā-shən\\ *n*

con·sump·tion \\kən-'səmp-shən\\ *n* 1 : progressive bodily wasting away;

also : TUBERCULOSIS 2 : the act of consuming or using up 3 : the use of economic goods

¹**con·sump·tive** \\-'səmp-tiv\\ *adj* 1 : tending to consume 2 : relating to or affected with consumption

²**consumptive** *n* : a person who has consumption

cont *abbr* 1 containing 2 contents 3 continent; continental 4 continued 5 control

¹**con·tact** \\'kän-ˌtakt\\ *n* 1 : a touching or meeting of bodies 2 : ASSOCIATION, RELATIONSHIP; *also* : CONNECTION, COMMUNICATION 3 : CONTACT LENS

²**contact** *vb* 1 : to come or bring into contact : TOUCH 2 : to get in communication with

contact lens *n* : a thin lens fitting over the cornea

con·ta·gion \\kən-'tā-jən\\ *n* 1 : the passing of disease by contact 2 : a contagious disease; *also* : its causative agent 3 : transmission of an influence on the mind or emotions

con·ta·gious \\-jəs\\ *adj* 1 : communicable by contact; *also* : relating to contagion or to contagious diseases 2 : exciting similar emotion or conduct in others

con·tain \\kən-'tān\\ *vb* 1 : RESTRAIN 2 : to have within : HOLD 3 : COMPRISE, INCLUDE — **con·tain·ment** *n*

con·tain·er \\kən-'tā-nər\\ *n* : RECEPTACLE: *esp* : one for shipment of goods

con·tain·er·ship \\-nər-ˌship\\ *n* : a ship esp. designed or equipped for carrying very large containers of cargo

con·tam·i·nant \\kən-'tam-ə-nənt\\ *n* : something that contaminates

con·tam·i·nate \\kən-'tam-ə-ˌnāt\\ *vb* **-nat·ed; -nat·ing** : to soil, stain, or infect by contact or association — **con·tam·i·na·tion** \\-ˌtam-ə-'nā-shən\\ *n*

contd *abbr* continued

con·temn \\kən-'tem\\ *vb* : to view or treat with contempt

con·tem·plate \\'känt-əm-ˌplāt\\ *vb* **-plat·ed; -plat·ing** [L *contemplari,* fr. *templum* space marked out for observation of auguries] 1 : to view or consider with continued attention 2 : INTEND — **con·tem·pla·tion** \\ˌkänt-əm-'plā-shən\\ *n* — **con·tem·pla·tive** \\kən-'tem-plət-iv; 'känt-əm-ˌplāt-\\ *adj*

con·tem·po·ra·ne·ous \\kən-ˌtem-pə-'rā-nē-əs\\ *adj* : CONTEMPORARY

con·tem·po·rary \\kən-'tem-pə-ˌrer-ē\\ *adj* 1 : occurring or existing at the same time 2 : marked by characteristics of the present period — **contemporary** *n*

con·tempt \\kən-'tempt\\ *n* 1 : the act of despising : the state of mind of one who despises : DISDAIN 2 : the state of being despised 3 : disobedience to or open disrespect of a court or legislature

con·tempt·ible \\kən-'temp-tə-bəl\\ *adj*

: deserving contempt : DESPICABLE — **con·tempt·ibly** \-blē\ adv

con·temp·tu·ous \-'temp-chə(-wə)s\ adj : feeling or expressing contempt — **con·temp·tu·ous·ly** adv

con·tend \kən-'tend\ vb 1 : to strive against rivals or difficulties; also : ARGUE, DEBATE 2 : MAINTAIN, ASSERT — **con·tend·er** n

¹**con·tent** \kən-'tent\ adj : SATISFIED

²**content** vb : SATISFY; esp : to limit (oneself) in requirements or actions

³**content** n : CONTENTMENT

⁴**con·tent** \'kän-,tent\ n 1 : something contained ⟨~s of a room⟩ ⟨~s of a bottle⟩ 2 : subject matter or topics treated (as in a book) 3 : MEANING, SIGNIFICANCE 4 : the amount of material contained

con·tent·ed \kən-'tent-əd\ adj : SATISFIED — **con·tent·ed·ly** adv — **con·tent·ed·ness** n

con·ten·tion \kən-'ten-chən\ n 1 : CONTEST, STRIFE 2 : an idea or point for which a person argues — **con·ten·tious** \-chəs\ adj

con·tent·ment \kən-'tent-mənt\ n : ease of mind : SATISFACTION

con·ter·mi·nous \kən-'tər-mə-nəs, kän-\ adj : having the same or a common boundary — **con·ter·mi·nous·ly** adv

¹**con·test** \kən-'test\ vb 1 : to engage in strife : FIGHT 2 : CHALLENGE, DISPUTE — **con·tes·tant** \-'tes-tənt\ n

²**con·test** \'kän-,test\ n : STRUGGLE, COMPETITION

con·text \'kän-,tekst\ n [ME, weaving together of words, fr. L contextus coherence, fr. contexere to weave together] : the part of a discourse surrounding a word or group of words that helps to explain the meaning of the word or word group; also : the circumstances surrounding an act or event

con·tig·u·ous \kən-'tig-yə-wəs\ adj : being in contact : TOUCHING; also : NEXT, ADJOINING — **con·ti·gu·i·ty** \,känt-ə-'gyü-ət-ē\ n

con·ti·nence \'känt-ʰn-əns\ n 1 : SELF-RESTRAINT; esp : voluntary refraining from sexual intercourse 2 : the ability to retain urine or feces voluntarily within the body — **con·ti·nent** \-ʰn-ənt\ adj

con·ti·nent \'känt-(ʰ)nənt\ n 1 : one of the great divisions of land on the globe 2 cap : the continent of Europe

¹**con·ti·nen·tal** \,känt-ʰn-'ent-ʰl\ adj 1 : of or relating to a continent; esp, often cap : of or relating to the continent of Europe 2 often cap : of or relating to the colonies later forming the U.S.

²**continental** n often cap : a soldier in the Continental army 2 : EUROPEAN

continental shelf n : a shallow submarine plain forming a border to a continent

continental slope n : a usu. steep slope

from a continental shelf to the ocean floor

con·tin·gen·cy \kən-'tin-jən-sē\ n, pl -cies : a chance or possible event

¹**con·tin·gent** \-jənt\ adj 1 : liable but not certain to happen : POSSIBLE 2 : happening by chance : not planned 3 : dependent on something that may or may not occur 4 : CONDITIONAL syn accidental, casual, incidental, odd

²**contingent** n : a quota (as of troops) supplied from an area or group

con·tin·u·al \kən-'tin-yə-(wə)l\ adj 1 : CONTINUOUS, UNBROKEN 2 : steadily recurring — **con·tin·u·al·ly** \-ē\ adv

con·tin·u·ance \-yə-wəns\ n 1 : unbroken succession : a continuing in a state or course of action : DURATION 3 : adjournment of legal proceedings

con·tin·u·a·tion \kən-,tin-yə-'wā-shən\ n 1 : extension or prolongation of a state or activity 2 : resumption after an interruption; also : something that carries on after a pause or break

con·tin·ue \kən-'tin-yü\ vb -tin·ued; -tin·u·ing 1 : PERSEVERE 2 : ENDURE, LAST 3 : to remain in a place or condition : ABIDE, STAY 4 : to resume (a story) after an intermission 5 : EXTEND; also : to persist in 6 : to allow to remain in 7 : to keep (a legal case) on the calendar or undecided

con·ti·nu·i·ty \,känt-ʰn-'(y)ü-ət-ē\ n, pl -ities 1 : the condition of being continuous 2 : something that has or provides continuity

con·tin·u·ous \kən-'tin-yə-wəs\ adj : continuing without interruption : UNBROKEN — **con·tin·u·ous·ly** adv

con·tin·u·um \-yə-wəm\ n, pl -ua \-yə-wə\ also -uums : something that is the same throughout or consists of a series of variations or of a sequence of things in regular order

con·tort \kən-'tórt\ vb : to twist out of shape — **con·tor·tion** \-'tór-shən\ n

con·tor·tion·ist \-'tór-sh(ə-)nəst\ n : an acrobat able to twist the body into unusual postures

con·tour \'kän-,túr\ n [F, fr. It contorno fr. contornare to round off, sketch in outline, fr. L com- together + tornare to turn in a lathe, fr. tornus lathe] 1 : OUTLINE 2 : SHAPE, FORM — often used in pl. ⟨the ~s of a statue⟩

contr abbr contract; contraction

con·tra·band \'kän-trə-,band\ n : goods legally prohibited in trade; also : smuggled goods

con·tra·cep·tion \,kän-trə-'sep-shən\ n : intentional prevention of conception and pregnancy — **con·tra·cep·tive** \-'sep-tive\ adj or n

¹**con·tract** \'kän-,trakt\ n 1 : a binding agreement : COVENANT 2 : an undertaking to win a specified number of tricks in contract bridge — **con·trac·tu·al** \kən-'trak-chə-(wə)l\ adj — **con·trac·tu·al·ly** \-ē\ adv

²**con·tract** \kən-'trakt, 1 usu 'kän-,trakt\ vb 1 : to become affected with ⟨~ a

disease) **2** : to establish or undertake by contract **3** : SHRINK, LESSEN; *esp* : to draw together esp. so as to shorten (~ a muscle) **4** : to shorten (a word) by omitting letters or sounds in the middle — **con·trac·tion** \kən-ˈtrak-shən\ *n* — **con·trac·tor** \ˈkän-ˌtrak-tər, kən-ˈtrak-\ *n*

con·trac·tile \kən-ˈtrak-tᵊl\ *adj* : able to contract — **con·trac·til·i·ty** \ˌkän-ˌtrak-ˈtil-ət-ē\ *n*

con·tra·dict \ˌkän-trə-ˈdikt\ *vb* : to state the contrary of : deny the truth of — **con·tra·dic·tion** \-ˈdik-shən\ *n* — **con·tra·dic·to·ry** \-ˈdik-t(ə-)rē\ *adj*

con·tra·dis·tinc·tion \ˌkän-trə-dis-ˈtiŋk-shən\ *n* : distinction by contrast

con·trail \ˈkän-ˌtrāl\ *n* : streaks of condensed water vapor created in the air by an airplane or rocket at high altitudes

con·tral·to \kən-ˈtral-tō\ *n, pl* **-tos** : the lowest female voice; *also* : a singer having such a voice

con·trap·tion \kən-ˈtrap-shən\ *n* : CONTRIVANCE, DEVICE

con·tra·pun·tal \ˌkän-trə-ˈpənt-ᵊl\ *adj* : of or relating to counterpoint

con·tra·ri·ety \ˌkän-trə-ˈrī-ət-ē\ *n, pl* **-eties** : the state of being contrary : DISAGREEMENT, INCONSISTENCY

con·trari·wise \ˈkän-ˌtrer-ē-ˌwīz, kən-ˈtrer-\ *adv* **1** : on the contrary **2** : VICE VERSA

con·trary \ˈkän-ˌtrer-ē; **4** *often* kən-ˈtre(ə)r-ē\ *adj* **1** : opposite in nature or position **2** : COUNTER, OPPOSED **3** : UNFAVORABLE **4** : unwilling to accept control or advice — **con·trari·ly** \-ˌtrer-ə-lē, -ˈtrer-\ *adv* — **con·trary** \ˈkän-ˌtrer-ē, *adv like adj* \ *n or adv*

¹**con·trast** \kən-ˈtrast\ *vb* [F *contraster*, fr. MF, to oppose, resist, fr. (assumed) VL *contrastare*, fr. L *contra-against + stare* to stand] **1** : to show differences when compared **2** : to compare in such a way as to show differences

²**con·trast** \ˈkän-ˌtrast\ *n* **1** : diversity of adjacent parts in color, emotion, tone, or brightness (the ~ of a photograph) **2** : unlikeness as shown when things are compared : DIFFERENCE

con·tra·vene \ˌkän-trə-ˈvēn\ *vb* **-vened; -ven·ing 1** : to go or act contrary to (~ a law) **2** : CONTRADICT

con·tre·temps \ˈkän-trə-ˌtäⁿ, kōⁿ-trə-täⁿ\ *n, pl* **con·tre·temps** \-ˌtäⁿ(z)\ : an inopportune embarrassing occurrence

contrib *abbr* contribution; contributor

con·trib·ute \kən-ˈtrib-yət\ *vb* **-ut·ed; -ut·ing** : to give along with others (as to a fund) : supply or furnish a share to : HELP, ASSIST — **con·tri·bu·tion** \ˌkän-trə-ˈbyü-shən\ *n* — **con·trib·u·tor** \kən-ˈtrib-yət-ər\ *n* — **con·trib·u·to·ry** \-yə-ˌtōr-ē\ *adj*

con·trite \ˈkän-ˌtrīt, kən-ˈtrīt\ *adj* : PENITENT, REPENTANT — **con·tri·tion** \kən-ˈtrish-ən\ *n*

con·triv·ance \kən-ˈtrī-vəns\ *n* **1** : a mechanical device : APPLIANCE **2** : SCHEME, PLAN

con·trive \kən-ˈtrīv\ *vb* **con·trived; con·triv·ing 1** : PLAN, DEVISE **2** : FRAME, MAKE **3** : to bring about with difficulty — **con·triv·er** *n*

¹**con·trol** \kən-ˈtrōl\ *vb* **con·trolled; con·trol·ling 1** : to exercise restraining or directing influence over : REGULATE **2** : DOMINATE, RULE

²**control** *n* **1** : power to direct or regulate **2** : RESERVE, RESTRAINT **3** : a device for regulating a mechanism

con·trol·ler \kən-ˈtrō-lər, ˈkän-ˌtrō-lər\ *n* **1** : COMPTROLLER **2** : one that controls

con·tro·ver·sy \ˈkän-trə-ˌvər-sē\ *n, pl* **-sies** : a clash of opposing views : DISPUTE — **con·tro·ver·sial** \ˌkän-trə-ˈvər-shəl, -sē-əl\ *adj*

con·tro·vert \ˈkän-trə-ˌvərt, ˌkän-trə-ˈvərt\ *vb* : DENY, CONTRADICT — **con·tro·vert·ible** *adj*

con·tu·ma·cious \ˌkän-t(y)ə-ˈmā-shəs\ *adj* : stubbornly resisting or disobeying authority syn rebellious, insubordinate, seditious — **con·tu·ma·cy** \kən-ˈt(y)ü-mə-sē, ˈkän-t(y)ə-\ *n* — **con·tu·ma·cious·ly** *adv*

con·tu·me·ly \kən-ˈt(y)ü-mə-lē, ˈkän-t(y)ə-ˌmē-lē\ *n, pl* **-lies** : contemptuous treatment : INSULT

con·tu·sion \kən-ˈt(y)ü-zhən\ *n* : BRUISE — **con·tuse** \-ˈt(y)üz\ *vb*

co·nun·drum \kə-ˈnən-drəm\ *n* : RIDDLE

con·ur·ba·tion \ˌkän-(ˌ)ər-ˈbā-shən\ *n* : a continuous network of urban communities

conv *abbr* **1** convention **2** convertible

con·va·lesce \ˌkän-və-ˈles\ *vb* **-lesced; -lesc·ing** : to recover health gradually — **con·va·les·cence** \-ˈles-ᵊns\ *n* — **con·va·les·cent** \-ᵊnt\ *adj or n*

con·vec·tion \kən-ˈvek-shən\ *n* : circulatory motion in a fluid due to warmer portions rising and cooler denser portions sinking; *also* : the transfer of heat by such motion — **con·vec·tion·al** \-ˈvek-sh(ə-)nəl\ *adj* — **con·vec·tive** \-ˈvek-tiv\ *adj*

convection oven *n* : an oven with a fan that circulates hot air uniformly and continuously around the food

con·vene \kən-ˈvēn\ *vb* **con·vened; con·ven·ing** : ASSEMBLE, MEET

con·ve·nience \kən-ˈvē-nyəns\ *n* **1** : SUITABLENESS **2** : a laborsaving device **3** : a suitable time **4** : personal comfort : EASE

con·ve·nient \-nyənt\ *adj* **1** : suited to one's comfort or ease **2** : placed near at hand — **con·ve·nient·ly** *adv*

con·vent \ˈkän-vənt, -ˌvent\ *n* [ME *covent*, fr. OF, fr. ML *conventus*, fr. L, assembly, fr. *convenire* come together] : a local community or house of a religious order esp. of nuns — **con·ven·tu·al** \kən-ˈven-chə-wəl, kän-\ *adj*

con·ven·ti·cle \kən-ˈvent-i-kəl\ *n* : MEET-

ING; *esp* : a secret meeting for worship

con·ven·tion \kən-'ven-chən\ *n* 1 : an agreement esp. between states on a matter of common concern 2 : MEETING, ASSEMBLY 3 : an assembly of delegates convened for some purpose 4 : generally accepted custom, practice, or belief

con·ven·tion·al \-'vench-(ə-)nəl\ *adj* 1 : sanctioned by general custom 2 : COMMONPLACE, ORDINARY *syn* formal, ceremonial, solemn — **con·ven·tion·al·i·ty** \-ven-chə-'nal-ət-ē\ *n* — **con·ven·tion·al·ize** \-'vench-(ə-)nə-,līz\ *vb* — **con·ven·tion·al·ly** \-'vench-(ə-)nəl-ē\ *adv*

con·verge \kən-'vərj\ *vb* **con·verged; con·verg·ing** : to approach one common center or single point — **con·ver·gence** \kən-'vər-jəns\ *or* **con·ver·gen·cy** \-jən-sē\ *n* — **con·ver·gent** \-jənt\ *adj*

con·ver·sant \kən-'vərs-ᵊnt\ *adj* : having knowledge and experience

con·ver·sa·tion \,kän-vər-'sā-shən\ *n* : an informal talking together — **con·ver·sa·tion·al** \-sh(ə-)nəl\ *adj*

¹con·verse \'kän-,vərs\ *n* : CONVERSATION

²con·verse \kən-'vərs\ *vb* **con·versed; con·vers·ing** : to engage in conversation

³con·verse \'kän-,vərs\ *n* : a statement related to another statement by having its hypothesis and conclusion or its subject and predicate reversed or interchanged

⁴con·verse \kən-'vərs, 'kän-,vərs\ *adj* : reversed in order or relation — **con·verse·ly** *adv*

con·ver·sion \kən-'vər-zhən\ *n* 1 : a change in nature or form 2 : an experience associated with a decisive adoption of religion

¹con·vert \kən-'vərt\ *vb* 1 : to turn from one belief or party to another 2 : TRANSFORM, CHANGE 3 : MISAPPROPRIATE 4 : EXCHANGE — **con·vert·er** *or* **con·ver·tor** \-ər\ *n* — **con·vert·ible** *adj*

²con·vert \'kän-,vərt\ *n* : one who has undergone religious conversion

con·vert·ible \kən-'vərt-ə-bəl\ *n* : an automobile with a top that may be lowered or removed

con·vex \kän-'veks, 'kän-,veks\ *adj* : curved or rounded like the exterior of a sphere or circle — **con·vex·i·ty** \kən-'vek-sət-ē, kän-\ *n*

con·vey \kən-'vā\ *vb* 1 : CARRY, TRANSPORT 2 : TRANSMIT, TRANSFER — **con·vey·er** *or* **con·vey·or** \-ər\ *n*

con·vey·ance \-'vā-əns\ *n* 1 : the act of conveying 2 : a legal paper transferring ownership of property 3 : VEHICLE

¹con·vict \kən-'vikt\ *vb* : to prove or find guilty

²con·vict \'kän-,vikt\ *n* : a person serving a prison sentence

con·vic·tion \kən-'vik-shən\ *n* 1 : the

act of convicting esp. in a court 2 : the state of being convinced : strong belief

con·vince \kən-'vins\ *vb* **con·vinced; con·vinc·ing** : to bring by demonstration or argument to a sure belief — **con·vinc·ing** *adj* — **con·vinc·ing·ly** *adv*

con·viv·ial \kən-'viv-yəl, -'viv-ē-əl\ *adj* [LL *convivialis*, fr. L *convivium* banquet, fr. *com-* together + *vivere* to live] : enjoying companionship and the pleasures of feasting and drinking : JOVIAL, FESTIVE — **con·viv·i·al·i·ty** \-,viv-ē-'al-ət-ē\ *n* — **con·viv·ial·ly** \-'viv-yə-lē, -'viv-ē-ə-lē\ *adv*

con·vo·ca·tion \,kän-və-'kā-shən\ *n* 1 : a ceremonial assembly (as of clergymen) 2 : the act of convoking

con·voke \kən-'vōk\ *vb* **con·voked; con·vok·ing** : to call together to a meeting

con·vo·lut·ed \'kän-və-,lüt-əd\ *adj* 1 : folded in curved or tortuous windings 2 : INVOLVED, INTRICATE

con·vo·lu·tion \,kän-və-'lü-shən\ *n* : a tortuous or sinuous structure; *esp* : one of the ridges of the brain

¹con·voy \'kän-,vói, kən-'vói\ *vb* : to accompany for protection

²con·voy \'kän-,vói\ *n* 1 : one that convoys; *esp* : a protective escort for ships, persons, or goods 2 : the act of convoying 3 : a group of moving vehicles

con·vulse \kən-'vəls\ *vb* **con·vulsed; con·vuls·ing** : to agitate violently

con·vul·sion \kən-'vəl-shən\ *n* 1 : an abnormal and violent involuntary contraction or series of contractions of muscle 2 : a violent disturbance — **con·vul·sive** \-'vəl-siv\ *adj* — **con·vul·sive·ly** *adv*

cony *var of* CONEY

coo \'kü\ *n* : a soft low sound made by doves or pigeons; *also* : a sound like this — **coo** *vb*

¹cook \'kuk\ *n* : one who prepares food for eating

²cook *vb* 1 : to prepare food for eating 2 : to subject to heat or fire — **cook·er** *n* — **cook·ware** \-,waər\ *n*

cook·book \-,buk\ *n* : a book of cooking directions and recipes

cook·ery \'kuk-(ə-)rē\ *n, pl* **-er·ies** : the art or practice of cooking

cook·ie *or* **cooky** \'kuk-ē\ *n, pl* **cook·ies** : a small sweet flat cake

cook·out \'kuk-,aut\ *n* : an outing at which a meal is cooked and served in the open

¹cool \'kül\ *adj* 1 : moderately cold 2 : not excited : CALM 3 : not ardent 4 : IMPUDENT 5 : protecting from heat 6 *slang* : very good 7 : employing understatement in style *syn* unflappable, composed, collected, unruffled, nonchalant — **cool·ly** \'kül-(l)ē\ *adv* — **cool·ness** *n*

²cool *vb* : to make or become cool

³cool *n* 1 : a cool time or place 2 : INDIFFERENCE; *also* : SELF-ASSURANCE, COMPOSURE (kept his ~)

cool·ant \'kü-lənt\ *n* : a usu. fluid cooling agent

cool·er \'kü-lər\ *n* **1** : a container for keeping food or drink cool **2** : JAIL, PRISON **3** : a tall iced drink

coo·lie \'kü-lē\ *n* [Hindi *kulī*] : an unskilled laborer usu. in or from the Far East

coon \'kün\ *n* : RACCOON

coon·hound \-,haùnd\ *n* : a sporting dog trained to hunt raccoons

coon·skin \-,skin\ *n* : the pelt of a raccoon; *also* : something (as a cap) made of this

¹coop \'küp, 'kùp\ *n* : a small enclosure or building usu. for poultry

²coop *vb* : to confine in or as if in a coop

co-op \'kō-,äp\ *n* : COOPERATIVE

coop·er \'kü-pər, 'kùp-ər\ *n* : one who makes or repairs barrels or casks — **cooper** *vb* — **coop·er·age** \'kü-p(ə-)rij, 'kùp-(ə-)\ *n*

co·op·er·ate \kō-'äp-ə-,rāt\ *vb* : to act jointly with another or others — **co·op·er·a·tion** \-,äp-ə-'rā-shən\ *n* — **co·op·er·a·tor** \-'äp-ə-,rāt-ər\ *n*

¹co·op·er·a·tive \kō-'äp-(ə-)rət-iv, -'äp-ə-,rāt-\ *adj* **1** : willing to work with others **2** : of or relating to an association formed to enable its members to buy or sell to better advantage by eliminating middlemen's profits

²cooperative *n* : a cooperative association

co-opt \kō-'äpt\ *vb* **1** : to choose or elect as a colleague **2** : ABSORB, ASSIMILATE; *also* : TAKE OVER

¹co·or·di·nate \kō-'ord-(ə-)nət\ *adj* **1** : equal in rank or order **2** : of equal rank in a compound sentence (~ clause) **3** : joining words or word groups of the same rank

²coordinate *n* **1** : one of a set of numbers used in specifying the location of a point on a surface or in space **2** *pl* : articles (as of clothing) designed to be used together and to attain their effect through pleasing contrast

³co·or·di·nate \kō-'ord-²n-,āt\ *vb* **-nat·ed; -nat·ing 1** : to make or become coordinate **2** : to work or act together harmoniously — **co·or·di·na·tion** \-,ord-²n-'ā-shən\ *n* — **co·or·di·na·tor** \-'ord-²n-,āt-ər\ *n*

coot \'küt\ *n* **1** : a dark-colored ducklike bird related to the rails **2** : any of several No. American sea ducks **3** : a harmless simple person

coo·tie \'küt-ē\ *n* : a body louse

cop \'käp\ *n* : POLICEMAN

co·part·ner \'kō-'pärt-nər\ *n* : PARTNER

¹cope \'kōp\ *n* : a long cloaklike ecclesiastical vestment

²cope *vb* **coped; cop·ing** : to struggle to overcome problems or difficulties

copi·er \'käp-ē-ər\ *n* : one that copies; *esp* : a machine for making copies

co·pi·lot \'kō-,pī-lət\ *n* : an assistant pilot of an aircraft or spacecraft

cop·ing \'kō-pin\ *n* : the top layer of a wall

co·pi·ous \'kō-pē-əs\ *adj* : LAVISH, ABUNDANT — **co·pi·ous·ly** *adv* — **co·pi·ous·ness** *n*

cop-out \'käp-,aùt\ *n* : an excuse for copping out; *also* : an act of copping out

cop out \(')käp-'aùt\ *vb* : to back out (as of an unwanted responsibility)

cop·per \'käp-ər\ *n* **1** : a malleable reddish metallic chemical element that is one of the best conductors of heat and electricity **2** : a coin or token made of copper — **cop·pery** *adj*

cop·per·head \'käp-ər-,hed\ *n* : a largely coppery brown venomous snake esp. of the eastern and central U.S.

cop·pice \'käp-əs\ *n* : THICKET

co·pra \'kō-prə\ *n* : dried coconut meat yielding coconut oil

copse \'käps\ *n* : THICKET

cop·ter \'käp-tər\ *n* : HELICOPTER

cop·u·la \'käp-yə-lə\ *n* : LINKING VERB — **cop·u·la·tive** \-,lāt-iv\ *adj*

cop·u·late \'käp-yə-,lāt\ *vb* **-lat·ed; -lat·ing** : to engage in sexual intercourse — **cop·u·la·tion** \,käp-yə-'lā-shən\ *n* — **cop·u·la·to·ry** \'käp-yə-lə-,tōr-ē\ *adj*

¹copy \'käp-ē\ *n, pl* **cop·ies 1** : an imitation or reproduction of an original work **2** : material to be set in type **syn** duplicate, reproduction, facsimile, replica

²copy *vb* **cop·ied; copy·ing 1** : to make a copy of **2** : IMITATE — **copy·ist** *n*

copy·book \'käp-ē-,bùk\ *n* : a book containing copies esp. of penmanship for learners to imitate

copy·boy \-,bói\ *n* : one who carries copy and runs errands (as in a newspaper office)

copy·cat \-,kat\ *n* : a slavish imitator

copy·desk \-,desk\ *n* : the desk at which newspaper copy is edited

copy editor *n* : one who edits newspaper copy and writes headlines; *also* : one who reads and corrects manuscript copy in a publishing house

copy·read·er \-,rēd-ər\ *n* : COPY EDITOR

¹copy·right \-,rīt\ *n* : the sole right to reproduce, publish, and sell a literary or artistic work

²copyright *vb* : to secure a copyright on

copy·writ·er \'käp-ē-,rīt-ər\ *n* : a writer of advertising copy

co·quet *or* **co·quette** \kō-'ket\ *vb* **co·quet·ted; co·quet·ting** : FLIRT — **co·quet·ry** \'kō-kə-trē, kō-'ke-trē\ *n*

co·quette \kō-'ket\ *n* [F, fem. of *coquet*, dim. of *coq* cock] : FLIRT — **co·quett·ish** *adj*

cor *abbr* corner

Cor *abbr* Corinthians

cor·a·cle \'kór-ə-kəl\ *n* [W *corwgl*] : a boat made of hoops covered with horsehide or canvas

cor·al \'kór-əl\ *n* **1** : a stony or horny material that forms the skeleton of colonies of tiny sea polyps and includes a red form used in jewelry; *also* : a coral-forming polyp or polyp colony **2** : a deep pink color — **coral** adj

coral snake n : any of several venomous chiefly tropical New World snakes brilliantly banded in red, black, and yellow or white

cor·bel \'kȯr-bəl\ n : a bracket-shaped architectural member that projects from a wall and supports a weight

¹**cord** \'kȯrd\ n **1** : a usu. heavy string consisting of several strands woven or twisted together **2** : a long slender anatomical structure (as a tendon or nerve) **3** : a small flexible insulated electrical cable used to connect an appliance with a receptacle **4** : a cubic measure used esp. for firewood and equal to a stack 4×4×8 feet (about 3.6 cubic meters) **5** : a rib or ridge on cloth

²**cord** vb **1** : to tie or furnish with a cord **2** : to pile (wood) in cords

cord·age \'kȯrd-ij\ n : ROPES, CORDS; esp : ropes in the rigging of a ship

¹**cor·dial** \'kȯr-jəl\ n **1** : a stimulating medicine or drink **2** : LIQUEUR

²**cordial** adj [ME, fr. ML cordialis, fr. L cord-, cor heart] : warmly receptive or welcoming : HEARTFELT, HEARTY — **cor·di·al·i·ty** \ˌkȯr-jē-'al-ət-ē, ˌkȯr-'jal-; ˌkȯrd-'yal-\ n — **cor·dial·ly** \'kȯr-jə-lē\ adv

cor·dil·le·ra \ˌkȯrd-ᵊl-'(y)er-ə\ n [Sp] : a group of mountain ranges — **cor·dil·le·ran** adj

cord·less \'kȯrd-ləs\ adj : having no cord; esp : powered by a battery ⟨∼ tools⟩

cor·do·ba \'kȯrd-ə-bə, -ə-və\ n — see MONEY table

cor·don \'kȯrd-ᵊn\ n **1** : an ornamental cord or ribbon **2** : an encircling line composed of individual units — **cordon** vb

cor·do·van \'kȯrd-ə-vən\ n : a soft fine-grained leather

cor·du·roy \'kȯrd-ə-ˌrȯi\ n, pl **-roys** : a heavy ribbed fabric; also, pl : trousers of this material

cord·wain·er \'kȯrd-ˌwā-nər\ n : SHOEMAKER

¹**core** \'kȯr\ n **1** : the central usu. inedible part of some fruits (as the apple); also : an inmost part of something **2** : GIST, ESSENCE

²**core** vb cored; cor·ing : to take out the core of — **cor·er** n

CORE \'kȯr\ abbr Congress of Racial Equality

co·re·spon·dent \ˌkō-ri-'spän-dənt\ n : a person named as guilty of adultery with the defendant in a divorce suit

co·ri·an·der \'kȯr-ē-ˌan-dər\ n : an herb related to the carrot; also : its aromatic dried fruit used as a flavoring

Cor·in·thi·ans \kə-'rin-thē-ənz\ n — see BIBLE table

¹**cork** \'kȯrk\ n **1** : the tough elastic bark of a European oak (**cork oak**) used esp. for stoppers and insulation; also : a stopper of this **2** : a tissue of a

woody plant making up most of the bark — **corky** adj

²**cork** vb : to furnish with or stop up with cork or a cork

cork·screw \'kȯrk-ˌskrü\ n : a device for drawing corks from bottles

corm \'kȯrm\ n : a solid bulblike underground part of a stem (as of the crocus or gladiolus)

cor·mo·rant \'kȯrm-(ə-)rənt, 'kȯr-məˌrant\ n [ME cormeraunt, fr. MF cormorant, fr. OF cormareng, fr. corp raven + marenc of the sea, fr. L marinus] : a dark seabird used in the Orient to catch fish

¹**corn** \'kȯrn\ n **1** : the seeds of a cereal grass and esp. of the chief cereal crop of a region (as wheat in Britain and Indian corn in the U.S.); also : a cereal grass **2** : sweet corn served as a vegetable

²**corn** vb : to salt (as beef) in brine and preservatives

³**corn** n : a local hardening and thickening of skin (as on a toe)

corn bread n : bread made with cornmeal

corn·cob \-ˌkäb\ n : the woody core on which the kernels of Indian corn are arranged

corn·crib \-ˌkrib\ n : a crib for storing ears of Indian corn

cor·nea \'kȯr-nē-ə\ n : the transparent part of the coat of the eyeball covering the iris and the pupil — **cor·ne·al** adj

corn earworm n : a moth whose larva is esp. destructive to Indian corn

¹**cor·ner** \'kȯ-nər\ n [ME, fr. OF cornere, fr. corne horn, corner, fr. L cornu horn, point] **1** : the point or angle formed by the meeting of lines, edges, or sides **2** : the place where two streets come together **3** : a quiet secluded place **4** : a position from which retreat or escape is impossible **5** : control of enough of the available supply (as of a commodity) to permit manipulation of the price

²**cor·ner** vb **cor·nered; cor·ner·ing** \'kȯrn-(ə-)riŋ\ **1** : to drive into a corner **2** : to get a corner on ⟨∼ the wheat market⟩ **3** : to turn a corner

cor·ner·stone \'kȯr-nər-ˌstōn\ n **1** : a stone forming part of a corner in a wall; esp : such a stone laid with special ceremonies **2** : something of basic importance

cor·net \kȯr-'net\ n : a brass band instrument resembling the trumpet

corn flour n, Brit : CORNSTARCH

corn·flow·er \'kȯrn-ˌflau̇(-ə)r\ n : BACHELOR'S BUTTON

cor·nice \'kȯr-nəs\ n : the horizontal projecting part crowning the wall of a building

corn·meal \'kȯrn-ˌmēl, -ˌmēl\ n : meal ground from corn

corn·row \'kȯrn-ˌrō\ vb : to braid (sections of hair) flat to the scalp in rows — **cornrow** n

corn·stalk \\'kȯrn-ˌstȯk\ *n* : a stalk of Indian corn

corn·starch \-ˌstärch\ *n* : a starch made from corn and used in cookery as a thickening agent

corn syrup *n* : a syrup obtained by partial hydrolysis of cornstarch

cor·nu·co·pia \ˌkȯr-n(y)ə-ˈkō-pē-ə\ *n* [LL, fr. L *cornu copiae* horn of plenty] : a horn-shaped container filled with fruits and grain emblematic of abundance

corny \'kȯr-nē\ *adj* **corn·i·er; -est** : tiresomely simple or sentimental

co·rol·la \kə-ˈräl-ə, -ˈrōl-\ *n* : the petals of a flower

cor·ol·lary \'kȯr-ə-ˌler-ē\ *n, pl* **-lar·ies** 1 : a deduction from a proposition already proved true 2 : CONSEQUENCE, RESULT

co·ro·na \kə-ˈrō-nə\ *n* 1 : a colored ring surrounding the sun or moon; *esp* : a shining ring around the sun seen during eclipses 2 : a faint glow adjacent to the surface of a conductor at high voltage — **co·ro·nal** \'kȯr-ən-ᵊl, kə-ˈrōn-ᵊl\ *adj*

co·ro·nal \'kȯr-ən-ᵊl\ *n* : a circlet for the head

¹**cor·o·nary** \'kȯr-ə-ˌner-ē\ *adj* : of or relating to the heart or its blood vessels

²**coronary** *n, pl* **-nar·ies** 1 : a coronary blood vessel 2 : CORONARY THROMBOSIS

coronary thrombosis *n* : the blocking by a thrombus of one of the arteries supplying the heart tissues

cor·o·na·tion \ˌkȯr-ə-ˈnā-shən\ *n* : the act or ceremony of crowning a monarch

cor·o·ner \'kȯr-ə-nər\ *n* : a public official whose chief duty is to investigate the causes of deaths possibly not due to natural causes

cor·o·net \ˌkȯr-ə-ˈnet\ *n* 1 : a small crown indicating rank lower than sovereignty 2 : an ornamental band worn around the temples

corp *abbr* 1 corporal 2 corporation

¹**cor·po·ral** \'kȯr-p(ə-)rəl\ *adj* : of or relating to the body (~ *punishment*)

²**corporal** *n* : a noncommissioned officer (as in the army) ranking next below a sergeant

cor·po·rate \'kȯr-p(ə-)rət\ *adj* 1 : INCORPORATED; *also* : belonging to an incorporated body 2 : combined into one body

cor·po·ra·tion \ˌkȯr-pə-ˈrā-shən\ *n* 1 : the municipal authorities of a town or city 2 : a legal creation authorized to act with the rights and liabilities of a person (a business ~)

cor·po·re·al \kȯr-ˈpōr-ē-əl\ *adj* 1 : PHYSICAL, MATERIAL 2 *archaic* : BODILY — **cor·po·re·al·i·ty** \(ˌ)kȯr-ˌpōr-ē-ˈal-ət-ē\ *n* — **cor·po·re·al·ly** \-ˈē-ə-lē\ *adv*

corps \'kȯr\ *n, pl* **corps** \'kȯrz\ [F, fr. L *corpus* body] 1 : an organized subdivision of a country's military forces 2 : a group acting under common direction

corpse \'kȯrps\ *n* : a dead body

corps·man \'kȯr(z)-mən\ *n* : an enlisted man trained to give first aid

cor·pu·lence \'kȯr-pyə-ləns\ *or* **cor·pu·len·cy** \-lən-sē\ *n* : excessive fatness — **cor·pu·lent** \-lənt\ *adj*

cor·pus \'kȯr-pəs\ *n, pl* **cor·po·ra** \-pə-rə\ [ME, fr. L] 1 : BODY; *esp* : CORPSE 2 : a body of writings or works

cor·pus·cle \'kȯr-(ˌ)pəs-əl\ *n* 1 : a minute particle 2 : a living cell (as in blood or cartilage) not aggregated into continuous tissues — **cor·pus·cu·lar** \kȯr-ˈpəs-kyə-lər\ *adj*

cor·pus de·lic·ti \ˌkȯr-pəs-di-ˈlik-ˌtī, -tē\ *n, pl* **corpora delicti** [NL, lit., body of the crime] 1 : the substantial fact establishing that a crime has been committed; *also* : the body of a victim of murder

corr *abbr* 1 correct; corrected; correction 2 correspondence; correspondent; corresponding

cor·ral \kə-ˈral\ *n* [Sp] : an enclosure for confining or capturing animals; *also* : an enclosure for defense — **corral** *vb*

¹**cor·rect** \kə-ˈrekt\ *vb* 1 : to make right 2 : REPROVE, CHASTISE — **cor·rect·able** \-ˈrek-tə-bəl\ *adj* — **cor·rec·tion** \-ˈrek-shən\ *n* — **cor·rec·tion·al** \-ˈrek-sh(ə-)nəl\ *adj* — **cor·rec·tive** \-ˈrek-tiv\ *adj*

²**correct** *adj* 1 : conforming to a conventional standard 2 : agreeing with fact or truth — **cor·rect·ly** \-ˈrek-(t)lē\ *adv* — **cor·rect·ness** \-ˈrek(t)-nəs\ *n*

cor·re·late \'kȯr-ə-ˌlāt\ *vb* **-lat·ed; -lat·ing** : to connect in a systematic way : establish the mutual relations of — **cor·re·late** \-lət, -ˌlāt\ *n* — **cor·re·la·tion** \ˌkȯr-ə-ˈlā-shən\ *n*

cor·rel·a·tive \kə-ˈrel-ət-iv\ *adj* 1 : reciprocally related 2 : regularly used together (as *either* and *or*) — **correlative** *n*

cor·re·spond \ˌkȯr-ə-ˈspänd\ *vb* 1 : to be in agreement : SUIT, MATCH 2 : to communicate by letter — **cor·re·spond·ing·ly** \-ˈspän-diŋ-lē\ *adv*

cor·re·spon·dence \-ˈspän-dəns\ *n* 1 : agreement between particular things 2 : communication by letters; *also* : the letters exchanged

¹**cor·re·spon·dent** \-ˈspän-dənt\ *adj* 1 : SIMILAR 2 : FITTING, CONFORMING

²**correspondent** *n* 1 : something that corresponds 2 : a person with whom one communicates by letter 3 : a person employed to contribute news regularly from a place

cor·ri·dor \'kȯr-əd-ər, -ə-ˌdȯr\ *n* 1 : a passageway into which compartments or rooms open (as in a hotel or school) 2 : a narrow strip of land esp. through foreign-held territory 3 : a densely populated strip of land including two or more major cities

cor·ri·gen·dum \ˌkȯr-ə-ˈjen-dəm\ *n, pl* **-da** \-də\ [L] : an error in a printed work discovered after printing and shown with its correction on a separate sheet

cor·ri·gi·ble \'kȯr-ə-jə-bəl\ *adj* : CORRECTABLE

cor·rob·o·rate \kə-'räb-ə-ˌrāt\ *vb* **-rated; -rat·ing** [L *corroborare*, fr. *robur* strength] : to support with evidence : CONFIRM — **cor·rob·o·ra·tion** \-ˌräb-ə-'rā-shən\ *n* — **cor·rob·o·ra·tive** \-'räb-ə-ˌrāt-iv, -'räb-(ə-)rət-\ *adj* — **cor·rob·o·ra·to·ry** \-'räb-(ə-)rə-ˌtȯr-ē\ *adj*

cor·rode \kə-'rōd\ *vb* **cor·rod·ed; cor·rod·ing** : to eat or be eaten away gradually (as by chemical action) — **cor·ro·sion** \-'rō-zhən\ *n* — **cor·ro·sive** \-'rō-siv\ *adj or n*

cor·ru·gate \'kȯr-ə-ˌgāt\ *vb* **-gat·ed; -gat·ing** : to form into wrinkles or ridges and grooves — **cor·ru·gat·ed** *adj* — **cor·ru·ga·tion** \ˌkȯr-ə-'gā-shən\ *n*

¹**cor·rupt** \kə-'rəpt\ *vb* **1** : to make evil : DEPRAVE; *esp* : BRIBE **2** : ROT, SPOIL — **cor·rupt·ible** *adj* — **cor·rup·tion** \-'rəp-shən\ *n*

²**corrupt** *adj* : DEPRAVED, DEBASED

cor·sage \kȯr-'säzh, -'säj\ *n* [F, bust, bodice, fr. OF, bust, fr. *cors* body, fr. L *corpus*] **1** : the waist or bodice of a dress **2** : a bouquet to be worn or carried

cor·sair \'kȯr-ˌsaər\ *n* : PIRATE

cor·set \'kȯr-sət\ *n* : a stiffened undergarment worn for support or to give shape to the waist and hips

cor·tege *also* **cor·tège** \kȯr-'tezh, 'kȯr-ˌtezh\ *n* [F] : PROCESSION; *esp* : a funeral procession

cor·tex \'kȯr-ˌteks\ *n, pl* **cor·ti·ces** \'kȯr-tə-ˌsēz\ *or* **cor·tex·es** : an outer or covering layer of an organism or one of its parts (the adrenal ∼) (∼ of a plant stem); *esp* : the outer layer of gray matter of the brain — **cor·ti·cal** \'kȯrt-i-kəl\ *adj*

cor·ti·sone \'kȯrt-ə-ˌsōn, -ˌzōn\ *n* : an adrenal hormone used in treating rheumatoid arthritis

co·run·dum \kə-'rən-dəm\ *n* : a very hard aluminum-containing mineral used as an abrasive or in some crystalline forms as a gem

cor·us·cate \'kȯr-ə-ˌskāt\ *vb* **-cat·ed; -cat·ing** : FLASH, SPARKLE — **cor·us·ca·tion** \ˌkȯr-ə-'skā-shən\ *n*

cor·vette \kȯr-'vet\ *n* **1** : a naval sailing ship smaller than a frigate **2** : an armed escort ship smaller than a destroyer

co·ry·za \kə-'rī-zə\ *n* : an inflammatory disorder of the upper respiratory tract; *esp* : COMMON COLD

COS *abbr* **1** cash on shipment **2** chief of staff

co·sig·na·to·ry \kō-'sig-nə-ˌtōr-ē\ *n* : a joint signer

co·sign·er \'kō-ˌsī-nər\ *n* : COSIGNATORY; *esp* : a joint signer of a promissory note

¹**cos·met·ic** \käz-'met-ik\ *n* : a cosmetic preparation

²**cosmetic** *adj* [Gk *kosmētikos* skilled in adornment, fr. *kosmein* to arrange, adorn, fr. *kosmos* order, ornament, universe] **1** : intended to beautify the hair or complexion **2** : SUPERFICIAL

cos·me·tol·o·gist \ˌkäz-mə-'täl-ə-jəst\ *n* : one who gives beauty treatments — **cos·me·tol·o·gy** \-jē\ *n*

cos·mic \'käz-mik\ *also* **cos·mi·cal** \-mi-kəl\ *adj* **1** : of or relating to the cosmos **2** : VAST, GRAND — **cos·mi·cal·ly** \-mi-k(ə-)lē\ *adv*

cosmic ray *n* : a stream of very penetrating atomic nuclei that enter the earth's atmosphere from outer space

cos·mog·o·ny \käz-'mäg-ə-nē\ *n, pl* **-nies** : the origin or creation of the world or universe

cos·mol·o·gy \käz-'mäl-ə-jē\ *n, pl* **-gies** : a branch of astronomy dealing with the origin and structure of the universe — **cos·mo·log·i·cal** \ˌkäz-mə-'läj-i-kəl\ *adj* — **cos·mol·o·gist** \käz-'mäl-ə-jəst\ *n*

cos·mo·naut \'käz-mə-ˌnȯt\ *n* : a Soviet astronaut

cos·mo·pol·i·tan \ˌkäz-mə-'päl-ət-ᵊn\ *adj* : belonging to all the world : not local syn universal, global, catholic — **cosmopolitan** *n*

cos·mos \'käz-məs, **1** *also* -ˌmōs, -ˌmäs\ *n* **1** : UNIVERSE **2** : a tall garden herb related to the daisies

co·spon·sor \'kō-ˌspän-sər, -'spän-\ *n* : a joint sponsor — **cosponsor** *vb*

cos·sack \'käs-ˌak, -ək\ *n* [Russ *kazak* & Ukrainian *kozak*, fr. Turk *kazak* free person] : a member of a group of frontiersmen of southern Russia organized as cavalry in the czarist army

¹**cost** \'kȯst\ *n* **1** : the amount paid or charged for something : PRICE **2** : the loss or penalty incurred in gaining something **3** *pl* : expenses incurred in a law suit

²**cost** *vb* **cost; cost·ing 1** : to require a specified amount in payment **2** : to cause to pay, suffer, or lose

co-star \'kō-ˌstär\ *n* : one of two leading players in a motion picture or play — **co-star** *vb*

cos·tive \'käs-tiv\ *adj* : affected with or causing constipation

cost·ly \'kȯst-lē\ *adj* **cost·li·er; -est** : of great cost or value : not cheap syn dear, valuable, expensive — **cost·li·ness** *n*

cos·tume \'käs-ˌt(y)üm\ *n* : CLOTHES, ATTIRE; *also* : a suit or dress characteristic of a period or country — **cos·tum·er** \'käs-ˌt(y)ü-mər\ *n* — **cos·tu·mi·er** \käs-'t(y)ü-mē-ər\ *n, chiefly Brit*

costume jewelry *n* : inexpensive jewelry

co·sy \'kō-zē\ *var of* COZY

¹**cot** \'kät\ *n* : a small house : COTTAGE

²**cot** *n* : a small often collapsible bed

cote \'kōt, 'kät\ *n* : a small shed or coop (as for sheep or doves)

co·te·rie \'kōt-ə-ˌrē, ˌkōt-ə-'rē\ *n* [F] : an intimate often exclusive group of persons with a common interest

co·ter·mi·nous \-mə-nəs\ *adj* : having the same scope or duration

co·til·lion \kō-'til-yən, kə-\ *n* 1 : a complicated formal dance with frequent changing of partners 2 : a formal ball

cot·tage \'kät-ij\ *n* : a small house — cot·tag·er *n*

cottage cheese *n* : a soft uncured cheese made from soured skim milk

cot·ter *or* cot·tar \'kät-ər\ *n* : a farm laborer occupying a cottage and often a small holding

cotter pin *n* : a metal strip bent into a pin whose ends can be spread apart after insertion through a hole or slot

cot·ton \'kät-ᵊn\ *n* [ME *coton*, fr. MF, fr. Ar *quṭn*] 1 : a soft fibrous usu. white substance composed of hairs attached to the seeds of a plant related to the mallow; *also* : this plant 2 : thread or cloth made of cotton — cot·tony *adj*

cot·ton·mouth \'kät-ᵊn-ˌmaùth\ *n* : WATER MOCCASIN

cot·ton·seed \-ˌsēd\ *n* : the seed of the cotton plant yielding a protein-rich meal and a fixed oil (cottonseed oil) used esp. in cooking

cot·ton·tail \-ˌtāl\ *n* : an American rabbit with a white-tufted tail

cot·ton·wood \-ˌwùd\ *n* : a poplar with cottony hair on its seed

cot·y·le·don \ˌkät-ᵊl-'ēd-ᵊn\ *n* : the first leaf or one of the first pair or whorl of leaves developed by a seed plant

¹couch \'kaùch\ *vb* 1 : to lie or place on a couch 2 : to phrase in a certain manner

²couch *n* : a piece of furniture (as a bed or sofa) that one can sit or lie on

couch·ant \'kaù-chənt\ *adj* : lying down with the head raised (coat of arms with lion ∼)

cou·gar \'kü-gər, -ˌgär\ *n, pl* cougars *also* cougar [F *couguar*, fr. NL *cuguacuarana*, modif. of Tupi (a Brazilian Indian language) *suasuarana*, lit., false deer, fr. *suasú* deer + *rana* false] : a large tawny wild American cat

cough \'kóf\ *vb* : to force air from the lungs with short sharp noises; *also* : to expel by coughing — cough *n*

could \kəd, (ˈ)kùd\ *past of* CAN — used as an auxiliary in the past or as a polite or less forceful alternative to *can* in the present

cou·lee \'kü-lē\ *n* 1 : a small stream 2 : a dry streambed 3 : GULLY

cou·lomb \'kü-ˌläm, -ˌlōm\ *n* : a unit of electric charge equal to the electricity transferred by a current of one ampere in one second

coun·cil \'kaùn-səl\ *n* 1 : ASSEMBLY, MEETING 2 : an official body of lawmakers ⟨a city ∼⟩ — coun·cil·lor *or*

coun·cil·or \-s(ə-)lər\ *n* — coun·cil·man \-səl-mən\ *n* — coun·cil·wom·an \-ˌwùm-ən\ *n*

¹coun·sel \'kaùn-səl\ *n* 1 : ADVICE 2 : a plan of action 3 : deliberation together 4 *pl* counsel : LAWYER

²counsel *vb* -seled *or* -selled; -sel·ing *or* -sel·ling \-s(ə-)liŋ\ 1 : ADVISE, RECOMMEND 2 : CONSULT

coun·sel·or *or* coun·sel·lor \'kaùn-s(ə-)lər\ *n* 1 : ADVISER 2 : LAWYER

¹count \'kaùnt\ *vb* [ME *counten*, fr. MF *compter*, fr. L *computare*, fr. *com-* with + *putare* to consider] 1 : to name or indicate one by one in order to find the total number 2 : to recite numbers in order 3 : CONSIDER, ACCOUNT 4 : RELY ⟨you can ∼ on him⟩ 5 : to be of value or account — count·able *adj*

²count *n* 1 : the act of counting; *also* : the total obtained by counting 2 : a particular charge in an indictment or legal declaration

³count *n* [MF *comte*, fr. LL *comes*, fr. L, companion, one of the imperial court, fr. *com-* with + *ire* to go] : a European nobleman whose rank corresponds to that of a British earl

count·down \'kaùnt-ˌdaùn\ *n* : a backward counting in fixed units (as seconds) to indicate the time remaining before an event (as the launching of a rocket) — count down \'daùn\ *vb*

¹coun·te·nance \'kaùnt-(ə-)nəns\ *n* : the human face esp. as an indicator of mood or character 2 : FAVOR, APPROVAL

²countenance *vb* -nanced; -nanc·ing : SANCTION, TOLERATE

¹coun·ter \'kaùnt-ər\ *n* 1 : a piece (as of metal or ivory) used in reckoning or in games 2 : a level surface over which business is transacted, food is served, or work is conducted

²coun·ter *vb* : to act in opposition to

³coun·ter *n* : a device for recording a number or amount

⁴coun·ter *adv* : in an opposite direction : CONTRARY

⁵coun·ter *n* 1 : OPPOSITE, CONTRARY 2 : an answering or offsetting force or blow

⁶coun·ter *adj* : CONTRARY, OPPOSITE

coun·ter·act \ˌkaùnt-ər-'akt\ *vb* : to lessen the force of : OFFSET — coun·ter·ac·tive \-'ak-tiv\ *adj*

coun·ter·at·tack \'kaùnt-ər-ə-ˌtak\ *n* : an attack made to oppose an enemy's attack — counterattack *vb*

¹coun·ter·bal·ance \'kaùnt-ər-ˌbal-əns\ *n* : a weight or influence that balances another

²counterbalance \ˌkaùnt-ər-'bal-əns\ *vb* : to oppose with equal weight or influence

coun·ter·claim \'kaùnt-ər-ˌklām\ *n* : an opposing claim esp. in law

coun·ter·clock·wise \ˌkaùnt-ər-'kläk-ˌwīz\ *adv* : in a direction opposite to that in which the hands of a clock rotate — **counterclockwise** *adj*

coun·ter·cul·ture \'kaùnt-ər-ˌkəl-chər\ *n* : a culture esp. of the young with values and mores that run counter to those of established society

coun·ter·es·pi·o·nage \ˌkaùnt-ər-'es-pē-ə-ˌnäzh, -nij\ *n* : activities intended to discover and defeat enemy espionage

¹coun·ter·feit \'kaùnt-ər-ˌfit\ *vb* **1** : to copy or imitate in order to deceive **2** : PRETEND, FEIGN — **coun·ter·feit·er** *n*

²counterfeit *adj* : SHAM, SPURIOUS; *also* : FORGED

³counterfeit *n* : something counterfeit : FORGERY **syn** fraud, sham, fake, imposture, deceit, deception

coun·ter·in·sur·gen·cy \ˌkaùnt-ər-in-'sər-jən-sē\ *n* : military activity designed to deal with insurgents

coun·ter·in·tel·li·gence \ˌkaùnt-ər-in-'tel-ə-jəns\ *n* : organized activities of an intelligence service designed to counter the activities of an enemy's intelligence service

coun·ter·man \'kaùnt-ər-ˌman, -mən\ *n* : one who tends a counter

coun·ter·mand \'kaùnt-ər-ˌmand\ *vb* : to withdraw (an order already given) by a contrary order

coun·ter·mea·sure \-ˌmezh-ər\ *n* : an action undertaken to counter another

coun·ter·of·fen·sive \-ə-ˌfen-siv\ *n* : a large-scale counterattack

coun·ter·pane \'kaùnt-ər-ˌpān\ *n* : BEDSPREAD

coun·ter·part \-ˌpärt\ *n* : a person or thing very closely like or corresponding to another person or thing

coun·ter·point \-ˌpòint\ *n* : music in which one melody is accompanied by one or more other melodies all woven into a harmonious whole

coun·ter·poise \-ˌpòiz\ *n* : COUNTERBALANCE

coun·ter·rev·o·lu·tion \ˌkaùnt-ə(r)-ˌrev-ə-'lü-shən\ *n* : a revolution opposed to a current or earlier one — **coun·ter·rev·o·lu·tion·ary** \-sha-ˌner-ē\ *adj or n*

coun·ter·sign \'kaùnt-ər-ˌsīn\ *n* **1** : a confirmatory signature added to a writing already signed by another person **2** : a secret signal that must be given by a person who wishes to pass a guard — **countersign** *vb*

coun·ter·sink \'kaùnt-ər-ˌsiŋk\ *vb* **-sunk** \-ˌsəŋk\ ; **-sink·ing 1** : to form a funnel-shaped enlargement at the outer end of a drilled hole **2** : to set the head of (as a screw) at or below the surface — **countersink** *n*

coun·ter·spy \-ˌspī\ *n* : a spy engaged in counterespionage

coun·ter·ten·or \-ˌten-ər\ *n* : a tenor with an unusually high range

coun·ter·vail \ˌkaùnt-ər-'vāl\ *vb* : COUNTERACT

coun·ter·weight \'kaùnt-ər-ˌwāt\ *n* : COUNTERBALANCE

count·ess \'kaùnt-əs\ *n* **1** : the wife or widow of a count or an earl **2** : a woman holding the rank of a count or an earl in her own right

count·ing·house \'kaùnt-iŋ-ˌhaùs\ *n* : a building or office for keeping books and conducting business

count·less \'kaùnt-ləs\ *adj* : INNUMERABLE

coun·tri·fied *also* **coun·try·fied** \'kən-tri-ˌfīd\ *adj* **1** : RURAL, RUSTIC **2** : UNSOPHISTICATED **3** : played or sung in the manner of country music

¹coun·try \'kən-trē\ *n, pl* **countries** [ME *contree*, fr. OF *contrée*, fr. ML *contrata*, fr. L *contra* against, on the opposite side] **1** : REGION, DISTRICT **2** : FATHERLAND **3** : a nation or its territory **4** : rural regions as opposed to towns and cities

²country *adj* **1** : RURAL **2** : of or relating to country music ⟨a ~ singer⟩

country and western *n* : COUNTRY MUSIC

country club *n* : a suburban club for social life and recreation; *esp* : one having a golf course

coun·try·dance \'kən-trē-ˌdans\ *n* : an English dance in which partners face each other esp. in rows

coun·try·man \'kən-trē-mən, *2 often* -ˌman\ *n* **1** : an inhabitant of a certain country **2** : COMPATRIOT **3** : one raised in the country : RUSTIC

country music *n* : music derived from or imitating the folk style of the southern U.S. or of the Western cowboy

coun·try·side \'kən-trē-ˌsīd\ *n* : a rural area or its people

coun·ty \'kaùnt-ē\ *n, pl* **counties 1** : the domain of a count **2** : a territorial division of a country or state for purposes of local government

coup \'kü\ *n, pl* **coups** \'küz\ [F, blow, stroke] **1** : a brilliant sudden stroke or stratagem **2** : COUP D'ÉTAT

coup de grace \ˌküd-ə-'gräs\ *n, pl* **coups de grace** \ˌküd-ə-\ [F *coup de grâce*, lit., stroke of mercy] : a deathblow or final decisive stroke or event

coup d'état \ˌküd-ə-'tä\ *n, pl* **coups d'état** \ˌküd-ə-'tä(z)\ [F, lit., stroke of state] : a sudden violent overthrow of a government by a small group

cou·pé *or* **coupe** \kü-'pā, *2 often* 'küp\ *n* [F *coupé*, fr. *couper* to cut] **1** : a closed carriage for two persons inside with an outside seat for the driver in front **2** *usu* **coupe** : a 2-door automobile with an enclosed body

¹cou·ple \'kəp-əl\ *vb* **cou·pled; cou·pling** \-(ə-)liŋ\ : to link together

²couple *n* **1** : two persons closely associated; *esp* : a man and a woman married or otherwise paired **2** : PAIR **3** : BOND, TIE **4** : an indefinite small number : FEW ⟨a ~ of days ago⟩

cou·plet \'kəp-lət\ *n* : two successive rhyming lines of verse

cou·pling \'kəp-liŋ *(usual for 2)*, -ə-liŋ\ *n* **1** : CONNECTION **2** : a device for connecting two parts or things

cou·pon \'k(y)ü-ˌpän\ *n* **1** : a statement attached to a bond showing interest due and designed to be cut off and presented for payment **2** : a certificate given to a purchaser of goods and redeemable in merchandise, cash, or services; *also* : a similar ticket or form surrendered for other purposes (a ration ~) **3** : a part of an advertisement to be cut off to use as an order blank or inquiry form or to obtain a discount on merchandise

cour·age \'kər-ij\ *n* : ability to conquer fear or depair : BRAVERY, VALOR — **cou·ra·geous** \kə-'rā-jəs\ *adj* — **cou·ra·geous·ly** *adv*

cou·ri·er \'kur-ē-ər, 'kər-ē-\ *n* : one who bears messages or information esp. for the diplomatic or military services

¹**course** \'kōrs\ *n* **1** : PROGRESS, PASSAGE; *also* : direction of progress **2** : the ground or path over which something moves **3** : method of procedure : CONDUCT, BEHAVIOR **4** : an ordered series of acts or proceedings : sequence of events **5** : a series of instruction periods dealing with a subject **6** : the series of studies leading to graduation from a school or college **7** : the part of a meal served at one time — **of course** : as might be expected

²**course** *vb* **coursed; cours·ing 1** : to hunt with dogs (~ a rabbit) **2** : to run or go speedily

cours·er \'kōr-sər\ *n* : a swift or spirited horse

¹**court** \'kōrt\ *n* **1** : the residence of a sovereign or similar dignitary **2** : a sovereign and his officials and advisers as a governing power **3** : an assembly of the retinue of a sovereign **4** : an open space enclosed by a building or buildings **5** : a space walled or marked off for playing a game (as in tennis or basketball) **6** : the place where justice is administered; *also* : a judicial body or a meeting of a judicial body **7** : HOMAGE, COURTSHIP

²**court** *vb* **1** : to try to gain the favor of **2** : WOO **3** : ATTRACT, TEMPT

cour·te·ous \'kərt-ē-əs\ *adj* : marked by respect for others : CIVIL, POLITE — **cour·te·ous·ly** *adv*

cour·te·san \'kōrt-ə-zən, 'kərt-\ *n* : PROSTITUTE

cour·te·sy \'kərt-ə-sē\ *n, pl* **-sies 1** : courteous behavior : POLITENESS **2** : a favor courteously performed

court·house \'kōrt-,haus\ *n* : a building in which courts of law are held or county offices are located

court·ier \'kōrt-ē-ər, 'kōrt-yər\ *n* : a person in attendance at a royal court

court·ly \'kōrt-lē\ *adj* **court·li·er; -est** : REFINED, ELEGANT, POLITE **syn** gallant, gracious — **court·li·ness** *n*

court–mar·tial \'kōrt-,mär-shəl\ *n, pl* **courts–martial** : a military or naval court for trial of offenses against military or naval law; *also* : a trial by this court — **court–martial** *vb*

court·room \-,rüm, -,rùm\ *n* : a room in which a court of law is held

court·ship \-,ship\ *n* : the act of courting : WOOING

court·yard \-,yärd\ *n* : an enclosure next to a building

cous·in \'kəz-ᵊn\ *n* [ME *cosin*, fr. OF, fr. L *consobrinus*, fr. *com-* with + *sobrinus* cousin on the mother's side, fr. *soror* sister] : a child of one's uncle or aunt

cou·ture \kü-'tür, -'tuer\ *n* [F] : the business of designing fashionable custom-made women's clothing; *also* : the designers and establishments engaged in this business

cou·tu·ri·er \kü-'tür-ē-ər, -ē-,ā\ *n* [F, dressmaker] : the owner of an establishment engaged in couture

cove \'kōv\ *n* **1** : a trough for lights at the upper part of a wall **2** : a small sheltered inlet or bay

co·ven \'kəv-ən\ *n* : an assembly or band of witches

cov·e·nant \'kəv-(ə-)nənt\ *n* : a formal binding agreement : COMPACT — **cov·e·nant** \'kəv-(ə-)nənt, -ə-,nant\ *vb*

¹**cov·er** \'kəv-ər\ *vb* **cov·ered; cov·er·ing** \'kəv-(ə-)riŋ\ **1** : to bring or hold within range of a firearm **2** : PROTECT, SHIELD **3** : HIDE, CONCEAL **4** : to place something over or upon **5** : INCLUDE, COMPRISE **6** : to have as one's field of activity (one salesman ~s the state) **7** : to buy (stocks) in order to have them for delivery on a previous short sale

²**cover** *n* **1** : something that protects or shelters **2** : LID, TOP **3** : CASE, BINDING **4** : TABLECLOTH **5** : a cloth used on a bed **6** : SCREEN, DISGUISE **7** : an envelope or wrapper for mail

cov·er·age \'kəv-(ə-)rij\ *n* **1** : the act or fact of covering **2** : the total group covered : SCOPE

cov·er·all \'kəv-ər-,ol\ *n* : a one-piece outer garment worn to protect one's clothes — usu. used in pl.

cover charge *n* : a charge made by a restaurant or nightclub in addition to the charge for food and drink

cover crop *n* : a crop planted to prevent soil erosion and to provide humus

cov·er·let \'kəv-ər-lət\ *n* : BEDSPREAD

¹**co·vert** \'kō-(,)vərt, 'kəv-ərt\ *adj* **1** : HIDDEN, SECRET **2** : SHELTERED — **co·vert·ly** *adv*

²**co·vert** \'kəv-ərt, 'kō-vərt\ *n* **1** : a secret or sheltered place; *esp* : a thicket sheltering game **2** : a feather covering the bases of the quills of the wings and tail of a bird **3** : a firm durable twilled cloth usu. of mixed-color yarns

cov·er–up \'kəv-ər-,əp\ *n* **1** : a device for masking or concealing **2** : a usu. concerted effort to keep an illegal or unethical act or situation from being made public

cov·et \'kəv-ət\ *vb* : to desire enviously (what belongs to another) — **cov·et·ous** *adj* — **cov·et·ous·ness** *n*

cov·ey \'kəv-ē\ *n, pl* **coveys** [ME, fr. MF

covee, fr. OF, fr. *cover* to sit on, brood over, fr. L *cubare* to lie] **1** : a bird with her brood of young **2** : a small flock (as of quail)

¹**cow** \'kaù\ *n* **1** : the mature female of cattle or of an animal (as the moose) of which the male is called *bull* **2** : any domestic bovine animal irrespective of sex or age

²**cow** *vb* : INTIMIDATE, DAUNT, OVERAWE

cow·ard \'kaù-(ə)rd\ *n* [ME, fr. OF *coart,* fr. *coe* tail, fr. L *cauda*] : one who lacks courage or shows shameful fear or timidity — **coward** *adj* — **cow·ard·ice** \-əs\ *n* — **cow·ard·ly** *adv or adj*

cow·bird \'kaù-₁bərd\ *n* : a small No. American bird that lays its eggs in the nests of other birds

cow·boy \-₁bòi\ *n* : one (as a mounted ranch hand) who tends cattle or horses

cow·er \'kaù-(ə)r\ *vb* : to shrink or crouch down from fear or cold : QUAIL

cow·girl \'kaù-₁gərl\ *n* : a girl or woman who tends cattle or horses

cow·hand \'kaù-₁hand\ *n* : COWBOY

cow·hide \-₁hīd\ *n* **1** : the hide of a cow; *also* : leather made from it **2** : a coarse whip of braided rawhide

cowl \'kaùl\ *n* **1** : a monk's hood **2** : the top part of the front of the body of an automobile to which the windshield is attached

cow·lick \'kaù-₁lik\ *n* : a turned-up tuft of hair that resists control

cowl·ing \'kaù-liŋ\ *n* : a usu. metal covering for the engine or another part of an airplane

cow·man \'kaù-mən, -₁man\ *n* : COWBOY; *also* : a cattle owner or rancher

co·work·er \'kō-₁wər-kər\ *n* : a fellow worker

cow·poke \'kaù-₁pōk\ *n* : COWBOY

cow pony *n* : a strong and agile horse trained for herding cattle

cow·pox \'kaù-₁päks\ *n* : a mild disease of the cow when communicated to man protects against smallpox

cow·punch·er \-₁pən-chər\ *n* : COWBOY

cow·slip \'kaù-₁slip\ *n* **1** : a yellow-flowered European primrose **2** : MARSH MARIGOLD

cox·comb \'käks-₁kōm\ *n* : a conceited foolish person : FOP

cox·swain \'käk-sən, -₁swän\ *n* : the steersman of a ship's boat or a racing shell

coy \'kòi\ *adj* [ME, quiet, shy, fr. MF *coi* calm, fr. L *quietus* quiet] : BASHFUL, SHY; *esp* : pretending shyness — **coy·ly** *adv* — **coy·ness** *n*

coy·ote \kī-₁ōt, kī-'ōt-ē\ *n, pl* **coyotes** *or* **coyote** : a mammal of No. America related to the domestic dog and the wolves

coy·pu \'kòi-pü\ *n* : NUTRIA 2

coz·en \'kəz-ᵊn\ *vb* [obs. It *cozzonare,* fr. It *cozzone* horse trader, fr. L *cocio* trader] : CHEAT, DEFRAUD — **coz·en·age** \-ij\ *n*

¹**co·zy** \'kō-zē\ *adj* **co·zi·er; -est** : SNUG,

COMFORTABLE — **co·zi·ly** \'kō-zə-lē\ *adv* — **co·zi·ness** \-zē-nəs\ *n*

²**cozy** *n, pl* **cozies** : a padded covering for a vessel (as a teapot) to keep the contents hot

cp *abbr* **1** compare **2** coupon

CP *abbr* **1** chemically pure **2** command post **3** communist party

CPA *abbr* certified public accountant

cpd *abbr* compound

CPI *abbr* consumer price index

Cpl *abbr* corporal

CPO *abbr* chief petty officer

CPOM *abbr* master chief petty officer

CPOS *abbr* senior chief petty officer

CPR *abbr* cardiopulmonary resuscitation

CPT *abbr* captain

CQ *abbr* charge of quarters

cr *abbr* credit; creditor

Cr *symbol* chromium

¹**crab** \'krab\ *n* : any of various crustaceans with a short broad shell and small abdomen

²**crab** *n* : an ill-natured person

crab apple *n* : a small often highly colored sour apple; *also* : a tree that produces crab apples

crab·bed \'krab-əd\ *adj* **1** : MOROSE, PEEVISH **2** : CRAMPED, IRREGULAR

crab·by \'krab-ē\ *adj* **crab·bi·er; -est** : CROSS, ILL-NATURED

crab·grass \'krab-₁gras\ *n* : a weedy grass with creeping or sprawling stems that root freely at the nodes

crab louse *n* : a louse infesting the pubic region in man

¹**crack** \'krak\ *vb* **1** : to break with a sharp sudden sound **2** : to break with or without completely separating into parts **3** : to fail in tone or become harsh (her voice ~ed) **4** : to subject (as a petroleum oil) to heat for breaking down into lighter products (as gasoline)

²**crack** *n* **1** : a sudden sharp noise **2** : a witty or sharp remark **3** : a narrow break or opening : FISSURE **4** : a sharp blow : ATTEMPT, TRY **6** : highly purified cocaine in the form of small chips used for smoking

³**crack** *adj* : extremely proficient

crack·down \'krak-₁daùn\ *n* : an act or instance of taking positive disciplinary action ⟨a ~ on gambling⟩ — **crack down** \'daùn\ *vb*

crack·er \'krak-ər\ *n* **1** : FIRECRACKER **2** : a dry thin crispy baked bread product made of flour and water

crack·er·jack \-₁jak\ *n* : something very excellent — **crackerjack** *adj*

crack·le \'krak-əl\ *vb* **crack·led; crack·ling** \-(ə-)liŋ\ **1** : to make small snapping noises **2** : to develop fine cracks in a surface — **crackle** *n* — **crack·ly** \-(ə-)lē\ *adj*

crack·pot \'krak-₁pät\ *n* : an eccentric person

crack–up \'krak-₁əp\ *n* : CRASH, WRECK; *also* : BREAKDOWN

¹**cra·dle** \'krād-ᵊl\ *n* **1** : a baby's bed or

cot **2** : INFANCY (from ~ to the grave) **3** : a place of origin **4** : a framework or support (as for a telephone receiver)

²**cradle** *vb* **cra·dled; cra·dling** \'krād-(ª-)lin\ **1** : to place in or as if in a cradle **2** : NURSE, REAR

cra·dle·song \'krād-ªl-,sȯn\ *n* : LULLABY

craft \'kraft\ *n* **1** : ART, SKILL; *also* : an occupation requiring special skill **2** : CUNNING, GUILE **3** *pl usu* **craft** : a boat esp. of small size; *also* : AIRCRAFT, SPACECRAFT

crafts·man \'krafts-mən\ *n* : a skilled artisan — **crafts·man·ship** *n*

crafty \'kraf-tē\ *adj* **craft·i·er; -est** : CUNNING, DECEITFUL, SUBTLE — **craft·i·ly** \'kraf-tə-lē\ *adv* — **craft·i·ness** \-tē-nəs\ *n*

crag \'krag\ *n* : a steep rugged cliff or rock — **crag·gy** \-ē\ *adj*

¹**cram** \'kram\ *vb* **crammed; cram·ming 1** : to pack in tight : JAM **2** : to eat greedily **3** : to study rapidly under pressure for an examination

¹**cramp** \'kramp\ *n* **1** : a sudden painful contraction of muscle : sharp abdominal pain — usu. used in pl.

²**cramp** *vb* **1** : to affect with a cramp or cramps **2** : to restrain from free action : HAMPER **3** : to turn (the front wheels) sharply to the side

cran·ber·ry \'kran-,ber-ē, -b(ə-)rē\ *n* : the red acid berry of any of several trailing plants related to the heaths; *also* : one of these plants

¹**crane** \'krān\ *n* **1** : any of a family of tall wading birds related to the rails; *also* : any of several herons **2** : a machine for lifting and carrying heavy objects

²**crane** *vb* **craned; cran·ing** : to stretch one's neck to see better

crane fly *n* : any of numerous longlegged slender two-winged flies that resemble large mosquitoes but do not bite

cranial nerve *n* : any of the nerves that arise in pairs from the lower surface of the brain and pass through openings in the skull to the periphery of the body

cra·ni·um \'krā-nē-əm\ *n, pl* **-ni·ums** or **-nia** \-nē-ə\ : SKULL; *esp* : the part enclosing the brain — **cra·ni·al** \-əl\ *adj*

¹**crank** \'kraŋk\ *n* **1** : a bent part of an axle or shaft or an arm at right angles to the end of a shaft by which circular motion is imparted to or received from it **2** : an eccentric person **3** : a bad-tempered person : GROUCH

²**crank** *vb* : to start or operate by turning a crank

crank·case \'kraŋk-,kās\ *n* : the housing of a crankshaft

crank out *vb* : to produce in a mechanical manner

crank·shaft \'kraŋk-,shaft\ *n* : a shaft turning or driven by a crank

cranky \'kraŋ-kē\ *adj* **crank·i·er; -est 1** : IRRITABLE **2** : operating uncertainly or imperfectly

cran·ny \'kran-ē\ *n, pl* **crannies** : CREVICE, CHINK

crape \'krāp\ *n* : CREPE; *esp* : black crepe used in mourning

craps \'kraps\ *n* : a gambling game played with two dice

crap·shoot·er \'krap-,shüt-ər\ *n* : a person who plays craps

¹**crash** \'krash\ *vb* **1** : to break noisily : SMASH **2** : to damage an airplane in landing **3** : to enter or attend without invitation or without paying (~ a party)

²**crash** *n* **1** : a loud noise (as of things smashing) **2** : an instance of crashing (a plane ~); *also* : COLLISION **3** : a sudden failure (as of a business)

³**crash** *adj* : marked by concerted effort over the shortest possible time

⁴**crash** *n* : coarse linen fabric used for towels and draperies

crash-land \'krash-,land\ *vb* : to land an aircraft or spacecraft under emergency conditions usu. with damage to the craft — **crash landing** *n*

crass \'kras\ *adj* : STUPID, GROSS — **crass·ly** *adv*

crate \'krāt\ *n* : a container often of wooden slats — **crate** *vb*

cra·ter \'krāt-ər\ *n* [L, mixing bowl, crater, fr. Gk *kratēr*, fr. *kerannynai* to mix] **1** : the depression around the opening of a volcano **2** : a depression formed by the impact of a meteorite or by the explosion of a bomb or shell

cra·vat \krə-'vat\ *n* : NECKTIE

crave \'krāv\ *vb* **craved; crav·ing 1** : to ask for earnestly : BEG **2** : to long for : DESIRE

cra·ven \'krā-vən\ *adj* : COWARDLY — **craven** *n*

crav·ing \'krā-viŋ\ *n* : an urgent or abnormal desire

craw·fish \'krȯ-,fish\ *n* **1** : CRAYFISH 1 **2** : SPINY LOBSTER

¹**crawl** \'krȯl\ *vb* **1** : to move slowly by drawing the body along the ground **2** : to advance feebly, cautiously, or slowly **3** : to be swarming with or feel as if swarming with creeping things (a place ~ing with ants) (her flesh ~ed)

²**crawl** *n* **1** : a very slow pace **2** : a prone speed swimming stroke

cray·fish \'krā-,fish\ *n* **1** : any of numerous freshwater crustaceans usu. much smaller than the related lobsters **2** : SPINY LOBSTER

cray·on \'krā-,än, -ən\ *n* : a stick of chalk or wax used for writing, drawing, or coloring; *also* : a drawing made with such material — **crayon** *vb*

¹**craze** \'krāz\ *vb* **crazed; craz·ing** [ME *crasen* to crush, craze] : to make or become insane

²**craze** *n* : FAD, MANIA

cra·zy \'krā-zē\ *adj* **cra·zi·er; -est 1** : mentally disordered : INSANE **2** : wildly impractical; *also* : ERRATIC — **cra·zi·ly** \'krā-zə-lē\ *adv* — **cra·zi·ness** \-zē-nəs\ *n*

CRC *abbr* Civil Rights Commission

creak \'krēk\ *vb* : to make a prolonged

squeaking or grating sound — **creak** n
— **creaky** adj

¹**cream** \'krēm\ n **1** : the yellowish fat-rich part of milk **2** : a thick smooth sauce, confection, or cosmetic **3** : the choicest part **4** : a pale yellow color — **creamy** adj

²**cream** vb **1** : to prepare with a cream sauce **2** : to beat or blend into creamy consistency **3** : to defeat decisively

cream cheese n : a cheese made from whole milk enriched with cream

cream·ery \'krēm-(ə-)rē\ n, pl **-er·ies** : an establishment where butter and cheese are made or milk and cream are prepared for sale

crease \'krēs\ n : a mark or line made by or as if by folding — **crease** vb

cre·ate \krē-'āt\ vb **cre·at·ed; cre·at·ing** : to bring into being : cause to exist : MAKE, PRODUCE — **cre·ative** \-'āt-iv\ adj — **cre·ativ·i·ty** \krē-(ˌ)ā-'tiv-ət-ē, ˌkrē-ə-\ n

cre·ation \krē-'ā-shən\ n **1** : the act of creating or producing ⟨∼ of the world⟩ **2** : something that is created **3** : all created things : WORLD

cre·ation·ism \krē-'ā-shə-ˌniz-əm\ n : a doctrine or theory holding that matter, the various forms of life, and the world were created by God out of nothing — **cre·ation·ist** \-shə-nəst\ n or adj

cre·ator \krē-'āt-ər\ n **1** : one that creates : MAKER, AUTHOR **2** cap : GOD

crea·ture \'krē-chər\ n : a lower animal; also : a human being

crèche \'kresh\ n [F, manger, crib] : a representation of the Nativity scene

cre·dence \'krēd-ᵊns\ n : BELIEF

cre·den·tial \kri-'den-chəl\ n : something that gives a basis for credit or confidence

cre·den·za \kri-'den-zə\ n [It, lit., belief, confidence] : a sideboard, buffet, or bookcase usu. without legs

cred·i·ble \'kred-ə-bəl\ adj : TRUSTWOR-THY, BELIEVABLE — **cred·i·bil·i·ty** \ˌkred-ə-'bil-ət-ē\ n

¹**cred·it** \'kred-ət\ vb **1** : BELIEVE **2** : to give credit to

²**credit** n [MF, fr. It credito, fr. L creditum something entrusted to another, loan, fr. credere to believe, entrust] **1** : the balance (as in a bank) in a person's favor **2** : time given for payment for goods sold on trust **3** : an accounting entry of payment received **4** : BE-LIEF, FAITH **5** : financial trustworthiness **6** : ESTEEM **7** : a source of honor or distinction **8** : a unit of academic work

cred·it·able \'kred-ət-ə-bəl\ adj : worthy of esteem or praise — **cred·it·ably** \-blē\ adv

credit card n : a card authorizing purchases on credit

cred·i·tor \'kred-ət-ər\ n : a person to whom money is owed

cre·do \'krēd-ō, 'krād-\ n, pl **credos** [ME, fr. L, I believe] : CREED

cred·u·lous \'krej-ə-ləs\ adj : inclined to believe esp. on slight evidence — **cre·du·li·ty** \kri-'d(y)ü-lət-ē\ n

Cree \'krē\ n, pl Cree or Crees : a member of an American Indian people of Manitoba and Saskatchewan

creed \'krēd\ n [ME crede, fr. OE crēda, fr. L credo I believe, first word of the Apostles' and Nicene Creeds] : a statement of the essential beliefs of a religious faith

creek \'krēk, 'krik\ n **1** chiefly Brit : a small inlet **2** : a stream smaller than a river and larger than a brook

Creek \'krēk\ n : a member of an American Indian people of Alabama, Georgia, and Florida

creel \'krēl\ n : a wicker basket esp. for carrying fish

creep \'krēp\ vb **crept** \'krept\; **creep·ing** **1** : CRAWL **2** : to grow over a surface like ivy **3** : to feel as though insects were crawling on the skin — **creep** n — **creep·er** n

creep·ing \'krē-piŋ\ adj : developing or advancing by imperceptible degrees

creepy \'krē-pē\ adj **creep·i·er; -est** : having or producing a nervous shivery fear

cre·mate \'krē-ˌmāt\ vb **cre·mat·ed; cre·mat·ing** : to reduce (a dead body) to ashes with fire — **cre·ma·tion** \kri-'mā-shən\ n

cre·ma·to·ry \'krē-mə-ˌtōr-ē, 'krem-ə-\ n, pl **-ries** : a furnace for cremating; also : a structure containing such a furnace

crème \'krem, 'krēm\ n, pl **crèmes** \'krem(z), 'krēmz\ [F, lit., cream] : a sweet liqueur

cren·el·at·ed or **cren·el·lat·ed** \'kren-ᵊl-ˌāt-əd\ adj : having battlements ⟨a ∼ tower⟩ — **cren·el·la·tion** \ˌkren-ᵊl-'ā-shən\ n

Cre·ole \'krē-ˌōl\ n : a descendant of early French or Spanish settlers of the U.S. Gulf states preserving their speech and culture; also : a person of mixed French or Spanish and Negro descent speaking a dialect of French or Spanish

cre·o·sote \'krē-ə-ˌsōt\ n : an oily liquid obtained by distillation of coal tar and used in preserving wood

crepe or **crêpe** \'krāp\ n : a light crinkled fabric of any of various fibers

crepe su·zette \ˌkrāp-sü-'zet\ n, pl **crepes suzette** \ˌkrāp(s)-sü-'zet\ or **crepe suzettes** \ˌkrāp-sü-'zets\ : a thin folded or rolled pancake in a hot orange-butter sauce that is sprinkled with a liqueur and set ablaze for serving

cre·pus·cu·lar \kri-'pəs-kyə-lər\ adj **1** : of, relating to, or resembling twilight **2** : active in the twilight ⟨∼ insects⟩

cre·scen·do \krə-'shen-dō\ adv or adj [It] : increasing in loudness — used as a direction in music — **crescendo** n

cres·cent \'kres-ᵊnt\ n [ME cressant, fr. MF creissant, fr. creistre to grow, increase, fr. L *crescere*] : the moon at any stage between new moon and first quarter and between last quarter and new moon; *also* : something shaped like the figure of the crescent moon with a convex and a concave edge — **cres·cen·tic** \kre-'sent-ik, krə-\ *adj*

cress \'kres\ *n* : any of several salad plants related to the mustards

¹**crest** \'krest\ *n* **1** : a tuft or process on the head of an animal (as a bird) **2** : a heraldic device **3** : an upper part, edge, or limit (the ~ of a hill) — **crest·ed** \'kres-təd\ *adj* — **crest·less** *adj*

²**crest** *vb* **1** : CROWN **2** : to reach the crest of **3** : to rise to a crest

crest·fall·en \'krest-ˌfȯ-lən\ *adj* : DISPIRITED, DEJECTED

Cre·ta·ceous \kri-'tā-shəs\ *adj* : of, relating to, or being the latest period of the Mesozoic era — **Cretaceous** *n*

cre·tin \'krēt-³n\ *n* [F *crétin*, fr. F dial. *cretin* Christian, human being, kind of idiot found in the Alps, fr. L *christianus* Christian] **1** : one affected with cretinism **2** : a stupid person

cre·tin·ism \-ˌiz-əm\ *n* : a usu. congenital abnormal condition characterized by physical stunting and mental deficiency

cre·tonne \'krē-ˌtän\ *n* : a strong unglazed cotton cloth for curtains and upholstery

cre·vasse \kri-'vas\ *n* : a deep fissure esp. in a glacier

crev·ice \'krev-əs\ *n* : a narrow fissure

¹**crew** \'krü\ *chiefly Brit past of* CROW

²**crew** \'krü\ *n* [ME *crue*, lit., reinforcement, fr. MF *creue* increase, fr. *creistre* to grow, fr. L *crescere*] **1** : a body of people trained to work together for certain purposes **2** : a group of people who operate a ship, train, aircraft, or spacecraft **3** : the rowers and coxswain of a racing shell; *also* : the sport of rowing engaged in by a crew — **crew·man** \-mən\ *n*

crew cut *n* : a very short bristly haircut

crew·el \'krü-əl\ *n* : slackly twisted worsted yarn used for embroidery — **crew·el·work** \-ˌwərk\ *n*

¹**crib** \'krib\ *n* **1** : a manger for feeding animals **2** : a small bedstead for a child **3** : a building or bin for storage (as of grain) **4** : a translation prepared to aid a student in preparing a lesson

²**crib** *vb* **cribbed; crib·bing 1** : to put in a crib **2** : STEAL, PLAGIARIZE — **crib·ber** *n*

crib·bage \'krib-ij\ *n* : a card game usu. played by two players and scored on a board (**cribbage board**)

crib death *n* : SUDDEN INFANT DEATH SYNDROME

crick \'krik\ *n* : a painful spasm of muscles (as of the neck)

¹**crick·et** \'krik-ət\ *n* : any of various leaping insects related to the grasshoppers and noted for the chirping noises of the male

²**cricket** *n* : a game played with a bat and ball by two teams on a field centering upon two wickets each defended by a batsman

cri·er \'krī(-ə)r\ *n* : one who calls out proclamations and announcements

crime \'krīm\ *n* : a serious offense against the public law

¹**crim·i·nal** \'krim-ən-³l\ *adj* **1** : involving or being a crime **2** : relating to crime or its punishment — **crim·i·nal·i·ty** \ˌkrim-ə-'nal-ət-ē\ *n* — **crim·i·nal·ly** \'krim-ən-³l-ē\ *adv*

²**criminal** *n* : one who has committed a crime

crim·i·nol·o·gy \ˌkrim-ə-'näl-ə-jē\ *n* : the scientific study of crime and criminals — **crim·i·nol·o·gist** \ˌkrim-ə-'näl-ə-jəst\ *n*

¹**crimp** \'krimp\ *vb* : to cause to become crinkled, wavy, or bent

²**crimp** *n* : something (as a curl in hair) produced by or as if by crimping

¹**crim·son** \'krim-zən\ *n* : a deep purplish red — **crimson** *adj*

²**crimson** *vb* : to make or become crimson

cringe \'krinj\ *vb* **cringed; cring·ing** : to shrink in fear : WINCE, COWER

crin·kle \'kriŋ-kəl\ *vb* **crin·kled; crin·kling** \-k(ə-)liŋ\ : to turn or wind in many short bends or curves; *also* : WRINKLE, RIPPLE — **crinkle** *n* — **crin·kly** \-k(ə-)lē\ *adj*

crin·o·line \'krin-³l-ən\ *n* **1** : an openweave cloth used for stiffening and lining **2** : a full stiff skirt or underskirt made of crinoline

¹**crip·ple** \'krip-əl\ *n* : a lame or disabled person

²**cripple** *vb* **crip·pled; crip·pling** \-(ə-)liŋ\ **1** : to make lame **2** : to make useless or imperfect

cri·sis \'krī-səs\ *n, pl* **cri·ses** \'krī-ˌsēz\ [L, fr. Gk *krisis*, lit., decision, fr. *krinein* to decide] **1** : the turning point for better or worse in an acute disease or fever **2** : a decisive or critical moment

crisp \'krisp\ *adj* **1** : CURLY, WAVY **2** : BRITTLE **3** : FIRM, FRESH (~ lettuce) **4** : being sharp and clear **5** : LIVELY, SPARKLING **6** : FROSTY, SNAPPY; *also* : BRACING — **crisp** *vb* — **crisp·ly** *adv* — **crisp·ness** *n* — **crispy** *adj*

¹**criss·cross** \'kris-ˌkrȯs\ *vb* **1** : to mark with crossed lines **2** : to go or pass back and forth

²**crisscross** *adj* : marked or characterized by crisscrossing — **crisscross** *adv*

³**crisscross** *n* : a pattern formed by crossed lines

crit *abbr* critical; criticism

cri·te·ri·on \krī-'tir-ē-ən\ *n, pl* **-ria** \-ē-ə\ : a standard on which a judgment may be based

¹**crit·ic** \'krit-ik\ *n* **1** : a person who judges literary or artistic works **2** : one inclined to find fault

crit·i·cal \'krit-i-kəl\ *adj* **1** : inclined to criticize **2** : relating to criticism or critics **3** : requiring careful judgment

4 : being or relating to a condition or disease involving danger of death 5 : being a crisis 6 : UNCERTAIN — **crit·i·cal·ly** \-i-k(ə-)lē\ *adv*

crit·i·cism \'krit-ə-ˌsiz-əm\ *n* 1 : the act of criticizing; *esp* : CENSURE 2 : a judgment or review 3 : the art of judging works of literature or art

crit·i·cize \'krit-ə-ˌsīz\ *vb* **-cized; -ciz·ing** 1 : to judge as a critic : EVALUATE 2 : to find fault : express criticism syn blame, censure, condemn

cri·tique \krə-'tēk\ *n* : a critical estimate or discussion

crit·ter \'krit-ər\ *n* : CREATURE

croak \'krōk\ *n* : a hoarse harsh cry (as of a frog) — **croak** *vb*

cro·chet \krō-'shā\ *n* [F, hook, crochet, fr. MF, dim. of *croche* hook] : needlework done with a single thread and hooked needle — **crochet** *vb*

crock \'kräk\ *n* : a thick earthenware pot or jar

crock·ery \'kräk-(ə-)rē\ *n* : EARTHENWARE

croc·o·dile \'kräk-ə-ˌdīl\ *n* [ME & L; ME *cocodrille*, fr. OF, fr. ML *cocodrillus*, alter. of L *crocodilus*, fr. Gk *krokodilos* lizard, crocodile, fr. *krokē* pebble + *drillos* worm] : any of several thick-skinned long-bodied reptiles of tropical and subtropical waters

cro·cus \'krō-kəs\ *n, pl* **cro·cus·es** also **crocus** or **cro·ci** \-ˌkī\ : any of a large genus of low herbs related to the irises and having brightly colored flowers borne singly in early spring

crois·sant \k(r)ə-ˌwä-'säⁿ\ *n, pl* **croissants** \-'säⁿ(z)\ : a rich crescent-shaped roll

crone \'krōn\ *n* : WITCH 2

cro·ny \'krō-nē\ *n, pl* **cronies** : a close friend esp. of long standing

¹**crook** \'kruk\ *vb* : to curve or bend sharply

²**crook** *n* 1 : a bent or curved implement 2 : SWINDLER, THIEF 3 : a bent or curved part; *also* : BEND, CURVE

crook·ed \'kruk-əd\ *adj* 1 : having a crook : BENT, CURVED 2 : DISHONEST — **crook·ed·ly** *adv* — **crook·ed·ness** *n*

croon \'krün\ *vb* : to sing or hum in a gentle murmuring voice — **croon·er** *n*

¹**crop** \'kräp\ *n* 1 : the handle of a whip; *also* : a short riding whip 2 : a pouch in the throat of many birds and insects where food is received 3 : something that can be harvested; *also* : the yield at harvest

²**crop** *vb* **cropped; crop·ping** 1 : to remove the tips of : cut off short; *also* : TRIM 2 : to feed on by cropping 3 : to devote (land) to crops 4 : to appear unexpectedly

crop·land \-ˌland\ *n* : land devoted to the production of plant crops

crop·per \'kräp-ər\ *n* : a raiser of crops; *esp* : SHARECROPPER

cro·quet \krō-'kā\ *n* : a game in which mallets are used to drive wooden balls

through a series of wickets set out on a lawn

cro·quette \krō-'ket\ *n* [F] : a small often rounded mass of minced meat, fish, or vegetables fried in deep fat

cro·sier \'krō-zhər\ *n* : a staff carried by bishops and abbots

¹**cross** \'krós\ *n* 1 : a structure consisting of an upright beam and a crossbar used esp. by the ancient Romans for execution 2 : a figure of the cross on which Christ was crucified used as a Christian symbol 3 : a hybridizing of unlike individuals or strains; *also* : product of this 4 : a punch delivered with a circular motion over an opponent's lead

²**cross** *vb* 1 : to lie or place across; *also* : INTERSECT 2 : to cancel by marking a cross on or by lining through 3 : THWART, OBSTRUCT 4 : to go or extend across : TRAVERSE 5 : HYBRIDIZE 6 : to meet and pass on the way

³**cross** *adj* 1 : lying across 2 : CONTRARY, OPPOSED 3 : marked by bad temper 4 : HYBRID — **cross·ly** *adv*

cross·bar \'krós-ˌbär\ *n* : a transverse bar or piece

cross·bones \-ˌbōnz\ *n pl* : two leg or arm bones placed or depicted crosswise

cross·bow \-ˌbō\ *n* : a short bow mounted crosswise at the end of a wooden stock that shoots short arrows

cross·breed \'krós-ˌbrēd, -'brēd\ *vb* **-bred** \-'bred\; **-breed·ing** : HYBRIDIZE

cross-coun·try \-'kən-trē\ *adj* 1 : extending or moving across a country 2 : proceeding over the countryside (as fields and woods) rather than by roads 3 : of or relating to racing or skiing over the countryside instead of over a track or run — **cross-country** *adv*

cross·cur·rent \-'kər-ənt\ *n* 1 : a current running counter to another 2 : a conflicting tendency — usu. used in pl.

¹**cross·cut** \-ˌkət\ *vb* : to cut or saw crosswise esp. of the grain of wood

²**crosscut** *adj* 1 : made or used for crosscutting (a ~ saw) 2 : cut across the grain

³**crosscut** *n* : something that cuts through transversely

cross-ex·am·ine \ˌkrós-ig-'zam-ən\ *vb* : to examine with questions to check the answers to previous questions — **cross-ex·am·i·na·tion** \-ˌzam-ə-'nā-shən\ *n*

cross-eyed \'krós-ˌīd\ *adj* : having one or both eyes turned inward toward the nose

cross-fer·til·iza·tion \-ˌfərt-ᵊl-ə-'zā-shən\ *n* 1 : fertilization between sex cells produced by separate individuals or sometimes by individuals of different kinds; *also* : CROSS-POLLINATION 2 : a broadening or productive interchange (as between cultures) — **cross-fer·til·ize** \-'fərt-ᵊl-ˌīz\ *vb*

cross fire *n* 1 : crossing lines of fire in combat 2 : rapid or angry interchange

cross hair *n* : one of the fine wires or threads in the eyepiece of an optical instrument used as a reference line

cross-hatch \'kròs-ˌhach\ *vb* : to mark with a series of parallel lines that cross esp. obliquely — **cross-hatching** *n*

cross·ing \'krò-siŋ\ *n* 1 : a place or structure for crossing something (as a street or river) 2 : a point of intersection (as of a street and a railroad track)

cross·over \'kròs-ˌō-vər\ *n* 1 : CROSSING 2 : a member of one political party who votes in the primary of the other party

cross·piece \'kròs-ˌpēs\ *n* : a crosswise member

cross-pol·li·na·tion \ˌkròs-ˌpäl-ə-ˈnā-shən\ *n* : transfer of pollen from one flower to the stigma of another — **cross-pol·li·nate** \'kròs-ˈpäl-ə-ˌnāt\ *vb*

cross-pur·pose \'kròs-ˈpər-pəs\ *n* : a purpose contrary to another purpose (working at ~s)

cross-ques·tion \-ˈkwes-chən\ *vb* : CROSS-EXAMINE

cross-re·fer \ˌkròs-ri-ˈfər\ *vb* : to refer by a notation or direction from one place to another (as in a book or list) — **cross-ref·er·ence** \'kròs-ˈref-(ə-)rəns\ *n*

cross·road \'kròs-ˌrōd\ *n* 1 : a road that crosses a main road or runs between main roads 2 : a place where roads meet — usu. used in pl. 3 : a crucial point where a decision must be made

cross section *n* 1 : a section cut across something; *also* : a representation made by or as if by such cutting 2 : a number of persons or things selected from a group that show the general nature of the whole group — **cross-sec·tion·al** *adj*

cross·walk \'kròs-ˌwok\ *n* : a specially marked path for pedestrians crossing a street

cross·ways \-ˌwāz\ *adv* : CROSSWISE

cross·wise \-ˌwīz\ *adv* : so as to cross something : ACROSS — **crosswise** *adj*

cross·word \'kròs-ˌwərd\ *n* : a puzzle in which words are fitted into a pattern of numbered squares in answer to clues

crotch \'kräch\ *n* : an angle formed by the parting of two legs, branches, or members

crotch·et \'kräch-ət\ *n* : an odd notion : WHIM — **crotch·ety** *adj*

crouch \'kraùch\ *vb* 1 : to stoop or bend low 2 : CRINGE, COWER — **crouch** *n*

croup \'krüp\ *n* : laryngitis esp. of infants marked by a hoarse ringing cough and difficult breathing — **croupy** *adj*

crou·pi·er \'krü-pē-ər, -pē-ˌā\ *n* [F, lit., rider on the rump of a horse, fr. *croupe* rump] : an employee of a gambling casino who collects and pays bets at a gaming table

crou·ton \'krü-ˌtän\ *n* [F *croûton*, dim.

of *croûte* crust] : a small cube of bread toasted or fried crisp

¹crow \'krō\ *n* 1 : any of various large glossy black birds related to the jays 2 *cap* : a member of an American Indian people of the region between the Platte and Yellowstone rivers; *also* : the language of the Crow people

²crow *vb* 1 : to make the loud shrill sound characteristic of the cock 2 : to utter a sound expressive of pleasure 3 : EXULT, GLOAT; *also* : BRAG, BOAST

³crow *n* : the cry of the cock

crow·bar \'krō-ˌbär\ *n* : a metal bar usu. wedge-shaped at the end for use as a pry or lever

¹crowd \'kraùd\ *vb* 1 : to press close 2 : to collect in numbers : THRONG 3 : CRAM, STUFF

²crowd *n* : a large number of people gathered together at random : THRONG

¹crown \'kraùn\ *n* 1 : a mark of victory or honor; *esp* : the title of a champion in a sport 2 : a royal headdress 3 : the top of the head 4 : the highest part (as of a tree or tooth) 5 *often cap* : sovereign power; *also* : MONARCH 6 : a formerly used British silver coin — **crowned** \'kraùnd\ *adj*

²crown *vb* 1 : to place a crown on 2 : HONOR 3 : TOP, SURMOUNT 4 : to fit (a tooth) with an artificial crown

crown vetch *n* : a European leguminous herb with umbels of pink-and-white flowers and sharp-angled pods

crow's-foot \'krōz-ˌfùt\ *n, pl* **crow's-feet** \-ˌfēt\ : any of the wrinkles around the outer corners of the eyes — usu. used in pl.

crow's nest *n* : a partly enclosed platform high on a ship's mast for use as a lookout

CRT *abbr* cathode-ray tube

cru·cial \'krü-shəl\ *adj* : DECISIVE; *also* : IMPORTANT, SIGNIFICANT

cru·ci·ble \'krü-sə-bəl\ *n* : a heat-resistant container in which material can be subjected to great heat

cru·ci·fix \'krü-sə-ˌfiks\ *n* : a representation of Christ on the cross

cru·ci·fix·ion \ˌkrü-sə-ˈfik-shən\ *n* : the act of crucifying; *esp, cap* : the crucifying of Christ

cru·ci·form \'krü-sə-ˌfòrm\ *adj* : cross-shaped

cru·ci·fy \'krü-sə-ˌfī\ *vb* **-fied; -fy·ing** 1 : to put to death by nailing or binding the hands and feet to a cross 2 : MORTIFY 1 3 : TORTURE, PERSECUTE

¹crude \'krüd\ *adj* **crud·er; crud·est** 1 : not refined : RAW (~ oil) (~ statistics) 2 : lacking grace, taste, tact, or polish : RUDE — **crude·ly** *adv* — **cru·di·ty** \'krüd-ət-ē\ *n*

²crude *n* : unrefined petroleum

cru·el \'krü-əl\ *adj* **cru·el·er or cru·el·ler; cru·el·est or cru·el·lest** : causing pain and suffering to others : MERCILESS — **cru·el·ly** \-ē\ *adv* — **cru·el·ty** \-tē\ *n*

cru·et \'krü-ət\ *n* : a small usu. glass bottle for vinegar, oil, or sauce

cruise \'krüz\ *vb* **cruised**; **cruis·ing** [D *kruisen* to make a cross, cruise, fr. L *crux* cross] **1** : to sail about touching at a series of ports **2** : to travel for enjoyment **3** : to travel about the streets at random **4** : to travel at the most efficient operating speed (the *cruising* speed of an airplane) — **cruise** *n*

cruis·er \'krü-zər\ *n* **1** : SQUAD CAR **2** : a large fast moderately armored and gunned warship **3** : a motorboat equipped for living aboard

crul·ler \'krəl-ər\ *n* **1** : a small sweet cake in the form of a twisted strip fried in deep fat **2** *North & Midland* : an unraised doughnut

¹crumb \'krəm\ *n* : a small fragment

²crumb *vb* **1** : to break into crumbs **2** : to cover with crumbs

crum·ble \'krəm-bəl\ *vb* **crum·bled**; **crum·bling** \-b(ə-)liŋ\ : to break into small pieces : DISINTEGRATE — **crum·bly** \-b(ə-)lē\ *adj*

crum·my *or* **crumby** \'krəm-ē\ *adj* **crum·mi·er** *or* **crumb·i·er**; **-est 1** : MISERABLE, FILTHY **2** : CHEAP, WORTHLESS

crum·pet \'krəm-pət\ *n* : a small round unsweetened bread cooked on a griddle

crum·ple \'krəm-pəl\ *vb* **crum·pled**; **crum·pling** \-p(ə-)liŋ\ **1** : to crush together : RUMPLE **2** : COLLAPSE

¹crunch \'krənch\ *vb* : to chew with a grinding noise; *also* : to grind or press with a crushing noise

²crunch *n* **1** : an act of or a sound made by crunching **2** : a tight or critical situation — **crunchy** *adj*

cru·sade \krü-'sād\ *n* **1** *cap* : any of the expeditions in the 11th, 12th, and 13th centuries undertaken by Christian countries to take the Holy Land from the Muslims **2** : a reforming enterprise undertaken with zeal — **crusade** *vb* — **cru·sad·er** *n*

cruse \'krüz, 'krüs\ *n* : a jar for water or oil

¹crush \'krəsh\ *vb* **1** : to squeeze out of shape **2** : HUG, EMBRACE **3** : to grind or pound to small bits **4** : OVERWHELM, SUPPRESS

²crush *n* **1** : an act of crushing **2** : a violent crowding **3** : INFATUATION

crust \'krəst\ *n* **1** : the outside part of bread; *also* : a piece of old dry bread **2** : the cover of a pie **3** : a hard surface layer — **crust·al** *adj*

crus·ta·cean \ˌkrəs-'tā-shən\ *n* : any of a large class of mostly aquatic arthropods (as lobsters or crabs) having a firm crustlike shell

crusty *adj* **crust·i·er**; **-est 1** : having or being a crust **2** : CROSS, GRUMPY

crutch \'krəch\ *n* : a supporting device; *esp* : a support fitting under the armpit for use by the disabled in walking

crux \'krəks, 'krüks\ *n*, *pl* **crux·es 1** : a puzzling or difficult problem **2** : a crucial point

cru·za·do \krü-'zäd-ō\ *n* — SEE MONEY table

¹cry \'krī\ *vb* **cried**; **cry·ing 1** : to call out : SHOUT **2** : WEEP **3** : to proclaim publicly; *also* : to advertise wares by calling out

²cry *n*, *pl* **cries 1** : a loud outcry **2** : APPEAL, ENTREATY **3** : a fit of weeping **4** : the characteristic sound uttered by an animal

cry·ba·by \'krī-ˌbā-bē\ *n* : one who cries easily or often

cryo·gen·ic \ˌkrī-ə-'jen-ik\ *adj* : of or relating to the production of very low temperatures; *also* : involving the use of a very low temperature — **cryo·gen·i·cal·ly** \-i-k(ə-)lē\ *adv*

cryo·gen·ics \-iks\ *n* : a branch of physics that relates to the production and effects of very low temperatures

cryo·lite \'krī-ə-ˌlīt\ *n* : a usu. white mineral used in making aluminum

crypt \'kript\ *n* : a chamber wholly or partly underground

cryp·tic \'krip-tik\ *adj* : meant to be puzzling or mysterious

cryp·to·gram \'krip-tə-ˌgram\ *n* : a communication in cipher or code

cryp·tog·ra·phy \krip-'täg-rə-fē\ *n* : the coding and decoding of secret messages — **cryp·tog·ra·pher** \-fər\ *n*

crys·tal \'kris-t³l\ *n* [ME *cristal*, fr. OF, fr. L *crystallum*, fr. Gk *krystallos* ice, crystal] **1** : transparent quartz **2** : something resembling crystal (as in transparency); *esp* : a clear glass used for table articles **3** : a body that is formed by solidification of a substance and has a regular repeating arrangement of atoms and often of external plane faces (a snow ~) (a salt ~) **4** : the transparent cover of a watch dial — **crys·tal·line** \-tə-lən\ *adj*

crys·tal·lize \'kris-tə-ˌlīz\ *vb* **-lized**; **-liz·ing 1** : to assume or cause to assume a crystalline form **2** : to take or cause to take a fixed and definite form — **crys·tal·li·za·tion** \ˌkris-tə-lə-'zā-shən\ *n*

crys·tal·log·ra·phy \ˌkris-tə-'läg-rə-fē\ *n* : the science dealing with the forms and structures of crystals — **crys·tal·log·ra·pher** \-fər\ *n*

cs *abbr* case; cases

Cs *symbol* cesium

CS *abbr* **1** civil service **2** county seat

C/S *abbr* cycles per second

CSA *abbr* Confederate States of America

CSM *abbr* command sergeant major

CST *abbr* central standard time

ct *abbr* **1** carat **2** cent **3** count **4** county **5** court

CT *abbr* **1** central time **2** Connecticut

ctg *or* **ctge** *abbr* cartage

ctn *abbr* carton

ctr *abbr* **1** center **2** counter

cu *abbr* cubic

Cu *symbol* [L *cuprum*] copper

cub \'kəb\ *n* : a young individual of some animals (as a fox, bear, or lion)

Cu·ban \'kyü-bən\ *n* : a native or inhabitant of Cuba — **Cuban** *adj*

cub·by·hole \'kəb-ē-,hōl\ *n* : a snug place (as for storing things)

¹cube \'kyüb\ *n* 1 : a solid having 6 equal square sides 2 : the product obtained by taking a number 3 times as a factor (27 is the ~ of 3)

²cube *vb* **cubed; cub·ing** 1 : to raise to the third power 2 : to form into a cube 3 : to cut into cubes

cube root *n* : a number whose cube is a given number

cu·bic \'kyü-bik\ *also* **cu·bi·cal** *adj* 1 : having the form of a cube 2 : having length, width, and height 3 : being the volume of a cube whose edge is a specified unit

cu·bi·cle \'kyü-bi-kəl\ *n* : a small separate space (as for sleeping or studying)

cubic measure *n* : a unit (as cubic inch) for measuring volume — see METRIC SYSTEM table, WEIGHT table

cub·ism \'kyü-,biz-əm\ *n* : a style of art characterized by the abstraction of natural forms into fragmented geometric shapes

cu·bit \'kyü-bət\ *n* : an ancient unit of length equal to about 18 inches (46 centimeters)

Cub Scout *n* : a member of the program of the Boy Scouts of America for boys 8–10 years of age

cuck·old \'kək-əld, 'kük-\ *n* : a man whose wife is unfaithful

¹cuck·oo \'kük-ü, 'kük-\ *n, pl* **cuckoos** : a largely grayish brown European bird that lays its eggs in the nests of other birds for them to hatch

²cuckoo *adj* : SILLY, FOOLISH

cu·cum·ber \'kyü-(,)kəm-bər\ *n* : the long fleshy many-seeded fruit of a vine of the gourd family that is grown as a garden vegetable; *also* : this vine

cud \'kəd\ *n* : food brought up into the mouth by ruminating animals (as cows) from the first stomach to be chewed again

cud·dle \'kəd-ᵊl\ *vb* **cud·dled; cud·dling** \'kəd-(ᵊ)liŋ\ : to lie close

cud·gel \'kəj-əl\ *n* : a short heavy club — **cudgel** *vb*

¹cue \'kyü\ *n* 1 : a word, phrase, or action in a play serving as a signal for the next actor to speak or act 2 : HINT — **cue** *vb*

²cue *n* : a tapered rod for striking the balls in billiards or pool

cue ball *n* : the ball a player strikes with a cue in billiards or pool

¹cuff \'kəf\ *n* 1 : a part (as of a sleeve or glove) encircling the wrist 2 : the folded hem of a trouser leg

²cuff *vb* : to strike esp. with the open hand : SLAP

³cuff *n* : a blow with the hand esp. when open

cui·sine \kwi-'zēn\ *n* : manner of cooking; *also* : the food so prepared

cuke \'kyük\ *n* : CUCUMBER

cul–de–sac \,kəl-di-'sak, ,kul-\ *n, pl* **culs–de–sac** \,kəl(z)-, ,kul(z)-\ *also* **cul–de–sacs** \,kəl-də-'saks, ,kul-\ [F, lit., bottom of the bag] : a street or passage closed at one end

cu·li·nary \'kəl-ə-,ner-ē, 'kyü-lə-\ *adj* : of or relating to cookery

¹cull \'kəl\ *vb* : to pick out from a group : CHOOSE

²cull *n* : something rejected from a group or lot as worthless or inferior

cul·mi·nate \'kəl-mə-,nāt\ *vb* **-nat·ed; -nat·ing** : to reach the highest point — **cul·mi·na·tion** \,kəl-mə-'nā-shən\ *n*

cu·lotte \'k(y)ü-,lät, k(y)ü-'lät\ *n* [F, breeches, fr. dim. of *cul* backside] : a divided skirt; *also* : a garment having a divided skirt — often used in pl.

cul·pa·ble \'kəl-pə-bəl\ *adj* : deserving blame — **cul·pa·bil·i·ty** \,kəl-pə-'bil-ət-ē\ *n*

cul·prit \'kəl-prət\ *n* [Anglo-French (the French of medieval England) *cul.* (abbr. of *culpable* guilty) + *prest*, *prit* ready (i.e. to prove it), fr. L *praestus*] : one accused or guilty of a crime

cult \'kəlt\ *n* 1 : formal religious veneration 2 : a religious system; *also* : its adherents 3 : faddish devotion; *also* : a group of persons showing such devotion — **cult·ist** *n*

cul·ti·vate \'kəl-tə-,vāt\ *vb* **-vat·ed; -vat·ing** 1 : to prepare for the raising of crops 2 : to foster the growth of ⟨~ vegetables⟩ 3 : REFINE, IMPROVE 4 : ENCOURAGE, FURTHER — **cul·ti·va·ble** \-və-bəl\ *adj* — **cul·ti·vat·able** \-,vāt-ə-bəl\ *adj* — **cul·ti·va·tion** \,kəl-tə-'vā-shən\ *n* — **cul·ti·va·tor** \'kəl-tə-,vāt-ər\ *n*

cul·ture \'kəl-chər\ *n* 1 : TILLAGE, CULTIVATION; *also* : the growing of a particular crop (grape ~) 2 : the act of developing by education and training 3 : refinement of intellectual and artistic taste 4 : a particular form or stage of civilization; *also* : a society characterized by such a culture — **cul·tur·al** \'kəlch-(ə)-rəl\ *adj* — **cul·tur·al·ly** \-ē\ *adv* — **cul·tured** \'kəl-chərd\ *adj*

cul·vert \'kəl-vərt\ *n* : a drain crossing under a road or railroad

cum *abbr* cumulative

cum·ber \'kəm-bər\ *vb* **cum·bered; cum·ber·ing** \-b(ə-)riŋ\ : to weigh down : BURDEN

cum·ber·some \'kəm-bər-səm\ *adj* : hard to handle or manage because of size or weight

cum·brous \'kəm-brəs\ *adj* : CUMBERSOME

cum·mer·bund \'kəm-ər-,bənd\ *n* [Hindi *kamarband*, fr. Per, fr. *kamar* waist + *band*] : a broad sash worn as a waistband

cu·mu·la·tive \'kyü-myə-lət-iv, -,lāt-\ *adj* : increasing in force or value by successive additions

cu·mu·lo·nim·bus \,kyü-myə-lō-'nim-bəs\ *n* : an anvil-shaped cumulus cloud extending to great heights

cu·mu·lus \'kyü-myə-ləs\ *n, pl* **-li** \-ֽlī, -ֽlē\ : a massive cloud having a flat base and rounded outlines

cu·ne·i·form \kyu̇-'nē-ə-ֽfȯrm\ *adj* **1** : wedge-shaped **2** : composed of wedge-shaped characters (~ alphabet)

cun·ner \'kən-ər\ *n* : a small American food fish of the New England coast

cun·ni·lin·gus \ֽkən-i-'liŋ-gəs\ *also* **cun·ni·linc·tus** \-'liŋk-təs\ *n* : oral stimulation of the vulva or clitoris

¹**cun·ning** \'kən-iŋ\ *adj* **1** : SKILLFUL, DEXTEROUS **2** : marked by wiliness and trickery **3** : CUTE — **cun·ning·ly** *adv*

²**cunning** *n* **1** : SKILL **2** : CRAFTINESS, SLYNESS

¹**cup** \'kəp\ *n* **1** : a small bowl-shaped drinking vessel **2** : the contents of a cup **3** : communion wine **4** : something resembling a cup : a small bowl or hollow — **cup·ful** *n*

²**cup** *vb* **cupped; cup·ping** : to curve into the shape of a cup

cup·bear·er \'kəp-ֽbar-ər\ *n* : one who has the duty of filling and serving cups of wine

cup·board \'kəb-ərd\ *n* : a small storage closet

cup·cake \'kəp-ֽkāk\ *n* : a small cake baked in a cuplike mold

Cu·pid \'kyü-pəd\ *n* : a winged naked figure of an infant often with a bow and arrow that represents the god Cupid

cu·pid·i·ty \kyu̇-'pid-ət-ē\ *n, pl* **-ties** : excessive desire for money : AVARICE

cu·po·la \'kyü-pə-lə, -ֽlō\ *n* : a small structure on top of a roof or building

cu·prite \'k(y)ü-ֽprīt\ *n* : a mineral that is an ore of copper

¹**cur** \'kər\ *n* : a mongrel dog

²**cur** *abbr* **1** currency **2** current

cu·rate \'kyu̇r-ət\ *n* **1** : a clergyman in charge of a parish **2** : a clergyman who assists a rector or vicar — **cu·ra·cy** \-ə-sē\ *n*

cu·ra·tive \'kyu̇r-ət-iv\ *adj* : relating to or used in the cure of diseases — **curative** *n*

cu·ra·tor \kyu̇-'rāt-ər\ *n* : CUSTODIAN; *esp* : one in charge of a place of exhibit (as a museum or ZOO)

¹**curb** \'kərb\ *n* **1** : a bit that exerts pressure on a horse's jaws **2** : CHECK, RESTRAINT **3** : a raised edging (as of stone or concrete) along a paved street

²**curb** *vb* : to hold in or back : RESTRAIN

curb·ing \'kər-biŋ\ *n* : the material for a curb **2** : CURB

curd \'kərd\ *n* : the thick protein-rich part of coagulated milk

cur·dle \'kərd-ᵊl\ *vb* **cur·dled; cur·dling** \'kərd-(ᵊ-)liŋ\ : to form curds; *also* : SPOIL, SOUR

¹**cure** \'kyu̇r\ *n* **1** : spiritual care **2** : recovery or relief from disease **3** : a

curative agent : REMEDY **4** : a course or period of treatment

²**cure** *vb* **cured; cur·ing 1** : to restore to health : HEAL, REMEDY **2** : to process for storage or use (~ bacon) : *also* : to become cured — **cur·able** *adj*

cu·ré \kyu̇-'rā\ *n* [F] : a parish priest

cure-all \'kyu̇r-ֽȯl\ *n* : a remedy for all ills : PANACEA

cu·ret·tage \ֽkyu̇r-ə-'täzh\ *n* : a surgical scraping and cleaning by means of a scoop, loop, or ring

cur·few \'kər-ֽfyü\ *n* [ME, fr. MF *covrefeu*, signal given to bank the hearth fire, curfew, fr. *covrir* to cover + *feu* fire, fr. L *focus* hearth] : a regulation that specified persons (as children) be off the streets at a set hour of the evening; *also* : the sounding of a signal (as a bell) at this hour

cu·ria \'k(y)u̇r-ē-ə\ *n, pl* **cu·ri·ae** \'kyu̇r-ē-ֽē, 'ku̇r-ē-ֽī\ *often cap* : the body of congregations, tribunals, and offices through which the pope governs the Roman Catholic Church

cu·rie \'kyu̇r-ē\ *n* : a unit of radioactivity equal to 37 billion disintegrations per second

cu·rio \'kyu̇r-ē-ֽō\ *n, pl* **cu·ri·os** : an object or article valued because it is strange or rare

cu·ri·ous \'kyu̇r-ē-əs\ *adj* **1** : having a desire to investigate and learn **2** : STRANGE, UNUSUAL, ODD — **cu·ri·os·i·ty** \ֽkyu̇r-ē-'äs-ət-ē\ *n* — **cu·ri·ous·ly** *adv*

cu·ri·um \'kyu̇r-ē-əm\ *n* : a metallic radioactive element produced artificially

¹**curl** \'kərl\ *vb* **1** : to form into ringlets **2** : CURVE, COIL — **curl·er** *n*

²**curl** *n* **1** : a lock of hair that coils : RINGLET **2** : something having a spiral or twisted form — **curly** *adj*

cur·lew \'kərl-(y)ü\ *n, pl* **curlews** *or* **curlew** : any of various long-legged brownish birds that have a down-curved bill and are related to the woodcocks

curli·cue \'kər-li-ֽkyü\ *n* : a fancifully curved or spiral figure

cur·rant \'kər-ənt\ *n* **1** : a small seedless raisin **2** : the acid berry of a shrub related to the gooseberry; *also* : this plant

cur·ren·cy \'kər-ən-sē\ *n, pl* **-cies 1** : general use or acceptance **2** : something that is in circulation as a medium of exchange : MONEY

¹**cur·rent** \'kər-ənt\ *adj* **1** : occurring in or belonging to the present **2** : used as a medium of exchange **3** : generally accepted or practiced

²**current** *n* **1** : the part of a body of fluid moving continuously in a certain direction; *also* : the swiftest part of a stream **2** : a flow of electric charge; *also* : the rate of such flow

cur·ric·u·lum \kə-'rik-yə-ləm\ *n, pl* **-la** \-lə\ *also* **-lums** [L, racecourse, fr. *currere* to run] : a course of study offered by a school or one of its divisions

cur·ry \\'kər-ē\\ *vb* **cur·ried; cur·ry·ing 1** : to clean the coat of (a horse) with a currycomb **2** : to treat (tanned leather) esp. by incorporating oil or grease — **curry fa·vor** \\-'fā-vər\\ : to seek to gain favor by flattery or attention

²**cur·ry** \\'kər-ē\\ *n, pl* **curries** : a powder of blended spices used in cooking; *also* : a food seasoned with curry

cur·ry·comb \\-,kōm\\ *n* : a comb used esp. to curry horses — **currycomb** *vb*

¹**curse** \\'kərs\\ *n* **1** : a prayer for harm to come upon one **2** : something that is cursed **3** : something that comes as if in response to a curse : SCOURGE

²**curse** *vb* **cursed; curs·ing 1** : to call on divine power to send injury upon **2** : BLASPHEME **3** : AFFLICT *syn* execrate, damn, anathematize, objurgate

cur·sive \\'kər-siv\\ *adj* : written or formed with the strokes of the letters joined together and the angles rounded

cur·sor \\'kər-sər\\ *n* : a bright figure (as a pointer) on a computer screen to indicate a character to be revised or a position where data is to be entered

cur·so·ry \\'kərs-(ə-)rē\\ *adj* : hastily and often superficially done : HASTY — **cur·so·ri·ly** \\-rə-lē\\ *adv*

curt \\'kərt\\ *adj* : rudely short or abrupt — **curt·ly** *adv*

cur·tail \\(,)kər-'tāl\\ *vb* : to cut off the end of : SHORTEN — **cur·tail·ment** *n*

cur·tain \\'kərt-³n\\ *n* **1** : a hanging screen that can be drawn back esp. at a window **2** : the screen between the stage and auditorium of a theater — **curtain** *vb*

curt·sy *or* **curt·sey** \\'kərt-sē\\ *n, pl* **curtsies** *or* **curtseys** : a courteous bow made by women chiefly by bending the knees — **curtsy** *or* **curtsey** *vb*

cur·va·ceous *also* **cur·va·cious** \\,kər-'vā-shəs\\ *adj* : having a well-proportioned feminine figure marked by pronounced curves

cur·va·ture \\'kər-və-,chūr\\ *n* : a measure or amount of curving : BEND

¹**curve** \\'kərv\\ *vb* **curved; curv·ing** : to bend from a straight line or course

²**curve** *n* **1** : a line esp. when curved **2** : something that bends or curves without angles (a ~ in the road) **3** : a ball thrown so that it swerves from a normal course

cur·vet \\(,)kər-'vet\\ *n* : a prancing leap of a horse — **curvet** *vb*

¹**cush·ion** \\'kush-ən\\ *n* **1** : a soft pillow or pad to rest on or against **2** : the springy pad inside the rim of a billiard table **3** : something soft that prevents discomfort or protects against injury

²**cushion** *vb* **cush·ioned; cush·ion·ing** \\-(ə-)niŋ\\ **1** : to provide (as a seat) with a cushion **2** : to soften or lessen the force or shock of

cusp \\'kəsp\\ *n* : a pointed end or part (as of a tooth)

cus·pid \\'kəs-pəd\\ *n* : a canine tooth

cus·pi·dor \\'kəs-pə-,dòr\\ *n* : SPITTOON

cus·tard \\'kəs-tərd\\ *n* : a sweetened mixture of milk and eggs baked, boiled, or frozen

cus·to·di·al \\,kəs-'tōd-ē-əl\\ *adj* : marked by watching and protecting rather than seeking to cure (~ care)

cus·to·di·an \\,kəs-'tōd-ē-ən\\ *n* : one who has custody (as of a building)

cus·to·dy \\'kəs-təd-ē\\ *n, pl* **-dies** : immediate care or charge

¹**cus·tom** \\'kəs-təm\\ *n* **1** : habitual course of action : recognized usage **2** *pl* : taxes levied on imports **3** : business patronage

²**custom** *adj* **1** : made to personal order **2** : doing work only on order

cus·tom·ary \\'kəs-tə-,mer-ē\\ *adj* **1** : based on or established by custom (~ rent) **2** : commonly practiced or observed : HABITUAL — **cus·tom·ar·i·ly** \\,kəs-tə-'mer-ə-lē\\ *adv*

cus·tom–built \\,kəs-təm-'bilt\\ *adj* : built to individual order

cus·tom·er \\'kəs-tə-mər\\ *n* : BUYER, PURCHASER; *esp* : a regular or frequent buyer

cus·tom·house \\'kəs-təm-,haüs\\ *n* : the building where customs are paid

cus·tom·ize \\'kəs-tə-,mīz\\ *vb* **-ized; -iz·ing** : to build, fit, or alter according to individual specifications

cus·tom–made \\,kəs-təm-'m)ād\\ *adj* : made to individual order

¹**cut** \\'kət\\ *vb* **cut; cut·ting 1** : to penetrate or divide with a sharp edge : CLEAVE, GASH; *also* : to experience the growth of (a tooth) through the gum **2** : to hurt the feelings of **3** : to strike sharply **4** : SHORTEN, REDUCE **5** : to remove by severing or paring **6** : INTERSECT, CROSS **7** : to divide into parts **8** : to go quickly or change direction abruptly **9** : to cause to stop

²**cut** *n* **1** : a customary segment of a meat carcass **2** : SHARE **3** : something made by cutting : GASH, CLEFT **4** : an excavated channel or roadway **5** : BAND **4 6** : a sharp stroke or blow **7** : REDUCTION (~ in wages) **8** : the shape or manner in which a thing is cut

cut–and–dried \\,kət-³n-'drīd\\ *also* **cut–and–dry** \\-'drī\\ *adj* : according to a plan, set procedure, or formula

cu·ta·ne·ous \\kyü-'tā-nē-əs\\ *adj* : of, relating to, or affecting the skin

cut·back \\'kət-,bak\\ *n* **1** : something cut back **2** : REDUCTION

cute \\'kyüt\\ *adj* **cut·er; cut·est** [short for *acute*] **1** : CLEVER, SHREWD **2** : daintily attractive : PRETTY

cu·ti·cle \\'kyüt-i-kəl\\ *n* **1** : an outer layer (as of skin) **2** : dead or horny epidermis esp. around a fingernail — **cu·tic·u·lar** \\kyü-'tik-yə-lər\\ *adj*

cut in \\,kət-'in\\ *vb* **1** : to thrust oneself between others **2** : to interrupt a dancing couple and take one as one's partner

cut·lass \'kət-ləs\ *n* : a short heavy curved sword

cut·ler \'kət-lər\ *n* : one who makes, deals in, or repairs cutlery

cut·lery \'kət-lə-rē\ *n* : edged or cutting tools; *esp* : implements for cutting and eating food

cut·let \'kət-lət\ *n* : a slice of meat (as veal) for broiling or frying

cut·off \'kət-ˌȯf\ *n* **1** : the channel formed when a stream cuts through the neck of an oxbow; *also* : SHORT-CUT **2** : a device for cutting off **3** *pl* : shorts orig. made from jeans with the legs cut off at the knees or higher

cut·out \'kət-ˌau̇t\ *n* : something cut out or prepared for cutting out from something else ⟨a page of animal ~s⟩

cut out \'kət-'au̇t\ *vb* **1** : to be all that one can handle ⟨had her work *cut out* for her⟩ **2** : DISCONNECT **3** : to cease operating ⟨the engine *cut out*⟩ **4** : ELIMINATE ⟨*cut out* unnecessary expense⟩

cut–rate \'kət-'rāt\ *adj* : relating to or dealing in goods sold at reduced rates

cut·ter \'kət-ər\ *n* **1** : a tool or a machine for cutting **2** : a ship's boat for carrying stores and passengers **3** : a small armed boat in government service **4** : a light sleigh

¹cut·throat \'kət-ˌthrōt\ *n* : MURDERER

²cutthroat *adj* **1** : MURDEROUS, CRUEL **2** : MERCILESS, RUTHLESS ⟨~ competition⟩

cutthroat trout *n* : a large American trout with a red mark under the jaw

¹cut·ting \'kət-iŋ\ *n* : a piece of a plant able to grow into a new plant

²cutting *adj* **1** : SHARP, EDGED **2** : marked by piercing cold **3** : likely to hurt the feelings : SARCASTIC

cut·tle·fish \'kət-ᵊl-ˌfish\ *n* : a 10-armed mollusk related to the squid with an internal shell ⟨**cut·tle·bone** \-ˌbōn\⟩ composed of calcium compounds

cut·up \'kət-ˌəp\ *n* : one that clowns or acts boisterously — **cut up** \ˌkət-'əp\ *vb*

cut·worm \-ˌwərm\ *n* : any of various smooth-bodied moth larvae that feed on plants at night

cw *abbr* clockwise

CWO *abbr* **1** cash with order **2** chief warrant officer

cwt *abbr* hundredweight

-cy \sē\ *n suffix* **1** : action : practice ⟨mendancy⟩ **2** : rank : office ⟨chaplaincy⟩ **3** : body : class ⟨magistracy⟩ **4** : state : quality ⟨accuracy⟩

cy·an \'sī-ˌan, -ən\ *n* : a greenish blue color

cy·a·nide \'sī-ə-ˌnīd, -nəd\ *n* : a poisonous compound of carbon and nitrogen with either sodium or potassium

cy·ber·net·ics \ˌsī-bər-'net-iks\ *n* : the science of communication and control theory that is concerned esp. with the comparative study of automatic control systems — **cy·ber·net·ic** *adj*

cyc *or* **cycl** *abbr* cyclopedia

cy·cla·men \'sī-klə-mən\ *n* : any of a genus of plants related to the primroses and grown for their showy nodding flowers

¹cy·cle \'sī-kəl\ *n* **1** : a period of time occupied by a series of events that repeat themselves regularly and in the same order **2** : a recurring round of operations or events **3** : one complete occurrence of a periodic process (as a vibration or current alternation) **4** : a circular or spiral arrangement **5** : a long period of time : AGE **6** : BICYCLE **7** : MOTORCYCLE — **cy·clic** \'sī-klik, 'sik-lik\ *or* **cy·cli·cal** \'sī-kli-kəl, 'sik-li-\ *adj* — **cy·cli·cal·ly** \-k(ə-)lē\ *also* **cy·clic·ly** \'sī-kli-klē, 'sik-li-\ *adv*

²cy·cle \'sī-kəl\ *vb* **cy·cled; cy·cling** \'sī-k(ə-)liŋ, 'sik-(ə-)-\ : to ride a cycle

cy·clist \'sī-k(ə-)ləst\ *n* : one who rides a cycle

cy·clone \'sī-ˌklōn\ *n* **1** : a storm or system of winds that rotates about a center of low atmospheric pressure and advances at 20 to 30 miles an hour (about 30 to 50 kilometers per hour) **2** : TORNADO — **cy·clon·ic** \sī-'klän-ik\ *adj*

cy·clo·pe·dia *or* **cy·clo·pae·dia** \ˌsī-klə-'pēd-ē-ə\ *n* : ENCYCLOPEDIA

cy·clo·tron \'sī-klə-ˌträn\ *n* : a device for giving high speed to charged particles by magnetic and electric fields

cyg·net \'sig-nət\ *n* : a young swan

cyl *abbr* cylinder

cyl·in·der \'sil-ən-dər\ *n* : the solid figure formed by turning a rectangle about one side as an axis; *also* : a body or space of this form ⟨an engine ~⟩ ⟨a bullet in the ~ of a revolver⟩ — **cy·lin·dri·cal** \sə-'lin-dri-kəl\ *adj*

cym·bal \'sim-bəl\ *n* : one of a pair of concave brass plates clashed together

cyme \'sīm\ *n* : an inflorescence of several flowers each on a stem with the first-opening central flower on the main stem and later-opening flowers developing from lateral buds

cyn·ic \'sin-ik\ *n* [MF *or* L, MF *cynique*, fr. L *cynicus*, fr. Gk *kynikos*, lit., like a dog, fr. *kyōn* dog] : one who attributes all actions to selfish motives — **cyn·i·cal** \-i-kəl\ *adj* — **cyn·i·cal·ly** \-k(ə-)lē\ *adv* — **cyn·i·cism** \'sin-ə-ˌsiz-əm\ *n*

cy·no·sure \'sī-nə-ˌshu̇r, 'sin-ə-\ *n* [MF & L; MF, Ursa Minor, guide, fr. L *cynosura* Ursa Minor, fr. Gk *kynosoura*, fr. *kynos oura* dog's tail] : a center of attraction

CYO *abbr* Catholic Youth Organization

cy·press \'sī-prəs\ *n* **1** : any of a genus of scaly-leaved evergreen trees related to the pines **2** : either of two large swamp trees of the southern U.S. with hard red wood **3** : the wood of a cypress

cyst \'sist\ *n* : an abnormal closed bodily sac usu. containing liquid — **cys·tic** \'sis-tik\ *adj*

cystic fibrosis *n* : a common hereditary disease marked esp. by deficiency of pancreatic enzymes and by respiratory symptoms

cy·tol·o·gy \sī-'täl-ə-jē\ *n* : a branch of biology dealing with cells — **cy·to·log·i·cal** \ˌsīt-ᵊl-'äj-i-kəl\ *or* **cy·to·log·ic** \-'äj-ik\ *adj* — **cy·tol·o·gist** \sī-'täl-ə-jəst\ *n*

cy·to·plasm \'sīt-ə-ˌplaz-əm\ *n* : the protoplasm of a cell that lies external to the nucleus — **cy·to·plas·mic** \ˌsīt-ə-'plaz-mik\ *adj*

cy·to·sine \'sīt-ə-ˌsēn\ *n* : a chemical base that is a pyrimidine coding genetic information in DNA and RNA

CZ *abbr* Canal Zone

czar \'zär\ *n* : the ruler of Russia until 1917; *also* : one having great authority — **czar·ist** *n or adj*

cza·ri·na \zä-'rē-nə\ *n* : the wife of a czar

Czech \'chek\ *n* **1** : a native or inhabitant of Czechoslovakia **2** : the language of the Czechs — **Czech** *adj*

Czecho·slo·vak \ˌchek-ə-'slō-ˌväk, -ˌvak\ *or* **Czecho·slo·va·ki·an** \-slō-'väk-ē-ən, -'vak-\ *adj* : of, relating to, or characteristic of Czechoslovakia or its people — **Czechoslovak** *or* **Czechoslovakian** *n*

D

¹d \'dē\ *n, pl* **d's** *or* **ds** \'dēz\ *often cap* **1** : the 4th letter of the English alphabet **2** : a grade rating a student's work as poor

²d *abbr, often cap* **1** date **2** daughter **3** day **4** dead **5** deceased **6** degree **7** [L *denarius*] penny; pence **8** depart; departure **9** diameter

D *symbol* deuterium

DA *abbr* **1** deposit account **2** district attorney **3** don't answer

¹dab \'dab\ *n* **1** : a sudden blow or thrust : POKE; *also* : PECK **2** : a gentle touch or stroke : PAT

²dab *vb* **dabbed; dab·bing 1** : to strike or touch gently : PAT **2** : to apply lightly or irregularly : DAUB

³dab *n* **1** : DAUB **2** : a small amount

dab·ble \'dab-əl\ *vb* **dab·bled; dab·bling** \-(ə-)liŋ\ **1** : to wet by splashing : SPATTER **2** : to paddle or play in or as if in water **3** : to work or concern oneself without serious effort

dace \'dās\ *n, pl* **dace** : any of various small No. American freshwater fishes related to the carp

da·cha \'däch-ə\ *n* [Russ, lit., gift; fr. its frequently being the gift of a ruler] : a Russian country house

dachs·hund \'däks-ˌhu̇nt\ *n, pl* **dachshunds** [G, fr. *dachs* badger + *hund* dog] : a small dog of a breed of German origin with a long body, short legs, and long drooping ears

dac·tyl \'dak-tᵊl\ *n* [ME *dactile*, fr. L *dactylus*, fr. Gk *daktylos*, lit., finger; fr. the fact that the three syllables have the first one longest like the joints of the finger] : a metrical foot of one accented syllable followed by two unaccented syllables — **dac·tyl·ic** \dak-'til-ik\ *adj or n*

dad \'dad\ *n* : FATHER

Da·da \'däd-(ˌ)ä\ *n* : a movement in art and literature based on deliberate irrationality and negation of traditional artistic values — **da·da·ism** \-ˌiz-əm\ *n, often cap* — **da·da·ist** \-ˌist\ *n or adj, often cap*

dad·dy \'dad-ē\ *n, pl* **daddies** : FATHER

dad·dy long·legs \ˌdad-ē-'lȯŋ-ˌlegz\ *n, pl* **daddy longlegs** : any of various arachnids resembling the true spiders but having small rounded bodies and long slender legs

dae·mon *var of* DEMON

daf·fo·dil \'daf-ə-ˌdil\ *n* : any of a genus of bulbous herbs with usu. large flowers having a trumpetlike center

daf·fy \'daf-ē\ *adj* **daf·fi·er; -est** : DAFT

daft \'daft\ *adj* : FOOLISH; *also* : INSANE — **daft·ness** *n*

dag·ger \'dag-ər\ *n* **1** : a sharp pointed knife for stabbing **2** : a character † used as a reference mark or to indicate a death date

da·guerre·o·type \də-'ger-(ē-)ə-ˌtīp\ *n* : an early photograph produced on a silver or a silver-covered copper plate

dahl·ia \'dal-yə, 'däl-\ *n* : any of a genus of tuberous herbs related to the daisies and having showy flowers

¹dai·ly \'dā-lē\ *adj* **1** : occurring, done, or used every day or every weekday **2** : of or relating to every day ⟨~ visitors⟩ **3** : computed in terms of one day ⟨~ wages⟩ — **daily** *adv*

²daily *n, pl* **dailies** : a newspaper published every weekday

daily double *n* : a system of betting on races in which the bettor must pick the winners of two stipulated races in order to win

¹dain·ty \'dānt-ē\ *n, pl* **dainties** [ME *deinte*, fr. OF *deintié*, fr. L *dignitas* dignity, worth] : something delicious or pleasing to the taste : DELICACY

²dainty *adj* **dain·ti·er; -est 1** : pleasing to the taste **2** : delicately pretty **3** : having or showing delicate taste; *also* : FASTIDIOUS — **dain·ti·ly** \'dānt-ᵊl-ē\ *adv* — **dain·ti·ness** \-ē-nəs\ *n*

dai·qui·ri \'dī-kə-rē, 'dak-ə-rē\ *n* [*Daiquiri*, Cuba] : a cocktail made of rum, lime juice, and sugar

dairy \'de(ə)r-ē\ *n, pl* **dair·ies** [ME *deyerie*, fr. *deye* dairymaid, fr. OE *dæge* kneader of bread] **1** : CREAMERY **2** : a farm specializing in milk production

dairy·ing \'der-ē-iŋ\ n : the business of operating a dairy

dairy·maid \-ˌmād\ n : a woman employed in a dairy

dairy·man \-mən, -ˌman\ n : a person who operates a dairy farm or works in a dairy

da·is \'dā-əs\ n : a raised platform usu. above the floor of a hall or large room

dai·sy \'dā-zē\ n, pl **daisies** [ME *dayeseye*, fr. OE *dægeseage*, fr. *dæg* day + *ēage* eye] : any of numerous composite plants having flower heads in which the marginal flowers resemble petals

daisy wheel n : a printing element for an electric typewriter or computer printer that consists of a disk having spokes with type on the end

Da·ko·ta \də-'kōt-ə\ n, pl **Dakotas** also **Dakota** : a member of an American Indian people of the northern Mississippi valley; also : their language

da·la·si \dä-'läs-ē\ n, pl **dalasi** or **dalasis** — see MONEY table

dale \'dāl\ n : VALLEY

dal·ly \'dal-ē\ vb **dal·lied; dal·ly·ing** : to act playfully; esp : to dally amorously 2 : to waste time 3 : LINGER, DAWDLE — **dal·li·ance** \-əns\ n

dal·ma·tian \dal-'mā-shən\ n, often cap : any of a breed of medium-sized dogs having a white short-haired coat with black or brown spots

¹**dam** \'dam\ n : a female parent — used esp. of a domestic animal

²**dam** n : a barrier (as across a stream) to prevent the flow of water — dam vb

¹**dam·age** \'dam-ij\ n 1 : loss or harm due to injury to persons, property, or reputation 2 pl : compensation in money imposed by law for loss or injury (bring a suit for ~s)

²**damage** vb **dam·aged; dam·ag·ing** : to cause damage to

dam·a·scene \'dam-ə-ˌsēn\ vb **-scened; -scen·ing** : to ornament (as iron or steel) with wavy patterns or with inlaid work of precious metals

dam·ask \'dam-əsk\ n 1 : a firm lustrous reversible figured fabric used for household linen 2 : a tough steel having decorative wavy lines

dame \'dām\ n 1 : a woman of rank, station, or authority 2 : an elderly woman 3 : WOMAN

damn \'dam\ vb **damned; damn·ing** \'dam-iŋ\ [ME *dampnen*, fr. OF *dampner*, fr. L *damnare*, fr. *damnum* damage, loss, fine] 1 : to condemn esp. to hell 2 : CURSE — **damned** adj

dam·na·ble \'dam-nə-bəl\ adj 1 : liable to or deserving punishment 2 : DETESTABLE (~ weather) — **dam·na·bly** \-blē\ adv

dam·na·tion \dam-'nā-shən\ n 1 : the act of damning 2 : the state of being damned

¹**damp** \'damp\ n 1 : a noxious gas 2 : MOISTURE

²**damp** vb : DAMPEN

³**damp** adj : MOIST — **damp·ness** n

damp·en \'dam-pən\ vb **damp·ened; damp·en·ing** \'damp-(ə-)niŋ\ 1 : to check or diminish in activity or vigor 2 : to make or become damp

damp·er \'dam-pər\ n : one that damps; esp : a valve or movable plate (as in the flue of a stove, furnace, or fireplace) to regulate the draft

dam·sel \'dam-zəl\ n : GIRL, MAIDEN

dam·sel·fly \-ˌflī\ n : any of a group of insects that are closely related to the dragonflies but fold their wings above the body when at rest

dam·son \'dam-zən\ n : a plum with acid purple fruit; also : its fruit

Dan abbr Daniel

¹**dance** \'dans\ vb **danced; danc·ing** 1 : to glide, step, or move through a set series of movements usu. to music 2 : to move quickly up and down or about 3 : to perform or take part in as a dancer — **danc·er** n

²**dance** n 1 : an act or instance of dancing 2 : a social gathering for dancing 3 : a piece of music (as a waltz) by which dancing may be guided 4 : the art of dancing

D & C abbr dilation and curettage

dan·de·li·on \'dan-dᵊl-ˌī-ən\ n [MF *dent de lion*, lit., lion's tooth] : any of a genus of common yellow-flowered composite herbs

dan·der \'dan-dər\ n : ANGER, TEMPER

dan·di·fy \'dan-di-ˌfī\ vb **-fied; -fy·ing** : to cause to resemble a dandy

dan·dle \'dan-dᵊl\ vb **dan·dled; dan·dling** : to move up and down in one's arms or on one's knee in affectionate play

dan·druff \'dan-drəf\ n : a whitish scurf on the scalp that comes off in small scales

¹**dan·dy** \'dan-dē\ n, pl **dandies** 1 : a man unduly attentive to dress 2 : something excellent in its class

²**dandy** adj **dan·di·er; -est** : very good : FIRST-RATE

Dane \'dān\ n : a native or inhabitant of Denmark

dan·ger \'dān-jər\ n 1 : exposure or liability to injury, harm, or evil 2 : something that may cause injury or harm syn peril, risk, jeopardy

dan·ger·ous \'dānj-(ə-)rəs\ adj 1 : HAZARDOUS, PERILOUS 2 : able or likely to inflict injury — **dan·ger·ous·ly** adv

dan·gle \'daŋ-gəl\ vb **dan·gled; dan·gling** \-g(ə-)liŋ\ 1 : to hang loosely esp. with a swinging motion : SWING 2 : to be a hanger-on or dependent 3 : to be left without proper grammatical connection in a sentence 4 : to keep hanging uncertainly

Dan·iel \'dan-yəl\ n — see BIBLE table

Dan·ish \'dā-nish\ n : the language of the Danes — **Danish** adj

Danish pastry n : a pastry made of a rich yeast-raised dough

dank \\'daŋk\\ *adj* : disagreeably wet or moist : DAMP

dan·seuse \\dän-ˈsə(r)z, dän-ˈsüz\\ *n* [F] : a female ballet dancer

dap·per \\'dap-ər\\ *adj* 1 : SPRUCE, TRIM 2 : being alert and lively in movement and manners : JAUNTY

dap·ple \\'dap-əl\\ *vb* **dap·pled; dap·pling** : to mark with different-colored spots

DAR *abbr* Daughters of the American Revolution

¹dare \\'daər\\ *vb* **dared; dar·ing** 1 : to have sufficient courage : be bold enough to 2 : CHALLENGE 3 : to confront boldly

²dare *n* : an act or instance of daring : CHALLENGE

dare·dev·il \\-ˌdev-əl\\ *n* : a recklessly bold person

dar·ing \\'da(ə)r-iŋ\\ *n* : venturesome boldness — **daring** *adj* — **dar·ing·ly** *adv*

¹dark \\'därk\\ *adj* 1 : being without light or without much light 2 : not light in color (a ∼ suit) 3 : GLOOMY 4 : being without knowledge and culture (the *Dark* Ages) 5 : SECRETIVE — **dark·ly** *adv* — **dark·ness** *n*

²dark *n* 1 : absence of light : DARKNESS; *esp* : NIGHT 2 : a dark or deep color — **in the dark** 1 : in secrecy 2 : in ignorance

dark adaptation *n* : the process by which the eye adapts to seeing in weak light — **dark–adapt·ed** \\ˌdär-kə-ˈdap-təd\\ *adj*

dark·en \\'där-kən\\ *vb* **dark·ened; dark·en·ing** \\'där-k(ə-)niŋ\\ 1 : to make or grow dark or darker 2 : DIM 3 : BESMIRCH, TARNISH 4 : to make or become gloomy or forbidding

dark horse *n* : a contestant or a political figure whose abilities and chances as a contender are not known

dark·ling \\'där-kliŋ\\ *adj* 1 : DARK (a ∼ plain) 2 : MYSTERIOUS

dark·room \\'därk-ˌrüm, -ˌrüm\\ *n* : a room which is protected from light and in which photographic plates and film are developed

dark·some \\'därk-səm\\ *adj* : DARK

¹dar·ling \\'där-liŋ\\ *n* 1 : a dearly loved person 2 : FAVORITE

²darling *adj* 1 : dearly loved : FAVORITE 2 : very pleasing : CHARMING

darn \\'därn\\ *vb* : to mend with interlacing stitches — **darn·er** *n*

darning needle *n* 1 : a needle for darning 2 : DRAGONFLY

¹dart \\'därt\\ *n* 1 : a small missile with a point on one end and feathers on the other; *also, pl* : a game in which darts are thrown at a target 2 : something causing a sudden pain 3 : a stitched tapering fold in a garment 4 : a quick movement

²dart *vb* 1 : to throw with a sudden movement 2 : to thrust or move suddenly or rapidly

dart·er \\'därt-ər\\ *n* : any of numerous small American freshwater fishes related to the perches

Dar·win·ism \\'där-wə-ˌniz-əm\\ *n* : a theory of the origin and perpetuation of new species of plants and animals through the action of natural selection on chance variations — **Dar·win·ist** \\-nəst\\ *n or adj*

¹dash \\'dash\\ *vb* 1 : to knock, hurl, or thrust violently 2 : SMASH 3 : SPLASH, SPATTER 4 : RUIN 5 : DEPRESS, SADDEN 6 : to perform or finish hastily 7 : to move with sudden speed

²dash *n* 1 : a sudden burst or splash 2 : a stroke of a pen 3 : a punctuation mark — that is used esp. to indicate a break in the thought or structure of a sentence 4 : a small addition (add a ∼ of salt) 5 : flashy showiness 6 : animation in style and action 7 : a sudden rush or attempt (made a ∼ for the door) 8 : a short foot race

dash·board \\-ˌbòrd\\ *n* : an instrument panel below the windshield in an automobile or aircraft

dash·er \\'dash-ər\\ *n* : a device (as in a churn) that agitates or stirs up something

da·shi·ki \\də-ˈshē-kē\\ *or* **dai·shi·ki** \\dī-\\ *n* [modif. of Yoruba *danshiki* (an African language) *danshiki*] : a usu. brightly colored loose-fitting pullover garment

dash·ing \\'dash-iŋ\\ *adj* 1 : marked by vigorous action 2 : marked by smartness esp. in dress and manners

das·tard \\'das-tərd\\ *n* : COWARD; *esp* : one who sneakingly commits malicious acts — **das·tard·ly** *adj*

dat *abbr* dative

da·ta \\'dāt-ə, 'dat-\\ *n sing or pl* : factual information (as measurements or statistics) used as a basis for reasoning, discussion, or calculation

data processing *n* : the action or process of supplying a computer with information and having the computer use it to produce a desired result

¹date \\'dāt\\ *n* [ME, fr. OF, deriv. of L *dactylus*, fr. Gk *daktylos*, lit., finger] : the edible fruit of a tall Old World palm; *also* : this palm

²date *n* [ME, fr. MF, fr. LL *data*, fr. *data* (as in *data Romae* given at Rome), fr. L *dare* to give] 1 : the day, month, or year of an event 2 : a statement giving the time of execution or making (as of a coin or check) 3 : the period to which something belongs 4 : APPOINTMENT; *esp* : a social engagement between two persons of opposite sex 5 : a person of the opposite sex with whom one has a social engagement — **to date** : up to the present moment

³date *vb* **dat·ed; dat·ing** 1 : to record the date of or on 2 : to determine, mark, or reveal the date, age, or period of 3 : to make or have a date with 4 : ORIGINATE (∼s from ancient times) 5 : EXTEND (*dating* back to childhood) 6 : to show qualities typical of a past period

dat·ed \'dāt-əd\ *adj* **1** : provided with a date **2** : OLD-FASHIONED

date·less \'dāt-ləs\ *adj* **1** : ENDLESS **2** : having no date **3** : too ancient to be dated **4** : TIMELESS

date·line \'dāt-,līn\ *n* : a line in a publication giving the date and place of composition or issue — **dateline** *vb*

da·tive \'dāt-iv\ *adj* : of, relating to, or constituting a grammatical case marking typically the indirect object of a verb — **dative** *n*

da·tum \'dāt-əm, 'dat-, 'dät-\ *n, pl* **da·ta** \-ə\ *or* **datums** : a single piece of data : FACT

dau *abbr* daughter

¹daub \'dob\ *vb* **1** : to cover with soft adhesive matter **2** : SMEAR, SMUDGE **3** : to paint crudely — **daub·er** *n*

²daub *n* : something daubed on : SMEAR **2** : a crude picture

daugh·ter \'dot-ər\ *n* **1** : a female offspring esp. of human beings **2** : a human female having a specified ancestor or belonging to a group of common ancestry

daugh·ter–in–law \'dot-ə-rən-,lo, -ərn-,lo\ *n, pl* **daugh·ters–in–law** \-ər-zən-\ : the wife of one's son

daunt \'dont\ *vb* [ME *daunten*, fr. OF *danter*, alter. of *donter*, fr. L *domitare* to tame] : to lessen the courage of : INTIMIDATE, OVERWHELM

daunt·less \-ləs\ *adj* : FEARLESS, UNDAUNTED

dau·phin \'do-fən\ *n, often cap* : the eldest son of a king of France

DAV *abbr* Disabled American Veterans

dav·en·port \'dav-ən-,port\ *n* : a large upholstered sofa

da·vit \'dā-vət, 'dav-ət\ *n* : either of a pair of small cranes used esp. on ships for raising and lowering small boats

daw·dle \'dod-ᵊl\ *vb* **daw·dled; daw·dling** \'dod-(ə-)lin\ **1** : to spend time wastefully or idly **2** : LOITER — **daw·dler** \'dod-(ᵊ-)lər\ *n*

¹dawn \'don\ *vb* **1** : to begin to grow light as the sun rises **2** : to begin to appear or develop **3** : to begin to be understood (the solution ~ed on him)

²dawn *n* **1** : the first appearance of light in the morning **2** : a first appearance : BEGINNING (the ~ of a new era)

day \'dā\ *n* **1** : the period of light between one night and the next; *also* : DAYLIGHT **2** : the period of the earth's rotation on its axis **3** : a period of 24 hours beginning at midnight **4** : a specified day or date (wedding ~) **5** : a specified time or period : AGE (in olden ~s) **6** : the conflict or contention of the day **7** : the time set apart by usage or law for work (the 8-hour ~)

day·bed \'dā-,bed\ *n* : a couch that can be converted into a bed

day·book \-,buk\ *n* : DIARY, JOURNAL

day·break \-,brāk\ *n* : DAWN

day–care \'dā-,keər\ *adj* : relating to or providing supervision and facilities for preschool children during the day

day·dream \'dā-,drēm\ *n* : a pleasant reverie — **daydream** *vb*

day·light \'dā-,līt\ *n* **1** : the light of day **2** : DAYTIME **3** : DAWN **4** : understanding of something that has been obscure **5** *pl* : CONSCIOUSNESS; *also* : WITS

daylight saving time : time usu. one hour ahead of standard time

Day of Atonement : YOM KIPPUR

day school *n* : a private school without boarding facilities

day student *n* : a student who attends regular classes at a college or preparatory school but does not live there

day·time \'dā-,tīm\ *n* : the period of daylight

daze \'dāz\ *vb* **dazed; daz·ing** **1** : to stupefy esp. by a blow **2** : DAZZLE — **daze** *n*

daz·zle \'daz-əl\ *vb* **daz·zled; daz·zling** \-(ə-)lin\ **1** : to overpower with light **2** : to impress greatly or confound with brilliance — **dazzle** *n*

db *or* **dB** *abbr* decibel

d/b/a *abbr* doing business as

dbl *abbr* double

DC *abbr* **1** [It *da capo*] from the beginning **2** direct current **3** District of Columbia **4** doctor of chiropractic

DD *abbr* **1** days after date **2** demand draft **3** dishonorable discharge **4** doctor of divinity

D day *n* [*D*, abbr. for *day*] : a day set for launching an operation (as an invasion)

DDS *abbr* **1** doctor of dental science **2** doctor of dental surgery

DDT \,dē-(,)dē-'tē\ *n* : a persistent insecticide poisonous to many higher animals

DE *abbr* Delaware

dea·con \'dē-kən\ *n* [ME *dekene*, fr. OE *dēacon*, fr. LL *diaconus*, fr. Gk *diakonos*, lit., servant] : a subordinate officer in a Christian church

dea·con·ess \'dē-kə-nəs\ *n* : a woman chosen to assist in the church ministry

de·ac·ti·vate \dē-'ak-tə-,vāt\ *vb* : to make inactive or ineffective

¹dead \'ded\ *adj* **1** : LIFELESS **2** : DEATHLIKE, DEADLY (in a ~ faint) **3** : NUMB **4** : very tired **5** : UNRESPONSIVE **6** : EXTINGUISHED (~ coals) **7** : INANIMATE, INERT **8** : no longer active or functioning : EXHAUSTED, EXTINCT (a ~ battery) (a ~ volcano) **9** : lacking power, significance, or effect (a ~ custom) **10** : OBSOLETE (a ~ language) **11** : lacking in gaiety or animation (a ~ party) **12** : QUIET, IDLE, UNPRODUCTIVE (~ capital) **13** : lacking elasticity (a ~ tennis ball) **14** : not circulating : STAGNANT (~ air) **15** : lacking warmth, vigor, or taste (~ wine) **16** : absolutely uniform (~ level) **17** : UNERRING, EXACT (a ~ shot) **18** : ABRUPT (a ~ stop) **19** : COMPLETE (a ~ loss)

²dead *n, pl* **dead** **1** : one that is dead — usu. used collectively (the living and the ∼) **2** : the time of greatest quiet (the ∼ of the night)

³**dead** *adv* **1** : UTTERLY (∼ right) **2** : in a sudden and complete manner (stopped ∼) **3** : DIRECTLY (∼ ahead)

dead·beat \-ˌbēt\ *n* : one who persistently fails to pay his debts or his way

dead·en \ˈded-ᵊn\ *vb* **dead·ened; dead·en·ing** \ˈded-(ᵊ-)niŋ\ **1** : to impair in force, activity, or sensation : BLUNT (∼ pain) **2** : to lessen the luster or spirit of **3** : to make (as a wall) soundproof

dead end *n* **1** : an end (as of a street) without an exit **2** : a position, situation, or course of action that leads to nothing further — **dead–end** \ˈded-ˌend\ *adj*

dead heat *n* : a contest in which two or more contestants tie (as by crossing the finish line simultaneously)

dead letter *n* **1** : something that has lost its force or authority without being formally abolished **2** : a letter that cannot be delivered or returned

dead·line \ˈded-ˌlīn\ *n* : a date or time before which something must be done

dead·lock \ˈded-ˌläk\ *n* : a stoppage of action because neither faction in a struggle will give in — **deadlock** *vb*

¹**dead·ly** \ˈded-lē\ *adj* **dead·li·er; -est 1** : likely to cause or capable of causing death **2** : HOSTILE, IMPLACABLE **3** : very accurate : UNERRING **4** : tending to deprive of force or vitality (a ∼ habit) **5** : suggestive of death **6** : very great : EXTREME — **dead·li·ness** *n*

²**deadly** *adv* **1** : suggesting death (∼ pale) **2** : EXTREMELY (∼ dull)

deadly sin *n* : one of seven sins of pride, covetousness, lust, anger, gluttony, envy, and sloth held to be fatal to spiritual progress

dead·pan \ˈded-ˌpan\ *adj* : marked by an impassive manner or expression — **deadpan** *vb*

dead reckoning *n* : the determination of the position of a ship or aircraft solely from the record of the direction and distance of its course

dead·weight \ˈded-ˈwāt\ *n* **1** : the unrelieved weight of an inert mass **2** : a ship's load including the weight of cargo, fuel, crew, and passengers

dead·wood \-ˌwu̇d\ *n* **1** : wood dead on the tree **2** : useless personnel or material

deaf \ˈdef\ *adj* **1** : unable to hear **2** : unwilling to hear or listen (∼ to all suggestions) — **deaf·ness** *n*

deaf·en \ˈdef-ən\ *vb* **deaf·ened; deaf·en·ing** \-(ə-)niŋ\ : to make deaf

deaf–mute \ˈdef-ˌmyüt\ *n* : a deaf person who cannot speak

¹**deal** \ˈdēl\ *n* **1** : a usu. large or indefinite quantity or degree (a great ∼ of support) **2** : the act or right of distributing cards to players in a card game; *also* : HAND

²**deal** *vb* **dealt** \ˈdelt\; **deal·ing** \ˈdē-liŋ\ **1** : DISTRIBUTE; *esp* : to distribute playing cards to players in a game **2** : ADMINISTER, DELIVER (*dealt* him a blow) **3** : to concern itself : TREAT (the book ∼s with crime) **4** : to take action in regard to something (∼ with offenders) **5** : TRADE; *also* : to sell or distribute something as a business (∼ in used cars) — **deal·er** *n*

³**deal** *n* **1** : BARGAINING, NEGOTIATION; *also* : TRANSACTION **2** : treatment received (a raw ∼)

⁴**deal** *n* : wood or a board of fir or pine

deal·er·ship \ˈdē-lər-ˌship\ *n* : an authorized sales agency

deal·ing \ˈdē-liŋ\ *n* **1** *pl* : friendly or business transactions **2** : a way of acting or of doing business

dean \ˈdēn\ *n* [ME *deen*, fr. MF *deien*, fr. LL *decanus*, lit., chief of ten, fr. L *decem* ten] **1** : a clergyman who is head of a group of canons or joint pastors of a church **2** : the head of a division, faculty, college, or school of a university **3** : a college or secondary school administrator in charge of counseling and disciplining students **4** : the senior member of a group (the ∼ of a diplomatic corps) — **dean·ship** *n*

dean·ery \ˈdēn-(ə-)rē\ *n*, *pl* **-er·ies** : the office, jurisdiction, or official residence of a clerical dean

¹**dear** \ˈdiər\ *adj* **1** : highly valued : PRECIOUS **2** : AFFECTIONATE, FOND **3** : EXPENSIVE **4** : HEARTFELT — **dear·ly** *adv* — **dear·ness** *n*

²**dear** *n* : a loved one : DARLING

Dear John \-ˈjän\ *n* : a letter (as to a soldier) in which a woman breaks off a marital or romantic relationship

dearth \ˈdərth\ *n* : SCARCITY, FAMINE

death \ˈdeth\ *n* **1** : the end of life **2** : the cause of loss of life **3** : the state of being dead **4** : DESTRUCTION, EXTINCTION **5** : SLAUGHTER — **death·like** *adj*

death·bed \ˈdeth-ˈbed\ *n* **1** : the bed in which a person dies **2** : the last hours of life

death·blow \ˈdeth-ˈblō\ *n* : a destructive or killing stroke or event

death·less \ˈdeth-ləs\ *adj* : IMMORTAL, IMPERISHABLE (∼ fame)

death·ly \ˈdeth-lē\ *adj* **1** : FATAL **2** : of, relating to, or suggestive of death (a ∼ pallor) — **deathly** *adv*

death rattle *n* : a sound produced by air passing through mucus in the lungs and air passages of a dying person

death's–head \ˈdeths-ˌhed\ *n* : a human skull emblematic of death

death·watch \ˈdeth-ˌwäch\ *n* : a vigil kept over the dead or dying

deb \ˈdeb\ *n* : DEBUTANTE

de·ba·cle \di-ˈbäk-əl, -ˈbak-əl\ *n* [F *débâcle*] : DISASTER, FAILURE, ROUT (stock market ∼)

de·bar \di-ˈbär\ *vb* : to bar from having or doing something : PRECLUDE

de·bark \di-ˈbärk\ *vb* : DISEMBARK — **de·bar·ka·tion** \ˌdē-ˌbär-ˈkā-shən\ *n*

de·base \di-ˈbās\ *vb* : to lower in character, quality, or value syn degrade, corrupt, deprave — **de·base·ment** n

de·bate \di-'bāt\ vb **de·bat·ed; de·bat·ing** **1** : to discuss or examine a question by presenting and considering arguments on both sides **2** : to take part in a debate — **de·bat·able** adj — debate n — **de·bat·er** n

de·bauch \di-'bóch\ vb : SEDUCE, CORRUPT — **de·bauch·ery** \-(ə-)rē\ n

de·ben·ture \di-'ben-chər\ n : a certificate of indebtedness; esp : a bond secured only by the general assets of the issuing government or company

de·bil·i·tate \di-'bil-ə-‚tāt\ vb **-tat·ed; -tat·ing** : to impair the health or strength of

de·bil·i·ty \di-'bil-ət-ē\ n, pl **-ties** : an infirm or weakened state

¹deb·it \'deb-ət\ vb : to enter as a debit : charge with or as a debit

²debit n **1** : an entry in an account showing money paid out or owed **2** : a disadvantageous or unfavorable quality or character

deb·o·nair \‚deb-ə-'naər\ adj [ME debonere, fr. OF debonaire, fr. de bon aire of good family or nature] : gaily and gracefully charming : LIGHTHEARTED

de·bouch \di-'bauch, -'bûsh\ vb [F déboucher, fr. dé- out of + bouche mouth] : to come out into an open area

de·brief \di-'brēf\ vb : to question (as a pilot back from a mission) in order to obtain useful information

de·bris \də-'brē, dā-; 'dā-‚brē\ n, pl **debris** \-'brēz, -‚brēz\ **1** : the remains of something broken down or destroyed : RUINS **2** : an accumulation of fragments of rock

debt \'det\ n **1** : SIN, TRESPASS **2** : a condition of owing; esp : the state of owing money in amounts greater than one can pay **3** : something owed : OBLIGATION

debt·or \'det-ər\ n **1** : one guilty of neglect or violation of duty **2** : one that owes a debt

de·bunk \di-'bəŋk\ vb : to expose the sham or falseness of ⟨~ a rumor⟩

de·but \'dā-‚byü, dā-'byü\ n **1** : a first appearance **2** : a formal entrance into society

deb·u·tante \'deb-yù-‚tänt\ n : a young woman making her formal entrance into society

dec abbr **1** deceased **2** decrease

Dec abbr December

de·cade \'dek-‚ād, -əd; de-'kād\ n : a period of 10 years

dec·a·dence \'dek-əd-əns, di-'kād-²ns\ n : DETERIORATION, DECLINE — **dec·a·dent** \'dek-əd-ənt, di-'kād-²nt\ adj or n

deca·gon \'dek-ə-‚gän\ n : a plane polygon of 10 angles and 10 sides

de·cal \'dē-‚kal\ n : a picture, design, or label made to be transferred (as to glass) from specially prepared paper

de·cal·co·ma·nia \di-‚kal-kə-'mā-nē-ə\ n

[F décalcomanie, fr. décalquer to copy by tracing (fr. calquer to trace, fr. It calcare, lit., to trample, fr. L) + manie mania, fr. LL mania] : DECAL

Deca·logue \'dek-ə-‚lòg\ n : the ten commandments of God given to Moses on Mount Sinai

de·camp \di-'kamp\ vb **1** : to break up a camp **2** : to depart suddenly

de·cant \di-'kant\ vb : to pour (liquor) gently

de·cant·er \di-'kant-ər\ n : an ornamental glass bottle for serving wine

de·cap·i·tate \di-'kap-ə-‚tāt\ vb **-tat·ed; -tat·ing** : BEHEAD — **de·cap·i·ta·tion** \-‚kap-ə-'tā-shən\ n

deca·syl·lab·ic \‚dek-ə-sə-'lab-ik\ adj : having or composed of verses having 10 syllables — **decasyllabic** n

de·cath·lon \di-'kath-lən, -‚län\ n : an athletic contest in which each competitor participates in each of a series of 10 track-and-field events

de·cay \di-'kā\ vb **1** : to decline from a sound or prosperous condition **2** : to cause or undergo decomposition ⟨radium ~s slowly⟩ ; esp : to break down while spoiling : ROT — decay n

decd abbr deceased

de·cease \di-'sēs\ n : DEATH

¹de·ceased \-'sēst\ adj : no longer living; esp : recently dead

²deceased n, pl **deceased** : a dead person

de·ce·dent \di-'sēd-²nt\ n : a deceased person

de·ceit \di-'sēt\ n **1** : DECEPTION **2** : TRICK **3** : DECEITFULNESS

de·ceit·ful \-fəl\ adj **1** : practicing or tending to practice deceit **2** : MISLEADING, DECEPTIVE ⟨a ~ answer⟩ — **de·ceit·ful·ly** adv — **de·ceit·ful·ness** n

de·ceive \di-'sēv\ vb **de·ceived; de·ceiv·ing** **1** : to cause to believe an untruth **2** : to use or practice deceit — **de·ceiv·er** n

de·cel·er·ate \dē-'sel-ə-‚rāt\ vb **-at·ed; -at·ing** : to slow down

De·cem·ber \di-'sem-bər\ n [ME Decembre, fr. OF, fr. L December (tenth month), fr. decem ten] : the 12th month of the year having 31 days

de·cen·cy \'dēs-²n-sē\ n, pl **-cies** **1** : PROPRIETY **2** : conformity to standards of taste, propriety, or quality **3** : standard of propriety — usu. used in pl.

de·cen·ni·al \di-'sen-ē-əl\ adj **1** : consisting of 10 years **2** : happening every 10 years ⟨~ census⟩

de·cent \'dēs-²nt\ adj **1** : conforming to standards of propriety, good taste, or morality **2** : modestly clothed **3** : free from immodesty or obscenity **4** : ADEQUATE ⟨~ housing⟩ — **de·cent·ly** adv

de·cen·tral·iza·tion \dē-‚sen-trə-lə-'zā-shən\ n **1** : the distribution of powers from a central authority to regional and local authorities **2** : the redistribution of population and industry from urban centers to outlying areas — **de·cen·tral·ize** \-'sen-trə-‚līz\ vb

de·cep·tion \di-'sep-shən\ n **1** : the act

of deceiving **2** : the fact or condition of being deceived **3** : FRAUD, TRICK — **de·cep·tive** \-'sep-tiv\ *adj* — **de·cep·tive·ly** *adv*

deci·bel \'des-ə-ˌbel, -bəl\ *n* : a unit for measuring the relative loudness of sounds

de·cide \di-'sīd\ *vb* **de·cid·ed; de·cid·ing** [ME *deciden*, fr. MF *decider*, fr. L *decidere*, lit., to cut off, fr. *caedere* to cut] **1** : to arrive at a solution that ends uncertainty or dispute about **2** : to bring to a definitive end ⟨one blow *decided* the fight⟩ **3** : to induce to come to a choice **4** : to make a choice or judgment

de·cid·ed \di-'sīd-əd\ *adj* **1** : CLEAR, UNMISTAKABLE **2** : FIRM, DETERMINED — **de·cid·ed·ly** *adv*

de·cid·u·ous \di-'sij-ə-wəs\ *adj* **1** : falling off usu. at the end of a period of growth or function ⟨~ leaves⟩ ⟨a ~ tooth⟩ **2** : having deciduous parts ⟨~ trees⟩

deci·gram \'des-ə-ˌgram\ *n* — see METRIC SYSTEM table

deci·li·ter \'des-ə-ˌlēt-ər\ *n* — see METRIC SYSTEM table

¹deci·mal \'des-ə-məl\ *adj* : based on the number 10 : reckoning by tens

²decimal *n* : any number expressed in base 10; *esp* : DECIMAL FRACTION

decimal fraction *n* : a fraction (as .25 = $^{25}/100$ or .025 = $^{25}/1000$) or mixed number (as 3.025 = 3 $^{25}/1000$) in which the denominator is a power of 10 usu. expressed by use of the decimal point

decimal point *n* : the dot at the left of a decimal fraction (as .678) less than one or between the parts of a mixed number (as 3.678) composed of a whole number and a decimal fraction

deci·mate \'des-ə-ˌmāt\ *vb* **-mat·ed; -mat·ing 1** : to take or destroy the 10th part of **2** : to destroy a large part of

deci·me·ter \'des-ə-ˌmēt-ər\ *n* — see METRIC SYSTEM table

de·ci·pher \di-'sī-fər\ *vb* **1** : to translate from secret writing (as code) **2** : to make out the meaning of despite indistinctness — **de·ci·pher·able** *adj*

de·ci·sion \di-'sizh-ən\ *n* **1** : the act or result of deciding **2** : promptness and firmness in deciding : DETERMINATION

de·ci·sive \-'sī-siv\ *adj* **1** : having the power to decide ⟨the ~ vote⟩ **2** : RESOLUTE, DETERMINED **3** : CONCLUSIVE ⟨a ~ victory⟩ — **de·ci·sive·ly** *adv* — **de·ci·sive·ness** *n*

¹deck \'dek\ *n* **1** : a floorlike platform of a ship; *also* : something resembling the deck of a ship **2** : a pack of playing cards

²deck *vb* **1** : ARRAY **2** : DECORATE **3** : to furnish with a deck **4** : KNOCK DOWN, FLOOR

deck·hand \'dek-ˌhand\ *n* : a sailor who performs manual duties

deck·le edge \ˌdek-əl-\ *n* : the rough untrimmed edge of paper — **deck·le-edged** \ˌdek-ə-'lejd\ *adj*

de·claim \di-'klām\ *vb* : to speak or deliver in the manner of a formal speech — **dec·la·ma·tion** \ˌdek-lə-'mā-shən\ *n* — **de·clam·a·to·ry** \di-'klam-ə-ˌtōr-ē\ *adj*

de·clar·a·tive \di-'klar-ət-iv\ *adj* : making a declaration ⟨~ sentence⟩

de·clare \di-'klaər\ *vb* **de·clared; de·clar·ing 1** : to make known formally or explicitly : ANNOUNCE ⟨~ war⟩ **2** : to state emphatically : AFFIRM **3** : to make a full statement of — **dec·la·ra·tion** \ˌdek-lə-'rā-shən\ *n* — **de·clar·a·to·ry** \di-'klar-ə-ˌtōr-ē\ *adj* — **de·clar·er** *n*

de·clas·si·fy \dē-'klas-ə-ˌfī\ *vb* : to remove or reduce the security classification of

de·clen·sion \di-'klen-chən\ *n* **1** : the inflectional forms of a noun, pronoun, or adjective **2** : DECLINE, DETERIORATION **3** : DESCENT, SLOPE

¹de·cline \di-'klīn\ *vb* **de·clined; de·clin·ing 1** : to slope downward : DESCEND **2** : DROOP **3** : RECEDE **4** : WANE **5** : to withhold consent; *also* : REFUSE, REJECT **6** : INFLECT **2** ⟨~ a noun⟩ — **de·clin·able** *adj* — **dec·li·na·tion** \ˌdek-lə-'nā-shən\ *n*

²decline *n* **1** : a gradual sinking and wasting away **2** : a change to a lower state or level **3** : the time when something is approaching its end **4** : a descending slope **5** : a wasting disease; *esp* : pulmonary tuberculosis

de·cliv·i·ty \di-'kliv-ət-ē\ *n, pl* **-ties** : a steep downward slope

de·code \dē-'kōd\ *vb* : to convert (a coded message) into ordinary language — **de·cod·er** *n*

dé·col·le·té \dā-ˌkäl-ə-'tā\ *adj* [F] **1** : wearing a strapless or low-necked gown **2** : having a low-cut neckline

de·com·mis·sion \ˌdē-kə-'mish-ən\ *vb* : to take out of commission

de·com·pose \ˌdē-kəm-'pōz\ *vb* **1** : to separate into constituent parts **2** : to break down in decay : ROT — **de·com·po·si·tion** \dē-ˌkäm-pə-'zish-ən\ *n*

de·com·press \ˌdē-kəm-'pres\ *vb* : to release (as a diver) from pressure or compression — **de·com·pres·sion** \-'presh-ən\ *n*

de·con·ges·tant \ˌdē-kən-'jes-tənt\ *n* : an agent that relieves congestion (as of mucous membranes)

de·con·tam·i·nate \ˌdē-kən-'tam-ə-ˌnāt\ *vb* : to rid of contamination (as radioactive material) — **de·con·tam·i·na·tion** \-ˌtam-ə-'nā-shən\ *n*

de·con·trol \ˌdē-kən-'trōl\ *vb* : to end control of ⟨~ prices⟩

de·cor *or* **dé·cor** \dā-ˌkȯr, 'dā-ˌkȯr\ *n* : DECORATION; *esp* : the arrangement of accessories in interior decoration

dec·o·rate \'dek-ə-ˌrāt\ *vb* **-rat·ed; -rat·ing 1** : to make more attractive by adding something beautiful or becoming : ADORN, EMBELLISH **2** : to award a mark of honor (as a medal) to

dec·o·ra·tion \ˌdek-ə-'rā-shən\ *n* **1** : the

act or process of decorating **2** : ORNA-MENT **3** : a badge of honor

dec·o·ra·tive \'dek-(ə-)rət-iv\ *adj* : OR-NAMENTAL

dec·o·ra·tor \'dek-ə-,rāt-ər\ *n* : one that decorates; *esp* : a person who designs or executes the interiors of buildings and their furnishings

dec·o·rous \'dek-ə-rəs, di-'kōr-əs\ *adj* : PROPER, SEEMLY, CORRECT

de·co·rum \di-'kōr-əm\ *n* [L] **1** : conformity to accepted standards of conduct **2** : ORDERLINESS, PROPRIETY

¹de·coy \'dē-,kói, di-'kói\ *n* : something that lures or entices; *esp* : an artificial bird used to attract live birds within shot

²de·coy \di-'kói, 'dē-,kói\ *vb* : to lure by or as if by a decoy : ENTICE

¹de·crease \di-'krēs\ *vb* **de·creased; de·creas·ing** : to grow or cause to grow less : DIMINISH

²de·crease \'dē-,krēs\ *n* **1** : the process of decreasing **2** : REDUCTION

¹de·cree \di-'krē\ *n* **1** : ORDER, EDICT **2** : a judicial decision

²decree *vb* **de·creed; de·cree·ing 1** : COMMAND **2** : to determine or order judicially

dec·re·ment \'dek-rə-mənt\ *n* **1** : gradual decrease **2** : the quantity lost by diminution or waste

de·crep·it \di-'krep-ət\ *adj* : broken down with age : WORN-OUT — **de·crep·i·tude** \-ə-,t(y)üd\ *n*

de·cre·scen·do \,dā-krə-'shen-dō\ *adv or adj* : with a decrease in volume — used as a direction in music

de·crim·i·nal·ize \dē-'krim-ən-ᵊl-,īz\ *vb* : to remove or reduce the criminal status of

de·cry \di-'krī\ *vb* **1** : to belittle publicly **2** : to find fault with : CONDEMN

ded·i·cate \'ded-i-,kāt\ *vb* **-cat·ed; -cat·ing 1** : to devote to the worship of a divine being esp. with sacred rites **2** : to set apart for a definite purpose **3** : to inscribe or address as a compliment — **ded·i·ca·tion** \,ded-i-'kā-shən\ *n* — **ded·i·ca·to·ry** \'ded-i-kə-,tōr-ē\ *adj*

de·duce \di-'d(y)üs\ *vb* **de·duced; de·duc·ing 1** : to derive by reasoning : IN-FER **2** : to trace the course of ⟨~ their lineage⟩ — **de·duc·ible** *adj*

de·duct \di-'dəkt\ *vb* : SUBTRACT — **de·duct·ible** *adj*

de·duc·tion \di-'dək-shən\ *n* **1** : SUB-TRACTION **2** : something that is or may be subtracted : ABATEMENT **3** : the deriving of a conclusion by reasoning : the conclusion so reached — **de·duc·tive** \-'dək-tiv\ *adj*

¹deed \'dēd\ *n* **1** : something done **2** : FEAT, EXPLOIT **3** : a document containing some legal transfer, bargain, or contract

²deed *vb* : to convey or transfer by deed

dee·jay \'dē-'jā\ *n* : DISC JOCKEY

deem \'dēm\ *vb* : THINK, JUDGE

de–em·pha·size \dē-'em-fə-,sīz\ *vb* : to refrain from emphasizing — **de–em·pha·sis** \-fə-səs\ *n*

¹deep \'dēp\ *adj* **1** : extending far down, back, within, or outward **2** : having a specified extension downward or backward **3** : difficult to understand; *also* : MYSTERIOUS, OBSCURE ⟨a ~ dark secret⟩ **4** : WISE **5** : ENGROSSED, IN-VOLVED ⟨~ in thought⟩ **6** : INTENSE, PROFOUND ⟨~ sleep⟩ **7** : dark and rich in color ⟨a ~ red⟩ **8** : having a low musical pitch or range ⟨a ~ voice⟩ **9** : situated well within **10** : covered, enclosed, or filled often to a specified degree — **deep·ly** *adv*

deep *adv* **1** : DEEPLY **2** : far on : LATE ⟨~ in the night⟩

³deep *n* **1** : an extremely deep place or part; *esp* : OCEAN **2** : the middle or most intense part ⟨the ~ of winter⟩

deep·en \'dē-pən\ *vb* **deep·ened; deep·en·ing** \'dēp-(ə-)niŋ\ : to make or become deep or deeper

deep–freeze \'dēp-'frēz\ *vb* **-froze** \-'frōz\; **-fro·zen** \-'frōz-ᵊn\ : QUICK-FREEZE

deep–root·ed \-'rüt-əd, -'rüt-\ *adj* : deeply implanted or established

deep–sea \,dēp-'sē\ *adj* : of, relating to, or occurring in the deeper parts of the sea ⟨~ fishing⟩

deep–seat·ed \'dēp-'sēt-əd\ *adj* **1** : situated far below the surface **2** : firmly established ⟨~ convictions⟩

deer \'diər\ *n, pl* **deer** [ME, *deer*, animal, fr. OE *dēor* beast] : any of a family of ruminant mammals with cloven hoofs and usu. antlers esp. in the males

deer·fly \-,flī\ *n* : any of numerous small horseflies

deer·skin \-,skin\ *n* : leather made from the skin of a deer; *also* : a garment of such leather

de·es·ca·late \dē-'es-kə-,lāt\ *vb* : to decrease in extent, volume, or scope : REDUCE ⟨~ the war⟩ — **de·es·ca·la·tion** \,dē-,es-kə-'lā-shən\ *n*

def *abbr* **1** defendant **2** definite **3** definition

de·face \di-'fās\ *vb* : to destroy or mar the face or surface of — **de·face·ment** *n*

de fac·to \di-'fak-tō, dā-\ *adj or adv* **1** : actually existing ⟨*de facto* segregation⟩ **2** : actually exercising power ⟨*de facto* government⟩

de·fal·ca·tion \,dē-,fal-'kā-shən, ,dē-,fól-; ,def-əl-\ *n* : EMBEZZLEMENT

de·fame \di-'fām\ *vb* **de·famed; de·fam·ing** : to injure or destroy the reputation of by libel or slander — **def·a·ma·tion** \,def-ə-'mā-shən\ *n* — **de·fam·a·to·ry** \di-'fam-ə-,tōr-ē\ *adj*

de·fault \di-'fólt\ *n* **1** : failure to do something required by duty or law ⟨the defendant failed to appear and was held in ~⟩ **2** : failure to compete in or to finish an appointed contest ⟨lose a race by ~⟩ — **default** *vb* — **de·fault·er** *n*

¹de·feat \di-ˈfēt\ *vb* **1** : FRUSTRATE, NULLIFY **2** : to win victory over : BEAT

²defeat *n* **1** : FRUSTRATION **2** : an overthrow of an army in battle **3** : loss of a contest

de·feat·ism \-ˌiz-əm,\ *n* : acceptance of or resignation to defeat — **de·feat·ist** \-əst\ *n or adj*

def·e·cate \ˈdef-i-ˌkāt\ *vb* -cat·ed; -cat·ing **1** : to free from impurity or corruption : REFINE **2** : to discharge feces from the bowels — **def·e·ca·tion** \ˌdef-i-ˈkā-shən\ *n*

¹de·fect \ˈdē-ˌfekt, di-ˈfekt\ *n* : BLEMISH, FAULT, IMPERFECTION

²de·fect \di-ˈfekt\ *vb* : to desert a cause or party esp. in order to espouse another — **de·fec·tion** \-ˈfek-shən\ *n* — **de·fec·tor** \-ˈfek-tər\ *n*

de·fec·tive \di-ˈfek-tiv\ *adj* : FAULTY, DEFICIENT — **defective** *n*

de·fend \di-ˈfend\ *vb* [ME *defenden,* fr. OF *defendre,* fr. L *defendere,* fr. *de-* from + *-fendere* to strike] **1** : to repel danger or attack from **2** : to act as attorney for **3** : to oppose the claim of another in a lawsuit : CONTEST **4** : to maintain against opposition ⟨~ an idea⟩ — **de·fend·er** *n*

de·fen·dant \di-ˈfen-dənt\ *n* : a person required to make answer in a legal action or suit

de·fense *or* **de·fence** \di-ˈfens\ *n* **1** : the act of defending : resistance against attack **2** : means, method, or capability of defending **3** : an argument in support **4** : the answer made by the defendant in a legal action **5** : a defending party, group, or team — **de·fense·less** *adj* — **de·fen·si·ble**

defense mechanism *n* : an often unconscious mental process (as repression or sublimation) that assists in reaching compromise solutions to personal problems

¹de·fen·sive \di-ˈfen-siv\ *adj* **1** : serving or intended to defend or protect **2** : of or relating to the attempt to keep an opponent from scoring (as in a game) — **de·fen·sive·ly** *adv* — **de·fen·sive·ness** *n*

²defensive *n* : a defensive position

¹de·fer \di-ˈfər\ *vb* **de·ferred; de·fer·ring** [ME *defferen, differen,* fr. MF *differer,* fr. L *differre* to postpone, be different] : POSTPONE, PUT OFF

²defer *vb* **deferred; deferring** [ME *deferren, differen,* fr. MF *deferer, deffer-er,* fr. LL *deferre,* fr. L, to bring down, bring, fr. *ferre* to carry] : to submit or yield to the opinion or wishes of another

def·er·ence \ˈdef-(ə-)rəns\ *n* : courteous, respectful, or ingratiating regard for another's wishes — **def·er·en·tial** \ˌdef-ə-ˈren-chəl\ *adj*

de·fer·ment \di-ˈfər-mənt\ *n* : the act of delaying; *esp* : official postponement of military service

de·fi·ance \di-ˈfī-əns\ *n* **1** : CHALLENGE **2** : a tendency to resist : contempt of opposition

de·fi·ant \-ənt\ *adj* : full of defiance ⟨a ~ gesture⟩ — **de·fi·ant·ly** *adv*

de·fi·bril·la·tor \dē-ˈfib-rə-ˌlāt-ər, -ˈfib-\ *n* : an electronic device used to restore the rhythm of a fibrillating heart by applying an electric shock to it — **de·fi·bril·late** \-ˌlāt\ *vb* — **de·fi·bril·la·tion** \dē-ˌfib-rə-ˈlā-shən, -ˌfib-\ *n*

deficiency disease *n* : a disease (as scurvy or beriberi) caused by a lack of essential dietary elements and esp. a vitamin or mineral

de·fi·cient \di-ˈfish-ənt\ *adj* : lacking in something necessary (as for completeness or health) : DEFECTIVE — **de·fi·cien·cy** \-ˈfish-ən-sē\ *n*

def·i·cit \ˈdef-ə-sət\ *n* : a deficiency in amount; *esp* : an excess of expenditures over revenue

¹de·file \di-ˈfīl\ *vb* **de·filed; de·fil·ing 1** : to make filthy **2** : CORRUPT **3** : to violate the chastity of **4** : to violate the sanctity of : DESECRATE **5** : DISHONOR — **de·file·ment** *n*

²de·file \di-ˈfīl, ˈdē-ˌfīl\ *n* : a narrow passage or gorge

de·fine \di-ˈfīn\ *vb* **de·fined; de·fin·ing 1** : to set forth the meaning of ⟨~ a word⟩ **2** : to fix or mark the limits of **3** : to clarify in outline or character — **de·fin·able** *adj* — **de·fin·er** *n*

def·i·nite \ˈdef-(ə-)nət\ *adj* **1** : having distinct limits : FIXED **2** : clear in meaning **3** : typically designating an identified or immediately identifiable person or thing — **def·i·nite·ly** *adv* — **def·i·nite·ness** *n*

def·i·ni·tion \ˌdef-ə-ˈnish-ən\ *n* **1** : an act of determining or settling **2** : a statement of the meaning of a word or word group; *also* : the action or process of stating such a meaning **3** : the action or the power of making definite and clear : CLARITY, DISTINCTNESS

de·fin·i·tive \di-ˈfin-ət-iv\ *adj* **1** : DECISIVE, CONCLUSIVE **2** : being authoritative and apparently exhaustive **3** : serving to define or specify precisely

de·flate \di-ˈflāt\ *vb* **de·flat·ed; de·flat·ing 1** : to release air or gas from **2** : to cause to contract from an abnormally high level : reduce from a state of inflation **3** : to become deflated

de·fla·tion \-ˈflā-shən\ *n* **1** : an act or instance of deflating : the state of being deflated **2** : reduction in the volume of available money or credit resulting in a decline of the general price level

de·flect \di-ˈflekt\ *vb* : to turn aside — **de·flec·tion** \-ˈflek-shən\ *n*

de·flo·ra·tion \ˌdef-lə-ˈrā-shən\ *n* : rupture of the hymen

de·flow·er \dē-ˈflaù(-ə)r\ *vb* : to deprive of virginity : RAVISH

de·fog \dē-ˈfòg, -ˈfäg\ *vb* : to remove fog or condensed moisture from — **de·fog·ger** *n*

de·fo·li·ant \dē-ˈfō-lē-ənt\ *n* : a chemical spray or dust applied to plants to cause the leaves to drop off prematurely

de·fo·li·ate \-lē-ıāt\ *vb* : to deprive of leaves esp. prematurely — **de·fo·li·a·tion** \dē-ıfō-lē-'ā-shən\ *n* — **de·fo·li·a·tor** \dē-'fō-lē-ıāt-ər\ *n*

de·for·es·ta·tion \dē-ıfōr-ə-'stā-shən\ *n* : the action or process of clearing an area of forests; *also* : the state of having been cleared of forests — **de·for·est** \(')dē-'fōr-əst, -'fär-\ *vb*

de·form \di-'fōrm\ *vb* 1 : DISFIGURE, DEFACE 2 : to make or become misshapen or changed in shape — **de·for·ma·tion** \ıdē-ıfōr-'mā-shən, ıdef-ər-\ *n*

de·for·mi·ty \di-'fōr-mət-ē\ *n, pl* -ties 1 : the state of being deformed 2 : a physical blemish or distortion

de·fraud \di-'frȯd\ *vb* : CHEAT

de·fray \di-'frā\ *vb* : to provide for the payment of : PAY — **de·fray·al** *n*

de·frost \dē-'frȯst\ *vb* 1 : to thaw out 2 : to free from ice — **de·frost·er** *n*

deft \'deft\ *adj* : quick and neat in action — **deft·ly** *adv* — **deft·ness** *n*

de·funct \di-'fəŋkt\ *adj* : DEAD, EXTINCT 〈a ~ organization〉

de·fuse \dē-'fyüz\ *vb* 1 : to remove the fuse from (as a bomb) 2 : to make less harmful, potent, or tense

de·fy \di-'fī\ *vb* **de·fied; de·fy·ing** [ME *defyen* to renounce faith in, challenge, fr. OF *defier*, fr. *de-* from + *fier* to entrust, fr. L *fidere* to trust] 1 : CHALLENGE, DARE 2 : to refuse boldly to obey or to yield to : DISREGARD 〈~ the law〉 3 : WITHSTAND, BAFFLE 〈a scene that *defies* description〉

deg *abbr* degree

de·gas \dē-'gas\ *vb* : to remove gas from

de·gen·er·a·cy \di-'jen-(ə-)rə-sē\ *n, pl* -cies 1 : the state of being degenerate 2 : the process of becoming degenerate

¹**de·gen·er·ate** \di-'jen-(ə-)rət\ *adj* : fallen or deteriorated from a former, higher, or normal condition — **de·gen·er·a·cy** \-rə-sē\ *n* — **de·gen·er·a·tion** \-ıjen-ə-'rā-shən\ *n* — **de·gen·er·a·tive** \-'jen-ə-ırāt-iv\ *adj*

²**de·gen·er·ate** \di-'jen-ə-ırāt\ *vb* : to undergo deterioration (as in morality, intelligence, structure, or function)

³**de·gen·er·ate** \-(ə-)rət\ *n* : a degenerate person; *esp* : a sexual pervert

de·grad·able \di-'grād-ə-bəl\ *adj* : capable of being chemically degraded 〈~ detergents〉

de·grade \di-'grād\ *vb* 1 : to reduce from a higher to a lower rank or degree 2 : DEBASE, CORRUPT — **deg·ra·da·tion** \ıdeg-rə-'dā-shən\ *n*

de·gree \di-'grē\ *n* [ME, fr. OF *degré*, fr. (assumed) VL *degradus*, fr. L *gradus* step, grade] 1 : a step in a series 2 : the extent, intensity, or scope of something esp. as measured by a graded series 3 : one of the forms or sets of forms used in the comparison

of an adjective or adverb 4 : a rank or grade of official, ecclesiastical, or social position; *also* : the civil condition of a person 5 : a title conferred upon students by a college, university, or professional school upon completion of a unified program of study 6 : a unit of measure for angles and arcs that for angles is equal to an angle with its vertex at the center of a circle and its sides cutting off ¹⁄₃₆₀ of the circumference and that for an arc of a circle is equal to ¹⁄₃₆₀ of the circumference 7 : a line or space of the musical staff; *also* : a note or tone of a musical scale

de·horn \dē-'hȯrn\ *vb* : to deprive of horns

de·hu·man·ize \dē-'hyü-mə-ınīz\ *vb* : to divest of human qualities or personality — **de·hu·man·iza·tion** \ıdē-ıhyü-mə-nə-'zā-shən\ *n*

de·hu·mid·i·fy \ıdē-hyü-'mid-ə-ıfī\ *vb* : to remove moisture from (as the air) — **de·hu·mid·i·fi·er** \-'mid-ə-ıfī(-ə)r\ *n*

de·hy·drate \dē-'hī-ıdrāt\ *vb* : to remove water from 〈*dehydrated* by fever〉 〈~ fruits〉; *also* : to lose liquid — **de·hy·dra·tion** \ıdē-hī-'drā-shən\ *n*

de·hy·dro·ge·nate \ıdē-hī-'dräj-ə-ınāt\ *vb* : to remove hydrogen from — **de·hy·dro·ge·na·tion** \ıdē-hī-ıdräj-ə-'nā-shən\ *n*

de·ice \dē-'īs\ *vb* : to keep free or rid of ice — **de·ic·er** *n*

de·i·fy \'dē-ə-ıfī\ *vb* -**fied; -fy·ing** 1 : to make a god of 2 : WORSHIP, GLORIFY — **de·i·fi·ca·tion** \ıdē-ə-fə-'kā-shən\ *n*

deign \'dān\ *vb* [ME *deignen*, fr. OF *deignier*, fr. L *dignare, dignari*, fr. *dignus* worthy] : CONDESCEND

de·ion·ize \dē-'ī-ə-ınīz\ *vb* : to remove ions from

de·ism \'dē-ıiz-əm\ *n, often cap* : a system of thought advocating natural religion based on human reason rather than revelation — **de·ist** \'dē-əst\ *n, often cap* — **de·is·tic** \dē-'is-tik\ *adj*

de·i·ty \'dē-ət-ē\ *n, pl* -ties 1 : DIVINITY 2 2 *cap* : GOD 1 3 : a god or goddess

de·ject·ed \di-'jek-təd\ *adj* : low in spirits : SAD — **de·ject·ed·ly** *adv*

de·jec·tion \di-'jek-shən\ *n* : lowness of spirits : DEPRESSION

de ju·re \dē-'jùr-ē\ *adv or adj* : existing or exercising power by legal right 〈*de jure* government〉

deka·gram \'dek-ə-ıgram\ *n* — see METRIC SYSTEM table

deka·li·ter \-ılēt-ər\ *n* — see METRIC SYSTEM table

deka·me·ter \-ımēt-ər\ *n* — see METRIC SYSTEM table

del *abbr* delegate; delegation

Del *abbr* Delaware

Del·a·ware \'del-ə-ıwaər\ *n, pl* **Delaware** *or* **Delawares** : a member of an American Indian people orig. of the Delaware valley; *also* : their language

¹**de·lay** \di-'lā\ *n* 1 : the act of delaying : the state of being delayed 2 : the

time for which something is delayed
²**delay** vb 1 : POSTPONE, PUT OFF 2 : to stop, detain, or hinder for a time 3 : to move or act slowly

de·lec·ta·ble \di-'lek-tə-bəl\ adj 1 : highly pleasing : DELIGHTFUL 2 : DELICIOUS

de·lec·ta·tion \,dē-,lek-'tā-shən\ n : DELIGHT, PLEASURE, DIVERSION

¹**del·e·gate** \'del-i-gət, -,gāt\ n 1 : DEPUTY, REPRESENTATIVE 2 : a member of the lower house of the legislature of Maryland, Virginia, or West Virginia
²**del·e·gate** \-,gāt\ vb -gat·ed; -gat·ing 1 : to entrust to another ⟨delegated his authority⟩ 2 : to appoint as one's delegate

del·e·ga·tion \,del-i-'gā-shən\ n 1 : the act of delegating 2 : one or more persons chosen to represent others

de·lete \di-'lēt\ vb de·let·ed; de·let·ing [L delēre to wipe out, destroy] : to eliminate esp. by blotting out, cutting out, or erasing — **de·le·tion** \-'lē-shən\ n

del·e·te·ri·ous \,del-ə-'tir-ē-əs\ adj : HARMFUL, NOXIOUS

delft \'delft\ n 1 : a Dutch pottery with an opaque white glaze and predominantly blue decoration 2 : glazed pottery esp. when blue and white

delft·ware \-,waər\ n : DELFT

deli \'del-ē\ n, pl **del·is** : DELICATESSEN
¹**de·lib·er·ate** \di-'lib-ə-,rāt\ vb -at·ed; -at·ing : to consider carefully — **de·lib·er·a·tion** \-,lib-ə-'rā-shən\ n
²**de·lib·er·ate** \di-'lib-(ə-)rət\ adj [L deliberare to weigh in mind, ponder, fr. libra scale, pound] 1 : determined after careful thought 2 : done or said intentionally 3 : UNHURRIED, SLOW — **de·lib·er·ate·ly** adv — **de·lib·er·ate·ness** n

de·lib·er·a·tive \-'lib-ə-,rāt-iv, -'lib-(ə-)rət-\ adj : of, relating to, or marked by deliberation ⟨~ assembly⟩ — **de·lib·er·a·tive·ly** adv

del·i·ca·cy \'del-i-kə-sē\ n, pl -cies 1 : something pleasing to eat because it is rare or luxurious 2 : FINENESS, DAINTINESS; also : FRAILTY 3 : nicety or expressiveness of touch 4 : precise perception and discrimination : SENSITIVITY 5 : sensibility in feeling or conduct; also : SQUEAMISHNESS 6 : the quality or state of requiring delicate handling

del·i·cate \'del-i-kət\ adj 1 : pleasing to the senses of taste or smell esp. in a mild or subtle way 2 : marked by daintiness or charm : EXQUISITE 3 : FASTIDIOUS, SQUEAMISH, SCRUPULOUS 4 : easily damaged : FRAGILE; also : SICKLY 5 : requiring skill or tact 6 : marked by care, skill, or tact 7 : marked by minute precision : very sensitive — **del·i·cate·ly** adv

del·i·ca·tes·sen \,del-i-kə-'tes-ᵊn\ n pl [G, pl. of delicatesse delicacy, fr. F délicatesse] 1 : ready-to-eat food products (as cooked meats and prepared salads) 2 sing, pl **delicatessens**

: a store where delicatessen are sold
de·li·cious \di-'lish-əs\ adj : affording great pleasure : DELIGHTFUL ; esp : very pleasing to the taste or smell — **de·li·cious·ly** adv

¹**de·light** \di-'līt\ n 1 : great pleasure or satisfaction : JOY 2 : something that gives great pleasure — **de·light·ful** \-fəl\ adj — **de·light·ful·ly** \-ē\ adv
²**delight** vb 1 : to take great pleasure 2 : to satisfy greatly : PLEASE

de·light·ed \-əd\ adj : highly pleased : GRATIFIED — **de·light·ed·ly** adv

de·lim·it \di-'lim-ət\ vb : to fix the limits of : BOUND

de·lin·e·ate \di-'lin-ē-,āt\ vb -at·ed; -at·ing 1 : SKETCH, PORTRAY 2 : to picture in words : DESCRIBE — **de·lin·e·a·tion** \-,lin-ē-'ā-shən\ n

de·lin·quen·cy \di-'liŋ-kwən-sē\ n, pl -cies : the quality or state of being delinquent
¹**de·lin·quent** \-kwənt\ n : a delinquent person
²**delinquent** adj 1 : offending by neglect or violation of duty or of law 2 : being overdue in payment

del·i·quesce \,del-i-'kwes\ vb -quesced; -quesc·ing : MELT, DISSOLVE; esp : to become liquid by absorbing moisture from the air — **del·i·ques·cent** \-'kwes-ᵊnt\ adj

de·lir·i·um \di-'lir-ē-əm\ n [L, fr. delirare to be crazy, fr. de- from + lira furrow] : mental disturbance marked by confusion, disordered speech, and hallucinations; also : violent excitement — **de·lir·i·ous** \-ē-əs\ adj — **de·lir·i·ous·ly** adv

delirium tre·mens \-'trē-mənz, -'trem-ənz\ n : a violent delirium with tremors that is induced by excessive and prolonged use of alcoholic liquors

de·liv·er \di-'liv-ər\ vb -ered; -er·ing \-(ə-)riŋ\ 1 : to set free : SAVE 2 : CONVEY, TRANSFER ⟨~ a letter⟩ 3 : to assist in giving birth or at the birth of 4 : UTTER, COMMUNICATE 5 : to send to an intended target or destination — **de·liv·er·ance** n — **de·liv·er·er** n

de·liv·ery \di-'liv-(ə-)rē\ n, pl -er·ies : the act of delivering something; also : something delivered

dell \'del\ n : a small secluded valley
de·louse \dē-'laùs\ vb : to remove lice from

del·phin·i·um \del-'fin-ē-əm\ n : any of a genus of mostly perennial herbs related to the buttercups with tall branching spikes of irregular flowers

del·ta \'del-tə\ n [Gk, fr. delta, fourth letter of the Gk alphabet, Δ, which an alluvial delta resembles in shape] : triangular silt-formed land at the mouth of a river — **del·ta·ic** \del-'tā-ik\ adj

de·lude \di-'lüd\ vb de·lud·ed; de·lud·ing : MISLEAD, DECEIVE, TRICK

¹**del·uge** \'del-yüj\ n 1 : a flooding of land by water 2 : a drenching rain 3

: a great amount or number ⟨a ∼ of Christmas mail⟩

²**deluge** vb **del·uged; del·ug·ing 1** : INUNDATE, FLOOD **2** : to overwhelm as if with a deluge

de·lu·sion \di-'lü-zhən\ n : a deluding or being deluded; esp : a persistent belief in something false typical of some mental disorders — **de·lu·sion·al** \-'lüzh-(ə-)nəl\ adj — **de·lu·sive** \-'lü-siv\ adj

de·luxe \di-'lùks, -'ləks, -'lüks\ adj : notably luxurious or elegant

delve \'delv\ vb **delved; delv·ing 1** : DIG **2** : to seek laboriously for information

dely abbr delivery

Dem abbr Democrat; Democratic

de·mag·ne·tize \dē-'mag-nə-ˌtīz\ vb : to cause to lose magnetic properties — **de·mag·ne·ti·za·tion** \ˌdē-ˌmag-nət-ə-'zā-shən\ n

dem·a·gogue or **dem·a·gog** \'dem-ə-ˌgäg\ n [Gk dēmagōgos, fr. dēmos people + agōgos leading, fr. agein to lead] : a person who appeals to the emotions and prejudices of people esp. in order to gain political power — **dem·a·gogu·ery** \-ˌgäg-(ə-)rē\ n — **dem·a·gogy** \-ˌgäg-ē, -ˌgäj-ē\ n

¹**de·mand** \di-'mand\ n **1** : an act of demanding or asking esp. with authority; also : something claimed as due **2** : the ability and desire to buy goods or services; also : the quantity of goods wanted at a stated price **3** : a seeking or being sought after : urgent need **4** : a pressing need or requirement

²**demand** vb **1** : to ask for with authority : claim as due **2** : to ask earnestly or in the manner of a command **3** : REQUIRE, NEED ⟨an illness that ∼s care⟩

de·mar·cate \di-'mär-ˌkāt, 'dē-ˌmär-\ vb **-cat·ed; -cat·ing 1** : to mark the limits of **2** : SEPARATE — **de·mar·ca·tion** \ˌdē-ˌmär-'kā-shən\ n

de·marche \dā-'märsh\ n : a course of action : MANEUVER

¹**de·mean** \di-'mēn\ vb **de·meaned; de·mean·ing** : to behave or conduct (oneself) usu. in a proper manner

²**demean** vb **de·meaned; de·mean·ing** : DEGRADE, DEBASE

de·mean·or \di-'mē-nər\ n : CONDUCT, BEARING

de·ment·ed \di-'ment-əd\ adj : MAD, INSANE — **de·ment·ed·ly** adv

de·men·tia \di-'men-chə\ n **1** : mental deterioration **2** : INSANITY

de·mer·it \di-'mer-ət\ n **1** : FAULT **2** : a mark placed against a person's record for some fault or offense

de·mesne \di-'mān, -'mēn\ n **1** : REALM **2** : manorial land actually possessed by the lord and not held by free tenants **3** : ESTATE **4** : REGION

demi·god \'dem-i-ˌgäd\ n : a mythological being with more power than a mortal but less than a god

demi·john \'dem-i-ˌjän\ n [F dame-jeanne, lit., Lady Jane] : a large glass or pottery bottle enclosed in wickerwork

de·mil·i·ta·rize \dē-'mil-ə-tə-ˌrīz\ vb : to strip of military forces, weapons, or fortifications — **de·mil·i·tar·iza·tion** \ˌdē-ˌmil-ə-t(ə-)rə-'zā-shən\ n

demi·mon·daine \ˌdem-i-ˌmän-'dān\ n : a woman of the demimonde

demi·monde \'dem-i-ˌmänd\ n [F demi-monde, fr. demi- half + monde world] **1** : a class of women on the fringes of respectable society supported by wealthy lovers **2** : a group engaged in activity of doubtful legality or propriety

de·min·er·al·ize \dē-'min-(ə-)rə-ˌlīz\ vb : to remove the mineral matter from

de·mise \di-'mīz\ n **1** : LEASE **2** : transfer of sovereignty to a successor ⟨∼ of the crown⟩ **3** : DEATH **4** : loss of status

demi·tasse \'dem-i-ˌtas\ n [F demitasse, fr. demi- half + tasse cup, fr. MF, fr. Ar tass, fr. Per tast] : a small cup of black coffee; also : the cup used to serve it

de·mo·bi·lize \di-'mō-bə-ˌlīz, dē-\ vb **1** : to discharge from military service **2** : to change from a state of war to a state of peace — **de·mo·bi·li·za·tion** \di-ˌmō-bə-lə-'zā-shən, dē-\ n

de·moc·ra·cy \di-'mäk-rə-sē\ n, pl **-cies 1** : government by the people; esp : rule of the majority **2** : a government in which the supreme power is held by the people **3** : a political unit that has a democratic government **4** cap : the principles and policies of the Democratic party in the U.S. **5** : the common people esp. when constituting the source of political authority **6** : the absence of hereditary or arbitrary class distinctions or privileges

dem·o·crat \'dem-ə-ˌkrat\ n **1** : one who believes in or practices democracy **2** cap : a member of the Democratic party of the U.S.

dem·o·crat·ic \ˌdem-ə-'krat-ik\ adj **1** : of, relating to, or favoring democracy **2** often cap : of or relating to one of the two major political parties in the U.S. associated in modern times with policies of broad social reform and internationalism **3** : relating to or appealing to the common people ⟨∼ art⟩ **4** : not snobbish

de·moc·ra·tize \di-'mäk-rə-ˌtīz\ vb **-tized; -tiz·ing** : to make democratic

dé·mo·dé \ˌdā-mō-'dā\ adj [F] : no longer fashionable : OUT-OF-DATE

de·mo·graph·ics \ˌdē-mə-'graf-iks, ˌdem-\ n pl : the statistical characteristics of human populations

de·mog·ra·phy \di-'mäg-rə-fē\ n : the statistical study of human populations and esp. their size and distribution and the number of births and deaths — **de·mog·ra·pher** \-fər\ n — **de·mo·graph·ic** \ˌdem-ə-'graf-ik, ˌdēm-\ adj — **de·mo·graph·i·cal·ly** \-i-k(ə-)lē\ adv

dem·oi·selle \ˌdem-(w)ə-'zel\ n [F] : a young woman

de·mol·ish \di-'mäl-ish\ *vb* **1** : to destroy by breaking apart : RAZE **2** : SMASH **3** : to put an end to

de·mo·li·tion \,dem-ə-'lish-ən, ,dē-mə-\ *n* : the act of demolishing; *esp* : destruction by means of explosives

de·mon *or* **dae·mon** \'dē-mən\ *n* **1** : an evil spirit : DEVIL **2** *usu daemon* : an attendant power or spirit **3** : one that has unusual drive or effectiveness

de·mon·e·tize \dē-'män-ə-,tīz, -'mən-\ *vb* : to stop using as money or as a monetary standard ⟨~ silver⟩ — **de·mon·e·ti·za·tion** \dē-,män-ət-ə-'zā-shən, -,mən-\ *n*

de·mo·ni·ac \di-'mō-nē-,ak\ *also* **de·mo·ni·a·cal** \,dē-mə-'nī-ə-kəl\ *adj* **1** : possessed or influenced by a demon **2** : DEVILISH, FIENDISH

de·mon·ic \di-'män-ik\ *also* **de·mon·i·cal** \-i-kəl\ *adj* : DEMONIAC 2

de·mon·ol·o·gy \,dē-mə-'näl-ə-jē\ *n* **1** : the study of demons **2** : belief in demons

de·mon·stra·ble \di-'män-strə-bəl\ *adj* **1** : capable of being demonstrated or proved **2** : APPARENT, EVIDENT

dem·on·strate \'dem-ən-,strāt\ *vb* **-strat·ed; -strat·ing 1** : to show clearly **2** : to prove or make clear by reasoning or evidence **3** : to explain esp. with many examples **4** : to show publicly ⟨~ a new car⟩ **5** : to make a public display (as of feelings or military force) ⟨~ in protest⟩ — **dem·on·stra·tion** \,dem-ən-'strā-shən\ *n* — **dem·on·stra·tor** \'dem-ən-,strāt-ər\ *n*

¹**de·mon·stra·tive** \di-'män-strət-iv\ *adj* **1** : demonstrating as real or true **2** : characterized by demonstration **3** : pointing out the one referred to and distinguishing it from others of the same class ⟨~ pronoun⟩ ⟨~ adjective⟩ **4** : marked by display of feeling : EFFUSIVE — **de·mon·stra·tive·ly** *adv* — **de·mon·stra·tive·ness** *n*

²**demonstrative** *n* : a demonstrative word and esp. a pronoun

de·mor·al·ize \di-'mȯr-ə-,līz\ *vb* **1** : to corrupt in morals **2** : to weaken in discipline or spirit : DISORGANIZE — **de·mor·al·iza·tion** \di-,mȯr-ə-lə-'zā-shən\ *n*

de·mote \di-'mōt\ *vb* **de·mot·ed; de·mot·ing** : to reduce to a lower grade or rank — **de·mo·tion** \-'mō-shən\ *n*

de·mot·ic \di-'mät-ik\ *adj* : of or relating to the people ⟨~ Greek⟩

¹**de·mul·cent** \di-'məl-sənt\ *adj* : SOOTHING

²**demulcent** *n* : a usu. mucilaginous or oily substance used to soothe or protect an irritated mucous membrane

de·mur \di-'mər\ *vb* **de·murred; de·mur·ring** [ME *demoren* to linger, fr. OF *demorer*, fr. L *demorari*, fr. *morari* to linger, fr. *mora* delay] : to take exception : OBJECT — **de·mur** *n*

de·mure \di-'myu̇r\ *adj* **1** : quietly modest : DECOROUS **2** : affectedly modest,

reserved, or serious : PRIM — **de·mure·ly** *adv*

de·mur·rage \di-'mər-ij\ *n* : the detention of a ship by the shipper or receiver beyond the time allowed for loading, unloading, or sailing; *also* : a charge for detaining a ship, freight car, or truck for such a delay

de·mur·rer \di-'mər-ər\ *n* : a claim by the defendant in a legal action that the plaintiff does not have sufficient grounds to proceed

den \'den\ *n* **1** : a shelter or resting place of a wild animal **2** : a hiding place (as for thieves) **3** : a dirty wretched place in which people live or gather ⟨~s of misery⟩ **4** : a cozy private little room

Den *abbr* Denmark

de·na·ture \dē-'nā-chər\ *vb* **de·na·tured; de·na·tur·ing** \-'nāch-(ə-)riŋ\ : to remove the natural qualities of; *esp* : to make (alcohol) unfit for drinking

den·drol·o·gy \den-'dräl-ə-jē\ *n* : the study of trees — **den·drol·o·gist** \-ə-jəst\ *n*

den·gue \'deŋ-gē, -,gā\ *n* [Sp] : an acute infectious disease characterized by headache, severe joint pain, and rash

de·ni·al \di-'nī(-ə)l\ *n* **1** : rejection of a request **2** : refusal to admit the truth of a statement or charge; *also* : assertion that something alleged is false **3** : DISAVOWAL **4** : restriction on one's own activity or desires

de·nier \'den-yər\ *n* : a unit of fineness for silk, rayon, or nylon yarn

den·i·grate \'den-i-,grāt\ *vb* **-grat·ed; -grat·ing** [L *denigrare*, fr. *nigrare* to blacken, fr. *niger* black] : to cast aspersions on : DEFAME

den·im \'den-əm\ *n* [F (*serge*) *de Nîmes* serge of Nîmes, France] **1** : a firm durable twilled usu. cotton fabric woven with colored warp and white filling threads **2** *pl* : overalls or trousers of usu. blue denim

den·i·zen \'den-ə-zən\ *n* : INHABITANT

de·nom·i·nate \di-'näm-ə-,nāt\ *vb* : to give a name to : DESIGNATE

de·nom·i·nate number \di-,näm-ə-nət-\ *n* : a number (as 7 in *7 feet*) that specifies a quantity in terms of a unit of measurement

de·nom·i·na·tion \di-,näm-ə-'nā-shən\ *n* **1** : an act of denominating **2** : a value or size of a series of related values (as of money) **3** : NAME, DESIGNATION; *esp* : a general name for a class of things **4** : a religious body comprising a number of local congregations having similar beliefs — **de·nom·i·na·tion·al** \-shə(-nə)l\ *adj*

de·nom·i·na·tor \di-'näm-ə-,nāt-ər\ *n* : the part of a fraction that is below the line

de·no·ta·tive \'dē-nō-,tāt-iv, di-'nōt-ət-iv\ *adj* **1** : denoting or tending to denote **2** : relating to denotation

de·note \di-'nōt\ *vb* **1** : to mark out plainly : INDICATE **2** : to make known

3 : MEAN, NAME — **de·no·ta·tion** \ˌdē-nō-ˈtā-shən\ n

de·noue·ment \ˌdā-ˌnü-ˈmäⁿ\ n [F *dénouement*, lit., untying, fr. MF *desnouement*, fr. *desnouer* to untie, fr. OF *desnoer*, fr. *noer* to tie, fr. L *nodare*, fr. *nodus* knot] : the final outcome of the dramatic complications in a literary work

de·nounce \di-ˈnauns\ vb **de·nounced; de·nounc·ing** 1 : to point out as deserving blame or punishment 2 : to inform against : ACCUSE 3 : to announce formally the termination of (as a treaty) — **de·nounce·ment** n

de no·vo \di-ˈnō-vō\ adv [L] : ANEW, AGAIN

dense \ˈdens\ adj **dens·er; dens·est** 1 : marked by compactness or crowding together of parts : THICK (a ~ forest) (a ~ fog) 2 : DULL, STUPID — **dense·ly** adv — **dense·ness** n

den·si·ty \ˈden-sət-ē\ n, pl **-ties** 1 : the quality or state of being dense 2 : the quantity of something per unit volume, unit area, or unit length

dent \ˈdent\ n 1 : a small depressed place made by a blow or by pressure 2 : an impression or effect made usu. against resistance 3 : initial progress — **dent** vb

den·tal \ˈdent-ᵊl\ adj : of or relating to the teeth or dentistry — **den·tal·ly** \-ē\ adv

dental floss n : a thread used to clean between the teeth

dental hygienist n : one who is licensed in the cleaning and examining of teeth

den·tate \ˈden-ˌtāt\ adj : having pointed projections : NOTCHED

den·ti·frice \ˈdent-ə-frəs\ n [MF, fr. L *dentifricium*, fr. *dent-, dens* tooth + *fricare* to rub] : a powder, paste, or liquid for cleaning the teeth

den·tin \ˈdent-ᵊn\ or **den·tine** \ˈden-ˌtēn, den-ˈtēn\ n : a calcareous material like bone but harder and denser that composes the principal mass of a tooth — **den·tin·al** \den-ˈtēn-ᵊl, ˈdent-ᵊn-əl\ adj

den·tist \ˈdent-əst\ n : one who is licensed in the care, treatment, and replacement of teeth — **den·tist·ry** n

den·ti·tion \den-ˈtish-ən\ n : the character of a set of teeth esp. with regard to number, kind, and arrangement; also : TEETH

den·ture \ˈden-chər\ n : an artificial replacement for teeth

de·nude \di-ˈn(y)üd\ vb **de·nud·ed; de·nud·ing** : to strip the covering from — **de·nu·da·tion** \ˌdē-(ˌ)n(y)ü-ˈdā-shən\ n

de·nun·ci·a·tion \di-ˌnən-sē-ˈā-shən\ n : the act of denouncing; esp : a public accusation

de·ny \di-ˈnī\ vb **de·nied; de·ny·ing** 1 : to declare untrue 2 : to refuse to recognize or acknowledge : DISAVOW 3 : to refuse to grant (~ a request) 4 : to reject as false (~ a theory)

de·o·dar \ˈdē-ə-ˌdär\ also **de·o·da·ra** \ˌdē-ə-ˈdär-ə\ n [Hindi *deodar*, fr. Skt *devadāru*, lit., timber of the gods, fr. *deva* god + *dāru* wood] : an East Indian cedar

de·odor·ant \dē-ˈōd-ə-rənt\ n : a preparation that destroys or masks unpleasant odors

de·odor·ize \dē-ˈōd-ə-ˌrīz\ vb : to eliminate the offensive odor of

de·ox·i·dize \dē-ˈäk-sə-ˌdīz\ vb : to remove oxygen from

de·oxy·ri·bo·nu·cle·ic acid \dē-ˈäk-si-ˌrī-bō-n(y)ü-ˌklē-ik-\ : DNA

de·oxy·ri·bose \dē-ˌäk-si-ˈrī-ˌbōs\ n : a sugar with five carbon and four oxygen atoms in each molecule that is part of DNA

dep abbr 1 depart; departure 2 deposit 3 deputy

de·part \di-ˈpärt\ vb 1 : to go away : go away from : LEAVE 2 : DIE 3 : to turn aside : DEVIATE

de·part·ment \di-ˈpärt-mənt\ n 1 : a distinct sphere : PROVINCE 2 : a functional or territorial division (as of a government, business, or college) — **de·part·men·tal** \di-ˌpärt-ˈment-ᵊl, ˌdē-\ adj

department store n : a store selling a wide variety of goods arranged in several departments

de·par·ture \di-ˈpär-chər\ n 1 : the act of going away 2 : a starting out (as on a journey) 3 : DIVERGENCE

de·pend \di-ˈpend\ vb 1 : to be determined by or based on some action or condition (our success ~s on his cooperation) 2 : TRUST, RELY (you can ~ on me) 3 : to be dependent esp. for financial support 4 : to hang down (a vine ~ing from a tree)

de·pend·able \di-ˈpen-də-bəl\ adj : TRUSTWORTHY, RELIABLE — **de·pend·abil·i·ty** \-ˌpen-də-ˈbil-ət-ē\ n

de·pen·dence also **de·pen·dance** \di-ˈpen-dəns\ n 1 : the quality or state of being dependent; esp : the quality or state of being influenced by or subject to another 2 : RELIANCE, TRUST 3 : something on which one relies 4 : drug addiction; also : HABITUATION 2

de·pen·den·cy \-dən-sē\ n, pl **-cies** 1 : DEPENDENCE 2 : a territory under the jurisdiction of a nation but not formally annexed by it

¹**de·pen·dent** \di-ˈpen-dənt\ adj 1 : hanging down 2 : determined or conditioned by another; also : affected with drug dependence 3 : relying on another for support 4 : subject to another's jurisdiction 5 : SUBORDINATE 4

²**dependent** also **de·pen·dant** \-dənt\ n : one that is dependent; esp : a person who relies on another for support

de·pict \di-ˈpikt\ vb 1 : to represent by a picture 2 : to describe in words — **de·pic·tion** \-ˈpik-shən\ n

de·pil·a·to·ry \di-ˈpil-ə-ˌtōr-ē\ n, pl **-ries** : an agent for removing hair, wool, or bristles

de·plane \dē-ˈplān\ vb : to get out of an airplane

de·plete \di-ˈplēt\ vb **de·plet·ed; de·plet·ing** : to exhaust esp. of strength or resources — **de·ple·tion** \-ˈplē-shən\ n

de·plor·able \di-ˈplōr-ə-bəl\ adj **1** : LAMENTABLE **2** : WRETCHED — **de·plor·ably** \-blē\ adv

de·plore \-ˈplōr\ vb **de·plored; de·plor·ing 1** : to feel or express grief for **2** : to regret strongly **3** : to consider unfortunate or deserving of disapproval

de·ploy \di-ˈplȯi\ vb : to spread out (as troops or ships) in order for battle — **de·ploy·ment** \-mənt\ n

de·po·nent \di-ˈpō-nənt\ n : one who gives evidence esp. in writing

de·pop·u·late \dē-ˈpäp-yə-ˌlāt\ vb : to reduce greatly the population of by destroying or driving away the inhabitants — **de·pop·u·la·tion** \dē-ˌpäp-yə-ˈlā-shən\ n

de·port \di-ˈpōrt\ vb **1** : CONDUCT, BEHAVE **2** : BANISH, EXILE — **de·por·ta·tion** \ˌdē-ˌpōr-ˈtā-shən\ n

de·port·ment \di-ˈpōrt-mənt\ n : BEHAVIOR, BEARING

de·pose \di-ˈpōz\ vb **de·posed; de·pos·ing 1** : to remove from high office (as of king) **2** : to testify under oath or by affidavit

¹de·pos·it \di-ˈpäz-ət\ vb **de·pos·it·ed** \-ˈpäz-ət-əd\ ; **de·pos·it·ing 1** : to place for safekeeping or as a pledge; esp : to put money in a bank **2** : to lay down : PUT **3** : to let fall or sink ⟨sand and silt ∼ed by a flood⟩ — **de·pos·i·tor** \-ˈpäz-ət-ər\ n

²deposit n **1** : the state of being deposited ⟨money on ∼⟩ **2** : something placed for safekeeping; esp : money deposited in a bank **3** : money given as a pledge **4** : an act of depositing **5** : something laid or thrown down ⟨a ∼ of silt by a river⟩ **6** : an accumulation of mineral matter (as ore, oil, or gas) in nature

de·po·si·tion \ˌdep-ə-ˈzish-ən, ˌdē-pə-\ n **1** : an act of removing from a position of authority **2** : TESTIMONY **3** : the process of depositing **4** : DEPOSIT

de·pos·i·to·ry \di-ˈpäz-ə-ˌtōr-ē\ n, pl **-ries** : a place where something is deposited esp. for safekeeping

de·pot \1 usu ˈdep-ō, 3 usu ˈdēp-ō\ n **1** : STOREHOUSE **2** : a place where military supplies are kept or where troops are assembled and trained **3** : a building for railroad or bus passengers : STATION

depr abbr depreciation

de·prave \di-ˈprāv\ vb **de·praved; de·prav·ing** [ME depraven, fr. MF depraver, fr. L depravare to pervert, fr. pravus crooked, bad] : CORRUPT, PERVERT — **de·praved** adj — **de·prav·i·ty** \-ˈprav-ət-ē\ n

dep·re·cate \ˈdep-ri-ˌkāt\ vb **-cat·ed; -cat·ing** [L deprecari to avert by prayer, fr. precari to pray] **1** : to express disapproval of **2** : DEPRECIATE — **dep·re·ca·to·ry** \ˈdep-ri-kə-ˌtōr-ē\ adj **1** : expressing deprecation : APOLOGETIC **2** : serving to deprecate

de·pre·ci·ate \di-ˈprē-shē-ˌāt\ vb **-at·ed; -at·ing** [LL depretiare, fr. L pretium price] **1** : to lessen in price or value **2** : UNDERVALUE, BELITTLE, DISPARAGE — **de·pre·ci·a·tion** \-ˌprē-shē-ˈā-shən\ n

dep·re·da·tion \ˌdep-rə-ˈdā-shən\ n : a laying waste or plundering — **dep·re·date** \ˈdep-rə-ˌdāt\ vb

de·press \di-ˈpres\ vb **1** : to press down : cause to sink to a lower position **2** : to lessen the activity or force of **3** : SADDEN, DISCOURAGE **4** : to lessen in price or value — **de·pres·sor** \di-ˈpres-ər\ n

de·pres·sant \di-ˈpres-ᵊnt\ n : one that depresses; esp : an agent that reduces bodily functional activity — **depressant** adj

de·pressed \di-ˈprest\ adj **1** : low in spirits; also : affected with emotional depression **2** : suffering from economic depression

de·pres·sion \di-ˈpresh-ən\ n **1** : an act of depressing : a state of being depressed **2** : a pressing down : LOWERING **3** : a state of feeling sad **4** : an emotional disorder marked esp. by sadness, inactivity, difficulty in thinking and concentration, and feelings of dejection **5** : a depressed area or part **6** : a period of low general economic activity with widespread unemployment

¹de·pres·sive \di-ˈpres-iv\ adj **1** : tending to depress **2** : characterized or affected by psychological depression

²depressive n : one who is psychologically depressed

de·pri·va·tion \ˌdep-rə-ˈvā-shən\ n : an act or instance of depriving : LOSS; also : PRIVATION

de·prive \di-ˈprīv\ vb **de·prived; de·priv·ing 1** : to take something away from ⟨∼ a king of his power⟩ **2** : to stop from having something

dept abbr department

depth \ˈdepth\ n, pl **depths** \ˈdep(th)s\ **1** : something that is deep; esp : the deep part of a body of water **2** : a part that is far from the outside or surface ⟨the ∼s of the woods⟩ **3** : ABYSS **4** : the middle or innermost part ⟨the ∼ of winter⟩ **5** : an extreme state (as of misery); also : the worst part ⟨the ∼s of despair⟩ **6** : the perpendicular distance downward from a surface; also : the distance from front to back **7** : the quality of being deep **8** : the degree of intensity

depth charge n : an explosive device for use underwater esp. against submarines

dep·u·ta·tion \ˌdep-yə-ˈtā-shən\ n **1** : the act of appointing a deputy **2** : DELEGATION

de·pute \di-ˈpyüt\ vb **de·put·ed; de·put·ing** : DELEGATE

dep·u·tize \ˈdep-yə-ˌtīz\ vb **-tized; -tiz·ing** : to appoint as deputy

dep·u·ty \ˈdep-yət-ē\ n, pl **-ties 1** : a person appointed to act for or in place of another **2** : an assistant empowered to act as a substitute in the absence of his superior **3** : a member of a lower house of a legislative assembly

der or **deriv** abbr derivation; derivative

de·rail \di-ˈrāl\ vb : to cause to run off the rails — **de·rail·ment** n

de·rail·leur \di-ˈrā-lər\ n [F dérailleur] : a device for shifting gears on a bicycle by moving the chain from one set of exposed gears to another

de·range \di-ˈrānj\ vb **de·ranged; de·rang·ing 1** : DISARRANGE, UPSET **2** : to make insane — **de·range·ment** n

der·by \ˈdər-bē, Brit ˈdär-\ n, pl **derbies 1** : a horse race usu. for three-year-olds held annually **2** : a race or contest open to all **3** : a man's stiff felt hat with dome-shaped crown and narrow brim

¹der·e·lict \ˈder-ə-ˌlikt\ adj **1** : abandoned by the owner or occupant ⟨a ∼ ship⟩ **2** : NEGLIGENT ⟨∼ in his duty⟩

²derelict n **1** : something voluntarily abandoned; esp : a ship abandoned on the high seas **2** : a destitute homeless social misfit : VAGRANT, BUM

der·e·lic·tion \ˌder-ə-ˈlik-shən\ n **1** : the act of abandoning : the state of being abandoned **2** : a failure in duty

de·ride \di-ˈrīd\ vb **de·rid·ed; de·rid·ing** [L deridēre, fr. ridēre to laugh] : to laugh at scornfully : make fun of : RIDICULE — **de·ri·sion** \-ˈrizh-ən\ n — **de·ri·sive** \-ˈrī-siv\ adj — **de·ri·sive·ly** adv — **de·ri·so·ry** \-ˈrī-sə-rē\ adj

de ri·gueur \də-rē-ˈgər\ adj [F] : prescribed or required by fashion, etiquette, or custom

der·i·va·tion \ˌder-ə-ˈvā-shən\ n **1** : the formation of a word from an earlier word or root; also : an act of ascertaining or stating the derivation of a word **2** : ETYMOLOGY **3** : SOURCE, ORIGIN; also : DESCENT **4** : an act or process of deriving

¹de·riv·a·tive \di-ˈriv-ət-iv\ n **1** : a word formed by derivation **2** : something derived

²derivative adj : derived from something else

de·rive \di-ˈrīv\ vb **de·rived; de·riv·ing** [ME deriven, fr. MF deriver, fr. L derivare, fr. de- from + rivus stream] **1** : to receive or obtain from a source **2** : to obtain from a parent substance **3** : INFER, DEDUCE **4** : to trace the origin, descent, or derivation of **5** : to come from a certain source

der·mal \ˈdər-məl\ adj : of or relating to the skin

der·ma·ti·tis \ˌdər-mə-ˈtīt-əs\ n : skin inflammation

der·ma·tol·o·gy \-ˈtäl-ə-jē\ n : a branch of science dealing with the skin and its

disorders — **der·ma·tol·o·gist** \-jəst\ n

der·mis \ˈdər-məs\ n : the sensitive vascular inner layer of the skin

der·o·gate \ˈder-ə-ˌgāt\ vb **-gat·ed; -gat·ing 1** : to cause to seem inferior : DISPARAGE **2** : DETRACT — **der·o·ga·tion** \ˌder-ə-ˈgā-shən\ n

de·rog·a·to·ry \di-ˈräg-ə-ˌtōr-ē\ adj : intended to lower the reputation of a person or thing : DISPARAGING

der·rick \ˈder-ik\ n [obs. derrick hangman, gallows, fr. Derick, name of 17th cent. E hangman] **1** : a hoisting apparatus : CRANE **2** : a framework over a drill hole (as for oil) supporting machinery

der·ri·ere or **der·ri·ère** \ˌder-ē-ˈeər\ n : BUTTOCKS

der·ring-do \ˌder-iŋ-ˈdü\ n : daring action : DARING

der·rin·ger \ˈder-ən-jər\ n : a short-barreled pocket pistol

der·vish \ˈdər-vish\ n [Turk derviş, lit., beggar, fr. Per darvēsh] : a member of a Muslim religious order noted for devotional exercises (as bodily movements leading to a trance)

de·sal·i·nate \dē-ˈsal-ə-ˌnāt\ vb **-nat·ed; -nat·ing** : DESALT — **de·sal·i·na·tion** \-ˌsal-ə-ˈnā-shən\ n

de·sal·i·nize \dē-ˈsal-ə-ˌnīz\ vb **-nized; -niz·ing** : DESALT — **de·sal·i·ni·za·tion** \-ˌsal-ə-nə-ˈzā-shən\ n

de·salt \dē-ˈsȯlt\ vb : to remove salt from ⟨∼ seawater⟩ — **de·salt·er** n

des·cant \ˈdes-ˌkant\ vb **1** : to sing or play past music : SING **2** : to discourse or write at length

de·scend \di-ˈsend\ vb **1** : to pass from a higher to a lower place or level : pass, move, or climb down or down along **2** : DERIVE ⟨∼ed from royalty⟩ **3** : to pass by inheritance or transmission **4** : to incline, lead, or extend downward **5** : to swoop down in a sudden attack

¹de·scen·dant or **de·scen·dent** \di-ˈsen-dənt\ adj **1** : DESCENDING **2** : proceeding from an ancestor or source

²descendant or **descendent** n **1** : one descended from another or from a common stock **2** : one deriving directly from a precursor or prototype

de·scent \di-ˈsent\ n **1** : ANCESTRY, BIRTH, LINEAGE **2** : the act or process of descending **3** : SLOPE **4** : a descending way (as a downgrade) **5** : a sudden hostile raid or assault **6** : a downward step (as in station or value) : DECLINE

de·scribe \di-ˈskrīb\ vb **de·scribed; de·scrib·ing 1** : to represent or give an account of in words **2** : to trace the outline of — **de·scrib·able** adj

de·scrip·tion \di-ˈskrip-shən\ n **1** : an account of something; esp : an account that presents a picture to a person who reads or hears it **2** : KIND, SORT — **de·scrip·tive** \-ˈskrip-tiv\ adj

de·scry \di-ˈskrī\ vb **de·scried; de·scry·ing 1** : to catch sight of **2** : to discover by observation or investigation

des·e·crate \'des-i-₁krāt\ vb **-crat·ed;** **-crat·ing** : PROFANE — **des·e·cra·tion** \₁des-i-'krā-shən\ n

de·seg·re·gate \dē-'seg-ri-₁gāt\ vb : to eliminate segregation in; *esp* : to free of any law, provision, or practice requiring isolation of the members of a particular race in separate units — **de·seg·re·ga·tion** \dē-₁seg-ri-'gā-shən\ n

de·sen·si·tize \dē-'sen-sə-₁tīz\ vb : to make (a sensitized or hypersensitive individual) insensitive or nonreactive to a sensitizing agent — **de·sen·si·ti·za·tion** \dē-₁sen-sət-ə-'zā-shən\ n

¹**des·ert** \'dez-ərt\ n : a dry barren region incapable of supporting a population without an artificial water supply

²**des·ert** \'dez-ərt\ adj : of, relating to, or resembling a desert; *esp* : being barren and without life (a ~ island)

³**de·sert** \di-'zərt\ n 1 : worthiness of reward or punishment 2 : a just reward or punishment

⁴**de·sert** \di-'zərt\ vb 1 : to withdraw from 2 : FORSAKE — **de·sert·er** n — **de·ser·tion** \-'zər-shən\ n

de·serve \di-'zərv\ vb **de·served;** **de·serv·ing** : to be worthy of : MERIT — **de·serv·ing** adj

de·serv·ed·ly \-'zər-vəd-lē\ adv : according to merit : JUSTLY

des·ic·cate \'des-i-₁kāt\ vb **-cat·ed;** **-cat·ing** : DRY, DEHYDRATE — **des·ic·ca·tor** \'des-i-₁kāt-ər\ n

de·sid·er·a·tum \di-₁sid-ə-'rät-əm, -₁zid-, -'rät-\ n, pl **-ta** \-ə\ [L] : something desired as essential or needed

¹**de·sign** \di-'zīn\ vb 1 : to conceive and plan out in the mind 2 : INTEND 3 : to devise for a specific function or end 4 : to make a pattern or sketch of 5 : to conceive and draw the plans for (~ an airplane)

²**design** n 1 : a particular purpose : deliberate planning 2 : a mental project or scheme : PLAN 3 : a secret project or scheme : PLOT 4 pl : aggressive or evil intent — used with on or against 5 : a preliminary sketch or plan : DELINEATION 6 : an underlying scheme that governs functioning, developing, or unfolding : MOTIF 7 : the arrangement of elements or details in a product or a work of art 8 : a decorative pattern 9 : the art of executing designs

¹**des·ig·nate** \'dez-ig-₁nāt, -nət\ adj : chosen for an office but not yet installed (ambassador ~)

²**des·ig·nate** \-₁nāt\ vb **-nat·ed; -nat·ing** 1 : to appoint or choose by name for a special purpose 2 : to mark or point out : INDICATE; *also* : SPECIFY, STIPULATE 3 : to call by a name or title — **des·ig·na·tion** \₁dez-ig-'nā-shən\ n

designated hitter n : a baseball player designated at the start of the game to bat in place of the pitcher without causing the pitcher to be removed from the game

de·sign·er \di-'zī-nər\ n 1 : one who creates plans for a project or structure 2 : one who designs and manufactures high-fashion clothing — **designer** adj

de·sign·ing \di-'zī-niŋ\ adj : CRAFTY, SCHEMING

de·sir·able \di-'zī-rə-bəl\ adj 1 : PLEASING, ATTRACTIVE (a ~ woman) 2 : ADVISABLE (~ legislation) — **de·sir·abil·i·ty** \-₁zī-rə-'bil-ət-ē\ n

¹**de·sire** \di-'zī(ə)r\ vb **-sired; de·sir·ing** [ME desiren, fr. OF desirer, fr. L desiderare, fr. sider-, sidus star] 1 : to long, hope, or wish for : COVET 2 : REQUEST

²**desire** n 1 : a strong wish : LONGING, CRAVING 2 : an expressed wish : REQUEST 3 : something desired

de·sir·ous \di-'zīr-əs\ adj : eagerly wishing : DESIRING

de·sist \di-'zist, -'sist\ vb : to cease to proceed or act

desk \'desk\ n [ME deske, fr. ML desca, fr. It desco table, fr. L discus dish, disc] 1 : a table, frame, or case esp. for writing and reading 2 : a counter, stand, or booth at which a person performs duties 3 : a specialized division of an organization (as a newspaper) (city ~)

¹**des·o·late** \'des-ə-lət, 'dez-\ adj 1 : DESERTED, ABANDONED 2 : FORSAKEN, LONELY 3 : DILAPIDATED 4 : BARREN, LIFELESS 5 : CHEERLESS, GLOOMY — **des·o·late·ly** adv

²**des·o·late** \-₁lāt\ vb **-lat·ed; -lat·ing** : to make desolate : lay waste : make wretched

des·o·la·tion \₁des-ə-'lā-shən, ₁dez-\ n 1 : the action of desolating 2 : GRIEF, SADNESS 3 : LONELINESS 4 : DEVASTATION, RUIN 5 : barren wasteland

des·oxy·ri·bo·nu·cle·ic acid \dē-₁zäk-sē-'rī-bō-n(y)ù-₁klē-ik-\ : DNA

¹**de·spair** \di-'spaər\ vb : to lose all hope or confidence — **de·spair·ing** adj — **de·spair·ing·ly** adv

²**despair** n 1 : utter loss of hope 2 : a cause of hopelessness

des·patch \dis-'pach\ var of DISPATCH

des·per·a·do \₁des-pə-'räd-ō, -'räd-\ n, pl **-does** or **-dos** : a bold or reckless criminal

des·per·ate \'des-p(ə-)rət\ adj 1 : being beyond or almost beyond hope : causing despair 2 : RASH 3 : extremely intense — **des·per·ate·ly** adv

des·per·a·tion \₁des-pə-'rā-shən\ n 1 : a loss of hope and surrender to despair 2 : a state of hopelessness leading to rashness

de·spi·ca·ble \di-'spik-ə-bəl, 'des-pik-\ adj : deserving to be despised — **de·spi·ca·bly** \-blē\ adv

de·spise \di-'spīz\ vb **de·spised; de·spis·ing** 1 : to look down on with contempt or aversion : DISDAIN, DETEST 2 : to regard as negligible, worthless, or distasteful

de·spite \di-'spīt\ prep : in spite of

de·spoil \di-'spòil\ vb : to strip of belongings, possessions, or value — **de-spoil·er** n — **de·spoil·ment** n

de·spo·li·a·tion \di-ˌspō-lē-ˈā-shən\ n : the act of plundering : the state of being despoiled

¹de·spond \di-ˈspänd\ vb : to become discouraged or disheartened

²despond n : DESPONDENCY

de·spon·den·cy \di-ˈspän-dən-sē\ n : DEJECTION, HOPELESSNESS — **de·spon·dent** \-dənt\ adj

des·pot \ˈdes-pət, -ˌpät\ n [MF despote, fr. Gk despotēs master] 1 : a ruler with absolute power and authority : AUTOCRAT, TYRANT 2 : a person exercising power abusively, oppressively, or tyrannously — **des·pot·ic** \des-ˈpät-ik\ adj — **des·po·tism** \ˈdes-pə-ˌtiz-əm\ n

des·sert \di-ˈzərt\ n : a course of sweet food, fruit, or cheese served at the close of a meal

des·ti·na·tion \ˌdes-tə-ˈnā-shən\ n 1 : a purpose for which something is destined 2 : an act of appointing, setting aside for a purpose, or predetermining 3 : a place to which one is journeying or to which something is sent

des·tine \ˈdes-tən\ vb **des·tined; des·tin·ing** 1 : to settle in advance 2 : to designate, assign, or dedicate in advance 3 : to be bound or directed (freight destined for English ports)

des·ti·ny \ˈdes-tə-nē\ n, pl **-nies** 1 : something to which a person or thing is destined : FATE, FORTUNE 2 : a predetermined course of events

des·ti·tute \ˈdes-tə-ˌt(y)üt\ adj 1 : lacking something needed or desirable 2 : extremely poor — **des·ti·tu·tion** \ˌdes-tə-ˈt(y)ü-shən\ n

de·stroy \di-ˈstrȯi\ vb 1 : to put an end to : RUIN 2 : KILL

de·stroy·er \di-ˈstrȯi-(-ə)r\ n 1 : one that destroys 2 : a small speedy warship

¹de·struct \di-ˈstrəkt\ vb : DESTROY

²destruct n : the deliberate destruction of a rocket after launching

de·struc·ti·ble \di-ˈstrək-tə-bəl\ adj : capable of being destroyed — **de·struc·ti·bil·i·ty** \di-ˌstrək-tə-ˈbil-ət-ē\ n

de·struc·tion \di-ˈstrək-shən\ n 1 : RUIN 2 : the action or process of destroying something 3 : a destroying agency

de·struc·tive \di-ˈstrək-tiv\ adj 1 : causing destruction : RUINOUS 2 : designed or tending to destroy — **de·struc·tive·ly** adv — **de·struc·tive·ness** n

de·struc·tor \di-ˈstrək-tər\ n : a furnace for burning refuse : INCINERATOR

de·sue·tude \ˈdes-wi-ˌt(y)üd\ n : DISUSE

des·ul·to·ry \ˈdes-əl-ˌtōr-ē\ adj : passing aimlessly from one thing or subject to another : DISCONNECTED

det $abbr$ 1 detached; detachment 2 detail

de·tach \di-ˈtach\ vb 1 : to separate esp. from a larger mass 2 : DISENGAGE, WITHDRAW — **de·tach·able** adj

de·tached \di-ˈtacht\ adj 1 : not joined or connected : SEPARATE 2 : ALOOF, IMPARTIAL ⟨a ~ attitude⟩

de·tach·ment \di-ˈtach-mənt\ n 1 : SEPARATION 2 : the dispatching of a body of troops or part of a fleet from the main body for special service; *also* : the portion so dispatched 3 : a small permanent military unit different in composition from normal units 4 : indifference to worldly concerns : ALOOFNESS, UNWORLDLINESS 5 : IMPARTIALITY

¹de·tail \di-ˈtāl, ˈdē-ˌtāl\ n [F détail, fr. OF detail slice, piece, fr. detaillier to cut in pieces, fr. taillier to cut] 1 : a dealing with something item by item ⟨go into ~⟩; *also* : ITEM, PARTICULAR ⟨the ~s of a story⟩ 2 : selection (as of soldiers) for special duty; *also* : the persons thus selected

²detail vb 1 : to report in detail 2 : ENUMERATE, SPECIFY 3 : to select for some special duty

de·tain \di-ˈtān\ vb 1 : to hold in or as if in custody : STOP, DELAY

de·tect \di-ˈtekt\ vb : to discover the nature, existence, presence, or fact of — **de·tect·able** adj — **de·tec·tion** \-ˈtek-shən\ n — **de·tec·tor** \-tər\ n

¹de·tec·tive \di-ˈtek-tiv\ adj 1 : fitted or used for detection ⟨a ~ device for coal gas⟩ 2 : of or relating to detectives

²detective n : a person employed or engaged in detecting lawbreakers or getting information that is not readily accessible

dé·tente \dā-ˈtänt\ n [F] : a relaxation of strained relations or tensions (as between nations)

de·ten·tion \di-ˈten-chən\ n 1 : the act or fact of detaining : CONFINEMENT; *esp* : a period of temporary custody prior to disposition by a court 2 : a forced delay

de·ter \di-ˈtər\ vb **de·terred; de·ter·ring** [L deterrēre, fr. terrēre to frighten] 1 : to turn aside, discourage, or prevent from acting (as by fear) 2 : INHIBIT

de·ter·gent \di-ˈtər-jənt\ n : a cleansing agent; *esp* : a chemical product similar to soap in its cleaning ability

de·te·ri·o·rate \di-ˈtir-ē-ə-ˌrāt\ vb **-rat·ed; -rat·ing** : to make or grow worse : DEGENERATE — **de·te·ri·o·ra·tion** \-ˌtir-ē-ə-ˈrā-shən\ n

de·ter·mi·na·ble \-ˈtər-mə-nə-bəl\ adj : capable of being determined; *esp* : ASCERTAINABLE

de·ter·mi·nant \-mə-nənt\ n 1 : something that determines or conditions 2 : a hereditary factor : GENE

de·ter·mi·nate \di-ˈtər-mə-nət\ adj 1 : having fixed limits : DEFINITE 2 : definitely settled — **de·ter·mi·na·cy** \-nə-sē\ n — **de·ter·mi·nate·ness** n

de·ter·mi·na·tion \di-ˌtər-mə-ˈnā-shən\ n 1 : the act of coming to a decision; *also* : the decision or conclusion reached 2 : the act of fixing the extent, position, or character of something **3** : accurate measurement (as of length or volume) **4** : firm or fixed purpose

de·ter·mine \di-'tər-mən\ *vb* -**mined**; -**min·ing** \-'tərm-(ə-)niŋ\ **1** : to fix conclusively or authoritatively **2** : to come to a decision : SETTLE, RESOLVE **3** : to fix the form or character of beforehand : ORDAIN; *also* : REGULATE **4** : to find out the limits, nature, dimensions, or scope of (~ a position at sea) **5** : to be the cause of or reason for : DECIDE

de·ter·mined \-'tər-mənd\ *adj* **1** : DECIDED, RESOLVED **2** : FIRM, RESOLUTE — **de·ter·mined·ly** \-mən-dlē, -mə-nəd-lē\ *adv* — **de·ter·mined·ness** \-mən(d)-nəs\ *n*

de·ter·min·ism \di-'tər-mə-ˌniz-əm\ *n* : a doctrine that acts of the will, natural events, or social changes are determined by preceding events or natural causes — **de·ter·min·ist** \-nəst\ *n or adj*

de·ter·rence \di-'tər-əns\ *n* : the act, process, or capacity of deterring

de·ter·rent \-ənt\ *adj* **1** : serving to deter **2** : relating to deterrence — **deterrent** *n*

de·test \di-'test\ *vb* [ME *detesten*, fr. L *detestari*, lit., to curse while calling a deity to witness, fr. *de-* from + *testari* to call to witness] : LOATHE, HATE — **de·test·able** *adj* — **de·tes·ta·tion** \ˌdē-ˌtes-'tā-shən\ *n*

de·throne \di-'thrōn\ *vb* : to remove from a throne : DEPOSE — **de·throne·ment** *n*

det·o·nate \'det-ᵊn-ˌāt, 'det-ə-ˌnāt\ *vb* -**nat·ed**; -**nat·ing** : to explode or cause to explode with violence — **det·o·na·tion** \ˌdet-ᵊn-'ā-shən, ˌdet-ə-'nā-\ *n*

det·o·na·tor \'det-ᵊn-ˌāt-ər, -ə-ˌnāt-\ *n* : a device for detonating a high explosive

¹de·tour \'dē-ˌtu̇r\ *n* : a roundabout way temporarily replacing part of a route

²detour *vb* : to go by detour

de·tox·i·fy \dē-'täk-sə-ˌfī\ *vb* -**fied**; -**fy·ing 1** : to remove a poison or toxin or the effect of such from **2** : to free (as a drug user or alcoholic) from an intoxicating or addictive substance or from dependence on it — **de·tox·i·fi·ca·tion** \dē-ˌtäk-sə-fə-'kā-shən\ *n*

de·tract \di-'trakt\ *vb* **1** : to take away : WITHDRAW, SUBTRACT **2** : DISTRACT — **de·trac·tion** \-'trak-shən\ *n* — **de·trac·tor** \-'trak-tər\ *n*

de·train \dē-'trān\ *vb* : to leave or cause to leave a railroad train

det·ri·ment \'de-trə-mənt\ *n* : injury or damage or its cause : HURT — **det·ri·men·tal** \ˌde-trə-'ment-ᵊl\ *adj* — **det·ri·men·tal·ly** \-ē\ *adv*

de·tri·tus \di-'trīt-əs\ *n, pl* **de·tri·tus** : fragments resulting from disintegration (as of rocks) : DEBRIS

deuce \'d(y)üs\ *n* **1** : a two in cards or dice **2** : a tie in tennis with both sides at 40 **3** : DEVIL — used chiefly as a mild oath

Deut *abbr* Deuteronomy

deu·te·ri·um \d(y)ü-'tir-ē-əm\ *n* : the isotope of hydrogen that is of twice the mass of ordinary hydrogen

Deu·ter·on·o·my \ˌd(y)üt-ə-'rän-ə-mē\ *n* — see BIBLE table

deut·sche mark \ˌdȯi-chə-'märk\ *n* — see MONEY table

dev *abbr* deviation

de·val·ue \dē-'val-yü\ *vb* : to reduce the international exchange value of (~ a currency) — **de·val·u·a·tion** \dē-ˌval-yə-'wā-shən\ *n*

dev·as·tate \'dev-ə-ˌstāt\ *vb* -**tat·ed**; -**tat·ing 1** : to bring to ruin : lay waste **2** : to reduce to chaos, disorder, or helplessness — **dev·as·ta·tion** \ˌdev-ə-'stā-shən\ *n*

de·vel·op \di-'vel-əp\ *vb* **1** : to unfold gradually or in detail **2** : to place (exposed photographic material) in chemicals in order to make the image visible **3** : to bring out the possibilities of **4** : to make more available or usable (~ natural resources) **5** : to acquire gradually (~ a taste for olives) **6** : to go through a natural process of growth and differentiation : EVOLVE **7** : to become apparent — **de·vel·op·er** *n* — **de·vel·op·ment** *n* — **de·vel·op·men·tal** \-ˌvel-əp-'ment-ᵊl\ *adj*

de·vi·ant \'dē-vē-ənt\ *adj* : deviating esp. from some accepted norm (as of behavior) — **de·vi·ance** \-əns\ *n* — **de·vi·an·cy** \-ən-sē\ *n* — **deviant** *n*

de·vi·ate \'dē-vē-ˌāt\ *vb* -**at·ed**; -**at·ing** [LL *deviare*, fr. L *de-* from + *via* way] : to turn aside from a course, standard, principle, or topic — **de·vi·ate** \-vē-ət, -vē-ˌāt\ *n* — **de·vi·a·tion** \ˌdē-vē-'ā-shən\ *n*

de·vice \di-'vīs\ *n* **1** : SCHEME, STRATAGEM **2** : a piece of equipment or a mechanism for a special purpose **3** : DESIRE, INCLINATION (left to his own ~s) **4** : an emblematic design

¹dev·il \'dev-əl\ *n* [ME *devel*, fr. OE *dēofol*, fr. LL *diabolus*, fr. Gk *diabolos*, lit., slanderer, fr. *diaballein* to throw across, slander, fr. *dia-* across + *ballein* to throw] **1** *often cap* : the personal supreme spirit of evil **2** : DEMON **3** : a wicked person **4** : a reckless or dashing person **5** : FELLOW (poor ~) (lucky ~)

²devil *vb* -**iled** *or* -**illed**; -**il·ing** *or* -**il·ling** \'dev-(ə-)liŋ\ **1** : to chop fine and season highly (~ed eggs) **2** : TEASE, ANNOY

dev·il·ish \'dev-(ə-)lish\ *adj* **1** : resembling or befitting a devil **2** : EXTREME, EXCESSIVE — **dev·il·ish·ly** *adv* — **dev·il·ish·ness** *n*

dev·il·ment \'dev-əl-mənt, -ˌment\ *n* : MISCHIEF

dev·il·ry \-rē\ *or* **dev·il·try** \-trē\ *n, pl* -**il·ries** *or* -**il·tries 1** : action performed with the help of the devil **2** : reckless mischievousness

de·vi·ous \'dē-vē-əs\ *adj* **1** : deviating

from a straight line : ROUNDABOUT **2** : ERRING **3** : TRICKY

¹de·vise \di-ˈvīz\ *vb* **de·vised; de·vis·ing 1** : INVENT **2** : PLOT **3** : to give (real estate) by will

²devise *n* **1** : a disposing of real property by will **2** : a will or clause of a will disposing of real property **3** : property given by will

de·vi·tal·ize \dē-ˈvīt-ᵊl-ˌīz\ *vb* : to deprive of life or vitality

de·void \di-ˈvȯid\ *adj* : entirely lacking : DESTITUTE (a book ~ of interest)

de·voir \dəv-ˈwär\ *n* **1** : DUTY **2** : a formal act of civility or respect

de·volve \di-ˈvälv\ *vb* **de·volved; de·volv·ing** : to pass from one person to another by succession or transmission — **dev·o·lu·tion** \ˌdev-ə-ˈlü-shən, ˌdē-və-\ *n*

De·vo·ni·an \di-ˈvō-nē-ən\ *adj* : of, relating to, or being the period of the Paleozoic era between the Silurian and the Mississippian — **Devonian** *n*

de·vote \di-ˈvōt\ *vb* **de·vot·ed; de·vot·ing 1** : to set apart for a special purpose : DEDICATE **2** : to give up to wholly or chiefly

de·vot·ed \-ˈvōt-əd\ *adj* : characterized by loyalty and devotion

dev·o·tee \ˌdev-ə-ˈtē, -ˈtā\ *n* : an ardent follower, supporter, or enthusiast (as of a religion, art form, or sport)

de·vo·tion \di-ˈvō-shən\ *n* **1** : religious fervor **2** : an act of prayer or private worship — usu. used in pl. **3** : a religious exercise for private use **4** : the act of devoting or quality of being devoted (~ to music) **5** : strong love or affection — **de·vo·tion·al** \-sh(ə-)nəl\ *adj*

de·vour \di-ˈvau̇(ə)r\ *vb* **1** : to eat up greedily or ravenously **2** : WASTE, ANNIHILATE **3** : to take in eagerly by the senses or mind (~ a book) — **de·vour·er** *n*

de·vout \di-ˈvau̇t\ *adj* **1** : devoted to religion : PIOUS **2** : expressing devotion or piety **3** : EARNEST, SINCERE — **de·vout·ly** *adv* — **de·vout·ness** *n*

dew \ˈd(y)ü\ *n* : moisture that condenses on the surfaces of cool bodies at night — **dewy** *adj*

DEW *abbr* distant early warning

dew·ber·ry \ˈd(y)ü-ˌber-ē\ *n* : any of several sweet edible berries related to and resembling blackberries

dew·claw \-ˌklȯ\ *n* : a digit on the foot of a mammal that does not reach the ground; *also* : its claw or hoof

dew·drop \-ˌdräp\ *n* : a drop of dew

dew·lap \-ˌlap\ *n* : loose skin hanging under the neck of various animals (as a bovine)

dew point *n* : the temperature at which the moisture in the air begins to condense

dex·ter·i·ty \dek-ˈster-ət-ē\ *n, pl* **-ties 1** : mental skill or quickness **2** : readiness and grace in physical activity; *esp* : skill and ease in using the hands

dex·ter·ous *or* **dex·trous** \ˈdek-strəs\ *adj* **1** : CLEVER **2** : done with skillfulness **3** : skillful and competent with the hands — **dex·ter·ous·ly** *adv*

dex·trose \ˈdek-ˌstrōs\ *n* : the naturally occurring form of glucose found in plants and blood

DFC *abbr* Distinguished Flying Cross

DFM *abbr* Distinguished Flying Medal

DG *abbr* **1** [LL *Dei gratia*] by the grace of God **2** director general

DH *abbr* designated hitter

dhow \ˈdau̇\ *n* : an Arab sailing ship usu. having a long overhang forward and a high poop

DI *abbr* drill instructor

di·a·be·tes \ˌdī-ə-ˈbēt-ēz, -ˈbēt-əs\ *n* : an abnormal state marked by passage of excessive amounts of urine; *esp* : one (diabetes mel·li·tus \-ˈmel-ət-əs\) in which insulin is deficient and the urine and blood contain excess sugar — **di·a·bet·ic** \-ˈbet-ik\ *adj or n*

di·a·bol·ic \ˌdī-ə-ˈbäl-ik\ *or* **di·a·bol·i·cal** \-i-kəl\ *adj* : DEVILISH, FIENDISH — **di·a·bol·i·cal·ly** \-k(ə-)lē\ *adv*

di·a·crit·ic \ˌdī-ə-ˈkrit-ik\ *n* : a mark accompanying a letter and indicating a sound value different from that of the same letter when unmarked — **di·a·crit·i·cal** \-ˈkrit-i-kəl\ *adj*

di·a·dem \ˈdī-ə-ˌdem\ *n* : CROWN; *esp* : a band worn on or around the head as a badge of royalty

di·aer·e·sis \dī-ˈer-ə-səs\ *n, pl* **-e·ses** \-ˌsēz\ : a mark ¨ placed over a vowel to show that it is pronounced in a separate syllable (as in *naïve*)

diag *abbr* **1** diagonal **2** diagram

di·ag·no·sis \ˌdī-ig-ˈnō-səs, -əg-\ *n, pl* **-no·ses** \-ˌsēz\ : the art or act of identifying a disease from its signs and symptoms; *also* : the decision reached by diagnosis — **di·ag·nose** \ˈdī-ig-ˌnōs, -əg-\ *vb* — **di·ag·nos·tic** \ˌdī-ig-ˈnäs-tik, -əg-\ *adj* — **di·ag·nos·ti·cian** \-ˌnäs-ˈtish-ən\ *n*

¹di·ag·o·nal \dī-ˈag-ə-)nəl\ *adj* **1** : extending from one corner to the opposite corner in a 4-sided figure **2** : running in a slanting direction (~ stripes) **3** : having slanting markings or parts (a ~ weave) — **di·ag·o·nal·ly** \-ē\ *adv*

²diagonal *n* **1** : a diagonal line **2** : a diagonal direction **3** : a diagonal row, arrangement, or pattern

¹di·a·gram \ˈdī-ə-ˌgram\ *n* : a drawing, sketch, plan, or chart that makes something easier to understand — **di·a·gram·mat·ic** \ˌdī-ə-grə-ˈmat-ik\ *adj* — **di·a·gram·mat·i·cal·ly** \-i-k(ə-)lē\ *adv*

²diagram *vb* **-gramed** \-ˌgramd\ *or* **-grammed; -gram·ing** \-ˌgram-iŋ\ *or* **-gram·ming** : to represent by a diagram

¹di·al \ˈdī(-ə)l\ *n* [ME, fr. L *dies* day] **1** : the face of a sundial **2** : the face of a timepiece **3** : a plate or face with a pointer and numbers that indicate something ⟨the ~ of a gauge⟩ **4** : a disk with a knob or slots that is turned for making connections (as on a telephone) or for regulating operation (as of a radio)

²**dial** *vb* **di·aled** *or* **di·alled; di·al·ing** *or* **di·al·ling** **1** : to manipulate a dial so as to operate or select **2** : to make a telephone call or connection

³**dial** *abbr* dialect

di·a·lect \'dī-ə-ˌlekt\ *n* : a regional variety of a language

di·a·lec·tic \ˌdī-ə-'lek-tik\ *n* : the process or art of reasoning correctly

di·a·logue *also* **di·a·log** \'dī-ə-ˌlȯg\ *n* **1** : a conversation between two or more persons **2** : the parts of a literary or dramatic composition that represent conversation

di·al·y·sis \dī-'al-ə-səs\ *n, pl* **-y·ses** \-ˌsēz\ : the separation of substances from solution by means of their unequal diffusion through semipermeable membranes

diam *abbr* diameter

di·am·e·ter \dī-'am-ət-ər\ *n* [ME *diametre,* fr. MF, fr. L *diametros,* fr. Gk, fr. *dia-* through + *metron* measure] **1** : a straight line passing through the center of a figure or body; *esp* : a straight line that passes through the center of a circle and divides it in half **2** : the length of a diameter

di·a·met·ric \ˌdī-ə-'me-trik\ *or* **di·a·met·ri·cal** \-tri-kəl\ *adj* **1** : of, relating to, or constituting a diameter **2** : completely opposed or opposite — **di·a·met·ri·cal·ly** \-tri-k(ə-)lē\ *adv*

di·a·mond \'dī-(ə-)mənd\ *n* **1** : a hard brilliant mineral that consists of crystalline carbon and is used as a gem **2** : a flat figure having four equal sides, two acute angles, and two obtuse angles **3** : any of a suit of playing cards marked with a red diamond **4** : INFIELD; *also* : the entire playing field in baseball

di·a·mond·back rattlesnake \'dī-(ə-)mən(d)-ˌbak-\ *n* : a large and very deadly rattlesnake

di·an·thus \dī-'an-thəs\ *n* : ¹PINK 1

di·a·pa·son \ˌdī-ə-'pāz-ᵊn, -'pās-\ *n* **1** : an organ stop covering the range of the organ **2** : the range of notes sounded by a voice or instrument

¹**di·a·per** \'dī-(ə-)pər\ *n* **1** : a cotton or linen fabric woven in a simple geometric pattern **2** : a piece of folded cloth drawn up between the legs of a baby and fastened about the waist

²**diaper** *vb* **di·a·pered; di·a·per·ing** \-p(ə-)riŋ\ **1** : to ornament with diaper designs **2** : to put a diaper on

di·aph·a·nous \dī-'af-ə-nəs\ *adj* : so fine of texture as to be transparent

di·a·pho·ret·ic \ˌdī-ə-fə-'ret-ik\ *adj* : having the power to increase perspiration — **diaphoretic** *n*

di·a·phragm \'dī-ə-ˌfram\ *n* **1** : a sheet of muscle between the chest and ab-

dominal cavities of a mammal **2** : a vibrating disk (as in a telephone receiver) **3** : a cup-shaped device usu. of thin rubber fitted over the uterine cervix to act as a mechanical contraceptive barrier — **di·a·phrag·mat·ic** \ˌdī-ə-fra(g)-'mat-ik, -ˌfrag-\ *adj*

di·a·rist \'dī-ə-rəst\ *n* : one who keeps a diary

di·ar·rhea *or* **di·ar·rhoea** \ˌdī-ə-'rē-ə\ *n* : abnormally frequent and watery bowel movements

di·a·ry \'dī-(ə-)rē\ *n, pl* **-ries** : a daily record esp. of personal experiences and observations; *also* : a book for keeping such private notes and records

di·as·to·le \dī-'as-tə-(ˌ)lē\ *n* : the stretching of the cavities of the heart during which they fill with blood — **di·a·stol·ic** \ˌdī-ə-'stäl-ik\ *adj*

di·as·tro·phism \dī-'as-trə-ˌfiz-əm\ *n* : the process of deformation of the earth's crust by which major relief features are formed — **di·a·stroph·ic** \ˌdī-ə-'sträf-ik\ *adj*

di·a·ther·my \'dī-ə-ˌthər-mē\ *n* : the generation of heat in tissue by electric currents for medical or surgical purposes

di·a·tom \'dī-ə-ˌtäm\ *n* : any of a class of planktonic one-celled or colonial algae with skeletons of silica

di·atom·ic \ˌdī-ə-'täm-ik\ *adj* : having two atoms in the molecule

di·at·o·mite \dī-'at-ə-ˌmīt\ *n* : a light crumbly siliceous material derived chiefly from diatom remains and used esp. as a filter

di·a·tribe \'dī-ə-ˌtrīb\ *n* : a bitter or violent attack in speech or writing

dib·ble \'dib-əl\ *n* : a pointed hand tool for making holes (as for planting bulbs) in the ground — **dibble** *vb*

¹**dice** \'dīs\ *n, pl* **dice** : DIE 1

²**dice** *vb* **diced; dic·ing** **1** : to cut into small cubes ⟨~ carrots⟩ **2** : to play games with dice

di·chot·o·my \dī-'kät-ə-mē\ *n, pl* **-mies** : a division or the process of dividing into two esp. mutually exclusive or contradictory groups — **di·chot·o·mous** \-məs\ *adj*

dick·er \'dik-ər\ *vb* **dick·ered; dick·er·ing** \'dik-(ə-)riŋ\ : BARGAIN, HAGGLE

dick·ey *or* **dicky** \'dik-ē\ *n, pl* **dickeys** *or* **dick·ies** : a small fabric insert worn to fill in the neckline

di·cot·y·le·don \ˌdī-ˌkät-ᵊl-'ēd-ᵊn\ *n* : any of a group of seed plants having an embryo with two cotyledons — **di·cot·y·le·don·ous** *adj*

dict *abbr* dictionary

¹**dic·tate** \'dik-ˌtāt\ *vb* **dic·tat·ed; dic·tat·ing** **1** : to speak or read for a person to transcribe or for a machine to record **2** : COMMAND, ORDER — **dic·ta·tion** \dik-'tā-shən\ *n*

²**dic·tate** \'dik-ˌtāt\ *n* : an authoritative rule, prescription, or injunction : COMMAND ⟨the ~s of conscience⟩

dic·ta·tor \'dik-ˌtāt-ər\ n 1 : a person ruling absolutely and often brutally and oppressively 2 : one that dictates

dic·ta·to·ri·al \ˌdik-tə-'tōr-ē-əl\ adj : of, relating to, or characteristic of a dictator or a dictatorship

dic·ta·tor·ship \dik-'tāt-ər-ˌship, 'dik-ˌtāt-\ n 1 : the office or term of office of a dictator 2 : autocratic rule, control, or leadership 3 : a government or country in which absolute power is held by a dictator or a small clique

dic·tion \'dik-shən\ n 1 : choice of words esp. with regard to correctness, clearness, or effectiveness : WORDING 2 : ENUNCIATION

dic·tio·nary \'dik-shə-ˌner-ē\ n, pl -nar·ies : a reference book containing words usu. alphabetically arranged along with information about their forms, pronunciations, functions, etymologies, meanings, and syntactical and idiomatic uses

dic·tum \'dik-təm\ n, pl **dic·ta** \-tə\ also **dictums** : a formal authoritative statement : PRONOUNCEMENT

did past of DO

di·dac·tic \dī-'dak-tik\ adj 1 : intended primarily to instruct; esp : intended to teach a moral lesson 2 : making moral observations

di·do \'dīd-ō\ n, pl **didoes** or **didos** : a foolish or mischievous act

¹die \'dī\ vb **died; dy·ing** \'dī-iŋ\ 1 : to stop living : EXPIRE 2 : to pass out of existence (a dying race) 3 : to disappear or subside gradually (the wind died down) 4 : to long keenly (dying to go) 5 : STOP (the motor died)

²die \'dī\ n, pl **dice** \'dīs\ or **dies** \'dīz\ 1 pl **dice** : a small cube marked on each face with one to six spots and used usu. in pairs in various games and gambling 2 pl **dies** : a device used in shaping or stamping an object or material

die-hard \'dī-ˌhärd\ n : one who resists against hopeless odds

diel·drin \'dē(ə)l-drən\ n : a persistent chlorinated hydrocarbon insecticide

die·sel \'dē-zəl, -səl\ n 1 : DIESEL ENGINE 2 : a vehicle driven by a diesel engine

diesel engine n : an internal-combustion engine in whose cylinders air is compressed to a temperature sufficiently high to ignite the fuel

die·sel·ing \'dēz-(ə-)liŋ\ n : an instance of an internal-combustion engine continuing to operate after the ignition has been turned off

¹di·et \'dī-ət\ n [ME diete, fr. OF, fr. L diaeta prescribed diet, fr. Gk diaita, lit., manner of living] 1 : the food and drink regularly consumed (as by a person or group) : FARE 2 : an allowance of food prescribed with reference to a particular state (as ill health) — **di·etary** \'dī-ə-ˌter-ē\ adj or n

²diet vb : to eat or cause to eat less or according to a prescribed rule — **di·et·er** n

di·etet·ics \ˌdī-ə-'tet-iks\ n sing or pl : the science or art of applying the principles of nutrition to diet — **dietet·ic** adj

di·eti·tian or **di·eti·cian** \ˌdī-ə-'tish-ən\ n : a specialist in dietetics

dif or **diff** abbr difference

dif·fer \'dif-ər\ vb **dif·fered; dif·fer·ing** \-(ə-)riŋ\ 1 : to be unlike 2 : DISAGREE

dif·fer·ence \'dif-(ə-)rəns, 'dif-ərns\ n 1 : UNLIKENESS (~ in their looks) 2 : distinction or discrimination in preference 3 : DISAGREEMENT, DISSENSION; also : an instance or cause of disagreement (unable to settle their ~s) 4 : the amount by which one number or quantity differs from another

dif·fer·ent \'dif-(ə-)rənt, 'dif-ərnt\ adj 1 : UNLIKE, DISSIMILAR 2 : not the same (~ age groups) (seen at ~ times) (try a ~ book) 3 : UNUSUAL, SPECIAL — **dif·fer·ent·ly** adv

¹dif·fer·en·tial \ˌdif-ə-'ren-chəl\ adj : showing, creating, or relating to a difference

²differential n 1 : the amount or degree by which things differ 2 : DIFFERENTIAL GEAR

differential gear n : an arrangement of gears in an automobile that allows one wheel to go faster than another (as in rounding curves)

dif·fer·en·ti·ate \ˌdif-ə-'ren-chē-ˌāt\ vb **-at·ed; -at·ing** 1 : to make or become different 2 : to recognize or state the difference (~ between two plants) — **dif·fer·en·ti·a·tion** \-ˌren-chē-'ā-shən\ n

dif·fi·cult \'dif-i-(ˌ)kəlt\ adj 1 : hard to do or make 2 : hard to understand or deal with (~ reading) (a ~ child)

dif·fi·cul·ty \'dif-i-(ˌ)kəl-tē\ n, pl -ties 1 : difficult nature (the ~ of a task) 2 : DISAGREEMENT (settled their difficulties) 3 : OBSTACLE (overcome difficulties) 4 : TROUBLE (in financial difficulties) syn hardship, rigor, vicissitude

dif·fi·dent \'dif-əd-ənt\ adj 1 : lacking confidence : TIMID 2 : RESERVED, UNASSERTIVE — **dif·fi·dence** \-əns\ n — **dif·fi·dent·ly** adv

dif·frac·tion \dif-'rak-shən\ n : the bending or spreading of a light beam esp. when passing through narrow slits or when reflecting from a ruled surface

¹dif·fuse \dif-'yüs\ adj 1 : VERBOSE, WORDY (~ writing) 2 : not concentrated : SCATTERED (~ light)

²dif·fuse \dif-'yüz\ vb **dif·fused; dif·fus·ing** : to pour out or spread widely — **dif·fu·sion** \-'yü-zhən\ n

dig \'dig\ vb **dug** \'dəg\ ; **dig·ging** 1 : to turn up the soil (as with a spade) 2 : to hollow out or form by removing earth (~ a hole) 3 : to uncover or seek by turning up earth (~ potatoes) 4 : DISCOVER (~ up information) 5 : POKE, THRUST (~ a person in the ribs) 6 : to work hard 7 : NOTICE, APPRECIATE; also : LIKE, ADMIRE

²**dig** n **1** : THRUST, POKE **2** : a cutting remark : GIBE

³**dig** abbr digest

di·gest \'dī-ˌjest\ n : a summation or condensation of a body of information or of a literary work

²**di·gest** \dī-'jest, də-\ vb **1** : to think over and arrange in the mind **2** : to convert (food) into simpler forms that can be absorbed by the body **3** : to compress into a short summary — **di·gest·ibil·i·ty** \-ˌjes-tə-'bil-ət-ē\ n — **di·gest·ible** adj — **di·ges·tion** \-'jes-chən\ n — **di·ges·tive** \-'jes-tiv\ adj

dig in vb **1** : to dig defensive trenches **2** : to go resolutely to work **3** : to begin eating

dig·it \'dij-ət\ n [ME, fr. L digitus finger, toe] **1** : any of the Arabic numerals 1 to 9 and usu. the symbol 0 **2** : FINGER, TOE

dig·i·tal \'dij-ət-ᵊl\ adj **1** : of, relating to, or done with a finger or toe **2** : of, relating to, or using calculation directly with digits rather than through measurable physical quantities (a ~ computer) **3** : providing a readout in numerical digits (a ~ watch) — **dig·i·tal·ly** \-ē\ adv

dig·i·tal·is \ˌdij-ə-'tal-əs\ n : a drug from the common foxglove that is a powerful heart stimulant; also : FOXGLOVE

dig·ni·fied \'dig-nə-ˌfīd\ adj : showing or expressing dignity

dig·ni·fy \-ˌfī\ vb -fied; -fy·ing : to give dignity or distinction to : HONOR

dig·ni·tary \'dig-nə-ˌter-ē\ n, pl -tar·ies : a person of high position or honor

dig·ni·ty \'dig-nət-ē\ n, pl -ties **1** : the quality or state of being worthy, honored, or esteemed : true worth : EXCELLENCE **2** : high rank, office, or position **3** : formal reserve of manner or language

di·graph \'dī-ˌgraf\ n : a group of two successive letters whose phonetic value is a single sound (as ea in bread)

di·gress \dī-'gres, də-\ vb : to turn aside esp. from the main subject in writing or speaking — **di·gres·sion** \-'gresh-ən\ n — **di·gres·sive** \-'gres-iv\ adj

dike \'dīk\ n : a bank of earth to control water : LEVEE

dil abbr dilute

di·lap·i·dat·ed \də-'lap-ə-ˌdāt-əd\ adj : fallen into partial ruin or decay — **di·lap·i·da·tion** \-ˌlap-ə-'dā-shən\ n

di·late \dī-'lāt, 'dī-ˌlāt\ vb di·lat·ed; di·lat·ing : SWELL, DISTEND, EXPAND — **dil·a·ta·tion** \ˌdil-ə-'tā-shən\ n — **di·la·tion** \dī-'lā-shən\ n

dil·a·to·ry \'dil-ə-ˌtōr-ē\ adj **1** : DELAYING **2** : TARDY, SLOW

di·lem·ma \də-'lem-ə\ n : a choice between equally unsatisfactory alternatives

dil·et·tante \ˌdil-ə-'tänt(-ē), -'tänt(-ē)\ n, pl -tantes or -tan·ti \-'tänt-ē, -'tänt-ē\ [It, fr. dilettare to delight, fr. L dilectare] : a person having a superficial interest in an art or a branch of knowledge

dil·i·gent \'dil-ə-jənt\ adj : characterized by steady, earnest, and energetic application and effort : PAINSTAKING — **dil·i·gence** \-jəns\ n — **dil·i·gent·ly** adv

dill \'dil\ n : an herb related to the carrot with aromatic leaves and seeds used in pickles

dil·ly \'dil-ē\ n, pl dil·lies : one that is remarkable or outstanding

dil·ly-dal·ly \'dil-ē-ˌdal-ē\ vb : to waste time by loitering or delay

di·lute \dī-'lüt, də-\ vb di·lut·ed; di·lut·ing : to lessen the consistency or strength of by mixing with something else — **di·lu·tion** \-'lü-shən\ n

²**dilute** adj : DILUTED, WEAK

¹**dim** \'dim\ adj dim·mer; dim·mest **1** : LUSTERLESS, DULL **2** : not bright or distinct : OBSCURE, FAINT **3** : not seeing or understanding clearly — **dim·ly** adv — **dim·ness** n

²**dim** vb dimmed; dim·ming **1** : to make or become dim or lusterless **2** : to reduce the light from (headlights) by switching to the low beam

³**dim** abbr **1** dimension **2** diminished **3** diminutive

dime \'dīm\ n [ME, tenth part, tithe, fr. MF, fr. L decima, fr. fem. of decimus tenth, fr. decem ten] : a U.S. coin worth ¹/₁₀ dollar

di·men·sion \də-'men-chən, dī-\ n **1** : measurement of extension (as in length, height, or breadth) **2** : EXTENT, SCOPE, PROPORTIONS — usu. used in pl. — **di·men·sion·al** \-'mench-(ə-)nəl\ adj — **di·men·sion·al·i·ty** \-ˌmen-chə-'nal-ət-ē\ n

di·min·ish \də-'min-ish\ vb **1** : to make less or cause to appear less **2** : BELITTLE **3** : DWINDLE **4** : TAPER — **dim·i·nu·tion** \ˌdim-ə-'n(y)ü-shən\ n

di·min·u·en·do \də-ˌmin-(y)ə-'wen-dō\ adv or adj : DECRESCENDO

¹**di·min·u·tive** \də-'min-yət-iv\ n **1** : a diminutive word or affix **2** : a diminutive individual

²**diminutive** adj **1** : indicating small size and sometimes the state or quality of being lovable, pitiable, or contemptible (the ~ suffixes -ette and -ling) **2** : extremely small : TINY

dim·i·ty \'dim-ət-ē\ n, pl -ties : a thin usu. corded cotton fabric

dim·mer \'dim-ər\ n : a device for controlling the amount of light from an electric lighting unit

di·mor·phic \(')dī-'mòr-fik\ adj : occurring in two distinct forms — **di·mor·phism** \-ˌfiz-əm\ n

¹**dim·ple** \'dim-pəl\ n : a small depression esp. in the cheek or chin

²**dimple** vb dim·pled; dim·pling : to form dimples (as in smiling)

din \'din\ n : a loud confused mixture of noises

di·nar \di-'när\ n **1** — see MONEY table **2** — see rial at MONEY table

dine \\'dīn\ *vb* **dined; din·ing** [ME *dinen*, fr. OF *diner*, fr. (assumed) VL *disjejunare* to break one's fast, deriv. of L *jejunus* fasting] **1** : to eat dinner **2** : to give a dinner to : FEED

din·er \\'dī-nər\ *n* **1** : one that dines **2** : a railroad dining car **3** : a restaurant usu. resembling a dining car

di·nette \dī-'net\ *n* : an alcove or small room used for dining

din·ghy \\'diŋ-ē\ *n, pl* **dinghies 1** : a small rowboat **2** : LIFE RAFT

din·gle \\'diŋ-gəl\ *n* : a small wooded valley

din·go \\'diŋ-gō\ *n, pl* **dingoes** : a reddish brown wild dog of Australia

din·gus \\'diŋ-(g)əs\ *n* : DOODAD

din·gy \\'din-jē\ *adj* **din·gi·er; -est 1** : DARK, DULL **2** : not fresh or clean : GRIMY — **din·gi·ness** *n*

dink·y \\'diŋ-kē\ *adj* **din·ki·er; -est** : SMALL, INSIGNIFICANT

din·ner \\'din-ər\ *n* : the main meal of the day; *also* : a formal banquet

din·ner·ware \-ˌwaər, -ˌwaər\ *n* : china, glassware, or tableware used in table service

di·no·fla·gel·late \ˌdī-nō-'flaj-ə-lət, -ˌlāt\ *n* : any of an order of planktonic plantlike flagellates of which some cause red tide

di·no·saur \\'dī-nə-ˌsȯr\ *n* [fr. Gk *deinos* terrible + *sauros* lizard] : any of a group of extinct long-tailed reptiles often of huge size

dint \\'dint\ *n* **1** : FORCE (reached the top by ~ of sheer grit) **2** : DENT

di·o·cese \\'dī-ə-səs, -ˌsēz, -ˌsēs\ *n, pl* **-ces·es** \-sə-səz, -ˌsē-zəz, -ˌsē-səz, -ə-ˌsēz\ : the territorial jurisdiction of a bishop — **di·oc·e·san** \dī-'äs-ə-sən, ˌdī-ə-'sēz-ºn\ *adj or n*

di·ode \\'dī-ˌōd\ *n* **1** : an electron tube having a cathode and anode **2** : a semiconductor device that functions as a rectifier

di·ox·in \dī-'äk-sən\ *n* : a hydrocarbon that occurs esp. as a persistent toxic impurity in herbicides (as Agent Orange)

¹dip \\'dip\ *vb* **dipped; dip·ping 1** : to plunge temporarily or partially under the surface (as of a liquid) **2** : to thrust in a way to suggest immersion **3** : to scoop up or out : LADLE **4** : to lower and then raise quickly (~ a flag in salute) **5** : to drop or slope down esp. suddenly (the moon *dipped* below the crest) **6** : to decrease moderately and usu. temporarily (prices *dipped*) **7** : to reach inside or as if inside or below a surface (*dipped* into their savings) **8** : to delve casually into something; *esp* : to read superficially (~ into a book)

²dip *n* **1** : an act of dipping; *esp* : a short swim **2** : inclination downward : DROP **3** : something obtained by or used in dipping **4** : a sauce or soft mixture into which food may be dipped **5** : a liquid into which something may be dipped (as for cleansing or coloring)

diph·the·ria \dif-'thir-ē-ə, dip-\ *n* : an acute contagious bacterial disease marked by fever and by coating of the air passages with a membrane that interferes with breathing

diph·thong \\'dif-ˌthȯŋ, 'dip-\ *n* : two vowel sounds joined in one syllable to form one speech sound (as *ou* in *out*)

dip·loid \\'dip-ˌlȯid\ *adj* : having the basic chromosome number doubled — **diploid** *n*

di·plo·ma \də-'plō-mə\ *n, pl* **diplomas** : an official record of graduation from or of a degree conferred by a school

di·plo·ma·cy \də-'plō-mə-sē\ *n* **1** : the art and practice of conducting negotiations between nations **2** : TACT

dip·lo·mat \\'dip-lə-ˌmat\ *n* : one employed or skilled in diplomacy — **dip·lo·mat·ic** \ˌdip-lə-'mat-ik\ *adj*

di·plo·ma·tist \də-'plō-mət-əst\ *n* : DIPLOMAT

dip·per \\'dip-ər\ *n* **1** : any of a genus of birds that are related to the thrushes and are skilled in diving **2** : something (as a ladle or scoop) that dips or is used for dipping **3** *cap* : the seven bright stars of Ursa Major arranged in a form resembling a dipper **4** *cap* : the seven bright stars of Ursa Minor arranged in a form resembling a dipper with the North Star forming the outer end of the handle

dip·so·ma·nia \ˌdip-sə-'mā-nē-ə\ *n* : an uncontrollable craving for alcoholic liquors — **dip·so·ma·ni·ac** \-nē-ˌak\ *n*

dip·stick \\'dip-ˌstik\ *n* : a graduated rod for indicating depth

dip·ter·ous \\'dip-tə-rəs\ *adj* : of, relating to, or being a two-winged fly — **dip·ter·an** \-rən\ *adj or n*

dir *abbr* director

dire \\'dī(ə)r\ *adj* **dir·er; dir·est 1** : very horrible : DREADFUL **2** : warning of disaster **3** : EXTREME

¹di·rect \də-'rekt, dī-\ *vb* **1** : ADDRESS (~ a letter) ; *also* : to impart orally : AIM (~ a remark to the gallery) **2** : to regulate the activities or course of : guide the supervision, organizing, or performance of **3** : to cause to turn, move, or point or to follow a certain course **4** : to point, extend, or project in a specified line or course **5** : to request or instruct with authority **6** : to show or point out the way

²direct *adj* **1** : stemming immediately from a source, cause, or reason (~ result) **2** : being or passing in a straight line of descent : LINEAL (~ ancestor) **3** : leading from one point to another in time or space without turn or stop : STRAIGHT **4** : NATURAL, STRAIGHTFORWARD (a ~ manner) **5** : operating without an intervening agency or step (~ action) **6** : effected by the action of the people or the electorate and not by representatives (~ legislation) **7** : consisting of or reproducing the exact words of a speaker

⟨~ discourse⟩ — **direct** *adv* — **di·rect·ly** \də-'rek-(t)lē, dī-\ *adv* — **di·rect·ness** \-'rek(t)-nəs\ *n*

direct current *n* : an electric current flowing in one direction only

di·rec·tion \də-'rek-shən, dī-\ *n* 1 : MANAGEMENT, GUIDANCE 2 : COMMAND, ORDER, INSTRUCTION 3 : the course or line along which something moves, lies, or points 4 : TENDENCY, TREND — **di·rec·tion·al** \-sh(ə-)nəl\ *adj*

di·rec·tive \də-'rek-tiv, dī-\ *n* : a general instruction as to procedure

di·rec·tor \də-'rek-tər, dī-\ *n* 1 : one that directs : MANAGER, SUPERVISOR, CONDUCTOR 2 : one of a group of persons who direct the affairs of an organized body — **di·rec·tor·ship** *n*

di·rec·tor·ate \də-'rek-t(ə-)rət\ *n* 1 : the office or position of director 2 : a board of directors; *also* : membership on such a board 3 : an executive staff

di·rec·to·ry \-t(ə-)rē\ *n, pl* **-ries** : an alphabetical or classified list of names and addresses

dire·ful \'dī(ə)r-fəl\ *adj* : producing dire effects

dirge \'dərj\ *n* : a song of lamentation; *also* : a slow mournful piece of music

dir·ham \'dir-həm\ *n* 1 — see MONEY table 2 — see *dinar, riyal* at MONEY table

di·ri·gi·ble \'dir-ə-jə-bəl, də-'rij-ə-\ *n* : AIRSHIP

dirk \'dərk\ *n* : DAGGER 1

dirndl \'dərn-d⁹l\ *n* [short for G *dirndlkleid,* fr. G dial. *dirndl* girl + G *kleid* dress] : a full skirt with a tight waistband

dirt \'dərt\ *n* 1 : a filthy or soiling substance (as mud, dust, or grime) 2 : loose or packed earth : SOIL 3 : moral uncleanness 4 : scandalous gossip 5 : embarrassing or incriminating information

¹**dirty** \'dərt-ē\ *adj* **dirt·i·er; -est** 1 : SOILED, FILTHY 2 : INDECENT, SMUTTY ⟨~ talk⟩ 3 : BASE, UNFAIR ⟨a ~ trick⟩ 4 : STORMY, FOGGY ⟨~ weather⟩ 5 : not clear in color : DULL ⟨a ~ red⟩ — **dirt·i·ness** \'dərt-ē-nəs\ *n* — **dirty** *adv*

²**dirty** *vb* **dirt·ied; dirty·ing** : to make or become dirty

dis·able \dis-'ā-bəl\ *vb* **dis·abled; disabling** \-b(ə-)liŋ\ 1 : to disqualify legally 2 : to make unable to perform by or as if by illness, injury, or malfunction — **dis·abil·i·ty** \,dis-ə-'bil-ət-ē\ *n*

dis·abuse \,dis-ə-'byüz\ *vb* : to free from error or fallacy

dis·sac·cha·ride \dī-'sak-ə-,rīd\ *n* : a sugar that yields two molecules of simple sugar upon hydrolysis

dis·ad·van·tage \,dis-əd-'vant-ij\ *n* 1 : loss or damage esp. to reputation or finances 2 : an unfavorable, inferior, or prejudicial condition; *also* : HANDICAP — **dis·ad·van·ta·geous** \,dis-,ad-,van-'tā-jəs, -vən-\ *adj*

dis·af·fect \,dis-ə-'fekt\ *vb* : to alienate the affection or loyalty of : cause discontent in ⟨the troops were ~ed⟩ — **dis·af·fec·tion** \-'fek-shən\ *n*

dis·agree \,dis-ə-'grē\ *vb* 1 : to fail to agree 2 : to differ in opinion 3 : to have an unpleasant effect ⟨fried foods ~ with her⟩ — **dis·agree·ment** *n*

dis·agree·able \-ə-bəl\ *adj* 1 : causing discomfort : UNPLEASANT, OFFENSIVE 2 : ILL-TEMPERED, PEEVISH — **dis·agree·able·ness** *n* — **dis·agree·ably** \-blē\ *adv*

dis·al·low \,dis-ə-'lau\ *vb* : to refuse to admit or recognize : REJECT ⟨~ a claim⟩ — **dis·al·low·ance** *n*

dis·ap·pear \,dis-ə-'piər\ *vb* 1 : to pass out of sight 2 : to cease to be : become lost — **dis·ap·pear·ance** *n*

dis·ap·point \,dis-ə-'point\ *vb* : to fail to fulfill the expectation or hope of — **dis·ap·point·ment** *n*

dis·ap·pro·ba·tion \dis-,ap-rə-'bā-shən\ *n* : DISAPPROVAL

dis·ap·prov·al \,dis-ə-'prü-vəl\ *n* : adverse judgment : CENSURE

dis·ap·prove \-'prüv\ *vb* 1 : CONDEMN 2 : to feel or express disapproval ⟨~s of smoking⟩ 3 : REJECT

dis·arm \dis-'ärm\ *vb* 1 : to take arms or weapons from 2 : to reduce the size and strength of the armed forces of a country 3 : to make harmless, peaceable, or friendly : win over ⟨a ~ing smile⟩ — **dis·ar·ma·ment** \-'är-mə-mənt\ *n*

dis·ar·range \,dis-ə-'rānj\ *vb* : to disturb the arrangement or order of — **dis·ar·range·ment** *n*

dis·ar·ray \-'rā\ *n* 1 : DISORDER, CONFUSION 2 : disorderly or careless dress

dis·as·sem·ble \,dis-ə-'sem-bəl\ *vb* : to take apart

dis·as·so·ci·ate \-'sō-s(h)ē-,āt\ *vb* : to detach from association

di·sas·ter \diz-'as-tər, dis-\ *n* [MF *desastre,* fr. It *disastro,* fr. *astro* star, fr. L *astrum*] : a sudden or great misfortune — **di·sas·trous** \-'as-trəs\ *adj* — **di·sas·trous·ly** *adv*

dis·avow \,dis-ə-'vau\ *vb* : to deny responsibility for : REPUDIATE — **dis·avow·al** \-'vau(-ə)l\ *n*

dis·band \dis-'band\ *vb* : to break up the organization of : DISPERSE

dis·bar \dis-'bär\ *vb* : to expel from the legal profession — **dis·bar·ment** *n*

dis·be·lieve \,dis-bə-'lēv\ *vb* 1 : to hold not to be true or real ⟨*disbelieved* his testimony⟩ 2 : to withhold or reject belief — **dis·be·lief** \-'lēf\ *n* — **dis·be·liev·er** *n*

dis·bur·den \dis-'bərd-⁹n\ *vb* : to rid of a burden

dis·burse \dis-'bərs\ *vb* **dis·bursed; dis·burs·ing** : to pay out : EXPEND — **dis·burse·ment** *n*

¹**disc** *var of* DISK

²**disc** *abbr* discount

³**dis·card** \dis-'kärd, 'dis-,kärd\ *vb* 1 : to let go a playing card from one's hand; *also* : to play (a card) from a suit other than a trump but different from the

one led **2** : to get rid of as unwanted — **dis·card** \\'dis-ˌkärd\ *n*

disc brake *n* : a brake that operates by the friction of a pair of plates pressing against the sides of a rotating disc

dis·cern \dis-'ərn, diz-\ *vb* **1** : to detect with the eyes : DISTINGUISH **2** : DISCRIMINATE **3** : to come to know or recognize mentally — **dis·cern·ible** *adj* — **dis·cern·ment** *n*

dis·cern·ing \-iŋ\ *adj* : revealing insight and understanding

¹**dis·charge** \dis-'chärj, 'dis-ˌchärj\ *vb* **1** : to relieve of a charge, load, or burden : UNLOAD; *esp* : to remove the electrical energy from ⟨~ a storage battery⟩ **2** : SHOOT ⟨~ a gun⟩ ⟨~ an arrow⟩ **3** : to set free ⟨~ a prisoner⟩ **4** : to dismiss from service or employment ⟨~ a soldier⟩ **5** : to let go or let off ⟨~ passengers⟩ **6** : to give forth fluid (the river ~s into the ocean) **7** : to get rid of by paying or doing ⟨~ a debt⟩

²**dis·charge** \'dis-ˌchärj, dis-'chärj\ *n* **1** : the act of discharging, unloading, or releasing **2** : something that discharges; *esp* : a certification of release or payment **3** : a firing off (as of a gun) **4** : a flowing out (as of blood from a wound); *also* : something that is emitted (a purulent ~) **5** : release or dismissal esp. from an office or employment; *also* : complete separation from military service **6** : a flow of electricity (as through a gas)

dis·ci·ple \dis-'ī-pəl\ *n* **1** : one who accepts and helps to spread the teachings of another; *also* : a convinced adherent **2** *cap* : a member of the Disciples of Christ

dis·ci·pli·nar·i·an \ˌdis-ə-plə-'ner-ē-ən\ *n* : one who enforces order

dis·ci·plin·ary \'dis-ə-plə-ˌner-ē\ *adj* : of or relating to discipline; *also* : CORRECTIVE (take ~ action)

¹**dis·ci·pline** \'dis-ə-plən\ *n* **1** : PUNISHMENT **2** : a field of study : SUBJECT **3** : training that corrects, molds, or perfects **4** : control gained by obedience or training : orderly conduct **5** : a system of rules governing conduct

²**discipline** *vb* **-plined; -plin·ing 1** : PUNISH **2** : to train or develop by instruction and exercise esp. in self-control **3** : to bring under control ⟨~ troops⟩ ; *also* : to impose order upon

disc jockey *n* : a person who conducts a radio show of popular recorded music

dis·claim \dis-'klām\ *vb* : to deny having a connection with or responsibility for : DISAVOW — **dis·claim·er** *n*

dis·close \dis-'klōz\ *vb* : to expose to view — **dis·clo·sure** \-'klō-zhər\ *n*

dis·co \'dis-ˌkō\ *n, pl* **discos 1** : DISCOTHEQUE **2** : popular dance music characterized by hypnotic rhythm, repetitive lyrics, and electronically produced sounds

dis·col·or \dis-'kəl-ər\ *vb* : to alter or change in hue or color : STAIN — **dis·col·or·ation** \dis-ˌkəl-ə-'rā-shən\ *n*

dis·com·bob·u·late \ˌdis-kəm-'bäb-(y)ə-ˌlāt\ *vb* **-lat·ed; -lat·ing** : UPSET, CONFUSE

dis·com·fit \dis-'kəm-fət, *esp South* ˌdis-kəm-'fit\ *vb* **1** : UPSET, FRUSTRATE — **dis·com·fi·ture** \dis-'kəm-fə-ˌchùr\ *n*

¹**dis·com·fort** \dis-'kəm-fərt\ *vb* : to make uncomfortable or uneasy

²**discomfort** *n* : lack of comfort : uneasiness of mind or body : DISTRESS

dis·com·mode \ˌdis-kə-'mōd\ *vb* **-mod·ed; -mod·ing** : INCONVENIENCE, TROUBLE

dis·com·pose \-kəm-'pōz\ *vb* **1** : AGITATE **2** : DISARRANGE — **dis·com·po·sure** \-'pō-zhər\ *n*

dis·con·cert \ˌdis-kən-'sərt\ *vb* : CONFUSE, UPSET

dis·con·nect \ˌdis-kə-'nekt\ *vb* : to undo the connection of — **dis·con·nec·tion** \-'nek-shən\ *n*

dis·con·nect·ed \-əd\ *adj* : not connected : RAMBLING, INCOHERENT — **dis·con·nect·ed·ly** *adv*

dis·con·so·late \dis-'kän-sə-lət\ *adj* **1** : CHEERLESS **2** : hopelessly sad — **dis·con·so·late·ly** *adv*

dis·con·tent \ˌdis-kən-'tent\ *n* : uneasiness of mind : DISSATISFACTION — **dis·con·tent·ed** *adj*

dis·con·tin·ue \ˌdis-kən-'tin-yü\ *vb* **1** : to break the continuity of : cease to operate, use, or take **2** : END — **dis·con·tin·u·ance** \-yə-wəns\ *n* — **dis·con·ti·nu·i·ty** \ˌdis-ˌkänt-ᵊn-'(y)ü-ət-ē\ *n* — **dis·con·tin·u·ous** \ˌdis-kən-'tin-yə-wəs\ *adj*

dis·cord \'dis-ˌkórd\ *n* **1** : lack of agreement or harmony : DISSENSION, CONFLICT **2** : a harsh combination of musical sounds **3** : a harsh or unpleasant sound — **dis·cor·dant** \dis-'kórd-ᵊnt\ *adj* — **dis·cor·dant·ly** *adv*

dis·co·theque \'dis-kə-ˌtek\ *n* : a nightclub for dancing to live or recorded music

¹**dis·count** \'dis-ˌkaùnt\ *n* **1** : a reduction made from a regular or list price **2** : a deduction of interest in advance when lending money

²**dis·count** \'dis-ˌkaùnt, dis-'kaùnt\ *vb* **1** : to deduct from the amount of a bill, debt, or charge usu. for cash or prompt payment; *also* : to sell or offer for sale at a discount **2** : to lend money after deducting the discount ⟨~ a note⟩ **3** : DISREGARD; *also* : MINIMIZE **4** : to make allowance for bias or exaggeration; *also* : DISBELIEVE **5** : to take into account (as a future event) in present calculations — **dis·count·able** *adj* — **dis·count·er** *n*

dis·coun·te·nance \dis-'kaùnt-(ᵊ)nəns\ *vb* **1** : EMBARRASS, DISCONCERT **2** : to look with disfavor on

dis·cour·age \dis-'kər-ij\ *vb* **-aged; -ag·ing 1** : to deprive of courage or confidence : DISHEARTEN **2** : to hinder by inspiring fear of consequences : DE-TER 3 : to attempt to dissuade — **dis·cour·age·ment** *n* — **dis·cour·ag·ing·ly** \-ij-iŋ-lē\ *adv*

¹**dis·course** \'dis-ˌkōrs\ *n* [ME *discours*, fr. ML & LL *discursus*; ML, argument, fr. LL, conversation, fr. L, act of running about, fr. *discurrere* to run about, fr. *currere* to run] 1 : CONVERSATION 2 : formal and usu. extended expression of thought on a subject

²**dis·course** \dis-'kōrs\ *vb* **dis·coursed**; **dis·cours·ing** 1 : to express oneself in esp. oral discourse 2 : TALK, CONVERSE

dis·cour·te·ous \dis-'kərt-ē-əs\ *adj* : lacking courtesy : UNCIVIL, RUDE — **dis·cour·te·ous·ly** *adv*

dis·cour·te·sy \-'kərt-ə-sē\ *n* : RUDENESS; *also* : a rude act

dis·cov·er \dis-'kəv-ər\ *vb* 1 : to make known or visible 2 : to obtain sight or knowledge of for the first time : FIND — **dis·cov·er·er** *n*

dis·cov·ery \dis-'kəv-(e-)rē\ *n, pl* **-er·ies** 1 : the act or process of discovering 2 : something discovered 3 : the disclosure usu. before a civil trial of pertinent facts or documents

¹**dis·cred·it** \dis-'kred-ət\ *vb* 1 : DISBELIEVE 2 : to cause disbelief in the accuracy or authority of 3 : DISGRACE — **dis·cred·it·able** *adj*

²**discredit** *n* 1 : loss of reputation 2 : lack or loss of belief or confidence

dis·creet \dis-'krēt\ *adj* : showing good judgment; *esp* : capable of observing prudent silence — **dis·creet·ly** *adv*

dis·crep·an·cy \dis-'krep-ən-sē\ *n, pl* **-cies** 1 : DIFFERENCE, DISAGREEMENT 2 : an instance of being discrepant

dis·crep·ant \-ənt\ *adj* [L *discrepans*, prp. of *discrepare* to sound discordantly, fr. *crepare* to rattle, creak] : being at variance : DISAGREEING

dis·crete \dis-'krēt, 'dis-ˌkrēt\ *adj* 1 : individually distinct 2 : NONCONTINUOUS

dis·cre·tion \dis-'kresh-ən\ *n* 1 : the quality of being discreet : PRUDENCE 2 : individual choice or judgment 3 : power of free decision or latitude of choice — **dis·cre·tion·ary** *adj*

dis·crim·i·nate \dis-'krim-ə-ˌnāt\ *vb* **-nat·ed; -nat·ing** 1 : DISTINGUISH, DIFFERENTIATE 2 : to make a distinction in favor of or against one person or thing as compared with others — **dis·crim·i·na·tion** \-ˌkrim-ə-'nā-shən\ *n*

dis·crim·i·nat·ing \-ˌnāt-iŋ\ *adj* : marked by discrimination; *esp* : DISCERNING, JUDICIOUS

dis·crim·i·na·to·ry \dis-'krim-ə-nə-ˌtōr-ē\ *adj* : marked by esp. unjust discrimination ⟨~ treatment⟩

dis·cur·sive \dis-'kər-siv\ *adj* : passing from one topic to another : RAMBLING — **dis·cur·sive·ly** *adv* — **dis·cur·sive·ness** *n*

dis·cus \'dis-kəs\ *n, pl* **dis·cus·es** : a disk that is hurled for distance in a track-and-field contest

dis·cuss \dis-'kəs\ *vb* [ME *discussen*, fr. L *discutere*, fr. *dis-* apart + *quatere* to shake] 1 : to argue or consider carefully by presenting the various sides 2 : to talk about — **dis·cus·sion** \-'kəsh-ən\ *n*

dis·cus·sant \dis-'kəs-ᵊnt\ *n* : one who takes part in a formal discussion

¹**dis·dain** \dis-'dān\ *n* : CONTEMPT, SCORN — **dis·dain·ful** \-fəl\ *adj* — **dis·dain·ful·ly** \-ē\ *adv*

²**disdain** *vb* 1 : to look upon with scorn 2 : to reject or refrain from because of disdain

dis·ease \diz-'ēz\ *n* : an abnormal bodily condition that impairs functioning and can usu. be recognized by signs and symptoms : SICKNESS — **dis·eased** \-'ēzd\ *adj*

dis·em·bark \ˌdis-əm-'bärk\ *vb* : to go or put ashore from a ship — **dis·em·bar·ka·tion** \dis-ˌem-ˌbär-'kā-shən\ *n*

dis·em·body \ˌdis-əm-'bäd-ē\ *vb* : to deprive of bodily existence

dis·em·bow·el \-'bau(-ə)l\ *vb* : EVISCERATE 1 — **dis·em·bow·el·ment** *n*

dis·en·chant \ˌdis-ᵊn-'chant\ *vb* : DISILLUSION — **dis·en·chant·ment** *n*

dis·en·cum·ber \ˌdis-ᵊn-'kəm-bər\ *vb* : to free from something that burdens

dis·en·fran·chise \ˌdis-ᵊn-'fran-ˌchīz\ *vb* : DISFRANCHISE — **dis·en·fran·chise·ment** *n*

dis·en·gage \ˌdis-ᵊn-'gāj\ *vb* : RELEASE, EXTRICATE, DISENTANGLE — **dis·en·gage·ment** *n*

dis·en·tan·gle \ˌdis-ᵊn-'taŋ-gəl\ *vb* : to free from entanglement : UNRAVEL

dis·equi·lib·ri·um \ˌdis-ˌē-kwə-'lib-rē-əm\ *n* : loss or lack of equilibrium

dis·es·tab·lish \ˌdis-ə-'stab-lish\ *vb* : to end the establishment of; *esp* : to deprive of the status of an established church — **dis·es·tab·lish·ment** *n*

dis·es·teem \ˌdis-ə-'stēm\ *n* : lack of esteem : DISFAVOR, DISREPUTE

di·seuse \dē-'zə(r)z, -'züz\ *n, pl* **diseuses** \-'zə(r)z(-əz), -'züz(-əz)\ [F] : a skilled and usu. professional woman reciter

dis·fa·vor \dis-'fā-vər\ *n* 1 : DISAPPROVAL, DISLIKE 2 : the state or fact of being no longer favored

dis·fig·ure \dis-'fig-yər\ *vb* : to spoil the appearance of ⟨*disfigured* by a scar⟩ — **dis·fig·ure·ment** *n*

dis·fran·chise \dis-'fran-ˌchīz\ *vb* : to deprive of a franchise, a legal right, or a privilege; *esp* : to deprive of the right to vote — **dis·fran·chise·ment** *n*

dis·gorge \-'gōrj\ *vb* : VOMIT; *also* : to discharge forcefully or confusedly

¹**dis·grace** \dis-'grās\ *vb* : to bring reproach or shame to

²**disgrace** *n* 1 : SHAME, DISHONOR; *also* : a cause of shame 2 : the condition of being out of favor : loss of respect — **dis·grace·ful** \-fəl\ *adj* — **dis·grace·ful·ly** \-ē\ *adv*

dis·grun·tle \dis-'grənt-ᵊl\ *vb* **dis·grun-**

tled; **dis·grun·tling** : to put in bad humor

¹dis·guise \dis-ˈgīz\ vb **dis·guised; disguis·ing 1** : to change the appearance of to conceal the identity or to resemble another **2** : HIDE, CONCEAL

²disguise n **1** : clothing put on to conceal one's identity or counterfeit another's **2** : an outward appearance that hides what something really is

¹dis·gust \dis-ˈgəst\ n : AVERSION, REPUGNANCE

²disgust vb : to provoke to loathing, repugnance, or aversion : be offensive to — **dis·gust·ed·ly** adv — **dis·gust·ing·ly** \-ˈgəs-tiŋ-lē\ adv

¹dish \ˈdish\ n [ME, fr. OE disc plate, fr. L discus quoit, disk, dish, fr. Gk diskos, fr. dikein to throw] **1** : a vessel used for serving food **2** : the food served in a dish (a ~ of berries) **3** : food prepared in a particular way **4** : something resembling a dish esp. in being shallow and concave

²dish vb **1** : to put into a dish **2** : to make concave like a dish

dis·ha·bille \ˌdis-ə-ˈbēl\ n [F déshabillé] : the state of being dressed in a casual or careless manner

dis·har·mo·ny \dis-ˈhär-mə-nē\ n : lack of harmony — **dis·har·mo·ni·ous** \ˌdis-(ˌ)här-ˈmō-nē-əs\ adj

dish·cloth \ˈdish-ˌklȯth\ n : a cloth for washing dishes

dis·heart·en \dis-ˈhärt-ᵊn\ vb : DISCOURAGE, DEJECT

dished \ˈdisht\ adj : CONCAVE

di·shev·el \dish-ˈev-əl\ vb **-shev·eled** or **-shev·elled; -shev·el·ing** or **-shev·el·ling** [ME discheveled, fr. MF deschevelé, fr. descheveler to disarrange the hair, fr. chevel hair, fr. L capillus] : to let hang or fall loosely in disorder : DISARRAY — **di·shev·eled** or **di·shev·elled** adj

dis·hon·est \dis-ˈän-əst\ adj : not honest : UNTRUSTWORTHY, DECEITFUL — **dis·hon·est·ly** adv — **dis·hon·es·ty** \-ə-stē\ n

¹dis·hon·or \dis-ˈän-ər\ vb **1** : DISGRACE **2** : to refuse to accept or pay (a ~ check)

²dishonor n **1** : lack or loss of honor **2** : SHAME, DISGRACE **3** : something dishonorable : a cause of disgrace **4** : the act of dishonoring a negotiable instrument when presented for payment — **dis·hon·or·able** \-ˈän-(ə-)rə-bəl, -ˈän-ər-bəl\ adj — **dis·hon·or·ably** \-blē\ adv

dish out vb : to give freely

dish·rag \ˈdish-ˌrag\ n : DISHCLOTH

dish·wash·er \-ˌwȯsh-ər, -ˌwäsh-\ n : a person or machine that washes dishes

dish·wa·ter \-ˌwȯt-ər, -ˌwät-\ n : water in which dishes have been or are to be washed

dis·il·lu·sion \ˌdis-ə-ˈlü-zhən\ vb **-sioned; -sion·ing** \-ˈlüzh-(ə-)niŋ\ : to free from mistaken beliefs or foolish hopes — **dis·il·lu·sion·ment** n

dis·in·cli·na·tion \dis-ˌin-klə-ˈnā-shən\ n

: a feeling of unwillingness or aversion : DISTASTE

dis·in·cline \ˌdis-ᵊn-ˈklīn\ vb : to make or be unwilling

dis·in·fect \ˌdis-ᵊn-ˈfekt\ vb : to cleanse of infection-causing germs — **dis·in·fec·tant** \-ˈfek-tənt\ n — **dis·in·fec·tion** \-ˈfek-shən\ n

dis·in·gen·u·ous \ˌdis-ᵊn-ˈjen-yə-wəs\ adj : lacking in candor : not frank or naive

dis·in·her·it \ˌdis-ᵊn-ˈher-ət\ vb : to deprive of the right to inherit

dis·in·te·grate \dis-ˈint-ə-ˌgrāt\ vb **1** : to break or decompose into constituent parts or small particles **2** : to destroy the unity or integrity of — **dis·in·te·gra·tion** \ˌdis-ˌint-ə-ˈgrā-shən\ n

dis·in·ter \ˌdis-ᵊn-ˈtər\ vb **1** : to take from the grave or tomb **2** : UNEARTH

dis·in·ter·est·ed \dis-ˈin-t(ə-)rəs-təd, -tə-ˌres-\ adj **1** : not interested **2** : free from selfish motive or interest : UNBIASED — **dis·in·ter·est·ed·ness** n

dis·join \dis-ˈjȯin\ vb : SEPARATE

dis·joint \dis-ˈjȯint\ vb : to separate the parts of : DISCONNECT; also : to separate at the joints

dis·joint·ed \-əd\ adj **1** : DISCONNECTED; esp : INCOHERENT **2** : separated at or as if at the joint

disk or **disc** \ˈdisk\ n **1** : something round and flat; esp : a flat rounded anatomical structure (as the central part of the flower head of a composite plant or a pad of cartilage between vertebrae) **2** usu **disc** : a phonograph record **3** : a round flat plate coated with a magnetic substance on which data for a computer is stored

¹dis·like \dis-ˈlīk\ n : a feeling of distaste or disapproval

²dislike vb : to regard with dislike : DISAPPROVE

dis·lo·cate \ˈdis-lō-ˌkāt, dis-ˈlō-\ vb **1** : to put out of place; esp : to displace (a bone or joint) from normal connections (~ a shoulder) **2** : DISRUPT — **dis·lo·ca·tion** \ˌdis-(ˌ)lō-ˈkā-shən\ n

dis·lodge \dis-ˈläj\ vb : to force out of a place esp. of rest, hiding, or defense

dis·loy·al \dis-ˈlȯi(-ə)l\ adj : lacking in loyalty — **dis·loy·al·ty** n

dis·mal \ˈdiz-məl\ adj [ME, fr. dismal, n., days marked as unlucky in medieval calendars, fr. ML dies mali, lit., evil days] **1** : showing or causing gloom or depression **2** : lacking interest or merit — **dis·mal·ly** \-ē\ adv

dis·man·tle \dis-ˈmant-ᵊl\ vb **-tled; -tling** \-ˈmant-(ə-)liŋ\ **1** : to take apart **2** : to strip of furniture and equipment — **dis·man·tle·ment** n

dis·may \dis-ˈmā\ vb : to cause to lose courage or resolution from alarm or fear : DAUNT — **dismay** n — **dis·may·ing·ly** \-iŋ-lē\ adv

dis·mem·ber \dis-ˈmem-bər\ vb **-bered; -ber·ing** \-b(ə-)riŋ\ **1** : to cut off or separate the limbs or parts of **2** : to break up or tear into pieces — **dis·mem·ber·ment** n

dis·miss \dis-'mis\ *vb* **1** : to send away **2** : to send or remove from office, service, or employment **3** : to put aside or out of mind **4** : to refuse further judicial hearing or consideration to ⟨the judge ∼ed the charge⟩ — **dis·miss·al** *n*

dis·mount \dis-'maůnt\ *vb* **1** : to get down from something (as a horse or bicycle) **2** : UNHORSE **3** : DISASSEMBLE

dis·obe·di·ence \ˌdis-ə-'bēd-ē-əns\ *n* : neglect or refusal to obey — **dis·obe·di·ent** \-ənt\ *adj*

dis·obey \ˌdis-ə-'bā\ *vb* : to fail to obey : be disobedient

dis·oblige \ˌdis-ə-'blīj\ *vb* **1** : to go counter to the wishes of **2** : INCONVENIENCE

¹**dis·or·der** \dis-'ȯrd-ər\ *vb* **1** : to disturb the order of **2** : to cause disorder in ⟨a ∼ed digestion⟩

²**disorder** *n* **1** : lack of order : CONFUSION **2** : breach of the peace or public order : TUMULT **3** : an abnormal state of body or mind : AILMENT

dis·or·der·ly \-lē\ *adj* **1** : offensive to public order or decency; *also* : guilty of disorderly conduct **2** : marked by disorder : DISARRANGED ⟨a ∼ desk⟩ — **dis·or·der·li·ness** *n*

dis·or·ga·nize \dis-'ȯr-gə-ˌnīz\ *vb* : to break up the regular system of : throw into disorder — **dis·or·ga·ni·za·tion** \dis-ˌȯrg-(ə-)nə-'zā-shən\ *n*

dis·ori·ent \dis-'ȯr-ē-ˌent\ *vb* : to cause to be confused or lost — **dis·ori·en·ta·tion** \dis-ˌȯr-ē-ən-'tā-shən\ *n*

dis·own \-'ōn\ *vb* : REPUDIATE, RENOUNCE, DISCLAIM

dis·par·age \dis-'par-ij\ *vb* **-aged; -ag·ing** [ME *disparagen* to degrade by marriage below one's class, disparage, fr. MF *desparagier* to marry below one's class, fr. OF, fr. *parage* extraction, lineage, fr. *per* peer] **1** : to lower in rank or reputation : DEGRADE **2** : BELITTLE — **dis·par·age·ment** *n* — **dis·par·ag·ing·ly** \-ij-iŋ-lē\ *adv*

dis·pa·rate \dis-p(ə-)rət, dis-'par-ət\ *adj* : distinct in quality or character — **dis·par·i·ty** \dis-'par-ət-ē\ *n*

dis·pas·sion·ate \dis-'pash-(ə-)nət\ *adj* : not influenced by strong feeling : CALM, IMPARTIAL — **dis·pas·sion** \-ən\ *n* — **dis·pas·sion·ate·ly** *adv*

¹**dis·patch** \dis-'pach\ *vb* **1** : to send off or away with promptness or speed esp. on official business **2** : to put to death **3** : to attend to rapidly or efficiently — **dis·patch·er** *n*

²**dispatch** *n* **1** : the act of dispatching; *esp* : SHIPMENT **2** : the act of putting to death **3** : MESSAGE **4** : a news item sent in by a correspondent to a newspaper **5** : promptness and efficiency in performing a task

dis·pel \dis-'pel\ *vb* **dis·pelled; dis·pel·ling** : to drive away by scattering : DISSIPATE

dis·pens·able \dis-'pen-sə-bəl\ *adj* : capable of being dispensed with

dis·pen·sa·ry \dis-'pens-(ə-)rē\ *n. pl* **-ries** : a place where medicine or medical or dental aid is dispensed

dis·pen·sa·tion \ˌdis-pən-'sā-shən\ *n* **1** : a system of rules for ordering affairs **2** : a particular arrangement or provision esp. of nature **3** : an exemption from a rule or from a vow or oath **4** : the act of dispensing **5** : something dispensed or distributed

dis·pense \dis-'pens\ *vb* **dis·pensed; dis·pens·ing 1** : to portion out **2** : ADMINISTER ⟨∼ justice⟩ **3** : EXEMPT **4** : to make up and give out ⟨remedies⟩ — **dis·pens·er** *n* — **dispense with 1** : SUSPEND **2** : to do without

dis·perse \dis-'pərs\ *vb* **dis·persed; dis·pers·ing** : to break up and scatter about : SPREAD — **dis·per·sal** \-'pər-səl\ *n* — **dis·per·sion** \-'pər-zhən\ *n*

dis·pir·it \dis-'pir-ət\ *vb* : DEPRESS, DISCOURAGE, DISHEARTEN

dis·place \dis-'plās\ *vb* **1** : to remove from the usual or proper place; *esp* : to expel or force to flee from home or native land ⟨displaced persons⟩ **2** : to move out of position ⟨water *displaced* by a floating object⟩ **3** : to take the place of : REPLACE

dis·place·ment \dis-'plās-mənt\ *n* **1** : the act of displacing : the state of being displaced **2** : the volume or weight of a fluid displaced by a floating body (as a ship) **3** : the difference between the initial position of an object and a later position

¹**dis·play** \dis-'plā\ *vb* : to present to view

²**display** *n* **1** : a displaying of something **2** : an electronic device (as a cathode-ray tube) that gives information in visual form; *also* : the visual information

dis·please \dis-'plēz\ *vb* **1** : to arouse the disapproval and dislike of **2** : to be offensive to : give displeasure

dis·plea·sure \dis-'plezh-ər\ *n* : a feeling of dislike and irritation

dis·port \dis-'pōrt\ *vb* **1** : DIVERT, AMUSE **2** : FROLIC **3** : DISPLAY

dis·pos·able \dis-'pō-zə-bəl\ *adj* **1** : remaining after deduction of taxes ⟨∼ income⟩ **2** : designed to be used once and then thrown away ⟨∼ diapers⟩ — **disposable** *n*

dis·pos·al \dis-'pō-zəl\ *n* **1** : CONTROL, COMMAND **2** : an orderly arrangement **3** : a getting rid of **4** : MANAGEMENT, ADMINISTRATION **5** : the transfer of something into new hands

dis·pose \dis-'pōz\ *vb* **dis·posed; dis·pos·ing 1** : to give a tendency to : INCLINE ⟨*disposed* to accept⟩ **2** : to put in place : ARRANGE ⟨troops *disposed* for withdrawal⟩ **3** : SETTLE — **dis·pos·er** *n* — **dispose of 1** : to transfer to the control of another **2** : to get rid of **3** : to deal with conclusively

dis·po·si·tion \ˌdis-pə-'zish-ən\ *n* **1** : the act or power of disposing : DISPOSAL ⟨funds at their ∼⟩ **2** : RELINQUISHMENT

3 : ARRANGEMENT 4 : TENDENCY, INCLINATION 5 : natural attitude toward things ⟨a cheerful ~⟩

dis·pos·sess \ˌdis-pə-ˈzes\ *vb* : to put out of possession or occupancy — **dis·pos·ses·sion** \-ˈzesh-ən\ *n*

dis·praise \dis-ˈprāz\ *vb* : DISPARAGE — **dispraise** *n*

dis·pro·por·tion \ˌdis-prə-ˈpōr-shən\ *n* : lack of proportion, symmetry, or proper relation — **dis·pro·por·tion·ate** \-shə-)nət\ *adj*

dis·prove \dis-ˈprüv\ *vb* : to prove to be false — **dis·proof** \-ˈprüf\ *n*

dis·pu·tant \dis-ˈpyüt-ᵊnt, ˈdis-pyət-ənt\ *n* : one that is engaged in a dispute

dis·pu·ta·tion \ˌdis-pyə-ˈtā-shən\ *n* 1 : DEBATE 2 : an oral defense of an academic thesis

dis·pu·ta·tious \-shəs\ *adj* : inclined to dispute : ARGUMENTATIVE

¹**dis·pute** \dis-ˈpyüt\ *vb* **dis·put·ed; dis·put·ing** 1 : ARGUE, DEBATE 2 : WRANGLE 3 : to deny the truth or rightness of 4 : to struggle against or over : CONTEST — **dis·put·able** \dis-ˈpyüt-ə-bəl, ˈdis-pyət-ə-bəl\ *adj* — **dis·put·er** \dis-ˈpyüt-ər\ *n*

²**dispute** *n* 1 : DEBATE 2 : QUARREL

dis·qual·i·fy \dis-ˈkwäl-ə-ˌfī\ *vb* : to make or declare unfit or not qualified — **dis·qual·i·fi·ca·tion** \-ˌkwäl-ə-fə-ˈkā-shən\ *n*

¹**dis·qui·et** \dis-ˈkwī-ət\ *vb* : to make uneasy or restless : DISTURB

²**disquiet** *n* : lack of peace or tranquillity : ANXIETY

dis·qui·etude \dis-ˈkwī-ə-ˌt(y)üd\ *n* : AGITATION, ANXIETY

dis·qui·si·tion \ˌdis-kwə-ˈzish-ən\ *n* : a formal inquiry or discussion

¹**dis·re·gard** \ˌdis-ri-ˈgärd\ *vb* : to pay no attention to : treat as unworthy of notice or regard

²**disregard** *n* : the act of disregarding : the state of being disregarded : NEGLECT — **dis·re·gard·ful** *adj*

dis·re·pair \ˌdis-ri-ˈpaər\ *n* : the state of being in need of repair

dis·rep·u·ta·ble \dis-ˈrep-yət-ə-bəl\ *adj* : not reputable : DISCREDITABLE; *esp* : having a bad reputation

dis·re·pute \ˌdis-ri-ˈpyüt\ *n* : loss or lack of reputation : low esteem

dis·re·spect \ˌdis-ri-ˈspekt\ *n* : DISCOURTESY — **dis·re·spect·ful** *adj*

dis·robe \dis-ˈrōb\ *vb* : UNDRESS

dis·rupt \dis-ˈrəpt\ *vb* 1 : to break apart 2 : to throw into disorder — **dis·rup·tion** \-ˈrəp-shən\ *n* — **dis·rup·tive** \-ˈrəp-tiv\ *adj*

dis·sat·is·fac·tion \ˌdis-ˌat-əs-ˈfak-shən\ *n* : DISCONTENT

dis·sat·is·fy \dis-ˈat-əs-ˌfī\ *vb* : to fail to satisfy : DISPLEASE — **dis·sat·is·fied** *adj*

dis·sect \dis-ˈekt\ *vb* 1 : to divide into parts esp. for examination and study 2 : ANALYZE — **dis·sec·tion** \-ˈek-shən\ *n*

dis·sect·ed *adj* : cut deeply into narrow lobes ⟨a ~ leaf⟩

dis·sem·ble \dis-ˈem-bəl\ *vb* **-bled; -bling** \-b(ə-)liŋ\ 1 : to hide under or put on a false appearance : conceal facts, intentions, or feelings under some pretense 2 : SIMULATE — **dis·sem·bler** \-b(ə-)lər\ *n*

dis·sem·i·nate \dis-ˈem-ə-ˌnāt\ *vb* **-nat·ed; -nat·ing** : to spread abroad as if sowing seed ⟨~ ideas⟩ — **dis·sem·i·na·tion** \-ˌem-ə-ˈnā-shən\ *n*

dis·sen·sion \dis-ˈen-chən\ *n* : disagreement in opinion : DISCORD

¹**dis·sent** \dis-ˈent\ *vb* 1 : to withhold assent 2 : to differ in opinion

²**dissent** *n* 1 : difference of opinion; *esp* : religious nonconformity 2 : a written statement in which a justice disagrees with the opinion of the majority — **dis·sen·tient** \-ˈen-chənt\ *adj or n*

dis·sent·er \dis-ˈent-ər\ *n* 1 : one that dissents 2 *cap* : an English Nonconformist

dis·ser·ta·tion \ˌdis-ər-ˈtā-shən\ *n* : an extended usu. written treatment of a subject; *esp* : one submitted for a doctorate

dis·ser·vice \dis-ˈər-vəs\ *n* : INJURY, HARM, MISCHIEF

dis·sev·er \dis-ˈev-ər\ *vb* : SEPARATE, DISUNITE

dis·si·dent \ˈdis-əd-ənt\ *adj* [L *dissidens,* prp. of *dissidēre* to sit apart, disagree, fr. *dis-* apart + *sedēre* to sit] : disagreeing with an opinion or a group — **dis·si·dence** \-əns\ *n* — **dissident** *n*

dis·sim·i·lar \dis-ˈim-ə-lər\ *adj* : UNLIKE — **dis·sim·i·lar·i·ty** \dis-ˌim-ə-ˈlar-ət-ē\ *n*

dis·sim·u·late \dis-ˈim-yə-ˌlāt\ *vb* : to hide under a false appearance : DISSEMBLE — **dis·sim·u·la·tion** \dis-ˌim-yə-ˈlā-shən\ *n*

dis·si·pate \ˈdis-ə-ˌpāt\ *vb* **-pat·ed; -pat·ing** 1 : to break up and drive off : DISPERSE, SCATTER ⟨~ a crowd⟩ 2 : DISPEL, DISSOLVE ⟨the breeze *dissipated* the fog⟩ 3 : SQUANDER 4 : to break up and vanish 5 : to be dissolute; *esp* : to drink alcoholic beverages to excess — **dis·si·pat·ed** *adj* — **dis·si·pa·tion** \ˌdis-ə-ˈpā-shən\ *n*

dis·so·ci·ate \dis-ˈō-s(h)ē-ˌāt\ *vb* **-at·ed; -at·ing** : DISCONNECT, DISUNITE — **dis·so·ci·a·tion** \-ˌō-s(h)ē-ˈā-shən\ *n*

dis·so·lute \ˈdis-ə-ˌlüt\ *adj* : loose in morals or conduct — **dis·so·lute·ly** *adv* — **dis·so·lute·ness** *n*

dis·so·lu·tion \ˌdis-ə-ˈlü-shən\ *n* 1 : the action or process of dissolving 2 : separation of a thing into its parts 3 : DECAY; *also* : DEATH 4 : the termination or breaking up of an assembly or a partnership

dis·solve \diz-ˈälv\ *vb* 1 : to separate into component parts 2 : to pass or cause to pass into solution ⟨sugar ~s in water⟩ 3 : TERMINATE, DISPERSE ⟨~ parliament⟩ 4 : to waste or fade away ⟨his courage *dissolved*⟩ 5 : to be overcome emotionally ⟨∼ in tears⟩ **6** : to resolve itself as if by dissolution

dis·so·nance \'dis-ə-nəns\ n : DISCORD — **dis·so·nant** \-nənt\ adj

dis·suade \dis-'wād\ vb **dis·suad·ed; dis·suad·ing** : to advise against a course of action : persuade or try to persuade not to do something — **dis·sua·sion** \-'wā-zhən\ n — **dis·sua·sive** \-'wā-siv\ adj

dist abbr **1** distance **2** district

¹**dis·taff** \'dis-ˌtaf\ n, pl **dis·taffs** \-ˌtafs, -ˌtavz\ **1** : a staff for holding the flax, tow, or wool in spinning **2** : a woman's work or domain **3** : the female branch or side of a family

²**distaff** adj : MATERNAL, FEMALE

dis·tal \'dis-t°l\ adj **1** : away from the point of attachment or origin **2** : of, relating to, or being the surface of a tooth that faces the back of the mouth — **dis·tal·ly** \-ē\ adv

¹**dis·tance** \'dis-təns\ n **1** : measure of separation in space or time **2** : EX-PANSE **3** : the full length (go the ∼) **4** : spatial remoteness **5** : COLDNESS, RE-SERVE **6** : DIFFERENCE, DISPARITY **7** : a distant point

²**distance** vb **dis·tanced; dis·tanc·ing** : to leave far behind : OUTSTRIP

dis·tant \'dis-tənt\ adj **1** : separate in space : AWAY **2** : FAR-OFF **3** : far apart **4** : not close in relationship ⟨a ∼ cousin⟩ **5** : different in kind **6** : RESERVED, ALOOF, COLD ⟨∼ politeness⟩ **7** : coming from or going to a distance — **dis·tant·ly** adv — **dis·tant·ness** n

dis·taste \dis-'tāst\ n : DISINCLINATION, DISLIKE — **dis·taste·ful** adj

dis·tem·per \dis-'tem-pər\ n : a bodily disorder usu. of a domestic animal; esp : a contagious often fatal virus disease of dogs

dis·tend \dis-'tend\ vb : EXPAND, SWELL — **dis·ten·si·ble** \-'ten-sə-bəl\ adj — **dis·ten·sion** or **dis·ten·tion** \-chən\ n

dis·tich \'dis-(ˌ)tik\ n : a strophic unit of two lines

dis·till also **dis·til** \dis-'til\ vb **dis·tilled; dis·till·ing** **1** : to fall or let fall drop by drop **2** : to obtain or purify by distillation — **dis·till·er** n — **dis·till·ery** \-(ə-)rē\ n

dis·til·late \'dis-tə-ˌlāt, -lət\ n : a liquid product condensed from vapor during distillation

dis·til·la·tion \ˌdis-tə-'lā-shən\ n : the driving off of gas or vapor from liquids or solids by heat and then condensing to a liquid product

dis·tinct \dis-'tiŋkt\ adj **1** : SEPARATE, INDIVIDUAL **2** : presenting a clear unmistakable impression — **dis·tinct·ly** adv — **dis·tinct·ness** n

dis·tinc·tion \dis-'tiŋk-shən\ n **1** : the act of distinguishing a difference **2** : DIFFERENCE **3** : a distinguishing quality or mark **4** : special honor or recognition

dis·tinc·tive \dis-'tiŋk-tiv\ adj **1** : clearly marking a person or a thing as dif-

ferent from others **2** : having or giving style or distinction — **dis·tinc·tive·ly** adv — **dis·tinc·tive·ness** n

dis·tin·guish \dis-'tiŋ-gwish\ vb [MF distinguer, fr. L distinguere, lit., to separate by pricking] **1** : to recognize by some mark or characteristic **2** : to hear or see clearly : DISCERN **3** : to make distinctions ⟨∼ between right and wrong⟩ **4** : to set apart : mark as different — **dis·tin·guish·able** adj

dis·tin·guished \-gwisht\ adj **1** : marked by eminence or excellence **2** : befitting an eminent person

dis·tort \dis-'tȯrt\ vb **1** : to twist out of the true meaning **2** : to twist out of a natural, normal, or original shape or condition — **dis·tor·tion** \-'tȯr-shən\ n

distr abbr distribute; distribution

dis·tract \dis-'trakt\ vb **1** : to draw (the attention or mind) to a different object : DIVERT **2** : to stir up or confuse with conflicting emotions or motives : HA-RASS — **dis·trac·tion** \-'trak-shən\ n

dis·trait \di-'strā\ adj [F, fr. L distractus] : ABSENTMINDED, DISTRAUGHT

dis·traught \dis-'trȯt\ adj : PERPLEXED, CONFUSED; also : CRAZED

¹**dis·tress** \dis-'tres\ n **1** : suffering of body or mind : PAIN, ANGUISH **2** : TROUBLE, MISFORTUNE **3** : a condition of danger or desperate need — **dis·tress·ful** adj

²**distress** vb **1** : to subject to great strain or difficulties **2** : UPSET

dis·trib·ute \dis-'trib-yət\ vb **-ut·ed; -ut·ing** **1** : to divide among several or many : APPORTION **2** : to spread out : SCATTER; also : DELIVER **3** : CLASSIFY — **dis·tri·bu·tion** \ˌdis-trə-'byü-shən\ n

dis·trib·u·tive \dis-'trib-yət-iv\ adj **1** : of or relating to distribution **2** : being or concerned with a mathematical operation (as multiplication in $a(b + c) = ab + ac$) that produces the same result when operating on a whole mathematical expression as when operating on each part and collecting the results — **dis·trib·u·tive·ly** adv

dis·trib·u·tor \dis-'trib-yət-ər\ n **1** : one that distributes **2** : an agent or agency for marketing goods **3** : a device for directing current to the spark plugs of an engine

dis·trict \'dis-(ˌ)trikt\ n **1** : a fixed territorial division (as for administrative or electoral purposes) **2** : an area, region, or section with a distinguishing character

district attorney n : the prosecuting attorney of a judicial district

¹**dis·trust** \dis-'trəst\ vb : to feel no confidence in : SUSPECT

²**distrust** n : a lack of trust or confidence : SUSPICION, WARINESS — **dis·trust·ful** \-fəl\ adj — **dis·trust·ful·ly** \-ē\ adv

dis·turb \dis-'tərb\ vb **1** : to interfere with : INTERRUPT **2** : to alter the position or arrangement of **3** : to destroy the tranquillity or composure of

: make uneasy **4** : to throw into disorder **5** : INCONVENIENCE — **dis·tur·bance** \-'tər-bəns\ *n*

dis·turbed \-'tərbd\ *adj* : showing symptoms of mental or emotional illness

dis·unite \,dis-yü-'nīt\ *vb* : DIVIDE, SEPARATE

dis·uni·ty \dis-'yü-nət-ē\ *n* : lack of unity; *esp* : DISSENSION

dis·use \-'yüs\ *n* : a cessation of use or practice

¹**ditch** \'dich\ *n* : a long narrow channel or trench dug in the earth

²**ditch** *vb* **1** : to enclose with a ditch; *also* : to dig a ditch in **2** : to get rid of : DISCARD **3** : to make a forced landing of an airplane on water

dith·er \'dith-ər\ *n* : a highly nervous, excited, or agitated state

dit·to \'dit-ō\ *n, pl* **dittos** [It dial., pp. of It *dire* to say, fr. L *dicere*] **1** : the same or more of the same : ANOTHER — used to avoid repeating a word ⟨lost: one book (new); ∼ (old)⟩ **2** : a mark composed of a pair of inverted commas or apostrophes used as a symbol for the word *ditto*

dit·ty \'dit-ē\ *n, pl* **ditties** : a short simple song

di·uret·ic \,dī-(y)ə-'ret-ik\ *adj* : tending to increase urine flow — **diuretic** *n*

di·ur·nal \dī-'ərn-ᵊl\ *adj* **1** : DAILY **2** : of, relating to, or occurring in the daytime

div *abbr* **1** divided **2** dividend **3** division **4** divorced

di·va \'dē-və\ *n, pl* **divas** *or* **di·ve** \-,vā\ [It, lit., goddess, fr. L, fem. of *divus* divine, god] : PRIMA DONNA

di·va·gate \'dī-və-,gāt\ *vb* **-gat·ed; -gat·ing** : to wander about or stray from a course or subject : DIVERGE — **di·va·ga·tion** \,dī-və-'gā-shən\ *n*

di·van \'dī-,van, di-'van\ *n* : COUCH, SOFA

¹**dive** \'dīv\ *vb* **dived** \'dīvd\ *or* **dove** \'dōv\; **dived; div·ing 1** : to plunge into water headfirst **2** : SUBMERGE **3** : to descend or fall precipitously **4** : to descend in an airplane at a steep angle **5** : to plunge into some matter or activity **6** : DART, LUNGE — **div·er** *n*

²**dive** *n* **1** : the act or an instance of diving **2** : a sharp decline **3** : a disreputable bar or place of amusement

di·verge \də-'vərj, dī-\ *vb* **di·verged; di·verg·ing 1** : to move or extend in different directions from a common point : draw apart **2** : to differ in character, form, or opinion **3** : DEVIATE **4** : DEFLECT — **di·ver·gence** \-'vər-jəns\ *n* — **di·ver·gent** \-jənt\ *adj*

di·vers \'dī-vərz\ *adj* : VARIOUS

di·verse \dī-'vərs, də-, 'dī-,vərs\ *adj* **1** : UNLIKE **2** : composed of distinct forms or qualities ⟨the ∼ nature of man⟩ — **di·verse·ly** *adv*

di·ver·si·fy \də-'vər-sə-,fī, dī-\ *vb* **-fied; -fy·ing** : to make different or various

in form or quality — **di·ver·si·fi·ca·tion** \-,vər-sə-fə-'kā-shən\ *n*

di·ver·sion \də-'vər-zhən, dī-\ *n* **1** : a turning aside from a course, activity, or use : DEVIATION **2** : something that diverts or amuses : PASTIME

di·ver·si·ty \-'vər-sət-ē, dī-\ *n, pl* **-ties 1** : the condition of being different : VARIETY **2** : an instance or a point of difference

di·vert \də-'vərt, dī-\ *vb* **1** : to turn from a course or purpose : DEFLECT **2** : DISTRACT **3** : ENTERTAIN, AMUSE

di·vest \dī-'vest, də-\ *vb* **1** : to strip esp. of clothing, ornament, or equipment **2** : to deprive or dispossess esp. of property, authority, or rights

¹**di·vide** \də-'vīd\ *vb* **di·vid·ed; di·vid·ing 1** : SEPARATE; *also* : CLASSIFY **2** : CLEAVE, PART **3** : DISTRIBUTE, APPORTION **4** : to possess or make use of in common : share in **5** : to cause to be separate, distinct, or apart from one another **6** : to separate into opposing sides or parties **7** : to mark divisions on **8** : to subject to or use in mathematical division **9** : to branch out

²**divide** *n* : WATERSHED

div·i·dend \'div-ə-,dend\ *n* **1** : an individual share of something distributed **2** : BONUS **3** : a number to be divided by another **4** : a sum or fund to be divided or distributed

di·vid·er \də-'vīd-ər\ *n* **1** : one that divides (as a partition) ⟨room ∼⟩ **2** *pl* : COMPASS **5**

div·i·na·tion \,div-ə-'nā-shən\ *n* **1** : the art or practice of using omens or magic powers to foretell the future **2** : unusual insight or intuitive perception

¹**di·vine** \də-'vīn\ *adj* **di·vin·er; -est 1** : of, relating to, or being God or a god **2** : supremely good : SUPERB; *also* : HEAVENLY — **di·vine·ly** *adv*

²**divine** *n* **1** : CLERGYMAN **2** : THEOLOGIAN

³**divine** *vb* **di·vined; di·vin·ing 1** : INFER, CONJECTURE **2** : PROPHESY **3** : DOWSE — **di·vin·er** *n*

di·vin·ing rod \də-'vī-nin-\ *n* : a forked rod believed to reveal the presence of water or minerals by dipping downward when held over a vein

di·vin·i·ty \də-'vin-ət-ē\ *n, pl* **-ties 1** : THEOLOGY **2** : the quality or state of being divine **3** : a divine being; : GOD

di·vis·i·ble \də-'viz-ə-bəl\ *adj* : capable of being divided — **di·vis·i·bil·i·ty** \-,bil-ət-ē\ *n*

di·vi·sion \də-'vizh-ən\ *n* **1** : DISTRIBUTION, SEPARATION **2** : one of the parts or groupings into which a whole is divided **3** : DISAGREEMENT, DISUNITY **4** : something that divides or separates **5** : the mathematical operation of finding how many times one number or quantity is contained in another **6** : a large self-contained military unit **7** : an administrative or operating unit of a governmental, business, or educational organization — **di·vi·sion·al** \-'vizh-(ə-)nəl\ *adj*

di·vi·sive \də-'vī-siv, -'viz-iv\ *adj* : creating disunity or dissension — **di·vi·sive·ly** *adv* — **di·vi·sive·ness** *n*

di·vi·sor \də-'vī-zər\ *n* : the number by which a dividend is divided

di·vorce \də-'vörs\ *n* **1** : a complete legal breaking up of a marriage **2** : SEPARATION, SEVERANCE — **divorce** *vb* — **di·vorce·ment** *n*

di·vor·cé \də-ˌvör-'sā\ *n* [F] : a divorced man

di·vor·cée \də-ˌvör-'sā, -'sē\ *n* : a divorced woman

div·ot \'div-ət\ *n* : a piece of turf dug from a golf fairway in making a stroke

di·vulge \də-'vəlj, dī-\ *vb* **di·vulged; di·vulg·ing** : REVEAL, DISCLOSE

Dix·ie·land \'dik-sē-ˌland\ *n* : lively jazz music in a style developed in New Orleans

diz·zy \'diz-ē\ *adj* **diz·zi·er; -est** [ME *disy*, fr. OE *dysig* stupid] **1** : having a sensation of whirling : GIDDY **2** : causing or caused by giddiness — **diz·zi·ly** \'diz-ə-lē\ *adv* — **diz·zi·ness** \-ē-nəs\ *n*

DJ *abbr* disc jockey

dk *abbr* **1** dark **2** deck **3** dock

dl *abbr* deciliter

DLitt *or* **DLit** *abbr* [L *doctor litterarum*] doctor of letters; doctor of literature

DLO *abbr* dead letter office

dm *abbr* decimeter

DMD *abbr* [NL *dentariae medicinae doctor*] doctor of dental medicine

DMZ *abbr* demilitarized zone

dn *abbr* down

DNA \ˌdē-ˌen-'ā\ *n* : any of various nucleic acids usu. of cell nuclei that are the molecular basis of heredity in many organisms

¹do \'dü\ *vb* **did** \'did\ ; **done** \'dən\ ; **do·ing** \'dü-iŋ\ ; **does** \(')dəz\ **1** : to bring to pass : ACCOMPLISH **2** : ACT, BEHAVE ⟨~ as I say⟩ **3** : to be active or busy ⟨up and ~ing⟩ **4** : HAPPEN ⟨what's ~ing?⟩ **5** : to work at ⟨he does tailoring⟩ **6** : PREPARE ⟨did his homework⟩ **7** : to put in order (as by cleaning or arranging) ⟨~ the dishes⟩ **8** : DECORATE ⟨did the hall in blue⟩ **9** : GET ALONG ⟨he does well⟩ **10** : CARRY ON, MANAGE **11** : to feel or function better ⟨could ~ with some food⟩ **12** : RENDER ⟨sleep will ~ you good⟩ **13** : FINISH ⟨when he had done⟩ **14** : EXERT ⟨did my best⟩ **15** : PRODUCE ⟨did a poem⟩ **16** : to play the part of **17** : CHEAT ⟨did him out of his share⟩ **18** : TRAVERSE, TOUR **19** : TRAVEL **20** : to serve out in prison **21** : to serve the needs or purpose of : SUIT **22** : to be fitting or proper **23** — used as an auxiliary verb (1) before the subject in an interrogative sentence ⟨*does* he work?⟩ and after some adverbs ⟨*did* he say so⟩ , (2) in a negative statement ⟨I *don't* know⟩ , (3) for emphasis ⟨he *does* know⟩ , and (4) as a substi-

tute for a preceding predicate ⟨he works harder than I ~⟩ — **do away with 1** : to put an end to **2** : DESTROY, KILL — **do by** : to act toward in a specified way : TREAT ⟨*did* right *by* her⟩ — **do for** : to bring about the death or ruin of — **do one's thing** : to do what is personally satisfying

²do *abbr* ditto

DOA *abbr* dead on arrival

DOB *abbr* date of birth

dob·bin \'däb-ən\ *n* [*Dobbin*, nickname for *Robert*] **1** : a farm horse **2** : a quiet plodding horse

Do·ber·man pin·scher \ˌdō-bər-mən-'pin-chər\ *n* : a short-haired medium-sized dog of a breed of German origin

do·bra \'dō-brə\ *n* — see MONEY table

dob·son·fly \'däb-sən-ˌflī\ *n* : a large-eyed winged insect with long slender mandibles in the male and a large carnivorous aquatic larva

¹doc \'däk\ *n* : DOCTOR

²doc *abbr* document

do·cent \'dōs-ᵊnt, dō(t)-'sent\ *n* [obs. G (now *dozent*), deriv. of L *docēre* to teach] : TEACHER, LECTURER

doc·ile \'däs-əl\ *adj* [L *docilis*, fr. *docēre* to teach] : easily taught, led, or managed : TRACTABLE — **do·cil·i·ty** \dä-'sil-ət-ē\ *n*

¹dock \'däk\ *n* : any of a genus of coarse weedy herbs related to buckwheat

²dock *vb* **1** : to cut off the end of : cut short **2** : to take away a part of : deduct from ⟨~ a man's wages⟩

³dock *n* **1** : an artificial basin to receive ships **2** : a slip between two piers to receive ships **3** : a wharf or platform for loading or unloading materials

⁴dock *vb* **1** : to bring or come into dock **2** : to join (as two spacecraft) mechanically in space

⁵dock *n* : the place in a court where a prisoner stands or sits during trial

dock·age \'däk-ij\ *n* : the provision or use of a dock; *also* : the charge for using a dock

dock·et \'däk-ət\ *n* **1** : a formal abridged record of the proceedings in a legal action; *also* : a register of such records **2** : a list of legal causes to be tried **3** : a calendar of matters to be acted on : AGENDA **4** : a label attached to a document containing identification or directions — **docket** *vb*

dock·hand \'däk-ˌhand\ *n* : LONGSHOREMAN

dock·work·er \-ˌwər-kər\ *n* : LONGSHOREMAN

dock·yard \-ˌyärd\ *n* : SHIPYARD

¹doc·tor \'däk-tər\ *n* [ME *doctour* teacher, doctor, fr. MF & ML; MF, fr. ML *doctor*, fr. L, teacher, fr. *docēre* to teach] **1** : a person holding one of the highest academic degrees (as a PhD) conferred by a university **2** : one skilled in healing arts : *esp* : an academically and legally qualified physician, surgeon, dentist, or veterinarian **3** : a person who restores or repairs things — **doc·tor·al** \-t(ə-)rəl\ *adj*

²**doctor** *vb* **doc·tored; doc·tor·ing** \-t(ə-)riŋ\ **1** : to give medical treatment to **2** : to practice medicine **3** : REPAIR **4** : to adapt or modify for a desired end **5** : to alter deceptively

doc·tor·ate \'däk-t(ə-)rət\ *n* : the degree, title, or rank of a doctor

doc·tri·naire \ˌdäk-trə-'naər\ *n* [F] : one who attempts to put an abstract theory into effect without regard to practical difficulties — **doctrinaire** *adj*

doc·trine \'däk-trən\ *n* **1** : something that is taught **2** : DOGMA, TENET — **doc·tri·nal** \-trən-ᵊl\ *adj*

docu·dra·ma \'däk-yə-ˌdräm-ə, -ˌdram-ə\ *n* : a television or motion-picture drama that deals with historical events

doc·u·ment \'däk-yə-mənt\ *n* : a paper that furnishes information, proof, or support of something else — **doc·u·ment** \-ˌment\ *vb* — **doc·u·men·ta·tion** \ˌdäk-yə-mən-'tā-shən\ *n*

doc·u·men·ta·ry \ˌdäk-yə-'men-t(ə-)rē\ *adj* **1** : consisting of documents; *also* : being in writing (∼ proof) **2** : giving a factual presentation in artistic form (a ∼ movie) — **documentary** *n*

DOD *abbr* Department of Defense

¹**dod·der** \'däd-ər\ *n* : any of a genus of leafless elongated wiry parasitic herbs deficient in chlorophyll

²**dodder** *vb* **dod·dered; dod·der·ing** \'däd-(ə-)riŋ\ **1** : to tremble or shake usu. from age **2** : to progress feebly and unsteadily

¹**dodge** \'däj\ *vb* **dodged; dodg·ing 1** : to move suddenly aside; *also* : to avoid or evade by so doing **2** : to avoid by trickery or evasion

²**dodge** *n* **1** : an act of evading by sudden bodily movement **2** : an artful device to evade, deceive, or trick **3** : EXPEDIENT

do·do \'dōd-ō\ *n, pl* **dodoes** *or* **dodos** [Port *doudo*, fr. *doudo* silly, stupid] **1** : a heavy flightless extinct bird related to the pigeons but larger than a turkey and formerly found on the island of Mauritius **2** : one hopelessly behind the times; *also* : a stupid person

doe \'dō\ *n, pl* **does** *or* **doe** : an adult female deer; *also* : the female of a mammal of which the male is called buck — **doe·skin** \-ˌskin\ *n*

DOE *abbr* Department of Energy

do·er \'dü-ər\ *n* : one that does

does *pres 3d sing of* DO, *pl of* DOE

doff \'däf\ *vb* [ME *doffen*, fr. *don* to do + *of* off] **1** : to take off (the hat) in greeting or as a sign of respect **2** : to rid oneself of

¹**dog** \'dȯg\ *n* **1** : a flesh-eating domestic mammal related to the wolves; *esp* : a male of this animal **2** : a worthless person **3** : FELLOW, CHAP (you lucky ∼) **4** : a mechanical device for holding something **5** : uncharacteristic or

affected stylishness or dignity (put on the ∼) **6** *pl* : RUIN (gone to the ∼s)

²**dog** *vb* **dogged; dog·ging 1** : to hunt or track like a hound **2** : to worry as if by pursuit with dogs : HOUND

dog·bane \'dȯg-ˌbān\ *n* : any of a genus of mostly poisonous herbs with milky juice and often showy flowers

dog·cart \-ˌkärt\ *n* : a light one-horse carriage with two seats back to back

dog·catch·er \-ˌkach-ər, -ˌkech-\ *n* : a community official assigned to catch and dispose of stray dogs

dog–ear \'dȯg-ˌiər\ *n* : the turned-down corner of a leaf of a book — **dog–eared** \-ˌiərd\ *adj*

dog·fight \'dȯg-ˌfīt\ *n* : a fight between two or more fighter planes usu. at close quarters

dog·fish \-ˌfish\ *n* : any of various small sharks

dogged \'dȯg-əd\ *adj* : stubbornly determined : TENACIOUS — **dog·ged·ly** *adv* — **dog·ged·ness** *n*

dog·ger·el \'dȯg-(ə-)rəl\ *n* : verse that is loosely styled and irregular in measure esp. for comic effect

doggie bag *or* **doggy bag** \'dȯg-ē-\ *n* : a bag provided by a restaurant to a customer for carrying home leftover food

¹**dog·gy** *or* **dog·gie** \'dȯg-ē\ *n, pl* **doggies** : a small dog

²**dog·gy** *adj* **dog·gi·er; -est** : of or resembling a dog (a ∼ odor)

dog·house \'dȯg-ˌhau̇s\ *n* : a shelter for a dog — **in the doghouse** : in a state of disfavor

do·gie \'dō-gē\ *n, chiefly West* : a motherless calf in a range herd

dog·leg \'dȯg-ˌleg\ *n* : a sharp bend or angle (as in a road) — **dogleg** *vb*

dog·ma \'dȯg-mə\ *n* **1** : a tenet or code of tenets **2** : a doctrine or body of doctrines formally proclaimed by a church

dog·ma·tism \'dȯg-mə-ˌtiz-əm\ *n* : positiveness in stating matters of opinion esp. when unwarranted or arrogant — **dog·mat·ic** \dȯg-'mat-ik\ *adj* — **dog·mat·i·cal·ly** \-i-k(ə-)lē\ *adv*

dog·tooth violet \'dȯg-ˌtüth-\ *n* : any of a genus of wild spring-flowering bulbous herbs related to the lilies

dog·trot \'dȯg-ˌträt\ *n* : a gentle trot — **dogtrot** *vb*

dog·wood \'dȯg-ˌwu̇d\ *n* : any of a genus of trees and shrubs having heads of small flowers often with showy bracts

doi·ly \'dȯi-lē\ *n, pl* **doilies** : a small often decorative mat

do in *vb* **1** : RUIN **2** : KILL **3** : TIRE, EXHAUST **4** : CHEAT

do·ings \'dü-iŋz\ *n pl* : ACTS, DEEDS, EVENTS

do-it-your·self \ˌdü-ə-chər-'self\ *adj* : of, relating to, or designed for use by or as if by an amateur or hobbyist — **do-it-your·self·er** \-'sel-fər\ *n*

dol *abbr* dollar

dol·drums \'dōl-drəmz, 'däl-\ *n pl* **1** : a

spell of listlessness or despondency **2** : a part of the ocean near the equator abounding in calms **3** : a state of inactivity, stagnation, or slump ⟨business is in the ∼⟩

¹dole \'dōl\ *n* **1** : a distribution esp. of food, money, or clothing to the needy; *also* : something so distributed **2** : a grant of government funds to the unemployed

²dole *vb* **doled; dol·ing 1** : to give or distribute as a charity **2** : to give in small portions : PARCEL ⟨∼ out food⟩

dole·ful \'dōl-fəl\ *adj* : full of grief : SAD — **dole·ful·ly** \-ē\ *adv*

doll \'däl, 'dȯl\ *n* **1** : a small figure of a human being used esp. as a child's plaything **2** : a pretty woman **3** : an attractive person

dol·lar \'däl-ər\ *n* [Dutch or LG *daler*, fr. G *taler*, short for *joachimstaler*, fr. Sankt *Joachimsthal*, Bohemia, where talers were first made] **1** : any of various basic monetary units (as in the U.S. and Canada) — see MONEY table **2** : a coin, note, or token representing one dollar

dol·lop \'däl-əp\ *n* : LUMP, BLOB

doll up *vb* **1** : to dress elegantly or extravagantly **2** : to make more attractive

dol·ly \'däl-ē\ *n, pl* **dollies** : a small wheeled truck used in moving heavy loads; *esp* : a wheeled platform for a television or movie camera

dol·men \'dōl-mən, 'däl-\ *n* : a prehistoric monument consisting of two or more upright stones supporting a horizontal stone slab

do·lo·mite \'dō-lə-ˌmīt, 'däl-ə-\ *n* : a mineral found in broad layers as a compact limestone

do·lor \'dō-lər, 'däl-ər\ *n* : mental suffering or anguish : SORROW — **do·lor·ous** *adj* — **do·lor·ous·ly** *adv* — **do·lor·ous·ness** *n*

dol·phin \'däl-fən\ *n* **1** : any of various small toothed whales with the snout more or less elongated into a beak **2** : either of two active food fishes of tropical and temperate seas

dolt \'dōlt\ *n* : a stupid fellow — **dolt·ish** *adj*

dom *abbr* **1** domestic **2** dominant **3** dominion

-dom \dəm\ *n suffix* **1** : dignity : office ⟨duke*dom*⟩ **2** : realm : jurisdiction ⟨king*dom*⟩ **3** : state or fact of being ⟨free*dom*⟩ **4** : those having a (specified) office, occupation, interest, or character ⟨official*dom*⟩

do·main \dō-'mān, də-\ *n* **1** : complete and absolute ownership of land **2** : land completely owned **3** : a territory over which dominion is exercised **4** : a sphere of influence or action ⟨the ∼ of science⟩

dome \'dōm\ *n* **1** : a large hemispherical roof or ceiling **2** : a structure or natural formation that resembles the dome of a building

¹do·mes·tic \də-'mes-tik\ *adj* **1** : living near or about the habitations of humans **2** : TAME, DOMESTICATED **3** : relating and limited to one's own country or the country under consideration **4** : of or relating to the household or the family **5** : devoted to home duties and pleasures **6** : INDIGENOUS — **do·mes·ti·cal·ly** \-ti-k(ə-)lē\ *adv*

²domestic *n* : a household servant

do·mes·ti·cate \də-'mes-ti-ˌkāt\ *vb* **-cat·ed; -cat·ing** : to adapt to life in association with and to the use of human beings — **do·mes·ti·ca·tion** \-ˌmes-ti-'kā-shən\ *n*

do·mes·tic·i·ty \ˌdō-ˌmes-'tis-ət-ē, də-\ *n, pl* **-ties 1** : the quality or state of being domestic or domesticated **2** : domestic activities or life

do·mi·cile \'däm-ə-ˌsīl, 'dō-mə-; 'däm-ə-səl\ *n* : a dwelling place : HOME — **domicile** *vb* — **dom·i·cil·i·ary** \ˌdäm-ə-'sil-ē-ˌer-ē, ˌdō-mə-\ *adj*

dom·i·nance \'däm-ə-nəns\ *n* **1** : AUTHORITY, CONTROL **2** : the property of a genetic dominant that prevents expression of a genetic recessive

¹dom·i·nant \'däm-ə-nənt\ *adj* **1** : controlling or prevailing over all others **2** : overlooking from a high elevation **3** : producing or being a bodily characteristic that is expressed when a contrasting recessive gene or trait is present

²dominant *n* : a dominant gene or a character which it controls

dom·i·nate \'däm-ə-ˌnāt\ *vb* **-nat·ed; -nat·ing 1** : RULE, CONTROL **2** : to have a commanding position or controlling power over **3** : to rise high above in a position suggesting power to dominate

dom·i·na·tion \ˌdäm-ə-'nā-shən\ *n* **1** : supremacy or preeminence over another **2** : exercise of mastery or preponderant influence

dom·i·neer \ˌdäm-ə-'niər\ *vb* **1** : to rule in an arrogant manner **2** : to be overbearing

do·mi·nie *1* oftenest 'däm-ə-nē, *2* oftenest 'dō-mə-\ *n* **1** *chiefly Scot* : SCHOOLMASTER **2** : CLERGYMAN

do·min·ion \də-'min-yən\ *n* **1** : DOMAIN **2** : supreme authority : SOVEREIGNTY **3** *often cap* : a self-governing nation of the Commonwealth

dom·i·no \'däm-ə-ˌnō\ *n, pl* **-noes** *or* **-nos 1** : a long loose hooded cloak usu. worn with a half mask as a masquerade costume **2** : a flat rectangular block used as a piece in a game (dominoes)

¹don \'dän\ *vb* **donned; don·ning** [*do* + *on*] : to put on (as clothes)

²don *n* [Sp, fr. L *dominus* lord, master] **1** : a Spanish nobleman or gentleman — used as a title prefixed to the Christian name **2** : a head, tutor, or fellow in an English university

do·ña \'dō-nyə\ *n* : a Spanish woman of

rank — used as a title prefixed to the Christian name

do·nate \'dō-ˌnāt\ *vb* **do·nat·ed; do·nat·ing** **1** : to make a gift of : CONTRIBUTE **2** : to make a donation

do·na·tion \dō-'nā-shən\ *n* **1** : the action of making a gift esp. to a charity **2** : a free contribution : GIFT

¹done \'dən\ *past part of* DO

²done *adj* **1** : doomed to failure, defeat, or death **2** : gone by : OVER ⟨when day is ∼⟩ **3** : cooked sufficiently **4** : conformable to social convention

dong \'dȯŋ, 'däŋ\ *n* — see MONEY table

don·key \'däŋ-kē, 'dəŋ-\ *n, pl* **donkeys 1** : a domestic mammal classified with the asses **2** : a stupid or obstinate person

don·ny·brook \'dän-ē-ˌbru̇k\ *n, often cap* [Donnybrook Fair, annual Irish event once known for its brawls] : an uproarious brawl

do·nor \'dō-nər\ *n* : one that gives, donates, or presents

donut *var of* DOUGHNUT

doo·dad \'dü-ˌdad\ *n* : a small article whose common name is unknown or forgotten

doo·dle \'düd-ᵊl\ *vb* **doo·dled; doo·dling** \'düd-(ᵊ-)liŋ\ : to draw or scribble aimlessly while occupied with something else — **doodle** *n* — **doo·dler** \'düd-(ᵊ-)lər\ *n*

doom \'düm\ *n* **1** : JUDGMENT, SENTENCE; *esp* : a judicial condemnation or sentence **2** : DESTINY, FATE **3** : RUIN, DEATH — **doom** *vb*

dooms·day \'dümz-ˌdā\ *n* : JUDGMENT DAY

door \'dȯr\ *n* **1** : a barrier by which an entry is closed and opened; *also* : a similar part of a piece of furniture **2** : DOORWAY **3** : a means of access

door·jamb \-ˌjam\ *n* : an upright piece forming the side of a door opening

door·keep·er \-ˌkē-pər\ *n* : one who tends a door

door·knob \-ˌnäb\ *n* : a knob that when turned releases a door latch

door·man \-ˌman, -mən\ *n* : one who tends a door and assists people by calling taxis and helping them in and out of cars

door·mat \-ˌmat\ *n* : a mat placed before or inside a door for wiping dirt from the shoes

door·plate \-ˌplāt\ *n* : a nameplate on a door

door·step \-ˌstep\ *n* : a step or series of steps before an outer door

door·way \-ˌwā\ *n* **1** : the opening that a door closes **2** : a means of gaining access

door·yard \-ˌyärd\ *n* : a yard outside the door of a house

do·pa \'dō-pə\ *n* : a form of an amino acid that is used esp. in the treatment of Parkinson's disease

¹dope \'dōp\ *n* **1** : a preparation for giving a desired quality **2** : a drug preparation esp. when narcotic or addictive and used illegally **3** : a stupid person **4** : INFORMATION

²dope *vb* **doped; dop·ing 1** : to treat with dope; *esp* : to give a narcotic to **2** : FIGURE OUT — usu. used with *out*

dop·ey *also* **dopy** \'dō-pē\ *adj* **dop·i·er; -est 1** : dulled by alcohol or a narcotic **2** : SLUGGISH **3** : STUPID

dorm \'dȯrm\ *n* : DORMITORY

dor·mant \'dȯr-mənt\ *adj* : INACTIVE; *esp* : not actively growing or functioning ⟨∼ buds⟩ — **dor·man·cy** \-mən-sē\ *n*

dor·mer \'dȯr-mər\ *n* [MF *dormeor* dormitory, fr. L *dormitorium*, fr. *dormire* to sleep] : a window built upright in a sloping roof

dor·mi·to·ry \'dȯr-mə-ˌtōr-ē\ *n, pl* **-ries 1** : a room for sleeping; *esp* : a large room containing a number of beds **2** : a residence hall providing sleeping rooms

dor·mouse \'dȯr-ˌmau̇s\ *n* : any of numerous Old World squirrellike rodents

dor·sal \'dȯr-səl\ *adj* : of, relating to, or located near or on the surface of the body that in man is the back but in most other animals is the upper surface — **dor·sal·ly** \-ē\ *adv*

do·ry \'dȯr-ē\ *n, pl* **dories** : a flat-bottomed boat with high flaring sides and a sharp bow

DOS *abbr* disk operating system

¹dose \'dōs\ *n* [F, fr. LL *dosis*, fr. Gk, lit., act of giving, fr. *didonai* to give] **1** : a measured quantity (as of medicine) to be taken or administered at one time **2** : the quantity of radiation administered or absorbed — **dos·age** \'dō-sij\ *n*

²dose *vb* **dosed; dos·ing 1** : to give in doses **2** : to give medicine to

do·sim·e·ter \dō-'sim-ət-ər\ *n* : a device for measuring doses of X rays or of radioactivity — **do·sim·e·try** \-ə-trē\ *n*

dos·sier \'däs-ˌyā, 'dȯs-ē-ˌā\ *n* [F, bundle of documents labeled on the back, dossier, fr. *dos* back, fr. L *dorsum*] : a file of papers containing a detailed report or detailed information

¹dot \'dät\ *n* **1** : a small spot : SPECK **2** : a small round mark **3** : a precise point esp. in time ⟨be here on the ∼⟩

²dot *vb* **dot·ted; dot·ting 1** : to mark with a dot ⟨∼ an *i*⟩ **2** : to cover with or as if with dots

DOT *abbr* Department of Transportation

dot·age \'dōt-ij\ *n* : feebleness of mind esp. in old age : SENILITY

dot·ard \-ərd\ *n* : a person in dotage

dote \'dōt\ *vb* **dot·ed; dot·ing 1** : to be feebleminded esp. from old age **2** : to be lavish or excessive in one's attention, affection, or fondness ⟨doted on her niece⟩

dot matrix *n* : a rectangular arrangement of dots from which alphanumeric characters can be formed (as by a computer printer)

Dou·ay Ver·sion \dü-ʹā-\ n : an English translation of the Vulgate used by Roman Catholics

¹**dou·ble** \ʹdəb-əl\ adj 1 : TWOFOLD, DUAL 2 : consisting of two members or parts 3 : being twice as great or as many 4 : folded in two 5 : having more than one whorl of petals (~ roses)

²**double** vb **dou·bled; dou·bling** \ʹdəb-(ə-)liŋ\ 1 : to make, be, or become twice as great or as many 2 : to make a call in bridge that increases the trick values and penalties of (an opponent's bid) 3 : FOLD 4 : CLENCH 5 : to be or cause to be bent over 6 : to take the place of another 7 : to hit a double 8 : to turn sharply and suddenly; esp : to turn back on one's course

³**double** adv 1 : DOUBLY 2 : two together (sleep ~)

⁴**double** n 1 : something twice another in size, strength, speed, quantity, or value 2 : a hit in baseball that enables the batter to reach second base 3 : COUNTERPART, DUPLICATE; esp : a person who closely resembles another 4 : UNDERSTUDY, SUBSTITUTE 5 : a sharp turn : REVERSAL 6 : FOLD 7 : a combined bet placed on two different contests 8 pl : a game between two pairs of players 9 : an act of doubling in a card game

double bond n : a chemical bond in which two atoms in a molecule share two pairs of electrons

double cross n : an act of betraying or cheating esp. an associate — **dou·ble-cross** \ˌdəb-əl-ʹkrós\ vb — **dou·ble-cross·er** n

dou·ble-deal·ing \-ʹdē-liŋ\ n : DUPLICITY — **dou·ble-deal·er** \-ʹdē-lər\ n — **double-dealing** adj

dou·ble-deck·er \-ʹdek-ər\ n : something having two decks, levels, or layers

dou·ble-dig·it \ˌdəb-əl-ʹdij-ət\ adj : amounting to 10 percent or more

dou·ble en·ten·dre \ˌdüb-(ə-)ˌlän-ʹtänʹdrᵊ, ˌdəb-ə-\ n, pl **double entendres** \-ʹtänʹdrᵊ, -ʹtänʹd-rəz\ [obs. F, lit., double meaning] : a word or expression capable of two interpretations one of which is usu. risqué

dou·ble-head·er \ˌdəb-əl-ʹhed-ər\ n : two games played consecutively on the same day

double helix n : a helix or spiral consisting of two strands (as of DNA) in the surface of a cylinder which coil around its axis

dou·ble-joint·ed \-ʹjóint-əd\ adj : having a joint that permits an exceptional degree of freedom of motion of the parts joined

double play n : a play in baseball by which two players are put out

double pneumonia n : pneumonia involving both lungs

dou·blet \ʹdəb-lət\ n 1 : a man's close-fitting jacket worn in Europe esp. in the 16th century 2 : one of two similar or identical things

dou·ble take \ʹdəb-əl-ˌtāk\ n : a delayed reaction to a surprising or significant situation after an initial failure to notice anything unusual

dou·ble-talk \-ˌtók\ n : language that appears to be meaningful but in fact is a mixture of sense and nonsense

double up vb : to share accommodations designed for one

dou·bloon \ˌdəb-ʹlün\ n : a former gold coin of Spain and Spanish America

dou·bly \ʹdəb-lē\ adv 1 : in a twofold manner 2 : to twice the degree

¹**doubt** \ʹdaùt\ vb 1 : to be uncertain about 2 : to lack confidence in : DISTRUST, FEAR 3 : to consider unlikely — **doubt·able** adj — **doubt·er** n

²**doubt** n 1 : uncertainty of belief or opinion 2 : a condition causing uncertainty, hesitation, or suspense (the outcome was in ~) 3 : DISTRUST 4 : an inclination not to believe or accept

doubt·ful \ʹdaùt-fəl\ adj 1 : QUESTIONABLE 2 : UNDECIDED — **doubt·ful·ly** \-ē\ adv

¹**doubt·less** \ʹdaùt-ləs\ adv 1 : without doubt 2 : PROBABLY

²**doubtless** adj : free from doubt

douche \ʹdüsh\ n [F] 1 : a jet of fluid (as water) directed against a part or into a cavity of the body; also : a cleansing with a douche 2 : a device for giving douches — **douche** vb

dough \ʹdō\ n 1 : a mixture that consists of flour or meal and a liquid (as milk or water) and is stiff enough to knead or roll 2 : something resembling dough esp. in consistency 3 : MONEY — **doughy** \ʹdō-ē\ adj

dough·boy \-ˌbói\ n : an American infantryman esp. in World War I

dough·nut \-(ˌ)nət\ n : a small usu. ring-shaped cake fried in fat

dough·ty \ʹdaùt-ē\ adj **dough·ti·er; -est** : ABLE, STRONG, VALIANT

Doug·las fir \ˌdəg-ləs-\ n : a tall evergreen timber tree of the western U.S.

do up vb 1 : to prepare (as by cleaning) for use 2 : to wrap up

dour \ʹdaù(ə)r, ʹdùr\ adj [ME, fr. L durus hard] 1 : STERN, HARSH 2 : GLOOMY, SULLEN

douse \ʹdaùs, ʹdaùz\ vb **doused; dous·ing** 1 : to plunge into water 2 : DRENCH 3 : EXTINGUISH

¹**dove** \ʹdəv\ n 1 : any of numerous pigeons; esp : a small wild pigeon 2 : an advocate of peace or of a peaceful policy — **dove·cote** \-ˌkōt, -ˌkät\ also **dove·cot** \-ˌkät\ n — **dov·ish** \ʹdəv-ish\ adj

²**dove** \ʹdōv\ past of DIVE

¹**dove·tail** \ʹdəv-ˌtāl\ n : something that resembles a dove's tail; esp : a flaring tenon and a mortise into which it fits tightly

²**dovetail** vb 1 : to join (as timbers) by means of dovetails 2 : to fit skillfully

together to form a whole (our plans ～ perfectly)

dow·a·ger \'daù-i-jər\ *n* 1 : a widow owning property or a title from her deceased husband 2 : a dignified elderly woman

dowdy \'daùd-ē\ *adj* **dowd·i·er; -est** : lacking neatness and charm — SHABBY, UNTIDY; *also* : lacking smartness

dow·el \'daù-(-ə)l\ *n* : a pin used for fastening together two pieces (as of board) — **dowel** *vb*

¹**dow·er** \'daù-(-ə)r\ *n* 1 : the part of a deceased husband's real estate which the law gives for life to his widow 2 : DOWRY

²**dower** *vb* : to supply with a dower or dowry : ENDOW

dow·itch·er \'daù-i-chər\ *n, pl* **dow·itch·ers** : any of several long-billed wading birds related to the sandpipers

¹**down** \'daùn\ *n* : a rolling usu. treeless upland with sparse soil — usu. used in pl.

²**down** *adv* 1 : toward or in a lower physical position 2 : to a lying or sitting position 3 : toward or to the ground, floor, or bottom 4 : as a down payment (paid $5 ～) 5 : on paper (put ～ what he says) 6 : in a direction that is the opposite of up 7 : SOUTH 8 : to or in a lower or worse condition or status 9 : from a past time 10 : to or in a state of less activity 11 : into defeat (voted the motion ～)

³**down** *prep* : down in, on, along, or through : toward the bottom of

⁴**down** *vb* 1 : to go or cause to go or come down 2 : DEFEAT 3 : to cause (a football) to be out of play

⁵**down** *adj* 1 : occupying a low position; *esp* : lying on the ground 2 : directed or going downward 3 : being in a state of reduced or low activity 4 : DEPRESSED, DEJECTED 5 : SICK (～ with a cold) 6 : FINISHED, DONE

⁶**down** *n* 1 : a low or falling period (as in activity, emotional life, or fortunes) 2 : one of a series of attempts to advance a football

⁷**down** *n* 1 : a covering of soft fluffy feathers; *also* : such feathers 2 : a downlike covering or material

down·beat \'daùn-,bēt\ *n* : the downward stroke of a conductor indicating the principally accented note of a measure of music

down·cast \-,kast\ *adj* 1 : DEJECTED 2 : directed down (a ～ glance)

down·draft \-,draft\ *n* : a downward current of gas (as air in a chimney)

down·er \'daù-nər\ *n* 1 : a depressant drug; *esp* : BARBITURATE 2 : a depressing experience or situation

down·fall \'daùn-,fòl\ *n* 1 : a sudden fall (as from high rank) 2 : a fall (as of rain) esp. when sudden or heavy 3 : something that causes a downfall — **down·fall·en** \-,fò-lən\ *adj*

¹**down·grade** \'daùn-,grād\ *n* 1 : a down-

ward grade or slope (as of a road) 2 : a decline toward a worse condition

²**downgrade** *vb* : to lower in grade, rank, position, or status

down·heart·ed \-'härt-əd\ *adj* : DEJECTED

down·hill \'daùn-'hil\ *adv* : toward the bottom of a hill — **downhill** \-,hil\ *adj*

down·load \'daùn-,lōd\ *vb* : to transfer (as data) from one computer to another device

down payment *n* : a part of the full price paid at the time of purchase or delivery with the balance to be paid later

down·pour \'daùn-,pōr\ *n* : a heavy rain

down·range \-'rānj\ *adv or adj* : toward the target area of a firing range

¹**down·right** \-,rīt\ *adv* : THOROUGHLY

²**downright** *adj* 1 : ABSOLUTE, UTTER (a ～ lie) 2 : PLAIN, BLUNT (a ～ man)

down·shift \-,shift\ *vb* : to shift an automotive vehicle into a lower gear

down·size \-,sīz\ *vb* : to design or produce in smaller size

Down's syndrome *or* **Down syndrome** \'daùn(z)-\ *n* : a birth defect characterized by mental deficiency, slanting eyes, a broad short skull, broad hands with short fingers, and the presence of an extra chromosome

down·stage \'daùn-'stāj\ *adv or adj* : toward or at the front of a theatrical stage

down·stairs \'daùn-'staərz\ *adv* : on or to a lower floor and esp. the main or ground floor — **downstairs** *adj or n*

down·stream \'daùn-'strēm\ *adv or adj* : in the direction of flow of a stream

down·stroke \-,strōk\ *n* : a stroke made in a downward direction

down·swing \-,swing\ *n* 1 : a swing downward 2 : DOWNTURN

down-to-earth \,daùn-tə-'(w)ərth\ *adj* : PRACTICAL, REALISTIC

down·town \'daùn-,taùn\ *n* : the main business district of a town or city — **downtown** \,daùn-,taùn\ *adj or adv*

down·trod·den \'daùn-'träd-³n\ *adj* : suffering oppression

down·turn \-,tərn\ *n* : a turning downward esp. in business activity

¹**down·ward** \'daùn-wərd\ *or* **down·wards** \-wərdz\ *adv* 1 : from a higher to a lower place or condition 2 : from an earlier time 3 : from an ancestor or predecessor

²**downward** *adj* : directed toward or situated in a lower place or condition

down·wind \'daùn-'wind\ *adv or adj* : in the direction toward which the wind is blowing

downy \'daù-nē\ *adj* **down·i·er; -est** : resembling or covered with down

downy mildew *n* : any of various parasitic fungi producing whitish masses esp. on the underside of plant leaves; *also* : a plant disease caused by downy mildew

downy woodpecker *n* : a small black-

and-white woodpecker of No. America

dow·ry \'daù(ə)r-ē\ *n, pl* **dowries** : the property that a woman brings to her husband in marriage

dowse \'daùz\ *vb* **dowsed; dows·ing** : to use a divining rod esp. to find water — **dows·er** *n*

dox·ol·o·gy \däk-'säl-ə-jē\ *n, pl* **-gies** : a usu. short hymn of praise to God

doy·en \'dȯi-ən, 'dwä-'yaⁿ(n)\ *n* : the senior or most experienced person in a group

doy·enne \dȯi-'(y)en, dwä-'yen\ *n* : a woman who is a doyen

doz *abbr* dozen

doze \'dōz\ *vb* **dozed; doz·ing** : to sleep lightly — **doze** *n*

doz·en \'dəz-ⁿn\ *n, pl* **dozens** *or* **dozen** [ME *dozeine*, fr. OF *dozaine*, fr. *doze* twelve, fr. L *duodecim*, fr. *duo* two + *decem* ten] : a group of twelve — **doz·enth** \-ⁿnth\ *adj*

¹DP \'dē-'pē\ *n, pl* **DP's** *or* **DPs** : a displaced person

²DP *abbr* **1** data processing **2** double play

dpt *abbr* department

DPT *abbr* diphtheria-pertussis-tetanus (vaccines)

dr *abbr* **1** debtor **2** dram **3** drive **4** drum

Dr *abbr* doctor

DR *abbr* **1** dead reckoning **2** dining room

drab \'drab\ *adj* **drab·ber; drab·best** **1** : being of a light olive-brown color **2** : DULL, MONOTONOUS, CHEERLESS — **drab·ness** *n*

drach·ma \'drak-mə\ *n, pl* **drach·mas** *or* **drach·mai** \-ˌmī\ *or* **drach·mae** \-ˌmē\ — see MONEY table

dra·co·ni·an \drā-'kō-nē-ən, drə-\ *adj, often cap* : HARSH, CRUEL

¹draft \'draft, 'dráft\ *n* **1** : the act of drawing or hauling **2** : the act or an instance of drinking or inhaling; *also* : the portion drunk or inhaled in one such act **3** : DOSE, POTION **4** : the force required to pull an implement **5** : DELINEATION, PLAN, DESIGN; *also* : a preliminary sketch, outline, or version (a rough ~ of a speech) **6** : the act of drawing (as from a cask); *also* : a portion of liquid so drawn **7** : the depth of water a ship draws esp. when loaded **8** : the selection of a person esp. for compulsory military service; *also* : the persons so selected **9** : an order for the payment of money drawn by one person or bank on another **10** : a heavy demand : STRAIN **11** : a current of air; *also* : a device to regulate air supply (as to a fire) — **on draft** : ready to be drawn from a receptacle (beer *on draft*)

²draft *adj* **1** : used or adapted for drawing loads (~ animals) **2** : being or having been on draft (~ beer) **3** : constituting a preliminary sketch, outline, or version

³draft *vb* **1** : to select usu. on a compulsory basis; *esp* : to conscript for military service **2** : to draw the preliminary sketch, version, or plan of **3** : COMPOSE, PREPARE **4** : to draw off or away — **draft·ee** \draf-'tē, dráf-\ *n*

drafts·man \'draft-smən, 'dráft-\ *n* : one who draws plans (as for buildings or machinery)

drafty \'draf-tē, 'dráf-\ *adj* **draft·i·er; -est** : exposed to a draft

¹drag \'drag\ *n* **1** : something (as a harrow, grapnel, sledge, or clog) that is dragged along over a surface **2** : the act or an instance of dragging **3** : something that hinders progress **4** : STREET (the main ~) **5** : woman's dress worn by a man **6** : something boring (the party was a ~)

²drag *vb* **dragged; drag·ging 1** : HAUL **2** : to move with painful slowness or difficulty **3** : to force into or out of some situation, condition, or course of action **4** : to pass (time) in pain or tedium **5** : PROTRACT (~ a story out) **6** : to hang or lag behind **7** : to trail along on the ground **8** : to explore, search, or fish with a drag **9** : DRAW, PUFF (~ on a cigarette) — **drag·ger** *n*

drag·net \-ˌnet\ *n* **1** : NET, TRAWL **2** : a network of planned actions for pursuing and catching (a police ~)

drag·o·man \'drag-ə-mən\ *n, pl* **-mans** *or* **-men** \-mən\ : an interpreter employed esp. in the Near East

drag·on \'drag-ən\ *n* [ME, fr. OF, fr. L *dracon-, draco* serpent, dragon, fr. Gk *drakōn* serpent] : a fabulous animal usu. represented as a huge winged scaly serpent with a crested head and large claws

drag·on·fly \-ˌflī\ *n* : any of a group of large harmless 4-winged insects

¹dra·goon \drə-'gün, dra-\ *n* [F *dragon* dragon, dragoon, fr. MF] : a heavily armed mounted soldier

²dragoon *vb* : to force or attempt to force into submission by violent measures

drag race *n* : an acceleration contest between vehicles

drag strip *n* : a site for drag races

¹drain \'drān\ *vb* **1** : to draw off or flow off gradually or completely **2** : to exhaust physically or emotionally **3** : to make or become gradually dry or empty **4** : to carry away the surface water of : discharge surface or surplus water **5** : EMPTY, EXHAUST — **drain·er** *n*

²drain *n* **1** : a means (as a channel or sewer) of draining **2** : the act of draining **3** : DEPLETION **4** : BURDEN, STRAIN (a ~ on his savings)

drain·age \-ij\ *n* **1** : the act or process of draining; *also* : something that is drained off **2** : a means for draining : DRAIN, SEWER **3** : an area drained

drain·pipe \'drān-ˌpīp\ *n* : a pipe for drainage

drake \'drāk\ *n* : a male duck

dram \'dram\ *n* **1** — see WEIGHT table **2** : FLUIDRAM **3** : a small drink

dra·ma \'dräm-ə, 'dram-\ *n* [LL, fr. Gk, deed, drama, fr. *dran* to do, act] **1** : a literary composition designed for theatrical presentation **2** : dramatic art, literature, or affairs **3** : a series of events involving conflicting forces — **dra·mat·ic** \drə-'mat-ik\ *adj* — **dra·mat·i·cal·ly** \-i-k(ə-)lē\ *adv* — **dram·a·tist** \'dram-ət-əst, 'dräm-\ *n*

dra·ma·tize \'dram-ə-ˌtīz, 'dräm-\ *vb* **-tized; -tiz·ing** **1** : to adapt for or be suitable for theatrical presentation **2** : to present or represent in a dramatic manner — **dram·a·ti·za·tion** \ˌdram-ət-ə-'zā-shən, ˌdräm-\ *n*

drank *past and past part of* DRINK

¹drape \'drāp\ *n* **1** : CURTAIN **2** : arrangement in or of folds **3** : the cut or hang of clothing

²drape *vb* **draped; drap·ing** **1** : to cover or adorn with or as if with folds of cloth **2** : to cause to hang or stretch out loosely or carelessly **3** : to arrange or become arranged in flowing lines or folds

drap·er \'drā-pər\ *n, chiefly Brit* : a dealer in cloth and sometimes in clothing and dry goods

drap·ery \'drā-p(ə-)rē\ *n, pl* **-er·ies** **1** *Brit* : DRY GOODS **2** : a decorative fabric esp. when hung loosely and in folds : HANGINGS **3** : the draping or arranging of materials

dras·tic \'dras-tik\ *adj* : HARSH, RIGOROUS, SEVERE \(~ punishment\) — **dras·ti·cal·ly** \-ti-k(ə-)lē\ *adv*

draught \'draft\, **draughty** \'draf-tē\ *chiefly Brit var of* DRAFT, DRAFTY

draughts \'drafts\ *n, Brit* : CHECKERS

¹draw \'dró\ *vb* **drew** \'drü\; **drawn** \'drón\; **draw·ing** **1** : HAUL, DRAG **2** : to cause to go in a certain direction \(*drew* him aside\) **3** : to move or go steadily or gradually \(night ~s near\) **4** : ATTRACT, ENTICE **5** : PROVOKE, ROUSE \(*drew* enemy fire\) **6** : INHALE \(~ a deep breath\) **7** : to bring or pull out **8** : to force out from cover or possession \(~ trumps\) **9** : to extract the essence from \(~ tea\) **10** : EVISCERATE **11** : to require \(a specified depth\) to float in **12** : ACCUMULATE, GAIN \(~ing interest\) **13** : to take money from a place of deposit : WITHDRAW **14** : to receive regularly from a source \(~ a salary\) **15** : to take \(cards\) from a stack or the dealer **16** : to receive or take at random \(~ a winning number\) **17** : to bend \(a bow\) by pulling back the string **18** : WRINKLE, SHRINK **19** : to change shape by or as if by pulling or stretching \(a face *drawn* with sorrow\) **20** : to leave \(a contest\) undecided : TIE **21** : DELINEATE, SKETCH **22** : to write out in due form : DRAFT \(~ up a will\) **23** : FORMULATE \(~ comparisons\) **24** : DEDUCE **25** : to spread or elongate \(metal\) by hammering or by pulling through dies **26** : to produce or allow a draft or current of air \(the furnace ~s well\) **27** : to swell out in a wind \(all sails ~ing\)

²draw *n* **1** : the act, process, or result of drawing **2** : a lot or chance drawn at random **3** : a contest left undecided or deadlocked : TIE **4** : ATTRACTION

draw·back \'dró-ˌbak\ *n* : HINDRANCE, HANDICAP

draw·bridge \-ˌbrij\ *n* : a bridge made to be drawn up, down, or aside

draw·er \'dró(-ə)r\ *n* **1** : one that draws **2** *pl* : an undergarment for the lower part of the body **3** : a sliding boxlike compartment \(as in a table or desk\)

draw·ing \'dró(-)iŋ\ *n* **1** : an act or instance of drawing; *esp* : an occasion when something is decided by drawing lots **2** : the act or art of making a figure, plan, or sketch by means of lines **3** : a representation made by drawing : SKETCH

drawing card *n* : one that attracts attention or patronage

drawing room *n* : a formal reception room

drawl \'dról\ *vb* : to speak or utter slowly with vowels greatly prolonged — **drawl** *n*

draw on *vb* : APPROACH \(night *draws* on\)

draw out *vb* **1** : PROLONG **2** : to cause to speak freely

draw·string \'dró-ˌstriŋ\ *n* : a string, cord, or tape for use in closing a bag or controlling fullness in garments or curtains

draw up *vb* **1** : to prepare a draft or version of **2** : to pull oneself erect **3** : to bring or come to a stop

dray \'drā\ *n* : a strong low cart for carrying heavy loads

¹dread \'dred\ *vb* **1** : to fear greatly **2** : to feel extreme reluctance to meet or face

²dread *n* : great fear esp. of some harm to come

³dread *adj* **1** : causing great fear or anxiety **2** : inspiring awe

dread·ful \'dred-fəl\ *adj* **1** : inspiring dread or awe : FRIGHTENING **2** : extremely distasteful, unpleasant, or shocking — **dread·ful·ly** \-ē\ *adv*

dread·locks \'dred-ˌläks\ *n pl* : long braids of hair over the entire head

dread·nought \'dred-ˌnót\ *n* : a battleship armed with big guns of the same caliber

¹dream \'drēm\ *n* [ME *dreem*, fr. OE *drēam* noise, joy] **1** : a series of thoughts, images, or emotions occurring during sleep **2** : a dreamlike vision : DAYDREAM, REVERIE **3** : something notable for its beauty, excellence, or enjoyable quality **4** : IDEAL — **dream·like** *adj* — **dreamy** *adj*

²dream \'drēm\ *vb* **dreamed** \'dremt, 'drēmd\ *or* **dreamt** \'dremt\; **dream·ing** **1** : to have a dream of **2** : to indulge in daydreams or fantasies : pass (time) in reverie or inaction **3** : IMAG-INE — **dream·er** *n*

dream·land \\'drēm-ˌland\ *n* : an unreal delightful country that exists in imagination or in dreams

dream up *vb* : INVENT, CONCOCT

dream-world \-ˌwərld\ *n* : a world of illusion or fantasy

drear \\'drir\ *adj* : DREARY

drea·ry \\'dri(ə)r-ē\ *adj* **drea·ri·er**; **-est** [ME *drery*, fr. OE *drēorig* sad, bloody, fr. *drēor* gore] **1** : DOLEFUL, SAD **2** : DISMAL, GLOOMY — **drea·ri·ly** \\'drir-ə-lē\ *adv*

¹dredge \\'drej\ *vb* **dredged**; **dredg·ing** : to gather or search with or as if with a dredge — **dredg·er** *n*

²dredge *n* : a machine or barge for removing earth or silt

³dredge *vb* **dredged**; **dredg·ing** : to coat (food) by sprinkling (as with flour)

dregs \\'dregz\ *n pl* **1** : SEDIMENT 1 2 : the most undesirable part (the ∼ of humanity)

drench \\'drench\ *vb* : to wet through

¹dress \\'dres\ *vb* **1** : to make or set straight : ALIGN **2** : to prepare for use; *esp* : BUTCHER **3** : TRIM, EMBELLISH ⟨∼ a store window⟩ **4** : to put clothes on : CLOTHE; *also* : to put on or wear formal or fancy clothes **5** : to apply dressings or medicine to **6** : to arrange (the hair) by combing, brushing, or curling **7** : to apply fertilizer to **8** : SMOOTH, FINISH ⟨∼ leather⟩

²dress *n* **1** : APPAREL, CLOTHING **2** : FROCK, GOWN — **dress-mak·er** \-ˌmā-kər\ *n* — **dress-mak·ing** \-ˌmā-kiŋ\ *n*

³dress *adj* : suitable for a formal occasion; *also* : requiring formal dress

dres·sage \drə-'säzh\ *n* [F] : the execution by a trained horse of complex movements in response to barely perceptible signals from its rider

dress down *vb* : to scold severely

¹dress·er \\'dres-ər\ *n* : a chest of drawers or bureau with a mirror

²dresser *n* : one that dresses

dress·ing \-iŋ\ *n* **1** : the act or process of one who dresses **2** : a sauce for adding to a dish (as a salad) **3** : a seasoned mixture usu. used as a stuffing (as for poultry) **4** : material used to cover an injury

dressing gown *n* : a loose robe worn esp. while dressing or resting

dressy \\'dres-ē\ *adj* **dress·i·er**; **-est** **1** : showy in dress **2** : STYLISH, SMART

drew *past of* DRAW

¹drib·ble \\'drib-əl\ *vb* **drib·bled**; **drib·bling** \-(ə-)liŋ\ **1** : to fall or flow in drops : TRICKLE **2** : DROOL **3** : to propel by successive slight taps or bounces

²dribble *n* **1** : a small trickling stream or flow **2** : a drizzling shower **3** : the dribbling of a ball or puck

drib·let \\'drib-lət\ *n* **1** : a trifling amount **2** : a drop of liquid

dri·er *also* **dry·er** \\'drī-(ə)r\ *n* **1** : a substance dissolved in paints, varnishes, or inks to speed drying **2** *usu* **dryer** : a device for drying

¹drift \\'drift\ *n* **1** : the motion or course of something drifting **2** : a mass of matter (as snow or sand) blown up by wind **3** : earth, gravel, and rock deposited by a glacier or by running water **4** : a general underlying design or tendency : MEANING

²drift *vb* **1** : to float or be driven along by or as if by a current of water or air **2** : to pile up under the force of wind or water

drift·er \\'drif-tər\ *n* : a person without aim, ambition, or initiative

drift-wood \\'drift-ˌwùd\ *n* : wood drifted or floated by water

¹drill \\'dril\ *n* **1** : a boring tool **2** : the training of soldiers in marching and the manual of arms **3** : strict training and instruction in a subject

²drill *vb* **1** : to instruct and exercise by repetition **2** : to train in or practice military drill **3** : to bore with a drill — **drill·er** *n*

³drill *n* **1** : a shallow furrow or trench in which seed is sown **2** : an agricultural implement for making furrows and dropping seed into them

⁴drill *n* : a firm cotton fabric in twill weave

drill·mas·ter \\'dril-ˌmas-tər\ *n* : one who drills; *esp* : an instructor in military drill

drill press *n* : an upright drilling machine in which the drill is pressed to the work usu. by a hand lever

drily *var of* DRYLY

¹drink \\'driŋk\ *vb* **drank** \\'draŋk\ ; **drunk** \\'drəŋk\ *or* **drank**; **drink·ing** : to swallow liquid : IMBIBE **2** : ABSORB **3** : to take in through the senses ⟨∼ in the beautiful scenery⟩ **4** : to give or join in a toast **5** : to drink alcoholic beverages esp. to excess — **drink·able** *adj* — **drink·er** *n*

²drink *n* **1** : BEVERAGE **2** : alcoholic liquor **3** : a draft or portion of liquid **4** : excessive consumption of alcoholic beverages

¹drip \\'drip\ *vb* **dripped**; **drip·ping 1** : to fall or let fall in drops **2** : to let fall drops of moisture or liquid ⟨a *dripping* faucet⟩ **3** : to overflow with or as if with moisture

²drip *n* **1** : a falling in drops **2** : liquid that falls, overflows, or is extruded in drops **3** : the sound made by or as if by falling drops

¹drive \\'drīv\ *vb* **drove** \\'drōv\ ; **driv·en** \\'driv-ən\ ; **driv·ing 1** : to urge, push, or force onward **2** : to direct the movement or course of **3** : to convey in a vehicle **4** : to set or keep in motion or operation **5** : to carry through strongly ⟨∼ a bargain⟩ **6** : FORCE, COMPEL ⟨*driven* by hunger to steal⟩ **7** : to project, inject, or impress forcefully ⟨*drove* the lesson home⟩ **8** : to bring into a specified condition ⟨the noise ∼s me crazy⟩ **9** : to produce by opening a way ⟨∼ a well⟩ **10** : to rush and press with violence ⟨a *driving* rain⟩ **11** : to propel an object of play (as a golf ball) by a hard blow — **driv·er** *n*

²drive *n* **1** : a trip in a carriage or automobile **2** : a driving together of animals (as for capture or slaughter) **3** : the guiding of logs downstream to a mill **4** : the act of driving a ball; *also* : the flight of a ball **5** : DRIVEWAY **6** : a public road for driving (as in a park) **7** : an offensive or aggressive move **:** a military attack **8** : an intensive campaign ⟨membership∼⟩ **9** : the state of being hurried and under pressure **10** : NEED, LONGING **11** : dynamic quality **12** : the apparatus by which motion is imparted to a machine **13** : a device for reading and writing on magnetic media (as magnetic tape or disks)

drive–in \'drī-ˌvin\ *adj* : accommodating patrons while they remain in their automobiles — **drive–in** *n*

¹driv·el \'driv-əl\ *vb* **-eled** *or* **-elled; -el·ing** *or* **-el·ling** \-(ə-)liŋ\ **1** : DROOL, SLAVER **2** : to talk or utter stupidly, carelessly, or in an infantile way — **driv·el·er** \-(ə-)lər\ *n*

²drivel *n* : NONSENSE

drive shaft *n* : a shaft that transmits mechanical power

drive·way \'drīv-ˌwā\ *n* : a short private road leading from the street to a house, garage, or parking lot

¹driz·zle \'driz-əl\ *n* : a fine misty rain

²drizzle *vb* **driz·zled; driz·zling** \-(ə-)liŋ\ : to rain in very small drops

drogue \'drōg\ *n* : a small parachute for slowing down or stabilizing something (as an astronaut's capsule)

droll \'drōl\ *adj* [F *drôle,* fr. *drôle* scamp, fr. MF *drolle,* fr. Middle Dutch, imp] : having a humorous, whimsical, or odd quality ⟨a ∼ expression⟩ — **droll·ery** \-(ə-)rē\ *n* — **droll·ly** \'drō(l)-lē\ *adv*

drom·e·dary \'dräm-ə-ˌder-ē\ *n, pl* **-dar·ies** [ME *dromedarie,* fr. MF *dromedaire,* fr. LL *dromedarius,* fr. L *dromad-, dromas,* fr. Gk, running] : CAMEL; *esp* : a domesticated one-humped camel of western Asia and northern Africa

¹drone \'drōn\ *n* **1** : a male honeybee **2** : one that lives on the labors of others : PARASITE **3** : a pilotless aircraft or ship controlled by radio

²drone *vb* **droned; dron·ing** : to sound with a low dull monotonous murmuring sound : speak monotonously

³drone *n* : a deep monotonous sound

drool \'drül\ *vb* **1** : to let liquid flow from the mouth **2** : to talk foolishly

droop \'drüp\ *vb* **1** : to hang or incline downward **2** : to sink gradually **:** LANGUISH — **droop** *n*

¹drop \'dräp\ *n* **1** : the quantity of fluid that falls in one spherical mass **2** *pl* : a dose of medicine measured by drops **3** : a small quantity of drink **4** : the smallest practical unit of liquid mea-

sure **5** : something (as a pendant or a small round candy) that resembles a liquid drop **6** : FALL **7** : a decline in quantity or quality **8** : a descent by parachute **9** : the distance through which something drops **10** : a slot into which something is to be dropped **11** : something that drops or has dropped

²drop *vb* **dropped; drop·ping 1** : to fall or let fall in drops **2** : to let fall : LOWER ⟨∼ a glove⟩ ⟨*dropped* his voice⟩ **3** : SEND ⟨∼ me a note⟩ **4** : to let go : DISMISS ⟨∼ the subject⟩ **5** : to knock down : cause to fall **6** : to go lower : become less ⟨prices *dropped*⟩ **7** : to come or go unexpectedly or informally ⟨∼ in to call⟩ **8** : to pass from one state into a less active one ⟨∼ off to sleep⟩ **9** : to move downward or with a current **10** : QUIT ⟨*dropped* out of the race⟩ — **drop back** : to move toward the rear — **drop behind** : to fail to keep up

drop–kick \-ˈkik\ *n* : a kick made by dropping a ball to the ground and kicking it at the moment it starts to rebound — **drop–kick** *vb*

drop·let \'dräp-lət\ *n* : a tiny drop

drop–off \'dräp-ˌȯf\ *n* **1** : a steep or perpendicular descent **2** : a marked decline ⟨a ∼ in attendance⟩

drop off \dräp-ˈȯf\ *vb* : to fall asleep

drop out \dräp-ˈaút\ *vb* : to withdraw from participation or membership; *esp* : to leave school before graduation — **drop·out** \'dräp-ˌaút\ *n*

drop·per \'dräp-ər\ *n* **1** : one that drops **2** : a short glass tube with a rubber bulb used to measure out liquids by drops

drop·pings *n pl* : DUNG

drop·sy \'dräp-sē\ *n* [ME *dropesie,* short for *ydropesie,* fr. OF, fr. L *hydropisis,* fr. Gk *hydrōps,* fr. *hydōr* water] : EDEMA — **drop·si·cal** \-si-kəl\ *adj*

dross \'dräs\ *n* **1** : the scum that forms on the surface of a molten metal **2** : waste matter : REFUSE

drought *also* **drouth** \'draút(h)\ *n* : a long spell of dry weather

¹drove \'drōv\ *n* **1** : a group of animals driven or moving in a body **2** : a crowd of people moving or acting together

²drove *past of* DRIVE

drov·er \'drō-vər\ *n* : one that drives domestic animals usu. to market

drown \'draún\ *vb* **drowned** \'draúnd\; **drown·ing 1** : to suffocate by submersion esp. in water **2** : to become drowned **3** : to cover with water **4** : OVERCOME, OVERPOWER

drowse \'draúz\ *vb* **drowsed; drows·ing** : DOZE — **drowse** *n*

drowsy \'draú-zē\ *adj* **drows·i·er; -est 1** : ready to fall asleep **2** : making one sleepy — **drows·i·ly** \'draú-zə-lē\ *adv* — **drows·i·ness** \-zē-nəs\ *n*

drub \'drəb\ *vb* **drubbed; drub·bing 1** : to beat severely : PUMMEL, THRASH **2** : to defeat decisively

drudge \'drəj\ *vb* **drudged; drudg·ing** : to do hard, menial, or monotonous work — **drudge** *n* — **drudg·ery** \-(ə-)rē\ *n*

¹drug \'drəg\ *n* **1** : a substance used as or in medicine **2** : a substance (as heroin or marijuana) affecting bodily activities often in a harmful way and taken for other than medical reasons

²drug *vb* **drugged; drug·ging** : to affect with drugs; *esp* : to stupefy with a narcotic

drug·gist \'drəg-əst\ *n* : a dealer in drugs and medicines; *also* : PHARMACIST

drug·store \'drəg-ˌstōr\ *n* : a retail shop where medicines and miscellaneous articles are sold

dru·id \'drü-əd\ *n, often cap* : one of an ancient Celtic priesthood of Gaul, Britain, and Ireland appearing in legends as magicians and wizards

¹drum \'drəm\ *n* **1** : a percussion instrument usu. consisting of a hollow cylinder with a skin or plastic head stretched over one or both ends that is beaten with the hands or with a stick **2** : the sound of a drum; *also* : a similar sound **3** : a drum-shaped object

²drum *vb* **drummed; drum·ming 1** : to beat a drum **2** : to sound rhythmically : THROB, BEAT **3** : to summon or assemble by or as if by beating a drum **4** : EXPEL (*drummed* out of camp) **5** : to drive or force by steady effort (~ a lesson into his head) **6** : to strike or tap repeatedly so as to produce rhythmic sounds

drum·beat \'drəm-ˌbēt\ *n* : a stroke on a drum or its sound

drum·lin \'drəm-lən\ *n* : an oval hill of glacial drift

drum major *n* : the leader of a marching band

drum ma·jor·ette \ˌdrəm-ˌmā-jə-'ret\ *n* : a girl or woman who leads a marching band; *also* : a baton twirler who accompanies a marching band

drum·mer \'drəm-ər\ *n* **1** : one that plays a drum **2** : a traveling salesman

drum·stick \-ˌstik\ *n* **1** : a stick for beating a drum **2** : the lower segment of a fowl's leg

drum up *vb* **1** : to bring about by persistent effort (*drum up* business) **2** : INVENT, ORIGINATE

¹drunk *past part of* DRINK

²drunk \'drəŋk\ *adj* **1** : having the faculties impaired by alcohol **2** : dominated by an intense feeling (~ with power) **3** : of, relating to, or caused by intoxication

³drunk *n* **1** : a period of excessive drinking **2** : a drunken person : DRUNKARD

drunk·ard \'drəŋ-kərd\ *n* : one who is habitually drunk

drunk·en \'drəŋ-kən\ *adj* **1** : DRUNK **2** : given to habitual excessive use of alcohol **3** : of, relating to, or resulting from intoxication **4** : unsteady or lurching as if from intoxication —

drunk·en·ly *adv* — **drunk·en·ness** \-kən-nəs\ *n*

drupe \'drüp\ *n* : a partly fleshy one-seeded fruit (as a plum or cherry) that remains closed at maturity

¹dry \'drī\ *adj* **dri·er** \'drī(-ə)r\ ; **dri·est** \'drī-əst\ **1** : free or freed from water or liquid **2** : characterized by loss or lack of water or moisture **3** : lacking freshness : WITHERED; *also* : low in or deprived of succulence (~ fruits) **4** : not being in or under water (~ land) **5** : THIRSTY **6** : marked by the absence of alcoholic beverages **7** : no longer liquid or sticky (the ink is ~) **8** : containing or employing no liquid **9** : not giving milk (a ~ cow) **10** : lacking natural lubrication (a ~ cough) **11** : solid as opposed to liquid (~ groceries) **12** : SEVERE **13** : not productive : BARREN **14** : marked by a matter-of-fact, ironic, or terse manner of expression (~ humor) **15** : UNINTERESTING, WEARISOME **16** : not ·sweet (~ wine) **17** : relating to, favoring, or practicing prohibition of alcoholic beverages — **dry·ly** *adv* — **dry·ness** *n*

²dry *vb* **dried; dry·ing** : to make or become dry

³dry *n, pl* **drys** : PROHIBITIONIST

dry·ad \'drī-əd, -ˌad\ *n* : WOOD NYMPH

dry cell *n* : a battery whose contents are not spillable

dry-clean \'drī-ˌklēn\ *vb* : to clean (fabrics) chiefly with solvents (as naphtha) other than water — **dry cleaning** *n*

dry dock \'drī-ˌdäk\ *n* : a dock that can be kept dry during ship construction or repair

dry·er *var of* DRIER

dry farm·ing *n* : farming without irrigation in areas of limited rainfall — **dry·farm** *vb* — **dry farm·er** *n*

dry goods \'drī-ˌgudz\ *n pl* : cloth goods (as fabrics, ribbon, and ready-to-wear clothing)

dry ice *n* : solid carbon dioxide used chiefly as a refrigerant

dry measure *n* : a series of units of capacity for dry commodities — see METRIC SYSTEM table, WEIGHT table

dry run *n* : REHEARSAL, TRIAL

dry·wall \'drī-ˌwȯl\ *n* : PLASTERBOARD

DSC *abbr* **1** Distinguished Service Cross **2** doctor of surgical chiropody

DSM *abbr* Distinguished Service Medal

DSO *abbr* Distinguished Service Order

DST *abbr* daylight saving time

DTP *abbr* diphtheria, tetanus, pertussis (vaccines)

d.t.'s \(ˈ)dē-ˈtēz\ *n pl, often cap D&T* : DELIRIUM TREMENS

du·al \'d(y)ü-əl\ *adj* **1** : TWOFOLD, DOUBLE **2** : having a double character or nature — **du·al·ism** \-ˌliz-əm\ *n* — **du·al·i·ty** \d(y)ü-'al-ət-ē\ *n*

¹dub \'dəb\ *vb* **dubbed; dub·bing 1** : to confer knighthood upon **2** : NAME, NICKNAME

²dub *n* : a clumsy person : DUFFER

³**dub** *vb* **dubbed; dub·bing** : to add (sound effects) to a motion picture or to a radio or television production

du·bi·e·ty \d(y)ü-'bī-ət-ē\ *n, pl* **-eties 1** : UNCERTAINTY **2** : a matter of doubt

du·bi·ous \'d(y)ü-bē-əs\ *adj* **1** : occasioning doubt : UNCERTAIN **2** : feeling doubt : UNDECIDED **3** : QUESTIONABLE — **du·bi·ous·ly** *adv* — **du·bi·ous·ness** *n*

du·cal \'d(y)ü-kəl\ *adj* : of or relating to a duke or dukedom

duc·at \'dək-ət\ *n* : a gold coin formerly used in various European countries

duch·ess \'dəch-əs\ *n* **1** : the wife or widow of a duke **2** : a woman holding the rank of duke in her own right

duchy \'dəch-ē\ *n, pl* **duch·ies** : the territory of a duke or duchess : DUKEDOM

¹**duck** \'dək\ *n, pl* **ducks** : any of various swimming birds related to but smaller than geese and swans

²**duck** *vb* **1** : to thrust or plunge under water **2** : to lower the head or body suddenly **3** : BOW, BOB **4** : DODGE **5** : to evade a duty, question, or responsibility (~ the issue)

³**duck** *n* **1** : a durable closely woven usu. cotton fabric **2** *pl* : clothes made of duck

duck·bill \'dək-ˌbil\ *n* : PLATYPUS

duck·ling \'dək-liŋ\ *n* : a young duck

duck·pin \-ˌpin\ *n* **1** : a small bowling pin shorter and wider in the middle than a tenpin **2** *pl but sing in constr* : a bowling game using duckpins

duct \'dəkt\ *n* : a tube or canal for conveying a bodily fluid; *also* : a pipe or tube for electrical conductors — **duct·less** \'dək-tləs\ *adj*

duc·tile \'dək-t³l\ *adj* **1** : capable of being drawn out (as into wire) or hammered thin **2** : DOCILE — **duc·til·i·ty** \ˌdək-'til-ət-ē\ *n*

ductless gland *n* : an endocrine gland

dud \'dəd\ *n* **1** : one that fails completely **2** : a missile that fails to explode

dude \'d(y)üd\ *n* **1** : FOP, DANDY **2** : a city person; *esp* : an Easterner in the West

dude ranch *n* : a vacation resort offering activities (as horseback riding) typical of western ranches

dud·geon \'dəj-ən\ *n* : ill humor : RESENTMENT (in high ~)

duds \'dədz\ *n pl* : CLOTHES

¹**due** \'d(y)ü\ *adj* [ME, fr. MF *deu*, pp. of *devoir* to owe, fr. L *debēre*] **1** : owed or owing as a debt **2** : owed or owing as a right **3** : APPROPRIATE, FITTING **4** : SUFFICIENT, ADEQUATE **5** : REGULAR, LAWFUL (~ process of law) **6** : ATTRIBUTABLE, ASCRIBABLE (~ to negligence) **7** : PAYABLE (a bill ~ today) **8** : required or expected to happen (~ to arrive soon)

²**due** *n* **1** : something that rightfully belongs to one (give to each his ~) **2** : something owed : DEBT **3** *pl* : FEES, CHARGES

³**due** *adv* : DIRECTLY, EXACTLY (~ north)

du·el \'d(y)ü-əl\ *n* : a combat between two persons; *esp* : one fought with weapons in the presence of witnesses — **duel** *vb* — **du·el·ist** *n*

du·en·de \dü-'en-dā\ *n* [Sp dial., charm, fr. Sp, ghost, goblin, fr. *duen de casa*, prob. fr. *dueño de casa* owner of a house] : the power to attract through personal magnetism and charm

du·en·na \d(y)ü-'en-ə\ *n* **1** : an elderly woman in charge of the younger ladies in a Spanish or Portuguese family **2** : CHAPERON

du·et \d(y)ü-'et\ *n* : a musical composition for two performers

due to *prep* : BECAUSE OF

duf·fel bag \'dəf-əl-\ *n* : a large cylindrical bag for personal belongings

duf·fer \'dəf-ər\ *n* : an incompetent or clumsy person

dug *past and past part of* DIG

dug·out \'dəg-ˌaut\ *n* **1** : a boat made by hollowing out a log **2** : a shelter dug in the ground **3** : a low shelter facing a baseball diamond that contains the players' bench

DUI *abbr* driving under the influence

duke \'d(y)ük\ *n* **1** : a sovereign ruler of a continental European duchy **2** : a nobleman of the highest rank; *esp* : a member of the highest grade of the British peerage **3** *slang* : FIST 1 — usu. used in pl. — **duke·dom** *n*

dul·cet \'dəl-sət\ *adj* **1** : sweet to the ear **2** : AGREEABLE, SOOTHING

dul·ci·mer \'dəl-sə-mər\ *n* **1** : a wire-stringed instrument of trapezoidal shape played with light hammers held in the hands **2** *or* **dul·ci·more** \-ˌmȯr, -ˌmȯr\ : an American folk instrument with three or four strings held on the lap and played by plucking or strumming

¹**dull** \'dəl\ *adj* **1** : mentally slow : STUPID **2** : slow in perception or sensibility **3** : LISTLESS **4** : slow in action : SLUGGISH (a ~ market) **5** : BLUNT **6** : lacking brilliance or luster **7** : DIM, INDISTINCT **8** : not resonant or ringing **9** : low in saturation and lightness (~ color) **10** : TEDIOUS, UNINTERESTING **11** : CLOUDY, OVERCAST — **dull·ness** *or* **dul·ness** *n* — **dul·ly** \'dəl-(l)ē\ *adv*

²**dull** *vb* : to make or become dull

dull·ard \'dəl-ərd\ *n* : a stupid person

du·ly \'d(y)ü-lē\ *adv* : in a due manner, time, or degree

du·ma \'dü-mə\ *n* : the principal legislative assembly in czarist Russia

dumb \'dəm\ *adj* **1** : lacking the power of speech **2** : SILENT **3** : STUPID — **dumb·ly** *adv*

dumb·bell \'dəm-ˌbel\ *n* **1** : a bar with weights at the end used for gymnastic exercises **2** : one who is stupid

dumb·found *or* **dum·found** \ˌdəm-'faund\ *vb* : ASTONISH, AMAZE

dumb·wait·er \'dəm-'wāt-ər\ *n* : a small elevator for conveying food and dishes or small goods from one story of a building to another

dum·dum \'dəm-ˌdəm\ *n* : a bullet (as

one with a hollow point) that expands more than usual upon hitting an object

dum·my \\'dəm-ē\\ *n, pl* **dummies** 1 : a dumb person 2 : the exposed hand in bridge played by the declarer in addition to his own hand; *also* : a bridge player whose hand is a dummy 3 : an imitation of something used as a substitute 4 : one seeming to act for itself but really acting for another 5 : a pattern arrangement of matter to be reproduced esp. by printing

¹**dump** \\'dəmp\\ *vb* : to let fall in a mass : UNLOAD (~ coal)

²**dump** *n* 1 : a place for dumping something (as refuse) 2 : a reserve supply; *esp* : one of military materials (an ammunition ~) 3 : a slovenly or dilapidated place

dump·ing \\-iŋ\\ *n* : the selling of goods in quantity at below market price esp. in international trade

dump·ling \\'dəm-pliŋ\\ *n* 1 : a small mass of boiled or steamed dough 2 : a dessert of fruit baked in biscuit dough

dumps \\'dəmps\\ *n pl* : a dull gloomy state of mind : low spirits (in the ~)

dump truck *n* : a truck for transporting and dumping loose materials

dump·y \\'dəm-pē\\ *adj* **dump·i·er; -est** : short and thick in build

¹**dun** \\'dən\\ *n* : a slightly brownish dark gray

²**dun** *vb* **dunned; dun·ning** 1 : to make persistent demands for payment 2 : PLAGUE, PESTER — **dun** *n*

dunce \\'dəns\\ *n* [John *Duns* Scotus, whose once accepted writings were ridiculed in the 16th cent.] : a dullwitted and stupid person

dun·der·head \\'dən-dər-,hed\\ *n* : DUNCE, BLOCKHEAD

dune \\'d(y)ün\\ *n* : a hill or ridge of sand piled up by the wind

dune buggy *n* : a motor vehicle with oversize tires for use on sand

¹**dung** \\'dəŋ\\ *n* : MANURE

²**dung** *vb* : to dress (land) with dung

dun·ga·ree \\,dəŋ-gə-'rē\\ *n* 1 : a heavy coarse cotton twill; *esp* : blue denim 2 *pl* : clothes made of blue denim

dun·geon \\'dən-jən\\ *n* [ME *donjon*, fr. MF, fr. (assumed) ML *dominion-, dominio*, fr. L *dominus* lord] : a dark prison commonly underground

dung·hill \\'dəŋ-,hil\\ *n* : a manure pile

dunk \\'dəŋk\\ *vb* 1 : to dip or submerge temporarily in liquid 2 : to submerge oneself in water

duo \\'d(y)ü-(,)ō\\ *n, pl* **du·os** 1 : DUET 2 : PAIR

duo·dec·i·mal \\,d(y)ü-ə-'des-ə-məl\\ *adj* : of, relating to, or being a system of numbers with a base of 12

du·o·de·num \\,d(y)ü-ə-'dē-nəm, d(y)ü-'äd-ən-əm\\ *n, pl* **-de·na** \\-'dē-nə, -ən-ə\\ *or* **-denums** : the part of the small intestine extending from the stomach to the jejunum — **du·o·de·nal** \\-'dēn-əl, -ən-əl\\ *adj*

dup *abbr* 1 duplex 2 duplicate

¹**dupe** \\'d(y)üp\\ *n* : one who is easily deceived or cheated : FOOL

²**dupe** *vb* **duped; dup·ing** : to make a dupe of : DECEIVE, FOOL

du·ple \\'d(y)ü-pəl\\ *adj* : having two beats or a multiple of two beats to the measure (~ time)

du·plex \\'d(y)ü-,pleks\\ *adj* : DOUBLE

¹**duplex** *n* : something duplex; *esp* : a 2-family house

¹**du·pli·cate** \\'d(y)ü-pli-kət\\ *adj* 1 : consisting of or existing in two corresponding or identical parts or examples 2 : being the same as another

²**du·pli·cate** \\'d(y)ü-pli-,kāt\\ *vb* **-cat·ed; -cat·ing** 1 : to make double or twofold 2 : to make an exact copy of — **du·pli·ca·tion** \\,d(y)ü-pli-'kā-shən\\ *n*

³**du·pli·cate** \\-kət\\ *n* : a thing that exactly resembles another in appearance, pattern, or content : COPY

du·pli·ca·tor \\'d(y)ü-pli-,kāt-ər\\ *n* : COPIER

du·plic·i·ty \\d(y)ü-'plis-ət-ē\\ *n, pl* **-ties** : deception by pretending to feel and act one way while acting another

du·ra·ble \\'d(y)ür-ə-bəl\\ *adj* : able to exist for a long time without significant deterioration (~ clothing) — **du·ra·bil·i·ty** \\,d(y)ür-ə-'bil-ət-ē\\ *n*

durable press *n* : PERMANENT PRESS

du·rance \\'d(y)ür-əns\\ *n* : IMPRISONMENT

du·ra·tion \\d(y)ü-'rā-shən\\ *n* : the time during which something exists or lasts

du·ress \\d(y)ü-'res\\ *n* : compulsion by threat (confession made under ~)

dur·ing \\'d(y)ur-iŋ\\ *prep* 1 : THROUGHOUT (swims every day ~ the summer) 2 : at some point in (broke in ~ the night)

dusk \\'dəsk\\ *n* 1 : the darker part of twilight esp. at night 2 : partial darkness

dusk·y \\'dəs-kē\\ *adj* **dusk·i·er; -est** 1 : somewhat dark in color 2 : SHADOWY — **dusk·i·ness** *n*

¹**dust** \\'dəst\\ *n* 1 : particles of powdery matter 2 : the particles into which something disintegrates 3 : something worthless 4 : the surface of the ground — **dust·less** *adj* — **dust·y** *adj*

²**dust** *vb* 1 : to make free of or remove dust 2 : to sprinkle with fine particles 3 : to sprinkle in the form of dust

dust bowl *n* : a region suffering from long droughts and dust storms

dust devil *n* : a small whirlwind containing sand or dust

dust·er \\'dəs-tər\\ *n* 1 : one that removes dust 2 : a dress-length housecoat 3 : one that scatters fine particles; *esp* : a device for applying insecticides to crops

dust·pan \\'dəst-,pan\\ *n* : a shovelshaped pan for sweepings

dust storm *n* : a violent wind carrying dust across a dry region

dutch \\'dəch\\ *adv, often cap* : with each person paying his or her own way (go ~)

Dutch \\'dəch\ *n* **1** Dutch *pl* : the people of the Netherlands **2** : the language of the Netherlands — **Dutch** *adj* — **Dutch·man** \-mən\ *n*

Dutch elm disease *n* : a fungous disease of elms characterized by yellowing of the foliage, defoliation, and death

Dutch treat *n* : an entertainment (as a meal) for which each person pays his or her own way

du·te·ous \\'d(y)üt-ē-əs\ *adj* : DUTIFUL, OBEDIENT

du·ti·able \\'d(y)üt-ē-ə-bəl\ *adj* : subject to a duty ⟨∼ imports⟩

du·ti·ful \\'d(y)üt-i-fəl\ *adj* **1** : motivated by a sense of duty ⟨a ∼ son⟩ **2** : coming from or showing a sense of duty ⟨∼ affection⟩ — **du·ti·ful·ly** \-f(ə-)lē\ *adv* — **du·ti·ful·ness** *n*

du·ty \\'d(y)üt-ē\ *n, pl* **duties 1** : conduct or action required by one's occupation or position **2** : assigned service or business; *esp* : active military service **3** : a moral or legal obligation **4** : TAX **5** : the service required (as of a machine) : USE ⟨a heavy-*duty* tire⟩

DV *abbr* [L *Deo volente*] God willing **2** Douay Version

DVM *abbr* doctor of veterinary medicine

¹**dwarf** \\'dwȯrf\ *n, pl* **dwarfs** \\'dwȯ(ə)rfs\ *or* **dwarves** \\'dwȯrvz\ : one that is much below normal size — **dwarf·ish** *adj*

²**dwarf** *vb* **1** : to restrict the growth or development of : STUNT **2** : to cause to appear smaller ⟨people *dwarfed* by tall trees⟩

dwell \\'dwel\ *vb* **dwelt** \\'dwelt\ *or* **dwelled** \\'dweld, 'dwelt\ ; **dwell·ing** [ME *dwellen*, fr. OE *dwellan* to go astray, hinder] **1** : ABIDE, REMAIN **2** : RESIDE, EXIST **3** : to keep the attention directed **4** : to write or speak at length or insistently — **dwell·er** *n*

dwell·ing \\'dwel-iŋ\ *n* : RESIDENCE

DWI *abbr* driving while intoxicated

dwin·dle \\'dwin-d²l\ *vb* **dwin·dled**; **dwin·dling** \\'dwin-d(²-)liŋ\ : to make or become steadily less : DIMINISH

dwt *abbr* pennyweight

Dy *symbol* dysprosium

dyb·buk \\'dib-ək\ *n, pl* **dyb·bu·kim** \,dib-ù-'kēm\ *also* **dybbuks** : a wandering soul believed in Jewish folklore to enter and possess a person

¹**dye** \\'dī\ *n* **1** : color produced by dyeing **2** : material used for coloring or staining

²**dye** *vb* **dyed**; **dye·ing 1** : to impart a new color to esp. by impregnating with a dye **2** : to take up or impart color in dyeing

dye·stuff \\'dī-,stəf\ *n* : DYE 2

dying *pres part of* DIE

dyke *var of* DIKE

dy·nam·ic \dī-'nam-ik\ *also* **dy·nam·i·cal** \-i-kəl\ *adj* : of or relating to physical force producing motion : ENERGETIC, FORCEFUL

¹**dy·na·mite** \\'dī-nə-,mīt\ *n* : an explosive made of nitroglycerin absorbed in a porous material; *also* : a blasting explosive made without nitroglycerin

²**dynamite** *vb* **-mit·ed**; **-mit·ing** : to blow up with dynamite

dy·na·mo \\'dī-nə-,mō\ *n, pl* **-mos** : an electrical generator

dy·na·mom·e·ter \,dī-nə-'mäm-ət-ər\ *n* : an instrument for measuring mechanical power (as of an engine)

dy·nas·ty \\'dī-nəs-tē, -,nas-\ *n, pl* **-ties 1** : a succession of rulers of the same family **2** : a powerful group or family that maintains its position for a long time — **dy·nas·tic** \dī-'nas-tik\ *adj*

dys·en·tery \\'dis-³n-,ter-ē\ *n, pl* **-ter·ies** : a disorder marked by diarrhea with blood and mucus in the feces

dys·lex·ia \dis-'lek-sē-ə\ *n* : a disturbance of the ability to read — **dys·lex·ic** \-sik\ *adj or n*

dys·pep·sia \dis-'pep-shə, -sē-ə\ *n* : INDIGESTION — **dys·pep·tic** \-'pep-tik\ *adj or n*

dys·pro·si·um \dis-'prō-zē-əm\ *n* : a metallic chemical element that forms highly magnetic compounds

dys·tro·phy \\'dis-trə-fē\ *n, pl* **-phies** : any of several disorders involving atrophy of muscular tissue; *esp* : MUSCULAR DYSTROPHY

dz *abbr* dozen

E

¹**e** \\'ē\ *n, pl* **e's** *or* **es** \\'ēz\ *often cap* **1** : the 5th letter of the English alphabet **2** : the base of the system of natural logarithms having the approximate value 2.71828 **3** : a grade rating a student's work as poor or failing

²**e** *abbr, often cap* **1** east; eastern **2** error **3** excellent

E *symbol* einsteinium

ea *abbr* each

¹**each** \\'ēch\ *adj* : being one of the class named ⟨∼ man⟩

²**each** *pron* : every individual one

³**each** *adv* : APIECE ⟨cost five cents ∼⟩

each other *pron* : each of two or more in reciprocal action or relation ⟨looked at *each other*⟩

ea·ger \\'ē-gər\ *adj* : marked by urgent or enthusiastic desire or interest ⟨∼ to learn⟩ *syn* avid, anxious, ardent, keen — **ea·ger·ly** *adv* — **ea·ger·ness** *n*

ea·gle \\'ē-gəl\ *n* **1** : a large bird of prey related to the hawks **2** : a score of two under par on a hole in golf

ea·glet \\'ē-glət\ *n* : a young eagle

-ean — *see* -AN

E and OE *abbr* errors and omissions excepted

¹**ear** \ˈiər\ *n* **1** : the organ of hearing; *also* : the outer part of this in a vertebrate **2** : something resembling a mammal's ear in shape, position, or function **3** : an ability to understand and appreciate something heard (a good ∼ for music) **4** : sympathetic attention

²**ear** *n* : the fruiting spike of a cereal (as wheat)

ear·ache \-ˌāk\ *n* : an ache or pain in the ear

ear·drum \-ˌdrəm\ *n* : a thin membrane that receives and transmits sound waves in the ear

eared \ˈiərd\ *adj* : having ears — used esp. in combination (a long-*eared* dog)

earl \ˈərl\ *n* [ME *erl*, fr. OE *eorl* warrior, nobleman] : a member of the British peerage ranking below a marquess and above a viscount — **earl·dom** \-dəm\ *n*

ear·lobe \ˈiər-ˌlōb\ *n* : the pendent part of the ear

¹**ear·ly** \ˈər-lē\ *adv* **ear·li·er; -est** : at an early time (as in a period or series)

²**early** *adj* **ear·li·er; -est 1** : of, relating to, or occurring near the beginning **2** : ANCIENT, PRIMITIVE **3** : occurring before the usual time (an ∼ breakfast); *also* : occurring in the near future

¹**ear·mark** \ˈiər-ˌmärk\ *n* : an identification mark (as on the ear of an animal)

²**earmark** *vb* : to designate for a specific purpose

ear·muff \-ˌməf\ *n* : one of a pair of ear coverings worn as protection against cold

earn \ˈərn\ *vb* **1** : to receive as a return for service **2** : DESERVE, MERIT **syn** gain, secure, get, obtain, acquire, win

¹**ear·nest** \ˈər-nəst\ *n* : an intensely serious state of mind (spoke in ∼)

²**earnest** *adj* **1** : seriously intent and sober (an ∼ face) (an ∼ attempt) **2** : GRAVE, IMPORTANT **syn** solemn, sedate, staid, sober — **ear·nest·ly** *adv* — **ear·nest·ness** \-nəs(t)-nəs\ *n*

³**earnest** *n* **1** : something of value given by a buyer to a seller to bind a bargain **2** : PLEDGE

earn·ings \ˈər-niŋz\ *n pl* **1** : something (as wages) earned **2** : the balance of revenue after deduction of costs and expenses

ear·phone \ˈiər-ˌfōn\ *n* : a device that reproduces sound and is worn over or in the ear

ear·plug \-ˌpləg\ *n* : a protective device for insertion into the opening of the ear

ear·ring \-ˌriŋ\ *n* : an ornament for the earlobe

ear·shot \-ˌshät\ *n* : range of hearing

ear·split·ting \-ˌsplit-iŋ\ *adj* : intolerably loud or shrill

earth \ˈərth\ *n* **1** : SOIL, DIRT **2** : LAND, GROUND **3** : the planet inhabited by man : WORLD

earth·en \ˈər-thən\ *adj* : made of earth or baked clay

earth·en·ware \-ˌwaər\ *n* : slightly porous opaque pottery fired at low heat

earth·ling \ˈərth-liŋ\ *n* : an inhabitant of the earth

earth·ly \ˈərth-lē\ *adj* : having to do with the earth esp. as distinguished from heaven — **earth·li·ness** *n*

earth·quake \-ˌkwāk\ *n* : a shaking or trembling of a portion of the earth

earth science *n* : any of the sciences (as geology or meteorology) that deal with the earth or one of its parts

earth·shak·ing \ˈərth-ˌshā-kiŋ\ *adj* : of fundamental importance

earth·ward \-wərd\ *or* **earth·wards** \-wərdz\ *adv* : toward the earth

earth·work \ˈərth-ˌwərk\ *n* : an embankment or fortification of earth

earth·worm \-ˌwərm\ *n* : a long segmented worm found in damp soil

earthy \ˈər-thē\ *adj* **earth·i·er; -est 1** : consisting of or resembling soil **2** : PRACTICAL **3** : COARSE, GROSS — **earth·i·ness** \-thē-nəs\ *n*

ear·wax \ˈiər-ˌwaks\ *n* : the yellow waxy secretion from the ear

ear·wig \-ˌwig\ *n* : any of numerous insects with slender many-jointed antennae and a pair of appendages resembling forceps at the end of the body

¹**ease** \ˈēz\ *n* **1** : comfort of body or mind **2** : naturalness of manner **3** : freedom from difficulty or effort **syn** relaxation, rest, repose, comfort, leisure

²**ease** *vb* **eased; eas·ing 1** : to relieve from distress **2** : to lessen the pressure or tension of **3** : to make or become less difficult (∼ credit)

ea·sel \ˈē-zəl\ *n* [Dutch, lit., ass] : a frame to hold a painter's canvas or a picture

¹**east** \ˈēst\ *adv* : to or toward the east

²**east** *adj* **1** : situated toward or at the east **2** : coming from the east

³**east** *n* **1** : the general direction of sunrise **2** : the compass point directly opposite to west **3** *cap* : regions or countries east of a specified or implied point — **east·er·ly** \ˈē-stər-lē\ *adv or adj* — **east·ward** *adv or adj* — **east·wards** *adv*

Eas·ter \ˈē-stər\ *n* : a church feast observed on a Sunday in March or April in commemoration of Christ's resurrection

east·ern \ˈē-stərn\ *adj* **1** *often cap* : of, relating to, or characteristic of a region designated East **2** *cap* : of, relating to, or being the Christian churches originating in the Church of the Eastern Roman Empire **3** : lying toward or coming from the east — **East·ern·er** *n*

easy \ˈē-zē\ *adj* **eas·i·er; -est 1** : marked by ease (an ∼ life) ; *esp* : not causing distress or difficulty (∼ tasks) **2** : MILD, LENIENT (be ∼ on him) **3**

: GRADUAL ⟨an ~ slope⟩ **4** : free from pain, trouble, or worry ⟨rest ~⟩ **5** : LEISURELY ⟨an ~ pace⟩ **6** : NATURAL ⟨an ~ manner⟩ **7** : COMFORTABLE ⟨an ~ chair⟩ syn facile, simple, effortless — **eas·i·ly** \'ēz-(ə-)lē\ adv — **eas·i·ness** \-ē-nəs\ n

easy·go·ing \ˌē-zē-'gō-iŋ\ adj : taking life easy : CAREFREE

eat \'ēt\ vb **ate** \'āt\; **eat·en** \'ēt-ᵊn\; **eat·ing** **1** : to take in as food : take food **2** : to use up : DEVOUR **3** : COR-RODE — **eat·able** adj or n — **eat·er** n

eat·ery \'ēt-ə-rē\ n, pl **-er·ies** : LUN-CHEONETTE, RESTAURANT

eaves \'ēvz\ n pl : the overhanging low-er edge of a roof

eaves·drop \'ēvz-ˌdräp\ vb : to listen secretly — **eaves·drop·per** n

¹**ebb** \'eb\ n **1** : the flowing back of wa-ter brought in by the tide **2** : a point or state of decline

²**ebb** vb **1** : to recede from the flood state **2** : DECLINE ⟨as his fortunes ~ed⟩

EBCDIC \'ep-sə-ˌdik\ n [extended binary coded decimal interchange code] : a computer code for repre-senting alphanumeric information

eb·o·ny \'eb-ə-nē\ n, pl **-nies** : a hard heavy wood of Old World tropical trees (**ebony trees**) related to the per-simmon

²**ebony** adj **1** : made of or resembling ebony **2** : BLACK, DARK

ebul·lient \i-'bul-yənt, -'bəl-\ adj **1** : BOILING, AGITATED **2** : EXUBERANT — **ebul·lience** \-yəns\ n

ec·cen·tric \ik-'sen-trik\ adj **1** : deviat-ing from a usual or accepted pattern **2** : deviating from a circular path ⟨~ or-bits⟩ **3** : set with axis or support off center ⟨an ~ cam⟩ ; also : being off center syn erratic, queer, singular, curious, odd — **eccentric** n — **ec·cen·tri·cal·ly** \-tri-k(ə-)lē\ adv — **ec·cen·tric·i·ty** \ˌek-ˌsen-'tris-ət-ē\ n

Eccles abbr Ecclesiastes

Ec·cle·si·as·tes \ik-ˌklē-zē-'as-tēz\ — see BIBLE table

ec·cle·si·as·tic \ik-ˌklē-zē-'as-tik\ n : CLERGYMAN

ec·cle·si·as·ti·cal \-ti-kəl\ or **ec·cle·si·as·tic** \-tik\ adj : of or relating to a church esp. as an institution ⟨~ art⟩ — **ec·cle·si·as·ti·cal·ly** \-ti-k(ə-)lē\ adv

Ec·cle·si·as·ti·cus \ik-ˌklē-zē-'as-ti-kəs\ n — see BIBLE table

Ecclus abbr Ecclesiasticus

ECG abbr electrocardiogram

ech·e·lon \'esh-ə-ˌlän\ n [F échelon, lit., rung of a ladder] **1** : a steplike ar-rangement (as of troops or airplanes) **2** : a level (as of authority or respon-sibility) within an organization

echi·no·derm \i-'kī-nə-ˌdərm\ n : any of a phylum of marine animals (as star-fishes and sea urchins) having similar body parts (as the arms of a starfish) arranged around a central axis and of-ten having a calcium-containing outer skeleton

echo \'ek-ō\ n, pl **ech·oes** : repetition of a sound caused by a reflection of the sound waves; also : the reflection of a radar signal by an object — **echo** vb

echo·lo·ca·tion \ˌek-ō-lō-'kā-shən\ n : a process for locating distant or invisi-ble objects by means of sound waves reflected back to the sender (as a bat or submarine) by the objects

éclair \ā-'klaər\ n [F, lit., lightning] : an oblong shell of light pastry with whipped cream or custard filling

éclat \ā-'klä\ n [F] **1** : a dazzling effect or success **2** : ACCLAIM

eclec·tic \e-'klek-tik, i-\ adj : selecting or made up of what seems best of var-ied sources — **eclectic** n

¹**eclipse** \i-'klips\ n **1** : the total or partial obscuring of one heavenly body by another; also : a passing into the shadow of a heavenly body **2** : a fall-ing into obscurity, decline, or dis-grace

²**eclipse** vb **eclipsed**; **eclips·ing** : to cause an eclipse of

eclip·tic \i-'klip-tik\ n : the great circle of the celestial sphere that is the ap-parent path of the sun

ec·logue \'ek-ˌlóg, -ˌläg\ n : a pastoral poem

ECM abbr European Common Market

ecol abbr ecological; ecology

ecol·o·gy \i-'käl-ə-jē, e-\ n, pl **-gies** [G ōkologie, fr. Gk oikos house] **1** : a branch of science concerned with the relationships between organisms and their environment **2** : the pattern of relations between organisms and their environment — **eco·log·i·cal** \ˌē-kə-'läj-i-kəl, ˌek-ə-\ also **eco·log·ic** \-ik\ adj — **eco·log·i·cal·ly** \-i-k(ə-)lē\ adv — **ecol·o·gist** \i-'käl-ə-jəst, e-\ n

econ abbr economics; economist; econ-omy

eco·nom·ic \ˌek-ə-'näm-ik, ˌē-kə-\ adj : of or relating to the satisfaction of material needs of humans

eco·nom·i·cal \-'näm-i-kəl\ adj **1** : THRIFTY **2** : operating with little waste or at a saving syn frugal, spar-ing, provident, thrifty — **eco·nom·i·cal·ly** \-k(ə-)lē\ adv

eco·nom·ics \ˌek-ə-'näm-iks, ˌē-kə-\ n : a branch of knowledge dealing with the production, distribution, and con-sumption of goods and services — **econ·o·mist** \i-'kän-ə-məst\ n

econ·o·mize \i-'kän-ə-ˌmīz\ vb **-mized**; **-miz·ing** : to practice economy : be frugal

¹**econ·o·my** \i-'kän-ə-mē\ n, pl **-mies** [MF yconomie, fr. ML oeconomia, fr. Gk oikonomia, fr. oikonomos household manager, fr. oikos house + nemein to manage] **1** : thrifty management or use of resources; also : an instance of this **2** : manner of arrangement or functioning : ORGANIZATION **3** : an economic system ⟨a money ~⟩

²**economy** adj : ECONOMICAL ⟨~ cars⟩

eco·sys·tem \'ē-kō-ˌsis-təm, 'ek-ō-\ n

: the complex of an ecological community and its environment functioning as a unit in nature

ecru \'ek-rü, 'ā-krü\ *n* [F *écru* unbleached] : BEIGE

ec·sta·sy \'ek-stə-sē\ *n, pl* **-sies** : extreme and usu. rapturous emotional excitement — **ec·stat·ic** \ek-'stat-ik, ik-'stat-\ *adj* — **ec·stat·i·cal·ly** \-i-k(ə-)lē\ *adv*

Ecua *abbr* Ecuador

ec·u·men·i·cal \ˌek-yə-'men-i-kəl\ *adj* : general in extent or influence; *esp* : promoting or tending toward worldwide Christian unity — **ec·u·men·i·cal·ly** \-k(ə-)lē\ *adv*

ec·ze·ma \ig-'zē-mə, 'eg-zə-mə, 'ek-sə-\ *n* : an itching skin inflammation with crusted lesions — **ec·zem·a·tous** \ig-'zem-ət-əs\ *adj*

ed *abbr* 1 edited; edition; editor 2 education

¹**-ed** \d *after a vowel or* b, g, j, l, m, n, ŋ, r, th, v, z, zh; əd, id *after* d, t; t *after other sounds*\ *vb suffix or adj suffix* 1 — used to form the past participle of regular weak verbs (ended) (faded) (tried) (patted) 2 — used to form adjectives of identical meaning from Latin-derived adjectives ending in *-ate* (pinnated) 3 : having : characterized by (cultured) (two-legged) ; *also* : having the characteristics of (bigoted)

²**-ed** *vb suffix* — used to form the past tense of regular weak verbs (judged) (denied) (dropped)

Edam \'ēd-əm, 'ē-ˌdam\ *n* : a yellow Dutch pressed cheese made in balls

ed·dy \'ed-ē\ *n, pl* **eddies** : WHIRLPOOL — **eddy** *vb*

edel·weiss \'ād-ᵊl-ˌwīs, -ˌvīs\ *n* [G, fr. *edel* noble + *weiss* white] : a small perennial woolly herb that is related to the thistles and grows high in the Alps

edema \i-'dē-mə\ *n* : abnormal accumulation of watery fluid in connective tissue or in a serous cavity; *also* : a condition marked by such accumulation — **edem·a·tous** \-'dem-ət-əs\ *adj*

Eden \'ēd-ᵊn\ *n* : PARADISE 2

¹**edge** \'ej\ *n* 1 : the cutting side of a blade 2 : power to cut or penetrate : SHARPNESS 3 : the line where something begins or ends; *also* : the area adjoining such an edge 4 : ADVANTAGE — **edged** \'ejd\ *adj*

²**edge** *vb* **edged; edg·ing** 1 : to give or form an edge 2 : to move or force gradually (~ into a crowd) — **edg·er** *n*

edge·ways \'ej-ˌwāz\ *adv* : SIDEWAYS

edg·ing \'ej-iŋ\ *n* : something that forms an edge or border (a lace ~)

edgy \'ej-ē\ *adj* **edg·i·er; -est** 1 : SHARP (an ~ tone) 2 : TENSE, NERVOUS — **edg·i·ness** \'ej-ē-nəs\ *n*

ed·i·ble \'ed-ə-bəl\ *adj* : fit or safe to be eaten — **ed·i·bil·i·ty** \ˌed-ə-'bil-ət-ē\ *n* — **edible** *n*

edict \'ē-ˌdikt\ *n* : DECREE

ed·i·fi·ca·tion \ˌed-ə-fə-'kā-shən\ *n* : instruction and improvement esp. in morality — **ed·i·fy** \'ed-ə-ˌfī\ *vb*

ed·i·fice \'ed-ə-fəs\ *n* : a usu. large building

ed·it \'ed-ət\ *vb* 1 : to revise and prepare for publication 2 : to direct the publication and policies of (as a newspaper) — **ed·i·tor** \'ed-ət-ər\ *n* — **ed·i·tor·ship** *n*

edi·tion \i-'dish-ən\ *n* 1 : the form in which a text is published 2 : the total number of copies (as of a book) published at one time 3 : VERSION

¹**ed·i·to·ri·al** \ˌed-ə-'tōr-ē-əl\ *adj* 1 : of, relating to, or functioning as an editor 2 : being an editorial; *also* : expressing opinion — **ed·i·to·ri·al·ly** \-ē\ *adv*

²**editorial** *n* : an article (as in a newspaper) giving the views of a publisher; *also* : an expression of opinion resembling an editorial (a television ~)

ed·i·to·ri·al·ize \ˌed-ə-'tōr-ē-ə-ˌlīz\ *vb* **-ized; -iz·ing** 1 : to express an opinion in an editorial 2 : to introduce opinions into factual reporting 3 : to express an opinion — **ed·i·to·ri·al·iza·tion** \-ˌtōr-ē-ə-lə-'zā-shən\ *n* — **ed·i·to·ri·al·iz·er** *n*

EDP *abbr* electronic data processing

EDT *abbr* Eastern daylight (saving) time

educ *abbr* education; educational

ed·u·ca·ble \'ej-ə-kə-bəl\ *adj* : capable of being educated

ed·u·cate \'ej-ə-ˌkāt\ *vb* **-cat·ed; -cat·ing** 1 : to provide with schooling 2 : to develop mentally and morally **syn** train, discipline, school, instruct, teach — **ed·u·ca·tor** \-ˌkāt-ər\ *n*

ed·u·ca·tion \ˌej-ə-'kā-shən\ *n* 1 : the action or process of educating or being educated 2 : a field of knowledge dealing with technical aspects of teaching — **ed·u·ca·tion·al** \-sh(ə-)nəl\ *adj*

educational television *n* : PUBLIC TELEVISION

educe \i-'d(y)üs\ *vb* **educed; educ·ing** 1 : ELICIT, EVOKE 2 : DEDUCE **syn** extract, evince, extort

EE *abbr* electrical engineer

EEC *abbr* European Economic Community

EEG *abbr* 1 electroencephalogram 2 electroencephalograph

eel \'ēl\ *n* : any of numerous snakelike fishes with a smooth slimy skin

EEO *abbr* equal employment opportunity

ee·rie *also* **ee·ry** \'i(ə)r-ē\ *adj* **ee·ri·er; -est** : WEIRD, UNCANNY — **ee·ri·ly** \'ir-ə-lē\ *adv*

eff *abbr* efficiency

ef·face \i-'fās, e-\ *vb* **ef·faced; ef·fac·ing** : to obliterate or obscure by or as if by rubbing out **syn** erase, delete, annul, cancel, expunge — **ef·face·able** *adj* — **ef·face·ment** *n*

¹**ef·fect** \i-'fekt\ *n* 1 : RESULT 2 : MEANING, INTENT 3 : APPEARANCE 4 : FUL-

FILLMENT **5** : INFLUENCE **6** *pl* : GOODS, POSSESSIONS **7** : the quality or state of being operative : OPERATION *syn* consequence, outcome, upshot, aftermath, result, issue

²**effect** *vb* **1** : ACCOMPLISH (~ repairs) **2** : to put into effect (~ changes)

ef·fec·tive \i-'fek-tiv\ *adj* **1** : producing a decisive or desired effect **2** : IMPRESSIVE, STRIKING **3** : ready for service or action **4** : being in effect — **ef·fec·tive·ly** *adv* — **ef·fec·tive·ness** *n*

ef·fec·tu·al \i-'fek-chə-(-wə)l\ *adj* : producing an intended effect : ADEQUATE — **ef·fec·tu·al·ly** \-ē\ *adv*

ef·fec·tu·ate \i-'fek-chə-ˌwāt\ *vb* **-at·ed; -at·ing** : BRING ABOUT, EFFECT

ef·fem·i·nate \ə-'fem-ə-nət\ *adj* : marked by qualities more typical of and suitable to women than men; : UNMANLY \ē-'fen-dē\ — **ef·fem·i·na·cy** \-nə-sē\ *n*

ef·fen·di \e-'fen-dē\ *n* [Turk *efendi* master, fr. NGk *aphentēs*, alter. of Gk *authentēs*] : a man of property, authority, or education in an eastern Mediterranean country

ef·fer·ent \'ef-ə-rənt\ *adj* : bearing or conducting outward from a more central part (~ nerves)

ef·fer·vesce \ˌef-ər-'ves\ *vb* **-vesced; -vesc·ing** : to bubble and hiss as gas escapes; *also* : to be exhilarated — **ef·fer·ves·cence** \-'ves-ᵊns\ *n* — **ef·fer·ves·cent** \-ᵊnt\ *adj* — **ef·fer·ves·cent·ly** *adv*

ef·fete \e-'fēt\ *adj* : worn out : EXHAUSTED; *also* : DECADENT

ef·fi·ca·cious \ˌef-ə-'kā-shəs\ *adj* : producing an intended effect (~ remedies) *syn* effectual, effective, efficient — **ef·fi·ca·cy** \'ef-i-kə-sē\ *n*

ef·fi·cient \i-'fish-ənt\ *adj* : productive of desired effects esp. without loss or waste : COMPETENT — **ef·fi·cien·cy** \-ən-sē\ *n* — **ef·fi·cient·ly** *adv*

ef·fi·gy \'ef-ə-jē\ *n, pl* **-gies** : IMAGE; *esp* : a crude figure of a hated person

ef·flo·resce \ˌef-lə-'res\ *vb* **-resced; -resc·ing** : to burst forth : BLOOM

ef·flo·res·cence \-'res-ᵊns\ *n* **1** : the period or state of flowering **2** : the action or process of developing **3** : fullness of manifestation : CULMINATION — **ef·flo·res·cent** \-ᵊnt\ *adj*

ef·flu·ence \'ef-ˌlü-əns\ *n* **1** : something that flows out **2** : an action or process of flowing out — **ef·flu·ent** \-ənt\ *adj or n*

ef·flu·vi·um \e-'flü-vē-əm\ *n, pl* **-via** \-vē-ə\ *or* **-vi·ums** [L outflow] **1** : a usu. unpleasant emanation **2** : a by-product usu. in the form of waste

ef·fort \'ef-ərt\ *n* **1** : EXERTION, ENDEAVOR; *also* : a product of effort **2** : active or applied force — **ef·fort·less** *adj* — **ef·fort·less·ly** *adv*

ef·fron·tery \i-'frənt-ə-rē\ *n, pl* **-ter·ies** : shameless boldness : IMPUDENCE *syn* temerity, audacity, brass, gall, nerve

ef·ful·gence \i-'fùl-jəns, -'fəl-\ *n* : radi-

ant splendor : BRILLIANCE — **ef·ful·gent** \-jənt\ *adj*

ef·fu·sion \i-'fyü-zhən, e-\ *n* : a gushing forth; *also* : unrestrained utterance — **ef·fuse** \-'fyüz, e-\ *vb* — **ef·fu·sive** \i-'fyü-siv, e-\ *adj*

eft \'eft\ *n* : NEWT

EFT *or* **EFTS** *abbr* electronic funds transfer (system)

e.g. \f(ə-)rig-'zam-pəl, (')ē-'jē\ *abbr* [L *exempli gratia*] for example

Eg *abbr* Egypt; Egyptian

egal·i·tar·i·an·ism \i-ˌgal-ə-'ter-ē-ə-ˌniz-əm\ *n* : a belief in human equality esp. in social, political, and economic affairs — **egal·i·tar·i·an** *adj or n*

¹**egg** \'eg\ *vb* [ME, fr. ON *eggja*; akin to OE *ecg* edge] : to urge to action

²**egg** *n* [ME *egge*, fr. ON *egg*; akin to OE *æg* egg, L *ovum*] **1** : a rounded usu. hard-shelled reproductive body esp. of birds and reptiles from which the young hatches; *also* : the egg of domestic poultry as an article of food (allergic to ~s) **2** : a germ cell produced by a female

egg·beat·er \'eg-ˌbēt-ər\ *n* : a hand-operated kitchen utensil for beating, stirring, or whipping

egg cell *n* : EGG 2

egg·head \-ˌhed\ *n* : INTELLECTUAL, HIGHBROW

egg·nog \-ˌnäg\ *n* : a drink consisting of eggs beaten up with sugar, milk or cream, and often alcoholic liquor

egg·plant \-ˌplant\ *n* : the edible usu. large and purplish fruit of a plant related to the potato; *also* : the plant

egg roll *n* : a thin egg-dough casing filled with minced vegetables and often bits of meat and usu. fried in deep fat

egg·shell \'eg-ˌshel\ *n* : the hard exterior or covering of an egg

egis \'ē-jəs\ *var of* AEGIS

eg·lan·tine \'eg-lən-ˌtīn, -ˌtēn\ *n* : SWEETBRIER

ego \'ē-gō\ *n, pl* **egos** [L, I] **1** : the self as distinguished from others **2** : the one of the three divisions of the psyche in psychoanalytic theory that serves as the organized conscious mediator between the person and reality

ego·cen·tric \ˌē-gō-'sen-trik\ *adj* : concerned or overly concerned with the self; *esp* : SELF-CENTERED

ego·ism \'ē-gə-ˌwiz-əm\ *n* **1** : a doctrine holding self-interest to be the motive or the valid end of action **2** : excessive concern for oneself usu. without exaggerated feelings of self-importance — **ego·ist** \-wəst\ *n* — **ego·is·tic** \ˌē-gə-'wis-tik\ *adj* — **ego·is·ti·cal·ly** \-ē\ *adv*

ego·tism \'ē-gə-ˌtiz-əm\ *n* **1** : the practice of talking about oneself too much **2** : an exaggerated sense of self-importance : CONCEIT — **ego·tist** \-təst\ *n* — **ego·tis·tic** \ˌē-gə-'tis-tik\ *or* **ego·tis-**

ti·cal \-ti-kəl\ *adj* — **ego·tis·ti·cal·ly** \-ē\ *adv*

ego trip *n* : an act that enhances and satisfies one's ego

egre·gious \i-ˈgrē-jəs\ *adj* [L *egregius* outstanding from the herd, fr. *ex*, *e* out of + *greg-*, *grex* flock, herd] : notably bad : FLAGRANT — **egre·gious·ly** *adv* — **egre·gious·ness** *n*

egress \ˈē-ˌgres\ *n* : a way out : EXIT

egret \ˈē-grət, i-ˈgret\ *n* : any of various herons that bear long plumes during the breeding season

Egyp·tian \i-ˈjip-shən\ *n* 1 : a native or inhabitant of Egypt 2 : the language of the ancient Egyptians from earliest times to about the 3d century A.D. — **Egyptian** *adj*

EHF *abbr* extremely high frequency

ei·der \ˈīd-ər\ *n* : any of several northern sea ducks that yield a soft down

ei·der·down \-ˌdaùn\ *n* 1 : the down of the eider 2 : a quilt filled with eiderdown

ei·do·lon \ī-ˈdō-lən\ *n, pl* **-lons** *or* **-la** \-lə\ 1 : an insubstantial image : PHANTOM 2 : IDEAL

eight \ˈāt\ *n* 1 : one more than seven 2 : the 8th in a set or series 3 : something having eight units; *esp* : an 8-cylinder engine or automobile — **eight** *adj or pron* — **eighth** \ˈātth\ *adj or adv or n*

eight ball *n* : a black pool ball numbered 8 — **behind the eight ball** : in a highly disadvantageous position or baffling situation

eigh·teen \ˈā(t)-ˈtēn\ *n* : one more than 17 — **eighteen** *adj or pron* — **eigh·teenth** \-ˈtēnth\ *adj or n*

eighty \ˈāt-ē\ *n, pl* **eight·ies** : eight times 10 — **eight·i·eth** \ˈāt-ē-əth\ *adj or n* — **eighty** *adj or pron*

ein·stein·i·um \īn-ˈstī-nē-əm\ *n* : an artificially produced radioactive element

¹**ei·ther** \ˈē-thər, ˈī-\ *adj* 1 : being the one and the other of two : EACH ⟨trees on ∼ side⟩ 2 : being the one or the other of two ⟨take ∼ road⟩

²**either** *pron* : the one or the other

³**either** *conj* — used as a function word before the first of two or more words or word groups of which the last is preceded by *or* to indicate that they represent alternatives ⟨a statement is ∼ true or false⟩

ejac·u·late \i-ˈjak-yə-ˌlāt\ *vb* **-lat·ed; -lat·ing** 1 : to eject a fluid (as semen) 2 : to utter suddenly : EXCLAIM — **ejac·u·la·tion** \-ˌjak-yə-ˈlā-shən\ *n* — **ejac·u·la·to·ry** \-ˈjak-yə-lə-ˌtōr-ē\ *adj*

eject \i-ˈjekt\ *vb* : to drive or throw out or off **syn** expel, oust, evict, dismiss — **ejec·tion** \-ˈjek-shən\ *n*

ejection seat *n* : an emergency escape seat for propelling an occupant out of an airplane

eke \ˈēk\ *vb* **eked; ek·ing** : to gain, supplement, or extend usu. with effort — usu. used with *out* ⟨∼ out a living⟩

EKG *abbr* [G *elektrokardiogramm*] 1

: electrocardiogram 2 : electrocardiograph

ekue·le \ā-ˈkwā-(ˌ)lā\ *n, pl* **ekuele** — see MONEY table

el *abbr* elevation

¹**elab·o·rate** \i-ˈlab-(ə-)rət\ *adj* 1 : planned or carried out with care and in detail 2 : being complex and usu. ornate — **elab·o·rate·ly** *adv* — **elab·o·rate·ness** *n*

²**elab·o·rate** \i-ˈlab-ə-ˌrāt\ *vb* **-rat·ed; -rat·ing** 1 : to build up from simpler ingredients 2 : to work out in detail : develop fully — **elab·o·ra·tion** \-ˌlab-ə-ˈrā-shən\ *n*

élan \ā-ˈläⁿ\ *n* [F] : ARDOR, SPIRIT

eland \ˈē-lənd, -ˌland\ *n, pl* **eland** *also* **elands** [Afrikaans, elk] : either of two large African antelopes with spirally twisted horns

elapse \i-ˈlaps\ *vb* **elapsed; elaps·ing** : to slip by : PASS

¹**elas·tic** \i-ˈlas-tik\ *adj* 1 : SPRINGY 2 : FLEXIBLE, PLIABLE 3 : ADAPTABLE **syn** resilient, supple, stretch — **elas·tic·i·ty** \-ˌlas-ˈtis-ət-ē, ˌē-ˌlas-\ *n*

²**elastic** *n* 1 : elastic material 2 : a rubber band

elate \i-ˈlāt\ *vb* **elat·ed; elat·ing** : to fill with joy — **ela·tion** \-ˈlā-shən\ *n*

¹**el·bow** \ˈel-ˌbō\ *n* 1 : the joint of the arm; *also* : the outer curve of the bent arm 2 : a bend or joint resembling an elbow in shape

²**elbow** *vb* : to push aside with the elbow; *also* : to make one's way by elbowing

el·bow·room \ˈel-ˌbō-ˌrüm, -ˌrùm\ *n* 1 : room for moving the elbows freely 2 : enough space for work or operation

¹**el·der** \ˈel-dər\ *n* : ELDERBERRY 2

²**elder** *adj* 1 : OLDER 2 : EARLIER, FORMER 3 : of higher rank : SENIOR

³**elder** *n* 1 : an older individual : SENIOR 2 : one having authority by reason of age and experience 3 : a church officer

el·der·ber·ry \ˈel-də(r)-ˌber-ē\ *n* 1 : the edible black or red fruit of a shrub or tree related to the honeysuckle and bearing flat clusters of small white or pink flowers 2 : a tree or shrub bearing elderberries

el·der·ly \ˈel-dər-lē\ *adj* 1 : rather old; *esp* : past middle age 2 : of, relating to, or characteristic of later life

el·dest \ˈel-dəst\ *adj* : of the greatest age

El Do·ra·do \ˌel-də-ˈräd-ō, -ˈrad-\ *n* [Sp, lit., the gilded one] : a place of vast riches or abundance

elec *abbr* electric; electrical; electricity

¹**elect** \i-ˈlekt\ *adj* 1 : CHOSEN, SELECT 2 : elected but not yet installed in office ⟨the president-*elect*⟩

²**elect** *n, pl* **elect** 1 : a selected person 2 *pl* : a select or exclusive group

³**elect** *vb* 1 : to select by vote (as for office or membership) 2 : CHOOSE, PICK **syn** prefer, select

elec·tion \i-ˈlek-shən\ *n* 1 : an act or

process of electing **2** : the fact of being elected

elec·tion·eer \i-ˌlek-shə-ˈniər\ *vb* : to work for the election of a candidate or party

¹elec·tive \i-ˈlek-tiv\ *adj* **1** : chosen or filled by election **2** : permitting a choice : OPTIONAL

²elective *n* : an elective course or subject of study

elec·tor \i-ˈlek-tər\ *n* **1** : one qualified to vote in an election **2** : one elected to an electoral college — **elec·tor·al** \i-ˈlek-t(ə-)rəl\ *adj*

electoral college *n* : a body of electors who elect the president and vice president of the U.S.

elec·tor·ate \i-ˈlek-t(ə-)rət\ *n* : a body of persons entitled to vote

elec·tric \i-ˈlek-trik\ *or* **elec·tri·cal** \-tri-kəl\ *adj* [NL *electricus* produced from amber by friction, electric, fr. ML, of amber, fr. L *electrum* amber, fr. Gk *ēlektron*] **1** : of, relating to, operated by, or produced by electricity **2** : ELECTRIFYING, THRILLING — **elec·tri·cal·ly** \-k(ə-)lē\ *adv*

electrical storm *n* : THUNDERSTORM

electric chair *n* : a chair used in legal electrocution

electric eye *n* : PHOTOELECTRIC CELL

elec·tri·cian \i-ˌlek-ˈtrish-ən\ *n* : one who installs, operates, or repairs electrical equipment

elec·tric·i·ty \i-ˌlek-ˈtris-(ə-)tē\ *n, pl* **-ties 1** : a form of energy that occurs in nature and is observable in natural phenomena (as lightning) and that can be produced by friction, chemical reaction, or mechanical effort **2** : electric current

elec·tri·fy \i-ˈlek-trə-ˌfī\ *vb* **-fied; -fy·ing 1** : to charge with electricity **2** : to equip for use of electric power **3** : THRILL — **elec·tri·fi·ca·tion** \-ˌlek-trə-fə-ˈkā-shən\ *n*

elec·tro·car·dio·gram \i-ˌlek-trō-ˈkärd-ē-ə-ˌgram\ *n* : the tracing made by an electrocardiograph

elec·tro·car·dio·graph \-ˌgraf\ *n* : an instrument for recording the changes of electrical potential occurring during the heartbeat — **elec·tro·car·dio·graph·ic** \-ˌkärd-ē-ə-ˈgraf-ik\ *adj* — **elec·tro·car·di·og·ra·phy** \-ē-ˈäg-rə-fē\ *n*

elec·tro·chem·is·try \-ˈkem-ə-strē\ *n* : a branch of chemistry that deals with the relation of electricity to chemical changes — **elec·tro·chem·i·cal** \-ˈkem-i-kəl\ *adj*

elec·tro·cute \i-ˈlek-trə-ˌkyüt\ *vb* **-cut·ed; -cut·ing** : to kill by an electric shock; *esp* : to kill (a criminal) in this way — **elec·tro·cu·tion** \-ˌlek-trə-ˈkyü-shən\ *n*

elec·trode \i-ˈlek-ˌtrōd\ *n* : a conductor used to establish electrical contact with a nonmetallic part of a circuit

elec·tro·en·ceph·a·lo·gram \-in-ˈsef-ə-lə-ˌgram\ *n* : the tracing of

the electrical activity of the brain that is made by an electroencephalograph

elec·tro·en·ceph·a·lo·graph \-ˌgraf\ *n* : an apparatus for detecting and recording the electrical activity of the brain — **elec·tro·en·ceph·a·lo·graph·ic** \-ˌsef-ə-lə-ˈgraf-ik\ *adj* — **elec·tro·en·ceph·a·log·ra·phy** \-ˈläg-rə-fē\ *n*

elec·trol·o·gist \i-ˌlek-ˈträl-ə-jəst\ *n* : one that uses electrical means to remove hair, warts, moles, and birthmarks from the body

elec·trol·y·sis \i-ˌlek-ˈträl-ə-səs\ *n* **1** : the production of chemical changes by passage of an electric current through an electrolyte **2** : the destruction of hair roots with an electric current — **elec·tro·lyt·ic** \-trə-ˈlit-ik\ *adj*

elec·tro·lyte \i-ˈlek-trə-ˌlīt\ *n* : a nonmetallic electric conductor in which current is carried by the movement of ions; *also* : a substance whose solution or molten form is such a conductor

elec·tro·mag·net \i-ˌlek-trō-ˈmag-nət\ *n* : a core of magnetic material surrounded by a coil of wire through which an electric current is passed to magnetize the core

elec·tro·mag·net·ic \-mag-ˈnet-ik\ *adj* : of, relating to, or produced by electromagnetism

electromagnetic radiation *n* : a series of electromagnetic waves

electromagnetic wave *n* : a wave (as a radio wave, an X ray, or a wave of visible light) that consists of associated electric and magnetic effects and that travels at the speed of light

elec·tro·mag·ne·tism \i-ˌlek-trō-ˈmag-nə-ˌtiz-əm\ *n* **1** : magnetism developed by a current of electricity **2** : physics dealing with the relations between electricity and magnetism

elec·tro·mo·tive force \i-ˌlek-trə-ˌmōt-iv-\ *n* : the work per unit charge required to carry a positive charge around a closed path in an electric field

elec·tron \i-ˈlek-ˌträn\ *n* : a negatively charged elementary particle that forms the part of an atom outside the nucleus

elec·tron·ic \i-ˌlek-ˈträn-ik\ *adj* : of or relating to electrons or electronics — **elec·tron·i·cal·ly** \-i-k(ə-)lē\ *adv*

electronic mail *n* : messages sent and received electronically

elec·tron·ics \i-ˌlek-ˈträn-iks\ *n* **1** : the physics of electrons and their utilization **2** : electronic devices or equipment

electron microscope *n* : an instrument in which a focused beam of electrons is used to produce an enlarged image of a minute object on a fluorescent screen or photographic plate

electron tube *n* : a device in which electrical conduction by electrons takes place within a container and which is used for the controlled flow of electrons

elec·tro·pho·re·sis \i-ˌlek-trə-fə-ˈrē-səs\ n : the movement of suspended particles through a fluid by an electromotive force — **elec·tro·pho·ret·ic** \-ˈret-ik\ adj

elec·tro·plate \i-ˈlek-trə-ˌplāt\ vb : to coat (as with metal) by electrolysis

elec·tro·pos·i·tive \i-ˌlek-trō-ˈpäz-ət-iv\ adj : having a tendency to give up electrons

elec·tro·shock therapy \-trō-ˌshäk-\ n : the treatment of mental disorder by the induction of coma with an electric current

elec·tro·stat·ics \i-ˌlek-trə-ˈstat-iks\ n : physics dealing with the interactions of stationary electric charges

el·ee·mos·y·nary \ˌel-i-ˈmäs-ᵊn-ˌer-ē\ adj : CHARITABLE

el·e·gance \ˈel-i-gəns\ n 1 : refined gracefulness; also : tasteful richness (as of design) 2 : something marked by elegance — **el·e·gant** \-gənt\ adj — **el·e·gant·ly** adv

el·e·gy \ˈel-ə-jē\ n, pl **-gies** : a poem expressing grief for one who is dead; also : a reflective poem usu. melancholy in tone — **el·e·gi·ac** \ˌel-ə-ˈjī-ək, -ˌak\ adj

elem abbr elementary

el·e·ment \ˈel-ə-mənt\ n 1 pl : weather conditions; esp : severe weather (boards exposed to the ∼s) 2 : natural environment (in her ∼) 3 : a constituent part 4 pl : the simplest principles (as of an art or science) : RUDIMENTS 5 : a basic member of a mathematical set 6 : a substance not separable into substances different from itself syn component, ingredient, factor, constituent — **el·e·men·tal** \ˌel-ə-ˈment-ᵊl\ adj

el·e·men·ta·ry \ˌel-ə-ˈmen-t(ə-)rē\ adj : SIMPLE, RUDIMENTARY; also : of, relating to, or teaching the basic subjects of education

elementary particle n : a subatomic particle (as the electron or photon) of matter and energy that does not appear to be made up of other smaller particles

elementary school n : a school usu. including the first six or the first eight grades

el·e·phant \ˈel-ə-fənt\ n : any of a family of huge thickset nearly hairless mammals that have the snout lengthened into a trunk and two long curving pointed tusks which furnish ivory

el·e·phan·ti·a·sis \ˌel-ə-fən-ˈtī-ə-səs\ n, pl **-a·ses** \-ˌsēz\ : enlargement and thickening of tissues in response esp. to infection by minute parasitic worms

el·e·phan·tine \ˌel-ə-ˈfan-ˌtēn, -ˌtīn, ˈel-ə-fən-\ adj 1 : of great size or strength 2 : CLUMSY, PONDEROUS

elev abbr elevation

el·e·vate \ˈel-ə-ˌvāt\ vb **-vat·ed; -vat·ing** 1 : to lift up : RAISE 2 : EXALT, ENNOBLE 3 : ELATE

el·e·va·tion \ˌel-ə-ˈvā-shən\ n 1 : the height to which something is raised (as above sea level) 2 : a lifting up 3 : something (as a hill or swelling) that is elevated syn altitude, height

el·e·va·tor \ˈel-ə-ˌvāt-ər\ n 1 : a cage or platform for conveying something from one level to another 2 : a building for storing and discharging grain 3 : a movable surface on an airplane to produce motion up or down

elev·en \i-ˈlev-ən\ n 1 : one more than 10 2 : the 11th in a set or series 3 : something having 11 units; esp : a football team — **eleven** adj or pron — **elev·enth** \-ᵊnth\ adj or n

elf \ˈelf\ n, pl **elves** \ˈelvz\ : a mischievous fairy — **elf·in** \ˈel-fən\ adj — **elf·ish** \ˈel-fish\ adj

ELF abbr extremely low frequency

elic·it \i-ˈlis-ət\ vb : to draw out or forth syn evoke, educe, extract, extort

elide \i-ˈlīd\ vb **elid·ed; elid·ing** : to suppress or alter by elision

el·i·gi·ble \ˈel-ə-jə-bəl\ adj : qualified to participate or to be chosen — **el·i·gi·bil·i·ty** \ˌel-ə-jə-ˈbil-ət-ē\ n — **eligible** n

elim·i·nate \i-ˈlim-ə-ˌnāt\ vb **-nat·ed; -nat·ing** [L eliminatus, pp. of eliminare, fr. limen threshold] 1 : EXCLUDE, EXPEL; esp : to pass (wastes) from the body 2 : to leave out : IGNORE — **elim·i·na·tion** \-ˌlim-ə-ˈnā-shən\ n

eli·sion \i-ˈlizh-ən\ n : the omission of a final or initial sound or a word; esp : the omission of an unstressed vowel or syllable in a verse to achieve a uniform rhythm

elite \ā-ˈlēt\ n [F élite] 1 : the choice part; also : a superior group 2 : a typewriter type providing 12 characters to the inch

elit·ism \ā-ˈlēt-ˌiz-əm\ n : leadership or rule by an elite; also : advocacy of such elitism

elix·ir \i-ˈlik-sər\ n [ME, fr. ML, fr. Ar al-iksīr the elixir, fr. al the + iksīr elixir] 1 : a substance held capable of prolonging life indefinitely; also : PANACEA 2 : a sweetened alcoholic medicinal solution

Eliz·a·be·than \i-ˌliz-ə-ˈbē-thən\ adj : of, relating to, or characteristic of Elizabeth I of England or her times

elk \ˈelk\ n, pl **elks** 1 : the largest existing deer of Europe and Asia related to the American moose and having broad spreading antlers 2 : a large North American deer with curved antlers having many branches

¹ell \ˈel\ n : a unit of length; esp : a former English cloth measure of 45 inches (1.1 meters)

²ell n : an extension at right angles to a building syn wing, annex, arm

el·lipse \i-ˈlips, e-\ n : a closed curve of oval shape

el·lip·sis \i-ˈlip-səs, e-\ n, pl **el·lip·ses** \-ˌsēz\ **1** : omission from an expression of a word clearly implied **2** : marks (as . . . or """) to show omission

el·lip·soid \i-ˈlip-ˌsóid, e-\ n : a surface all plane sections of which are circles or ellipses — **ellipsoid** or **el·lip·soi·dal** \-ˌlip-ˈsóid-ᵊl\ adj

el·lip·tic \i-ˈlip-tik, e-\ or **el·lip·ti·cal** \-ti-kəl\ adj **1** : of, relating to, or shaped like an ellipse **2** : of, relating to, or marked by ellipsis — **el·lip·ti·cal·ly** \-ti-k(ə-)lē\ adv

elm \ˈelm\ n : any of a genus of large graceful trees that have toothed leaves and nearly circular one-seeded winged fruits and are often grown as shade trees; also : the wood of an elm

el·o·cu·tion \ˌel-ə-ˈkyü-shən\ n : the art of effective public speaking — **el·o·cu·tion·ist** \-sh(ə-)nəst\ n

elon·gate \i-ˈlóŋ-ˌgāt\ vb **-gat·ed; -gat·ing** : to make or grow longer syn extend, lengthen, prolong, protract — **elon·ga·tion** \(ˌ)ē-ˌlóŋ-ˈgā-shən\ n

elope \i-ˈlóp\ vb **eloped; elop·ing** : to run away esp. to be married — **elope·ment** n

el·o·quent \ˈel-ə-kwənt\ adj **1** : having or showing clear and forceful expression **2** : clearly showing some feeling or meaning — **el·o·quence** \-kwəns\ n — **el·o·quent·ly** adv

¹else \ˈels\ adv **1** : in a different manner or place or at a different time ⟨where ∼ can we meet⟩ **2** : OTHERWISE ⟨obey or ∼ you'll be sorry⟩

²else adj : OTHER; esp : being in addition ⟨what ∼ do you want⟩

else·where \-ˌhwear\ adv : in or to another place

elu·ci·date \i-ˈlü-sə-ˌdāt\ vb **-dat·ed; -dat·ing** : to make clear usu. by explanation syn clarify, explain, illuminate — **elu·ci·da·tion** \-ˌlü-sə-ˈdā-shən\ n

elude \ē-ˈlüd\ vb **elud·ed; elud·ing 1** : EVADE **2** : to escape the notice of

elu·sive \ē-ˈlü-siv\ adj : tending to elude : EVASIVE — **elu·sive·ly** adv — **elu·sive·ness** n

el·ver \ˈel-vər\ n [alter. of eelfare (migration of eels)] : a young eel

elves pl of ELF

Ely·si·um \i-ˈliz(h))-ē-əm\ n, pl **-si·ums** or **-sia** \-ē-ə\ **1** : PARADISE **2** — **Ely·sian** \-ˈlizh-ən\ adj

em \ˈem\ n : a length approximately the width of the letter M

EM abbr **1** electromagnetic **2** electron microscope **3** enlisted man

ema·ci·ate \i-ˈmā-shē-ˌāt\ vb **-at·ed; -at·ing** : to become or cause to become very thin — **ema·ci·a·tion** \-ˌmā-s(h)ē-ˈā-shən\ n

emalangeni pl of LILANGENI

em·a·nate \ˈem-ə-ˌnāt\ vb **-nat·ed; -nat·ing** : to come out from a source syn proceed, spring, rise, arise, originate — **em·a·na·tion** \ˌem-ə-ˈnā-shən\ n

eman·ci·pate \i-ˈman-sə-ˌpāt\ vb **-pat-**

ed; **-pat·ing** : to set free syn liberate, release, deliver, discharge — **eman·ci·pa·tion** \-ˌman-sə-ˈpā-shən\ n — **eman·ci·pa·tor** \-ˈman-sə-ˌpāt-ər\ n

emas·cu·late \i-ˈmas-kyə-ˌlāt\ vb **-lat·ed; -lat·ing** : CASTRATE, GELD; also : WEAKEN — **emas·cu·la·tion** \-ˌmas-kyə-ˈlā-shən\ n

em·balm \im-ˈbäm, -ˈbälm\ vb : to treat (a corpse) with preservative preparations — **em·balm·er** n

em·bank \im-ˈbaŋk\ vb : to enclose or confine by an embankment

em·bank·ment \-mənt\ n : a raised structure (as of earth) to hold back water or carry a roadway

em·bar·go \im-ˈbär-gō\ n, pl **-goes** [Sp, fr. embargar to bar] : a prohibition on commerce — **embargo** vb

em·bark \im-ˈbärk\ vb **1** : to put or go on board a ship or airplane **2** : to make a start — **em·bar·ka·tion** \ˌem-ˌbär-ˈkā-shən\ n

em·bar·rass \im-ˈbar-əs\ vb **1** : CONFUSE, DISCONCERT **2** : to involve in financial difficulties **3** : HINDER, IMPEDE — **em·bar·rass·ing·ly** adv — **em·bar·rass·ment** n

em·bas·sy \ˈem-bə-sē\ n, pl **-sies 1** : the function, position, or mission of an ambassador **2** : a group of representatives headed by an ambassador **3** : the official residence and offices of an ambassador

em·bat·tle \im-ˈbat-ᵊl\ vb **-tled; -tling** \-ˈbat-(ᵊ-)liŋ\ : to arrange in order for battle

em·bat·tled adj **1** : engaged in battle, conflict, or controversy **2** : being a site of battle, conflict, or controversy **3** : characterized by conflict or controversy

em·bed \im-ˈbed\ vb **em·bed·ded; em·bed·ding** : to enclose closely in a surrounding mass

em·bel·lish \im-ˈbel-ish\ vb **1** : ADORN, DECORATE **2** : to add ornamental details to syn beautify, deck, bedeck, garnish, ornament, dress — **em·bel·lish·ment** n

em·ber \ˈem-bər\ n **1** : a glowing or smoldering fragment from a fire **2** pl : smoldering remains of a fire

em·bez·zle \im-ˈbez-əl\ vb **-zled; -zling** \-(ə-)liŋ\ : to steal (as money) by falsifying records — **em·bez·zle·ment** n — **em·bez·zler** \-(ə-)lər\ n

em·bit·ter \im-ˈbit-ər\ vb **1** : to make bitter **2** : to arouse bitter feelings in

em·bla·zon \-ˈblāz-ᵊn\ vb **1** : to adorn with heraldic devices **2** : to display conspicuously

em·blem \ˈem-bləm\ n : something (as an object or picture) suggesting another object or an idea : SYMBOL — **em·blem·at·ic** \ˌem-blə-ˈmat-ik\ also **em·blem·at·i·cal** \-i-kəl\ adj

em·body \im-ˈbäd-ē\ vb **em·bod·ied; em·body·ing 1** : INCARNATE **2** : to express in definite form **3** : to incorporate into a system or body syn combine, incor-

porate, integrate — **em·bodi·ment**
\-'bäd-i-mənt\ *n*

em·bold·en \im-'bōl-dən\ *vb* : to inspire
with courage

em·bo·lism \'em-bə-ˌliz-əm\ *n* : the obstruction of a blood vessel by a foreign or abnormal particle

em·bon·point \äⁿ-bōⁿ-pwäⁿ\ *n* [F]
: plumpness of person : STOUTNESS

em·boss \im-'bäs, -'bȯs\ *vb* : to ornament with raised work

em·bou·chure \ˌäm-bù-'shùr\ *n* [F,
deriv. of *bouche* mouth] : the position
and use of the lips in producing a musical tone on a wind instrument

em·bow·er \im-'baù-(-ə)r\ *vb* : to shelter or enclose in a bower

¹**em·brace** \im-'brās\ *vb* **em·braced; em-
brac·ing 1** : to clasp in the arms; *also*
: CHERISH, LOVE **2** : ENCIRCLE **3** : TAKE
UP, ADOPT; *also* : WELCOME **4** : IN-
CLUDE **5** : to participate in an embrace
syn comprehend, involve, encom-
pass, embody

²**embrace** *n* : an encircling with the arms

em·bra·sure \im-'brā-zhər\ *n* **1** : a recess of a door or window **2** : an opening in a wall through which a cannon is
fired

em·bro·ca·tion \ˌem-brə-'kā-shən\ *n*
: LINIMENT

em·broi·der \im-'brȯid-ər\ *vb* -**dered;
-der·ing** \-(ə-)riŋ\ **1** : to ornament with
or do needlework **2** : to elaborate
with exaggerated detail

em·broi·dery \im-'brȯid-(ə-)rē\ *n, pl*
-**der·ies 1** : the forming of decorative
designs with needlework **2** : something embroidered

em·broil \im-'brȯil\ *vb* **1** : to throw into
confusion or strife **2** : to involve in
conflict or difficulties — **em·broil-
ment** *n*

em·bryo \'em-brē-ˌō\ *n, pl* **embryos** : a
living thing in its earliest stages of development — **em·bry·on·ic** \ˌem-brē-
'än-ik\ *adj*

em·bry·ol·o·gy \ˌem-brē-'äl-ə-jē\ *n* : a
branch of biology dealing with embryos and their development —
em·bry·o·log·i·cal \-i-kəl\ *adj* — **em·
bry·ol·o·gist** \-brē-'äl-ə-jəst\ *n*

em·cee \'em-'sē\ *n* : MASTER OF CEREMO-
NIES — **emcee** *vb*

emend \ē-'mend\ *vb* : to correct usu. by
altering the text of **syn** rectify, revise,
amend — **emen·da·tion** \ˌē-
ˌmen-'dā-shən\ *n*

emer *abbr* emeritus

¹**em·er·ald** \'em-(ə-)rəld\ *n* : a green beryl prized as a gem

²**emerald** *adj* : brightly or richly green

emerge \i-'mərj\ *vb* **emerged; emerg·ing**
: to rise, come forth, or come out into
view **syn** appear, loom, show — **emergence** \-'mər-jəns\ *n* — **emer·gent**
\-jənt\ *adj*

emer·gen·cy \i-'mər-jən-sē\ *n, pl* -**cies**
: an unforeseen event or condition requiring prompt action **syn** exigency,
contingency, crisis, juncture

emer·i·ta \i-'mer-ət-ə\ *adj* : EMERITUS —
used of a woman

emer·i·tus \i-'mer-ət-əs\ *adj* [L]
: retired from active duty (professor
~)

em·ery \'em-(ə-)rē\ *n, pl* **em·er·ies** : a
dark granular corundum used esp. for
grinding and polishing

emet·ic \i-'met-ik\ *n* : an agent that induces vomiting — **emetic** *adj*

emf *abbr* electromotive force

em·i·grate \'em-ə-ˌgrāt\ *vb* -**grat·ed;
-grat·ing** : to leave a place (as a country) to settle elsewhere — **em·i·grant**
\-i-grənt\ *n* — **em·i·gra·tion** \ˌem-ə-
'grā-shən\ *n*

émi·gré *also* **emi·gré** \'em-i-ˌgrā, ˌem-i-
'grā\ *n* [F] : a person who emigrates
esp. because of political conditions

em·i·nence \'em-ə-nəns\ *n* **1** : high rank
or position; *also* : a person of high
rank or attainments **2** : a lofty place

em·i·nent \'em-ə-nənt\ *adj* **1** : CONSPIC-
UOUS, EVIDENT **2** : DISTINGUISHED,
PROMINENT (~ men) — **em·i·nent·ly**
adv

eminent domain *n* : a right of a government to take private property for public use

emir \i-'miər, ā-\ *n* [Ar *amīr* command-
er] : a native ruler in parts of Africa
and Asia — **emir·ate** \'em-ər-ət\ *n*

em·is·sary \'em-ə-ˌser-ē\ *n, pl* -**sar·ies**
: AGENT; *esp* : a secret agent

emit \ē-'mit\ *vb* **emit·ted; emit·ting 1**
: to give off or out (~ light) ; *also*
: EJECT **2** : EXPRESS, UTTER — **emis·sion**
\-'mish-ən\ *n* — **emit·ter** *n*

emol·lient \i-'mäl-yənt\ *adj* : making
soft or supple; *also* : soothing esp. to
the skin or mucous membrane —
emollient *n*

emol·u·ment \i-'mäl-yə-mənt\ *n* [ME,
fr. L *emolumentum*, lit., miller's fee,
fr. *emolere* to grind up] : the product
(as salary or fees) of an employment

emote \i-'mōt\ *vb* **emot·ed; emot·ing** : to
give expression to emotion in or as if
in a play

emo·tion \i-'mō-shən\ *n* : a usu. intense
feeling (as of love, hate, or despair) —
emo·tion·al \-sh(ə-)nəl\ *adj* — **emo·
tion·al·ly** \-ē\ *adv*

emp *abbr* emperor; empress

em·pa·thy \'em-pə-thē\ *n* : the capacity
for experiencing as one's own the
feelings of another — **em·path·ic** \em-
'path-ik\ *adj*

em·pen·nage \ˌäm-pə-'näzh, ˌem-\ *n* [F]
: the tail assembly of an airplane

em·per·or \'em-pər-ər\ *n* : the sovereign ruler of an empire

em·pha·sis \'em-fə-səs\ *n, pl* -**pha·ses**
\-ˌsēz\ : particular stress or prominence given (as to a phrase in speaking or to a phase of action)

em·pha·size \-ˌsīz\ *vb* -**sized; -siz·ing** : to
place emphasis on : STRESS

em·phat·ic \im-'fat-ik, em-\ *adj* : uttered with emphasis : STRESSED — **em·
phat·i·cal·ly** \-'fat-i-k(ə-)lē\ *adv*

em·phy·se·ma \,em-fə-'zē-mə, -'sē-\ *n* : a condition marked esp. by abnormal expansion of the air spaces of the lungs and often by impairment of heart action

em·pire \'em-ˌpī(ə)r\ *n* **1** : a large state or a group of states under a single sovereign who is usu. an emperor **2** : imperial sovereignty or dominion

em·pir·i·cal \im-'pir-i-kəl\ *also* **em·pir·ic** \-ik\ *adj* : based on observation; *also* : subject to verification by observation or experiment ⟨~ laws⟩ — **em·pir·i·cal·ly** \-i-k(ə-)lē\ *adv*

em·pir·i·cism \im-'pir-ə-ˌsiz-əm, em-\ *n* : the practice of relying on observation and experiment esp. in the natural sciences — **em·pir·i·cist** \-səst\ *n*

em·place·ment \im-'plās-mənt\ *n* **1** : a prepared position for weapons or military equipment **2** : PLACEMENT

¹em·ploy \im-'plói\ *vb* **1** : to make use of **2** : to use the services of **3** : OCCUPY, DEVOTE — **em·ploy·er** *n*

²employ *n* : EMPLOYMENT

em·ploy·ee *or* **em·ploye** \im-ˌplói-'ē, ˌem-; im-'plói-ē, em-\ *n* : a person who works for another

em·ploy·ment \im-'plói-mənt\ *n* **1** : OCCUPATION, ACTIVITY **2** : the act of employing : the condition of being employed

em·po·ri·um \im-'pōr-ē-əm, em-\ *n, pl* **-ri·ums** *also* **-ria** \-ē-ə\ [L, fr. Gk *emporion*, fr. *emporos* traveler, trader] : a commercial center; *esp* : a store carrying varied articles

em·pow·er \im-'paú(-ə)r\ *vb* : AUTHORIZE

em·press \'em-prəs\ *n* **1** : the wife or widow of an emperor **2** : a woman holding an imperial title

¹emp·ty \'emp-tē\ *adj* **emp·ti·er; -est** **1** : containing nothing **2** : UNOCCUPIED, UNINHABITED **3** : lacking value, force, sense, or purpose **syn** vacant, blank, void, stark, vacuous — **emp·ti·ness** \-tē-nəs\ *n*

²empty *vb* **emp·tied; emp·ty·ing 1** : to make or become empty **2** : to discharge contents; *also* : to transfer by emptying

³empty *n, pl* **empties** : an empty container or vehicle

emp·ty-hand·ed \ˌemp-tē-'han-dəd\ *adj* **1** : having nothing in the hands **2** : having acquired or gained nothing

em·py·re·an \ˌem-ˌpī-'rē-ən, -pə-\ *n* : the highest heaven; *also* : FIRMAMENT

EMT \ˌē-ˌem-'tē\ *n* [*emergency medical technician*] : a person trained and certified to provide basic medical services before and during transportation to a hospital

¹emu \'ē-myü\ *n* : a swift-running flightless Australian bird smaller than the related ostrich

²emu *abbr* electromagnetic unit

em·u·late \'em-yə-ˌlāt\ *vb* **-lat·ed; -lat·ing** : to strive to equal or excel — **em·u·la·tion** \ˌem-yə-'lā-shən\ *n* — **em·u·lous** \'em-yə-ləs\ *adj*

emul·si·fi·er \i-'məl-sə-ˌfī(-ə)r\ *n* : something promoting the formation and stabilizing of an emulsion

emul·si·fy \-ˌfī\ *vb* **-fied; -fy·ing** : to convert (as an oil) into an emulsion — **emul·si·fi·ca·tion** \i-ˌməl-sə-fə-'kā-shən\ *n*

emul·sion \i-'məl-shən\ *n* **1** : a mixture of mutually insoluble liquids in which one is dispersed in droplets throughout the other (an ~ of oil in water) **2** : a light-sensitive coating on photographic film or paper

en \'en\ *n* : a length approximately half the width of the letter M

¹-en \ən, ᵊn\ *also* **-n** \n\ *adj suffix* : made of : consisting of (earthen)

²-en *vb suffix* **1** : become or cause to be (sharpen) **2** : cause or come to have (lengthen)

en·able \in-'ā-bəl\ *vb* **en·abled; en·abling** \-b(ə-)liŋ\ **1** : to make able or feasible **2** : to give legal power, capacity, or sanction to

en·act \in-'akt\ *vb* **1** : to make into law **2** : to act out — **en·act·ment** *n*

enam·el \in-'am-əl\ *n* **1** : a glasslike substance used for coating the surface of metal or pottery **2** : the hard outer layer of a tooth **3** : a usu. glossy paint that forms a hard coat — **enamel** *vb*

enam·el·ware \-ˌwaər\ *n* : metal utensils coated with enamel

en·am·or \in-'am-ər\ *vb* **-ored; -or·ing** \-(ə-)riŋ\ : to inflame with love

en·am·our *chiefly Brit var of* ENAMOR

en bloc \äⁿ-'bläk\ *adv or adj* : as a whole : in a mass

enc *or* **encl** *abbr* enclosure

en·camp \in-'kamp\ *vb* : to make camp — **en·camp·ment** *n*

en·cap·su·late \in-'kap-sə-ˌlāt\ *vb* **-lated; -lat·ing 1** : to encase or become encased in a capsule **2** : to condense (as a report) into a few words — **en·cap·su·la·tion** \-ˌkap-sə-'lā-shən\ *n*

en·case \in-'kās\ *vb* : to enclose in or as if in a case

-ence \əns, ᵊns\ *n suffix* **1** : action or process (emergence) : instance of an action or process (reference) **2** : quality or state (dependence)

en·ceinte \äⁿ-'sant\ *adj* : PREGNANT

en·ceph·a·li·tis \in-ˌsef-ə-'līt-əs\ *n, pl* **-lit·i·des** \-'lit-ə-ˌdēz\ : inflammation of the brain — **en·ceph·a·lit·ic** \-'lit-ik\ *adj*

en·ceph·a·lo·my·eli·tis \in-ˌsef-ə-lō-ˌmī-ə-'līt-əs\ *n* : concurrent inflammation of the brain and spinal cord

en·chain \in-'chān\ *vb* : FETTER, CHAIN

en·chant \in-'chant\ *vb* **1** : BEWITCH **2** : ENRAPTURE, FASCINATE — **en·chant·er** *n* — **en·chant·ing·ly** *adv* — **en·chant·ment** *n* — **en·chant·ress** \-'chan-trəs\ *n*

en·chi·la·da \ˌen-chə-'läd-ə\ *n* : a tortilla rolled with meat filling and served with chili-seasoned sauce

en·ci·pher \in-'sī-fər, en-\ *vb* : ENCODE

en·cir·cle \in-'sər-kəl\ vb : to pass completely around : SURROUND — **en·cir·cle·ment** n

en·clave \'en-ˌklāv; 'än-ˌklāv\ n : a territorial or culturally distinct unit enclosed within foreign territory

en·close \in-'klōz\ vb 1 : to shut up or in; esp : to surround with a fence 2 : to include along with something else in a parcel or envelope ⟨∼ a check⟩ — **en·clo·sure** \in-'klō-zhər\ n

en·code \in-'kōd, en-\ vb : to convert (a message) into code

en·co·mi·um \en-'kō-mē-əm\ n, pl **-mi·ums** or **-mia** \-mē-ə\ [L] : high or glowing praise

en·com·pass \in-'kəm-pəs\ vb 1 : ENCIRCLE 2 : ENVELOP, INCLUDE

¹**en·core** \'än-ˌkōr\ n : a demand for repetition or reappearance; also : a further performance (as of a singer) in response to such a demand

²**encore** vb **en·cored; en·cor·ing** : to request an encore from

¹**en·coun·ter** \in-'kaunt-ər\ n 1 : a hostile meeting; esp : COMBAT 2 : a chance meeting

²**encounter** vb 1 : to meet as an enemy : FIGHT 2 : to meet usu. unexpectedly

en·cour·age \in-'kər-ij\ vb **-aged; -ag·ing** 1 : to inspire with courage and hope 2 : STIMULATE, INCITE 3 : FOSTER — **en·cour·age·ment** n — **en·cour·ag·ing·ly** adv

en·croach \in-'krōch\ vb [ME encrochen to seize, fr. MF encrochier, fr. OF, fr. croche hook] : to enter or force oneself gradually upon another's property or rights — **en·croach·ment** n

en·crust \in-'krəst\ vb : to provide with or form a crust

encrustation var of INCRUSTATION

en·cum·ber \in-'kəm-bər\ vb **-bered; -ber·ing** \-b(ə-)riŋ\ 1 : to weigh down : BURDEN 2 : to hinder the function or activity of — **en·cum·brance** \-brəns\ n

ency or **encyc** abbr encyclopedia

-en·cy \ən-sē, ⁿn-\ n suffix : quality or state ⟨despondency⟩

¹**en·cyc·li·cal** \in-'sik-li-kəl, en-\ adj : addressed to all the individuals of a group

²**encyclical** n : an encyclical letter; esp : a papal letter to the bishops of the church

en·cy·clo·pe·dia also **en·cy·clo·pae·dia** \in-ˌsī-klə-'pēd-ē-ə\ n [ML encyclopaedia course of general education, fr. Gk enkyklios paideia general education] : a work treating the various branches of learning — **en·cy·clo·pe·dic** \-'pēd-ik\ adj

en·cyst \in-'sist, en-\ vb : to form or become enclosed in a cyst — **en·cyst·ment** n

¹**end** \'end\ n 1 : the part of an area that lies at the boundary; also : a point which marks the extent or limit of something or at which something ceases to exist 2 : a ceasing of a course (as of action or activity); also : DEATH 3 : the ultimate state; also : RESULT, ISSUE 4 : REMNANT 5 : PURPOSE, OBJECTIVE 6 : a player stationed at the extremity of a line (as in football) 7 : a share, operation, or aspect of an undertaking

²**end** vb 1 : to bring or come to an end 2 : DESTROY; also : DIE 3 : to form or be at the end of syn close, conclude, terminate, finish, complete

en·dan·ger \in-'dān-jər\ vb **-gered; -ger·ing** \-'dānj-(ə-)riŋ\ : to bring into danger

en·dan·gered \-jərd\ adj : threatened with extinction ⟨∼ species⟩

en·dear \in-'diər\ vb : to cause to become an object of affection

en·dear·ment \-mənt\ n : a sign of affection : CARESS

en·deav·or \in-'dev-ər\ vb **-ored; -or·ing** \-(ə-)riŋ\ : TRY, ATTEMPT — **endeavor** n

en·dem·ic \en-'dem-ik, in-\ adj : restricted or peculiar to a particular place ⟨∼ plants⟩ ⟨an ∼ disease⟩ — **endemic** n

end·ing \'en-diŋ\ n : something that forms an end; esp : SUFFIX

en·dive \'en-ˌdīv\ n 1 : an herb related to chicory and grown as a salad plant 2 : the blanched shoot of chicory

end·less \'end-ləs\ adj 1 : having no end : ETERNAL 2 : united at the ends : CONTINUOUS ⟨an ∼ belt⟩ syn interminable, everlasting, unceasing, ceaseless, unending — **end·less·ly** adv

end·most \'end-ˌmōst\ adj : situated at the very end

end·note \-ˌnōt\ n : a note placed at the end of the text (as of an article, chapter, or book)

en·do·crine \'en-də-krən, -ˌkrīn, -ˌkrēn\ adj : producing secretions that are distributed by way of the bloodstream ⟨∼ glands⟩ — **endocrine** n — **en·do·cri·nol·o·gist** \ˌen-də-kri-'näl-ə-jəst\ n — **en·do·cri·nol·o·gy** \-jē\ n

en·dog·e·nous \en-'däj-ə-nəs\ adj : caused or produced by factors inside the organism or system ⟨∼ psychic depression⟩ — **en·dog·e·nous·ly** adv

en·dorse \in-'dors\ vb **en·dorsed; en·dors·ing** 1 : to sign one's name on the back of (as a check) for some purpose 2 : APPROVE, SANCTION syn accredit, certify — **en·dorse·ment** n

en·do·scope \'en-də-ˌskōp\ n : an instrument with which the interior of a hollow organ (as the rectum) may be visualized — **en·do·scop·ic** \ˌen-də-'skäp-ik\ adj — **en·dos·co·py** \en-'däs-kə-pē\ n

en·do·ther·mic \ˌen-də-'thər-mik\ also **en·do·ther·mal** \-məl\ adj : characterized by or formed with absorption of heat

en·dow \in-'dau\ vb 1 : to furnish with funds for support ⟨∼ a school⟩ 2 : to furnish with something freely or naturally — **en·dow·ment** n

end run n : a football play in which the

ballcarrier attempts to run wide around the end

en·due \in-'d(y)ü\ *vb* **en·dued; en·du·ing** : to provide with some quality or power

en·dur·ance \in-'d(y)ùr-əns\ *n* 1 : DURATION 2 : the ability to withstand hardship or stress : FORTITUDE

en·dure \in-'d(y)ùr\ *vb* **en·dured; en·dur·ing** 1 : LAST, PERSIST 2 : to suffer firmly or patiently : BEAR 3 : TOLERATE **syn** continue, abide, persist — **en·dur·able** *adj*

end·ways \'end-,wāz\ *adv or adj* 1 : with the end forward 2 : LENGTHWISE 3 : on end

end·wise \-,wīz\ *adv or adj* : ENDWAYS

ENE *abbr* east-northeast

en·e·ma \'en-ə-mə\ *n, pl* enemas *also* ene·ma·ta \,en-ə-'mät-ə, 'en-ə-mə-tə\ : injection of liquid into the rectum; *also* : material so injected

en·e·my \'en-ə-mē\ *n, pl* **-mies** : one that attacks or tries to harm another : FOE; *esp* : a military opponent

en·er·get·ic \,en-ər-'jet-ik\ *adj* : marked by energy : ACTIVE, VIGOROUS **syn** strenuous, lusty, dynamic, vital — **en·er·get·i·cal·ly** \-i-k(ə-)lē\ *adv*

en·er·gize \'en-ər-,jīz\ *vb* **-gized; -giz·ing** : to give energy to

en·er·giz·er \-,jī-zər\ *n* : ANTIDEPRESSANT

en·er·gy \'en-ər-jē\ *n, pl* **-gies** 1 : vigorous action : EFFORT 2 : capacity for action 3 : capacity for performing work 4 : usable power (as heat or electricity); *also* : the resources for producing such power **syn** strength, might, vigor

energy level *n* : one of the stable states of constant energy that may be assumed by a physical system (as the electrons in an atom)

en·er·vate \'en-ər-,vāt\ *vb* **-vat·ed; -vat·ing** : to lessen the strength or vigor of : weaken in mind or body — **en·er·va·tion** \,en-ər-'vā-shən\ *n*

en·fee·ble \in-'fē-bəl\ *vb* **-bled; -bling** \-b(ə-)liŋ\ : to make feeble **syn** weaken, debilitate, sap, undermine, cripple — **en·fee·ble·ment** *n*

en·fi·lade \'en-fə-,lād, -,läd\ *n* : gunfire directed along the length of an enemy battle line

en·fold \in-'fōld\ *vb* 1 : ENVELOP 2 : EMBRACE

en·force \in-'fōrs\ *vb* 1 : COMPEL ⟨∼ obedience by threats⟩ 2 : to execute effectively ⟨∼ the law⟩ — **en·force·able** *adj* — **en·force·ment** *n*

en·fran·chise \in-'fran-,chīz\ *vb* **-chised; -chis·ing** 1 : to set free (as from slavery) 2 : to admit to citizenship; *also* : to grant the vote to — **en·fran·chise·ment** \-,chīz-mənt, -,chəz-\ *n*

eng *abbr* engine; engineer; engineering

Eng *abbr* England; English

en·gage \in-'gāj\ *vb* **en·gaged; en·gag·ing** 1 : PLEDGE; *esp* : to bind by a pledge to marry 2 : EMPLOY, HIRE 3 : to attract and hold esp. by interesting ⟨*engaged* his friend's attention⟩; *also* : to cause to participate 4 : to commence or take part in a venture 5 : to bring or enter into conflict 6 : to connect or interlock with : MESH; *also* : to cause to mesh

en·gage·ment \in-'gāj-mənt\ *n* 1 : APPOINTMENT 2 : EMPLOYMENT 3 : a mutual promise to marry 4 : a hostile encounter

en·gag·ing *adj* : ATTRACTIVE — **en·gag·ing·ly** *adv*

en·gen·der \in-'jen-dər\ *vb* **-dered; -der·ing** \-d(ə-)riŋ\ 1 : BEGET 2 : BRING ABOUT, CREATE **syn** generate, breed, occasion, produce

en·gine \'en-jən\ *n* [ME *engin*, fr. OF. fr. L *ingenium* natural disposition, talent] 1 : a mechanical device 2 : a machine for converting energy into mechanical motion 3 : LOCOMOTIVE

¹**en·gi·neer** \,en-jə-'niər\ *n* 1 : a member of a military group devoted to engineering work 2 : a designer or builder of engines 3 : one trained in engineering 4 : one that operates an engine

²**engineer** *vb* : to lay out or manage as an engineer **syn** guide, pilot, lead, steer

en·gi·neer·ing \-iŋ\ *n* : the practical applications of scientific and mathematical principles

En·glish \'iŋ-glish\ *n* 1 : the language of England, the U.S., and many areas now or formerly under British rule 2 **English** *pl* : the people of England — **English** *adj* — **En·glish·man** \-mən\ *n* — **En·glish·wom·an** \-,wùm-ən\ *n*

English horn *n* : a woodwind instrument longer than and having a range lower than the oboe

English setter *n* : any of a breed of bird dogs with a flat silky coat of white with flecks or patches of black or brown

English sparrow *n* : HOUSE SPARROW

English system *n* : a system of weights and measures in which the foot is the principal unit of length and the pound is the principal unit of weight

engr *abbr* 1 engineer 2 engraved

en·gram \'en-,gram\ *n* : a hypothetical change in neural tissue postulated in order to account for persistence of memory

en·grave \in-'grāv\ *vb* **en·graved; en·grav·ing** 1 : to produce (as letters or lines) by incising a surface 2 : to incise (as stone or metal) to produce a representation (as of letters or figures) esp. that may be printed from 3 : PHOTOENGRAVE — **en·grav·er** *n*

en·grav·ing \in-'grā-viŋ\ *n* 1 : the art of one who engraves 2 : an engraved plate; *also* : a print made from it

en·gross \in-'grōs\ *vb* : to take up the whole interest or attention of **syn** monopolize, absorb, consume

en·gulf \in-'gəlf\ *vb* : to flow over and enclose

en·hance \in-'hans\ *vb* **en·hanced; en-**

hanc·ing : to make greater (as in value or desirability) **syn** heighten, intensify, magnify — **en·hance·ment** n

enig·ma \i-'nig-mə\ n [L *aenigma,* fr. Gk *ainigma,* fr. *ainissesthai* to speak in riddles, fr. *ainos* fable] : something obscure or hard to understand — PUZZLE

enig·mat·ic \,en-ig-'mat-ik\ adj : resembling an enigma **syn** obscure, cryptic, mystifying — **en·ig·mat·i·cal·ly** \-i-k(ə-)lē\ adv

en·isle \in-'īl\ vb : ISOLATE

en·jamb·ment \in-'jam-mənt\ or **en·jambe·ment** *same,* or än-zhäⁿb-(ə-)mäⁿ\ n [F *enjambement*] : the running over of a sentence from one verse or couplet into another so that closely related words fall in different lines

en·join \in-'jóin\ vb 1 : COMMAND, ORDER 2 : FORBID **syn** direct, bid, charge, command, instruct

en·joy \in-'jói\ vb 1 : to have for one's benefit or use (⟨~ good health⟩) 2 : to take pleasure or satisfaction in (⟨~ed the concert⟩) **syn** like, love, relish, fancy — **en·joy·able** adj — **en·joy·ment** n

enl abbr 1 enlarged 2 enlisted

en·large \in-'lärj\ vb **en·larged; en·larg·ing** 1 : to make or grow larger 2 : ELABORATE **syn** increase, augment, multiply, expand — **en·large·ment** n

en·light·en \in-'līt-²n\ vb **-ened; -en·ing** \-'līt-(²-)niŋ\ 1 : INSTRUCT, INFORM 2 : to give spiritual insight to **syn** illuminate, edify — **en·light·en·ment** n

en·list \in-'list\ vb 1 : to engage for service in the armed forces 2 : to secure the aid or support of — **en·list·ee** \-,lis-'tē\ n — **en·list·ment** \-'lis(t)-mənt\ n

en·list·ed \in-'lis-təd\ adj : of, relating to, or forming the part of a military force below commissioned or warrant officers

en·liv·en \in-'lī-vən\ vb : to give life, action, or spirit to : ANIMATE

en masse \äⁿ-'mas\ adv [F] : in a body : as a whole

en·mesh \in-'mesh\ vb : to catch or entangle in or as if in meshes

en·mi·ty \'en-mət-ē\ n, pl **-ties** : ILL WILL; *esp* : mutual hatred **syn** hostility, antipathy, animosity, rancor, antagonism

en·no·ble \in-'ō-bəl\ vb **-bled; -bling** \-b(ə-)liŋ\ : ELEVATE, EXALT; *esp* : to raise to noble rank — **en·no·ble·ment** n

en·nui \'än-'wē\ n [F] : BOREDOM

enor·mi·ty \i-'nór-mət-ē\ n, pl **-ties** 1 : a grave offense against order, right, or decency 2 : great wickedness 3 : IMMENSITY

enor·mous \i-'nór-məs\ adj [L *enormis,* fr. *e, ex* out of + *norma* rule] 1 : exceedingly wicked 2 : great in size, number, or degree : HUGE **syn** immense, vast, gigantic, colossal, mammoth, elephantine

¹**enough** \i-'nəf\ adj : SUFFICIENT **syn** adequate, satisfactory, sufficing

²**enough** adv 1 : SUFFICIENTLY 2 : FULLY, QUITE 3 : TOLERABLY

³**enough** pron : a sufficient number, quantity, or amount

en·plane \in-'plān\ vb : to board an airplane

en·quire \in-'kwī(ə)r\, **en·qui·ry** \'in-,kwī(ə)r-ē, in-'kwī(ə)r-; 'in-kwə-rē, 'iŋ-\ *var of* INQUIRE, INQUIRY

en·rage \in-'rāj\ vb : to fill with rage

en·rap·ture \in-'rap-chər\ vb **en·rap·tured; en·rap·tur·ing** : DELIGHT

en·rich \in-'rich\ vb 1 : to make rich or richer 2 : ORNAMENT, ADORN — **en·rich·ment** n

en·roll or **en·rol** \in-'rōl\ vb **en·rolled; en·roll·ing** 1 : to enter or register on a roll or list 2 : to offer (oneself) for membership — **en·roll·ment** n

en route \än-'rüt, en-\ adv or adj : on or along the way

ENS abbr ensign

en·sconce \in-'skäns\ vb **en·sconced; en·sconc·ing** 1 : SHELTER, CONCEAL 2 : to settle snugly or securely **syn** secrete, hide, cache, stash

en·sem·ble \än-'säm-bəl\ n [F, fr. *ensemble* together, fr. L *insimul* at the same time] 1 : SET, WHOLE 2 : integrated music of two or more parts 3 : a complete costume of harmonizing garments 4 : a group of persons (as musicians) acting together to produce a particular effect or end

en·sheathe \in-'shēth\ vb : to cover with or as if with a sheath

en·shrine \in-'shrīn\ vb 1 : to enclose in or as if in a shrine 2 : to cherish as sacred

en·shroud \in-'shraúd\ vb : SHROUD, OBSCURE

¹**en·sign** \'en-sən, 1 also 'en-,sīn\ n 1 : FLAG; *also* : BADGE, EMBLEM 2 : a commissioned officer in the navy ranking next below a lieutenant junior grade

en·si·lage \'en-sə-lij\ n : the process of converting feed crops into silage; *also* : SILAGE

en·sile \en-'sīl\ vb **en·siled; en·sil·ing** : to prepare and store (fodder) for silage

en·slave \in-'slāv\ vb : to make a slave of — **en·slave·ment** n

en·snare \in-'snaər\ vb : SNARE, TRAP **syn** entrap, bag, catch, capture

en·sue \in-'sü\ vb **en·sued; en·su·ing** : to follow as a consequence or in time : RESULT

en·sure \in-'shúr\ vb **en·sured; en·sur·ing** : INSURE, GUARANTEE **syn** assure, secure

en·tail \in-'tāl\ vb 1 : to limit the inheritance of (property) to the owner's lineal descendants or to a class thereof 2 : to include or involve as a necessary step or result — **en·tail·ment** n

en·tan·gle \in-'taŋ-gəl\ vb : TANGLE, CONFUSE — **en·tan·gle·ment** n

en·tente \än-'tänt\ n [F agreement, understanding] : an understanding providing for joint action; *also* : parties linked by such an entente

en•ter \'ent-ər\ *vb* **en•tered; en•ter•ing** \'ent-ə-riŋ, 'en-triŋ\ **1** : to go or come in or into **2** : to become a member of : JOIN (~ the ministry) **3** : BEGIN **4** : to take part in : CONTRIBUTE **5** : to go into or upon and take possession **6** : to set down (as in a list) : REGISTER **7** : to place (a complaint) before a court; *also* : to put on record (~ed his objections)

en•ter•i•tis \,ent-ə-'rīt-əs\ *n* : intestinal inflammation; *also* : a disease marked by this

en•ter•prise \'ent-ər-,prīz\ *n* **1** : UNDERTAKING, PROJECT **2** : readiness for daring action : INITIATIVE **3** : a business organization

en•ter•pris•ing \-,prī-ziŋ\ *adj* : bold and vigorous in action : ENERGETIC

en•ter•tain \,ent-ər-'tān\ *vb* **1** : to treat or receive as a guest **2** : AMUSE, DIVERT **3** : to hold in mind *syn* harbor, shelter, lodge, house, billet — **en•ter•tain•er** *n* — **en•ter•tain•ment** *n*

en•thrall *or* **en•thral** \in-'thrȯl\ *vb* **en•thralled; en•thrall•ing 1** : to hold spellbound **2** : ENSLAVE

en•throne \in-'thrōn\ *vb* **1** : to seat on or as if on a throne **2** : EXALT

en•thuse \in-'th(y)üz\ *vb* **en•thused; en•thus•ing 1** : to make enthusiastic **2** : to show enthusiasm

en•thu•si•asm \in-'th(y)ü-zē-,az-əm\ *n* [Gk *enthousiasmos,* fr. *enthousiazein* to be inspired, fr. *entheos* inspired, fr. *theos* god] **1** : strong warmth of feeling : keen interest : FERVOR **2** : a cause of fervor — **en•thu•si•ast** \-,ast, -əst\ *n* — **en•thu•si•as•tic** \in-,th(y)ü-zē-'as-tik\ *adj* — **en•thu•si•as•ti•cal•ly** \-ti-k(ə-)lē\ *adv*

en•tice \in-'tīs\ *vb* **en•ticed; en•tic•ing** : ALLURE, TEMPT — **en•tice•ment** *n*

en•tire \in-'tī(ə)r\ *adj* : COMPLETE, WHOLE *syn* sound, perfect, intact, undamaged — **en•tire•ly** *adv*

en•tire•ty \in-'tī-rət-ē, -'tī-(ə)rt-ē\ *n, pl* **-ties 1** : COMPLETENESS **2** : WHOLE, TOTALITY

en•ti•tle \in-'tīt-ᵊl\ *vb* **en•ti•tled; en•ti•tling** \-'tīt-(ᵊ-)liŋ\ **1** : NAME, DESIGNATE **2** : to give a right or claim to

en•ti•tle•ment \in-'tīt-ᵊl-mənt\ *n* : a government program providing benefits to members of a specified group

en•ti•ty \'ent-ət-ē\ *n, pl* **-ties 1** : EXISTENCE, BEING **2** : something with separate and real existence

en•tomb \in-'tüm\ *vb* : to place in a tomb : BURY — **en•tomb•ment** \-'tüm-mənt\ *n*

en•to•mol•o•gy \,ent-ə-'mäl-ə-jē\ *n* : a branch of zoology that deals with insects — **en•to•mo•log•i•cal** \-mə-'läj-i-kəl\ *adj* — **en•to•mol•o•gist** \,ent-ə-'mäl-ə-jəst\ *n*

en•tou•rage \,än-tù-'räzh\ *n* [F] : RETINUE

en•tr'acte \'än-ᵊ,trakt\ *n* [F] **1** : something (as a dance) performed between two acts of a play **2** : the interval between two acts of a play

en•trails \'en-ᵊträlz\ *n pl* : VISCERA; *esp* : INTESTINES

en•train \in-'trān\ *vb* : to put or go aboard a railroad train

¹en•trance \'en-trəns\ *n* **1** : a means or place of entry **2** : the act of entering **3** : permission or right to enter

²en•trance \in-'trans\ *vb* **en•tranced; en•tranc•ing** : CHARM, DELIGHT

en•trant \'en-trənt\ *n* : one that enters esp. as a competitor

en•trap \in-'trap\ *vb* : ENSNARE, TRAP — **en•trap•ment** *n*

en•treat \in-'trēt\ *vb* : to ask earnestly or urgently : BESEECH *syn* beg, implore, plead, supplicate — **en•treaty** \-'trēt-ē\ *n*

en•trée *or* **en•tree** \'än-,trā, än-'trā\ *n* [F *entrée*] **1** : the principal dish of the meal in the U.S. **2** : ENTRANCE *syn* entry, access, admission, admittance

en•trench \in-'trench\ *vb* **1** : to surround with a trench; *also* : to establish in a strong defensive position (~ed customs) **2** : ENCROACH, TRESPASS — **en•trench•ment** *n*

en•tre•pre•neur \,än-trə-prə-'nər\ *n* [F, fr. OF, fr. *entreprendre* to undertake] : one who organizes and assumes the risk of a business or enterprise

en•tro•py \'en-trə-pē\ *n, pl* **-pies 1** : a measure of the unavailable energy of a closed thermodynamic system **2** : an ultimate state of inert uniformity

en•trust \in-'trəst\ *vb* **1** : to commit something to as a trust **2** : to commit to another with confidence *syn* confide, consign, relegate, commend

en•try \'en-trē\ *n, pl* **entries 1** : ENTRANCE 1, 2; *also* : VESTIBULE **2 2** : an entering in a record; *also* : an item so entered **3** : a headword with its definition or identification; *also* : VOCABULARY ENTRY 4 **4** : one entered in a contest

en•twine \in-'twīn\ *vb* : to twine together or around

enu•mer•ate \i-'n(y)ü-mə-,rāt\ *vb* **-at•ed; -at•ing 1** : to determine the number of : COUNT **2** : LIST — **enu•mer•a•tion** \-,n(y)ü-mə-'rā-shən\ *n*

enun•ci•ate \ē-'nən-sē-,āt\ *vb* **-at•ed; -at•ing 1** : to state definitely; *also* : ANNOUNCE, PROCLAIM **2** : PRONOUNCE, ARTICULATE — **enun•ci•a•tion** \-,nən-sē-'ā-shən\ *n*

en•ure•sis \,en-yù-'rē-səs\ *n* : involuntary discharge of urine : BED-WETTING

env *abbr* envelope

en•vel•op \in-'vel-əp\ *vb* : to enclose completely with or as if with a covering — **en•vel•op•ment** *n*

en•ve•lope \'en-və-,lōp, 'än-\ *n* **1** : a usu. paper container for a letter **2** : WRAPPER, COVERING **3** : the bag containing the gas in a balloon or airship

en·ven·om \in-'ven-əm\ *vb* 1 : to poison with venom 2 : EMBITTER

en·vi·able \'en-vē-ə-bəl\ *adj* : highly desirable — **en·vi·ably** \-blē\ *adv*

en·vi·ous \'en-vē-əs\ *adj* : feeling or showing envy — **en·vi·ous·ly** *adv* — **en·vi·ous·ness** *n*

en·vi·ron·ment \in-'vī-rən-mənt\ *n* 1 : SURROUNDINGS 2 : the whole complex of factors (as soil, climate, and living things) that influence the form and the ability to survive of a plant or animal or ecological community — **en·vi·ron·men·tal** \-,vī-rən-'ment-ᵊl\ *adj*

en·vi·ron·men·tal·ist \-ᵊl-əst\ *n* : a person concerned about the quality of the human environment

en·vi·rons \in-'vī-rənz\ *n pl* 1 : SUBURBS 2 : SURROUNDINGS; *also* : VICINITY

en·vis·age \in-'viz-ij\ *vb* -**aged**; -**ag·ing** : to have a mental picture of

en·voy \'en-,vȯi, 'än-\ *n* 1 : a diplomatic agent 2 : REPRESENTATIVE, MESSENGER

¹en·vy \'en-vē\ *n, pl* **envies** [ME *envie,* fr. OF, fr. L *invidia,* fr. *invidus* envious, fr. *invidēre* to look askance at, envy, fr. *vidēre* to see] : grudging desire for or discontent at the sight of another's excellence or advantages; *also* : an object of envy

²envy *vb* **en·vied; en·vy·ing** : to feel envy toward or on account of

en·zyme \'en-,zīm\ *n* : any of various complex proteins produced by living cells that induce or accelerate chemical reactions (as in the digestion of food) at body temperatures without being permanently altered — **en·zy·mat·ic** \,en-zə-'mat-ik\ *adj*

Eo·cene \'ē-ə-,sēn\ *adj* : of, relating to, or being the epoch of the Tertiary between the Paleocene and the Oligocene — **Eocene** *n*

eo·lian \ē-'ō-lē-ən\ *adj* : borne, deposited, or produced by the wind

EOM *abbr* end of month

eon \'ē-ən, 'ē-,än\ *var of* AEON

EP *abbr* European plan

EPA *abbr* Environmental Protection Agency

ep·au·let *also* **ep·au·lette** \,ep-ə-'let\ *n* [F *épaulette,* dim. of *épaule* shoulder] : a shoulder ornament esp. on a uniform

épée \'ep-,ā, ā-'pā\ *n* [F] : a fencing or dueling sword

Eph *or* **Ephes** *abbr* Ephesians

ephed·rine \i-'fed-rən\ *n* : a drug used in relieving hay fever, asthma, and nasal congestion

ephem·er·al \i-'fem-(ə-)rəl\ *adj* [Gk *ephēmeros* lasting a day, daily, fr. *hēmera* day] : SHORT-LIVED, TRANSITORY **syn** passing, fleeting, transient, evanescent

Ephe·sians \i-'fē-zhənz\ *n* — see BIBLE table

ep·ic \'ep-ik\ *n* : a long poem in elevated style narrating the deeds of a hero — **epic** *adj*

epi·cen·ter \'ep-i-,sent-ər\ *n* : the point on the earth's surface directly above the point of origin of an earthquake

epi·cure \'ep-i-,kyu̇r\ *n* : a person with sensitive and discriminating tastes esp. in food and wine

epi·cu·re·an \,ep-i-kyu̇-'rē-ən, -'kyu̇r-ē-\ *n* : EPICURE — **epicurean** *adj*

¹epi·dem·ic \,ep-ə-'dem-ik\ *adj* : affecting many persons at one time (~ disease); *also* : excessively prevalent

²epidemic *n* : an epidemic outbreak esp. of disease

epi·der·mis \,ep-ə-'dər-məs\ *n* : an outer layer esp. of skin — **epi·der·mal** \-məl\ *adj*

epi·glot·tis \,ep-ə-'glät-əs\ *n* : a thin plate of flexible tissue protecting the tracheal opening during swallowing

epi·gram \'ep-ə-,gram\ *n* : a short witty poem or saying — **epi·gram·mat·ic** \,ep-ə-grə-'mat-ik\ *adj*

epi·lep·sy \'ep-ə-,lep-sē\ *n, pl* -**sies** : a disorder typically marked by disturbed electrical rhythms of the central nervous system, by attacks of convulsions, and by loss of consciousness — **epi·lep·tic** \,ep-ə-'lep-tik\ *adj or n*

epi·logue *or* **epi·log** \'ep-ə-,lȯg, -,läg\ *n* : a speech addressed to the spectators by an actor at the end of a play

epi·neph·rine *also* **epi·neph·rin** \,ep-ə-'nef-rən\ *n* : an adrenal hormone used medicinally esp. as a heart stimulant, a muscle relaxant, and a vasoconstrictor

Epiph·a·ny \i-'pif-ə-nē\ *n, pl* -**nies** : January 6 observed as a church festival in commemoration of the coming of the Magi to Jesus at Bethlehem

epis·co·pa·cy \i-'pis-kə-pə-sē\ *n, pl* -**cies** 1 : government of a church by bishops 2 : EPISCOPATE

epis·co·pal \i-'pis-kə-pəl\ *adj* 1 : of or relating to a bishop or episcopacy 2 *cap* : or or relating to the Protestant Episcopal Church

Epis·co·pa·lian \i-,pis-kə-'pāl-yən\ *n* : a member of the Protestant Episcopal Church

epis·co·pate \i-'pis-kə-pət, -,pāt\ *n* 1 : the rank, office, or term of a bishop 2 : a body of bishops

ep·i·sode \'ep-ə-,sōd, -,zōd\ *n* [Gk *epeisodion,* fr. *epeisodios* coming in besides, fr. *eisodios* coming in, fr. *eis* into + *hodos* road, journey] 1 : a unit of action in a dramatic or literary work 2 : an incident in a course of events : OCCURRENCE (a feverish ~) — **ep·i·sod·ic** \,ep-ə-'säd-ik, -'zäd-\ *adj*

epis·tle \i-'pis-əl\ *n* 1 *cap* : one of the letters of the New Testament 2 : LETTER — **epis·to·lary** \i-'pis-tə-,ler-ē\ *adj*

ep·i·taph \'ep-ə-,taf\ *n* : an inscription in memory of a dead person

ep·i·tha·la·mi·um \,ep-ə-thə-'lā-mē-əm\ *or* **ep·i·tha·la·mi·on** \-mē-ən\ *n pl* -**mi·ums** *or* -**mia** \-mē-ə\ : a song or poem in honor of a bride and bridegroom

ep·i·the·li·um \,ep-ə-'thē-lē-əm\ *n, pl* **-lia** \-lē-ə\ : a cellular membrane covering a bodily surface or lining a cavity — **ep·i·the·li·al** \-lē-əl\ *adj*

ep·i·thet \'ep-ə-,thet, -thət\ *n* : a characterizing and often abusive word or phrase

epit·o·me \i-'pit-ə-mē\ *n* **1** : ABSTRACT, SUMMARY **2** : EMBODIMENT — **epit·o·mize** \-,mīz\ *vb*

ep·och \'ep-ək, 'ep-,äk\ *n* : a usu. extended period : ERA, AGE — **ep·och·al** \'ep-ə-kəl, 'ep-,äk-əl\ *adj*

ep·oxy \i-'päk-sē\ *vb* **ep·ox·ied** *or* **ep·oxyed**; **ep·oxy·ing** : to glue with epoxy resin

epoxy resin *n* : a synthetic resin used in coatings and adhesives

Ep·som salts \'ep-səm-\ *n* : a bitter colorless or white magnesium salt with cathartic properties

eq *abbr* **1** equal **2** equation

equa·ble \'ek-wə-bəl, 'ē-kwə-\ *adj* : UNIFORM, EVEN; *esp* : free from unpleasant extremes — **eq·ua·bil·i·ty** \,ek-wə-'bil-ət-ē, ,ē-kwə-\ *n* — **equa·bly** \'ek-wə-blē, 'ē-kwə-\ *adv*

¹equal \'ē-kwəl\ *adj* **1** : of the same measure, quantity, value, quality, number, or degree as another **2** : IMPARTIAL **3** : free from extremes **4** : able to cope with a situation or task syn same, identical, equivalent, tantamount — **equal·i·ty** \i-'kwäl-ət-ē\ *n* — **equal·ly** \'ē-kwə-lē\ *adv*

²equal *vb* **equaled** *or* **equalled**; **equal·ing** *or* **equal·ling** : to be or become equal to : MATCH

³equal *n* : one that is equal; *esp* : a person of like rank, abilities, or age

equal·ize \'ē-kwə-,līz\ *vb* **-ized**; **-iz·ing** : to make equal, uniform, or constant — **equal·iza·tion** \,ē-kwə-lə-'zā-shən\ *n* — **equal·iz·er** \'ē-kwə-,lī-zər\ *n*

equa·nim·i·ty \,ē-kwə-'nim-ət-ē, ,ek-wə-\ *n, pl* **-ties** : COMPOSURE

equate \i-'kwāt\ *vb* **equat·ed**; **equat·ing** : to make, treat, or regard as equal or comparable

equa·tion \i-'kwā-zhən, -shən\ *n* **1** : an act of equating : the state of being equated **2** : a usu. formal statement of equivalence (as between mathematical or logical expressions) with the relation typically symbolized by the sign =

equa·tor \i-'kwāt-ər\ *n* : an imaginary circle around the earth that is everywhere equally distant from the two poles — **equa·to·ri·al** \,ē-kwə-'tōr-ē-əl, ,ek-wə-\ *adj*

equer·ry \'ek-wə-rē, i-'kwer-ē\ *n, pl* **-ries** : an officer in charge of the horses of a prince or nobleman **2** : a personal attendant of a member of the British royal family

¹eques·tri·an \i-'kwes-trē-ən\ *adj* **1** : of or relating to horses, horsemen, or horsemanship **2** : representing a person on horseback

²equestrian *n* : one that rides on horseback

eques·tri·enne \i-,kwes-trē-'en\ *n* : a female rider on horseback

equi·dis·tant \,ē-kwə-'dis-tənt\ *adj* : equally distant

equi·lat·er·al \,ē-kwə-'lat-(ə-)rəl\ *adj* : having all sides or faces equal ⟨~ triangles⟩

equi·lib·ri·um \,ē-kwə-'lib-rē-əm, ,ek-wə-\ *n, pl* **-ri·ums** *or* **-ria** \-rē-ə\ : a state of balance between opposing forces or actions syn poise, balance, equipoise

equine \'ē-,kwīn, 'ek-,wīn\ *adj* [L *equinus*, fr. *equus* horse] : of or relating to the horse — **equine** *n*

equi·nox \'ē-kwə-,näks, 'ek-wə-\ *n* : either of the two times each year when the sun appears directly overhead at the equator and day and night are everywhere of equal length that occur about March 21 and September 23 — **equi·noc·tial** \,ē-kwə-'näk-shəl, ,ek-wə-\ *adj*

equip \i-'kwip\ *vb* **equipped**; **equip·ping** : to supply with needed resources

equi·page \'ek-wə-pij\ *n* : a horse-drawn carriage usu. with its attendant servants

equip·ment \i-'kwip-mənt\ *n* **1** : things used in equipping : SUPPLIES, OUTFIT **2** : the equipping of a person or thing : the state of being equipped

equi·poise \'ek-wə-,poiz, 'ē-kwə-\ *n* **1** : BALANCE, EQUILIBRIUM **2** : COUNTERBALANCE

eq·ui·ta·ble \'ek-wət-ə-bəl\ *adj* : JUST, FAIR — **eq·ui·ta·bly** \-blē\ *adv*

eq·ui·ta·tion \,ek-wə-'tā-shən\ *n* : the act or art of riding on horseback

eq·ui·ty \'ek-wət-ē\ *n, pl* **-ties** **1** : JUSTNESS, IMPARTIALITY **2** : value of a property or of an interest in it in excess of claims against it

equiv *abbr* equivalent

equiv·a·lent \i-'kwiv-(ə-)lənt\ *adj* : EQUAL; *also* : virtually identical syn same, tantamount — **equiv·a·lence** \-ləns\ *n* — **equivalent** *n*

equiv·o·cal \i-'kwiv-ə-kəl\ *adj* **1** : AMBIGUOUS **2** : UNCERTAIN **3** : SUSPICIOUS, DUBIOUS ⟨~ behavior⟩ syn obscure, dark, vague, enigmatic — **equiv·o·cal·ly** \-ē\ *adv*

equiv·o·cate \i-'kwiv-ə-,kāt\ *vb* **-cat·ed**; **-cat·ing** **1** : to use misleading language **2** : to avoid giving a definite answer — **equiv·o·ca·tion** \-,kwiv-ə-'kā-shən\ *n*

¹-er \ər\ *adj suffix or adv suffix* — used to form the comparative degree of adjectives and adverbs of one syllable ⟨hotter⟩ ⟨drier⟩ and of some adjectives and adverbs of two syllables ⟨completer⟩ and sometimes of longer ones

²-er \ər\ *also* **-ier** \ē-ər, yər\ *or* **-yer** \yər\ *n suffix* **1** : a person occupationally connected with ⟨hatter⟩ ⟨lawyer⟩ **2** : a person or thing belonging to or associated with ⟨old-timer⟩ **3** : a native of : resident of ⟨New Yorker⟩ **4** : one that has ⟨double-deck*er*⟩ **5** : one that produces or yields ⟨pork*er*⟩ **6** : one that does or performs (a specified action) ⟨report*er*⟩ **7** : one that is a suitable object of (a specified action) ⟨broil*er*⟩ **8** : one that is (foreign*er*⟩

Er *symbol* erbium

ER *abbr* emergency room

era \'ir-ə, 'er-ə, 'ē-rə\ *n* [LL *aera,* fr. L, counters, pl. of *aes* copper, money] **1** : a chronological order or system of notation reckoned from a given date as basis **2** : a period typified by some special feature **3** : any of the five major divisions of geologic time *syn* age, epoch, period, time

ERA *abbr* Equal Rights Amendment

erad·i·cate \i-'rad-ə-ˌkāt\ *vb* **-cat·ed; -cat·ing** [L *eradicatus,* pp. of *eradicare,* fr. *e-* out + *radix* root] : UPROOT, ELIMINATE *syn* exterminate, annihilate, abolish, extinguish — **erad·i·ca·ble** \-'rad-i-kə-bəl\ *adj*

erase \i-'rās\ *vb* **erased; eras·ing** : to rub or scratch out (as written words); *also* : OBLITERATE *syn* cancel, efface, delete, expunge — **eras·er** \i-'rā-sər\ *n* — **era·sure** \i-'rā-shər\ *n*

er·bi·um \'ər-bē-əm\ *n* : a rare metallic element

¹ere \(ˌ)eər\ *prep* : BEFORE

²ere *conj* : BEFORE

¹erect \i-'rekt\ *adj* **1** : not leaning or lying down : UPRIGHT **2** : being in a state of physiological erection

²erect *vb* **1** : BUILD **2** : to fix or set in an upright position **3** : SET UP; *also* : ESTABLISH, DEVELOP

erec·tile \i-'rek-t°l, -ˌtīl\ *adj* : capable of becoming erect ⟨∼ tissue⟩ ⟨∼ feathers of a bird⟩

erec·tion \i-'rek-shən\ *n* **1** : the turgid state of a previously flaccid bodily part when it becomes dilated with blood **2** : CONSTRUCTION

ere·long \eər-'lȯŋ\ *adv* : before long

er·e·mite \'er-ə-ˌmīt\ *n* : HERMIT

er·go \'er-gō, 'ər-\ *adv* [L] : THEREFORE

er·got \'ər-gət, -ˌgät\ *n* **1** : a disease of rye and other cereals caused by a fungus; *also* : this fungus **2** : a medicinal compound or preparation derived from an ergot fungus

Erie \'i(ə)r-ē\ *n* : a member of an American Indian people of the Lake Erie region; *also* : their language

er·mine \'ər-mən\ *n, pl* **ermines 1** : any of several weasels with winter fur mostly white; *also* : the white fur of an ermine **2** : a rank or office whose official robe is ornamented with ermine

erode \i-'rōd\ *vb* **erod·ed; erod·ing** : to diminish or destroy by degrees; *esp* : to gradually eat into or wear away ⟨soil *eroded* by wind and water⟩ — **erod·ible** \-'rōd-ə-bəl\ *adj*

erog·e·nous \i-'räj-ə-nəs\ *adj* **1** : sexually sensitive ⟨∼ zones⟩ **2** : of, relating to, or arousing sexual feelings

ero·sion \i-'rō-zhən\ *n* : the process or

state of being eroded — **ero·sion·al** \-'rōzh-(ə-)nəl\ *adj* — **ero·sion·al·ly** \-ē\ *adv*

ero·sive \i-'rō-siv\ *adj* : tending to erode — **ero·sive·ness** *n*

erot·ic \i-'rät-ik\ *adj* : relating to or dealing with sexual love : AMATORY — **erot·i·cal·ly** \-i-k(ə-)lē\ *adv* — **erot·i·cism** \i-'rät-ə-ˌsiz-əm\ *n*

err \'ər, 'er\ *vb* : to be or do wrong

er·rand \'er-ənd\ *n* : a short trip taken to do something; *also* : the object or purpose of such a trip

er·rant \'er-ənt\ *adj* **1** : WANDERING **2** : straying outside proper bounds **3** : deviating from an accepted pattern or standard

er·ra·ta \e-'rät-ə\ *n* : a list of corrigenda

er·rat·ic \ir-'at-ik\ *adj* **1** : IRREGULAR, CAPRICIOUS **2** : ECCENTRIC, UNUSUAL — **er·rat·i·cal·ly** \-i-k(ə-)lē\ *adv*

er·ra·tum \e-'rät-əm\ *n, pl* **-ta** \-ə\ : CORRIGENDUM

er·ro·ne·ous \ir-'ō-nē-əs, e-'rō-\ *adj* : INCORRECT — **er·ro·ne·ous·ly** *adv*

er·ror \'er-ər\ *n* **1** : a usu. ignorant or unintentional deviating from accuracy or truth ⟨made an ∼ in adding⟩ **2** : a defensive misplay in baseball **3** : the state of one that errs ⟨to be in ∼⟩ **4** : a product of mistake ⟨a typographical ∼⟩ — **er·ror·less** *adj*

er·satz \'er-ˌzäts\ *adj* [G] : SUBSTITUTE, SYNTHETIC ⟨∼ flour⟩

erst \'ərst\ *adv, archaic* : ERSTWHILE

¹erst·while \-ˌhwīl\ *adv* : in the past : FORMERLY

²erstwhile *adj* : FORMER, PREVIOUS

er·u·di·tion \ˌer-(y)ə-'dish-ən\ *n* : LEARNING, SCHOLARSHIP — **er·u·dite** \'er-(y)ə-ˌdīt\ *adj*

erupt \i-'rəpt\ *vb* **1** : to burst forth or cause to burst forth : EXPLODE **2** : to break through a surface ⟨teeth ∼*ing* through the gum⟩ **3** : to break out with or as if with a skin rash — **erup·tion** \-'rəp-shən\ *n* — **erup·tive** \-tiv\ *adj*

-ery \(ə-)rē\ *n suffix* **1** : qualities collectively : character : **-NESS** ⟨snobb*ery*⟩ **2** : art : practice ⟨cook*ery*⟩ **3** : place of doing, keeping, producing, or selling ⟨the thing specified⟩ ⟨fish*ery*⟩ ⟨bak*ery*⟩ **4** : collection : aggregate ⟨fin*ery*⟩

ery·sip·e·las \ˌer-ə-'sip-(ə-)ləs, ˌir-\ *n* : an acute bacterial disease marked by fever and severe skin inflammation

ery·the·ma \ˌer-ə-'thē-mə\ *n* : abnormal redness of the skin due to capillary congestion (as in inflammation)

eryth·ro·cyte \i-'rith-rə-ˌsīt\ *n* : RED BLOOD CELL

Es *symbol* einsteinium

¹-es \əz, iz *after* s, z, sh, ch; z *after* v or a vowel\ *n pl suffix* — used to form the plural of most nouns that end in s ⟨glass*es*⟩, z ⟨fuzz*es*⟩, sh ⟨bush*es*⟩, ch ⟨peach*es*⟩, or a final y that changes to *i* ⟨lad*ies*⟩ and of some nouns ending in f that changes to v ⟨loav*es*⟩

²-es *adv suffix* : **²-s**

³-es *vb suffix* — used to form the third

person singular present of most verbs that end in s (blesses), z (fizzes), sh (hushes), ch (catches), or a final y that changes to i (defies)

es·ca·late \'es-kə-ˌlāt\ *vb* **-lat·ed; -lat·ing :** to increase in extent, volume, number, intensity, or scope — **es·ca·la·tion** \ˌes-kə-'lā-shən\ *n*

es·ca·la·tor \'es-kə-ˌlāt-ər\ *n* : a power-driven set of stairs

es·cal·lop \is-'käl-əp, -'kal-\ *var of* SCALLOP

es·ca·pade \'es-kə-ˌpād\ *n* [F, action of escaping] : a mischievous adventure : PRANK

¹**es·cape** \is-'kāp\ *vb* **es·caped; es·cap·ing** [ME *escapen*, fr. OF *escaper*, fr. (assumed) VL *excappare*, fr. L *ex-* out + LL *cappa* head covering, cloak] 1 : to get free or away 2 : to avoid a threatening evil 3 : to miss or succeed in averting (~ injury) 4 : ELUDE (his name ~s me) 5 : to be produced or uttered involuntarily by (let a sob ~ him)

²**escape** *n* 1 : flight from or avoidance of something unpleasant 2 : LEAKAGE 3 : a means of escape

³**escape** *adj* : providing a means or way of escape

es·cap·ee \is-ˌkā-'pē, ˌes-(ˌ)kā-\ *n* : one that has escaped esp. from prison

escape velocity *n* : the minimum velocity needed by a body (as a rocket) to escape from the gravitational field of a celestial body (as the earth)

es·cap·ism \is-'kā-ˌpiz-əm\ *n* : diversion of the mind to imaginative activity as an escape from routine — **es·cap·ist** \-pəst\ *adj or n*

es·ca·role \'es-kə-ˌrōl\ *n* : ENDIVE 1

es·carp·ment \is-'kärp-mənt\ *n* 1 : a steep slope in front of a fortification 2 : a long cliff

es·chew \is-'chü\ *vb* : SHUN, AVOID

¹**es·cort** \'es-ˌkȯrt\ *n* : one (as a person or warship) accompanying another esp. as a protection or courtesy

²**es·cort** \is-'kȯrt, es-\ *vb* : to accompany as an escort

es·crow \'es-ˌkrō\ *n* : something (as a deed or a sum of money) delivered by one person to another to be delivered to a third party only upon the fulfillment of a condition; *also* : a fund or deposit serving as an escrow

es·cu·do \is-'küd-ō\ *n, pl* **-dos** — see MONEY table

es·cutch·eon \is-'kəch-ən\ *n* : the usu. shield-shaped surface on which a coat of arms is shown

Esd *abbr* Esdras

Es·dras \'ez-drəs\ *n* — see BIBLE table

ESE *abbr* east-southeast

Es·ki·mo \'es-kə-ˌmō\ *n* 1 : a member of a group of peoples of northern Canada, Greenland, Alaska, and eastern Siberia 2 : the language of the Eskimo people

Eskimo dog *n* : a sled dog of American origin

ESL *abbr* English as a second language

esoph·a·gus \i-'säf-ə-gəs\ *n, pl* **-gi** \-ˌgī, -ˌjī\ : a muscular tube that leads from the cavity behind the mouth to the stomach — **esoph·a·geal** \-ˌsäf-ə-'jē-əl\ *adj*

es·o·ter·ic \ˌes-ə-'ter-ik\ *adj* 1 : designed for or understood only by the specially initiated 2 : PRIVATE, SECRET

esp *abbr* especially

ESP \ˌē-ˌes-'pē\ *n* : extrasensory perception

es·pa·drille \'es-pə-ˌdril\ *n* [F] : a flat sandal usu. having a fabric upper and a flexible sole

es·pal·ier \is-'pal-yər, -ˌyā\ *n* : a plant (as a fruit tree) trained to grow flat against a support — **espalier** *vb*

es·pe·cial \is-'pesh-əl\ *adj* : SPECIAL, PARTICULAR — **es·pe·cial·ly** \-'pesh-ə-)lē\ *adv*

Es·pe·ran·to \ˌes-pə-'rant-ō, -'rän-tō\ *n* : an artificial international language based as far as possible on words common to the chief European languages

es·pi·o·nage \'es-pē-ə-ˌnäzh, -nij\ *n* [F *espionnage*] : the practice of spying

es·pla·nade \'es-plə-ˌnäd\ *n* : a level open stretch or area; *esp* : one for walking or driving along a shore

es·pous·al \is-'paù-zəl\ *n* 1 : BETROTHAL; *also* : WEDDING 2 : a taking up (as of a cause) as a supporter — **es·pouse** \-'paùz\ *vb*

espres·so \e-'spres-ō\ *n, pl* **-sos** [It (*caffè*) *espresso*, lit., pressed out coffee] : coffee brewed by forcing steam through finely ground darkly roasted coffee beans

es·prit \is-'prē\ *n* : sprightly wit

es·prit de corps \is-ˌprēd-ə-'kȯr\ *n* [F] : the common spirit existing in the members of a group

es·py \is-'pī\ *vb* **es·pied; es·py·ing** : to catch sight of *syn* behold, see, view, descry

Esq *or* **Esqr** *abbr* esquire

es·quire \'es-ˌkwī(ə)r\ *n* [ME, fr. MF *esquier* squire, fr. LL *scutarius*, fr. L *scutum* shield] 1 : a man of the English gentry ranking next below a knight 2 : a candidate for knighthood serving as attendant to a knight 3 — used as a title of courtesy

-ess \əs, ˌes\ *n suffix* : female (authoress)

¹**es·say** \e-'sā, 'es-ˌā\ *vb* : ATTEMPT, TRY

²**es·say** *n* 1 \'es-ˌā, e-'sā\ : ATTEMPT 2 \'es-ˌā\ : a literary composition usu. dealing with a subject from a limited or personal point of view — **es·say·ist** \'es-ˌā-əst\ *n*

es·sence \'es-ᵊns\ *n* 1 : fundamental nature or quality 2 : a substance distilled or extracted from another substance (as a plant or drug) and having the special qualities of the original substance (~ of peppermint) 3 : PERFUME

¹**es·sen·tial** \i-'sen-chəl\ *adj* 1 : contain-

ing or constituting an essence ⟨free speech is an ~ right of citizenship⟩ ⟨~ oils⟩ 2 : of the utmost importance : IN-DISPENSABLE **syn** imperative, necessary, necessitous — **es·sen·tial·ly** \-ē\ *adv*

²**essential** *n* : something essential

est *abbr* 1 established 2 estimate; estimated

EST *abbr* eastern standard time

¹**-est** \əst, ist\ *adj suffix or adv suffix* — used to form the superlative degree of adjectives and adverbs of one syllable ⟨fatt*est*⟩ ⟨lat*est*⟩, of some adjectives and adverbs of two syllables ⟨luck*iest*⟩ ⟨oft*enest*⟩, and less often of longer ones ⟨beggarl*iest*⟩

²**-est** \əst, ist\ *or* **-st** \st\ *vb suffix* — used to form the archaic second person singular of English verbs (with *thou*) ⟨gett*est*⟩ ⟨did*st*⟩

es·tab·lish \is-'tab-lish\ *vb* 1 : to make firm or stable 2 : ORDAIN 3 : FOUND ⟨~ a settlement⟩; *also* : to put on a firm basis : SET UP ⟨~ a son in business⟩ 5 : to gain acceptance or recognition of (as a claim or fact) ⟨~ed his right to help⟩; *also* : PROVE

es·tab·lish·ment \-mənt\ *n* 1 : something established 2 : a place of residence or business with its furnishings and staff 3 : an established ruling or controlling group ⟨the literary ~⟩ 4 : the act or state of establishing or being established

es·tate \is-'tāt\ *n* 1 : STATE, CONDITION; *also* : social standing : STATUS 2 : a social or political class ⟨the three ~s of nobility, clergy, and commons⟩ 3 : a person's possessions : FORTUNE 4 : a landed property

¹**es·teem** \is-'tēm\ *n* : high regard

²**esteem** *vb* 1 : REGARD 2 : to set a high value on **syn** respect, admire, revere

es·ter \'es-tər\ *n* : an often fragrant organic compound formed by the reaction of an acid and an alcohol

Esth *abbr* Esther

Es·ther \'es-tər\ *n* — see BIBLE table

esthete, esthetic, esthetics *var of* AESTHETE, AESTHETIC, AESTHETICS

es·ti·ma·ble \'es-tə-mə-bəl\ *adj* : worthy of esteem

¹**es·ti·mate** \'es-tə-,māt\ *vb* **-mat·ed; -mat·ing** 1 : to give or form an approximation (as of value, size, or cost) 2 : JUDGE, CONCLUDE **syn** evaluate, value, rate, appraise, assay, assess — **es·ti·ma·tor** \-,mā-tər\ *n*

²**es·ti·mate** \'es-tə-mət\ *n* 1 : OPINION, JUDGMENT 2 : a rough or approximate calculation 3 : a statement of the cost of work to be done

es·ti·ma·tion \,es-tə-'mā-shən\ *n* 1 : JUDGMENT, OPINION 2 : ESTIMATE 3 : ESTEEM, HONOR

es·ti·vate \'es-tə-,vāt\ *vb* **-vat·ed; -vat·ing** : to pass the summer in an inactive or resting state — **es·ti·va·tion** \,es-tə-'vā-shən\ *n*

Es·to·nian \e-'stō-nē-ən\ *n* : a native or inhabitant of Estonia

es·trange \is-'trānj\ *vb* **es·tranged; es·trang·ing** : to alienate the affections or confidence of — **es·trange·ment** *n*

es·tro·gen \'es-trə-jən\ *n* : a substance (as a sex hormone) that tends to cause estrus and the development of secondary sex characteristics in the female — **es·tro·gen·ic** \,es-trə-'jen-ik\ *adj*

estrous cycle *n* : the cycle of changes in the endocrine and reproductive systems of a female mammal from the beginning of one period of estrus to the beginning of the next

es·trus \'es-trəs\ *n* : a periodic state of sexual excitability during which the female of most mammals is willing to mate with the male and is capable of becoming pregnant : HEAT — **es·trous** \-trəs\ *adj*

es·tu·ary \'es-chə-,wer-ē\ *n, pl* **-ar·ies** : an arm of the sea at the mouth of a river

ET *abbr* eastern time

ETA *abbr* estimated time of arrival

et al \et-'al\ *abbr* [L *et alii* (masc.), *et aliae* (fem.), *or et alia* (neut.)] and others

etc \ən-'sō-,fōrth, et-'set-ə-rə, -'se-trə\ *abbr* et cetera

et cet·era \et-'set-ə-rə, -'se-trə\ [L] and others esp. of the same kind

etch \'ech\ *vb* [Dutch *etsen*, fr G *ätzen*, lit., to feed] 1 : to make lines on (as metal) usu. by the action of acid; *also* : to produce (as a design) by etching 2 : to delineate clearly — **etch·er** *n*

etch·ing \-iŋ\ *n* 1 : the act, process, or art of etching 2 : a design produced on or print made from an etched plate

ETD *abbr* estimated time of departure

eter·nal \i-'tərn-əl\ *adj* : EVERLASTING, PERPETUAL — **eter·nal·ly** \-ē\ *adv*

eter·ni·ty \i-'tər-nət-ē\ *n, pl* **-ties** 1 : infinite duration 2 : IMMORTALITY

¹**-eth** \əth, ith\ *or* **-th** \th\ *vb suffix* — used to form the archaic third person singular present of verbs ⟨go*eth*⟩ ⟨do*th*⟩

²**-eth** — see ²-TH

eth·ane \'eth-,ān\ *n* : a colorless odorless gaseous hydrocarbon found in natural gas and used esp. as a fuel

eth·a·nol \'eth-ə-,nōl\ *n* : ALCOHOL 1

ether \'ē-thər\ *n* 1 : the upper regions of space; *also* : the gaseous element formerly held to fill these regions 2 : a light flammable liquid used as an anesthetic and solvent

ethe·re·al \i-'thir-ē-əl\ *adj* 1 : CELESTIAL, HEAVENLY 2 : exceptionally delicate AIRY, DAINTY — **ethe·re·al·ly** \-ē\ *adv* — **ethe·re·al·ness** *n*

eth·i·cal \'eth-i-kəl\ *adj* 1 : of or relating to ethics 2 : conforming to accepted and esp. professional standards of conduct **syn** virtuous, moral, principled — **eth·i·cal·ly** \-i-k(ə-)lē\ *adv*

eth·ics \'eth-iks\ *n sing or pl* 1 : a discipline dealing with good and evil and with moral duty **2** : moral principles or practice

Ethi·o·pi·an \ˌē-thē-'ō-pē-ən\ *n* : a native or inhabitant of Ethiopia — **Ethiopian** *adj*

¹**eth·nic** \'eth-nik\ *n* : a member of a minority ethnic group who retains its customs, language, or social views

²**ethnic** *adj* : of or relating to races or large groups of people classed according to common traits and customs — **eth·ni·cal·ly** \-ni-k(ə-)lē\ *adv*

eth·nol·o·gy \eth-'näl-ə-jē\ *n* : a science dealing with the races of man, their origin, distribution, characteristics, and relations — **eth·no·log·i·cal** \ˌeth-nə-'läj-i-kəl\ *adj* — **eth·nol·o·gist** \eth-'näl-ə-jəst\ *n*

ethol·o·gy \ē-'thäl-ə-jē\ *n* : the scientific and objective study of animal behavior — **etho·log·i·cal** \ˌē-thə-'läj-i-kəl, ˌeth-ə-\ *adj* — **ethol·o·gist** \ē-'thäl-ə-jəst\ *n*

ethos \'ē-ˌthäs\ *n* : the distinguishing character, sentiment, moral nature, or guiding beliefs of a person, group, or institution

ethyl alcohol *n* : ALCOHOL 1

eth·yl·ene \'eth-ə-ˌlēn\ *n* : a colorless flammable gas found in coal gas or obtained from petroleum

eti·ol·o·gy \ˌēt-ē-'äl-ə-jē\ *n* **1** : CAUSE, ORIGIN; *esp* : the causes of a disease or abnormal condition **2** : a branch of medicine concerned with the causes and origins of diseases — **eti·o·log·ic** \ˌēt-ē-ə-'läj-ik\ *or* **eti·o·log·i·cal** \-i-kəl\ *adj*

et·i·quette \'et-i-kət, -ˌket\ *n* [F *étiquette*, lit., ticket] : the forms prescribed by custom or authority to be observed in social, official, or professional life **syn** propriety, decorum, decency, dignity

Etrus·can \i-'trəs-kən\ *n* **1** : the language of the Etruscans **2** : an inhabitant of ancient Etruria — **Etruscan** *adj*

et seq *abbr* [L *et sequens*] and the following one; [L *et sequentes* (masc. & fem. pl.) *or et sequentia* (neut. pl.)] and the following ones

-ette \'et, ˌet, ət, it\ *n suffix* **1** : little one (din*ette*) **2** : female (major*ette*)

étude \'ā-ˌt(y)üd\ *n* [F, lit., study] : a musical composition for practice to develop technical skill

ety *abbr* etymology

et·y·mol·o·gy \ˌet-ə-'mäl-ə-jē\ *n, pl* **-gies** **1** : the history of a linguistic form (as a word) shown by tracing its development and relationships **2** : a branch of linguistics dealing with etymologies — **et·y·mo·log·i·cal** \-mə-'läj-i-kəl\ *adj* — **et·y·mol·o·gist** \-'mäl-ə-jəst\ *n*

Eu *symbol* europium

eu·ca·lyp·tus \ˌyü-kə-'lip-təs\ *n, pl* **-ti** \-ˌtī\ *or* **-tus·es** : any of a genus of mostly Australian evergreen trees widely grown for shade or their wood, oils, resins, and gums

Eu·cha·rist \'yü-k(ə-)rəst\ *n* : COMMUNION 2 — **eu·cha·ris·tic** \ˌyü-kə-'ris-tik\ *adj, often cap*

¹**euchre** \'yü-kər\ *n* : a card game in which the side naming the trump must take three of five tricks to win

²**euchre** *vb* **eu·chred; eu·chring** \-k(ə-)riŋ\ : CHEAT, TRICK

eu·clid·e·an *also* **eu·clid·i·an** \yù-'klid-ē-ən\ *adj, often cap* : of or relating to the geometry of Euclid or a geometry based on similar axioms

eu·gen·ics \yü-'jen-iks\ *n* : a science dealing with the improvement (as by selective breeding) of hereditary qualities esp. of human beings — **eu·gen·ic** \-ik\ *adj*

eu·lo·gy \'yü-lə-jē\ *n, pl* **-gies 1** : a speech in praise of some person or thing **2** : high praise — **eu·lo·gis·tic** \ˌyü-lə-'jis-tik\ *adj* — **eu·lo·gize** \'yü-lə-ˌjīz\ *vb*

eu·nuch \'yü-nək\ *n* : a castrated man

eu·phe·mism \'yü-fə-ˌmiz-əm\ *n* [Gk *euphēmismos*, fr. *euphēmos* auspicious, sounding good, fr. *eu-* good + *phēmē* speech] : the substitution of a mild or pleasant expression for one offensive or unpleasant; *also* : the expression substituted — **eu·phe·mis·tic** \ˌyü-fə-'mis-tik\ *adj*

eu·pho·ni·ous \yù-'fō-nē-əs\ *adj* : pleasing to the ear

eu·pho·ny \'yü-fə-nē\ *n, pl* **-nies** : the effect produced by words so combined as to please the ear

eu·pho·ria \yù-'fōr-ē-ə\ *n* : a marked feeling of well-being or elation — **eu·phor·ic** \-'fōr-ik\ *adj*

Eur *abbr* Europe; European

Eur·asian \yù-'rā-zhən, -shən\ *adj* **1** : of mixed European and Asian origin **2** : of or relating to Europe and Asia — **Eurasian** *n*

eu·re·ka \yù-'rē-kə\ *interj* [Gk *heurēka* I have found, fr. *heuriskein* to find; fr. the exclamation attributed to Archimedes on discovering a method for determining the purity of gold] — used to express triumph on a discovery

Eu·ro·bond \'yùr-ō-ˌbänd\ *n* : a bond of a U.S. corporation that is sold outside the U.S. but that is valued and paid for in dollars and yields interest in dollars

Eu·ro·cur·ren·cy \ˌyùr-ō-'kər-ən-sē, -'kə-rən-\ *n* : moneys (as of the U.S. and Japan) held outside their countries of origin and used in the money markets of Europe

Eu·ro·dol·lar \'yùr-ō-ˌdäl-ər\ *n* : a U.S. dollar held (as by a bank) outside the U.S. and esp. in Europe

Eu·ro·pe·an \ˌyùr-ə-'pē-ən\ *n* : a native or inhabitant of Europe — **European** *adj*

European plan *n* : a hotel plan whereby the daily rates cover only the cost of the room eu·ro·pi·um \yù-'rō-pē-əm\ n : a metallic chemical element

eu·sta·chian tube \yù-'stā-shən-\ n, often cap E : a tube connecting the inner cavity of the ear with the throat and equalizing air pressure on both sides of the eardrum

eu·tha·na·sia \,yü-thə-'nā-zh(ē-)ə\ n [Gk, easy death, fr. eu- good + thanatos death] : MERCY KILLING

eu·tro·phi·ca·tion \yù-,trō-fə-'kā-shən\ n : the process by which a body of water becomes rich in dissolved nutrients (as phosphates) and often shallow with a seasonal deficiency in dissolved oxygen — eu·tro·phic \yù-'trō-fik\ adj

EVA abbr extravehicular activity

evac·u·ate \i-'vak-yə-,wāt\ vb -at·ed; -at·ing 1 : EMPTY 2 : to discharge wastes from the body 3 : to remove or withdraw from : VACATE — evac·u·a·tion \-,vak-yə-'wā-shən\ n

evac·u·ee \i-,vak-yə-'wē\ n : an evacuated person

evade \i-'vād\ vb evad·ed; evad·ing : to manage to avoid esp. by dexterity or slyness : ELUDE, ESCAPE

eval·u·ate \i-'val-yə-,wāt\ vb -at·ed; -at·ing : APPRAISE, VALUE — eval·u·a·tion \-,val-yə-'wā-shən\ n

ev·a·nes·cent \,ev-ə-'nes-°nt\ adj : tending to vanish like vapor syn passing, transient, transitory, momentary — ev·a·nes·cence \-°ns\ n

evan·gel·i·cal \,ē-,van-'jel-i-kəl, ,ev-ən-\ adj [LL evangelium gospel, fr. Gk evangelion, fr. eu- good + angelos messenger] 1 : of or relating to the Christian gospel esp. as presented in the four Gospels 2 : of or relating to certain Protestant churches emphasizing the authority of Scripture and the importance of preaching as contrasted with ritual 3 : ZEALOUS ⟨~ fervor⟩ — Evangelical n — evan·gel·i·cal·ism \-kə-,liz-əm\ n — evan·gel·i·cal·ly \-k(ə-)lē\ adv

evan·ge·lism \i-'van-jə-,liz-əm\ n 1 : the winning or revival of personal commitments to Christ 2 : militant or crusading zeal — evan·ge·lis·tic \-,van-jə-'lis-tik\ adj — evan·ge·lis·ti·cal·ly \-ti-k(ə-)lē\ adv

evan·ge·list \i-'van-jə-ləst\ n 1 often cap : the writer of any of the four Gospels 2 : one who evangelizes; esp : a preacher who conducts revival services

evan·ge·lize \i-'van-jə-,līz\ vb -lized; -liz·ing 1 : to preach the gospel 2 : to convert to Christianity

evap abbr evaporate

evap·o·rate \i-'vap-ə-,rāt\ vb -rat·ed; -rat·ing 1 : to pass off or cause to pass off in vapor 2 : to disappear quickly 3 : to drive out the moisture from (as by heat) — evap·o·ra·tion \-,vap-ə-'rā-shən\ n — evap·o·ra·tor \-'vap-ə-,rā-tər\ n

evap·o·rite \i-'vap-ə-,rīt\ n : a sedimentary rock that originates by the evapo-

ration of seawater in an enclosed basin

eva·sion \i-'vā-zhən\ n 1 : an act or instance of evading 2 : a means of evading; esp : an equivocal statement used in evading — eva·sive \i-'vā-siv\ adj — eva·sive·ness n

eve \'ēv\ n 1 : EVENING 2 : the period just before some important event

¹even \'ē-vən\ adj 1 : LEVEL, FLAT 2 : REGULAR, SMOOTH 3 : EQUAL, FAIR 4 : BALANCED; also : fully revenged 5 : divisible by two 6 : EXACT syn stable, uniform, steady, constant — even·ly adv — even·ness \-vən-nəs\ n

²even adv 1 : EXACTLY, PRECISELY 2 : FULLY, QUITE 3 : at the very time 4 — used as an intensive to stress identity ⟨~ we know that⟩ 5 — used as an intensive to stress the comparative degree ⟨did ~ better⟩

³even vb evened; even·ing \'ēv-(ə-)niŋ\ : to make or become even

even·hand·ed \,ē-vən-'han-dəd\ adj : FAIR, IMPARTIAL

eve·ning \'ēv-niŋ\ n : the end of the day and early part of the night

evening primrose n : a coarse biennial herb with yellow flowers that open in the evening

evening star n : a bright planet seen esp. in the western sky at or after sunset

even·song \'ē-vən-,sȯŋ\ n, often cap 1 : VESPERS 2 : evening prayer esp. when sung

event \i-'vent\ n [MF or L; MF, fr. L eventus, fr. evenire to happen, fr. venire to come] 1 : OCCURRENCE 2 : a noteworthy happening 3 : CONTINGENCY ⟨in the ~ of rain⟩ 4 : a contest in a program of sports — event·ful adj

even·tide \'ē-vən-,tīd\ n : EVENING

even·tu·al \i-'vench-(ə-w)əl\ adj : coming at some later time : ULTIMATE — even·tu·al·ly \-ē\ adv

even·tu·al·i·ty \i-,ven-chə-'wal-ət-ē\ n, pl -ties : a possible event or outcome

even·tu·ate \i-'ven-chə-,wāt\ vb -at·ed; -at·ing : to result finally

ev·er \'ev-ər\ adv 1 : ALWAYS 2 : at any time 3 : in any way : AT ALL

ev·er·bloom·ing \,ev-ər-'blü-miŋ\ adj : blooming more or less continuously throughout the growing season

ev·er·glade \'ev-ər-,glād\ n : a low-lying tract of swampy or marshy land

ev·er·green \-,grēn\ adj : having foliage that remains green ⟨coniferous trees are mostly ~⟩ — evergreen n

¹ev·er·last·ing \,ev-ər-'las-tiŋ\ adj 1 : enduring forever : ETERNAL 2 : keeping form or color for a long time when dried ⟨~ flowers⟩ — ev·er·last·ing·ly adv

²everlasting n 1 : ETERNITY ⟨from ~⟩ 2 : a plant with everlasting flowers; also : its flower

ev·er·more \,ev-ər-'mōr\ adv : FOREVER

ev·ery \'ev-rē\ adj 1 : being each one of a group 2 : all possible ⟨given ~

chance); *also* : COMPLETE (have ∼ confidence)

ev·ery·body \'ev-ri-ˌbäd-ē, -bəd-\ *pron* : every person

ev·ery·day \'ev-rē-ˌdā\ *adj* : used or fit for daily use : ORDINARY

ev·ery·one \-(ˌ)wən\ *pron* : EVERYBODY

ev·ery·thing \'ev-rē-ˌthiŋ\ *pron* : all that exists; *also* : all that is relevant

ev·ery·where \'ev-rē-ˌhweər\ *adv* : in every place or part

evg *abbr* evening

evict \i-'vikt\ *vb* : to put (a person) out from a property by legal process; *also* : EXPEL syn eject, oust, dismiss — **evic·tion** \-'vik-shən\ *n*

ev·i·dence \'ev-əd-əns\ *n* 1 : an outward sign 2 : PROOF, TESTIMONY; *esp* : matter submitted in court to determine the truth of alleged facts

ev·i·dent \'ev-əd-ənt\ *adj* : clear to the vision and understanding syn manifest, distinct, obvious, apparent, plain — **ev·i·dent·ly** \'ev-əd-ənt-lē, -ə-ˌdent-\ *adv*

¹**evil** \'ē-vəl\ *adj* **evil·er** or **evil·ler**; **evil·est** or **evil·lest** 1 : WICKED 2 : causing or threatening distress or harm : PERNICIOUS — **evil·ly** *adv*

²**evil** *n* 1 : a source of sorrow or distress : CALAMITY 2 : the fact of suffering, misfortune, and wrongdoing — **evil·do·er** \ˌē-vəl-'dü-ər\ *n*

evil-mind·ed \ˌē-vəl-'mīn-dəd\ *adj* : having an evil disposition or evil thoughts

evince \i-'vins\ *vb* **evinced; evinc·ing** : SHOW, REVEAL

evis·cer·ate \i-'vis-ə-ˌrāt\ *vb* **-at·ed; -at·ing** 1 : to remove the entrails of 2 : to deprive of vital content or force — **evis·cer·a·tion** \-ˌvis-ə-'rā-shən\ *n*

evoke \i-'vōk\ *vb* **evoked; evok·ing** : to call forth or up — **evo·ca·tion** \ˌē-vō-'kā-shən, ˌev-ə-\ *n* — **evoc·a·tive** \i-'väk-ət-iv\ *adj*

evo·lu·tion \ˌev-ə-'lü-shən\ *n* 1 : a process of change in a particular direction 2 : one of a series of prescribed movements (as in a dance or military exercise) 3 : a theory that the various kinds of plants and animals are descended from other kinds that lived in earlier times and that the differences are due to inherited changes that took place over many generations — **evo·lu·tion·ary** \-shə-ˌner-ē\ *adj* — **evo·lu·tion·ist** \-sh(ə-)nəst\ *n*

evolve \i-'välv\ *vb* **evolved; evolv·ing** [L *evolvere* to unroll] : to develop by or as if by evolution

EW *abbr* enlisted woman

ewe \'yü\ *n* : a female sheep

ew·er \'yü-ər\ *n* : a vase-shaped jug

¹**ex** \(ˌ)eks\ *prep* [L] : out of : FROM

²**ex** \'eks\ *n* : a former spouse

³**ex** *abbr* 1 example 2 express 3 extra

Ex *abbr* Exodus

ex- \e *also* occurs in this prefix where only i is shown below (as in "express") and ks sometimes occurs where only gz is shown (as in "exact")\ *prefix* 1 : out of : outside 2 : former ⟨*ex*-president⟩

ex·ac·er·bate \ig-'zas-ər-ˌbāt\ *vb* **-bat·ed; -bat·ing** : to make more violent, bitter, or severe — **ex·ac·er·ba·tion** \-ˌzas-ər-'bā-shən\ *n*

¹**ex·act** \ig-'zakt\ *vb* 1 : to compel to furnish 2 : to call for as suitable or necessary — **ex·ac·tion** \-'zak-shən\ *n*

²**exact** *adj* : precisely accurate or correct syn right, precise, proper, nice — **ex·act·ly** \-zak-(t)lē\ *adv* — **ex·act·ness** \-'zak(t)-nəs\ *n*

ex·act·ing \ig-'zak-tiŋ\ *adj* 1 : greatly demanding ⟨an ∼ taskmaster⟩ 2 : requiring close attention and precision

ex·ac·ti·tude \ig-'zak-tə-ˌt(y)üd\ *n* : the quality or state of being exact

ex·ag·ger·ate \ig-'zaj-ə-ˌrāt\ *vb* **-at·ed; -at·ing** [L *exaggeratus*, pp. of *exaggerare*, lit., to heap up, fr. *agger* heap] : to enlarge (as a statement) beyond bounds : OVERSTATE — **ex·ag·ger·at·ed·ly** *adv* — **ex·ag·ger·a·tion** \-ˌzaj-ə-'rā-shən\ *n* — **ex·ag·ger·a·tor** \-'zaj-ə-ˌrāt-ər\ *n*

ex·alt \ig-'zōlt\ *vb* 1 : to raise up esp. in rank, power, or dignity 2 : GLORIFY 3 : to elate the mind or spirits — **ex·al·ta·tion** \ˌeg-ˌzōl-'tā-shən, ˌek-ˌsôl-\ *n*

ex·am \ig-'zam\ *n* : EXAMINATION

ex·am·ine \ig-'zam-ən\ *vb* **ex·am·ined; ex·am·in·ing** \-(ə-)niŋ\ 1 : to inspect closely 2 : QUESTION; *esp* : to test by questioning syn interrogate, query, quiz, catechize — **ex·am·i·na·tion** \-ˌzam-ə-'nā-shən\ *n*

ex·am·ple \ig-'zam-pəl\ *n* 1 : something forming a model to be followed or avoided 2 : a representative sample 3 : a problem to be solved in order to show the application of some rule

ex·as·per·ate \ig-'zas-pə-ˌrāt\ *vb* **-at·ed; -at·ing** : VEX, IRRITATE — **ex·as·per·a·tion** \ig-ˌzas-pə-'rā-shən\ *n*

exc *abbr* 1 excellent 2 except

ex·ca·vate \'ek-skə-ˌvāt\ *vb* **-vat·ed; -vat·ing** 1 : to hollow out; *also* : to form by hollowing out 2 : to dig out and remove (as earth) 3 : to reveal to view by digging away a covering — **ex·ca·va·tion** \ˌek-skə-'vā-shən\ *n* — **ex·ca·va·tor** \'ek-skə-ˌvāt-ər\ *n*

ex·ceed \ik-'sēd\ *vb* 1 : to go or be beyond the limit of 2 : SURPASS

ex·ceed·ing·ly \-iŋ-lē\ *or* **ex·ceed·ing** *adv* : EXTREMELY, VERY

ex·cel \ik-'sel\ *vb* **-celled; -cel·ling** : SURPASS, OUTDO

ex·cel·lence \'ek-s(ə-)ləns\ *n* 1 : the quality of being excellent 2 : an excellent or valuable quality : VIRTUE 3 : EXCELLENCY 2

ex·cel·len·cy \-s(ə-)lən-sē\ *n, pl* **-cies** 1 : EXCELLENCE 2 — used as a title of honor

ex·cel·lent \'ek-s(ə-)lənt\ *adj* : very good of its kind : FIRST-CLASS — **ex·cel·lent·ly** *adv*

ex·cel·si·or \ik-'sel-sē-ər\ *n* : fine curled

wood shavings used esp. for packing fragile items

¹ex·cept \ik-ˈsept\ *also* **ex·cept·ing** \-ˈsep-tiŋ\ *prep* **1** : not including ⟨daily ∼ Sundays⟩ **2** : other than : BUT ⟨saw no one ∼ him⟩

²except *vb* **1** : to take or leave out **2** : OBJECT

³except *also* **excepting** *conj* : ONLY ⟨I'd go, ∼ it's too far⟩

ex·cep·tion \ik-ˈsep-shən\ *n* **1** : the act of excepting **2** : something excepted **3** : OBJECTION

ex·cep·tion·able \ik-ˈsep-sh(ə-)nə-bəl\ *adj* : OBJECTIONABLE

ex·cep·tion·al \ik-ˈsep-sh(ə-)nəl\ *adj* **1** : UNUSUAL **2** : SUPERIOR — **ex·cep·tion·al·ly** \-ˈsep-sh(ə-)nə-lē\ *adv*

ex·cerpt \ˈek-ˌsərpt, ˈeg-ˌzərpt\ *n* : a passage selected or copied : EXTRACT — **excerpt** \ek-ˈsərpt, eg-ˈzərpt; ˈek-ˌsərpt, ˈeg-ˌzərpt\ *vb*

ex·cess \ik-ˈses, ˈek-ˌses\ *n* **1** : SUPERFLUITY, SURPLUS **2** : the amount by which one quantity exceeds another **3** : INTEMPERANCE — **excess** *adj* — **ex·ces·sive** \ik-ˈses-iv\ *adj* — **ex·ces·sive·ly** *adv*

exch *abbr* exchange; exchanged

¹ex·change \iks-ˈchānj, ˈeks-ˌchānj\ *n* **1** : the giving or taking of one thing in return for another : TRADE **2** : a substituting of one thing for another **3** : interchange of valuables and esp. of bills of exchange or money of different countries **4** : a place where things and services are exchanged; *esp* : a marketplace for securities **5** : a central office in which telephone lines are connected for communication

²exchange *vb* **ex·changed; ex·chang·ing** : to transfer in return for some equivalent : BARTER, SWAP — **ex·change·able** \iks-ˈchān-jə-bəl\ *adj*

ex·che·quer \ˈeks-ˌchek-ər\ *n* [ME *escheker*, fr. OF *eschequier* chessboard, counting table] : TREASURY; *esp* : a national treasury

ex·cise \ˈek-ˌsīz, -ˌsīs\ *n* : a tax on the manufacture, sale, or consumption of goods within a country

ex·ci·sion \ik-ˈsizh-ən\ *n* : removal by or as if by cutting out esp. by surgical means — **ex·cise** \ik-ˈsīz\ *vb*

ex·cit·able \ik-ˈsīt-ə-bəl\ *adj* : easily excited — **ex·cit·abil·i·ty** \-ˌsīt-ə-ˈbil-ət-ē\ *n*

ex·cite \ik-ˈsīt\ *vb* **ex·cit·ed; ex·cit·ing** **1** : to stir up the emotions of : ROUSE **2** : to increase the activity of : STIMULATE *syn* provoke, stimulate, pique, quicken — **ex·ci·ta·tion** \ˌek-ˌsī-ˈtā-shən, ˌek-sə-\ *n* — **ex·cit·ed·ly** *adv*

ex·cite·ment \ik-ˈsīt-mənt\ *n* : AGITATION, STIR

ex·claim \iks-ˈklām\ *vb* : to cry out, speak, or utter sharply or vehemently — **ex·cla·ma·tion** \ˌeks-klə-ˈmā-shən\ *n* — **ex·clam·a·to·ry** \iks-ˈklam-ə-ˌtōr-ē\ *adj*

exclamation point *n* : a punctuation mark ! used esp. after an interjection or exclamation

ex·clude \iks-ˈklüd\ *vb* **ex·clud·ed; ex·clud·ing** **1** : to shut out (as from using or participating) : BAR **2** : to put out : EXPEL — **ex·clu·sion** \-ˈklü-zhən\ *n*

ex·clu·sive \iks-ˈklü-siv\ *adj* **1** : reserved for particular persons **2** : snobbishly aloof; *also* : STYLISH **3** : SOLE ⟨∼ rights⟩; *also* : UNDIVIDED *syn* chic, modish, smart, swank, fashionable — **ex·clu·sive·ly** *adv* — **ex·clu·sive·ness** *n*

exclusive of *prep* : not taking into account

ex·cog·i·tate \ek-ˈskäj-ə-ˌtāt\ *vb* : to think out : DEVISE

ex·com·mu·ni·cate \ˌek-skə-ˈmyü-nə-ˌkāt\ *vb* : to cut off officially from communion with the church — **ex·com·mu·ni·ca·tion** \-ˌmyü-nə-ˈkā-shən\ *n*

ex·co·ri·ate \ek-ˈskōr-ē-ˌāt\ *vb* **-at·ed; -at·ing** : to criticize severely — **ex·co·ri·a·tion** \(ˌ)ek-ˌskōr-ē-ˈā-shən\ *n*

ex·cre·ment \ˈek-skrə-mənt\ *n* : waste discharged from the body and esp. from the alimentary canal — **ex·cre·men·tal** \ˌek-skrə-ˈment-ᵊl\ *adj*

ex·cres·cence \ik-ˈskres-ᵊns\ *n* : OUTGROWTH; *esp* : an abnormal outgrowth (as a wart) — **ex·cres·cent** \-ᵊnt\ *adj*

ex·cre·ta \ik-ˈskrēt-ə\ *n pl* : waste matter separated or eliminated from an organism

ex·crete \ik-ˈskrēt\ *vb* **ex·cret·ed; ex·cret·ing** : to separate and eliminate wastes from the body esp. in urine — **ex·cre·tion** \-ˈskrē-shən\ *n* — **ex·cre·to·ry** \ˈek-skrə-ˌtōr-ē\ *adj*

ex·cru·ci·at·ing \ik-ˈskrü-shē-ˌāt-iŋ\ *adj* [L *excruciare*, fr. *cruciare* to crucify, fr. *crux* cross] : intensely painful or distressing *syn* agonizing, harrowing, torturous — **ex·cru·ci·at·ing·ly** *adv*

ex·cul·pate \ˈek-(ˌ)skəl-ˌpāt\ *vb* **-pat·ed; -pat·ing** : to clear from alleged fault or guilt *syn* absolve, exonerate, acquit, vindicate, clear

ex·cur·sion \ik-ˈskər-zhən\ *n* **1** : EXPEDITION; *esp* : a pleasure trip **2** : DIGRESSION — **ex·cur·sion·ist** \-ˈskərzh-(ə-)nəst\ *n*

ex·cur·sive \-ˈskər-siv\ *adj* : constituting or characterized by digression

¹ex·cuse \ik-ˈskyüz\ *vb* **ex·cused; ex·cus·ing** [ME *excusen*, fr. OF *excuser*, fr. L *excusare*, fr. *causa* cause, explanation] **1** : to offer excuse for **2** : PARDON **3** : to release from an obligation **4** : JUSTIFY — **ex·cus·able** *adj*

²excuse \ik-ˈskyüs\ *n* **1** : an act of excusing **2** : grounds for being excused : JUSTIFICATION **3** : something that excuses or is a reason for excusing

exec *abbr* executive

ex·e·cra·ble \ˈek-si-krə-bəl\ *adj* **1** : DETESTABLE **2** : very bad ⟨∼ spelling⟩

ex·e·crate \ˈek-sə-ˌkrāt\ *vb* **-crat·ed; -crat·ing** [L *exsecratus*, pp. of *exse-*

crari to put under a curse, fr. *ex-* out of + *sacer* sacred] : to denounce as evil or detestable; *also* : DETEST — **ex•e•cra•tion** \,ek-sə-'krā-shən\ *n*

¹**ex•e•cute** \'ek-si-,kyüt\ *vb* -**cut•ed**; -**cut•ing 1** : to carry to completion : PERFORM **2** : to do what is called for by (as a law) **3** : to put to death in accordance with a legal sentence **4** : to produce in accordance with a plan or design **5** : to do what is needed to give legal force to (as a deed) — **ex•e•cu•tion** \,ek-si-'kyü-shən\ *n* — **ex•e•cu•tion•er** \-sh(ə-)nər\ *n*

¹**ex•ec•u•tive** \ig-'zek-(y)ət-iv\ *adj* **1** : designed for or related to carrying out plans or purposes **2** : of or relating to the enforcement of laws and the conduct of affairs

²**executive** *n* **1** : the branch of government with executive duties **2** : one having administrative or managerial responsibility

ex•ec•u•tor \ig-'zek-(y)ət-ər\ *n* : the person named in a will to carry out its provisions

ex•ec•u•trix \ig-'zek-(y)ə-,triks\ *n, pl* **ex•ec•u•tri•ces** \-,zek-(y)ə-'trī-,sēz\ *or* **ex•ec•u•trix•es** \-'zek-(y)ə-,trik-səz\ : a woman who is an executor

ex•e•ge•sis \,ek-sə-'jē-səs\ *n, pl* -**ge•ses** \-'jē-,sēz\ : explanation or critical interpretation of a text

ex•e•gete \'ek-sə-,jēt\ *n* : one who practices exegesis

ex•em•plar \ig-'zem-,plär, -plər\ *n* **1** : one that serves as a model or pattern; *esp* : an ideal model **2** : a typical instance or example

ex•em•pla•ry \ig-'zem-plə-rē\ *adj* : serving as a pattern; *also* : COMMENDABLE

ex•em•pli•fy \ig-'zem-plə-,fī\ *vb* -**fied**; -**fy•ing** : to illustrate by example : serve as an example of — **ex•em•pli•fi•ca•tion** \-,zem-plə-fə-'kā-shən\ *n*

¹**ex•empt** \ig-'zempt\ *adj* : free from some liability to which others are subject

²**exempt** *vb* : to make exempt : EXCUSE — **ex•emp•tion** \ig-'zemp-shən\ *n*

¹**ex•er•cise** \'ek-sər-,sīz\ *n* **1** : EMPLOYMENT, USE (⟨~ of authority⟩) **2** : exertion made for the sake of training **3** : a task or problem done to develop skill **4** *pl* : a public exhibition or ceremony

²**exercise** *vb* -**cised**; -**cis•ing 1** : EXERT (⟨~ control⟩) **2** : to train by or engage in exercise **3** : WORRY, DISTRESS — **ex•er•cis•er** *n*

ex•ert \ig-'zərt\ *vb* : to bring or put into action (⟨~ influence⟩) (⟨~ed⟩ himself) — **ex•er•tion** \-'zər-shən\ *n*

ex•hale \eks-'hāl\ *vb* **ex•haled**; **ex•hal•ing 1** : to breathe out **2** : to give or pass off in the form of vapor — **ex•ha•la•tion** \,eks-(h)ə-'lā-shən\ *n*

¹**ex•haust** \ig-'zóst\ *vb* **1** : to use up wholly **2** : to tire or wear out **3** : to draw out completely (as air from a jar); *also* : EMPTY **4** : to develop (a subject) completely

²**exhaust** *n* **1** : the escape of used vapor or gas from an engine; *also* : the gas that escapes **2** : a system of pipes through which exhaust escapes

ex•haus•tion \ig-'zós-chən\ *n* : extreme weariness : FATIGUE

ex•haus•tive \ig-'zó-stiv\ *adj* : covering all possibilities : THOROUGH

¹**ex•hib•it** \ig-'zib-ət\ *vb* **1** : to display esp. publicly **2** : to present to a court in legal form syn display, show, parade, flaunt — **ex•hi•bi•tion** \,ek-sə-'bish-ən\ *n* — **ex•hib•i•tor** \ig-'zib-ət-ər\ *n*

²**exhibit** *n* : an act or instance of exhibiting; *also* : something exhibited **2** : something produced and identified in court for use as evidence

ex•hi•bi•tion•ism \,ek-sə-'bish-ə-,niz-əm\ *n* : the act or practice of so behaving as to attract undue attention sometimes by indecent exposure — **ex•hi•bi•tion•ist** \-'bish-(ə-)nəst\ *n or adj*

ex•hil•a•rate \ig-'zil-ə-,rāt\ *vb* -**rat•ed**; -**rat•ing** : ENLIVEN, STIMULATE — **ex•hil•a•ra•tion** \-,zil-ə-'rā-shən\ *n*

ex•hort \ig-'zórt\ *vb* : to urge, advise, or warn earnestly — **ex•hor•ta•tion** \,eks-,ór-tā-shən, ,egz-, -ər-\ *n*

ex•hume \igz-'(y)üm, iks-'(h)yüm\ *vb* **ex•humed**; **ex•hum•ing** [F or ML; F *exhumer*, fr. ML *exhumare*, fr. L *ex* out of + *humus* earth] : DISINTER — **ex•hu•ma•tion** \,eks-(h)yü-'mā-shən, ,egz-(y)ü-\ *n*

ex•i•gen•cy \'ek-sə-jən-sē, ig-'zij-ən-\ *n, pl* -**cies 1** : urgent need **2** *pl* : REQUIREMENTS — **ex•i•gent** \'ek-sə-jənt\ *adj*

ex•ig•u•ous \ig-'zig-yə-wəs\ *adj* : scanty in amount — **ex•i•gu•i•ty** \,eg-zi-'gyü-ət-ē\ *n*

¹**ex•ile** \'eg-,zīl, 'ek-,sīl\ *n* **1** : BANISHMENT **2** : a person driven from his native place

²**exile** *vb* **ex•iled**; **ex•il•ing** : BANISH, EXPEL syn expatriate, deport, ostracize

ex•ist \ig-'zist\ *vb* **1** : to have being **2** : to continue to be : LIVE

ex•is•tence \ig-'zis-təns\ *n* **1** : continuance in living **2** : actual occurrence **3** : something existing — **ex•is•tent** \-tənt\ *adj*

ex•is•ten•tial \,eg-zis-'ten-chəl, ,ek-sis-\ *adj* **1** : of or relating to existence **2** : EMPIRICAL **3** : having being in time and space **4** : of or relating to existentialism or existentialists

ex•is•ten•tial•ism \,eg-zis-'ten-chə-,liz-əm\ *n* : a philosophy centered upon the analysis of existence and stressing the freedom, responsibility, and usu. the isolation of the individual — **ex•is•ten•tial•ist** \-ləst\ *adj or n*

ex•it \'eg-zət, 'ek-sət\ *n* **1** : a departure from a stage **2** : a going out or away; *also* : DEATH **3** : a way out of an enclosed space **4** : a point of departure from an expressway — **exit** *vb*

exo•bi•ol•o•gy \,ek-sō-bī-'äl-ə-jē\ *n* : biology concerned with life originating or existing outside the earth or its atmosphere — **exo·bi·ol·o·gist** \-bī-ˈäl-ə-jəst\ n

exo·crine gland \ˈek-sə-krən-, -ˌkrīn-, -ˌkrēn-\ n : a gland (as a sweat gland or a kidney) that releases a secretion externally by means of a canal or duct

Exod abbr Exodus

ex·o·dus \ˈek-səd-əs\ n : a mass departure : EMIGRATION

Ex·o·dus n — see BIBLE table

ex of·fi·cio \ˌek-sə-ˈfish-ē-ˌō\ adv or adj : by virtue of or because of an office (ex officio chairman)

ex·og·e·nous \ek-ˈsäj-ə-nəs\ adj : caused or produced by factors outside the organism or system — **ex·og·e·nous·ly** adv

ex·on·er·ate \ig-ˈzän-ə-ˌrāt\ vb **-at·ed; -at·ing** [ME exoneraten, fr. L exoneratus to unburden, fr. ex- out + onus load] : to free from blame syn acquit, absolve, exculpate, vindicate — **ex·on·er·a·tion** \-ˌzän-ə-ˈrā-shən\ n

ex·or·bi·tant \ig-ˈzor-bət-ənt\ adj : exceeding what is usual or proper

ex·or·cise \ˈek-ˌsor-ˌsīz, -sər-\ vb **-cised; -cis·ing** 1 : to get rid of by or as if by solemn command 2 : to free of an evil spirit — **ex·or·cism** \-ˌsiz-əm\ n — **ex·or·cist** \-ˌsist\ n

exo·sphere \ˈek-sō-ˌsfiər\ n : the outermost region of the atmosphere

exo·ther·mic \ˌek-sō-ˈthər-mik\ adj : characterized by or formed with evolution of heat

ex·ot·ic \ig-ˈzät-ik\ adj : FOREIGN, STRANGE — **exotic** n — **ex·ot·i·cal·ly** \-i-k(ə-)lē\ adv — **ex·ot·i·cism** \-ˈzät-ə-ˌsiz-əm\ n

exp abbr 1 expense 2 experiment 3 export 4 express

ex·pand \ik-ˈspand\ vb 1 : to open up : UNFOLD 2 : ENLARGE 3 : to develop in detail syn amplify, swell, distend, inflate, dilate — **ex·pand·er** n

ex·panse \ik-ˈspans\ n : a broad extent (as of land or sea)

ex·pan·sion \ik-ˈspan-chən\ n 1 : the act or process of expanding 2 : the quality or state of being expanded 3 : an expanded part or thing

ex·pan·sive \ik-ˈspan-siv\ adj 1 : tending to expand or to cause expansion 2 : warmly benevolent or emotional 3 : of large extent or scope — **ex·pan·sive·ly** adv — **ex·pan·sive·ness** n

ex parte \eks-ˈpärt-ē\ adv or adj [ML] : from a one-sided point of view

ex·pa·ti·ate \ek-ˈspā-shē-ˌāt\ vb **-at·ed; -at·ing** : to talk or write at length — **ex·pa·ti·a·tion** \ek-ˌspā-shē-ˈā-shən\ n

¹**ex·pa·tri·ate** \ek-ˈspā-trē-ˌāt\ vb **-at·ed; -at·ing** : EXILE — **ex·pa·tri·a·tion** \ek-ˌspā-trē-ˈā-shən\ n

²**ex·pa·tri·ate** \ek-ˈspā-trē-ˌāt, -trē-ət\ adj : living in a foreign country — **expatriate** n

ex·pect \ik-ˈspekt\ vb 1 : SUPPOSE, THINK 2 : to look forward to : ANTICIPATE 3 : to consider reasonable, due,

or necessary 4 : to consider to be obliged

ex·pec·tan·cy \-ˈspek-tən-sē\ n, pl **-cies** 1 : EXPECTATION 2 : the expected amount (as of years of life)

ex·pec·tant \-tənt\ adj : EXPECTING; esp : expecting the birth of a child — **ex·pec·tant·ly** adv

ex·pec·ta·tion \ˌek-ˌspek-ˈtā-shən\ n 1 : the act or state of expecting 2 : prospect of good or bad fortune — usu. used in pl. 3 : something expected

ex·pec·to·rant \ik-ˈspek-t(ə-)rənt\ n : an agent that promotes the discharge or expulsion of mucus from the respiratory tract — **expectorant** adj

ex·pec·to·rate \-tə-ˌrāt\ vb **-rat·ed; -rat·ing** : SPIT — **ex·pec·to·ra·tion** \-ˌspek-tə-ˈrā-shən\ n

ex·pe·di·ence \ik-ˈspēd-ē-əns\ n : EXPEDIENCY

ex·pe·di·en·cy \-ən-sē\ n, pl **-cies** 1 : fitness to some end 2 : use of expedient means and methods; also : something expedient

¹**ex·pe·di·ent** \ik-ˈspēd-ē-ənt\ adj [ME, fr. MF or L; MF, fr. L expediens prp. of expedire to extricate, arrange, be advantageous, fr. ex- out + ped-, pes foot] 1 : adapted for achieving a particular end 2 : marked by concern with what is advantageous; esp : governed by self-interest

²**expedient** n : something expedient; esp : a temporary means to an end

ex·pe·dite \ˈek-spə-ˌdīt\ vb **-dit·ed; -dit·ing** : to carry out promptly; also : to speed up

ex·pe·dit·er \-ˌdīt-ər\ n : one that expedites; esp : one employed to ensure efficient movement of goods or supplies in a business

ex·pe·di·tion \ˌek-spə-ˈdish-ən\ n 1 : a journey for a particular purpose; also : the persons making it 2 : efficient promptness

ex·pe·di·tion·ary \-ˈdish-ə-ˌner-ē\ adj : of, relating to, or constituting an expedition; also : sent on military service abroad

ex·pe·di·tious \ˌek-spə-ˈdish-əs\ adj : marked by or acting with prompt efficiency syn swift, fast, rapid, speedy

ex·pel \ik-ˈspel\ vb **ex·pelled; ex·pel·ling** : to drive or force out : EJECT

ex·pend \ik-ˈspend\ vb 1 : to pay out : SPEND 2 : UTILIZE; also : USE UP — **ex·pend·able** adj

ex·pen·di·ture \ik-ˈspen-di-chər, -də-ˌchùr\ n 1 : the act or process of expending 2 : something expended

ex·pense \ik-ˈspens\ n 1 : EXPENDITURE 2 : COST 3 : a cause of expenditure 4 : SACRIFICE

ex·pen·sive \ik-ˈspen-siv\ adj : COSTLY, DEAR — **ex·pen·sive·ly** adv

¹**ex·pe·ri·ence** \ik-ˈspir-ē-əns\ n 1 : observation or practice resulting in or tending toward knowledge; also : the resulting state of enhanced comprehension and efficiency 2 : a state of

being affected from without (as by events) ; *also* : an affecting event ⟨a startling ∼⟩ **3** : something or the totality experienced (as by a person or community)

²**experience** *vb* **-enced; -enc·ing 1** : FIND OUT, DISCOVER **2** : to know as an experience : SUFFER, UNDERGO

ex·pe·ri·enced \-ənst\ *adj* : made capable by repeated experience

¹**ex·per·i·ment** \ik-ˈsper-ə-mənt\ *n* : a controlled procedure carried out to discover, test, or demonstrate something; *also* : the process of testing — **ex·per·i·men·tal** \-ˌsper-ə-ˈment-ᵊl\ *adj*

²**ex·per·i·ment** \-ˌment\ *vb* : to make experiments — **ex·per·i·men·ta·tion** \ik-ˌsper-ə-mən-ˈtā-shən\ *n* — **ex·per·i·men·ter** \-ˈsper-ə-ˌment-ər\ *n*

¹**ex·pert** \ˈek-ˌspərt\ *adj* : showing special skill or knowledge — **ex·pert·ly** *adv* — **ex·pert·ness** *n*

²**ex·pert** \ˈek-ˌspərt\ *n* : an expert person : SPECIALIST

ex·per·tise \ˌek-(ˌ)spər-ˈtēz\ *n* : the skill of an expert

ex·pi·ate \ˈek-spē-ˌāt\ *vb* **-at·ed; -at·ing** : to make amends : ATONE — **ex·pi·a·tion** \ˌek-spē-ˈā-shən\ *n*

ex·pi·a·to·ry \ˈek-spē-ə-ˌtōr-ē\ *adj* : serving to expiate

ex·pire \ik-ˈspī(ə)r, ek-\ *vb* **ex·pired; ex·pir·ing 1** : to breathe one's last breath : DIE **2** : to come to an end **3** : to breathe out from or as if from the lungs — **ex·pi·ra·tion** \ˌek-spə-ˈrā-shən\ *n*

ex·plain \ik-ˈsplān\ *vb* [ME *explanen*, fr. L *explanare*, lit., to make level, fr. *planus* level, flat] **1** : to make clear **2** : to give the reason for — **ex·pla·na·tion** \ˌek-splə-ˈnā-shən\ *n* — **ex·plan·a·to·ry** \ik-ˈsplan-ə-ˌtōr-ē\ *adj*

ex·ple·tive \ˈek-splət-iv\ *n* : a usu. profane exclamation

ex·pli·ca·ble \ek-ˈsplik-ə-bəl, ˈek-(ˌ)splik-\ *adj* : capable of being explained

ex·pli·cate \ˈek-splə-ˌkāt\ *vb* **-cat·ed; -cat·ing** : to give a detailed explanation of

ex·plic·it \ik-ˈsplis-ət\ *adj* : clearly and precisely expressed — **ex·plic·it·ly** *adv* — **ex·plic·it·ness** *n*

ex·plode \ik-ˈsplōd\ *vb* **ex·plod·ed; ex·plod·ing** [L *explodere* to drive off the stage by clapping, fr. *ex-* out + *plaudere* to clap] **1** : DISCREDIT ⟨∼ a belief⟩ **2** : to burst or cause to burst violently and noisily ⟨∼ a bomb⟩ ⟨the boiler *exploded*⟩ **3** : to undergo a rapid chemical or nuclear reaction with production of heat and violent expansion of gas ⟨∼ dynamite⟩ **4** : to give forth a sudden strong and noisy outburst of emotion ⟨∼ with rage⟩

ex·plod·ed \-əd\ *adj* : showing the parts separated but in correct relationship to each other ⟨an ∼ view of a carburetor⟩

¹**ex·ploit** \ˈek-ˌsplóit\ *n* : DEED; *esp* : a notable or heroic act

²**ex·ploit** \ik-ˈsplóit\ *vb* **1** : to put to productive use ⟨∼ resources⟩ ; *also* : UTILIZE **2** : to use unfairly for one's own advantage — **ex·ploi·ta·tion** \ˌek-ˌsplói-ˈtā-shən\ *n*

ex·plore \ik-ˈsplōr\ *vb* **ex·plored; ex·plor·ing 1** : to look into or travel over thoroughly **2** : to examine carefully ⟨∼ a wound⟩ — **ex·plo·ra·tion** \ˌek-splə-ˈrā-shən\ *n* — **ex·plor·a·to·ry** \ik-ˈsplōr-ə-ˌtōr-ē\ *adj* — **ex·plor·er** *n*

ex·plo·sion \ik-ˈsplō-zhən\ *n* : the act or an instance of exploding

ex·plo·sive \ik-ˈsplō-siv\ *adj* **1** : relating to or able to cause explosion **2** : tending to explode — **explosive** *n* — **ex·plo·sive·ly** *adv*

ex·po \ˈek-ˌspō\ *n, pl* **expos** : EXPOSITION 2

ex·po·nent \ik-ˈspō-nənt, ˈek-ˌspō-\ *n* **1** : a symbol written above and to the right of a mathematical expression to signify how many times it is to be used as a factor (in a^3 the ∼ 3 indicates that *a* is to be used three times in the product *a·a·a*) **2** : INTERPRETER, EXPOUNDER **3** : ADVOCATE, CHAMPION — **ex·po·nen·tial** \ˌek-spə-ˈnen-chəl\ *adj* — **ex·po·nen·tial·ly** \-ē\ *adv*

ex·po·nen·ti·a·tion \ˌek-spə-ˌnen-chē-ˈā-shen\ *n* : the mathematical operation of raising a quantity to a power

¹**ex·port** \ek-ˈspōrt, ˈek-ˌspōrt\ *vb* : to send (as merchandise) to foreign countries — **ex·por·ta·tion** \ˌek-ˌspōr-ˈtā-shən, -spər-\ *n* — **ex·port·er** \ek-ˈspōrt-ər, ˈek-ˌspōrt-\ *n*

²**ex·port** \ˈek-ˌspōrt\ *n* **1** : something exported esp. for trade **2** : an act or the business of exporting

ex·pose \ik-ˈspōz\ *vb* **ex·posed; ex·pos·ing 1** : to deprive of shelter or protection **2** : to submit or subject to an action or influence; *esp* : to subject (as photographic film) to radiant energy (as light) **3** : to display esp. for sale **4** : to bring to light : DISCLOSE

ex·po·sé *or* **ex·po·se** \ˌek-spō-ˈzā\ *n* : an exposure of something discreditable

ex·po·si·tion \ˌek-spə-ˈzish-ən\ *n* **1** : a setting forth of the meaning or purpose (as of a writing); *also* : discourse designed to convey information **2** : a public exhibition

ex·pos·i·tor \ik-ˈspäz-ət-ər\ *n* : one who explains : COMMENTATOR

ex·pos·tu·late \ik-ˈspäs-chə-ˌlāt\ *vb* : to reason earnestly with a person esp. in dissuading : REMONSTRATE — **ex·pos·tu·la·tion** \-ˌspäs-chə-ˈlā-shən\ *n*

ex·po·sure \ik-ˈspō-zhər\ *n* **1** : the fact or condition of being exposed **2** : the act or an instance of exposing **3** : the length of time for which a film is exposed **4** : a section of a photographic film for one picture

ex·pound \ik-ˈspaùnd\ *vb* **1** : STATE **2** : INTERPRET, EXPLAIN — **ex·pound·er** *n*

¹**ex·press** \ik-ˈspres\ *adj* **1** : EXPLICIT;

also : EXACT, PRECISE **2** : SPECIFIC (his ~ purpose) **3** : traveling at high speed and esp. with few stops (~ train) ; *also* : adapted to high speed use (~ roads) — **ex·press·ly** *adv*

²**express** *adv* : by express (ship it ~)

³**express** *n* **1** : a system for the prompt transportation of goods; *also* : a company operating such a service or the shipments so transported **2** : an express vehicle

⁴**express** *vb* **1** : to make known : SHOW, STATE (~ regret) ; *also* : SYMBOLIZE **2** : to squeeze out : extract by pressing **3** : to send by express

ex·pres·sion \ik-ᵇspresh-ən\ *n* **1** : UTTERANCE **2** : something that represents or symbolizes : SIGN; *esp* : a mathematical symbol or combination of signs and symbols representing a quantity or operation **3** : a significant word or phrase; *also* : manner of expressing (as in writing or music) **4** : facial aspect or vocal intonation indicative of feeling — **ex·pres·sion·less** *adj*

ex·pres·sion·ism \ik-ᵇspresh-ə-ₑniz-əm\ *n* : a theory or practice in art of seeking to depict the artist's subjective responses to objects and events — **ex·pres·sion·ist** \-ᵇspresh-(ə-)nəst\ *n or adj* — **ex·pres·sion·is·tic** \-ₑspresh-ə-ᵇnis-tik\ *adj*

ex·pres·sive \ik-ᵇspres-iv\ *adj* **1** : of or relating to expression **2** : serving to express — **ex·pres·sive·ly** *adv* — **ex·pres·sive·ness** *n*

ex·press·way \ik-ᵇspres-ₑwā\ *n* : a divided superhighway with limited access

ex·pro·pri·ate \ek-ᵇsprō-prē-ₑāt\ *vb* -at·ed; -at·ing : to deprive of possession or the right to own — **ex·pro·pri·a·tion** \(ₑ)ek-ₑsprō-prē-ᵇā-shən\ *n*

expt *abbr* experiment

ex·pul·sion \ik-ᵇspəl-shən\ *n* : an expelling or being expelled : EJECTION

ex·punge \ik-ᵇspənj\ *vb* **ex·punged; ex·pung·ing** [L *expungere* to mark for deletion by dots, fr. *ex-* out + *pungere* to prick] : OBLITERATE, ERASE

ex·pur·gate \ᵇek-spər-ₑgāt\ *vb* -gat·ed; -gat·ing : to clear (as a book) of objectionable passages — **ex·pur·ga·tion** \ₑek-spər-ᵇgā-shən\ *n*

ex·qui·site \ek-ᵇskwiz-ət, ᵇek-(ₑ)skwiz-\ *adj* [ME *exquisit,* fr. L *exquisitus,* fr. pp. of *exquirere* to search out, fr. *quaerere* to seek] **1** : excellent in form or workmanship **2** : keenly appreciative **3** : pleasingly beautiful or delicate **4** : INTENSE

ext *abbr* **1** extension **2** exterior **3** external **4** extra **5** extract

ex·tant \ᵇek-stənt; ek-ᵇstant\ *adj* : EXISTENT; *esp* : not lost or destroyed

ex·tem·po·ra·ne·ous \ek-ₑstem-pə-ᵇrā-nē-əs\ *adj* : not planned beforehand : IMPROMPTU — **ex·tem·po·ra·ne·ous·ly** *adv*

ex·tem·po·rary \ik-ᵇstem-pə-ₑrer-ē\ *adj* : EXTEMPORANEOUS

ex·tem·po·re \ik-ᵇstem-pə-(ₑ)rē\ *adv* : EXTEMPORANEOUSLY

ex·tem·po·rize \ik-ᵇstem-pə-ₑrīz\ *vb* -rized; -riz·ing : to do something extemporaneously

ex·tend \ik-ᵇstend\ *vb* **1** : to spread or stretch forth or out (as in reaching or straightening) **2** : to exert or cause to exert to full capacity **3** : PROFFER (~ credit) **4** : PROLONG (~ a note) **5** : to make greater or broader (~ knowledge) (~ a business) **6** : to stretch out or reach across a distance, space, or time **syn** lengthen, elongate, protract — **ex·tend·able** *or* **ex·tend·ible** \-ᵇstendə-bəl\ *adj*

ex·ten·sion \ik-ᵇsten-chən\ *n* **1** : an extending or being extended **2** : educational programs (as correspondence courses) that reach beyond the campus of a school **3** : an additional part (~ on a house)

ex·ten·sive \ik-ᵇsten-siv\ *adj* : of considerable extent : FAR-REACHING, BROAD — **ex·ten·sive·ly** *adv*

ex·tent \ik-ᵇstent\ *n* **1** : the size, length, or bulk of something (a property of large ~) **2** : the degree or measure of something (the ~ of his guilt)

ex·ten·u·ate \ik-ᵇsten-yə-ₑwāt\ *vb* -at·ed; -at·ing : to lessen the seriousness of — **ex·ten·u·a·tion** \-ₑsten-yə-ᵇwā-shən\ *n*

¹**ex·te·ri·or** \ek-ᵇstir-ē-ər\ *adj* **1** : EXTERNAL **2** : suitable for use on an outside surface (~ paint)

²**exterior** *n* : an exterior part or surface

ex·ter·mi·nate \ik-ᵇstər-mə-ₑnāt\ *vb* -nat·ed; -nat·ing : to get rid of completely **syn** extirpate, eradicate, abolish, annihilate — **ex·ter·mi·na·tion** \-ₑstər-mə-ᵇnā-shən\ *n*

ex·ter·mi·na·tor \ik-ᵇstər-mə-ₑnāt-ər\ *n* : one that exterminates; *esp* : a person whose occupation is destroying household vermin with chemicals

¹**ex·ter·nal** \ek-ᵇstərn-ᵊl\ *adj* **1** : outwardly perceivable; *also* : SUPERFICIAL **2** : of, relating to, or located on the outside or an outer part **3** : arising or acting from without; *also* : FOREIGN (~ affairs) — **ex·ter·nal·ly** \-ē\ *adv*

²**external** *n* : an external feature

ex·tinct \ik-ᵇstiŋkt\ *adj* **1** : EXTINGUISHED (with hope ~) ; *also* : no longer active (as a volcano) **2** : no longer existing (as a kind of plant or animal) or in use (as a language) — **ex·tinc·tion** \ik-ᵇstiŋk-shən\ *n*

ex·tin·guish \ik-ᵇstiŋ-gwish\ *vb* : to put out (as a fire); *also* : to bring to an end (as by destroying) — **ex·tin·guish·able** *adj* — **ex·tin·guish·er** *n*

ex·tir·pate \ᵇek-stər-ₑpāt\ *vb* -pat·ed; -pat·ing [L *exstirpatus,* pp. *exstirpare,* fr. *ex-* out + *stirps* trunk, root] **1** : UPROOT **2** : to destroy completely **syn** exterminate, eradicate, abolish, annihilate — **ex·tir·pa·tion** \ₑek-stər-ᵇpā-shən\ *n*

ex·tol *also* **ex·toll** \ik-ᵇstōl\ *vb* **ex·tolled;**

ex·tol·ling : to praise highly : GLORIFY syn laud, eulogize

ex·tort \ik-'stȯrt\ *vb* [L *extortus,* pp. of *extorquēre* to wrench out, extort, fr. *ex-* out + *torquēre* to twist] : to obtain by force or improper pressure ⟨~ a bribe⟩ — **ex·tor·tion** \-'stȯr-shən\ *n* — **ex·tor·tion·er** *n* — **ex·tor·tion·ist** *n*

ex·tor·tion·ate \ik-'stȯr-sh(ə-)nət\ *adj* : EXCESSIVE, EXORBITANT — **ex·tor·tion·ate·ly** *adv*

¹**ex·tra** \'ek-strə\ *adj* **1** : ADDITIONAL **2** : SUPERIOR syn spare, surplus, superfluous

²**extra** *n* **1** : something (as a charge) added **2** : a special edition of a newspaper **3** : an additional worker or performer (as in a group scene)

³**extra** *adv* : beyond what is usual

¹**ex·tract** \ik-'strakt, *esp for 3* 'ek-ˌstrakt\ *vb* **1** : to draw out; *esp* : to pull out forcibly ⟨~ a tooth⟩ **2** : to withdraw (as a juice or a constituent) by a physical or chemical process **3** : to select for citation : QUOTE — **ex·tract·able** *adj* — **ex·trac·tion** \-'strak-shən\ *n* — **ex·trac·tor** \-tər\ *n*

²**ex·tract** \'ek-ˌstrakt\ *n* **1** : EXCERPT, CITATION **2** : a product (as a juice or concentrate) obtained by extracting

ex·tra·cur·ric·u·lar \ˌek-strə-kə-'rik-yə-lər\ *adj* : lying outside the regular curriculum; *esp* : of or relating to school-connected activities (as sports) carrying no academic credit

ex·tra·dite \'ek-strə-ˌdīt\ *vb* **-dit·ed; -dit·ing** : to obtain by or deliver up to extradition

ex·tra·di·tion \ˌek-strə-'dish-ən\ *n* : surrendering an alleged criminal to a different jurisdiction for trial

ex·tra·mar·i·tal \ˌek-strə-'mar-ət-ᵊl\ *adj* : of or relating to sexual intercourse by a married person with someone other than his or her spouse

ex·tra·mu·ral \-'myůr-əl\ *adj* : existing or functioning beyond the bounds of an organized unit

ex·tra·ne·ous \ek-'strā-nē-əs\ *adj* **1** : coming from without ⟨~ moisture⟩ **2** : not intrinsic ⟨~ incidents in a story⟩ ; *also* : IRRELEVANT ⟨~ digressions⟩ — **ex·tra·ne·ous·ly** *adv*

ex·traor·di·nary \ik-'strȯrd-ᵊn-ˌer-ē, ˌek-strə-'ȯrd-\ *adj* **1** : notably unusual or exceptional **2** : employed on special service — **ex·traor·di·nar·i·ly** \ik-ˌstrȯrd-ᵊn-'er-ə-lē, ˌek-strə-ˌȯrd-\ *adv*

ex·trap·o·late \ik-'strap-ə-ˌlāt\ *vb* **-lat·ed; -lat·ing** : to infer (unknown data) from known data — **ex·trap·o·la·tion** \-ˌstrap-ə-'lā-shən\ *n*

ex·tra·sen·so·ry \ˌek-strə-'sens-(ə-)rē\ *adj* : not acting or occurring through the known senses ⟨~ perception⟩

ex·tra·ter·res·tri·al \-tə-'res-trē-əl\ *adj* : originating or existing outside the earth or its atmosphere ⟨~ life⟩ — **extraterrestrial** *n*

ex·tra·ter·ri·to·ri·al \-ˌter-ə-'tȯr-ē-əl\ *adj* : existing or taking place outside the territorial limits of a jurisdiction

ex·tra·ter·ri·to·ri·al·i·ty \-ˌtȯr-ē-ʾal-ət-ē\ *n* : exemption from the application or jurisdiction of local law or tribunals ⟨diplomats enjoy ~⟩

ex·trav·a·gant \ik-'strav-i-gənt\ *adj* **1** : EXCESSIVE ⟨~ claims⟩ **2** : unduly lavish : WASTEFUL **3** : too costly syn immoderate, exorbitant, extreme, inordinate, undue — **ex·trav·a·gance** \-gəns\ *n* — **ex·trav·a·gant·ly** *adv*

ex·trav·a·gan·za \ik-ˌstrav-ə-'gan-zə\ *n* **1** : a literary or musical work marked by extreme freedom of style and structure **2** : a spectacular show

ex·tra·ve·hic·u·lar \ˌek-strə-vē-'hik-yə-lər\ *adj* : taking place outside a vehicle (as a spacecraft) ⟨~ activity⟩

¹**ex·treme** \ik-'strēm\ *adj* **1** : very great or intense ⟨~ cold⟩ **2** : very severe or drastic ⟨~ measures⟩ **3** : going to great lengths or beyond normal limits ⟨politically ~⟩ **4** : most remote ⟨the ~ end⟩ **5** : UTMOST; *also* : MAXIMUM ⟨an ~ effort⟩ — **ex·treme·ly** *adv*

²**extreme** *n* **1** : something located at one end or the other of a range or series **2** : EXTREMITY **4**

extremely high frequency *n* : a radio frequency in the highest range of the radio frequency spectrum

ex·trem·ism \ik-'strē-ˌmiz-əm\ *n* : the quality or state of being extreme; *esp* : advocacy of extreme political measures : RADICALISM — **ex·trem·ist** \-məst\ *n or adj*

ex·trem·i·ty \ik-'strem-ət-ē\ *n, pl* **-ties 1** : the most remote part or point **2** : a limb of the body; *esp* : a human hand or foot **3** : the greatest need or danger **4** : the utmost degree; *also* : a drastic or desperate measure

ex·tri·cate \'ek-strə-ˌkāt\ *vb* **-cat·ed; -cat·ing** [L *extricatus,* pp. of *extricare,* fr. *ex-* out + *tricae* trifles, perplexities] : to free from an entanglement or difficulty syn disentangle, untangle, disencumber — **ex·tri·ca·ble** \ik-'strik-ə-bəl, ek-; 'ek-(ˌ)strik-\ *adj* — **ex·tri·ca·tion** \ˌek-strə-'kā-shən\ *n*

ex·trin·sic \ek-'strin-zik, -sik\ *adj* **1** : not forming part of or belonging to a thing **2** : EXTERNAL — **ex·trin·si·cal·ly** \-zi-k(ə-)lē, -si-\ *adv*

ex·tro·vert *or* **ex·tra·vert** \'ek-strə-ˌvərt\ *n* : a person who is interested only or mostly in things outside the self — **ex·tro·ver·sion** *or* **ex·tra·ver·sion** \ek-strə-'vər-zhən\ *n* — **ex·tro·vert·ed** *or* **ex·tra·vert·ed** *adj*

ex·trude \ik-'strüd\ *vb* **ex·trud·ed; ex·trud·ing 1** : to force, press, or push out **2** : to shape (as plastic) by forcing through a die — **ex·tru·sion** \-'strü-zhən\ *n* — **ex·trud·er** *n*

ex·tru·sive \ik-'strü-siv\ *adj* : relating to or formed by geological extrusion from the earth in a molten state or as volcanic ash

ex·u·ber·ant \ig-'zü-b(ə-)rənt\ *adj* **1** : joyously unrestrained **2** : PROFUSE—

ex·u·ber·ance \-b(ə-)rəns\ *n* — **ex·u·ber·ant·ly** *adv*

ex·ude \ig-'züd\ *vb* **ex·ud·ed; ex·ud·ing** [L *exsudare,* fr. *ex-* out + *sudare* to sweat] 1 : to discharge slowly through pores or cuts : OOZE 2 : to give off or out conspicuously or abundantly (~s charm) — **ex·u·date** \'ek-s(y)ù-ˌdāt\ *n* — **ex·u·da·tion** \ˌek-s(y)ù-'dā-shən\ *n*

ex·ult \ig-'zəlt\ *vb* : to rejoice in triumph : GLORY — **ex·ul·tant** \-'zəlt-ᵊnt\ *adj* — **ex·ul·tant·ly** *adv* — **ex·ul·ta·tion** \ˌek-(ˌ)səl-'tā-shən, ˌeg-(ˌ)zəl-\ *n*

ex·urb \'ek-ˌsərb, 'eg-ˌzərb\ *n* : a region outside a city and its suburbs inhabited chiefly by well-to-do families — **ex·ur·bia** \ek-'sər-bē-ə, eg-'zər-\ *n*

ex·ur·ban·ite \ek-'sər-bə-ˌnīt; eg-'zər-\ *n* : one who lives in an exurb

-ey — see -Y

¹**eye** \'ī\ *n* 1 : an organ of sight typically consisting of a globular structure in a socket of the skull with thin movable covers bordered with hairs 2 : VISION, PERCEPTION; *also* : faculty of discrimination (a good ~ for bargains) 3 : POINT OF VIEW, JUDGMENT — often used in pl. (an offender in the ~s of the law) 4 : something suggesting an eye (the ~ of a needle) ; *esp* : an undeveloped bud (as on a potato) — **eyed** \'īd\ *adj*

²**eye** *vb* **eyed; eye·ing** or **ey·ing** : to look at : WATCH

eye·ball \'ī-ˌbȯl\ *n* : the globular capsule of the vertebrate eye

eye·brow \-ˌbraù\ *n* : the bony arch forming the upper edge of the eye socket; *also* : the hair growing on this

eye·drop·per \'ī-ˌdräp-ər\ *n* : DROPPER 2

eye·glass \'ī-ˌglas\ *n* 1 : a lens variously mounted for personal use as an aid to vision 2 *pl* : GLASSES, SPECTACLES

eye·lash \'ī-ˌlash\ *n* 1 : the fringe of hair edging the eyelid — usu. used in pl. 2 : a single hair of the eyelashes

eye·let \'ī-lət\ *n* 1 : a small reinforced hole in material intended for ornament or for passage of something (as a cord or lace) 2 : a typically metal ring for reinforcing an eyelet : GROMMET

eye·lid \'ī-ˌlid\ *n* : either of the movable lids of skin and muscle that can be closed over the eyeball

eye·lin·er \'ī-ˌlī-nər\ *n* : makeup used to emphasize the contour of the eyes

eye-open·er \'ī-ˌōp(-ə)-nər\ *n* : something startling or surprising — **eye-open·ing** \-niŋ\ *adj*

eye·piece \'ī-ˌpēs\ *n* : the lens or combination of lenses at the eye end of an optical instrument

eye shadow *n* : a colored cosmetic applied to the eyelids to accent the eyes

eye·sight \'ī-ˌsīt\ *n* : SIGHT, VISION

eye·sore \'ī-ˌsȯr\ *n* : something offensive to view

eye·strain \'ī-ˌstrān\ *n* : weariness or a strained state of the eye

eye·tooth \'ī-'tüth\ *n* : a canine tooth of the upper jaw

eye·wash \'ī-ˌwȯsh, -ˌwäsh\ *n* 1 : an eye lotion 2 : misleading or deceptive statements, actions, or procedures

eye·wit·ness \'ī-'wit-nəs\ *n* : a person who actually sees something happen

ey·rie \'ī(ə)r-ē, *or like* AERIE\ *var of* AER-IE

ey·rir \'ā-ˌriər\ *n, pl* **au·rar** \'aù-ˌrär\ — see *krona* at MONEY table

Ez *or* **Ezr** *abbr* Ezra

Ezech *abbr* Ezechiel

Eze·chiel \i-'zē-kyəl\ *n* — see BIBLE table

Ezek *abbr* Ezekiel

Eze·kiel \i-'zē-kyəl\ *n* — see BIBLE table

Ez·ra \'ez-rə\ *n* — see BIBLE table

F

¹**f** \'ef\ *n, pl* **f's** *or* **fs** \'efs\ *often cap* 1 : the 6th letter of the English alphabet 2 : a grade rating a student's work as failing

²**f** *abbr, often cap* 1 Fahrenheit 2 false 3 family 4 farad 5 female 6 feminine 7 forte 8 French 9 frequency

³**f** *symbol* 1 focal length 2 the relative aperture of a photographic lens — often written *f/* 3 function

F *symbol* fluorine

FAA *abbr* Federal Aviation Agency

Fa·bi·an \'fā-bē-ən\ *adj* : of, relating to, or being a society of socialists organized in England in 1884 to spread socialist principles gradually — **Fabian** *n* — **Fa·bi·an·ism** *n*

fa·ble \'fā-bəl\ *n* 1 : a legendary story of supernatural happenings 2 : a narration intended to teach a lesson; *esp*

: one in which animals speak and act like people 3 : FALSEHOOD

fa·bled \'fā-bəld\ *adj* 1 : FICTITIOUS 2 : told or celebrated in fable

fab·ric \'fab-rik\ *n* [MF *fabrique,* fr. L *fabrica* workshop, structure] 1 : STRUCTURE, FRAMEWORK (the ~ of society) 2 : CLOTH; *also* : a material that resembles cloth

fab·ri·cate \'fab-ri-ˌkāt\ *vb* **-cat·ed; -cat·ing** 1 : CONSTRUCT, MANUFACTURE 2 : INVENT, CREATE 3 : to make up for the sake of deception — **fab·ri·ca·tion** \ˌfab-ri-'kā-shən\ *n*

fab·u·lous \'fab-yə-ləs\ *adj* 1 : resembling a fable : LEGENDARY 2 : told in or based on fable 3 : INCREDIBLE, MARVELOUS — **fab·u·lous·ly** *adv*

fac *abbr* 1 facsimile 2 faculty

fa·cade *also* **fa·çade** \fə-'säd\ *n* [F *façade,* fr. It *facciata,* fr. *faccia* face]

1 : the principal face or front of a building **2** : a false, superficial, or artificial appearance ⟨a ∼ of composure⟩

¹face \'fās\ *n* **1** : the front part of the head **2** : PRESENCE ⟨in the ∼ of danger⟩ **3** : facial expression : LOOK ⟨put a sad ∼ on⟩ **4** : GRIMACE ⟨made a ∼⟩ **5** : outward appearance ⟨looks easy on the ∼ of it⟩ **6** : BOLDNESS **7** : DIGNITY, PRESTIGE ⟨afraid to lose ∼⟩ **8** : the surface of something : *esp* : the front or principal surface — **faced** \'fāst\ *adj* — **face·less** *adj* — **face·less·ness** *n*

²face *vb* **faced; fac·ing 1** : to confront brazenly **2** : to line near the edge esp. with a different material; *also* : to cover the front or surface of ⟨∼ a building with marble⟩ **3** : to bring face to face ⟨*faced* him with proof⟩ **4** : to stand or sit with the face toward ⟨∼ the sun⟩ **5** : to front on ⟨a house *facing* the park⟩ **6** : to oppose firmly ⟨*faced* up to his foe⟩ **7** : to turn the face or body in a specified direction

face-down \'fās-'daūn\ *adv* : with the face downward

face-lift·ing \-ˌlif-tiṅ\ *n* **1** : a plastic operation for removal of facial defects (as wrinkles or sagging) usu. associated with aging **2** : MODERNIZATION

face-off \'fās-ˌȯf\ *n* **1** : a method of putting a puck in play in ice hockey by dropping it between two opposing players each of whom attempts to control it **2** : CONFRONTATION

fac·et \'fas-ət\ *n* [F *facette*, dim. of *face*] **1** : one of the small plane surfaces of a cut gem **2** : ASPECT, PHASE

fa·ce·tious \fə-'sē-shəs\ *adj* **1** : FLIPPANT **2** : JOCULAR, JOCOSE — **fa·ce·tious·ly** *adv* — **fa·ce·tious·ness** *n*

¹fa·cial \'fā-shəl\ *adj* : of or relating to the face

²facial *n* : a facial treatment

fac·ile \'fas-əl\ *adj* **1** : easily accomplished, handled, or attained **2** : SUPERFICIAL **3** : readily manifested and often insincere ⟨∼ prose⟩ **4** : READY, FLUENT ⟨a ∼ writer⟩

fa·cil·i·tate \fə-'sil-ə-ˌtāt\ *vb* **-tat·ed; -tat·ing** : to make easier

fa·cil·i·ty \fə-'sil-ət-ē\ *n, pl* **-ties 1** : the quality of being easily performed **2** : ease in performance : APTITUDE **3** : PLIANCY **4** : something that makes easier an action, operation, or course of conduct **5** : something (as a hospital) built or installed for a particular purpose

fac·ing \'fā-siṅ\ *n* **1** : a lining at the edge esp. of a garment **2** *pl* : the collar, cuffs, and trimmings of a uniform coat **3** : an ornamental or protective layer **4** : material for facing

fac·sim·i·le \fak-'sim-ə-lē\ *n* [L *fac simile* make similar] **1** : an exact copy **2** : the transmitting of printed matter or pictures by wire or radio for reproduction

fact \'fakt\ *n* **1** : DEED; *esp* : CRIME

⟨accessory after the ∼⟩ **2** : the quality of being actual **3** : something that exists or occurs : EVENT; *also* : a piece of information about such a fact

fac·tion \'fak-shən\ *n* : a group or combination (as in a government) acting together within and usu. against a larger body : CLIQUE — **fac·tion·al·ism** \-sh(ə-)nəl-ˌiz-əm\ *n*

fac·tious \'fak-shəs\ *adj* **1** : of, relating to, or caused by faction **2** : inclined to faction or the formation of factions : causing dissension

fac·ti·tious \fak-'tish-əs\ *adj* : ARTIFICIAL, SHAM ⟨a ∼ display of grief⟩

¹fac·tor \'fak-tər\ *n* **1** : AGENT **2** : something that actively contributes to a result **3** : GENE **4** : any of the numbers or symbols in mathematics that when multiplied together form a product; *esp* : any of the integers that divide a given integer without a remainder

²factor *vb* **fac·tored; fac·tor·ing** \-t(ə-)riṅ\ **1** : to work as a factor **2** : to find the mathematical factors of and esp. the prime mathematical factors of

¹fac·to·ri·al \fak-'tōr-ē-əl\ *adj* : of, relating to, or being a factor

²factorial *n* : the product of all the positive integers from one to a given integer

fac·to·ry \'fak-t(ə-)rē\ *n, pl* **-ries 1** : a trading post where resident factors trade **2** : a building or group of buildings used for manufacturing

fac·to·tum \fak-'tōt-əm\ *n* [NL, lit., do everything, fr. L *fac* do + *totum* everything] : an employee with numerous varied duties

facts of life : the physiological processes and behavior involved in sex and reproduction

fac·tu·al \'fak-chə(-wə)l\ *adj* : of or relating to facts; *also* : based on fact — **fac·tu·al·ly** \-ē\ *adv*

fac·ul·ty \'fak-əl-tē\ *n, pl* **-ties 1** : ability to act or do : POWER; *also* : natural aptitude **2** : one of the powers of the mind or body ⟨the ∼ of hearing⟩ **3** : the teachers in a school or college or one of its divisions

fad \'fad\ *n* : a practice or interest followed for a time with exaggerated zeal : CRAZE — **fad·dish** *adj* — **fad·dist** *n*

fade \'fād\ *vb* **fad·ed; fad·ing 1** : WITHER **2** : to lose or cause to lose freshness or brilliance of color **3** : VANISH **4** : to grow dim or faint

FADM *abbr* fleet admiral

fae·cal, fae·ces *var of* FECAL, FECES

fa·er·ie *also* **fa·ery** \'fā-rē, 'fa(ə)r-ē\ *n, pl* **fa·er·ies 1** : FAIRYLAND **2** : FAIRY

¹fag \'fag\ *vb* **fagged; fag·ging 1** : DRUDGE **2** : to act as a fag **3** : TIRE, EXHAUST

²fag *n* **1** : an English public-school boy who acts as servant to another **2** : MENIAL, DRUDGE

³fag *n* : CIGARETTE

fag end *n* : the last part or coarser end of a web of cloth **2** : the untwisted end of a rope **3** : REMNANT **4** : the extreme end

fag·ot *or* **fag·got** \'fag-ət\ *n* : a bundle of sticks or twigs esp. as used for fuel

fag·ot·ing *or* **fag·got·ing** *n* : an embroidery produced by tying threads in hourglass-shaped clusters

Fah *or* **Fahr** *abbr* Fahrenheit

Fahr·en·heit \'far-ən-ˌhīt\ *adj* : relating to, conforming to, or having a thermometer scale with the boiling point of water at 212 degrees and the freezing point at 32 degrees above zero

fa·ience *or* **fa·ience** \fä-'äns\ *n* [F] : earthenware decorated with opaque colored glazes

¹fail \'fāl\ *vb* **1** : to become feeble; *esp* : to decline in health **2** : to die away **3** : to stop functioning **4** : to fall short (*~ed* in his duty) **5** : to be or become absent or inadequate **6** : to be unsuccessful **7** : to become bankrupt *n* : DISAPPOINT, DESERT **9** : NEGLECT

²fail *n* : FAILURE (without *~*)

¹fail·ing \'fā-liŋ\ *n* : WEAKNESS, SHORTCOMING

²failing *prep* : in the absence or lack of

faille \'fīl\ *n* : a somewhat shiny closely woven ribbed silk, rayon, or cotton fabric

fail–safe \'fāl-ˌsāf\ *adj* **1** : incorporating a counteractive feature for a possible source of failure **2** : having no chance of failure

fail·ure \'fāl-yər\ *n* **1** : a failing to do or perform **2** : a state of inability to perform a normal function adequately (heart *~*) **3** : a fracturing under or yielding to stress **4** : a lack of success **5** : BANKRUPTCY **6** : DEFICIENCY **7** : DETERIORATION, BREAKDOWN **8** : one that has failed

¹fain \'fān\ *adj, archaic* **1** : GLAD **2** : INCLINED **3** : OBLIGED

²fain *adv, archaic* **1** : WILLINGLY **2** : RATHER

¹faint \'fānt\ *adj* [ME *faint, feint*, fr. OF, fr. *faindre, feindre* to feign, shirk] **1** : COWARDLY, SPIRITLESS **2** : weak, dizzy, and likely to faint **3** : lacking vigor or strength : FEEBLE (*~* praise) **4** : INDISTINCT, DIM — **faint·ly** *adv* — **faint·ness** *n*

²faint *vb* : to lose consciousness

³faint *n* : the action of fainting; *also* : the resulting condition

faint-heart·ed \'fānt-'härt-əd\ *adj* : lacking courage : TIMID

¹fair \'faər\ *adj* **1** : attractive in appearance : BEAUTIFUL **2** : superficially pleasing : SPECIOUS **3** : CLEAN, PURE **4** : CLEAR, LEGIBLE **5** : not stormy or cloudy (*~* weather) **6** : JUST **7** : conforming with the rules : ALLOWED; *also* : being within the foul lines (*~* ball) **8** : open to legitimate pursuit or attack (*~* game) **9** : PROMISING, LIKELY (a *~* chance of winning) **10** : favorable to a ship's course (a *~* wind) **11** : light in coloring : BLOND **12** : ADEQUATE — **fair·ness** *n*

²fair *adv* : FAIRLY

³fair *n* **1** : a gathering of buyers and sellers at a stated time and place for trade **2** : a competitive exhibition (as of farm products) **3** : a sale of assorted articles usu. for a charitable purpose

fair·ground \-ˌgraund\ *n* : an area where outdoor fairs, circuses, or exhibitions are held

fair·ing \'fa(ə)r-iŋ\ *n* : a structure for producing a smooth outline and reducing drag (as on an airplane)

fair·ly \'fa(ə)r-lē\ *adv* **1** : HANDSOMELY, FAVORABLY (*~* situated) **2** : QUITE, COMPLETELY **3** : in a fair manner : JUSTLY **4** : MODERATELY, TOLERABLY (a *~* easy job)

fair–spo·ken \'faər-'spō-kən\ *adj* : pleasant and courteous in speech

fair–trade \-'trād\ *adj* : of, relating to, or being an agreement between a producer and a seller that branded merchandise will be sold at or above a specified price (*~* items) — **fair–trade** *vb*

fair·way \-ˌwā\ *n* : the mowed part of a golf course between tee and green

fairy \'fa(ə)r-ē\ *n, pl* **fair·ies** [ME *fairie* fairyland, fairy people, fr. OF *faerie*, fr. *feie, fee* fairy, fr. L *Fata*, goddess of fate, fr. *fatum* fate] : an imaginary being of folklore and romance usu. having diminutive human form and magic powers

fairy·land \-ˌland\ *n* **1** : the land of fairies **2** : a beautiful or charming place

fairy tale *n* **1** : a simple children's story about fairies **2** : FIB

fait ac·com·pli \ˌfāt-ˌak-ō"-plē\ *n, pl* **faits accomplis** *same, or* -"plēz\ [F, accomplished fact] : a thing accomplished and presumably irreversible

faith \'fāth\ *n, pl* **faiths** \'fāths, 'fāthz\ [deriv. of L *fides*] **1** : allegiance to duty or a person : LOYALTY **2** : belief and trust in God **3** : complete trust **4** : a system of religious beliefs — **faith·ful** \-fəl\ *adj* — **faith·ful·ly** \-ē\ *adv* — **faith·ful·ness** *n*

faith·less \'fāth-ləs\ *adj* **1** : DISLOYAL **2** : not to be relied on : UNTRUSTWORTHY — **faith·less·ly** *adv* — **faith·less·ness** *n*

¹fake \'fāk\ *adj* : COUNTERFEIT, SHAM

²fake *vb* **faked; fak·ing 1** : to treat so as to falsify **2** : COUNTERFEIT **3** : PRETEND, SIMULATE — **fak·er** *n*

³fake *n* **1** : IMITATION, FRAUD, COUNTERFEIT **2** : IMPOSTOR

fa·kir \fə-'kiər\ *n* [Ar *faqīr*, lit., poor man] **1** : a Muslim mendicant : DERVISH **2** : a wandering Hindu holy man who performs tricks

fal·chion \'fol-chən\ *n* : a broad-bladed slightly curved medieval sword

fal·con \'fal-kən, 'fo(l)-\ *n* **1** : a hawk trained for use in falconry **2** : any of various swift long-winged dark-eyed hawks having a beak adapted to snapping the spine of prey

fal·con·ry \'fal-kən-rē, 'fol-, 'fo-\ *n* **1** : the art of training hawks to hunt in cooperation with a person **2** : the sport of hunting with hawks — **fal-con-er** \-ər\ *n*

¹fall \'fȯl\ *vb* **fell** \'fel\ ; **fall-en** \'fȯ-lən\ ; **fall-ing** **1** : to descend freely by the force of gravity **2** : to hang freely **3** : to come as if by descending ⟨darkness *fell*⟩ **4** : to become uttered **5** : to lower or become lowered ⟨her eyes *fell*⟩ **6** : to leave an erect position suddenly and involuntarily **7** : STUMBLE, STRAY **8** : to drop down wounded or dead : die in battle **9** : to become captured or defeated **10** : to suffer ruin or failure **11** : to commit an immoral act **12** : to move or extend in a downward direction **13** : SUBSIDE, ABATE **14** : to decline in quality, activity, quantity, or value **15** : to assume a look of shame or dejection ⟨her face *fell*⟩ **16** : to occur at a certain time **17** : to come by chance **18** : DEVOLVE **19** : to have the proper place or station ⟨the accent ∼s on the first syllable⟩ **20** : to come within the scope of something **21** : to pass from one condition to another ⟨*fell* ill⟩ **22** : to set about heartily or actively ⟨∼ to work⟩ — **fall flat** : to produce no response or result — **fall for 1** : to fall in love with **2** : to become a victim of — **fall foul 1** : to have a collision **2** : to have a quarrel : CLASH — **fall from grace** : BACKSLIDE — **fall into line** : to comply with a certain course of action — **fall over oneself** *or* **fall over backward** : to display excessive eagerness — **fall short 1** : to be deficient in quantity **2** : to fail to attain

²fall *n* **1** : the act of falling **2** : a falling out, off, or away **3** : DROPPING **4** : AUTUMN **4** : a thing or quantity that falls ⟨a light ∼ of snow⟩ **5** : COLLAPSE, DOWNFALL **6** : the surrender or capture of a besieged place **7** : departure from virtue or goodness **8** : SLOPE **9** : WATERFALL — usu. used in pl. **10** : a decrease in size, quantity, degree, or value ⟨a ∼ in price⟩ **11** : the distance which something falls **12** : an act of forcing a wrestler's shoulders to the mat; *also* : a bout of wrestling

fal-la-cious \fə-'lā-shəs\ *adj* **1** : embodying a fallacy ⟨a ∼ argument⟩ **2** : MISLEADING, DECEPTIVE

fal-la-cy \'fal-ə-sē\ *n, pl* **-cies** **1** : a false or mistaken idea **2** : an often plausible argument using false or illogical reasoning

fall back \'fȯl-'bak\ *vb* : RETREAT, RECEDE

fall guy *n* **1** : one that is easily duped **2** : SCAPEGOAT

fal-li-ble \'fal-ə-bəl\ *adj* **1** : liable to be erroneous **2** : capable of making a mistake

fall-ing-out \,fȯ-liŋ-'au̇t\ *n, pl* **fallings-out** *or* **falling-outs** : QUARREL

falling star *n* : METEOR

fal-lo-pi-an tube \fə-,lō-pē-ən-\ *n, often cap F* : either of the pair of anatomical

tubes that carry the egg from the ovary to the uterus

fall-out \'fȯl-,au̇t\ *n* **1** : the often radioactive particles that result from a nuclear explosion and descend through the air **2** : an incidental result : BYPRODUCT

fall out \('¹)fȯl-'au̇t\ *vb* : QUARREL

fal-low \'fal-ō\ *n* **1** : land for crops allowed to lie idle during the growing season **2** : the tilling of land without sowing it for a season — **fal-low** *vb* — **fallow** *adj*

false \'fȯls\ *adj* **fals-er**; **fals-est 1** : not genuine : ARTIFICIAL **2** : intentionally untrue **3** : adjusted or made so as to deceive ⟨∼ scales⟩ **4** : tending to mislead : DECEPTIVE ⟨∼ promises⟩ **5** : not true ⟨∼ concepts⟩ **6** : not faithful or loyal : TREACHEROUS **7** : not essential or permanent ⟨∼ front⟩ **8** : inaccurate in pitch **9** : based on mistaken ideas — **false·ly** *adv* — **false·ness** *n* — **fal·si·ty** \'fȯl-sət-ē\ *n*

false·hood \'fȯls-,hu̇d\ *n* **1** : LIE **2** : absence of truth or accuracy **3** : the practice of lying

fal·set·to \fȯl-'set-ō\ *n, pl* **-tos** [It, fr. dim. of *falso* false] : an artificially high voice; *esp* : an artificial singing voice that overlaps and extends above the range of the full voice esp. of a tenor

fal·si·fy \'fȯl-sə-,fī\ *vb* **-fied**; **-fy·ing 1** : to make false : change so as to deceive **2** : LIE **3** : MISREPRESENT **4** : to prove to be false — **fal·si·fi·ca·tion** \,fȯl-sə-fə-'kā-shən\ *n*

fal·ter \'fȯl-tər\ *vb* **fal·tered**; **fal·ter·ing** \-t(ə-)riŋ\ **1** : to move unsteadily : STUMBLE, TOTTER **2** : to hesitate in speech : STAMMER **3** : to hesitate in purpose or action : WAVER, FLINCH — **fal·ter·ing·ly** \-t(ə-)riŋ-lē\ *adv*

fam *abbr* **1** familiar **2** family

fame \'fām\ *n* : public reputation : RENOWN — **famed** \'fāmd\ *adj*

fa·mil·ial \fə-'mil-yəl\ *adj* **1** : of, relating to, or characteristic of a family **2** : tending to occur in more members of a family than expected by chance alone ⟨a ∼ disorder⟩

¹fa·mil·iar \fə-'mil-yər\ *n* **1** : COMPANION **2** : a spirit held to attend and serve or guard a person **3** : one who frequents a place

²familiar *adj* **1** : closely acquainted : INTIMATE **2** : of or relating to a family **3** : INFORMAL **4** : FORWARD, PRESUMPTUOUS **5** : frequently seen or experienced **6** : of everyday occurrence — **fa·mil·iar·ly** *adv*

fa·mil·iar·i·ty \fə-,mil-'yar-ət-ē, -,mil-ē-'(y)ar-\ *n, pl* **-ties 1** : close friendship : INTIMACY **2** : INFORMALITY **3** : an unduly bold or forward act or expression : IMPROPRIETY **4** : close acquaintance with something

fa·mil·iar·ize \fə-'mil-yə-,rīz\ *vb* **-ized**; **-iz·ing 1** : to make known or familiar **2**

: to make thoroughly acquainted : AC-CUSTOM

fam·i·ly \'fam-(ə-)lē\ *n, pl* **-lies** [ME *familie*, fr. L *familia* household] **1** : a group of persons of common ancestry : CLAN **2** : a group of individuals living under one roof and under one head : HOUSEHOLD **3** : a group of things having common characteristics; *esp* : a group of related plants or animals ranking in biological classification above a genus and below an order **4** : a social group composed of parents and their children

family planning *n* : planning intended to determine the number and spacing of one's children through effective methods of birth control

family tree *n* : GENEALOGY; *also* : a genealogical diagram

fam·ine \'fam-ən\ *n* **1** : an extreme scarcity of food **2** : a great shortage

fam·ish \'fam-ish\ *vb* **1** : STARVE **2** : to suffer for lack of something necessary

fa·mous \'fā-məs\ *adj* **1** : widely known **2** : honored for achievement **3** : EXCELLENT, FIRST-RATE **syn** renowned, celebrated, noted, notorious, distinguished, eminent, illustrious

fa·mous·ly *adv* : SPLENDIDLY, EXCELLENTLY

¹fan \'fan\ *n* : a device (as a hand-waved triangular piece or a mechanism with blades) for producing a current of air

²fan *vb* **fanned; fan·ning 1** : to drive away the chaff from grain by winnowing **2** : to move (air) with or as if with a fan **3** : to direct a current of air upon ⟨~ a fire⟩ **4** : to stir up to activity : STIMULATE **5** : to spread like a fan **6** : to strike out in baseball

³fan *n* : an enthusiastic follower or admirer

fa·nat·ic \fə-'nat-ik\ *or* **fa·nat·i·cal** \-i-kəl\ *adj* [L *fanaticus* inspired by a deity, frenzied, fr. *fanum* temple] : marked by excessive enthusiasm and often intense uncritical devotion — **fanatic** *n* — **fa·nat·i·cism** \fə-'nat-ə-,siz-əm\ *n*

fan·ci·er \'fan-sē-ər\ *n* : a person who breeds or grows some kind of animal or plant for points of excellence

¹fan·ci·ful \'fan-si-fəl\ *adj* **1** : full of fancy : guided by fancy : WHIMSICAL **2** : coming from the fancy rather than from the reason **3** : curiously made or shaped — **fan·ci·ful·ly** \-f(ə-)lē\ *adv*

¹fan·cy \'fan-sē\ *n, pl* **fancies** [ME *fantasie, fantsy* fantasy, fancy, fr. MF *fantasie,* fr. L *phantasia,* fr. Gk, appearance, imagination] **1** : LIKING, INCLINATION; *also* : LOVE **2** : NOTION, IDEA, WHIM ⟨a passing ~⟩ **3** : IMAGINATION **4** : TASTE, JUDGMENT

²fancy *vb* **fan·cied; fan·cy·ing 1** : LIKE **2** : IMAGINE **3** : to believe without evidence **4** : to believe without being certain

³fancy *adj* **fan·ci·er; -est 1** : WHIMSICAL **2** : not plain : ORNAMENTAL **3** : of particular excellence **4** : bred esp. for a showy appearance **5** : above the usual price or the real value : EXTRAVAGANT **6** : executed with technical skill and superior grace — **fan·ci·ly** \'fan-sə-lē\ *adv*

fancy dress *n* : a costume (as for a masquerade) chosen to suit a fancy

fan·cy-free \'fan-sē-'frē\ *adj* : not centering the attention on any one person or thing; *esp* : not in love

fan·cy·work \'fan-sē-,wərk\ *n* : ornamental needlework (as embroidery)

fan·dan·go \fan-'daŋ-gō\ *n, pl* **-gos** : a lively Spanish or Spanish-American dance

fane \'fān\ *n* : TEMPLE

fan·fare \'fan-,faər\ *n* **1** : a flourish of trumpets **2** : a showy display

fang \'faŋ\ *n* : a long sharp tooth; *esp* : a grooved or hollow tooth of a venomous snake

fan-jet \'fan-,jet\ *n* **1** : a jet engine having a fan in its forward end that draws in extra air whose compression and expulsion provide extra thrust **2** : an airplane powered by a fan-jet

fan·light \'fan-,līt\ *n* : a semicircular window with radiating bars like the ribs of a fan set over a door or window

fan·tail \'fan-,tāl\ *n* **1** : a fan-shaped tail or end **2** : an overhang at the stern of a ship

fan·ta·sia \fan-'tā-zhə, -z(h)ē-ə; ,fant-ə-'zē-ə\ *also* **fan·ta·sie** \,fant-ə-'zē ,fänt-\ *n* : a musical composition free and fanciful in form

fan·ta·size \'fant-ə-,sīz\ *vb* **-sized; -siz·ing** : IMAGINE, DAYDREAM

fan·tas·tic \fan-'tas-tik\ *also* **fan·tas·ti·cal** \-ti-kəl\ *adj* **1** : IMAGINARY, UNREAL, UNREALISTIC **2** : conceived by unrestrained fancy : GROTESQUE **3** : exceedingly or unbelievably great **4** : ECCENTRIC — **fan·tas·ti·cal·ly** \-ti-k(ə-)lē\ *adv*

fan·ta·sy \'fant-ə-sē\ *n, pl* **-sies 1** : IMAGINATION, FANCY **2** : a product of the imagination : ILLUSION **3** : FANTASIA — **fantasy** *vb*

¹far \'fär\ *adv* **far·ther** \-thər\ *or* **fur·ther** \'fər-\; **far·thest** *or* **fur·thest** \-thəst\ **1** : at or to a considerable distance in space or time ⟨~ from home⟩ **2** : by a broad interval : WIDELY, MUCH ⟨~ better⟩ **3** : to or at a definite distance, point, or degree ⟨as ~ as I know⟩ **4** : to an advanced point or extent ⟨go ~ in his field⟩ — **by far** : GREATLY — **far and away** : DECIDEDLY — **so far** : until now

²far *adj* **farther** *or* **further; farthest** *or* **furthest 1** : remote in space or time : DISTANT **2** : DIFFERENT ⟨a ~ cry from former methods⟩ **3** : LONG ⟨a ~ journey⟩ **4** : being the more distant of two ⟨on the ~ side of the lake⟩

far·ad \'far-,ad, -əd\ *n* : a unit of capacitance equal to the capacitance of a capacitor having a potential difference of one volt between its plates when it is charged with one coulomb of electricity

far·away \ˌfär-ə-ˌwā\ *adj* **1** : DISTANT, REMOTE **2** : DREAMY

farce \ˈfärs\ *n* **1** : a broadly satirical comedy with an improbable plot **2** : the humor characteristic of farce or pretense **3** : a ridiculous action, display, or pretense — **far·ci·cal** \ˈfär-si-kəl\ *adj*

¹fare \ˈfaər\ *vb* **fared; far·ing 1** : GO, TRAVEL **2** : GET ALONG, SUCCEED **3** : EAT, DINE

²fare *n* **1** : the price charged to transport a person **2** : a person paying a fare : PASSENGER **3** : range of food : DIET; *also* : material provided for use, consumption, or enjoyment

¹fare·well \faər-ˈwel\ *vb imper* : get along well — used interjectionally to or by one departing

²farewell *n* **1** : a wish of well-being at parting : GOOD-BYE **2** : LEAVE-TAKING

³fare·well \faər-ˈwel\ *adj* : PARTING, FINAL (a ~ concert)

far-fetched \ˈfär-ˈfecht\ *adj* : not easily or naturally deduced or introduced : IMPROBABLE

far-flung \-ˈfləŋ\ *adj* : widely spread or distributed

fa·ri·na \fə-ˈrē-nə\ *n* [L, meal, flour] : a fine meal (as of wheat) used in puddings or as a breakfast cereal

far·i·na·ceous \ˌfar-ə-ˈnā-shəs\ *adj* **1** : containing or rich in starch **2** : having a mealy texture or surface

¹farm \ˈfärm\ *n* [ME *ferme* rent, lease, fr. OF. lease, fr. *fermer* to fix, make a contract, fr. L *firmare* to make firm, fr. *firmus* firm] **1** : a tract of land used for raising crops or livestock **2** : a minor-league baseball team

²farm *vb* : to use (land) as a farm (~ed 200 acres); *also* : to raise crops or livestock esp. as a business — **farm·er** *n*

farm·hand \ˈfärm-ˌhand\ *n* : a farm laborer

farm·house \-ˌhaùs\ *n* : a dwelling on a farm

farm·ing \ˈfär-miŋ\ *n* : the practice of agriculture

farm·land \ˈfärm-ˌland\ *n* : land used or suitable for farming

farm out *vb* : to turn over (as a task) to another

farm·stead \ˈfärm-ˌsted\ *also* **farm-stead·ing** \-iŋ\ *n* : the buildings and adjacent service areas of a farm

farm·yard \-ˌyärd\ *n* : space around or enclosed by farm buildings

far-off \ˈfär-ˈȯf\ *adj* : remote in time or space : DISTANT

fa·rouche \fə-ˈrüsh\ *adj* [F] **1** : marked by shyness and lack of polish **2** : WILD

far-out \ˈfär-ˈaùt\ *adj* : very unconventional : EXTREME (~ clothes)

far·ra·go \fə-ˈräg-ō, -ˈrä-gō\ *n, pl* **-goes** [L, mixed fodder] : a confused collection : MIXTURE

far-reach·ing \ˈfär-ˌrē-chiŋ\ *adj* : having a wide range or effect

far·ri·er \ˈfar-ē-ər\ *n* : one that shoes horses

¹far·row \ˈfar-ō\ *vb* : to give birth to a farrow

²farrow *n* : a litter of pigs

far-see·ing \ˈfär-ˌsē-iŋ\ *adj* : FARSIGHTED

far·sight·ed \ˈfär-ˈsīt-əd\ *adj* **1** : seeing or able to see to a great distance **2** : JUDICIOUS, WISE, SHREWD **3** : affected with an eye condition in which the image comes into focus behind the retina — **far·sight·ed·ness** *n*

¹far·ther \ˈfär-thər\ *adv* **1** : at or to a greater distance or more advanced point **2** : more completely

²farther *adj* **1** : more distant **2** : ADDITIONAL

far·ther·most \-ˌmōst\ *adj* : most distant

¹far·thest \ˈfär-thəst\ *adj* : most distant

²farthest *adv* **1** : to or at the greatest distance : REMOTEST **2** : to the most advanced point **3** : by the greatest degree or extent : MOST

far·thing \ˈfär-thiŋ\ *n* : a former British monetary unit equal to ¼ of a penny; *also* : a coin representing this unit

far·thin·gale \ˈfär-thən-ˌgāl, -thiŋ-\ *n* [modif. of MF *verdugale*, fr. Sp *verdugado*, fr. *verdugo* young shoot of a tree, fr. *verde* green, fr. L *viridis*] : a support (as of hoops) worn esp. in the 16th century to swell out a skirt

fas·ci·cle \ˈfas-i-kəl\ *n* **1** : a small bundle or cluster (as of flowers or roots) **2** : one of the divisions of a book published in parts — **fas·ci·cled** \-kəld\ *adj*

fas·ci·nate \ˈfas-ᵊn-ˌāt\ *vb* **-nat·ed; -nat·ing** [L *fascinare*, fr. *fascinum* witchcraft] **1** : to transfix and hold spellbound by an irresistible power **2** : ALLURE **3** : to be irresistibly attractive — **fas·ci·na·tion** \ˌfas-ᵊn-ˈā-shən\ *n*

fas·cism \ˈfash-ˌiz-əm\ *n, often cap* : a political philosophy, movement, or regime that exalts nation and often race and stands for a centralized autocratic government headed by a dictatorial leader, severe economic and social regimentation, and forcible suppression of opposition — **fas·cist** \-əst\ *n or adj, often cap* — **fas·cis·tic** \fa-ˈshis-tik\ *adj, often cap*

¹fash·ion \ˈfash-ən\ *n* **1** : the make or form of something **2** : MANNER, WAY **3** : a prevailing custom, usage, or style **4** : the prevailing style (as in dress) *syn* mode, vogue, rage, trend

²fashion *vb* **fash·ioned; fash·ion·ing** \ˈfash-(ə-)niŋ\ **1** : MOLD, CONSTRUCT **2** : FIT, ADAPT

fash·ion·able \ˈfash-(ə-)nə-bəl\ *adj* **1** : dressing or behaving according to fashion : STYLISH **2** : of or relating to the world of fashion (~ resorts) — **fash·ion·ably** \-blē\ *adv*

¹fast \ˈfast\ *adj* **1** : firmly fixed **2** : tightly shut **3** : adhering firmly **4** : STUCK **5**

: STAUNCH ⟨∼ friends⟩ **6** : characterized by quick motion, operation, or effect ⟨a ∼ trip⟩ ⟨a ∼ track⟩ **7** : indicating ahead of the correct time ⟨the clock is ∼⟩ **8** : not easily disturbed : SOUND ⟨a ∼ sleep⟩ **9** : permanently dyed; *also* : being proof against fading ⟨colors ∼ to sunlight⟩ **10** : DISSIPATED, WILD **11** : sexually promiscuous **syn** rapid, swift, fleet, quick, speedy, hasty

²**fast** *adv* **1** : in a firm or fixed manner ⟨stuck ∼ in the mud⟩ **2** : SOUNDLY, DEEPLY ⟨∼ asleep⟩ **3** : SWIFTLY **4** : RECKLESSLY

³**fast** *vb* **1** : to abstain from food **2** : to eat sparingly or abstain from some foods

⁴**fast** *n* **1** : the act or practice of fasting **2** : a time of fasting

fast-back \'fas(t)-ˌbak\ *n* : an automobile having a roof with a long slope to the rear

fast-ball \'fas(t)-ˌból\ *n* : a baseball pitch thrown at full speed

fas-ten \'fas-ⁿn\ *vb* **fas-tened; fas-ten-ing** \'fas-(ə-)niŋ\ **1** : to attach or join by or as if by pinning, tying, or nailing **2** : to make fast : fix securely **3** : to fix or set steadily ⟨∼ed his eyes on her⟩ **4** : to become fixed or joined — **fas-ten-er** \'fas-(ə-)nər\ *n*

fas-ten-ing \'fas-(ə-)niŋ\ *n* : something that fastens : FASTENER

fast-food \ˌfas(t)-'füd\ *adj* : specializing in food that is prepared and served quickly ⟨a ∼ restaurant⟩ — **fast-food** *n*

fas-tid-i-ous \fas-'tid-ē-əs\ *adj* **1** : overly difficult to please **2** : showing or demanding excessive delicacy or care — **fas-tid-i-ous-ly** *adv* — **fas-tid-i-ous-ness** *n*

fast-ness \'fas(t)-nəs\ *n* **1** : the quality or state of being fast **2** : a fortified or secure place : STRONGHOLD

fast-talk \'fas(t)-'tók\ *vb* : to influence by persuasive and usu. deceptive talk

¹**fat** \'fat\ *adj* **fat-ter; fat-test 1** : FLESHY, PLUMP **2** : OILY, GREASY **3** : well filled out : BIG **4** : well stocked : ABUNDANT **5** : PROFITABLE — **fat-ness** *n*

²**fat** *n* **1** : animal tissue rich in greasy or oily matter **2** : any of numerous energy-rich esters that occur naturally in animal fats and in plants and are soluble in organic solvents (as ether) but not in water **3** : the best or richest portion (lived on the ∼ of the land) **4** : OBESITY **5** : excess matter

fa-tal \'fāt-ⁿl\ *adj* **1** : FATEFUL **2** : MORTAL, DEADLY, DISASTROUS — **fa-tal-ly** \-ē\ *adv*

fa-tal-ism \-ˌiz-əm\ *n* : the belief that events are determined by **fate** — **fa-tal-ist** \-əst\ *n* — **fa-tal-is-tic** \ˌfāt-ⁿl-'is-tik\ *adj*

fa-tal-i-ty \fā-'tal-ət-ē, fə-\ *n, pl* -ties **1** : DEADLINESS **2** : the quality or state of being destined for disaster **3** : FATE **4** : death resulting from a disaster or accident

fat-back \'fat-ˌbak\ *n* : a fatty strip from the back of the hog usu. cured by salting and drying

fat cat *n* **1** : a wealthy contributor to a political campaign **2** : a wealthy privileged person

fate \'fāt\ *n* [ME, fr. MF or L; fr. L *fatum*, lit., what has been spoken, fr. *fari* to speak] **1** : the cause beyond man's control that is held to determine events : DESTINY **2** : LOT, FORTUNE **3** : DISASTER; *esp* : DEATH **4** : END, OUTCOME **5** *cap, pl* : the three goddesses of classical mythology who determine the course of human life

fat-ed \'fā-təd\ *adj* : decreed, controlled, or marked by fate

fate-ful \'fāt-fəl\ *adj* **1** : OMINOUS, PROPHETIC **2** : IMPORTANT, DECISIVE **3** : DEADLY, DESTRUCTIVE **4** : determined by fate — **fate-ful-ly** \-ē\ *adv*

fat-head \'fat-ˌhed\ *n* : a stupid person — **fat-head-ed** \-ˌhed-əd\ *adj*

fa-ther \'fäth-ər\ *n* **1** : a male parent **2** *cap* : God esp. as the first person of the Trinity **3** : FOREFATHER **4** : one deserving the respect and love given to a father **5** *often cap* : an early Christian writer accepted by the church as an authoritative witness to its teaching and practice **6** : ORIGINATOR ⟨the ∼ of modern radio⟩; *also* : SOURCE **7** : PRIEST — used esp. as a title **8** : one of the leading men ⟨city ∼s⟩ — **fa-ther-hood** \-ˌhùd\ *n* — **fa-ther-less** *adj* — **fa-ther-ly** *adj*

²**father** *vb* **1** : BEGET **2** : to be the founder, producer, or author of **3** : to treat or care for as a father

father-in-law \'fäth-(ə-)rən-ˌló\ *n, pl* **fa-thers-in-law** \-ər-zən-\ : the father of one's husband or wife

fa-ther-land \'fäth-ər-ˌland\ *n* **1** : one's native land **2** : the native land of one's ancestors

¹**fath-om** \'fath-əm\ *n* [ME *fadme*, fr. OE *fæthm* outstretched arms, fathom] : a unit of length equal to 6 feet (about 1.8 meters) used esp. for measuring the depth of water

²**fathom** *vb* **1** : to measure by a sounding line **2** : PROBE **3** : to penetrate and come to understand — **fath-om-able** \'fath-ə-mə-bəl\ *adj*

fath-om-less \'fath-əm-ləs\ *adj* : incapable of being fathomed

¹**fa-tigue** \fə-'tēg\ *n* [F] **1** : manual or menial work performed by military personnel **2** *pl* : the uniform or work clothing worn on fatigue and in the field **3** : weariness from labor or use **4** : the tendency of a material to break under repeated stress

²**fatigue** *vb* **fa-tigued; fa-tigu-ing** : WEARY, TIRE

fat-ten \'fat-ⁿn\ *vb* : to make or grow fat

¹**fat-ty** \'fat-ē\ *adj* **fat-ti-er; -est 1** : containing fat esp. in unusual amounts **2** : GREASY

²**fatty** *n, pl* **fatties** : a fat person

fatty acid *n* : any of numerous acids that contain only carbon, hydrogen, and oxygen and that occur naturally in fats and various oils

fa·tu·ity \fə-'t(y)ü-ət-ē\ *n, pl* **-ities** : FOOLISHNESS, STUPIDITY

fat·u·ous \'fach-(ə-)wəs\ *adj* : FOOLISH, INANE, SILLY — **fat·u·ous·ly** *adv*

fau·bourg \fō-'bùr\ *n* 1 : SUBURB; *esp* : a suburb of a French city 2 : a city quarter

fau·ces \'fò-ˌsēz\ *n pl* [L, throat] : the narrow passage located between the soft palate and the base of the tongue that joins the mouth to the pharynx

fau·cet \'fòs-ət, 'fäs-\ *n* : a fixture for drawing off a liquid (as from a pipe)

¹fault \'fòlt\ *n* 1 : a weakness in character : FAILING 2 : IMPERFECTION, IMPAIRMENT 3 : an error esp. in service in a net or racket game 4 : MISDEMEANOR; *also* : MISTAKE 5 : responsibility for something wrong 6 : a fracture in the earth's crust accompanied by a displacement of one side relative to the other — **fault·i·ly** \'fòl-tə-lē\ *adv* — **fault·less** *adj* — **fault·less·ly** *adv* — **faulty** *adj*

²fault *vb* 1 : to commit a fault : ERR 2 : to fracture so as to produce a geologic fault 3 : to find a fault in

fault·find·er \'fòlt-ˌfīn-dər\ *n* : a person who tends to find fault or complain — **fault·find·ing** \-diŋ\ *n or adj*

faun \'fòn\ *n* : a Roman god of fields and herds represented as part goat and part man

fau·na \'fòn-ə\ *n, pl* **faunas** *also* **fau·nae** \-ˌē, -ˌī\ [LL *Fauna*, sister of Faunus (the Roman god of animals)] : animals or animal life esp. of a region, period, or environment — **fau·nal** \-ᵊl\ *adj*

fau·vism \'fō-ˌviz-əm\ *n, often cap* : a movement in painting characterized by vivid colors, free treatment of form, and a vibrant and decorative effect — **fau·vist** \-vəst\ *n, often cap*

faux pas \'fō-'pä\ *n, pl* **faux pas** \-'pä(z)\ [F, lit., false step] : BLUNDER; *esp* : a social blunder

¹fa·vor \'fā-vər\ *n* 1 : friendly regard shown toward another esp. by a superior 2 : APPROVAL 3 : PARTIALITY 4 : POPULARITY 5 : gracious kindness; *also* : an act of such kindness 6 : effort in one's behalf : ATTENTION 7 : a token of love (as a ribbon) as worn conspicuously 8 : a small gift or decorative item given out at a party 9 : a special privilege 10 *archaic* : LETTER 11 : BEHALF, INTEREST

²favor *vb* **fa·vored; fa·vor·ing** \'fā-v(ə-)riŋ\ 1 : to regard or treat with favor 2 : OBLIGE 3 : ENDOW ⟨~ed by nature⟩ 4 : to treat gently or carefully : SPARE ⟨~ a lame leg⟩ 5 : PREFER 6 : SUPPORT, SUSTAIN 7 : FACILITATE ⟨darkness ~s attack⟩ 8 : RESEMBLE ⟨he ~s his father⟩

fa·vor·able \'fāv-(ə-)rə-bəl\ *adj* 1 : APPROVING 2 : HELPFUL, PROMISING, AD-VANTAGEOUS ⟨~ weather⟩ — **fa·vor·ably** \-blē\ *adv*

fa·vor·ite \'fāv-(ə-)rət\ *n* 1 : a person or a thing that is favored above others 2 : a competitor regarded as most likely to win — **favorite** *adj*

favorite son *n* : a candidate supported by the delegates of his state at a presidential nominating convention

fa·vor·it·ism \'fāv-(ə-)rət-ˌiz-əm\ *n* : PARTIALITY, BIAS

fa·vour *chiefly Brit var of* FAVOR

¹fawn \'fòn, 'fän\ *vb* 1 : to show affection ⟨a dog ~ing on its master⟩ 2 : to court favor by a cringing or flattering manner

²fawn *n* 1 : a young deer 2 : a variable color averaging a light grayish brown

fax \'faks\ *n* : FACSIMILE 2

fay \'fā\ *n* : FAIRY, ELF — **fay** *adj*

faze \'fāz\ *vb* **fazed; faz·ing** : to disturb the composure or courage of : DAUNT

FBI *abbr* Federal Bureau of Investigation

FCC *abbr* Federal Communications Commission

FD *abbr* fire department

FDA *abbr* Food and Drug Administration

FDIC *abbr* Federal Deposit Insurance Corporation

Fe *symbol* [L *ferrum*] iron

fe·al·ty \'fē-(ə)l-tē\ *n, pl* **-ties** : LOYALTY, ALLEGIANCE

¹fear \'fi(ə)r\ *vb* 1 : to have a reverent awe of ⟨~ God⟩ 2 : to be afraid of : have fear 3 : to be apprehensive

²fear *n* 1 : an unpleasant often strong emotion caused by expectation or awareness of danger; *also* : an instance of or a state marked by this emotion 2 : anxious concern : SOLICITUDE 3 : profound reverence esp. toward God **syn** dread, fright, alarm, panic, terror, trepidation

fear·ful \-fəl\ *adj* 1 : causing fear 2 : filled with fear 3 : showing or caused by fear 4 : extremely bad, intense, or large — **fear·ful·ly** \-ē\ *adv*

fear·less \-ləs\ *adj* : free from fear : BRAVE — **fear·less·ly** *adv* — **fear·less·ness** *n*

fear·some \-səm\ *adj* 1 : causing fear 2 : TIMID

fea·si·ble \'fē-zə-bəl\ *adj* 1 : capable of being done or carried out ⟨a ~ plan⟩ 2 : SUITABLE 3 : REASONABLE, LIKELY — **fea·si·bil·i·ty** \ˌfē-zə-'bil-ət-ē\ *n* — **fea·si·bly** \'fē-zə-blē\ *adv*

¹feast \'fēst\ *n* 1 : an elaborate meal : BANQUET 2 : FESTIVAL 1

²feast *vb* 1 : to take part in a feast; *also* : to give a feast for 2 : to enjoy some unusual pleasure or delight 3 : DELIGHT, GRATIFY

feat \'fēt\ *n* : DEED, EXPLOIT, ACHIEVEMENT; *esp* : an act notable for courage, skill, endurance, or ingenuity

feath·er \'feth-ər\ *n* 1 : one of the light horny outgrowths that form the external covering of the body of a bird 2

feather·feeding 276

: PLUME **3** : PLUMAGE **4** : KIND, NATURE (birds of a ~) **5** : ATTIRE, DRESS (in full ~) **6** : CONDITION, MOOD (in fine ~) — **feath·ered** \-ərd\ *adj* — **feath·er·less** *adj* — **feath·ery** *adj* — **a feather in one's cap** : a mark of distinction : HONOR

²**feather** *vb* **1** : to furnish with a feather (~ an arrow) **2** : to cover, clothe, line, or adorn with feathers — **feather one's nest** : to provide for oneself esp. while in a position of trust

feath·er·bed·ding \'feth-ər-ˌbed-iŋ\ *n* : the requiring of an employer usu. under a union rule or safety statute to employ more workers than are needed

feath·er·edge \-ˌej\ *n* : a very thin sharp edge; *esp* : one that is easily broken or bent over

feath·er·weight \-ˌwāt\ *n* : one that is very light in weight; *esp* : a boxer weighing more than 118 but not over 126 pounds

¹**fea·ture** \'fē-chər\ *n* **1** : the shape or appearance of the face or its parts **2** : a part of the face : LINEAMENT **3** : a prominent part or characteristic **4** : a special attraction (as in a motion picture or newspaper) **5** : something offered to the public or advertised as particularly attractive — **fea·ture·less** *adj*

²**feature** *vb* **1** : to picture in the mind : IMAGINE **2** : to give special prominence to (~ a story in a newspaper) **3** : to play an important part

feaze \'fēz, 'fāz\ *var of* FAZE

Feb *abbr* February

feb·ri·fuge \'feb-rə-ˌfyüj\ *n* : a medicine for relieving fever — **febrifuge** *adj*

fe·brile \'feb-rəl, -ˌrīl; 'fēb-\ *adj* : FEVERISH

Feb·ru·ary \'feb-(y)ə-ˌwer-ē, 'feb-rə-\ *n* [ME *Februarie*, fr. L *Februarius*, fr. *Februa*, pl., feast of purification] : the second month of the year having 28 and in leap years 29 days

fe·ces \'fē-ˌsēz\ *n pl* : bodily waste discharged from the intestine — **fe·cal** \-kəl\ *adj*

feck·less \'fek-ləs\ *adj* **1** : WEAK, INEFFECTIVE **2** : WORTHLESS, IRRESPONSIBLE

fe·cund \'fek-ənd, 'fēk-\ *adj* : FRUITFUL, PROLIFIC — **fe·cun·di·ty** \fi-'kən-dət-ē, fe-\ *n*

fe·cun·date \'fek-ən-ˌdāt, 'fē-kən-\ *vb* **-dat·ed; -dat·ing 1** : to make fecund **2** : IMPREGNATE — **fe·cun·da·tion** \ˌfek-ən-'dā-shən, ˌfē-kən-\ *n*

fed *abbr* federal; federation

fed·er·al \'fed-(ə-)rəl\ *adj* **1** : formed by a compact between political units that surrender individual sovereignty to a central authority but retain certain limited powers **2** : of or constituting a form of government in which power is distributed between a central authority and constituent territorial units **3** : of or relating to the central government of a federation **4** *cap* : FEDERAL-

IST **5** *often cap* : of, relating to, or loyal to the federal government or the Union armies of the U.S. in the American Civil War — **fed·er·al·ly** \-ē\ *adv*

Federal *n* : a supporter of the U.S. government in the Civil War; *esp* : a soldier in the federal armies

federal district *n* : a district (as the District of Columbia) set apart as the seat of the central government of a federation

fed·er·al·ism \'fed-(ə-)rə-ˌliz-əm\ *n* **1** *often cap* : the distribution of power in an organization (as a government) between a central authority and the constituent units **2** : support or advocacy of federalism **3** *cap* : the principles of the Federalists

fed·er·al·ist \-ləst\ *n* **1** : an advocate of federalism **2** *often cap* : an advocate of a federal union between the American colonies after the Revolution and of adoption of the U.S. Constitution **3** *cap* : a member of a major political party in the early years of the U.S. favoring a strong centralized national government — **federalist** *adj, often cap*

fed·er·al·ize \'fed(-ə)-rə-ˌlīz\ *vb* **-ized; -iz·ing 1** : to unite in or under a federal system **2** : to bring under the jurisdiction of a federal government

fed·er·ate \'fed-ə-ˌrāt\ *vb* **-at·ed; -at·ing** : to join in a federation

fed·er·a·tion \ˌfed-ə-'rā-shən\ *n* **1** : the act of federating; *esp* : the forming of a federal union **2** : a federal government **3** : a union of organizations

fedn *abbr* federation

fe·do·ra \fi-'dōr-ə\ *n* : a low soft felt hat with the crown creased lengthwise

fed up *adj* : satiated, tired, or disgusted beyond endurance

fee \'fē\ *n* **1** : an estate in land held from a feudal lord **2** : an inherited or heritable estate in land **3** : a fixed charge; *also* : a charge for a professional service **4** : TIP

fee·ble \'fē-bəl\ *adj* **fee·bler** \-b(ə-)lər\ ; **fee·blest** \-b(ə-)ləst\ [ME *feble*, fr. OF. fr. L *flebilis* lamentable, wretched, fr. *flēre* to weep] **1** : DECREPIT, FRAIL **2** : INEFFECTIVE, INADEQUATE (a ~ protest) — **fee·ble·ness** *n* — **fee·bly** \-blē\ *adv*

fee·ble·mind·ed \ˌfē-bəl-'mīn-dəd\ *adj* : lacking normal intelligence — **fee·ble·mind·ed·ness** *n*

¹**feed** \'fēd\ *vb* **fed** \'fed\ ; **feed·ing 1** : to give food to; *also* : to give as food **2** : EAT; *also* : PREY **3** : to furnish what is necessary to the growth or function of — **feed·er** *n*

²**feed** *n* **1** : a usu. large meal **2** : food for livestock **3** : material supplied (as to a furnace) **4** : a mechanism for feeding material to a machine

feed·back \'fēd-ˌbak\ *n* **1** : the return to the input of a part of the output of a machine, system, or process **2** : response esp. to one in authority about an activity or policy

feed·lot \'fēd-ˌlät\ *n* : land on which cattle are fattened for market

feed·stuff \-ˌstəf\ *n* : ²FEED 2

¹**feel** \'fēl\ *vb* felt \'felt\ ; feel·ing 1 : to perceive or examine through physical contact : TOUCH, HANDLE 2 : EXPERIENCE; *also* : to suffer from 3 : to ascertain by cautious trial (∼ out public sentiment) 4 : to be aware of 5 : to be conscious of an inward impression, state of mind, or physical condition 6 : BELIEVE, THINK 7 : to search for something with the fingers : GROPE 8 : to seem esp. to the touch 9 : to have sympathy or pity

²**feel** *n* 1 : the sense of touch 2 : SENSATION, FEELING 3 : the quality of a thing as imparted through touch

feel·er \'fē-lər\ *n* 1 : one that feels; *esp* : a tactile organ (as on the head of an insect) 2 : a proposal or remark made to find out the views of other people

¹**feel·ing** \'fē-liŋ\ *n* 1 : the sense of touch; *also* : a sensation perceived by this 2 : a state of mind (a ∼ of loneliness) 3 *pl* : general emotional condition : SENSIBILITIES (hurt their ∼s) 4 : OPINION, BELIEF, SENTIMENT 5 : capacity to respond emotionally

²**feeling** *adj* 1 : SENSITIVE; *esp* : easily moved emotionally 2 : expressing emotion or sensitivity — feel·ing·ly *adv*

feet *pl of* FOOT

feign \'fān\ *vb* 1 : to give a false appearance of : SHAM (∼ illness) 2 : to assert as if true : PRETEND

feint \'fānt\ *n* : something feigned; *esp* : a mock blow or attack intended to distract attention from the real point of attack — feint *vb*

feld·spar \'feld-ˌspär\ *n* : any of a group of crystalline minerals consisting of silicates of aluminum with either potassium, sodium, calcium, or barium

fe·lic·i·tate \fi-'lis-ə-ˌtāt\ *vb* -tat·ed; -tat·ing : CONGRATULATE — fe·lic·i·ta·tion \-ˌlis-ə-'tā-shən\ *n*

fe·lic·i·tous \fi-'lis-ət-əs\ *adj* 1 : suitably expressed : APT 2 : PLEASANT, DELIGHTFUL — fe·lic·i·tous·ly *adv*

fe·lic·i·ty \fi-'lis-ət-ē\ *n, pl* -ties 1 : the quality or state of being happy; *esp* : great happiness 2 : something that causes happiness 3 : a pleasing manner or quality esp. in art or language : APTNESS 4 : an apt expression

fe·line \'fē-ˌlīn\ *adj* [L *felinus,* fr. *felis* cat] 1 : of or relating to cats or their kin 2 : SLY, TREACHEROUS 3 : STEALTHY — feline *n*

¹**fell** \'fel\ *vb* : SKIN, HIDE, PELT

²**fell** *vb* 1 : to cut, beat, or knock down (∼ trees) ; *also* : KILL 2 : to sew (a seam) by folding one raw edge under the other

³**fell** *past of* FALL

⁴**fell** *adj* : CRUEL, FIERCE; *also* : DEADLY

fel·lah \'fel-ə, fə-'lä\ *n, pl* fel·la·hin or fel·la·heen \ˌfel-ə-'hēn\ : a peasant or agricultural laborer in Arab countries (as Egypt or Syria)

fel·la·tio \fə-'lā-shē-ˌō\ *also* fel·la·tion \-'lā-shən\ *n* [deriv. of L *fellare* to suck] : oral stimulation of the penis

fel·low \'fel-ō\ *n* [ME *felawe,* fr. OE *fēolaga,* fr. ON *fēlagi,* fr. *fēlag* partnership, fr. *fē* cattle, money + *lag* act of laying] 1 : COMRADE, ASSOCIATE 2 : EQUAL, PEER 3 : one of a pair : MATE 4 : a member of an incorporated literary or scientific society 5 : MAN, BOY 6 : BOYFRIEND 7 : a person granted a stipend for advanced study

fel·low·man \ˌfel-ō-'man\ *n* : a kindred human being

fel·low·ship \'fel-ō-ˌship\ *n* 1 : the condition of friendly relationship existing among persons : COMRADESHIP 2 : a community of interest or feeling 3 : a group with similar interests 4 : the position of a fellow (as of a university) 5 : the stipend granted a fellow

fellow traveler *n* : a person who sympathizes with and often furthers the ideals and program of an organized group (as the Communist party) without joining it or regularly participating in its activities

fel·on \'fel-ən\ *n* 1 : one who has committed a felony 2 : WHITLOW

fel·o·ny \'fel-ə-nē\ *n, pl* -nies : a serious crime punishable by a heavy sentence — fe·lo·ni·ous \fə-'lō-nē-əs\ *adj*

¹**felt** \'felt\ *n* 1 : a cloth made of wool and fur often mixed with natural or synthetic fibers 2 : a material resembling felt

²**felt** *past and past part of* FEEL

fem *abbr* 1 female 2 feminine

fe·male \'fē-ˌmāl\ *adj* [ME, alter. of *femel,* deriv. of ML *femella,* fr. L, girl, dim. of *femina* woman] : of, relating to, or being the sex that bears young; *also* : PISTILLATE **syn** feminine, womanly, womanlike, womanish, effeminate — female *n*

¹**fem·i·nine** \'fem-ə-nən\ *adj* 1 : of the female sex; *also* : characteristic of or appropriate or peculiar to women 2 : of, relating to, or constituting the gender that includes most words or grammatical forms referring to females — fem·i·nin·i·ty \ˌfem-ə-'nin-ət-ē\ *n*

²**feminine** *n* : a noun, pronoun, adjective, or inflectional form or class of the feminine gender; *also* : the feminine gender

fem·i·nism \'fem-ə-ˌniz-əm\ *n* 1 : the theory of the political, economic, and social equality of the sexes 2 : organized activity on behalf of women's rights and interests — fem·i·nist \-nəst\ *n or adj*

femme fa·tale \ˌfem-fə-'tal\ *n, pl* femmes fa·tales \-'tal(z)\ [F, lit., disastrous woman] : a seductive woman : SIREN fe·mur \'fē-mər\ n, pl fe·murs or fem·o·ra \'fem-(ə-)rə\ : the long bone of the thigh — fem·o·ral \'fem-(ə-)rəl\ adj

¹fen \'fen\ n : low swampy land

²fen \'fən\ n, pl fen — see yuan at MONEY table

¹fence \'fens\ n [ME fens, short for defens defense] 1 : a barrier (as of wood or wire) to prevent escape or entry or to mark a boundary 2 : a person who receives stolen goods; also : a place where stolen goods are disposed of — on the fence : in a position of neutrality or indecision

²fence vb fenced; fenc·ing 1 : to enclose with a fence 2 : to keep in or out with a fence 3 : to practice fencing 4 : to use tactics of attack and defense esp. in debate — fenc·er n

fenc·ing \'fen-siŋ\ n 1 : the art or practice of attack and defense with the foil, épée, or saber 2 : the fences of a property or region 3 : material used for building fences

fend \'fend\ vb 1 : to keep or ward off : REPEL 2 : SHIFT ⟨~ for himself⟩

fend·er \'fen-dər\ n : a protective device (as a guard over the wheel of an automobile or as a screen before a fire)

fen·es·tra·tion \ˌfen-ə-'strā-shən\ n : the arrangement and design of windows and doors in a building

Fe·ni·an \'fē-nē-ən\ n : a member of a secret 19th century Irish and Irish-American organization dedicated to the overthrow of British rule in Ireland

fen·nel \'fen-ᵊl\ n : a garden plant related to the carrot and grown for its aromatic foliage and seeds

FEPC abbr Fair Employment Practices Commission

fe·ral \'fir-əl, 'fer-\ adj 1 : SAVAGE 2 : WILD 1 3 : having escaped from domestication and become wild

fer-de-lance \'ferd-ᵊl-'ans\ n, pl fer-de-lance [F, lit., lance iron, spearhead] : a large venomous pit viper of Central and So. America

¹fer·ment \fər-'ment\ vb 1 : to cause or undergo fermentation 2 : to be or cause to be in a state of agitation or intense activity

²fer·ment \'fər-ˌment\ n 1 : a living organism (as a yeast) causing fermentation by its enzymes; also : ENZYME 2 : AGITATION, TUMULT

fer·men·ta·tion \ˌfər-mən-'tā-shən, -ˌmen-\ n 1 : chemical decomposition of an organic substance (as in the souring of milk or the formation of alcohol from sugar) in the absence of oxygen by enzymatic action often with formation of gas 2 : AGITATION, UNREST

fer·mi·um \'fer-mē-əm, 'fər-\ n : an artificially produced radioactive metallic chemical element

fern \'fərn\ n : any of an order of vascular plants resembling seed plants in having root, stem, and leaflike fronds but reproducing by spores instead of by flowers and seeds

fern·ery \'fərn-(ə-)rē\ n, pl -er·ies 1 : a place for growing ferns 2 : a collection of growing ferns

fe·ro·cious \fə-'rō-shəs\ adj 1 : FIERCE, SAVAGE 2 : extremely intense ⟨~ heat⟩ — fe·ro·cious·ly adv — fe·ro·cious·ness n

fe·roc·i·ty \fə-'räs-ət-ē\ n : the quality or state of being ferocious

¹fer·ret \'fer-ət\ n : a partially domesticated usu. white European mammal related to the weasels and used esp. for hunting rodents

²ferret vb 1 : to hunt game with ferrets 2 : to drive out of a hiding place 3 : to find and bring to light by searching ⟨~ out the truth⟩

fer·ric \'fer-ik\ adj : of, relating to, or containing iron

ferric oxide n : an oxide of iron that is found in nature as hematite and as rust and that is used as a pigment and for polishing

Fer·ris wheel \'fer-əs-\ n : an amusement device consisting of a large upright power-driven wheel carrying seats that remain horizontal around its rim

fer·ro·mag·net·ic \ˌfer-ō-mag-'net-ik\ adj : of or relating to substances that are easily magnetized

fer·rous \'fer-əs\ adj : of, relating to, or containing iron

fer·rule \'fer-əl\ n : a metal ring or cap around a slender wooden shaft to prevent splitting

¹fer·ry \'fer-ē\ vb fer·ried; fer·ry·ing [ME ferien, fr. OE ferian to carry, convey] 1 : to carry by boat over a body of water 2 : to cross by a ferry 3 : to convey from one place to another

²ferry n, pl ferries 1 : a place where persons or things are ferried 2 : FERRYBOAT

fer·ry·boat \'fer-ē-ˌbōt\ n : a boat used in ferrying

fer·tile \'fərt-ᵊl\ adj 1 : producing plentifully : PRODUCTIVE ⟨~ soils⟩ 2 : capable of developing or reproducing ⟨~ eggs⟩ ⟨a ~ family⟩ syn fruitful, prolific, fecund, productive — fer·til·i·ty \(ˌ)fər-'til-ət-ē\ n

fer·til·ize \'fərt-ᵊl-ˌīz\ vb -ized; -iz·ing 1 : to unite with in the process of fertilization (one sperm ~s each egg) 2 : to apply fertilizer to — fer·til·iza·tion \ˌfərt-ᵊl-ə-'zā-shən\ n

fer·til·iz·er \-ˌī-zər\ n : material (as manure or a chemical mixture) for enriching land

fer·ule \'fer-əl\ also fer·u·la \'fer-(y)ə-lə\ n : a rod or ruler used to punish children

fer·ven·cy \'fər-vən-sē\ n, pl -cies : FERVOR

fer·vent \'fər-vənt\ adj 1 : very hot : GLOWING 2 : marked by great intensity of feeling — fer·vent·ly adv

fer·vid \\-vəd\\ *adj* **1** : very hot **2** : AR-DENT, ZEALOUS — **fer·vid·ly** *adv*

fer·vor \\'fər-vər\\ *n* **1** : intense heat **2** : intensity of feeling or expression

fes·tal \\'fest-ᵊl\\ *adj* : FESTIVE

¹fes·ter \\'fes-tər\\ *n* : a pus-filled sore

²fester *vb* **fes·tered; fes·ter·ing** \\-t(ə-)riŋ\\ **1** : to form pus **2** : PUTREFY, ROT **3** : RANKLE

fes·ti·val \\'fes-tə-vəl\\ *n* **1** : a time of celebration marked by special observances; *esp* : an occasion marked with religious ceremonies **2** : a periodic season or program of cultural events or entertainment ⟨a dance ∼⟩

fes·tive \\'fes-tiv\\ *adj* **1** : of, relating to, or suitable for a feast or festival **2** : JOYFUL, GAY — **fes·tive·ly** *adv*

fes·tiv·i·ty \\fes-'tiv-ət-ē\\ *n, pl* **-ties 1** : FESTIVAL **1 2** : the quality or state of being festive **3** : festive activity

¹fes·toon \\fes-'tün\\ *n* [F *feston,* fr. It *festone,* fr. *festa* festival] **1** : a decorative chain or strip hanging between two points **2** : a carved, molded, or painted ornament representing a decorative chain

²festoon *vb* **1** : to hang or form festoons on **2** : to shape into festoons

fe·tal \\'fēt-ᵊl\\ *adj* : of, relating to, or being a fetus

fetal position *n* : a resting position with body curved, legs bent and drawn toward the chest, head bowed forward, and arms tucked in in the manner of the fetus in the womb that is assumed in some forms of psychic disorder

fetch \\'fech\\ *vb* **1** : to go or come after and bring or take back ⟨teach a dog to ∼ a stick⟩ **2** : to cause to come : bring out ⟨∼ed tears from the eyes⟩ **3** : to sell for **4** : to give by striking ⟨∼ him a blow⟩

fetch·ing \\'fech-iŋ\\ *adj* : ATTRACTIVE, PLEASING — **fetch·ing·ly** *adv*

¹fete *or* **fête** \\'fāt, 'fet\\ *n* [F *fête,* fr. OF *feste*] **1** : FESTIVAL **2** : a large elaborate entertainment or party

²fete *or* **fête** *vb* **fet·ed** *or* **fêt·ed; fet·ing** *or* **fêt·ing 1** : to honor or commemorate with a fete **2** : to pay high honor to

fet·id \\'fet-əd\\ *adj* : having an offensive smell : STINKING

fe·tish *also* **fe·tich** \\'fet-ish, 'fēt-\\ *n* [F & Pg; F *fétiche,* fr. Pg *feitiço,* fr. *feitiço* artificial, false, fr. L *facticius* factitious] **1** : an object (as an idol or image) believed to have magical powers (as in curing disease) **2** : an object of unreasoning devotion or concern **3** : an object whose real or fantasied presence is psychologically necessary for sexual gratification

fe·tish·ism \\-ish-ˌiz-əm\\ *n* : belief in, devotion to, or pathological attachment to fetishes — **fe·tish·ist** \\-ish-əst\\ *n* — **fe·tish·is·tic** \\ˌfet-ish-'is-tik, ˌfēt-\\ *adj*

fet·lock \\'fet-ˌläk\\ *n* : a projection on the back of a horse's leg above the hoof; *also* : a tuft of hair on this

fet·ter \\'fet-ər\\ *n* **1** : a chain or shackle

for the feet **2** : something that confines : RESTRAINT — **fetter** *vb*

fet·tle \\'fet-ᵊl\\ *n* : a state of fitness or order : CONDITION ⟨in fine ∼⟩

fe·tus \\'fēt-əs\\ *n* : an unborn or unhatched vertebrate esp. after its basic structure is laid down; *esp* : a developing human being in the uterus from usu. three months after pregnancy occurs to birth

feud \\'fyüd\\ *n* : a prolonged quarrel; *esp* : a lasting conflict between families or clans marked by violent attacks undertaken for revenge — **feud** *vb*

feu·dal \\'fyüd-ᵊl\\ *adj* **1** : of, relating to, or having the characteristics of a medieval fee **2** : of, relating to, or characteristic of feudalism

feu·dal·ism \\'fyüd-ᵊl-ˌiz-əm\\ *n* : a system of political organization prevailing in medieval Europe in which a vassal renders service to a lord and receives protection and land in return; *also* : a similar political or social system — **feu·dal·is·tic** \\ˌfyüd-ᵊl-'is-tik\\ *adj*

¹feu·da·to·ry \\'fyüd-ə-ˌtōr-ē\\ *adj* : owing feudal allegiance

²feudatory *n, pl* **-ries 1** : a person who holds lands by feudal law or usage **2** : FIEF

fe·ver \\'fē-vər\\ *n* **1** : a rise in body temperature above the normal; *also* : a disease of which this is a chief symptom **2** : a state of heightened emotion or activity **3** : CRAZE — **fe·ver·ish** *adj* — **fe·ver·ish·ly** *adv*

¹few \\'fyü\\ *pron* : not many : a small number

²few *adj* **1** : consisting of or amounting to a small number **2** : not many but some ⟨caught a ∼ fish⟩ — **few·ness** *n*

³few *n* **1** : a small number of units or individuals ⟨a ∼ of them⟩ **2** : a special limited number ⟨among the ∼⟩

few·er \\'fyü-ər\\ *pron* : a smaller number of persons or things

fey \\'fā\\ *adj* **1** *chiefly Scot* : fated to die; *also* : marked by a foreboding of death or calamity **2** : able to see into the future : VISIONARY **3** : marked by an otherworldly air or attitude **4** : CRAZY, TOUCHED

fez \\'fez\\ *n, pl* **fez·zes** *also* **fez·es** : a round red felt hat that has a flat top and a tassel but no brim

ff *abbr* **1** folios **2** [following] and the following ones **3** fortissimo

FHA *abbr* Federal Housing Administration

fi·an·cé \\ˌfē-ˌän-'sā\\ *n* [F, fr. MF, fr. *fiancer* to promise, betroth, fr. OF *fiancier,* fr. *fiance* promise, trust, fr. *fier* to trust, fr. L *fidere*] : a man engaged to be married

fi·an·cée \\ˌfē-ˌän-'sā\\ *n* : a woman engaged to be married

fi·as·co \\fē-'as-kō\\ *n, pl* **-coes** [F] : a complete failure

fi·at \\'fē-ət, -ˌat, -ˌät; 'fī-ət, -ˌat\\ *n* [L,

let it be done] : an authoritative and often arbitrary order or decree

fiat money *n* : paper currency backed only by the authority of the government and not by metal

¹**fib** \'fib\ *n* : a trivial or childish lie

²**fib** *vb* **fibbed; fib·bing** : to tell a fib — **fib·ber** *n*

fi·ber *or* **fi·bre** \'fī-bər\ *n* **1** : a thread-like substance or structure (as a muscle cell or fine root); *esp* : a natural (as wool or flax) or artificial (as rayon) filament capable of being spun or woven **2** : ROUGHAGE **3** : an element that gives texture or substance **4** : basic toughness : STRENGTH — **fi·brous** \-brəs\ *adj*

fi·ber·board \-ˌbōrd\ *n* : a material made by compressing fibers (as of wood) into stiff sheets

fi·ber·fill \-ˌfil\ *n* : man-made fibers used as a filling material (as for cushions)

fi·ber·glass \-ˌglas\ *n* : glass in fibrous form used in making various products (as yarn and insulation)

fiber optics *n pl* : thin transparent fibers of glass or plastic that are enclosed by a less refractive material and that transmit light by internal reflection; *also* : a bundle of such fibers used in an instrument **2** : the technique of the use of fiber optics — **fiber–optic** *adj*

fi·bril \'fīb-rəl, 'fib-\ *n* : a small fiber

fi·bril·la·tion \ˌfib-rə-'lā-shən, ˌfīb-\ *n* : rapid irregular contractions of muscle fibers (as of the heart) — **fib·ril·late** \'fib-rə-ˌlāt, 'fīb-\ *vb*

fi·brin \'fī-brən\ *n* : a white insoluble fibrous protein formed from fibrinogen in the clotting of blood

fi·brin·o·gen \fī-'brin-ə-jən\ *n* : a globulin produced in the liver, present esp. in blood plasma, and converted into fibrin during clotting of blood

fi·broid \'fī-ˌbroid, 'fib-\ *adj* : resembling, forming, or consisting of fibrous tissue (~ tumors)

fi·bro·sis \fī-'brō-səs\ *n* : a condition marked by abnormal increase of fiber-containing tissue

fib·u·la \'fib-yə-lə\ *n, pl* **-lae** \-ˌlē, -ˌlī\ *or* **-las** : the outer and usu. the smaller of the two bones of the hind limb below the knee — **fib·u·lar** \-lər\ *adj*

FICA *abbr* Federal Insurance Contributions Act

fiche \'fēsh, 'fish\ *n, pl* **fiche** : MICROFICHE

fi·chu \'fish-ü\ *n* [F] : a woman's light triangular scarf draped over the shoulders and fastened in front

fick·le \'fik-əl\ *adj* : not firm or steadfast in disposition or character : INCONSTANT — **fick·le·ness** *n*

fic·tion \'fik-shən\ *n* **1** : something (as a story) invented by the imagination **2** : fictitious literature (as novels) — **fic·tion·al** \-sh(ə-)nəl\ *adj* — **fic·tion·al·ly** \-ē\ *adv*

fic·ti·tious \fik-'tish-əs\ *adj* **1** : of, relating to, or characteristic of fiction : IMAGINARY **2** : FEIGNED **syn** chimerical, fanciful, fantastic, unreal

¹**fid·dle** \'fid-ᵊl\ *n* : VIOLIN

²**fiddle** *vb* **fid·dled; fid·dling** \'fid-(ᵊ-)liŋ\ **1** : to play on a fiddle **2** : to move the hands or fingers restlessly **3** : PUTTER **4** : MEDDLE, TAMPER — **fid·dler** \'fid-(ᵊ-)lər\ *n*

fiddler crab *n* : a burrowing crab with one claw much enlarged in the male

fid·dle·stick \'fid-ᵊl-ˌstik\ *n* **1** *archaic* : a violin bow **2** *pl* : NONSENSE — used as an interjection

fi·del·i·ty \fə-'del-ət-ē, fī-\ *n, pl* **-ties 1** : the quality or state of being faithful **2** : ACCURACY (~ of a news report) (~ in sound reproduction) **syn** allegiance, loyalty, devotion, fealty

¹**fidg·et** \'fij-ət\ *n* **1** *pl* : uneasiness or restlessness as shown by nervous movements **2** : one that fidgets — **fidg·ety** *adj*

²**fidget** *vb* : to move or cause to move or act restlessly or nervously

fi·du·ci·ary \fə-'d(y)ü-shē-ˌer-ē, -shə-rē\ *adj* **1** : involving a confidence or trust **2** : held or holding in trust for another (~ accounts) — **fiduciary** *n*

fie \'fī\ *interj* — used to express disgust or disapproval

fief \'fēf\ *n* : a feudal estate : FEE

¹**field** \'fēld\ *n* **1** : open country **2** : a piece of cleared land for cultivation or pasture **3** : a piece of land yielding some special product **4** : the place where a battle is fought; *also* : BATTLE **5** : an area, division, or sphere of activity (the ~ of science) (salesmen in the ~) **6** : an area for military exercises **7** : an area for sports **8** : a background on which something is drawn or projected (a flag with white stars on a ~ of blue) **9** : a region or space in which a given effect (as magnetism) exists — **field** *adj*

²**field** *vb* **1** : to handle a batted or thrown baseball while on defense **2** : to put into the field **3** : to answer satisfactorily (~ a tough question) — **field·er** *n*

field day *n* **1** : a day devoted to outdoor sports and athletic competition **2** : a time of extraordinary pleasure or opportunity

field event *n* : a track-and-field event (as weight-throwing) other than a race

field glass *n* : a hand-held binocular telescope — usu. used in pl.

field hockey *n* : a field game played between two teams of 11 players each whose object is to knock a ball into the opponent's goal with a curved stick

field marshal *n* : an officer (as in the British army) of the highest rank

field–test \-ˌtest\ *vb* : to test (as a new product) in a natural environment — **field test** *n*

fiend \'fēnd\ *n* **1** : DEVIL 1 **2** : DEMON **3**

: an extemely wicked or cruel person **4** : a person excessively devoted to a pursuit **5** : ADDICT ⟨dope ∼⟩ — **fiend·ish** *adj* — **fiend·ish·ly** *adv*

fierce \'fiərs\ *adj* **fierc·er; fierc·est 1** : violently hostile or aggressive in temperament **2** : PUGNACIOUS **3** : IN-TENSE **4** : furiously active or determined **5** : wild or menacing in appearance **syn** ferocious, barbarous, savage, cruel — **fierce·ly** *adv* — **fierce·ness** *n*

fiery \'fī(-ə)-rē\ *adj* **fi·er·i·er; -est 1** : consisting of fire **2** : BURNING, BLAZ-ING **3** : FLAMMABLE **4** : hot like a fire : INFLAMED, FEVERISH **5** : RED **6** : full of emotion or spirit **7** : IRRITABLE — **fi·eri·ness** \'fī(-ə)-rē-nəs\ *n*

fi·es·ta \fē-'es-tə\ *n* [Sp] : FESTIVAL

fife \'fīf\ *n* [G *pfeife* pipe, fife] : a small shrill flutelike musical instrument

FIFO *abbr* first in, first out

fif·teen \fif-'tēn\ *n* : one more than 14 — **fifteen** *adj or pron* — **fif·teenth** \-'tēnth\ *adj or n*

fifth \'fifth\ *n* **1** : one that is number five in a countable series **2** : one of five equal parts of something **3** : a unit of measure for liquor equal to 1/5 U.S. gallon (about 0.75 liter) — **fifth** *adj or adv*

fifth column *n* : a group of secret supporters of a nation's enemy that engage in espionage or sabotage within the country — **fifth col·um·nist** \-'käl-əm-(n)əst\ *n*

fifth wheel *n* : one that is unnecessary and often burdensome

fif·ty \'fif-tē\ *n, pl* **fifties** : five times 10 — **fif·ti·eth** \-tē-əth\ *adj or n* — **fifty** *adj or pron*

fif·ty-fif·ty \,fif-tē-'fif-tē\ *adj* **1** : shared equally ⟨a ∼ proposition⟩ **2** : half favorable and half unfavorable

¹fig \'fig\ *n* : a usu. pear-shaped edible fruit of warm regions; *also* : a tree related to the mulberry that bears this fruit

²fig *abbr* **1** figurative; figuratively **2** figure

¹fight \'fīt\ *vb* **fought** \'fōt\; **fight·ing 1** : to contend against another in battle or physical combat **2** : BOX **3** : to put forth a determined effort **4** : STRUG-GLE, CONTEND **5** : to attempt to prevent the success or effectiveness of **6** : WAGE **7** : to gain by struggle

²fight *n* **1** : a hostile encounter : BATTLE **2** : a boxing match **3** : a verbal disagreement **4** : a struggle for a goal or an objective **5** : strength or disposition for fighting ⟨full of ∼⟩

fight·er \-ər\ *n* **1** : one that fights; *esp* : WARRIOR **2** : BOXER **3** : a fast maneuverable airplane armed for destroying enemy aircraft

fig·ment \'fig-mənt\ *n* : something imagined or made up

fig·u·ra·tion \,fig-(y)ə-'rā-shən\ *n* **1** : FORM, OUTLINE **2** : an act or instance of representation in figures and shapes

fig·u·ra·tive \'fig-(y)ə-rət-iv\ *adj* **1** : EM-BLEMATIC **2** : SYMBOLIC, METAPHORICAL ⟨∼ language⟩ **3** : characterized by figures of speech — **fig·u·ra·tive·ly** *adv*

¹fig·ure \'fig-yər\ *n* **1** : NUMERAL **2** *pl* : arithmetical calculations **3** : a written or printed character **4** : PRICE, AMOUNT **5** : SHAPE, FORM, OUTLINE **6** : the graphic representation of a form and esp. of a person **7** : a diagram or pictorial illustration of textual matter **8** : a combination of points, lines, or surfaces in geometry ⟨a circle is a closed plane ∼⟩ **9** : PATTERN, DESIGN **10** : appearance made or impression produced ⟨they cut quite a ∼⟩ **11** : a series of movements (as in a dance) **12** : PERSONAGE

²figure *vb* **fig·ured; fig·ur·ing** \'fig-yə-riŋ\ **1** : to represent by or as if by a figure or outline : PORTRAY **2** : to decorate with a pattern **3** : to indicate or represent by numerals **4** : REGARD, CONSIDER **5** : to be or appear important or conspicuous **6** : COMPUTE, CALCU-LATE

fig·ure·head \'fig-(y)ər-,hed\ *n* **1** : a figure on the bow of a ship **2** : a head or chief in name only

figure of speech : a form of expression (as a simile or metaphor) that uses words in other than a plain or literal way

figure out *vb* **1** : FIND OUT, DISCOVER **2** : SOLVE

fig·u·rine \,fig-(y)ə-'rēn\ *n* : a small carved or molded figure

Fi·ji·an \'fē-,jē-ən, fi-'jē-ən\ *n* : a native or inhabitant of the Pacific island country of Fiji — **Fijian** *adj*

fil·a·ment \'fil-ə-mənt\ *n* : a fine thread or threadlike object, part, or process — **fil·a·men·tous** \,fil-ə-'ment-əs\ *adj*

fil·bert \'fil-bərt\ *n* : the sweet thick-shelled nut of either of two European hazels; *also* : a shrub or small tree bearing filberts

filch \'filch\ *vb* : to steal furtively

¹file \'fīl\ *n* : a usu. steel tool with a ridged or toothed surface used esp. for smoothing a hard substance

²file *vb* **filed; fil·ing** : to rub, smooth, or cut away with a file

³file *vb* **filed; fil·ing** [ME *filen*, fr. MF *filer* to string documents on a string or wire, fr. *fil* thread, fr. L *filum*] **1** : to arrange in order **2** : to enter or record officially or as prescribed by law ⟨∼ a lawsuit⟩ **3** : to send (copy) to a newspaper

⁴file *n* **1** : a device (as a folder or cabinet) by means of which papers may be kept in order **2** : a collection of papers or publications usu. arranged or classified

⁵file *n* : a row of persons, animals, or things arranged one behind the other

⁶file *vb* **filed; fil·ing** : to march or proceed in file

fi-let mi-gnon \ˌfil-(ˌ)ā-mēn-ˈyōⁿ, fi-ˌlā-\ *n, pl* **filets mignons** \-(ˌ)ā-mēn-ˈyōⁿz, -ˌlā-\ [F, lit., dainty fillet] : a fillet of beef cut from the thick end of a beef tenderloin

fil-ial \ˈfil-ē-əl, ˈfil-yəl\ *adj* : of, relating to, or befitting a son or daughter

fil-i-bus-ter \ˈfil-ə-ˌbəs-tər\ *n* [Sp *filibustero*, lit., freebooter] **1** : a military adventurer; *esp* : an American engaged in fomenting 19th century Latin American uprisings **2** : the use of delaying tactics (as extremely long speeches) esp. in a legislative assembly; *also* : an instance of this practice — **filibuster** *vb* — **fil-i-bus-ter-er** *n*

fil-i-gree \ˈfil-ə-ˌgrē\ *n* [F *filigrane*] : ornamental openwork (as of fine wire)

fil-ing \ˈfī-liŋ\ *n* **1** : the act of one who files **2** : a small piece scraped off by a file ⟨iron ∼s⟩

Fil-i-pi-no \ˌfil-ə-ˈpē-nō\ *n, pl* **Filipinos** : a native or inhabitant of the Philippines — **Filipino** *adj*

¹fill \ˈfil\ *vb* **1** : to make or become full **2** : to stop up : PLUG ⟨∼ a cavity⟩ **3** : FEED, SATIATE **4** : SATISFY, FULFILL ⟨∼ all requirements⟩ **5** : to occupy fully **6** : to spread through ⟨laughter ∼ed the room⟩ **7** : OCCUPY ⟨∼ the office of president⟩ **8** : to put a person in ⟨∼ a vacancy⟩ **9** : to supply as directed ⟨∼ a prescription⟩

²fill *n* **1** : a full supply; *esp* : a quantity that satisfies or satiates **2** : material used esp. for filling a low place

¹fill-er \ˈfil-ər\ *n* **1** : one that fills **2** : a substance added to another substance (as to increase bulk or weight) **3** : a material used for filling cracks and pores in wood before painting

²fil-ler \ˈfil-ər, *in sense 2* fi-ˈler\ *n, pl* **fillers** *or* **filler** — see *forint* at MONEY table

¹fil-let \ˈfil-ət, *in sense 2 also* fi-ˈlā, ˈfil-(ˌ)ā\ *also* **fi-let** \fi-ˈlā, ˈfil-(ˌ)ā\ *n* [ME *filet*, fr. MF, dim. of *fil* thread] **1** : a narrow band, strip, or ribbon **2** : a piece or slice of boneless meat or fish; *esp* : the tenderloin of beef

²fil-let \ˈfil-ət, *in sense 2 also* fi-ˈlā, ˈfil-(ˌ)ā\ *vb* **1** : to bind or adorn with or as if with a fillet **2** : to cut into fillets

fill in \(ˈ)fil-ˈin\ *vb* **1** : to provide necessary or recent information **2** : to serve as a temporary substitute

fill-ing \ˈfil-iŋ\ *n* **1** : material used to fill something ⟨a ∼ for a tooth⟩ **2** : the yarn interlacing the warp in a fabric **3** : a food mixture used to fill pastry or sandwiches

filling station *n* : SERVICE STATION

fil-lip \ˈfil-əp\ *n* **1** : a blow or gesture made by a flick or snap of the finger across the thumb **2** : something that serves to arouse or stimulate — **fillip** *vb*

fil-ly \ˈfil-ē\ *n, pl* **fillies** : a young female horse usu. less than four years old

¹film \ˈfilm\ *n* **1** : a thin skin or membrane **2** : a thin coating or layer **3** : a flexible strip of chemically treated material used in taking pictures **4** : MOTION PICTURE — **filmy** *adj*

²film *vb* **1** : to cover with a film **2** : to make a motion picture of

film-dom \ˈfilm-dəm\ *n* : the motion-picture industry

film-og-ra-phy \fil-ˈmäg-rə-fē\ *n, pl* **-phies** : a list or catalog of motion pictures relating usu. to a particular actor or director

film-strip \ˈfilm-ˌstrip\ *n* : a strip of film bearing images to be projected on a screen as still pictures

fils \ˈfils\ *n, pl* **fils** — see *dinar, dirham, rial* at MONEY table

¹fil-ter \ˈfil-tər\ *n* **1** : a porous material through which a fluid is passed to separate out matter in suspension; *also* : a device containing such material **2** : a device for suppressing waves of certain frequencies; *esp* : one (as for a camera) that absorbs light of certain colors

²filter *vb* **fil-tered; fil-ter-ing** \-t(ə-)riŋ\ **1** : to remove by means of a filter **2** : to pass through a filter — **fil-ter-able** *also* **fil-tra-ble** \-t(ə-)rə-bəl\ *adj* — **fil-tra-tion** \fil-ˈtrā-shən\ *n*

filter bed *n* : a bed of sand or gravel for filtering water or sewage

filth \ˈfilth\ *n* [ME, fr. OE *fylth*, fr. *fūl* foul] **1** : foul matter; *esp* : loathsome dirt or refuse **2** : moral corruption **3** : OBSCENITY — **filth-i-ness** \ˈfil-thē-nəs\ *n* — **filthy** \ˈfil-thē\ *adj*

fil-trate \ˈfil-ˌtrāt\ *n* : material that has passed through a filter

¹fin \ˈfin\ *n* **1** : one of the thin external processes by which an aquatic animal (as a fish) moves through water **2** : a fin-shaped part (as on an airplane) **3** : FLIPPER **2** — **finned** \ˈfind\ *adj*

²fin *abbr* **1** finance; financial **2** finish

fi-na-gle \fə-ˈnā-gəl\ *vb* **-gled; -gling** \-g(ə-)liŋ\ **1** : to obtain by indirect or dishonest means : WANGLE **2** : to use devious dishonest methods to achieve one's ends — **fi-na-gler** \-g(ə-)lər\ *n*

¹fi-nal \ˈfīn-ᵊl\ *adj* **1** : not to be altered or undone : ULTIMATE **3** : relating to or occurring at the end or conclusion — **fi-nal-i-ty** \fī-ˈnal-ət-ē, fə-\ *n* — **fi-nal-ly** \ˈfīn-(ᵊ-)lē\ *adv*

²final *n* **1** : a deciding match, game, or trial — usu. used in pl. **2** : the last examination in a course — usu. used in pl.

fi-na-le \fə-ˈnal-ē, fi-ˈnäl-\ *n* : the close or end of something; *esp* : the last section of a musical composition

fi-nal-ist \ˈfīn-ᵊl-əst\ *n* : a contestant in the finals of a competition

fi-nal-ize \ˈfīn-ᵊl-ˌīz\ *vb* **-ized; -iz-ing** : to put in final or finished form

¹fi-nance \fə-ˈnans, ˈfī-ˌnans\ *n* [ME, payment, ransom, fr. MF, fr. *finer* to end, pay, fr. *fin* end, fr. L *finis* boundary, end] **1** *pl* : money resources available esp. to a government or business **2** : management of money affairs

²**finance** *vb* **fi·nanced; fi·nanc·ing 1** : to raise or provide funds for **2** : to furnish with necessary funds **3** : to sell or supply on credit

finance company *n* : a company that makes usu. small short-term loans usu. to individuals

fi·nan·cial \fə-ˈnan-chəl, fī-\ *adj* : having to do with finance or financiers (in ~ circles) — **fi·nan·cial·ly** \-ˈnanch-(ə-)lē\ *adv*

fi·nan·cier \ˌfin-ən-ˈsiər, ˌfī-ˌnan-\ *n* **1** : a person skilled in managing public moneys **2** : a person who invests large sums of money

finch \ˈfinch\ *n* : any of numerous songbirds (as sparrows, linnets, or buntings) with strong conical bills

¹**find** \ˈfīnd\ *vb* **found** \ˈfaůnd\; **find·ing 1** : to meet with either by chance or by searching or study : ENCOUNTER, DISCOVER **2** : to obtain by effort or management (~ time to read) **3** : to arrive at : REACH (the bullet *found* its mark) **4** : EXPERIENCE, DETECT, PERCEIVE, FEEL **5** : to gain or regain the use of (*found* his voice again) **6** : PROVIDE, SUPPLY **7** : to settle upon and make a statement about (~ a verdict)

²**find** *n* **1** : an act or instance of finding **2** : something found; *esp* : a valuable item of discovery

find·er \ˈfīn-dər\ *n* : one that finds; *esp* : a device on a camera showing the view being photographed

fin de siè·cle \ˌfaⁿ-də-sē-ˈeklᵊ\ *adj* [F, end of century] : of, relating to, or characteristic of the close of the 19th century

find·ing \ˈfīn-diŋ\ *n* **1** : the act of finding **2** : FIND **2 3** : the result of a judicial proceeding or inquiry

find out *vb* : to learn by study, observation, or search : DISCOVER

¹**fine** \ˈfīn\ *n* : money exacted as a penalty for an offense

²**fine** *vb* **fined; fin·ing** : to impose a fine on : punish by a fine

³**fine** *adj* **fin·er; fin·est 1** : free from impurity **2** : very thin in gauge or texture **3** : not coarse **4** : SUBTLE, SENSITIVE (a ~ distinction) **5** : superior in quality, conception, or appearance **6** : ELEGANT, REFINED — **fine·ly** *adv* — **fine·ness** \ˈfīn-nəs\ *n*

⁴**fine** *adv* : FINELY

fine art *n* : art (as painting, sculpture, or music) concerned primarily with the creation of beautiful objects — usu. used in pl.

fin·ery \ˈfīn-(ə-)rē\ *n, pl* **-er·ies** : ORNAMENT, DECORATION; *esp* : showy clothing and jewels

fine-spun \ˈfīn-ˈspən\ *adj* : developed with extremely or excessively fine delicacy or detail

fi·nesse \fə-ˈnes\ *n* **1** : refinement or delicacy of workmanship, structure, or texture **2** : CUNNING, SUBTLETY — **finesse** *vb*

fine-tune \ˈfīn-ˈtün\ *vb* : to adjust so as

to bring to the highest level of performance or effectiveness

fin·fish \ˈfin-ˌfish\ *n* : FISH 2

¹**fin·ger** \ˈfiŋ-gər\ *n* **1** : any of the five divisions at the end of the hand; *esp* : one other than the thumb **2** : something that resembles or does the work of a finger **3** : a part of a glove into which a finger is inserted

²**finger** *vb* **fin·gered; fin·ger·ing** \-g(ə-)riŋ\ **1** : to perform with the fingers or with a certain fingering **2** : to mark the notes of a piece of music as a guide in playing **3** : to touch or feel with the fingers : HANDLE **4** : to point out

fin·ger·board \ˈfiŋ-gər-ˌbȯrd\ *n* : the part of a stringed instrument against which the fingers press the strings to vary the pitch

finger bowl *n* : a basin to hold water for rinsing the fingers at table

fin·ger·ing \ˈfiŋ-g(ə-)riŋ\ *n* **1** : handling or touching with the fingers **2** : the act or method of using the fingers in playing an instrument **3** : the marking of the method of fingering

fin·ger·ling \ˈfiŋ-gər-liŋ\ *n* : a small fish

fin·ger·nail \ˈfiŋ-gər-ˌnāl\ *n* : the nail of a finger

fin·ger·print \-ˌprint\ *n* : the pattern of marks made by pressing the tip of a finger or thumb on a surface; *esp* : an ink impression of such a pattern taken for the purpose of identification — **fingerprint** *vb*

fin·ger·tip \-ˌtip\ *n* : the tip of a finger

fin·i·al \ˈfin-ē-əl\ *n* : an ornamental projection or end (as on a spire)

fin·ick·ing \ˈfin-i-kiŋ\ *adj* : FINICKY

fin·icky \ˈfin-i-kē\ *adj* : excessively particular in tastes or standards

fi·nis \ˈfin-əs\ *n* : END, CONCLUSION

¹**fin·ish** \ˈfin-ish\ *vb* **1** : TERMINATE **2** : to use or dispose of entirely **3** : to bring to completion : ACCOMPLISH; *also* : PERFECT **4** : to put a final coat or surface on **5** : to come to the end of a course or undertaking — **fin·ish·er** *n*

²**finish** *n* **1** : END, CONCLUSION **2** : something that completes or perfects **3** : the final treatment or coating of a surface

fi·nite \ˈfī-ˌnīt\ *adj* **1** : having definite or definable limits **2** : having a limited nature or existence **3** : being neither infinite nor infinitesimal

fink \ˈfiŋk\ *n* **1** : a contemptible person **2** : STRIKEBREAKER **3** : INFORMER

Finn \ˈfin\ *n* : a native or inhabitant of Finland

fin·nan had·die \ˌfin-ən-ˈhad-ē\ *n* : smoked haddock

¹**Finn·ish** \ˈfin-ish\ *adj* : of or relating to Finland, the Finns, or Finnish

²**Finnish** *n* : the language of Finland

fin·ny \ˈfin-ē\ *adj* **1** : having or characterized by fins **2** : relating to or being fish

fiord *var of* FJORD

fir \ˈfər\ *n* : an erect evergreen tree related to the pines; *also* : its light soft wood

¹fire \'fī(ə)r\ *n* **1** : the light or heat and esp. the flame of something burning **2** : ENTHUSIASM, ZEAL **3** : fuel that is burning (as in a stove or fireplace) **4** : destructive burning of something (as a house) **5** : the discharge of firearms — **fire·less** *adj*

²fire *vb* **fired; fir·ing 1** : KINDLE, IGNITE ⟨~ a house⟩ **2** : STIR, ENLIVEN ⟨~ the imagination⟩ **3** : to dismiss from employment **4** : SHOOT ⟨~ a gun⟩ ⟨~ an arrow⟩ **5** : BAKE ⟨*firing* pottery in a kiln⟩ **6** : to apply fire or fuel to something ⟨~ a furnace⟩

fire ant *n* : either of two small fiercely stinging South American ants that are pests in the southeastern U.S. esp. in fields used to grow crops

fire·arm \'fī(ə)r-ˌärm\ *n* : a weapon (as a rifle or pistol) from which a shot is discharged by an explosion of gunpowder

fire·ball \'fī(ə)r-ˌbȯl\ *n* **1** : a ball of fire **2** : a very bright meteor **3** : the highly luminous cloud of vapor and dust created by a nuclear explosion **4** : a highly energetic person

fire·boat \'fī(ə)r-ˌbōt\ *n* : a boat equipped for fighting fires

fire·bomb \-ˌbäm\ *n* : an incendiary bomb — **firebomb** *vb*

fire·box \-ˌbäks\ *n* **1** : a chamber (as of a furnace) that contains a fire **2** : a box containing a fire alarm

fire·brand \-ˌbrand\ *n* **1** : a piece of burning wood **2** : a person who creates unrest or strife : AGITATOR

fire·break \-ˌbrāk\ *n* : a barrier of cleared or plowed land intended to check a forest or grass fire

fire·brick \-ˌbrik\ *n* : a brick capable of withstanding great heat and used for lining furnaces or fireplaces

fire·bug \'fī(ə)r-ˌbəg\ *n* : a person who deliberately sets destructive fires

fire·clay \-ˌklā\ *n* : clay capable of withstanding high temperatures and used esp. for firebrick and crucibles

fire·crack·er \'fī(ə)r-ˌkrak-ər\ *n* : a paper tube containing an explosive and a fuse and usu. set off for amusement

fire·damp \-ˌdamp\ *n* : a combustible mine gas that consists chiefly of methane

fire engine *n* : a motor vehicle with equipment for extinguishing fires

fire escape *n* : a stairway or ladder for escape from a burning building

fire·fly \'fī(ə)r-ˌflī\ *n* : any of various small night-flying beetles that produce flashes of light for courtship purposes

fire·house \'fī(ə)r-ˌhau̇s\ *n* : FIRE STATION

fire irons *n pl* : tools for tending a fire esp. in a fireplace

fire·man \-mən\ *n* **1** : a member of a company organized to put out fires **2** : STOKER

fire·place \'fī(ə)r-ˌplās\ *n* **1** : a framed opening made in a chimney to hold an open fire : HEARTH **2** : an outdoor structure of brick or stone for an open fire

fire·plug \-ˌpləg\ *n* : HYDRANT

fire·pow·er \-ˌpau̇(-ə)r\ *n* : the ability to deliver gunfire or warheads on a target

¹fire·proof \-'prüf\ *adj* : proof against or resistant to fire

²fireproof *vb* : to make fireproof

fire screen *n* : a protecting wire screen before a fireplace

¹fire·side \'fī(ə)r-ˌsīd\ *n* **1** : a place near the fire or hearth **2** : HOME

²fireside *adj* : having an informal or intimate quality

fire station *n* : a building housing fire engines and usu. firemen

fire tower *n* : a tower (as in a forest) from which a watch for fires is kept

fire·trap \'fī(ə)r-ˌtrap\ *n* : a building or place apt to catch on fire or difficult to escape from in case of fire

fire truck *n* : FIRE ENGINE

fire·wa·ter \'fī(ə)r-ˌwȯt-ər, -ˌwät-\ *n* : intoxicating liquor

fire·wood \-ˌwu̇d\ *n* : wood cut for fuel

fire·work \-ˌwərk\ *n* : a device designed to produce a display of light, noise, and smoke by the burning of explosive or flammable materials

firing line *n* **1** : a line from which fire is delivered against a target **2** : the forefront of an activity

¹firm \'fərm\ *adj* **1** : securely fixed in place **2** : SOLID, VIGOROUS ⟨a ~ handshake⟩ **3** : having a solid or compact texture ⟨~ flesh⟩ **4** : not subject to change of fluctuation : STEADY ⟨~ prices⟩ **5** : STEADFAST **6** : indicating firmness or resolution ⟨a ~ mouth⟩ — **firm·ly** *adv* — **firm·ness** *n*

²firm *vb* : to make or become firm

³firm *n* [G *firma*, fr. It, signature, deriv. of L *firmare* to make firm, confirm] **1** : the name under which a company transacts business **2** : a business partnership of two or more persons **3** : a business enterprise

fir·ma·ment \'fər-mə-mənt\ *n* : the arch of the sky : HEAVENS

firm·ware \'firm-ˌwaər\ *n* : computer programs contained permanently in a hardware device (as read-only memory)

¹first \'fərst\ *adj* : preceding all others as in time, order, or importance

²first *adv* **1** : before any other **2** : for the first time **3** : in preference to something else

³first *n* **1** : number one in a countable series **2** : something that is first **3** : the lowest forward gear in an automotive vehicle

first aid *n* : emergency care or treatment given an injured or ill person

first·born \'fərs(t)-'bȯrn\ *adj* : ELDEST — **firstborn** *n*

first class *n* : the best or highest group

in a classification — **first-class** *adj or adv*

first·hand \'fərst-'hand\ *adj* : coming directly from the original source (~ knowledge) — **firsthand** *adv*

first lady *n, often cap F&L* : the wife or hostess of the chief executive of a political unit (as a country)

first lieutenant *n* : a commissioned officer (as in the army) ranking next below a captain

first·ling \'fərst-liŋ\ *n* : one that comes or is produced first

first·ly \-lē\ *adv* : in the first place : FIRST

first-rate \-'rāt\ *adj* : of the first order of size, importance, or quality — **first-rate** *adv*

first sergeant *n* 1 : a noncommissioned officer serving as the chief assistant to the commander of a military unit (as a company) 2 : a rank in the army below a command sergeant major and in the marine corps below a sergeant major

first-string \'fərs(t)-'striŋ\ *adj* : being a regular as distinguished from a substitute

firth \'fərth\ *n* [ME, fr. ON *fjörthr*] : a narrow arm of the sea

fis·cal \'fis-kəl\ *adj* [L *fiscalis*, fr. *fiscus* basket, treasury] 1 : of or relating to taxation, public revenues, or public debt 2 : of or relating to financial matters

¹fish \'fish\ *n, pl* **fish** *or* **fish·es** 1 : a water-dwelling animal — usu. used in combination (star*fish*) (shell*fish*) 2 : any of numerous cold-blooded water-breathing vertebrates with fins, gills, and usu. scales 3 : the flesh of fish used as food

²fish *vb* 1 : to attempt to catch fish 2 : to seek something by roundabout means (~ for praise) 3 : to search for something underwater 4 : to engage in a search by groping 5 : to draw forth

fish-and-chips \,fish-ən-'chips\ *n pl* : fried fish and french fried potatoes

fish·bowl \'fish-,bōl\ *n* 1 : a bowl for the keeping of live fish 2 : a place or condition that affords no privacy

fish·er \'fish-ər\ *n* 1 : one that fishes 2 : a large dark brown No. American arboreal carnivorous mammal related to the weasels

fish·er·man \-mən\ *n* : a person engaged in fishing; *also* : a fishing boat

fish·ery \'fish-(ə-)rē\ *n, pl* **-er·ies** : the business of catching fish; *also* : a place for catching fish

fish·hook \'fish-,hůk\ *n* : a usu. barbed hook for catching fish

fish·ing \'fish-iŋ\ *n* : the business or sport of catching fish

fish ladder *n* : an arrangement of pools by which fish can pass around a dam

fish protein concentrate *n* : flour made of pulverized dried fish

fish·wife \'fish-,wīf\ *n* 1 : a woman who sells fish 2 : a vulgar abusive woman

fishy \'fish-ē\ *adj* **fish·i·er; -est** 1 : of or resembling fish 2 : QUESTIONABLE

fis·sion \'fish-ən, 'fizh-\ *n* [L *fissio*, fr. *fissus*, pp. of *findere* to split] 1 : a cleaving into parts 2 : a method of reproduction in which a living cell or body divides into two or more parts each of which grows into a whole new individual 3 : the splitting of an atomic nucleus resulting in the release of large amounts of energy — **fis·sion·able** \'fish-(ə-)nə-bəl, 'fizh-\ *adj*

fis·sure \'fish-ər\ *n* : a narrow opening or crack

fist \'fist\ *n* 1 : the hand with fingers doubled into the palm 2 : INDEX 6

fist·ful \-,fůl\ *n* : HANDFUL

fist·i·cuffs \'fis-ti-,kəfs\ *n pl* : a fight with usu. bare fists

fis·tu·la \'fis-chə-lə\ *n, pl* **-las** *or* **-lae** : an abnormal passage leading from an abscess or hollow organ — **fis·tu·lous** \-ləs\ *adj*

¹fit \'fit\ *adj* **fit·ter; fit·test** 1 : adapted to a purpose : APPROPRIATE 2 : PROPER, RIGHT, BECOMING 3 : PREPARED, READY 4 : physically and mentally sound — **fit·ly** *adv* — **fit·ness** *n*

²fit *n* 1 : a sudden violent attack (as of bodily disorder) 2 : a sudden outburst (as of laughter)

³fit *vb* **fit·ted** *also* **fit; fit·ting** 1 : to be suitable for or to : BEFIT 2 : to be correctly adjusted to or shaped for 3 : to insert or adjust until correctly in place 4 : to make a place or room for 5 : to be in agreement or accord with 6 : PREPARE 7 : ADJUST 8 : SUPPLY, EQUIP 9 : BELONG — **fit·ter** *n*

⁴fit *n* : the fact, condition, or manner of fitting or being fitted

fit·ful \'fit-fəl\ *adj* : not regular : INTERMITTENT (~ sleep) — **fit·ful·ly** \-ē\ *adv*

¹fit·ting \'fit-iŋ\ *adj* : APPROPRIATE, SUITABLE — **fit·ting·ly** *adv*

²fitting *n* 1 : the action or act of one that fits; *esp* : a trying on of clothes being made or altered 2 : a small often standardized part (a plumbing ~)

five \'fīv\ *n* 1 : one more than four 2 : the 5th in a set or series 3 : something having five units; *esp* : a basketball team — **five** *adj or pron*

¹fix \'fiks\ *vb* 1 : to make firm, stable, or fast 2 : to give a permanent or final form to (~ a photographic film) 3 : AFFIX, ATTACH 4 : to hold or direct steadily (~es his eyes on the horizon) 5 : ESTABLISH (~ a date) 6 : ASSIGN (~ blame) 7 : to set in order : ADJUST 8 : PREPARE 9 : to make whole or sound again 10 : to get even with 11 : to influence by improper or unfair methods (~ a horse race) — **fix·er** *n*

²fix *n* 1 : PREDICAMENT 2 : a determination of position (as of a ship) 3 : an accurate determination or understanding 4 : an act of improper influence (as bribery) 5 : a shot of a narcotic 6 : something that fixes or restores

fix·a·tion \fik-'sā-shən\ *n* : an obsessive or unhealthy preoccupation or attachment — **fix·ate** \'fik-,sāt\ *vb*

fix·a·tive \'fik-sət-iv\ *n* : something (as a varnish) for crayon drawings) that stabilizes or sets

fixed \'fikst\ *adj* **1** : securely placed or fastened : STATIONARY **2** : not volatile **3** : SETTLED, FINAL **4** : INTENT, CONCENTRATED (a ~ stare) **5** : supplied with a definite amount of something needed (as money) — **fixed·ly** \'fik-səd-lē\ *adv* — **fixed·ness** \-nəs\ *n*

fixed star : a star so distant that its motion can be measured only by very precise observations over long periods

fix·i·ty \'fik-sət-ē\ *n, pl* **-ties** : the quality or state of being fixed or stable

fix·ture \'fiks-chər\ *n* : something firmly attached as a permanent part of some other thing (an electrical ~)

¹fizz \'fiz\ *vb* : to make a hissing or sputtering sound

²fizz *n* : an effervescent beverage

fiz·zle \'fiz-əl\ *vb* **fiz·zled; fiz·zling** \-(ə-)liŋ\ **1** : FIZZ **2** : to fail after a good start

²fizzle *n* : FAILURE

fjord \fē-'ȯrd\ *n* : a narrow inlet of the sea between cliffs or steep slopes

fl *abbr* **1** [L *floruit*] flourished **2** fluid

FL *or* **Fla** *abbr* Florida

flab \'flab\ *n* : soft flabby body tissue

flab·ber·gast \'flab-ər-,gast\ *vb* : ASTOUND

flab·by \'flab-ē\ *adj* **flab·bi·er; -est** : lacking firmness and substance : FLACCID (~ muscles) — **flab·bi·ness** \'flab-ē-nəs\ *n*

flac·cid \'flak-səd, 'flas-əd\ *adj* : deficient in firmness (~ plant stems)

fla·con \'flak-ən\ *n* : a small usu. ornamental bottle with a tight cap

¹flag \'flag\ *n* : any of various irises: *esp* : a wild iris

²flag *n* **1** : a usu. rectangular piece of fabric of distinctive design that is used as a symbol (as of a nation) or as a signaling device **2** : something used like a flag to signal or attract attention **3** : one of the cross strokes of a musical note less that a quarter note in value

³flag *vb* **flagged; flag·ging** **1** : to signal with or as if with a flag; *esp* : to signal to stop (~ a taxi) **2** : to put a flag on

⁴flag *vb* **flagged; flag·ging** **1** : to be loose, yielding, or limp : DROOP **2** : to become unsteady, feeble, or spiritless (his interest *flagged*) **3** : to decline in interest or attraction (the topic *flagged*)

⁵flag *n* : a hard flat stone suitable for paving

flag·el·late \'flaj-ə-,lāt\ *vb* **-lat·ed; -lat·ing** : to punish by whipping — **flag·el·la·tion** \,flaj-ə-'lā-shən\ *n*

fla·gel·lum \flə-'jel-əm\ *n, pl* **-la** \-ə\ *also* **-lums** : a tapering process that projects singly or in groups from a cell

and is the primary organ of motion of many microorganisms — **fla·gel·lar** \-əl-ər\ *adj*

fla·geo·let \,flaj-ə-'let, -'lā\ *n* [F] : a small woodwind instrument belonging to the flute class

fla·gi·tious \flə-'jish-əs\ *adj* : grossly wicked : VILLAINOUS

flag·on \'flag-ən\ *n* : a container for liquids usu. with a handle, spout, and lid

flag·pole \'flag-,pōl\ *n* : a pole to raise a flag on

fla·grant \'flā-grənt\ *adj* [L *flagrans*, prp. of *flagrare* to burn] : conspicuously bad — **fla·grant·ly** *adv*

fla·gran·te de·lic·to \flə-,grant-ē-di-'lik-tō\ *adv* [ML, lit., while the crime is blazing] : in the very act of committing a misdeed

flag·ship \'flag-,ship\ *n* **1** : the ship that carries the commander of a fleet or subdivision thereof and flies his flag **2** : the most important one of a group (a ~ store)

flag·staff \-,staf\ *n* : FLAGPOLE

flag·stone \-,stōn\ *n* : ⁵FLAG

¹flail \'flāl\ *n* : a tool for threshing grain by hand

²flail *vb* **1** : to beat with or as if with a flail **2** : to move as if swinging a flail

flair \'flaər\ *n* [F, lit., sense of smell, fr. OF, odor, fr. *flairier* to give off an odor, fr. LL *flagrare*, fr. L *fragrare*] **1** : discriminating sense **2** : natural aptitude : BENT (a ~ for acting)

flak \'flak\ *n, pl* **flak** [G, fr. *flieger-abwehrkanonen*, fr. *flieger* flyer + *abwehr* defense + *kanonen* cannons] : antiaircraft guns or bursting shells fired from them

¹flake \'flāk\ *n* **1** : a small loose mass or bit **2** : a thin flattened piece or layer : CHIP — **flaky** *adj*

²flake *vb* **flaked; flak·ing** : to form or separate into flakes

flam·beau \'flam-,bō\ *n, pl* **flambeaux** \-,bōz\ *or* **flambeaus** [F, fr. MF, fr. *flambe* flame] : a flaming torch

flam·boy·ant \flam-'bȯi-ənt\ *adj* : FLORID, SHOWY — **flam·boy·ance** \-əns\ *n* — **flam·boy·an·cy** \-ən-sē\ *n* — **flam·boy·ant·ly** *adv*

flame \'flām\ *n* **1** : the glowing gaseous part of a fire **2** : a state of blazing combustion **3** : a flamelike condition **4** : burning zeal or passion **5** : BRILLIANCE **6** : SWEETHEART — **flame** *vb* — **flam·ing·ly** \'flā-miŋ\ *adv*

fla·men·co \flə-'meŋ-kō\ *n, pl* **-cos** [Sp, Flemish, like a Gypsy, fr. Dutch *Vlaminc* Fleming] : a vigorous rhythmic dance style of the Spanish Gypsies

flame·throw·er \'flām-,thrō(-ə)r\ *n* : a device that expels from a nozzle a burning stream of liquid or semiliquid fuel under pressure

fla·min·go \flə-'miŋ-gō\ *n, pl* **-gos** *also* **-goes** : any of several long-legged long-necked tropical water birds with scarlet wings and a broad bill bent downward

flam·ma·ble \'flam-ə-bəl\ *adj* : easily ignited and quick-burning — **flam·ma·bil·i·ty** *n* — **flammable** *n*

flange \'flanj\ *n* : a rim used for strengthening or guiding something or for attachment to another object

¹**flank** \'flaŋk\ *n* 1 : the fleshy part of the side between the ribs and the hip; *also* : the side of a quadruped 2 : SIDE 3 : the right or left of a formation

²**flank** *vb* 1 : to attack or threaten the flank of 2 : to be situated on the side of : BORDER

flank·er \'flaŋ-kər\ *n* : a football player stationed wide of the formation slightly behind the line of scrimmage as a pass receiver

flan·nel \'flan-əl\ *n* 1 : a soft twilled wool or worsted fabric with a napped surface 2 : a stout cotton fabric napped on one side 3 *pl* : flannel underwear or trousers

flan·nel·ette \,flan-əl-'et\ *n* : a light-weight cotton flannel

¹**flap** \'flap\ *n* 1 : a stroke with something broad : SLAP 2 : something broad, limber, or flat and usu. thin that hangs loose (the ~ of a pocket) 3 : the motion or sound of something broad and limber as it swings to and fro 4 : a state of excitement or confusion

²**flap** *vb* **flapped; flap·ping** 1 : to beat with something broad and flat 2 : FLING 3 : to move (as wings) with a beating motion 4 : to sway loosely usu. with a noise of striking

flap·jack \-,jak\ *n* : PANCAKE

flap·per \'flap-ər\ *n* 1 : one that flaps 2 : a young woman of the 1920s who showed freedom from conventions (as in conduct)

¹**flare** \'flaər\ *vb* **flared; flar·ing** 1 : to flame with a sudden unsteady light 2 : to become suddenly excited or angry (~ up) 3 : to spread outward

²**flare** *n* 1 : an unsteady glaring light 2 : a blaze of light used to signal or illuminate; *also* : a device for producing such a blaze

flare–up \-,əp\ *n* : a sudden outburst or intensification

¹**flash** \'flash\ *vb* 1 : to break forth in or like a sudden flame 2 : to appear or pass suddenly or with great speed 3 : to send out in or as if in flashes (~ a message) 4 : to make a sudden display (as of brilliance or feeling) 5 : to gleam or glow intermittently 6 : to fill by a sudden rush of water 7 : to expose to view very briefly (~ a badge) **syn** glance, glint, sparkle, twinkle — **flash·er** *n*

²**flash** *n* 1 : a sudden burst of light 2 : a movement of a flag or light in signaling 3 : a sudden and brilliant burst (as of wit) 4 : a brief time 5 : SHOW, DISPLAY; *esp* : ostentatious display *n* : one that attracts notice; *esp* : an outstanding athlete. 7 : GLIMPSE, LOOK 8 : a first brief news report 9 : a device

for producing a brief and very bright flash of light for taking photographs 10 : a quick-spreading flame or momentary intense outburst of radiant heat

³**flash** *adj* 1 : of sudden origin and short duration (a ~ fire) 2 : involving brief exposure to an intense agent (as heat or cold) (~ freezing of food)

flash·back \'flash-,bak\ *n* : introduction into the chronological sequence of events (as in a literary or theatrical work) of an event of earlier occurrence

flash·bulb \-,bəlb\ *n* : an electric light bulb in which metal foil or wire is burned to produce a brief and very bright flash of light for taking photographs

flash card *n* : a card bearing words, numbers, or pictures briefly displayed usu. by a teacher as a learning aid

flash·cube \'flash-,kyüb\ *n* : a cubical device incorporating four flashbulbs

flash·gun \-,gən\ *n* : a device for holding and operating a flashbulb

flash·ing \'flash-iŋ\ *n* : sheet metal used in waterproofing roof valleys or the angle between a chimney and a roof

flash·light \'flash-,līt\ *n* : a small battery-operated portable electric light

flash point *n* : the lowest temperature at which vapors above a volatile combustible substance ignite in air when exposed to flame

flashy \'flash-ē\ *adj* **flash·i·er; -est** 1 : momentarily dazzling 2 : BRIGHT 3 : SHOWY — **flash·i·ly** \'flash-ə-lē\ *adv* — **flash·i·ness** \-ē-nəs\ *n*

flask \'flask\ *n* : a flattened bottle-shaped container (a whiskey ~)

¹**flat** \'flat\ *n* 1 : a level surface of land : PLAIN 2 : a flat part or surface 3 : a musical tone one half step lower than a specified tone; *also* : a character b on the musical staff indicating a flat 4 : something flat 5 : an apartment on one floor 6 : a deflated tire

²**flat** *adj* **flat·ter; flat·test** 1 : having a smooth, level, or even surface 2 : spread out along a surface; *also* : being or characterized by a horizontal line 3 : having a broad smooth surface and little thickness 4 : DOWNRIGHT, POSITIVE (a ~ refusal) 5 : FIXED, UNCHANGING (charge a ~ rate) 6 : EXACT, PRECISE (in four minutes ~) 7 : DULL, UNINTERESTING (a ~ story) ; *also* : INSIPID (a ~ taste) 8 : DEFLATED 9 : lower that the true pitch; *also* : lower by a half step (a ~ note) 10 : free from gloss — **flat·ly** *adv* — **flat·ness** *n*

³**flat** *adv* 1 : FLATLY 2 : COMPLETELY (~ broke) 3 : below the true musical pitch

⁴**flat** *vb* **flat·ted; flat·ting** 1 : FLATTEN 2 : to lower in pitch esp. by a half step 3 : to sing or play below the true pitch

flat·bed \'flat-,bed\ *n* : a truck or trailer with a body in the form of a platform or shallow box

flat·boat \-ˌbōt\ *n* : a flat-bottomed boat used esp. for carrying bulky freight

flat·car \-ˌkär\ *n* : a railroad freight car without sides or roof

flat·fish \-ˌfish\ *n* : any of a group of flattened bony sea fishes with both eyes on the upper side

flat·foot \-ˌfůt, -ˈfůt\ *n, pl* **flat·feet** \-ˌfēt, -ˈfēt\ : a condition in which the arch of the foot is flattened so that the entire sole rests upon the ground — **flat·foot·ed** \-ˈfůt-əd\ *adj*

Flat·head \-ˌhed\ *n, pl* **Flatheads** *or* **Flathead** : a member of an American Indian people of Montana

flat·iron \-ˌī(-ə)rn\ *n* : IRON 3

flat·land \-ˌland\ *n* : land lacking significant variation in elevation

flat out \-ˈaůt\ *adv* 1 : BLUNTLY, DIRECTLY 2 : at top speed

flat·ten \ˈflat-ᵊn\ *vb* **flat·tened; flat·ten·ing** \ˈflat-(ᵊ-)niŋ\ : to make or become flat

flat·ter \ˈflat-ər\ *vb* [ME *flateren*, fr. OF *flater* to lick, flatter] 1 : to praise too much or without sincerity 2 : to represent too favorably ⟨the picture ~s her⟩ 3 : to judge (oneself) favorably or too favorably — **flat·ter·er** *n*

flat·tery \ˈflat-ə-rē\ *n, pl* **-ter·ies** : flattering speech or attentions : insincere or excessive praise

flat·top \ˈflat-ˌtäp\ *n* 1 : AIRCRAFT CARRIER 2 : CREW CUT

flat·u·lent \ˈflach-ə-lənt\ *adj* 1 : full of gas ⟨a ~ stomach⟩ 2 : TURGID ⟨~ oratory⟩ — **flat·u·lence** \-ləns\ *n*

fla·tus \ˈflāt-əs\ *n* : gas formed in the intestine or stomach

flat·ware \ˈflat-ˌwaər\ *n* : eating and serving utensils (as forks, spoons, and knives)

flat·worm \-ˌwůrm\ *n* : any of a phylum of flattened mostly parasitic segmented worms (as trematodes and tapeworms)

flaunt \ˈflȯnt\ *vb* 1 : to display oneself to public notice 2 : to wave or flutter showily 3 : to display ostentatiously or impudently : PARADE — **flaunt** *n*

flau·tist \ˈflȯt-əst, ˈflaůt-\ *n* [It *flautista*] : FLUTIST

¹fla·vor \ˈflā-vər\ *n* 1 : the quality of something that affects the sense of taste or of taste and smell; *also* : the resulting sensation 2 : a substance that adds flavor 3 : characteristic or predominant quality — **fla·vor·ful** *adj* — **fla·vor·less** *adj* — **fla·vor·some** *adj*

²flavor *vb* **fla·vored; fla·vor·ing** \ˈflāv-(ə-)riŋ\ : to give or add flavor to

fla·vor·ing *n* : FLAVOR 2

fla·vour *chiefly Brit var of* FLAVOR

flaw \ˈflȯ\ *n* : a small often hidden defect — **flaw·less** *adj*

flax \ˈflaks\ *n* : a fiber that is the source of linen; *also* : a blue-flowered plant grown for this fiber and its oily seeds

flax·en \ˈflak-sən\ *adj* 1 : made of flax 2

: resembling flax esp. in pale soft straw color

flay \ˈflā\ *vb* 1 : to strip off the skin or surface of 2 : to criticize harshly

flea \ˈflē\ *n* : any of an order of small wingless leaping bloodsucking insects

flea·bane \-ˌbān\ *n* : any of various plants of the daisy family once believed to drive away fleas

flea–bit·ten \-ˌbit-ᵊn\ *adj* : bitten by or infested with fleas

flea market *n* : a usu. open-air market for secondhand articles and antiques

¹fleck \ˈflek\ *vb* : STREAK, SPOT

²fleck *n* 1 : SPOT, MARK 2 : FLAKE, PARTICLE

fledg·ling \ˈflej-liŋ\ *n* 1 : a young bird with flight feathers newly developed 2 : an immature or inexperienced person

flee \ˈflē\ *vb* **fled** \ˈfled\; **flee·ing** 1 : to run away often from danger or evil 2 : to run away from 3 : VANISH

¹fleece \ˈflēs\ *n* 1 : the woolly coat of an animal and esp. a sheep 2 : a soft or woolly covering — **fleecy** *adj*

²fleece *vb* **fleeced; fleec·ing** 1 : to strip of money or property by fraud or extortion 2 : SHEAR

fleer \ˈfliər\ *vb* : to laugh or grimace in a coarse manner : SNEER

¹fleet \ˈflēt\ *vb* : to pass rapidly

²fleet *n* [ME *flete*, fr. OE *flēot* ship, fr. *flēotan* to float] 1 : a group of warships under one command 2 : a group of ships or vehicles (as trucks or airplanes) under one management

³fleet *adj* 1 : SWIFT, NIMBLE 2 : not enduring : FLEETING — **fleet·ness** *n*

fleet admiral *n* : a commissioned officer of the highest rank in the navy

fleet·ing \ˈflēt-iŋ\ *adj* : passing swiftly

Flem·ing \ˈflem-iŋ\ *n* : a member of a Germanic people inhabiting chiefly northern Belgium

Flem·ish \ˈflem-ish\ *n* 1 : the Germanic language of the Flemings 2 **Flemish** *pl* : FLEMINGS — **Flemish** *adj*

flesh \ˈflesh\ *n* 1 : the soft parts of an animal's body; *esp* : muscular tissue 2 : MEAT 3 : the physical being of man as distinguished from the soul 4 : human beings; *also* : living beings 5 : STOCK, KINDRED 6 : fleshy plant tissue (as fruit pulp) — **fleshed** \ˈflesht\ *adj*

flesh fly *n* : a two-winged fly whose maggots feed on flesh

flesh·ly \ˈflesh-lē\ *adj* 1 : CORPOREAL, BODILY 2 : CARNAL, SENSUAL 3 : not spiritual : WORLDLY

flesh·pot \ˈflesh-ˌpät\ *n* 1 *pl* : bodily comfort : LUXURY 2 : a place of lascivious entertainment — usu. used in pl.

fleshy \ˈflesh-ē\ *adj* **flesh·i·er; -est** 1 : consisting of or resembling animal flesh 2 : PLUMP, FAT

flew *past of* FLY

flex \ˈfleks\ *vb* : to bend esp. repeatedly

flexiblility·flock

flex·i·ble \\'flek-sə-bəl\\ *adj* **1** : capable of being flexed : PLIANT **2** : yielding to influence : TRACTABLE **3** : readily changed or changing : ADAPTABLE **syn** elastic, supple, resilient, springy — **flex·i·bil·i·ty** \\,flek-sə-'bil-ət-ē\\ *n*

flex·ure \\'flek-shər\\ *n* : TURN, FOLD, BEND

flib·ber·ti·gib·bet \\,flib-ərt-ē-'jib-ət\\ *n* : a silly flighty person

¹flick \\'flik\\ *n* **1** : a light sharp jerky stroke or movement **2** : a sound produced by a flick **3** : FLICKER

²flick *vb* **1** : to strike lightly with a quick sharp motion **2** : FLUTTER, DART, FLIT

¹flick·er \\'flik-ər\\ *vb* **flick·ered; flick·er·ing** \\-(ə-)riŋ\\ **1** : to move irregularly or unsteadily : FLUTTER **2** : to burn fitfully or with a fluctuating light (a ~ing candle)

²flicker *n* **1** : an act of flickering **2** : a sudden brief movement (a ~ of an eyelid) **3** : a momentary stirring (a ~ of interest) **4** : a slight indication : HINT **5** : a wavering light

³flicker *n* : a large insect-eating North American woodpecker with yellow or red on the underside of the wings and tail

flied *past of* FLY

fli·er \\'flī(-ə)r\\ *n* **1** : one that flies; *esp* : PILOT **2** : a reckless or speculative undertaking **3** : an advertising circular for mass distribution

¹flight \\'flīt\\ *n* **1** : an act or instance of flying **2** : the ability to fly **3** : a passing through the air or through space **4** : the distance covered in a flight **5** : swift movement **6** : a trip made by or in an airplane or spacecraft **7** : a group of similar individuals (as birds or airplanes) flying as a unit **8** : a passing (as of the imagination) beyond ordinary limits **9** : a series of stairs from one landing to another — **flight·less** *adj*

²flight *n* : an act or instance of running away

flight bag *n* **1** : a lightweight traveling bag with zippered outside pockets **2** : a small canvas satchel

flight line *n* : a parking and servicing area for airplanes

flighty \\'flīt-ē\\ *adj* **flight·i·er; -est** **1** : easily upset : VOLATILE **2** : easily excited : SKITTISH **3** : IRRESPONSIBLE, SILLY

flim·flam \\'flim-,flam\\ *n* : DECEPTION, FRAUD

flim·sy \\'flim-zē\\ *adj* **flim·si·er; -est** **1** : lacking strength or substance **2** : of inferior materials and workmanship **3** : having little worth or plausibility (a ~ excuse) — **flim·si·ly** \\'flim-zə-lē\\ *adv* — **flim·si·ness** \\-zē-nəs\\ *n*

flinch \\'flinch\\ *vb* [MF *flenchir* to bend] : to shrink from or as if from physical pain : WINCE

¹fling \\'fliŋ\\ *vb* **flung** \\'fləŋ\\; **fling·ing** \\'fliŋ-iŋ\\ **1** : to move hastily, brusquely, or violently (*flung* out of the room)

2 : to kick or plunge vigorously **3** : to throw with force or recklessness : HURL; *also* : to cast as if by throwing **4** : to put suddenly into a state or condition

²fling *n* **1** : an act or instance of flinging **2** : a casual try : ATTEMPT **3** : a period of self-indulgence

flint \\'flint\\ *n* **1** : a hard quartz that produces a spark when struck by steel **2** : an alloy used for producing a spark in lighters — **flinty** *adj*

flint glass *n* : heavy glass containing an oxide of lead that is used for optical structures (as lenses)

flint·lock \\'flint-,läk\\ *n* **1** : a lock for a firearm using a flint to ignite the charge **2** : a firearm fitted with a flintlock

¹flip \\'flip\\ *vb* **flipped; flip·ping** **1** : to turn by tossing (~ a coin) **2** : to turn over; *also* : to leaf through **3** : FLICK, JERK (~ a light switch) **4** : to lose self-control — **flip** *n*

²flip *adj* : FLIPPANT, IMPERTINENT

flip·pant \\'flip-ənt\\ *adj* : lacking proper respect or seriousness — **flip·pan·cy** \\'flip-ən-sē\\ *n*

flip·per \\'flip-ər\\ *n* **1** : a broad flat limb (as of a seal) adapted for swimming **2** : a paddlelike shoe used in skin diving

flip side *n* : the reverse and usu. less popular side of a phonograph record

¹flirt \\'flərt\\ *vb* **1** : to move erratically : FLIT **2** : to behave amorously without serious intent **3** : to show casual interest (~ed with the idea of quitting) — **flir·ta·tion** \\,flər-'tā-shən\\ *n* — **flir·ta·tious** \\-shəs\\ *adj*

²flirt *n* **1** : an act or instance of flirting **2** : a person who flirts

flit \\'flit\\ *vb* **flit·ted; flit·ting** : to pass or move quickly or abruptly from place to place : DART

flitch \\'flich\\ *n* : a side of pork cured and smoked as bacon

fliv·ver \\'fliv-ər\\ *n* : a small cheap usu. old automobile

¹float \\'flōt\\ *n* **1** : something (as a raft) that floats **2** : a cork buoying up the baited end of a fishing line **3** : a hollow ball that floats at the end of a lever in a cistern or tank and regulates the level of the liquid **4** : a vehicle with a platform to carry an exhibit **5** : a soft drink with ice cream floating in it

²float *vb* **1** : to rest on the surface of or be suspended in a fluid **2** : to move gently on or through a fluid **3** : to cause to float **4** : to wander esp. without a permanent home (the ~ing population) **5** : FLOOD **6** : to offer (securities) in order to finance an enterprise **7** : to finance by floating an issue of stocks or bonds **8** : to arrange for (~ a loan) — **float·er** *n*

¹flock \\'fläk\\ *n* **1** : a group of birds or mammals assembled or herded together **2** : a group of people under the guidance of a leader; *esp* : CONGREGATION **3** : a large number

²**flock** *vb* : to gather or move in a flock

floe \'flō\ *n* : a flat mass of floating ice

flog \'fläg\ *vb* **flogged; flog·ging** : to beat severely with a rod or whip : LASH — **flog·ger** *n*

¹**flood** \'fləd\ *n* **1** : a great flow of water over the land **2** : the flowing in of the tide **3** : an overwhelming volume

²**flood** *vb* **1** : to cover or become filled with a flood **2** : to fill abundantly or excessively; *esp* : to supply (a carburetor) with too much fuel **3** : to pour forth in a flood

flood·gate \'fləd-,gāt\ *n* : a gate for controlling a body of water : SLUICE

flood·light \-,līt\ *n* : a lamp that throws a broad beam of light; *also* : the beam itself — **floodlight** *vb*

flood·plain \-,plān\ *n* : a plain that may be submerged by floodwaters

flood tide *n* **1** : a rising tide **2** : an overwhelming quantity **3** : a high point : PEAK

flood·wa·ter \'fləd-,wot-ər, -,wät-\ *n* : the water of a flood

¹**floor** \'flōr\ *n* **1** : the bottom of a room on which one stands **2** : a ground surface **3** : a story of a building **4** : a main level space (as in a legislative chamber) distinguished from a platform or gallery **5** : AUDIENCE **6** : the right to speak from one's place in an assembly **7** : a lower limit (put a ~ under wheat prices) — **floor·ing** \-iŋ\ *n*

²**floor** *vb* **1** : to furnish with a floor **2** : to knock down **3** : SHOCK, OVERWHELM **4** : DEFEAT

floor·board \-,bōrd\ *n* **1** : a board in a floor **2** : the floor of an automobile

floor leader *n* : a member of a legislative body who has charge of a party's organization and strategy on the floor

floor show *n* : a series of acts presented in a nightclub

floor·walk·er \'flōr-,wo-kər\ *n* : a person employed in a retail store to oversee the sales force and aid customers

floo·zy *or* **floo·zie** \'flü-zē\ *n, pl* **floozies** : a tawdry or immoral woman

flop \'fläp\ *vb* **flopped; flop·ping 1** : FLAP **2** : to throw oneself down heavily, clumsily, or in a relaxed manner (*flopped* into a chair) **3** : FAIL — **flop** *n*

flop·house \'fläp-,haus\ *n* : a cheap hotel

flop·py \'fläp-ē\ *adj* **flop·pi·er; -est** : tending to flop; *esp* : soft and flexible

floppy disk *n* : a small flexible disk with a magnetic coating on which computer data can be stored

flo·ra \'flōr-ə\ *n, pl* **floras** *also* **flo·rae** \-,ē, -,ī\ [L *Flora*, Roman goddess of flowers] : plants or plant life esp. of a region or period

flo·ral \'flōr-əl\ *adj* : of or relating to flowers or a flora

flo·res·cence \flō-'res-∍ns, flə-\ *n* : a state or period of being in bloom or flourishing — **flo·res·cent** \-∍nt\ *adj*

flor·id \'flōr-əd\ *adj* **1** : excessively flowery in style : ORNATE (~ writing) **2** : tinged with red : RUDDY

flo·rin \'flōr-ən\ *n* **1** : an old gold coin first struck at Florence in 1252 **2** : a gold coin of a European country patterned after the Florentine florin **3** : a modern silver coin in the Netherlands and in Great Britain **4** : GULDEN

flo·rist \'flōr-əst\ *n* : one who deals in flowers

floss \'fläs\ *n* **1** : waste or short silk fibers that cannot be reeled **2** : soft thread of silk or mercerized cotton used for embroidery; *also* : DENTAL FLOSS **3** : a lightweight wool knitting yarn **4** : a fluffy filamentous mass esp. of plant fiber (milkweed ~)

²**floss** *vb* : to use dental floss on (one's teeth)

flossy \'fläs-ē\ *adj* **floss·i·er; -est 1** : of, relating to, or having the characteristics of floss; *also* : DOWNY **2** : STYLISH, GLAMOROUS

flo·ta·tion \flō-'tā-shən\ *n* : the process or an instance of floating

flo·til·la \flō-'til-ə\ *n* [Sp, dim. of *flota* fleet] : FLEET **1**; *esp* : a fleet of small ships

flot·sam \'flät-səm\ *n* : floating wreckage of a ship or its cargo

¹**flounce** \'flauns\ *vb* **flounced; flounc·ing 1** : to move with exaggerated jerky motions **2** : to go with sudden determination

²**flounce** *n* : an act or instance of flouncing

³**flounce** *n* : a strip of fabric attached by one edge (as to a skirt)

¹**floun·der** \'flaun-dər\ *n, pl* **flounder** *or* **flounders** : FLATFISH; *esp* : one important as food

²**flounder** *vb* **floun·dered; floun·der·ing** \-d(ə-)riŋ\ **1** : to struggle to move or obtain footing **2** : to proceed clumsily (~ed through his speech)

¹**flour** \'flau(ə)r\ *n* : finely ground and sifted meal of a grain (as wheat); *also* : a fine soft powder (~ed about 1850) **3** : to reach a height of development or influence **4** : to make bold and sweeping gestures **5** : BRANDISH

²**flour** *vb* : to coat with or as if with flour

¹**flour·ish** \'flər-ish\ *vb* **1** : THRIVE, PROSPER **2** : to be in a state of activity or production (~ed about 1850) **3** : to reach a height of development or influence **4** : to make bold and sweeping gestures **5** : BRANDISH

²**flourish** *n* **1** : a florid embellishment or passage (a ~ of drums) **2** : WAVE (with a ~ of his cane) **3** : a dramatic action (introduced her with a ~)

¹**flout** \'flaut\ *vb* **1** : SCORN **2** : to indulge in scornful behavior : MOCK

²**flout** *n* : INSULT, MOCKERY

¹**flow** \'flō\ *vb* **1** : to issue or move in a stream **2** : RISE (the tide ebbs and ~s) **3** : ABOUND **5** : to proceed smoothly and readily **5** : to have a smooth continuity **6** : to hang loose and billowing **7** : COME, ARISE **8** : MENSTRUATE

²**flow** *n* **1** : an act of flowing **2** : FLOOD **1**,

ment 4 : STREAM; *also* : a mass of material that has flowed when molten 5 : the quantity that flows in a certain time 6 : MENSTRUATION 7 : YIELD, PRODUCTION 8 : a continuous flow of energy

flow·chart \'flō-,chärt\ *n* : a symbolic diagram showing step-by-step progression through a procedure

flow diagram *n* : FLOWCHART

¹**flow·er** \'flaù(-ə)r\ *n* 1 : a plant branch modified for seed production and bearing leaves specialized into floral organs (as petals) 2 : a plant cultivated or outstanding for its blossoms 3 : the best part or example 4 : the finest most vigorous period 5 : a state of blooming or flourishing — **flow·ered** \'flaù(-ə)rd\ *adj* — **flow·er·less** *adj*

²**flower** *vb* 1 : to produce flowers : BLOOM 2 : DEVELOP; *also* : FLOURISH

flower girl *n* : a little girl who carries flowers at a wedding

flower head *n* : a very short compact flower cluster suggesting a single flower

flow·er·pot \'flaù(-ə)r-,pät\ *n* : a pot in which to grow plants

flow·ery \'flaù(-ə)r-ē\ *adj* 1 : full of or covered with flowers 2 : full of fine words or phrases — **flow·er·i·ness** *n*

flown \'flōn\ *past part of* FLY

fl oz *abbr* fluidounce

flu \'flü\ *n* 1 : INFLUENZA 2 : any of several minor virus ailments usu. with respiratory symptoms

flub \'fləb\ *vb* **flubbed; flub·bing** : BOTCH, BLUNDER — **flub** *n*

fluc·tu·ate \'flək-chə-,wāt\ *vb* **-at·ed; -at·ing** 1 : to move up and down or back and forth 2 : WAVER, VACILLATE — **fluc·tu·a·tion** \,flək-chə-'wā-shən\ *n*

flue \'flü\ *n* : a passage (as in a chimney) for directing a current (as of smoke or gases)

flu·ent \'flü-ənt\ *adj* 1 : capable of flowing : FLUID 2 : ready or facile in speech (~ in French) 3 : effortlessly smooth and rapid (~ speech) — **flu·en·cy** \-ən-sē\ *n* — **flu·ent·ly** *adv*

¹**fluff** \'fləf\ *n* 1 : NAP, DOWN (~ from a pillow) 2 : something fluffy 3 : something inconsequential 4 : BLUNDER; *esp* : an actor's lapse of memory

²**fluff** *vb* 1 : to make or become fluffy (~ up a pillow) 2 : to make a mistake

fluffy \'fləf-ē\ *adj* **fluff·i·er; -est** 1 : having, covered with, or resembling fluff or down 2 : being light and soft or airy (a ~ omelet) 3 : FATUOUS, SILLY

¹**flu·id** \'flü-əd\ *adj* 1 : capable of flowing like a liquid or gas 2 : likely to change or move 3 : showing a smooth easy style (~ movements) 4 : available for a different use; *esp* : easily converted into cash (~ assets) — **flu·id·i·ty** \flü-'id-ət-ē\ *n*

²**fluid** *n* : a substance tending to flow or

take the shape of its container (liquids and gases are ~s)

flu·id·ounce \,flü-əd-'aùns\ *n* — see WEIGHT table

flu·idram \,flü-ə(d)-'dram\ *n* — see WEIGHT table

¹**fluke** \'flük\ *n* : any of various trematode flatworms

²**fluke** *n* 1 : the part of an anchor that fastens in the ground 2 : a barbed head (as of a harpoon) 3 : a lobe of a whale's tail

³**fluke** *n* : a stroke of luck (won by a ~)

flume \'flüm\ *n* 1 : an inclined channel for carrying water (as for power) 2 : a ravine or gorge with a stream running through it

flung *past and past part of* FLING

flunk \'fləŋk\ *vb* : to fail esp. in an examination or course

flun·ky *or* **flun·key** \'fləŋ-kē\ *n, pl* **flunkies** *or* **flunkeys** 1 : a liveried servant; *also* : one performing menial duties 2 : YES-MAN

flu·o·res·cence \,flù(-ə)r-'es-°ns\ *n* : emission of radiation usu. as visible light during exposure to radiation from some other source; *also* : the emitted radiation — **flu·o·resce** \-'es\ *vb* — **flu·o·res·cent** \-'es-°nt\ *adj*

fluorescent lamp *n* : a tubular electric lamp in which light is produced by the action of ultraviolet light on a fluorescent material that coats the inner surface of the lamp

flu·o·ri·date \'flùr-ə-,dāt\ *vb* **-dat·ed; -dat·ing** : to add a fluoride to (as drinking water) to reduce tooth decay — **flu·o·ri·da·tion** \,flùr-ə-'dā-shən\ *n*

flu·o·ride \'flù(-ə)r-,īd\ *n* : a compound of fluorine with another chemical element or group

flu·o·ri·nate \'flùr-ə-,nāt\ *vb* **-nat·ed; -nat·ing** : to treat or cause to combine with fluorine or a compound of fluorine — **flu·o·ri·na·tion** \,flùr-ə-'nā-shən\ *n*

flu·o·rine \'flù(-ə)r-,ēn, -ən\ *n* : a pale yellowish flammable irritating toxic gaseous chemical element

flu·o·rite \'flù(-ə)r-,īt\ *n* : a mineral that consists of a fluoride of calcium used as a flux and in making glass

flu·o·ro·car·bon \,flù(-ə)r-ō-'kär-bən\ *n* : a compound containing fluorine and carbon used chiefly as a lubricant, refrigerant, or nonstick-coating material

flu·o·ro·scope \'flùr-ə-,skōp\ *n* : an instrument for observing the internal structure of an opaque object (as the living body) by means of X rays — **flu·o·ro·scop·ic** \,flùr-ə-'skäp-ik\ *adj* — **flu·o·ros·co·py** \-pē\ *n*

flu·o·ro·sis \,flùr-'ō-səs\ *n* : an abnormal condition (as spotting of the tooth enamel) caused by fluorine or its compounds

flur·ry \'flər-ē\ *n, pl* **flurries** 1 : a gust of wind 2 : a brief light snowfall 3 : COMMOTION, BUSTLE 4 : a brief outburst of activity ⟨a ~ of trading⟩ — **flurry** *vb*

¹**flush** \'fləsh\ *vb* : to cause (a bird) to take wing suddenly

²**flush** *n* : a hand of cards all of the same suit

³**flush** *n* **1** : a sudden flow (as of water) **2** : a surge esp. of emotion ⟨a ~ of triumph⟩ **3** : a tinge of red : BLUSH **4** : a fresh and vigorous state ⟨in the ~ of youth⟩ **5** : a passing sensation of extreme heat

⁴**flush** *vb* **1** : to flow and spread suddenly and freely **2** : to glow brightly **3** : BLUSH **4** : to wash out with a rush of fluid **5** : INFLAME, EXCITE **6** : to cause to blush

⁵**flush** *adj* **1** : full of life and vigor **2** : of a ruddy healthy color **3** : filled to overflowing **4** : AFFLUENT **5** : readily available **6** : ABUNDANT **6** : having an unbroken or even surface **7** : directly abutting : immediately adjacent **8** : set even with the left edge of the type page or column

⁶**flush** *adv* **1** : in a flush manner **2** : SQUARELY ⟨a blow ~ on the chin⟩

⁷**flush** *vb* : to make flush

flus·ter \'fləs-tər\ *vb* : to put into a state of agitated confusion : UPSET — **fluster** *n*

flute \'flüt\ *n* **1** : a hollow pipelike musical instrument **2** : a grooved pleat **3** : CHANNEL, GROOVE — **flute** *vb* — **fluted** *adj*

flut·ing \'flüt-iŋ\ *n* : fluted decoration

flut·ist \'flüt-əst\ *n* : a flute player

flut·ter \'flət-ər\ *vb* [ME *floteren* to float, flutter, fr. OE *floterian*, fr. *flotian* to float] **1** : to flap the wings rapidly **2** : to move with quick wavering or flapping motions **3** : to vibrate in irregular spasms **4** : to move about or behave in an agitated aimless manner — **flut·tery** \-ə-rē\ *adj*

²**flutter** *n* **1** : an act of fluttering **2** : a state of nervous confusion **3** : FLURRY, COMMOTION

¹**flux** \'fləks\ *n* **1** : an act of flowing **2** : a state of continuous change **3** : a substance used to aid in fusing metals

²**flux** *vb* : FUSE

¹**fly** \'flī\ *vb* **flew** \'flü\; **flown** \'flōn\; **fly·ing 1** : to move in or pass through the air with wings **2** : to move through the air or before the wind **3** : to float or cause to float, wave, or soar in the air **4** : FLEE **5** : to fade and disappear : VANISH **6** : to move or pass swiftly **7** : to become expended or dissipated rapidly **8** : to pursue or attack in flight **9** : to operate or travel in an aircraft or spacecraft **10** : to journey over by flying **11** : AVOID, SHUN **12** : to transport by flying

²**fly** *n, pl* **flies 1** : the action or process of flying : FLIGHT **2** *pl* : the space over a theater stage **3** : a garment closing concealed by a fold of cloth extending over the fastener **4** : the outer canvas of a tent with a double top **5** : the

length of an extended flag from its staff or support **6** : a baseball hit high into the air — **on the fly** : while still in the air

³**fly** *vi* **flied; fly·ing** : to hit a fly in baseball

⁴**fly** *n, pl* **flies 1** : a winged insect — usu. used in combination ⟨butter*fly*⟩ **2** : TWO-WINGED FLY; *esp* : one (as a housefly) that is large and stout-bodied **3** : a fishhook dressed to suggest an insect

fly·able \'flī-ə-bəl\ *adj* : suitable for flying or being flown

fly ball *n* : ²FLY 6

fly-blown \'flī-₁blōn\ *adj* : not pure : TAINTED, CORRUPT

fly·by \'flī-₁bī\ *n, pl* **flybys** : a usu. low-altitude flight past a designated point by an aircraft **2** : a flight of a spacecraft past a heavenly body (as Jupiter) close enough to obtain scientific data; *also* : a spacecraft that makes a flyby

fly-by-night \'flī-bə-₁nīt\ *adj* **1** : seeking a quick profit usu. by shady acts **2** : TRANSITORY, PASSING

fly casting *n* : the act or practice of throwing the lure in angling with artificial flies

fly·catch·er \'flī-₁kach-ər, -₁kech-\ *n* : a small bird that feeds on insects caught in flight

fly·er *var of* FLIER

flying boat *n* : a seaplane with a hull designed for floating

flying buttress *n* : a projecting arched structure to support a wall or building

flying fish *n* : any of numerous fishes with long fins suggesting wings that enable them to glide some distance through the air

flying saucer *n* : an unidentified flying object reported to be saucer-shaped or disk-shaped

flying squirrel *n* : any of several No. American squirrels with folds of skin connecting the forelegs and hind legs that enable them to make long gliding leaps

fly·leaf \'flī-₁lēf\ *n* : a blank leaf at the beginning or end of a book

fly·pa·per \-₁pā-pər\ *n* : paper poisoned or coated with a sticky substance for killing or catching flies

fly·speck \-₁spek\ *n* **1** : a speck of fly dung **2** : something small and insignificant — **flyspeck** *vb*

fly·way \-₁wā\ *n* : an established air route of migratory birds

fly·wheel \-₁hwēl\ *n* : a heavy wheel for regulating the speed of machinery

fm *abbr* fathom

Fm *symbol* fermium

FM \'ef-'em\ *n* : a broadcasting system using frequency modulation; *also* : a radio receiver of such a system — **FM** *adj*

fn *abbr* footnote

fo *or* **fol** *abbr* folio

FO *abbr* foreign office

foal \'fōl\ n : the young of a horse or related animal; *esp* : one under one year — **foal** vb

¹**foam** \'fōm\ n 1 : a mass of bubbles formed on the surface of a liquid : FROTH, SPUME 2 : material (as rubber) in a lightweight cellular form — **foamy** adj

²**foam** vb : to form foam : FROTH

fob \'fäb\ n 1 : a short strap, ribbon, or chain attached esp. to a pocket watch 2 : a small ornament worn on a fob

FOB abbr free on board

fob off vb 1 : to put off with a trick, excuse, or inferior substitute 2 : to pass or offer as genuine 3 : to put aside

FOC abbr free of charge

focal length n : the distance of a focus from a lens or concave mirror

fo'c'sle var of FORECASTLE

¹**fo·cus** \'fō-kəs\ n, pl **fo·ci** \-ˌsī\ also **fo·cus·es** [L, hearth] 1 : a point at which rays (as of light, heat, or sound) meet or diverge or appear to diverge; *esp* : the point at which an image is formed by a mirror, lens, or optical system 2 : FOCAL LENGTH 3 : adjustment (as of eyes or eyeglasses) that gives clear vision 4 : central point : CENTER — **fo·cal** \'fō-kəl\ adj — **fo·cal·ly** \-ē\ adv

²**focus** vb **-cused** also **-cussed; -cus·ing** also **cus·sing** 1 : to bring or come to a focus (~ rays of light) 2 : CENTER (~ attention on a problem) 3 : to adjust the focus of

fod·der \'fäd-ər\ n : coarse dry food (as cornstalks) for livestock

foe \'fō\ n [ME *fo*, fr. OE *fāh*, fr. *fāh* hostile] : ENEMY

FOE abbr Fraternal Order of Eagles

foehn or **föhn** \'fā(r)n, 'fœn, 'fän\ n [G föhn] : a warm dry wind blowing down a mountainside

foe·man \'fō-mən\ n : FOE

foe·tal, foe·tus *chiefly Brit var of* FETAL, FETUS

¹**fog** \'fóg, 'fäg\ n 1 : fine particles of water suspended in the lower atmosphere 2 : mental confusion — **fog·gy** adj

²**fog** vb **fogged; fog·ging** : to obscure or become obscured with or as if with fog

fog·horn \-ˌhórn\ n : a horn sounded in a fog to give warning

fo·gy also **fo·gey** \'fō-gē\ n, pl **fogies** also **fogeys** : a person with old-fashioned ideas (he's an old ~)

foi·ble \'fói-bəl\ n : a minor failing or weakness in character or behavior

¹**foil** \'fói(ə)l\ vb [ME *foilen* to trample, full cloth, fr. MF *fouler*] 1 : to prevent from attaining an end : DEFEAT 2 : to bring to naught : THWART

²**foil** n : a fencing weapon with a light flexible blade tapering to a blunt point

³**foil** n [ME, leaf, fr. MF *foille*, foil, fr. L *folium*] 1 : a very thin sheet of metal 2

: one that serves as a contrast to another

foist \'fóist\ vb : to pass off (something false or worthless) as genuine

¹**fold** \'fōld\ n 1 : an enclosure for sheep 2 : a group of people with a common faith, belief, or interest

²**fold** vb : to house (sheep) in a fold

³**fold** vb 1 : to lay one part over or against another part 2 : to clasp together 3 : EMBRACE 4 : to bend (as a layer of rock) into folds 5 : to incorporate into a mixture by overturning repeatedly without stirring or beating 6 : to become doubled or pleated 7 : FAIL, COLLAPSE

⁴**fold** n 1 : a doubling or folding over 2 : a part doubled or laid over another part

fold·away \ˌfōl-də-ˌwā\ adj : designed to fold out of the way or out of sight

fold·er \'fōl-dər\ n 1 : one that folds 2 : a folded printed circular 3 : a folded cover or large envelope for loose papers

fol·de·rol \'fäl-də-ˌräl\ n 1 : a useless trifle 2 : NONSENSE

fold-out \'fōld-ˌaút\ n : a folded leaf (as in a magazine) larger in some dimensions than the page

fo·liage \'fō-l(ē-)ij\ n : a mass of leaves (as of a plant or forest)

fo·li·at·ed \'fō-lē-ˌāt-əd\ adj : separable into layers

fo·lio \'fō-lē-ˌō\ n, pl **fo·li·os** 1 : a leaf of a book; also : a page number 2 : the size of a piece of paper cut two from a sheet 3 : a book printed on folio pages

folk \'fōk\ n, pl **folk** or **folks** 1 : a group of people forming a tribe or nation; also : the largest number or most characteristic part of such a group 2 pl : PEOPLE, PERSONS (country ~) (old ~s) 3 **folks** pl : the persons of one's own family

folk adj : of, relating to, or originating among the common people (~ music)

folk·lore \-ˌlór\ n : customs, beliefs, stories, and sayings of a people handed down from generation to generation — **folk·lor·ist** \-əst\ n

folk mass n : a mass in which traditional liturgical music is replaced by folk music

folk·sing·er \'fōk-ˌsin̩-ər\ n : a singer of folk songs — **folk·sing·ing** \-ˌsin̩-in̩\ n

folk·sy \'fōk-sē\ adj **folks·i·er; -est** 1 : SOCIABLE, FRIENDLY 2 : informal, casual, or familiar in manner or style

folk·way \'fōk-ˌwā\ n : a way of thinking, feeling, or acting common to a given group of people; *esp* : a traditional social custom

fol·li·cle \'fäl-i-kəl\ n 1 : a small anatomical cavity or gland (a hair ~) 2 : a small fluid-filled cavity in the ovary of a mammal enclosing a developing egg

fol·low \'fäl-ō\ vb 1 : to go or come after 2 : PURSUE 3 : OBEY 4 : to proceed along 5 : to engage in as a way of life

(~ the sea) (~ a profession) **6** : to come after in order or rank or natural sequence **7** : to keep one's attention fixed on **8** : to result from syn succeed, ensue, supervene — **fol·low·er** n — **follow suit 1** : to play a card of the same suit as the card led **2** : to follow an example set

¹**fol·low·ing** \ˈfäl-ə-wiŋ\ adj **1** : next after : SUCCEEDING **2** : that immediately follows

²**following** n : a group of followers, adherents, or partisans

³**following** prep : subsequent to : AFTER

follow-up \ˈfäl-ə-ˌwəp\ n : a system or instance of pursuing an initial effort by supplementary action

fol·ly \ˈfäl-ē\ n, pl **follies** [ME folie, fr. OF, fr. fol fool] **1** : lack of good sense **2** : a foolish act or idea : FOOLISHNESS **3** : an excessively costly or unprofitable undertaking

fo·ment \fō-ˈment\ vb : to stir up : INSTIGATE

fo·men·ta·tion \ˌfō-mən-ˈtā-shən, -ˌmen-\ n **1** : a hot moist material (as a damp cloth) applied to the body to ease pain **2** : the act of fomenting : INSTIGATION

fond \ˈfänd\ adj [ME, fr. fonne fool] **1** : FOOLISH, SILLY (~ pride) **2** : prizing highly : DESIROUS (~ of praise) **3** : strongly attracted or predisposed (~ of music) **4** : foolishly tender : INDULGENT; also : LOVING, AFFECTIONATE **5** : CHERISHED, DEAR (his ~est hopes) — **fond·ly** \ˈfän-(d)lē\ adv — **fond·ness** \ˈfän(d)-nəs\ n

fon·dant \ˈfän-dənt\ n : a creamy preparation of sugar used as a basis for candies or icings

fon·dle \ˈfän-dᵊl\ vb **fon·dled; fon·dling** \-(d)liŋ, -dᵊl-iŋ\ : to touch or handle lovingly : CARESS, PET

fon·due also **fon·du** \fän-ˈd(y)ü\ n [F] : a preparation of melted cheese usu. flavored with wine or brandy

¹**font** \ˈfänt\ n **1** : a receptacle for baptismal or holy water **2** : FOUNTAIN, SOURCE

²**font** n : an assortment of printing type of one size and style

food \ˈfüd\ n **1** : material taken into an organism and used for growth, repair, and vital processes and as a source of energy; also : organic material produced by green plants and used by them as food **2** : solid nutritive material as distinguished from drink **3** : something that nourishes, sustains, or supplies (~ for thought)

food chain n : a hierarchical arrangement of organisms in an ecological community such that each uses the next usu. lower member as a food source

food poisoning n : a digestive illness caused by bacteria or by chemicals in food

food·stuff \ˈfüd-ˌstəf\ n : something

with food value; esp : a specific nutrient (as fat or protein)

food web n : the interacting food chains of an ecological community

¹**fool** \ˈfül\ n [ME, fr. OF fol, fr. LL follis, fr. L, bellows, bag] **1** : a person who lacks sense or judgment **2** : JESTER **3** : DUPE **4** : IDIOT

²**fool** vb **1** : to spend time idly or aimlessly **2** : to meddle or tamper thoughtlessly or ignorantly **3** : JOKE **4** : DECEIVE **5** : FRITTER (~ed away his time)

fool·ery \ˈfül-(ə-)rē\ n, pl **-er·ies 1** : the habit of fooling : the behavior of a fool **2** : a foolish act : HORSEPLAY

fool·har·dy \ˈfül-ˌhärd-ē\ adj : foolishly daring : RASH — **fool·har·di·ness** \-ˌhärd-ē-nəs\ n

fool·ish \ˈfü-lish\ adj **1** : showing or arising from folly or lack of judgment **2** : ABSURD, RIDICULOUS **3** : ABASHED — **fool·ish·ly** adv — **fool·ish·ness** n

fool·proof \ˈfül-ˌprüf\ adj : so simple or reliable as to leave no opportunity for error, misuse, or failure

fools·cap \ˈfül-ˌskap\ n [fr. the watermark of a fool's cap formerly applied to such paper] : a size of paper typically 16 × 13 inches

¹**foot** \ˈfut\ n, pl **feet** \ˈfēt\ also **foot 1** : the terminal part of a leg on which one stands **2** — see WEIGHT table **3** : a group of syllables forming the basic unit of verse meter **4** : something resembling an animal's foot in position or use **5** foot pl, chiefly Brit : INFANTRY **6** : the lowest part : BOTTOM **7** : the part at the opposite end from the head **8** : the part (as of a stocking) that covers the foot

²**foot** vb **1** : DANCE **2** : to go on foot **3** : to add up **4** : to pay or provide for paying

foot·age \ˈfut-ij\ n : length expressed in feet

foot·ball \ˈfut-ˌbol\ n **1** : any of several games played by two teams on a rectangular field with goalposts at each end; esp : one in which the ball is in possession of one team at a time and is advanced by running or passing **2** : the ball used in football

foot·board \-ˌbōrd\ n **1** : a narrow platform on which to stand or brace the feet **2** : a board forming the foot of a bed

foot·bridge \-ˌbrij\ n : a bridge for pedestrians

foot·ed \ˈfut-əd\ adj : having a foot or feet of a specified kind or number (flat-footed) (four-footed)

-foot·er \ˈfut-ər\ comb form : one that is a specified number of feet in height, length, or breadth (a six-footer)

foot·fall \ˈfut-ˌfol\ n : the sound of a footstep

foot·hill \-ˌhil\ n : a hill at the foot of higher hills or mountains

foot·hold \-ˌhōld\ n **1** : a hold for the feet : FOOTING **2** : a position usable as a base for further advance

foot·ing \ˈfut-iŋ\ n **1** : the placing of

one's feet in a stable position **2** : the act of moving on foot **3** : a place or space for standing : FOOTHOLD **4** : position with respect to one another : STATUS **5** : BASIS **6** : the sum of a column of figures

foot·less \'fút-ləs\ *adj* **1** : having no feet **2** : INEPT

foot·lights \-ˌlīts\ *n pl* **1** : a row of lights along the front of a stage floor **2** : the stage as a profession

foo·tling \'fút-liŋ\ *adj* **1** : INEPT **2** : TRIVIAL

foot·lock·er \'fút-ˌläk-ər\ *n* : a small trunk designed to be placed at the foot of a bed (as in a barracks)

foot·loose \-ˌlüs\ *adj* : having no ties : FREE, UNTRAMMELED

foot·man \-mən\ *n* : a male servant who attends a carriage, waits on table, admits visitors, and runs errands

foot·note \-ˌnōt\ *n* **1** : a note of reference, explanation, or comment placed usu. at the bottom of a page **2** : COMMENTARY

foot·pad \-ˌpad\ *n* : a round somewhat flat foot on the leg of a spacecraft for distributing weight to minimize sinking into a surface

foot·path \'fút-ˌpath, -ˌpåth\ *n* : a narrow path for pedestrians

foot·print \-ˌprint\ *n* : an impression of the foot

foot·race \-ˌrās\ *n* : a race run on foot

foot·rest \-ˌrest\ *n* : a support for the feet

foot·sore \-ˌsōr\ *adj* : having sore or tender feet (as from much walking)

foot·step \-ˌstep\ *n* **1** : the mark of the foot : TRACK **2** : TREAD **3** : distance covered by a step : PACE **4** : a step on which to ascend or descend **5** : a way of life, conduct, or action

foot·stool \-ˌstül\ *n* : a low stool to support the feet

foot·wear \-ˌwaər\ *n* : apparel (as shoes or boots) for the feet

foot·work \-ˌwərk\ *n* : the management of the feet (as in boxing)

fop \'fäp\ *n* : DANDY **1** — **fop·pery** \-(ə-)rē\ *n* — **fop·pish** *adj*

¹**for** \fər, (ˈ)fȯr\ *prep* **1** : as a preparation toward ⟨dress ~ dinner⟩ **2** : toward the purpose or goal of ⟨need time ~ study⟩ ⟨money ~ a trip⟩ **3** : so as to reach or attain ⟨run ~ cover⟩ **4** : as being ⟨took him ~ a fool⟩ **5** : because of ⟨cry ~ joy⟩ **6** — used to indicate a recipient ⟨a letter ~ you⟩ **7** : in support of ⟨fought ~ his country⟩ **8** : directed at : AFFECTING ⟨a cure ~ what ails you⟩ **9** — used with a noun or pronoun followed by an infinitive to form the equivalent of a noun clause ⟨~ you to go would be silly⟩ **10** : in exchange as equal to : so as to return the value of ⟨a lot of trouble ~ nothing⟩ ⟨pay $10 ~ a hat⟩ **11** : CONCERNING ⟨a stickler ~ detail⟩ **12** : CONSIDERING ⟨tall ~ his age⟩ **13** : through the

period of ⟨served ~ three years⟩ **14** : in honor of

²**for** *conj* : BECAUSE

³**for** *abbr* **1** foreign **2** forestry

fora *pl of* FORUM

¹**for·age** \'fȯr-ij\ *n* **1** : food for animals esp. when taken by browsing or grazing **2** : a search for provisions

²**forage** *vb* **for·aged; for·ag·ing 1** : to collect forage from **2** : to wander in search of provisions **3** : to get by foraging **4** : to make a search : RUMMAGE

for·ay \'fȯr-ˌā\ *vb* : to raid esp. in search of plunder : PILLAGE — **foray** *n*

¹**for·bear** \fȯr-'baər\ *vb* **-bore** \-'bōr\; **-borne** \-'bōrn\; **-bear·ing 1** : to refrain from : ABSTAIN **2** : to be patient — **for·bear·ance** \-'bar-əns\ *n*

²**forbear** *var of* FOREBEAR

for·bid \fər-'bid\ *vb* **-bade** \-'bad, -'bād\ *or* **-bad** \-'bad\; **-bid·den** \-'bid-ᵊn\; **-bid·ding 1** : to command against : PROHIBIT **2** : HINDER, PREVENT **syn** enjoin, interdict, inhibit, ban

for·bid·ding \-iŋ\ *adj* : DISAGREEABLE, REPELLENT

forbode *var of* FOREBODE

¹**force** \'fōrs\ *n* **1** : strength or energy esp. of an exceptional degree : active power **2** : capacity to persuade or convince **3** : military strength; *also*, *pl* : the whole military strength (as of a nation) **4** : a body (as of persons or ships) available for a particular purpose **5** : VIOLENCE, COMPULSION **6** : an influence (as a push or pull) that causes motion or a change of motion — **force·ful** \-fəl\ *adj* — **force·ful·ly** \-ē\ *adv* — **in force 1** : in great numbers **2** : VALID, OPERATIVE

²**force** *vb* **forced; forc·ing 1** : COMPEL, CO-ERCE **2** : to cause through necessity ⟨*forced* to admit defeat⟩ **3** : to press, attain to, or effect against resistance or inertia ⟨~ your way through⟩ **4** : to raise or accelerate to the utmost ⟨~ the pace⟩ **5** : to produce with unnatural or unwilling effort ⟨*forced* laughter⟩ **6** : to hasten (as in growth) by artificial means

for·ceps \'fȯr-səps\ *n*, *pl* **forceps** [L] : a hand-held instrument for grasping, holding, or pulling objects esp. for delicate operations (as by a surgeon)

forc·ible \'fȯr-sə-bəl\ *adj* **1** : obtained or done by force **2** : showing force or energy : POWERFUL — **forc·i·bly** \-blē\ *adv*

¹**ford** \'fōrd\ *n* : a place where a stream may be crossed by wading

²**ford** *vb* : to cross (a body of water) by wading

¹**fore** \'fōr\ *adv* : in, toward, or adjacent to the front : FORWARD

²**fore** *adj* : being or coming before in time, order, or space

³**fore** *n* : something that occupies a front position

⁴**fore** *interj* — used by a golfer to warn anyone within range of the probable line of flight of his ball

fore-and-aft \ˌfōr-ə-ˈnaft\ *adj* : lying, running, or acting along the length of a structure (as a ship)

¹fore-arm \ˈfōr-ˌärm\ *vb* : to arm in advance : PREPARE

²fore-arm \ˈfōr-ˌärm\ *n* : the part of the arm between the elbow and the wrist

fore-bear *or* **for-bear** \-ˌbaər\ *n* : ANCESTOR, FOREFATHER

fore-bode *also* **for-bode** \fōr-ˈbōd, fōr-\ *vb* **1** : to have a premonition esp. of misfortune **2** : FORETELL, PREDICT *syn* augur, bode, foreshadow, portend, promise — **fore-bod-ing** *n*

fore-cast \ˈfōr-ˌkast\ *vb* **-cast** *also* **-casted; -cast-ing 1** : PREDICT, CALCULATE ⟨∼ weather conditions⟩ **2** : to indicate as likely to occur — **forecast** *n* — **fore-cast-er** *n*

fore-cas-tle \ˈfōk-səl\ *n* **1** : the forward part of the upper deck of a ship **2** : the living area for the crew in the forward part of a ship

fore-close \fōr-ˈklōz\ *vb* **1** : to shut out : PRECLUDE **2** : to take legal measures to terminate a mortgage and take possession of the mortgaged property

fore-clo-sure \-ˈklō-zhər\ *n* : the act of foreclosing; *esp* : the legal procedure of foreclosing a mortgage

fore-doom \fōr-ˈdüm\ *vb* : to doom beforehand

fore-fa-ther \ˈfōr-ˌfäth-ər\ *n* **1** : ANCESTOR **2** : a person of an earlier period and common heritage

forefend *var of* FORFEND

fore-fin-ger \-ˌfiŋ-gər\ *n* : the finger next to the thumb

fore-foot \-ˌfu̇t\ *n* : either of the front feet of a quadruped

fore-front \-ˌfrənt\ *n* : the foremost part or place : VANGUARD

fore-gath-er *var of* FORGATHER

¹fore-go \fōr-ˈgō\ *vb* **-went** \-ˈwent\; **-gone** \-ˈgȯn\; **-go-ing** \-ˈgō-iŋ\ : PRECEDE

²forego *var of* FORGO

fore-go-ing \-ˈgō-iŋ\ *adj* : PRECEDING

fore-gone \ˈfōr-ˌgȯn\ *adj* : determined in advance ⟨a ∼ conclusion⟩

fore-ground \ˈfōr-ˌgrau̇nd\ *n* **1** : the part of a scene or representation that appears nearest to and in front of the spectator **2** : a position of prominence

fore-hand \-ˌhand\ *n* : a stroke (as in tennis) made with the palm of the hand turned in the direction in which the hand is moving; *also* : the side on which such a stroke is made — **forehand** *adj*

fore-hand-ed \-ˈhan-dəd\ *adj* : mindful of the future : THRIFTY, PRUDENT

fore-head \ˈfōr-əd, ˈfōr-ˌhed\ *n* : the part of the face above the eyes

for-eign \ˈfȯr-ən\ *adj* [ME *forein*, fr. OF, fr. LL *foranus* on the outside, fr. L *foris* outside] **1** : situated outside a place or country and esp. one's own country **2** : born in, belonging to, or characteristic of some place or country other than the one under consider-

ation ⟨∼ language⟩ **3** : not connected or pertinent **4** : related to or dealing with other nations ⟨∼ affairs⟩ **5** : occurring in an abnormal situation in the living body ⟨a ∼ body in the eye⟩

for-eign-er \ˈfȯr-ə-nər\ *n* : a person belonging to or owing allegiance to a foreign country

foreign minister *n* : a governmental minister for foreign affairs

fore-know \fōr-ˈnō\ *vb* **-knew** \-ˈn(y)ü\; **-known** \-ˈnōn\; **-know-ing** : to have previous knowledge of — **fore-knowl-edge** \-ˈnäl-ij\ *n*

fore-la-dy \ˈfōr-ˌlād-ē\ *n* : a woman who acts as a foreman

fore-leg \-ˌleg\ *n* : a front leg

fore-limb \-ˌlim\ *n* : either of an anterior or pair of limbs (as wings, arms, or fins)

fore-lock \-ˌläk\ *n* : a lock of hair growing from the front part of the head

fore-man \ˈfōr-mən\ *n* **1** : a spokesperson of a jury **2** : a person in charge of a group of workers

fore-mast \-ˌmast\ *n* : the mast nearest the bow of a ship

fore-most \-ˌmōst\ *adj* : first in time, place, or order : most important : PREEMINENT — **foremost** *adv*

fore-name \-ˌnām\ *n* : a first name

fore-named \-ˌnāmd\ *adj* : previously named : AFORESAID

fore-noon \-ˌnün\ *n* : MORNING

¹fo-ren-sic \fə-ˈren-sik\ *adj* [L *forensis* public, forensic, fr. *forum* forum] : belonging to, used in, or suitable to courts of law or to public speaking or debate

²forensic *n* **1** : an argumentative exercise **2** *pl* : the art or study of argumentative discourse

fore-or-dain \ˌfōr-ȯr-ˈdān\ *vb* : to ordain or decree beforehand : PREDESTINE

fore-part \ˈfōr-ˌpärt\ *n* **1** : the anterior part of something **2** : the earlier part of a period of time

fore-quar-ter \-ˌkwȯrt-ər\ *n* : the front half of a lateral half of the body or carcass of a quadruped ⟨a ∼ of beef⟩

fore-run-ner \ˈfōr-ˌrən-ər\ *n* **1** : one that goes before to give notice of the approach of others : HARBINGER **2** : PREDECESSOR, ANCESTOR *syn* precursor, herald

fore-sail \ˈfōr-ˌsāl, -səl\ *n* : the largest sail on the foremast of a square-rigged ship or schooner

fore-see \fōr-ˈsē\ *vb* **-saw** \-ˈsȯ\; **-seen** \-ˈsēn\; **-see-ing** : to see or realize beforehand : EXPECT *syn* foreknow, divine, apprehend, anticipate — **fore-see-able** *adj*

fore-shad-ow \-ˈshad-ō\ *vb* : to give a hint or suggestion of beforehand

fore-short-en \fōr-ˈshȯrt-ᵊn\ *vb* : to shorten (a detail) in a drawing or painting so that it appears to have depth

fore-sight \ˈfōr-ˌsīt\ *n* **1** : the act or

power of foreseeing **2** : an act of looking forward; *also* : a view forward **3** : care or provision for the future : PRUDENCE — **fore·sight·ed** \-əd\ *adj* — **fore·sight·ed·ness** *n*

fore·skin \-ˌskin\ *n* : a fold of skin enclosing the end of the penis

for·est \ˈfȯr-əst\ *n* [ME, fr. OF, fr. ML *forestis*, fr. L *foris* outside] : a large thick growth of trees and underbrush — **for·est·ed** \ˈfȯr-ə-stəd\ *adj* — **for·est·land** \ˈfȯr-əst-ˌland\ *n*

fore·stall \fȯr-ˈstȯl, fȯr-\ *vb* **1** : to keep out, hinder, or prevent by measures taken in advance **2** : ANTICIPATE

forest ranger *n* : a person in charge of the management and protection of a portion of a forest

for·est·ry \ˈfȯr-ə-strē\ *n* : the science of growing and caring for forests — **for·est·er** \ˈfȯr-ə-stər\ *n*

foreswear *var of* FORSWEAR

¹**fore·taste** \ˈfȯr-ˌtāst\ *n* : an advance indication, warning, or notion

²**fore·taste** \fȯr-ˈtāst\ *vb* : to taste beforehand : ANTICIPATE

fore·tell \fȯr-ˈtel\ *vb* **-told** \-ˈtōld\ ; **-tell·ing** : to tell of beforehand : PREDICT *syn* forecast, prophesy, prognosticate

fore·thought \ˈfȯr-ˌthȯt\ *n* **1** : PREMEDITATION **2** : consideration for the future

fore·to·ken \fȯr-ˈtō-kən\ *vb* **-kened**; **-ken·ing** \-ˈtōk-(ə-)niŋ\ : to indicate in advance

fore·top \ˈfȯr-ˌtäp\ *n* : a platform near the top of a ship's foremast

for·ev·er \fȯr-ˈev-ər\ *adv* **1** : for a limitless time **2** : at all times : ALWAYS

for·ev·er·more \-ˌev-ər-ˈmȯr\ *adv* : FOREVER

fore·warn \fȯr-ˈwȯrn\ *vb* : to warn beforehand

forewent *past of* FOREGO

fore·wing \ˈfȯr-ˌwiŋ\ *n* : either of the anterior wings of a 4-winged insect

fore·wom·an \ˈfȯr-ˌwu̇m-ən\ *n* : FORELADY

fore·word \-ˌwərd\ *n* : PREFACE

¹**for·feit** \ˈfȯr-fət\ *n* **1** : something forfeited : PENALTY, FINE **2** : FORFEITURE **3** : something deposited and then redeemed on payment of a fine **4** *pl* : a game in which forfeits are exacted

²**forfeit** *vb* : to lose or lose the right to by some error, offense, or crime

for·fei·ture \ˈfȯr-fə-ˌchu̇r\ *n* **1** : the act of forfeiting **2** : something forfeited : PENALTY

for·fend \fȯr-ˈfend\ *vb* **1** : PREVENT **2** : PROTECT, PRESERVE

for·gath·er *or* **fore·gath·er** \fȯr-ˈgath-ər, fȯr-, -ˈgeth-\ *vb* **1** : to come together : ASSEMBLE **2** : to meet someone usu. by chance

¹**forge** \ˈfȯrj\ *n* [ME, fr. OF, fr. L *fabrica*, fr. *faber* smith] : a furnace or shop with its furnace where metal is heated and worked

²**forge** *vb* **forged**; **forg·ing 1** : to form (metal) by heating and hammering **2** : FASHION, SHAPE (~ an agreement) **3**

: to make or imitate falsely esp. with intent to defraud (~ a signature) — **forg·er** *n* — **forg·ery** \ˈfȯrj-(ə-)rē\ *n*

³**forge** *vb* **forged**; **forg·ing** : to move ahead steadily but gradually

for·get \fər-ˈget\ *vb* **-got** \-ˈgät\ ; **-got·ten** \-ˈgät-ᵊn\ *or* **-got**; **-get·ting 1** : to be unable to think of or recall **2** : to fail to become mindful of at the proper time **3** : NEGLECT, DISREGARD — **for·get·ful** \-ˈget-fəl\ *adj* — **for·get·ful·ly** \-ē\ *adv*

for·get-me-not \fər-ˈget-mē-ˌnät\ *n* : any of a genus of small herbs having bright-blue or white flowers usu. arranged in a curving spike

forg·ing \ˈfȯr-jiŋ\ *n* : a piece of forged work

for·give \fər-ˈgiv\ *vb* **-gave** \-ˈgāv\ ; **-giv·en** \-ˈgiv-ən\ ; **-giv·ing 1** : PARDON, ABSOLVE **2** : to give up resentment of **3** : to grant relief from payment of — **for·giv·able** *adj* — **for·give·ness** *n*

for·giv·ing \-iŋ\ *adj* **1** : showing forgiveness : inclined or ready to forgive **2** : allowing room for error or weakness

for·go *or* **fore·go** \fȯr-ˈgō, fȯr-\ *vb* **-went** \-ˈwent\ ; **-gone** \-ˈgȯn\ ; **-go·ing** \-ˈgō-iŋ\ : to abstain from : GIVE UP, RENOUNCE

fo·rint \ˈfȯr-int\ *n, pl* **forints** *also* **forint** — see MONEY table

¹**fork** \ˈfȯrk\ *n* **1** : an implement with two or more prongs for taking up (as in eating), piercing, pitching, or digging **2** : a forked part, tool, or piece of equipment **3** : a dividing into branches or a place where something branches; *also* : a branch of such a fork

²**fork** *vb* **1** : to divide into two or more branches **2** : to give the form of a fork to (~ing her fingers) **3** : to raise or pitch with a fork (~ hay)

forked \ˈfȯrkt, ˈfȯr-kəd\ *adj* : having a fork : shaped like a fork (~ lightning)

fork·lift \ˈfȯrk-ˌlift\ *n* : a machine for hoisting heavy objects by means of steel fingers inserted under the load

for·lorn \fər-ˈlȯrn\ *adj* **1** : sad and lonely because of isolation or desertion **2** : WRETCHED **3** : nearly hopeless — **for·lorn·ly** *adv*

forlorn hope *n* [modif. of Dutch *verloren hoop*, lit., lost band] **1** : a body of men selected to perform a perilous service **2** : a desperate or extremely difficult enterprise

¹**form** \ˈfȯrm\ *n* **1** : SHAPE, STRUCTURE **2** : a body esp. of a person : FIGURE **3** : the essential nature of a thing **4** : established manner of doing or saying something **5** : FORMULA **6** : a document with blank spaces for insertion of information (tax ~) **7** : CEREMONY, CONVENTIONALITY **8** : manner of performing according to recognized standards **9** : a long seat : BENCH **10** : a model of the human figure used for displaying clothes **11** : MOLD (a ~ for concrete) **12** : type or plates in a frame ready for printing **13** : MODE,

KIND, VARIETY ⟨coal is a ~ of carbon⟩
14 : orderly method of arrangement;
also : a particular kind or instance of
such arrangement ⟨the sonnet ~ in
poetry⟩ **15** : the structural element,
plan, or design of a work of art **16** : a
bounded surface or volume **17** : a
grade in a British secondary school or
in some American private schools **18**
: RACING FORM **19** : known ability to
perform; *also* : condition (as of an
athlete) suitable for performing **20**
: one of the ways in which a word is
changed to show difference in use ⟨the
plural ~ of a noun⟩

²**form** *vb* **1** : to give form or shape to
2 : FASHION, MAKE **2** : TRAIN, INSTRUCT **3**
: DEVELOP, ACQUIRE ⟨~ a habit⟩ **4**
: CONSTITUTE, COMPOSE **5** : to arrange
in order ⟨~ a battle line⟩ **6** : to take
form : ARISE ⟨clouds are ~ing⟩ **7** : to
take a definite form, shape, or arrangement

¹**for·mal** \'for-məl\ *adj* **1** : based on conventional forms and rules; *also* : being or requiring elegant dress and
manners ⟨a ~ reception⟩ **2** : done in
due or lawful form ⟨a ~ contract⟩ **3**
: CEREMONIOUS, PRIM ⟨a ~ manner⟩ **4**
: NOMINAL — **for·mal·ly** \-ē\ *adv*

²**formal** *n* : something (as a social event)
formal in character

form·al·de·hyde \for-'mal-də-ˌhīd\ *n* : a
colorless pungent gas used in water
solution as a preservative and disinfectant

for·mal·ism \'for-mə-ˌliz-əm\ *n* : strict
adherence to set forms

for·mal·i·ty \for-'mal-ət-ē\ *n, pl* **-ties 1**
: the quality or state of being formal **2**
: compliance with formal or conventional rules **3** : an established form
that is required or conventional

for·mal·ize \'for-mə-ˌlīz\ *vb* **-ized; -iz-
ing 1** : to give a certain or definite
form to **2** : to make formal; *also* : to
give formal status or approval to

¹**for·mat** \'for-ˌmat\ *n* **1** : the general
composition or style of a publication **2**
: the general plan or arrangement of
something

²**format** *vb* **for·mat·ted; for·mat·ting** : to
produce (as a book, printed matter, or
data) in a particular form

for·ma·tion \for-'mā-shən\ *n* **1** : a giving
form to something : DEVELOPMENT **2**
: something that is formed **3** : STRUC-
TURE, SHAPE **4** : an arrangement of
persons, ships, or airplanes

for·ma·tive \'for-mət-iv\ *adj* **1** : giving
or capable of giving form : CONSTRUC-
TIVE **2** : of, relating to, or characterized by important growth and formation ⟨a child's ~ years⟩

¹**for·mer** \'for-mər\ *adj* **1** : PREVIOUS,
EARLIER **2** : FOREGOING **3** : being first
mentioned or in order of two things

for·mer·ly \-lē\ *adv* : in time past
: HERETOFORE, PREVIOUSLY

form-fit·ting \'form-ˌfit-iŋ\ *adj* : conforming to the outline of the body

for·mi·da·ble \'for-məd-ə-bəl, for-'mid-\
adj **1** : exciting fear, dread, or awe **2**
: imposing serious difficulties — **for-
mi·da·bly** \-blē\ *adv*

form·less \'form-ləs\ *adj* : having no
definite shape or form

form letter *n* **1** : a letter on a frequently
recurring topic that can be sent to different people at different times **2** : a
letter sent out in many printed copies
to a large number of people

for·mu·la \'for-myə-lə\ *n, pl* **-las** *or* **-lae**
\-ˌlē, -ˌlī\ **1** : a set form of words for
ceremonial use **2** : RECIPE, PRESCRIP-
TION **3** : a milk mixture or substitute
for a baby **4** : a group of symbols or
figures joined to express information
concisely **5** : a prescribed or set form
or method

for·mu·late \-ˌlāt\ *vb* **-lat·ed; -lat·ing 1**
: to express in a formula **2** : to state
definitely and clearly **3** : to prepare
according to a formula — **for·mu·la-
tion** \ˌfor-myə-'lā-shən\ *n*

for·ni·ca·tion \ˌfor-nə-'kā-shən\ *n* : human sexual intercourse other than between a man and his wife — **for·ni·cate**
\'for-nə-ˌkāt\ *vb* — **for·ni·ca·tor** \-ˌkāt-
ər\ *n*

for·sake \fər-'sāk\ *vb* **for·sook** \-'sūk\;
for·sak·en \-'sā-kən\; **for·sak·ing** [ME
forsaken, fr. OE *forsacan*, fr. *sacan*
to dispute] **1** : GIVE UP, RENOUNCE **2**
: to quit or leave entirely : ABANDON

for·sooth \fər-'süth\ *adv* : in truth : IN-
DEED

for·swear *or* **fore·swear** \for-'swaər\ *vb*
-swore \-'swōr\; **-sworn** \-'swōrn\;
-swear·ing 1 : to renounce earnestly
or under oath **2** : to deny under oath **3**
: to swear falsely : commit perjury

for·syth·ia \fər-'sith-ē-ə\ *n* : any of a
genus of shrubs related to the olive
and having yellow bell-shaped flowers appearing before the leaves in early spring

fort \'fort\ *n* [ME *forte*, fr. MF *fort*, fr.
fort strong, fr. L *fortis*] **1** : a fortified
place **2** : a permanent army post

¹**forte** \'fort, 'for-ˌtā\ *n* [F *fort*, fr. *fort*,
adj., strong] : something in which a
person excels

²**for·te** \'for-ˌtā\ *adv or adj* [It, fr. *forte*
strong] : LOUDLY, POWERFULLY —
used as a direction in music

forth \'forth\ *adv* **1** : FORWARD, ONWARD
⟨from that day ~⟩ **2** : out into view
⟨put ~ leaves⟩

forth·com·ing \forth-'kəm-iŋ\ *adj*
1 : coming or available soon ⟨the ~
holidays⟩ ⟨the funds will be ~⟩

forth·right \'forth-ˌrīt\ *adj* : free from
ambiguity or evasiveness : going
straight to the point ⟨a ~ answer⟩ —
forth·right·ly *adv* — **forth·right·ness** *n*

forth·with \forth-'with, -'with\ *adv* : IM-
MEDIATELY

for·ti·fy \'fort-ə-ˌfī\ *vb* **-fied; -fy·ing 1**
: to strengthen by military defenses **2**
: to give physical strength or endurance to **3** : ENCOURAGE **4** : ENRICH ⟨~

bread with vitamins) — **for·ti·fi·ca·tion** \ˌfȯrt-ə-fə-ˈkā-shən\ n

for·tis·si·mo \fȯr-ˈtis-ə-ˌmō\ adv or adj : very loud — used as a direction in music

for·ti·tude \ˈfȯrt-ə-ˌt(y)üd\ n : strength of mind that enables a person to meet danger or bear pain or adversity with courage syn grit, backbone, pluck, guts

fort·night \ˈfȯrt-ˌnīt\ n [ME *fourtenight*, fr. *fourtene night* fourteen nights] : two weeks — **fort·night·ly** \-lē\ adj or adv

for·tress \ˈfȯr-trəs\ n : FORT 1

for·tu·itous \fȯr-ˈt(y)ü-ət-əs\ adj 1 : happening by chance 2 : FORTUNATE

for·tu·ity \-ət-ē\ n, pl **-ities** 1 : the quality or state of being fortuitous 2 : a chance event or occurrence

for·tu·nate \ˈfȯrch-(ə-)nət\ adj 1 : coming by good luck 2 : LUCKY — **for·tu·nate·ly** adv

for·tune \ˈfȯr-chən\ n 1 : an apparent cause of something that happens to one suddenly and unexpectedly : CHANCE, LUCK 2 : what happens to a person : good or bad luck 3 : FATE, DESTINY 4 : RICHES, WEALTH

fortune hunter n : a person who seeks wealth esp. by marriage

for·tune-tell·er \-ˌtel-ər\ n : a person who professes to tell future events — **for·tune-tell·ing** \-iŋ\ n or adj

for·ty \ˈfȯrt-ē\ n, pl **forties** : four times 10 — **for·ti·eth** \ˈfȯrt-ē-əth\ adj or n — **forty** adj or pron

for·ty-five \ˌfȯrt-ē-ˈfīv\ n 1 : a .45 caliber handgun — usu. written .45 2 : a phonograph record designed to be played at 45 revolutions per minute

for·ty-nin·er \ˌfȯrt-ē-ˈnī-nər\ n : a person in the rush to California for gold in 1849

forty winks n sing or pl : a short sleep

fo·rum \ˈfȯr-əm\ n, pl **forums** also **fo·ra** \-ə\ [L] 1 : the marketplace or central meeting place of an ancient Roman city 2 : a medium (as a publication) of open discussion 3 : COURT 4 : a public assembly, lecture, or program involving audience or panel discussion

¹**for·ward** \ˈfȯr-wərd\ adj 1 : being near or at or belonging to the front 2 : EAGER, READY 3 : BRASH, BOLD 4 : notably advanced or developed 5 : moving, tending, or leading toward a position in front (a ∼ movement) 6 : EXTREME, RADICAL 7 : of, relating to, or getting ready for the future — **for·ward·ness** n

²**forward** adv : to or toward what is before or in front

³**forward** n : a player stationed near the front of his team (as in hockey) or in the corner (as in basketball)

⁴**forward** vb 1 : to help onward : ADVANCE 2 : to send forward : TRANSMIT 3 : to send or ship onward

for·ward·er \-wərd-ər\ n : one that forwards; esp : an agent who forwards goods — **for·ward·ing** \-iŋ\ n

for·wards \ˈfȯr-wərdz\ adv : FORWARD

¹**fos·sil** \ˈfäs-əl\ adj [L *fossilis* dug up, fr. *fossus*, pp. of *fodere* to dig] 1 : being or resembling a fossil (∼ plants) 2 : of or relating to fossil feuls

²**fossil** n 1 : a trace or impression or the remains of a plant or animal preserved in the earth's crust from past ages 2 : a person whose ideas are out-of-date — **fos·sil·ize** vb

fossil fuel n : a fuel (as coal or oil) that is formed in the earth from plant or animal remains

¹**fos·ter** \ˈfȯs-tər\ adj [ME, fr. OE *fōstor*-, fr. *fōstor* food, feeding] : affording, receiving, or sharing nourishment or parental care though not related by blood or legal ties (∼ parent) (∼ child)

²**foster** vb : fos·tered; fos·ter·ing \-t(ə-)riŋ\ 1 : to give parental care to : NURTURE 2 : to promote the growth or development of : ENCOURAGE

fos·ter·ling \-tər-liŋ\ n : a foster child

Fou·cault pendulum \ˌfü-ˈkō-\ n : a device that consists of a heavy weight hung by a long wire and that swings in a constant direction which appears to change showing that the earth rotates

fought past and past part of FIGHT

¹**foul** \ˈfau̇l\ adj 1 : offensive to the senses : LOATHSOME; also : clogged with dirt 2 : ODIOUS, DETESTABLE 3 : OBSCENE, ABUSIVE 4 : DISAGREEABLE, STORMY (∼ weather) 5 : TREACHEROUS, DISHONORABLE, UNFAIR 6 : marking the bounds of a playing field (∼ lines) ; also : being outside the foul line (∼ ball) (∼ territory) 7 : containing marked-up corrections 8 : ENTANGLED — **foul·ly** \-ē\ adv — **foul·ness** n

²**foul** n 1 : an entanglement or collision in fishing or sailing 2 : an infraction of the rules in a game or sport; also : a baseball hit outside the foul line

³**foul** vb 1 : to make or become foul or filthy 2 : to make or hit a foul 3 : to entangle or become entangled 4 : OBSTRUCT, BLOCK 5 : to collide with

⁴**foul** adv : in a foul manner

fou·lard \fu̇-ˈlärd\ n : a lightweight silk of plain or twill weave usu. decorated with a printed pattern

foul-mouthed \ˈfau̇l-ˈmau̇t͟hd, -ˈmau̇tht\ adj : given to the use of obscene, profane, or abusive language

foul play n : VIOLENCE; esp : MURDER

foul-up \ˈfau̇l-ˌəp\ n 1 : a state of being fouled up 2 : a mechanical difficulty

foul up \(ˈ)fau̇l-ˈəp\ vb 1 : to spoil by mistakes or poor judgment 2 : to make a mistake : BUNGLE

¹**found** \ˈfau̇nd\ past and past part of FIND

²**found** vb 1 : to take the first steps in building (∼ a colony) 2 : to set or ground on something solid : BASE 3 : to establish and often to provide for

the future maintenance of ⟨~ a col-lege⟩ — **found·er** n

³**found** vb : to melt (metal) and pour into a mold — **found·er** n

foun·da·tion \faun-'dā-shən\ n 1 : the act of founding 2 : a basis upon which something stands or is supported (sus-picions without ~) 3 : funds given for the permanent support of an institu-tion : ENDOWMENT; also : an institu-tion so endowed 4 : supporting struc-ture : BASE 5 : CORSET — **foun·da·tion·al** \-sh(ə-)nəl\ adj

foun·der \'faun-dər\ vb **foun·dered**; **foun·der·ing** \-d(ə-)riŋ\ 1 : to make or become lame ⟨~ a horse⟩ 2 : COLLAPSE 3 : SINK ⟨a ~ing ship⟩ 4 : FAIL

found·ling \'faun-(d)liŋ\ n : an infant found after its unknown parents have abandoned it

found·ry \'faun-drē\ n, pl **foundries** : a building or works where metal is cast

fount \'faunt\ n : SOURCE, FOUNTAIN

foun·tain \'faunt-ᵊn\ n 1 : a spring of water 2 : SOURCE 3 : an artificial jet of water 4 : a container for liquid that can be drawn off as needed

foun·tain·head \-ˌhed\ n : SOURCE

fountain pen n : a pen with a reservoir that feeds the writing point with ink

four \'fōr\ n 1 : one more than three 2 : the 4th in a set or series 3 : some-thing having four units — **four** adj or pron

four·flush \-ˌfləsh\ vb : to make a false claim : BLUFF — **four-flush·er** \-ər\ n

four·fold \-ˌfōld, -'fōld\ adj 1 : being four times as great or as many 2 : hav-ing four units or members — **four·fold** \-'fōld\ adv

4-H \'fōr-'āch\ adj : of or relating to a program set up by the U.S. Depart-ment of Agriculture to help young people become productive citizens — **4-H'er** \-ər\ n

Four Hundred or **400** n : the exclusive social set of a community — used with the

four-in-hand \'fōr-ən-ˌhand\ n 1 : a necktie tied in a slipknot with long ends overlapping vertically in front 2 : a team of four horses driven by one person; also : a vehicle drawn by such a team

four-o'clock \'fōr-ə-ˌkläk\ n : a garden plant with fragrant yellow, red, or white flowers without petals that open late in the afternoon

four-post·er \'fōr-'pō-stər\ n : a bed with tall corner posts orig. designed to support curtains or a canopy

four·score \'fōr-'skōr\ adj : being four times twenty : EIGHTY

four·some \'fōr-səm\ n 1 : a group of four persons or things 2 : a golf match between two pairs of partners

four·square \-'skwaər\ adj 1 : SQUARE 2 : marked by boldness and conviction; also : FORTHRIGHT — **foursquare** adv

four·teen \'fōr-'tēn\ n : one more than

13 — **fourteen** adj or pron — **four·teenth** \-'tēnth\ adj or n

fourth \'fōrth\ n 1 : one that is number four in a countable series 2 : one of four equal parts of something — **fourth** adj or adv

fourth estate n, often cap F&E : the public press

4WD abbr four-wheel drive

four-wheel \'fōr-ˌhwēl\ or **four-wheeled** \-ˌhwēld\ adj : acting on or by means of four wheels of an automotive ve-hicle

¹**fowl** \'faul\ n, pl **fowl** or **fowls** 1 : BIRD 2 : a cock or hen of the domestic chick-en; also : the flesh of these used as food

²**fowl** vb : to hunt wildfowl

¹**fox** \'fäks\ n, pl **fox·es** also **fox** 1 : any of various flesh-eating mammals related to the wolves but smaller and with shorter legs and a more pointed muz-zle; also : the fur of a fox 2 : a clever crafty person 3 cap : a member of an American Indian people formerly liv-ing in Wisconsin

²**fox** vb : TRICK, OUTWIT

foxed \'fäkst\ adj : discolored with yel-lowish brown stains

fox·glove \'fäks-ˌgləv\ n : a plant relat-ed to the snapdragons and grown for its showy spikes of dotted white or purple tubular flowers and as a source of digitalis

fox·hole \-ˌhōl\ n : a pit dug for protec-tion against enemy fire

fox·hound \-ˌhaund\ n : any of various large swift powerful hounds used in hunting foxes

fox terrier n : a small lively terrier that occurs in varieties with smooth dense coats or with harsh wiry coats

fox-trot \'fäks-ˌträt\ n 1 : a short bro-ken slow trotting gait 2 : a ballroom dance in duple time

foxy \'fäk-sē\ adj **fox·i·er**; **-est** 1 : re-sembling or suggestive of a fox 2 : WILY; also : CLEVER

foy·er \'fȯi-ər, 'fȯi-(ˌ)yā\ n [F, lit., fire-place, fr. ML focarius, fr. L focus hearth] : LOBBY; also : an entrance hallway

FPC abbr fish protein concentrate

fpm abbr feet per minute

FPO abbr fleet post office

fps abbr feet per second

fr abbr 1 father 2 franc 3 friar 4 from

¹**Fr** abbr French

²**Fr** symbol francium

fra·cas \'frāk-əs, 'frak-\ n, pl **fra·cas·es** \-ə-səz\ [F, din, row, fr. It fracasso, fr. fracassare to shatter] : BRAWL

frac·tion \'frak-shən\ n 1 : a number (as ½ or ¾) indicating one or more equal parts of a whole or the division of one number by another; also : a number (as 3.323) consisting of a whole number and a decimal 2 : FRAGMENT 3 : PORTION — **frac·tion·al** \-sh(ə-)nəl\ adj — **frac·tion·al·ly** \-ē\ adv

frac·tious \'frak-shəs\ adj 1 : tending to

be troublesome : hard to handle or control **2** : QUARRELSOME, IRRITABLE

frac·ture \'frak-chər\ *n* **1** : a breaking of something and esp. a bone **2** : CRACK, CLEFT — **fracture** *vb*

frag·ile \'fraj-əl, -ˌil\ *adj* : easily broken : DELICATE — **fra·gil·i·ty** \fra-'jil-ət-ē\ *n*

¹**frag·ment** \'frag-mənt\ *n* : a part broken off, detached, or incomplete

²**frag·ment** \-ˌment\ *vb* : to break into fragments — **frag·men·ta·tion** \ˌfrag-mən-'tā-shən, -mən-\ *n*

frag·men·tary \'frag-mən-ˌter-ē\ *adj* : made up of fragments : INCOMPLETE

fra·grant \'frā-grənt\ *adj* : sweet or agreeable in smell — **fra·grance** \-grəns\ *n* — **fra·grant·ly** *adv*

frail \'frāl\ *adj* **1** : morally or physically weak **2** : FRAGILE, DELICATE

frail·ty \'frāl-(ə)l-tē\ *n, pl* **frailties 1** : the quality or state of being frail **2** : a fault due to weakness

¹**frame** \'frām\ *vb* **framed; fram·ing 1** : PLAN, CONTRIVE **2** : FORMULATE **3** : SHAPE, CONSTRUCT **4** : DRAW UP (~ a constitution) **5** : to fit or adjust for a purpose : ARRANGE **6** : to provide with or enclose in a frame **7** : to make appear guilty — **fram·er** *n*

²**frame** *n* **1** : something made of parts fitted and joined together **2** : the physical makeup of the body **3** : an arrangement of structural parts that gives form or support **4** : a supporting or enclosing border or open case (as for a window or picture) **5** : a particular state or disposition (as of mind) : MOOD **6** : one picture of a series (as on a length of motion-picture film or of television images) **7** : FRAME-UP

³**frame** *adj* : having a wood frame

frame-up \'frām-ˌəp\ *n* : a scheme to cause an innocent person to be accused of a crime; *also* : the action resulting from such a scheme

frame·work \-ˌwərk\ *n* : a basic supporting part or structure

franc \'frank\ *n* — see MONEY table

fran·chise \'fran-ˌchīz\ *n* [ME, fr. OF, fr. *franchir* to free, fr. *franc* free] **1** : a special privilege granted to an individual or group (a ~ to operate a ferry) **2** : a constitutional or statutory right or privilege; *esp* : the right to vote

fran·chi·see \ˌfran-ˌchī-'zē, -chə-\ *n* : one who is granted a marketing franchise

fran·chis·er \'fran-ˌchī-zər\ *n* **1** : FRANCHISEE **2** : FRANCHISOR

fran·chi·sor \ˌfran-ˌchī-'zór, -chə-\ *n* : one that grants a marketing franchise

fran·ci·um \'fran-sē-əm\ *n* : a radioactive metallic chemical element

Fran·co–Amer·i·can \ˌfran-kō-ə-'mer-ə-kən\ *n* : an American of French or esp. French-Canadian descent — **Franco–American** *adj*

fran·gi·ble \'fran-jə-bəl\ *adj* : BREAKABLE — **fran·gi·bil·i·ty** \ˌfran-jə-'bil-ət-ē\ *n*

¹**frank** \'frank\ *adj* : marked by free,

forthright, and sincere expression — **frank·ly** *adv* — **frank·ness** *n*

²**frank** *vb* : to mark (a piece of mail) with an official signature or sign indicating that it can be mailed free; *also* : to mail in this manner

³**frank** *n* **1** : a signature, mark, or stamp on a piece of mail indicating that it can be mailed free **2** : the privilege of sending mail free of charge

Fran·ken·stein \'fran-kən-ˌstīn\ *n* **1** : a creation that ruins its originator **2** : a monster in the shape of a man

frank·furt·er *or* **frank·fort·er** \'frank-fə(r)t-ər, -ˌfərt-\ *or* **frank·furt** *or* **frank·fort** \-fərt\ *n* : a seasoned sausage (as of beef or beef and pork)

frank·in·cense \'fran-kən-ˌsens\ *n* : a fragrant resin burned as incense

fran·tic \'frant-ik\ *adj* : wildly excited — **fran·ti·cal·ly** \-i-k(ə-)lē\ *adv* — **fran·tic·ly** \-i-klē\ *adv*

frap·pé \fra-'pā\ *or* **frappe** \'frap, fra-'pā\ [F *frappé*, fr. pp. of *frapper* to strike, chill] *n* **1** : an iced or frozen mixture or drink **2** : a thick milk shake — **frap·pé** *or* **frap·pe** \fra-'pā\ *adj*

fra·ter·nal \frə-'tərn-ᵊl\ *adj* **1** : of, relating to, or involving brothers **2** : of, relating to, or being a fraternity or society **3** : FRIENDLY, BROTHERLY — **fra·ter·nal·ly** \-ē\ *adv*

fra·ter·ni·ty \frə-'tər-nət-ē\ *n, pl* **-ties 1** : a social, honorary, or professional organization; *esp* : a social club of male college students **2** : BROTHERLINESS, BROTHERHOOD **3** : men of the same class, profession, or tastes

frat·er·nize \'frat-ər-ˌnīz\ *vb* **-nized; -niz·ing 1** : to mingle as friends **2** : to associate on intimate terms with citizens or troops of a hostile nation — **frat·er·ni·za·tion** \ˌfrat-ər-nə-'zā-shən\ *n*

frat·ri·cide \'fra-trə-ˌsīd\ *n* **1** : one that kills his brother or sister **2** : the act of a fratricide — **frat·ri·cid·al** \ˌfra-trə-'sīd-ᵊl\ *adj*

fraud \'fród\ *n* **1** : DECEIT, TRICKERY **2** : TRICK **3** : IMPOSTOR, CHEAT

fraud·u·lent \'fró-jə-lənt\ *adj* : characterized by, based on, or done by fraud : DECEITFUL — **fraud·u·lent·ly** *adv*

fraught \'frót\ *adj* : full of or accompanied by something specified (~ with danger)

¹**fray** \'frā\ *n* : BRAWL, FIGHT; *also* : DISPUTE

²**fray** *vb* **1** : to wear (as an edge of cloth) by rubbing **2** : to separate the threads at the edge of **3** : STRAIN, IRRITATE (~ed nerves)

fraz·zle \'fraz-əl\ *vb* **fraz·zled; fraz·zling** \'fraz-(ə-)lin\ **1** : FRAY **2** : to put in a state of extreme physical or nervous fatigue — **frazzle** *n*

¹**freak** \'frēk\ *n* **1** : WHIM, CAPRICE **2** : a strange, abnormal, or unusual person or thing **3** : a person who uses an illicit drug **4** : an ardent enthusiast — **freak·ish** *adj*

²**freak** vb **1** : to experience or appear to experience the effects (as hallucinations) of taking illicit drugs — often used with *out* **2** : to disturb one's calmness of mind : UPSET — often used with *out* — **freak-out** \'frēk-ˌaȯt\ n

freck-le \'frek-əl\ n : a brownish spot on the skin — **freckle** vb

¹**free** \'frē\ adj **fre-er; fre-est 1** : having liberty **2** : not controlled by others : INDEPENDENT; also : not allowing slavery **3** : made or done voluntarily : SPONTANEOUS **4** : released or not suffering from something unpleasant **5** : not subject to a duty, tax, or other charge **6** : not obstructed : CLEAR **7** : not being used or occupied **8** : not fastened **9** : LAVISH **10** : OPEN, FRANK **11** : given without charge **12** : not literal or exact **13** : not restricted by conventional forms — **free-ly** adv

²**free** vb **freed; free-ing 1** : to set free **2** : RELIEVE, RID **3** : DISENTANGLE, CLEAR syn release, liberate, discharge, emancipate, loose

³**free** adv **1** : FREELY **2** : without charge

free-bie or **free-bee** \'frē-bē\ n : something given without charge

free-board \'frē-ˌbōrd\ n : the vertical distance between the waterline and the upper edge of the side of a boat

free-boot-er \'frē-ˌbüt-ər\ n [D *vrijbuiter*, fr. *vrijbuit* plunder, fr. *vrij* free + *buit* booty] : PLUNDERER, PIRATE

free-born \-ˈbȯrn\ adj **1** : not born in vassalage or slavery **2** : of, relating to, or befitting one that is freeborn

freed-man \'frēd-mən, -ˌman\ n : a man freed from slavery

free-dom \'frēd-əm\ n **1** : the quality or state of being free : INDEPENDENCE **2** : EXEMPTION, RELEASE **3** : EASE, FACILITY **4** : FRANKNESS **5** : unrestricted use **6** : a political right; also : FRANCHISE, PRIVILEGE

free-for-all \'frē-fə-ˌrȯl\ n : a competition or fight open to all comers and usu. with no rules : BRAWL — **free-for-all** adj

free-hand \'frē-ˌhand\ adj : done without mechanical aids or devices

free-hold \ˌfrē-ˌhōld\ n : ownership of an estate for life usu. with the right to bequeath it to one's heirs; also : an estate thus owned — **free-hold-er** n

free lance n : one who pursues a profession (as writing) without long-term contractual commitments to any one employer — **free-lance** adj or vb

free-living \'frē-'liv-iŋ\ adj : being neither parasitic nor symbiotic (∼ organisms)

free-load \'frē-ˌlōd\ vb : to impose upon another's generosity or hospitality — **free-load-er** n

free love n : the practice of living openly with one of the opposite sex without marriage

free-man \'frē-mən, -ˌman\ n **1** : one ~ho has civil or political liberty **2**

: one having the full rights of a citizen

Free-ma-son \-ˌmās-ᵊn\ n : a member of a secret fraternal society called Free and Accepted Masons — **Free-ma-son-ry** \-rē\ n

free-stand-ing \'frē-'stan-diŋ\ adj : standing alone or on its own foundation

free-stone \'frē-ˌstōn\ n **1** : a stone that may be cut freely without splitting **2** : a fruit stone to which the flesh does not cling; also : a fruit (as a peach or cherry) having such a stone

free-think-er \-'thiŋ-kər\ n : one who forms opinions on the basis of reason independently of authority; esp : one who doubts or denies religious dogma — **free-think-ing** n or adj

free trade n : trade between nations without restrictions (as high taxes on imports)

free verse n : verse whose meter is irregular or whose rhythm is not metrical

free-way \'frē-ˌwā\ n : an expressway with fully controlled access

free-wheel \-'hwēl\ vb : to move, live, or drift along freely or irresponsibly

free-will \'frē-ˌwil\ adj : VOLUNTARY

free will n : voluntary choice or decision

¹**freeze** \'frēz\ vb **froze** \'frōz\ ; **fro-zen** \'frōz-ᵊn\ ; **freez-ing 1** : to harden or cause to harden into a solid (as ice) by loss of heat **2** : to chill or become chilled with cold **3** : to become coldly formal in manner; also : to act toward in a stiff and formal way **4** : to damage by frost **5** : to adhere solidly by freezing **6** : to cause to grip tightly or remain in immovable contact **7** : to become clogged with ice **8** : to become fixed or motionless **9** : to fix at a certain stage or level

²**freeze** n **1** : a state of weather marked by low temperature **2** : an act or instance of freezing (a price ∼) **3** : the state of being frozen

freeze-dry \'frēz-ˌdrī\ vb : to dry in a frozen state under vacuum esp. for preservation — **freeze-dried** adj

freez-er \'frē-zər\ n : a compartment, device, or room for freezing food or keeping it frozen

¹**freight** \'frāt\ n **1** : payment for carrying goods **2** : CARGO **3** : BURDEN **4** : the carrying of goods by a common carrier **5** : a train that carries freight

²**freight** vb **1** : to load with goods for transportation **2** : BURDEN, CHARGE **3** : to ship or transport by freight

freight-er \'frāt-ər\ n : a ship or airplane used chiefly to carry freight

French \'french\ n **1** : the language of France **2** French pl : the people of France — **French** adj — **French-man** \-mən\ n — **French-wom-an** \-ˌwu̇m-ən\ n

french fry vb, often cap 1st F : to fry (as strips of potato) in deep fat until brown — **french fry** n, often cap 1st F

French horn *n* : a curved brass instrument with a funnel-shaped mouthpiece and a flaring bell

fre·net·ic \fri-'net-ik\ *adj* : FRENZIED, FRANTIC — **fre·net·i·cal·ly** \-i-k(ə-)lē\ *adv*

fren·zy \'fren-zē\ *n, pl* **frenzies** : temporary madness or a violently agitated state — **fren·zied** \-zēd\ *adj*

freq *abbr* frequency, frequent, frequently

fre·quen·cy \'frē-kwən-sē\ *n, pl* **-cies** **1** : the fact or condition of occurring frequently **2** : rate of occurrence **3** : the number of cycles per second of an alternating current **4** : the number of waves (as of sound or electromagnetic energy) that pass a fixed point each second

frequency modulation *n* : variation of the frequency of a carrier wave according to another signal; *also* : a broadcasting system using such modulation

¹fre·quent \'frē-kwənt\ *adj* **1** : happening often or at short intervals **2** : HABITUAL — **fre·quent·ly** *adv*

²fre·quent \frē-'kwent, 'frē-kwənt\ *vb* : to associate with, be in, or resort to habitually — **fre·quent·er** *n*

fres·co \'fres-kō\ *n, pl* **frescoes** [It. fr. *fresco* fresh] : the art of painting on fresh plaster; *also* : a painting done by this method

fresh \'fresh\ *adj* **1** : not salt (~ water) **2** : PURE, INVIGORATING **3** : fairly strong : BRISK (~ breeze) **4** : not altered by processing (as freezing or canning) **5** : VIGOROUS, REFRESHED (~ not stale, sour, or decayed (~ bread) **7** : not faded **8** : not worn or rumpled **9** : experienced, made, or received newly or anew **10** : ADDITIONAL, ANOTHER (made a ~ start) **11** : ORIGINAL, VIVID **12** : INEXPERIENCED **13** : newly come or arrived (~ from school) **14** : IMPUDENT — **fresh·ly** *adv* — **fresh·ness** *n*

fresh·en \'fresh-ən\ *vb* **fresh·ened**; **fresh·en·ing** \-(ə-)niŋ\ : to make, grow, or become more fresh

fresh·et \'fresh-ət\ *n* : an overflowing of a stream (as by heavy rains)

fresh·man \'fresh-mən\ *n* **1** : BEGINNER, NEWCOMER **2** : a 1st-year student

fresh·wa·ter \'fresh-,wȯt-ər, -,wät-\ *adj* : of, relating to, or living in fresh water

¹fret \'fret\ *vb* **fret·ted**; **fret·ting** [ME *freten* to devour, fret, fr. OE *fretan* to devour] **1** : to become irritated : WORRY, VEX **2** : WEAR, CORRODE; *also* : FRAY **3** : RUB, CHAFE **4** : to make by wearing away **5** : GRATE (the siren *fretted* at their nerves) **6** : AGITATE, RIPPLE

²fret *n* : an irritated or worried state (in a ~)

³fret *n* : ornamental work esp. of straight lines in symmetrical patterns

⁴fret *n* : one of a series of ridges across the fingerboard of a stringed musical instrument — **fret·ted** *adj*

fret·ful \'fret-fəl\ *adj* : IRRITABLE — **fret·ful·ly** \-ē\ *adv* — **fret·ful·ness** *n*

fret·saw \-,sȯ\ *n* : a narrow-bladed saw used for cutting curved outlines

fret·work \-,wərk\ *n* **1** : decoration consisting of frets **2** : ornamental openwork or work in relief

Fri *abbr* Friday

fri·a·ble \'frī-ə-bəl\ *adj* : easily pulverized (~ soil)

fri·ar \'frī(-ə)r\ *n* [ME *frere, fryer,* fr. OF *frere,* lit., brother, fr. L *frater*] : a member of a mendicant religious order

fri·ary \'frī(-ə)r-ē\ *n, pl* **-ar·ies** : a monastery of friars

¹fric·as·see \'frik-ə-,sē, ,frik-ə-'sē\ *n* : a dish made of meat (as chicken or veal) cut into pieces and stewed in a gravy

²fricassee *vb* **-seed**; **-see·ing** : to cook as a fricassee

fric·tion \'frik-shən\ *n* **1** : the rubbing of one body against another **2** : the force that resists motion between bodies in contact **3** : clash in opinions between persons or groups : DISAGREEMENT — **fric·tion·al** *adj*

friction tape *n* : a usu. cloth tape impregnated with insulating material and an adhesive and used esp. to protect and insulate electrical conductors

Fri·day \'frīd-ē\ *n* : the sixth day of the week

fried·cake \'frīd-,kāk\ *n* : DOUGHNUT, CRULLER

friend \'frend\ *n* **1** : a person attached to another by respect or affection **2** : ACQUAINTANCE **3** : one who is not hostile **4** : one who supports or favors something (a ~ of art) **5** *cap* : a member of the Society of Friends : QUAKER — **friend·less** \'fren-(d)ləs\ *adj* — **friend·li·ness** \'fren-(d)lē-nəs\ *n* — **friend·ly** *adj* — **friend·ship** \'fren(d)-,ship\ *n*

frieze \'frēz\ *n* : an ornamental often sculptured band extending around something (as a building or room)

frig·ate \'frig-ət\ *n* **1** : a square-rigged warship **2** : a warship smaller than a destroyer used for escort and patrol duties

fright \'frīt\ *n* **1** : sudden terror : ALARM **2** : something that is ugly or shocking

fright·en \'frīt-ᵊn\ *vb* **fright·ened**; **fright·en·ing** \'frīt-(ᵊ-)niŋ\ **1** : to make afraid **2** : to drive away or out by frightening **3** : to become frightened — **fright·en·ing·ly** *adv*

fright·ful \'frīt-fəl\ *adj* **1** : TERRIFYING **2** : STARTLING **3** : EXTREME (~ thirst) — **fright·ful·ly** \-ē\ *adv* — **fright·ful·ness** *n*

frig·id \'frij-əd\ *adj* **1** : intensely cold **2** : lacking warmth or ardor : INDIFFERENT **3** : abnormally averse to or unable to achieve orgasm during sexual intercourse — used esp. of women — **fri·gid·i·ty** \frij-'id-ət-ē\ *n*

frigid zone *n* : the area or region between the arctic circle and the north pole or between the antarctic circle and the south pole

frill \'fril\ *n* **1** : a gathered, pleated, or ruffled edging **2** : an ornamental addition : something unessential — **frilly** \-ē\ *adj*

fringe \'frinj\ *n* **1** : an ornamental border consisting of short threads or strips hanging from an edge or band **2** : something that resembles a fringe : BORDER **3** : something on the margin of an activity, process, or subject matter — **fringe** *vb*

fringe benefit *n* : an employment benefit paid for by an employer without affecting basic wage rates **2** : any additional benefit

frip·pery \'frip-(ə-)rē\ *n, pl* **-per·ies** [MF *friperie*] **1** : cheap showy finery **2** : pretentious display

frisk \'frisk\ *vb* **1** : to leap, skip, or dance in a lively or playfuly way : GAMBOL **2** : to search (a person) esp. for concealed weapons by running the hand rapidly over the clothing

frisky \'fris-kē\ *adj* **frisk·i·er; -est** : FROLICSOME — **frisk·i·ly** \'fris-kə-lē\ *adv* — **frisk·i·ness** \-kē-nəs\ *n*

¹frit·ter \'frit-ər\ *n* : a small lump of fried batter often containing fruit or meat

²fritter *vb* **1** : to reduce or waste piecemeal **2** : to break into small fragments

fritz \'frits\ *n* : a state of disorder or disrepair — used in the phrase *on the fritz*

friv·o·lous \'friv-(ə-)ləs\ *adj* **1** : of little importance : TRIVIAL **2** : lacking in seriousness — **fri·vol·i·ty** \friv-'äl-ət-ē\ *n* — **friv·o·lous·ly** *adv*

frizz \'friz\ *vb* : to curl in small tight curls — **frizz** *n* — **frizzy** *adj*

¹friz·zle \'friz-əl\ *vb* **friz·zled; friz·zling** \-(ə-)liŋ\ : FRIZZ, CURL — **frizzle** *n*

²frizzle *vb* **friz·zled; friz·zling** **1** : to fry until crisp and curled **2** : to cook with a sizzling noise

fro \'frō\ *adv* : BACK, AWAY — used in the phrase *to and fro*

frock \'fräk\ *n* **1** : an outer garment worn by monks and friars **2** : an outer garment worn esp. by men **3** : a woman's or girl's dress

frock coat *n* : a man's usu. double-breasted coat with knee-length skirts

frog \'frog, 'fräg\ *n* **1** : any of various largely aquatic smooth-skinned tailless leaping amphibians **2** : an ornamental braiding for fastening the front of a garment by a loop through which a button passes **3** : a condition in the throat causing hoarseness **4** : a small holder (as of metal, glass, or plastic) with perforations or spikes that is placed in a bowl or vase to keep cut flowers in position

frog·man \'frog-,man, 'fräg-, -mən\ *n* : a swimmer equipped to work underwater for long periods of time

¹frol·ic \'fräl-ik\ *vb* **frol·icked; frol·ick-**

ing **1** : to make merry **2** : to play about happily : ROMP

²frolic *n* **1** : a playful or mischievous action **2** : FUN, MERRIMENT — **frol·ic·some** \-səm\ *adj*

from \(')frəm, 'främ\ *prep* **1** — used to show a starting point (a letter ~ home) **2** — used to show removal or separation (subtract 3 ~ 9) **3** — used to show a material, source, or cause (suffering ~ a cold)

frond \'fränd\ *n* : a usu. large divided leaf esp. of a fern or palm tree

¹front \'frənt\ *n* **1** : FOREHEAD; *also* : the whole face **2** : external and often feigned appearance **3** : a region of active fighting; *also* : a sphere of activity **4** : a political coalition **5** : the side of a building containing the main entrance **6** : the forward part or surface **7** : FRONTAGE **8** : a boundary between two dissimilar air masses **9** : a position directly before or ahead of something else **10** : a person, group, or thing used to mask the identity or true character or activity of the actual controlling agent

²front *vb* **1** : FACE **2** : to serve as a front **3** : CONFRONT

front·age \'frənt-ij\ *n* **1** : a piece of land that fronts something (as on a river or road) **2** : the front side of a building **3** : the extent or measure of a frontage

front·al \'frənt-ᵊl\ *adj* **1** : of, relating to, or next to the forehead **2** : of, relating to, or directed at the front (a ~ attack) — **front·al·ly** \-ᵊl-ē\ *adv*

fron·tier \,frən-'tiər\ *n* **1** : a border between two countries **2** : a region that forms the margin of settled territory **3** : the outer limits of knowledge or achievement (the ~s of science) — **fron·tiers·man** \-'tiərz-mən\ *n*

fron·tis·piece \'frənt-ə-,spēs\ *n* : an illustration preceding and usu. facing the title page of a book

front man *n* : a person serving as a front or figurehead

front·ward \'frənt-wərd\ *or* **front·wards** \-wərdz\ *adv or adj* : toward the front

¹frost \'frost\ *n* **1** : freezing temperature **2** : a covering of tiny ice crystals on a cold surface — **frosty** *adj*

²frost *vb* **1** : to cover with frost **2** : to put icing on (as a cake) **3** : to produce a slightly roughened surface on (as glass) **4** : to injure or kill by frost

frost·bite \'fros(t)-,bīt\ *vb* **-bit** \-,bit\; **-bit·ten** \-,bit-ᵊn\; **-bit·ing** \-,bīt-iŋ\ : to injure by frost or frostbite

²frostbite *n* : the freezing or the local effect of a partial freezing of some part of the body

frost heave *n* : an upthrust of pavement caused by freezing of moist soil

frost·ing \'frō-stiŋ\ *n* **1** : ICING **2** : dull finish on metal or glass

froth \'froth\ *n, pl* **froths** \'froths, 'frothz\ **1** : bubbles formed in or on a liquid **2** : something light or frivolous — **frothy** *adj*

frou·frou \'frü-frü\ *n* [F] **1** : a rustling esp. of a woman's skirts **2** : frilly ornamentation esp. in women's clothing

fro·ward \'frō-(w)ərd\ *adj* : DISOBEDIENT, WILLFUL

frown \'fraùn\ *vb* **1** : to wrinkle the forehead (as in anger, displeasure, or thought) : SCOWL **2** : to look with disapproval **3** : to express with a frown — **frown** *n*

frow·sy *or* **frow·zy** \'fraù-zē\ *adj* **frow·si·er** *or* **frow·zi·er; -est** : having a slovenly or uncared-for appearance

froze *past of* FREEZE

fro·zen \'frōz-ᵊn\ *adj* **1** : treated, affected, or crusted over by freezing **2** : subject to long and severe cold **3** : expressing or characterized by cold unfriendliness **4** : incapable of being changed, moved, or undone : FIXED (~ wages) **5** : not available for present use (~ capital)

FRS *abbr* Federal Reserve System

frt *abbr* freight

fruc·ti·fy \'frək-tə-₁fī, 'frùk-\ *vb* **-fied; -fy·ing** **1** : to bear fruit **2** : to make fruitful or productive

fru·gal \'frü-gəl\ *adj* : ECONOMICAL, THRIFTY — **fru·gal·i·ty** \frü-'gal-ət-ē\ *n* — **fru·gal·ly** \'frü-gə-lē\ *adv*

¹fruit \'früt\ *n* [ME, fr. OF, fr. L *fructus* fruit, use, fr. *frui* to enjoy, have the use of] **1** : a usu. useful product of plant growth; *esp* : a usu. edible and sweet reproductive body (as a strawberry or apple) of a seed plant **2** : a product of fertilization in a plant; *esp* : the ripe ovary of a seed plant with its contents and appendages **3** : CONSEQUENCE, RESULT — **fruit·ed** \-əd\ *adj*

²fruit *vb* : to bear or cause to bear fruit

fruit·cake \'früt-₁kāk\ *n* : a rich cake containing nuts, dried or candied fruits, and spices

fruit fly *n* : any of various small two-winged flies whose larvae feed on fruit or decaying vegetable matter

fruit·ful \'früt-fəl\ *adj* **1** : yielding or producing fruit **2** : very productive (a ~ soil) ; *also* : bringing results (a ~ idea) — **fruit·ful·ly** \-fə-lē\ *adv* — **fruit·ful·ness** *n*

fru·ition \frü-'ish-ən\ *n* **1** : ENJOYMENT **2** : the state of bearing fruit **3** : REALIZATION, ACCOMPLISHMENT

fruit·less \'früt-ləs\ *adj* **1** : not bearing fruit **2** : producing no good results : UNSUCCESSFUL (a ~ attempt) — **fruit·less·ly** *adv*

fruity \'früt-ē\ *adj* **fruit·i·er; -est** : resembling a fruit esp. in flavor

frumpy \'frəm-pē\ *adj* **frump·i·er; -est** : DRAB, DOWDY

frus·trate \'frəs-₁trāt\ *vb* **frus·trat·ed; frus·trat·ing** **1** : to balk in an endeavor : BLOCK **2** : to bring to nothing **3** : to fill with dissatisfaction due to unresolved problems or unfulfilled needs — **frus·trat·ing·ly** \-iŋ-lē\ *adv* — **frus·tra·tion** \₁frəs-'trā-shən\ *n*

frus·tum \'frəs-təm\ *n, pl* **frustums** *or*

frus·ta \-tə\ : the part of a cone or pyramid formed by cutting off the top by a plane parallel to the base

frwy *abbr* freeway

¹fry \'frī\ *vb* **fried; fry·ing** **1** : to cook in a pan or on a griddle over a fire esp. with the use of fat **2** : to undergo frying

²fry *n, pl* **fries** **1** : a dish of something fried **2** : a social gathering where fried food is eaten

³fry *n, pl* **fry** **1** : recently hatched fishes; *also* : very small adult fishes **2** : members of a group or class (small ~)

fry·er \'frī(-ə)r\ *n* **1** : something (as a young chicken) suitable for frying **2** : a deep utensil for frying foods

FSLIC *abbr* Federal Savings and Loan Insurance Corporation

ft *abbr* **1** feet; foot **2** fort

FTC *abbr* Federal Trade Commission

fuch·sia \'fyü-shə\ *n* **1** : any of a genus of shrubs related to the evening primrose and grown for their showy nodding often red or purple flowers **2** : a vivid reddish purple

fud·dle \'fəd-ᵊl\ *vb* **fud·dled; fud·dling** : MUDDLE, CONFUSE

fud·dy-dud·dy \'fəd-ē-₁dəd-ē\ *n, pl* **-dies** : a person who is old-fashioned, pompous, unimaginative, or fussy

¹fudge \'fəj\ *vb* **fudged; fudg·ing** **1** : to cheat or exaggerate by blurring or overstepping a boundary **2** : to avoid coming to grips with something

²fudge *n* **1** : NONSENSE **2** : a soft creamy candy of milk, sugar, butter, and flavoring

¹fu·el \'fyü-əl\ *n* : a substance (as coal) used to produce heat or power by combustion; *also* : a substance from which nuclear energy can be liberated

²fuel *vb* **-eled** *or* **-elled; -el·ing** *or* **-el·ling** : to provide with or take in fuel

fuel cell *n* : a device that continuously changes the chemical energy of a fuel directly into electrical energy

¹fu·gi·tive \'fyü-jət-iv\ *n* **1** : one who flees or tries to escape **2** : something elusive or hard to find

²fugitive *adj* **1** : running away or trying to escape **2** : likely to vanish suddenly : not fixed or lasting

fugue \'fyüg\ *n* **1** : a musical composition in which different parts successively repeat the theme **2** : a disturbed state of consciousness characterized by acts that are not recalled upon recovery

füh·rer *or* **fueh·rer** \'fyùr-ər, 'fir-\ *n* : LEADER — used chiefly of the leader of the German Nazis

¹-ful \fəl\ *adj suffix, sometimes* **-ful·er;** *sometimes* **-ful·est** **1** : full of (event*ful*) **2** : characterized by (peace*ful*) **3** : having the qualities of (master*ful*) **4** : tending, given, or liable to (mourn*ful*)

²-ful \₁fùl\ *n suffix* : number or quantity that fills or would fill (room*ful*)

ful·crum \'fùl-krəm, 'fəl-\ *n, pl* **ful-**

crums or **ful·cra** \-krə\ [LL, fr. L, bedpost] : the support on which a lever turns

ful·fill or **ful·fil** \fu̇l-ˈfil\ vb **ful·filled; ful·fill·ing** 1 : to put into effect 2 : to bring to an end 3 : SATISFY — **ful·fill·ment** n

¹**full** \ˈfu̇l\ adj 1 : FILLED 2 : complete esp. in detail, number, or duration 3 : having all the distinguishing characteristics (a ~ member) 4 : MAXIMUM 5 : rounded in outline (a ~ figure) 6 : possessing or containing an abundance (~ of wrinkles) 7 : having an abundance of material (a ~ skirt) 8 : satisfied esp. with food or drink 9 : having volume or depth of sound 10 : completely occupied with a thought or plan — **full·ness** also **ful·ness** \ˈfu̇l-nəs\ n

²**full** adv 1 : VERY, EXTREMELY 2 : ENTIRELY 3 : STRAIGHT, SQUARELY (hit him ~ in the face)

³**full** n 1 : the utmost extent 2 : the highest or fullest state or degree 3 : the requisite or complete amount

⁴**full** vb : to shrink and thicken (woolen cloth) by moistening, heating, and pressing — **full·er** n

full·back \-ˌbak\ n : a football back stationed between the halfbacks

full-blood·ed \ˈfu̇l-ˈbləd-əd\ adj : of unmixed ancestry : PUREBRED

full-blown \-ˈblōn\ adj 1 : being at the height of bloom 2 : fully mature or developed

full-bod·ied \-ˈbäd-ēd\ adj : marked by richness and fullness

full dress n : the style of dress worn for ceremonial or formal occasions

full-fledged \ˈfu̇l-ˈflejd\ adj 1 : fully developed 2 : having full plumage

full moon n : the moon with its whole disk illuminated

full-scale \ˈfu̇l-ˈskāl\ adj 1 : identical to an original in proportion and size (~ drawing) 2 : involving full use of available resources (a ~ revolt)

full tilt adv : at high speed

full-time \ˈfu̇l-ˈtīm\ adj or adv : involving or working a full or regular schedule

ful·ly \ˈfu̇l-ē\ adv 1 : in a full manner or degree : COMPLETELY 2 : at least

ful·mi·nate \ˈfu̇l-mə-ˌnāt, ˈfəl-\ vb **-nat·ed; -nat·ing** [ME fulminaten, fr. ML fulminare, fr. L, to flash with lightning, strike with lightning, fr. fulmen lightning] 1 : to utter or send out censure or invective : condemn severely 2 : EXPLODE — **ful·mi·na·tion** \ˌfu̇l-mə-ˈnā-shən, ˌfəl-\ n

ful·some \ˈfu̇l-səm\ adj 1 : COPIOUS, ABUNDANT (~ detail) 2 : OFFENSIVE, DISGUSTING 3 : excessively flattering (~ praise)

fu·ma·role \ˈfyü-mə-ˌrōl\ n : a hole in a volcanic region from which hot gases issue

fum·ble \ˈfəm-bəl\ vb **fum·bled; fum·bling** \-b(ə-)liŋ\ 1 : to grope about

clumsily 2 : to fail to hold, catch, or handle properly — **fumble** n

¹**fume** \ˈfyüm\ n : a usu. irritating smoke, vapor, or gas

²**fume** vb **fumed; fum·ing** 1 : to treat with fumes 2 : to give off fumes 3 : to express anger or annoyance

fu·mi·gant \ˈfyü-mi-gənt\ n : a substance used for fumigation

fu·mi·gate \ˈfyü-mə-ˌgāt\ vb **-gat·ed; -gat·ing** : to treat with fumes to disinfect or destroy pests — **fu·mi·ga·tion** \ˌfyü-mə-ˈgā-shən\ n — **fu·mi·ga·tor** \ˈfyü-mə-ˌgāt-ər\ n

fun \ˈfən\ n [E dial. fun to hoax] 1 : something that provides amusement or enjoyment 2 : ENJOYMENT

¹**func·tion** \ˈfəŋk-shən\ n 1 : OCCUPATION 2 : special purpose 3 : the particular purpose for which a person or thing is specially fitted or used or for which a thing exists (the ~ of a knife is cutting); also : the natural or proper action of a bodily part in a living thing (the ~ of the heart) 4 : a formal ceremony or social affair 5 : the mathematical relationship that assigns to each element of a set one and only one element of the same or another set 6 : a variable (as a quality, trait, or measurement) that depends on and varies with another (height is a ~ of age in children) — **func·tion·al** \-sh(ə-)nəl\ adj — **func·tion·al·ly** \-ē\ adv — **func·tion·less** adj

²**function** vb **func·tioned; func·tion·ing** \-sh(ə-)niŋ\ 1 : SERVE 2 : OPERATE, WORK

func·tion·ary \ˈfəŋk-shə-ˌner-ē\ n, pl **-ar·ies** : one who performs a certain function; esp : OFFICIAL

function word n : a word (as a preposition, auxiliary verb, or conjunction) expressing the grammatical relationship between other words

¹**fund** \ˈfənd\ n [L fundus bottom, piece of landed property] 1 : STORE, SUPPLY 2 : a sum of money or resources intended for a special purpose 3 pl : available money 4 : an organization administering a special fund

²**fund** vb 1 : to provide funds for 2 : to convert (a short-term obligation) into a long-term interest-bearing debt

fun·da·men·tal \ˌfən-də-ˈment-ᵊl\ adj 1 : serving as an origin : PRIMARY 2 : BASIC, ESSENTIAL 3 : RADICAL (~ change) 4 : of central importance : PRINCIPAL — **fundamental** n — **fun·da·men·tal·ly** \-ē\ adv

fun·da·men·tal·ism \-ˌiz-əm\ n, often cap : a Protestant religious movement emphasizing the literal infallibility of the Bible — **fun·da·men·tal·ist** \-əst\ adj or n

¹**fu·ner·al** \ˈfyün-(ə-)rəl\ adj 1 : of, relating to, or constituting a funeral 2 : FUNEREAL 2

²**funeral** n : the ceremonies held for a dead person usu. before burial

fu·ner·ary \'fyü-nə-ˌrer-ē\ *adj* : of, used for, or associated with burial

fu·ne·re·al \fyu̇-'nir-ē-əl\ *adj* **1** : of or relating to a funeral **2** : suggesting a funeral

fun·gi·cide \'fən-jə-ˌsīd, 'fəŋ-gə-\ *n* : an agent that kills or checks the growth of fungi — **fun·gi·cid·al** \ˌfən-jə-'sīd-ᵊl, ˌfəŋ-gə-\ *adj*

fun·gus \'fəŋ-gəs\ *n, pl* **fun·gi** \'fən-ˌjī, 'fəŋ-ˌgī\ *also* **fun·gus·es** \'fəŋ-gə-səz\ : any of a large group of lower plants that lack chlorophyll and include molds, mildews, mushrooms, and yeasts — **fun·gal** \-gəl\ *adj* — **fun·gous** \-gəs\ *adj*

fu·nic·u·lar \fyu̇-'nik-yə-lər, fə-\ *n* : a cable railway ascending a mountain

funk \'fəŋk\ *n* : a depressed state of mind

funky \'fəŋ-kē\ *adj* **funk·i·er; -est 1** : having an earthy, unsophisticated style and feeling; *esp* : having the style and feeling of blues **2** : odd or quaint in appearance or style

¹fun·nel \'fən-ᵊl\ *n* **1** : a cone-shaped utensil with a tube used for catching and directing a downward flow (as of liquid) **2** : FLUE, SMOKESTACK

²funnel *vb* **-neled** *also* **-nelled; -nel·ing** *also* **-nel·ling 1** : to pass through or as if through a funnel **2** : to move to a central point or into a central channel

¹fun·ny \'fən-ē\ *adj* **fun·ni·er; -est 1** : AMUSING **2** : FACETIOUS **3** : QUEER, ODD **4** : UNDERHANDED

²funny *n, pl* **funnies 2** : a comic strip or a comic section (as of a newspaper)

funny bone *n* : a place at the back of the elbow where a blow compresses a nerve and causes a painful tingling sensation

¹fur \'fər\ *n* **1** : an article of clothing made of or with fur **2** : the hairy coat of a mammal esp. when fine, soft, and thick; *also* : this coat dressed for human use — **fur** *adj* — **furred** \'fərd\ *adj*

²fur *abbr* furlong

fur·be·low \'fər-bə-ˌlō\ *n* **1** : FLOUNCE, RUFFLE **2** : showy trimming

fur·bish \'fər-bish\ *vb* **1** : to make lustrous : POLISH **2** : to give a new look to : RENOVATE

fu·ri·ous \'fyu̇r-ē-əs\ *adj* **1** : FIERCE, ANGRY, VIOLENT **2** : BOISTEROUS **3** : INTENSE — **fu·ri·ous·ly** *adv*

furl \'fərl\ *vb* **1** : to wrap or roll (as a sail or a flag) close to or around something **2** : to curl in furls — **furl** *n*

fur·long \'fər-ˌlȯŋ\ *n* [ME, fr. OE *furlang*, fr. *furh* furrow + *lang* long] : a unit of length equal to 220 yards (about 201 meters)

fur·lough \'fər-lō\ *n* [Dutch *verlof*, lit., permission] : a leave of absence from duty granted esp. to a soldier — **furlough** *vb*

fur·nace \'fər-nəs\ *n* : an enclosed structure in which heat is produced

fur·nish \'fər-nish\ *vb* **1** : to provide with what is needed : EQUIP **2** : SUPPLY, GIVE

fur·nish·ings \-iŋs\ *n pl* **1** : articles or accessories of dress **2** : FURNITURE

fur·ni·ture \'fər-ni-chər\ *n* : equipment that is necessary, useful, or desirable; *esp* : movable articles (as chairs, tables, or beds) for a room

fu·ror \'fyu̇r-ˌȯr\ *n* **1** : ANGER, RAGE **2** : a contagious excitement; *esp* : a fashionable craze **3** : UPROAR

fu·rore \-ˌȯr\ *n* [It] : FUROR 2, 3

fur·ri·er \'fər-ē-ər\ *n* : one who prepares or deals in fur

fur·ring \'fər-iŋ\ *n* : wood or metal strips applied to a wall or ceiling to form a level surface or an air space

fur·row \'fər-ō\ *n* **1** : a trench in the earth made by or as if by a plow **2** : a narrow groove or wrinkle — **furrow** *vb*

fur·ry \'fər-ē\ *adj* **fur·ri·er; -est 1** : resembling or consisting of fur **2** : covered with fur

¹fur·ther \'fər-thər\ *adv* **1** : FARTHER 1 **2** : in addition : MOREOVER **3** : to a greater extent or degree

²further *vb* **fur·thered; fur·ther·ing** \'fərth-(ə-)riŋ\ : to help forward — **fur·ther·ance** \'fərth-(ə-)rəns\ *n*

³further *adj* **1** : ²FARTHER 1 **2** : ADDITIONAL

fur·ther·more \'fər-thə(r)-ˌmȯr\ *adv* : in addition to what precedes : BESIDES

fur·ther·most \-ˌmȯst\ *adj* : most distant : FARTHEST

fur·thest \'fər-thəst\ *adv or adj* : FARTHEST

fur·tive \'fərt-iv\ *adj* [F or L; F *furtif*, fr. L *furtivus*, fr. *furtum* theft, fr. *fur* thief] : done by stealth : SLY — **fur·tive·ly** *adv* — **fur·tive·ness** *n*

fu·ry \'fyu̇r-ē\ *n, pl* **furies 1** : violent anger : RAGE **2** : extreme fierceness or violence **3** : FRENZY

furze \'fərz\ *n* : GORSE

¹fuse \'fyüz\ *n* **1** : a cord or cable that is set afire to ignite an explosive charge **2** *usu* **fuze** : a mechanical or electrical device for setting off the explosive charge of a projectile, bomb, or torpedo

²fuse *or* **fuze** \'fyüz\ *vb* **fused** *or* **fuzed; fus·ing** *or* **fuz·ing** : to equip with a fuse

³fuse *vb* **fused; fus·ing 1** : MELT **2** : to unite by or as if by melting together — **fus·ible** *adj*

⁴fuse *n* : an electrical safety device having a metal wire or strip that melts and interrupts the circuit when the current becomes too strong

fu·se·lage \'fyü-sə-ˌläzh, -zə-\ *n* : the central body portion of an airplane that holds the crew, passengers, and cargo

fu·sil·lade \'fyü-sə-ˌläd, -zə-ˌläd\ *n* : a number of shots fired simultaneously or in rapid succession

fu·sion \'fyü-zhən\ *n* **1** : the act or process of melting or making plastic by heat **2** : union by or as if by melting **3** : the union of light atomic nuclei to form heavier nuclei with the release of huge quantities of energy

¹fuss \'fəs\ *n* **1** : needless bustle or excitement : COMMOTION **2** : effusive praise **3** : a state of agitation **4** : OBJECTION, PROTEST **5** : DISPUTE

²fuss *vb* : to make a fuss

fuss·bud·get \'fəs-ˌbəj-ət\ *n* : one who fusses about trifles

fussy \'fəs-ē\ *adj* fuss·i·er; -est **1** : IRRITABLE **2** : requiring or giving close attention to details **3** : revealing a sometimes extreme concern for niceties : FASTIDIOUS (not ~ about food) — fuss·i·ly \'fəs-ə-lē\ *adv* — fuss·i·ness \-ē-nəs\ *n*

fus·tian \'fəs-chən\ *n* **1** : a strong cotton and linen cloth **2** : pretentious writing or speech

fus·ty \'fəs-tē\ *adj* fus·ti·er; -est [ME, fr. *fust* wine cask, fr. MF, club, cask, fr. L *fustis*] **1** : MUSTY **2** : OLD-FASHIONED

fut *abbr* future

fu·tile \'fyüt-ᵊl, 'fyü-ˌtīl\ *adj* **1** : USELESS, VAIN **2** : FRIVOLOUS, TRIVIAL — fu·til·i·ty \fyü-'til-ət-ē\ *n*

¹fu·ture \'fyü-chər\ *adj* **1** : of, relating to, or constituting a verb tense that expresses time yet to come **2** : coming after the present

²future *n* **1** : time that is to come **2** : what is going to happen **3** : an expectation of advancement or progressive development **4** : the future tense; *also* : a verb form in it

fu·tur·ism \'fyü-chə-ˌriz-əm\ *n* : a modern movement in art, music, and literature that tries esp. to express the energy and activity of mechanical processes — fu·tur·ist \'fyüch-(ə-)rəst\ *n*

fu·tur·is·tic \ˌfyü-chə-'ris-tik\ *adj* : of or relating to the future or to futurism; *also* : very modern

fu·tu·ri·ty \fyü-'t(y)ùr-ət-ē\ *n, pl* -ties **1** : FUTURE **2** : the quality or state of being future **3** *pl* : future events or prospects

fuze *var of* FUSE

fuzz \'fəz\ *n* : fine light particles or fibers (as of down or fluff)

fuzzy \'fəz-ē\ *adj* fuzz·i·er; -est **1** : having or resembling fuzz **2** : INDISTINCT — fuzz·i·ness \'fəz-ē-nəs\ *n*

fwd *abbr* forward

FWD *abbr* front-wheel drive

FY *abbr* fiscal year

-fy \ˌfī\ *vb suffix* : make : form into ⟨dandify⟩

FYI *abbr* for your information

G

¹g \'jē\ *n, pl* g's *or* gs \'jēz\ *often cap* **1** : the 7th letter of the English alphabet **2** : a unit of force equal to the force exerted by gravity on a body at rest and used to indicate the force to which a body is subjected when accelerated **3** *slang* : a sum of $1000

²g *abbr, often cap* **1** game **2** gauge **3** good **4** gram **5** gravity

ga *abbr* gauge

¹Ga *abbr* Georgia

²Ga *symbol* gallium

GA *abbr* **1** general assembly **2** general average **3** general of the army **4** Georgia

gab \'gab\ *vb* gabbed; gab·bing : to talk in a rapid or thoughtless manner : CHATTER — gab *n*

gab·ar·dine \'gab-ər-ˌdēn\ *n* **1** : GABERDINE 1, 2 **2** : a firm durable twilled fabric having diagonal ribs and made of various fibers; *also* : a garment of gabardine

gab·ble \'gab-əl\ *vb* gab·bled; gab·bling \-(ə-)liŋ\ : JABBER, BABBLE

gab·by \'gab-ē\ *adj* gab·bi·er; -est : TALKATIVE, GARRULOUS

gab·er·dine \'gab-ər-ˌdēn\ *n* **1** : a long coat or smock worn chiefly by Jews in medieval times **2** : an English laborer's smock **3** : GABARDINE

gab·fest \'gab-ˌfest\ *n* **1** : an informal gathering for general talk **2** : an extended conversation

ga·ble \'gā-bəl\ *n* : the triangular part of the end of a building formed by the sides of the roof sloping from the ridgepole down to the eaves — ga·bled \-bəld\ *adj*

gad \'gad\ *vb* gad·ded; gad·ding : to be on the go to little purpose — usu. used with *about* — gad·der *n*

gad·about \'gad-ə-ˌbaùt\ *n* : a person who flits about in social activity

gad·fly \'gad-ˌflī\ *n* **1** : a fly that bites or harasses livestock **2** : a usu. intentionally annoying and persistently critical person

gad·get \'gaj-ət\ *n* : DEVICE, CONTRIVANCE — gad·ge·teer \ˌgaj-ə-'tiər\ *n* — gad·get·ry \'gaj-ə-trē\ *n*

gad·o·lin·i·um \ˌgad-ᵊl-'in-ē-əm\ *n* : a magnetic metallic chemical element

¹Gael \'gāl\ *n* : a Celtic inhabitant of Ireland or Scotland

²Gael *abbr* Gaelic

Gael·ic \'gā-lik\ *adj* : of or relating to the Gaels or their languages — Gaelic *n*

gaff \'gaf\ *n* **1** : a spear used in taking fish or turtles; *also* : a metal hook for holding or lifting heavy fish **2** : the spar supporting the top of a fore- and-aft sail **3** : rough treatment : ABUSE — gaff *vb*

gaffe \'gaf\ *n* : a social blunder

gaf·fer \'gaf-ər\ *n* : an old man

¹gag \'gag\ *vb* gagged; gag·ging **1** : to

prevent from speaking or crying out by stopping up the mouth 2 : to prevent from speaking freely 3 : to retch or cause to retch 4 : OBSTRUCT, CHOKE 5 : BALK 6 : to make quips
²**gag** *n* 1 : something thrust into the mouth esp. to prevent speech or outcry 2 : an official check or restraint on free speech 3 : a laugh-provoking remark or act 4 : PRANK, TRICK
¹**gage** \'gāj\ *n* 1 : a token of defiance; *esp* : a glove or cap cast on the ground as a pledge of combat 2 : SECURITY
²**gage** *var of* GAUGE
gag·gle \'gag-əl\ *n* [ME *gagyll*, fr. *ga-gelen* to cackle] 1 : a flock of geese 2 : GROUP, CLUSTER
gai·ety \'gā-ət-ē\ *n, pl* **-eties** 1 : MERRYMAKING 2 : MERRIMENT 3 : FINERY
gai·ly \'gā-lē\ *adv* : in a gay manner
¹**gain** \'gān\ *n* 1 : PROFIT 2 : ACQUISITION, ACCUMULATION 3 : INCREASE
²**gain** *vb* 1 : to get possession of : EARN 2 : WIN ⟨∼ a victory⟩ 3 : ACHIEVE ⟨∼ strength⟩ 4 : to arrive at 5 : PERSUADE 6 : to increase in ⟨∼ momentum⟩ 7 : to run fast ⟨the watch ∼s a minute a day⟩ 8 : PROFIT 9 : INCREASE 10 : to improve in health — **gain·er** *n*
gain·ful \'gān-fəl\ *adj* : PROFITABLE — **gain·ful·ly** \-ē\ *adv*
gain·say \gān-'sā\ *vb* **-said** \-'sād, -'sed\; **-say·ing** \-'sā-iŋ\; **-says** \-'sāz, -'sez\ [ME *gainsayen*, fr. *gain-against + -sayen* to say] 1 : DENY, DISPUTE 2 : to speak against — **gain·say·er** *n*
gait \'gāt\ *n* : manner of moving on foot; *also* : a particular pattern or style of such moving — **gait·ed** \-əd\ *adj*
gai·ter \'gāt-ər\ *n* 1 : a leg covering reaching from the instep to ankle, mid-calf, or knee 2 : an ankle-high shoe with elastic gores in the sides 3 : an overshoe with a fabric upper
¹**gal** \'gal\ *n* : GIRL
²**gal** *abbr* gallon
Gal *abbr* Galatians
ga·la \'gā-lə, 'gal-ə, 'gäl-ə\ *n* : a gay celebration : FESTIVITY — **gala** *adj*
ga·lac·tose \gə-'lak-₁tōs\ *n* : a sugar less soluble and less sweet than glucose
Ga·la·tians \gə-'lā-shənz\ *n* — see BIBLE table
gal·axy \'gal-ək-sē\ *n, pl* **-ax·ies** [ME *galaxie, galaxias*, fr. LL *galaxias*, fr. Gk, fr. *galakt-, gala* milk] 1 *often cap* : MILKY WAY GALAXY — used with *the* 2 : a very large group of stars 3 : an assemblage of brilliant or famous persons or things — **ga·lac·tic** \gə-'lak-tik\ *adj*
¹**gale** \'gāl\ *n* 1 : a strong wind 2 : an emotional outburst (as of laughter)
ga·le·na \gə-'lē-nə\ *n* : a lustrous bluish gray mineral that consists of the sulfide of lead and is the chief ore of lead
¹**gall** \'gol\ *n* 1 : BILE 2 : something bitter to endure 3 : RANCOR 4 : IMPUDENCE

²**gall** *n* : a sore on the skin caused by chafing
³**gall** *vb* 1 : CHAFE; *esp* : to become sore or worn by rubbing 2 : VEX, HARASS
⁴**gall** *n* : a swelling of plant tissue caused by parasites (as fungi or mites)
¹**gal·lant** \gə-'lant, gə-'länt, 'gal-ənt\ *n* 1 : a young man of fashion 2 : a man who shows a marked fondness for the company of women and who is esp. attentive to them 3 : SUITOR
²**gal·lant** \'gal-ənt (*usual for 2, 3, 4*); gə-'lant, gə-'länt (*usual for 5*)\ *adj* 1 : showy in dress or bearing : SMART 2 : SPLENDID, STATELY 3 : SPIRITED, BRAVE 4 : CHIVALROUS, NOBLE 5 : polite and attentive to women — **gal·lant·ly** *adv*
gal·lant·ry \'gal-ən-trē\ *n, pl* **-ries** 1 *archaic* : gallant appearance 2 : an act of marked courtesy 3 : courteous attention to a woman 4 : conspicuous bravery
gall·blad·der \'gol-₁blad-ər\ *n* : a membranous muscular sac attached to the liver in which bile is stored
gal·le·on \'gal-ē-ən\ *n* : a large square-rigged sailing ship formerly used esp. by the Spanish
gal·le·ria \₁gal-ə-'rē-ə\ *n* [It] : a roofed and usu. glass-enclosed promenade or court
gal·lery \'gal-(ə)-rē\ *n, pl* **-ler·ies** 1 : an outdoor balcony; *also* : PORCH, VERANDA 2 : a long narrow room or hall; *esp* : one with windows along one side 3 : a narrow passage (as one made underground by a miner or through wood by an insect) 4 : a room where works of art are exhibited; *also* : an organization dealing in works of art 5 : a balcony in a theater, auditorium, or church; *esp* : the highest one in a theater 6 : a body of spectators (as at a tennis match) 7 : a photographer's studio — **gal·ler·ied** \-rēd\ *adj*
gal·ley \'gal-ē\ *n, pl* **galleys** 1 : a long low ship propelled esp. by oars and formerly used esp. in the Mediterranean sea 2 : the kitchen esp. of a boat or airplane 3 : a tray to hold printer's type that has been set; *also* : proof from type in such a tray
Gal·lic \'gal-ik\ *adj* : of or relating to Gaul or France
gal·li·mau·fry \₁gal-ə-'mó-frē\ *n, pl* **-fries** [MF *galimafree* hash] : HODGEPODGE
gal·li·nule \'gal-ə-₁n(y)ü(ə)l\ *n* : any of several aquatic birds related to the rails
gal·li·um \'gal-ē-əm\ *n* : a rare bluish white metallic chemical element
gal·li·vant \'gal-ə-₁vant\ *vb* : to go roaming about for pleasure
gal·lon \'gal-ən\ *n* — see WEIGHT table
¹**gal·lop** \gal-əp\ *vb* 1 : to go or cause to go at a gallop 2 : to run fast — **gal·lop·er** *n*
²**gallop** *n* 1 : a springing gait of a quad-

ruped; *esp* : a fast 3-beat gait of a horse **2** : a ride or run at a gallop

gal·lows \'gal-ōz\ *n, pl* **gallows** *or* **gallows·es** : a frame usu. of two upright posts and a crosspiece from which criminals are hanged

gall·stone \'gȯl-ˌstōn\ *n* : an abnormal concretion occurring in the gallbladder or bile passages

gal·lus·es \'gal-ə-səz\ *n pl, chiefly dial* : SUSPENDERS

ga·lore \gə-'lōr\ *adj* [IrGael *go leor* enough] : ABUNDANT, PLENTIFUL

ga·losh \gə-'läsh\ *n* : a high overshoe

galv *abbr* galvanized

gal·va·nize \'gal-və-ˌnīz\ *vb* **-nized; -niz·ing** **1** : to stimulate as if by an electric shock **2** : to coat (iron or steel) with zinc — **gal·va·ni·za·tion** \ˌgal-və-nə-'zā-shən\ *n* — **gal·va·niz·er** \'gal-və-ˌnī-zər\ *n*

gal·va·nom·e·ter \ˌgal-və-'näm-ət-ər\ *n* : an instrument for detecting or measuring a small electric current

Gam·bi·an \'gam-bē-ən\ *n* : a native or inhabitant of Gambia — **Gambian** *adj*

gam·bit \'gam-bət\ *n* [It *gambetto*, lit., act of tripping someone, fr. *gamba* leg] **1** : a chess opening in which a player risks one or more minor pieces to gain an advantage in position **2** : a calculated move : STRATAGEM

¹gam·ble \'gam-bəl\ *vb* **gam·bled; gam·bling** \-b(ə-)liŋ\ **1** : to play a game for money or other stakes **2** : SPECULATE, BET, WAGER **3** : VENTURE, HAZARD — **gam·bler** \-blər\ *n*

²gamble *n* : a risky undertaking

gam·bol \'gam-bəl\ *vb* **-boled** *or* **-bolled; -bol·ing** *or* **-bol·ling** \-b(ə-)liŋ\ : to skip about in play : FRISK — **gambol** *n*

gam·brel roof \'gam-brəl-\ *n* : a roof with a lower steeper slope and an upper flatter one on each side

¹game \'gām\ *n* **1** : AMUSEMENT, DIVERSION **2** : SPORT, FUN **3** : SCHEME, PROJECT **4** : a line of work : PROFESSION **5** : CONTEST **6** : animals hunted for sport or food; *also* : the flesh of a game animal

²game *vb* **gamed; gam·ing** : to play for a stake : GAMBLE

³game *adj* : PLUCKY — **game·ly** *adv* — **game·ness** *n*

⁴game *adj* : LAME (a ~ leg)

game·cock \'gām-ˌkäk\ *n* : a rooster trained for fighting

game fish *n* : SPORT FISH

game·keep·er \'gām-ˌkē-pər\ *n* : a person in charge of the breeding and protection of game animals or birds on a private preserve

game·some \'gām-səm\ *adj* : MERRY

game·ster \'gām-stər\ *n* : GAMBLER

gam·ete \'gam-ˌēt\ *n* : a matured germ cell — **ga·met·ic** \gə-'met-ik\ *adj*

game theory *n* : the analysis of a situation involving conflicting interests (as in business) in terms of gains and losses among opposing players

gam·in \'gam-ən\ *n* [F] **1** : a boy who

---

hangs out on the streets **2** : GAMINE 2

ga·mine \ga-'mēn\ *n* **1** : a girl who hangs out on the streets **2** : a small playfully mischievous girl

gam·ma globulin \'gam-ə-\ *n* : a blood protein fraction rich in antibodies; *also* : a solution of this from human blood donors that is given to provide immunity against some infectious diseases (as measles)

gamma rays *n pl* : very penetrating radiation similar to X rays but of shorter wavelength

gam·mer \'gam-ər\ *n, archaic* : an old woman

gam·mon \'gam-ən\ *n, chiefly Brit* : a cured ham or side of bacon

gam·ut \'gam-ət\ *n* [ML *gamma*, lowest note of a medieval scale (fr. LL, 3d letter of the Greek alphabet) + *ut*, lowest of each series of six tones in the scale] : an entire range or series

gamy *or* **gam·ey** \'gā-mē\ *adj* **gam·i·er; -est** **1** : GAME, PLUCKY **2** : having the flavor of game esp. when slightly tainted (~ meat) **3** : SCANDALOUS; *also* : DISREPUTABLE — **gam·i·ness** \-mē-nəs\ *n*

¹gan·der \'gan-dər\ *n* : a male goose

²gander *n* : LOOK, GLANCE

¹gang \'gaŋ\ *n* **1** : a set of implements or devices arranged to operate together **2** : a group of persons working or associated together; *esp* : a group of criminals or young delinquents

²gang *vb* **1** : to attack in a gang — usu. used with *up* **2** : to form into or move or act as a gang

gang·land \'gaŋ-ˌland\ *n* : the world of organized crime

gan·gling \'gaŋ-gliŋ\ *adj* : LANKY, SPINDLING

gan·gli·on \'gaŋ-glē-ən\ *n, pl* **-glia** \-glē-ə\ *also* **-gli·ons** : a mass of nerve cells outside the central nervous system; *also* : NUCLEUS 3 — **gan·gli·on·ic** \ˌgaŋ-glē-'än-ik\ *adj*

gang·plank \'gaŋ-ˌplaŋk\ *n* : a movable bridge from a ship to the shore

gang·plow \-ˌplaù\ *n* : a plow that turns two or more furrows at one time

gan·grene \'gaŋ-ˌgrēn, gaŋ-'grēn\ *n* : the death of soft tissues in a local area of the body due to loss of the blood supply — **gangrene** *vb* — **gan·gre·nous** \'gaŋ-grə-nəs\ *adj*

gang·ster \'gaŋ-stər\ *n* : a member of a gang of criminals : RACKETEER

gang·way \'gaŋ-ˌwā\ *n* **1** : a passage into, through, or out of an enclosed place **2** : GANGPLANK

gan·net \'gan-ət\ *n, pl* **gannets** *also* **gannet** : any of several large fish-eating usu. white and black marine birds that breed on offshore islands

gant·let \'gȯnt-lət\ *var of* GAUNTLET

gan·try \'gan-trē\ *n, pl* **gantries** : a frame structure on side supports over or around something

GAO *abbr* General Accounting Office

gaol \'jāl\, **gaol·er** \'jā-lər\ *chiefly Brit var of* JAIL, JAILER

gap \'gap\ *n* **1** : BREACH, CLEFT **2** : a mountain pass **3** : a blank space **4** : a wide difference in character or attitude

gape \'gāp, 'gap\ *vb* **gaped; gap·ing** **1** : to open the mouth wide **2** : to open or part widely **3** : to stare with mouth open **4** : YAWN — **gape** *n*

¹**gar** \'gär\ *n* : any of several fishes that have a long body resembling that of a pike and long narrow jaws

²**gar** *abbr* garage

GAR *abbr* Grand Army of the Republic

¹**ga·rage** \gə-'räzh, -'räj\ *n* [F] : a building for housing or repairing automobiles

²**garage** *vb* **ga·raged; ga·rag·ing** : to keep or put in a garage

garage sale *n* : a sale of used household articles held on one's own premises

garb \'gärb\ *n* **1** : style of dress **2** : outward form : APPEARANCE — **garb** *vb*

gar·bage \'gär-bij\ *n* **1** : food waste **2** : unwanted or useless material

gar·ble \'gär-bəl\ *vb* **gar·bled; gar·bling** \-b(ə-)liŋ\ [ME *garbelen*, fr. It *garbellare* to sift, fr. Ar *ghirbāl* sieve] : to distort the meaning or sound of \~ a story\ \~ words\

gar·çon \gär-'sōⁿ\ *n, pl* **garçons** \-'sōⁿ(z)\ [F, boy, waiter] : WAITER

¹**gar·den** \'gärd-ᵊn\ *n* **1** : a plot for growing fruits, flowers, or vegetables **2** : a public recreation area; *esp* : one for displaying plants or animals

²**garden** *vb* **gar·dened; gar·den·ing** \'gärd-(ᵊ-)niŋ\ : to develop or work in a garden — **gar·den·er** \'gärd-(ᵊ-)nər\ *n*

gar·de·nia \gär-'dē-nyə\ *n* [NL, genus name, fr. Alexander *Garden* †1791 Scot. naturalist] : the fragrant white or yellow flower of any of a genus of trees or shrubs of the madder family; *also* : one of these trees

garden–variety *adj* : COMMONPLACE, ORDINARY

gar·fish \'gär-ˌfish\ *n* : GAR

gar·gan·tuan \gär-'ganch-(ə-)wən\ *adj, often cap* : of tremendous size or volume

gar·gle \'gär-gəl\ *vb* **gar·gled; gar·gling** \-g(ə-)liŋ\ : to rinse the throat with liquid agitated by air forced through it from the lungs — **gargle** *n*

gar·goyle \'gär-ˌgȯil\ *n* **1** : a waterspout in the form of a grotesque human or animal figure projecting from the roof or eaves of a building **2** : a grotesquely carved figure

gar·ish \'ga(ə)r-ish\ *adj* : FLASHY, GLARING, SHOWY, GAUDY

¹**gar·land** \'gär-lənd\ *n* : a wreath or rope of leaves or flowers

²**garland** *vb* : to form into or deck with a garland

gar·lic \'gär-lik\ *n* [ME *garlek*, fr. OE *gārlēac*, fr. *gār* spear + *lēac* leek] : an herb related to the lilies and grown for its pungent bulbs used in cooking; *also* : its bulb — **gar·licky** \-li-kē\ *adj*

gar·ment \'gär-mənt\ *n* : an article of clothing

gar·ner \'gär-nər\ *vb* **gar·nered; gar·ner·ing** \'gärn-(ə-)riŋ\ **1** : to gather into storage **2** : to acquire by effort **3** : ACCUMULATE, COLLECT

gar·net \'gär-nət\ *n* [ME *grenat*, fr. MF, fr. *grenat*, adj., red like a pomegranate, fr. *(pomme) grenate* pomegranate] : a transparent deep red mineral sometimes used as a gem

gar·nish \'gär-nish\ *vb* **1** : DECORATE, EMBELLISH **2** : to add decorative or savory touches to (food) — **garnish** *n*

gar·nish·ee \ˌgär-nə-'shē\ *vb* **-eed; -ee·ing** **1** : to serve with a garnishment **2** : to take (as a debtor's wages) by legal authority

gar·nish·ment \'gär-nish-mənt\ *n* **1** : GARNISH **2** : a legal warning to the holder of property of a debtor to give it to a creditor; *also* : the attachment of such property to satisfy a creditor

gar·ni·ture \-ni-chər, -nə-ˌchù(ə)r\ *n* : EMBELLISHMENT, TRIMMING

gar·ret \'gar-ət\ *n* [ME *garette* watchtower, fr. MF *garite*] : the part of a house just under the roof : ATTIC

gar·ri·son \'gar-ə-sən\ *n* **1** : a military post; *esp* : a permanent military installation **2** : the troops stationed at a garrison — **garrison** *vb*

garrison state *n* : a state organized on a primarily military basis

gar·rote *or* **ga·rotte** \gə-'rät, -'rōt\ *n* [Sp *garrote*] **1** : a method of execution by strangling with an iron collar; *also* : the iron collar used **2** : strangulation esp. for the purpose of robbery; *also* : an implement for this purpose — **garrote** *or* **garotte** *vb*

gar·ru·lous \'gar-ə-ləs\ *adj* : CHATTERING, TALKATIVE, WORDY — **gar·ru·li·ty** \gə-'rü-lət-ē\ *n* — **gar·ru·lous·ly** \'gar-ə-ləs-lē\ *adv* — **gar·ru·lous·ness** *n*

gar·ter \'gärt-ər\ *n* : a band or strap worn to hold up a stocking or sock

garter snake *n* : any of numerous harmless American snakes with longitudinal stripes on the back

¹**gas** \'gas\ *n, pl* **gas·es** *also* **gas·ses** [NL, alter. of L *chaos* space, chaos] **1** : a fluid (as hydrogen or air) that tends to expand indefinitely **2** : a gas or mixture of gases used as a fuel or anesthetic **3** : a substance that can be used to produce a poisonous, asphyxiating, or irritant atmosphere **4** : GASOLINE — **gas·eous** \-ē-əs, 'gash-əs\ *adj*

²**gas** *vb* **gassed; gas·sing** **1** : to treat with gas; *also* : to poison with gas **2** : to fill with gasoline

gash \'gash\ *n* : a deep long cut — **gash** *vb*

gas·ket \'gas-kət\ *n* : material (as rubber or metal) used to prevent a joint from leaking

gas·light \'gas-ˌlīt\ *n* **1** : light made by

burning illuminating gas **2** : a gas flame; *also* : a gas lighting fixture

gas mask *n* : a mask connected to a chemical air filter and used to protect the face and lungs against poison gases

gas·o·line *also* **gas·o·lene** \'gas-ə-ˌlēn, ˌgas-ə-'lēn\ *n* : a flammable liquid made esp. by blending products from natural gas and petroleum and used as a motor fuel

gasp \'gasp\ *vb* **1** : to catch the breath with emotion (as shock) **2** : to breathe laboriously : PANT **3** : to utter in a gasping manner — **gasp** *n*

gas·tric \'gas-trik\ *adj* : of, relating to, or located near the stomach

gastric juice *n* : the acid digestive secretion of the stomach

gas·tri·tis \gas-'trīt-əs\ *n* : inflammatory disorder of the stomach

gas·tro·en·ter·ol·o·gy \ˌgas-trō-ˌent-ə-'räl-ə-jē\ *n* : a branch of medicine dealing with the alimentary canal — **gas·tro·en·ter·ol·o·gist** \-jəst\ *n*

gas·tro·in·tes·ti·nal \ˌgas-trō-in-'tes-tən-ᵊl\ *adj* : of, relating to, affecting, or including both stomach and intestine

gas·tron·o·my \gas-'trän-ə-mē\ *n* [F *gastronomie*, fr. Gk *Gastronomia*, title of a 4th cent. B.C. poem, fr. *gastēr* belly] : the art of good eating — **gas·tro·nom·ic** \ˌgas-trə-'näm-ik\ *also* **gas·tro·nom·i·cal** \-i-kəl\ *adj*

gas·tro·pod \'gas-trə-ˌpäd\ *n* : any of a large class of mollusks (as snails, whelks, and slugs) with a muscular foot and a spiral shell or none

gas·works \'gas-ˌwərks\ *n pl* : a plant for manufacturing gas

gate \'gāt\ *n* **1** : an opening for passage in a wall or fence **2** : a city or castle entrance often with defensive structures **3** : the frame or door that closes a gate **4** : a device (as a valve) for controlling the passage of a fluid or signal **5** : the total admission receipts or the number of people at an event

gate-crash·er \'gāt-ˌkrash-ər\ *n* : one who enters without paying admission or attends without invitation

gate·keep·er \-ˌkē-pər\ *n* : a person who tends or guards a gate

gate·post \'gāt-ˌpōst\ *n* : the post to which a gate is hung or the one against which it closes

gate·way \-ˌwā\ *n* **1** : an opening for a gate **2** : a means of entrance or exit

¹**gath·er** \'gath-ər\ *vb* **gath·ered; gath·er·ing** \-(ə-)riŋ\ **1** : to bring together : COLLECT **2** : PICK, HARVEST **3** : to pick up little by little **4** : to gain or win by gradual increase : ACCUMULATE (~ speed) **5** : to summon up (~ courage to dive) **6** : to draw about or close to something **7** : to pull (fabric) along a line of stitching into puckers **8** : GUESS, DEDUCE, INFER **9** : ASSEMBLE **10** : to swell out and fill with pus **11**

: GROW, INCREASE — **gath·er·er** *n* — **gath·er·ing** *n*

²**gather** *n* : a puckering in cloth made by gathering

GATT *abbr* General Agreement on Tariffs and Trade

gauche \'gōsh\ *adj* [F, lit., left] : lacking social experience or grace

gau·che·rie \ˌgōsh-(ə-)'rē\ *n* : a tactless or awkward action

gau·cho \'gaù-chō\ *n, pl* **gauchos** : a cowboy of the So. American pampas

gaud \'gòd\ *n* : ORNAMENT, TRINKET

gaudy \'gòd-ē\ *adj* **gaud·i·er; -est** : ostentatiously or tastelessly ornamented **syn** garish, flashy, glaring, tawdry — **gaud·i·ly** \'gòd-ᵊl-ē\ *adv* — **gaud·i·ness** \-ē-nəs\ *n*

¹**gauge** *or* **gage** \'gāj\ *n* **1** : measurement according to some standard or system **2** : DIMENSIONS, SIZE **3** *usu* **gage** : an instrument for measuring, testing, or registering

²**gauge** *or* **gage** *vb* **gauged** *or* **gaged; gaug·ing** *or* **gag·ing 1** : MEASURE **2** : to determine the capacity or contents of **3** : ESTIMATE, JUDGE

gaunt \'gònt\ *adj* **1** : being thin and angular (as from hunger or suffering) **2** : BARREN, DESOLATE — **gaunt·ness** *n*

¹**gaunt·let** \'gònt-lət\ *n* **1** : a protective glove **2** : a challenge to combat **3** : a dress glove extending above the wrist

²**gauntlet** *n* **1** : a double file of men armed with weapons (as clubs) with which to strike at an individual who is made to run between them **2** : ORDEAL

gauze \'gòz\ *n* : a very thin often transparent fabric used esp. for draperies and surgical dressings — **gauzy** *adj*

gave *past of* GIVE

gav·el \'gav-əl\ *n* : the mallet of a presiding officer or auctioneer

ga·votte \gə-'vät\ *n* : a dance of French peasant origin marked by the raising rather than sliding of the feet

gawk \'gòk\ *vb* : to gape or stare stupidly

gawky \'gò-kē\ *adj* **gawk·i·er; -est** : AWKWARD, CLUMSY

gay \'gā\ *adj* **1** : MERRY **2** : BRIGHT, LIVELY **3** : brilliant in color **4** : given to social pleasures; *also* : LICENTIOUS **5** : HOMOSEXUAL

gay·ety, gay·ly *var of* GAIETY, GAILY

gaz *abbr* gazette

gaze \'gāz\ *vb* **gazed; gaz·ing** : to fix the eyes in a steady intent look — **gaze** *n* — **gaz·er** *n*

ga·ze·bo \gə-'zā-bō, -'zē-\ *n, pl* **-bos 1** : BELVEDERE **2** : a freestanding roofed structure usu. open on the sides

ga·zelle \gə-'zel\ *n, pl* **gazelles** *also* **gazelle** : any of several small swift graceful antelopes

¹**ga·zette** \gə-'zet\ *n* **1** : NEWSPAPER **2** : an official journal

²**gazette** *vb* **ga·zett·ed; ga·zett·ing** *chiefly Brit* : to announce or publish in a gazette

gaz·et·teer \ˌgaz-ə-ˈtiər\ *n* : a geographical dictionary

GB *abbr* Great Britain

GCA *abbr* ground-controlled approach

gd *abbr* good

Gd *symbol* gadolinium

GDR *abbr* German Democratic Republic

Ge *symbol* germanium

gear \ˈgiər\ *n* **1** : CLOTHING **2** : movable property (as GOODS **3** : EQUIPMENT ⟨fishing ∼⟩ ⟨photographic ∼⟩ **4** : a mechanism that performs a specific function (steering ∼) **5** : a toothed wheel that interlocks with another toothed wheel or shaft for transmitting motion **6** : working adjustment of gears (in ∼) **7** : an adjustment of transmission gears (as of an automobile or bicycle) that determines speed and direction of travel — **gear** *vb* — **gear·ing** \-iŋ\ *n*

gear·box \ˈgiər-ˌbäks\ *n* : TRANSMISSION 3

gear·shift \-ˌshift\ *n* : a mechanism by which transmission gears are shifted

gear wheel *n* : COGWHEEL

GED *abbr* general equivalency diploma

geese *pl of* GOOSE

gee·zer \ˈgē-zər\ *n* : an odd or eccentric man

Gei·ger counter \ˈgī-gər-\ *or* **Gei·ger–Mül·ler counter** \-ˈmyül-ər-, -ˈmil-, -ˈməl-\ *n* : an electronic instrument for detecting the presence of cosmic rays or radioactive substances

gei·sha \ˈgā-shə, ˈgē-\ *n, pl* **geisha** *or* **geishas** [Jp, fr. *gei* art + *-sha* person] : a Japanese girl who is trained to provide entertaining company for men

gel \ˈjel\ *n* : a solid jellylike colloid (as gelatin dessert) — **gel** *vb*

gel·a·tin *also* **gel·a·tine** \ˈjel-ət-ᵊn\ *n* : glutinous material and esp. protein obtained from animal tissues by boiling and used as a food, in dyeing, and in photography; *also* : an edible jelly formed with gelatin — **ge·lat·i·nous** \jə-ˈlat-(ᵊ-)nəs\ *adj*

geld \ˈgeld\ *vb* : CASTRATE

geld·ing \ˈgel-diŋ\ *n* : a gelded individual; *esp* : a castrated male h.

gel·id \ˈjel-əd\ *adj* : extremely cold

gem \ˈjem\ *n* **1** : JEWEL **2** : a usu. valuable stone cut and polished for ornament **3** : something valued for beauty or perfection

Gem·i·ni \ˈjem-ə-(ˌ)nē, -ˌnī; ˈgem-ə-ˌnē\ *n* **1** : a zodiacal constellation between Taurus and Cancer usu. pictured as twins sitting together **2** : the 3d sign of the zodiac in astrology; *also* : one born under this sign

gem·ol·o·gy *or* **gem·mol·o·gy** \je-ˈmäl-ə-jē, jə-\ *n* : the science of gems — **gem·olog·i·cal** *or* **gem·mo·log·i·cal** \ˌjem-ə-ˈläj-i-kəl\ *adj* — **gem·ol·o·gist** *or* **gem·mol·o·gist** \-jəst\ *n*

gem·stone \ˈjem-ˌstōn\ *n* : a mineral or petrified material that when cut and polished can be used in jewelry

gen *abbr* **1** general **2** genitive

Gen *abbr* Genesis

Gen AF *abbr* general of the air force

gen·darme \ˈzhän-ˌdärm, ˈjän-\ *n* [F, intended as sing. of *gensdarmes*, pl. of *gent d'armes*, lit., armed people] : one of a body of soldiers esp. in France serving as an armed police force

gen·dar·mer·ie *or* **gen·dar·mery** \jän-ˈdärm-ə-rē, zhän-\ *n, pl* **-mer·ies** : a body of gendarmes

gen·der \ˈjen-dər\ *n* **1** : SEX 1 **2** : any of two or more divisions within a grammatical class that determine agreement with and selection of other words or grammatical forms

gene \ˈjēn\ *n* : a part of DNA or sometimes RNA that contains chemical information needed to make a particular protein (as an enzyme) controlling or influencing an inherited bodily trait or activity (as eye color) or that influences or controls the activity of another gene or genes — **gen·ic** \ˈjē-nik, ˈjen-\ *adj*

ge·ne·al·o·gy \ˌjē-nē-ˈäl-ə-jē, -ˈal-\ *n, pl* **-gies** : PEDIGREE, LINEAGE; *also* : the study of family pedigrees — **ge·ne·alog·i·cal** \ˌjē-nē-ə-ˈläj-i-kəl, ˌjen-ē-\ *adj* — **ge·ne·alog·i·cal·ly** \-k(ə-)lē\ *adv* — **ge·ne·al·o·gist** \ˌjē-nē-ˈäl-ə-jəst, ˌjen-ē-; -ˈal-\ *n*

genera *pl of* GENUS

¹**gen·er·al** \ˈjen-(ə-)rəl\ *adj* **1** : of or relating to the whole : not local **2** : taken as a whole **3** : relating to or covering all instances (a ∼ conclusion) **4** : not limited in meaning : not specific (a ∼ outline) **5** : common to many (a ∼ custom) **6** : not special or specialized **7** : holding superior rank (inspector ∼) — **gen·er·al·ly** \-ē\ *adv*

²**general** *n* **1** : something that involves or is applicable to the whole **2** : a commissioned officer ranking next below a general of the army or a general of the air force **3** : a commissioned officer of the highest rank in the marine corps — **in general** : for the most part

general assembly *n* **1** : a legislative assembly; *esp* : a U.S. state legislature **2** *cap G&A* : the supreme deliberative body of the United Nations

gen·er·a·lis·si·mo \ˌjen-(ə-)rə-ˈlis-ə-ˌmō\ *n, pl* **-mos** [It, fr. *generale* general] : COMMANDER IN CHIEF

gen·er·al·i·ty \ˌjen-ə-ˈral-ət-ē\ *n, pl* **-ties** **1** : the quality or state of being general **2** : GENERALIZATION **2 3** : a vague or inadequate statement **4** : the greatest part : BULK

gen·er·al·iza·tion \ˌjen-(ə-)rə-lə-ˈzā-shən\ *n* **1** : the act or process of generalizing **2** : a general statement, law, principle, or proposition

gen·er·al·ize \ˈjen-(ə-)rə-ˌlīz\ *vb* **-ized; -iz·ing 1** : to make general **2** : to draw general conclusions from **3** : to reach a general conclusion esp. on the basis of particular instances **4** : to extend throughout the body

general of the air force : a commissioned officer of the highest rank in the air force

general of the army : a commissioned officer of the highest rank in the army

general practitioner *n* : a physician or veterinarian who does not limit his practice to a specialty

gen·er·al·ship \'jen-(ə-)rəl-,ship\ *n* **1** : office or tenure of office of a general **2** : military skill as a high commander **3** : LEADERSHIP

general store *n* : a retail store that carries a wide variety of goods but is not divided into departments

gen·er·ate \'jen-ə-,rāt\ *vb* **-at·ed; -at·ing** : to bring into existence : PRODUCE

gen·er·a·tion \,jen-ə-'rā-shən\ *n* **1** : a body of living beings constituting a single step in the line of descent from an ancestor; *also* : the average period between generations **2** : PRODUCTION (~ of electric current)

gen·er·a·tive \'jen-(ə-)rət-iv, 'jen-ə-,rāt-iv\ *adj* : having the power or function of generating, originating, producing, or reproducing (~ organs)

gen·er·a·tor \'jen-ə-,rāt-ər\ *n* : one that generates; *esp* : a machine by which mechanical energy is changed into electrical energy

ge·ner·ic \jə-'ner-ik\ *adj* **1** : not specific : GENERAL **2** : not protected by a trademark (a ~ drug) **3** : of or relating to a genus — **generic** *n*

gen·er·ous \'jen-(ə-)rəs\ *adj* **1** : free in giving or sharing **2** : HIGH-MINDED, NOBLE **3** : ABUNDANT, AMPLE, COPIOUS — **gen·er·os·i·ty** \,jen-ə-'räs-ət-ē\ *n* — **gen·er·ous·ly** \'jen-(ə-)rəs-lē\ *adv* — **gen·er·ous·ness** *n*

gen·e·sis \'jen-ə-səs\ *n, pl* **-e·ses** \-,sēz\ : the origin or coming into existence of something

Gen·e·sis \'jen-ə-səs\ *n* — see BIBLE table

gene–splic·ing \-,splī-siŋ\ *n* : the technique by which recombinant DNA is produced and made to function in an organism

ge·net·ic \jə-'net-ik\ *adj* : of or relating to the origin, development, or causes of something; *also* : of or relating to genetics — **ge·net·i·cal·ly** \-i-k(ə-)lē\ *adv*

genetic code *n* : the chemical code that is the basis of genetic inheritance and consists of triplets of three linked chemical groups which specify particular kinds of amino acids used to make proteins or which start or stop the process of making proteins

genetic engineering *n* : the directed alteration of genetic material by intervention in genetic processes; *esp* : GENE-SPLICING

ge·net·ics \jə-'net-iks\ *n* : a branch of biology dealing with heredity and variation — **ge·net·i·cist** \-'net-ə-səst\ *n*

ge·nial \'jē-nyəl\ *adj* **1** : favorable to

growth or comfort (~ sunshine) **2** : CHEERFUL, KINDLY (a ~ host) — **ge·nial·i·ty** \,jē-nē-'al-ət-ē, jēn-'yal-\ *n* — **ge·nial·ly** \'jē-nyə-lē\ *adv*

-gen·ic \'jen-ik\ *adj comb form* **1** : producing : forming **2** : produced by : formed from **3** : suitable for production or reproduction by (such) a medium

ge·nie \'jē-nē\ *n, pl* **ge·nies** *also* **ge·nii** \'jē-nē-,ī\ [F *génie*, fr. Ar *jinnīy*] : a supernatural spirit that often takes human form

gen·i·tal \'jen-ə-t³l\ *adj* **1** : concerned with reproduction (~ organs) **2** : of, relating to, or characterized by the stage of psychosexual development in which oral and anal impulses are subordinated to adaptive interpersonal mechanisms — **gen·i·tal·ly** \-tə-lē\ *adv*

gen·i·ta·lia \,jen-ə-'tāl-yə\ *n pl* : reproductive organs; *esp* : the external genital organs — **gen·i·ta·lic** \-'tal-ik, -'tāl-\ *adj*

gen·i·tals \'jen-ə-t³lz\ *n pl* : GENITALIA

gen·i·tive \'jen-ət-iv\ *adj* : of, relating to, or constituting a grammatical case marking typically a relationship of possessor or source — **genitive** *n*

gen·i·to·uri·nary \,jen-ə-tō-'yùr-ə-,ner-ē\ *adj* : of or relating to the genital and urinary organs or functions

ge·nius \'jē-nyəs\ *n, pl* **ge·nius·es** *or* **ge·nii** \-nē-,ī\ [L, tutelary spirit, fondness for social enjoyment, fr. *gignere* to beget] **1** *pl* **genii** : an attendant spirit of a person or place; *also* : a person who influences another for good or evil **2** : a strong leaning or inclination **3** : a peculiar or distinctive character or spirit (as of a nation or a language) **4** *pl usu* **genii** : SPIRIT, GENIE **5** : a single strongly marked capacity or aptitude **6** : extraordinary intellectual power; *also* : a person having such power

genl *abbr* general

geno·cide \'jen-ə-,sīd\ *n* : the deliberate and systematic destruction of a racial, political, or cultural group

-ge·nous \j-ə-nəs\ *adj comb form* **1** : producing : yielding **2** : having (such) an origin

genre \'zhän-rə, 'zhä⁻-; 'zhä⁻(-ə)r\ *n* **1** : a distinctive type or category esp. of literary composition **2** : a style of painting in which everyday subjects are treated realistically

gens \'jenz, 'gens\ *n, pl* **gen·tes** \'jen-,tēz, 'gen-,tās\ : a Roman clan embracing the families of the same stock in the male line

gent *n* : GENTLEMAN

gen·teel \jen-'tēl\ *adj* **1** : ARISTOCRATIC **2** : ELEGANT, STYLISH **3** : POLITE, REFINED **4** : maintaining the appearance of superior or middle-class social status **5** : marked by false delicacy, prudery, or affectation

gen·tian \'jen-chən\ *n* : any of numerous herbs with opposite leaves and showy usu. blue flowers in the fall

gen·tile \'jen-,tīl\ *n* [LL *gentilis* heathen, pagan, lit., belonging to the nations, fr. L *gent-, gens* family, clan, nation] **1** *often cap* : a person who is not Jewish **2** : HEATHEN, PAGAN — **gentile** *adj, often cap*

gen·til·i·ty \jen-'til-ət-ē\ *n, pl* **-ties 1** : good birth and family **2** : the qualities characteristic of a well-bred person **3** : good manners **4** : maintenance of the appearance of superior or middle-class social status

¹gen·tle \'jent-ᵊl\ *adj* **gen·tler** \'jent-(ᵊ-)lər\; **gen·tlest** \'jent-(ᵊ-)ləst\ **1** : belonging to a family of high social station **2** : of, relating to, or characteristic of a gentleman **3** : KIND, AMIABLE **4** : TRACTABLE, DOCILE **5** : not harsh, stern, or violent **6** : SOFT, DELICATE **7** : MODERATE — **gen·tly** \'jent-lē\ *adv*

²gentle *vb* **gen·tled**; **gen·tling** \'jent-(ᵊ-)liŋ\ **1** : to make mild, docile, soft, or moderate **2** : MOLLIFY, PLACATE

gen·tle·folk \'jent-ᵊl-,fōk\ *also* **gen·tle·folks** \-,fōks\ *n* : persons of good family and breeding

gen·tle·man \'jent-ᵊl-mən\ *n* **1** : a man of good family **2** : a well-bred man **3** : MAN — used in pl. as a form of address — **gen·tle·man·ly** *adj*

gen·tle·wom·an \'jent-ᵊl-,wum-ən\ *n* **1** : a woman of good family **2** : a woman attending a lady of rank **3** : a woman with very good manners : LADY

gen·tri·fi·ca·tion \,jen-trə-fə-'kā-shən\ *n* : the immigration of middle-class people into a run-down or recently renewed city area — **gen·tri·fy** \'jen-trə-fī\ *vb*

gen·try \'jen-trē\ *n, pl* **gentries 1** : people of good birth, breeding, and education : ARISTOCRACY **2** : the class of English people between the nobility and the yeomanry **3** : PEOPLE; *esp* : persons of a designated class

gen·u·flect \'jen-yə-,flekt\ *vb* : to bend the knee esp. in worship — **gen·u·flec·tion** \,jen-yə-'flek-shən\ *n*

gen·u·ine \'jen-yə-wən\ *adj* **1** : AUTHENTIC, REAL **2** : SINCERE, HONEST — **gen·u·ine·ly** *adv* — **gen·u·ine·ness** \-wən-(n)əs\ *n*

ge·nus \'jē-nəs\ *n, pl* **gen·era** \'jen-ə-rə\ [L, birth, race, kind] : a category of biological classification that ranks between the family and the species and contains related species

geo·cen·tric \,jē-ō-'sen-trik\ *adj* **1** : relating to or measured from the earth's center **2** : having or relating to the earth as a center

geo·chem·is·try \-'kem-ə-strē\ *n* : a branch of geology that deals with the chemical composition of and chemical changes in the earth — **geo·chem·i·cal** \-'kem-i-kəl\ *adj* — **geo·chem·ist** \-'kem-əst\ *n*

ge·ode \'jē-,ōd\ *n* : a nodule of stone having a cavity lined with mineral matter

¹geo·des·ic \,jē-ə-'des-ik\ *adj* : made of a framework of light straight-sided polygons in tension ⟨a ~ dome⟩

²geodesic *n* : the shortest line between two points on a surface

ge·od·e·sy \jē-'äd-ə-sē\ *n* : a branch of applied mathematics that determines the exact positions of points and the figures and areas of large portions of the earth's surface, the shape and size of the earth, and the variations of terrestrial gravity and magnetism — **geo·det·ic** \,jē-ə-'det-ik\ *adj*

geodetic survey *n* : a survey of a large land area in which corrections are made for the curving of the earth's surface

geog *abbr* geographic; geographical; geography

ge·og·ra·phy \jē-'äg-rə-fē\ *n, pl* **-phies 1** : a science that deals with the natural features of the earth and the climate, products, and inhabitants **2** : the natural features of a region — **ge·og·ra·pher** \-fər\ *n* — **geo·graph·ic** \,jē-ə-'graf-ik\ *or* **geo·graph·i·cal** \-i-kəl\ *adj* — **geo·graph·i·cal·ly** \-i-k(ə-)lē\ *adv*

geol *abbr* geologic; geological; geology

ge·ol·o·gy \jē-'äl-ə-jē\ *n, pl* **-gies 1** : a science that deals with the history of the earth and its life esp. as recorded in rocks; *also* : a study of the solid matter of a celestial body (as the moon) **2** : the geologic features of an area — **ge·o·log·ic** \jē-ə-'läj-ik\ *or* **ge·o·log·i·cal** \-i-kəl\ *adj* — **ge·o·log·i·cal·ly** \-i-k(ə-)lē\ *adv* — **ge·ol·o·gist** \jē-'äl-ə-jəst\ *n*

geom *abbr* geometric; geometrical; geometry

geo·mag·net·ic \,jē-ō-mag-'net-ik\ *adj* : of or relating to the magnetism of the earth — **geo·mag·ne·tism** \-'mag-nə-,tiz-əm\ *n*

geometric mean *n* : the *n*th root of the product of *n* numbers; *esp* : a number that is the second term of three consecutive terms of a geometric progression ⟨the *geometric mean* of 9 and 4 is 6⟩

geometric progression *n* : a progression (as 1, ½, ¼) in which the ratio of a term to its predecessor is always the same

ge·om·e·try \jē-'äm-ə-trē\ *n, pl* **-tries** : a branch of mathematics dealing with the relations, properties, and measurements of solids, surfaces, lines, points, and angles — **ge·om·e·ter** \jē-'äm-ət-ər\ *n* — **geo·met·ric** \,jē-ə-'me-trik\ *or* **geo·met·ri·cal** \-tri-kəl\ *adj*

geo·phys·ics \,jē-ō-'fiz-iks\ *n* : the physics of the earth — **geo·phys·i·cal** \-i-kəl\ *adj* — **geo·phys·i·cist** \-'fiz-ə-səst\ *n*

geo·pol·i·tics \-'päl-ə-,tiks\ *n* : a combination of political and geographic factors relating to a state

geo·ther·mal \-'thər-məl\ also **geo·ther·mic** \-mik\ adj : of, relating to, or using the heat of the earth's interior

ger abbr gerund

Ger abbr German; Germany

ge·ra·ni·um \jə-'rā-nē-əm\ n [L, fr. Gk geranion, fr. geranos crane] **1** : any of a genus of herbs with usu. deeply cut leaves and pink, purple, or white flowers followed by long slender dry fruits **2** : any of a genus of herbs of the same family as the geraniums that have clusters of scarlet, pink, or white flowers with the sepals joined at the base into a hollow tube closed at one end

ger·bil also **ger·bile** \'jər-bəl\ n : any of numerous Old World burrowing desert rodents with long hind legs

ge·ri·at·ric \,jer-ē-'a-trik\ adj : of or relating to aging, the aged, or geriatrics

ge·ri·at·rics \-triks\ n : a branch of medicine dealing with the problems and diseases of old age and aging

germ \'jərm\ n **1** : a bit of living matter capable of growth and development (as into an organism) **2** : SOURCE, RUDIMENTS **3** : MICROORGANISM; esp : one causing disease

Ger·man \'jər-mən\ n **1** : a native or inhabitant of Germany **2** : the language of Germany, Austria, and parts of Switzerland — **German** adj — **German·ic** \jər-'man-ik\ adj

ger·mane \jər-'mān\ adj [ME germain, lit., having the same parents, fr. MF] : RELEVANT, PERTINENT

ger·ma·ni·um \jər-'mā-nē-əm\ n : a grayish white hard chemical element used as a semiconductor

German measles n sing or pl : an acute contagious virus disease milder than typical measles but damaging to the fetus when occurring early in pregnancy

German shepherd n : an intelligent responsive working dog often used in police work and as a guide dog for the blind

germ cell n : an egg or sperm or one of their antecedent cells

ger·mi·cide \'jər-mə-,sīd\ n : an agent that destroys germs — **ger·mi·cid·al** \,jər-mə-'sīd-ᵊl\ adj

ger·mi·nal \'jərm-(ə-)nəl\ adj : of or relating to a germ or germ cell; also : EMBRYONIC

ger·mi·nate \'jər-mə-,nāt\ vb **-nat·ed; -nat·ing 1** : to begin to develop : SPROUT **2** : to come into being : EVOLVE — **ger·mi·na·tion** \,jər-mə-'nā-shən\ n

ger·on·tol·o·gy \,jer-ən-'täl-ə-jē\ n : a scientific study of aging and the problems of the aged — **ge·ron·to·log·i·cal** \jə-,ränt-ᵊl-'äj-i-kəl\ adj — **ger·on·tol·o·gist** \,jer-ən-'täl-ə-jəst\ n

ger·ry·man·der \'jer-ē-,man-dər\ vb **-man·dered; -man·der·ing** \-d(ə-)riŋ\ : to divide into election districts so as to give one political party an advantage — **gerrymander** n

ger·und \'jer-ənd\ n : a word having the characteristics of both verb and noun

ge·sta·po \gə-'stäp-ō\ n, pl **-pos** [G, fr. Geheime Staatspolizei, lit., secret state police] : a secret-police organization operating esp. against suspected political criminals

ges·ta·tion \je-'stā-shən\ n : PREGNANCY, INCUBATION — **ges·tate** \'jes-,tāt\ vb

ges·tic·u·late \je-'stik-yə-,lāt\ vb **-lat·ed; -lat·ing** : to make gestures esp. when speaking — **ges·tic·u·la·tion** \-,stik-yə-'lā-shən\ n

ges·ture \'jes-chər\ n **1** : a movement usu. of the body or limbs that expresses or emphasizes an idea, sentiment, or attitude **2** : something said or done by way of formality or courtesy, as a symbol or token, or for its effect on the attitudes of others — **ges·tur·al** \-chə-rəl\ adj — **gesture** vb

ge·sund·heit \gə-'zunt-,hīt\ interj [G, lit., health] — used to wish good health esp. to one who has just sneezed

¹get \'get\ vb **got** \'gät\ ; **got** or **got·ten** \'gät-ᵊn\ ; **get·ting 1** : to gain possession of (as by receiving, acquiring, earning, buying, or winning) : PROCURE, OBTAIN, FETCH **2** : to succeed in coming or going (got home early) **3** : to cause to come or go (got the car to the station) **4** : BEGET **5** : to cause to be in a certain condition or position (don't ~ wet) **6** : BECOME (~ sick) **7** : PREPARE **8** : SEIZE **9** : to move emotionally; also : IRRITATE **10** : BAFFLE, PUZZLE **11** : HIT **12** : KILL **13** : to be subjected to (~ the measles) **14** : to receive as punishment **15** : to find out by calculation **16** : HEAR; also : UNDERSTAND **17** : PERSUADE, INDUCE **18** : HAVE (he's got no money) **19** : to have as an obligation or necessity (he has got to come) **20** : to establish communication with **21** : to be able : CONTRIVE, MANAGE **22** : to leave at once

²get \'get\ n : OFFSPRING, PROGENY

get along vb **1** : GET BY **2** : to be on friendly terms

get·away \'get-ə-,wā\ n **1** : START **2** : ESCAPE

get by vb : to meet one's needs

get-to·geth·er \'get-tə-,geth-ər\ n : an informal social gathering

get·up \'get-,əp\ n **1** : general composition or structure **2** : OUTFIT, COSTUME

gew·gaw \'g(y)ü-,gȯ\ n : a showy trifle : BAUBLE, TRINKET

gey·ser \'gī-zər\ n [Icelandic geysir gusher] : a spring that intermittently shoots up hot water and steam

Gha·na·ian \gä-'nä-(y)ən\ n : a native or inhabitant of Ghana — **Ghanaian** adj

ghast·ly \'gast-lē\ adj **ghast·li·er; -est 1**

: HORRIBLE, SHOCKING **2** : resembling a ghost : DEATHLIKE, PALE **syn** gruesome, grim, lurid, grisly, macabre

ghat \'gȯt\ n [Hindi] : a broad flight of steps that is situated on an Indian riverbank and provides access to the water

gher·kin \'gər-kən\ n : a small young cucumber used to make pickles; *also* : a small prickly fruit of a vine related to the cucumber used for the same purpose

ghet·to \'get-ō\ n, pl **ghettos** or **ghettoes** : a quarter of a city in which members of a minority group live because of social, legal, or economic pressure

¹**ghost** \'gōst\ n **1** : the seat of life : SOUL **2** : a disembodied soul; *esp* : the soul of a dead person believed to be an inhabitant of the unseen world or to appear in bodily form to living people **3** : SPIRIT, DEMON **4** : a faint trace (a ∼ of a smile) **5** : a false image in a photographic negative or on a television screen — **ghost·ly** adv

²**ghost** vb : GHOSTWRITE

ghost·write \-ˌrīt\ vb **-wrote** \-ˌrōt\ ; **-writ·ten** \-ˌrit-ⁿn\ : to write for and in the name of another — **ghost·writ·er** n

ghoul \'gül\ n [Ar ghūl] : a legendary evil being that robs graves and feeds on corpses — **ghoul·ish** adj

GHQ abbr general headquarters

gi abbr gill

¹**GI** \(ˌ)jē-'ī\ adj [galvanized iron; fr. abbr. used in listing such articles as garbage cans, but taken as abbr. for government issue] **1** : provided by an official U.S. military supply department (∼ shoes) **2** : of, relating to, or characteristic of U.S. military personnel **3** : conforming to military regulations or customs (a ∼ haircut)

²**GI** n, pl **GI's** or **GIs** \-'īz\ : a member or former member of the U.S. armed forces; *esp* : an enlisted man

³**GI** abbr **1** galvanized iron **2** gastrointestinal **3** general issue **4** government issue

gi·ant \'jī-ənt\ n **1** : a huge legendary manlike being of great strength **2** : a living being or thing of extraordinary size or powers — **giant** adj

gi·ant·ess \-əs\ n : a female giant

gib·ber \'jib-ər\ vb **gib·bered**; **gib·ber·ing** \-(ə-)riŋ\ : to speak rapidly, inarticulately, and often foolishly

gib·ber·ish \'jib-(ə-)rish\ n : unintelligible or confused speech or language

¹**gib·bet** \'jib-ət\ n : GALLOWS

²**gibbet** vb **1** : to hang on a gibbet **2** : to expose to public scorn **3** : to execute by hanging

gib·bon \'gib-ən\ n : any of several tailless apes of southeastern Asia and the East Indies

gib·bous \'jib-əs, 'gib-\ adj **1** : convexly rounded in form : PROTUBERANT **2** : seen with more than half but not all of the apparent disk illuminated (∼

moon) **3** : having a hump : HUMP-BACKED

gibe \'jīb\ vb **gibed**; **gib·ing** : to utter taunting words : SNEER — **gibe** n

gib·lets \'jib-ləts\ n pl : the edible viscera of a fowl

Gib·son \'gib-sən\ n : a martini with a small onion

gid·dy \'gid-ē\ adj **gid·di·er; -est 1** : DIZZY **2** : causing dizziness **3** : not serious : FRIVOLOUS, SILLY — **gid·di·ness** \'gid-ē-nəs\ n

gift \'gift\ n **1** : a special ability : TALENT **2** : something given : PRESENT **3** : the act or power of giving

gift·ed \'gif-təd\ adj : TALENTED

¹**gig** \'gig\ n **1** : a long light ship's boat **2** : a light 2-wheeled one-horse carriage

²**gig** n : a pronged spear for catching fish — **gig** vb

³**gig** n : JOB; *esp* : an entertainer's engagement for a specified time

⁴**gig** n : a military demerit — **gig** vb

gi·gan·tic \jī-'gant-ik\ adj : resembling a giant : IMMENSE, HUGE

gig·gle \'gig-əl\ vb **gig·gled; gig·gling** \-(ə-)liŋ\ : to laugh with repeated short catches of the breath — **giggle** n — **gig·gly** \-(ə-)lē\ adj

GIGO abbr garbage in, garbage out

gig·o·lo \'jig-ə-ˌlō\ n, pl **-los 1** : a man supported by a woman usu. in return for his attentions **2** : a professional dancing partner or male escort

Gi·la monster \ˌhē-lə-\ n : a large orange and black venomous lizard of the southwestern U.S.

¹**gild** \'gild\ vb **gild·ed** \'gil-dəd\ or **gilt** \'gilt\ ; **gild·ing 1** : to overlay with or as if with a thin covering of gold **2** : to give an attractive but often deceptive outward appearance to — **gild·ing** n

²**gild** var of GUILD

¹**gill** \'jil\ n — see WEIGHT table

²**gill** \'gil\ n : an organ (as of a fish) for obtaining oxygen from water

¹**gilt** \'gilt\ adj : of the color of gold

²**gilt** n : gold or a substance resembling gold laid on the surface of an object

³**gilt** n : a young female swine

gim·crack \'jim-ˌkrak\ n : a showy object of little use or value

gim·let \'gim-lət\ n : a small tool with screw point and cross handle for boring

gim·mick \'gim-ik\ n **1** : CONTRIVANCE, GADGET **2** : an important feature that is not immediately apparent : CATCH **3** : a new and ingenious scheme — **gim·micky** \-i-kē\ adj

gim·mick·ry \'gim-i-krē\ n, pl **-ries** : an array of or the use of gimmicks

gimpy \'gim-pē\ adj : CRIPPLED, LAME

¹**gin** \'jin\ n [ME gin, modif. of OF engin] **1** : TRAP, SNARE **2** : a machine to separate seeds from cotton — **gin** vb

²**gin** \'jin\ n [by shortening & alter. fr. geneva] : a liquor distilled from a grain mash and flavored with juniper berries

gin·ger \'jin-jər\ n : the pungent aromatic rootstock of a tropical plant used esp. as a spice and in medicine; *also* : the spice or the plant

ginger ale *n* : a carbonated soft drink flavored with ginger

gin·ger·bread \'jin-jər-ˌbred\ *n* **1** : a cake made with molasses and flavored with ginger **2** : tawdry, gaudy, or superfluous ornament

gin·ger·ly \'jin-jər-lē\ *adj* : very cautious or careful — **gingerly** *adv*

gin·ger·snap \-ˌsnap\ *n* : a thin brittle molasses cookie flavored with ginger

ging·ham \'giŋ-əm\ *n* : a clothing fabric usu. of yarn-dyed cotton in plain weave

gin·gi·vi·tis \ˌjin-jə-'vīt-əs\ *n* : inflammation of the gums

gink·go *also* **ging·ko** \'giŋ-(ˌ)kō\ *n, pl* **ginkgoes** *or* **ginkgos** : a tree of eastern China with fan-shaped leaves often grown as a shade tree

gin·seng \'jin-ˌseŋ\ *n* : an aromatic root of a Chinese or No. American herb used esp. in Oriental medicine; *also* : one of these herbs

Gipsy *var of* GYPSY

gi·raffe \jə-'raf\ *n, pl* **giraffes** [It *giraffa*, fr. Ar *zirāfah*] : an African ruminant mammal with an extraordinarily long neck

gird \'gərd\ *vb* **gird·ed** \'gərd-əd\ *or* **girt** \'gərt\; **gird·ing** **1** : to encircle or fasten with or as if with a belt : GIRDLE (~ on a sword) **2** : to clothe or invest esp. with power or authority **3** : PREPARE, BRACE

gird·er \'gərd-ər\ *n* : a horizontal main supporting beam

gir·dle \'gərd-ᵊl\ *n* **1** : something (as a belt or sash) that encircles or confines **2** : a woman's supporting undergarment that extends from the waist to below the hips — **girdle** *vb*

girl \'gərl\ *n* **1** : a female child **2** : a typically young woman **3** : a female servant or employee **4** : SWEETHEART — **girl·hood** \-ˌhud\ *n* — **girl·ish** *adj*

girl Friday *n* : a female assistant (as in an office) entrusted with a wide variety of tasks

girlfriend *n* **1** : a female friend **2** : a frequent or regular female companion of a boy or man

Girl Scout *n* : a member of the Girl Scouts of the United States of America

girth \'gərth\ *n* **1** : a band around an animal by which something (as a saddle) may be fastened on its back **2** : a measure around something

gist \'jist\ *n* [MF, it lies, fr. *gesir* to lie, fr. L *jacēre*] : the main point of a matter

¹give \'giv\ *vb* **gave** \'gāv\; **giv·en** \'giv-ən\; **giv·ing 1** : to make a present of **2** : to bestow by formal action **3** : to accord or yield to another **4** : to put into the possession or keeping of another **5** : PROFFER **6** : DELIVER; *esp* : to deliver in exchange **7** : PAY **8** : to present in

public performance or to view **9** : PROVIDE **10** : ATTRIBUTE **11** : to make, form, or yield as a product or result (cows ~ milk) **12** : to deliver by some bodily action (*gave* me a push) **13** : UTTER, PRONOUNCE **14** : DEVOTE **15** : to cause to have or receive **16** : CONTRIBUTE, DONATE **17** : to yield to force, strain, or pressure

²give *n* **1** : capacity or tendency to yield to force or strain **2** : the quality or state of being springy

give-and-take \ˌgiv-ən-'tāk\ *n* : an exchange (as of remarks or ideas) esp. on fair or equal terms

give·away \'giv-ə-ˌwā\ *n* **1** : an unintentional revelation or betrayal **2** : something given away free; *esp* : PREMIUM

give in *vb* : SURRENDER, SUBMIT

giv·en \'giv-ən\ *adj* **1** : DISPOSED, INCLINED (~ to swearing) **2** : SPECIFIED, FIXED (at a ~ time) **3** : granted as true : ASSUMED

given name *n* : a name that precedes one's surname

give out *vb* **1** : EMIT **2** : to become exhausted : COLLAPSE **3** : BREAK DOWN

give up *vb* **1** : SURRENDER **2** : to abandon (oneself) to a feeling, influence, or activity **3** : QUIT

giz·mo *or* **gis·mo** \'giz-mō\ *n, pl* **gizmos** *or* **gismos** : GADGET

giz·zard \'giz-ərd\ *n* : a muscular usu. horny-lined enlargement of the alimentary canal of a bird used for churning and grinding up food

gla·brous \'glā-brəs\ *adj* : SMOOTH; *esp* : having a surface without hairs or projections (a ~ leaf)

gla·cial \'glā-shəl\ *adj* **1** : extremely cold **2** : of or relating to glaciers **3** : being or relating to a past period of time when a large part of the earth was covered by glaciers **4** *cap* : PLEISTOCENE — **gla·cial·ly** \-ē\ *adv*

gla·ci·ate \'glā-shē-ˌāt\ *vb* **-at·ed; -at·ing 1** : to subject to glacial action **2** : to produce glacial effects in or on — **gla·ci·a·tion** \ˌglā-s(h)ē-'ā-shən\ *n*

gla·cier \'glā-shər\ *n* : a large body of ice moving slowly down a slope or spreading outward on a land surface

¹glad \'glad\ *adj* **glad·der; glad·dest 1** : experiencing pleasure, joy, or delight **2** : PLEASED **3** : very willing **4** : PLEASANT, JOYFUL **5** : CHEERFUL — **glad·ly** *adv* — **glad·ness** *n*

²glad *n* : GLADIOLUS

glad·den \'glad-ᵊn\ *vb* : to make glad

glade \'glād\ *n* : a grassy open space surrounded by woods

glad·i·a·tor \'glad-ē-ˌāt-ər\ *n* **1** : a person engaged in a fight to the death for public entertainment in ancient Rome **2** : a person engaging in a fierce fight or controversy — **glad·i·a·to·ri·al** \ˌglad-ē-ə-'tōr-ē-əl\ *adj*

glad·i·o·lus \ˌglad-ē-'ō-ləs\ *n, pl* **-li** \-(ˌ)lē, -ˌlī\ [L, fr. dim. of *gladius* sword] : any of a genus of chiefly African plants related to the irises and having erect sword-shaped leaves and stalks of brilliantly colored flowers

glad·some \'glad-səm\ *adj* : giving or showing joy : CHEERFUL

glad·stone \'glad-ˌstōn\ *n, often cap* : a traveling bag with flexible sides on a rigid frame that opens flat into two compartments

glam·or·ize *also* **glam·our·ize** \'glam-ə-ˌrīz\ *vb* **-ized; -iz·ing** : to make or look upon as glamorous

glam·our *or* **glam·or** \'glam-ər\ *n* [Sc *glamour*, alter. of E *grammar*; fr. the popular association of erudition with occult practices] : an exciting and often illusory and romantic attractiveness; *esp* : alluring personal attraction — **glam·or·ous** *also* **glam·our·ous** \-(ə-)rəs\ *adj*

¹**glance** \'glans\ *vb* **glanced; glanc·ing** 1 : to strike and fly off to one side 2 : GLEAM 3 : to give a quick look

²**glance** *n* 1 : a quick intermittent flash or gleam 2 : a glancing impact or blow 3 : a quick look

gland \'gland\ *n* : a cell or group of cells that prepares and secretes a substance (as saliva or sweat) for further use in or discharge from the body — **glan·du·lar** \'glan-jə-lər\ *adj*

glans \'glanz\ *n, pl* **glan·des** \'glan-ˌdēz\ [L, lit., acorn] : a conical vascular body forming the extremity of the penis or clitoris

¹**glare** \'glaər\ *vb* **glared; glar·ing** 1 : to shine with a harsh dazzling light 2 : to stare fiercely or angrily — **glar·ing** \'gla(ə)r-iŋ\ *adj* — **glar·ing·ly** *adv*

²**glare** *n* 1 : a harsh dazzling light 2 : an angry or fierce stare

glass \'glas\ *n* 1 : a hard brittle usu. transparent or translucent substance made by melting sand and other materials and cooling to hardness 2 : something made of glass 3 *pl* : a pair of lenses used to correct defects of vision : SPECTACLES 4 : the quantity held by a glass — **glass** *adj* — **glass·ful** \-ˌfûl\ *n* — **glass·ware** \-ˌwaər\ *n* — **glassy** *adj*

glass-blow·ing \-ˌblō-iŋ\ *n* : the art of shaping a mass of glass that has been softened by heat by blowing air into it through a tube — **glass·blow·er** \-ˌblō-(ə)r\ *n*

glau·co·ma \glaù-'kō-mə, glò-\ *n* : a disease of the eye marked by increased pressure within the eyeball resulting in damage to the retina and gradual loss of vision

¹**glaze** \'glāz\ *vb* **glazed; glaz·ing** 1 : to furnish (as a window frame) with glass 2 : to apply glaze to

²**glaze** *n* : a glassy coating or surface

gla·zier \'glā-zhər\ *n* : a person who sets glass in window frames

¹**gleam** \'glēm\ *n* 1 : a transient subdued or partly obscured light 2 : GLINT 3 : a faint trace (a ~ of hope)

²**gleam** *vb* 1 : to shine with subdued light

or moderate brightness 2 : to appear briefly or faintly

glean \'glēn\ *vb* 1 : to gather grain left by reapers 2 : to collect little by little or with patient effort — **glean·able** *adj* — **glean·er** *n*

glean·ings \'glē-niŋz\ *n pl* : things acquired by gleaning

glee \'glē\ *n* [ME, fr. OE *glēo* entertainment, music] 1 : JOY, HILARITY 2 : an unaccompanied song for three or more solo usu. male voices — **glee·ful** *adj*

glee club *n* : a chorus organized for singing usu. short choral pieces

glen \'glen\ *n* : a secluded narrow valley

glen·gar·ry \glen-'gar-ē\ *n, pl* **-ries** *often cap* : a woolen cap of Scottish origin

glib \'glib\ *adj* **glib·ber; glib·best** : speaking or spoken with careless ease — **glib·ly** *adv*

glide \'glīd\ *vb* **glid·ed; glid·ing** 1 : to move smoothly and effortlessly 2 : to descend gradually without engine power (~ in an airplane) — **glide** *n*

glid·er \'glīd-ər\ *n* 1 : one that glides 2 : an aircraft resembling an airplane but having no engine 3 : a porch seat suspended from an upright framework by short chains or straps

¹**glim·mer** \'glim-ər\ *vb* **glim·mered; glim·mer·ing** \-(ə-)riŋ\ : to shine faintly or unsteadily

²**glimmer** *n* 1 : a faint unsteady light 2 : INKLING 3 : a small amount : BIT

¹**glimpse** \'glimps\ *vb* **glimpsed; glimps·ing** : to take a brief look : see momentarily or incompletely

²**glimpse** *n* 1 : a faint idea : GLIMMER 2 : a short hurried look

glint \'glint\ *vb* 1 : to shine by reflection : SPARKLE, GLITTER, GLEAM 2 : to appear briefly or faintly — **glint** *n*

glis·san·do \gli-'sän-(ˌ)dō\ *n, pl* **-di** \-(ˌ)dē\ *or* **-dos** : a rapid sliding up or down the musical scale

glis·ten \'glis-ᵊn\ *vb* **glis·tened; glis·ten·ing** \'glis-(ᵊ-)niŋ\ : to shine by reflection with a soft luster or sparkle

²**glisten** *n* : GLITTER, SPARKLE

glis·ter \'glis-tər\ *vb* : GLITTER

glitch \'glich\ *n* : MALFUNCTION; *also* : SNAG 2

¹**glit·ter** \'glit-ər\ *vb* 1 : to shine with brilliant or metallic luster : SPARKLE 2 : to shine with strong emotion : FLASH (eyes ~*ing* in anger) 3 : to be brilliantly attractive esp. in a superficial way

²**glitter** *n* 1 : sparkling brilliancy, showiness, or attractiveness 2 : small glittering objects used for ornamentation — **glit·tery** \'glit-ə-rē\ *adj*

gloam·ing \'glō-miŋ\ *n* : TWILIGHT, DUSK

gloat \'glōt\ *vb* : to think about something with great and often malicious delight

glob \'gläb\ *n* 1 : a small drop 2 : a large rounded mass

glob·al \'glō-bəl\ *adj* 1 : WORLDWIDE 2

: COMPREHENSIVE, GENERAL — **glob·al·ly** \-ē\ *adv*

globe \'glōb\ *n* **1** : BALL, SPHERE **2** : EARTH; *also* : a spherical representation of the earth

globe–trot·ter \-ˌträt-ər\ *n* : one that travels widely — **globe–trot·ting** \-ˌträt-iŋ\ *n or adj*

glob·u·lar \'gläb-yə-lər\ *adj* : having the shape of a globe or globule

glob·ule \'gläb-yül\ *n* : a tiny globe or ball

glob·u·lin \'gläb-yə-lən\ *n* : any of a class of simple proteins insoluble in pure water but soluble in dilute salt solutions that occur widely in plant and animal tissues

glock·en·spiel \'gläk-ən-ˌs(h)pēl\ *n* [G, fr. *glocke* bell + *spiel* play] : a percussion musical instrument consisting of a series of metal bars played with two hammers

gloom \'glüm\ *n* **1** : partial or total darkness **2** : lowness of spirits : DEJECTION **3** : an atmosphere of despondency — **gloom·i·ly** \'glü-mə-lē\ *adv* — **gloom·i·ness** \-mē-nəs\ *n* — **gloomy** \'glü-mē\ *adj*

glop \'gläp\ *n* : a messy mass or mixture

glo·ri·fy \'glōr-ə-ˌfī\ *vb* **-fied; -fy·ing** **1** : to raise to heavenly glory **2** : to light up brilliantly **3** : EXTOL **4** : to give glory to (as in worship) — **glo·ri·fi·ca·tion** \ˌglōr-ə-fə-'kā-shən\ *n*

glo·ri·ous \'glōr-ē-əs\ *adj* **1** : possessing or deserving glory : PRAISEWORTHY **2** : conferring glory **3** : RESPLENDENT, MAGNIFICENT **4** : DELIGHTFUL, WONDERFUL — **glo·ri·ous·ly** *adv*

¹**glo·ry** \'glōr-ē\ *n, pl* **glories 1** : RENOWN **2** : honor and praise rendered in worship **3** : something that secures praise or renown **4** : a distinguishing quality or asset **5** : RESPLENDENCE, MAGNIFICENCE **6** : heavenly bliss **7** : a height of prosperity or achievement

²**glory** *vb* **glo·ried; glo·ry·ing** : to rejoice proudly : EXULT

¹**gloss** \'gläs, 'glós\ *n* **1** : LUSTER, SHEEN, BRIGHTNESS **2** : outward show — **glossy** *adj*

²**gloss** *vb* **1** : to give a deceptive appearance to **2** : to deal with too lightly or not at all (~ over inadequacies)

³**gloss** *n* [ME *glose*, fr. OF, fr. L *glossa* unusual word requiring explanation, fr. Gk *glōssa, glōtta* tongue, language, unusual word] **1** : an explanatory note (as in the margin of a text) **2** : GLOSSARY **3** : an interlinear translation **4** : a continuous commentary accompanying a text

⁴**gloss** *vb* : to furnish glosses for

glos·sa·ry \'gläs-(ə-)rē, 'glós-\ *n, pl* **-ries** : a collection of difficult or specialized terms with their meanings — **glos·sar·i·al** \glä-'sar-ē-əl, glô-\ *adj*

glos·so·la·lia \ˌgläs-ə-'lā-lē-ə, ˌglós-\ *n* [Gk *glōssa* tongue, language + *lalia*

chatter, fr. *lalein* to chatter, talk] : TONGUE 6

¹**glossy** \'gläs-ē, 'glós-\ *adj* **gloss·i·er; -est** : having a surface luster or brightness — **gloss·i·ly** \-ə-lē\ *adv* — **gloss·i·ness** \-ē-nəs\ *n*

²**glossy** *n, pl* **gloss·ies** : a photograph printed on smooth shiny paper

glot·tis \'glät-əs\ *n, pl* **glot·tis·es** or **glot·ti·des** \-ə-ˌdēz\ : the slitlike opening between the vocal cords in the larynx — **glot·tal** \-ᵊl\ *adj*

glove \'gləv\ *n* **1** : a covering for the hand having separate sections for each finger **2** : a padded leather covering for the hand for use in a sport

¹**glow** \'glō\ *vb* **1** : to shine with or as if with intense heat **2** : to have a rich warm usu. ruddy color : FLUSH, BLUSH **3** : to feel hot **4** : to show exuberance or elation (~ with pride)

²**glow** *n* **1** : brightness or warmth of color; *esp* : REDNESS **2** : warmth of feeling or emotion **3** : a sensation of warmth **4** : light such as is emitted from a heated substance

glow·er \'glau̇(-ə)r\ *vb* : to stare angrily : SCOWL — **glower** *n*

glow·worm \'glō-ˌwərm\ *n* : any of various insect larvae or adults that give off light

glox·in·ia \gläk-'sin-ē-ə\ *n* : any of a genus of Brazilian herbs related to the African violets; *esp* : one with showy bell-shaped or slipper-shaped flowers

gloze \'glōz\ *vb* **glozed; gloz·ing** : to make appear right or acceptable

glu·cose \'glü-ˌkōs\ *n* **1** : a sugar known in three different forms; *esp* : DEXTROSE **2** : a sweet light-colored syrup made from cornstarch

glue \'glü\ *n* : a jellylike protein substance made from animal materials and used for sticking things together; *also* : any of various other strong adhesives — **glue** *vb* — **glu·ey** \'glü-ē\ *adj*

glum \'gləm\ *adj* **glum·mer; glum·mest** **1** : MOROSE, SULLEN **2** : DREARY, GLOOMY

¹**glut** \'glət\ *vb* **glut·ted; glut·ting 1** : to fill esp. with food to satiety : SATIATE **2** : OVERSUPPLY

²**glut** *n* : an excessive supply

glu·ten \'glüt-ᵊn\ *n* : a gluey protein substance that causes dough to be sticky

glu·ti·nous \'glüt-(ᵊ-)nəs\ *adj* : STICKY

glut·ton \'glət-ᵊn\ *n* : one that eats to excess — **glut·ton·ous** \'glət-(ᵊ-)nəs\ *adj* — **glut·tony** \'glət-(ᵊ-)nē\ *n*

glyc·er·in or **glyc·er·ine** \'glis-(ə-)rən\ *n* : GLYCEROL

glyc·er·ol \'glis-ə-ˌról, -ˌrōl\ *n* : a sweet colorless syrupy liquid obtained from fats or synthesized and used as a solvent, moistener, and lubricant

gly·co·gen \'glī-kə-jən\ *n* : a white tasteless substance that is the chief storage carbohydrate of animals

gm *abbr* gram

GM *abbr* **1** general manager **2** guided missile

G–man \'jē-ˌman\ *n* : a special agent of the Federal Bureau of Investigation

GMT *abbr* Greenwich mean time

gnarled \'när-əld\ *adj* **1** : KNOTTY **2** : GLOOMY, SULLEN

gnash \'nash\ *vb* : to grind (as teeth) together

gnat \'nat\ *n* : any of various small usu. biting two-winged flies

gnaw \'nȯ\ *vb* **1** : to consume, wear away, or make by persistent biting or nibbling **2** : to affect as if by gnawing — **gnaw·er** \'nȯ(-ə)r\ *n*

gneiss \'nīs\ *n* : a layered granitelike rock

gnome \'nōm\ *n* : a dwarf of folklore who lives inside the earth and guards precious ore or treasure — **gnom·ish** \'nō-mish\ *adj*

GNP *abbr* gross national product

gnu \'nü\ *n, pl* **gnu** *or* **gnus** : any of several large African antelopes with an oxlike head and horns and a horse-like mane and tail

¹go \'gō\ *vb* **went** \'went\ ; **gone** \'gȯn, 'gän\ ; **go·ing** \'gō-iŋ\ ; **goes** \'gōz\ **1** : to move on a course : PROCEED ⟨~ slow⟩ **2** : LEAVE, DEPART **3** : to take a certain course or follow a certain procedure **4** : EXTEND, RUN ⟨his land ~es to the river⟩ ; *also* : LEAD ⟨that door ~es to the cellar⟩ **5** : to be habitually in a certain state ⟨~es armed after dark⟩ **6** : to become lost, consumed, or spent; *also* : DIE **7** : ELAPSE, PASS **8** : to pass by sale ⟨went for a good price⟩ **9** : to become impaired or weakened **10** : to give way under force or pressure : BREAK **11** : HAPPEN ⟨what's ~ing on⟩ **12** : to be in general or on an average ⟨cheap, as yachts ~⟩ **13** : to become esp. as the result of a contest ⟨the decision went against him⟩ **14** : to put or subject oneself ⟨~ to great expense⟩ **15** : RESORT ⟨went to court to recover damages⟩ **16** : to begin or maintain an action or motion ⟨here ~es⟩ **17** : to function properly ⟨the clock doesn't ~⟩ **18** : to have currency : CIRCULATE ⟨the report ~es⟩ **19** : to be or act in accordance ⟨a good rule to ~ by⟩ **20** : to come to be applied **21** : to pass by award, assignment, or lot **22** : to contribute to a result ⟨qualities that ~ to make a hero⟩ **23** : to be about, intending, or expecting something ⟨is ~ing to leave town⟩ **24** : to arrive at a certain state or condition ⟨~ to sleep⟩ **25** : to come to be ⟨the tire went flat⟩ **26** : to be capable of being sung or played ⟨the tune ~es like this⟩ **27** : to be suitable or becoming : HARMONIZE **28** : to be capable of passing, extending, or being contained or inserted ⟨this coat will ~ in the trunk⟩ **29** : to have a usual or proper place or position : BELONG ⟨these books ~ on the top shelf⟩ **30** : to be capable of being divided ⟨3 ~es into 6 twice⟩ **31** : to have a tendency ⟨that ~es to show that is honest⟩ **32** : to be acceptable, satisfactory, or adequate **33** : to proceed along or according to : FOLLOW **34** : TRAVERSE **35** : BET, BID ⟨willing to ~ $50⟩ **36** : to assume the function or obligation of ⟨~ bail for a friend⟩ **37** : to participate to the extent of ⟨~ halves⟩ **38** : WEIGH **39** : ENDURE, TOLERATE **40** : AFFORD ⟨can't ~ the price⟩ — **go at 1** : ATTACK, ATTEMPT **2** : UNDERTAKE — **go back on 1** : ABANDON **2** : BETRAY **3** : FAIL — **go by the board** : to be discarded — **go down the line** : to give wholehearted support — **go for 1** : to pass for or serve as **2** : to try to secure **3** : FAVOR — **go one better** : OUTDO, SURPASS — **go over 1** : EXAMINE **2** : REPEAT **3** : STUDY, REVIEW — **go places** : to be on the way to success — **go to bat for** : DEFEND, CHAMPION — **go to town 1** : to work or act efficiently **2** : to be very successful

²go \'gō\ *n, pl* **goes 1** : the act or manner of going **2** : the height of fashion ⟨boots are all the ~⟩ **3** : a turn of affairs : OCCURRENCE **4** : ENERGY, VIGOR **5** : ATTEMPT, TRY **6** : a spell of activity — **no go** : USELESS, HOPELESS — **on the go** : constantly active

³go *adj* : functioning properly

GO *abbr* general order

goad \'gōd\ *n* [ME *gode*, fr. OE *gād* spear, goad] **1** : a pointed rod used to urge on an animal **2** : something that urges : SPUR — **goad** *vb*

go–ahead \'gō-ə-ˌhed\ *n* : authority to proceed

goal \'gōl\ *n* **1** : the mark set as limit to a race; *also* : an area to be reached safely in children's games **2** : AIM, PURPOSE **3** : an area or object toward which play is directed in order to score; *also* : a successful attempt to score

goal·ie \'gō-lē\ *n* : GOALKEEPER

goal·keep·er \'gōl-ˌkē-pər\ *n* : a player who defends the goal in various games

goal·post \'gōl-ˌpōst\ *n* : one of the two vertical posts with a crossbar that constitute the goal (as in soccer)

goat \'gōt\ *n, pl* **goats** *or* **goat** : any of various hollow-horned ruminant mammals related to the sheep that have backward-curving horns, a short tail, and usu. straight hair

goa·tee \gō-'tē\ *n* : a small trim pointed or tufted beard on a man's chin

goat·herd \'gōt-ˌhərd\ *n* : one who tends goats

goat·skin \-ˌskin\ *n* : the skin of a goat or a leather made from it

¹gob \'gäb\ *n* : LUMP, MASS

²gob *n* : SAILOR

gob·bet \'gäb-ət\ *n* : LUMP, MASS

¹gob·ble \'gäb-əl\ *vb* **gob·bled**; **gob·bling** \-(ə-)liŋ\ **1** : to swallow or eat greedily **2** : to take eagerly : GRAB

²gobble *vb* **gob·bled**; **gob·bling** \-(ə-)liŋ\

: to make the natural guttural noise of a male turkey

gob·ble·dy·gook *or* **gob·ble·de·gook** \ˈgäb-əl-dē-ˌgŭk, -ˌgŭk\ *n* : generally unintelligible jargon

gob·bler \ˈgäb-lər\ *n* : a male turkey

go-be·tween \ˈgō-bə-ˌtwēn\ *n* : an intermediate agent : BROKER

gob·let \ˈgäb-lət\ *n* : a drinking glass with a foot and stem

gob·lin \ˈgäb-lən\ *n* : an ugly or grotesque sprite that is mischievous and sometimes evil and malicious

god \ˈgäd, ˈgȯd\ *n* **1** *cap* : the supreme reality : *esp* : the Being worshiped as the creator and ruler of the universe **2** : a being or object believed to have supernatural attributes and powers and to require worship **3** : a person or thing of supreme value

god·child \-ˌchīld\ *n* : a person for whom one stands as sponsor at baptism

god·daugh·ter \-ˌdȯt-ər\ *n* : a female godchild

god·dess \ˈgäd-əs\ *n* **1** : a female god **2** : a woman whose charm or beauty arouses adoration

god·fa·ther \ˈgäd-ˌfäth-ər, ˈgȯd-\ *n* : a man who sponsors a person at baptism

god·head \-ˌhed\ *n* **1** : divine nature or essence **2** *cap* : GOD **1**; *also* : the nature of God esp. as existing in three persons

god·hood \-ˌhŭd\ *n* : DIVINITY

god·less \ˈgäd-ləs, ˈgȯd-\ *adj* : not acknowledging a deity or divine law — **god·less·ness** *n*

god·like \-ˌlīk\ *adj* : resembling or having the qualities of God or a god

god·ly \-lē\ *adj* **god·li·er; -est 1** : DIVINE **2** : PIOUS, DEVOUT — **god·li·ness** \-lē-nəs\ *n*

god·moth·er \-ˌməth-ər\ *n* : a woman who sponsors a person at baptism

god·par·ent \-ˌpar-ənt\ *n* : a sponsor at baptism

god·send \-ˌsend\ *n* : a desirable or needed thing that comes unexpectedly

god·son \-ˌsən\ *n* : a male godchild

go-fer \ˈgō-fər\ *n* [alter. of *go for*] : an employee whose duties include running errands

go-get·ter \ˈgō-ˌget-ər\ *n* : an aggressively enterprising person — **go-get·ting** \-ˌget-iŋ\ *adj or n*

gog·gle \ˈgäg-əl\ *vb* **gog·gled; gog·gling** \-(ə-)liŋ\ : to stare with wide or protuberant eyes

gog·gles \ˈgäg-əlz\ *n pl* : protective glasses set in a flexible frame that fits snugly against the face

go-go \ˈgō-ˌgō\ *adj* [a *go-go*] **1** : related to, being, or employed to entertain in a discotheque (∼ *dancers*) **2** : aggressively enterprising and energetic

go·ings-on \ˌgō-iŋz-ˈȯn, -ˈän\ *n pl* : ACTIONS, EVENTS

goi·ter \ˈgȯit-ər\ *n* : an abnormally en-

larged thyroid gland visible as a swelling at the base of the neck — **goi·trous** \-(ə-)rəs\ *adj*

goi·tre *chiefly Brit var of* GOITER

gold \ˈgōld\ *n* **1** : a malleable yellow metallic chemical element used esp. for coins and jewelry **2** : gold coins; *also* : MONEY **3** : a yellow color

gold·brick \-ˌbrik\ *n* : a person (as a soldier) who shirks assigned work — **goldbrick** *vb*

Gold Coast *n* : an exclusive residential district

gold digger *n* : a woman who uses feminine charm to extract money or gifts from men

gold·en \ˈgōl-dən\ *adj* **1** : made of or relating to gold **2** : having the color of gold; *also* : BLOND **3** : SHINING, LUSTROUS **4** : SUPERB **5** : FLOURISHING, PROSPEROUS **6** : radiantly youthful and vigorous **7** : FAVORABLE, ADVANTAGEOUS (a ∼ *opportunity*) **8** : MELLOW, RESONANT

gold·en·ag·er \ˈgōl-dən-ˌā-jər\ *n* : an elderly and often retired person usu. engaging in club activities

golden hamster *n* : a small tawny hamster often kept as a pet

gold·en·rod \ˈgōl-dən-ˌräd\ *n* : any of numerous plants related to the daisies but having tall slender stalks with many tiny usu. yellow flower heads

gold·field \ˈgōld-ˌfēld\ *n* : a gold-mining district

gold·finch \-ˌfinch\ *n* **1** : a small largely red, black, and yellow European finch often kept in a cage **2** : any of several small American finches of which the males usu. become bright yellow and black in summer

gold·fish \-ˌfish\ *n* : a small usu. yellow or golden carp often kept as an aquarium fish

gold·smith \ˈgōld-ˌsmith\ *n* : one who makes or deals in articles of gold

golf \ˈgälf, ˈgȯlf\ *n* : a game played with a small ball and various clubs on a course having 9 or 18 holes — **golf** *vb* — **golf·er** *n*

-gon \ˌgän\ *n comb form* : figure having (so many) angles (hexa*gon*)

go·nad \ˈgō-ˌnad\ *n* : a sperm- or egg-producing gland : OVARY, TESTIS — **go·nad·al** \gō-ˈnad-ᵊl\ *adj*

go·nad·o·trop·ic \gō-ˌnad-ə-ˈträp-ik\ *or* **go·nad·o·tro·phic** \-ˈtrō-fik, -ˈträf-ik\ *adj* : acting on or stimulating the gonads (∼ *hormones*)

go·nad·o·tro·pin \-ˈtrō-pən\ *or* **go·nad·o·tro·phin** \-fən\ *n* : a gonadotropic hormone

gon·do·la \ˈgän-də-lə (*usual for I*), gän-ˈdō-\ *n* **1** : a long narrow boat used on the canals of Venice **2** : a railroad car with no top used for hauling loose freight (as coal) **3** : an enclosure attached to the underside of an airship or balloon **4** : an enclosed car suspended from a cable and used esp. for transporting skiers

gon·do·lier \ˌgän-də-ˈliər\ *n* : one who propels a gondola

gone \ˈgȯn\ *adj* **1** : DEAD **2** : LOST, RUINED **3** : SINKING, WEAK **4** : INVOLVED, ABSORBED **5** : INFATUATED **6** : PREGNANT **7** : PAST

gon·er \ˈgȯn-ər\ *n* : one whose case is hopeless

gon·fa·lon \ˈgän-fə-ˌlän\ *n* : a flag that hangs from a crosspiece or frame

gong \ˈgäŋ, ˈgȯŋ\ *n* : a metallic disk that produces a resounding tone when struck

gono·coc·cus \ˌgän-ə-ˈkäk-əs\ *n, pl* **-coc·ci** \-ˈkäk-ˌ(s)ī, -ˈkäk-ˌ(ˌ)(s)ē\ : a pus-producing bacterium that causes gonorrhea — **gono·coc·cal** \-ˈkäk-əl\ *or* **gono·coc·cic** \-ˈkäk-(s)ik\ *adj*

gon·or·rhea \ˌgän-ə-ˈrē-ə\ *n* : a contagious sexually transmitted inflammation of the genital tract caused by a bacterium — **gon·or·rhe·al** \-ˈrē-əl\ *adj*

goo \ˈgü\ *n* **1** : a viscid or sticky substance **2** : sentimental tripe — **gooey** \-ē\ *adj*

goo·ber \ˈgü-bər, ˈgüb-ər\ *n, South & Midland* : PEANUT

¹**good** \ˈgu̇d\ *adj* **bet·ter** \ˈbet-ər\ ; **best** \ˈbest\ **1** : of a favorable character or tendency **2** : BOUNTIFUL, FERTILE **3** : COMELY, ATTRACTIVE **4** : SUITABLE, FIT **5** : SOUND, WHOLE **6** : AGREEABLE, PLEASANT **7** : SALUTARY, WHOLESOME **8** : CONSIDERABLE, AMPLE **9** : FULL **10** : WELL-FOUNDED **11** : TRUE (holds ~ for everybody) **12** : recognized or valid esp. in law **13** : ADEQUATE, SATISFACTORY **14** : conforming to a standard **15** : DISCRIMINATING **16** : COMMENDABLE, VIRTUOUS **17** : KIND **18** : UPPER-CLASS **19** : COMPETENT **20** : LOYAL — **good-heart·ed** \-ˈhärt-əd\ *adj* **13** : ADEQUATE, SATISFACTORY — **good·ish** *adj* — **good-look·ing** \ˌgu̇d-ˈlu̇k-iŋ\ *adj* — **good-na·tured** \-ˈnā-chərd\ *adj* — **good-tem·pered** \-ˈtem-pərd\ *adj*

²**good** *n* **1** : something good **2** : GOODNESS **3** : BENEFIT, WELFARE (for the ~ of mankind) **4** : something that has economic utility **5** *pl* : personal property **6** *pl* : CLOTH **7** *pl* : WARES, COMMODITIES **8** : good persons (the ~ die young) **9** *pl* : proof of wrongdoing — **for good** : FOREVER, PERMANENTLY — **to the good** : in a position of net gain or profit ($10 *to the good*)

³**good** *adv* : WELL

good-bye *or* **good-by** \gu̇d-ˈbī, gə(d)-\ *n* : a concluding remark at parting

good-for-noth·ing \ˈgu̇d-fər-ˌnəth-iŋ\ *n* : an idle worthless person

Good Friday *n* : the Friday before Easter observed as the anniversary of the crucifixion of Christ

good·ly \ˈgu̇d-lē\ *adj* **good·li·er; -est 1** : of pleasing appearance **2** : LARGE, CONSIDERABLE

good·man \ˈgu̇d-mən\ *n, archaic* : MR.

good·ness \ˈgu̇d-nəs\ *n* : EXCELLENCE, VIRTUE

good·wife \ˈgu̇d-ˌwīf\ *n, archaic* : MRS.

good·will \ˈgu̇d-ˈwil\ *n* **1** : BENEVOLENCE **2** : the value of the trade a business has built up over time **3** : cheerful consent **4** : willing effort

goody \ˈgu̇d-ē\ *n, pl* **good·ies** : something that is good esp. to eat

goody-goody \ˌgu̇d-ē-ˈgu̇d-ē\ *adj* : affectedly good — **goody-goody** *n*

goof \ˈgüf\ *vb* **1** : BLUNDER **2** : to spend time idly or foolishly — often used with *off* — **goof** *n*

goof·ball \ˈgüf-ˌbȯl\ *n* **1** *slang* : a barbiturate sleeping pill **2** *slang* : a goofy person

go off *vb* **1** : EXPLODE **2** : to follow a course (the party *went off* well)

goof-off \ˈgüf-ˌȯf\ *n* : one who evades work or responsibility

goofy \ˈgü-fē\ *adj* **goof·i·er; -est** : CRAZY, SILLY — **goof·i·ness** \ˈgü-fē-nəs\ *n*

goon \ˈgün\ *n* : a man hired to terrorize or kill opponents

go on *vb* **1** : to continue in a course of action **2** : to take place : HAPPEN

goose \ˈgüs\ *n, pl* **geese** \ˈgēs\ **1** : any of numerous long-necked web-footed birds related to the swans and ducks; *esp* : a female goose as distinguished from a gander **2** : a foolish person **3** *pl* **goos·es** : a tailor's smoothing iron

goose·ber·ry \ˈgüs-ˌber-ē, ˈgüz-, -b(ə-)rē\ *n* : the acid berry of any of several shrubs related to the currant and used esp. in jams and pies

goose·flesh \ˈgüs-ˌflesh\ *n* : a roughening of the skin caused usu. by cold or fear

goose pimples *n pl* : GOOSEFLESH

go out *vb* **1** : to become extinguished **2** : to become a candidate (*went out* for the football team)

go over *vb* : SUCCEED

GOP *abbr* Grand Old Party (Republican)

go·pher \ˈgō-fər\ *n* **1** : a burrowing American land tortoise **2** : any of several No. American burrowing rodents with large cheek pouches opening beside the mouth **3** : any of numerous small ground squirrels of the prairie region of No. America

¹**gore** \ˈgōr\ *n* : BLOOD

²**gore** *n* : a tapering or triangular piece (as of cloth in a skirt)

³**gore** *vb* **gored; gor·ing** : to pierce or wound with something pointed

¹**gorge** \ˈgȯrj\ *n* **1** : THROAT **2** : a narrow ravine **3** : a mass of matter that chokes up a passage

²**gorge** *vb* **gorged; gorg·ing** : to eat greedily : stuff to capacity : GLUT

gor·geous \ˈgȯr-jəs\ *adj* [ME *gorgayse*, fr. MF *gorgias* elegant] : resplendently beautiful

Gor·gon·zo·la \ˌgȯr-gən-ˈzō-lə\ *n* : a blue cheese of Italian origin

go·ril·la \gə-ˈril-ə\ *n* [fr. Gk *Gorillai*, an African tribe of hairy women] : an African manlike ape related to but much larger than the chimpanzee

gor·man·dize \\'gȯr-mən-ˌdīz\\ vb **-dized;**
-diz·ing : to eat ravenously — **gor·**
man·diz·er n

gorp \\'gȯrp\\ n : a snack consisting of
high-calorie food (as raisins and nuts)

gorse \\'gȯrs\\ n : a prickly mostly leafless evergreen Old World shrub of the
legume family that bears yellow flowers

gory \\'gȯr-ē\\ adj **gor·i·er; -est 1** : BLOOD-
STAINED **2** : HORRIBLE, SENSATIONAL

gos·hawk \\'gäs-ˌhȯk\\ n : any of several
long-tailed hawks with short rounded
wings

gos·ling \\'gäz-liŋ, 'gȯz-\\ n : a young
goose

¹gos·pel \\'gäs-pəl\\ n [ME, fr. OE
gōdspel, fr. *gōd* good + *spell* tale] **1**
: the teachings of Christ and the apostles **2** cap : any of the first four books
of the New Testament **3** : something
accepted as infallible truth

²gospel adj **1** : of, relating to, or emphasizing the gospel **2** : relating to or being American religious songs associated with evangelism

gos·sa·mer \\'gäs-ə-mər, 'gäz-(ə-)mər\\ n
[ME *gossomer*, fr. *gos* goose + *so-*
mer summer] **1** : a film of cobwebs
floating in the air **2** : something light,
delicate, or tenuous

¹gos·sip \\'gäs-əp\\ n **1** : a person who
habitually reveals personal or sensational facts **2** : rumor or report of an
intimate nature **3** : an informal conversation — **gos·sipy** adj

²gossip vb : to spread gossip

got past and past part of GET

Goth \\'gäth\\ n : a member of a Germanic race that early in the Christian era
overran the Roman Empire

¹Goth·ic \\'gäth-ik\\ adj **1** : of or relating
to the Goths **2** : of or relating to a
style of architecture prevalent in
western Europe from the middle 12th
to the earth 16th century

²Gothic n **1** : the Germanic language of
the Goths **2** : the Gothic architectural
style or decoration

gotten past part of GET

Gou·da \\'güd-ə\\ n : a mild Dutch milk
cheese shaped in balls

¹gouge \\'gauj\\ n **1** : a rounded troughlike
chisel **2** : a hole or groove made with
or as if with a gouge

²gouge vb **gouged; goug·ing 1** : to cut
holes or grooves in with or as if with a
gouge **2** : DEFRAUD, CHEAT

gou·lash \\'gü-ˌläsh, -ˌlash\\ n [Hungari-
an *gulyás*] : a stew made with meat,
assorted vegetables, and paprika

go under vb : to be overwhelmed, defeated, or destroyed : FAIL

gourd \\'gȯrd, 'gurd\\ n **1** : any of a family of tendril-bearing vines including
the cucumber, squash, and melon **2**
: the fruit of a gourd; esp : any of various inedible hard-shelled fruits used
esp. for ornament or implements

gourde \\'gurd\\ n — see MONEY table

gour·mand \\'gur-ˌmänd\\ n **1** : one who

is excessively fond of eating and
drinking **2** : GOURMET

gour·met \\'gur-ˌmā, gur-'mā\\ n [F, fr.
MF, fr. *gromet* boy servant, vintner's
assistant] : a connoisseur in eating
and drinking

gout \\'gaut\\ n : a disease marked by
painful inflammation and swelling of
the joints — **gouty** adj

gov abbr **1** government **2** governor

gov·ern \\'gəv-ərn\\ vb **1** : to control and
direct the making and administration
of policy in : RULE **2** : CONTROL, DI-
RECT, INFLUENCE **3** : DETERMINE, REGU-
LATE **4** : RESTRAIN — **gov·er·nance**
\\'gəv-ər-nəns\\ n

gov·ern·ess \\'gəv-ər-nəs\\ n : a woman
who teaches and trains a child esp. in
a private home

gov·ern·ment \\'gəv-ər(n)-mənt\\ n **1**
: authoritative direction or control
: RULE **2** : the making of policy **3** : the
organization or agency through which
a political unit exercises authority **4**
: the complex of institutions, laws,
and customs through which a political
unit is governed **5** : the governing
body — **gov·ern·men·tal** \\ˌgəv-
ər(n)-¹ment-ᵊl\\ adj

gov·er·nor \\'gəv-(ə-)nər, 'gəv-ər-nər\\ n
1 : one that governs; esp : a ruler,
chief executive, or head of a political
unit (as a state) **2** : an attachment to a
machine for automatic control of
speed — **gov·er·nor·ship** n

govt abbr government

gown \\'gaun\\ n **1** : a loose flowing outer
garment **2** : an official robe worn esp.
by a judge, clergyman, or teacher **3**
: a woman's dress (evening ∼s) **4** : a
loose robe — **gown** vb

gp abbr group

GP abbr general practitioner

GPO abbr **1** general post office **2** Government Printing Office

GQ abbr general quarters

gr abbr **1** grade **2** grain **3** gram **4** gravity
5 gross

grab \\'grab\\ vb **grabbed; grab·bing** : to
take hastily : SNATCH — **grab** n

¹grace \\'grās\\ n **1** : help given man by
God (as in overcoming temptation) **2**
: freedom from sin through divine
grace **3** : a virtue coming from God **4**
: a short prayer at a meal **5** : a temporary respite (as from the payment of a
debt) **6** : APPROVAL, ACCEPTANCE (in his
good ∼s) **7** : CHARM **8** : ATTRACTIVE-
NESS, BEAUTY **9** : fitness or proportion
of line or expression **10** : ease of
movement **11** : a musical trill or ornament **12** — used as a title for a duke, a
duchess, or an archbishop — **grace·ful**
\\-fəl\\ adj — **grace·ful·ly** \\-ē\\ adv —
grace·ful·ness n — **grace·less** adj

²grace vb **graced; grac·ing 1** : HONOR **2**
: ADORN, EMBELLISH

gra·cious \\'grā-shəs\\ adj **1** : marked by
kindness and courtesy **2** : GRACEFUL **3**
: characterized by charm and good

taste **4** : MERCIFUL — **gra·cious·ly** *adv*
— **gra·cious·ness** *n*

grack·le \'grak-əl\ *n* **1** : an Old World
starling **2** : an American blackbird
with glossy iridescent plumage

grad *abbr* graduate

gra·da·tion \grā-'dā-shən, grə-\ *n* **1** : a
series forming successive stages **2** : a
step, degree, or stage in a series **3** : an
advance by regular degrees **4** : the act
or process of grading

1grade \'grād\ *vb* **grad·ed; grad·ing 1** : to
arrange in grades : SORT **2** : to make
level or evenly sloping ⟨∼ a highway⟩
3 : to give a grade to ⟨∼ a pupil in
history⟩ **4** : to assign to a grade

2grade *n* **1** : a degree or stage in a series,
order, or ranking **2** : a position in a
scale of rank, quality, or order **3** : a
class of persons or things of the same
rank or quality **4** : a division of the
school course representing one year's
work; *also* : the pupils in such a division **5** *pl* : the elementary school system **6** : a mark or rating esp. of accomplishment in school **7** : the degree
of slope (as of a road); *also* : SLOPE

grad·er \'grād-ər\ *n* : a machine for leveling earth

grade school *n* : ELEMENTARY SCHOOL

gra·di·ent \'grād-ē-ənt\ *n* : SLOPE, GRADE

grad·u·al \'graj-(ə-w)əl\ *adj* : proceeding or changing by steps or degrees —
grad·u·al·ly \-ē\ *adv*

grad·u·al·ism \-,iz-əm\ *n* : the policy of
approaching a desired end gradually

1grad·u·ate \'graj-(ə-)wət, -ə-,wāt\ *n* **1**
: a holder of an academic degree or
diploma **2** : a graduated container for
measuring contents

2graduate *adj* **1** : holding an academic
degree or diploma **2** : of or relating to
studies beyond the first or bachelor's
degree ⟨∼ school⟩

3grad·u·ate \'graj-ə-,wāt\ *vb* **-at·ed; -at-
ing 1** : to grant or receive an academic
degree or diploma **2** : to admit to a
particular standing or grade **3** : to divide into grades, classes, or intervals
⟨*graduated* thermometer⟩

grad·u·a·tion \,graj-ə-'wā-shən\ *n* **1** : a
mark that graduates something **2** : an
act or process of graduating **3** : COM-
MENCEMENT 2

graf·fi·to \gra-'fēt-ō, grə-\ *n*, *pl* **-ti** \-(,)ē\
: an inscription or drawing made on a
public surface (as a wall)

1graft \'graft\ *n* **1** : a grafted plant; *also*
: the point of union in this **2** : material
(as skin) used in grafting **3** : the getting of money or advantage dishonestly; *also* : the money or advantage so
gained

2graft *vb* **1** : to insert a shoot from one
plant into another so that they join
and grow; *also* : to join one thing to
another as in plant grafting ⟨∼ skin
over a burn⟩ **2** : to get (as money) dishonestly — **graft·er** *n*

gra·ham cracker \'grā-əm-, 'gram-\ *n*

: a slightly sweet cracker made chiefly
of whole wheat flour

Grail \'grāl\ *n* : the cup or platter used
according to medieval legend by
Christ at the Last Supper and thereafter the object of knightly quests

grain \'grān\ *n* **1** : a seed or fruit of a
cereal grass **2** : seeds or fruits of various food plants and esp. cereal
grasses; *also* : a plant producing grain
3 : a small hard particle **4** : a unit of
weight based on the weight of a grain
of wheat — see WEIGHT table **5** : TEX-
TURE; *also* : the arrangement of fibers
in wood **6** : natural disposition —
grained \'grānd\ *adj*

grain alcohol *n* : ALCOHOL 1

grain·field \'grān-,fēld\ *n* : a field
where grain is grown

grainy \'grā-nē\ *adj* **grain·i·er; -est 1**
: resembling or having some characteristic of grain : not smooth or fine
2 *of a photograph* : appearing to be
composed of grain-like particles

1gram \'gram\ *n* [F *gramme*, fr. LL
gramma, a weight, fr. Gk *gramma* letter, writing, a small weight, fr.
graphein to write] : a metric unit of
mass and weight equal to 1/1000 kilogram and nearly equal to one cubic
centimeter of water at its maximum
density — see METRIC SYSTEM table

2gram *abbr* grammar; grammatical

-gram \,gram\ *n comb form* : drawing
: writing : record ⟨telegram⟩

gram·mar \'gram-ər\ *n* **1** : the study of
the classes of words, their inflections,
and their functions and relations in the
sentence **2** : a study of what is to be
preferred and what avoided in inflection and syntax; *also* : speech or writing evaluated according to its conformity to the principles of grammar —
gram·mar·i·an \grə-'mer-ē-ən, -'mar-\
n — **gram·mat·i·cal** \-'mat-i-kəl\ *adj*—
gram·mat·i·cal·ly \-k(ə-)lē\ *adv*

grammar school *n* **1** : a secondary
school emphasizing Latin and Greek
in preparation for college; *also* : a
British college preparatory school **2**
: a school intermediate between the
primary grades and high school **3** : EL-
EMENTARY SCHOOL

gramme \'gram\ *chiefly Brit var of*
GRAM

gram·o·phone \'gram-ə-,fōn\ *n*
: PHONOGRAPH

gra·na·ry \'grān-(ə-)rē, 'gran-\ *n*, *pl*
-ries 1 : a storehouse for grain **2** : a
region producing grain in abundance

1grand \'grand\ *adj* **1** : higher in rank or
importance : FOREMOST, CHIEF **2**
: great in size **3** : INCLUSIVE, COMPLETE
⟨a ∼ total⟩ **4** : MAGNIFICENT, SPLENDID
5 : showing wealth or high social
standing **6** : IMPRESSIVE, STATELY **7**
: very good : FINE — **grand·ly** \'gran-
(d)lē\ *adv* — **grand·ness** \'gran(d)-nəs\
n

2grand *n, slang* : a thousand dollars

gran·dam \'gran-,dam, -dəm\ *or* **gran-**

dame \-ˌdām, -dəm\ *n* : an old woman

grand·child \ˈgran(d)-ˌchīld\ *n* : a child of one's son or daughter

grand·daugh·ter \ˈgran-ˌdȯt-ər\ *n* : a daughter of one's son or daughter

grande dame \ˈgrän-ˈdäm\ *n, pl* **grandes dames** : a usu. elderly woman of great prestige or ability

gran·dee \gran-ˈdē\ *n* : a high-ranking Spanish or Portuguese nobleman

gran·deur \ˈgran-jər\ *n* 1 : the quality or state of being grand : MAGNIFICENCE 2 : something that is grand

grand·fa·ther \ˈgran(d)-ˌfäth-ər\ *n* : the father of one's father or mother; *also* : ANCESTOR

grandfather clock *n* : a tall clock standing directly on the floor

gran·dil·o·quence \gran-ˈdil-ə-kwəns\ *n* : pompous eloquence — **gran·dil·o·quent** \-kwənt\ *adj*

gran·di·ose \ˈgran-dē-ˌōs, ˌgran-dē-ˈōs\ *adj* : IMPRESSIVE, IMPOSING; *also* : affectedly splendid — **gran·di·ose·ly** *adv* — **gran·di·os·i·ty** \ˌgran-dē-ˈäs-ət-ē\ *n*

grand mal \ˈgrän(d)-ˌmäl; ˈgran(d)-ˌmal\ *n* [F, lit., great illness] : severe epilepsy

grand·moth·er \ˈgran(d)-ˌməth-ər\ *n* : the mother of one's father or mother; *also* : a female ancestor

grand·par·ent \-ˌpar-ənt\ *n* : a parent of one's father or mother

grand piano *n* : a piano with horizontal frame and strings

grand prix \ˈgrän-ˈprē\ *n, pl* **grand prix** \-ˈprē(z)\ *often cap G&P* : a long-distance auto race over a road course

grand slam *n* 1 : a total victory or success 2 : a home run hit with three runners on base

grand·son \ˈgran(d)-ˌsən\ *n* : a son of one's son or daughter

grand·stand \-ˌstand\ *n* : a usu. roofed stand for spectators at a racecourse or stadium

grange \ˈgrānj\ *n* 1 : a farm or farmhouse with its various buildings 2 *cap* : one of the lodges of a national association originally made up of farmers; *also* : the association itself — **grang·er** \ˈgrān-jər\ *n*

gran·ite \ˈgran-ət\ *n* : a hard igneous rock that takes a polish and is used for building — **gra·nit·ic** \gra-ˈnit-ik\ *adj*

gran·ite·ware \-ˌwaər\ *n* : enameled ironware

gra·no·la \grə-ˈnō-lə\ *n* : a mixture of rolled oats and usu. raisins and nuts eaten esp. for breakfast

¹**grant** \ˈgrant\ *vb* 1 : to consent to : ALLOW, PERMIT 2 : GIVE, BESTOW 3 : to admit as true — **grant·er** \-ər\ *n* — **grant·or** \ˈgrant-ər, -ˌȯr\ *n*

²**grant** *n* 1 : the act of granting 2 : something granted; *esp* : a gift for a particular purpose (a ~ for study abroad) 3 : a transfer of property by deed or writing; *also* : the instrument by which such a transfer is made 4 : the property transferred by grant

grant·ee \grant-ˈē\ *n* : one to whom a grant is made

grants·man·ship \ˈgrants-mən-ˌship\ *n* : the art of obtaining grants (as for research) — **grants·man** *n*

gran·u·lar \ˈgran-yə-lər\ *adj* : consisting of or appearing to consist of granules — **gran·u·lar·i·ty** \ˌgran-yə-ˈlar-ət-ē\ *n*

gran·u·late \ˈgran-yə-ˌlāt\ *vb* **-lat·ed**; **-lat·ing** : to form into grains or crystals — **gran·u·la·tion** \ˌgran-yə-ˈlā-shən\ *n*

gran·ule \ˈgran-yül\ *n* : a small grain or particle

grape \ˈgrāp\ *n* [ME, fr. OF *crape*, *grape* hook, grape stalk, bunch of grapes, grape] 1 : a smooth-skinned juicy edible greenish white, deep red, or purple berry that is the chief source of wine 2 : any of numerous woody vines widely grown for their bunches of grapes

grape·fruit \ˈgrāp-ˌfrüt\ *n* : a large edible yellow-skinned citrus fruit; *also* : a tree bearing grapefruit

grape hyacinth *n* : any of several small bulbous spring-flowering herbs with racemes of usu. blue flowers that are related to the lilies

grape·shot \ˈgrāp-ˌshät\ *n* : a cluster of small iron balls formerly fired at people from short range by a cannon

grape·vine \ˈgrāp-ˌvīn\ *n* 1 : GRAPE 2 2 : RUMOR; *also* : an informal means of circulating information or gossip

graph \ˈgraf\ *n* : a diagram that usu. by means of dots and lines shows relationships between things — **graph** *vb*

-graph \ˌgraf\ *n comb form* 1 : something written (autograph) 2 : instrument for making or transmitting records (seismograph)

graph·ic \ˈgraf-ik\ *also* **graph·i·cal** \-i-kəl\ *adj* 1 : being written, drawn, or engraved 2 : vividly described 3 : of or relating to the arts (**graphic arts**) of representation, decoration, and printing on flat surfaces — **graph·i·cal·ly** \-i-k(ə-)lē\ *adv* — **graph·ics** \-iks\ *n*

graphics tablet *n* : a computer input device for entering graphics information by drawing or tracing

graph·ite \ˈgraf-ˌīt\ *n* [G *Graphit*, fr. Gk *graphein* to write] : soft carbon used esp. for lead pencils and lubricants

grap·nel \ˈgrap-nᵊl\ *n* : a small anchor with two or more claws used esp. in dragging or grappling operations

¹**grap·ple** \ˈgrap-əl\ *n* [MF *grappelle*, dim. of *grape* hook] 1 : GRAPNEL 2 : the act of grappling

²**grapple** *vb* **grap·pled**; **grap·pling** \ˈgrap-(ə-)liŋ\ 1 : to seize or hold with or as if with a hooked implement 2 : to come to grips with : WRESTLE 3 : COPE (~ with a problem)

¹**grasp** \ˈgrasp\ *vb* 1 : to make the motion of seizing 2 : to take or seize firm-

ly **3** : to enclose and hold with the fingers or arms **4** : COMPREHEND

²**grasp** n **1** : HANDLE **2** : EMBRACE **3** : HOLD, CONTROL **4** : the reach of the arms **5** : the power of seizing and holding **6** : COMPREHENSION

grasp·ing \-iŋ\ adj : GREEDY, AVARICIOUS

grass \'gras\ n **1** : herbage for grazing animals **2** : any of a large family of plants (as wheat, bamboo, or sugarcane) with jointed stems and narrow leaves **3** : grass-covered land **4** : MARIJUANA — **grassy** adj

grass·hop·per \-ˌhäp-ər\ n : any of numerous leaping plant-eating insects

grass·land \-ˌland\ n : land covered naturally or under cultivation with grasses and low-growing herbs

grass roots n pl : society at the local level as distinguished from the centers of political leadership

¹**grate** \'grāt\ vb **grat·ed; grat·ing** **1** : to pulverize by rubbing against something rough **2** : to grind or rub against with a rasping noise **3** : IRRITATE — **grat·er** n — **grat·ing·ly** \'grāt-iŋ-lē\ adv

²**grate** n **1** : a framework with bars across it (as in a window) **2** : a frame of iron bars for holding fuel while it is burning

grate·ful \'grāt-fəl\ adj **1** : THANKFUL, APPRECIATIVE; also : expressing gratitude **2** : PLEASING — **grate·ful·ly** \-ē\ adv — **grate·ful·ness** n

grat·i·fy \'grat-ə-ˌfī\ vb **-fied; -fy·ing** : to afford pleasure to — **grat·i·fi·ca·tion** \ˌgrat-ə-fə-'kā-shən\ n

grat·ing \'grāt-iŋ\ n : GRATE

gra·tis \'grat-əs, 'grāt-\ adv or adj : without charge or recompense : FREE

grat·i·tude \'grat-ə-ˌt(y)üd\ n : THANKFULNESS

gra·tu·itous \grə-'t(y)ü-ət-əs\ adj **1** : done or provided without recompense : FREE **2** : UNWARRANTED

gra·tu·ity \-ət-ē\ n, pl **-ities** : TIP

gra·va·men \grə-'vā-mən\ n, pl **-vamens** or **-vam·i·na** \-'vam-ə-nə\ [LL burden] : the basic or significant part of a grievance or complaint

¹**grave** \'grāv\ vb **graved; grav·en** \'grā-vən\ or **graved; grav·ing** : SCULPTURE, ENGRAVE

²**grave** n : an excavation in the earth as a place of burial; also : TOMB

³**grave** \'grāv; 5 also 'gräv\ adj **1** : IMPORTANT **2** : threatening serious harm or danger **3** : DIGNIFIED, SOLEMN **4** : drab in color : SOMBER **5** : of, marked by, or being an accent mark having the form ` — **grave·ly** adv — **grave·ness** n

grav·el \'grav-əl\ n : pebbles and small pieces of rock larger than grains of sand — **grav·el·ly** \-ē\ adj

grave·stone \'grāv-ˌstōn\ n : a burial monument

grave·yard \-ˌyärd\ n : CEMETERY

grav·id \'grav-əd\ adj [L gravidus, fr. gravis heavy] : PREGNANT

gra·vim·e·ter \gra-'vim-ət-ər, 'grav-ə-ˌmēt-\ n : a device for measuring variations in a gravitational field

grav·i·tate \'grav-ə-ˌtāt\ vb **-tat·ed; -tat·ing** : to move or tend to move toward something

grav·i·ta·tion \ˌgrav-ə-'tā-shən\ n **1** : a natural force of attraction that tends to draw bodies together **2** : the action or process of gravitating — **grav·i·ta·tion·al** \-sh(ə-)nəl\ adj — **grav·i·ta·tion·al·ly** \-ē\ adv — **grav·i·ta·tive** \'grav-ə-ˌtāt-iv\ adj

grav·i·ty \'grav-ət-ē\ n, pl **-ties** **1** : IMPORTANCE; esp : SERIOUSNESS **2** : ²MASS **5** **3** : the gravitational attraction of the mass of a celestial object (as earth) for bodies close to it; also : GRAVITATION **1**

gra·vure \grə-'vyùr\ n [F] : PHOTOGRAVURE

gra·vy \'grā-vē\ n, pl **gravies** **1** : a sauce made from the thickened and seasoned juices of cooked meat **2** : unearned or illicit gain : GRAFT

¹**gray** \'grā\ adj **1** : of the color gray; also : dull in color **2** : having gray hair **3** : CHEERLESS, DISMAL **4** : intermediate in position or character — **gray·ish** adj — **gray·ness** n

²**gray** n **1** : something of a gray color **2** : a neutral color ranging between black and white

³**gray** vb : to make or become gray

gray·beard \'grā-ˌbiərd\ n : an old man

gray birch n : a small No. American birch with many lateral branches, grayish white bark, and soft wood

gray·ling \'grā-liŋ\ n, pl **grayling** also **graylings** : any of several slender freshwater food and sport fishes related to the trouts

gray matter n **1** : the grayish part of nervous tissue consisting mostly of nerve cell bodies **2** : INTELLIGENCE

¹**graze** \'grāz\ vb **grazed; graz·ing** **1** : to feed on herbage or pasture **2** : to feed (livestock) on grass or pasture — **graz·er** n

²**graze** vb **grazed; graz·ing** **1** : to touch lightly in passing : SCRATCH, ABRADE

¹**grease** \'grēs\ n **1** : rendered animal fat **2** : oily material **3** : a thick lubricant — **greasy** \'grē-sē, -zē\ adj

²**grease** \'grēs, 'grēz\ vb **greased; greas·ing** : to smear or lubricate with grease

grease·paint \'grēs-ˌpānt\ n : theater makeup

great \'grāt\ adj **1** : large in size : BIG **2** : ELABORATE, AMPLE **3** : large in number : NUMEROUS **4** : being beyond the average · : MIGHTY, INTENSE ⟨a ~ weight⟩ ⟨in ~ pain⟩ **5** : EMINENT, GRAND **6** : long continued ⟨a ~ while⟩ **7** : MAIN, PRINCIPAL **8** : more distant in a family relationship by one generation ⟨a great-grandfather⟩ **9** : markedly superior in character, quality, or skill ⟨~ at bridge⟩ **10** : EXCELLENT, FINE ⟨had a ~ time⟩ — **great·ly** adv — **great·ness** n

great circle n : a circle on the surface of

a sphere that has the same center as the sphere; *esp* : one on the surface of the earth an arc of which is the shortest travel distance between two points

great-coat \'grāt-ˌkōt\ *n* : a heavy overcoat

Great Dane *n* : any of a breed of tall massive powerful smooth-coated dogs

great-heart-ed \'grāt-'härt-əd\ *adj* 1 : COURAGEOUS 2 : MAGNANIMOUS

great power *n, often cap G&P* : one of the nations that figure most decisively in international affairs

great white shark *n* : WHITE SHARK

grebe \'grēb\ *n* : any of a family of lobe-toed diving birds related to the loons

Gre-cian \'grē-shən\ *adj* : GREEK

greed \'grēd\ *n* : acquisitive or selfish desire beyond reason — **greed·i·ly** \'grēd-əl-ē\ *adv* — **greed·i·ness** \-ē-nəs\ *n* — **greedy** \'grēd-ē\ *adj*

¹Greek \'grēk\ *n* 1 : a native or inhabitant of Greece 2 : the ancient or modern language of Greece

²Greek *adj* 1 : of, relating to, or characteristic of Greece, the Greeks, or Greek 2 : ORTHODOX 3

¹green \'grēn\ *adj* 1 : of the color green 2 : covered with verdure; *also* : consisting of green plants or of the leafy parts of plants (a ~ salad) 3 : UNRIPE; *also* : IMMATURE 4 : having a sickly appearance 5 : not fully processed or treated (~ liquor) (~ hides) 6 : INEXPERIENCED; *also* : NAIVE — **green·ish** *adj* — **green·ness** \'grēn-nəs\ *n*

²green *vb* : to make or become green

³green *n* 1 : a color between blue and yellow in the spectrum : the color of growing fresh grass or of the emerald 2 : something of a green color 3 *pl* : leafy parts of plants 4 : a grassy plot; *esp* : a smooth grassy area around the hole into which the ball must be played in golf

green·back \'grēn-ˌbak\ *n* : a U.S. legal-tender note

green bean *n* : a kidney bean that is used as a snap bean when the pods are colored green

green·belt \'grēn-ˌbelt\ *n* : a belt of parkways or farmlands that encircles a community

green·ery \'grēn-(ə-)rē\ *n, pl* **-er·ies** : green foliage or plants

green–eyed \'grēn-'īd\ *adj* : JEALOUS

green·gro·cer \'grēn-ˌgrō-sər\ *n* : a retailer of fresh vegetables and fruit

green·horn \-ˌhȯrn\ *n* : an inexperienced person; *esp* : one easily tricked or cheated

green·house \-ˌhaȯs\ *n* : a glass structure for the growing of tender plants

green manure *n* : an herbaceous crop (as clover) plowed under when green to enrich the soil

green onion *n* : a young onion pulled before the bulb has enlarged and used esp. in salads

green pepper *n* : SWEET PEPPER

green–room \'grēn-ˌrüm, -ˌrum\ *n* : a room in a theater or concert hall where actors or musicians relax before, between, or after appearances

green·sward \-ˌswȯrd\ *n* : turf that is green with growing grass

green thumb *n* : an unusual ability to make plants grow

Green·wich mean time \'grin-ij-, 'gren-, -ich-\ *n* [*Greenwich*, England] : GREENWICH TIME

Greenwich time *n* : the time of the meridian of Greenwich used as the basis of worldwide standard time

green·wood \'grēn-ˌwùd\ *n* : a forest green with foliage

greet \'grēt\ *vb* 1 : to address with expressions of kind wishes 2 : to meet or react to in a specified manner 3 : to be perceived by — **greet·er** *n*

greet·ing \-iŋ\ *n* 1 : a salutation on meeting 2 *pl* : best wishes : REGARDS

greeting card *n* : a card that bears a message usu. sent on a special occasion

gre·gar·i·ous \gri-'gar-ē-əs\ *adj* [L *gregarius* of a herd or flock, fr. *greg-, grex* flock, herd] 1 : SOCIAL, COMPANIONABLE 2 : tending to flock together — **gre·gar·i·ous·ly** *adv* — **gre·gar·i·ous·ness** *n*

grem·lin \'grem-lən\ *n* : a small gnome held to be responsible for malfunction of equipment esp. in aircraft

gre·nade \grə-'nād\ *n* [MF, pomegranate, fr. LL *granata*, fr. L *granatus* seedy, fr. *granum* grain] : a small bomb that is thrown by hand or launched (as by a rifle)

gren·a·dier \ˌgren-ə-'diər\ *n* : a member of a European regiment formerly armed with grenades

gren·a·dine \ˌgren-ə-'dēn, 'gren-ə-ˌdēn\ *n* : a syrup flavored with pomegranates and used in mixed drinks

grew *past of* GROW

grey *var of* GRAY

grey·hound \'grā-ˌhaȯnd\ *n* : a tall slender dog noted for speed and keen sight

grid \'grid\ *n* 1 : GRATE 2 : a metal plate used as a conductor in a storage battery 3 : an element in an electron tube consisting of a mesh of fine wire 4 : GRIDIRON 2; *also* : FOOTBALL

grid·dle \'grid-ᵊl\ *n* : a flat usu. metal surface for cooking food

griddle cake *n* : PANCAKE

grid·iron \'grid-ˌī(-ə)rn\ *n* 1 : a grate (as of parallel bars) for broiling food 2 : something resembling a gridiron in appearance; *esp* : a football field

grid·lock \'grid-ˌläk\ *n* : a traffic jam in which an intersection is so blocked that no vehicular movement is possible

grief \'grēf\ *n* 1 : emotional suffering caused by or as if by bereavement; *also* : a cause of such suffering 2 : MISHAP 3 : DISASTER

griev·ance \'grē-vəns\ *n* 1 : a cause of

distress affording reason for complaint or resistance 2 : COMPLAINT

grieve \'grēv\ vb **grieved; griev·ing** [ME *greven*, fr. OF *grever*, fr. L *gravare* to burden, fr. *gravis* heavy, grave] 1 : to cause grief or sorrow to : DISTRESS 2 : to feel grief : SORROW

griev·ous \'grē-vəs\ adj 1 : OPPRESSIVE, ONEROUS 2 : causing suffering, grief, or sorrow : SEVERE (a ~ wound) 3 : SERIOUS, GRAVE — **griev·ous·ly** adv

¹**grill** \'gril\ vb 1 : to broil on a grill; *also* : to fry or toast on a griddle 2 : to question intensely

²**grill** n 1 : a cooking utensil of parallel bars on which food is grilled 2 : an informal restaurant

grille *or* **grill** \'gril\ n : a grating that forms a barrier or screen

grill·work \'gril-ˌwərk\ n : work constituting or resembling a grille

grim \'grim\ adj **grim·mer; grim·mest** 1 : CRUEL, FIERCE 2 : harsh and forbidding in appearance 3 : RELENTLESS 4 : ghastly or repellent in character — **grim·ly** adv — **grim·ness** n

gri·mace \'grim-əs, grim-ˈās\ n : a facial expression usu. of disgust or disapproval — **grimace** vb

grime \'grim\ n : soot, smut, or dirt adhering to or embedded in a surface; *also* : accumulated dirtiness and disorder — **grimy** adj

grin \'grin\ vb **grinned; grin·ning** : to draw back the lips so as to show the teeth esp. in amusement — **grin** n

¹**grind** \'grind\ vb **ground** \'graund\; **grind·ing** 1 : to reduce to small particles 2 : to wear down, polish, or sharpen by friction 3 : to press with a grating noise : GRIT (~ the teeth) 4 : OPPRESS 5 : to operate or produce by turning a crank 6 : DRUDGE; *esp* : to study hard 7 : to move with difficulty or friction (gears ~ing)

²**grind** n 1 : monotonous labor or routine; *esp* : intensive study 2 : one who works or studies excessively

grind·er \'grin-dər\ n 1 : MOLAR 2 pl : TEETH 3 : one that grinds 4 : SUBMARINE 2

grind·stone \'grin-ˌstōn\ n : a flat circular stone of natural sandstone that revolves on an axle and is used for grinding, shaping, or smoothing

¹**grip** \'grip\ vb **gripped; grip·ping** 1 : to seize or hold firmly 2 : to hold strongly the interest of

²**grip** n 1 : GRASP; *also* : strength in gripping 2 : a firm tenacious hold 3 : UNDERSTANDING 4 : a device for grasping and holding 5 : TRAVELING BAG

gripe \'grip\ vb **griped; grip·ing** 1 : SEIZE, GRIP 2 : IRRITATE, VEX 3 : to cause or experience spasmodic pains in the bowels 4 : COMPLAIN — **gripe** n

grippe \'grip\ n : INFLUENZA

gris-gris \'grē-ˌgrē\ n, pl **gris-gris** \-ˌgrēz\ [F] : an amulet or incantation used chiefly by people of African Negro ancestry

gris·ly \'griz-lē\ adj **gris·li·er; -est** : HORRIBLE, GRUESOME

grist \'grist\ n : grain to be ground or already ground

gris·tle \'gris-əl\ n : CARTILAGE — **gristly** \-(ə-)lē\ adj

grist·mill \'grist-ˌmil\ n : a mill for grinding grain

¹**grit** \'grit\ n 1 : a hard sharp granule (as of sand); *also* : material composed of such granules 2 : unyielding courage — **grit·ty** adj

²**grit** vb **grit·ted; grit·ting** : GRIND, GRATE

grits \'grits\ n pl : coarsely ground hulled grain ⟨hominy ~⟩

griz·zled \'griz-əld\ adj : streaked or mixed with gray

griz·zly \'griz-lē\ adj **griz·zli·er; -est** : GRIZZLED

grizzly bear n : a large pale-coated bear of western No. America

gro abbr gross

groan \'grōn\ vb 1 : MOAN 2 : to make a harsh sound under sudden or prolonged strain ⟨the chair ~ed under his weight⟩ — **groan** n

groat \'grōt\ n : an old British coin worth four pennies

gro·cer \'grō-sər\ n [ME, fr. MF *grossier* wholesaler, fr. *gros* coarse, wholesale, fr. L *grossus* coarse] : a dealer esp. in staple foodstuffs — **gro·cery** \'grōs-(ə-)rē\ n

grog \'gräg\ n [*Old Grog*, nickname of Edward Vernon †1757 Eng. admiral responsible for diluting the sailors' rum] : alcoholic liquor; *esp* : liquor (as rum) mixed with water

grog·gy \'gräg-ē\ adj **grog·gi·er; -est** : weak and unsteady on the feet or in action — **grog·gi·ly** \'gräg-ə-lē\ adv — **grog·gi·ness** \-ē-nəs\ n

groin \'groin\ n 1 : the fold marking the juncture of the abdomen and thigh; *also* : the region of this fold 2 : the curved line or rib on a ceiling along which two vaults meet

grom·met \'gräm-ət, 'grəm-\ n 1 : a ring of rope 2 : an eyelet of firm material to strengthen or protect an opening

¹**groom** \'grüm, 'grum\ n 1 : a male servant; *esp* : one in charge of horses 2 : BRIDEGROOM

²**groom** vb 1 : to attend to the cleaning of (an animal) 2 : to make neat, attractive, or acceptable : POLISH

grooms·man \'grümz-mən, 'grumz-\ n : a male friend who attends a bridegroom at his wedding

¹**groove** \'grüv\ n 1 : a long narrow channel 2 : a fixed routine — **groove** vb

groovy \'grü-vē\ adj **groov·i·er; -est** : very good : EXCELLENT

grope \'grōp\ vb **groped; grop·ing** 1 : to feel about blindly or uncertainly in search ⟨~ for the right word⟩ 2 : to feel one's way by groping

gros·beak \'grōs-ˌbēk\ n : any of several finches of Europe or America with large stout conical bills

gro·schen \'grō-shən\ *n, pl* **groschen** — see *schilling* at MONEY table

gros·grain \'grō-ˌgrān\ *n* [F *gros grain* coarse texture] : a silk or rayon fabric with crosswise cotton ribs

¹**gross** \'grōs\ *adj* **1** : glaringly noticeable **2** : OUT-AND-OUT, UTTER **3** : BIG, BULKY; *esp* : excessively fat **4** : excessively luxuriant : RANK **5** : GENERAL, BROAD **6** : consisting of an overall total exclusive of deductions ⟨~ earnings⟩ **7** : EARTHY, CARNAL ⟨~ pleasures⟩ **8** : lacking knowledge or culture : UNREFINED **9** : OBSCENE — **gross·ly** *adv* — **gross·ness** *n*

²**gross** *n* : an overall total exclusive of deductions — **gross** *vb*

³**gross** *n, pl* **gross** : a total of 12 dozen things ⟨a ~ of pencils⟩

gross national product *n* : the total value of the goods and services produced in a nation during a year

gro·szy \'grō-shē\ *n, pl* **groszy** — see *zloty* at MONEY table

grot \'grät\ *n* : GROTTO

gro·tesque \grō-'tesk\ *adj* **1** : FANCIFUL, BIZARRE **2** : absurdly incongruous **3** : ECCENTRIC — **gro·tesque·ly** *adv*

grot·to \'grät-ō\ *n, pl* **grottoes** *also* **grottos 1** : CAVE **2** : an artificial cave-like structure

grouch \'grau̇ch\ *n* **1** : a fit of bad temper **2** : an habitually irritable or complaining person — **grouch** *vb* — **grouchy** *adj*

¹**ground** \'grau̇nd\ *n* **1** : the bottom of a body of water **2** *pl* : sediment at the bottom of a liquid : DREGS, LEES **3** : a basis for belief, action, or argument **4** : BACKGROUND **5** : FOUNDATION **6** : the surface of the earth; *also* : SOIL **7** : an area with a particular use ⟨fishing ~s⟩ **8** *pl* : the area about and belonging to a building **9** : a conductor that makes electrical connection with the earth — **ground·less** \'grau̇n-(d)ləs\ *adj*

²**ground** *vb* **1** : to bring to or place on the ground **2** : to provide a reason or justification for **3** : to instruct in fundamental principles **4** : to connect electrically with a ground **5** : to restrict to the ground **6** : to run aground

³**ground** *past and past part of* GRIND

ground ball *n* : a batted baseball that rolls or bounces along the ground

ground cover *n* : low plants that grow over and cover the soil; *also* : a plant suitable for this use

ground·er \'grau̇n-dər\ *n* : GROUND BALL

ground glass *n* : glass with a light-diffusing surface produced by etching or abrading

ground·hog \'grau̇nd-ˌhȯg, -ˌhäg\ *n* : WOODCHUCK

ground·ling \'grau̇nd-liŋ\ *n* **1** : a spectator in the cheaper part of a theater **2** : a person of inferior judgment or taste

ground rule *n* **1** : a sports rule adopted to modify play on a particular field, court, or course **2** : a rule of procedure

ground squirrel *n* : any of various burrowing rodents that are related to the squirrels and live in colonies in open areas

ground swell *n* **1** : a broad deep ocean swell caused by an often distant gale or earthquake **2** : a rapid spontaneous growth (as of political opinion)

ground·wa·ter \'grau̇nd-ˌwȯt-ər, -ˌwät-\ *n* : water within the earth that supplies wells and springs

ground·work \-ˌwərk\ *n* : FOUNDATION, BASIS

ground zero *n* : the point above, below, or at which a nuclear explosion occurs

¹**group** \'grüp\ *n* **1** : a number of individuals related by a common factor (as physical association, community of interests, or blood) **2** : a combination of atoms commonly found together in a molecule ⟨a methyl ~⟩

²**group** *vb* : to associate in groups : CLUSTER, AGGREGATE

grou·per \'grü-pər\ *n, pl* **groupers** *also* **grouper** : any of numerous large solitary bottom fishes of warm seas

group·ie \'grü-pē\ *n* : a fan of a rock group who usu. follows the group around on concert tours

group therapy *n* : therapy in the presence of a therapist in which several patients discuss their personal problems

¹**grouse** \'grau̇s\ *n, pl* **grouse** *or* **grouses** : any of numerous plump-bodied ground-dwelling game birds related to but usu. less brightly colored than the pheasants

²**grouse** *vb* **groused; grous·ing** : COMPLAIN, GRUMBLE

grout \'grau̇t\ *n* : material (as mortar) used for filling spaces — **grout** *vb*

grove \'grōv\ *n* : a small wood usu. without underbrush

grov·el \'gräv-əl, 'grəv-\ *vb* **-eled** *or* **-elled; -el·ing** *or* **-el·ling** \-(ə-)liŋ\ **1** : to creep or lie with the body prostrate in fear or humility **2** : to abase oneself

grow \'grō\ *vb* **grew** \'grü\ ; **grown** \'grōn\ ; **grow·ing 1** : to spring up and come to maturity **2** : to be able to grow : THRIVE **3** : to take on some relation through or as if through growth ⟨tree limbs grown together⟩ **4** : INCREASE, EXPAND **5** : RESULT, ORIGINATE **6** : to come into existence : ARISE **7** : BECOME **8** : to have an increasing influence **9** : to cause to grow — **grow·er** \'grō-(ə)r\ *n*

growl \'grau̇l\ *vb* **1** : RUMBLE **2** : to utter a deep throaty threatening sound **3** : GRUMBLE — **growl** *n*

grown-up \'grōn-ˌəp\ *adj* : not childish : ADULT — **grown-up** *n*

growth \'grōth\ *n* **1** : stage or condition attained in growing **2** : a process of growing esp. through progressive development or increase **3** : a result or product of growing ⟨a fine ~ of hair⟩ ; *also* : an abnormal mass of tissue (as a tumor)

¹**grub** \'grəb\ vb **grubbed; grub•bing 1** : to clear or root out by digging **2** : to dig in the ground usu. for a hidden object **3** : RUMMAGE

²**grub** n **1** : a soft thick wormlike larva (beetle ~s) **2** : DRUDGE; also : a slovenly person **3** : FOOD

grub•by \'grəb-ē\ adj **grub•bi•er; -est** : DIRTY, SLOVENLY — **grub•bi•ness** \'grəb-ē-nəs\ n

grub•stake \'grəb-ˌstāk\ n : supplies or funds furnished a mining prospector in return for a share in his finds

¹**grudge** \'grəj\ vb **grudged; grudg•ing** : to be reluctant to give : BEGRUDGE

²**grudge** n : a feeling of deep-seated resentment or ill will

gru•el \'grü-əl\ n : a thin porridge

gru•el•ing or **gru•el•ling** \-ə-liŋ\ adj : requiring extreme effort : EXHAUSTING

grue•some \'grü-səm\ adj [fr. earlier *growsome*, fr. E dial. *grow*, *grue* to shiver] : inspiring horror or repulsion : GRISLY

gruff \'grəf\ adj **1** : rough in speech or manner **2** : being deep and harsh : HOARSE — **gruff•ly** adv

grum•ble \'grəm-bəl\ vb **grum•bled; grum•bling** \-b(ə-)liŋ\ **1** : to mutter in discontent **2** : GROWL, RUMBLE — **grum•bler** \-b(ə-)lər\ n

grumpy \'grəm-pē\ adj **grump•i•er; -est** : moodily cross : SURLY — **grump•i•ly** \'grəm-pə-lē\ adv — **grump•i•ness** \-pē-nəs\ n

grun•gy \'grən-jē\ adj **grun•gi•er; -est** : shabby or dirty in character or condition

grun•ion \'grən-yən\ n : a fish of the California coast which comes inshore to spawn at nearly full moon

grunt \'grənt\ n : a deep throaty sound (as that of a hog) — **grunt** vb

GSA abbr **1** General Services Administration **2** Girl Scouts of America

G suit n [*gravity suit*] : an astronaut's or aviator's suit designed to counteract the physiological effects of acceleration

gt abbr great

Gt Brit abbr Great Britain

gtd abbr guaranteed

GU abbr Guam

gua•ca•mo•le \ˌgwäk-ə-'mō-lē\ n [AmerSp] : mashed and seasoned avocado

gua•nine \'gwän-ˌēn\ n : a purine base that codes genetic information in the molecular chain of DNA or RNA

gua•no \'gwän-ō\ n [Sp, fr. Quechua (a South American Indian language) *huanu* dung] : a substance composed chiefly of the excrement of seabirds and used as a fertilizer

gua•ra•ni \ˌgwär-ə-'nē\ n, pl **guaranies** also **guaranis** — see MONEY table

¹**guar•an•tee** \ˌgar-ən-'tē\ n **1** : GUARANTOR **2** : GUARANTY **3** : an agreement by which one person undertakes to secure another in the possession or enjoyment of something **4** : an assurance of the quality of or of the length of use to be expected from a product offered for sale **5** : GUARANTY **3**

²**guarantee** vb **-teed; -tee•ing 1** : to undertake to answer for the debt, failure to perform, or faulty performance of (another) **2** : to undertake an obligation to establish, perform, or continue **3** : to give security to

guar•an•tor \ˌgar-ən-'tȯr\ n : one who gives a guarantee

¹**guar•an•ty** \'gar-ən-tē\ n, pl **-ties 1** : an undertaking to answer for another's failure to pay a debt or perform a duty **2** : GUARANTEE **3 3** : PLEDGE, SECURITY **4** : GUARANTOR

²**guaranty** vb **-tied; -ty•ing** : GUARANTEE

¹**guard** \'gärd\ n **1** : one assigned to protect or oversee another **2** : a man or a body of men on sentinel duty **3** pl : troops attached to the person of the sovereign **4** : a defensive position (as in boxing) **5** : the act or duty of protecting or defending **6** : PROTECTION **7** : a football lineman playing between center and tackle; also : a basketball player stationed toward the rear **8** : a protective or safety device — **on guard** : WATCHFUL, ALERT

²**guard** vb **1** : PROTECT, DEFEND **2** : to watch over **3** : to be on guard

guard•house \'gärd-ˌhaůs\ n **1** : a building occupied by a guard or used as a headquarters by soldiers on guard duty **2** : a military jail

guard•ian \'gärd-ē-ən\ n **1** : CUSTODIAN **2** : one who has the care of the person or property of another — **guard•ian•ship** n

guard•room \'gärd-ˌrüm\ n **1** : a room used by a military guard while on duty **2** : a room where military prisoners are confined

guards•man \'gärdz-mən\ n : a member of a military body called *guard* or *guards*

gua•va \'gwäv-ə\ n : the sweet yellow acid fruit of a shrubby tropical American tree of the myrtle family used esp. for making jam and jelly; also : the tree

gu•ber•na•to•ri•al \ˌgüb-ə(r)-nə-'tȯr-ē-əl\ adj : of or relating to a governor

guer•don \'gərd-ⁿn\ n [ME, fr. MF, fr. Old High German *widarlōn*, fr. *widar* back + *lōn* reward] : REWARD, RECOMPENSE

guern•sey \'gərn-zē\ n, pl **guernseys** often cap : any of a breed of fawn and white dairy cattle that produce rich yellowish milk

guer•ril•la or **gue•ril•la** \gə-'ril-ə\ n [Sp *guerrilla*, fr. dim. of *guerra* war, of Gmc origin] : one who engages in irregular warfare esp. as a member of an independent unit

guess \'ges\ vb **1** : to form an opinion from little or no evidence **2** : to conjecture correctly about : DISCOVER **3** : BELIEVE, SUPPOSE — **guess** n

guest \'gest\ n **1** : a person to whom

hospitality (as of a house or a club) is extended **2** : a patron of a commercial establishment (as of a hotel or restaurant) **3** : a person not a regular member of a cast who appears on a program

guf·faw \gə-'fò\ n : a loud burst of laughter — **guf·faw** \(ˌ)gə-'fò\ vb

guid·ance \'gïd-²ns\ n **1** : the act or process of guiding **2** : ADVICE, DIRECTION

¹**guide** \'gïd\ n **1** : one who leads or directs another on a course **2** : one who shows and explains points of interest **3** : something that provides guiding information; also : SIGNPOST **4** : a device to direct the motion of something

²**guide** vb **guid·ed; guid·ing 1** : CONDUCT **2** : MANAGE, DIRECT **3** : to superintend the training of — **guid·able** \'gïd-ə-bəl\ adj

guide·book \'gïd-ˌbùk\ n : a book of information for travelers

guided missile n : a missile whose course may be altered during flight

guide·line \'gïd-ˌlïn\ n : an indication or outline of policy or conduct

guide word n : a term at the head of a page of an alphabetical reference work that indicates the alphabetically first or last word on that page

gui·don \'gïd-ˌän, -²n\ n : a small flag (as of a military unit)

guild \'gïld\ n : an association of people with common aims and interests; esp : a medieval association of merchants or craftsmen — **guild·hall** \-ˌhòl\ n

guil·der \'gil-dər\ n : GULDEN

guile \'gïl\ n : deceitful cunning : DUPLICITY — **guile·ful** adj — **guile·less** \'gïl-ləs\ adj — **guile·less·ness** n

guil·lo·tine \'gil-ə-ˌtēn, ˌgē-(y)ə-¹tēn\ n : a machine for beheading persons — **guillotine** vb

guilt \'gilt\ n **1** : the fact of having committed an offense esp. against the law **2** : BLAMEWORTHINESS **3** : a feeling of responsibility for wrongdoing — **guilt·less** adj

guilty \'gil-tē\ adj **guilt·i·er; -est 1** : having committed a breach of conduct **2** : suggesting or involving guilt **3** : aware of or suffering from guilt — **guilt·i·ly** \'gil-tə-lē\ adv — **guilt·i·ness** \-tē-nəs\ n

guin·ea \'gin-ē\ n **1** : a British gold coin no longer issued worth 21 shillings **2** : a unit of value equal to 21 shillings

guinea fowl n : a gray and white spotted West African bird related to the pheasants and widely raised for food; also : any of several related birds

guinea hen n : a female guinea fowl; also : GUINEA FOWL

guinea pig n : a small stocky short-eared and nearly tailless So. American rodent

guise \'gïz\ n **1** : a form or style of dress : COSTUME **2** : external appearance : SEMBLANCE

gui·tar \gi-'tär\ n : a musical instru-

ment with usu. six strings plucked with a pick or with the fingers

gulch \'gəlch\ n : RAVINE

gul·den \'gül-dən, 'gùl-\ n, pl **guldens** or **gulden** — see MONEY table

gulf \'gəlf\ n [ME goulf, fr. MF golfe, fr. It golfo, fr. LL colpus, fr. Gk kolpos bosom, gulf] **1** : an extension of an ocean or a sea into the land **2** : ABYSS, CHASM **3** : a wide separation

¹**gull** \'gəl\ n : any of numerous mostly white or gray long-winged web-footed seabirds

²**gull** vb : to make a dupe of : DECEIVE — **gull·ible** adj

³**gull** n : DUPE

gul·let \'gəl-ət\ n : ESOPHAGUS; also : THROAT

gul·ly \'gəl-ē\ n, pl **gullies** : a trench worn in the earth by running water after rains

gulp \'gəlp\ vb **1** : to swallow hurriedly or greedily **2** : SUPPRESS (~ down a sob) **3** : to catch the breath as if in taking a long drink — **gulp** n

¹**gum** \'gəm\ n : the tissue along the jaws that surrounds the necks of the teeth

²**gum** n **1** : a sticky plant exudate; esp : one that hardens on drying and is soluble in or swells in water and that includes substances used as emulsifiers, adhesives, and thickeners and in inks **2** : a sticky substance **3** : a preparation usu. of a plant gum sweetened and flavored and used for chewing — **gum·my** adj

gum arabic n : a water-soluble gum obtained from several acacias and used esp. in adhesives, in confectionery, and in pharmacy

gum·bo \'gəm-bō\ n [AmerF gombo, of Bantu origin] : a rich thick soup usu. thickened with okra

gum·drop \'gəm-ˌdräp\ n : a candy made usu. from corn syrup with gelatin and coated with sugar crystals

gump·tion \'gəmp-shən\ n **1** : shrewd common sense **2** : ENTERPRISE, INITIATIVE

gum·shoe \'gəm-ˌshü\ n : DETECTIVE — **gumshoe** vb

¹**gun** \'gən\ n **1** : CANNON **2** : a portable firearm **3** : a discharge of a gun **4** : something suggesting a gun in shape or function **5** : THROTTLE

²**gun** vb **gunned; gun·ning 1** : to hunt with a gun **2** : SHOOT **3** : to open up the throttle of so as to increase speed

gun·boat \'gən-ˌbōt\ n : a small lightly armed ship for use in shallow waters

gun·fight \-ˌfït\ n : a duel with guns — **gun·fight·er** \-ər\ n

gun·fire \-ˌfï(ə)r\ n : the firing of guns

gung ho \'gəŋ-'hō\ adj [Gung ho!, motto (interpreted as meaning "work together") of certain U.S. marine raiders in World War II, fr. Chin kung¹-ho², short for chung¹-kuo² kung¹-yeh⁴ ho²-tso⁴ she⁴ Chinese Industrial Cooperatives Society] : extremely zealous

gun·lock \'gən-ˌläk\ *n* : a device on a firearm by which the charge is ignited

gun·man \-mən\ *n* : a man armed with a gun; *esp* : an armed bandit or gangster

gun·ner \'gən-ər\ *n* 1 : a soldier or airman who operates or aims a gun 2 : one who hunts with a gun

gun·nery \'gən-(ə-)rē\ *n* : the use of guns; *esp* : the science of the flight of projectiles and effective use of guns

gunnery sergeant *n* : a noncommissioned officer in the marine corps ranking next below a first sergeant

gun·ny \'gən-ē\ *n* : coarse jute or hemp material for making sacks

gun·ny·sack \-ˌsak\ *n* : a sack made of gunny

gun·point \-ˌpȯint\ *n* : the muzzle of a gun — **at gunpoint** : under a threat of death by being shot

gun·pow·der \-ˌpaȯd-ər\ *n* : an explosive powder used in guns and blasting

gun·shot \'gən-ˌshät\ *n* 1 : shot fired from a gun 2 : the range of a gun (within ~)

gun-shy \-ˌshī\ *adj* 1 : afraid of a loud noise 2 : markedly distrustful

gun·sling·er \-ˌsliṇ-ər\ *n* : a gunman esp. in the old West

gun·smith \-ˌsmith\ *n* : one who designs, makes, or repairs firearms

gun·wale *also* **gun·nel** \'gən-ᵊl\ *n* : the upper edge of a ship's or boat's side

gup·py \'gəp-ē\ *n, pl* **guppies** [after R.J.L. *Guppy* †1916 Trinidadian naturalist] : a tiny brightly colored tropical fish

gur·gle \'gər-gəl\ *vb* **gur·gled; gur·gling** \-g(ə-)liṇ\ : to make a sound like that of a flowing and gently splashing liquid — **gurgle** *n*

Gur·kha \'gu̇r-kə, 'gər-\ *n* : a soldier from Nepal in the British or Indian army

gur·ney \'gər-nē\ *n, pl* **gurneys** : a wheeled cot or stretcher

gu·ru \'gu̇r-ü, gə-'rü\ *n, pl* **gurus** [Hindi] 1 : a personal religious and spiritual teacher in Hinduism 2 : a teacher in matters of fundamental concern

gush \'gəsh\ *vb* 1 : to issue or pour forth copiously or violently : SPOUT 2 : to make an effusive display of affection or enthusiasm

gush·er \'gəsh-ər\ *n* : one that gushes; *esp* : an oil well with a large natural flow

gushy \'gəsh-ē\ *adj* **gush·i·er; -est** : marked by effusive sentimentality

gus·set \'gəs-ət\ *n* [ME, piece of armor covering the joints in a suit of armor, fr. MF *gousset*] : a triangular insert (as in a seam of a sleeve) to give width or strength — **gusset** *vb*

gus·sy up \ˌgəs-ē-\ *vb* : to dress up

¹**gust** \'gəst\ *n* 1 : a sudden brief rush of wind 2 : a sudden outburst : SURGE — **gusty** *adj*

²**gust** *vb* : to blow in gusts

gus·ta·to·ry \'gəs-tə-ˌtōr-ē\ *adj* : of, re-

lating to, or being the sense or sensation of taste

gus·to \'gəs-tō\ *n, pl* **gustoes** : RELISH, ZEST

¹**gut** \'gət\ *n* 1 *pl* : BOWELS, ENTRAILS 2 : the alimentary canal or a part of it (as the intestine); *also* : BELLY, ABDOMEN 3 *pl* : the inner essential parts 4 *pl* : COURAGE, STAMINA

²**gut** *vb* **gut·ted; gut·ting** 1 : EVISCERATE 2 : to destroy the inside of

gut·sy \'gət-sē\ *adj* **guts·i·er; -est** : aggressively tough : COURAGEOUS

gut·ter \'gət-ər\ *n* : a channel or low area for carrying off rainwater

gut·ter·snipe \-ˌsnīp\ *n* : a street urchin

gut·tur·al \'gət-ə-rəl\ *adj* 1 : sounded in the throat 2 : being or marked by an utterance that is strange, unpleasant, or disagreeable — **guttural** *n*

gut·ty \'gət-ē\ *adj* **gut·ti·er; -est** 1 : GUTSY 2 : having a vigorous challenging quality

¹**guy** \'gī\ *n* : a rope, chain, or rod attached to something as a brace or guide

²**guy** *vb* : to steady or reinforce with a guy

³**guy** *n* : MAN, FELLOW

⁴**guy** *vb* : to make fun of : RIDICULE

Guy·a·nese \ˌgī-ə-'nēz\ *n, pl* **Guyanese** : a native or inhabitant of Guyana — **Guyanese** *adj*

guz·zle \'gəz-əl\ *vb* **guz·zled; guz·zling** \-(ə-)liṇ\ : to drink greedily

gym \'jim\ *n* : GYMNASIUM

gym·kha·na \jim-'kän-ə\ *n* : a meet featuring sports contests; *esp* : a contest of automobile-driving skill

gym·na·si·um *for 1* jim-'nä-zē-əm, -zhəm, *for 2* gim-'nä-zē-əm\ *n, pl* **-si·ums** *or* **-na·sia** \-'nä-zē-ə, -'nä-zhə; -ˈnä-zē-ə\ [L, exercise ground, school, fr. Gk *gymnasion*, fr. *gymnazein* to exercise naked, fr. *gymnos* naked] 1 : a room or building for indoor sports activities 2 : a German secondary school that prepares students for the university

gym·nas·tics \jim-'nas-tiks\ *n* : physical exercises performed in or adapted to performance in a gymnasium — **gymnast** \'jim-ˌnast\ *n* — **gym·nas·tic** *adj*

gym·no·sperm \'jim-nə-ˌspərm\ *n* : any of a class or subdivision of woody vascular seed plants (as conifers) that produce naked seeds not enclosed in an ovary

gyn *or* **gynecol** *abbr* gynecology

gy·ne·col·o·gy \ˌgīn-ə-'käl-ə-jē, ˌjin-\ *n* : a branch of medicine dealing with the diseases and hygiene of women — **gy·ne·co·log·ic** \ˌgīn-i-kə-'läj-ik, ˌjin-\ *or* **gy·ne·co·log·i·cal** \-i-kəl\ *adj* — **gy·ne·col·o·gist** \ˌgīn-ə-'käl-ə-jəst, ˌjin-\ *n*

gyp \'jip\ *n* 1 : CHEAT, SWINDLER 2 : FRAUD, SWINDLE — **gyp** *vb*

gyp·sum \'jip-səm\ *n* : a calcium-containing mineral used in making plaster of paris

Gyp·sy \'jip-sē\ *n, pl* **Gypsies** [by shortening & alter. fr. *Egyptian*] : one of a dark Caucasian race coming orig. from India and living chiefly in Europe and the U.S.; *also* : the language of the Gypsies

gypsy moth *n* : an Old World moth that was introduced into the U.S. where its caterpillar is a destructive defoliator of many trees

gy·rate \'jī-ˌrāt\ *vb* **gy·rat·ed; gy·rat·ing 1** : to revolve around a point or axis **2** : to oscillate with or as if with a circular or spiral motion — **gy·ra·tion** \jī-'rā-shən\ *n*

gyr·fal·con \'jər-ˌfal-kən, -ˌfö(l)-\ *n* : an arctic falcon that is the largest of all falcons and occurs in several forms

gy·ro \'jī-rō\ *n, pl* **gyros 1** : GYROSCOPE **2** : GYROCOMPASS

gy·ro·com·pass \-ˌkəm-pəs, -ˌkäm-\ *n* : a compass in which the axis of a spinning gyroscope points to the north

gy·ro·scope \-ˌskōp\ *n* : a wheel or disk mounted to spin rapidly about an axis that is free to turn in various directions

Gy Sgt *abbr* gunnery sergeant

gyve \'jīv, 'gīv\ *n* : FETTER — **gyve** *vb*

H

¹h \'āch\ *n, pl* **h's** *or* **hs** \'ā-chəz\ *often cap* : the 8th letter of the English alphabet

²h *abbr, often cap* **1** hard; hardness **2** heroin **3** hit **4** husband

H *symbol* hydrogen

ha *abbr* hectare

Hab *abbr* Habacuc; Habakkuk

Ha·ba·cuc \'hab-ə-ˌkək, hə-'bak-ək\ *n* — see BIBLE table

Hab·ak·kuk \'hab-ə-ˌkək, hə-'bak-ək\ *n* — see BIBLE table

ha·ba·ne·ra \ˌ(h)äb-ə-'ner-ə\ *n* [Sp (*danza*) *habanera*, lit., dance of Havana] : a Cuban dance in slow time; *also* : the music for this dance

ha·be·as cor·pus \ˌhā-bē-əs-'kör-pəs\ *n* [ME, fr. ML, lit., you should have the body (the opening words of the writ)] : a writ issued to bring a party before a court

hab·er·dash·er \'hab-ə(r)-ˌdash-ər\ *n* : a dealer in men's clothing and accessories

hab·er·dash·ery \-ˌdash-(ə-)rē\ *n, pl* **-er·ies 1** : goods sold by a haberdasher **2** : a haberdasher's shop

ha·bil·i·ment \hə-'bil-ə-mənt\ *n* **1** *pl* : TRAPPINGS, EQUIPMENT **2** : DRESS; *esp* : the dress characteristic of an occupation or occasion — usu. used in pl.

hab·it \'hab-ət\ *n* **1** : DRESS, GARB **2** : BEARING, CONDUCT **3** : PHYSIQUE **4** : mental makeup **5** : a usual manner of behavior : CUSTOM **6** : a behavior pattern acquired by frequent repetition **7** : ADDICTION **8** : mode of growth or occurrence

hab·it·able \'hab-ət-ə-bəl\ *adj* : capable of being lived in — **hab·it·abil·i·ty** \ˌhab-ət-ə-'bil-ət-ē\ *n*

hab·i·tant \'hab-ət-ənt\ *n* : INHABITANT, RESIDENT

hab·i·tat \'hab-ə-ˌtat\ *n* [L, it inhabits] : the place or kind of place where a plant or animal naturally occurs

hab·i·ta·tion \ˌhab-ə-'tā-shən\ *n* **1** : OCCUPANCY **2** : a dwelling place : RESIDENCE **3** : SETTLEMENT

hab·it-form·ing \'hab-ət-ˌför-miŋ\ *adj* : inducing the formation of an addiction

ha·bit·u·al \hə-'bich-(ə-w)əl\ *adj* **1** : CUSTOMARY **2** : doing, practicing, or acting by force of habit **3** : inherent in an individual — **ha·bit·u·al·ly** \-ē\ *adv* — **ha·bit·u·al·ness** *n*

ha·bit·u·ate \hə-'bich-ə-ˌwāt\ *vb* **-at·ed; -at·ing 1** : ACCUSTOM **2** : to cause habituation

ha·bit·u·a·tion \hə-ˌbich-ə-'wā-shən\ *n* **1** : the process of making habitual **2** : psychological dependence on a drug after a period of use

ha·bi·tué \hə-'bich-ə-ˌwā\ *n* [F] : one who frequents a place or class of places

ha·ci·en·da \ˌ(h)äs-ē-'en-də\ *n* **1** : a large estate in a Spanish-speaking country **2** : the main building of a farm or ranch

¹hack \'hak\ *vb* **1** : to cut with repeated irregular blows : CHOP **2** : to cough in a short dry manner **3** : to manage successfully — **hack·er** *n*

²hack *n* **1** : an implement for hacking **2** : a short dry cough **3** : a hacking blow

³hack *n* **1** : a horse hired or used for varied work **2** : a horse worn out in service **3** : a light easy often 3-gaited saddle horse **4** : HACKNEY **2**, TAXICAB **5** : a writer who works mainly for hire **6** : one who serves a cause merely for reward — **hack** *adj*

⁴hack *vb* : to operate a taxicab

hack·ie \'hak-ē\ *n* : a taxicab driver

hack·le \'hak-əl\ *n* **1** : one of the long feathers on the neck or back of a bird **2** *pl* : hairs (as on a dog's neck) that can be erected **3** *pl* : TEMPER, DANDER

hack·man \'hak-mən\ *n* : HACKIE

¹hack·ney \'hak-nē\ *n, pl* **hackneys 1** : a horse for riding or driving **2** : a carriage or automobile kept for hire

²hackney *vb* : to make trite

hack·neyed \'hak-nēd\ *adj* : lacking in freshness or originality

hack·saw \-ˌsö\ *n* : a fine-tooth saw in a frame for cutting metal

hack·work \-₁wərk\ n : work done on order usu. according to a formula

had past and past part of HAVE

had·dock \'had-ək\ n, pl **haddock** also **haddocks** : an Atlantic food fish usu. smaller than the related cod

Ha·des \'hād-(₁)ēz\ n 1 : the abode of the dead in Greek mythology 2 often not cap : HELL

haf·ni·um \'haf-nē-əm\ n : a gray metallic chemical element

haft \'haft\ n : the handle of a weapon or tool

hag \'hag\ n 1 : an ugly, slatternly, or evil-looking old woman 2 : WITCH 2

Hag abbr Haggai

Hag·gai \'hag-ē-₁ī, 'hag-₁ī\ n — see BIBLE table

hag·gard \'hag-ərd\ adj : having a worn or emaciated appearance syn careworn, wasted, drawn — **hag·gard·ly** adv

hag·gis \'hag-əs\ n : a traditionally Scottish dish made of the heart, liver, and lungs of a sheep or a calf minced with suet, onions, oatmeal, and seasonings

hag·gle \'hag-əl\ vb **hag·gled; hag·gling** \-(ə-)liŋ\ : to argue in bargaining — **hag·gler** \-(ə-)lər\ n

ha·gi·og·ra·phy \₁hag-ē-'äg-rə-fē, ₁hā-jē-\ n 1 : biography of saints or venerated persons 2 : idealizing or idolizing biography — **ha·gi·og·ra·pher** \-fər\ n

hai·ku \'hī-(₁)kü\ n, pl **haiku** : an unrhymed Japanese verse form of three lines containing usu. 5, 7, and 5 syllables respectively; also : a poem in this form

¹hail \'hāl\ n 1 : precipitation in the form of small lumps of ice 2 : something that gives the effect of falling hail

²hail vb 1 : to precipitate hail 2 : to hurl forcibly

³hail interj [ME, fr. ON heill, fr. heill healthy] — used to express acclamation

⁴hail vb 1 : SALUTE, GREET 2 : SUMMON

⁵hail n 1 : an expression of greeting, approval, or praise 2 : hearing distance

Hail Mary n : a salutation and prayer to the Virgin Mary

hail·stone \'hāl-₁stōn\ n : a pellet of hail

hail·storm \-₁storm\ n : a storm accompanied by hail

hair \'haər\ n : a threadlike outgrowth esp. of the skin of a mammal; also : a covering (as of the head) consisting of such hairs — **haired** \'haərd\ adj — **hair·less** adj

hair·breadth \-₁bredth\ or **hairs·breadth** \'haərz-\ n : a very small distance or margin

hair·brush \-₁brəsh\ n : a brush for the hair

hair·cloth \-₁klȯth\ n : a stiff wiry fabric used esp. for upholstery

hair·cut \-₁kət\ n : the act, process, or style of cutting and shaping the hair

hair·do \-₁dü\ n, pl **hairdos** : a way of dressing the hair

hair·dress·er \-₁dres-ər\ n : one who dresses or cuts hair — **hair·dress·ing** n

hair·line \-'līn\ n 1 : a very slender line 2 : the outline of the hair on the head

hair·piece \-₁pēs\ n 1 : TOUPEE 2 : supplementary hair (as a switch) used in some women's hairdos

hair·pin \-₁pin\ n 1 : a U-shaped pin to hold the hair in place 2 : a sharp U-shaped turn in a road — **hairpin** adj

hair–rais·ing \'haər-₁rā-ziŋ\ adj : causing terror or astonishment

hair·split·ter \-₁split-ər\ n : a person who makes unnecessarily fine distinctions in reasoning or argument — **hair·split·ting** \-₁split-iŋ\ adj or n

hair·style \-₁stīl\ n : a way of wearing the hair

hair·styl·ist \-₁stī-ləst\ n : HAIRDRESSER — **hair·styl·ing** \-₁stī-liŋ\ n

hair–trigger adj : immediately responsive to the slightest stimulus

hairy \'ha(ə)r-ē\ adj **hair·i·er; -est** : covered with or as if with hair — **hair·i·ness** \'har-ē-nəs\ n

hairy woodpecker n : a common No. American woodpecker with a white back that is larger than the similarly marked downy woodpecker

hajj \'haj\ n : the Islamic religious pilgrimage to Mecca

hajji \'haj-ē\ n : one who has made a pilgrimage to Mecca — often used as a title

hake \'hāk\ n : a marine food fish related to the cod

ha·la·la \hə-'läl-ə\ n, pl **halala** or **halalas** — see riyal at MONEY table

hal·berd \'hal-bərd, 'hȯl-\ or **hal·bert** \-bərt\ n : a weapon esp. of the 15th and 16th centuries consisting of a battle-ax and pike on a long handle

hal·cy·on \'hal-sē-ən\ adj [Gk halkyōn, a mythical bird believed to nest at sea and to calm the waves] : CALM, PEACEFUL

¹hale \'hāl\ adj : free from defect, disease, or infirmity syn healthy, sound, robust, well

²hale vb **haled; hal·ing** : HAUL, PULL 2 : to compel to go ⟨haled him into court⟩

ha·ler \'häl-ər\ n, pl **ha·le·ru** \'häl-ə-₁rü\ — see koruna at MONEY table

¹half \'haf, 'håf\ n, pl **halves** \'havz, 'håvz\ 1 : one of two equal parts into which something is divisible 2 : one of a pair

²half adj 1 : being one of two equal parts 2 : amounting to nearly half 3 : PARTIAL, IMPERFECT — **half** adv

half–and–half \₁haf-ən-'haf, ₁håf-ən-'håf\ n : something that is half one thing and half another

half·back \'haf-₁bak, 'håf-\ n 1 : a football back stationed on or near the flank 2 : a player stationed immediately behind the forward line

half–baked \-'bākt\ adj 1 : not thoroughly baked **2** : poorly planned; *also* : lacking common sense

half boot *n* : a boot with a top reaching above the ankle

half-breed \'haf-ˌbrēd, 'hȧf-\ *n* : the offspring of parents of different races — **half–breed** *adj*

half brother *n* : a brother by one parent only

half–caste \'haf-ˌkast, 'hȧf-\ *n* : one of mixed racial descent — **half–caste** *adj*

half–dol·lar \-ˈdäl-ər\ *n* **1** : a coin representing one half of a dollar **2** : the sum of fifty cents

half–heart·ed \-ˈhärt-əd\ *adj* : lacking spirit or interest — **half–heart·ed·ly** *adv* — **half–heart·ed·ness** *n*

half–life \-ˌlīf\ *n* : the time required for half of something (as atoms or a drug) to undergo a process

half–mast \-ˈmast\ *n* : a point some distance but not necessarily halfway down below the top of a mast or staff or the peak of a gaff (flags hanging at ⁓)

half note *n* : a musical note equal in time to ½ of a whole note

half–pen·ny \'hāp-(ə-)nē\ *n, pl* **half·pence** \'hā-pəns\ *or* **halfpennies** : a formerly used British coin representing one half of a penny

half–pint \'haf-ˌpīnt, 'hȧf-\ *adj* : of less than average size — **half–pint** *n*

half sister *n* : a sister by one parent only

half sole *n* : a shoe sole extending from the shank forward — **half–sole** *vb*

half–staff \'haf-ˈstaf, 'hȧf-\ *n* : HALF–MAST

half step *n* : the pitch interval between any two adjacent keys on a keyboard instrument

half–time \'haf-ˌtīm, 'hȧf-\ *n* : an intermission between halves of a game

half–track \-ˌtrak\ *n* **1** : an endless chain-track drive system that propels a vehicle supported in front by a pair of wheels **2** : a motor vehicle propelled by half-tracks; *esp* : such a vehicle lightly armored for military use

half–truth \-ˌtrüth\ *n* : a statement that is only partially true; *esp* : one that deliberately mixes truth and falsehood

half·way \-ˈwā\ *adj* **1** : midway between two points **2** : PARTIAL — **halfway** *adv*

half–wit \'haf-ˌwit, 'hȧf-\ *n* : a foolish or imbecilic person — **half–wit·ted** \-ˈwit-əd\ *adj*

hal·i·but \'hal-ə-bət\ *n, pl* **halibut** *also* **halibuts** [ME *halybutte,* fr. *haly, holy* + *butte* flatfish, fr. its being eaten on holy days] : a large edible marine flatfish

ha·lite \'hal-ˌīt, 'hā-ˌlīt\ *n* : ROCK SALT

hal·i·to·sis \ˌhal-ə-ˈtō-səs\ *n* : a condition of having fetid breath

hall \'hȯl\ *n* **1** : the residence of a medieval king or noble; *also* : the house of a landed proprietor **2** : a large public building **3** : a college or university

building **4** : LOBBY; *also* : CORRIDOR **5** : AUDITORIUM

hal·le·lu·jah \ˌhal-ə-ˈlü-yə\ *interj* [Heb *hallĕlūyāh* praise (ye) the Lord] — used to express praise, joy, or thanks

hall·mark \'hȯl-ˌmärk\ *n* **1** : a mark put on an article to indicate origin, purity, or genuineness **2** : a distinguishing characteristic

hal·low \'hal-ō\ *vb* **1** : CONSECRATE **2** : REVERE — **hal·lowed** \-ōd, -ə-wəd\ *adj*

Hal·low·een \ˌhal-ə-ˈwēn, ˌhäl-\ *n* : the evening of October 31 observed esp. by children in merrymaking and masquerading

hal·lu·ci·nate \hə-ˈlüs-ᵊn-ˌāt\ *vb* **-nat·ed; -nat·ing** : to perceive or experience as an hallucination

hal·lu·ci·na·tion \hə-ˌlüs-ᵊn-ˈā-shən\ *n* : perception of objects or events with no existence in reality due usu. to use of drugs or to disorder of the nervous system; *also* : something so perceived syn delusion, illusion, mirage — **hal·lu·ci·na·to·ry** \-ᵊn-ə-ˌtōr-ē\ *adj*

hal·lu·ci·no·gen \hə-ˈlüs-ᵊn-ə-jən\ *n* : a substance that induces hallucinations — **hal·lu·ci·no·gen·ic** \-ˌlüs-ᵊn-ə-ˈjen-ik\ *adj or n*

hall·way \'hȯl-ˌwā\ *n* **1** : an entrance hall **2** : CORRIDOR

ha·lo \'hā-lō\ *n, pl* **halos** *or* **haloes** [L *halos,* fr. Gk *halōs* threshing floor, disk, halo] **1** : a circle of light appearing to surround a shining body (as the sun) **2** : the aura of glory surrounding an idealized person or thing

¹**halt** \'hȯlt\ *adj* : LAME

²**halt** *n* : STOP

³**halt** *vb* **1** : to stop marching or traveling **2** : DISCONTINUE, END

¹**hal·ter** \'hȯl-tər\ *n* **1** : a rope or strap for leading or tying an animal; *also* : HEADSTALL **2** : NOOSE **3** : a brief blouse held in place by straps around the neck and across the back

²**halter** *vb* **hal·tered; hal·ter·ing** \-t(ə-)riŋ\ **1** : to catch with or as if with a halter; *also* : to put a halter on (as a horse) **2** : IMPEDE, RESTRAIN

halt·ing \'hȯl-tiŋ\ *adj* : UNCERTAIN, FALTERING — **halt·ing·ly** *adv*

halve \'hav, 'hȧv\ *vb* **halved; halv·ing 1** : to divide into two equal parts **2** : to reduce to one half

halv·ers \'hav-ərz, 'hȧv-\ *n pl* : half shares

halves *pl of* HALF

hal·yard \'hal-yərd\ *n* : a rope or tackle for hoisting and lowering something (as sails)

¹**ham** \'ham\ *n* **1** : a buttock with its associated thigh **2** : a cut of meat and esp. pork from this region **3** : a showy performer **4** : an operator of an amateur radio station — **ham** *adj*

²**ham** *vb* **hammed; ham·ming** : to overplay a part : OVERACT

ham·burg·er \'ham-ˌbər-gər\ *or* **ham·burg** \-ˌbərg\ *n* [G *Hamburger* of

Hamburg, West Germany] **1** : ground beef **2** : a sandwich consisting of a ground-beef patty in a round roll

ham·let \'ham-lət\ *n* : a small village

¹ham·mer \'ham-ər\ *n* **1** : a hand tool used for pounding; *also* : something resembling a hammer in form or function **2** : the part of a gun whose striking action causes explosion of the charge **3** : a metal sphere with a flexible wire handle that is hurled for distance in a track-and-field event (**hammer throw**) **4** : ACCELERATOR 2

²hammer *vb* **ham·mered; ham·mer·ing** \'ham-(ə-)riŋ\ **1** : to beat, drive, or shape with repeated blows of a hammer : POUND **2** : to produce or bring about as if by repeated blows

ham·mer·head \'ham-ər-,hed\ *n* **1** : the striking part of a hammer **2** : any of various medium-sized sharks with eyes at the ends of lateral extensions of the flattened head

ham·mer·lock \-,läk\ *n* : a wrestling hold in which an opponent's arm is held bent behind his back

ham·mer·toe \-'tō\ *n* : a deformed toe with the 2d and 3d joints permanently flexed

¹ham·mock \'ham-ək\ *n* [Sp *hamaca*, of AmerInd origin] : a swinging couch hung by cords at each end

²hammock *n* : a fertile elevated area of the southern U.S. and esp. Florida with hardwood vegetation and soil rich in humus

¹ham·per \'ham-pər\ *vb* **ham·pered; ham·per·ing** \-p(ə-)riŋ\ : IMPEDE **syn** trammel, clog, fetter, shackle

²hamper *n* : a large basket

ham·ster \'ham-stər\ *n* [G, fr. OHG *hamustro*, of Slavic origin] : a stocky short-tailed Old World rodent with large cheek pouches

¹ham·string \'ham-,striŋ\ *vb* **-strung** \-,strəŋ\; **-string·ing** \-,striŋ-iŋ\ **1** : to cripple by cutting the leg tendons **2** : to make ineffective or powerless

²hamstring *n* : any of several muscles at the back of the thigh or tendons at the back of the knee

¹hand \'hand\ *n* **1** : the end of a front limb when modified (as in humans) for grasping **2** : personal possession — usu. used in pl; *also* : CONTROL **3** : SIDE **5 4** : a pledge esp. of betrothal **5** : HANDWRITING **6** : SKILL, ABILITY; *also* : a significant part **7** : ASSISTANCE; *also* : PARTICIPATION **8** : an outburst of applause **9** : a single round in a card game; *also* : the cards held by a player after a deal **10** : WORKER, EMPLOYEE; *also* : a member of a ship's crew — **hand·less** \'han-(d)ləs\ *adj* — **at hand** : near in time or place

²hand *vb* **1** : to lead, guide, or assist with the hand **2** : to give, pass, or transmit with the hand

hand·bag \'han(d)-,bag\ *n* : a bag for carrying small personal articles and money

hand·ball \-,bȯl\ *n* : a game played by striking a small rubber ball against a wall with the hand

hand·bar·row \-,bar-ō\ *n* : a flat rectangular frame with handles at both ends that is carried by two persons

hand·bill \-,bil\ *n* : a small printed sheet for distribution by hand

hand·book \-,bu̇k\ *n* : a concise reference book : MANUAL

hand·car \'han(d)-,kär\ *n* : a small 4-wheeled railroad car propelled by hand or by a small motor

hand·clasp \-,klasp\ *n* : HANDSHAKE

hand·craft \-,kraft\ *vb* : to fashion by manual skill

¹hand·cuff \-,kəf\ *n* : a metal fastening that can be locked around a wrist and is usu. connected with another such fastening

²handcuff *vb* : MANACLE

hand·ful \'han(d)-,fu̇l\ *n, pl* **hand·fuls** \-,fu̇lz\ *also* **hands·ful** \'han(d)z-,fu̇l\ **1** : as much or as many as the hand will grasp **2** : a small number (a ~ of people) **3** : as much as one can manage

hand·gun \-,gən\ *n* : a firearm held and fired with one hand

¹hand·i·cap \'han-di-,kap\ *n* [obs. E *handicap* (a game in which forfeits were held in a cap), fr. *hand in cap*] **1** : a contest in which an artificial advantage is given or disadvantage imposed on a contestant to equalize chances of winning; *also* : the advantage given or disadvantage imposed **2** : a disadvantage that makes achievement difficult

²handicap *vb* **-capped; -cap·ping 1** : to give a handicap to **2** : to put at a disadvantage

hand·i·capped *adj* : having a physical or mental disability that limits activity

hand·i·cap·per \-,kap-ər\ *n* : one who predicts the winners in a horse race usu. for a publication

hand·i·craft \'han-di-,kraft\ *n* **1** : manual skill **2** : an occupation requiring manual skill **3** : the articles fashioned by those engaged in handicraft — **hand·i·craft·er** *n* — **hand·i·crafts·man** \-,krafts-mən\ *n*

hand in glove *or* **hand and glove** *adv* : in an extremely close relationship

hand·i·work \'han-di-,wərk\ *n* : work done personally

hand·ker·chief \'haŋ-kər-chəf, -,chēf\ *n, pl* **-chiefs** \-chəfs, -,chēfs\ *also* **-chieves** \-,chēvz\ : a small piece of cloth used for various personal purposes (as the wiping of the face)

¹han·dle \'han-dᵊl\ *n* : a part (as of a tool) designed to be grasped by the hand — **han·dled** \-dᵊld\ *adj* — **off the handle** : into a state of sudden and violent anger

²handle *vb* **han·dled; han·dling** \'han-dliŋ\ **1** : to touch, hold, or manage with the hands **2** : to have responsibility for **3** : to deal or trade in **4** : to behave in a certain way when managed or directed ⟨a car that ∼s well⟩ — **han·dler** \'han-dlər\ n

han·dle·bar \-də̇l-ˌbär\ n : a straight or bent bar with a handle at each end (as for steering a bicycle) — usu. used in pl.

hand·made \'han(d)-'mād\ adj : made by hand or a hand process

hand·maid·en \-ˌmād-ᵊn\ or **hand·maid** \-ˌmād\ n : a female attendant

hand–me–down \-me-ˌdaůn\ adj : used by one person after being used by another ⟨∼ clothes⟩ — **hand–me–down** n

hand·out \'hand-ˌaůt\ n 1 : a portion (as of food) given to a beggar 2 : a piece of printed information for free distribution; also : a prepared statement released to the press

hand·pick \'han(d)-'pik\ vb : to select personally ⟨a ∼ed candidate⟩

hand·rail \'hand-ˌrāl\ n : a narrow rail for grasping as a support

hand·saw \'han(d)-ˌsȯ\ n : a saw usu. operated with one hand

hands down \'han(d)z-'daůn\ adv 1 : with little effort 2 : without question

hand·sel \'han-səl\ n 1 : a gift made as a token of good luck 2 : a first installment : earnest money

hand·set \'han(d)-ˌset\ n : a combined telephone transmitter and receiver mounted on a handle

hand·shake \-ˌshāk\ n : a clasping of right hands by two people

hand·some \'han-səm\ adj [ME *handsom* easy to manipulate] 1 : SIZABLE, AMPLE 2 : GENEROUS, LIBERAL 3 : pleasing and usu. impressive in appearance syn beautiful, lovely, pretty, comely, fair — **hand·some·ly** adv — **hand·some·ness** n

hands–on \'han(d)-'zȯn, -'zän\ adj : being or providing direct practical experience in the operation of something

hand·spring \-ˌspriŋ\ n : an acrobatic feat in which the body turns forward or backward in a full circle from a standing position and lands first on the hands and then on the feet

hand·stand \-ˌstand\ n : an act of supporting the body on the hands with the trunk and legs balanced in the air

hand–to–hand \ˌhan-tə-ˌhand\ adj : being at very close quarters — **hand to hand** adv

hand–to–mouth \-ˌmaůth\ adj : having or providing nothing to spare

hand·wo·ven \'hand-ˌwō-vən\ adj : produced on a hand-operated loom

hand·writ·ing \-ˌrīt-iŋ\ n : writing done by hand; also : the form of writing peculiar to a person — **hand·writ·ten** \-ˌrit-ᵊn\ adj

handy \'han-dē\ adj **hand·i·er; -est** 1 : conveniently near 2 : easily used 3 : DEXTEROUS — **hand·i·ly** \'han-də-lē\ adv — **hand·i·ness** \-dē-nəs\ n

handy·man \-ˌman\ n 1 : one who does odd jobs 2 : one competent in a variety of small skills or repair work

¹**hang** \'haŋ\ vb hung \'həŋ\ also hanged \'haŋd\; hang·ing \'haŋ-iŋ\ 1 : to fasten or remain fastened to an elevated point without support from below; also : to fasten or be fastened so as to allow free motion on the point of suspension ⟨∼ a door⟩ 2 : to put or come to death by suspension (as from a gallows) 3 : DROOP ⟨hung his head in shame⟩ 4 : to fasten to a wall ⟨∼ wallpaper⟩ 5 : to prevent (a jury) from coming to a decision 6 : to display (pictures) in a gallery 7 : to remain stationary in the air 8 : to be imminent 9 : DEPEND 10 : to take hold for support 11 : to be burdensome 12 : to undergo delay 13 : to incline downward; also : to fit or fall from the figure in easy lines 14 : to be raptly attentive 15 : LINGER, LOITER — **hang·er** n

²**hang** n 1 : the manner in which a thing hangs 2 : peculiar and significant meaning 3 : KNACK

han·gar \'haŋ-ər\ n [F] : a covered and usu. enclosed area for housing and repairing aircraft

hang·dog \'haŋ-ˌdȯg\ adj 1 : ASHAMED, GUILTY 2 : ABJECT, COWED

hang·er–on \ˌhaŋ-ər-'ȯn, -'än\ n, pl **hangers–on** : one who hangs around a person or place esp. for personal gain

hang in vb : to persist tenaciously

hang·ing \'haŋ-iŋ\ n 1 : an execution by strangling or snapping the neck by a suspended noose 2 : something hung — **hanging** adj

hang·man \-mən\ n : a public executioner

hang·nail \-ˌnāl\ n : a bit of skin hanging loose at the side or base of a fingernail

hang on vb 1 : HANG IN 2 : to keep a telephone connection open

hang·out \'haŋ-ˌaůt\ n : a favorite or usual place of resort

hang·over \-ˌō-vər\ n 1 : something that remains from what is past 2 : disagreeable physical effects following heavy drinking

hang–up \'haŋ-ˌəp\ n : a source of mental or emotional difficulty

hang up \(')haŋ-'əp\ vb 1 : to place on a hook or hanger 2 : to end a telephone conversation by replacing the receiver on the cradle 3 : to keep delayed or suspended

hank \'haŋk\ n : COIL, LOOP

han·ker \'haŋ-kər\ vb **han·kered; han·ker·ing** \-k(ə-)riŋ\ : to desire strongly or persistently : LONG — **han·ker·ing** n

han·kie or **han·ky** \'haŋ-kē\ n, pl **hankies** : HANDKERCHIEF

han·ky–pan·ky \ˌhaŋ-kē-'paŋ-kē\ n : questionable or underhanded activity

han·sel var of HANDSEL

han·som \'han-səm\ n : a 2-wheeled covered carriage with the driver's seat elevated at the rear

¹**Ha·nuk·kah** \'kän-ə-kə, 'hän-\ n [Heb

hănukkāh dedication] : an 8-day Jewish holiday commemorating the rededication of the Temple of Jerusalem after its defilement by Antiochus of Syria

hap \'hap\ n 1 : HAPPENING 2 : CHANCE, FORTUNE

¹**hap·haz·ard** \hap-'haz-ərd\ n : CHANCE

²**haphazard** adj : marked by lack of plan or order : AIMLESS — **hap·haz·ard·ly** adv — **hap·haz·ard·ness** n

hap·less \'hap-ləs\ adj : UNFORTUNATE — **hap·less·ly** adv — **hap·less·ness** n

hap·loid \'hap-,lȯid\ adj : having the number of chromosomes characteristic of gametic cells — **haploid** n

hap·ly \'hap-lē\ adv : by chance

hap·pen \'hap-ən\ vb **hap·pened; hap·pen·ing** \'hap-(ə-)niŋ\ 1 : to occur by chance 2 : to take place 3 : CHANCE 2

hap·pen·ing \'hap-(ə-)niŋ\ n 1 : OCCURRENCE 2 : an event that is especially interesting, entertaining, or important

hap·pi·ly \'hap-ə-lē\ adv 1 : LUCKILY 2 : in a happy manner or state (lived ~ ever after) 3 : APTLY, SUCCESSFULLY

hap·pi·ness \'hap-i-nəs\ n 1 : a state of well-being and contentment; also : a pleasurable satisfaction 2 : APTNESS

hap·py \'hap-ē\ adj **hap·pi·er; -est** 1 : FORTUNATE 2 : APT, FELICITOUS 3 : enjoying well-being and contentment 4 : PLEASANT; also : PLEASED, GRATIFIED syn glad, cheerful, lighthearted, joyful, joyous

hap·py-go-lucky \,hap-ē-gō-'lək-ē\ adj : CAREFREE

happy hour n : a period of time when the price of drinks at a bar is reduced

ha·ra-kiri \,har-ə-'kir-ē, ,her-ē-'ker-ē\ n [Jp harakiri, fr. hara belly + kiri cutting] : suicide by disembowelment

ha·rangue \hə-'raŋ\ n 1 : LECTURE 2 : a bombastic ranting speech — **harangue** vb — **ha·rangu·er** \-'raŋ-ər\ n

ha·rass \hə-'ras, 'har-əs\ vb [F harasser, fr. MF, fr. harer to set a dog on, fr. OF hare, interj. used to incite dogs] 1 : to worry and impede by repeated raids 2 : EXHAUST, FATIGUE 3 : to annoy continually syn harry, plague, pester, tease, bedevil — **ha·rass·ment** n

har·bin·ger \'här-bən-jər\ n : one that announces or foreshadows what is coming : PRECURSOR; also : PORTENT

¹**har·bor** \'här-bər\ n 1 : a place of security and comfort 2 : a part of a body of water protected and deep enough to furnish anchorage : PORT

²**harbor** vb **har·bored; har·bor·ing** \-b(ə-)riŋ\ 1 : to give or take refuge : SHELTER 2 : to be the home or habitat of; also : LIVE 3 : to hold a thought or feeling (~ a grudge)

har·bor·age \-bə-rij\ n : HARBOR

har·bour chiefly Brit var of HARBOR

hard \'härd\ adj 1 : not easily penetrated 2 : high in alcoholic content; also : containing salts that prevent lathering with soap (~ water) 3 : stable in value (~ currency) 4 : physically fit; also : free from flaw 5 : FIRM, DEFINITE (~ agreement) ; also : based on clear fact (~ evidence) 6 : CLOSE, SEARCHING (~ look) 7 : REALISTIC (good ~ sense) 8 : OBDURATE, UNFEELING (~ heart) 9 : difficult to bear (~ times) ; also : HARSH, SEVERE 10 : RESENTFUL (~ feelings) 11 : STRICT, UNRELENTING (~ bargain) 12 : INCLEMENT (~ winter) 13 : intense in force or manner (~ blow) 14 : ARDUOUS, STRENUOUS (~ work) 15 : sounding as in *arcing* and *geese* respectively — used of c and g 16 : TROUBLESOME (~ problem) 17 : having difficulty in doing something (~ of hearing) 18 : addictive and gravely detrimental to health (~ drugs) — **hard** adv — **hard·ness** n

hard-and-fast \,härd-ən-'fast\ adj : rigidly binding : STRICT (a ~ rule)

hard·back \'härd-,bak\ n : a book bound in hard covers

hard·ball \-,bȯl\ n 1 : BASEBALL 2 : forceful uncompromising methods

hard-bit·ten \-'bit-ən\ adj : SEASONED, TOUGH (~ campaigners)

hard·board \-,bȯrd\ n : a very dense fiberboard

hard-boiled \-'bȯild\ adj 1 : boiled until both white and yolk have solidified 2 : lacking sentiment : CALLOUS; also : HARDHEADED

hard·bound \-,baúnd\ adj : HARDCOVER

hard copy n : copy produced on paper in normal-size type

hard-core \'härd-'kōr\ adj 1 : extremely resistant to solution or improvement 2 : being the most determined or dedicated members of a specified group 3 : containing explicit depictions of sex acts — **hard core** n

hard-cov·er \-'kəv-ər\ adj : having rigid boards on the sides covered in cloth or paper (~ books)

hard·en \'härd-ən\ vb **hard·ened; hard·en·ing** \'härd-(ə-)niŋ\ 1 : to make or become hard or harder 2 : to confirm or become confirmed in disposition or action — **hard·en·er** n

hard·hack \'härd-,hak\ n : an American spirea with rusty hairy leaves and dense clusters of pink or white flowers

hard hat n 1 : a protective hat worn esp. by construction workers 2 : a construction worker

hard·head·ed \'härd-'hed-əd\ adj 1 : STUBBORN, WILLFUL 2 : SOBER, REALISTIC — **hard·head·ed·ly** adv — **hard·head·ed·ness** n

hard·heart·ed \-'härt-əd\ adj : PITILESS, CRUEL — **hard·heart·ed·ly** adv — **hard·heart·ed·ness** n

har·di·hood \'härd-ē-,húd\ n 1 : resolute courage and fortitude 2 : VIGOR, ROBUSTNESS

hard-line \'härd-'līn\ adj : advocating

or involving a persistently firm course of action — **hard·lin·er** \-'lī-nər\ *n*

hard·ly \'härd-lē\ *adv* 1 : with force 2 : SEVERELY 3 : with difficulty 4 : only just : BARELY 5 : certainly not

hard palate *n* : the bony anterior part of the palate forming the roof of the mouth

hard·pan \'härd-,pan\ *n* : a compact often clayey layer in soil that is impenetrable by roots

hard-pressed \-'prest\ *adj* : HARD PUT; *esp* : being under financial strain

hard put *adj* 1 : barely able 2 : faced with difficulty or perplexity

hard rock *n* : rock music marked by a heavy beat, high amplification, and usu. frenzied performances

hard-shell \'härd-,shel\ *adj* : CONFIRMED, UNCOMPROMISING ⟨a ~ conservative⟩

hard·ship \-,ship\ *n* 1 : SUFFERING, PRIVATION 2 : something that causes suffering or privation

hard·stand \-,stand\ *n* : a hard-surfaced area for parking an airplane

hard-sur·face \-'sər-fəs\ *vb* : to provide (as a road) with a paved surface

hard·tack \-,tak\ *n* : a hard biscuit made of flour and water without salt

hard·top \-,täp\ *n* : an automobile resembling a convertible but having a rigid top

hard·ware \-,waər\ *n* 1 : ware (as cutlery or tools) made of metal 2 : the physical components (as electronic devices) of a vehicle (as a spacecraft) or an apparatus (as a computer)

¹**hard·wood** \'härd-,wùd\ *n* : the wood of a broad-leaved usu. deciduous tree as distinguished from that of a conifer; *also* : such a tree

²**hardwood** *adj* 1 : having or made of hardwood ⟨~ floors⟩ 2 : consisting of mature woody tissue ⟨~ cuttings⟩

hard-work·ing \'härd-'wər-kiŋ\ *adj* : INDUSTRIOUS

har·dy \'härd-ē\ *adj* **har·di·er; -est** 1 : BOLD, BRAVE 2 : AUDACIOUS, BRAZEN 3 : ROBUST; *also* : able to withstand adverse conditions (as of weather) ⟨~ shrubs⟩ — **har·di·ly** \'härd-ə-lē\ *adv* — **har·di·ness** \-ē-nəs\ *n*

hare \'haər\ *n, pl* **hare** *or* **hares** : a swift timid long-eared mammal distinguished from the related rabbit by being open-eyed and furry at birth

hare·bell \-,bel\ *n* : a slender herb with blue bell-shaped flowers

hare·brained \-'brānd\ *adj* : FLIGHTY, FOOLISH

hare·lip \-'lip\ *n* : a deformity in which the upper lip is vertically split — **hare·lipped** \-'lipt\ *adj*

ha·rem \'har-əm\ *n* [Ar ḥarīm, lit., something forbidden & ḥaram, lit., sanctuary] 1 : a house or part of a house allotted to women in a Muslim household 2 : the women and servants occupying a harem 3 : a group of females associated with one male

hark \'härk\ *vb* : LISTEN

harken *var of* HEARKEN

har·le·quin \'här-li-k(w)ən\ *n* 1 *cap* : a character (as in comedy) with a shaved head, masked face, variegated tights, and wooden sword 2 : CLOWN 2

¹**har·lot** \'här-lət\ *n* : PROSTITUTE

¹**harm** \'härm\ *n* 1 : physical or mental damage : INJURY 2 : MISCHIEF, HURT — **harm·ful** \-fəl\ *adj* — **harm·ful·ly** \-ē\ *adv* — **harm·ful·ness** *n* — **harm·less** *adj* — **harm·less·ly** *adv* — **harm·less·ness** *n*

²**harm** *vb* : to cause harm to : INJURE

¹**har·mon·ic** \här-'män-ik\ *adj* 1 : of or relating to musical harmony or harmonics 2 : pleasing to the ear — **har·mon·i·cal·ly** \-i-k(ə-)lē\ *adv*

²**harmonic** *n* : a musical overtone

har·mon·i·ca \här-'män-i-kə\ *n* : a small wind instrument played by breathing through metallic reeds

har·mo·ni·ous \här-'mō-nē-əs\ *adj* 1 : musically concordant 2 : CONGRUOUS 3 : marked by accord in sentiment or action — **har·mo·ni·ous·ly** *adv* — **har·mo·ni·ous·ness** *n*

har·mo·ni·um \här-'mō-nē-əm\ *n* : a keyboard wind instrument in which the wind acts on a set of metal reeds

har·mo·nize \'här-mə-,nīz\ *vb* **-nized; -niz·ing** 1 : to play or sing in harmony 2 : to be in harmony 3 : to bring into consonance or accord — **har·mo·ni·za·tion** \,här-mə-nə-'zā-shən\ *n*

har·mo·ny \'här-mə-nē\ *n, pl* **-nies** 1 : musical agreement of sounds; *esp* : the combination of tones into chords and progressions of chords 2 : a pleasing arrangement of parts; *also* : ACCORD 3 : internal calm

¹**har·ness** \'här-nəs\ *n* 1 : the gear other than a yoke of a draft animal 2 : something that resembles a harness

²**harness** *vb* 1 : to put a harness on; *also* : YOKE 2 : UTILIZE

¹**harp** \'härp\ *n* : a musical instrument consisting of a triangular frame set with strings plucked by the fingers — **harp·ist** *n*

²**harp** *vb* 1 : to play on a harp 2 : to dwell on a subject tiresomely — **harp·er** *n*

har·poon \här-'pün\ *n* : a barbed spear used esp. in hunting large fish or whales — **harpoon** *vb* — **har·poon·er** *n*

harp·si·chord \'härp-si-,kòrd\ *n* : a keyboard instrument producing tones by the plucking of its strings with quills or with leather or plastic points

har·py \'här-pē\ *n, pl* **harpies** [L *Harpyia*, a mythical predatory monster having a woman's head and a vulture's body, fr. Gk] 1 : a predatory person : LEECH 2 : a shrewish woman

har·ri·dan \'har-əd-³n\ *n* : a scolding woman

¹**har·ri·er** \'har-ē-ər\ *n* 1 : a small hound used esp. in hunting rabbits 2 : a runner on a cross-country team

²**harrier** *n* : a slender long-legged hawk

¹har·row \'har-ō\ *n* : a cultivating tool that has spikes, spring teeth, or disks and is used esp. to pulverize and smooth the soil

²harrow *vb* **1** : to cultivate with a harrow **2** : TORMENT, VEX

har·ry \'har-ē\ *vb* **har·ried; har·ry·ing 1** : RAID, PILLAGE **2** : to torment by or as if by constant attack *syn* worry, annoy, plague, pester

harsh \'härsh\ *adj* **1** : disagreeably rough **2** : causing discomfort or pain **3** : unduly exacting : SEVERE — **harsh·ly** *adv* — **harsh·ness** *n*

hart \'härt\ *n* : STAG

har·um–scar·um \,har-əm-'skar-əm\ *adj* : RECKLESS, IRRESPONSIBLE

¹har·vest \'här-vəst\ *n* **1** : the season for gathering in crops; *also* : the act of gathering in a crop **2** : a mature crop **3** : the product or reward of exertion

²harvest *vb* : to gather in a crop : REAP — **har·vest·er** *n*

has *pres 3d sing of* HAVE

has–been \'haz-,bin\ *n* : one that has passed the peak of ability, power, effectiveness, or popularity

¹hash \'hash\ *vb* [F *hacher*, fr. OF *hachier*, fr. *hache* battle-ax] **1** : to chop into small pieces **2** : to talk about

²hash *n* **1** : chopped meat mixed with potatoes and browned **2** : HODGEPODGE, JUMBLE

³hash *n* : HASHISH

hash browns *n pl* : boiled potatoes that have been diced, mixed with chopped onions and shortening, and fried

hash·ish \'hash-,ēsh, ha-'shēsh\ [Ar] *n* : an intoxicating preparation of resin from the hemp plant

hasp \'hasp\ *n* : a fastener (as for a door) consisting of a hinged metal strap that fits over a staple and is secured by a pin or padlock

has·sle \'has-əl\ *n* **1** : WRANGLE; *also* : FIGHT **2** : an annoying or troublesome concern — **hassle** *vb*

has·sock \'has-ək\ *n* [ME, sedge, fr. OE *hassuc*] : a cushion that serves as a seat or leg rest; *also* : a cushion to kneel on in prayer

haste \'hāst\ *n* **1** : rapidity of motion or action : SPEED **2** : rash or headlong action **3** : excessive eagerness — **hast·i·ly** \'hā-stə-lē\ *adv* — **hast·i·ness** \-stē-nəs\ *n* — **hasty** \'hā-stē\ *adj*

has·ten \'hās-ᵊn\ *vb* **has·tened; has·ten·ing** \'hās-(ᵊ-)niŋ\ **1** : to urge on **2** : to move or act quickly : HURRY *syn* speed, accelerate, quicken

hat \'hat\ *n* : a covering for the head usu. having a shaped crown and brim

hat·box \'hat-,bäks\ *n* : a round piece of luggage esp. for carrying hats

¹hatch \'hach\ *n* **1** : a small door or opening **2** : a door or cover for access down into a compartment of a ship

²hatch *vb* **1** : to produce by incubation; *also* : INCUBATE **2** : to emerge from an egg or pupa; *also* : to give forth young **3** : ORIGINATE — **hatch·ery** \-(ə-)rē\ *n*

hatch·back \'hach-,bak\ *n* **1** : a back on an automobile having an upward-opening hatch **2** : an automobile having a hatchback

hatch·et \'hach-ət\ *n* **1** : a short-handled ax with a hammerlike part opposite the blade **2** : TOMAHAWK

hatchet man *n* : a person hired for murder, coercion, or unscrupulous attack

hatch·ing \'hach-iŋ\ *n* : the engraving or drawing of fine lines in close proximity chiefly to give an effect of shading; *also* : the pattern so created

hatch·way \'hach-,wā\ *n* : an opening having a hatch

¹hate \'hāt\ *n* **1** : intense hostility and aversion **2** : an object of hatred — **hate·ful** \-fəl\ *adj* — **hate·ful·ly** \-ē\ *adv* — **hate·ful·ness** *n*

²hate *vb* **hat·ed; hat·ing 1** : to express or feel extreme enmity **2** : to find distasteful *syn* detest, abhor, abominate, loathe — **hat·er** *n*

ha·tred \'hā-trəd\ *n* : HATE; *also* : prejudiced hostility or animosity

hat·ter \'hat-ər\ *n* : one that makes, sells, or cleans or repairs hats

hau·berk \'hȯ-bərk\ *n* : a coat of mail

haugh·ty \'hȯt-ē\ *adj* **haugh·ti·er; -est** [obs. *haught*, fr. ME *haute*, fr. MF *haut*, lit., high, fr. L *altus*] : disdainfully proud *syn* insolent, lordly, overbearing, arrogant — **haugh·ti·ly** \'hȯt-ə-lē\ *adv* — **haugh·ti·ness** \-ē-nəs\ *n*

¹haul \'hȯl\ *vb* **1** : to exert traction on : DRAW, PULL **2** : to furnish transportation : CART — **haul·er** *n*

²haul *n* **1** : PULL, TUG **2** : the result of an effort to collect : TAKE **3** : the distance over which a load is transported; *also* : LOAD

haul·age \-ij\ *n* **1** : the act or process of hauling **2** : a charge for hauling

haunch \'hȯnch\ *n* **1** : HIP **1 2** : HINDQUARTER **2** — usu. used in pl. **3** : HINDQUARTER **1**

¹haunt \'hȯnt\ *vb* **1** : to visit often : FREQUENT **2** : to recur constantly and spontaneously to; *also* : to reappear continually in **3** : to visit or inhabit as a ghost — **haunt·er** *n* — **haunt·ing·ly** \-iŋ-lē\ *adv*

²haunt \'hȯnt, 2 is usu 'hant\ *n* **1** : a place habitually frequented **2** *chiefly dial* : GHOST

haut·bois *or* **haut·boy** \'(h)ō-,bȯi\ *n, pl* **hautbois** \-,bȯiz\ *or* **hautboys** : OBOE

haute cou·ture \,ōt-kù-'tü(ə)r\ *n* [F] : the establishments or designers that create fashions for women; *also* : the fashions created

haute cui·sine \-kwi-'zēn\ *n* : artful or elaborate cuisine

hau·teur \hō-'tər, (h)ō-\ *n* : HAUGHTINESS

have \(')hav, (h)əv, v; *in sense 2 before* "*to*" *usu* 'haf\ *vb* **had** \(')had, (h)əd\ ; **hav·ing** \'hav-iŋ\ ; **has** \(')haz, (h)əz, *in sense 2 before* "*to*" *usu* 'has\ **1** : to hold in possession; *also* : to hold in one's use, service, or regard : to be compelled or forced to **3** : to stand in relationship to ⟨*has* many enemies⟩ **4** : OBTAIN; *also* : RECEIVE, ACCEPT **5** : to be marked by **6** : SHOW; *also* : USE, EXERCISE **7** : EXPERIENCE; *also* : TAKE ⟨~ a look⟩ **8** : to entertain in the mind **9** : to cause to **10** : ALLOW **11** : to be competent in **12** : to hold in a disadvantageous position; *also* : TRICK **13** : BEGET **14** : to partake of **15** — used as an auxiliary with the past participle to form the present perfect, past perfect, or future perfect — **have at** : ATTACK — **have coming** : DESERVE — **have done with** : to be finished with — **have had it** : to have endured all one will permit or can stand — **have to do with 1** : to deal with **2** : to have in the way of connection or relation with or effect on

²**have** \'hav\ *n* : one that has material wealth

ha·ven \'hā-vən\ *n* **1** : HARBOR, PORT **2** : a place of safety **3** : a place offering favorable conditions ⟨a tourist's ~⟩

have-not \'hav-ˌnät, -ˈnät\ *n* : one that is poor in material wealth

haver·sack \'hav-ər-ˌsak\ *n* [F *haversac*, fr. G *habersack* bag for oats] : a bag similar to a knapsack but worn over one shoulder

hav·oc \'hav-ək\ *n* **1** : wide and general destruction **2** : great confusion and disorder

haw \'hȯ\ *n* : a hawthorn berry; *also* : HAWTHORN

Ha·wai·ian \hə-'wä-yən, -'wī-(y)ən\ *n* : the Polynesian language of Hawaii

¹**hawk** \'hȯk\ *n* **1** : any of numerous mostly small or medium-sized day-flying birds of prey (as a falcon or kite) **2** : a supporter of a war or a warlike policy — **hawk·ish** *adj*

²**hawk** *vb* : to offer goods for sale by calling out in the street — **hawk·er** *n*

hawk·weed \'hȯk-ˌwēd\ *n* : any of several plants related to the daisies usu. having red or orange flower heads

haw·ser \'hȯ-zər\ *n* : a large rope for towing, mooring, or securing a ship

haw·thorn \'hȯ-ˌthȯrn\ *n* : a spiny shrub or tree related to the apple and having white or pink fragrant flowers

¹**hay** \'hā\ *n* **1** : herbage (as grass) mowed and cured for fodder **2** : REWARD **3** *slang* : BED ⟨hit the ~⟩ **4** : a small amount of money

²**hay** *vb* : to cut, cure, and store for hay

hay·cock \'hā-ˌkäk\ *n* : a small conical pile of hay

hay fever *n* : an acute allergic catarrh

hay·fork \'hā-ˌfȯrk\ *n* : a fork for loading or unloading hay

hay·loft \-ˌlȯft\ *n* : a loft for hay

hay·mow \-ˌmau̇\ *n* : a mow of or for hay

hay·rick \-ˌrik\ *n* : a large sometimes thatched outdoor stack of hay

hay·seed \-ˌsēd\ *n*, *pl* **hayseed** or **hayseeds 1** : clinging bits of straw or chaff from hay **2** : BUMPKIN, YOKEL

hay·stack \-ˌstak\ *n* : a stack of hay

hay·wire \-ˌwī(ə)r\ *adj* : being out of order or control : CRAZY

¹**haz·ard** \'haz-ərd\ *n* [ME, a dice game, fr. MF *hasard*, fr. Ar *az-zahr* the die] **1** : a source of danger **2** : CHANCE; *also* : ACCIDENT **3** : an obstacle on a golf course — **haz·ard·ous** *adj*

²**hazard** *vb* : VENTURE, RISK

¹**haze** \'hāz\ *n* **1** : fine dust, smoke, or light vapor causing lack of transparency in the air **2** : vagueness of mind or perception

²**haze** *vb* **hazed; haz·ing** : to harass by abusive and humiliating tricks

ha·zel \'hā-zəl\ *n* **1** : any of a genus of shrubs or small trees related to the birches and bearing edible nuts (**ha·zel·nuts** \-ˌnəts\) **2** : a light brown color

hazy \'hā-zē\ *adj* **haz·i·er; -est 1** : obscured or darkened by haze **2** : VAGUE, INDEFINITE — **haz·i·ly** \'hā-zə-lē\ *adv* — **haz·i·ness** \-zē-nəs\ *n*

Hb *abbr* hemoglobin

HBM *abbr* Her Britannic Majesty; His Britannic Majesty

H-bomb \'āch-ˌbäm\ *n* : HYDROGEN BOMB

HC *abbr* **1** Holy Communion **2** House of Commons

hd *abbr* head

HD *abbr* heavy-duty

hdbk *abbr* handbook

hdkf *abbr* handkerchief

hdwe *abbr* hardware

he \(')hē, ē\ *pron* **1** : that male one **2** : a or the person ⟨~ who hesitates is lost⟩

He *symbol* helium

HE *abbr* **1** Her Excellency **2** His Eminence **3** His Excellency

¹**head** \'hed\ *n* **1** : the front or upper part of the body containing the brain, the chief sense organs, and the mouth **2** : MIND; *also* : natural aptitude **3** : POISE **4** : the obverse of a coin **5** : INDIVIDUAL; *also*, *pl* **head** : one of a number (as of cattle) **6** : the end that is upper or higher or opposite the foot; *also* : either end of something (as a drum) whose two ends need not be distinguished **7** : DIRECTOR, LEADER; *also* : a leading element (as of a procession) **8** : a projecting part; *also* : the striking part of a weapon **9** : the place of leadership or honor **10** : a separate part or topic **11** : the foam on a fermenting or effervescing liquid **12** : CRISIS — **head·ed** \-əd\ *adj* — **head·less** *adj*

²**head** *adj* : PRINCIPAL, CHIEF

³**head** *vb* **1** : to cut back the upper growth of **2** : to provide with or form a head; *also* : to form the head of **3** : LEAD, CONDUCT **4** : to get in front of esp. so as to stop; *also* : SURPASS **5** : to put or stand at the head of **6** : to point or proceed in a certain direction **7** : ORIGINATE

head·ache \-ˌāk\ *n* **1** : pain in the head **2** : a baffling situation or problem

head·band \-‚band\ *n* : a band worn on or around the head

head·board \-‚bȯrd\ *n* : a board forming the head (as of a bed)

head cold *n* : a common cold centered in the nasal passages and adjacent mucous tissues

head·dress \'hed-‚dres\ *n* : an often elaborate covering for the head

head·first \-'fərst\ *adv* : HEADLONG — **headfirst** *adj*

head·gear \-‚gir\ *n* : a covering or protective device for the head

head·hunt·ing \-‚hənt-iŋ\ *n* : the act or custom of seeking out and decapitating enemies and preserving their heads as trophies — **head·hunt·er** \-ər\ *n*

head·ing \'hed-iŋ\ *n* 1 : the compass direction in which the longitudinal axis of a ship or airplane points 2 : something that forms or serves as a head

head·land \'hed-lənd, -‚land\ *n* : PROMONTORY

head·light \-‚līt\ *n* : a light with a reflector and special lens mounted on the front of a vehicle

head·line \-‚līn\ *n* : a head of a newspaper story or article usu. printed in large type

head·lock \-‚läk\ *n* : a wrestling hold in which one encircles his opponent's head with one arm

¹**head·long** \-‚lȯŋ\ *adv* 1 : with the head foremost 2 : RECKLESSLY 3 : without delay

²**head·long** \-‚lȯŋ\ *adj* 1 : PRECIPITATE, RASH 2 : plunging with the head foremost

head·man \'hed-'man, -‚man\ *n* : one who is a leader : CHIEF

head·mas·ter \-‚mas-tər\ *n* : a man heading the staff of a private school

head·mis·tress \-‚mis-trəs\ *n* : a woman head of a private school

head–on \'hed-'ȯn, -'än\ *adj* : having the front facing in the direction of initial contact or line of sight (∼ collision) — **head–on** *adv*

head·phone \-‚fōn\ *n* : an earphone held on by a band over the head

head·piece \-‚pēs\ *n* 1 : a covering for the head 2 : an ornament esp. at the beginning of a chapter

head·pin \-‚pin\ *n* : a bowling pin that stands foremost in the arrangement of pins

head·quar·ters \-‚kwȯrt-ərz\ *n sing or pl* 1 : a place from which a commander exercises command 2 : the administrative center of an enterprise

head·rest \-‚rest\ *n* 1 : a support for the head 2 : a pad at the top of the back of an automobile seat

head·room \'hed-‚rüm, -‚rum\ *n* : vertical space in which to stand, sit, or move

head·set \-‚set\ *n* : a pair of headphones

head·ship \-‚ship\ *n* : the position, office, or dignity of a head

heads·man \'hedz-mən\ *n* : EXECUTIONER

head·stall \'hed-‚stȯl\ *n* : an arrangement of straps or rope encircling the head of an animal and forming part of a bridle or halter

head·stone \-‚stōn\ *n* : a memorial stone at the head of a grave

head·strong \-‚strȯŋ\ *adj* 1 : not easily restrained 2 : directed by ungovernable will syn unruly, intractable, willful, pertinacious, refractory, stubborn

head·wait·er \-'wāt-ər\ *n* : the head of the dining-room staff of a restaurant or hotel

head·wa·ter \-‚wȯt-ər, -‚wät-\ *n* : the source of a stream — usu. used in pl.

head·way \-‚wā\ *n* : forward motion; *also* : PROGRESS

head wind *n* : a wind blowing in a direction opposite to a course esp. of a ship or aircraft

head·word \'hed-‚wərd\ *n* 1 : a word or term placed at the beginning 2 : a word qualified by a modifier

head·work \-‚wərk\ *n* : mental work or effort : THINKING

heady \'hed-ē\ *adj* **head·i·er; -est** 1 : WILLFUL, RASH; *also* : IMPETUOUS 2 : INTOXICATING 3 : SHREWD

heal \'hēl\ *vb* 1 : to make or become sound or whole; *also* : to restore to health 2 : CURE, REMEDY — **heal·er** *n*

health \'helth\ *n* 1 : sound physical or mental condition; *also* : overall condition of the body (in poor ∼) 2 : WELL-BEING 3 : a toast to someone's health or prosperity

health·ful \'helth-fəl\ *adj* 1 : beneficial to health 2 : HEALTHY — **health·ful·ly** \-ē\ *adv* — **health·ful·ness** *n*

healthy \'hel-thē\ *adj* **health·i·er; -est** 1 : enjoying or typical of good health : WELL 2 : evincing or conducive to health 3 : PROSPEROUS; *also* : CONSIDERABLE — **health·i·ly** \'hel-thə-lē\ *adv* — **health·i·ness** \-thē-nəs\ *n*

¹**heap** \'hēp\ *n* : PILE; *also* : LOT

²**heap** *vb* 1 : to throw or lay in a heap 2 : to give in large quantities; *also* : to fill more than full

hear \'hir\ *vb* **heard** \'hərd\ ; **hear·ing** \'hi(ə)r-iŋ\ 1 : to perceive by the ear 2 : HEED; *also* : ATTEND 3 : to give a legal hearing to or take testimony from 4 : LEARN — **hear·er** \'hir-ər\ *n*

hear·ing *n* 1 : the process, function, or power of perceiving sound; *esp* : the special sense by which noises and tones are received as stimuli 2 : EARSHOT 3 : opportunity to be heard 4 : a listening to arguments (as in a court); *also* : a session in which witnesses are heard (as by a legislative committee)

hear·ken \'här-kən\ *vb* : to give attention : LISTEN syn hear, hark, heed

hear·say \'hir-‚sā\ *n* : RUMOR

hearse \'hərs\ *n* [ME *herse*, fr. MF *herce* harrow, frame for holding candles] : a vehicle for carrying the dead to the grave

heart \'härt\ n 1 : a hollow muscular organ that by rhythmic contraction keeps up the circulation of the blood in the body; *also* : something resembling a heart in shape 2 : any of a suit of playing cards marked with a red figure of a heart; *also, pl* : a card game in which the object is to avoid taking tricks containing hearts 3 : the whole personality; *also* : the emotional or moral as distinguished from the intellectual nature 4 : COURAGE 5 : one's innermost being 6 : CENTER; *also* : the essential part 7 : the younger central part of a compact leafy cluster (as of lettuce) — **heart·ed** \-ǝd\ *adj* — **by heart** : by rote or from memory

heart·ache \-ˌāk\ n : anguish of mind

heart attack n : an acute episode of heart disease due to insufficient blood supply to the heart muscle itself

heart·beat \'härt-ˌbēt\ n : one complete pulsation of the heart

heart·break \-ˌbrāk\ n : crushing grief

heart·break·ing \-ˌbrā-kiŋ\ *adj* : causing extreme sorrow or distress — **heart·break·er** \-ˌbrā-kǝr\ n

heart·bro·ken \-ˌbrō-kǝn\ *adj* : overcome by sorrow

heart·burn \-ˌbǝrn\ n : a burning distress behind the lower sternum usu. due to spasm of the esophagus or upper stomach

heart disease n : an abnormal organic condition of the heart or of the heart and circulation

heart·en \'härt-ǝn\ vb **heart·ened; heart·en·ing** \'härt-(ǝ-)niŋ\ : ENCOURAGE

heart·felt \'härt-ˌfelt\ *adj* : deeply felt : SINCERE

hearth \'härth\ n 1 : an area (as of brick) in front of a fireplace; *also* : the floor of a fireplace 2 : HOME

hearth·stone \-ˌstōn\ n 1 : a stone forming a hearth 2 : HOME

heart·less \'härt-lǝs\ *adj* : CRUEL

heart·rend·ing \-ˌren-diŋ\ *adj* : HEARTBREAKING

heart·sick \-ˌsik\ *adj* : very despondent — **heart·sick·ness** n

heart·strings \-ˌstriŋz\ n pl : the deepest emotions or affections

heart·throb \-ˌthräb\ n 1 : the throb of a heart 2 : sentimental emotion 3 : SWEETHEART

heart-to-heart \ˌhärt-tǝ-ˈhärt\ *adj* : SINCERE, FRANK (a ~ talk)

heart·warm·ing \'härt-ˌwȯr-miŋ\ *adj* : inspiring sympathetic feeling

heart·wood \-ˌwu̇d\ n : the older harder nonliving central portion of wood

¹**hearty** \'härt-ē\ *adj* **heart·i·er; -est** 1 : THOROUGHGOING; *also* : JOVIAL 2 : vigorously healthy 3 : ABUNDANT; *also* : NOURISHING *syn* sincere, wholehearted, unfeigned, heartfelt — **heart·i·ly** \'härt-ǝ-lē\ *adv* — **heart·i·ness** \-ē-nǝs\ n

²**hearty** n, pl **heart·ies** : COMRADE; *also* : SAILOR

¹**heat** \'hēt\ vb 1 : to make or become warm or hot 2 : EXCITE — **heat·ed·ly** \-ǝd-lē\ *adv* — **heat·er** n

²**heat** n 1 : a condition of being hot : WARMTH 2 : a form of energy that causes a body to rise in temperature, to fuse, to evaporate, or to expand 3 : high temperature 4 : intensity of feeling; *also* : sexual excitement esp. in a female mammal 5 : pungency of flavor 6 : a single continuous effort; *also* : a preliminary race for eliminating less competent contenders 7 : PRESSURE, COERCION; *also* : ABUSE, CRITICISM — **heat·less** *adj*

heat engine n : a mechanism for converting heat energy into mechanical energy

heat exchanger n : a device (as an automobile radiator) for transferring heat from one fluid to another without allowing them to mix

heat exhaustion n : a condition marked by weakness, nausea, dizziness, and profuse sweating that results from physical exertion in a hot environment

heath \'hēth\ n 1 : any of a large family of often evergreen shrubby plants (as a blueberry or heather) of wet acid soils 2 : a tract of wasteland — **heathy** *adj*

hea·then \'hē-thǝn\ n, pl **heathens** or **heathen** 1 : an unconverted member of a people or nation that does not acknowledge the God of the Bible 2 : an uncivilized or irreligious person — **heathen** *adj* — **hea·then·dom** n — **hea·then·ish** *adj* — **hea·then·ism** n

heath·er \'heth-ǝr\ n : a northern evergreen heath with usu. lavender flowers — **heath·ery** *adj*

heat lightning n : flashes of light without thunder ascribed to distant lightning reflected by high clouds

heat·stroke \'hēt-ˌströk\ n : a disorder marked esp. by high body temperature without sweating and by collapse that follows prolonged exposure to excessive heat

¹**heave** \'hēv\ vb **heaved** or **hove** \'hōv\ ; **heav·ing** 1 : to rise or lift upward 2 : THROW 3 : to rise and fall rhythmically; *also* : PANT 4 : RETCH 5 : PULL, PUSH — **heav·er** n

²**heave** n 1 : an effort to lift or raise 2 : THROW, CAST 3 : an upward motion 4 pl : a chronic lung disease of horses marked by difficult breathing and persistent cough

heav·en \'hev-ǝn\ n 1 : FIRMAMENT — usu. used in pl. 2 *often cap* : the abode of the Deity and of the blessed dead; *also* : a spiritual state of everlasting communion with God 3 *cap* : GOD 1 4 : a place of supreme happiness — **heav·en·ly** *adj* — **heav·en·ward** *adv* or *adj*

heavy \'hev-ē\ *adj* **heavi·er; -est** 1 : having great weight 2 : hard to bear 3 : SERIOUS 4 : DEEP, PROFOUND 5 : burdened with something oppressive;

also : PREGNANT **6** : SLUGGISH **7** : DRAB; *also* : DOLEFUL **8** : DROWSY **9** : greater than the average of its kind or class **10** : digested with difficulty; *also* : not properly raised or leavened **11** : producing goods (as steel) used in the production of other goods **12** : heavily armed or armored — **heavi·ly** \'hev-ə-lē\ *adv* — **heavi·ness** \-ē-nəs\ *n*

²**heavy** *n, pl* **heav·ies** : a theatrical role representing a dignified or imposing person; *also* : a villain esp. in a story or a play

heavy-du·ty \ˌhev-ē-ˈd(y)üt-ē\ *adj* : able to withstand unusual strain

heavy-hand·ed \-ˈhan-dəd\ *adj* **1** : CLUMSY, UNGRACEFUL **2** : OPPRESSIVE, HARSH

heavy-heart·ed \-ˈhärt-əd\ *adj* : SADDENED, DESPONDENT

heavy metal *n* : highly amplified electronic rock with elements of the fantastic

heavy-set \ˌhev-ē-ˈset\ *adj* : stocky and compact in build

heavy water *n* : water enriched in deuterium

heavy·weight \'hev-ē-ˌwāt\ *n* : one above average in weight; *esp* : a boxer weighing over 175 pounds

Heb *abbr* Hebrews

He·bra·ism \'hē-brā-ˌiz-əm\ *n* : the thought, spirit, or practice characteristic of the Hebrews — **He·bra·ic** \hi-ˈbrā-ik\ *adj*

He·bra·ist \'hē-ˌbrā-əst\ *n* : a specialist in Hebrew and Hebraic studies

He·brew \'hē-brü\ *n* **1** : the language of the Hebrews **2** : a member of or descendant from a group of Semitic peoples; *esp* : ISRAELITE — **Hebrew** *adj*

He·brews \'hē-(ˌ)brüz\ *n* — see BIBLE table

hec·a·tomb \'hek-ə-ˌtōm\ *n* : an ancient Greek and Roman sacrifice of 100 oxen or cattle

heck·le \'hek-əl\ *vb* **heck·led; heck·ling** \-(ə-)liŋ\ : to harass with questions or gibes : BADGER — **heck·ler** \-(ə-)lər\ *n*

hect·are \'hek-ˌtaər\ *n* — see METRIC SYSTEM table

hec·tic \'hek-tik\ *adj* **1** : being hot and flushed **2** : filled with excitement or confusion — **hec·ti·cal·ly** \-ti-k(ə-)lē\ *adv*

hec·to·gram \'hek-tə-ˌgram\ *n* — see METRIC SYSTEM table

hec·to·li·ter \'hek-tə-ˌlēt-ər\ *n* — see METRIC SYSTEM table

hec·to·me·ter \'hek-tə-ˌmēt-ər, hek-ˈtäm-ət-ər\ *n* — see METRIC SYSTEM table

hec·tor \'hek-tər\ *vb* **hec·tored; hec·tor·ing** \-t(ə-)riŋ\ **1** : SWAGGER **2** : to intimidate by bluster or personal pressure

¹**hedge** \'hej\ *n* **1** : a fence or boundary formed of shrubs or small trees **2** : BARRIER **3** : a means of protection (as against financial loss)

²**hedge** *vb* **hedged; hedg·ing 1** : ENCIRCLE **2** : HINDER **3** : to protect oneself financially by a counterbalancing transaction **4** : to evade the risk of commitment — **hedg·er** *n*

hedge·hog \-ˌhȯg, -ˌhäg\ *n* : a small Old World insect-eating mammal covered with spines; *also* : PORCUPINE

hedge·hop \-ˌhäp\ *vb* : to fly an airplane very close to the ground

²**hedge·row** \-ˌrō\ *n* : a row of shrubs or trees bounding or separating fields

he·do·nism \'hēd-ˀn-ˌiz-əm\ *n* [Gk *hēdonē* pleasure] : the doctrine that pleasure is the chief good in life; *also* : a way of life based on this — **he·do·nist** \-ˀn-əst\ *n* — **he·do·nis·tic** \ˌhēd-ˀn-ˈis-tik\ *adj*

¹**heed** \'hēd\ *vb* : to pay attention

²**heed** *n* : ATTENTION, NOTICE — **heed·ful** \-fəl\ *adj* — **heed·ful·ly** \-ē\ *adv* — **heed·ful·ness** *n* — **heed·less** *adj* — **heed·less·ly** *adv* — **heed·less·ness** *n*

¹**heel** \'hēl\ *n* **1** : the hind part of the foot **2** : one of the crusty ends of a loaf of bread **3** : a solid attachment forming the back of the sole of a shoe **4** : a rear, low, or bottom part **5** : a contemptible person — **heel·less** \'hēl-ləs\ *adj*

²**heel** *vb* : to tilt to one side : LIST

¹**heft** \'heft\ *n* : WEIGHT, HEAVINESS

²**heft** *vb* : to test the weight of by lifting

hefty \'hef-tē\ *adj* **heft·i·er; -est 1** : marked by bigness, bulk, and usu. strength **2** : impressively large

he·ge·mo·ny \hi-ˈjem-ə-nē\ *n* : preponderant influence or authority esp. of one nation over others

he·gi·ra \hi-ˈjī-rə\ *n* [the *Hegira,* flight of Muhammad from Mecca in A.D. 622, fr. ML, fr. Ar *hijrah,* lit., flight] : a journey esp. when undertaken to seek refuge away from a dangerous or undesirable environment

heif·er \'hef-ər\ *n* : a young cow; *esp* : one that has not had a calf

height \'hīt, 'hītth\ *n* **1** : the highest part or point **2** : the distance from the bottom to the top of something standing upright **3** : ALTITUDE

height·en \'hīt-ˀn\ *vb* **height·ened; height·en·ing** \'hīt-(ˀ-)niŋ\ **1** : to increase in amount or degree : AUGMENT **2** : to make or become high or higher *syn* enhance, intensify, aggravate, magnify

Heim·lich maneuver \'hīm-lik-\ [Henry J. *Heimlich* b1920 Am. surgeon] : the manual application of sudden upward pressure on the upper abdomen of a choking victim to force a foreign object from the windpipe

hei·nous \'hā-nəs\ *adj* [ME, fr. MF *haineus,* fr. *haine* hate, fr. *hair* to hate] : hatefully or shockingly evil — **hei·nous·ly** *adv* — **hei·nous·ness** *n*

heir \'aər\ *n* : one who inherits or is entitled to inherit property, rank, title, or office — **heir·ship** *n*

heir apparent *n, pl* **heirs apparent** : an

heir whose right to succeed (as to a title) cannot be taken away if he or she survives the present holder

heir·ess \'ar-əs\ *n* : a female heir esp. to great wealth

heir·loom \'aər-ˌlüm\ *n* **1** : a piece of personal property that descends by inheritance **2** : something handed on from one generation to another

heir presumptive *n, pl* **heirs presumptive** : an heir whose present right to inherit could be lost through the birth of a nearer relative

heist \'hīst\ *vb, slang* : to commit armed robbery on; *also* : STEAL — **heist** *n, slang*

held *past and past part of* HOLD

he·li·cal \'hel-i-kəl, 'hē-li-\ *adj* : SPIRAL

he·li·coid \'hel-ə-ˌkȯid, 'hē-lə-\ *or* **he·li·coi·dal** \ˌhel-ə-'kȯid-ᵊl, ˌhē-lə-\ *adj* : forming or arranged in a spiral

he·li·cop·ter \'hel-ə-ˌkäp-tər, 'hē-lə-\ *n* [F *hélicoptère*, fr. Gk *helix* spiral + *pteron* wing] : an aircraft that is supported in the air by one or more rotors revolving on substantially vertical axes

he·lio·cen·tric \ˌhē-lē-ō-'sen-trik\ *adj* : having or relating to the sun as center

he·lio·trope \'hēl-yə-ˌtrōp\ *n* [L *heliotropium*, fr. Gk *hēliotropion*, fr. *hēliosun* + *tropos* turn; fr. its flowers' turning toward the sun] : a hairy-leaved garden herb related to the forget-me-not that has clusters of small fragrant white or purple flowers

he·li·port \'hel-ə-ˌpȯrt\ *n* : a landing and takeoff place for a helicopter

he·li·um \'hē-lē-əm\ *n* [NL, fr. Gk *hēlios* sun; so called from the fact that its existence in the sun's atmosphere was inferred before it was identified on the earth] : a very light nonflammable gaseous chemical element occurring in various natural gases

he·lix \'hē-liks\ *n, pl* **he·li·ces** \'hel-ə-ˌsēz, 'hē-lə-\ *also* **he·lix·es** \'hē-lik-səz\ : something spiral in form

hell \'hel\ *n* **1** : a nether world in which the dead continue to exist **2** : the realm of the devil in which the damned suffer everlasting punishment **3** : a place or state of torment or destruction — **hell·ish** *adj*

hell-bent \-ˌbent\ *adj* : stubbornly determined

hell·cat \-ˌkat\ *n* **1** : WITCH **2 2** : TORMENTOR; *esp* : SHREW 2

hel·le·bore \'hel-ə-ˌbȯr\ *n* **1** : a plant related to the buttercup; *also* : its roots used formerly in medicine **2** : a poisonous plant related to the lilies; *also* : its dried roots used in medicine and insecticides

Hel·lene \'hel-ˌēn\ *n* : GREEK

Hel·le·nism \'hel-ə-ˌniz-əm\ *n* : a body of humanistic and classical ideals associated with ancient Greece — **Hellen·ic** \he-'len-ik\ *adj* — **Hel·le·nist** \'hel-ə-nəst\ *n*

Hel·le·nis·tic \ˌhel-ə-'nis-tik\ *adj* : of or relating to Greek history, culture, or art after Alexander the Great

hell-for-leather *adv* : at full speed

hell·gram·mite \'hel-grə-ˌmīt\ *n* : an aquatic insect larva that is used as bait in fishing

hell·hole \'hel-ˌhōl\ *n* : a place of extreme misery or squalor

hell·ion \'hel-yən\ *n* : a troublesome or mischievous person

hel·lo \hə-'lō, he-\ *n, pl* **hellos** : an expression of greeting — used interjectionally

helm \'helm\ *n* **1** : a lever or wheel for steering a ship **2** : a position of control

hel·met \'hel-mət\ *n* : a protective covering for the head

helms·man \'helmz-mən\ *n* : the person at the helm : STEERSMAN

hel·ot \'hel-ət\ *n* : SLAVE, SERF

¹help \'help\ *vb* **1** : AID, ASSIST **2** : REMEDY, RELIEVE **3** : to be of use; *also* : PROMOTE **4** : to change for the better **5** : to refrain from; *also* : PREVENT **6** : to serve with food or drink — **help·er** *n*

²help *n* **1** : AID, ASSISTANCE; *also* : a source of aid **2** : REMEDY, RELIEF **3** : one who assists another **4** : the services of a paid worker — **help·ful** \-fəl\ *adj* — **help·ful·ly** \-ē\ *adv* — **help·ful·ness** *n* — **help·less** *adj* — **help·less·ly** *adv* — **help·less·ness** *n*

help·ing \'hel-piŋ\ *n* : a portion of food (asked for a second ∼ of potatoes)

help·mate \'help-ˌmāt\ *n* **1** : HELPER **2** : WIFE

help·meet \-ˌmēt\ *n* : HELPMATE

hel·ter-skel·ter \ˌhel-tər-'skel-tər\ *adv* **1** : in headlong disorder **2** : HAPHAZARDLY

helve \'helv\ *n* : a handle of a tool or weapon

Hel·ve·tian \hel-'vē-shən\ *adj* : SWISS — **Helvetian** *n*

¹hem \'hem\ *n* **1** : a border of an article (as of cloth) doubled back and stitched down **2** : RIM, MARGIN

²hem *vb* **hemmed; hem·ming 1** : to make a hem in sewing; *also* : BORDER, EDGE **2** : to surround restrictively

he-man \'hē-ˌman\ *n* : a strong virile man

he·ma·tite \'hē-mə-ˌtīt\ *n* : a mineral that consists of an oxide of iron and that constitutes an important iron ore

he·ma·tol·o·gy \ˌhē-mə-'täl-ə-jē\ *n* : a branch of biology that deals with the blood and blood-forming organs — **he·ma·to·log·ic** \-mət-ᵊl-'äj-ik\ *also* **he·ma·to·log·i·cal** \-i-kəl\ *adj* — **he·ma·tol·o·gist** \-'täl-ə-jəst\ *n*

heme \'hēm\ *n* : the deep red iron-containing part of hemoglobin

hemi·sphere \'hem-ə-ˌsfiər\ *n* **1** : one of the halves of the earth as divided by the equator into northern and southern parts (**northern hemisphere, southern hemisphere**) or by a meridian into two parts so that one half (eastern hemisphere) to the east of the Atlantic ocean includes Europe, Asia, and Africa and the half (western hemisphere) to the west includes No. and So. America and surrounding waters 2 : either of two half spheres formed by a plane through the sphere's center — **hemi·spher·ic** \hem-ə-¹sfiər-ik, -¹sfer-\ *or* **hemi·spher·i·cal** \-¹sfir-i-kəl, -¹sfer-\ *adj*

hem·line \¹hem-₁līn\ *n* : the line formed by the lower edge of a dress, skirt, or coat

hem·lock \¹hem-₁läk\ *n* 1 : any of several poisonous herbs related to the carrot 2 : an evergreen tree related to the pines; *also* : its soft light wood

he·mo·glo·bin \¹hē-mə-₁glō-bən\ *n* : an iron-containing compound found in red blood cells that carries oxygen from the lungs to the body tissues

he·mo·phil·ia \₁hē-mə-¹fil-ē-ə\ *n* : a usu. hereditary tendency to severe prolonged bleeding — **he·mo·phil·i·ac** \-ē-₁ak\ *adj or n* — **he·mo·phil·ic** \-¹fil-ik\ *n or adj*

hem·or·rhage \¹hem-(ə-)rij\ *n* : a large discharge of blood from the blood vessels — **hemorrhage** *vb* — **hem·or·rhag·ic** \₁hem-ə-¹raj-ik\ *adj*

hem·or·rhoid \¹hem-(ə-)₁roid\ *n* : a swollen mass of dilated veins situated at or just within the anus — usu. used in pl.

hemp \¹hemp\ *n* : a tall widely grown Asian herb related to the mulberry that is the source of a tough fiber used in cordage and of marijuana and hashish from its flowers and leaves — **hemp·en** \¹hem-pən\ *adj*

hem·stitch \¹hem-₁stich\ *vb* : to embroider (fabric) by drawing out parallel threads and stitching the exposed threads in groups to form designs

hen \¹hen\ *n* : a female chicken esp. over a year old; *also* : a female bird

hence \¹hens\ *adv* 1 : AWAY 2 : from this time 3 : CONSEQUENTLY 4 : from this source or origin

hence·forth \-₁fōrth\ *adv* : from this point on

hence·for·ward \hens-¹fōr-wərd\ *adv* : HENCEFORTH

hench·man \¹hench-mən\ *n* [ME *hengestman* groom, fr. *hengest* stallion] : a trusted follower or supporter

hen·na \¹hen-ə\ *n* 1 : an Old World tropical shrub with fragrant white flowers; *also* : a reddish brown dye obtained from its leaves and used esp. for the hair 2 : the color of henna dye

hen·peck \¹hen-₁pek\ *vb* : to nag and boss one's husband

hep \¹hep\ *var of* HIP

hep·a·rin \¹hep-ə-rən\ *n* : a compound found esp. in liver that slows the clotting of blood and is used medically

he·pat·ic \hi-¹pat-ik\ *adj* : of, relating to, or associated with the liver

he·pat·i·ca \hi-¹pat-i-kə\ *n* : any of a genus of herbs related to the buttercups that have lobed leaves and delicate flowers

hep·a·ti·tis \₁hep-ə-¹tīt-əs\ *n, pl* **-tit·i·des** \-¹tit-ə-₁dēz\ : inflammation of the liver; *also* : an acute virus disease of which this is a feature

hep·tam·e·ter \hep-¹tam-ət-ər\ *n* : a line of verse containing seven metrical feet

¹**her** \(h)ər, ₁hər\ *adj* : of or relating to her or herself

²**her** \ər, (¹)hər\ *pron, objective case of* SHE

¹**her·ald** \¹her-əld\ *n* 1 : an official crier or messenger 2 : HARBINGER 3 : ANNOUNCER, SPOKESMAN

²**herald** *vb* 1 : to give notice of 2 : HAIL, GREET; *also* : PUBLICIZE

he·ral·dic \he-¹ral-dik, hə-\ *adj* : of or relating to heralds or heraldry

her·ald·ry \¹her-əl-drē\ *n, pl* **-ries** 1 : the practice of devising and granting armorial insignia and of tracing a person's family to find out its coat of arms 2 : COAT OF ARMS 3 : PAGEANTRY

herb \¹(h)ərb\ *n* 1 : a seed plant that lacks woody tissue and dies to the ground at the end of a growing season 2 : a plant or plant part valued for medicinal or savory qualities — **her·ba·ceous** \₁(h)ər-¹bā-shəs\ *adj*

herb·age \¹(h)ər-bij\ *n* : green plants esp. when used or fit for grazing

herb·al·ist \¹(h)ər-bə-ləst\ *n* 1 : one that collects, grows, or deals in herbs 2 : one who practices healing by the use of herbs

her·bar·i·um \₁(h)ər-¹bar-ē-əm\ *n, pl* **-ia** \-ē-ə\ 1 : a collection of dried plant specimens 2 : a place that houses an herbarium

her·bi·cide \¹(h)ər-bə-₁sīd\ *n* : an agent used to destroy unwanted plants — **her·bi·cid·al** \₁(h)ər-bə-¹sīd-ᵊl\ *adj*

her·biv·o·rous \₁(h)ər-¹biv-ə-rəs\ *adj* : feeding on plants — **her·bi·vore** \¹(h)ər-bə-₁vōr\ *n*

her·cu·le·an \₁hər-kyə-¹lē-ən, ₁hər-¹kyü-lē-\ *adj, often cap* : of extraordinary power, size, or difficulty

¹**herd** \¹hərd\ *n* 1 : a group of animals of one kind kept or living together 2 : a group of people with a common bond 3 : MOB

²**herd** *vb* : to assemble or move in a herd — **herd·er** *n*

herds·man \¹hərdz-mən\ *n* : one who manages, breeds, or tends livestock

¹**here** \¹hiər\ *adv* 1 : in or at this place; *also* : NOW 2 : at or in this point, particular, or case 3 : in the present life or state 4 : HITHER

²**here** *n* : this place (get away from ~)

here·abouts \¹hir-ə-₁bauts\ *or* **here·about** \-₁baut\ *adv* : in this vicinity : about or near this place

¹**here·af·ter** \hir-¹af-tər\ *adv* 1 : after this in sequence or in time 2 : in some future time or state

²**hereafter** *n, often cap* 1 : FUTURE 2 : an existence beyond earthly life

here·by \hiər-'bī\ adv : by means of this

he·red·i·tary \hə-'red-ə-,ter-ē\ adj 1 : genetically passed or passable from parent to offspring 2 : passing by inheritance; also : having title or possession through inheritance 3 : of a kind established by tradition

he·red·i·ty \-ət-ē\ n : the qualities and potentialities genetically derived from one's ancestors; also : the passing of these from ancestor to descendant

Here·ford \'hər-fərd\ n : any of an English breed of hardy red beef cattle with white faces and markings

here·in \hir-'in\ adv : in this

here·of \-'əv, -'äv\ adv : of this

here·on \-'ȯn, -'än\ adv : on this

her·e·sy \'her-ə-sē\ n, pl -sies [ME heresie, fr. OF, fr. LL haeresis, fr. LGk hairesis, fr. Gk, action of taking, choice, sect, fr. hairein to take] 1 : adherence to a religious opinion contrary to church dogma 2 : an opinion or doctrine contrary to church dogma 3 : dissent from a dominant theory, opinion, or practice — her·e·tic \-,tik\ n — he·ret·i·cal \hə-'ret-i-kəl\ adj

here·to \-'tü\ adv : to this document

here·to·fore \'hirt-ə-,fȯr\ adv : up to this time

here·un·der \hir-'ən-dər\ adv : under this or according to this writing

here·un·to \hir-'ən-tü\ adv : to this

here·upon \'hir-ə-,pȯn, -,pän\ adv : on this or immediately after this

here·with \'hiər-'with, -'with\ adv 1 : with this 2 : HEREBY

her·i·ta·ble \'her-ət-ə-bəl\ adj : capable of being inherited

her·i·tage \'her-ət-ij\ n 1 : property that descends to an heir 2 : LEGACY 3 : BIRTHRIGHT

her·maph·ro·dite \(,)hər-'maf-rə-,dīt\ n : an animal or plant having both male and female reproductive organs — hermaphrodite adj — her·maph·ro·dit·ic \(,)hər-,maf-rə-'dit-ik\ adj

her·met·ic \hər-'met-ik\ also her·met·i·cal \-i-kəl\ adj : tightly sealed : AIRTIGHT — her·met·i·cal·ly \-i-k(ə-)lē\ adv

her·mit \'hər-mət\ n [ME eremite, fr. OF, fr. LL eremita, fr. Gk erēmitēs, adj., living in the desert, fr. erēmia desert, fr. erēmos lonely] : one who lives in solitude esp. for religious reasons

her·mit·age \-ij\ n 1 : the dwelling of a hermit 2 : a secluded dwelling

her·nia \'hər-nē-ə\ n, pl -ni·as or -ni·ae \-nē-,ē, -nē-,ī\ : a protruding of a bodily part (as a loop of intestine) into a pouch of the weakened wall of a cavity in which it is normally enclosed; also : the protruded mass — her·ni·ate \-nē-,āt\ vb — her·ni·a·tion \,hər-nē-'ā-shən\ n

he·ro \'hē-rō\ n, pl heroes 1 : a mythological or legendary figure of great strength or ability 2 : a man admired for his achievements and qualities 3

: the chief male character in a literary or dramatic work 4 pl usu heros : SUBMARINE 2 — he·ro·ic \hi-'rō-ik\ adj — he·ro·i·cal·ly \-i-k(ə-)lē\ adv

heroic couplet n : a rhyming couplet in iambic pentameter

he·ro·ics \hi-'rō-iks\ n pl : heroic or showy behavior

her·o·in \'her-ə-wən\ n : an illicit addictive narcotic drug made from morphine

her·o·ine \'her-ə-wən\ n 1 : a woman admired for her achievements and qualities 2 : the chief female character in a literary or dramatic work

her·o·ism \'her-ə-,wiz-əm\ n 1 : heroic conduct 2 : the qualities of a hero syn valor, prowess, gallantry

her·on \'her-ən\ n, pl herons also heron : a long-legged long-billed wading bird with soft plumage

her·pes \'hər-,pēz\ n : any of several virus diseases characterized by the formation of blisters on the skin or mucous membranes

herpes sim·plex \-'sim-,pleks\ n : either of two forms of herpes marked in one by watery blisters above the waist (as on the mouth and lips) and in the other on the genitalia

herpes zos·ter \-'zäs-tər\ n : SHINGLES

her·pe·tol·o·gy \,hər-pə-'täl-ə-jē\ n : a branch of zoology dealing with reptiles and amphibians — her·pe·tol·o·gist \,hər-pə-'täl-ə-jəst\ n

her·ring \'her-iŋ\ n, pl herring or herrings : a soft-finned narrow-bodied food fish of the north Atlantic; also : any of various similar or related fishes

her·ring·bone \'her-iŋ-,bōn\ n : a pattern made up of rows of parallel lines with adjacent rows slanting in reverse directions; also : a twilled fabric with this pattern

hers \'hərz\ pron : one or the ones belonging to her

her·self \(h)ər-'self\ pron : SHE, HER — used reflexively, for emphasis, or in absolute constructions

hertz \'hərts, 'herts\ n, pl hertz : a unit of frequency equal to one cycle per second

hes·i·tant \'hez-ə-tənt\ adj : tending to hesitate — hes·i·tance \-tən(t)s\ n — hes·i·tan·cy \-tən-sē\ n — hes·i·tant·ly adv

hes·i·tate \'hez-ə-,tāt\ vb -tat·ed; -tat·ing 1 : to hold back (as in doubt) 2 : PAUSE syn waver, vacillate, falter, shilly-shally — hes·i·ta·tion \,hez-ə-'tā-shən\ n

het·ero·dox \'het-(ə-)rə-,däks\ adj 1 : differing from an acknowledged standard 2 : holding unorthodox opinions — het·er·o·doxy \-,däk-sē\ n

het·er·o·ge·neous \,het-(ə-)rə-'jē-nē-əs, -nyəs\ adj : consisting of dissimilar ingredients or constituents : MIXED — het·er·o·ge·ne·ity \-jə-'nē-ət-ē\ n —

het•er•o•ge•neous•ly adv — het•er•o•ge-
neous•ness n

het•ero•sex•u•al \ˌhet-ə-rō-¹sek-
sh(ə-w)əl\ adj : tending to direct sexual desire toward the opposite sex; also
: of or relating to different sexes —
heterosexual n — het•ero•sex•u•al•i•ty
\-ˌsek-shə-¹wal-ət-ē\ n

hew \¹hyü\ vb hewed; hewed or hewn
\¹hyün\; hew•ing 1 : to cut or fell with
blows (as of an ax) 2 : to give shape to
with or as if with an ax 3 : to conform
strictly — hew•er n

HEW abbr Department of Health, Education, and Welfare

¹hex \¹heks\ vb 1 : to practice witchcraft
2 : JINX

²hex n : SPELL, JINX

³hex abbr hexagon; hexagonal

hexa•gon \¹hek-sə-ˌgän\ n : a polygon
having six angles and six sides — hex-
ag•o•nal \hek-¹sag-ən-°l\ adj

hex•am•e•ter \hek-¹sam-ət-ər\ n : a line
of verse containing six metrical feet

hey•day \¹hā-ˌdā\ n : a period of greatest strength, vigor, or prosperity

hf abbr half

Hf symbol hafnium

HF abbr high frequency

hg abbr hectogram

Hg symbol [NL hydrargyrum, lit., water silver] mercury

hgt abbr height

hgwy abbr highway

HH abbr 1 Her Highness; His Highness
ness 2 His Holiness

HHS abbr Department of Health and
Human Services

HI abbr 1 Hawaii 2 humidity index

hi•a•tus \hī-¹āt-əs\ n [L, fr. hiatus, pp.
of hiare to yawn] 1 : a break in an
object : GAP 2 : a lapse in continuity

hi•ba•chi \hi-¹bäch-ē\ n [Jp] : a charcoal
brazier

hi•ber•nate \¹hī-bər-ˌnāt\ vb -nat•ed;
-nat•ing : to pass the winter in a torpid
or resting state — hi•ber•na•tion \ˌhī-
bər-¹nā-shən\ n — hi•ber•na•tor \¹hī-
bər-ˌnāt-ər\ n

hi•bis•cus \hī-¹bis-kəs, hə-\ n : any of a
genus of herbs, shrubs, and trees related to the mallows and noted for
large showy flowers

hic•cup also hic•cough \¹hik-(ˌ)əp\ n : a
spasmodic breathing movement
checked by sudden closing of the glot-
tis accompanied by a peculiar sound;
also : this sound — hiccup vb

hick \¹hik\ n [Hick, nickname for Rich-
ard] : an awkward provincial person
— hick adj

hick•o•ry \¹hik-(ə-)rē\ n, pl -ries : any of
a genus of No. American hardwood
trees related to the walnuts; also : the
wood of a hickory — hickory adj

hi•dal•go \hid-¹al-gō\ n, pl -gos often cap
[Sp, fr. earlier fijo dalgo, lit., son of
something, son of property] : a member of the lower nobility of Spain

hidden tax n 1 : a tax ultimately paid by
someone other than the person on

whom it is formally levied 2 : an economic injustice that reduces one's income or buying power

¹hide \¹hīd\ vb hid \¹hid\; hid•den \¹hid-
°n\ or hid; hid•ing \¹hīd-iŋ\ 1 : to put
or remain out of sight 2 : to conceal
for shelter or protection; also : to
seek protection 3 : to keep secret 4
: to turn away in shame or anger

²hide n : the skin of an animal

hide-and-seek \ˌhīd-°n-¹sēk\ n : a children's game in which everyone hides
from one player who tries to find them

hide•away \¹hīd-ə-ˌwā\ n : HIDEOUT

hide•bound \-ˌbaùnd\ adj : obstinately
conservative

hid•eous \¹hid-ē-əs\ adj [ME hidous, fr.
OF, fr. hisde, hide terror] 1 : offensive to one of the senses : UGLY 2
: morally offensive : SHOCKING — hid-
eous•ly adv — hid•eous•ness n

hide•out \¹hīd-ˌaùt\ n : a place of refuge
or concealment

hie \¹hī\ vb hied; hy•ing or hie•ing : HAS-
TEN

hi•er•ar•chy \¹hī-(ə-)ˌrär-kē\ n, pl -chies
1 : a ruling body of clergy organized
into ranks 2 : persons or things arranged in a graded series — hi•er•ar-
chi•cal \ˌhī-ə-¹rär-ki-kəl\ adj — hi•er-
ar•chi•cal•ly \-k(ə-)lē\ adv

hi•er•o•glyph•ic \ˌhī-(ə-)rə-¹glif-ik\ n
[MF hieroglyphique, adj., deriv. of
Gk hieroglyphikos, fr. hieros sacred
+ glyphein to carve] 1 : a character in
a system of picture writing (as of the
ancient Egyptians) 2 : a symbol or
sign difficult to decipher

hi-fi \¹hī-¹fī\ n 1 : HIGH FIDELITY 2
: equipment for reproduction of sound
with high fidelity

hig•gle•dy-pig•gle•dy \ˌhig-əl-dē-¹pig-əl-
dē\ adv : in confusion

¹high \¹hī\ adj 1 : ELEVATED; also : TALL
2 : advanced toward fullness or culmination; also : slightly tainted 3 : long
past 4 : SHRILL, SHARP 5 : far from the
equator ⟨∼ latitudes⟩ 6 : exalted in
character 7 : of greater degree, size,
or amount than average 8 : of relatively great importance 9 : FORCIBLE,
STRONG ⟨∼ winds⟩ 10 : BOASTFUL, AR-
ROGANT 11 : showing elation or excitement 12 : COSTLY, DEAR 13 : advanced esp. in complexity ⟨∼er
mathematics⟩ 14 : INTOXICATED; also
: excited or stupefied by or as if by a
drug (as heroin) — high•ly adv

²high adv 1 : at or to a high place or
degree 2 : LUXURIOUSLY (living ∼)

³high n 1 : an elevated place 2 : a high
point or level 3 : the arrangement of
gears in an automobile that gives the
highest speed 4 : an excited or stupefied state produced by or as if by a
drug

high•ball \¹hī-ˌbòl\ n : a usu. tall drink
of liquor mixed with water or a carbonated beverage

high beam n : the long-range focus of a
vehicle headlight

high·born \'hī-'bórn\ *adj* : of noble birth

high·boy \-,bòi\ *n* : a high chest of drawers mounted on a base with legs

high·bred \-'bred\ *adj* : coming from superior stock

high·brow \-,braú\ *n* : a person of superior learning or culture — **highbrow** *adj*

high·er-up \,hī-ər-'əp\ *n* : a superior officer of official

high·fa·lu·tin \,hī-fə-'lüt-³n\ *adj* : PRETENTIOUS, POMPOUS

high fashion *n* 1 : HIGH STYLE 2 : HAUTE COUTURE

high fidelity *n* : the reproduction of sound or image with a high degree of faithfulness to the original

high five *n* : a slapping of upraised right hands by two people (as in celebration) — **high-five** *vb*

high-flown \'hī-'flōn\ *adj* 1 : EXALTED 2 : BOMBASTIC

high frequency *n* : a radio frequency between 3 and 30 megahertz

high gear *n* 1 : HIGH 3 2 : a state of intense or maximum activity

high-hand·ed \'hī-'han-dəd\ *adj* : OVERBEARING — **high-hand·ed·ly** *adv* — **high-hand·ed·ness** *n*

high-hat \-'hat\ *adj* : SUPERCILIOUS, SNOBBISH — **high-hat** *vb*

high·land \-lənd\ *n* : elevated or mountainous land

high·land·er \-lən-dər\ *n* 1 : an inhabitant of a highland 2 *cap* : an inhabitant of the Scottish Highlands

¹high·light \-,līt\ *n* : an event or detail of major importance

²highlight *vb* 1 : EMPHASIZE 2 : to constitute a highlight of

high-mind·ed \'hī-'mīn-dəd\ *adj* : marked by elevated principles and feelings — **high-mind·ed·ness** *n*

high·ness \'hī-nəs\ *n* 1 : the quality or state of being high 2 — used as a title (as for kings)

high-pres·sure \-'presh-ər\ *adj* : using or involving aggressive and insistent sales techniques

high-rise \-'rīz\ *adj* : having several stories and being equipped with elevators (~ apartments) ; *also* : of or relating to high-rise buildings

high-road \-,rōd\ *n* : HIGHWAY

high school *n* : a school usu. including grades 9 to 12 or 10 to 12

high sea *n* : the open sea outside territorial waters — usu. used in pl.

high-sound·ing \'hī-'saún-diŋ\ *adj* : POMPOUS, IMPOSING

high-spir·it·ed \-'spir-ət-əd\ *adj* : characterized by a bold or lofty spirit

high-strung \-'strəŋ\ *adj* : having an extremely nervous or sensitive temperament

high style *n* : the newest in fashion or design usu. adopted by a limited number of people

high·tail \'hī-,tāl\ *vb* : to retreat at full speed

high tech \-'tek\ *n* : HIGH TECHNOLOGY

high technology *n* : technology involving the use of advanced devices or techniques

high-ten·sion \'hī-'ten-chən\ *adj* : having, using, or relating to high voltage

high-test \-'test\ *adj* : having a high octane number

high-toned \-'tōnd\ *adj* 1 : high in social, moral, or intellectual quality 2 : PRETENTIOUS, POMPOUS

high·way \'hī-,wā\ *n* : a main direct road

high·way·man \-mən\ *n* : a person who robs travelers on a road

hi·jack *or* **high·jack** \'hī-,jak\ *vb* : to steal esp. by stopping a vehicle on the highway; *also* : to commandeer a flying airplane — **hijack** *n* — **hi·jack·er** *n*

¹hike \'hīk\ *vb* **hiked**; **hik·ing** 1 : to move or raise with a sudden motion 2 : to take a long walk — **hik·er** *n*

²hike *n* 1 : a long walk 2 : RISE, INCREASE

hi·lar·i·ous \hil-'ar-ē-əs, hī-'lar-\ *adj* : marked by or providing boisterous merriment — **hi·lar·i·ous·ly** *adv* — **hi·lar·i·ty** \-ət-ē\ *n*

hill \'hil\ *n* 1 : a usu. rounded elevation of land 2 : a little heap or mound (as of earth) — **hilly** *adj*

hill·bil·ly \'hil-,bil-ē\ *n*, *pl* **-lies** : a person from a backwoods area

hill·ock \'hil-ək\ *n* : a small hill

hill·side \-,sīd\ *n* : the part of a hill between the summit and the foot

hill·top \-,täp\ *n* : the top of a hill

hilt \'hilt\ *n* : a handle esp. of a sword or dagger

him \im, (')him\ *pron*, *objective case of* HE

Hi·ma·la·yan \,him-ə-'lā-ən, him-'äl-yən\ *adj* : of, relating to, or characteristic of the Himalaya mountains or the people living there

him·self \(h)im-'self\ *pron* : HE, HIM — used reflexively, for emphasis, or in absolute constructions

¹hind \'hind\ *n*, *pl* **hinds** *also* **hind** : a female deer : DOE

²hind *adj* : REAR

hin·der \'hin-dər\ *vb* **hin·dered**; **hin·der·ing** \-d(ə-)riŋ\ 1 : to impede the progress of 2 : to hold back **syn** obstruct, block, bar, impede

²hind·er \'hīn-dər\ *adj* : HIND

Hin·di \'hin-dē\ *n* : a literary and official language of northern India

hind·most \'hīn(d)-,mōst\ *adj* : farthest to the rear

hind·quar·ter \-,kwórt-ər\ *n* 1 : one side of the back half of the carcass of a quadruped 2 *pl* : the part of the body of a quadruped behind the junction of hind limbs and trunk

hin·drance \'hin-drəns\ *n* 1 : the state of being hindered; *also* : the action of hindering 2 : IMPEDIMENT

hind·sight \'hīn(d)-,sīt\ *n* : understanding of an event after it has happened

Hin·du·ism \'hin-dü-,iz-əm\ *n* : a body

of religious beliefs and practices native to India — **Hin·du** *n or adj*

hind wing *n* : either of the posterior wings of a 4-winged insect

¹**hinge** \'hinj\ *n* : a jointed piece on which one piece (as a door, gate, or lid) turns or swings on another

²**hinge** *vb* **hinged; hing·ing 1** : to attach by or furnish with hinges **2** : to be contingent on a single consideration

hint \'hint\ *n* **1** : an indirect or summary suggestion **2** : CLUE **3** : a very small amount — **hint** *vb*

hin·ter·land \'hint-ər-,land\ *n* **1** : a region behind a coast **2** : a region remote from cities

¹**hip** \'hip\ *n* : the fruit of a rose

²**hip** *n* **1** : the part of the body on either side below the waist consisting of the side of the pelvis and the upper thigh **2** : the joint between pelvis and femur

³**hip** *also* **hep** *adj* **hip·per; hip·pest** : keenly aware of or interested in the newest developments

⁴**hip** *vb* **hipped; hip·ping** : TELL, INFORM

hip·bone \-'bōn, -,bōn\ *n* : the large flaring bone that makes a lateral half of the pelvis in mammals

hip joint *n* : the articulation between the femur and the hipbone

hipped \'hipt\ *adj* : having hips esp. of a specified kind (broad-*hipped*)

hip·pie *or* **hip·py** \'hip-ē\ *n, pl* **hippies** : a usu. young person who rejects established mores, advocates nonviolence, and often uses psychedelic drugs or marijuana; *also* : a long-haired unconventionally dressed young person

hip·po·drome \'hip-ə-,drōm\ *n* : an arena for equestrian performances

hip·po·pot·a·mus \,hip-ə-'pät-ə-məs\ *n, pl* **-mus·es** *or* **-mi** \-,mī\ [L, fr. Gk *hippopotamos*, fr. *hippos* horse + *potamos* river] : a large thick-skinned African river animal related to the swine

¹**hire** \'hī(ə)r\ *n* **1** : payment for labor or personal services : WAGES **2** : EMPLOYMENT

²**hire** *vb* **hired; hir·ing 1** : to employ for pay **2** : to engage the temporary use of for pay

hire·ling \'hī(ə)r-liŋ\ *n* : a hired person; *esp* : one whose motives are mercenary

hir·sute \'hər-,süt, 'hiər-\ *adj* : HAIRY

¹**his** \(h)iz, ,hiz\ *adj* : of or relating to him or himself

²**his** \'hiz\ *pron* : one or the ones belonging to him

His·pan·ic \his-'pan-ik\ *adj* : of or relating to the people, speech, or culture of Spain or Latin America

hiss \'his\ *vb* : to make a sharp sibilant sound; *also* : to express disapproval of by hissing — **hiss** *n*

hist *abbr* historian; historical; history

his·ta·mine \'his-tə-,mēn, -mən\ *n* : a chemical compound widespread in animal tissues and playing a major role in allergic reactions

his·to·gram \'his-tə-,gram\ *n* : representation of statistical data by means of rectangles whose widths represent class intervals and whose heights represent corresponding frequencies

his·to·ri·an \his-'tōr-ē-ən\ *n* : a student or writer of history

his·to·ric·i·ty \,his-tə-'ris-ət-ē\ *n* : historical actuality

his·to·ri·og·ra·pher \his-,tōr-ē-'äg-rə-fər\ *n* : HISTORIAN

his·to·ry \'his-t(ə-)rē\ *n, pl* **-ries** [L *historia*, fr. Gk, inquiry, history, fr. *histōr, istōr* knowing, learned] **1** : a chronological record of significant events often with an explanation of their causes **2** : a branch of knowledge that records and explains past events **3** : events that form the subject matter of history — **his·tor·ic** \his-'tōr-ik\ *adj* — **his·tor·i·cal** \-i-kəl\ *adj* — **his·tor·i·cal·ly** \-k(ə-)lē\ *adv*

his·tri·on·ic \,his-trē-'än-ik\ *adj* [LL *histrionicus*, fr. L *histrio* actor] **1** : deliberately affected **2** : of or relating to actors or the theater — **his·tri·on·i·cal·ly** \-i-k(ə-)lē\ *adv*

his·tri·on·ics \-iks\ *n pl* **1** : theatrical performances **2** : deliberate display of emotion for effect

¹**hit** \'hit\ *vb* **hit; hit·ting 1** : to reach with a blow : STRIKE **2** : to make or bring into contact : COLLIDE **3** : to affect detrimentally **4** : to make a request of **5** : to come upon **6** : to accord with : SUIT **7** : REACH, ATTAIN **8** : to indulge in often to excess — **hit·ter** *n*

²**hit** *n* **1** : BLOW; *also* : COLLISION **2** : something highly successful **3** : a stroke in an athletic contest; *esp* : BASE HIT **4** : a dose of an illegal drug **5** : a murder committed by a gangster

¹**hitch** \'hich\ *vb* **1** : to move by jerks **2** : to catch or fasten esp. by a hook or knot **3** : HITCHHIKE

²**hitch** *n* **1** : JERK, PULL **2** : a sudden halt **3** : a connection between something towed and its mover **4** : KNOT

hitch·hike \'hich-,hīk\ *vb* : to travel by securing free rides from passing vehicles — **hitch·hik·er** *n*

¹**hith·er** \'hith-ər\ *adv* : to this place

²**hither** *adj* : being on the near or adjacent side

hith·er·to \-,tü\ *adv* : up to this time

HIV *n* [*human immunodeficiency virus*] : AIDS VIRUS

hive \'hīv\ *n* **1** : a container for housing honeybees **2** : a colony of bees **3** : a place swarming with busy occupants — **hive** *vb*

hives \'hīvz\ *n sing or pl* : an allergic disorder marked by the presence of itching wheals

HJ *abbr* [L *hic jacet*] here lies — used in epitaphs

hl *abbr* hectoliter

HL *abbr* House of Lords

hm *abbr* hectometer

HM *abbr* **1** Her Majesty; Her Majesty's **2** His Majesty; His Majesty's

HMS *abbr* Her Majesty's ship; His Majesty's ship

Ho *symbol* holmium

hoa·gie *also* **hoa·gy** \'hō-gē\ *n*, *pl* **hoagies** : SUBMARINE 2

hoard \'hōrd\ *n* : a hidden accumulation — **hoard** *vb* — **hoard·er** *n*

hoar·frost \'hōr-,frȯst\ *n* : FROST 2

hoarse \'hōrs\ *adj* **hoars·er**; **hoars·est 1** : rough and harsh in sound **2** : having a grating voice — **hoarse·ly** *adv* — **hoarse·ness** *n*

hoary \'hōr-ē\ *adj* **hoar·i·er**; **-est 1** : gray or white with age **2** : ANCIENT — **hoar·i·ness** *n*

hoax \'hōks\ *n* : an act intended to trick or dupe; *also* : something accepted or established by fraud — **hoax** *vb* — **hoax·er** *n*

hob \'häb\ *n* : MISCHIEF, TROUBLE

¹**hob·ble** \'häb-əl\ *vb* **hob·bled**; **hob·bling** \-(ə-)liŋ\ **1** : to limp along; *also* : to make lame **2** : FETTER

²**hobble** *n* **1** : a hobbling movement **2** : something used to hobble an animal

hob·by \'häb-ē\ *n*, *pl* **hobbies** : a pursuit or interest engaged in for relaxation — **hob·by·ist** \-ē-əst\ *n*

hob·by·horse \'häb-ē-,hȯrs\ *n* **1** : a stick with a horse's head on which children pretend to ride **2** : a toy horse mounted on rockers **3** : a favorite topic to which one constantly reverts

hob·gob·lin \'häb-,gäb-lən\ *n* **1** : a mischievous goblin **2** : BOGEY 1

hob·nail \-,nāl\ *n* : a short large-headed nail for studding shoe soles — **hob·nailed** \-,nāld\ *adj*

hob·nob \-,näb\ *vb* **hob·nobbed**; **hob·nob·bing** : to associate familiarly

ho·bo \'hō-bō\ *n*, *pl* **hoboes** *also* **hobos** : TRAMP 2

¹**hock** \'häk\ *n* : a joint or region in the hind limb of a quadruped just above the foot and corresponding to the human ankle

²**hock** *n* [D *hok* pen, prison] : PAWN; *also* : DEBT 2 — **hock** *vb*

hock·ey \'häk-ē\ *n* **1** : FIELD HOCKEY **2** : ICE HOCKEY

ho·cus-po·cus \,hō-kəs-'pō-kəs\ *n* **1** : SLEIGHT OF HAND **2** : nonsense or sham used to conceal deception

hod \'häd\ *n* **1** : a long-handled tray or trough for carrying a load esp. of mortar or bricks **2** : a coal scuttle

hodge·podge \'häj-,päj\ *n* : a heterogeneous mixture

hoe \'hō\ *n* : a long-handled implement with a thin flat blade used esp. for cultivating, weeding, or loosening the earth around plants — **hoe** *vb*

hoe·cake \'hō-,kāk\ *n* : a small cornmeal cake

hoe·down \-,daůn\ *n* **1** : SQUARE DANCE **2** : a gathering featuring hoedowns

¹**hog** \'hȯg, 'häg\ *n*, *pl* **hogs** *also* **hog 1** : a domestic swine esp. when grown **2** : a selfish, gluttonous, or filthy person — **hog·gish** *adj*

²**hog** *vb* **hogged**; **hog·ging** : to take or hold selfishly

ho·gan \'hō-,gän\ *n* : an earth-covered dwelling of the Navaho Indians

hog·back \'hȯg-,bak, 'häg-\ *n* : a ridge with a sharp summit and steep sides

hog·nose snake \'hȯg-,nōz-, ,häg-\ *or* **hog-nosed snake** \-,nōz(d)-\ *n* : any of several rather small harmless stout-bodied No. American snakes with an upturned snout that play dead when their threatening display is ineffective

hogs·head \'hȯgz-,hed, 'hägz-\ *n* **1** : a large cask or barrel; *esp* : one holding from 63 to 140 gallons **2** : a liquid measure equal to 63 U.S. gallons

hog-tie \'hȯg-,tī, 'häg-\ *vb* **1** : to tie together the feet of (~ a calf) **2** : to make helpless

hog·wash \-,wȯsh, -,wäsh\ *n* **1** : SWILL 1, SLOP **2** : NONSENSE, BALONEY

hog-wild \-'wīld\ *adj* : lacking in restraint

hoi pol·loi \,hȯi-pə-'lȯi\ *n pl* [Gk, the many] : the general populace

¹**hoist** \'hȯist\ *vb* : RAISE, LIFT

²**hoist** *n* **1** : LIFT **2** : an apparatus for hoisting

hoke \'hōk\ *vb* **hoked**; **hok·ing** : FAKE — usu. used with *up*

ho·kum \'hō-kəm\ *n* : NONSENSE

¹**hold** \'hōld\ *vb* **held** \'held\; **hold·ing 1** : POSSESS; *also* : KEEP **2** : RESTRAIN **3** : to have a grasp on **4** : to remain or keep in a particular situation or position **5** : SUSTAIN; *also* : RESERVE **6** : BEAR, COMPORT **7** : to maintain in being or action : PERSIST **8** : CONTAIN, ACCOMMODATE **9** : HARBOR, ENTERTAIN; *also* : CONSIDER, REGARD **10** : to carry on by concerted action; *also* : CONVOKE **11** : to occupy esp. by appointment or election **12** : to be valid **13** : HALT, PAUSE — **hold·er** *n* — **hold forth** : to speak at length — **hold to** : to adhere to : MAINTAIN — **hold with** : to agree with or approve of

²**hold** *n* **1** : STRONGHOLD **2** : CONFINEMENT; *also* : PRISON **3** : the act or manner of holding : GRIP **4** : a restraining, dominating, or controlling influence **5** : something that may be grasped as a support **6** : an order or indication that something is to be reserved or delayed

³**hold** *n* **1** : the interior of a ship below decks; *esp* : a ship's cargo deck **2** : an airplane's cargo compartment

hold·ing \'hōl-diŋ\ *n* **1** : land or other property owned **2** : a ruling of a court esp. on an issue of law

holding pattern *n* : a course flown by an aircraft waiting to land

hold out \(')hōl-'daůt\ *vb* **1** : to continue to fight or work **2** : to refuse to come to an agreement — **hold·out** \'hōl-,daůt\ *n*

hold·over \'hōl-,dō-vər\ *n* : a person who continues in office

hold-up \'hōl-,dəp\ *n* 1 : DELAY 2 : robbery at the point of a gun

hole \'hōl\ *n* 1 : an opening into or through something 2 : a hollow place (as a pit or cave) 3 : DEN, BURROW 4 : a unit of play from tee to cup in golf 5 : a wretched or dingy place 6 : an awkward position — **hole** *vb*

hol·i·day \'häl-ə-,dā\ *n* [ME, fr. OE *hāligdæg*, fr. *hālig* holy + *dæg* day] 1 : a day observed in Judaism with commemorative ceremonies 2 : a day of freedom from work; *esp* : one in commemoration of an event 3 : VACATION — **holiday** *vb*

ho·li·ness \'hō-lē-nəs\ *n* 1 : the quality or state of being holy 2 — used as a title for various high religious officials

hol·ler \'häl-ər\ *vb* **hol·lered; hol·ler·ing** \-(ə-)riŋ\ : to cry out : SHOUT — **holler** *n*

¹**hol·low** \'häl-ō\ *adj* **hol·low·er** \'häl-ə-wər\; **hol·low·est** \-ə-wəst\ 1 : CONCAVE, SUNKEN 2 : having a cavity within 3 : MUFFLED (a ~ sound) 4 : lacking in real value, sincerity, or substance; *also* : FALSE — **hol·low·ness** *n*

²**hollow** *n* 1 : a surface depression 2 : CAVITY, HOLE

³**hollow** *vb* : to make or become hollow

hol·low·ware *or* **hol·lo·ware** \'häl-ə-,waər\ *n* : vessels (as bowls or cups) that have a significant depth and volume

hol·ly \'häl-ē\ *n, pl* **hollies** : a tree or shrub with usu. evergreen glossy spiny-margined leaves and red berries

hol·ly·hock \-,häk, -,hók\ *n* [ME *holihoc*, fr. *holi* holy + *hoc* mallow] : a tall perennial herb related to the mallows that is widely grown for its showy flowers

hol·mi·um \'hōl-mē-əm\ *n* : a metallic chemical element

ho·lo·caust \'häl-ə-,kóst, 'hō-lə-, 'hó-lə-\ *n* 1 : a thorough destruction esp. by fire 2 *often cap* : the killing of European Jews by the Nazis during World War II

Ho·lo·cene \'hō-lə-,sēn\ *adj* : RECENT 3 — **Holocene** *n*

ho·lo·gram \'hō-lə-,gram, 'häl-ə-\ *n* : a three-dimensional picture made by reflected laser light on a photographic film without the use of a camera

ho·lo·graph \'hō-lə-,graf, 'häl-ə-\ *n* : a document wholly in the handwriting of its author

ho·log·ra·phy \hō-'läg-rə-fē\ *n* : the process of making or using a hologram — **ho·lo·graph·ic** \,hō-lə-'graf-ik, ,häl-ə-\ *adj*

hol·stein \'hōl-,stēn, -,stīn\ *n* : any of a breed of large black-and-white dairy cattle that produce large quantities of comparatively low-fat milk

hol·stein-frie·sian \-'frē-zhən\ *n* : HOLSTEIN

hol·ster \'hōl-stər\ *n* [Dutch] : a usu. leather case for a firearm

ho·ly \'hō-lē\ *adj* **ho·li·er; -est** 1 : worthy of absolute devotion 2 : SACRED 3 : having a divine quality **syn** hallowed, blessed, sacred, sanctified, consecrated

Holy Spirit *n* : the active presence of God in human life constituting the third person of the Trinity

ho·ly·stone \'hō-lē-,stōn\ *n* : a soft sandstone used to scrub a ship's decks — **holy-stone** *vb*

hom·age \'(h)äm-ij\ *n* [ME, fr. OF *hommage*, fr. *homme* man, vassal, fr. L *homo* man] : reverential regard

hom·bre \'äm-brē, 'əm-, -,brā\ *n* : GUY, FELLOW

hom·burg \'häm-,bərg\ *n* [*Homburg*, Germany] : a man's felt hat with a stiff curled brim and a high crown creased lengthwise

¹**home** \'hōm\ *n* 1 : one's residence; *also* : HOUSE 2 : the social unit formed by a family living together 3 : a congenial environment; *also* : HABITAT 4 : a place of origin 5 : the objective in various games — **home·less** *adj*

²**home** *vb* **homed; hom·ing** 1 : to go or return home 2 : to proceed to or toward a source of radiated energy used as a guide

home·body \'hōm-,bäd-ē\ *n* : one whose life centers in the home

home-bred \-'bred\ *adj* : produced at home : INDIGENOUS

home·com·ing \-,kəm-iŋ\ *n* 1 : a return home 2 : the return of a group of people esp. on a special occasion to a place formerly frequented

home computer *n* : a small inexpensive microcomputer

home economics *n* : the theory and practice of homemaking

home·grown \'hōm-'grōn\ *adj* 1 : grown domestically (~ corn) 2 : LOCAL, INDIGENOUS

home·land \-,land\ *n* 1 : native land 2 : an area set aside to be a state for a people of a particular national, cultural, or racial origin

home·ly \'hōm-lē\ *adj* **home·li·er; -est** 1 : FAMILIAR 2 : unaffectedly natural 3 : lacking beauty or proportion — **home·li·ness** *n*

home·made \'hōm-'(m)ād\ *adj* : made in the home, on the premises, or by one's own efforts

home·mak·er \-,mā-kər\ *n* : one who manages a household esp. as a wife and mother — **home·mak·ing** \-kiŋ\ *n*

ho·me·op·a·thy \,hō-mē-'äp-ə-thē\ *n* : a system of medical practice that treats disease esp. with minute doses of a remedy that would in healthy persons produce symptoms of the disease treated — **ho·meo·path** \'hō-mē-ə-,path\ *n* — **ho·meo·path·ic** \,hō-mē-ə-'path-ik\ *adj*

ho·meo·sta·sis \,hō-mē-ō-'stā-səs\ *n* : a tendency toward a stable state of equilibrium between interrelated physiological, psychological, or social factors characteristic of an individual or group — **ho·meo·stat·ic** \-'stat-ik\ *adj*

home plate *n* : a slab at the apex of a baseball diamond that a base runner must touch in order to score

hom·er \'hō-mər\ *n* : HOME RUN — **homer** *vb*

home·room \'hōm-,rüm, -,rům\ *n* : a classroom where pupils report at the beginning of each school day

home run *n* : a hit in baseball that enables the batter to make a circuit of the bases and score a run

home·sick \'hōm-,sik\ *adj* : longing for home and family while absent from them — **home·sick·ness** *n*

home·spun \-,spən\ *adj* 1 : spun or made at home; *also* : made of a loosely woven usu. woolen or linen fabric 2 : SIMPLE, HOMELY

[1]**home·stead** \'hōm-,sted\ *n* : the home and land occupied by a family

[2]**homestead** *vb* : to acquire or settle on public land — **home·stead·er** \-,sted-ər\ *n*

home·stretch \'hōm-'strech\ *n* 1 : the part of a racecourse between the last curve and the winning post 2 : a final stage (as of a project)

[1]**home·ward** \'hōm-wərd\ *or* **home·wards** \-wərdz\ *adv* : in the direction of home

[2]**homeward** *adj* : being or going in the direction of home

home·work \'hōm-,wərk\ *n* 1 : an assignment given a student to be completed outside the classroom 2 : preparatory reading or research

hom·ey \'hō-mē\ *adj* **hom·i·er; -est** : intimate or homelike

ho·mi·cide \'häm-ə-,sīd, 'hō-mə-\ *n* [L *homicida* manslayer & *homicidium* manslaughter; both fr. *homo* man + *caedere* to cut, kill] 1 : a person who kills another 2 : a killing of one human being by another — **hom·i·cid·al** \,häm-ə-'sīd-²l\ *adj*

hom·i·ly \'häm-ə-lē\ *n, pl* **-lies** : SERMON — **hom·i·let·ic** \,häm-ə-'let-ik\ *adj*

homing pigeon *n* : a racing pigeon trained to return home

hom·i·ny \'häm-ə-nē\ *n* : hulled corn with the germ removed

ho·mo \'hō-mō\ *n, pl* **homos** : any of the genus of primate mammals that includes all surviving and various extinct human beings

ho·mo·ge·neous \,hō-mə-'jē-nē-əs, -nyəs\ *adj* : of the same or a similar kind; *also* : of uniform structure — **ho·mo·ge·ne·i·ty** \-jə-'nē-ət-ē\ *n* — **ho·mo·ge·neous·ly** *adv* — **ho·mo·ge·neous·ness** *n*

ho·mo·ge·nize \hō-'mäj-ə-,nīz, hə-\ *vb* **-nized; -niz·ing** 1 : to make homogeneous 2 : to reduce the particles in (as milk or paint) to uniform size and distribute them evenly throughout the liquid — **ho·mo·ge·ni·za·tion** \-,mäj-ə-nə-'zā-shən\ *n* — **ho·mo·ge·niz·er** *n*

ho·mo·graph \'häm-ə-,graf, 'hō-mə-\ *n* : one of two or more words spelled alike but different in origin or meaning or pronunciation (the noun *conduct* and the verb *conduct* are ~s)

ho·mol·o·gy \hō-'mäl-ə-jē, hə-\ *n, pl* **-gies** 1 : structural likeness between corresponding parts of different plants or animals due to evolution from a common ancestor 2 : structural likeness between different parts of the same individual — **ho·mol·o·gous** \-'mäl-ə-gəs\ *adj*

hom·onym \'häm-ə-,nim, 'hō-mə-\ *n* : HOMOPHONE, HOMOGRAPH 2 : one of two or more words spelled and pronounced alike but different in meaning (*pool* of water and *pool* the game are ~s)

ho·mo·phone \'häm-ə-,fōn, 'hō-mə-\ *n* : one of two or more words (as *to, too, two*) pronounced alike but different in meaning or derivation or spelling

Ho·mo sa·pi·ens \,hō-mō-'sā-pē-ənz, -'sap-ē-\ *n* : the totality of human beings : MANKIND 1

ho·mo·sex·u·al \,hō-mō-'sek-sh(ə-w)əl\ *adj* : of, relating to, or exhibiting sexual desire toward another of the same sex — **homosexual** *n* — **ho·mo·sex·u·al·i·ty** \-,sek-shə-'wal-ət-ē\ *n*

hon *abbr* honor; honorable; honorary

hone \'hōn\ *n* : a fine-grit stone for sharpening a cutting implement — **hone** *vb* — **hon·er** *n*

hon·est \'än-əst\ *adj* 1 : free from deception : TRUTHFUL; *also* : GENUINE, REAL 2 : REPUTABLE 3 : CREDITABLE 4 : marked by integrity 5 : FRANK *syn* upright, just, conscientious, honorable — **hon·est·ly** *adv* — **hon·esty** \-ə-stē\ *n*

hon·ey \'hən-ē\ *n, pl* **honeys** : a sweet sticky substance made by bees (**hon·ey·bees** \-,bēz\) from the nectar of flowers

[1]**hon·ey·comb** \-,kōm\ *n* : a mass of 6-sided wax cells built by honeybees; *also* : something of similar structure or appearance

[2]**honeycomb** *vb* : to make or become full of cavities like a honeycomb

hon·ey·dew \-,d(y)ü\ *n* : a sweetish deposit secreted on plants by aphids, scale insects, or fungi

honeydew melon *n* : a smooth-skinned muskmelon with sweet green flesh

honey locust *n* : a tall usu. spiny No. American leguminous tree with hard durable wood and long twisted pods

hon·ey·moon \'hən-ē-,mün\ *n* 1 : a holiday taken by an newly married couple 2 : a period of harmony esp. just after marriage — **honeymoon** *vb*

hon·ey·suck·le \'hən-ē-,sək-əl\ *n* : any of various shrubs, vines, or herbs with tube-shaped flowers rich in nectar

honk \'häŋk, 'hȯŋk\ *n* : the cry of a goose; *also* : a similar sound (as of a horn) — **honk** *vb* — **honk·er** *n*

hon·ky-tonk \'häŋ-kē-,täŋk, 'hȯŋ-kē-

tonk \ n : a tawdry nightclub or dance hall

¹hon·or \'än-ər\ n 1 : good name : REPUTATION; also : outward respect 2 : PRIVILEGE 3 : a person of superior standing — used esp. as a title 4 : one who brings respect or fame 5 : an evidence or symbol of distinction 6 : CHASTITY, PURITY 7 : INTEGRITY syn homage, reverence, deference, obeisance

²honor vb **hon·ored; hon·or·ing** \-(ə-)riŋ\ 1 : to regard or treat with honor 2 : to confer honor on 3 : to fulfill the terms of; also : to accept as payment — **hon·or·er** \'än-ər-ər\ n

hon·or·able \'än-(ə-)rə-bəl\ adj 1 : deserving of honor 2 : accompanied with marks of honor 3 : of great renown 4 : doing credit to the possessor 5 : characterized by integrity — **hon·or·able·ness** n — **hon·or·ably** \-blē\ adv

hon·o·rar·i·um \,än-ə-'rer-ē-əm\ n, pl **-ia** \-ē-ə\ also **-iums** : a reward usu. for services on which custom or propriety forbids a price to be set

hon·or·ary \'än-ə-,rer-ē\ adj 1 : having or conferring distinction 2 : conferred in recognition of achievement without the usual prerequisites (~ degree) 3 : UNPAID, VOLUNTARY — **hon·or·ar·i·ly** \,än-ə-'rer-ə-lē\ adv

hon·or·if·ic \,än-ə-'rif-ik\ adj : conferring or conveying honor (~ titles)

hon·our \'än-ər\ chiefly Brit var of HONOR

¹hood \'hud\ n 1 : a covering for the head and neck and sometimes the face 2 : an ornamental fold (as at the back of an ecclesiastical vestment) 3 : a cover for parts of mechanisms; esp : the metal covering over an automobile engine — **hood·ed** \-əd\ adj

²hood \'hud, 'hud\ n : HOODLUM

-hood \,hud\ n suffix 1 : state : condition : quality : character ⟨boyhood⟩ ⟨hardihood⟩ 2 : instance of a (specified) state or quality ⟨falsehood⟩ 3 : individuals sharing a (specified) state or character ⟨brotherhood⟩

hood·lum \'hud-ləm, 'hud-\ n 1 : THUG 2 : a young ruffian

hoo·doo \'hud-ü\ n, pl **hoodoos** 1 : VOODOO 2 : something that brings bad luck — **hoodoo** vb

hood·wink \'hud-,wiŋk\ vb : to deceive by false appearance

hoo·ey \'hü-ē\ n : NONSENSE

hoof \'huf, 'huf\ n, pl **hooves** \'huvz, 'huvz\ or **hoofs** : a horny covering that protects the ends of the toes of ungulate mammals (as horses or cattle); also : a hoofed foot — **hoofed** \'huft, 'huft\ adj

¹hook \'huk\ n 1 : a curved or bent device for catching, holding, or pulling 2 : something curved or bent like a hook 3 : a flight of a ball (as in golf) that curves in a direction opposite to the dominant hand of the player propelling it 4 : a short punch delivered with

a circular motion and with the elbow bent and rigid

²hook vb 1 : CURVE, CROOK 2 : to seize or make fast with a hook 3 : STEAL 4 : to work as a prostitute

hoo·kah \'huk-ə, 'hü-kə\ n [Ar huqqah bottle of a water pipe] : a pipe for smoking that has a long flexible tube whereby the smoke is cooled by passing through water

hook·er \'huk-ər\ n 1 : one that hooks 2 : PROSTITUTE

hook·up \'huk-,əp\ n : an assemblage (as of apparatus or circuits) used for a specific purpose (as in radio)

hook·worm \'huk-,wərm\ n : a parasitic intestinal nematode worm having hooks or plates around the mouth

hoo·li·gan \'hü-li-gən\ n : RUFFIAN, HOODLUM

hoop \'hup, 'hup\ n 1 : a circular strip used esp. for holding together the staves of a barrel 2 : a circular figure or object : RING 3 : a circle or flexible material for expanding a woman's skirt

hoop·la \'hup-,lä, 'hup-,lä\ n [F houp-lä, interj.] 1 : TO-DO; also : BALLYHOO 2 : bewildering language

hoose·gow \'hüs-,gau\ n [Sp juzgado panel of judges, courtroom] slang : JAIL

hoot \'hut\ vb 1 : to shout or laugh usu. in contempt 2 : to make the natural throat noise of an owl — **hoot** n — **hoot·er** n

¹hop \'häp\ vb **hopped; hop·ping** 1 : to move by quick springy leaps 2 : to make a quick trip 3 : to ride on esp. surreptitiously and without authorization

²hop n 1 : a short brisk leap esp. on one leg 2 : DANCE 3 : a short trip by air

³hop n : a vine belonging to the mulberry whose ripe dried pistillate catkins are used in medicine and in flavoring malt liquors; also : its pistillate catkin

⁴hop vb **hopped; hop·ping** : to increase the power of (~ up an engine)

¹hope \'hop\ vb **hoped; hop·ing** : to desire with expectation of fulfillment

²hope n 1 : TRUST, RELIANCE 2 : desire accompanied by expectation of fulfillment; also : something hoped for 3 : one that gives promise for the future — **hope·ful** \-fəl\ adj — **hope·ful·ly** \-ē\ adv — **hope·ful·ness** n — **hope·less** adj — **hope·less·ly** adv — **hope·less·ness** n

HOPE abbr Health Opportunity for People Everywhere

Ho·pi \'hō-pē\ n, pl **Hopi** also **Hopis** [Hopi Hópi, lit., good, peaceful] : a member of an American Indian people of Arizona; also : the language of the Hopi people

hop·per \'häp-ər\ n 1 : a usu. immature hopping insect 2 : a usu. funnel-shaped container for delivering material (as grain) 3 : a freight car with hinged doors in a sloping bottom 4 : a box into which a bill to be considered by a legislative body is dropped **5** : a tank holding a liquid and having a device for releasing its contents through a pipe

hop·scotch \'häp-ˌskäch\ *n* : a child's game in which a player tosses an object (as a stone) consecutively into areas of a figure outlined on the ground and hops through the figure and back to regain the object

hor *abbr* horizontal

horde \'hȯrd\ *n* : THRONG, SWARM

hore·hound \'hȯr-ˌhau̇nd\ *n* [ME *horhoune*, fr. OE *hārhūne*, fr. *hār* hoary + *hūne* horehound] : an aromatic bitter mint with downy leaves used esp. in candy or as an extract in cold and cough remedies

ho·ri·zon \hə-'rīz-ᵊn\ *n* [Gk *horizont-, horizōn*, fr. prp. of *horizein* to bound, fr. *horos* limit, boundary] **1** : the line marking the apparent junction of earth and sky **2** : range of outlook or experience

hor·i·zon·tal \ˌhȯr-ə-'zänt-ᵊl\ *adj* : parallel to the horizon : LEVEL — **horizontal** *n* — **hor·i·zon·tal·ly** \-ē\ *adv*

hor·mon·al \hȯr-'mōn-ᵊl\ *adj* : of, relating to, or resembling a hormone

hor·mone \'hȯr-ˌmōn\ *n* [Gk *hormōn*, prp. of *horman* to stir up, fr. *hormē* impulse, assault] : a product of living cells that circulates in body fluids and has a specific effect on some other cells; *esp* : the secretion of an endocrine gland

horn \'hȯrn\ *n* **1** : one of the hard projections of bone or keratin on the head of many hoofed animals **2** : something resembling or suggesting a horn **3** : a brass wind instrument **4** : a usu. electrical device that makes a noise (automobile ∼) — **horned** \'hȯrnd\ *adj* — **horn·less** *adj* — **horny** *adj*

horn·book \'hȯrn-ˌbuk\ *n* **1** : a child's primer consisting of a sheet of parchment or paper protected by a sheet of transparent horn **2** : a rudimentary treatise

horned toad *n* : any of several small harmless insect-eating lizards with spines on the head resembling horns and spiny scales on the body

hor·net \'hȯr-nət\ *n* : any of the larger social wasps

horn in *vb* : to participate without invitation : INTRUDE

horn·pipe \'hȯrn-ˌpīp\ *n* : a lively folk dance of the British Isles

ho·rol·o·gy \hə-'räl-ə-jē\ *n* : the science of measuring time or constructing time-indicating instruments — **ho·ro·log·ic** \ˌhȯr-ə-'läj-ik\ *adj* — **ho·rol·o·gist** \hə-'räl-ə-jəst\ *n*

horo·scope \'hȯr-ə-ˌskōp\ *n* [MF, fr. L *horoscopus*, fr. Gk *hōroskopos*, fr. *hōra* hour + *skopein* to look at] **1** : a diagram of the relative positions of planets and signs of the zodiac at a particular time for use by astrologers

to foretell events of a person's life **2** : an astrological forecast

hor·ren·dous \hȯ-'ren-dəs\ *adj* : DREADFUL, HORRIBLE

hor·ri·ble \'hȯr-ə-bəl\ *adj* **1** : marked by or conducive to horror **2** : highly disagreeable — **hor·ri·ble·ness** *n* — **hor·ri·bly** \-blē\ *adv*

hor·rid \'hȯr-əd\ *adj* **1** : HIDEOUS **2** : REPULSIVE — **hor·rid·ly** *adv*

hor·ri·fy \'hȯr-ə-ˌfī\ *vb* **-fied; -fy·ing** : to cause to feel horror **syn** appall, daunt, dismay

hor·ror \'hȯr-ər\ *n* **1** : painful and intense fear, dread, or dismay **2** : intense repugnance **3** : something that horrifies

hors de com·bat \ˌȯrd-ə-kōⁿ-'bä\ *adv or adj* : in a disabled condition

hors d'oeuvre \ȯr-'dərv\ *n, pl* **hors d'oeuvres** *also* **hors d'oeuvre** \-'dərv(z)\ [F *hors-d'oeuvre*, lit., outside of work] : any of various savory foods usu. served as appetizers

horse \'hȯrs\ *n, pl* **hors·es** *also* **horse 1** : a large solid-hoofed herbivorous mammal domesticated as a draft and saddle animal **2** : a supporting framework usu. with legs — **horse·less** *adj*

¹horse·back \'hȯrs-ˌbak\ *adv* : on horseback

²horseback *n* : the back of a horse

horse chestnut *n* : a large Asian tree with palmate leaves, erect conical clusters of showy flowers, and large glossy brown seeds enclosed in a prickly bur

horse·flesh \'hȯrs-ˌflesh\ *n* : horses for riding, driving, or racing

horse·fly \-ˌflī\ *n* : any of a group of large two-winged flies with bloodsucking females

horse·hair \-ˌhaər\ *n* **1** : the hair of a horse esp. from the mane or tail **2** : cloth made from horsehair

horse·hide \-ˌhīd\ *n* **1** : the dressed or raw hide of a horse **2** : the ball used in baseball

horse latitudes *n pl* : either of two calm regions near 30°N and 30°S latitude

horse·laugh \'hȯrs-ˌlaf, -ˌläf\ *n* : a loud boisterous laugh

horse·man \-mən\ *n* **1** : one who rides horseback; *also* : one skilled in managing horses **2** : a breeder or raiser of horses — **horse·man·ship** *n*

horse·play \-ˌplā\ *n* : rough boisterous play

horse·play·er \-ər\ *n* : a bettor on horse races

horse·pow·er \'hȯrs-ˌpau̇(-ə)r\ *n* : a unit of power equal in the U.S. to 746 watts

horse·rad·ish \-ˌrad-ish\ *n* : a tall white-flowered herb related to the mustards whose pungent root is used as a condiment

horse·shoe \'hȯrs(h)-ˌshü\ *n* **1** : a protective metal plate fitted to the rim of a horse's hoof **2** *pl* : a game in which horseshoes are pitched at a fixed object — **horse-sho-er** \-,shü-ər\ n

horseshoe crab n : any of several marine arthropods with a broad crescent-shaped combined head and thorax

horse-tail \'hórs-,tāl\ n : any of a genus of perennial flowerless plants related to the ferns

horse-whip \-,hwip\ vb : to flog with a whip made to be used on a horse

horse-wom-an \-,wùm-ən\ n : a woman skilled in riding horseback or in caring for or managing horses; also : a woman who breeds or raises horses

hors-ey or **horsy** \'hór-sē\ adj **hors-i-er**; **-est** 1 : of, relating to, or suggesting a horse 2 : having to do with horses or horse racing

hort abbr horticultural; horticulture

hor-ta-tive \'hórt-ət-iv\ adj : giving exhortation

hor-ta-to-ry \'hórt-ə-,tōr-ē\ adj : HORTATIVE

hor-ti-cul-ture \'hórt-ə-,kəl-chər\ n : the science and art of growing fruits, vegetables, flowers, and ornamental plants — **hor-ti-cul-tur-al** \,hórt-ə-'kəlch-(ə)-rəl\ adj — **hor-ti-cul-tur-ist** \-rəst\ n

Hos abbr Hosea

ho-san-na \hō-'zan-ə, -'zän-\ interj [Gk hōsanna, fr. Heb hōshī'āh-nnā pray, save (us)!] — used as a cry of acclamation and adoration

¹hose \'hōz\ n, pl **hose** or **hos-es** pl **hose** : STOCKING, SOCK; also : a close-fitting garment covering the legs and waist 2 : a flexible tube for conveying fluids (as from a faucet)

²hose vb **hosed**; **hos-ing** : to spray, water, or wash with a hose

Ho-sea \hō-'zā-ə, -'zē-\ n — see BIBLE table

ho-siery \'hōzh-(ə)-rē, 'hōz(-ə)-\ n : STOCKINGS, SOCKS

hosp abbr hospital

hos-pice \'häs-pəs\ n 1 : a lodging for travelers or for young persons or the underprivileged 2 : a facility or program supplying a caring environment for those with fatal illnesses

hos-pi-ta-ble \hä-'spit-ə-bəl, 'häs-(,)pit-\ adj 1 : given to generous and cordial reception of guests 2 : readily receptive — **hos-pi-ta-bly** \-blē\ adv

hos-pi-tal \'häs-,pit-ºl\ n [ME, fr. OF, fr. ML hospitale, fr. LL, hospice, fr. L, guest room, fr. hospit-, hospes guest, host, fr. hostis stranger, enemy] : an institution where the sick or injured receive medical or surgical care

hos-pi-tal-i-ty \,häs-pə-'tal-ət-ē\ n, pl **-ties** : hospitable treatment, reception, or disposition

hos-pi-tal-ize \'häs-,pit-ºl-,īz\ vb **-ized**; **-iz-ing** : to place in a hospital for care and treatment — **hos-pi-tal-iza-tion** \,häs-,pit-ºl-ə-'zā-shən\ n

¹host \'hōst\ n [ME, fr. OF, fr. LL hos-

tis, fr. L, stranger, enemy] 1 : ARMY 2 : MULTITUDE

²host n [ME hoste host, guest, fr. OF, fr. L hospit-, hospes] 1 : one who receives or entertains guests 2 : an animal or plant on or in which a parasite lives — **host** vb

³host n, often cap [deriv. of L hostia sacrifice] : the eucharistic bread

hos-tage \'häs-tij\ n : a person kept as a pledge pending the fulfillment of an agreement

hos-tel \'häs-tºl\ n [ME, fr. OF, fr. LL hospitale hospice] 1 : INN 2 : a supervised lodging for youth — **hos-tel-er** n

hos-tel-ry \-rē\ n, pl **-ries** : INN, HOTEL

host-ess \'hō-stəs\ n : a woman who acts as host

hos-tile \'häs-tºl, -,tīl\ adj : marked by usu. overt antagonism : UNFRIENDLY — **hostile** n — **hos-tile-ly** \-lē\ adv

hos-til-i-ty \hä-'stil-ət-ē\ n, pl **-ties** 1 : an unfriendly state or action 2 pl : overt acts of war

hos-tler \'(h)äs-lər\ n : one who takes care of horses or mules

hot \'hät\ adj **hot-ter**; **hot-test** 1 : marked by a high temperature or an uncomfortable degree of body heat 2 : giving a sensation of heat or of burning 3 : ARDENT, FIERY 4 : LUSTFUL 5 : EAGER 6 : newly made or received 7 : PUNGENT 8 : unusually lucky or favorable (∼ dice) 9 : recently and illegally obtained (∼ jewels) — **hot** adv — **hot-ly** adv — **hot-ness** n

hot-bed \-,bed\ n 1 : a glass-covered bed of soil heated (as by fermenting manure) and used esp. for raising seedlings 2 : an environment that favors rapid growth or development

hot-blood-ed \-'bləd-əd\ adj : easily roused or excited

hot-box \-,bäks\ n : a journal bearing (as of a railroad car) overheated by friction

hot-cake \-,kāk\ n : PANCAKE

hot dog \'hät-,dóg\ n : a cooked frankfurter usu. served in a long split roll

ho-tel \hō-'tel\ n [F hôtel, fr. OF hostel, fr. LL hospitale hospice] : a building where lodging and usu. meals, entertainment, and various personal services are provided for the public

hot flash n : a sudden brief flushing and sensation of heat caused by dilation of skin capillaries usu. associated with menopausal endocrine imbalance

hot-head-ed \'hät-'hed-əd\ adj : FIERY, IMPETUOUS — **hot-head** \-,hed\ n — **hot-head-ed-ly** adv — **hot-head-ed-ness** n

hot-house \-,haùs\ n : a heated glass-enclosed house for raising plants

hot line n : a telephone line for emergency use (as between governments or to a counseling service)

hot plate n : a simple portable appliance for heating or for cooking

hot potato n : an embarrassing or controversial issue

hot rod *n* : an automobile modified for high speed and fast acceleration — **hot-rod-der** \ˈhät-ˌräd-ər\ *n*

hots \ˈhäts\ *n pl* : strong sexual desire — usu. used with *the*

hot seat *n* : a position of anxiety or embarrassment

hot-shot \ˈhät-ˌshät\ *n* : a showily skillful person

hot tub *n* : a large wooden tub of hot water for soaking and socializing

hot-wire \ˈhät-ˌwī(ə)r\ *vb* : to start (an automobile) by short-circuiting the ignition system

¹**hound** \ˈhaünd\ *n* **1** : : a long-eared hunting dog that follows its prey by scent **2** : FAN, ADDICT

²**hound** *vb* : to pursue relentlessly

hour \ˈaü(ə)r\ *n* **1** : the 24th part of a day **2** : the time of day **3** : a particular or customary time **4** : a class session — **hour-ly** *adv or adj*

hour-glass \ˈaü(ə)r-ˌglas\ *n* : a glass vessel for measuring time in which sand, water, or mercury runs from an upper compartment to a lower compartment in an hour

hou-ri \ˈhür-ē\ *n* [F, fr. Per *hūri*, fr. Ar *hūrīyah*] : one of the beautiful maidens of the Muslim paradise

¹**house** \ˈhaüs\ *n, pl* **hous-es** \ˈhaü-zəz\ **1** : a building for human habitation **2** : a shelter for an animal **3** : a building in which something is stored **4** : HOUSEHOLD; *also* : FAMILY **5** : a residence for a religious community or for students; *also* : those in residence **6** : a legislative body **7** : a place of business or entertainment **8** : a business organization **9** : the audience in a theater or concert hall — **house-ful** *n*

²**house** \ˈhaüz\ *vb* **housed; hous-ing 1** : to provide with or take shelter : LODGE **2** : STORE

house-boat \ˈhaüs-ˌbōt\ *n* : a roomy pleasure boat fitted for use as a dwelling or for leisurely cruising

house-boy \-ˌbȯi\ *n* : a boy or man hired to act as a household servant

house-break \-ˌbrāk\ *vb* **-broke; -broken; -break-ing** : to train in excretory habits acceptable in indoor living

house-break-ing \-ˌbrā-kiŋ\ *n* : the act of breaking into a dwelling with the intent of committing a felony

house-clean \-ˌklēn\ *vb* : to clean a house and its furniture — **house-clean-ing** *n*

house-coat \ˈhaüs-ˌkōt\ *n* : a woman's often long-skirted informal garment for wear around the house

house-fly \-ˌflī\ *n* : a two-winged fly that is common about human habitations and acts as a vector of diseases (as typhoid fever)

¹**house-hold** \ˈhaüs-ˌhōld\ *n* : those who dwell as a family under the same roof — **house-hold-er** *n*

²**household** *adj* **1** : DOMESTIC **2** : FAMILIAR, COMMON (a ~ name)

house-keep-er \-ˌkē-pər\ *n* : a woman employed to take care of a house — **house-keep-ing** \-piŋ\ *n*

house-lights \-ˌlīts\ *n pl* : the lights that illuminate the parts of a theater occupied by the audience

house-maid \-ˌmād\ *n* : a female servant employed to do housework

house-moth-er \-ˌməth-ər\ *n* : a woman acting as hostess, chaperon, and often housekeeper in a residence for young people

house-plant \ˈhaüs-ˌplant\ *n* : a plant grown or kept indoors

house sparrow *n* : a sparrow native to Europe and parts of Asia that has been widely introduced elsewhere

house-top \ˈhaüs-ˌtäp\ *n* : ROOF

house-wares \-ˌwaərz\ *n pl* : small articles of household equipment

house-warm-ing \-ˌwȯr-miŋ\ *n* : a party to celebrate the taking possession of a house or premises

house-wife \ˈhaüs-ˌwīf\ *n* : a married woman in charge of a household — **house-wife-ly** \-lē\ *adj* — **house-wif-ery** \-ˌwīf-(ə)-rē\ *n*

house-work \ˈhaüs-ˌwərk\ *n* : the work of housekeeping

¹**hous-ing** \ˈhaü-ziŋ\ *n* **1** : SHELTER; *also* : dwellings provided for people **2** : something that covers or protects

²**housing** *n* **1** : CAPARISON **1 2** *pl* : decorative trappings and harness

hove *past and past part of* HEAVE

hov-el \ˈhəv-əl, ˈhäv-\ *n* : a small, wretched, and often dirty house : HUT

hov-er \ˈhəv-ər, ˈhäv-\ *vb* **hov-ered; hov-er-ing** \-(ə-)riŋ\ **1** : FLUTTER; *also* : to move to and fro **2** : to be in an uncertain state

¹**how** \(ˈ)haü\ *adv* **1** : in what way or manner (~ was it done) **2** : with what meaning (~ do we interpret such behavior) **3** : for what reason (~ could you have done such a thing) **4** : to what extent or degree (~ deep is it) **5** : in what state or condition (~ are you) — **how about** : what do you say to or think of (how about coming with me) — **how come** : why is it that

²**how** *conj* **1** : in what manner or condition (remember ~ they fought) **2** : HOWEVER (do it ~ you like)

¹**how-be-it** \haü-ˈbē-ət\ *adv* : NEVERTHELESS

²**howbeit** *conj* : ALTHOUGH

how-dah \ˈhaüd-ə\ *n* [Hindi *hauda*] : a seat or covered pavilion on the back of an elephant or camel

¹**how-ev-er** \haü-ˈev-ər\ *conj* : in whatever manner

²**however** *adv* **1** : to whatever degree; *also* : in whatever manner **2** : in spite of that

how-it-zer \ˈhaü-ət-sər\ *n* : a short cannon that shoots shells at a high angle of fire

howl \ˈhaül\ *vb* **1** : to emit a loud long doleful sound characteristic of dogs **2** : to cry loudly — **howl** *n*

howl-er \ˈhaü-lər\ *n* **1** : one that howls **2**

: a humorous and ridiculous blunder

howl·ing \ˈhau̇-liŋ\ *adj* **1** : DESOLATE, WILD **2** : very great (a ~ success)

how·so·ev·er \ˌhau̇-sə-ˈwev-ər\ *adv* : HOWEVER 1

hoy·den \ˈhȯid-ᵊn\ *n* : a girl or woman of saucy, boisterous, or carefree behavior

HP *abbr* **1** high pressure **2** horsepower

HPF *abbr* highest possible frequency

HQ *abbr* headquarters

hr *abbr* **1** here **2** hour

HR *abbr* House of Representatives

HRH *abbr* Her Royal Highness; His Royal Highness

hrzn *abbr* horizon

HS *abbr* high school

HST *abbr* Hawaiian standard time

ht *abbr* height

HT *abbr* high-tension

hua·ra·che \wə-ˈräch-ē\ *n* [MexSp] : a sandal with an upper made of interwoven leather thongs

hub \ˈhəb\ *n* **1** : the central part of a wheel, propeller, or fan **2** : a center of activity

hub·bub \ˈhəb-əb\ *n* : UPROAR; *also* : TURMOIL

hub·cap \ˈhəb-ˌkap\ *n* : a removable metal cap over the end of an axle

hu·bris \ˈhyü-brəs\ *n* : exaggerated pride or self-confidence

huck·le·ber·ry \ˈhək-əl-ˌber-ē\ *n* **1** : an American shrub related to the blueberry; *also* : its edible dark blue berry **2** : BLUEBERRY

huck·ster \ˈhək-stər\ *n* : PEDDLER, HAWKER

HUD *abbr* Department of Housing and Urban Development

¹hud·dle \ˈhəd-ᵊl\ *vb* **hud·dled; hud·dling** \ˈhəd-(ə-)liŋ\ **1** : to crowd together **2** : CONFER

²huddle *n* **1** : a closely packed group **2** : MEETING, CONFERENCE

hue \ˈhyü\ *n* **1** : a color as distinct from white, gray, and black; *also* : gradation of color **2** : the attribute of colors that permits them to be classed as red, yellow, green, blue, or an intermediate color — **hued** \ˈhyüd\ *adj*

hue and cry *n* : a clamor of pursuit or protest

huff \ˈhəf\ *n* : a fit of anger or pique — **huffy** *adj*

hug \ˈhəg\ *vb* **hugged; hug·ging 1** : EMBRACE **2** : to stay close to (the road ~s the river) — **hug** *n*

huge \ˈhyüj\ *adj* **hug·er; hug·est** : very large or extensive — **huge·ly** *adv* — **huge·ness** *n*

hug·ger-mug·ger \ˈhəg-ər-ˌməg-ər\ *n* **1** : SECRECY **2** : CONFUSION, MUDDLE

Hu·gue·not \ˈhyü-gə-ˌnät\ *n* : a French Protestant in the 16th and 17th centuries

hu·la \ˈhü-lə\ *n* : a sinuous Polynesian dance usu. accompanied by chants

hulk \ˈhəlk\ *n* **1** : a heavy clumsy ship **2** : an old ship unfit for service **3** : a bulky or unwieldy person or thing

hulk·ing \ˈhəl-kiŋ\ *adj* : BURLY, MASSIVE

¹hull \ˈhəl\ *n* **1** : the outer covering of a fruit or seed **2** : the frame or body esp. of a ship

²hull *vb* : to remove the hulls of — **hull·er** *n*

hul·la·ba·loo \ˈhəl-ə-bə-ˌlü\ *n, pl* **-loos** : a confused noise : UPROAR

hum \ˈhəm\ *vb* **hummed; hum·ming 1** : to utter a sound like that of the speech sound \m\ prolonged **2** : DRONE **3** : to be busily active **4** : to sing with closed lips — **hum** *n* — **hum·mer** *n*

hu·man \ˈ(h)yü-mən\ *adj* **1** : of, relating to, being, or characteristic of man **2** : having human form or attributes — **human** *n* — **hu·man·ly** *adv* — **hu·man·ness** \-mən-nəs\ *n*

hu·mane \(h)yü-ˈmān\ *adj* **1** : marked by compassion, sympathy, or consideration for others **2** : HUMANISTIC — **hu·mane·ly** *adv* — **hu·mane·ness** \-ˈmān-nəs\ *n*

human immunodeficiency virus *n* : AIDS VIRUS

hu·man·ism \ˈ(h)yü-mə-ˌniz-əm\ *n* **1** : devotion to the humanities; *also* : the revival of classical letters characteristic of the Renaissance **2** : a doctrine or way of life centered on human interests or values — **hu·man·ist** \-nəst\ *n or adj* — **hu·man·is·tic** \ˌ(h)yü-mə-ˈnis-tik\ *adj*

hu·man·i·tar·i·an \(h)yü-ˌman-ə-ˈter-ē-ən\ *n* : one who practices philanthropy — **humanitarian** *adj* — **hu·man·i·tar·i·an·ism** *n*

hu·man·i·ty \(h)yü-ˈman-ət-ē\ *n, pl* **-ties 1** : the quality or state of being human or humane **2** *pl* : the branches of learning dealing with human concerns (as philosophy) as opposed to natural processes (as physics) **3** : MANKIND 1

hu·man·ize \ˈ(h)yü-mə-ˌnīz\ *vb* **-ized; -iz·ing** : to make human or humane — **hu·man·iza·tion** \ˌ(h)yü-mə-nə-ˈzā-shən\ *n*

hu·man·kind \ˈ(h)yü-mən-ˌkīnd\ *n* : MANKIND 1

hu·man·oid \ˈ(h)yü-mə-ˌnȯid\ *adj* : having human form or characteristics — **humanoid** *n*

¹hum·ble \ˈhəm-bəl\ *adj* **hum·bler** \-b(ə-)lər\; **hum·blest** \-b(ə-)ləst\ [ME, fr. OF, fr. L *humilis* low, humble, fr. *humus* earth] **1** : not proud or haughty **2** : not pretentious : UNASSUMING **3** : INSIGNIFICANT **syn** meek, modest, lowly, unassuming — **hum·ble·ness** *n* — **hum·bly** \-blē\ *adv*

²humble *vb* **hum·bled; hum·bling** \-b(ə-)liŋ\ **1** : to make humble **2** : to destroy the power or prestige of — **hum·bler** \-b(ə-)lər\ *n*

¹hum·bug \ˈhəm-ˌbəg\ *n* **1** : HOAX, FRAUD **2** : NONSENSE

²humbug *vb* **hum·bugged; hum·bug·ging** : DECEIVE

hum·ding·er \ˈhəm-ˈdiŋ-ər\ *n* : a person or thing of striking excellence

hum·drum \'həm-ˌdrəm\ *adj* : MONOTO-NOUS, DULL

hu·mer·us \'hyüm-(ə-)rəs\ *n, pl* **hu·meri** \'hyü-mə-ˌrī, -ˌrē\ : the long bone extending from elbow to shoulder

hu·mid \'(h)yü-məd\ *adj* : containing or characterized by perceptible moisture : DAMP — **hu·mid·ly** *adv*

hu·mid·i·fy \(h)yü-'mid-ə-ˌfī\ *vb* -**fied**; -**fy·ing** : to make humid — **hu·mid·i·fi·ca·tion** \-ˌmid-ə-fə-'kā-shən\ *n* — **hu·mid·i·fi·er** \-'mid-ə-ˌfī(-ə)r\ *n*

hu·mid·i·ty \(h)yü-'mid-ət-ē\ *n, pl* -**ties** : the amount of atmospheric moisture

hu·mi·dor \'(h)yü-mə-ˌdȯr\ *n* : a case usu. for storing cigars in which the air is kept properly humidified

hu·mil·i·ate \(h)yü-'mil-ē-ˌāt\ *vb* -**at·ed**; -**at·ing** : to injure the self-respect of : MORTIFY — **hu·mil·i·at·ing·ly** \-ˌāt-iŋ-lē\ *adv* — **hu·mil·i·a·tion** \-ˌmil-ē-'ā-shən\ *n*

hu·mil·i·ty \(h)yü-'mil-ət-ē\ *n* : the quality or state of being humble

hum·ming·bird \'həm-iŋ-ˌbərd\ *n* : a tiny American bird related to the swifts

hum·mock \'həm-ək\ *n* : a rounded mound : KNOLL

hu·mon·gous \hyü-'məŋ-gəs, -'mäŋ-\ *adj* [prob. alter. of *huge* + *monstrous*] *slang* : extremely large

¹**hu·mor** \'(h)yü-mər\ *n* 1 : TEMPERA-MENT 2 : MOOD 3 : WHIM 4 : a quality that appeals to a sense of the ludicrous or incongruous; *also* : a keen perception of the ludicrous or incongruous 5 : comical or amusing entertainment — **hu·mor·ist** \'(h)yüm-(ə-)rəst\ *n* — **hu·mor·less** \'(h)yü-mər-ləs\ *adj* — **hu·mor·less·ly** *adv* — **hu·mor·less·ness** *n* — **hu·mor·ous** \'(h)yüm-(ə-)rəs\ *adj* — **hu·mor·ous·ly** *adv* — **hu·mor·ous·ness** *n*

²**humor** *vb* **hu·mored**; **hu·mor·ing** \'(h)yüm-(ə-)riŋ\ : to comply with the wishes or mood of

hu·mour *chiefly Brit var of* HUMOR

hump \'həmp\ *n* 1 : a rounded protuberance (as on the back of a camel) 2 : a difficult phase (over the ~)

hump·back \-ˌbak\; *1 also* -'bak\ *n* 1 : HUNCHBACK 2 : HUMPBACK WHALE — **hump·backed** *adj*

humpback whale *n* : a large whalebone whale having very long flippers

hu·mus \'(h)yü-məs\ *n* : the dark organic part of soil formed from decaying matter

Hun \'hən\ *n* : a member of an Asian people that invaded Europe in the 5th century A.D.

¹**hunch** \'hənch\ *vb* 1 : to thrust oneself forward 2 : to assume or cause to assume a bent or crooked posture

²**hunch** *n* 1 : PUSH 2 : a strong intuitive feeling as to how something will turn out

hunch·back \'hənch-ˌbak\ *n* : a back with a hump; *also* : a person with a crooked back — **hunch·backed** *adj*

hun·dred \'hən-drəd\ *n, pl* **hundreds** *or* **hundred** : 10 times 10 — **hundred** *adj* — **hun·dredth** \-drədth\ *adj or n*

hun·dred·weight \-ˌwāt\ *n, pl* **hun·dredweight** *or* **hundredweights** — see WEIGHT table

hung *past and past part of* HANG

Hung *abbr* Hungarian; Hungary

Hun·gar·i·an \ˌhəŋ-'ger-ē-ən\ *n* 1 : a native or inhabitant of Hungary 2 : the language of Hungary — **Hungarian** *adj*

hun·ger \'həŋ-gər\ *n* 1 : a craving or urgent need for food 2 : a strong desire — **hunger** *vb* — **hun·gri·ly** \-grə-lē\ *adv* — **hun·gry** *adj*

hung over *adj* : having a hangover

hung up *adj* 1 : DELAYED 2 : ENTHUSIAS-TIC; *also* : PREOCCUPIED

hunk \'həŋk\ *n* 1 : a large piece 2 : an attractive well-built man

hun·ker \'həŋ-kər\ *vb* **hun·kered**; **hun·ker·ing** \-k(ə-)riŋ\ : CROUCH, SQUAT — usu. used with *down*

hun·kers \'həŋ-kərz\ *n pl* : HAUNCHES

hun·ky-do·ry \ˌhəŋ-kē-'dȯr-ē\ *adj* : quite satisfactory : FINE

¹**hunt** \'hənt\ *vb* 1 : to pursue for food or in sport; *also* : to take part in a hunt 2 : to try to find : SEEK 3 : to drive or chase esp. by harrying 4 : to traverse in search of prey — **hunt·er** *n*

²**hunt** *n* : an act, practice, or instance of hunting

hunt·ress \'hən-trəs\ *n* : a woman who hunts

hunts·man \'hənts-mən\ *n* 1 : HUNTER 2 : one who manages a hunt and looks after the hounds

hur·dle \'hərd-ᵊl\ *n* 1 : an artificial barrier to leap over in a race 2 : OBSTACLE — **hurdle** *vb* — **hur·dler** \'hərd-(ᵊ-)lər\ *n*

hur·dy-gur·dy \ˌhərd-ē-'gərd-ē, 'hərd-ē-ˌgərd-ē\ *n, pl* -**gur·dies** : a musical instrument in which the sound is produced by turning a crank

hurl \'hərl\ *vb* 1 : to move or cause to move vigorously 2 : to throw down with violence 3 : FLING; *also* : PITCH — **hurl** *n* — **hurl·er** *n*

hur·ly-bur·ly \ˌhər-lē-'bər-lē\ *n* : UP-ROAR, TUMULT

Hu·ron \'hyu̇r-ən, 'hyu̇r-ˌän\ *n, pl* **Hurons** *or* **Huron** : a member of an American Indian people orig. of the St. Lawrence valley

hur·rah \hu̇-'rȯ, -'rä\ *also* **hur·ray** \-'rä\ *interj* — used to express joy, approval, or encouragement

hur·ri·cane \'hər-ə-ˌkān\ *n* [Sp *huracán*, of AmerInd origin] : a tropical cyclone that has winds of 74 miles per hour (117 kilometers per hour) or greater and is usu. accompanied by rain, thunder, and lightning

¹**hur·ry** \'hər-ē\ *vb* **hur·ried**; **hur·ry·ing** 1 : to carry or cause to go with haste 2 : to impel to a greater speed 3 : to move or act with haste — **hur·ried·ly** *adv* — **hur·ried·ness** *n*

²**hurry** *n* : extreme haste or eagerness

¹**hurt** \'hǝrt\ *vb* **hurt; hurt·ing 1** : to feel or cause to feel pain **2** : to do harm to : DAMAGE **3** : OFFEND **4** : HAMPER

²**hurt** *n* **1** : a bodily injury or wound **2** : SUFFERING **3** : HARM, WRONG — **hurt·ful** *adj*

hur·tle \'hǝrt-ᵊl\ *vb* **hur·tled; hur·tling** \'hǝrt-(ᵊ-)liŋ\ **1** : to move with a rushing sound **2** : : HURL, FLING

¹**hus·band** \'hǝz-bǝnd\ *n* [ME *husbonde*, fr. OE *hūsbonda* master of a house, fr. ON *hūsbōndi*, fr. *hūs* house + *bōndi* householder] : a married man

²**husband** *vb* : to manage prudently

hus·band·man \'hǝz-bǝn(d)-mǝn\ *n* : FARMER

hus·band·ry \'hǝz-bǝn-drē\ *n* **1** : the control or judicious use of resources **2** : AGRICULTURE

¹**hush** \'hǝsh\ *vb* **1** : to make or become quiet or calm **2** : SUPPRESS

²**hush** *n* : SILENCE, QUIET

hush-hush \'hǝsh-,hǝsh\ *adj* : SECRET, CONFIDENTIAL

¹**husk** \'hǝsk\ *n* **1** : a usu. thin dry outer covering of a seed or fruit **2** : an outer layer : SHELL

²**husk** *vb* : to strip the husk from — **husk·er** *n*

¹**hus·ky** \'hǝs-kē\ *adj* **husk·i·er; -est** : HOARSE — **hus·ki·ly** \'hǝs-kǝ-lē\ *adv* — **hus·ki·ness** \-kē-nǝs\ *n*

²**husky** *adj* **1** : BURLY, ROBUST **2** : LARGE

³**husky** *n*, *pl* **huskies** : a heavy-coated working dog of the New World arctic

hus·sar \(,)hǝ-'zär\ *n* [Hung *huszár* hussar, (obs.) highway robber, fr. Serb *husar* pirate, fr. ML *cursarius*, fr. *cursus* course] : a member of any of various European cavalry units

hus·sy \'hǝz-ē, 'hǝs-\ *n*, *pl* **hussies** [alter. of *housewife*] **1** : a lewd or brazen woman **2** : a pert or mischievous girl

hus·tings \'hǝs-tiŋz\ *n pl* : a place where political campaign speeches are made; *also* : the proceedings in an election campaign

hus·tle \'hǝs-ǝl\ *vb* **hus·tled; hus·tling** \'hǝs-(ǝ-)liŋ\ **1** : JOSTLE, SHOVE **2** : HASTEN, HURRY **3** : to work energetically — **hustle** *n* — **hus·tler** \'hǝs-lǝr\ *n*

hut \'hǝt\ *n* : a small and often temporary dwelling : SHACK

hutch \'hǝch\ *n* **1** : a chest or compartment for storage **2** : a low cupboard usu. surmounted with open shelves **3** : a pen or coop for an animal **4** : HUT, SHACK

huz·zah *or* **huz·za** \(,)hǝ-'zä\ *n* : a cheer of acclaim — often used interjectionally to express joy or approbation

HV *abbr* **1** high velocity **2** high voltage

hvy *abbr* heavy

HW *abbr* hot water

hwy *abbr* highway

hy·a·cinth \'hī-ǝ-(,)sinth\ *n* : a bulbous herb related to the lilies and widely grown for its spikes of fragrant bell-shaped flowers

hy·ae·na *var of* HYENA

hy·brid \'hī-brǝd\ *n* **1** : an offspring of genetically differing parents (as members of different breeds or species) **2** : one of mixed origin or composition — **hybrid** *adj* — **hy·brid·iza·tion** \,hī-brǝd-ǝ-'zā-shǝn\ *n* — **hy·brid·ize** \'hī-brǝd-,īz\ *vb* — **hy·brid·iz·er** \-,īz-ǝr\ *n*

hy·dra \'hī-drǝ\ *n* : any of numerous small tubular freshwater polyps having at one end a mouth surrounded by tentacles

hy·dran·gea \hī-'drän-jǝ\ *n* : any of a genus of shrubs related to the currants and grown for their large clusters of white or tinted flowers

hy·drant \'hī-drǝnt\ *n* : a pipe with a valve and spout at which water may be drawn from a main pipe

hy·drate \'hī-,drāt\ *n* : a compound formed by union of water with some other substance — **hydrate** *vb*

hy·drau·lic \hī-'drò-lik\ *adj* **1** : operated, moved, or effected by means of water **2** : of or relating to hydraulics **3** : operated by the resistance offered or the pressure transmitted when a quantity of liquid is forced through a small orifice or through a tube **4** : hardening or setting under water

hy·drau·lics \hī-'drò-liks\ *n* : a science that deals with practical applications of liquids in motion

hydro \'hī-drō\ *adj* : HYDROELECTRIC

hy·dro·car·bon \,hī-drǝ-'kär-bǝn\ *n* : an organic compound (as acetylene) containing only carbon and hydrogen

hy·dro·ceph·a·lus \,hī-drō-'sef-ǝ-lǝs\ *n* : abnormal increase in the amount of fluid in the cranial cavity accompanied by expansion of the ventricles, enlargement of the skull, and atrophy of the brain

hy·dro·chlo·ric acid \,hī-drǝ-,klōr-ik-\ *n* : a sharp-smelling corrosive acid used in the laboratory and in industry and present in dilute form in gastric juice

hy·dro·dy·nam·ics \,hī-drō-dī-'nam-iks\ *n* : a science that deals with the motion of fluids and the forces acting on moving bodies immersed in fluids — **hy·dro·dy·nam·ic** *adj*

hy·dro·elec·tric \,hī-drō-i-'lek-trik\ *adj* : of, relating to, or used in the production of electricity by waterpower — **hy·dro·elec·tric·i·ty** \-,lek-'tris-ǝt-ē\ *n*

hy·dro·flu·or·ic acid \,hī-drō-,flu̇-ȯr-ik-\ *n* : a weak poisonous acid used esp. in finishing and etching glass

hy·dro·foil \'hī-drǝ-,fȯil\ *n* : a boat that has fins attached to the bottom by struts for lifting the hull clear of the water to allow faster speeds

hy·dro·gen \'hī-drǝ-jǝn\ *n* [F *hydrogène*, fr. Gk *hydōr* water + *-genēs* born, fr. the fact that water is generated by its combustion] : a gaseous colorless odorless highly flammable chemical element that is the lightest of the elements — **hy·drog·e·nous** \hī-'dräj-ǝ-nǝs\ *adj*

hy·dro·ge·nate \hī-'dräj-ǝ-,nāt, hī-drǝ-jə-\ *vb* **-nat·ed; -nat·ing** : to combine or treat with hydrogen; *esp* : to add hydrogen to the molecule of — **hy·dro·ge·na·tion** \ˌhī-ˌdräj-ə-ˈnā-shən, ˌhī-drə-jə-\ *n*

hydrogen bomb *n* : a bomb whose violent explosive power is due to the sudden release of atomic energy resulting from the union of light nuclei (as of hydrogen atoms)

hydrogen peroxide *n* : an unstable compound of hydrogen and oxygen used as an oxidizing and bleaching agent, an antiseptic, and a propellant

hy·drog·ra·phy \hī-ˈdräg-rə-fē\ *n* : the description and study of bodies of water — **hy·drog·ra·pher** \-fər\ *n* — **hy·dro·graph·ic** \ˌhī-drə-ˈgraf-ik\ *adj*

hy·drol·o·gy \hī-ˈdräl-ə-jē\ *n* : a science dealing with the properties, distribution, and circulation of water — **hy·dro·log·ic** \ˌhī-drə-ˈläj-ik\ *or* **hy·dro·log·i·cal** \-i-kəl\ *adj* — **hy·drol·o·gist** \hī-ˈdräl-ə-jəst\ *n*

hy·dro·ly·sis \hī-ˈdräl-ə-səs\ *n* : a chemical decomposition involving the addition of the elements of water

hy·drom·e·ter \hī-ˈdräm-ət-ər\ *n* : a floating instrument for determining specific gravities of liquids and hence the strength (as of alcoholic liquors)

hy·dro·pho·bia \ˌhī-drə-ˈfō-bē-ə\ *n* [LL, fr. Gk, fr. *hydōr* water + *phobos* fear] : RABIES

hy·dro·phone \ˈhī-drə-ˌfōn\ *n* : an underwater listening device

¹**hy·dro·plane** \ˈhī-drə-ˌplān\ *n* **1** : a speedboat usu. with a stepped bottom so that the hull is raised wholly or partly out of the water **2** : SEAPLANE

²**hydroplane** *vb* : to skid on a wet road due to loss of contact between the tires and road

hy·dro·pon·ics \ˌhī-drə-ˈpän-iks\ *n* : the growing of plants in nutrient solutions — **hy·dro·pon·ic** *adj*

hy·dro·pow·er \ˈhī-drə-ˌpau̇(-ə)r\ *n* : hydroelectric power

hy·dro·sphere \ˈhī-drə-ˌsfiər\ *n* : the water (as vapor or lakes) of the earth

hy·dro·stat·ic \ˌhī-drə-ˈstat-ik\ *adj* : of or relating to fluids at rest or to the pressures they exert or transmit

hy·dro·ther·a·py \ˌhī-drə-ˈther-ə-pē\ *n* : the external application of water in the treatment of disease or disability

hy·dro·ther·mal \ˌhī-drə-ˈthər-məl\ *adj* : of or relating to hot water

hy·drous \ˈhī-drəs\ *adj* : containing water

hy·drox·ide \hī-ˈdräk-ˌsīd\ *n* **1** : a negatively charged ion consisting of one atom of oxygen and one atom of hydrogen **2** : a compound of hydroxide with an element or group

hy·e·na \hī-ˈē-nə\ *n* [L *hyaena*, fr. Gk *hyaina*, fr. *hys* hog] : a large nocturnal carnivorous mammal of Asia and Africa

hy·giene \ˈhī-ˌjēn\ *n* **1** : a science dealing with the establishment and

maintenance of health **2** : conditions or practices conducive to health — **hy·gien·ic** \ˌhī-jē-ˈen-ik, hī-ˈjen-, hī-ˈjēn-\ *adj* — **hy·gien·i·cal·ly** \-i-k(ə-)lē\ *adv* — **hy·gien·ist** \hī-ˈjēn-əst, ˈhī-ˌjēn-, hī-ˈjen-\ *n*

hy·grom·e·ter \hī-ˈgräm-ət-ər\ *n* : any of several instruments for measuring the humidity of the atmosphere

hy·gro·scop·ic \ˌhī-grə-ˈskäp-ik\ *adj* : readily taking up and retaining moisture

hying *pres part of* HIE

hy·men \ˈhī-mən\ *n* : a fold of mucous membrane partly or wholly closing the orifice of the vagina

hy·me·ne·al \ˌhī-mə-ˈnē-əl\ *adj* : NUPTIAL

hymn \ˈhim\ *n* : a song of praise esp. to God — **hymn** *vb* — **hym·nal** \ˈhim-nəl\ *n*

hyp *abbr* hypothesis; hypothetical

hype \ˈhīp\ *n* **1** *slang* : HYPODERMIC **2** *slang* : DECEPTION, PUT-ON

hy·per \ˈhī-pər\ *adj* : EXCITABLE, HIGH-STRUNG

hy·per·acid·i·ty \ˌhī-pə-rə-ˈsid-ət-ē\ *n* : the condition of containing excessive acid esp. in the stomach — **hy·per·ac·id** \-pə-ˈras-əd\ *adj*

hy·per·ac·tive \ˌhī-pə-ˈrak-tiv\ *adj* : excessively or pathologically active — **hy·per·ac·tiv·i·ty** \-ˌrak-ˈtiv-ət-ē\ *n*

hy·per·bar·ic \ˌhī-pər-ˈbar-ik\ *adj* : of, relating to, or utilizing greater than normal pressure esp. of oxygen

hy·per·bo·la \hī-ˈpər-bə-lə\ *n, pl* **-las** *or* **-lae** \-(ˌ)lē\ : a curve formed by the intersection of a double right circular cone with a plane that cuts both halves of the cone — **hy·per·bol·ic** \ˌhī-pər-ˈbäl-ik\ *adj*

hy·per·bo·le \hī-ˈpər-bə-(ˌ)lē\ *n* : extravagant exaggeration used as a figure of speech

hy·per·crit·i·cal \ˌhī-pər-ˈkrit-i-kəl\ *adj* : excessively critical — **hy·per·crit·i·cal·ly** \-k(ə-)lē\ *adv*

hy·per·sen·si·tive \ˌhī-ˈsen-sət-iv\ *adj* **1** : excessively or abnormally sensitive **2** : abnormally susceptible physiologically to a specific agent (as a drug or antigen) — **hy·per·sen·si·tive·ness** *n* — **hy·per·sen·si·tiv·i·ty** \-ˌsen-sə-ˈtiv-ət-ē\ *n*

hy·per·ten·sion \ˈhī-pər-ˌten-chən\ *n* : high blood pressure — **hy·per·ten·sive** \ˌhī-pər-ˈten-siv\ *adj or n*

hy·per·thy·roid·ism \ˌhī-pər-ˈthī-ˌroid-ˌiz-əm\ *n* : excessive functional activity of the thyroid gland; *also* : the resulting bodily condition — **hy·per·thy·roid** \-ˈthī-ˌroid\ *adj*

hy·per·tro·phy \hī-ˈpər-trə-fē\ *n, pl* **-phies** : excessive growth or development of a body part — **hy·per·tro·phic** \ˌhī-pər-ˈtrō-fik\ *adj* — **hypertrophy** *vb*

hy·phen \ˈhī-fən\ *n* : a punctuation mark - used to divide or to compound words or word elements — **hyphen** *vb*

hy·phen·ate \'hī-fə-ˌnāt\ *vb* **-at·ed; -at·ing** : to connect or divide with a hyphen — **hy·phen·ation** \ˌhī-fə-'nā-shən\ *n*

hyp·no·sis \hip-'nō-səs\ *n, pl* **-no·ses** \-ˌsēz\ : an induced state that resembles sleep and in which the subject is responsive to suggestions of the inducer (**hyp·no·tist** \'hip-nə-təst\) — **hyp·no·tism** \'hip-nə-ˌtiz-əm\ *n* — **hyp·no·tiz·able** \'hip-nə-ˌtī-zə-bəl\ *adj* — **hyp·no·tize** \-ˌtīz\ *vb*

¹**hyp·not·ic** \hip-'nät-ik\ *adj* **1** : inducing sleep : SOPORIFIC **2** : of or relating to hypnosis or hypnotism — **hyp·not·i·cal·ly** \-i-k(ə-)lē\ *adv*

²**hypnotic** *n* : a sleep-inducing drug

¹**hy·po** \'hī-pō\ *n, pl* **hypos** [short for *hyposulfite*] : SODIUM THIOSULFATE

²**hypo** *n, pl* **hypos** : HYPODERMIC

hy·po·cen·ter \'hī-pə-ˌsent-ər\ *n* : EPICENTER

hy·po·chon·dria \ˌhī-pə-'kän-drē-ə\ *n* [NL, fr. LL, pl., upper abdomen (formerly regarded as the seat of hypochondria), fr. Gk, lit., the parts under the cartilage (of the breastbone), fr. *hypo-* under + *chondros* cartilage] : depression of mind usu. centered on imaginary physical ailments — **hy·po·chon·dri·ac** \-drē-ˌak\ *adj or n*

hy·poc·ri·sy \hip-'äk-rə-sē\ *n, pl* **-sies** : a feigning to be what one is not or to believe what one does not; *esp* : the false assumption of an appearance of virtue or religion — **hypo·crite** \'hip-ə-ˌkrit\ *n* — **hypo·crit·i·cal** \ˌhip-ə-'krit-i-kəl\ *adj* — **hypo·crit·i·cal·ly** \-k(ə-)lē\ *adv*

¹**hy·po·der·mic** \ˌhī-pə-'dər-mik\ *adj* : adapted for use in or administered by injection beneath the skin (~ injection) (~ syringe)

²**hypodermic** *n* : a small syringe with a hollow needle for injecting material into or through the skin; *also* : an injection made with this

hypodermic needle *n* **1** : NEEDLE 3 **2** : a hypodermic syringe complete with needle

hy·po·gly·ce·mia \ˌhī-pō-glī-'sē-mē-ə\ *n* : abnormal decrease of sugar in the blood — **hy·po·gly·ce·mic** \-mik\ *adj*

hy·pot·e·nuse \hī-'pät-ᵊn-ˌ(y)üs, -ˌ(y)üz\ *n* : the side of a triangle having a right angle that is opposite the right angle

hy·poth·e·sis \hī-'päth-ə-səs\ *n, pl* **-e·ses** \-ˌsēz\ : an assumption made esp. in order to test its logical or empirical consequences — **hy·po·thet·i·cal** \ˌhī-pə-'thet-i-kəl\ *adj* — **hy·po·thet·i·cal·ly** \-k(ə-)lē\ *adv*

hy·poth·e·size \-ˌsīz\ *vb* **-sized; -siz·ing** : to adopt as a hypothesis

hy·po·thy·roid·ism \ˌhī-pō-'thī-ˌròid-ˌiz-əm\ *n* : deficient activity of the thyroid gland; *also* : a resultant lowered metabolic rate and general loss of vigor — **hy·po·thy·roid** *adj*

hys·sop \'his-əp\ *n* : a European mint used in medicine

hys·ter·ec·to·my \ˌhis-tə-'rek-tə-mē\ *n, pl* **-mies** : surgical removal of the uterus

hys·te·ria \his-'ter-ē-ə, -'tir-\ *n* [NL, fr. E *hysteric*, adj., fr. L *hystericus*, fr. Gk *hysterikos*, fr. *hystera* womb; fr. the former notion that hysteric women were suffering from disturbances of the womb] **1** : a nervous disorder marked esp. by defective emotional control **2** : uncontrollable fear or emotion — **hys·ter·i·cal** \-'ter-i-kəl\ *also* **hys·ter·ic** \-ik\ *adj* — **hys·ter·i·cal·ly** \-k(ə-)lē\ *adv*

hys·ter·ics \-'ter-iks\ *n, pl* a fit of uncontrollable laughter or crying

Hz *abbr* hertz

I

¹**i** \'ī\ *n, pl* **i's** or **is** \'īz\ *often cap* : the 9th letter of the English alphabet

²**i** *abbr, often cap* island; isle

¹**I** \(ᵊ)ī, ə\ *pron* : the one speaking or writing

²**I** *abbr* interstate highway

³**I** *symbol* iodine

Ia or **IA** *abbr* Iowa

iamb \'ī-ˌam\ or **iam·bus** \ī-'am-bəs\ *n, pl* **iambs** \'ī-ˌamz\ or **iam·bus·es** : a metrical foot of one unaccented syllable followed by one accented syllable — **iam·bic** \ī-'am-bik\ *adj or n*

-ian — see -AN

-i·at·ric \ē-'a-trik\ *also* **-i·at·ri·cal** \-tri-kəl\ *adj comb form* : of or relating to (such) medical treatment or healing

-i·at·rics \ē-'a-triks\ *n pl comb form* : medical treatment

ib or **ibid** *abbr* ibidem

ibex \'ī-ˌbeks\ *n, pl* **ibex·es** [L]: an Old World wild goat with large curved horns

ibi·dem \'ib-ə-ˌdem, ib-'īd-əm\ *adv* [L] : in the same place

ibis \'ī-bəs\ *n, pl* **ibis** or **ibis·es** [L, fr. Gk, fr. Egypt *hyb*] : any of several wading birds related to the herons but having a downwardly curved bill

-ible — see -ABLE

¹**-ic** \ik\ *adj suffix* **1** : of, relating to, or being : having the form of (panoram*ic*) **2** : related to, derived from, or containing (alcohol*ic*) **3** : in the manner of : like that of : characteristic of **4** : associated or dealing with : utilizing (electron*ic*) **5** : characterized by : exhibiting (nostalg*ic*) : affected with (allerg*ic*) **6** : caused by **7** : tending to produce

²**-ic** *n suffix* : one having the character or nature of : one belonging to or associ-

ated with : one exhibiting or affected by : one that produces

-i·cal \i-kəl\ *adj suffix* : -IC (symmetr*ical*) (geolog*ical*) — **-i·cal·ly** \i-k(ə-)lē\ *adv suffix*

ICBM \ˌī-ˌsē-(ˌ)bē-'em\ *n, pl* **ICBM's** *or* **ICBMs** \-'emz\ : an intercontinental ballistic missile

ICC *abbr* Interstate Commerce Commission

¹**ice** \'īs\ *n* **1** : frozen water **2** : a state of coldness (as from formality or reserve) **3** : a substance resembling ice **4** : a frozen dessert; *esp* : one containing no milk or cream

²**ice** *vb* **iced; ic·ing 1** : FREEZE **2** : CHILL **3** : to cover with or as if with icing

ice age *n* : a time of widespread glaciation

ice bag *n* : a waterproof bag to hold ice for local application of cold to the body

ice·berg \'īs-ˌbərg\ *n* : a large floating mass of ice broken off from a glacier

iceberg lettuce *n* : any of various crisp light green lettuces that when mature have the leaves arranged in a compact head resembling a cabbage

ice·boat \'īs-ˌbōt\ *n* **1** : a boatlike frame on runners propelled on ice usu. by sails **2** : ICEBREAKER 2

ice·bound \-ˌbau̇nd\ *adj* : surrounded or obstructed by ice

ice·box \-ˌbäks\ *n* : REFRIGERATOR

ice·break·er \-ˌbrā-kər\ *n* : a ship equipped to make a channel through ice

ice cap *n* : a glacier forming on relatively level land and flowing outward from its center

ice cream *n* : a frozen food containing sweetened or flavored cream or butterfat

ice hockey *n* : a game in which two teams of ice-skating players try to shoot a puck into the opponent's goal

ice·house \'īs-ˌhau̇s\ *n* : a building in which ice is made or stored

ice·land·er \-ˌlan-dər, -lən-\ *n* : a native or inhabitant of Iceland

¹**Ice·lan·dic** \īs-'lan-dik\ *adj* : of, relating to, or characteristic of Iceland, the Icelanders, or their language

²**Icelandic** *n* : the language of Iceland

ice·man \'īs-ˌman\ *n* : one who sells or delivers ice

ice milk *n* : a sweetened frozen food made of skim milk

ice pick *n* : a hand tool ending in a spike for chipping ice

ice-skate \'īs-ˌskāt\ *vb* : to skate on ice — **ice skater** *n*

ice storm *n* : a storm in which falling rain freezes on contact

ice water *n* : chilled or iced water esp. for drinking

ich·thy·ol·o·gy \ˌik-thē-'äl-ə-jē\ *n* : a branch of zoology dealing with fishes — **ich·thy·ol·o·gist** \-jəst\ *n*

ici·cle \'ī-ˌsik-əl\ *n* : a hanging mass of

ice formed by the freezing of dripping water

ic·ing \'ī-siŋ\ *n* : a sweet usu. creamy mixture used to coat baked goods

ICJ *abbr* International Court of Justice

icky \'ik-ē\ *adj* **ick·i·er; -est** : OFFENSIVE, DISTASTEFUL

icon \'ī-ˌkän\ *n* : IMAGE; *esp* : a religious image painted on a wood panel

icon·o·clasm \ī-'kän-ə-ˌklaz-əm\ *n* : the doctrine, practice, or attitude of an iconoclast

icon·o·clast \-ˌklast\ *n* [ML *iconoclastes*, fr. MGk *eikonoklastēs*, lit., image destroyer, fr. Gk *eikōn* image + *klan* to break] **1** : one who destroys religious images or opposes their veneration **2** : one who attacks cherished beliefs or institutions

-ics \iks\ *n sing or pl suffix* **1** : study : knowledge : skill : practice (lingu*istics*) (electron*ics*) **2** : characteristic actions or activities (acrobat*ics*) **3** : characteristic qualities, operations, or phenomena (mechan*ics*)

ic·tus \'ik-təs\ *n* : the recurring stress or beat in a rhythmic or metrical series of sounds

ICU *abbr* intensive care unit

icy \'ī-sē\ *adj* **ic·i·er; -est 1** : covered with, abounding in, or consisting of ice **2** : intensely cold **3** : being cold and unfriendly — **ic·i·ly** \'ī-sə-lē\ *adv* — **ic·i·ness** \-sē-nəs\ *n*

¹**id** \'id\ *n* [L, it] : the part of the psyche in psychoanalytic theory that is completely unconscious and is the source of psychic energy derived from instinctual needs and drives

²**id** *abbr* idem

ID *abbr* **1** Idaho **2** identification

idea \ī-'dē-ə\ *n* **1** : a plan for action : DESIGN, PROJECT **2** : something imagined or pictured in the mind **3** : a central meaning or purpose *syn* concept, conception, notion, impression

¹**ide·al** \ī-'dē(-ə)l\ *adj* **1** : existing only in the mind : IMAGINARY; *also* : lacking practicality **2** : of or relating to an ideal or to perfection : PERFECT

²**ideal** *n* **1** : a standard of excellence **2** : one regarded as a model worthy of imitation **3** : GOAL

ide·al·ism \ī-'dē-(ə-)ˌliz-əm\ *n* **1** : the practice of forming or living according to ideals **2** : the tendency to see things as they should be — **ide·al·ist** \-(ə-)ləst\ *n* — **ide·al·is·tic** \ī-ˌdē-(ə-)'lis-tik\ *adj* — **ide·al·is·ti·cal·ly** \-ti-k(ə-)lē\ *adv*

ide·al·ize \ī-'dē-(ə-)ˌlīz\ *vb* **-ized; -iz·ing** : to think of or represent as ideal — **ide·al·iza·tion** \ī-ˌdē-(ə-)lə-'zā-shən\ *n*

ide·al·ly \ī-'dē-(ə-)lē\ *adv* **1** : in idea or imagination : MENTALLY **2** : in agreement with an ideal : PERFECTLY

ide·ation \ˌī-dē-'ā-shən\ *n* : the capacity for or process of forming ideas — **ide·ate** \'īd-ē-ˌāt\ *vb* — **ide·ation·al** \ˌīd-ē-'āsh(ə-)nəl\ *adj*

idem \'īd-ˌem, 'ēd-, 'id-\ *pron* [L,

same] : something previously mentioned

iden·ti·cal \ī-'dent-i-kəl\ *adj* 1 : being the same 2 : exactly or essentially alike **syn** equivalent, equal, tantamount

iden·ti·fi·ca·tion \ī-,dent-ə-fə-'kā-shən\ *n* 1 : an act of identifying : the state of being identified 2 : evidence of identity 3 : an unconscious psychological process by which an individual models thoughts, feelings, and actions after another person or an object

iden·ti·fy \ī-'dent-ə-,fī\ *vb* -fied; -fy·ing 1 : to regard as identical 2 : ASSOCIATE 3 : to establish the identity of 4 : to practice psychological identification — **iden·ti·fi·able** \-,fī-ə-bəl\ *adj* — **iden·ti·fi·ably** \-blē\ *adv* — **iden·ti·fi·er** \-,fī(-ə)r\ *n*

iden·ti·ty \ī-'dent-ət-ē\ *n, pl* -ties 1 : sameness of essential character 2 : INDIVIDUALITY 3 : the fact of being the same person or thing as claimed

identity crisis *n* : psychological conflict esp. in adolescence involving confusion about one's social role and one's personality

ideo·gram \'id-ē-ə-,gram, 'īd-\ *n* 1 : a picture or symbol used in a system of writing to represent a thing or an idea 2 : a character or symbol used in a system of writing to represent an entire word

ide·ol·o·gy \,īd-ē-'äl-ə-jē, ,id-\ *also* **ide·al·o·gy** \-'äl-ə-jē, -'al-\ *n, pl* -gies 1 : the body of ideas characteristic of a particular individual, group, or culture 2 : the assertions, theories, and aims that constitute a political, social, and economic program — **ide·o·log·i·cal** \,īd-ē-ə-'läj-i-kəl, ,id-\ *adj* — **ide·ol·o·gist** \-ē-'äl-ə-jəst\ *n*

ides \'īdz\ *n sing or pl* : the 15th day of March, May, July, or October or the 13th day of any other month in the ancient Roman calendar

id·i·o·cy \'id-ē-ə-sē\ *n, pl* -cies 1 : extreme mental deficiency 2 : something notably stupid or foolish

id·i·om \'id-ē-əm\ *n* 1 : the language peculiar to a person or group 2 : the characteristic form or structure of a language 3 : an expression that cannot be understood from the meanings of its separate words (as *give way*) — **id·i·om·at·ic** \,id-ē-ə-'mat-ik\ *adj* — **id·i·om·at·i·cal·ly** \-i-k(ə-)lē\ *adv*

id·i·o·path·ic \,id-ē-ə-'path-ik\ *adj* : arising spontaneously or from an obscure or unknown cause (an ~ disease)

id·io·syn·cra·sy \,id-ē-ə-'siŋ-krə-sē\ *n, pl* -sies : personal peculiarity — **id·io·syn·crat·ic** \,id-ē-ō-sin-'krat-ik\ *adj* — **id·io·syn·crat·i·cal·ly** \-'krat-i-k(ə-)lē\ *adv*

id·i·ot \'id-ē-ət\ *n* [ME, fr. L *idiota* ignorant person, fr. Gk *idiōtēs* one in a private station, ignorant person, fr. *idios* one's own, private] 1 : a feebleminded person 2 : a silly or foolish

person — **id·i·ot·ic** \,id-ē-'ät-ik\ *adj* — **id·i·ot·i·cal·ly** \-i-k(ə-)lē\ *adv*

¹idle \'īd-²l\ *adj* **idler** \'īd-(ə-)lər\ ; **idlest** \'īd-(ə-)ləst\ 1 : GROUNDLESS, WORTHLESS, USELESS (~ rumor) (~ talk) 2 : not occupied or employed : INACTIVE 3 : LAZY (~ fellows) — **idle·ness** *n* — **idly** \'īd-lē\ *adv*

²idle *vb* **idled; idling** \'īd-(²-)liŋ\ 1 : to spend time doing nothing 2 : to make idle 3 : to run without being connected so that power is not used for useful work — **idler** \'īd-(ə-)lər\ *n*

idol \'īd-²l\ *n* 1 : an image worshiped as a god 2 : a false god 3 : an object of passionate devotion

idol·a·ter \ī-'däl-ət-ər\ *n* : a worshiper of idols

idol·a·try \-ə-trē\ *n, pl* -tries 1 : the worship of a physical object as a god 2 : immoderate devotion — **idol·a·trous** \-trəs\ *adj*

idol·ize \'īd-²l-,īz\ *vb* -ized; -iz·ing : to make an idol of — **idol·iza·tion** \,īd-²l-ə-'zā-shən\ *n*

idyll *or* **idyl** \'īd-²l\ *n* 1 : a simple descriptive or narrative composition; *esp* : a poem about country life 2 : a fit subject for an idyll — **idyl·lic** \ī-'dil-ik\ *adj*

i.e. \'that-'iz, (')ī-'ē\ *abbr* [L *id est* that is]

IE *abbr* 1 Indo-European 2 industrial engineer

-ier — see -ER

if \(,)if, əf\ *conj* 1 : in the event that (~ he stays, I leave) 2 : WHETHER (ask ~ he left) 3 — used as a function word to introduce an exclamation expressing a wish (~ it would only rain) 4 : even though (an interesting ~ untenable argument)

IF *abbr* intermediate frequency

if·fy \'if-ē\ *adj* : full of contingencies or unknown conditions

-i·fy \ə-,fī\ *vb suffix* : -FY

IG *abbr* inspector general

ig·loo \'ig-lü\ *n, pl* **igloos** [Eskimo *iglu* house] : an Eskimo house or hut often made of snow blocks and in the shape of a dome

ig·ne·ous \'ig-nē-əs\ *adj* 1 : FIERY 2 : formed by solidification of molten rock

ig·nite \ig-'nīt\ *vb* **ig·nit·ed; ig·nit·ing** : to set afire or catch fire — **ig·nit·able** \-'nīt-ə-bəl\ *adj*

ig·ni·tion \ig-'nish-ən\ *n* 1 : a setting on fire 2 : the process or means (as an electric spark) of igniting the fuel mixture in an engine

ig·no·ble \ig-'nō-bəl\ *adj* 1 : of low birth : PLEBEIAN 2 : not honorable : BASE, MEAN — **ig·no·bly** \-blē\ *adv*

ig·no·min·i·ous \,ig-nə-'min-ē-əs\ *adj* 1 : DISHONORABLE 2 : DESPICABLE 3 : HUMILIATING, DEGRADING — **ig·no·min·i·ous·ly** *adv* — **ig·no·mi·ny** \'ig-nə-,min-ē, ig-'näm-ə-nē\ *n*

ig·no·ra·mus \,ig-nə-'rā-məs\ *n* [*Ignoramus*, ignorant lawyer in *Ig-*

noramus (1615), play by George Ruggle] : an utterly ignorant person : DUNCE

ig·no·rance \'ig-nə-rəns\ *n* : the state of being ignorant : lack of knowledge

ig·no·rant \'ig-nə-rənt\ *adj* 1 : lacking knowledge : UNEDUCATED 2 : resulting from or showing lack of knowledge or intelligence 3 : UNAWARE, UNINFORMED — **ig·no·rant·ly** *adv*

ig·nore \ig-'nōr\ *vb* **ig·nored**; **ig·nor·ing** : to refuse to take notice of *syn* overlook, slight, neglect

igua·na \i-'gwän-ə\ *n* : a large edible tropical American lizard

IGY *abbr* International Geophysical Year

IHP *abbr* indicated horsepower

IHS \ˌī-ˌā-'ches\ [LL, part transliteration of Gk IHΣ, abbreviation for IHΣOYΣ *Iēsous* Jesus] — used as a Christian symbol and monogram for Jesus

ikon *var of* ICON

IL *abbr* Illinois

il·e·itis \ˌil-ē-'īt-əs\ *n* : inflammation of the ileum

il·e·um \'il-ē-əm\ *n, pl* **il·ea** \-ē-ə\ : the part of the small intestine between the jejunum and the large intestine — **il·e·al** \-ē-əl\ *adj*

il·i·ac \'il-ē-ˌak\ *adj* : of, relating to, or located near the ilium

il·i·um \'il-ē-əm\ *n* : the upper one of the three bones making up either half of the pelvis

ilk \'ilk\ *n* : SORT, FAMILY

¹ill \'il\ *adj* **worse** \'wərs\ ; **worst** \'wərst\ 1 : not normal or sound (~ health) ; *also* : suffering ill health : SICK 2 : BAD, UNLUCKY (~ omen) 3 : not right or proper (~ manners) 4 : UNFRIENDLY, HOSTILE (~ feeling) 5 : HARSH, CRUEL (~ treatment)

²ill *adv* **worse**; **worst** 1 : with displeasure 2 : in a harsh manner 3 : HARDLY, SCARCELY (can ~ afford it) 4 : BADLY, UNLUCKILY 5 : in a faulty way

³ill *n* 1 : EVIL 2 : MISFORTUNE, DISTRESS 3 : AILMENT, SICKNESS; *also* : TROUBLE

⁴ill *abbr* illustrated; illustration; illustrator

Ill *abbr* Illinois

ill-ad·vised \ˌil-əd-'vīzd\ *adj* : not well counseled (~ efforts) — **ill-ad·vis·ed·ly** \-'vī-zəd-lē\ *adv*

ill-bred \-'bred\ *adj* : badly brought up : IMPOLITE

il·le·gal \il-'(l)ē-gəl\ *adj* : not lawful; *also* : not sanctioned by official rules — **il·le·gal·i·ty** \ˌil-i-'gal-ət-ē\ *n* — **il·le·gal·ly** \il-'(l)ē-gə-lē\ *adv*

il·leg·i·ble \il-'(l)ej-ə-bəl\ *adj* : not legible — **il·leg·i·bil·i·ty** \il-'(l)ej-ə-'bil-ət-ē\ *n* — **il·leg·i·bly** \il-'(l)ej-ə-blē\ *adv*

il·le·git·i·mate \ˌil-i-'jit-ə-mət\ *adj* 1 : born of unmarried parents 2 : ILLOGICAL 3 : ILLEGAL — **il·le·git·i·ma·cy** \-'jit-ə-mə-sē\ *n* — **il·le·git·i·mate·ly** \-'jit-ə-mət-lē\ *adv*

ill-fat·ed \'il-'fāt-əd\ *adj* : having or

destined to an evil fate : UNFORTUNATE

ill-fa·vored \-'fā-vərd\ *adj* : UGLY, UNATTRACTIVE

ill-got·ten \-'gät-ᵊn\ *adj* : acquired by evil means (~ gains)

ill-hu·mored \-'(h)yü-mərd\ *adj* : SURLY, IRRITABLE

il·lib·er·al \il-'(l)ib-(ə-)rəl\ *adj* : not liberal : NARROW, BIGOTED

il·lic·it \il-'(l)is-ət\ *adj* : not permitted : UNLAWFUL — **il·lic·it·ly** *adv*

il·lim·it·able \il-'(l)im-ət-ə-bəl\ *adj* : BOUNDLESS, MEASURELESS — **il·lim·it·ably** \-blē\ *adv*

Il·li·nois \ˌil-ə-'nòi *also* -'nòiz\ *n, pl* **Illinois** : a member of an American Indian people of Illinois, Iowa, and Wisconsin

il·lit·er·ate \il-'(l)it-(ə-)rət\ *adj* 1 : having little or no education; *esp* : unable to read or write 2 : showing a lack of familiarity with the fundamentals of a particular field of knowledge — **il·lit·er·a·cy** \-'(l)it-(ə-)rə-sē\ *n* — **illiterate** *n*

ill-man·nered \'il-'man-ərd\ *adj* : marked by bad manners : RUDE

ill-na·tured \-'nā-chərd\ *adj* : CROSS, SURLY — **ill-na·tured·ly** *adv*

ill·ness \'il-nəs\ *n* : SICKNESS

il·log·i·cal \il-'(l)äj-i-kəl\ *adj* : not according to good reasoning; *also* : SENSELESS — **il·log·i·cal·ly** \-i-k(ə-)lē\ *adv*

ill-starred \'il-'stärd\ *adj* : ILL-FATED, UNLUCKY

ill-tem·pered \-'tem-pərd\ *adj* : ILL-NATURED, QUARRELSOME

ill-treat \-'trēt\ *vb* : to treat cruelly or improperly : MALTREAT — **ill-treat·ment** \-mənt\ *n*

il·lume \il-'üm\ *vb* **il·lumed**; **il·lum·ing** : ILLUMINATE

il·lu·mi·nate \il-'ü-mə-ˌnāt\ *vb* **-nat·ed**; **-nat·ing** 1 : to supply or brighten with light : light up 2 : to make clear : ELUCIDATE 3 : to decorate (as a manuscript) with designs or pictures in gold or colors — **il·lu·mi·nat·ing·ly** \-ˌnāt-iŋ-lē\ *adv* — **il·lu·mi·na·tion** \-ˌü-mə-'nā-shən\ *n* — **il·lu·mi·na·tor** \-'ü-mə-ˌnāt-ər\ *n*

il·lu·mine \il-'ü-mən\ *vb* **-mined**; **-min·ing** : ILLUMINATE

ill-us·age \il-'yü-sij, -zij\ *n* : harsh, unkind, or abusive treatment

ill-use \-'yüz\ *vb* : MALTREAT, ABUSE

il·lu·sion \il-'ü-zhən\ *n* [ME, fr. MF, fr. LL *illusio*, fr. L, action of mocking, fr. *illudere* to mock at, fr. *ludere* to play, mock] 1 : a mistaken idea : MISAPPREHENSION, MISCONCEPTION, FANCY 2 : a misleading visual image : HALLUCINATION

il·lu·sion·ist \il-'üzh-(ə-)nəst\ *n* : one that produces illusions; *esp* : a sleight-of-hand performer

il·lu·sive \il-'ü-siv\ *adj* : ILLUSORY

il·lu·so·ry \il-'üs-(ə-)rē, -'üz-\ *adj* : based on or producing illusion

illust *or* **illus** *abbr* illustrated; illustration

il·lus·trate \'il-əs-ˌtrāt\ *vb* **-trat·ed; -trat·ing** [L *illustrare,* fr. *lustrare* to purify, make bright] **1** : to explain by use of examples : CLARIFY; *also* : DEMONSTRATE **2** : to provide with pictures or figures that explain or decorate **3** : to serve to explain or decorate — **il·lus·tra·tor** \'il-əs-ˌtrāt-ər\ *n*

il·lus·tra·tion \ˌil-əs-'trā-shən\ *n* **1** : the act of illustrating : the condition of being illustrated **2** : an example or instance that helps make something clear **3** : a picture or diagram that explains or decorates

il·lus·tra·tive \il-'əs-trət-iv\ *adj* : serving, tending, or designed to illustrate — **il·lus·tra·tive·ly** *adv*

il·lus·tri·ous \il-'əs-trē-əs\ *adj* : notably outstanding because of rank or achievement : EMINENT — **il·lus·tri·ous·ness** *n*

ill will *n* : unfriendly feeling

ILS *abbr* instrument landing system

¹im·age \'im-ij\ *n* **1** : a likeness or imitation of a person or thing; *esp* : STATUE **2** : a picture of an object formed by a device (as a mirror or lens) **3** : a person strikingly like another person (he is the ~ of his father) **4** : a mental picture or conception : IMPRESSION, IDEA, CONCEPT **5** : a vivid representation or description

²image *vb* **im·aged; im·ag·ing 1** : to call up a mental picture of **2** : to describe or portray in words **3** : to create a representation of **4** : REFLECT, MIRROR **5** : to make appear : PROJECT

im·ag·ery \'im-ij-(ə-)rē\ *n* **1** : IMAGES; *also* : the art of making images **2** : figurative language **3** : mental images; *esp* : the products of imagination

imag·in·able \im-'aj-(ə-)nə-bəl\ *adj* : capable of being imagined : CONCEIVABLE — **imag·in·ably** \-blē\ *adv*

imag·i·nary \im-'aj-ə-ˌner-ē\ *adj* **1** : existing only in the imagination **2** : containing or relating to the imaginary unit

imaginary number *n* : a complex number (as $2 + 3i$) whose imaginary part is not zero

imaginary part *n* : the part of a complex number (as $3i$ in $2 + 3i$) that has the imaginary unit as a factor

imaginary unit *n* : the positive square root of minus 1 : $+\sqrt{-1}$

imag·i·na·tion \im-ˌaj-ə-'nā-shən\ *n* **1** : the act or power of forming a mental image of something not present to the senses or not previously known or experienced **2** : creative ability **3** : RESOURCEFULNESS **4** : a mental image : a creation of the mind — **imag·i·na·tive** \im-'aj-(ə)-nat-iv, -ə-ˌnāt-iv\ *adj* — **imag·i·na·tive·ly** *adv*

imag·ine \im-'aj-ən\ *vb* **imag·ined; imag·in·ing** \-'aj-(ə-)nin\ **1** : to form a mental picture of something not present **2** : THINK, GUESS (I ~ it will rain)

im·ag·ism \'im-ij-ˌiz-əm\ *n, often cap* : a movement in poetry advocating free verse and the expression of ideas and emotions through clear precise images — **im·ag·ist** \-ij-əst\ *n*

ima·go \im-'ā-gō, -'āg-ō\ *n, pl* **imagoes** *or* **ima·gi·nes** \-'ā-gə-ˌnēz, -'āg-ə-\ [L, image] : an insect in its final adult stage — **ima·gi·nal** \im-'ā-gən-ᵊl, -'āg-ən-\ *adj*

im·bal·ance \(')im-'bal-əns\ *n* : lack of balance : the state of being out of equilibrium or out of proportion

im·be·cile \'im-bə-səl, -ˌsil\ *n* **1** : a feebleminded person; *esp* : one capable of performing routine personal care under supervision **2** : FOOL, IDIOT — **imbecile** *or* **im·be·cil·ic** \ˌim-bə-'sil-ik\ *adj* — **im·be·cil·i·ty** \ˌim-bə-'sil-ət-ē\ *n*

imbed *var of* EMBED

im·bibe \im-'bīb\ *vb* **im·bibed; im·bib·ing 1** : to receive and retain in the mind **2** : DRINK **3** : to drink in : ABSORB — **im·bib·er** *n*

im·bi·bi·tion \ˌim-bə-'bish-ən\ *n* : the act or action of imbibing; *esp* : the taking up of fluid by a colloidal system resulting in swelling

im·bri·ca·tion \ˌim-brə-'kā-shən\ *n* **1** : an overlapping of edges (as of tiles) **2** : a pattern showing imbrication — **im·bri·cate** \'im-bri-kət\ *adj*

im·bro·glio \im-'brōl-yō\ *n, pl* **-glios** [It, fr. *imbrogliare* to entangle] **1** : a confused mass **2** : a difficult or embarrassing situation; *also* : a serious or embarrassing misunderstanding

im·brue \im-'brü\ *vb* **im·brued; im·bru·ing** : DRENCH, STAIN (a nation *imbrued* with the blood of executed men)

im·bue \-'byü\ *vb* **im·bued; im·bu·ing 1** : to permeate or influence as if by dyeing **2** : to tinge or dye deeply

IMF *abbr* International Monetary Fund

imit *abbr* imitative

im·i·ta·ble \'im-ət-ə-bəl\ *adj* : capable or worthy of being imitated or copied

im·i·tate \'im-ə-ˌtāt\ *vb* **-tat·ed; -tat·ing 1** : to follow as a model : COPY **2** : RESEMBLE **3** : REPRODUCE **4** : MIMIC, COUNTERFEIT — **im·i·ta·tor** \-ˌtāt-ər\ *n*

im·i·ta·tion \ˌim-ə-'tā-shən\ *n* **1** : an act of imitating **2** : COPY, COUNTERFEIT **3** : a literary work that reproduces the style of another author — **imitation** *adj*

im·i·ta·tive \'im-ə-ˌtāt-iv\ *adj* **1** : marked by imitation **2** : exhibiting mimicry **3** : inclined to imitate or copy **4** : COUNTERFEIT

im·mac·u·late \im-'ak-yə-lət\ *adj* **1** : being without stain or blemish : PURE **2** : spotlessly clean (~ linen) — **im·mac·u·late·ly** *adv*

im·ma·nent \'im-ə-nənt\ *adj* : having existence only in the mind — **im·ma·nence** \-nəns\ *n* — **im·ma·nen·cy** \-nən-sē\ *n*

im·ma·te·ri·al \ˌim-ə-'tir-ē-əl\ *adj* **1** : not consisting of matter : SPIRITUAL **2**

: UNIMPORTANT, TRIFLING — **im·ma·te·ri·al·i·ty** \-ˌtir-ē-'al-ət-ē\ n

im·ma·ture \ˌim-ə-'t(y)ùr\ adj : lacking complete development : not yet mature — **im·ma·tu·ri·ty** \-'t(y)ùr-ət-ē\ n

im·mea·sur·able \(')im-'ezh-(ə-)rə-bəl\ adj : not capable of being measured : indefinitely extensive : ILLIMITABLE — **im·mea·sur·ably** \-blē\ adv

im·me·di·a·cy \im-'ēd-ē-ə-sē\ n, pl -cies 1 : the quality or state of being immediate 2 : URGENCY 3 : something that is of immediate importance

im·me·di·ate \im-'ēd-ē-ət\ adj 1 : acting directly and alone : DIRECT ⟨the ~ cause of death⟩ 2 : being next in line or relation ⟨members of the ~ family attended⟩ 3 : not distant : CLOSE 4 : made or done at once ⟨an ~ response⟩ 5 : near to or related to the present time ⟨the ~ future⟩ — **im·me·di·ate·ly** adv

im·me·mo·ri·al \ˌim-ə-'mōr-ē-əl\ adj : extending beyond the reach of memory, record, or tradition

im·mense \im-'ens\ adj [MF, fr. L immensus immeasurable, fr. mensus, pp. of metiri to measure] 1 : very great in size or degree : VAST, HUGE 2 : EXCELLENT — **im·mense·ly** adv — **im·men·si·ty** \-'en-sət-ē\ n

im·merse \im-'ərs\ vb im·mersed; im·mers·ing 1 : to plunge or dip esp. into a fluid 2 : ENGROSS, ABSORB 3 : to baptize by immersing — **im·mer·sion** \-'ər-zhən\ n

im·mi·grant \'im-i-grənt\ n 1 : a person who immigrates 2 : a plant or animal that becomes established where it did not previously occur

im·mi·grate \'im-ə-ˌgrāt\ vb -grat·ed; -grat·ing : to come into a foreign country and take up residence — **im·mi·gra·tion** \ˌim-ə-'grā-shən\ n

im·mi·nent \'im-ə-nənt\ adj : ready to take place; esp : hanging threateningly over one's head — **im·mi·nence** \-nəns\ n — **im·mi·nent·ly** adv

im·mis·ci·ble \(')im-'is-ə-bəl\ adj : incapable of mixing — **im·mis·ci·bil·i·ty** \(ˌ)im-ˌis-ə-'bil-ət-ē\ n

im·mo·bile \(')im-'ō-bəl\ adj : incapable of being moved : IMMOVABLE, FIXED — **im·mo·bil·i·ty** \ˌim-ō-'bil-ət-ē\ n

im·mo·bi·lize \im-'ō-bə-ˌlīz\ vb : to make immobile — **im·mo·bi·li·za·tion** \im-ˌō-bə-lə-'zā-shən\ n

im·mod·er·ate \(')im-'äd-(ə-)rət\ adj : lacking in moderation : EXCESSIVE — **im·mod·er·a·cy** \-(ə-)rə-sē\ n — **im·mod·er·ate·ly** adv

im·mod·est \(')im-'äd-əst\ adj : not modest : BRAZEN, INDECENT ⟨an ~ dress⟩ ⟨~ conduct⟩ — **im·mod·est·ly** adv — **im·mod·es·ty** \-ə-stē\ n

im·mo·late \'im-ə-ˌlāt\ vb -lat·ed; -lat·ing [L immolare, fr. mola grits; fr. the custom of sprinkling victims with sacrificial meal] : to offer in sacrifice; esp : to kill as a sacrificial victim — **im·mo·la·tion** \ˌim-ə-'lā-shən\ n

im·mor·al \(')im-'ȯr-əl\ adj : not moral : WICKED — **im·mor·al·ly** \-ē\ adv

im·mo·ral·i·ty \ˌim-ȯ-'ral-ət-ē, ˌim-ə-'ral-\ n 1 : WICKEDNESS; esp : UNCHASTITY 2 : an immoral act or practice

[1]**im·mor·tal** \(')im-'ȯrt-ᵊl\ adj 1 : not mortal : exempt from death ⟨~ gods⟩ 2 : exempt from oblivion ⟨those ~ words⟩ — **im·mor·tal·ly** \-ē\ adv

[2]**immortal** n 1 : one exempt from death 2 pl, often cap : the gods in Greek and Roman mythology 3 : a person whose fame is lasting ⟨an ~ of baseball⟩

im·mor·tal·i·ty \ˌim-ȯr-'tal-ət-ē\ n : the quality or state of being immortal; esp : unending existence

im·mor·tal·ize \im-'ȯrt-ᵊl-ˌīz\ vb -ized; -iz·ing : to make immortal

im·mov·able \(')im-'ü-və-bəl\ adj 1 : firmly fixed, settled, or fastened : FAST, STATIONARY ⟨~ mountains⟩ 2 : STEADFAST, UNYIELDING 3 : IMPASSIVE — **im·mov·abil·i·ty** \(ˌ)im-ˌü-və-'bil-ət-ē\ n — **im·mov·ably** \-blē\ adv

im·mune \im-'yün\ adj 1 : EXEMPT 2 : having a special capacity for resistance ⟨as to a disease⟩ — **im·mu·ni·ty** \im-'yü-nət-ē\ n

immune response n : a response of the body to an antigen resulting in the formation of antibodies and cells capable of reacting with the antigen and rendering it harmless

im·mu·nize \'im-yə-ˌnīz\ vb -nized; -niz·ing : to make immune — **im·mu·ni·za·tion** \ˌim-yə-nə-'zā-shən\ n

im·mu·no·de·fi·cien·cy \ˌim-yə-nō-di-'fish-ən-sē\ n : inability to produce the normal number of antibodies or immunologically sensitized cells esp. in response to specific antigens — **im·mu·no·de·fi·cient** \-ənt\ adj

im·mu·no·glob·u·lin \ˌim-yə-nō-'gläb-yə-lən\ n : any of a group of vertebrate serum proteins that include all known antibodies

im·mu·nol·o·gy \ˌim-yə-'näl-ə-jē\ n : a science that deals with the phenomena and causes of immunity — **im·mu·no·log·ic** \-yən-ᵊl-'äj-ik\ or **im·mu·no·log·i·cal** \-i-kəl\ adj — **im·mu·no·log·i·cal·ly** \-i-k(ə-)lē\ adv — **im·mu·nol·o·gist** \ˌim-yə-'näl-ə-jəst\ n

im·mu·no·sup·pres·sion \ˌim-yə-nō-sə-'presh-ən\ n : suppression ⟨as by drugs⟩ of natural immune responses — **im·mu·no·sup·press** \-sə-'pres\ vb — **im·mu·no·sup·pres·sant** \-sə-'pres-ᵊnt\ n or adj — **im·mu·no·sup·pres·sive** \-sə-'pres-iv\ adj

im·mure \im-'yü(ə)r\ vb im·mured; im·mur·ing 1 : to enclose within or as if within walls 2 : to build into a wall; esp : to entomb in a wall

im·mu·ta·ble \(')im-'yüt-ə-bəl\ adj : UNCHANGEABLE, UNCHANGING — **im·mu·ta·bil·i·ty** \(ˌ)im-ˌyüt-ə-'bil-ət-ē\ n — **im·mu·ta·bly** \(')im-'yüt-ə-blē\ adv

¹**imp** \'imp\ n **1** : a small demon : FIEND **2** : a mischievous child

²**imp** abbr **1** imperative **2** imperfect **3** imperial **4** import; imported

¹**im·pact** \im-'pakt\ vb **1** : to press together **2** : to have an impact on

²**im·pact** \'im-,pakt\ n **1** : a forceful contact, collision, or onset; also : the impetus communicated in or as if in a collision **2** : EFFECT

im·pact·ed \im-'pak-təd\ adj : wedged between the jawbone and another tooth

im·pair \im-'paər\ vb : to diminish in quantity, value, excellence, or strength : DAMAGE, LESSEN — **im·pair·ment** n

im·pa·la \im-'pal-ə\ n : a large brownish African antelope that in the male has slender lyre-shaped horns

im·pale \im-'pāl\ vb im·paled; im·pal·ing : to pierce with or as if with something pointed — **im·pale·ment** n

im·pal·pa·ble \(')im-'pal-pə-bəl\ adj **1** : unable to be felt by touch : INTANGIBLE **2** : not easily seen or understood — **im·pal·pa·bly** \(,)im-'pal-pə-blē\ adv

im·pan·el \im-'pan-ᵊl\ vb : to enter in or on a panel : ENROLL (~ a jury)

im·part \im-'pärt\ vb **1** : to give from one's store or abundance (the sun ~s warmth) **2** : to make known

im·par·tial \(')im-'pär-shəl\ adj : not partial : UNBIASED, JUST — **im·par·ti·al·i·ty** \(,)im-,pär-shē-'al-ət-ē, -,pär-'shal-\ n — **im·par·tial·ly** \(')im-'pärsh-(ə-)lē\ adv

im·pass·able \(')im-'pas-ə-bəl\ adj : incapable of being passed, traversed, or circulated (~ roads) — **im·pass·ably** \(')im-'pas-ə-blē\ adv

im·passe \'im-,pas\ n **1** : an impassable road or way **2** : a predicament from which there is no obvious escape

im·pas·si·ble \(')im-'pas-ə-bəl\ adj : UNFEELING, IMPASSIVE

im·pas·sioned \im-'pash-ənd\ adj : filled with passion or zeal : showing great warmth or intensity of feeling syn passionate, ardent, fervent, fervid

im·pas·sive \(')im-'pas-iv\ adj : showing no signs of feeling, emotion, or interest : EXPRESSIONLESS, INDIFFERENT syn stoic, phlegmatic, apathetic, stolid — **im·pas·sive·ly** adv — **im·pas·siv·i·ty** \,im-,pas-'iv-ət-ē\ n

im·pas·to \im-'pas-tō, -'päs-\ n : the thick application of a pigment to a canvas or panel in painting; also : the body of pigment so applied

im·pa·tience \(')im-'pā-shən(t)s\ n **1** : restlessness of spirit esp. under irritation, delay, or opposition **2** : restless or eager desire or longing

im·pa·tiens \im-'pā-shənz, -shəns\ n : any of a genus of watery-juiced annual herbs with spurred flowers and seed capsules that readily split open

im·pa·tient \(')im-'pā-shənt\ adj **1** : not patient : restless or short of temper esp. under irritation, delay, or opposition **2** : INTOLERANT (~ of poverty) **3** : prompted or marked by impatience **4** : ANXIOUS — **im·pa·tient·ly** adv

im·peach \im-'pēch\ vb [ME empechen, fr. MF empeechier to hinder, fr. LL impedicare to fetter, fr. L pedica fetter, fr. ped-, pes foot] **1** : to charge (a public official) before an authorized tribunal with misbehavior in office **2** : to challenge the credibility or validity of — **im·peach·ment** n

im·pec·ca·ble \(')im-'pek-ə-bəl\ adj **1** : not capable of sinning or wrongdoing **2** : FAULTLESS, FLAWLESS, IRREPROACHABLE (a man of ~ character) — **im·pec·ca·bil·i·ty** \(,)im-,pek-ə-'bil-ət-ē\ n — **im·pec·ca·bly** \(')im-'pek-ə-blē\ adv

im·pe·cu·nious \,im-pi-'kyü-nyəs, -nē-əs\ adj : having little or no money — **im·pe·cu·nious·ness** n

im·ped·ance \im-'pēd-ᵊns\ n : the opposition in an electrical circuit to the flow of an alternating current

im·pede \im-'pēd\ vb im·ped·ed; im·ped·ing [L impedire, fr. ped-, pes foot] : to interfere with the progress of

im·ped·i·ment \im-'ped-ə-mənt\ n : OBSTRUCTION, BLOCK; esp : a speech defect

im·ped·i·men·ta \im-,ped-ə-'ment-ə\ n pl : things that impede

im·pel \im-'pel\ vb im·pelled; im·pel·ling : to urge or drive forward or on : FORCE; also : PROPEL

im·pel·ler also **im·pel·lor** \im-'pel-ər\ n : ROTOR

im·pend \im-'pend\ vb **1** : to hover or hang over threateningly : MENACE **2** : to be about to occur

im·pen·e·tra·ble \(')im-'pen-ə-trə-bəl\ adj **1** : incapable of being penetrated or pierced (an ~ jungle) **2** : incapable of being comprehended : INSCRUTABLE (an ~ mystery) — **im·pen·e·tra·bil·i·ty** \(,)im-,pen-ə-trə-'bil-ət-ē\ n — **im·pen·e·tra·bly** \(')im-'pen-ə-trə-blē\ adv

im·pen·i·tent \(')im-'pen-ə-tənt\ adj : not penitent : not repenting of sin — **im·pen·i·tence** \-təns\ n

im·per·a·tive \im-'per-ət-iv\ adj **1** : expressing a command, request, or encouragement (~ sentence) **2** : having power to restrain, control, or direct **3** : NECESSARY — **imperative** n — **im·per·a·tive·ly** adv

im·per·cep·ti·ble \,im-pər-'sep-tə-bəl\ adj : not perceptible by the senses or by the mind (~ changes) — **im·per·cep·ti·bly** \-'sep-tə-blē\ adv

im·per·cep·tive \,im-pər-'sep-tiv\ adj : not perceptive

imperf abbr **1** imperfect **2** imperforate

¹**im·per·fect** \(')im-'pər-fikt\ adj **1** : not perfect : DEFECTIVE, INCOMPLETE **2** : of, relating to, or being a verb tense used to designate a continuing state or an incomplete action esp. in the past — **im·per·fect·ly** adv

imperfect · imponderable

370

²**im·per·fect** *n* : the imperfect tense; *also* : a verb form in it

im·per·fec·tion \ˌim-pər-ˈfek-shən\ *n* : the quality or state of being imperfect; *also* : DEFICIENCY, FAULT, BLEMISH

im·per·fo·rate \im-ˈpər-fə-rət\ *adj* : lacking perforations or tiny slits ⟨~ postage stamps⟩

¹**im·pe·ri·al** \im-ˈpir-ē-əl\ *adj* 1 : of, relating to, or befitting an empire or an emperor; *also* : of or relating to the United Kingdom or to the Commonwealth or British Empire 2 : ROYAL, SOVEREIGN; *also* : REGAL, IMPERIOUS 3 : of unusual size or excellence

²**imperial** *n* : a pointed beard growing below the lower lip

im·pe·ri·al·ism \im-ˈpir-ē-ə-ˌliz-əm\ *n* : the policy of seeking to extend the power, dominion, or territories of a nation — **im·pe·ri·al·ist** \-ləst\ *n or adj* — **im·pe·ri·al·is·tic** \-ˌpir-ē-ə-ˈlis-tik\ *adj* — **im·pe·ri·al·is·ti·cal·ly** \-ti-k(ə-)lē\ *adv*

im·per·il \im-ˈper-əl\ *vb* **-iled** *or* **-illed; -il·ing** *or* **-il·ling** : ENDANGER

im·pe·ri·ous \im-ˈpir-ē-əs\ *adj* 1 : COMMANDING, LORDLY 2 : ARROGANT, DOMINEERING 3 : IMPERATIVE, URGENT — **im·pe·ri·ous·ly** *adv*

im·per·ish·able \(ˈ)im-ˈper-ish-ə-bəl\ *adj* : not perishable or subject to decay

im·per·ma·nent \(ˈ)im-ˈpər-mə-nənt\ *adj* : not permanent : TRANSIENT — **im·per·ma·nent·ly** *adv*

im·per·me·able \(ˈ)im-ˈpər-mē-ə-bəl\ *adj* : not permitting passage (as of a fluid) through its substance

im·per·mis·si·ble \ˌim-pər-ˈmis-ə-bəl\ *adj* : not permissible

im·per·son·al \(ˈ)im-ˈpərs-(ə-)nəl\ *adj* 1 : not referring to any particular person or thing 2 : not involving human emotions — **im·per·son·al·i·ty** \(ˌ)im-ˌpərs-ᵊn-ˈal-ət-ē\ *n* — **im·per·son·al·ly** \-ē\ *adv*

im·per·son·ate \im-ˈpərs-ᵊn-ˌāt\ *vb* **-at·ed; -at·ing** : to assume or act the character of — **im·per·son·ation** \-ˌpərs-ᵊn-ˈā-shən\ *n* — **im·per·son·ator** \-ˈpərs-ᵊn-ˌāt-ər\ *n*

im·per·ti·nent \(ˈ)im-ˈpərt-ᵊn-ənt\ *adj* 1 : IRRELEVANT 2 : not restrained within due or proper bounds : RUDE, INSOLENT, SAUCY — **im·per·ti·nence** \-ᵊn-əns\ *n* — **im·per·ti·nent·ly** *adv*

im·per·turb·able \ˌim-pər-ˈtər-bə-bəl\ *adj* : marked by extreme calm, impassivity, and steadiness : SERENE

im·per·vi·ous \(ˈ)im-ˈpər-vē-əs\ *adj* 1 : incapable of being penetrated (as by moisture) 2 : not capable of being affected or disturbed ⟨~ to criticism⟩

im·pe·ti·go \ˌim-pə-ˈtē-gō, -ˈtī-\ *n* : a contagious skin disease characterized by vesicles, pustules, and yellowish crusts

im·pet·u·ous \im-ˈpech-(ə-)wəs\ *adj* 1 : marked by impulsive vehemence ⟨~

temper⟩ 2 : marked by force and violence ⟨with ~ speed⟩ — **im·pet·u·os·i·ty** \(ˌ)im-ˌpech-ə-ˈwäs-ət-ē\ *n* — **im·pet·u·ous·ly** *adv*

im·pe·tus \ˈim-pət-əs\ *n* [L, assault, impetus, fr. *impetere* to attack, fr. *petere* to go to, seek] 1 : a driving force : IMPULSE 2 : INCENTIVE 3 : MOMENTUM

im·pi·ety \(ˈ)im-ˈpī-ət-ē\ *n, pl* **-eties** 1 : the quality or state of being impious 2 : an impious act

im·pinge \im-ˈpinj\ *vb* **im·pinged; im·ping·ing** 1 : to strike or dash esp. with a sharp collision 2 : ENCROACH, INFRINGE — **im·pinge·ment** \-ˈpinj-mənt\ *n*

im·pi·ous \ˈim-pē-əs, (ˈ)im-ˈpī-\ *adj* : not pious : IRREVERENT, PROFANE

imp·ish \ˈim-pish\ *adj* : of, relating to, or befitting an imp; *esp* : MISCHIEVOUS — **imp·ish·ly** *adv* — **imp·ish·ness** *n*

im·pla·ca·ble \(ˈ)im-ˈplak-ə-bəl, -ˈplā-kə-\ *adj* : not capable of being appeased, pacified, mitigated, or changed ⟨an ~ enemy⟩ — **im·pla·ca·bil·i·ty** \(ˌ)im-ˌplak-ə-ˈbil-ət-ē, -ˌplā-kə-\ *n* — **im·pla·ca·bly** \(ˈ)im-ˈplak-ə-blē\ *adv*

im·plant \im-ˈplant\ *vb* 1 : to set firmly or deeply 2 : to fix in the mind or spirit 3 : to insert in a living site — **im·plant** \ˈim-ˌplant\ *n* — **im·plan·ta·tion** \ˌim-ˌplan-ˈtā-shən\ *n*

im·plau·si·ble \(ˈ)im-ˈplȯ-zə-bəl\ *adj* : not plausible — **im·plau·si·bil·i·ty** \(ˌ)im-ˌplȯ-zə-ˈbil-ət-ē\ *n* — **im·plau·si·bly** \(ˈ)im-ˈplȯ-zə-blē\ *adv*

¹**im·ple·ment** \ˈim-plə-mənt\ *n* [ME, fr. LL *implementum* action of filling up, fr. L *implēre* to fill up] : TOOL, UTENSIL, INSTRUMENT

²**im·ple·ment** \-ˌment\ *vb* 1 : to carry out; *esp* : to put into practice 2 : to provide implements for — **im·ple·men·ta·tion** \ˌim-plə-mən-ˈtā-shən\ *n*

im·pli·cate \ˈim-plə-ˌkāt\ *vb* **-cat·ed; -cat·ing** 1 : IMPLY 2 : INVOLVE — **im·pli·ca·tion** \ˌim-plə-ˈkā-shən\ *n*

im·plic·it \im-ˈplis-ət\ *adj* 1 : understood though not directly stated or expressed : IMPLIED; *also* : POTENTIAL 2 : COMPLETE, UNQUESTIONING, ABSOLUTE ⟨~ faith⟩ — **im·plic·it·ly** *adv*

im·plode \im-ˈplōd\ *vb* **im·plod·ed; im·plod·ing** : to burst or collapse inward — **im·plo·sion** \-ˈplō-zhən\ *n* — **im·plo·sive** \-ˈplō-siv\ *adj*

im·plore \im-ˈplȯr\ *vb* **im·plored; im·plor·ing** : BESEECH, ENTREAT *syn* supplicate, beg, importune, plead

im·ply \im-ˈplī\ *vb* **im·plied; im·ply·ing** 1 : to involve or indicate by inference, association, or necessary consequence rather than by direct statement ⟨war *implies* fighting⟩ 2 : to express indirectly : hint at : SUGGEST

im·po·lite \ˌim-pə-ˈlīt\ *adj* : not polite : RUDE, DISCOURTEOUS

im·pol·i·tic \(ˈ)im-ˈpäl-ə-ˌtik\ *adj* : not politic : RASH

im·pon·der·a·ble \(ˈ)im-ˈpän-d(ə-)rə-bər\ *adj* : incapable of being weighed or evaluated with exactness — **imponderable** *n*

¹im·port \im-ˈpōrt\ *vb* 1 : MEAN, SIGNIFY 2 : to bring (as merchandise) into a place or country from a foreign or external source — **im·port·er** *n*

²im·port \ˈim-ˌpōrt\ *n* 1 : IMPORTANCE, SIGNIFICANCE 2 : MEANING, SIGNIFICATION 3 : something (as merchandise) brought in from another country

im·por·tance \im-ˈpōrt-ᵊns\ *n* : the quality or state of being important : MOMENT, SIGNIFICANCE **syn** consequence, import, weight

im·por·tant \im-ˈpōrt-ᵊnt\ *adj* 1 : marked by importance : SIGNIFICANT 2 : giving an impression of importance — **im·por·tant·ly** *adv*

im·por·ta·tion \ˌim-ˌpōr-ˈtā-shən, -pər-\ *n* 1 : the act or practice of importing 2 : something imported

im·por·tu·nate \im-ˈpōrch-(ə-)nət\ *adj* 1 : troublesomely urgent 2 : BURDENSOME, TROUBLESOME

im·por·tune \ˌim-pər-ˈt(y)ün, im-ˈpōrchən\ *vb* -tuned; -tun·ing : to urge or beg with troublesome persistence — **im·por·tu·ni·ty** \ˌim-pər-ˈt(y)ü-nət-ē\ *n*

im·pose \im-ˈpōz\ *vb* **im·posed; im·pos·ing** 1 : to establish or apply by authority (~ a tax) ; *also* : INFLICT (*imposed* himself as leader) 2 : to make public or offer for sale with intent to deceive (~ fake antiques on buyers) 3 : OBTRUDE (*imposed* herself upon others) 4 : to take unwarranted advantage of something (~ on her good nature) — **im·po·si·tion** \ˌim-pə-ˈzish-ən\ *n*

im·pos·ing \im-ˈpō-ziŋ\ *adj* : impressive because of size, bearing, dignity, or grandeur — **im·pos·ing·ly** *adv*

im·pos·si·ble \(ˈ)im-ˈpäs-ə-bəl\ *adj* 1 : incapable of being or of occurring 2 : felt to be too difficult 3 : extremely undesirable : UNACCEPTABLE — **im·pos·si·bil·i·ty** \(ˌ)im-ˌpäs-ə-ˈbil-ət-ē\ *n* — **im·pos·si·bly** \(ˈ)im-ˈpäs-ə-blē\ *adv*

¹im·post \ˈim-ˌpōst\ *n* : TAX, DUTY

²impost *n* : a block, capital, or molding from which an arch springs

im·pos·tor *or* **im·pos·ter** \im-ˈpäs-tər\ *n* : one that assumes an identity or title not his own in order to deceive

im·pos·ture \im-ˈpäs-chər\ *n* : DECEPTION; *esp* : fraudulent impersonation

im·po·tent \ˈim-pət-ənt\ *adj* 1 : lacking in power or strength : HELPLESS 2 : unable to copulate; *also* : STERILE — **im·po·tence** \-pət-əns\ *n* — **im·po·ten·cy** \-ən-sē\ *n* — **im·po·tent·ly** *adv*

im·pound \im-ˈpaund\ *vb* 1 : CONFINE, ENCLOSE (~ stray dogs) 2 : to seize and hold in legal custody 3 : to collect in a reservoir (~ water) — **im·pound·ment** \-ˈpaun(d)-mənt\ *n*

im·pov·er·ish \im-ˈpäv-(ə-)rish\ *vb* : to make poor; *also* : to deprive of

strength, richness, or fertility — **im·pov·er·ish·ment** *n*

im·prac·ti·ca·ble \(ˈ)im-ˈprak-ti-kə-bəl\ *adj* : not practicable : incapable of being put into practice or use

im·prac·ti·cal \(ˈ)im-ˈprak-ti-kəl\ *adj* 1 : not practical 2 : IMPRACTICABLE

im·pre·cate \ˈim-pri-ˌkāt\ *vb* **-cat·ed; -cat·ing** : CURSE — **im·pre·ca·tion** \ˌim-pri-ˈkā-shən\ *n*

im·pre·cise \ˌim-pri-ˈsīs\ *adj* : not precise — **im·pre·cise·ly** *adv* — **im·pre·cise·ness** *n* — **im·pre·ci·sion** \-ˈsizh-ən\ *n*

im·preg·na·ble \im-ˈpreg-nə-bəl\ *adj* : able to resist attack : UNCONQUERABLE, UNASSAILABLE — **im·preg·na·bil·i·ty** \(ˌ)im-ˌpreg-nə-ˈbil-ət-ē\ *n*

im·preg·nate \im-ˈpreg-ˌnāt\ *vb* **-nat·ed; -nat·ing** 1 : to fertilize or make pregnant 2 : to fill or soak with some other substance — **im·preg·na·tion** \ˌim-ˌpreg-ˈnā-shən\ *n*

im·pre·sa·rio \ˌim-prə-ˈsär-ē-ˌō\ *n, pl* **-ri·os** [It, fr. *impresa* undertaking, fr. *imprendere* to undertake] 1 : the manager or conductor of an opera or concert company 2 : one who puts on an entertainment 3 : MANAGER, PRODUCER

¹im·press \im-ˈpres\ *vb* 1 : to apply with or produce (as a mark) by pressure : IMPRINT 2 : to press, stamp, or print in or upon 3 : to produce a vivid impression of 4 : to affect esp. forcibly or deeply — **im·press·ible** *adj*

²im·press \ˈim-ˌpres\ *n* 1 : a characteristic or distinctive mark : STAMP 2 : IMPRESSION, EFFECT 3 : a mark made by pressure : IMPRINT 4 : an image of something formed by or as if by pressure; *esp* : SEAL 5 : a product of pressure or influence

³im·press \im-ˈpres\ *vb* 1 : to force into naval service 2 : to get the aid or services of by forcible argument or persuasion — **im·press·ment** *n*

im·pres·sion \im-ˈpresh-ən\ *n* 1 : a stamp, form, or figure made by impressing : IMPRINT 2 : an esp. marked influence or effect on feeling, sense, or mind 3 : a characteristic trait or feature resulting from influence : IMPRESS 4 : a single print or copy (as from type or from an engraved plate or book) 5 : all the copies of a publication (as a book) printed for one issue : PRINTING 6 : a usu. vague notion, recollection, belief, or opinion 7 : an imitation in caricature of a noted personality as a form of entertainment

im·pres·sion·able \im-ˈpresh-(ə-)nə-bəl\ *adj* : capable of being easily impressed : easily molded or influenced

im·pres·sion·ism \im-ˈpresh-ə-ˌniz-əm\ *n* 1 *often cap* : a theory or practice in modern art of depicting the natural appearances of objects by dabs or strokes of primary unmixed colors in order to simulate actual reflected light 2 : the depiction of scene, emotion, or character by details intended to achieve a vividness or effectiveness esp. by evoking subjective and sensory impressions — **im·pres·sion·is·tic** \(,)im-ˌpresh-ə-ˈnis-tik\ adj

im·pres·sion·ist \im-ˈpresh-(ə-)nəst\ n 1 often cap : a painter who practices impressionism 2 : an entertainer who does impressions

im·pres·sive \im-ˈpres-iv\ adj : making or tending to make a marked impression (an ∼ speech) — **im·pres·sive·ly** adv — **im·pres·sive·ness** n

im·pri·ma·tur \ˌim-prə-ˈmä-ˌtu̇(ə)r\ n [NL, let it be printed] 1 : a license to print or publish; also : official approval of a publication by a censor 2 : SANCTION, APPROVAL

¹**im·print** \im-ˈprint, ˈim-ˌprint\ vb 1 : to stamp or mark by or as if by pressure : IMPRESS 2 : to fix firmly (as on the memory)

²**im·print** \ˈim-ˌprint\ n 1 : something imprinted or printed : IMPRESS 2 : a publisher's name printed at the foot of a title page 3 : an indelible distinguishing effect or influence

im·pris·on \im-ˈpriz-ⁿn\ vb : to put in or as if in prison : CONFINE — **im·pris·on·ment** \im-ˈpriz-n-mənt\ n

im·prob·a·ble \(ˈ)im-ˈpräb-ə-bəl\ adj : unlikely to be true or to occur — **im·prob·a·bil·i·ty** \(,)im-ˌpräb-ə-ˈbil-ət-ē\ n — **im·prob·a·bly** \(ˈ)im-ˈpräb-ə-blē\ adv

im·promp·tu \im-ˈprämp-t(y)ü\ adj [F, fr. impromptu extemporaneously, fr. L in promptu in readiness] 1 : made or done on or as if on the spur of the moment 2 : EXTEMPORANEOUS, UNREHEARSED — **impromptu** adv or n

im·prop·er \(ˈ)im-ˈpräp-ər\ adj 1 : not proper, fit, or suitable 2 : INCORRECT, INACCURATE 3 : not in accord with propriety, modesty, or good manners — **im·prop·er·ly** adv

improper fraction n : a fraction whose numerator is equal to or larger than the denominator

im·pro·pri·e·ty \ˌim-prə-ˈprī-ət-ē\ n, pl **-eties** 1 : the quality or state of being improper 2 : an improper act or remark; esp : an unacceptable use of a word or of language

im·prove \im-ˈprüv\ vb **im·proved; im·prov·ing** 1 : INCREASE, AUGMENT (education improved his chances) 2 : to enhance or increase in value or quality (∼ farmlands by cultivation) 3 : to grow or become better (∼ in health) 4 : to make good use of (∼ the time by reading) — **im·prov·able** \-ˈprü-və-bəl\ adj

im·prove·ment \im-ˈprüv-mənt\ n 1 : the act or process of improving 2 : increased value or excellence of something 3 : something that adds to the value or appearance of a thing

im·prov·i·dent \(ˈ)im-ˈpräv-əd-ənt\ adj : not providing for the future — **im·prov·i·dence** \-əns\ n

im·pro·vise \ˈim-prə-ˌvīz\ vb **-vised;**

-vis·ing [F improviser, fr. It improvvisare, fr. improvviso sudden, fr. L improvisus, lit., unforeseen] 1 : to compose, recite, play, or sing on the spur of the moment 2 : EXTEMPORIZE (∼ on the piano) 2 : to make, invent, or arrange offhand (∼ a sail out of shirts) — **im·pro·vi·sa·tion** \im-ˌpräv-ə-ˈzā-shən, ˌim-prə-və-\ n — **im·pro·vis·er** or **im·pro·vi·sor** \ˈim-prə-ˌvī-zər, ˈim-prə-ˌvī-\ n

im·pru·dent \(ˈ)im-ˈprüd-ⁿnt\ adj : not prudent : lacking discretion — **im·pru·dence** \-ⁿns\ n

im·pu·dent \ˈim-pyəd-ənt\ adj : marked by contemptuous boldness or disregard of others — **im·pu·dence** \-əns\ n — **im·pu·dent·ly** adv

im·pugn \im-ˈpyün\ vb [ME, deriv. of L impugnare, deriv. of pugnare to fight] : to attack by words or arguments : oppose or attack as false (∼ the motives of an opponent)

im·puis·sance \im-ˈpwis-ⁿns, -ˈpyü-ə-səns\ n [ME, fr. MF] : the quality or state of being powerless : WEAKNESS

im·pulse \ˈim-ˌpəls\ n 1 : a force that starts a body into motion; also : the motion produced by such a force 2 : an arousing of the mind and spirit to action; also : a wave of nervous excitation 3 : a natural tendency

im·pul·sion \im-ˈpəl-shən\ n 1 : the act of impelling : the state of being impelled 2 : a force that impels 3 : IMPETUS 4 : a sudden inclination

im·pul·sive \im-ˈpəl-siv\ adj 1 : having the power of or actually driving or impelling 2 : acting or prone to act on impulse (∼ buying) — **im·pul·sive·ly** adv — **im·pul·sive·ness** n

im·pu·ni·ty \im-ˈpyü-nət-ē\ n [MF or L; MF impunité, fr. L impunitas, fr. impune without punishment, fr. poena pain, punishment] : exemption from punishment, harm, or loss

im·pure \(ˈ)im-ˈpyu̇r\ adj 1 : not pure : UNCHASTE, OBSCENE 2 : DIRTY, FOUL 3 : ADULTERATED, MIXED — **im·pu·ri·ty** \-ˈpyu̇r-ət-ē\ n

im·pute \im-ˈpyüt\ vb **im·put·ed; im·put·ing** 1 : to lay the responsibility or blame for often falsely or unjustly : CHARGE 2 : to credit to a person or a cause : ATTRIBUTE — **im·put·able** \-ˈpyüt-ə-bəl\ adj — **im·pu·ta·tion** \ˌim-pyə-ˈtā-shən\ n

¹**in** \ˈin\ prep 1 — used to indicate physical surroundings (swim ∼ the lake) 2 : INTO 1 (ran ∼ the house) 3 : DURING (∼ the summer) 4 : WITH (written ∼ pencil) 5 — used to indicate one's situation or state of being (∼ luck) (∼ love) 6 — used to indicate manner or purpose (∼ a hurry) (said ∼ reply) 7 : INTO 2 (broke ∼ pieces)

²**in** \ˈin\ adv 1 : to or toward the inside (come ∼) 2 : to or toward some destination or place (flew ∼ from the South) 2 : at close quarters : NEAR (the enemy closed ∼) 3 : into the

midst of something ⟨mix ∼ the flour⟩ 4 : to or at its proper place ⟨fit a piece ∼⟩ 5 : WITHIN ⟨locked ∼⟩ 6 : in vogue or season; *also* : at hand 7 : in a completed or terminated state

³in \'in\ *adj* 1 : located inside or within 2 : that is in position, connection, operation, or power ⟨the ∼ party⟩ 3 : directed inward : INCOMING ⟨the ∼ train⟩ 4 : keenly aware of and responsive to what is new and smart ⟨the ∼ crowd⟩ 5 : extremely fashionable ⟨the ∼ thing to do⟩

⁴in \'in\ *n* 1 : one who is in office or power or on the inside 2 : INFLUENCE, PULL ⟨he has an ∼ with the owner⟩

⁵in *abbr* 1 inch 2 inlet

In *symbol* indium

IN *abbr* Indiana

in- \(')in, ₁in\ *prefix* 1 : not : NON-, UN- 2 : opposite of : contrary to

inacceptable	indefensible
inaccessibility	indemonstrable
inaccessible	indestructible
inaccuracy	indeterminable
inaccurate	indiscernible
inaction	indistinguishable
inactive	inedible
inactivity	ineducable
inadmissibility	inefficacious
inadmissible	inefficacy
inadvisability	inelastic
inadvisable	inelasticity
inapplicable	inequitable
inapposite	inequity
inappreciative	ineradicable
inapproachable	inexpedient
inappropriate	inexpensive
inapt	inexpressive
inartistic	inextinguishable
inattentive	infeasible
inaudible	inharmonious
inaudibly	inhospitable
inauspicious	injudicious
incautious	inoffensive
incomprehension	insanitary
inconceivable	insensitive
inconclusive	insensitivity
inconsistency	insignificance
inconsistent	insignificant
incoordination	insuppressible
indecipherable	insusceptible

in·a·bil·i·ty \₁in-ə-'bil-ət-ē\ *n* : the quality or state of being unable

in ab·sen·tia \₁in-ab-'sen-ch(ē-)ə\ *adv* : in one's absence

in·ac·ti·vate \(')in-'ak-tə-₁vāt\ *vb* : to make inactive — **in·ac·ti·va·tion** \(₁)in-₁ak-tə-'vā-shən\ *n*

in·ad·e·quate \(')in-'ad-i-kwət\ *adj* : not adequate : INSUFFICIENT — **in·ad·e·qua·cy** \-kwə-sē\ *n* — **in·ad·e·quate·ly** *adv* — **in·ad·e·quate·ness** *n*

in·ad·ver·tent \₁in-əd-'vərt-ᵊnt\ *adj* 1 : HEEDLESS, INATTENTIVE 2 : UNINTENTIONAL — **in·ad·ver·tence** \-ᵊns\ *n* — **in·ad·ver·ten·cy** \-ᵊn-sē\ *n* — **in·ad·ver·tent·ly** *adv*

in·alien·able \(')in-'āl-yə-nə-bəl, -'ā-lē-ə-nə-\ *adj* : incapable of being alienated, surrendered, or transferred ⟨∼

rights⟩ — **in·alien·abil·i·ty** \(₁)in-₁āl-yə-nə-'bil-ət-ē, -₁ā-lē-ə-nə-\ *n* — **in·alien·ably** \(')in-'āl-yə-nə-blē, -'ā-lē-ə-nə-\ *adv*

in·amo·ra·ta \in-₁am-ə-'rät-ə\ *n* : a woman with whom one is in love

inane \in-'ān\ *adj* **inan·er; -est** : EMPTY, INSUBSTANTIAL; *also* : SHALLOW, SILLY — **inan·i·ty** \in-'an-ət-ē\ *n*

in·an·i·mate \(')in-'an-ə-mət\ *adj* : not animate or animated : lacking the qualities of living things — **in·an·i·mate·ly** *adv* — **in·an·i·mate·ness** *n*

in·ap·pre·cia·ble \₁in-ə-'prē-shə-bəl\ *adj* : too small to be perceived — **in·ap·pre·cia·bly** \-blē\ *adv*

in·ap·ti·tude \(')in-'ap-tə-₁t(y)üd\ *n* : lack of aptitude

in·ar·tic·u·late \₁in-är-'tik-yə-lət\ *adj* 1 : not understandable as spoken words 2 : MUTE 3 : incapable of being expressed by speech; *also* : UNSPOKEN 4 : not having the power of distinct utterance or effective expression — **in·ar·tic·u·late·ly** *adv*

in·as·much as \₁in-əz-₁məch-əz\ *conj* : seeing that : SINCE

in·at·ten·tion \₁in-ə-'ten-chən\ *n* : failure to pay attention : DISREGARD

¹in·au·gu·ral \in-'ȯ-gyə-rəl, -g(ə-)rəl\ *adj* 1 : of or relating to an inauguration 2 : marking a beginning

²inaugural *n* 1 : an inaugural address 2 : INAUGURATION

in·au·gu·rate \in-'ȯ-g(y)ə-₁rāt\ *vb* **-rat·ed; -rat·ing** 1 : to introduce into an office with suitable ceremonies : INSTALL 2 : to dedicate ceremoniously 3 : BEGIN, INITIATE — **in·au·gu·ra·tion** \-₁ȯ-g(y)ə-'rā-shən\ *n*

in·board \'in-₁bȯrd\ *adv* 1 : inside the hull of a ship 2 : close or closest to the center line of a ship or aircraft — **inboard** *adj*

in·born \'in-'bȯrn\ *adj* : present from birth rather than acquired : NATURAL syn innate, congenital, native

in·bound \'in-₁baúnd\ *adj* : inward bound ⟨∼ traffic⟩

in·bred \'in-'bred\ *adj* 1 : INBORN, INNATE 2 : subjected to or produced by inbreeding

in·breed·ing \'in-₁brēd-iŋ\ *n* 1 : the interbreeding of closely related individuals esp. to preserve and fix desirable characters of and to eliminate unfavorable characters from a stock 2 : confinement to a narrow range or a local or limited field of choice — **in·breed** \-'brēd\ *vb*

inc *abbr* 1 incomplete 2 incorporated 3 increase

In·ca \'iŋ-kə\ *n* [Sp, fr. Quechua (a So. American Indian language) *inka* king, prince] 1 : a noble or a member of the ruling family of an Indian empire of Peru, Bolivia, and Ecuador until the Spanish conquest 2 : a member of any people under Inca influence

in·cal·cu·la·ble \(')in-'kal-kyə-lə-bəl\ *adj* : not capable of being calculated;

esp : too large or numerous to be calculated — **in·cal·cu·la·bly** \-blē\ *adv*

in·can·des·cent \,in-kən-ˈdes-ᵊnt\ *adj* **1** : glowing with heat **2** : SHINING, BRILLIANT — **in·can·des·cence** \-ᵊns\ *n*

incandescent lamp *n* : a lamp in which an electrically heated filament emits light

in·can·ta·tion \,in-,kan-ˈtā-shən\ *n* : a use of spells or verbal charms spoken or sung as a part of a ritual of magic; *also* : a formula of words used in or as if in such a ritual

in·ca·pa·ble \(ˈ)in-ˈkā-pə-bəl\ *adj* : lacking ability or qualification for a particular purpose; *also* : UNQUALIFIED — **in·ca·pa·bil·i·ty** \(,)in-,kā-pə-ˈbil-ət-ē\ *n*

in·ca·pac·i·tate \,in-kə-ˈpas-ə-,tāt\ *vb* **-tat·ed; -tat·ing** : to make incapable or unfit : DISQUALIFY, DISABLE

in·ca·pac·i·ty \,in-kə-ˈpas-ət-ē\ *n, pl* **-ties** : the quality or state of being incapable

in·car·cer·ate \in-ˈkär-sə-,rāt\ *vb* **-at·ed; -at·ing** : IMPRISON, CONFINE — **in·car·cer·a·tion** \(,)in-,kär-sə-ˈrā-shən\ *n*

in·car·na·dine \in-ˈkär-nə-,dīn, -,dēn\ *vb* **-dined; -din·ing** : REDDEN

in·car·nate \in-ˈkär-nət, -,nāt\ *adj* **1** : having bodily and esp. human form and substance **2** : PERSONIFIED — **in·car·nate** \-,nāt\ *vb*

in·car·na·tion \,in-,kär-ˈnā-shən\ *n* **1** : the embodiment of a deity or spirit in an earthly form **2** *cap* : the union of divine and human natures in Jesus Christ **3** : a person showing a trait or typical character to a marked degree **4** : the act of incarnating : the state of being incarnate

incase *var of* ENCASE

in·cen·di·ary \in-ˈsen-dē-,er-ē\ *adj* **1** : of or relating to a deliberate burning of property **2** : tending to excite or inflame **3** : designed to kindle fires ⟨an ~ bomb⟩ **incendiary** *n*

¹in·cense \ˈin-,sens\ *n* **1** : material used to produce a fragrant odor when burned **2** : the perfume or smoke from some spices and gums when burned

²in·cense \in-ˈsens\ *vb* **in·censed; in·cens·ing** : to make extremely angry

in·cen·tive \in-ˈsent-iv\ *n* [ME, fr. LL *incentivum*, fr. *incentivus* stimulating, fr. L, setting the tune, fr. *incinere* to set the tune, fr. *canere* to sing] : something that incites or is likely to incite to determination or action

in·cep·tion \in-ˈsep-shən\ *n* : BEGINNING, COMMENCEMENT

in·cer·ti·tude \(ˈ)in-ˈsərt-ə-,t(y)üd\ *n* **1** : UNCERTAINTY, DOUBT, INDECISION **2** : INSECURITY, INSTABILITY

in·ces·sant \(ˈ)in-ˈses-ᵊnt\ *adj* : continuing or flowing without interruption ⟨~ rains⟩ — **in·ces·sant·ly** *adv*

in·cest \ˈin-,sest\ *n* [ME, fr. L *incestum*, fr. *incestus* impure, fr. *castus* pure] : sexual intercourse between persons so closely related that marriage is illegal — **in·ces·tu·ous** \in-ˈses-chə-wəs\ *adj*

¹inch \ˈinch\ *n* [ME, fr. OE *ynce*, fr. L *uncia* twelfth part, inch, ounce] — see WEIGHT table

²inch *vb* : to move by small degrees

in·cho·ate \in-ˈkō-ət, in-kə-,wāt\ *adj* [L *inchoatus*, pp. of *inchoare*, lit., to hitch up, fr. *cohum* fastening a plow beam to the yoke] : being only partly in existence or operation : INCOMPLETE, INCIPIENT

inch·worm \ˈinch-,wərm\ *n* : LOOPER

in·ci·dence \ˈin-səd-əns\ *n* : rate of occurrence or effect

¹in·ci·dent \ˈin-səd-ənt\ *n* **1** : OCCURRENCE, HAPPENING **2** : an action likely to lead to grave consequences esp. in diplomatic matters

²incident *adj* **1** : occurring or likely to occur esp. in connection with some other happening **2** : falling or striking on something ⟨~ light rays⟩

¹in·ci·den·tal \,in-sə-ˈdent-ᵊl\ *adj* **1** : subordinate, nonessential, or attendant in position or significance ⟨~ expenses⟩ **2** : CASUAL, CHANCE — **in·ci·den·tal·ly** \-ē\ *adv*

²incidental *n* **1** *pl* : minor items (as of expense) that are not individually accounted for **2** : something that is incidental

in·cin·er·ate \in-ˈsin-ə-,rāt\ *vb* **-at·ed; -at·ing** : to burn to ashes

in·cin·er·a·tor \in-ˈsin-ə-,rāt-ər\ *n* : a furnace for burning waste

in·cip·i·ent \in-ˈsip-ē-ənt\ *adj* : beginning to be or become apparent

in·cise \in-ˈsīz\ *vb* **in·cised; in·cis·ing** : to cut into : CARVE, ENGRAVE

in·ci·sion \in-ˈsizh-ən\ *n* : CUT, GASH; *esp* : a surgical wound

in·ci·sive \in-ˈsī-siv\ *adj* : impressively direct and decisive — **in·ci·sive·ly** *adv*

in·ci·sor \in-ˈsī-zər\ *n* : a tooth for cutting; *esp* : one of the cutting teeth in front of the canines of a mammal

in·cite \in-ˈsīt\ *vb* **in·cit·ed; in·cit·ing** : to arouse to action : stir up — **in·cite·ment** *n*

in·ci·vil·i·ty \,in-sə-ˈvil-ət-ē\ *n* **1** : DISCOURTESY, RUDENESS **2** : a rude or discourteous act

incl *abbr* including; inclusive

in·clem·ent \(ˈ)in-ˈklem-ənt\ *adj* : SEVERE, STORMY ⟨~ weather⟩ — **in·clem·en·cy** \-ən-sē\ *n*

in·cli·na·tion \,in-klə-ˈnā-shən\ *n* **1** : PROPENSITY, BENT; *esp* : LIKING **2** : BOW, NOD ⟨an ~ of the head⟩ **3** : a tilting of something **4** : SLANT, SLOPE

¹in·cline \in-ˈklīn\ *vb* **in·clined; in·clin·ing** **1** : BOW, BEND **2** : to be drawn toward an opinion or course of action **3** : to deviate from the vertical or horizontal : SLOPE **4** : INFLUENCE, PERSUADE

²in·cline \ˈin-,klīn\ *n* : SLOPE

inclose, inclosure *var of* ENCLOSE, ENCLOSURE

in·clude \in-ˈklüd\ *vb* **in·clud·ed; in·clud·ing** : to take in or comprise as a part of a whole ⟨the price ∼s tax⟩ — **in·clu·sion** \in-'klü-zhən\ n — **in·clu·sive** \-'klü-siv\ adj

incog abbr incognito

¹**in·cog·ni·to** \in-₁käg-'nēt-ō, in-'käg-nə-₁tō\ adv or adj [It, fr. L incognitus unknown, fr. cognoscere to know] : with one's identity concealed

²**incognito** n, pl **-tos 1** : one appearing or living incognito **2** : the state or disguise of an incognito

in·co·her·ent \in-kō-'hir-ənt, -'her-\ adj **1** : not sticking closely or compactly together : LOOSE **2** : not clearly or logically connected : RAMBLING — **in·co·her·ence** \-əns\ n — **in·co·her·ent·ly** adv

in·com·bus·ti·ble \in-kəm-'bəs-tə-bəl\ adj : incapable of being burned — **incombustible** n

in·come \'in-₁kəm\ n : a gain usu. measured in money that derives from labor, business, or property

income tax \-in-(₁)kəm-\ n : a tax on the net income of an individual or business concern

in·com·ing \'in-₁kəm-iŋ\ adj : coming in ⟨the ∼ tide⟩ ⟨∼ freshmen⟩

in·com·men·su·rate \₁in-kə-'mens-(ə-)rət, -'mench-(ə-)rət\ adj : not commensurate; esp : INADEQUATE

in·com·mode \₁in-kə-'mōd\ vb **-mod·ed; -mod·ing** : INCONVENIENCE, DISTURB

in·com·mu·ni·ca·ble \₁in-kə-'myü-ni-kə-bəl\ adj : not communicable : not capable of being communicated or imparted; also : UNCOMMUNICATIVE

in·com·mu·ni·ca·do \₁in-kə-₁myü-nə-'käd-ō\ adv or adj : without means of communication; also : in solitary confinement ⟨a prisoner held ∼⟩

in·com·pa·ra·ble \(')in-'käm-p(ə-)rə-bəl\ adj **1** : eminent beyond comparison : MATCHLESS **2** : not suitable for comparison

in·com·pat·i·ble \₁in-kəm-'pat-ə-bəl\ adj : incapable of or unsuitable for association or use together ⟨∼ colors⟩ ⟨temperamentally ∼⟩ — **in·com·pat·i·bil·i·ty** \₁in-kəm-₁pat-ə-'bil-ət-ē\ n

in·com·pe·tent \(')in-'käm-pət-ənt\ adj **1** : not legally qualified **2** : not competent : lacking sufficient knowledge, skill, or ability — **in·com·pe·tence** \-pət-əns\ n — **in·com·pe·ten·cy** \-ən-sē\ n — **incompetent** n

in·com·plete \₁in-kəm-'plēt\ adj : lacking a part or parts : UNFINISHED, IMPERFECT — **in·com·plete·ly** adv — **in·com·plete·ness** n

in·com·pre·hen·si·ble \₁in-₁käm-pē-'hen-sə-bəl adj : impossible to comprehend : UNINTELLIGIBLE

in·com·press·ible \₁in-kəm-'pres-ə-bəl\ adj : not capable of or resistant to compression

in·con·gru·ent \in-kən-'grü-ənt, (')in-'käŋ-grə-wənt\ adj : not congruent

in·con·gru·ous \(')in-'käŋ-grə-wəs\ adj : not consistent with or suitable to the surroundings or associations — **in·con·gru·ity** \in-kən-'grü-ət-ē, -₁kän-\ n — **in·con·gru·ous·ly** \(')in-'käŋ-grə-wəs-lē\ adv

in·con·se·quen·tial \in-₁kän-sə-'kwen-chəl\ adj **1** : ILLOGICAL: also : IRRELEVANT **2** : of no significance : UNIMPORTANT — **in·con·se·quence** \(')in-'kän-sə-₁kwens\ n — **in·con·se·quen·tial·ly** \in-₁kän-sə-'kwench-(ə-)lē\ adv

in·con·sid·er·able \in-kən-'sid-ər-(ə-)bəl, -'sid-rə-bəl\ adj : SLIGHT, TRIVIAL

in·con·sid·er·ate \in-kən-'sid-(ə-)rət\ adj : HEEDLESS, THOUGHTLESS; esp : not respecting the rights or feelings of others — **in·con·sid·er·ate·ly** adv — **in·con·sid·er·ate·ness** n

in·con·sol·able \in-kən-'sō-lə-bəl\ adj : incapable of being consoled — **in·con·sol·ably** \-blē\ adv

in·con·spic·u·ous \in-kən-'spik-yə-wəs\ adj : not readily noticeable — **in·con·spic·u·ous·ly** adv

in·con·stant \(')in-'kän-stənt\ adj : not constant : CHANGEABLE syn fickle, capricious, mercurial, unstable, volatile — **in·con·stan·cy** \-stən-sē\ n — **in·con·stant·ly** adv

in·con·test·able \in-kən-'tes-tə-bəl\ adj : not contestable : INDISPUTABLE — **in·con·test·ably** \-'tes-tə-blē\ adv

in·con·ti·nent \(')in-'känt-ᵊn-ənt\ adj **1** : lacking self-restraint **2** : unable to retain a bodily discharge (as urine) voluntarily — **in·con·ti·nence** \-ᵊn-əns\ n

in·con·tro·vert·ible \₁in-₁kän-trə-'vərt-ə-bəl\ adj : not open to question : INDISPUTABLE ⟨∼ evidence⟩ — **in·con·tro·vert·ibly** \-blē\ adv

¹**in·con·ve·nience** \in-kən-'vē-nyəns\ n **1** : something that is inconvenient **2** : the quality or state of being inconvenient

²**inconvenience** vb : to subject to inconvenience

in·con·ve·nient \in-kən-'vē-nyənt\ adj : not convenient : causing trouble or annoyance : INOPPORTUNE — **in·con·ve·nient·ly** adv

in·cor·po·rate \in-'kór-pə-₁rāt\ vb **-rat·ed; -rat·ing 1** : to unite closely or so as to form one body : BLEND **2** : to form, form into, or become a corporation **3** : to give material form to : EMBODY — **in·cor·po·ra·tion** \-₁kór-pə-'rā-shən\ n

in·cor·po·re·al \₁in-kór-'pōr-ē-əl\ adj : having no material body or form

in·cor·rect \₁in-kə-'rekt\ adj **1** : INACCURATE, FAULTY **2** : not true : WRONG **3** : UNBECOMING, IMPROPER — **in·cor·rect·ly** \-'rek-(t)lē\ adv — **in·cor·rect·ness** \-'rek(t)-nəs\ n

in·cor·ri·gi·ble \(')in-'kór-ə-jə-bəl\ adj : incapable of being corrected, amended, or reformed — **in·cor·ri·gi·bil·i·ty** \(₁)in-₁kór-ə-jə-'bil-ət-ē\ n — **in·cor·ri·gi·bly** \(')in-'kór-ə-jə-blē\ adv

in·cor·rupt·ible \₁in-kə-'rəp-tə-bəl\ adj **1** : not subject to decay or dissolution **2** : incapable of being bribed or morally corrupted — **in·cor·rupt·ibil·i·ty** \-ˌrəp-tə-ˈbil-ət-ē\ n —**in·cor·rupt·ibly** \-ˈrəp-tə-blē\ adv

incr abbr increase; increased

¹**in·crease** \in-ˈkrēs, ˈin-ˌkrēs\ vb **increased; in·creas·ing** 1 : to become greater : GROW 2 : to multiply by the production of young (rabbits ~ rapidly) 3 : to make greater — **in·creas·ing·ly** \-ˈkrē-siŋ-lē\ adv

²**in·crease** \ˈin-ˌkrēs, in-ˈkrēs\ n 1 : addition or enlargement in size, extent, or quantity : GROWTH 2 : something (as offspring, produce, or profit) that is added

in·cred·i·ble \(ˈ)in-ˈkred-ə-bəl\ adj : too extraordinary and improbable to be believed; also : hard to believe — **in·cred·i·bil·i·ty** \(ˌ)in-ˌkred-ə-ˈbil-ət-ē\ n — **in·cred·i·bly** \(ˈ)in-ˈkred-ə-blē\ adv

in·cred·u·lous \(ˈ)in-ˈkrej-ə-ləs\ adj 1 : SKEPTICAL 2 : expressing disbelief — **in·cre·du·li·ty** \ˌin-kri-ˈd(y)ü-lət-ē\ n — **in·cred·u·lous·ly** adv

in·cre·ment \ˈiŋ-krə-mənt, ˈin-\ n 1 : the action or process of increasing esp. in quantity or value : ENLARGEMENT; also : QUANTITY 2 : something gained or added; esp : one of a series of regular consecutive additions — **in·cre·men·tal** \ˌiŋ-krə-ˈment-ᵊl, ˌin-\ adj — **in·cre·men·tal·ly** \-ᵊl-ē\ adv

in·crim·i·nate \in-ˈkrim-ə-ˌnāt\ vb **-nat·ed; -nat·ing** : to charge with or prove involvement in a crime or fault : ACCUSE — **in·crim·i·na·tion** \-ˌkrim-ə-ˈnā-shən\ n — **in·crim·i·na·to·ry** \-ˈkrim-(ə)-nə-ˌtōr-ē\ adj

incrust var of ENCRUST

in·crus·ta·tion \ˌin-ˌkrəs-ˈtā-shən\ n 1 : the act of encrusting : the state of being encrusted 2 : CRUST; also : something resembling a crust ⟨~ of habits⟩

in·cu·bate \ˈiŋ-kyə-ˌbāt, ˈin-\ vb **-bat·ed; -bat·ing** : to sit on eggs to hatch them; also : to keep (as eggs) under conditions favorable for development — **in·cu·ba·tion** \ˌiŋ-kyə-ˈbā-shən, ˌin-\ n

in·cu·ba·tor \ˈiŋ-kyə-ˌbāt-ər, ˈin-\ n : one that incubates; esp : an apparatus providing suitable conditions (as of warmth and moisture) for incubating something

in·cu·bus \ˈiŋ-kyə-bəs, ˈin-\ n, pl **-bi** \-ˌbī, -ˌbē\ also **-bus·es** [ME, fr. LL, fr. L incubare to lie on] 1 : a spirit supposed to work evil on persons in their sleep : NIGHTMARE 3 : one that oppresses like a nightmare

in·cul·cate \in-ˈkəl-ˌkāt, ˈin-(ˌ)kəl-\ vb **-cat·ed; -cat·ing** [L inculcare, lit., to tread on, fr. calcare to trample, fr. calx heel] : to teach and impress by frequent repetitions or admonitions — **in·cul·ca·tion** \ˌin-(ˌ)kəl-ˈkā-shən\ n

in·cul·pa·ble \(ˈ)in-ˈkəl-pə-bəl\ adj : free from guilt : BLAMELESS

in·cul·pate \in-ˈkəl-ˌpāt, ˈin-(ˌ)kəl-\ vb **-pat·ed; -pat·ing** : to involve or implicate in guilt : INCRIMINATE

in·cum·ben·cy \in-ˈkəm-bən-sē\ n, pl **-cies** 1 : something that is incumbent 2 : the quality of state of being incumbent 3 : the office or period of office of an incumbent

¹**in·cum·bent** \in-ˈkəm-bənt\ n : the holder of an office or position

²**incumbent** adj 1 : imposed as a duty 2 : occupying a specified office 3 : lying or resting on something else

incumber var of ENCUMBER

in·cu·nab·u·lum \ˌin-kyə-ˈnab-yə-ləm, ˌiŋ-\ n, pl **-la** \-lə\ [NL, fr. L incunabula, pl., swaddling clothes, cradle, fr. cunae cradle] : a book printed before 1501

in·cur \in-ˈkər\ vb **in·curred; in·cur·ring** 1 : to meet with (as an inconvenience) 2 : to become liable or subject to : bring down upon oneself

in·cur·able \(ˈ)in-ˈkyúr-ə-bəl\ adj : not subject to cure — **in·cur·abil·i·ty** \(ˌ)in-ˌkyúr-ə-ˈbil-ət-ē\ n — **incurable** n — **in·cur·ably** \(ˈ)in-ˈkyúr-ə-blē\ adv

in·cu·ri·ous \(ˈ)in-ˈkyúr-ē-əs\ adj : not curious or inquisitive

in·cur·sion \in-ˈkər-zhən\ n : a sudden usu. temporary invasion : RAID

in·cus \ˈiŋ-kəs\ n, pl **in·cu·des** \iŋ-ˈkyüd-(ˌ)ēz\ [NL, fr. L, anvil] : the middle of a chain of three small bones in the ear of a mammal

ind abbr 1 independent 2 index 3 industrial; industry

Ind abbr 1 Indian 2 Indiana

in·debt·ed \in-ˈdet-əd\ adj 1 : owing money 2 : owing gratitude or recognition to another — **in·debt·ed·ness** n

in·de·cent \(ˈ)in-ˈdēs-ᵊnt\ adj : not decent : UNBECOMING, UNSEEMLY; also : morally offensive — **in·de·cen·cy** \-ᵊn-sē\ n — **in·de·cent·ly** adv

in·de·ci·sion \ˌin-di-ˈsizh-ən\ n : a wavering between two or more possible courses of action : IRRESOLUTION

in·de·ci·sive \ˌin-di-ˈsī-siv\ adj 1 : not decisive : INCONCLUSIVE 2 : marked by or prone to indecision 3 : INDEFINITE — **in·de·ci·sive·ly** adv — **in·de·ci·sive·ness** n

in·de·co·rous \(ˈ)in-ˈdek-(ə)-rəs; ˌin-di-ˈkōr-əs\ adj : not decorous syn improper, unseemly, indecent, unbecoming, indelicate — **in·de·co·rous·ly** adv — **in·de·co·rous·ness** n

in·deed \in-ˈdēd\ adv 1 : without any question : TRULY — often used interjectionally to express irony, disbelief, or surprise 2 : in reality 3 : all things considered

indef abbr indefinite

in·de·fat·i·ga·ble \ˌin-di-ˈfat-i-gə-bəl\ adj : UNTIRING — **in·de·fat·i·ga·bly** \-blē\ adv

in·de·fea·si·ble \-ˈfē-zə-bəl\ adj : not capable of or not liable to being annulled, made void, or forfeited — **in·de·fea·si·bly** \-ˈfē-zə-blē\ adv

in·de·fin·able \-ˈfī-nə-bəl\ adj : incapable of being precisely described or analyzed

in·def·i·nite \(¹)in-ˈdef-(ə-)nət\ adj 1 : not defining or identifying ⟨an is an ~ article⟩ 2 : not precise : VAGUE 3 : having no fixed limit or amount — in·def·i·nite·ly adv — in·def·i·nite·ness n

in·del·i·ble \in-ˈdel-ə-bəl\ adj [ML indelibilis, fr. L indelebilis, fr. delēre to delete, destroy] 1 : not capable of being removed or erased ⟨~impression⟩ 2 : making marks that cannot easily be removed ⟨an ~ pencil⟩ — in·del·i·bly \in-ˈdel-ə-blē\ adv

in·del·i·cate \in-ˈdel-i-kət\ adj : not delicate; esp : IMPROPER, COARSE, TACTLESS syn indecent, unseemly, indecorous, unbecoming — in·del·i·ca·cy \in-ˈdel-ə-kə-sē\ n

in·dem·ni·fy \in-ˈdem-nə-ˌfī\ vb -fied; -fy·ing [L indemnis unharmed, fr. in- not + damnum damage] 1 : to secure against hurt, loss, or damage 2 : to make compensation to for some loss or damage — in·dem·ni·fi·ca·tion \-ˌdem-nə-fə-ˈkā-shən\ n

in·dem·ni·ty \in-ˈdem-nət-ē\ n, pl -ties 1 : security against hurt, loss, or damage; also : exemption from incurred penalties or liabilities 2 : something that indemnifies

¹in·dent \in-ˈdent\ vb [ME indenten, fr. MF endenter, fr. OF, fr. dent tooth, fr. L dent-, dens] 1 : INDENTURE 2 : to make a toothlike cut on the edge of 3 : to space in (as the first line of a paragraph) from the margin

²indent vb 1 : to force inward so as to form a depression : IMPRESS ⟨~ a pattern in metal⟩ 2 : to form a dent in

in·den·ta·tion \ˌin-ˌden-ˈtā-shən\ n 1 : NOTCH; also : a usu. deep recess (as in a coastline) 2 : the action of indenting : the condition of being indented 3 : DENT 4 : INDENTION

in·den·tion \in-ˈden-chən\ n 1 : the action of indenting : the condition of being indented 2 : the blank space produced by indenting

¹in·den·ture \in-ˈden-chər\ n 1 : a written certificate or agreement; esp : a contract binding one person (as an apprentice) to work for another for a given period of time — usu. used in pl. 2 : INDENTATION 1 3 : DENT

²indenture vb in·den·tured; in·den·tur·ing : to bind (as an apprentice) by indentures

in·de·pen·dence \ˌin-də-ˈpen-dəns\ n : the quality or state of being independent : FREEDOM

Independence Day n : July 4 observed as a legal holiday in commemoration of the adoption of the Declaration of Independence in 1776

in·de·pen·dent \ˌin-də-ˈpen-dənt\ adj 1 : SELF-GOVERNING; also : not affiliated with a larger controlling unit 2 : not requiring or relying on something else or somebody else ⟨an ~ conclusion⟩ ⟨an ~ source of income⟩ 3 : not easily influenced : showing self-reliance ⟨an

~ mind⟩ 4 : not committed to a political party ⟨an ~ voter⟩ 5 : refusing or disliking to look to others for help ⟨too ~ to accept charity⟩ 6 : MAIN ⟨an ~ clause⟩ — independent n — in·de·pen·dent·ly adv

in·de·scrib·able \ˌin-di-ˈskrī-bə-bəl\ adj 1 : that cannot be described ⟨an ~ sensation⟩ 2 : being too intense or great for description — in·de·scrib·ably \-blē\ adv

in·de·ter·mi·nate \ˌin-di-ˈtərm-(ə-)nət\ adj 1 : VAGUE; also : not known in advance 2 : not limited in advance; also : not leading to a definite end or result — in·de·ter·mi·na·cy \-(ə-)nə-sē\ n — in·de·ter·mi·nate·ly adv

¹in·dex \ˈin-ˌdeks\ n, pl in·dex·es or in·di·ces \-də-ˌsēz\ 1 : POINTER, INDICATOR 2 : SIGN, TOKEN ⟨an ~ of character⟩ 3 : a guide for facilitating references; esp : an alphabetical list of items (as topics or names) treated in a printed work with the page number where each item may be found 4 : a list of restricted or prohibited material ⟨an ~ of forbidden books⟩ 5 pl usu indices : a number or symbol or expression (as an exponent) associated with another to indicate a mathematical operation or use or position in an arrangement or expansion 6 : a character ☞ used to direct attention (as to a note) 7 : INDEX NUMBER

²index vb 1 : to provide with or put into an index 2 : to serve as an index of 3 : to regulate by indexation

in·dex·a·tion \ˌin-ˌdek-ˈsā-shən\ n : a system of economic control in which a body of variables (as wages and interest) rise or fall at the same rate as an index of the cost of living

index finger n : FOREFINGER

in·dex·ing n : INDEXATION

index number n : a number used to indicate change in magnitude (as of cost) as compared with the magnitude at some specified time usu. taken as 100

index of refraction : the ratio of the velocity of radiation in the first of two media to its velocity in the second

in·dia ink \ˌin-dē-ə-\ n, often cap 1st I 1 : a black solid pigment used in drawing 2 : a fluid made from india ink

In·di·an \ˈin-dē-ən\ n 1 : a native or inhabitant of the subcontinent of India 2 : AMERICAN INDIAN — Indian adj

Indian corn n : a tall widely grown American cereal grass bearing seeds on long ears; also : its ears or seeds

Indian meal n : CORNMEAL

Indian paintbrush n : any of a genus of herbaceous plants with brightly colored bracts that are related to the snapdragon

Indian pipe n : a waxy white leafless saprophytic herb of Asia and the U.S.

Indian summer n : a period of mild weather in late autumn or early winter

In·dia paper \ˌin-dē-ə-\ n 1 : a thin absorbent paper used esp. for taking impressions (as of steel engravings) 2 : a thin tough opaque printing paper

indic *abbr* indicative

in·di·cate \'in-də-ˌkāt\ *vb* **-cat·ed; -cat·ing** **1** : to point out or to **2** : to state briefly : show indirectly : SUGGEST — **in·di·ca·tion** \ˌin-də-ˈkā-shən\ *n* — **in·di·ca·tor** \'in-də-ˌkāt-ər\ *n*

¹in·dic·a·tive \in-ˈdik-ət-iv\ *adj* **1** : of, relating to, or being a verb form that represents an act or state as a fact ⟨~ mood⟩ **2** : serving to indicate ⟨actions ~ of fear⟩

²indicative *n* **1** : the indicative mood of a language **2** : a form in the indicative mood

in·di·cia \in-ˈdish-(ē-)ə\ *n pl* **1** : distinctive marks **2** : postal markings often imprinted on mail or mailing labels

in·dict \in-ˈdīt\ *vb* **1** : to charge with an offense **2** : to charge with a crime by the finding of a grand jury — **in·dict·able** *adj* — **in·dict·ment** *n*

in·dif·fer·ent \in-ˈdif-ərnt, -ˈdif-(ə-)rənt\ *adj* **1** : UNBIASED, UNPREJUDICED **2** : of no importance one way or the other **3** : marked by no special liking for or dislike of something **4** : being neither excessive nor defective **5** : PASSABLE, MEDIOCRE **6** : being neither right nor wrong — **in·dif·fer·ence** \in-ˈdif-ərns, -ˈdif-(ə-)rəns\ *n* — **in·dif·fer·ent·ly** *adv*

in·dig·e·nous \in-ˈdij-ə-nəs\ *adj* : produced, growing, or living naturally in a particular region

in·di·gent \'in-di-jənt\ *adj* : IMPOVERISHED, NEEDY — **in·di·gence** \-jəns\ *n*

in·di·gest·ible \ˌin-dī-ˈjes-tə-bəl, -də-\ *adj* : not readily digested

in·di·ges·tion \-ˈjes-chən\ *n* : inadequate or difficult digestion : DYSPEPSIA

in·dig·nant \in-ˈdig-nənt\ *adj* : filled with or marked by indignation — **in·dig·nant·ly** *adv*

in·dig·na·tion \ˌin-dig-ˈnā-shən\ *n* : anger aroused by something unjust, unworthy, or mean

in·dig·ni·ty \in-ˈdig-nət-ē\ *n, pl* **-ties** : an offense against personal dignity or self-respect; *also* : humiliating treatment

in·di·go \'in-di-ˌgō\ *n, pl* **-gos** *or* **-goes** [It dial., fr. L *indicum*, fr. L *indikon*, fr. *indikos* Indic, fr. *Indos* India] **1** : a blue dye obtained from plants or synthesized **2** : a color between blue and violet

indigo bunting *n* : a common small finch of the eastern U.S. of which the male is largely indigo-blue

indigo snake *n* : a large harmless blue-black snake of the southern U.S.

in·di·rect \ˌin-də-ˈrekt, -dī-\ *adj* **1** : not straight ⟨an ~ route⟩ **2** : not straightforward and open ⟨~ methods⟩ **3** : not having a plainly seen connection ⟨an ~ cause⟩ **4** : not directly to the point ⟨an ~ answer⟩ — **in·di·rec·tion** \-ˈrek-shən\ *n* — **in·di·rect·ly** \-ˈrek-(t)lē\ *adv* — **in·di·rect·ness** \-ˈrek(t)-nəs\ *n*

in·dis·creet \ˌin-dis-ˈkrēt\ *adj* : not discreet : IMPRUDENT — **in·dis·cre·tion** \-dis-ˈkresh-ən\ *n*

in·dis·crim·i·nate \ˌin-dis-ˈkrim-ə-nət\ *adj* **1** : not marked by discrimination or careful distinction **2** : HAPHAZARD, RANDOM **3** : UNRESTRAINED **4** : JUMBLED, CONFUSED — **in·dis·crim·i·nate·ly** *adv*

in·dis·pens·able \ˌin-dis-ˈpen-sə-bəl\ *adj* : absolutely essential : REQUISITE — **in·dis·pens·abil·i·ty** \-ˌpen-sə-ˈbil-ət-ē\ *n* — **indispensable** *n* — **in·dis·pens·ably** \-ˈpen-sə-blē\ *adv*

in·dis·posed \-ˈpōzd\ *adj* **1** : slightly ill **2** : AVERSE — **in·dis·po·si·tion** \ˌ(ˌ)in-ˌdis-pə-ˈzish-ən\ *n*

in·dis·put·able \ˌin-dis-ˈpyüt-ə-bəl, (ˈ)in-dis-pyət-\ *adj* : not disputable : UNQUESTIONABLE ⟨~ proof⟩ — **in·dis·put·ably** \-blē\ *adv*

in·dis·sol·u·ble \ˌin-dis-ˈäl-yə-bəl\ *adj* : not capable of being dissolved, undone, or broken : PERMANENT

in·dis·tinct \ˌin-dis-ˈtiŋkt\ *adj* **1** : not sharply outlined or separable : BLURRED, FAINT, DIM **2** : not readily distinguishable : UNCERTAIN — **in·dis·tinct·ly** *adv* — **in·dis·tinct·ness** *n*

in·dite \in-ˈdīt\ *vb* **in·dit·ed; in·dit·ing** : COMPOSE ⟨~ a poem⟩; *also* : to put in writing ⟨~ a letter⟩

in·di·um \'in-dē-əm\ *n* : a malleable silvery metallic chemical element

indiv *abbr* individual

¹in·di·vid·u·al \ˌin-də-ˈvij-(ə-w)əl\ *adj* **1** : of, relating to, or used by an individual ⟨~ traits⟩ **2** : being an individual : existing as an indivisible whole **3** : intended for one person ⟨an ~ serving⟩ **4** : SEPARATE ⟨~ copies⟩ **5** : having marked individuality ⟨an ~ style⟩ — **in·di·vid·u·al·ly** \-ē\ *adv*

²individual *n* **1** : a single member of a category : a particular person, animal, or thing **2** : PERSON ⟨a disagreeable ~⟩

in·di·vid·u·al·ism \ˌin-də-ˈvij-ə-(wə-)ˌliz-əm\ *n* **1** : EGOISM **2** : a doctrine that the interests of the individual are primary **3** : a doctrine holding that the individual has political or economic rights with which the state must not interfere

in·di·vid·u·al·ist \-ləst\ *n* **1** : one that pursues a markedly independent course in thought or action **2** : one that advocates or practices individualism — **individualist** *or* **in·di·vid·u·al·is·tic** \-ˌvij-ə-(wə-)ˈlis-tik\ *adj*

in·di·vid·u·al·i·ty \-ˌvij-ə-ˈwal-ət-ē\ *n, pl* **-ties** **1** : the sum of qualities that characterize and distinguish an individual from all others; *also* : PERSONALITY **2** : INDIVIDUAL, PERSON **3** : separate or distinct existence

in·di·vid·u·al·ize \-ˈvij-ə-(wə-)ˌlīz\ *vb* **-ized; -iz·ing** **1** : to make individual in character **2** : to treat or notice individually : PARTICULARIZE **3** : to adapt to the needs of an individual

in·di·vid·u·ate \ˌin-də-ˈvij-ə-ˌwāt\ *vb* **-at·ed; -at·ing** : to give individuality to : form into an individual — **in·di·vid·u·a·tion** \-ˌvij-ə-ˈwā-shən\ *n*

in·di·vis·i·ble \ˌin-də-ˈviz-ə-bəl\ *adj* : not divisible — **in·di·vis·i·bil·i·ty** \-ˌviz-ə-ˈbil-ət-ē\ *n* — **in·di·vis·i·bly** \-ˈviz-ə-blē\ *adv*

in·doc·tri·nate \in-ˈdäk-trə-ˌnāt\ *vb* **-nat·ed; -nat·ing 1** : to instruct esp. in fundamentals or rudiments : TEACH **2** : to teach the beliefs and doctrines of a particular group — **in·doc·tri·na·tion** \(ˌ)in-ˌdäk-trə-ˈnā-shən\ *n*

In·do-Eu·ro·pe·an \ˌin-dō-ˌyùr-ə-ˈpē-ən\ *adj* : of, relating to, or constituting a family of languages comprising those spoken in most of Europe and in the parts of the world colonized by Europeans since 1500 and also in Persia, the subcontinent of India, and some other parts of Asia

in·do·lent \ˈin-də-lənt\ *adj* [LL *indolens* insensitive to pain, fr. L *dolēre* to feel pain] **1** : slow to develop or heal (~ ulcers) **2** : LAZY — **in·do·lence** \-ləns\ *n*

in·dom·i·ta·ble \in-ˈdäm-ət-ə-bəl\ *adj* : UNCONQUERABLE (~ courage) — **in·dom·i·ta·bly** \-blē\ *adv*

In·do·ne·sian \ˌin-də-ˈnē-zhən\ *n* : a native or inhabitant of the Republic of Indonesia — **Indonesian** *adj*

in·door \ˈin-ˌdȯr\ *adj* **1** : of or relating to the inside of a building **2** : living, located, or carried on within a building

in·doors \in-ˈdȯrz\ *adv* : in or into a building

indorse *var of* ENDORSE

in·du·bi·ta·ble \(ˈ)in-ˈd(y)ü-bət-ə-bəl\ *adj* : UNQUESTIONABLE — **in·du·bi·ta·bly** \-blē\ *adv*

in·duce \in-ˈd(y)üs\ *vb* **in·duced; in·duc·ing 1** : PERSUADE, INFLUENCE **2** : BRING ABOUT (illness *induced* by overwork) **3** : to produce (as an electric current) by induction **4** : to determine by induction; *esp* : to infer from particulars — **in·duc·er** *n*

in·duce·ment \in-ˈd(y)üs-mənt\ *n* **1** : something that induces : MOTIVE **2** : the act or process of inducing

in·duct \in-ˈdəkt\ *vb* **1** : to place in office **2** : to admit as a member **3** : to enroll for military training or service

in·duc·tance \in-ˈdək-təns\ *n* : a property of an electric circuit by which a varying current produces an electromotive force in that circuit or in a nearby circuit

in·duct·ee \(ˌ)in-ˌdək-ˈtē\ *n* : a person inducted into military service

in·duc·tion \in-ˈdək-shən\ *n* **1** : INSTALLATION; *also* : INITIATION **2** : the formality by which a civilian is inducted into military service **3** : inference of a generalized conclusion from particular instances; *also* : a conclusion so reached **4** : the act of causing or bringing on or about **5** : the process

by which an electric current, an electric charge, or magnetism is produced in a body by the proximity of an electric or magnetic field

in·duc·tive \in-ˈdək-tiv\ *adj* : of, relating to, or employing induction

indue *var of* ENDUE

in·dulge \in-ˈdəlj\ *vb* **in·dulged; in·dulg·ing 1** : to give free rein to : GRATIFY (~ a taste for exotic dishes) **2** : to yield to the desire of (~ a sick child) **3** : to gratify one's taste or desire for (~ in alcohol)

in·dul·gence \in-ˈdəl-jəns\ *n* **1** : remission of temporal punishment due in Roman Catholic doctrine for sins whose eternal punishment has been remitted by reception of the sacrifice of penance **2** : the act of indulging : the state of being indulgent **3** : an indulgent act **4** : the thing indulged in **5** : SELF-INDULGENCE — **in·dul·gent** \-jənt\ *adj* — **in·dul·gent·ly** *adv*

in·du·rate \ˈin-d(y)ə-rət\ *adj* : physically or morally hardened

²in·du·rate \ˈin-d(y)ə-ˌrāt\ *vb* **-rat·ed; -rat·ing 1** : to make unfeeling, stubborn, or obdurate **2** : to make hardy : INURE **3** : to make hard **4** : to grow hard : HARDEN — **in·du·ra·tion** \ˌin-d(y)ə-ˈrā-shən\ *n*

in·dus·tri·al \in-ˈdəs-trē-əl\ *adj* : of, relating to, or having to do with industry — **in·dus·tri·al·ly** \-ē\ *adv*

in·dus·tri·al·ist \-ə-ləst\ *n* : a person owning or engaged in the management of an industry : MANUFACTURER

in·dus·tri·al·ize \in-ˈdəs-trē-ə-ˌlīz\ *vb* **-ized; -iz·ing** : to make or become industrial — **in·dus·tri·al·iza·tion** \-ˌdəs-trē-ə-lə-ˈzā-shən\ *n*

in·dus·tri·ous \in-ˈdəs-trē-əs\ *adj* : DILIGENT, BUSY — **in·dus·tri·ous·ly** *adv* — **in·dus·tri·ous·ness** *n*

in·dus·try \ˈin-(ˌ)dəs-trē\ *n, pl* **-tries 1** : DILIGENCE **2** : a department or branch of a craft, art, business, or manufacture; *esp* : one that employs a large personnel and capital **3** : a distinct group of productive enterprises **4** : manufacturing activity as a whole

in·dwell \(ˈ)in-ˈdwel\ *vb* : to exist within as an activating spirit, force, or principle

¹ine·bri·ate \in-ˈē-brē-ˌāt\ *vb* **-at·ed; -at·ing** : to make drunk : INTOXICATE — **ine·bri·a·tion** \-ˌē-brē-ˈā-shən\ *n*

²ine·bri·ate \-ət\ *n* : one that is drunk; *esp* : an habitual drunkard

in·ef·fa·ble \(ˈ)in-ˈef-ə-bəl\ *adj* **1** : incapable of being expressed in words : INDESCRIBABLE (~ joy) **2** : UNSPEAKABLE (~ disgust) **3** : not to be uttered : TABOO (the ~ name of Jehovah) — **in·ef·fa·bly** \-blē\ *adv*

in·ef·face·able \ˌinə-ˈfā-sə-bəl\ *adj* : not effaceable : INERADICABLE

in·ef·fec·tive \ˌin-ə-ˈfek-tiv\ *adj* **1** : not effective : INEFFECTUAL **2** : INCAPABLE — **in·ef·fec·tive·ly** *adv*

in·ef·fec·tu·al \ˌin-ə-ˈfek-chə-(wə)l\ *adj*

: not producing the proper or usual effect — **in·ef·fec·tu·al·ly** \-ē\ adv

in·ef·fi·cient \ˌin-ə-ˈfish-ənt\ adj 1 : not producing the effect intended or desired 2 : INCAPABLE, INCOMPETENT — **in·ef·fi·cien·cy** \-ˈfish-ən-sē\ n — **in·ef·fi·cient·ly** adv

in·el·e·gant \(ˈ)in-ˈel-i-gənt\ adj : lacking in refinement, grace, or good taste — **in·el·e·gance** \-gəns\ n

in·el·i·gi·ble \(ˈ)in-ˈel-ə-jə-bəl\ adj : not qualified to be chosen for an office — **in·el·i·gi·bil·i·ty** \(ˌ)in-ˌel-ə-jə-ˈbil-ət-ē\ n — **ineligible** n

in·eluc·ta·ble \ˌin-i-ˈlək-tə-bəl\ adj : not to be avoided, changed, or resisted

in·ept \in-ˈept\ adj 1 : lacking in fitness or aptitude : UNFIT 2 : FOOLISH 3 : being out of place : INAPPROPRIATE 4 : generally incompetent : BUNGLING — **in·ep·ti·tude** \in-ˈep-tə-ˌt(y)üd\ n — **in·ept·ly** adv — **in·ept·ness** n

in·equal·i·ty \ˌin-i-ˈkwäl-ət-ē\ n 1 : the quality of being unequal or uneven; esp : UNEVENNESS, DISPARITY, CHANGEABLENESS 2 : an instance of being unequal

in·er·rant \(ˈ)in-ˈer-ənt\ adj : INFALLIBLE

in·ert \in-ˈərt\ adj [L inert-, iners unskilled, idle, fr. art-, ars skill] 1 : powerless to move itself 2 : SLUGGISH 3 : lacking in active properties ⟨chemically ∼⟩ — **in·ert·ly** adv — **in·ert·ness** n

in·er·tia \in-ˈər-sh(ē-)ə\ n 1 : a property of matter whereby it remains at rest or continues in uniform motion unless acted upon by some outside force 2 : INERTNESS, SLUGGISHNESS — **in·er·tial** \-shəl\ adj

in·es·cap·able \ˌin-ə-ˈskā-pə-bəl\ adj : incapable of being escaped : INEVITABLE — **in·es·cap·ably** \-blē\ adv

in·es·ti·ma·ble \(ˈ)in-ˈes-tə-mə-bəl\ adj 1 : incapable of being estimated or computed ⟨∼ errors⟩ 2 : too valuable or excellent to be fully appreciated — **in·es·ti·ma·bly** \-blē\ adv

in·ev·i·ta·ble \in-ˈev-ət-ə-bəl\ adj : incapable of being avoided or evaded : bound to happen — **in·ev·i·ta·bil·i·ty** \(ˌ)in-ˌev-ət-ə-ˈbil-ət-ē\ n — **in·ev·i·ta·bly** \in-ˈev-ət-ə-blē\ adv

in·ex·act \ˌin-ig-ˈzakt\ adj 1 : not precisely correct or true : INACCURATE 2 : not rigorous and careful — **in·ex·act·ly** \-ˈzak-(t)lē\ adv

in·ex·cus·able \ˌin-ik-ˈskyü-zə-bəl\ adj : being without excuse or justification — **in·ex·cus·ably** \-blē\ adv

in·ex·haust·ible \ˌin-ig-ˈzó-stə-bəl\ adj 1 : incapable of being used up ⟨an ∼ supply⟩ 2 : UNTIRING — **in·ex·haust·ibly** \-blē\ adv

in·ex·o·ra·ble \(ˈ)in-ˈeks-(ə-)rə-bəl\ adj : not to be moved by entreaty : RELENTLESS — **in·ex·o·ra·bly** adv

in·ex·pe·ri·ence \ˌin-ik-ˈspir-ē-əns\ n : lack of experience or of knowledge or proficiency gained by experience — **in·ex·pe·ri·enced** \-ənst\ adj

in·ex·pert \(ˈ)in-ˈek-ˌspərt\ adj : not expert : UNSKILLED — **in·ex·pert·ly** adv

in·ex·pi·a·ble \(ˈ)in-ˈek-spē-ə-bəl\ adj : not capable of being atoned for

in·ex·pli·ca·ble \ˌin-ik-ˈsplik-ə-bəl, (ˈ)in-ˈek-(ˌ)splik-\ adj : incapable of being explained or accounted for — **in·ex·pli·ca·bly** \-blē\ adv

in·ex·press·ible \-ˈspres-ə-bəl\ adj : not capable of being expressed — **in·ex·press·ibly** \-blē\ adv

in ex·tre·mis \ˌin-ik-ˈstrā-məs, -ˈstrē-\ adv : in extreme circumstances; esp : at the point of death

in·ex·tri·ca·ble \ˌin-ik-ˈstrik-ə-bəl, (ˈ)in-ˈek-(ˌ)strik-\ adj 1 : forming a maze or tangle from which it is impossible to get free 2 : incapable of being disentangled or untied : UNSOLVABLE — **in·ex·tri·ca·bly** \-blē\ adv

inf abbr 1 infantry 2 infinitive

in·fal·li·ble \(ˈ)in-ˈfal-ə-bəl\ adj : incapable of error : UNERRING 2 : SURE, CERTAIN ⟨an ∼ remedy⟩ — **in·fal·li·bil·i·ty** \(ˌ)in-ˌfal-ə-ˈbil-ət-ē\ n — **in·fal·li·bly** \(ˈ)in-ˈfal-ə-blē\ adv

in·fa·mous \ˈin-fə-məs\ adj 1 : having a reputation of the worst kind 2 : DISGRACEFUL — **in·fa·mous·ly** adv

in·fa·my \-mē\ n, pl -mies 1 : evil reputation brought about by something grossly criminal, shocking, or brutal 2 : an extreme and publicly known criminal or evil act 3 : the state of being infamous

in·fan·cy \ˈin-fən-sē\ n, pl -cies 1 : early childhood 2 : a beginning or early period of existence

in·fant \ˈin-fənt\ n [ME enfaunt, fr. MF enfant, fr. L infant-, infans incapable of speech, young, fr. fant-, fans, prp. of fari to speak] : BABY; also : a person who is a legal minor

in·fan·ti·cide \in-ˈfant-ə-ˌsīd\ n : the killing of an infant; also : one who kills an infant

in·fan·tile \ˈin-fən-ˌtīl, -tᵊl, -ˌtēl\ adj : of or relating to infants; also : CHILDISH

infantile paralysis n : POLIOMYELITIS

in·fan·try \ˈin-fən-trē\ n, pl -tries [MF & It; MF infanterie, fr. It infanteria, fr. infante boy, foot soldier] : soldiers trained, armed, and equipped for service on foot — **in·fan·try·man** \-mən\ n

in·farct \ˈin-ˌfärkt\ n [L infarctus, pp. of infarcire to stuff] : an area of dead tissue (as of the heart wall) caused by blocking of local blood circulation — **in·farc·tion** \in-ˈfärk-shən\ n

in·fat·u·ate \in-ˈfach-ə-ˌwāt\ vb -at·ed; -at·ing : to inspire with a foolish or extravagant love or admiration — **in·fat·u·a·tion** \-ˌfach-ə-ˈwā-shən\ n

in·fect \in-ˈfekt\ vb 1 : to contaminate with disease-producing matter 2 : to communicate a germ or disease to 3 : to cause to share one's feelings

in·fec·tion \in-ˈfek-shən\ n 1 : an act of infecting : the state of being infected

2 : a communicable disease; *also* : an infective agent (as a germ) — **in·fec·tious** \-shəs\ *adj* — **in·fec·tive** \-'fek-tiv\ *adj*

in·fe·lic·i·tous \,in-fi-'lis-ət-əs\ *adj* : not apt in application or expression — **in·fe·lic·i·ty** \-ət-ē\ *n*

in·fer \in-'fər\ *vb* **in·ferred; in·fer·ring** 1 : to derive as a conclusion from facts or premises 2 : GUESS, SURMISE 3 : to lead to as a conclusion or consequence 4 : HINT, SUGGEST *syn* deduce, conclude, judge, gather — **in·fer·ence** \'in-f(ə-)rəns\ *n* — **in·fer·en·tial** \,in-fə-'ren-chəl\ *adj*

in·fe·ri·or \in-'fir-ē-ər\ *adj* 1 : situated lower down 2 : of low or lower degree or rank 3 : of little or less importance, value, or merit — **inferior** *n* — **in·fe·ri·or·i·ty** \(,)in-,fir-ē-'ȯr-ət-ē\ *n*

in·fer·nal \in-'fərn-ᵊl\ *adj* 1 : of or relating to hell (~ fires) 2 : HELLISH, FIENDISH (~ schemes) 3 : DAMNABLE, DAMNED (~) — **in·fer·nal·ly** \-ē\ *adv*

in·fer·no \in-'fər-nō\ *n, pl* **-nos** [It, hell, fr. LL *infernus* hell, fr. L, lower] : a place or a state that resembles or suggests hell

in·fer·tile \(')in-'fərt-ᵊl\ *adj* : not fertile or productive : BARREN — **in·fer·til·i·ty** \,in-fər-'til-ət-ē\ *n*

in·fest \in-'fest\ *vb* : to trouble by spreading or swarming in or over; *also* : to live in or on as a parasite — **in·fes·ta·tion** \,in-,fes-'tā-shən\ *n*

in·fi·del \'in-fəd-ᵊl, -fə-,del\ *n* 1 : one who is not a Christian or opposes Christianity 2 : an unbeliever esp. with respect to a particular religion

in·fi·del·i·ty \,in-fə-'del-ət-ē, -fī-\ *n, pl* **-ties** 1 : lack of belief in a religion 2 : UNFAITHFULNESS, DISLOYALTY

in·field \'in-,fēld\ *n* : the part of a baseball field inside the baselines — **in·field·er** *n*

in·fight·ing \'in-,fīt-iŋ\ *n* 1 : fighting or boxing at close quarters 2 : dissension or rivalry among members of a group

in·fil·trate \in-'fil-,trāt, 'in-(,)fil-\ *vb* **-trat·ed; -trat·ing** 1 : to enter or filter into or through something 2 : to pass into or through by or as if by filtering or permeating — **in·fil·tra·tion** \,in-(,)fil-'trā-shən\ *n*

in·fi·nite \'in-fə-nət\ *adj* 1 : LIMITLESS, BOUNDLESS, ENDLESS (~ space) (~ wisdom) (~ patience) 2 : VAST, IMMENSE; *also* : INEXHAUSTIBLE (~ wealth) 3 : greater than any preassigned finite value however large (~ number of positive integers); *also* : extending to infinity (~ plane surface) — **infinite** *n* — **in·fi·nite·ly** *adv*

in·fin·i·tes·i·mal \(,)in-,fin-ə-'tes-ə-məl\ *adj* : immeasurably or incalculably small : very minute — **in·fin·i·tes·i·mal·ly** \-ē\ *adv*

in·fin·i·tive \in-'fin-ət-iv\ *n* : a verb form having the characteristics of

both verb and noun and in English usu. being used with *to*

in·fin·i·tude \in-'fin-ə-,t(y)üd\ *n* 1 : the quality or state of being infinite 2 : something that is infinite esp. in extent

in·fin·i·ty \in-'fin-ət-ē\ *n, pl* **-ties** 1 : the quality of being infinite 2 : unlimited extent of time, space, or quantity : BOUNDLESSNESS 3 : an indefinitely great number or amount

in·firm \in-'fərm\ *adj* 1 : deficient in vitality; *esp* : feeble from age 2 : not solid or stable : INSECURE

in·fir·ma·ry \in-'fərm-(ə-)rē\ *n, pl* **-ries** : a place for the care of the infirm or sick

in·fir·mi·ty \in-'fər-mət-ē\ *n, pl* **-ties** 1 : FEEBLENESS 2 : DISEASE, AILMENT 3 : a personal failing : FOIBLE

infl *abbr* influenced

in·flame \in-'flām\ *vb* **in·flamed; in·flam·ing** 1 : KINDLE 2 : to excite to excessive or uncontrollable action or feeling; *also* : INTENSIFY 3 : to affect or become affected with inflammation

in·flam·ma·ble \in-'flam-ə-bəl\ *adj* 1 : FLAMMABLE 2 : easily inflamed, excited, or angered : IRASCIBLE

in·flam·ma·tion \,in-flə-'mā-shən\ *n* : a bodily response to injury in which an affected area becomes red, hot, and painful and congested with blood

in·flam·ma·to·ry \in-'flam-ə-,tōr-ē\ *adj* 1 : tending to excite the senses or to arouse anger, disorder, or tumult : SEDITIOUS 2 : causing or accompanied by inflammation (an ~ disease)

in·flate \in-'flāt\ *vb* **in·flat·ed; in·flat·ing** 1 : to swell with air or gas (~ a balloon) 2 : to puff up : ELATE (*inflated* with pride) 3 : to expand or increase abnormally (~ prices) — **in·flat·able** *adj*

in·fla·tion \in-'flā-shən\ *n* 1 : an act of inflating : the state of being inflated 2 : empty pretentiousness : POMPOSITY 3 : an abnormal increase in the volume of money and credit resulting in a substantial and continuing rise in the general price level

in·fla·tion·ary \-shə-,ner-ē\ *adj* : of, characterized by, or productive of inflation

in·flect \in-'flekt\ *vb* 1 : to turn from a direct line or course : CURVE 2 : to vary a word by inflection 3 : to change or vary the pitch of the voice

in·flec·tion \in-'flek-shən\ *n* 1 : the act or result of curving or bending 2 : a change in pitch or loudness of the voice 3 : the change of form that words undergo to mark case, gender, number, tense, person, mood, or voice — **in·flec·tion·al** \-sh(ə-)nəl\ *adj*

in·flex·i·ble \(')in-'flek-sə-bəl\ *adj* 1 : UNYIELDING 2 : RIGID 3 : UNALTERABLE — **in·flex·i·bil·i·ty** \(,)in-,flek-sə-'bil-ət-ē\ *n* — **in·flex·i·bly** \(')in-'flek-sə-blē\ *adv*

in·flex·ion \in-ˈflek-shən\ *chiefly Brit var of* INFLECTION

in·flict \in-ˈflikt\ *vb* : IMPOSE, AFFLICT; *also* : to give or deliver by or as if by striking — **in·flic·tion** \-ˈflik-shən\ *n*

in·flo·res·cence \ˌin-flə-ˈres-ᵊns\ *n* : the manner of development and arrangement of flowers on a stem; *also* : a flowering stem with its appendages : a flower cluster

in·flow \ˈin-ˌflō\ *n* : a flowing in

¹in·flu·ence \ˈin-ˌflü-əns\ *n* 1 : the act or power of producing an effect without apparent force or direct authority 2 : the power or capacity of causing an effect in indirect or intangible ways (under the ∼ of liquor) 3 : a person or thing that exerts influence — **in·flu·en·tial** \ˌin-flü-ˈen-chəl\ *adj*

²influence *vb* **-enced; -enc·ing** 1 : to affect or alter by influence : SWAY 2 : to have an effect on the condition or development of : MODIFY

in·flu·en·za \ˌin-flü-ˈen-zə\ *n* [It, lit., influence, fr. ML *influentia*; fr. the belief that epidemics were due to the influence of the stars] : an acute and very contagious virus disease marked by fever, prostration, aches and pains, and respiratory inflammation; *also* : any of various feverish usu. virus diseases typically with respiratory symptoms

in·flux \ˈin-ˌfləks\ *n* : a coming in

in·fo \ˈin-(ˌ)fō\ *n* : INFORMATION

in·fold \in-ˈfōld\ *vb* 1 : ENFOLD 2 : to fold inward or toward one another

in·form \in-ˈfȯrm\ *vb* 1 : to communicate knowledge to : TELL 2 : to give information or knowledge 3 : to act as an informer *syn* acquaint, apprise, advise, notify

in·for·mal \(ˈ)in-ˈfȯr-məl\ *adj* 1 : conducted or carried out without formality or ceremony (an ∼ party) 2 : characteristic of or appropriate to ordinary, casual, or familiar use (∼ clothes) — **in·for·mal·i·ty** \ˌin-fȯr-ˈmal-ət-ē, -fər-\ *n* — **in·for·mal·ly** \(ˈ)in-ˈfȯr-mə-lē\ *adv*

in·for·mant \in-ˈfȯr-mənt\ *n* : one who gives information : INFORMER

in·for·ma·tion \ˌin-fər-ˈmā-shən\ *n* 1 : the communication or reception of knowledge or intelligence 2 : knowledge obtained from investigation, study, or instruction : FACTS, DATA — **in·for·ma·tion·al** \-sh(ə-)nəl\ *adj*

in·for·ma·tive \in-ˈfȯr-mət-iv\ *adj* : imparting knowledge : INSTRUCTIVE

in·formed \in-ˈfȯrmd\ *adj* : EDUCATED, KNOWLEDGEABLE

informed consent *n* : consent to a medical procedure by a subject who understands what is involved

in·form·er \-ˈfȯr-mər\ *n* : one that informs; *esp* : a person who secretly provides information about the activities of another

in·frac·tion \in-ˈfrak-shən\ *n* [deriv. of L *infractus*, pp. of *infringere* to break

off] : the act of infringing : VIOLATION

in·fra dig \ˌin-frə-ˈdig\ *adj* [short for L *infra dignitatem*] : being beneath one's dignity

in·fra·red \ˌin-frə-ˈred\ *adj* : being, relating to, or using radiation having wavelengths longer than those of red light — **infrared** *n*

in·fra·son·ic \-ˈsän-ik\ *adj* : having a frequency too low to hear (∼ vibration)

in·fre·quent \(ˈ)in-ˈfrē-kwənt\ *adj* 1 : seldom happening : RARE 2 : placed or occurring at considerable distances or intervals : OCCASIONAL *syn* uncommon, scarce, rare, sporadic — **in·fre·quent·ly** *adv*

in·fringe \in-ˈfrinj\ *vb* **in·fringed; in·fring·ing** [L *infringere*] 1 : VIOLATE, TRANSGRESS (∼ a patent) 2 : ENCROACH, TRESPASS — **in·fringe·ment** *n*

in·fu·ri·ate \in-ˈfyu̇r-ē-ˌāt\ *vb* **-at·ed; -at·ing** : to make furious : ENRAGE — **in·fu·ri·at·ing·ly** \-ˌāt-iŋ-lē\ *adv*

in·fuse \in-ˈfyüz\ *vb* **in·fused; in·fus·ing** 1 : to instill a principle or quality in : INTRODUCE 2 : INSPIRE, ANIMATE 3 : to steep (as tea) without boiling — **in·fu·sion** \-ˈfyü-zhən\ *n*

in·fus·ible \(ˈ)in-ˈfyü-zə-bəl\ *adj* : very difficult or impossible to fuse

¹-ing \iŋ\ *vb suffix or adj suffix* — used to form the present participle (sailing) and sometimes to form an adjective resembling a present participle but not derived from a verb (swashbuckling)

²-ing *n suffix* : one of a (specified) kind

³-ing *n suffix* 1 : action or process (sleeping) : instance of an action or process (a meeting) 2 : product or result of an action or process (an engraving) (earnings) 3 : something used in an action or process (a bed covering) 4 : something connected with, consisting of, or used in making (a specified thing) (scaffolding) 5 : something related to (a specified concept) (offing)

in·gath·er·ing \ˈin-ˌgath-(ə-)riŋ\ *n* 1 : COLLECTION, HARVEST 2 : ASSEMBLY

in·ge·nious \in-ˈjēn-yəs\ *adj* 1 : marked by special aptitude at discovering, inventing, or contriving 2 : marked by originality, resourcefulness, and cleverness in conception or execution — **in·ge·nious·ly** *adv* — **in·ge·nious·ness** *n*

in·ge·nue *or* **in·gé·nue** \ˈan-jə-ˌnü, ˈän-; ˈaⁿ-zhə-\ *n* : a naive girl or young woman; *esp* : an actress representing such a person

in·ge·nu·ity \ˌin-jə-ˈn(y)ü-ət-ē\ *n, pl* **-ities** : skill or cleverness in planning or inventing : INVENTIVENESS

in·gen·u·ous \in-ˈjen-yə-wəs\ *adj* [L *ingenuus* native, freeborn, fr. *gignere* to beget] 1 : STRAIGHTFORWARD, FRANK 2 : NAIVE — **in·gen·u·ous·ly** *adv* — **in·gen·u·ous·ness** *n*

in·gest \in-ˈjest\ *vb* : to take in for or as

if for digestion : ABSORB — **in·ges·tion**
\-'jes-chən\ n

in·gle·nook \-'nùk\ n 1 : a corner by the
fire or chimney 2 : a high-backed
wooden settee placed close to a fireplace

in·glo·ri·ous \(')in-'glōr-ē-əs\ adj 1
: SHAMEFUL 2 : not glorious : lacking
fame or honor — **in·glo·ri·ous·ly** adv

in·got \'iŋ-gət\ n : a mass of metal cast
in a form convenient for storage or
transportation

¹**in·grain** \(')in-'grān\ vb : to work indel-
ibly into the natural texture or mental
or moral constitution : IMBUE — **in-
grained** adj

²**in·grain** \'in-grān\ adj 1 : made of fiber that is dyed before being spun into
yarn 2 : made of yarn that is dyed
before being woven or knitted 3 : IN-
NATE — **ingrain** \'in-grān\ n

in·grate \'in-grāt\ n : an ungrateful
person

in·gra·ti·ate \in-'grā-shē-,āt\ vb -at·ed;
-at·ing : to gain favor by deliberate effort

in·gra·ti·at·ing adj 1 : capable of winning favor : PLEASING (an ~ smile) 2
: FLATTERING (an ~ manner)

in·grat·i·tude \(')in-'grat-ə-,t(y)üd\ n
: lack of gratitude : UNGRATEFULNESS

in·gre·di·ent \in-'grēd-ē-ənt\ n : one of
the substances that make up a mixture
or compound : CONSTITUENT

in·gress \'in-,gres\ n : ENTRANCE, AC-
CESS

in·grow·ing \'in-,grō-iŋ\ adj : growing
or tending inward

in·grown \-,grōn\ adj : grown in; esp
: having the free tip or edge embedded
in the flesh (~ toenail)

in·gui·nal \'iŋ-gwən-ᵊl\ adj : of, relating
to, or situated in the region of the
groin

in·hab·it \in-'hab-ət\ vb : to live or
dwell in — **in·hab·it·able** adj

in·hab·it·ant \in-'hab-ət-ənt\ n : a permanent resident in a place

in·hal·ant \in-'hā-lənt\ n : something
(as a medicine) that is inhaled

in·ha·la·tor \'in-(h)ə-,lāt-ər\ n : a device that provides a mixture of carbon
dioxide and oxygen for breathing

in·hale \in-'hāl\ vb **in·haled**; **in·hal·ing**
: to draw in by breathing : draw air
into the lungs — **in·ha·la·tion** \,in-(h)ə-
'lā-shən\ n

in·hal·er \in-'hā-lər\ n : a device by
means of which medicinal material is
inhaled

in·here \in-'hiər\ vb **in·hered**; **in·her·ing**
: to be inherent in : BELONG

in·her·ent \in-'hir-ənt, -'her-\ adj : established as an essential part of something : INTRINSIC — **in·her·ent·ly** adv

in·her·it \in-'her-ət\ vb : to receive esp.
from one's ancestors — **in·her·it·able**
\-ə-bəl\ adj — **in·her·i·tance** \-ət-əns\ n
— **in·her·i·tor** \-ət-ər\ n

in·hib·it \in-'hib-ət\ vb 1 : PROHIBIT,
FORBID 2 : to hold in check : RESTRAIN

in·hi·bi·tion \,in-(h)ə-'bish-ən\ n 1
: PROHIBITION, RESTRAINT 2 : a usu. inner check on free activity, expression, or functioning

in·house \'in-,haùs, 'in-'haùs\ adj : existing, originating, or carried on within a group or organization

in·hu·man \(')in-'(h)yü-mən\ adj 1
: lacking pity or kindness : CRUEL,
SAVAGE 2 : COLD, IMPERSONAL 3 : not
worthy of or conforming to the needs
of human beings 4 : of or suggesting a
nonhuman class of beings — **in·hu·
man·ly** adv

in·hu·mane \,in-(h)yü-'mān\ adj : not
humane : INHUMAN 1

in·hu·man·i·ty \-'man-ət-ē\ n, pl -ities 1
: the quality or state of being cruel or
barbarous 2 : a cruel or barbarous act

in·hu·ma·tion \,in-hyü-'mā-shən\ n
: BURIAL

in·im·i·cal \in-'im-i-kəl\ adj 1 : being
adverse often by reason of hostility 2
: HOSTILE, UNFRIENDLY — **in·im·i·cal·ly**
\-ē\ adv

in·im·i·ta·ble \(')in-'im-ət-ə-bəl\ adj
: not capable of being imitated

in·iq·ui·ty \in-'ik-wət-ē\ n, pl -ties [ME
iniquite, fr. MF iniquité, fr. L iniqui-
tas, fr. iniquus uneven, fr. aequus
equal] 1 : WICKEDNESS 2 : a wicked act
— **in·iq·ui·tous** \-wət-əs\ adj

¹**ini·tial** \in-'ish-əl\ adj 1 : of or relating
to the beginning : INCIPIENT 2 : FIRST
— **ini·tial·ly** \-ē\ adv

²**initial** n : the first letter of a word or
name

³**initial** vb -tialed or -tialled; -tial·ing or
-tial·ling \-'ish-(ə-)liŋ\ : to affix an initial to

¹**ini·ti·ate** \in-'ish-ē-,āt\ vb -at·ed; -at·ing
1 : START, BEGIN 2 : to induct into
membership by or as if by special ceremonies 3 : to instruct in the first
principles of something — **ini·ti·a·tion**
\-,ish-ē-'ā-shən\ n

²**ini·ti·ate** \in-'ish-(ē-)ət\ n 1 : a person
who is undergoing or has passed an
initation 2 : a person who is instructed or adept in some special field

ini·tia·tive \in-'ish-ət-iv\ n 1 : an introductory step 2 : self-reliant enterprise
3 : a process by which laws may be
introduced or enacted directly by vote
of the people

ini·tia·to·ry \in-'ish-(ē-)ə-,tōr-ē\ adj 1
: INTRODUCTORY 2 : tending or serving
to initiate (~ rites)

in·ject \in-'jekt\ vb 1 : to force into
something (~ serum with a needle) 2
: to introduce into some situation or
subject (~ a note of suspicion) — **injection** \-'jek-shən\ n

in·junc·tion \in-'jəŋk-shən\ n 1 : ORDER,
ADMONITION 2 : a court writ whereby
one is required to do or to refrain from
doing a specified act

in·jure \'in-jər\ vb **in·jured**; **in·jur·ing**
\'inj-(ə-)riŋ\ 1 : WRONG, DAMAGE, HURT
syn harm, impair, mar, spoil

in·ju·ry \'inj-(ə-)rē\ n, pl -ries 1 : an act

that damages or hurts : WRONG 2 : hurt, damage, or loss sustained — **in·ju·ri·ous** \in-ˈju̇r-ē-əs\ adj

in·jus·tice \(ˈ)in-ˈjəs-təs\ n 1 : violation of a person's rights : UNFAIRNESS, WRONG 2 : an unjust act or deed

¹ink \ˈiŋk\ n [ME enke, fr. OF, fr. LL encaustum, fr. L encaustus burned in, fr. Gk enkaustos, verbal of enkaiein to burn in] : a usu. liquid and colored material for writing and printing — **inky** adj

²ink vb : to put ink on; esp : SIGN

ink·blot test \ˈiŋ-ˌblät-\ n : any of several psychological tests based on the interpretation of irregular figures

ink·horn \ˈiŋk-ˌhȯrn\ n : a small bottle (as of horn) for holding ink

ink·ling \ˈiŋ-kliŋ\ n 1 : HINT, INTIMATION 2 : a vague idea

ink·stand \ˈiŋk-ˌstand\ n : INKWELL; also : a pen and ink stand

ink·well \-ˌwel\ n : a container for ink

in·laid \ˈin-ˈlād\ adj : decorated with material set into a surface

in·land \ˈin-ˌland, -lənd\ n : the interior of a country

²inland adj 1 chiefly Brit : not foreign : DOMESTIC (~ revenue) 2 : of or relating to the interior of a country

³inland adv : into or toward the interior

in·law \ˈin-ˌlȯ\ n : a relative by marriage

¹in·lay \(ˈ)in-ˈlā, ˈin-ˌlā\ vb **in·laid** \-ˈlād\; **in·lay·ing** : to set (one material into another) by way of decoration

²in·lay \ˈin-ˌlā\ n 1 : inlaid work 2 : a shaped filling cemented into a tooth

in·let \ˈin-ˌlet, -lət\ n 1 : a bay in the shore of a sea, lake, or river 2 : a narrow strip of water running into the land

in·mate \ˈin-ˌmāt\ n : a person who lives in the same house or institution with another; esp : a person confined to an institution (as a hospital or prison)

in me·di·as res \in-ˌmād-ē-əs-ˈrās\ adv [L, lit., into the midst of things] : in or into the middle of a narrative or plot

in memo·ri·am \ˌin-mə-ˈmȯr-ē-əm\ prep : in memory of

in·most \ˈin-ˌmōst\ adj : deepest within : INNERMOST

inn \ˈin\ n : HOTEL, TAVERN

in·nards \ˈin-ərdz\ n pl 1 : the internal organs of a man or animal; esp : VISCERA 2 : the internal parts of a structure or mechanism

in·nate \in-ˈāt\ adj 1 : existing in, belonging to, or determined by factors present in an individual from birth : NATIVE 2 : belonging to the essential nature of something : INHERENT — **in·nate·ly** adv

in·ner \ˈin-ər\ adj 1 : situated farther in (the ~ bark) 2 : near a center esp. of influence (the ~ circle) 3 : of or relating to the mind or spirit

in·ner-di·rect·ed \ˌin-ər-də-ˈrek-təd, -(ˌ)dī-\ adj : directed in thought and action by one's own scale of values as opposed to external norms

inner ear n : the part of the ear that consists of a complex membranous labyrinth located in a cavity in the temporal bone and contains sense organs of hearing and of awareness of position in space

in·ner·most \ˈin-ər-ˌmōst\ adj : farthest inward : INMOST

in·ner·sole \ˈin-ər-ˌsōl\ n : INSOLE

in·ner·spring \ˌin-ər-ˌspriŋ\ adj : having coil springs inside a padded casing

inner tube n : TUBE 5

in·ning \ˈin-iŋ\ n : a baseball team's turn at bat; also : a division of a baseball game consisting of a turn at bat for each team

in·nings \ˈin-iŋz\ n sing or pl : a division of a cricket match

inn·keep·er \ˈin-ˌkē-pər\ n 1 : the landlord of an inn 2 : a hotel manager

in·no·cence \ˈin-ə-səns\ n 1 : BLAMELESSNESS; also : freedom from legal guilt 2 : GUILELESSNESS, SIMPLICITY; also : IGNORANCE

in·no·cent \-sənt\ adj [ME, fr. MF, fr. L innocens, fr. nocens, wicked, fr. nocēre to harm] 1 : free from guilt or sin : BLAMELESS 2 : harmless in effect or intention; also : CANDID 3 : free from legal guilt or fault : LAWFUL 4 : INGENUOUS 5 : DESTITUTE — **innocent** n — **in·no·cent·ly** adv

in·noc·u·ous \in-ˈäk-yə-wəs\ adj 1 : HARMLESS 2 : INOFFENSIVE, INSIPID

in·nom·i·nate \in-ˈäm-ə-nət\ adj : having no name; also : ANONYMOUS

in·no·vate \ˈin-ə-ˌvāt\ vb -vat·ed; -vat·ing : to introduce as or as if new : make changes — **in·no·va·tive** \-ˌvāt-iv\ adj — **in·no·va·tor** \-ˌvāt-ər\ n

in·no·va·tion \ˌin-ə-ˈvā-shən\ n 1 : the introduction of something new 2 : a new idea, method, or device

in·nu·en·do \ˌin-yə-ˈwen-dō\ n, pl -dos or -does [L, by hinting, fr. innuere to hint, fr. nuere to nod] : HINT, INSINUATION; esp : a veiled reflection on character or reputation

in·nu·mer·a·ble \in-ˈ(y)üm-(ə)-rə-bəl\ adj : too many to be numbered

in·oc·u·late \in-ˈäk-yə-ˌlāt\ vb -lat·ed; -lat·ing [ME inoculaten to insert a bud in a plant, fr. L inoculare, fr. oculus eye, bud] : to introduce something into; esp : to treat with a serum or antibody to prevent or cure a disease — **in·oc·u·la·tion** \-ˌäk-yə-ˈlā-shən\ n

in·op·er·a·ble \(ˈ)in-ˈäp-(ə-)rə-bəl\ adj 1 : not suitable for surgery 2 : not operable

in·op·er·a·tive \-ˈäp-(ə-)rət-iv, -ˈäp-ə-ˌrāt-\ adj : not functioning

in·op·por·tune \(ˌ)in-ˌäp-ər-ˈt(y)ün\ adj : happening or coming at the wrong time — **in·op·por·tune·ly** adv

in·or·di·nate \in-ˈȯrd-(ə-)nət\ adj 1 : UNREGULATED, DISORDERLY 2 : EXTRAORDINARY, IMMODERATE (an ~ curiosity) — **in·or·di·nate·ly** adv

in·or·gan·ic \,in-,ȯr-'gan-ik\ *adj* : being or composed of matter of other than plant or animal origin : MINERAL

in·pa·tient \'in-,pā-shǝnt\ *n* : a hospital patient who receives lodging and food as well as treatment

in·put \'in-,pu̇t\ *n* **1** : something put in **2** : power or energy put into a machine or system **3** : information fed into a data processing system or computer **4** : ADVICE, OPINION — **input** *vb*

in·quest \'in-,kwest\ *n* **1** : an official inquiry or examination esp. before a jury **2** : INQUIRY, INVESTIGATION

in·qui·e·tude \(')in-'kwī-ǝ-,t(y)üd\ *n* : UNEASINESS, RESTLESSNESS

in·quire \in-'kwī(ǝ)r\ *vb* **in·quired;** **in·quir·ing 1** : to ask about : ASK **2** : INVESTIGATE, EXAMINE — **in·quir·er** *n* — **in·quir·ing·ly** *adv*

in·qui·ry \in-'kwī(ǝ)r-ē, in-'kwī(ǝ)r-ē; 'in-kwǝ-rē, 'iŋ-\ *n, pl* **-ries 1** : a request for information; *also* : a search for truth or knowledge **2** : a systematic investigation of a matter of public interest

in·qui·si·tion \,in-kwǝ-'zish-ǝn, ,iŋ-\ *n* **1** : a judicial or official inquiry usu. before a jury **2** *cap* : a former Roman Catholic tribunal for the discovery and punishment of heretics **3** : a severe questioning — **in·quis·i·tor** \in-'kwiz-ǝt-ǝr\ *n* — **in·quis·i·to·ri·al** \-,kwiz-ǝ-'tȯr-ē-ǝl\ *adj*

in·quis·i·tive \in-'kwiz-ǝt-iv\ *adj* **1** : given to examination or investigation (an ~ mind) **2** : unduly curious — **in·quis·i·tive·ly** *adv* — **in·quis·i·tive·ness** *n*

in re \in-'rā, -'rē\ *prep* : in the matter of

INRI *abbr* [L *Iesus Nazarenus Rex Iudaeorum*] Jesus of Nazareth, King of the Jews

in·road \'in-,rōd\ *n* **1** : INVASION, RAID **2** : ENCROACHMENT

in·rush \'in-,rǝsh\ *n* : a crowding or flooding in

ins *abbr* **1** inches **2** insurance

INS *abbr* Immigration and Naturalization Service

in·sa·lu·bri·ous \,in-sǝ-'lü-brē-ǝs\ *adj* : UNWHOLESOME, NOXIOUS

ins and outs *n pl* : characteristic peculiarities : RAMIFICATIONS

in·sane \(')in-'sān\ *adj* **1** : not mentally sound; *also* : MAD; *also* : used by or for the insane **2** : FOOLISH, WILD — **in·sane·ly** *adv* — **in·san·i·ty** \in-'san-ǝt-ē\ *n*

in·sa·tia·ble \(')in-'sā-shǝ-bǝl\ *adj* : incapable of being satisfied

in·sa·tiate \(')in-'sā-sh(ē-)ǝt\ *adj* : INSATIABLE

in·scribe \in-'skrīb\ *vb* **1** : to write, engrave, or print esp. as a lasting record **2** : ENROLL **3** : to write, engrave, or print characters upon **4** : to dedicate to someone **5** : to stamp deeply or impress esp. on the memory **6** : to draw within a figure so as to touch in as many places as possible — **in·scrip·tion** \-'skrip-shǝn\ *n*

in·scru·ta·ble \in-'skrüt-ǝ-bǝl\ *adj* : not readily comprehensible : MYSTERIOUS (an ~ smile) — **in·scru·ta·bly** \-blē\ *adv*

in·seam \'in-,sēm\ *n* : the seam on the inside of the leg of a pair of pants; *also* : the length of this seam

in·sect \'in-,sekt\ *n* [L *insectum*, fr. *insectus*, pp. of *insecare* to cut into, fr. *secare* to cut] : any of a major group of small usu. winged animals (as flies, bees, beetles, and moths) with three pairs of legs

in·sec·ti·cide \in-'sek-tǝ-,sīd\ *n* : a preparation for destroying insects — **in·sec·ti·cid·al** \(,)in-,sek-tǝ-'sīd-ᵊl\ *adj*

in·sec·tiv·o·rous \,in-,sek-'tiv-(ǝ-)rǝs\ *adj* : depending on insects as food

in·se·cure \,in-si-'kyu̇r\ *adj* **1** : UNCERTAIN **2** : UNPROTECTED, UNSAFE **3** : LOOSE, SHAKY **4** : INFIRM **5** : beset by fear or anxiety — **in·se·cure·ly** *adv* — **in·se·cu·ri·ty** \-'kyu̇r-ǝt-ē\ *n*

in·sem·i·nate \in-'sem-ǝ-,nāt\ *vb* **-nat·ed; -nat·ing** : to introduce semen into the genital tract of (a female) — **in·sem·i·na·tion** \-,sem-ǝ-'nā-shǝn\ *n*

in·sen·sate \(')in-'sen-,sāt, -sǝt\ *adj* **1** : INANIMATE **2** : lacking sense or understanding; *also* : FOOLISH **3** : BRUTAL, INHUMAN (~ rage)

in·sen·si·ble \(,)in-'sen-sǝ-bǝl\ *adj* **1** : IMPERCEPTIBLE; *also* : SLIGHT, GRADUAL **2** : INANIMATE **3** : UNCONSCIOUS **4** : lacking sensory perception or ability to react (~ to pain) (~ from cold) **5** : APATHETIC, INDIFFERENT; *also* : UNAWARE (~ of their danger) **6** : MEANINGLESS **7** : lacking delicacy or refinement — **in·sen·si·bil·i·ty** \(,)in-,sen-sǝ-'bil-ǝt-ē\ *n* — **in·sen·si·bly** \(')in-'sen-sǝ- blē\ *adv*

in·sen·tient \(')in-'sen-ch(ē-)ǝnt\ *adj* : lacking perception, consciousness, or animation — **in·sen·tience** \-ch(ē-)ǝns\ *n*

in·sep·a·ra·ble \(')in-'sep-(ǝ-)rǝ-bǝl\ *adj* : incapable of being separated or disjoined — **in·sep·a·ra·bil·i·ty** \(,)in-,sep-(ǝ-)rǝ-'bil-ǝt-ē\ *n* — **inseparable** *n* — **in·sep·a·ra·bly** \(')in-'sep-(ǝ-)rǝ- blē\ *adv*

¹in·sert \in-'sǝrt\ *vb* **1** : to put or thrust in (~ a key in a lock) (~ a comma) **2** : INTERPOLATE **3** : to set in (as a piece of fabric) and make fast

²in·sert \'in-,sǝrt\ *n* : something that is inserted or is for insertion; *esp* : written or printed material inserted (as between the leaves of a book)

in·ser·tion \in-'sǝr-shǝn\ *n* **1** : something that is inserted **2** : the act or process of inserting

in·set \'in-,set\ *vb* **inset** *or* **in·set·ted; in·set·ting** : to set in : INSERT — **inset** *n*

¹in·shore \'in-'shōr\ *adj* **1** : situated or carried on near shore **2** : moving toward shore

²inshore *adv* : to or toward shore

¹in·side \'in-'sīd, 'in-,sīd\ *n* **1** : an inner side or surface : INTERIOR **2** : inward nature, thoughts, or feeling **3** *pl* : VIS-

CERA, ENTRAILS **4** : a position of power or confidence — **inside** adj

²**inside** prep **1** : in or into the inside of **2** : before the end of ⟨~ an hour⟩

³**inside** adv **1** : on the inner side **2** : in or into the interior

inside of prep : INSIDE

in·sid·er \in-ˈsīd-ər\ n : a person who is in a position of power or has access to confidential information

in·sid·i·ous \in-ˈsid-ē-əs\ adj [L insidiosus, fr. insidiae ambush, fr. insidēre to sit in, sit on, fr. sedēre to sit] **1** : SLY, TREACHEROUS **2** : SEDUCTIVE **3** : having a gradual and cumulative effect : SUBTLE — **in·sid·i·ous·ly** adv — **in·sid·i·ous·ness** n

in·sight \ˈin-ˌsīt\ n : the power or act of seeing into a situation : UNDERSTANDING, PENETRATION; also : INTUITION — **in·sight·ful** \ˈin-ˌsīt-fəl, in-ˈsīt-\ adj

in·sig·nia \in-ˈsig-nē-ə\ or **in·sig·ne** \-(ˌ)nē\ n, pl -nia or -ni·as : a distinguishing mark esp. of authority, office, or honor : BADGE, EMBLEM

in·sin·cere \ˌin-sin-ˈsiər\ adj : not sincere : HYPOCRITICAL — **in·sin·cere·ly** adv — **in·sin·cer·i·ty** \-ˈser-ət-ē\ n

in·sin·u·ate \in-ˈsin-yə-ˌwāt\ vb -at·ed; -at·ing [L insinuare, fr. sinuare to bend, curve, fr. sinus curve] **1** : to introduce gradually or in a subtle, indirect, or artful way **2** : to imply in a subtle or devious way — **in·sin·u·a·tion** \(ˌ)in-ˌsin-yə-ˈwā-shən\ n

in·sin·u·at·ing adj **1** : tending gradually to cause doubt, distrust, or change of outlook **2** : winning favor and confidence by imperceptible degrees

in·sip·id \in-ˈsip-əd\ adj **1** : lacking savor **2** : DULL, UNINTERESTING — **in·si·pid·i·ty** \ˌin-sə-ˈpid-ət-ē\ n

in·sist \in-ˈsist\ vb [MF or L; MF insister, fr. L insistere to stand upon, persist, fr. sistere to stand] : to take a resolute stand

in·sis·tence \in-ˈsis-təns\ n : the act of insisting; also : an insistent attitude or quality : URGENCY

in·sis·tent \in-ˈsis-tənt\ adj : disposed to insist — **in·sis·tent·ly** adv

in si·tu \in-ˈsī-tü\ adv or adj [L, in position] : in the natural or original position

in·so·far as \ˌin-sə-ˌfär-əz\ conj : to the extent or degree that

insol abbr insoluble

in·so·la·tion \ˌin-(ˌ)sō-ˈlā-shən\ n : solar radiation that has been received

in·sole \ˈin-ˌsōl\ n **1** : an inside sole of a shoe **2** : a loose thin strip placed inside a shoe for warmth or comfort

in·so·lent \ˈin-sə-lənt\ adj : contemptuous, rude, disrespectful, or brutal in behavior or language : OVERBEARING, BOLD — **in·so·lence** \-ləns\ n

in·sol·u·ble \(ˈ)in-ˈsäl-yə-bəl\ adj **1** : having of admitting of no solution or explanation **2** : difficult or impossible to dissolve — **in·sol·u·bil·i·ty** \(ˌ)ˌsäl-yə-ˈbil-ət-ē\ n

in·solv·able \(ˈ)in-ˈsäl-və-bəl\ adj : not capable of being solved

in·sol·vent \(ˈ)in-ˈsäl-vənt\ adj **1** : unable to pay one's debts **2** : insufficient to pay all debts charged against it ⟨an ~ estate⟩ **3** : IMPOVERISHED, DEFICIENT — **in·sol·ven·cy** \-vən-sē\ n

in·som·nia \in-ˈsäm-nē-ə\ n : prolonged and usu. abnormal sleeplessness

in·so·much as \ˌin-sə-ˌməch-əz\ conj : INASMUCH AS

insomuch that conj : to such a degree that : so

in·sou·ci·ance \in-ˈsü-sē-əns, aⁿ-süs-yäⁿs\ n [F] : lighthearted unconcern — **in·sou·ci·ant** \in-ˈsü-sē-ənt, aⁿ-süs-yäⁿ\ adj

insp abbr inspector

in·spect \in-ˈspekt\ vb : to view closely and critically : EXAMINE — **in·spec·tion** \ˈspek-shən\ n — **in·spec·tor** \-tər\ n

in·spi·ra·tion \ˌin-spə-ˈrä-shən\ n **1** : INHALATION **2** : the act or power of moving the intellect or emotions **3** : the quality or state of being inspired; also : something that is inspired **4** : an inspiring agent or influence — **in·spi·ra·tion·al** \-sh(ə-)nəl\ adj

in·spire \in-ˈspī(ə)r\ vb **in·spired; in·spir·ing 1** : INHALE **2** : to influence, move, or guide by divine or supernatural inspiration **3** : exert an animating, enlivening, or exalting influence upon **4** : AFFECT **5** : to communicate to an agent supernaturally; also : CREATE **6** : to bring about; also : INCITE **7** : to spread by indirect means — **in·spir·er** n

in·spir·it \in-ˈspir-ət\ vb : ANIMATE, HEARTEN

inst abbr **1** instant **2** institute; institution; institutional

in·sta·bil·i·ty \ˌin-stə-ˈbil-ət-ē\ n : lack of firmness or steadiness

in·stall or **in·stal** \in-ˈstȯl\ vb **in·stalled; in·stall·ing 1** : to place formally in office : induct into an office, rank, or order **2** : to establish in an indicated place, condition, or status **3** : to set up for use or service — **in·stal·la·tion** \ˌin-stə-ˈlā-shən\ n

¹**in·stall·ment** or **in·stal·ment** \in-ˈstȯl-mənt\ n : INSTALLATION

²**installment** also **instalment** n **1** : one of the parts into which a debt or sum is divided for payment **2** : one of several parts presented at intervals

¹**in·stance** \ˈin-stəns\ n **1** : INSTIGATION, REQUEST ⟨entered the contest at the ~ of friends⟩ **2** : EXAMPLE ⟨an ~ of heroism⟩ ⟨for ~⟩ **3** : an event or step that is part of a process or series syn case, illustration, sample, specimen

²**instance** vb **in·stanced; in·stanc·ing** : to mention as a case or example

¹**in·stant** \ˈin-stənt\ n **1** : MOMENT ⟨the ~ we met⟩ **2** : the present or current month ⟨your letter of the 10th ~⟩

²**instant** adj **1** : URGENT **2** : PRESENT, CURRENT **3** : IMMEDIATE ⟨~ relief⟩ **4** : partially prepared by the manufacturer to

make final preparation easy ⟨~ cake mix⟩ ; *also* : immediately soluble in water ⟨~ coffee⟩

in·stan·ta·neous \ˌin-stən-ˈtā-nē-əs\ *adj* : done or occurring in an instant or without delay — **in·stan·ta·neous·ly** *adv*

in·stan·ter \in-ˈstant-ər\ *adv* : at once

in·stan·ti·ate \in-ˈstan-chē-ˌāt\ *vb* -at·ed; -at·ing : to represent by a concrete example — **in·stan·ti·a·tion** \-ˌstan-chē-ˈā-shən\ *n*

in·stant·ly \ˈin-stənt-lē\ *adv* : at once : IMMEDIATELY

in·state \in-ˈstāt\ *vb* : to establish in a rank or office : INSTALL

in·stead \in-ˈsted\ *adv* 1 : as a substitute or equivalent 2 : as an alternative : RATHER

instead of \in-ˌsted-ə(v), -ˌstid-\ *prep* : as a substitute for or alternative to

in·step \ˈin-ˌstep\ *n* : the arched part of the human foot in front of the ankle joint

in·sti·gate \ˈin-stə-ˌgāt\ *vb* -gat·ed; -gat·ing : to goad or urge forward : PROVOKE, INCITE ⟨~ a revolt⟩ — **in·sti·ga·tion** \ˌin-stə-ˈgā-shən\ *n* — **in·sti·ga·tor** \ˈin-stə-ˌgāt-ər\ *n*

in·still *also* **in·stil** \in-ˈstil\ *vb* **in·stilled; in·still·ing** 1 : to cause to enter drop by drop 2 : to impart gradually

¹**in·stinct** \ˈin-ˌstiŋkt\ *n* 1 : a natural aptitude 2 : a largely inheritable and unalterable tendency of an organism to make a complex and specific response to environmental stimuli without involving reason; *also* : behavior originating below the conscious level — **in·stinc·tive** \in-ˈstiŋk-tiv\ *adj* — **in·stinc·tive·ly** *adv*

²**in·stinct** \in-ˈstiŋkt, ˈin-ˌstiŋkt\ *adj* : IMBUED, INFUSED

in·stinc·tu·al \in-ˈstiŋ(k)-chə(-wə)l\ *adj* : of, relating to, or based on instinct

¹**in·sti·tute** \ˈin-stə-ˌt(y)üt\ *vb* -tut·ed; -tut·ing 1 : to establish in a position or office 2 : to originate and get established 3 : INAUGURATE, INITIATE

²**institute** *n* 1 : an elementary principle recognized as authoritative; *also*, *pl* : a collection of such principles and precepts 2 : an organization for the promotion of a cause : ASSOCIATION 3 : an educational institution 4 : a meeting for instruction or a brief course of such meetings

in·sti·tu·tion \ˌin-stə-ˈt(y)ü-shən\ *n* 1 : an act of originating, setting up, or founding 2 : an established practice, law, or custom 3 : a society or corporation esp. of a public character ⟨a charitable ~⟩; *also* : the building which houses it — **in·sti·tu·tion·al** \-ˈt(y)ü-sh(ə-)nəl\ *adj* — **in·sti·tu·tion·al·ize** \-ˌīz\ *vb* — **in·sti·tu·tion·al·ly** \-ē\ *adv*

instr *abbr* 1 instructor 2 instrument; instrumental

in·struct \in-ˈstrəkt\ *vb* [ME *instructen*,

fr. L *instructus*, pp. of *instruere*, fr. *struere* to build] 1 : TEACH 2 : INFORM 3 : to give directions or commands to

in·struc·tion \in-ˈstrək-shən\ *n* 1 : LESSON, PRECEPT 2 : COMMAND, ORDER 3 *pl* : DIRECTIONS 4 : the action, practice, or profession of a teacher — **in·struc·tion·al** \-sh(ə-)nəl\ *adj*

in·struc·tive \in-ˈstrək-tiv\ *adj* : carrying a lesson : ENLIGHTENING

in·struc·tor \in-ˈstrək-tər\ *n* : one that instructs; *esp* : a college teacher below professorial rank — **in·struc·tor·ship** *n*

¹**in·stru·ment** \ˈin-strə-mənt\ *n* 1 : a device used to produce music 2 : a means by which something is done 3 : TOOL, UTENSIL 4 : a legal document (as a deed) 5 : a device used in navigating an airplane

²**in·stru·ment** \-ˌment\ *vb* : to equip with instruments

in·stru·men·tal \ˌin-strə-ˈment-ᵊl\ *adj* 1 : acting as an agent or means 2 : of, relating to, or done with an instrument 3 : relating to, composed for, or performed on a musical instrument

in·stru·men·tal·ist \-əst\ *n* : a player on a musical instrument

in·stru·men·tal·i·ty \ˌin-strə-mən-ˈtal-ət-ē, -ˌmen-\ *n*, *pl* -ties 1 : the quality or state of being instrumental 2 : MEANS, AGENCY

in·stru·men·ta·tion \ˌin-strə-mən-ˈtā-shən, -ˌmen-\ *n* 1 : the arrangement or composition of music for instruments (as for an orchestra) 2 : the use or application of instruments

instrument flying *n* : airplane navigation by instruments only

instrument panel *n* : DASHBOARD

in·sub·or·di·nate \ˌin-sə-ˈbȯrd-(ᵊ-)nət\ *adj* : disobedient to authority — **in·sub·or·di·na·tion** \-ˌbȯrd-ᵊn-ˈā-shən\ *n*

in·sub·stan·tial \ˌin-səb-ˈstan-chəl\ *adj* 1 : lacking substance or reality 2 : lacking firmness or solidity

in·suf·fer·able \(ˈ)in-ˈsəf-(ə-)rə-bəl\ *adj* : not to be endured : INTOLERABLE ⟨an ~ bore⟩ — **in·suf·fer·ably** \-blē\ *adv*

in·suf·fi·cient \ˌin-sə-ˈfish-ənt\ *adj* : not sufficient; *also* : INCOMPETENT — **in·suf·fi·cien·cy** \-ˈfish-ən-sē\ *n* — **in·suf·fi·cient·ly** *adv*

in·su·lar \ˈins-(y)ə-lər, ˈin-shə-lər\ *adj* 1 : of, relating to, or forming an island 2 : ISOLATED, DETACHED 3 : of or relating to island people 4 : NARROW, PREJUDICED — **in·su·lar·i·ty** \ˌins-(y)ə-ˈlar-ət-ē, ˌin-shə-ˈlar-\ *n*

in·su·late \ˈin-sə-ˌlāt\ *vb* -lat·ed; -lat·ing [L *insula* island] : ISOLATE; *esp* : to separate a conductor of electricity, heat, or sound from other conducting bodies by means of a nonconductor — **in·su·la·tion** \ˌin-sə-ˈlā-shən\ *n* — **in·su·la·tor** \ˈin-sə-ˌlāt-ər\ *n*

in·su·lin \ˈin-s(ə-)lən\ *n* : a pancreatic hormone essential for bodily use of sugars and used in the control of diabetes mellitus

insulin shock *n* : hypoglycemia associated with the presence of excessive insulin in the system

¹in·sult \in-'səlt\ *vb* [MF or L; MF *insulter*, fr. L *insultare*, lit., to spring upon, fr. *saltare* to leap] : to treat with insolence or contempt : AFFRONT — **in·sult·ing·ly** \-iŋ-lē\ *adv*

²in·sult \'in-ˌsəlt\ *n* : a gross indignity

in·su·per·a·ble \(')in-'sü-p(ə-)rə-bəl\ *adj* : incapable of being surmounted, overcome, or passed over — **in·su·per·a·bly** \-blē\ *adv*

in·sup·port·able \ˌin-sə-'pōrt-ə-bəl\ *adj* 1 : UNENDURABLE 2 : UNJUSTIFIABLE

in·sur·able \in-'shùr-ə-bəl\ *adj* : capable of being or proper to be insured

in·sur·ance \in-'shùr-əns\ *n* 1 : the business of insuring persons or property 2 : coverage by contract whereby one party agrees to indemnify or guarantee another against loss by a specified contingent event or peril 3 : the state of being insured; *also* : means of insuring 4 : the sum for which something is insured

in·sure \in-'shùr\ *vb* **in·sured; in·sur·ing** 1 : to provide or obtain insurance on or for : UNDERWRITE 2 : to make certain : ENSURE

in·sured \in-'shùrd\ *n* : a person whose life or property is insured

in·sur·er \in-'shùr-ər\ *n* : one that insures; *esp* : a company issuing insurance

in·sur·gent \in-'sər-jənt\ *n* 1 : a person who revolts against civil authority or an established government : REBEL 2 : one who acts contrary to the policies and decisions of his political party — **in·sur·gen·cy** \-jəns\ *n* — **in·sur·gen·cy** \-jən-sē\ *n* — **in·sur·gent** *adj*

in·sur·mount·able \ˌin-sər-maùnt-ə-bəl\ *adj* : INSUPERABLE — **in·sur·mount·ably** \-blē\ *adv*

in·sur·rec·tion \ˌin-sə-'rek-shən\ *n* : an act or instance of revolting against civil authority or an established government — **in·sur·rec·tion·ist** *n*

int *abbr* 1 interest 2 interior 3 intermediate 4 internal 5 international 6 intransitive

in·tact \in-'takt\ *adj* : untouched esp. by anything that harms or diminishes

in·ta·glio \in-'tal-yō\ *n, pl* **-glios** [It] : an engraving cut deeply into the surface of a hard material

in·take \'in-ˌtāk\ *n* 1 : an opening through which fluid enters 2 : the act of taking in 3 : the amount taken in

in·tan·gi·ble \(')in-'tan-jə-bəl\ *adj* 1 : incapable of being touched : not tangible : IMPALPABLE 2 : impossible to define or determine with certainty or precision : VAGUE — **intangible** *n* — **in·tan·gi·bly** \-blē\ *adv*

in·te·ger \'int-i-jər\ *n* [L, adj., whole, entire] : a number (as 1, 2, 3, 12, 432) that is not a fraction and does not include a fraction, is the negative of such a number, or is 0

in·te·gral \'int-i-grəl\ *adj* 1 : essential to completeness : CONSTITUENT 2 : formed as a unit with another part 3 : composed of parts that make up a whole 4 : ENTIRE

in·te·grate \'int-ə-ˌgrāt\ *vb* **-grat·ed; -grat·ing** 1 : to form, coordinate, or blend into a functioning or unified whole : UNITE 2 : to incorporate into a larger unit 3 : to end the segregation of and bring into common and equal membership in society or an organization; *also* : DESEGREGATE — **in·te·gra·tion** \ˌint-ə-'grā-shən\ *n*

integrated circuit *n* : a group of tiny electronic components and their connections in or on a small slice of material (as silicon)

in·teg·ri·ty \in-'teg-rət-ē\ *n* 1 : SOUNDNESS 2 : adherence to a code of values : utter sincerity, honesty, and candor 3 : COMPLETENESS

in·teg·u·ment \in-'teg-yə-mənt\ *n* : a covering layer (as a skin or cuticle) of an organism

in·tel·lect \'int-əl-ˌekt\ *n* 1 : the power of knowing : the capacity for knowledge 2 : the capacity for rational or intelligent thought esp. when highly developed 3 : a person with great intellectual powers

in·tel·lec·tu·al \ˌint-əl-'ek-ch(ə-w)əl\ *adj* 1 : of, relating to, or performed by the intellect : RATIONAL 2 : given to study, reflection, and speculation 3 : engaged in activity requiring the creative use of the intellect — **intellectual** *n* — **in·tel·lec·tu·al·ly** \-ē\ *adv*

in·tel·lec·tu·al·ism \-chə(-wə)-ˌliz-əm\ *n* : devotion to the exercise of intellect or to intellectual pursuits

in·tel·li·gence \in-'tel-ə-jəns\ *n* 1 : ability to learn and understand or to deal with new or trying situations 2 : relative intellectual capacity 3 : INFORMATION, NEWS 4 : an agency engaged in obtaining information esp. concerning an enemy or possible enemy; *also* : the information so gained

intelligence quotient *n* : a number expressing the intelligence of a person determined by dividing the person's mental age by his or her chronological age and multiplying by 100

in·tel·li·gent \in-'tel-ə-jənt\ *adj* : having or showing intelligence or intellect — **in·tel·li·gent·ly** *adv*

in·tel·li·gen·tsia \in-ˌtel-ə-'jent-sē-ə, -ˌgent-\ *n* [Russ *intelligentsiya,* fr. L *intelligentia* intelligence] : intellectual people as a group : the educated class

in·tel·li·gi·ble \in-'tel-ə-jə-bəl\ *adj* : capable of being understood or comprehended — **in·tel·li·gi·bil·i·ty** \-ˌtel-ə-jə-'bil-ət-ē\ *n* — **in·tel·li·gi·bly** \-'tel-ə-jə-blē\ *adv*

in·tem·per·ance \(')in-'tem-p(ə-)rəns\ *n* : lack of moderation; *esp* : habitual or excessive drinking of intoxicants — **in·tem·per·ate** \-p(ə-)rət\ *adj* — **in·tem·per·ate·ness** *n*

in·tend \in-'tend\ *vb* [ME *entenden, intenden,* fr. MF *entendre* to purpose, fr. L *indendere* to stretch out, to purpose, fr. *tendere* to stretch] **1** : to have in mind as a purpose or aim **2** : to design for a specified use or future

in·ten·dant \in-'ten-dənt\ *n* : a governor or similar administrative official esp. under the French, Spanish, or Portuguese monarchies

¹in·tend·ed \-'ten-dəd\ *adj* **1** : expected to be such in the future; *esp* : BETROTHED **2** : INTENTIONAL

²intended *n* : an affianced person

in·tense \in-'tens\ *adj* **1** : existing in an extreme degree **2** : very large : CONSIDERABLE **3** : strained or straining to the utmost **4** : feeling deeply; *also* : deeply felt — **in·tense·ly** *adv*

in·ten·si·fy \in-'ten-sə-ˌfī\ *vb* **-fied; -fy·ing 1** : to make or become intense or more intensive **2** : to make more acute : SHARPEN *syn* aggravate, heighten, enhance, magnify — **in·ten·si·fi·ca·tion** \-ˌten-sə-fə-'kā-shən\ *n*

in·ten·si·ty \in-'ten-sət-ē\ *n, pl* **-ties 1** : the quality or state of being intense **2** : degree of strength, energy, or force

¹in·ten·sive \in-'ten-siv\ *adj* **1** : involving or marked by special effort **2** : serving to give emphasis — **in·ten·sive·ly** *adv*

²intensive *n* : an intensive word, particle, or prefix

intensive care *adj* : having special medical facilities, services, and equipment to meet the needs of gravely ill patients — **intensive care** *n*

¹in·tent \in-'tent\ *n* **1** : PURPOSE, AIM **2** : the state of mind with which an act is done : VOLITION **3** : MEANING, SIGNIFICANCE

²intent *adj* **1** : directed with keen or eager attention (an ~ gaze) **2** : ENGROSSED; *also* : DETERMINED — **in·tent·ly** *adv* — **in·tent·ness** *n*

in·ten·tion \in-'ten-chən\ *n* **1** : a determination to act in a certain way **2** : PURPOSE, AIM, END *syn* intent, design, object, objective, goal

in·ten·tion·al \in-'tench-(ə-)nəl\ *adj* : done by intention or design : INTENDED — **in·ten·tion·al·ly** *adv*

in·ter \in-'tər\ *vb* **in·terred; in·ter·ring** [ME *enteren,* fr. OF *enterrer,* fr. L *in* in + *terra* earth] : BURY

in·ter·ac·tion \ˌint-ər-'ak-shən\ *n* : mutual or reciprocal action or influence — **in·ter·act** \-'akt\ *vb*

in·ter·ac·tive \-'ak-tiv\ *adj* **1** : mutually or reciprocally active **2** : allowing two-way electronic communications (as between a person and a computer) — **in·ter·ac·tive·ly** *adv*

in·ter alia \ˌint-ər-'ā-lē-ə, -'äl-ē-\ *adv* : among other things

in·ter·atom·ic \ˌint-ər-ə-'täm-ik\ *adj* : existing or acting between atoms

in·ter·breed \-'brēd\ *vb* **-bred** \-'bred\ ; **-breed·ing** : to breed together

in·ter·ca·la·ry \in-'tər-kə-ˌler-ē\ *adj* **1** : INTERCALATED (February 29 is an ~ day) **2** : INTERPOLATED

in·ter·ca·late \-ˌlāt\ *vb* **-lat·ed; -lat·ing 1** : to insert (as a day) in a calendar **2** : to insert between or among existing elements or layers — **in·ter·ca·la·tion** \-ˌtər-kə-'lā-shən\ *n*

in·ter·cede \ˌint-ər-'sēd\ *vb* **-ced·ed; -ced·ing** : to act between parties with a view to reconciling differences

¹in·ter·cept \ˌint-ər-'sept\ *vb* **1** : to stop or interrupt the progress or course of **2** : to include (as part of a curve or solid) between two points, curves, or surfaces **3** : to gain possession of (an opponent's pass in football) — **in·ter·cep·tion** \-'sep-shən\ *n*

²in·ter·cept \'int-ər-ˌsept\ *n* : INTERCEPTION; *esp* : the interception of a target by an interceptor or missile

in·ter·cep·tor \ˌint-ər-'sep-tər\ *n* : a fighter plane or missile designed for defense against attacking bombers or missiles

in·ter·ces·sion \ˌint-ər-'sesh-ən\ *n* **1** : MEDIATION **2** : prayer or petition in favor of another — **in·ter·ces·sor** \-'ses-ər\ *n* — **in·ter·ces·so·ry** \-'ses-(ə-)rē\ *adj*

¹in·ter·change \ˌint-ər-'chānj\ *vb* **1** : to put each in the place of the other **2** : EXCHANGE **3** : to change places mutually — **in·ter·change·able** \-'chān-jə-bəl\ *adj* — **in·ter·change·ably** \-blē\ *adv*

²in·ter·change \'int-ər-ˌchānj\ *n* **1** : EXCHANGE **2** : a highway junction that by separated levels permits passage between highways without crossing traffic streams

in·ter·col·le·giate \ˌint-ər-kə-'lē-j(ē-)ət\ *adj* : existing or carried on between colleges

in·ter·com \'int-ər-ˌkäm\ *n* : INTERCOMMUNICATION SYSTEM

in·ter·com·mun·i·ca·tion system \ˌint-ər-kə-ˌmyü-nə-'kā-shən-\ *n* : a two-way communication system with microphone and loudspeaker at each station for localized use

in·ter·con·ti·nen·tal \-ˌkänt-ᵊn-'ent-ᵊl\ *adj* **1** : extending among or carried on between continents (~ trade) **2** : capable of traveling between continents (~ ballistic missiles)

in·ter·course \'int-ər-ˌkōrs\ *n* **1** : connection or dealings between persons or nations **2** : physical sexual contact between individuals that involves the genitalia of at least one person (oral ~) (heterosexual ~) ; *esp* : SEXUAL INTERCOURSE

in·ter·de·nom·i·na·tion·al \ˌint-ər-di-ˌnäm-ə-'nā-sh(ə-)nəl\ *adj* : involving different denominations

in·ter·de·part·men·tal \ˌint-ər-di-ˌpärt-'ment-ᵊl, -ˌdē-\ *adj* : carried on between or involving different departments (as of a college)

in·ter·de·pen·dent \ˌint-ər-di-ˈpen-dənt\ *adj* : dependent upon one another — **in·ter·de·pen·dence** \-dəns\ *n*

in·ter·dict \ˌint-ər-ˈdikt\ *vb* 1 : to prohibit by decree 2 : to destroy, cut, or damage (as an enemy line of supply) — **in·ter·dic·tion** \-ˈdik-shən\ *n*

in·ter·dis·ci·plin·ary \-ˈdis-ə-plə-ˌner-ē\ *adj* : involving two or more academic, scientific, or artistic disciplines

¹**in·ter·est** \ˈin-t(ə-)rəst, -tə-ˌrest\ *n* 1 : right, title, or legal share in something 2 : a charge for borrowed money that is generally a percentage of the amount borrowed : the return received by capital on its investment 3 : WELFARE, BENEFIT; *also* : SELF-INTEREST 4 *pl* : a group financially interested in an industry or enterprise 5 : CURIOSITY, CONCERN 6 : readiness to be concerned with or moved by an object or class of objects 7 : a quality in a thing that arouses interest

²**interest** *vb* 1 : to persuade to participate or engage 2 : to engage the attention of

in·ter·est·ing *adj* : holding the attention — **in·ter·est·ing·ly** *adv*

in·ter·face \ˈint-ər-ˌfās\ *n* 1 : a surface forming a common boundary of two bodies, spaces, or phases (an oil-water ∼) 2 : the place at which two independent systems meet and act on or communicate with each other (the man-machine ∼) 3 : the means by which interaction or communication is effected at an interface — **in·ter·fa·cial** \ˌint-ər-ˈfā-shəl\ *adj*

in·ter·faith \ˌint-ər-ˈfāth\ *adj* : involving persons of different religious faiths

in·ter·fere \ˌint-ə(r)-fiər\ *vb* -**fered**; -**fering** [MF (*s'*)*entreferir* to strike one another, fr. OF, fr. *entre* between, among + *ferir* to strike, fr. L *ferire*] 1 : to come in collision or be in opposition : CLASH 2 : to enter into the affairs of others 3 : to affect one another

in·ter·fer·ence \-ˈfir-əns\ *n* 1 : the act or process of interfering 2 : something that interferes : OBSTRUCTION 3 : the mutual effect on meeting of two waves resulting in areas of increased and decreased amplitude 4 : the blocking of an opponent in football to make way for the ballcarrier 5 : the illegal hindering of an opponent in sports

in·ter·fer·om·e·ter \ˌint-ə(r)-fə-ˈräm-ət-ər\ *n* : a device that uses the interference of waves for making precise measurements — **in·ter·fer·om·e·try** \-fə-ˈräm-ə-trē\ *n*

in·ter·fer·on \ˌint-ər-ˈfiər-ˌän\ *n* : an antiviral protein of low molecular weight produced usu. by animal cells in response to a virus, a parasite in the cell, or a chemical

in·ter·fuse \ˌint-ər-ˈfyüz\ *vb* 1 : to combine by fusing : BLEND 2 : INFUSE

in·ter·ga·lac·tic \ˌint-ər-gə-ˈlak-tik\ *adj* : relating to or situated in the spaces between galaxies

in·ter·gla·cial \-ˈglā-shəl\ *adj* : occurring between successive glaciations

in·ter·gov·ern·men·tal \-ˌgəv-ər(n)-ˈment-ᵊl\ *adj* : existing or occurring between two governments or levels of government

in·ter·im \ˈin-tə-rəm\ *n* [L, adv., meanwhile, fr. *inter* between] : a time intervening : INTERVAL — **interim** *adj*

¹**in·te·ri·or** \in-ˈtir-ē-ər\ *adj* 1 : lying, occurring, or functioning within the limiting boundaries : INSIDE, INNER 2 : remote from the surface, border, or shore : INLAND

²**interior** *n* 1 : INSIDE 2 : the inland part (as of a country) 3 : the internal affairs of a state or nation 4 : a scene or view of the interior of a building

interior decoration *n* : INTERIOR DESIGN — **interior decorator** *n*

interior design *n* : the art or practice of planning and supervising the design and execution of architectural interiors and their furnishings — **interior designer** *n*

interj *abbr* interjection

in·ter·ject \ˌint-ər-ˈjekt\ *vb* : to throw in between or among other things

in·ter·jec·tion \ˌint-ər-ˈjek-shən\ *n* : an exclamatory word (as *ouch*) — **in·ter·jec·tion·al·ly** \-sh(ə-)nəl-ē\ *adv*

in·ter·lace \ˌint-ər-ˈlās\ *vb* 1 : to unite by or as if by lacing together : INTERWEAVE 2 : INTERSPERSE

in·ter·lard \ˌint-ər-ˈlärd\ *vb* : to insert or introduce at intervals : INTERSPERSE

in·ter·leave \ˌint-ər-ˈlēv\ *vb* -**leaved**; -**leav·ing** : to arrange in alternate layers

¹**in·ter·line** \ˌint-ər-ˈlīn\ *vb* : to insert between lines already written or printed

²**interline** *vb* : to provide (as a coat) with an interlining

in·ter·lin·ear \ˌint-ər-ˈlin-ē-ər\ *adj* : inserted between lines already written or printed (an ∼ translation of a text)

in·ter·lin·ing \ˈint-ər-ˌlī-niŋ\ *n* : a lining (as of a coat) between the ordinary lining and the outside fabric

in·ter·link \ˌint-ər-ˈliŋk\ *vb* : to link together

in·ter·lock \ˌint-ər-ˈläk\ *vb* 1 : to engage or interlace together : lock together : UNITE 2 : to connect in such a way that action of one part affects action of another part — **in·ter·lock** \ˈint-ər-ˌläk\ *n*

in·ter·loc·u·tor \ˌint-ər-ˈläk-yət-ər\ *n* : one who takes part in dialogue or conversation

in·ter·loc·u·to·ry \-yə-ˌtōr-ē\ *adj* : pronounced during the progress of a legal action and having only provisional force (an ∼ decree)

in·ter·lope \ˌint-ər-ˈlōp\ *vb* -**loped**; -**lop·ing** 1 : to encroach on the rights (as in

trade) of others **2** : INTRUDE, INTER-
FERE — **in·ter·lop·er** n

in·ter·lude \'int-ər-ˌlüd\ n **1** : a usu.
short simple play or dramatic entertainment **2** : an intervening period,
space, or event **3** : a short piece of
music inserted between the parts of a
longer composition or a religious service

in·ter·mar·riage \ˌint-ər-'mar-ij\ n
: marriage between members of different groups; also : marriage within
one's own group

in·ter·mar·ry \-'mar-ē\ vb **1** : to marry
each other **2** : to marry within a group
3 : to become connected by intermar-
riage

in·ter·med·dle \ˌint-ər-'med-ᵊl\ vb
: MEDDLE, INTERFERE

¹in·ter·me·di·ary \ˌint-ər-'mēd-ē-ˌer-ē\
adj **1** : INTERMEDIATE **2** : acting as a
mediator

²intermediary n, pl **-ar·ies** : MEDIATOR,
GO-BETWEEN

¹in·ter·me·di·ate \ˌint-ər-'mēd-ē-ət\
adj : being or occurring at the middle
place or degree or between extremes

²intermediate n **1** : an intermediate
term, object, or class **2** : INTERMEDI-
ARY

intermediate school n **1** : JUNIOR HIGH
SCHOOL **2** : a school usu. comprising
grades 4–6

in·ter·ment \in-'tər-mənt\ n : BURIAL

in·ter·mez·zo \ˌint-ər-'met-sō, -'med-
zō\ n, pl **-zi** \-sē, -zē\ or **-zos** [It, deriv.
of L intermedius intermediate] : a
short movement connecting major
sections of an extended musical work
(as a symphony); also : a short independent instrumental composition

in·ter·mi·na·ble \(')in-'tərm-(ə-)nə-bəl\
adj : ENDLESS; esp : wearisomely protracted — **in·ter·mi·na·bly** \-blē\
adv

in·ter·min·gle \ˌint-ər-'miŋ-gəl\ vb : to
mingle or mix together

in·ter·mis·sion \ˌint-ər-'mish-ən\ n **1**
: INTERRUPTION, BREAK **2** : a temporary halt esp. in a public performance

in·ter·mit \-'mit\ vb **-mit·ted; -mit·ting**
: DISCONTINUE; also : to be intermittent

in·ter·mit·tent \-'mit-ᵊnt\ adj : coming
and going at intervals syn recurrent,
periodic, alternate — **in·ter·mit·tent·ly**
adv

in·ter·mix \ˌint-ər-'miks\ vb : to mix together : INTERMINGLE — **in·ter·mix-
ture** \-'miks-chər\ n

in·ter·mo·lec·u·lar \-mə-'lek-yə-lər\ adj
: existing or acting between molecules

in·ter·mon·tane \ˌint-ər-'män-ˌtān\ or
in·ter·mont \'int-ər-ˌmänt\ adj : situated between mountains

¹in·tern \'in-ˌtərn, in-'tərn\ vb : to confine or impound esp. during a war —
in·tern·ee \(ˌ)in-ˌtər-'nē\ n — **in·tern-
ment** \in-'tərn-mənt\ n

²in·tern or **in·terne** \'in-ˌtərn\ n : an ad-

vanced student or recent graduate (as
in medicine) gaining supervised practical experience — **in·tern·ship** n

³in·tern \'in-ˌtərn\ vb : to act as an in-
tern

in·ter·nal \in-'tərn-ᵊl\ adj **1** : INWARD,
INTERIOR **2** : having to do with or situated in the inside of the body ⟨~ pain⟩
3 : of or relating to the domestic affairs of a country or state ⟨~ revenue⟩
4 : of, relating to, or existing within
the mind **5** : INTRINSIC, INHERENT —
in·ter·nal·ly \-ē\ adv

internal–combustion engine n : a heat
engine in which the combustion that
generates the heat takes place inside
the engine proper

internal medicine n : a branch of medicine that deals with the diagnosis and
treatment of nonsurgical diseases

¹in·ter·na·tion·al \ˌint-ər-'nash-(ə-)nəl\
adj **1** : common to or affecting two or
more nations ⟨~ trade⟩ **2** : of, relating
to, or constituting a group having
members in two or more nations —
in·ter·na·tion·al·ly \-ē\ adv

²international n : one that is international; esp : an organization of international scope

in·ter·na·tion·al·ism \-'nash-(ə-)nəl-ˌiz-
əm\ n : a policy of political and economic cooperation among nations;
also : an attitude favoring such a
policy

in·ter·na·tion·al·ize \ˌint-ər-'nash-
(ə-)nəl-ˌīz\ vb : to make international;
esp : to place under international control

in·ter·ne·cine \ˌint-ər-'nes-ˌēn, -'nē-
ˌsīn\ adj [L internecinus, fr. inter-
necare to destroy, kill, fr. necare to
kill, fr. nec-, nex violent death] **1**
: DEADLY; esp : mutually destructive **2**
: of, relating to, or involving conflict
within a group ⟨~ feuds⟩

in·ter·nist \'in-ˌtər-nəst\ n : a specialist
in internal medicine esp. as distinguished from a surgeon

in·ter·node \'int-ər-ˌnōd\ n : an interval
or part between two nodes (as of a
stem)

in·ter·nun·cio \ˌint-ər-'nən-sē-ˌō,
-'nün-\ n [It internunzio] : a papal le-
gate of lower rank than a nuncio

in·ter·of·fice \-'of-əs\ adj : functioning
or communicating between the offices
of an organization

in·ter·per·son·al \-'pərs-(ᵊ-)nəl\ adj : being, relating to, or involving relations
between persons — **in·ter·per·son·al·ly**
\-ē\ adv

in·ter·plan·e·tary \ˌint-ər-'plan-ə-ˌter-ē\
adj : existing, carried on, or operating
between planets ⟨~ space⟩

in·ter·play \'int-ər-ˌplā\ n : INTERAC-
TION

in·ter·po·late \in-'tər-pə-ˌlāt\ vb **-lat·ed;
-lat·ing** **1** : to change (as a text) by
inserting new or foreign matter **2** : to
insert (as words) into a text or into a
conversation **3** : to estimate values of

(a function) between two known values — **in·ter·po·la·tion** \-ˌtər-pə-ˈlā-shən\ n

in·ter·pose \ˌint-ər-ˈpōz\ vb **-posed; -pos·ing 1** : to place between **2** : to thrust in : INTRUDE, INTERRUPT **3** : to inject between parts of a conversation or argument **4** : to be or come between syn interfere, intercede, intermediate, intervene — **in·ter·po·si·tion** \-pə-ˈzish-ən\ n

in·ter·pret \in-ˈtər-prət\ vb **1** : to explain the meaning of; also : to act as an interpreter : TRANSLATE **2** : to understand according to individual belief, judgment, or interest **3** : to represent artistically — **in·ter·pret·er** n — **in·ter·pre·tive** \-ˈtər-prət-iv\ adj

in·ter·pre·ta·tion \in-ˌtər-prə-ˈtā-shən\ n **1** : EXPLANATION **2** : an instance of artistic interpretation in performance or adaptation — **in·ter·pre·ta·tive** \-ˈtər-prə-ˌtāt-iv\ adj

in·ter·ra·cial \-ˈrā-shəl\ adj : of, involving, or designed for members of different races

in·ter·reg·num \ˌint-ə-ˈreg-nəm\ n, pl **-nums** or **-na** \-nə\ **1** : the time during which a throne is vacant between two successive reigns or regimes **2** : a pause in a continuous series

in·ter·re·late \ˌint-ə(r)-ri-ˈlāt\ vb : to bring into or have a mutual relationship — **in·ter·re·lat·ed·ness** \-lāt-əd-nəs\ n — **in·ter·re·la·tion** \-ˈlā-shən\ n — **in·ter·re·la·tion·ship** n

interrog abbr interrogative

in·ter·ro·gate \in-ˈter-ə-ˌgāt\ vb **-gat·ed; -gat·ing** : to question esp. formally and systematically : ASK — **in·ter·ro·ga·tion** \-ˌter-ə-ˈgā-shən\ n — **in·ter·ro·ga·tor** \-ˈter-ə-ˌgāt-ər\ n

in·ter·rog·a·tive \ˌint-ə-ˈräg-ət-iv\ adj : asking a question (~ sentence) — **interrogative** n

in·ter·rog·a·to·ry \ˌint-ə-ˈräg-ə-ˌtōr-ē\ adj : INTERROGATIVE

in·ter·rupt \ˌint-ə-ˈrəpt\ vb **1** : to stop or hinder by breaking in **2** : to break the uniformity or continuity of **3** : to break in with questions or remarks while another is speaking — **in·ter·rupt·er** n — **in·ter·rup·tion** \-ˈrəp-shən\ n — **in·ter·rup·tive** \-ˈrəp-tiv\ adv

in·ter·scho·las·tic \ˌint-ər-skə-ˈlas-tik\ adj : existing or carried on between schools

in·ter·sect \ˌint-ər-ˈsekt\ vb : to cut or divide by passing through : cut across : meet and cross : OVERLAP — **in·ter·sec·tion** \-ˈsek-shən\ n

in·ter·sperse \ˌint-ər-ˈspərs\ vb **-spersed; -spers·ing 1** : to place something at intervals in or among **2** : to insert at intervals among other things — **in·ter·sper·sion** \-ˈspər-zhən\ n

¹**in·ter·state** \ˌint-ər-ˈstāt\ adj : relating to, including, or connecting two or more states esp. of the U.S.

²**in·ter·state** \ˈint-ər-ˌstāt\ n : an interstate highway

in·ter·stel·lar \ˌint-ər-ˈstel-ər\ adj : located or taking place among the stars

in·ter·stice \in-ˈtər-stəs\ n, pl **-stic·es** \-stə-ˌsēz, -stə-səz\ : a space that intervenes between things : CHINK — **in·ter·sti·tial** \ˌint-ər-ˈstish-əl\ adj

in·ter·tid·al \ˌint-ər-ˈtīd-ᵊl\ adj : of, relating to, or being the area that is above low-tide mark but exposed to tidal flooding

in·ter·twine \-ˈtwīn\ vb : to twine or cause to twine about one another : INTERLACE

in·ter·twist \-ˈtwist\ vb : INTERTWINE

in·ter·ur·ban \-ˈər-bən\ adj : going between cities or towns

in·ter·val \ˈint-ər-vəl\ n [ME intervalle, fr. MF, fr. L intervallum space between ramparts, interval, fr. inter- between + vallum rampart] **1** : a space of time between events or states : PAUSE **2** : a space between objects, units, or states **3** : the difference in pitch between two tones

in·ter·vene \ˌint-ər-ˈvēn\ vb **-vened; -ven·ing 1** : to occur, fall, or come between points of time or between events **2** : to enter or appear as an unrelated feature or circumstance (rain intervened and we postponed the trip) **3** : to come in or between in order to stop, settle, or modify (~ in a quarrel) **4** : to occur or lie between two things — **in·ter·ven·tion** \-ˈven-chən\ n

in·ter·ven·tion·ism \-ˈven-chə-ˌniz-əm\ n : interference by one country in the political affairs of another — **in·ter·ven·tion·ist** \-ˈvench-(ə-)nəst\ n or adj

in·ter·view \ˈint-ər-ˌvyü\ n **1** : a formal consultation **2** : a meeting at which a writer or reporter obtains information from a person; also : the recorded or written account of such a meeting — **interview** vb — **in·ter·view·er** n

in·ter·vo·cal·ic \ˌint-ər-vō-ˈkal-ik\ adj : immediately preceded and immediately followed by a vowel

in·ter·weave \ˌint-ər-ˈwēv\ vb **-wove** \-ˈwōv\ also **-weaved; -wo·ven** \-ˈwō-vən\ also **-weaved; -weav·ing** : to weave or blend together : INTERTWINE, INTERMINGLE — **in·ter·wo·ven** \-ˈwō-vən\ adj

in·tes·tate \in-ˈtes-ˌtāt, -tət\ adj **1** : having made no valid will (died ~) **2** : not disposed of by will (~ estate)

in·tes·tine \in-ˈtes-tən\ n : the tubular part of the alimentary canal that extends from stomach to anus and consists of a long narrow upper part (small intestine) followed by a broader shorter lower part (large intestine) — **in·tes·ti·nal** \-tən-ᵊl\ adj

in·ti \ˈint-ē\ n — see MONEY table

¹**in·ti·mate** \ˈint-ə-ˌmāt\ vb **-mat·ed; -mat·ing 1** : ANNOUNCE, NOTIFY **2** : to communicate indirectly : HINT — **in·ti·ma·tion** \ˌint-ə-mā-shən\ n

²in·ti·mate \'int-ə-mət\ adj 1 : INTRINSIC; also : INNERMOST 2 : marked by very close association, contact, or familiarity 3 : marked by a warm friendship 4 : suggesting informal warmth or privacy 5 : of a very personal or private nature — in·ti·ma·cy \'int-ə-mə-sē\ n — in·ti·mate·ly adv

³in·ti·mate \'int-ə-mət\ n : an intimate friend, associate, or confidant

in·tim·i·date \in-'tim-ə-ˌdāt\ vb -dat·ed; -dat·ing : to make timid or fearful ; FRIGHTEN; esp : to compel or deter by or as if by threats syn cow, bulldoze, bully, browbeat — in·tim·i·da·tion \-ˌtim-ə-'dā-shən\ n

intl or intnl abbr international

in·to \'in-tə, 'in-tü\ prep 1 : to the inside of ⟨ran ~ the house⟩ 2 : to the state, condition, or form of ⟨got ~ trouble⟩ 3 : AGAINST ⟨ran ~ a wall⟩

in·tol·er·a·ble \(')in-'täl-(ə-)rə-bəl\ adj 1 : UNBEARABLE 2 : EXCESSIVE — in·tol·er·a·bly \-blē\ adv

in·tol·er·ant \(')in-'täl-ə-rənt\ adj 1 : unable to endure 2 : unwilling to endure 3 : unwilling to grant equality, freedom, or other social rights : BIGOTED — in·tol·er·ance \-rəns\ n

in·to·na·tion \ˌin-tə-'nā-shən\ n 1 : the act of intoning and esp. of chanting 2 : something that is intoned 3 : the manner of singing, playing, or uttering tones 4 : the rise and fall in pitch of the voice in speech

in·tone \in-'tōn\ vb in·toned; in·ton·ing : to utter in musical or prolonged tones : CHANT

in to·to \in-'tōt-ō\ adv [L, on the whole] : TOTALLY, ENTIRELY

in·tox·i·cant \in-'täk-si-kənt\ n : something that intoxicates; esp : an alcoholic drink — intoxicant adj

in·tox·i·cate \-sə-ˌkāt\ vb -cat·ed; -cat·ing [ML intoxicare, fr. L toxicum poison] 1 : to make drunk 2 : to excite or elate greatly — in·tox·i·ca·tion \-ˌtäk-sə-'kā-shən\ n

in·trac·ta·ble \(')in-'trak-tə-bəl\ adj : not easily controlled : OBSTINATE

in·tra·mo·lec·u·lar \ˌin-trə-mə-'lek-yə-lər\ adj : exciting or acting within a molecule

in·tra·mu·ral \-'myùr-əl\ adj : being or occurring within the walls or limits (as of a city or college) ⟨~ sports⟩

in·tra·mus·cu·lar \-'məs-kyə-lər\ adj : situated within or administered by entering a muscle — in·tra·mus·cu·lar·ly adv

intrans abbr intransitive

in·tran·si·geance \in-'trans-ə-jəns, -'tranz-\ n : INTRANSIGENCE

in·tran·si·gence \-jəns\ n : the quality or state of being intransigent

in·tran·si·gent \-jənt\ adj : UNCOMPROMISING; also : IRRECONCILABLE — intransigent n

in·tran·si·tive \(')in-'trans-ət-iv, -'tranz-\ adj : not transitive; esp : not having or containing an object ⟨an ~

verb⟩ — in·tran·si·tive·ly adv — in·tran·si·tive·ness n

in·tra·state \ˌin-trə-'stāt\ adj : existing or occurring within a state

in·tra·uter·ine device \-'yüt-ə-rən-, -ˌrīn\ n : a device (as a spiral of plastic or a ring of stainless steel) inserted and left in the uterus to prevent pregnancy

in·tra·ve·nous \ˌin-trə-'vē-nəs\ adj : being within or entering by way of the veins — in·tra·ve·nous·ly adv

intrench var of ENTRENCH

in·trep·id \in-'trep-əd\ adj : characterized by resolute fearlessness, fortitude, and endurance — in·tre·pid·i·ty \ˌin-trə-'pid-ət-ē\ n

in·tri·cate \'in-tri-kət\ adj [ME, fr. L intricatus, pp. of intricare to entangle, fr. tricae trifles, impediments] 1 : having many complexly interrelated parts : COMPLICATED 2 : difficult to follow, understand, or solve — in·tri·ca·cy \-tri-kə-sē\ n — in·tri·cate·ly adv

¹in·trigue \in-'trēg\ vb in·trigued; in·trigu·ing 1 : to accomplish by intrigue 2 : to carry on an intrigue; esp : PLOT, SCHEME 3 : to arouse the interest, desire, or curiosity of — in·trigu·ing·ly \-iŋ-lē\ adv

²in·trigue \'in-ˌtrēg, in-'trēg\ n 1 : a secret scheme : MACHINATION 2 : a clandestine love affair

in·trin·sic \in-'trin-zik, -sik\ adj : belonging to the essential nature or constitution of a thing — in·trin·si·cal·ly \-zi-k(ə-)lē, -si-\ adv

introd abbr introduction

in·tro·duce \ˌin-trə-'d(y)üs\ vb -duced; -duc·ing 1 : to lead or bring in esp. for the first time 2 : to bring into practice or use 3 : to cause to be acquainted 4 : to present for discussion 5 : to put in syn insinuate, interpolate, interpose, interject — in·tro·duc·tion \-'dək-shən\ n — in·tro·duc·to·ry \-'dək-t(ə-)rē\ adj

in·troit \'in-ˌtrō-ət, -ˌtròit\ n 1 often cap : the first part of the traditional proper of the Mass 2 : a piece of music sung or played at the beginning of a worship service

in·tro·mit \ˌin-trə-'mit\ vb -mit·ted; -mit·ting : to send or put in : INSERT — in·tro·mis·sion \-'mish-ən\ n

in·tro·spec·tion \-'spek-shən\ n : a reflective looking inward : an examination of one's own thoughts or feelings — in·tro·spect \ˌin-trə-'spekt\ vb — in·tro·spec·tive \-'spek-tiv\ adj — in·tro·spec·tive·ly adv

in·tro·vert \'in-trə-ˌvərt\ n : a person more interested in his own mental life than in the world about him — in·tro·ver·sion \ˌin-trə-'vər-zhən\ n — introvert adj — in·tro·vert·ed \'in-trə-ˌvərt-əd\ adj

in·trude \in-'trüd\ vb in·trud·ed; in·trud·ing 1 : to thrust, enter, or force in or upon 2 : ENCROACH, TRESPASS — in·trud·er n — in·tru·sion \-'trü-zhən\

n — in·tru·sive \-'trü-siv\ *adj* — in·tru·sive·ness *n*

intrust *var of* ENTRUST

in·tu·it \in-'t(y)ü-ət\ *vb* : to apprehend by intuition

in·tu·ition \,in-t(y)ú-'ish-ən\ *n* 1 : the power or faculty of knowing things without conscious reasoning 2 : quick and ready insight — in·tu·i·tive \in-'t(y)ü-ət-iv\ *adj* — in·tu·i·tive·ly *adv*

in·tu·mes·cence \,in-t(y)ü-'mes-²ns\ *n* 1 : the state of being or the action of becoming swollen 2 : something swollen or enlarged — in·tu·mesce \-'mes\ *vb* — in·tu·mes·cent \-'²nt\ *adj*

In·u·it \'in-(y)ə-wət\ *n* [Aleut *inuit*, pl. of *inuk* person] 1 : a member of the Eskimo people of America 2 : the language of the Inuit people

in·un·date \'in-ən-,dāt\ *vb* -dat·ed; -dat·ing : to cover with or as if with a flood : OVERFLOW — in·un·da·tion \,in-ən-'dā-shən\ *n*

in·ure \in-'(y)úr\ *vb* in·ured; in·ur·ing [ME *enuren*, fr. *en-* in + *ure* n., use, custom, fr. MF *uevre* work, practice, fr. L *opera* work] 1 : to accustom to accept something undesirable 2 : to become of advantage : ACCRUE

inv *abbr* 1 inventor 2 invoice

in vac·uo \in-'vak-yə-,wō\ *adv* [L] : in a vacuum

in·vade \in-'vād\ *vb* in·vad·ed; in·vad·ing 1 : to enter for conquest or plunder 2 : to encroach upon 3 : to spread through and usu. harm (germs ~ the tissues) — in·vad·er *n*

¹**in·val·id** \(')in-'val-əd\ *adj* : being without foundation or force in fact, reason, or law — in·va·lid·i·ty \,in-və-'lid-ət-ē\ *n* — in·val·id·ly *adv*

²**in·val·id** \in-və-ləd\ *adj* : defective in health : SICKLY

³**in·va·lid** \'in-və-ləd\ *n* : a person in usu. chronic ill health — in·va·lid·ism \-,iz-əm\ *n*

⁴**in·va·lid** \'in-və-ləd, -,lid\ *vb* 1 : to remove from active duty by reason of sickness or disability 2 : to make sickly or disabled

in·val·i·date \(')in-'val-ə-,dāt\ *vb* : to make invalid; *esp* : to weaken or make valueless

in·valu·able \(')in-'val-yə(-wə)-bəl\ *adj* : valuable beyond estimation

in·vari·able \(')in-'ver-ē-ə-bəl\ *adj* : not changing or capable of change : CONSTANT — in·vari·ably \-blē\ *adv*

in·va·sion \in-'vā-zhən\ *n* : an act or instance of invading; *esp* : entry of an army into a country for conquest

in·vec·tive \in-'vek-tiv\ *n* 1 : an abusive expression or speech 2 : abusive language — invective *adj*

in·veigh \in-'vā\ *vb* : to protest or complain bitterly or vehemently : RAIL

in·vei·gle \in-'vā-gəl, -'vē-\ *vb* in·vei·gled; in·vei·gling \-g(ə-)liŋ\ [modif. of MF *aveugler* to blind, hoodwink] 1 : to win over by flattery : ENTICE 2 : to acquire by ingenuity or flattery

in·vent \in-'vent\ *vb* 1 : to think up 2 : to create or produce for the first time — in·ven·tor \-'vent-ər\ *n*

in·ven·tion \in-'ven-chən\ *n* 1 : INVENTIVENESS 2 : a creation of the imagination; *esp* : a false conception 3 : a device, contrivance, or process originated after study and experiment 4 : the act or process of inventing

in·ven·tive \in-'vent-iv\ *adj* 1 : CREATIVE, INGENIOUS (an ~ composer) 2 : characterized by invention (an ~ turn of mind) — in·ven·tive·ness *n*

in·ven·to·ry \'in-vən-,tōr-ē\ *n, pl* -ries 1 : an itemized list of current goods or assets 2 : SURVEY, SUMMARY 3 : STOCK, SUPPLY 4 : the act or process of taking an inventory — inventory *vb*

in·verse \(')in-'vərs, 'in-,vərs\ *adj* : opposite in order, nature, or effect : REVERSED — in·verse·ly *adv*

in·ver·sion \in-'vər-zhən\ *n* 1 : a reversal of position, order, or relationship; *esp* : an increase of temperature with altitude through a layer of air 2 : the act or process of inverting

in·vert \in-'vərt\ *vb* 1 : to reverse in position, order, or relationship 2 : to turn upside down or inside out 3 : to turn inward

¹**in·ver·te·brate** \(')in-'vərt-ə-brət, -,brāt\ *adj* : lacking a backbone; *also* : of or relating to invertebrates

²**invertebrate** *n* : an invertebrate animal

¹**in·vest** \in-'vest\ *vb* 1 : to install formally in an office or honor 2 : to furnish with power or authority : VEST 3 : to cover completely : ENVELOP 4 : CLOTHE, ADORN 5 : BESIEGE 6 : to endow with a quality or characteristic

²**invest** *vb* 1 : to commit money in order to earn a financial return 2 : to expend for future benefits or advantages 3 : to make an investment — in·ves·tor \-'ves-tər\ *n*

in·ves·ti·gate \in-'ves-tə-,gāt\ *vb* -gat·ed; -gat·ing [L *investigare* to track, investigate, fr. *vestigium* footprint, track] : to study by close examination and systematic inquiry — in·ves·ti·ga·tion \-,ves-tə-'gā-shən\ *n* — in·ves·ti·ga·tor \in-'ves-tə-,gāt-ər\ *n*

in·ves·ti·ture \in-'ves-tə-,chúr, -chər\ *n* 1 : the act of ratifying or establishing in office : CONFIRMATION 2 : something that covers or adorns

¹**in·vest·ment** \in-'ves(t)-mənt\ *n* 1 : an outer layer : ENVELOPE 2 : INVESTITURE 3 : BLOCKADE, SIEGE

²**investment** *n* : the outlay of money for income or profit; *also* : the sum invested or the property purchased

in·vet·er·ate \in-'vet-(ə-)rət\ *adj* 1 : firmly established by age or long persistence 2 : confirmed in a habit — in·vet·er·a·cy \-(ə-)rə-sē\ *n*

in·vi·a·ble \(')in-'vī-ə-bəl\ *adj* : incapable of surviving

in·vid·i·ous \in-'vid-ē-əs\ *adj* 1 : tending to cause discontent, animosity, or envy 2 : ENVIOUS 3 : INJURIOUS — **in·vid·i·ous·ly** adv

in·vig·o·rate \in-ˈvig-ə-ˌrāt\ vb **-rat·ed; -rat·ing** : to give life and energy to : ANIMATE — **in·vig·o·ra·tion** \-ˌvig-ə-ˈrā-shən\ n

in·vin·ci·ble \(ˈ)in-ˈvin-sə-bəl\ adj : incapable of being conquered, overcome, or subdued — **in·vin·ci·bil·i·ty** \(ˌ)in-ˌvin-sə-ˈbil-ət-ē\ n — **in·vin·ci·bly** \(ˈ)in-ˈvin-sə-blē\ adv

in·vi·o·la·ble \(ˈ)in-ˈvī-ə-lə-bəl\ adj 1 : safe from violation or profanation 2 : UNASSAILABLE — **in·vi·o·la·bil·i·ty** \(ˌ)in-ˌvī-ə-lə-ˈbil-ət-ē\ n

in·vi·o·late \(ˈ)in-ˈvī-ə-lət\ adj : not violated or profaned : PURE

in·vis·i·ble \(ˈ)in-ˈviz-ə-bəl\ adj 1 : incapable of being seen (∼ to the naked eye) 2 : HIDDEN 3 : IMPERCEPTIBLE, INCONSPICUOUS — **in·vis·i·bil·i·ty** \(ˌ)in-ˌviz-ə-ˈbil-ət-ē\ n — **in·vis·i·bly** \(ˈ)in-ˈviz-ə-blē\ adv

in·vi·ta·tion·al \ˌin-və-ˈtā-sh(ə-)nəl\ adj : limited to invited participants

in·vite \in-ˈvīt\ vb **in·vit·ed; in·vit·ing** 1 : ENTICE, TEMPT 2 : to increase the likelihood of 3 : to request the presence or participation of : ASK 4 : to request formally 5 : ENCOURAGE — **in·vi·ta·tion** \ˌin-və-ˈtā-shən\ n

in·vit·ing \in-ˈvīt-iŋ\ adj : ATTRACTIVE, TEMPTING

in·vo·ca·tion \ˌin-və-ˈkā-shən\ n 1 : SUPPLICATION; esp : a prayer at the beginning of a service 2 : a formula for conjuring : INCANTATION

¹**in·voice** \ˈin-ˌvȯis\ n [modif. of MF envois, pl. of envoi message] 1 : an itemized list of goods shipped usu. specifying the price and the terms of sale : BILL 2 : a consignment of merchandise

²**invoice** vb **in·voiced; in·voic·ing** : to make an invoice for : BILL

in·voke \in-ˈvōk\ vb **in·voked; in·vok·ing** 1 : to petition for help or support 2 : to appeal to or cite as authority (∼ a law) 3 : to call forth by incantation : CONJURE (∼ spirits) 4 : to make an earnest request for : SOLICIT 5 : to put into effect or operation 6 : to bring about : CAUSE

in·vo·lu·cre \ˈin-və-ˌlü-kər\ n : one or more whorls of bracts below and close to a flower or fruit

in·vol·un·tary \(ˈ)in-ˈväl-ən-ˌter-ē\ adj 1 : done contrary to or without choice 2 : COMPULSORY 3 : not subject to control by the will (∼ muscles) — **in·vol·un·tar·i·ly** \(ˌ)in-ˌväl-ən-ˈter-ə-lē\ adv

in·vo·lute \ˈin-və-ˌlüt\ adj 1 : curled spirally and usu. closely (∼ shell) 2 : INVOLVED, INTRICATE

in·vo·lu·tion \ˌin-və-ˈlü-shən\ n 1 : the act or an instance of enfolding or entangling 2 : COMPLEXITY, INTRICACY

in·volve \in-ˈvälv\ vb **in·volved; in·volv·ing** 1 : to draw in as a participant 2 : ENVELOP 3 : to relate closely : CONNECT 4 : to have as part of itself : IN-CLUDE 5 : ENTAIL, IMPLY 6 : to have an effect on — **in·volve·ment** n

in·volved \-ˈvälvd\ adj : INTRICATE, COMPLEX (an ∼ assassination plot)

in·vul·ner·a·ble \(ˈ)in-ˈvəl-nə-rə-bəl\ adj 1 : incapable of being wounded, injured, or damaged 2 : immune to or proof against attack — **in·vul·ner·a·bil·i·ty** \(ˌ)in-ˌvəl-nə-rə-ˈbil-ət-ē\ n — **in·vul·ner·a·bly** \(ˈ)in-ˈvəl-nə-rə-blē\ adv

¹**in·ward** \ˈin-wərd\ adj 1 : situated on the inside 2 : MENTAL; also : SPIRITUAL 3 : directed toward the interior

²**inward** or **in·wards** \-wərdz\ adv 1 : toward the inside, center, or interior 2 : toward the inner being

in·ward·ly \ˈin-wərd-lē\ adv 1 : MENTALLY, SPIRITUALLY 2 : INTERNALLY (bled ∼) 3 : to oneself (cursed ∼) 4 : toward the center or interior

IOC abbr International Olympic Committee

io·dide \ˈī-ə-ˌdīd\ n : a compound of iodine with another element or group

io·dine \ˈī-ə-ˌdīn, -əd-ᵊn\ n : a nonmetallic chemical element used in medicine and photography

io·dize \ˈī-ə-ˌdīz\ vb **io·dized; io·diz·ing** : to treat with iodine or an iodide

ion \ˈī-ən, ˈī-ˌän\ n [Gk, neut. of iōn, prp. of ienai to go; so called because in electrolysis it goes to one of the two poles] : an electrically charged particle or group of atoms — **ion·ic** \ī-ˈän-ik\ adj

ion·ize \ˈī-ə-ˌnīz\ vb **ion·ized; ion·iz·ing** 1 : to convert wholly or partly into ions 2 : to become ionized — **ion·iz·able** \-ˌnī-zə-bəl\ adj — **ion·iza·tion** \ˌī-ə-nə-ˈzā-shən\ n — **ion·iz·er** \ˈī-ə-ˌnī-zər\ n

ion·o·sphere \ī-ˈän-ə-ˌsfiər\ n : the part of the earth's atmosphere beginning at an altitude of about 30 miles and extending outward 300 miles or more that contains free electrically charged particles — **ion·o·spher·ic** \ī-ˌän-ə-ˈsfiə(ə)r-ik, -ˈsfer-\ adj

IOOF abbr Independent Order of Odd Fellows

io·ta \ī-ˈōt-ə\ n [L, fr. Gk iōta, the 9th letter of the Greek alphabet] : a very small quantity : JOT

IOU \ˌī-(ˌ)ō-ˈyü\ n : an acknowledgement of a debt

IP abbr innings pitched

ip·e·cac \ˈip-i-ˌkak\ n [Pg ipecacuanha] 1 : the dried rhizome and roots of ipecac used esp. as the source of an emetic 2 : a tropical So. American creeping plant related to the madder

ip·so fac·to \ˌip-sō-ˈfak-tō\ adv [NL, lit., by the fact itself] : by the very nature of the case

iq abbr [L idem quod] the same as

IQ \ˈī-ˈkyü\ n : INTELLIGENCE QUOTIENT

¹**Ir** abbr Irish

²**Ir** symbol iridium

IR abbr 1 information retrieval 2 internal revenue

IRA *abbr* **1** individual retirement account **2** Irish Republican Army

Ira·ni·an \ir-ˈā-nē-ən *also* -ˈā-\ *n* : a native or inhabitant of Iran — **Iranian** *adj*

Iraqi \i-ˈräk-ē, -ˈrak-\ *n* : a native or inhabitant of Iraq — **Iraqi** *adj*

iras·ci·ble \ir-ˈas-ə-bəl, ī-ˈras-\ *adj* : marked by hot temper and easily provoked anger **syn** choleric, testy, touchy, cranky, cross — **iras·ci·bil·i·ty** \-ˌas-ə-ˈbil-ət-ē, -ˌras-\ *n*

irate \ī-ˈrāt\ *adj* **1** : roused to ire **2** : arising from anger ⟨∼ words⟩ — **irate·ly** *adv*

IRBM *abbr* intermediate range ballistic missile

ire \ˈī(ə)r\ *n* : ANGER, WRATH — **ire·ful** *adj*

Ire *abbr* Ireland

iren·ic \i-ˈren-ik\ *adj* : conducive to or operating toward peace or conciliation

ir·i·des·cence \ir-ə-ˈdes-ᵊns\ *n* : a rainbowlike play of colors — **ir·i·des·cent** \-ᵊnt\ *adj*

irid·i·um \ir-ˈid-ē-əm\ *n* : a hard brittle very heavy metallic chemical element used in alloys

iris \ˈī-rəs\ *n, pl* **iris·es** *or* **iri·des** \ˈī-rə-ˌdēz, ˈir-ə-\ [ME, fr. L *iris* rainbow, iris plant, fr. Gk, rainbow, iris plant, iris of the eye] **1** : the colored part around the pupil of the eye **2** : any of a large genus of plants with linear basal leaves and large showy flowers

Irish \ˈīr-ish\ *n* **1** *Irish pl* : the people of Ireland **2** : the Celtic language of Ireland — **Irish** *adj* — **Irish·man** \-mən\ *n* — **Irish·wom·an** \-ˌwum-ən\ *n*

Irish bull *n* : an incongruous statement (as "it was hereditary in his family to have no children")

Irish coffee *n* : hot sugared coffee with Irish whiskey and whipped cream

Irish moss *n* : the dried and bleached plants of two red algae; *also* : either of these two red algae

Irish setter *n* : any of a breed of bird dogs with a mahogany-red coat

irk \ˈərk\ *vb* : to make weary, irritated, or bored : ANNOY

irk·some \ˈərk-səm\ *adj* : tending to irk : ANNOYING — **irk·some·ly** *adv*

¹iron \ˈī(-ə)rn\ *n* **1** : a heavy magnetic metallic chemical element that rusts easily, can be readily shaped, and is vital to biological processes **2** : something made of metal and esp. iron; *also* : something (as handcuffs) used to bind or restrain (put them in ∼s) **3** : a household device with a flat base that is heated and used for pressing cloth **4** : STRENGTH, HARDNESS

²iron *vb* **1** : to press or smooth with or as if with a heated flatiron **2** : to remove (as wrinkles) by ironing — **iron·er** *n*

iron·bound \ˈī(-ə)rn-ˈbaund\ *adj* **1** : HARSH, RUGGED ⟨∼ coast⟩ **2** : STERN, RIGOROUS ⟨∼ traditions⟩

¹iron·clad \-ˈklad\ *adj* **1** : sheathed in

iron armor **2** : so firm or secure as to be unbreakable

²iron·clad \-ˌklad\ *n* : an armored naval vessel

iron curtain *n* : a political, military, and ideological barrier that cuts off and isolates an area; *esp* : one between an area under Soviet control and other areas

iron·ic \ī-ˈrän-ik\ *or* **iron·i·cal** \-i-kəl\ *adj* **1** : of, relating to, or marked by irony **2** : given to irony — **iron·i·cal·ly** \-i-k(ə-)lē\ *adv*

iron·ing \ˈī(-ə)r-niŋ\ *n* : clothes ironed or to be ironed

iron lung *n* : a device for artificial respiration (as in polio) that encloses the chest or body in a chamber in which changes of pressure force air into and out of the lungs

iron out *vb* : to remove or lessen difficulties in or extremes of

iron oxide *n* : FERRIC OXIDE

iron·stone \ˈī(-ə)rn-ˌstōn\ *n* **1** : a hard iron-rich sedimentary rock **2** : a hard heavy durable pottery developed in England in the 19th century

iron·ware \-ˌwaər\ *n* : articles made of iron

iron·weed \-ˌwēd\ *n* : any of several weedy American plants related to the daisy that have terminal heads of red or purple tubular flowers

iron·wood \-ˌwud\ *n* : a tree or shrub with exceptionally hard wood; *also* : its wood

iron·work \-ˌwərk\ *n* **1** : work in iron **2** *pl* : a mill or building where iron or steel is smelted or heavy iron or steel products are made — **iron·work·er** *n*

iro·ny \ˈī-rə-nē\ *n, pl* **-nies** [L *ironia*, fr. Gk *eirōnia*, fr. *eirōn* dissembler] **1** : the use of words to express the opposite of what one really means **2** : incongruity between the actual result of a sequence of events and the expected result

Ir·o·quois \ˈir-ə-ˌkwȯi\ *n, pl* **Iroquois** \-ˌkwȯi(z)\ [F, fr. Algonquin (a No. American Indian dialect) *Irinakhoiw*, lit., real adders] **1** *pl* : an American Indian confederacy of New York that consisted of the Cayuga, Mohawk, Oneida, Onondaga, and Seneca and later included the Tuscarora **2** : a member of any of the Iroquois peoples

ir·ra·di·ate \ir-ˈād-ē-ˌāt\ *vb* **-at·ed; -at·ing** **1** : ILLUMINATE **2** : ENLIGHTEN **3** : to treat by exposure to radiation **4** : RADIATE — **ir·ra·di·a·tion** \-ˌād-ē-ˈā-shən\ *n*

ir·ra·tio·nal \(ˈ)ir-ˈash-(ə-)nəl\ *adj* **1** : incapable of reasoning ⟨∼ beasts⟩; *also* : defective in mental power ⟨∼ with fever⟩ **2** : not based on reason ⟨∼ fears⟩ **3** : relating to, consisting of, or being one or more irrational numbers — **ir·ra·tio·nal·i·ty** \(ˌ)ir-ˌash-ə-ˈnal-ət-ē\ *n* — **ir·ra·tio·nal·ly** \(ˈ)ir-ˈash-(ə-)nə-lē\ *adv*

²**irrational** *n* : IRRATIONAL NUMBER

irrational number *n* : a real number that cannot be expressed as the quotient of two integers

ir·rec·on·cil·able \(̣)ir-ˌek-ən-ˈsī-lə-bəl, (ˈ)ir-ˈek-ən-ˌsī-\ *adj* : impossible to reconcile, adjust, or harmonize — **ir·rec·on·cil·abil·i·ty** \(̣)ir-ˌek-ən-ˌsī-lə-ˈbil-ət-ē\ *n*

ir·re·cov·er·able \ˌir-i-ˈkəv-(ə-)rə-bəl\ *adj* : not capable of being recovered or rectified : IRREPARABLE — **ir·re·cov·er·ably** \-blē\ *adv*

ir·re·deem·able \ˌir-i-ˈdē-mə-bəl\ *adj* 1 : not redeemable; *esp* : not terminable by payment of the principal (an ∼ bond) 2 : not convertible into gold or silver at the will of the holder 3 : being beyond remedy : HOPELESS

ir·re·den·tism \-ˈden-ˌtiz-əm\ *n* : a principle or policy directed toward the incorporation of a territory historically or ethnically part of another into that other — **ir·re·den·tist** \-ˈdent-əst\ *n or adj*

ir·re·duc·ible \ˌir-i-ˈd(y)ü-sə-bəl\ *adj* : not reducible — **ir·re·duc·ibly** \-ˈd(y)ü-sə-blē\ *adv*

ir·re·fra·ga·ble \(ˈ)ir-ˈ(r)ef-rə-gə-bəl\ *adj* : IRREFUTABLE

ir·re·fut·able \ˌir-i-ˈfyüt-ə-bəl, (ˈ)ir-ˈ(r)ef-yət-\ *adj* : impossible to refute

irreg *abbr* irregular

ir·reg·u·lar \(ˈ)ir-ˈeg-yə-lər\ *adj* 1 : not regular : not natural or uniform 2 : not conforming to the normal or usual manner of inflection (∼ verbs) 3 : not belonging to a regular or organized army organization (∼ troops) — **irregular** *n* — **ir·reg·u·lar·i·ty** \(̣)ir-ˌeg-yə-ˈlar-ət-ē\ *n* — **ir·reg·u·lar·ly** \(ˈ)ir-ˈeg-yə-lər-lē\ *adv*

ir·rel·e·vant \(ˈ)ir-ˈel-ə-vənt\ *adj* : not relevant — **ir·rel·e·vance** \-vəns\ *n*

ir·re·li·gious \ˌir-i-ˈlij-əs\ *adj* : lacking religious emotions, doctrines, or practices

ir·re·me·di·a·ble \ˌir-i-ˈmēd-ē-ə-bəl\ *adj* : impossible to remedy or correct : INCURABLE

ir·re·mov·able \-ˈmü-və-bəl\ *adj* : not removable

ir·rep·a·ra·ble \(ˈ)ir-ˈep-(ə-)rə-bəl\ *adj* : impossible to make good, undo, repair, or remedy (∼ damage)

ir·re·place·able \ˌir-i-ˈplā-sə-bəl\ *adj* : not replaceable

ir·re·press·ible \-ˈpres-ə-bəl\ *adj* : impossible to repress or control

ir·re·proach·able \-ˈprō-chə-bəl\ *adj* : not reproachable : BLAMELESS

ir·re·sist·ible \ˌir-i-ˈzis-tə-bəl\ *adj* : impossible to successfully resist — **ir·re·sist·ibly** \-blē\ *adv*

ir·res·o·lute \(ˈ)ir-ˈez-ə-ˌlüt\ *adj* : uncertain how to act or proceed : VACILLATING — **ir·res·o·lute·ly** \-ˌlüt-lē; (ˌ)ir-ˌez-ə-ˈlüt\ *adv* — **ir·res·o·lu·tion** \(̣)ir-ˌez-ə-ˈlü-shən\ *n*

ir·re·spec·tive of \ˌir-i-ˈspek-tiv-\ *prep* : without regard to

ir·re·spon·si·ble \-ˈspän-sə-bəl\ *adj* : not responsible — **ir·re·spon·si·bil·i·ty** \-ˌspän-sə-ˈbil-ət-ē\ *n* — **ir·re·spon·si·bly** \-ˈspän-sə-blē\ *adv*

ir·re·triev·able \ˌir-i-ˈtrē-və-bəl\ *adj* : not retrievable : IRRECOVERABLE

ir·rev·er·ence \(ˈ)ir-ˈev-(ə-)rəns\ *n* 1 : lack of reverence 2 : an irreverent act or utterance — **ir·rev·er·ent** \-(ə-)rənt\ *adj*

ir·re·vers·ible \ˌir-i-ˈvər-sə-bəl\ *adj* : incapable of being reversed

ir·re·vo·ca·ble \(ˈ)ir-ˈev-ə-kə-bəl\ *adj* : incapable of being revoked or recalled — **ir·re·vo·ca·bly** \-blē\ *adv*

ir·ri·gate \ˈir-ə-ˌgāt\ *vb* -**gat·ed**; -**gat·ing** : to supply (as land) with water by artificial means; *also* : to flush with liquid — **ir·ri·ga·tion** \ˌir-ə-ˈgā-shən\ *n*

ir·ri·ta·ble \ˈir-ət-ə-bəl\ *adj* : capable of being irritated; *esp* : readily or easily irritated — **ir·ri·ta·bil·i·ty** \ˌir-ət-ə-ˈbil-ət-ē\ *n* — **ir·ri·ta·bly** \ˈir-ət-ə-blē\ *adv*

ir·ri·tate \ˈir-ə-ˌtāt\ *vb* -**tat·ed**; -**tat·ing** 1 : to excite to anger : EXASPERATE 2 : to act as a stimulus toward : STIMULATE; *also* : to make sore or inflamed — **ir·ri·tant** \ˈir-ə-tənt\ *adj or n* — **ir·ri·tat·ing·ly** \-ˌtāt-iŋ-lē\ *adv* — **ir·ri·ta·tion** \ˌir-ə-ˈtā-shən\ *n*

ir·rupt \(ˈ)ir-ˈəpt\ *vb* 1 : to rush in forcibly or violently 2 : to increase suddenly in numbers (rabbits ∼ in cycles) — **ir·rup·tion** \-ˈəp-shən\ *n*

IRS *abbr* Internal Revenue Service

is *pres 3d sing of* BE

Isa *or* **Is** *abbr* Isaiah

Isa·iah \ī-ˈzā-ə\ *n* — see BIBLE table

Isa·ias \ī-ˈzā-əs\ *n* — see BIBLE table

ISBN *abbr* International Standard Book Number

-ish \ish\ *adj suffix* 1 : of, relating to, or being (Finnish) 2 : characteristic of (boyish) (mulish) 3 : having a touch or trace of : somewhat (purplish) 4 : having the approximate age of (fortyish) 5 : being or occurring at the approximate time of (eightish)

isin·glass \ˈīz-ᵊn-ˌglas, ˈī-ziŋ-\ *n* 1 : a gelatin obtained from various fish 2 : MICA

isl *abbr* island

Is·lam \is-ˈläm, iz-, -ˈlam, ˈis-ˌ, ˈiz-ˌ\ *n* [Ar *islām* submission (to the will of God)] : the religious faith of Muslims; *also* : the civilization built on this faith — **Is·lam·ic** \is-ˈläm-ik, iz-, -ˈlam-\ *adj*

is·land \ˈī-lənd\ *n* 1 : a body of land surrounded by water and smaller than a continent 2 : something resembling an island in its isolation

is·land·er \ˈī-lən-dər\ *n* : a native or inhabitant of an island

isle \ˈīl\ *n* : ISLAND; *esp* : a small island

is·let \ˈī-lət\ *n* : a small island

ism \ˈiz-əm\ *n* : a distinctive doctrine, cause, or theory

-ism \ˌiz-əm\ *n suffix* 1 : act : practice : process (criticism) 2 : manner of action or behavior characteristic of a (specified) person or thing **3** : state : condition : property ⟨barbarian*ism*⟩ **4** : abnormal state or condition resulting from excess of a (specified) thing or marked by resemblance to (such) a person or thing ⟨alcohol*ism*⟩ ⟨mongol*ism*⟩ **5** : doctrine : theory : cult ⟨Buddh*ism*⟩ **6** : adherence to a set of principles ⟨stoic*ism*⟩ **7** : characteristic or peculiar feature or trait ⟨colloqui-al*ism*⟩

iso·bar \'ī-sə-ˌbär\ *n* : a line on a map connecting places of equal barometric pressure — **iso·bar·ic** \ˌī-sə-'bär-ik, -'bar-\ *adj*

iso·late \'ī-sə-ˌlāt, 'is-ə-\ *vb* **-lat·ed; -lat·ing** [fr. *isolated* set apart, fr. F *isolé*, fr. It *isolato*, fr. *isola* island, fr. L *insula*] : to place or keep by itself : separate from others — **iso·la·tion** \ˌī-sə-'lā-shən, ˌis-ə-\ *n*

iso·lat·ed *adj* **1** : occurring alone or once : UNIQUE **2** : SPORADIC

iso·la·tion·ism \ˌī-sə-'lā-shə-ˌniz-əm, ˌis-ə-\ *n* : a policy of national isolation by abstention from international political and economic relations — **iso·la·tion·ist** \-sh(ə-)nəst\ *n or adj*

iso·mer \'ī-sə-mər\ *n* : any of two or more chemical compounds that contain the same numbers of atoms of the same elements but differ in structural arrangement and properties — **iso·mer·ic** \ˌī-sə-'mer-ik\ *adj* — **isom·er·ism** \ī-'säm-ə-ˌriz-əm\ *n*

iso·met·rics \ˌī-sə-'me-triks\ *n sing or pl* : exercise involving contraction of muscles taking place against resistance but without significant shortening of muscle fibers — **isometric** *adj*

iso·prene \'ī-sə-ˌprēn\ *n* : a hydrocarbon used esp. in making synthetic rubber

isos·ce·les \ī-'säs-ə-ˌlēz\ *adj* : having two equal sides ⟨an ∼ triangle⟩

isos·ta·sy \ī-'säs-tə-sē\ *n* : general equilibrium in the earth's crust maintained by the gravity-induced flow of deep rock material — **iso·stat·ic** \ˌī-sə-'stat-ik\ *adj* — **iso·stat·i·cal·ly** \-i-k(ə-)lē\ *adv*

iso·therm \'ī-sə-ˌthərm\ *n* : a line on a map connecting points having the same temperature

iso·ther·mal \ˌī-sə-'thər-məl\ *adj* : of, relating to, or marked by equality of temperature

iso·ton·ic \ˌī-sə-'tän-ik\ *adj* : having the same or equal osmotic pressure ⟨a salt solution ∼ with red blood cells⟩

iso·tope \'ī-sə-ˌtōp\ *n* [Gk *isos* equal + *topos* place] : any of the forms of a chemical element that differ chiefly in the number of neutrons in an atom — **iso·to·pic** \ˌī-sə-'täp-ik, -'tō-pik\ *adj* — **iso·to·pi·cal·ly** \-'täp-i-k(ə-)lē, -'tō-pi-\ *adv*

Isr \abbr\ Israel; Israeli

Is·rae·li \iz-'rā-lē\ *n, pl* **Israelis** *also*

Israeli : a native or inhabitant of Israel — **Israeli** *adj*

Is·ra·el·ite \'iz-rē-ə-ˌlīt\ *n* : a member of the Hebrew people descended from Jacob

is·su·ance \'ish-ə-wəns\ *n* : the act of issuing or giving out esp. officially

¹**is·sue** \'ish-ü\ *n* **1** *pl* : proceeds from a source of revenue (as an estate) **2** : the action of going, coming, or flowing out : EGRESS, EMERGENCE **3** : EXIT, OUTLET, VENT **4** : OFFSPRING, PROGENY **5** : OUTCOME, RESULT **6** : a point of debate or controversy; *also* : the point at which an unsettled matter is ready for a decision **7** : a discharge (as of blood) from the body **8** : something coming forth from a specified source **9** : the act of officially giving out or printing : PUBLICATION; *also* : the quantity of things given out at one time

²**issue** *vb* **is·sued; is·su·ing 1** : to go, come, or flow out **2** : to come forth or cause to come forth : EMERGE, DISCHARGE, EMIT **3** : ACCRUE **4** : to descend from a specified parent or ancestor **5** : to result in **6** : to put forth or distribute officially **7** : PUBLISH **8** : EMANATE, RESULT — **is·su·er** *n*

¹**-ist** \əst\ *n suffix* **1** : one that performs a (specified) action ⟨cycl*ist*⟩ : one that makes or produces ⟨novel*ist*⟩ **2** : one that plays a (specified) musical instrument ⟨harp*ist*⟩ **3** : one that operates a (specified) mechanical instrument or contrivance ⟨automobil*ist*⟩ **4** : one that specializes in a (specified) art or science or skill ⟨geolog*ist*⟩ **5** : one that adheres to or advocates a (specified) doctrine or system or code of behavior ⟨social*ist*⟩ or that of a (specified) individual ⟨Darwin*ist*⟩

²**-ist** *adj suffix* : -ISTIC

isth·mi·an \'is-mē-ən\ *adj* : of, relating to, or situated in or near an isthmus

isth·mus \'is-məs\ *n* : a narrow strip of land connecting two larger portions of land

-is·tic \'is-tik\ *or* **-is·ti·cal** \'is-ti-kəl\ *adj suffix* : of, relating to, or characteristic of ⟨altru*istic*⟩

ISV *abbr* International Scientific Vocabulary

¹**it** \(')it, ət\ *pron* **1** : that one — used of a lifeless thing, a plant, a person or animal, or an abstract entity ⟨∼'s a big building⟩ ⟨∼'s a shade tree⟩ ⟨who is ∼⟩ ⟨beauty is everywhere and ∼ is a source of joy⟩ **2** — used as an anticipatory subject or object ⟨∼'s good to see you⟩

²**it** \'it\ *n* : the player in a game who performs a function (as trying to catch others in a game of tag) essential to the nature of the game

It *abbr* Italian; Italy

ital *abbr* italic; italicized

Ital *abbr* Italian

Ital·ian \ə-'tal-yən, i-\ *n* **1** : a native or

inhabitant of Italy **2** : the language of Italy — **Italian** *adj*

Italian sandwich *n* : SUBMARINE 2

ital·ic \i-ˈtal-ik, ī-\ *adj* : relating to type in which the letters slope up toward the right (as in *"italic"*) — **italic** *n*

ital·i·cize \i-ˈtal-ə-ˌsīz, ī-\ *vb* **-cized; -ciz·ing** : to print in italics

itch \ˈich\ *n* **1** : an uneasy irritating skin sensation related to pain **2** : a skin disorder accompanied by an itch **3** : a persistent desire — **itch** *vb* — **itchy** *adj*

-ite \ˌīt\ *n suffix* **1** : native : resident (Brooklyn*ite*) **2** : descendant (Ishmael*ite*) **3** : adherent : follower (Lenin*ite*) **4** : product (metabol*ite*) **5** : mineral : rock (quartz*ite*)

item \ˈīt-əm\ *n* [L, likewise, also] **1** : a separate particular in a list, account, or series : ARTICLE **2** : a separate piece of news (as in a newspaper)

item·ize \ˈīt-ə-ˌmīz\ *vb* **-ized; -iz·ing** : to set down in detail : LIST — **item·iza·tion** \ˌīt-ə-mə-ˈzā-shən\ *n*

it·er·ate \ˈit-ə-ˌrāt\ *vb* **-at·ed; -at·ing** : REITERATE, REPEAT

it·er·a·tion \ˌit-ə-ˈrā-shən\ *n* : REPETITION; *esp* : a computational process in which a series of operations is repeated a number of times

itin·er·ant \ī-ˈtin-ə-rənt, ə-\ *adj* : traveling from place to place; *esp* : covering a circuit (an ~ preacher)

itin·er·ary \ī-ˈtin-ə-ˌrer-ē, ə-\ *n, pl* **-ar·ies 1** : the route of a journey or the proposed outline of one **2** : a travel diary **3** : GUIDEBOOK

its \(ˌ)its, əts\ *adj* : of or relating to it or itself

it·self \it-ˈself, ət-\ *pron* : that identical one — used reflexively, for emphasis, or in absolute constructions

-ity \ət-ē\ *n suffix* : quality : state : degree (alkalin*ity*)

IUD \ˌī-ˌyü-ˈdē\ *n* : INTRAUTERINE DEVICE

IV *abbr* intravenous; intravenously

-ive \iv\ *adj suffix* : that performs or tends toward an (indicated) action (correct*ive*)

ivo·ry \ˈīv-(ə-)rē\ *n, pl* **-ries** [ME *ivorie*, fr. OF *ivoire*, fr. L *eboreus* of ivory, fr. *ebur* ivory] **1** : the hard creamywhite material composing elephants' tusks **2** : a variable door averaging a pale yellow **3** : something made of ivory or of a similar substance

ivory tower *n* **1** : an impractical lack of concern with urgent problems **2** : a place of learning

ivy \ˈī-vē\ *n, pl* **ivies** : a trailing woody vine with evergreen leaves and small black berries

IWW *abbr* Industrial Workers of the World

-ize \ˌīz\ *vb suffix* **1** : cause to be or conform to or resemble (American*ize*) : cause to be formed into (union*ize*) **2** : subject to a (specified) action (satir*ize*) **3** : saturate, treat, or combine with (macadam*ize*) **4** : treat like (idol*ize*) **5** : become : become like (crystall*ize*) **6** : be productive in or of : engage in a (specified) activity (philosoph*ize*) **7** : adopt or spread the manner of activity or the teaching of (Christian*ize*)

J

¹j \ˈjā\ *n, pl* **j's** *or* **js** \ˈjāz\ *often cap* : the 10th letter of the English alphabet

²j *abbr, often cap* **1** jack **2** journal **3** judge **4** justice

¹jab \ˈjab\ *vb* **jabbed; jab·bing** : to thrust quickly or abruptly : POKE

²jab *n* : a usu. short straight punch

jab·ber \ˈjab-ər\ *vb* **jab·bered; jab·ber·ing** \ˈjab-(ə-)riŋ\ : to talk rapidly, indistinctly, or unintelligibly : CHATTER — **jabber** *n*

jab·ber·wocky \ˈjab-ər-ˌwäk-ē\ *n* : meaningless speech or writing

ja·bot \zha-ˈbō, ˈjab-ˌō\ *n* : a ruffle worn down the front of a dress or shirt

jac·a·ran·da \ˌjak-ə-ˈran-də\ *n* : any of a genus of pinnate-leaved tropical American trees with clusters of showy blue flowers

ja·cinth \ˈjās-ᵊnth\ *n* : HYACINTH

¹jack \ˈjak\ *n* **1** : a mechanical device; *esp* : one used to raise a heavy body a short distance **2** : a male donkey **3** : a small target ball in lawn bowling **4** : a small national flag flown by a ship **5** : a small 6-pointed metal object used

in a game (jacks) **6** : a playing card bearing the figure of a soldier or servant **7** : a socket into which a plug is inserted for connecting electric circuits

²jack *vb* **1** : to raise by means of a jack **2** : INCREASE (~ up prices)

jack·al \ˈjak-əl, -ˌȯl\ *n* [Turk *çakal*, fr. Per *shagāl*, fr. Skt *sṛgāla*] : an Old World wild dog smaller than the related wolves

jack·a·napes \ˈjak-ə-ˌnāps\ *n* **1** : MONKEY, APE **2** : an impudent or conceited person

jack·ass \-ˌas\ *n* **1** : a male ass; *also* : DONKEY **2** : a stupid person : FOOL

jack·boot \-ˌbüt\ *n* **1** : a heavy military boot of glossy black leather extending above the knee **2** : a military boot reaching to the calf and having no laces

jack·daw \ˈjak-ˌdȯ\ *n* : a black and gray Eurasian crowlike bird

jack·et \ˈjak-ət\ *n* [ME *jaket*, fr. MF *jaquet*, dim. of *jaque* short jacket, fr. *jacque* peasant, fr. the name *Jacques*

James] **1** : a garment for the upper body usu. having a front opening, collar, and sleeves **2** : an outer covering or casing (a book ~)

Jack Frost *n* : frost or frosty weather personified

jack·ham·mer \'jak-‚ham-ər\ *n* : a pneumatic percussion tool for drilling rock or breaking pavement

jack-in-the-box \'jak-ən-thə-‚bäks\ *n*, *pl* **jack-in-the-box·es** *or* **jacks-in-the-box** : a toy consisting of a small box out of which a figure springs when the lid is raised

jack-in-the-pul·pit \‚jak-ən-thə-'pul-‚pit, -pət, -'pəl-\ *n*, *pl* **jack-in-the-pulpits** *or* **jacks-in-the-pulpit** : an American spring-flowering woodland herb having an upright club-shaped spadix arched over by a green and purple spathe

¹**jack·knife** \'jak-‚nīf\ *n* **1** : a large pocketknife **2** : a dive in which the diver bends from the waist and touches his ankles before straightening out

²**jackknife** *vb* : to fold like a jackknife (the trailer truck *jackknifed*)

jack·leg \'jak-‚leg\ *adj* **1** : lacking skill or training **2** : MAKESHIFT

jack-of-all-trades \‚jak-əv-'ól-'trädz\ *n*, *pl* **jacks-of-all-trades** : one who is able to do passable work at various tasks

jack-o'-lan·tern \'jak-ə-‚lant-ərn\ *n* : a lantern made of a pumpkin cut to look like a human face

jack·pot \'jak-‚pät\ *n* **1** : a large sum of money formed by the accumulation of stakes from previous play (as in poker) **2** : an impressive and often unexpected success or reward

jack·rab·bit \-‚rab-ət\ *n* : a large hare of western No. America with very long hind legs

jack·screw \-‚skrü\ *n* : a screw-operated jack

jack·straw \-‚stró\ *n* **1** : a straw or a thin strip used in the game of jackstraws **2** *pl* : a game in which jackstraws are let fall in a heap and each player in turn tries to remove them one at a time without disturbing the rest

jack-tar \-'tär\ *n*, *often cap* : SAILOR

Ja·cob's ladder \‚jā-kəbz-\ *n* : any of several perennial herbs related to phlox that have pinnate leaves and bright blue or white bell-shaped flowers

jac·quard \'jak-‚ärd\ *n*, *often cap* : a fabric of intricate variegated weave or pattern

¹**jade** \'jād\ *n* **1** : a broken-down, vicious, or worthless horse **2** : a disreputable woman

²**jade** *vb* **jad·ed**; **jad·ing** **1** : to wear out by overwork or abuse **2** : to become weary *syn* exhaust, fatigue, tire

³**jade** *n* [F, fr. obs. Sp (*piedra de la*) *ijada*, lit., loin stone; fr. the belief that jade cures renal colic] : a usu. green gemstone that takes a high polish

jad·ed \'jäd-əd\ *adj* : dulled by a surfeit or excess

¹**jag** \'jag\ *n* : a sharp projecting part

²**jag** *n* : SPREE

jag·ged \'jag-əd\ *adj* : sharply notched

jag·uar \'jag-(yə-)‚wär\ *n* : a black-spotted tropical American cat that is larger and stockier than the Old World leopard

jai alai \'hī-‚lī\ *n* [Sp, fr. Basque, fr. *jai* festival + *alai* merry] : a court game played by usu. two or four players with a ball and a curved wicker basket strapped to the right wrist

¹**jail** \'jāl\ *n* [ME *jaiole*, fr. OF, fr. LL *caveola*, dim. of L *cavea* cage] : PRISON; *esp* : one for persons held in lawful custody

²**jail** *vb* : to confine in a jail

jail·bird \-‚bərd\ *n* : an habitual criminal

jail·break \-‚brāk\ *n* : a forcible escape from jail

jail·er *or* **jail·or** \'jā-lər\ *n* : a keeper of a jail

jal·ap \'jal-əp, 'jäl-\ *n* : a purgative drug from the root of a Mexican plant related to the morning glory; *also* : this root or plant

ja·la·pe·ño \‚häl-ə-'pān-(‚)yō\ *n* : a Mexican hot pepper

ja·lopy \jə-'läp-ē\ *n*, *pl* **ja·lop·ies** : a dilapidated automobile

jal·ou·sie \'jal-ə-sē\ *n* [F, lit., jealousy] : a blind, window, or door with adjustable horizontal slats or louvers

¹**jam** \'jam\ *vb* **jammed**; **jam·ming** **1** : to press into a close or tight position **2** : to cause to become wedged so as to be unworkable; *also* : to make or become unworkable through the jamming of a movable part **3** : to push forcibly (~ on the brakes) **4** : CRUSH, BRUISE **5** : to make unintelligible by sending out interfering signals or messages **6** : to take part in a jam session

²**jam** *n* **1** : a crowded mass that impedes or blocks (traffic ~) **2** : a difficult state of affairs

³**jam** *n* : a food made by boiling fruit and sugar to a thick consistency

Jam *abbr* Jamaica

jamb \'jam\ *n* [ME *jambe*, fr. MF, lit., leg] : an upright piece forming the side of an opening (as of a door)

jam·ba·laya \‚jəm-bə-'lī-ə\ *n* [LaF] : rice cooked with ham, sausage, chicken, shrimp, or oysters and seasoned with herbs

jam·bo·ree \‚jam-bə-'rē\ *n* : a large festive gathering

James \'jāmz\ *n* — see BIBLE table

jam-pack \'jam-'pak\ *vb* : to pack tightly or to excess

jam session *n* : an impromptu performance by jazz musicians

Jan *abbr* January

jan·gle \'jaŋ-gəl\ *vb* **jan·gled**; **jan·gling** \-g(ə-)liŋ\ : to make a harsh or discordant sound — **jangle** *n*

jan·i·tor \'jan-ət-ər\ *n* [L, fr. *janua*

door] : a person who has the care of a building — **jan·i·to·ri·al** \ˌjan-ə-ˈtōr-ē-əl\ adj

Jan·u·ary \ˈjan-yə-ˌwer-ē\ n [ME Januarie, fr. L Januarius, first month of the ancient Roman year, fr. Janus, two-faced god of gates and beginnings] : the 1st month of the year having 31 days

¹**ja·pan** \jə-ˈpan\ n : a varnish giving a hard brilliant finish

²**japan** vb **ja·panned; ja·pan·ning** : to cover with a coat of japan

Jap·a·nese \ˌjap-ə-ˈnēz, -ˈnēs\ n, pl **Japanese 1** : a native or inhabitant of Japan **2** : the language of Japan — **Japanese** adj

Japanese beetle n : a small metallic green and brown beetle introduced from Japan that is a pest on the roots of grasses as a grub and on foliage and fruits as an adult

¹**jape** \ˈjāp\ vb **japed; jap·ing 1** : JOKE **2** : MOCK

²**jape** n : JEST, GIBE

¹**jar** \ˈjär\ vb **jarred; jar·ring 1** : to make a harsh or discordant sound **2** : to have a harsh or disagreeable effect **3** : VIBRATE, SHAKE

²**jar** n **1** : a harsh discordant sound **2** : QUARREL, DISPUTE **3** : JOLT **4** : a painful effect : SHOCK

³**jar** n : a broad-mouthed container usu. of glass or earthenware

jar·di·niere \ˌjärd-ᵊn-ˈiər\ n : an ornamental stand or pot for plants or flowers

jar·gon \ˈjär-gən, -ˌgän\ n **1** : confused unintelligible language **2** : the special vocabulary of a particular group or activity **3** : obscure and often pretentious language

Jas abbr James

jas·mine \ˈjaz-mən\ n [F jasmin, fr. Ar yāsamīn] : any of various climbing shrubs with fragrant flowers

jas·per \ˈjas-pər\ n : a red, yellow, or brown opaque quartz

jaun·dice \ˈjȯn-dəs\ n : yellowish discoloration of skin, tissues, and body fluids by bile pigments; also : a disorder marked by jaundice

jaun·diced \-dəst\ adj **1** : affected with or as if with jaundice **2** : exhibiting envy, distaste, or hostility

jaunt \ˈjȯnt\ n : a short trip usu. for pleasure

jaun·ty \ˈjȯnt-ē\ adj **jaun·ti·er; -est** : sprightly in manner or appearance : LIVELY — **jaun·ti·ly** \ˈjȯnt-ᵊl-ē\ adv — **jaun·ti·ness** \-ē-nəs\ n

Ja·va·nese \ˌjav-ə-ˈnēz, ˌjäv-, -ˈnēs\ n : a native or inhabitant of the Indonesian island of Java

jav·e·lin \ˈjav-(ə-)lən\ n **1** : a light spear **2** : a slender shaft thrown for distance in a track-and-field contest

¹**jaw** \ˈjȯ\ n **1** : either of the bony or cartilaginous structures that support the soft tissues enclosing the mouth and that usu. bear teeth **2** : the parts forming the walls of the mouth and serving to open and close it — usu. used in pl. **3** : one of a pair of movable parts for holding or crushing something — **jaw·bone** \-ˈbōn, -ˌbōn\ n — **jawed** \ˈjȯd\ adj

²**jaw** vb : to talk abusively, indignantly, or at length

jaw·break·er \-ˌbrā-kər\ n **1** : a word difficult to pronounce **2** : a round hard candy

jay \ˈjā\ n : any of various noisy brightly colored birds smaller than the related crows

jay·bird \ˈjā-ˌbərd\ n : JAY

jay·gee \ˈjā-ˈjē\ n : LIEUTENANT JUNIOR GRADE

jay·vee \ˈjā-ˈvē\ n **1** : JUNIOR VARSITY **2** : a member of a junior varsity team

jay·walk \ˈjā-ˌwȯk\ vb : to cross a street carelessly without regard for traffic regulations — **jay·walk·er** n

¹**jazz** \ˈjaz\ n **1** : American music characterized by improvisation, syncopated rhythms, and contrapuntal ensemble playing **2** : empty talk **3** : similar but unspecified things : STUFF

²**jazz** vb : ENLIVEN ⟨~ things up⟩

jazzy \ˈjaz-ē\ adj **jazz·i·er; -est 1** : having the characteristics of jazz **2** : marked by unrestraint, animation, or flashiness

JCS abbr joint chiefs of staff

jct abbr junction

JD abbr **1** [L juris doctor] doctor of jurisprudence; doctor of law **2** [L jurum doctor] doctor of laws **3** justice department **4** juvenile delinquent

jeal·ous \ˈjel-əs\ adj **1** : demanding complete devotion **2** : suspicious of a rival or of one believed to enjoy an advantage **3** : VIGILANT — **jeal·ous·ly** adv — **jeal·ou·sy** \-ə-sē\ n

jeans \ˈjēnz\ n pl [short for jean fustian, fr. ME Gene Genoa] : pants made of durable twilled cotton cloth

jeep \ˈjēp\ n [alter. of gee pee, fr. general-purpose] : a small four-wheel drive general-purpose motor vehicle used by the U.S. army in World War II

¹**jeer** \ˈjiər\ vb : to speak or cry out in derision : MOCK

²**jeer** n : TAUNT

Je·ho·vah \ji-ˈhō-və\ n : GOD 1

je·hu \ˈjē-h(y)ü\ n : a driver of a coach or cab

je·june \ji-ˈjün\ adj : lacking interest or significance : DULL

je·ju·num \ji-ˈjü-nəm\ n [L] : the section of the small intestine between the duodenum and the ileum — **je·ju·nal** \-ˈjün-ᵊl\ adj

jell \ˈjel\ vb **1** : to come to the consistency of jelly **2** : to take shape

jel·ly \ˈjel-ē\ n, pl **jellies 1** : a food with a soft elastic consistency due usu. to the presence of gelatin or pectin; esp : a fruit product made by boiling sugar and the juice of a fruit **2** : a substance resembling jelly — **jelly** vb

jelly bean n : a bean-shaped candy

jel·ly·fish \'jel-ē-ˌfish\ n : an invertebrate sea animal with a saucer-shaped jellylike body

jen·net \'jen-ət\ n 1 : a small Spanish horse 2 : a female donkey

jen·ny \'jen-ē\ n, pl **jennies** : a female bird or donkey

je·on \jä-ˈon\ n, pl **jeon** — see **won** at MONEY table

jeop·ar·dy \'jep-ərd-ē\ n [ME jeopardie, fr. OF jeu parti alternative, lit., divided game] : exposure to death, loss, or injury syn peril, hazard, risk, danger — **jeop·ar·dize** \-ər-ˌdīz\ vb

Jer abbr Jeremiah; Jeremias

jer·e·mi·ad \ˌjer-ə-ˈmī-əd, -ˌad\ n : a prolonged lamentation or complaint

Jer·e·mi·ah \ˌjer-ə-ˈmī-ə\ n — see BIBLE table

Jer·e·mi·as \ˌjer-ə-ˈmī-əs\ n — see BIBLE table

¹**jerk** \'jərk\ n 1 : a short quick pull or twist : TWITCH 2 : a stupid, foolish, or eccentric person — **jerk·i·ly** \'jər-kə-lē\ adv — **jerky** \'jər-kē\ adj

²**jerk** vb 1 : to give a sharp quick push, pull, or twist 2 : to move in short abrupt motions

jer·kin \'jər-kən\ n : a close-fitting usu. sleeveless jacket

jerk·wa·ter \'jərk-ˌwȯt-ər, -ˌwät-\ adj [fr. jerkwater (rural train); fr. the fact that it took on water carried in buckets from the source of supply] : of minor importance : INSIGNIFICANT (~ towns)

jer·ry-built \'jer-ē-ˌbilt\ adj : built cheaply and flimsily

jer·sey \'jər-zē\ n, pl **jerseys** [Jersey, one of the Channel islands] 1 : a plain weft-knitted fabric 2 : a close fitting knitted shirt 3 : any of a breed of small usu. fawn-colored dairy cattle

jess \'jes\ n : a leg strap by which a captive bird of prey may be controlled

jes·sa·mine \'jes-ə-mən\ var of JASMINE

jest \'jest\ n 1 : an act intended to provoke laughter 2 : a witty remark 3 : a frivolous mood (spoken in ~) — **jest** vb

jest·er \'jes-tər\ n : a retainer formerly kept to provide casual entertainment

¹**jet** \'jet\ n : a velvet-black coal that takes a good polish and is used for jewelry

²**jet** vb **jet·ted; jet·ting** : to spout or emit in a stream

³**jet** n 1 : a forceful rush (as of liquid or gas) through a narrow opening; also : a nozzle for a jet of fluid 2 : a jet-propelled airplane

⁴**jet** vb **jet·ted; jet·ting** : to travel by jet

jet ▮ n : a condition that is marked esp. by fatigue and irritability and occurs following a long flight through several time zones

jet·lin·er \'jet-ˌlī-nər\ n : a jet-propelled airliner

jet·port \'jet-ˌpȯrt\ n : an airport designed to handle jets

jet–propelled \ˌjet-prə-ˈpeld\ adj : driven by an engine (**jet engine**) that produces propulsion (**jet propulsion**) by the rearward discharge of a jet of fluid (as heated air and exhaust gases)

jet·sam \'jet-səm\ n : jettisoned goods; esp : such goods washed ashore

jet set n : an international group of wealthy people who frequent fashionable resorts

jet stream n : a long narrow high-altitude current of high-speed winds blowing generally from the west

jet·ti·son \'jet-ə-sən\ vb 1 : to throw (goods) overboard to lighten a ship or aircraft in distress 2 : DISCARD — **jettison** n

jet·ty \'jet-ē\ n, pl **jetties** 1 : a pier built to influence the current or to protect a harbor 2 : a landing wharf

jeu d'es·prit \zhœ-des-prē\ n, pl **jeux d'esprit** \same\ [F, lit., play of the mind] : a witty comment or composition

Jew \'jü\ n 1 : ISRAELITE 2 : one whose religion is Judaism — **Jew·ish** adj

¹**jew·el** \'jü-əl\ n [ME juel, fr. OF, dim. of jeu game, play, fr. L jocus game, joke] 1 : an ornament of precious metal 2 : GEMSTONE, GEM

²**jewel** vb **-eled** or **-elled; -el·ing** or **-el·ling** : to adorn or equip with jewels

jew·el·er or **jew·el·ler** \'jü-ə-lər\ n : a person who makes or deals in jewelry and related articles

jew·el·ry \'jü-əl-rē\ n : JEWELS; esp : objects of precious metal set with gems and worn for personal adornment

jew·el·weed \-ˌwēd\ n : IMPATIENS

Jew·ry \'jü(ə)r-ē, 'jü-rē\ n : the Jewish people

jg abbr junior grade

¹**jib** \'jib\ n : a triangular sail set on a line running from the bow to the mast

²**jib** vb **jibbed; jib·bing** : to refuse to proceed further

jibe \'jīb\ vb **jibed; jib·ing** : to be in accord : AGREE

jif·fy \'jif-ē\ n, pl **jiffies** : MOMENT, INSTANT (I'll be ready in a ~)

¹**jig** \'jig\ n 1 : a lively dance in triple rhythm 2 : TRICK, GAME (the ~ is up) 3 : a device used to hold work during manufacture or assembly

²**jig** vb **jigged; jig·ging** : to dance a jig

jig·ger \'jig-ər\ n : a measure usu. holding 1½ ounces used in mixing drinks

jig·gle \'jig-əl\ vb **jig·gled; jig·gling** \-(ə-)liŋ\ : to move with quick little jerks — **jiggle** n

jig·saw \'jig-ˌsȯ\ n : a machine saw with a narrow vertically reciprocating blade for cutting curved lines

jigsaw puzzle n : a puzzle consisting of small irregularly cut pieces to be fitted together to form a picture

ji·had \ji-ˈhäd, -ˈhad\ n 1 : a Muslim holy war 2 : CRUSADE 2

¹**jilt** \'jilt\ vb : to drop (one's lover) unfeelingly

²**jilt** n : one who jilts a lover

jim crow \'jim-ˌkrō\ *n, often cap J&C* : discrimination against blacks esp. by legal enforcement or traditional sanctions — **jim crow** *adj, often cap J&C* — **jim crow·ism** *n, often cap J&C*

jim-dan-dy \'jim-'dan-dē\ *n* : something excellent of its kind

jim-mies \'jim-ēz\ *n pl* : tiny rod-shaped bits of usu. chocolate-flavored candy often sprinkled on ice cream

¹**jim·my** \'jim-ē\ *n, pl* **jimmies** : a small crowbar

²**jimmy** *vb* **jim·mied**; **jim·my·ing** : to force open with a jimmy

jim·son·weed \'jim-sən-ˌwēd\ *n, often cap* : a coarse poisonous weed that is related to the potato and tomato and has large trumpet-shaped white or violet flowers

¹**jin·gle** \'jiŋ-gəl\ *vb* **jin·gled**; **jin·gling** \-g(ə-)liŋ\ : to make a light clinking or tinkling sound

²**jingle** *n* **1** : a light clinking or tinkling sound **2** : a short verse or song with catchy repetition

jin·go·ism \'jiŋ-gō-ˌiz-əm\ *n* : extreme chauvinism or nationalism marked esp. by a belligerent foreign policy — **jin·go·ist** \-əst\ *n* — **jin·go·is·tic** \ˌjiŋ-gō-'is-tik\ *adj*

jin·rik·i·sha \jin-'rik-ˌshô\ *n* : RICKSHA

¹**jinx** \'jiŋks\ *n* : one that brings bad luck

²**jinx** *vb* : to foredoom to failure or misfortune

jit·ney \'jit-nē\ *n, pl* **jitneys** : a small bus that serves a regular route according to a flexible schedule

jit·ter·bug \'jit-ər-ˌbəg\ *n* : a dance in which couples two-step, balance, and twirl vigorously in standardized patterns — **jitterbug** *vb*

jit·ters \'jit-ərz\ *n pl* : extreme nervousness — **jit·tery** \-ə-rē\ *adj*

¹**jive** \'jīv\ *n* **1** : swing music or dancing performed to it **2** : glib, deceptive, or foolish talk **3** : the jargon of jazz enthusiasts

²**jive** *vb* **jived**; **jiv·ing 1** : KID, TEASE; *also* : DECEIVE, SWINDLE **2** : to dance to or play jive

Jn *or* **Jno** *abbr* John

Jo *abbr* Joel

¹**job** \'jäb\ *n* **1** : a piece of work **2** : something that has to be done : DUTY **3** : a regular remunerative position — **job·less** *adj*

²**job** *vb* **jobbed**; **job·bing 1** : to do occasional pieces of work for hire **2** : to hire or let by the job

Job \'jōb\ *n* — see BIBLE table

job action *n* : a protest action by workers to force compliance with demands

job·ber \'jäb-ər\ *n* **1** : a person who buys goods and then sells them to other dealers : MIDDLEMAN **2** : a person who does work by the job

job·hold·er \'jäb-ˌhōl-dər\ *n* : one having a regular job

jock \'jäk\ *n* [*jockstrap*] : ATHLETE; *esp* : a college athlete

¹**jock·ey** \'jäk-ē\ *n, pl* **jockeys** : one who

rides a horse esp. as a professional in a race

²**jockey** *vb* **jock·eyed**; **jock·ey·ing** : to maneuver or manipulate by adroit or devious means

jock·strap \'jäk-ˌstrap\ *n* [E slang *jock* (penis)] : ATHLETIC SUPPORTER

jo·cose \jō-'kōs\ *adj* : MERRY, HUMOROUS syn jocular, facetious, witty

joc·u·lar \'jäk-yə-lər\ *adj* : marked by jesting : PLAYFUL — **joc·u·lar·i·ty** \ˌjäk-yə-'lar-ət-ē\ *n*

jo·cund \'jäk-ənd\ *adj* : marked by mirth or cheerfulness

jodh·pur \'jäd-pər\ *n* **1** *pl* : riding breeches loose above the knee and tight-fitting below **2** : an ankle-high boot fastened with a strap

Jo·el \'jō-əl\ *n* — see BIBLE table

¹**jog** \'jäg\ *vb* **jogged**; **jog·ging 1** : to give a slight shake or push to **2** : to go at a slow monotonous pace **3** : to run or ride at a slow trot — **jog·ger** *n*

²**jog** *n* **1** : a slight shake **2** : a jogging movement or pace

³**jog** *n* **1** : a projecting or retreating part of a line or surface **2** : a brief abrupt change in direction

jog·gle \'jäg-əl\ *vb* **jog·gled**; **jog·gling** \-(ə-)liŋ\ : to shake slightly — **joggle** *n*

john \'jän\ *n* **1** : TOILET **2** : a prostitute's client

John \'jän\ *n* — see BIBLE table

john·ny \'jän-ē\ *n, pl* **johnnies** : a short gown opening in the back that is worn by hospital patients

John·ny–jump–up \ˌjän-ē-'jəm-ˌpəp\ *n* : any of various small-flowered cultivated pansies

joie de vi·vre \ˌzhwäd-ə-'vēvrᵊ\ *n* [F] : keen enjoyment of life

join \'jóin\ *vb* **1** : to come or bring together so as to form a unit **2** : to come or bring into close association **3** : to become a member of ⟨~ a church⟩ **4** : ADJOIN **5** : to take part in a collective activity

join·er \'jói-nər\ *n* **1** : a worker who constructs articles by joining pieces of wood **2** : a gregarious person who joins many organizations

¹**joint** \'jóint\ *n* **1** : the point of contact between bones of an animal skeleton with the parts that surround and support it **2** : a cut of meat suitable for roasting **3** : a place where two things or parts are connected **4** : ESTABLISHMENT; *esp* : a shabby or disreputable establishment **5** : a marijuana cigarette

²**joint** *adj* **1** : UNITED **2** : common to two or more — **joint·ly** *adv*

³**joint** *vb* **1** : to unite by or provide with a joint **2** : to separate the joints of

joist \'jóist\ *n* : any of the small beams ranged parallel from wall to wall in a building to support the floor or ceiling

¹**joke** \'jōk\ *n* : something said or done to provoke laughter; *esp* : a brief narrative with a humorous climax

²joke *vb* **joked; jok·ing** : to make jokes — **jok·ing·ly** \'jō-kiŋ-lē\ *adv*

jok·er \'jō-kər\ *n* **1** : a person who jokes **2** : an extra card used in some card games **3** : a misleading part of an agreement that works to one party's disadvantage

jol·li·fi·ca·tion \ˌjäl-i-fə-'kā-shən\ *n* : a festive celebration

jol·li·ty \'jäl-ət-ē\ *n, pl* **-ties** : GAIETY, MERRIMENT

jol·ly \'jäl-ē\ *adj* **jol·li·er; -est** : full of high spirits : MERRY

¹jolt \'jōlt\ *vb* **1** : to give a quick hard knock or blow to **2** : to move with a sudden jerky motion — **jolt·er** *n*

²jolt *n* **1** : an abrupt jerky blow or movement **2** : a sudden shock

Jo·nah \'jō-nə\ *n* — see BIBLE table

Jo·nas \'jō-nəs\ *n* — see BIBLE table

jon·gleur \zhōⁿ-'glər\ *n* : an itinerant medieval minstrel

jon·quil \'jän-kwəl\ *n* [F *jonquille,* fr. Sp *junquillo,* dim. of *junco* reed, fr. L *juncus*] : a narcissus with fragrant clustered white or yellow flowers

josh \'jäsh\ *vb* : TEASE, JOKE

Josh *abbr* Joshua

Josh·ua \'jäsh-(ə-)wə\ *n* — see BIBLE table

Joshua tree *n* : a tall branched yucca of the southwestern U.S.

jos·tle \'jäs-əl\ *vb* **jos·tled; jos·tling** \-(ə-)liŋ\ **1** : to come in contact or into collision **2** : to make one's way by pushing and shoving

Jos·ue \'jäsh-ə-ˌwē\ *n* — see BIBLE table

¹jot \'jät\ *n* : the least bit : IOTA

²jot *vb* **jot·ted; jot·ting** : to write briefly and hurriedly

jot·ting \'jät-iŋ\ *n* : a brief note

joule \'jül\ *n* : a unit of work or energy equal to the work done by a force of one newton acting through a distance of one meter

jounce \'jauns\ *vb* **jounced; jounc·ing** : JOLT — **jounce** *n*

jour *abbr* **1** journal **2** journeyman

jour·nal \'jərn-əl\ *n* [ME, service book containing the day hours, fr. MF, fr. *journal* daily, fr. L *diurnalis,* fr. *dies* day] **1** : a brief account of daily events **2** : a record of proceedings (as of a legislative body) **3** : a periodical (as a newspaper) dealing esp. with current events **4** : the part of a rotating axle or spindle that turns in a bearing

jour·nal·ese \ˌjərn-əl-'ēz, -'ēs\ *n* : a style of writing held to be characteristic of newspapers

jour·nal·ism \'jərn-əl-ˌiz-əm\ *n* **1** : the business of writing for, editing, or publishing periodicals (as newspapers) **2** : writing designed for or characteristic of newspapers — **jour·nal·ist** \-əst\ *n* — **jour·nal·is·tic** \ˌjərn-əl-'is-tik\ *adj*

¹jour·ney \'jər-nē\ *n, pl* **journeys** [ME, fr. OF *journee* day's journey, fr. *jour* day] : travel from one place to another

²journey *vb* **jour·neyed; jour·ney·ing** : to go on a journey : TRAVEL

jour·ney·man \-mən\ *n* **1** : a worker who has learned a trade and works for another person **2** : an experienced reliable worker

¹joust \'jaust\ *n* : a combat on horseback between two knights with lances esp. as part of a tournament

²joust *vb* : to engage in a joust

jo·vial \'jō-vē-əl\ *adj* : marked by good humor — **jo·vi·al·i·ty** \ˌjō-vē-'al-ət-ē\ *n* — **jo·vi·al·ly** \'jō-vē-ə-lē\ *adv*

¹jowl \'jaul\ *n* **1** : the lower jaw **2** : CHEEK

²jowl *n* : loose flesh about the lower jaw or throat

¹joy \'joi\ *n* [ME, fr. OF *joie,* fr. L *gaudia*] **1** : a feeling of happiness that comes from success, good fortune, or a sense of well-being **2** : a source of happiness **syn** bliss, delight, enjoyment, pleasure — **joy·less** *adj*

²joy *vb* : REJOICE

joy·ful \-fəl\ *adj* : experiencing, causing, or showing joy — **joy·ful·ly** \-ē\ *adv*

joy·ous \'joi-əs\ *adj* : JOYFUL — **joy·ous·ly** *adv* — **joy·ous·ness** *n*

joy·ride \-ˌrīd\ *n* : a ride for pleasure often marked by reckless driving — **joy·rid·er** *n* — **joy·rid·ing** *n*

JP *abbr* **1** jet propulsion **2** justice of the peace

Jr *abbr* junior

JRC *abbr* Junior Red Cross

jt *or* **jnt** *abbr* joint

ju·bi·lant \'jü-bə-lənt\ *adj* [L *jubilans,* prp. of *jubilare* to rejoice] : EXULTANT — **ju·bi·lant·ly** *adv*

ju·bi·la·tion \ˌjü-bə-'lā-shən\ *n* : EXULTATION

ju·bi·lee \'jü-bə-ˌlē\ *n* [ME, fr. MF & LL; MF *jubilé,* fr. LL *jubilaeus,* fr. LGk *iōbēlaios,* fr. Heb *yōbhēl* ram's horn, trumpet, jubilee] **1** : a 50th anniversary **2** : a season or occasion of celebration

Jud *abbr* Judith

Ju·da·ic \jü-'dā-ik\ *also* **Ju·da·i·cal** \-'dā-ə-kəl\ *adj* : of, relating to, or characteristic of Jews or Judaism

Ju·da·ism \'jüd-ə-ˌiz-əm\ *n* : a religion developed among the ancient Hebrews and marked by belief in one God and by the moral and ceremonial laws of the Old Testament and the rabinic tradition

Ju·das tree \'jüd-əs-\ *n* : a Eurasian leguminous tree with purplish rosy flowers

Jude \'jüd\ *n* — see BIBLE table

Judg *abbr* Judges

¹judge \'jəj\ *vb* **judged; judg·ing** **1** : to form an authoritative opinion **2** : to decide as a judge : TRY **3** : to form an estimate or evaluation about something : THINK **syn** conclude, deduce, gather, infer

²judge *n* **1** : a public official authorized to decide questions brought before a court 2 : UMPIRE 3 : one who gives an authoritative opinion : CRITIC — **judge·ship** n

Judges n — see BIBLE table

judg·ment or **judge·ment** \'jəj-mənt\ n 1 : a decision or opinion given after judging; esp : a formal decision given by a court 2 cap : the final judging of mankind by God 3 : the process of forming an opinion by discerning and comparing 4 : the capacity for judging : DISCERNMENT

Judgment Day n : the day of the final judging of all human beings by God

ju·di·ca·ture \'jüd-i-kə-,chùr\ n 1 : the administration of justice 2 : JUDICIARY 1

ju·di·cial \ju-'dish-əl\ adj 1 : of or relating to the administration of justice or by a court 2 : CRITICAL — **ju·di·cial·ly** \-ē\ adv

ju·di·cia·ry \ju-'dish-ē-,er-ē, -'dish-ə-rē\ n 1 : a system of courts of law; also : the judges of these courts 2 : a branch of government in which judicial power is vested — **judiciary** adj

ju·di·cious \ju-'dish-əs\ adj : having, exercising, or characterized by sound judgment syn prudent, sage, sane, sensible, wise — **ju·di·cious·ly** adv

Ju·dith \'jüd-əth\ n — see BIBLE table

ju·do \'jüd-ō\ n [Jp, lit., gentleness art] : a sport derived from jujitsu that emphasizes the use of quick movement and leverage to throw an opponent — **ju·do·ist** n

¹**jug** \'jəg\ n 1 : a large deep container with a narrow mouth and a handle 2 : JAIL, PRISON

²**jug** vb **jugged; jug·ging** : JAIL, IMPRISON

jug·ger·naut \'jəg-ər-,nȯt\ n [Hindi Jagannāth, title of Vishnu (a Hindu god), lit., lord of the world] : a massive inexorable force or object that crushes everything in its path

jug·gle \'jəg-əl\ vb **jug·gled; jug·gling** \-(ə-)liŋ\ 1 : to keep several objects in motion in the air at the same time 2 : to manipulate esp. in order to achieve a desired and often fraudulent end — **jug·gler** \'jəg-lər\ n

jug·u·lar \'jəg-yə-lər\ adj : of, relating to, or situated in or on the throat or neck (the ~ veins)

juice \'jüs\ n 1 : the extractable fluid contents of cells or tissues 2 pl : the natural fluids of an animal body 3 : a medium (as electricity) that supplies power

juic·er \'jü-sər\ n : an appliance for extracting juice (as from fruit)

juice up vb : to give life, energy, or spirit to

juicy \'jü-sē\ adj **juic·i·er; -est** 1 : SUCCULENT 2 : rich in interest; also : RACY — **juic·i·ly** \'jü-sə-lē\ adv — **juic·i·ness** \-sē-nəs\ n

ju·jit·su or **ju·jut·su** \jü-'jit-sü\ n [Jp jūjutsu, fr. jū weakness, gentleness + jutsu art, skill] : an art of fighting em-

ploying holds, throws, and paralyzing blows

ju·jube \'jü-,jüb, 'jü-jù-,bē\ n : a fruit-flavored gumdrop or lozenge

juke·box \'jük-,bäks\ n : a coin-operated automatic record player

Jul abbr July

ju·lep \'jü-ləp\ n [ME sweetened water, fr. MF, fr. Ar julāb, fr. Per gulāb, fr. gul rose + āb water] : a drink made of bourbon, sugar, and mint served over crushed ice in a tall glass

Ju·ly \ju-'lī\ n [ME Julie, fr. OE Julius, fr. L, fr. Gaius Julius Caesar] : the 7th month of the year having 31 days

¹**jum·ble** \'jəm-bəl\ vb **jum·bled; jum·bling** \-b(ə-)liŋ\ : to mix in a confused mass

²**jumble** n : a disorderly mass or pile

jum·bo \'jəm-bō\ n, pl **jumbos** [Jumbo, a huge elephant exhibited by P.T. Barnum] : a very large specimen of its kind — **jumbo** adj

¹**jump** \'jəmp\ vb 1 : to spring into the air : leap over 2 : to give a start 3 : to rise or increase suddenly or sharply 4 : to make a sudden attack 5 : ANTICIPATE (~ the gun) 6 : to leave hurriedly and often furtively (~ town) 7 : to act or move before (as a signal)

²**jump** n 1 : a spring into the air; esp : one made for height or distance in a track meet 2 : a sharp sudden increase 3 : an initial advantage

¹**jump·er** \'jəm-pər\ n : one that jumps

²**jumper** n 1 : a loose blouse 2 : a sleeveless one-piece dress worn usu. with a blouse 3 pl : a child's sleeveless coverall

jumping bean n : a seed of any of several Mexican shrubs that tumbles about because of the movements of the larva of a small moth inside it

jumping-off place \,jəm-piŋ-'ȯf-\ n 1 : a remote or isolated place 2 : a place from which an enterprise is launched

jump·suit \'jəmp-,süt\ n 1 : a uniform worn by parachutists in jumping 2 : a one-piece garment consisting of a blouse or shirt with attached trousers or shorts

jumpy \'jəm-pē\ adj **jump·i·er; -est** : NERVOUS, JITTERY

¹**jun** \'jən\ n, pl **jun** — see won at MONEY table

²**jun** abbr junior

Jun abbr June

junc abbr junction

jun·co \'jəŋ-kō\ n, pl **juncos** or **juncoes** : any of several small common pink-billed American finches that are largely gray with conspicuous white feathers in the tail

junc·tion \'jəŋk-shən\ n 1 : an act of joining 2 : a place or point of meeting (a railroad ~)

junc·ture \'jəŋk-chər\ n 1 : JOINT, CONNECTION 2 : UNION 3 : a critical time or state of affairs

June \'jün\ n [ME, fr. L Junius] : the 6th month of the year having 30 days

jun·gle \'jəŋ-gəl\ *n* **1** : a thick tangled mass of tropical vegetation; *also* : a tract overgrown with vegetation **2** : a place of ruthless struggle for survival

¹ju·nior \'jü-nyər\ *adj* **1** : YOUNGER **2** : lower in rank **3** : of or relating to juniors

²junior *n* **1** : a person who is younger or of lower rank than another **2** : a student in his next-to-last year (as at a college)

junior college *n* : a school that offers studies corresponding to those of the 1st two years of college

junior high school *n* : a school usu. including grades 7-9

junior varsity *n* : a team whose members lack the experience or qualifications required for the varsity

ju·ni·per \'jü-nə-pər\ *n* : any of various evergreen shrubs or trees related to the pines

¹junk \'jəŋk\ *n* **1** : old iron, glass, paper, or waste; *also* : discarded articles **2** : a shoddy product **3** *slang* : NARCOTICS; *esp* : HEROIN — **junky** *adj*

²junk *vb* : DISCARD, SCRAP

³junk *n* : a ship of Chinese waters with a high poop and overhanging stem

junk·er \'jəŋ-kər\ *n* : something (as an old automobile) ready for scrapping

Jun·ker \'yuṅ-kər\ *n* [G] : a member of the Prussian landed aristocracy

jun·ket \'jəŋ-kət\ *n* **1** : a dessert of sweetened flavored milk set by rennet as a pudding **2** : a trip made by an official at public expense

junk food *n* : food that is high in calories but low in nutritional content

junk·ie *or* **junky** \'jəŋ-kē\ *n, pl* **junkies 1** *slang* : a narcotics peddler or addict **2** : one that derives inordinate pleasure from or is dependent on something (sugar ~)

jun·ta \'huṅ-tə, 'jənt-ə, 'hən-tə\ *n* [Sp, fr. *junto* joined, fr. L *jungere* to join] : a group of persons controlling a government esp. after a revolutionary seizure of power

Ju·pi·ter \'jü-pət-ər\ *n* : the largest of the planets and the one 5th in order of distance from the sun

Ju·ras·sic \ju̇-'ras-ik\ *adj* : of, relating to, or being the period of the Mesozoic era between the Triassic and the Cretaceous — **Jurassic** *n*

ju·rid·i·cal \ju̇-'rid-i-kəl\ *or* **ju·rid·ic** \-ik\ *adj* **1** : of or relating to the administration of justice **2** : LEGAL — **ju·rid·i·cal·ly** \-i-k(ə-)lē\ *adv*

ju·ris·dic·tion \ˌju̇r-əs-'dik-shən\ *n* **1** : the power, right, or authority to interpret and apply the law **2** : the authority of a sovereign power **3** : the limits or territory within which authority may be exercised — **ju·ris·dic·tion·al** \-sh(ə-)nəl\ *adj*

ju·ris·pru·dence \-'prüd-əns\ *n* **1** : a system of laws **2** : the science or philosophy of law

ju·rist \'ju̇r-əst\ *n* : one having a thorough knowledge of law

ju·ris·tic \ju̇-'ris-tik\ *adj* **1** : of or relating to a jurist or jurisprudence **2** : of, relating to, or recognized in law

ju·ror \'ju̇r-ər\ *n* : a member of a jury

ju·ry \'ju̇r-ē\ *n, pl* **juries 1** : a body of persons sworn to inquire into a matter submitted to them and to give their verdict **2** : a committee for judging and awarding prizes (as at a contest)

²jury *adj* : improvised for temporary use esp. in an emergency ⟨a ~ mast⟩

jury-rig \'ju̇r-ē-ˌrig\ *vb* : to erect, construct, or arrange in a makeshift fashion

¹just \'jəst\ *adj* **1** : having a basis in or conforming to fact or reason : REASONABLE ⟨~ comment⟩ **2** : CORRECT, PROPER ⟨~ proportions⟩ **3** : morally or legally right ⟨a ~ title⟩ **4** : DESERVED, MERITED ⟨~ punishment⟩ **syn** upright, honorable, conscientious, honest — **just·ly** *adv* — **just·ness** *n*

²just \(ˌ)jəst, (ˌ)jist\ *adv* **1** : EXACTLY ⟨~ right⟩ **2** : very recently ⟨has ~ left⟩ **3** : BARELY ⟨lives ~ outside the city⟩ **4** : DIRECTLY ⟨~ across the street⟩ **5** : VERY ⟨~ a note⟩ **6** : VERY

jus·tice \'jəs-təs\ *n* **1** : the administration of what is just (as by assigning merited rewards or punishments) **2** : JUDGE **3** : the administration of law **4** : FAIRNESS; *also* : RIGHTEOUSNESS

justice of the peace : a local magistrate empowered chiefly to try minor cases, to administer oaths, and to perform marriages

jus·ti·fy \'jəs-tə-ˌfī\ *vb* **-fied; -fy·ing 1** : to prove to be just, right, or reasonable **2** : to pronounce free from guilt or blame **3** : to adjust or arrange spaces in a line of printed text so the margins are even — **jus·ti·fi·able** *adj* — **jus·ti·fi·ca·tion** \ˌjəs-tə-fə-'kā-shən\ *n*

jut \'jət\ *vb* **jut·ted; jut·ting** : PROJECT, PROTRUDE

jute \'jüt\ *n* : a strong glossy fiber from a tropical herb used esp. for making sacks and twine

juv *abbr* juvenile

¹ju·ve·nile \'jü-və-ˌnīl, -vən-ªl\ *adj* **1** : showing incomplete development **2** : of, relating to, or characteristic of children or young people

²juvenile *n* **1** : a young person **2** : a young lower animal (as a fish or a bird) **3** : an actor or actress who plays youthful parts

jux·ta·pose \'jək-stə-ˌpōz\ *vb* **-posed; -pos·ing** : to place side by side — **jux·ta·po·si·tion** \ˌjək-stə-pə-'zish-ən\ *n*

JV *abbr* junior varsity

K

¹k \'kā\ *n, pl* k's *or* ks \'kāz\ *often cap* : the 11th letter of the English alphabet

²k *abbr* 1 karat 2 kilogram 3 kitchen 4 knit 5 kosher

¹K *abbr* Kelvin

²K *symbol* 1 [NL *kalium*] potassium 2 strikeout

ka·bob \'kä-ˌbäb, kə-'bäb\ *n* : cubes of meat cooked with vegetables usu. on a skewer

Ka·bu·ki \kə-'bü-kē\ *n* : traditional Japanese popular drama with highly stylized singing and dancing

kad·dish \'käd-ish\ *n, often cap* : a Jewish prayer recited in the daily synagogue ritual and by mourners at public services after the death of a close relative

kaf·fee·klatsch \'kȯf-ē-ˌklach, 'käf-\ *n, often cap* : an informal social gathering for coffee and talk

kai·ser \'kī-zər\ *n* : EMPEROR; *esp* : the ruler of Germany from 1871 to 1918

kale \'kāl\ *n* : a hardy cabbage with curled leaves that do not form a head

ka·lei·do·scope \kə-'līd-ə-ˌskōp\ *n* : an instrument containing loose bits of colored glass between two flat plates and two plane mirrors so placed that changes of position of the bits of glass are reflected in an endless variety of patterns — ka·lei·do·scop·ic \-ˌlīd-ə-'skäp-ik\ *adj* — ka·lei·do·scop·i·cal·ly \-i-k(ə-)lē\ *adv*

ka·ma·ai·na \ˌkäm-ə-'ī-nə\ *n* [Hawaiian *kama'aina,* fr. *kama* child + *'aina* land] : one who has lived in Hawaii for a long time

kame \'kām\ *n* [Sc, lit., comb] : a short ridge or mound of material deposited by glacial meltwater

ka·mi·ka·ze \ˌkäm-i-'käz-ē\ *n* [Jp, lit., divine wind] : a member of a corps of Japanese pilots assigned to make a suicidal crash on a target; *also* : an airplane flown in such an attack

Kan *or* Kans *abbr* Kansas

kan·ga·roo \ˌkaŋ-gə-'rü\ *n, pl* -roos : any of several large leaping marsupial mammals of Australia with powerful hind legs and a long thick tail

kangaroo court *n* : a court or an illegal self-appointed tribunal characterized by irresponsible, perverted, or irregular procedures

ka·olin \'kā-ə-lən\ *n* : a fine usu. white clay used in ceramics and refractories and in medicine in the treatment of diarrhea

ka·pok \'kā-ˌpäk\ *n* : silky fiber from the seeds of a tropical tree used esp. as a filling (as for life preservers)

Kap·o·si's sar·co·ma \'kap-ə-sēz-sär-'kō-mə\ *n* : a serious disease now usu. associated with AIDS that affects esp. the skin and mucous membranes and is characterized usu. by the formation of pink to reddish-brown or bluish plaques

ka·put *also* ka·putt \kä-'pùt, kə-, -'püt\ *adj* [G, fr. F *capot* not having made a trick at piquet] 1 : utterly defeated or destroyed 2 : made useless or unable to function

kar·a·kul \'kar-ə-kəl\ *n* : the dark tightly curled pelt of the newborn lamb of an Asian sheep

kar·at \'kar-ət\ *n* : a unit for expressing proportion of gold in an alloy equal to ¹⁄₂₄ part of pure gold

ka·ra·te \kə-'rät-ē\ *n* [Jp, lit., empty hand] : an art of self-defense in which an attacker is disabled by crippling kicks and punches

kar·ma \'kär-mə\ *n, often cap* [Skt] : the force generated by a person's actions held in Hinduism and Buddhism to perpetuate transmigration and to determine his destiny in his next existence — kar·mic \-mik\ *adj, often cap*

karst \'kärst\ *n* [G] : an irregular limestone region with sinks, underground streams, and caverns

ka·ty·did \'kāt-ē-ˌdid\ *n* : any of several large green tree-dwelling American grasshoppers

kay·ak \'kī-ˌak\ *n* : an Eskimo canoe made of a skin-covered frame with a small opening and propelled by a double-bladed paddle; *also* : a similar portable boat

kayo \(')kā-'ō, 'kā-ō\ *n* : KNOCKOUT — kayo *vb*

ka·zoo \kə-'zü\ *n, pl* kazoos : a toy musical instrument consisting of a tube with a membrane sealing one end and a side hole to sing or hum into

KB *abbr* kilobyte

kc *abbr* kilocycle

KC *abbr* 1 Kansas City 2 King's Counsel 3 Knights of Columbus

kc/s *abbr* kilocycles per second

KD *abbr* knocked down

ke·bab *or* ke·bob \kə-'bäb\ *var of* KABOB

¹kedge \'kej\ *vb* kedged; kedg·ing : to move a ship by hauling on a line attached to a small anchor dropped at the distance and in the direction desired

²kedge *n* : a small anchor

keel \'kēl\ *n* 1 : a timber or plate running lengthwise along the center of the bottom of a ship 2 : something (as a bird's breastbone) like a ship's keel in form or use — keeled \'kēld\ *adj*

keel·boat \'kēl-ˌbōt\ *n* : a shallow covered keeled riverboat for freight that is usu. rowed, poled, or towed

keel·haul \-ˌhȯl\ *vb* : to haul under the keel of a ship as punishment

keel over *vb* 1 : OVERTURN, CAPSIZE 2 : FAINT, SWOON

keel·son \'kel-sən, 'kēl-\ *n* : a reinforcing structure above and fastened to a ship's keel

¹**keen** \'kēn\ *adj* 1 : SHARP ⟨a ~ knife⟩ 2 : SEVERE ⟨a ~ wind⟩ 3 : ENTHUSIASTIC ⟨~ about swimming⟩ 4 : mentally alert ⟨a ~ mind⟩ 5 : STRONG, ACUTE ⟨~ eyesight⟩ 6 : WONDERFUL, EXCELLENT — **keen·ly** *adv* — **keen·ness** \'kēn-nəs\ *n*

²**keen** *n* : a lamentation for the dead uttered in a loud wailing voice or in a wordless cry — **keen** *vb*

¹**keep** \'kēp\ *vb* **kept** \'kept\ ; **keep·ing** 1 : FULFILL, OBSERVE ⟨~ a promise⟩ ⟨~ a holiday⟩ 2 : GUARD ⟨~ us from harm⟩ ; *also* : to take care of ⟨~ a neighbor's children⟩ 3 : MAINTAIN ⟨~ silence⟩ 4 : to have in one's service or at one's disposal ⟨~ a horse⟩ 5 : to preserve a record in ⟨~ a diary⟩ 6 : to have in stock for sale 7 : to retain in one's possession ⟨~ what you find⟩ 8 : to carry on (as a business) : CONDUCT 9 : HOLD, DETAIN ⟨~ him in jail⟩ 10 : to refrain from revealing ⟨~ a secret⟩ 11 : to continue in good condition ⟨meat will ~ in a freezer⟩ 12 : ABSTAIN, REFRAIN — **keep·er** *n*

²**keep** *n* 1 : FORTRESS 2 : the means or provisions by which one is kept — **for keeps** 1 : with the provision that one keeps what he wins ⟨play marbles *for keeps*⟩ 2 : PERMANENTLY

keep·ing \'kē-piŋ\ *n* : CONFORMITY ⟨in ~ with good taste⟩

keep·sake \'kēp-,sāk\ *n* : MEMENTO

keep up *vb* 1 : to persevere in 2 : MAINTAIN, SUSTAIN 3 : to keep informed 4 : to continue without interruption

keg \'keg\ *n* : a small cask or barrel

keg·ler \'keg-lər\ *n* : BOWLER

kelp \'kelp\ *n* : any of various coarse brown seaweeds; *also* : a mass of these or their ashes often used as fertilizer

Kelt \'kelt\ *var of* CELT

kel·vin \'kel-vən\ *n* : a unit of temperature equal to 1/273.16 of the Kelvin scale temperature of the triple point of water and equal to the Celsius degree in size

Kelvin *adj* : relating to, conforming to, or being a temperature scale according to which absolute zero is 0 K, the equivalent of —273.15°C

ken \'ken\ *n* 1 : range of vision : SIGHT 2 : range of understanding

ken·nel \'ken-ᵊl\ *n* : a shelter for a dog or cat; *also* : an establishment for the breeding or boarding of dogs or cats — **kennel** *vb*

ke·no \'kē-nō\ *n* : a game resembling bingo

Ken·tucky bluegrass \kən-,tək-ē-\ *n* : a valuable pasture and meadow grass of both Europe and America

Ke·ogh plan \'kē-(,)ō-\ *n* [Eugene James *Keogh* b1907 Am. politician]

: an individual retirement account for the self-employed

ke·pi \'kā-pē, 'kep-ē\ *n* [F] : a military cap with a round flat top sloping toward the front and a visor

ker·a·tin \'ker-ət-ᵊn\ *n* : any of various sulfur-containing fibrous proteins that form the chemical basis of hair and horny tissues — **ke·ra·ti·nous** \kə-'rat-ᵊn-əs, ,ker-ə-'tī-nəs\ *adj*

kerb \'kərb\ *n, Brit* : CURB

ker·chief \'kər-chəf, -,chēf\ *n, pl* **kerchiefs** \-chəfs, -,chēfs\ *also* **kerchieves** \-,chēvz\ [ME *courchef*, fr. OF *cuevrechief*, fr. *covrir* to cover + *chief* head] 1 : a square of cloth worn by women esp. as a head covering 2 : HANDKERCHIEF

kerf \'kərf\ *n* : a slit or notch made by a saw or cutting torch

ker·nel \'kərn-ᵊl\ *n* 1 : the inner softer part of a seed, fruit stone, or nut 2 : a whole seed of a cereal 3 : a central or essential part : CORE

ker·o·sene *or* **ker·o·sine** \'ker-ə-,sēn, ,ker-ə-'sēn, 'kar-, ,kar-\ *n* : a thin oil produced from petroleum and used for a fuel and as a solvent

ketch \'kech\ *n* : a large fore-and-aft rigged boat with two masts

ketch·up *var of* CATSUP

ket·tle \'ket-ᵊl\ *n* : a metallic vessel for boiling liquids

ket·tle·drum \-,drəm\ *n* : a brass or copper drum with parchment stretched across the top

¹**key** \'kē\ *n* 1 : a usu. metal instrument by which the bolt of a lock is turned; *also* : a device having the form or function of a key 2 : a means of gaining or preventing entrance, possession, or control 3 : EXPLANATION, SOLUTION 4 : one of the levers pressed by a finger in operating or playing an instrument 5 : a leading individual or principle 6 : a system of seven tones based on their relationship to a tonic; *also* : the tone or pitch of a voice 7 : a small switch for opening or closing an electric circuit

²**key** *vb* 1 : SECURE, FASTEN 2 : to regulate the musical pitch of 3 : to bring into harmony or conformity 4 : to make nervous — usu. used with *up*

³**key** *adj* : BASIC, CENTRAL ⟨~ issues⟩

⁴**key** *n* : a low island or reef (as off the southern coast of Florida)

⁵**key** *n, slang* : a kilogram esp. of marijuana or heroin

key·board \-,bōrd\ *n* 1 : a row of keys (as on a piano) 2 : an assemblage of keys for operating a machine

key club : a private club serving liquor and providing entertainment

key·hole \'kē-,hōl\ *n* : a hole for receiving a key

¹**key·note** \-,nōt\ *n* 1 : the first and harmonically fundamental tone of a scale 2 : the central fact, idea, or mood

²**keynote** *vb* 1 : to set the keynote of 2

: to deliver the major address (as at a convention) — **key·not·er** n

key·punch \'kē-ˌpənch\ n : a machine with a keyboard used to cut holes or notches in punch cards — **keypunch** vb — **key·punch·er** n

key·stone \'kē-ˌstōn\ n : the wedge-shaped piece at the crown of an arch that locks the other pieces in place

key word n : a word that is a key; esp : a word exemplifying the meaning or value of a letter or symbol

kg abbr kilogram

KGB abbr [Russ Komitet Gosudarst-vennoi Bezopasnosti] (Soviet) State Security Committee

kha·ki \'kak-ē, 'käk-\ n [Hindi khaki dust-colored, fr. khāk dust, fr. Per] 1 : a light yellowish brown 2 : a khaki-colored cloth; also : a military uniform of this cloth

khan \'kän, 'kan\ n : a Mongol leader; esp : a successor of Genghis Khan

khe·dive \kə-'dēv\ n : a ruler of Egypt from 1867 to 1914 governing as a viceroy of the sultan of Turkey

khoum \'küm\ n — see ouguiya at MONEY table

kHz abbr kilohertz

KIA abbr killed in action

kib·ble \'kib-əl\ vb **kib·bled; kib·bling** : to grind coarsely — **kibble** n

kib·butz \kib-'ùts, -'ūts\ n, pl **kib·but·zim** \-ˌùt-'sēm, -ūt-\ [NHeb qibbūṣ] : a collective farm or settlement in Israel

ki·bitz·er \'kib-ət-sər, kə-'bit-\ n [Yiddish] : one who looks on and usu. offers unwanted advice esp. at a card game — **kib·itz** \'kib-əts\ vb

ki·bosh \'kī-ˌbäsh\ n : something that serves as a check or stop (put the ~ on his plan)

¹**kick** \'kik\ vb 1 : to strike out or hit with the foot; also : to score by kicking a ball 2 : to object strongly 3 : to recoil when fired — **kick·er** n

²**kick** n 1 : a blow or thrust with the foot; esp : a propelling of a ball with the foot 2 : the recoil of a gun 3 : a feeling or expression of objection 4 : stimulating effect esp. of pleasure

kick·back \'kik-ˌbak\ n 1 : a sharp violent reaction 2 : a secret return of a part of a sum received

kick in vb 1 : CONTRIBUTE 2 slang : DIE

kick·off \'kik-ˌóf\ n 1 : a kick that puts the ball in play (as in football) 2 : COMMENCEMENT

kick off vb 1 : to start or resume play with a placekick 2 : to begin proceedings 3 slang : DIE

kick over vb : to begin or cause to begin to fire — used of an internal-combustion engine

kick·shaw \'kik-ˌshó\ n [fr. F quelque chose something] 1 : DELICACY 2 : BAUBLE

kick·stand \'kik-ˌstand\ n : a swiveling metal bar attached to a 2-wheeled vehicle for holding it up when not in use

kicky \'kik-ē\ adj : providing a kick or thrill : EXCITING

¹**kid** \'kid\ n 1 : a young goat 2 : the flesh, fur, or skin of a young goat; also : something (as leather) made of kid 3 : CHILD, YOUNGSTER — **kid·dish** \'kid-ish\ adj

²**kid** vb **kid·ded; kid·ding** 1 : FOOL 2 : TEASE — **kid·der** n — **kid·ding·ly** \'kid-iŋ-lē\ adv

kid·nap \'kid-ˌnap\ vb **-napped** or **-naped** \-ˌnapt\; **-nap·ping** or **-nap·ing** : to hold or carry a person away by unlawful force or by fraud and against his will — **kid·nap·per** or **kid·nap·er** n

kid·ney \'kid-nē\ n, pl **kidneys** 1 : either of a pair of organs lying near the backbone that excrete waste products of the body in the form of urine 2 : TEMPERAMENT; also : SORT

kidney bean n 1 : an edible seed of the common cultivated bean; esp : one that is large and dark red 2 : a plant bearing kidney beans

kid·skin \'kid-ˌskin\ n : the skin of a young goat used for leather

kiel·ba·sa \k(y)el-'bäs-ə, kil-\ n, pl **-basas** also **-ba·sy** \-'bäs-ē\ : a smoked sausage of Polish origin

kie·sel·guhr or **kie·sel·gur** \'kē-zəl-ˌgùr\ n : loose or porous diatomite

¹**kill** \'kil\ vb 1 : to deprive of life 2 : to put an end to (~ competition) ; also : DEFEAT (~ a proposed amendment) 3 : USE UP (~ time) 4 : to mark for omission syn slay, murder, assassinate, execute — **kill·er** n

²**kill** n 1 : an act of killing 2 : an animal or animals killed (as in a hunt); also : an aircraft, ship, or vehicle destroyed by military action

kill·deer \'kil-ˌdiər\ n, pl **killdeers** or **killdeer** [imit.] : a plover of temperate No. America with a plaintive penetrating cry

kill·ing \'kil-iŋ\ n : a sudden notable gain or profit

kill·joy \'kil-ˌjói\ n : one who spoils the pleasures of others

kiln \'kil(n)\ n : a heated enclosure (as an oven) for processing a substance by burning, firing, or drying — **kiln** vb

ki·lo \'kē-lō\ n, pl **kilos** : KILOGRAM

ki·lo·byte \'kil-ə-ˌbīt, 'kē-lə-\ n : 1024 bytes

kilo·cy·cle \'kil-ə-ˌsī-kəl\ n : KILOHERTZ

ki·lo·gram \'kil-ə-ˌgram, 'kē-lə-\ n : the basic metric unit of mass and weight — see METRIC SYSTEM table

ki·lo·hertz \'kil-ə-ˌhərts, 'kē-lə-, -ˌherts\ n : 1000 hertz

kilo·li·ter \'kil-ə-ˌlēt-ər\ n — see METRIC SYSTEM table

ki·lo·me·ter \kil-'äm-ət-ər, 'kil-ə-ˌmēt-\ n — see METRIC SYSTEM table

ki·lo·ton \'kil-ə-ˌtən, 'kē-lō-\ n 1 : 1000 tons 2 : an explosive force equivalent to that of 1000 tons of TNT

ki·lo·volt \-ˌvōlt\ n : 1000 volts

ki·lo·watt \'kil-ə-ˌwät\ n : 1000 watts

kilowatt–hour n : a unit of energy equal

to that expended by one kilowatt in one hour

kilt \'kilt\ n : a knee-length pleated skirt usu. of tartan worn by men in Scotland

kil·ter \'kil-tər\ n : proper condition ⟨out of ~⟩

ki·mo·no \kə-'mō-nə\ n, pl **-nos** 1 : a loose robe with wide sleeves traditionally worn with a wide sash as an outer garment by the Japanese 2 : a loose dressing gown or jacket

kin \'kin\ n 1 : an individual's relatives 2 : KINSMAN

ki·na \'kē-nə\ n — see MONEY table

¹**kind** \'kīnd\ n 1 : essential quality or character 2 : a group united by common traits or interests : CATEGORY; also : VARIETY 3 : goods or commodities as distinguished from money

²**kind** adj 1 : of a sympathetic, forbearing, or pleasant nature ⟨~ friends⟩ 2 : arising from sympathy or forbearance ⟨~ deeds⟩ syn benevolent, benign, benignant, kindly — **kind·ness** \'kīn(d)-nəs\ n

kin·der·gar·ten \'kin-dər-,gärt-ᵊn\ n [Ger., lit., children's garden] : a school or class for children usu. from four to six years old

kin·der·gart·ner \-,gärt-nər\ n 1 : a kindergarten pupil 2 : a kindergarten teacher

kind·heart·ed \'kīnd-'härt-əd\ adj : marked by a sympathetic nature

kin·dle \'kin-dᵊl\ vb **kin·dled; kin·dling** \-(d)liŋ, -dᵊl-iŋ\ 1 : to set on fire : start burning 2 : to stir up : AROUSE 3 : ILLUMINATE, GLOW

kin·dling \'kin-(d)liŋ, 'kin-lən\ n : easily combustible material for starting a fire

¹**kind·ly** \'kīn-dlē\ adj **kind·li·er; -est** 1 : of an agreeable or beneficial nature 2 : of a sympathetic or generous nature ⟨~ men⟩ — **kind·li·ness** n

²**kindly** adv 1 : READILY ⟨does not take ~ to criticism⟩ 2 : SYMPATHETICALLY 3 : COURTEOUSLY, OBLIGINGLY

kind of \'kīn-də(v)\ adv : to a moderate degree ⟨it's kind of late to begin⟩

¹**kin·dred** \'kin-drəd\ n 1 : a group of related individuals 2 : one's relatives

²**kindred** adj : of a like nature or character

kine \'kīn\ archaic pl of COW

ki·ne·mat·ics \,kin-ə-'mat-iks\ n : a science that deals with motion apart from considerations of mass and force — **ki·ne·mat·ic** \-ik\ or **ki·ne·mat·i·cal** \-i-kəl\ adj

kin·e·scope \'kin-ə-,skōp\ n 1 : PICTURE TUBE 2 : a moving picture made from the image on a picture tube

kin·es·the·sia \,kin-əs-'thē-zh(ē-)ə\ or **kin·es·the·sis** \-'thē-səs\ n, pl **-the·sias** or **-the·ses** \-,sēz\ : a sense mediated by nervous elements in muscles, tendons, and joints and stimulated by bodily movements and tensions; also : sensory experience derived from

this source — **kin·es·thet·ic** \-'thet-ik\ adj

ki·net·ic \kə-'net-ik\ adj : of or relating to the motion of material bodies and the forces and energy (**kinetic energy**) associated with them

ki·net·ics \kə-'net-iks\ n sing or pl : a science that deals with the effects of forces upon the motions of material bodies or with changes in a physical or chemical system

kin·folk \'kin-,fōk\ or **kinfolks** n pl : RELATIVES

king \'kiŋ\ n 1 : a male sovereign 2 : a chief among competitors ⟨home-run ~⟩ 3 : the principal piece in the game of chess 4 : a playing card bearing the figure of a king 5 : a checker that has been crowned — **king·less** adj — **king·ly** adj — **king·ship** n

king·bolt \-,bōlt\ n : a vertical bolt by which the forward axle and wheels of a vehicle are connected to the other parts

king crab n 1 : HORSESHOE CRAB 2 : any of several very large crabs

king·dom \'kiŋ-dəm\ n 1 : a country whose head is a king or queen 2 : a realm or region in which something or someone is dominant ⟨a cattle ~⟩ 3 : one of the three primary divisions of lifeless material, plants, and animals into which natural objects are grouped

king·fish·er \-,fish-ər\ n : a bright-colored crested bird that feeds chiefly on fish

king·pin \'kiŋ-,pin\ n 1 : any of several bowling pins 2 : the leader in a group or undertaking 3 : KINGBOLT

Kings n — see BIBLE table

king-size \'kiŋ-,sīz\ or **king-sized** \-,sīzd\ adj 1 : longer than the regular or standard size 2 : unusually large 3 : having dimensions of about 76 by 80 inches ⟨a ~ bed⟩; also : of a size that fits a king-size bed

kink \'kiŋk\ n 1 : a short tight twist or curl 2 : a mental peculiarity : QUIRK 3 : CRAMP ⟨a ~ in the back⟩ 4 : an imperfection likely to cause difficulties in operation — **kinky** adj

kin·ship \'kin-,ship\ n : RELATIONSHIP

kins·man \'kinz-mən\ n : RELATIVE; esp : a male relative

kins·wom·an \-,wùm-ən\ n : a female relative

ki·osk \'kē-,äsk\ n : a small structure with one or more open sides

Ki·o·wa \'kī-ə-,wó, -,wä, -,wā\ n, pl **Kiowa** or **Kiowas** : a member of an American Indian people of Colorado, Kansas, New Mexico, Oklahoma, and Texas

¹**kip** \'kip\ n : the undressed hide of a young or small animal

²**kip** \'kip, 'gip\ n, pl **kip** or **kips** — see MONEY table

kip·per \'kip-ər\ n : a fish (as a herring) preserved by salting and drying or smoking — **kipper** vb

kirk \'kərk\, 'kirk\ n, *chiefly Scot* : CHURCH

kir·tle \'kərt-²l\ n : a long gown or dress worn by women

kis·met \'kiz-,met, -mət\ n, *often cap* [Turk, fr. Ar *qismah* portion, lot] : FATE

¹kiss \'kis\ vb 1 : to touch or caress with the lips as a mark of affection or greeting 2 : to touch gently or lightly

²kiss n 1 : a caress with the lips 2 : a gentle touch or contact 3 : a bite-size candy

kiss·er \'kis-ər\ n 1 : one that kisses 2 *slang* : MOUTH 3 *slang* : FACE

kit \'kit\ n 1 : a set of articles for personal use; *also* : a set of tools or implements or of parts to be assembled 2 : a container (as a case) for a kit

kitch·en \'kich-ən\ n 1 : a room with cooking facilities 2 : the personnel that prepares, cooks, and serves food

kitch·en·ette \,kich-ə-'net\ n : a small kitchen or an alcove containing cooking facilities

kitchen police n 1 : KP 2 : the work of KPs

kitch·en·ware \'kich-ən-,waər\ n : utensils and appliances for use in a kitchen

kite \'kit\ n 1 : any of various hawks with deeply forked tails 2 : a light frame covered with paper or cloth and designed to be flown in the air at the end of a long string

kith \'kith\ n [ME, fr. OE *cȳthth*, fr. *cūth* known] : familiar friends, neighbors, or relatives (~ and kin)

kitsch \'kich\ n [G] : shoddy or cheap artistic or literary material

kit·ten \'kit-²n\ n : a young cat — **kit·ten·ish** adj

¹kit·ty \'kit-ē\ n, pl **kitties** : CAT; *esp* : KITTEN

²kitty n, pl **kitties** : a fund in a poker game made up of contributions from each pot; *also* : POOL

kit·ty-cor·ner or **kit·ty-cor·nered** var of CATERCORNER

ki·wi \'kē-(,)wē\ n : a flightless New Zealand bird

ki·wi·fruit \-,früt\ n : a brownish hairy egg-shaped fruit with sweet bright green flesh and small edible black seeds

KJV abbr King James Version

KKK abbr Ku Klux Klan

kl abbr kiloliter

klatch or **klatsch** \'klach\ n [G *klatsch* gossip] : a gathering marked by informal conversation

klep·to·ma·nia \,klep-tə-'mā-nē-ə\ n : a persistent neurotic impulse to steal esp. without economic motive — **klep·to·ma·ni·ac** \-nē-,ak\ n

klieg light or **kleig light** \'klēg-\ n : a very bright lamp used in making motion pictures

km abbr kilometer

kn abbr knot

knack \'nak\ n 1 : a clever way of doing something 2 : natural aptitude

knap·sack \'nap-,sak\ n : a usu. canvas or leather bag or case strapped on the back and used esp. for carrying supplies (as on a hike)

knave \'nāv\ n 1 : ROGUE 2 : JACK 6 — **knav·ery** \'nāv-(ə-)rē\ n — **knav·ish** \'nā-vish\ adj

knead \'nēd\ vb : to work and press into a mass with the hands; *also* : MASSAGE — **knead·er** n

knee \'nē\ n : the joint in the middle part of the leg — **kneed** \'nēd\ adj

knee·cap \'nē-,kap\ n : a thick flat movable bone forming the front of the knee

knee·hole \-,hōl\ n : a space (as under a desk) for the knees

kneel \'nēl\ vb **knelt** \'nelt\ or **kneeled**; **kneel·ing** : to bend the knee : fall or rest on the knees

¹knell \'nel\ vb 1 : to ring esp. for a death or disaster 2 : to summon, announce, or proclaim by a knell

²knell n 1 : a stroke of a bell esp. when tolled (as for a funeral) 2 : an indication of the end or failure of something

knew past of KNOW

knick·ers \'nik-ərz\ n pl : loose-fitting short pants gathered at the knee

knick·knack \'nik-,nak\ n : a small trivial article intended for ornament

¹knife \'nīf\ n, pl **knives** \'nīvz\ 1 : a cutting instrument consisting of a sharp blade fastened to a handle 2 : a sharp cutting tool in a machine

²knife vb **knifed**; **knif·ing** : to stab, slash, or wound with a knife

¹knight \'nīt\ n 1 : a mounted warrior of feudal times serving a king 2 : a man honored by a sovereign for merit and in Great Britain ranking below a baronet 3 : a man devoted to the service of a lady 4 : a member of an order or society 5 : a chess piece having a move of two squares to a square of the opposite color — **knight·ly** adj

²knight vb : to make a knight of

knight·hood \'nīt-,hùd\ n 1 : the rank, dignity, or profession of a knight 2 : CHIVALRY 3 : knights as a class or body

knish \kə-'nish\ n [Yiddish] : a small round or square of dough stuffed with a filling (as of meat or fruit) and baked or fried

¹knit \'nit\ vb **knit** or **knit·ted**; **knit·ting** 1 : to link firmly or closely 2 : WRINKLE (~ her brows) 3 : to form a fabric by interlacing yarn or thread in connected loops with needles 4 : to grow together — **knit·ter** n

²knit n 1 : a basic knitting stitch 2 : a knitted garment or fabric

knit·wear \-,waər\ n : knitted clothing

knob \'näb\ n 1 : a rounded protuberance; *also* : a small rounded ornament or handle 2 : a rounded usu. isolated hill — **knobbed** \'näbd\ adj — **knob·by** \'näb-ē\ adj

¹knock \\'näk\ *vb* **1** : to strike with a sharp blow **2** : BUMP, COLLIDE **3** : to make a pounding noise; *esp* : to have engine knock **4** : to find fault with an engine

²knock *n* **1** : a sharp blow **2** : a pounding noise; *esp* : one caused by abnormal ignition in an engine

knock-down \\'näk-ˌdaün\ *n* **1** : the action of knocking down **2** : something (as a blow) that knocks down **3** : something that can be easily assembled or disassembled

knock down \-ˈdaün\ *vb* **1** : to strike to the ground with or as if with as sharp blow **2** : to take apart : DISASSEMBLE **3** : to receive an income or salary : EARN **4** : to make a reduction in

knock-er \\'näk-ər\ *n* : one that knocks; *esp* : a device hinged to a door for use in knocking

knock–knee \\'näk-ˈnē, -ˌnē\ *n* : a condition in which the legs curve inward at the knees — **knock–kneed** \-ˈnēd\ *adj*

knock off *vb* **1** : to stop doing something **2** : to do quickly, carelessly, or routinely **3** : to deduct from a price **4** : KILL **5** : ROB

knock-out \\'näk-ˌaüt\ *n* **1** : a blow that fells and immobilizes an opponent (as in boxing) **2** : something sensationally striking or attractive

knock out \-ˈaüt\ *vb* **1** : to defeat by a knockout **2** : to make unconscious or inoperative **3** : to tire out : EXHAUST

knock-wurst *or* **knack-wurst** \\'näk-ˌwərst, -ˌvu̇(r)st\ *n* : a short thick heavily seasoned sausage

knoll \\'nōl\ *n* : a small round hill

¹knot \\'nät\ *n* **1** : an interlacing (as of string or ribbon) that forms a lump or knob **2** : PROBLEM **3** : a bond of union; *esp* : the marriage bond **4** : a protuberant lump or swelling in tissue; *also* : the base of a woody branch enclosed in the stem from which it arises **5** : GROUP, CLUSTER **6** : an ornamental bow of ribbon **7** : one nautical mile per hour; *also* : one nautical mile — **knot-ty** *adj*

²knot *vb* **knot-ted; knot-ting 1** : to tie in or with a knot **2** : ENTANGLE

knot-hole \-ˌhōl\ *n* : a hole in a board or tree trunk where a knot has come out

knout \\'naüt, 'nüt\ *n* : a whip used for flogging

know \\'nō\ *vb* **knew** \\'n(y)ü\; **known** \\'nōn\; **know-ing 1** : to perceive directly : have understanding or direct cognition of; *also* : to recognize the nature of **2** : to be acquainted or familiar with **3** : to be aware of the truth of **4** : to have a practical understanding of — **know-able** *adj* — **know-er** *n* — **in the know** : possessing confidential information

know–how \\'nō-ˌhaü\ *n* : knowledge of how to do something smoothly and efficiently

know-ing \\'nō-iŋ\ *adj* **1** : having or reflecting knowledge, intelligence, or information **2** : shrewdly and keenly

alert **3** : DELIBERATE, INTENTIONAL syn intelligent, clever, bright, smart — **know-ing-ly** *adv*

knowl-edge \\'näl-ij\ *n* **1** : understanding gained by actual experience (a ~ of carpentry) **2** : range of information (within my ~) **3** : clear perception of truth **4** : something learned and kept in the mind

knowl-edge-able \-ə-bəl\ *adj* : having or showing knowledge or intelligence

knuck-le \\'nək-əl\ *n* : the rounded knob at a joint and esp. at a finger joint

knuck-le-bone \\'nək-əl-ˌbōn\ *n* : one of the bones forming a knuckle

knuckle down *vb* : to apply oneself earnestly

knuckle under *vb* : SUBMIT, SURRENDER

knurl \\'nərl\ *n* **1** : KNOB **2** : one of a series of small ridges on a metal surface to aid in gripping — **knurled** \\'nərld\ *adj*

¹KO \(ˈ)kā-ˈō, ˈkā-ō\ *n* : KNOCKOUT

²KO *vb* **KO'd** \-ˈōd, ˈkā-ˈōd\; **KO'-ing** \-ˈō-iŋ, -ō-\ : to knock out in boxing

ko-ala \kō-ˈäl-ə\ *n* : a gray furry Australian marsupial with large hairy ears that feeds on eucalyptus leaves

ko-bo \\'kō-(ˌ)bō\ *n, pl* **kobo** — see **naira** at MONEY table

K of C *abbr* Knights of Columbus

kohl-ra-bi \kōl-ˈräb-ē\ *n, pl* **-bies** [G, fr. It *cavolo rapa*, lit., cabbage turnip] : a cabbage that forms no head but has a swollen fleshy edible stem

ko-lin-sky \kə-ˈlin-skē\ *n, pl* **-skies** : the fur of various Asian minks

kook \\'kük\ *n* : SCREWBALL 2

kooky *also* **kook-ie** \\'kü-kē\ *adj* **kook-i-er; -est** : having the characteristics of a kook — **kook-i-ness** *n*

ko-peck *or* **ko-pek** \\'kō-ˌpek\ *n* — see **ruble** at MONEY table

Ko-ran \kə-ˈran, -ˈrän\ *n* [Ar *qurʾān*] : a book of sacred writings accepted by Muslims as revelations made to Muhammad by Allah

Ko-re-an \kə-ˈrē-ən\ *n* : a native or inhabitant of Korea — **Korean** *adj*

ko-ru-na \\'kȯr-ə-ˌnä\ *n, pl* **ko-ru-ny** \-ə-nē\ *or* **korunas** *or* **ko-run** \\'kȯr- əm\ — see MONEY table

ko-sher \\'kō-shər\ *adj* [Yiddish, fr. Heb *kāshēr* fit, proper] : ritually fit for use according to Jewish law; *also* : selling or serving such food

kow-tow \kau̇-ˈtau̇, ˈkau̇-ˌtau̇\ *vb* [Chin *k'o¹ t'ou²*, fr. *k'o¹* to bump + *t'ou²* head] **1** : to show obsequious deference **2** : to kneel and touch the forehead to the ground as a sign of homage or deep respect

KP \(ˈ)kā-ˈpē\ *n* **1** : enlisted persons detailed to help the cooks in a military mess **2** : the work of KPs

kph *abbr* kilometers per hour

Kr *symbol* krypton

kraal \\'kräl, ˈkrȯl\ *n* **1** : a village of southern African natives **2** : an enclosure for domestic animals in southern Africa

kraut \\'kraut\\ *n* : SAUERKRAUT

Krem·lin \\'krem-lən\\ *n* : the Russian government

Krem·lin·ol·o·gist \\,krem-lə-'näl-ə-jəst\\ *n* : a specialist in the policies and practices of the Soviet government

¹**kro·na** \\'krō-nə\\ *n, pl* **kro·nor** \\-,nȯr\\ [Sw] — see MONEY table

²**kro·na** \\'krō-nə\\ *n, pl* **kro·nur** \\-,nər\\ [Icel] — see MONEY table

kro·ne \\'krō-nə\\ *n, pl* **kro·ner** \\-nər\\ — see MONEY table

Kru·ger·rand \\'krü-gə(r)-,rand, -,ränd\\ *n* : a 1-ounce gold coin of the Republic of South Africa equal in bullion value to 25 rand and having an official price of 31 rand

kryp·ton \\'krip-,tän\\ *n* : a gaseous chemical element that occurs in small quantities in air and is used in electric lamps

KS *abbr* Kansas

kt *abbr* **1** karat **2** knight

ku·do \\'k(y)üd-ō\\ *n, pl* **kudos** [fr. *kudos* (taken as pl.)] **1** : AWARD, HONOR **2** : COMPLIMENT, PRAISE

ku·dos \\'k(y)ü-,däs\\ *n* : fame and renown resulting from achievement

kud·zu \\'kùd-zü\\ *n* [Jp *kuzu*] : a creeping vine widely grown for hay and forage and for erosion control

ku·lak \\k(y)ü-'lak\\ *n* [Russ, lit., fist] **1** : a wealthy peasant farmer in 19th century Russia **2** : a farmer characterized by Communists as too wealthy

kum·quat \\'kəm-,kwät\\ *n* [Chin *kam kwat*, fr. *kam* gold + *kwat* orange] : a small citrus fruit with sweet spongy rind and acid pulp

kung fu \\,kəŋ-'fü, ,kuŋ-\\ *n* : a Chinese art of self-defense resembling karate

ku·rus \\kə-'rüsh\\ *n, pl* **kurus** — see lira at MONEY table

kv *abbr* kilovolt

kw *abbr* kilowatt

kwa·cha \\'kwäch-ə\\ *n, pl* **kwacha** — see MONEY table

kwan·za \\'kwän-zə\\ *n, pl* **kwanzas** *or* **kwanza** — see MONEY table

kwash·i·or·kor \\,kwäsh-ē-'ȯr-kȯr, -ȯr-'kȯr\\ *n* : a disease of young children resulting from deficient intake of protein

kwhr *or* **kwh** *abbr* kilowatt-hour

Ky *or* **KY** *abbr* Kentucky

kyat \\'chät\\ *n* — see MONEY table

L

¹\\'el\\ *n, pl* **l's** *or* **ls** \\'elz\\ *often cap* : the 12th letter of the English alphabet

²*abbr, often cap* **1** lake **2** large **3** left **4** [L *libra*] pound **5** line **6** liter

¹**La** *abbr* Louisiana

²**La** *symbol* lanthanum

LA *abbr* **1** law agent **2** Los Angeles **3** Louisiana

lab \\'lab\\ *n* : LABORATORY

Lab *abbr* Labrador

¹**la·bel** \\'lā-bəl\\ *n* **1** : a slip attached to something for identification or description **2** : a descriptive or identifying word or phrase **3** : BRAND

²**label** *vb* **-beled** *or* **-belled; -bel·ing** *or* **-bel·ling** \\-b(ə-)liŋ\\ **1** : to affix a label to **2** : to describe or name with a label

la·bi·al \\'lā-bē-əl\\ *adj* : of or relating to the lips or labia

la·bia ma·jo·ra \\,lā-bē-ə-mə-'jōr-ə\\ *n pl* : the outer fatty folds of the vulva

labia mi·no·ra \\-mə-'nōr-ə\\ *n pl* : the inner highly vascular folds of the vulva

la·bile \\'lā-,bīl, -bəl\\ *adj* **1** : UNSTABLE **2** : ADAPTABLE

la·bi·um \\'lā-bē-əm\\ *n, pl* **la·bia** \\-ə\\ [NL, fr. L, lip] : any of the folds at the margin of the vulva

¹**la·bor** \\'lā-bər\\ *n* **1** : physical or mental effort; *also* : human activity that provides the goods or services in an economy **2** : the physical activities involved in parturition **3** : TASK **4** : those who do manual labor or work for wages; *also* : labor unions or their officials

²**labor** *vb* **la·bored; la·bor·ing** \\-b(ə-)riŋ\\

1 : WORK **2** : to move with great effort **3** : to be in the labor of giving birth **4** : to suffer from some disadvantage or distress ⟨~ under a delusion⟩ **5** : to treat or work out laboriously — **la·bor·er** *n*

lab·o·ra·to·ry \\'lab-(ə-)rə-,tōr-ē\\ *n, pl* **-ries** : a place equipped for making scientific experiments or tests

Labor Day *n* : the 1st Monday in September observed as a legal holiday in recognition of the working people

la·bored \\'lā-bərd\\ *adj* : not freely or easily done ⟨~ breathing⟩

la·bo·ri·ous \\lə-'bȯr-ē-əs\\ *adj* **1** : INDUSTRIOUS **2** : requiring great effort — **la·bo·ri·ous·ly** *adv*

la·bor-sav·ing \\'lā-bər-,sā-viŋ\\ *adj* : designed to replace or decrease labor

la·bour *chiefly Brit var of* LABOR

lab·ra·dor·ite \\'lab-rə-,dȯr-,īt\\ *n* : a feldspar showing a play of several colors

Lab·ra·dor retriever \\'lab-rə-,dȯr-\\ *n* : a strongly built retriever having a short dense black, yellow, or chocolate coat

la·bur·num \\lə-'bər-nəm\\ *n* : a leguminous shrub or tree with hanging clusters of yellow flowers

lab·y·rinth \\'lab-ə-,rin(t)th\\ *n* : a place constructed of or filled with confusing intricate passageways : MAZE — **lab·y·rin·thine** \\,lab-ə-'rin-thən\\ *adj*

lac \\'lak\\ *n* : a resinous substance secreted by a scale insect and used in the manufacture of shellac and lacquers

¹lace \'lās\ *vb* **laced; lac·ing 1** : TIE **2** : to adorn with lace **3** : INTERTWINE **4** : BEAT, LASH **5** : to give zest or savor to

²lace *n* [ME, fr. OF *laz*, fr. L *laqueus* snare, noose] **1** : a cord or string used for drawing together two edges **2** : an ornamental braid **3** : a fine openwork usu. figured fabric made of thread — **lacy** \'lā-sē\ *adj*

lac·er·ate \'las-ə-ˌrāt\ *vb* **-at·ed; -at·ing** : to tear roughly — **lac·er·a·tion** \ˌlas-ə-'rā-shən\ *n*

lace·wing \'lās-ˌwiŋ\ *n* : any of various insects with delicate wing veins, long antennae, and brilliant eyes

lach·ry·mose \'lak-rə-ˌmōs\ *adj* **1** : TEARFUL **2** : MOURNFUL

¹lack \'lak\ *vb* **1** : to be wanting or missing **2** : to be deficient in

²lack *n* : the fact or state of being wanting or deficient : NEED

lack·a·dai·si·cal \ˌlak-ə-'dā-zi-kəl\ *adj* : lacking life, spirit, or zest — **lack·a·dai·si·cal·ly** \-k(ə-)lē\ *adv*

lack·ey \'lak-ē\ *n, pl* **lackeys 1** : a liveried retainer **2** : TOADY

lack·lus·ter \'lak-ˌləs-tər\ *adj* : DULL

la·con·ic \lə-'kän-ik\ *adj* [L *laconicus* Spartan, fr. Gk *lakōnikos*; fr. the Spartan reputation for terseness of speech] : sparing of words : TERSE — **la·con·i·cal·ly** \-i-k(ə-)lē\ *adv*

lac·quer \'lak-ər\ *n* : a clear or colored usu. glossy and quick-drying surface coating that contains natural or synthetic substances — **lacquer** *vb*

lac·ri·mal *also* **lach·ry·mal** \'lak-rə-məl\ *adj* : of, relating to, or being the glands that produce tears

lac·ri·ma·tion \ˌlak-rə-'mā-shən\ *n* : secretion of tears

la·crosse \lə-'krós\ *n* [CanF *la crosse*, lit., the crosier] : a game played on a field by two teams with a hard ball and long-handled rackets

lac·tate \'lak-ˌtāt\ *vb* **lac·tat·ed; lac·tat·ing** : to secrete milk — **lac·ta·tion** \lak-'tā-shən\ *n*

lac·tic \'lak-tik\ *adj* **1** : of or relating to milk **2** : formed in the souring of milk

lactic acid *n* : a syrupy acid present in blood and muscle tissue, produced by bacterial fermentation of carbohydrates, and used in food and medicine

lac·tose \'lak-ˌtōs\ *n* : a sugar present in milk

la·cu·na \lə-'k(y)ü-nə\ *n, pl* **la·cu·nae** \-nē\ *or* **la·cu·nas** [L, pool, pit, gap, fr. *lacus* lake] : a blank space or missing part : GAP

lad \'lad\ *n* : YOUTH; *also* : FELLOW

lad·der \'lad-ər\ *n* : a device for climbing that consists of two parallel side-pieces joined at intervals by cross-pieces

lad·die \'lad-ē\ *n* : a young lad

lad·en \'lād-ᵊn\ *adj* : LOADED, BURDENED

lad·ing \'lād-iŋ\ *n* : CARGO, FREIGHT

la·dle \'lād-ᵊl\ *n* : a deep-bowled long-handled spoon used in taking up and conveying liquids — **ladle** *vb*

la·dy \'lād-ē\ *n, pl* **ladies** [ME, fr. OE *hlǣfdīge*, fr. *hlāf* bread + *-dīge* (akin to *dǣge* kneader of bread)] **1** : a woman of property, rank, or authority; *also* : a woman of superior social position or of refinement **2** : WOMAN **3** : WIFE

lady beetle *n* : LADYBUG

la·dy·bird \'lād-ē-ˌbərd\ *n* : LADYBUG

la·dy·bug \-ˌbəg\ *n* : any of various small nearly hemispherical and usu. brightly colored beetles that feed mostly on other insects

la·dy·fin·ger \'lād-ē-ˌfiŋ-gər\ *n* : a small finger-shaped sponge cake

la·dy-in-wait·ing \ˌlād-ē-in-'wāt-iŋ\ *n, pl* **ladies-in-waiting** : a lady appointed to attend or wait on a queen or princess

la·dy·like \'lād-ē-ˌlīk\ *adj* : WELL-BRED

la·dy·love \-ˌləv\ *n* : SWEETHEART

la·dy·ship \'lād-ē-ˌship\ *n* : the condition of being a lady : rank of lady

lady's slipper \'lād-ē(z)-ˌslip-ər\ *n* : any of several No. American orchids with slipper-shaped flowers

¹lag \'lag\ *n* **1** : a slowing up or falling behind; *also* : the amount by which one lags **2** : INTERVAL

²lag *vb* **lagged; lag·ging 1** : to fail to keep up : stay behind **2** : to slacken gradually syn dawdle, dally, tarry, loiter

la·ger \'läg-ər\ *n* : a light-colored usu. dry beer

lag·gard \'lag-ərd\ *adj* : DILATORY, SLOW — **lag·gard·ly** *adv or adj* — **lag·gard·ness** *n*

²laggard *n* : one that lags or lingers

la·gniappe \'lan-ˌyap\ *n* : something given free esp. with a purchase

la·goon \lə-'gün\ *n* : a shallow sound, channel, or pond near or communicating with a larger body of water

laid *past and past part of* LAY

laid-back \'lād-'bak\ *adj* : having a relaxed style or character ⟨~ music⟩

lain *past part of* ¹LIE

lair \'laər\ *n* : the resting or living place of a wild animal : DEN

laird \'laərd\ *n, Scot* : a landed proprietor

lais·sez-faire \ˌles-ˌā-'far\ *n* [F *laissez faire* let do] : a doctrine opposing governmental interference in economic affairs beyond that necessary to maintain peace and property rights

la·ity \'lā-ət-ē\ *n* **1** : the people of a religious faith who are not members of its clergy **2** : the mass of people who are of a particular field

lake \'lāk\ *n* : an inland body of standing water of considerable size; *also* : a pool of liquid (as lava or pitch)

¹lam \'lam\ *vb* **lammed; lam·ming** : to flee hastily — **lam** *n*

²lam *abbr* laminated

Lam *abbr* Lamentations

la·ma \'läm-ə\ *n* : a Buddhist monk of Tibet or Mongolia

la·ma·sery \'läm-ə-ˌser-ē\ *n, pl* **-ser·ies** : a monastery for lamas

¹lamb \'lam\ *n* **1** : a young sheep; *also* : its flesh used as food **2** : an innocent or gentle person

²lamb *vb* : to bring forth a lamb

lam·baste *or* **lam·bast** \lam-ˈbāst, -ˈbast\ *vb* **1** : BEAT **2** : EXCORIATE

lam·bent \'lam-bənt\ *adj* [L *lambens*, prp. of *lambere* to lick] **1** : FLICKERING **2** : softly radiant ⟨∼ eyes⟩ **3** : marked by lightness or brilliance ⟨∼ humor⟩ — **lam·ben·cy** \-bən-sē\ *n* — **lam·bent·ly** *adv*

lamb·skin \'lam-ˌskin\ *n* : a lamb's skin or a small fine-grade sheepskin or the leather made from either

¹lame \'lām\ *adj* **lam·er; lam·est 1** : having a body part and usu. a limb so disabled as to impair freedom of movement; *also* : marked by stiffness and soreness **2** : lacking substance : WEAK — **lame·ly** *adv* — **lame·ness** *n*

²lame *vb* **lamed; lam·ing** : to make lame : CRIPPLE

la·mé \lä-ˈmā, la-\ *n* [F] : a brocaded clothing fabric with tinsel filling threads (as of gold or silver)

lame·brain \'lām-ˌbrān\ *n* : a stupid person

lame duck *n* : an elected official continuing to hold office between an election and the inauguration of a successor

¹la·ment \lə-ˈment\ *vb* **1** : to mourn aloud : WAIL **2** : to express sorrow for : BEWAIL — **lam·en·ta·ble** \'lam-ən-tə-bəl, lə-ˈment-ə-\ *adj* — **lam·en·ta·bly** \-blē\ *adv* — **lam·en·ta·tion** \ˌlam-ən-ˈtā-shən\ *n*

²lament *n* **1** : a crying out in grief : WAIL **2** : DIRGE, ELEGY

Lamentations *n* — see BIBLE table

la·mia \'lā-mē-ə\ *n* : a female demon

lam·i·na \'lam-ə-nə\ *n, pl* **-nae** \-ˌnē\ *or* **-nas** : a thin plate or scale

lam·i·nar \'lam-ə-nər\ *adj* : arranged in or consisting of laminae

lam·i·nat·ed \-ˌnāt-əd\ *adj* : consisting of laminae; *esp* : composed of layers of firmly united material — **lam·i·nate** \-ˌnāt\ *vb* — **lam·i·nate** \-nət\ *n or adj* — **lam·i·na·tion** \ˌlam-ə-ˈnā-shən\ *n*

lamp \'lamp\ *n* **1** : a vessel with a wick for burning a flammable liquid (as oil) to produce light **2** : a device for producing light or heat

lamp·black \-ˌblak\ *n* : black soot made by incomplete burning of carbonaceous matter and used esp. as a pigment

lamp·light·er \-ˌlīt-ər\ *n* : a person employed to light gas streetlights

lam·poon \lam-ˈpün\ *n* : SATIRE; *esp* : one that is harsh and usu. directed against an individual — **lampoon** *vb*

lam·prey \'lam-prē\ *n, pl* **lampreys** : an eellike aquatic vertebrate animal with sucking mouth and no jaws

la·nai \lə-ˈnī\ *n* [Hawaiian] : a porch furnished for use as a living room

lance \'lans\ *n* **1** : a spear carried by mounted soldiers **2** : any of various sharp-pointed implements; *esp* : LANCET

²lance *vb* **lanced; lanc·ing** : to pierce or open with a lance ⟨∼ a boil⟩

lance corporal *n* : an enlisted man in the marine corps ranking above a private first class and below a corporal

lanc·er \'lan-sər\ *n* : a cavalryman of a unit formerly armed with lances

lan·cet \'lan-sət\ *n* : a sharp-pointed and usu. 2-edged surgical instrument

¹land \'land\ *n* **1** : the solid part of the surface of the earth; *also* : a part of the earth's surface (fenced ∼) (marshy ∼) **2** : NATION **3** : REALM, DOMAIN — **land·less** *adj*

²land *vb* **1** : DISEMBARK; *also* : to touch at a place on shore **2** : to alight or cause to alight on a surface **3** : to bring to or arrive at a destination **4** : to catch with a hook and bring in ⟨∼ a fish⟩ ; *also* : GAIN, SECURE ⟨∼ a job⟩

lan·dau \'lan-ˌdau\ *n* **1** : a 4-wheeled carriage with a top divided into two sections that can be lowered, thrown back, or removed **2** : an automobile with a folding top over the rear passenger compartment

land·ed \'lan-dəd\ *adj* : having an estate in land ⟨∼ gentry⟩

land·er \'lan-dər\ *n* : a space vehicle designed to land on a celestial body

land·fall \'lan(d)-ˌfól\ *n* : a sighting or making of land (as after a voyage); *also* : the land first sighted

land·fill \-ˌfil\ *n* : a low-lying area on which trash and garbage is buried between layers of earth

land·form \-ˌfórm\ *n* : a natural feature of a land surface

land·hold·er \'land-ˌhōl-dər\ *n* : a holder or owner of land — **land·hold·ing** \-diŋ\ *adj or n*

land·ing \'lan-diŋ\ *n* **1** : the action of one that lands **2** : a place for discharging or taking on passengers and cargo **3** : a level part of a staircase

landing gear *n* : the part that supports the weight of an airplane or spacecraft

land·la·dy \'land-ˌlād-ē\ *n* : a woman who is a landlord

land·locked \-ˌläkt\ *adj* **1** : enclosed or nearly enclosed by land ⟨a ∼ country⟩ **2** : confined to fresh water by some barrier ⟨∼ salmon⟩

land·lord \-ˌlórd\ *n* **1** : the owner of property leased or rented to another **2** : a person who rents lodgings : INNKEEPER

land·lub·ber \-ˌləb-ər\ *n* : one who knows little of the sea or seamanship

land·mark \'lan(d)-ˌmärk\ *n* **1** : an object that marks a course or boundary or serves as a guide **2** : an event that marks a turning point **3** : a structure of unusual historical and usu. aesthetic interest

land·mass \-ˌmas\ *n* : a large area of land

landowner · lares and penates

land·own·er \'land-ˌō-nər\ *n* : an owner of land

¹land·scape \'lan(d)-ˌskāp\ *n* **1** : a picture of natural inland scenery **2** : a portion of land that can be seen in one glance

²landscape *vb* **land·scaped; land·scap·ing** : to improve the natural beauties of a tract of land by grading, clearing, or decorative planting

land·slide \'lan(d)-ˌslīd\ *n* **1** : the slipping down of a mass of rocks or earth on a steep slope; *also* : the mass of material that slides **2** : an overwhelming victory esp. in a political contest

lands·man \'lan(d)z-mən\ *n* : a person who lives or works on land

land·ward \'land-wərd\ *adv or adj* : to or toward the land

lane \'lān\ *n* **1** : a narrow passageway (as between fences) **2** : a relatively narrow way or track ⟨traffic ~⟩

lang *abbr* language

lan·guage \'laŋ-gwij\ *n* [ME, fr. OF, fr. *langue* tongue, language, fr. L *lingua*] **1** : the words, their pronunciation, and the methods of combining them used and understood by a considerable community **2** : form or style of verbal expression **3** : a system of signs and symbols and rules for using them that is used to carry information

lan·guid \'laŋ-gwəd\ *adj* **1** : WEAK **2** : sluggish in character or disposition : LISTLESS **3** : SLOW — **lan·guid·ly** *adv* — **lan·guid·ness** *n*

lan·guish \'laŋ-gwish\ *vb* **1** : to become languid **2** : to become dispirited : PINE **3** : to appeal for sympathy by assuming an expression of grief

lan·guor \'laŋ-(g)ər\ *n* **1** : a languid feeling : SLUGGISHNESS **syn** lethargy, lassitude, torpidity, torpor — **lan·guor·ous** *adj* — **lan·guor·ous·ly** *adv*

lank \'laŋk\ *adj* **1** : not well filled out **2** : hanging straight and limp

lanky \'laŋ-kē\ *adj* **lank·i·er; -est** : ungracefully tall and thin

lan·o·lin \'lan-ᵊl-ən\ *n* : the fatty coating of sheep's wool esp. when refined for use in ointments and cosmetics

lan·ta·na \lan-'tän-ə\ *n* : any of a genus of tropical shrubs related to the vervains with heads of small bright flowers

lan·tern \'lant-ərn\ *n* **1** : a usu. portable light with a protective covering **2** : the chamber in a lighthouse containing the light **3** : a projector for slides

lan·tha·num \'lan-thə-nəm\ *n* : a soft malleable metallic chemical element

lan·yard \'lan-yərd\ *n* : a piece of rope for fastening something in ships; *also* : any of various cords

¹lap \'lap\ *n* **1** : a loose panel of a garment **2** : the clothing that lies on the knees, thighs, and lower part of the trunk when one sits; *also* : the front part of the lower trunk and thighs of a seated person **3** : an environment of nurture ⟨the ~ of luxury⟩ **4** : CHARGE, CONTROL ⟨in the ~ of the gods⟩

²lap *vb* **lapped; lap·ping 1** : FOLD **2** : WRAP **3** : to lay over or near so as to partly cover

³lap *n* **1** : the amount by which an object overlaps another; *also* : the part of an object that overlaps another **2** : a smoothing and polishing tool **3** : one circuit around a racecourse **4** : one complete turn (as of a rope around a drum)

⁴lap *vb* **lapped; lap·ping 1** : to scoop up food or drink with the tip of the tongue; *also* : DEVOUR — usu. used with *up* **2** : to splash gently ⟨lapping waves⟩

⁵lap *n* **1** : an act or instance of lapping **2** : a gentle splashing sound

lap·board \'lap-ˌbōrd\ *n* : a board used on the lap as a table or desk

lap·dog \-ˌdóg\ *n* : a small dog that may be held in the lap

la·pel \lə-'pel\ *n* : the fold of the front of a coat that is usu. a continuation of the collar

lap·i·dary \'lap-ə-ˌder-ē\ *n, pl* **-dar·ies** : one who cuts, polishes, and engraves precious stones

²lapidary *adj* **1** : of, relating to, or suitable for engraved inscriptions **2** : of or relating to precious stones or the art of cutting them

lap·in \'lap-ən\ *n* : rabbit fur usu. sheared and dyed

la·pis la·zu·li \ˌlap-əs-'laz(h)-ə-lē\ *n* : a usu. blue semiprecious stone often having sparkling bits of pyrite

Lapp \'lap\ *n* : a member of a people of northern Scandinavia, Finland, and the Kola peninsula of Russia

lap·pet \'lap-ət\ *n* : a fold or flap on a garment

¹lapse \'laps\ *n* [L *lapsus*, fr. *labi* to slip] **1** : a slight error **2** : a fall from a higher to a lower state **3** : the termination of a right or privilege through failure to meet requirements **4** : a passage of time; *also* : INTERVAL

²lapse *vb* **lapsed; laps·ing 1** : to commit apostasy **2** : to sink or slip gradually : SUBSIDE **3** : CEASE

lap·wing \'lap-ˌwiŋ\ *n* : an Old World crested plover

lar·board \'lär-bərd\ *n* : ⁵PORT

lar·ce·ny \'lärs-(ə)-nē\ *n, pl* **-nies** [ME, fr. MF *larcin* theft, fr. L *latrocinium* robbery, fr. *latro* mercenary soldier] : THEFT — **lar·ce·nous** \-nəs\ *adj*

larch \'lärch\ *n* : a conical tree related to the pines that sheds its needles in the fall

¹lard \'lärd\ *vb* **1** : to insert strips of usu. pork fat into (meat) before cooking; *also* : GREASE **2** *obs* : ENRICH

²lard *n* : a soft white fat obtained by rendering fatty tissue of the hog

lar·der \'lärd-ər\ *n* : a place where foods (as meat) are kept

lar·es and pe·na·tes \ˌlar-ēz-ən-pə-ˈnāt-ēz\ *n pl* **1** : household gods **2** : personal or household effects

large \ˈlärj\ *adj* **larg·er; larg·est** **1** : having more than usual power, capacity, or scope **2** : exceeding most other things of like kind in quantity or size syn big, great, oversize — **large·ness** *n* — **at large 1** : UNCONFINED **2** : as a whole

large·ly \ˈlärj-lē\ *adv* : to a large extent

lar·gess *or* **lar·gesse** \lär-ˈzhes, -ˈjes\ *n* **1** : liberal giving **2** : a generous gift

¹**lar·go** \ˈlär-gō\ *adv or adj* [It, slow, broad, fr. L *largus* abundant] : in a very slow and stately manner — used as a direction in music

²**largo** *n, pl* **largos** : a largo movement

lar·i·at \ˈlar-ē-ət\ *n* [AmerSp *la reata* the lasso, fr. Sp *la* the + AmerSp *reata* lasso, fr. Sp *reatar* to tie again] : a long rope used to catch or tether livestock

¹**lark** \ˈlärk\ *n* : any of various small songbirds; *esp* : SKYLARK

²**lark** *n* : something done solely for fun or adventure : ESCAPADE

³**lark** *vb* : to engage in harmless fun or mischief — usu. used with *about*

lark·spur \ˈlärk-ˌspər\ *n* : any of various mostly annual delphiniums

lar·va \ˈlär-və\ *n, pl* **lar·vae** \-(ˌ)vē\ *also* **larvas** [L, specter, mask] : the wingless often wormlike form in which insects hatch from the egg; *also* : any young animal (as a tadpole) that is fundamentally unlike its parent — **lar·val** \-vəl\ *adj*

lar·yn·gi·tis \ˌlar-ən-ˈjīt-əs\ *n* : inflammation of the larynx

lar·ynx \ˈlar-iŋks\ *n, pl* **la·ryn·ges** \lə-ˈrin-ˌjēz\ *or* **lar·ynx·es** : the upper part of the trachea containing the vocal cords — **la·ryn·ge·al** \ˌlar-ən-ˈjē-əl, lə-ˈrin-jē-əl\ *adj*

la·sa·gna \lə-ˈzän-yə\ *n* [It] : boiled broad flat noodles baked with a sauce usu. of tomatoes, cheese, and meat

las·car \ˈlas-kər\ *n* : an Indian sailor

las·civ·i·ous \lə-ˈsiv-ē-əs\ *adj* : LEWD, LUSTFUL — **las·civ·i·ous·ness** *n*

la·ser \ˈlā-zər\ *n* [*l*ight *a*mplification by *s*timulated *e*mission of *r*adiation] : a device that produces an intense monochromatic beam of light

¹**lash** \ˈlash\ *vb* **1** : to move vigorously **2** : WHIP **3** : to attack verbally

²**lash** *n* **1** : a stroke esp. with a whip **2** : a stinging rebuke **3** : EYELASH

³**lash** *vb* : to bind with a rope, cord, or chain

lass \ˈlas\ *n* : GIRL

lass·ie \ˈlas-ē\ *n* : LASS

las·si·tude \ˈlas-ə-ˌt(y)üd\ *n* **1** : WEARINESS, FATIGUE **2** : LANGUOR

las·so \ˈlas-ō, la-ˈsü\ *n, pl* **lassos** *or* **lassoes** [Sp *lazo*] : a rope or long leather thong with a noose used for catching livestock — **lasso** *vb*

¹**last** \ˈlast\ *vb* **1** : to continue in existence or operation **2** : to remain valid, valuable, or important : ENDURE **3** : to be enough for the needs of

²**last** *n* : a foot-shaped form on which a shoe is shaped or repaired

³**last** *vb* : to shape with a last

⁴**last** *adj* **1** : following all the rest : FINAL **2** : next before the present **3** : least likely ⟨the ∼ thing he wants⟩ **4** : CONCLUSIVE; *also* : SUPREME — **last·ly** *adv*

⁵**last** *adv* **1** : at the end **2** : most recently **3** : in conclusion

⁶**last** *n* : something that is last — **at last** : FINALLY

Last Supper *n* : the supper eaten by Jesus and his disciples on the night of his betrayal

lat *abbr* latitude

Lat *abbr* Latin

lat·a·kia \ˌlat-ə-ˈkē-ə\ *n* : an aromatic Turkish smoking tobacco

¹**latch** \ˈlach\ *vb* : to catch or get hold

²**latch** *n* : a catch that holds a door or gate closed

³**latch** *vb* : CATCH, FASTEN

latch·et \ˈlach-ət\ *n* : a strap, thong, or lace for fastening a shoe or sandal

latch·key \ˈlach-ˌkē\ *n* : a key for opening a door latch esp. from the outside

latch·string \-ˌstriŋ\ *n* : a string on a latch that may be left hanging outside the door for raising the latch

¹**late** \ˈlāt\ *adj* **lat·er; lat·est** **1** : coming or remaining after the due, usual, or proper time : TARDY **2** : far advanced toward the close or end **3** : recently deceased ⟨her ∼ husband⟩ **4** : made, appearing, or happening just previous to the present : RECENT — **late·ly** *adv* — **late·ness** *n*

²**late** *adv* **lat·er; lat·est** **1** : after the usual or proper time; *also* : at or to an advanced point in time **2** : RECENTLY

late·com·er \ˈlāt-ˌkəm-ər\ *n* : one who arrives late

la·teen \lə-ˈtēn\ *adj* : relating to or being a triangular sail extended by a long spar slung to a low mast

la·tent \ˈlāt-ᵊnt\ *adj* : present but not visible or active syn dormant, quiescent, potential — **la·ten·cy** \-ᵊn-sē\ *n*

¹**lat·er·al** \ˈlat-(ə-)rəl\ *adj* : situated on, directed toward, or coming from the side — **lat·er·al·ly** \-ē\ *adv*

²**lateral** *n* **1** : a lateral passage (as a drainage ditch) **2** : a football pass thrown parallel to the line of scrimmage or away from the opponent's goal

la·tex \ˈlā-ˌteks\ *n, pl* **la·ti·ces** \ˈlāt-ə-ˌsēz, ˈlat-\ *or* **la·tex·es** **1** : a milky plant juice esp. of members of the milkweed group (rubber is made from a ∼) **2** : a water emulsion of a synthetic rubber or plastic used esp. as a paint

lath \ˈlath, ˈláth\ *n, pl* **laths** *or* **lath** : a thin narrow strip of wood used esp. as a base for plaster; *also* : a building material in sheets used for the same purpose — **lath·ing** \-iŋ\ *n*

lathe \ˈlāth\ *n* : a machine in which a

piece of material is held and turned while being shaped by a tool

¹lath·er \'lath-ər\ *n* **1** : a foam or froth formed when a detergent is agitated in water; *also* : foam from profuse sweating (as by a horse) **2** : DITHER

²lather *vb* **lath·ered; lath·er·ing** \-(ə-)riŋ\ : to spread lather over; *also* : to form a lather

Lat·in \'lat-³n\ *n* **1** : the language of ancient Rome **2** : a member of any of the peoples whose languages derive from Latin — **Latin** *adj*

Latin American *n* : a native or inhabitant of any of the countries of No., Central, or So. America whose official language is Spanish or Portuguese — **Latin–American** *adj*

La·ti·no \lə-'tē-nō\ *n, pl* **-nos** : a native or inhabitant of Latin America; *also* : a person of Latin-American origin living in the U.S.

lat·i·tude \'lat-ə-,t(y)üd\ *n* **1** : angular distance north or south from the earth's equator measured in degrees **2** : a region marked by its latitude **3** : freedom of action or choice

lat·i·tu·di·nar·i·an \,lat-ə-,t(y)üd-³n-'er-ē-ən\ *n* : a person who is broad and liberal in religious belief and conduct

la·trine \lə-'trēn\ *n* : TOILET

lat·ter \'lat-ər\ *adj* **1** : more recent; *also* : FINAL **2** : of, relating to, or being the second of two things referred to — **lat·ter·ly** *adv*

lat·ter–day *adj* **1** : of present or recent times **2** : of a later or subsequent time

Latter–day Saint *n* : a member of a religious body founded by Joseph Smith in 1830 and accepting the Book of Mormon as divine revelation : MORMON

lat·tice \'lat-əs\ *n* **1** : a framework of crossed wood or metal strips; *also* : a window, door, or gate having a lattice **2** : a regular geometrical arrangement

lat·tice·work \-,wərk\ *n* : LATTICE; *also* : work made of lattices

¹laud \'lȯd\ *n* **1** : PRAISE, ACCLAIM

²laud *vb* : PRAISE, EXTOL — **laud·able** *adj* — **laud·ably** *adv*

lau·da·num \'lȯd-(ə-)nəm\ *n* : OPIATE; *esp* : a tincture of opium

lau·da·to·ry \'lȯd-ə-,tōr-ē\ *adj* : of, relating to, or expressive of praise

¹laugh \'laf, 'läf\ *vb* : to show mirth, joy, or scorn with a smile and chuckle or explosive sound; *also* : to become amused or derisive — **laugh·able** *adj* — **laugh·ing·ly** \-iŋ-lē\ *adv*

²laugh *n* **1** : the act of laughing **2** : JOKE; *also* : JEER

laugh·ing·stock \'laf-iŋ-,stäk, 'läf-\ *n* : an object of ridicule

laugh·ter \'laf-tər, 'läf-\ *n* : the action or sound of laughing

¹launch \'lȯnch\ *vb* [ME *launchen*, fr. OF *lancher*, fr. LL *lanceare* to wield a lance] **1** : THROW, HURL; *also* : to send off (~ a rocket) **2** : to set afloat **3** : to set in operation : START

²launch *n* : an act or instance of launching

³launch *n* : a small open or half-decked motorboat

launch·er \'lȯn-chər\ *n* **1** : one that launches **2** : a device for firing a grenade from a rifle **3** : a device for launching a rocket or rocket shell

launch·pad \'lȯnch-,pad\ *n* : a platform from which a rocket is launched

laun·der \'lȯn-dər\ *vb* **laun·dered; laun·der·ing** \-d(ə-)riŋ\ : to wash or wash and iron clothing and household linens — **laun·der·er** *n* — **laun·dress** \-drəs\ *n*

laun·dry \'lȯn-drē\ *n, pl* **laundries** [fr. obs. *launder* launderer, fr. MF *lavandier*, fr. ML *lavandarius*, fr. L *lavandus* needing to be washed, fr. *lavare* to wash] **1** : a place where laundering is done **2** : clothes or linens that have been or are to be laundered — **laun·dry·man** \-mən\ *n* — **laun·dry·wom·an** \-,wum-ən\ *n*

lau·re·ate \'lȯr-ē-ət\ *n* : the recipient of honor for achievement in an art or science — **lau·re·ate·ship** *n*

lau·rel \'lȯr-əl\ *n* **1** : any of several trees or shrubs related to the sassafras and cinnamon; *esp* : a small evergreen tree of southern Europe **2** : MOUNTAIN LAUREL **3** : a crown of laurel : HONOR, DISTINCTION — usu. used in pl.

lav *abbr* lavatory

la·va \'läv-ə, 'lav-\ *n* [It] : melted rock coming from a volcano; *also* : such rock solidified

la·vage \lə-'väzh\ *n* [F] : WASHING; *esp* : the washing out (as of an organ) for medicinal reasons

la·va·liere *or* **la·val·liere** \,läv-ə-'liər\ *n* [F *lavallière* necktie with a large bow] : a pendant on a fine chain that is worn as a necklace

lav·a·to·ry \'lav-ə-,tōr-ē\ *n, pl* **-ries** **1** : a fixed washbowl with running water and drainpipe **2** : BATHROOM

lave \'lāv\ *vb* **laved; lav·ing** : WASH

lav·en·der \'lav-ən-dər\ *n* **1** : a European mint or its dried leaves and flowers used to perfume clothing and bed linen **2** : a pale purple

¹lav·ish \'lav-ish\ *adj* [ME *lavas* abundance, fr. MF *lavasse* downpour, fr. *laver* to wash] **1** : expending or bestowing profusely **2** : expended or produced in abundance — **lav·ish·ly** *adv*

²lavish *vb* : to expend or give freely

law \'lȯ\ *n* **1** : a rule of conduct or action established by custom or laid down and enforced by a governing authority; *also* : the whole body of such rules **2** : the control brought about by enforcing rules **3** *cap* : the revelation of the divine will set forth in the Old Testament; *also* : the first part of the Jewish scriptures **4** : a rule or principle of construction or procedure **5** : the science that deals with laws and their interpretation and application **6**

: the profession of a lawyer **7** : a rule or principle stating something that always works in the same way under the same conditions

law·break·er \'lȯ-ˌbrā-kər\ *n* : one who violates the law

law·ful \'lȯ-fəl\ *adj* **1** : permitted by law **2** : RIGHTFUL — **law·ful·ly** \-ē\ *adv*

law·giv·er \-ˌgiv-ər\ *n* : LEGISLATOR

law·less \'lȯ-ləs\ *adj* **1** : having no laws **2** : UNRULY, DISORDERLY ⟨a ∼ mob⟩ — **law·less·ness** *n*

law·mak·er \-ˌmā-kər\ *n* : LEGISLATOR

law·man \'lȯ-mən\ *n* : a law enforcement official (as a sheriff or marshal)

¹lawn \'lȯn\ *n* : ground (as around a house) covered with closely mowed grass

²lawn *n* : a fine sheer linen or cotton fabric

law·ren·ci·um \lȯ-'ren-sē-əm\ *n* : a short-lived radioactive element

law·suit \'lȯ-ˌsüt\ *n* : a suit in law

law·yer \'lȯ-yər\ *n* : one who conducts lawsuits for clients or advises as to legal rights and obligations in other matters

lax \'laks\ *adj* **1** : not strict ⟨∼ discipline⟩ **2** : not tense or rigid syn remiss, negligent, neglectful, delinquent, derelict — **lax·i·ty** \'lak-sət-ē\ *n* — **lax·ly** *adv*

¹lax·a·tive \'lak-sət-iv\ *adj* : relieving constipation

²laxative *n* : a usu. mild laxative drug

¹lay \'lā\ *vb* **laid** \'lād\; **lay·ing 1** : to beat or strike down **2** : to put on or against a surface : PLACE **3** : to produce and deposit eggs **4** : SETTLE; *also* : ALLAY **5** : SPREAD **6** : PREPARE, CONTRIVE **7** : WAGER **8** : to impose esp. as a duty or burden **9** : to set in order or position **10** : to bring to a specified condition **11** : to put forward : SUBMIT

²lay *n* : the way in which something lies or is laid in relation to something else

³lay *past of* ¹LIE

⁴lay *n* **1** : a simple narrative poem **2** : SONG

⁵lay *adj* : of or relating to the laity

lay·away \'lā-ə-ˌwā\ *n* : a purchasing agreement by which a retailer agrees to hold merchandise secured by a deposit until the price is paid in full by the customer

lay·er \'lā-ər\ *n* **1** : one that lays **2** : one thickness, course, or fold laid or lying over or under another

lay·ette \lā-'et\ *n* [F, fr. MF, dim. of *laye* box] : an outfit of clothing and equipment for a newborn infant

lay·man \'lā-mən\ *n* : a member of the laity

lay·off \'lā-ˌȯf\ *n* **1** : the act of dismissing an employee temporarily **2** : a period of inactivity

lay·out \'lā-ˌaut\ *n* **1** : ARRANGEMENT : SET, OUTFIT

lay·wom·an \'lā-ˌwum-ən\ *n* : a woman who is a member of the laity

la·zar \'laz-ər, 'lā-zər\ *n* : LEPER

laze \'lāz\ *vb* **lazed; laz·ing** : to pass time in idleness or relaxation

la·zy \'lā-zē\ *adj* **la·zi·er; -est 1** : disliking activity or exertion **2** : SLUGGISH — **la·zi·ly** \'lā-zə-lē\ *adv* — **la·zi·ness** \-zē-nəs\ *n*

la·zy·bones \'lā-zē-ˌbōnz\ *n* : a lazy person

lazy Su·san \ˌlā-zē-'süz-ᵊn\ *n* : a revolving tray placed on a dining table

lb *abbr* [L *libra*] pound

lc *abbr* lowercase

LC *abbr* Library of Congress

¹LCD \'el-ˌsē-'dē\ *n* [*liquid crystal display*] : a display (as of the time in a watch) that consists of segments of a liquid crystal whose reflectivity varies with the voltage applied to them

²LCD *abbr* least common denominator; lowest common denominator

LCDR *abbr* lieutenant commander

LCM *abbr* least common multiple; lowest common multiple

LCpl *abbr* lance corporal

ld *abbr* **1** load **2** lord

LD *abbr* lethal dose

LDC *abbr* less developed country

ldg *abbr* **1** landing **2** loading

LDS *abbr* Latter-day Saints

lea \'lē, 'lā\ *n* : PASTURE, MEADOW

leach \'lēch\ *vb* : to pass a liquid (as water) through to carry off the soluble components; *also* : to dissolve out by such means ⟨∼ alkali from ashes⟩

¹lead \'lēd\ *vb* **led** \'led\; **lead·ing 1** : to guide on a way; *also* : to run in a specified direction ⟨∼ a quiet life⟩ **3** : to direct the operations, activity, or performance of ⟨∼ an orchestra⟩ **4** : to go at the head of : be first ⟨∼ a parade⟩ **5** : to begin play with; *also* : BEGIN, OPEN **6** : to tend toward a definite result ⟨study ∼*ing* to a degree⟩ — **lead·er** *n* — **lead·er·less** *adj* — **lead·er·ship** *n*

²lead \'lēd\ *n* **1** : a position at the front; *also* : a margin by which one leads **2** : the privilege of leading in cards; *also* : the card or suit led **3** : EXAMPLE **4** : one that leads **5** : a principal role (as in a play); *also* : one who plays such a role **6** : INDICATION, CLUE **7** : an insulated electrical conductor

³lead \'led\ *n* **1** : a heavy bluish white chemical element that is easily bent and shaped **2** : an article made of lead; *esp* : a weight for sounding at sea **3** : a thin strip of metal used to separate lines of type in printing **4** : a thin stick of marking substance in or for a pencil

⁴lead \'led\ *vb* **1** : to cover, line, or weight with lead **2** : to fix (glass) in position with lead **3** : to treat or mix with lead or a lead compound

lead·en \'led-ᵊn\ *adj* **1** : made of lead; *also* : of the color of lead **2** : SLUGGISH, DULL

lead off \ˌlēd-'ȯf\ *vb* : OPEN, BEGIN; *esp* : to bat first in an inning — **lead-off** \'lēd-ˌȯf\ *adj*

lead poisoning *n* : chronic intoxication produced by the absorption of lead into the system

¹**leaf** \'lēf\ *n, pl* **leaves** \'lēvz\ **1** : a usu. flat and green outgrowth of a plant stem that is a unit of foliage and functions esp. in photosynthesis; *also* : FOLIAGE **2** : something that is suggestive of a leaf — **leaf·less** *adj* — **leafy** *adj*

²**leaf** *vb* **1** : to produce leaves **2** : to turn the pages of a book

leaf·age \'lē-fij\ *n* : FOLIAGE

leafed \'lēft\ *adj* : LEAVED

leaf·hop·per \'lēf-,häp-ər\ *n* : any of numerous small leaping insects related to the cicadas that suck the juices of plants

leaf·let \'lēf-lət\ *n* **1** : a division of a compound leaf **2** : PAMPHLET, FOLDER

leaf mold *n* : a compost or layer composed chiefly of decayed vegetable matter

leaf·stalk \'lēf-,stök\ *n* : PETIOLE

¹**league** \'lēg\ *n* : a measure of distance equal to about three miles

²**league** *n* **1** : an association or alliance for a common purpose **2** : CLASS, CATEGORY — **league** *vb*

leagu·er \'lē-gər\ *n* : a member of a league

¹**leak** \'lēk\ *vb* **1** : to enter or escape through a leak **2** : to let a substance in or out through an opening **3** : to become or make known

²**leak** *n* **1** : a crack or hole that accidentally admits a fluid or light or lets it escape; *also* : something that secretly or accidentally permits the admission or escape of something else **2** : LEAKAGE — **leaky** *adj*

leak·age \'lē-kij\ *n* **1** : the act of leaking **2** : the thing or amount that leaks

leal \'lēl\ *adj, chiefly Scot* : LOYAL

¹**lean** \'lēn\ *vb* **1** : to bend from a vertical position : INCLINE **2** : to cast one's weight to one side for support **3** : to rely on for support **4** : to incline in opinion, taste, or desire — **lean** *n*

²**lean** *adj* **1** : lacking or deficient in flesh and esp. in fat **2** : lacking richness or productiveness **3** : low in fuel content — **lean·ness** \'lēn-nəs\ *n*

lean–to \'lēn-,tü\ *n, pl* **lean–tos** \-,tüz\ : a wing or extension of a building having a roof of only one slope; *also* : a rough shed or shelter with a similar roof

¹**leap** \'lēp\ *vb* **leapt** \'lēpt, 'lept\ *or* **leaped**; **leap·ing** : to spring free from a surface or over an obstacle : JUMP

²**leap** *n* : JUMP

leap·frog \'lēp-,frög, -,fräg\ *n* : a game in which one player bends down and another vaults over him — **leapfrog** *vb*

leap year *n* : a year containing 366 days with February 29 as the extra day

learn \'lərn\ *vb* **learned** \'lərnd, 'lərnt\; **learn·ing** **1** : to gain knowledge, understanding, or skill by study or experience; *also* : MEMORIZE **2** : to find out : ASCERTAIN — **learn·er** *n*

learn·ed \'lər-nəd\ *adj* : SCHOLARLY, ERUDITE

learn·ing \'lər-niŋ\ *n* : KNOWLEDGE, ERUDITION

learnt \'lərnt\ *chiefly Brit past & past part of* LEARN

¹**lease** \'lēs\ *n* : a contract transferring real estate for a term of years or at will usu. for a specified rent

²**lease** *vb* **leased**; **leas·ing** **1** : to grant by lease **2** : to hold under a lease **syn** let, charter, hire, rent

lease·hold \'lēs-,hōld\ *n* **1** : a tenure by lease **2** : land held by lease — **lease·hold·er** *n*

leash \'lēsh\ *n* [ME *lees, leshe,* fr. OF *laisse,* fr. *laissier* to let go, fr. L *laxare* to loosen, fr. *laxus* slack] : a line for leading or restraining an animal — **leash** *vb*

¹**least** \'lēst\ *adj* **1** : lowest in importance or position **2** : smallest in size or degree **3** : SLIGHTEST

²**least** *n* : one that is least

³**least** *adv* : in the smallest or lowest degree

least common denominator *n* : the least common multiple of two or more denominators

least common multiple *n* : the smallest common multiple of two or more numbers

least·wise \'lēst-,wīz\ *adv* : at least

leath·er \'leth-ər\ *n* : animal skin dressed for use — **leath·ern** \-ərn\ *adj* — **leath·ery** *adj*

leath·er·neck \-,nek\ *n* : MARINE

¹**leave** \'lēv\ *vb* **left** \'left\; **leav·ing** **1** : to allow or cause to remain behind; *also* : DELIVER **2** : to have as a remainder **3** : BEQUEATH **4** : to let stay without interference **5** : to go away : depart from **6** : to give up : ABANDON

²**leave** *n* **1** : PERMISSION; *also* : authorized absence from duty **2** : DEPARTURE

³**leave** *vb* **leaved**; **leav·ing** : LEAF

leaved \'lēvd\ *adj* : having leaves

leav·en \'lev-ən\ *n* **1** : a substance (as yeast) used to produce fermentation (as in dough) **2** : something that modifies or lightens a mass or aggregate

²**leaven** *vb* **leav·ened**; **leav·en·ing** \'lev-(ə-)niŋ\ : to raise (dough) with a leaven; *also* : to permeate with a modifying or vivifying element

leav·en·ing \'lev-(ə-)niŋ\ *n* : LEAVEN

leaves *pl of* LEAF

leave–tak·ing \'lēv-,tā-kiŋ\ *n* : DEPARTURE, FAREWELL

leav·ings \'lē-viŋz\ *n pl* : REMNANT, RESIDUE

lech·ery \'lech-ə-rē\ *n* : inordinate indulgence in sexual activity — **lech·er** \'lech-ər\ *n* — **lech·er·ous** *adj* — **lech·er·ous·ness** *n*

lec·i·thin \'les-ə-thən\ *n* : any of several waxy phosphorus-containing substances that are common in animals and plants, form colloidal solutions in water, and have emulsifying and wetting properties

lect *abbr* lecture; lecturer

lec·tern \'lek-tərn\ *n* : a desk to support a book in a convenient position for a standing reader

lec·tor \-tər\ *n* : one whose chief duty is to read the lessons in a church service

lec·ture \'lek-chər\ *n* **1** : a discourse given before an audience or a class esp. for instruction **2** : REPRIMAND — **lec·ture** *vb* — **lec·tur·er** *n* — **lec·ture·ship** *n*

led *past and past part of* LEAD

LED \'el-ˌē-'dē\ *n* [*light-emitting diode*] : a semiconductor diode that emits light when a voltage is applied to it and is used esp. for electronic displays

le·der·ho·sen \'lād-ər-ˌhōz-ᵊn\ *n pl* : leather shorts often with suspenders worn esp. in Bavaria

ledge \'lej\ *n* [ME *legge* bar of a gate] **1** : a shelflike projection from a top or an edge **2** : REEF

led·ger \'lej-ər\ *n* : a book containing accounts to which debits and credits are transferred in final form

lee \'lē\ *n* **1** : a protecting shelter **2** : the side (as of a ship) that is sheltered from the wind — **lee** *adj*

leech \'lēch\ *n* [ME *leche* physician, fr. OE *lǣce*] **1** : any of various segmented usu. freshwater worms related to the earthworms; *esp* : one formerly used by physicians to draw blood **2** : a hanger-on who seeks gain

leek \'lēk\ *n* : an onionlike herb grown for its mildly pungent leaves and stalk

leer \'liər\ *n* : a suggestive, knowing, or malicious look — **leer** *vb*

leery \'li(ə)r-ē\ *adj* : SUSPICIOUS, WARY

lees \'lēz\ *n pl* : DREGS

¹lee·ward \'lē-wərd, 'lü-ərd\ *n* : the lee side

²leeward *adj* : situated away from the wind

lee·way \'lē-ˌwā\ *n* **1** : lateral movement of a ship when under way **2** : an allowable margin of freedom or variation

¹left \'left\ *adj* [ME, fr. OE, weak; fr. the left hand's being the weaker in most individuals] **1** : of, relating to, or being the side of the body in which the heart is mostly located; *also* : located nearer to this side than to the right **2** *often cap* : of, adhering to, or constituted by the political Left — **left** *adv*

²left *n* **1** : the left hand; *also* : the side or part that is on or toward the left side **2** *cap* : those professing political views marked by desire to reform the established order and usu. to give greater freedom to the common man

³left *past and past part of* LEAVE

left-hand *adj* **1** : LEFT-HANDED **2** : situated on the left

left-hand·ed \'left-'han-dəd\ *adj* **1** : using the left hand habitually or better than the right **2** : designed for or done

with the left hand **3** : INSINCERE, BACKHANDED **4** : COUNTERCLOCKWISE — **left-handed** *adv*

left·ism \'lef-ˌtiz-əm\ *n* **1** : the principles and views of the Left; *also* : the movement embodying these principles **2** : advocacy of or adherence to the doctrines of the Left — **left·ist** \-təst\ *n or adj*

left·over \'left-ˌō-vər\ *n* : an unused or unconsumed residue

¹leg \'leg\ *n* **1** : a limb of an animal used esp. for supporting the body and in walking; *esp* : the part of the vertebrate leg between knee and foot **2** : something resembling or analogous to an animal leg (table ∼) **3** : the part of an article of clothing that covers the leg **4** : a portion of a trip — **legged** \'leg-əd\ *adj* — **leg·less** *adj*

²leg *vb* **legged**; **leg·ging** : to use the legs in walking or esp. in running

³leg *abbr* **1** legal **2** legislative; legislature

leg·a·cy \'leg-ə-sē\ *n, pl* **-cies** : INHERITANCE, BEQUEST; *also* : something that has come from an ancestor or predecessor or the past

le·gal \'lē-gəl\ *adj* **1** : of or relating to law or lawyers **2** : LAWFUL; *also* : STATUTORY **3** : enforced in courts of law — **le·gal·i·ty** \li-'gal-ət-ē\ *n* — **le·gal·ize** \'lē-gə-ˌlīz\ *vb* — **le·gal·ly** \-gə-lē\ *adv*

le·gal·ism \'lē-gə-ˌliz-əm\ *n* : strict, literal, or excessive conformity to the law or to a religious or moral code — **le·gal·is·tic** \ˌlē-gə-'lis-tik\ *adj*

leg·ate \'leg-ət\ *n* : an official representative; *esp* : AMBASSADOR

leg·a·tee \ˌleg-ə-'tē\ *n* : a person to whom a legacy is bequeathed

le·ga·tion \li-'gā-shən\ *n* **1** : a diplomatic mission headed by a minister **2** : the official residence and office of a minister to a foreign government

le·ga·to \li-'gät-ō\ *adv or adj* [It, lit., tied] : in a smooth and connected manner — used as a direction in music

leg·end \'lej-ənd\ *n* [ME *legende*, fr. MF & ML; MF *legende*, fr. ML *legenda*, fr. L *legere* to gather, select, read] **1** : a story coming down from the past; *esp* : one popularly accepted as historical though not verifiable **2** : an inscription on an object; *also* : CAPTION **3** : an explanatory list of the symbols on a map or chart

leg·end·ary \'lej-ən-ˌder-ē\ *adj* : of, relating to, or characteristic of a legend

leg·er·de·main \ˌlej-ərd-ə-'mān\ *n* [ME, fr. MF *leger de main* light of hand] : SLEIGHT OF HAND

leg·ging *or* **leg·gin** \'leg-ən, -in\ *n* : a covering for the leg

leg·gy \'leg-ē\ *adj* **leg·gi·er**; **-est** **1** : having unusually long legs **2** : having attractive legs **3** : SPINDLY — used of a plant

leg·horn \'leg-ˌ(h)ȯrn, 'leg-ərn\ *n* **1** : a fine plaited straw; *also* : a hat made of this straw **2** : any of a Mediterranean breed of small hardy fowls

leg·i·ble \'lej-ə-bəl\ *adj* : capable of being read : CLEAR — **leg·i·bil·i·ty** \,lej-ə-'bil-ət-ē\ *n* — **leg·i·bly** \'lej-ə-blē\ *adv*

¹le·gion \'lē-jən\ *n* **1** : a unit of the Roman army comprising 3000 to 6000 soldiers **2** : MULTITUDE **3** : an association of ex-servicemen — **le·gion·ary** \-,er-ē\ *n* — **le·gion·naire** \,lē-jən-'aər\ *n*

²legion *adj* : MANY, NUMEROUS

Le·gion·naires' disease *also* **Le·gion·naire's disease** \,lē-jə-'nerz-\ *n* [so called fr. its first recognized occurrence during the 1976 American Legion convention] : a pneumonia that is caused by a bacterium and affects one or more lobes of the lung

legis *abbr* legislation; legislative; legislature

leg·is·late \'lej-ə-,slāt\ *vb* **-lat·ed**; **-lat·ing** : to make or enact laws; *also* : to bring about by legislation — **leg·is·la·tor** \-,slāt-ər\ *n*

leg·is·la·tion \,lej-ə-'slā-shən\ *n* **1** : the action of legislating **2** : laws made by a legislative body

leg·is·la·tive \'lej-ə-,slāt-iv\ *adj* **1** : having the power of legislating **2** : of or relating to a legislature

leg·is·la·ture \'lej-ə-,slā-chər\ *n* : an organized body of persons having the authority to make laws

le·git \li-'jit\ *adj, slang* : LEGITIMATE

le·git·i·mate \li-'jit-ə-mət\ *adj* **1** : lawfully begotten **2** : GENUINE **3** : LAWFUL **4** : conforming to recognized principles or accepted rules or standards — **le·git·i·ma·cy** \-mə-sē\ *n* — **le·git·i·mate·ly** *adv*

le·git·i·mize \li-'jit-ə-,mīz\ *vb* **-mized**; **-miz·ing** : LEGITIMATE

leg·man \'leg-,man\ *n* **1** : a reporter assigned usu. to gather information **2** : an assistant who gathers information and runs errands

le·gume \'leg-,yüm, li-'gyüm\ *n* [F] **1** : any of a large group of plants having fruits that are dry pods and split when ripe and including important food and forage plants (as beans and clover) **2** : the part of a legume used as food; *also* : VEGETABLE 2 — **le·gu·mi·nous** \li-'gyü-mə-nəs\ *adj*

¹lei \'lā(-,)ē\ *n* : a wreath or necklace usu. of flowers

²lei \'lā\ *pl of* LEU

lei·sure \'lēzh-ər, 'lezh-, 'lāzh-\ *n* **1** : time free from work or duties **2** : EASE; *also* : CONVENIENCE syn relaxation, rest, repose — **lei·sure·ly** *adj*

leit·mo·tiv *or* **leit·mo·tif** \'līt-mō-,tēf\ *n* [G *leitmotiv*, fr. *leiten* to lead + *motiv* motive] : a dominant recurring theme

lek \'lek\ *n, pl* **leks** *or* **le·ke** *also* **lek** *or* **le·ku** — see MONEY table

lem·ming \'lem-iŋ\ *n* [Norw] : any of several short-tailed northern rodents

lem·on \'lem-ən\ *n* **1** : an acid yellow usu. nearly oblong citrus fruit; *also* : a

citrus tree that bears lemons **2** : something unsatisfactory or defective (as an automobile) : DUD — **lem·ony** *adj*

lem·on·ade \,lem-ə-'nād\ *n* : a beverage of lemon juice, sugar, and water

lem·pi·ra \lem-'pir-ə\ *n* — see MONEY table

le·mur \'lē-mər\ *n* : any of numerous arboreal mammals largely of Madagascar usu. with a muzzle like a fox, large eyes, very soft woolly fur, and a long furry tail

lend \'lend\ *vb* **lent** \'lent\; **lend·ing 1** : to give for temporary use on condition that the same or its equivalent be returned **2** : AFFORD, FURNISH **3** : ACCOMMODATE — **lend·er** *n*

lend-lease \-'lēs\ *n* : the transfer of goods and services to an ally to aid in a common cause with payment being made by a return of the items or their use in the common cause or by a similar transfer of other goods and services

length \'leŋth\ *n* **1** : the longer or longest dimension of an object; *also* : a measured distance **2** : duration or extent in time or space **3** : the length of something taken as a unit of measure (the horse won by a ~) **4** : PIECE; *esp* : one in a series of pieces designed to be joined

length·en \'leŋ-thən\ *vb* **length·ened**; **length·en·ing** \'leŋth-(ə-)niŋ\ : to make or become longer syn extend, elongate, prolong, protract

length·wise \-,wīz\ *adv* : in the direction of the length — **lengthwise** *adj*

lengthy \'leŋ-thē\ *adj* **length·i·er**; **-est 1** : protracted excessively **2** : EXTENDED, LONG

le·nient \'lē-nē-ənt, -nyənt\ *adj* : of mild and tolerant disposition or effect syn indulgent, forbearing, merciful, tolerant — **le·ni·en·cy** \'lē-nē-ən-sē, -nyən-sē\ *n* — **le·ni·ent·ly** *adv*

len·i·tive \'len-ət-iv\ *adj* : alleviating pain or acrimony

len·i·ty \'len-ət-ē\ *n* : LENIENCY, MILDNESS

lens \'lenz\ *n* [L *lent-, lens* lentil; so called fr. the shape of a convex lens] **1** : a curved piece of glass or plastic used singly or combined in an optical instrument for forming an image; *also* : a device for focusing radiation other than light **2** : a transparent body in the eye that focuses light rays on receptors at the back of the eye

Lent \'lent\ *n* : a 40-day period of penitence and fasting observed from Ash Wednesday to Easter by many churches — **Lent·en** \-ᵊn\ *adj*

len·til \'lent-ᵊl\ *n* : an Old World legume grown for its flat edible seeds and for fodder; *also* : its seed

Leo \'lē-ō\ *n* [L, lit., lion] : the 5th sign of the zodiac in astrology

le·one \lē-'ōn\ *n, pl* **leones** *or* **leone** — see MONEY table

le·o·nine \'lē-ə-ˌnīn\ *adj* : of, relating to, or resembling a lion

leop·ard \'lep-ərd\ *n* : a large strong usu. tawny and black-spotted cat of southern Asia and Africa

le·o·tard \'lē-ə-ˌtärd\ *n* : a close-fitting garment worn esp. by dancers and people doing exercises

lep·er \'lep-ər\ *n* 1 : a person affected with leprosy 2 : OUTCAST

lep·re·chaun \'lep-rə-ˌkän\ *n* : a mischievous elf of Irish folklore

lep·ro·sy \'lep-rə-sē\ *n* : a chronic bacterial disease marked esp. by slow-growing swellings with deformity and loss of sensation of affected parts — **lep·rous** \-rəs\ *adj*

lep·ton \lep-'tän\ *n*, *pl* **lep·ta** \-'tä\ — see *drachma* at MONEY table

les·bi·an \'lez-bē-ən\ *n*, *often cap* [fr. the reputed homosexual group associated with the poet Sappho of Lesbos] : a female homosexual — **lesbian** *adj* — **les·bi·an·ism** \-ˌiz-əm\ *n*

lèse ma·jes·té *or* **lese maj·es·ty** \'lēz-'maj-ə-stē\ *n* [MF *lese majesté*, fr. L *laesa majestas*, lit., injured majesty] : an offense violating the dignity of a sovereign

le·sion \'lē-zhən\ *n* : an abnormal structural change in the body due to injury or disease

¹less \'les\ *adj* 1 : FEWER ⟨∼ than six⟩ 2 : of lower rank, degree, or importance 3 : SMALLER; *also* : more limited in quantity

²less *adv* : to a lesser extent or degree

³less *prep* : diminished by : MINUS

⁴less *n*, *pl* **less** 1 : a smaller portion 2 : something of less importance

-less \ləs\ *adj suffix* 1 : destitute of : not having ⟨child*less*⟩ 2 : unable to be acted on or to act (in a specified way) ⟨daunt*less*⟩

les·see \le-'sē\ *n* : a tenant under a lease

less·en \'les-ᵊn\ *vb* **less·ened; less·en·ing** \'les-(ᵊ-)niŋ\ : to make or become less syn decrease, diminish, dwindle, abate

less·er \'les-ər\ *adj* : of less size, quality, or significance

les·son \'les-ᵊn\ *n* 1 : a passage from sacred writings read in a service of worship 2 : a reading or exercise to be studied by a pupil; *also* : something learned 3 : a period of instruction 4 : an instructive example

les·sor \'les-ˌor, le-'sor\ *n* : one who conveys property by a lease

lest \ˌlest\ *conj* : for fear that

¹let \'let\ *n* [ME *lette*, fr. *letten* to delay, hinder, fr. OE *lettan*] 1 : HINDRANCE, OBSTACLE 2 : a shot or point in racket games that does not count

²let *vb* **let; let·ting** [ME *leten*, fr. OE *lǣtan*] 1 : to cause to : MAKE ⟨∼ it be known⟩ 2 : RENT, LEASE; *also* : to assign esp. after bids 3 : ALLOW, PERMIT ⟨∼ me go⟩

-let \lət\ *n suffix* 1 : small one ⟨book*let*⟩ 2 : article worn on ⟨wrist*let*⟩

let·down \'let-ˌdaún\ *n* 1 : DISAPPOINTMENT 2 : a slackening of effort 3 : the descent of an aircraft to the beginning of a landing approach

le·thal \'lē-thəl\ *adj* : DEADLY, FATAL — **le·thal·ly** \-ē\ *adv*

leth·ar·gy \'leth-ər-jē\ *n* 1 : abnormal drowsiness 2 : the quality or state of being lazy or indifferent syn languor, lassitude, torpidity, torpidness — **le·thar·gic** \li-'thär-jik\ *adj*

let on *vb* 1 : REVEAL, ADMIT 2 : PRETEND

¹let·ter \'let-ər\ *n* 1 : a symbol that stands for a speech sound and constitutes a unit of an alphabet 2 : a written or printed communication 3 *pl* : LITERATURE; *also* : LEARNING 4 : the literal meaning ⟨the ∼ of the law⟩ 5 : a single piece of type

²letter *vb* : to mark with letters : INSCRIBE — **let·ter·er** *n*

let·ter·head \'let-ər-ˌhed\ *n* : stationery with a printed or engraved heading; *also* : the heading itself

let·ter-per·fect \ˌlet-ər-'pər-fikt\ *adj* : correct to the smallest detail

let·ter·press \'let-ər-ˌpres\ *n* 1 : printing done directly by impressing the paper on an inked raised surface 2 *chiefly Brit* : TEXT

letters patent *n pl* : a written grant from a government to a person in a form readily open for inspection by all

let·tuce \'let-əs\ *n* [ME *letuse*, fr. OF *laitues*, pl. of *laitue*, fr. L *lactuca*, fr. *lac* milk; fr. its milky juice] : a garden plant with crisp leaves used esp. in salads

let·up \'let-ˌəp\ *n* : a lessening of effort

leu \'leú\ *n*, *pl* **lei** \'lā\ — see MONEY table

leu·ke·mia \lü-'kē-mē-ə\ *n* : a cancerous disease in which white blood cells increase greatly — **leu·ke·mic** \-mik\ *adj or n*

leu·ko·cyte *also* **leu·co·cyte** \'lü-kə-ˌsīt\ *n* : WHITE BLOOD CELL

lev \'lef\ *n*, *pl* **le·va** \'lev-ə\ — see MONEY table

Lev *or* **Levit** *abbr* Leviticus

¹le·vee \'lev-ē; lə-'vē, -'vā\ *n* [F *lever* act of arising] : a reception held by a person of distinction

²lev·ee \'lev-ē\ *n* : an embankment to prevent or confine flooding (as by a river); *also* : a river landing place

¹lev·el \'lev-əl\ *n* 1 : a device for establishing a horizontal line or plane 2 : horizontal condition 3 : a horizontal position, line, or surface often taken as an index of altitude; *also* : a flat area of ground 4 : height, position, rank, or size in a scale

²level *vb* **-eled** *or* **-elled; -el·ing** *or* **-el·ling** \-(ə-)liŋ\ 1 : to make flat or level; *also* : to come to a level 2 : AIM, DIRECT 3 : EQUALIZE 4 : RAZE — **lev·el·er** *n*

³level *adj* 1 : having a flat even surface 2 : HORIZONTAL 3 : of the same height or rank; *also* : UNIFORM 4 : steady and cool in judgment — **lev·el·ly** \'lev-əl-(l)ē\ *adv* — **lev·el·ness** *n*

lev·el·head·ed \ˌlev-əl-'hed-əd\ *adj* : having sound judgment : SENSIBLE

le·ver \'lev-ər, 'lē-vər\ *n* 1 : a bar used for prying or dislodging something; *also* : a means for achieving one's purpose 2 : a rigid piece turning about an axis and used for transmitting and changing force and motion

le·ver·age \'lev-(ə-)rij, 'lēv-\ *n* : the action or mechanical effect of a lever

le·vi·a·than \li-'vī-ə-thən\ *n* 1 : a large sea animal 2 : something very large or formidable of its kind

lev·i·tate \'lev-ə-ˌtāt\ *vb* **-tat·ed; -tat·ing** : to rise or cause to rise in the air in seeming defiance of gravitation — **lev·i·ta·tion** \ˌlev-ə-'tā-shən\ *n*

Le·vit·i·cus \li-'vit-ə-kəs\ *n* — see BIBLE table

lev·i·ty \'lev-ət-ē\ *n* : lack of earnestness **syn** lightness, flippancy, frivolity

¹**levy** \'lev-ē\ *n, pl* **lev·ies** 1 : the imposition or collection of an assessment; *also* : an amount levied 2 : the enlistment of men for military service; *also* : troops raised by levy

²**levy** *vb* **lev·ied; levy·ing** 1 : to impose or collect by legal authority 2 : to enlist for military service 3 : WAGE (~ war) 4 : to seize property in satisfaction of a legal claim

lewd \'lüd\ *adj* [ME *lewed* vulgar, fr. OE *lǣwede* lay, ignorant] 1 : sexually unchaste 2 : OBSCENE, SALACIOUS — **lewd·ly** *adv* — **lewd·ness** *n*

lex·i·cog·ra·phy \ˌlek-sə-'käg-rə-fē\ *n* 1 : the editing or making of a dictionary 2 : the principles and practices of dictionary making — **lex·i·cog·ra·pher** \-fər\ *n* — **lex·i·co·graph·i·cal** \-kō-'graf-i-kəl\ *or* **lex·i·co·graph·ic** \-ik\ *adj*

lex·i·con \'lek-sə-ˌkän\ *n, pl* **lex·i·ca** \-si-kə\ *or* **lexicons** : DICTIONARY

LF *abbr* low frequency

lg *abbr* 1 large 2 long

LH *abbr* 1 left hand 2 lower half

li *abbr* link

Li *symbol* lithium

LI *abbr* Long Island

li·a·bil·i·ty \ˌlī-ə-'bil-ət-ē\ *n, pl* **-ties** 1 : the quality or state of being liable 2 *pl* : DEBTS 3 : DISADVANTAGE

li·a·ble \'lī-ə-bəl\ *adj* 1 : legally obligated : RESPONSIBLE 2 : LIKELY, APT (~ to fall) 3 : SUSCEPTIBLE

li·ai·son \'lē-ə-ˌzän, lē-'ā-\ *n* [F] 1 : a close bond : INTERRELATIONSHIP 2 : an illicit sexual relationship 3 : communication for mutual understanding (as between parts of an armed force)

li·ar \'lī-ər\ *n* : a person who lies

¹**lib** \'lib\ *n* : LIBERATION

²**lib** *abbr* 1 liberal 2 librarian; library

li·ba·tion \lī-'bā-shən\ *n* 1 : an act of pouring a liquid as a sacrifice (as to a god); *also* : the liquid poured 2 : DRINK — **li·ba·tion·ary** *adj*

¹**li·bel** \'lī-bəl\ *n* [ME, written declaration, fr. MF, fr. L *libellus*, dim. of

liber book] 1 : a spoken or written statement or a representation that gives an unjustly unfavorable impression of a person or thing 2 : the action or crime of publishing a libel — **li·bel·ous** *or* **li·bel·lous** \-bə-ləs\ *adj*

²**libel** *vb* **-beled** *or* **-belled; -bel·ing** *or* **-bel·ling** : to make or publish a libel — **li·bel·er** *n* — **li·bel·ist** *n*

¹**lib·er·al** \'lib-(ə-)rəl\ *adj* [ME, fr. MF, fr. L *liberalis* suitable for a freeman, generous, fr. *liber* free] 1 : of, relating to, or based on the liberal arts 2 : GENEROUS, BOUNTIFUL 3 : not literal 4 : not narrow in opinion or judgment : TOLERANT; *also* : not orthodox 5 : not conservative — **lib·er·al·i·ty** \ˌlib-ə-'ral-ət-ē\ *n* — **lib·er·al·ize** \'lib-(ə-)rə-ˌlīz\ *vb* — **lib·er·al·ly** \-rə-lē\ *adv*

²**liberal** *n* : a person who holds liberal views

liberal arts *n pl* : the studies (as language, philosophy, history, literature, or abstract science) in a college or university intended to provide chiefly general knowledge and to develop the general intellectual capacities

lib·er·al·ism \'lib-(ə-)rə-ˌliz-əm\ *n* : liberal principles and theories

lib·er·ate \'lib-ə-ˌrāt\ *vb* **-at·ed; -at·ing** 1 : to free from bondage or restraint; *also* : to raise to equal rights and status 2 : to free (as a gas) from combination — **lib·er·a·tion** \ˌlib-ə-'rā-shən\ *n* — **lib·er·a·tor** \'lib-ə-ˌrāt-ər\ *n*

lib·er·at·ed *adj* : freed from or opposed to traditional social and sexual attitudes or roles (a ~ woman)

lib·er·tar·i·an \ˌlib-ər-'ter-ē-ən\ *n* 1 : an advocate of the doctrine of free will 2 : one who upholds the principles of liberty

lib·er·tine \'lib-ər-ˌtēn\ *n* : one who leads a dissolute life

lib·er·ty \'lib-ərt-ē\ *n, pl* **-ties** 1 : FREEDOM 2 : an action going beyond normal limits; *esp* : FAMILIARITY 3 : a short leave from naval duty

li·bid·i·nous \lə-'bid-ᵊn-əs\ *adj* 1 : LASCIVIOUS 2 : LIBIDINAL

li·bi·do \lə-'bēd-ō, -'bid-\ *n, pl* **-dos** [NL, fr. L *libido*, desire, lust] : psychic energy derived from basic biological urges; *also* : sexual drive — **li·bid·i·nal** \lə-'bid-ᵊn-əl\ *adj*

Li·bra \'lē-brə\ *n* [L, lit., scales] : the 7th sign of the zodiac in astrology

li·brar·i·an \lī-'brer-ē-ən\ *n* : a specialist in the management of a library

li·brary \'lī-ˌbrer-ē\ *n, pl* **-brar·ies** 1 : a place in which books and related materials are kept for use but not for sale 2 : a collection of books

li·bret·to \lə-'bret-ō\ *n, pl* **-tos** *or* **-ti** \-ē\ [It, dim. of *libro* book, fr. L *liber*] : the text of a work (as an opera) for the musical theater — **li·bret·tist** \-əst\ *n*

Lib·y·an \'lib-ē-ən\ *n* : a native or inhabitant of Libya — **Libyan** *adj*

lice *pl of* LOUSE

li·cense *or* **li·cence** \'līs-ᵊns\ *n* 1 : permission to act; *esp* : legal permission to engage in an activity 2 : a document, plate, or tag evidencing a license granted 3 : freedom used irresponsibly — **license** *vb*

licensed practical nurse *n* : a specially trained person who is licensed (as by a state) to provide routine care for the sick

li·cens·ee \,līs-ᵊn-'sē\ *n* : a licensed person

li·cen·te \lǝ-'sent-ē\ *n, pl* **licente** *or* **li·cen·ti** \-ē\ — see *loti* at MONEY table

li·cen·ti·ate \lī-'sen-chē-ǝt\ *n* : one licensed to practice a profession

li·cen·tious \lī-'sen-chǝs\ *adj* : LEWD, LASCIVIOUS — **li·cen·tious·ly** *adv* — **li·cen·tious·ness** *n*

li·chee *var of* LITCHI

li·chen \'lī-kǝn\ *n* : any of various complex lower plants made up of an alga and a fungus growing as a unit on a solid surface — **li·chen·ous** *adj*

lic·it \'lis-ǝt\ *adj* : LAWFUL

¹lick \'lik\ *vb* 1 : to draw the tongue over; *also* : to flicker like a tongue 2 : THRASH; *also* : DEFEAT

²lick *n* 1 : a stroke of the tongue 2 : a small amount 3 : a hasty careless effort 4 : BLOW 5 : a natural deposit of salt that animals lick

lick·e·ty-split \,lik-ǝt-ē-'split\ *adv* : at great speed

lick·spit·tle \'lik-,spit-ᵊl\ *n* : a fawning subordinate : TOADY

lic·o·rice \'lik-(ǝ)-rish, -rǝs\ *n* [ME *licorice*, fr. OF, fr. LL *liquiritia*, alter. of L *glycyrrhiza*, fr. Gk *glykyrrhiza*, fr. *glykys* sweet + *rhiza* root] 1 : the dried root of a European leguminous plant; *also* : an extract from it used esp. as a flavoring and in medicine 2 : a confection flavored with licorice 3 : a plant yielding licorice

lid \'lid\ *n* 1 : a movable cover 2 : EYELID 3 : a force that represses — **lid·ded** \'lid-ǝd\ *adj*

li·do \'lēd-ō\ *n, pl* **lidos** : a fashionable beach resort

¹lie \'lī\ *vb* **lay** \'lā\; **lain** \'lān\; **ly·ing** \'lī-iŋ\ 1 : to be in, stay at rest in, or assume a horizontal position; *also* : to be in a helpless or defenseless state 2 : EXTEND 3 : to occupy a certain relative position 4 : to have an effect esp. through mere presence

²lie *n* : the position in which something lies

³lie *vb* **lied**; **ly·ing** \'lī-iŋ\ : to tell a lie

⁴lie *n* : an untrue statement made with intent to deceive

lied \'lēt\ *n, pl* **lie·der** \'lēd-ǝr\ [G] : a German song esp. of the 19th century

lief \'lēv, 'lēf\ *adv* : GLADLY, WILLINGLY

¹liege \'lēj\ *adj* [ME, fr. OF, fr. LL *laeticus*, fr. *laetus* serf] : LOYAL, FAITHFUL

²liege *n* 1 : VASSAL 2 : a feudal superior

lien \'lēn, 'lē-ǝn\ *n* : a legal claim on the property of another for the satisfaction of a debt or the fulfillment of a duty

lieu \'lü\ *n, archaic* : PLACE, STEAD — **in lieu of** : in the place of

lieut *abbr* lieutenant

lieu·ten·ant \lü-'ten-ǝnt\ *n* [ME, fr. MF, fr. *lieu* place + *tenant* holding, fr. *tenir* to hold, fr. L *tenēre*] 1 : a representative of another in the performance of duty 2 : FIRST LIEUTENANT; *also* : SECOND LIEUTENANT 3 : a commissioned officer in the navy ranking next below a lieutenant commander — **lieu·ten·an·cy** \-ǝn-sē\ *n*

lieutenant colonel *n* : a commissioned officer (as in the army) ranking next below a colonel

lieutenant commander *n* : a commissioned officer in the navy ranking next below a commander

lieutenant general *n* : a commissioned officer (as in the army) ranking next below a general

lieutenant governor *n* : a deputy or subordinate governor

lieutenant junior grade *n, pl* **lieutenants junior grade** : a commissioned officer in the navy ranking next below a lieutenant

life \'līf\ *n, pl* **lives** \'līvz\ 1 : the quality that distinguishes a vital and functional being from a dead body or inanimate matter; *also* : a state of an organism characterized esp. by capacity for metabolism, growth, reaction to stimuli, and reproduction 2 : the physical and mental experiences of an individual 3 : BIOGRAPHY 4 : the period of existence 5 : manner of living 6 : PERSON 7 : ANIMATION, SPIRIT; *also* : LIVELINESS 8 : animate activity (signs of ~) 9 : one providing interest and vigor — **lifeless** *adj* — **life·like** *adj*

life·blood \'līf-'blǝd, -,blǝd\ *n* : a basic source of strength and vitality

life·boat \-,bōt\ *n* : a sturdy boat designed for use in saving lives at sea

life·guard \-,gärd\ *n* : a usu. expert swimmer employed to safeguard bathers

life·line \-,līn\ *n* 1 : a line to which persons may cling for safety 2 : a trade route or means of communication considered indispensable

life·long \-,lȯŋ\ *adj* : continuing through life

life preserver *n* : a device designed to save a person from drowning by providing buoyancy in water

lif·er \'lī-fǝr\ *n* 1 : a person sentenced to life imprisonment 2 : a person who makes a career in the armed forces

life raft *n* : a raft for use by people forced into the water

life·sav·ing \'līf-,sā-viŋ\ *n* : the skill or practice of saving or protecting lives esp. of drowning persons — **life·sav·er** \-,sā-vǝr\ *n*

life science *n* : a branch of science (as biology, medicine, anthropology, or sociology) that deals with living organisms and life processes — usu. used in pl

life·time \-ˌtīm\ *n* : the duration of an individual's existence

life·work \-ˈwərk\ *n* : the entire or principal work of one's lifetime; *also* : a work extending over a lifetime

LIFO *abbr* last in, first out

¹**lift** \ˈlift\ *vb* 1 : RAISE, ELEVATE; *also* : RISE, ASCEND 2 : to put an end to : STOP 3 : to pay off (∼ a mortgage)

²**lift** *n* 1 : LOAD 2 : the action or an instance of lifting 3 : HELP; *also* : a ride along one's way 4 : RISE, ADVANCE 5 *chiefly Brit* : ELEVATOR 6 : an elevation of the spirits 7 : the upward force that is developed by a moving airfoil and that opposes the pull of gravity

lift-off \ˈlif-ˌtȯf\ *n* : a vertical takeoff (as by a rocket)

lift truck *n* : a small truck for lifting and transporting loads

lig·a·ment \ˈlig-ə-mənt\ *n* : a band of tough tissue that holds bones together

li·gate \ˈlī-ˌgāt\ *vb* **li·gat·ed; li·gat·ing** : to tie with a ligature — **li·ga·tion** \lī-ˈgā-shən\ *n*

lig·a·ture \ˈlig-ə-ˌchu̇r, -chər\ *n* 1 : something that binds or ties; *also* : a thread used in surgery esp. for tying blood vessels 2 : a printed or written character consisting of two or more letters or characters (as *æ*) united

¹**light** \ˈlīt\ *n* 1 : something that makes vision possible : electromagnetic radiation visible to the human eye; *also* : BRIGHTNESS 2 : DAYLIGHT 3 : a source of light (as a candle) 4 : ENLIGHTENMENT; *also* : TRUTH 5 : public knowledge 6 : a particular aspect or appearance presented to view (now saw the matter in a different ∼) 7 : WINDOW 8 *pl* : STANDARDS (according to his ∼s) 9 : CELEBRITY 10 : LIGHTHOUSE, BEACON; *also* : a traffic signal 11 : a flame for lighting something

²**light** *adj* 1 : BRIGHT 2 : PALE (∼ blue) — **light·ness** *n*

³**light** *vb* **light·ed** *or* **lit** \ˈlit\; **light·ing** 1 : to make or become light 2 : to cause to burn : BURN 3 : to conduct with a light 4 : ILLUMINATE

⁴**light** *adj* 1 : not heavy 2 : not serious (∼ reading) 3 : SCANTY (∼ rain) 4 : GENTLE (a ∼ blow) 5 : easily endurable (∼ cold) ; *also* : requiring little effort (∼ exercise) 6 : SWIFT, NIMBLE 7 : FRIVOLOUS 8 : DIZZY 9 : producing goods for direct consumption by the consumer (∼ industry) — **light·ly** *adv* — **light·ness** *n*

⁵**light** *adv* 1 : LIGHTLY 2 : with little baggage (travel ∼)

⁶**light** *vb* **light·ed** *or* **lit** \ˈlit\; **light·ing** 1 : SETTLE, ALIGHT 2 : to fall unexpectedly 3 : HAPPEN

light adaptation *n* : the whole process by which the eye adapts to seeing in strong light — **light-adapt·ed** \ˈlīt-ə-ˌdap-təd\ *adj*

light-emitting diode *n* : LED

¹**light·en** \ˈlīt-ᵊn\ *vb* **light·ened; light·en·ing** \ˈlīt-(ᵊ-)niŋ\ 1 : ILLUMINATE, BRIGHTEN 2 : to give out flashes of lightning

²**lighten** *vb* **light·ened; light·en·ing** \ˈlīt-(ᵊ-)niŋ\ 1 : to relieve of a burden 2 : GLADDEN 3 : to become lighter

light·er \ˈlīt-ər\ *n* : a barge used esp. in loading or unloading ships

²**light·er** \ˈlīt-ər\ *n* : a device for lighting (a cigarette ∼)

light·face \ˈlīt-ˌfās\ *n* : a type having light thin lines — **light-faced** \-ˈfāst\ *adj*

light-head·ed \ˈlīt-ˈhed-əd\ *adj* 1 : feeling confused or dizzy 2 : lacking maturity or seriousness

light-heart·ed \-ˈhärt-əd\ *adj* : free from worry — **light-heart·ed·ly** *adv* — **light-heart·ed·ness** *n*

light·house \-ˌhau̇s\ *n* : a structure with a powerful light for guiding mariners

light meter *n* : a small portable device for measuring illumination; *esp* : a device for indicating correct photographic exposure

¹**light·ning** \ˈlīt-niŋ\ *n* : the flashing of light produced by a discharge of atmospheric electricity from one cloud to another or between a cloud and the earth; *also* : the discharge itself

²**lightning** *adj* : extremely fast

lightning bug *n* : FIREFLY

lightning rod *n* : a grounded metallic rod set up on a structure to protect it from lightning

light out *vb* : to leave in a hurry

light-proof \ˈlīt-ˈprüf\ *adj* : impenetrable by light

lights \ˈlīts\ *n pl* : the lungs esp. of a slaughtered animal

light·ship \ˈlīt-ˌship\ *n* : a ship with a powerful light moored at a place dangerous to navigation

light show *n* : a kaleidoscopic display (as of colored lights) imitating the effects of psychedelic drugs

light·some \ˈlīt-səm\ *adj* 1 : free from care 2 : NIMBLE

¹**light·weight** \ˈlīt-ˌwāt\ *n* : one of less than average weight; *esp* : a boxer weighing more than 126 but not over 135 pounds

²**lightweight** *adj* 1 : INCONSEQUENTIAL 2 : of less than average weight

light-year \ˈlīt-ˌyiər\ *n* 1 : an astronomical unit of distance equal to the distance that light travels in one year or about 5,878,000,000,000 miles 2 : an extremely long distance esp. as a measure of progress

lig·ne·ous \ˈlig-nē-əs\ *adj* : WOODY

lig·ni·fy \ˈlig-nə-ˌfī\ *vb* **-fied; -fy·ing** : to convert into or become wood or woody tissue — **lig·ni·fi·ca·tion** \ˌlig-nə-fə-ˈkā-shən\ *n*

lig·nite \ˈlig-ˌnīt\ *n* : brownish black soft coal esp. of a slightly woody texture

¹**like** \ˈlīk\ *vb* **liked; lik·ing** 1 : ENJOY (∼s

baseball) **2** : WANT **3** : CHOOSE ⟨does as she ∼s⟩ — **lik·able** *or* **like·able** \'lī-kə-bəl\ *adj*

²**like** *n* : PREFERENCE

³**like** *adj* : SIMILAR **syn** alike, analogous, comparable, parallel, uniform

⁴**like** *prep* **1** : similar or similarly to **2** : typical of **3** : inclined to ⟨looks ∼ rain⟩ **4** : such as ⟨a subject ∼ physics⟩

⁵**like** *n* : COUNTERPART

⁶**like** *conj* : in the same way that

-**like** \ˌlīk\ *adj comb form* : resembling or characteristic of ⟨lady*like* behavior⟩ ⟨a life*like* statue⟩

like·li·hood \'lī-klē-ˌhùd\ *n* : PROBABILITY

¹**like·ly** \'lī-klē\ *adj* **like·li·er; -est 1** : PROBABLE **2** : BELIEVABLE **3** : PROMISING ⟨a ∼ place to fish⟩

²**likely** *adv* : in all probability

lik·en \'lī-kən\ *vb* **lik·ened; lik·en·ing** \'līk-(ə-)niŋ\ : COMPARE

like·ness \'līk-nəs\ *n* **1** : COPY, PORTRAIT **2** : APPEARANCE, GUISE **3** : RESEMBLANCE

like·wise \-ˌwīz\ *adv* **1** : in like manner **2** : in addition : ALSO

lik·ing \'lī-kiŋ\ *n* : favorable regard; *also* : TASTE

li·ku·ta \li-'küt-ə\ *n, pl* **ma·ku·ta** \mä-\ — see MONEY table

li·lac \'lī-lək, -ˌlak, -ˌläk\ *n* [obs. F (now *lilas*), fr. Ar *līlak*, fr. Per *nīlak* bluish, fr. *nīl* blue, fr. Skt *nīla* dark blue] **1** : a shrub with large clusters of fragrant grayish pink, purple, or white flowers **2** : a moderate purple

lil·an·ge·ni \ˌlil-ən-'gen-ē\ *n, pl* **em·a·lan·ge·ni** \ˌem-ə-lən-'gen-ē\ — see MONEY table

lil·li·pu·tian \ˌlil-ə-'pyü-shən\ *adj, often cap* **1** : SMALL, MINIATURE **2** : PETTY

lilt \'lilt\ *n* **1** : a cheerful lively song or tune **2** : a rhythmical swing, flow, or cadence

lily \'lil-ē\ *n, pl* **lil·ies** : any of numerous tall bulbous herbs with leafy stems and usu. funnel-shaped flowers; *also* : any of various related plants (as the onion, amaryllis, or iris)

lily of the valley : a low perennial herb of the lily family that produces a raceme of fragrant nodding bell-shaped white flowers

li·ma bean \ˌlī-mə-\ *n* : any of various bushy or tall-growing beans that have flat edible usu. pale green or whitish seeds; *also* : the seed of a lima bean

limb \'lim\ *n* **1** : one of the projecting paired appendages (as legs, arms, or wings) that an animal uses esp. in moving or grasping **2** : a large branch of a tree : BOUGH — **limb·less** *adj*

¹**lim·ber** \'lim-bər\ *adj* **1** : FLEXIBLE, SUPPLE **2** : LITHE, NIMBLE

²**limber** *vb* **lim·bered; lim·ber·ing** \-b(ə-)riŋ\ : to make or become limber

¹**lim·bo** \'lim-bō\ *n, pl* **limbos** [ME, fr. ML, abl. of *limbus* limbo, fr. L, border] **1** *often cap* : an abode of souls barred from heaven through no fault

of their own **2** : a place or state of confinement or oblivion

²**limbo** *n, pl* **limbos** [native name in West Indies] : a West Indian acrobatic dance orig. for men

Lim·burg·er \'lim-ˌbər-gər\ *n* : a creamy semisoft surface-ripened cheese with a pungent odor and strong flavor

¹**lime** \'līm\ *n* : a caustic infusible white substance that consists of calcium and oxygen, is obtained by heating limestone or shells until they crumble to powder, and is used in making cement and in fertilizer — **limy** \'lī-mē\ *adj*

²**lime** *n* : a small lemonlike greenish yellow citrus fruit with juicy acid pulp

lime·ade \ˌlīm-'ād\ *n* : a beverage of lime juice, sugar, and water

lime·light \'līm-ˌlīt\ *n* **1** : a device in which flame is directed against a cylinder of lime formerly used in the theater to cast a strong white light on the stage **2** : the center of public attention

lim·er·ick \'lim-(ə-)rik\ *n* : a light or humorous poem of 5 lines

lime·stone \'līm-ˌstōn\ *n* : a rock that is formed by accumulation of organic remains (as shells), is used in building, and yields lime when burned

¹**lim·it** \'lim-ət\ *vb* **1** : to set limits to **2** : to reduce in quantity or extent — **lim·i·ta·tion** \ˌlim-ə-'tā-shən\ *n*

²**limit** *n* **1** : BOUNDARY; *also, pl* : BOUNDS **2** : something that restrains or confines; *also* : the utmost extent **3** : a prescribed maximum or minimum — **lim·it·less** *adj*

lim·it·ed \'lim-ət-əd\ *adj* **1** : confined within limits **2** : offering superior and faster service and transportation

limn \'lim\ *vb* **limned; limn·ing** \lim-(n)iŋ\ **1** : DRAW; *also* : PAINT **2** : DELINEATE **3** : DESCRIBE

li·mo·nite \'lī-mə-ˌnīt\ *n* : a ferric oxide that is a major ore of iron — **li·mo·nit·ic** \ˌlī-mə-'nit-ik\ *adj*

lim·ou·sine \'lim-ə-ˌzēn, ˌlim-ə-'zēn\ *n* [F] **1** : a large luxurious often chauffeur-driven sedan **2** : a large vehicle for transporting passengers to and from an airport

¹**limp** \'limp\ *vb* : to walk lamely; *also* : to proceed with difficulty

²**limp** *n* : a limping movement or gait

³**limp** *adj* **1** : having no defined shape; *also* : not stiff or rigid **2** : lacking in strength or firmness — **limp·ly** *adv* — **limp·ness** *n*

lim·pet \'lim-pət\ *n* : a sea mollusk with a conical shell that clings to rocks or timbers

lim·pid \'lim-pəd\ *adj* [F or L; F *limpide*, fr. L *limpidus*, fr. *lympha, limpa* water] : CLEAR, TRANSPARENT

lin *abbr* **1** lineal **2** linear

lin·age \'lī-nij\ *n* : the number of lines of written or printed matter

linch·pin \'linch-ˌpin\ *n* : a locking pin inserted crosswise (as through the end of an axle)

lin·den \'lin-dən\ *n* : any of a genus of trees with large heart-shaped leaves and clustered yellowish flowers rich in nectar

¹line \'līn\ *vb* **lined; lin·ing** : to cover the inner surface of

²line *n* **1** : CORD, ROPE, WIRE; *also* : a length of material used in measuring and leveling **2** : pipes for conveying a fluid (a gas ~) **3** : a horizontal row of written or printed characters; *also* : VERSE **4** : NOTE **5** : the words making up a part in a drama — usu. used in pl. **6** : something distinct, long, and narrow; *also* : ROUTE **7** : a state of agreement **8** : a course of conduct, action, or thought; *also* : OCCUPATION **9** : LIMIT **10** : an arrangement of persons or objects of one kind in an orderly series (a ~ of trees) (waiting in ~) **11** : a transportation system **12** : the football players who are stationed on the line of scrimmage **13** : a long narrow mark; *also* : EQUATOR **14** : a geometric element that is the path of a moving point **15** : CONTOUR **16** : a general plan **17** : an indication based on insight or investigation

³line *vb* **lined; lin·ing 1** : to mark with a line **2** : to place or form a line along **3** : ALIGN

lin·eage \'lin-ē-ij\ *n* : lineal descent from a common progenitor; *also* : FAMILY

lin·eal \'lin-ē-əl\ *adj* **1** : LINEAR **2** : consisting of or being in a direct line of ancestry; *also* : HEREDITARY

lin·ea·ment \'lin-ē-ə-mənt\ *n* : an outline, feature, or contour of a body and esp. of a face — usu. used in pl.

lin·ear \'lin-ē-ər\ *adj* **1** : of, relating to, or consisting of a line **2** : STRAIGHT **2** : composed of simply drawn lines with little attempt at pictorial representation (~ script) **3** : being long and uniformly narrow

line·back·er \'līn-ˌbak-ər\ *n* : a defensive football player who lines up immediately behind the line of scrimmage

line drive *n* : a baseball hit in a nearly straight line not far above the ground

line·man \'līn-mən\ *n* **1** : one who sets up or repairs communication or power lines **2** : a player in the line in football

lin·en \'lin-ən\ *n* **1** : cloth made of flax; *also* : thread or yarn spun from flax **2** : clothing or household articles made of linen cloth or similar fabric

line of scrimmage : an imaginary line in football parallel to the goal lines and tangent to the nose of the ball laid on the ground before a scrimmage

¹lin·er \'lī-nər\ *n* : a ship or airplane of a regular transportation line

²liner *n* : one that lines or is used as a lining

line score *n* : a score of a baseball game giving the runs, hits, and errors made by each team

lines·man \'līnz-mən\ *n* **1** : LINEMAN **2** : an official who assists a referee

line·up \'līn-ˌəp\ *n* **1** : a list of players taking part in a game (as of baseball) **2** : a line of persons arranged esp. for identification by police

ling \'liŋ\ *n* : any of several fishes related to the cod

lin·ger \'liŋ-gər\ *vb* **lin·gered; lin·ger·ing** \-g(ə-)riŋ\ : TARRY; *also* : PROCRASTINATE

lin·ge·rie \ˌlän-jə-ˈrā, ˌlaⁿ-zhə-, -ˈrē\ *n* [F, fr. MF, fr. *linge* linen, fr. L *lineus* made of linen, fr. *linum* flax, linen] : women's intimate apparel

lin·go \'liŋ-gō\ *n*, *pl* **lingoes** : usu. strange or incomprehensible language

lin·gua fran·ca \ˌliŋ-gwə-ˈfraŋ-kə\ *n*, *pl* **lingua francas** *or* **lin·guae fran·cae** \-gwē-ˈfraŋ-ˌkē\ [It] **1** : a common language that consists of Italian mixed with French, Spanish, Greek, and Arabic and is spoken in Mediterranean ports **2** : any of various languages used as common or commercial tongues among speakers of different languages

lin·gual \'liŋ-gwəl\ *adj* : of, relating to, or produced by the tongue

lin·guist \'liŋ-gwəst\ *n* **1** : a person skilled in languages **2** : one who specializes in linguistics

lin·guis·tics \liŋ-ˈgwis-tiks\ *n* : the study of human speech including the units, nature, structure, and development of language or a language — **lin·guis·tic** *adj*

lin·i·ment \'lin-ə-mənt\ *n* : a liquid preparation rubbed on the skin esp. to relieve pain

lin·ing \'lī-niŋ\ *n* : material used to line esp. an inner surface

link \'liŋk\ *n* **1** : a connecting structure; *esp* : a single ring of a chain **2** : BOND, TIE — **link** *vb*

link·age \'liŋ-kij\ *n* **1** : the manner or style of being united **2** : the quality or state of being linked **3** : a system of links

linking verb *n* : a word or expression (as a form of *be, become, feel,* or *seem*) that links a subject with its predicate

links \'liŋks\ *n pl* : a golf course

link·up \'liŋk-ˌəp\ *n* **1** : MEETING **2** : something that serves as a linking device or factor

lin·net \'lin-ət\ *n* : an Old World finch

li·no·le·um \lə-ˈnō-lē-əm\ *n* [L *linum* flax + *oleum* oil] : a floor covering with a canvas back and a surface of hardened linseed oil and a filler (as cork dust)

lin·seed \'lin-ˌsēd\ *n* : the seeds of flax yielding a yellowish oil (**linseed oil**) used esp. in paints and linoleum

lin·sey-wool·sey \ˌlin-zē-ˈwul-zē\ *n* : a coarse sturdy fabric of wool and linen or cotton

lint \'lint\ *n* **1** : linen made into a soft fleecy substance for use in surgical dressings **2** : fine ravels, fluff, or loose short fibers from yarn or fabrics **3** : the fibers that surround cotton seeds and form the cotton staple

lin·tel \'lint-ᵊl\ *n* : a horizontal piece across the top of an opening (as of a door) that carries the weight of the structure above it

li·on \'lī-ən\ *n, pl* **lions** : a large flesh-eating cat of Africa and southern Asia with a shaggy mane in the male

li·on·ess \'lī-ə-nəs\ *n* : a female lion

li·on-heart·ed \,lī-ən-'härt-əd\ *adj* : COURAGEOUS, BRAVE

li·on·ize \'lī-ə-,nīz\ *vb* **-ized; iz·ing** : to treat as an object of great interest or importance — **li·on·iza·tion** \lī-ə-nə-'zā-shən\ *n*

lip \'lip\ *n* **1** : either of the two fleshy folds that surround the mouth; *also* : a part or projection suggesting such a lip **2** : the edge of a hollow vessel or cavity — **lipped** \'lipt\ *adj*

lip-read·ing \'lip-,rēd-iŋ\ *n* : the interpreting of a speaker's words without hearing the voice by watching lip and facial movements

lip service *n* : avowal of allegiance that goes no further than verbal expression

lip·stick \'lip-,stik\ *n* : a waxy solid colored cosmetic in stick form for the lips

liq *abbr* **1** liquid **2** liquor

liq·ue·fy *also* **liq·ui·fy** \'lik-wə-,fī\ *vb* **-fied; -fy·ing** : to make or become liquid — **liq·ue·fac·tion** \,lik-wə-'fak-shən\ *n* — **liq·ue·fi·a·ble** \-,fī-ə-bəl\ *adj* — **liq·ue·fier** \-,fī(-ə)r\ *n*

li·queur \li-'kər\ *n* [F] : a distilled alcoholic liquor flavored with aromatic susbtances and usu. sweetened

¹liq·uid \'lik-wəd\ *adj* **1** : flowing freely like water **2** : neither solid nor gaseous **3** : shining and clear (large ~ eyes) **4** : smooth and musical in tone; *also* : smooth and unconstrained in movement **5** : consisting of or capable of ready conversion into cash (~ assets) — **li·quid·i·ty** \lik-'wid-ət-ē\ *n*

²liquid *n* : a liquid substance

liq·ui·date \'lik-wə-,dāt\ *vb* **-dat·ed; -dat·ing 1** : to pay off (~ a debt) **2** : to settle the accounts and distribute the assets of (as a business) **3** : to get rid of; *esp* : KILL — **liq·ui·da·tion** \,lik-wə-'dā-shən\ *n*

liquid crystal *n* : an organic liquid that resembles a crystal in having ordered molecular arrays

liquid crystal display *n* : LCD

liquid measure *n* : a unit or series of units for measuring liquid capacity — see METRIC SYSTEM table, WEIGHT table

li·quor \'lik-ər\ *n* : a liquid substance; *esp* : a distilled alcoholic beverage

li·ra \'lir-ə, 'lē-rə\ *n* — see MONEY table

lisle \'līl\ *n* : a smooth tightly twisted thread usu. made of long-staple cotton

lisp \'lisp\ *vb* : to pronounce \s\ and \z\ imperfectly esp. by giving them the

sounds of \th\ and \<u>th</u>\; *also* : to speak childishly — **lisp** *n*

lis·some *also* **lis·som** \'lis-əm\ *adj* : LITHE; *also* : NIMBLE

¹list \'list\ *vb, archaic* : PLEASE; *also* : WISH

²list *vb, archaic* : LISTEN

³list *n* **1** : a simple series of words or numerals; *also* : an official roster **2** : CATALOG, CHECKLIST

⁴list *vb* : to make a list of; *also* : to include on a list

⁵list *vb* : TILT

⁶list *n* : a leaning to one side : TILT

lis·ten \'lis-ᵊn\ *vb* **lis·tened; lis·ten·ing** \'lis-(ə-)niŋ\ **1** : to pay attention in order to hear **2** : HEED — **lis·ten·er** \'lis-(ə-)nər\ *n*

lis·ten·er·ship \'lis-(ə-)nər-,ship\ *n* : the audience for a radio program or record album

list·ing \'lis-tiŋ\ *n* **1** : an act or instance of making or including in a list **2** : something that is listed

list·less \'list-ləs\ *adj* : LANGUID, SPIRITLESS — **list·less·ly** *adv* — **list·less·ness** *n*

list price *n* : the price of an item as published in a catalog, price list, or advertisement but subject to discounts

lists \'lists\ *n pl* : an arena for combat (as jousting)

¹lit \'lit\ *past and past part of* LIGHT

²lit *abbr* **1** liter **2** literal; literally **3** literary **4** literature

lit·a·ny \'lit-ᵊn-ē\ *n, pl* **-nies** [ME *letanie*, fr. OF, fr. LL *litania*, fr. LGk *litaneia*, fr. Gk. entreaty, fr. *litanos* entreating] : a prayer consisting of a series of supplications and responses said alternately by a leader and a group

li·tchi \'lī-chē, 'lē-\ *n* [Chin (Peking dialect) *li⁴ chih¹*] **1** : an oval fruit with a hard scaly outer covering, a small hard seed, and edible flesh **2** : a tree bearing litchis

li·ter \'lēt-ər\ *n* — see METRIC SYSTEM table

lit·er·al \'lit-(ə-)rəl\ *adj* **1** : adhering to fact or to the ordinary or usual meaning (as of a word) **2** : UNADORNED; *also* : PROSAIC **3** : VERBATIM

lit·er·al·ism \'lit-(ə-)rə-,liz-əm\ *n* **1** : adherence to the explicit substance (as of an idea) **2** : fidelity to observable fact — **lit·er·al·is·tic** \,lit-(ə-)rə-'lis-tik\ *adj*

lit·er·al·ly \'lit-ər-(ə-)lē, 'li-trə-lē\ *adv* **1** : ACTUALLY (was ~ insane) **2** : VIRTUALLY (~ poured out new ideas)

lit·er·ary \'lit-ə-,rer-ē\ *adj* **1** : of or relating to literature **2** : versed in literature : WELL-READ

lit·er·ate \'lit-(ə-)rət\ *adj* **1** : EDUCATED; *also* : able to read and write **2** : LITERARY; *also* : POLISHED, LUCID — **lit·er·a·cy** \'lit-(ə-)rə-sē\ *n*

li·te·ra·ti \,lit-ə-'rät-ē\ *n pl* **1** : the educated class **2** : persons interested in literature or the arts lit·er·a·tim \,lit-ə-'rät-əm, -'rät-\ *adv or adj* : letter for letter

lit·er·a·ture \'lit-(ə-)rə-,chùr, -chər\ *n* 1 : the production of written works having excellence of form or expression and dealing with ideas of permanent interest 2 : the written works produced in a particular language, country, or age

lithe \'līth, 'līth\ *adj* 1 : SUPPLE, RESILIENT 2 : characterized by effortless grace

lithe·some \'līth-səm, 'līth-\ *adj* : LISSOME

lith·i·um \'lith-ē-əm\ *n* : a light silver-white chemical element

li·thog·ra·phy \lith-'äg-rə-fē\ *n* : the process of printing from a plane surface (as a smooth stone or metal plate) on which the image to be printed is ink-receptive and the blank area ink-repellent — lith·o·graph \'lith-ə-,graf\ *vb* — lithograph *n* — li·thog·ra·pher \lith-'äg-rə-fər, 'lith-ə-,graf-ər\ *n* — lith·o·graph·ic \,lith-ə-'graf-ik\ *adj* — lith·o·graph·i·cal·ly \-i-k(ə-)lē\ *adv*

li·thol·o·gy \lith-'äl-ə-jē\ *n, pl* -gies : the study of rocks — lith·o·log·ic \,lith-ə-'läj-ik\ *adj*

lith·o·sphere \'lith-ə-,sfiər\ *n* : the outer part of the solid earth

Lith·u·a·nian \,lith-(y)ə-'wā-nē-ən\ *n* 1 : a native or inhabitant of Lithuania 2 : the language of the Lithuanians — Lithuanian *adj*

lit·i·gant \'lit-i-gənt\ *n* : a party to a lawsuit

lit·i·gate \'lit-ə-,gāt\ *vb* -gat·ed; -gat·ing : to carry on a legal contest by judicial process; *also* : to contest at law — lit·i·ga·tion \,lit-ə-'gā-shən\ *n*

li·ti·gious \lə-'tij-əs\ *adj* 1 : CONTENTIOUS 2 : prone to engage in lawsuits 3 : of or relating to litigation — li·ti·gious·ness *n*

lit·mus \'lit-məs\ *n* : a coloring matter from lichens that turns red in acid solutions and blue in alkaline

litmus test *n* : a test in which a single factor (as an attitude) is decisive

Litt D *or* Lit D *abbr* [ML *litterarum doctor*] : doctor of letters; doctor of literature

¹lit·ter \'lit-ər\ *n* [ME, fr. OF *litiere*, fr. *lit* bed, fr. L *lectus*] 1 : a covered and curtained couch with shafts used to carry a single passenger; *also* : a device (as a stretcher) for carrying a sick or injured person 2 : material used as bedding for animals; *also* : the uppermost layer of organic debris on the forest floor 3 : the offspring of an animal at one birth 4 : RUBBISH

²litter *vb* 1 : to give birth to young 2 : to strew with litter

lit·ter·a·teur \,lit-ə-rə-'tər\ *n* [F] : a literary person; *esp* : a professional writer

lit·ter·bug \'lit-ər-,bəg\ *n* : one who litters a public area

¹lit·tle \'lit-ᵊl\ *adj* lit·tler \'lit-(ᵊ-)lər\ *or*

less \'les\ *or* less·er \'les-ər\ ; lit·tlest \'lit-(ᵊ-)ləst\ *or* least \'lēst\ 1 : not big 2 : not important 3 : not much 4 : NARROW, MEAN — lit·tle·ness *n*

²little *adv* less \'les\ ; least \'lēst\ 1 : SLIGHTLY; *also* : not at all 2 : INFREQUENTLY

³little *n* 1 : a small amount or quantity 2 : a short time or distance

Little Dipper *n* : DIPPER 4

little theater *n* : a small theater for low-cost usu. experimental drama designed for a limited audience

lit·to·ral \'lit-ə-rəl; ,lit-ə-'ral\ *adj* : of, relating to, or growing on or near a shore esp. of the sea — littoral *n*

lit·ur·gy \'lit-ər-jē\ *n, pl* -gies : a rite or body of rites prescribed for public worship — li·tur·gi·cal \lə-'tər-ji-kəl\ *adj* — li·tur·gi·cal·ly \-k(ə-)lē\ *adv* — lit·ur·gist \'lit-ər-jəst\ *n*

liv·able *also* live·able \'liv-ə-bəl\ *adj* 1 : suitable for living in or with 2 : ENDURABLE — liv·a·bil·i·ty \,liv-ə-'bil-ət-ē\ *n*

¹live \'liv\ *vb* lived; liv·ing 1 : to be or continue alive 2 : SUBSIST 3 : RESIDE 4 : to conduct one's life 5 : to remain in human memory or record

²live \'līv\ *adj* 1 : having life 2 : BURNING, GLOWING (a ~ cigar) 3 : connected to electric power (a ~ wire) 4 : UNEXPLODED (a ~ bomb) 5 : of continuing interest (a ~ issue) 6 : of or involving the actual presence of real people (~ audience); *also* : broadcast directly at the time of production (a ~ radio program) 7 : being in play (a ~ ball)

lived-in \'livd-,in\ *adj* : of or suggesting long-term human habitation or use

live down *vb* : to live so as to wipe out the memory or effects of

live in \(')liv-'in\ *vb* : to live in one's place of employment — used of a servant — live-in \,liv-,in\ *adj*

live·li·hood \'līv-lē-,hùd\ *n* : means of support or subsistence

live·long \,liv-,lòŋ\ *adj* [ME *lef long*, fr. *lef* dear + *long* long] : WHOLE, ENTIRE (the ~ day)

live·ly \'līv-lē\ *adj* live·li·er; -est 1 : full of life 2 : KEEN, VIVID (~ interest) 3 : ANIMATED (~ debate) 4 : showing activity or vigor (a ~ manner) 5 : quick to rebound (a ~ ball) *syn* vivacious, sprightly, gay, animated, spirited — live·li·ness *n*

liv·en \'lī-vən\ *vb* liv·ened; liv·en·ing \'līv-(ə-)niŋ\ : ENLIVEN

¹liv·er \'liv-ər\ *n* : a large glandular organ of vertebrates that secretes bile and is a center of metabolic activity — liv·ered \'liv-ərd\ *adj*

²liver *n* : one that lives esp. in a specified way (a fast ~)

liv·er·ish \'liv-(ə-)rish\ *adj* 1 : resembling liver esp. in color 2 : BILIOUS 3 : MELANCHOLY

liv·er·wort \'liv-ər-,wərt\ *n* : any of various plants resembling the related mosses

liv·er·wurst \-,wərst, -,wu̇(r)st\ *n* [part trans. of G *leberwurst*, fr. *leber* liver + *wurst* sausage] : a sausage consisting chiefly of liver

liv·ery \'liv-(ə-)rē\ *n, pl* **-er·ies** 1 : a special uniform worn by the servants of a wealthy household; *also* : distinctive dress 2 : the feeding, care, and stabling of horses for pay; *also* : the keeping of horses and vehicles for hire — **liv·er·ied** \-rēd\ *adj*

liv·ery·man \-mən\ *n* : the keeper of a livery stable

lives *pl of* LIFE

live·stock \'līv-,stäk\ *n* : farm animals kept for use and profit

live wire *n* : an alert active aggressive person

liv·id \'liv-əd\ *adj* [F *livide*, fr. L *lividus*, fr. *livēre* to be blue] 1 : discolored by bruising 2 : ASHEN, PALLID 3 : REDDISH 4 : ENRAGED

¹liv·ing \'liv-iŋ\ *adj* 1 : having life 2 : NATURAL 3 : full of life and vigor; *also* : VIVID

²living *n* 1 : the condition of being alive; *also* : manner of life 2 : LIVELIHOOD

living room *n* : a room in a residence used for the common social activities of the occupants

living wage *n* : a wage sufficient to provide the necessities and comforts held to comprise an acceptable standard of living

liz·ard \'liz-ərd\ *n* : a 4-legged scaly reptile with a long tapering tail

Lk *abbr* Luke

ll *abbr* lines

lla·ma \'läm-ə\ *n* [Sp] : any of several wild or domesticated So. American mammals related to the camel but smaller and without a hump

lla·no \'län-ō\ *n, pl* **llanos** : an open grassy plain esp. of Latin America

LLD *abbr* [NL *legum doctor*] doctor of laws

LNG *abbr* liquefied natural gas

¹load \'lōd\ *n* 1 : PACK; *also* : CARGO 2 : a mass of weight supported by something 3 : something that burdens the mind or spirits 4 : a large quantity — usu. used in pl. 5 : a standard, expected, or authorized burden

²load *vb* 1 : to put a load in or on; *also* : to receive a load 2 : BURDEN 3 : to increase the weight of by adding something 4 : to supply abundantly 5 : to put a charge in (as a firearm)

load·ed \'lōd-əd\ *adj* 1 *slang* : DRUNK 2 : having a large amount of money

load·stone *var of* LODESTONE

¹loaf \'lōf\ *n, pl* **loaves** \'lōvz\ : a shaped or molded mass esp. of bread

²loaf *vb* : to spend time in idleness : LOUNGE — **loaf·er** *n*

loam \'lōm, 'lüm\ *n* : SOIL; *esp* : a loose soil of mixed clay, sand, and silt — **loamy** *adj*

¹loan \'lōn\ *n* 1 : money lent at interest; *also* : something lent for the borrower's temporary use 2 : the grant of temporary use

²loan *vb* : LEND

loan shark *n* : a person who lends money at excessive rates of interest — **loan·shark·ing** \'lōn-,shär-kiŋ\ *n*

loan·word \'lōn-,wərd\ *n* : a word taken from another language and at least partly naturalized

loath \'lōth, 'lōth\ *also* **loathe** \'lōth, 'lōth\ *adj* : RELUCTANT

loathe \'lōth\ *vb* **loathed; loath·ing** : to dislike greatly syn abominate, abhor, detest, hate

loath·ing \'lō-thiŋ\ *n* : extreme disgust

loath·some \'lōth-səm, 'lōth-\ *adj* : exciting loathing : REPULSIVE

lob \'läb\ *vb* **lobbed; lob·bing** : to throw, hit, or propel something in a high arc — **lob** *n*

¹lob·by \'läb-ē\ *n, pl* **lobbies** 1 : a corridor or hall used esp. as a passageway or waiting room 2 : a group of persons engaged in lobbying

²lobby *vb* **lob·bied; lob·by·ing** : to try to influence public officials and esp. legislators — **lob·by·ist** *n*

lobe \'lōb\ *n* : a curved or rounded projection or division — **lo·bar** \'lō-bər\ *adj* — **lobed** \'lōbd\ *adj*

lo·bot·o·my \lō-'bät-ə-mē\ *n, pl* **-mies** : severance of nerve fibers by incision into the brain for the relief of some mental disorders

lob·ster \'läb-stər\ *n* [ME, fr. OE *loppestre*, fr. *loppe* spider] : an edible marine crustacean with two large pincerlike claws and four other pairs of legs; *also* : SPINY LOBSTER

lob·ule \'läb-yül\ *n* : a small lobe; *also* : a subdivision of a lobe — **lob·u·lar** \'läb-yə-lər\ *adj*

¹lo·cal \'lō-kəl\ *adj* 1 : of, relating to, or occupying a particular place 2 : serving a particular limited district; *also* : making all stops ⟨a ~ train⟩ 3 : affecting a small part of the body ⟨~ infection⟩ — **lo·cal·ly** \-ē\ *adv*

²local *n* : one that is local

lo·cale \lō-'kal\ *n* : a place that is the setting for a particular event

lo·cal·i·ty \lō-'kal-ət-ē\ *n, pl* **-ties** : a particular spot, situation, or location

lo·cal·ize \'lō-kə-,līz\ *vb* **-ized; -iz·ing** : to fix in or confine to a definite place or locality — **lo·cal·iza·tion** \,lō-kə-lə-'zā-shən\ *n*

lo·cate \'lō-,kāt, lō-'kāt\ *vb* **lo·cat·ed; lo·cat·ing** 1 : STATION, SETTLE 2 : to determine the site of 3 : to find or fix the place of in a sequence

lo·ca·tion \lō-'kā-shən\ *n* 1 : SITUATION, PLACE 2 : the process of locating 3 : a place outside a studio where a motion picture is filmed

loc cit *abbr* [L *loco citato*] in the place cited

loch \'läk, 'läḵ\ *n, Scot* : LAKE; *also* : a bay or arm of the sea esp. when nearly landlocked

¹lock \\'läk\ *n* : a tuft, strand, or ringlet of hair; *also* : a cohering bunch (as of wool or flax)

²lock *n* **1** : a fastening in which a bolt is operated **2** : the mechanism of a firearm by which the charge is exploded **3** : an enclosure (as in a canal) used in raising or lowering boats from level to level **4** : a wrestling hold

³lock *vb* **1** : to fasten the lock of; *also* : to make fast with a lock **2** : to confine or exclude by means of a lock **3** : INTERLOCK

lock·er \\'läk-ər\ *n* **1** : a drawer, cupboard, or compartment for individual storage use **2** : an insulated compartment for storing frozen food

lock·et \\'läk-ət\ *n* : a small usu. metal case for a memento worn suspended from a chain or necklace

lock·jaw \\'läk-‚jò\ *n* : TETANUS

lock·nut \-‚nət\ *n* **1** : a nut screwed tight on another to prevent it from slacking back **2** : a nut designed to lock itself when screwed tight

lock·out \\'läk-‚aüt\ *n* : the suspension of work by an employer during a labor dispute in order to make employees accept the terms being offered

lock·smith \\'läk-‚smith\ *n* : one who makes or repairs locks

lock·step \\'läk-‚step\ *n* : a mode of marching in step by a body of men moving in a very close single file

lock·up \\'läk-‚əp\ *n* : JAIL

lo·co \\'lō-kō\ *adj, slang* [Sp] : CRAZY, FRENZIED

lo·co·mo·tion \‚lō-kə-'mō-shən\ *n* **1** : the act or power of moving from place to place : TRAVEL

¹lo·co·mo·tive \‚lō-kə-'mōt-iv\ *adj* : of or relating to locomotion or a locomotive

²locomotive *n* : a self-propelled vehicle used to move railroad cars

lo·co·mo·tor \‚lō-kə-'mōt-ər\ *adj* : of or relating to locomotion or organs used in locomotion

lo·co·weed \\'lō-kō-‚wēd\ *n* : any of several leguminous plants of western No. America that are poisonous to livestock

lo·cus \\'lō-kəs\ *n, pl* **lo·ci** \\'lō-‚sī\ [L] **1** : PLACE, LOCALITY **2** : the set of all points whose location is determined by stated conditions

lo·cust \\'lō-kəst\ *n* **1** : a usu. destructive migratory grasshopper **2** : CICADA **3** : any of various leguminous trees with hard wood

lo·cu·tion \lō-'kyü-shən\ *n* : a particular form of expression; *also* : PHRASEOLOGY

lode \\'lōd\ *n* : an ore deposit

lode·star \\'lōd-‚stär\ *n* [ME *lode sterre*, fr. *lode* course, fr. OE *lād*] : a guiding star; *esp* : NORTH STAR

lode·stone \-‚stōn\ *n* : an iron-containing rock with magnetic properties

¹lodge \\'läj\ *vb* **lodged; lodg·ing 1** : to provide quarters for; *also* : to settle in a place **2** : CONTAIN **3** : to come to a

rest and remain **4** : to deposit for safekeeping **5** : to vest (as authority) in an agent **6** : FILE ⟨~ a complaint⟩

²lodge *n* **1** : a house set apart for residence in a special season or by an employee on an estate; *also* : INN **2** : the meeting place of a branch of a fraternal organization; *also* : the members of such a branch **3** : a den or lair esp. of gregarious animals

lodg·er \\'läj-ər\ *n* : a person who occupies a rented room in another's house

lodg·ing \\'läj-iŋ\ *n* **1** : DWELLING **2** : a room or suite of rooms in another's house rented as a dwelling place — usu. used in pl.

lodg·ment *or* **lodge·ment** \\'läj-mənt\ *n* **1** : a lodging place **2** : the act or manner of lodging **3** : DEPOSIT

loess \\'les, 'lə(r)s, 'lō-əs\ *n* : a usu. yellowish brown loamy deposit believed to be chiefly deposited by the wind

¹loft \\'lòft\ *n* [ME, fr. OE, fr. ON *lopt* air] **1** : ATTIC **2** : GALLERY ⟨organ ~⟩ **3** : an upper floor (as in a warehouse or barn) esp. when not partitioned **4** : the thickness of a fabric or insulated material (as of a sleeping bag)

²loft *vb* : to strike or throw a ball so that it rises high in the air

lofty \\'lòf-tē\ *adj* **loft·i·er; -est 1** : NOBLE; *also* : SUPERIOR **2** : extremely proud **3** : HIGH, TALL — **loft·i·ly** \\'lòf-tə-lē\ *adv* — **loft·i·ness** \-tē-nəs\ *n*

¹log \\'lóg, 'läg\ *n* **1** : a bulky piece of unshaped timber **2** : an apparatus for measuring a ship's speed **3** : the daily record of a ship's progress; *also* : a regularly kept record of performance (as of an airplane)

²log *vb* **logged; log·ging 1** : to cut trees for lumber **2** : to enter in a log **3** : to sail a ship or fly an airplane for (an indicated distance or period of time) **4** : to have (an indicated record) to one's credit : ACHIEVE — **log·ger** \\'lòg-ər, 'läg-\ *n*

³log *n* : LOGARITHM

lo·gan·ber·ry \\'lō-gən-‚ber-ē\ *n* : a redfruited upright-growing dewberry; *also* : its fruit

log·a·rithm \\'lòg-ə-‚rith-əm, 'läg-\ *n* : the exponent that indicates the power to which a base number is raised to produce a given number (the ~ of 100 to the base number of 10 is 2) — **log·a·rith·mic** \‚lòg-ə-'rith-mik, ‚läg-\ *adj*

loge \\'lōzh\ *n* **1** : a small compartment; *also* : a box in a theater **2** : a small partitioned area; *also* : the forward section of a theater mezzanine

log·ger·head \\'lòg-ər-‚hed, 'läg-\ *n* : a large sea turtle of the warmer parts of the Atlantic — **at loggerheads** : in a state of quarrelsome disagreement

log·gia \\'lō-jē-ə, 'lō-jä\ *n, pl* **loggias** \\'lō-jē-əz, 'lō-jäz\ : a roofed open gallery

log·ic \\'läj-ik\ *n* **1** : a science that deals with the rules and tests of sound thinking and proof by reasoning **2** : sound reasoning **3** : the fundamental principles and the connection of circuit elements for arithmetical computation in a computer — **log·i·cal** \-i-kəl\ *adj* — **log·i·cal·ly** \-i-k(ə)lē\ *adv* — **lo·gi·cian** \lō-ˈjish-ən\ *n*

lo·gis·tics \lō-ˈjis-tiks\ *n sing or pl* : the procurement, maintenance, and transportation of matériel, facilities, and personnel — **lo·gis·tic** *adj*

log·jam \ˈlóg-ˌjam, ˈlȧg-\ *n* 1 : a deadlocked jumble of logs in a watercourse 2 : DEADLOCK

logo \ˈlóg-ō, ˈlȧg-\ *n, pl* **log·os** \-ōz\ : LOGOTYPE

logo·type \ˈlóg-ə-ˌtīp, ˈlȧg-\ *n* : an identifying symbol (as for advertising)

log·roll·ing \-ˌrō-liŋ\ *n* : the trading of votes by legislators to secure favorable action on projects of individual interest

lo·gy \ˈlō-gē\ *also* **log·gy** \ˈlóg-ē, ˈlȧg-\ *adj* **lo·gi·er; -est** : deficient in vitality : SLUGGISH

loin \ˈlóin\ *n* 1 : the part of the body on each side of the spinal column and between the hip and the lower ribs; *also* : a cut of meat from this part of an animal 2 *pl* : the upper and lower abdominal regions and the region about the hips

loin·cloth \-ˌklóth\ *n* : a cloth worn about the loins often as the sole article of clothing in warm climates

loi·ter \ˈlóit-ər\ *vb* 1 : LINGER 2 : to hang around idly *syn* dawdle, dally, procrastinate, lag, tarry — **loi·ter·er** *n*

loll \ˈlȧl\ *vb* 1 : DROOP, DANGLE 2 : LOUNGE

lol·li·pop *or* **lol·ly·pop** \ˈläl-i-ˌpäp\ *n* : a lump of hard candy on a stick

lol·ly·gag \ˈläl-ē-ˌgag\ *vb* **-gagged; -gagging** : DAWDLE

Lond *abbr* London

lone \ˈlōn\ *adj* 1 : SOLITARY ⟨a ~ sentinel⟩ 2 : SOLE, ONLY ⟨the ~ theater in town⟩ 3 : ISOLATED ⟨a ~ tree⟩

lone·ly \ˈlōn-lē\ *adj* **lone·li·er; -est** 1 : being without company 2 : UNFREQUENTED ⟨a ~ spot⟩ 3 : LONESOME — **lone·li·ness** *n*

lon·er \ˈlō-nər\ *n* : one that avoids others

lone·some \ˈlōn-səm\ *adj* 1 : sad from lack of companionship 2 : REMOTE; *also* : SOLITARY — **lone·some·ly** *adv* — **lone·some·ness** *n*

¹**long** \ˈlóŋ\ *adj* **lon·ger** \ˈlóŋ-gər\ ; **lon·gest** \ˈlóŋ-gəst\ 1 : extending for a considerable distance; *also* : TALL, ELONGATED 2 : having a specified length 3 : extending over a considerable time; *also* : TEDIOUS 4 : containing many items in a series 5 : being a syllable or speech sound of relatively great duration 6 : extending far into the future 7 : well furnished with something — used with *on*

²**long** *adv* : for or during a long time

³**long** *n* : a long period of time

⁴**long** *vb* **longed; long·ing** \ˈlóŋ-iŋ\ : to feel a strong desire or wish *syn* yearn, hanker, pine, hunger, thirst

⁵**long** *abbr* longitude

long·boat \ˈlóŋ-ˌbōt\ *n* : the largest boat carried by a merchant sailing ship

long·bow \-ˌbō\ *n* : a wooden bow drawn by hand and usu. 5 to 6 feet long

lon·gev·i·ty \län-ˈjev-ət-ē\ *n* [LL *longaevitas*, fr. L *longaevus* long-lived, fr. *longus* long + *aevum* age] : a long duration of individual life; *also* : length of life

long·hair \ˈlóŋ-ˌha(ə)r\ *n* 1 : a lover of classical music 2 : HIPPIE 3 : a domestic cat having long outer fur

long·hand \-ˌhand\ *n* : HANDWRITING

long·horn \-ˌhórn\ *n* : any of the cattle with long horns formerly common in the southwestern U.S.

long hundredweight *n* — see WEIGHT table

long·ing \ˈlóŋ-iŋ\ *n* : an eager desire esp. for something unattainable — **long·ing·ly** *adv*

lon·gi·tude \ˈlän-jə-ˌt(y)üd\ *n* : angular distance expressed usu. in degrees east or west from the meridian that runs between the north and south poles and passes through Greenwich, England

lon·gi·tu·di·nal \ˌlän-jə-ˈt(y)üd-(ə-)nəl\ *adj* 1 : extending lengthwise 2 : of or relating to length — **lon·gi·tu·di·nal·ly** \-ē\ *adv*

long·shore·man \ˈlóŋ-ˈshór-mən\ *n* : a laborer at a wharf who loads and unloads cargo

long–suf·fer·ing \-ˈsəf-(ə-)riŋ\ *n* : long and patient endurance of offense

long–term \ˈlóŋ-ˈtərm\ *adj* 1 : extending over or involving a long period of time 2 : constituting a financial obligation based on a term usu. of more than 10 years ⟨a ~ mortgage⟩

long–time \ˌlóŋ-ˈtīm\ *adj* : of long duration ⟨~ friends⟩

long ton *n* — see WEIGHT table

lon·gueur \lōⁿ-ˈgœr\ *n, pl* **longueurs** \-ˈgœr(z)\ [F, lit., length] : a dull tedious passage or section

long–wind·ed \ˈlóŋ-ˈwin-dəd\ *adj* : tediously long in speaking or writing

loo·fah \ˈlü-fə\ *n* : a sponge consisting of the fibrous skeleton of a gourd

¹**look** \ˈlùk\ *vb* 1 : to exercise the power of vision : SEE 2 : EXPECT 3 : to have an appearance that befits ⟨~s the part⟩ 4 : SEEM ⟨~s thin⟩ 5 : to direct one's attention : HEED 6 : POINT, FACE 7 : to show a tendency — **look after** : to take care of — **look for** : EXPECT

²**look** *n* 1 : the action of looking : GLANCE 2 : EXPRESSION; *also* : physical appearance 3 : ASPECT

look down \(ˈ)lùk-ˈdaùn\ *vb* : DESPISE — used with *on* or *upon*

looking glass *n* : MIRROR

look·out \ˈlùk-ˌaùt\ *n* 1 : a person assigned to watch (as on a ship) 2 : a careful watch **3** : VIEW **4** : a matter of concern

look up \(ˈ)lu̇k-ˈəp\ vb **1** : IMPROVE (business is *looking up*) **2** : to search for in or as if in a reference work **3** : to seek out esp. for a brief visit

¹**loom** \ˈlüm\ n : a frame or machine for weaving together threads or yarns into cloth

²**loom** vb **1** : to come into sight in an unnaturally large, indistinct, or distorted form **2** : to appear in an impressively exaggerated form

loon \ˈlün\ n : a web-footed black-and-white fish-eating diving bird

loo·ny or **loo·ney** \ˈlü-nē\ adj **loo·ni·er**; **-est** : CRAZY, FOOLISH

loony bin n : an insane asylum

loop \ˈlüp\ n **1** : a fold or doubling of a line through which another line or hook can be passed; *also* : a loop-shaped figure or course (a ∼ in a river) **2** : a circular airplane maneuver involving flying upside down **3** : a ring-shaped intrauterine device **4** : a piece of film whose ends are spliced together to project continuously — **loop** vb

loop·er \ˈlü-pər\ n : any of numerous rather small hairless moth caterpillars that move with a looping movement

loop·hole \ˈlüp-ˌhōl\ n **1** : a small opening in a wall through which firearms may be discharged **2** : a means of escape; *esp* : an ambiguity or omission that allows one to evade the intent of a law or contract

¹**loose** \ˈlüs\ adj **loos·er**; **loos·est** **1** : not rigidly fastened **2** : free from restraint or obligation **3** : not dense or compact in structure **4** : not chaste : LEWD **5** : SLACK **6** : not precise or exact — **loose·ly** adv — **loose·ness** n

²**loose** vb **loosed**; **loos·ing** **1** : RELEASE **2** : UNTIE **3** : DETACH **4** : DISCHARGE **5** : RELAX, SLACKEN

³**loose** adv : LOOSELY

loos·en \ˈlüs-ᵊn\ vb **loos·ened**; **loos·en·ing** \ˈlüs-(ᵊ-)niŋ\ **1** : FREE **2** : to make or become loose **3** : to relax the severity of

loot \ˈlüt\ n [Hindi *lūṭ*, fr. Skt *luṇṭati* he robs] : goods taken in war or by robbery : PLUNDER — **loot** vb — **loot·er** n

¹**lop** \ˈläp\ vb **lopped**; **lop·ping** : to cut branches or twigs from : TRIM; *also* : to cut off

²**lop** vb **lopped**; **lop·ping** : to hang downward; *also* : to flop or sway loosely

lope \ˈlōp\ n : an easy bounding gait — **lope** vb

lop·sid·ed \ˈläp-ˈsīd-əd\ adj **1** : leaning to one side **2** : UNSYMMETRICAL — **lop·sid·ed·ly** adv — **lop·sid·ed·ness** n

lo·qua·cious \lō-ˈkwā-shəs\ adj : excessively talkative — **lo·quac·i·ty** \-ˈkwas-ət-ē\ n

lord \ˈlȯrd\ n [ME *loverd, lord*, fr. OE *hlāford*, fr. *hlāf* loaf + *weard* keeper] **1** : one having power and authority over others; *esp* : a person from

whom a feudal fee or estate is held **2** : a man of rank or high position; *esp* : a British nobleman **3** *pl, cap* : the upper house of the British parliament **4** : a person of great power in some field

²**lord** vb : to act like a lord; *esp* : to put on airs — usu. used with *it*

lord chancellor n, *pl* **lords chancellor** : a British officer of state who presides over the House of Lords, serves as head of the British judiciary, and is usu. a leading member of the cabinet

lord·ly \-lē\ adj **lord·li·er**; **-est** **1** : DIGNIFIED; *also* : NOBLE **2** : HAUGHTY

lord·ship \-ˌship\ n **1** : the rank or dignity of a lord — used as a title **2** : the authority or territory of a lord

Lord's Supper n : COMMUNION

lore \ˈlōr\ n : KNOWLEDGE; *esp* : traditional knowledge or belief

lor·gnette \lȯrn-ˈyet\ n [F, fr. *lorgner* to take a sidelong look at, fr. MF, fr. *lorgne* cross-eyed] : a pair of eyeglasses or opera glasses with a handle

lorn \ˈlȯrn\ adj : FORSAKEN, DESOLATE

lor·ry \ˈlȯr-ē\ n, *pl* **lorries 1** : a large low horse-drawn wagon without sides **2** *Brit* : MOTORTRUCK

lose \ˈlüz\ vb **lost** \ˈlȯst\; **los·ing** \ˈlü-ziŋ\ **1** : DESTROY **2** : to miss from a customary place : MISLAY **3** : to suffer deprivation of **4** : to fail to use : WASTE **5** : to fail to win or obtain (∼ the game) **6** : to fail to keep or maintain (∼ his balance) **7** : to wander from (∼ his way) **8** : to get rid of (∼ weight) — **los·er** n

loss \ˈlȯs\ n **1** : the harm resulting from losing **2** : something that is lost **3** *pl* : killed, wounded, or captured soldiers **4** : failure to win **5** : an amount by which the cost exceeds the selling price **6** : decrease in amount or degree **7** : RUIN

loss leader n : an article sold at a loss in order to draw customers

lost \ˈlȯst\ adj **1** : not used, won, or claimed **2** : no longer possessed or known **3** : ruined or destroyed physically or morally **4** : DENIED; *also* : HARDENED **5** : unable to find the way; *also* : HELPLESS **6** : ABSORBED, RAPT

lot \ˈlät\ n **1** : an object used in deciding something by chance; *also* : the use of lots to decide something **2** : SHARE, PORTION; *also* : FORTUNE, FATE **3** : a plot of land **4** : a group of individuals : SET **5** : a considerable quantity

loth \ˈlōth, ˈlōth\ *var of* LOATH

lo·ti \ˈlōt-ē\ n, *pl* **ma·lo·ti** \mə-ˈlōt-ē\ — see MONEY table

lo·tion \ˈlō-shən\ n : a liquid preparation for cosmetic and external medicinal use

lot·tery \ˈlät-ə-rē\ n, *pl* **-ter·ies 1** : a drawing of lots in which prizes are given to the winning names or numbers **2** : a matter determined by chance

lo·tus \ˈlōt-əs\ n **1** : a fruit held in Greek

legend to cause dreamy content and forgetfulness **2** : a water lily used in ancient Egyptian and Hindu art and religious symbolism **3** : any of several forage plants related to the clovers

loud \'laud\ *adj* **1** : marked by intensity or volume of sound **2** : CLAMOROUS, NOISY **3** : obtrusive or offensive in color or pattern (a ~ suit) — **loud** *adv* — **loud·ly** *adv* — **loud·ness** *n*

loud–mouthed \-ˌmauᵗhd, -ˈmauᵗht\ *adj* : given to loud offensive talk

loud·speak·er \'laud-ˌspē-kər\ *n* : a device that changes electrical signals into sound

¹**lounge** \'launj\ *vb* **lounged; loung·ing** : to act or move lazily or listlessly

²**lounge** *n* **1** : a room with comfortable furniture; *also* : a room (as in a theater) with lounging, smoking, and toilet facilities **2** : a long couch

lour \'lau̇(-ə)r\, **loury** \'lau̇(ə)r-ē\ *var of* LOWER, LOWERY

louse \'laus\ *n, pl* **lice** \'līs\ **1** : a small wingless insect parasitic on warm-blooded animals **2** : a plant pest (as an aphid) **3** : a contemptible person

lousy \'lau̇-zē\ *adj* **lous·i·er; -est 1** : infested with lice **2** : POOR, INFERIOR **3** : amply supplied (~ with money) — **lous·i·ly** \'lau̇-zə-lē\ *adv* — **lous·i·ness** \-zē-nəs\ *n*

lout \'laut\ *n* : a stupid awkward fellow — **lout·ish** *adj* — **lout·ish·ly** *adv*

lou·ver *or* **lou·vre** \'lü-vər\ *n* **1** : an opening having parallel slanted slats to allow flow of air but to exclude rain or sun or to provide privacy; *also* : a slat in such an opening **2** : a device with movable slats for controlling the flow of air or light

¹**love** \'ləv\ *n* **1** : strong affection **2** : warm attachment (~ of the sea) **3** : attraction based on sexual desire **4** : a beloved person **5** : a score of zero in tennis — **love·less** *adj*

²**love** *vb* **loved; lov·ing 1** : CHERISH **2** : to feel a passion, devotion, or tenderness for **3** : CARESS **4** : to take pleasure in (~s to play bridge) — **lov·able** \'ləv-ə-bəl\ *adj* — **lov·er** *n*

love·bird \'ləv-ˌbərd\ *n* : any of various small usu. gray or green parrots that seemingly show great affection for their mates

love·lorn \-ˌlȯrn\ *adj* : deprived of love or of a lover

love·ly \'ləv-lē\ *adj* **love·li·er; -est** : BEAUTIFUL — **love·li·ness** *n*

love·mak·ing \-ˌmā-kiŋ\ *n* **1** : COURTSHIP **2** : sexual activity; *esp* : COPULATION

love·sick \-ˌsik\ *adj* **1** : YEARNING **2** : expressing a lover's longing — **love·sick·ness** *n*

lov·ing \'ləv-iŋ\ *adj* : AFFECTIONATE — **lov·ing·ly** *adv*

¹**low** \'lō\ *vb* : MOO

²**low** *n* : MOO

³**low** *adj* **low·er** \'lō(-ə)r\; **low·est** \'lō-əst\ **1** : not high or tall (~ wall) ; *also* : DÉCOLLETÉ **2** : situated or passing be-

low the normal level or surface (~ ground); *also* : marking a nadir **3** : STRICKEN, PROSTRATE **4** : not loud (~ voice) **5** : being near the equator **6** : humble in status **7** : WEAK; *also* : DEPRESSED **8** : less than usual **9** : falling short of a standard **10** : UNFAVORABLE — **low** *adv* — **low·ness** *n*

⁴**low** *n* **1** : something that is low **2** : a region of low barometric pressure **3** : the arrangement of gears in an automobile transmission that gives the slowest speed and greatest power

low beam *n* : the short-range focus of a vehicle headlight

low blow *n* : an unprincipled attack

low·brow \'lō-ˌbrau̇\ *n* : a person without intellectual interests or culture

low·down \'lō-ˌdau̇n\ *n* : pertinent and esp. guarded information

low–down \'lō-ˈdau̇n\ *adj* **1** : MEAN, CONTEMPTIBLE **2** : deeply emotional

low–end \-ˌend\ *adj* : of, relating to, or being the lowest-priced merchandise in a manufacturer's line

¹**low·er** \'lau̇(-ə)r\ *vb* **1** : FROWN **2** : to become dark, gloomy, and threatening

²**low·er** \'lō(-ə)r\ *adj* **1** : relatively low (as in rank) **2** : constituting the popular and more representative branch of a bicameral legislative body **3** : situated beneath the earth's surface

³**low·er** \'lō(-ə)r\ *vb* **1** : DROP; *also* : DIMINISH **2** : to let descend by its own weight; *also* : to reduce the height of **3** : to reduce in value, number, or amount **4** : DEGRADE; *also* : HUMBLE

low·er·case \ˌlō(-ə)r-ˈkās\ *adj* : being a letter that belongs to or conforms to the series a, b, c, etc., rather than A, B, C, etc. — **lowercase** *n*

lower class *n* : a social class occupying a position below the middle class and having the lowest status in a society — **lower–class** \-ˈklas\ *adj*

low·er·most \'lō(-ə)r-ˌmōst\ *adj* : LOWEST

low·ery \'lau̇-(ə-)rē\ *adj* : GLOOMY, LOWERING

lowest common denominator *n* **1** : LEAST COMMON DENOMINATOR **2** : something acceptable to the greatest number of people

lowest common multiple *n* : LEAST COMMON MULTIPLE

low frequency *n* : a frequency of a radio wave in the range between 30 and 300 kilohertz

low–key \'lō-'kē\ *also* **low–keyed** \-'kēd\ *adj* : of low intensity : restrained

low·land \'lō-lənd, -ˌland\ *n* : low and usu. level country

low·life \'lō-ˌlīf\ *n, pl* **low·lifes** \-ˌlīfs\ *also* **low·lives** \-ˌlīvz\ : a person of low social status or moral character

low·ly \'lō-lē\ *adj* **low·li·er; -est 1** : HUMBLE, MEEK **2** : ranking low in some hierarchy — **low·li·ness** *n*

low–rise \'lō-ˈrīz\ *adj* : being one or

two stories and not equipped with elevators ⟨a ~ building⟩

¹lox \ˈläks\ *n* : liquid oxygen

²lox *n, pl* **lox** *or* **lox·es** : smoked salmon

loy·al \ˈlȯi-(ə)l\ *adj* [MF, fr. OF *leial, leel,* fr. L *legalis* legal] **1** : faithful in allegiance to one's government **2** : faithful esp. to a cause or ideal : CONSTANT — **loy·al·ly** \ˈlȯi-ə-lē\ *adv* — **loy·al·ty** \ˈlȯi-(ə)l-tē\ *n*

loy·al·ist \ˈlȯi-ə-ləst\ *n* : one who is or remains loyal to a political party, government, or sovereign

loz·enge \ˈläz-ᵊnj\ *n* **1** : a diamond-shaped figure **2** : a small flat often medicated candy

LP *abbr* low pressure

LPG *abbr* liquefied petroleum gas

LPN \ˈel-ˈpē-ˈen\ *n* : LICENSED PRACTICAL NURSE

LSD \ˌel-ˌes-ˈdē\ *n* [*l*ysergic acid *d*iethylamide] : a crystalline compound that causes psychotic symptoms similar to those of schizophrenia

lt *abbr* light

Lt *abbr* lieutenant

LT *abbr* long ton

LTC *or* **Lt Col** *abbr* lieutenant colonel

Lt Comdr *abbr* lieutenant commander

ltd *abbr* limited

LTG *or* **Lt Gen** *abbr* lieutenant general

LTJG *abbr* lieutenant, junior grade

ltr *abbr* letter

Lu *symbol* lutetium

lu·au \ˈlü-ˌaù\ *n* : a Hawaiian feast

lub *abbr* lubricant; lubricating

lub·ber \ˈlab-ər\ *n* **1** : LOUT **2** : an unskilled seaman — **lub·ber·ly** *adj*

lube \ˈlüb\ *n* : lubricant; *also* : an application of a lubricant

lu·bri·cant \ˈlü-bri-kənt\ *n* : a material (as grease) capable of reducing friction when applied between moving parts

lu·bri·cate \ˈlü-brə-ˌkāt\ *vb* **-cat·ed; -cat·ing** : to apply a lubricant to — **lu·bri·ca·tion** \ˌlü-brə-ˈkā-shən\ *n* — **lu·bri·ca·tor** \ˈlü-brə-ˌkāt-ər\ *n*

lu·bri·cious \lü-ˈbrish-əs\ *or* **lu·bri·cous** \ˈlü-bri-kəs\ *adj* **1** : SMOOTH, SLIPPERY **2** : LECHEROUS; *also* : SALACIOUS — **lu·bric·i·ty** \lü-ˈbris-ət-ē\ *n*

lu·cent \ˈlüs-ᵊnt\ *adj* **1** : LUMINOUS **2** : CLEAR, LUCID

lu·cerne \lü-ˈsərn\ *n, chiefly Brit* : ALFALFA

lu·cid \ˈlü-səd\ *adj* **1** : SHINING **2** : clear-minded **3** : easily understood — **lu·cid·i·ty** \lü-ˈsid-ət-ē\ *n* — **lu·cid·ly** *adv* — **lu·cid·ness** *n*

Lu·ci·fer \ˈlü-sə-fər\ *n* [ME, the morning star, a fallen rebel archangel, the Devil, fr. OE, fr. L, the morning star, fr. *lucifer* light-bearing] : DEVIL, SATAN

¹luck \ˈlək\ *n* **1** : CHANCE, FORTUNE **2** : good fortune — **luck·less** *adj*

²luck *vb* **1** : to prosper or succeed esp. through chance or good fortune **2** : to come upon something desirable by chance — usu. used with *out, on, onto,* or *into*

lucky \ˈlək-ē\ *adj* **luck·i·er; -est 1** : favored by luck : FORTUNATE **2** : FORTUITOUS **3** : seeming to bring good luck — **luck·i·ly** \ˈlək-ə-lē\ *adv* — **luck·i·ness** \-ē-nəs\ *n*

lu·cra·tive \ˈlü-krət-iv\ *adj* : PROFITABLE — **lu·cra·tive·ly** *adv* — **lu·cra·tive·ness** *n*

lu·cre \ˈlü-kər\ *n* [ME, fr. L *lucrum*] : PROFIT; *also* : MONEY

lu·cu·bra·tion \ˌlü-k(y)ə-ˈbrā-shən\ *n* : laborious study : MEDITATION

lu·di·crous \ˈlüd-ə-krəs\ *adj* : LAUGHABLE, RIDICULOUS — **lu·di·crous·ly** *adv* — **lu·di·crous·ness** *n*

luff \ˈləf\ *vb* : to sail a ship closer to the wind — **luff** *n*

¹lug \ˈləg\ *vb* **lugged; lug·ging 1** : DRAG, PULL **2** : to carry laboriously

²lug *n* **1** : a projecting piece (as for fastening, support, or traction) **2** : a heavy nut used with a bolt

lug·gage \ˈləg-ij\ *n* **1** : BAGGAGE **2** : containers (as suitcases) for carrying personal belongings

lu·gu·bri·ous \lu-ˈgü-brē-əs\ *adj* : mournful often to an exaggerated degree — **lu·gu·bri·ous·ly** *adv* — **lu·gu·bri·ous·ness** *n*

Luke \ˈlük\ *n* — see BIBLE table

luke·warm \ˈlük-ˈwȯrm\ *adj* **1** : moderately warm : TEPID **2** : not enthusiastic — **luke·warm·ly** *adv*

¹lull \ˈləl\ *vb* **1** : SOOTHE, CALM **2** : to cause to relax vigilance

²lull *n* **1** : a temporary calm (as during a storm) **2** : a temporary drop in activity

lul·la·by \ˈlə l-ə-ˌbī\ *n, pl* **-bies** : a song to lull children to sleep

lum·ba·go \ˌləm-ˈbā-gō\ *n* : rheumatic pain in the lower back and loins

lum·bar \ˈləm-bər, -ˌbär\ *adj* : of, relating to, or constituting the loins or the vertebrae between the thoracic vertebrae and sacrum ⟨~ region⟩

¹lum·ber \ˈləm-bər\ *vb* **lum·bered; lum·ber·ing** \-b(ə-)riŋ\ : to move heavily or clumsily

²lumber *n* **1** : surplus or disused articles that are stored away **2** : timber esp. when dressed for use

³lumber *vb* **lum·bered; lum·ber·ing** \-b(ə-)riŋ\ : to cut logs; *also* : to saw logs into lumber — **lum·ber·man** \-mən\ *n*

lum·ber·jack \-ˌjak\ *n* : LOGGER

lum·ber·yard \-ˌyärd\ *n* : a place where lumber is kept for sale

lu·mi·nary \ˈlü-mə-ˌner-ē\ *n, pl* **-nar·ies 1** : a very famous person **2** : a source of light; *esp* : a celestial body

lu·mi·nes·cence \ˌ-ˈnes-ᵊns\ *n* : the low-temperature emission of light (as by a chemical or physiological process) — **lu·mi·nes·cent** \-ᵊnt\ *adj*

lu·mi·nous \ˈlü-mə-nəs\ *adj* **1** : emitting light; *also* : LIGHTED **2** : CLEAR, INTELLIGIBLE — **lu·mi·nance** \-nəns\ *n* — **lu·mi·nos·i·ty** \ˌlü-mə-ˈnäs-ət-ē\ *n* — **lu·mi·nous·ly** *adv*

lum·mox \'ləm-əks\ *n* : a clumsy person

¹lump \'ləmp\ *n* **1** : a piece or mass of irregular shape **2** : AGGREGATE, TOTALITY **3** : a usu. abnormal swelling — **lump·ish** *adj* — **lumpy** *adj*

²lump *vb* **1** : to leap together in a lump **2** : to form into lumps

³lump *adj* : not divided into parts (a ~ sum)

lu·na·cy \'lü-nə-sē\ *n, pl* **-cies 1** : INSANITY **2** : extreme folly

lu·nar \'lü-nər\ *adj* : of or relating to the moon

lu·na·tic \'lü-nə-ˌtik\ *adj* [ME *lunatik,* fr. LL *lunaticus,* fr. L *luna;* fr. the belief that lunacy fluctuated with the phases of the moon] **1** : INSANE; *also* : used for insane persons **2** : extremely foolish — **lunatic** *n*

¹lunch \'lənch\ *n* **1** : a light meal usu. eaten in the middle of the day **2** : the food prepared for a lunch

²lunch *vb* : to eat lunch

lun·cheon \'lən-chən\ *n* : a usu. formal lunch

lun·cheon·ette \ˌlən-chə-'net\ *n* : a small restaurant serving light lunches

lunch·room \'lənch-ˌrüm, -ˌrüm\ *n* **1** : LUNCHEONETTE **2** : a room (as in a school) where lunches are sold and eaten or lunches brought from home may be eaten

lu·nette \lü-'net\ *n* : something shaped like a crescent

lung \'ləŋ\ *n* **1** : one of the usu. paired baglike breathing organs in the chest of an air-breathing vertebrate **2** : a mechanical device for introducing fresh air into and removing stale air from the lungs — **lunged** \'ləŋd\ *adj*

lunge \'lənj\ *n* **1** : a sudden thrust or pass (as with a sword) **2** : a sudden forward stride or leap — **lunge** *vb*

lu·pine \'lü-pən\ *n* : any of a genus of leguminous plants with long upright clusters of pealike flowers

lu·pus \'lü-pəs\ *n* [ML, fr. L *wolf*] : any of several diseases (as systemic lupus erythematosus) characterized by skin lesions

lupus er·y·the·ma·to·sus \-ˌer-ə-ˌthē-mə-'tō-səs\ *n* : a disorder characterized by skin inflammation; *esp* : SYSTEMIC LUPUS ERYTHEMATOSUS

lurch \'lərch\ *n* : a sudden swaying or tipping movement — **lurch** *vb*

¹lure \'lu̇r\ *n* **1** : ENTICEMENT; *also* : APPEAL **2** : an artificial bait for catching fish

²lure *vb* **lured; lur·ing** : to draw on with a promise of pleasure or gain

lu·rid \'lu̇r-əd\ *adj* **1** : LIVID **2** : shining with the red glow of fire seen through smoke or cloud **3** : GRUESOME; *also* : SENSATIONAL **syn** ghastly, grisly, grim, horrible, macabre — **lu·rid·ly** *adv*

lurk \'lərk\ *vb* **1** : to move furtively : SNEAK **2** : to lie concealed

lus·cious \'ləsh-əs\ *adj* **1** : having a

pleasingly sweet taste or smell **2** : sensually appealing — **lus·cious·ly** *adv* — **lus·cious·ness** *n*

¹lush \'ləsh\ *adj* : having or covered with abundant growth (~ pastures)

²lush *n* : an habitual heavy drinker

lust \'ləst\ *n* **1** : sexual desire often to an intense or unrestrained degree **2** : an intense longing — **lust** *vb* — **lustful** *adj*

lus·ter *or* **lus·tre** \'ləs-tər\ *n* **1** : a shine or sheen esp. from reflected light **2** : BRIGHTNESS, GLITTER **3** : GLORY, SPLENDOR — **lus·ter·less** *adj* — **lus·trous** \-trəs\ *adj*

lus·tral \'ləs-trəl\ *adj* : PURIFICATORY

lusty \'ləs-tē\ *adj* **lust·i·er; -est** : full of vitality : ROBUST — **lust·i·ly** \'ləs-tə-lē\ *adv* — **lust·i·ness** \-tē-nəs\ *n*

lute \'lüt\ *n* : a stringed musical instrument with a large pear-shaped body and a fretted fingerboard — **lu·te·nist** *or* **lu·ta·nist** \'lüt-ᵊn-əst\ *n*

lu·te·tium *also* **lu·te·cium** \lü-'tē-sh(ē-)əm\ *n* : a rare metallic chemical element

Lu·ther·an \'lü-th(ə-)rən\ *n* : a member of a Protestant denomination adhering to the doctrines of Martin Luther — **Lu·ther·an·ism** \-ˌiz-əm\ *n*

lux·u·ri·ant \(ˌ)ləg-'zhu̇r-ē-ənt, ˌlək-'shu̇r-\ *adj* **1** : yielding or growing abundantly : LUSH, PRODUCTIVE **2** : abundantly rich and varied; *also* : FLORID — **lux·u·ri·ance** \-ē-əns\ *n* — **lux·u·ri·ant·ly** *adv*

lux·u·ri·ate \-ē-ˌāt\ *vb* **-at·ed; -at·ing 1** : to grow profusely **2** : REVEL

lux·u·ry \'ləksh-(ə-)rē, 'ləgzh-\ *n, pl* **-ries 1** : great ease and comfort **2** : something desirable but costly or hard to get **3** : something adding to pleasure or comfort but not absolutely necessary — **lux·u·ri·ous** \ˌləg-'zhu̇r-ē-əs, ˌlək-'shu̇r-\ *adj* — **lux·u·ri·ous·ly** *adv*

lv *abbr* leave

lwei \lə-'wā\ *n, pl* **lwei** — see *kwanza* at MONEY table

LWV *abbr* League of Women Voters

¹-ly \lē\ *adj suffix* **1** : like in appearance, manner, or nature (queen*ly*) **2** : characterized by regular recurrence in (specified) units of time : every (hour*ly*)

²-ly \lē *(corresponding adjectives may end in* əl, *as* "double"); *-ically is* i-k(ə-)lē\ *adv suffix* **1** : in a (specified) manner (slow*ly*) **2** : from a (specified) point of view (grammatical*ly*)

ly·ce·um \lī-'sē-əm, 'lī-sē-\ *n* **1** : a hall for public lectures **2** : an association providing public lectures, concerts, and entertainments

lye \'lī\ *n* : a white crystalline corrosive alkaline substance used in making rayon and soap

ly·ing \'lī-iŋ\ *adj* : UNTRUTHFUL, FALSE

ly·ing-in \ˌlī-iŋ-'in\ *n, pl* **lyings-in** *or* **lying-ins** : the state during and consequent to childbirth : CONFINEMENT

lymph \'limf\ *n* [L *lympha,* water goddess, water, fr. Gk *nymphē* nymph] : a pale liquid consisting chiefly of blood plasma and white blood cells, circulating in thin-walled tubes (**lymphatic vessels**), and bathing the body tissues — **lym·phat·ic** \lim-'fat-ik\ *adj*

lymph·ade·nop·a·thy \,lim-,fad-ᵊn-'äp-ə-thē\ *n, pl* **-thies** : abnormal enlargement of the lymph nodes

lymph node *n* : one of the rounded masses of lymphoid tissue surrounded by a capsule

lym·pho·cyte \'lim-fə-,sīt\ *n* : any of the weakly motile leukocytes produced in lymphoid tissue that are the typical cells in lymph and include the cellular mediators (as a B cell or a T cell) of immunity

lym·phoid \'lim-,fȯid\ *adj* **1** : of, relating to, or constituting the tissue characteristic of the lymph nodes **2** : of, relating to, or resembling lymph

lynch \'linch\ *vb* : to put to death by mob action without legal sanction or due process of law — **lynch·er** *n*

lynx \'liŋks\ *n, pl* **lynx** *or* **lynx·es** : a wildcat with a short tail, long legs, and usu. tufted ears

lyre \'lī(ə)r\ *n* : a stringed musical instrument of the harp class used by the ancient Greeks

¹lyr·ic \'lir-ik\ *n* **1** : a lyric poem **2** *pl* : the words of a popular song — **lyr·i·cal** \-i-kəl\ *adj*

²lyric *adj* **1** : suitable for singing : MELODIC **2** : expressing direct and usu. intense personal emotion

ly·ser·gic acid di·eth·yl·am·ide \lə-,sər-jik . . . ,dī-,eth-ə-'lam-,īd, lī-, -'lam-əd\ *n* : LSD

LZ *abbr* landing zone

M

¹m \'em\ *n, pl* **m's** *or* **ms** \'emz\ *often cap* : the 13th letter of the English alphabet

²m *abbr, often cap* **1** Mach **2** male **3** married **4** masculine **5** medium **6** [L *meridies*] noon **7** meter **8** mile **9** [L *mille*] thousand **10** minute **11** month **12** moon

ma \'mä, 'mȯ\ *n* **1** : MOTHER

MA *abbr* **1** [ML *magister artium*] master of arts **2** Massachusetts **3** mental age

ma'am \'mam, *after* "yes" *often* əm\ *n* : MADAM

Mac *or* **Macc** *abbr* Maccabees

ma·ca·bre \mə-'käb(-rə), -'käb-ər\ *adj* [F] **1** : having death as a subject **2** : GRUESOME **3** : HORRIBLE

mac·ad·am \mə-'kad-əm\ *n* **1** : a roadway or pavement of small closely packed broken stone **2** : the broken stone used in macadamizing — **mac·ad·am·ize** \-,īz\ *vb*

ma·caque \mə-'kak, -'käk\ *n* : any of several short-tailed Asian and East Indian monkeys

mac·a·ro·ni \,mak-ə-'rō-nē\ *n* **1** : a food made chiefly of wheat flour dried in the form of usu. slender tubes **2** *pl* **-nis** *or* **-nies** : FOP, DANDY

mac·a·roon \,mak-ə-'rün\ *n* : a small cookie made chiefly of egg whites, sugar, and ground almonds or coconut

ma·caw \mə-'kȯ\ *n* : a large long-tailed parrot of Central and So. America

Mac·ca·bees \'mak-ə-,bēz\ *n* — see BIBLE table

Mc·Coy \mə-'kȯi\ *n* [alter. of *Mackay* (in the phrase *the real Mackay* the true chief of the Mackay clan, a position often disputed)] : something that is neither imitation nor substitute (the real ∼)

¹mace \'mās\ *n* **1** : a heavy often spiked

club used as a weapon esp. in the Middle Ages **2** : an ornamental staff carried as a symbol of authority

²mace *n* : a spice from the fibrous coating of the nutmeg

mac·er·ate \'mas-ə-,rāt\ *vb* **-at·ed; -at·ing 1** : to cause to waste away **2** : to soften by steeping or soaking so as to separate the parts — **mac·er·a·tion** \,mas-ə-'rā-shən\ *n*

mach *abbr* machine; machinery; machinist

Mach \'mäk\ *n* : MACH NUMBER

Mach·a·bees \'mak-ə-,bēz\ *n* — see BIBLE table

ma·che·te \mə-'shet-ē\ *n* : a large heavy knife used for cutting sugarcane and underbrush and as a weapon

Ma·chi·a·vel·lian \,mak-ē-ə-'vel-ē-ən\ *adj* [Niccolo *Machiavelli,* †1527 Ital. political philosopher] : characterized by cunning, duplicity, and bad faith — **Ma·chi·a·vel·lian·ism** *n*

mach·i·na·tion \,mak-ə-'nā-shən, ,mash-ə-\ *n* : an act of planning esp. to do harm; *esp* : PLOT — **mach·i·nate** \'mak-ə-,nāt, 'mash-\ *vb*

¹ma·chine \mə-'shēn\ *n* **1** : CONVEYANCE, VEHICLE; *esp* : AUTOMOBILE **2** : a combination of mechanical parts that transmit forces, motion, and energy to do some desired work (a sewing ∼) **3** : an instrument (as a pulley or lever) for transmitting or modifying force or motion **4** : an electrical, electronic, or mechanical device for performing a task (a calculating ∼) **5** : a highly organized political group under the leadership of a boss or small clique

²machine *vb* **ma·chined; ma·chin·ing** : to shape or finish by machine-operated tools — **ma·chin·able** \-'shē-nə-bəl\ *adj*

machine gun *n* : an automatic gun capable of rapid continuous firing —

machine–gun *vb* — **machine gunner** *n*

machine language *n* : the set of symbolic instruction codes usu. in binary form that is used to represent operations and data in a machine (as a computer)

machine–readable *adj* : directly usable by a computer

ma·chin·ery \mə-'shēn-(ə-)rē\ *n, pl* **-eries 1** : MACHINES; *also* : the working parts of a machine **2** : the means by which something is done

ma·chin·ist \mə-'shē-nəst\ *n* : a person who makes or works on machines

ma·chis·mo \mä-'chēz-(ˌ)mō, -'chiz-\ *n* : a strong or exaggerated pride in one's masculinity

Mach number \'mäk-\ *n* : a number representing the ratio of the speed of a body to the speed of sound in the surrounding atmosphere (a *Mach number* of 2 indicates a speed that is twice the speed of sound)

ma·cho \'mä-chō\ *adj* [Sp, male, fr. L *masculus*] : characterized by machismo

mack·er·el \'mak-(ə-)rəl\ *n, pl* **mackerel** *or* **mackerels** : a No. Atlantic food fish greenish above and silvery below

mack·i·naw \'mak-ə-ˌnȯ\ *n* : a short heavy plaid coat

mack·in·tosh *also* **mac·in·tosh** \'mak-ən-ˌtäsh\ *n* **1** *chiefly Brit* : RAINCOAT **2** : a lightweight waterproof fabric

mac·ra·mé *also* **mac·ra·me** \'mak-rə-ˌmā\ *n* [deriv. of Ar *miqramah* embroidered veil] : a coarse lace or fringe made by knotting threads or cords in a geometrical pattern

mac·ro \'mak-(ˌ)rō\ *adj* : very large; *also* : involving large quantities or being on a large scale

mac·ro·bi·ot·ic \ˌmak-rō-bī-'ät-ik, -bē-\ *adj* : relating to or being a very restricted diet (as one containing chiefly whole grains)

mac·ro·cosm \'mak-rə-ˌkäz-əm\ *n* : the great world : UNIVERSE

ma·cron \'māk-ˌrän, 'mak-\ *n* : a mark placed over a vowel (as in \mäk\) to show that the vowel is long

mac·ro·scop·ic \ˌmak-rə-'skäp-ik\ *adj* : visible to the naked eye — **mac·ro·scop·i·cal·ly** \-i-k(ə-)lē\ *adv*

mad \'mad\ *adj* **mad·der; mad·dest 1** : disordered in mind : INSANE **2** : being rash and foolish **3** : FURIOUS, ENRAGED **4** : carried away by enthusiasm **5** : RABID **6** : marked by wild gaiety and merriment **7** : FRANTIC — **mad·ly** *adv* — **mad·ness** *n*

Mad·a·gas·can \ˌmad-ə-'gas-kən\ *n* : a native or inhabitant of Madagascar

mad·am \'mad-əm\ *n* **1** *pl* **mes·dames** \mā-'däm\ — used as a form of polite address to a woman **2** *pl* **madams** : the female head of a house of prostitution

ma·dame \mə-'dam, *before a surname also* ˌmad-əm\ *n, pl* **mes·dames** \mā-'däm\ : MISTRESS — used as a title for

a woman not of English-speaking nationality

mad·cap \'mad-ˌkap\ *adj* : WILD, RECKLESS — **madcap** *n*

mad·den \'mad-ᵊn\ *vb* **mad·dened; mad·den·ing** \'mad-(ᵊ-)niŋ\ : to make mad — **mad·den·ing·ly** *adv*

mad·der \'mad-ər\ *n* : a Eurasian plant with yellow flowers and fleshy red roots; *also* : its root or a dye prepared from it

made *past and past part of* MAKE

Ma·dei·ra \mə-'dir-ə\ *n* : an amber-colored dessert wine

ma·de·moi·selle \ˌmad-(ə-)m(w)ə-'zel, mam-'zel\ *n, pl* **ma·de·moi·selles** \-'zelz\ *or* **mes·de·moi·selles** \ˌmād-(ə-)m(w)ə-'zel\ : an unmarried girl or woman — used as a title for an unmarried woman not of English-speaking and esp. of French nationality

made–up \'mād-'əp\ *adj* **1** : marked by the use of makeup **2** : fancifully conceived or falsely devised

mad·house \'mad-ˌhau̇s\ *n* **1** : a place for the detention and care of the insane **2** : a place of great uproar

mad·man \'mad-ˌman, -mən\ *n* : LUNATIC

ma·don·na \mə-'dän-ə\ *n* : a representation (as a picture or statue) of the Virgin Mary

ma·dras \'mad-rəs; mə-'dras, -'dräs\ *n* [*Madras*, India] : a fine usu. cotton fabric with various designs (as plaid)

mad·ri·gal \'mad-ri-gəl\ *n* [It *madrigale*] : a somewhat elaborate part-song esp. of the 16th century; *also* : a love poem suitable for a musical setting

mad·wom·an \'mad-ˌwu̇m-ən\ *n* : a woman who is insane

mael·strom \'māl-strəm\ *n* : a violent whirlpool

mae·stro \'mī-strō\ *n, pl* **maestros** *or* **mae·stri** \-ˌstrē\ [It] : a master in an art; *esp* : an eminent composer, conductor, or teacher of music

Ma·fia \'mäf-ē-ə\ *n* [It] **1** : a secret society of political terrorists **2** : a secret criminal organization

ma·fi·o·so \ˌmäf-ē-'ō-(ˌ)sō\ *n, pl* **-si** \-(ˌ)sē\ : a member of the Mafia

¹mag *abbr* **1** magnetism **2** magneto **3** magnitude

²mag \'mag\ *n* : MAGAZINE

mag·a·zine \'mag-ə-ˌzēn\ *n* **1** : a storehouse esp. for military supplies **2** : a place for keeping gunpowder in a fort or ship **3** : a publication usu. containing stories, articles, or poems and issued periodically **4** : a container in a gun for holding cartridges; *also* : a chamber (as on a camera) for film

ma·gen·ta \mə-'jent-ə\ *n* : a deep purplish red

mag·got \'mag-ət\ *n* : the legless wormlike larva of a two-winged fly — **mag·goty** *adj*

ma·gi \'mā-ˌjī\ *n pl, often cap* : the three

wise men from the East who paid homage to the infant Jesus

mag·ic \'maj-ik\ *n* **1** : the art of persons who claim to be able to do things by the help of supernatural powers or by their own knowledge of nature's secrets **2** : an extraordinary power or influence seemingly from a supernatural force **3** : SLEIGHT OF HAND — **magic** *adj* — **mag·i·cal** \-i-kəl\ *adj* — **mag·i·cal·ly** \-i-k(ə-)lē\ *adv*

ma·gi·cian \mə-'jish-ən\ *n* : one skilled in magic

mag·is·te·ri·al \,maj-ə-'stir-ē-əl\ *adj* **1** : AUTHORITATIVE **2** : of or relating to a magistrate or his office or duties

ma·gis·tral \'maj-ə-strəl\ *adj* : AUTHORITATIVE

mag·is·trate \'maj-ə-,strāt\ *n* : an official entrusted with administration of the laws — **mag·is·tra·cy** \-strə-sē\ *n*

mag·ma \'mag-mə\ *n* : molten rock material within the earth — **mag·mat·ic** \mag-'mat-ik\ *adj*

mag·nan·i·mous \mag-'nan-ə-məs\ *adj* **1** : showing or suggesting a lofty and courageous spirit **2** : NOBLE, GENEROUS — **mag·na·nim·i·ty** \,mag-nə-'nim-ət-ē\ *n* — **mag·nan·i·mous·ly** *adv* — **mag·nan·i·mous·ness** *n*

mag·nate \'mag-,nāt\ *n* : a person of rank, influence, or distinction

mag·ne·sia \mag-'nē-shə, -zhə\ *n* [NL, fr. *magnes carneus*, a white earth, lit., flesh magnet] : a light white substance that is an oxide of magnesium and is used as a laxative

mag·ne·sium \mag-'nē-zē-əm, -zhəm\ *n* : a silver-white light and easily worked metallic chemical element

mag·net \'mag-nət\ *n* **1** : LODESTONE **2** : a body that is able to attract iron **3** : something that attracts

mag·net·ic \mag-'net-ik\ *adj* **1** : of or relating to a magnet or magnetism **2** : magnetized or capable of being magnetized **3** : having an unusual ability to attract (a ~ leader) — **mag·net·i·cal·ly** \-i-k(ə-)lē\ *adv*

magnetic disk *n* : DISK 3

magnetic north *n* : the northerly direction in the earth's magnetic field indicated by the north-seeking pole of a horizontal magnetic needle

magnetic tape *n* : a ribbon coated with a magnetic material on which information (as sound) may be stored

mag·ne·tism \'mag-nə-,tiz-əm\ *n* **1** : the power to attract as possessed by a magnet **2** : the science that deals with magnetic phenomena **3** : an ability to attract

mag·ne·tite \'mag-nə-,tīt\ *n* : a black mineral that is an important iron ore

mag·ne·tize \'mag-nə-,tīz\ *vb* **-tized; -tiz·ing 1** : to induce magnetic properties in **2** : to attract like a magnet : CHARM — **mag·ne·tiz·able** *adj* — **mag·ne·ti·za·tion** \,mag-nət-ə-'zā-shən\ *n* — **mag·ne·tiz·er** *n*

mag·ne·to \mag-'nēt-ō\ *n, pl* **-tos** : a

generator used to produce sparks in an internal-combustion engine

mag·ne·tom·e·ter \,mag-nə-'täm-ət-ər\ *n* : an instrument for measuring the strength of a magnetic field

mag·ne·to·sphere \mag-'nēt-ə-,sfiər, -'net-\ *n* : a region of the upper atmosphere that extends out for thousands of miles and in which charged particles are trapped by the earth's magnetic field — **mag·ne·to·spher·ic** \-,nēt-ə-'sfiər-ik, -'sfer-\ *adj*

mag·nif·i·cent \mag-'nif-ə-sənt\ *adj* **1** : characterized by grandeur or beauty : SPLENDID **2** : EXALTED, NOBLE **syn** imposing, stately, noble, grand, majestic — **mag·nif·i·cence** \-səns\ *n* — **mag·nif·i·cent·ly** *adv*

mag·nif·i·co \mag-'nif-i-,kō\ *n, pl* **-coes** *or* **-cos 1** : a nobleman of Venice **2** : a person of high position

mag·ni·fy \'mag-nə-,fī\ *vb* **-fied; -fy·ing 1** : EXTOL, LAUD; *also* : to cause to be held in greater esteem **2** : INTENSIFY; *also* : EXAGGERATE **3** : to enlarge in fact or in appearance (a microscope *magnifies* an object) — **mag·ni·fi·ca·tion** \,mag-nə-fə-'kā-shən\ *n* — **mag·ni·fi·er** \'mag-nə-,fī(-ə)r\ *n*

mag·nil·o·quent \mag-'nil-ə-kwənt\ *adj* : characterized by an exalted and often bombastic style or manner — **mag·nil·o·quence** \-kwəns\ *n*

mag·ni·tude \'mag-nə-,t(y)üd\ *n* **1** : greatness of size or extent **2** : SIZE **3** : QUANTITY **4** : a number representing the brightness of a celestial body

mag·no·lia \mag-'nōl-yə\ *n* : any of several spring-flowering shrubs and trees with large often fragrant flowers

mag·num opus \,mag-nəm-'ō-pəs\ *n* [L] : the greatest achievement of an artist or writer

mag·pie \'mag-,pī\ *n* : a long-tailed black-and-white bird related to the jays

Mag·yar \'mag-,yär, 'mäg-; 'mäj-,är\ *n* : a member of the dominant people of Hungary — **Magyar** *adj*

ma·ha·ra·ja *or* **ma·ha·ra·jah** \,mä-hə-'räj-ə\ *n* : a Hindu prince ranking above a raja

ma·ha·ra·ni *or* **ma·ha·ra·nee** \-'rän-ē\ *n* : the wife of a maharaja; *also* : a Hindu princess ranking above a rani

ma·ha·ri·shi \,mä-hə-'rē-shē\ *n* : a Hindu teacher of mystical knowledge

ma·hat·ma \mə-'hät-mə, -'hat-\ *n* [Skt *mahātman*, fr. *mahātman* great-souled, fr. *mahat* great + *ātman* soul] : a person revered for high-mindedness, wisdom, and selflessness

Ma·hi·can \mə-'hē-kən\ *n, pl* **Mahican** *or* **Mahicans** : a member of an American Indian people of the upper Hudson river valley

ma·hog·a·ny \mə-'häg-ə-nē\ *n, pl* **-nies** : any of various tropical trees with reddish wood used in furniture; *esp* : an American evergreen tree or its durable lustrous brown wood

ma·hout \mə-ˈhau̇t\ n [Hindi mahāut] : a keeper and driver of an elephant

maid \ˈmād\ n 1 : an unmarried girl or young woman 2 : a female servant

¹**maid·en** \ˈmād-ᵊn\ n : MAID 1 — **maid·en·ly** adj

²**maiden** adj 1 : UNMARRIED; also : VIRGIN 2 : of, relating to, or befitting a maiden 3 : FIRST ⟨~ voyage⟩

maid·en·hair \-ˌhaer\ n : a fern with delicate feathery fronds

maid·en·head \ˈmād-ᵊn-ˌhed\ n 1 : VIRGINITY 2 : HYMEN

maid·en·hood \-ˌhu̇d\ n : the condition or time of being a maiden

maid–in–wait·ing \ˌmād-ᵊn-ˈwāt-iŋ\ n, pl **maids–in–wait·ing** \ˌmād-zᵊn-\ : a young woman appointed to attend a queen or princess

maid of honor : a bride's principal unmarried wedding attendant

maid·ser·vant \ˈmād-ˌsər-vənt\ n : a female servant

¹**mail** \ˈmāl\ n [ME male, fr. OF] 1 : something sent or carried in the postal system 2 : a nation's postal system — often used in pl.

²**mail** vb : to send by mail

³**mail** n [ME maille, fr. MF, fr. L macula spot, mesh] : armor made of metal links or plates

mail·box \-ˌbäks\ n 1 : a public box for the collection of mail 2 : a private box for the delivery of mail

mail·man \-ˌman\ n : a man who delivers mail

maim \ˈmām\ vb : to mutilate, disfigure, or wound seriously : CRIPPLE

¹**main** \ˈmān\ n 1 : FORCE ⟨with might and ~⟩ 2 : MAINLAND; also : HIGH SEA 3 : the chief part 4 : a principal pipe, duct, or circuit of a utility system

²**main** adj 1 : CHIEF, PRINCIPAL 2 : fully exerted ⟨~ force⟩ 3 : expressing the chief predication in a complex sentence ⟨the ~ clause⟩ — **main·ly** adv

main·frame \ˈmān-ˌfrām\ n : a large fast computer

main·land \ˈmān-ˌland, -lənd\ n : a continuous body of land constituting the chief part of a country or continent

main·line \ˈmān-ˈlīn\ vb, slang : to inject a narcotic drug into a vein

main line n : a principal highway or railroad line

main·mast \ˈmān-ˌmast, -məst\ n : the principal mast on a sailing ship

main·sail \ˈmān-ˌsāl, -səl\ n : the largest sail on the mainmast

main·spring \-ˌspriŋ\ n 1 : the chief spring in a mechanism (as of a watch) 2 : the chief motive, agent, or cause

main·stay \-ˌstā\ n 1 : a stay running from the head of the mainmast to the foot of the foremast 2 : a chief support

main·stream \-ˌstrēm\ n : a prevailing current or direction of activity or influence — **mainstream** adj

main·tain \mān-ˈtān\ vb [ME maintenen, fr. OF maintenir, fr. ML manu-

tenēre, fr. L manu tenēre to hold in the hand] 1 : to keep in an existing state (as of repair) 2 : to sustain against opposition or danger 3 : to continue in : CARRY ON 4 : to provide for : SUPPORT 5 : ASSERT — **main·tain·abil·i·ty** \-ˌtā-nə-ˈbil-ət-ē\ n — **main·tain·able** \-ˈtā-nə-bəl\ adj — **main·te·nance** \ˈmānt-(ᵊ-)nəns\ n

main·top \ˈmān-ˌtäp\ n : a platform at the head of the mainmast of a square-rigged ship

mai·son·ette \ˌmāz-ᵊn-ˈet\ n 1 : a small house 2 : an apartment often on two floors

maî·tre d' or **mai·tre d'** \ˌmā-trə-ˈdē, ˌme-\ n, pl **maître d's** or **maitre d's** \-ˈdēz\ : MAÎTRE D'HÔTEL

maî·tre d'hô·tel \ˌmā-trə-dō-ˈtel, ˌme-\ n, pl **maîtres d'hôtel** \same\ [F, lit., master of house] 1 : MAJORDOMO 2 : the head of a dining-room staff (as of a hotel)

maize \ˈmāz\ n : INDIAN CORN

Maj abbr major

maj·es·ty \ˈmaj-ə-stē\ n, pl **-ties** 1 : sovereign power, authority, or dignity; also : the person of a sovereign — used as a title 2 : GRANDEUR, SPLENDOR — **ma·jes·tic** \mə-ˈjes-tik\ adj — **ma·jes·ti·cal·ly** \-ti-k(ə-)lē\ adv

Maj Gen abbr Major General

ma·jol·i·ca \mə-ˈjäl-i-kə\ also **ma·iol·i·ca** \-ˈyäl-\ n : any of several faiences; esp : an Italian tin-glazed pottery

¹**ma·jor** \ˈmā-jər\ adj 1 : greater in number, extent, or importance ⟨a ~ poet⟩ 2 : notable or conspicuous in effect or scope ⟨a ~ campaign⟩ 3 : SERIOUS ⟨a ~ illness⟩ 4 : having half steps between the 3d and 4th and the 7th and 8th degrees ⟨~ scale⟩; also : based on a major scale ⟨~ key⟩ ⟨~ chord⟩

²**major** n 1 : a commissioned officer (as in the army) ranking next below a lieutenant colonel 2 : a subject of academic study chosen as a field of specialization; also : a student specializing in such a field

³**major** vb **ma·jored; ma·jor·ing** \ˈmāj-(ə-)riŋ\ : to pursue an academic major

ma·jor·do·mo \ˌmā-jər-ˈdō-mō\ n, pl **-mos** [Sp mayordomo or obs. It maiordomo, fr. ML major domus, lit., chief of the house] 1 : a head steward 2 : BUTLER

majorette n : DRUM MAJORETTE

major general n : a commissioned officer (as in the army) ranking next below a lieutenant general

ma·jor·i·ty \mə-ˈjȯr-ət-ē\ n, pl **-ties** 1 : the age at which full civil rights are accorded; also : the status of one who has attained this age 2 : a number greater than half of a total; also : the excess of this greater number over the remainder 3 : the military rank of a major

major–medical adj : of, relating to, or being a form of insurance designed to pay all or part of the medical bills of major illnesses usu. after deduction of a fixed initial sum

ma·jus·cule \'maj-əs-ˌkyül, mə-'jəs-\ *n* : a large letter (as a capital)

¹**make** \'māk\ *vb* **made** \'mād\ ; **mak·ing** **1** : to cause to exist, occur, or appear; *also* : DESTINE (was *made* to be an actor) **2** : FASHION (~ a dress) ; *also* : COMPOSE **3** : to formulate in the mind (~ plans) **4** : CONSTITUTE (house *made* of stone) **5** : to compute to be **6** : to set in order : PREPARE (~ a bed) **7** : to cause to be or become; *also* : APPOINT **8** : ENACT; *also* : EXECUTE (~ a will) **9** : CONCLUDE (didn't know what to ~ of it) **10** : to carry out : PERFORM (~ a speech) **11** : COMPEL **12** : to assure the success of (anyone he likes is *made*) **13** : to amount to in significance (~s no difference) **14** : to be capable of developing or being fashioned into **15** : REACH, ATTAIN; *also* : GAIN **16** : to start out : GO **17** : to have weight or effect (courtesy ~s for safer driving) **syn** form, shape, fabricate, manufacture — **mak·er** *n* — **make believe** : PRETEND — **make do** : to manage with the means at hand — **make fun of** : RIDICULE, MOCK — **make good 1** : INDEMNIFY (*make good* the loss) ; *also* : to carry out successfully (*make good* his promise) **2** : SUCCEED — **make way 1** : to give room for passing, entering, or occupying **2** : to make progress

²**make** *n* **1** : the manner or style of construction; *also* : BRAND **3 2** : MAKEUP **3** : the action of manufacturing — **on the make** : in search of wealth, social status, or sexual adventure

¹**make–be·lieve** \'māk-bə-ˌlēv\ *n* : a pretending to believe : PRETENSE

²**make–believe** *adj* : IMAGINED, PRETENDED

make–do \-ˌdü\ *adj* : MAKESHIFT

make out *vb* **1** : to draw up in writing (*make out* a shopping list) **2** : to find or grasp the meaning of (how do you *make* that out) **3** : to pretend to be true **4** : DISCERN (*make out* a form in the fog) **5** : GET ALONG, FARE (*make out* well in business) **6** : to engage in amorous kissing and caressing

make over *vb* : REMAKE, REMODEL

make·shift \'māk-ˌshift\ *n* : a temporary expedient — **makeshift** *adj*

make–up \-ˌəp\ *n* **1** : the way in which something is put together; *also* : physical, mental, and moral constitution **2** : cosmetics esp. for the face; *also* : materials (as wigs and cosmetics) used in costuming (as for a play)

make up \(ˈ)māk-'əp\ *vb* **1** : FORM, COMPOSE **2** : to compensate for a deficiency **3** : SETTLE (*made up* my mind) **4** : INVENT, IMPROVISE **5** : to become reconciled **6** : to put on makeup

make–work \'māk-ˌwərk\ *n* : assigned busywork

mak·ings \'mā-kiŋz\ *n pl* : the material from which something is made

makuta *pl of* LIKUTA

Mal *abbr* Malachi

Mal·a·chi \'mal-ə-ˌkī\ *n* — see BIBLE table

Mal·a·chias \ˌmal-ə-'kī-əs\ *n* — see BIBLE table

mal·a·chite \'mal-ə-ˌkīt\ *n* : a mineral that is a green carbonate of copper used for making ornamental objects

mal·adapt·ed \ˌmal-ə-'dap-təd\ *adj* : poorly suited to a particular use, purpose, or situation

mal·ad·just·ed \ˌmal-ə-'jəs-təd\ *adj* : poorly or inadequately adjusted (as to one's environment) — **mal·ad·just·ment** \-'jəs(t)-mənt\ *n*

mal·adroit \ˌmal-ə-'droit\ *adj* : not adroit : INEPT

mal·a·dy \'mal-əd-ē\ *n, pl* **-dies** : a disease or disorder of body or mind

mal·aise \mə-'lāz, ma-\ *n* [F] : a vague feeling of bodily or mental disorder

mal·a·mute \'mal-ə-ˌmyüt\ *n* : a dog often used to draw sleds esp. in northern No. America

mal·a·prop·ism \'mal-ə-ˌpräp-ˌiz-əm\ *n* : a usu. humorous misuse of a word

mal·ap·ro·pos \ˌmal-ˌap-rə-'pō, ˌmal-'ap-rə-ˌpō\ *adv* : in an inappropriate or inopportune way — **malapropos** *adj*

ma·lar·ia \mə-'ler-ē-ə\ *n* [It, fr. *mala aria* bad air] : a disease marked by recurring chills and fever and caused by a parasite carried by a mosquito — **ma·lar·i·al** \-ē-əl\ *adj*

ma·lar·key \mə-'lär-kē\ *n* : insincere or foolish talk

mal·a·thi·on \ˌmal-ə-'thī-ən, -ˌän\ *n* : an insecticide with a relatively low toxicity for mammals

Ma·la·wi·an \mə-'lä-wē-ən\ *n* : a native or inhabitant of Malawi — **Malawian** *adj*

Ma·lay \mə-'lā, 'mā-ˌlā\ *n* **1** : a member of a people of the Malay peninsula and archipelago **2** : the language of the Malays — **Malay** *adj* — **Ma·lay·an** \mə-'lā-ən, 'mā-ˌlā-\ *n or adj*

Ma·lay·sian \mə-'lā-zhən, -shən\ *n* : a native or inhabitant of Malaysia — **Malaysian** *adj*

mal·con·tent \ˌmal-kən-'tent\ *adj* : marked by a dissatisfaction with the existing state of affairs : DISCONTENTED — **malcontent** *n*

mal de mer \ˌmal-də-'meər\ *n* : SEASICKNESS

¹**male** \'māl\ *adj* **1** : of, relating to, or being the sex that begets young; *also* : STAMINATE **2** : MASCULINE — **male·ness** *n*

²**male** *n* : a male individual

male·dic·tion \ˌmal-ə-'dik-shən\ *n* : CURSE, EXECRATION

male·fac·tor \'mal-ə-ˌfak-tər\ *n* : EVILDOER; *esp* : one who commits an offense against the law — **male·fac·tion** \ˌmal-ə-'fak-shən\ *n*

ma·lef·ic \mə-'lef-ik\ *adj* **1** : BALEFUL **2** : MALICIOUS

ma·lef·i·cent \-ə-sənt\ *adj* : working or productive of harm or evil

ma·lev·o·lent \mə-'lev-ə-lənt\ *adj* : having, showing, or arising from ill will, spite, or hatred syn malignant, malign, malicious, spiteful — **ma·lev·o·lence** \-ləns\ *n*

mal·fea·sance \mal-'fēz-ᵊns\ *n* : wrongful conduct esp. by a public official

mal·for·ma·tion \ˌmal-fȯr-'mā-shən\ *n* : an irregular or faulty formation or structure — **mal·formed** \-'fȯrmd\ *adj*

mal·func·tion \mal-'fəŋk-shən\ *vb* : to fail to operate in the normal or usual manner — **malfunction** *n*

Ma·li·an \'mäl-ē-ən\ *n* : a native or inhabitant of Mali — **Malian** *adj*

mal·ice \'mal-əs\ *n* : ILL WILL — **ma·li·cious** \mə-'lish-əs\ *adj* — **ma·li·cious·ly** *adv*

¹**ma·lign** \mə-'līn\ *adj* **1** : evil in nature, influence, or effect (hindered by ~ influences) ; *also* : MALIGNANT **2 2** : moved by ill will toward others

²**malign** *vb* : to speak evil of : DEFAME

ma·lig·nant \mə-'lig-nənt\ *adj* **1** : INJURIOUS, MALIGN **2** : tending or likely to cause death : VIRULENT — **ma·lig·nan·cy** \-nən-sē\ *n* — **ma·lig·nant·ly** *adv* — **ma·lig·ni·ty** \-nət-ē\ *n*

ma·lin·ger \mə-'liŋ-gər\ *vb* -**gered**; -**ger·ing** \-g(ə-)riŋ\ [F *malingre* sickly] : to pretend illness so as to avoid duty — **ma·lin·ger·er** *n*

mal·i·son \'mal-ə-sən, -zən\ *n* : CURSE

mall \'mȯl, 'mal\ *n* **1** : a shaded walk : PROMENADE **2** : an urban shopping area featuring a variety of shops surrounding a concourse **3** : a usu. large enclosed suburban shopping area containing various shops

mal·lard \'mal-ərd\ *n, pl* **mallard** *or* **mallards** : a common wild duck that is the ancestor of domestic ducks

mal·lea·ble \'mal-ē-ə-bəl\ *adj* **1** : capable of being extended or shaped by beating with a hammer or by the pressure of rollers **2** : ADAPTABLE, PLIABLE syn plastic, pliant, ductile, supple — **mal·le·a·bil·i·ty** \ˌmal-ē-ə-'bil-ət-ē\ *n*

mal·let \'mal-ət\ *n* **1** : a tool with a large head for driving another tool or for striking a surface without marring it **2** : a hammerlike implement for striking a ball (as in polo or croquet)

mal·le·us \'mal-ē-əs\ *n, pl* **mal·lei** \-ē-ˌī -ē-ˌē\ [NL, fr. L, hammer] : the outermost of the three small bones of the mammalian ear

mal·low \'mal-ō\ *n* : any of several tall herbs with lobed leaves and 5-petaled white, yellow, rose, or purplish flowers

malm·sey \'mä(l)m-zē\ *n, often cap* : the sweetest variety of Madeira wine

mal·nour·ished \mal-'nər-isht\ *adj* : poorly nourished

mal·nu·tri·tion \ˌmal-n(y)ü-'trish-ən\ *n* : faulty and esp. inadequate nutrition

mal·oc·clu·sion \ˌmal-ə-'klü-zhən\ *n* : faulty coming together of teeth in biting

mal·odor·ous \mal-'ōd-ə-rəs\ *adj* : ill-smelling — **mal·odor·ous·ly** *adv* — **mal·odor·ous·ness** *n*

ma·lo·ti \mə-'lōt-ē\ *pl of* LOTI

mal·prac·tice \mal-'prak-təs\ *n* : a dereliction of professional duty or a failure of professional skill that results in injury, loss, or damage

malt \'mȯlt\ *n* **1** : grain and esp. barley steeped in water until it has sprouted and used in brewing and distilling **2** : liquor made with malt — **malty** *adj*

malted milk \ˌmȯl-təd-\ *n* : a powder prepared from dried milk and an extract from malt; *also* : a beverage of this powder in milk or other liquid

Mal·thu·sian \mal-'th(y)ü-zhən\ *adj* : of or relating to Malthus or his theory that population unless checked (as by war) tends to increase faster than its means of subsistence — **Malthusian** *n* — **Mal·thu·sian·ism** \-zhə-ˌniz-əm\ *n*

malt·ose \'mȯl-ˌtōs\ *n* : a sugar formed esp. from starch by the action of enzymes and used in brewing and distilling

mal·treat \mal-'trēt\ *vb* : to treat cruelly or roughly : ABUSE — **mal·treat·ment** *n*

ma·ma *or* **mam·ma** \'mäm-ə\ *n* : MOTHER

mam·bo \'mäm-bō\ *n, pl* **mambos** : a dance of Cuban origin related to the rumba — **mambo** *vb*

mam·mal \'mam-əl\ *n* : any of the group of vertebrate animals that includes man and all others which nourish their young with milk — **mam·ma·li·an** \mə-'mā-lē-ən, ma-\ *adj or n*

mam·ma·ry \'mam-ə-rē\ *adj* : of, relating to, or being the glands (**mammary glands**) that in female mammals secrete milk

mam·mo·gram \'mam-ə-ˌgram\ *n* : a photograph of the breasts made by X rays

mam·mog·ra·phy \ma-'mäg-rə-fē\ *n, pl* -**phies** : X-ray examination of the breasts (as for early detection of cancer)

mam·mon \'mam-ən\ *n, often cap* : material wealth having a debasing influence

¹**mam·moth** \'mam-əth\ *n* : any of various large hairy extinct elephants

²**mammoth** *adj* : of very great size : GIGANTIC syn colossal, enormous, immense, vast, elephantine

¹**man** \'man\ *n, pl* **men** \'men\ **1** : a human being; *esp* : an adult male **2** : MANKIND **3** : one possessing in high degree the qualities considered distinctive of manhood; *also* : HUSBAND **4** : an adult male servant or employee **5** : one of the pieces with which various games (as chess) are played **6** *often cap* : white society or people

²**man** *vb* **manned**; **man·ning 1** : to supply with men (~ a fleet) **2** : FORTIFY, BRACE

³**man** *abbr* manual

Man *abbr* Manitoba

man–about–town \,man-ə-,baut-'taun\ *n, pl* **men–about–town** \,men-\ : a worldly and socially active man

man·a·cle \'man-i-kəl\ *n* 1 : a shackle for the hand or wrist 2 : something used as a restraint

man·age \'man-ij\ *vb* **man·aged; man·ag·ing** 1 : HANDLE, CONTROL; *also* : to direct or carry on business or affairs 2 : to make and keep submissive 3 : to treat with care : HUSBAND 4 : to achieve one's purpose : CONTRIVE — **man·age·abil·i·ty** \,man-ij-ə-'bil-ət-ē\ *n* — **man·age·able** \'man-ij-ə-bəl\ *adj* — **man·age·able·ness** *n* — **man·age·ably** \-blē\ *adv*

man·age·ment \'man-ij-mənt\ *n* 1 : the act or art of managing : CONTROL 2 : judicious use of means to accomplish an end 3 : executive ability 4 : the group of those who manage or direct an enterprise

man·ag·er \'man-ij-ər\ *n* : one that manages — **man·a·ge·ri·al** \,man-ə-'jir-ē-əl\ *adj*

ma·ña·na \mən-'yän-ə\ [Sp., lit., to-morrow] *n* : an indefinite time in the future

man–at–arms \,man-ət-'ärmz\ *n, pl* **men–at–arms** \,men-\ : SOLDIER; *esp* : one who is heavily armed and mounted

Man·chu·ri·an \man-'chur-ē-ən\ *n* : a native or inhabitant of Manchuria, China — **Manchurian** *adj*

man·ci·ple \'man-sə-pəl\ *n* : a steward or purveyor esp. for a college or monastery

man·da·mus \man-'dä-məs\ *n* [L, we enjoin, fr. *mandare*] : a writ issued by a superior court commanding that an official act or duty be performed

man·da·rin \'man-də-rən\ *n* 1 : a public official of high rank under the Chinese Empire 2 *cap* : the chief dialect of China 3 : a reddish orange to yellow loose-skinned citrus fruit; *also* : a tree that bears mandarins

man·date \'man-,dāt\ *n* 1 : an authoritative command 2 : an authorization to act given to a representative 3 : a commission granted by the League of Nations to a member nation for governing conquered territory; *also* : a territory so governed

man·da·to·ry \'man-də-,tōr-ē\ *adj* 1 : containing or constituting a command : OBLIGATORY 2 : of or relating to a League of Nations mandate

man·di·ble \'man-də-bəl\ *n* 1 : JAW; *esp* : a lower jaw 2 : either segment of a bird's bill — **man·dib·u·lar** \man-'dib-yə-lər\ *adj*

man·do·lin \'man-də-'lin, 'man-dəl-ən\ *n* : a stringed musical instrument with a pear-shaped body and a fretted neck

man·drag·o·ra \man-'drag-ə-rə\ : MANDRAKE 1

man·drake \'man-,drāk\ *n* 1 : an Old World herb of the nightshade family

or its large forked root superstitiously credited with human and medicinal attributes 2 : MAYAPPLE

man·drel *also* **man·dril** \'man-drəl\ *n* 1 : an axle or spindle inserted into a hole in a piece of work to support it during machining 2 : a metal bar used as a core around which material may be cast, shaped, or molded

man·drill \'man-drəl\ *n* : a large fierce gregarious baboon of western Africa

mane \'mān\ *n* : long heavy hair growing about the neck of some mammals (as a horse) — **maned** \'mānd\ *adj*

man·eat·er \'man-,ēt-ər\ *n* : one (as a shark or cannibal) that has or is thought to have an appetite for human flesh — **man·eat·ing** \-,ēt-iŋ\ *adj*

ma·nège \ma-'nezh, mə-\ *n* : the art of horsemanship or of training horses

ma·nes \'män-,ās, 'mä-,nēz\ *n pl, often cap* : the spirits of the dead and gods of the lower world in ancient Roman belief

ma·neu·ver \mə-'n(y)ü-vər\ *n* [F *man-œuvre*, fr. OF *maneuvre* work done by hand, fr. ML *manuopera*, fr. L *manu operare* to work by hand] 1 : a military or naval movement; *also* : an armed forces training exercise — often used in pl. 2 : a procedure involving expert physical movement 3 : an evasive movement or shift of tactics; *also* : an action taken to gain a tactical end — **maneuver** *vb* — **ma·neu·ver·abil·i·ty** \-,n(y)üv-(ə-)rə-'bil-ət-ē\ *n*

man Fri·day \'man-'frīd-ē\ *n* : an efficient and devoted aide or employee

man·ful \'man-fəl\ *adj* : having or showing courage and resolution — **man·ful·ly** \-ē\ *adv*

man·ga·nese \'maŋ-gə-,nēz, -,nēs\ *n* : a grayish white metallic chemical element resembling iron but not magnetic

mange \'mānj\ *n* : a contagious itchy skin disease esp. of domestic animals — **mangy** \'mān-jē\ *adj*

man·ger \'mān-jər\ *n* : a trough or open box for livestock feed or fodder

¹**man·gle** \'maŋ-gəl\ *vb* **man·gled; man·gling** \-g(ə-)liŋ\ 1 : to cut, bruise, or hack with repeated blows 2 : to spoil or injure in making or performing — **man·gler** \-g(ə-)lər\ *n*

²**mangle** *n* : a machine for ironing laundry by passing it between heated rollers

man·go \'maŋ-gō\ *n, pl* **mangoes** *also* **mangos** [Pg *manga*] : a yellowish red tropical fruit with juicy slightly acid pulp; *also* : an evergreen tree related to the sumacs that bears this fruit

man·grove \'man-,grōv\ *n* : a tropical maritime tree that sends out many prop roots and forms dense thickets important in coastal land building

man·han·dle \'man-,han-dəl\ *vb* : to handle roughly

man·hat·tan \man-'hat-ᵊn\ *n, often cap*

: a cocktail made of whiskey and vermouth

man·hole \'man-ˌhōl\ n : a hole through which a person may go esp. to gain access to an underground or enclosed structure

man·hood \-ˌhud\ n 1 : the condition of being an adult male 2 : manly qualities : COURAGE 3 : MEN (the nation's ∼)

man–hour \-'aû(-ə)r\ n : a unit of one hour's work by one person

man–hunt \-ˌhənt\ n : an organized hunt for a person and esp. for one charged with a crime

ma·nia \'mā-nē-ə, -nyə\ n 1 : insanity esp. when marked by extreme excitement 2 : excessive enthusiasm

ma·ni·ac \'mā-nē-ˌak\ n : LUNATIC, MADMAN

ma·ni·a·cal \mə-'nī-ə-kəl\ also **ma·ni·ac** \'mā-nē-ak\ adj 1 : affected with or suggestive of madness 2 : FRANTIC

man·ic \'man-ik\ adj : affected with, relating to, or resembling mania — **manic** n

man·ic–de·pres·sive \ˌman-ik-di-'pres-iv\ adj : characterized by mania, by psychotic depression, or by alternating mania and depression — **manic-depressive** n

¹man·i·cure \'man-ə-ˌkyur\ n 1 : MANICURIST 2 : a treatment for the care of the hands and nails

²manicure vb **-cured; -cur·ing** 1 : to do manicure work on 2 : to trim closely and evenly

man·i·cur·ist \-ˌkyur-əst\ n : a person who gives manicure treatments

¹man·i·fest \'man-ə-ˌfest\ adj [ME, fr. MF or L; MF manifeste, fr. L manifestus, lit., hit by the hand, fr. manus hand + -festus (akin to L infestus hostile)] 1 : readily perceived by the senses and esp. by the sight 2 : easily understood : OBVIOUS — **man·i·fest·ly** adv

²manifest vb : to make evident or certain by showing or displaying syn evince, demonstrate, exhibit

³manifest n : a list of passengers or an invoice of cargo for a ship or plane

man·i·fes·ta·tion \ˌman-ə-fə-'stā-shən\ n : DISPLAY, DEMONSTRATION

man·i·fes·to \ˌman-ə-'fes-tō\ n, pl **-tos** or **-toes** : a public declaration of intentions, motives, or views

¹man·i·fold \'man-ə-ˌfōld\ adj 1 : marked by diversity or variety 2 : consisting of or operating many of one kind combined

²manifold n : a pipe fitting with several lateral outlets for connecting with other pipes

³manifold vb 1 : to make a number of copies of (as a letter) 2 : MULTIPLY

man·i·kin or **man·ni·kin** \'man-i-kən\ n 1 : MANNEQUIN 2 : a little man : DWARF, PYGMY

Ma·nila hemp \mə-ˌnil-ə-\ n : a tough

fiber from a Philippine banana plant used esp. for cordage

manila paper \mə-ˌnil-ə-\ n, often cap M : a tough brownish paper made orig. from Manila hemp

man·i·oc \'man-ē-ˌäk\ n : CASSAVA

ma·nip·u·late \mə-'nip-yə-ˌlāt\ vb **-lat·ed; -lat·ing** [fr. manipulation, fr. F, fr. manipule handful, fr. L manipulus] 1 : to treat or operate manually or mechanically esp. with skill 2 : to manage or use skillfully 3 : to influence esp. with intent to deceive — **ma·nip·u·la·tion** \mə-ˌnip-yə-'lā-shən\ n — **ma·nip·u·la·tive** \-'nip-yə-ˌlāt-iv\ adj — **ma·nip·u·la·tor** \-ˌlāt-ər\ n

man·kind n 1 \'man-'kīnd\ : the human race 2 \-ˌkīnd\ : men as distinguished from women

¹man·ly \'man-lē\ adj **man·li·er; -est** : having qualities appropriate to or generally associated with a man : BOLD, RESOLUTE — **man·li·ness** n

²manly adv : in a manly manner

man–made \'man-'mād\ adj : made by man rather than nature (∼ systems); esp : SYNTHETIC (∼ fibers)

man·na \'man-ə\ n 1 : food miraculously supplied to the Israelites in the wilderness 2 : something of value that comes unexpectedly : WINDFALL

manned \'mand\ adj : carrying or performed by a person (∼ spaceflight)

man·ne·quin \'man-i-kən\ n 1 : a form representing the human figure used esp. for displaying clothes 2 : a person employed to model clothing

man·ner \'man-ər\ n 1 : KIND, SORT 2 : a way of acting or proceeding (worked in a brisk ∼); also : normal behavior (spoke bluntly as was his ∼) 3 : a method of artistic execution 4 pl : social conduct; also : BEARING 5 pl : BEHAVIOR (taught the child good ∼s)

man·nered \'man-ərd\ adj 1 : having manners of a specified kind (well-mannered) 2 : having an artificial character (a highly ∼ style)

man·ner·ism \'man-ə-ˌriz-əm\ n 1 : ARTIFICIALITY, PRECIOSITY 2 : a peculiarity of action, bearing, or treatment syn pose, air, affectation

man·ner·ly \'man-ər-lē\ adj : showing good manners : POLITE — **man·ner·li·ness** n

man·nish \'man-ish\ adj 1 : resembling or suggesting a man rather than a woman 2 : generally associated with or characteristic of a man — **man·nish·ly** adv — **man·nish·ness** n

ma·noeu·vre \mə-'n(y)ü-vər\ chiefly Brit var of MANEUVER

man–of–war \ˌman-ə(v)-'wȯr\ n, pl **men–of–war** \ˌmen-\ : WARSHIP

ma·nom·e·ter \mə-'näm-ət-ər\ n : an instrument for measuring the pressure of gases — **mano·met·ric** \ˌman-ə-'me-trik\ adj

man·or \'man-ər\ n 1 : the house or hall of an estate; also : a landed estate 2 : an English estate of a feudal lord —

ma·no·ri·al \mə-ˈnōr-ē-əl\ *adj* — **ma·no·ri·al·ism** \-ə-ˌliz-əm\ *n*

man power *n* 1 : power available from or supplied by the physical effort of human beings 2 *usu* **man·pow·er** : the total supply of persons available and fitted for service

man·qué \mäⁿ-ˈkā\ *adj* [F, fr. pp. of *manquer* to lack, fail] : short of or frustrated in the fulfillment of one's aspirations or talents ⟨a poet ∼⟩

man·sard \ˈman-ˌsärd, -sərd\ *n* : a roof having two slopes on all sides with the lower slope steeper than the upper one

manse \ˈmans\ *n* : the residence esp. of a Presbyterian clergyman

man·ser·vant \ˈman-ˌsər-vənt\ *n, pl* **men·ser·vants** \ˈmen-ˌsər-vənts\ : a male servant

man·sion \ˈman-chən\ *n* : a large imposing residence; *also* : a separate apartment in a large structure

man–size \ˈman-ˌsīz\ *or* **man–sized** \-ˌsīzd\ *adj* : suitable for or requiring a man

man·slaugh·ter \-ˌslȯt-ər\ *n* : the unlawful killing of a human being without express or implied malice

man·slay·er \-ˌslā-ər\ *n* : one who slays a man

man·ta \ˈmant-ə\ *n* : a square piece of cloth or blanket used in southwestern U.S. and Latin America as a cloak or shawl

man·teau \man-ˈtō\ *n* : a loose cloak, coat, or robe

man·tel \ˈmant-ᵊl\ *n* : a beam, stone, or arch serving as a lintel to support the masonry above a fireplace; *also* : a shelf above a fireplace

man·tel·piece \ˈmant-ᵊl-ˌpēs\ *n* : the shelf of a mantel

man·til·la \man-ˈtē-(y)ə, -ˈtil-ə\ *n* : a light scarf worn over the head and shoulders esp. by Spanish and Latin-American women

man·tis \ˈmant-əs\ *n, pl* **man·tis·es** *or* **man·tes** \ˈman-ˌtēz\ [NL, fr. Gk. lit., diviner, prophet] : a large insect related to the grasshoppers that feeds on other insects which it holds in forelimbs folded as if in prayer

man·tis·sa \man-ˈtis-ə\ *n* : the decimal part of a logarithm

¹**man·tle** \ˈmant-ᵊl\ *n* 1 : a loose sleeveless garment worn over other clothes 2 : something that covers, enfolds, or envelopes 3 : a lacy sheath that gives light by incandescence when placed over a flame 4 : the portion of the earth lying between the crust and the core 5 : MANTEL

²**mantle** *vb* **man·tled**; **man·tling** \ˈmant-(ᵊ-)liŋ\ 1 : to cover with a mantle 2 : BLUSH

man·tra \ˈman-trə\ *n* : a Hindu or Buddhist mystical formula of incantation

¹**man·u·al** \ˈman-yə(-wə)l\ *adj* 1 : of, relating to, or involving the hands; *also* : worked by hand ⟨a ∼ choke⟩ 2 : re-

quiring or using physical skill and energy — **man·u·al·ly** \-ē\ *adv*

²**manual** *n* 1 : a small book; *esp* : HANDBOOK 2 : the prescribed movements in the handling of a military item and esp. a weapon during a drill or ceremony ⟨the ∼ of arms⟩ 3 : a keyboard esp. of an organ

man·u·fac·to·ry \ˌman-(y)ə-ˈfak-t(ə-)rē\ *n* : FACTORY

¹**man·u·fac·ture** \ˌman-(y)ə-ˈfak-chər\ *n* [MF, fr. L *manu factus* made by hand] 1 : something made from raw materials 2 : the process of making wares by hand or by machinery; *also* : a productive industry using mechanical power and machinery

²**manufacture** *vb* **-tured**; **-tur·ing** 1 : to make from raw materials by hand or by machinery; *also* : to engage in manufacture 2 : INVENT, FABRICATE; *also* : CREATE — **man·u·fac·tur·er** *n*

man·u·mit \ˌman-yə-ˈmit\ *vb* **-mit·ted**; **-mit·ting** : to free from slavery — **man·u·mis·sion** \-ˈmish-ən\ *n*

¹**ma·nure** \mə-ˈn(y)u̇r\ *vb* **ma·nured**; **ma·nur·ing** : to fertilize land with manure

²**manure** *n* : FERTILIZER; *esp* : refuse from stables and barnyards — **ma·nu·ri·al** \-ˈn(y)u̇r-ē-əl\ *adj*

man·u·script \ˈman-yə-ˌskript\ *n* [L *manu scriptus* written by hand] 1 : a written or typewritten composition or document 2 : writing as opposed to print

Manx \ˈmaŋks\ *n pl* : the people of the Isle of Man — **Manx** *adj*

¹**many** \ˈmen-ē\ *adj* **more** \ˈmōr\ ; **most** \ˈmōst\ : consisting of or amounting to a large but indefinite number

²**many** *pron* : a large number

³**many** *n* : a large but indefinite number

many·fold \ˌmen-ē-ˈfōld\ *adv* : by many times

many–sid·ed \-ˈsīd-əd\ *adj* 1 : having many sides or aspects 2 : VERSATILE

Mao·ism \ˈmau̇-ˌiz-əm\ *n* : the theory and practice of Communism developed in China chiefly by Mao Tse-tung — **Mao·ist** \ˈmau̇-əst\ *n or adj*

Mao·ri \ˈmau̇(ə)r-ē\ *n, pl* **Maori** *or* **Maoris** : a member of a Polynesian people native to New Zealand

¹**map** \ˈmap\ *n* [ML *mappa*, fr. L, napkin, towel] 1 : a representation usu. on a flat surface of the whole or part of an area 2 : a representation of the celestial sphere or part of it

²**map** *vb* **mapped**; **map·ping** 1 : to make a map of 2 : to plan in detail ⟨∼ out a program⟩ — **map·pa·ble** \ˈmap-ə-bəl\ *adj* — **map·per** *n*

ma·ple \ˈmā-pəl\ *n* : any of various trees or shrubs with 2-winged dry fruit and opposite leaves; *also* : the hard light-colored wood of a maple used esp. for floors and furniture

maple sugar *n* : sugar made by boiling maple syrup

maple syrup *n* : syrup made by concentrating the sap of maple trees and esp. the sugar maple

mar \\'mär\\ *vb* **marred; mar·ring** : to detract from the wholeness or perfection of : SPOIL **syn** injure, hurt, harm, damage, impair, blemish

Mar *abbr* March

ma·ra·ca \\mə-'räk-ə, -'rak-\\ *n* [Pg *maracá*] : a dried gourd or a rattle like a gourd that contains dried seeds or pebbles and is used as a percussion instrument

mar·a·schi·no \\,mar-ə-'skē-nō, -'shē-\\ *n, pl* **-nos** *often cap* [It] : a cherry preserved in a true or imitation sweet cherry liqueur

mar·a·thon \\'mar-ə-,thän\\ *n* [*Marathon*, Greece, site of a victory of Greeks over Persians in 490 B.C. the news of which was carried to Athens by a long-distance runner] **1** : a long-distance race esp. on foot **2** : an endurance contest

mar·a·thon·er \\'mar-ə-,thän-ər\\ *n* : one who takes part in a marathon — **mar·a·thon·ing** *n*

ma·raud \\mə-'rȯd\\ *vb* : to roam about and raid in search of plunder : PILLAGE — **ma·raud·er** *n*

mar·ble \\'mär-bəl\\ *n* **1** : a limestone that can be polished and used in fine building work **2** : something resembling marble (as in coldness) **3** : a small ball (as of glass) used in various games; *also, pl* : a children's game played with these small balls — **marble** *adj*

mar·bling \\-b(ə-)liŋ\\ *n* : an intermixture of fat through the lean of a cut of meat

mar·cel \\mär-'sel\\ *n* : a deep soft wave made in the hair by the use of a heated curling iron — **marcel** *vb*

¹march \\'märch\\ *n* : a border region : FRONTIER

²march *vb* **1** : to move along in or as if in military formation **2** : to walk in a direct purposeful manner; *also* : PROGRESS, ADVANCE **3** : TRAVERSE — **march·er** *n*

³march *n* **1** : the action of marching; *also* : the distance covered (as by a military unit) in a march **2** : a regular measured stride or rhythmic step used in marching **3** : forward movement **4** : a piece of music with marked rhythm suitable for marching

March *n* [ME, fr. OF, fr. L *martius*, fr. *Mart-, Mars*, Roman god of war] : the third month of the year having 31 days

mar·chio·ness \\'mär-shə-nəs\\ *n* **1** : the wife or widow of a marquess **2** : a woman holding the rank of a marquess in her own right

march-past \\'märch-,past\\ *n* : a marching by esp. of troops in review

Mar·di Gras \\'märd-ē-,grä\\ *n* [F, lit., fat Tuesday] : the Tuesday before Ash Wednesday often observed with parades and merrymaking

¹mare \\'maər\\ *n* : a female of an animal of the horse group

²ma·re \\'mär-(,)ā\\ *n, pl* **ma·ria** \\'mär-ē-ə\\ : any of several large dark areas on the surface of the moon or Mars

mar·ga·rine \\'märj-(ə-)rən, -ə-,rēn\\ *n* : a food product made usu. from vegetable oils churned with skimmed milk and used as a substitute for butter

mar·gin \\'mär-jən\\ *n* **1** : the part of a page outside the main body of printed or written matter **2** : EDGE **3** : a spare amount, measure, or degree allowed for use if needed **4** : measure or degree of difference (passed the bill by a ~ of one vote) — **mar·gin·al** \\-ᵊl\\ *adj* — **mar·gin·al·ly** \\-ē\\ *adv*

mar·gi·na·lia \\,mär-jə-'nā-lē-ə\\ *n pl* : marginal notes

mar·grave \\'mär-,grāv\\ *n* : the military governor esp. of a medieval German border province

mar·gue·rite \\,mär-g(y)ə-'rēt\\ *n* [F] : any of several daisies or chrysanthemums

ma·ri·a·chi \\,mär-ē-'äch-ē\\ *n* : a Mexican street band; *also* : a member of or the music of such a band

mar·i·gold \\'mar-ə-,gōld, 'mer-\\ *n* : a garden plant related to the daisies with double yellow, orange, or reddish flower heads

mar·i·jua·na *also* **mar·i·hua·na** \\,mar-ə-'(h)wän-ə\\ *n* [MexSp *marihuana*] : the dried leaves and flowering tops of the female hemp plant that are sometimes smoked for their intoxicating effect; *also* : HEMP

ma·rim·ba \\mə-'rim-bə\\ *n* : a xylophone of southern Africa and Central America; *also* : a modern version of it

ma·ri·na \\mə-'rē-nə\\ *n* : a dock or basin providing secure moorings for motorboats and yachts

mar·i·na·ra \\,mar-ə-'nar-ə\\ *adj* [It (*alla*) *marinara*, lit., in sailor style] : made with tomatoes, onions, garlic, and spices; *also* : served with marinara sauce

mar·i·nate \\'mar-ə-,nāt\\ *vb* **-nat·ed; -nat·ing** : to steep (as meat or fish) in a brine or pickle

¹ma·rine \\mə-'rēn\\ *adj* **1** : of or relating to the sea or its navigation or commerce **2** : of or relating to marines

²marine *n* **1** : the mercantile and naval shipping of a country **2** : any of a class of soldiers serving on shipboard or with a naval force

mar·i·ner \\'mar-ə-nər\\ *n* : SAILOR

mar·i·o·nette \\,mar-ē-ə-'net, ,mer-\\ *n* : a puppet moved by strings or by hand

mar·i·tal \\'mar-ət-ᵊl\\ *adj* : of or relating to marriage : CONJUGAL **syn** matrimonial, connubial, nuptial

mar·i·time \\'mar-ə-,tīm\\ *adj* **1** : of, relating to, or bordering on the sea **2** : of or relating to navigation or commerce of the sea

mar·jo·ram \\'märj-(ə-)rəm\\ *n* : a fragrant aromatic mint used esp. as a seasoning

¹**mark** \'märk\ *n* **1** : TARGET; *also* : GOAL, OBJECT **2** : something (as a line or fixed object) designed to record position; *also* : the starting line or position in a track event **3** : an object of abuse or ridicule **4** : the question under discussion **5** : NORM (not up to the ∼) **6** : a visible sign : INDICATION; *also* : CHARACTERISTIC **7** : a written or printed symbol **8** : GRADE (a ∼ of B+) **9** : IMPORTANCE, DISTINCTION **10** : a lasting impression (made his ∼ in the world); *also* : a damaging impression left on a surface

²**mark** *vb* **1** : to set apart by a line or boundary **2** : to designate by a mark or make a mark on **3** : CHARACTERIZE (the vehemence that ∼s his speeches); *also* : SIGNALIZE (this year ∼s the 50th anniversary) **4** : to take notice of : OBSERVE — **mark·er** *n*

³**mark** *n* — see MONEY table

Mark \'märk\ *n* — see BIBLE table

mark·down \'märk-ˌdaun\ *n* **1** : a lowering of price **2** : the amount by which an original price is reduced

mark down \(ˈ)märk-ˈdaun\ *vb* : to put a lower price on

marked \'märkt\ *adj* : NOTICEABLE — **mark·ed·ly** \'mär-kəd-lē\ *adv*

¹**mar·ket** \'mär-kət\ *n* **1** : a meeting together of people for trade by purchase and sale; *also* : a public place where such a meeting is held **2** : the rate or price offered for a commodity or security **3** : a geographical area of demand for commodities; *also* : extent of demand **4** : a retail establishment usu. of a specific kind (a meat ∼)

²**market** *vb* : to go to a market to buy or sell; *also* : SELL — **mar·ket·able** *adj*

mar·ket·place \'mär-kət-ˌplās\ *n* **1** : an open square in a town where markets are held **2** : the world of trade or economic activity

mark·ka \'mär-ˌkä\ *n, pl* **mark·kaa** \'mär-ˌkä\ *or* **markkas** \-ˌkäz\ — see MONEY table

marks·man \'märks-mən\ *n* : a person skillful at hitting a target — **marks·man·ship** *n*

mark·up \'märk-ˌəp\ *n* **1** : a raising of price **2** : an amount added to the cost price of an article to determine the selling price

mark up \(ˈ)märk-ˈəp\ *vb* : to put a higher price on

marl \'märl\ *n* : an earthy deposit rich in lime used as fertilizer — **marly** \'mär-lē\ *adj*

mar·lin \'mär-lən\ *n* : a large oceanic sport fish

mar·line·spike *also* **mar·lin·spike** \'mär-lən-ˌspīk\ *n* : a pointed iron tool used to separate strands of rope or wire (as in splicing)

mar·ma·lade \'mär-mə-ˌlād\ *n* : a clear jelly holding in suspension pieces of fruit and fruit rind

mar·mo·re·al \mär-ˈmōr-ē-əl\ *adj* : of, relating to, or resembling marble

mar·mo·set \'mär-mə-ˌset\ *n* : any of various small bushy-tailed tropical American monkeys

mar·mot \'mär-mət\ *n* : a stout short-legged burrowing No. American rodent

¹**ma·roon** \mə-ˈrün\ *vb* **1** : to put ashore (as on a desolate island) and leave to one's fate **2** : to leave in isolation and without hope of escape

²**maroon** *n* : a dark red

mar·plot \'mär-ˌplät\ *n* : one who endangers the success of an enterprise by his meddling

mar·quee \mär-ˈkē\ *n* [modif. of F *marquise*, lit., marchioness] **1** : a large tent set up (as for an outdoor party) **2** : a usu. metal and glass canopy over an entrance (as of a theater)

mar·quess \'mär-kwəs\ *n* **1** : a nobleman of hereditary rank in Europe and Japan **2** : a member of the British peerage ranking below a duke and above an earl

mar·que·try \'mär-kə-trē\ *n* : inlaid work of wood, shell, or ivory (as on a table or cabinet)

mar·quis \'mär-kwəs, mär-ˈkē\ *n* : MARQUESS

mar·quise \mär-ˈkēz\ *n, pl* **mar·quises** \-ˈkēz(-əz)\ : MARCHIONESS

mar·qui·sette \ˌmär-k(w)ə-ˈzet\ *n* : a sheer meshed fabric

mar·riage \'mar-ij\ *n* **1** : the state of being married **2** : a wedding ceremony and attendant festivities **3** : a close union — **mar·riage·able** *adj*

mar·row \'mar-ō\ *n* : a soft vascular tissue that fills the cavities of most bones

mar·row·bone \'mar-ə-ˌbōn, -ō-ˌbōn\ *n* : a bone (as a shinbone) rich in marrow

mar·ry \'mar-ē\ *vb* **mar·ried; mar·ry·ing** **1** : to join as husband and wife according to law or custom **2** : to take as husband or wife : WED **3** : to enter into a close union — **mar·ried** *adj or n*

Mars \'märz\ *n* : the planet fourth from the sun conspicuous for its red appearance

marsh \'märsh\ *n* : a tract of soft wet land — **marshy** *adj*

¹**mar·shal** \'mär-shəl\ *n* **1** : a high official in a medieval household; *also* : a person in charge of the ceremonial aspects of a gathering **2** : a general officer of the highest military rank **3** : an administrative officer (as of a U.S. judicial district) having duties similar to a sheriff's **4** : the administrative head of a city police or fire department

²**marshal** *vb* **-shaled** *or* **-shalled; -shal·ing** *or* **-shal·ling** \'märsh-(ə-)liŋ\ **1** : to arrange in order, rank, or position **2** : to lead with ceremony : USHER

marsh gas *n* : METHANE

marsh·mal·low \'märsh-ˌmel-ō, -ˌmal-\ *n* : a light creamy confection made from corn syrup, sugar, albumen, and gelatin

marsh marigold *n* : a swamp herb related to the buttercups that has bright yellow flowers

mar·su·pi·al \mär-'sü-pē-əl\ *n* : any of a large group of mostly Australian primitive mammals that bear very immature young which are nourished in a pouch on the abdomen of the female — **marsupial** *adj*

mart \'märt\ *n* : MARKET

mar·ten \'märt-ᵊn\ *n, pl* **marten** *or* **martens** : a slender weasel-like mammal with fine gray or brown fur; *also* : this fur

mar·tial \'mär-shəl\ *adj* [L *martialis* of Mars, fr. *Mart-, Mars* Mars, Roman god of war] 1 : of, relating to, or suited for war or a warrior ⟨~ music⟩ 2 : of or relating to an army or military life 3 : WARLIKE

martial law *n* 1 : the law applied in occupied territory by the occupying military forces 2 : the established law of a country administered by military forces in an emergency when civilian law enforcement agencies are unable to maintain public order and safety

mar·tian \'mär-shən\ *adj, often cap* : of or relating to the planet Mars or its hypothetical inhabitants — **martian** *n, often cap*

mar·tin \'märt-ᵊn\ *n* : any of several small swallows and flycatchers

mar·ti·net \,märt-ᵊn-'et\ *n* : a strict disciplinarian

mar·tin·gale \'märt-ᵊn-,gäl\ *n* : a strap connecting a horse's girth to the bit or reins so as to hold down its head

mar·ti·ni \mär-'tē-nē\ *n* : a cocktail made of gin or vodka and dry vermouth

¹mar·tyr \'märt-ər\ *n* [ME, fr. OE, fr. LL, fr. Gk *martyr-, martys,* lit., witness] 1 : a person who dies rather than renounce his religion; *also* : one who makes a great sacrifice for the sake of principle 2 : a great or constant sufferer

²martyr *vb* 1 : to put to death for adhering to a belief 2 : TORTURE

mar·tyr·dom \'märt-ər-dəm\ *n* 1 : the suffering and death of a martyr 2 : TORTURE

¹mar·vel \'mär-vəl\ *n* 1 : something that causes wonder or astonishment 2 : intense surprise or interest

²marvel *vb* **-veled** *or* **-velled; -vel·ing** *or* **-vel·ling** \'märv-(ə-)liŋ\ : to feel surprise, wonder, or amazed curiosity

mar·vel·ous *or* **mar·vel·lous** \'märv-(ə-)ləs\ *adj* 1 : causing wonder 2 : of the highest kind or quality : SPLENDID — **mar·vel·ous·ly** *adv* — **mar·vel·ous·ness** *n*

Marx·ism \'märk-,siz-əm\ *n* : the political, economic, and social principles and policies advocated by Karl Marx — **Marx·ist** \-səst\ *n or adj*

mar·zi·pan \'märt-sə-,pän, -,pan; 'mär-zə-,pan\ *n* [G] : a confection of almond paste, sugar, and egg whites

masc *abbr* masculine

mas·cara \mas-'kar-ə\ *n* : a cosmetic for coloring the eyelashes and eyebrows

mas·cot \'mas-,kät, -kət\ *n* [F *mascotte,* fr. Provençal *mascoto,* fr. *masco* witch, fr. ML *masca*] : a person, animal, or object believed to bring good luck

¹mas·cu·line \'mas-kyə-lən\ *adj* 1 : MALE; *also* : MANLY 2 : of, relating to, or constituting the gender that includes most words or grammatical forms referring to males — **mas·cu·lin·i·ty** \,mas-kyə-'lin-ət-ē\ *n*

²masculine *n* 1 : a male person 2 : a noun, pronoun, adjective, or inflectional form or class of the masculine gender; *also* : the masculine gender

ma·ser \'mā-zər\ *n* [*m*icrowave *a*mplification by *s*timulated *e*mission of *r*adiation] : a device that utilizes the natural oscillation of atoms or molecules between energy levels for generating microwaves

¹mash \'mash\ *n* 1 : crushed malt or grain steeped in hot water to make wort 2 : a mixture of ground feeds for livestock 3 : a soft pulpy mass

²mash *vb* 1 : to reduce to a soft pulpy state 2 : CRUSH, SMASH ⟨~ a finger⟩ — **mash·er** *n*

MASH *abbr* mobile army surgical hospital

¹mask \'mask\ *n* 1 : a cover for the face usu. for disguise or protection 2 : MASQUE 3 : a figure of a head worn on the stage in antiquity 4 : a copy of a face made by means of a mold ⟨death ~⟩ 5 : something that conceals or disguises 6 : the face of an animal (as a fox)

²mask *vb* 1 : to conceal from view : DISGUISE 2 : to cover for protection

mask·er \'mas-kər\ *n* : a participant in a masquerade

mas·och·ism \'mas-ə-,kiz-əm, 'maz-\ *n* 1 : a sexual perversion characterized by pleasure in being subjected to pain and humiliation 2 : pleasure in being abused or dominated — **mas·och·ist** \-kəst\ *n* — **mas·och·is·tic** \,mas-ə-'kis-tik, ,maz-\ *adj*

ma·son \'mās-ᵊn\ *n* 1 : a skilled worker who builds with stone, brick, or concrete 2 *cap* : FREEMASON

Ma·son·ic \mə-'sän-ik\ *adj* : of or relating to Freemasons or Freemasonry

ma·son·ry \'mās-ᵊn-rē\ *n, pl* **-ries** 1 : something constructed of materials used by masons 2 : the art, trade, or work of a mason 3 *cap* : FREEMASONRY

masque \'mask\ *n* 1 : MASQUERADE 2 : a short allegorical dramatic performance (as of the 17th century)

¹mas·quer·ade \,mas-kə-'rād\ *n* 1 : a social gathering of persons wearing masks; *also* : a costume for wear at such a gathering 2 : DISGUISE

²masquerade *vb* **-ad·ed; -ad·ing** 1 : to disguise oneself : POSE 2 : to take part in a masquerade — **mas·quer·ad·er** *n*

¹mass \'mas\ *n* **1** *cap* : a sequence of prayers and ceremonies forming the eucharistic service of the Roman Catholic Church **2** *often cap* : a celebration of the Eucharist **3** : a musical setting for parts of the Mass

²mass *n* **1** : a quantity or aggregate of matter usu. of considerable size **2** : EXPANSE, BULK; *also* : MASSIVENESS **3** : the principal part **4** : AGGREGATE, WHOLE (people in the ~) **5** : the quantity of matter that a body possesses as evidenced by inertia **6** : a large quantity, amount, or number **7** : the great body of people — usu. used in pl. — **massy** *adj*

³mass *vb* : to form or collect into a mass

Mass *abbr* Massachusetts

mas·sa·cre \'mas-i-kər\ *n* **1** : the killing of many persons under cruel or atrocious circumstances **2** : a wholesale slaughter — **massacre** *vb*

¹mas·sage \mə-'säzh, -'säj\ *n* : remedial or hygienic treatment of the body by manipulation (as rubbing and kneading)

²massage *vb* **mas·saged; mas·sag·ing 1** : to subject to massage **2** : to treat flatteringly; *also* : MANIPULATE (~ data)

mas·seur \ma-'sər\ *n* : a man who practices massage

mas·seuse \-'sə(r)z, -'süz\ *n* : a woman who practices massage

mas·sif \ma-'sēf\ *n* : a principal mountain mass

mas·sive \'mas-iv\ *adj* **1** : forming or consisting of a large mass **2** : large in structure, scope, or degree — **mas·sive·ly** *adv* — **mas·sive·ness** *n*

mass·less \'mas-ləs\ *adj* : having no mass (~ particles)

mass medium *n*, *pl* **mass media** : a medium of communication (as the newspapers or television) that is designed to reach the mass of the people

mass·pro·duce \,mas-prə-'d(y)üs\ *vb* : to produce in quantity usu. by machinery — **mass production** *n*

¹mast \'mast\ *n* **1** : a long pole or spar rising from the keel or deck of a ship and supporting the yards, booms, and rigging **2** : a vertical pole — **mast·ed** \'mas-təd\ *adj*

²mast *n* : nuts (as acorns) accumulated on the forest floor and often serving as food for hogs

¹mas·ter \'mas-tər\ *n* **1** : a male teacher; *also* : a person holding an academic degree higher than a bachelor's but lower than a doctor's **2** : one highly skilled (as in an art or profession) **3** : one having authority or control **4** : VICTOR, SUPERIOR **5** : the commander of a merchant ship **6** : a youth or boy too young to be called *mister* — used as a title **7** : an original (as of a phonograph record) from which copies are made

²master *vb* **mas·tered; mas·ter·ing**

\-t(ə-)riŋ\ **1** : OVERCOME, SUBDUE **2** : to become skilled or proficient in **3** : to produce a master record or tape of (as a musical performance)

master chief petty officer *n* : a petty officer of the highest rank in the navy

mas·ter·ful \'mas-tər-fəl\ *adj* **1** : inclined and usu. competent to act as a master **2** : having or reflecting the skill of a master (did a ~ job of reporting) — **mas·ter·ful·ly** \-ē\ *adv*

master gunnery sergeant *n* : a noncommissioned officer in the marine corps ranking above a master sergeant

master key *n* : a key designed to open several different locks

mas·ter·ly \'mas-tər-lē\ *adj* : indicating thorough knowledge or superior skill (~ performance)

mas·ter·mind \-,mīnd\ *n* : a person who provides the directing or creative intelligence for a project — **mastermind** *vb*

master of ceremonies : a person who acts as host at a formal event or a program of entertainment

mas·ter·piece \'mas-tər-,pēs\ *n* : a work done with extraordinary skill

master plan *n* : an overall plan

master sergeant *n* **1** : a noncommissioned officer in the army ranking next below a sergeant major **2** : a noncommissioned officer in the air force ranking next below a senior master sergeant **3** : a noncommissioned officer in the marine corps ranking next below a master gunnery sergeant

mas·ter·stroke \'mas-tər-,strōk\ *n* : a masterly performance or move

mas·ter·work \-,wərk\ *n* : MASTERPIECE

mas·tery \'mas-t(ə-)rē\ *n* **1** : DOMINION; *also* : SUPERIORITY **2** : possession or display of great skill or knowledge

mast·head \'mast-,hed\ *n* **1** : the top of a mast **2** : the printed matter in a newspaper giving the title and details of ownership and rates

mas·tic \'mas-tik\ *n* : a pasty material used as a protective coating or cement

mas·ti·cate \'mas-tə-,kāt\ *vb* **-cat·ed; -cat·ing** : CHEW — **mas·ti·ca·tion** \,mas-tə-'kā-shən\ *n*

mas·tiff \'mas-təf\ *n* : a large smooth-coated dog used esp. as a guard dog

mast·odon \'mas-tə-,dän\ *n* [NL, fr. Gk *mastos* breast + *odōn, odous* tooth] : a huge elephantlike extinct animal

mas·toid \'mas-,tȯid\ *n* : a bony prominence behind the ear — **mastoid** *adj*

mas·tur·ba·tion \,mas-tər-'bā-shən\ *n* : stimulation of the genital organs to a climax of excitement by contact (as manual) exclusive of sexual intercourse — **mas·tur·bate** \'mas-tər-,bāt\ *vb*

¹mat \'mat\ *n* **1** : a piece of coarse woven or plaited fabric **2** : something made up of many intertwined strands **3** : a large thick pad used as a surface for wrestling and gymnastics

²**mat** *vb* **mat·ted; mat·ting** : to form into a tangled mass

³**mat** *or* **matt** *or* **matte** *adj* [F, fr. OF, defeated, fr. L *mattus* drunk] : not shiny : DULL

⁴**mat** *or* **matt** *or* **matte** *n* **1** : a border going around a picture between picture and frame or serving as the frame **2** : a dull finish

mat·a·dor \'mat-ə-ˌdȯr\ *n* [Sp, fr. *matar* to kill] : a bullfighter whose role is to kill the bull in a bullfight

¹**match** \'mach\ *n* **1** : a person or thing equal or similar to another : COUNTERPART **2** : a pair of persons or objects that harmonize **3** : a contest or game between two or more individuals **4** : a marriage union; *also* : a prospective marriage partner — **match·less** *adj*

²**match** *vb* **1** : to meet as an antagonist; *also* : PIT (~*ing* his strength against his enemy's) **2** : to provide with a worthy competitor; *also* : to set in comparison with **3** : MARRY **4** : to combine suitably or congenially; *also* : ADAPT, SUIT **5** : to provide with a counterpart

³**match** *n* : a short slender piece of flammable material (as wood) tipped with a combustible mixture that ignites through friction

match·book \-ˌbùk\ *n* : a small folder containing rows of paper matches

match·lock \-ˌläk\ *n* : a musket with a slow-burning cord lowered over a hole in the breech to ignite the charge

match·mak·er \-ˌmā-kər\ *n* : one who arranges a match and esp. a marriage

match·wood \-ˌwùd\ *n* : small pieces of wood

¹**mate** \'māt\ *vb* **mat·ed; mat·ing** : CHECKMATE — **mate** *n*

²**mate** *n* **1** : ASSOCIATE, COMPANION; *also* : HELPER **2** : a deck officer on a merchant ship ranking below the captain **3** : one of a pair; *esp* : either member of a married couple or a breeding pair of animals

³**mate** *vb* **mat·ed; mat·ing 1** : to join or fit together : COUPLE **2** : to come or bring together as mates

ma·té *or* **ma·te** \'mä-ˌtā\ *n* : a tealike beverage used esp. in So. America

¹**ma·te·ri·al** \mə-'tir-ē-əl\ *adj* **1** : PHYSICAL (~ world); *also* : BODILY (~ needs) **2** : of or relating to matter rather than form (~ cause); *also* : EMPIRICAL (~ knowledge) **3** : highly important : SIGNIFICANT **4** : of a physical or worldly nature (~ progress) — **ma·te·ri·al·ly** \-ē\ *adv*

²**material** *n* **1** : the elements or substance of which something is composed or made **2** : apparatus necessary for doing or making something

ma·te·ri·al·ism \mə-'tir-ē-ə-ˌliz-əm\ *n* **1** : a theory that everything can be explained as being or coming from matter **2** : a preoccupation with material rather than intellectual or spiritual things — **ma·te·ri·al·ist** \-ləst\ *n or adj*

— **ma·te·ri·al·is·tic** \-ˌtir-ē-ə-'lis-tik\ *adj* — **ma·te·ri·al·is·ti·cal·ly** \-ti-k(ə-)lē\ *adv*

ma·te·ri·al·ize \mə-'tir-ē-ə-ˌlīz\ *vb* **-ized; -iz·ing 1** : to give material form to; *also* : to assume bodily form **2** : to make an often unexpected appearance — **ma·te·ri·al·iza·tion** \mə-ˌtir-ē-ə-lə-'zā-shən\ *n*

ma·te·ri·el *or* **ma·té·ri·el** \mə-ˌtir-ē-'el\ *n* [F *matériel*] : equipment, apparatus, and supplies used by an organization

ma·ter·nal \mə-'tərn-ᵊl\ *adj* **1** : MOTHERLY **2** : related through or inherited or derived from a mother — **ma·ter·nal·ly** \-ē\ *adv*

ma·ter·ni·ty \mə-'tər-nət-ē\ *n, pl* **-ties 1** : the quality or state of being a mother; *also* : MOTHERLINESS **2** : a hospital facility for the care of women before and during childbirth and for newborn babies — **maternity** *adj*

¹**math** \'math\ *n* : MATHEMATICS

²**math** *abbr* mathematical; mathematician

math·e·mat·ics \ˌmath-ə-'mat-iks\ *n pl* : the science of numbers and their operations and the relations between them and of space configurations and their structure and measurement — **math·e·mat·i·cal** \-'mat-i-kəl\ *adj* — **math·e·mat·i·cal·ly** \-i-k(ə-)lē\ *adv* — **math·e·ma·ti·cian** \ˌmath-ə-mə-'tish-ən\ *n*

mat·i·nee *or* **mat·i·née** \ˌmat-ᵊn-'ā\ *n* [F *matinée*, lit., morning, fr. OF, fr. *matin* morning, fr. L *matutinum*, fr. neut. of *matutinus* of the morning, fr. *Matuta*, goddess of morning] : a musical or dramatic performance usu. in the afternoon

mat·ins \'mat-ᵊnz\ *n pl, often cap* **1** : special prayers said between midnight and 4 a.m. **2** : a morning service of liturgical prayer in Anglican churches

ma·tri·arch \'mā-trē-ˌärk\ *n* : a female who rules or dominates a family, group, or state — **ma·tri·ar·chal** \ˌmā-trē-'är-kəl\ *adj* — **ma·tri·ar·chy** \'mā-trē-ˌär-kē\ *n*

ma·tri·cide \'ma-trə-ˌsīd, 'mā-\ *n* **1** : the murder of a mother by her child **2** : one who kills his mother — **ma·tri·cid·al** \ˌma-trə-'sīd-ᵊl, ˌmā-\ *adj*

ma·tric·u·late \mə-'trik-yə-ˌlāt\ *vb* **-lat·ed; -lat·ing** : to enroll as a member of a body and esp. of a college or university — **ma·tric·u·la·tion** \-ˌtrik-yə-'lā-shən\ *n*

mat·ri·mo·ny \'mat-rə-ˌmō-nē\ *n* [ME, fr. MF *matremoine*, fr. L *matrimonium*, fr. *mater* mother, matron] : MARRIAGE — **mat·ri·mo·nial** \ˌmat-rə-'mō-nē-əl\ *adj* — **mat·ri·mo·nial·ly** *adv*

ma·trix \'mā-triks\ *n, pl* **ma·tri·ces** \'mā-trə-ˌsēz, 'ma-\ *or* **ma·trix·es** \'mā-trik-səz\ **1** : something within which something else originates or develops **2** : a mold from which a relief surface (as a piece of type) is made

ma·tron \'mā-trən\ *n* **1** : a married woman usu. of dignified maturity or social distinction **2** : a woman supervisor (as in a school or police station) — **ma·tron·ly** *adj*

Matt *abbr* Matthew

¹mat·ter \'mat-ər\ *n* **1** : a subject of interest or concern **2** *pl* : events or circumstances of a particular situation; *also* : elements that constitute material for treatment (as in writing) **3** : TROUBLE, DIFFICULTY ⟨what's the ∼⟩ **4** : the substance of which a physical object is composed **5** : PUS **6** : an indefinite amount or quantity ⟨a ∼ of a few days⟩ **7** : something written or printed **8** : MAIL

²matter *vb* : to be of importance : SIGNIFY

mat·ter-of-fact \,mat-ə-rə(v)-'fakt\ *adj* : adhering to or concerned with fact — **mat·ter-of-fact·ly** *adv* — **mat·ter-of-fact·ness** *n*

Mat·thew \'math-yü\ *n* — see BIBLE table

mat·tins *often cap, chiefly Brit var of* MATINS

mat·tock \'mat-ək\ *n* : a digging and grubbing tool with features of an adz and an ax or pick

mat·tress \'ma-trəs\ *n* **1** : a fabric case filled with resilient material used either alone as a bed or on a bedstead **2** : an inflatable airtight sack for use as a mattress

mat·u·rate \'mach-ə-,rāt\ *vb* **-rat·ed; -rat·ing** : MATURE

mat·u·ra·tion \,mach-ə-'rā-shən\ *n* **1** : the process of becoming mature **2** : the emergence of personal and behavioral characteristics through growth processes — **mat·u·ra·tion·al** \-sh(ə-)nəl\ *adj*

¹ma·ture \mə-'t(y)ùr\ *adj* **ma·tur·er; -est** **1** : based on slow careful consideration **2** : having attained a final or desired state ⟨∼ wine⟩ **3** : of or relating to a condition of full development **4** : due for payment ⟨a ∼ loan⟩

²mature *vb* **ma·tured; ma·tur·ing** : to bring to maturity or completion

ma·tu·ri·ty \mə-'t(y)ùr-ət-ē\ *n* : the quality or state of being mature; *esp* : full development

ma·tu·ti·nal \,mach-ù-'tīn-ᵊl; mə-'t(y)üt-(ᵊ-)nəl\ *adj* : of, relating to, or occurring in the morning : EARLY

mat·zo \'mät-sə\ *n, pl* **mat·zoth** \-,sōt(h), -sōs\ *or* **mat·zos** [Yiddish *matse*] : unleavened bread eaten esp. at the Passover

maud·lin \'mod-lən\ *adj* [alter. of Mary *Magdalene;* fr. the practice of depicting her as a weeping, penitent sinner] **1** : weakly and effusively sentimental **2** : drunk enough to be emotionally silly : FUDDLED

¹maul \'mol\ *n* : a heavy hammer often with a wooden head used esp. for driving wedges or piles

²maul *vb* **1** : BEAT, BRUISE; *also* : MANGLE **2** : to handle roughly

maun·der \'mon-dər\ *vb* **maun·dered; maun·der·ing** \-d(ə-)riŋ\ **1** : to wander slowly and idly **2** : to speak indistinctly or disconnectedly

mau·so·le·um \,mó-sə-'lē-əm, ,mó-zə-\ *n, pl* **-leums** *or* **-lea** \-'lē-ə\ [L, fr. Gk *mausōleion,* fr. *Mausōlos* Mausolus † *ab* 353 B.C. ruler of Caria whose tomb was one of the seven wonders of the ancient world] : a large tomb; *esp* : a usu. stone building for entombment of the dead above ground

mauve \'mōv, 'móv\ *n* : a moderate purple, violet, or lilac color

ma·ven *or* **ma·vin** \'mā-vən\ *n* [Yiddish *meyvn,* fr. LHeb *mēbhīn,* fr. Heb *l'havin* to understand] : EXPERT

mav·er·ick \'mav-(ə-)rik\ *n* [Samuel A. *Maverick* † 1870 Am. pioneer who did not brand his calves] **1** : an unbranded range animal **2** : NONCONFORMIST

ma·vis \'mā-vəs\ *n* : an Old World thrush

maw \'mo\ *n* **1** : STOMACH; *also* : the crop of a bird **2** : the throat, gullet, or jaws usu. of a carnivore

mawk·ish \'mó-kish\ *adj* [ME *mawke* maggot, fr. ON *mathkr*] : sickly sentimental — **mawk·ish·ly** *adv* — **mawk·ish·ness** *n*

max *abbr* maximum

maxi \'mak-sē\ *n, pl* **max·is** : a long skirt, dress, or coat that usu. extends to the ankle

maxi- *comb form* **1** : extra long ⟨*maxi*-kilt⟩ **2** : extra large ⟨*maxi*-problems⟩

max·il·la \mak-'sil-ə\ *n, pl* **max·il·lae** \-'sil-(,)ē\ *or* **maxillas** : JAW 1; *esp* : an upper jaw — **max·il·lary** \'mak-sə-,ler-ē\ *adj*

max·im \'mak-səm\ *n* : a proverbial saying

max·i·mal \'mak-s(ə-)məl\ *adj* : MAXIMUM — **max·i·mal·ly** \-ē\ *adv*

max·i·mize \'mak-sə-,mīz\ *vb* **-mized; -miz·ing** **1** : to increase to a maximum **2** : to make the most of

max·i·mum \'mak-s(ə-)məm\ *n, pl* **max·i·ma** \-sə-mə\ *or* **maximums** \-s(ə-)məmz\ **1** : the greatest quantity, value, or degree **2** : an upper limit allowed by authority **3** : the largest of a set of numbers — **maximum** *adj*

may \(')mā\ *verbal auxiliary, past* **might** \(')mīt\ *; pres sing & pl* **may** **1** : have permission or liberty to ⟨you ∼ go now⟩ **2** : be in some degree likely to ⟨you ∼ be right⟩ **3** — used as an auxiliary to express a wish, purpose, contingency, or concession

May \'mā\ *n* [ME, fr. OF *mai,* fr. L *Maius,* fr. *Maia,* Roman goddess] : the fifth month of the year having 31 days

Ma·ya \'mī-ə\ *n, pl* **Maya** *or* **Mayas** : a member of a group of peoples of the Yucatan peninsula and adjacent areas — **Ma·yan** \'mī-ən\ *adj*

may·ap·ple \'mā-ˌap-əl\ *n* : a No. American woodland herb related to the barberry that has a poisonous root, large leaf, and edible but insipid yellow fruit

may·be \'mā-bē, 'meb-ē\ *adv* : PERHAPS

May Day \'mā-ˌdā\ *n* : May 1 celebrated as a springtime festival and in some countries as Labor Day

may·flow·er \'mā-ˌflau(-ə)r\ *n* : any of several spring blooming herbs (as the trailing arbutus or anemone)

may·fly \'mā-ˌflī\ *n* : any of an order of insects with an aquatic nymph and a short-lived fragile adult having membranous wings

may·hem \'mā-ˌhem, 'mā-əm\ *n* 1 : willful and permanent crippling, mutilation, or disfigurement of a person 2 : needless or willful damage

may·on·naise \'mā-ə-ˌnāz\ *n* [F] : a dressing made of raw eggs or egg yolks, vegetable oil, and vinegar or lemon juice

may·or \'mā-ər\ *n* : an official elected to act as chief executive or nominal head of a city or borough — **may·or·al** \-əl\ *adj* — **may·or·al·ty** \-əl-tē\ *n*

may·pole \'mā-ˌpōl\ *n, often cap* : a tall flower-wreathed pole forming a center for May Day sports and dances

maze \'māz\ *n* : a confusing intricate network of passages — **mazy** *adj*

ma·zur·ka \mə-'zər-kə\ *n* : a Polish dance in moderate triple measure

MB *abbr* Manitoba

MBA *abbr* master of business administration

mc *abbr* megacycle

¹**MC** *n* : MASTER OF CEREMONIES

²**MC** *abbr* member of Congress

MCPO *abbr* master chief petty officer

¹**Md** *abbr* Maryland

²**Md** *symbol* mendelevium

MD *abbr* 1 [NL *medicinae doctor*] doctor of medicine 2 Maryland 3 muscular dystrophy

mdnt *abbr* midnight

mdse *abbr* merchandise

MDT *abbr* mountain daylight (saving) time

me \(')mē\ *pron, objective case of* I

Me *abbr* Maine

ME *abbr* 1 Maine 2 mechanical engineer 3 medical examiner 4 Middle English

¹**mead** \'mēd\ *n* : an alcoholic beverage brewed from water and honey, malt, and yeast

²**mead** *n, archaic* : MEADOW

mead·ow \'med-ō\ *n* : land in or mainly in grass; *esp* : a tract of moist low-lying usu. level grassland — **mead·ow·land** \-ˌland\ *n* — **mead·owy** \'med-ə-wē\ *adj*

mead·ow·lark \'med-ō-ˌlärk\ *n* : any of several No. American songbirds that are largely brown and buff above and have a yellow breast marked with a black crescent

mead·ow·sweet \-ˌswēt\ *n* : a No. American native or naturalized spirea

mea·ger *or* **mea·gre** \'mē-gər\ *adj* 1 : THIN 2 : lacking richness, fertility, or strength : POOR *syn* scanty, scant, spare, sparse — **mea·ger·ly** *adv* — **mea·ger·ness** *n*

¹**meal** \'mēl\ *n* 1 : the portion of food taken at one time : REPAST 2 : an act or the time of eating a meal

²**meal** *n* 1 : usu. coarsely ground seeds of a cereal (as Indian corn) 2 : a product resembling seed meal — **mealy** *adj*

meal·time \'mēl-ˌtīm\ *n* : the usual time at which a meal is served

mealy·bug \'mē-lē-ˌbəg\ *n* : any of numerous scale insects with a white powdery covering that are destructive pests esp. of fruit trees

mealy·mouthed \ˌmē-lē-'mauthd, -'mautht\ *adj* : not plain and straightforward : DEVIOUS

¹**mean** \'mēn\ *adj* 1 : HUMBLE 2 : lacking power or acumen : ORDINARY 3 : SHABBY, CONTEMPTIBLE 4 : IGNOBLE, BASE 5 : STINGY 6 : pettily selfish or malicious — **mean·ly** *adv* — **mean·ness** \'mēn-nəs\ *n*

²**mean** \'mēn\ *vb* **meant** \'ment\; **mean·ing** \'mē-niŋ\ 1 : to have in the mind as a purpose 2 : to serve to convey, show, or indicate : SIGNIFY 3 : to have importance to the degree of ⟨health ∼*s* everything⟩ 4 : to direct to a particular individual

³**mean** *adj* 1 : occupying a middle position (as in space, order, or time) 2 : being a mean ⟨a ∼ value⟩

⁴**mean** *n* 1 : a middle point between extremes 2 *pl* : something helpful in achieving a desired end 3 *pl* : material resources affording a secure life 4 : ARITHMETIC MEAN

¹**me·an·der** \mē-'an-dər\ *n* [L *maeander*, fr. Gk *maiandros*, fr. *Maiandros* (now *Menderes*), river in Asia Minor] 1 : a turn or winding of a stream 2 : a winding course

²**meander** *vb* **-dered; -der·ing** \-d(ə-)riŋ\ 1 : to follow a winding course 2 : to wander aimlessly or casually

mean·ing \'mē-niŋ\ *n* 1 : the thing one intends to convey esp. by language; *also* : the thing that is thus conveyed 2 : PURPOSE 3 : SIGNIFICANCE 4 : CONNOTATION; *also* : DENOTATION — **mean·ing·ful** \-fəl\ *adj* — **mean·ing·ful·ly** \-ē\ *adv* — **mean·ing·less** *adj*

¹**mean·time** \'mēn-ˌtīm\ *n* : the intervening time

²**meantime** *adv* : MEANWHILE

¹**mean·while** \-ˌhwīl\ *n* : MEANTIME

²**meanwhile** *adv* : during the intervening time

meas *abbr* measure

mea·sles \'mē-zəlz\ *n pl* : an acute virus disease marked by fever and an eruption of distinct circular red spots

mea·sly \'mēz-(ə-)lē\ *adj* **mea·sli·er; -est** : contemptibly small or insignificant

¹**mea·sure** \'mezh-ər, 'māzh-\ *n* 1 : an adequate or moderate portion; *also*

: a suitable limit **2** : the dimensions, capacity, or amount of something ascertained by measuring; *also* : an instrument for measuring **3** : a unit of measurement; *also* : a system of such units ⟨metric ∼⟩ **4** : the act or process of measuring **5** : rhythmic structure or movement **6** : the part of a musical staff between two adjacent bars **7** : CRITERION **8** : a means to an end **9** : a legislative bill — **mea·sure·less** *adj*

²**measure** *vb* **mea·sured; mea·sur·ing** \'mezh-(ə-)riŋ, 'mäzh-\ **1** : to regulate esp. by a standard **2** : to apportion by measure **3** : to mark off by making measurements **4** : to ascertain the measurements of **5** : to bring into comparison or competition **6** : to serve as a means of measuring **7** : to have a specified measurement — **mea·sur·able** \'mezh-(ə-)rə-bəl, 'mäzh-\ *adj* — **mea·sur·ably** \-blē\ *adv* — **mea·sur·er** *n*

mea·sure·ment \'mezh-ər-mənt, 'mäzh-\ *n* **1** : the act or process of measuring **2** : a figure, extent, or amount obtained by measuring

measure up *vb* **1** : to have necessary qualifications **2** : to equal esp. in ability

meat \'mēt\ *n* **1** : FOOD; *esp* : solid food as distinguished from drink **2** : animal and esp. mammal flesh considered as food **3** : the edible part inside a covering (as a shell or rind) — **meaty** *adj*

meat·ball \-,bol\ *n* : a small ball of chopped or ground meat

mec·ca \'mek-ə\ *n, often cap* [*Mecca*, Saudi Arabia, birthplace of Muhammad and holy city of Islam] : a center of activity sought as a goal by people sharing a common interest

mech *abbr* mechanical; mechanics

¹**me·chan·ic** \mi-'kan-ik\ *adj* : of or relating to manual work or skill

²**mechanic** *n* **1** : a manual worker **2** : MACHINIST; *esp* : one who repairs machines

me·chan·i·cal \mi-'kan-i-kəl\ *adj* **1** : of or relating to machinery, to manual operations, or to mechanics **2** : done as if by a machine : AUTOMATIC **syn** instinctive, impulsive, spontaneous — **me·chan·i·cal·ly** \-k(ə-)lē\ *adv*

mechanical drawing *n* : drawing done with the aid of instruments

me·chan·ics \mi-'kan-iks\ *n sing or pl* **1** : a branch of physics that deals with energy and forces and their effect on bodies **2** : the practical application of mechanics (as to the operation of machines) **3** : mechanical or functional details

mech·a·nism \'mek-ə-,niz-əm\ *n* **1** : a piece of machinery; *also* : a process or technique for achieving a result **2** : mechanical operation or action **3** : the fundamental processes involved in or responsible for a natural phenomenon ⟨the visual ∼⟩

mech·a·nis·tic \,mek-ə-'nis-tik\ *adj*

: mechanically determined ⟨∼ universe⟩ — **mech·a·nis·ti·cal·ly** \-ti-k(ə-)lē\ *adv*

mech·a·nize \'mek-ə-,nīz\ *vb* **-nized; -niz·ing 1** : to make mechanical **2** : to equip with machinery esp. in order to replace human or animal labor **3** : to equip with armed and armored motor vehicles — **mech·a·ni·za·tion** \,mek-ə-nə-'zā-shən\ *n* — **mech·a·niz·er** \'mek-ə-,nī-zər\ *n*

med *abbr* **1** medical; medicine **2** medieval **3** medium

MEd *abbr* master of education

med·al \'med-ᵊl\ *n* [MF *medaille*, fr. OIt *medaglia* coin worth half a denarius, medal, fr. (assumed) VL *medalis* half, fr. LL *medialis* middle, fr. L *medius*] **1** : a small usu. metal object bearing a religious emblem or picture **2** : a piece of metal issued to commemorate a person or event or awarded for excellence or achievement

med·al·ist *or* **med·al·list** \'med-ᵊl-əst\ *n* **1** : a designer or maker of medals **2** : a recipient of a medal

me·dal·lion \mə-'dal-yən\ *n* **1** : a large medal **2** : a tablet or panel bearing a portrait or an ornament

med·dle \'med-ᵊl\ *vb* **med·dled; med·dling** \'med-(ᵊ-)liŋ\ : to interfere without right or propriety — **med·dler** \'med-(ᵊ-)lər\ *n*

med·dle·some \'med-ᵊl-səm\ *adj* : inclined to meddle in the affairs of others

me·dia \'mēd-ē-ə\ *n, pl* **me·di·as** : MEDIUM **4**

me·di·al \'mēd-ē-əl\ *adj* **1** : occurring in or extending toward the middle : MEDIAN **2** : MEAN, AVERAGE

¹**me·di·an** \'mēd-ē-ən\ *n* **1** : a medial part **2** : a value in an ordered set of values below and above which there are an equal number of values

²**median** *adj* **1** : MEDIAL **1 2** : relating to or constituting a statistical median

median strip *n* : a strip dividing a highway into lanes according to the direction of travel

¹**me·di·ate** \'mēd-ē-ət\ *adj* **1** : occupying a middle or mediating position **2** : acting through a mediate agency — **me·di·ate·ly** *adv*

²**me·di·ate** \'mēd-ē-,āt\ *vb* **-at·ed; -at·ing** : to act as an intermediary (as in settling a dispute or promoting a chemical or physiological result or activity) **syn** intercede, intervene, interpose, interfere — **me·di·a·tion** \,mēd-ē-'ā-shən\ *n* — **me·di·a·tor** \'mēd-ē-,āt-ər\ *n*

med·ic \'med-ik\ *n* : one engaged in medical work; *esp* : CORPSMAN

med·i·ca·ble \'med-i-kə-bəl\ *adj* : CURABLE, REMEDIABLE — **med·i·ca·bly** \-blē\ *adv*

med·ic·aid \'med-i-,kād\ *n, often cap* : a program of financial assistance for medical care designed for those unable to afford regular medical service and financed jointly by the state and federal governments

med·i·cal \'med-i-kəl\ *adj* : of or relating to the science or practice of medicine or the treatment of disease — **med·i·cal·ly** \-k(ə-)lē\ *adv*

medical examiner *n* : a public officer who makes postmortem examinations of bodies to find the cause of death

me·di·ca·ment \mi-'dik-ə-mənt, 'med-i-kə-\ *n* : a medicine or healing application

medi·care \'med-i-ˌkeər\ *n, often cap* : a government program of financial assistance for medical care esp. for the aged

med·i·cate \'med-ə-ˌkāt\ *vb* **-cat·ed; -cat·ing** : to treat with medicine — **med·i·ca·tion** \ˌmed-ə-'kā-shən\ *n*

me·dic·i·nal \mə-'dis-(ə-)nəl\ *adj* : tending or used to cure disease or relieve pain — **me·dic·i·nal·ly** \-ē\ *adv*

med·i·cine \'med-ə-sən\ *n* **1** : a substance or preparation used in treating disease **2** : a science or art dealing with the prevention or cure of disease

medicine ball *n* : a heavy stuffed leather ball used for conditioning exercises

medicine man *n* : a priestly healer or sorcerer esp. among the American Indians

med·i·co \'med-i-ˌkō\ *n, pl* **-cos** : a medical practitioner or student

me·di·eval *or* **me·di·ae·val** \ˌmēd-ē-'ē-vəl, ˌmed-, med-, ˌmē'dē-vəl\ *adj* : of, relating to, or characteristic of the Middle Ages — **me·di·eval·ism** \-ˌiz-əm\ *n* — **me·di·eval·ist** \-əst\ *n*

me·di·o·cre \ˌmēd-ē-'ō-kər\ *adj* [MF, fr. L *mediocris*, lit., halfway up a mountain, fr. *medius* middle + *ocris* stony mountain] : of moderate or low quality : ORDINARY — **me·di·oc·ri·ty** \-'äk-rət-ē\ *n*

med·i·tate \'med-ə-ˌtāt\ *vb* **-tat·ed; -tat·ing 1** : to muse over : CONTEMPLATE, PONDER **2** : INTEND, PURPOSE — **med·i·ta·tion** \ˌmed-ə-'tā-shən\ *n* — **med·i·ta·tive** \'med-ə-ˌtāt-iv\ *adj* — **med·i·ta·tive·ly** *adv*

Med·i·ter·ra·nean \ˌmed-ə-tə-'rā-nē-ən, -'rā-nyən\ *adj* : of or relating to the Mediterranean sea or to the lands or people around it

¹me·di·um \'mēd-ē-əm\ *n, pl* **mediums** *or* **me·dia** \-ē-ə\ [L] **1** : something in a middle position; *also* : a middle position or degree **2** : a means of effecting or conveying something **3** : a surrounding or enveloping substance **4** : a channel or system of communication, information, or entertainment **5** : a mode of artistic expression **6** : an individual held to be a channel of communication between the earthly world and a world of spirits **7** : a condition in which something may function or flourish

²medium *adj* : intermediate in amount, quality, position, or degree

me·di·um·is·tic \ˌmēd-ē-ə-'mis-tik\ *adj* : of, relating to, or being a spiritualistic medium

med·ley \'med-lē\ *n, pl* **medleys 1** : HODGEPODGE **2** : a musical composition made up esp. of a series of songs

me·dul·la \mə-'dəl-ə\ *n, pl* **-las** *or* **-lae** \-(ˌ)ē, -ˌī\ [L] : an inner or deep anatomical part; *also* : the posterior part (**medulla ob·lon·ga·ta** \-ˌäb-ˌlõŋ-gät-ə\) of the brain

meed \'mēd\ *n* **1** *archaic* : REWARD **2** : a fitting return

meek \'mēk\ *adj* **1** : characterized by patience and long-suffering **2** : deficient in spirit and courage **3** : MODERATE — **meek·ly** *adv* — **meek·ness** *n*

meer·schaum \'mir-shəm, -ˌshȯm\ *n* [G, fr. *meer* sea + *schaum* foam] : a tobacco pipe made of a light white clayey mineral

¹meet \'mēt\ *vb* **met** \'met\; **meet·ing 1** : to come upon : FIND **2** : JOIN, INTERSECT **3** : to appear to the perception of **4** : OPPOSE, FIGHT **5** : to join in conversation or discussion; *also* : ASSEMBLE **6** : to conform to **7** : to pay fully **8** : to cope with **9** : to provide for **10** : to be introduced to

²meet *n* : an assembling esp. for a hunt or for competitive sports

³meet *adj* : SUITABLE, PROPER

meet·ing \'mēt-iŋ\ *n* **1** : an act of coming together : ASSEMBLY **2** : JUNCTION, INTERSECTION

meet·ing·house \-ˌhaȯs\ *n* : a building for public assembly and esp. for Protestant worship

mega·byte \'meg-ə-ˌbīt\ *n* : a unit of computer storage capacity approximately equal to one million bytes

mega·cy·cle \-ˌsī-kəl\ *n* : MEGAHERTZ

mega·death \-ˌdeth\ *n* : one million deaths — used as a unit in reference to atomic warfare

mega·hertz \'meg-ə-ˌhərts, -ˌheərts\ *n* : a unit of frequency equal to one million hertz

mega·lith \'meg-ə-ˌlith\ *n* : one of the huge stones used in various prehistoric monuments — **mega·lith·ic** \ˌmeg-ə-'lith-ik\ *adj*

meg·a·lo·ma·nia \ˌmeg-ə-lō-'mā-nē-ə, -nyə\ *n* : a disorder of mind marked by feelings of personal omnipotence and grandeur — **meg·a·lo·ma·ni·ac** \-'mā-nē-ˌak\ *adj or n*

meg·a·lop·o·lis \ˌmeg-ə-'läp-ə-ləs\ *n* : a very large urban unit

mega·phone \'meg-ə-ˌfōn\ *n* : a cone-shaped device used to intensify or direct the voice — **megaphone** *vb*

mega·ton \-ˌtən\ *n* : an explosive force equivalent to that of one million tons of TNT

mega·vi·ta·min \-ˌvīt-ə-mən\ *adj* : relating to or consisting of very large doses of vitamins — **mega·vi·ta·mins** *n pl*

mei·o·sis \mī-'ō-səs\ *n* : the cellular process that results in the number of chromosomes in gamete-producing cells being reduced to one half — **mei·ot·ic** \mī-'ät-ik\ *adj*

mel·an·cho·lia \,mel-ən-'kō-lē-ə\ *n* : a mental condition marked by extreme depression often with delusions

mel·an·chol·ic \,mel-ən-'käl-ik\ *adj* 1 : DEPRESSED 2 : of or relating to melancholia

mel·an·choly \'mel-ən-,käl-ē\ *n, pl* **-chol·ies** [ME *malencolie*, fr. MF *melancolie*, fr. LL *melancholia*, fr. Gk, fr. *melan-, melas* black + *cholē* bile; so called fr. the former belief that it was caused by an excess in the system of black bile, a substance supposedly secreted by the kidneys or spleen] : depression of spirits : DEJECTION, GLOOM — **melancholy** *adj*

Mel·a·ne·sian \,mel-ə-'nē-zhən\ *n* : a member of the dominant native group of the Pacific island grouping of Melanesia — **Melanesian** *adj*

mé·lange \mā-'läⁿzh, -'länj\ *n* : a mixture esp. of incongruous elements

me·lan·ic \mə-'lan-ik\ *adj* 1 : having black pigment 2 : affected with or characterized by melanism — **melanic** *n*

mel·a·nin \'mel-ə-nən\ *n* : a dark brown or black animal or plant pigment

mel·a·nism \'mel-ə-,niz-əm\ *n* : an increased amount of black or nearly black pigmentation

mel·a·no·ma \,mel-ə-'nō-mə\ *n, pl* **-mas** *also* **-ma·ta** \-'mät-ə\ : a usu. malignant tumor containing black pigment

¹**meld** \'meld\ *vb* : to show or announce for a score in a card game

²**meld** *n* : a card or combination of cards that is or can be melded

me·lee \'mā-,lā, mā-'lā\ *n* [F *mêlée*] : a confused struggle **syn** fracas, row, brawl, donnybrook

me·lio·rate \'mēl-yə-,rāt, 'mē-lē-ə-\ *vb* **-rat·ed; -rat·ing** : to make or become better — **me·lio·ra·tion** \,mēl-yə-'rā-shən, ,mē-lē-ə-\ *n* — **me·lio·ra·tive** \'mēl-yə-,rāt-iv, 'mē-lē-ə-\ *adj*

mel·lif·lu·ous \me-'lif-lə-wəs, mə-\ *adj* [LL *mellifluus*, fr. L *mel* honey + *fluere* to flow] : sweetly flowing — **mel·lif·lu·ous·ly** *adv* — **mel·lif·lu·ous·ness** *n*

¹**mel·low** \'mel-ō\ *adj* 1 : soft and sweet because of ripeness ⟨~ apple⟩ ; *also* : well aged and pleasingly mild ⟨~ wine⟩ 2 : made gentle by age or experience 3 : being rich and full but not garish or strident ⟨~ colors⟩ 4 : of soft loamy consistency ⟨~ soil⟩ — **mel·low·ness** *n*

²**mellow** *vb* : to make or become mellow

me·lo·de·on \mə-'lōd-ē-ən\ *n* : a small reed organ in which a suction bellows draws air inward through the reeds

me·lo·di·ous \mə-'lōd-ē-əs\ *adj* : pleasing to the ear — **me·lo·di·ous·ly** *adv* — **me·lo·di·ous·ness** *n*

melo·dra·ma \'mel-ə-,dräm-ə, -,dram-\ *n* : an extravagantly theatrical play in which action and plot predominate over characterization — **melo·dra·mat·ic** \,mel-ə-drə-'mat-ik\ *adj* — **melo·dra·ma·tist** \,mel-ə-'dram-ət-əst, -'dräm-\ *n*

mel·o·dy \'mel-əd-ē\ *n, pl* **-dies** 1 : sweet or agreeable sound ⟨birds making ~⟩ 2 : a particular succession of notes : TUNE, AIR — **me·lod·ic** \mə-'läd-ik\ *adj* — **me·lod·i·cal·ly** \-i-k(ə-)lē\ *adv*

mel·on \'mel-ən\ *n* : any of certain fruits (as a muskmelon or watermelon) of the gourd family usu. eaten raw

¹**melt** \'melt\ *vb* 1 : to change from a solid to a liquid state usu. by heat 2 : DISSOLVE, DISINTEGRATE; *also* : to cause to disperse or disappear 3 : to make or become tender or gentle

²**melt** *n* : a melted substance

melt·down \'melt-,daun\ *n* : the melting of the core of a nuclear reactor

melt·wa·ter \'melt-,wòt-ər, -,wät-\ *n* : water derived from the melting of ice and snow

mem *abbr* 1 member 2 memoir 3 memorial

mem·ber \'mem-bər\ *n* 1 : a part (as an arm, leg, or branch) of a person, lower animal, or plant 2 : one of the individuals composing a group 3 : a constituent part of a whole

mem·ber·ship \-,ship\ *n* 1 : the state or status of being a member 2 : the body of members

mem·brane \'mem-,brān\ *n* : a thin pliable layer esp. of animal or plant tissue — **mem·bra·nous** \-brə-nəs\ *adj*

me·men·to \mə-'ment-ō\ *n, pl* **-tos** *or* **-toes** [ME, fr. L remember] : something that serves to warn or remind : SOUVENIR

memo \'mem-ō\ *n, pl* **mem·os** : MEMORANDUM

mem·oir \'mem-,wär\ *n* 1 : MEMORANDUM 2 : AUTOBIOGRAPHY — usu. used in pl. 3 : an account of something noteworthy; *also, pl* : the record of the proceedings of a learned society

mem·o·ra·bil·ia \,mem-ə-rə-'bil-ē-ə, -'bil-yə\ *n pl* [L] : things worthy of remembrance; *also* : a record of such things

mem·o·ra·ble \'mem-(ə-)rə-bəl\ *adj* : worth remembering : NOTABLE — **mem·o·ra·bil·i·ty** \,mem-ə-rə-'bil-ət-ē\ *n* — **mem·o·ra·ble·ness** *n* — **mem·o·ra·bly** \-blē\ *adv*

mem·o·ran·dum \,mem-ə-'ran-dəm\ *n, pl* **-dums** *or* **-da** \-də\ 1 : an informal record; *also* : a written reminder 2 : an informal written note

¹**me·mo·ri·al** \mə-'mòr-ē-əl\ *adj* : serving to preserve remembrance

²**memorial** *n* 1 : something designed to keep remembrance alive; *esp* : MONUMENT 2 : a statement of facts often accompanied with a petition — **me·mo·ri·al·ize** *vb*

Memorial Day *n* : the last Monday in May or formerly May 30 observed as a legal holiday in honor of those who died in war

mem•o•rize \'mem-ə-ˌrīz\ vb -rized; -riz•ing : to learn by heart — **mem•o•ri•za•tion** \ˌmem-(ə-)rə-'zā-shən\ n — **mem•o•riz•er** \'mem-ə-ˌrīz-ər\ n

mem•o•ry \'mem-(ə-)rē\ n, pl -ries **1** : the power or process of remembering **2** : the store of things remembered **3** : COMMEMORATION **4** : something remembered **5** : the time within which past events are remembered **6** : a device (as in a computer) in which information can be stored syn remembrance, recollection, reminiscence

men pl of MAN

¹men•ace \'men-əs\ n **1** : THREAT **2** : DANGER; also : NUISANCE

²menace vb **men•aced; men•ac•ing 1** : THREATEN **2** : ENDANGER — **men•ac•ing•ly** adv

mé•nage \mā-'näzh\ n [F] : HOUSEHOLD

me•nag•er•ie \mə-'naj-(ə-)rē\ n : a collection of wild animals esp. for exhibition

¹mend \'mend\ vb **1** : to improve in manners or morals **2** : to put into good shape : REPAIR **3** : to restore to health : HEAL — **mend•er** n

²mend n **1** : an act of mending **2** : a mended place

men•da•cious \men-'dā-shəs\ adj : given to deception or falsehood : UNTRUTHFUL syn dishonest, deceitful — **men•da•cious•ly** adv — **men•dac•i•ty** \-'das-ət-ē\ n

men•de•le•vi•um \ˌmen-də-'lē-vē-əm, -'lā-\ n : a radioactive chemical element artificially produced

men•di•cant \'men-di-kənt\ n **1** : BEGGAR **2** often cap : FRIAR — **men•di•can•cy** \-kən-sē\ n — **mendicant** adj

men•folk \'men-ˌfōk\ or **men•folks** \-ˌfōks\ n pl **1** : men in general **2** : the men of a family or community

men•ha•den \men-'hād-ᵊn, mən-\ n, pl **-den** also **-dens** : a marine fish related to the herring that is abundant along the Atlantic coast of the U.S.

¹me•nial \'mē-nē-əl, -nyəl\ adj **1** : of or relating to servants **2** : HUMBLE; also : SERVILE — **me•ni•al•ly** \-ē\ adv

²menial n : a domestic servant

men•in•gi•tis \ˌmen-ən-'jīt-əs\ n, pl **-git•i•des** \-'jit-ə-ˌdēz\ : inflammation of the membranes enclosing the brain and spinal cord; also : a usu. bacterial disease marked by this

me•ninx \'mē-niŋks, 'men-iŋks\ n, pl **me•nin•ges** \mə-'nin-(ˌ)jēz\ : any of the three membranes that envelop the brain and spinal cord — **men•in•ge•al** \ˌmen-ən-'jē-əl\ adj

me•nis•cus \mə-'nis-kəs\ n, pl **me•nis•ci** \-'nis-ˌ(k)ī, -ˌkē\ also **me•nis•cus•es 1** : CRESCENT **2** : the curved upper surface of a column of liquid

meno•pause \'men-ə-ˌpȯz\ n : the period of natural cessation of menstruation — **meno•paus•al** \ˌmen-ə-'pȯ-zəl\ adj

men•ses \'men-ˌsēz\ n pl : the menstrual flow

men•stru•a•tion \ˌmen-strə-'wā-shən, men-'strā-\ n : a discharging of bloody matter at approximately monthly intervals from the uterus of breeding-age nonpregnant primate females — **men•stru•al** \'men-strə(-wə)l\ adj — **men•stru•ate** \'men-strə-ˌwāt, -ˌstrāt\ vb

men•su•ra•ble \'mens-(ə-)rə-bəl, 'mench-(ə-)rə-\ adj : MEASURABLE

men•su•ra•tion \ˌmen-sə-'rā-shən, ˌmen-chə-\ n : MEASUREMENT

-ment \mənt\ n suffix **1** : concrete result, object, or agent of a (specified) action (embankment) (entanglement) **2** : concrete means or instrument of a (specified) action (entertainment) **3** : action : process (encirclement) (development) **4** : place of a (specified) action (encampment) **5** : state : condition (amazement)

men•tal \'ment-ᵊl\ adj **1** : of or relating to the mind **2** : of, relating to, or affected with a disorder of the mind — **men•tal•ly** \-ē\ adv

mental age n : a measure used in psychological testing that expresses a person's mental attainment in terms of the number of years it takes the average child to reach the same level

mental deficiency n : failure in intellectual development that results in social incompetence and is considered to be the result of a defective central nervous system

men•tal•i•ty \men-'tal-ət-ē\ n, pl -ties **1** : mental power or capacity **2** : mode or way of thought

men•thol \'men-ˌthȯl, -ˌthōl\ n : a white soothing substance from oil of peppermint — **men•tho•lat•ed** \-thə-ˌlāt-əd\ adj

¹men•tion \'men-chən\ n **1** : a brief or casual reference **2** : a formal citation for outstanding achievement

²mention vb **men•tioned; men•tion•ing** \'mench-(ə-)niŋ\ **1** : to refer to : CITE **2** : to cite for outstanding achievement — **not to mention** : AS WELL AS

men•tor \'men-ˌtȯr, 'ment-ər\ n : a trusted counselor or guide; also : TUTOR, COACH

menu \'men-yü, 'mān-\ n, pl **menus** [F, fr. menu small, detailed, fr. L minutus minute (adj.)] : a list of the dishes available (as in a restaurant) for a meal; also : the dishes served

me•ow \mē-'au̇\ vb : to make the characteristic cry of a cat — **meow** n

me•phit•ic \mə-'fit-ik\ adj : foul-smelling

mer abbr meridian

mer•can•tile \'mər-kən-ˌtēl, -ˌtīl\ adj : of or relating to merchants or trading

¹mer•ce•nary \'mərs-ᵊn-ˌer-ē\ n, pl **-nar•ies** : one who serves merely for wages; esp : a soldier serving in a foreign army

²mercenary adj **1** : serving merely for

pay or gain **2** : hired for service in a foreign army — **mer·ce·nari·ly** \,mərs-ᵊn-ᵊer-ə-lē\ adv — **mer·ce·nari·ness** \'mərs-ᵊn-,er-ē-nəs\ n

mer·cer \'mər-sər\ n : a dealer in usu. expensive fabrics

mer·cer·ize \'mər-sə-,rīz\ vb **-ized; -iz·ing** : to treat cotton yarn or cloth with alkali so that it looks silky or takes a better dye

¹**mer·chan·dise** \'mər-chən-,dīz, -,dīs\ n : the commodities or goods that are bought and sold in business

²**mer·chan·dise** \-,dīz\ vb **-dised; -dis·ing** : to buy and sell in business : TRADE — **mer·chan·dis·er** n

mer·chant \'mər-chənt\ n **1** : a buyer and seller of commodities for profit **2** : STOREKEEPER

mer·chant·able \'mər-chənt-ə-bəl\ : acceptable to buyers : MARKETABLE

mer·chant·man \'mər-chənt-mən\ n : a ship used in commerce

merchant marine n : the commercial ships of a nation

merchant ship n : MERCHANTMAN

mer·cu·ri·al \,mər-'kyùr-ē-əl\ adj **1** : unpredictably changeable **2** : MER-CURIC — **mer·cu·ri·al·ly** \-ē\ adv — **mer·cu·ri·al·ness** n

mer·cu·ric \,mər-'kyùr-ik\ adj : of, relating to, or containing mercury

mercuric chloride n : a poisonous compound of mercury and chlorine used as an antiseptic and fungicide

mer·cu·ry \'mər-kyə-rē\ n, pl **-ries 1** : a heavy silver-white liquid metallic chemical element used esp. in scientific instruments **2** cap : the planet nearest the sun

mer·cy \'mər-sē\ n, pl **mercies** [ME, fr. OF merci, fr. ML merces, fr. L, price paid, wages, fr. merc-, merx merchandise] **1** : compassion shown to an offender; also : imprisonment rather than death for first-degree murder **2** : a blessing resulting from divine favor or compassion; also : a fortunate circumstance **3** : compassion shown to victims of misfortune — **mer·ci·ful** \-si-fəl\ adj — **mer·ci·ful·ly** \-ē\ adv — **mer·ci·less** \-si-ləs\ adj — **mer·ci·less·ly** adv — **mercy** adj

mercy killing n : the act or practice of killing or permitting the death of hopelessly sick or injured persons or animals with as little pain as possible for reasons of mercy

¹**mere** \'miər\ n : LAKE, POOL

²**mere** adj mer·est **1** : being nothing more than : BARE **2** : not diluted : PURE — **mere·ly** adv

mer·e·tri·cious \,mer-ə-'trish-əs\ adj [L meretricius, fr. meretrix prostitute, fr. merēre to earn] : tawdrily attractive; also : SPECIOUS — **mer·e·tri·cious·ly** adv — **mer·e·tri·cious·ness** n

mer·gan·ser \(,)mər-'gan-sər\ n : any of various fish-eating ducks with a crested head and a slender bill hooked at the end and serrated along the margins

merge \'mərj\ vb **merged; merg·ing 1** : to blend gradually **2** : to combine, unite, or coalesce into one syn mingle, amalgamate, fuse, interfuse, intermingle

merg·er \'mər-jər\ n **1** : the act or process of merging **2** : absorption by a corporation of one or more others

me·rid·i·an \mə-'rid-ē-ən\ n [ME, fr. MF meridien, fr. meridien of noon, fr. L meridianus, fr. meridies noon, south, irreg. fr. medius mid + dies day] **1** : the highest point : CULMINA-TION **2** : one of the imaginary circles on the earth's surface passing through the north and south poles — **meridian** adj

me·ringue \mə-'raŋ\ n [F] : a dessert topping of baked beaten egg whites and powdered sugar

me·ri·no \mə-'rē-nō\ n, pl **-nos** [Sp] **1** : any of a breed of sheep noted for fine soft wool; also : its wool or fleece **2** : a fine soft fabric or yarn of wool or wool and cotton

¹**mer·it** \'mer-ət\ n **1** : laudable or blameworthy traits or actions **2** : a praiseworthy quality; also : character or conduct deserving reward or honor **3** pl : the intrinsic nature of a legal case; also : legal significance

²**merit** vb : EARN, DESERVE

mer·i·toc·ra·cy \,mer-ə-'täk-rə-sē\ n, pl **-cies** : an educational system whereby the talented are chosen and moved ahead on the basis of their achievement; also : leadership by the talented

mer·i·to·ri·ous \,mer-ə-'tōr-ē-əs\ adj : deserving honor or esteem — **mer·i·to·ri·ous·ly** adv — **mer·i·to·ri·ous·ness** n

mer·maid \'mər-,mād\ n : a legendary sea creature with a woman's upper body and a fish's tail

mer·man \-,man, -mən\ n : a legendary sea creature with a man's upper body and a fish's tail

mer·ri·ment \'mer-i-mənt\ n **1** : HILARI-TY **2** : FESTIVITY

mer·ry \'mer-ē\ adj mer·ri·er; -est **1** : full of gaiety or high spirits **2** : marked by festivity **3** : BRISK (a ~ pace) syn blithe, jocund, jovial, jolly, mirthful — **mer·ri·ly** \'mer-ə-lē\ adv

merry-go-round \'mer-ē-gō-,raûnd\ n **1** : a circular revolving platform with benches and figures of animals on which people sit for a ride **2** : a busy round of activities

mer·ry·mak·ing \'mer-ē-,mā-kiŋ\ n **1** : CONVIVIALITY **2** : a festive occasion — **mer·ry·mak·er** \-,kər\ n

me·sa \'mā-sə\ n [Sp, lit., table, fr. L mensa] : a flat-topped hill with steep sides

més·al·liance \,mā-,zal-'yäⁿs, ,mā-zə-'lī-əns\ n, pl **més·al·liances** \-'yäⁿs(-,əz), -'lī-ən-səz\ [F] : a marriage with a person of inferior social position

mes·cal \me-'skal, mə-\ *n* **1** : a small cactus that is the source of a stimulant used esp. by Mexican Indians **2** : a usu. colorless liquor distilled from the leaves of an agave; *also* : AGAVE

mes·ca·line \'mes-kə-lən, -ˌlēn\ *n* : a hallucinatory alkaloid from the mescal cactus

mesdames *pl of* MADAM *or of* MADAME *or of* MRS.

mesdemoiselles *pl of* MADEMOISELLE

¹mesh \'mesh\ *n* **1** : one of the openings between the threads or cords of a net; *also* : one of the similar spaces in a network **2** : the fabric of a net **3** : NETWORK **4** : working contact (as of the teeth of gears) (in ~) — **meshed** \'mesht\ *adj*

²mesh *vb* **1** : to catch in or as if in a mesh **2** : to be in or come into mesh : ENGAGE **3** : to fit together properly

mesh·work \'mesh-ˌwərk\ *n* : NETWORK

me·si·al \'mē-zē-əl, -sē-\ *adj* : of, relating to, or being the surface of a tooth that is closest to the middle of the front of the jaw

mes·mer·ize \'mez-mə-ˌrīz\ *vb* **-ized; -iz·ing** : HYPNOTIZE — **mes·mer·ic** \mez-'mer-ik\ *adj* — **mes·mer·ism** \'mez-mə-ˌriz-əm\ *n*

Me·so·lith·ic \ˌmez-ə-'lith-ik\ *adj* : of, relating to, or being a transitional period of the Stone Age between the Paleolithic and the Neolithic periods

me·so·sphere \'mez-ə-ˌsfiər\ *n* : a layer of the atmosphere above the stratosphere

Me·so·zo·ic \ˌmez-ə-'zō-ik, ˌmēz-\ *adj* : of, relating to, or being the era of geologic history between the Paleozoic and the Cenozoic and extending from about 230 million years ago to about 70 million years ago — **Mesozoic** *n*

mes·quite \mə-'skēt, me-\ *n* : a thorny leguminous shrub of Mexico and the southwestern U.S. with sugar-rich pods important as fodder

¹mess \'mes\ *n* **1** : a quantity of food; *also* : enough food of a specified kind for a dish or meal (a ~ of beans) **2** : a group of persons who regularly eat together; *also* : a meal eaten by such a group **3** : a confused, dirty, or offensive state — **messy** *adj*

²mess *vb* **1** : to supply with meals; *also* : to take meals with a mess **2** : to make dirty or untidy; *also* : BUNGLE **3** : INTERFERE, MEDDLE **4** : PUTTER, TRIFLE

mes·sage \'mes-ij\ *n* : a communication sent by one person to another

messeigneurs *pl of* MONSEIGNEUR

mes·sen·ger \'mes-ᵊn-jər\ *n* : one who carries a message or does an errand

messenger RNA *n* : an RNA that carries the code for a particular protein from the nuclear DNA to a ribosome in the cytoplasm and acts as a template for the formation of that protein

Mes·si·ah \mə-'sī-ə\ *n* **1** : the expected king and deliverer of the Jews **2** : Jesus **3** *not cap* : a professed or accepted leader of a cause — **mes·si·an·ic** \ˌmes-ē-'an-ik\ *adj*

messieurs *pl of* MONSIEUR

mess·mate \'mes-ˌmāt\ *n* : a member of a group who eat regularly together

Messrs. \'mes-ərz\ *pl of* MR.

mes·ti·zo \me-'stē-zō\ *n, pl* **-zos** [Sp, fr. *mestizo* mixed, fr. LL *mixticius*, fr. L *mixtus*, pp. of *miscēre* to mix] : a person of mixed blood

¹met *past and past part of* MEET

²met *abbr* metropolitan

me·tab·o·lism \mə-'tab-ə-ˌliz-əm\ *n* : the sum of the processes in the building up and breaking down of the substance of plants and animals incidental to life; *also* : the processes by which a substance is handled in the body (~ of sugar) — **met·a·bol·ic** \ˌmet-ə-'bäl-ik\ *adj* — **me·tab·o·lize** \mə-'tab-ə-ˌlīz\ *vb*

me·tab·o·lite \-ˌlīt\ *n* **1** : a product of metabolism **2** : a substance essential to the metabolism of a particular organism

meta·car·pal \ˌmet-ə-'kär-pəl\ *n* : any of usu. five more or less elongated bones of the part of the hand or forefoot between the carpus and the bones of the digits — **metacarpal** *adj*

meta·car·pus \-'kär-pəs\ *n* : the part of the hand or forefoot that contains the metacarpals

met·al \'met-ᵊl\ *n* **1** : any of various opaque, fusible, ductile, and typically lustrous substances; *esp* : one that is a chemical element **2** : METTLE; *also* : the material out of which a person or thing is made — **me·tal·lic** \mə-'tal-ik\ *adj* — **met·al·loid** \'met-ᵊl-ˌȯid\ *n or adj*

met·al·lur·gy \'met-ᵊl-ˌər-jē\ *n* : the science and technology of metals — **met·al·lur·gi·cal** \ˌmet-ᵊl-'ər-ji-kəl\ *adj* — **met·al·lur·gist** \'met-ᵊl-ˌər-jəst\ *n*

met·al·ware \'met-ᵊl-ˌwaər\ *n* : metal utensils for household use

met·al·work \-ˌwərk\ *n* : work and esp. artistic work made of metal — **met·al·work·er** \-ˌwər-kər\ *n* — **met·al·work·ing** \-ˌwər-kiŋ\ *n*

meta·mor·phism \ˌmet-ə-'mȯr-ˌfiz-əm\ *n* : a change in the structure of rock; *esp* : a change to a more compact highly crystalline condition produced by pressure, heat, and water — **meta·mor·phic** \-'mȯr-fik\ *adj*

meta·mor·pho·sis \ˌmet-ə-'mȯr-fə-səs\ *n, pl* **-pho·ses** \-ˌsēz\ **1** : a change of physical form, structure, or substance esp. by supernatural means; *also* : a striking alteration (as in appearance or character) **2** : a fundamental change in form and often habits of an animal accompanying the transformation of a larva into an adult — **meta·mor·phose** \-ˌfōz, -ˌfōs\ *vb*

meta·phor \'met-ə-ˌfȯr\ *n* : a figure of speech in which a word denoting one subject or idea is used in place of another to suggest a likeness between them (as in "the ship plows the sea") — **met·a·phor·i·cal** \,met-ə-'fȯr-i-kəl\ adj

meta·phys·ics \,met-ə-'fiz-iks\ n [ML *Metaphysica*, title of Aristotle's treatise on the subject, fr. Gk (*ta*) *meta* (*ta*) *physika*, lit., the (works) after the physical (works); fr. its position in his collected works] : the part of philosophy concerned with the study of the ultimate causes and underlying nature of things — **meta·phys·i·cal** \-'fiz-i-kəl\ adj — **meta·phy·si·cian** \-fə-'zish-ən\ n

me·tas·ta·sis \mə-'tas-tə-səs\ n, pl **-ta·ses** \-,sēz\ : transfer of a health-impairing agency (as tumor cells) to a new site in the body; also : a secondary growth of a malignant tumor — **met·a·stat·ic** \,met-ə-'stat-ik\ adj

meta·tar·sal \,met-ə-'tär-səl\ n : any of the bones of the foot between the tarsus and the bones of the digits that in human beings include five more or less elongated bones — **metatarsal** adj

meta·tar·sus \-'tär-səs\ n : the part of the foot in man or of the hind foot in quadrupeds that contains the metatarsals

¹**mete** \'mēt\ vb **met·ed; met·ing** 1 archaic : MEASURE 2 : ALLOT

²**mete** n : BOUNDARY (~s and bounds)

me·tem·psy·cho·sis \mə-,tem(p)-si-'kō-səs, ,met-əm-,sī-\ n : the passing of the soul at death into another body either human or animal

me·te·or \'mēt-ē-ər, -ē-ȯr\ n 1 : a usu. small particle of matter in the solar system observable only when it falls into the earth's atmosphere where friction causes it to glow 2 : the streak of light produced by passage of a meteor

me·te·or·ic \,mēt-ē-'ȯr-ik\ adj 1 : of, relating to, or resembling a meteor 2 : transiently brilliant (a ~ career) — **me·te·or·i·cal·ly** \-i-k(ə-)lē\ adv

me·te·or·ite \'mēt-ē-ə-,rīt\ n : a meteor that reaches the surface of the earth

me·te·or·oid \'mēt-ē-ə-,rȯid\ n : a meteor in orbit around the sun

me·te·o·rol·o·gy \,mēt-ē-ə-'räl-ə-jē\ n : a science that deals with the atmosphere and its phenomena and esp. with weather and weather forecasting — **me·te·o·ro·log·ic** \,mēt-ē-,ȯr-ə-'läj-ik\ or **me·te·o·ro·log·i·cal** \-'läj-i-kəl\ adj — **me·te·o·rol·o·gist** \,mēt-ē-ə-'räl-ə-jəst\ n

¹**me·ter** \'mēt-ər\ n : rhythm in verse or music

²**me·ter** \'mēt-ər\ n : the basic metric unit of length — see METRIC SYSTEM table

³**me·ter** \'mēt-ər\ n : a measuring and sometimes recording instrument

⁴**me·ter** vb 1 : to measure by means of a meter 2 : to print postal indicia on by means of a postage meter (~ed mail)

meter–kilogram–second adj : MKS

meter maid n : a female member of a police department who is assigned to write tickets for parking violations

meth·a·done \'meth-ə-,dōn\ also **meth·a·don** \-,dän\ n : a synthetic addictive narcotic drug used esp. as a substitute narcotic in the treatment of heroin addiction

meth·am·phet·amine \,meth-am-'fet-ə-,mēn, ,meth-əm-, -mən\ n : a drug used in the form of its hydrochloride as a stimulant for the central nervous system and in the treatment of obesity

meth·ane \'meth-,ān\ n : a colorless odorless flammable gas produced by decomposition of organic matter (as in marshes) or from coal and used as a fuel

meth·a·nol \'meth-ə-,nȯl, -,nōl\ n : a volatile flammable poisonous liquid alcohol that consists of carbon, hydrogen, and oxygen and that is used esp. as a solvent and as an antifreeze

meth·aqua·lone \me-'thak-wə-,lōn\ n : a sedative and hypnotic habit-forming drug that is not a barbiturate

meth·od \'meth-əd\ n [MF *methode*, fr. L *methodus*, fr. Gk *methodos*, fr. *meta* with + *hodos* way] 1 : a procedure or process for achieving an end 2 : orderly arrangement : PLAN syn mode, manner, way, fashion, system — **me·thod·i·cal** \mə-'thäd-i-kəl\ adj — **me·thod·i·cal·ly** \-k(ə-)lē\ adv — **me·thod·i·cal·ness** n

Meth·od·ist \'meth-əd-əst\ n : a member of a Protestant denomination adhering to the doctrines of John Wesley — **Meth·od·ism** \-ə-,diz-əm\ n

meth·od·ize \'meth-ə-,dīz\ vb **-ized; -iz·ing** : SYSTEMATIZE

meth·od·ol·o·gy \,meth-ə-'däl-ə-jē\ n, pl **-gies** 1 : a body of methods and rules followed in a science or discipline 2 : the study of the principles or procedures of inquiry in a particular field

meth·yl \'meth-əl\ n : a chemical group consisting of carbon and hydrogen

methyl alcohol n : METHANOL

meth·yl·mer·cury \,meth-əl-'mər-kyə-rē\ n : any of various toxic compounds of mercury that tend to accumulate in animals esp. at the top of a food chain

met·i·cal \'met-i-kəl\ n — see MONEY table

me·tic·u·lous \mə-'tik-yə-ləs\ adj [L *meticulosus* timid, fr. *metus* fear] : extremely careful in attending to details — **me·tic·u·lous·ly** adv — **me·tic·u·lous·ness** n

mé·tier \'me-,tyā, me-'tyā\ n : an area of activity in which one is expert or successful

me·tre \'mēt-ər\ chiefly Brit var of METER

met·ric \'me-trik\ adj 1 : of or relating to measurement; esp : of or relating to the metric system 2 : METRICAL 1

met·ri·cal \'me-tri-kəl\ adj 1 : of, relating to, or composed in meter 2 : MET-

METRIC SYSTEM[1]

LENGTH

unit	number of meters	approximate U.S. equivalent
kilometer	1.000	0.62 mile
hectometer	100	109.36 yards
dekameter	10	32.81 feet
meter	1	39.37 inches
decimeter	0.1	3.94 inches
centimeter	0.01	0.39 inch
millimeter	0.001	0.039 inch

AREA

unit	number of square meters	approximate U.S. equivalent
square kilometer	1.000.000	0.3861 square mile
hectare	10.000	2.47 acres
are	100	119.60 square yards
square centimeter	0.0001	0.155 square inch

VOLUME

unit	number of cubic meters	approximate U.S. equivalent
cubic meter	1	1.307 cubic yards
cubic decimeter	0.10	61.023 cubic inches
cubic centimeter	0.000001	0.061 cubic inch

CAPACITY

unit	number of liters	approximate U.S. equivalent		
		cubic	dry	liquid
kiloliter	1.000	1.31 cubic yards		
hectoliter	100	3.53 cubic feet	2.84 bushels	
dekaliter	10	0.35 cubic foot	1.14 pecks	2.64 gallons
liter	1	61.02 cubic inches	0.908 quart	1.057 quarts
deciliter	0.1	6.1 cubic inches	0.18 pint	0.21 pint
centiliter	0.01	0.61 cubic inch		0.338 fluidounce
milliliter	0.001	0.061 cubic inch		0.27 fluidram

MASS AND WEIGHT

unit	number of grams	approximate U.S. equivalent
metric ton	1.000.000	1.102 short tons
kilogram	1.000	2.2046 pounds
hectogram	100	3.527 ounces
dekagram	10	0.353 ounce
gram	1	0.035 ounce
decigram	0.10	1.543 grains
centigram	0.01	0.154 grain
milligram	0.001	0.015 grain

[1]For metric equivalents of U.S. units see Weights and Measures table

RIC 1 — **met·ri·cal·ly** \-tri-k(ə-)lē\ *adv*
met·ri·ca·tion \ˌme-tri-ˈkā-shən\ *n* : the act or process of converting into or expressing in the metric system
met·ri·cize \ˈme-trə-ˌsīz\ *vb* **-cized; -ciz·ing** : to change into or express in the metric system
metric system *n* : a decimal system of weights and measures based on the meter and on the kilogram
metric ton *n* — see METRIC SYSTEM table
[1]**met·ro** \ˈme-trō\ *n, pl* **metros** : SUBWAY
[2]**metro** *adj* : of, relating to, or characteristic of a metropolis and sometimes

including its suburbs
me·trol·o·gy \me-ˈträl-ə-jē\ *n* : the science of weights and measures or of measurement
met·ro·nome \ˈme-trə-ˌnōm\ *n* : an instrument for marking exact time by a regularly repeated tick
me·trop·o·lis \mə-ˈträp-(ə-)ləs\ *n* [LL, fr. Gk *mētropolis*, fr. *mētēr* mother + *polis* city] : the chief or capital city of a country, state, or region — **met·ro·pol·i·tan** \ˌme-trə-ˈpäl-ət-ᵊn\ *adj*
met·tle \ˈmet-ᵊl\ *n* 1 : quality of temperament 2 : SPIRIT, COURAGE

met·tle·some \\'met-ᵊl-səm\ *adj* : full of mettle

MeV *abbr* million electron volts

mew \\'myü\ *vb* : CONFINE

mews \\'myüz\ *n pl, chiefly Brit* : stables usu. with living quarters built around a court; *also* : a narrow street with dwellings converted from stables

Mex *abbr* Mexican; Mexico

Mex·i·can \\'mek-si-kən\ *n* : a native or inhabitant of Mexico — **Mexican** *adj*

mez·za·nine \\'mez-ᵊn-ᵊen, ˌmez-ᵊn-'en\ *n* **1** : a low-ceilinged story between two main stories of a building **2** : the lowest balcony in a theater; *also* : the first few rows of such a balcony

mez·zo·so·pra·no \ˌmet-sō-sə-'pran-ō, ˌme(d)z-\ *n* : a woman's voice having a range between that of the soprano and contralto; *also* : a singer having such a voice

MF *abbr* medium frequency

MFA *abbr* master of fine arts

mg *abbr* milligram

Mg *symbol* magnesium

MG *abbr* **1** machine gun **2** major general **3** military government

mgr *abbr* **1** manager **2** monseigneur **3** monsignor

mgt *or* **mgmt** *abbr* management

MGy Sgt *abbr* master gunnery sergeant

MHz *abbr* megahertz

mi *abbr* **1** mile; mileage **2** mill

MI *abbr* **1** Michigan **2** military intelligence

MIA \\'em-ᵊi-'ā\ *n* [*missing in action*] : a member of the armed forces whose whereabouts following a combat mission are unknown

Mi·ami \mi-'am-ē, -'am-ə\ *n, pl* **Miami** *or* **Mi·am·is** : a member of an American Indian people orig. of Wisconsin and Indiana

mi·as·ma \mi-'az-mə, mē-\ *n, pl* **-mas** *also* **-ma·ta** \-'mət-ə\ : an exhalation formerly held to cause disease : a noxious vapor — **mi·as·mic** \-mik\ *adj*

Mic *abbr* Micah

mi·ca \\'mi-kə\ *n* [NL, fr. L, grain, crumb] : any of various minerals readily separable into thin transparent sheets

Mi·cah \\'mi-kə\ *n* — see BIBLE table

mice *pl of* MOUSE

Mich *abbr* Michigan

Mi·che·as \\'mi-kē-əs, mi-'kē-əs\ *n* — see BIBLE table

Mic·mac \\'mik-ˌmak\ *n, pl* **Micmac** *or* **Micmacs** : a member of an American Indian people of eastern Canada

micr- *or* **micro-** *comb form* **1** : small : minute **2** : one millionth part of a specified unit (*microsecond*)

¹mi·cro \\'mi-krō\ *adj* **1** : very small; *esp* : MICROSCOPIC **2** : involving minute quantities or variations

²micro *n* : MICROCOMPUTER

mi·crobe \\'mi-ˌkrōb\ *n* : MICROORGANISM; *esp* : one causing disease — **mi·cro·bi·al** \mi-'krō-bē-əl\ *adj*

mi·cro·bi·ol·o·gy \ˌmi-krō-bi-'äl-ə-jē\

n : a branch of biology dealing esp. with microscopic forms of life — **mi·cro·bi·o·log·i·cal** \'mi-krō-ˌbi-ə-'läj-i-kəl\ *adj* — **mi·cro·bi·ol·o·gist** \ˌmi-krō-bi-'äl-ə-jəst\ *n*

mi·cro·bus \\'mi-krō-ˌbəs\ *n* : a station wagon shaped like a bus

mi·cro·cap·sule \-ˌkap-səl, -ˌsül\ *n* : a tiny capsule containing material (as a medicine) that is released when the capsule is broken, melted, or dissolved

mi·cro·chip \-ˌchip\ *n* : INTEGRATED CIRCUIT

mi·cro·cir·cuit \-ˌsər-kət\ *n* : a compact electronic circuit

mi·cro·com·put·er \-kəm-ˌpyüt-ər\ *n* : a very small computer

mi·cro·copy \-ˌkäp-ē\ *n* : a photographic copy (as of print) on a reduced scale — **microcopy** *vb*

mi·cro·cosm \\'mi-krə-ˌkäz-əm\ *n* : an individual or community thought of as a miniature world or universe

mi·cro·elec·tron·ics \ˌmi-krō-i-ˌlek-'trän-iks\ *n* : a branch of electronics that deals with the miniaturization of electronic circuits and components — **mi·cro·elec·tron·ic** \-ik\ *adj*

mi·cro·en·cap·su·late \ˌmi-krō-in-'kap-sə-ˌlāt\ *vb* : to enclose in a microcapsule (*microencapsulated* aspirin) — **mi·cro·en·cap·su·la·tion** \-in-ˌkap-sə-'lā-shən\ *n*

mi·cro·fiche \\'mi-krō-ˌfēsh, -ˌfish\ *n, pl* **-fiche** *or* **-fiches** \-ˌfēsh(-əz), -ˌfish(-əz)\ : a sheet of microfilm containing rows of images of pages of printed matter

mi·cro·film \-ˌfilm\ *n* : a film bearing a photographic record (as of print) on a reduced scale — **microfilm** *vb*

mi·cro·graph \\'mi-krə-ˌgraf\ *n* : a graphic reproduction of the image of an object formed by a microscope — **micrograph** *vb*

mi·cro·me·te·or·ite \ˌmi-krō-'mēt-ē-ə-ˌrīt\ *n* **1** : a meteorite particle of very small size **2** : a very small particle in interplanetary space

mi·crom·e·ter \mi-'kräm-ət-ər\ *n* : an instrument used with a telescope or microscope for measuring minute distances

mi·cro·min·ia·ture \ˌmi-krō-'min-ē-ə-ˌchùr, -'min-i-ˌchùr, -chər\ *adj* : MICROMINIATURIZED

mi·cro·min·ia·tur·iza·tion \-ˌmin-ē-ə-ˌchùr-ə-'zā-shən, -ˌmin-i-ˌchùr-, -chər-\ *n* : the process of producing microminiaturized things

mi·cro·min·ia·tur·ized \-'min-ē-ə-chə-ˌrīzd, -'min-i-chə-\ *adj* : reduced to or produced in a very small size and esp. in a size smaller than one considered miniature

mi·cron \\'mi-ˌkrän\ *n, pl* **microns** *also* **mi·cra** \-krə\ : one millionth of a meter

mi·cro·or·gan·ism \ˌmi-krō-'òr-gə-ˌniz-əm\ *n* : a living being (as a bacterium) too tiny to be seen by the unaided eye

mi·cro·phone \'mī-krə-ˌfōn\ n : an instrument for converting sound waves into variations of an electric current for transmitting or recording sound

mi·cro·pho·to·graph \ˌmī-krə-'fōt-ə-ˌgraf\ n : PHOTOMICROGRAPH

mi·cro·pro·ces·sor \ˌmī-krō-'präs-ˌes-ər\ n : a computer processor contained on a microchip

mi·cro·scope \'mī-krə-ˌskōp\ n : an instrument for making magnified images of minute objects usu. using light — **mi·cros·co·py** \mī-'kräs-kə-pē\ n

mi·cro·scop·ic \ˌmī-krə-'skäp-ik\ or **mi·cro·scop·i·cal** \-i-kəl\ adj 1 : of, relating to, or involving the use of the microscope 2 : too tiny to be seen without the use of a microscope : very small — **mi·cro·scop·i·cal·ly** \-i-k(ə-)lē\ adv

mi·cro·sec·ond \ˌmī-krō-'sek-ənd\ n : one millionth of a second

mi·cro·state \'mī-krō-ˌstāt\ n : a nation that is extremely small in area and population

mi·cro·sur·gery \ˌmī-krō-'sərj-(ə-)rē\ n : minute dissection or manipulation (as by a laser beam) of living structures (as cells) for surgical or experimental purposes — **mi·cro·sur·gi·cal** \-'sər-ji-kəl\ adj

mi·cro·wave \'mī-krō-ˌwāv\ n : a radio wave between one millimeter and one meter in wavelength

microwave oven n : an oven in which food is cooked by the heat produced from microwave penetration of the food

¹mid \'mid\ adj : MIDDLE

²mid abbr middle

mid·air \'mid-'aər\ n : a point or region in the air well above the ground

mid·day \'mid-ˌdā, -'dā\ n : NOON

mid·den \'mid-ᵊn\ n : a refuse heap

¹mid·dle \'mid-ᵊl\ adj 1 : equally distant from the extremes : MEDIAL, CENTRAL 2 : being at neither extreme : INTERMEDIATE 3 cap : constituting an intermediate period

²middle n 1 : a middle part, point, or position 2 : WAIST

middle age n : the period of life from about 40 to about 60 — **mid·dle–aged** \ˌmid-ᵊl-'ājd\ adj

Middle Ages n pl : the period of European history from about A.D. 500 to about 1500

mid·dle·brow \'mid-ᵊl-ˌbraủ\ n : a person who is moderately but not highly cultivated

middle class n : a social class holding a position between the upper class and the lower class — **middle–class** adj

middle ear n : a small membrane-lined cavity of the ear through which sound waves are transmitted by a chain of tiny bones

middle finger n : the midmost of the five digits of the hand

mid·dle·man \'mid-ᵊl-ˌman\ n : INTER-

MEDIARY; esp : one intermediate between the producer of goods and the retailer or consumer

middle–of–the–road adj : standing for or following a course of action midway between extremes; also : being neither liberal nor conservative in politics — **mid·dle–of–the–road·er** \-'rōd-ər\ n — **midd·le–of–the–road·ism** \-'rōd-ˌiz-əm\ n

middle school n : a school usu. including grades 5 to 8 or 6 to 8

mid·dle·weight \'mid-ᵊl-ˌwāt\ n : one of average weight; esp : a boxer weighing more than 147 but not over 160 pounds

mid·dling \'mid-liŋ, -lən\ adj 1 : of middle, medium, or moderate size, degree, or quality 2 : MEDIOCRE

mid·dy \'mid-ē\ n, pl mid·dies : MIDSHIPMAN

midge \'mij\ n : a very small fly : GNAT

midg·et \'mij-ət\ n 1 : a very small person : DWARF 2 : something (as an animal) very small of its kind

midi \'mid-ē\ n : a calf-length dress, coat, or skirt

mid·land \'mid-lənd, -ˌland\ n : the interior or central region of a country

mid–life \'mid-'līf\ n : MIDDLE AGE

mid·most \-ˌmōst\ adj : being in or near the exact middle — **midmost** adv

mid·night \-ˌnīt\ n : 12 o'clock at night

midnight sun n : the sun above the horizon at midnight in the arctic or antarctic summer

mid·point \'mid-ˌpȯint, -'pȯint\ n : a point at or near the center or middle

mid·riff \'mid-ˌrif\ n [ME midrif, fr. OE midhrif, fr. midde mid + hrif belly] 1 : DIAPHRAGM 1 2 : the mid-region of the human torso

mid·ship·man \'mid-ˌship-mən, (')mid-'ship-mən\ n : a student in a naval academy

mid·ships \-ˌships\ adv : AMIDSHIPS

midst \'midst\ n 1 : the interior or central part or point 2 : a position of proximity to the members of a group (in our ∼) 3 : the condition of being surrounded or beset — **midst** prep

mid·stream \'mid-'strēm, -ˌstrēm\ n : the middle of a stream

mid·sum·mer \-'səm-ər, -ˌsəm-\ n 1 : the middle of summer 2 : the summer solstice

mid·town \'mid-ˌtaủn, -'taủn\ n : a central section of a city; esp : one situated between sections called downtown and uptown — **midtown** adj

¹mid·way \'mid-ˌwā, -'wā\ adv : in the middle of the way or distance

²mid·way \-ˌwā\ n : an avenue (as at a carnival) for concessions and light amusements

mid·week \-ˌwēk\ n : the middle of the week — **mid·week·ly** \-ˌwē-klē, -'wē-\ adj or adv

mid·wife \'mid-ˌwīf\ n : a woman who helps other women in childbirth — **mid·wife·ry** \-ˌwī-f(ə-)rē\ n

mid·win·ter \'mid-'wint-ər, -,wint-\ n 1 : the middle of winter 2 : the winter solstice

mid·year \-,yiər\ n 1 : the middle of a year 2 : a midyear examination — **midyear** adj

mien \'mēn\ n 1 : air or bearing esp. as expressive of mood or personality : DEMEANOR 2 : APPEARANCE, ASPECT

miff \'mif\ vb : to put into an ill humor

¹**might** \(')mīt\ past of MAY — used as an auxiliary to express permission or possibility in the past, a present condition contrary to fact, less probability or possibility than may, or as a polite alternative to may, ought, or should

²**might** \'mīt\ n : the power, authority, or resources of an individual or a group

mighty \'mīt-ē\ adj might·i·er; -est 1 : very strong : POWERFUL 2 : GREAT, NOTABLE — **might·i·ly** \'mīt-ə-lē\ adv — **might·i·ness** n — **mighty** adv

mi·gnon·ette \,min-yə-'net\ n : a garden plant with spikes of tiny fragrant flowers

mi·graine \'mī-,grān\ n [F, fr. LL hemicrania pain in one side of the head, fr. Gk hēmikrania, fr. hēmi- half + kranion cranium] : a condition marked by recurrent severe headache and often nausea

mi·grant \'mī-grənt\ n : one that migrates; esp : a person who moves in order to find work (as picking crops)

mi·grate \'mī-,grāt\ vb **mi·grat·ed; mi·grat·ing** 1 : to move from one country or place to another 2 : to pass usu. periodically from one region or climate to another for feeding or breeding — **mi·gra·tion** \mī-'grā-shən\ n — **mi·gra·tion·al** \-sh(ə-)nəl\ adj — **mi·gra·to·ry** \'mī-grə-,tōr-ē\ adj

mi·ka·do \mə-'käd-ō\ n, pl -dos : an emperor of Japan

mike \'mīk\ n : MICROPHONE

¹**mil** \'mil\ n 1 : a unit of length equal to ¹⁄₁₀₀₀ inch 2 — see pound at MONEY table

²**mil** abbr military

milch \'milk, 'milch\ adj : giving milk ⟨~ cow⟩

mild \'mīld\ adj 1 : gentle in nature or behavior 2 : moderate in action or effect 3 : TEMPERATE syn easy, complaisant, amiable, lenient — **mild·ly** adv — **mild·ness** n

mil·dew \'mil-,d(y)ü\ n : a superficial usu. whitish growth produced on organic matter and on plants by a fungus; also : a fungus producing this growth — **mildew** vb

mile \'mī(ə)l\ n [ME, fr. OE mīl, fr. L milia miles, fr. milia passuum, lit., thousands of paces] 1 — see WEIGHT table 2 : NAUTICAL MILE

mile·age \'mī-lij\ n 1 : an allowance for traveling expenses at a certain rate per mile 2 : distance in miles traveled (as in a day) 3 : the amount of service yielded (as by a tire) expressed in terms of miles of travel 4 : the average number of miles a car will travel on a gallon of gasoline

mile·post \'mīl-,pōst\ n : a post indicating the distance in miles from a given point

mile·stone \'mīl-,stōn\ n 1 : a stone serving as a milepost 2 : a significant point in development

mi·lieu \mēl-'yə(r), -'yü\ n, pl **mi·lieus** or **mi·lieux** \-'yə(r)(z), -'yüz\ [F] : ENVIRONMENT, SETTING

mil·i·tant \'mil-ə-tənt\ adj 1 : engaged in warfare 2 : aggressively active esp. in a cause — **militant** \-təns\ n — **mil·i·tan·cy** \-tən-sē\ n — **militant** n — **mil·i·tant·ly** adv

mil·i·ta·rism \'mil-ə-tə-,riz-əm\ n 1 : predominance of the military class or its ideals 2 : a policy of aggressive military preparedness — **mil·i·ta·rist** \-rəst\ n — **mil·i·ta·ris·tic** \,mil-ə-tə-'ris-tik\ adj

mil·i·ta·rize \'mil-ə-tə-,rīz\ vb **-rized; -riz·ing** 1 : to equip with military forces and defenses 2 : to give a military character to

¹**mil·i·tary** \'mil-ə-,ter-ē\ adj 1 : of or relating to soldiers, arms, war, or the army 2 : performed by armed forces; also : supported by armed force syn martial, warlike — **mil·i·tar·i·ly** \,mil-ə-'ter-ə-lē\ adv

²**military** n, pl military also **mil·i·tar·ies** 1 : the military, naval, and air forces of a nation 2 : military persons

mil·i·tate \'mil-ə-,tāt\ vb **-tat·ed; -tat·ing** : to have weight or effect

mi·li·tia \mə-'lish-ə\ n : a part of the organized armed forces of a country liable to call only in emergency — **mi·li·tia·man** \-mən\ n

¹**milk** \'milk\ n 1 : a nutritive usu. whitish fluid secreted by female mammals for feeding their young 2 : a milklike liquid (as a plant juice) — **milk·i·ness** \-ē-nəs\ n — **milky** adj

²**milk** vb 1 : to draw off the milk of ⟨~ a cow⟩ 2 : to draw something from as if by milking — **milk·er** n

milk·maid \'milk-,mād\ n : DAIRYMAID

milk·man \-,man, -mən\ n : a person who sells or delivers milk

milk of magnesia : a milk-white mixture of hydroxide of magnesium and water used as an antacid and laxative

milk shake n : a thoroughly blended drink made of milk, a flavoring syrup, and often ice cream

milk·sop \'milk-,säp\ n : an unmanly man

milk·weed \-,wēd\ n : any of a genus of coarse herbs with milky juice and clustered flowers

Milky Way n 1 : a broad irregular band of light that stretches across the sky and is caused by the light of a very great number of faint stars 2 : MILKY WAY GALAXY

Milky Way galaxy *n* : the galaxy of which the sun is a member and which includes the stars that comprise the Milky Way

¹**mill** \'mil\ *n* **1** : a building with machinery for grinding grain into flour **2** : a machine used in processing (as by grinding, stamping, cutting, or finishing) raw material **3** : FACTORY

²**mill** *vb* **1** : to process in a mill **2** : to move in a circle or in an eddying mass

³**mill** *n* : one tenth of a cent

mill·age \'mil-ij\ *n* : a rate (as of taxation) expressed in mills

mill·dam \'mil-ˌdam\ *n* : a dam to make a millpond; *also* : MILLPOND

mil·len·ni·um \mə-'len-ē-əm\ *n, pl* **-nia** \-ē-ə\ *or* **-niums** **1** : a period of 1000 years; *also* : a 1000th anniversary or its celebration **2** : the 1000 years mentioned in Revelation 20 when holiness is to prevail and Christ is to reign on earth **3** : a period of great happiness or perfect government

mill·er \'mil-ər\ *n* **1** : one that operates a mill and esp. a flour mill **2** : any of various moths having powdery wings

mil·let \'mil-ət\ *n* : any of several small-seeded cereal and forage grasses cultivated for grain or hay; *also* : the grain of a millet

mil·li·am·pere \ˌmil-ē-'am-ˌpiər\ *n* : one thousandth of an ampere

mil·liard \'mil-ˌyärd, 'mil-ē-ˌärd\ *n, Brit* : a thousand millions

mil·li·bar \'mil-ə-ˌbär\ *n* : a unit of atmospheric pressure

mil·li·gram \'mil-ə-ˌgram\ *n* — see METRIC SYSTEM table

mil·li·li·ter \-ˌlēt-ər\ *n* — see METRIC SYSTEM table

mil·lime \mə-'lēm\ *n* — see *dinar* at MONEY table

mil·li·me·ter \'mil-ə-ˌmēt-ər\ *n* — see METRIC SYSTEM table

mil·li·ner \'mil-ə-nər\ *n* [fr. *Milan*, Italy; fr. the importation of women's finery from Italy in the 16th century] : one who designs, makes, trims, or sells women's hats

mil·li·nery \'mil-ə-ˌner-ē\ *n* **1** : women's apparel for the head **2** : the business or work of a milliner

mill·ing \'mil-iŋ\ *n* : a corrugated edge on a coin

mil·lion \'mil-yən\ *n, pl* **millions** *or* **million** : a thousand thousands — **million** *adj* — **mil·lionth** \-yənth\ *adj or n*

mil·lion·aire \ˌmil-yə-'ner, 'mil-yə-ˌner\ *n* : one whose wealth is estimated at a million or more (as of dollars or pounds)

mil·li·pede \'mil-ə-ˌpēd\ *n* : any of a class of arthropods related to the centipedes and having a long segmented body with a hard covering, two pairs of legs on most segments, and no poison fangs

mil·li·sec·ond \'mil-ə-ˌsek-ənd\ *n* : one thousandth of a second

mil·li·volt \-ˌvōlt\ *n* : one thousandth of a volt

mill·pond \'mil-ˌpänd\ *n* : a pond made by damming a stream to produce a fall of water for operating a mill

mill·race \-ˌrās\ *n* : a canal in which water flows to and from a mill wheel

mill·stone \-ˌstōn\ *n* : either of two round flat stones used for grinding grain

mill·stream \-ˌstrēm\ *n* : a stream whose flow is used to run a mill; *also* : the stream in a millrace

mill wheel *n* : a waterwheel that drives a mill

mill·wright \'mil-ˌrīt\ *n* : one whose occupation is planning and building mills or setting up their machinery

milt \'milt\ *n* : the male reproductive glands of fishes when filled with secretion; *also* : the secretion itself

mime \'mīm, 'mēm\ *n* **1** : MIMIC **2** : the art of characterization or of narration by body movement; *also* : a performance of mime — **mime** *vb*

mim·eo·graph \'mim-ē-ə-ˌgraf\ *n* : a machine for making many copies by means of a stencil through which ink is pressed — **mimeograph** *vb*

mi·me·sis \mə-'mē-səs, mī-\ *n* : IMITATION, MIMICRY

mi·met·ic \-'met-ik\ *adj* **1** : IMITATIVE **2** : relating to, characterized by, or exhibiting mimicry

¹**mim·ic** \'mim-ik\ *n* : one that mimics

²**mimic** *vb* **mim·icked** \-ikt\ ; **mim·ick·ing** **1** : to imitate closely **2** : to ridicule by imitation **3** : to resemble by biological mimicry

mim·ic·ry \'mim-i-krē\ *n, pl* **-ries** **1** : an instance of mimicking **2** : a superficial resemblance of one organism to another or to natural objects among which it lives that gives it an advantage (as protection from predation)

mi·mo·sa \mə-'mō-sə, mī-, -zə\ *n* : any of various leguminous trees, shrubs, and herbs of warm regions with globular heads of small white or pink flowers

min *abbr* **1** minim **2** minimum **3** mining **4** minister **5** minor **6** minute

min·a·ret \ˌmin-ə-'ret\ *n* [F, fr. Turk *minare*, fr. Ar *manārah* lighthouse] : a slender lofty tower attached to a mosque

mi·na·to·ry \'min-ə-ˌtōr-ē, 'mī-nə-\ *adj* : THREATENING, MENACING

mince \'mins\ *vb* **minced** ; **minc·ing** **1** : to cut into small pieces **2** : to restrain (words) within the bounds of decorum **3** : to walk in a prim affected manner — **minc·ing** *adj*

mince·meat \'mins-ˌmēt\ *n* : a finely chopped mixture esp. of raisins, apples, spices, and often meat used as a filling for a pie

mince pie *n* : a pie filled with mincemeat

¹**mind** \'mīnd\ *n* **1** : MEMORY **2** : the part of an individual that feels, perceives,

thinks, wills, and esp. reasons **3** : IN-TENTION, DESIRE **4** : normal mental condition **5** : OPINION, VIEW **6** : mental qualities of a person or group **7** : intellectual ability

²**mind** vb **1** chiefly dial : REMEMBER **2** : to attend to ⟨~ your own business⟩ **3** : HEED, OBEY **4** : to be concerned about : WORRY; also : DISLIKE **5** : to be careful or cautious **6** : to take charge of **7** : to regard with attention

mind–bend·ing \'mīn(d)-,ben-diŋ\ adj : MIND-BLOWING

mind–blow·ing \-,blō-iŋ\ adj : PSYCHEDELIC; also : MIND-BOGGLING

mind–bog·gling \-,bäg-(ə-)liŋ\ adj : mentally or emotionally exciting

mind·ed \'mīn-dəd\ adj **1** : having a mind of a specified kind — usu. used in combination ⟨narrow-*minded*⟩ **2** : INCLINED, DISPOSED

mind·ful \'mīnd-fəl\ adj : bearing in mind : AWARE — **mind·ful·ly** \-ē\ adv — **mind·ful·ness** n

mind·less \'mīn-dləs\ adj **1** : destitute of mind or consciousness; esp : UNINTELLIGENT **2** : UNTHINKING, HEEDLESS — **mind·less·ly** adv — **mind·less·ness** n

¹**mine** \'mīn\ pron : one or the ones belonging to me

²**mine** \'mīn\ n **1** : an excavation in the earth from which mineral substances are taken; also : an ore deposit **2** : a subterranean passage under an enemy position; also : an encased explosive for destroying enemy personnel, vehicles, or ships **3** : a rich source of supply

³**mine** \'mīn\ vb **mined**; **min·ing 1** : to dig a mine **2** : UNDERMINE **3** : to get ore from the earth **4** : to place military mines in — **min·er** n

mine·lay·er \'mīn-,lā-ər\ n : a naval vessel for laying underwater mines

min·er·al \'min-(ə-)rəl\ n **1** : a solid homogeneous crystalline substance (as diamond, gold, or quartz) not of animal or vegetable origin **2** : any of various naturally occurring homogeneous substances (as coal, salt, water, or gas) obtained usu. from the ground **3** pl, Brit : MINERAL WATER — **mineral** adj

min·er·al·ize \'min-(ə-)rə-,līz\ vb **-ized**; **-iz·ing 1** : to transform (a metal) into an ore **2** : to impregnate or supply with minerals

min·er·al·o·gy \,min-ə-'räl-ə-jē, -'ral-\ n : a science dealing with minerals — **min·er·al·og·i·cal** \,min-(ə-)rə-'läj-i-kəl\ adj — **min·er·al·o·gist** \,min-ə-'räl-ə-jəst, -'ral-\ n

mineral oil n : an oil of mineral origin; esp : a refined petroleum oil used as a laxative

mineral water n : water infused with mineral salts or gases

min·e·stro·ne \,min-ə-'strō-nē, -'strōn\ n [It, fr. minestra, fr. minestrare to serve, dish up, fr. L ministrare, fr.

minister servant] : a rich thick vegetable soup

mine·sweep·er \'mīn-,swē-pər\ n : a warship designed for removing or neutralizing underwater mines

min·gle \'miŋ-gəl\ vb **min·gled**; **min·gling** \-g(ə-)liŋ\ **1** : to bring or combine together : MIX **2** : CONCOCT

ming tree \'miŋ-\ n : a dwarfed usu. evergreen tree grown in a pot; also : an artificial imitation of this made from plant materials

mini \'min-ē\ n, pl **min·is** : something small of its kind — **mini** adj

mini- comb form : miniature : of small dimensions

min·ia·ture \'min-ē-ə-,chur, 'min-i-,chur, -chər\ n [It miniatura art of illuminating a manuscript, fr. ML, fr. L miniare to color with red lead, fr. minium red lead] **1** : a copy on a much reduced scale; also : something small of its kind **2** : a small painting (as on ivory or metal) — **miniature** adj — **min·ia·tur·ist** \-,chur-əst, -,chər-\ n

min·ia·tur·ize \'min-ē-ə-,chə-,rīz, 'min-i-\ vb **-ized**; **iz·ing** : to design or construct in small size — **min·ia·tur·iza·tion** \,min-ē-ə-,chur-ə-'zā-shən, ,min-i-, -,chər-\ n

mini·bike \'min-ē-,bīk\ n : a small one-passenger motorcycle

mini·bus \-,bəs\ n : a small bus

mini·com·put·er \-kəm-,pyüt-ər\ n : a computer intermediate between a mainframe and a microcomputer in size and speed

min·im \'min-əm\ n — see WEIGHT table

min·i·mal \'min-ə-məl\ adj **1** : relating to or being a minimum : LEAST **2** : of or relating to minimal art — **min·i·mal·ly** \-ē\ adv

minimal art n : an impersonal style of abstract art and esp. sculpture consisting primarily of simple geometric forms — **minimal artist** n

min·i·mal·ist \'min-ə-mə-ləst\ n : MINIMAL ARTIST

min·i·mize \'min-ə-,mīz\ vb **-mized**; **-miz·ing 1** : to reduce to a minimum **2** : to estimate at a minimum; also : BELITTLE **syn** depreciate, decry, disparage

min·i·mum \'min-ə-məm\ n, pl **-ma** \-mə\ or **-mums 1** : the least quantity assignable, admissible, or possible **2** : the least of a set of numbers **3** : the lowest degree or amount of variation (as of temperature) reached or recorded — **minimum** adj

min·ion \'min-yən\ n [MF mignon darling] **1** : a servile dependent **2** : one highly favored **3** : a subordinate official

min·is·cule \'min-əs-,kyül\ var of MINUSCULE

mini·se·ries \'min-ē-,sir-ēz\ n : a motion picture made for television and presented in several parts

mini·skirt \-,skərt\ n : a skirt with the

hemline several inches above the knee

mini-state \-,stāt\ *n* : MICROSTATE

¹min-is-ter \'min-ə-stər\ *n* 1 : AGENT 2 : CLERGYMAN; *esp* : a Protestant clergyman 3 : a high officer of state who heads a division of governmental activities 4 : a diplomatic representative to a foreign state — **min-is-te-ri-al** \,min-ə-'stir-ē-əl\ *adj*

²minister *vb* **min-is-tered; min-is-ter-ing** \-st(ə-)riŋ\ 1 : to perform the functions of a minister of religion 2 : to give aid — **min-is-tra-tion** \,min-ə-'strā-shən\ *n*

min-is-trant \'min-ə-strənt\ *adj, archaic* : performing service as a minister — **ministrant** *n*

min-is-try \'min-ə-strē\ *n, pl* **-tries** 1 : MINISTRATION 2 : the office, duties, or functions of a minister; *also* : his period of service or office 3 : CLERGY 4 : AGENCY 5 *often cap* : the body of ministers governing a nation or state; *also* : a government department headed by a minister

mink \'miŋk\ *n, pl* **mink** *or* **minks** : a slender mammal resembling the related weasels; *also* : its soft lustrous typically dark brown fur

Minn *abbr* Minnesota

min-ne-sing-er \'min-i-,sin-ər, 'min-ə-,ziŋ-\ *n* [G, fr. Middle High German, fr. *minne* love + *singer*] : one of a class of German lyric poets and musicians of the 12th to the 14th centuries

min-now \'min-ō\ *n, pl* **minnows** *also* **minnow** : any of numerous small freshwater fishes

¹mi-nor \'mī-nər\ *adj* 1 : inferior in importance, size, or degree 2 : not having reached majority 3 : having the third, sixth, and sometimes the seventh degrees lowered by a half step (~ scale); *also* : based on a minor scale (~ key)

²minor *n* 1 : a person who has not attained majority 2 : a subject of academic study chosen as a secondary field of specialization

³minor *vb* : to pursue an academic minor

mi-nor-i-ty \mə-'nȯr-ət-ē, mī-\ *n, pl* **-ties** 1 : the period or state of being a minor 2 : the smaller in number of two groups; *esp* : a group having less than the number of votes necessary for control 3 : a part of a population differing from others (as in race or religion); *also* : a member of a minority

min-ster \'min-stər\ *n* 1 : a church attached to a monastery 2 : a large or important church

min-strel \'min-strəl\ *n* 1 : a medieval singer of verses; *also* : MUSICIAN, POET 2 : one of a group of performers in a program usu. of black American songs, jokes, and impersonations — **min-strel-sy** \-sē\ *n*

¹mint \'mint\ *n* 1 : a place where coins

are made 2 : a vast sum — **mint** *vb* — **mint-age** \-ij\ *n* — **mint-er** *n*

²mint *adj* : unmarred as if fresh from a mint (~ coins)

³mint *n* : any of a large family of square-stemmed herbs and shrubs; *esp* : one (as spearmint) with fragrant aromatic foliage used in flavoring — **minty** *adj*

min-u-end \'min-yə-,wend\ *n* : a number from which another is to be subtracted

min-u-et \,min-yə-'wet\ *n* : a slow graceful dance

¹mi-nus \'mī-nəs\ *prep* 1 : diminished by : LESS (7 ~ 3 equals 4) 2 : LACKING, WITHOUT (~ his hat)

²minus *n* : a negative quantity or quality

³minus *adj* 1 : requiring subtraction 2 : algebraically negative (~ quantity) 3 : having negative qualities

¹mi-nus-cule \'min-əs-,kyül\ *n* : a lowercase letter

²minuscule *adj* : very small

minus sign *n* : a sign — used in mathematics to indicate subtraction or a negative quantity

¹min-ute \'min-ət\ *n* 1 : the 60th part of an hour or of a degree 2 : a short space of time 3 *pl* : the official record of the proceedings of a meeting

²mi-nute \mī-'n(y)üt, mə-\ *adj* **mi-nut-er; -est** 1 : very small 2 : of little importance : TRIFLING 3 : marked by close attention to details syn diminutive, tiny, miniature, wee — **mi-nute-ly** *adv* — **mi-nute-ness** *n*

min-ute-man \'min-ət-,man\ *n* : a member of a group of armed men pledged to take the field at a minute's notice during and immediately before the American Revolution

mi-nu-tia \mə-'n(y)ü-sh(ē-)ə, mī-\ *n, pl* **-ti-ae** \-shē-,ē\ [L] : a minute or minor detail — usu. used in pl.

minx \'miŋks\ *n* : a pert girl

Mio-cene \'mī-ə-,sēn\ *adj* : of, relating to, or being the epoch of the Tertiary between the Oligocene and the Pliocene — **Miocene** *n*

mir-a-cle \'mir-i-kəl\ *n* 1 : an extraordinary event manifesting a supernatural work of God 2 : an unusual event, thing, or accomplishment : WONDER, MARVEL — **mi-rac-u-lous** \mə-'rak-yə-ləs\ *adj* — **mi-rac-u-lous-ly** *adv*

miracle drug *n* : a usu. newly discovered drug capable of producing a marked and favorable change in a patient's condition

mi-rage \mə-'räzh\ *n* 1 : an illusion visible at sea, in deserts, or above a hot pavement of some distant object often in distorted form as a result of atmospheric conditions 2 : something illusory and unattainable

¹mire \'mī(ə)r\ *n* : heavy and often deep mud or slush — **miry** *adj*

²mire *vb* **mired; mir-ing** : to stick or sink in or as if in mire

¹mir-ror \'mir-ər\ *n* 1 : a polished or

smooth substance (as of glass) that forms images by reflection **2** : a true representation; *also* : MODEL

²**mirror** *vb* : to reflect in or as if in a mirror

mirth \'mərth\ *n* : gladness or gaiety accompanied with laughter syn glee, jollity, hilarity, merriment — **mirth·ful** \-fəl\ *adj* — **mirth·ful·ly** \-ē\ *adv* — **mirth·ful·ness** *n* — **mirth·less** *adj*

MIRV \'mərv\ *n* [*multiple independently targeted reentry vehicle*] : an ICBM with multiple warheads that have different targets — **MIRV** *vb*

mis·ad·ven·ture \,mis-əd-'ven-chər\ *n* : MISFORTUNE, MISHAP

mis·aligned \,mis-ə-'līnd\ *adj* : not properly aligned — **mis·align·ment** \-'līn-mənt\ *n*

mis·al·li·ance \,mis-ə-'lī-əns\ *n* : MÉSALLIANCE; *also* : a marriage between persons unsuited to each other

mis·al·lo·ca·tion \,mis-,al-ō-'kā-shən\ *n* : faulty or improper allocation

mis·an·thrope \'mis-ᵊn-,thrōp\ *n* : one who hates mankind — **mis·an·throp·ic** \,mis-ᵊn-'thräp-ik\ *adj* — **mis·an·throp·i·cal·ly** \-i-k(ə-)lē\ *adv* — **mis·an·thro·py** \mis-'an-thrə-pē\ *n*

mis·ap·ply \,mis-ə-'plī\ *vb* : to apply wrongly — **mis·ap·pli·ca·tion** \,mis-,ap-lə-'kā-shən\ *n*

mis·ap·pre·hend \,mis-,ap-ri-'hend\ *vb* : MISUNDERSTAND — **mis·ap·pre·hen·sion** \-'hen-chən\ *n*

mis·ap·pro·pri·ate \,mis-ə-'prō-prē-,āt\ *vb* : to appropriate wrongly; *esp* : to take dishonestly for one's own use — **mis·ap·pro·pri·a·tion** \-,prō-prē-'ā-shən\ *n*

mis·be·got·ten \-bi-'gät-ᵊn\ *adj* : ILLEGITIMATE

mis·be·have \,mis-bi-'hāv\ *vb* : to behave improperly — **mis·be·hav·er** *n* — **mis·be·hav·ior** \-'hā-vyər\ *n*

mis·be·liev·er \-bə-'lē-vər\ *n* : one who holds a false or unorthodox belief

mis·brand \mis-'brand\ *vb* : to brand falsely or in a misleading manner

misc *abbr* miscellaneous

mis·cal·cu·late \mis-'kal-kyə-,lāt\ *vb* : to calculate wrongly — **mis·cal·cu·la·tion** \,mis-,kal-kyə-'lā-shən\ *n*

mis·call \mis-'kȯl\ *vb* : MISNAME

mis·car·riage \-'kar-ij\ *n* **1** : a corrupt or incompetent administration (∼ of justice) **2** : expulsion of a fetus before it is capable of independent life

mis·car·ry \-'kar-ē\ *vb* **1** : to give birth prematurely and esp. before the fetus is capable of living independently **2** : to go wrong; *also* : to be unsuccessful

mis·ce·ge·na·tion \,mis-,ej-ə-'nā-shən, ,mis-i-jə-'nā-\ *n* [L *miscēre* to mix + *genus* race] : a mixture of races; *esp* : marriage or cohabitation between a white person and a member of another race

mis·cel·la·neous \,mis-ə-'lā-nē-əs\ *adj* **1** : consisting of diverse things or members; *also* : having various traits **2** : dealing with or interested in diverse subjects — **mis·cel·la·neous·ly** *adv* — **mis·cel·la·neous·ness** *n*

mis·cel·la·ny \'mis-ə-,lā-nē\ *n, pl* -nies **1** : a collection of writings on various subjects **2** : HODGEPODGE

mis·chance \mis-'chans\ *n* : bad luck; *also* : MISHAP

mis·chief \'mis-chəf\ *n* **1** : injury caused by a human agency **2** : a source of harm or irritation **3** : action that annoys; *also* : MISCHIEVOUSNESS

mis·chie·vous \'mis-chə-vəs\ *adj* **1** : HARMFUL, INJURIOUS **2** : causing annoyance or minor injury **3** : irresponsibly playful — **mis·chie·vous·ly** *adv* — **mis·chie·vous·ness** *n*

mis·ci·ble \'mis-ə-bəl\ *adj* : capable of being mixed or dissolved

mis·com·mu·ni·ca·tion \,mis-kə-,myü-nə-'kā-shən\ *n* : failure to communicate clearly

mis·con·ceive \,mis-kən-'sēv\ *vb* : to interpret incorrectly — **mis·con·cep·tion** \-'sep-shən\ *n*

mis·con·duct \mis-'kän-(,)dəkt\ *n* **1** : MISMANAGEMENT **2** : intentional wrongdoing **3** : improper behavior

mis·con·strue \,mis-kən-'strü\ *vb* : MISINTERPRET — **mis·con·struc·tion** \-'strək-shən\ *n*

mis·count \mis-'kaúnt\ *vb* : to count incorrectly : MISCALCULATE

mis·cre·ant \'mis-krē-ənt\ *n* : one who behaves criminally or viciously — **miscreant** *adj*

mis·cue \mis-'kyü\ *n* : MISTAKE, ERROR — **miscue** *vb*

mis·deed \mis-'dēd\ *n* : a wrong deed

mis·de·mean·or \,mis-di-'mē-nər\ *n* **1** : a crime less serious than a felony **2** : MISDEED

mis·di·rect \,mis-də-'rekt, -dī-\ *vb* : to give a wrong direction to — **mis·di·rec·tion** \-'rek-shən\ *n*

mis·do·ing \mis-'dü-iŋ\ *n* : WRONGDOING — **mis·do·er** \-'dü-ər\ *n*

mise-en-scène \,mē-,zäⁿ-'sen, -'sän\ *n, pl* **mise-en-scènes** \-'sen(z), -'sän(z)\ [F] **1** : the arrangement of the scenery, property, and actors on a stage **2** : SETTING; *also* : ENVIRONMENT

mi·ser \'mī-zər\ *n* [L *miser* miserable] : a person who hoards his money — **mi·ser·li·ness** \-lē-nəs\ *n* — **mi·ser·ly** *adj*

mis·er·a·ble \'miz-(ə-)rə-bəl, 'miz-ər-bəl\ *adj* **1** : wretchedly deficient; *also* : causing extreme discomfort **2** : extremely poor **3** : SHAMEFUL — **mis·er·a·ble·ness** *n* — **mis·er·a·bly** \-blē\ *adv*

mis·ery \'miz-(ə-)rē\ *n, pl* -er·ies **1** : suffering and want caused by poverty or affliction **2** : a cause of suffering or discomfort **3** : emotional distress

mis·fea·sance \mis-'fēz-ᵊns\ *n* : the performance of a lawful action in an illegal or improper manner

mis·file \-'fīl\ *vb* : to file in an inappropriate place

mis·fire \-'fī(ə)r\ vb 1 : to fail to fire 2 : to miss an intended effect — **misfire** n

mis·fit \'mis-,fit, mis-'fit\ n 1 : an imperfect fit 2 : a person poorly adjusted to his environment

mis·for·tune \mis-'fȯr-chən\ n 1 : bad fortune : ill luck 2 : an unfortunate condition or event

mis·giv·ing \-'giv-iŋ\ n : a feeling of doubt or suspicion esp. concerning a future event

mis·gov·ern \-'gəv-ərn\ vb : to govern badly — **mis·gov·ern·ment** \-'gəv-ər(n)-mənt\ n

mis·guid·ance \mis-'gīd-ᵊns\ n : faulty guidance — **mis·guide** \-'gīd\ vb — **mis·guid·ed·ly** \-'gīd-əd-lē\ adv

mis·han·dle \-'han-dᵊl\ vb 1 : MALTREAT 2 : to manage wrongly

mis·hap \'mis-,hap\ n : an unfortunate accident

mish·mash \'mish-,mash, -,mäsh\ n : HODGEPODGE, JUMBLE

mis·in·form \,mis-ᵊn-'fȯrm\ vb : to give false or misleading information to — **mis·in·for·ma·tion** \,mis-,in-fər-'mā-shən\ n

mis·in·ter·pret \,mis-ᵊn-'tər-prət\ vb : to understand or explain wrongly — **mis·in·ter·pre·ta·tion** \-,tər-prə-'tā-shən\ n

mis·judge \mis-'jəj\ vb 1 : to estimate wrongly 2 : to have an unjust opinion of — **mis·judg·ment** \mis-'jəj-mənt\ n

mis·la·bel \-'lā-bəl\ vb : to label incorrectly or falsely

mis·lay \mis-'lā\ vb -laid \-'lād\ ; -lay·ing : MISPLACE, LOSE

mis·lead \mis-'lēd\ vb -led \-'led\ ; -lead·ing : to lead in a wrong direction or into a mistaken action or belief — **mis·lead·ing·ly** adv

mis·like \-'līk\ vb : DISLIKE — **mislike** n

mis·man·age \-'man-ij\ vb : to manage badly — **mis·man·age·ment** n

mis·match \-'mach\ vb : to match unsuitably or badly — **mismatch** \mis-'mach, 'mis-,mach\ n

mis·name \-'nām\ vb : to name incorrectly : MISCALL

mis·no·mer \mis-'nō-mər\ n : a wrong name or designation

mi·sog·y·nist \mə-'säj-ə-nəst\ n : one who hates women — **mi·sog·y·nis·tic** \mə-,säj-ə-'nis-tik\ adj — **mi·sog·y·ny** \mə-'säj-ə-nē\ n

mis·ori·ent \mis-'ȯr-ē-,ent\ vb : to orient improperly or incorrectly — **mis·ori·en·ta·tion** \mis-,ȯr-ē-ən-'tā-shən\ n

mis·place \-'plās\ vb 1 : to put in a wrong place; also : MISLAY 2 : to set on a wrong object (~ trust)

mis·play \-'plā\ n : a wrong or unskillful play — **mis·play** \mis-'plā, 'mis-,plā\ vb

mis·print \mis-'print\ vb : to print incorrectly — **misprint** \'mis-,print, mis-'print\ n

mis·pro·nounce \,mis-prə-'naùns\ vb : to pronounce incorrectly — **mis·pro·**nun·ci·a·tion \-,prə-,nən-sē-'ā-shən\ n

mis·quote \mis-'kwōt\ vb : to quote incorrectly — **mis·quo·ta·tion** \,mis-kwō-'tā-shən\ n

mis·read \-'rēd\ vb -read \-'red\ ; -read·ing \-'rēd-iŋ\ : to read or interpret incorrectly

mis·rep·re·sent \,mis-,rep-ri-'zent\ vb : to represent falsely or unfairly — **mis·rep·re·sen·ta·tion** \-,zen-'tā-shən\ n

¹**mis·rule** \mis-'rül\ vb : MISGOVERN

²**misrule** n 1 : MISGOVERNMENT 2 : DISORDER

¹**miss** \'mis\ vb 1 : to fail to hit, reach, or contact 2 : to feel the absence of 3 : to fail to obtain 4 : AVOID (just ~ed hitting the other car) 5 : OMIT 6 : to fail to understand 7 : to fail to perform or attend; also : MISFIRE

²**miss** n 1 : a failure to hit or to attain a result 2 : MISFIRE

³**miss** n 1 cap — used as a title prefixed to the name of an unmarried woman or girl 2 : a young unmarried woman or girl

Miss abbr Mississippi

mis·sal \'mis-əl\ n : a book containing all that is said or sung at mass during the entire year

mis·send \mis-'send\ vb : to send incorrectly ⟨missent mail⟩

mis·shap·en \-'shā-pən\ adj : badly shaped : having an ugly shape

mis·sile \'mis-əl\ n [L, fr. neut. of missilis capable of being thrown, fr. mittere to let go, send] : an object (as a stone, bullet, or rocket) thrown or projected usu. so as to strike a target

mis·sil·ery also **mis·sil·ry** \'mis-əl-rē\ n 1 : MISSILES 2 : the science of the making and use of guided missiles

miss·ing \'mis-iŋ\ adj : ABSENT; also : LOST

mis·sion \'mish-ən\ n 1 : a group of missionaries; also : a place where missionaries work 2 : a group of envoys to a foreign country; also : a team of specialists or cultural leaders sent to a foreign country 3 : TASK

¹**mis·sion·ary** \'mish-ə-,ner-ē\ adj : of, relating to, or engaged in church missions

²**missionary** n, pl -ar·ies : a person commissioned by a church to propagate its faith or carry on humanitarian work

mis·sion·er \'mish-(ə-)nər\ n : MISSIONARY

Mis·sis·sip·pi·an \,mis-ə-'sip-ē-ən\ adj : of, relating to, or being the period of the Paleozoic era between the Devonian and the Pennsylvanian — **Mississippian** n

mis·sive \'mis-iv\ n : LETTER

mis·spell \mis-'spel\ vb : to spell incorrectly — **mis·spell·ing** n

mis·spend \mis-'spend\ vb -spent \-'spent\ ; -spend·ing : WASTE, SQUANDER ⟨a misspent youth⟩

mis·state \-'stāt\ vb : to state incorrectly — **mis·state·ment** n

mis·step \-ˈstep\ *n* **1** : a wrong step **2** : MISTAKE, BLUNDER

mist \ˈmist\ *n* **1** : water in the form of particles suspended or falling in the air **2** : something that dims or obscures

mis·tak·able \mə-ˈstā-kə-bəl\ *adj* : capable of being misunderstood or mistaken

mis·take \mə-ˈstāk\ *n* **1** : a misunderstanding of the meaning or implication of something **2** : a wrong action or statement : ERROR — **mistake** *vb*

mis·tak·en \-ˈstā-kən\ *adj* **1** : MISUNDERSTOOD **2** : having a wrong opinion or incorrect information **3** : ERRONEOUS — **mis·tak·en·ly** *adv*

mis·ter \ˈmis-tər\ *n* **1** *cap* — used sometimes instead of *Mr.* **2** : SIR — used without a name in addressing a man

mis·tle·toe \ˈmis-əl-ˌtō\ *n* : a parasitic green plant with yellowish flowers and waxy white berries that grows on trees

mis·tral \ˈmis-trəl, mi-ˈsträl\ *n* [F, fr. Provençal, fr. *mistral* masterful, fr. L *magistralis*, fr. *magister* master] : a strong cold dry northerly wind of southern Europe

mis·treat \mis-ˈtrēt\ *vb* : to treat badly : ABUSE — **mis·treat·ment** *n*

mis·tress \ˈmis-trəs\ *n* **1** : a woman who has power, authority, or ownership (∼ of the house) **2** : a country or state having supremacy (∼ of the seas) **3** : a woman with whom a man has sexual relations outside of marriage; *also*, *archaic* : SWEETHEART **4** — used archaically as a title prefixed to the name of a married or unmarried woman

mis·tri·al \ˈmis-ˌtrīl\ *n* : a trial that has no legal effect (as by reason of an error)

¹mis·trust \mis-ˈtrəst\ *n* : a lack of confidence : DISTRUST — **mis·trust·ful** \-fəl\ *adj* — **mis·trust·ful·ly** \-ē\ *adv* — **mis·trust·ful·ness** *n*

²mistrust *vb* : to have no trust or confidence in : SUSPECT

misty \ˈmis-tē\ *adj* **mist·i·er; -est** : obscured by or as if by mist : INDISTINCT — **mist·i·ly** \ˈmis-tə-lē\ *adv* — **mist·i·ness** \-tē-nəs\ *n*

mis·un·der·stand \ˌmis-ˌən-dər-ˈstand\ *vb* **-stood** \-ˈstůd\ ; **-stand·ing 1** : to fail to understand **2** : to interpret incorrectly

mis·un·der·stand·ing \-ˈstan-diŋ\ *n* **1** : MISINTERPRETATION **2** : DISAGREEMENT, QUARREL

mis·us·age \mish-ˈü-sij, mis(h)-ˈyü-zij\ *n* **1** : bad treatment : ABUSE **2** : wrong or improper use

mis·use \mish-ˈüz, mis(h)-ˈyüz\ *vb* **1** : to use incorrectly **2** : ABUSE, MISTREAT — **mis·use** \-ˈyüs\ *n*

mite \ˈmīt\ *n* **1** : any of various tiny animals related to the spiders that often live and feed on animals or plants

2 : a small coin or sum of money **3** : a small amount : BIT

¹mi·ter *or* **mi·tre** \ˈmīt-ər\ *n* [ME *mitre*, fr. MF, fr. L *mitra* headband, turban, fr. Gk] **1** : a headdress worn by bishops and abbots **2** : a joint or corner made by cutting two pieces of wood at an angle and fitting the cut edges together

²miter *or* **mitre** *vb* **mi·tered** *or* **mi·tred; mi·ter·ing** *or* **mi·tring** \ˈmīt-ə-riŋ\ **1** : to match or fit together in a miter joint **2** : to bevel the ends of for making a miter joint

mit·i·gate \ˈmit-ə-ˌgāt\ *vb* **-gat·ed; -gat·ing 1** : to make less harsh or hostile **2** : to make less severe or painful — **mit·i·ga·tion** \ˌmit-ə-ˈgā-shən\ *n* — **mit·i·ga·tive** \ˈmit-ə-ˌgāt-iv\ *adj*

mi·to·sis \mī-ˈtō-səs\ *n, pl* **-to·ses** \-ˌsēz\ : a process that takes place in the nucleus of a dividing cell and results in the formation of two new nuclei each having the same number of chromosomes as the parent nucleus; *also* : cell division in which mitosis occurs — **mi·tot·ic** \-ˈtät-ik\ *adj*

mitt \ˈmit\ *n* : a baseball glove (as for a catcher)

mit·ten \ˈmit-ᵊn\ *n* : a covering for the hand having a separate section for the thumb only

¹mix \ˈmiks\ *vb* **1** : to combine into one mass **2** : ASSOCIATE **3** : to form by mingling components **4** : to produce (a recording) by electronically combining sounds from different sources **5** : CROSSBREED **6** : CONFUSE (∼*es* up the facts) **7** : to become involved **syn** blend, merge, coalesce, amalgamate, fuse — **mix·able** *adj* — **mix·er** *n*

²mix *n* : a product of mixing; *esp* : a commercially prepared mixture of food ingredients

mixed number *n* : a number (as 5⅔) composed of an integer and a fraction

mixed–up \ˈmikst-ˈəp\ *adj* : marked by bewilderment, perplexity, or disorder : CONFUSED

mixt *abbr* mixture

mix·ture \ˈmiks-chər\ *n* **1** : the act or process of mixing; *also* : the state of being mixed **2** : a product of mixing

mix–up \ˈmiks-ˌəp\ *n* : an instance of confusion (a ∼ about the train)

miz·zen *or* **miz·en** \ˈmiz-ᵊn\ *n* **1** : a fore-and-aft sail set on the mizzenmast **2** : MIZZENMAST — **mizzen** *or* **mizen** *adj*

miz·zen·mast \-ˌmast, -məst\ *n* : the mast aft or next aft of the mainmast

mk *abbr* **1** mark **2** markka

Mk *abbr* Mark

mks \ˈem-ˌkā-ˈes\ *adj, often cap* M&K&S : of, relating to, or being a system of units based on the meter, the kilogram, and the second

mktg *abbr* marketing

ml *abbr* milliliter

MLD *abbr* **1** median lethal dose **2** minimum lethal dose

Mlle *abbr* [F] mademoiselle

Mlles *abbr* [F] mesdemoiselles

mm *abbr* millimeter

MM *abbr* [F] messieurs

Mme *abbr* [F] madame

Mn *symbol* manganese

MN *abbr* Minnesota

mne·mon·ic \nə-ˈmän-ik\ *adj* : assisting or designed to assist memory

mo *abbr* month

¹**Mo** *abbr* Missouri

²**Mo** *symbol* molybdenum

MO *abbr* **1** mail order **2** medical officer **3** Missouri **4** modus operandi **5** money order

moan \ˈmōn\ *n* : a low prolonged sound indicative of pain or grief — **moan** *vb*

moat \ˈmōt\ *n* : a deep wide usu. water-filled trench around a castle

¹**mob** \ˈmäb\ *n* [L *mobile vulgus* vacillating crowd] **1** : MASSES, RABBLE **2** : a large disorderly crowd **3** : a criminal gang

²**mob** *vb* **mobbed**; **mob·bing 1** : to crowd around and attack or annoy **2** : to crowd into or around ⟨shoppers *mobbed* the stores⟩

¹**mo·bile** \ˈmō-bəl, -ˌbīl, -ˌbēl\ *adj* **1** : capable of moving or being moved **2** : changeable in appearance, mood, or purpose; *also* : ADAPTABLE **3** : having the opportunity for or undergoing a shift in social status **4** : using vehicles for transportation ⟨~ warfare⟩ — **mo·bil·i·ty** \mō-ˈbil-ət-ē\ *n*

²**mo·bile** \ˈmō-ˌbēl\ *n* : a construction (as of wire and sheet metal) with parts that can be set in motion by air currents; *also* : a similar structure suspended so that it is moved by a current of air

mobile home *n* : a trailer used as a permanent dwelling

mo·bi·lize \ˈmō-bə-ˌlīz\ *vb* **-lized**; **-liz·ing 1** : to put into movement or circulation **2** : to assemble and make ready for action ⟨~ army reserves⟩ — **mo·bi·li·za·tion** \ˌmō-bə-lə-ˈzā-shən\ *n* — **mo·bi·liz·er** \ˈmō-bə-ˌlī-zər\ *n*

mob·ster \ˈmäb-stər\ *n* : a member of a criminal gang

moc·ca·sin \ˈmäk-ə-sən\ *n* **1** : a soft leather heelless shoe **2** : WATER MOCCASIN

¹**mock** \ˈmäk, ˈmȯk\ *vb* **1** : to treat with contempt or ridicule **2** : DELUDE **3** : DEFY **4** : to mimic in sport or derision — **mock·er** *n* — **mock·ery** \-(ə-)rē\ *n* — **mock·ing·ly** *adv*

²**mock** *adj* : SHAM, PSEUDO

mock-he·ro·ic \ˌmäk-hi-ˈrō-ik, ˌmȯk-\ *adj* : ridiculing or burlesquing the heroic style, character, or action ⟨a ~ poem⟩

mock·ing·bird \ˈmäk-iŋ-ˌbərd, ˈmȯk-\ *n* : a songbird of the southern U.S. that mimics the calls of other birds

mock-up \ˈmäk-ˌəp, ˈmȯk-\ *n* : a full-sized structural model built for study, testing, or display ⟨a ~ of an airplane⟩

¹**mod** \ˈmäd\ *adj* : MODERN; *esp* : bold,

free, and unconventional in style, behavior, or dress

²**mod** *abbr* **1** moderate **2** modern

mode \ˈmōd\ *n* **1** : a particular form or variety of something; *also* : STYLE **2** : a manner of doing something **3** : the most frequent value of a set of data — **mod·al** \ˈmōd-ᵊl\ *adj*

¹**mod·el** \ˈmäd-ᵊl\ *n* **1** : structural design **2** : a miniature representation; *also* : a pattern of something to be made **3** : an example for imitation or emulation **4** : one who poses for an artist; *also* : MANNEQUIN **5** : TYPE, DESIGN — **model** *adj*

²**model** *vb* **-eled** *or* **-elled**; **-el·ing** *or* **-el·ling** \-(ə-)liŋ\ **1** : SHAPE, FASHION, CONSTRUCT **2** : to work as a fashion model

³**model** *adj* **1** : serving as or worthy of being a pattern ⟨a ~ student⟩ **2** : being a miniature representation of something ⟨a ~ airplane⟩

¹**mod·er·ate** \ˈmäd-(ə-)rət\ *adj* **1** : avoiding extremes; *also* : TEMPERATE **2** : AVERAGE; *also* : MEDIOCRE **3** : limited in scope or effect **4** : not expensive — **moderate** *n* — **mod·er·ate·ly** *adv* — **mod·er·ate·ness** *n*

²**mod·er·ate** \ˈmäd-ə-ˌrāt\ *vb* **-at·ed**; **-at·ing 1** : to lessen the intensity of : TEMPER **2** : to act as a moderator — **mod·er·a·tion** \ˌmäd-ə-ˈrā-shən\ *n*

mod·er·a·tor \ˈmäd-ə-ˌrāt-ər\ *n* **1** : MEDIATOR **2** : one who presides over an assembly, meeting, or discussion

mod·ern \ˈmäd-ərn\ *adj* [LL *modernus*, fr. L *modo* just now, fr. *modus* measure] : of, relating to, or characteristic of the present or the immediate past : CONTEMPORARY — **modern** *n* — **mo·der·ni·ty** \mə-ˈdər-nət-ē\ *n* — **mod·ern·ly** \ˈmäd-ərn-lē\ *adv* — **mod·ern·ness** \-ərn-nəs\ *n*

mod·ern·ism \ˈmäd-ər-ˌniz-əm\ *n* : a practice, movement, or belief peculiar to modern times

mod·ern·ize \ˈmäd-ər-ˌnīz\ *vb* **-ized**; **-iz·ing** : to make or become modern — **mod·ern·iza·tion** \ˌmäd-ər-nə-ˈzā-shən\ *n* — **mod·ern·iz·er** \ˈmäd-ər-ˌnī-zər\ *n*

mod·est \ˈmäd-əst\ *adj* **1** : having a moderate estimate of oneself; *also* : DIFFIDENT **2** : observing the proprieties of dress and behavior **3** : limited in size, amount, or scope — **mod·est·ly** *adv* — **mod·es·ty** \-ə-stē\ *n*

mod·i·cum \ˈmäd-i-kəm\ *n* : a small amount

modif *abbr* modification

mod·i·fy \ˈmäd-ə-ˌfī\ *vb* **-fied**; **-fy·ing 1** : MODERATE **2** : to limit the meaning of esp. in a grammatical construction **3** : CHANGE, ALTER — **mod·i·fi·ca·tion** \ˌmäd-ə-fə-ˈkā-shən\ *n* — **mod·i·fi·er** \ˈmäd-ə-ˌfī(-ə)r\ *n*

mod·ish \ˈmōd-ish\ *adj* : FASHIONABLE, STYLISH — **mod·ish·ly** *adv* — **mod·ish·ness** *n*

mo·diste \mō-ˈdēst\ *n* : a maker of fashionable dresses

mod·u·lar \\'mäj-ə-lər\\ *adj* : constructed with standardized units

mod·u·lar·ized \\'mäj-ə-lə-ˌrīzd\\ *adj* : containing or consisting of modules

mod·u·late \\'mäj-ə-ˌlāt\\ *vb* **-lat·ed; -lat·ing 1** : to tune to a key or pitch **2** : to keep in proper measure or proportion : TEMPER **3** : to vary the amplitude or frequency of a carrier wave for the transmission of intelligence (as in radio or television) — **mod·u·la·tion** \\ˌmäj-ə-'lā-shən\\ *n* — **mod·u·la·tor** \\'mäj-ə-ˌlāt-ər\\ *n* — **mod·u·la·to·ry** \\-lə-ˌtōr-ē\\ *adj*

mod·ule \\'mäj-ül\\ *n* **1** : any in a series of standardized units for use together **2** : an assembly of wired electronic parts for use with other such assemblies **3** : an independent unit that constitutes a part of the total structure of a space vehicle (a propulsion ~)

mo·dus op·e·ran·di \\ˌmō-dəs-ˌäp-ə-'ran-dē, -ˌdī\\ *n, pl* **mo·di operandi** \\'mō-ˌdē-ˌäp-, 'mō-ˌdī-\\ [NL] : a method of procedure

¹mo·gul \\'mō-gəl, mō-'gəl\\ *n* [fr. *Mogul*, one of the Mongol conquerors of India or their descendants, fr. Per *Mughul* Mongol, fr. Mongolian *Moṅgol*] : an important person : magnate

²mogul \\'mō-gəl\\ *n* : a bump in a ski run

mo·hair \\'mō-ˌhaər\\ *n* [modif. of obs. It *mocaiarro*, fr. Ar *mukhayyar*, lit., choice] : a fabric or yarn made wholly or in part from the long silky hair of the Angora goat

Mo·ham·med·an *var of* MUHAMMADAN

Mo·hawk \\'mō-ˌhók\\ *n, pl* **Mohawk** or **Mohawks** : a member of an American Indian people of the Mohawk river valley, New York; *also* : the language of the Mohawk people

Mo·he·gan \\mō-'hē-gən, mə-\\ or **Mo·hi·can** \\-'hē-kən\\ *n, pl* **Mohegan** or **Mohegans** or **Mohican** or **Mohicans** : a member of an American Indian people of southeastern Connecticut

Mo·hi·can \\mō-'hē-kən, mə-\\ *var of* MAHICAN

moi·e·ty \\'mói-ət-ē\\ *n, pl* **-eties** : one of two equal or approximately equal parts

moil \\'móil\\ *vb* : to work hard : DRUDGE — **moil** *n* — **moil·er** *n*

moi·ré \\mó-'rā, mwä-\\ or **moire** *same*, or 'mói(-ə)r, 'mwär\\ *n* : a fabric (as silk) having a watered appearance

moist \\'móist\\ *adj* : slightly or moderately wet — **moist·ly** *adv* — **moist·ness** *n*

moist·en \\'mói-sən\\ *vb* **moist·ened; moist·en·ing** \\'mói-s(ə-)niŋ\\ : to make or become moist — **moist·en·er** \\'mói-s(ə-)nər\\ *n*

mois·ture \\'mói-schər\\ *n* : the small amount of liquid that causes dampness

mol *abbr* molecular; molecule

mo·lar \\'mō-lər\\ *n* [L *molaris*, fr. *mola* of a mill, fr. *mola* millstone] : one of the broad teeth adapted to grinding food and located in the back of the jaw — **molar** *adj*

mo·las·ses \\mə-'las-əz\\ *n* : the thick brown syrup that is separated from raw sugar in sugar manufacture

¹mold \\'mōld\\ *n* : crumbly soil rich in organic matter

²mold *n* **1** : distinctive nature or character **2** : the frame on or around which something is constructed **3** : a cavity in which something is shaped; *also* : an object so shaped **4** : MOLDING

³mold *vb* **1** : to shape in or as if in a mold **2** : to ornament with molding — **mold·er** *n*

⁴mold *n* : a surface growth of fungus on damp or decaying matter; *also* : a fungus that forms molds — **mold·i·ness** \\'mōl-dē-nəs\\ *n* — **moldy** *adj*

⁵mold *vb* : to become moldy

mold·board \\'mōl(d)-ˌbōrd\\ *n* : a curved iron plate attached above the plowshare to lift and turn the soil

mold·er \\'mōl-dər\\ *vb* **mold·ered; mold·er·ing** \\-d(ə-)riŋ\\ : to crumble into small pieces

mold·ing \\'mōl-diŋ\\ *n* **1** : an act or process of shaping in a mold; *also* : an object so shaped **2** : a decorative surface, plane, or curved strip

¹mole \\'mōl\\ *n* : a small often pigmented spot or protuberance on the skin

²mole *n* : a small burrowing mammal with tiny eyes, hidden ears, and soft fur

³mole *n* : a massive breakwater or jetty

mo·lec·u·lar biology \\mə-'lek-yə-lər-\\ : a branch of biology dealing with the ultimate physical and chemical organization of living matter and esp. with the molecular basis of inheritance and protein synthesis — **molecular biologist** *n*

mol·e·cule \\'mäl-i-ˌkyül\\ *n* : the smallest particle of matter that is the same chemically as the whole mass — **mo·lec·u·lar** \\mə-'lek-yə-lər\\ *adj*

mole·hill \\'mōl-ˌhil\\ *n* : a little ridge of earth thrown up by a mole

mole·skin \\-ˌskin\\ *n* **1** : the skin of the mole used as fur **2** : a heavy durable cotton fabric for industrial, medical, or clothing use

mo·lest \\mə-'lest\\ *vb* **1** : ANNOY, DISTURB **2** : to make annoying sexual advances to — **mo·les·ta·tion** \\ˌmōl-ˌes-'tā-shən\\ *n* — **mo·lest·er** \\mə-'les-tər\\ *n*

moll \\'mäl\\ *n* : a gangster's girlfriend

mol·li·fy \\'mäl-ə-ˌfī\\ *vb* **-fied; -fy·ing 1** : to soothe in temper : APPEASE **2** : SOFTEN **3** : to reduce in intensity : ASSUAGE — **mol·li·fi·ca·tion** \\ˌmäl-ə-fə-'kā-shən\\ *n*

mol·lusk or **mol·lusc** \\'mäl-əsk\\ *n* : any of a large group of mostly shelled and aquatic invertebrate animals including snails, clams, and squids — **mol·lus·can** *also* **mol·lus·kan** \\mə-'ləs-kən\\ *adj*

¹**mol·ly·cod·dle** \ˈmäl-ē-ˌkäd-ᵊl\ *n* : a pampered man or boy

²**mollycoddle** *vb* **mol·ly·cod·dled; mol·ly·cod·dling** \-ˌkäd-(ᵊ-)liŋ\ : PAMPER

Mo·lo·tov cocktail \ˈmäl-ə-ˌtóf-, ˌmól-\ *n* : a crude bomb made of a bottle filled usu. with gasoline and fitted with a wick or saturated rag and ignited usu. just prior to hurling

¹**molt** \ˈmōlt\ *vb* : to shed hair, feathers, outer skin, or horns periodically with the parts being replaced by new growth — **molt·er** *n*

²**molt** *n* : the act or process of molting

mol·ten \ˈmōlt-ᵊn\ *adj* **1** : fused or liquefied by heat **2** : GLOWING

mo·ly \ˈmō-lē\ *n* : a mythical herb with black root, white flowers, and magic powers

mo·lyb·de·num \mə-ˈlib-də-nəm\ *n* : a metallic chemical element used in strengthening and hardening steel

mom \ˈmäm, ˈməm\ *n* : MOTHER

mom–and–pop *adj* : being a small owner-operated business

mo·ment \ˈmō-mənt\ *n* **1** : a minute portion of time : INSTANT **2** : a time of excellence (he has his ~s) **3** : IMPORTANCE **syn** consequence, significance, weight, import

mo·men·tar·i·ly \ˌmō-mən-ˈter-ə-lē\ *adv* **1** : for a moment **2** : INSTANTLY **3** : at any moment : SOON

mo·men·tary \ˈmō-mən-ˌter-ē\ *adj* **1** : continuing only a moment; *also* : EPHEMERAL **2** : recurring at every moment — **mo·men·tar·i·ness** \ˈmō-mən-ˌter-ē-nəs\ *n*

mo·men·tous \mō-ˈment-əs\ *adj* : very important — **mo·men·tous·ly** *adv* — **mo·men·tous·ness** *n*

mo·men·tum \mō-ˈment-əm\ *n, pl* **mo·men·ta** \-ˈment-ə\ *or* **momentums** : a property that a moving body has due to its mass and motion; *also* : IMPETUS

mom·my \ˈmäm-ē, ˈməm-\ *n, pl* **mommies** : MOTHER

Mon *abbr* Monday

mon·arch \ˈmän-ərk, -ˌärk\ *n* **1** : a person who reigns over a kingdom or an empire **2** : one holding preeminent position or power — **mo·nar·chi·cal** \mə-ˈnär-ki-kəl\ *also* **mo·nar·chic** \-ˈnär-kik\ *adj*

monarch butterfly *n* : a large orange and black migratory American butterfly whose larva feeds on milkweed

mon·ar·chist \ˈmän-ər-kəst\ *n* : a believer in monarchical government — **mon·ar·chism** \-ˌkiz-əm\ *n*

mon·ar·chy \ˈmän-ər-kē\ *n, pl* **-chies** : a nation or state governed by a monarch

mon·as·tery \ˈmän-ə-ˌster-ē\ *n, pl* **-ter·ies** : a house for persons under religious vows (as monks)

mo·nas·tic \mə-ˈnas-tik\ *adj* : of or relating to monasteries or to monks or nuns — **monastic** *n* — **mo·nas·ti·cal·ly** \-ti-k(ə-)lē\ *adv*

mo·nas·ti·cism \mə-ˈnas-tə-ˌsiz-əm\ *n* : the monastic life, system, or condition

mon·au·ral \mä-ˈnór-əl\ *adj* : MONOPHONIC — **mon·au·ral·ly** \-ē\ *adv*

Mon·day \ˈmən-dē, -ˌdā\ *n* : the second day of the week

mon·e·tary \ˈmän-ə-ˌter-ē, ˈmən-\ *adj* : of or relating to money or to the mechanisms by which it is supplied and circulated in the economy

mon·ey \ˈmən-ē\ *n, pl* **moneys** *or* **monies** \ˈmən-ēz\ **1** : something (as metal currency) accepted as a medium of exchange **2** : wealth reckoned in monetary terms **3** : the 1st, 2d, and 3d places in a horse or dog race

MONEY

NAME	SUBDIVISIONS	COUNTRY
afghani	100 puls	Afghanistan
austral		Argentina
baht *or* tical	100 satang	Thailand
balboa	100 centesimos	Panama
birr	100 cents	Ethiopia
bolivar	100 centimos	Venezuela
cedi	100 pesewas	Ghana
colon	100 centimos	Costa Rica
colon	100 centavos	El Salvador
cordoba	100 centavos	Nicaragua
cruzado		Brazil
dalasi	100 bututs	Gambia
deutsche mark	100 pfennigs	West Germany
dinar	100 centimes	Algeria
dinar	1000 fils	Bahrain
dinar	1000 fils	Iraq
dinar	1000 fils	Jordan
dinar	1000 fils	Kuwait
dinar	1000 dirhams	Libya
dinar	1000 fils	Southern Yemen (People's Democratic Republic of Yemen)
dinar	1000 millimes	Tunisia
dinar	100 paras	Yugoslavia
dirham	100 centimes	Morocco
dirham	1000 fils	United Arab Emirates
dobra	100 centavos	Sao Tome and Principe
dollar	100 cents	Australia
dollar	100 cents	Bahamas
dollar	100 cents	Barbados
dollar	100 cents	Belize
dollar	100 cents	Bermuda
dollar	100 sen	Brunei
dollar	100 cents	Canada
dollar *or* yuan	100 cents	China (Taiwan)
dollar	100 cents	Ethiopia
dollar	100 cents	Fiji
dollar	100 cents	Grenada
dollar	100 cents	Guyana
dollar	100 cents	Hong Kong
dollar	100 cents	Jamaica

NAME	SUBDIVISIONS	COUNTRY	NAME	SUBDIVISIONS	COUNTRY
dollar	100 cents	Liberia	lempira	100 centavos	Honduras
dollar	100 cents	New Zealand	leone	100 cents	Sierra Leone
dollar	100 cents	St. Vincent and the Grenadines	leu	100 bani	Romania
			lev	100 stotinki	Bulgaria
dollar	100 cents	Singapore	lilangeni (pl emalangeni)	100 cents	Swaziland
dollar	100 cents	Trinidad and Tobago	lira	100 centesimi	Italy
dollar	100 cents	United States	lira or pound	100 kurus or piasters	Turkey
dollar	100 cents	Zimbabwe	lira—see POUND, below		
dong	100 xu	Vietnam	loti (pl maloti)	100 licente	Lesotho
drachma	100 lepta	Greece	mark or ostmark	100 pfennigs	East Germany
ekuele	100 centimos	Equatorial Guinea	mark—see DEUTSCHE MARK, above		
escudo	100 centavos	Cape Verde	markka	100 pennia	Finland
escudo	100 centavos	Portugal	metical	100 centavos	Mozambique
escudo—see PESO, below			naira	100 kobo	Nigeria
florin—see GULDEN, below			ngultrum	100 chetrums	Bhutan
forint	100 filler	Hungary	ostmark—see MARK, above		
franc	100 centimes	Belgium	ouguiya	5 khoums	Mauritania
franc	100 centimes	Benin	pa'anga	100 seniti	Tonga
franc	100 centimes	Burkina Faso	pataca	100 avos	Macao
franc	100 centimes	Burundi	peseta	100 centimos	Spain
franc	100 centimes	Cameroon	peso	100 centavos	Bolivia
franc	100 centimes	Central African Republic	peso	100 centavos	Chile
			peso	100 centavos	Colombia
franc	100 centimes	Chad	peso	100 centavos	Cuba
franc	100 centimes	Congo	peso	100 centavos	Dominican Republic
franc	100 centimes	Djibouti	peso	100 centavos	Guinea-Bissau
franc	100 centimes	France			
franc	100 centimes	Gabon	peso	100 centavos	Mexico
franc	100 centimes	Ivory Coast	peso	100 sentimos or centavos	Philippines
franc	100 centimes	Luxembourg			
franc	100 centimes	Madagascar	peso	100 centesimos	Uruguay
franc	100 centimes	Mali	pound	1000 mils	Cyprus
franc	100 centimes	Niger	pound	100 piasters	Egypt
franc	100 centimes	Rwanda	pound	100 pence	Ireland
franc	100 centimes	Senegal	pound	100 piasters	Lebanon
franc	100 centimes or rappen	Switzerland	pound or lira	100 pence	Malta
franc	100 centimes	Togo	pound	100 piasters	Sudan
gourde	100 centimes	Haiti	pound	100 piasters	Syria
guarani	100 centimos	Paraguay	pound	100 pence	United Kingdom
gulden or guilder or florin	100 cents	Netherlands	pound—see LIRA, above		
			pula	100 thebe	Botswana
			quetzal	100 centavos	Guatemala
gulden or guilder or florin	100 cents	Suriname	rand	100 cents	South Africa
			rial	100 dinars	Iran
inti		Peru	rial	1000 baizas	Oman
kina	100 toea	Papua New Guinea	rial or riyal	100 fils	Yemen Arab Republic
kip	100 at	Laos			
koruna	100 halers	Czechoslovakia	riel	100 sen	Cambodia
			ringgit	100 sen	Malaysia
krona	100 aurar (sing eyrir)	Iceland	riyal	100 dirhams	Qatar
krona	100 ore	Sweden	riyal	20 qursh 100 halala	Saudi Arabia
krone	100 ore	Denmark	riyal—see RIAL, above		
krone	100 ore	Norway	ruble	100 kopecks	U.S.S.R.
kwacha	100 tambala	Malawi	rupee	100 paise	India
kwacha	100 ngwee	Zambia	rupee	100 cents	Mauritius
kwanza	100 lwei	Angola	rupee	100 paisa	Nepal
kyat	100 pyas	Burma	rupee	100 paisa	Pakistan
lek	100 qindarka	Albania	rupee	100 cents	Seychelles
			rupee	100 cents	Sri Lanka
			rupiah	100 sen	Indonesia

NAME	SUBDIVISIONS	COUNTRY
schilling	100 groschen	Austria
shekel	100 agorot	Israel
shilingi—see SHILLING, below		
shilling	100 cents	Kenya
shilling	100 cents	Somalia
shilling *or* shilingi	100 senti *or* cents	Tanzania
shilling	100 cents	Uganda
sucre	100 centavos	Ecuador
syli	100 cauris	Guinea
taka	100 paisa	Bangladesh
tala	100 sene	Western Samoa
tical—see BAHT, above		
tugrik	100 mongo	Mongolia
vatu		Vanuatu
won	100 jun	North Korea
won	100 jeon	South Korea
yen	100 sen	Japan
yuan	100 fen	China (mainland)
yuan—see DOLLAR, above		
zaire	100 makuta (*sing.* likuta) 10,000 sengi	Zaire
zloty	100 groszy	Poland

mon·eyed \'mən-ēd\ *adj* **1** : having money : WEALTHY **2** : consisting in or derived from money

mon·ey·lend·er \'mən-ē-ˌlen-dər\ *n* : one whose business is lending money; *specif* : PAWNBROKER

money market *n* : the trade in short-term negotiable financial instruments

money of account : a denominator of value or basis of exchange used in keeping accounts

money order *n* : an order purchased at a post office, bank, or telegraph office directing another office to pay a sum of money to a party named on it

mon·ger \'məŋ-gər, 'məŋ-\ *n* **1** : DEALER **2** : one who tries to stir up or spread something

mon·go \'məŋ-(ˌ)gō\ *n, pl* **mongo** — see *tugrik* at MONEY table

Mon·gol \'mäŋ-gəl, 'män-ˌgōl\ *n* : a person of Mongoloid racial stock and esp. of the chiefly pastoral Mongoloid peoples of Mongolia — **Mongol** *adj*

Mon·go·lian \män-'gōl-yən, mäŋ-, -ˌgō-lē-ən\ *n* **1** : a native or inhabitant of Mongolia **2** : a member of the Mongoloid racial stock — **Mongolian** *adj*

mon·gol·ism \'mäŋ-gə-ˌliz-əm\ *n* : DOWN'S SYNDROME

Mon·gol·oid \'mäŋ-gə-ˌlöid\ *adj* **1** : of or relating to a major racial stock native to Asia that includes peoples of northern and eastern Asia, Malaysians, Eskimos, and often American Indians **2** *often not cap* : of, relating to, or affected with Down's syndrome — **Mongoloid** *n*

mon·goose \'mäŋ-ˌgüs, 'mäŋ-\ *n, pl* **mon·goos·es** *also* **mon·geese** \-ˌgēs\ : a small agile mammal of India that is related to the civet cats and feeds on snakes and rodents

mon·grel \'mäŋ-grəl, 'məŋ-\ *n* : an offspring of parents of different breeds or uncertain ancestry

mo·nism \'mō-ˌniz-əm, 'män-iz-\ *n* : a view that reality is basically one — **mo·nist** \'mō-nəst, 'män-əst\ *n*

mo·ni·tion \mō-'nish-ən, mə-\ *n* : WARNING, CAUTION

¹mon·i·tor \'män-ət-ər\ *n* **1** : a student appointed to assist a teacher **2** : one that monitors; *esp* : a video display screen (as for a computer)

²monitor *vb* **mon·i·tored; mon·i·tor·ing** \'män-ət-ə-riŋ, 'män-ə-triŋ\ : to watch, check, or observe for a special purpose

mon·i·to·ry \'män-ə-ˌtōr-ē\ *adj* : giving admonition : WARNING

¹monk \'məŋk\ *n* [ME, fr. OE *munuc,* fr. LL *monachus,* fr. LGk *monachos,* fr. Gk, adj., single, fr. *monos* single, alone] : a man belonging to a religious order and living in a monastery — **monk·ish** *adj*

²monk *n* : MONKEY

¹mon·key \'məŋ-kē\ *n, pl* **monkeys** : a primate mammal other than man; *esp* : one of the smaller, longer-tailed, and usu. more arboreal primates as contrasted with the apes

²monkey *vb* **mon·keyed; mon·key·ing 1** : FOOL, TRIFLE **2** : TAMPER

monkey bars *n pl* : a framework of bars on which children can play

mon·key·shine \'män-kē-ˌshīn\ *n* : PRANK — usu. used in pl.

monkey wrench *n* : a wrench with one fixed and one adjustable jaw at right angles to a handle

monks·hood \'məŋks-ˌhůd\ *n* : any of a genus of poisonous plants related to the buttercups; *esp* : a tall Old World plant grown for its white or purplish flowers or as a source of drugs (as aconite)

¹mono \'män-ō\ *adj* : MONOPHONIC

²mono *n* : MONONUCLEOSIS

mono·chro·mat·ic \ˌmän-ə-krō-'mat-ik\ *adj* **1** : having or consisting of one color **2** : consisting of radiation (as light) of a single wavelength

mono·chrome \'män-ə-ˌkrōm\ *adj* : characterized by the reproduction or transmission of visual images in tones of gray (~ television)

mon·o·cle \'män-i-kəl\ *n* : an eyeglass for one eye

mono·clo·nal \ˌmän-ə-'klō-nəl\ *adj* : produced by, being, or composed of cells derived from a single cell (~ antibodies)

mono·cot·y·le·don \ˌmän-ə-ˌkät-ᵊl-'ēd-ᵊn\ *n* : any of a subclass of seed plants having an embryo with a single cotyledon and usu. parallel-veined leaves — **mono·cot·y·le·don·ous** *adj*

mon·o·dy \'män-əd-ē\ *n, pl* **-dies** : ELEGY, DIRGE — **mo·nod·ic** \mə-'näd-ik\ *or* **mo·nod·i·cal** \-i-kəl\ *adj* — **mon·o·dist** \'män-əd-əst\ *n*

mo·nog·a·my \mə-'näg-ə-mē\ *n* : mar-

mo·nog·a·mist \mə-ˈnäg-ə-məst\ *n* — **mo·nog·a·mous** \mə-ˈnäg-ə-məs\ *adj*

riage with but one person at a time —

mono·gram \ˈmän-ə-ˌgram\ *n* : a sign of identity composed of the combined initials of a name — **monogram** *vb*

mono·graph \ˈmän-ə-ˌgraf\ *n* : a learned treatise on a small area of learning

mono·lin·gual \ˌmän-ə-ˈliŋ-gwəl\ *adj* : expressed in or knowing or using only one language

mono·lith \ˈmän-ᵊl-ˌith\ *n* 1 : a single great stone often in the form of a monument or column 2 : something large and powerful that acts as a single unified force — **mono·lith·ic** \ˌmän-ᵊl-ˈith-ik\ *adj*

mono·logue *also* **mono·log** \ˈmän-ᵊl-ˌȯg\ *n* : a dramatic soliloquy; *also* : a long speech monopolizing conversation — **mono·logu·ist** \-ˌȯg-əst\ *or* **mo·nol·o·gist** \mə-ˈnäl-ə-jəst; ˈmän-ᵊl-ˌȯg-əst\ *n*

mono·ma·nia \ˌmän-ə-ˈmä-nē-ə, -nyə\ *n* 1 : mental derangement involving a single idea or area of thought 2 : excessive concentration on a single object or idea — **mono·ma·ni·ac** \-nē-ˌak\ *n or adj*

mono·mer \ˈmän-ə-mər\ *n* : a simple chemical compound that can be polymerized

mono·nu·cle·o·sis \ˌmän-ō-ˌn(y)ü-klē-ˈō-səs\ *n* : an acute infectious disease characterized by fever, swelling of lymph glands, and increased numbers of lymph cells in the blood

mono·phon·ic \ˌmän-ə-ˈfän-ik\ *adj* : of or relating to sound transmission, recording, or reproduction by techniques that provide a single transmission path

mono·plane \ˈmän-ə-ˌplän\ *n* : an airplane with only one set of wings

mo·nop·o·ly \mə-ˈnäp-(ə-)lē\ *n, pl* **-lies** [L *monopolium*, fr. Gk *monopōlion*, fr. *monos* alone, single + *pōlein* to sell] 1 : exclusive ownership (as through command of supply) 2 : a commodity controlled by one party 3 : one that has a monopoly — **mo·nop·o·list** \-ləst\ *n* — **mo·nop·o·lis·tic** \mə-ˌnäp-ə-ˈlis-tik\ *adj* — **mo·nop·o·li·za·tion** \-lə-ˈzā-shən\ *n* — **mo·nop·o·lize** \mə-ˈnäp-ə-ˌlīz\ *vb*

mono·rail \ˈmän-ə-ˌrāl\ *n* : a single rail serving as a track for a wheeled vehicle; *also* : a vehicle traveling on such a track

mono·so·di·um glu·ta·mate \ˌmän-ə-ˌsōd-ē-əm-ˈglüt-ə-ˌmāt\ *n* : a crystalline salt used for seasoning foods

mono·syl·la·ble \ˈmän-ə-ˌsil-ə-bəl\ *n* : a word of one syllable — **mono·syl·lab·ic** \ˌmän-ə-sə-ˈlab-ik\ *adj* — **mono·syl·lab·i·cal·ly** \-i-k(ə-)lē\ *adv*

mono·the·ism \ˈmän-ə-(ˌ)thē-ˌiz-əm\ *n* : a doctrine or belief that there is only one deity — **mono·the·ist** \-ˌthē-əst\ *n*

mono·tone \ˈmän-ə-ˌtōn\ *n* : a succes-

sion of syllables, words, or sentences in one unvaried key or pitch

mo·not·o·nous \mə-ˈnät-ᵊn-əs\ *adj* 1 : uttered or sounded in one unvarying tone 2 : tediously uniform — **mo·not·o·nous·ly** *adv* — **mo·not·o·nous·ness** *n* — **mo·not·o·ny** \-ᵊn-ē\ *n*

mon·ox·ide \mə-ˈnäk-ˌsīd\ *n* : an oxide containing one atom of oxygen in the molecule

mon·sei·gneur \ˌmōⁿ-ˌsān-ˈyər\ *n, pl* **mes·sei·gneurs** \ˌmā-ˌsān-ˈyər(z)\ : a French dignitary — used as a title

mon·sieur \məs-ˈya(r), Fr mə-ˈsyœ\ *n, pl* **mes·sieurs** \məs(h)-ˈ(ᵊ)ya(r)(z), mäs-; mə-ˈsi(ə)r(z)\ : a Frenchman of high rank or station — used as a title equivalent to *Mister*

mon·si·gnor \män-ˈsē-nyər\ *n, pl* **monsignors** *or* **mon·si·gno·ri** \ˌmän-ˌsēn-ˈyȯr-ē\ [It *monsignore*] : a Roman Catholic prelate — used as a title

mon·soon \män-ˈsün\ *n* [obs. Dutch *monssoen*, fr. Pg *monção*, fr. Ar *mawsim* time, season] 1 : a periodic wind esp. in the Indian ocean and southern Asia 2 : the season of the southwest monsoon esp. in India 3 : rainfall associated with the monsoon

¹**mon·ster** \ˈmän-stər\ *n* 1 : an abnormally developed plant or animal 2 : an animal of strange or terrifying shape; *also* : one unusually large of its kind 3 : an extremely ugly, wicked, or cruel person — **mon·stros·i·ty** \män-ˈsträs-ət-ē\ *n* — **mon·strous** \ˈmän-strəs\ *adj* — **mon·strous·ly** *adv*

²**monster** *adj* : very large : ENORMOUS

mon·strance \ˈmän-strəns\ *n* : a vessel in which the consecrated Host is exposed for the adoration of the faithful

Mont *abbr* Montana

mon·tage \män-ˈtäzh\ *n* [F] 1 : a composite photograph made by combining several separate pictures 2 : an artistic composition made up of several different kinds of items (as strips of newspaper, pictures, bits of wood) arranged together

month \ˈmənth\ *n, pl* **months** \ˈməns, ˈmənths\ [OE *mōnath*, fr. *mōna* moon] : one of the 12 parts into which the year is divided — **month·ly** *adv or adj or n*

month·long \ˈmənth-ˈlȯŋ\ *adj* : lasting a month

mon·u·ment \ˈmän-yə-mənt\ *n* 1 : a lasting reminder; *esp* : a structure erected in remembrance of a person or event 2 : a natural feature or area of special interest set aside by the government as public property

mon·u·men·tal \ˌmän-yə-ˈment-ᵊl\ *adj* 1 : of or relating to a monument 2 : MASSIVE; *also* : OUTSTANDING 3 : very great — **mon·u·men·tal·ly** \-ē\ *adv*

moo \ˈmü\ *vb* : to make the natural throat noise of a cow — **moo** *n*

¹**mood** \ˈmüd\ *n* 1 : a conscious state of mind or predominant emotion : FEEL-

ING **2** : a prevailing attitude : DISPOSITION

²**mood** n : distinction of form of a verb to express whether its action or state is conceived as fact or in some other manner (as wish)

moody \'müd-ē\ adj **mood·i·er; -est 1** : GLOOMY **2** : subject to moods : TEMPERAMENTAL — **mood·i·ly** \'müd-ᵊl-ē\ adv — **mood·i·ness** \-ē-nəs\ n

¹**moon** \'mün\ n **1** : the earth's natural satellite **2** : SATELLITE **2**

²**moon** vb : to engage in idle reverie

moon·beam \'mün-ˌbēm\ n : a ray of light from the moon

¹**moon·light** \-ˌlīt\ n : the light of the moon — **moon·lit** \-ˌlit\ adj

²**moonlight** vb **moon·light·ed; moon·light·ing** : to hold a second job in addition to a regular one — **moon·light·er** n

moon·scape \-ˌskāp\ n : the surface of the moon as seen or as pictured

moon·shine \-ˌshīn\ n **1** : MOONLIGHT **2** : empty talk **3** : intoxicating liquor usu. illegally distilled

moon·stone \-ˌstōn\ n : a transparent or translucent feldspar of pearly luster used as a gem

moon·struck \-ˌstrək\ adj **1** : mentally unbalanced **2** : romantically sentimental

¹**moor** \'mùr\ n : an area of open and usu. infertile and wet or peaty wasteland

²**moor** vb : to make fast with or as if with cables, lines, or anchors

Moor \'mùr\ n : one of a North African people of Arab and Berber ancestry that conquered Spain in the 8th century — **Moor·ish** adj

moor·ing \'mùr-iŋ\ n **1** : a place where or an object to which a craft can be made fast **2** : an established practice or stabilizing influence — usu. used in pl.

moor·land \-lənd, -ˌland\ n : land consisting of moors

moose \'müs\ n, pl **moose** : a large heavy-antlered American deer; also : the European elk

¹**moot** \'müt\ vb : to bring up for debate or discussion; also : DEBATE

²**moot** adj **1** : open to question; also : DISPUTED **2** : having no practical significance

¹**mop** \'mäp\ n : an implement made of absorbent material fastened to a handle and used esp. for cleaning floors

²**mop** vb **mopped; mop·ping** : to use a mop on : clean with a mop

mope \'mōp\ vb **moped; mop·ing 1** : to become dull, dejected, or listless **2** : DAWDLE

mop·pet \'mäp-ət\ n [obs. E mop fool, child] : CHILD

mop-up \'mäp-ˌəp\ n : a final clearance or disposal

mo·raine \mə-'rān\ n : an accumulation of earth and stones left by a glacier

¹**mor·al** \'mòr-əl\ adj **1** : of or relating to principles of right and wrong **2** : con-

forming to a standard of right behavior; also : capable of right and wrong action **3** : probable but not proved ⟨a ~ certainty⟩ **4** : having the effects of such on the mind, confidence, or will ⟨a ~ victory⟩ syn virtuous, righteous, noble, ethical, principled — **mor·al·ly** \-ē\ adv

²**moral** n **1** : the practical meaning (as of a story) **2** pl : moral practices or teachings

mo·rale \mə-'ral\ n **1** : MORALITY **2** : the mental and emotional attitudes of an individual to the tasks at hand; also : ESPRIT DE CORPS

mor·al·ist \'mòr-ə-ləst\ n **1** : a teacher or student of morals **2** : one concerned with regulating the morals of others — **mor·al·is·tic** \ˌmòr-ə-'lis-tik\ adj — **mor·al·is·ti·cal·ly** \-ti-k(ə-)lē\ adv

mo·ral·i·ty \mə-'ral-ət-ē\ n, pl **-ties** : moral conduct : VIRTUE

mor·al·ize \'mòr-ə-ˌlīz\ vb **-ized; -iz·ing** : to make moral reflections — **mor·al·iza·tion** \ˌmòr-ə-lə-'zā-shən\ n — **mor·al·iz·er** \'mòr-ə-ˌlī-zər\ n

mo·rass \mə-'ras\ n : SWAMP

mor·a·to·ri·um \ˌmòr-ə-'tōr-ē-əm\ n, pl **-ri·ums** or **-ria** \-ē-ə\ [deriv. of L mora delay] : a suspension of activity

mo·ray \mə-'rā, 'mòr-ˌā\ n : any of numerous often brightly colored savage eels occurring in warm seas

mor·bid \'mòr-bəd\ adj **1** : of, relating to, or typical of disease; also : DISEASED, SICKLY **2** : characterized by gloomy or unwholesome ideas or feelings **3** : GRISLY, GRUESOME ⟨~ details⟩ — **mor·bid·i·ty** \mòr-'bid-ət-ē\ n — **mor·bid·ly** \'mòr-bəd-lē\ adv — **mor·bid·ness** n

mor·dant \'mòrd-ᵊnt\ adj **1** : INCISIVE **2** : BURNING, PUNGENT — **mor·dant·ly** adv

¹**more** \'mòr\ adj **1** : GREATER **2** : ADDITIONAL

²**more** adv **1** : in addition ⟨a couple of times ~⟩ **2** : to a greater or higher degree

³**more** n **1** : a greater quantity, number, or amount ⟨the ~ the merrier⟩ **2** : an additional amount ⟨too full to eat ~⟩

⁴**more** pron : additional persons or things ⟨~ were found in the road⟩

mo·rel \mə-'rel\ n : any of several pitted edible fungi

more·over \mōr-'ō-vər\ adv : in addition : FURTHER

mo·res \'mòr-ˌāz\ n pl **1** : the fixed morally binding customs of a group **2** : HABITS, MANNERS

Mor·gan \'mòr-gən\ n : any of an American breed of lightly built horses

morgue \'mòrg\ n : a place where the bodies of dead persons are kept until released for burial

mor·i·bund \'mòr-ə-(ˌ)bənd\ adj : being in a dying condition — **mor·i·bun·di·ty** \ˌmòr-ə-'bən-dət-ē\ n

Mor·mon \'mòr-mən\ n : a member of

Mormonism·mot

the Church of Jesus Christ of Latter-day Saints — **Mor·mon·ism** \-mə-ˌniz-əm\ n

morn \ˈmȯrn\ n : MORNING

morn·ing \ˈmȯr-niŋ\ n **1** : the early part of the day; esp : the time from the sunrise to noon **2** : BEGINNING

morning glory n : any of various twining plants related to the sweet potato that have often showy bell-shaped or funnel-shaped flowers

morning sickness n : nausea and vomiting that occur in the morning esp. during early pregnancy

morning star n : a bright planet (as Venus) seen in the eastern sky before or at sunrise

Mo·roc·can \mə-ˈräk-ən\ n : a native or inhabitant of Morocco

mo·roc·co \mə-ˈräk-ō\ n : a fine leather made of goatskins tanned with sumac

mo·ron \ˈmȯr-ˌän\ n : a defective person having a potential mental age of between 8 and 12 years and capable of doing routine work under supervision; also : a stupid person — **mo·ron·ic** \mə-ˈrän-ik\ adj — **mo·ron·i·cal·ly** \-i-k(ə-)lē\ adv

mo·rose \mə-ˈrōs\ adj [L morosus, lit., capricious, fr. mor-, mos will] : having a sullen disposition; also : GLOOMY — **mo·rose·ly** adv — **mo·rose·ness** n

mor·pheme \ˈmȯr-ˌfēm\ n : a meaningful linguistic unit that contains no smaller meaningful parts — **mor·phe·mic** \mȯr-ˈfē-mik\ adj

mor·phia \ˈmȯr-fē-ə\ n : MORPHINE

mor·phine \ˈmȯr-ˌfēn\ n [F, fr. Gk Morpheus Greek god of dreams] : an addictive drug obtained from opium and used to ease pain or induce sleep

mor·phol·o·gy \mȯr-ˈfäl-ə-jē\ n **1** : a branch of biology dealing with the form and structure of organisms **2** : a study and description of word formation in a language — **mor·pho·log·i·cal** \ˌmȯr-fə-ˈläj-i-kəl\ adj — **mor·phol·o·gist** \mȯr-ˈfäl-ə-jəst\ n

mor·ris \ˈmȯr-əs\ n : a vigorous English dance performed traditionally by men wearing costumes and bells

mor·row \ˈmär-ō\ n : the next day

Morse code \ˈmȯrs-\ n : either of two codes consisting of dots and dashes or long and short sounds used for transmitting messages

mor·sel \ˈmȯr-səl\ n [ME, fr. OF, dim. of mors bite, fr. L morsus, fr. mordēre to bite] **1** : a small piece or quantity **2** : a tasty dish

mor·tal \ˈmȯrt-ᵊl\ adj **1** : causing death : FATAL; also : leading to eternal punishment (⟨~ sin⟩ **2** : subject to death (⟨~ man⟩ **3** : implacably hostile (⟨~ foe⟩ **4** : very great : EXTREME (⟨~ fear⟩ **5** : HUMAN (⟨~ limitations⟩ — mortal n — **mor·tal·i·ty** \mȯr-ˈtal-ət-ē\ n — **mor·tal·ly** \ˈmȯrt-ᵊl-ē\ adv

¹mor·tar \ˈmȯrt-ər\ n **1** : a strong bowl in which substances are pounded or crushed with a pestle **2** : a short-barreled cannon used to fire shells at high angles

²mortar n : a plastic building material (as a mixture of cement, lime, or gypsum plaster with sand and water) that is spread between bricks or stones to bind them together as it hardens — mortar vb

mor·tar·board \ˈmȯrt-ər-ˌbȯrd\ n **1** : a board or platform about three feet square for holding mortar **2** : an academic cap with a broad square top

mort·gage \ˈmȯr-gij\ n [ME morgage, fr. MF, fr. OF, fr. mort dead + gage gage] : a transfer of rights to a piece of property usu. as security for the payment of a loan or debt that becomes void when the debt is paid — mortgage vb — **mort·gag·ee** \ˌmȯr-gi-ˈjē\ n — **mort·ga·gor** \ˌmȯr-gi-ˈjȯr\ n

mor·ti·cian \mȯr-ˈtish-ən\ n [L mort-, mors death + E -ician (as in physician)] : UNDERTAKER

mor·ti·fy \ˈmȯrt-ə-ˌfī\ vb -fied; -fy·ing **1** : to subdue (as the body) esp. by abstinence or self-inflicted pain **2** : HUMILIATE **3** : to become necrotic or gangrenous — **mor·ti·fi·ca·tion** \ˌmȯrt-ə-fə-ˈkā-shən\ n

mor·tise also **mor·tice** \ˈmȯrt-əs\ n : a hole cut in a piece of wood into which another piece fits to form a joint

mor·tu·ary \ˈmȯr-chə-ˌwer-ē\ n, pl -ar·ies : a place in which dead bodies are kept until burial

mos abbr months

mo·sa·ic \mō-ˈzā-ik\ n : a surface decoration made by inlaying small pieces (as of colored glass or stone) to form figures or patterns; also : a design made in mosaic

mo·sey \ˈmō-zē\ vb mo·seyed; mo·sey·ing : SAUNTER

Mos·lem \ˈmäz-ləm\ var of MUSLIM

mosque \ˈmäsk\ n : a building used for public worship by Muslims

mos·qui·to \mə-ˈskēt-ō\ n, pl -toes also -tos : a two-winged fly the female of which sucks the blood of man and lower animals

mosquito net n : a net or screen for keeping out mosquitoes

moss \ˈmȯs\ n : any of a large group of green plants without flowers but with small leafy stems growing in clumps — mossy adj

moss·back \ˈmȯs-ˌbak\ n : an extremely conservative person : FOGY

¹most \ˈmōst\ adj **1** : the majority of (⟨~ people⟩ **2** : GREATEST (the ~ ability)

²most adv **1** : to the greatest or highest degree (⟨~ beautiful⟩ **2** : to a very great degree (a ~ careful driver)

³most n : the greatest amount (the ~ he can do)

⁴most pron : the greatest number or part (⟨~ became discouraged⟩

-most \ˌmōst\ adj suffix : most (innermost)

most·ly \ˈmōst-lē\ adv : MAINLY

mot \ˈmō\ n, pl mots \ˈmō(z)\ [F, word,

saying, fr. L *muttum* grunt] : a witty saying

mote \'mōt\ *n* : a small particle

mo·tel \mō-'tel\ *n* [blend of *motor* and *hotel*] : a hotel in which the rooms are accessible from an outdoor parking area

mo·tet \mō-'tet\ *n* : a choral work on a sacred text for several voices usu. without instrumental accompaniment

moth \'mȯth\ *n, pl* **moths** \'mȯthz, 'mȯths\ : any of various insects belonging to the same order as the butterflies but usu. night-flying and with a stouter body and smaller wings: *esp* : CLOTHES MOTH

moth·ball \'mȯth-ˌbȯl\ *n* 1 : a ball (as of naphthalene) used to keep moths out of clothing 2 *pl* : protective storage (ships put in ∼s after the war)

¹**moth·er** \'məth-ər\ *n* 1 : a female parent 2 : the superior of a religious community of women 3 : SOURCE, ORIGIN — **moth·er·hood** \-ˌhu̇d\ *n* — **moth·er·less** *adj* — **moth·er·li·ness** \-lē-nəs\ *n* — **moth·er·ly** *adj*

²**mother** *vb* **moth·ered; moth·er·ing** \'məth-(ə-)riŋ\ 1 : to give birth to; *also* : PRODUCE 2 : to protect like a mother

moth·er–in–law \'məth-ə-rən-ˌlȯ, 'məth-ərn-ˌlȯ\ *n, pl* **mothers–in–law** \'məth-ər-zən-\ : the mother of one's spouse

moth·er·land \'məth-ər-ˌland\ *n* 1 : the land of origin of something 2 : the native land of one's ancestors

moth·er–of–pearl \ˌməth-ə-rə(v)-'pərl\ *n* : the hard pearly matter forming the inner layer of a mollusk shell

mo·tif \mō-'tēf\ *n* [F, motive, motif] : a dominant idea or central theme (as in a work of art)

mo·tile \'mōt-ᵊl, 'mō-ˌtīl\ *adj* : capable of spontaneous movement — **mo·til·i·ty** \mō-'til-ət-ē\ *n*

¹**mo·tion** \'mō-shən\ *n* 1 : a proposal for action (as by a deliberative body) 2 : an act, process, or instance of moving 3 *pl* : ACTIVITIES, MOVEMENTS — **mo·tion·less** *adj* — **mo·tion·less·ly** *adv* — **mo·tion·less·ness** *n*

²**motion** *vb* **mo·tioned; mo·tion·ing** \'mō-sh(ə-)niŋ\ : to direct or signal by a motion

motion picture *n* : a series of pictures thrown on a screen so rapidly that they produce a continuous picture in which persons and objects seem to move

motion sickness *n* : sickness induced by motion and characterized by nausea

mo·ti·vate \'mōt-ə-ˌvāt\ *vb* **-vat·ed; -vat·ing** : to provide with a motive : IMPEL — **mo·ti·va·tion** \ˌmōt-ə-'vā-shən\ *n*

¹**mo·tive** \'mōt-iv, 2 *also* mō-'tēv\ *n* 1 : something (as a need or desire) that causes a person to act 2 : a recurrent theme in a musical composition — **mo·tive·less** *adj*

²**mo·tive** \'mōt-iv\ *adj* 1 : moving to action 2 : of or relating to motion

mot·ley \'mät-lē\ *adj* 1 : variegated in color 2 : made up of diverse often incongruous elements **syn** heterogeneous, miscellaneous, assorted, mixed, varied

¹**mo·tor** \'mōt-ər\ *n* 1 : one that imparts motion 2 : a machine that produces motion or power for doing work 3 : AUTOMOBILE

²**motor** *vb* : to travel or transport by automobile : DRIVE — **mo·tor·ist** *n*

mo·tor·bike \'mōt-ər-ˌbīk\ *n* : a small lightweight motorcycle

mo·tor·boat \-ˌbōt\ *n* : a boat propelled by a motor

mo·tor·cade \-ˌkād\ *n* : a procession of motor vehicles

mo·tor·car \-ˌkär\ *n* : AUTOMOBILE

motor court *n* : MOTEL

mo·tor·cy·cle \'mōt-ər-ˌsī-kəl\ *n* : a 2-wheeled automotive vehicle — **mo·tor·cy·clist** \-k(ə-)ləst\ *n*

motor home *n* : a motor vehicle built on a truck or bus chassis and equipped as a self-contained traveling home

mo·tor·ize \'mōt-ə-ˌrīz\ *vb* **-ized; -iz·ing** 1 : to equip with a motor 2 : to equip with motor-driven vehicles

mo·tor·man \'mōt-ər-mən\ *n* : an operator of a motor-driven vehicle (as a streetcar or subway train)

motor scooter *n* : a low 2- or 3-wheeled automotive vehicle resembling a child's scooter but having a seat

mo·tor·truck \'mōt-ər-ˌtrək\ *n* : an automotive truck

motor vehicle *n* : an automotive vehicle (as an automobile) not operated on rails

mot·tle \'mät-ᵊl\ *vb* **mot·tled; mot·tling** \'mät-(ᵊ-)liŋ\ : to mark with spots of different color : BLOTCH

mot·to \'mät-ō\ *n, pl* **mottoes** *also* **mottos** [It, fr. L *muttum* grunt, fr. *muttire* to mutter] 1 : a sentence, phrase, or word inscribed on something to indicate its character or use 2 : a short expression of a guiding rule of conduct

moue \'mü\ *n* : a little grimace

mould \'mōld\ *var of* MOLD

moult \'mōlt\ *var of* MOLT

mound \'mau̇nd\ *n* 1 : an artificial bank or hill of earth or stones 2 : KNOLL

¹**mount** \'mau̇nt\ *n* : a high hill

²**mount** *vb* 1 : to increase in amount or extent; *also* : RISE, ASCEND 2 : to get up on something; *esp* : to seat oneself on (as a horse) for riding 3 : to put in position (∼ artillery) 4 : to set on something that elevates 5 : to attach to a support 6 : to prepare esp. for examination or display : ARRANGE — **mount·able** *adj* — **mount·er** *n*

³**mount** *n* 1 : FRAME, SUPPORT 2 : a means of conveyance; *esp* : SADDLE HORSE

moun·tain \'mau̇nt-ᵊn\ *n* : a landmass higher than a hill — **moun·tain·ous** \-(ᵊ-)nəs\ *adj*

mountain ash *n* : any of various trees related to the roses that have pinnate leaves and red or orange-red fruits

moun·tain·eer \ˌmaunt-ᵊn-'iər\ *n* **1** : a native or inhabitant of a mountainous region **2** : one who climbs mountains for sport

mountain goat *n* : an antelope of mountainous northwestern No. America that resembles a goat

mountain laurel *n* : a No. American evergreen shrub of the heath family that has glossy leaves and clusters of rose-colored or white flowers

mountain lion *n* : COUGAR

moun·tain·side \'maunt-ᵊn-ˌsīd\ *n* : the side of a mountain

moun·tain·top \-ˌtäp\ *n* : the summit of a mountain

moun·te·bank \'maunt-i-ˌbaŋk\ *n* [It *montimbanco*, fr. *montare* to mount + *in* in, on + *banco, banca* bench] : QUACK, CHARLATAN

Mount·ie \'maunt-ē\ *n* : a member of the Royal Canadian Mounted Police

mount·ing \'maunt-iŋ\ *n* : something that serves as a frame or support

mourn \'mōrn\ *vb* : to feel or express grief or sorrow — **mourn·er** *n*

mourn·ful \-fəl\ *adj* : expressing, feeling, or causing sorrow — **mourn·ful·ly** \-ē\ *adv* — **mourn·ful·ness** *n*

mourn·ing \'mōr-niŋ\ *n* **1** : an outward sign (as black clothes) of grief for a person's death **2** : a period of time during which signs of grief are shown

mouse \'maus\ *n, pl* **mice** \'mīs\ : any of various small rodents with pointed snout, long body, and slender tail

mous·er \'mau-zər\ *n* : a cat proficient at catching mice

mouse·trap \'maus-ˌtrap\ *n* **1** : a trap for catching mice **2** : a stratagem that lures one to defeat or destruction — **mousetrap** *vb*

mousse \'müs\ *n* [F, lit., froth] : a molded chilled dessert made with sweetened and flavored whipped cream or egg whites and gelatin

mous·tache \'məs-ˌtash, (ˌ)məs-'tash\ *var of* MUSTACHE

mousy *or* **mous·ey** \'mau-sē, -zē\ *adj* **mous·i·er; -est 1** : QUIET, STEALTHY **2** : TIMID — **mous·i·ness** \'mau-sē-nəs, -zē-\ *n*

¹**mouth** \'mauth\ *n, pl* **mouths** \'mauthz, 'mauths\ **1** : the opening through which an animal takes in food; *also* : the space between the mouth and the pharynx **2** : something resembling a mouth (as in affording entrance) — **mouthed** \'mauthd, 'mautht\ *adj* — **mouth·ful** *n*

²**mouth** \'mauth\ *vb* : SPEAK; *also* : DECLAIM

mouth·part \'mauth-ˌpärt\ *n* : a structure or appendage near the mouth (as of an insect) esp. when adapted for eating

mouth·piece \-ˌpēs\ *n* **1** : a part (as of a musical instrument) that goes in the mouth or to which the mouth is applied **2** : SPOKESMAN

mouth·wash \-ˌwosh, -ˌwäsh\ *n* : a usu. antiseptic liquid preparation for cleaning the mouth and teeth

mou·ton \'mü-ˌtän\ *n* : processed sheepskin that has been sheared or dyed to resemble beaver or seal

¹**move** \'müv\ *vb* **moved; mov·ing 1** : to change or cause to change position or posture : SHIFT **2** : to go or cause to go from one point to another : ADVANCE; *also* : DEPART **3** : to take or cause to take action : PROMPT **4** : to show marked activity **5** : to stir the emotions **6** : to make a formal request, application, or appeal **7** : to change one's residence **8** : EVACUATE **2** — **mov·able** *or* **move·able** \-ə-bəl\ *adj*

²**move** *n* **1** : an act of moving **2** : a calculated procedure : MANEUVER

move·ment \'müv-mənt\ *n* **1** : the act or process of moving : MOVE **2** : TENDENCY, TREND; *also* : a series of organized activities working toward an objective **3** : the moving parts of a mechanism (as of a watch) **4** : RHYTHM **5** : a unit or division of an extended musical composition **6** : CADENCE **7** : an act of voiding the bowels; *also* : STOOL **4**

mov·er \'mü-vər\ *n* : one that moves; *esp* : a person or company that moves the belongings of others from one home or place of business to another

mov·ie \'mü-vē\ *n* **1** : MOTION PICTURE **2** *pl* : a showing of a motion picture **3** *pl* : the motion-picture industry

¹**mow** \'mau\ *n* : the part of a barn where hay or straw is stored

²**mow** \'mō\ *vb* **mowed; mowed** *or* **mown** \'mōn\; **mow·ing 1** : to cut (as grass) with a scythe or machine **2** : to cut the standing herbage of (~ the lawn) — **mow·er** *n*

Mo·zam·bi·can \ˌmō-zəm-'bē-kən\ *n* : a native or inhabitant of Mozambique

moz·za·rel·la \ˌmät-sə-'rel-ə\ *n* [It] : a moist white unsalted unripened mild cheese of a smooth rubbery texture

MP *abbr* **1** melting point **2** member of parliament **3** metropolitan police **4** military police; military policeman

mpg *abbr* miles per gallon

mph *abbr* miles per hour

Mr. \'mis-tər\ *n, pl* **Messrs.** \'mes-ərz\ — used as a conventional title of courtesy before a man's surname or his title of office

Mrs. \'mis-əz, -əs, *esp Southern* ˌmiz-əz, -əs, *or* (ˌ)miz, *or before given names* (ˌ)mis\ *n, pl* **Mes·dames** \mā-'däm, -'dam\ — used as a conventional title of courtesy before a married woman's surname

Ms. \(ˌ)miz\ *n* — used instead of *Miss* or *Mrs.*

MS *abbr* **1** manuscript **2** master of science **3** military science **4** Mississippi **5** motor ship **6** multiple sclerosis

msec *abbr* millisecond

msg *abbr* message

MSG *abbr* **1** master sergeant **2** monosodium glutamate

msgr *abbr* **1** monseigneur **2** monsignor

MSgt *abbr* master sergeant

MSS *abbr* manuscripts

MST *abbr* mountain standard time

mt *abbr* mount; mountain

Mt *abbr* Matthew

MT *abbr* **1** metric ton **2** Montana **3** mountain time

mtg *abbr* **1** meeting **2** mortgage

mtge *abbr* mortgage

¹**much** \\'məch\ *adj* **more** \\'mōr\ : **most** \\'mōst\ : great in quantity, amount, extent, or degree ⟨~ money⟩

²**much** *adv* **more; most** **1** : to a great degree or extent ⟨~ happier⟩ **2** : APPROXIMATELY, NEARLY ⟨looks ~ as he did years ago⟩

³**much** *n* **1** : a great quantity, amount, extent, or degree **2** : something considerable or impressive

mu·ci·lage \\'myü-s(ə-)lij\ *n* : a watery sticky solution (as of a gum) used esp. as an adhesive — **mu·ci·lag·i·nous** \\,myü-sə-'laj-ə-nəs\ *adj*

muck \\'mək\ *n* **1** : soft moist barnyard manure **2** : FILTH, DIRT **3** : a dark richly organic soil; *also* : MUD, MIRE — **mucky** *adj*

muck·rak·er \\-,rā-kər\ *n* : one who exposes publicly real or apparent misconduct of prominent individuals — **muck·rak·ing** \\-,rā-kiŋ\ *n*

mu·cus \\'myü-kəs\ *n* : a slimy slippery protective secretion of membranes (**mucous membranes**) lining some body cavities — **mu·cous** \\-kəs\ *adj*

mud \\'məd\ *n* : soft wet earth : MIRE — **mud·di·ly** \\'məd-ᵊl-ē\ *adv* — **mud·di·ness** \\-ē-nəs\ *n* — **mud·dy** *adj or vb*

mud·dle \\'məd-ᵊl\ *vb* **mud·dled; mud·dling** \\'məd-(ᵊ-)liŋ\ **1** : to make muddy **2** : to confuse esp. with liquor **3** : to mix up or make a mess of **4** : to think or act in a confused way

mud·dle·head·ed \\,məd-ᵊl-'hed-əd\ *adj* **1** : mentally confused **2** : INEPT

mud·guard \\'məd-,gärd\ *n* : a guard over or a flap behind a wheel of a vehicle to catch or deflect mud

mud·room \\'məd-,rüm, -,rüm\ *n* : a room in a house for removing dirty or wet footwear and clothing

mud·sling·er \\-,sliŋ-ər\ *n* : one who uses invective esp. against a political opponent — **mud·sling·ing** \\-,sliŋ-iŋ\ *n*

Muen·ster \\'mən-stər, 'm(y)ün-, 'mün-\ *n* : a semisoft bland or sharp cheese

mu·ez·zin \\m(y)ü-'ez-ᵊn\ *n* : a Muslim crier who calls the hour of daily prayer

¹**muff** \\'məf\ *n* : a warm tubular covering for the hands

²**muff** *n* : a bungling performance; *esp* : a failure to hold a ball in attempting a catch — **muff** *vb*

muf·fin \\'məf-ən\ *n* : a small soft biscuit baked in a small cup-shaped container

muf·fle \\'məf-əl\ *vb* **muf·fled; muf·fling**

\\'məf-(ə-)liŋ\ **1** : to wrap up so as to conceal or protect **2** : to wrap or pad with something to dull the sound of **3** : to keep down : SUPPRESS

muf·fler \\'məf-lər\ *n* **1** : a scarf worn around the neck **2** : a device to deaden noise

muf·ti \\'məf-tē\ *n* : civilian clothes

¹**mug** \\'məg\ *n* : a usu. metal or earthenware cylindrical drinking cup

²**mug** *vb* **mugged; mug·ging** **1** : to make faces esp. in order to attract the attention of an audience **2** : PHOTOGRAPH

³**mug** *vb* **mugged; mug·ging** : to assault usu. with intent to rob — **mug·ger** *n*

mug·gy \\'məg-ē\ *adj* **mug·gi·er; -est** : being warm and humid — **mug·gi·ness** \\'məg-ē-nəs\ *n*

mug·wump \\'məg-,wəmp\ *n* [obs. slang *mugwump* (kingpin), fr. Natick (a No. American Indian dialect) *mugwomp* captain] : an independent in politics

Mu·ham·mad·an \\mō-'ham-əd-ən, -'häm-; mü-\ *n* : MUSLIM — **Mu·ham·mad·an·ism** \\-,iz-əm\ *n*

muk·luk \\'mək-,lək\ *n* [Esk *muklok* large seal] **1** : an Eskimo boot of sealskin or reindeer skin **2** : a boot with a soft leather sole worn over several pairs of socks

mu·lat·to \\m(y)ü-'lat-ō, -'lät-\ *n, pl* **-toes** *or* **-tos** [Sp *mulato*, fr. *mulo* mule, fr. L *mulus*; so called because the mule is the offspring of parents of different species] : a first-generation offspring of a Negro and a white; *also* : a person of mixed Caucasian and Negro ancestry

mul·ber·ry \\'məl-,ber-ē\ *n* : a tree grown for its leaves that are used as food for silkworms or for its edible berrylike fruit; *also* : this fruit

mulch \\'məlch\ *n* : a protective covering (as of straw or leaves) spread on the ground esp. to reduce evaporation or control weeds — **mulch** *vb*

¹**mulct** \\'məlkt\ *vb* **1** : FINE **2** : DEFRAUD

²**mulct** *n* : FINE, PENALTY

¹**mule** \\'myül\ *n* **1** : a hybrid offspring of a male donkey and a female horse **2** : a very stubborn person — **mul·ish** \\'myü-lish\ *adj* — **mul·ish·ly** *adv* — **mul·ish·ness** *n*

²**mule** *n* : a slipper whose upper does not extend around the heel of the foot

mule deer *n* : a long-eared deer of western No. America

mu·le·teer \\,myü-lə-'tiər\ *n* : one who drives mules

¹**mull** \\'məl\ *vb* : PONDER, MEDITATE

²**mull** *vb* : to heat, sweeten, and flavor (as wine) with spices

mul·lein \\'məl-ən\ *n* : a tall herb with coarse woolly leaves and flowers in spikes

mul·let \\'məl-ət\ *n, pl* **mullet** *or* **mullets** **1** : any of various largely gray marine food fishes **2** : any of various red or golden mostly tropical marine food fishes

mul·li·gan stew \,məl-i-gən-\ *n* : a stew made from whatever ingredients are available

mul·li·ga·taw·ny \,məl-i-gə-'tȯ-nē\ *n* : a soup usu. of chicken stock seasoned with curry

mul·lion \'məl-yən\ *n* : a vertical strip separating windowpanes

multi- *comb form* **1** : many : multiple ⟨*multi*unit⟩ **2** : many times over ⟨*multi*millionaire⟩

mul·ti·col·ored \,məl-ti-'kəl-ərd\ *adj* : having many colors

mul·ti·di·men·sion·al \-ti-də-'mench-nəl, -dī-; -,tī-də-\ *adj* : of, relating to, or having many dimensions ⟨a ∼ problem⟩

mul·ti·fac·et·ed \-'fas-ət-əd\ *adj* : having several distinct facets

mul·ti·fam·i·ly \-'fam-(ə-)lē\ *adj* : designed for use by several families

mul·ti·far·i·ous \,məl-tə-'far-ē-əs\ *adj* : having great variety : DIVERSE — **mul·ti·far·i·ous·ly** *adv*

mul·ti·flo·ra rose \,məl-tə-,flȯr-ə-\ *n* : a vigorous thorny rose with clusters of small flowers

mul·ti·form \'məl-ti-,fȯrm\ *adj* : having many forms or appearances — **mul·ti·for·mi·ty** \,məl-ti-'fȯr-mət-ē\ *n*

mul·ti·lat·er·al \,məl-ti-'lat-ə-rəl, -,tī-, -'la-trəl\ *adj* : having many sides or participants ⟨∼ treaty⟩

mul·ti·lev·el \-'lev-əl\ *adj* : having several levels

mul·ti·lin·gual \-'liŋ-gwəl\ *adj* : containing, expressed in, or able to use several languages — **mul·ti·lin·gual·ism** \-gwə-,liz-əm\ *n*

mul·ti·me·dia \-'mēd-ē-ə\ *adj* : using, involving, or encompassing several media ⟨a ∼ advertising campaign⟩

mul·ti·mil·lion·aire \,məl-ti-,mil-yə-'naər, -,tī-, -'mil-yə-,naər\ *n* : a person worth several million dollars

mul·ti·na·tion·al \-'nash-(ə-)nəl\ *adj* **1** : of or relating to several nationalities ⟨a ∼ society⟩ **2** : relating to or involving several nations **3** : having divisions in several countries

¹**mul·ti·ple** \'məl-tə-pəl\ *adj* **1** : more than one; *also* : MANY **2** : VARIOUS, COMPLEX

²**multiple** *n* : the product of a quantity by an integer ⟨35 is a ∼ of 7⟩

multiple-choice *adj* : having several answers given from which the correct one is to be chosen ⟨a ∼ question⟩

multiple sclerosis : a disease marked by patches of hardened tissue in the brain or spinal cord resulting in partial or complete paralysis and muscular twitching

mul·ti·pli·cand \,məl-tə-pli-'kand\ *n* : a number that is to be multiplied by another

mul·ti·pli·ca·tion \,məl-tə-plə-'kā-shən\ *n* **1** : INCREASE **2** : a short method of finding out what would be the result of adding a figure the number of times indicated by another figure

multiplication sign *n* **1** : TIMES SIGN **2** : a centered dot used to indicate multiplication

mul·ti·plic·i·ty \,məl-tə-'plis-ət-ē\ *n, pl* **-ties** : a great number or variety

mul·ti·pli·er \'məl-tə-,plī-(ə-)r\ *n* : one that multiplies; *esp* : a number by which another number is multiplied

mul·ti·ply \'məl-tə-,plī\ *vb* **-plied; -ply·ing 1** : to increase in number (as by breeding) **2** : to find the product of by multiplication

mul·ti·pur·pose \,məl-ti-'pər-pəs, -,tī-\ *adj* : having or serving several purposes

mul·ti·ra·cial \-'rā-shəl\ *adj* : composed of, involving, or representing several races

mul·ti·sense \-,sen(t)s\ *adj* : having several meanings ⟨∼ words⟩

mul·ti·stage \-,stāj\ *adj* : having successive operating stages ⟨∼ rockets⟩

mul·ti·story \-,stōr-ē\ *adj* : having several stories ⟨∼ buildings⟩

mul·ti·tude \'məl-tə-,t(y)üd\ *n* : a great number — **mul·ti·tu·di·nous** \,məl-tə-'t(y)üd-(ə-)nəs\ *adj*

mul·ti·unit \,məl-ti-'yü-nət, -,tī-\ *adj* : having several units

mul·ti·ver·si·ty \,məl-ti-'vər-s(ə-)tē\ *n, pl* **-ties** : a very large university with many divisions and diverse functions

mul·ti·vi·ta·min \-'vīt-ə-mən\ *adj* : containing several vitamins and esp. all known to be essential to health

¹**mum** \'məm\ *adj* : SILENT

²**mum** *n* : CHRYSANTHEMUM

mum·ble \'məm-bəl\ *vb* **mum·bled; mum·bling** \-b(ə-)liŋ\ : to speak in a low indistinct manner — **mumble** *n* — **mum·bler** \-b(ə-)lər\ *n* — **mum·bly** \-b(ə-)lē\ *adj*

mum·ble·ty·peg *or* **mum·ble-the-peg** \'məm-bəl-(tē-),peg\ *n* : a game in which the players try to flip a knife from various positions so that the blade will stick into the ground

mum·bo jum·bo \,məm-bō-'jəm-bō\ *n* **1** : a complicated ritual with elaborate trappings **2** : confusing or meaningless talk : NONSENSE

mum·mer \'məm-ər\ *n* **1** : an actor esp. in a pantomime **2** : one who goes merrymaking in disguise during festivals — **mum·mery** *n*

mum·my \'məm-ē\ *n, pl* **mummies** [ME *mummie* powdered parts of a mummified body used as a drug, fr. MF *momie*, fr. ML *mumia* mummy, powdered mummy, fr. Ar *mūmiyah* bitumen, mummy, fr. Per *mūm* wax] : a body embalmed for burial in the manner of the ancient Egyptians — **mum·mi·fi·ca·tion** \,məm-i-fə-'kā-shən\ *n* — **mum·mi·fy** \'məm-i-,fī\ *vb*

mumps \'məmps\ *n sing or pl* [fr. pl. of obs. *mump* (grimace)] : a virus disease marked by fever and swelling esp. of the salivary glands

mun *or* **munic** *abbr* municipal

munch \\'mənch\\ vb : to chew with a crunching sound

munch·ies \\'mən-chēz\\ n pl 1 : hunger pangs 2 : light snack foods

mun·dane \\,mən-'dān, 'mən-,dān\\ adj 1 : of or relating to the world 2 : concerned with the practical details of everyday life — **mun·dane·ly** adv

mu·nic·i·pal \\myu̇-'nis-ə-pəl\\ adj 1 : of, relating to, or characteristic of a municipality 2 : restricted to one locality — **mu·nic·i·pal·ly** \\-ē\\ adv

mu·nic·i·pal·i·ty \\myu̇-,nis-ə-'pal-ət-ē\\ n, pl **-ties** : an urban political unit with corporate status and usu. powers of self-government

mu·nif·i·cent \\myu̇-'nif-ə-sənt\\ adj : liberal in giving : GENEROUS — **mu·nif·i·cence** \\-səns\\ n

mu·ni·tions \\myu̇-'nish-ənz\\ n pl : military materiel; esp : AMMUNITION

¹mu·ral \\'myu̇r-əl\\ adj 1 : of or relating to a wall 2 : applied to and made part of a wall surface

²mural n : a mural painting — **mu·ral·ist** n

¹mur·der \\'mərd-ər\\ n 1 : the crime of unlawfully killing a person esp. with malice aforethought 2 : something unusually difficult or dangerous

²murder vb 1 : to commit a murder; also : to kill brutally 2 : to put an end to 3 : to spoil by performing poorly (~ a song) — **mur·der·er** n

mur·der·ess \\'mərd-ə-rəs\\ n : a woman who murders

mur·der·ous \\'mərd-ər-əs\\ adj 1 : marked by or causing murder or bloodshed (~ gunfire) 2 : having or appearing to have the purpose of murder — **mur·der·ous·ly** adv

murk \\'mərk\\ n : DARKNESS, GLOOM — **murk·i·ly** \\'mər-kə-lē\\ adv — **murk·i·ness** \\-kē-nəs\\ n — **murky** adj

mur·mur \\'mər-mər\\ n 1 : a muttered complaint 2 : a low indistinct often continuous sound — **murmur** vb — **mur·mur·er** n — **mur·mur·ous** adj

mur·rain \\'mər-ən\\ n : PLAGUE

mus abbr 1 museum 2 music

mus·ca·tel \\,məs-kə-'tel\\ n : a sweet dessert wine

¹mus·cle \\'məs-əl\\ n [MF, fr. L musculus, fr. dim. of mus mouse] 1 : body tissue consisting of long cells that contract when stimulated; also : an organ consisting of this tissue and functioning in moving a body part 2 : STRENGTH, BRAWN — **mus·cled** \\'məs-əld\\ adj — **mus·cu·lar** \\'məs-kyə-lər\\ adj — **mus·cu·lar·i·ty** \\,məs-kyə-'lar-ət-ē\\ n

²muscle vb **mus·cled; mus·cling** \\'məs-(ə-)liŋ\\ : to force one's way (~ in on another racketeer)

mus·cle-bound \\'məs-əl-,bau̇nd\\ adj : having some of the muscles abnormally enlarged and lacking in elasticity (as from excessive athletic exercise)

muscular dystrophy n : a disease characterized by progressive wasting of muscles

mus·cu·la·ture \\'məs-kyə-lə-,chu̇r\\ n : the muscles of the body or its parts

¹muse \\'myu̇z\\ vb **mused; mus·ing** [ME musen, fr. MF muser to gape, idle, muse, fr. muse mouth of an animal, fr. ML musus] : to become absorbed in thought — **mus·ing·ly** adv

²muse n [fr. Muse any of the nine sister goddesses of learning and the arts in Greek mythology, fr. ME, fr. MF, fr. L Musa, fr. Gk Mousa] : a source of inspiration

mu·sette \\myu̇-'zet\\ n [F] : a small knapsack with a shoulder strap used esp. by soldiers for carrying provisions and personal belongings

musette bag n : MUSETTE

mu·se·um \\myu̇-'zē-əm\\ n : an institution devoted to the procurement, care, and display of objects of lasting interest or value

¹mush \\'məsh\\ n 1 : cornmeal boiled in water 2 : sentimental drivel

²mush vb : to travel esp. over snow with a sled drawn by dogs

¹mush·room \\'məsh-,rüm, -,ru̇m\\ n : the fleshy usu. caplike spore-bearing organ of various fungi esp. when edible

²mushroom vb 1 : to grow rapidly 2 : to spread out : EXPAND

mushy \\'məsh-ē\\ adj **mush·i·er; -est** 1 : soft like mush 2 : weakly sentimental

mu·sic \\'myü-zik\\ n 1 : the science or art of combining tones into a composition having structure and continuity; also : vocal or instrumental sounds having rhythm, melody, or harmony 2 : an agreeable sound 3 : the unpleasant consequences of one's actions (face the ~)

¹mu·si·cal \\'myü-zi-kəl\\ adj 1 : of or relating to music or musicians 2 : having the pleasing tonal qualities of music 3 : having an interest in or a talent for music — **mu·si·cal·ly** \\-k(ə-)lē\\ adv

²musical n : a film or theatrical production consisting of musical numbers and dialogue based on a unifying plot

mu·si·cale \\,myü-zi-'kal\\ n : a usu. private social gathering featuring music

mu·si·cian \\myu̇-'zish-ən\\ n : a composer, conductor, or performer of music — **mu·si·cian·ly** adj — **mu·si·cian·ship** n

mu·si·col·o·gy \\,myü-zi-'käl-ə-jē\\ n : a study of music as a field of knowledge or research — **mu·si·co·log·i·cal** \\-kə-'läj-i-kəl\\ adj — **mu·si·col·o·gist** \\-'käl-ə-jəst\\ n

musk \\'məsk\\ n : a substance obtained esp. from a small Asian deer (**musk deer**) and used as a perfume fixative — **musk·i·ness** \\'məs-kē-nəs\\ n — **musky** adj

mus·keg \\'məs-,keg\\ n : BOG; esp : a mossy bog in northern No. America

mus·kel·lunge \\'məs-kə-,lənj\\ n, pl

mus·kel·lunge : a large No. American pike prized as a sport fish

mus·ket \'məs-kət\ n [MF *mousquet*, fr. It *moschetto* arrow for a crossbow, musket, fr. dim. of *mosca* fly, fr. L *musca*] : a heavy large-caliber usu. muzzle-loading shoulder firearm — **mus·ke·teer** \,məs-kə-'tiər\ n

mus·ket·ry \'məs-kə-trē\ n 1 : MUSKETS 2 : MUSKETEERS 3 : musket fire

musk·mel·on \'məsk-,mel-ən\ n : a small round to oval melon that has usu. a sweet edible green or orange flesh

musk-ox \'məsk-,äks\ n : a heavyset shaggy-coated wild ox of Greenland and the arctic tundra of northern No. America

musk·rat \'məs-,krat\ n, pl muskrat or muskrats : a large No. American water rodent with webbed feet and dark brown fur; *also* : its fur

Mus·lim \'məz-ləm\ n : an adherent of the religion founded by the Arab prophet Muhammad

mus·lin \'məz-lən\ n : a plain-woven sheer to coarse cotton fabric

¹muss \'məs\ n : a state of disorder — **muss·i·ly** \'məs-ə-lē\ adv — **muss·i·ness** \-ē-nəs\ n — **mussy** adj

²muss vb : to make untidy : DISARRANGE

mus·sel \'məs-əl\ n 1 : a dark edible saltwater bivalve mollusk 2 : any of various freshwater bivalve mollusks of the central U.S. having shells with a pearly lining

¹must \(')məst\ vb — used as an auxiliary esp. to express a command, requirement, obligation, or necessity

²must \'məst\ n 1 : an imperative duty 2 : an indispensable item

mus·tache \'məs-,tash, (,)məs-'tash\ n : the hair growing on the human upper lip

mus·tang \'məs-,taŋ\ n [MexSp *mestengo*, fr. Sp, stray, fr. *mesteño* strayed, fr. *mesta* annual roundup of cattle that disposed of strays, fr. ML (*animalia*) *mixta* mixed animals] : a small hardy naturalized horse of the western plains of America

mus·tard \'məs-tərd\ n 1 : a pungent yellow powder obtained from the seeds of an herb related to the turnips and used as a condiment or in medicine 2 : the mustard plant; *also* : a closely related plant

mustard gas n : an irritant vesicant poisonous gas used in warfare

¹mus·ter \'məs-tər\ vb mustered; mustering \-t(ə-)riŋ\ [ME *mustren*, to show, muster, fr. OF *monstrer*, fr. L *monstrare* to show, fr. *monstrum* evil omen, monster] 1 : CONVENE, ASSEMBLE; *also* : to call the roll of 2 : ACCUMULATE 3 : to call forth : ROUSE 4 : to amount to : COMPRISE

²muster n 1 : an act of assembling (as for military inspection); *also* : critical examination 2 : an assembled group

muster out vb : to discharge from military service

musty \'məs-tē\ adj **mus·ti·er; -est** : MOLDY, STALE; *also* : tasting or smelling of damp or decay — **must·i·ly** \'məs-tə-lē\ adv — **must·i·ness** \-tē-nəs\ n

mu·ta·ble \'myüt-ə-bəl\ adj 1 : prone to change : FICKLE 2 : liable to mutation : VARIABLE — **mu·ta·bil·i·ty** \,myüt-ə-'bil-ət-ē\ n

mu·tant \'myüt-³nt\ adj : of, relating to, or produced by mutation — **mutant** n

mu·tate \'myü-,tāt\ vb **mu·tat·ed; mu·tat·ing** : to undergo or cause to undergo mutation — **mu·ta·tive** \'myü-,tāt-iv, 'myüt-ət-iv\ adj

mu·ta·tion \myü-'tā-shən\ n 1 : CHANGE 2 : a sudden and relatively permanent change in a hereditary character; *also* : the process of producing a mutation 3 : an individual or strain resulting from mutation — **mu·ta·tion·al** adj

¹mute \'myüt\ adj **mut·er; -est** 1 : unable to speak : DUMB 2 : SILENT — **mute·ly** adv — **mute·ness** n

²mute n 1 : a person who cannot or does not speak 2 : a device on a musical instrument that reduces, softens, or muffles the tone

³mute vb **mut·ed; mut·ing** : to muffle or reduce the sound of

mu·ti·late \'myüt-³l-,āt\ vb **-lat·ed; -lat·ing** 1 : MAIM, CRIPPLE 2 : to cut up or alter radically so as to make imperfect — **mu·ti·la·tion** \,myüt-³l-'ā-shən\ n — **mu·ti·la·tor** \'myüt-³l-,āt-ər\ n

mu·ti·ny \'myüt-³n-ē\ n, pl **-nies** : willful refusal to obey constituted authority; *esp* : revolt against a superior officer — **mu·ti·neer** \,myüt-³n-'iər\ n — **mu·ti·nous** \'myüt-³n-əs\ adj — **mu·ti·nous·ly** adv

mutt \'mət\ n : MONGREL, CUR

mut·ter \'mət-ər\ vb 1 : to speak indistinctly or with a low voice and lips partly closed 2 : GRUMBLE — **mutter** n

mut·ton \'mət-³n\ n [ME *motoun*, fr. OF *moton* ram] : the flesh of a mature sheep used for food — **mut·tony** adj

mut·ton·chops \'mət-³n-,chäps\ n pl : whiskers on the side of the face that are narrow at the temple and broad and round by the lower jaws

mu·tu·al \'myü-chə(-wə)l\ adj 1 : given and received in equal amount ⟨~ trust⟩ 2 : having the same feelings one for the other ⟨~ enemies⟩ 3 : COMMON, JOINT ⟨a ~ friend⟩ — **mu·tu·al·ly** \-ē\ adv

mutual fund n : an investment company that invests money of its shareholders in a usu. diversified group of securities of other corporations

muu-muu \'mü-,mü\ n : a loose dress of Hawaiian origin for informal wear

¹muz·zle \'məz-əl\ n 1 : the nose and jaws of an animal; *also* : a covering for the muzzle to prevent the animal from biting or eating 2 : the mouth of a gun

²**muzzle** vb **muz·zled; muz·zling** \-(ə-)liŋ\ 1 : to put a muzzle on 2 : to restrain from expression : GAG

mv or **mV** abbr millivolt

MV abbr motor vessel

MVP abbr most valuable player

MW abbr megawatt

my \(ᵗ)mī, mə\ adj 1 : of or relating to me or myself 2 — used interjectionally esp. to express surprise

my·col·o·gy \mī-ˈkäl-ə-jē\ n : the study of fungi — **my·co·log·i·cal** \ˌmī-kə-ˈläj-i-kəl\ adj — **my·col·o·gist** \mī-ˈkäl-ə-jəst\ n

my·elo·ma \ˌmī-ə-ˈlō-mə\ n, pl **-mas** or **-ma·ta** \-mət-ə\ : a primary tumor of the bone marrow

my·nah or **my·na** \ˈmī-nə\ n : any of several Asian starlings; esp : a dark brown slightly crested bird sometimes taught to mimic speech

my·o·pia \mī-ˈō-pē-ə\ n : SHORTSIGHTEDNESS — **my·o·pic** \-ˈō-pik, -ˈäp-ik\ adj — **my·o·pi·cal·ly** \-(ə-)lē\ adv

¹**myr·i·ad** \ˈmir-ē-əd\ n [Gk myriad-, myrias, fr. myrioi countless, ten thousand] : an indefinitely large number

²**myriad** adj : consisting of a very great but indefinite number

myr·mi·don \ˈmər-mə-ˌdän\ n : a loyal follower; esp : one who executes orders without protest or pity

myrrh \ˈmər\ n : a fragrant aromatic plant gum used in perfumes and formerly for incense

myr·tle \ˈmərt-ᵊl\ n : an evergreen shrub of southern Europe with shiny leaves, fragrant flowers, and black berries; also : PERIWINKLE

my·self \mī-ˈself, mə-\ pron : I, ME — used reflexively, for emphasis, or in absolute constructions (I hurt ~) (I ~ did it) (~ busy, I sent him instead)

mys·tery \ˈmis-t(ə-)rē\ n, pl **-ter·ies** 1 : a religious truth known by revelation alone 2 : something not understood or beyond understanding 3 : enigmatic quality or character 4 : a work of fiction dealing with the solution of a mysterious crime — **mys·te·ri·ous** \mis-ˈtir-ē-əs\ adj — **mys·te·ri·ous·ly** adv — **mys·te·ri·ous·ness** n

¹**mys·tic** \ˈmis-tik\ adj 1 : of or relating to mystics or mysticism 2 : MYSTERIOUS; also : MYSTIFYING

²**mystic** n : a person who experiences mystical union or direct communion with God or ultimate reality

mys·ti·cal \ˈmis-ti-kəl\ adj 1 : SPIRITUAL, SYMBOLIC 2 : of or relating to an intimate knowledge of or direct communion with God (as through contemplation or visions)

mys·ti·cism \ˈmis-tə-ˌsiz-əm\ n : the belief that direct knowledge of God or ultimate reality is attainable through immediate intuition or insight

mys·ti·fy \ˈmis-tə-ˌfī\ vb **-fied; -fy·ing** 1 : to perplex the mind of 2 : to make mysterious — **mys·ti·fi·ca·tion** \ˌmis-tə-fə-ˈkā-shən\ n

mys·tique \mis-ˈtēk\ n [F] 1 : an air or attitude of mystery and reverence developing around something 2 : the special esoteric skill essential in a calling or activity

myth \ˈmith\ n 1 : a usu. legendary narrative that presents part of the beliefs of a people or explains a practice or natural phenomenon 2 : an imaginary or unverifiable person or thing — **myth·i·cal** \-i-kəl\ adj

my·thol·o·gy \mith-ˈäl-ə-jē\ n, pl **-gies** : a body of myths and esp. of those dealing with the gods and heroes of a people — **myth·o·log·i·cal** \ˌmith-ə-ˈläj-i-kəl\ adj — **my·thol·o·gist** \mith-ˈäl-ə-jəst\ n

N

¹**n** \ˈen\ n, pl **n's** or **ns** \ˈenz\ often cap 1 : the 14th letter of the English alphabet 2 : an unspecified quantity

²**n** abbr, often cap 1 net 2 neuter 3 noon 4 normal 5 north; northern 6 note 7 noun 8 number

N symbol nitrogen

-n- — see -EN

Na symbol [NL natrium] sodium

NA abbr 1 no account 2 North America 3 not applicable 4 not available

NAACP \ˌen-ˌdəb-əl-ˌā-ˌā-ˌsē-ˈpē, ˌen-ˌā-ˌā-ˌsē-\ abbr National Association for the Advancement of Colored People

nab \ˈnab\ vb **nabbed; nab·bing** : SEIZE; esp : ARREST

na·bob \ˈnā-ˌbäb\ n [Hindi & Urdu nawwāb, fr. Ar nuwwāb, pl. of nā'ib governor] : a man of great wealth or prominence

na·celle \nə-ˈsel\ n : an enclosed shelter on an aircraft (as for an engine)

na·cre \ˈnā-kər\ n : MOTHER-OF-PEARL

na·dir \ˈnā-ˌdir, ˈnād-ər\ n [ME, fr. MF, fr. Ar naẓīr opposite] 1 : the point of the celestial sphere that is directly opposite the zenith and directly beneath the observer 2 : the lowest point

¹**nag** \ˈnag\ n : HORSE; esp : an old or decrepit horse

²**nag** vb **nagged; nag·ging** 1 : to find fault incessantly : COMPLAIN 2 : to irritate by constant scolding or urging 3 : to be a continuing source of annoyance (a nagging toothache)

³**nag** n : one who nags habitually

Nah abbr Nahum

Na·hua·tl \ˈnä-ˌwät-ᵊl\ n : an American Indian language of southern Mexico

Na·hum \ˈnā-(h)əm\ n — see BIBLE table

na·iad \ˈnā-əd, ˈnī-, -ˌad\ n, pl naiads or

na·ia·des \-ə-ˌdēz\ *n* 1 : one of the nymphs in ancient mythology living in lakes, rivers, springs, and fountains 2 : an aquatic young of some insects (as a dragonfly)

na·if *or* **na·if** \nä-ˈēf\ *adj* : NAIVE

¹nail \ˈnāl\ *n* 1 : a horny sheath protecting the end of each finger and toe in man and related primates 2 : a slender pointed fastener with a head designed to be pounded in

²nail *vb* : to fasten with or as if with a nail — **nail·er** *n*

nail down *vb* : to settle or establish clearly and unmistakably

nain·sook \ˈnān-ˌsůk\ *n* [Hindi *nainsukh*, fr. *nain* eye + *sukh* delight] : a soft lightweight muslin

nai·ra \ˈnī-rə\ *n* — see MONEY table

na·ive *or* **na·ïve** \nä-ˈēv\ *adj* **na·iv·er; -est** [F *naïve*, fem. of *naïf*, fr. OF, inborn, natural, fr. L *nativus* native] 1 : marked by unaffected simplicity : ARTLESS, INGENUOUS 2 : CREDULOUS — **na·ive·ly** *adv* — **na·ive·ness** *n*

na·ive·té *or* **na·ïve·té** \ˌnä-ˌēv(-ə)-ˈtā, nä-ˈē-və-ˌtā\ *n* 1 : a naive remark or action 2 : the quality or state of being naive

na·ive·ty *also* **na·ïve·ty** \nä-ˈēv-ə-(ə)tē\ *n*, *pl* **-ties**

na·ked \ˈnā-kəd\ *adj* 1 : having no clothes on : NUDE 2 : UNSHEATHED (a ~ sword) 3 : lacking a usual or natural covering (as of foliage or feathers) 4 : PLAIN, UNADORNED (the ~ truth) 5 : not aided by artificial means (seen by the ~ eye) — **na·ked·ly** *adv* — **na·ked·ness** *n*

nam·by–pam·by \ˌnam-bē-ˈpam-bē\ *adj* 1 : INSIPID 2 : WEAK, INDECISIVE

¹name \ˈnām\ *n* 1 : a word or words by which a person or thing is known 2 : a disparaging epithet (call someone ~s) 3 : REPUTATION; *esp* : distinguished reputation (made a ~ for himself) 4 : FAMILY, CLAN (was a disgrace to his ~) 5 : appearance as opposed to reality (a friend in ~ only)

²name *vb* **named; nam·ing** 1 : to give a name to : CALL 2 : to mention or identify by name 3 : NOMINATE, APPOINT 4 : to decide on : CHOOSE 5 : to speak about : MENTION (~ a price) — **name·able** *adj*

³name *adj* 1 : of, relating to, or bearing a name (~ tag) 2 : having an established reputation (~ brands)

name day *n* : the church feast day of the saint after whom one is named

name·less \ˈnām-ləs\ *adj* 1 : having no name 2 : not marked with a name (a ~ grave) 3 : not known by name (a ~ hero) 4 : too distressing to be described (~ fears) — **name·less·ly** *adv*

name·ly \ˈnām-lē\ *adv* : that is to say : AS (the cat family, ~, lions, tigers, and similar animals)

name·plate \-ˌplāt\ *n* : a plate or plaque bearing a name (as of a resident)

name·sake \-ˌsāk\ *n* : one that has the same name as another; *esp* : one named after another

nan·keen \nan-ˈkēn\ *n* : a durable brownish yellow cotton fabric orig. woven by hand in China

nan·ny goat \ˈnan-ē-\ *n* : a female domestic goat

nano·me·ter \ˈnan-ə-ˌmēt-ər\ *n* : one billionth of a meter

nano·sec·ond \-ˌsek-ənd\ *n* : one billionth of a second

¹nap \ˈnap\ *vb* **napped; nap·ping** 1 : to sleep briefly esp. during the day : DOZE 2 : to be off guard (was caught napping)

²nap *n* : a short sleep esp. during the day

³nap *n* : a soft downy fibrous surface (as on yarn and cloth) — **nap·less** *adj*

na·palm \ˈnā-ˌpä(l)m\ *n* [*naph*thalene + *palm*itate salt of a fatty acid] 1 : a thickener used in jelling gasoline (as for incendiary bombs) 2 : fuel jelled with napalm

nape \ˈnāp, ˈnap\ *n* : the back of the neck

na·pery \ˈnā-p(ə)rē\ *n* : household linen esp. for the table

naph·tha \ˈnaf-thə, ˈnap-\ *n* : any of various liquid hydrocarbon mixtures used chiefly as solvents

naph·tha·lene \-ˌlēn\ *n* : a crystalline substance obtained from coal tar used in organic synthesis and as a moth repellent

nap·kin \ˈnap-kən\ *n* 1 : a piece of material (as cloth) used at table to wipe the lips or fingers and protect the clothes 2 : a small cloth or towel

na·po·le·on \nə-ˈpōl-yən, -ˈpō-lē-ən\ *n* : an oblong pastry with a filling of cream, custard, or jelly between layers of puff paste

Na·po·le·on·ic \nə-ˌpō-lē-ˈän-ik\ *adj* : of, relating to, or characteristic of Napoleon I or his family

narc \ˈnärk\ *n*, *slang* : one (as a government agent) who investigates narcotics violations

nar·cis·sism \ˈnär-sə-ˌsiz-əm\ *n* [G *narzissmus*, fr. *Narziss* Narcissus, fr. L *Narcissus*, fr. Gk *Narkissos*, beautiful youth of Greek mythology who fell in love with his own image] 1 : undue dwelling on one's own self or attainments 2 : love of or sexual desire for one's own body — **nar·cis·sist** \-səst\ *n* *or adj* — **nar·cis·sis·tic** \ˌnär-sə-ˈsis-tik\ *adj*

nar·cis·sus \när-ˈsis-əs\ *n*, *pl* **-cis·sus** *or* **-cis·sus·es** *or* **-cis·si** \-ˈsis-ˌī, -ē\ : DAFFODIL; *esp* : one with short-tubed flowers usu. borne separately

nar·co·sis \när-ˈkō-səs\ *n*, *pl* **-co·ses** \-ˌsēz\ : a state of stupor, unconsciousness, or arrested activity produced by the influence of chemicals (as narcotics)

nar·cot·ic \när-ˈkät-ik\ *n* [ME *narkotik*, fr. MF *narcotique*, fr. *narcotique*, adj., fr. ML *narcoticus*, fr. Gk *narkōtikos*, fr. *narkoun* to benumb, fr.

narkē numbness] : a drug (as opium) that dulls the senses and induces sleep — **narcotic** *adj*

nar·co·tize \\'när-kə-ˌtīz\\ *vb* **-tized; -tiz·ing 1** : to treat with or subject to a narcotic: *also* : to put into a state of narcosis **2** : to soothe to unconsciousness or unawareness

nard \\'närd\\ *n* : a fragment ointment of the ancients

na·ris \\'nar-əs\\ *n, pl* **na·res** \\'nar-(ˌ)ēz\\ [L] : an opening of the nose : NOSTRIL

nark *var of* NARC

Nar·ra·gan·set \\ˌnar-ə-'gan-sət\\ *n, pl* **Narraganset** *or* **Narragansets** : a member of an American Indian people of Rhode Island

nar·rate \\'nar-ˌāt\\ *vb* **nar·rat·ed; nar·rat·ing** : to recite the details of (as a story) : RELATE, TELL — **nar·ra·tion** \\na-'rā-shən\\ *n* — **nar·ra·tor** \\'nar-ˌāt-ər\\ *n*

nar·ra·tive \\'nar-ət-iv\\ *n* **1** : something that is narrated : STORY **2** : the art or practice of narrating

¹**nar·row** \\'nar-ō\\ *adj* **1** : of slender or less than standard width **2** : limited in size or scope : RESTRICTED **3** : not liberal in views : PREJUDICED **4** : interpreted or interpreting strictly **5** : CLOSE ⟨a ~ escape⟩; *also* : barely successful ⟨won by a ~ margin⟩ — **nar·row·ly** *adv* — **nar·row·ness** *n*

²**narrow** *n* : a narrow passage : STRAIT — usu. used in pl.

³**narrow** *vb* : to lessen in width or extent

nar·row-mind·ed \\ˌnar-ō-'mīn-dəd\\ *adj* : not liberal or broad-minded

nar·whal \\'när-ˌhwäl, 'när-wəl\\ *n* : an arctic sea animal about 20 feet (6 meters) long that is related to the dolphin and in the male has a long twisted ivory tusk

NAS *abbr* naval air station

NASA \\'nas-ə\\ *abbr* National Aeronautics and Space Administration

¹**na·sal** \\'nā-zəl\\ *n* **1** : a nasal part **2** : a nasal consonant or vowel

²**nasal** *adj* **1** : of or relating to the nose **2** : uttered through the nose — **na·sal·ly** \\-ē\\ *adv*

na·sal·ize \\'nā-zə-ˌlīz\\ *vb* **-ized; -iz·ing 1** : to make nasal **2** : to speak in a nasal manner — **na·sal·iza·tion** \\ˌnā-zə-lə-'zā-shən\\ *n*

na·scent \\'nas-ᵊnt, 'nās\\ *adj* : coming into existence : beginning to grow or develop — **na·scence** \\-ᵊns\\ *n*

nas·tur·tium \\nə-'stər-shəm, na-\\ *n* : a watery-stemmed herb with showy spurred flowers and pungent seeds

nas·ty \\'nas-tē\\ *adj* **nas·ti·er; -est 1** : FILTHY **2** : INDECENT, OBSCENE **3** : DISHONORABLE ⟨a ~ trick⟩ **4** : HARMFUL, DANGEROUS ⟨took a ~ fall⟩ **5** : DISAGREEABLE ⟨~ weather⟩ **6** : MEAN, ILL-NATURED ⟨a ~ temper⟩ — **nas·ti·ly** \\'nas-tə-lē\\ *adv* — **nas·ti·ness** \\-tē-nəs\\ *n*

nat *abbr* **1** national **2** native **3** natural

na·tal \\'nāt-ᵊl\\ *adj* **1** : NATIVE **2** : of, relating to, or present at birth

na·tal·i·ty \\nā-'tal-ət-ē, nə-\\ *n, pl* **-ties** : BIRTHRATE

na·ta·to·ri·um \\ˌnāt-ə-'tōr-ē-əm, ˌnat-\\ *n* : a swimming pool esp. indoors

na·tion \\'nā-shən\\ *n* [ME *nacioun*, fr. MF *nation*, fr. L *nation-, natio* birth, race, nation, fr. *natus*, pp. of *nasci* to be born] **1** : NATIONALITY **5**; *also* : a politically organized nationality **2** : a community of people composed of one or more nationalities with its own territory and government **3** : the territory of a nation **4** : a federation of tribes (as of American Indians) — **na·tion·hood** *n*

¹**na·tion·al** \\'nash-(ə-)nəl\\ *adj* **1** : of or relating to a nation **2** : comprising or characteristic of a nationality **3** : FEDERAL **3** — **na·tion·al·ly** \\-ē\\ *adv*

²**national** *n* **1** : one who is under the protection of a nation without regard to the more formal status of citizen or subject **2** : an organization (as a labor union) having local units throughout a nation **3** : a competition that is national in scope — usu. used in pl.

National Guard *n* **1** : a militia force recruited by each state, equipped by the federal government, and jointly maintained subject to the call of either **2** : a military force serving as a national constabulary and defense force

na·tion·al·ism \\'nash-(ə-)nəl-ˌiz-əm\\ *n* : devotion to national interests, unity, and independence

na·tion·al·ist \\-əst\\ *n* **1** : an advocate of or believer in nationalism **2** *cap* : a member of a political party or group advocating national independence or strong national government — **nationalist** *adj, often cap* — **na·tion·al·is·tic** \\ˌnash-(ə-)nəl-'is-tik\\ *adj*

na·tion·al·i·ty \\ˌnash-(ə-)'nal-ət-ē\\ *n, pl* **-ties 1** : national character **2** : a legal relationship involving allegiance of an individual and his protection by the state **3** : membership in a particular nation **4** : political independence or existence as a separate nation **5** : a people having a common origin, tradition, and language and capable of forming a state **6** : an ethnic group within a larger unit (as a nation)

na·tion·al·ize \\'nash-(ə-)nəl-ˌīz\\ *vb* **-ized; -iz·ing 1** : to make national : make a nation of **2** : to remove from private ownership and place under government control — **na·tion·al·iza·tion** \\ˌnash-(ə-)nəl-ə-'zā-shən\\ *n*

national park *n* : an area of special scenic, historical, or scientific importance set aside and maintained by a national government esp. for recreation or study

national seashore *n* : a recreational area adjacent to a seacoast and maintained by the federal government

na·tion·wide \\ˌnā-shən-'wīd\\ *adj* : extending throughout a nation

¹na·tive \'nāt-iv\ adj 1 : INBORN, NATURAL 2 : born in a particular place or country 3 : belonging to a person because of the place or circumstances of his birth ⟨his ~ language⟩ 4 : grown, produced, or originating in a particular place : INDIGENOUS

²native n : one that is native; esp : a person who belongs to a particular country by birth

Native American n : AMERICAN INDIAN

na·tiv·ism \'nāt-iv-₁iz-əm\ n 1 : a policy of favoring native inhabitants over immigrants 2 : the revival or perpetuation of a native culture esp. in opposition to acculturation

Na·tiv·i·ty \nə-'tiv-ət-ē, nā-\ n, pl -ties 1 : the birth of Christ 2 not cap : the process or circumstances of being born : BIRTH

natl abbr national

NATO \'nāt-(₁)ō\ abbr North Atlantic Treaty Organization

nat·ty \'nat-ē\ adj nat·ti·er; -est : trimly neat and tidy : SMART — nat·ti·ly \'nat-ʰl-ē\ adv — nat·ti·ness \-ē-nəs\ n

¹nat·u·ral \'nach-(ə-)rəl\ adj 1 : determined by nature : INBORN, INNATE ⟨~ ability⟩ 2 : BORN ⟨a ~ fool⟩ 3 : ILLEGITIMATE 4 : HUMAN 5 : of or relating to nature 6 : not artificial 7 : being simple and sincere : not affected 8 : LIFELIKE 9 : having neither sharps nor flats in the key signature syn ingenuous, naive, unsophisticated, artless, guileless — nat·u·ral·ness n

²natural n 1 : IDIOT 2 : a character placed on a line or space of the musical staff to nullify the effect of a preceding sharp or flat 3 : one obviously suitable for a specific purpose 4 : AFRO

natural childbirth n : a system of managing childbirth in which the mother prepares to remain conscious and assist in delivery with little or no use of drugs

natural gas n : gas coming from the earth's crust through natural openings or bored wells; esp : a combustible mixture of hydrocarbons and esp. methane used chiefly as a fuel and raw material

natural history n 1 : a treatise on some aspect of nature 2 : the study of natural objects esp. from an amateur or popular point of view

nat·u·ral·ism \'nach-(ə-)rə-₁liz-əm\ n 1 : action or thought based only on natural desires and instincts 2 : a doctrine that denies a supernatural explanation of the origin or development of the universe and holds that scientific laws account for all of nature 3 : realism in art and literature — nat·u·ral·is·tic \₁nach-(ə-)rə-'lis-tik\ adj

nat·u·ral·ist \-ləst\ n 1 : one that advocates or practices naturalism 2 : a student of animals or plants esp. in the field

nat·u·ral·ize \-₁līz\ vb -ized; -iz·ing 1 : to

become or cause to become established as if native ⟨~ new forage crops⟩ 2 : to confer the rights of a citizen on — nat·u·ral·i·za·tion \₁nach-(ə-)rə-lə-'zā-shən\ n

nat·u·ral·ly \'nach-(ə-)rə-lē, 'nach-ər-lē\ adv 1 : by nature : by natural character or ability 2 : as might be expected 3 : without artificial aid: also : without affectation 4 : REALISTICALLY

natural science n : a science (as physics, chemistry, or biology) that deals with matter, energy, and their interrelations and transformations or with objectively measurable phenomena — natural scientist n

natural selection n : the natural process that results in the survival of individuals or groups best adjusted to the conditions under which they live

na·ture \'nā-chər\ n [ME, fr. MF, fr. L natura, fr. natus, pp. of nasci to be born] 1 : the inherent quality or basic constitution of a person or thing 2 : KIND, SORT 3 : DISPOSITION, TEMPERAMENT 4 : the physical universe 5 : one's natural instincts or way of life ⟨quirks of human ~⟩; also : primitive state ⟨a return to ~⟩ 6 : natural scenery or environment ⟨beauties of ~⟩

naught \'nȯt, 'nät\ n 1 : NOTHING 2 : the arithmetical symbol 0 : ZERO

naugh·ty \'nȯt-ē, 'nät-\ adj naugh·ti·er; -est 1 : guilty of disobedience or misbehavior 2 : lacking in taste or propriety — naugh·ti·ly \'nȯt-ʰl-ē, 'nät-\ adv — naugh·ti·ness \-ē-nəs\ n

nau·sea \'nȯ-zē-ə, 'nȯ-shə\ n [L, seasickness, nausea, fr. Gk nautia, nausia, fr. nautēs sailor] 1 : sickness of the stomach with a desire to vomit 2 : extreme disgust

nau·se·ate \'nȯ-z(h)ē-₁āt, -s(h)ē-\ vb -at·ed; -at·ing : to affect or become affected with nausea — nau·se·at·ing·ly \-₁āt-iŋ-lē\ adv

nau·seous \'nȯ-shəs, -zē-əs\ adj 1 : causing nausea or disgust 2 : affected with nausea or disgust

naut abbr nautical

nau·ti·cal \'nȯt-i-kəl\ adj : of or relating to seamen, navigation, or ships — nau·ti·cal·ly \-k(ə-)lē\ adv

nautical mile n : a unit of distance equal to about 6076.115 feet

nau·ti·lus \'nȯt-ʰl-əs\ n, pl -lus·es or -li \-ʰl-₁ī, -₁ē\ : a sea mollusk related to the octopuses but having a spiral shell divided into chambers

nav abbr 1 naval 2 navigable; navigation

Na·va·ho or Na·va·jo \'nav-ə-₁hō, 'näv-\ n, pl Navaho or Navahos or Navajo or Navajos : a member of an American Indian people of northern New Mexico and Arizona; also : their language

na·val \'nā-vəl\ adj : of, relating to, or possessing a navy

naval stores n pl : products (as pitch,

turpentine, or rosin) obtained from resinous conifers (as pines)

nave \\'nāv\ *n* [ML *navis*, fr. L, ship] : the central part of a church running lengthwise

na·vel \\'nā-vəl\ *n* : a depression in the middle of the abdomen that marks the ȋnt of attachment of fetus and moth-e.

navel orange *n* : a seedless orange having a pit at the blossom end where the fruit encloses a small secondary fruit

nav·i·ga·ble \\'nav-i-gə-bəl\ *adj* 1 : capable of being navigated ⟨a ~ river⟩ 2 : capable of being steered ⟨a ~ balloon⟩ — **nav·i·ga·bil·i·ty** \\,nav-i-gə-'bil-ət-ē\ *n*

nav·i·gate \\'nav-ə-,gāt\ *vb* **-gat·ed; -gat·ing** 1 : to sail on or through ⟨~ the Atlantic ocean⟩ 2 : to steer or direct the course of a ship or aircraft 3 : MOVE; *esp* : WALK ⟨could hardly ~⟩ — **nav·i·ga·tion** \\,nav-ə-'gā-shən\ *n* — **nav·i·ga·tor** \\'nav-ə-,gāt-ər\

na·vy \\'nā-vē\ *n, pl* **navies** FLEET; *also* : the warships belonging to a nation 2 *often cap* : a nation's organization for naval warfare

navy exchange *n* : a post exchange at a navy installation

navy yard *n* : a yard where naval vessels are built or repaired

¹**nay** \\'nā\ *adv* 1 : NO 2 : not merely this but also : not only so but ⟨the letter made him happy, ~, ecstatic⟩

²**nay** *n* : a negative vote; *also* : a person casting such a vote

nay·say·er \\'nā-,sā-ər\ : one who denies, refuses, or opposes something

Na·zi \\'nät-sē, 'nat-\ *n* [G, fr. *nationalsozialist*, lit., national socialist] : a member of a German fascist party controlling Germany from 1933 to 1945 under Adolf Hitler — **Nazi** *adj* — **Na·zism** \\'nät-,siz-əm, 'nat-\ *or* **Na·zi·ism** \-sē-,iz-əm\ *n*

Nb *symbol* niobium

NB *abbr* 1 New Brunswick 2 nota bene

NBA *abbr* 1 National Basketball Association 2 National Boxing Association

NBC *abbr* National Broadcasting Company

NBS *abbr* National Bureau of Standards

NC *abbr* 1 no charge 2 North Carolina

NCAA *abbr* National Collegiate Athletic Association

NCE *abbr* New Catholic Edition

NCO \\,en-,sē-'ō\ *n* : NONCOMMISSIONED OFFICER

Nd *symbol* neodymium

ND *abbr* 1 no date 2 North Dakota

N Dak *abbr* North Dakota

Ne *symbol* neon

NE *abbr* 1 Nebraska 2 New England 3 northeast

Ne·an·der·thal \ni-ˈan-dər-,t(h)ȯl, nā-ˈän-dər-,täl\ *adj* : of, relating to, or being an extinct primitive Old World man; *also* : crudely primitive (as in

manner or conduct) — **Neanderthal** *n*

neap tide \\'nēp-\ *n* : a tide of minimum range occurring at the first and third quarters of the moon

¹**near** \\'niər\ *adv* 1 : at, within, or to a short distance or time 2 : ALMOST

²**near** *prep* : close to

³**near** *adj* 1 : closely related or associated; *also* : INTIMATE 2 : not far away; *also* : being the closer or left-hand member of a pair 3 : barely avoided ⟨a ~ accident⟩ 4 : DIRECT, SHORT ⟨by the ~est route⟩ 5 : STINGY 6 : not real but very like ⟨~ silk⟩ — **near·ly** *adv* — **near·ness** *n*

⁴**near** *vb* : APPROACH

near beer *n* : any of various malt liquors low in alcohol

near·by \niər-'bī, 'niər-,bī\ *adv or adj* : close at hand

near·sight·ed \\'niər-'sīt-əd\ *adj* : seeing distinctly at short distances only : SHORTSIGHTED — **near·sight·ed·ly** *adv* — **near·sight·ed·ness** *n*

neat \\'nēt\ *adj* [MF *net*, fr. L *nitidus* bright, neat, fr. *nitēre* to shine] 1 : being orderly and clean 2 : not mixed or diluted ⟨~ brandy⟩ 3 : marked by tasteful simplicity 4 : PRECISE, SYSTEMATIC 5 : SKILLFUL, ADROIT 6 : FINE, ADMIRABLE — **neat** *adv* — **neat·ly** *adv* — **neat·ness** *n*

neath \\'nēth\ *prep, dial* : BENEATH

neat's–foot oil \\'nēts-,fut-\ *n* [*neat* (bovine)] : a pale yellow fatty oil made esp. from the bones of cattle and used chiefly as a leather dressing

neb \\'neb\ *n* 1 : the beak of a bird or tortoise; *also* : NOSE, SNOUT 2 : NIB

Neb *or* **Nebr** *abbr* Nebraska

NEB *abbr* New English Bible

neb·u·la \\'neb-yə-lə\ *n, pl* **-las** *or* **-lae** \-,lē, -,lī\ [NL, fr. L, mist, cloud] 1 : any of many vast cloudlike masses of gas or dust among the stars 2 : GALAXY — **neb·u·lar** \-lər\ *adj*

neb·u·lize \\'neb-yə-,līz\ *vb* **-lized; -lizing** : to reduce to a fine spray — **neb·u·liz·er** \-,lī-zər\ *n*

neb·u·los·i·ty \,neb-yə-'läs-ət-ē\ *n, pl* **-ties** 1 : the quality or state of being nebulous 2 : nebulous matter

neb·u·lous \\'neb-yə-ləs\ *adj* 1 : of or relating to a nebula 2 : HAZY, INDISTINCT ⟨a ~ memory⟩

¹**nec·es·sary** \\'nes-ə-,ser-ē\ *n, pl* **-saries** : an indispensable item

²**necessary** *adj* [ME *necessarie*, fr. L *necessarius*, fr. *necesse* necessary, fr. *ne-* not + *cedere* to withdraw] 1 : INEVITABLE, INESCAPABLE; *also* : CERTAIN 2 : PREDETERMINED 3 : COMPULSORY 4 : positively needed : INDISPENSABLE **syn** imperative, necessitous, essential — **nec·es·sar·i·ly** \,nes-ə-'ser-ə-lē\ *adv*

ne·ces·si·tate \ni-'ses-ə-,tāt\ *vb* **-tated; -tat·ing** : to make necessary

ne·ces·si·tous \ni-'ses-ət-əs\ *adj* 1 : NEEDY, IMPOVERISHED 2 : URGENT 3 : NECESSARY

ne·ces·si·ty \ni-'ses-ət-ē\ *n, pl* **-ties** 1

: conditions that cannot be changed **2** : WANT, POVERTY **3** : something that is necessary **4** : very great need

¹neck \'nek\ *n* **1** : the part of the body connecting the head and the trunk **2** : the part of a garment covering or near to the neck **3** : a relatively narrow part suggestive of a neck (∼ of a bottle) (∼ of land) **4** : a narrow margin esp. of victory (won by a ∼) — **necked** \'nekt\ *adj*

²neck *vb* : to kiss and caress amorously

neck and neck *adv or adj* : very close (as in a race)

neck·er·chief \'nek-ər-chəf, -ˌchēf\ *n, pl* **-chiefs** \-chəfs, -ˌchēfs\ *also* **-chieves** \-ˌchēvz\ : a square of cloth worn folded about the neck like a scarf

neck·lace \'nek-ləs\ *n* : an ornamental chain or a string (as of jewels or beads) worn around the neck

neck·line \-ˌlīn\ *n* : the outline of the neck opening of a garment

neck·tie \-ˌtī\ *n* : a strip of cloth worn around the neck and tied in front

ne·crol·o·gy \nə-'kräl-ə-jē\ *n, pl* **-gies 1** : a list of the recently dead **2** : OBITUARY

nec·ro·man·cy \'nek-rə-ˌman-sē\ *n* **1** : the art or practice of conjuring up the spirits of the dead for purposes of magically revealing the future **2** : MAGIC, SORCERY — **nec·ro·man·cer** \-sər\ *n*

ne·crop·o·lis \nə-'kräp-ə-ləs, ne-\ *n, pl* **-lis·es** *or* **-les** \-ˌlēz\ *or* **-leis** \-ˌlās\ *or* **-li** \-ˌlī, -ˌlē\ : CEMETERY; *esp* : a large elaborate cemetery of an ancient city

ne·cro·sis \nə-'krō-səs, ne-\ *n, pl* **ne·cro·ses** \-ˌsēz\ : usu. local death of body tissue — **ne·crot·ic** \-'krät-ik\ *adj*

nec·tar \'nek-tər\ *n* **1** : the drink of the Greek and Roman gods; *also* : any delicious drink **2** : a sweet plant secretion that is the raw material of honey

nec·tar·ine \ˌnek-tə-'rēn\ *n* : a smooth-skinned peach

née *or* **nee** \'nā\ *adj* [F, lit., born] — used to identify a woman by her maiden family name

¹need \'nēd\ *n* **1** : OBLIGATION (no ∼ to hurry) **2** : a lack of something requisite, desirable, or useful **3** : a condition requiring supply or relief (when the ∼ arises) **4** : POVERTY *syn* necessity, exigency

²need *vb* **1** : to be in want **2** : to have cause or occasion for : REQUIRE (he ∼s advice) **3** : to be under obligation or necessity (we ∼ to know the truth)

need·ful \'nēd-fəl\ *adj* : NECESSARY, REQUISITE

¹nee·dle \'nēd-əl\ *n* **1** : a slender pointed usu. steel implement used in sewing **2** : a slender rod (as for knitting, controlling a small opening, or transmitting vibrations to or from a recording) (a phonograph ∼) **3** : a slender hollow instrument by which material is introduced into or withdrawn from the body **4** : a slender indicator on a

dial **5** : a needle-shaped leaf (as of a pine)

²needle *vb* **nee·dled; nee·dling** \'nēd-(ə-)liŋ\ : PROD, GOAD; *esp* : to incite to action by repeated gibes

nee·dle·point \'nēd-əl-ˌpoint\ *n* **1** : lace worked with a needle over a paper pattern **2** : embroidery done on canvas across counted threads — **needlepoint** *adj*

need·less \'nēd-ləs\ *adj* : UNNECESSARY — **need·less·ly** *adv* — **need·less·ness** *n*

nee·dle·wom·an \'nēd-əl-ˌwùm-ən\ *n* : a woman who does needlework; *esp* : SEAMSTRESS

nee·dle·work \-ˌwərk\ *n* : work done with a needle; *esp* : work (as embroidery) other than plain sewing

needs \'nēdz\ *adv* : of necessity : NECESSARILY (must ∼ be recognized)

needy \'nēd-ē\ *adj* **need·i·er; -est** : being in want : POVERTY-STRICKEN

ne'er \'neər\ *adv* : NEVER

ne'er-do-well \'neər-dù-ˌwel\ *n* : an idle worthless person — **ne'er-do-well** *adj*

ne·far·i·ous \ni-'far-ē-əs\ *adj* [L nefarius, fr. nefas crime, fr. ne- not + fas right, divine law] : very wicked : EVIL — **ne·far·i·ous·ly** *adv*

neg *abbr* negative

ne·gate \ni-'gāt\ *vb* **ne·gat·ed; ne·gat·ing** **1** : to deny the existence or truth of **2** : to cause to be ineffective or invalid : NULLIFY

ne·ga·tion \ni-'gā-shən\ *n* **1** : the action or operation of negating or making negative **2** : a negative doctrine or statement

¹neg·a·tive \'neg-ət-iv\ *adj* **1** : marked by denial, prohibition, or refusal (a ∼ reply) **2** : not positive or constructive; *esp* : not affirming the presence of what is sought or suspected to be present (a ∼ test) **3** : less than zero (a ∼ number) **4** : being, relating to, or charged with electricity of which the electron is the elementary unit (a ∼ particle) **5** : having the light and dark parts opposite to what they were in the original photographic subject — **neg·a·tive·ly** *adv*

²negative *n* **1** : a negative word or statement **2** : a negative vote or reply; *also* : REFUSAL **3** : something that is the opposite or negation of something else **4** : the side that votes or argues for the opposition (as in a debate) **5** : a negative photographic image on transparent material

³negative *vb* **-tived; -tiv·ing 1** : to refuse to accept or approve **2** : to vote against **3** : DISPROVE

negative income tax *n* : a system of federal subsidy payments to families with incomes below a stipulated level

neg·a·tiv·ism \'neg-ət-iv-ˌiz-əm\ *n* : an attitude of skepticism and denial of nearly everything affirmed or suggested by others

¹ne·glect \ni-'glekt\ *vb* [L *neglegere*,

neclegere, fr. *nec-* not + *legere* to gather] **1** : DISREGARD **2** : to leave undone or unattended to esp. through carelessness *syn* omit, ignore, overlook, slight, forget, miss

²**neglect** *n* **1** : an act or instance of neglecting something **2** : the condition of being neglected — **neg·lect·ful** *adj*

neg·li·gee *also* **neg·li·gé** \ˌneg-lə-ˈzhā\ *n* : a woman's long flowing dressing gown

neg·li·gent \ˈneg-li-jənt\ *adj* : marked by neglect *syn* neglectful, remiss, delinquent, derelict — **neg·li·gence** \-jəns\ *n* — **neg·li·gent·ly** *adv*

neg·li·gi·ble \ˈneg-li-jə-bəl\ *adj* : so small as to be neglected or disregarded

ne·go·tiant \ni-ˈgō-sh(ē-)ənt\ *n* : NEGOTIATOR

ne·go·ti·ate \ni-ˈgō-shē-ˌāt\ *vb* **-at·ed; -at·ing** [L *negotiari* to carry on business, fr. *negotium* business, fr. *neg-* not + *otium* leisure] **1** : to confer with another so as to arrive at the settlement of some matter; *also* : to arrange for or bring about by such conferences (∼ a treaty) **2** : to transfer to another by delivery or endorsement in return for equivalent value (∼ a check) **3** : to get through, around, or over successfully (∼ a turn) — **ne·go·tia·ble** \-sh(ē-)ə-bəl\ *adj* — **ne·go·ti·a·tion** \ni-ˌgō-s(h)ē-ˈā-shən\ *n* — **ne·go·ti·a·tor** \-ˈgō-shē-ˌāt-ər\ *n*

ne·gri·tude \ˈneg-rə-ˌt(y)üd, ˈnē-grə-\ *n* : a consciousness and pride in one's African heritage

Ne·gro \ˈnē-grō\ *n, pl* **Negroes** [Sp or Pg, fr. *negro* black] : a member of the black race — **Negro** *adj* — **Ne·groid** \ˈnē-ˌgroid\ *n or adj, often not cap*

Neh *abbr* Nehemiah

Ne·he·mi·ah \ˌnē-(h)ə-ˈmī-ə\ *n* — see BIBLE table

NEI *abbr* not elsewhere included

neigh \ˈnā\ *n* : a loud prolonged cry of a horse — **neigh** *vb*

¹**neigh·bor** \ˈnā-bər\ *n* **1** : one living or located near another **2** : FELLOWMAN

²**neighbor** *vb* **neigh·bored; neigh·bor·ing** \-b(ə-)riŋ\ : to be next to or near to : border on

neigh·bor·hood \ˈnā-bər-ˌhùd\ *n* **1** : NEARNESS **2** : a place or region near : VICINITY; *also* : a number or amount near (costs in the ∼ of $10) **3** : the people living near one another **4** : a section lived in by neighbors and usu. having distinguishing characteristics

neigh·bor·ly \-lē\ *adj* : befitting congenial neighbors; *esp* : FRIENDLY — **neigh·bor·li·ness** *n*

¹**nei·ther** \ˈnē-thər, ˈnī-\ *pron* : neither one : not the one and not the other (∼ of the two)

²**neither** *conj* **1** : not either (∼ good nor bad) **2** : NOR (∼ did I)

³**neither** *adj* : not either (∼ hand)

nel·son \ˈnel-sən\ *n* : a wrestling hold in which one applies leverage against an opponent's arm, neck, and head

nem·a·tode \ˈnem-ə-ˌtōd\ *n* : any of a group of elongated cylindrical worms parasitic in animals or plants or free-living in soil or water

nem·e·sis \ˈnem-ə-səs\ *n, pl* **-e·ses** \-ə-ˌsēz\ [L *Nemesis,* goddess of divine retribution, fr. Gk] **1** : one that inflicts retribution or vengeance **2** : a formidable and usu. victorious rival **3** : an act or effect of retribution; *also* : CURSE

neo·clas·sic \ˌnē-ō-ˈklas-ik\ *or* **neo·clas·si·cal** \-i-kəl\ *adj* : of or relating to a revival or adaptation of the classical style esp. in literature, art, or music

neo·co·lo·nial·ism \ˌnē-ō-kə-ˈlō-nyəl-ˌiz-əm, -ˈlō-nē-ə-ˌliz-əm\ *n* : the economic and political policies by which a nation indirectly maintains or extends its influence over other areas or peoples — **neo·co·lo·nial** *adj* — **neo·co·lo·nial·ist** \-əst\ *n or adj*

neo·con·ser·va·tive \-kən-ˈsər-vət-iv\ *n* : a former liberal espousing political conservatism — **neo·con·ser·va·tism** \-və-ˌtiz-əm\ *n* — **neoconservative** *adj*

neo·dym·i·um \ˌnē-ō-ˈdim-ē-əm\ *n* : a yellow metallic chemical element

neo-im·pres·sion·ism \ˌnē-ō-im-ˈpresh-ə-ˌniz-əm\ *n, often cap N&I* : a late 19th century French art movement that attempted to make impressionism more precise and to use a pointillist painting technique

Neo·lith·ic \ˌnē-ə-ˈlith-ik\ *adj* : of or relating to the latest period of the Stone Age characterized by polished stone implements

ne·ol·o·gism \nē-ˈäl-ə-ˌjiz-əm\ *n* : a new word or expression

ne·on \ˈnē-ˌän\ *n* [Gk, neut. of *neos* new] **1** : a gaseous colorless chemical element used in electric lamps **2** : a lamp in which a discharge through neon gives a reddish glow — **neon** *adj*

neo·na·tal \ˌnē-ō-ˈnāt-ᵊl\ *adj* : of, relating to, or affecting the newborn — **neo·na·tal·ly** \-ē\ *adv* — **ne·o·nate** \ˈnē-ō-ˌnāt\ *n*

neo·phyte \ˈnē-ə-ˌfīt\ *n* **1** : a new convert : PROSELYTE **2** : NOVICE **3** : BEGINNER

neo·plasm \ˈnē-ə-ˌplaz-əm\ *n* : TUMOR — **neo·plas·tic** \ˌnē-ə-ˈplas-tik\ *adj*

Ne·pali \nə-ˈpȯl-ē, -ˈpäl-\ *n, pl* **Nepali** : a native or inhabitant of Nepal

ne·pen·the \nə-ˈpen-thē\ *n* **1** : a potion used by the ancients to dull pain and sorrow **2** : something capable of making one forget grief or suffering

neph·ew \ˈnef-yü, *chiefly Brit* ˈnev-\ *n* : a son of one's brother, sister, brother-in-law, or sister-in-law

ne·phrit·ic \ni-ˈfrit-ik\ *adj* **1** : RENAL **2** : of, relating to, or affected with nephritis

ne·phri·tis \ni-ˈfrīt-əs\ *n, pl* **ne·phrit·i·des** \-ˈfrit-ə-ˌdēz\ : kidney inflammation

ne plus ul·tra \ˌnē-ˌpləs-'əl-trə\ *n* [NL, (go) no more beyond] : the highest point capable of being attained

nep·o·tism \'nep-ə-ˌtiz-əm\ *n* [F *népotisme*, fr. It *nepotismo*, fr. *nepote* nephew, fr. L *nepot-*, *nepos* grandson, nephew] : favoritism shown to a relative (as in the granting of jobs)

Nep·tune \'nep-ˌt(y)ün\ *n* : the 8th planet in order of distance from the sun — **Nep·tu·ni·an** \nep-'t(y)ü-nē-ən\ *adj*

nep·tu·ni·um \nep-'t(y)ü-nē-əm\ *n* : a short-lived radioactive chemical element artificially produced as a by-product in the production of plutonium

Ne·re·id \'nir-ē-əd\ *n* : a sea nymph in Greek mythology

¹**nerve** \'nərv\ *n* **1** : one of the strands of nervous tissue that carry nervous impulses between the brain and spinal cord and every part of the body **2** : power of endurance or control : FORTITUDE; *also* : BOLDNESS, DARING **3** *pl* : NERVOUSNESS **4** : a vein of a leaf or insect wing — **nerved** \'nərvd\ *adj* — **nerve·less** *adj*

²**nerve** *vb* **nerved; nerv·ing** : to give strength or courage to

nerve cell *n* : NEURON; *also* : the nucleus-containing central part of a neuron exclusive of its processes

nerve gas *n* : a war gas damaging esp. to the nervous and respiratory systems

nerve–rack·ing *or* **nerve–wrack·ing** \'nərv-ˌrak-iŋ\ *adj* : extremely trying on the nerves

ner·vous \'nər-vəs\ *adj* **1** : FORCIBLE, SPIRITED **2** : of, relating to, or made up of nerve cells or nerves **3** : easily excited or annoyed : JUMPY **4** : TIMID, APPREHENSIVE ⟨a ~ smile⟩ **5** : UNEASY, UNSTEADY — **ner·vous·ly** *adv* — **ner·vous·ness** *n*

nervous breakdown *n* : an attack of mental or emotional disorder of sufficient severity to be incapacitating esp. when requiring hospitalization

nervous system *n* : a bodily system that in vertebrates is made up of the brain and spinal cord, nerves, ganglia, and parts of the sense organs and that receives and interprets stimuli and transmits impulses

nervy \'nər-vē\ *adj* **nerv·i·er; -est 1** : showing calm courage **2** : marked by impudence or presumption ⟨a ~ salesman⟩ **3** : EXCITABLE, NERVOUS

-ness \nəs\ *n suffix* : state : condition : quality : degree ⟨good*ness*⟩

¹**nest** \'nest\ *n* **1** : the shelter prepared by a bird for its eggs and young **2** : a place where eggs (as of insects or fish) are laid and hatched **3** : a place of rest, retreat, or lodging **4** : DEN, HANGOUT ⟨a ~ of thieves⟩ **5** : the occupants of a nest **6** : a series of objects (as bowls or tables) fitting inside or under one another

²**nest** *vb* **1** : to build or occupy a nest **2** : to fit compactly together or within one another

nest egg *n* : a fund of money accumulated as a reserve

nes·tle \'nes-əl\ *vb* **nes·tled; nes·tling** \-(ə-)liŋ\ **1** : to settle snugly or comfortably **2** : to press closely and affectionately : CUDDLE **3** : to settle, shelter, or house as if in a nest

nest·ling \'nest-liŋ\ *n* : a bird too young to leave its nest

¹**net** \'net\ *n* **1** : a meshed fabric twisted, knotted, or woven together at regular intervals; *esp* : a device of net used esp. to catch birds, fish, or insects **2** : something made of net used esp. for protecting, confining, carrying, or dividing ⟨a tennis ~⟩ **3** : SNARE, TRAP

²**net** *vb* **net·ted; net·ting 1** : to cover or enclose with or as if with a net **2** : to catch in or as if in a net

³**net** *adj* : free from all charges or deductions ⟨~ profit⟩ ⟨~ weight⟩

⁴**net** *vb* **net·ted; net·ting** to gain or produce as profit : CLEAR, YIELD ⟨his business netted $50,000 a year⟩

⁵**net** *n* : a net amount, profit, weight, or price

NET *abbr* National Educational Television

Neth *abbr* Netherlands

neth·er \'neth-ər\ *adj* : situated down or below ⟨the ~ regions of the earth⟩

Neth·er·land·er \'neth-ər-ˌland-ər\ *n* : a native or inhabitant of the Netherlands

neth·er·most \-ˌmōst\ *adj* : LOWEST

neth·er·world \-ˌwərld\ *n* **1** : the world of the dead **2** : UNDERWORLD

net·ting \'net-iŋ\ *n* **1** : NETWORK **2** : the act or process of making a net or network **3** : the act, process, or right of fishing with a net

¹**net·tle** \'net-ᵊl\ *n* : any of various coarse herbs with stinging hairs

²**nettle** *vb* **net·tled; net·tling** : PROVOKE, VEX, IRRITATE

net·tle·some \'net-ᵊl-səm\ *adj* : causing vexation : IRRITATING

net·work \'net-ˌwərk\ *n* **1** : NET **2** : a system of elements (as lines or channels) that cross in the manner of the threads in a net **3** : a group or system of related or connected parts; *esp* : a chain of radio or television stations

net·work·ing \'net-ˌwərk-iŋ\ *n* : the exchange of information or services among individuals, groups, or institutions

neu·ral \'n(y)ùr-əl\ *adj* : of, relating to, or involving a nerve or the nervous system

neu·ral·gia \n(y)ù-'ral-jə\ *n* : acute pain that follows the course of a nerve — **neu·ral·gic** \-jik\ *adj*

neur·as·the·nia \ˌn(y)ùr-əs-'thē-nē-ə\ *n* : an emotional and psychic disorder characterized esp. by easy susceptibility to fatigue and often by lack of motivation, feelings of inadequacy,

and psychosomatic symptoms —
neur·as·then·ic \-¹then-ik\ *adj or n*

neu·ri·tis \n(y)ù-¹rīt-əs\ *n, pl* **-rit·i·des**
\-¹rit-ə-,dēz\ *or* **-ri·tis·es** : inflammation of a nerve — **neu·rit·ic** \-¹rit-ik\
adj or n

neu·rol·o·gy \n(y)ù-¹räl-ə-jē\ *n* : the scientific study of the nervous system —
neu·ro·log·i·cal \,n(y)ùr-ə-¹läj-i-kəl\ *or* **neu·ro·log·ic** \-ik\ *adj* — **neu·ro·log·i·cal·ly** \-i-k(ə-)lē\ *adv* — **neu·rol·o·gist** \n(y)ù-¹räl-ə-jəst\ *n*

neu·ron \¹n(y)ù-,rän\ *also* **neu·rone** \-,rōn\ *n* : a cell with specialized processes that is the fundamental functional unit of nervous tissue

neu·ro·sci·ence \,n(y)ùr-ō-¹sī-ən(t)s\ *n* : a branch of the life sciences that deals with the anatomy, physiology, biochemistry, or molecular biology of nerves and nervous tissue and esp. with their relation to behavior and learning — **neu·ro·sci·en·tist** \-ənt-əst\ *n*

neu·ro·sis \n(y)ù-¹rō-səs\ *n, pl* **-ro·ses** \-,sēz\ : a mental and emotional disorder that is less serious than a psychosis, is not characterized by disturbance of the use of language, and is accompanied by various bodily and mental disturbances (as visceral symptoms, anxieties, or phobias)

¹**neu·rot·ic** \n(y)ù-¹rät-ik\ *adj* : of, relating to, being, or affected with a neurosis; *also* : NERVOUS — **neu·rot·i·cal·ly** \-i-k(ə-)lē\ *adv*

²**neurotic** *n* : an emotionally unstable or neurotic person

neut *abbr* neuter

¹**neu·ter** \¹n(y)üt-ər\ *adj* [ME *neutre*, fr. MF & L; MF *neutre*, fr. L *neuter*, lit., neither, fr. *ne-* not + *uter* which of two] **1** : of, relating to, or constituting the gender that includes most words or grammatical forms referring to things classed as neither masculine nor feminine **2** : having imperfectly developed or no sex organs

²**neuter** *n* **1** : a noun, pronoun, adjective, or inflectional form or class of the neuter gender; *also* : the neuter gender **2** : WORKER **2**: *also* : a spayed or castrated animal

¹**neu·tral** \¹n(y)ù-trəl\ *n* **1** : one that is neutral **2** : a neutral color **3** : the position of machine gears in which power is not transmitted

²**neutral** *adj* **1** : not favoring either side in a quarrel, contest, or war **2** : of or relating to a neutral state or power **3** : MIDDLING, INDIFFERENT **4** : having no hue : GRAY; *also* : not decided in color **5** : neither acid nor basic (a ∼ solution) **6** : not electrically charged

neu·tral·ism \¹n(y)ù-trə-,liz-əm\ *n* : a policy or the advocacy of neutrality esp. in international affairs

neu·tral·i·ty \n(y)ù-¹tral-ət-ē\ *n* : the quality or state of being neutral; *esp* : immunity from invasion or from use by belligerents

neu·tral·ize \¹n(y)ù-trə-,līz\ *vb* **-ized**; **-iz·ing** : to make neutral; *esp* : COUNTERACT — **neu·tral·iza·tion** \,n(y)ù-trə-lə-¹zā-shən\ *n*

neu·tri·no \n(y)ù-¹trē-nō\ *n, pl* **-nos** : an uncharged elementary particle held to be massless

neu·tron \¹n(y)ù-,trän\ *n* : an uncharged atomic particle that is nearly equal in mass to the proton and is present in all atomic nuclei except hydrogen

neutron bomb *n* : a nuclear bomb designed to produce lethal neutrons but less blast and fire damage than other nuclear bombs

Nev *abbr* Nevada

nev·er \¹nev-ər\ *adv* **1** : not ever **2** : not in any degree, way, or condition

nev·er·more \,nev-ər-¹mōr\ *adv* : never again

nev·er-nev·er land \,nev-ər-¹nev-ər-\ *n* : an ideal or imaginary place

nev·er·the·less \,nev-ər-thə-¹les\ *adv* : in spite of that : HOWEVER

ne·vus \¹nē-vəs\ *n, pl* **ne·vi** \-,vī\ : a usu. pigmented birthmark

¹**new** \¹n(y)ü\ *adj* **1** : not old : RECENT, MODERN **2** : recently discovered, recognized, or learned about (∼ drugs) **3** : not formerly known or experienced : UNFAMILIAR **4** : different from the former **5** : not accustomed (∼ to the work) **6** : beginning as a repetition of a previous act or thing (a ∼ year) **7** : REFRESHED, REGENERATED (rest made a ∼ man of him) **8** : being in a position or place for the first time (a ∼ member) **9** *cap* : having been in use after medieval times : MODERN (*New* Latin) **syn** novel, modern, newfangled, fresh — **new·ish** *adj* — **new·ness** *n*

²**new** *adv* : NEWLY (*new*-mown hay)

¹**new·born** \-¹bȯrn\ *adj* **1** : recently born **2** : born anew (∼ hope)

²**newborn** *n, pl* **newborn** *or* **newborns** : a newborn individual

new·com·er \¹n(y)ü-,kəm-ər\ *n* **1** : one recently arrived **2** : BEGINNER

New Deal *n* : the legislative and administrative program of President F. D. Roosevelt to promote economic recovery and social reform during the 1930s — **New Deal·er** \-¹dē-lər\ *n*

new·el \¹n(y)ü-əl\ *n* [ME *nowell*, fr. MF *nouel* stone of a fruit, fr. LL *nucalis* like a nut, fr. L *nuc-*, *nux* nut] : a post about which the steps of a circular staircase wind; *also* : a post at the foot of a stairway or one at a landing

new-fan·gled \¹n(y)ü-¹faŋ-gəld\ *adj* [ME, fr. *newefangel*, fr. *new* + OE *fangen*, pp. of *fōn* to take, seize] **1** : attracted to novelty **2** : of the newest style : NOVEL

new-fash·ioned \-¹fash-ənd\ *adj* **1** : made in a new fashion or form **2** : UP-TO-DATE

new·found \-¹faúnd\ *adj* : newly found

New Left *n* : a political movement originating in the 1960s that advocates radical change in prevailing political, social, and educational practices

new·ly \'n(y)ü-lē\ *adv* 1 : LATELY, RE-CENTLY 2 : ANEW, AFRESH

new·ly·wed \-, wed\ *n* : one recently married

new math *n* : mathematics based on the theory of sets

new mathematics *n* : NEW MATH

new moon *n* : the phase of the moon with its dark side toward the earth; *also* : the thin crescent moon seen for a few days after the new moon phase

news \'n(y)üz\ *n* 1 : a report of recent events : TIDINGS 2 : material reported in a newspaper or news periodical or on a newscast

news·boy \'n(y)üz-, bȯi\ *n* : one who delivers or sells newspapers

news·cast \-, kast\ *n* : a radio or television broadcast of news — **news·cast·er** \-, kas-tər\ *n*

news·let·ter \-, let-ər\ *n* : a small newspaper containing news or information of interest chiefly to a special group

news·mag·a·zine \'n(y)üz-, mag-ə-, zēn\ *n* : a usu. weekly magazine devoted chiefly to summarizing and analyzing the news

news·man \-mən, -, man\ *n* : one who gathers, reports, or comments on the news

news·pa·per \'n(y)üz-, pā-pər\ *n* : a paper that is published at regular intervals and contains news, articles of opinion, features, and advertising

news·pa·per·man \'n(y)üz-, pā-pər-, man\ *n* : one who owns or is employed by a newspaper

news·print \'n(y)üz-, print\ *n* : cheap paper made chiefly from wood pulp and used mostly for newspapers

news·reel \-, rēl\ *n* : a short motion picture portraying current events

news·stand \-, stand\ *n* : a place where newspapers and periodicals are sold

news·week·ly \-, wēk-lē\ *n* : a weekly newspaper or newsmagazine

news·wor·thy \-, wər-thē\ *adj* : sufficiently interesting to the general public to warrant reporting (as in a newspaper)

newsy \'n(y)ü-zē\ *adj* **news·i·er**; **-est** : filled with news; *esp* : CHATTY

newt \'n(y)üt\ *n* : any of various small salamanders living chiefly in the water

New Testament *n* : the second of the two chief divisions of the Bible — see BIBLE table

new·ton \'n(y)üt-ᵊn\ *n* : the unit of force in the metric system equal to the force required to impart an acceleration of one meter per second per second to a mass of one kilogram

new wave *n*, *often cap N&W* : a cinematic movement characterized by improvisation, abstraction, subjective symbolism, and often experimental photographic techniques

New World *n* : the western hemi-

sphere; *esp* : the continental landmass of No. and So. America

New Year *n* : NEW YEAR'S DAY; *also* : the first days of the year

New Year's Day *n* : January 1 observed as a legal holiday

New Zea·land·er \n(y)ü-'zē-lən-dər\ *n* : a native or inhabitant of New Zealand

¹**next** \'nekst\ *adj* : immediately preceding or following : NEAREST

²**next** *prep* : nearest or adjacent to

³**next** *adv* 1 : in the time, place, or order nearest or immediately succeeding 2 : on the first occasion to come

nex·us \'nek-səs\ *n*, *pl* **nex·us·es** \-sə-səz\ *or* **nex·us** \-səs, -, süs\ : CONNECTION, LINK

Nez Percé \'nez-'pərs, *F* nā-per-sā\ *n* : a member of an American Indian people of Idaho, Washington, and Oregon

NF *abbr* Newfoundland

NFC *abbr* National Football Conference

NFL *abbr* National Football League

Nfld *abbr* Newfoundland

NG *abbr* 1 National Guard 2 no good

ngul·trum \eŋ-'gül-trəm\ *n* — see MONEY table

ngwee \eŋ-'gwē\ *n*, *pl* **ngwee** — see *kwacha* at MONEY table

NH *abbr* New Hampshire

NHL *abbr* National Hockey League

Ni *symbol* nickel

ni·a·cin \'nī-ə-sən\ *n* : NICOTINIC ACID

nib \'nib\ *n* : POINT; *esp* : a pen point

¹**nib·ble** \'nib-əl\ *vb* **nib·bled**; **nib·bling** \-(ə-)liŋ\ : to bite gently or bit by bit

²**nibble** *n* : a small or cautious bite

nice \'nīs\ *adj* **nic·er**; **nic·est** [ME, foolish, wanton, fr. OF, fr. L *nescius* ignorant, fr. *nescire* not to know] 1 : FASTIDIOUS, DISCRIMINATING 2 : marked by delicate discrimination or treatment 3 : PLEASING, AGREEABLE; *also* : well-executed 4 : WELL-BRED ⟨~ people⟩ 5 : VIRTUOUS, RESPECTABLE — **nice·ly** *adv* — **nice·ness** *n*

nice-nel·ly \'nīs-'nel-ē\ *adj*, *often cap 2d N* 1 : PRUDISH 2 : having the nature of or containing a euphemism — **nice nelly** *n*, *often cap 2d N* — **nice–nel·ly·ism** \-, iz-əm\ *n*, *often cap 2d N*

nice·ty \'nī-sət-ē\ *n*, *pl* **-ties** 1 : a dainty, delicate, or elegant thing ⟨enjoy the *niceties* of life⟩ 2 : a fine detail ⟨*niceties* of workmanship⟩ 3 : EXACTNESS, PRECISION, ACCURACY

niche \'nich\ *n* [F] 1 : a recess (as for a statue) in a wall 2 : a place, work, or use for which a person or thing is best fitted

¹**nick** \'nik\ *n* 1 : a small notch or groove 2 : the final critical moment ⟨in the ~ of time⟩

²**nick** *vb* : NOTCH, CHIP

¹**nick·el** \'nik-əl\ *n* 1 : a hard silver-white metallic chemical element capable of a high polish and used in alloys 2 *also* **nick·le** : the U.S. 5-cent piece made of

copper and nickel; *also* : the Canadian 5-cent piece

²**nick·el** *vb* **-eled** *or* **-elled; -el·ing** *or* **-el·ling** : to plate with nickel

nick·el·ode·on \ˌnik-ə-ˈlōd-ē-ən\ *n* **1** : an early movie theater charging an admission price of five cents **2** : a coin-operated musical device

nickel silver *n* : a silver-white alloy of copper, zinc, and nickel

nick·er \ˈnik-ər\ *vb* **nick·ered; nick·er·ing** : NEIGH, WHINNY

nick·name \ˈnik-ˌnām\ *n* [ME *nekename* additional name, alter. (resulting from incorrect division of *an ekename*) of *ekename*, fr. *eke* addition + *name*] **1** : a usu. descriptive name given instead of or in addition to the one belonging to a person, place, or thing **2** : a familiar form of a proper name — **nickname** *vb*

nic·o·tine \ˈnik-ə-ˌtēn\ *n* : a poisonous substance found in tobacco and used as an insecticide

nicotinic acid *n* : an organic acid of the vitamin B complex found in plants and animals and used against pellagra

niece \ˈnēs\ *n* : a daughter of one's brother, sister, brother-in-law, or sister-in-law

nif·ty \ˈnif-tē\ *adj* **nif·ti·er; -est** : very good : very attractive

Ni·ge·ri·an \nī-ˈjir-ē-ən\ *n* : a native or inhabitant of Nigeria — **Nigerian** *adj*

Ni·ge·rois \ˌnē-zhər-ˈwä\ *n, pl* **Nigerois** : a native or inhabitant of Niger

nig·gard \ˈnig-ərd\ *n* : a stingy person : MISER — **nig·gard·li·ness** \-lē-nəs\ *n* — **nig·gard·ly** *adj or adv*

nig·gling \ˈnig-(ə-)liŋ\ *adj* **1** : PETTY **2** : bothersome in a petty way

¹**nigh** \ˈnī\ *adv* **1** : near in place, time, or relationship **2** : NEARLY, ALMOST

²**nigh** *adj* : CLOSE, NEAR

³**nigh** *prep* : NEAR

night \ˈnīt\ *n* **1** : the period between dusk and dawn **2** : the darkness of night **3** : a period of misery or unhappiness **4** : NIGHTFALL — **night** *adj*

night blindness *n* : reduced visual capacity in faint light (as at night)

night·cap \ˈnīt-ˌkap\ *n* **1** : a cloth cap worn with nightclothes **2** : a usu. alcoholic drink taken at bedtime

night·clothes \-ˌklō(th)z\ *n pl* : garments worn in bed

night·club \-ˌkləb\ *n* : a place of entertainment open at night usu. serving food and liquor and providing music for dancing

night crawler *n* : EARTHWORM; *esp* : a large earthworm found on the soil surface at night

night·dress \ˈnīt-ˌdres\ *n* : NIGHTGOWN

night·fall \-ˌfol\ *n* : the coming of night

night·gown \-ˌgaůn\ *n* : a loose garment designed for wear in bed

night·hawk \-ˌhok\ *n* : any of several birds related to and resembling the whippoorwill

night·in·gale \ˈnīt-ᵊn-ˌgāl, -iŋ-\ *n* [ME, fr. OE *nihtegale*, fr. *niht* night + *galan* to sing] : any of several Old World thrushes noted for the sweet nocturnal song of the male

night·life \ˈnīt-ˌlīf\ *n* : the activity of pleasure-seekers at night

night·ly \ˈnīt-lē\ *adj* **1** : happening, done, or produced by night or every night **2** : of or relating to the night or every night — **nightly** *adv*

night·mare \ˈnīt-ˌmar\ *n* : a frightening oppressive dream or state occurring during sleep — **nightmare** *adj* — **night·mar·ish** \-ˌmar-ish\ *adj*

night rider *n* : a member of a secret band who ride masked at night doing violence to punish or terrorize

night·shade \ˈnīt-ˌshād\ *n* : any of a large genus of woody or herbaceous plants having alternate leaves, flowers in clusters, and fruits that are berries and including poisonous forms (as belladonna) and important food plants (as potato, tomato, or eggplant)

night·shirt \-ˌshərt\ *n* : a nightgown esp. for a man or a boy

night soil *n* : human excrement collected for fertilizing the soil

night·stick \-ˌstik\ *n* : a policeman's club

night·time \-ˌtīm\ *n* : the time from dusk to dawn

night-walk·er \-ˌwo-kər\ *n* : a person who roves about at night esp. with criminal or immoral intent

ni·hil·ism \ˈnī-(h)ə-ˌliz-əm, ˈnē-\ *n* **1** : an attitude or doctrine that traditional values and beliefs are unfounded and that existence is senseless and useless **2** : ANARCHISM **3** : TERRORISM — **ni·hil·ist** \-ləst\ *n or adj* — **ni·hil·is·tic** \ˌnī-(h)ə-ˈlis-tik, ˌnē-\ *adj*

nil \ˈnil\ *n* : NOTHING, ZERO

nim·ble \ˈnim-bəl\ *adj* **nim·bler** \-b(ə-)lər\; **nim·blest** \-b(ə-)ləst\ [ME *nimel*, fr. OE *numol* holding much, fr. *niman* to take] **1** : quick and light in motion : AGILE (a ~ dancer) **2** : quick in understanding and learning : CLEVER (a ~ mind) — **nim·ble·ness** *n* — **nim·bly** \-blē\ *adv*

nim·bus \ˈnim-bəs\ *n, pl* **nim·bi** \-ˌbī, -ˌbē\ *or* **nim·bus·es** **1** : a figure (as a disk) suggesting radiant light about the head of a drawn or sculptured divinity, saint, or sovereign **2** : a rain cloud that is of uniform grayness and extends over the entire sky

nim·rod \ˈnim-ˌräd\ *n* : HUNTER

nin·com·poop \ˈnin-kəm-ˌpüp\ *n* : FOOL, SIMPLETON

nine \ˈnīn\ *n* **1** : one more than eight **2** : the 9th in a set or series **3** : something having nine units; *esp* : a baseball team — **nine** *adj or pron* — **ninth** \ˈnīnth\ *adj or adv or n*

nine days' wonder *n* : something that creates a short-lived sensation

nine·pins \ˈnīn-ˌpinz\ *n* : tenpins played without the headpin

nine·teen \ˈnīn-ˈtēn\ *n* : one more than

18 — **nineteen** *adj or pron* — **nineteenth** \-ˈtēnth\ *adj or n*

nine·ty \ˈnīnt-ē\ *n, pl* **nineties** : nine times 10 — **nine·ti·eth** \-ē-əth\ *adj or n* — **ninety** *adj or pron*

nin·ny \ˈnin-ē\ *n, pl* **ninnies** : FOOL

ni·o·bi·um \nī-ˈō-bē-əm\ *n* : a gray metallic chemical element used in alloys

¹**nip** \ˈnip\ *vb* **nipped; nip·ping 1** : to catch hold of and squeeze tightly between two surfaces, edges, or points **2** : CLIP **3** : to destroy the growth, progress, or fulfillment of ⟨nipped in the bud⟩ **4** : to injure or make numb with cold ⟨CHILL **5** : SNATCH, STEAL

²**nip** *n* **1** : a sharp stinging cold **2** : a biting or pungent flavor **3** : PINCH, BITE **4** : a small portion : BIT

³**nip** *n* : a small quantity of liquor : SIP

⁴**nip** *vb* **nipped; nip·ping** : to take liquor in nips : TIPPLE

nip and tuck \ˌnip-ən-ˈtək\ *adj or adv* : so close that the lead shifts rapidly from one contestant to another

nip·per \ˈnip-ər\ *n* **1** : one that nips **2** *pl* : PINCERS **3** : a small boy

nip·ple \ˈnip-əl\ *n* : the protuberance of a mammary gland through which milk is drawn off : TEAT; *also* : something resembling a nipple

nip·py \ˈnip-ē\ *adj* **nip·pi·er; -est 1** : PUNGENT, SHARP **2** : CHILLY

nir·va·na \nir-ˈvän-ə\ *n, often cap* [Skt *nirvāṇa*, lit., act of extinguishing, fr. *nis-* out + *vāti* it blows] **1** : the final freeing of a soul from all that enslaves it; *esp* : the supreme happiness that according to Buddhism comes when all passion, hatred, and delusion die out and the soul is released from the necessity of further purification **2** : OBLIVION; *also* : PARADISE

ni·sei \ˈnē-ˈsā\ *n, pl* **nisei** *also* **niseis** : a son or daughter of immigrant Japanese parents who is born and educated in America

ni·si \ˈnī-ˌsī\ *adj* [L, unless, fr. *ne-* not + *si* if] : taking effect at a specified time unless previously modified or voided ⟨a divorce decree ∼⟩

nit \ˈnit\ *n* : the egg of a parasitic insect (as a louse); *also* : the young insect

ni·ter \ˈnīt-ər\ *n* **1** : POTASSIUM NITRATE **2** : SODIUM NITRATE

nit-pick·ing \ˈnit-ˌpik-iŋ\ *n* : minute and usu. unjustified criticism — **nit-pick·er** \-ər\ *n*

¹**ni·trate** \ˈnī-ˌtrāt, -trət\ *n* **1** : a salt or ester of nitric acid **2** : sodium nitrate or potassium nitrate used as a fertilizer

²**ni·trate** \-ˌtrāt\ *vb* **ni·trat·ed; ni·trat·ing** : to treat or combine with nitric acid or a nitrate — **ni·tra·tion** \nī-ˈtrā-shən\ *n*

ni·tric acid \ˌnī-trik-\ *n* : a corrosive liquid acid used in making dyes, explosives, and fertilizers

ni·tri·fi·ca·tion \ˌnī-trə-fə-ˈkā-shən\ *n* : the process of nitrifying; *esp* : the oxidation (as by bacteria) of ammonium salts to nitrites and then to nitrates

ni·tri·fy \ˈnī-trə-ˌfī\ *vb* **-fied; -fy·ing 1** : to combine with nitrogen or a nitrogen compound **2** : to subject to or produce by nitrification

ni·trite \ˈnī-ˌtrīt\ *n* : a salt of nitrous acid

ni·tro \ˈnī-trō\ *n, pl* **nitros** : any of various nitrated products; *esp* : NITROGLYCERIN

ni·tro·gen \ˈnī-trə-jən\ *n* : a tasteless odorless gaseous chemical element constituting 78 percent of the atmosphere by volume — **ni·trog·e·nous** \nī-ˈträj-ə-nəs\ *adj*

ni·tro·glyc·er·in *or* **ni·tro·glyc·er·ine** \ˌnī-trə-ˈglis-(ə-)rən\ *n* : a heavy oily explosive liquid used in making dynamite and in medicine

ni·trous acid \ˌnī-trəs-\ *n* : an unstable nitrogen-containing acid known only in solution or in the form of its salts

nitrous oxide *n* : a colorless gas used esp. as an anesthetic in dentistry

nit·ty-grit·ty \ˈnit-ē-ˌgrit-ē, ˌnit-ē-ˈgrit-ē\ *n* : the actual state of things : what is ultimately essential and true

nit·wit \ˈnit-ˌwit\ *n* : a flighty stupid person

¹**nix** \ˈniks\ *n* : NOTHING

²**nix** *vb* : VETO, REJECT

³**nix** *adv* : NO

NJ *abbr* New Jersey

NL *abbr* National League

NLRB *abbr* National Labor Relations Board

NM *abbr* **1** nautical mile **2** New Mexico

N Mex *abbr* New Mexico

NNE *abbr* north-northeast

NNW *abbr* north-northwest

¹**no** \(ˈ)nō\ *adv* **1** — used to express the negative of an alternative ⟨shall we continue or ∼⟩ **2** : in no respect or degree ⟨he is ∼ better than the others⟩ **3** : not so ⟨∼, I'm not ready⟩ **4** — used with adjective to imply a meaning opposite to the positive statement ⟨in ∼ uncertain terms⟩ **5** — used to introduce a more emphatic or explicit statement ⟨has the right, ∼, the duty to continue⟩ **6** — used as an interjection to express surprise or doubt ⟨∼—you don't say⟩ **7** — used in combination with a verb to form a compound adjective ⟨no-bake pie⟩

²**no** *adj* **1** : not any; *also* : hardly any **2** : not a ⟨she's ∼ expert⟩

³**no** \ˈnō\ *n, pl* **noes** *or* **nos** \ˈnōz\ **1** : REFUSAL, DENIAL **2** : a negative vote or decision; *also, pl* : persons voting in the negative

⁴**no** *abbr* **1** north; northern **2** [L *numero*, abl. of *numerus*] number

¹**No** *or* **Noh** \ˈnō\ *n, pl* **No** *or* **Noh** : classic Japanese dance-drama having a heroic theme, a chorus, and highly stylized action, costuming, and scenery

²**No** *symbol* nobelium

No·bel·ist \nō-ˈbel-əst\ *n* : a winner of a Nobel prize

no·bel·i·um \nō-ˈbel-ē-əm\ *n* : a radioactive chemical element produced artificially

No·bel prize \(ₒ)nō-ˈbel-\ *n* : any of various annual prizes (as in peace, literature, or medicine) established by the will of Alfred Nobel for the encouragement of persons who work for the interests of humanity

no·bil·i·ty \nō-ˈbil-ət-ē\ *n* 1 : the quality or state of being noble ⟨∼ of character⟩ 2 : nobles considered as forming a class

¹no·ble \ˈnō-bəl\ *adj* **no·bler** \-b(ə-)lər\ ; **no·blest** \-b(ə-)ləst\ [ME, fr. OF, fr. L *nobilis* knowable, well known, noble, fr. *noscere* to come to know] 1 : ILLUSTRIOUS; *also* : FAMOUS, NOTABLE 2 : of high birth, rank, or station : ARISTOCRATIC 3 : EXCELLENT 4 : STATELY, IMPOSING ⟨a ∼ edifice⟩ 5 : of a magnanimous nature — **no·ble·ness** *n* — **no·bly** \-blē\ *adv*

²noble *n* : a person of noble rank or birth

no·ble·man \ˈnō-bəl-mən\ *n* : a member of the nobility : PEER

no·blesse oblige \nō-ˌbles-ə-ˈblēzh\ : the obligation of honorable, generous, and responsible behavior associated with high rank or birth

¹no·body \ˈnō-ˌbäd-ē, -bəd-ē\ *pron* : no person

²nobody *n, pl* **no·bod·ies** : a person of no influence, importance, or worth

noc·tur·nal \näk-ˈtərn-ᵊl\ *adj* 1 : of, relating to, or occurring in the night 2 : active at night ⟨a ∼ bird⟩

noc·turne \ˈnäk-ˌtərn\ *n* 1 : a dreamy pensive composition for the piano 2 : a work of art dealing with night

noc·u·ous \ˈnäk-yə-wəs\ *adj* : likely to cause injury : HARMFUL

nod \ˈnäd\ *vb* **nod·ded; nod·ding** 1 : to bend the head downward or forward (as in bowing, going to sleep, or giving assent) 2 : to move up and down ⟨tulips *nodding* in the breeze⟩ 3 : to show by a nod of the head ⟨∼ agreement⟩ 4 : to make a slip or error in a moment of abstraction — **nod** *n*

nod·dle \ˈnäd-ᵊl\ *n* : HEAD

nod·dy \ˈnäd-ē\ *n, pl* **noddies** 1 : SIMPLETON 2 : a stout-bodied tropical tern

node \ˈnōd\ *n* : a thickened, swollen, or differentiated area (as of tissue): *esp* : the part of a stem from which a leaf arises — **nod·al** \-ᵊl\ *adj*

nod·ule \ˈnäj-ül\ *n* : a small lump or swelling — **nod·u·lar** \ˈnäj-ə-lər\ *adj*

no·el \nō-ˈel\ *n* [F *noël* Christmas, carol, fr. L *natalis* birthday] 1 : a Christmas carol 2 *cap* : the Christmas season

noes *pl of* NO

no-fault \ˈnō-ˈfolt\ *adj* 1 : of, relating to, or being a motor vehicle insurance plan under which an accident victim is compensated usu. up to a stipulated limit for actual losses by his own insurance company regardless of who is responsible 2 : of, relating to, or being a divorce law according to which neither party is held responsible for the breakup of the marriage

nog·gin \ˈnäg-ən\ *n* 1 : a small mug or cup; *also* : a small quantity of drink 2 : a person's head

no-good \ˌnō-ˈgud\ *adj* : having no worth, use, or chance of success — **no-good** \ˈnō-ˌgud\ *n*

Noh *var of* NO

no-hit·ter \ˈnō-ˈhit-ər\ *n* : a baseball game or part of a game in which a pitcher allows the opposition no base hits

no-how \ˈnō-ˌhaù\ *adv* : in no manner

¹noise \ˈnoiz\ *n* [ME, fr. OF, strife, quarrel, noise, fr. L *nausea* nausea] 1 : loud, confused, or senseless shouting or outcry 2 : SOUND; *esp* : one that lacks agreeable musical quality or is noticeably unpleasant 3 : unwanted electronic signal or disturbance — **noise·less** *adj* — **noise·less·ly** *adv*

²noise *vb* **noised; nois·ing** : to spread by rumor or report ⟨the story was *noised* abroad⟩

noise·mak·er \ˈnoiz-ˌmā-kər\ *n* : one that makes noise; *esp* : a device used to make noise at parties

noise pollution *n* : environmental pollution consisting of annoying or harmful noise

noi·some \ˈnoi-səm\ *adj* 1 : HARMFUL, UNWHOLESOME 2 : offensive to the senses (as smell) : DISGUSTING

noisy \ˈnoi-zē\ *adj* **nois·i·er; -est** 1 : making loud noises 2 : full of noises : LOUD — **nois·i·ly** \ˈnoi-zə-lē\ *adv* — **nois·i·ness** \-zē-nəs\ *n*

nol·le pro·se·qui \ˌnäl-ē-ˈpräs-ə-ˌkwī\ *n* [L, to be unwilling to pursue] : an entry on the record of a legal action that the prosecutor or plaintiff will proceed no further in an action or suit or in some aspect of it

no·lo con·ten·de·re \ˌnō-lō-kən-ˈten-də-rē\ *n* [L, I do not wish to contend] : a plea in a criminal prosecution that subjects the defendant to conviction but does not admit guilt or preclude denying the charges in another proceeding

nol-pros \ˈnäl-ˈpräs\ *vb* **nol-prossed; nol-pros·ing** : to discontinue by entering a nolle prosequi

nom *abbr* nominative

no·mad \ˈnō-ˌmad\ *n* 1 : a member of a people with no fixed residence but wandering from place to place 2 : an individual who roams about aimlessly — **nomad** *adj* — **no·mad·ic** \nō-ˈmad-ik\ *adj*

no-man's-land \ˈnō-ˌmanz-ˌland\ *n* 1 : an area of unowned, unclaimed, or uninhabited land 2 : an unoccupied area between opposing troops

nom de guerre \ˌnäm-di-ˈgeər\ *n, pl* **noms de guerre** \ˌnäm(z)-di-\ [F, lit., war name] : PSEUDONYM

nom de plume \-ˈplüm\ *n, pl* **noms de**

plume \‚nӓm(z)-di-\ [F *nom* name + *de* of + *plume* pen] : PSEUDONYM

no·men·cla·ture \'nō-mən-‚klā-chər\ *n* **1** : NAME, DESIGNATION **2** : a system of names used in a science or art

nom·i·nal \'näm-ən-ᵊl\ *adj* **1** : being something in name or form only ⟨∼ head of a party⟩ **2** : TRIFLING ⟨a ∼ price⟩ — **nom·i·nal·ly** \-ē\ *adv*

nom·i·nate \'näm-ə-‚nāt\ *vb* **-nat·ed; -nat·ing** : to choose as a candidate for election, appointment, or honor — **nom·i·na·tion** \‚näm-ə-'nā-shən\ *n*

nom·i·na·tive \'näm-(ə-)nət-iv\ *adj* : of, relating to, or constituting a grammatical case marking typically the subject of a verb — **nominative** *n*

nom·i·nee \‚näm-ə-'nē\ *n* : a person nominated for an office, duty, or position

non- \(')nän, ‚nän\ *prefix* : not : reverse of : absence of

nonabrasive	nondelivery
nonabsorbent	nondemocratic
nonacademic	nondenominational
nonacceptance	nondepartmental
nonacid	nondestructive
nonactivated	nondevelopment
nonadaptive	nondiscrimination
nonaddicting	nondiscriminitory
nonadhesive	nondistinctive
nonadjacent	nondistribution
nonadjustable	nondivided
nonaggression	nondurable
nonalcoholic	noneconomic
nonappearance	noneducational
nonaromatic	nonelastic
nonathletic	nonelection
nonattendance	nonelective
nonbeliever	nonelectric
nonbelligerent	nonelectrical
nonbreakable	nonemotional
nonburnable	nonenforceable
noncancerous	nonenforcement
noncandidate	nonessential
noncellular	nonethical
nonchargeable	nonexchangeable
nonclerical	nonexempt
noncoital	nonexistence
noncombat	nonexistent
noncombustible	nonexplosive
noncommercial	nonfarm
noncommunicable	nonfatal
non-Communist	nonfattening
noncompeting	nonfederated
noncompetitive	nonferrous
noncompliance	nonfiction
noncomplying	nonfictional
nonconcurrence	nonfilamentous
nonconcurrent	nonfilterable
nonconducting	nonflammable
nonconflicting	nonflowering
nonconformance	nonfood
nonconforming	nonfreezing
nonconstructive	nonfulfillment
noncontagious	nonfunctional
noncontinuous	nongraded
noncontributing	nonhereditary
noncorroding	nonhomogeneous
noncorrosive	nonhomologous
noncrystalline	nonhuman
nondeductible	nonidentical

nonimportation	nonreligious
nonindustrial	nonrenewable
noninfectious	nonresidential
noninflammable	nonrestricted
nonintellectual	nonreturnable
nonintercourse	nonreversible
noninterference	nonruminant
nonintoxicant	nonsalable
nonintoxicating	nonscientific
nonionizing	nonscientist
nonirritating	nonseasonal
nonlegal	nonsectarian
nonlife	nonsegregated
nonlinear	nonselective
nonliterary	non-self-governing
nonliving	nonsexist
nonlogical	nonsexual
nonmagnetic	nonshrinkable
nonmalignant	nonsinkable
nonmaterial	nonskid
nonmember	nonslip
nonmembership	nonsmoker
nonmigratory	nonsmoking
nonmilitary	nonsocial
nonmoral	nonspeaking
nonmotile	nonspecialist
nonmoving	nonspecialized
nonnegotiable	nonstaining
nonobservance	nonstriated
nonoccurrence	nonstriker
nonofficial	nonsubscriber
nonoily	nonsuccess
nonorthodox	nonsurgical
nonparallel	nontaxable
nonparasitic	nonteaching
nonparticipant	nontechnical
nonparticipating	nontemporal
nonpathogenic	nontenured
nonpaying	nontheistic
nonpayment	nonthreatening
nonperformance	nontoxic
nonperishable	nontraditional
nonphysical	nontransferable
nonpoisonous	nontransparent
nonpolar	nontypical
nonpolitical	nonuniform
nonporous	nonuser
nonpregnant	nonvascular
nonproductive	nonvenomous
nonprofessional	nonviable
nonprotein	nonviolation
nonradioactive	nonvisual
nonrandom	nonvocal
nonreactive	nonvolatile
nonreciprocal	nonvoter
nonrecognition	nonvoting
nonrecoverable	nonworker
nonrecurrent	nonworking
nonrecurring	nonzero
nonrefillable	

non·age \'nän-ij, 'nō-nij\ *n* **1** : legal minority **2** : a period of youth **3** : IMMATURITY

no·na·ge·nar·i·an \‚nō-nə-jə-'ner-ē-ən, ‚nän-ə-\ *n* : a person who is in his nineties

non·aligned \‚nän-ᵊl-'īnd\ *adj* : not allied with other nations

non·book \'nän-‚buk\ *n* : a book of little literary merit which is often a compilation (as of press clippings)

¹**nonce** \'näns\ *n* : the one, particular, or present occasion or purpose ⟨for the ~⟩

²**nonce** *adj* : occurring, used, or made only once or for a special occasion ⟨a ~ word⟩

non·cha·lant \ˌnän-shə-'länt\ *adj* [F, fr. OF, fr. prp. of *nonchaloir* to disregard, fr. *non-* not + *chaloir* to concern, fr. L *calēre* to be warm] : giving an effect of unconcern or indifference — **non·cha·lance** \-'läns\ *n* — **non·cha·lant·ly** *adv*

non·com \'nän-ˌkäm\ *n* : NONCOMMISSIONED OFFICER

non·com·ba·tant \ˌnän-kəm-'bat-ᵊnt, nän-'käm-bət-ənt\ *n* : a member (as a chaplain) of the armed forces whose duties do not include fighting; *also* : CIVILIAN — **noncombatant** *adj*

non·com·mis·sioned officer \ˌnän-kəˌmish-ənd-\ *n* : a subordinate officer in the armed forces appointed from enlisted personnel

non·com·mit·tal \ˌnän-kə-'mit-ᵊl\ *adj* : indicating neither consent nor dissent

non com·pos men·tis \ˌnän-ˌkäm-pəs-'ment-əs\ *adj* : not of sound mind

non·con·duc·tor \ˌnän-kən-'dək-tər\ *n* : a substance that is a very poor conductor of heat, electricity, or sound

non·con·form·ist \-kən-'for-məst\ *n* *often cap* : a person who does not conform to an established church and esp. the Church of England 2 : a person who does not conform to a generally accepted pattern of thought or action — **non·con·for·mi·ty** \-'for-mət-ē\ *n*

non·co·op·er·a·tion \ˌnän-kō-ˌäp-ə-'rā-shən\ *n* : failure or refusal to cooperate; *esp* : refusal through civil disobedience of a people to cooperate with the government of a country

non·cred·it \(ˈ)nän-'kred-ət\ *adj* : not offering credit toward a degree

non·dairy \'nän-'de(ə)r-ē\ *adj* : containing no milk or milk products

non·de·script \ˌnän-di-'skript\ *adj* : not belonging to any particular class or kind : not easily described

non·drink·er \-'driŋ-kər\ *n* : one who abstains from alcoholic beverages

¹**none** \'nən\ *pron* 1 : not any ⟨~ of them went⟩ 2 : not one ⟨~ of the family⟩ 3 : not any such thing or person ⟨half a loaf is better than ~⟩

²**none** *adj, archaic* : not any : NO

³**none** *adv* : by no means : not at all ⟨he got there ~ too soon⟩

non·en·ti·ty \ˌnän-'ent-ət-ē\ *n* 1 : something that does not exist or exists only in the imagination 2 : one of no consequence or significance

nones \'nōnz\ *n sing or pl* 1 : the 7th day of March, May, July, or October or the 5th day of any other month in the ancient Roman calendar

none·such \'nən-ˌsəch\ *n* : one without an equal — **nonesuch** *adj*

none·the·less \ˌnən-t͟hə-'les\ *adv* : NEVERTHELESS

non-eu·clid·e·an \ˌnän-yü-'klid-ē-ən\ *adj, often cap E* : not assuming or in accordance with all the postulates of Euclid's *Elements* ⟨~ geometry⟩

non·event \'nän-i-ˌvent\ *n* 1 : an event that fails to take place or to satisfy expectations 2 : a highly promoted event of little or no consequence

non·fat \-'fat\ *adj* : lacking fat solids : having fat solids removed ⟨~ milk⟩

non·gono·coc·cal \'nän-ˌgän-ə-'käk-əl\ *adj* : not caused by the gonococcus

non·he·ro \-'hē-rō\ *n* : ANTIHERO

non·in·ter·ven·tion \ˌnän-ˌint-ər-'ven-chən\ *n* : refusal or failure to intervene (as in the affairs of another state)

non·met·al \'nän-'met-ᵊl\ *n* : a chemical element (as carbon, phosphorus, or oxygen) that lacks metallic properties — **non·me·tal·lic** \ˌnän-mə-'tal-ik\ *adj*

non·neg·a·tive \-'neg-ət-iv\ *adj* : not negative : being either positive or zero

non·ob·jec·tive \ˌnän-əb-'jek-tiv\ *adj* 1 : not objective 2 : representing no natural or actual object, figure, or scene ⟨~ art⟩

¹**non·pa·reil** \ˌnän-pə-'rel\ *adj* : having no equal : PEERLESS

²**nonpareil** *n* 1 : an individual of unequaled excellence : PARAGON 2 : a small flat disk of chocolate covered with white sugar pellets

non·par·ti·san \'nän-'pärt-ə-zən\ *adj* : not partisan; *esp* : not influenced by political party spirit or interests

non·per·son \-'pərs-ᵊn\ *n* 1 : UNPERSON 2 : a person having no social or legal status

non·plus \'nän-'pləs\ *vb* -**plussed** *also* -**plused** \-'pləst\; -**plus·sing** *also* -**plus·ing** : PUZZLE, PERPLEX

non·pre·scrip·tion \ˌnän-pri-'skrip-shən\ *adj* : available for sale legally without a doctor's prescription

non·prof·it \'nän-'präf-ət\ *adj* : not conducted or maintained for the purpose of making a profit

non·pro·lif·er·a·tion \ˌnän-prə-ˌlif-ə-'rā-shən\ *adj* : providing for the stoppage of proliferation (as of nuclear arms) ⟨a ~ treaty⟩

non·read·er \'nän-'rēd-ər\ *n* : one who does not read

non·rep·re·sen·ta·tion·al \ˌnän-ˌrep-ri-ˌzen-'tā-sh(ə)nəl\ *adj* : NONOBJECTIVE 2

non·res·i·dent \'nän-'rez-əd-ənt\ *adj* : not living in a particular place — **non·res·i·dence** \-əd-əns\ *n* — **nonresident** *n*

non·re·sis·tance \ˌnän-ri-'zis-təns\ *n* : the principles or practice of passive submission to authority even when unjust or oppressive

non·re·stric·tive \-ri-'strik-tiv\ *adj* 1 : not serving or tending to restrict 2 : not limiting the reference of the word or phrase modified ⟨a ~ clause⟩

non·rig·id \nän-'rij-əd\ *adj* : maintaining form by pressure of contained gas ⟨a ~ airship⟩

non·sched·uled \nän-'skej-üld\ *adj* : licensed to carry passengers or freight by air without a regular schedule

non·sense \'nän-,sens, -səns\ *n* **1** : foolish or meaningless words or actions **2** : things of no importance or value : TRIFLES — **non·sen·si·cal** \nän-'sen-si-kəl\ *adj* — **non·sen·si·cal·ly** \-k(ə-)lē\ *adv*

non seq *abbr* non sequitur

non se·qui·tur \nän-'sek-wət-ər\ *n* [L, it does not follow] : an inference that does not follow from the premises

non-sked \'nän-'sked\ *n* : a nonscheduled airline or transport plane

non·stan·dard \,nän-'stan-dərd\ *adj* : not standard **1** : not conforming to the usage characteristic of educated native speakers of a language

non·start·er \'nän-'stärt-ər\ *n* : one that does not start or gets off to a poor start

non·stick \-'stik\ *adj* : allowing easy removal of cooked food particles

non·stop \-'stäp\ *adj* : done or made without a stop — **nonstop** *adv*

non·sup·port \,nän-sə-'pōrt\ *n* : failure to support; *esp* : failure on the part of one under obligation to provide maintenance

non trop·po \'nän-'trō-pō\ *adv or adj* [It] : not too much so : moderately so — used as a direction in music

non-U \'nän-'yü\ *adj* : not characteristic of the upper classes

non·union \-'yü-nyən\ *adj* **1** : not belonging to a trade union ⟨~ carpenters⟩ **2** : not recognizing or favoring trade unions or their members ⟨~ employers⟩

non·us·er \-'yü-zər\ *n* : one who does not make use of something (as drugs)

non·vi·o·lence \-'nän-'vī-ə-ləns\ *n* **1** : abstention from violence as a matter of principle **2** : avoidance of violence **3** : nonviolent political demonstrations — **non·vi·o·lent** \-lənt\ *adj*

non·white \,nän-'hwīt, -'wīt\ *adj* : a person whose features and esp. skin color are different from those of Caucasians of northwestern Europe — **nonwhite** *adj*

non·wo·ven \'nän-'wō-vən\ *adj* : made of fibers held together by interlocking or bonding (as by chemical or thermal means) — **nonwoven** *n*

noo·dle \'nüd-ᵊl\ *n* : a food paste made with egg and shaped typically in ribbon form

nook \'nůk\ *n* **1** : an interior angle or corner formed usu. by two walls ⟨a chimney ~⟩ **2** : a sheltered or hidden place ⟨a shady ~⟩

noon \'nün\ *n* : the middle of the day : 12 o'clock in the daytime — **noon** *adj*

noon·day \-,dā\ *n* : NOON, MIDDAY

no one *pron* : NOBODY

noon·tide \'nün-,tīd\ *n* : NOON

noon·time \-,tīm\ *n* : NOON

noose \'nüs\ *n* : a loop with a running knot (as in a lasso) that binds closer the more it is drawn

no-par \'no-'pär\ *or* **no-par-val·ue** *adj* : having no nominal value ⟨~ stock⟩

nope \'nōp\ *adv* : NO

nor \nər, (')nór\ *conj* : and not ⟨not for you ~ for me⟩ — used esp. to introduce and negate the second member and each later member of a series of items preceded by *neither* ⟨neither here ~ there⟩

Nor *abbr* Norway; Norwegian

Nor·dic \'nórd-ik\ *adj* **1** : of or relating to the Germanic peoples of northern Europe and esp. of Scandinavia **2** : of or relating to a physical type characterized by tall stature, long head, light skin and hair, and blue eyes — **Nordic** *n*

nor·epi·neph·rine \'nor-,ep-ə-'nef-rən\ *n* [*normal* + *epinephrine*] : a nitrogen-containing compound that is the chemical means of transmission across synapses in parts of the sympathetic and central nervous systems

norm \'nórm\ *n* [L *norma*, lit., carpenter's square] : AVERAGE; *esp* : a set standard of development or achievement usu. derived from the average or median achievement of a large group

¹nor·mal \'nór-məl\ *adj* **1** : REGULAR, STANDARD, NATURAL **2** : of average intelligence; *also* : sound in mind and body — **nor·mal·cy** \-sē\ *n* — **nor·mal·i·ty** \nór-'mal-ət-ē\ *n* — **nor·mal·ly** \'nór-mə-lē\ *adv*

²normal *n* **1** : one that is normal **2** : the usual condition, level, or quantity

nor·mal·ize \'nór-mə-,līz\ *vb* **-ized; -iz·ing** : to make normal or average — **nor·mal·iza·tion** \,nór-mə-lə-'zā-shən\ *n*

normal school *n* : a usu. 2-year school for training chiefly elementary teachers

Nor·man \'nór-mən\ *n* **1** : a native or inhabitant of Normandy **2** : one of the 10th century Scandinavian conquerors of Normandy **3** : one of the Norman-French conquerors of England in 1066 — **Norman** *adj*

nor·ma·tive \'nór-mət-iv\ *adj* : of, relating to, or prescribing norms — **nor·ma·tive·ly** *adv* — **nor·ma·tive·ness** *n*

Norse \'nórs\ *n, pl* **Norse 1** *pl* : SCANDINAVIANS; *also* : NORWEGIANS **2** : NORWEGIAN; *also* : any of the western Scandinavian dialects or languages

Norse·man \-mən\ *n* : one of the ancient Scandinavians

¹north \'nórth\ *adv* : to or toward the north

²north *adj* **1** : situated toward or at the north **2** : coming from the north

³north *n* **1** : the direction to the left of one facing east **2** : the compass point directly opposite to south **3** *cap* : regions or countries north of a specified or implied point — **north·er·ly** \'nórth-**

ər-lē\ *adv or adj* — **north·ern** \-ərn\ *adj* — **North·ern·er** \-ə(r)n-ər\ *n* — **north·ern·most** \-ərn-ˌmōst\ *adj* — **north·ward** \'nȯrth-wərd\ *adv or adj* — **north·wards** \-wərdz\ *adv*

north·east \nȯrth-'ēst\ *n* **1** : the general direction between north and east **2** : the compass point midway between north and east **3** *cap* : regions or countries northeast of a specified or implied point — **northeast** *adj or adv* — **north·east·er·ly** \-ər-lē\ *adv or adj* — **north·east·ern** \-ərn\ *adj*

north·east·er \-ər\ *n* **1** : a strong northeast wind **2** : a storm with northeast winds

north·er \'nȯr-thər\ *n* **1** : a strong north wind **2** : a storm with north winds

northern lights *n pl* : AURORA BOREALIS

north pole *n, often cap N&P* : the northernmost point of the earth

North Star *n* : the star toward which the northern end of the earth's axis points

north·west \nȯrth-'west\ *n* **1** : the general direction between north and west **2** : the compass point midway between north and west **3** *cap* : regions or countries northwest of a specified or implied point — **northwest** *adj or adv* — **north·west·er·ly** \-ər-lē\ *adv or adj* — **north·west·ern** \-ərn\ *adj*

Norw *abbr* Norway; Norwegian

Nor·we·gian \nȯr-'wē-jən\ *n* **1** : a native or inhabitant of Norway **2** : the language of Norway — **Norwegian** *adj*

nos *abbr* numbers

¹**nose** \'nōz\ *n* **1** : the part of the face containing the nostrils and covering the front of the nasal cavity **2** : the organ or sense of smell **3** : something (as a point, edge, or projecting front part) that resembles a nose ⟨the ~ of a plane⟩ — **nosed** \'nōzd\ *adj*

²**nose** *vb* **nosed; nos·ing 1** : to detect by or as if by smell : SCENT **2** : to push or move with the nose **3** : to touch or rub with the nose : NUZZLE **4** : PRY **5** : to move slowly ⟨the ship *nosed* into her berth⟩

nose·bleed \-ˌblēd\ *n* : a bleeding from the nose

nose cone *n* : a protective cone constituting the forward end of a rocket or missile

nose dive *n* **1** : a downward nose-first plunge (as of an airplane) **2** : a sudden extreme drop (as in prices)

nose·gay \'nōz-ˌgā\ *n* : a small bunch of flowers : POSY

nose out *vb* : to defeat by a narrow margin

nose·piece \-ˌpēs\ *n* **1** : a fitting at the lower end of a microscope tube to which the objectives are attached **2** : the bridge of a pair of eyeglasses

no-show \'nō-'shō\ *n* : a person who reserves space (as on an airplane or at a concert) but neither uses nor cancels the reservation

nos·tal·gia \nä-'stal-jə\ *n* [NL, fr. Gk *nostos* return home + *algos* pain, grief] **1** : HOMESICKNESS **2** : a wistful yearning for something past or irrecoverable — **nos·tal·gic** \-jik\ *adj*

nos·tril \'näs-trəl\ *n* [ME *nosethirl*, fr. OE *nosthyrl*, fr. *nosu* nose + *thyrel* hole] : an external naris ins. with the adjoining nasal wall and passage

nos·trum \'näs-trəm\ *n* [L, neut. of *noster* our, ours, fr. *nos* we] : a questionable medicine or remedy

nosy *or* **nos·ey** \'nō-zē\ *adj* **nos·i·er; -est** : INQUISITIVE, PRYING

not \(')nät\ *adv* **1** — used to make negative a group of words or a word ⟨the boys are ~ here⟩ **2** — used to stand for the negative of a preceding group of words ⟨sometimes hard to see and sometimes ~⟩

no·ta be·ne \ˌnōt-ə-'bē-nē, -'ben-ē\ [L, mark well] — used to call attention to something important

no·ta·bil·i·ty \ˌnōt-ə-'bil-ət-ē\ *n, pl* **-ties 1** : the quality or state of being notable **2** : NOTABLE

¹**no·ta·ble** \'nōt-ə-bəl\ *adj* **1** : NOTEWORTHY, REMARKABLE ⟨a ~ achievement⟩ **2** : DISTINGUISHED, PROMINENT ⟨two ~ politicians made speeches⟩

²**no·ta·ble** *n* : a person of note

no·ta·bly \'nōt-ə-blē\ *adv* **1** : in a notable manner **2** : ESPECIALLY, PARTICULARLY

no·tar·i·al \nō-'ter-ē-əl\ *adj* : of, relating to, or done by a notary public

no·ta·rize \'nōt-ə-ˌrīz\ *vb* **-rized; -riz·ing** : to acknowledge or make legally authentic as a notary public

no·ta·ry public \ˌnōt-ə-rē-\ *n, pl* **notaries public** *or* **notary publics** : a public official who attests or certifies writings (as deeds) to make them legally authentic

no·ta·tion \nō-'tā-shən\ *n* **1** : ANNOTATION, NOTE **2** : the act, process, or method of representing data by marks, signs, figures, or characters; *also* : a system of symbols (as letters, numerals, or musical notes) used in such notation

¹**notch** \'näch\ *n* **1** : a V-shaped hollow in an edge or surface **2** : a narrow pass between two mountains

²**notch** *vb* **1** : to cut or make notches in **2** : to score or record by or as if by cutting a series of notches ⟨~ed 20 points for the team⟩

notch·back \'näch-ˌbak\ *n* : an automobile with a trunk whose lid forms a distinct deck

¹**note** \'nōt\ *vb* **not·ed; not·ing 1** : to notice or observe with care; *also* : to record or preserve in writing **2** : to make special mention of : REMARK

²**note** *n* **1** : a musical sound **2** : a cry, call, or sound esp. of a bird **3** : a special tone in a person's words or voice ⟨a ~ of fear⟩ **4** : a character in music used to indicate duration of a tone by its shape and pitch by its position on the staff **5** : a characteristic feature

: MOOD, QUALITY ⟨a ∼ of optimism⟩ 6
: MEMORANDUM 7 : a brief and informal record; *also* : a written or printed comment or explanation 8 : a written promise to pay a debt 9 : a piece of paper money 10 : a short informal letter 11 : a formal diplomatic or official communication 12 : DISTINCTION, REPUTATION ⟨an artist of ∼⟩ 13 : OBSERVATION, NOTICE, HEED ⟨take ∼ of the time⟩

note·book \'nōt-ˌbuk\ *n* : a book for notes or memoranda

not·ed \'nōt-əd\ *adj* : well known by reputation : EMINENT, CELEBRATED

note·wor·thy \-ˌwər-thē\ *adj* : worthy of note : REMARKABLE

¹noth·ing \'nəth-iŋ\ *pron* 1 : no thing ⟨leaves ∼ to the imagination⟩ 2 : no part 3 : one of no interest, value, or importance ⟨she's ∼ to me⟩

²nothing *adv* : not at all : in no degree

³nothing *n* 1 : something that does not exist 2 : ZERO 3 : a person or thing of little or no value or importance

⁴nothing *adj* : of no account : worthless

noth·ing·ness \-nəs\ *n* 1 : the quality or state of being nothing 2 : NONEXISTENCE; *also* : utter insignificance 3 : something insignificant or valueless

¹no·tice \'nōt-əs\ *n* 1 : WARNING, ANNOUNCEMENT 2 : notification of the termination of an agreement or contract at a specified time 3 : ATTENTION, HEED ⟨bring the matter to my ∼⟩ 4 : a written or printed announcement 5 : a short critical account or examination ⟨as of a play⟩ : REVIEW

²notice *vb* **no·ticed; no·tic·ing** 1 : to make mention of : remark on : NOTE 2 : to take notice of : OBSERVE, MARK

no·tice·able \'nōt-ə-sə-bəl\ *adj* 1 : worthy of notice 2 : capable of being or likely to be noticed — **not·tice·ably** \-blē\ *adv*

no·ti·fy \'nōt-ə-ˌfī\ *vb* **-fied; -fy·ing** 1 : to give notice of : report the occurrence of 2 : to give notice to — **no·ti·fi·ca·tion** \ˌnōt-ə-fə-'kā-shən\ *n*

no·tion \'nō-shən\ *n* 1 : IDEA, CONCEPTION ⟨have a ∼ of what he means⟩ 2 : a belief held : OPINION, VIEW 3 : WHIM, FANCY ⟨a sudden ∼ to go⟩ 4 *pl* : small useful articles ⟨as pins, needles, or thread⟩

no·tion·al \'nō-sh(ə-)nəl\ *adj* 1 : existing in the mind only : IMAGINARY, UNREAL 2 : given to foolish or fanciful moods or ideas : WHIMSICAL

no·to·ri·ous \nō-'tōr-ē-əs\ *adj* : generally known and talked of; *esp* : widely and unfavorably known — **no·to·ri·ety** \ˌnōt-ə-'rī-ət-ē\ *n* — **no·to·ri·ous·ly** \nō-'tōr-ē-əs-lē\ *adv*

¹not·with·stand·ing \ˌnät-with-'stan-diŋ, -with-\ *prep* : in spite of

²notwithstanding *adv* : NEVERTHELESS

³notwithstanding *conj* : ALTHOUGH

nou·gat \'nü-gət\ *n* [F, fr. Provençal, fr. Old Provençal *nogat*, fr. *noga* nut, fr.

L *nuc-, nux*] : a confection of nuts or fruit pieces in a sugar paste

nought \'not, 'nät\ *var of* NAUGHT

noun \'naun\ *n* : a word that is the name of a subject of discourse ⟨as a person or place⟩

nour·ish \'nər-ish\ *vb* : to cause to grow and develop ⟨as by care and feeding⟩

nour·ish·ing *adj* : giving nourishment

nour·ish·ment \'nər-ish-mənt\ *n* 1 : FOOD, NUTRIMENT 2 : the action or process of nourishing

nou·veau riche \ˌnü-ˌvō-'rēsh\ *n, pl* **nou·veaux riches** *same*\ [F] : a person newly rich : PARVENU

Nov *abbr* November

no·va \'nō-və\ *n, pl* **novas** *or* **no·vae** \-(ˌ)vē, -ˌvī\ [NL, fem. of L *novus* new] : a star that suddenly increases greatly in brightness and then within a few months or years grows dim again

¹nov·el \'näv-əl\ *adj* 1 : having no precedent : NEW 2 : STRANGE, UNUSUAL

²novel *n* : a long invented prose narrative dealing with human experience through a connected sequence of events — **nov·el·ist** \-(ə-)ləst\ *n*

nov·el·ette \ˌnäv-ə-'let\ *n* : a brief novel or long short story

nov·el·ize \'näv-ə-ˌlīz\ *vb* **-ized; -iz·ing** : to convert into the form of a novel — **nov·el·iza·tion** \ˌnäv-ə-lə-'zā-shən\ *n*

no·vel·la \nō-'vel-ə\ *n, pl* **novellas** *or* **no·vel·le** \-'vel-ē\ : NOVELETTE

nov·el·ty \'näv-əl-tē\ *n, pl* **-ties** 1 : something new or unusual : NEWNESS 2 : a small manufactured article intended mainly for personal or household adornment — usu. used in pl.

No·vem·ber \nō-'vem-bər\ *n* [ME *Novembre*, fr. OF, fr. L *November* (ninth month), fr. *novem* nine] : the 11th month of the year having 30 days

no·ve·na \nō-'vē-nə\ *n* : a Roman Catholic nine days' devotion

nov·ice \'näv-əs\ *n* 1 : a new member of a religious order who is preparing to take the vows of religion 2 : one who is inexperienced or untrained

no·vi·tiate \nō-'vish-ət\ *n* 1 : the period or state of being a novice : NOVICE 2 : a house where novices are trained

¹now \(')naù\ *adv* 1 : at the present time or moment 2 : in the time immediately before the present 3 : FORTHWITH 4 — used with the sense of present time weakened or lost ⟨as to express command, introduce an important point, or indicate a transition⟩ ⟨∼ hear this⟩ 5 : SOMETIMES ⟨∼ one and ∼ another⟩ 6 : under the present circumstances 7 : at the time referred to

²now *conj* : in view of the fact ⟨∼ that you're here, we'll start⟩

³now \'naù\ *n* : the present time or moment : PRESENT

⁴now \'naù\ *adj* 1 : of or relating to the present time ⟨the ∼ president⟩ 2 : excitingly new ⟨∼ clothes⟩ : *also* : constantly aware of what is new ⟨∼ people⟩

NOW *abbr* **1** National Organization for Women **2** negotiable order of withdrawal

now·a·days \'naů-(ə-)ˌdāz\ *adv* : at the present time

no·way \'nō-ˌwā\ *or* **no·ways** \-ˌwāz\ *adv* : NOWISE

no·where \-ˌhwe͟ər\ *adv* : not anywhere — **no·where** *n*

nowhere near *adv* : not nearly

no·wise \'nō-ˌwīz\ *adv* : in no way

nox·ious \'näk-shəs\ *adj* : harmful esp. to health or morals

noz·zle \'näz-əl\ *n* : a short tube constricted in the middle or at one end and used (as on a hose) to speed up or direct a flow of fluid

np *abbr* **1** no pagination **2** no place (of publication)

Np *symbol* neptunium

NP *abbr* **1** notary public **2** noun phrase

NS *abbr* **1** not specified **2** Nova Scotia **3** nuclear ship

NSA *abbr* National Security Agency

NSC *abbr* National Security Council

NSF *abbr* **1** National Science Foundation **2** not sufficient funds

NSW *abbr* New South Wales

NT *abbr* **1** New Testament **2** Northern Territory **3** Northwest Territories

nth \'enth\ *adj* **1** : numbered with an unspecified or indefinitely large ordinal number **2** : EXTREME, UTMOST ⟨to the ∼ degree⟩

NTP *abbr* normal temperature and

net *or* **n wt** *abbr* net weight

NU *abbr* name unknown

nu·ance \'n(y)ü-ˌäns, n(y)ü-'äns\ *n* [F] : a shade of difference : a delicate variation (as in tone or meaning)

nub \'nəb\ *n* **1** : KNOB, LUMP **2** : GIST, POINT ⟨the ∼ of the story⟩

nub·bin \'nəb-ən\ *n* **1** : something (as an ear of Indian corn) that is small for its kind, stunted, undeveloped, or imperfect **2** : a small projecting knob

nub·ble \'nəb-əl\ *n* : a small knob or lump — **nub·bly** \-(ə-)lē\ *adj*

nu·bile \'n(y)ü-bəl, -ˌbīl\ *adj* : of marriageable condition or age ⟨∼ girls⟩

nu·cle·ar \'n(y)ü-klē-ər\ *adj* **1** : of, relating to, or constituting a nucleus **2** : of, relating to, or using the atomic nucleus or energy derived from it

nu·cle·ate \'n(y)ü-klē-ˌāt\ *vb* **-at·ed; -at·ing** : to form, act as, or have a nucleus — **nu·cle·ation** \ˌn(y)ü-klē-'ā-shən\ *n*

nu·cle·ic acid \n(y)ü-ˌklē-ik-, -ˌklā-\ *n* : any of various complex organic acids (as DNA) found esp. in cell nuclei

nu·cle·on \'n(y)ü-klē-ˌän\ *n* : a proton or a neutron esp. in the atomic nucleus — **nu·cle·on·ic** \ˌn(y)ü-klē-'än-ik\ *adj*

nu·cle·us \'n(y)ü-klē-əs\ *n, pl* **nu·clei** \-klē-ˌī\ *also* **nu·cle·us·es** [NL, fr. L, kernel, dim. of *nuc-, nux* nut] **1** : a

central mass or part about which matter gathers or is collected : CORE **2** : a cell part that is characteristic of all living things except viruses, bacteria, and certain algae, that is necessary for heredity and for making proteins, that contains the chromosomes with their genes, and that is enclosed in a membrane **3** : a mass of gray matter or group of nerve cells in the central nervous system **4** : the central part of an atom that comprises nearly all of the atomic mass

nu·clide \'n(y)ü-ˌklīd\ *n* : a species of atom characterized by the constitution of its nucleus

¹**nude** \'n(y)üd\ *adj* **nud·er; nud·est** : BARE, NAKED, UNCLOTHED — **nu·di·ty** \'n(y)üd-ət-ē\ *n*

²**nude** *n* **1** : a nude human figure esp. as depicted in art **2** : the condition of being nude (in the ∼)

nudge \'nəj\ *vb* **nudged; nudg·ing** : to touch or push gently (as with the elbow) usu. in order to seek attention — **nudge** *n*

nud·ism \'n(y)üd-ˌiz-əm\ *n* : the practice of going nude esp. in mixed groups at specially secluded places — **nud·ist** \'n(y)üd-əst\ *n*

nu·ga·to·ry \'n(y)ü-gə-ˌtōr-ē\ *adj* **1** : INCONSEQUENTIAL, WORTHLESS **2** : having no force : INOPERATIVE

nug·get \'nəg-ət\ *n* : a lump of precious metal (as gold)

nui·sance \'n(y)üs-°ns\ *n* : an annoying or troublesome person or thing

nuisance tax *n* : an excise tax collected in small amounts directly from the consumer

null \'nəl\ *adj* **1** : having no legal or binding force : INVALID, VOID **2** : amounting to nothing **2** : INSIGNIFICANT — **nul·li·ty** \'nəl-ət-ē\ *n*

null and void *adj* : having no force, binding power, or validity

nul·li·fy \'nəl-ə-ˌfī\ *vb* **-fied; -fy·ing** : to make null or valueless; *also* : ANNUL — **nul·li·fi·ca·tion** \ˌnəl-ə-fə-'kā-shən\ *n*

num *abbr* numeral

Num *or* **Numb** *abbr* Numbers

numb \'nəm\ *adj* : lacking sensation or emotion : BENUMBED — **numb** *vb* — **numb·ly** *adv* — **numb·ness** *n*

¹**num·ber** \'nəm-bər\ *n* **1** : the total of individuals or units taken together **2** : a group or aggregate not specif. enumerated ⟨a small ∼ of tickets remain unsold⟩ **3** : the possibility of being counted ⟨the sands of the desert are without ∼⟩ **4** : a distinction of word form to denote reference to one or more than one **5** : a unit belonging to a mathematical system and subject to its laws; *also, pl* : ARITHMETIC **6** : a symbol used to represent a mathematical number; *also* : such a number used to identify or designate ⟨a phone ∼⟩ **7** : one in a series ⟨the best ∼ on the program⟩

²**number** vb **num·bered; num·ber·ing** \-b(ə-)riŋ\ 1 : COUNT, ENUMERATE 2 : to include with or be one of a group 3 : to restrict to a small or definite number 4 : to assign a number to 5 : to comprise in number : TOTAL

num·ber·less \-ləs\ adj : INNUMERABLE, COUNTLESS

Numbers n — see BIBLE table

nu·mer·al \'n(y)üm-(ə-)rəl\ n : a word or symbol representing a number — numeral adj

nu·mer·ate \'n(y)ü-mə-ˌrāt\ vb -at·ed; -at·ing : ENUMERATE

nu·mer·a·tor \'n(y)ü-mə-ˌrāt-ər\ n : the part of a fraction above the line

nu·mer·ic \n(y)u̇-'mer-ik\ adj : NUMERICAL; esp : denoting a number or a system of numbers

nu·mer·i·cal \n(y)u̇-'mer-i-kəl\ adj 1 : of or relating to numbers 2 : denoting a number or expressed in numbers — **nu·mer·i·cal·ly** \-k(ə-)lē\ adv

nu·mer·ol·o·gy \ˌn(y)ü-mə-'räl-ə-jē\ n : the study of the occult significance of numbers — **nu·mer·ol·o·gist** \-jəst\ n

nu·mer·ous \'n(y)üm-(ə-)rəs\ adj : consisting of, including, or relating to a great number : MANY

nu·mis·mat·ics \ˌn(y)ü-məz-'mat-iks\ n : the study or collection of monetary objects — **nu·mis·mat·ic** \-ik\ adj — **nu·mis·ma·tist** \n(y)ü-'miz-mət-əst\ n

num·skull \'nəm-ˌskəl\ n : a stupid person : DUNCE

nun \'nən\ n : a woman belonging to a religious order; esp : one under solemn vows of poverty, chastity, and obedience

nun·cio \'nən-sē-ˌō, 'nən-\ n, pl -ci·os [It, fr. L nuntius messenger] : a permanent high-ranking papal representative to a civil government

nun·nery \'nən-ə-rē\ n, pl -ner·ies : a convent of nuns

¹**nup·tial** \'nəp-shəl\ adj : of or relating to marriage or a wedding

²**nuptial** n : MARRIAGE, WEDDING — usu. used in pl.

¹**nurse** \'nərs\ n [ME, fr. OF nurice, fr. LL nutricia, fr. L, fem. of nutricius nourishing] 1 : a girl or woman employed to take care of children 2 : a person trained to care for sick people

²**nurse** vb **nursed; nurs·ing** 1 : SUCKLE 2 : to take charge of and watch over 3 : TEND (~ an invalid) 4 : to treat with special care (~ a headache) 5 : to hold in one's mind or consideration (~ a grudge) 6 : to act or serve as a nurse

nurse·maid \-ˌmād\ n : a girl or woman employed to look after children

nurs·ery \'nərs-(ə-)rē\ n, pl -er·ies 1 : a room for children 2 : a place where children are temporarily cared for in their parents' absence 3 : a place where young plants are grown usu. for transplanting

nurs·ery·man \-mən\ n : a man who keeps or works in a plant nursery

nursery school n : a school for children under kindergarten age

nursing home n : a private establishment where care is provided for persons (as the chronically ill) who are unable to care for themselves

nurs·ling \'nərs-liŋ\ n 1 : one that is solicitously cared for 2 : a nursing child

¹**nur·ture** \'nər-chər\ n 1 : TRAINING, UPBRINGING; also : the influences that modify the expression of an individual's heredity 2 : FOOD, NOURISHMENT

²**nurture** vb **nur·tured; nur·tur·ing** 1 : to care for : FEED, NOURISH 2 : EDUCATE, TRAIN 3 : FOSTER

nut \'nət\ n 1 : a dry fruit or seed with a hard shell and a firm inner kernel; also : its kernel 2 : a metal block with a hole through it that is fastened to a bolt or screw by means of a screw thread within the hole 3 : the ridge on the upper end of the fingerboard in a stringed musical instrument over which the strings pass 4 : a foolish, eccentric, or crazy person 5 : ENTHUSIAST

nut·crack·er \-ˌkrak-ər\ n : an instrument for cracking nuts

nut·hatch \'nət-ˌhach\ n [ME note-hache, fr. note nut + hache ax, fr. OF, battle-ax] : any of various small birds that creep on tree trunks in search of food and resemble titmice

nut·meg \'nət-ˌmeg, -ˌmäg\ n [ME notemuge, deriv. of Old Provençal noz muscada, fr. noz nut (fr. L nuc-nux) + muscada, fem. of musky] : the nutlike aromatic seed of a tropical tree that is ground for use as a spice; also : this spice

nut·pick \'nət-ˌpik\ n : a small sharp-pointed table implement for extracting the kernels from nuts

nu·tria \'n(y)ü-trē-ə\ n [Sp] 1 : the durable usu. light brown fur of a nutria 2 : a So. American aquatic rodent with webbed feet and dorsal mammary glands

¹**nu·tri·ent** \'n(y)ü-trē-ənt\ adj : NOURISHING

²**nutrient** n : a nutritive substance or ingredient

nu·tri·ment \-trə-mənt\ n : NUTRIENT

nu·tri·tion \n(y)u̇-'trish-ən\ n : the act or process of nourishing; esp : the processes by which an individual takes in and utilizes food material — **nu·tri·tion·al** \-'trish-(ə-)nəl\ adj — **nu·tri·tious** \-'trish-əs\ adj — **nu·tri·tive** \'n(y)ü-trət-iv\ adj

nuts \'nəts\ adj 1 : ENTHUSIASTIC, KEEN 2 : CRAZY, DEMENTED

nut·shell \'nət-ˌshel\ n : the shell of a nut — **in a nutshell** : in a few words (that's the story in a nutshell)

nut·ty \'nət-ē\ adj **nut·ti·er; -est** 1 : containing or suggesting nuts (a ~ flavor) 2 : mentally unbalanced

nuz·zle \'nəz-əl\ vb **nuz·zled; nuz·zling** \-(ə-)liŋ\ 1 : to root around, push, or

touch with or as if with the nose **2**
: NESTLE, SNUGGLE

NV *abbr* Nevada

NW *abbr* northwest

NWT *abbr* Northwest Territories

NY *abbr* New York

NYC *abbr* New York City

ny·lon \'nī-,län\ *n* **1** : any of numerous strong tough elastic synthetic materials used esp. in textiles and plastics **2** *pl* : stockings made of nylon

nymph \'nimf\ *n* **1** : any of the lesser goddesses in ancient mythology represented as maidens living in the mountains, forests, meadows, and waters **2** : an immature insect; *esp* : one that resembles the adult but is smaller and less differentiated and usu. lacks wings

nym·pho·ma·nia \,nim-fə-¹mā-nē-ə, -nyə\ *n* : excessive sexual desire by a female — **nym·pho·ma·ni·ac** \-nē-,ak\ *n or adj*

NZ *abbr* New Zealand

O

¹o \'ō\ *n, pl* **o's** *or* **os** \'ōz\ *often cap* : the 15th letter of the English alphabet

²o *abbr, often cap* **1** ocean **2** Ohio **3** ohm

¹O \'ō\ *var of* OH

²O *symbol* oxygen

o/a *abbr* on or about

oaf \'ōf\ *n* : a stupid or awkward person — **oaf·ish** \'ō-fish\ *adj*

oak \'ōk\ *n, pl* **oaks** *or* **oak** : any of various trees or shrubs related to the beech and chestnut and having a rounded thin-shelled nut surrounded at the base by a hardened cup; *also* : the usu. tough hard durable wood of an oak — **oak·en** \'ō-kən\ *adj*

oa·kum \'ō-kəm\ *n* : loosely twisted hemp or jute fiber impregnated with tar and used esp. in caulking ships

oar \'ōr\ *n* : a long pole with a broad blade at one end used for propelling or steering a boat

oar·lock \-,läk\ *n* : a U-shaped device for holding an oar in place

oars·man \'ōrz-mən\ *n* : one who rows esp. in a racing crew

OAS *abbr* Organization of American States

oa·sis \ō-¹ā-səs\ *n, pl* **oa·ses** \-,sēz\ : a fertile or green area in an arid region

oat \'ōt\ *n* : a cereal grass widely grown for its edible seed; *also* : this seed — **oat·en** \-³n\ *adj*

oat·cake \'ōt-,kāk\ *n* : a thin flat oatmeal cake

oath \'ōth\ *n, pl* **oaths** \'ō̲t̲h̲z̲, 'ōths\ **1** : a solemn appeal to God to witness to the truth of a statement or the sacredness of a promise **2** : an irreverent or careless use of a sacred name

oat·meal \'ōt-,mēl\ *n* **1** : meal made from oats **2** : porridge made from ground or rolled oats

Ob *or* **Obad** *abbr* Obadiah

Oba·di·ah \,ō-bə-¹dī-əh\ *n* — see BIBLE table

ob·bli·ga·to \,äb-lə-¹gät-ō\ *n, pl* **-tos** *also* **-ti** \-¹gät-ē\ [It] : an accompanying part usu. played by a solo instrument

ob·du·rate \'äb-d(y)ə-rət\ *adj* : stubbornly resistant : UNYIELDING **syn** inflexible, adamant, rigid, uncompromising — **ob·du·ra·cy** \-rə-sē\ *n*

obe·di·ent \ō-¹bēd-ē-ənt\ *adj* : submissive to the restraint or command of authority **syn** docile, tractable, amenable, biddable — **obe·di·ence** \-əns\ *n* — **obe·di·ent·ly** *adv*

obei·sance \ō-¹bās-əns, -¹bēs-\ *n* : a bow made to show respect or submission; *also* : DEFERENCE, HOMAGE

obe·lisk \'äb-ə-,lisk\ *n* [MF *obelisque*, fr. L *obeliscus*, fr. Gk *obeliskos*, fr. dim. of *obelos* spit, pointed pillar] : a 4-sided pillar that tapers toward the top and ends in a pyramid

obese \ō-¹bēs\ *adj* [L *obesus*, fr. pp. of *obedere* to eat up, fr. *ob-* against + *edere* to eat] : excessively fat — **obe·si·ty** \-¹bē-sət-ē\ *n*

obey \ō-¹bā\ *vb* **obeyed; obey·ing 1** : to follow the commands or guidance of : behave obediently **2** : to comply with (~ orders)

ob·fus·cate \'äb-fə-,skāt\ *vb* **-cat·ed; -cat·ing 1** : to make dark or obscure **2** : CONFUSE — **ob·fus·ca·tion** \,äb-fəs-¹kā-shən\ *n*

obi \'ō-bē\ *n* : a broad sash worn with a Japanese kimono

obit \'ō-¹bit, 'ō-bət\ *n* : OBITUARY

obi·ter dic·tum \,ō-bət-ər-¹dik-təm\ *n, pl* **obiter dic·ta** \-tə\ [LL, lit., something said in passing] : an incidental remark or observation

obit·u·ary \ə-¹bich-ə-,wer-ē\ *n, pl* **-ar·ies** : a notice of a person's death usu. with a short biographical account

obj *abbr* object; objective

¹ob·ject \'äb-jikt\ *n* **1** : something that may be seen or felt; *also* : something that may be perceived or examined mentally **2** : something that arouses an emotional response (as of affection or pity) **3** : AIM, PURPOSE **4** : a word or word group denoting that on or toward which the action of a verb is directed; *also* : a noun or noun equivalent in a prepositional phrase

²ob·ject \əb-¹jekt\ *vb* **1** : to offer in opposition **2** : to oppose something; *also* : DISAPPROVE **syn** protest, remonstrate, expostulate — **ob·jec·tor** \-¹jek-tər\ *n*

ob·jec·ti·fy \əb-¹jek-tə-,fī\ *vb* **-fied; -fy·ing** : to make objective

ob·jec·tion \əb-¹jek-shən\ *n* **1** : the act of objecting **2** : a reason for or a feeling of disapproval

ob·jec·tion·able \əb-¹jek-sh(ə-)nə-bəl\

adj : UNDESIRABLE, OFFENSIVE — **ob·jec·tion·ably** \-blē\ *adv*

¹**ob·jec·tive** \əb-'jek-tiv\ *adj* 1 : of or relating to an object or end 2 : existing outside and independent of the mind 3 : of, relating to, or constituting a grammatical case marking typically the object of a verb or preposition 4 : treating or dealing with facts without distortion by personal feelings or prejudices — **ob·jec·tive·ly** *adv* — **ob·jec·tive·ness** *n* — **ob·jec·tiv·i·ty** \,äb-jek-'tiv-ət-ē\ *n*

²**objective** *n* 1 : the lens (as in a microscope) nearest the object and forming an image of it 2 : an aim, goal, or end of action

ob·jet d'art \,ôb-,zhā-'där\ *n, pl* **ob·jets d'art** *same*\ [F] : an article of artistic worth; *also* : CURIO

ob·jet trou·vé \'ôb-,zhā-trü-'vā\ *n, pl* **objets trouvés** *same*\ [F, lit., found object] : a found natural object (as a piece of driftwood) held to have aesthetic value; *also* : an artifact not orig. intended as art but displayed as a work of art

ob·jur·gate \'äb-jər-,gāt\ *vb* **-gat·ed; -gat·ing** : to denounce harshly — **ob·jur·ga·tion** \,äb-jər-'gā-shən\ *n*

obl *abbr* 1 oblique 2 oblong

ob·late \äb-'lāt\ *adj* : flattened or depressed at the poles (an ~ spheroid)

ob·la·tion \ə-'blā-shən\ *n* : a religious offering

ob·li·gate \'äb-lə-,gāt\ *vb* **-gat·ed; -gat·ing** : to bind legally or morally; *also* : to bind by a favor

ob·li·ga·tion \,äb-lə-'gā-shən\ *n* 1 : an act of obligating oneself to a course of action 2 : something (as a promise or a contract) that binds one to a course of action 3 : INDEBTEDNESS; *also* : LIABILITY 4 : DUTY — **oblig·a·to·ry** \ə-'blig-ə-,tōr-ē, 'äb-li-gə-\ *adj*

oblige \ə-'blīj\ *vb* **obliged; oblig·ing** 1 : FORCE, COMPEL 2 : to bind by a favor; *also* : to do a favor for or do something as a favor

oblig·ing \ə-'blī-jiŋ\ *adj* : willing to do favors — **oblig·ing·ly** *adv*

oblique \ō-'blēk *also* ō-'blīk\ *adj* 1 : neither perpendicular nor parallel : SLANTING 2 : not straightforward : INDIRECT — **oblique·ly** *adv* — **oblique·ness** *n* — **obliq·ui·ty** \-'blik-wət-ē\ *n*

oblit·er·ate \ə-'blit-ə-,rāt\ *vb* **-at·ed; -at·ing** [L *oblitterare,* fr. *ob* in the way of + *littera* letter] 1 : to make undecipherable by wiping out or covering over 2 : to remove from recognition or memory 3 : CANCEL — **oblit·er·a·tion** \-,blit-ə-'rā-shən\ *n*

obliv·i·on \ə-'bliv-ē-ən\ *n* 1 : the condition of being oblivious 2 : the condition or state of being forgotten

obliv·i·ous \-ē-əs\ *adj* 1 : lacking memory or mindful attention 2 : UNAWARE — **obliv·i·ous·ly** *adv* — **obliv·i·ous·ness** *n*

ob·long \'äb-,lȯŋ\ *adj* : deviating from a square, circular, or spherical form by elongation in one dimension ⟨the ~ fruit of a lemon tree⟩ — **oblong** *n*

ob·lo·quy \'äb-lə-kwē\ *n, pl* **-quies** 1 : strongly condemnatory utterance or language 2 : bad repute : DISGRACE syn dishonor, shame, infamy, disrepute, ignominy

ob·nox·ious \äb-'näk-shəs, əb-\ *adj* : REPUGNANT, OFFENSIVE — **ob·nox·ious·ly** *adv* — **ob·nox·ious·ness** *n*

oboe \'ō-bō\ *n* [It, fr. F *hautbois,* fr. *haut* high + *bois* wood] : a woodwind instrument shaped like a slender conical tube with holes and keys and a reed mouthpiece — **obo·ist** \'ō-bō-əst\ *n*

ob·scene \äb-'sēn, əb-\ *adj* 1 : REPULSIVE 2 : deeply offensive to morality or decency; *esp* : designed to incite to lust or depravity syn gross, vulgar, coarse, crude, indecent — **ob·scene·ly** *adv* — **ob·scen·i·ty** \-'sen-ət-ē\ *n*

ob·scu·ran·tism \äb-'skyur-ən-,tiz-əm, ,äb-skyù-'ran-\ *n* 1 : opposition to the spread of knowledge 2 : deliberate vagueness or abstruseness — **ob·scu·ran·tist** \-ən-təst, -'rant-əst\ *n or adj*

¹**ob·scure** \äb-'skyur, əb-\ *adj* 1 : DIM, GLOOMY 2 : not readily understood : VAGUE 3 : REMOTE; *also* : HUMBLE — **ob·scure·ly** *adv* — **ob·scu·ri·ty** \-'skyùr-ət-ē\ *n*

²**obscure** *vb* **ob·scured; ob·scur·ing** 1 : to make dark, dim, or indistinct 2 : to conceal or hide by or as if by covering

ob·se·qui·ous \əb-'sē-kwē-əs\ *adj* : humbly or excessively attentive (as to a person in authority) : FAWNING, SYCOPHANTIC — **ob·se·qui·ous·ly** *adv* — **ob·se·qui·ous·ness** *n*

ob·se·quy \'äb-sə-kwē\ *n, pl* **-quies** : a funeral or burial rite — usu. used in pl.

ob·serv·able \əb-'zər-və-bəl\ *adj* 1 : necessarily or customarily observed 2 : NOTICEABLE

ob·ser·vance \əb-'zər-vəns\ *n* 1 : a customary practice or ceremony 2 : an act or instance of following a custom, rule, or law 3 : OBSERVATION

ob·ser·vant \-vənt\ *adj* 1 : WATCHFUL ⟨~ spectators⟩ 2 : KEEN, PERCEPTIVE 3 : MINDFUL ⟨~ of the amenities⟩

ob·ser·va·tion \,äb-sər-'vā-shən, -zər-\ *n* 1 : an act or the power of observing 2 : the gathering of information (as for scientific studies) by noting facts or occurrences 3 : *also* : a conclusion drawn from observing; *also* : REMARK, STATEMENT 4 : the fact of being observed

ob·ser·va·to·ry \əb-'zər-və-,tōr-ē\ *n, pl* **-ries** : a place or institution equipped for observation of natural phenomena (as in astronomy)

ob·serve \əb-'zərv\ *vb* **ob·served; ob·serv·ing** 1 : to conform one's action or practice to 2 : CELEBRATE 3 : to make a scientific observation of 4 : to see or sense esp. through careful attention 5 : to come to realize esp. through consideration of noted facts **6** : REMARK — **ob·serv·er** *n*

ob·sess \əb-'ses\ *vb* : to preoccupy intensely or abnormally

ob·ses·sion \äb-'sesh-ən, əb-\ *n* : a persistent disturbing preoccupation with an idea or feeling; *also* : an emotion or idea causing such a preoccupation — **ob·ses·sive** \-'ses-iv\ *adj or n* — **ob·ses·sive·ly** *adv*

ob·sid·i·an \əb-'sid-ē-ən\ *n* : a dark natural glass formed by the cooling of molten lava

ob·so·les·cent \,äb-sə-'les-ᵊnt\ *adj* : going out of use : becoming obsolete — **ob·so·les·cence** \-ᵊns\ *n*

ob·so·lete \,äb-sə-'lēt, 'äb-sə-,lēt\ *adj* : no longer in use; *also* : OLD-FASHIONED **syn** extinct, outworn, passé, superseded

ob·sta·cle \'äb-sti-kəl\ *n* : something that stands in the way or opposes

ob·stet·rics \əb-'stet-riks\ *n sing or pl* : a branch of medicine that deals with childbirth — **ob·stet·ric** \-rik\ *or* **ob·stet·ri·cal** \-ri-kəl\ *adj* — **ob·ste·tri·cian** \,äb-stə-'trish-ən\ *n*

ob·sti·nate \'äb-stə-nət\ *adj* : fixed and unyielding (as in an opinion or course) despite reason or persuasion : STUBBORN — **ob·sti·na·cy** \-nə-sē\ *n* — **ob·sti·nate·ly** *adv*

ob·strep·er·ous \əb-'strep-(ə-)rəs\ *adj* **1** : uncontrollably noisy **2** : stubbornly resistant to control : UNRULY — **ob·strep·er·ous·ness** *n*

ob·struct \əb-'strəkt\ *vb* **1** : to block by an obstacle **2** : to impede the passage, action, or operation of **3** : to shut off from sight — **ob·struc·tive** \-'strək-tiv\ *adj* — **ob·struc·tor** \-tər\ *n*

ob·struc·tion \əb-'strək-shən\ *n* **1** : an act of obstructing : the state of being obstructed **2** : something that obstructs : HINDRANCE

ob·struc·tion·ist \-sh(ə-)nəst\ *n* : a person who hinders progress or business esp. in a legislative body — **ob·struc·tion·ism** \-shə-,niz-əm\ *n*

ob·tain \əb-'tān\ *vb* **1** : to gain or attain usu. by planning or effort **2** : to be generally recognized or established **syn** procure, secure, win, earn, acquire — **ob·tain·able** *adj*

ob·trude \əb-'trüd\ *vb* **ob·trud·ed; ob·trud·ing 1** : to thrust out **2** : to thrust forward without warrant or request **3** : INTRUDE — **ob·tru·sion** \-'trü-zhən\ *n* — **ob·tru·sive** \-'trü-siv\ *adj* — **ob·tru·sive·ly** *adv* — **ob·tru·sive·ness** *n*

ob·tuse \äb-'t(y)üs, əb-\ *adj* **ob·tus·er; -est 1** : not sharp or quick of wit **2** : exceeding 90 degrees but less than 180 degrees (~ angle) **3** : not pointed or acute : BLUNT — **ob·tuse·ly** *adv* — **ob·tuse·ness** *n*

obv *abbr* obverse

¹**ob·verse** \'äb-,vərs, 'äb-,vərs\ *adj* **1** : facing the observer or opponent **2** : having the base narrower than the top **3** : being a counterpart or complement — **ob·verse·ly** *adv*

²**ob·verse** \'äb-,vərs, äb-'vərs\ *n* **1** : the side (as of a coin) bearing the principal design and lettering **2** : a front or principal surface **3** : a similar but contrasting element or condition

ob·vi·ate \'äb-vē-,āt\ *vb* **-at·ed; -at·ing** : to anticipate and prevent (as a situation) or make unnecessary (as an action) **syn** prevent, avert, forestall, forfend, preclude — **ob·vi·a·tion** \,äb-vē-'ā-shən\ *n*

ob·vi·ous \'äb-vē-əs\ *adj* [L *obvius*, fr. *obviam* in the way, fr. *ob* in the way of + *viam*, acc. of *via* way] : easily found, seen, or understood : PLAIN **syn** evident, manifest, patent, clear — **ob·vi·ous·ly** *adv* — **ob·vi·ous·ness** *n*

OC *abbr* officer candidate

oc·a·ri·na \,äk-ə-'rē-nə\ *n* [It, fr. *oca* goose, fr. LL *auca*, deriv. of L *avis* bird] : a simple wind instrument with holes that may be opened or closed by the finger to vary the pitch

occas *abbr* occasionally

¹**oc·ca·sion** \ə-'kā-zhən\ *n* **1** : a favorable opportunity **2** : a direct or indirect cause **3** : the time of an event **4** : EXIGENCY **5** *pl* : AFFAIRS, BUSINESS **6** : a special event : CELEBRATION

²**occasion** *vb* **-sioned; -sion·ing** \-'käzh-(ə-)niŋ\ : CAUSE

oc·ca·sion·al \ə-'kāzh-(ə-)nəl\ *adj* **1** : happening or met with now and then (~ references to the war) **2** : used or designed for a special occasion (~ verse) **syn** infrequent, rare, sporadic — **oc·ca·sion·al·ly** \-ē\ *adv*

oc·ci·den·tal \,äk-sə-'dent-ᵊl\ *adj, often cap* [fr. *Occident* West, fr. ME, fr. L *occident-, occidens,* fr. prp. of *occidere* to fall, set (of the sun)] : WESTERN — **Occidental** *n*

oc·clude \ə-'klüd\ *vb* **oc·clud·ed; oc·clud·ing 1** : OBSTRUCT **2** : to shut in or out **3** : to come together with opposing surfaces in contact — **oc·clu·sion** \-'klü-zhən\ *n* — **oc·clu·sive** \-'klü-siv\ *adj*

¹**oc·cult** \ə-'kəlt\ *adj* **1** : not revealed : SECRET **2** : ABSTRUSE, MYSTERIOUS **3** : of or relating to supernatural agencies, their effects, or knowledge of them

²**occult** *n* : occult matters — used with *the*

oc·cult·ism \ə-'kəl-,tiz-əm\ *n* : occult theory or practice — **oc·cult·ist** \-təst\ *n*

oc·cu·pan·cy \'äk-yə-pən-sē\ *n, pl* **-cies 1** : the act of occupying : the state of being occupied **2** : an occupied building or part of a building

oc·cu·pant \-pənt\ *n* : one who occupies something; *esp* : RESIDENT

oc·cu·pa·tion \,äk-yə-'pā-shən\ *n* **1** : an activity in which one engages; *esp* : VOCATION **2** : the taking possession of property; *also* : the taking possession of an area by a foreign military force — **oc·cu·pa·tion·al** \-sh(ə-)nəl\ *adj* — **oc·cu·pa·tion·al·ly** \-ē\ *adv*

occupational therapy *n* : therapy by means of activity; *esp* : creative activity prescribed for its effect in promoting recovery or rehabilitation — **occupational therapist** *n*

oc·cu·py \'äk-yə-ˌpī\ *vb* **-pied; -py·ing** 1 : to engage the attention or energies of 2 : to fill up (an extent in space or time) 3 : to take or hold possession of 4 : to reside in as owner or tenant — **oc·cu·pi·er** \-ˌpī(-ə)r\ *n*

oc·cur \ə-'kər\ *vb* **oc·curred; oc·cur·ring** \-'kər-iŋ\ 1 : to be found or met with : APPEAR 2 : HAPPEN 3 : to come to mind

oc·cur·rence \ə-'kər-əns\ *n* 1 : something that takes place 2 : the action or process of occurring

ocean \'ō-shən\ *n* 1 : the whole body of salt water that covers nearly three fourths of the surface of the earth 2 : one of the large bodies of water into which the great ocean is divided — **oce·an·ic** \ˌō-shē-'an-ik\ *adj*

ocean·ar·i·um \ˌō-shə-'nar-ē-əm\ *n, pl* **-iums** *or* **-ia** \-ē-ə\ : a large marine aquarium

ocean·front \'ō-shən-ˌfrənt\ *n* : a shore area on the ocean

ocean·go·ing \-ˌgō-iŋ\ *adj* : of, relating to, or suitable for travel on the ocean

ocean·og·ra·phy \ˌō-shə-'näg-rə-fē\ *n* : a science dealing with the ocean and its phenomena — **ocean·og·ra·pher** \-fər\ *n* — **ocean·o·graph·ic** \-nə-'graf-ik\ *adj*

ocean·ol·o·gy \ˌō-shə-'näl-ə-jē\ *n* : OCEANOGRAPHY — **ocean·ol·o·gist** \-jəst\ *n*

oce·lot \'äs-ə-ˌlät, 'ō-sə-\ *n* : a medium-sized American wildcat ranging southward from Texas and having a tawny yellow or gray coat with black markings

ocher *or* **ochre** \'ō-kər\ *n* : an earthy usu. red or yellow iron ore used as a pigment; *also* : the color esp. of yellow ocher

o'clock \ə-'kläk\ *adv* : according to the clock

OCS *abbr* officer candidate school

oct *abbr* octavo

Oct *abbr* October

oc·ta·gon \'äk-tə-ˌgän\ *n* : a polygon of eight angles and eight sides — **oc·tag·o·nal** \äk-'tag-ən-ᵊl\ *adj*

oc·tane \'äk-ˌtān\ *n* 1 : any of several isomeric liquid hydrocarbons containing 8 carbon atoms per molecule 2 : OCTANE NUMBER

octane number *n* : a number that is used to measure the antiknock properties of gasoline and that increases as the likelihood of knocking decreases

oc·tave \'äk-tiv\ *n* 1 : a musical interval embracing eight degrees; *also* : a tone or note at this interval or the whole series of notes, tones, or keys within this interval 2 : a group of eight

oc·ta·vo \äk-'tā-vō, -'täv-ō\ *n, pl* **-vos** 1 : the size of a piece of paper cut eight from a sheet 2 : a book printed on octavo pages

oc·tet \äk-'tet\ *n* 1 : a musical composition for eight voices or eight instruments; *also* : the performers of such a composition 2 : a group or set of eight

Oc·to·ber \äk-'tō-bər\ *n* [ME *Octobre*, fr. OF, fr. L *October* (eighth month), fr. *octo* eight] : the 10th month of the year having 31 days

oc·to·ge·nar·i·an \ˌäk-tə-jə-'ner-ē-ən\ *n* : a person who is in his eighties

oc·to·pus \'äk-tə-pəs\ *n, pl* **-pus·es** *or* **-pi** \-ˌpī\ : any of various sea mollusks with eight long arms furnished with two rows of suckers

oc·to·syl·lab·ic \ˌäk-tə-sə-'lab-ik\ *adj* : having or composed of verses having eight syllables — **octosyllabic** *n*

¹**oc·u·lar** \'äk-yə-lər\ *adj* 1 : VISUAL 2 : of or relating to the eye or the eyesight

²**ocular** *n* : EYEPIECE

oc·u·list \'äk-yə-ləst\ *n* 1 : OPHTHALMOLOGIST 2 : OPTOMETRIST

¹**OD** \(')ō-'dē\ *n* : an overdose of a narcotic

²**OD** *abbr* 1 doctor of optometry 2 [L *oculus dexter*] right eye 3 officer of the day 4 olive drab 5 overdraft 6 overdrawn

odd \'äd\ *adj* [ME *odde*, fr. ON *oddi* point of land, triangle, odd number] 1 : being only one of a pair or set (an ~ shoe) 2 : somewhat more than the number mentioned (forty ~ years ago) 3 : not divisible by two without leaving a remainder (~ numbers) 4 : additional to what is usual (~ jobs) 5 : STRANGE (an ~ way of behaving) — **odd·ly** *adv* — **odd·ness** *n*

odd·ball \'äd-ˌbȯl\ *n* : one that is eccentric

odd·i·ty \'äd-ət-ē\ *n, pl* **-ties** 1 : one that is odd 2 : the quality or state of being odd

odd·ment \'äd-mənt\ *n* : something left over : REMNANT

odds \'ädz\ *n pl* 1 : a difference by which one thing is favored over another 2 : DISAGREEMENT — usu. used with *at* 3 : an equalizing allowance made to one believed to have a smaller chance of winning

odds and ends *n pl* : miscellaneous things or matters

odds-on \'ädz-'ȯn, -'än\ *adj* : having a better than even chance to win

ode \'ōd\ *n* : a lyric poem that expresses a noble feeling with dignity

odi·ous \'ōd-ē-əs\ *adj* : causing or deserving hatred or repugnance — **odi·ous·ly** *adv* — **odi·ous·ness** *n*

odi·um \'ōd-ē-əm\ *n* 1 : merited loathing : HATRED 2 : DISGRACE

odom·e·ter \ō-'däm-ət-ər\ *n* [F *odomètre*, fr. Gk *hodometron*, fr. *hodos* way, road + *metron* measure]

: an instrument for measuring distance traveled (as by a vehicle)

odor \'ōd-ər\ *n* **1** : the quality of something that stimulates the sense of smell; *also* : a sensation resulting from such stimulation **2** : REPUTE, ESTIMATION — **odor·less** *adj* — **odor·ous** *adj*

od·ys·sey \'äd-ə-sē\ *n, pl* **-seys** [the *Odyssey*, epic poem attributed to Homer recounting the long wanderings of Odysseus] : a long wandering marked usu. by many changes of fortune

OED *abbr* Oxford English Dictionary

oe·di·pal \'ed-ə-pəl, 'ēd-\ *adj, often cap* : of or relating to the Oedipus complex

Oe·di·pus complex \-pəs-\ *n* : the positive sexual feelings of a child toward the parent of the opposite sex that may be a source of adult personality disorder when unresolved

OEO *abbr* Office of Economic Opportunity

o'er \'ō(ə)r\ *adv or prep* : OVER

OES *abbr* Order of the Eastern Star

oe·soph·a·gus *chiefly Brit var of* ESOPHAGUS

oeu·vre \œvrᵉ\ *n, pl* **oeuvres** *same*\ : a substantial body of work constituting the lifework of a writer, an artist, or a composer

of \(')əv, 'äv\ *prep* **1** : FROM ⟨a man ∼ the West⟩ **2** : having as a significant background or character element ⟨a man ∼ noble birth⟩ ⟨a woman ∼ ability⟩ **3** : owing to ⟨died ∼ flu⟩ **4** : BY ⟨the plays ∼ Shakespeare⟩ **5** : having as component parts or material, contents, or members ⟨a house ∼ brick⟩ ⟨a glass ∼ water⟩ ⟨a pack ∼ fools⟩ **6** : belonging to or included by the front ⟨the house⟩ ⟨a time ∼ life⟩ ⟨one ∼ you⟩ ⟨the best ∼ his kind⟩ ⟨the son ∼ a doctor⟩ **7** : ABOUT ⟨tales ∼ the West⟩ **8** : connected with : OVER ⟨the king ∼ England⟩ **9** : that is : signified as ⟨the city ∼ Rome⟩ **10** — used to indicate apposition of the words it joins ⟨that fool ∼ a husband⟩ **11** : as concerns : FOR ⟨love ∼ country⟩ **12** — used to indicate the application of an adjective ⟨fond ∼ candy⟩ **13** : BEFORE ⟨five minutes ∼ ten⟩

OF *abbr* outfield

¹off \'òf\ *adv* **1** : from a place or position ⟨drove ∼ in a new car⟩; *also* : ASIDE ⟨turned ∼ into a side road⟩ **2** : at a distance in time or space ⟨stood ∼ a few yards⟩ ⟨several years ∼⟩ **3** : so as to be unattached or removed ⟨the lid blew ∼⟩ **4** : to a state of discontinuance, exhaustion, or completion ⟨shut the radio ∼⟩ **5** : away from regular work ⟨took time ∼ for lunch⟩

²off \(')òf\ *prep* **1** : away from ⟨just ∼ the highway⟩ ⟨take it ∼ the table⟩ **2** : to seaward of ⟨sail ∼ the Maine coast⟩ **3** : FROM ⟨borrowed a dollar ∼ me⟩ **4** : at the expense of ⟨lives ∼ his

sister⟩ **5** : not now engaged in ⟨∼ duty⟩ **6** : abstaining from ⟨∼ liquor⟩ **7** : below the usual level of ⟨∼ his game⟩

³off \'òf\ *adj* **1** : more removed or distant **2** : started on the way **3** : not operating **4** : not correct **5** : REMOTE, SLIGHT **6** : INFERIOR **7** : provided for ⟨well ∼⟩

⁴off *abbr* office; officer; official

of·fal \'ò-fəl\ *n* : the waste or by-product of a process; *esp* : the viscera and trimmings of a butchered animal removed in dressing

off and on *adv* : with periodic cessation

¹off·beat \'òf-ˌbēt\ *n* : the unaccented part of a musical measure

²offbeat *adj* : ECCENTRIC, UNCONVENTIONAL

off-col·or \'òf-'kəl-ər\ *or* **off-col·ored** \-ərd\ *adj* **1** : not having the right or standard color **2** : of doubtful propriety : RISQUÉ

of·fend \ə-'fend\ *vb* **1** : SIN, TRANSGRESS **2** : to cause discomfort or pain : HURT **3** : to cause dislike or vexation : ANNOY *syn* affront, insult, outrage — **of·fend·er** *n*

of·fense *or* **of·fence** \ə-'fens, *esp for 2 &* **3** 'äf-ˌens\ *n* **1** : something that outrages the senses **2** : ATTACK, ASSAULT **3** : the offensive team or members of a team playing offensive positions **4** : DISPLEASURE **5** : SIN, MISDEED **6** : an infraction of law : CRIME

¹of·fen·sive \ə-'fen-siv *esp for 1 & 2* 'äf-ˌen-\ *adj* **1** : AGGRESSIVE **2** : of or relating to an attempt to score in a game; *also* : of or relating to a team in possession of the ball or puck **3** : OBNOXIOUS **4** : INSULTING — **of·fen·sive·ly** *adv* — **of·fen·sive·ness** *n*

²offensive *n* : ATTACK

¹of·fer \'òf-ər\ *vb* **of·fered**; **of·fer·ing** \-(ə-)riŋ\ **1** : SACRIFICE **2** : to present for acceptance : TENDER; *also* : to propose as payment **3** : PROPOSE, SUGGEST; *also* : to declare one's readiness **4** : to try or begin to exert ⟨∼ resistance⟩ **5** : to place on sale — **of·fer·ing** *n*

²offer *n* **1** : PROPOSAL **2** : BID **3** : TRY

of·fer·to·ry \'òf-ə(r)-ˌtōr-ē\ *n, pl* **-ries** : the presentation of offerings at a church service; *also* : the musical accompaniment during it

off·hand \'òf-'hand\ *adv or adj* : without previous thought or preparation

off-hour \-ˌaù-(ə)r\ *n* : a period of time other than a rush hour; *also* : a period of time other than business hours

of·fice \'òf-əs\ *n* **1** : a special duty or position; *esp* : a position of authority in government ⟨run for ∼⟩ **2** : a prescribed form or service of worship; *also* : RITE **3** : an assigned or assumed duty or role **4** : a place where a business is transacted or a service is supplied

of·fice·hold·er \-ˌhōl-dər\ *n* : one holding a public office

of·fi·cer \'òf-ə-sər\ *n* **1** : one charged

with the enforcement of law **2** : one who holds an office of trust or authority **3** : one who holds a commission in the armed forces

¹**of·fi·cial** \ə-'fish-əl\ *n* : OFFICER

²**official** *adj* **1** : of or relating to an office or to officers **2** : AUTHORIZED, AUTHORITATIVE **3** : befitting or characteristic of a person in office — **of·fi·cial·ly** \-ē\ *adv*

of·fi·cial·dom \ə-'fish-əl-dəm\ *n* : officials as a class

of·fi·cial·ism \ə-'fish-ə-,liz-əm\ *n* : lack of flexibility and initiative combined with excessive adherence to regulations

of·fi·ci·ant \ə-'fish-ē-ənt\ *n* : an officiating clergyman

of·fi·ci·ate \ə-'fish-ē-,āt\ *vb* **-at·ed; -at·ing 1** : to perform a ceremony, function, or duty **2** : to act in an official capacity

of·fi·cious \ə-'fish-əs\ *adj* : volunteering one's services where they are neither asked for nor needed — **of·fi·cious·ly** *adv* — **of·fi·cious·ness** *n*

off·ing \'of-iŋ\ *n* : the near or foreseeable future

off·ish \'of-ish\ *adj* : inclined to stand aloof

off–line \'of-'līn\ *adj or adv* : not controlled directly by a computer

off of *prep* : OFF

off–print \'of-,print\ *n* : a separately printed excerpt (as from a magazine)

off–sea·son \-,sēz-ᵊn\ *n* : a time of suspended or reduced activity

¹**off·set** \-,set\ *n* **1** : a sharp bend (as in a pipe) by which one part is turned aside out of line **2** : a printing process in which an inked impression is first made on a rubber-blanketed cylinder and then transferred to the paper

²**off·set** *vb* **-set; -set·ting 1** : to place over against : BALANCE **2** : to compensate for **3** : to form an offset in (as a wall)

off·shoot \'of-,shüt\ *n* **1** : a collateral or derived branch, descendant, or member **2** : a branch of a main stem (as of a plant)

¹**off·shore** \'of-'shōr\ *adv* : at a distance from the shore

²**off·shore** \'of-,shōr\ *adj* **1** : moving away from the shore **2** : situated off the shore but within waters under a country's control

off·side \-'sīd\ *adv or adj* : illegally in advance of the ball or puck

off·spring \-,spriŋ\ *n, pl* **offspring** *also* **offsprings** : PROGENY, YOUNG

off·stage \'of-'stāj, -,stāj\ *adv or adj* : off or away from the stage

off–the–record *adj* : given or made in confidence and not for publication

off–the–shelf *adj* : available as a stock item : not specially designed or made

off–white \'of-'hwīt\ *n* : a yellowish or grayish white

off year *n* **1** : a year in which no major election is held **2** : a year of diminished activity or production

oft \'oft\ *adv* : OFTEN

of·ten \'of-(t)ən\ *adv* : many times : FREQUENTLY

of·ten·times \-,tīmz\ *or* **oft·times** \'of(t)-,tīmz\ *adv* : OFTEN

ogle \'ōg-əl\ *vb* **ogled; ogling** \-(ə-)liŋ\ : to look at in a flirtatious way — **ogle** *n* — **ogler** \-(ə-)lər\ *n*

ogre \'ō-gər\ *n* **1** : a monster of fairy tales and folklore that feeds on human beings **2** : a dreaded person or object

ogress \'ō-g(ə-)rəs\ *n* : a female ogre

oh \'ō\ *interj* **1** — used to express an emotion or in response to physical stimuli **2** — used in direct address

OH *abbr* Ohio

ohm \'ōm\ *n* : a unit of electrical resistance equal to the resistance of a circuit in which a potential difference of one volt produces a current of one ampere — **ohm·ic** \'ō-mik\ *adj*

ohm·me·ter \'ō(m)-,mēt-ər\ *n* : an instrument for indicating resistance in ohms directly

¹**oil** \'oil\ *n* [ME *oile*, fr. OF, fr. L *oleum* olive oil, fr. Gk *elaion*, fr. *elaia* olive] **1** : a fatty or greasy liquid substance obtained from plants, animals, or minerals and used for fuel, food, medicines, and manufacturing : PETROLEUM **3** : artists' colors made with oil; *also* : a painting in such colors — **oil·i·ness** \'oi-lē-nəs\ *n* — **oily** \'oi-lē\ *adj*

²**oil** *vb* : to put oil in or on — **oil·er** *n*

oil·cloth \-,kloth\ *n* : cloth treated with oil or paint and used for table and shelf coverings

oil shale *n* : a rock (as shale) from which oil can be recovered by distillation

oil·skin \'oil-,skin\ *n* **1** : an oiled waterproof cloth **2** : an oilskin raincoat **3** *pl* : an oilskin coat and trousers

oink \'oiŋk\ *n* : the natural noise of a hog — **oink** *vb*

oint·ment \'oint-mənt\ *n* : a medicinal or cosmetic preparation usu. with a fatty or greasy base for use on the skin

OJ *abbr* orange juice

Ojib·wa *or* **Ojib·way** \ō-'jib-,wä\ *n, pl* **Ojibwa** *or* **Ojibwas** *or* **Ojibway** *or* **Ojibways** : a member of an American Indian people orig. of Michigan

OJT *abbr* on-the-job training

¹**OK** *or* **okay** \ō-'kā\ *adv or adj* : all right

²**OK** *or* **okay** *vb* **OK'd** *or* **okayed; OK'-ing** *or* **okay·ing** : APPROVE, AUTHORIZE — **OK** *or* **okay** *n*

³**OK** *abbr* Oklahoma

Okla *abbr* Oklahoma

okra \'ō-krə, *Southern also* -krē\ *n* : a tall annual plant related to the hollyhocks that has edible green pods; *also* : these pods

¹**old** \'ōld\ *adj* **1** : ANCIENT; *also* : of long standing **2** *cap* : belonging to an early period (*Old* Irish) **3** : having existed for a specified period of time **4** : of or relating to a past era **5** : advanced in years **6** : showing the effects of age or

use 7 : no longer in use — **old·ish** \'ōl-dish\ adj

²**old** n : old or earlier time ⟨days of ∼⟩

old·en \'ōl-dən\ adj : of or relating to a bygone era

¹**old–fash·ioned** \'ōl(d)-'fash-ənd\ adj 1 : OUT-OF-DATE, ANTIQUATED 2 : CONSERVATIVE

²**old–fashioned** n : a cocktail usu. made with whiskey, bitters, sugar, a twist of lemon peel, and water or soda water

old guard n, often cap O&G : the conservative members of an organization

old hat adj 1 : OLD-FASHIONED 2 : STALE, TRITE

old·ie \'ōl-dē\ n : something old; esp : a popular song from the past

old–line \'ōl(d)-'līn\ adj 1 : ORIGINAL, ESTABLISHED ⟨an ∼ business⟩ 2 : adhering to old policies or practices

old maid n 1 : SPINSTER 2 : a prim fussy person — **old–maid·ish** \'ōl(d)-'mād-ish\ adj

old man n 1 : HUSBAND 2 : FATHER

old·ster \'ōl(d)-stər\ n : an old or elderly person

Old Testament n : the first of the two chief divisions of the Bible — see BIBLE table

old–time \,ōl(d)-'tīm\ adj 1 : of, relating to, or characteristic of an earlier period 2 : of long standing

old–tim·er \ōl(d)-'tī-mər\ n : VETERAN; also : OLDSTER

old–world \'ōl(d)-'wərld\ adj : having old-fashioned charm

Old World n : the eastern hemisphere; esp : continental Europe

ole·ag·i·nous \,ō-lē-'aj-ə-nəs\ adj : OILY

ole·an·der \'ō-lē-,an-dər\ n : a poisonous evergreen shrub often grown for its fragrant red or white flowers

oleo \'ō-lē-,ō\ n, pl **oleos** : MARGARINE

oleo·mar·ga·rine \,ō-lē-ō-'märj-(ə-)rən, -'märj-ə-,rēn\ n : MARGARINE

ol·fac·to·ry \äl-'fak-t(ə-)rē, ōl-\ adj : of or relating to the sense of smell

oli·gar·chy \'äl-ə-,gär-kē, 'ō-lə-\ n, pl **-chies** 1 : a government in which power is in the hands of a few 2 : a state having an oligarchy; also : the group holding power in such a state — **oli·garch** \-,gärk\ n — **oli·gar·chic** \,äl-ə-'gär-kik, ,ō-lə-\ or **oli·gar·chi·cal** \-ki-kəl\ adj

Oli·go·cene \'äl-i-gō-,sēn, ə-'lig-ə-,sēn\ adj : of, relating to, or being the epoch of the Tertiary between the Eocene and the Miocene — **Oligocene** n

olio \'ō-lē-,ō\ n, pl **oli·os** : HODGEPODGE, MEDLEY

ol·ive \'äl-iv, -əv\ n 1 : an Old World evergreen tree grown in warm regions for its fruit that is important as food and for its edible oil (**olive oil**) 2 : a dull yellow to yellowish green color

olive drab n 1 : a variable color averaging a grayish olive 2 : a wool or cotton fabric of an olive drab color; also : a uniform of this fabric

ol·iv·ine \'äl-ə-,vēn\ n : a usu. greenish mineral that is a complex silicate of magnesium and iron

Olym·pic Games \ə-'lim-pik-, ō-\ n pl : a modified revival of an ancient Greek festival held every four years and consisting of international athletic contests

om \'ōm\ n : a mantra consisting of the sound "om" used in contemplating ultimate reality

Oma·ha \'ō-mə-,hä, -,hò\ n, pl **Omaha** or **Omahas** : a member of an American Indian people of northeastern Nebraska

om·buds·man \'äm-,bùdz-mən, äm-'bùdz-\ n, pl **-men** \-mən\ 1 : a government official appointed to investigate complaints made by individuals against abuses or capricious acts of public officials 2 : one that investigates reported complaints (as from students or consumers)

om·elet or **om·elette** \'äm-(ə-)lət\ n [F omelette, alter. of MF alumelle, lit., knife blade, modif. of L lamella, dim. of lamina thin plate] : eggs beaten with milk or water, cooked without stirring until set, and folded over

omen \'ō-mən\ n : an event or phenomenon believed to be a sign or warning of a future occurrence

om·i·nous \'äm-ə-nəs\ adj : foretelling evil : THREATENING — **om·i·nous·ly** adv — **om·i·nous·ness** n

omis·sion \ō-'mish-ən\ n 1 : something neglected or left undone 2 : the act of omitting : the state of being omitted

omit \ō-'mit\ vb **omit·ted; omit·ting** 1 : to leave out or leave unmentioned 2 : to fail to perform : NEGLECT

¹**om·ni·bus** \'äm-ni-(,)bəs\ n : BUS

²**omnibus** adj : of, relating to, or providing for many things at once ⟨an ∼ bill⟩

om·nip·o·tent \äm-'nip-ət-ənt\ adj : having unlimited authority or influence : ALMIGHTY — **om·nip·o·tence** \-əns\ n — **om·nip·o·tent·ly** adv

om·ni·pres·ent \,äm-ni-'prez-ənt\ adj : present in all places at all times — **om·ni·pres·ence** \-əns\ n

om·ni·scient \äm-'nish-ənt\ adj : having infinite awareness, understanding, and insight — **om·ni·science** \-əns\ n — **om·ni·scient·ly** adv

om·ni·um–gath·er·um \,äm-nē-əm-'gath-ə-rəm\ n, pl **omnium–gatherums** : a miscellaneous collection

om·niv·o·rous \äm-'niv-(ə-)rəs\ adj : feeding on both animal and vegetable substances; also : AVID ⟨an ∼ reader⟩ — **om·niv·o·rous·ly** adv

¹**on** \(')òn, (')än\ prep 1 : in or to a position over and in contact with ⟨a book ∼ the table⟩ ⟨jumped ∼ his horse⟩ 2 : touching the surface of ⟨shadows ∼ the wall⟩ 3 : AT, TO ⟨∼ the right were the mountains⟩ 4 : IN, ABOARD ⟨went ∼ the train⟩ 5 : during or at the time of ⟨came ∼ Monday⟩ ⟨every hour ∼

the hour) **6** : through the agency of ⟨was cut ~ a tin can⟩ **7** : in a state or process of ⟨~ fire⟩ ⟨~ the wane⟩ **8** : connected with as a member or participant ⟨~ a committee⟩ ⟨~ tour⟩ **9** — used to indicate a basis, source, or standard of computation ⟨has it ~ good authority⟩ ⟨10 cents ~ the dollar⟩ **10** : with regard to ⟨a monopoly ~ wheat⟩ **11** : at or toward as an object ⟨crept up ~ her⟩ ⟨smiled ~ him⟩ **12** : ABOUT, CONCERNING ⟨a book ~ minerals⟩

²**on** \'ȯn, 'än\ *adv* **1** : in or into a position of contact with or attachment to a surface **2** : FORWARD **3** : into operation

³**on** \'ȯn, 'än\ *adj* : being in operation or in progress

ON *abbr* Ontario

¹**once** \'wəns\ *adv* **1** : one time only **2** : at any one time **3** : FORMERLY **4** : by one degree of relationship

²**once** *n* : one single time — **at once 1** : at the same time **2** : IMMEDIATELY

³**once** *adj* : FORMER

⁴**once** *conj* : AS SOON AS

once-over \-ˌō-vər\ *n* : a swift examination or survey

on·com·ing \'ȯn-ˌkəm-iŋ, 'än-\ *adj* : APPROACHING ⟨~ traffic⟩

¹**one** \'wən\ *adj* **1** : being a single unit or thing ⟨~ person went⟩ **2** : being one in particular ⟨early ~ morning⟩ **3** : being the same in kind or quality ⟨members of ~ race⟩ ; *also* : UNITED **4** : being not specified or fixed ⟨at ~ time or another⟩

²**one** *n* **1** : the number denoting unity **2** : the 1st in a set or series **3** : a single person or thing — **one·ness** \'wən-nəs\ *n*

³**one** *pron* **1** : a single member or specimen ⟨saw ~ of his friends⟩ **2** : a person in general ⟨~ never knows⟩ **3** — used in place of a first-person pronoun

Onei·da \ō-'nīd-ə\ *n, pl* **Oneida** *or* **Oneidas** : a member of an American Indian people orig. of New York

oner·ous \'än-ə-rəs, 'ō-nə-\ *adj* : imposing or constituting a burden : TROUBLESOME **syn** oppressive, exacting, burdensome, weighty

one·self \(ˌ)wən-'self, (ˌ)ȯn-\ *pron* : one's own self — usu. used reflexively or for emphasis

one-sid·ed \'wən-'sīd-əd\ *adj* **1** : having or occurring on one side only; *also* : having one side prominent or more developed **2** : UNEQUAL ⟨a ~ game⟩ **3** : PARTIAL ⟨a ~ attitude⟩

one·time \'wən-ˌtīm\ *adv* : FORMER

one-to-one \ˌwən-tə-'wən\ *adj* : pairing each element of a class uniquely with an element of another class

one up *adj* : being in a position of advantage ⟨was *one up* on the others⟩

one-way *adj* : moving, allowing movement, or functioning in only one direction ⟨~ streets⟩

on·go·ing \'ȯn-ˌgō-iŋ, 'än-\ *adj* : continuously moving forward

on·ion \'ən-yən\ *n* : a plant related to the lilies and grown for its pungent edible bulb; *also* : this bulb

on·ion·skin \-ˌskin\ *n* : a thin strong translucent paper of very light weight

on-line *adj or adv* : controlled directly by a computer ⟨~ equipment⟩

on·look·er \'ȯn-ˌlu̇k-ər, 'än-\ *n* : SPECTATOR

¹**on·ly** \'ȯn-lē\ *adj* **1** : unquestionably the best **2** : SOLE

²**only** *adv* **1** : MERELY, JUST ⟨~ $2⟩ **2** : SOLELY ⟨known ~ to me⟩ **3** : at the very least ⟨was ~ too true⟩ **4** : as a final result ⟨will ~ make you sick⟩

³**only** *conj* : except that

on·o·mato·poe·ia \ˌän-ə-ˌmat-ə-'pē-(y)ə\ *n* **1** : formation of words in imitation of natural sounds ⟨as *buzz* or *hiss*⟩ **2** : the use of words whose sound suggests the sense — **on·o·mato·poe·ic** \-'pē-ik\ *or* **on·o·mato·po·et·ic** \-ˌpō-'et-ik\ *adj* — **on·o·mato·poe·i·cal·ly** \-'pē-ə-k(ə-)lē\ *or* **on·o·mato·po·et·i·cal·ly** \-ˌpō-'et-i-k(ə-)lē\ *adv*

On·on·da·ga \ˌän-ə(n)-'dȯ-gə\ *n, pl* **-ga** *or* **-gas** : a member of an American Indian people of New York and Canada

on·rush \'ȯn-ˌrəsh, 'än-\ *n* : a rushing onward — **on·rush·ing** \-iŋ\ *adj*

on·set \-ˌset\ *n* **1** : ATTACK **2** : BEGINNING

on·shore \-ˌshȯr\ *adj* **1** : moving toward the shore **2** : situated on or near the shore — **on·shore** \-'shȯr\ *adv*

on·slaught \'ȯn-ˌslȯt, 'än-\ *n* : a fierce attack

Ont *abbr* Ontario

on·to \ˌȯn-tə, 'än-; 'ȯn-tü, 'än-\ *prep* : to a position or point on

onus \'ō-nəs\ *n* **1** : BURDEN **2** : OBLIGATION **3** : BLAME

¹**on·ward** \'ȯn-wərd, 'än-\ *also* **on·wards** \-wərdz\ *adv* : FORWARD

²**onward** *adj* : directed or moving onward : FORWARD

on·yx \'än-iks\ *n* [ME *onix,* fr. OF & L; OF, fr. L *onyx,* fr. Gk, lit., claw, nail] : a translucent chalcedony in parallel layers of different colors

oo·dles \'üd-²lz\ *n pl* : a great quantity

oo·lite \'ō-ə-ˌlīt\ *n* : a rock consisting of small round grains cemented together — **oo·lit·ic** \ˌō-ə-'lit-ik\ *adj*

¹**ooze** \'üz\ *n* **1** : a soft deposit ⟨as of mud⟩ on the bottom of a body of water **2** : soft wet ground : MUD — **oozy** \'ü-zē\ *adj*

²**ooze** *n* : something that oozes

³**ooze** *vb* **oozed; ooz·ing** **1** : to flow or leak out slowly or imperceptibly **2** : EXUDE

op *abbr* opus

OP *abbr* **1** observation post **2** out of print

opac·i·ty \ō-'pas-ət-ē\ *n, pl* **-ties 1** : the quality or state of being opaque **2**

: obscurity of meaning **3** : mental dullness **4** : an opaque spot in a normally transparent structure

opal \'ō-pəl\ *n* : a mineral with soft changeable colors that is used as a gem

opal·es·cent \,ō-pə-'les-ᵊnt\ *adj* : IRIDESCENT — **opal·es·cence** \-ᵊns\ *n*

opaque \ō-'pāk\ *adj* **1** : not allowing radiant energy and esp. light to pass through **2** : not easily understood **3** : OBTUSE — **opaque·ly** *adv* — **opaque·ness** *n*

op art \'äp-\ *n* : OPTICAL ART — **op artist** *n*

op cit *abbr* [L *opere citato*] in the work cited

ope \'ōp\ *vb* **oped; op·ing** *archaic* : OPEN

OPEC *abbr* Organization of Petroleum Exporting Countries

¹**open** \'ō-pən\ *adj* **open·er** \'ōp-(ə-)nər\ ; **open·est** \'ōp-(ə-)nəst\ **1** : not shut or shut up (an ~ door) **2** : not secret or hidden; *also* : FRANK **3** : not enclosed or covered (an ~ fire) ; *also* : not protected **4** : free to be entered or used (an ~ tournament) **5** : easy to get through or see (~ country) **6** : spread out : EXTENDED **7** : not decided (an ~ question) **8** : readily accessible and cooperative; *also* : GENEROUS **9** : having components separated by a space in writing and printing (the name *Spanish moss* is an ~ compound) **10** : ready to operate (stores are ~) **11** : free from restraints or controls (~ season) — **open·ly** *adv* — **open·ness** \-pən-nəs\ *n*

²**open** \'ō-pən\ *vb* **opened** \'ō-pənd\ ; **open·ing** \'ōp-(ə-)niŋ\ **1** : to change or move from a shut position; *also* : to make open by clearing away obstacles **2** : to make accessible **3** : to make openings in **4** : to make or become functional (~ a store) **5** : REVEAL; *also* : ENLIGHTEN **6** : BEGIN — **open·er** \'ōp-(ə-)nər\ *n*

³**open** *n* **1** : OUTDOORS **2** : a contest or tournament open to all

open–air *adj* : OUTDOOR (~ theaters)

open–hand·ed \,ō-pən-'han-dəd\ *adj* : GENEROUS

open–heart *adj* : of, relating to, or performed on a heart temporarily relieved of circulatory function and laid open for inspection and treatment

open–hearth *adj* : of, relating to, or being a process of making steel in a furnace that reflects the heat from the roof onto the material

open·ing \'ōp-(ə-)niŋ\ *n* **1** : an act or instance of making or becoming open **2** : BEGINNING **3** : something that is open **4** : OCCASION; *also* : an opportunity for employment

open–mind·ed \,ō-pən-'mīn-dəd\ *adj* : free from rigidly fixed preconceptions

open sentence *n* : a statement (as in mathematics) containing at least one blank or unknown so that when the blank is filled or a quantity substituted for the unknown the statement becomes a complete statement that is either true or false

open shop *n* : an establishment having members and nonmembers of a labor union on the payroll

open·work \'ō-pən-,wərk\ *n* : work so made as to show openings through its substance (a railing of wrought-iron ~) — **open–worked** \-,wərkt\ *adj*

¹**op·era** *pl of* OPUS

²**op·era** \'äp-(ə-)rə\ *n* : a drama set to music — **op·er·at·ic** \,äp-ə-'rat-ik\ *adj*

op·er·a·ble \'äp-(ə-)rə-bəl\ *adj* **1** : fit, possible, or desirable to use **2** : likely to result in a favorable outcome upon surgical treatment

opera glasses *n pl* : small binoculars for use in a theater

op·er·ate \'äp-ə-,rāt\ *vb* **-at·ed; -at·ing 1** : to perform work : FUNCTION **2** : to produce an effect **3** : to put or keep in operation **4** : to perform an operation — **op·er·a·tor** \-,rāt-ər\ *n*

op·er·a·tion \,äp-ə-'rā-shən\ *n* **1** : a doing or performing of a practical work **2** : an exertion of power or influence; *also* : method or manner of functioning **3** : a surgical procedure **4** : a process of deriving one mathematical expression from others according to a rule **5** : a military action or mission — **op·er·a·tion·al** \-sh(ə-)nəl\ *adj*

¹**op·er·a·tive** \'äp-(ə-)rət-iv, 'äp-ə-,rāt-\ *adj* **1** : producing an appropriate effect **2** : OPERATING (an ~ force) **3** : having to do with physical operations; *also* : WORKING (an ~ craftsman) **4** : based on or consisting of an operation

²**operative** *n* : OPERATOR; *esp* : a secret agent

op·er·et·ta \,äp-ə-'ret-ə\ *n* [It, dim. of *opera*] : a light musical-dramatic work with a romantic plot, spoken dialogue, and dancing scenes

oph·thal·mic \äf-'thal-mik, äp-\ *adj* : of, relating to, or located near the eye

oph·thal·mol·o·gy \,äf-,thal-'mäl-ə-jē, ,äp-\ *n* : a branch of medicine dealing with the structure, functions, and diseases of the eye — **oph·thal·mol·o·gist** \-jəst\ *n*

oph·thal·mo·scope \äf-'thal-mə-,skōp, äp-\ *n* : an instrument with a mirror centrally perforated for use in viewing the interior of the eye

opi·ate \'ō-pē-ət, -pē-,āt\ *n* : a preparation or derivative of opium; *also* : NARCOTIC — **opiate** *adj*

opine \ō-'pīn\ *vb* **opined; opin·ing** : to express an opinion : STATE

opin·ion \ə-'pin-yən\ *n* **1** : a belief stronger than impression and less strong than positive knowledge **2** : JUDGMENT **3** : a formal statement by an expert after careful study

opin·ion·at·ed \ə-'pin-yə-,nāt-əd\ *adj* : obstinately adhering to personal opinions

opi·um \ˈō-pē-əm\ n [ME, fr. L, fr. Gk *opion*, fr. dim. of *opos* sap] : an addictive narcotic drug that is the dried juice of a poppy

opos·sum \ə-ˈpäs-əm\ n, pl **opossums** *also* **opossum** [fr. *âpäsûm*, lit., white animal (in some American Indian language of Virginia)] : any of various American marsupial mammals; *esp* : a common omnivorous tree-dwelling animal of the eastern U.S.

opp *abbr* opposite

op·po·nent \ə-ˈpō-nənt\ n : one that opposes : ADVERSARY

op·por·tune \ˌäp-ər-ˈt(y)ün\ adj [ME, fr. MF *opportun*, fr. L *opportunus*, fr. *ob-* toward + *portus* port, harbor] : SUITABLE — **op·por·tune·ly** adv

op·por·tun·ism \ˌäp-ər-ˈt(y)ü-ˌniz-əm\ n : a taking advantage of opportunities or circumstances esp. with little regard for principles or ultimate consequences — **op·por·tun·ist** \-nəst\ n — **op·por·tun·is·tic** \-t(y)ü-ˈnis-tik\ adj

op·por·tun·i·ty \ˌäp-ər-ˈt(y)ü-nət-ē\ n, pl **-ties** 1 : a favorable combination of circumstances, time, and place 2 : a chance for advancement or progress

op·pose \ə-ˈpōz\ vb **op·posed; op·pos·ing** 1 : to place opposite or against something (as to provide resistance or contrast) 2 : to strive against : RESIST — **op·po·si·tion** \ˌäp-ə-ˈzish-ən\ n

¹**op·po·site** \ˈäp-ə-zət\ n : one that is opposed or contrary

²**opposite** adj 1 : set over against something that is at the other end or side 2 : OPPOSED, HOSTILE; *also* : CONTRARY 1 : contrarily turned or moving — **op·po·site·ly** adv — **op·po·site·ness** n

³**opposite** adv : on opposite sides

⁴**opposite** prep : across from and usu. facing ⟨the house ∼ ours⟩

op·press \ə-ˈpres\ vb 1 : to crush by abuse of power or authority 2 : to weigh down : BURDEN syn aggrieve, wrong, persecute — **op·pres·sive** \-ˈpres-iv\ adj — **op·pres·sive·ly** adv — **op·pres·sor** \-ˈpres-ər\ n

op·pres·sion \ə-ˈpresh-ən\ n 1 : unjust or cruel exercise of power or authority 2 : DEPRESSION

op·pro·bri·ous \ə-ˈprō-brē-əs\ adj : expressing or deserving opprobrium — **op·pro·bri·ous·ly** adv

op·pro·bri·um \-brē-əm\ n 1 : something that brings disgrace 2 : INFAMY

¹**opt** \ˈäpt\ vb : to make a choice

²**opt** abbr 1 optical; optician; optics 2 optional

op·tic \ˈäp-tik\ adj : of or relating to vision or the eye

op·ti·cal \ˈäp-ti-kəl\ adj 1 : relating to optics 2 : OPTIC 3 : of, relating to, or using light 4 : of or relating to optical art

optical art n : nonobjective art characterized by the use of geometric patterns often for an illusory effect

optical disc n : a disc on which information has been recorded digitally and which is read using a laser

optical fiber n : a single fiber-optic strand

op·ti·cian \äp-ˈtish-ən\ n 1 : a maker of or dealer in optical items and instruments 2 : one that grinds lenses to prescription and dispenses spectacles

op·tics \ˈäp-tiks\ n pl : a science that deals with the nature and properties of light and the effects that it undergoes and produces

op·ti·mal \ˈäp-tə-məl\ adj : most desirable or satisfactory — **op·ti·mal·ly** \-ē\ adv

op·ti·mism \ˈäp-tə-ˌmiz-əm\ n [F *optimisme*, fr. L *optimum*, n., best, fr. neut. of *optimus* best] 1 : a doctrine that this world is the best possible world 2 : an inclination to anticipate the best possible outcome of actions or events — **op·ti·mist** \-məst\ n — **op·ti·mis·tic** \ˌäp-tə-ˈmis-tik\ adj — **op·ti·mis·ti·cal·ly** \-ti-k(ə-)lē\ adv

op·ti·mum \ˈäp-tə-məm\ n, pl **-ma** \-mə\ *also* **-mums** [L] : the amount or degree of something most favorable to an end; *also* : greatest degree attained under implied or specified conditions

op·tion \ˈäp-shən\ n 1 : the power or right to choose 2 : a right to buy or sell something at a specified price during a specified period 3 : something offered for choice — **op·tion·al** \-sh(ə-)nəl\ adj

op·tom·e·try \äp-ˈtäm-ə-trē\ n : the art or profession of examining the eyes for defects of refraction and of prescribing lenses to correct these — **op·tom·e·trist** \-trəst\ n

opt out vb : to choose not to participate

op·u·lence \ˈäp-yə-ləns\ n 1 : WEALTH 2 : ABUNDANCE

op·u·lent \ˈäp-yə-lənt\ adj 1 : WEALTHY 2 : richly abundant

opus \ˈō-pəs\ n, pl **opera** \ˈō-pə-rə, ˈäp-ə-\ *also* **opus·es** \ˈō-pə-səz\ : WORK; *esp* : a musical composition

or \ər, (ˌ)ȯr\ conj — used as a function word to indicate an alternative ⟨sink ∼ swim⟩

OR abbr 1 operating room 2 Oregon

-or \ər\ n suffix : one that does a (specified) thing ⟨calculat*or*⟩ ⟨elevat*or*⟩

or·a·cle \ˈȯr-ə-kəl\ n 1 : one held to give divinely inspired answers or revelations 2 : an authoritative or wise utterance; *also* : a person of great authority or wisdom — **orac·u·lar** \ȯ-ˈrak-yə-lər\ adj

¹**oral** \ˈȯr-əl, ˈȯr-\ adj 1 : SPOKEN 2 : of or relating to the mouth 3 : of, relating to, or characterized by the first stage of psychosexual development in which libidinal gratification is derived from intake (as of food), by sucking, and later by biting 4 : relating to or characterized by personality traits of passive dependency and aggressiveness — **oral·ly** \ˈȯr-ə-lē, ˈȯr-\ adv

²**oral** *n* : an oral examination — usu. used in pl.

orang \ə-ˈraŋ\ *n* : ORANGUTAN

or·ange \ˈör-inj\ *n* 1 : a juicy citrus fruit with reddish yellow rind; *also* : the evergreen tree with fragrant white flowers that bears this fruit 2 : a color between red and yellow

or·ange·ade \ˌör-inj-ˈād\ *n* : a beverage of orange juice, sugar, and water

orange hawkweed *n* : a weedy herb related to the daisies with bright orange-red flower heads

or·ange·ry \ˈör-inj-(ə-)rē\ *n*, *pl* **-ries** : a protected place (as a greenhouse) for raising oranges in cool climates

orang·utan \ə-ˈraŋ-ə-ˌtaŋ, -ˌtan\ *n* [Malay *orang hutan*, fr. *orang* man + *hutan* forest] : a reddish brown manlike tree-living ape of Borneo and Sumatra

orate \ȯ-ˈrāt\ *vb* **orat·ed; orat·ing** : to speak in a declamatory manner

ora·tion \ə-ˈrā-shən\ *n* : an elaborate discourse delivered in a formal dignified manner

or·a·tor \ˈör-ət-ər\ *n* : one noted for skill and power as a public speaker

or·a·tor·i·cal \ˌör-ə-ˈtör-i-kəl\ *adj* : of, relating to, or characteristic of an orator or oratory

or·a·to·rio \ˌör-ə-ˈtör-ē-ˌō\ *n*, *pl* **-rios** : a lengthy choral work usu. on a scriptural subject

¹**or·a·to·ry** \ˈör-ə-ˌtör-ē\ *n*, *pl* **-ries** : a private or institutional chapel

²**oratory** *n* : the art of speaking eloquently and effectively in public **syn** rhetoric, elocution

orb \ˈörb\ *n* : a spherical body; *esp* : a celestial body (as a planet)

or·bic·u·lar \ör-ˈbik-yə-lər\ *adj* : SPHERICAL

¹**or·bit** \ˈör-bət\ *n* [L *orbita*, lit., track, rut] 1 : a path described by one body or object in its revolution about another 2 : range or sphere of activity — **or·bit·al** \-ᵊl\ *adj*

²**orbit** *vb* 1 : CIRCLE 2 : to send up and make revolve in an orbit (~ a satellite) — **or·bit·er** \-bət-ər\ *n*

orch *abbr* orchestra

or·chard \ˈör-chərd\ *n* : a place where fruit trees or nut trees are grown; *also* : the trees of such a place — **or·chard·ist** \-əst\ *n*

or·ches·tra \ˈör-kə-strə\ *n* [L, fr. Gk *orchēstra*, fr. *orcheisthai* to dance] 1 : a group of instrumentalists organized to perform ensemble music 2 : the front section of seats on the main floor of a theater — **or·ches·tral** \ör-ˈkes-trəl\ *adj*

or·ches·trate \ˈör-kə-ˌstrāt\ *vb* **-trat·ed; -trat·ing** : to compose or arrange for an orchestra — **or·ches·tra·tion** \ˌör-kə-ˈstrā-shən\ *n*

or·chid \ˈör-kəd\ *n* [irreg. from L *orchis*, fr. Gk, testicle] : any of numerous related plants having often showy flowers with three petals of which the middle one is enlarged into a lip; *also* : a flower of an orchid

ord *abbr* 1 order 2 ordnance

or·dain \ör-ˈdān\ *vb* 1 : to admit to the ministry or priesthood by the ritual of a church 2 : DECREE, ENACT; *also* : DESTINE

or·deal \ör-ˈdē(-ə)l, ˈör-ˌdē(-ə)l\ *n* : a severe trial or experience

¹**or·der** \ˈörd-ər\ *vb* **or·dered; or·der·ing** \ˈörd-(ə-)riŋ\ 1 : ARRANGE, REGULATE 2 : COMMAND 3 : to place an order

²**order** *n* 1 : a group of people formally united; *also* : a badge or medal of such a group 2 : any of the several grades of the Christian ministry; *also*, *pl* : ORDINATION 3 : a rank, class, or special group of persons or things 4 : a category of biological classification ranking above the family and below the class 5 : ARRANGEMENT, SEQUENCE; *also* : the prevailing mode of things 6 : a customary mode of procedure; *also* : the rule of law or proper authority 7 : a specific rule, regulation, or authoritative direction 8 : a style of building; *also* : an architectural column forming the unit of a style 9 : condition esp. with regard to repair 10 : a written direction to pay money or to buy or sell goods; *also* : goods bought or sold

¹**or·der·ly** \ˈörd-ər-lē\ *adj* 1 : arranged according to some order; *also* : NEAT, TIDY 2 : well behaved ⟨an ~ crowd⟩ **syn** methodical, systematic, regular — **or·der·li·ness** *n*

²**orderly** *n*, *pl* **-lies** 1 : a soldier who attends a superior officer 2 : a hospital attendant who does general work

¹**or·di·nal** \ˈörd-(ᵊ-)nəl\ *n* : an ordinal number

²**ordinal** *adj* : indicating order or rank (as sixth) in a series

or·di·nance \ˈörd-(ᵊ-)nəns\ *n* : an authoritative decree or law; *esp* : a municipal regulation

or·di·nary \ˈörd-ᵊn-ˌer-ē\ *adj* 1 : to be expected; *usual* 2 : of common quality, rank, or ability; *also* : POOR, INFERIOR **syn** customary, routine, normal, everyday — **or·di·nar·i·ly** \ˌörd-ᵊn-ˈer-ə-lē\ *adv*

or·di·nate \ˈörd-(ᵊ-)nət, ˈörd-ᵊn-ˌāt\ *n* : the coordinate of a point in a plane coordinate system that is the distance of the point measured from the horizontal axis found by measuring along a line parallel to the vertical axis

or·di·na·tion \ˌörd-ᵊn-ˈā-shən\ *n* : the act or ceremony by which a person is ordained

ord·nance \ˈörd-nəns\ *n* 1 : military supplies (as weapons, ammunition, or vehicles) 2 : CANNON, ARTILLERY

Or·do·vi·cian \ˌörd-ə-ˈvish-ən\ *adj* : of, relating to, or being the period of the Paleozoic era between the Cambrian and the Silurian — **Ordovician** *n*

or·dure \ˈör-jər\ *n* : EXCREMENT

¹ore \'ōr\ *n* : a mineral mined to obtain a substance that it contains

²ore \'ər-ə\ *n, pl* **ore** — see *krona, krone* at MONEY table

Oreg *or* **Ore** *abbr* Oregon

oreg·a·no \ə-'reg-ə-,nō\ *n* [AmerSp] : a bushy perennial mint used as a seasoning and a source of oil

org *abbr* organization; organized

or·gan \'ōr-gən\ *n* **1** : a musical instrument having sets of pipes sounded by compressed air and controlled by keyboards; *also* : an instrument in which the sounds of the pipe organ are approximated by electronic devices **2** : a differentiated animal or plant structure made up of cells and tissues and performing some bodily function **3** : a means of performing a function or accomplishing an end **4** : PERIODICAL

or·gan·dy *also* **or·gan·die** \'ōr-gən-dē\ *n, pl* **-dies** [F *organdi*] : a fine transparent muslin with a stiff finish

or·gan·ic \ōr-'gan-ik\ *adj* **1** : of, relating to, or arising in a bodily organ **2** : ORGANIZED (an ~ whole) **3** : of, relating to, or derived from living things **4** : of, relating to, or containing carbon compounds **5** : of or relating to a branch of chemistry dealing with carbon compounds **6** : involving, producing, or dealing in foods produced without the use of laboratory-made fertilizers, growth substances, antibiotics, or pesticides (~ gardeners) — **or·gan·i·cal·ly** \-i-k(ə-)lē\ *adv*

or·gan·ism \'ōr-gə-,niz-əm\ *n* : a living person, animal, or plant — **or·gan·is·mic** \ōr-gə-'niz-mik\ *adj*

or·gan·ist \'ōr-gə-nəst\ *n* : one who plays an organ

or·ga·ni·za·tion \ōrg-(ə-)nə-'zā-shən\ *n* **1** : the act or process of organizing or of being organized; *also* : the condition or manner of being organized **2** : ASSOCIATION, SOCIETY **3** : MANAGEMENT — **or·ga·ni·za·tion·al** *adj*

or·ga·nize \'ōr-gə-,nīz\ *vb* **-nized; -niz·ing** **1** : to develop an organic structure **2** : to arrange or form into a complete and functioning whole **3** : to set up an administrative structure for **4** : to arrange by systematic planning and united effort **5** : to join in a union; *also* : UNIONIZE *syn* institute, found, establish, constitute — **or·ga·niz·er** *n*

or·gano·chlo·rine \ōr-,gan-ə-'klōr-,ēn\ *adj* : of or relating to the chlorinated hydrocarbon pesticides (as DDT) — **organochlorine** *n*

or·gano·phos·phate \-'fäs-,fāt\ *n* : an organophosphorus pesticide — **organophosphate** *adj*

or·gano·phos·pho·rus \-'fäs-f(ə-)rəs\ *also* **or·gano·phos·pho·rous** \-,fäs-'fōr-əs\ *adj* : of, relating to, or being a phosphorus-containing organic pesticide (as malathion)

or·gan·za \ōr-'gan-zə\ *n* : a sheer dress fabric resembling organdy and usu. made of silk, rayon, or nylon

or·gasm \'ōr-,gaz-əm\ *n* : a climax of sexual excitement

or·gi·as·tic \,ōr-jē-'as-tik\ *adj* : of, relating to, or marked by orgies

or·gu·lous \'ōr-g(y)ə-ləs\ *adj* : PROUD

or·gy \'ōr-jē\ *n, pl* **orgies** : a gathering marked by unrestrained indulgence (as in alcohol, drugs, or sexual practices)

ori·el \'ōr-ē-əl\ *n* : a window built out from a wall and usu. supported by a bracket

ori·ent \'ōr-ē-,ent\ *vb* **1** : to set in a definite position esp. in relation to the points of the compass **2** : to acquaint with an existing situation or environment — **ori·en·ta·tion** \,ōr-ē-ən-'tā-shən\ *n*

Orient *n* **1** EAST 3: *esp* : the countries of eastern Asia

ori·en·tal \,ōr-ē-'ent-ᵊl\ *adj* [fr. *Orient* East, fr. ME, fr. MF, fr. L *orient-, oriens,* fr. prp. of *oriri* to rise] *often cap* : of or situated in the Orient — **Oriental** *n*

ori·en·tate \'ōr-ē-ən-,tāt\ *vb* **-tat·ed; -tat·ing** **1** : ORIENT **2** : to face east

or·i·fice \'ōr-ə-fəs\ *n* : OPENING, MOUTH

ori·flamme \'ōr-ə-,flam\ *n* : a brightly colored banner used as a standard or ensign in battle

orig *abbr* original; originally

ori·ga·mi \,ōr-ə-'gäm-ē\ *n* : the art or process of Japanese paper folding

or·i·gin \'ōr-ə-jən\ *n* **1** : ANCESTRY **2** : rise, beginning, or derivation from a source; *also* : CAUSE **3** : the intersection of coordinate axes

¹orig·i·nal \ə-'rij-(ə-)nəl\ *n* : something from which a copy, reproduction, or translation is made : PROTOTYPE

²original *adj* **1** : FIRST, INITIAL **2** : not copied from something else : FRESH **3** : INVENTIVE — **orig·i·nal·i·ty** \-,rij-ə-'nal-ət-ē\ *n* — **orig·i·nal·ly** \-'rij-ən-ᵊl-ē\ *adv*

orig·i·nate \ə-'rij-ə-,nāt\ *vb* **-nat·ed; -nat·ing** **1** : to give rise to : INITIATE **2** : to come into existence : BEGIN — **orig·i·na·tor** \-,nāt-ər\ *n*

ori·ole \'ōr-ē-,ōl\ *n* [F *oriol,* fr. L *aureolus,* dim. of *aureus* golden, fr. *aurum* gold] : any of a family of New World birds of which the males are usually black and yellow or orange and the females chiefly greenish or yellowish

ori·son \'ōr-ə-sən\ *n* : PRAYER

or·mo·lu \'ōr-mə-,lü\ *n* : a brass made to imitate gold and used for decorative purposes

¹or·na·ment \'ōr-nə-mənt\ *n* : something that lends grace or beauty — **or·na·men·tal** \,ōr-nə-'ment-ᵊl\ *adj*

²or·na·ment \-,ment\ *vb* : to provide with ornament : ADORN — **or·na·men·ta·tion** \,ōr-nə-mən-'tā-shən\ *n*

or·nate \ōr-'nāt\ *adj* : elaborately decorated — **or·nate·ly** *adv* — **or·nate·ness** *n*

or·nery \'ȯrn-(ə-)rē, 'än-\ *adj* : having an irritable disposition

ornith *abbr* ornithology

or·ni·thol·o·gy \,ȯr-nə-'thäl-ə-jē\ *n, pl* **-gies** : a branch of zoology dealing with birds — **or·ni·tho·log·i·cal** \-thə-'läj-i-kəl\ *adj* — **or·ni·thol·o·gist** \-'thäl-ə-jəst\ *n*

oro·tund \'ȯr-ə-,tənd\ *adj* 1 : SONOROUS 2 : POMPOUS

or·phan \'ȯr-fən\ *n* : a child deprived by death of one or usu. both parents — **orphan** *vb*

or·phan·age \'ȯrf-(ə-)nij\ *n* : an institution for the care of orphans

or·ris \'ȯr-əs\ *n* : a European iris with a fragrant rootstock (**orrisroot**) used in perfume and sachets

orth·odon·tia \,ȯr-thə-'dän-ch(ē-)ə\ *n* : ORTHODONTICS

or·tho·don·tics \,ȯr-thə-'dänt-iks\ *n* : a branch of dentistry dealing with faulty tooth occlusion and its correction — **or·tho·don·tist** \-'dänt-əst\ *n*

or·tho·dox \'ȯr-thə-,däks\ *adj* [MF or LL; MF *orthodoxe*, fr. LL *orthodox-us*, fr. LGk *orthodoxos*, fr. Gk *orthos* right + *doxa* opinion] 1 : conforming to established doctrine esp. in religion 2 : CONVENTIONAL 3 *cap* : of or relating to a Christian church originating in the church of the Eastern Roman Empire — **or·tho·doxy** \-,däk-sē\ *n*

or·thog·ra·phy \ȯr-'thäg-rə-fē\ *n* : SPELLING — **or·tho·graph·ic** \,ȯr-thə-'graf-ik\ *adj*

or·tho·pe·dics \,ȯr-thə-'pēd-iks\ *n sing or pl* : the correction or prevention of skeletal deformities — **or·tho·pe·dic** \-ik\ *adj* — **or·tho·pe·dist** \-'pēd-əst\ *n*

or·to·lan \'ȯrt-ᵊl-ən\ *n* : a European bunting valued as a table delicacy

-ory \-ȯr-ē, (ə-)rē\ *adj suffix* 1 : of, relating to, or characterized by 2 : serving for, producing, or maintaining

Os *symbol* osmium

OS *abbr* 1 [L *oculus sinister*] left eye 2 out of stock

Osage \ō-'sāj\ *n, pl* **Osag·es** *or* **Osage** : a member of an American Indian people orig. of Missouri

os·cil·late \'äs-ə-,lāt\ *vb* **-lat·ed; -lat·ing** 1 : to swing backward and forward like a pendulum 2 : to move or travel back and forth between two points 3 : VARY, FLUCTUATE — **os·cil·la·tion** \,äs-ə-'lā-shən\ *n* — **os·cil·la·tor** \'äs-ə-,lāt-ər\ *n* — **os·cil·la·to·ry** \'ä-'sil-ə-,tōr-ē\ *adj*

os·cil·lo·scope \ä-'sil-ə-,skōp\ *n* : an instrument in which variations in current or voltage appear as a visible wave form on a fluorescent screen

os·cu·late \'äs-kyə-,lāt\ *vb* **-lat·ed; -lat·ing** : KISS — **os·cu·la·tion** \,äs-kyə-'lā-shən\ *n*

Osee \'ō-,zē, ō-'zā-ə\ *n* — see BIBLE table

OSHA *abbr* Occupational Safety and Health Administration

osier \'ō-zhər\ *n* : a willow tree with pliable twigs used esp. in making baskets and furniture; *also* : a twig from an osier

os·mi·um \'äz-mē-əm\ *n* : a heavy hard brittle metallic chemical element used in alloys

os·mo·sis \äz-'mō-səs, äs-\ *n* : diffusion of a solvent through a partially permeable membrane into a solution of higher concentration that tends to equalize the concentrations of the solutions on either side of the membrane — **os·mot·ic** \-'mät-ik\ *adj*

os·prey \'äs-prē, -,prā\ *n, pl* **ospreys** : a large brown and white fish-eating hawk

os·si·fy \'äs-ə-,fī\ *vb* **-fied; -fy·ing** : to change into bone — **os·si·fi·ca·tion** \,äs-ə-fə-'kā-shən\ *n*

os·su·ary \'äsh-ə-,wer-ē, 'äs-(y)ə-\ *n, pl* **-ar·ies** : a depository for the bones of the dead

os·ten·si·ble \ä-'sten-sə-bəl\ *adj* : shown outwardly : PROFESSED, APPARENT — **os·ten·si·bly** \-blē\ *adv*

os·ten·ta·tion \,äs-tən-'tā-shən\ *n* : pretentious or excessive display — **os·ten·ta·tious** \-shəs\ *adj* — **os·ten·ta·tious·ly** *adv*

os·teo·path \'äs-tē-ə-,path\ *n* : a practitioner of osteopathy

os·te·op·a·thy \,äs-tē-'äp-ə-thē\ *n* : a system of healing that emphasizes manipulation (as of joints) but does not exclude other agencies (as the use of medicine and surgery) — **os·teo·path·ic** \,äs-tē-ə-'path-ik\ *adj*

os·teo·po·ro·sis \,äs-tē-ō-pə-'rō-səs\ *n, pl* **-ro·ses** \-,sēz\ : a bodily disorder occurring esp. after age 45, characterized by fragile and porous bones, and caused by faulty nutrition and mineral metabolism

ostler *var of* HOSTLER

ost·mark \'ōst-,märk, 'ȯst-\ *n* — see MONEY table

os·tra·cize \'äs-trə-,sīz\ *vb* **-cized; -ciz·ing** [Gk *ostrakizein* to banish by voting with potsherds, fr. *ostrakon* shell, potsherd] : to exclude from a group by common consent — **os·tra·cism** \-,siz-əm\ *n*

os·trich \'äs-trich, 'ȯs-\ *n* : a very large swift-footed flightless bird of Africa and Arabia

Os·we·go tea \ä-,swē-gō-\ *n* : a No. American mint with showy scarlet flowers

OT *abbr* 1 Old Testament 2 overtime

¹oth·er \'əth-ər\ *adj* 1 : being the one left; *also* : being the ones distinct from those first mentioned 2 : ALTERNATE ⟨every ~ day⟩ 3 : DIFFERENT 4 : ADDITIONAL 5 : recently past ⟨the ~ night⟩

²other *pron* 1 : remaining one or ones ⟨one foot and then the ~⟩ 2 : a different or additional one ⟨something or ~⟩

oth·er·wise \-,wīz\ *adv* 1 : in a different

way **2** : in different circumstances **3** : in other respects — **otherwise** *adj*

oth·er·world \-ˌwərld\ *n* : a world beyond death or beyond present reality

oth·er·world·ly \-ˌwərl-(d)lē\ *adj* : not worldly : concerned with spiritual, intellectual, or imaginative matters

oti·ose \ˈō-shē-ˌōs, ˈōt-ē-\ *adj* **1** : IDLE **2** : STERILE **3** : USELESS

oto·lar·yn·gol·o·gist \ˌōt-ō-ˌlar-ən-ˈgäl-ə-jəst\ *n* : a specialist in otorhinolaryngology — **oto·lar·yn·gol·o·gy** \-ə-jē\ *n*

oto·rhi·no·lar·yn·gol·o·gy \ˌōt-ō-ˌrī-nō-ˌlar-ən-ˈgäl-ə-jē\ *n* : a medical specialty concerned esp. with the ear, nose, and throat — **oto·rhi·no·lar·yn·gol·o·gist** \-jəst\ *n*

OTS *abbr* officers' training school

Ot·ta·wa \ˈät-ə-wə, -ˌwä, -ˌwô\ *n, pl* **Ottawas** *or* **Ottawa** : a member of an American Indian people of Michigan and southern Ontario

ot·ter \ˈät-ər\ *n, pl* **otters** *also* **otter** : a web-footed fish-eating mammal that is related to the weasels and has dark brown fur; *also* : its fur

ot·to·man \ˈät-ə-mən\ *n* : an upholstered seat or couch; *also* : an overstuffed footstool

ou·bli·ette \ˌü-blē-ˈet\ *n* [F, fr. MF, fr. *oublier* to forget, fr. L *oblivisci*] : a dungeon with an opening at the top

ought \ˈȯt\ *verbal auxiliary* — used to express moral obligation, advisability, natural expectation, or logical consequence

ou·gui·ya \ü-ˈg(w)ē-(y)ə\ *n, pl* **ouguiya** — see MONEY table

ounce \ˈau̇ns\ *n* [ME, fr. MF *unce*, fr. L *uncia* twelfth part, ounce, fr. *unus* one] : a unit of avoirdupois, troy, and apothecaries' weight — see WEIGHT table

our \är, (ˈ)au̇(ə)r\ *adj* : of or relating to us or ourselves

ours \(ˈ)au̇(ə)rz, ärz\ *pron* : one or the ones belonging to us

our·selves \är-ˈselvz, au̇(ə)r-\ *pron* : our own selves — used reflexively, for emphasis, or in absolute constructions (we pleased ∼) (we'll do it ∼) (∼ tourists, we avoided other tourists)

-ous \əs\ *adj suffix* : full of : abounding in : having : possessing the qualities of (clamor*ous*) (poison*ous*)

oust \ˈau̇st\ *vb* : to eject from or deprive of property or position : EXPEL **syn** evict, dismiss, banish, deport

oust·er \ˈau̇s-tər\ *n* : EXPULSION

¹out \ˈau̇t\ *adv* **1** : in a direction away from the inside or center **2** : beyond control **3** : to extinction, exhaustion, or completion **4** : in or into the open **5** : so as to retire a batter or base runner; *also* : so as to be retired

²out *vb* : to become known (the truth will ∼)

³out *prep* **1** : out through (looked ∼ the window) **2** : outward on or along (drive ∼ the river road)

⁴out *adj* **1** : situated outside or at a distance **2** : not in : ABSENT; *also* : not being in power **3** : not successful in reaching base **4** : not being in vogue or fashion : not up-to-date

⁵out *n* **1** : one who is out of office **2** : the retiring of a batter or base runner

out-and-out \ˌau̇t-ᵊn(d)-ˈau̇t\ *adj* : COMPLETE, THOROUGHGOING (an ∼ fraud)

out·bid \ˈau̇t-ˈbid\ *vb* : to make a higher bid than

¹out·board \ˈau̇t-ˌbȯrd\ *adj* **1** : situated outboard **2** : having or using an outboard motor

²outboard *adv* **1** : outside a ship's hull : away from the long axis of a ship **2** : in a position closer to the wing tip of an airplane

outboard motor *n* : a small internal-combustion engine with propeller attached for mounting at the stern of a small boat

out·bound \ˈau̇t-ˌbau̇nd\ *adj* : outward bound (∼ traffic)

out·break \-ˌbrāk\ *n* **1** : a sudden or violent breaking out **2** : something (as an epidemic) that breaks out

out·build·ing \-ˌbil-diŋ\ *n* : a building separate from but accessory to a main house

out·burst \-ˌbərst\ *n* : ERUPTION; *esp* : a violent expression of feeling

out·cast \-ˌkast\ *n* : one who is cast out by society : PARIAH

out·class \au̇t-ˈklas\ *vb* : SURPASS

out·come \ˈau̇t-ˌkəm\ *n* : a final consequence : RESULT

out·crop \-ˌkräp\ *n* : a coming out of bedrock to the surface of the ground; *also* : the part of a rock formation that thus appears — **outcrop** *vb*

out·cry \-ˌkrī\ *n* : a loud cry : CLAMOR

out·dat·ed \au̇t-ˈdāt-əd\ *adj* : OUTMODED

out·dis·tance \-ˈdis-təns\ *vb* : to go far ahead of (as in a race) : OUTSTRIP

out·do \-ˈdü\ *vb* **-did** \-ˈdid\ ; **-done** \-ˈdən\ ; **-do·ing** \-ˈdü-iŋ\ ; **-does** \-ˈdəz\ : to go beyond in action or performance : EXCEL

out·door \ˈau̇t-ˌdȯr\ *also* **out·doors** \-ˌdȯrz\ *adj* **1** : of or relating to the outdoors **2** : performed outdoors **3** : not enclosed (as by a roof)

¹out·doors \au̇t-ˈdȯrz\ *adv* : in or into the open air

²outdoors *n* **1** : the open air **2** : the world away from human habitation

out·draw \au̇t-ˈdrȯ\ *vb* **-drew** \-ˈdrü\ ; **-drawn** \-ˈdrȯn\ ; **-draw·ing** **1** : to attract a larger audience than **2** : to draw a handgun more quickly than

out·er \ˈau̇t-ər\ *adj* **1** : EXTERNAL **2** : situated farther out; *also* : being away from a center

out·er·most \-ˌmōst\ *adj* : farthest out

outer space *n* : SPACE 5; *esp* : the region beyond the solar system

out·face \aut-'fās\ vb 1 : to cause to waver or submit 2 : DEFY

out·field \'aut-,fēld\ n : the part of a baseball field beyond the infield and within the foul lines; also : players in the outfield — **out·field·er** \-,fēl-dər\ n

out·fight \aut-'fīt\ vb : to surpass in fighting : DEFEAT

¹**out·fit** \'aut-,fit\ n 1 : the equipment or apparel for a special purpose or occasion 2 : GROUP

²**outfit** vb out·fit·ted; out·fit·ting : EQUIP — **out·fit·ter** n

out·flank \aut-'flank\ vb : to get around the flank of (an opposing force)

out·flow \'aut-,flō\ n 1 : a flowing out 2 : something that flows out

out·fox \aut-'fäks\ vb : OUTWIT

out·gen·er·al \-'jen-(ə-)rəl\ vb : to surpass in generalship

out·go \'aut-,gō\ n, pl outgoes : EXPENDITURES, OUTLAY

out·go·ing \-,gō-iŋ\ adj 1 : going out ⟨∼ tide⟩ 2 : retiring from a place or position 3 : FRIENDLY

out·grow \aut-'grō\ vb -grew \-'grü\ ; -grown \-'grōn\ ; -grow·ing : to grow faster than 2 : to grow too large for

out·growth \'aut-,grōth\ n : a product of growing out : OFFSHOOT; also : CONSEQUENCE

out·guess \aut-'ges\ vb : OUTWIT

out·gun \-'gən\ vb : to surpass in firepower

out·house \'aut-,haus\ n : OUTBUILDING; esp : an outdoor toilet

out·ing \'aut-iŋ\ n : a brief stay or trip in the open

out·land·ish \aut-'lan-dish\ adj 1 : of foreign appearance or manner; also : BIZARRE 2 : remote from civilization — **out·land·ish·ly** adv

out·last \-'last\ vb : to last longer than

¹**out·law** \'aut-,lo\ n 1 : a person excluded from the protection of the law 2 : a lawless person

²**outlaw** vb 1 : to deprive of the protection of the law 2 : to make illegal — **out·law·ry** \aut-,lo(ə)r-ē\ n

out·lay \'aut-,lā\ n 1 : the act of spending 2 : EXPENDITURE

out·let \'aut-,let, -lət\ n 1 : EXIT, VENT 2 : a means of release (as for an emotion) 3 : a market for a commodity 4 : a receptacle for the plug of an electrical device

¹**out·line** \'aut-,līn\ n 1 : a line marking the outer limits of an object or figure 2 : a drawing in which only contours are marked 3 : SUMMARY, SYNOPSIS 4 : PLAN

²**outline** vb 1 : to draw the outline of 2 : to indicate the chief features or parts of

out·live \aut-'liv\ vb : to live longer than syn outlast, survive

out·look \'aut-,luk\ n 1 : a place offering a view; also : VIEW 2 : STANDPOINT 3 : the prospect for the future

out·ly·ing \-,lī-iŋ\ adj : distant from a center or main body

out·ma·neu·ver \,aut-mə-'n(y)ü-vər\ vb 1 : to defeat by more skillful maneuvering 2 : to surpass in maneuverability

out·mod·ed \aut-'mōd-əd\ adj 1 : being out of style 2 : no longer acceptable or approved

out·num·ber \-'nəm-bər\ vb : to exceed in number

out of prep 1 : out from within or behind ⟨walk *out* of the room⟩ ⟨look *out* of the window⟩ 2 : from a state of ⟨wake up *out* of a deep sleep⟩ 3 : beyond the limits of ⟨*out* of sight⟩ 4 : BECAUSE OF ⟨came *out* of curiosity⟩ 5 : FROM, WITH ⟨built it *out* of scrap⟩ 6 : in or into a state of loss or not having ⟨cheated him *out* of $5000⟩ ⟨we're *out* of matches⟩ 7 : from among ⟨one *out* of four⟩ — **out of it** : SQUARE, OLD-FASHIONED

out-of-bounds \,aut-ə(v)-'baun(d)z\ adv or adj : outside the prescribed boundaries or limits

out-of-date \-'dāt\ adj : no longer in fashion or in use : OUTMODED

out-of-door \-'dōr\ or **out-of-doors** \-'dōrz\ adj : OUTDOOR

out-of-the-way \-thə-'wā\ adj 1 : being off the beaten track 2 : UNUSUAL

out·pa·tient \'aut-,pā-shənt\ n : a person not an inmate of a hospital who visits it for diagnosis or treatment

out·per·form \,aut-pər-'fórm\ vb : to perform better than

out·play \aut-'plā\ vb : to play more skillfully than

out·point \-'póint\ vb : to win more points than

out·post \'aut-,pōst\ n 1 : a military detachment stationed at some distance from a main force to protect it from surprise attack; also : a military base established (as by treaty) in a foreign country 2 : an outlying or frontier settlement

out·pour·ing \-,pōr-iŋ\ n : something that pours out or is poured out

out·pull \aut-'pul\ vb : OUTDRAW 1

¹**out·put** \'aut-,put\ n 1 : the amount produced (as by a machine or factory) : PRODUCTION 2 : the information fed out by a computer

²**output** vb out·put·ted or output; out·put·ting : to produce as output

¹**out·rage** \'aut-,rāj\ n [ME, fr. OF, excess, outrage, fr. *outre* beyond, in excess, fr. L *ultra*] 1 : a violent or shameful act 2 : INJURY, INSULT 3 : the anger or resentment aroused by an outrage

²**outrage** vb out·raged; out·rag·ing 1 : RAPE 2 : to subject to violent injury or gross insult 3 : to arouse to extreme resentment

out·ra·geous \aut-'rā-jəs\ adj : extremely offensive, insulting, or shameful : SHOCKING — **out·ra·geous·ly** adv

out·rank \-'raŋk\ vb : to rank higher than

ou·tré \ü-ˈtrā\ *adj* [F] : violating convention or propriety : BIZARRE

¹**out·reach** \aut-ˈrēch\ *vb* **1** : to surpass in reach **2** : to get the better of by trickery

²**out·reach** \ˈaut-ˌrēch\ *n* **1** : the act of reaching out **2** : the extent of reach **3** : the extending of services beyond usual limits

out·rid·er \-ˌrīd-ər\ *n* : a mounted attendant

out·rig·ger \-ˌrig-ər\ *n* **1** : a frame that extends from the side of a canoe or boat to prevent upsetting **2** : a craft equipped with an outrigger

¹**out·right** \(ˈ)aut-ˈrīt\ *adv* **1** : COMPLETELY **2** : INSTANTANEOUSLY

²**outright** *adj* **1** : being exactly what is stated (~ lie) **2** : given or made without reservation or encumbrance (~ sale)

out·run \aut-ˈrən\ *vb* **-ran** \-ˈran\ ; **-run;** **-run·ning** : to run faster than; *also* : EXCEED

out·sell \-ˈsel\ *vb* **-sold** \-ˈsōld\ ; **-sell·ing** : to exceed in sales

out·set \ˈaut-ˌset\ *n* : BEGINNING, START

out·shine \aut-ˈshīn\ *vb* **-shone** \-ˈshōn\ *or* **-shined; -shin·ing 1** : to shine brighter than **2** : SURPASS

¹**out·side** \-ˈsīd, ˈaut-ˌsīd\ *n* **1** : a place or region beyond an enclosure or boundary **2** : EXTERIOR **3** : the utmost limit or extent

²**outside** *adj* **1** : OUTER **2** : coming from without (~ influences) **3** : being apart from one's regular duties (~ activities) **4** : REMOTE (an ~ chance)

³**outside** *adv* : on or to the outside

⁴**outside** *prep* **1** : on or to the outside of **2** : beyond the limits of **3** : EXCEPT

outside of *prep* **1** : OUTSIDE **2** : BESIDES

out·sid·er \aut-ˈsīd-ər\ *n* : one who does not belong to a group

out·size \ˈaut-ˌsīz\ *n* : an unusual size; *esp* : a size larger than the standard

out·skirts \-ˌskərts\ *n pl* : the outlying parts (as of a city) : BORDERS

out·smart \-ˈsmärt\ *vb* : OUTWIT

out·spend \-ˈspend\ *vb* **1** : to exceed the limits of in spending (~s his income) **2** : to surpass in spending

out·spo·ken \aut-ˈspō-kən\ *adj* : direct and open in speech or expression — **out·spo·ken·ness** \-kən-nəs\ *n*

out·spread \-ˈspred\ *vb* **-spread; -spread·ing** : to spread out : EXTEND

out·stand·ing \-ˈstan-diŋ\ *adj* **1** : PROJECTING **2** : UNPAID; *also* : UNRESOLVED **3** : publicly issued and sold **4** : CONSPICUOUS; *also* : DISTINGUISHED — **out·stand·ing·ly** *adv*

out·stay \-ˈstā\ *vb* **1** : OVERSTAY **2** : to surpass in endurance

out·stretched \-ˈstrecht\ *adj* : stretched out : EXTENDED

out·strip \-ˈstrip\ *vb* **1** : to go faster than **2** : EXCEL, SURPASS

out·vote \-ˈvōt\ *vb* : to defeat by a majority of votes

¹**out·ward** \ˈaut-wərd\ *adj* **1** : moving or directed toward the outside **2** : showing outwardly

²**outward** *or* **out·wards** \-wərdz\ *adv* : toward the outside

out·ward·ly \-wərd-lē\ *adv* : on the outside : EXTERNALLY

out·wear \aut-ˈwaar\ *vb* **-wore** \-ˈwōr\ ; **-worn** \-ˈwōrn\ ; **-wear·ing** : to wear longer than : OUTLAST

out·weigh \-ˈwā\ *vb* : to exceed in weight, value, or importance

out·wit \-ˈwit\ *vb* : to get the better of by superior cleverness

¹**out·work** \-ˈwərk\ *vb* : to outdo in working

²**out·work** \ˈaut-ˌwərk\ *n* : a minor defensive position outside a fortified area

out·worn \aut-ˈwōrn\ *adj* : OUTMODED

ou·zo \ˈü-(ˌ)zō, -(ˌ)zō\ *n* : a colorless anise-flavored unsweetened Greek liqueur

ova *pl of* OVUM

oval \ˈō-vəl\ *adj* [ML ovalis, fr. LL, of an egg, fr. L ovum] : egg-shaped; *also* : broadly elliptical — **oval** *n*

ova·ry \ˈōv-(ə-)rē\ *n, pl* **-ries 1** : a usu. paired organ of a female animal in which eggs and often sex hormones are produced **2** : the part of a flower in which seeds are produced — **ovar·i·an** \ō-ˈvar-ē-ən, -ˈver-\ *adj*

ovate \ˈō-ˌvāt\ *adj* : egg-shaped

ova·tion \ō-ˈvā-shən\ *n* [L ovation-, ovatio, fr. ovatus, pp. of ovare to exult] : an enthusiastic popular tribute

ov·en \ˈəv-ən\ *n* : a chamber (as in a stove) for baking, heating, or drying

oven·bird \-ˌbərd\ *n* : a large American warbler that builds its dome-shaped nest on the ground

¹**over** \ˈō-vər\ *adv* **1** : across a barrier or intervening space **2** : across the brim (boil ~) **3** : so as to bring the underside up **4** : out of a vertical position **5** : beyond some quantity, limit, or norm **6** : ABOVE **7** : at an end **8** : THROUGH; *also* : THOROUGHLY **9** : AGAIN

²**over** \ˈō-vər, ˈō-\ *prep* **1** : above in position, authority, or scope (towered ~ her) (obeyed those ~ him) (the talk was ~ their heads) **2** : more than (paid ~ $100 for it) **3** : ON, UPON (a cape ~ his shoulders) **4** : along the length of (~ the road) **5** : through the medium of : ON (spoke ~ TV) **6** : all through (showed me ~ the house) **7** : on or above so as to cross (walk ~ the bridge) (jump ~ a ditch) **8** : DURING (~ the past 25 years) **9** : on account of (fought ~ a woman)

³**over** \ˈō-vər, ˈō-\ *adj* **1** : UPPER, HIGHER **2** : REMAINING **3** : ENDED

over- *prefix* **1** : so as to exceed or surpass **2** : excessive; excessively

overabundance	overanxious
overabundant	overbid
overactive	overbold
overaggressive	overbuild
overambitious	overburden

overbuy
overcapacity
overcapitalize
overcareful
overcautious
overcompensation
overconfidence
overconfident
overconscientious
overcook
overcritical
overcrowd
overdecorated
overdetermined
overdevelop
overdose
overdress
overeager
overeat
overemphasis
overemphasize
overenthusiastic
overestimate
overexcite
overexert
overexertion
overextend
overfatigued
overfeed
overfill
overgenerous
overgraze
overhasty
overheat
overindulge
overindulgence
overindulgent
overlarge
overlearn
overliberal

overload
overlong
overmodest
overnice
overoptimism
overoptimistic
overpay
overpopulated
overpopulation
overpraise
overprice
overproduce
overproduction
overprotect
overproud
overrate
overreact
overrefinement
overrepresented
overripe
oversell
oversensitive
oversensitiveness
oversimple
oversimplification
oversimplify
overspecialization
overspecialize
overspend
overstock
overstrict
oversubtle
oversupply
overtax
overtired
overtrain
overuse
overvalue
overzealous

over-act \ˌō-vər-ˈakt\ vb : to exaggerate in acting

¹over-age \-ˈāj\ adj 1 : too old to be useful 2 : older than is normal for one's position, function, or grade

²over-age \ˈōv-(ə-)rij\ n : SURPLUS

over-all \ˌō-vər-ˈȯl\ adj : including everything (∼ expenses)

over-alls \ˈō-vər-ˌȯlz\ n pl : trousers of strong material usu. with a piece extending up to cover the chest

over-arm \-ˌärm\ adj : done with the arm raised above the shoulder

over-awe \ˌō-vər-ˈȯ\ vb : to restrain or subdue by awe

over-bal-ance \-ˈbal-əns\ vb 1 : OUTWEIGH 2 : to cause to lose balance

over-bear-ing \-ˈba(ə)r-iŋ\ adj : ARROGANT, DOMINEERING

over-blown \-ˈblōn\ adj 1 : PORTLY 2 : INFLATED, PRETENTIOUS

over-board \ˈō-vər-ˌbōrd\ adv 1 : over the side of a ship into the water 2 : to extremes of enthusiasm

¹over-cast \ˈō-vər-ˌkast\ adj : clouded over : GLOOMY

²over-cast n : COVERING; esp : a covering of clouds

over-charge \ˌō-vər-ˈchärj\ vb 1 : to charge too much 2 : to fill or load too full — **over-charge** \ˈō-vər-ˌchärj\ n

over-coat \ˈō-vər-ˌkōt\ n : a warm coat worn over indoor clothing

over-come \ˌō-vər-ˈkəm\ vb **-came** \-ˈkām\ : **-come**; **-com-ing** 1 : CONQUER 2 : to make helpless or exhausted

over-do \ˌō-vər-ˈdü\ vb **-did** \-ˈdid\ : **-done** \-ˈdən\ : **-do-ing** \-ˈdü-iŋ\ : **-does** \-ˈdəz\ 1 : to do too much; also : to tire oneself 2 : EXAGGERATE 3 : to cook too long

over-draft \ˈō-vər-ˌdraft, -ˌdräft\ n : an overdrawing of a bank account; also : the sum overdrawn

over-draw \ˌō-vər-ˈdrȯ\ vb **-drew** \-ˈdrü\ : **-drawn** \-ˈdrȯn\ : **-draw-ing** 1 : to draw checks on a bank account for more than the balance 2 : EXAGGERATE

over-drive \ˈō-vər-ˌdrīv\ n : an automotive transmission gear that transmits to the drive shaft a speed greater than the engine speed

over-dub \ˌō-vər-ˈdəb\ vb : to transfer (recorded sound) onto an earlier recording for a combined effect — **over-dub** \ˈō-vər-ˌdəb\ n

over-due \-ˈd(y)ü\ adj 1 : unpaid when due; also : not appearing or presented on time 2 : more than ready

over-ex-pose \ˌō-vər-ik-ˈspōz\ vb : to expose (a photographic plate or film) for more time than is needed — **over-ex-po-sure** \-ˈspō-zhər\ n

¹over-flow \-ˈflō\ vb 1 : INUNDATE; also : to pour forth in a flood 2 : to flow over the brim or top of

²over-flow \ˈō-vər-ˌflō\ n 1 : FLOOD; also : SURPLUS 2 : an outlet for surplus liquid

over-fly \ˌō-vər-ˈflī\ vb **-flew** \-ˈflü\ : **-flown** \-ˈflōn\ : **-fly-ing** : to fly over in an airplane or spacecraft — **over-flight** \ˈō-vər-ˌflīt\ n

over-grow \ˌō-vər-ˈgrō\ vb **-grew** \-ˈgrü\ : **-grown** \-ˈgrōn\ : **-grow-ing** 1 : to grow over so as to cover 2 : OUTGROW 3 : to grow excessively

over-hand \ˈō-vər-ˌhand\ adj : made with the hand brought down from above — **overhand** adv

¹over-hang \ˈō-vər-ˌhaŋ, ˌō-vər-ˈhaŋ\ vb **-hung** \-ˌhəŋ, -ˈhəŋ\ : **-hang-ing** 1 : to project over : jut out 2 : to hang over threateningly

²over-hang \ˈō-vər-ˌhaŋ\ n : a part (as of a roof) that overhangs

over-haul \ˌō-vər-ˈhȯl\ vb 1 : to examine thoroughly and make necessary repairs and adjustments 2 : OVERTAKE

¹over-head \ˌō-vər-ˈhed\ adv : ALOFT

²over-head \ˈō-vər-ˌhed\ adj : operating or lying above (∼ door)

³over-head \ˈō-vər-ˌhed\ n : business expenses not chargeable to a particular part of the work

over-hear \ˌō-vər-ˈhiər\ vb **-heard** \-ˈhərd\ : **-hear-ing** \-ˈhi(ə)r-iŋ\ : to hear without the speaker's knowledge or intention

over-joyed \ˌō-vər-ˈjȯid\ adj : filled with great joy

over·kill \'ō-vər-ˌkil\ n 1 : a capacity for destruction of a target greatly exceeding that required 2 : a large excess

over·land \'ō-vər-ˌland, -lənd\ adv or adj : by, on, or across land

over·lap \ˌō-vər-'lap\ vb 1 : to lap over 2 : to have something in common

over·lay \ˌō-vər-'lā\ vb **-laid** \-'lād\ ; **-lay·ing** : to lay or spread over or across — **over·lay** \'ō-vər-ˌlā\ n

over·leap \ˌō-vər-'lēp\ vb **-leaped** or **-leapt** \-'lept, 'lept\ ; **-leap·ing** \-'lē-piŋ\ 1 : to leap over or across 2 : to defeat (oneself) by going too far

over·lie \ˌō-vər-'lī\ vb **-lay** \-'lā\ ; **-lain** \-'lān\ ; **-ly·ing** \-'lī-iŋ\ : to lie over or upon

¹over·look \ˌō-vər-'lùk\ vb 1 : INSPECT 2 : to look down on from above 3 : to fail to see 4 : IGNORE; also : EXCUSE 5 : SUPERVISE

²over·look \'ō-vər-ˌlùk\ n : a place from which to look down upon a scene below

over·lord \-ˌlórd\ n : a lord who has supremacy over other lords

over·ly \'ō-vər-lē\ adv : EXCESSIVELY

over·mas·ter \ˌō-vər-'mas-tər\ vb : OVERPOWER, SUBDUE

over·match \-'mach\ vb : to be more than a match for : DEFEAT

over·much \-'məch\ adj or adv : too much

¹over·night \-'nīt\ adv 1 : on or during the night 2 : SUDDENLY (became famous ~)

²overnight adj : of, lasting, or staying the night (~ guests)

over·pass \'ō-vər-ˌpas\ n 1 : a crossing (as of two highways) at different levels by means of a bridge 2 : the upper level of an overpass

over·play \ˌō-vər-'plā\ vb 1 : EXAGGERATE; also : OVEREMPHASIZE 2 : to rely too much on the strength of

over·pow·er \-'paù(-ə)r\ vb 1 : to overcome by superior force 2 : OVERWHELM (~ed by hunger)

over·print \-'print\ vb : to print over with something additional — **over·print** \'ō-vər-ˌprint\ n

over·qual·i·fied \-'kwäl-ə-ˌfīd\ adj : having more education, training, or experience than a job calls for

over·reach \ˌō-və(r)-'rēch\ vb 1 : to reach above or beyond 2 : to defeat (oneself) by too great an effort

over·ride \-'rīd\ vb **-rode** \-'rōd\ ; **-rid·den** \-'rid-ᵊn\ ; **-rid·ing** \-'rīd-iŋ\ 1 : to ride over or across 2 : to prevail over; also : to set aside

over·rule \-'rül\ vb 1 : to prevail over 2 : to rule against 3 : to set aside

¹over·run \-'rən\ vb **-ran** \-'ran\ ; **-running** 1 : to defeat and occupy the positions of 2 : OVERSPREAD; also : INFEST 3 : to go beyond 4 : to flow over

²over·run \'ō-və(r)-ˌrən\ n 1 : an act or instance of overrunning; esp : an exceeding of estimated costs 2 : the

amount by which something overruns

over·sea \ˌō-vər-'sē, 'ō-vər-ˌsē\ adj or adv : OVERSEAS

over·seas \ˌō-vər-'sēz, -ˌsēz\ adv or adj : beyond or across the sea : ABROAD

over·see \ˌō-vər-'sē\ vb **-saw** \-'sò\ ; **-seen** \-'sēn\ ; **-see·ing** 1 : OVERLOOK 2 : INSPECT; also : SUPERVISE — **over·seer** \'ō-vər-ˌsiər\ n

over·sexed \ˌō-vər-'sekst\ adj : exhibiting excessive sexual drive or interest

over·shad·ow \-'shad-ō\ vb 1 : DARKEN 2 : to exceed in importance

over·shoe \'ō-vər-ˌshü\ n : a protective outer shoe; esp : GALOSH

over·shoot \ˌō-vər-'shüt\ vb **-shot** \-'shät\ ; **-shoot·ing** 1 : to pass swiftly beyond 2 : to shoot over or beyond (as a target)

over·sight \'ō-vər-ˌsīt\ n 1 : SUPERVISION 2 : an inadvertent omission or error

over·size \ˌō-vər-'sīz\ or **over·sized** \-'sīzd\ adj : of more than ordinary size

over·sleep \ˌō-vər-'slēp\ vb **-slept** \-'slept\ ; **-sleep·ing** : to sleep beyond the time for waking

over·spread \-'spred\ vb **-spread; -spread·ing** : to spread over or above

over·state \-'stāt\ vb : EXAGGERATE — **over·state·ment** n

over·stay \-'stā\ vb : to stay beyond the time or limits of

over·step \-'step\ vb : EXCEED

over·sub·scribe \-səb-'skrīb\ vb : to subscribe for more of than is available, asked for, or offered for sale

overt \ō-'vərt, 'ō-ˌvərt\ adj [ME, fr. MF ouvert, overt, fr. pp. of ouvrir to open] : not secret

over·take \ˌō-vər-'tāk\ vb **-took** \-'tùk\ ; **-tak·en** \-'tā-kən\ ; **-tak·ing** : to catch up with; also : to catch up with and pass by

over·throw \ˌō-vər-'thrō\ vb **-threw** \-'thrü\ ; **-thrown** \-'thrōn\ ; **-throw·ing** 1 : UPSET 2 : to bring down : DEFEAT (~ a government) 3 : to throw over or past — **over·throw** \'ō-vər-ˌthrō\ n

over·time \'ō-vər-ˌtīm\ n : time beyond a set limit; esp : working time in excess of a standard day or week — **overtime** adv

over·tone \-ˌtōn\ n 1 : one of the higher tones in a complex musical tone 2 : IMPLICATION, SUGGESTION

over·top \ˌō-vər-'täp\ vb 1 : to tower above 2 : SURPASS

over·trick \'ō-vər-ˌtrik\ n : a card trick won in excess of the number bid

over·ture \'ō-vər-ˌchùr, -chər\ n [ME, lit., opening, fr. MF, fr. (assumed) VL opertura, alter. of L apertura] 1 : an opening offer 2 : an orchestral introduction to a musical dramatic work

over·turn \ˌō-vər-'tərn\ vb 1 : to turn over : UPSET 2 : OVERTHROW

over·view \'ō-vər-ˌvyü\ n : a general survey : SUMMARY

over·ween·ing \,ō-vər-'wē-niŋ\ adj 1
: ARROGANT 2 : IMMODERATE

over·weigh \-'wā\ vb 1 : to exceed in
weight 2 : OPPRESS

over·weight \'ō-vər-,wāt\ n 1 : weight
above what is required or allowed 2
: bodily weight greater than normal
for one's age, height, and build —
overweight adj

over·whelm \,ō-vər-'hwelm\ vb 1
: OVERTHROW 2 : SUBMERGE 3 : to
overcome completely

over·whelm·ing adj : EXTREME, GREAT
⟨~ indifference⟩ — **over·whelm·ing·ly**
adv

over·win·ter \-'wint-ər\ vb : to survive
the winter

over·work \-'wərk\ vb 1 : to work or
cause to work too hard or long 2 : to
use too much — **overwork** n

over·wrought \,ō-və(r)-'rȯt\ adj 1 : extremely excited 2 : elaborated to excess

ovi·duct \'ō-və-,dəkt\ n : a tube that
serves for the passage of eggs from an
ovary

ovip·a·rous \ō-'vip-ə-rəs\ adj : reproducing by eggs that hatch outside the
parent's body

ovoid \'ō-,vȯid\ or **ovoi·dal** \ō-'vȯid-ᵊl\
adj : egg-shaped : OVAL

ovu·late \'äv-yə-,lāt, 'ōv-\ vb **-lat·ed;**
-lat·ing : to produce eggs or discharge
them from an ovary — **ovu·la·tion**
\,äv-yə-'lā-shən, ,ōv-\ n

ovule \'äv-yül, 'ōv-\ n : any of the bodies in a plant ovary that after fertilization become seeds

ovum \'ō-vəm\ n, pl **ova** \-və\ : EGG 2

ow \'au̇\ interj — used esp. to express
sudden pain

owe \'ō\ vb **owed; ow·ing** 1 : to be under
obligation to pay or render 2 : to be
indebted to or for; also : to be in debt

owing to prep : BECAUSE OF

owl \'au̇l\ n : a nocturnal bird of prey
with large head and eyes and strong
talons — **owl·ish** adj — **owl·ish·ly** adv

owl·et \'au̇-lət\ n : a young or small owl

¹own \'ōn\ adj : belonging to oneself —
used as an intensive after a possessive
adjective ⟨his ~ car⟩

²own vb 1 : to have or hold as property
2 : ACKNOWLEDGE; also : CONFESS —
own·er n — **own·er·ship** n

³own pron : one or ones belonging to
oneself

ox \'äks\ n, pl **ox·en** \'äk-sən\ also **ox**
: one of the common large domestic

cattle kept for milk, draft, and meat;
esp : an adult castrated male

ox·blood \'äks-,bləd\ n : a moderate
reddish brown

ox·bow \'äks-,bō\ n 1 : a U-shaped collar worn by a draft ox 2 : a U-shaped
bend in a river — **oxbow** adj

ox·ford \'äks-fərd\ n : a low shoe laced
or tied over the instep

oxi·dant \'äk-səd-ənt\ n : OXIDIZING
AGENT — **oxidant** adj

oxi·da·tion \,äk-sə-'dā-shən\ n : the act
or process of oxidizing; also : the
condition of being oxidized — **oxi·da·**
tive \'äk-sə-,dāt-iv\ adj

ox·ide \'äk-,sīd\ n : a compound of oxygen with another element or group

ox·i·dize \'äk-sə-,dīz\ vb **-dized; -diz·ing**
: to combine with oxygen ⟨iron rusts
because it is oxidized by exposure to
the air⟩ — **ox·i·diz·er** n

oxidizing agent n : a substance (as oxygen or nitric acid) that oxidizes by taking up electrons

oxy·acet·y·lene \,äk-sē-ə-'set-ᵊl-ən, -ᵊl-
,ēn\ adj : of, relating to, or utilizing a
mixture of oxygen and acetylene

ox·y·gen \'äk-si-jən\ n [F oxygène, fr.
Gk oxys, adj., acid, lit., sharp +
-genēs born; so called because it was
once thought to be an essential element of all acids] : a colorless odorless gaseous chemical element that is
found in the air, is essential to life, and
is involved in combustion

ox·y·gen·ate \'äk-si-jə-,nāt\ vb **-at·ed;**
-at·ing : to impregnate, combine, or
supply with oxygen — **ox·y·gen·ation**
\,äk-si-jə-'nā-shən\ n

oxygen tent n : a canopy which can be
placed over a bedridden person and
within which a flow of oxygen can be
maintained

oys·ter \'ȯi-stər\ n : any of various mollusks with an irregular 2-valved shell
that live on stony bottoms in shallow
seas and include edible shellfish and
pearl producers — **oys·ter·ing** \'ȯi-
st(ə-)riŋ\ n — **oys·ter·man** \'ȯi-stər-
mən\ n

oz abbr [obs. It onza (now oncia)]
ounce; ounces

ozone \'ō-,zōn\ n 1 : a faintly blue form
of oxygen that is produced by the silent discharge of electricity in air or
oxygen and is used for disinfecting,
deodorizing, and bleaching 2 : pure
and refreshing air

P

¹p \'pē\ n, pl **p's** or **ps** \'pēz\ often cap
: the 16th letter of the English alpha-
bet

²p abbr, often cap 1 page 2 participle 3
past 4 pawn 5 pence; penny 6 per 7
petite 8 pint 9 pressure 10 purl

P symbol phosphorus

pa \'pä, 'pȯ\ n : FATHER

¹Pa abbr Pennsylvania

²Pa symbol protactinium

PA abbr 1 Pennsylvania 2 per annum 3
physician's assistant 4 power of attor-

ney **5** press agent **6** private account **7** professional association **8** public address **9** purchasing agent

pa-'an-ga \pä-'äŋ-(g)ə\ *n* — see MONEY table

pab-u-lum \'pab-yə-ləm\ *n* [L, food, fodder] : usu. soft digestible food

Pac *abbr* Pacific

PAC *abbr* political action committee

¹**pace** \'pās\ *n* **1** : rate of movement or progress (as in walking or working) **2** : a step in walking; *also* : the length of such a step **3** : GAIT; *esp* : a horse's gait in which the legs on the same side move together

²**pace** *vb* **paced; pac-ing 1** : to go or cover at a pace or with slow steps **2** : to measure off by paces **3** : to set or regulate the pace of

³**pace** \'pä-sē\ *prep* : with due respect to

pace-mak-er \'pās-,mā-kər\ *n* **1** : one that sets the pace for another **2** : a body part (as of the heart) that serves to establish and maintain a rhythmic activity **3** : an electrical device for stimulating or steadying the heartbeat

pac-er \'pā-sər\ *n* **1** : a horse that paces **2** : PACEMAKER

pachy-derm \'pak-i-,dərm\ *n* [F *pachyderme*, fr. Gk *pachydermos* thick-skinned, fr. *pachys* thick + *derma* skin] : any of various thick-skinned hoofed mammals (as an elephant)

pachy-san-dra \,pak-i-'san-drə\ *n* : any of a genus of low evergreen plants used as a ground cover

pa-cif-ic \pə-'sif-ik\ *adj* **1** : tending to lessen conflict **2** : CALM, PEACEFUL **3** *cap* : of or relating to the Pacific Ocean

pac-i-fi-er \'pas-ə-,fī(-ə)r\ *n* : one that pacifies; *esp* : a device for a baby to chew or suck on

pac-i-fism \'pas-ə-,fiz-əm\ *n* : opposition to war or violence as a means of settling disputes — **pac-i-fist** \-fəst\ *n or adj* — **pac-i-fis-tic** \,pas-ə-'fis-tik\ *adj*

pac-i-fy \'pas-ə-,fī\ *vb* **-fied; -fy-ing 1** : to allay anger or agitation in **2** : SETTLE; *also* : SUBDUE — **pac-i-fi-ca-tion** \,pas-ə-fə-'kā-shən\ *n*

¹**pack** \'pak\ *n* **1** : a compact bundle; *also* : a flexible container for carrying a bundle esp. on the back **2** : a large amount : HEAP **3** : a set of playing cards **4** : a group or band of people or animals **5** : wet absorbent material for application to the body

²**pack** *vb* **1** : to stow goods in for transportation **2** : to fill in or surround so as to prevent passage of air, steam, or water **3** : to put into a protective container **4** : to load with a pack ⟨~ a mule⟩ **5** : to crowd in **6** : to make into a pack **7** : to cause to go without ceremony ⟨~ them off to school⟩ **8** : WEAR, CARRY ⟨~ a gun⟩

³**pack** *vb* : to make up fraudulently so as to secure a desired result ⟨~ a jury⟩

¹**pack-age** \'pak-ij\ *n* **1** : BUNDLE, PARCEL **2** : a group of related things offered as a whole

²**package** *vb* **pack-aged; pack-ag-ing** : to make into or enclose in a package

package deal *n* : an offer containing several items all or none of which must be accepted

package store *n* : a store that sells alcoholic beverages in sealed containers for consumption off the premises

pack-er \'pak-ər\ *n* : one that packs; *esp* : a wholesale food dealer

pack-et \'pak-ət\ *n* **1** : a passenger boat carrying mail and cargo on a regular schedule **2** : a small bundle or package

pack-horse \'pak-,hórs\ *n* : a horse used to carry goods or supplies

pack-ing \'pak-iŋ\ *n* : material used to pack something

pack-ing-house \-,haús\ *n* : an establishment for processing and packing food and esp. meat and its by-products

pack rat *n* : a bushy-tailed rodent of the Rocky Mountain area that hoards food and miscellaneous objects

pack-sad-dle \'pak-,sad-ᵊl\ *n* : a saddle for supporting packs on the back of an animal

pack-thread \-,thred\ *n* : strong thread for tying

pact \'pakt\ *n* : AGREEMENT, TREATY

¹**pad** \'pad\ *n* **1** : a cushioning part or thing : CUSHION **2** : the cushioned part of the foot of some mammals **3** : the floating leaf of a water plant **4** : a writing tablet **5** : LAUNCHPAD **6** : living quarters; *also* : BED

²**pad** *vb* **pad-ded; pad-ding 1** : to furnish with a pad or padding **2** : to expand with needless or fraudulent matter

pad-ding \'pad-iŋ\ *n* : the material with which something is padded

¹**pad-dle** \'pad-ᵊl\ *vb* **pad-dled; pad-dling** : to move the hands and feet about in shallow water

²**paddle** *n* **1** : an implement with a flat blade used in propelling and steering a small craft (as a canoe) **2** : an implement used for stirring, mixing, or beating **3** : a broad board on the outer rim of a waterwheel or a paddle wheel

³**paddle** *vb* **pad-dled; pad-dling** \'pad-(ᵊ-)liŋ\ **1** : to move on or through water by or as if by using a paddle **2** : to beat or stir with a paddle

paddle wheel *n* : a wheel with boards around its outer edge used to move a water craft

paddle wheeler *n* : a steam-driven vessel propelled by a paddle wheel

pad-dock \'pad-ək\ *n* : a usu. enclosed area for pasturing or exercising animals; *esp* : one where racehorses are saddled and paraded before a race

pad-dy \'pad-ē\ *n*, *pl* **paddies** : wet land where rice is grown

pad-dy wagon \'pad-ē-\ *n* : PATROL WAGON

pad·lock \'pad-ˌläk\ n : a removable lock with a curved piece that snaps into a catch — **padlock** vb

pa·dre \'päd-rā\ n [Sp or It or Pg, lit., father, fr. L pater] **1** : PRIEST, CLERGYMAN **2** : a military chaplain

pae·an \'pē-ən\ n : an exultant song of praise or thanksgiving

pa·gan \'pā-gən\ n [ME, fr. LL paganus, fr. L, country dweller, fr. pagus country district] : HEATHEN — **pagan** adj — **pa·gan·ism** \-ˌiz-əm\ n

¹page \'pāj\ n : ATTENDANT: esp : one employed to deliver messages

²page vb **paged; pag·ing** : to summon by repeatedly calling out the name of

³page n : a single leaf (as of a book); also : a single side of such a leaf

⁴page vb **paged; pag·ing** : to mark or number the pages of

pag·eant \'paj-ənt\ n [ME pagyn, padgeant, lit., scene of a play, fr. ML pagina, fr. L, page] : an elaborate spectacle, show, or procession esp. with tableaux or floats — **pag·eant·ry** \-ən-trē\ n

page·boy \'pāj-ˌboi\ n [¹page] : an often shoulder-length hairdo with the ends of the hair turned under in a smooth roll

pag·er \'pā-jər\ n : one that pages; esp : BEEPER

pag·i·nate \'paj-ə-ˌnāt\ vb **-nat·ed; -nat·ing** : ²PAGE

pag·i·na·tion \ˌpaj-ə-'nā-shən\ n **1** : the paging of written or printed matter **2** : the number and arrangement of pages (as of a book)

pa·go·da \pə-'gōd-ə\ n : a tower with roofs curving upward at the division of each of several stories (Chinese ∼)

paid past and past part of PAY

pail \'pāl\ n : a usu. cylindrical vessel with a handle — **pail·ful** \-ˌfûl\ n

¹pain \'pān\ n **1** : PUNISHMENT, PENALTY **2** : suffering or distress of body or mind; also : a sensation marked by discomfort (as throbbing or aching) **3** pl : great care — **pain·ful** \-fəl\ adj — **pain·ful·ly** \-ē\ adv — **pain·less** adj — **pain·less·ly** adv

²pain vb : to cause or experience pain

pain·kill·er \'pān-ˌkil-ər\ n : something (as a drug) that relieves pain — **pain·kill·ing** \-iŋ\ adj

pains·tak·ing \'pān-ˌstā-kiŋ\ adj : taking pains : showing care — **pains·taking** n — **pains·tak·ing·ly** adv

¹paint \'pānt\ vb **1** : to apply color, pigment, or paint to **2** : to produce or portray in lines or colors on a surface; also : to practice the art of painting **3** : to decorate with colors **4** : to use cosmetics **5** : to describe vividly **6** : SWAB — **paint·er** n

²paint n **1** : something produced by painting **2** : MAKEUP **3** : a mixture of a pigment and a liquid that forms a thin adherent coating when spread on a surface; also : the dry pigment used in making this mixture **4** : an applied coating of paint

paint·brush \'pānt-ˌbrəsh\ n : a brush for applying paint

paint·ing \'pānt-iŋ\ n **1** : a work (as a picture) produced by painting **2** : the art or occupation of painting

¹pair \'paər\ n, pl **pairs** also **pair** [ME paire, fr. OF, fr. L paria equal things, fr. neut. pl. of par equal] **1** : two things of a kind designed for use together **2** : something made up of two corresponding pieces ⟨a ∼ of trousers⟩ **3** : a set of two people or animals ⟨a carriage and ∼⟩ ⟨a married ∼⟩

²pair vb **1** : to arrange in pairs **2** : to form a pair : MATCH **3** : to become associated with another

pai·sa \pī-'sä\ n, pl **paisa** or **pai·se** \-'sā\ — see rupee, taka at MONEY table

pais·ley \'pāz-lē\ adj, often cap : decorated with colorful curved abstract figures ⟨a ∼ shawl⟩

Pai·ute \'pī-ˌ(y)üt\ n : a member of an American Indian people orig. of Utah, Arizona, Nevada, and California

pa·ja·mas \pə-'jäm-əz, -'jam-\ n pl : a loose suit for sleeping or lounging

Pak·i·stani \ˌpak-i-'stan-ē, ˌpäk-i-'stän-ē\ n : a native or inhabitant of Pakistan — **Pakistani** adj

pal \'pal\ n : a close friend

pal·ace \'pal-əs\ n [ME palais, fr. OF, fr. L palatium, fr. Palatium, the Palatine Hill in Rome where the emperors' residences were built] **1** : the official residence of a sovereign **2** : MANSION

pal·a·din \'pal-əd-ən\ n : a knightly supporter of a medieval prince

pa·laes·tra \pə-'les-trə\ n, pl **-trae** \-(ˌ)trē\ : a school in ancient Greece or Rome for sports (as wrestling)

pa·lan·quin \ˌpal-ən-'kēn\ n : an enclosed couch for one person borne on the shoulders of men by means of poles

pal·at·able \'pal-ət-ə-bəl\ adj : agreeable to the taste **syn** appetizing, savory, tasty, toothsome

pal·a·tal \'pal-ət-ᵊl\ adj **1** : of or relating to the palate **2** : pronounced with the front of the tongue near or touching the hard palate (the \y\ in yeast and the \sh\ in she are ∼ sounds)

pal·a·tal·ize \'pal-ət-ᵊl-ˌīz\ vb **-ized; -iz·ing** : to pronounce as or change into a palatal sound — **pal·a·tal·iza·tion** \ˌpal-ət-ᵊl-ə-'zā-shən\ n

pal·ate \'pal-ət\ n **1** : the roof of the mouth consisting of an anterior bony part and a posterior membranous fold **2** : TASTE

pa·la·tial \pə-'lā-shəl\ adj **1** : of, relating to, or being a palace **2** : MAGNIFICENT

pa·lat·i·nate \pə-'lat-ᵊn-ət\ n : the territory of a palatine

¹pal·a·tine \'pal-ə-ˌtīn\ adj **1** : of or relating to a palace : PALATIAL **2** : possessing royal privileges; also : of or relating to a palatine or a palatinate

²**pal·a·tine** *n* **1** : a high officer of an imperial palace **2** : a feudal lord having sovereign power within his domains

pa·la·ver \pə-ˈlav-ər, -ˈläv-\ *n* [Pg *palavra* word, speech, fr. LL *parabola* parable, speech] : a long parley : TALK — **palaver** *vb*

¹**pale** \ˈpāl\ *adj* **pal·er; pal·est 1** : deficient in color : WAN (~ face) **2** : lacking in brightness : DIM (~ star) **3** : light in color or shade (~ blue) — **pale·ness** *n*

²**pale** *vb* **paled; pal·ing** : to make or become pale

³**pale** *vb* **paled; pal·ing** : to enclose with or as if with pales : FENCE

⁴**pale** *n* **1** : a stake or picket of a fence **2** : an enclosed place; *also* : a district or territory within certain bounds or under a particular jurisdiction **3** : LIMITS, BOUNDS (conduct beyond the ~)

pale·face \ˈpāl-ˌfās\ *n* : a white person

Pa·leo·cene \ˈpā-lē-ə-ˌsēn\ *adj* : of, relating to, or being the earliest epoch of the Tertiary — **Paleocene** *n*

pa·le·og·ra·phy \ˌpā-lē-ˈäg-rə-fē\ *n* : the study of ancient writings and inscriptions — **pa·le·og·ra·pher** \-fər\ *n*

Pa·leo·lith·ic \ˌpā-lē-ə-ˈlith-ik\ *adj* : of or relating to an early period of the Stone Age characterized by rough or chipped stone implements

pa·le·on·tol·o·gy \ˌpā-lē-ˌän-ˈtäl-ə-jē\ *n* : a science dealing with the life of past geologic periods esp. as known from fossil remains — **pa·le·on·tol·o·gist** \-ˌän-ˈtäl-ə-jəst, -ən-\ *n*

Pa·leo·zo·ic \ˌpā-lē-ə-ˈzō-ik\ *adj* : of, relating to, or being the era of geologic history between the Proterozoic and Mesozoic and extending from about 620 million years ago to about 230 million years ago — **Paleozoic** *n*

pal·ette \ˈpal-ət\ *n* : a thin often oval board on which a painter lays and mixes colors; *also* : the colors on a palette

pal·frey \ˈpȯl-frē\ *n, pl* **palfreys** *archaic* : a saddle horse; *esp* : one suitable for a woman

pa·limp·sest \ˈpal-əmp-ˌsest\ *n* [L *palimpsestus*, fr. Gk *palimpsēstos* scraped again] : writing material (as a parchment) used after the erasure of earlier writing

pal·in·drome \ˈpal-ən-ˌdrōm\ *n* : a word, verse, or sentence (as 'Able was I ere I saw Elba') that reads the same backward or forward

pal·ing \ˈpā-liŋ\ *n* **1** : a fence of pales **2** : material for pales **3** : PALE, PICKET

pal·in·ode \ˈpal-ə-ˌnōd\ *n* : an ode or song of recantation or retraction

pal·i·sade \ˌpal-ə-ˈsād\ *n* **1** : a high fence of stakes esp. for defense **2** : a line of steep cliffs

¹**pall** \ˈpȯl\ *vb* **1** : to lose in interest or attraction **2** : SATIATE, CLOY

²**pall** *n* **1** : a heavy cloth draped over a coffin **2** : something that produces a gloomy atmosphere

pal·la·di·um \pə-ˈlād-ē-əm\ *n* : a silver-white metallic chemical element used esp. as a catalyst and in alloys

pall·bear·er \ˈpȯl-ˌbar-ər\ *n* : a person who attends the coffin at a funeral

¹**pal·let** \ˈpal-ət\ *n* : a small, hard, or makeshift bed

²**pallet** *n* : a portable platform for transporting and storing materials

pal·li·ate \ˈpal-ē-ˌāt\ *vb* **-at·ed; -at·ing 1** : to ease without curing **2** : to cover by excuses and apologies — **pal·li·a·tion** \ˌpal-ē-ˈā-shən\ *n* — **pal·li·a·tive** \ˈpal-ē-ˌāt-iv\ *adj or n*

pal·lid \ˈpal-əd\ *adj* : PALE, WAN

pal·lor \ˈpal-ər\ *n* : PALENESS

¹**palm** \ˈpäm, ˈpälm\ *n* [ME, fr. OE, fr. L *palma* palm of the hand, palm tree; fr. the resemblance of the tree's leaves to the outstretched hand] **1** : any of a family of mostly tropical trees, shrubs, or vines usu. with a tall unbranched stem topped by a crown of large leaves **2** : a symbol of victory; *also* : VICTORY

²**palm** *n* : the underpart of the hand between the fingers and the wrist

³**palm** *vb* **1** : to conceal in or with the hand (~ a card) **2** : to impose by fraud

pal·mate \ˈpal-ˌmāt, ˈpäl)m-ˌāt\ *also* **pal·mat·ed** \-ˌmāt-əd, -ˌāt-\ *adj* : resembling a hand with the fingers spread

palm·er \ˈpäm-ər, ˈpäl-mər\ *n* : a person wearing two crossed palm leaves as a sign of having gone on a pilgrimage to the Holy Land

pal·met·to \pal-ˈmet-ō\ *n, pl* **-tos** *or* **-toes** : any of several usu. small palms with fan-shaped leaves

palm·is·try \ˈpäm-ə-strē, ˈpäl-mə-\ *n* : the practice of reading a person's character or future from the markings on the palms — **palm·ist** \ˈpäm-əst, ˈpäl-məst\ *n*

Palm Sunday *n* : the Sunday preceding Easter and commemorating Christ's triumphal entry into Jerusalem

palmy \ˈpäm-ē, ˈpäl-mē\ *adj* **palm·i·er; -est 1** : abounding in or bearing palms **2** : FLOURISHING, PROSPEROUS

pal·o·mi·no \ˌpal-ə-ˈmē-nō\ *n, pl* **-nos** [AmerSp, fr. Sp, like a dove, fr. L *palumbinus*, fr. *palumbes* wood pigeon] : a horse with a pale cream to golden coat and cream or white mane and tail

pal·pa·ble \ˈpal-pə-bəl\ *adj* **1** : capable of being touched or felt : TANGIBLE **2** : OBVIOUS, PLAIN *syn* perceptible, sensible, appreciable, tangible, detectable — **pal·pa·bly** \-blē\ *adv*

pal·pate \ˈpal-ˌpāt\ *vb* **pal·pat·ed; pal·pat·ing** : to examine by touch esp. medically — **pal·pa·tion** \pal-ˈpā-shən\ *n*

pal·pi·tate \ˈpal-pə-ˌtāt\ *vb* **-tat·ed; -tat·ing** : to beat strongly and irregularly : THROB, QUIVER — **pal·pi·ta·tion** \ˌpal-pə-ˈtā-shən\ *n*

pal·sy \ˈpȯl-zē\ *n, pl* **palsies 1** : PA-

RALYSIS **2** : a condition marked by tremor — **pal·sied** \-zēd\ *adj*

pal·ter \'pȯl-tər\ *vb* **pal·tered; pal·ter·ing** \-t(ə-)riŋ\ **1** : to act insincerely : EQUIVOCATE **2** : HAGGLE

pal·try \'pȯl-trē\ *adj* **pal·tri·er; -est 1** : TRASHY (a ~ pamphlet) **2** : MEAN (a ~ trick) **3** : TRIVIAL (~ excuses) **4** : MEAGER, MEASLY (a ~ sum)

pam *abbr* pamphlet

pam·pa \'pam-pə, 'päm-\ *n, pl* **pam·pas** \-pəz, -pəs\ : a grassy So. American plain

pam·per \'pam-pər\ *vb* **pam·pered; pam·per·ing** \-p(ə-)riŋ\ : to treat with excessive attention : INDULGE *syn* coddle, humor, baby, spoil

pam·phlet \'pam-flət\ *n* [ME *pamflet* unbound booklet, fr. *Pamphilus seu De Amore* Pamphilus or On Love, popular Latin love poem of the 12th cent.] : an unbound printed publication

pam·phle·teer \ˌpam-flə-'tir\ *n* : a writer of pamphlets attacking something or urging a cause

¹pan \'pan\ *n* **1** : a usu. broad, shallow, and open container for domestic use; *also* : something resembling such a container **2** : a basin or depression in land **3** : HARDPAN

²pan *vb* **panned; pan·ning 1** : to wash earth or gravel in a pan in searching for gold **2** : to criticize severely (a new play *panned* by the critics)

Pan *abbr* Panama

pan·a·cea \ˌpan-ə-'sē-ə\ *n* : a remedy for all ills or difficulties

pa·nache \pə-'nash, -'näsh\ *n* [MF *pennache,* deriv. of LL *pinnaculum* small wing] **1** : an ornamental tuft (as of feathers) esp. on a helmet **2** : dash or flamboyance in style and action

pan·a·ma \'pan-ə-ˌmä, -ˌmȯ\ *n, often cap* : a handmade hat braided from strips of the leaves from a tropical American tree

pan·a·tela \ˌpan-ə-'tel-ə\ *n* [Sp, fr. AmerSp, a long thin biscuit, deriv. of L *panis* bread] : a long slender cigar with straight sides rounded off at the sealed end

pan·cake \'pan-ˌkāk\ *n* : a flat cake made of thin batter and fried on both sides

pan·chro·mat·ic \ˌpan-krō-'mat-ik\ *adj* : sensitive to light of all colors (~ film)

pan·cre·as \'paŋ-krē-əs, 'pan-\ *n* : a large gland that produces insulin and discharges enzymes into the intestine — **pan·cre·at·ic** \ˌpaŋ-krē-'at-ik, ˌpan-\ *adj*

pan·da \'pan-də\ *n* **1** : a long-tailed Himalayan mammal related to and resembling the racoon **2** : a large black-and-white mammal of western China usu. classified with the bears

pan·dem·ic \pan-'dem-ik\ *n* : a widespread outbreak of disease — **pandemic** *adj*

pan·de·mo·ni·um \ˌpan-də-'mō-nē-əm\ *n* : a wild uproar : TUMULT

¹pan·der \'pan-dər\ *n* **1** : a go-between in love intrigues **2** : PIMP **3** : someone who caters to or exploits others' desires or weaknesses

²pander *vb* **pan·dered; pan·der·ing** \-d(ə-)riŋ\ : to act as a pander

P and L *abbr* profit and loss

pan·dow·dy \pan-'daúd-ē\ *n, pl* **-dies** : a deep-dish apple dessert spiced, sweetened, and covered with a crust

pane \'pān\ *n* : a sheet of glass (as in a door or window)

pan·e·gyr·ic \ˌpan-ə-'jir-ik\ *n* : a eulogistic oration or writing — **pan·e·gyr·ist** \-'jir-əst\ *n*

¹pan·el \'pan-ᵊl\ *n* **1** : a list of persons appointed for special duty (a jury ~); *also* : a group of people taking part in a discussion or quiz program **2** : a section of something (as a wall or door) often sunk below the level of the frame; *also* : a flat piece of construction material **3** : a flat piece of wood on which a picture is painted **4** : a board housing instruments or controls

²panel *vb* **-eled** *or* **-elled; -el·ing** *or* **-el·ling** : to decorate with panels

pan·el·ing \'pan-ᵊl-iŋ\ *n* : decorative panels

pan·el·ist \'pan-ᵊl-əst\ *n* : a member of a discussion or quiz panel

panel truck *n* : a small motortruck with a fully enclosed body

pang \'paŋ\ *n* : a sudden sharp attack (as of pain)

¹pan·han·dle \'pan-ˌhan-dᵊl\ *n* : a narrow projection of a larger territory (as a state)

²panhandle *vb* **-dled; -dling** \-ˌhan-d(ᵊ-)liŋ\ : to ask for money on the street — **pan·han·dler** \-d(ᵊ-)lər\ *n*

¹pan·ic \'pan-ik\ *n* : a sudden overpowering fright *syn* terror, consternation, dismay, alarm, dread, fear — **pan·icky** \-i-kē\

²panic *vb* **pan·icked** \-ikt\ ; **pan·ick·ing** : to affect or be affected with panic

pan·i·cle \'pan-i-kəl\ *n* : a compound loosely branched racemose flower cluster

pan·jan·drum \pan-'jan-drəm\ *n, pl* **-drums** *also* **-dra** \-drə\ : a powerful personage or pretentious official

pan·nier *also* **pan·ier** \'pan-yər\ *n* : a large basket esp. for bearing on the back

pan·o·ply \'pan-ə-plē\ *n, pl* **-plies 1** : a full suit of armor **2** : a protective covering **3** : an impressive array

pan·ora·ma \ˌpan-ə-'ram-ə, -'räm-\ *n* **1** : a picture unrolled before one's eyes **2** : a complete view in every direction — **pan·oram·ic** \-'ram-ik\ *adj*

pan out *vb* : TURN OUT; *esp* : SUCCEED

pan·sy \'pan-zē\ *n, pl* **pansies** [MF *pensée,* fr. *pensée* thought, fr. *penser* to think, fr. L *pensare* to ponder] : a low-growing garden herb related to the violet; *also* : its showy flower

¹**pant** \'pant\ *vb* [ME *panten*, fr. MF *pantaisier*, fr. (assumed) VL *phantasiare* to have hallucinations, fr. Gk *phantasioun*, fr. *phantasia* appearance, imagination] **1** : to breathe in a labored manner **2** : YEARN **3** : THROB

²**pant** *n* : a panting breath or sound

³**pant** *n* **1** : an outer garment covering each leg separately and usu. extending from the waist to the ankle — usu. used in pl. **2** *pl* : PANTIE

pan·ta·loons \,pant-ᵊl-'ünz\ *n pl* **1** : close-fitting trousers of the 19th century usu. having straps passing under the instep **2** : loose-fitting usu. shorter than ankle-length trousers

pan·the·ism \'pan-thē-ˌiz-əm\ *n* : a doctrine that equates God with the forces and laws of the universe — **pan·the·ist** \-əst\ *n* — **pan·the·is·tic** \,pan-thē-'is-tik\ *adj*

pan·the·on \'pan-thē-ˌän, -ən\ *n* **1** : a temple dedicated to all the gods **2** : a building serving as the burial place of or containing memorials to famous dead **3** : the gods of a people

pan·ther \'pan-thər\ *n, pl* **panthers** *also* **panther 1** : LEOPARD; *esp* : one of a black form **2** : COUGAR **3** : JAGUAR

pant·ie *or* **panty** \'pant-ē\ *n, pl* **pant·ies** : a woman's or child's undergarment covering the lower trunk and made with closed crotch — usu. used in pl.

pan·to·mime \'pant-ə-ˌmīm\ *n* **1** : a play in which the actors use no words **2** : expression of something by bodily or facial movements only — **pantomime** *vb* — **pan·to·mim·ic** \,pant-ə-'mim-ik\ *adj*

pan·try \'pan-trē\ *n, pl* **pantries** : a storage room for food or dishes

pant·suit \'pant-ˌsüt\ *n* : a woman's outfit consisting usu. of a long jacket and pants of the same material

panty hose *n pl* : a one-piece undergarment for women consisting of hosiery combined with a panty

panty·waist \'pant-ē-ˌwāst\ *n* : SISSY

pap \'pap\ *n* : soft food for infants or invalids

pa·pa \'päp-ə\ *n* : FATHER

pa·pa·cy \'pā-pə-sē\ *n, pl* **-cies 1** : the office of pope **2** : a succession of popes **3** : the term of a pope's reign **4** *cap* : the system of government of the Roman Catholic Church

pa·pa·in \pə-'pā-ən, -'pī-ən\ *n* : an enzyme in the juice of unripe papayas that is used esp. as a meat tenderizer and in medicine

pa·pal \'pā-pəl\ *adj* : of or relating to the pope or to the Roman Catholic Church

pa·paw *n* **1** \pə-'pȯ\ : PAPAYA **2** \'päp-ˌȯ\ : a No. American tree with yellow edible fruit; *also* : its fruit

pa·pa·ya \pə-'pī-ə\ *n* : a tropical American tree with large yellow black-seeded edible fruit; *also* : its fruit

pa·per \'pā-pər\ *n* [ME *papir*, fr. MF *papier*, fr. L *papyrus* papyrus, paper, fr. Gk *papyros* papyrus] **1** : a pliable substance made usu. of vegetable matter and used to write or print on, to wrap things in, or to cover walls; *also* : a single sheet of this substance **2** : a printed or written document **3** : NEWSPAPER **4** : WALLPAPER — **paper** *adj or vb* — **pa·pery** \'pā-p(ə-)rē\ *adj*

pa·per·back \-ˌbak\ *n* : a paper-covered book

pa·per·board \-ˌbȯrd\ *n* : a material made from cellulose fiber (as wood pulp) like paper but usu. thicker

pa·per·hang·er \'pā-pər-ˌhaŋ-ər\ *n* : one that applies wallpaper — **pa·per·hang·ing** \-iŋ\ *n*

pa·per·weight \-ˌwāt\ *n* : an object used to hold down loose papers by its weight

pa·pier-mâ·ché \,pā-pər-mə-'shā, ,pap-ˌyä-mə-, -ma-\ *n* [F, lit., chewed paper] : a molding material of wastepaper and additives (as glue) — **papier-mâché** *adj*

pa·pil·la \pə-'pil-ə\ *n, pl* **pa·pil·lae** \-'pil-(ˌ)ē, -ˌī\ [L, nipple] : a small projecting bodily part — **pap·il·lary** \'pap-ə-ˌler-ē, pə-'pil-ə-rē\ *adj*

pa·pil·lote \'päp-ē-ᵊl(y)ōt\ *n* [F] : a greased paper wrapper in which food is cooked

pa·poose \pa-'püs, pə-\ *n* : a young child of No. American Indian parents

pa·pri·ka \pə-'prē-kə, pa-\ *n* [Hung] : a mild red spice made from the fruit of some sweet peppers

Pap smear \'pap-\ *n* : a method for the early detection of cancer

Pap test \'pap-\ *n* : PAP SMEAR

pap·ule \'pap-yül\ *n* : a small solid usu. conical lesion of the skin — **pap·u·lar** \-yə-lər\ *adj*

pa·py·rus \pə-'pī-rəs\ *n, pl* **pa·py·rus·es** *or* **pa·py·ri** \-(ˌ)rē, -ˌrī\ **1** : a tall grassy Egyptian sedge **2** : paper made from papyrus pith

¹**par** \'pär\ *n* **1** : a stated value (as of a security) **2** : a common level : EQUALITY **3** : an accepted standard or normal condition **4** : the score standard set for each hole of a golf course — **par** *adj*

²**par** *abbr* **1** paragraph **2** parallel **3** parish

pa·ra \'pär-ə\ *n, pl* **paras** *or* **para** — see *dinar* at MONEY table

par·a·ble \'par-ə-bəl\ *n* : a simple story told to illustrate a moral truth

pa·rab·o·la \pə-'rab-ə-lə\ *n* : a plane curve generated by a point moving so that its distance from a fixed point is equal to its distance from a fixed line : a curve formed by the intersection of a cone with a plane parallel to its side — **par·a·bol·ic** \,par-ə-'bäl-ik\ *adj*

para·chute \'par-ə-ˌshüt\ *n* : a device for slowing the descent of a person or object through the air that consists of a usu. hemispherical canopy beneath which the person or object is suspended — **parachute** *vb* — **par·a·chut·ist** \-ˌshüt-əst\ *n*

¹pa·rade \pə-ˈrād\ *n* **1** : a pompous display : EXHIBITION ⟨a ∼ of wealth⟩ **2** : MARCH, PROCESSION; *esp* : a ceremonial formation and march (as of troops) **3** : a place for strolling

²parade *vb* **pa·rad·ed; pa·rad·ing 1** : to march in a parade **2** : PROMENADE **3** : SHOW OFF **4** : MASQUERADE

par·a·digm \ˈpar-ə-ˌdīm, -ˌdim\ *n* **1** : MODEL, PATTERN **2** : a systematic inflection of a verb or noun showing a complete conjugation or declension

par·a·dise \ˈpar-ə-ˌdīs, -ˌdīz\ *n* [ME *paradis*, fr. OF, fr. LL *paradisus*, fr. Gk *paradeisos*, lit., enclosed park, of Iranian origin] **1** : HEAVEN **2** : a place or state of bliss

par·a·di·si·a·cal \ˌpar-ə-də-ˈsī-ə-kəl\ *or* **par·a·dis·i·ac** \-ˈdiz-ē-ˌak, -ˈdis-\ *adj* : of, relating to, or resembling paradise

par·a·dox \ˈpar-ə-ˌdäks\ *n* : a statement that seems contrary to common sense and yet is perhaps true — **par·a·dox·i·cal** \ˌpar-ə-ˈdäk-si-kəl\ *adj* — **par·a·dox·i·cal·ly** \-k(ə-)lē\ *adv*

par·af·fin \ˈpar-ə-fən\ *n* : a waxy substance used esp. for making candles and sealing foods

par·a·gon \ˈpar-ə-ˌgän, -gən\ *n* : a model of perfection : PATTERN

¹para·graph \ˈpar-ə-ˌgraf\ *n* : a subdivision of a written composition that deals with one point or gives the words of one speaker; *also* : a character (as ¶) marking the beginning of a paragraph

²paragraph *vb* : to divide into paragraphs

par·a·keet \ˈpar-ə-ˌkēt\ *n* : any of numerous usu. small slender parrots with a long graduated tail

para·le·gal \ˌpar-ə-ˈlē-gəl\ *adj* : of, relating to, or being a paraprofessional who assists a lawyer — **paralegal** *n*

Par·a·li·pom·e·non \ˌpar-ə-lə-ˈpäm-ə-ˌnän\ *n* — see BIBLE table

par·al·lax \ˈpar-ə-ˌlaks\ *n* : the difference in apparent direction of an object as seen from two different points

¹par·al·lel \ˈpar-ə-ˌlel\ *adj* [L *parallelus*, fr. Gk *parallēlos*, fr. *para* beside + *allēlōn* of one another, fr. *allos* . . . *allos*, *allos* one . . . another, fr. *allos* other] **1** : lying or moving in the same direction but always the same distance apart **2** : similar in essential parts : LIKE — **par·al·lel·ism** \-ˌiz-əm\ *n*

²parallel *n* **1** : a parallel line, curve, or surface **2** : one of the imaginary circles on the earth's surface that parallel the equator and mark the latitude **3** : something essentially similar to another **4** : LIKENESS, SIMILARITY

³parallel *vb* **1** : COMPARE **2** : to correspond to **3** : to extend in a parallel direction with

par·al·lel·o·gram \ˌpar-ə-ˈlel-ə-ˌgram\ *n*

: a 4-sided geometrical figure with opposite sides equal and parallel

pa·ral·y·sis \pə-ˈral-ə-səs\ *n, pl* **-y·ses** \-ˌsēz\ : loss of function and esp. of feeling or the power of voluntary motion — **par·a·lyt·ic** \ˌpar-ə-ˈlit-ik\ *adj or n*

par·a·lyze \ˈpar-ə-ˌlīz\ *vb* **-lyzed; -lyz·ing 1** : to affect with paralysis **2** : to make powerless or inactive — **par·a·lyz·ing·ly** \-ˌlī-ziŋ-lē\ *adv*

par·a·me·cium \ˌpar-ə-ˈmē-sh(ē-)əm, -sē-əm\ *n, pl* **-cia** \-sh(ē-)ə, -sē-ə\ *also* **-ci·ums** : any of a genus of slipper-shaped protozoans that move by cilia

para·med·i·cal \ˌpar-ə-ˈmed-i-kəl\ *adj* : concerned with supplementing the work of trained medical professionals — **para·med·ic** \ˌpar-ə-ˈmed-ik\ *n*

pa·ram·e·ter \pə-ˈram-ət-ər\ *n* **1** : an arbitrary constant whose value characterizes a member of a system (as a family of curves) **2** : a physical property whose value determines the characteristics or behavior of a system **3** : a characteristic element : FACTOR — **para·met·ric** \ˌpar-ə-ˈme-trik\ *adj*

para·mil·i·tary \ˌpar-ə-ˈmil-ə-ˌter-ē\ *adj* : formed on a military pattern esp. as an auxiliary military force

par·a·mount \ˈpar-ə-ˌmaůnt\ *adj* : superior to all others : SUPREME **syn** preponderant, predominant, dominant, chief, sovereign

par·amour \ˈpar-ə-ˌmůr\ *n* : an illicit lover

para·noia \ˌpar-ə-ˈnȯi-ə\ *n* : a psychosis marked by delusions and irrational suspicion usu. without hallucinations — **par·a·noid** \ˈpar-ə-ˌnȯid\ *adj or n*

par·a·pet \ˈpar-ə-pət, -ˌpet\ *n* **1** : a protecting rampart **2** : a low wall or railing (as at the edge of a bridge)

par·a·pher·na·lia \ˌpar-ə-fə(r)-ˈnāl-yə\ *n sing or pl* **1** : personal belongings **2** : EQUIPMENT, APPARATUS

para·phrase \ˈpar-ə-ˌfrāz\ *n* : a restatement of a text giving the meaning in different words — **paraphrase** *vb*

para·ple·gia \ˌpar-ə-ˈplē-j(ē-)ə\ *n* : paralysis of the lower trunk and legs — **para·ple·gic** \-jik\ *adj or n*

para·pro·fes·sion·al \-prə-ˈfesh-(ə-)nəl\ *n* : a trained aide who assists a professional

para·psy·chol·o·gy \ˌpar-ə-sī-ˈkäl-ə-jē\ *n* : a branch of study involving the investigation of telepathy and related subjects — **para·psy·chol·o·gist** \-jəst\ *n*

par·a·site \ˈpar-ə-ˌsīt\ *n* [MF, fr. L *parasitus*, fr. Gk *parasitos*, fr. *para-* beside + *sitos* grain, food] **1** : a plant or animal living in or on another organism usu. to its harm **2** : one depending on another and not making adequate return — **par·a·sit·ic** \ˌpar-ə-ˈsit-ik\ *adj* — **par·a·sit·ism** \ˈpar-ə-sə-ˌtīz-əm, -ˌsīt-ˌiz-\ *n* — **par·a·sit·ize** \-sə-ˌtīz\ *vb*

par·a·si·tol·o·gy \ˌpar-ə-sə-ˈtäl-ə-jē\ *n*

: a branch of biology dealing with parasites and parasitism esp. among animals — **par·a·si·tol·o·gist** \-jəst\ n

parasol \'par-ə-ˌsȯl\ n [F, fr. It *parasole*, fr. *parare* to shield + *sole* sun, fr. L *sol*] : a lightweight umbrella used as a shield against the sun

para·sym·pa·thet·ic nervous system \ˌpar-ə-ˌsim-pə-ˈthet-ik-\ n : the part of the autonomic nervous system that tends to induce secretion, to increase the tone and contractility of smooth muscle, and to cause the dilatation of blood vessels

para·thi·on \ˌpar-ə-ˈthī-ən, -ˌän\ n : an extremely toxic insecticide

para·thy·roid \-ˈthī-ˌrȯid\ n : PARATHYROID GLAND — **parathyroid** adj

parathyroid gland n : any of usu. four small endocrine glands that are adjacent to or embedded in the thyroid gland and produce a hormone concerned with calcium metabolism

para·troop·er \'par-ə-ˌtrü-pər\ n : a member of the paratroops

para·troops \-ˌtrüps\ n pl : troops trained to parachute from an airplane

para·ty·phoid \ˌpar-ə-ˈtī-ˌfȯid, -tī-ˈfȯid\ n : a food poisoning resembling typhoid fever

par·boil \'pär-ˌbȯil\ vb : to boil briefly

¹par·cel \'pär-səl\ n 1 : a tract or plot of land 2 : COLLECTION, LOT 3 : a wrapped bundle : PACKAGE

²parcel vb **-celed** or **-celled; -cel·ing** or **-cel·ling** \'pär-s(ə-)liŋ\ : to divide into portions

parcel post n 1 : a mail service handling parcels 2 : packages handled by parcel post

parch \'pärch\ vb 1 : to toast under dry heat 2 : to shrivel with heat

parch·ment \'pärch-mənt\ n : the skin of an animal prepared for writing on; *also* : a writing on such material

pard \'pärd\ n : LEOPARD

¹par·don \'pärd-ᵊn\ n : excuse of an offense without penalty; *esp* : an official release from legal punishment

²pardon vb **par·doned; par·don·ing** \'pärd-(ᵊ-)niŋ\ : to free from penalty : EXCUSE, FORGIVE — **par·don·able** \'pärd-(ᵊ-)nə-bəl\ adj

par·don·er \'pärd-(ᵊ-)nər\ n 1 : a medieval preacher delegated to raise money for religious works by soliciting offerings and granting indulgences 2 : one that pardons

pare \'paər\ vb **pared; par·ing** 1 : to trim or shave off an outside part (as the skin or rind) of (∼ an apple) 2 : to reduce as if by paring (∼ expenses) — **par·er** n

par·e·gor·ic \ˌpar-ə-ˈgȯr-ik\ n : an alcoholic preparation of opium and camphor

par·ent \'par-ənt\ n 1 : one that begets or brings forth offspring : FATHER, MOTHER 2 : SOURCE, ORIGIN — **par·ent·age** \-ij\ n — **pa·ren·tal** \pə-ˈrent-ᵊl\ adj — **par·ent·hood** n

pa·ren·the·sis \pə-ˈren-thə-səs\ n, pl **-the·ses** \-ˌsēz\ 1 : a word, phrase, or sentence inserted in a passage to explain or modify the thought 2 : one of a pair of punctuation marks () used esp. to enclose parenthetic matter — **par·en·thet·ic** \ˌpar-ən-ˈthet-ik\ or **par·en·thet·i·cal** \-i-kəl\ adj — **par·en·thet·i·cal·ly** \-k(ə-)lē\ adv

pa·ren·the·size \pə-ˈren-thə-ˌsīz\ vb **-sized; -siz·ing** : to make a parenthesis of

par·ent·ing \'par-ənt-iŋ, 'per-\ n : the raising of a child by its parents

pa·re·sis \pə-ˈrē-səs, 'par-ə-\ n, pl **pa·re·ses** \-ˌsēz\ : a usu. incomplete paralysis: *also* : insanity caused by syphilitic alteration of the brain that leads to dementia and paralysis

par ex·cel·lence \ˌpär-ˌek-sə-ˈläⁿs\ adj [F, lit., by excellence] : being the best of a kind : PREEMINENT

par·fait \pär-ˈfā\ n [F, lit., something perfect, fr. *parfait* perfect, fr. L *perfectus*] 1 : a flavored custard containing whipped cream and a syrup frozen without stirring 2 : a cold dessert made of layers of fruit, syrup, ice cream, and whipped cream

pa·ri·ah \pə-ˈrī-ə\ n : OUTCAST

pa·ri·etal \pə-ˈrī-ət-ᵊl\ adj 1 : of, relating to, or forming the walls of an anatomical structure 2 : of or relating to college living or its regulation

pari·mu·tu·el \ˌpar-i-ˈmyü-chə(-wə)l\ n : a betting system in which winners share the total stakes minus a percentage for the management

par·ing \'par-iŋ\ n : something pared off (potato ∼s)

pa·ri pas·su \ˌpar-i-ˈpas-ü\ adv or adj [L, with equal step] : at an equal rate or pace

Paris green \ˌpar-əs-\ n : a poisonous bright green powder used as a pigment and as an insecticide

par·ish \'par-ish\ n 1 : a church district in the care of one pastor; *also* : the residents of such an area 2 : a local church community 3 : a civil division of the state of Louisiana : COUNTY

pa·rish·io·ner \pə-ˈrish-(ə-)nər\ n : a member or resident of a parish

par·i·ty \'par-ət-ē\ n, pl **-ties** : EQUALITY, EQUIVALENCE

¹park \'pärk\ n 1 : a tract of ground kept as a game preserve or recreation area 2 : a level valley between mountain ranges 3 : a place where vehicles (as automobiles) are parked 4 : an enclosed stadium used esp. for ball games

²park vb 1 : to leave a vehicle temporarily (as in a parking lot or garage) 2 : to set and leave temporarily

par·ka \'pär-kə\ n : a very warm jacket with a hood

Par·kin·son's disease \'pär-kən-sənz-\ n : a chronic progressive nervous disease of later life that is marked by tremor and weakness of resting muscles and by a peculiar gait

Par·kin·son's Law *n* 1 : an observation in office organization: the number of subordinates increases at a fixed rate regardless of the amount of work produced 2 : an observation in office organization: work expands so as to fill the time available for its completion

park·way \\'pärk-ˌwā\ *n* : a broad landscaped thoroughfare

par·lance \\'pär-ləns\ *n* 1 : SPEECH 2 : manner of speaking ⟨military ∼⟩

¹par·lay \\'pär-ˌlā, -lē\ *vb* : to increase or change into something of much greater value

²parlay *n* : a series of bets in which the original stake plus its winnings are risked on successive wagers

par·ley \\'pär-lē\ *n, pl* **parleys** : a conference usu. over matters in dispute — **DISCUSSION — parley** *vb*

par·lia·ment \\'pär-lə-mənt\ *n* 1 : a formal governmental conference 2 *cap* : an assembly that constitutes the supreme legislative body of a country (as the United Kingdom) — **par·lia·men·ta·ry** \ˌpär-lə-ˈment-(ə-)rē\ *adj*

par·lia·men·tar·i·an \ˌpär-lə-ˌmen-ˈter-ē-ən\ *n* 1 *often cap* : an adherent of the parliament in opposition to the king during the English Civil War 2 : an expert in parliamentary procedure

par·lor \\'pär-lər\ *n* 1 : a room for conversation or the reception of guests 2 : a place of business ⟨beauty ∼⟩

par·lour \\'pär-lər\ *chiefly Brit var of* PARLOR

par·lous \\'pär-ləs\ *adj* : full of danger or risk : PRECARIOUS ⟨∼ state of a country's finances⟩ — **par·lous·ly** *adv*

Par·me·san \\'pär-mə-ˌzän, -ˌzän\ *n* : a hard dry cheese with a sharp flavor

par·mi·gia·na \ˌpär-mi-ˈjän-ə, ˌpär-mi-ˈzhän\ *or* **par·mi·gia·no** \-ˈjän-(ˌ)ō\ *adj* : made or covered with Parmesan cheese ⟨veal ∼⟩

pa·ro·chi·al \pə-ˈrō-kē-əl\ *adj* 1 : of or relating to a church parish 2 : limited in scope : NARROW, PROVINCIAL — **pa·ro·chi·al·ism** \-ə-ˌliz-əm\ *n*

parochial school *n* : a school maintained by a religious body

par·o·dy \\'par-əd-ē\ *n, pl* **-dies** [L *parodia*, fr. Gk *parōidia*, fr. *para-* beside + *aidein* to sing] : a humorous or satirical imitation — **parody** *vb*

pa·role \pə-ˈrōl\ *n* : a conditional release of a prisoner before his sentence expires — **parole** *vb* — **pa·rol·ee** \-ˌrō-ˈlē, -ˈrō-ˌlē\ *n*

par·ox·ysm \\'par-ək-ˌsiz-əm, pə-ˈräk-\ *n* : a sudden sharp attack (as of pain or coughing) : SPASM *syn* convulsion, fit — **par·ox·ys·mal** \ˌpar-ək-ˈsiz-məl, pə-ˌräk-\ *adj*

par·quet \\'pär-ˌkā, ˌkā\ *n* [F] 1 : a flooring of parquetry 2 : the lower floor of a theater; *esp* : the forward part of the orchestra

par·que·try \\'pär-kə-trē\ *n, pl* **-tries** : fine woodwork inlaid in patterns

par·ra·keet *var of* PARAKEET

par·ri·cide \\'par-ə-ˌsīd\ *n* 1 : one that murders his or her father, mother, or a close relative 2 : the act of a parricide

par·rot \\'par-ət\ *n* : any of numerous bright-colored tropical birds that have a stout hooked bill

parrot fever *n* : an infectious disease of birds that is marked by diarrhea and wasting and is transmissible to man

par·ry \\'par-ē\ *vb* **par·ried**; **par·ry·ing** 1 : to ward off a weapon or blow 2 : to evade esp. by an adroit answer — **parry** *n*

parse \\'pärs *also* 'pärz\ *vb* **parsed**; **pars·ing** : to give a grammatical description of a word or a group of words

par·sec \\'pär-ˌsek\ *n* : a unit of measure for interstellar space equal to 3.26 light-years or 19.2 trillion miles

par·si·mo·ny \\'pär-sə-ˌmō-nē\ *n* : extreme or excessive frugality — **par·si·mo·ni·ous** \ˌpär-sə-ˈmō-nē-əs\ *adj* — **par·si·mo·ni·ous·ly** *adv*

pars·ley \\'pär-slē\ *n* : a garden plant with finely divided leaves used as a seasoning or garnish

pars·nip \\'pär-snəp\ *n* : a garden plant with a long edible root; *also* : this root

par·son \\'pärs-ᵊn\ *n* [ME *persone*, fr. OF, fr. ML *persona*, lit., person, fr. L] : a usu. Protestant clergyman

par·son·age \\'pärs-(ᵊ-)nij\ *n* : a house provided by a church for its pastor

¹part \\'pärt\ *n* 1 : a division or portion of a whole 2 : the melody or score for a particular voice or instrument ⟨the alto ∼⟩ 3 : a spare piece for a machine 4 : DUTY, FUNCTION 5 : one of the sides in a dispute ⟨took his friend's ∼⟩ 6 : ROLE; *also* : an actor's lines in a play 7 *pl* : TALENTS, ABILITY 8 : the line where one's hair divides (as in combing)

²part *vb* 1 : to take leave of someone 2 : to divide or break into parts : SEPARATE 3 : to go away : DEPART; *also* : DIE 4 : to give up possession ⟨∼ed with her jewels⟩ 5 : APPORTION, SHARE

³part *abbr* 1 participial; participle 2 particular

par·take \pär-ˈtāk, pər-\ *vb* **-took** \-ˈtùk\ ; **-tak·en** \-ˈtā-kən\ ; **-tak·ing** 1 : to have a share or part 2 : to take a portion (as of food) — **par·tak·er** *n*

par·terre \pär-ˈteər\ *n* [F, fr. MF, fr. *par terre* on the ground] 1 : an ornamental arrangement of flower beds 2 : the part of a theater floor behind the orchestra

par·the·no·gen·e·sis \ˌpär-thə-nō-ˈjen-ə-səs\ *n* [NL, fr. Gk *parthenos* virgin + L *genesis* genesis] : development of a new individual from an unfertilized egg — **par·the·no·ge·net·ic** \-jə-ˈnet-ik\ *adj*

par·tial \\'pär-shəl\ *adj* 1 : favoring one party over the other : BIASED 2

: markedly or foolishly fond — used with *to* **3** : not total or general : affecting a part only — **par·tial·i·ty** \ˌpärsh-(ē-)ˈal-ət-ē\ *n* — **par·tial·ly** \ˈpärsh-(ə-)lē\ *adv*

par·tic·i·pate \pər-ˈtis-ə-ˌpāt, pär-\ *vb* **-pat·ed; -pat·ing** **1** : to take part in something (∼ in a game) **2** : SHARE — **par·tic·i·pant** \-pənt\ *adj or n* — **par·tic·i·pa·tion** \-ˌtis-ə-ˈpā-shən\ *n* — **par·tic·i·pa·tor** \-ˈtis-ə-ˌpāt-ər\ *n* — **par·tic·i·pa·to·ry** \-ˌtis-ə-pə-ˌtōr-ē\ *adj*

par·ti·ci·ple \ˈpärt-ə-ˌsip-əl\ *n* : a word having the characteristics of both verb and adjective — **par·ti·cip·i·al** \ˌpärt-ə-ˈsip-ē-əl\ *adj*

par·ti·cle \ˈpärt-i-kəl\ *n* **1** : a very small bit of matter **2** : ELEMENTARY PARTICLE **3** : a unit of speech (as an article, preposition, or conjunction) expressing some general aspect of meaning or some connective or limiting relation

par·ti·cle·board \-ˌbōrd\ *n* : a board made of very small pieces of wood bonded together

par·ti·col·or \ˈpärt-ē-ˌkəl-ər\ *or* **par·ti·col·ored** \-ərd\ *adj* : showing different colors or tints : *esp* : having patches of two or more colors

¹**par·tic·u·lar** \pə(r)-ˈtik-yə-lər\ *adj* **1** : of or relating to a specific person or thing (the laws of a ∼ state) **2** : DISTINCTIVE, SPECIAL (the ∼ point of his talk) **3** : SEPARATE, INDIVIDUAL (each ∼ hair) **4** : attentive to details : PRECISE **5** : hard to please : EXACTING **syn** single, sole, unique, lone, solitary — **par·tic·u·lar·i·ty** \-ˌtik-yə-ˈlar-ət-ē\ *n* — **par·tic·u·lar·ly** \-ˈtik-yə-lər-lē\ *adv*

²**particular** *n* : an individual fact or detail

par·tic·u·lar·ize \pə(r)-ˈtik-yə-lə-ˌrīz\ *vb* **-ized; -iz·ing** **1** : to state in detail : SPECIFY **2** : to go into details

par·tic·u·late \pər-ˈtik-yə-lət, pär-, -ˌlāt\ *adj* : relating to or existing as minute separate particles

¹**part·ing** \ˈpärt-iŋ\ *n* **1** : SEPARATION, DIVISION **2** : the action of leaving one another (lovers' ∼) **3** : a place of separation or divergence

²**parting** *adj* : given, taken, or performed at parting (a ∼ kiss)

par·ti·san *or* **par·ti·zan** \ˈpärt-ə-zən, -sən\ *n* **1** : one that takes the part of another : ADHERENT **2** : GUERRILLA — **partisan** *adj* — **par·ti·san·ship** *n*

par·tite \ˈpär-ˌtīt\ *adj* : divided into a usu. specified number of parts

par·ti·tion \pər-ˈtish-ən, pär-\ *n* **1** : DIVISION **2** : something that divides or separates; *esp* : an interior wall dividing one part of a house from another — **partition** *vb*

par·ti·tive \ˈpärt-ət-iv\ *adj* : of, relating to, or denoting a part (a ∼ construction)

part·ly \ˈpärt-lē\ *adv* : in part : in some measure or degree

part·ner \ˈpärt-nər\ *n* **1** : ASSOCIATE, COLLEAGUE **2** : either of two persons

who dance together **3** : one who plays on the same team with another **4** : HUSBAND, WIFE **5** : one of two or more persons contractually associated as joint principals in a business — **part·ner·ship** *n*

part of speech : a traditional class of words distinguished according to the kind of idea denoted and the function performed in a sentence

par·tridge \ˈpär-trij\ *n, pl* **partridge** *or* **par·tridg·es** : any of various stout-bodied game birds

part-song \ˈpärt-ˌsòŋ\ *n* : a song with two or more voice parts

part-time \-ˈtīm\ *adj or adv* : involving or working less than a full or regular schedule

par·tu·ri·tion \ˌpärt-ə-ˈrish-ən, ˌpär-chə-, ˌpär-tyü-\ *n* : CHILDBIRTH

part·way \ˈpärt-ˈwā\ *adv* : to some extent : PARTLY

par·ty \ˈpärt-ē\ *n, pl* **parties** **1** : a person or group taking one side of a question; *esp* : a group of persons organized for the purpose of directing the policies of a government **2** : a person or group concerned in an action or affair : PARTICIPANT **3** : a group of persons detailed for a common task **4** : a social gathering

par·ve·nu \ˈpär-və-ˌn(y)ü\ *n* [F, fr. pp. of *parvenir* to arrive, fr. L *pervenire*, fr. *per* through + *venire* to come] : one who has recently or suddenly risen to wealth or power and has not yet secured the social position associated with it

¹**pas** \ˈpä\ *n, pl* **pas** \ˈpä(z)\ *n* : a dance step or combination of steps

pas·cal \pas-ˈkal\ *n* : a unit of pressure in the metric system equal to one newton per square meter

pas·chal \ˈpas-kəl\ *adj* [deriv. of Heb *pesaḥ* Passover] : of, relating to, appropriate for, or used during Passover or Easter ceremonies

pa·sha \ˈpäsh-ə, ˈpash-; pə-ˈshä\ *n* : a man (as formerly a governor in Turkey) of high rank

¹**pass** \ˈpas\ *vb* **1** : MOVE, PROCEED **2** : to go away; *also* : DIE **3** : to move past, beyond, or over **4** : to allow to elapse : SPEND **5** : to go or make way through **6** : to go or allow to go unchallenged **7** : to undergo transfer **8** : to render a legal judgment **9** : OCCUR **10** : to secure the approval of (as a legislature) **11** : to go or cause to go through an inspection, test, or course of study successfully **12** : to be regarded **13** : CIRCULATE **14** : VOID **15** : to transfer the ball or puck to another player **16** : to decline to bid or bet on one's hand in a card game **17** : to permit to reach first base by a base on balls — **pass·er** *n*

²**pass** *n* : a gap in a mountain range

³**pass** *n* **1** : the act or an instance of passing **2** : REALIZATION, ACCOMPLISHMENT **3** : a state of affairs **4** : a written au-

thorization to leave, enter, or move about freely **5** : a transfer of a ball or puck from one player to another **6** : BASE ON BALLS **7** : EFFORT, TRY **8** : a sexually inviting gesture or approach

⁴**pass** *abbr* **1** passenger **2** passive

pass·able \'pas-ə-bəl\ *adj* **1** : capable of being passed or traveled on **2** : just good enough : TOLERABLE — **pass·ably** \-blē\ *adv*

pas·sage \'pas-ij\ *n* **1** : the action or process of passing **2** : a means (as a road or corridor) of passing **3** : a voyage esp. by sea or air **4** : a right or permission to pass **5** : ENACTMENT **6** : a mutual act (as an exchange of blows) **7** : a usu. brief portion or section (as of a book)

pas·sage·way \-ˌwā\ *n* : a way that allows passage

pass·book \'pas-ˌbuk\ *n* : BANKBOOK

pas·sé \pa-'sā\ *adj* **1** : past one's prime **2** : not up-to-date : OUTMODED

pas·sel \'pas-əl\ *n* : a large number

pas·sen·ger \'pas-ᵊn-jər\ *n* : a traveler in a public or private conveyance

passe-par·tout \ˌpas-pər-'tü\ *n* [F] : something that passes or enables one to pass everywhere

pass·er-by \'pas-ər-ˌbī\ *n, pl* **pass·ers-by** \-ᵊrz-\ : one who passes by

pas·ser·ine \'pas-ə-ˌrīn\ *adj* : of or relating to the large order of birds comprising singing birds that perch

pas·sim \'pas-əm\ *adv* [L, fr. *passus* scattered, fr. pp. of *pandere* to spread] : here and there : THROUGHOUT

pass·ing \'pas-iŋ\ *n* : the act of one that passes or causes to pass; *esp* : DEATH

pas·sion \'pash-ən\ *n* **1** *often cap* : the sufferings of Christ between the night of the Last Supper and his death **2** : strong feeling; *also pl* : the emotions as distinguished from reason **3** : RAGE, ANGER **4** : LOVE; *also* : an object of affection or enthusiasm **5** : sexual desire — **pas·sion·ate** \'pash-(ə-)nət\ *adj* — **pas·sion·ate·ly** *adv* — **pas·sion·less** *adj*

pas·sion-flow·er \'pash-ən-ˌflaù-(ə)r\ *n* [trans. of L *flos passionis*; fr. the fancied resemblance of parts of the flower to the instruments of Christ's crucifixion] : any of a genus of chiefly tropical woody climbing vines or erect herbs with showy flowers and pulpy often edible berries

passion fruit *n* : the edible fruit of a passionflower

pas·sive \'pas-iv\ *adj* **1** : not active : acted upon **2** : asserting that the grammatical subject is subjected to or affected by the action represented by the verb ⟨~ voice⟩ **3** : making use of the sun's heat usu. without the aid of mechanical devices **4** : SUBMISSIVE, PATIENT — **passive** *n* — **pas·sive·ly** *adv* — **pas·siv·i·ty** \pa-'siv-ət-ē\ *n*

pass·key \'pas-ˌkē\ *n* : a key for opening two or more locks

pass out *vb* : to lose consciousness

Pass·over \'pas-ˌō-vər\ *n* [fr. the exemption of the Israelites from the slaughter of the firstborn in Egypt (Exod 12:23–27)] : a Jewish holiday celebrated in March or April in commemoration of the Hebrews' liberation from slavery in Egypt

pass·port \'pas-ˌpōrt\ *n* : an official document issued by a country upon request to a citizen requesting protection during travel abroad

pass up *vb* : DECLINE, REJECT

pass·word \'pas-ˌwərd\ *n* **1** : a word or phrase that must be spoken by a person before he is allowed to pass a guard **2** : a sequence of characters required for access to a computer system

¹**past** \'past\ *adj* **1** : AGO ⟨10 years ~⟩ **2** : just gone or elapsed ⟨the ~ month⟩ **3** : having existed or taken place in a period before the present : BYGONE **4** : of, relating to, or constituting a verb tense that expresses time gone by

²**past** *prep or adv* : BEYOND

³**past** *n* **1** : time gone by **2** : something that happened or was done in a former time **3** : the past tense; *also* : a verb form in it **4** : a secret past life

pas·ta \'päs-tə\ *n* [It] **1** : a paste in processed form (as spaghetti) or in the form of fresh dough (as ravioli) **2** : a dish of cooked pasta

¹**paste** \'pāst\ *n* **1** : DOUGH **2** : a smooth food product made by evaporation or grinding ⟨almond ~⟩ **3** : a shaped dough (as spaghetti or ravioli) **4** : a preparation (as of flour and water) for sticking things together **5** : a brilliant glass of high lead content used in imitation gems

²**paste** *vb* **past·ed; past·ing** : to cause to adhere by paste : STICK

paste·board \'pās(t)-ˌbōrd\ *n* : a stiff material made of sheets of paper pasted together; *also* : PAPERBOARD

¹**pas·tel** \pas-'tel\ *n* **1** : a paste made of powdered pigment; *also* : a crayon of such paste **2** : a drawing in pastel **3** : a pale or light color

²**pastel** *adj* **1** : of or relating to a pastel **2** : pale and light in color

pas·tern \'pas-tərn\ *n* : the part of a horse's foot extending from the fetlock to the top of the hoof

pas·teur·iza·tion \ˌpas-chə-rə-'zā-shən, ˌpas-tə-\ *n* : partial sterilization of a substance (as milk) by heat or radiation — **pas·teur·ize** \'pas-chə-ˌrīz, 'pas-tə-\ *vb* — **pas·teur·iz·er** *n*

pas·tiche \pas-'tēsh\ *n* : a composition (as in literature or music) made up of selections from different works

pas·tille \pas-'tēl\ *n* **1** : a small mass of aromatic paste for fumigating or scenting the air of a room **2** : an aromatic or medicated lozenge

pas·time \'pas-ˌtīm\ *n* : DIVERSION

pas·tor \'pas-tər\ *n* [ME *pastour*, fr. OF, fr. L *pastor*, herdsman, fr. *pas-*

tus, pp. of *pascere* to feed] : a clergyman serving a local church or parish — **pas·tor·ate** \-t(ə-)rət\ *n*

¹**pas·to·ral** \'pas-t(ə-)rəl\ *adj* 1 : of or relating to shepherds or to rural life 2 : of or relating to spiritual guidance esp. of a congregation 3 : of or relating to the pastor of a church

²**pastoral** \'pas-t(ə-)rəl\ *n* : a literary work dealing with shepherds or rural life

pas·to·rale \,pas-tə-'räl, -'ral\ *n* [It] : a musical composition having a pastoral theme

past participle *n* : a participle that typically expresses completed action, that is one of the principal parts of the verb, and that is used in the formation of perfect tenses in the active voice and of all tenses in the passive voice

pas·tra·mi *also* **pas·tro·mi** \pə-'sträm-ē\ *n* [Yiddish] : a highly seasoned smoked beef prepared esp. from shoulder cuts

pas·try \'pā-strē\ *n, pl* **pastries** : sweet baked goods made of dough or with a crust made of enriched dough

pas·tur·age \'pas-chə-rij\ *n* : PASTURE

¹**pas·ture** \'pas-chər\ *n* 1 : plants (as grass) for the feeding of grazing livestock 2 : land or a plot of land used for grazing

²**pasture** *vb* **pas·tured; pas·tur·ing** 1 : GRAZE 2 : to use as pasture

pasty \'pā-stē\ *adj* **past·i·er; -est** : resembling paste; *esp* : pallid and unhealthy in appearance

¹**pat** \'pat\ *n* 1 : a light tap esp. with the hand or a flat instrument; *also* : the sound made by it 2 : something (as butter) shaped into a small flat usu. square individual portion

²**pat** *adv* : in a pat manner : APTLY, PERFECTLY

³**pat** *vb* **pat·ted; pat·ting** 1 : to strike lightly with a flat instrument 2 : to flatten, smooth, or put into place or shape with a pat 3 : to tap gently or lovingly with the hand

⁴**pat** *adj* 1 : exactly suited to the occasion 2 : memorized exactly 3 : UNYIELDING

⁵**pat** *abbr* patent

pa·ta·ca \pə-'täk-ə\ *n* — see MONEY table

¹**patch** \'pach\ *n* 1 : a piece used to cover a torn or worn place; *also* : one worn on a garment as an ornament or insignia 2 : a small area distinct from that about it 3 : a shield worn over the socket of an injured or missing eye

²**patch** *vb* 1 : to mend or cover with a patch 2 : to make of fragments 3 : to repair usu. in hasty fashion

patch test *n* : a test for allergic sensitivity made by applying to the unbroken skin small pads soaked with the allergen to be tested

patch·work \'pach-,wərk\ *n* : something made of pieces of different materials, shapes, or colors

pate \'pāt\ *n* : HEAD; *esp* : the crown of the head

pâ·té \pä-'tā\ *n* [F] 1 : a meat or fish pie or patty 2 : a spread of finely mashed seasoned and spiced meat

pa·tel·la \pə-'tel-ə\ *n, pl* **-lae** \-'tel-(,)ē, -,ī\ *or* **-las** [L] : KNEECAP

pat·en \'pat-ᵊn\ *n* 1 : PLATE; *esp* : one of precious metal for the eucharistic bread 2 : a thin disk

¹**pa·tent** \1 & 4 *are* 'pat-ᵊnt, *Brit also* 'pāt-, 2 & 3 *are* 'pat-ᵊnt, 'pāt-\ *adj* 1 : open to public inspection — used chiefly in the phrase *letters patent* 2 : free from obstruction 3 : EVIDENT, OBVIOUS 4 : protected by a patent **syn** manifest, distinct, apparent, palpable, plain, clear — **pat·ent·ly** *adv*

²**pat·ent** \'pat-ᵊnt, *Brit also* 'pāt-\ *n* 1 : an official document conferring a right or privilege 2 : a document securing to an inventor for a term of years exclusive right to his invention 3 : something patented — **pat·en·tee** \,pat-ᵊn-'tē, *Brit also* ,pāt-\

³**patent** *vb* : to secure by patent

pa·ter·fa·mil·i·as \,pāt-ər-fə-'mil-ē-əs\ *n, pl* **pa·tres·fa·mil·i·as** \,pā-,trēz-\ [L] : the father of a family : the male head of a household

pa·ter·nal \pə-'tərn-ᵊl\ *adj* 1 : FATHERLY 2 : related through or inherited or derived from a father — **pa·ter·nal·ly** \-ē\ *adv*

pa·ter·nal·ism \-,iz-əm\ *n* : a system under which an authority treats those under its control paternally (as by regulating their conduct and supplying their needs)

pa·ter·ni·ty \pə-'tər-nət-ē\ *n* 1 : FATHERHOOD 2 : descent from a father

path \'path, 'páth\ *n, pl* **paths** \'pathz, 'paths, 'páthz, 'páths\ 1 : a trodden way 2 : ROUTE, COURSE — **path·less** *adj*

path *or* **pathol** *abbr* pathology

pa·thet·ic \pə-'thet-ik\ *adj* : evoking tenderness, pity, or sorrow **syn** pitiful, piteous, pitiable, poor — **pa·thet·i·cal·ly** \-i-k(ə-)lē\ *adv*

path·find·er \'path-,fīn-dər, 'páth-\ *n* : one that discovers a way; *esp* : one that explores untraveled regions to mark out a new route

patho·gen \'path-ə-jən\ *n* : a specific cause (as a bacterium or virus) of disease — **patho·gen·ic** \,path-ə-'jen-ik\ *adj* — **patho·ge·nic·i·ty** \-jə-'nis-ət-ē\ *n*

pa·thol·o·gy \pə-'thäl-ə-jē\ *n, pl* **-gies** 1 : the study of the essential nature of disease 2 : the abnormality of structure and function characteristic of a disease — **path·o·log·i·cal** \,path-ə-'läj-i-kəl\ *adj* — **pa·thol·o·gist** \pə-'thäl-ə-jəst\ *n*

pa·thos \'pā-,thäs\ *n* : an element in experience or artistic representation evoking pity or compassion

path·way \'path-,wā, 'páth-\ *n* : PATH

pa·tience \'pā-shəns\ *n* 1 : the capacity, habit, or fact of being patient 2 *chiefly Brit* : SOLITAIRE 2

¹pa·tient \'pā-shənt\ *adj* 1 : bearing pain or trials without complaint 2 : showing self-control : CALM 3 : STEADFAST, PERSEVERING — **pa·tient·ly** *adv*

²patient *n* : a person under medical care

pa·ti·na \'pat-ə-nə, pə-'tē-nə\ *n, pl* **pa·ti·nas** \-nəz\ *or* **pa·ti·nae** \'pat-ə-,nē, -,nī\ : a green film formed on copper and bronze by exposure to moist air

pa·tio \'pat-ē-,ō, 'pät-\ *n, pl* **pa·ti·os** 1 : COURTYARD 2 : a paved recreation area near a house

pa·tois \'pa-,twä\ *n, pl* **pa·tois** \-,twäz\ [F] 1 : a dialect other than the standard dialect; *esp* : illiterate or provincial speech 2 : JARGON 2

pa·tri·arch \'pā-trē-,ärk\ *n* 1 : a man revered as father or founder (as of a tribe) 2 : a venerable old man 3 : an ecclesiastical dignitary (as the bishop of an Eastern Orthodox see) — **pa·tri·ar·chal** \,pā-trē-'är-kəl\ *adj* — **pa·tri·arch·ate** \'pā-trē-,är-kət, -,kāt\ *n* — **pa·tri·ar·chy** \-,är-kē\ *n*

pa·tri·cian \pə-'trish-ən\ *n* : a person of high birth : ARISTOCRAT — **patrician** *adj*

pat·ri·cide \'pa-trə-,sīd\ *n* 1 : one who murders his own father 2 : the murder of one's own father

pat·ri·mo·ny \'pa-trə-,mō-nē\ *n* : something (as an estate) inherited or derived esp. from one's father : HERITAGE — **pat·ri·mo·ni·al** \,pat-rə-'mō-nē-əl\ *adj*

pa·tri·ot \'pā-trē-ət, -,ät\ *n* [MF *patriote*, fr. LL *patriota*, fr. Gk *patriōtēs*, fr. *patrios* of one's father, fr. *patr-*, *patēr* father] : one who loves his country — **pa·tri·ot·ic** \,pā-trē-'ät-ik\ *adj* — **pa·tri·ot·i·cal·ly** \-i-k(ə-)lē\ *adv* — **pa·tri·o·tism** \'pā-trē-ə-,tiz-əm\ *n*

pa·tris·tic \pə-'tris-tik\ *adj* : of or relating to the church fathers or their writings

¹pa·trol \pə-'trōl\ *n* : the action of going the rounds (as of an area) for observation or the maintenance of security; *also* : a person or group performing such an action

²patrol *vb* **pa·trolled; pa·trol·ling** [F *patrouiller*, fr. MF, to tramp around in the mud, fr. *patte* paw] : to carry out a patrol

pa·trol·man \pə-'trōl-mən\ *n* : a policeman assigned to a beat

patrol wagon *n* : an enclosed motor-truck for carrying prisoners

pa·tron \'pā-trən\ *n* [ME, fr. MF, fr. ML & L; ML *patronus* patron saint, patron of a benefice, pattern, fr. L, defender, fr. *patr-*, *pater* father] 1 : a person chosen or named as special protector 2 : a wealthy or influential supporter (~ of poets); *also* : BENEFACTOR 3 : a regular client or customer **syn** sponsor, guarantor, angel, backer

pa·tron·ess \'pā-trə-nəs\ *n* : a woman who is a patron

pa·tron·age \'pa-trə-nij, 'pā-\ *n* 1 : the support or influence of a patron 2 : the trade of customers 3 : control of appointment to government jobs

pa·tron·ize \'pā-trə-,nīz, 'pa-\ *vb* **-ized; -iz·ing** 1 : to be a customer of 2 : to treat condescendingly

pat·ro·nym·ic \,pa-trə-'nim-ik\ *n* : a name derived from the name of one's father or paternal ancestor usu. by the addition of a prefix or suffix

pa·troon \pə-'trün\ *n* : the proprietor of a manorial estate esp. in New York under Dutch rule

pat·sy \'pat-sē\ *n, pl* **pat·sies** : one who is duped or victimized

¹pat·ter \'pat-ər\ *vb* : to talk glibly or mechanically **syn** chatter, prate, chat, prattle, babble

²patter *n* 1 : a specialized lingo 2 : extremely rapid talk (a comedian's ~)

³patter *vb* : to strike, pat, or tap rapidly

⁴patter *n* : a quick succession of taps or pats (the ~ of rain)

¹pat·tern \'pat-ərn\ *n* [ME *patron*, fr. MF, fr. ML *patronus*, fr. L, defender, fr. *patr-*, *pater* father] 1 : an ideal model 2 : something used as a model for making things (a dressmaker's ~) 3 : SAMPLE 4 : an artistic design 5 : CONFIGURATION

²pattern *vb* : to form according to a pattern

pat·ty *also* **pat·tie** \'pat-ē\ *n, pl* **patties** 1 : a little pie 2 : a small flat cake esp. of chopped food

pau·ci·ty \'pȯ-sət-ē\ *n* : smallness of number or quantity

paunch \'pȯnch\ *n* : a usu. large belly : POTBELLY — **paunchy** *adj*

pau·per \'pȯ-pər\ *n* : a person without means of support except from charity — **pau·per·ism** \-pə-,riz-əm\ *n* — **pau·per·ize** \-pə-,rīz\ *vb*

¹pause \'pȯz\ *n* 1 : a temporary stop; *also* : a period of inaction 2 : a brief suspension of the voice 3 : a sign ⌢ or ⌣ above or below a musical note or rest to show it is to be prolonged 4 : a reason for pausing

²pause *vb* **paused; paus·ing** : to stop, rest, or linger for a time

pave \'pāv\ *vb* **paved; pav·ing** : to cover (as a road) with hard material in order to smooth or firm the surface

pave·ment \'pāv-mənt\ *n* 1 : a paved surface 2 : the material with which something is paved

pa·vil·ion \pə-'vil-yən\ *n* [ME *pavilon*, fr. OF *paveillon*, fr. L *papilion-*, *papilio* butterfly] 1 : a large tent 2 : a light structure (as in a park) used for entertainment or shelter

pav·ing \'pā-vin\ *n* : PAVEMENT

paw \'pȯ\ *n* : the foot of a quadruped (as a dog or lion) having claws

²paw *vb* 1 : to feel or handle clumsily or rudely 2 : to touch or strike with a paw; *also* : to scrape with a hoof 3 : to flail about or grab for with the hands

pawl \'pȯl\ *n* : a pivoted tongue or sliding bolt designed to fall into notches on another machine part to permit motion in one direction only

¹**pawn** \'pȯn\ n 1 : goods deposited as security for a loan; *also* : HOSTAGE 2 : the state of being pledged

²**pawn** vb : to deposit as a pledge

³**pawn** n [ME *pown*, fr. MF *poon*, fr. ML *pedon-*, *pedo* foot soldier, fr. LL, one with broad feet, fr. L *ped-*, *pes* foot] : a chessman of the least value

pawn·bro·ker \'pȯn-ˌbrō-kər\ n : one who loans money on goods pledged

Paw·nee \pȯ-'nē\ n, pl **Pawnee** or **Pawnees** : a member of an American Indian people orig. of Kansas and Nebraska

pawn·shop \'pȯn-ˌshäp\ n : a pawnbroker's place of business

paw·paw var of PAPAW

¹**pay** \'pā\ vb **paid** \'pād\ *also in sense 7* **payed**; **pay·ing** [ME *payen*, fr. OF *paier*, fr. L *pacare* to pacify, fr. *pac-*, *pax* peace] 1 : to make due return to for goods or services 2 : to discharge indebtedness for : SETTLE (~ a bill) 3 : to give in forfeit (~ the penalty) 4 : REQUITE 5 : to give, offer, or make freely or as fitting (~ attention) 6 : to be profitable to : RETURN 7 : to make slack and allow to run out (~ out a rope) — **pay·able** adj — **pay·ee** \pā-'ē\ n — **pay·er** n

²**pay** n 1 : the status of being paid by an employer : EMPLOY 2 : something paid; *esp* : WAGES

³**pay** adj 1 : containing something valuable (as gold) (~ dirt) 2 : equipped to receive a fee for use (~ telephone)

pay·check \'pā-ˌchek\ n 1 : a check in payment of wages or salary 2 : WAGES, SALARY

pay·load \'pā-ˌlōd\ n : the load carried by a vehicle in addition to what is necessary for its operation

pay·mas·ter \-ˌmas-tər\ n : one who distributes the payroll

pay·ment \'pā-mənt\ n 1 : the act of paying 2 : something paid

pay·off \-ˌȯf\ n 1 : payment at the outcome of an enterprise (a big ~ from an investment) 2 : the climax of an incident or enterprise (the ~ of a story)

pay·roll \'pā-ˌrōl\ n : a list of persons entitled to receive pay; *also* : the money to pay those on such a list

payt abbr payment

pay up vb : to pay what is due; *also* : to pay in full

Pb symbol [L *plumbum*] lead

PBX abbr private branch exchange

PC abbr 1 Peace Corps 2 percent; percentage 3 personal computer 4 postcard 5 [L *post cibum*] after meals 6 professional corporation

PCB \ˈpē-ˌsē-ˈbē\ n : POLYCHLORINATED BIPHENYL

PCP \ˈpē-ˌsē-ˈpē\ n : PHENCYCLIDINE

pct abbr percent; percentage

pd abbr paid

Pd symbol palladium

PD abbr 1 per diem 2 police department 3 potential difference

PDQ \ˌpē-ˌdē-ˈkyü\ adv, *often not cap* [abbr. of *pretty damned quick*] : IMMEDIATELY

PDT abbr Pacific daylight time

PE abbr 1 physical education 2 printer's error 3 professional engineer

pea \'pē\ n, pl **peas** *also* **pease** \'pēz\ 1 : the round edible protein-rich seed borne in the pod of a widely grown leguminous vine; *also* : this vine 2 : any of various plants resembling or related to the pea

peace \'pēs\ n 1 : a state of calm and quiet; *esp* : public security under law 2 : freedom from disturbing thoughts or emotions 3 : a state of concord (as between persons or governments); *also* : an agreement to end hostilities — **peace·able** \-ə-bəl\ adj — **peace·ably** \-blē\ adv — **peace·ful** \-fəl\ adj — **peace·ful·ly** \-ē\ adv

peace·keep·ing \'pēs-ˌkē-piŋ\ n : the preserving of peace; *esp* : international enforcement and supervision of a truce — **peace·keep·er** \-pər\ n

peace·mak·er \-ˌmā-kər\ n : one who settles an argument or stops a fight

peace·time \-ˌtīm\ n : a time when a nation is not at war

peach \'pēch\ n [ME *peche*, fr. MF (the fruit), fr. LL *persica*, fr. L *persicum*, fr. neut. of *persicus* Persian, fr. *Persia*] : a sweet juicy fruit of a low tree with pink blossoms; *also* : this tree

pea·cock \'pē-ˌkäk\ n : the male peafowl having long tail coverts which can be spread at will displaying brilliant colors

pea·fowl \-ˌfau̇l\ n : a very large domesticated Asian pheasant

pea·hen \-ˌhen\ n : the female peafowl

¹**peak** \'pēk\ n 1 : a pointed or projecting part 2 : the top of a hill or mountain; *also* : MOUNTAIN 3 : the front projecting part of a cap 4 : the narrow part of a ship's bow or stern 5 : the highest level or greatest degree — **peak** adj

²**peak** vb : to bring to or reach a maximum

peak·ed \'pē-kəd\ adj : THIN, SICKLY

¹**peal** \'pēl\ n 1 : the loud ringing of bells 2 : a set of tuned bells 3 : a loud sound or succession of sounds

²**peal** vb : to give out peals : RESOUND

pea·nut \'pē-(ˌ)nət\ n : an annual herb related to the pea but having pods that ripen underground; *also* : this pod or one of the edible seeds it bears

pear \'paər\ n : the fleshy fruit of a tree related to the apple; *also* : this tree

pearl \'pərl\ n 1 : a small hard often lustrous body formed within the shell of some mollusks and used as a gem 2 : one that is choice or precious (~s of wisdom) 3 : a slightly bluish medium gray — **pearly** \'pər-lē\ adj

peas·ant \'pez-²nt\ n 1 : any of a class

of small landowners or laborers tilling the soil **2** : a person of low social or cultural status — **peas·ant·ry** \-ᵊn-trē\ *n*

pea·shoot·er \'pē-ˌshüt-ər\ *n* : a toy blowgun for shooting peas

peat \'pēt\ *n* : a dark substance formed by partial decay of plants (as mosses) in water — **peaty** *adj*

peat moss *n* : SPHAGNUM

¹**peb·ble** \'peb-əl\ *n* : a small usu. round stone — **peb·bly** \-(ə-)lē\ *adj*

²**pebble** *vb* **peb·bled; peb·bling** \-(ə-)liŋ\ : to produce a rough surface texture in (∼ leather)

pe·can \pi-'kän, -'kan\ *n* : a large American hickory tree bearing a smooth-shelled edible nut; *also* : this nut

pec·ca·dil·lo \ˌpek-ə-'dil-ō\ *n, pl* **-loes** *or* **-los** : a slight offense

pec·ca·ry \'pek-ə-rē\ *n, pl* **-ries** : an American chiefly tropical mammal resembling but smaller than the related pigs

pec·ca·vi \pe-'kä-ˌvē\ *n* [L, I have sinned, fr. *peccare* to sin] : an acknowledgment of sin

¹**peck** \'pek\ *n* — see WEIGHT table

²**peck** *vb* **1** : to strike or pierce with or as if with the bill **2** : to make (as a hole) by pecking **3** : to pick up with or as if with the bill

³**peck** *n* **1** : an impression made by pecking **2** : a quick sharp stroke; *also* : KISS

pecking order *also* **peck order** *n* : a basic pattern of social organization within a flock of poultry in which each bird pecks another lower in the scale without fear of retaliation and submits to pecking by one of higher rank; *also* : a social hierarchy

pec·tin \'pek-tən\ *n* : any of various water-soluble plant substances that cause fruit jellies to set — **pec·tic** \-tik\ *adj*

pec·to·ral \'pek-t(ə-)rəl\ *adj* : of or relating to the breast or chest

pec·u·late \'pek-yə-ˌlāt\ *vb* **-lat·ed; -lat·ing** : EMBEZZLE — **pec·u·la·tion** \ˌpek-yə-'lā-shən\ *n*

pe·cu·liar \pi-'kyül-yər\ *adj* [ME *peculier*, fr. L *peculiaris* of private property, special, fr. *peculium* private property, fr. *pecus* cattle] **1** : belonging exclusively to one person or group **2** : CHARACTERISTIC, DISTINCTIVE **3** : QUEER, ODD syn idiosyncratic, eccentric, singular, strange, weird — **pe·cu·liar·i·ty** \-ˌkyül-'yar-ət-ē, -ˌkyü-lē-'ar-\ *n* — **pe·cu·liar·ly** \-'kyül-yər-lē\ *adv*

pe·cu·ni·ary \pi-'kyü-nē-ˌer-ē\ *adj* : of or relating to money : MONETARY

ped·a·gogue *also* **ped·a·gog** \'ped-ə-ˌgäg\ *n* : TEACHER, SCHOOLMASTER

ped·a·go·gy \'ped-ə-ˌgōj-ē, -ˌgäj-\ *n* : the art or profession of teaching; *esp* : EDUCATION **2** — **ped·a·gog·ic** \ˌped-ə-'gäj-ik, -'gōj-\ *or* **ped·a·gog·i·cal** \-i-kəl\ *adj*

¹**pedal** \'ped-ᵊl\ *n* : a lever worked by the foot

²**ped·al** *adj* : of or relating to the foot

³**ped·al** \'ped-ᵊl\ *vb* **-aled** *also* **-alled; -al·ing** *also* **-al·ling** \-(ᵊ-)liŋ\ **1** : to use or work a pedal (as of a piano or bicycle) **2** : to ride a bicycle

ped·ant \'ped-ᵊnt\ *n* **1** : a person who makes a display of his learning **2** : a formal uninspired teacher — **pe·dan·tic** \pi-'dant-ik\ *adj* — **ped·ant·ry** \'ped-ᵊn-trē\ *n*

ped·dle \'ped-ᵊl\ *vb* **ped·dled; ped·dling** \'ped-(ᵊ-)liŋ\ : to sell or offer for sale from place to place — **ped·dler** *also* **ped·lar** \'ped-lər\ *n*

ped·er·ast \'ped-ə-ˌrast\ *n* [Gk *paiderastēs*, lit., lover of boys] : one that practices anal intercourse esp. with a boy — **ped·er·as·ty** \'ped-ə-ˌras-tē\ *n*

ped·es·tal \'ped-əs-tᵊl\ *n* : the support or foot of something (as a column, statue, or vase) that is upright

¹**pe·des·tri·an** \pə-'des-trē-ən\ *adj* **1** : COMMONPLACE **2** : going on foot

²**pedestrian** *n* : WALKER

pe·di·at·rics \ˌpēd-ē-'a-triks\ *n* : a branch of medicine dealing with the care and diseases of children — **pe·di·at·ric** \-trik\ *adj* — **pe·di·a·tri·cian** \ˌpēd-ē-ə-'trish-ən\ *n*

pedi·cab \'ped-i-ˌkab\ *n* : a pedal-driven tricycle with seats for a driver and two passengers

ped·i·cure \'ped-i-ˌkyúr\ *n* : care of the feet, toes, and nails; *also* : a single treatment of these parts — **ped·i·cur·ist** \-ˌkyúr-əst\ *n*

ped·i·gree \'ped-ə-ˌgrē\ *n* [ME *pedegru*, fr. MF *pie de grue* crane's foot; fr. the shape made by the lines of genealogical chart] **1** : a record of a line of ancestors **2** : an ancestral line — **ped·i·greed** \-ˌgrēd\ *adj*

ped·i·ment \'ped-ə-mənt\ *n* : a low triangular gablelike decoration (as over a door or window) on a building

pe·dom·e·ter \pi-'däm-ət-ər\ *n* : an instrument that measures the distance one walks

pe·dun·cle \'pē-ˌdəŋ-kəl\ *n* : a narrow supporting stalk

peek \'pēk\ *vb* **1** : to look furtively **2** : to peer from a place of concealment **3** : GLANCE — **peek** *n*

¹**peel** \'pēl\ *n* : a skin or rind esp. of a fruit

²**peel** *vb* [ME *pelen*, fr. MF *peler*, fr. L *pilare* to remove the hair from, fr. *pilus* hair] **1** : to strip the skin, bark, or rind from **2** : to strip off (as a coat); *also* : to come off **3** : to lose the skin, bark, or rind

peel·ing \'pē-liŋ\ *n* : a peeled-off piece or strip (as of skin or rind)

peen \'pēn\ *n* : the usu. hemispherical or wedge-shaped end of the head of a hammer opposite the face

¹**peep** \'pēp\ *vb* : to utter a feeble shrill sound

²**peep** *n* : a feeble shrill sound

³**peep** \'pēk\ *vb* **1** : to look slyly esp. through an aperture : PEEK **2** : to begin to emerge — **peep·er** *n*

⁴**peep** *n* **1** : a first faint appearance **2** : a brief or furtive look

peep·hole \'pēp-ˌhōl\ *n* : a hole to peep through

¹**peer** \'piər\ *n* **1** : one of equal standing with another : EQUAL **2** : NOBLE — **peer·age** \-ij\ *n*

²**peer** *vb* **1** : to look intently or curiously **2** : to come slightly into view

peer·ess \'pir-əs\ *n* : a woman who is a peer

peer·less \'piər-ləs\ *adj* : having no equal : MATCHLESS **syn** supreme, un-equalled, unparalleled, incomparable

¹**peeve** \'pēv\ *vb* **peeved; peev·ing** : to make resentful : ANNOY

²**peeve** *n* **1** : a feeling or mood of resent-ment **2** : a particular grievance

pee·vish \'pē-vish\ *adj* : querulous in temperament : FRETFUL **syn** irritable, petulant, huffy — **pee·vish·ly** *adv* — **pee·vish·ness** *n*

pee·wee \'pē-(ˌ)wē\ *n* : one that is diminutive or tiny

¹**peg** \'peg\ *n* **1** : a small pointed piece (as of wood) used to pin down or fas-ten things or to fit into holes **2** : a projecting piece used as a support or boundary marker **3** : SUPPORT, PRE-TEXT **4** : STEP, DEGREE **5** : THROW

²**peg** *vb* **pegged; peg·ging 1** : to put a peg into : fasten, pin down, or attach with or as if with pegs **2** : to work hard and steadily : PLUG **3** : HUSTLE **4** : to mark by pegs **5** : to hold (as prices) at a set level or rate **6** : THROW

peg·ma·tite \'peg-mə-ˌtīt\ *n* : a coarse variety of granite occurring in veins

PEI *abbr* Prince Edward Island

pei·gnoir \pān-'wär, pen-\ *n* [F, lit., gar-ment worn while combing the hair, fr. MF, fr. *peigner* to comb the hair, fr. L *pectinare*, fr. *pectin-*, *pecten* comb] : NEGLIGEE

pe·jo·ra·tive \pi-'jor-ət-iv, 'pej-(ə-)rət-\ *adj* : having a tendency to make or become worse : DISPARAGING

peke \'pēk\ *n, often cap* : PEKINGESE

Pe·king·ese *or* **Pe·kin·ese** \ˌpē-kən-'ēz, -kiŋ-, -'ēs\ *n, pl* **Pekingese** *or* **Pekinese** : a small short-legged long-haired Chi-nese dog

pe·koe \'pē-(ˌ)kō\ *n* : a black tea made from small-sized tea leaves esp. in In-dia and Ceylon

pel·age \'pel-ij\ *n* : the hairy covering of a mammal

pe·lag·ic \pə-'laj-ik\ *adj* : OCEANIC

pelf \'pelf\ *n* : MONEY, RICHES

pel·i·can \'pel-i-kən\ *n* : a large web-footed bird having a pouched lower bill used to scoop in fish

pel·la·gra \pə-'lag-rə, -'lāg-\ *n* : a chronic disease marked by skin and digestive disorders and nervous symptoms and caused by a faulty diet

pel·let \'pel-ət\ *n* **1** : a little ball (as of medicine) **2** : BULLET — **pel·let·al** \-ᵊl\ *adj* — **pel·let·ize** \-ˌīz\ *vb*

pell-mell \'pel-'mel\ *adv* **1** : in mingled confusion **2** : HEADLONG

pel·lu·cid \pə-'lü-səd\ *adj* : extremely clear : LIMPID, TRANSPARENT **syn** trans-lucent, lucid, lucent

¹**pelt** \'pelt\ *n* : a skin esp. of a fur-bear-ing animal

²**pelt** *vb* : to strike with a succession of blows or missiles

pel·vis \'pel-vəs\ *n, pl* **pel·vis·es** \-və-səz\ *or* **pel·ves** \-ˌvēz\ : a basin-shaped part of the vertebrate skeleton consisting chiefly of the two large bones of the hip — **pel·vic** \-vik\ *adj*

pem·mi·can *also* **pem·i·can** \'pem-i-kən\ *n* : dried meat pounded fine and mixed with melted fat

¹**pen** \'pen\ *n* **1** : a small enclosure for animals **2** : a small place of confine-ment or storage

²**pen** *vb* **penned; pen·ning** : to shut in a pen : ENCLOSE

³**pen** *n* : an instrument with a split point to hold ink used for writing; *also* : a fluid-using writing instrument

⁴**pen** *vb* **penned; pen·ning** : WRITE

⁵**pen** *n* : PENITENTIARY

⁶**pen** *abbr* peninsula

PEN *abbr* International Association of Poets, Playwrights, Editors, Essay-ists and Novelists

pe·nal \'pēn-ᵊl\ *adj* : of or relating to punishment

pe·nal·ize \'pēn-ᵊl-ˌīz, 'pen-\ *vb* **-ized; -iz·ing** : to put a penalty on

pen·al·ty \'pen-ᵊl-tē\ *n, pl* **-ties 1** : pun-ishment for crime or offense **2** : some-thing forfeited when a person fails to do something agreed to **3** : disadvan-tage, loss, or hardship due to some action

pen·ance \'pen-əns\ *n* **1** : an act per-formed to show sorrow or repentance for sin **2** : a sacrament (as in the Ro-man Catholic Church) consisting of repentance, confession, a penance, and absolution

Pe·na·tes \pə-'nāt-ēz\ *n pl* : the Roman gods of the household

pence \'pens\ *pl of* PENNY

pen·chant \'pen-chənt\ *n* [F, fr. prp. of *pencher* to incline, fr. (assumed) VL *pendicare*, fr. L *pendere* to weigh] : a strong inclination : LIKING **syn** lean-ing, propensity, predilection, predis-position

¹**pen·cil** \'pen-səl\ *n* : a writing or draw-ing tool consisting of or having a slen-der cylinder of a solid marking sub-stance

²**pencil** *vb* **-ciled** *or* **-cilled; -cil·ing** *or* **-cil·ling** \-s(ə-)liŋ\ : to paint, draw, or write with a pencil

pen·dant *also* **pen·dent** \'pen-dənt\ *n* : a hanging ornament (as an earring)

pen·dent *or* **pen·dant** \'pen-dənt\ *adj* : SUSPENDED, OVERHANGING

¹**pend·ing** \'pen-diŋ\ *prep* **1** : DURING **2** : while awaiting

²**pend·ing** *adj* **1** : not yet decided **2** : IMMINENT

pen·du·lous \'pen-jə-ləs, -də-\ *adj* : hanging loosely : DROOPING

pen·du·lum \-ləm\ *n* : a body that swings freely from a fixed point

pe·ne·plain *also* **pe·ne·plane** \'pēn-i-ˌplān\ *n* : a large almost flat land surface shaped by erosion

pen·e·trate \'pen-ə-ˌtrāt\ *vb* **-trat·ed; -trat·ing 1** : to enter into : PIERCE **2** : PERMEATE **3** : to see into : UNDERSTAND **4** : to affect deeply — **pen·e·tra·ble** \-trə-bəl\ *adj* — **pen·e·tra·tion** \ˌpen-ə-'trā-shən\ *n* — **pen·e·tra·tive** \'pen-ə-ˌtrāt-iv\ *adj*

pen·e·trat·ing \-ˌtrāt-iŋ\ *adj* **1** : having the power of entering, piercing, or pervading (a ∼ shriek) (a ∼ odor) **2** : ACUTE, DISCERNING (a ∼ look)

pen·guin \'peŋ-gwən, 'pen-\ *n* : any of several erect short-legged flightless seabirds of the southern hemisphere

pen·hold·er \'pen-ˌhōl-dər\ *n* : a holder or handle for a pen

pen·i·cil·lin \ˌpen-ə-'sil-ən\ *n* : any of several antibiotics produced by a green mold and used against various bacteria

pen·in·su·la \pə-'nin-sə-lə\ *n* [L *paeninsula*, fr. *paene* almost + *insula* island] : a long narrow portion of land extending out into the water — **pen·in·su·lar** \-lər\ *adj*

pe·nis \'pē-nəs\ *n, pl* **pe·nes** \-ˌnēz\ *or* **pe·nis·es** [L, penis, tail] : a male organ of copulation that in the human male also functions as the channel by which urine leaves the body

¹**pen·i·tent** \'pen-ə-tənt\ *adj* : feeling sorrow for sins or offenses : REPENTANT — **pen·i·tence** \-təns\ *n* — **pen·i·ten·tial** \ˌpen-ə-'ten-chəl\ *adj*

²**penitent** *n* : a penitent person

¹**pen·i·ten·tia·ry** \ˌpen-ə-'tench-(ə-)rē\ *n, pl* **-ries** : a state or federal prison

²**pen·i·ten·tia·ry** *adj* : of, relating to, or incurring confinement in a penitentiary

pen·knife \'pen-ˌnīf\ *n* : a small pocketknife

pen·light *or* **pen·lite** \'pen-ˌlīt\ *n* : a small flashlight resembling a fountain pen in size or shape

pen·man \'pen-mən\ *n* **1** : COPYIST **2** : one skilled in penmanship **3** : AUTHOR

pen·man·ship \-ˌship\ *n* : the art or practice of writing with the pen

Penn *or* **Penna** *abbr* Pennsylvania

pen name *n* : an author's pseudonym

pen·nant \'pen-ənt\ *n* **1** : a tapering flag used esp. for signaling **2** : a flag symbolic of championship

pen·ni \'pen-ē\ *n, pl* **pen·nia** \-ē-ə\ *or* **pen·nis** \-ēz\ — see *markka* at MONEY table

pen·non \'pen-ən\ *n* **1** : a long narrow ribbonlike flag borne on a lance **2** : WING

Penn·syl·va·nian \ˌpen-səl-'vā-nyən\

adj : of, relating to, or being the period of the Paleozoic era between the Mississippian and the Permian — **Pennsylvanian** *n*

pen·ny \'pen-ē\ *n, pl* **pennies** \-ēz\ *or* **pence** \'pens\ **1** : a British monetary unit formerly equal to ¹⁄₁₂ shilling but now equal to ¹⁄₁₀₀ pound; *also* : a coin of this value — see *pound* at MONEY table **2** *pl* **pennies** : a cent of the U.S. or Canada — **pen·ni·less** \'pen-i-ləs\ *adj*

pen·ny-pinch·ing \'pen-ē-ˌpin-chiŋ\ *n* : FRUGALITY, PARSIMONY — **pen·ny-pinch·er** \-chər\ *n* — **penny-pinching** *adj*

pen·ny·roy·al \ˌpen-ē-'rȯi-əl, 'pen-i-ˌrȯil\ *n* : a hairy perennial mint with small pungently aromatic leaves

pen·ny·weight \'pen-ē-ˌwāt\ *n* — see WEIGHT table

pen·ny-wise \'pen-ē-ˌwīz\ *adj* : wise or prudent only in small matters

pe·nol·o·gy \pi-'näl-ə-jē\ *n* : a branch of criminology dealing with prisons and the treatment of offenders

¹**pen·sion** \'pen-chən\ *n* : a fixed sum paid regularly esp. to a person retired from service

²**pen·sion** \'pen-chən\ *vb* **pen·sioned; pen·sion·ing** \'pench-(ə-)niŋ\ : to pay a pension to — **pen·sion·er** *n*

pen·sive \'pen-siv\ *adj* : musingly, dreamily, or sadly thoughtful syn reflective, speculative, contemplative, meditative — **pen·sive·ly** *adv*

pen·stock \'pen-ˌstäk\ *n* **1** : a sluice or gate for regulating a flow **2** : a conduit for conducting water

pent \'pent\ *adj* : shut up : CONFINED

pen·ta·gon \'pent-ə-ˌgän\ *n* : a polygon of five angles and five sides — **pen·tag·o·nal** \pen-'tag-ən-²l\ *adj*

pen·tam·e·ter \pen-'tam-ət-ər\ *n* : a line consisting of five metrical feet

Pen·te·cost \'pent-i-ˌkȯst\ *n* : the 7th Sunday after Easter observed as a church festival commemorating the descent of the Holy Spirit on the apostles — **Pen·te·cos·tal** \ˌpent-i-'käst-²l\ *adj*

Pentecostal *n* : a member of a fundamentalist Christian religious body that stresses religious revivals — **Pen·te·cos·tal·ism** \ˌpent-i-'käst-²l-ˌiz-əm\ *n*

pent·house \'pent-ˌhau̇s\ *n* [ME *pentis*, fr. MF *appentis*, prob. fr. ML *appenticium* appendage, fr. L *appendic-, appendix*] **1** : a shed or sloping roof attached to a wall or building **2** : an apartment built on the roof of a building

pen·ul·ti·mate \pi-'nəl-tə-mət\ *adj* : next to the last (∼ syllable)

pen·um·bra \pə-'nəm-brə\ *n, pl* **-brae** \-(ˌ)brē\ *or* **-bras** : the partial shadow surrounding a complete shadow (as in an eclipse)

pe·nu·ri·ous \pə-'n(y)u̇r-ē-əs\ *adj* **1** : marked by penury **2** : MISERLY syn stingy, close, tightfisted, parsimonious

pen·u·ry \'pen-yə-rē\ *n* : extreme poverty

pe·on \'pē-ˌän, -ən\ *n*, *pl* **peons** or **pe·ones** \pā-'ō-ˌnēz\ 1 : a member of the landless laboring class in Spanish America 2 : one bound to service for payment of a debt — **pe·on·age** \-ə-nij\ *n*

pe·o·ny \'pē-ə-nē\ *n*, *pl* **-nies** : a garden plant with large usu. double red, pink, or white flowers; *also* : its flower

¹peo·ple \'pē-pəl\ *n*, *pl* **people** [ME *peple*, fr. OF *peuple*, fr. L *populus*] 1 *pl* : human beings making up a group or linked by a common characteristic or interest 2 *pl* : human beings — often used in compounds instead of *persons* (sales*people*) 3 *pl* : the mass of persons in a community : POPULACE; *also* : ELECTORATE (the ~'s choice) 4 *pl* **peoples** : a body of persons (as a tribe, nation, or race) united by a common culture, sense of kinship, or political organization

²people *vb* **peo·pled; peo·pling** \-p(ə-)liŋ\ : to supply or fill with or as if with people

¹pep \'pep\ *n* : brisk energy or initiative — **pep·py** *adj*

²pep *vb* **pepped; pep·ping** : to put pep into : STIMULATE

¹pep·per \'pep-ər\ *n* 1 : a pungent condiment from the berry (**pep·per·corn** \-ˌkȯrn\) of an East Indian climbing plant; *also* : this plant 2 : a plant related to the tomato and widely grown for its hot or mild sweet fruit; *also* : this fruit

²pepper *vb* **pep·pered; pep·per·ing** \'pep-(ə-)riŋ\ 1 : to sprinkle or season with or as if with pepper 2 : to shower with missiles or rapid blows

pep·per·mint \-ˌmint, -mənt\ *n* : a pungent aromatic mint; *also* : candy flavored with its oil

pep·per·o·ni \ˌpep-ə-'rō-nē\ *n* : a highly seasoned beef and pork sausage

pep·pery \'pep-(ə-)rē\ *adj* 1 : having the qualities of pepper : PUNGENT, HOT 2 : having a hot temper 3 : FIERY

pep·sin \'pep-sən\ *n* : an enzyme of the stomach that begins the digestion of proteins; *also* : a preparation of this used medicinally

pep·tic \'pep-tik\ *adj* 1 : relating to or promoting digestion 2 : resulting from the action of digestive juices (a ~ ulcer)

Pe·quot \'pē-ˌkwät\ *n* : a member of an American Indian people of eastern Connecticut

¹per \(')pər\ *prep* 1 : by means of 2 : to or for each 3 : ACCORDING TO

²per *adv* : for each : APIECE

³per *abbr* 1 period 2 person

per·ad·ven·ture \ˌpər-əd-ˌven-chər\ *adv*, *archaic* : PERHAPS

²peradventure *n* : DOUBT, CHANCE

per·am·bu·late \pə-'ram-byə-ˌlāt\ *vb*

-lat·ed; -lat·ing : to travel over esp. on foot — **per·am·bu·la·tion** \-ˌram-byə-'lā-shən\ *n*

per·am·bu·la·tor \pə-'ram-byə-ˌlāt-ər\ *n*, *chiefly Brit* : a baby carriage

per an·num \(ˌ)pər-'an-əm\ *adv* [ML] : in or for each year : ANNUALLY

per·cale \(ˌ)pər-'kāl, 'pər-; (ˌ)pər-'kal\ *n* : a fine woven cotton cloth

per cap·i·ta \(ˌ)pər-'kap-ət-ə\ *adv or adj* [ML, by heads] : by or for each person

per·ceive \pər-'sēv\ *vb* **per·ceived; per·ceiv·ing** 1 : to attain awareness : REALIZE 2 : to become aware of through the senses — **per·ceiv·able** *adj*

¹per·cent \pər-'sent\ *adv* [fr. *per* + L *centum* hundred] : in each hundred

²percent *n*, *pl* **percent** or **percents** 1 : one part in a hundred : HUNDREDTH 2 : PERCENTAGE

per·cent·age \pər-'sent-ij\ *n* 1 : a part of a whole expressed in hundredths 2 : the result obtained by multiplying a number by a percent 3 : ADVANTAGE, PROFIT 4 : PROBABILITY; *also* : favorable odds

per·cen·tile \pər-'sen-ˌtīl\ *n* : a statistical measure expressing the standing of a score or grade in terms of the percentage of scores or grades falling with or below it

per·cept \'pər-ˌsept\ *n* : a sense impression of an object accompanied by an understanding of what it is

per·cep·ti·ble \pər-'sep-tə-bəl\ *adj* : capable of being perceived — **per·cep·ti·bly** \-blē\ *adv*

per·cep·tion \pər-'sep-shən\ *n* 1 : an act or result of perceiving 2 : awareness of environment through physical sensation 3 : ability to perceive : INSIGHT, COMPREHENSION *syn* penetration, discernment, discrimination

per·cep·tive \pər-'sep-tiv\ *adj* : of or relating to perception : having perception; *also* : DISCERNING — **per·cep·tive·ly** *adv*

per·cep·tu·al \-chə(-wə)l\ *adj* : of, relating to, or involving sensory stimulus as opposed to abstract concept — **per·cep·tu·al·ly** \-ē\ *adv*

¹perch \'pərch\ *n* 1 : a roost for birds 2 : a high station or vantage point

²perch *vb* : ROOST

³perch *n*, *pl* **perch** or **perch·es** : either of two small freshwater spiny-finned food fishes; *also* : any of various fishes resembling or related to these

per·chance \pər-'chans\ *adv* : PERHAPS

per·cip·i·ent \pər-'sip-ē-ənt\ *adj* : capable of or characterized by perception — **per·cip·i·ence** \-əns\ *n*

per·co·late \'pər-kə-ˌlāt\ *vb* **-lat·ed; -lat·ing** 1 : to trickle or filter through a permeable substance 2 : to filter hot water through to extract the essence (~ coffee) — **per·co·la·tor** \-ˌlāt-ər\ *n*

per con·tra \(ˌ)pər-'kän-trə\ *adv* [It, by the opposite side (of the ledger)] 1

: on the contrary **2** : by way of contrast

per·cus·sion \pər-'kəsh-ən\ *n* **1** : a sharp blow : IMPACT; *esp* : a blow upon a cap (**percussion cap**) filled with powder and designed to explode the charge in a firearm **2** : the beating or striking of a musical instrument; *also* : instruments sounded by striking, shaking, or scraping

per di·em \-'dē-əm, -'dī-\ *adv* [ML] : by the day — **per diem** *adj or n*

per·di·tion \pər-'dish-ən\ *n* [ME *perdicion*, fr. LL *perdition-, perditio*, fr. L *perdere* to destroy, fr. *per-* to destruction + *dare* to give] **1** : eternal damnation **2** : HELL

per·du·ra·ble \(,)pər-'d(y)ùr-ə-bəl\ *adj* : very durable — **per·du·ra·bil·i·ty** \-,d(y)ùr-ə-'bil-ət-ē\ *n*

per·e·gri·na·tion \,per-ə-grə-'nā-shən\ *n* : a journeying about from place to place

pe·remp·to·ry \pə-'remp-t(ə-)rē\ *adj* **1** : barring a right of action or delay : FINAL **2** : expressive of urgency or command : IMPERATIVE **3** : marked by self-assurance : DECISIVE *syn* imperious, masterful, domineering, magisterial — **pe·remp·to·ri·ly** \-t(ə-)rə-lē\ *adv*

¹pe·ren·ni·al \pə-'ren-ē-əl\ *adj* **1** : present at all seasons of the year (~ streams) **2** : continuing to live from year to year (~ plants) **3** : recurring regularly : PERMANENT (~ problems) *syn* lasting, perpetual, enduring, everlasting — **pe·ren·ni·al·ly** \-ē\ *adv*

²perennial *n* : a plant that lives for an indefinite number of years

perf *abbr* **1** perfect **2** perforated

¹per·fect \'pər-fikt\ *adj* **1** : being without fault or defect : EXACT, PRECISE **3** : COMPLETE **4** : relating to or being a verb tense that expresses an action or state completed at the time of speaking or at a time spoken of *syn* whole, entire, intact — **per·fect·ly** \-fik-(t)lē\ *adv* — **per·fect·ness** \-fik(t)-nəs\ *n*

²per·fect \pər-'fekt\ *vb* : to make perfect

³per·fect \'pər-fikt\ *n* : the perfect tense; *also* : a verb form in it

per·fect·ible \pər-'fek-tə-bəl, 'pər-fik-\ *adj* : capable of improvement or perfection — **per·fect·ibil·i·ty** \pər-,fek-tə-'bil-ət-ē, ,pər-fik-\ *n*

per·fec·tion \pər-'fek-shən\ *n* **1** : the quality or state of being perfect **2** : the highest degree of excellence **3** : the act or process of perfecting *syn* virtue, merit, excellence

per·fec·tion·ist \-sh(ə-)nəst\ *n* : a person who will not accept or be content with anything less than perfection

per·fec·to \pər-'fek-tō\ *n, pl* **-tos** : a cigar that is thick in the middle and tapers almost to a point at each end

per·fi·dy \'pər-fəd-ē\ *n, pl* **-dies** [L *perfidia*, fr. *perfidus* faithless, fr. *per fidem decipere* to betray, lit., to deceive by trust] : violation of faith or

loyalty : TREACHERY — **per·fid·i·ous** \pər-'fid-ē-əs\ *adj* — **per·fid·i·ous·ly** *adv*

per·fo·rate \'pər-fə-,rāt\ *vb* **-rat·ed; -rat·ing** : to bore through : PIERCE; *esp* : to make a line of holes in to facilitate separation *syn* puncture, punch, prick — **per·fo·ra·tion** \,pər-fə-'rā-shən\ *n*

per·force \pər-'fōrs\ *adv* : of necessity

per·form \pə(r)-'fōrm\ *vb* **1** : FULFILL **2** : to carry out : ACCOMPLISH **3** : FUNCTION **4** : to do in a set manner **5** : to give a performance : PLAY *syn* execute, discharge, achieve — **per·form·er** *n*

per·for·mance \pər-'fōr-məns\ *n* **1** : the act or process of performing **2** : DEED, FEAT **3** : a public presentation

¹per·fume \'pər-,fyüm, pər-'fyüm\ *n* **1** : a usu. pleasant odor : FRAGRANCE **2** : a preparation used for scenting

²per·fume \pər-'fyüm, 'pər-,fyüm\ *vb* **per·fumed; per·fum·ing** : to treat with a perfume; *also* : SCENT

per·fum·ery \,pər-'fyüm-(ə-)rē\ *n, pl* **-er·ies** : PERFUMES

per·func·to·ry \pər-'fəŋk-t(ə-)rē\ *adj* : done merely as a duty — **per·func·to·ri·ly** \-t(ə-)rə-lē\ *adv*

per·go·la \'pər-gə-lə\ *n* [It] : a structure consisting of posts supporting an open roof in the form of a trellis

perh *abbr* perhaps

per·haps \pər-'(h)aps, 'praps\ *adv* : possibly but not certainly

per·i·gee \'per-ə-,jē\ *n* [fr. *perigee* point in the orbit of a satellite of the earth when it is nearest the earth, fr. NL *perigeum*, fr. Gk *perigeion*, fr. *peri* around, near + *gē* earth] : the point at which an orbiting object is nearest the body (as the earth) being orbited

peri·he·lion \,per-ə-'hēl-yən\ *n, pl* **-he·lia** \-'hēl-yə\ : the point in the path of a celestial body (as a planet) that is nearest to the sun

per·il \'per-əl\ *n* : DANGER; *also* : a source of danger : RISK *syn* jeopardy, hazard — **per·il·ous** *adj* — **per·il·ous·ly** *adv*

peri·lune \'per-ə-,lün\ *n* : the point in a lunar orbit closest to the moon's surface

pe·rim·e·ter \pə-'rim-ət-ər\ *n* : the outer boundary of a body or figure; *also* : the length of a perimeter

¹pe·ri·od \'pir-ē-əd\ *n* **1** : SENTENCE; *also* : the full pause closing the utterance of a sentence **2** : END, STOP **3** : a punctuation mark . used esp. to mark the end of a declarative sentence or an abbreviation **4** : an extent of time; *esp* : one regarded as a stage or division in a process or development **5** : a portion or division of time in which something comes to an end and is ready to begin again **6** : a single cyclic occurrence of menstruation *syn* epoch, era, age

²period *adj* : of or relating to a particular historical period (~ furniture)

pe·ri·od·ic \ˌpir-ē-ˈäd-ik\ *adj* **1** : occurring at regular intervals of time **2** : happening repeatedly **3** : of or relating to a sentence that has no trailing elements following full grammatical statement of the essential idea

¹**pe·ri·od·i·cal** \ˌpir-ē-ˈäd-i-kəl\ *adj* **1** : PERIODIC **2** : published at regular intervals **3** : of or relating to a periodical — **pe·ri·od·i·cal·ly** \-k(ə-)lē\ *adv*

²**periodical** *n* : a periodical publication

peri·odon·tal \ˌper-ē-ō-ˈdänt-ᵊl\ *adj* : surrounding or occurring about the teeth

per·i·pa·tet·ic \ˌper-ə-pə-ˈtet-ik\ *adj* : performed or performing while moving about : ITINERANT

pe·riph·er·al \pə-ˈrif-(ə-)rəl\ *n* : a device connected to a computer to provide communication or auxiliary functions

peripheral nervous system *n* : the part of the nervous system that is outside the central nervous system and comprises the spinal nerves, the cranial nerves except the one supplying the retina, and the autonomic nervous system

pe·riph·ery \pə-ˈrif-(ə-)rē\ *n, pl* **-er·ies** **1** : the boundary of a rounded figure **2** : outward bounds : border area — **pe·riph·er·al** \-(ə-)rəl\ *adj*

pe·riph·ra·sis \pə-ˈrif-rə-səs\ *n, pl* **-ra·ses** \-ˌsēz\ : CIRCUMLOCUTION

pe·rique \pə-ˈrēk\ *n* [LaF] : a strong-flavored Louisiana tobacco used in smoking mixtures

peri·scope \ˈper-ə-ˌskōp\ *n* : a tubular optical instrument enabling an observer to get an otherwise blocked field of view

per·ish \ˈper-ish\ *vb* : to become destroyed or ruined : DIE

per·ish·able \ˈper-ish-ə-bəl\ *adj* : easily spoiled (~ foods) — **perishable** *n*

peri·stal·sis \ˌper-ə-ˈstôl-səs, -ˈstal-\ *n, pl* **-stal·ses** : waves of contraction passing along the intestine and forcing its contents onward — **per·i·stal·tic** \-ˈstôl-tik, -ˈstal-\ *adj*

peri·style \ˈper-ə-ˌstīl\ *n* : a row of columns surrounding a building or court

peri·to·ne·um \ˌper-ət-ᵊn-ˈē-əm\ *n, pl* **-ne·ums** *or* **-nea** : the smooth transparent serous membrane that lines the cavity of the abdomen — **peri·to·ne·al** \-ˈē-əl\ *adj*

peri·to·ni·tis \ˌper-ət-ᵊn-ˈīt-əs\ *n* : inflammation of the membrane lining the cavity of the abdomen

peri·wig \ˈper-i-ˌwig\ *n*

¹**per·i·win·kle** \ˈper-i-ˌwiŋ-kəl\ *n* : a usu. blue-flowered creeping plant cultivated as a ground cover

²**periwinkle** *n* : any of various small edible seashore snails

per·ju·ry \ˈpərj-(ə-)rē\ *n* : the voluntary violation of an oath to tell the truth : false swearing — **per·jure** \ˈpər-jər\ *vb* — **per·jur·er** *n*

¹**perk** \ˈpərk\ *vb* **1** : to thrust (as the head) up impudently or jauntily **2** : to make trim or brisk : FRESHEN **3** : to regain vigor or spirit — **perky** *adj*

²**perk** *vb* : PERCOLATE

per·lite \ˈpər-ˌlīt\ *n* : volcanic glass that when expanded by heat forms a lightweight material used esp. in concrete and plaster and for potting plants

¹**perm** \ˈpərm\ *n* : PERMANENT

²**perm** *vb* : to give (hair) a permanent

³**perm** *abbr* permanent

per·ma·frost \ˈpər-mə-ˌfrôst\ *n* : a permanently frozen layer below the surface in frigid regions of a planet (as earth)

¹**per·ma·nent** \ˈpər-mə-nənt\ *adj* : LASTING, STABLE — **per·ma·nence** \-nəns\ *n* — **per·ma·nen·cy** \-nən-sē\ *n* — **per·ma·nent·ly** *adv*

²**permanent** *n* : a long-lasting hair wave or straightening

permanent press *n* : the process of treating fabrics with chemicals (as resin) and heat for setting the shape and for aiding wrinkle resistance

per·me·able \ˈpər-mē-ə-bəl\ *adj* : having small openings that permit liquids or gases to seep through — **per·me·a·bil·i·ty** \ˌpər-mē-ə-ˈbil-ət-ē\ *n*

per·me·ate \ˈpər-mē-ˌāt\ *vb* **-at·ed; -at·ing 1** : PERVADE **2** : to seep through the pores of : PENETRATE — **per·me·ation** \ˌpər-mē-ˈā-shən\ *n*

Perm·ian \ˈpər-mē-ən\ *adj* : of, relating to, or being the latest period of the Paleozoic era — **Permian** *n*

per·mis·si·ble \pər-ˈmis-ə-bəl\ *adj* : that may be permitted : ALLOWABLE

per·mis·sion \pər-ˈmish-ən\ *n* : formal consent : AUTHORIZATION

per·mis·sive \pər-ˈmis-iv\ *adj* : granting permission; *esp* : INDULGENT — **per·mis·sive·ness** *n*

¹**per·mit** \pər-ˈmit\ *vb* **per·mit·ted; per·mit·ting 1** : to consent to : ALLOW **2** : to make possible

²**per·mit** \ˈpər-ˌmit, pər-ˈmit\ *n* : a written permission : LICENSE

per·mu·ta·tion \ˌpər-myü-ˈtā-shən\ *n* **1** : TRANSFORMATION **2** : any one of the total number of changes in position or order possible among the units or members of a group (~s of the alphabet) *syn* innovation, mutation, vicissitude

per·ni·cious \pər-ˈnish-əs\ *adj* [MF *pernicieus*, fr. L *perniciosus*, fr. *pernicies* destruction, fr. *per-* through + *nec-*, *nex* violent death] : very destructive or injurious — **per·ni·cious·ly** *adv*

per·ora·tion \ˈper-ər-ˌā-shən, ˈpər-\ *n* : the concluding part of a speech

¹**per·ox·ide** \pə-ˈräk-ˌsīd\ *n* : an oxide containing a large proportion of oxygen; *esp* : HYDROGEN PEROXIDE

²**peroxide** *vb* **-id·ed; -id·ing** : to bleach with hydrogen peroxide

perp *abbr* perpendicular

per·pen·dic·u·lar \ˌpər-pən-ˈdik-yə-lər\ *adj* **1** : standing at right angles to the plane of the horizon **2** : meeting another line at a right angle —

pe·pendicular *n* — **per·pen·dic·u·lar·i·ty** \-ˌdik-yə-ˈlar-ət-ē\ *n* — **per·pen·dic·u·lar·ly** *adv*

per·pe·trate \ˈpər-pə-ˌtrāt\ *vb* **-trat·ed; -trat·ing** : to be guilty of : COMMIT — **per·pe·tra·tion** \ˌpər-pə-ˈtrā-shən\ *n* — **per·pe·tra·tor** \ˈpər-pə-ˌtrāt-ər\ *n*

per·pet·u·al \pər-ˈpech-(ə-w)əl\ *adj* **1** : continuing forever : EVERLASTING **2** : occurring continually : CONSTANT 〈∼ annoyance〉 *syn* ceaseless, unceasing, continual, continuous, incessant, unremitting — **per·pet·u·al·ly** \-ē\ *adv*

per·pet·u·ate \pər-ˈpech-ə-ˌwāt\ *vb* **-at·ed; -at·ing** : to make perpetual : cause to last indefinitely — **per·pet·u·a·tion** \-ˌpech-ə-ˈwā-shən\ *n*

per·pe·tu·ity \ˌpər-pə-ˈt(y)ü-ət-ē\ *n, pl* **-it·ies** **1** : endless time : ETERNITY **2** : the quality or state of being perpetual

per·plex \pər-ˈpleks\ *vb* : to disturb mentally; *esp* : CONFUSE — **per·plex·i·ty** \-ət-ē\ *n*

per·plexed \-ˈplekst\ *adj* **1** : filled with uncertainty : PUZZLED **2** : full of difficulty : COMPLICATED — **per·plexed·ly** \-ˈplek-səd-lē\ *adv*

per·qui·site \ˈpər-kwə-zət\ *n* : a privilege or profit beyond regular pay

pers *abbr* person; personal

per se \(ˌ)pər-ˈsā\ *adv* [L] : by, of, or in itself : as such

per·se·cute \ˈpər-si-ˌkyüt\ *vb* **-cut·ed; -cut·ing** : to pursue in such a way as to injure or afflict : HARASS; *esp* : to cause to suffer because of belief *syn* oppress, wrong, aggrieve — **per·se·cu·tion** \ˌpər-si-ˈkyü-shən\ *n* — **per·se·cu·tor** \ˈpər-si-ˌkyüt-ər\ *n*

per·se·vere \ˌpər-sə-ˈviər\ *vb* **-vered; -ver·ing** : to persist (as in an undertaking) in spite of difficulties — **per·se·ver·ance** \-ˈvir-əns\ *n*

Per·sian \ˈpər-zhən\ *n* **1** : a native or inhabitant of ancient Persia **2** : a member of one of the peoples of modern Iran **3** : the language of the Persians

Persian cat *n* : a stocky round-headed domestic cat that has long and silky fur

Persian lamb *n* : a pelt that is obtained from lambs that are older than those yielding broadtail and that has very silky tightly curled fur

per·si·flage \ˈpər-si-ˌfläzh, ˈper-\ *n* [F, fr. *persifler* to banter, fr. *per-* thoroughly + *siffler* to whistle, hiss, boo, fr. L *sibilare*] : lightly jesting or mocking talk

per·sim·mon \pər-ˈsim-ən\ *n* : a tree related to the ebony; *also* : its edible orange-red plumlike fruit

per·sist \pər-ˈsist, -ˈzist\ *vb* **1** : to go on resolutely or stubbornly in spite of difficulties : PERSEVERE **2** : to continue to exist — **per·sis·tence** \-ˈsis-təns, -ˈzis-\ *n* — **per·sis·ten·cy** \-tən-sē\ *n* — **per-**

sis·tent \-tənt\ *adj* — **per·sis·tent·ly** *adv*

per·snick·e·ty \pər-ˈsnik-ət-ē\ *adj* : fussy about small details

per·son \ˈpər-sən\ *n* [ME, fr. OF *persone*, fr. L *persona* actor's mask, character in a play, person, prob. fr. Etruscan *phersu* mask] **1** : a human being : INDIVIDUAL — used in combination esp. by those who prefer to avoid *man* in compounds applicable to both sexes 〈chair*person*〉 **2** : one of the three modes of being in the Godhead as understood by Trinitarians **3** : the body of a human being **4** : the individual personality of a human being : SELF **5** : reference of a segment of discourse to the speaker, to one spoken to, or to one spoken of esp. as indicated by certain pronouns

per·son·able \ˈpər-s-(ə-)nə-bəl\ *adj* : pleasing in person : ATTRACTIVE

per·son·age \ˈpər-s-(ə-)nij\ *n* : a person of rank, note, or distinction

¹per·son·al \ˈpər-s-(ə-)nəl\ *adj* **1** : of, relating to, or affecting a person : PRIVATE 〈∼ correspondence〉 **2** : done in person 〈a ∼ inquiry〉 **3** : relating to the person or body 〈∼ injuries〉 **4** : relating to an individual esp. in an offensive way (resented such ∼ remarks) **5** : of or relating to temporary or movable property as distinguished from real estate **6** : denoting grammatical person — **per·son·al·ly** \-ē\ *adv*

²personal *n* **1** : a short newspaper paragraph relating to a person or group or to personal matters **2** : a short personal or private communication in the classified ads section of a newspaper

personal computer *n* : MICROCOMPUTER

per·son·al·i·ty \ˌpər-s-ᵊn-ˈal-ət-ē\ *n, pl* **-ties** **1** : an offensively personal remark (indulges in *personalities*) **2** : distinctive personal character **3** : distinction of personal and social traits; *also* : a person having such quality *syn* individuality, temperament, disposition, makeup

per·son·al·ize \ˈpər-s-(ə-)nə-ˌlīz\ *vb* **-ized; -iz·ing** : to make personal or individual; *esp* : to mark as belonging to a particular person

per·son·al·ty \ˈpər-s-(ə-)nəl-tē\ *n, pl* **-ties** : personal property

per·so·na non gra·ta \pər-ˌsō-nə-ˌnän-ˈgrat-ə, -ˈgrät-\ *adj* [L] : being personally unacceptable or unwelcome

per·son·ate \ˈpər-s-ᵊn-ˌāt\ *vb* **-at·ed; -at·ing** : IMPERSONATE, REPRESENT

per·son·i·fy \pər-ˈsän-ə-ˌfī\ *vb* **-fied; -fy·ing** **1** : to think of or represent as a person **2** : to be the embodiment of : INCARNATE 〈∼ the law〉 — **per·son·i·fi·ca·tion** \-ˌsän-ə-fə-ˈkā-shən\ *n*

per·son·nel \ˌpər-s-ᵊn-ˈel\ *n* : a body of persons employed in a service or an organization

per·spec·tive \pər-ˈspek-tiv\ *n* **1** : the science of painting and drawing so that objects represented have apparent depth and distance **2** : the aspect in which a subject or its parts are mentally viewed; *esp* : a view of things (as objects or events) in their true relationship or relative importance

per·spi·cac·i·ty \ˌpər-spə-ˈkas-ət-ē\ *n* : acuteness of understanding or judgment — **per·spi·ca·cious** \-ˈkā-shəs\ *adj*

per·spic·u·ous \pər-ˈspik-yə-wəs\ *adj* : plain to the understanding — **per·spi·cu·i·ty** \ˌpər-spə-ˈkyü-ət-ē\ *n*

per·spire \pər-ˈspīr\ *vb* **per·spired; per·spir·ing** : SWEAT — **per·spi·ra·tion** \ˌpər-spə-ˈrā-shən\ *n*

per·suade \pər-ˈswād\ *vb* **per·suad·ed; per·suad·ing** : to move by argument or entreaty to a belief or course of action — **per·sua·sive** \-ˈswā-siv, -ziv\ *adj* — **per·sua·sive·ly** *adv* — **per·sua·sive·ness** *n*

per·sua·sion \pər-ˈswā-zhən\ *n* **1** : the act or process of persuading **2** : OPINION, BELIEF

¹pert \ˈpərt\ *adj* [ME, open, bold, pert, modif. of OF *apert*, fr. L *apertus* open, fr. pp. of *aperire* to open] **1** : saucily free and forward : IMPUDENT **2** : stylishly trim : JAUNTY **3** : LIVELY

²pert *abbr* pertaining

per·tain \pər-ˈtān\ *vb* **1** : to belong to as a part, quality, or function (duties ~ing to the office) **2** : to have reference (facts that ~ to the case) *syn* bear, appertain, apply

per·ti·na·cious \ˌpərt-ᵊn-ˈā-shəs\ *adj* **1** : holding resolutely to an opinion or purpose **2** : obstinately persistent : TENACIOUS (a ~ bill collector) *syn* obstinate, dogged, mulish, headstrong, perverse — **per·ti·nac·i·ty** \-ˈas-ət-ē\ *n*

per·ti·nent \ˈpərt-ᵊn-ənt\ *adj* : relating to the matter under consideration *syn* relevant, germane, applicable, apropos — **per·ti·nence** \-əns\ *n*

per·turb \pər-ˈtərb\ *vb* : to disturb greatly esp. in mind : UPSET — **per·tur·ba·tion** \ˌpərt-ər-ˈbā-shən\ *n*

per·tus·sis *n* : WHOOPING COUGH

pe·ruke \pə-ˈrük\ *n* : WIG

pe·ruse \pə-ˈrüz\ *vb* **pe·rused; pe·rus·ing** : READ; *esp* : to read attentively — **pe·rus·al** \-ˈrü-zəl\ *n*

Pe·ru·vi·an \pə-ˈrü-vē-ən\ *n* : a native or inhabitant of Peru

per·vade \pər-ˈvād\ *vb* **per·vad·ed; per·vad·ing** : to spread through every part of : PERMEATE, PENETRATE — **per·va·sive** \-ˈvā-siv, -ziv\ *adj*

per·verse \pər-ˈvərs\ *adj* **1** : turned away from what is right or good : CORRUPT **2** : obstinate in opposing what is reasonable or accepted — **per·verse·ly** *adv* — **per·verse·ness** *n* — **per·ver·si·ty** \-ˈvər-sət-ē\ *n*

per·ver·sion \pər-ˈvər-zhən\ *n* **1** : the action of perverting : the condition of being perverted **2** : a perverted form of something; *esp* : aberrant sexual behavior

¹per·vert \pər-ˈvərt\ *vb* **1** : to lead astray : CORRUPT (~ the young) **2** : to divert

to a wrong purpose : MISAPPLY (~ evidence) *syn* deprave, debase, debauch, demoralize

²per·vert \ˈpər-ˌvərt\ *n* : one that is perverted; *esp* : a person given to sexual perversion

pe·se·ta \pə-ˈsāt-ə\ *n* — see MONEY table

pe·se·wa \pə-ˈsā-wə\ *n* — see *cedi* at MONEY table

pes·ky \ˈpes-kē\ *adj* **pes·ki·er; -est** : causing annoyance : TROUBLESOME

pe·so \ˈpā-sō\ *n, pl* **pesos** — see MONEY table

pes·si·mism \ˈpes-ə-ˌmiz-əm\ *n* [F *pessimisme*, fr. L *pessimus* worst] : an inclination to take the least favorable view (as of events) or to expect the worst possible outcome — **pes·si·mist** \-məst\ *n* — **pes·si·mis·tic** \ˌpes-ə-ˈmis-tik\ *adj*

pest \ˈpest\ *n* **1** : a destructive epidemic disease : PLAGUE **2** : a plant or animal detrimental to man **3** : one that pesters : NUISANCE

pes·ter \ˈpes-tər\ *vb* **pes·tered; pes·ter·ing** \-t(ə-)riŋ\ : to harass with petty irritations : ANNOY

pes·ti·cide \ˈpes-tə-ˌsīd\ *n* : an agent used to kill pests

pes·tif·er·ous \pes-ˈtif-(ə-)rəs\ *adj* **1** : PESTILENT **2** : ANNOYING

pes·ti·lence \ˈpes-tə-ləns\ *n* : a destructive infectious swiftly spreading disease; *esp* : PLAGUE

pes·ti·lent \-lənt\ *adj* **1** : dangerous to life : DEADLY; *also* : spreading or causing pestilence **2** : PERNICIOUS, HARMFUL **3** : TROUBLESOME

pes·ti·len·tial \ˌpes-tə-ˈlen-chəl\ *adj* **1** : causing or tending to cause pestilence : DEADLY **2** : morally harmful — **pes·ti·len·tial·ly** \-ē\ *adv*

pes·tle \ˈpes-əl, ˈpes-tᵊl\ *n* : an implement for grinding substances in a mortar

¹pet \ˈpet\ *n* **1** : FAVORITE, DARLING **2** : a domesticated animal kept for pleasure rather than utility

²pet *adj* **1** : kept or treated as a pet (~ dog) **2** : expressing fondness (~ name) **3** : particularly liked or favored

³pet *vb* **pet·ted; pet·ting** **1** : to stroke gently or lovingly **2** : to make a pet of : PAMPER **3** : to engage in amorous kissing and caressing

⁴pet *n* : a fit of peevishness, sulkiness, or anger

Pet *abbr* Peter

pet·al \ˈpet-ᵊl\ *n* : one of the modified leaves of a flower's corolla

pe·tard \pə-ˈtär(d)\ *n* : a case containing an explosive to break down a door or gate or breach a wall

pe·ter \ˈpēt-ər\ *vb* : to diminish gradually and come to an end (his energy ~ed out)

Pe·ter \ˈpēt-ər\ *n* — see BIBLE table

pet·i·ole \ˈpet-ē-ˌōl\ *n* : a stalk that supports a leaf

pe·tite \pə-ˈtēt\ *adj* [F] : small and trim of figure (a ~ woman)

pe·tit four \‚pet-ē-ˈfȯr\ *n, pl* **petits fours** *or* **petit fours** \-ˈfȯrz\ [F, lit., small oven] : a small cake cut from pound or sponge cake and frosted

¹pe·ti·tion \pə-ˈtish-ən\ *n* : an earnest request : ENTREATY; *esp* : a formal written request made to a superior

²petition *vb* **-tioned; -tion·ing** \-ˈtish-(ə-)niŋ\ : to make a petition — **pe·ti·tion·er** \-(ə-)nər\ *n*

pet·nap·ping \ˈpet-‚nap-iŋ\ *n* : the act of stealing a pet

pe·trel \ˈpe-trəl\ *n* : any of various small seabirds that fly far from land

pet·ri·fy \ˈpe-trə-‚fī\ *vb* **-fied; -fy·ing** 1 : to change into stony material 2 : to make rigid or inactive (as from fear or awe) — **pet·ri·fac·tion** \‚pe-trə-ˈfak-shən\ *n*

pet·ro·chem·i·cal \‚pe-trō-ˈkem-i-kəl\ *n* : a chemical isolated or derived from petroleum or natural gas — **pet·ro·chem·is·try** \-ˈkem-ə-strē\ *n*

pet·rol \ˈpe-trəl\ *n, Brit* : GASOLINE

pet·ro·la·tum \‚pe-trə-ˈlät-əm\ *n* : a tasteless, odorless, and oily or greasy substance from petroleum that is used esp. in ointments and dressings

pe·tro·leum \pə-ˈtrō-lē-əm\ *n* [ML, fr. L *petr-* stone, rock (fr. Gk, fr. *petros* stone & *petra* rock) + *oleum* oil] : an oily flammable liquid obtained from wells drilled in the ground and refined into gasoline, fuel oils, and other products

petroleum jelly *n* : PETROLATUM

¹pet·ti·coat \ˈpet-ē-‚kōt\ *n* 1 : a skirt worn under a dress 2 : an outer skirt

²petticoat *adj* : FEMALE (~ government)

pet·ti·fog \ˈpet-ē-‚fȯg, -‚fäg\ *vb* **-fogged; -fog·ging** 1 : to engage in legal trickery 2 : to quibble over insignificant details — **pet·ti·fog·ger** *n*

pet·tish \ˈpet-ish\ *adj* : PEEVISH **syn** irritable, petulant, fretful, huffy, querulous

pet·ty \ˈpet-ē\ *adj* **pet·ti·er; -est** [ME *pety* small, minor, alter. of *petit*, fr. MF, small] 1 : having secondary rank : MINOR (~ prince) 2 : of little importance : TRIFLING (~ faults) 3 : marked by narrowness or meanness — **pet·ti·ly** \ˈpet-ᵊl-ē\ *adv* — **pet·ti·ness** \-ē-nəs\ *n*

petty officer *n* : a subordinate officer in the navy or coast guard appointed from among the enlisted men

petty officer first class *n* : a petty officer ranking below a chief petty officer

petty officer second class *n* : a petty officer ranking below a petty officer first class

petty officer third class *n* : a petty officer ranking below a petty officer second class

pet·u·lant \ˈpech-ə-lənt\ *adj* : marked by capricious ill humor **syn** irritable, peevish, fretful, fractious, querulous — **pet·u·lance** \-ləns\ *n* — **pet·u·lant·ly** *adv*

pe·tu·nia \pi-ˈt(y)ün-yə\ *n* : a garden plant with bright funnel-shaped flowers

pew \ˈpyü\ *n* [ME *pewe*, fr. MF *puie* balustrade, fr. L *podia*, pl. of *podium* parapet, podium, fr. Gk *podion* base, dim. of *pod-, pous* foot] : one of the benches with backs fixed in rows in a church

pe·wee \ˈpē-(‚)wē\ *n* : any of various small flycatchers

pew·ter \ˈpyüt-ər\ *n* : an alloy of tin usu. with lead used esp. for kitchen or table utensils

pey·o·te \pā-ˈōt-ē\ *also* **pey·otl** \-ˈōt-ᵊl\ *n* : a stimulant drug derived from an American cactus; *also* : this cactus

pf *abbr* 1 pfennig 2 preferred

PFC *abbr* private first class

pfd *abbr* preferred

pfen·nig \ˈfen-ig\ *n, pl* **pfennig** *also* **pfennigs** *or* **pfen·ni·ge** \ˈfen-i-gə\ — see *deutsche mark, mark* at MONEY table

pg *abbr* page

PG *abbr* postgraduate

PGA *abbr* Professional Golfers' Association

pH \(ˈ)pē-ˈāch\ *n* : a value used to express acidity and alkalinity; *also* : the condition represented by such a value

PH *abbr* 1 pinch hit 2 public health

pha·eton \ˈfā-ət-ᵊn\ *n* [F *phaéton*, fr. Gk Phaethōn, son of the sun god who persuaded his father to let him drive the chariot of the sun but who lost control of the horses with disastrous consequences] 1 : a light 4-wheeled horse-drawn vehicle 2 : an open automobile with two cross seats

phage \ˈfāj\ *n* : BACTERIOPHAGE

pha·lanx \ˈfā-‚laŋks\ *n, pl* **pha·lanx·es** *or* **pha·lan·ges** \fə-ˈlan-‚jēz\ 1 : a group or body (as of troops) in compact formation 2 *pl* **phalanges** : one of the digital bones of the hand or foot of a vertebrate

phal·a·rope \ˈfal-ə-‚rōp\ *n, pl* **-ropes** *also* **-rope** : any of several small shorebirds

phal·lic \ˈfal-ik\ *adj* 1 : of, relating to, or resembling a phallus 2 : relating to or being the stage of psychosexual development in psychoanalytic theory during which children become interested in their own sexual organs

phal·lus \ˈfal-əs\ *n, pl* **phal·li** \ˈfal-‚ī\ *or* **phal·lus·es** : PENIS; *also* : a symbolic representation of the penis

phan·tasm \ˈfan-‚taz-əm\ *n* : a product of the imagination : ILLUSION

phan·tas·ma·go·ria \‚fan-‚taz-mə-ˈgōr-ē-ə\ *n* : a constantly shifting complex succession of things seen or imagined; *also* : a scene that constantly changes or fluctuates

phantasy *var of* FANTASY

phan·tom \ˈfant-əm\ *n* [deriv. of L *phantasma*] 1 : something (as a specter) that is apparent to sense but has no substantial existence 2 : a mere show : SHADOW 3 : a representation of something abstract, ideal, or incor-

poreal — phantom *adj* — phan·tom·
like *adv or adj*

pha·raoh \'fe(ə)r-ō, 'fā-rō\ *n, often cap*
: a ruler of ancient Egypt

phar·i·sa·i·cal \,far-ə-'sā-ə-kəl\ *adj*
: hypocritically self-righteous —
phar·i·sa·i·cal·ly \-k(ə-)lē\ *adv*

phar·i·see \'far-ə-,sē\ *n* 1 *cap* : a member of an ancient Jewish sect noted for
strict observance of rites and ceremonies of the traditional law 2 : a self-
righteous or hypocritical person —
phar·i·sa·ic \,far-ə-'sā-ik\ *adj*

pharm *abbr* pharmaceutical; pharmacist; pharmacy

phar·ma·ceu·ti·cal \,fär-mə-'süt-i-kəl\
adj 1 : of or relating to pharmacy or
pharmacists 2 : MEDICINAL —
pharmaceutical *n*

phar·ma·col·o·gy \,fär-mə-'käl-ə-jē\ *n* 1
: the science of drugs esp. as related
to medicinal uses 2 : the reactions
and properties of a drug — phar·ma·
co·log·i·cal \-i-kəl\ *also* phar·ma·co·
log·ic \-kə-'läj-ik\ *adj* — phar·ma·col·
o·gist \-'käl-ə-jəst\ *n*

phar·ma·co·poe·ia *also* phar·ma·co·pe·ia
\-kə-'pē-(y)ə\ *n* 1 : a book describing
drugs and medicinal preparations 2
: a stock of drugs

phar·ma·cy \'fär-mə-sē\ *n, pl* -cies 1
: the art or practice of preparing and
dispensing drugs 2 : DRUGSTORE —
phar·ma·cist \-səst\ *n*

phar·os \'faər-,äs\ *n* : LIGHTHOUSE

phar·ynx \'far-inks\ *n, pl* pha·ryn·ges
\fə-'rin-,jēz\ *also* pharynx·es : the
space just back of the mouth into
which the nostrils, esophagus, and
trachea open — pha·ryn·ge·al \fə-'rin-
j(ē-)əl, ,far-ən-'jē-əl\ *adj*

phase \'fāz\ *n* 1 : a particular appearance in a recurring series of changes
(~s of the moon) 2 : a stage or interval in a process or cycle (first ~ of an
experiment) 3 : an aspect or part under consideration

phase in *vb* : to introduce in stages

phase·out \'fāz-,aùt\ *n* : a gradual stopping of operations or production

phase out *vb* : to stop production or use of in stages

PhD *abbr* [L *philosophiae doctor*] doctor of philosophy

pheas·ant \'fez-ᵊnt\ *n, pl* pheasant *or*
pheasants : any of various long-tailed
brilliantly colored game birds related
to the domestic fowl

phen·cy·cli·dine \,fen-'sī-klə-,dēn\ *n* : a
drug used medicinally as an anesthetic and sometimes illicitly to induce
vivid mental imagery

phe·no·bar·bi·tal \,fē-nō-'bär-bə-,tòl\ *n*
: a crystalline drug used as a hypnotic
and sedative

phe·nol \'fē-,nòl, -,nòl, fi-'nòl, -'nòl\ *n*
: a caustic poisonous acidic compound in tar used as a disinfectant

phe·nom·e·non \fi-'näm-ə-,nän, -nən\ *n,
pl* -na \-nə\ *or* -nons [LL *phae-
nomenon*, fr. Gk *phainomenon*, fr.

neut. of *phainomenos*, prp. of *phai-
nesthai* to appear] 1 *pl* -na : an
observable fact or event 2 : an outward sign of the working of a law of
nature 3 *pl* -nons : an extraordinary
person or thing : PRODIGY — phe·nom·
e·nal \-'näm-ən-ᵊl\ *adj*

pher·o·mone \'fer-ə-,mōn\ *n* : a chemical substance that is produced by an
animal and serves to stimulate a
behavioral response in other individuals of the same species — pher·o·
mon·al \,fer-ə-'mōn-ᵊl\ *adj*

phi·al \'fī-(-)əl\ *n* : VIAL

Phil *abbr* Philippians

phi·lan·der \fə-'lan-dər\ *vb* -dered; -der·
ing \-d(ə-)riŋ\ : to make love without
serious intent : FLIRT — phi·lan·der·er
n

phi·lan·thro·py \fə-'lan-thrə-pē\ *n, pl*
-pies 1 : goodwill to fellowmen; *esp*
: effort to promote human welfare 2
: a charitable act or gift; *also* : an organization that distributes or is supported by donated funds — phil·an·
throp·ic \,fil-ən-'thräp-ik\ *adj* —
phi·lan·thro·pist \fə-'lan-thrə-pəst\ *n*

phi·lat·e·ly \fə-'lat-ᵊl-ē\ *n* : the collection and study of postage and imprinted stamps — phil·a·tel·ist \-ᵊl-əst\ *n*

Phi·le·mon \fī-'lē-mən, fī-\ *n* — see BI-
BLE table

Phi·lip·pi·ans \fə-'lip-ē-ənz\ *n* — see BI-
BLE table

phi·lip·pic \fə-'lip-ik\ *n* : TIRADE

phi·lis·tine \'fil-ə-,stēn; fə-'lis-tən\ *n,
often cap* [*Philistine*, inhabitant of ancient Philistia (Palestine)] : a materi-
alistic person; *esp* : one who is
smugly insensitive or indifferent to intellectual or artistic values —
philistine *adj, often cap*

philo·den·dron \,fil-ə-'den-drən\ *n, pl*
-drons *or* -dra \-drə\ [NL, fr. Gk,
neut. of *philodendros* loving trees, fr.
philos dear, friendly + *dendron* tree]
: any of various arums grown for their
showy foliage

phi·lol·o·gy \fə-'läl-ə-jē\ *n* 1 : the study
of literature and relevant fields 2
: LINGUISTICS; *esp* : historical and
comparative linguistics — phil·o·log·i·
cal \,fil-ə-'läj-i-kəl\ *adj* — phi·lol·o·gist
\fə-'läl-ə-jəst\ *n*

philos *abbr* philosopher; philosophy

phi·los·o·pher \fə-'läs-ə-fər\ *n* 1 : a reflective thinker : SCHOLAR 2 : a student of or specialist in philosophy 3
: one whose philosophical perspective enables him to meet trouble calmly

phi·los·o·phize \fə-'läs-ə-,fīz\ *vb*
-phized; -phiz·ing 1 : to reason like a
philosopher : THEORIZE 2 : to ex-
pound a philosophy esp. superficially

phi·los·o·phy \fə-'läs-ə-fē\ *n, pl* -phies 1
: a critical study of fundamental beliefs and the grounds for them 2
: sciences and liberal arts exclusive of
medicine, law, and theology (doctor
of ~) 3 : a system of philosophical

concepts ⟨Aristotelian ∼⟩ **4** : a basic theory concerning a particular subject or sphere of activity **5** : the sum of the ideas and convictions of an individual or group (his ∼ of life) **6** : calmness of temper and judgment — **phil·o·soph·ic** \ˌfil-ə-ˈsäf-ik\ *or* **phil·o·soph·i·cal** \-i-kəl\ *adj* — **phil·o·soph·i·cal·ly** \-k(ə-)lē\ *adv*

phil·ter *or* **phil·tre** \ˈfil-tər\ *n* **1** : a potion, drug, or charm held to arouse sexual passion **2** : a magic potion

phle·bi·tis \fli-ˈbīt-əs\ *n* : inflammation of a vein

phle·bot·o·my \fli-ˈbät-ə-mē\ *n, pl* **-mies** : the opening of a vein for removing or releasing blood

phlegm \ˈflem\ *n* : thick mucus secreted in abnormal quantity esp. in the nose and throat

phleg·mat·ic \fleg-ˈmat-ik\ *adj* : having or showing a slow and stolid temperament **syn** impassive, apathetic, stoic, stolid

phlo·em \ˈflō-ˌem\ *n* : a vascular plant tissue external to the xylem that carries dissolved food material downward

phlox \ˈfläks\ *n, pl* **phlox** *or* **phlox·es** : any of several American herbs; *esp* : one that has tall stalks with showy spreading terminal clusters of flowers

pho·bia \ˈfō-bē-ə\ *n* : an irrational persistent fear or dread

phoe·be \ˈfē-(ˌ)bē\ *n* : a flycatcher of the eastern U.S. that has a slight crest and is grayish brown above and yellowish white below

phoe·nix \ˈfē-niks\ *n* : a legendary bird held to live for centuries and then to burn itself to death and rise fresh and young from its ashes

phon *abbr* phonetics

¹phone \ˈfōn\ *n* **1** : EARPHONE **2** : TELEPHONE

²phone *vb* **phoned; phon·ing** : TELEPHONE

pho·neme \ˈfō-ˌnēm\ *n* : one of the smallest units of speech that distinguish one utterance from another — **pho·ne·mic** \fō-ˈnē-mik\ *adj*

pho·net·ics \fə-ˈnet-iks\ *n* : the study and systematic classification of the sounds made in spoken utterance — **pho·net·ic** \-ik\ *adj* — **pho·ne·ti·cian** \ˌfō-nə-ˈtish-ən\ *n*

pho·nic \ˈfän-ik\ *adj* **1** : of, relating to, or producing sound **2** : of or relating to the sounds of speech or to phonics — **pho·ni·cal·ly** \-i-k(ə-)lē\ *adv*

pho·nics \ˈfän-iks\ *n* : a method of teaching people to read and pronounce words by learning the phonetic value of letters, letter groups, and esp. syllables

pho·no·graph \ˈfō-nə-ˌgraf\ *n* : an instrument for reproducing sounds by means of the vibration of a needle following a spiral groove on a revolving disc — **pho·no·graph·ic** \ˌfō-nə-ˈgraf-ik\ *adj* — **pho·no·graph·i·cal·ly** \-i-k(ə-)lē\ *adv*

pho·nol·o·gy \fə-ˈnäl-ə-jē\ *n* : a study and description of the sound changes in a language — **pho·no·log·i·cal** \ˌfōn-əl-ˈäj-i-kəl\ *adj* — **pho·nol·o·gist** \fə-ˈnäl-ə-jəst\ *n*

pho·ny *or* **pho·ney** \ˈfō-nē\ *adj* **pho·ni·er; -est** : marked by empty pretension : FAKE — **phony** *n*

phosph- *or* **phospho-** *comb form* **1** : phosphorus **2** : phosphate

phos·phate \ˈfäs-ˌfāt\ *n* : a salt of a phosphoric acid — **phos·phat·ic** \fäs-ˈfat-ik\ *adj*

phos·phor \ˈfäs-fər\ *also* **phos·phore** \-ˌfōr, -fər\ *n* : a phosphorescent substance

phos·pho·res·cence \ˌfäs-fə-ˈres-ᵊns\ *n* **1** : luminescence caused by radiation absorption that continues after the radiation has stopped **2** : an enduring luminescence without sensible heat — **phos·pho·res·cent** \-ᵊnt\ *adj* — **phos·pho·res·cent·ly** *adv*

phosphoric acid \ˌfäs-ˌfōr-ik-, -ˌfär-\ *n* : any of several oxygen-containing acids of phosphorus

phos·pho·rus \ˈfäs-f(ə-)rəs\ *n* [NL, fr. Gk *phōsphoros* light-bearing, fr. *phōs* light + *pherein* to carry, bring] : a nonmetallic chemical element that has characteristics similar to nitrogen and occurs widely esp. as phosphates — **phos·phor·ic** \fäs-ˈfōr-ik\ *adj* — **phos·pho·rous** \ˈfäs-f(ə-)rəs-; fäs-ˈfōr-əs, -ˈfōr-\ *adj*

phot- *or* **photo-** *comb form* **1** : light **2** : photograph : photographic **3** : photoelectric

pho·to \ˈfōt-ō\ *n, pl* **photos** : PHOTOGRAPH — **photo** *vb* or *adj*

pho·to·cell \ˈfōt-ə-ˌsel\ *n* : PHOTOELECTRIC CELL

pho·to·chem·i·cal \ˌfōt-ō-ˈkem-i-kəl\ *adj* : of, relating to, or resulting from the chemical action of radiant energy.

pho·to·com·pose \-kəm-ˈpōz\ *vb* : to compose reading matter for reproduction by means of characters photographed on film — **pho·to·com·po·si·tion** \-ˌkäm-pə-ˈzish-ən\ *n*

pho·to·copy \ˈfōt-ə-ˌkäp-ē\ *n* : a photographic reproduction of graphic matter — **photocopy** *vb*

pho·to·elec·tric \ˌfōt-ō-i-ˈlek-trik\ *adj* : relating to an electrical effect due to the interaction of light with matter — **pho·to·elec·tri·cal·ly** \-tri-k(ə-)lē\ *adv*

photoelectric cell *n* : a device in which variations in light are converted into variations in an electric current

pho·to·en·grave \ˌfōt-ō-in-ˈgrāv\ *vb* : to make a photoengraving of

pho·to·en·grav·ing \-ˈgrā-viŋ\ *n* : a process by which an etched printing plate is made from a photograph or drawing; *also* : a print made from such a plate

photo finish *n* : a race finish so close that a photograph of the finish is used to determine the winner

¹pho·tog \fə-ˈtäg\ *n* : PHOTOGRAPHER

²photog *abbr* photographic; photography

pho·to·gen·ic \ˌfōt-ə-'jen-ik\ *adj* : eminently suitable esp. aesthetically for being photographed

pho·to·graph \'fōt-ə-ˌgraf\ *n* : a picture taken by photography — **pho·to·graph** *vb* — **pho·tog·ra·pher** \fə-'täg-rə-fər\ *n*

pho·tog·ra·phy \fə-'täg-rə-fē\ *n* : the art or process of producing images on a sensitized surface (as film in a camera) by the action of light — **pho·to·graph·ic** \ˌfōt-ə-'graf-ik\ *adj* — **pho·to·graph·i·cal·ly** \-i-k(ə-)lē\ *adv*

pho·to·gra·vure \ˌfōt-ə-grə-'vyùr\ *n* : a process for making prints from an intaglio plate prepared by photographic methods

pho·to·li·thog·ra·phy \ˌfōt-ō-lith-'äg-rə-fē\ *n* : the process of photographically transferring a pattern to a surface for etching (as in making an integrated circuit)

pho·tom·e·ter \fō-'täm-ət-ər\ *n* : an instrument for measuring luminous intensity — **pho·to·met·ric** \ˌfōt-ə-'me-trik\ *adj* — **pho·tom·e·try** \fō-'täm-ə-trē\ *n*

pho·to·mi·cro·graph \ˌfōt-ə-'mī-krə-ˌgraf\ *n* : a photograph of a magnified image of a small object — **pho·to·mi·crog·ra·phy** \-mī-'kräg-rə-fē\ *n*

pho·ton \'fō-ˌtän\ *n* : a quantum of radiant energy

pho·to·play \'fōt-ō-ˌplā\ *n* : MOTION PICTURE

pho·to·sen·si·tive \ˌfōt-ə-'sen-sət-iv\ *adj* : sensitive or sensitized to the action of radiant energy

pho·to·sphere \'fōt-ə-ˌsfiər\ *n* 1 : a sphere of light 2 : the luminous surface of a star — **pho·to·spher·ic** \ˌfōt-ə-'sfi(ə)r-ik, -'sfer-\ *adj*

pho·to·syn·the·sis \ˌfōt-ō-'sin-thə-səs\ *n* : formation of carbohydrates by chlorophyll-containing plants exposed to sunlight — **pho·to·syn·the·size** \-ˌsīz\ *vb* — **pho·to·syn·thet·ic** \-sin-'thet-ik\ *adj*

phr *abbr* phrase

¹phrase \'frāz\ *n* 1 : a brief expression 2 : a group of two or more grammatically related words that form a sense unit expressing a thought

²phrase *vb* **phrased; phras·ing** : to express in words

phrase·ol·o·gy \ˌfrā-zē-'äl-ə-jē\ *n, pl* **-gies** : a manner of phrasing : STYLE

phras·ing \'frā-ziŋ\ *n* : style of expression

phre·net·ic \fri-'net-ik\ *adj* : FRENETIC

phren·ic \'fren-ik\ *adj* : of or relating to the diaphragm (~ nerves)

phre·nol·o·gy \fri-'näl-ə-jē\ *n* : the study of the conformation of the skull as indicative of mental faculties and character traits

phy·lac·tery \fə-'lak-t(ə-)rē\ *n, pl* **-ter·ies** 1 : one of two small square leather boxes containing slips inscribed with scripture passages and traditionally worn on the left arm and forehead by Jewish men during morning weekday prayers 2 : AMULET

phy·lum \'fī-ləm\ *n, pl* **phy·la** \-lə\ : a major division of the animal and in some classifications the plant kingdom; *also* : a group (as of people) apparently of common origin

phys *abbr* 1 physical 2 physics

¹phys·ic \'fiz-ik\ *n* 1 : the profession of medicine 2 : MEDICINE; *esp* : CATHARTIC

²physic *vb* **phys·icked; phys·ick·ing** : PURGE

¹phys·i·cal \'fiz-i-kəl\ *adj* 1 : of or relating to nature or the laws of nature 2 : material as opposed to mental or spiritual 3 : of, relating to, or produced by the forces and operations of physics 4 : of or relating to the body — **phys·i·cal·ly** \-k(ə-)lē\ *adv*

²physical *n* : an examination of the bodily functions and condition of an individual

physical education *n* : instruction in the development and care of the body ranging from simple calisthenics to training in hygiene, gymnastics, and the performance and management of athletic games

physical examination *n* : PHYSICAL

physical science *n* : any of the sciences (as physics and astronomy) that deal primarily with nonliving materials — **physical scientist** *n*

physical therapy *n* : the treatment of disease by physical and mechanical means (as massage, exercise, water, or heat) — **physical therapist** *n*

phy·si·cian \fə-'zish-ən\ *n* : a doctor of medicine

phys·i·cist \'fiz-ə-səst\ *n* : a specialist in physics

phys·ics \'fiz-iks\ *n* 1 : the science of matter and energy and their interactions 2 : physical properties and composition

phys·i·og·no·my \ˌfiz-ē-'ä(g)-nə-mē\ *n, pl* **-mies** : facial appearance esp. as a reflection of inner character

phys·i·og·ra·phy \ˌfiz-ē-'äg-rə-fē\ *n* : geography dealing with physical features of the earth — **phys·io·graph·ic** \ˌfiz-ē-ō-'graf-ik\ *adj*

phys·i·ol·o·gy \ˌfiz-ē-'äl-ə-jē\ *n* 1 : a science dealing with the functions and functioning of living matter and beings 2 : functional processes in an organism or any of its parts — **phys·i·o·log·i·cal** \-ē-ə-'läj-i-kəl\ *or* **phys·i·o·log·ic** \-ik\ *adj* — **phys·i·o·log·i·cal·ly** \-i-k(ə-)lē\ *adv* — **phys·i·ol·o·gist** \-ē-'äl-ə-jəst\ *n*

phys·io·ther·a·py \ˌfiz-ē-ō-'ther-ə-pē\ *n* : treatment of disease by physical means (as massage or exercise) — **phys·io·ther·a·pist** \-pəst\ *n*

phy·sique \fə-'zēk\ *n* : the build of a person's body : bodily constitution

phy·to·plank·ton \'fīt-ō-ˌplaŋk-tən\ *n* : plant life of the plankton

¹**pi** *also* **pie** \'pī\ *n, pl* **pies** : jumbled type

²**pi** *n, pl* **pis** \'pīz\ : the symbol π denoting the ratio of the circumference of a circle to its diameter; *also* : the ratio itself

pi·a·nis·si·mo \,pē-ə-'nis-ə-,mō\ *adv or adj* : very softly — used as a direction in music

pi·a·nist \pē-'an-əst, 'pē-ə-nəst\ *n* : one who plays the piano

¹**pi·a·no** \pē-'än-ō\ *adv or adj* : SOFTLY — used as a direction in music

²**piano** \pē-'an-ō\ *n, pl* **pianos** [It, short for *pianoforte*, fr. *piano e forte* soft and loud, fr. *piano* soft (fr. L *planus* level, flat) + *forte* loud, fr. L *fortis* strong; fr. the fact that its tones could be varied in loudness] : a musical instrument having steel strings sounded by felt-covered hammers operated from a keyboard

pi·ano·forte \pē-,an-ō-'fōr-,tā, -tē; pē-'an-ə-,fōrt\ *n* : PIANO

pi·as·ter *or* **pi·as·tre** \pē-'as-tər\ *n* — see *lira, pound* at MONEY table

pi·az·za \pē-'az-ə, *esp for* 1 -'at-sə\ *n, pl* **piazzas** *or* **pi·az·ze** \-'at-(,)sā, -'ät-\ [It, fr. L *platea* broad street] 1 : an open square esp. in an Italian town 2 : a long hall with an arched roof; *also, dial* : VERANDA

pi·broch \'pē-,bräk\ *n* : a set of variations for the bagpipe

pic \'pik\ *n, pl* **pics** *or* **pix** \'piks\ 1 : PHOTOGRAPH 2 : MOTION PICTURE

pi·ca \'pī-kə\ *n* : a typewriter type providing 10 characters to the inch

pic·a·resque \,pik-ə-'resk, ,pē-kə-\ *adj* : of or relating to rogues (~ fiction)

pic·a·yune \,pik-ē-'(y)ün\ *adj* [F *picaillon* halfpenny] : of little value : TRIVIAL; *also* : PETTY

pic·ca·lil·li \,pik-ə-'lil-ē\ *n* : a pungent relish of chopped vegetables and spices

pic·co·lo \'pik-ə-,lō\ *n, pl* **-los** [It, short for *piccolo flauto* small flute] : a small shrill flute pitched an octave higher than the ordinary flute

pice \'pīs\ *n, pl* **pice** : PAISA

¹**pick** \'pik\ *vb* 1 : to pierce or break up with a pointed instrument 2 : to remove bit by bit (~ meat from bones) ; *also* : to remove covering matter from 3 : to gather by plucking (~ apples) 4 : CULL, SELECT 5 : ROB (~ a pocket) 6 : PROVOKE (~ a quarrel) 7 : to dig into or pull lightly at 8 : to pluck with fingers or a plectrum 9 : to loosen or pull apart with a sharp point (~ wool) 10 : to unlock with a wire 11 : to eat sparingly — **pick·er** *n*

²**pick** *n* 1 : the act or privilege of choosing 2 : the best or choicest one 3 : the part of a crop gathered at one time

³**pick** *n* 1 : PICKAX 2 : a pointed implement used for picking 3 : a small thin piece (as of metal) used to pluck the strings of a stringed instrument

pick·a·back \'pig-ē-,bak, 'pik-ə-\ *var of* PIGGYBACK

pick·ax \'pik-,aks\ *n* : a tool with a wooden handle and a blade pointed at one end or at both ends that is used by diggers and miners

pick·er·el \'pik(-ə)-rəl\ *n, pl* **pickerel** *or* **pickerels** : any of various small pikes; *also* : WALLEYE 2

pick·er·el·weed \-rəl-,wēd\ *n* : a blue=flowered American shallow-water herb

¹**pick·et** \'pik-ət\ *n* 1 : a pointed stake (as for a fence) 2 : a detached body of soldiers on outpost duty; *also* : SENTINEL 3 : a person posted by a labor union where workers are on strike; *also* : a person posted for a demonstration

²**picket** *vb* 1 : to guard with pickets 2 : TETHER 3 : to post pickets at (~ a factory) 4 : to serve as a picket

pick·ings \'pik-iŋz, -ənz\ *n pl* 1 : gleanable or eatable fragments : SCRAPS 2 : yield for effort expended : RETURN; *also* : share of spoils

pick·le \'pik-əl\ *n* 1 : a brine or vinegar solution for preserving foods; *also* : a food preserved in a pickle 2 : a difficult situation : PLIGHT — **pickle** *vb*

pick·lock \'pik-,läk\ *n* 1 : a tool for picking locks 2 : BURGLAR, THIEF

pick·pock·et \'pik-,päk-ət\ *n* : one who steals from pockets

pick·up \'pik-,əp\ *n* 1 : a picking up 2 : revival of activity : IMPROVEMENT 3 : ACCELERATION 4 : a temporary chance acquaintance 5 : the conversion of mechanical movements into electrical impulses in the reproduction of sound; *also* : a device for making such conversion 6 : a light truck having an enclosed cab and an open body with low sides and a tailgate

pick up \(')pik-'əp\ *vb* 1 : to take hold of and lift 2 : IMPROVE 3 : to put in order

picky \'pik-ē\ *adj* **pick·i·er; -est** : FUSSY, FINICKY

¹**pic·nic** \'pik-,nik\ *n* : an outing with food usu. provided by members of the group and eaten in the open

²**picnic** *vb* **pic·nicked; pic·nick·ing** : to go on a picnic : eat in picnic fashion

pi·co·sec·ond \'pē-kō-,sek-ənd\ *n* : one trillionth of a second

pi·cot \'pē-,kō\ *n* : one of a series of small loops forming an edging on ribbon or lace

pic·to·ri·al \pik-'tōr-ē-əl\ *adj* : of, relating to, or consisting of pictures

¹**pic·ture** \'pik-chər\ *n* 1 : a representation made by painting, drawing, or photography 2 : a vivid description in words 3 : IMAGE, COPY 4 : a transitory visual image or reproduction 5 : MOTION PICTURE 6 : SITUATION

²**picture** *vb* **pic·tured; pic·tur·ing** 1 : to paint or draw a picture of 2 : to describe vividly in words 3 : to form a mental image of

pic·tur·esque \,pik-chə-'resk\ *adj* 1 : resembling a picture (a ~ landscape)

2 : CHARMING, QUAINT ⟨a ∼ character⟩ **3** : GRAPHIC, VIVID ⟨a ∼ account⟩ — **pic·tur·esque·ness** *n*

picture tube *n* : a cathode-ray tube on which the picture in a television set appears

pid·dle \'pid-ᵊl\ *vb* **pid·dled; pid·dling** \'pid-(ᵊ-)liŋ\ : to act or work idly : DAWDLE

pid·dling \-(ᵊ-)lən, -(ᵊ-)liŋ\ *adj* : TRIVIAL, PALTRY

pid·gin \'pij-ən\ *n* [fr. *Pidgin English*, Pidgin E, modif. of E *business English*] : a simplified speech used for communication between people with different languages; *esp* : an English-based pidgin used in the Orient

¹**pie** \'pī\ *n* : a dish consisting of a pastry crust and a filling (as of fruit or meat)

²**pie** *var of* PI

¹**pie·bald** \'pī-ˌbȯld\ *adj* : of different colors; *esp* : blotched with white and black

²**piebald** *n* : a piebald animal (as a horse)

¹**piece** \'pēs\ *n* **1** : a part of a whole : FRAGMENT **2** : one of a group, set, or mass ⟨chess ∼⟩ : *also* : a single item ⟨a ∼ of news⟩ **3** : a length, weight, or size in which something is made or sold **4** : a product (as an essay) of creative work **5** : FIREARM **6** : COIN

²**piece** *vb* **pieced; piec·ing 1** : to repair or complete by adding pieces : PATCH **2** : to join into a whole

pièce de ré·sis·tance \pē-ˌes-də-rā-ˈstäⁿs\ *n, pl* **pièces de ré·sis·tance** *same*\ **1** : the chief dish of a meal **2** : an outstanding item

piece·meal \'pēs-ˌmēl\ *adv or adj* : one piece at a time : GRADUALLY

piece·work \-ˌwərk\ *n* : work done and paid for by the piece — **piece·work·er** *n*

pied \'pīd\ *adj* : of two or more colors in blotches : VARIEGATED

pied-à-terre \pē-ˌäd-ə-ˈter\ *n, pl* **pieds-à-terre** *same*\ [F, lit., foot to the ground] : a temporary or second lodging

pier \'piər\ *n* **1** : a support for a bridge span **2** : a structure built out into the water for use as a landing place or a promenade or to protect or form a harbor **3** : an upright supporting part (as a pillar) of a building or structure

pierce \'piərs\ *vb* **pierced; pierc·ing 1** : to enter or thrust into sharply or painfully : STAB **2** : to make a hole in or through : PERFORATE **3** : to force or make a way into or through : PENETRATE **4** : to see through : DISCERN

pies *pl of* PI *or of* PIE

pi·ety \'pī-ət-ē\ *n, pl* **pi·eties 1** : fidelity to natural obligations (as to parents) **2** : dutifulness in religion : DEVOUTNESS **3** : a pious act *syn* allegiance, devotion, loyalty

pif·fle \'pif-əl\ *n* : trifling talk or action

pig \'pig\ *n* **1** : SWINE; *esp* : a young swine **2** : PORK **3** : one thought to resemble a pig (as in dirtiness or greed) **4** : a casting of metal (as iron or lead) run directly from a smelting furnace into a mold

pi·geon \'pij-ən\ *n* : any of numerous stout-bodied short-legged birds with smooth thick plumage

¹**pi·geon·hole** \'pij-ən-ˌhōl\ *n* : a small open compartment (as in a desk) for keeping letters or documents

²**pigeonhole** *vb* **1** : to place in or as if in a pigeonhole : FILE **2** : to lay aside **3** : CLASSIFY

pi·geon-toed \'pij-ən-ˌtōd\ *adj* : having the toes turned in

pig·gish \'pig-ish\ *adj* **1** : GREEDY **2** : STUBBORN

pig·gy·back \'pig-ē-ˌbak\ *adv or adj* **1** : up on the back and shoulders **2** : on a railroad flatcar

pig·head·ed \'pig-ˈhed-əd\ *adj* : OBSTINATE, STUBBORN

pig latin *n, often cap L* : a jargon that is made by systematic alteration of English

pig·let \'pig-lət\ *n* : a small usu. young hog

pig·ment \'pig-mənt\ *n* **1** : coloring matter **2** : a powder mixed with a suitable liquid to give color (as in paints and enamels)

pig·men·ta·tion \ˌpig-mən-ˈtā-shən\ *n* : coloration with or deposition of pigment; *esp* : an excessive deposition of bodily pigment

pigmy *var of* PYGMY

pig·nut \'pig-ˌnət\ *n* : any of several bitter hickory nuts; *also* : a tree bearing these

pig·pen \-ˌpen\ *n* **1** : a pen for pigs **2** : a dirty place

pig·skin \-ˌskin\ *n* **1** : the skin of a pig; *also* : leather made from it **2** : FOOTBALL **2**

pig·sty \-ˌstī\ *n* : PIGPEN

pig·tail \-ˌtāl\ *n* : a tight braid of hair

pi·ka \'pī-kə\ *n* : any of various small short-eared mammals of the rocky uplands of Asia and western No. America that are related to the rabbits

¹**pike** \'pīk\ *n* : a sharp point or spike

²**pike** *n, pl* **pike** *or* **pikes** : a large slender long-snouted freshwater food fish; *also* : a related fish

³**pike** *n* : a long wooden shaft with a pointed steel head formerly used as a foot soldier's weapon

⁴**pike** *n* : TURNPIKE

pik·er \'pī-kər\ *n* **1** : one who does things in a small way or on a small scale **2** : TIGHTWAD, CHEAPSKATE

pike·staff \'pīk-ˌstaf\ *n* : the staff of a foot soldier's pike

pi·laf *or* **pi·laff** \pi-ˈläf, ˈpē-ˌläf\ *or* **pi·lau** \pi-ˈlȯ, -ˈlȯ, ˈpē-ˌlō, -ˌlȯ\ *n* : a dish made of seasoned rice often with meat

pi·las·ter \pi-ˈlas-tər, ˈpī-ˌlas-tər\ *n* : a slightly projecting upright column that ornaments or helps to support a wall

pil·chard \'pil-chərd\ *n* : any of several

fishes related to the herrings and often packed as sardines

¹pile \'pīl\ n : a long slender column (as of wood or steel) driven into the ground to support a vertical load

²pile n 1 : a quantity of things heaped together 2 : PYRE 3 : a great number or quantity : LOT

³pile vb **piled; pil·ing** 1 : to lay in a pile : STACK 2 : to heap up : ACCUMULATE 3 : to press forward in a mass : CROWD

⁴pile n : a velvety surface of fine short hairs or threads (as on cloth) — **piled** \'pīld\ adj — **pile·less** adj

piles \'pīlz\ n pl : HEMORRHOIDS

pil·fer \'pil-fər\ vb **pil·fered; pil·fer·ing** \-f(ə-)riŋ\ : to steal in small quantities

pil·grim \'pil-grəm\ n [ME, fr. OF peligrin, fr. LL pelegrinus, alter. of L peregrinus foreigner, fr. peregrinus foreign, fr. pereger being abroad, fr. per through + ager land] 1 : one who journeys in foreign lands : WAYFARER 2 : one who travels to a shrine or holy place as an act of devotion 3 cap : one of the English settlers founding Plymouth colony in 1620

pil·grim·age \-grə-mij\ n : a journey of a pilgrim esp. to a shrine or holy place

pil·ing \'pī-liŋ\ n : a structure of piles

pill \'pil\ n 1 : a medicine prepared in a little ball to be taken whole 2 : a disagreeable or tiresome person 3 : an oral contraceptive — usu. used with the

pil·lage \'pil-ij\ vb **pil·laged; pil·lag·ing** : to take booty : LOOT, PLUNDER — **pillage** n

pil·lar \'pil-ər\ n 1 : a strong upright support (as for a roof) 2 : a column or shaft standing alone esp. as a monument — **pil·lared** \-ərd\ adj

pill·box \'pil-‚bäks\ n 1 : a low usu. round box to hold pills 2 : something (as a low concrete emplacement for machine guns) shaped like a pillbox

pil·lion \'pil-yən\ n 1 : a pad or cushion placed behind a saddle for an extra rider 2 : a motorcycle or bicycle saddle for a passenger

¹pil·lo·ry \'pil-(ə-)rē\ n, pl **-ries** : a wooden frame for public punishment having holes in which the head and hands can be locked

²pillory vb **-ried; -ry·ing** 1 : to set in a pillory 2 : to expose to public scorn

¹pil·low \'pil-ō\ n : a case filled with springy material (as feathers) and used to support the head of a resting person

²pillow vb : to rest or place on or as if on a pillow; also : to serve as a pillow for

pil·low·case \'pil-ə-‚kās, -ō-\ n : a removable covering for a pillow

¹pi·lot \'pī-lət\ n 1 : HELMSMAN, STEERSMAN 2 : a person qualified and licensed to take ships into and out of a port 3 : GUIDE, LEADER 4 : one that flies an aircraft or spacecraft 5 : a television show filmed or taped as a

sample of a proposed series — **pi·lot·less** adj

²pilot vb : CONDUCT, GUIDE; esp : to act as pilot of

³pilot adj : serving as a guiding or activating device or as a testing or trial unit ⟨a ~ light⟩ ⟨a ~ factory⟩

pi·lot·house \'pī-lət-‚haús\ n : an enclosed place forward on the upper deck of a ship that shelters the steering gear and the helmsman

pil·sner also **pil·sen·er** \'pilz-(ə-)nər\ n [G, lit., of Pilsen, city in Czechoslovakia (now Plzeň)] 1 : a light beer with a strong flavor of hops 2 : a tall slender footed glass for beer

pi·men·to \pə-'ment-ō\ n, pl **pimentos** or **pimento** [Sp pimienta allspice, pepper, fr. LL pigmenta, pl. of pigmentum plant juice, fr. L, pigment] 1 : PIMIENTO 2 : ALLSPICE

pi·mien·to \pə-'m(y)ent-ō\ n, pl **-tos** : a mild red sweet pepper fruit that yields paprika

pimp \'pimp\ n : a man who solicits clients for a prostitute — **pimp** vb

pim·per·nel \'pim-pər-‚nel, -pər-nəl\ n : any of a genus of herbs related to the primroses and having flowers that close in rainy or cloudy weather

pim·ple \'pim-pəl\ n : a small inflamed swelling on the skin often containing pus — **pim·ply** \-p(ə-)lē\ adj

¹pin \'pin\ n 1 : a piece of wood or metal used esp. for fastening articles together or as a support by which one article may be suspended from another; esp : a small pointed piece of wire with a head used for fastening clothes or attaching papers 2 : an ornament or emblem fastened to clothing with a pin 3 : one of the wooden pieces constituting the target (as in bowling); also : the staff of the flag marking a hole on a golf course 4 : LEG

²pin vb **pinned; pin·ning** 1 : to fasten with a pin 2 : to press together and hold fast 3 : to make dependent ⟨pinned their hopes on one man⟩ 4 : to assign the blame for ⟨~ a crime on someone⟩ 5 : to define clearly : ESTABLISH ⟨~ down an idea⟩ 6 : to hold fast or immobile in a spot or position

pi·ña co·la·da \‚pēn-yə-kō-'läd-ə\ n [Sp, lit., strained pineapple] : a tall drink made of rum, cream of coconut, and pineapple juice mixed with ice

pin·afore \'pin-ə-‚fōr\ n : a sleeveless dress or apron fastened at the back

pince–nez \‚paⁿs-'nā\ n, pl **pince–nez** \-'nā(z)\ [F, lit., pinch-nose] : eyeglasses clipped to the nose by a spring

pin·cer \'pin-sər\ n 1 pl : a gripping instrument with two handles and two grasping jaws 2 : a claw (as of a lobster) resembling pincers

¹pinch \'pinch\ vb 1 : to squeeze between the finger and thumb or between the jaws of an instrument 2 : to compress painfully : CRAMP 3 : CONTRACT, SHRIVEL 4 : to be miserly; also

: to subject to strict economy **5**
: STEAL **6** : ARREST
²**pinch** n **1** : a critical point **2** : painful
effect **3** : an act of pinching **4** : a very
small quantity **5** : ARREST
³**pinch** adj : SUBSTITUTE (a ~ runner)
pinch–hit \(')pinch-'hit\ vb **1** : to bat in
the place of another player esp. when
a hit is particularly needed **2** : to act
or serve in place of another — **pinch
hit** n — **pinch hitter** n
pin curl n : a curl made usu. by damp-
ening a strand of hair, coiling it, and
securing it by a hairpin or clip
pin·cush·ion \'pin-ˌküsh-ən\ n : a cushion for pins not in use
¹**pine** \'pīn\ n : any of a genus of evergreen cone-bearing trees; also : the
light durable resinous wood of a pine
²**pine** vb **pined; pin·ing 1** : to lose vigor
or health through distress **2** : to long
for something intensely
pi·ne·al \'pī-nē-əl, pī-'nē-əl\ n : PINEAL
GLAND — **pineal** adj
pineal gland n : a small usu. conical
appendage of the brain of all vertebrates with a cranium that is variously
postulated to be a vestigial third eye,
an endocrine organ, or the seat of the
soul
pine·ap·ple \'pīn-ˌap-əl\ n : a tropical
plant bearing an edible juicy fruit; also
: its fruit
pin·feath·er \'pin-ˌfeth-ər\ n : a new
feather just coming through the skin
ping \'piŋ\ n **1** : a sharp sound like that
of a bullet striking **2** : engine knock
pin·hole \'pin-ˌhōl\ n : a small hole
made by, for, or as if by a pin
¹**pin·ion** \'pin-yən\ n : the end section of
a bird's wing; also : WING
²**pinion** vb : to restrain by binding the
arms; also : SHACKLE
³**pinion** n : a gear with a small number of
teeth designed to mesh with a larger
wheel or rack
¹**pink** \'piŋk\ n **1** : any of a genus of
plants with narrow leaves often grown
for their showy flowers **2** : the highest
degree : HEIGHT (the ~ of condition)
²**pink** n : a light tint of red
³**pink** adj **1** : of the color pink **2** : holding socialistic views — **pink·ish** adj
⁴**pink** vb **1** : PIERCE, STAB **2** : to perforate
in an ornamental pattern **3** : to cut a
saw-toothed edge on
pink elephants n pl : any of various hallucinations arising esp. from heavy
drinking or use of narcotics
pink·eye \'piŋk-ˌī\ n : an acute contagious eye inflammation
pin·kie or **pin·ky** \'piŋ-kē\ n, pl **pinkies**
: the smallest finger of the hand
pin·nace \'pin-əs\ n **1** : a light sailing
ship **2** : a ship's boat
pin·na·cle \'pin-i-kəl\ n [ME pinacle, fr.
MF, fr. LL pinnaculum gable, fr. dim.
of L pinna wing, battlement] **1** : a tur-
ret ending in a small spire **2** : a lofty
peak **3** : the highest point : ACME
pin·nate \'pin-ˌāt\ adj : having similar

parts arranged on each side of an axis
— **pin·nate·ly** adv
pi·noch·le \'pē-ˌnak-əl\ n : a card game
played with a 48-card deck
pi·ñon or **pin·yon** \'pin-ˌyōn, -ˌyän\ n,
pl **pi·ñons** or **pin·yons** or **pi·ño·nes** \pin-
'yō-nēz\ [AmerSp piñón] : any of var-
ious low-growing pines of western
No. America with edible seeds; also
: the edible seed of a piñon
pin·point \'pin-ˌpöint\ vb : to locate,
hit, or aim with great precision
pin·prick \-ˌprik\ n **1** : a small puncture
made by or as if by a pin **2** : a petty
irritation or annoyance
pins and needles n pl : a pricking tingling sensation in a limb growing
numb or recovering from numbness
— **on pins and needles** : in a nervous
or jumpy state of anticipation
pin·stripe \'pin-ˌstrīp\ n : a narrow
stripe on a fabric; also : a suit with
such stripes — **pin·striped** \-ˌstrīpt\
adj
pint \'pīnt\ n — see WEIGHT table
pin·to \'pin-ˌtō\ n, pl **pintos** also **pintoes**
: a spotted horse
pinto bean n : a mottled kidney bean
that is grown in the southwestern
U.S. for food and for stock feed
pin·up \'pin-ˌəp\ adj : suitable for pinning up on an admirer's wall (~
photo) ; also : suited (as by beauty) to
be the subject of a pinup photograph
pin·wheel \-ˌhwēl\ n **1** : a toy consisting
of lightweight vanes that revolve at
the end of a stick **2** : a fireworks device in the form of a revolving wheel
of colored fire
pin·worm \-ˌwərm\ n : a small worm
parasitic in the intestines of man
pin·yin \'pin-'yin\ n, often cap : a system for writing Chinese ideograms by
using Roman letters to represent the
sounds
¹**pi·o·neer** \ˌpī-ə-'niər\ n [MF pionier, fr.
OF peonier foot soldier, fr. peon foot
soldier, fr. ML pedon-, pedo, fr. LL
one with broad feet, fr. L ped-, pes
foot] **1** : one that originates or helps
open up a new line of thought or activity **2** : an early settler in a territory
²**pioneer** vb **1** : to act as a pioneer **2** : to
open or prepare for others to follow;
esp : SETTLE
pi·ous \'pī-əs\ adj **1** : marked by reverence for deity : DEVOUT **2** : excessively or affectedly religious **3** : SACRED,
DEVOTIONAL **4** : marked by sham or
hypocrisy **5** : showing loyal reverence for a person or thing : DUTIFUL —
pi·ous·ly adv
¹**pip** \'pip\ n **1** : a disease of birds **2** : a
usu. minor human ailment
²**pip** n : one of the dots or figures used
chiefly to indicate numerical value (as
of a playing card)
³**pip** n : a small fruit seed (as of an apple)
pipe \'pīp\ n **1** : a musical instrument
having a tube played by forcing air
through it **2** : BAGPIPE **3** : a tube de-

signed to conduct something (as water, steam, or oil) **4** : a device for smoking having a tube with a bowl at one end and a mouthpiece at the other

²**pipe** vb **piped; pip·ing 1** : to play on a pipe **2** : to speak in a high or shrill voice **3** : to convey by or as if by pipes — **pip·er** n

pipe down vb : to stop talking or making noise

pipe dream n : an illusory or fantastic hope

pipe·line \'pīp-₁līn\ n **1** : a line of pipe with pumps, valves, and control devices for conveying liquids, gases, or fine solids **2** : a channel for information

pi·pette or **pi·pet** \pī-¹pet\ n : a device for measuring and transferring small volumes of liquid

pipe up vb : to begin to play, sing, or speak

pip·ing \'pī-piŋ\ n **1** : the music of pipes **2** : a narrow fold of material used to decorate edges or seams

piping hot adj : so hot as to sizzle or hiss : very hot

pip·pin \'pip-ən\ n : any of several yellowish apples

pip-squeak \'pip-₁skwēk\ n : one that is small or insignificant

pi·quant \'pē-kənt\ adj **1** : pleasantly savory : PUNGENT **2** : engagingly provocative; also : having a lively charm — **pi·quan·cy** \-kən-sē\ n

¹**pique** \'pēk\ n [F] : offense taken by one slighted; also : a fit of resentment

²**pique** vb **piqued; piqu·ing 1** : to offend esp. by slighting **2** : to arouse by a provocation or challenge : GOAD

pi·qué or **pi·que** \pi-¹kā\ n : a durable ribbed clothing fabric

pi·quet \pi-¹kā\ n : a 2-handed card game played with 32 cards

pi·ra·cy \'pī-rə-sē\ n, pl **-cies 1** : robbery on the high seas or in the air **2** : the unauthorized use of another's production or invention

pi·ra·nha \pə-¹rän-yə, -¹rän-(y)ə\ n [Pg] : a small So. American fish that often attacks human beings and large animals

pi·rate \'pī-rət\ n [ME, fr. MF or L; MF, fr. L pirata, fr. Gk peiratēs, fr. peiran to attempt, attack] : one who commits piracy — **pirate** vb — **pi·rat·i·cal** \pə-¹rat-i-kəl, pī-\ adj

pir·ou·ette \₁pir-ə-¹wet\ n [F] : a full turn on the toe or ball of one foot in ballet; also : a rapid whirling about of the body — **pirouette** vb

pis pl of PI

pis·ca·to·ri·al \₁pis-kə-¹tōr-ē-əl\ adj : of or relating to fishing

Pi·sces \'pī-sēz\ n [ME, fr. L, lit., fishes] **1** : a zodiacal constellation between Aquarius and Aries usu. pictured as a fish **2** : the 12th sign of the zodiac in astrology; also : one born under this sign

pis·mire \'pis-₁mī(ə)r\ n : ANT

pis·ta·chio \pə-¹stash-(ē-)₁ō, -¹stäsh-\ n, pl **-chios** : the greenish edible seed of a small tree related to the sumacs; also : the tree

pis·til \'pis-t³l\ n : the female reproductive organ in a flower — **pis·til·late** \'pis-tə-₁lāt\ adj

pis·tol \'pis-t³l\ n : a handgun whose chamber is integral with the barrel

pistol–whip \-₁hwip\ vb : to beat with a pistol

pis·ton \'pis-tən\ n : a sliding piece that receives and transmits motion and that usu. consists of a short cylinder inside a large cylinder

¹**pit** \'pit\ n **1** : a hole, shaft, or cavity in the ground **2** : an often sunken area designed for a particular use; also : an enclosed place (as for cockfights) **3** : HELL; also, pl : WORST (it's the ∼s) **4** : a hollow or indentation esp. in the surface of the body **5** : a small indented scar (as from smallpox)

²**pit** vb **pit·ted; pit·ting 1** : to form pits in or become marred with pits **2** : to match for fighting

³**pit** n : the stony seed of some fruits (as the cherry, peach, and date)

⁴**pit** vb **pit·ted; pit·ting** : to remove the pit from

pi·ta \'pēt-ə\ n [NGk] : a thin flat bread

pit-a-pat \₁pit-i-¹pat\ n : PITTER-PATTER — **pit-a-pat** adv or adj

pit bull n : a powerful compact short-haired dog developed for fighting

¹**pitch** \'pich\ n **1** : a dark sticky substance left over esp. from distilling tar or petroleum **2** : resin from various conifers — **pitchy** adj

²**pitch** vb **1** : to erect and fix firmly in place (∼ a tent) **2** : THROW, FLING **3** : to deliver a baseball to a batter **4** : to toss (as coins) toward a mark **5** : to set at a particular level (∼ the voice low) **6** : to fall headlong **7** : to have the front end (as of a ship) alternately plunge and rise **8** : to incline downward : SLOPE

³**pitch** n **1** : the action or a manner of pitching **2** : degree of slope (∼ of a roof) **3** : the relative level of some quality or state (a high ∼ of excitement) **4** : highness or lowness of sound **5** : an often high-pressure sales talk **6** : the delivery of a baseball to a batter; also : the baseball delivered

pitch·blende \'pich-₁blend\ n : a dark mineral that is the chief source of uranium

¹**pitch·er** \'pich-ər\ n : a container for liquids that usu. has a lip and a handle

²**pitcher** n : one that pitches esp. in a baseball game

pitcher plant n : a plant with leaves modified to resemble pitchers in which insects are trapped and digested

pitch·fork \'pich-₁fork\ n : a long-handled fork used esp. in pitching hay

pitch in vb **1** : to begin to work **2** : to contribute to a common effort

pitch·man \'pich-mən\ *n* : SALESMAN; *esp* : one who vends novelties on the streets or from a concession

pit·e·ous \'pit-ē-əs\ *adj* : arousing pity : PITIFUL — **pit·e·ous·ly** *adv*

pit·fall \'pit-ˌfȯl\ *n* **1** : TRAP, SNARE; *esp* : a covered pit used for capturing animals **2** : a hidden danger or difficulty

pith \'pith\ *n* **1** : loose spongy tissue esp. in the center of the stem of vascular plants **2** : the essential part : CORE

pithy \'pith-ē\ *adj* **pith·i·er; -est 1** : consisting of or filled with pith **2** : being brief and to the point

piti·able \'pit-ē-ə-bəl\ *adj* : PITIFUL

piti·ful \'pit-i-fəl\ *adj* **1** : arousing or deserving pity (a ~ sight) **2** : MEAN, MEAGER — **piti·ful·ly** \-f(ə-)lē\ *adv*

piti·less \'pit-i-ləs\ *adj* : devoid of pity : MERCILESS — **piti·less·ly** *adv*

pi·ton \'pē-ˌtän\ *n* [F] : a spike, wedge, or peg that can be driven into a rock or ice surface as a support

pit·tance \'pit-ᵊns\ *n* : a small portion, amount, or allowance

pit·ter-pat·ter \'pit-ər-ˌpat-ər, 'pit-ē-\ *n* : a rapid succession of light taps or sounds — **pitter-patter** \ˌpit-ər-'pat-ər, ˌpit-ē-\ *adv or adj* — **pitter-patter** *like adv*\ *vb*

pi·tu·itary \pə-'t(y)ü-ə-ˌter-ē\ *n, pl* **-itar·ies** : PITUITARY GLAND — **pituitary** *adj*

pituitary gland *n* : a small oval endocrine gland attached to the brain which produces various hormones that affect most basic bodily functions

pit viper *n* : any of various mostly New World specialized venomous snakes with a sensory pit on each side of the head and hollow perforated fangs

¹pity \'pit-ē\ *n, pl* **pit·ies** [ME *pite*, fr. OF *pité*, fr. L *pietas* piety, fr. *pius* pious] **1** : sympathetic sorrow : COMPASSION **2** : something to be regretted

²pity *vb* **pit·ied; pity·ing** : to feel pity for

¹piv·ot \'piv-ət\ *n* : a fixed pin on which something turns — **pivot** *adj* — **piv·ot·al** \'piv-ət-ᵊl\ *adj*

²pivot *vb* : to turn on or as if on a pivot

pix *pl of* PIC

pix·el \'pik-səl, -ˌsel\ *n* : any of the small elements that together make up an image (as on a television screen)

pix·ie *or* **pixy** \'pik-sē\ *n, pl* **pix·ies** : FAIRY; *esp* : a mischievous sprite

piz·za \'pēt-sə\ *n* [It] : an open pie made of rolled bread dough spread with a spiced mixture (as of tomatoes, cheese, and ground meat) and baked

piz·zazz *or* **piz·zaz** \pə-'zaz\ *n* **1** : GLAMOUR **2** : VITALITY

piz·ze·ria \ˌpēt-sə-'rē-ə\ *n* : an establishment where pizzas are made and sold

piz·zi·ca·to \ˌpit-si-'kät-ō\ *adv or adj* [It] : by means of plucking instead of bowing — used as a direction in music

pj's \('¹)pē-'jāz\ *n pl* : PAJAMAS

pk *abbr* **1** park **2** peak **3** peck **4** pike

pkg *abbr* package

pkt *abbr* **1** packet **2** pocket

pkwy *abbr* parkway

pl *abbr* **1** place **2** plate **3** plural

¹plac·ard \'plak-ərd, -ˌärd\ *n* : a notice posted in a public place : POSTER

²plac·ard \-ˌärd, -ərd\ *vb* **1** : to cover with or as if with placards **2** : to announce by posting

pla·cate \'plā-ˌkāt, 'plak-ˌāt\ *vb* **pla·cat·ed; pla·cat·ing** : to soothe esp. by concessions : APPEASE — **pla·ca·ble** \'plak-ə-bəl, 'plā-kə-\ *adj*

¹place \'plās\ *n* [ME, fr. MF, open space, fr. L *platea* broad street, fr. Gk *plateia* (*hodos*), fr. fem. of *platys* broad, flat] **1** : SPACE, ROOM **2** : an indefinite region : AREA **3** : a building or locality used for a special purpose **4** : a center of population **5** : a particular part of a surface : SPOT **6** : relative position in a scale or sequence; *also* : high and esp. 2d position at the end of a competition **7** : ACCOMMODATION; *esp* : SEAT **8** : the position of a figure in a numeral ⟨12 is a two ~ number⟩ **9** : JOB; *esp* : public office **10** : a public square

²place *vb* **placed; plac·ing 1** : to distribute in an orderly manner : ARRANGE **2** : to put in a particular place : SET **3** : IDENTIFY **4** : to give an order for (~ a bet) **5** : to rank high and esp. 2d at the end of a competition

pla·ce·bo \plə-'sē-bō\ *n, pl* **-bos** [L, I shall please] : an inert medication used for its psychological effect or for purposes of comparison in an experiment

place·hold·er \'plās-ˌhōl-dər\ *n* : a symbol in a mathematical or logical expression that may be replaced by the name of any element of a set

place·kick \-ˌkik\ *n* : the kicking of a ball placed or held on the ground — **placekick** *vb* — **place·kick·er** *n*

place·ment \'plās-mənt\ *n* : an act or instance of placing

pla·cen·ta \plə-'sent-ə\ *n, pl* **-centas** *or* **-cen·tae** \-'sent-(ˌ)ē\ [NL, fr. L, flat cake] : the organ in most mammals by which the fetus is joined to the uterus of the mother and is nourished — **pla·cen·tal** \-'sent-ᵊl\ *adj*

plac·er \'plas-ər\ *n* : an alluvial or glacial deposit containing particles of valuable mineral

plac·id \'plas-əd\ *adj* : UNDISTURBED, PEACEFUL **syn** tranquil, serene, calm — **pla·cid·i·ty** \pla-'sid-ət-ē\ *n* — **plac·id·ly** \'plas-əd-lē\ *adv*

plack·et \'plak-ət\ *n* : a slit in a garment

pla·gia·rize \'plā-jə-ˌrīz\ *vb* **-rized; -riz·ing** : to present the ideas or words of another as one's own — **pla·gia·rism** \-ˌriz-əm\ *n* — **pla·gia·rist** \-rəst\ *n*

¹plague \'plāg\ *n* **1** : a disastrous evil or influx; *also* : NUISANCE **2** : PESTILENCE; *esp* : a destructive contagious bacterial disease (as bubonic plague)

²plague *vb* **plagued; plagu·ing 1** : to afflict with or as if with disease or disaster 2 : TEASE, TORMENT, HARASS

plaid \ˈplad\ *n* 1 : a rectangular length of tartan worn esp. over the left shoulder as part of the Scottish national costume 2 : a twilled woolen fabric with a tartan pattern 3 : a pattern of unevenly spaced repeated stripes crossing at right angles — **plaid** *adj*

1**plain** \ˈplān\ *n* : an extensive area of level or rolling treeless country

2**plain** *adj* 1 : lacking ornament ⟨a ~ dress⟩ 2 : free of extraneous matter 3 : OPEN, UNOBSTRUCTED ⟨~ view⟩ 4 : EVIDENT, OBVIOUS 5 : easily understood : CLEAR 6 : CANDID, BLUNT 7 : SIMPLE, UNCOMPLICATED ⟨~ cooking⟩ 8 : lacking beauty — **plain•ly** *adv* — **plain•ness** \ˈplān-nəs\ *n*

plain•clothes•man \ˈplān-ˈklō(th)z-mən, -ˌman\ *n* : a police officer who does not wear a uniform while on duty : DETECTIVE

plain•spo•ken \-ˈspō-kən\ *adj* : speaking or spoken plainly and esp. bluntly

plaint \ˈplānt\ *n* 1 : LAMENTATION, WAIL 2 : PROTEST, COMPLAINT

plain•tiff \ˈplānt-əf\ *n* : the complaining party in a lawsuit

plain•tive \ˈplānt-iv\ *adj* : expressive of suffering or woe : MELANCHOLY — **plain•tive•ly** *adv*

plait \ˈplāt, ˈplat\ *n* 1 : PLEAT 2 : a braid esp. of hair or straw — **plait** *vb*

1**plan** \ˈplan\ *n* 1 : a drawing or diagram showing the parts or outline of something 2 : a method for accomplishing something 3 : GOAL, AIM — **plan•less** *adj*

2**plan** *vb* **planned; plan•ning** 1 : to form a plan of ⟨~ a new city⟩ 2 : INTEND ⟨*planned* to go⟩ — **plan•ner** *n*

1**plane** \ˈplān\ *vb* **planed; plan•ing** : to smooth or level off with or as if with a plane — **plan•er** *n*

2**plane** *n* : PLANE TREE

3**plane** *n* : a tool for smoothing or shaping a wood surface

4**plane** *n* 1 : a level or flat surface 2 : a level of existence, consciousness, or development 3 : one of the main supporting surfaces of an airplane; *also* : AIRPLANE

5**plane** *adj* 1 : FLAT, LEVEL 2 : dealing with flat surfaces or figures ⟨~ geometry⟩

plane•load \ˈplān-ˌlōd\ *n* : a load that fills an airplane

plan•et \ˈplan-ət\ *n* [ME *planete,* fr. OF, fr. LL *planeta,* modif. of Gk *planēt-, planēs,* lit., wanderer, fr. *planasthai* to wander] : a celestial body other than a comet, asteroid, or satellite that revolves around the sun — **plan•e•tary** \-ə-ˌter-ē\ *adj*

plan•e•tar•i•um \ˌplan-ə-ˈter-ē-əm\ *n, pl* **-iums** *or* **-ia** \-ē-ə\ : a building or room housing a device to project images of celestial bodies

plan•e•tes•i•mal \ˌplan-ə-ˈtes-ə-məl\ *n* : any of numerous small solid celestial bodies which may have existed during the formation of the solar system

plan•e•toid \ˈplan-ə-ˌtȯid\ *n* : a body resembling a planet; *esp* : ASTEROID

plane tree *n* : SYCAMORE 2; *esp* : one of or introduced from the Old World

plan•gent \ˈplan-jənt\ *adj* 1 : having a loud reverberating sound 2 : having an expressive esp. plaintive quality — **plan•gen•cy** \-jən-sē\ *n*

1**plank** \ˈplaŋk\ *n* 1 : a heavy thick board 2 : an article in the platform of a political party

2**plank** *vb* 1 : to cover with planks 2 : to set or lay down forcibly 3 : to cook and serve on a board

plank•ing \ˈplaŋ-kiŋ\ *n* : a quantity or covering of planks

plank•ton \ˈplaŋk-tən\ *n* : the passively floating or weakly swimming animal and plant life of a body of water — **plank•ton•ic** \plaŋk-ˈtän-ik\ *adj*

1**plant** \ˈplant\ *vb* 1 : to set in the ground to grow 2 : ESTABLISH, SETTLE 3 : to stock or provide with something 4 : to place firmly or forcibly 5 : to hide or arrange with intent to deceive

2**plant** *n* 1 : any of a kingdom of living things that usu. have no locomotor ability or obvious sense organs and have cellulose cell walls and usu. capacity for indefinite growth 2 : the land, buildings, and machinery used in carrying on a trade or business

1**plan•tain** \ˈplant-ᵊn\ *n* [ME, fr. OF, fr. L *plantagin-, plantago,* fr. *planta* sole of the foot; fr. its broad leaves] : any

PLANETS

SYMBOL	NAME	MEAN DISTANCE FROM THE SUN: astronomical units	MEAN DISTANCE FROM THE SUN: million miles	PERIOD OF REVOLUTION IN DAYS OR YEARS	EQUATORIAL DIAMETER IN MILES
☿	Mercury	0.387	36.0	87.97 d.	3,031
♀	Venus	0.723	67.2	224.70 d.	7,521
⊕	Earth	1.000	92.9	365.26 d.	7,926
♂	Mars	1.524	141.5	686.98 d.	4,216
♃	Jupiter	5.203	483.4	11.86 y.	88,700
♄	Saturn	9.569	889.0	29.46 y.	74,500
⛢	Uranus	19.309	1793.8	84.01 y.	31,600
♆	Neptune	30.284	2813.4	164.79 y.	30,200
♇	Pluto	39.781	3695.7	247.69 y.	1,900

of a genus of short-stemmed weedy herbs with spikes of tiny greenish flowers

²**plan·tain** n [Sp *plántano* plane tree, banana tree, fr. ML *plantanus* plane tree, alter. of L *platanus*] : a banana plant with starchy greenish fruit; *also* : its fruit

plan·tar \'plant-ər, 'plan-ˌtär\ *adj* : of or relating to the sole of the foot

plan·ta·tion \plan-'tā-shən\ n 1 : a large group of trees under cultivation 2 : an agricultural estate worked by resident laborers

plant·er \'plant-ər\ n 1 : one that plants or sows; *esp* : an owner or operator of a plantation 2 : a container for a plant

plant louse n : APHID

plaque \'plak\ n [F] 1 : an ornamental brooch 2 : a flat thin piece (as of metal) used for decoration; *also* : a commemorative tablet 3 : a bacteria-containing film on a tooth

plash \'plash\ n : SPLASH — **plash** vb

plas·ma \'plaz-mə\ n 1 : the watery part of blood, lymph, or milk 2 : a gas composed of ionized particles — **plas·mat·ic** \plaz-'mat-ik\ *adj*

¹**plas·ter** \'plas-tər\ n 1 : a dressing consisting of a backing spread with an often medicated substance that clings to the skin (adhesive ~) 2 : a paste that hardens as it dries and is used for coating walls and ceilings

²**plaster** vb **plas·tered**; **plas·ter·ing** \-t(ə-)riŋ\ : to cover with or as if with plaster — **plas·ter·er** n

plas·ter·board \'plas-tər-ˌbȯrd\ n : a wallboard consisting of fiberboard, paper, or felt over a plaster core

plaster of par·is \-'par-əs\ *often cap 2d P* : a white powder made from gypsum and used as a quick-setting paste with water for casts and molds

¹**plas·tic** \'plas-tik\ *adj* [L *plasticus* of molding, fr. Gk *plastikos*, fr. *plassein* to mold, form] 1 : capable of being molded (~ clay) 2 : characterized by or using modeling (~ arts) 3 : made or consisting of a plastic syn pliable, pliant, ductile, malleable, adaptable — **plas·tic·i·ty** \plas-'tis-ət-ē\ n

²**plastic** n : a plastic substance; *esp* : a synthetic or processed material that can be formed into rigid objects or into films or filaments

plastic surgery n : a branch of surgery concerned with the repair, restoration, or improvement of lost, injured, defective, or misshapen body parts — **plastic surgeon** n

¹**plat** \'plat\ n 1 : a small plot of ground 2 : a plan of a piece of land with actual or proposed features (as lots)

²**plat** vb **plat·ted**; **plat·ting** : to make a plat of

¹**plate** \'plāt\ n 1 : a flat thin piece of material 2 : domestic hollowware made of or plated with gold, silver, or base metals 3 : DISH 4 : HOME PLATE 5 : the molded metal or plastic cast of a page of type to be printed from 6 : a thin sheet of material (as glass) that is coated with a chemical sensitive to light and is used in photography 7 : the part of a denture that fits to the mouth and holds the teeth 8 : something printed from an engraving 9 : a huge mobile segment of the earth's crust

²**plate** vb **plat·ed**; **plat·ing** 1 : to arm with armor plate 2 : to overlay with metal (as gold or silver) 3 : to make a printing plate of

pla·teau \pla-'tō\ n, pl **plateaus** or **plateaux** \-'tōz\ [F] : a large level area raised above adjacent land on at least one side : TABLELAND

plate glass n : rolled, ground, and polished sheet glass

plat·en \'plat-ən\ n 1 : a flat plate of metal; *esp* : one (as the part of a printing press which presses the paper against the type) that exerts or receives pressure 2 : the roller of a typewriter

plat·form \'plat-ˌform\ n 1 : a raised flooring or stage for speakers, performers, or workers 2 : a declaration of the principles on which a group of persons (as a political party) stands

plat·ing \'plāt-iŋ\ n : a coating of metal plates or plate (the ~ of a ship)

plat·i·num \'plat-(ə-)nəm\ n : a heavy silver-white metallic chemical element

plat·i·tude \'plat-ə-ˌt(y)üd\ n : a flat or trite remark — **plat·i·tu·di·nous** \-ˌt(y)üd-(ə-)nəs\ *adj*

pla·ton·ic love \plə-ˌtän-ik-, plā-\ n, *often cap P* : a close relationship between two persons in which sexual desire has been suppressed or sublimated

pla·toon \plə-'tün\ n [F *peloton* small detachment, lit., ball, fr. *pelote* little ball] 1 : a subdivision of a company-size military unit usu. consisting of two or more squads or sections 2 : a group of football players trained either for offense or for defense and sent into the game as a body

platoon sergeant n : a noncommissioned officer in the army ranking below a first sergeant

plat·ter \'plat-ər\ n 1 : a large serving plate 2 : a phonograph record

platy \'plat-ē\ n, pl **platy** or **plat·ys** or **plat·ies** : any of various small stocky often brilliantly colored fish that are popular for tropical aquariums

platy·pus \'plat-i-pəs\ n, pl **platy·pus·es** *also* **platy·pi** \-ˌpī\ [NL, fr. Gk *platypous* flat-footed, fr. *platys* broad, flat + *pous* foot] : a small aquatic egg-laying marsupial mammal of Australia with webbed feet and a fleshy bill like a duck's

plau·dit \'plȯd-ət\ n : an act of applause

plau·si·ble \'plȯ-zə-bəl\ *adj* [L *plausibilis* worthy of applause, fr. *plausus*, pp. of *plaudere*] : seemingly worthy of belief : PERSUASIVE — **plau·si·bil·i·ty** \ˌplȯ-zə-ˈbil-ət-ē\ *n* — **plau·si·bly** \ˈplȯ-zə-blē\ *adv*

¹play \ˈplā\ *n* **1** : brisk handling of something (as a weapon) **2** : the course of a game; *also* : a particular act or maneuver in a game **3** : recreational activity; *esp* : the spontaneous activity of children **4** : JEST (said in ~) **5** : the act or an instance of punning **6** : GAMBLING **7** : OPERATION (bring extra force into ~) **8** : a brisk or light movement **9** : free motion (as of part of a machine) **10** : scope for action **11** : PUBLICITY **12** : an effort to arouse liking (made a ~ for her) **13** : a stage representation of a drama; *also* : a dramatic composition — **play·ful** \-fəl\ *adj* — **play·ful·ly** \-ē\ *adv* — **play·ful·ness** *n* — **in play** : in condition or position to be played

²play *vb* **1** : to engage in recreation : FROLIC **2** : to handle or behave lightly or absentmindedly **3** : to make a pun (~ on words) **4** : to take advantage (~ on fears) **5** : to move or operate in a brisk or irregular manner (a flashlight ~ed over the wall) **6** : to perform music (~ on a violin); *also* : to perform (music) on an instrument (~ a waltz) **7** : to perform music upon (~ the piano); *also* : to sound in performance (the organ is ~ing) **8** : to cause to emit sounds (~ a radio) **9** : to act in a dramatic medium; *also* : to act in the character of (~ the hero) **10** : GAMBLE **11** : to behave in a specified way (~ safe); *also* : COOPERATE (~ along with him) **12** : to deal with; *also* : EMPHASIZE (~ up her good qualities) **13** : to perform for amusement (~ a trick) **14** : WREAK **15** : to contend with in a game; *also* : to fill (a certain position) on a team **16** : to make wagers on (~ the races) **17** : WIELD, PLY **18** : to keep in action — **play·er** *n*

play·act·ing \ˈplā-ˌak-tiŋ\ *n* **1** : performance in theatrical productions **2** : insincere or artificial behavior

play·back \ˈplā-ˌbak\ *n* : an act of reproducing a sound recording often immediately after recording — **play back** \(ˈ)plā-ˈbak\ *vb*

play·bill \-ˌbil\ *n* : a poster advertising the performance of a play

play·book \-ˌbu̇k\ *n* : a notebook containing diagramed football plays

play·boy \-ˌbȯi\ *n* : a man whose chief interest is the pursuit of pleasure

play·go·er \-ˌgō-(ə)r\ *n* : a person who frequently attends plays

play·ground \-ˌgrau̇nd\ *n* : an area used for games and recreation esp. by children

play·house \-ˌhau̇s\ *n* **1** : THEATER **2** : a small house for children to play in

playing card *n* : one of a set of 24 to 78 cards marked to show its rank and suit and used to play a game of cards

play·let \ˈplā-lət\ *n* : a short play

play·mate \-ˌmāt\ *n* : a companion in play

play-off \-ˌȯf\ *n* : a contest or series of contests to break a tie or determine a championship

play·pen \-ˌpen\ *n* : a portable enclosure in which a young child may play

play·suit \-ˌsüt\ *n* : a sports and play outfit for women and children

play·thing \-ˌthiŋ\ *n* : TOY

play·wright \-ˌrīt\ *n* : a writer of plays

pla·za \ˈplaz-ə, ˈpläz-\ *n* [Sp, fr. L *platea* broad street] **1** : a public square in a city or town **2** : a shopping center

plea \ˈplē\ *n* **1** : a defendant's answer in law to charges made against him **2** : something alleged as an excuse : PRETEXT **3** : ENTREATY, APPEAL

plead \ˈplēd\ *vb* **plead·ed** \ˈplēd-əd\ *or* **pled** \ˈpled\; **plead·ing** **1** : to argue before a court or authority (~ a case) **2** : to answer to a charge or indictment (~ guilty) **3** : to argue for or against something (~ for acquittal) **4** : to appeal earnestly (~s for help) **5** : to offer as a plea (as in defense) (~ed illness) — **plead·er** *n*

pleas·ant \ˈplez-ᵊnt\ *adj* **1** : giving pleasure : AGREEABLE (a ~ experience) **2** : marked by pleasing behavior or appearance (a ~ person) — **pleas·ant·ly** *adv* — **pleas·ant·ness** *n*

pleas·ant·ry \-ᵊn-trē\ *n, pl* **-ries** : a pleasant and casual act or speech

¹please \ˈplēz\ *vb* **pleased**; **pleas·ing** **1** : to give pleasure or satisfaction to **2** : LIKE (do as you ~) **3** : to be the will or pleasure of (may it ~ his Majesty)

²please *adv* — used as a function word to express politeness or emphasis in a request (~ come in)

pleas·ing \ˈplē-ziŋ\ *adj* : giving pleasure — **pleas·ing·ly** *adv*

plea·sur·able \ˈplezh-(ə-)rə-bəl\ *adj* : PLEASANT, GRATIFYING — **plea·sur·ably** \-blē\ *adv*

plea·sure \ˈplezh-ər\ *n* **1** : DESIRE, INCLINATION (await your ~) **2** : a state of gratification : ENJOYMENT **3** : a source of delight or joy

¹pleat \ˈplēt\ *vb* **1** : FOLD; *esp* : to arrange in pleats **2** : BRAID

²pleat *n* : a fold (as in cloth) made by doubling material over on itself : PLAIT

plebe \ˈplēb\ *n* : a freshman at a military or naval academy

¹ple·be·ian \pli-ˈbē-ən\ *n* **1** : a member of the Roman plebs **2** : one of the common people

²plebeian *adj* **1** : of or relating to plebeians **2** : COMMON, VULGAR

pleb·i·scite \ˈpleb-ə-ˌsīt, -sət\ *n* : a vote of the people (as of a country) on a proposal submitted to them

plebs \ˈplebz\ *n, pl* **ple·bes** \ˈplē-bēz\ **1** : the common people of ancient Rome **2** : the general populace

plec·trum \ˈplek-trəm\ *n, pl* **plec·tra** \-trə\ *or* **plec·trums** [L] : ³PICK 3

¹pledge \ˈplej\ *n* **1** : something given as

security for the performance of an act 2 : the state of being held as a security or guaranty 3 : TOAST 3 4 : PROMISE, VOW

²**pledge** vb **pledged; pledg·ing** 1 : to deposit as a pledge 2 : TOAST 3 : to bind by a pledge : PLIGHT 4 : PROMISE

Pleis·to·cene \'plī-stə-,sēn\ adj : of, relating to, or being the earlier epoch of the Quaternary — **Pleistocene** n

ple·na·ry \'plē-nə-rē, 'plen-ə-\ adj 1 : FULL (~ power) 2 : including all entitled to attend (~ session)

pleni·po·ten·tia·ry \,plen-ə-pə-'tench-(ə-)rē, -'ten-chē-,er-ē\ n, pl **-ries** : a diplomatic agent having full authority — **plenipotentiary** adj

plen·i·tude \'plen-ə-,t(y)üd\ n 1 : COMPLETENESS 2 : ABUNDANCE

plen·te·ous \'plent-ē-əs\ adj 1 : FRUITFUL 2 : existing in plenty

plen·ti·ful \'plent-i-fəl\ adj 1 : containing or yielding plenty 2 : ABUNDANT — **plen·ti·ful·ly** \-ē\ adv

plen·ty \'plent-ē\ n : a more than adequate number or amount

ple·num \'plen-əm, 'plēn-əm\ n, pl **-nums** or **-na** \-ə\ : a general assembly of all members esp. of a legislative body

pleth·o·ra \'pleth-ə-rə\ n : an excessive quantity or fullness; also : PROFUSION

pleu·ri·sy \'plur-ə-sē\ n : inflammation of the membrane that lines the chest and covers the lungs

plex·us \'plek-səs\ n : an interlacing network esp. of blood vessels or nerves

pli·able \'plī-ə-bəl\ adj 1 : FLEXIBLE 2 : yielding easily to others syn plastic, pliant, ductile, malleable, adaptable — **pli·abil·i·ty** \,plī-ə-'bil-ət-ē\ n

pli·ant \'plī-ənt\ adj 1 : FLEXIBLE 2 : easily influenced : PLIABLE — **pli·an·cy** \-ən-sē\ n

pli·ers \'plī(-ə)rz\ n pl : small pincers for bending wire or handling small objects

¹**plight** \'plīt\ vb : to put or give in pledge : ENGAGE

²**plight** n : CONDITION, STATE; esp : a bad state

plinth \'plinth\ n : the lowest part of the base of an architectural column

Plio·cene \'plī-ə-,sēn\ adj : of, relating to, or being the latest epoch of the Tertiary — **Pliocene** n

plod \'pläd\ vb **plod·ded; plod·ding** 1 : to walk heavily or slowly : TRUDGE 2 : to work laboriously and monotonously : DRUDGE — **plod·der** n — **plod·ding·ly** \-iŋ-lē\ adv

plop \'pläp\ vb **plopped; plop·ping** 1 : to make or move with a sound like that of something dropping into water 2 : to set, drop, or throw heavily — **plop** n

¹**plot** \'plät\ n 1 : a small area of ground 2 : a ground plan (as of an area) 3 : the main story (as of a book or movie) 4 : a secret scheme : INTRIGUE

²**plot** vb **plot·ted; plot·ting** 1 : to make a plot or plan of 2 : to mark on or as if on a chart 3 : to plan or contrive esp. secretly — **plot·ter** n

plo·ver \'pləv-ər, 'plō-vər\ n, pl **plover** or **plovers** : any of various shorebirds related to the sandpipers but with shorter stouter bills

¹**plow** or **plough** \'plau\ n 1 : an implement used to cut, turn over, and partly break up soil 2 : a device operating like a plow; esp : SNOWPLOW

²**plow** or **plough** vb 1 : to open, break up, or work with a plow 2 : to cleave or move through like a plow (a ship ~ing the waves) 3 : to proceed laboriously — **plow·able** adj — **plow·er** n

plow·boy \'plau-,bȯi\ n : a boy who guides a plow or leads the horse drawing it

plow·man \-mən, -,man\ n 1 : a man who guides a plow 2 : a farm laborer

plow·share \-,sheər\ n : the part of a plow that cuts the earth

ploy \'plȯi\ n : a tactic intended to embarrass or frustrate an opponent

¹**pluck** \'plək\ vb 1 : to pull off or out : PICK; also : to pull something from 2 : to play (an instrument) by pulling the strings 3 : TUG, TWITCH

²**pluck** n 1 : an act or instance of plucking 2 : SPIRIT, COURAGE

plucky \'plək-ē\ adj **pluck·i·er; -est** : COURAGEOUS, SPIRITED

¹**plug** \'pləg\ n 1 : STOPPER; also : an obstructing mass 2 : a cake of tobacco 3 : a poor or worn-out horse 4 : a device on the end of a cord for making an electrical connection 5 : a piece of favorable publicity

²**plug** vb **plugged; plug·ging** 1 : to stop, make tight, or secure by inserting a plug 2 : HIT, SHOOT 3 : to publicize insistently 4 : PLOD, DRUDGE

plum \'pləm\ n [ME, fr. OE plūme, fr. L prunum plum] 1 : a smooth-skinned juicy fruit borne by trees related to the peach and cherry; also : a tree bearing plums 2 : a raisin when used in desserts (as puddings) 3 : something excellent; esp : something desirable given in return esp. for a political favor

plum·age \'plü-mij\ n : the feathers of a bird

¹**plumb** \'pləm\ n : a weight on the end of a line (**plumb line**) used esp. by builders to show vertical direction

²**plumb** adv 1 : VERTICALLY 2 : EXACTLY; also : IMMEDIATELY 3 : COMPLETELY

³**plumb** vb : to sound, adjust, or test with a plumb (~ the depth of a well)

⁴**plumb** adj 1 : VERTICAL 2 : THOROUGH, COMPLETE

plumb·er \'pləm-ər\ n [ME, fr. MF plombier, fr. L plumbarius, deriv. of plumbum lead] : a worker who fits or repairs water and gas pipes and fixtures

plumb·ing \'pləm-iŋ\ n : a system of

pipes in a building for supplying and carrying off water

¹plume \'plüm\ n : FEATHER; esp : a large, conspicuous, or showy feather — plumed \'plümd\ adj — plumy \'plü-mē\ adj

²plume vb plumed; plum·ing 1 : to provide or deck with feathers 2 : to indulge (oneself) in pride

plum·met \'pləm-ət\ n : PLUMB; also : PLUMB LINE

²plummet vb : to drop or plunge straight down

¹plump \'pləmp\ vb 1 : to drop or fall suddenly or heavily 2 : to favor something strongly ⟨~s for the new method⟩

²plump n : a sudden heavy fall or blow; also : the sound made by it

³plump adv 1 : straight down; also : straight ahead 2 : UNQUALIFIEDLY

⁴plump adj : having a full rounded usu. pleasing form : CHUBBY syn fleshy, stout, roly-poly, rotund — plump·ness n

¹plun·der \'plən-dər\ vb plun·dered; plun·der·ing \-d(ə-)riŋ\ : to take the goods of by force or wrongfully : PILLAGE — plun·der·er n

²plunder n : something taken by force or theft : LOOT

¹plunge \'plənj\ vb plunged; plung·ing 1 : IMMERSE, SUBMERGE 2 : to enter or cause to enter a state or course of action suddenly or violently ⟨~ into war⟩ 3 : to cast oneself into or as if into water 4 : to gamble heavily and recklessly 5 : to descend suddenly

²plunge n : a sudden dive, leap, or rush

plung·er \'plən-jər\ n 1 : one that plunges 2 : a sliding piece driven by or against fluid pressure : PISTON 3 : a rubber cup on a handle pushed against an opening to free a waste outlet of an obstruction

plunk \'pləŋk\ vb 1 : to make or cause to make a hollow metallic sound 2 : to drop heavily or suddenly — plunk n

plu·per·fect \(')plü-'pər-fikt\ adj [modif. of LL plusquamperfectus, lit., more than perfect] : of, relating to, or constituting a verb tense that denotes an action or state as completed at or before a past time spoken of — pluperfect n

plu·ral \'plùr-əl\ adj [ME, fr. MF & L; MF plurel, fr. L pluralis, fr. plur-, plus more] : of, relating to, or constituting a word form used to denote more than one — plural n

plu·ral·i·ty \plù-'ral-ət-ē\ n, pl -ties 1 : the state of being plural 2 : an excess of votes over those cast for an opposing candidate 3 : the greatest number of votes cast when not a majority

plu·ral·ize \'plùr-ə-ˌlīz\ vb -ized; -iz·ing : to make plural or express in the plural form — plu·ral·iza·tion \ˌplùr-ə-lə-'zā-shən\ n

¹plus \'pləs\ adj [L, more] 1 : requiring addition or being in addition to what is anticipated or specified ⟨~ values⟩

²plus n, pl plus·es \'pləs-əz\ also plus·ses 1 : a sign + (plus sign) used in mathematics to require addition or designate a positive quantity 2 : an added quantity; also : a positive quantity 3 : ADVANTAGE

³plus prep : increased by : with the addition of ⟨3 ~ 4 equals 7⟩

¹plush \'pləsh\ n : a fabric with a pile longer and less dense than velvet pile — plushy adj

²plush adj : notably luxurious — plush·ly adv

Plu·to \'plüt-ō\ n : the planet farthest from the sun

plu·toc·ra·cy \plü-'täk-rə-sē\ n, pl -cies 1 : government by the wealthy 2 : a controlling class of the wealthy — plu·to·crat \'plüt-ə-ˌkrat\ n — plu·to·crat·ic \ˌplüt-ə-'krat-ik\ adj

plu·to·ni·um \plü-'tō-nē-əm\ n : a radioactive chemical element formed by the decay of neptunium

plu·vi·al \'plü-vē-əl\ adj 1 : of or relating to rain 2 : characterized by abundant rain

¹ply \'plī\ vb plied; ply·ing : to twist together ⟨~ yarns⟩

²ply n, pl plies : one of the folds, thicknesses, or strands of which something (as plywood or yarn) is made

³ply vb plied; ply·ing 1 : to use, practice, or work diligently ⟨plies her needle⟩ ⟨~ a trade⟩ 2 : to keep supplying something to ⟨plied them with liquor⟩ 3 : to go or travel regularly esp. by sea

Plym·outh Rock \ˌplim-əth-\ n : any of an American breed of medium-sized single-combed domestic fowls

ply·wood \'plī-ˌwùd\ n : material made of thin sheets of wood glued and pressed together

pm abbr premium

Pm symbol promethium

PM abbr 1 paymaster 2 police magistrate 3 postmaster 4 often not cap post meridiem 5 postmortem 6 prime minister 7 provost marshal

pmk abbr postmark

pmt abbr payment

PN abbr promissory note

pneu·mat·ic \n(y)ù-'mat-ik\ adj 1 : of, relating to, or using air or wind 2 : moved by air pressure 3 : filled with compressed air — pneu·mat·i·cal·ly \-i-k(ə-)lē\ adv

pneu·mo·co·ni·o·sis \ˌn(y)ü-mō-ˌkō-nē-'ō-səs\ n : a disease of the lungs caused by habitual inhalation of irritant mineral or metallic particles

pneu·mo·nia \n(y)ù-'mō-nyə\ n : an inflammatory disease of the lungs

Po symbol polonium

PO abbr 1 petty officer 2 post office

¹poach \'pōch\ vb [ME, fr. MF pocher, fr. OF pochier, lit., to put into a bag, fr. poche bag, pocket, of Gmc origin] : to cook (as an egg or fish) in simmering liquid

²**poach** *vb* : to hunt or fish unlawfully — **poach·er** *n*

POC *abbr* port of call

pock \'päk\ *n* : a small swelling on the skin (as in smallpox); *also* : its scar

¹**pock·et** \'päk-ət\ *n* **1** : a small bag open at the top or side inserted in a garment **2** : supply of money : MEANS **3** : RECEPTACLE, CONTAINER **4** : a small isolated area or group **5** : a small body of ore — **pock·et·ful** *n*

²**pocket** *vb* **1** : to put in or as if in a pocket **2** : STEAL

³**pocket** *adj* **1** : small enough to fit in a pocket; *also* : SMALL, MINIATURE **2** : carried in or paid from one's own pocket

¹**pock·et·book** \-ˌbùk\ *n* **1** : PURSE; *also* : HANDBAG **2** : financial resources

²**pocketbook** *adj* : relating to money

pocket gopher *n* : GOPHER 2

pock·et·knife \'päk-ət-ˌnīf\ *n* : a knife with a folding blade to be carried in the pocket

pocket veto *n* : an indirect veto of a legislative bill by an executive through retention of the bill unsigned until after adjournment of the legislature

pock·mark \'päk-ˌmärk\ *n* : a pit or scar caused by smallpox or acne — **pock·marked** \-ˌmärkt\ *adj*

po·co \'pō-kō, 'pò-\ *adv* [It, little, fr. L *paucus*] : SOMEWHAT — used to qualify a direction in music ⟨~ *allegro*⟩

po·co a po·co \ˌpō-kō-ä-'pō-kō, ˌpò-kō-ä-'pò-\ *adv* : little by little : by small degrees : GRADUALLY

pod \'päd\ *n* **1** : a dry fruit (as of a pea) that splits open when ripe **2** : an external streamlined compartment (as for a jet engine) on an airplane **3** : a detachable compartment (as for personnel, a power unit, or an instrument) on a spacecraft

POD *abbr* pay on delivery

po·di·a·try \pə-'dī-ə-trē, pō-\ *n* : the care and treatment of the human foot in health and disease — **po·di·a·trist** \pə-'dī-ə-trəst, pō-\ *n*

po·di·um \'pōd-ē-əm\ *n, pl* **podiums** *or* **po·dia** \-ē-ə\ **1** : a dais esp. for an orchestral conductor **2** : LECTERN

POE *abbr* **1** port of embarkation **2** port of entry

po·em \'pō-əm\ *n* : a composition in verse

po·esy \'pō-ə-zē\ *n* : POETRY

po·et \'pō-ət\ *n* [ME, fr. OF *poete*, fr. L *poeta*, fr. Gk *poiētēs* maker, poet, fr. *poiein* to make, create] : a writer of poetry; *also* : a creative artist of great sensitivity

po·et·as·ter \'pō-ət-ˌas-tər\ *n* : an inferior or poet

po·et·ess \'pō-ət-əs\ *n* : a girl or woman who writes poetry

poetic justice *n* : an outcome in which vice is punished and virtue rewarded usu. in a manner peculiarly or ironically appropriate

po·et·ry \'pō-ə-trē\ *n* **1** : metrical writing **2** : POEMS — **po·et·ic** \pō-'et-ik\ *or* **po·et·i·cal** \-i-kəl\ *adj*

po·grom \'pō-grəm, pō-'gräm\ *n* [Yiddish, fr. Russ, lit., devastation] : an organized massacre of helpless people and esp. of Jews

poi \'pòi\ *n, pl* **poi** *or* **pois** : a Hawaiian food of taro root cooked, pounded, and kneaded to a paste and often allowed to ferment

poi·gnant \'pòi-nyənt\ *adj* **1** : painfully affecting the feelings ⟨~ grief⟩ **2** : deeply moving ⟨~ scene⟩ — **poi·gnan·cy** \-nyən-sē\ *n*

poi·lu \pwäl-'(y)ü\ *n* : a French soldier

poin·ci·ana \ˌpòin-sē-'an-ə\ *n* : any of a genus of ornamental tropical leguminous trees or shrubs with bright orange or red flowers

poin·set·tia \pòin-'set-ē-ə, -'set-ə\ *n* : a showy tropical American spurge that has scarlet bracts around its small greenish flowers

¹**point** \'pòint\ *n* **1** : an individual detail; *also* : the most important essential **2** : PURPOSE **3** : a geometric element that has position but no size **4** : a particular place : LOCALITY **5** : a particular stage or degree **6** : a sharp end : TIP **7** : a projecting piece of land **8** : a punctuation mark; *esp* : PERIOD **9** : DECIMAL POINT **10** : one of the divisions of the compass **11** : a unit of counting (as in a game score) — **point·less** *adj* — **beside the point** : IRRELEVANT — **in point** : to the point — **to the point** : RELEVANT, PERTINENT

²**point** *vb* **1** : to furnish with a point : SHARPEN **2** : PUNCTUATE **3** : to separate (a decimal fraction) from an integer by a decimal point **4** : to indicate the position of esp. by extending a finger **5** : to direct attention to ⟨~ out an error⟩ **6** : AIM, DIRECT **7** : to lie extended, aimed, or turned in a particular direction : FACE, LOOK

point–blank \'pòint-'blaŋk\ *adj* **1** : so close to the target that a missile fired will travel in a straight line to the mark **2** : DIRECT, BLUNT — **point–blank** *adv*

point·ed \'pòint-əd\ *adj* **1** : having a point **2** : being to the point : DIRECT **3** : aimed at a particular person or group; *also* : CONSPICUOUS, MARKED — **point·ed·ly** *adv*

point·er \'pòint-ər\ *n* **1** : one that points out : INDICATOR **2** : a large short-haired hunting dog **3** : HINT, TIP

poin·til·lism \'pwaⁿ(n)-tē-ˌ(y)iz-əm, 'pòint-ᵊl-ˌiz-əm\ *n* [F *pointillisme*, fr. *pointiller* to stipple] : the theory or practice in painting of applying small strokes or dots of color to a surface so that from a distance they blend together — **poin·til·list** *also* **poin·til·liste** \ˌpwaⁿ(n)-tē-'(y)èst, 'pòint-ᵊl-əst\ *n or adj*

point of no return : a critical point (as in

a course of action) at which turning back or reversal is not possible

point of view : a position from which something is considered or evaluated

¹poise \'pȯiz\ vb **poised; pois·ing** : BALANCE

²poise n **1** : BALANCE **2** : self-possessed calmness; *also* : a particular way of carrying oneself

¹poi·son \'pȯiz-ᵊn\ n [ME, fr. OF, drink, poisonous drink, poison, fr. L *potion-, potio* drink] : a substance that through its chemical action can injure or kill — **poi·son·ous** \-(ᵊ-)nəs\ *adj*

²poison vb **poi·soned; poi·son·ing** \'pȯiz-(ᵊ-)niŋ\ **1** : to injure or kill with poison **2** : to treat or taint with poison **3** : to affect destructively : CORRUPT ⟨~ed her mind⟩ — **poi·son·er** \'pȯiz-(ᵊ-)nər\ n

poison hemlock n : a large branching poisonous herb with finely divided leaves and white flowers that is related to the carrot

poison ivy n : a usu. climbing plant related to sumac that has leaves composed of three shiny leaflets and produces an irritating oil causing a usu. intensely itching skin rash; *also* : any of several related plants

poison oak n : any of several plants closely related to poison ivy and with similar properties

poison sumac n : a smooth shrubby American swamp plant with pinnate leaves, greenish flowers, greenish white berries, and irritating properties similar to the related poison ivy

¹poke \'pōk\ n : BAG, SACK

²poke vb **poked; pok·ing 1** : PROD; *also* : to stir up by prodding **2** : to make a prodding or jabbing movement esp. repeatedly **3** : HIT, PUNCH **4** : to thrust forward obtrusively **5** : RUMMAGE **6** : MEDDLE, PRY **7** : DAWDLE — **poke fun at** : RIDICULE, MOCK

³poke n : a quick thrust; *also* : PUNCH

¹pok·er \'pō-kər\ n : a metal rod for stirring a fire

²po·ker \'pō-kər\ n : any of several card games played with a deck of 52 cards in which each player bets on the superiority of his hand

poke·weed \'pōk-ˌwēd\ n : a coarse American perennial herb with clusters of white flowers and dark purple juicy berries

poky *or* **pok·ey** \'pō-kē\ *adj* **pok·i·er; -est 1** : small and cramped **2** : SHABBY, DULL **3** : annoyingly slow

pol \'päl\ n : POLITICIAN

po·lar \'pō-lər\ *adj* **1** : of or relating to a geographical pole **2** : of or relating to a pole (as of a magnet)

polar bear n : a large creamy-white bear that inhabits arctic regions

Po·lar·is \pə-'lar-əs\ n : NORTH STAR

po·lar·i·ty \pō-'lar-ət-ē, pə-\ n, pl **-ties** : the condition of having poles and esp. magnetic or electrical poles

po·lar·iza·tion \ˌpō-lə-rə-'zā-shən\ n **1**

: the action of polarizing : the state of being polarized **2** : concentration about opposing extremes

po·lar·ize \'pō-lə-ˌrīz\ vb **-ized; -iz·ing 1** : to cause (light waves) to vibrate in a definite way **2** : to give physical polarity to **3** : to break up into opposing groups

pol·der \'pōl-dər, 'päl-\ n [D] : a tract of low land reclaimed from the sea

¹pole \'pōl\ n : a long slender piece of wood or metal (telephone ~)

²pole vb **poled; pol·ing** : to impel or push with a pole

³pole n **1** : either end of an axis esp. of the earth **2** : either of the terminals of an electric battery **3** : one of two or more regions in a magnetized body at which the magnetism is concentrated

Pole \'pōl\ n : a native or inhabitant of Poland

pole·ax \'pōl-ˌaks\ n : a battle-ax with a short handle and a hook or point opposite the blade

pole·cat \'pōl-ˌkat\ n, pl **polecats** *or* **polecat 1** : a European carnivorous mammal of which the ferret is considered a domesticated variety **2** : SKUNK

po·lem·ic \pə-'lem-ik\ n : the art or practice of disputation — usu. used in pl. — **po·lem·i·cal** \-i-kəl\ *also* **po·lem·ic** \-ik\ *adj* — **po·lem·i·cist** \-səst\ n

pole·star \'pōl-ˌstär\ n **1** : NORTH STAR **2** : a directing principle : GUIDE

pole vault n : a field contest in which each contestant uses a pole to vault for height over a crossbar — **pole·vault** vb — **pole-vault·er** n

¹po·lice \pə-'lēs\ vb **po·liced; po·lic·ing 1** : to control, regulate, or keep in order esp. by use of police ⟨~ a highway⟩ **2** : to make clean and put in order ⟨~ a camp⟩

²police n, pl **police** [MF, government, fr. LL *politia*, fr. Gk *politeia*, fr. *politeuein* to be a citizen, engage in political activity, fr. *politēs* citizen, fr. *polis* city, state] **1** : the department of government that keeps public order and safety and enforces the laws; *also* : the members of this department **2** : a private organization resembling a police force; *also* : its members **3** : military personnel detailed to clean and put in order

po·lice·man \-mən\ n : a member of a police force

police state n : a state characterized by repressive, arbitrary, totalitarian rule by means of secret police

po·lice·wom·an \pə-'lēs-ˌwu̇-mən\ n : a woman who is a member of a police force

¹pol·i·cy \'päl-ə-sē\ n, pl **-cies** : a definite course or method of action selected to guide and determine present and future decisions

²policy n, pl **-cies** : a writing whereby a contract of insurance is made

pol·i·cy·hold·er \'päl-ə-sē-ˌhōl-dər\ n : one granted an insurance policy

po·lio \'pō-lē-ˌō\ n : POLIOMYELITIS — **polio** adj

po·lio·my·eli·tis \-ˌmī-ə-'līt-əs\ n : an acute virus disease marked by inflammation of the nerve cells of the spinal cord

¹pol·ish \'päl-ish\ vb 1 : to make smooth and glossy usu. by rubbing 2 : to refine or improve in manners, condition, or style

²polish n 1 : a smooth glossy surface : LUSTER 2 : REFINEMENT, CULTURE 3 : the action or process of polishing

Pol·ish \'pō-lish\ n : the Slavic language of the Poles — **Polish** adj

polit abbr political; politician

po·lit·bu·ro \'päl-ət-ˌbyùr-ō, 'pō-lət-, pə-'lit-\ n [Russ politbyuro] : the principal policy-making committee of a Communist party

po·lite \pə-'līt\ adj po·lit·er; -est 1 : REFINED, CULTIVATED ⟨∼ society⟩ 2 : marked by correct social conduct : COURTEOUS; also : CONSIDERATE, TACTFUL — **po·lite·ly** adv — **po·lite·ness** n

po·li·tesse \ˌpäl-i-'tes\ n [F] : formal politeness

pol·i·tic \'päl-ə-ˌtik\ adj 1 : wise in promoting a policy ⟨a ∼ statesman⟩ 2 : shrewdly tactful ⟨a ∼ move⟩

po·lit·i·cal \pə-'lit-i-kəl\ adj 1 : of or relating to government or politics 2 : involving or charged or concerned with acts against a government or a political system ⟨∼ criminals⟩ — **po·lit·i·cal·ly** \-k(ə-)lē\ adv

pol·i·ti·cian \ˌpäl-ə-'tish-ən\ n : a person actively engaged in government or politics

pol·i·tick \'päl-ə-ˌtik\ vb : to engage in political discussion or activity

po·lit·i·co \pə-'lit-i-ˌkō\ n, pl -cos also -coes : POLITICIAN

pol·i·tics \'päl-ə-ˌtiks\ n sing or pl 1 : the art or science of government, of guiding or influencing governmental policy, or of winning and holding control over a government 2 : political affairs or business; esp : competition between groups or individuals for power and leadership 3 : political opinions

pol·i·ty \'päl-ət-ē\ n, pl -ties : a politically organized unit; also : the form or constitution of such a unit

pol·ka \'pōl-kə, 'pō-kə\ n [Czech, fr. Pol Polka Polish woman, fem. of Polak Pole] : a lively couple dance of Bohemian origin; also : music for this dance — **polka** vb

pol·ka dot \'pō-kə-ˌdät\ n : a dot in a pattern of regularly distributed dots — **polka-dot** or **polka-dot·ted** \-ˌdät-əd\ adj

¹poll \'pōl\ n 1 : HEAD 2 : the casting and recording of votes; also : the total vote cast 3 : the place where votes are cast — usu. used in pl. 4 : a questioning of persons to obtain information or opinions to be analyzed

²poll vb 1 : to cut off or shorten a growth or part of : CLIP, SHEAR 2 : to receive and record the votes of 3 : to receive (as votes) in an election 4 : to question in a poll

pol·lack or **pol·lock** \'päl-ək\ n, pl pollack or pollock : an important Atlantic food fish that is related to the cods

pol·len \'päl-ən\ n [NL fr. L, fine flour] : a mass of male spores of a seed plant usu. appearing as a yellow dust

pol·li·na·tion \ˌpäl-ə-'nā-shən\ n : the carrying of pollen to the female part of a plant to fertilize the seed — **pol·li·nate** \'päl-ə-ˌnāt\ vb — **pol·li·na·tor** \-ər\ n

poll·ster \'pōl-stər\ n : one that conducts a poll or compiles data obtained by a poll

poll tax n : a tax of a fixed amount per person levied on adults

pol·lute \pə-'lüt\ vb pol·lut·ed; pol·lut·ing : to make impure; esp : to contaminate with man-made waste — **pol·lut·ant** \-'lüt-ᵊnt\ n — **pol·lut·er** n — **pol·lu·tion** \-'lü-shən\ n

pol·ly·wog or **pol·li·wog** \'päl-ē-ˌwäg\ n : TADPOLE

po·lo \'pō-lō\ n : a game played by two teams on horseback using long-handled mallets to drive a wooden ball

po·lo·ni·um \pə-'lō-nē-əm\ n [NL, fr. ML Polonia Poland, birthplace of its discoverer, Mme. Curie] : a radioactive metallic chemical element

pol·ter·geist \'pōl-tər-ˌgīst\ n [G, fr. poltern to knock + geist spirit] : a noisy usu. mischievous ghost held to be responsible for unexplained noises

pol·troon \päl-'trün\ n : COWARD

poly·chlo·ri·nat·ed bi·phe·nyl \ˌpäl-i-'klōr-ə-ˌnāt-əd-ˌbī-'fen-ᵊl, -'fēn-\ n : any of several industrial compounds that are poisonous environmental pollutants

poly·clin·ic \ˌpäl-i-'klin-ik\ n : a clinic or hospital treating diseases of many sorts

poly·es·ter \'päl-ē-ˌes-tər\ n : a polymer composed of ester groups used esp. in making fibers or plastics

poly·eth·yl·ene \ˌpäl-ē-'eth-ə-ˌlēn\ n : a lightweight plastic resistant to chemicals and moisture and used chiefly in packaging

po·lyg·a·my \pə-'lig-ə-mē\ n : the practice of having more than one wife or husband at one time — **po·lyg·a·mist** \-məst\ n — **po·lyg·a·mous** \-məs\ adj

poly·glot \'päl-i-ˌglät\ adj 1 : speaking or writing several languages 2 : containing or made up of several languages — **polyglot** n

poly·gon \'päl-i-ˌgän\ n : a closed plane figure bounded by straight lines — **po·lyg·o·nal** \pə-'lig-ən-ᵊl\ adj

poly·graph \'päl-i-ˌgraf\ n : an instrument for recording variations of several bodily functions (as blood pressure) simultaneously — **po•lyg•ra•pher** \pə-ˈlig-rə-fər, ˈpäl-i-ˌgraf-ər\ *n*

poly•he•dron \ˌpäl-i-ˈhē-drən\ *n* : a solid formed by plane faces — **poly•he•dral** \-drəl\ *adj*

poly•math \ˈpäl-i-ˌmath\ *n* : a person of encyclopedic learning

poly•mer \ˈpäl-ə-mər\ *n* : a chemical compound formed by union of small molecules of the same kind — **poly•mer•ic** \ˌpäl-ə-ˈmer-ik\ *adj*

po•lym•er•iza•tion \pə-ˌlim-ə-rə-ˈzā-shən\ *n* : a chemical reaction in which two or more small molecules combine to form larger molecules with repeating structural units — **po•lym•er•ize** \pə-ˈlim-ə-ˌrīz\ *vb*

Poly•ne•sian \ˌpäl-ə-ˈnē-zhən\ *n* **1** : a member of any of the native peoples of Polynesia **2** : a group of Austronesian languages spoken in Polynesia — **Polynesian** *adj*

poly•no•mi•al \ˌpäl-ə-ˈnō-mē-əl\ *n* : an algebraic expression having two or more terms each of which consists of a constant multiplied by one or more variables raised to a nonnegative integral power — **polynomial** *adj*

pol•yp \ˈpäl-əp\ *n* **1** : an invertebrate animal (as a coral) that is a coelenterate having a hollow cylindrical body closed at one end **2** : a projecting mass of swollen and hypertrophied or tumorous membrane (a rectal ∼)

po•lyph•o•ny \pə-ˈlif-ə-nē\ *n* : music consisting of two or more melodically independent but harmonizing voice parts — **poly•phon•ic** \ˌpäl-i-ˈfän-ik\ *adj*

poly•sty•rene \ˌpäl-i-ˈstīr-ˌēn\ *n* : a rigid transparent nonconducting thermoplastic used esp. in molded products and foams

poly•syl•lab•ic \ˌpäl-i-sə-ˈlab-ik\ *adj* **1** : having more than three syllables **2** : characterized by polysyllabic words

poly•syl•la•ble \ˈpäl-i-ˌsil-ə-bəl\ *n* : a polysyllabic word

poly•tech•nic \ˌpäl-i-ˈtek-nik\ *adj* : of, relating to, or instructing in many technical arts or applied sciences

poly•the•ism \ˈpäl-i-thē-ˌiz-əm\ *n* : belief in or worship of many gods — **poly•the•ist** \-ˌthē-əst\ *adj or n* — **poly•the•is•tic** \ˌpäl-i-thē-ˈis-tik\ *adj*

poly•un•sat•u•rat•ed \ˌpäl-ē-ˌən-ˈsach-ə-ˌrāt-əd\ *adj, of an oil or fatty acid* : having many unsaturated chemical bonds between carbon atoms

poly•vi•nyl \ˌpäl-i-ˈvīn-ᵊl\ *adj* : of, relating to, or being a polymerized vinyl compound, resin, or plastic — often used in combination

po•made \pō-ˈmäd, -ˈmäd\ *n* : a perfumed ointment esp. for the hair or scalp

pome•gran•ate \ˈpäm-(ə-)ˌgran-ət\ *n* [ME *poumgarnet*, fr. MF *pomme grenate*, lit., seedy apple, fr. *pomme* apple (fr. LL *pomum*, fr. L, fruit) + *grenate* seedy, fr. L *granatus*, fr. *gra-*

num grain] : a tropical reddish fruit with many seeds and an edible crimson pulp; *also* : the tree that bears it

¹**pom•mel** \ˈpəm-əl, ˈpäm-\ *n* **1** : the knob on the hilt of a sword **2** : the knoblike bulge at the front and top of a saddlebow

²**pom•mel** \ˈpəm-əl\ *vb* -**meled** *or* -**melled**; -**mel•ing** *or* -**mel•ling** \-(ə-)liŋ\ : PUMMEL

pomp \ˈpämp\ *n* **1** : brilliant display : SPLENDOR **2** : OSTENTATION

pom•pa•dour \ˈpäm-pə-ˌdȯr\ *n* : a style of dressing the hair high over the forehead

pom•pa•no \ˈpäm-pə-ˌnō, ˈpəm-\ *n, pl* -**no** *or* -**nos** : a food fish of the southern Atlantic coast

pom–pom \ˈpäm-ˌpäm\ *n* : an ornamental ball or tuft used on a cap or costume

pom–pon \ˈpäm-ˌpän\ *n* **1** : POM-POM **2** : a chrysanthemum or dahlia with small rounded flower heads

pomp•ous \ˈpäm-pəs\ *adj* **1** : suggestive of pomp; *esp* : OSTENTATIOUS **2** : pretentiously dignified **3** : excessively elevated or ornate **syn** arrogant, magisterial, self-important — **pom•pos•i•ty** \päm-ˈpäs-ət-ē\ *n* — **pomp•ous•ly** *adv*

pon•cho \ˈpän-chō\ *n, pl* **ponchos** [AmerSp] **1** : a cloak like a blanket with a slit in the middle for the head **2** : a waterproof garment resembling a poncho

pond \ˈpänd\ *n* : a small body of water

pon•der \ˈpän-dər\ *vb* **pon•dered**; **pon•der•ing** \-d(ə-)riŋ\ **1** : to weigh in the mind **2** : to consider carefully

pon•der•o•sa pine \ˌpän-də-ˌrō-sə-, -zə-\ *n* : a tall timber tree of western No. America with long needles; *also* : its wood

pon•der•ous \ˈpän-d(ə-)rəs\ *adj* **1** : of very great weight (a ∼ stone) **2** : UNWIELDY, CLUMSY (a ∼ weapon) **3** : oppressively dull (a ∼ speech) **syn** cumbrous, cumbersome, weighty

pone \ˈpōn\ *n, Southern & Midland* : an oval-shaped cornmeal cake; *also* : corn bread in the form of pones

pon•gee \pän-ˈjē\ *n* : a thin soft silk, cotton, or rayon fabric

pon•iard \ˈpän-yərd\ *n* : DAGGER

pon•tiff \ˈpänt-əf\ *n* : BISHOP; *esp* : POPE — **pon•tif•i•cal** \pän-ˈtif-i-kəl\ *adj*

pon•tif•i•cals \pän-ˈtif-i-kəlz\ *n pl* : the insignia worn by a bishop when celebrating a pontifical mass

¹**pon•tif•i•cate** \pän-ˈtif-i-kət, -ə-ˌkāt\ *n* : the state, office, or term of office of a pontiff

²**pon•tif•i•cate** \pän-ˈtif-ə-ˌkāt\ *vb* -**cat•ed**; -**cat•ing** : to deliver dogmatic opinions

pon•toon \pän-ˈtün\ *n* **1** : a flat-bottomed boat **2** : a boat or float used in building a floating temporary bridge **3** : a float of an airplane

po•ny \ˈpō-nē\ *n, pl* **ponies** : a small horse

po·ny·tail \-ˌtāl\ *n* : a style of arranging hair to resemble the tail of a pony

pooch \ˈpüch\ *n* : DOG

poo·dle \ˈpüd-ᵊl\ *n* [G *pudel*, short for *pudelhund*, fr. *pudeln* to splash (fr. *pudel* puddle) + *hund* dog] : an active dog with a heavy curly coat

pooh–pooh \ˈpü-ˈpü\ *also* **pooh** \ˈpü\ *vb* **1** : to express contempt or impatience **2** : DERIDE, SCORN

¹**pool** \ˈpül\ *n* **1** : a small deep body of usu. fresh water **2** : a small body of standing liquid **3** : SWIMMING POOL

²**pool** *n* **1** : all the money bet on the result of a particular event **2** : any of several games of billiards played on a table having six pockets **3** : the amount contributed by the participants in a joint venture **4** : a combination between competing firms for mutual profit **5** : a readily available supply

³**pool** *vb* : to contribute to a common fund or effort

¹**poop** \ˈpüp\ *n* : an enclosed superstructure at the stern of a ship

²**poop** *n, slang* : INFORMATION

poop deck *n* : a partial deck above a ship's main afterdeck

poor \ˈpu̇r\ *adj* **1** : lacking material possessions ⟨~ people⟩ **2** : less than adequate : MEAGER ⟨~ crop⟩ **3** : arousing pity ⟨~ fellows⟩ **4** : inferior in quality or value ⟨~ sportsmanship⟩ **5** : UNPRODUCTIVE, BARREN ⟨~ soil⟩ **6** : fairly unsatisfactory ⟨~ prospects⟩ ; *also* : UNFAVORABLE ⟨~ opinion⟩ **syn** bad, wrong, unsatisfactory, rotten — **poor·ly** *adv*

poor boy \ˈpō(r)-ˌbȯi\ *n* : SUBMARINE 2

poor·house \-ˌhau̇s\ *n* : a publicly supported home for needy or dependent persons

poor–mouth \-ˌmau̇th, -ˌmau̇th\ *vb* : to plead poverty as a defense or excuse

¹**pop** \ˈpäp\ *vb* **popped**; **pop·ping 1** : to go, come, enter, or issue forth suddenly or quickly ⟨~ into bed⟩ **2** : to put or thrust suddenly ⟨~ questions⟩ **3** : to burst or cause to burst with or make a sharp sound **4** : to protrude from the sockets **5** : SHOOT **6** : to hit a pop-up

²**pop** *n* **1** : a sharp explosive sound **2** : SHOT **3** : a flavored soft drink

³**pop** *n* : FATHER

⁴**pop** *adj* **1** : POPULAR ⟨~ music⟩ **2** : of or relating to pop music ⟨~ singer⟩ **3** : of or relating to the popular culture disseminated through the mass media ⟨~ psychology⟩ **4** : of, relating to, or imitating pop art ⟨~ painter⟩

⁵**pop** *n* : pop music, art, or culture

⁶**pop** *abbr* population

pop art *n* : art in which commonplace objects (as comic strips or soup cans) are used as subject matter — **pop artist** *n*

pop·corn \ˈpäp-ˌkȯrn\ *n* : an Indian corn whose kernels burst open into a white starchy mass when heated; *also* : the burst kernels

pope \ˈpōp\ *n, often cap* : the head of the Roman Catholic Church

pop–eyed \ˈpäp-ˈīd\ *adj* : having eyes that bulge (as from disease)

pop fly *n* : a short high fly in baseball

pop·gun \ˈpäp-ˌgən\ *n* : a toy gun for shooting pellets with compressed air

pop·in·jay \ˈpäp-ən-ˌjā\ *n* [ME *papejay* parrot, fr. MF *papegai, papejai*, fr. Ar *babghā*] : a strutting supercilious person

pop·lar \ˈpäp-lər\ *n* : any of various slender quick-growing trees related to the willows

pop·lin \ˈpäp-lən\ *n* : a strong plain-woven fabric with crosswise ribs

pop·over \ˈpäp-ˌō-vər\ *n* : a biscuit made from a thin batter rich in egg and expanded by baking into a hollow shell

pop·per \ˈpäp-ər\ *n* : a utensil for popping corn

pop·py \ˈpäp-ē\ *n, pl* **poppies** : any of several herbs that have showy flowers including one that yields opium

pop·py·cock \ˈpäp-ē-ˌkäk\ *n* : empty talk : NONSENSE

pop·u·lace \ˈpäp-yə-ləs\ *n* **1** : the common people **2** : POPULATION

pop·u·lar \ˈpäp-yə-lər\ *adj* **1** : of or relating to the general public ⟨~ government⟩ **2** : easy to understand : PLAIN ⟨~ style⟩ **3** : INEXPENSIVE ⟨~ rates⟩ **4** : frequently encountered or widely accepted ⟨~ notion⟩ **5** : commonly liked or approved ⟨~ teacher⟩ — **pop·u·lar·i·ty** \ˌpäp-yə-ˈlar-ət-ē\ *n* — **pop·u·lar·ize** \ˈpäp-yə-lə-ˌrīz\ *vb* — **pop·u·lar·ly** \-lər-lē\ *adv*

pop·u·late \ˈpäp-yə-ˌlāt\ *vb* **-lat·ed; -lat·ing 1** : to have a place in : INHABIT **2** : PEOPLE

pop·u·la·tion \ˌpäp-yə-ˈlā-shən\ *n* **1** : the people or number of people in an area **2** : the individuals under consideration (as in statistical sampling)

population explosion *n* : a pyramiding of numbers of a biological population; *esp* : the recent great increase in human numbers resulting from both increased survival and exponential population growth

pop·u·list \ˈpäp-yə-ləst\ *n* : a believer in or advocate of the rights, wisdom, or virtues of the common people — **pop·u·lism** \-ˌliz-əm\ *n*

pop·u·lous \ˈpäp-yə-ləs\ *adj* **1** : densely populated; *also* : having a large population **2** : CROWDED — **pop·u·lous·ness** *n*

pop–up \ˈpäp-ˌəp\ *n* : a short high fly in baseball

POR *abbr* pay on return

por·ce·lain \ˈpȯr-s(ə-)lən\ *n* : a fine-grained translucent ceramic ware

porch \ˈpȯrch\ *n* : a covered entrance usu. with a separate roof : VERANDA

por·cine \ˈpȯr-ˌsīn\ *adj* : of, relating to, or suggesting swine

por·cu·pine \'pȯr-kyə-ˌpīn\ n [ME *porkepin,* fr. MF *porc espin,* fr. It *por-cospino,* fr. L *porcus* pig + *spina* spine, prickle] : a mammal having stiff sharp easily detachable spines mingled with its hair

¹**pore** \'pȯr\ vb **pored; por·ing 1** : to read studiously or attentively (~ over a book) **2** : PONDER, REFLECT

²**pore** n : a tiny hole or space (as in the skin or soil) — **pored** \'pȯrd\ adj

pork \'pȯrk\ n : the flesh of swine dressed for use as food

pork barrel n : a government project or appropriation yielding rich patronage benefits

pork·er \'pȯr-kər\ n : HOG; *esp* : a young pig suitable for use as fresh pork

por·nog·ra·phy \pȯr-'näg-rə-fē\ n [Gk *pornographos* writing of harlots] : the depiction of erotic behavior designed primarily to cause sexual excitement — **por·no·graph·ic** \ˌpȯr-nə-'graf-ik\ adj

po·rous \'pȯr-əs\ adj **1** : full of pores **2** : permeable to fluids : ABSORPTIVE — **po·ros·i·ty** \pə-'räs-ət-ē\ n

por·phy·ry \'pȯr-f(ə-)rē\ n, pl **-ries** : a rock consisting of feldspar crystals embedded in a compact fine-grained base material — **por·phy·rit·ic** \ˌpȯr-fə-'rit-ik\ adj

por·poise \'pȯr-pəs\ n [ME *porpoys,* fr. MF *porpois,* fr. ML *porcopiscis,* fr. L *porcus* pig + *piscis* fish] **1** : any of several small blunt-snouted whales **2** : any of several dolphins

por·ridge \'pȯr-ij\ n : a soft food made by boiling meal of grains or legumes in milk or water

por·rin·ger \-ən-jər\ n : a low one-handled metal bowl or cup

¹**port** \'pȯrt\ n **1** : HARBOR **2** : a city with a harbor **3** : AIRPORT

²**port** n **1** : an inlet or outlet (as in an engine) for a fluid **2** : PORTHOLE

³**port** n : BEARING, CARRIAGE

⁴**port** vb : to turn or put a helm to the left

⁵**port** n : the left side of a ship or airplane looking forward — **port** adj

⁶**port** n : a sweet fortified wine

por·ta·ble \'pȯrt-ə-bəl\ adj : capable of being carried — **portable** n

¹**por·tage** \'pȯrt-ij, pȯr-'täzh\ n [ME, MF] : the carrying of boats and goods overland between navigable bodies of water; *also* : a route for such carrying

²**por·tage** \'pȯrt-ij, pȯr-'täzh\ vb **por·taged; por·tag·ing** : to carry gear over a portage

por·tal \'pȯrt-ᵊl\ n : DOOR, ENTRANCE; *esp* : a grand or imposing one

portal-to-portal adj : of or relating to the time spent by a worker in traveling from the entrance to his employer's property to his actual working place (as in a mine) and in returning after the work shift

port·cul·lis \pȯrt-'kəl-əs\ n : a grating at the gateway of a castle or fortress that can be let down to stop entrance

porte co·chere \ˌpȯrt-kō-'sher\ n [F *porte cochère,* lit., coach door] : a roofed structure extending from the entrance of a building over an adjacent driveway and sheltering those getting in or out of vehicles

por·tend \pȯr-'tend\ vb **1** : to give a sign or warning of beforehand **2** : INDICATE, SIGNIFY *syn* augur, prognosticate, foretell, predict, forecast, prophesy

por·tent \'pȯr-ˌtent\ n **1** : something that foreshadows a coming event : OMEN **2** : MARVEL, PRODIGY

por·ten·tous \pȯr-'tent-əs\ adj **1** : of, relating to, or constituting a portent : PRODIGIOUS **3** : self-consciously weighty : POMPOUS

¹**por·ter** \'pȯrt-ər\ n, *chiefly Brit* : DOORKEEPER

²**porter** n **1** : one that carries burdens; *esp* : one employed (as at a terminal) to carry baggage **2** : an attendant in a railroad car **3** : a dark heavy ale

por·ter·house \'pȯrt-ər-ˌhaus\ n : a choice beefsteak with a large tenderloin

port·fo·lio \pȯrt-'fō-lē-ˌō\ n, pl **-li·os 1** : a portable case for papers or drawings **2** : the office and functions of a minister of state **3** : the securities held by an investor

port·hole \'pȯrt-ˌhōl\ n : an opening in the side of a ship or aircraft

por·ti·co \'pȯrt-i-ˌkō\ n, pl **-coes** or **-cos** [It] : a row of columns supporting a roof around or at the entrance of a building

por·tiere \pȯr-'tye(ə)r, -'ti(ə)r; pȯrt-ē-ər\ n : a curtain hanging across a doorway

¹**por·tion** \'pȯr-shən\ n **1** : one's part or share (a ~ of food) **2** : DOWRY **3** : an individual's lot **4** : a part of a whole (a ~ of the sky)

²**portion** vb **por·tioned; por·tion·ing** \-sh(ə-)niŋ\ **1** : to divide into portions **2** : to allot to as a portion

port·land cement \ˌpȯrt-lən(d)-\ n : a cement made by calcining and grinding a mixture of clay and limestone

port·ly \'pȯrt-lē\ adj **port·li·er; -est** : somewhat stout

port·man·teau \pȯrt-'man-ˌtō\ n, pl **-teaus** or **-teaux** \-ˌtōz\ [MF *porte-manteau,* fr. *porter* to carry + *man-teau* mantle, fr. L *mantellum*] : a large traveling bag

port of call : an intermediate port where ships customarily stop for supplies, repairs, or transshipment of cargo

port of entry 1 : a place where foreign goods may be cleared through a customhouse **2** : a place where an alien may enter a country

por·trait \'pȯr-trət, -ˌtrāt\ n : a picture (as a painting or photograph) of a person usu. showing the face

por•trait•ist \-əst\ *n* : a maker of portraits

por•trai•ture \ˈpōr-trə-ˌchu̇r\ *n* : the practice or art of making portraits

por•tray \pōr-ˈtrā\ *vb* **1** : to make a picture of : DEPICT **2** : to describe in words **3** : to play the role of — **por•tray•al** *n*

Por•tu•guese \ˈpōr-chə-ˌgēz, -ˌgēs; ˌpōr-chə-ˈgēz, -ˈgēs\ *n, pl* **Portuguese** **1** : a native or inhabitant of Portugal **2** : the language of Portugal and Brazil — **Portuguese** *adj*

Portuguese man-of-war *n* : any of several large colonial invertebrate animals that are related to the jellyfishes and have a large sac resembling a bladder by means of which the colony floats at the surface of the sea

por•tu•laca \ˌpōr-chə-ˈlak-ə\ *n* : a tropical succulent herb cultivated for its showy flowers

pos *abbr* **1** position **2** positive

[1]**pose** \ˈpōz\ *vb* **posed; pos•ing** **1** : to assume or cause to assume a posture usu. for artistic purposes **2** : to set forth : PROPOSE ⟨~ a question⟩ **3** : to affect an attitude or character

[2]**pose** *n* **1** : a sustained posture; *esp* : one assumed by a model **2** : an attitude assumed for effect : PRETENSE

[1]**pos•er** \ˈpō-zər\ *n* : a puzzling question

[2]**poser** *n* : a person who poses

po•seur \pō-ˈzər\ *n* [F, lit., poser] : an affected or insincere person

posh \ˈpäsh\ *adj* : FASHIONABLE

pos•it \ˈpäs-ət\ *vb* : to assume the existence of : POSTULATE

po•si•tion \pə-ˈzish-ən\ *n* **1** : an arranging in order **2** : the stand taken on a question **3** : the point or area occupied by something : SITUATION **4** : the arrangement of parts (as of the body) in relation to one another : POSTURE **5** : RANK, STATUS **6** : EMPLOYMENT, JOB — **position** *vb*

[1]**pos•i•tive** \ˈpäz-ət-iv\ *adj* **1** : expressed definitely ⟨~ views⟩ **2** : CONFIDENT, CERTAIN **3** : of, relating to, or constituting the degree of grammatical comparison that denotes no increase in quality, quantity, or relation **4** : not fictitious : REAL **5** : active and effective in function ⟨~ leadership⟩ **6** : having the light and shade as existing in the original subject ⟨a ~ photograph⟩ **7** : numerically greater than zero ⟨a ~ number⟩ **8** : being, relating to, or charged with electricity of which the proton is the elementary unit **9** : AFFIRMATIVE ⟨a ~ response⟩ — **pos•i•tive•ly** *adv* — **pos•i•tive•ness** *n*

[2]**positive** *n* **1** : the positive degree or a positive form in a language **2** : a positive photograph

pos•i•tron \ˈpäz-ə-ˌträn\ *n* : a positively charged particle having the same mass and magnitude of charge as the electron

poss *abbr* possessive

pos•se \ˈpäs-ē\ *n* [ML *posse comitatus*, lit., power or authority of the country] : a body of persons organized to assist a sheriff in an emergency

pos•sess \pə-ˈzes\ *vb* **1** : to have as property : OWN **2** : to have as an attribute, knowledge, or skill **3** : to enter into and control firmly ⟨~*ed* by a devil⟩ — **pos•ses•sor** \-ˈzes-ər\ *n*

pos•ses•sion \-ˈzesh-ən\ *n* **1** : control or occupancy of property **2** : OWNERSHIP **3** : something owned : PROPERTY **4** : domination by something **5** : SELF-CONTROL

pos•ses•sive \pə-ˈzes-iv\ *adj* **1** : of, relating to, or constituting a grammatical case denoting ownership **2** : showing the desire to possess ⟨a ~ nature⟩ — **possessive** *n* — **pos•ses•sive•ness** *n*

pos•si•ble \ˈpäs-ə-bəl\ *adj* **1** : being within the limits of ability, capacity, or realization ⟨a ~ task⟩ **2** : being something that may or may not occur ⟨~ dangers⟩ **3** : able or fitted to become ⟨a ~ site for a bridge⟩ — **pos•si•bil•i•ty** \ˌpäs-ə-ˈbil-ət-ē\ *n* — **pos•si•bly** \ˈpäs-ə-blē\ *adv*

pos•sum \ˈpäs-əm\ *n* : OPOSSUM

[1]**post** \ˈpōst\ *n* **1** : an upright piece of timber or metal serving esp. as a support : PILLAR **2** : a pole or stake set up as a mark or indicator

[2]**post** *vb* **1** : to affix to a usual place (as a wall) for public notices ⟨~ no bills⟩ **2** : to publish or announce by or as if by a public notice ⟨~ grades⟩ **3** : to forbid (property) to trespassers by putting up a notice **4** : SCORE 4

[3]**post** *n* **1** *obs* : COURIER **2** *chiefly Brit* : MAIL; *also* : POST OFFICE

[4]**post** *vb* **1** : to ride or travel with haste : HURRY **2** : MAIL ⟨~ a letter⟩ **3** : to enter in a ledger **4** : INFORM ⟨kept him ~*ed* on new developments⟩

[5]**post** *n* **1** : the place at which a soldier is stationed; *esp* : a sentry's beat or station **2** : a station or task to which a person is assigned **3** : the place at which a body of troops is stationed : CAMP **4** : OFFICE, POSITION **5** : a trading settlement or station

[6]**post** *vb* **1** : to station in a given place **2** : to put up (as bond)

post•age \ˈpōs-tij\ *n* : the fee for postal service; *also* : stamps representing this fee

post•al \ˈpōs-tᵊl\ *adj* : of or relating to the mails or the post office

postal card *n* : POSTCARD

postal service *n* : a government agency or department handling the transmission of mail

post•boy \ˈpōst-ˌbȯi\ *n* : POSTILION

post•card \-ˌkärd\ *n* : a card on which a message may be written for mailing without an envelope

post chaise *n* : a 4-wheeled closed carriage for two to four persons

post•con•so•nan•tal \ˌpōst-ˌkän-sə-ˈnant-ᵊl\ *adj* : immediately following a consonant

post•date \(ˈ)pōs(t)-ˈdāt\ *vb* : to date

with a date later than that of execution

post·doc·tor·al \(ˈ)pōs(t)-ˈdäk-t(ə-)rəl\ *also* **post·doc·tor·ate** \-t(ə-)rət\ *adj* : of, relating to, or engaged in advanced academic or professional work beyond a doctor's degree

post·er \ˈpō-stər\ *n* : a bill or placard for posting in a public place

¹pos·te·ri·or \pō-ˈstir-ē-ər, pä-\ *adj* **1** : later in time **2** : situated behind

²pos·te·ri·or \pä-ˈstir-ē-ər, pō-\ *n* : the hinder parts of the body : BUTTOCKS

pos·ter·i·ty \pä-ˈster-ət-ē\ *n* **1** : the descendants from one ancestor **2** : succeeding generations; *also* : future time

pos·tern \ˈpōs-tərn, ˈpäs-\ *n* **1** : a back door or gate **2** : a private or side entrance

post exchange *n* : a store at a military post that sells to military personnel and authorized civilians

post·grad·u·ate \(ˈ)pōst-ˈgraj-ə-wət\ *adj* : of or relating to studies beyond the bachelor's degree — **postgraduate** *n*

post·haste \ˈpōst-ˈhäst\ *adv* : with all possible speed

post·hole \ˈpōst-ˌhōl\ *n* : a hole for a post and esp. a fence post

post·hu·mous \ˈpäs-chə-məs\ *adj* **1** : born after the death of the father **2** : published after the death of the author

post·hyp·not·ic \ˌpōst-hip-ˈnät-ik\ *adj* : of, relating to, or characteristic of the period following a hypnotic trance

pos·til·ion *or* **pos·til·lion** \pō-ˈstil-yən, pə-\ *n* : a rider on the left-hand horse of a pair drawing a coach

Post·im·pres·sion·ism \ˌpōst-im-ˈpresh-ə-ˌniz-əm\ *n* : a late 19th century French theory or practice of art that stresses variously volume, picture structure, or expressionism

post·lude \ˈpōst-ˌlüd\ *n* : an organ solo played at the end of a church service

post·man \ˈpōst-mən, -ˌman\ *n* : MAILMAN

post·mark \-ˌmärk\ *n* : an official postal marking on a piece of mail; *esp* : the mark canceling the postage stamp — **postmark** *vb*

post·mas·ter \-ˌmas-tər\ *n* : one who has charge of a post office

postmaster general *n, pl* **postmasters general** : an official in charge of a national postal service

post me·ri·di·em \ˈpōst-mə-ˈrid-ē-əm\ *adj* [L] : being after noon

post·mis·tress \-ˌmis-trəs\ *n* : a woman in charge of a post office

¹post·mor·tem \(ˈ)pōst-ˈmȯrt-əm\ *adj* [L *post mortem* after death] **1** : done, occurring, or collected after death **2** : relating to a postmortem examination

²postmortem *n* : AUTOPSY

post·na·sal drip \ˈpōst-ˌnā-zəl-\ *n* : flow of mucous secretion from the posterior part of the nasal cavity onto the wall of the pharynx

post·na·tal \(ˈ)pōst-ˈnāt-əl\ *adj* : subsequent to birth; *also* : of or relating to a newborn child

post office *n* **1** : POSTAL SERVICE **2** : a local branch of a post office department

post·op·er·a·tive \(ˈ)pōst-ˈäp-(ə-)rət-iv, -ˈäp-ə-ˌrāt-\ *adj* : following a surgical operation (~ care)

post·paid \ˈpōst-ˈpād\ *adv* : with the postage paid by the sender and not chargeable to the receiver

post·par·tum \(ˈ)pōst-ˈpärt-əm\ *adj* [NL *post partum* after birth] : following parturition — **postpartum** *adv*

post·pone \pōs(t)-ˈpōn\ *vb* **post·poned**; **post·pon·ing** : to hold back to a later time — **post·pone·ment** *n*

post road *n* : a road over which mail is carried

post·script \ˈpōs(t)-ˌskript\ *n* : a note added esp. to a completed letter

post time *n* : the designated time for the start of a horse race

pos·tu·lant \ˈpäs-chə-lənt\ *n* : a probationary candidate for membership in a religious house

¹pos·tu·late \ˈpäs-chə-ˌlāt\ *vb* **-lat·ed**; **-lat·ing** : to assume as true

²pos·tu·late \ˈpäs-chə-lət, -ˌlāt\ *n* : a proposition taken for granted as true and made the starting point in a chain of reasoning

¹pos·ture \ˈpäs-chər\ *n* **1** : the position or bearing of the body or one of its parts **2** : STATE, CONDITION **3** : ATTITUDE

²posture *vb* **pos·tured**; **pos·tur·ing** : to strike a pose esp. for effect

post·war \ˈpōst-ˈwȯr\ *adj* : of or relating to the period after a war

po·sy \ˈpō-zē\ *n, pl* **posies** **1** : a brief sentiment : MOTTO **2** : a bunch of flowers; *also* : FLOWER

¹pot \ˈpät\ *n* **1** : a rounded container used chiefly for domestic purposes **2** : the total of the bets at stake at one time **3** : RUIN (go to ~) **4** : MARIJUANA — **pot·ful** *n*

²pot *vb* **pot·ted**; **pot·ting** **1** : to preserve in a pot **2** : SHOOT

po·ta·ble \ˈpōt-ə-bəl\ *adj* : suitable for drinking — **po·ta·bil·i·ty** \ˌpōt-ə-ˈbil-ət-ē\ *n*

po·tage \pō-ˈtäzh\ *n* : a thick soup

pot·ash \ˈpät-ˌash\ *n* [sing. of *pot ashes*] : potassium or any of its various compounds

po·tas·si·um \pə-ˈtas-ē-əm\ *n* : a silver-white metallic chemical element that occurs abundantly in nature esp. combined in minerals

potassium bromide *n* : a crystalline salt used as a sedative and in photography

potassium carbonate *n* : a white salt used in making glass and soap

potassium nitrate *n* : a soluble salt used in making gunpowder, in preserving meat, and in medicine

po·ta·tion \pō-ˈtā-shən\ *n* : a usu. alcoholic drink; *also* : the act of drinking

po·ta·to \pə-'tāt-ō\ *n, pl* **-toes** : the edible starchy tuber of a plant related to the tomato; *also* : this plant

potato beetle *n* : COLORADO POTATO BEETLE

potato bug *n* : COLORADO POTATO BEETLE

pot·bel·ly \'pät-ˌbel-ē\ *n* : a protruding abdomen — **pot·bel·lied** \-ēd\ *adj*

pot·boil·er \-ˌbȯi-lər\ *n* : a usu. inferior work of art or literature produced only to earn money

po·tent \'pōt-ᵊnt\ *adj* 1 : having authority or influence : POWERFUL 2 : chemically or medicinally effective 3 : able to copulate **syn** forceful, forcible, mighty, puissant — **po·ten·cy** \-ᵊn-sē\ *n*

po·ten·tate \'pōt-ᵊn-ˌtāt\ *n* : one who wields controlling power : RULER

¹**po·ten·tial** \pə-'ten-chəl\ *adj* : existing in possibility : capable of becoming actual (a ∼ champion) **syn** dormant, latent, quiescent — **po·ten·ti·al·i·ty** \pə-ˌten-chē-'al-ət-ē\ *n* — **po·ten·tial·ly** \-'tench-(ə-)lē\ *adv*

²**potential** *n* 1 : something that can develop or become actual 2 : the work required to move a unit positive charge from infinity to a point in question; *also* : POTENTIAL DIFFERENCE

potential difference *n* : the difference in potential between two points that represents the work involved in the transfer of a unit quantity of electricity from one point to the other

po·ten·ti·ate \pə-'ten-chē-ˌāt\ *vb* **-at·ed; -at·ing** : to make potent; *esp* : to augment the activity of (as a drug) synergistically — **po·ten·ti·a·tion** \-ˌten-chē-'ā-shən\ *n*

pot·head \'pät-ˌhed\ *n* : an individual who smokes marijuana

poth·er \'päth-ər\ *n* : a noisy disturbance; *also* : FUSS

pot·herb \'pät-ˌ(h)ərb\ *n* : an herb whose leaves or stems are boiled for greens or used to season food

pot·hole \'pät-ˌhōl\ *n* : a large pit or hole (as in a road surface)

pot·hook \-ˌhu̇k\ *n* : an S-shaped hook for hanging pots and kettles over an open fire

po·tion \'pō-shən\ *n* : a mixture of liquids (as liquor or medicine)

pot·luck \'pät-'lək\ *n* : the regular meal available to a guest for whom no special preparations have been made

pot·pie \-'pī\ *n* : pastry-covered meat and vegetables cooked in a deep dish

pot·pour·ri \ˌpō-pu̇-'rē\ *n* [F *pot pourri*, lit., rotten pot] : a miscellaneous collection : MEDLEY

pot·sherd \'pät-ˌshərd\ *n* : a pottery fragment

pot·shot \-ˌshät\ *n* 1 : a shot taken from ambush or at a random or easy target 2 : a critical remark made in a random or sporadic manner

pot·tage \'pät-ij\ *n* : a thick soup of vegetables or vegetables and meat

¹**pot·ter** \'pät-ər\ *n* : one that makes pottery

²**potter** *vb* : PUTTER

pot·tery \'pät-ə-rē\ *n, pl* **-ter·ies** 1 : a place where earthen pots and dishes are made 2 : the art of the potter 3 : dishes, pots, and vases made from clay

¹**pouch** \'pau̇ch\ *n* 1 : a small bag (as for tobacco) carried on the person 2 : a bag for storing or transporting goods (mail ∼) (diplomatic ∼) 3 : an anatomical sac; *esp* : one for carrying the young on the abdomen of a female marsupial (as a kangaroo)

²**pouch** *vb* : to make puffy or protuberant

poult \'pōlt\ *n* : a young fowl; *esp* : a young turkey

poul·ter·er \'pōl-tər-ər\ *n* : one that deals in poultry

poul·tice \'pōl-təs\ *n* : a soft usu. heated and medicated mass spread on cloth and applied to a sore or injury — **poultice** *vb*

poul·try \'pōl-trē\ *n* : domesticated birds kept for eggs or meat — **poul·try·man** \-mən\ *n*

pounce \'pau̇ns\ *vb* **pounced; pounc·ing** : to spring or swoop upon and seize something

¹**pound** \'pau̇nd\ *n, pl* **pounds** *also* **pound** 1 : a unit of avoirdupois, troy, and apothecaries' weight — see WEIGHT table 2 — see MONEY table

²**pound** *vb* 1 : to crush to a powder or pulp by beating 2 : to strike or beat heavily or repeatedly 3 : DRILL 4 : to move or move along heavily

³**pound** *n* : a public enclosure where stray animals are kept

pound·age \'pau̇n-dij\ *n* : POUNDS; *also* : weight in pounds

pound cake *n* : a rich cake made with a large amount of eggs and shortening in proportion to the flour used

pound-fool·ish \ˌpau̇nd-'fu̇l-ish\ *adj* : imprudent in dealing with large sums or large matters

pour \'pōr\ *vb* 1 : to flow or cause to flow in a stream or flood 2 : to rain hard 3 : to supply freely and copiously

pour·boire \pu̇r-'bwär\ *n* [F, fr. *pour boire* for drinking] : TIP, GRATUITY

pout \'pau̇t\ *vb* : to show displeasure by thrusting out the lips; *also* : to look sullen — **pout** *n*

pov·er·ty \'päv-ərt-ē\ *n* [ME *poverte*, fr. OF *poverté*, fr. L *paupertat-*, *paupertas*, fr. *pauper* poor] 1 : lack of money or material possessions : WANT 2 : poor quality (as of soil)

poverty line *n* : a level of personal or family income below which one is classified as poor according to government standards

pov·er·ty–strick·en \'päv-ərt-ē-ˌstrik-ən\ *adj* : very poor : DESTITUTE

POW \pē-(ˌ)ō-ˈdəb-əl-(ˌ)yü\ abbr prisoner of war

¹**powder** \ˈpaȯd-ər\ n [ME poudre, fr. OF, fr. L pulver-, pulvis dust] 1 : dry material made up of fine particles; also : a usu. medicinal or cosmetic preparation in this form 2 : a solid explosive (as gunpowder) — **pow·dery** adj

²**powder** vb **pow·dered; pow·der·ing** \ˈpaȯd-(ə-)riŋ\ 1 : to sprinkle or cover with or as if with powder 2 : to reduce to powder

powder room n : a rest room for women

¹**pow·er** \ˈpaȯ(-ə)r\ n 1 : a position of ascendancy over others : AUTHORITY 2 : the ability to act or produce an effect 3 : one that has control or authority; esp : a sovereign state 4 : physical might; also : mental or moral vigor 5 : the number of times as indicated by an exponent a number is to be multiplied by itself 6 : force or energy used to do work; also : the time rate at which work is done or energy transferred 7 : the amount by which an optical lens magnifies — **pow·er·ful** \-fəl\ adj — **pow·er·ful·ly** \-ē\ adv — **pow·er·less** adj

²**power** vb : to supply with power and esp. motive power

pow·er·boat \-ˌbōt\ n : MOTORBOAT

pow·er·house \ˈpaȯ(-ə)r-ˌhaȯs\ n 1 : POWER PLANT 1 2 : one having great drive, energy, or ability

power plant n 1 : a building in which electric power is generated 2 : an engine and related parts supplying the motive power of a self-propelled vehicle

pow·wow \ˈpaȯ-ˌwaȯ\ n 1 : a No. American Indian ceremony (as for victory in war) 2 : a meeting for discussion : CONFERENCE

pox \ˈpäks\ n, pl pox or pox·es : any of various diseases (as smallpox or syphilis) marked by a rash on the skin

pp abbr 1 pages 2 pianissimo

PP abbr 1 parcel post 2 past participle 3 postpaid 4 prepaid

ppd abbr 1 postpaid 2 prepaid

PPS abbr [L post postscriptum] an additional postscript

ppt abbr precipitate

PQ abbr Province of Quebec

pr abbr 1 pair 2 price

Pr symbol praseodymium

PR abbr 1 payroll 2 public relations 3 Puerto Rico

prac·ti·ca·ble \ˈprak-ti-kə-bəl\ adj : capable of being put into practice, done, or accomplished — **prac·ti·ca·bil·i·ty** \ˌprak-ti-kə-ˈbil-ət-ē\ n

prac·ti·cal \ˈprak-ti-kəl\ adj 1 : of, relating to, or shown in practice (~ questions) 2 : VIRTUAL (~ control) 3 : capable of being put to use (a ~ knowledge of French) 4 : inclined to action as opposed to speculation (a ~ person) 5 : qualified by practice (a good ~ mechanic) — **prac·ti·cal·i·ty**

\ˌprak-ti-ˈkal-ət-ē\ n — **prac·ti·cal·ly** \ˈprak-ti-k(ə-)lē\ adv

practical joke n : a prank intended to trick or embarrass someone or cause him physical discomfort

practical nurse n : a nurse who cares for the sick professionally without having the training or experience required of a registered nurse

¹**prac·tice** or **prac·tise** \ˈprak-təs\ vb **prac·ticed** or **prac·tised; prac·tic·ing** or **prac·tis·ing** 1 : to perform or work at repeatedly so as to become proficient (~ tennis strokes) 2 : CARRY OUT, APPLY (~ what he preaches) 3 : to do or perform customarily (~ politeness) 4 : to be professionally engaged in (~ law)

²**practice** also **practise** n 1 : actual performance or application 2 : customary action : HABIT 3 : systematic exercise for proficiency 4 : the exercise of a profession; also : a professional business

prac·ti·tio·ner \prak-ˈtish-(ə-)nər\ n : one that practices a profession

prae·tor \ˈprēt-ər\ n : an ancient Roman magistrate ranking below a consul — **prae·to·ri·an** \prē-ˈtōr-ē-ən, -ˈtȯr-\ adj

prag·mat·ic \prag-ˈmat-ik\ also **prag·mat·i·cal** \-i-kəl\ adj 1 : of or relating to practical affairs 2 : concerned with the practical consequences of actions or beliefs

prag·ma·tism \ˈprag-mə-ˌtiz-əm\ n : a practical approach to problems and affairs

prai·rie \ˈprer-ē\ n : a broad tract of level or rolling grassland

prairie dog n : an American burrowing rodent related to the marmots and living in colonies

prairie schooner n : a covered wagon used by pioneers in cross-country travel

praise \ˈprāz\ vb **praised; prais·ing** 1 : to express approval of : COMMEND 2 : to glorify (a divinity or a saint) esp. in song — **praise** n — **praise·wor·thy** \-ˌwər-thē\ adj

pra·line \ˈprä-ˌlēn, ˈprā-\ n [F] : a candy of nut kernels embedded in boiled brown sugar or maple sugar

pram \ˈpram\ n, chiefly Brit : PERAMBULATOR

prance \ˈprans\ vb **pranced; pranc·ing** 1 : to spring from the hind legs (a prancing horse) 2 : SWAGGER; also : CAPER — **prance** n — **pranc·er** n

prank \ˈpraŋk\ n : a playful or mildly mischievous act : TRICK — **prank·ster** \-stər\ n

pra·seo·dym·i·um \ˌprā-zē-ō-ˈdim-ē-əm\ n : a white metallic chemical element

prate \ˈprāt\ vb **prat·ed; prat·ing** : to talk long and idly : chatter foolishly

prat·fall \ˈprat-ˌfȯl\ n 1 : a fall on the buttocks 2 : a humiliating blunder

¹**prat·tle** \'prat-³l\ *vb* **prat·tled; prat·tling** \'prat-(³-)liŋ\ : PRATE, BABBLE

²**prattle** *n* : trifling or childish talk

prawn \'prȯn\ *n* : any of numerous edible shrimplike crustaceans; *also* : SHRIMP !

pray \'prā\ *vb* 1 : ENTREAT, IMPLORE 2 : to ask earnestly for something 3 : to address a divinity esp. with supplication

prayer \'praər\ *n* 1 : a supplication or expression addressed to God; *also* : a set order of words used in praying 2 : an earnest request or wish 3 : the act or practice of praying to God 4 : a religious service consisting chiefly of prayers — often used in pl. 5 : something prayed for 6 : a slight chance

prayer book *n* : a book containing prayers and often directions for worship

prayer·ful \'praər-fəl\ *adj* 1 : DEVOUT 2 : EARNEST — **prayer·ful·ly** \-ē\ *adv*

praying mantis *n* : MANTIS

preach \'prēch\ *vb* 1 : to deliver a sermon 2 : to set forth in a sermon 3 : to advocate earnestly — **preach·er** *n* — **preach·ment** *n*

pre·ad·o·les·cence \'prē-,ad-³l-'es-³ns\ *n* : the period of human development just preceding adolescence — **pre·ad·o·les·cent** \-³nt\ *adj or n*

pre·am·ble \'prē-am-bəl\ *n* [ME, fr. MF *preamble*, fr. ML *preambulum*, fr. LL, neut. of *praeambulus* walking in front of, fr. L *prae* in front of + *ambulare* to walk] : an introductory part (the ~ to a constitution)

pre·am·pli·fi·er \(')prē-'am-plə-,fī(-ə)r\ *n* : an amplifier that increases extremely weak signals before they are fed to additional amplifier circuits

pre·ar·range \,prē-ə-'rānj\ *vb* : to arrange beforehand — **pre·ar·range·ment** *n*

pre·as·signed \,prē-ə-'sīnd\ *adj* : assigned beforehand

prec *abbr* preceding

Pre·cam·bri·an \'prē-'kam-brē-ən, -'käm-\ *adj* : of, relating to, or being the period of geologic history preceding the Paleozoic era — **Precambrian** *n*

¹**pre·can·cel** \(')prē-'kan-səl\ *vb* : to cancel (a postage stamp) in advance of use — **pre·can·cel·la·tion** \,prē-,kan-sə-'lā-shən\ *n*

²**precancel** *n* : a precanceled postage stamp

pre·can·cer·ous \(')prē-'kans-(ə-)rəs\ *adj* : likely to become cancerous

pre·car·i·ous \pri-'kar-ē-əs\ *adj* : dependent on uncertain conditions : dangerously insecure : UNSTABLE (a ~ foothold) (~ prosperity) *syn* delicate, sensitive, ticklish, touchy, tricky — **pre·car·i·ous·ly** *adv* — **pre·car·i·ous·ness** *n*

pre·cau·tion \pri-'kȯ-shən\ *n* : a measure taken beforehand to prevent harm or secure good — **pre·cau·tion·ary** \-shə-,ner-ē\ *adj*

pre·cede \pri-'sēd\ *vb* **pre·ced·ed; pre·ced·ing** : to be, go, or come ahead or in front of (as in rank, sequence, or time)

pre·ce·dence \'pres-əd-əns, pri-'sēd-³ns\ *n* 1 : the act or fact of preceding 2 : consideration based on order of importance : PRIORITY

¹**pre·ce·dent** \pri-'sēd-³nt, 'pres-əd-ənt\ *adj* : prior in time, order, or significance

²**prec·e·dent** \'pres-əd-ənt\ *n* : something said or done that may serve to authorize or justify further words or acts of the same or a similar kind

pre·ced·ing \pri-'sēd-iŋ\ *adj* : that precedes *syn* antecedent, foregoing, prior, former, anterior

pre·cen·tor \pri-'sent-ər\ *n* : a leader of the singing of a choir or congregation

pre·cept \'prē-,sept\ *n* : a command or principle intended as a general rule of action or conduct

pre·cep·tor \pri-'sep-tər, 'prē-,sep-\ *n* : TUTOR

pre·ces·sion \prē-'sesh-ən\ *n* : a slow gyration of the rotation axis of a spinning body (as the earth) — **pre·cess** \'prē-'ses\ *vb*

pre·cinct \'prē-,siŋkt\ *n* 1 : an administrative subdivision (as of a city) : DISTRICT (police ~) (electoral ~) 2 : an enclosure bounded by the limits of a building or place — often used in pl. 3 *pl* : ENVIRONS

pre·ci·os·i·ty \,pres(h)-ē-'äs-ət-ē\ *n, pl* **-ties** : fastidious refinement

pre·cious \'presh-əs\ *adj* 1 : of great value (~ jewels) 2 : greatly cherished : DEAR (~ memories) 3 : AFFECTED (~ language)

prec·i·pice \'pres-ə-pəs\ *n* : a steep cliff

pre·cip·i·tan·cy \pri-'sip-ət-ən-sē\ *n* : undue hastiness or suddenness

¹**pre·cip·i·tate** \pri-'sip-ə-,tāt\ *vb* **-tat·ed; -tat·ing** 1 : to throw violently 2 : to throw down 3 : to cause to happen quickly or abruptly (~ a quarrel) 4 : to cause to separate from solution or suspension 5 : to fall as rain, snow, or hail *syn* speed, accelerate, quicken, hasten, hurry

²**pre·cip·i·tate** \pri-'sip-ət-ət, -ə-,tāt\ *n* : the solid matter that separates from a solution or suspension

³**pre·cip·i·tate** \pri-'sip-ət-ət\ *adj* 1 : showing extreme or unwise haste : RASH 2 : falling with steep descent; *also* : PRECIPITOUS — **pre·cip·i·tate·ly** *adv* — **pre·cip·i·tate·ness** *n*

pre·cip·i·ta·tion \pri-,sip-ə-'tā-shən\ *n* 1 : rash haste 2 : the process of precipitating or forming a precipitate 3 : water that falls to earth esp. as rain or snow; *also* : the quantity of this water

pre·cip·i·tous \pri-'sip-ət-əs\ *adj* 1 : PRECIPITATE 2 : having the character of a precipice : very steep (a ~ slope)

; *also* : containing precipices (∼ trails) — **pre·cip·i·tous·ly** *adv*

pré·cis \prā-'sē\ *n, pl* **pré·cis** \-'sēz\ [F] : a concise summary of essential points

pre·cise \pri-'sīs\ *adj* 1 : exactly defined or stated : DEFINITE 2 : highly accurate : EXACT 3 : conforming strictly to a standard : SCRUPULOUS — **pre·cise·ly** *adv* — **pre·cise·ness** *n*

pre·ci·sion \pri-'sizh-ən\ *n* : the quality or state of being precise

pre·clude \pri-'klüd\ *vb* **pre·clud·ed**; **pre·clud·ing** : to make impossible : BAR, PREVENT

pre·co·cious \pri-'kō-shəs\ *adj* [L *praecoc-, praecox* early ripening, precocious, fr. *prae-* ahead + *coquere* to cook] : early in development and esp. in mental development — **pre·co·cious·ly** *adv* — **pre·coc·i·ty** \pri-'käs-ət-ē\ *n*

pre·con·ceive \prē-kən-'sēv\ *vb* : to form an opinion of beforehand — **pre·con·cep·tion** \-'sep-shən\ *n*

pre·con·cert·ed \-'sərt-əd\ *adj* : arranged or agreed on in advance

pre·con·di·tion \-'dish-ən\ *n* : to put in proper or desired condition or frame of mind in advance

pre·cook \'prē-'kuk\ *vb* : to cook partially or entirely before final cooking or reheating

pre·cur·sor \pri-'kər-sər\ *n* : one that precedes and indicates the approach of another : FORERUNNER

pred *abbr* predicate

pre·da·ceous *or* **pre·da·cious** \pri-'dā-shəs\ *adj* : living by preying on others : PREDATORY

pre·date \'prē-'dāt\ *vb* : ANTEDATE

pre·da·tion \pri-'dā-shən\ *n* 1 : the act of preying or plundering 2 : a mode of life in which food is primarily obtained by killing and consuming animals

pred·a·tor \'pred-ət-ər\ *n* : an animal that lives by killing and consuming other animals

pred·a·to·ry \'pred-ə-ˌtōr-ē\ *adj* 1 : of or relating to plunder (∼ warfare) 2 : disposed to exploit others 3 : preying upon other animals

pre·de·cease \ˌprē-di-'sēs\ *vb* **-ceased**; **-ceas·ing** : to die before another person

pre·de·ces·sor \'pred-ə-ˌses-ər, 'prēd-\ *n* : one that has previously held a position to which another has succeeded

pre·des·ig·nate \(')prē-'dez-ig-ˌnāt\ *vb* : to designate beforehand

pre·des·ti·na·tion \ˌprē-ˌdes-tə-'nā-shən\ *n* : the act of foreordaining to an earthly lot or eternal destiny by divine decree; *also* : the state of being so foreordained — **pre·des·ti·nate** \prē-'des-tə-ˌnāt\ *vb*

pre·des·tine \prē-'des-tən\ *vb* : to settle beforehand : FOREORDAIN

pre·de·ter·mine \ˌprē-di-'tər-mən\ *vb* : to determine beforehand

pred·i·ca·ble \'pred-i-kə-bəl\ *adj* : capable of being predicated or affirmed

pre·dic·a·ment \pri-'dik-ə-mənt\ *n* : a difficult or trying situation syn dilemma, pickle, quagmire, jam

¹**pred·i·cate** \'pred-i-kət\ *n* : the part of a sentence or clause that expresses what is said of the subject

²**pred·i·cate** \'pred-ə-ˌkāt\ *vb* **-cat·ed**; **-cat·ing** 1 : AFFIRM 2 : to assert to be a quality or attribute (∼ intelligence of man) 3 : FOUND, BASE — **pred·i·ca·tion** \ˌpred-ə-'kā-shən\ *n*

pre·dict \pri-'dikt\ *vb* : to declare in advance — **pre·dict·able** \-'dik-tə-bəl\ *adj* — **pre·dict·ably** \-blē\ *adv* — **pre·dic·tion** \-'dik-shən\ *n*

pre·di·ges·tion \ˌprē-dī-'jes-chən, -də-\ *n* : artificial partial digestion of food esp. for use in cases of illness or impaired digestion — **pre·di·gest** \-'jest\ *vb*

pre·di·lec·tion \ˌpred-ᵊl-'ek-shən, ˌprēd-\ *n* : a favorable inclination

pre·dis·pose \ˌprē-dis-'pōz\ *vb* : to incline in advance : make susceptible — **pre·dis·po·si·tion** \ˌprē-ˌdis-pə-'zish-ən\ *n*

pre·dom·i·nant \pri-'däm-ə-nənt\ *adj* : greater in importance, strength, influence, or authority — **pre·dom·i·nance** \-nəns\ *n*

pre·dom·i·nant·ly \-nənt-lē\ *adv* : for the most part : MAINLY

pre·dom·i·nate \pri-'däm-ə-ˌnāt\ *vb* : to be superior esp. in power or numbers : PREVAIL

pree·mie \'prē-mē\ *n* : a baby born prematurely

pre·em·i·nent \prē-'em-ə-nənt\ *adj* : having highest rank : OUTSTANDING — **pre·em·i·nence** \-nəns\ *n* — **pre·em·i·nent·ly** *adv*

pre·empt \prē-'empt\ *vb* 1 : to settle upon (public land) with the right to purchase before others; *also* : to take by such right 2 : to seize upon before someone else can 3 : to take the place of syn usurp, confiscate, appropriate, expropriate — **pre·emp·tion** \-'emp-shən\ *n*

pre·emp·tive \prē-'emp-tiv\ *adj* : marked by the seizing of the initiative : initiated by oneself (∼ attack)

preen \'prēn\ *vb* 1 : to dress or smooth up : PRIMP 2 : to trim or dress with the beak 3 : to pride (oneself) for achievement

pre·ex·ist \ˌprē-ig-'zist\ *vb* : to exist before — **pre·ex·is·tence** \-'zis-təns\ *n* — **pre·ex·is·tent** \-tənt\ *adj*

pref *abbr* 1 preface 2 preference 3 preferred 4 prefix

pre·fab \'prē-ˌfab, 'prē-'fab\ *n* : a prefabricated structure

pre·fab·ri·cate \'prē-'fab-rə-ˌkāt\ *vb* : to manufacture the parts of (a structure) beforehand for later assembly — **pre·fab·ri·ca·tion** \ˌprē-ˌfab-ri-'kā-shən\ *n*

¹**pref·ace** \'pref-əs\ *n* : introductory

comments : FOREWORD — **pref·a·to·ry** \'pref-ə-ˌtōr-ē\ adj

²**preface** vb **pref·aced; pref·ac·ing** : to introduce with a preface

pre·fect \'prē-ˌfekt\ n 1 : a high official; esp : a chief officer or magistrate 2 : a student monitor — **pre·fec·ture** \-ˌfek-chər\ n

pre·fer \pri-'fər\ vb **pre·ferred; pre·fer·ring** 1 archaic : PROMOTE 2 : to like better : choose above another 3 : to bring (as a charge) against a person — **pref·er·a·ble** \'pref-(ə-)rə-bəl\ adj — **pref·er·a·bly** \-blē\ adv

pref·er·ence \'pref-(ə-)rəns\ n 1 : a special liking for one thing over another 2 : CHOICE, SELECTION — **pref·er·en·tial** \ˌpref-ə-'ren-chəl\ adj

pref·er·ment \pri-'fər-mənt\ n : PROMOTION, ADVANCEMENT

pre·fig·ure \prē-'fig-yər\ vb 1 : FORESHADOW 2 : to imagine beforehand

¹**pre·fix** \'prē-ˌfiks, prē-'fiks\ vb : to place before ⟨∼ a title to a name⟩

²**pre·fix** \'prē-ˌfiks\ n : an affix occurring at the beginning of a word

pre·flight \'prē-'flīt\ adj : preparing for or preliminary to flight

pre·form \'prē-'fōrm\ vb : to form or shape beforehand

preg·na·ble \'preg-nə-bəl\ adj : vulnerable to capture ⟨a ∼ fort⟩

preg·nant \'preg-nənt\ adj 1 : containing unborn young within the body 2 : rich in significance : MEANINGFUL — **preg·nan·cy** \-nən-sē\ n

pre·heat \'prē-'hēt\ vb : to heat beforehand; esp : to heat (an oven) to a designated temperature before using

pre·hen·sile \prē-'hen-səl, -ˌsīl\ adj : adapted for grasping esp. by wrapping around ⟨a monkey with a ∼ tail⟩

pre·his·tor·ic \ˌprē-(h)is-'tor-ik\ or **pre·his·tor·i·cal** \-i-kəl\ adj : of, relating to, or existing in the period before written history began

pre·ig·ni·tion \ˌprē-ig-'nish-ən\ n : ignition in an internal-combustion engine before the proper time

pre·in·duc·tion \ˌprē-in-'dək-shən\ adj : occurring prior to induction into military service

pre·judge \'prē-'jəj\ vb : to judge before full hearing or examination

¹**prej·u·dice** \'prej-əd-əs\ n 1 : DAMAGE; esp : detriment to one's rights or claims 2 : an opinion for or against something without adequate basis — **prej·u·di·cial** \ˌprej-ə-'dish-əl\ adj

²**prejudice** vb **-diced; -dic·ing** 1 : to damage by a judgment or action esp. at law 2 : to cause to have prejudice

prel·ate \'prel-ət\ n : an ecclesiastic (as a bishop) of high rank — **prel·a·cy** \-ə-sē\ n

pre·launch \'prē-'lónch\ adj : preparing for or preliminary to launch

pre·lim \'prē-ˌlim, pri-'lim\ n or adj : PRELIMINARY

¹**pre·lim·i·nary** \pri-'lim-ə-ˌner-ē\ n, pl **-nar·ies** : something that precedes or

introduces the main business or event

²**preliminary** adj : preceding the main discourse or business

pre·lude \'prel-ˌ(y)üd, 'prā-ˌlüd\ n 1 : an introductory performance or event 2 : a musical section or movement introducing the main theme; also : an organ solo played at the beginning of a church service

prem abbr premium

pre·mar·i·tal \ˌ(')prē-'mar-ət-ᵊl\ adj : existing or occurring before marriage

pre·ma·ture \ˌprē-mə-'t(y)ůər, -'chů(ə)r\ adj : happening, coming, born, or done before the usual or proper time syn untimely, early — **pre·ma·ture·ly** adv

pre·med \'prē-'med\ adj : PREMEDICAL — **premed** n

pre·med·i·cal \(')prē-'med-i-kəl\ adj : preceding and preparing for the professional study of medicine

pre·med·i·tate \pri-'med-ə-ˌtāt\ vb : to consider and plan beforehand — **pre·med·i·ta·tion** \-ˌmed-ə-'tā-shən\ n

pre·men·stru·al \(')prē-'men-strə(-wə)l\ adj : of, relating to, or occurring in the period just preceding menstruation

¹**pre·mier** \pri-'m(y)iər, 'prē-mē-ər\ adj [ME primier, fr. MF premier first, chief, fr. L primarius of the first rank] : first in rank or importance : CHIEF; also : first in time : EARLIEST

²**premier** n : PRIME MINISTER — **pre·mier·ship** n

¹**pre·miere** \pri-'miər, -'miər\ n : a first performance

²**premiere** or **pre·mier** \like ¹PREMIERE\ vb **pre·miered; pre·mier·ing** : to give or receive a first public performance

prem·ise \'prem-əs\ n 1 : a statement of fact or a supposition made or implied as a basis of argument 2 pl : a piece of land with the structures on it; also : the place of business of an enterprise

pre·mi·um \'prē-mē-əm\ n 1 : REWARD, PRIZE 2 : a sum over and above the stated value 3 : something paid over and above a fixed wage or price 4 : something given with a purchase 5 : the sum paid for a contract of insurance 6 : an unusually high value

pre·mix \'prē-'miks\ vb : to mix before use

¹**pre·mo·lar** \(')prē-'mō-lər\ adj : situated in front of or preceding the molar teeth

²**premolar** n : either of two double-pointed premolar teeth behind the canine on each side of each jaw in man

pre·mo·ni·tion \ˌprē-mə-'nish-ən, ˌprem-ə-\ n : previous notice : FOREWARNING; also : PRESENTIMENT — **pre·mon·i·to·ry** \pri-'män-ə-ˌtōr-ē\ adj

pre·na·tal \'prē-'nāt-ᵊl\ adj : occurring, existing, or taking place before birth

pre·oc·cu·pa·tion \prē-ˌäk-yə-'pā-shən\ n : complete absorption of the mind or interests; also : something that causes such absorption

pre·oc·cu·pied \prē-'äk-yə-ˌpīd\ adj 1

: last in thought; *also* : absorbed in some preoccupation 2 : already occupied syn abstracted, absent, absent-minded

pre·oc·cu·py \-ˌpī\ *vb* 1 : to occupy the attention of beforehand 2 : to take possession of before another

pre·op·er·a·tive \(ˈ)prē-ˈäp-(ə-)rət-iv, -ˈäp-ə-ˌrāt-\ *adj* : occurring before and usu. soon before a surgical operation

pre·or·dain \ˌprē-ôr-ˈdān\ *vb* : FOREORDAIN

pre-owned \ˈprē-ˈōnd\ *adj* : SECONDHAND

prep *abbr* 1 preparatory 2 preposition

pre·pack·age \(ˈ)prē-ˈpak-ij\ *vb* : to package (as food) before offering for sale to the customer

preparatory school *n* 1 : a usu. private school preparing students primarily for college 2 *Brit* : a private elementary school preparing students primarily for public schools

pre·pare \pri-ˈpaər\ *vb* **pre·pared; pre·par·ing** 1 : to make or get ready 〈~ dinner〉 〈~ a boy for college〉 2 : to get ready beforehand : PROVIDE 3 : to put together : COMPOUND 〈~ a vaccine〉 — **prep·a·ra·tion** \ˌprep-ə-ˈrā-shən\ *n* — **pre·par·a·to·ry** \pri-ˈpar-ə-ˌtōr-ē\ *adj*

pre·pared·ness \pri-ˈpar-əd-nəs\ *n* : a state of adequate preparation

pre·pay \ˈprē-ˈpā\ *vb* **-paid** \-ˈpād\ ; **-pay·ing** : to pay or pay the charge on in advance

pre·pon·der·ant \pri-ˈpän-d(ə-)rənt\ *adj* : having greater weight, force, influence, or frequency — **pre·pon·der·ance** \-d(ə-)rəns\ *n* — **pre·pon·der·ant·ly** *adv*

pre·pon·der·ate \pri-ˈpän-də-ˌrāt\ *vb* **-at·ed; -at·ing** [L *praeponderare*, fr. *prae-* ahead + *ponder-*, *pondus* weight] : to exceed in weight, force, influence, or frequency : PREDOMINATE

prep·o·si·tion \ˌprep-ə-ˈzish-ən\ *n* : a word that combines with a noun or pronoun to form a phrase — **prep·o·si·tion·al** \-ˈzish-(ə-)nəl\ *adj*

pre·pos·sess \ˌprē-pə-ˈzes\ *vb* 1 : to influence beforehand for or against someone or something 2 : to induce to a favorable opinion beforehand

pre·pos·sess·ing *adj* : tending to create a favorable impression : ATTRACTIVE 〈a ~ manner〉

pre·pos·ses·sion \-ˈzesh-ən\ *n* 1 : PREJUDICE 2 : an exclusive concern with one idea or object

pre·pos·ter·ous \pri-ˈpäs-t(ə-)rəs\ *adj* : contrary to nature or reason : ABSURD

prep·py *or* **prep·pie** \ˈprep-ē\ *n, pl* **prep·pies** 1 : a student at or a graduate of a preparatory school 2 : a person deemed to dress or behave like a preppy

pre·puce \ˈprē-ˌpyüs\ *n* : FORESKIN

pre·re·cord \ˌprē-ri-ˈkórd\ *vb* : to record for later broadcast

pre·req·ui·site \prē-ˈrek-wə-zət\ *n* : something required beforehand or for the end in view — **prerequisite** *adj*

pre·rog·a·tive \pri-ˈräg-ət-iv\ *n* : an exclusive or special right, power, or privilege

pres *abbr* 1 present 2 president

¹pres·age \ˈpres-ij\ *n* 1 : something that foreshadows a future event : OMEN 2 : FOREBODING

²pre·sage \ˈpres-ij, pri-ˈsāj\ *vb* **pre·saged; pre·sag·ing** 1 : to give an omen or warning of : FORESHADOW 2 : FORETELL, PREDICT

pres·by·opia \ˌprez-bē-ˈō-pē-ə\ *n* : a visual condition in which loss of elasticity of the lens of the eye causes defective accommodation and inability to focus sharply for near vision — **pres·by·opic** \-ˈō-pik, -ˈäp-ik\ *adj or n*

pres·by·ter \ˈprez-bət-ər\ *n* 1 : PRIEST, MINISTER 2 : an elder in a Presbyterian church

¹Pres·by·te·ri·an \ˌprez-bə-ˈtir-ē-ən\ *adj* 1 *often not cap* : characterized by a graded system of representative ecclesiastical bodies (as presbyteries) exercising legislative and judicial powers 2 : of or relating to a group of Protestant Christian bodies that are presbyterian in government

²Presbyterian *n* : a member of a Presbyterian church — **Pres·by·te·ri·an·ism** \-ˌiz-əm\ *n*

pres·by·tery \ˈprez-bə-ˌter-ē\ *n, pl* **-ter·ies** 1 : the part of a church reserved for the officiating clergy 2 : a ruling body in Presbyterian churches consisting of the ministers and representative elders of a district

pre·school \ˈprē-ˈskül\ *adj* : of, relating to, or constituting the period in a child's life from infancy to the age of five or six — **pre·school·er** \-ˈskü-lər\ *n*

pre·science \ˈpresh-əns, ˈprēsh-\ *n* : foreknowledge of events; *also* : FORESIGHT — **pre·scient** \-(ē-)ənt\ *adj*

pre·scribe \pri-ˈskrīb\ *vb* **pre·scribed; pre·scrib·ing** 1 : to lay down as a guide or rule of action 2 : to direct the use of something as a remedy

pre·scrip·tion \pri-ˈskrip-shən\ *n* 1 : the action of prescribing rules or directions 2 : a written direction for the preparation and use of a medicine; *also* : a medicine prescribed

pres·ence \ˈprez-ⁿns\ *n* 1 : the fact or condition of being present 2 : the space immediately around a person 3 : one that is present 4 : the bearing of a person; *esp* : stately bearing

¹pres·ent \ˈprez-ⁿnt\ *n* : something presented : GIFT

²pre·sent \pri-ˈzent\ *vb* 1 : to bring into the presence or acquaintance of : INTRODUCE 2 : to bring before the public 〈~ a play〉 3 : to make a gift to 4 : to give formally 5 : to lay (as a charge)

before a court for inquiry **6** : to aim or direct (as a weapon) so as to face in a particular direction — **pre·sen·ta·tion** \ˌprē-ˌzen-ˈtā-shən, ˌprez-ᵊn-\ *n* — **pre·sent·ment** \pri-ˈzent-mənt\ *n*

³**pres·ent** \ˈprez-ᵊnt\ *adj* **1** : now existing or in progress (∼ conditions) **2** : being in view or at hand (∼ at the meeting) **3** : under consideration (the ∼ problem) **4** : of, relating to, or constituting a verb tense that expresses present time or the time of speaking

⁴**pres·ent** \ˈprez-ᵊnt\ *n* **1** *pl* : the present legal document **2** : the present tense; *also* : a verb form in it **3** : the present time

pres·ent–day \ˈprez-ᵊnt-ˈdā\ *adj* : now existing or occurring : CURRENT

pre·sen·ti·ment \pri-ˈzent-ə-mənt\ *n* : a feeling that something is about to happen : PREMONITION

pres·ent·ly \ˈprez-ᵊnt-lē\ *adv* **1** : SOON **2** : NOW

present participle *n* : a participle that typically expresses present action and that in English is formed with the suffix -*ing* and is used in the formation of the progressive tenses

¹**pre·serve** \pri-ˈzərv\ *vb* **pre·served**; **pre·serv·ing 1** : to keep safe : GUARD, PROTECT **2** : to keep from decaying; *esp* : to process food (as by canning or pickling) to prevent spoilage **3** : MAINTAIN (∼ silence) — **pres·er·va·tion** \ˌprez-ər-ˈvā-shən\ *n* — **pre·ser·va·tive** \pri-ˈzər-vət-iv\ *adj or n* — **pre·serv·er** \-ˈzər-vər\ *n*

²**preserve** *n* **1** : preserved fruit — often used in pl. **2** : an area for the protection of natural resources (as animals)

pre·set \ˈprē-ˈset\ *vb* **-set**; **-set·ting** : to set beforehand

pre·shrunk \ˈprē-ˈshrəŋk\ *adj* : of, relating to, or being a fabric subjected to a shrinking process during manufacture usu. to reduce later shrinking

pre·side \pri-ˈzīd\ *vb* **pre·sid·ed**; **pre·sid·ing** [L *praesidēre* to guard, preside over, lit., to sit in front of, sit at the head of, fr. *prae* in front of + *sedēre* to sit] **1** : to occupy the place of authority; *esp* : to act as chairman **2** : to exercise guidance or control

pres·i·dent \ˈprez-əd-ənt\ *n* **1** : one chosen to preside (∼ of the assembly) **2** : the chief officer of an organization (as a corporation or society) **3** : an elected official serving as both chief of state and chief political executive; *also* : a chief of state often with only minimal political powers — **pres·i·den·cy** \-ən-sē\ *n* — **pres·i·den·tial** \ˌprez-ə-ˈden-chəl\ *adj*

pre·si·dio \pri-ˈsēd-ē-ˌō, -ˈsid-\ *n, pl* **-di·os** [Sp] : a garrisoned place; *esp* : a military post or fortified settlement in areas currently or orig. under Spanish control

pre·sid·i·um \pri-ˈsid-ē-əm\ *n, pl* **-ia** \-ē-ə\ *or* **-iums** [Russ *prezidium*, fr. L

praesidium garrison] : a permanent executive committee selected in Communist countries to act for a larger body

¹**pre·soak** \(ˈ)prē-ˈsōk\ *vb* : to soak beforehand

²**pre·soak** \ˈprē-ˌsōk\ *n* **1** : an instance of presoaking **2** : a preparation used in presoaking clothes

¹**press** \ˈpres\ *n* **1** : a crowded condition : THRONG **2** : a machine for exerting pressure; *esp* : PRINTING PRESS **3** : CLOSET, CUPBOARD **4** : PRESSURE **5** : the properly creased condition of a freshly pressed garment **6** : the act or the process of printing **7** : a printing or publishing establishment **8** : the media (as newspapers and magazines) of public news and comment; *also* : persons (as reporters) employed in these media **9** : comment in newspapers and periodicals **10** : a pressure device (as for keeping a tennis racket from warping)

²**press** *vb* **1** : to bear down upon : push steadily against **2** : ASSAIL, COMPEL **3** : to squeeze out the juice or contents of (∼ grapes) **4** : to squeeze to a desired density, shape, or smoothness; *esp* : IRON **5** : to try hard to persuade : URGE **6** : to follow through : PROSECUTE **7** : CROWD **8** : to force one's way **9** : to require haste or speed in action **10** : to make (a phonograph record) from a matrix — **press·er** *n*

press agent *n* : an agent employed to maintain good public relations through publicity

press·ing \ˈpres-iŋ\ *adj* : URGENT

press·man \ˈpres-mən, -ˌman\ *n* : the operator of a press and esp. a printing press

press·room \ˈpres-ˌrüm, -ˌrùm\ *n* : a room in a printing plant containing the printing presses; *also* : a room for the use of reporters

¹**pres·sure** \ˈpresh-ər\ *n* **1** : the burden of physical or mental distress : OPPRESSION **2** : the action of pressing; *esp* : the application of force to something by something else in direct contact with it **3** : the condition of being pressed or of exerting force over a surface **4** : the stress or urgency of matters demanding attention **syn** stress, strain, tension

²**pressure** *vb* **pres·sured**; **pres·sur·ing** \-(ə-)riŋ\ : to apply pressure to

pressure group *n* : a group that seeks to influence governmental policy but not to elect candidates to office

pressure suit *n* : an inflatable suit for high-altitude or space flight to protect the body from low pressure

pres·sur·ize \ˈpresh-ə-ˌrīz\ *vb* **-ized**; **-iz·ing 1** : to maintain normal atmospheric pressure within (an airplane cabin) during high-altitude flight **2** : to apply pressure to **3** : to design to withstand pressure — **pres·sur·iza·tion** \ˌpresh-(ə-)rə-ˈzā-shən\ *n*

pres·ti·dig·i·ta·tion \ˌpres-tə-ˌdij-ə-ˈtā-shən\ n : SLEIGHT OF HAND

pres·tige \pres-ˈtēzh, -ˈtēj\ n [F, fr. MF, conjuror's trick, illusion, fr. LL *praestigium*, fr. L *praestigiae*, pl., conjuror's tricks, irreg. fr. *praestringere* to tie up, blindfold, fr. *prae-* in front of + *stringere* to bind tight] : standing or estimation in the eyes of people : REPUTATION syn influence, authority, weight — **pres·ti·gious** \-ˈtij-əs, -ˈtēj-\ adj

pres·to \ˈpres-tō\ adv or adj [It] : suddenly as if by magic : IMMEDIATELY

pre·stress \(ˈ)prē-ˈstres\ vb : to introduce internal stresses into (as a structural beam) to counteract later load stresses

pre·sume \pri-ˈzüm\ vb **pre·sumed; pre·sum·ing** 1 : to take upon oneself without leave or warrant : DARE 2 : to take for granted : ASSUME 3 : to act or behave with undue boldness — **pre·sum·able** \-ˈzü-mə-bəl\ adj — **pre·sum·ably** \-blē\ adv

pre·sump·tion \pri-ˈzəmp-shən\ n 1 : presumptuous attitude or conduct : AUDACITY 2 : an attitude or belief dictated by probability; *also* : the grounds lending probability to a belief — **pre·sump·tive** \-tiv\ adj

pre·sump·tu·ous \pri-ˈzəmp-chə-(wə)s\ adj : overstepping due bounds : taking liberties : OVERBOLD

pre·sup·pose \ˌprē-sə-ˈpōz\ vb 1 : to suppose beforehand 2 : to require beforehand as a necessary condition syn presume, assume — **pre·sup·po·si·tion** \(ˌ)prē-ˌsəp-ə-ˈzish-ən\ n

pre·teen \ˈprē-ˈtēn\ n : a boy or girl not yet 13 years old — **preteen** adj

pre·tend \pri-ˈtend\ vb 1 : PROFESS ⟨doesn't ~ to be scientific⟩ 2 : FEIGN ⟨~ to be angry⟩ 3 : to lay claim ⟨~ to a throne⟩ — **pre·tend·er** n

pre·tense or **pre·tence** \ˈprē-ˌtens, pri-ˈtens\ n 1 : CLAIM; *esp* : one not supported by fact 2 : mere display : SHOW 3 : an attempt to attain a certain condition ⟨made a ~ at discipline⟩ 4 : false show : PRETEXT — **pre·ten·sion** \pri-ˈten-chən\ n

pre·ten·tious \pri-ˈten-chəs\ adj 1 : making or possessing claims (as to excellence) : OSTENTATIOUS ⟨a ~ literary style⟩ 2 : making demands on one's ability or means : AMBITIOUS ⟨too ~ an undertaking⟩ — **pre·ten·tious·ly** adv — **pre·ten·tious·ness** n

pret·er·it or **pret·er·ite** \ˈpret-ə-rət\ adj : PAST 3 — **preterit** n

pre·ter·nat·u·ral \ˌprēt-ər-ˈnach-(ə-)rəl\ adj 1 : exceeding what is natural 2 : inexplicable by ordinary means — **pre·ter·nat·u·ral·ly** \-ē\ adv

pre·text \ˈprē-ˌtekst\ n : a purpose stated or assumed to cloak the real intention or state of affairs

pret·ti·fy \ˈprit-i-ˌfī, ˈpùrt-\ vb **-fied; -fy·ing** : to make pretty — **pret·ti·fi·ca·tion** \ˌprit-i-fə-ˈkā-shən, ˌpùrt-\ n

¹**pret·ty** \ˈprit-ē, ˈpùrt\ adj **pret·ti·er; -est** [ME *praty, prety,* fr. OE *prættig* tricky, fr. *prætt* trick] 1 : pleasing by delicacy or grace : superficially appealing rather than strikingly beautiful ⟨~ flowers⟩ 2 : FINE, GOOD ⟨a ~ profit⟩ — often used ironically ⟨a ~ state of affairs⟩ syn comely, fair, beautiful, attractive, lovely — **pret·ti·ly** \ˈprit-ə-lē\ adv — **pret·ti·ness** \-ē-nəs\ n

²**pret·ty** \ˌpùrt-ē, pərt-, ˌprit-\ adv : in some degree : MODERATELY

³**pret·ty** \ˈprit-ē, ˈpùrt-ē\ vb **pret·tied; pret·ty·ing** : to make pretty

pret·zel \ˈpret-səl\ n [G *brezel,* deriv. of L *brachiatus* having branches like arms, fr. *brachium* arm] : a usu. brittle, glazed, salted, and usu. twisted cracker

prev abbr previous; previously

pre·vail \pri-ˈvāl\ vb 1 : to win mastery : TRIUMPH 2 : to be or become effective : SUCCEED 3 : to urge successfully ⟨~ed upon her to sing⟩ 4 : to be frequent : PREDOMINATE — **pre·vail·ing·ly** \-iŋ-lē\ adv

prev·a·lent \ˈprev-ə-lənt\ adj : generally or widely existent : WIDESPREAD — **prev·a·lence** \-ləns\ n

pre·var·i·cate \pri-ˈvar-ə-ˌkāt\ vb **-cat·ed; -cat·ing** : to deviate from the truth : EQUIVOCATE — **pre·var·i·ca·tion** \-ˌvar-ə-ˈkā-shən\ n — **pre·var·i·ca·tor** \-ˈvar-ə-ˌkāt-ər\ n

pre·vent \pri-ˈvent\ vb 1 : to keep from happening or existing ⟨steps to ~ war⟩ 2 : to hold back : HINDER, STOP ⟨~ us from going⟩ — **pre·vent·able** also **pre·vent·ible** \-ə-bəl\ adj — **pre·ven·tion** \-ˈven-chən\ n — **pre·ven·tive** \-ˈvent-iv\ or **pre·ven·ta·tive** \-ˈvent-ət-iv\ adj or n

pre·ver·bal \(ˈ)prē-ˈvər-bəl\ adj : having not yet acquired the faculty of speech

¹**pre·view** \ˈprē-ˌvyü\ vb : to see or discuss beforehand; *esp* : to view or show in advance of public presentation

²**preview** n 1 : an advance showing or viewing 2 also **pre·vue** \-ˌvyü\ : a showing of snatches from a motion picture advertised for future appearance 3 : FORETASTE

pre·vi·ous \ˈprē-vē-əs\ adj : going before : EARLIER, FORMER syn foregoing, prior, preceding, former, antecedent — **pre·vi·ous·ly** adv

pre·vi·sion \prē-ˈvizh-ən\ n 1 : FORESIGHT, PRESCIENCE 2 : FORECAST, PREDICTION

pre·war \ˈprē-ˈwòr\ adj : occurring or existing before a war

¹**prey** \ˈprā\ n, pl **preys** 1 : an animal taken for food by another; *also* : VICTIM 2 : the act or habit of preying

²**prey** vb 1 : to raid for booty 2 : to seize and devour something as prey 3 : to have a harmful or wearing effect

prf abbr proof

¹**price** \'prīs\ *n* **1** *archaic* : VALUE **2** : the amount of money paid or asked for the sale of a specified thing; *also* : the cost at which something is obtained

²**price** *vb* **priced; pric·ing 1** : to set a price on **2** : to ask the price of **3** : to drive by raising prices ⟨*priced* themselves out of the market⟩

price–fix·ing \'prīs-,fik-siŋ\ *n* : the setting of prices artificially (as by producers or government)

price·less \'prīs-ləs\ *adj* : having a value beyond any price : INVALUABLE **syn** precious, costly, expensive

price support *n* : artificial maintenance of prices of a commodity at a level usu. fixed through government action

price war *n* : a period of commercial competition in which prices are repeatedly cut by the competitors

pric·ey *also* **pricy** \'prī-sē\ *adj* **pric·i·er; -est** : EXPENSIVE

¹**prick** \'prik\ *n* **1** : a mark or small wound made by a pointed instrument **2** : something sharp or pointed **3** : an instance of pricking; *also* : a sensation of being pricked

²**prick** *vb* **1** : to pierce slightly with a sharp point; *also* : to have or cause a pricking sensation **2** : to affect with anguish or remorse ⟨∼s his conscience⟩ **3** : to outline with punctures ⟨∼ out a pattern⟩ **4** : to cause to stand erect ⟨the dog ∼*ed* up his ears⟩ **syn** punch, puncture, perforate, bore, drill

prick·er \'prik-ər\ *n* : BRIAR, THORN

¹**prick·le** \'prik-əl\ *n* **1** : a small sharp point (as on a plant) **2** : a slight stinging pain — **prick·ly** \'prik-lē\ *adj*

²**prickle** *vb* **prick·led; prick·ling** \-(ə-)liŋ\ **1** : to prick lightly **2** : TINGLE

prickly heat *n* : a red cutaneous eruption with intense itching and tingling caused by inflammation around the ducts of the sweat glands

prickly pear *n* : any of a genus of cacti with usu. yellow flowers and prickly flat or rounded joints; *also* : the pulpy pear-shaped edible fruit of a prickly pear

¹**pride** \'prīd\ *n* **1** : CONCEIT **2** : justifiable self-respect **3** : elation over an act or possession **4** : haughty behavior : DISDAIN **5** : ostentatious display — **pride·ful** *adj*

²**pride** *vb* **prid·ed; prid·ing** : to indulge in pride

priest \'prēst\ *n* [ME *preist*, fr. OE *prēost*, fr. LL *presbyter*, fr. Gk *presbyteros* elder, priest, fr. compar. of *presbys* old] : a person having authority to perform the sacred rites of a religion; *esp* : an Anglican, Eastern, or Roman Catholic clergyman ranking below a bishop and above a deacon — **priest·hood** *n* — **priest·li·ness** \-lē-nəs\ *n* — **priest·ly** *adj*

priest·ess \'prē-stəs\ *n* : a woman authorized to perform the sacred rites of a religion

prig \'prig\ *n* : one who irritates by rigid or pointed observance of proprieties — **prig·gish** \'prig-ish\ *adj* — **prig·gish·ly** *adv*

prim \'prim\ *adj* **prim·mer; prim·mest** : stiffly formal and precise — **prim·ly** *adv* — **prim·ness** *n*

prim *abbr* **1** primary **2** primitive

pri·ma·cy \'prī-mə-sē\ *n* **1** : the state of being first (as in rank) **2** : the office, rank, or character of an ecclesiastical primate

pri·ma don·na \,prim-ə-'dän-ə\ *n*, *pl* **prima donnas** [It, lit., first lady] **1** : a principal female singer (as in an opera company) **2** : an extremely sensitive, vain, or undisciplined person

pri·ma fa·cie \,prī-mə-'fā-shə, -s(h)ē\ *adj or adv* [L, at first view] **1** : based on immediate impression : APPARENT **2** : SELF-EVIDENT

pri·mal \'prī-məl\ *adj* **1** : ORIGINAL, PRIMITIVE **2** : first in importance

pri·mar·i·ly \prī-'mer-ə-lē\ *adv* **1** : FUNDAMENTALLY **2** : ORIGINALLY

¹**pri·ma·ry** \'prī-,mer-ē, 'prīm-(ə-)rē\ *adj* **1** : first in order of time or development; *also* : PREPARATORY **2** : of first rank or importance; *also* : FUNDAMENTAL **3** : not derived from or dependent on something else ⟨∼ sources⟩

²**primary** *n*, *pl* **-ries** : a preliminary election in which voters nominate or express a preference among candidates usu. of their own party

primary school *n* : a school usu. including grades 1-3 and sometimes kindergarten **2** : ELEMENTARY SCHOOL

pri·mate \'prī-,māt *or esp for 1* -mət\ *n* **1** *often cap* : the highest-ranking bishop of a province or nation **2** : any of an order of mammals that includes man, the apes, and monkeys

prime \'prīm\ *n* **1** : the earliest stage of something; *esp* : SPRINGTIME **2** : the most active, thriving, or successful stage or period (as of one's life) **3** : the best individual; *also* : the best part of something **4** : any integer that is not 0, +1, or −1 and is divisible by no integer except +1, −1, and plus or minus itself; *esp* : any such integer that is positive

²**prime** *adj* **1** : standing first (as in time, rank, significance, or quality) ⟨∼ requisite⟩ **2** : not capable of being divided without a remainder by any number except itself or 1 ⟨a ∼ number⟩

³**prime** *vb* **primed; prim·ing 1** : FILL, LOAD **2** : to lay a preparatory coating upon (as in painting) **3** : to put in working condition **4** : to instruct beforehand : COACH

prime meridian *n* : the meridian of 0° longitude from which other longitudes are reckoned east and west

prime minister *n* **1** : the chief minister of a ruler or state **2** : the chief executive of a parliamentary government

¹**prim·er** \'prim-ər\ *n* **1** : a small book for

teaching children to read **2** : a small introductory book on a subject

²**prim·er** \'prī-mər\ n **1** : one that primes **2** : a device for igniting an explosive **3** : material for priming a surface

prime rate n : an interest rate announced by a bank to be the lowest available to its most credit-worthy customers

prime time n : the evening period generally from 7 to 11 p.m. during which television has its largest number of viewers

pri·me·val \prī-'mē-vəl\ adj : of or relating to the earliest ages : PRIMITIVE

¹**prim·i·tive** \'prim-ət-iv\ adj **1** : ORIGINAL, PRIMEVAL **2** : of, relating to, or characteristic of an early stage of development or a relatively simple people or culture **3** : ELEMENTAL, NATURAL **4** : SELF-TAUGHT; also : produced by a self-taught artist — **prim·i·tive·ly** adv — **prim·i·tive·ness** n — **prim·i·tiv·i·ty** \ˌprim-ə-'tiv-ət-ē\ n

²**primitive** n **1** : a primitive artist **2** : a member of a primitive people

prim·i·tiv·ism \'prim-ət-iv-ˌiz-əm\ n : the style of art of primitive peoples or primitive artists

pri·mo·gen·i·tor \ˌprī-mō-'jen-ət-ər\ n : ANCESTOR, FOREFATHER

pri·mo·gen·i·ture \-'jen-ə-ˌchùr\ n **1** : the state of being the firstborn of a family **2** : an exclusive right of inheritance belonging to the eldest son

pri·mor·di·al \prī-'mórd-ē-əl\ adj : first created or developed : existing in its original state : PRIMEVAL

primp \'primp\ vb : to dress in a careful or finicky manner

prim·rose \'prim-ˌrōz\ n : any of a genus of herbs with large leaves arranged at the base of the stem and clusters of showy flowers on leafless stalks

prin abbr **1** principal **2** principle

prince \'prins\ n [ME, fr. OF, fr. L princeps, lit., one who takes the first part, fr. primus first + capere to take] **1** : MONARCH, KING **2** : a male member of a royal family; esp : a son of the monarch **3** : a person of high standing (as in a class) (a ~ of poets) — **prince·dom** \-dəm\ n — **prince·ly** adj

prince·ling \-liŋ\ n : a petty prince

prin·cess \'prin-səs, -ˌses\ n **1** : a female member of a royal family **2** : the consort of a prince

¹**prin·ci·pal** \'prin-sə-pəl\ adj : most important — **prin·ci·pal·ly** \-ē\ adv

²**principal** n **1** : a leading person (as in a play) **2** : the chief officer of an educational institution **3** : the person from whom an agent's authority derives **4** : a capital sum placed at interest or used as a fund

prin·ci·pal·i·ty \ˌprin-sə-'pal-ət-ē\ n, pl -ties : the position, territory, or jurisdiction of a prince

principal parts n pl : the inflected forms of a verb

prin·ci·ple \'prin-sə-pəl\ n **1** : a general or fundamental law, doctrine, or assumption **2** : a rule or code of conduct; also : devotion to such a code **3** : the laws or facts of nature underlying the working of an artificial device **4** : a primary source : ORIGIN; also : an underlying faculty or endowment **5** : the active part (as of a drug)

prin·ci·pled \-sə-pəld\ adj : exhibiting, based on, or characterized by principle ⟨high-principled⟩

prink \'priŋk\ vb : PRIMP

¹**print** \'print\ n **1** : a mark made by pressure **2** : something stamped with an impression **3** : printed state or form **4** : printed matter **5** : a copy made by printing **6** : cloth with a pattern applied by printing

²**print** vb **1** : to stamp (as a mark) in or on something **2** : to produce impressions of (as from type) **3** : to write in letters like those of printer's type **4** : to make (a positive picture) from a photographic negative — **print·er** n

print·able \'print-ə-bəl\ adj **1** : capable of being printed or of being printed from **2** : worthy or fit to be published

print·ing \'print-iŋ\ n **1** : reproduction in printed form **2** : the art, practice, or business of a printer **3** : IMPRESSION **5**

printing press n : a machine that produces printed copies

print·out \'print-ˌaùt\ n : a printed record produced by a computer — **print out** \(')print-'aùt\ vb

¹**pri·or** \'prī-(ə)r\ n : the superior of a religious house

²**prior** adj **1** : earlier in time or order **2** : taking precedence logically or in importance — **pri·or·i·ty** \prī-'ôr-ət-ē\ n

pri·or·ess \'prī-ə-rəs\ n : a nun corresponding in rank to a prior

pri·or·i·tize \prī-'ôr-ə-ˌtīz, 'prī-ə-rə-ˌtīz\ vb -tized; -tiz·ing : to list or rate in order of priority

prior to prep : in advance of : BEFORE

pri·o·ry \'prī-(ə-)rē\ n, pl -ries : a religious house under a prior or prioress

prism \'priz-əm\ n [LL prisma, fr. Gk, lit., anything sawed, fr. priein to saw] **1** : a solid whose sides are parallelograms and whose ends are parallel and alike in shape and size **2** : a usu. 3-sided transparent object that breaks up light into rainbow colors — **pris·mat·ic** \priz-'mat-ik\ adj

pris·on \'priz-ᵊn\ n : a place or state of confinement esp. for criminals

pris·on·er \'priz-(ᵊ-)nər\ n : a person deprived of his liberty; esp : one on trial or in prison

pris·sy \'pris-ē\ adj pris·si·er; -est : being overly prim and precise : PRIGGISH — **pris·si·ness** \'pris-ē-nəs\ n

pris·tine \'pris-ˌtēn\ adj **1** : PRIMITIVE **2** : having the purity of its original state : UNSPOILED

prith·ee \'prith-ē\ interj, archaic — used to express a wish or request

pri·va·cy \'prī-və-sē\ n, pl -cies **1** : the

quality or state of being apart from others **2** : SECRECY

¹pri·vate \'prī-vət\ *adj* **1** : belonging to or intended for a particular individual or group ⟨~ property⟩ **2** : restricted to the individual : PERSONAL ⟨~ opinion⟩ **3** : carried on by the individual independently ⟨~ study⟩ **4** : not holding public office ⟨a ~ citizen⟩ **5** : withdrawn from company or observation ⟨a ~ place⟩ **6** : not known publicly ⟨~ dealings⟩ — **pri·vate·ly** *adv*

²private *n* : an enlisted man of the lowest rank in the marine corps or of one of the two lowest ranks in the army — **in private** : not openly or in public

pri·va·teer \ˌprī-və-'tiər\ *n* : an armed private ship licensed to attack enemy shipping; *also* : a sailor on such a ship

private first class *n* : an enlisted man ranking next below a corporal in the army and next below a lance corporal in the marine corps

pri·va·tion \prī-'vā-shən\ *n* **1** : DEPRIVATION **2** : the state of being deprived; *esp* : lack of what is needed for existence

priv·et \'priv-ət\ *n* : a nearly evergreen shrub related to the olive and widely used for hedges

¹priv·i·lege \'priv-(ə-)lij\ *n* [ME, fr. OF, fr. L *privilegium* law for or against a private person, fr. *privus* private + *leg-*, *lex* law] : a right or immunity granted as an advantage or favor esp. to some and not others

²privilege *vb* **-leged; -leg·ing** : to grant a privilege to

priv·i·leged \-lijd\ *adj* **1** : having or enjoying one or more privileges ⟨~ classes⟩ **2** : not subject to disclosure in a court of law ⟨a ~ communication⟩

¹privy \'priv-ē\ *adj* **1** : PERSONAL, PRIVATE **2** : SECRET **3** : admitted as one sharing in a secret ⟨~ to the conspiracy⟩ — **priv·i·ly** \'priv-ə-lē\ *adv*

²privy *n, pl* **priv·ies** : TOILET; *esp* : OUTHOUSE

¹prize \'prīz\ *n* **1** : something offered or striven for in competition or in contests of chance **2** : something exceptionally desirable

²prize *adj* **1** : awarded or worthy of a prize ⟨a ~ essay⟩ ; *also* : awarded as a prize ⟨a ~ medal⟩ **2** : OUTSTANDING

³prize *vb* **prized; priz·ing** : to value highly : ESTEEM **syn** treasure, cherish, appreciate

⁴prize *n* : property (as a ship) lawfully captured in time of war

⁵prize \'prīz\ *vb* **prized; priz·ing** : PRY

prize·fight \'prīz-ˌfīt\ *n* : a professional boxing match — **prize·fight·er** *n* — **prize·fight·ing** \-iŋ\ *n*

prize·win·ner \'prīz-ˌwin-ər\ *n* : a winner of a prize — **prize·win·ning** \-ˌwin-iŋ\ *adj*

¹pro \'prō\ *n, pl* **pros** : a favorable argument, person, or position

²pro *adv* : in favor of : FOR

³pro *n or adj* : PROFESSIONAL

PRO *abbr* public relations officer

prob *abbr* **1** probable; probably **2** problem

prob·a·ble \'präb-ə-bəl\ *adj* **1** : apparently or presumably true ⟨a ~ hypothesis⟩ **2** : likely to be or become true or real ⟨a ~ result⟩ — **prob·a·bil·i·ty** \ˌpräb-ə-'bil-ət-ē\ *n* — **prob·a·bly** \'präb-ə-blē, 'präb-lē\ *adv*

¹pro·bate \'prō-ˌbāt\ *n* : the judicial determination of the validity of a will

²pro·bate *vb* **pro·bat·ed; pro·bat·ing** : to establish (a will) by probate as genuine and valid

pro·ba·tion \prō-'bā-shən\ *n* **1** : subjection of an individual to a period of testing and trial to ascertain fitness (as for a job) **2** : the action of giving a convicted offender freedom during good behavior under the supervision of a probation officer — **pro·ba·tion·ary** \-shə-ˌner-ē\ *adj*

pro·ba·tion·er \-sh(ə-)nər\ *n* **1** : one (as a newly admitted student nurse) whose fitness is being tested during a trial period **2** : a convicted offender on probation

pro·ba·tive \'prō-bət-iv\ *adj* **1** : serving to test or try **2** : serving to prove

¹probe \'prōb\ *n* **1** : a slender instrument for examining a cavity (as a wound) **2** : an information-gathering device sent into outer space **3** : a penetrating investigation **syn** inquiry, inquest, research, inquisition

²probe *vb* **probed; prob·ing** **1** : to examine with a probe **2** : to investigate thoroughly

pro·bi·ty \'prō-bət-ē\ *n* : UPRIGHTNESS, HONESTY

prob·lem \'präb-ləm\ *n* **1** : a question raised for consideration or solution **2** : an intricate unsettled question **3** : a source of perplexity or vexation — **problem** *adj*

prob·lem·at·ic \ˌpräb-lə-'mat-ik\ *or* **prob·lem·at·i·cal** \-i-kəl\ *adj* **1** : difficult to solve or decide : PUZZLING **2** : DUBIOUS, QUESTIONABLE

pro·bos·cis \prə-'bäs-əs, -bäs\ *n, pl* **-bos·cis·es** *also* **-bos·ci·des** \-'bäs-ə-ˌdēz\ [L, fr. Gk *proboskis*, fr. *pro-* before + *boskein* to feed] : a long flexible snout (as the trunk of an elephant)

proc *abbr* proceedings

pro·caine \'prō-ˌkān\ *n* : a compound used esp. as a local anesthetic

pro·ca·the·dral \ˌprō-kə-'thē-drəl\ *n* : a parish church used as a cathedral

pro·ce·dure \prə-'sē-jər\ *n* **1** : a particular way of doing something ⟨democratic ~⟩ **2** : a series of steps followed in a regular order ⟨surgical ~⟩ — **pro·ce·dur·al** \-'sēj-(ə-)rəl\ *adj*

pro·ceed \prō-'sēd\ *vb* **1** : to come forth : ISSUE **2** : to go on in an orderly way; *also* : CONTINUE **3** : to begin and carry on an action **4** : to take legal action **5** : to go forward : ADVANCE

pro·ceed·ing \-iŋ\ *n* **1** : PROCEDURE **2** *pl* : DOINGS **3** *pl* : legal action **4** : TRANS-

ACTION **5** *pl* : an official record of things said or done

pro·ceeds \'prō-ˌsēdz\ *n pl* : the total amount or the profit arising from a business deal — RETURN

¹**proc·ess** \'präs-ˌes, 'prōs-\ *n, pl* **proc·ess·es** \-ˌes-əz, -ə-səz, -ə-ˌsēz\ **1** : PROGRESS, ADVANCE **2** : something going on : PROCEEDING **3** : a natural phenomenon marked by gradual changes that lead toward a particular result (the ∼ of growth) **4** : a series of actions or operations directed toward a particular result ⟨a manufacturing ∼⟩ **5** : legal action **6** : a mandate issued by a court; *esp* : SUMMONS **7** : a projecting part of an organism or organic structure

²**process** *vb* : to subject to a special process

pro·ces·sion \prə-'sesh-ən\ *n* : a group of individuals moving along in an orderly often ceremonial way : PARADE

pro·ces·sion·al \-'sesh-(ə-)nəl\ *n* **1** : music for a procession **2** : a ceremonial procession

proc·es·sor \'präs-ˌes-ər, 'prōs-\ *n* **1** : one that processes **2** : the part of a computer that operates on data

pro·claim \prō-'klām\ *vb* : to make known publicly : DECLARE — **proc·la·ma·tion** \ˌpräk-lə-'mā-shən\ *n*

pro·cliv·i·ty \prō-'kliv-ət-ē\ *n, pl* **-ties** : an inherent inclination esp. toward something objectionable

pro·con·sul \prō-'kän-səl\ *n* **1** : a governor or military commander of an ancient Roman province **2** : an administrator in a modern colony, dependency, or occupied area usu. with wide powers — **pro·con·su·lar** \-sə-lər\ *adj* — **pro·con·su·late** \-sə-lət\ *n* — **pro·con·sul·ship** *n*

pro·cras·ti·nate \prə-'kras-tə-ˌnāt\ *vb* **-nat·ed; -nat·ing** [L *procrastinare,* fr. *pro-* forward + *crastinus* of tomorrow, fr. *cras* tomorrow] : to put off usu. habitually the doing of something that should be done syn dawdle, delay, loiter, linger — **pro·cras·ti·na·tion** \-ˌkras-tə-'nā-shən\ *n* — **pro·cras·ti·na·tor** \-'kras-tə-ˌnāt-ər\ *n*

pro·cre·ate \'prō-krē-ˌāt\ *vb* **-at·ed; -at·ing** : to beget or bring forth offspring syn reproduce, breed, generate, propagate — **pro·cre·ation** \ˌprō-krē-'ā-shən\ *n* — **pro·cre·ative** \'prō-krē-ˌāt-iv\ *adj* — **pro·cre·ator** \-ˌāt-ər\ *n*

pro·crus·te·an \prə-'krəs-tē-ən\ *adj, often cap* [deriv. of *Procrustes,* villain of Greek mythology who made victims fit his bed by stretching them or cutting off their legs] : marked by arbitrary often ruthless disregard of individual differences or special circumstances

proc·tor \'präk-tər\ *n* : one appointed to supervise students (as at an examination) — **proctor** *vb* — **proc·to·ri·al** \präk-'tōr-ē-əl\ *adj*

proc·u·ra·tor \'präk-yə-ˌrāt-ər\ *n* : ADMINISTRATOR; *esp* : an official of ancient Rome administering a province

pro·cure \prə-'kyù(ə)r\ *vb* **pro·cured; pro·cur·ing 1** : to get possession of : OBTAIN **2** : to make women available for promiscuous sexual intercourse **3** : to cause to happen or be done : ACHIEVE syn secure, acquire, gain, win, earn — **pro·cur·able** \-'kyùr-ə-bəl\ *adj* — **pro·cure·ment** \-'kyù(ə)r-mənt\ *n* — **pro·cur·er** *n*

¹**prod** \'präd\ *vb* **prod·ded; prod·ding 1** : to thrust a pointed instrument into : GOAD **2** : INCITE, STIR — **prod** *n*

²**prod** *abbr* product; production

prod·i·gal \'präd-i-gəl\ *adj* **1** : recklessly extravagant; *also* : LUXURIANT **2** : WASTEFUL, LAVISH syn profuse, lavish, lush, opulent — **prodigal** *n* — **prod·i·gal·i·ty** \ˌpräd-ə-'gal-ət-ē\ *n*

pro·di·gious \prə-'dij-əs\ *adj* **1** : exciting wonder **2** : extraordinary in size or degree : ENORMOUS syn monstrous, tremendous, stupendous, monumental — **pro·di·gious·ly** *adv*

prod·i·gy \'präd-ə-jē\ *n, pl* **-gies 1** : something extraordinary : WONDER **2** : a highly talented child

¹**pro·duce** \prə-'d(y)üs\ *vb* **pro·duced; pro·duc·ing 1** : to present to view : EXHIBIT **2** : to give birth or rise to : YIELD **3** : EXTEND, PROLONG **4** : to give being or form to : BRING ABOUT, MAKE; *esp* : MANUFACTURE **5** : to cause to accrue ⟨∼ a profit⟩ — **pro·duc·er** *n*

²**pro·duce** \'präd-(ˌ)üs, 'prōd-(ˌ)yüs\ *n* : PRODUCT **2**; *also* : agricultural products and esp. fresh fruits and vegetables

prod·uct \'präd-(ˌ)əkt\ *n* **1** : the number resulting from multiplication **2** : something produced (as by labor, thought, or growth)

pro·duc·tion \prə-'dək-shən\ *n* **1** : something produced : PRODUCT **2** : the act or process of producing — **pro·duc·tive** \-'dək-tiv\ *adj* — **pro·duc·tive·ness** *n* — **pro·duc·tiv·i·ty** \(ˌ)prō-ˌdək-'tiv-ət-ē, ˌpräd-(ˌ)ək-\ *n*

pro·em \'prō-ˌem\ *n* **1** : preliminary comment : PREFACE **2** : PRELUDE

prof *abbr* **1** professional **2** professor

¹**pro·fane** \prō-'fān\ *vb* **pro·faned; pro·fan·ing 1** : to treat (something sacred) with irreverence or contempt : DESECRATE **2** : to debase by an unworthy use — **prof·a·na·tion** \ˌpräf-ə-'nā-shən\ *n*

²**profane** *adj* [ME *prophane,* fr. MF, fr. L *profanus,* fr. *pro-* before + *fanum* temple] **1** : not concerned with religion : SECULAR **2** : not holy because unconsecrated, impure, or defiled **3** : serving to debase what is holy : IRREVERENT ⟨∼ language⟩ — **pro·fane·ly** *adv* — **pro·fane·ness** \-'fān-nəs\ *n*

pro·fan·i·ty \prō-'fan-ət-ē\ *n, pl* **-ties 1** : the quality or state of being profane **2** : the use of profane language **3** : profane language

pro·fess \prə-'fes\ *vb* **1** : to declare or admit openly : PRETEND **2** : to declare in words only : PRETEND **3** : to confess one's faith in **4** : to practice or claim to be versed in (a calling or occupation) — **pro·fess·ed·ly** \-əd-lē\ *adv*

pro·fes·sion \prə-'fesh-ən\ *n* **1** : an open declaration or avowal of a belief or opinion **2** : a calling requiring specialized knowledge and often long academic preparation **3** : the whole body of persons engaged in a calling

¹**pro·fes·sion·al** \prə-'fesh-(ə-)nəl\ *adj* **1** : of, relating to, or characteristic of a profession **2** : engaged in one of the learned professions **3** : participating for gain in an activity often engaged in by amateurs — **pro·fes·sion·al·ly** \-ē\ *adv*

²**professional** *n* : one that engages in an activity professionally

pro·fes·sion·al·ism \-,iz-əm\ *n* **1** : the conduct, aims, or qualities that characterize or mark a profession or a professional person **2** : the following of a profession (as athletics) for gain or livelihood

pro·fes·sion·al·ize \-,īz\ *vb* **-ized**; **-iz·ing** : to give a professional nature to

pro·fes·sor \prə-'fes-ər\ *n* : a teacher at a university or college; *esp* : a faculty member of the highest academic rank — **pro·fes·so·ri·al** \,prō-fə-'sōr-ē-əl, ,präf-ə-\ *adj* — **pro·fes·sor·ship** *n*

prof·fer \'präf-ər\ *vb* **prof·fered**; **prof·fer·ing** \-(ə-)riŋ\ : to present for acceptance : OFFER — **proffer** *n*

pro·fi·cient \prə-'fish-ənt\ *adj* : well advanced in an art, occupation, or branch of knowledge **syn** skillful, expert, masterful, masterly — **pro·fi·cien·cy** \-ən-sē\ *n* — **proficient** *n* — **pro·fi·cient·ly** *adv*

¹**pro·file** \'prō-,fīl\ *n* [It *profilo*, fr. *profilare* to draw in outline, fr. *pro-* forward (fr. L) + *filare* to spin, fr. LL, fr. L *filum* thread] **1** : a representation of something in outline: *esp* : a human head seen in side view **2** : a concise biographical sketch **3** : degree or level of public exposure ⟨keep a low ∼⟩ **syn** contour, silhouette, outline

²**profile** *vb* **pro·filed**; **pro·fil·ing** : to write or draw a profile of

¹**prof·it** \'präf-ət\ *n* **1** : a valuable return : GAIN **2** : the excess of the selling price of goods over their cost — **prof·it·less** *adj*

²**profit** *vb* **1** : to be of use : BENEFIT **2** : to derive benefit : GAIN — **prof·it·able** \'präf-ət-ə-bəl, 'präf-tə-bəl\ *adj* — **prof·it·ably** \-blē\ *adv*

prof·i·teer \,präf-ə-'tiər\ *n* : one who makes what is considered an unreasonable profit — **profiteer** *vb*

prof·li·gate \'präf-li-gət, -lə-,gāt\ *adj* **1** : completely given up to dissipation and licentiousness **2** : wildly extravagant — **prof·li·ga·cy** \-gə-sē\ *n* — **profligate** *n* — **prof·li·gate·ly** *adv*

pro for·ma \prō-'fōr-mə\ *adj* : done or existing as a matter of form

pro·found \prə-'faûnd\ *adj* **1** : marked by intellectual depth or insight ⟨a ∼ thought⟩ **2** : coming from or reaching to a depth ⟨a ∼ sigh⟩ **3** : deeply felt : INTENSE ⟨∼ sympathy⟩ — **pro·found·ly** *adv* — **pro·fun·di·ty** \-'fən-dət-ē\ *n*

pro·fuse \prə-'fyüs\ *adj* : pouring forth liberally : ABUNDANT **syn** lavish, prodigal, luxuriant, exuberant — **pro·fuse·ly** *adv* — **pro·fu·sion** \-'fyü-zhən\ *n*

pro·gen·i·tor \prō-'jen-ət-ər\ *n* **1** : a direct ancestor : FOREFATHER **2** : ORIGINATOR, PRECURSOR

prog·e·ny \'präj-ə-nē\ *n, pl* **-nies** : OFFSPRING, CHILDREN, DESCENDANTS

prog·na·thous \'präg-nə-thəs\ *adj* : having the jaws projecting beyond the upper part of the face

prog·no·sis \präg-'nō-səs\ *n, pl* **-no·ses** \-,sēz\ : a forecast esp. of the course of a disease

prog·nos·tic \präg-'näs-tik\ *n* **1** : PORTENT **2** : PROPHECY — **prognostic** *adj*

prog·nos·ti·cate \präg-'näs-tə-,kāt\ *vb* **-cat·ed; -cat·ing** : to foretell from signs or symptoms — **prog·nos·ti·ca·tion** \-,näs-tə-'kā-shən\ *n* — **prog·nos·ti·ca·tor** \-'näs-tə-,kāt-ər\ *n*

¹**pro·gram** \'prō-,gram, -grəm\ *n* **1** : a brief outline of the order to be pursued or the subjects included (as in a public entertainment); *also* : PERFORMANCE **2** : a plan of procedure **3** : coded instructions for a computer — **pro·gram·mat·ic** \,prō-grə-'mat-ik\ *adj*

²**program** *also* **programme** *vb* **-grammed** *or* **-gramed; -gram·ming** *or* **-gram·ing** **1** : to enter in a program **2** : to provide (as a computer) with a program — **pro·gram·ma·bil·i·ty** \(,)prō-,gram-ə-'bil-ət-ē\ *n* — **pro·gram·ma·ble** \'prō-,gram-ə-bəl\ *adj* — **pro·gram·mer** *or* **pro·gram·er** \'prō-,gram-ər, -grə-mər\ *n*

programmed instruction *n* : instruction through information given in small steps with each requiring a correct response by the learner before going on to the next step

pro·gram·ming *or* **pro·gram·ing** \-,gram-iŋ, -grə-miŋ\ *n* **1** : the process of instructing or learning by means of an instruction program **2** : the process of preparing an instruction program

¹**prog·ress** \'präg-rəs, -,res\ *n* **1** : a forward movement : ADVANCE **2** : a gradual betterment

²**pro·gress** \prə-'gres\ *vb* **1** : to move forward : PROCEED **2** : to develop to a more advanced stage : IMPROVE

pro·gres·sion \prə-'gresh-ən\ *n* **1** : an act of progressing : ADVANCE **2** : a continuous and connected series

¹**pro·gres·sive** \prə-'gres-iv\ *adj* **1** : of, relating to, or characterized by progress ⟨a ∼ city⟩ **2** : advancing by stages ⟨a ∼ disease⟩ **3** *often cap* : of or relating to political Progressives **4** : of, re-

lating to, or constituting a verb form that expresses action in progress at the time of speaking or a time spoken of — **pro·gres·sive·ly** adv

²**progressive** n 1 : one that is progressive 2 : a person believing in moderate political change and social improvement by government action; esp, cap : a member of a Progressive Party (as in the presidential campaigns of 1912, 1924, and 1948) in the U.S.

pro·hib·it \prō-'hib-ət\ vb 1 : to forbid by authority 2 : to prevent from doing something

pro·hi·bi·tion \,prō-ə-'bish-ən\ n 1 : the act of prohibiting 2 : the forbidding by law of the sale or manufacture of alcoholic beverages — **pro·hi·bi·tion·ist** \-'bish-(ə-)nəst\ n — **pro·hib·i·tive** \prō-'hib-ət-iv\ adj — **pro·hib·i·tive·ly** adv — **pro·hib·i·to·ry** \-'hib-ə-,tōr-ē\ adj

¹**proj·ect** \'präj-,ekt, -ikt\ n 1 : a specific plan or design : SCHEME 2 : a planned undertaking ⟨a research ~⟩

²**pro·ject** \prə-'jekt\ vb 1 : to devise in the mind : DESIGN 2 : to throw forward 3 : PROTRUDE 4 : to cause (light or shadow) to fall into space or (an image) to fall on a surface ⟨~ a beam of light⟩ 5 : to attribute (a thought, feeling, or personal characteristic) to a person, group, or object — **pro·jec·tion** \-'jek-shən\ n

pro·jec·tile \prə-'jek-t⁽ə⁾l\ n 1 : a body hurled or projected by external force; esp : a missile for a firearm 2 : a self-propelling weapon

pro·jec·tion·ist \prə-'jek-sh(ə-)nəst\ n : one that operates a motion-picture projector or television equipment

pro·jec·tor \-'jek-tər\ n : one that projects; esp : a device for projecting pictures on a screen

pro·le·gom·e·non \,prō-li-'gäm-ə-,nän, -nən\ n, pl **-e·na** \-nə\ : prefatory remarks

pro·le·tar·i·an \,prō-lə-'ter-ē-ən\ n : a member of the proletariat — **proletarian** adj

pro·le·tar·i·at \-ē-ət\ n : the laboring class; esp : industrial workers who sell their labor to live

pro·lif·er·ate \prə-'lif-ə-,rāt\ vb -at·ed; -at·ing : to grow or increase by rapid production of new units (as cells or offspring) — **pro·lif·er·a·tion** \-,lif-ə-'rā-shən\ n

pro·lif·ic \prə-'lif-ik\ adj 1 : producing young or fruit abundantly 2 : marked by abundant inventiveness or productivity ⟨a ~ writer⟩ — **pro·lif·i·cal·ly** \-i-k(ə-)lē\ adv

pro·lix \prō-'liks, 'prō-,liks\ adj : VERBOSE syn wordy, diffuse, redundant — **pro·lix·i·ty** \prō-'lik-sət-ē\ n

pro·logue also **pro·log** \'prō-,lòg, -,läg\ n : PREFACE ⟨~ of a play⟩

pro·long \prə-'lòŋ\ vb 1 : to lengthen in time : CONTINUE ⟨~ a meeting⟩ 2 : to lengthen in extent or range syn pro-tract, extend, elongate, stretch — **pro·lon·ga·tion** \,prō-,lòŋ-'gā-shən\ n

prom \'präm\ n : a formal dance given by a high school or college class

¹**prom·e·nade** \,präm-ə-'nād, -'näd\ n [F, fr. promener to take for a walk, fr. L prominare to drive forward] 1 : a leisurely walk for pleasure or display 2 : a place for strolling 3 : an opening grand march at a formal ball

²**promenade** vb **-nad·ed; -nad·ing** 1 : to take a promenade 2 : to walk about in or on

pro·me·thi·um \prə-'mē-thē-əm\ n : a metallic chemical element obtained from uranium or neodymium

prom·i·nence \'präm-(ə-)nəns\ n 1 : something prominent 2 : the quality, state, or fact of being prominent or conspicuous 3 : a mass of cloudlike gas that arises from the sun's chromosphere

prom·i·nent \-nənt\ adj 1 : jutting out : PROJECTING 2 : readily noticeable : CONSPICUOUS 3 : DISTINGUISHED, EMINENT syn remarkable, outstanding, striking, salient — **prom·i·nent·ly** adv

pro·mis·cu·ous \prə-'mis-kyə-wəs\ adj 1 : consisting of various sorts and kinds : MIXED 2 : not restricted to one class or person; esp : not restricted to one sexual partner syn miscellaneous, assorted, heterogeneous, motley, varied — **prom·is·cu·i·ty** \,präm-is-'kyü-ət-ē, ,prō-,mis-\ n — **pro·mis·cu·ous·ly** adv — **pro·mis·cu·ous·ness** n

¹**prom·ise** \'präm-əs\ n 1 : a pledge to do or not to do something specified 2 : ground for expectation of success or improvement 3 : something promised

²**promise** vb **prom·ised; prom·is·ing** 1 : to engage to do, bring about, or provide ⟨~ help⟩ 2 : to suggest beforehand ⟨dark clouds ~ rain⟩ 3 : to give ground for expectation ⟨the book ~s to be good⟩

prom·is·ing \'präm-ə-siŋ\ adj : likely to succeed or yield good results — **prom·is·ing·ly** adv

prom·is·so·ry \'präm-ə-,sōr-ē\ adj : containing a promise

prom·on·to·ry \'präm-ən-,tōr-ē\ n, pl **-ries** : a point of land jutting into the sea : HEADLAND

pro·mote \prə-'mōt\ vb **pro·mot·ed; pro·mot·ing** 1 : to advance in station, rank, or honor 2 : to contribute to the growth or prosperity of : FURTHER 3 : LAUNCH — **pro·mo·tion** \-'mō-shən\ n — **pro·mo·tion·al** \-'mōsh-(ə-)nəl\ adj

pro·mot·er \-'mōt-ər\ n : one that promotes; esp : one that assumes the financial responsibilities of a sports event

¹**prompt** \'prämpt\ vb 1 : INCITE 2 : to assist (one acting or reciting) by suggesting the next words 3 : INSPIRE, URGE — **prompt·er** n

²**prompt** adj 1 : being ready and quick to act; also : PUNCTUAL 2 : performed

readily or immediately ⟨∼ service⟩ — **prompt·ly** *adv* — **prompt·ness** *n*

prompt·book \-ˌbȯk\ *n* : a copy of a play with directions for performance used by a theater prompter

promp·ti·tude \ˈpräm(p)-təˌt(y)üd\ *n* : the quality or habit of being prompt : PROMPTNESS

pro·mul·gate \ˈpräm-əlˌgāt; prō-ˈməl-\ *vb* **-gat·ed; -gat·ing** : to make known or put into force by open declaration — **prom·ul·ga·tion** \ˌpräm-əl-ˈgā-shən, ˌprō-(ˌ)məl-\ *n*

pron *abbr* **1** pronoun **2** pronounced **3** pronunciation

prone \ˈprōn\ *adj* **1** : having a tendency or inclination : DISPOSED **2** : lying face downward: *also* : lying flat or prostrate *syn* subject, exposed, open, liable, susceptible — **prone·ness** \ˈprōn-nəs\ *n*

prong \ˈprȯŋ\ *n* : one of the sharp points of a fork : TINE; *also* : a slender projecting part (as of an antler)

prong·horn \ˈprȯŋ-ˌhȯrn\ *n, pl* **pronghorn** *also* **pronghorns** : a ruminant mammal of treeless parts of western No. America that resembles an antelope

pro·noun \ˈprō-ˌnaȯn\ *n* : a word used as a substitute for a noun

pro·nounce \prə-ˈnaȯns\ *vb* **pronounced; pro·nounc·ing 1** : to utter officially or as an opinion ⟨∼ sentence⟩ **2** : to employ the organs of speech in order to produce ⟨∼ a word⟩ ; *esp* : to say or speak correctly ⟨she can't ∼ his name⟩ — **pro·nounce·able** *adj* — **pro·nun·ci·a·tion** \-ˌnən-sē-ˈā-shən\ *n*

pro·nounced \-ˈnaȯnst\ *adj* : strongly marked : DECIDED

pro·nounce·ment \prə-ˈnaȯns-mənt\ *n* : a formal declaration of opinion: *also* : ANNOUNCEMENT

pron·to \ˈprän-ˌtō\ *adv* [Sp, fr. L *promptus* prompt] : QUICKLY

pro·nu·clear \ˈprō-ˈn(y)ü-klē-ər\ *adj* : supporting the use of nuclear-powered electric generating stations

pro·nun·cia·men·to \ˌprō-ˌnən-sē-ə-ˈment-ō\ *n, pl* **-tos** *or* **-toes** : PROCLAMATION, MANIFESTO

¹**proof** \ˈprüf\ *n* **1** : the evidence that compels acceptance by the mind of a truth or fact **2** : a process or operation that establishes validity or truth : TEST **3** : a trial impression (as from type) **4** : a trial print from a photographic negative **5** : alcoholic content (as of a beverage) indicated by a number that is twice the percent by volume of alcohol present ⟨whiskey of 90∼ is 45% alcohol⟩

²**proof** *adj* **1** : successful in resisting or repelling ⟨∼ against tampering⟩ **2** : of standard strength or quality or alcoholic content

proof·read \-ˌrēd\ *vb* : to read and mark corrections in (as a printer's proof) — **proof·read·er** *n*

¹**prop** \ˈpräp\ *n* : something that props

²**prop** *vb* **propped; prop·ping 1** : to support by placing something under or against ⟨∼ up a wall⟩ **2** : SUSTAIN, STRENGTHEN

³**prop** *n* : PROPERTY 4

⁴**prop** *n* : PROPELLER

⁵**prop** *abbr* **1** property **2** proposition **3** proprietor

pro·pa·gan·da \ˌpräp-ə-ˈgan-də, ˌprō-pə-\ *n* [NL, fr. *Congregatio de propaganda fide* Congregation for propagating the faith, organization established by Pope Gregory XV] : the spreading of ideas or information to further or damage a cause: *also* : ideas or allegations spread for such a purpose — **pro·pa·gan·dist** \-dəst\ *n*

pro·pa·gan·dize \-ˌdīz\ *vb* **-dized; -diz·ing** : to subject to or carry on propaganda

prop·a·gate \ˈpräp-ə-ˌgāt\ *vb* **-gat·ed; -gat·ing 1** : to reproduce or cause to reproduce biologically : MULTIPLY **2** : to cause to spread — **prop·a·ga·tion** \ˌpräp-ə-ˈgā-shən\ *n*

pro·pane \ˈprō-ˌpān\ *n* : a heavy flammable gas found in petroleum and natural gas and used as a fuel

pro·pel \prə-ˈpel\ *vb* **pro·pelled; pro·pelling 1** : to drive forward or onward **2** : to urge on : MOTIVATE *syn* push, shove, thrust, drive

pro·pel·lant *also* **pro·pel·lent** \-ˈpel-ənt\ *n* : something (as an explosive or fuel) that propels — **propellant** *or* **propellent** *adj*

pro·pel·ler \prə-ˈpel-ər\ *n* : a device consisting of a hub fitted with blades that is used to propel a vehicle (as a motorboat or an airplane)

pro·pen·si·ty \prə-ˈpen-sət-ē\ *n, pl* **-ties** : an often intense natural inclination or preference

¹**prop·er** \ˈpräp-ər\ *adj* **1** : referring to one individual only ⟨∼ noun⟩ **2** : belonging characteristically to a species or individual : PECULIAR **3** : very satisfactory : EXCELLENT **4** : strictly limited to a specified thing ⟨the city ∼⟩ **5** : CORRECT ⟨the ∼ way to proceed⟩ **6** : strictly decorous : GENTEEL **7** : marked by suitability or rightness ⟨∼ punishment⟩ *syn* meet, appropriate, fitting, seemly — **prop·er·ly** *adv*

²**proper** *n* : the parts of the Mass that vary according to the liturgical calendar

prop·er·tied \ˈpräp-ərt-ēd\ *adj* : owning property and esp. much property

prop·er·ty \ˈpräp-ərt-ē\ *n, pl* **-ties 1** : a quality peculiar to an individual or thing **2** : something owned: *esp* : a piece of real estate **3** : OWNERSHIP **4** : an article or object used in a play other than painted scenery and actor's costumes

proph·e·cy *also* **proph·e·sy** \ˈpräf-ə-sē\ *n, pl* **-cies** *also* **-sies 1** : an inspired utterance of a prophet **2** : PREDICTION

proph·e·sy \-ˌsī\ *vb* **-sied; -sy·ing 1** : to speak or utter by divine inspiration **2**

: PREDICT — **proph·e·si·er** \-ˌsī-(-ə)r\ n

proph·et \ˈpräf-ət\ n [ME *prophete*, fr. OF, fr. L *propheta*, fr. Gk *prophētēs*, fr. *pro* for + *phanai* to speak] 1 : one who utters divinely inspired revelations 2 : one who foretells future events

proph·et·ess \ˈpräf-ət-əs\ n : a woman who is a prophet

pro·phet·ic \prə-ˈfet-ik\ or **pro·phet·i·cal** \-i-kəl\ adj : of, relating to, or characteristic of a prophet or prophecy — **pro·phet·i·cal·ly** \-i-k(ə-)lē\ adv

¹**pro·phy·lac·tic** \ˌprō-fə-ˈlak-tik, ˌpräf-ə-\ adj 1 : preventing or guarding from disease 2 : PREVENTIVE

²**prophylactic** n : something (as a drug or device) that protects from disease

pro·phy·lax·is \-ˈlak-səs\ n, pl **-lax·es** \-ˈlak-ˌsēz\ : measures designed to preserve health and prevent the spread of disease

pro·pin·qui·ty \prə-ˈpiŋ-kwət-ē\ n 1 : KINSHIP 2 : nearness in place or time : PROXIMITY

pro·pi·ti·ate \prō-ˈpish-ē-ˌāt\ vb **-at·ed; -at·ing** : to gain or regain the favor of : APPEASE — **pro·pi·ti·a·tion** \-ˌpis(h)-ē-ˈā-shən\ n — **pro·pi·ti·a·to·ry** \-ˈpish-(ē-)ə-ˌtōr-ē\ adj

pro·pi·tious \prə-ˈpish-əs\ adj 1 : favorably disposed (~ deities) 2 : being of good omen (~ circumstances)

prop·man \ˈpräp-ˌman\ n : one who is in charge of theater or motion-picture stage properties

pro·po·nent \prə-ˈpō-nənt\ n : one who argues in favor of something

¹**pro·por·tion** \prə-ˈpōr-shən\ n 1 : the relation of one part to another or to the whole with respect to magnitude, quantity, or degree : RATIO 2 : BALANCE, SYMMETRY 3 : SHARE, QUOTA 4 : SIZE, DEGREE — **in proportion** : PROPORTIONAL

²**proportion** vb **-tioned; -tion·ing** \-sh(ə-)niŋ\ 1 : to adjust (a part or thing) in size relative to other parts or things 2 : to make the parts of harmonious

pro·por·tion·al \prə-ˈpōr-sh(ə-)nəl\ adj : corresponding in size, degree, or intensity; also : having the same or a constant ratio — **pro·por·tion·al·ly** \-ē\ adv

pro·por·tion·ate \prə-ˈpōr-sh(ə-)nət\ adj : PROPORTIONAL — **pro·por·tion·ate·ly** adv

pro·pose \prə-ˈpōz\ vb **pro·posed; pro·pos·ing** 1 : PLAN, INTEND (~s to buy a house) 2 : to make an offer of marriage 3 : to offer for consideration : SUGGEST (~ a policy) — **pro·pos·al** \-ˈpō-zəl\ n — **pro·pos·er** n

¹**prop·o·si·tion** \ˌpräp-ə-ˈzish-ən\ n 1 : something proposed for consideration : PROPOSAL; esp : a request for sexual intercourse 2 : a statement of something to be discussed, proved, or explained 3 : SITUATION, AFFAIR (a

tough ~) — **prop·o·si·tion·al** \-ˈzish-(ə-)nəl\ adj

²**proposition** vb **-tioned; -tion·ing** \-(ə-)niŋ\ : to make a proposal to; esp : to suggest sexual intercourse to

pro·pound \prə-ˈpaund\ vb : to set forth for consideration (~ a doctrine)

pro·pri·e·tary \prə-ˈprī-ə-ˌter-ē\ adj 1 : of, relating to, or characteristic of a proprietor (~ control) 2 : made and sold by one with the sole right to do so (~ medicines)

pro·pri·e·tor \prə-ˈprī-ət-ər\ n : OWNER — **pro·pri·e·tor·ship** n

pro·pri·e·tress \prə-ˈprī-ə-trəs\ n : a woman who is a proprietor

pro·pri·e·ty \prə-ˈprī-ət-ē\ n, pl **-eties** 1 : the standard of what is socially acceptable in conduct or speech 2 pl : the customs of polite society

pro·pul·sion \prə-ˈpəl-shən\ n 1 : the action or process of propelling 2 : something that propels — **pro·pul·sive** \-siv\ adj

pro ra·ta \prō-ˈrāt-ə, -ˈrät-\ adv : in proportion to the share of each : PROPORTIONATELY

pro·rate \ˈprō-ˈrāt\ vb **pro·rat·ed; pro·rat·ing** : to divide, distribute, or assess proportionately

pro·rogue \prə-ˈrōg\ vb **pro·rogued; pro·rogu·ing** : to suspend or end a session of (a legislative body) syn adjourn, dissolve, recess — **pro·ro·ga·tion** \ˌprōr-ō-ˈgā-shən\ n

pros pl of PRO

pro·sa·ic \prō-ˈzā-ik\ adj : lacking imagination or excitement : DULL

pro·sce·ni·um \prō-ˈsē-nē-əm\ n 1 : the part of a stage in front of the curtain 2 : the wall containing the arch that frames the stage

pro·scribe \prō-ˈskrīb\ vb **pro·scribed; pro·scrib·ing** 1 : OUTLAW 2 : to condemn or forbid as harmful — **pro·scrip·tion** \-ˈskrip-shən\ n

prose \ˈprōz\ n [ME, fr. MF, fr. L *prosa*, fr. fem. of *prorsus, prosus*, straightforward, being in prose, fr. *proversus*, pp. of *provertere* to turn forward] : the ordinary language people use in speaking or writing

pros·e·cute \ˈpräs-i-ˌkyüt\ vb **-cut·ed; -cut·ing** 1 : to follow to the end (~ an investigation) 2 : to seek legal punishment of (~ a forger) — **pros·e·cu·tion** \ˌpräs-i-ˈkyü-shən\ n — **pros·e·cu·tor** \ˈpräs-i-ˌkyüt-ər\ n

¹**pros·e·lyte** \ˈpräs-ə-ˌlīt\ n : a new convert to a religion, belief, or party — **pros·e·lyt·ism** \-ˌlīt-ˌiz-əm\ n

²**proselyte** vb **-lyt·ed; -lyt·ing** : PROSELYTIZE

pros·e·ly·tize \ˈpräs-(ə-)lə-ˌtīz\ vb **-tized; -tiz·ing** 1 : to induce someone to convert to one's faith 2 : to recruit someone to join one's party, institution, or cause

pros·o·dy \ˈpräs-əd-ē\ n, pl **-dies** : the study of versification and esp. of metrical structure

¹pros·pect \'präs-ˌpekt\ *n* **1** : an extensive view; *also* : OUTLOOK **2** : the act of looking forward **3** : a mental vision of something to come **4** : something that is awaited or expected : POSSIBILITY **5** : a potential buyer or customer; *also* : a likely candidate — **pro·spec·tive** \prə-'spek-tiv, 'präs-ˌpek-\ *adj* — **pro·spec·tive·ly** *adv*

²pros·pect \'präs-ˌpekt\ *vb* : to explore esp. for mineral deposits — **pros·pec·tor** \-ˌpek-tər, -'pek-\ *n*

pro·spec·tus \prə-'spek-təs\ *n* : a preliminary statement that describes an enterprise and is distributed to prospective buyers or participants

pros·per \'präs-pər\ *vb* **pros·pered; pros·per·ing** \-p(ə-)riŋ\ **2** : SUCCEED; *esp* : to achieve economic success

pros·per·i·ty \präs-'per-ət-ē\ *n* : thriving condition : SUCCESS; *esp* : economic well-being

pros·per·ous \'präs-p(ə-)rəs\ *adj* **1** : FAVORABLE (~ winds) **2** : marked by success or economic well-being ⟨a ~ business⟩

pros·tate \'präs-ˌtāt\ *also* **pros·tat·ic** \prä-'stat-ik\ *adj* : of, relating to, or being the prostate gland — **prostate** *n*

prostate gland *n* : a glandular body about the base of the male urethra that produces a secretion which is a major part of the fluid ejaculated during an orgasm

pros·ta·ti·tis \ˌpräs-tə-'tīt-əs\ *n* : inflammation of the prostate gland

pros·the·sis \präs-'thē-səs, 'präs-thə-\ *n, pl* **-the·ses** \-ˌsēz\ : an artificial replacement for a missing body part — **pros·thet·ic** \präs-'thet-ik\ *adj*

pros·thet·ics \-'thet-iks\ *n pl* : the surgical and dental specialties concerned with the artificial replacement of missing parts

¹pros·ti·tute \'präs-tə-ˌt(y)üt\ *vb* **-tut·ed; -tut·ing 1** : to offer indiscriminately for sexual intercourse esp. for money **2** : to devote to corrupt or unworthy purposes — **pros·ti·tu·tion** \ˌpräs-tə-'t(y)ü-shən\ *n*

²prostitute *n* : one who engages in promiscuous sexual intercourse for pay

¹pros·trate \'präs-ˌtrāt\ *adj* **1** : stretched out with face on the ground in adoration or submission **2** : lying flat **3** : completely overcome ⟨~ with a cold⟩

²prostrate \'präs-ˌtrāt\ *vb* **pros·trat·ed; pros·trat·ing 1** : to throw or put into a prostrate position **2** : to reduce to a weak or powerless condition — **pros·tra·tion** \präs-'trā-shən\ *n*

prosy \'prō-zē\ *adj* **pros·i·er; -est 1** : PROSAIC **2** : TEDIOUS

Prot *abbr* Protestant

prot·ac·tin·i·um \ˌprōt-ˌak-'tin-ē-əm\ *n* : a metallic radioactive element of relatively short life

pro·tag·o·nist \prō-'tag-ə-nəst\ *n* **1** : the principal character in a drama or story

2 : a spokesman for a cause : CHAMPION

pro·te·an \'prōt-ē-ən\ *adj* : able to assume different shapes or roles

pro·tect \prə-'tekt\ *vb* : to shield from injury : GUARD

pro·tec·tion \prə-'tek-shən\ *n* **1** : the act of protecting : the state of being protected **2** : one that protects ⟨wear a helmet as a ~⟩ **3** : the supervision or support of one that is smaller and weaker **4** : the freeing of producers from foreign competition in their home market by high duties on foreign competitive goods — **pro·tec·tive** \-'tek-tiv\ *adj*

pro·tec·tion·ist \-sh(ə-)nəst\ *n* : an advocate of government economic protection for domestic producers through restrictions on foreign competitors — **pro·tec·tion·ism** \-shə-ˌniz-əm\ *n*

pro·tec·tor \prə-'tek-tər\ *n* **1** : one that protects : GUARDIAN **2** : a device used to prevent injury : GUARD **3** : REGENT **1**

pro·tec·tor·ate \-t(ə-)rət\ *n* **1** : government by a protector **2** : the relationship of superior authority assumed by one state over a dependent one; *also* : the dependent political unit in such a relationship

pro·té·gé \'prōt-ə-ˌzhā\ *n* [F] : one who is protected, trained, or guided by an influential person

pro·tein \'prō-ˌtēn, 'prōt-ē-ən\ *n* [F *protéine*, fr. LGk *prōteios* primary, fr. Gk *prōtos* first] : any of numerous complex nitrogen-containing substances that consist of chains of amino acids, are present in all living matter, and are an essential part of the human diet

pro tem \prō-'tem\ *adv* : PRO TEMPORE

pro tem·po·re \prō-'tem-pə-rē\ *adv* [L] : for the time being

Pro·tero·zo·ic \ˌprät-ə-rə-'zō-ik, ˌprōt-\ *adj* : of, relating to, or being the era of geologic history between the Archeozoic and the Paleozoic and extending from about 1.4 billion years ago to about 620 million years ago — **Proterozoic** *n*

¹pro·test \'prō-ˌtest\ *n* **1** : the act of protesting; *esp* : an organized public demonstration of disapproval **2** : a complaint or objection against an idea, an act, or a course of action

²pro·test \prə-'test\ *vb* **1** : to assert positively : make solemn declaration of ⟨~s his innocence⟩ **2** : to object strongly : make a protest against ⟨~ a ruling⟩ — **prot·es·ta·tion** \ˌprät-əs-'tā-shən\ *n* — **pro·test·er** *or* **pro·tes·tor** \-ər\ *n*

Prot·es·tant \'prät-əs-tənt, **3** *also* prə-'tes-\ *n* **1** : a member or adherent of one of the Christian churches deriving from the Reformation **2** : a Christian not of a Catholic or Orthodox church **3** *not cap* : one who makes a protest

— **Prot·es·tant·ism**
\'prät-əs-tənt-ˌiz-əm\ *n*

pro·tha·la·mi·on \ˌprō-thə-'lā-mē-ən\ *or* **pro·tha·la·mi·um** \-mē-əm\ *n, pl* **-mia** \-mē-ə\ : a song in celebration of a marriage

pro·to·col \'prōt-ə-ˌkȯl\ *n* [MF *prothocole*, fr. ML *protocollum*, fr. LGk *prōtokollon* first sheet of a papyrus roll bearing data of manufacture, fr. Gk *prōtos* first + *kolla* glue] **1** : an original draft or record **2** : a preliminary memorandum of diplomatic negotiation **3** : a code of diplomatic or military etiquette

pro·ton \'prō-ˌtän\ *n* [Gk *prōton*, neut. of *prōtos* first] : a positively charged atomic particle present in all atomic nuclei

pro·to·plasm \'prōt-ə-ˌplaz-əm\ *n* : the complex colloidal largely protein substance of living plant and animal cells that is regarded as the only form of matter in which the vital phenomena are manifested — **pro·to·plas·mic** \ˌprōt-ə-'plaz-mik\ *adj*

pro·to·type \'prōt-ə-ˌtīp\ *n* : an original model : ARCHETYPE

pro·to·zo·an \ˌprōt-ə-'zō-ən\ *n* : any of a phylum or subkingdom of lower invertebrate animals that are not divided into cells or are considered as made up of a single cell

pro·tract \prō-'trakt\ *vb* : to prolong in time or space *syn* extend, lengthen, elongate, stretch

pro·trac·tor \-'trak-tər\ *n* : an instrument for drawing and measuring angles

pro·trude \prō-'trüd\ *vb* **pro·trud·ed; pro·trud·ing** : to stick out or cause to stick out : jut out — **pro·tru·sion** \-'trü-zhən\ *n*

pro·tu·ber·ance \prō-'t(y)ü-b-(ə-)rəns\ *n* : something that protrudes

pro·tu·ber·ant \-b(ə-)rənt\ *adj* : extending beyond the surrounding surface in a bulge

proud \'praud\ *adj* **1** : having or showing excessive self-esteem : HAUGHTY **2** : highly pleased : EXULTANT **3** : having proper self-respect (too ~ to beg) **4** : GLORIOUS (a ~ occasion) **5** : SPIRITED (a ~ steed) *syn* arrogant, insolent, overbearing, disdainful — **proud·ly** *adv*

prov *abbr* **1** province; provincial **2** provisional

Prov *abbr* Proverbs

prove \'prüv\ *vb* **proved; proved** *or* **prov·en** \'prü-vən\; **prov·ing** \'prü-viŋ\ **1** : to test by experiment or by a standard **2** : to establish the truth of by argument or evidence **3** : to show to be correct, valid, or genuine **4** : to turn out esp. after trial or test (the car *proved* to be a good choice) — **prov·able** \'prü-və-bəl\ *adj*

prov·e·nance \'präv-ə-nəns\ *n* : ORIGIN, SOURCE

Pro·ven·çal \ˌprō-ˌvän-'säl, ˌpräv-ən-\ *n* **1** : a native or inhabitant of Provence **2** : a Romance language spoken in southeastern France — **Provençal** *adj*

prov·en·der \'präv-ən-dər\ *n* **1** : dry food for domestic animals : FEED **2** : FOOD, VICTUALS

pro·ve·nience \prə-'vē-nyəns\ *n* : ORIGIN, SOURCE

prov·erb \'präv-ˌərb\ *n* : a pithy popular saying : ADAGE

pro·ver·bi·al \prə-'vər-bē-əl\ *adj* **1** : of, relating to, or resembling a proverb : commonly spoken of

Proverbs *n* — see BIBLE table

pro·vide \prə-'vīd\ *vb* **pro·vid·ed; pro·vid·ing** [ME *providen*, fr. L *providēre*, lit., to see ahead, fr. *pro*- forward + *vidēre* to see] **1** : to take measures beforehand (~ against inflation) **2** : to make a proviso or stipulation **3** : to supply what is needed (~ for a family) **4** : EQUIP **5** : to supply for use : YIELD — **pro·vid·er** *n*

pro·vid·ed \prə-'vīd-əd\ *conj* : on condition that : IF

prov·i·dence \'präv-əd-əns\ *n* **1** *often cap* : divine guidance or care **2** *cap* : GOD **1 3** : the quality or state of being provident

prov·i·dent \-əd-ənt\ *adj* **1** : making provision for the future : PRUDENT **2** : FRUGAL — **prov·i·dent·ly** *adv*

prov·i·den·tial \ˌpräv-ə-'den-chəl\ *adj* **1** : of, relating to, or determined by Providence **2** : OPPORTUNE, LUCKY

prov·ince \'präv-əns\ *n* **1** : an administrative district or division of a country **2** *pl* : all of a country except the metropolis **3** : proper business or scope : SPHERE

pro·vin·cial \prə-'vin-chəl\ *adj* **1** : of or relating to a province **2** : confined to a region : NARROW (~ ideas) — **pro·vin·cial·ism** \-ˌiz-əm\ *n*

proving ground *n* : a place for scientific experimentation or testing

¹pro·vi·sion \prə-'vizh-ən\ *n* **1** : the act or process of providing; *also* : a measure taken beforehand **2** : a stock of needed supplies; *esp* : a stock of food — usu. used in pl. **3** : PROVISO

²provision *vb* **-sioned; -sion·ing** \-'vizh-(ə-)niŋ\ : to supply with provisions

pro·vi·sion·al \-'vizh-(ə-)nəl\ *adj* : provided for a temporary need : CONDITIONAL

pro·vi·so \prə-'vī-zō\ *n, pl* **-sos** *or* **-soes** [ME, fr. ML *proviso quod* provided that] : an article or clause that introduces a condition : STIPULATION

prov·o·ca·tion \ˌpräv-ə-'kā-shən\ *n* **1** : the act of provoking **2** : something that provokes

pro·voke \prə-'vōk\ *vb* **pro·voked; pro·vok·ing** **1** : to incite to anger : INCENSE **2** : to call forth : EVOKE (a sally that *provoked* laughter) **3** : to stir up on purpose (~ an argument) *syn* irritate, exasperate, aggravate, inflame, rile, pique — **pro·vo·ca·tive** \prə-'väk-ət-iv\ adj

pro·vo·lo·ne \‚prō-və-'lō-nē\ n : a hard smooth often smoked Italian cheese that is made from heated and kneaded curd

pro·vost \'prō-‚vōst, 'präv-əst\ n : a high official : DIGNITARY; esp : a high-ranking university administrative officer

provost marshal \‚prō-‚vō-'mär-shəl\ : an officer who supervises the military police of a command

prow \'prau̇\ n : the bow of a ship

prow·ess \'prau̇-əs\ n 1 : military valor and skill 2 : extraordinary ability

prowl \'prau̇l\ vb : to roam about stealthily — **prowl** n — **prowl·er** n

prowl car n : SQUAD CAR

prox·i·mal \'präk-sə-məl\ adj 1 : next to or nearest the point of attachment or origin; esp : located toward the center of the body 2 : of, relating to, or being the mesial and distal surfaces of a tooth

prox·i·mate \'präk-sə-mət\ adj 1 : very near 2 : DIRECT ⟨the ~ cause⟩

prox·im·i·ty \präk-'sim-ət-ē\ n : NEARNESS

prox·i·mo \'präk-sə-‚mō\ adj [L proximo mense in the next month] : of or occurring in the next month after the present

proxy \'präk-sē\ n, pl **prox·ies** : the authority or power to act for another; also : a document giving such authorization — **proxy** adj

prude \'prüd\ n : one who shows or affects extreme modesty — **prud·ery** \'prüd-ə-rē\ n — **prud·ish** \'prüd-ish\ adj

pru·dent \'prüd-²nt\ adj 1 : shrewd in the management of practical affairs 2 : CAUTIOUS, DISCREET 3 : PROVIDENT, FRUGAL syn judicious, foresighted, sensible, sane — **pru·dence** \-²ns\ n — **pru·den·tial** \prü-'den-chəl\ adj — **pru·dent·ly** \'prüd-²nt-lē\ adv

¹**prune** \'prün\ n : a dried plum

²**prune** vb **pruned; prun·ing** : to cut off unwanted parts (as of a tree)

pru·ri·ent \'prür-ē-ənt\ adj : LASCIVIOUS; also : exciting to lasciviousness — **pru·ri·ence** \-ē-əns\ n

¹**pry** \'prī\ vb **pried; pry·ing** : to look closely or inquisitively; esp : SNOOP

²**pry** vb **pried; pry·ing** : to raise, move, or pull apart with a pry or lever 2 : to detach or open with difficulty

³**pry** n : a tool for prying

Ps or **Psa** abbr Psalms

PS abbr 1 [L postscriptum] postscript 2 public school

psalm \'säm, 'sälm\ n, often cap [ME, fr. OE psealm, fr. LL psalmus, fr. Gk psalmos, lit., twanging of a harp, fr. psallein to pluck, play a stringed instrument] : a sacred song or poem; esp : one of the hymns collected in the Book of Psalms — **psalm·ist** n

psalm·o·dy \'säm-əd-ē, 'säl-məd-\ n 1

: the singing of psalms in worship 2 : a collection of psalms

Psalms n — see BIBLE table

Psal·ter \'sȯl-tər\ n : the Book of Psalms; also : a collection of the Psalms arranged for devotional use

pseud abbr pseudonym; pseudonymous

pseu·do \'süd-ō\ adj : SPURIOUS, SHAM

pseud·onym \'süd-²n-‚im\ n : a fictitious name — **pseud·on·y·mous** \sü-'dän-ə-məs\ adj

PSG abbr platoon sergeant

psi abbr pounds per square inch

psi particle \'sī-, 'psī-\ n [psi (Greek letter)] : J PARTICLE

pso·ri·a·sis \sə-'rī-ə-səs\ n : a chronic skin disease characterized by red patches covered with white scales

PST abbr Pacific standard time

¹**psych** also **psyche** \'sīk\ vb **psyched; psych·ing** 1 : OUTGUESS; also : to analyze beforehand 2 : INTIMIDATE; also : to prepare oneself psychologically ⟨get psyched up for the game⟩

²**psych** abbr psychology

psy·che \'sī-kē\ n : SOUL, SELF; also : MIND

psy·che·del·ic \‚sī-kə-'del-ik\ adj 1 : of, relating to, or causing abnormal psychic effects ⟨~ drugs⟩ 2 : relating to the taking of psychedelic drugs ⟨~ experience⟩ 3 : imitating, suggestive of, or reproducing the effects of psychedelic drugs ⟨~ art⟩ ⟨~ colors⟩ — **psychedelic** n — **psy·che·del·i·cal·ly** \-i-k(ə-)lē\ adv

psy·chi·a·try \sə-'kī-ə-trē, sī-\ n : a branch of medicine dealing with mental disorders — **psy·chi·at·ric** \‚sī-kē-'a-trik\ adj — **psy·chi·a·trist** \sə-'kī-ə-trəst, sī-\ n

¹**psy·chic** \'sī-kik\ also **psy·chi·cal** \-ki-kəl\ adj 1 : of or relating to the psyche 2 : lying outside the sphere of physical science 3 : sensitive to nonphysical or supernatural forces — **psy·chi·cal·ly** \-k(ə-)lē\ adv

²**psychic** n : a person apparently sensitive to nonphysical forces; also : MEDIUM 6

psychic energizer n : ANTIDEPRESSANT

psy·cho \'sī-kō\ n, pl **psychos** : a mentally disturbed person — **psycho** adj

psy·cho·ac·tive \‚sī-kō-'ak-tiv\ adj : affecting the mind or behavior

psy·cho·anal·y·sis \‚sī-kō-ə-'nal-ə-səs\ n : a method of dealing with psychic disorders by having the patient talk freely about himself and esp. about dreams, problems, and early childhood memories and experiences — **psy·cho·an·a·lyst** \-'an-²l-əst\ n — **psy·cho·an·a·lyt·ic** \-‚an-²l-'it-ik\ adj — **psy·cho·an·a·lyze** \-'an-²l-‚īz\ vb

psy·cho·dra·ma \‚sī-kə-'dräm-ə, -'dram-\ n : an extemporized dramatization designed esp. to afford catharsis for one or more of the participants from whose life history the plot is abstracted

psy·cho·gen·ic \-ˈjen·ik\ *adj* : originating in the mind or in mental or emotional conflict

psychol *abbr* psychologist; psychology

psy·chol·o·gy \sī-ˈkäl-ə-jē\ *n, pl* **-gies** 1 : the science of mind and behavior 2 : the mental and behavioral characteristics of an individual or group — **psy·cho·log·i·cal** \ˌsī-kə-ˈläj-i-kəl\ *adj* — **psy·cho·log·i·cal·ly** \-i-k(ə-)lē\ *adv* — **psy·chol·o·gist** \sī-ˈkäl-ə-jəst\ *n*

psy·cho·path \ˈsī-kə-ˌpath\ *n* : a mentally ill or unstable person; *esp* : one who has a poorly balanced personality and does not feel guilty about not living up to normal moral and social responsibilities — **psy·cho·path·ic** \ˌsī-kə-ˈpath-ik\ *adj*

psy·cho·sex·u·al \ˌsī-kō-ˈsek-sh(ə-w)əl\ *adj* 1 : of or relating to the mental, emotional, and behavioral aspects of sexual development 2 : of or relating to the physiological psychology of sex

psy·cho·sis \sī-ˈkō-səs\ *n, pl* **-cho·ses** \-ˌsēz\ : a serious mental illness (as schizophrenia) characterized by defective or lost contact with reality — **psy·chot·ic** \-ˈkät-ik\ *adj or n*

psy·cho·so·mat·ic \ˌsī-kə-sə-ˈmat-ik\ *adj* : of, relating to, or caused by the interaction of mental and bodily phenomena (~ ulcers)

psy·cho·ther·a·py \ˌsī-kō-ˈther-ə-pē\ *n* : treatment of mental or emotional disorder or of related bodily ills by psychological means — **psy·cho·ther·a·pist** \-pəst\ *n*

psy·cho·tro·pic \ˌsī-kə-ˈtrō-pik\ *adj* : acting on the mind (~ drugs)

pt *abbr* 1 part 2 payment 3 pint 4 point 5 port

Pt *symbol* platinum

PT *abbr* 1 Pacific time 2 physical therapy 3 physical training

PTA *abbr* Parent-Teacher Association

ptar·mi·gan \ˈtär-mi-gən\ *n, pl* **-gan** or **-gans** : any of various grouses of northern regions with completely feathered feet

PT boat \(ˈ)pē-ˈtē-\ *n* [*patrol torpedo*] : a fast motorboat usu. armed with torpedos, machine guns, and depth charges

pte *abbr, Brit* private

ptg *abbr* printing

PTO *abbr* 1 Parent-Teacher Organization 2 please turn over

pto·maine \ˈtō-ˌmān\ *n* : any of various chemical substances formed by bacteria in decaying matter (as meat)

ptomaine poisoning *n* : food poisoning caused usu. by bacteria or their products

PTV *abbr* public television

Pu *symbol* plutonium

¹**pub** \ˈpəb\ *n, chiefly Brit* : PUBLIC HOUSE, TAVERN

²**pub** *abbr* 1 public 2 publication 3 published; publisher; publishing

pu·ber·ty \ˈpyü-bərt-ē\ *n* : the condition of being or period of becoming first capable of reproducing sexually — **pu·ber·tal** \-bərt-ᵊl\ *adj*

pu·bes \ˈpyü-bēz\ *n, pl* **pubes** 1 : the hair that appears upon the lower middle region of the abdomen at puberty 2 : the pubic region

pu·bes·cence \pyü-ˈbes-ᵊns\ *n* 1 : the quality or state of being pubescent 2 : a pubescent covering or surface

pu·bes·cent \-ᵊnt\ *adj* 1 : arriving at or having reached puberty 2 : covered with fine soft short hairs

pu·bic \ˈpyü-bik\ *adj* : of, relating to, or situated near the pubes or the pubis

pu·bis \ˈpyü-bəs\, *n, pl* **pubes** \-bēz\ : the ventral and anterior of the three principal bones composing either half of the pelvis

publ *abbr* 1 publication 2 published; publisher

¹**pub·lic** \ˈpəb-lik\ *adj* 1 : of, relating to, or affecting the people as a whole (~ opinion) 2 : CIVIC, GOVERNMENTAL (~ expenditures) 3 : of, relating to, or serving the community (~ officials) 4 : not private : SOCIAL (~ morality) 5 : open to all (~ library) 6 : exposed to general view (the story became ~) 7 : well known : PROMINENT (~ figures) — **pub·lic·ly** *adv*

²**public** *n* 1 : the people as a whole : POPULACE 2 : a group of people having common interests (wrote for his ~)

pub·li·can \ˈpəb-li-kən\ *n* 1 : a Jewish tax collector for the ancient Romans 2 *chiefly Brit* : the licensee of a public house

pub·li·ca·tion \ˌpəb-lə-ˈkā-shən\ *n* 1 : the act or process of publishing 2 : a published work

public house *n* 1 : INN 2 *chiefly Brit* : a licensed saloon or bar

pub·li·cist \ˈpəb-lə-səst\ *n* : one that publicizes; *esp* : PRESS AGENT

pub·lic·i·ty \(ˌ)pə-ˈblis-ət-ē\ *n* 1 : information with news value issued to gain public attention or support 2 : public attention or acclaim

pub·li·cize \ˈpəb-lə-ˌsīz\ *vb* **-cized; -ciz·ing** : to give publicity to

public relations *n sing or pl* : the business of fostering public goodwill toward a person, firm, or institution; *also* : the degree of goodwill and understanding achieved

public school *n* 1 : an endowed secondary boarding school in Great Britain offering a classical curriculum and preparation for the universities or public service 2 : a free tax-supported school controlled by a local governmental authority

pub·lic–spir·it·ed \ˌpəb-lik-ˈspir-ət-əd\ *adj* : motivated by devotion to the general or national welfare

public television *n* : television that provides cultural, informational, and instructive programs without commercials

pub·lish \ˈpəb-lish\ *vb* 1 : to make generally known : announce publicly

2 : to produce or release literature, information, musical scores or sometimes recordings, or art for sale to the public — **pub·lish·er** n

¹**puck** \'pək\ n : a mischievous sprite — **puck·ish** adj

²**puck** n : a disk used in ice hockey

¹**puck·er** \'pək-ər\ vb **puck·ered; puck·er·ing** \-(ə-)riŋ\ : to contract into folds or wrinkles

²**pucker** n : FOLD, WRINKLE

pud·ding \'pùd-iŋ\ n : a soft, spongy, or thick creamy dessert

pud·dle \'pəd-ᵊl\ n : a very small pool of usu. dirty or muddy water

pu·den·dum \pyü-'den-dəm\ n, pl **-da** \-də\ [NL, deriv. of L pudēre to be ashamed] : the human external genital organs esp. of a woman

pudgy \'pəj-ē\ adj **pudg·i·er; -est** : being short and plump : CHUBBY

pueb·lo \pù-'eb-lō, 'pweb-\ n, pl **-los** [Sp, village, lit., people, fr. L populus] 1 : an American Indian village of Arizona or New Mexico consisting of flat-roofed stone or adobe houses 2 cap : a member of an American Indian people of the southwestern U.S.

pu·er·ile \'pyù-ə-rəl\ adj : CHILDISH, SILLY — **pu·er·il·i·ty** \,pyü-ə-'ril-ət-ē\ n

pu·er·per·al \pyù-'ər-p(ə-)rəl\ adj : of, relating to, or occurring during childbirth or the period immediately following ⟨∼ infection⟩

puerperal fever n : an abnormal condition that results from infection of the placental site following childbirth or abortion

Puer·to Ri·can \,pòrt-ə-'rē-kən, ,pwert-\ n : a native or inhabitant of Puerto Rico — **Puerto Rican** adj

¹**puff** \'pəf\ vb 1 : to blow in short gusts 2 : PANT 3 : to emit small whiffs or clouds 4 : BLUSTER, BRAG 5 : INFLATE, SWELL 6 : to make proud or conceited 7 : to praise extravagantly

²**puff** n 1 : a short discharge (as of air or smoke); also : a slight explosive sound accompanying it 2 : a light fluffy pastry 3 : a slight swelling 4 : a fluffy mass; esp : a small pad for applying cosmetic powder 5 : a laudatory notice or review — **puffy** adj

puff·ball \'pəf-,bòl\ n : any of various globe-shaped and often edible fungi

puf·fin \'pəf-ən\ n : any of several seabirds having a short neck and a red-tipped triangular bill

¹**pug** \'pəg\ n 1 : any of a breed of small stocky short-haired dogs 2 : a close coil of hair

²**pug** n : BOXER

pu·gi·lism \'pyü-jə-,liz-əm\ n : BOXING — **pu·gi·list** \-ləst\ n — **pu·gi·lis·tic** \,pyü-jə-'lis-tik\ adj

pug·na·cious \,pəg-'nā-shəs\ adj : fond of fighting : COMBATIVE **syn** belligerent, quarrelsome, bellicose, contentious, truculent — **pug·nac·i·ty** \-'nas-ət-ē\ n

puis·sance \'pwis-ᵊns, 'pyü-ə-səns\ n

: POWER, STRENGTH — **puis·sant** \-ᵊnt, -sənt\ adj

puke \'pyük\ vb **puked; puk·ing** : VOMIT — **puke** n

puk·ka \'pək-ə\ adj [Hindi pakkā cooked, ripe, solid, fr. Skt pakva] : GENUINE, AUTHENTIC; also : FIRST-CLASS, COMPLETE

pul \'pül\ n, pl **puls** \'pülz\ or **pul** — see afghani at MONEY table

pu·la \'p(y)ü-lə\ n, pl **pula** — see MONEY table

pul·chri·tude \'pəl-krə-,t(y)üd\ n : BEAUTY — **pul·chri·tu·di·nous** \,pəl-krə-'t(y)üd-(ᵊ-)nəs\ adj

pule \'pyül\ vb **puled; pul·ing** : WHINE, WHIMPER

¹**pull** \'pùl\ vb 1 : PLUCK; also : EXTRACT ⟨∼ a tooth⟩ 2 : to exert force so as to draw (something) toward the force; also : MOVE ⟨∼ out of a driveway⟩ 3 : STRETCH, STRAIN ⟨∼ a tendon⟩ 4 : to draw apart : TEAR 5 : to make (as a proof) by printing 6 : REMOVE 7 : DRAW ⟨∼ a gun⟩ 8 : to carry out esp. with daring ⟨∼ a robbery⟩ 9 : to be guilty of : PERPETRATE 10 : ATTRACT 11 : to express strong sympathy — **pull·er** n

²**pull** n 1 : the act or an instance of pulling 2 : the effort expended in moving 3 : ADVANTAGE; esp : special influence 4 : a device for pulling something or for operating by pulling 5 : a force that attracts or compels

pull·back \'pùl-,bak\ n : an orderly withdrawal of troops

pul·let \'pùl-ət\ n : a young hen esp. of the domestic chicken when less than a year old

pul·ley \'pùl-ē\ n, pl **pulleys** 1 : a wheel with a grooved rim that forms part of a tackle for hoisting or for changing the direction of a force 2 : a wheel used to transmit power by means of a band, belt, rope, or chain

Pull·man \'pùl-mən\ n : a railroad passenger car with comfortable furnishings esp. for night travel

pull off vb : to accomplish successfully

pull·out \'pùl-,aùt\ n : PULLBACK

pull·over \,pùl-,ō-vər\ adj : put on by being pulled over the head ⟨∼ sweater⟩ — **pull·over** \'pùl-,ō-vər\ n

pull–up \'pùl-,əp\ n : CHIN-UP

pull up vb : to bring or come to a halt : STOP

pul·mo·nary \'pùl-mə-,ner-ē, 'pəl-\ adj : of, relating to, or carried on by the lungs (the ∼ circulation)

pul·mo·tor \-,mōt-ər\ n : an apparatus for pumping oxygen or air into and out of the lungs

pulp \'pəlp\ n 1 : the soft juicy or fleshy part of a fruit or vegetable 2 : a soft moist mass 3 : the soft sensitive tissue that fills the central cavity of a tooth 4 : a material (as from wood or rags) used in making paper 5 : a magazine using rough-surfaced paper and often dealing with sensational material — **pulpy** adj

pul·pit \\'pu̇l-ˌpit\\ n : a raised platform or high reading desk used in preaching or conducting a worship service

pulp·wood \\'pəlp-ˌwu̇d\\ n : wood (as of aspen or pine) used in making pulp for paper

pul·sar \\'pəl-ˌsär\\ n : a celestial source of pulsating electromagnetic radiation (as radio waves)

pul·sate \\'pəl-ˌsāt\\ vb **pul·sat·ed; pul·sat·ing** : to expand and contract rhythmically : BEAT — **pul·sa·tion** \\ˌpəl-'sā-shən\\ n

pulse \\'pəls\\ n 1 : the regular throbbing in the arteries caused by the contractions of the heart 2 : a brief change in electrical current or voltage — **pulse** vb

pul·ver·ize \\'pəl-və-ˌrīz\\ vb **-ized; -iz·ing** 1 : to reduce (as by crushing or grinding) or be reduced to very small particles 2 : DEMOLISH

pu·ma \\'p(y)ü-mə\\ n, pl **pumas** also **puma** : COUGAR

pum·ice \\'pəm-əs\\ n : a light porous volcanic glass used esp. for smoothing and polishing

pum·mel \\'pəm-əl\\ vb **-meled** also **-melled; -mel·ing** also **-mel·ling** \\-(ə-)liŋ\\ : POUND, BEAT

¹pump \\'pəmp\\ n : a device for raising, transferring, or compressing fluids esp. by suction or pressure

²pump vb 1 : to raise (as water) with a pump 2 : to draw water or air from by means of a pump; also : to fill by means of a pump ⟨~ up a tire⟩ 3 : to force or propel in the manner of a pump — **pump·er** n

³pump n : a low shoe that grips the foot chiefly at the toe and heel

pum·per·nick·el \\'pəm-pər-ˌnik-əl\\ n : a dark coarse somewhat sour rye bread

pump·kin \\'pəm(p)-kən, 'pəŋ-kən\\ n : the large usu. orange fruit of a vine of the gourd family that is widely used as food; also : this vine

pun \\'pən\\ n : the humorous use of a word in a way that suggests two interpretations — **pun** vb

¹punch \\'pənch\\ vb 1 : PROD, POKE; also : DRIVE, HERD ⟨~ing cattle⟩ 2 : to strike with the fist 3 : to emboss, perforate, or make with a punch — **punch·er** n

²punch n 1 : a quick blow with or as if with the fist 2 : effective energy or forcefulness

³punch n : a tool for piercing, stamping, cutting, or forming

⁴punch n [perh. fr. Hindi pāc five, fr. Skt pañca: fr. the number of ingredients] : a drink usu. composed of wine or alcoholic liquor and nonalcoholic beverages; also : a drink composed of nonalcoholic beverages (as fruit juices)

punch card n : a card with holes punched in particular positions to represent data

pun·cheon \\'pən-chən\\ n : a large cask

punch line n : the sentence or phrase in a joke that makes the point

punc·til·io \\ˌpəŋk-'til-ē-ˌō\\ n, pl **-i·os** 1 : a nice detail of conduct in a ceremony or in observance of a code 2 : careful observance of forms (as in social conduct)

punc·til·i·ous \\ˌpəŋk-'til-ē-əs\\ adj : marked by precise accordance with codes or conventions syn meticulous, scrupulous, careful, punctual

punc·tu·al \\'pəŋk-chə-(wə)l\\ adj : acting or habitually acting at an appointed time : PROMPT — **punc·tu·al·i·ty** \\ˌpəŋk-chə-'wal-ət-ē\\ n — **punc·tu·al·ly** \\'pəŋk-chə-(wə)-lē\\ adv

punc·tu·ate \\'pəŋk-chə-ˌwāt\\ vb **-at·ed; -at·ing** 1 : to mark or divide (written matter) with punctuation marks 2 : to break into at intervals 3 : EMPHASIZE

punc·tu·a·tion \\ˌpəŋk-chə-'wā-shən\\ n : the act, practice, or system of inserting standardized marks in written matter to clarify the meaning and separate structural units

¹punc·ture \\'pəŋk-chər\\ n 1 : an act of puncturing 2 : a small hole made by puncturing

²puncture vb **punc·tured; punc·tur·ing** 1 : to make a hole in : PIERCE 2 : to make useless as if by a puncture

pun·dit \\'pən-dət\\ n 1 : a learned person : TEACHER 2 : AUTHORITY

pun·gent \\'pən-jənt\\ adj 1 : having a sharp incisive quality : CAUSTIC ⟨a ~ editorial⟩ 2 : causing a sharp or irritating sensation; esp : ACRID ⟨~ smell of burning leaves⟩ — **pun·gen·cy** \\-jən-sē\\ n — **pun·gent·ly** adv

pun·ish \\'pən-ish\\ vb 1 : to impose a penalty on for a fault or crime ⟨~ an offender⟩ 2 : to inflict a penalty for ⟨~ treason with death⟩ 3 : to inflict injury on : HURT syn chastise, castigate, chasten, discipline, correct — **pun·ish·able** adj

pun·ish·ment \\-mənt\\ n 1 : retributive suffering, pain, or loss : PENALTY 2 : rough treatment

pu·ni·tive \\'pyü-nət-iv\\ adj : inflicting, involving, or aiming at punishment

¹punk \\'pəŋk\\ n 1 : a young inexperienced person 2 : a petty hoodlum

²punk adj : very poor : INFERIOR

³punk n : dry crumbly wood useful for tinder; also : a substance made from fungi for use as tinder

pun·kin \\'pəŋ-kən\\ var of PUMPKIN

pun·ster \\'pən-stər\\ n : one who is given to punning

¹punt \\'pənt\\ n : a long narrow flat-bottomed boat with square ends

²punt vb : to propel (as a punt) with a pole

³punt vb : to kick a football or soccer ball dropped from the hands before it touches the ground

⁴punt *n* : the act or an instance of punting a ball

pu·ny \'pyü-nē\ *adj* **pu·ni·er; -est** [MF *puisné* younger, lit., born afterward, fr. *puis* afterward (fr. L *post*) + *né* born, fr. L *natus*] : slight in power, size, or importance : WEAK

pup \'pəp\ *n* : a young dog; *also* : one of the young of some other animals

pu·pa \'pyü-pə\ *n, pl* **pu·pae** \-(ˌ)pē\ *or* **pupas** [NL, fr. L *pupa* girl, doll] : a form of some insects (as a bee, moth, or beetle) that occurs between the larva and the adult and is usu. enclosed in a cocoon or case — **pu·pal** \-pəl\ *adj*

¹pu·pil \'pyü-pəl\ *n* **1** : a child or young person in school or in the charge of a tutor **2** : DISCIPLE

²pupil *n* : the dark central opening of the iris of the eye

pup·pet \'pəp-ət\ *n* [ME *popet*, fr. MF deriv. of L *pupa*] **1** : a small figure of a person or animal moved by hand or by strings or wires **2** : DOLL **3** : one whose acts are controlled by an outside force

pup·pe·teer \ˌpəp-ə-'tiər\ *n* : one who manipulates puppets

pup·py \'pəp-ē\ *n, pl* **puppies** : a young dog

pur·blind \'pər-ˌblīnd\ *adj* **1** : partly blind **2** : lacking in insight : OBTUSE

¹pur·chase \'pər-chəs\ *vb* **pur·chased; pur·chas·ing** : to obtain by paying money or its equivalent : BUY — **pur·chas·er** *n*

²purchase *n* **1** : an act or instance of purchasing **2** : something purchased **3** : a secure hold or grasp; *also* : advantageous leverage

pur·dah \'pərd-ə\ *n* : seclusion of women from public observation among Muslims and some Hindus esp. in India

pure \'pyur\ *adj* **pur·er; pur·est 1** : unmixed with any other matter : free from taint (~ gold) (~ water) **2** : SHEER, ABSOLUTE (~ nonsense) **3** : ABSTRACT, THEORETICAL (~ mathematics) **4** : free from what vitiates, weakens, or pollutes (speaks a ~ French) **5** : free from moral fault : INNOCENT **6** : CHASTE, CONTINENT — **pure·ly** *adv*

pure·blood·ed \-'bləd-əd\ *or* **pure·blood** *adj* : of unmixed ancestry : PUREBRED — **pure·blood** *n*

pure·bred \-'bred\ *adj* : bred from members of a recognized breed, strain, or kind without crossbreeding over many generations — **pure·bred** \-ˌbred\ *n*

¹pu·ree \pyu̇-'rā, -'rē\ *n* [F, fr. MF, fr. fem. of *puré*, pp of *purer* to purify, strain, fr. L *purare* to purify] : a paste or thick liquid suspension usu. produced by rubbing cooked food through a sieve; *also* : a thick soup having vegetables so prepared as a base

²puree *vb* **pu·reed; pu·ree·ing** : to make a puree of

pur·ga·tion \ˌpər-'gā-shən\ *n* : the act or result of purging

¹pur·ga·tive \'pər-gət-iv\ *adj* : purging or tending to purge; *also* : being a purgative

²purgative *n* : a strong laxative : CATHARTIC

pur·ga·to·ry \'pər-gə-ˌtōr-ē\ *n, pl* **-ries 1** : an intermediate state after death for expiatory purification **2** : a place or state of temporary punishment — **pur·ga·tor·i·al** \ˌpər-gə-'tōr-ē-əl\ *adj*

¹purge \'pərj\ *vb* **purged; purg·ing 1** : to cleanse or purify esp. from sin **2** : to have or cause strong and usu. repeated emptying of the bowels **3** : to rid (as a political party) by a purge

²purge *n* **1** : something that purges; *esp* : PURGATIVE **2** : an act or result of purging; *esp* : a ridding of persons regarded as treacherous or disloyal

pu·ri·fy \'pyur-ə-ˌfī\ *vb* **-fied; -fy·ing** : to make or become pure — **pu·ri·fi·ca·tion** \ˌpyur-ə-fə-'kā-shən\ *n* — **pu·rif·i·ca·to·ry** \pyu̇-'rif-i-kə-ˌtōr-ē\ *adj* — **pu·ri·fi·er** \-ˌfī(-ə)r\ *n*

Pu·rim \'pur-(ˌ)im\ *n* : a Jewish holiday celebrated in February or March in commemoration of the deliverance of the Jews from the massacre plotted by Haman

pu·rine \'pyur-ˌēn\ *n* **1** : a base that is the parent of compounds of the uric-acid group **2** : a derivative of purine; *esp* : a base (as adenine or guanine) that is a constituent of DNA or RNA

pu·rism \'pyur-ˌiz-əm\ *n* : rigid adherence to or insistence on purity or nicety esp. in use of words — **pur·ist** \-əst\ *n*

pu·ri·tan \'pyur-ət-ᵊn\ *n* **1** *cap* : a member of a 16th and 17th century Protestant group in England and New England opposing the ceremonies and government of the Church of England **2** : one who practices or preaches a stricter or professedly purer moral code than that which prevails — **pu·ri·tan·i·cal** \ˌpyur-ə-'tan-i-kəl\ *adj*

pu·ri·ty \'pyur-ət-ē\ *n* : the quality or state of being pure

¹purl \'pərl\ *vb* : to knit in purl stitch

²purl *n* : a stitch in knitting

³purl *n* : a gentle murmur or movement (as of purling water)

⁴purl *vb* **1** : EDDY, SWIRL **2** : to make a soft murmuring sound

pur·lieu \'pərl-(y)ü\ *n* **1** : an outlying district : SUBURB **2** *pl* : ENVIRONS

pur·loin \(ˌ)pər-'lȯin, 'pər-ˌlȯin\ *vb* : to appropriate wrongfully : FILCH

pur·ple \'pər-pəl\ *adj* **pur·pler** \-p(ə-)lər\; **pur·plest** \-p(ə-)ləst\ **1** : of the color purple **2** : highly rhetorical (a ~ passage) **3** : PROFANE (~ language) — **pur·plish** \'pər-p(ə-)lish\ *adj*

purple *n* **1** : a bluish red color **2** : a purple robe emblematic esp. of regal rank or authority

¹**pur·port** \'pər-ˌpōrt\ *n* : meaning conveyed or implied; *also* : GIST

²**pur·port** \(ˌ)pər-'pōrt\ *vb* : to convey or profess outwardly as the meaning or intention : CLAIM — **pur·port·ed·ly** \-əd-lē\ *adv*

¹**pur·pose** \'pər-pəs\ *n* 1 : an object or result aimed at : INTENTION 2 : RESOLUTION, DETERMINATION — **pur·pose·ful** \-fəl\ *adj* — **pur·pose·ful·ly** \-ē\ *adv* — **pur·pose·less** *adj* — **pur·pose·ly** *adv*

²**purpose** *vb* **pur·posed; pur·pos·ing** : to propose as an aim to oneself

purr \'pər\ *n* : a low murmur typical of a contented cat — **purr** *vb*

¹**purse** \'pərs\ *n* 1 : a receptacle (as a pouch) to carry money and often other small objects in 2 : RESOURCES 3 : a sum of money offered as a prize or present

²**purse** *vb* **pursed; purs·ing** : PUCKER

purs·er \'pər-sər\ *n* : an official on a ship who keeps accounts and attends to the comfort of passengers

purs·lane \'pər-slən, -ˌslān\ *n* : a fleshy-leaved weedy trailing plant with tiny yellow flowers that is sometimes used in salads

pur·su·ance \pər-'sü-əns\ *n* : the act of carrying into effect

pur·su·ant to \-'sü-ənt-\ *prep* : in carrying out : ACCORDING TO ⟨*pursuant to* your instructions⟩

pur·sue \pər-'sü\ *vb* **pur·sued; pur·su·ing** 1 : to follow in order to overtake or overcome : CHASE 2 : to seek to accomplish ⟨∼s his aims⟩ 3 : to proceed along ⟨∼ a course⟩ 4 : to engage in ⟨∼ a vocation⟩ — **pur·su·er** *n*

pur·suit \pər-'süt\ *n* 1 : the act of pursuing 2 : OCCUPATION, BUSINESS

pu·ru·lent \'pyür-(y)ə-lənt\ *adj* : containing or accompanied by pus — **pu·ru·lence** \-ləns\ *n*

pur·vey \(ˌ)pər-'vā\ *vb* **pur·veyed; pur·vey·ing** : to supply (as provisions) usu. as a business — **pur·vey·ance** \-əns\ *n* — **pur·vey·or** \-ər\ *n*

pur·view \'pər-ˌvyü\ *n* 1 : the range or limit esp. of authority, responsibility, or intention 2 : range of vision, understanding, or cognizance

pus \'pəs\ *n* : thick yellowish white fluid matter (as in a boil) formed at a place of inflammation and infection (as an abscess) and containing germs, blood cells, and tissue debris

¹**push** \'push\ *vb* [ME *pusshen,* fr. OF *poulser* to beat, push, fr. L *pulsare,* fr. *pulsus,* pp. of *pellere* to drive, strike] 1 : to press against with force in order to drive or impel 2 : to thrust forward, downward, or outward 3 : to urge on : press forward 4 : to urge or press the advancement, adoption, or practice of: *esp* : to make aggressive efforts to sell 5 : to engage in the illicit sale of narcotics

²**push** *n* 1 : a vigorous effort : DRIVE 2 : an act of pushing : SHOVE 3 : vigorous enterprise : ENERGY

push–button *adj* : using or dependent on complex and more or less automatic mechanisms ⟨∼ warfare⟩

push button *n* : a small button or knob that when pushed operates something esp. by closing an electric circuit

push·cart \'push-ˌkärt\ *n* : a cart or barrow pushed by hand

push·er \-ər\ *n* : one that pushes; *esp* : one that pushes illegal drugs

push·over \-ˌō-vər\ *n* 1 : an opponent easy to defeat 2 : SUCKER 3 : something easily accomplished

push–up \-ˌəp\ *n* : a conditioning exercise performed in a prone position by raising and lowering the body with the straightening and bending of the arms while keeping the back straight and supporting the body on the hands and toes

pushy \'push-ē\ *adj* **push·i·er; -est** : aggressive often to an objectionable degree

pu·sil·lan·i·mous \ˌpyü-sə-'lan-ə-məs\ *adj* [LL *pusillanimis,* fr. L *pusillus* very small (dim. of *pusus* small child) + *animus* spirit] : contemptibly timid : COWARDLY — **pu·sil·la·nim·i·ty** \ˌpyü-sə-lə-'nim-ət-ē\ *n*

¹**puss** \'pus\ *n* : CAT

²**puss** *n* : FACE

pussy \'pus-ē\ *n, pl* **puss·ies** : CAT

²**pussy** \'pəs-ē\ *adj* **pus·si·er; -est** : full of or resembling pus

pussy·cat \-ē-ˌkat\ *n* : CAT

pussy·foot \'pus-ē-ˌfut\ *vb* 1 : to tread or move warily or stealthily 2 : to refrain from committing oneself

pussy willow \ˌpus-ē-\ *n* : a willow having large silky catkins

pus·tule \'pəs-chül\ *n* : a pus-filled pimple

put \'put\ *vb* **put; put·ting** 1 : to bring into a specified position : PLACE ⟨∼ the book on the table⟩ 2 : SEND, THRUST 3 : to throw with an upward pushing motion ⟨∼ the shot⟩ 4 : to bring into a specified state ⟨∼ the plan into effect⟩ 5 : SUBJECT ⟨∼ traitors to death⟩ 6 : IMPOSE 7 : to set before one for decision ⟨∼ the question⟩ 8 : EXPRESS, STATE 9 : TRANSLATE, ADAPT 10 : APPLY, ASSIGN ⟨∼ them to work⟩ 11 : to give as an estimate ⟨∼ the number at 20⟩ 12 : ATTACH, ATTRIBUTE ⟨∼ a high value on it⟩ 13 : to take a specified course ⟨the ship ∼ out to sea⟩

pu·ta·tive \'pyüt-ət-iv\ *adj* 1 : commonly accepted 2 : INFERRED

put–down \'put-ˌdaun\ *n* : a humiliating remark : SQUELCH

put in *vb* 1 : to come in with : INTERPOSE ⟨*put in* a good word for me⟩ 2 : to spend time at some occupation or job ⟨*put in* eight hours at the office⟩

put off *vb* : POSTPONE, DELAY

¹**put–on** \ˌput-ˌȯn, -ˌän\ *adj* : PRETENDED, ASSUMED

²**put–on** \'put-ˌȯn, -ˌän\ *n* : a deliberate act of misleading someone; *also* : PARODY, SPOOF

put-out \'put-ˌaut\ *n* : the retiring of a base runner or batter in baseball

put out \ˌput-'aut\ *vb* **1** : EXTINGUISH **2** : ANNOY; *also* : INCONVENIENCE **3** : to cause to be out (as in baseball)

pu-tre-fy \'pyü-trə-ˌfī\ *vb* **-fied; -fy-ing** : to make or become putrid : ROT — **pu-tre-fac-tion** \ˌpyü-trə-'fak-shən\ *n* — **pu-tre-fac-tive** \-tiv\ *adj*

pu-tres-cent \pyü-'tres-ᵊnt\ *adj* : becoming putrid : ROTTING — **pu-tres-cence** \-ᵊns\ *n*

pu-trid \'pyü-trəd\ *adj* **1** : ROTTEN, DECAYED **2** : VILE, CORRUPT — **pu-trid-i-ty** \pyü-'trid-ət-ē\ *n*

putsch \'puch\ *n* [G] : a secretly plotted and suddenly executed attempt to overthrow a government

putt \'pət\ *n* : a golf stroke made on the green to cause the ball to roll into the hole — **putt** *vb*

put-tee \ˌpə-'tē, 'pət-ē\ *n* [Hindi *paṭṭī* strip of cloth] **1** : a cloth strip wrapped around the lower leg **2** : a leather legging

¹put-ter \'put-ər\ *n* : one that puts

²put-ter \'pət-ər\ *n* : a golf club used in putting

³put-ter \'pət-ər\ *vb* **1** : to move or act aimlessly or idly **2** : TINKER

put-ty \'pət-ē\ *n, pl* **putties** [F *potée*, lit., potful, fr. OF, fr. *pot*, fr. *pot*, of Gmc origin] : a doughlike cement usu. of whiting and linseed oil used esp. to fasten glass in sashes — **putty** *vb*

¹puz-zle \'pəz-əl\ *vb* **puz-zled; puz-zling** \-(ə-)liŋ\ **1** : to bewilder mentally : CONFUSE, PERPLEX **2** : to solve with difficulty or ingenuity (~ out a mystery) **3** : to be in a quandary (~ over what to do) **4** : to attempt a solution of a puzzle (~ over a person's words) *syn* mystify, bewilder, nonplus, confound — **puz-zle-ment** *n* — **puz-zler** \-(ə-)lər\ *n*

²puzzle *n* **1** : something that puzzles **2** : a question, problem, or contrivance designed for testing ingenuity

PVC *abbr* polyvinyl chloride

pvt *abbr* private

PW *abbr* prisoner of war

PX *abbr* post exchange

pya \pē-'ä\ *n* — see *kyat* at MONEY table

pyg-my \'pig-mē\ *n, pl* **pygmies** [ME *pigmei*, fr. L *pygmaeus* of a pygmy, dwarfish, fr. Gk *pygmaios*, fr. *pygmē* fist, measure of length] **1** *cap* : any of a small people of equatorial Africa **2** : DWARF — **pygmy** *adj*

py-ja-mas \pə-'jä-məz\ *chiefly Brit var of* PAJAMAS

py-lon \'pī-ˌlän, -lən\ *n* **1** : a usu. massive gateway; *esp* : an Egyptian one flanked by flat-topped pyramids **2** : a tower that supports a long span of wire **3** : a post or tower marking a prescribed course of flight for an airplane

py-or-rhea \ˌpī-ə-'rē-ə\ *n* : an inflammation with pus of the sockets of the teeth

¹pyr-a-mid \'pir-ə-ˌmid\ *n* **1** : a massive structure with a square base and four triangular faces meeting at a point **2** : a geometrical solid having a polygon for its base and three or more triangles for its sides that meet at a point to form the top — **py-ra-mi-dal** \pə-'ram-əd-ᵊl, ˌpir-ə-'mid-ᵊl\ *adj*

²pyramid *vb* **1** : to build up in the form of a pyramid : heap up **2** : to increase rapidly on a broadening base

pyre \'pī(ə)r\ *n* : a combustible heap for burning a dead body as a funeral rite

py-re-thrum \pī-'rē-thrəm\ *n* : an insecticide consisting of the dried heads of any of several Old World chrysanthemums

py-rim-i-dine \pī-'rim-ə-ˌdēn\ *n* : any of a group of bases including several (as cytosine, thymine, or uracil) that are constituents of DNA or RNA

py-rite \'pī-ˌrīt\ *n* : a mineral containing sulfur and iron that is brass-yellow in color

py-rol-y-sis \pī-'räl-ə-səs\ *n* : chemical change brought about by the action of heat

py-ro-ma-nia \ˌpī-rō-'mā-nē-ə\ *n* : an irresistible impulse to start fires — **py-ro-ma-ni-ac** \-nē-ˌak\ *n*

py-ro-tech-nics \ˌpī-rə-'tek-niks\ *n pl* **1** : a display of fireworks **2** : a spectacular display (as of oratory) — **py-ro-tech-nic** \-nik\ *also* **py-ro-tech-ni-cal** \-ni-kəl\ *adj*

py-rox-ene \pī-'räk-ˌsēn\ *n* : any of various minerals that are silicates and usu. contain aluminum, calcium, sodium, magnesium, or iron

Pyr-rhic victory \ˌpir-ik-\ *n* [*Pyrrhus,* king of Epirus who sustained heavy losses in defeating the Romans] : a victory won at excessive cost

py-thon \'pī-ˌthän, -thən\ *n* [L, monstrous serpent killed by the god Apollo, fr. Gk *Pythōn*] : a large snake (as a boa) that squeezes and suffocates its prey; *esp* : any of an Old World genus including the largest snakes living at the present time

pyx \'piks\ *n* : a small case used to carry the Eucharist to the sick

Q

¹q \'kyü\ *n, pl* **q's** *or* **qs** \'kyüz\ *often cap*
: the 17th letter of the English alphabet

²q *abbr, often cap* **1** quart **2** quarto **3**
queen **4** query **5** question

QC *abbr* Queen's Counsel

QED *abbr* [L *quod erat demonstrandum*] which was to be demonstrated

QEF *abbr* [L *quod erat faciendum*]
which was to be done

QEI *abbr* [L *quod erat inveniendum*]
which was to be found out

qin·tar \kin-'tär\ *n, pl* **qin·dar·ka** \kin-'där-kə\ *or* **qintar** — see *lek* at MONEY
table

qi·vi·ut \'kē-vē-,üt\ *n* [Esk] : the wool
of the undercoat of the musk-ox

Qld *or* **Q'land** *abbr* Queensland

QM *abbr* quartermaster

QMC *abbr* quartermaster corps

QMG *abbr* quartermaster general

qq v *abbr* [L *quae vide*] which (*pl*) see

qr *abbr* quarter

¹**qt** \'kyü-'tē\ *n, often cap Q&T* : QUIET
— usu. used in the phrase *on the qt*

²**qt** *abbr* **1** quantity **2** quart

qto *abbr* quarto

qty *abbr* quantity

qu *or* **ques** *abbr* question

¹**quack** \'kwak\ *vb* : to make the characteristic cry of a duck

²**quack** *n* : the cry of a duck

³**quack** *n* **1** : CHARLATAN **2** : a pretender
to medical skill **syn** faker, impostor,
mountebank — **quack** *adj* — **quack·ery** \-ə-rē\ *n* — **quack·ish** *adj*

¹**quad** \'kwäd\ *n* : QUADRANGLE

²**quad** *n* : QUADRUPLET

³**quad** *abbr* quadrant

quad·ran·gle \'kwäd-,raŋ-gəl\ *n* **1** : a
flat geometrical figure having four angles and four sides **2** : a 4-sided courtyard or enclosure — **quad·ran·gu·lar** \kwä-'draŋ-gyə-lər\ *adj*

quad·rant \'kwäd-rənt\ *n* **1** : an instrument for measuring angular elevation
used esp. in astronomy and surveying
2 : one quarter of a circle : an arc of
90° **3** : any of the four quarters into
which something is divided by two
lines intersecting each other at right
angles

quad·ra·phon·ic \,kwäd-rə-'fän-ik\ *adj*
: of or relating to the transmission, recording, or reproduction of sound using four transmission channels

qua·drat·ic \kwä-'drat-ik\ *adj* : having
or being a term in which the variable
(as *x*) is squared but containing no
term in which the variable is raised to
a higher power than a square (a ~
equation) — **quadratic** *n*

qua·dren·ni·al \kwä-'dren-ē-əl\ *adj* **1**
: consisting of or lasting for four years
2 : occurring every four years

qua·dren·ni·um \-ē-əm\ *n, pl* **-ni·ums** *or*
-nia \-ē-ə\ : a period of four years

¹**quad·ri·lat·er·al** \,kwäd-rə-'lat-(ə-)rəl\
n : a polygon of four sides

²**quadrilateral** *adj* : having four sides

qua·drille \kwä-'dril, k(w)ə-\ *n* : a
square dance made up of five or six
figures in various rhythms

quad·ri·par·tite \,kwäd-rə-'pär-,tīt\ *adj*
1 : consisting of four parts **2** : shared
by four parties or persons

quad·ri·phon·ics \-'fän-iks\ *n* : QUADRIPHONY

quad·ri·phony \'kwäd-rə-,fän-ē\ *n*
: quadraphonic transmission, recording, or reproduction of sound

qua·driv·i·um \kwä-'driv-ē-əm\ *n* : the
four liberal arts of arithmetic, music,
geometry, and astronomy in a medieval university

quad·ru·ped \'kwäd-rə-,ped\ *n* : an animal having four feet — **qua·dru·pe·dal** \kwä-'drü-pəd-ᵊl, ,kwäd-rə-'ped-\ *adj*

¹**qua·dru·ple** \kwä-'drüp-əl, -'drəp-; 'kwäd-rəp-\ *vb* **qua·dru·pled; qua·dru·pling** \-(ə-)liŋ\ : to make or become
four times as great or as many

²**quadruple** *adj* : FOURFOLD

qua·dru·plet \kwä-'drəp-lət, -'drüp-; 'kwäd-rəp-\ *n* **1** : one of four offspring
born at one birth **2** : a group of four of
a kind

¹**qua·dru·pli·cate** \kwä-'drü-pli-kət\ *adj*
1 : repeated four times **2** : FOURTH

²**qua·dru·pli·cate** \-plə-,kāt\ *vb* **-cat·ed;
-cat·ing 1** : QUADRUPLE **2** : to provide
in quadruplicate — **qua·dru·pli·ca·tion** \-,drü-plə-'kā-shən\ *n*

³**qua·dru·pli·cate** \-'drü-pli-kət\ *n* **1**
: four copies all alike (typed in ~) **2**
: one of four like things

¹**quaff** \'kwäf, 'kwaf\ *vb* : to drink deeply or repeatedly — **quaff** *n*

quag·mire \'kwag-,mī(ə)r, 'kwäg-\ *n* **1**
: soft miry land that yields under the
foot **2** : a difficult situation from
which it is hard to escape

qua·hog \'kō-,hóg, 'kwó-, 'kwō-, -,häg\
n : a round thick-shelled American
clam

quai \'kā\ *n* : QUAY

¹**quail** \'kwāl\ *n, pl* **quail** *or* **quails** [ME
quaille, fr. MF, fr. ML *quaccula,* of
imit. origin] : any of various shortwinged stout-bodied game birds (as a
bobwhite) related to the domestic
chicken

²**quail** *vb* [ME *quailen* to curdle, fr. MF
quailler, fr. L *coagulare,* fr. *coagulum* curdling agent, fr. *cogere* to drive
together] : to lose heart : COWER **syn**
recoil, shrink, flinch, wince, blanch

quaint \'kwänt\ *adj* : unusual or different in character or appearance : *esp*
: pleasingly old-fashioned or unfamil-

iar syn odd, queer, curious, strange —
quaint·ly adv — **quaint·ness** n

¹**quake** \'kwāk\ vb **quaked; quak·ing 1** : to shake usu. from shock or instability **2** : to tremble usu. from cold or fear

²**quake** n : a shaking or trembling; esp : EARTHQUAKE

Quak·er \'kwā-kər\ n : FRIEND 5

quaking aspen n : an aspen of the U.S. and Canada that has small nearly circular leaves with flattened petioles and finely serrate margins

qual abbr quality

qual·i·fi·ca·tion \,kwäl-ə-fə-'kā-shən\ n **1** : LIMITATION, MODIFICATION **2** : a special skill that fits a person for some work or position

qual·i·fied \'kwäl-ə-,fīd\ adj **1** : fitted for a given purpose **2** : limited in some way

qual·i·fi·er \'kwäl-ə-,fī-ər\ n **1** : one that satisfies requirements **2** : a word or word group that limits the meaning of another word or word group

qual·i·fy \'kwäl-ə-,fī\ vb **-fied; -fy·ing 1** : to reduce from a general to a particular form : MODIFY **2** : to make less harsh **3** : to limit the meaning of (as a noun) **4** : to fit by skill or training for some purpose **5** : to give or have a legal right to do something **6** : to demonstrate the necessary ability (as in a preliminary race) syn moderate, temper

qual·i·ta·tive \'kwäl-ə-,tāt-iv\ adj : of, relating to, or involving quality — **qual·i·ta·tive·ly** adv

¹**qual·i·ty** \'kwäl-ət-ē\ n, pl **-ties 1** : peculiar and essential character : NATURE **2** : degree of excellence **3** : high social status **4** : a distinguishing attribute

²**quality** adj : being of high quality

qualm \'kwäm\ n **1** : a sudden attack (as of nausea) **2** : a sudden misgiving **3** : SCRUPLE

qualm·ish \-ish\ adj **1** : feeling qualms : NAUSEATED **2** : overly scrupulous : SQUEAMISH **3** : of, relating to, or producing qualms

quan·da·ry \'kwän-d(ə-)rē\ n, pl **-ries** : a state of perplexity or doubt

quan·ti·ta·tive \'kwän-tə-,tāt-iv\ adj : of, relating to, or involving quantity — **quan·ti·ta·tive·ly** adv

quan·ti·ty \'kwän-tət-ē\ n, pl **-ties 1** : AMOUNT, NUMBER **2** : a considerable amount

quan·tize \'kwän-,tīz\ vb **quan·tized; quan·tiz·ing** : to subdivide (as energy) into small units

quan·tum \'kwänt-əm\ n, pl **quan·ta** \-ə\ [L, neut. of quantus how much] **1** : QUANTITY, AMOUNT **2** : an elemental unit of energy

quantum mechanics n sing or pl : a general mathematical theory dealing with the interactions of matter and radiation in terms of observable quantities only — **quantum mechanical** adj — **quantum mechanically** adv

quar·an·tine \'kwȯr-ən-,tēn\ n [It qua-

rantina, lit., period of forty days, fr. MF quarantaine, fr. OF, fr. quarante forty, fr. L quadraginta] **1** : a period during which a ship suspected of carrying contagious disease is forbidden contact with the shore **2** : a restraint on the movements of persons or goods to prevent the spread of pests or disease **3** : a place or period of quarantine — **quarantine** vb

quark \'kwȯrk, 'kwärk\ n : a hypothetical particle that carries a fractional charge and is held to be a constituent of heavier particles (as protons and neutrons)

¹**quar·rel** \'kwȯr(-ə)l\ n **1** : a ground of dispute **2** : a verbal clash : CONFLICT — **quar·rel·some** \-səm\ adj

²**quarrel** vb **-reled** or **-relled; -rel·ing** or **-rel·ling 1** : to find fault **2** : to dispute angrily : WRANGLE

¹**quar·ry** \'kwȯr-ē\ n, pl **quarries** [ME querre entrails of game given to the hounds, fr. MF cuiree] **1** : game hunted with hawks **2** : PREY

²**quarry** n, pl **quarries** [ME quarey, alter. of quarrere, fr. MF quarriere, fr. (assumed) OF quarre squared stone, fr. L quadrum square] : an open excavation usu. for obtaining building stone, slate, or limestone — **quarry** vb

¹**quart** \'kwȯrt\ n — see WEIGHT table

²**quart** abbr quarterly

¹**quar·ter** \'kwȯrt-ər\ n **1** : one of four equal parts : a fourth of a dollar; also : a coin of this value **3** : a district of a city **4** pl : LODGINGS (moved into new ~s) **5** : MERCY, CLEMENCY (gave no ~) **6** : a fourth part of the moon's period

²**quarter** vb **1** : to divide into four equal parts **2** : to provide with shelter

¹**quar·ter·back** \-,bak\ n : a football player who calls the signals for his team

²**quarterback** vb **1** : to direct the offensive play of a football team **2** : LEAD, BOSS

quar·ter·deck \-,dek\ n : the stern area of a ship's upper deck

quarter horse n : a compact muscular saddle horse characterized by great endurance and by high speed for short distances

¹**quar·ter·ly** \'kwȯrt-ər-lē\ adv : at 3-month intervals

²**quarterly** adj : occurring, issued, or payable at 3-month intervals

³**quarterly** n, pl **-lies** : a periodical published four times a year

quar·ter·mas·ter \-,mas-tər\ n **1** : a petty officer who attends to a ship's helm, binnacle, and signals **2** : an army officer who provides clothing and subsistence for troops

quar·ter·staff \-,staf\ n, pl **-staves** \-,stavz, -,stāvz\ : a long stout staff formerly used as a weapon

quar·tet also **quar·tette** \kwȯr-'tet\ n **1** : a musical composition for four instruments or voices **2** : a group of four and esp. of four musicians

quar·to \'kwȯrt-ō\ *n, pl* **quartos 1** : the size of a piece of paper cut four from a sheet **2** : a book printed on quarto pages

quartz \'kwȯrts\ *n* : a common often transparent crystalline mineral that is a form of silica

quartz heater *n* : a portable electric heater whose heating elements are sealed in quartz-glass tubes

quartz·ite \'kwȯrt-ˌsīt\ *n* : a compact granular rock composed of quartz and derived from sandstone

qua·sar \'kwā-ˌzär, -ˌsär\ *n* : any of various distant starlike celestial objects that are powerful emitters of electromagnetic radiation (as blue light and radio waves)

quash \'kwäsh, 'kwȯsh\ *vb* **1** : to set aside by judicial action : VOID **2** : to suppress or extinguish summarily and completely : QUELL

qua·si \'kwā-ˌzī, -ˌsī; 'kwäz-ē, 'kwäs-\ *adj* : being in some sense or degree ⟨a ~ corporation⟩

quasi- *comb form* [L, as if, as it were, approximately, fr. *quam* as + *si* if] : in some sense or degree ⟨*quasi*-historical⟩

Qua·ter·na·ry \'kwät-ər-ˌner-ē, kwə-'tər-nə-rē\ *adj* : of, relating to, or being the geologic period from the end of the Tertiary to the present — **Quaternary** *n*

qua·train \'kwä-ˌtrān\ *n* : a unit of four lines of verse

qua·tre·foil \'kat-ər-ˌfȯil, 'kat-rə-\ *n* : a conventionalized representation of a flower with four petals or of a leaf with four leaflets

qua·ver \'kwā-vər\ *vb* **qua·vered; qua·ver·ing** \'kwāv-(ə-)riŋ\ **1** : TREMBLE, SHAKE **2** : TRILL **3** : to speak in tremulous tones *syn* shudder, quake, twitter, quiver, shiver — **quaver** *n*

quay \'kē, 'k(w)ā\ *n* : WHARF

Que *abbr* Quebec

quean \'kwēn\ *n* : PROSTITUTE

quea·sy \'kwē-zē\ *adj* **quea·si·er; -est** : NAUSEATED — **quea·si·ly** \-zə-lē\ *adv* — **quea·si·ness** \-zē-nəs\ *n*

queen \'kwēn\ *n* **1** : the wife or widow of a king **2** : a female monarch **3** : a woman notable for rank, power, or attractiveness **4** : the most privileged piece in the game of chess **5** : a playing card bearing the figure of a queen **6** : a fertile female of a social insect (as a bee or termite) — **queen·ly** *adj*

Queen Anne's lace \-'anz-\ *n* : WILD CARROT

queen consort *n, pl* **queens consort** : the wife of a reigning king

queen mother *n* : a dowager queen who is mother of the reigning sovereign

queen-size *adj* : having dimensions of approximately 60 inches by 80 inches ⟨~ bed⟩ ; *also* : of a size that fits a queen-size bed

¹queer \'kwiər\ *adj* **1** : differing from the usual or normal : PECULIAR, STRANGE **2** : COUNTERFEIT *syn* weird, bizarre, eccentric, curious — **queer** *n* — **queer·ly** *adv* — **queer·ness** *n*

²queer *vb* : to spoil the effect of : DISRUPT ⟨~ed our plans⟩

quell \'kwel\ *vb* : to put an end to by force : CRUSH ⟨~ a riot⟩

quench \'kwench\ *vb* **1** : PUT OUT, EXTINGUISH **2** : SUBDUE **3** : SLAKE, SATISFY ⟨~ed his thirst⟩ **4** : to cool (as heated steel) suddenly by immersion esp. in water or oil — **quench·able** *adj* — **quench·less** *adj*

quer·u·lous \'kwer-(y)ə-ləs\ *adj* **1** : constantly complaining **2** : FRETFUL, WHINING *syn* petulant, pettish, irritable, peevish, huffy — **quer·u·lous·ly** *adv* — **quer·u·lous·ness** *n*

que·ry \'kwi(ə)r-ē, 'kwe(ə)r-\ *n, pl* **queries** : QUESTION — **query** *vb*

quest \'kwest\ *n* : SEARCH — **quest** *vb*

¹ques·tion \'kwes-chən\ *n* **1** : an interrogative expression : QUERY **2** : a subject for discussion or debate; *also* : a proposition to be voted on in a meeting **3** : INQUIRY **4** : DISPUTE

²question *vb* **1** : to ask questions **2** : DOUBT, DISPUTE **3** : to subject to analysis : EXAMINE *syn* ask, interrogate, quiz, query — **ques·tion·er** *n*

ques·tion·able \'kwes-chə-nə-bəl\ *adj* **1** : not certain or exact : DOUBTFUL **2** : not believed to be true, sound, or moral *syn* dubious, problematical, moot, debatable

question mark *n* : a punctuation mark ? used esp. at the end of a sentence to indicate a direct question

ques·tion·naire \ˌkwes-chə-'na(ə)r\ *n* : a set of questions for obtaining information

quet·zal \ket-'säl, -'sal\ *n, pl* **quetzals** *or* **quet·za·les** \-'säl-äs, -'sal-\ **1** : a Central American bird with brilliant plumage **2** *pl* **quetzales** — see MONEY table

¹queue \'kyü\ *n* [F, lit., tail, fr. L *cauda*, *coda*] **1** : a braid of hair usu. worn hanging at the back of the head **2** : a line esp. of persons or vehicles

²queue *vb* **queued; queu·ing** *or* **queue·ing** : to line up in a queue

quib·ble \'kwib-əl\ *n* **1** : an evasion of or shifting from the point at issue **2** : a minor objection — **quibble** *vb*

¹quick \'kwik\ *adj* **1** *archaic* : LIVING **2** : RAPID, SPEEDY ⟨~ steps⟩ **3** : prompt to understand, think, or perceive : ALERT **4** : easily aroused ⟨a ~ temper⟩ **5** : turning or bending sharply ⟨a ~ turn in the road⟩ *syn* fleet, fast, hasty, expeditious — **quick** *adv* — **quick·ly** *adv* — **quick·ness** *n*

²quick *n* **1** : sensitive living flesh **2** : a vital part : HEART

quick bread *n* : a bread made with a leavening agent that permits immediate baking of the dough or batter mixture

quick·en \'kwik-ən\ *vb* **quick·ened;**

quick·en·ing \-(ə-)niŋ\ 1 : to come to life : REVIVE 2 : AROUSE, STIMULATE 3 : to increase in speed : HASTEN 4 : to show vitality (as by growing or moving) *syn* animate, enliven, liven, vivify

quick-freeze \ˈkwik-ˈfrēz\ *vb* **-froze** \-ˈfrōz\; **-fro·zen** \-ˈfrōz-ᵊn\; **-freez·ing** : to freeze (food) for preservation so rapidly that ice crystals formed are too small to rupture the cells

quick·ie \ˈkwik-ē\ *n* : something hurriedly done or made

quick·lime \ˈkwik-ˌlīm\ *n* : the first solid product obtained by calcining limestone

quick·sand \-ˌsand\ *n* : a deep mass of loose sand mixed with water

quick·sil·ver \-ˌsil-vər\ *n* : MERCURY

quick·step \-ˌstep\ *n* : a spirited march tune esp. accompanying a march in quick time

quick time *n* : a rate of marching in which 120 steps each 30 inches in length are taken in one minute

quick-wit·ted \ˈkwik-ˈwit-əd\ *adj* : mentally alert *syn* clever, bright, smart, intelligent

quid \ˈkwid\ *n* : a cut or wad of something chewable (a ~ of tobacco)

quid pro quo \ˌkwid-ˌprō-ˈkwō\ *n* [NL, something for something] : something given or received for something else

qui·es·cent \kwī-ˈes-ᵊnt\ *adj* : being at rest : QUIET *syn* latent, dormant, potential — **qui·es·cence** \-ᵊns\ *n*

¹qui·et \ˈkwī-ət\ *n* : REPOSE

²quiet *adj* 1 : marked by little motion or activity : CALM 2 : GENTLE, MILD (a man of ~ disposition) 3 : enjoyed in peace and relaxation (a ~ cup of tea) 4 : free from noise or uproar 5 : not showy : MODEST (~ clothes) 6 : SECLUDED (a ~ nook) — **quiet** *adv* — **qui·et·ly** *adv* — **qui·et·ness** *n*

³quiet *vb* 1 : CALM, PACIFY 2 : to become quiet (~ down)

qui·etude \ˈkwī-ə-ˌt(y)üd\ *n* : QUIETNESS, REPOSE

qui·etus \kwī-ˈēt-əs\ *n* [ME *quietus est*, fr. ML, he is quit, formula of discharge from obligation] 1 : final settlement (as of a debt) 2 : DEATH

quill \ˈkwil\ *n* 1 : a large stiff feather; *also* : the hollow tubular part of a feather 2 : one of the hollow sharp spines of a hedgehog or porcupine 3 : a pen made from a feather

¹quilt \ˈkwilt\ *n* : a padded bed coverlet

²quilt *vb* 1 : to fill, pad, or line like a quilt 2 : to stitch or sew in layers with padding in between 3 : to make quilts

quince \ˈkwins\ *n* : a hard yellow applelike fruit; *also* : a tree related to the roses that bears this fruit

qui·nine \ˈkwī-ˌnīn\ *n* : a bitter white drug obtained from cinchona bark and used esp. in treating malaria

quin·sy \ˈkwin-zē\ *n* : a severe inflammation of the throat or adjacent parts with swelling and fever

quint \ˈkwint\ *n* : QUINTUPLET

quin·tal \ˈkwint-ᵊl, ˈkant-\ *n* : HUNDREDWEIGHT

quin·tes·sence \kwin-ˈtes-ᵊns\ *n* 1 : the purest essence of something 2 : the most typical example — **quint·es·sen·tial** \ˌkwint-ə-ˈsen-chəl\ *adj*

quin·tet *also* **quin·tette** \kwin-ˈtet\ *n* 1 : a musical composition for five instruments or voices 2 : a group of five and esp. of five musicians; *also* : a basketball team

¹quin·tu·ple \kwin-ˈt(y)üp-əl, -ˈtəp-; ˈkwint-əp-\ *adj* 1 : having five units or members 2 : being five times as great or as many — **quintuple** *n*

²quintuple *vb* **quin·tu·pled; quin·tu·pling** : to make or become five times as great or as many

quin·tu·plet \kwin-ˈtəp-lət, -ˈt(y)üp-; ˈkwint-əp-\ *n* 1 : a group of five of a kind 2 : one of five offspring born at one birth

¹quin·tu·pli·cate \kwin-ˈt(y)ü-pli-kət\ *adj* 1 : repeated five times 2 : FIFTH

²quintuplicate *n* 1 : one of five like things : five copies all alike (typed in ~)

³quin·tu·pli·cate \-plə-ˌkāt\ *vb* **-cat·ed; -cat·ing** 1 : QUINTUPLE 2 : to provide in quintuplicate

¹quip \ˈkwip\ *n* : a clever remark : GIBE

²quip *vb* **quipped; quip·ping** 1 : to make quips : GIBE 2 : to jest or gibe at

quire \ˈkwī(ə)r\ *n* : a set of 24 or sometimes 25 sheets of paper of the same size and quality

quirk \ˈkwərk\ *n* : a peculiarity of action or behavior — **quirky** *adj*

quirt \ˈkwərt\ *n* : a riding whip with a short handle and a rawhide lash

quis·ling \ˈkwiz-liŋ\ *n* [Vidkun *Quisling* †1945 Norw. politician who collaborated with the Nazis] : a traitor who collaborates with the invaders of his country

quit \ˈkwit\ *vb* **quit** *also* **quit·ted; quit·ting** 1 : CONDUCT, BEHAVE (~ themselves well) 2 : to depart from : LEAVE, ABANDON *syn* acquit, comport, deport, demean — **quit·ter** *n*

quite \ˈkwīt\ *adv* 1 : COMPLETELY, WHOLLY 2 : to an extreme : POSITIVELY 3 : to a considerable extent : RATHER

quits \ˈkwits\ *adj* : even or equal with another (call it ~)

quit·tance \ˈkwit-ᵊns\ *n* : REQUITAL

¹quiv·er \ˈkwiv-ər\ *n* : a case for carrying arrows

²quiver *vb* **quiv·ered; quiv·er·ing** \-(ə-)riŋ\ : to shake with a slight trembling motion *syn* shiver, shudder, quaver, quake, tremble

³quiver *n* : the act or action of quivering : TREMOR

qui vive \kē-ˈvēv\ *n* [F *qui-vive*, fr. *qui vive?* long live who?, challenge of a French sentry] : ALERT (on the *qui vive* for prowlers)

quix·ot·ic \kwik-ˈsät-ik\ *adj* [fr. Don *Quixote*, hero of the novel *Don Quixote de la Mancha* by Cervantes]

: foolishly impractical esp. in the pursuit of ideals

¹quiz \'kwiz\ *n, pl* **quiz·zes 1** : an eccentric person **2** : PRACTICAL JOKE **3** : a short oral or written test

²quiz *vb* **quizzed; quiz·zing 1** : MOCK **2** : to look at inquisitively **3** : to question closely : EXAMINE **syn** ask, interrogate, query

quiz·zi·cal \'kwiz-i-kəl\ *adj* **1** : slightly eccentric **2** : marked by bantering or teasing **3** : INQUISITIVE, QUESTIONING

quoit \'kwät, 'k(w)ȯit\ *n* **1** : a flattened ring of iron or circle of rope used in a throwing game **2** *pl* : a game in which quoits are thrown at an upright pin in an attempt to ring the pin

quon·dam \'kwän-dəm, -ˌdam\ *adj* [L, at one time, formerly, fr. *quom, cum* when] : FORMER

quo·rum \'kwōr-əm\ *n* : the number of members required to be present for business to be legally transacted

quot *abbr* quotation

quo·ta \'kwōt-ə\ *n* : a proportional part esp. when assigned : SHARE

quot·able \'kwōt-ə-bəl\ *adj* : fit for or worth quoting

quo·ta·tion \kwō-'tā-shən\ *n* **1** : the act or process of quoting **2** : the price currently bid or offered for something **3** : something that is quoted

quotation mark *n* : one of a pair of punctuation marks " " or ' ' used esp. to indicate the beginning and end of a quotation in which exact phraseology is directly cited

quote \'kwōt\ *vb* **quot·ed; quot·ing** [ML *quotare* to mark the number of, number references, fr. L *quotus* how many, (as) many as] **1** : to speak or write a passage from another usu. with acknowledgment; *also* : to repeat a passage in substantiation or illustration **2** : to state the market price of a commodity, stock, or bond **3** : to inform a hearer or reader that matter following is quoted — **quote** *n*

quoth \('l)kwōth\ *vb past* [ME, past of *quethen* to say, fr. OE *cwethan*] *archaic* : SAID — usu. used in the 1st and 3d persons with the subject following

quo·tid·i·an \kwō-'tid-ē-ən\ *adj* **1** : DAILY **2** : COMMONPLACE, ORDINARY

quo·tient \'kwō-shənt\ *n* : the number obtained by the division of one number by another

qursh *n, pl* **qursh** \'kùrsh\ — see *riyal* at MONEY table

qv *abbr* [L *quod vide*] which see

qy *abbr* query

R

¹r \'är\ *n, pl* **r's** *or* **rs** \'ärz\ *often cap* : the 18th letter of the English alphabet

²r *abbr, often cap* **1** rabbi **2** radius **3** rare **4** Republican **5** rerun **6** resistance **7** right **8** river **9** roentgen **10** rook **11** run

Ra *symbol* radium

RA *abbr* **1** regular army **2** Royal Academy

¹rab·bet \'rab-ət\ *n* : a groove in the edge or face of a board esp. to receive another piece

²rabbet *vb* : to cut a rabbet in; *also* : to join by means of a rabbet

rab·bi \'rab-ˌī\ *n* [LL, fr. Gk *rhabbi*, fr. Heb *rabbī* my master, fr. *rabh* master + *-ī* my] **1** : MASTER, TEACHER — used by Jews as a term of address **2** : a Jew trained and ordained for professional religious leadership — **rab·bin·ic** \rə-'bin-ik\ *or* **rab·bin·i·cal** \-i-kəl\ *adj*

rab·bin·ate \'rab-ə-nət, -ˌnāt\ *n* **1** : the office of a rabbi **2** : the whole body of rabbis

rab·bit \'rab-ət\ *n, pl* **rabbit** *or* **rabbits** : a long-eared burrowing mammal related to the hare; *also* : its pelt

rabble \'rab-əl\ *n* **1** : MOB **2 2** : the lowest class of people

rab·ble-rous·er \'rab-əl-ˌraù-zər\ *n* : one that stirs up (as to hatred or violence) the masses of the people

ra·bid \'rab-əd\ *adj* **1** : VIOLENT, FURIOUS **2** : being fanatical or extreme **3**

: affected with rabies — **ra·bid·ly** *adv*

ra·bies \'rā-bēz\ *n, pl* **rabies** [NL, fr. L, madness] : an acute deadly virus disease of the nervous system transmitted by the bite of an affected animal

rac·coon \ra-'kün\ *n, pl* **raccoon** *or* **raccoons** : a gray No. American chiefly tree-dwelling mammal with a bushy ringed tail and nocturnal habits; *also* : its fur

¹race \'rās\ *n* **1** : a strong current of running water; *also* : its channel **2** : an onward course (as of time or life) **3** : a contest in speed **4** : a contest for a desired end (as election to office)

²race *vb* **raced; rac·ing 1** : to run in a race **2** : to run swiftly : RUSH **3** : to engage in a race with **4** : to drive at high speed — **rac·er** *n*

³race *n* **1** : a family, tribe, people, or nation of the same stock; *also* : MANKIND **2** : a group of individuals within a biological species able to breed together — **ra·cial** \'rā-shəl\ *adj* — **ra·cial·ly** \-ē\ *adv*

race·course \'rās-ˌkōrs\ *n* : a course for racing

race·horse \-ˌhȯrs\ *n* : a horse bred or kept for racing

ra·ceme \rā-'sēm\ *n* [L *racemus* bunch of grapes] : a flower cluster with flowers borne along a stem and blooming from the base toward the tip — **rac·e·mose** \'ras-ə-ˌmōs\ *adj*

race·track \'rās-ˌtrak\ *n* : a usu. oval course on which races are run

race·way \-ˌwā\ *n* 1 : a channel for a current of water 2 : RACECOURSE

ra·cial·ism \'rā-shə-ˌliz-əm\ *n* : RACISM — **ra·cial·ist** \-ləst\ *n* — **ra·cial·is·tic** \ˌrā-shə-'lis-tik\ *adj*

racing form *n* : an information sheet giving data about racehorses for use by bettors

rac·ism \'rās-ˌiz-əm\ *n* : a belief that some races are by nature superior to others; *also* : discrimination based on such belief — **rac·ist** \-əst\ *n*

¹rack \'rak\ *n* 1 : an instrument of torture on which a body is stretched 2 : a framework on or in which something may be placed (as for display or storage) 3 : a bar with teeth on one side to mesh with a pinion or worm gear

²rack *vb* 1 : to torture with or as if with a rack 2 : to stretch or strain by force 3 : TORMENT 4 : to place on or in a rack

rack·et *also* **rac·quet** \'rak-ət\ *n* [MF *raquette*, fr. Ar *rāhah* palm of the hand] : a light bat made of netting stretched across an oval open frame and used for striking a ball

²racket *n* 1 : confused noise : DIN 2 : a fraudulent or dishonest scheme or activity

³racket *vb* : to make a racket

rack·e·teer \ˌrak-ə-'tiər\ *n* : a person who obtains money by an illegal enterprise usu. involving intimidation — **rack·e·teer·ing** *n*

rack up *vb* : SCORE

ra·con·teur \ˌrak-ˌän-'tər\ *n* : one good at telling anecdotes

racy \'rā-sē\ *adj* **rac·i·er; -est** 1 : having the quality of something in its original or most characteristic form 2 : full of zest 3 : PUNGENT, SPICY 4 : RISQUÉ, SUGGESTIVE — **rac·i·ly** \'rā-sə-lē\ *adv* — **rac·i·ness** \-sē-nəs\ *n*

rad *abbr* 1 radical 2 radio 3 radius

ra·dar \'rā-ˌdär\ *n* [*radio detecting and ranging*] : a device that emits radio waves for detecting and locating an object by the reflection of the radio waves and that may use this reflection to determine the object's direction and speed

ra·dar·scope \'rā-ˌdär-ˌskōp\ *n* : a visual display for a radar receiver

¹ra·di·al \'rād-ē-əl\ *adj* : arranged or having parts arranged like rays coming from a common center (the ∼ form of a starfish) — **ra·di·al·ly** \-ē\ *adv*

²radial *n* : a pneumatic tire with cords laid perpendicular to the center line

radial engine *n* : an internal-combustion engine with cylinders arranged radially like the spokes of a wheel

ra·di·ant \'rād-ē-ənt\ *adj* 1 : SHINING, GLOWING 2 : beaming with happiness 3 : transmitted by radiation syn brilliant, bright, luminous, lustrous — **ra·di·ance** \-əns\ *n* — **ra·di·ant·ly** *adv*

radiant energy *n* : energy transmitted as electromagnetic waves

ra·di·ate \'rād-ē-ˌāt\ *vb* **-at·ed; -at·ing** 1 : to send out rays : SHINE, GLOW 2 : to issue in rays ⟨light ∼s⟩ ⟨heat ∼s⟩ 3 : to spread around as from a center — **ra·di·a·tion** \ˌrād-ē-'ā-shən\ *n*

radiation sickness *n* : sickness that results from exposure to radiation and is commonly marked by fatigue, nausea, vomiting, loss of teeth and hair, and in more severe cases by damage to blood-forming tissue

ra·di·a·tor \'rād-ē-ˌāt-ər\ *n* : any of various devices (as a set of pipes or tubes) for transferring heat from a fluid within to an area or object outside

¹rad·i·cal \'rad-i-kəl\ *adj* [ME, fr. LL *radicalis*, fr. L *radic-, radix* root] 1 : FUNDAMENTAL, EXTREME, THOROUGHGOING 2 : of or relating to radicals in politics — **rad·i·cal·ism** \-ˌiz-əm\ *n* — **rad·i·cal·ly** \-ē\ *adv*

²radical *n* 1 : a person who favors rapid and sweeping changes in laws and methods of government 2 : a group of atoms that is replaceable by a single atom or remains unchanged during reactions 3 : a mathematical expression indicating a root by means of a radical sign; *also* : RADICAL SIGN

rad·i·cal·ize \-kə-ˌlīz\ *vb* **-ized; -iz·ing** : to make radical esp. in politics — **rad·i·cal·iza·tion** \ˌrad-i-kə-lə-'zā-shən\ *n*

radical sign *n* : the sign √ placed over a mathematical expression to indicate that its root is to be taken

radii *pl of* RADIUS

¹ra·dio \'rād-ē-ˌō\ *n, pl* **ra·di·os** 1 : transmission or reception of signals using electromagnetic waves without a connecting wire 2 : a radio receiving set 3 : the radio broadcasting industry — **radio** *adj*

²radio *vb* : to communicate or send a message to by radio

ra·dio·ac·tiv·i·ty \ˌrād-ē-ō-ˌak-'tiv-ət-ē\ *n* : the property that some elements have of spontaneously emitting energetic particles by the disintegration of atomic nuclei — **ra·dio·ac·tive** \-'ak-tiv\ *adj*

radio astronomy *n* : astronomy dealing with radio waves received from outside the earth's atmosphere

ra·dio·car·bon \ˌrād-ē-ō-'kär-bən\ *n* : CARBON 14

radio frequency *n* : an electromagnetic wave frequency intermediate between audio frequency and infrared frequency used esp. in radio and television transmission

ra·dio·gen·ic \ˌrād-ē-ō-'jen-ik\ *adj* : produced by radioactivity

ra·dio·gram \'rād-ē-ō-ˌgram\ *n* 1 : RADIOGRAPH 2 : a message transmitted by radiotelegraphy

ra·dio·graph \-ˌgraf\ *n* : a photograph made by some form of radiation other than light; *esp* : an X-ray photograph — **radiograph** *vb* — **ra·dio·graph·ic** \ˌrād-ē-ō-ˈgraf-ik\ *adj* — **ra·dio·graph·i·cal·ly** \-i-k(ə-)lē\ *adv* — **ra·di·og·ra·phy** \ˌrād-ē-ˈäg-rə-fē\ *n*

ra·dio·iso·tope \ˌrād-ē-ō-ˈī-sə-ˌtōp\ *n* : a radioactive isotope

ra·di·ol·o·gy \ˌrād-ē-ˈäl-ə-jē\ *n* : the use of radiant energy (as X rays and radium radiations) in medicine — **ra·di·ol·o·gist** \-jəst\ *n*

ra·dio·man \ˈrād-ē-ō-ˌman\ *n* : a radio operator or technician

ra·di·om·e·ter \ˌrād-ē-ˈäm-ət-ər\ *n* : an instrument for measuring the intensity of radiant energy — **ra·di·om·e·try** \-ə-trē\ *n* — **ra·dio·met·ric** \ˌrād-ē-ō-ˈme-trik\ *adj*

ra·dio·phone \ˈrād-ē-ə-ˌfōn\ *n* : RADIO-TELEPHONE

ra·dio·sonde \ˈrād-ē-ō-ˌsänd\ *n* : a small radio transmitter carried aloft (as by balloon) and used to transmit meteorological data

ra·dio·tele·graph \ˌrād-ē-ō-ˈtel-ə-ˌgraf\ *n* : wireless telegraphy — **ra·dio·tele·graph·ic** \-ˌtel-ə-ˈgraf-ik\ *adj* — **ra·dio·te·leg·ra·phy** \-tə-ˈleg-rə-fē\ *n*

ra·dio·tele·phone \-ˈtel-ə-ˌfōn\ *n* : a telephone that uses radio waves wholly or partly instead of connecting wires — **ra·dio·te·le·pho·ny** \-ˈlef-ə-nē, -ˈtel-ə-ˌfō-nē\ *n*

radio telescope *n* : a radio receiver-antenna combination used for observation in radio astronomy

ra·dio·ther·a·py \ˌrād-ē-ō-ˈther-ə-pē\ *n* : the treatment of disease by means of X rays or radioactive substances — **ra·dio·ther·a·pist** \-pəst\ *n*

rad·ish \ˈrad-ish\ *n* [ME, alter. of OE *rædic*, fr. L *radic-, radix* root, radish] : a pungent fleshy root usu. eaten raw; *also* : a plant related to the mustards that produces this root

ra·di·um \ˈrād-ē-əm\ *n* : a strongly radioactive metallic chemical element that is used in the treatment of cancer

ra·di·us \ˈrād-ē-əs\ *n, pl* **ra·dii** \-ē-ˌī\ *also* **ra·di·us·es** 1 : the one of the two bones of the human forearm that is on the thumb side; 2 : a straight line extending from the center of a circle or a sphere to the circumference or surface 3 : a circular area defined by the length of its radius *syn* range, reach, scope, compass

RADM *abbr* rear admiral

ra·don \ˈrā-ˌdän\ *n* : a heavy radioactive gaseous chemical element

RAF *abbr* Royal Air Force

raf·fia \ˈraf-ē-ə\ *n* : fiber used esp. for making baskets and hats and obtained from the stalks of the leaves of a Madagascar palm (raffia palm)

raff·ish \ˈraf-ish\ *adj* : jaunty or sporty esp. in a flashy or vulgar manner — **raff·ish·ly** *adv* — **raff·ish·ness** *n*

¹raf·fle \ˈraf-əl\ *n* : a lottery in which the prize is won by one of a number of persons buying chances

²raffle *vb* **raf·fled; raf·fling** \ˈraf-(ə-)liŋ\ : to dispose of by a raffle

¹raft \ˈraft\ *n* 1 : a number of logs or timbers fastened together to form a float 2 : a flat structure for support or transportation on water

²raft *vb* 1 : to travel or transport by raft 2 : to make into a raft

³raft *n* : a large amount or number

raf·ter \ˈraf-tər\ *n* : a usu. sloping timber of a roof

¹rag \ˈrag\ *n* : a waste piece of cloth

²rag *n* : a composition in ragtime

ra·ga \ˈräg-ə\ *n* 1 : an ancient traditional melodic pattern or mode in Indian music 2 : an improvisation based on a raga

rag·a·muf·fin \ˈrag-ə-ˌməf-ən\ *n* [*Ragamoffyn*, a demon in *Piers Plowman* (1393), attributed to William Langland] : a ragged dirty person

¹rage \ˈrāj\ *n* 1 : violent and uncontrolled anger 2 : VOGUE, FASHION

²rage *vb* **raged; rag·ing** 1 : to be furiously angry : RAVE 2 : to be in violent tumult (the storm *raged*) 3 : to continue out of control

rag·ged \ˈrag-əd\ *adj* 1 : TORN, TATTERED; *also* : wearing tattered clothes 2 : done in an uneven way (a ~ performance) — **rag·ged·ly** *adv* — **rag·ged·ness** *n*

rag·lan \ˈrag-lən\ *n* : an overcoat with sleeves (raglan sleeves) sewn in with seams slanting from neck to underarm

ra·gout \ra-ˈgü\ *n* [F *ragoût*, fr. *ragoûter* to revive the taste, fr. *re-* + *a-* to (fr. L *ad-*) + *goût* taste, fr. L *gustus*] : a highly seasoned meat stew with vegetables

rag·pick·er \ˈrag-ˌpik-ər\ *n* : one who collects rags and refuse for a livelihood

rag·time \ˈrag-ˌtīm\ *n* : rhythm in which there is more or less continuous syncopation in the melody

rag·weed \-ˌwēd\ *n* : any of several coarse weedy herbs with allergenic pollen

¹raid \ˈrād\ *n* : a sudden usu. surprise attack or invasion : FORAY

²raid *vb* : to make a raid on — **raid·er** *n*

¹rail \ˈrāl\ *n* [ME *raile*, fr. MF *reille* ruler, bar, fr. L *regula* ruler, fr. *regere* to keep straight, direct, rule] 1 : a bar extending from one support to another as a guard or barrier 2 : a bar forming a track for wheeled vehicles 3 : RAILROAD

²rail *vb* : to provide with a railing : FENCE

³rail *n, pl* **rail** *or* **rails** : any of a family of small wading birds related to the cranes and often hunted as game birds

⁴rail *vb* [ME *railen*, fr. MF *railler* to mock, fr. Old Provençal *ralhar* to babble, joke] : to complain angrily : SCOLD, REVILE — **rail·er** *n*

rail·ing \ˈrā-liŋ\ *n* : a barrier of rails

rail·lery \ˈrā-lə-rē\ *n, pl* **-ler·ies** : good-natured ridicule : BANTER

¹rail·road \'rāl-ˌrōd\ n : a permanent road with rails fixed to ties providing a track for cars; also : such a road and its assets constituting a property

²railroad vb 1 : to send by rail 2 : to work on a railroad 3 : to put through (as a law) too hastily 4 : to convict hastily or with insufficient or improper evidence — **rail·road·er** n — **rail·road·ing** n

rail·way \-ˌwā\ n 1 : a line of track providing a runway for wheels 2 : RAILROAD

rai·ment \'rā-mənt\ n : CLOTHING

¹rain \'rān\ n 1 : water falling in drops from the clouds 2 : a shower of objects ⟨a ~ of bullets⟩ — rainy adj

²rain vb 1 : to fall as or like rain 2 : to send down rain 3 : to pour down

rain·bow \-ˌbō\ n : an arc or circle of colors formed by the refraction and reflection of the sun's rays in rain, spray, or mist

rainbow trout n : a large stout-bodied trout of western No. America that usu. has red or pink stripes with black dots along its sides

rain check n 1 : a ticket stub good for a later performance when the scheduled one is rained out 2 : an assurance of a deferred extension of an offer

rain·coat \-ˌkōt\ n : a waterproof or water-repellent coat

rain·drop \-ˌdräp\ n : a drop of rain

rain·fall \-ˌfȯl\ n 1 : a fall of rain 2 : amount of precipitation ⟨an annual ~ of 50 centimeters⟩

rain forest n : a tropical woodland that has an annual rainfall of at least 100 inches and that is marked by lofty broad-leaved evergreen trees forming a continuous canopy

rain·mak·ing \'rān-ˌmā-kiŋ\ n : the action or process of producing or attempting to produce rain by artificial means — **rain·mak·er** \-kər\ n

rain out vb : to interrupt or prevent by rain

rain·storm \'rān-ˌstȯrm\ n : a storm of or with rain

rain·wa·ter \-ˌwȯt-ər, -ˌwät-\ n : water fallen as rain

¹raise \'rāz\ vb raised; rais·ing 1 : to cause or help to rise : LIFT ⟨~ a window⟩ 2 : AWAKEN, AROUSE ⟨enough to ~ the dead⟩ 3 : BUILD, ERECT ⟨~ a monument⟩ 4 : PROMOTE ⟨was raised to captain⟩ 5 : COLLECT ⟨~ money⟩ 6 : BREED, GROW ⟨~ cattle⟩ ⟨~ corn⟩; also : BRING UP ⟨~ a family⟩ 7 : PROVOKE ⟨~ a laugh⟩ 8 : to bring to notice ⟨~ an objection⟩ 9 : INCREASE ⟨~ prices⟩; also : to bet more than 10 : to make light and spongy ⟨~ dough⟩ 11 : END ⟨~ a siege⟩ 12 : to cause to form ⟨~ a blister⟩ syn lift, hoist, boost, elevate — **rais·er** n

²raise n : an increase in amount (as of a bid or bet); also : an increase in pay

rai·sin \'rāz-ᵊn\ n [ME, fr. MF, grape, fr. L racemus cluster of grapes or berries] : a grape dried for food

rai·son d'être \ˌrā-ˌzōⁿ-ˈdetrᵊ\ n : reason or justification for existence

ra·ja or ra·jah \'räj-ə\ n [Hindi rājā, fr. Skt rājan king] : an Indian prince

¹rake \'rāk\ n : a long-handled garden tool having a crossbar with prongs

²rake vb raked; rak·ing 1 : to gather, loosen, or smooth with or as if with a rake 2 : to sweep the length of (as a trench or ship) with gunfire

³rake n : inclination from either perpendicular or horizontal : SLANT, SLOPE

⁴rake n : a dissolute man : LIBERTINE

rake-off \'rāk-ˌȯf\ n : a percentage or cut taken

rak·ish \'rā-kish\ adj : DISSOLUTE — rak·ish·ly adv — rak·ish·ness n

²rakish adj 1 : having a smart appearance indicative of speed ⟨a ~ sloop⟩ ⟨~ masts⟩ 2 : JAUNTY, SPORTY — rak·ish·ly adv — rak·ish·ness n

¹ral·ly \'ral-ē\ vb ral·lied; ral·ly·ing 1 : to bring together for a common purpose; also : to bring back to order ⟨a leader ~ing his forces⟩ 2 : to arouse to activity or from depression or weakness : REVIVE, RECOVER 3 : to come together again to renew an effort syn stir, rouse, awaken, waken, kindle

²rally n, pl rallies 1 : an act of rallying 2 : a mass meeting to arouse enthusiasm 3 : a competitive automobile event run over public roads

³rally vb ral·lied; ral·ly·ing : BANTER

¹ram \'ram\ n 1 : a male sheep 2 : BATTERING RAM

²ram vb rammed; ram·ming 1 : to force or drive in or through 2 : CRAM, CROWD 3 : to strike against violently

¹ram·ble \'ram-bəl\ vb ram·bled; ram·bling \-b(ə-)liŋ\ : to go about aimlessly : ROAM, WANDER

²ramble n : a leisurely excursion; esp : an aimless walk

ram·bler \'ram-blər\ n 1 : a person who rambles 2 : a hardy climbing rose with large clusters of small flowers

ram·bunc·tious \ram-ˈbəŋk-shəs\ adj : UNRULY

ra·mie \'rā-mē, 'ram-ē\ n : a strong lustrous bast fiber from an Asian nettle

ram·i·fy \'ram-ə-ˌfī\ vb -fied; -fy·ing : to branch out — **ram·i·fi·ca·tion** \ˌram-ə-fə-ˈkā-shən\ n

ramp \'ramp\ n : a sloping passage or roadway connecting different levels

¹ram·page \'ram-ˌpāj, (ˈ)ram-ˈpāj\ vb ram·paged; ram·pag·ing : to rush about wildly

²ram·page \'ram-ˌpāj\ n : a course of violent or riotous action or behavior — ram·pa·geous \ram-ˈpā-jəs\ adj

ram·pan·cy \'ram-pən-sē\ n : the quality or state of being rampant

ram·pant \'ram-pənt\ adj : unchecked in growth or spread : RIFE ⟨fear was ~ in the town⟩ — ram·pant·ly adv

ram·part \'ram-ˌpärt\ n 1 : a broad embankment raised as a fortification 2

: a protective barrier **3** : a wall-like ridge

¹ram·rod \'ram-ˌräd\ *n* **1** : a rod used to ram a charge into a muzzle-loading gun **2** : a cleaning rod for small arms **3** : BOSS, OVERSEER

²ramrod *vb* : to direct, supervise, and control

ram·shack·le \'ram-ˌshak-əl\ *adj* : RICKETY, TUMBLEDOWN

ran *past of* RUN

¹ranch \'ranch\ *n* [MexSp *rancho* small ranch, fr. Sp. *rancho* camp, hut & Sp dial., small farm, fr. Old Spanish *ranchear* (*se*) to take up quarters, fr. MF (*se*) *ranger* to take up a position, fr. *ranger* to set in a row] **1** : an establishment for the raising and grazing of livestock (as cattle, sheep, or horses) **2** : a large farm devoted to a specialty

²ranch *vb* : to live or work on a ranch — **ranch·er** *n*

ranch house *n* : a one-story house typically with a low-pitched roof

ran·cho \'ran-chō, 'rän-\ *n, pl* **ranchos** : RANCH

ran·cid \'ran-səd\ *adj* **1** : having a rank smell or taste **2** : ROTTEN, SPOILED — **ran·cid·i·ty** \ran-'sid-ət-ē\ *n*

ran·cor \'raŋ-kər\ *n* : deep hatred : intense ill will *syn* antagonism, animosity, antipathy, enmity, hostility — **ran·cor·ous** *adj*

rand \'rand, 'ränd, 'ränt\ *n, pl* **rand** — see MONEY table

R & B *abbr* rhythm and blues

R & D *abbr* research and development

ran·dom \'ran-dəm\ *adj* : CHANCE, HAPHAZARD — **ran·dom·ly** *adv* — **ran·dom·ness** *n*

random-access *adj* : allowing access to stored data in any order the user desires

random-access memory \ˌran-dəm-'ak-ˌses-\ *n* : a computer memory that provides the main internal storage available to the user for programs and data

ran·dom·ize \'ran-də-ˌmīz\ *vb* **-ized; -iz·ing** : to distribute, treat, or perform in a random way — **ran·dom·iza·tion** \ˌran-də-mə-'zā-shən\ *n*

R and R *abbr* rest and recreation; rest and recuperation

rang *past of* RING

¹range \'rānj\ *n* **1** : a series of things in a row **2** : the act of ranging or roaming **3** : open land where animals (as livestock) may roam and graze **4** : a cooking stove **5** : a variation within limits **6** : the distance a weapon will shoot or is to be shot **7** : a place where shooting is practiced; *also* : a course over which missiles are tested **8** : the space or extent included, covered, or used : SCOPE *syn* reach, compass, radius, circle

²range *vb* **ranged; rang·ing** **1** : to set in a row or in proper order **2** : to set in place among others of the same kind **3** : to roam over or through : EXPLORE **4**

: to roam at large or freely **5** : to correspond in direction or line **6** : to vary within limits **7** : to find the range of an object by instrument (as radar)

rang·er \'rān-jər\ *n* **1** : a warden who patrols forest lands **2** : a member of a body of troops who range over a region **3** : an expert in close-range fighting and raiding tactics

rangy \'rān-jē\ *adj* **rang·i·er; -est** : being long-limbed and slender — **rang·i·ness** \'rān-jē-nəs\ *n*

ra·ni *or* **ra·nee** \rä-'nē, 'rän-ˌē\ *n* : a raja's wife

¹rank \'raŋk\ *adj* **1** : strong and vigorous and usu. coarse in growth (∼ weeds) **2** : unpleasantly strong-smelling — **rank·ly** *adv* — **rank·ness** *n*

²rank *n* **1** : ROW **2** : a line of soldiers ranged side by side **3** *pl* : the body of enlisted men (rose from the ∼s) **4** : an orderly arrangement **5** : CLASS, DIVISION **6** : a grade of official standing (as in an army) **7** : position in a group **8** : superior position

³rank *vb* **1** : to arrange in lines or in regular formation **2** : to arrange according to classes **3** : to take or have a relative position **4** : to rate above (as in official standing)

rank and file *n* **1** : the enlisted men of an armed force **2** : the general membership of a body as contrasted with its leaders

rank·ing \'raŋ-kiŋ\ *adj* **1** : having a high position : FOREMOST **2** : being next to the chairman in seniority

ran·kle \'raŋ-kəl\ *vb* **ran·kled; ran·kling** \-k(ə-)liŋ\ [ME *ranclen* to fester, fr. MF *rancler*, fr. OF *draoncler*, *raoncler*, fr. *draoncle*, *raoncle* festering sore, fr. (assumed) VL *dracunculus*, fr. L, dim. of *draco* serpent] : to cause anger, irritation, or bitterness

ran·sack \'ran-ˌsak\ *vb* : to search thoroughly; *esp* : to search through and rob

¹ran·som \'ran-səm\ *n* [ME *ransoun*, fr. OF *rançon*, fr. L *redemption-*, *redemptio* act of buying back, fr. *redimere* to buy back, redeem] **1** : something paid or demanded for the freedom of a captive **2** : the act of ransoming

²ransom *vb* : to free from captivity or punishment by paying a price — **ran·som·er** *n*

rant \'rant\ *vb* **1** : to talk loudly and wildly **2** : to scold violently — **rant·er** *n* — **rant·ing·ly** \-iŋ-lē\ *adv*

¹rap \'rap\ *n* **1** : a sharp blow **2** : a sharp rebuke **3** *slang* : responsibility for or consequences of an action

²rap *vb* **rapped; rap·ping** **1** : to strike sharply : KNOCK **2** : to utter sharply **3** : to criticize sharply

³rap *vb* **rapped; rap·ping** : to talk freely and frankly — **rap** *n*

ra·pa·cious \rə-'pā-shəs\ *adj* **1** : excessively greedy or covetous **2** : living on prey **3** : RAVENOUS — **ra·pa·cious·ly**

adv — **ra·pa·cious·ness** *n* — **ra·pac·i·ty** \-'pas-ət-ē\ *n*

¹**rape** \'rāp\ *n* : a European herb related to the mustards that is grown as a forage crop and for its seeds (rapeseed \-,sēd\)

²**rape** *vb* **raped; rap·ing** : to commit rape on : RAVISH — **rap·er** *n* — **rap·ist** \'rā-pəst\ *n*

³**rape** *n* **1** : a carrying away by force **2** : sexual intercourse by a man with a woman without her consent and chiefly by force or deception; *also* : unlawful sexual intercourse of any kind by force or threat

¹**rap·id** \'rap-əd\ *adj* [L *rapidus* seizing, sweeping, rapid, fr. *rapere* to seize, sweep away] : very fast : SWIFT *syn* fleet, quick, speedy — **ra·pid·i·ty** \rə-'pid-ət-ē\ *n* — **rap·id·ly** \'rap-əd-lē\ *adv*

²**rapid** *n* : a place in a stream where the current flows very fast usu. over obstructions — usu. used in pl.

rapid eye movement *n* : rapid conjugate movement of the eyes associated with REM sleep

rapid transit *n* : fast passenger transportation (as by subway) in urban areas

ra·pi·er \'rā-pē-ər\ *n* : a straight 2-edged sword with a narrow pointed blade

rap·ine \'rap-ən, -,īn\ *n* : PILLAGE, PLUNDER

rap·pen \'räp-ən\ *n, pl* **rappen** : the centime of Switzerland

rap·port \ra-'pōr\ *n* : RELATION; *esp* : relation characterized by harmony

rap·proche·ment \,rap-,rōsh-'mä, ra-'prōsh-,mä°\ *n* : the establishment of or a state of having cordial relations

rap·scal·lion \rap-'skal-yən\ *n* : RASCAL, SCAMP

rapt \'rapt\ *adj* **1** : carried away with emotion **2** : ABSORBED, ENGROSSED — **rapt·ly** \'rap-(t)lē\ *adv* — **rapt·ness** \'rap(t)-nəs\ *n*

rap·ture \'rap-chər\ *n* : spiritual or emotional ecstasy — **rap·tur·ous** \-chə-rəs\ *adj*

rapture of the deep : a confused mental state caused by nitrogen forced into a diver's bloodstream from atmospheric air under pressure

ra·ra avis \,rar-ə-'ā-vəs\ *n* [L, rare bird] : a rare person or thing : RARITY

¹**rare** \'ra(ə)r\ *adj* **rar·er; rar·est** : not thick or dense : THIN ⟨~ air⟩ **2** : unusually fine : EXCELLENT, SPLENDID **3** : seldom met with — **rare·ly** *adv* — **rare·ness** *n* — **rar·i·ty** \'rar-ət-ē\ *n*

²**rare** *adj* **rar·er; rar·est** : cooked so that the inside is still red ⟨~ beef⟩

rare·bit \'ra(ə)r-bət\ *n* : WELSH RABBIT

rar·efac·tion \,rar-ə-'fak-shən\ *n* **1** : the action or process of rarefying **2** : the state of being rarefied **3** : a state or region of minimum pressure in a substance (as air) being traveled through

by a wave formed by compression (as sound)

rar·efy *also* **rar·i·fy** \'rar-ə-,fī\ *vb* **-efied; -efy·ing** : to make or become rare, thin, or less dense

rar·ing \'rar-ən, -iŋ\ *adj* : full of enthusiasm or eagerness

ras·cal \'ras-kəl\ *n* **1** : a mean or dishonest person **2** : a mischievous person — **ras·cal·i·ty** \ras-'kal-ət-ē\ *n* — **ras·cal·ly** \'ras-kə-lē\ *adj*

¹**rash** \'rash\ *adj* : having or showing little regard for consequences : too hasty in decision, action, or speech : RECKLESS *syn* daring, foolhardy, adventurous, venturesome — **rash·ly** *adv* — **rash·ness** *n*

²**rash** *n* : an eruption on the body

rash·er \'rash-ər\ *n* : a thin slice of bacon or ham broiled or fried; *also* : a portion consisting of several such slices

¹**rasp** \'rasp\ *vb* **1** : to rub with or as if with a rough file **2** : to grate harshly on (as one's nerves) **3** : to speak in a grating tone

²**rasp** *n* : a coarse file with cutting points instead of ridges

rasp·ber·ry \'raz-,ber-ē, -b(ə-)rē\ *n* **1** : an edible red or black berry produced by some brambles; *also* : such a bramble **2** : a sound of contempt made by protruding the tongue through the lips and expelling air forcibly

¹**rat** \'rat\ *n* **1** : any of numerous scaly-tailed rodents larger than the related mice **2** : a contemptible person; *esp* : one that betrays his associates

²**rat** *vb* **rat·ted; rat·ting 1** : to betray one's associates **2** : to hunt or catch rats

rat cheese *n* : CHEDDAR

ratch·et \'rach-ət\ *n* : a device that consists of a bar or wheel having slanted teeth into which a pawl drops so as to allow motion in only one direction

ratchet wheel *n* : a toothed wheel held in position or turned by a pawl

¹**rate** \'rāt\ *vb* **rat·ed; rat·ing** : to scold violently

²**rate** *n* **1** : quantity, amount, or degree measured by some standard **2** : an amount (as of payment) measured by its relation to some other amount (as of time) **3** : a charge, payment, or price fixed according to a ratio, scale, or standard ⟨tax ~⟩ **4** : RANK, CLASS

³**rate** *vb* **rat·ed; rat·ing 1** : CONSIDER, REGARD **2** : ESTIMATE **3** : to settle the relative rank or class of **4** : to be classed : RANK **5** : to be of consequence **6** : to have a right to : DESERVE — **rat·er** *n*

rath·er \'rath-ər, 'räth-, 'rəth-\ *adv* [ME, fr. OE *hrathor,* compar. of *hrathe* quickly] **1** : more properly **2** : PREFERABLY **3** : more correctly speaking **4** : to the contrary : INSTEAD **5** : SOMEWHAT

raths·kel·ler \'rät-,skel-ər, 'rat(h)-\ *n* [obs. G (now *ratskeller*), city-hall basement restaurant, fr. *rat* council + *keller* cellar] : a usu. basement tavern or restaurant

rat·i·fy \'rat-ə-ˌfī\ *vb* **-fied; -fy·ing** : to approve and accept formally — **rat·i·fi·ca·tion** \ˌrat-ə-fə-'kā-shən\ *n*

rat·ing \'rāt-iŋ\ *n* 1 : a classification according to grade : RANK 2 *Brit* : a naval enlisted man 3 : an estimate of the credit standing and business responsibility of a person or firm

ra·tio \'rā-sh(ē-)ō\ *n, pl* **ra·tios** 1 : the quotient of two numbers or mathematical expressions 2 : the relation in number, quantity, or degree between things

ra·ti·o·ci·na·tion \ˌrat-ē-ˌōs-ᵊn-'ā-shən, ˌrash-, -ˌās-\ *n* : exact thinking : REASONING — **ra·ti·o·ci·nate** \-'ōs-ᵊn-ˌāt, -'ās-\ *vb* — **ra·ti·o·ci·na·tive** \-'ōs-ᵊn-ˌāt-iv, -'ās-\ *adj* — **ra·ti·o·ci·na·tor** \-'ōs-ᵊn-ˌāt-ər, -'ās-\ *n*

¹**ra·tion** \'rash-ən, 'rā-shən\ *n* 1 : a food allowance for one day 2 : FOOD, PROVISIONS, DIET — usu. used in pl. 3 : SHARE, ALLOTMENT

²**ration** *vb* **ra·tioned; ra·tion·ing** \'rash-(ə-)niŋ, 'rāsh-\ 1 : to supply with or allot as rations 2 : to use or allot sparingly *syn* apportion, portion, prorate, parcel

¹**ra·tio·nal** \'rash-(ə-)nəl\ *adj* 1 : having reason or understanding; *also* : SANE 2 : of or relating to reason 3 : relating to, consisting of, or being one or more rational numbers — **ra·tio·nal·ly** \-ē\ *adv*

²**rational** *n* : RATIONAL NUMBER

ra·tio·nale \ˌrash-ə-'nal\ *n* 1 : an explanation of principles controlling belief or practice 2 : an underlying reason

ra·tio·nal·ism \'rash-(ə-)nə-ˌliz-əm\ *n* : the practice of guiding one's actions and opinions solely by what seems reasonable — **ra·tio·nal·ist** \-əst\ *n* — **rationalist** *or* **ra·tio·nal·is·tic** \ˌrash-(ə-)nə-'lis-tik\ *adj*

ra·tio·nal·i·ty \ˌrash-ə-'nal-ət-ē\ *n, pl* **-ties** : the quality or state of being rational

ra·tio·nal·ize \'rash-(ə-)nə-ˌlīz\ *vb* **-ized; -iz·ing** 1 : to make (something irrational) appear rational or reasonable 2 : to provide a natural explanation of (as a myth) 3 : to justify (as one's behavior or weaknesses) esp. to oneself 4 : to find plausible but untrue reasons for conduct — **ra·tio·nal·i·za·tion** \ˌrash-(ə-)nə-lə-'zā-shən\ *n*

rational number *n* : an integer or the quotient of two integers

rat·line \'rat-lən\ *n* : one of the small transverse ropes fastened to the shrouds of a ship and forming the steps of a rope ladder

rat race *n* : strenuous, tiresome, and usu. competitive activity or rush

rat·tan \ra-'tan, rə-\ *n* : an Asian climbing palm with long stems

rat·ter \'rat-ər\ *n* : a rat-catching dog or cat

¹**rat·tle** \'rat-ᵊl\ *vb* **rat·tled; rat·tling** \'rat-(ᵊ-)liŋ\ 1 : to make or cause to make a series of clattering sounds 2 : to move with a clattering sound 3 : to say or do in a brisk lively fashion (∼ off the answers) 4 : CONFUSE, UPSET (∼ a witness)

²**rattle** *n* 1 : a series of clattering and knocking sounds 2 : a toy that produces a rattle when shaken 3 : a rattling organ at the end of a rattlesnake's tail made up of horny joints

rat·tler \'rat-lər\ *n* : RATTLESNAKE

rat·tle·snake \'rat-ᵊl-ˌsnāk\ *n* : any of various American venomous snakes with a rattle at the end of the tail

rat·tle·trap \'rat-ᵊl-ˌtrap\ *n* : something rickety and full of rattles; *esp* : an old car

rat·tling \'rat-liŋ\ *adj* 1 : LIVELY, BRISK 2 : FIRST-RATE, SPLENDID

rat·trap \'rat-ˌtrap\ *n* 1 : a trap for rats 2 : a dilapidated building

rat·ty \'rat-ē\ *adj* **rat·ti·er; -est** 1 : infested with rats 2 : of, relating to, or suggestive of rats 3 : SHABBY

rau·cous \'ró-kəs\ *adj* 1 : HARSH, HOARSE, STRIDENT 2 : boisterously disorderly — **rau·cous·ly** *adv* — **rau·cous·ness** *n*

raun·chy \'rón-chē, 'rän-\ *adj* **raun·chi·er; -est** 1 : SLOVENLY, DIRTY 2 : OBSCENE, SMUTTY — **raun·chi·ness** \-chē-nəs\ *n*

rau·wol·fia \raù-'wùl-fē-ə, ró-\ *n* : a medicinal extract from the root of an Indian tree; *also* : this tree

¹**rav·age** \'rav-ij\ *n* [F] : an act or result of ravaging : DEVASTATION

²**ravage** *vb* **rav·aged; rav·ag·ing** : to lay waste : DEVASTATE — **rav·ag·er** *n*

¹**rave** \'rāv\ *vb* **raved; rav·ing** [ME *raven*] 1 : to talk wildly in or as if in delirium : STORM, RAGE 2 : to talk with extreme enthusiasm

²**rave** *n* 1 : an act or instance of raving 2 : an extravagantly favorable criticism

¹**rav·el** \'rav-əl\ *vb* **-eled** *or* **-elled; -el·ing** *or* **-el·ling** \-(ə-)liŋ\ 1 : UNRAVEL, UNTWIST 2 : TANGLE, CONFUSE

²**ravel** *n* 1 : something tangled 2 : something raveled out; *esp* : a loose thread

¹**ra·ven** \'rā-vən\ *n* : a large black bird related to the crow

²**raven** *adj* : black and glossy like a raven's feathers

rav·en·ing \'rav-(ə-)niŋ\ *adj* : GREEDY

rav·en·ous \'rav-(ə-)nəs\ *adj* 1 : RAPACIOUS, VORACIOUS 2 : eager for food : very hungry — **rav·en·ous·ly** *adv* — **rav·en·ous·ness** *n*

ra·vine \rə-'vēn\ *n* : a small narrow steep-sided valley larger than a gully and smaller than a canyon

rav·i·o·li \ˌrav-ē-'ō-lē\ *n* [It, fr. It dial., pl. of *raviolo*, lit., little turnip, dim. of *rava* turnip, fr. L *rapa*] : small cases of dough with a savory filling (as of meat or cheese)

rav·ish \'rav-ish\ *vb* 1 : to seize and take away by violence 2 : to over-

come with emotion and esp. with joy
or delight **3** : RAPE — **rav·ish·er** *n* —
rav·ish·ment *n*

¹**raw** \'ró\ *adj* **raw·er** \'ró-(-ə)r\ ; **raw·est**
\'ró-əst\ **1** : not cooked **2** : changed
little from the original form : not processed ⟨∼ materials⟩ **3** : having the
skin abraded or irritated ⟨a ∼ sore⟩ **4**
: not trained or experienced ⟨∼ re-
cruits⟩ **5** : VULGAR, COARSE **6** : disagreeably cold and damp ⟨a ∼ day⟩ **7**
: UNFAIR ⟨∼ deal⟩ — **raw·ness** *n*

²**raw** *n* : a raw place or state; *esp* : NUDI-
TY

raw-boned \'ró-'bōnd\ *adj* **1** : LEAN,
GAUNT **2** : having a heavy frame that
seems to have little flesh

raw·hide \'ró-₁hīd\ *n* : the untanned
skin of cattle; *also* : a whip made of
this

¹**ray** \'rā\ *n* : any of numerous large flat
fishes that are related to the sharks
and have the eyes on the upper surface and the hind end of the body slender and taillike

²**ray** *n* [ME, fr. MF *rai*, fr. L *radius* rod,
ray] **1** : one of the lines of light that
appear to radiate from a bright object
2 : a thin beam of radiant energy ⟨as
light⟩ **3** : light from a beam **4** : a thin
line like a beam of light **5** : an animal
or plant structure resembling a ray **6**
: a tiny bit : PARTICLE ⟨a ∼ of hope⟩

ray·on \'rā-₁än\ *n* : a yarn, thread, or
fabric made from fibers produced
chemically from cellulose

raze \'rāz\ *vb* **razed; raz·ing 1** : to destroy to the ground : DEMOLISH **2** : to
scrape, cut, or shave off

ra·zor \'rā-zər\ *n* : a sharp cutting instrument used to shave off hair

ra·zor–backed \₁rā-zər-'bakt\ *or* **ra·zor-
back** \'rā-zər-₁bak\ *adj* : having a
sharp narrow back ⟨∼ horse⟩

razor clam *n* : any of numerous marine
bivalve mollusks having a long narrow curved thin shell

¹**razz** \'raz\ *n* : RASPBERRY 2

²**razz** *vb* : RIDICULE, TEASE

Rb *symbol* rubidium

RBC *abbr* red blood cells; red blood
count

RBI \₁är-(₁)bē-'ī, 'rib-ē\ *n, pl* **RBIs** *or*
RBI [*run batted in*] : a run in baseball
that is driven in by a batter

RC *abbr* **1** Red Cross **2** Roman Catholic

RCAF *abbr* Royal Canadian Air Force

RCMP *abbr* Royal Canadian Mounted
Police

rct *abbr* recruit

rd *abbr* **1** road **2** rod **3** round

RD *abbr* rural delivery

RDA *abbr* recommended daily allowance; recommended dietary allowance

re \(')rā, (')rē\ *prep* : with regard to

Re *symbol* rhenium

re- \rē, ₁rē, 'rē\ *prefix* **1** : again : anew
2 : back : backward

reabsorb   reaccommodate

reacquire   recheck
reactivate   rechristen
reactivation   reclean
readapt   recoin
readdress   recolonization
readjust   recolonize
readjustment   recolor
readmission   recomb
readmit   recombine
readmittance   recommence
readopt   recommission
reaffirm   recommit
reaffirmation   recompile
realign   recompose
realignment   recompress
reallocate   recompression
reallocation   recomputation
reanalysis   recompute
reanalyze   reconceive
reanimate   reconcentrate
reanimation   reconception
reannex   recondensation
reannexation   recondense
reappear   recondition
reappearance   reconfirm
reapplication   reconfirmation
reapply   reconnect
reappoint   reconquer
reappointment   reconquest
reapportion   reconsecrate
reapportionment   reconsecration
reappraisal   reconsult
reappraise   reconsultation
rearm   recontact
rearmament   recontaminate
rearouse   recontamination
rearrange   recontract
rearrangement   reconvene
rearrest   reconvert
reascend   recook
reassail   recopy
reassemble   recouple
reassembly   recross
reassert   recrystallize
reassess   recut
reassessment   redecorate
reassign   redecoration
reassignment   rededicate
reassume   rededication
reattach   redefine
reattachment   redefinition
reattack   redeposit
reattempt   redesign
reauthorization   redetermination
reauthorize   redetermine
reawake   redevelop
reawaken   redevelopment
rebaptism   redigest
rebaptize   redip
rebid   redirect
rebind   rediscount
reboil   rediscover
rebroadcast   rediscovery
reburial   redissolve
rebury   redistill
recalculate   redistillation
recalculation   redistribute
rechannel   redistribution
recharge   redouble
recharter   redraft
                    redraw

reecho
reedit
reelect
reelection
reembodiment
reembody
reemerge
reemergence
reemphasis
reemphasize
reemploy
reemployment
reenact
reenactment
reenergize
reenlist
reenlistment
reenter
reequip
reestablish
reestablishment
reevaluate
reevaluation
reexamination
reexamine
reexchange
reexport
refashion
refasten
refight
refigure
refilm
refilter
refinance
refinish
refit
refix
refloat
refly
refold
reforge
reformulate
reformulation
refortify
refound
refreeze
refuel
refurnish
regather
regild
regive
reglue
regrade
regrind
regrowth
rehandle
rehear
reheat
rehouse
reimpose
reimposition
reincorporate
reinsert
reinsertion
reintegrate
reinterpret
reinterpretation
reintroduce
reintroduction
reinvent
reinvention

reinvest
reinvestment
reinvigorate
reinvigoration
reissue
rejudge
rekindle
reknit
relaunch
relearn
reletter
relight
reline
reload
remanufacture
remap
remarriage
remarry
remelt
remigration
remix
remold
rename
renegotiate
renegotiation
renominate
renomination
renumber
reoccupy
reopen
reorder
reorganization
reorganize
reorient
reorientation
repack
repaint
repass
repeople
rephotograph
rephrase
replant
repopulate
reprice
reprocess
republication
republish
repurchase
reradiate
reread
rerecord
resay
rescore
rescreen
reseal
reseed
resell
reset
resettle
resettlement
resew
reshipment
reshow
resow
respell
restaff
restate
restatement
restock
restraighten
restrengthen

restrike
restring
restructure
restudy
restuff
restyle
resubmit
resummon
resupply
resurface
resurvey
resynthesis
resynthesize
retaste
retell
retest
rethink
retool
retrain
retransmission
retransmit
retrial

¹reach \'rēch\ vb 1 : to stretch out 2 : to touch or attempt to touch or seize 3 : to extend to 4 : to arrive at 5 : to communicate with syn gain, realize, achieve, attain — reach·able adj — reach·er n

²reach n 1 : an unbroken stretch or expanse; esp : a straight part of a river 2 : the act of reaching 3 : the distance or extent of reaching or of ability to reach 4 : power to comprehend

re·act \rē-'akt\ vb 1 : to exert a return or counteracting influence 2 : to respond to a stimulus 3 : to act in opposition to a force or influence 4 : to turn back or revert to a former condition 5 : to undergo chemical reaction

re·ac·tant \-'tant\ n : a chemically reacting substance

re·ac·tion \rē-'ak-shən\ n 1 : a return or reciprocal action 2 : a counter tendency; esp : a tendency toward a former esp. outmoded political or social order or policy 3 : bodily, mental, or emotional response to a stimulus 4 : chemical change 5 : a process involving change in atomic nuclei

¹re·ac·tion·ary \rē-'ak-shə-ner-ē\ adj : relating to, marked by, or favoring esp. political reaction

²reactionary n, pl -ar·ies : a reactionary person

re·ac·tive \rē-'ak-tiv\ adj : reacting or tending to react

re·ac·tor \rē-'ak-tər\ n 1 : one that reacts 2 : a vessel for a chemical reaction 3 : a device for the controlled release of nuclear energy

¹read \'rēd\ vb read \'red\ ; read·ing \'rēd-iŋ\ 1 : to understand language by interpreting written symbols for speech sounds 2 : to utter aloud written or printed words 3 : to learn by observing (~ nature's signs) 4 : to discover the meaning of (~ the clues) 5 : to attribute (a meaning) to something (~ guilt in his manner) 6 : INDICATE (thermometer ~s 10°) 7 : to study by a course of reading (~s law)

reunification
reunify
reunite
reusable
reuse
revaluate
revaluation
revalue
reverify
revictual
revisit
rewarm
rewash
reweave
rewed
reweigh
reweld
rewind
rewire
rewrite
rezone

8 : to consist in phrasing or meaning ⟨the two versions ∼ differently⟩ — **read·abil·i·ty** \ˌrēd-ə-ˈbil-ət-ē\ *n* — **read·able** \ˈrēd-ə-bəl\ *adj* — **read·ably** \-blē\ *adv* — **read·er** *n*

²**read** \ˈred\ *adj* : informed by reading ⟨a widely ∼ man⟩

read·er·ship \ˈrēd-ər-ˌship\ *n* : the mass or a particular group of readers

read·ing \ˈrēd-iŋ\ *n* **1** : something read or for reading **2** : a particular version **3** : a particular interpretation (as of a law) **4** : a particular performance (as of a musical work) **5** : an indication of a certain state of affairs; *also* : an indication of data made by an instrument ⟨thermometer ∼⟩

read-only memory \ˌrēd-ˈōn-lē-\ *n* : a usu. small computer memory that contains special-purpose information (as a program) which cannot be altered

read·out \ˈrēd-ˌaut\ *n* : the process of removing information from an automatic device (as a computer) and displaying it in an understandable form; *also* : the information removed from such a device

read out \(ˈ)rēd-ˈaut\ *vb* : to expel from an organization

¹**ready** \ˈred-ē\ *adj* **read·i·er; -est** **1** : prepared for use or action **2** : likely to do something indicated; *also* : willingly disposed : INCLINED **3** : spontaneously prompt **4** : notably dexterous, adroit, or skilled **5** : immediately available : HANDY — **read·i·ly** \ˈred-ə-lē\ *adv* — **read·i·ness** \-ē-nəs\ *n*

²**ready** *vb* **read·ied; ready·ing** : to make ready : PREPARE

³**ready** *n* : the state of being ready

ready–made \ˌred-ē-ˈmād\ *adj* : already made up for general sale : not specially made — **ready–made** *n*

ready room *n* : a room in which pilots are briefed and await orders

re·agent \rē-ˈā-jənt\ *n* : a substance that takes part in or brings about a particular chemical reaction

¹**re·al** \ˈrē-(ə)l\ *adj* [ME, real, relating to things (in law), fr. MF, fr. ML & LL; ML *realis* relating to things (in law), fr. LL, real, fr. L *res* thing, fact] **1** : actually being or existent **2** : not artificial : GENUINE — **re·al·ness** *n* — **for real 1** : in earnest **2** : GENUINE

²**real** *adv* : VERY

real estate *n* : property in buildings and land

real image *n* : an image formed by rays of light coming to a focus

re·al·ism \ˈrē-ə-ˌliz-əm\ *n* **1** : the disposition to face facts and to deal with them practically **2** : true and faithful portrayal of nature and of people in art or literature — **re·al·ist** \-ləst\ *adj or n* — **re·al·is·tic** \ˌrē-ə-ˈlis-tik\ *adj* — **re·al·is·ti·cal·ly** \-ti-k(ə-)lē\ *adv*

re·al·i·ty \rē-ˈal-ət-ē\ *n, pl* **-ties** **1** : the quality or state of being real **2** : some-thing real **3** : the totality of real things and events

re·al·ize \ˈrē-ə-ˌlīz\ *vb* **-ized; -iz·ing** **1** : to make actual : ACCOMPLISH **2** : OBTAIN, GAIN ⟨∼ a profit⟩ **3** : to convert into money ⟨∼ assets⟩ **4** : to be aware of : UNDERSTAND — **re·al·iz·able** *adj* — **re·al·iza·tion** \ˌrē-ə-lə-ˈzā-shən\ *n*

re·al·ly \ˈrē-(ə-)lē, ˈril-ē\ *adv* : in truth : in fact : ACTUALLY

realm \ˈrelm\ *n* **1** : KINGDOM **2** : SPHERE, DOMAIN

real number *n* : any of the numbers (as -2, 3, $7/8$, $.25$, π) that are rational or irrational

re·al·po·li·tik \rā-ˈäl-ˌpō-li-ˌtēk\ *n* [G] : politics based on practical and material factors rather than on theoretical or ethical objectives

real time *n* : the actual time during which something takes place — **real–time** *adj*

re·al·ty \ˈrē(ə)l-tē\ *n* : REAL ESTATE

¹**ream** \ˈrēm\ *n* [ME *reme*, fr. MF *raime*, fr. Ar *rizmah*, lit., bundle] : a quantity of paper that is variously 480, 500, or 516 sheets

²**ream** *vb* **1** : to enlarge or shape with a reamer **2** : to clean or clear with a reamer

ream·er \ˈrē-mər\ *n* : a tool with cutting edges that is used to enlarge or shape a hole

reap \ˈrēp\ *vb* **1** : to cut or clear with a scythe, sickle, or machine **2** : to gather by or as if by cutting : HARVEST ⟨∼ a reward⟩ — **reap·er** *n*

¹**rear** \ˈriər\ *vb* **1** : to erect by building **2** : to set or raise upright **3** : to breed and raise for use or market ⟨∼ livestock⟩ **4** : BRING UP, FOSTER **5** : to lift or rise up; *esp* : to rise on the hind legs

²**rear** *n* **1** : the unit (as of an army) or area farthest from the enemy **2** : BACK; *also* : the position at the back of something

³**rear** *adj* : being at the back

rear admiral *n* : a commissioned officer in the navy or coast guard ranking next below a vice admiral

¹**rear·ward** \ˈriər-wərd\ *adj* **1** : being at or toward the rear **2** : directed toward the rear

²**rear·ward** *also* **rear·wards** \-wərdz\ *adv* : at or toward the rear

¹**rea·son** \ˈrēz-ᵊn\ *n* [ME *resoun*, fr. OF *raison*, fr. L *ration-, ratio* reason, computation] **1** : a statement offered in explanation or justification **2** : GROUND, CAUSE **3** : the power to think : INTELLECT **4** : a sane or sound mind **5** : due exercise of the faculty of logical thought

²**reason** *vb* **rea·soned; rea·son·ing** \ˈrēz-(ᵊ-)niŋ\ **1** : to talk with another to cause a change of mind **2** : to use the faculty of reason : THINK **3** : to discover or formulate by the use of reason — **rea·son·er** *n* — **rea·son·ing** *n*

rea·son·able \ˈrēz-(ᵊ-)nə-bəl\ *adj* **1** : being within the bounds of reason : not extreme : MODERATE, FAIR **2** : INEXPENSIVE **3** : able to reason : RATIONAL — **rea·son·able·ness** n — **rea·son·ably** \-blē\ adv

re·as·sure \ˌrē-ə-ˈshu̇r\ vb **1** : to assure again **2** : to restore confidence to : free from fear — **re·as·sur·ance** \-ˈshu̇r-əns\ n — **re·as·sur·ing·ly** \-ˈshu̇r-iŋ-lē\ adv

¹**re·bate** \ˈrē-ˌbāt\ vb re·bat·ed; re·bat·ing : to make or give a rebate

²**re·bate** n : a return of part of a payment syn deduction, abatement, discount

¹**reb·el** \ˈreb-əl\ adj [ME, fr. OF rebelle, fr. L rebellis, fr. re- + bellum war, fr. OL duellum] : of or relating to rebels

²**rebel** n : one that rebels against authority

³**re·bel** \ri-ˈbel\ vb re·belled; re·bel·ling **1** : to resist the authority of one's government **2** : to act in or show disobedience **3** : to feel or exhibit anger or revulsion

re·bel·lion \ri-ˈbel-yən\ n : resistance to authority; esp : defiance against a government through uprising or revolt

re·bel·lious \-yəs\ adj **1** : given to or engaged in rebellion **2** : inclined to resist authority — **re·bel·lious·ly** adv — **re·bel·lious·ness** n

re·birth \ˈrē-ˈbərth\ n **1** : a new or 2d birth **2** : RENAISSANCE, REVIVAL

re·born \-ˈbȯrn\ adj : born again : REGENERATED, REVIVED

¹**re·bound** \ˈrē-ˈbau̇nd, ri-\ vb **1** : to spring back on or as if on striking another body **2** : to recover from a setback or frustration

²**re·bound** \ˈrē-ˌbau̇nd\ n **1** : the action of rebounding **2** : a rebounding ball **3** : immediate spontaneous reaction to setback or frustration

re·buff \ri-ˈbəf\ vb : to reject or criticize sharply : SNUB — **rebuff** n

re·build \(ˈ)rē-ˈbild\ vb -built \-ˈbilt\ -build·ing **1** : REPAIR, RECONSTRUCT; also : REMODEL **2** : to build again

¹**re·buke** \ri-ˈbyük\ vb re·buked; re·buk·ing : to reprimand sharply : REPROVE

²**rebuke** n : a sharp reprimand

re·bus \ˈrē-bəs\ n [L, by things, abl. pl. of res thing] : a representation of syllables or words by means of pictures; also : a riddle composed of such pictures

re·but \ri-ˈbət\ vb re·but·ted; re·but·ting : to refute esp. formally (as in debate) by evidence and arguments syn disprove, controvert, confute — **re·but·ter** n

re·but·tal \ri-ˈbət-ᵊl\ n : the act of rebutting

rec abbr **1** receipt **2** record; recording **3** recreation

re·cal·ci·trant \ri-ˈkal-sə-trənt\ adj [LL recalcitrant-, recalcitrans, prp. of recalcitrare to be stubbornly disobedient, fr. L, to kick back, fr. re- back, again + calcitrare to kick, fr. calc-, calx heel] **1** : stubbornly resisting authority **2** : resistant to handling or treatment syn refractory, headstrong, willful, unruly, ungovernable — **re·cal·ci·trance** \-trəns\ n

¹**re·call** \ri-ˈkȯl\ vb **1** : to call back **2** : REMEMBER, RECOLLECT **3** : REVOKE, ANNUL

²**re·call** \ri-ˈkȯl, ˈrē-ˌkȯl\ n **1** : a summons to return **2** : the procedure of removing an official by popular vote **3** : remembrance of things learned or experienced **4** : the act of revoking

re·cant \ri-ˈkant\ vb : to take back (something one has said) publicly : make an open confession of error — **re·can·ta·tion** \ˌrē-ˌkan-ˈtā-shən\ n

¹**re·cap** \ˈrē-ˌkap, ri-ˈkap\ vb re·capped; re·cap·ping : RECAPITULATE — **re·cap** \ˈrē-ˌkap\ n

²**re·cap** \ˈrē-ˌkap\ vb re·capped; re·cap·ping : RETREAD — **re·cap** \ˈrē-ˌkap\ n

re·ca·pit·u·late \ˌrē-kə-ˈpich-ə-ˌlāt\ vb -lat·ed; -lat·ing : to restate briefly : SUMMARIZE — **re·ca·pit·u·la·tion** \-ˌpich-ə-ˈlā-shən\ n

re·cap·ture \(ˈ)rē-ˈkap-chər\ vb **1** : to capture again **2** : to experience again ⟨~ happy times⟩

re·cast \(ˈ)rē-ˈkast\ vb **1** : to cast again **2** : REVISE, REMODEL ⟨~ a sentence⟩

recd abbr received

re·cede \ri-ˈsēd\ vb re·ced·ed; re·ced·ing **1** : to move back or away : WITHDRAW **2** : to slant backward **3** : DIMINISH, CONTRACT

¹**re·ceipt** \ri-ˈsēt\ n **1** : RECIPE **2** : the act of receiving **3** : something received — usu. used in pl. **4** : a written acknowledgment of something received

²**receipt** vb **1** : to give a receipt for **2** : to mark as paid

re·ceiv·able \ri-ˈsē-və-bəl\ adj **1** : capable of being received; esp : acceptable as legal ⟨~ certificates⟩ **2** : subject to call for payment (notes ~)

re·ceive \ri-ˈsēv\ vb re·ceived; re·ceiv·ing **1** : to take in or accept (as something sent or paid) : come into possession of : GET **2** : CONTAIN, HOLD **3** : to permit to enter : GREET, WELCOME **4** : to be at home to visitors **5** : to accept as true or authoritative **6** : to be the subject of : UNDERGO, EXPERIENCE ⟨~ a shock⟩ **7** : to change incoming radio waves into sounds or pictures

re·ceiv·er \ri-ˈsē-vər\ n **1** : one that receives **2** : a person legally appointed to receive and have charge of property or money involved in a lawsuit **3** : a device for converting electromagnetic waves or signals into audio or visual form (telephone ~)

re·ceiv·er·ship \-ˌship\ n **1** : the office or function of a receiver **2** : the condition of being in the hands of a receiver

re·cen·cy \ˈrēs-ᵊn-sē\ n : RECENTNESS

re·cent \ˈrēs-ᵊnt\ adj **1** : of the present time or time just past ⟨~ history⟩ **2** : lately made or used : NEW, FRESH **3** cap : of, relating to, or being the

present geologic epoch — **re·cent·ly**
adv — **re·cent·ness** *n*

re·cep·ta·cle \ri-'sep-ti-kəl\ *n* 1 : something used to receive and hold something else : CONTAINER 2 : the enlarged end of a flower stalk upon which the parts of the flower grow 3 : an electrical fitting containing the live parts of a circuit

re·cep·tion \ri-'sep-shən\ *n* 1 : the act of receiving 2 : a social gathering at which guests are formally welcomed

re·cep·tion·ist \-sh(ə-)nəst\ *n* : one employed to greet callers

re·cep·tive \ri-'sep-tiv\ *adj* : able or inclined to receive; *esp* : open and responsive to ideas, impressions, or suggestions — **re·cep·tive·ly** *adv* — **re·cep·tive·ness** *n* — **re·cep·tiv·i·ty** \ˌrē-ˌsep-'tiv-ət-ē\ *n*

re·cep·tor \ri-'sep-tər\ *n* 1 : one that receives; *esp* : SENSE ORGAN 2 : a molecule in the outer cell membrane or in the cell interior that has an affinity for a specific chemical group, molecule, or virus

¹**re·cess** \'rē-ˌses, ri-'ses\ *n* 1 : a secret or secluded place 2 : an indentation in a line or surface (as an alcove in a room) 3 : a suspension of business or procedure for rest or relaxation

²**recess** *vb* 1 : to put into a recess 2 : to make a recess in 3 : to interrupt for a recess 4 : to take a recess

re·ces·sion \ri-'sesh-ən\ *n* 1 : the act of receding : WITHDRAWAL 2 : a departing procession (as at the end of a church service) 3 : a period of reduced economic activity

re·ces·sion·al \-(ə-)nəl\ *n* 1 : a hymn or musical piece at the conclusion of a service or program 2 : RECESSION 2

¹**re·ces·sive** \ri-'ses-iv\ *adj* 1 : tending to go back : RECEDING 2 : producing or being a bodily characteristic that is masked or not expressed when a contrasting dominant gene or trait is present ⟨∼ genes⟩

²**recessive** *n* 1 : a recessive characteristic or gene 2 : an individual that has one or more recessive characteristics

re·cher·ché \rə-ˌsher-'shā, -'sher(ˌ)-ˌshā\ *adj* [F] 1 : CHOICE, RARE 2 : excessively refined

re·cid·i·vism \ri-'sid-ə-ˌviz-əm\ *n* : a tendency to relapse into a previous condition; *esp* : relapse into criminal behavior — **re·cid·i·vist** \-vəst\ *n*

recip *abbr* reciprocal; reciprocity

rec·i·pe \'res-ə-(ˌ)pē\ *n* [L, take, imperative of *recipere* to receive, fr. *re-* back + *capere* to take] 1 : a set of instructions for making something (as a food dish) from various ingredients 2 : a method of procedure : FORMULA

re·cip·i·ent \ri-'sip-ē-ənt\ *n* : one that receives

¹**re·cip·ro·cal** \ri-'sip-rə-kəl\ *adj* 1 : inversely related 2 : MUTUAL, JOINT, SHARED 3 : so related to each other that one completes the other or is

equivalent to the other syn correspondent, complementary — **re·cip·ro·cal·ly** \-k(ə-)lē\ *adv*

²**reciprocal** *n* 1 : something in a reciprocal relationship to another 2 : one of a pair of numbers (as ⅔, 3⁄2) whose product is one

re·cip·ro·cate \-ˌkāt\ *vb* -**cat·ed**; -**cat·ing** 1 : to move backward and forward alternately ⟨a *reciprocating* piston⟩ 2 : to give and take mutually 3 : to make a return for something done or given — **re·cip·ro·ca·tion** \-ˌsip-rə-'kā-shən\ *n*

rec·i·proc·i·ty \ˌres-ə-'präs-ət-ē\ *n, pl* -**ties** 1 : the quality or state of being reciprocal 2 : mutual exchange of privileges (as trade advantages between countries)

re·cit·al \ri-'sīt-ᵊl\ *n* 1 : an act or instance of reciting : ACCOUNT 2 : a public reading or recitation ⟨a poetry ∼⟩ 3 : a concert given by a musician, dancer, or dance troupe 4 : a public exhibition of skill given by music or dance pupils — **re·cit·al·ist** \-ᵊl-əst\ *n*

rec·i·ta·tion \ˌres-ə-'tā-shən\ *n* 1 : RECITING, RECITAL 2 : delivery before an audience of something memorized 3 : a classroom exercise in which pupils answer questions on a lesson they have studied

re·cite \ri-'sīt\ *vb* **re·cit·ed**; **re·cit·ing** 1 : to repeat verbatim (as something memorized) 2 : to recount in some detail : RELATE 3 : to reply to a teacher's questions on a lesson — **re·cit·er** *n*

reck·less \'rek-ləs\ *adj* : lacking caution : RASH syn hasty, brash, hotheaded, thoughtless — **reck·less·ly** *adv* — **reck·less·ness** *n*

reck·on \'rek-ən\ *vb* **reck·oned**; **reck·on·ing** \-(ə-)niŋ\ 1 : COUNT, CALCULATE, COMPUTE 2 : CONSIDER, REGARD 3 *chiefly dial* : THINK, SUPPOSE, GUESS

reck·on·ing \-iŋ\ *n* 1 : an act or instance of reckoning 2 : a settling of accounts ⟨day of ∼⟩

re·claim \ri-'klām\ *vb* 1 : to recall from wrong conduct : REFORM 2 : to put into a desired condition (as by labor or discipline) ⟨∼ marshy land⟩ 3 : to obtain from a waste product or by-product 4 : to demand or obtain the return of syn save, redeem, rescue — **re·claim·able** *adj* — **rec·la·ma·tion** \ˌrek-lə-'mā-shən\ *n*

re·cline \ri-'klīn\ *vb* **re·clined**; **re·clin·ing** 1 : to lean or incline backward 2 : to lie down : REST

re·clin·er \ri-'klī-nər\ *n* : a chair with an adjustable back and footrest

re·cluse \'rek-ˌlūs, ri-'klūs\ *n* : a person who lives in seclusion or leads a solitary life : HERMIT

rec·og·ni·tion \ˌrek-əg-'nish-ən\ *n* 1 : the act of recognizing : the state of being recognized : ACKNOWLEDGMENT 2 : special notice or attention

re·cog·ni·zance \ri-'kä(g)-nə-zəns\ *n* : a promise recorded before a court or magistrate to do something (as to appear in court or to keep the peace) usu. under penalty of a money forfeiture

rec·og·nize \'rek-əg-ˌnīz\ vb **-nized; -niz·ing 1** : to acknowledge (as a speaker in a meeting) as one entitled to be heard at the time **2** : to acknowledge the existence or the independence of (a country or government) **3** : to take notice of **4** : to acknowledge with appreciation **5** : to acknowledge acquaintance with **6** : to identify as previously known **7** : to perceive clearly : REALIZE — **rec·og·niz·able** \'rek-əg-ˌnī-zə-bəl\ adj — **rec·og·niz·ably** \-blē\ adv

¹re·coil \ri-'kȯil\ vb **1** : to draw back : RETREAT **2** : to spring back to or as if to a starting point syn shrink, flinch, wince, quail, blanch

²re·coil \'rē-ˌkȯil, ri-'kȯil\ n : the action of recoiling (as by a gun or spring)

re·coil·less \-ˌkȯil-ləs, -'kȯil-\ adj : venting expanding propellant gas before recoil is produced (~ gun)

rec·ol·lect \ˌrek-ə-'lekt\ vb : to recall to mind : REMEMBER syn recall, remind, reminisce, bethink

rec·ol·lec·tion \ˌrek-ə-'lek-shən\ n **1** : the act or power of recollecting **2** : something recollected

re·com·bi·nant DNA \(')rē-ˌkäm-bə-nənt-\ n : DNA prepared in the laboratory by breaking up and splicing together DNA from several different species of organisms

rec·om·mend \ˌrek-ə-'mend\ vb **1** : to present as deserving of acceptance or trial **2** : to give in charge : COMMIT **3** : to cause to receive favorable attention **4** : ADVISE, COUNSEL — **rec·om·mend·able** \-'men-də-bəl\ adj

rec·om·men·da·tion \ˌrek-ə-mən-'dā-shən\ n **1** : the act of recommending **2** : a thing or a course of action recommended **3** : something that recommends

¹rec·om·pense \'rek-əm-ˌpens\ vb **-pensed; -pens·ing 1** : to give compensation to : pay for **2** : to return in kind : REQUITE syn reimburse, indemnify, repay, compensate

²recompense n : COMPENSATION

rec·on·cile \'rek-ən-ˌsīl\ vb **-ciled; -cil·ing 1** : to cause to be friendly or harmonious again **2** : ADJUST, SETTLE (~ differences) **3** : to bring to submission or acceptance syn conform, accommodate, harmonize, coordinate — **rec·on·cil·able** adj — **rec·on·cile·ment** n — **rec·on·cil·er** n — **rec·on·cil·i·a·tion** \ˌrek-ən-ˌsil-ē-'ā-shən\ n

re·con·dite \'rek-ən-ˌdīt\ adj **1** : hard to understand : PROFOUND, ABSTRUSE **2** : little known : OBSCURE

re·con·nais·sance \ri-'kän-ə-zəns, -səns\ n [F, lit., recognition] : a preliminary survey of an area; esp : an exploratory military survey of enemy territory

re·con·noi·ter or **re·con·noi·tre** \ˌrē-

kə-'nȯit-ər, ˌrek-ə-\ vb **-noi·tered** or **-noi·tred; -noi·ter·ing** or **-noi·tring** : to make a reconnaissance of : engage in reconnaissance

re·con·sid·er \ˌrē-kən-'sid-ər\ vb : to consider again with a view to changing or reversing; esp : to take up again in a meeting — **re·con·sid·er·a·tion** \-ˌsid-ə-'rā-shən\ n

re·con·sti·tute \'rē-'kän-stə-ˌt(y)üt\ vb : to restore to a former condition by adding water (~ powdered milk)

re·con·struct \ˌrē-kən-'strəkt\ vb : to construct again : REBUILD

re·con·struc·tion \ˌrē-kən-'strək-shən\ n **1** : the action of reconstructing : the state of being reconstructed **2** often cap : the reorganization and reestablishment of the seceded states in the Union after the American Civil War **3** : something reconstructed

¹re·cord \ri-'kȯrd\ vb **1** : to set down (as proceedings in a meeting) in writing **2** : to register permanently **3** : INDICATE, READ **4** : to give evidence of **5** : to cause (as sound or visual images) to be registered (as on magnetic tape) in a form that permits reproduction

²rec·ord \'rek-ərd\ n **1** : the act of recording **2** : a written account of proceedings **3** : known facts about a person **4** : an attested top performance **5** : something on which sound or visual images have been recorded

re·cord·er \ri-'kȯrd-ər\ n **1** : a judge in some city courts **2** : one who records transactions officially **3** : a recording device **4** : a wind instrument with a whistle mouthpiece and eight fingerholes

re·cord·ing \ri-'kȯrd-iŋ\ n : RECORD 5

re·cord·ist \ri-'kȯrd-əst\ n : one who records sound esp. on film

¹re·count \ri-'kaunt\ vb : to relate in detail : TELL syn recite, rehearse, narrate, describe, state, report

²re·count \'rē-'kaunt\ vb : to count again

³re·count \'rē-ˌkaunt, (')rē-'kaunt\ n : a second or fresh count

re·coup \ri-'küp\ vb : to get an equivalent or compensation for : make up for something lost syn retrieve, regain, recover

re·course \'rē-ˌkȯrs, ri-'kȯrs\ n **1** : a turning to someone or something for assistance or protection **2** : a source of aid : RESORT

re·cov·er \ri-'kəv-ər\ vb **-ered; -er·ing** \-(ə-)riŋ\ **1** : to get back again : REGAIN, RETRIEVE **2** : to regain normal health, poise, or status **3** : to make up for : RECOUP (~ed all his losses) **4** : RECLAIM (~ land from the sea) **5** : to obtain a legal judgment in one's favor — **re·cov·er·able** adj — **re·cov·ery** \-'kəv-(ə-)rē\ n

re-cov·er \'rē-'kəv-ər\ vb : to cover again

¹rec·re·ant \'rek-rē-ənt\ adj [ME, fr. MF, fr. prp. of recroire to renounce one's cause in a trial by battle, fr. re-back + *croire* to believe, fr. L *credere*] **1** : COWARDLY **2** : UNFAITHFUL

²recreant *n* **1** : COWARD **2** : DESERTER

rec·re·ate \'rek-rē-₁āt\ *vb* -at·ed; -at·ing **1** : to give new life or freshness to **2** : to take recreation — **rec·re·ative** \-₁āt-iv\ *adj*

re·cre·ate \₁rē-krē-'āt\ *vb* : to create again — **re-cre·ation** \-'ā-shən\ *n* — **re-cre·ative** \-'āt-iv\ *adj*

rec·re·ation \₁rek-rē-'ā-shən\ *n* : a refreshing of strength or spirits after work; *also* : a means of refreshment **syn** diversion, entertainment, amusement — **rec·re·ation·al** \-sh(ə-)nəl\ *adj*

recreational vehicle *n* : a vehicle designed for recreational use (as camping)

re·crim·i·nate \ri-'krim-ə-₁nāt\ *vb* -nat·ed; -nat·ing : to make an accusation against an accuser — **re·crim·i·na·tion** \-₁krim-ə-'nā-shən\ *n* — **re·crim·i·na·to·ry** \-'krim-(ə-)nə-₁tōr-ē\ *adj*

re·cru·des·cence \₁rē-krü-'des-ᵊns\ *n* : a new outbreak esp. of something unhealthful or dangerous after a period of abatement or inactivity — **re·cru·desce** \₁rē-krü-'des\ *vb*

¹re·cruit \ri-'krüt\ *vb* **1** : to form or strengthen with new members (∼ an army) **2** : to secure the services of (∼ engineers) **3** : to restore or increase in health or vigor (resting to ∼ his strength) — **re·cruit·er** *n* — **re·cruit·ment** *n*

²recruit *n* [F *recrute, recrue* fresh growth, new levy of soldiers, fr. MF, fr. *recroistre* to grow up again, fr. L *recrescere*] : a newcomer to an activity or field; *esp* : a newly enlisted member of the armed forces

rec sec *abbr* recording secretary

rect *abbr* **1** receipt **2** rectangle; rectangular **3** rectified

rec·tal \'rek-tᵊl\ *adj* : of or relating to the rectum — **rec·tal·ly** \-ē\ *adv*

rect·an·gle \'rek-₁taŋ-gəl\ *n* : a 4-sided figure with four right angles; *esp* : one with adjacent sides of unequal length — **rect·an·gu·lar** \rek-'taŋ-gyə-lər\ *adj*

rec·ti·fi·er \'rek-tə-₁fī(-ə)r\ *n* : one that rectifies; *esp* : a device for converting alternating current into direct current

rec·ti·fy \'rek-tə-₁fī\ *vb* -fied; -fy·ing **1** : to make or set right : CORRECT **2** : to convert alternating current into direct current **syn** emend, amend, mend, right — **rec·ti·fi·ca·tion** \₁rek-tə-fə-'kā-shən\ *n*

rec·ti·lin·ear \₁rek-tə-'lin-ē-ər\ *adj* **1** : moving in a straight line (∼ motion) **2** : characterized by straight lines

rec·ti·tude \'rek-tə-₁t(y)üd\ *n* **1** : moral integrity **2** : correctness of procedure **syn** virtue, goodness, morality, probity

rec·to \'rek-tō\ *n*, *pl* **rectos** : a right= hand page

rec·tor \'rek-tər\ *n* **1** : a clergyman in charge of a parish **2** : the head of a university or school — **rec·to·ri·al** \rek-'tōr-ē-əl\ *adj*

rec·to·ry \'rek-t(ə-)rē\ *n*, *pl* **-ries** : the residence of a rector or a parish priest

rec·tum \'rek-təm\ *n*, *pl* **rectums** or **rec·ta** \-tə\ [NL, fr. *rectum intestinum*, lit., straight intestine] : the last part of the intestine joining colon and anus

re·cum·bent \ri-'kəm-bənt\ *adj* : lying down : RECLINING

re·cu·per·ate \ri-'k(y)ü-pə-₁rāt\ *vb* -at·ed; -at·ing : to get back (as health, strength, or losses) : RECOVER — **re·cu·per·a·tion** \-₁k(y)ü-pə-'rā-shən\ *n* — **re·cu·per·a·tive** \-'k(y)ü-pə-₁rāt-iv\ *adj*

re·cur \ri-'kər\ *vb* **re·curred; re·cur·ring 1** : to go or come back in thought or discussion **2** : to occur or appear again esp. after an interval — **re·cur·rence** \-'kər-əns\ *n* — **re·cur·rent** \-ənt\ *adj*

re·cy·cle \rē-'sī-kəl\ *vb* **1** : to pass again through a cycle of changes or treatment **2** : to process (as liquid body waste, glass, or cans) in order to regain materials for human use — **recycle** *n*

¹red \'red\ *adj* **red·der; red·dest 1** : of the color red **2** : endorsing radical social or political change esp. by force **3** *often cap* : of or relating to the U.S.S.R. or its allies — **red·ly** *adv* — **red·ness** *n*

²red *n* **1** : the color of blood or of the ruby **2** : a revolutionary in politics **3** *cap* : COMMUNIST **4** : the condition of showing a loss (in the ∼)

re·dact \ri-'dakt\ *vb* **1** : to put in writing : FRAME **2** : EDIT — **re·dac·tor** \-'dak-tər\ *n*

re·dac·tion \-'dak-shən\ *n* **1** : an act or instance of redacting **2** : EDITION

red alga *n* : any of several reddish usu. marine algae

red blood cell *n* : one of the hemoglobin-containing cells that carry oxygen from the lungs to the tissues and are responsible for the red color of vertebrate blood

red·breast \'red-₁brest\ *n* : ROBIN

red·cap \'red-₁kap\ *n* : a baggage porter (as at a railroad station)

red-carpet *adj* : marked by ceremonial courtesy

red cedar *n* : an American juniper with fragrant close-grained red wood; *also* : its wood

red clover *n* : a Eurasian clover with globe-shaped heads of reddish flowers widely cultivated for hay and forage

red·coat \'red-₁kōt\ *n* : a British soldier esp. during the Revolutionary War

red·den \'red-ᵊn\ *vb* : to make or become red or reddish : FLUSH, BLUSH

red·dish \'red-ish\ *adj* : tinged with red — **red·dish·ness** *n*

re·deem \ri-'dēm\ *vb* [ME *redemen*, modif. of MF *redimer*, fr. L *redimere*, fr. *re-, red-* re- + *emere* to take, buy]

1 : to recover (property) by discharging an obligation 2 : to ransom, free, or rescue by paying a price 3 : to free from the consequences of sin 4 : to remove the obligation of by payment (the government ~s savings bonds) ; *also* : to convert into something of value 5 : to make good (a promise) by performing : FULFILL 6 : to atone for — **re·deem·able** *adj* — **re·deem·er** *n*

re·demp·tion \ri-ˈdemp-shən\ *n* : the act of redeeming : the state of being redeemed — **re·demp·tive** \-tiv\ *adj* — **re·demp·to·ry** \-t(ə-)rē\ *adj*

re·de·ploy \ˌrēd-i-ˈplȯi\ *vb* 1 : to transfer from one area or activity to another 2 : to relocate men or equipment — **re·de·ploy·ment** \-mənt\ *n*

red fox *n* : a fox with orange-red to reddish brown fur

red–hand·ed \ˈred-ˈhan-dəd\ *adv or adj* : in the act of committing a misdeed

red·head \-ˌhed\ *n* : a person having red hair — **red·head·ed** \-ˈhed-əd\ *adj*

red herring *n* : a diversion intended to distract attention from the real issue

red–hot \ˈred-ˈhät\ *adj* 1 : glowing red with heat (~ iron) 2 : EXCITED, FURIOUS 3 : very new (~ news)

re·dis·trict \ˈrē-ˈdis-(ˌ)trikt\ *vb* : to organize into new territorial and esp. political divisions

red–let·ter \ˌred-ˈlet-ər\ *adj* : of special significance : MEMORABLE

red–light district *n* : a district with many houses of prostitution

re·do \(ˈ)rē-ˈdü\ *vb* : to do over or again; *esp* : REDECORATE

red oak *n* : any of various American oaks with leaves usu. having spiny-tipped lobes and acorns that take two years to mature; *also* : the wood of a red oak

red·o·lent \ˈred-ᵊl-ənt\ *adj* 1 : FRAGRANT, AROMATIC 2 : having a specified fragrance 3 : REMINISCENT, SUGGESTIVE — **red·o·lence** \-əns\ *n* — **red·o·lent·ly** *adv*

re·doubt \ri-ˈdaȯt\ *n* [F *redoute*, fr. It *ridotto*, fr. ML *reductus* secret place, fr. L, withdrawn, fr. *reducere* to lead back, fr. *re-* back + *ducere* to lead] : a small usu. temporary fortification

re·doubt·able \ri-ˈdaȯt-ə-bəl\ *adj* [ME *redoutable*, fr. MF, fr. *redouter* to dread, fr. *re-* re- + *douter* to doubt] : arousing dread or fear : FORMIDABLE

re·dound \ri-ˈdaȯnd\ *vb* 1 : to have an effect 2 : to become added or transferred : ACCRUE

red pepper *n* : CAYENNE PEPPER

¹**re·dress** \ri-ˈdres\ *vb* 1 : to set right : REMEDY 2 : COMPENSATE 3 : to remove the cause of (a grievance) 4 : AVENGE

²**re·dress** *n* 1 : relief from distress 2 : a means or possibility of seeking a remedy 3 : compensation for loss or injury 4 : an act or instance of redressing

red snapper *n* : any of various fishes including several food fishes

red spider *n* : any of several small web-spinning mites that attack forage and crop plants

red squirrel *n* : a common American squirrel with the upper parts chiefly red

red–tailed hawk \ˌred-ˌtāld-\ *n* : a common hawk of eastern No. America with a rather short typically reddish tail

red tape *n* [fr. the red tape formerly used to bind legal documents in England] : official routine or procedure marked by excessive complexity which results in delay or inaction

red tide *n* : seawater discolored by the presence of large numbers of dinoflagellates which produce a toxin poisonous to many forms of marine life and to human beings who consume infected shellfish

re·duce \ri-ˈd(y)üs\ *vb* **re·duced; re·duc·ing** 1 : LESSEN 2 : to bring to a specified state or condition (~ chaos to order) 3 : to put in a lower rank or grade 4 : CONQUER (~ a fort) 5 : to bring into a certain order or classification 6 : to correct (as a fracture) by restoration of displaced parts 7 : to lessen one's weight syn decrease, diminish, abate, dwindle, lessen, recede — **re·duc·er** *n* — **re·duc·ible** \-ˈd(y)üs-ə-bəl\ *adj*

re·duc·tion \ri-ˈdək-shən\ *n* 1 : the act of reducing : the state of being reduced 2 : something made by reducing 3 : the amount taken off in reducing something

re·dun·dan·cy \ri-ˈdən-dən-sē\ *n, pl* **-cies** 1 : the quality or state of being redundant : SUPERFLUITY 2 : something redundant or in excess 3 : the use of surplus words

re·dun·dant \-dənt\ *adj* : exceeding what is needed or normal : SUPERFLUOUS; *esp* : using more words than necessary — **re·dun·dant·ly** *adv*

red–winged blackbird \ˈred-ˌwiŋd-\ *n* : a No. American blackbird of which the adult male is black with a patch of bright scarlet on the wings

red·wood \ˈred-ˌwu̇d\ *n* : a tall coniferous timber tree of California or its durable wood

reed \ˈrēd\ *n* 1 : any of various tall slender grasses of wet areas; *also* : a stem or growth of reed 2 : a musical instrument made from the hollow stem of a reed 3 : an elastic tongue of cane, wood, or metal by which tones are produced in organ pipes and certain other wind instruments — **reedy** *adj*

re·ed·u·cate \(ˈ)rē-ˈej-ə-ˌkāt\ *vb* : to train again; *esp* : to rehabilitate through education — **re·ed·u·ca·tion** *n*

¹**reef** \ˈrēf\ *n* 1 : a part of a sail taken in or let out in regulating the sail's size 2 : the reduction in sail area made by reefing

²**reef** *vb* : to reduce the area of a sail by rolling or folding part of it

³**reef** *n* : a ridge of rocks or sand at or near the surface of the water

¹**reef·er** \'rē-fər\ *n* 1 : one that reefs 2 : a close-fitting thick jacket

²**reefer** *n* : a marijuana cigarette

¹**reek** \'rēk\ *n* : a strong or disagreeable fume or odor

²**reek** *vb* 1 : to give off or become permeated with a strong or offensive odor 2 : to give a strong impression of some constituent quality — **reek·er** *n* — **reeky** \-kē\ *adj*

¹**reel** \'rēl\ *n* : a revolvable device on which something flexible (as film, tape, cord, or wire) may be wound: *also* : a quantity of something wound on such a device

²**reel** *vb* 1 : to wind on or as if on a reel 2 : to pull or draw (as a fish) by reeling a line — **reel·able** *adj* — **reel·er** *n*

³**reel** *vb* 1 : WHIRL; *also* : to be giddy 2 : to waver or fall back from a blow : RECOIL 3 : to walk or move unsteadily

⁴**reel** *n* : a reeling motion

⁵**reel** *n* : a lively Scottish dance or its music

re·en·force \ˌrē-ən-'fōrs\ *var of* REINFORCE

re·en·try \rē-'en-trē\ *n* 1 : a second or new entry 2 : the action of reentering the earth's atmosphere from space

reeve \'rēv\ *vb* **rove** \'rōv\ *or* **reeved**; **reev·ing** : to pass (as a rope) through a hole in a block or cleat

¹**ref** \'ref\ *n* : REFEREE

²**ref** *abbr* 1 reference 2 referred 3 reformed 4 refunding

re·fec·tion \ri-'fek-shən\ *n* 1 : refreshment esp. after hunger or fatigue 2 : food and drink together : REPAST

re·fec·to·ry \ri-'fek-t(ə-)rē\ *n, pl* **-ries** : a dining hall (as in a monastery or college)

re·fer \ri-'fər\ *vb* **re·ferred**; **re·fer·ring** 1 : to assign to a certain source, cause, or relationship 2 : to direct or send to some person or place (as for information or help) 3 : to submit to someone else for consideration or action 4 : to have recourse (as for information or aid) 5 : to have connection : RELATE 6 : to direct attention : speak of : MENTION, ALLUDE **syn** recur, resort, apply, go, turn — **re·fer·able** \'ref-(ə-)rə-bəl, ri-'fər-ə-\ *adj*

¹**ref·er·ee** \ˌref-ə-'rē\ *n* 1 : a person to whom an issue esp. in law is referred for investigation or settlement 2 : an umpire in certain games

²**referee** *vb* **-eed**; **-ee·ing** : to act as referee

ref·er·ence \'ref-ərns, 'ref-(ə-)rəns\ *n* 1 : the act of referring 2 : RELATION, RESPECT 3 : ALLUSION, MENTION 4 : a direction of the attention to another passage or book 5 : consultation esp. for obtaining information (books for ~) 6 : a person of whom inquiries as to character or ability can be made 7 : a written recommendation of a person for employment

ref·er·en·dum \ˌref-ə-'ren-dəm\ *n, pl* **-da** \-də\ *or* **-dums** [NL, fr. L] : the referring of legislative measures to the voters for approval or rejection; *also* : a vote on a measure so submitted

ref·er·ent \'ref-(ə-)rənt\ *n* [L *referent-, referens*, prp. of *referre*] : one that refers or is referred to; *esp* : the thing a word stands for — **referent** *adj*

re·fer·ral \ri-'fər-əl\ *n* 1 : the act or an instance of referring 2 : one that is referred

¹**re·fill** \'rē-'fil\ *vb* : to fill again : REPLENISH — **re·fill·able** *adj*

²**re·fill** \'rē-ˌfil\ *n* : a new or fresh supply of something

re·fine \ri-'fīn\ *vb* **re·fined**; **re·fin·ing** 1 : to free from impurities or waste matter 2 : IMPROVE, PERFECT 3 : to free or become free of what is coarse or uncouth 4 : to make improvements by introducing subtle changes — **re·fin·er** *n*

re·fined \ri-'fīnd\ *adj* 1 : freed from impurities 2 : CULTURED, CULTIVATED 3 : SUBTLE

re·fine·ment \ri-'fīn-mənt\ *n* 1 : the action of refining 2 : the quality or state of being refined 3 : a refined feature or method; *also* : something intended to improve or perfect

re·fin·ery \ri-'fīn-(ə-)rē\ *n, pl* **-er·ies** : a building and equipment for refining metals, oil, or sugar

refl *abbr* reflex; reflexive

re·flect \ri-'flekt\ *vb* [ME *reflecten*, fr. L *reflectere* to bend back, fr. *re-* back + *flectere* to bend] 1 : to bend or cast back (as light, heat, or sound) 2 : to give back a likeness or image of as a mirror does 3 : to bring as a result (~ed credit on him) 4 : to cast reproach or blame (their bad conduct ~ed on their training) 5 : PONDER, MEDITATE — **re·flec·tion** \-'flek-shən\ *n* — **re·flec·tive** \-tiv\ *adj* — **re·flec·tiv·i·ty** \ˌ(ˌ)rē-ˌflek-'tiv-ət-ē\

re·flec·tor \ri-'flek-tər\ *n* : one that reflects; *esp* : a polished surface for reflecting radiation (as light)

¹**re·flex** \'rē-ˌfleks\ *n* 1 : an automatic and usu. inborn response to a stimulus not involving higher mental centers 2 *pl* : the power of acting or responding with enough speed (an athlete with great ~es)

²**reflex** *adj* 1 : bent or directed back 2 : of or relating to a reflex — **re·flex·ly** *adv*

¹**re·flex·ive** \ri-'flek-siv\ *adj* : of or relating to an action directed back upon the doer or the grammatical subject (a ~ verb) (the ~ pronoun *himself*) — **re·flex·ive·ly** *adv* — **re·flex·ive·ness** *n*

²**reflexive** *n* : a reflexive verb or pronoun

re·fo·cus \(ˌ)rē-'fō-kəs\ *vb* 1 : to focus again 2 : to change the emphasis or direction of (~ed her life)

re·for·es·ta·tion \ˌrē-ˌfȯr-ə-'stā-shən\ *n*

: the action of renewing a forest by planting seeds or young trees — **re-for-est** \'rē-'fȯr-əst\ *vb*

¹**re-form** \ri-'fȯrm\ *vb* **1** : to make better or improve by removal of faults **2** : to correct or improve one's own character or habits **syn** correct, rectify, emend, remedy, redress, revise — **re-form-able** *adj* — **re-for-ma-tive** \-'fȯr-mət-iv\ *adj*

²**reform** *n* : improvement or correction of what is corrupt or defective

re-form \'rē-'fȯrm\ *vb* : to form again

ref-or-ma-tion \,ref-ər-'mā-shən\ *n* **1** : the act of reforming : the state of being reformed **2** *cap* : a 16th century religious movement marked by the establishment of the Protestant churches

¹**re-for-ma-to-ry** \ri-'fȯr-mə-,tōr-ē\ *adj* : aiming at or tending toward reformation : REFORMATIVE

²**reformatory** *n, pl* **-ries** : a penal institution for reforming young or first offenders or women

re-form-er \ri-'fȯr-mər\ *n* **1** : one that works for or urges reform **2** *cap* : a leader of the Protestant Reformation

refr *abbr* refraction

re-fract \ri-'frakt\ *vb* [L *refractus,* pp. of *refringere* to break open, break up, refract, fr. *re-* back + *frangere* to break] : to subject to refraction

re-frac-tion \ri-'frak-shən\ *n* : the bending of a ray (as of light) when it passes obliquely from one medium into another in which its speed is different — **re-frac-tive** \-tiv\ *adj*

re-frac-to-ry \ri-'frak-t(ə-)rē\ *adj* **1** : OBSTINATE, STUBBORN, UNMANAGEABLE **2** : difficult to melt, corrode, or draw out; *esp* : capable of enduring high temperature ⟨∼ bricks⟩ **syn** recalcitrant, intractable, ungovernable, unruly, headstrong, willful — **re-frac-to-ri-ness** \ri-'frak-t(ə-)rē-nəs\ *n* — **refractory** *n*

¹**re-frain** \ri-'frān\ *vb* : to hold oneself back : FORBEAR — **re-frain-ment** *n*

²**refrain** *n* : a phrase or verse recurring regularly in a poem or song

re-fresh \ri-'fresh\ *vb* **1** : to make or become fresh or fresher **2** : to revive by or as if by renewal of supplies ⟨∼ one's memory⟩ **3** : to freshen up **4** : to supply or take refreshment **syn** restore, rejuvenate, renovate, refurbish — **re-fresh-er** *n* — **re-fresh-ing-ly** *adv*

re-fresh-ment \-mənt\ *n* **1** : the act of refreshing : the state of being refreshed **2** : something that refreshes **3** *pl* : a light meal

re-fried beans \(,)rē-,frīd-\ *n pl* : beans cooked with seasonings, fried, then mashed and fried again

refrig *abbr* refrigerating; refrigeration

re-frig-er-ate \ri-'frij-ə-,rāt\ *vb* **-at-ed; -at-ing** : to make cool; *esp* : to chill or freeze (food) for preservation — **re-frig-er-ant** \-(ə-)rənt\ *adj or n* — **re-**

frig-er-a-tion \-,frij-ə-'rā-shən\ *n* — **re-frig-er-a-tor** \-'frij-ə-,rāt-ər\ *n*

ref-uge \'ref-,yüj\ *n* : shelter or protection from danger or distress **2** : a place that provides protection

ref-u-gee \,ref-yù-'jē\ *n* : one who flees for safety esp. to a foreign country

re-ful-gence \ri-'fùl-jəns, -'fəl-\ *n* : radiant or shining quality or state — **re-ful-gent** \-jənt\ *adj*

¹**re-fund** \ri-'fənd, 'rē-,fənd\ *vb* : to give or put back (money) : REPAY — **re-fund-able** *adj*

²**re-fund** \'rē-,fənd\ *n* **1** : the act of refunding **2** : a sum refunded

re-fur-bish \ri-'fər-bish\ *vb* : to brighten or freshen up : RENOVATE

¹**re-fuse** \ri-'fyüz\ *vb* **re-fused; re-fus-ing** **1** : to decline to accept : REJECT **2** : to decline to do, give, or grant : DENY — **re-fus-al** \-'fyü-zəl\ *n*

²**ref-use** \'ref-,yüs, -,yüz\ *n* : rejected or worthless matter : RUBBISH, TRASH

re-fuse-nik *or* **re-fus-nik** \ri-'fyüz-nik\ *n* : a Soviet citizen who is refused permission to emigrate

re-fute \ri-'fyüt\ *vb* **re-fut-ed; re-fut-ing** [L *refutare,* fr. *re-* back + *-futare* to beat] : to prove to be false by argument or evidence — **ref-u-ta-tion** \,ref-yù-'tā-shən\ *n* — **re-fut-er** \ri-'fyüt-ər\ *n*

¹**reg** \'reg\ *n* : REGULATION

²**reg** *abbr* **1** region **2** register; registered; registration **3** regular

re-gain \ri-'gān\ *vb* **1** : to gain or get again : get back ⟨∼ed his health⟩ **2** : to get back to : reach again ⟨∼ the shore⟩ **syn** recover, retrieve, recoup, repossess

re-gal \'rē-gəl\ *adj* **1** : of, relating to, or befitting a king : ROYAL **2** : STATELY, SPLENDID — **re-gal-ly** \-ē\ *adv*

re-gale \ri-'gāl\ *vb* **re-galed; re-gal-ing** **1** : to entertain richly or agreeably **2** : to give pleasure or amusement to **syn** gratify, delight, please, rejoice, gladden

re-ga-lia \ri-'gāl-yə\ *n pl* **1** : the emblems, symbols, or paraphernalia of royalty (as the crown and scepter) **2** : the insignia of an office or order **3** : special costume : FINERY

¹**re-gard** \ri-'gärd\ *n* **1** : CONSIDERATION, HEED; *also* : CARE, CONCERN **2** : GAZE, GLANCE, LOOK **3** : RESPECT, ESTEEM **4** *pl* : friendly greetings implying respect and esteem **5** : an aspect to be considered : PARTICULAR — **re-gard-ful** *adj* — **re-gard-less** *adj*

²**regard** *vb* **1** : to pay attention to **2** : to show respect for : HEED **3** : to hold in high esteem : care for **4** : to look at : gaze upon **5** *archaic* : to relate to **6** : to think of : CONSIDER

re-gard-ing \-iŋ\ *prep* : CONCERNING

regardless of \ri-'gärd-ləs-\ *prep* : in spite of

re-gat-ta \ri-'gät-ə, -'gat-\ *n* : a boat race or a series of boat races

regd *abbr* registered

re·gen·cy \ˈrē-jən-sē\ n, pl -cies 1 : the office or government of a regent or body of regents 2 : a body of regents 3 : the period during which a regent governs

re·gen·er·a·cy \ri-ˈjen-(ə-)rə-sē\ n : the state of being regenerated

¹re·gen·er·ate \ri-ˈjen-(ə-)rət\ adj 1 : formed or created again 2 : spiritually reborn or converted

²re·gen·er·ate \ri-ˈjen-ə-ˌrāt\ vb 1 : to cause to experience spiritual renewal 2 : to reform completely 3 : to give or gain new life; also : to renew by a new growth of tissue — re·gen·er·a·tion \-ˌjen-ə-ˈrā-shən\ n — re·gen·er·a·tive \-ˈjen-ə-ˌrāt-iv\ adj — re·gen·er·a·tor \-ˌrāt-ər\ n

re·gent \ˈrē-jənt\ n 1 : a person who rules during the childhood, absence, or incapacity of the sovereign 2 : a member of a governing board (as of a state university)

reg·gae \ˈreg-ˌā\ n : popular music that originated in Jamaica and combines indigenous styles with elements of rock and roll and soul music

reg·i·cide \ˈrej-ə-ˌsīd\ n 1 : one who murders a king 2 : murder of a king

re·gime also ré·gime \rā-ˈzhēm, ri-\ n 1 : REGIMEN 2 : a form or system of government 3 : a government in power; also : a period of rule

reg·i·men \ˈrej-ə-mən\ n 1 : a systematic course of treatment or behavior (a strict dietary ∼) 2 : GOVERNMENT

¹reg·i·ment \ˈrej-ə-mənt\ n : a military unit consisting usu. of a number of battalions — reg·i·men·tal \ˌrej-ə-ˈment-ᵊl\ adj

²reg·i·ment \ˈrej-ə-ˌment\ vb : to organize rigidly esp. for regulation or central control — reg·i·men·ta·tion \ˌrej-ə-mən-ˈtā-shən\ n

reg·i·men·tals \ˌrej-ə-ˈment-ᵊlz\ n pl 1 : a regimental uniform 2 : military dress

re·gion \ˈrē-jən\ n [ME, fr. MF, fr. L region-, regio, fr. regere to rule] : an often indefinitely defined part or area

re·gion·al \ˈrēj-(ə-)nəl\ adj 1 : of or relating to a geographical region 2 : of or relating to a bodily region — LOCALIZED — re·gion·al·ly \-ē\ adv

¹reg·is·ter \ˈrej-ə-stər\ n 1 : a record of items or details; also : a book or system for keeping such a record 2 : the range of a voice or instrument 3 : a device to regulate ventilation or heating 4 : an automatic device recording a number or quantity

²register vb -tered; -ter·ing \-st(ə-)riŋ\ 1 : to enter in a register (as in a list of guests) 2 : to record automatically 3 : to secure special care for (mail matter) by paying additional postage 4 : to show (emotions) by facial expression or gestures 5 : to correspond or adjust so as to correspond exactly

registered nurse n : a graduate trained nurse who has been licensed to prac-

tice by a state authority after passing qualifying examinations

reg·is·trant \ˈrej-ə-strənt\ n : one that registers or is registered

reg·is·trar \-ˌsträr\ n : an official recorder or keeper of records (as at an educational institution)

reg·is·tra·tion \ˌrej-ə-ˈstrā-shən\ n 1 : the act of registering 2 : an entry in a register 3 : the number of persons registered : ENROLLMENT 4 : a document certifying an act of registering

reg·is·try \ˈrej-ə-strē\ n, pl -tries 1 : ENROLLMENT, REGISTRATION 2 : the state or fact of being entered in a register 3 : a place of registration 4 : an official record book or an entry in one

reg·nant \ˈreg-nənt\ adj 1 : REIGNING 2 : DOMINANT 3 : of common or widespread occurrence : PREVALENT

reg·o·lith \ˈreg-ə-ˌlith\ n : unconsolidated residual or transported material that overlies the solid rock on the earth, moon, or a planet

¹re·gress \ˈrē-ˌgres\ n 1 : WITHDRAWAL 2 : RETROGRESSION

²re·gress \ri-ˈgres\ vb : to go or cause to go back or to a lower level — re·gressive adj — re·gres·sor \-ˈgres-ər\ n

re·gres·sion \ri-ˈgresh-ən\ n : the act or an instance of regressing; esp : reversion to an earlier mental or behavioral level

¹re·gret \ri-ˈgret\ vb re·gret·ted; re·gret·ting 1 : to mourn the loss or death of 2 : to be keenly sorry for 3 : to experience regret — re·gret·ta·ble \-ə-bəl\ adj — re·gret·ta·bly \-blē\ adv — re·gret·ter n

²regret n 1 : mental distress caused by something beyond one's power to remedy 2 : an expression of sorrow 3 pl : a note or oral message politely declining an invitation — re·gret·ful \-fəl\ adj — re·gret·ful·ly \-ē\ adv

re·group \(ˈ)rē-ˈgrüp\ vb : to form into a new grouping

regt abbr regiment

¹reg·u·lar \ˈreg-yə-lər\ adj [ME reguler, fr. MF, fr. LL regularis regular, fr. L, of a bar, fr. regula rule, straightedge, fr. regere to guide straight, rule] 1 : belonging to a religious order 2 : made, built, or arranged according to a rule, standard, or type; also : even or symmetrical in form or structure 3 : ORDERLY, METHODICAL (∼ habits); also : not varying : STEADY (a ∼ pace) 4 : made, selected, or conducted according to rule or custom 5 : properly qualified (not a ∼ lawyer) 6 : conforming to the normal or usual manner or inflection 7 : belonging to a permanent standing army and esp. to one maintained by a national government syn systematic, orderly, methodical — reg·u·lar·i·ty \ˌreg-yə-ˈlar-ət-ē\ n — reg·u·lar·ize \ˈreg-yə-lə-ˌrīz\ vb — reg·u·lar·ly adv

²regular n 1 : one that is regular (as in attendance) 2 : a member of the regu-

lar clergy **3** : a soldier in a regular army **4** : a player on an athletic team who is usu. in the starting lineup

reg·u·late \'reg-yə-ˌlāt\ *vb* **-lat·ed; -lat·ing 1** : to govern or direct according to rule : CONTROL **2** : to bring under the control of law or authority **3** : to put in good order **4** : to fix or adjust the time, amount, degree, or rate of — **reg·u·la·tive** \-ˌlāt-iv\ *adj* — **reg·u·la·tor** \-ˌlāt-ər\ *n* — **reg·u·la·to·ry** \-lə-ˌtōr-ē\ *adj*

reg·u·la·tion \ˌreg-yə-'lā-shən\ *n* **1** : the act of regulating : the state of being regulated **2** : a rule dealing with details of procedure **3** : an order issued by an executive authority of a government and having the force of law

re·gur·gi·tate \rē-'gər-jə-ˌtāt\ *vb* **-tat·ed; -tat·ing** [ML *regurgitare*, fr. L *re-* + LL *gurgitare* to engulf, fr. L *gurgit-, gurges* whirlpool] : to throw or be thrown back or out; *esp* : VOMIT — **re·gur·gi·ta·tion** \-ˌgər-jə-'tā-shən\ *n*

re·hab \'rē-ˌhab\ *n* **1** : REHABILITATION **2** : a rehabilitated building — **rehab** *vb*

re·ha·bil·i·tate \ˌrē-(h)ə-'bil-ə-ˌtāt\ *vb* **-tat·ed; -tat·ing 1** : to restore to a former capacity, rank, or right : REINSTATE **2** : to put into good condition again — **re·ha·bil·i·ta·tion** \-ˌbil-ə-'tā-shən\ *n* — **re·ha·bil·i·ta·tive** \-ˌtāt-iv\ *adj*

re·hash \'rē-'hash\ *vb* : to present again in another form without real change or improvement — **rehash** *n*

re·hear·ing \'rē-'hi(ə)r-iŋ\ *n* : a second or new hearing by the same tribunal

re·hears·al \ri-'hər-səl\ *n* **1** : something told again : RECITAL **2** : a private performance or practice session preparatory to a public appearance

re·hearse \ri-'hərs\ *vb* **re·hearsed; re·hears·ing 1** : to say again : REPEAT **2** : to recount in order : ENUMERATE **3** : to give a rehearsal of ⟨~ a play⟩ **4** : to train by rehearsal ⟨~ an actor⟩ **5** : to engage in a rehearsal — **re·hears·er** *n*

¹reign \'rān\ *n* **1** : the authority or rule of a sovereign **2** : the time during which a sovereign rules

²reign *vb* **1** : to rule as a sovereign **2** : to be predominant or prevalent

re·im·burse \ˌrē-əm-'bərs\ *vb* **-bursed; -burs·ing** [*re-* re- + obs. E *imburse* (to put in the pocket, pay), fr. ML *imbursare* to put into a purse, fr. L *in-* in + ML *bursa* purse, fr. LL, hide of an ox, fr. Gk *byrsa*] : to pay back : make restitution : REPAY **syn** indemnify, recompense, requite, compensate — **re·im·burs·able** *adj* — **re·im·burse·ment** *n*

¹rein \'rān\ *n* **1** : a line of a bridle by which a rider or driver directs an animal **2** : a restraining influence : CHECK **3** : position of control or command **4** : complete freedom — usu. used in the phrase *give free rein to*

²rein *vb* : to check or direct by reins

re·in·car·na·tion \ˌrē-ˌin-ˌkär-'nā-shən\ *n* : rebirth of the soul in a new body — **re·in·car·nate** \ˌrē-in-'kär-ˌnāt\ *vb*

rein·deer \'rān-ˌdiər\ *n* [ME *reindere*, fr. ON *hreinn* reindeer + ME *deer*] : any of several large deer of northern regions that are used for draft and meat, have antlers in both sexes, and are grouped with the caribou in a single species

reindeer moss *n* : a gray, erect, tufted, and much-branched lichen of northern regions that is consumed by reindeer and sometimes by man

re·in·fec·tion \ˌrē-ən-'fek-shən\ *n* : infection following another infection of the same type

re·in·force \ˌrē-ən-'fōrs\ *vb* **1** : to strengthen with additional forces (as troops or ships) **2** : to strengthen with new force, aid, material, or support — **re·in·force·ment** *n* — **re·in·forc·er** *n*

re·in·state \ˌrē-ən-'stāt\ *vb* **-stat·ed; -stat·ing** : to restore to a former position, condition, or capacity — **re·in·state·ment** *n*

re·it·er·ate \rē-'it-ə-ˌrāt\ *vb* **-at·ed; -at·ing** : to state or do over again or repeatedly **syn** repeat, iterate, reprise — **re·it·er·a·tion** \-ˌit-ə-'rā-shən\ *n*

¹re·ject \ri-'jekt\ *vb* **1** : to refuse to acknowledge or submit to **2** : to refuse to take or accept **3** : to refuse to grant, consider, or accede to **4** : to throw out esp. as useless or unsatisfactory — **re·jec·tion** \-'jek-shən\ *n*

²re·ject \'rē-ˌjekt\ *n* : a rejected person or thing

re·joice \ri-'jōis\ *vb* **re·joiced; re·joic·ing 1** : to give joy to : GLADDEN **2** : to feel joy or great delight — **re·joic·er** *n*

re·join \'rē-'jōin *for 1*, ri-*for 2*\ *vb* **1** : to join again : come together again : REUNITE **2** : to say in answer (as to a plaintiff's plea in court) : REPLY

re·join·der \ri-'join-dər\ *n* : REPLY; *esp* : an answer to a reply

re·ju·ve·nate \ri-'jü-və-ˌnāt\ *vb* **-nat·ed; -nat·ing** : to make young or youthful again : give new vigor to **syn** renew, refresh, renovate, restore — **re·ju·ve·na·tion** \-ˌjü-və-'nā-shən\ *n*

rel *abbr* relating; relative

¹re·lapse \ri-'laps, 'rē-ˌlaps\ *n* : the action or process of relapsing; *esp* : a recurrence of illness after a period of improvement

²re·lapse \ri-'laps\ *vb* **re·lapsed; re·laps·ing** : to slip back into a former condition (as of illness) after a change for the better

re·late \ri-'lāt\ *vb* **re·lat·ed; re·lat·ing 1** : to give an account of : TELL, NARRATE **2** : to show or establish logical or causal connection between **3** : to be connected : have reference **4** : to have meaningful social relationships **5** : to respond favorably — **re·lat·able** *adj* — **re·lat·er** *or* **re·la·tor** *n*

re·lat·ed \-əd\ *adj* **1** : connected by some understood relationship **2** : connected through membership in the same family — **re·lat·ed·ness** n

re·la·tion \ri-ˈlā-shən\ n 1 : NARRATION, ACCOUNT 2 : CONNECTION, RELATION-SHIP 3 : connection by blood or marriage : KINSHIP; also : RELATIVE 4 : REFERENCE, RESPECT (in ~ to this matter) 5 : the state of being mutually interested or involved (as in social or commercial matters) 6 pl : DEALINGS, AFFAIRS 7 pl : SEXUAL INTERCOURSE — **re·la·tion·al** \-sh(ə-)nəl\ adj

re·la·tion·ship \-ˌship\ n : the state of being related or interrelated

¹**rel·a·tive** \ˈrel-ət-iv\ n 1 : a word referring grammatically to an antecedent 2 : a thing having a relation to or a dependence upon another thing 3 : a person connected with another by blood or marriage; also : an animal or plant related to another by common descent

²**relative** adj 1 : introducing a subordinate clause qualifying an expressed or implied antecedent (~ pronoun) ; also : introduced by such a connective (~ clause) 2 : PERTINENT, RELEVANT 3 : not absolute or independent : COMPARATIVE 4 : expressed as the ratio of the specified quantity to the total magnitude or to the mean of all quantities involved syn dependent, contingent, conditional — **rel·a·tive·ly** adv — **rel·a·tive·ness** n

relative humidity n : the ratio of the amount of water vapor actually present in the air to the greatest amount possible at the same temperature

rel·a·tiv·is·tic \ˌrel-ət-iv-ˈis-tik\ adj 1 : of, relating to, or characterized by relativity 2 : moving at a velocity that is a significant fraction of the speed of light so that effects predicted by the theory of relativity become evident (a ~ electron) — **rel·a·tiv·is·ti·cal·ly** \-ti-k(ə-)lē\ adv

rel·a·tiv·i·ty \ˌrel-ə-ˈtiv-ət-ē\ n, pl -ties 1 : the quality or state of being relative 2 : a theory in physics that considers mass and energy to be equivalent and that states that a moving object will experience changes in size and time which are related to its speed but are only noticeable at speeds approaching that of light

re·lax \ri-ˈlaks\ vb 1 : to make or become less firm, tense, or rigid 2 : to make less severe or strict 3 : to seek rest or recreation — **re·lax·er** n

¹**re·lax·ant** \ri-ˈlak-sənt\ adj : producing relaxation

²**relaxant** n : a relaxing agent; esp : a drug that induces muscular relaxation

re·lax·ation \ˌrē-ˌlak-ˈsā-shən\ n 1 : the act of relaxing or state of being relaxed : a lessening of tension 2 : DIVERSION, RECREATION syn rest, repose, leisure, ease

¹**re·lay** \ˈrē-ˌlā\ n 1 : a fresh supply (as of horses or men) arranged beforehand

to relieve or replace others at various stages 2 : a race between teams in which each team member covers a specified part of a course 3 : an electromagnetic device in which the opening or closing of one circuit activates another device (as a switch in another circuit) 4 : the act of passing along by stages

²**re·lay** \ˈrē-ˌlā, ri-ˈlā\ vb **re·layed; re·lay·ing** 1 : to place in or provide with relays 2 : to pass along by relays 3 : to control or operate by a relay

³**re·lay** \ˈrē-ˈlā\ vb **-laid** \-ˈlād\ ; **-lay·ing** : to lay again

¹**re·lease** \ri-ˈlēs\ vb **re·leased; re·leas·ing** 1 : to set free from confinement or restraint 2 : to relieve from something (as pain, trouble, or penalty) that oppresses or burdens 3 : RELINQUISH (~ a claim) 4 : to permit publication or performance (as of a news story or a motion picture) on but not before a specified date syn emancipate, discharge, free, liberate

²**release** n 1 : relief or deliverance from sorrow, suffering, or trouble 2 : discharge from an obligation or responsibility 3 : an act of setting free : the state of being freed 4 : a document effecting a legal release 5 : a device for holding or releasing a mechanism as required 6 : a releasing for performance or publication; also : the matter released (as to the press)

rel·e·gate \ˈrel-ə-ˌgāt\ vb **-gat·ed; -gat·ing** 1 : to send into exile : BANISH 2 : to remove or dismiss to some less prominent position 3 : to assign to a particular class or sphere 4 : to submit or refer for judgment, decision, or execution : DELEGATE syn commit, entrust, consign, commend — **rel·e·ga·tion** \ˌrel-ə-ˈgā-shən\ n

re·lent \ri-ˈlent\ vb 1 : to become less stern, severe, or harsh 2 : SLACKEN

re·lent·less \-ləs\ adj : mercilessly hard or harsh : immovably stern or persistent — **re·lent·less·ly** adv — **re·lent·less·ness** n

rel·e·vance \ˈrel-ə-vəns\ n : relation to the matter at hand : practical and esp. social applicability

rel·e·van·cy \-vən-sē\ n : RELEVANCE

rel·e·vant \ˈrel-ə-vənt\ adj : bearing on the matter at hand : PERTINENT syn germane, material, applicable, apropos — **rel·e·vant·ly** adv

re·li·able \ri-ˈlī-ə-bəl\ adj : fit to be trusted or relied on : DEPENDABLE, TRUSTWORTHY — **re·li·abil·i·ty** \-ˌlī-ə-ˈbil-ət-ē\ n — **re·li·able·ness** n — **re·li·ably** \-ˈlī-ə-blē\ adv

re·li·ance \ri-ˈlī-əns\ n 1 : the act of relying 2 : the state of being reliant 3 : one relied on — **re·li·ant** \-ənt\ adj

rel·ic \ˈrel-ik\ n 1 : an object venerated because of its association with a saint or martyr 2 : SOUVENIR, MEMENTO 3 pl : REMAINS, RUINS 4 : a remaining trace : VESTIGE

rel·ict \'rel-ikt\ *n* : WIDOW

re·lief \ri-'lēf\ *n* **1** : removal or lightening of something oppressive, painful, or distressing **2** : aid in the form of money or necessities (as for the aged or handicapped) **3** : military assistance in or rescue from a position of difficulty **4** : release from a post or from performance of a duty : also : one that relieves another by taking his place **5** : legal remedy or redress **6** : projection of figures or ornaments from the background (as in sculpture) **7** : the elevations of a land surface

relief pitcher *n* : a baseball pitcher who takes over for another during a game

re·lieve \ri-'lēv\ *vb* **re·lieved; re·liev·ing** **1** : to free partly or wholly from a burden or from distress **2** : to bring about the removal or alleviation of : MITIGATE **3** : to release from a post or duty; *also* : to take the place of **4** : to break the monotony of (as by contrast in color) **5** : to raise in relief *syn* alleviate, lighten, assuage, allay — **re·liev·er** *n*

relig *abbr* religion

re·li·gion \ri-'lij-ən\ *n* **1** : the service and worship of God or the supernatural **2** : devotion to a religious faith **3** : an organized system of faith and worship; *also* : a personal set of religious beliefs and practices **4** : a cause, principle, or belief held to with faith and ardor — **re·li·gion·ist** *n*

¹re·li·gious \ri-'lij-əs\ *adj* **1** : relating or devoted to the divine or that which is held to be of ultimate importance **2** : of or relating to religious beliefs or observances **3** : scrupulously and conscientiously faithful **4** : FERVENT, ZEALOUS — **re·li·gious·ly** *adv*

²religious *n, pl* **religious** : one (as a monk) bound by vows and devoted to a life of piety

re·lin·quish \ri-'liŋ-kwish, -'lin-\ *vb* **1** : to withdraw or retreat from : ABANDON, QUIT **2** : GIVE UP ⟨~ a title⟩ **3** : to let go of : RELEASE *syn* yield, leave, resign, surrender, cede, waive — **re·lin·quish·ment** *n*

rel·i·quary \'rel-ə-ˌkwer-ē\ *n, pl* **-quar·ies** : a container for religious relics

¹rel·ish \'rel-ish\ *n* [ME *reles* aftertaste, fr. OF, release, something left over, fr. *relessier* to relax, release, fr. L *relaxare*] **1** : a characteristic flavor (as of food) : SAVOR **2** : keen enjoyment or delight in something : ENJOY **3** : APPETITE, INCLINATION **4** : a highly seasoned sauce (as of pickles) eaten with other food to add flavor

²relish *vb* **1** : to add relish to **2** : to take pleasure in : ENJOY **3** : to eat with pleasure — **rel·ish·able** *adj*

re·live \(ˈ)rē-'liv\ *vb* : to live again or over again; *esp* : to experience again in the imagination

re·lo·cate \(ˈ)rē-'lō-ˌkāt, ˌrē-lō-'kāt\ *vb* **1** : to locate again **2** : to move to a

new location — **re·lo·ca·tion** \ˌrē-lō-'kā-shən\ *n*

re·luc·tant \ri-'lək-tənt\ *adj* : holding back (as from acting) : UNWILLING; *also* : showing unwillingness ⟨~ obedience⟩ *syn* disinclined, indisposed, hesitant, loath, averse — **re·luc·tance** \-təns\ — **re·luc·tant·ly** *adv*

re·ly \ri-'lī\ *vb* **re·lied; re·ly·ing** [ME *relien* to rally, fr. MF *relier* to connect, rally, fr. L *religare* to tie back, fr. *re-* back + *ligare* to tie] : to place faith or confidence in : DEPEND *syn* trust, count

REM \'rem\ *n* : RAPID EYE MOVEMENT

re·main \ri-'mān\ *vb* **1** : to be left after others have been removed, subtracted, or destroyed **2** : to be something yet to be shown, done, or treated (it ~s to be seen) **3** : to stay after others have gone **4** : to continue unchanged

re·main·der \ri-'mān-dər\ *n* **1** : that which is left over : a remaining group, part, or trace **2** : the number left after a subtraction **3** : the number that is left over from the dividend after division and that is less than the divisor **4** : a book sold at a reduced price by the publisher after sales have slowed *syn* leavings, rest, balance, remnant, residue

re·mains \-'mānz\ *n pl* **1** : a remaining part or trace ⟨the ~ of a meal⟩ **2** : writings left unpublished at an author's death **3** : a dead body

¹re·make \(ˈ)rē-'māk\ *vb* **-made** \-'mād\ ; **-mak·ing** : to make anew or in a different form

²re·make \(ˈ)rē-ˌmāk\ *n* : one that is remade; *esp* : a new version of a motion picture

re·mand \ri-'mand\ *vb* : to order back; *esp* : to return to custody pending trial or for further detention

¹re·mark \ri-'märk\ *vb* **1** : to take notice of : OBSERVE **2** : to express as an observation or comment : SAY

²remark *n* **1** : the act of remarking : OBSERVATION, NOTICE **2** : a passing observation or comment

re·mark·able \ri-'mär-kə-bəl\ *adj* : worthy of being or likely to be noticed : UNUSUAL, EXTRAORDINARY, NOTEWORTHY — **re·mark·able·ness** *n* — **re·mark·ably** \-blē\ *adv*

re·me·di·a·ble \ri-'mēd-ē-ə-bəl\ *adj* : capable of being remedied ⟨~ speech defects⟩

re·me·di·al \ri-'mēd-ē-əl\ *adj* : intended to remedy or improve

¹rem·e·dy \'rem-əd-ē\ *n, pl* **-dies** **1** : a medicine or treatment that cures or relieves **2** : something that corrects or counteracts an evil or compensates for a loss

²remedy *vb* **-died; -dy·ing** : to provide or serve as a remedy for

re·mem·ber \ri-'mem-bər\ *vb* **-bered; -ber·ing** \-b(ə-)riŋ\ **1** : to have come into the mind again : think of again : RECOLLECT **2** : to keep from forgetting : keep in mind 3 : to convey greetings from 4 : COMMEMORATE

re·mem·brance \-brəns\ *n* 1 : an act of remembering : RECOLLECTION 2 : the ability to remember : MEMORY 3 : the power of remembering; *also* : the period over which one's memory extends 4 : a memory of a person, thing, or event 5 : something that serves to bring to mind : REMINDER, MEMENTO 6 : a greeting or gift recalling or expressing friendship or affection

re·mind \ri-'mīnd\ *vb* : to put in mind of someone or something : cause to remember — **re·mind·er** *n*

rem·i·nisce \,rem-ə-'nis\ *vb* **-nisced**; **-nisc·ing** : to indulge in reminiscence

rem·i·nis·cence \-'nis-əns\ *n* 1 : a recalling or telling of a past experience 2 : an account of a memorable experience

rem·i·nis·cent \-'ənt\ *adj* 1 : of or relating to reminiscence 2 : marked by or given to reminiscence 3 : serving to remind : SUGGESTIVE — **rem·i·nis·cent·ly** *adv*

re·miss \ri-'mis\ *adj* 1 : negligent or careless in the performance of work or duty 2 : showing neglect or inattention **syn** lax, neglectful, delinquent, derelict — **re·miss·ly** *adv* — **re·miss·ness** *n*

re·mis·sion \ri-'mish-ən\ *n* 1 : the act or process of remitting 2 : a state or period during which something is remitted

re·mit \ri-'mit\ *vb* **re·mit·ted**; **re·mit·ting** 1 : FORGIVE, PARDON 2 : to give or gain relief from (as pain) 3 : to refer for consideration, report, or decision 4 : to refrain from exacting or enforcing (as a penalty) 5 : to send (money) in payment of a bill **syn** excuse, condone

re·mit·tal \ri-'mit-²l\ *n* : REMISSION

re·mit·tance \ri-'mit-²ns\ *n* 1 : a sum of money remitted 2 : transmittal of money (as to a distant place)

rem·nant \'rem-nənt\ *n* 1 : a usu. small part or trace remaining 2 : an unsold or unused end of fabrics that are sold by the yard **syn** remainder, residue, rest

re·mod·el \'rē-'mäd-²l\ *vb* : to alter the structure of : MAKE OVER

re·mon·strance \ri-'män-strəns\ *n* : an act or instance of remonstrating

re·mon·strant \-strənt\ *adj* : vigorously objecting or opposing — **remonstrant** *n* — **re·mon·strant·ly** *adv*

re·mon·strate \ri-'män-,strāt\ *vb* **-strat·ed**; **-strat·ing** : to plead in opposition to something : speak in protest or reproof **syn** expostulate, object, protest — **re·mon·stra·tion** \ri-,män-'strā-shən, ,rem-ən-\ *n* — **re·mon·stra·tive** \ri-'män-strət-iv\ *adj* — **re·mon·stra·tor** \ri-'män-,strāt-ər\ *n*

rem·o·ra \'rem-ə-rə\ *n* : any of several fishes with sucking organs on the head by means of which they cling to other fishes and ships

re·morse \ri-'mórs\ *n* [ME, fr. MF *re-*

mors, fr. ML *remorsus*, fr. LL, act of biting again, fr. L *remorsus*, pp. of *remordēre* to bite again, fr. *re-* again + *mordēre* to bite] : regret for one's sins or for acts that wrong others : distress arising from a sense of guilt **syn** penitence, repentance, contrition — **re·morse·ful** *adj*

re·morse·less \-ləs\ *adj* 1 : MERCILESS 2 : PERSISTENT, RELENTLESS

re·mote \ri-'mōt\ *adj* **re·mot·er; -est** 1 : far off in place or time : not near 2 : not closely related : DISTANT 3 : located out of the way : SECLUDED 4 : small in degree : SLIGHT (a ~ chance) 5 : distant in manner — **re·mote·ly** *adv* — **re·mote·ness** *n*

¹**re·mount** \'rē-'maŭnt\ *vb* 1 : to mount again 2 : to furnish remounts to

²**re·mount** \'rē-,maŭnt\ *n* : a fresh horse to replace one disabled or exhausted

¹**re·move** \ri-'mūv\ *vb* **re·moved; re·mov·ing** 1 : to move from one place to another : TRANSFER 2 : to move by lifting or taking off or away 3 : DISMISS, DISCHARGE 4 : to get rid of : ELIMINATE (~ a fire hazard) 5 : to change one's residence or location 6 : to go away : DEPART 7 : to be capable of being removed — **re·mov·able** *adj* — **re·mov·al** \-vəl\ *n* — **re·mov·er** *n*

²**remove** *n* 1 : a transfer from one location to another : MOVE 2 : a degree or stage of separation

REM sleep *n* : a state of sleep associated with rapid eye movements and occurring approximately at 90-minute intervals that is characterized by changes in the electrical activity of the brain, changes in heart rhythm, relaxed muscles, vascular congestion of the sex organs, and dreaming

re·mu·ner·ate \ri-'myü-nə-,rāt\ *vb* **-at·ed; -at·ing** : to pay an equivalent for or to : RECOMPENSE — **re·mu·ner·a·tor** \-,rāt-ər\ *n*

re·mu·ner·a·tion \ri-,myü-nə-'rā-shən\ *n* : COMPENSATION, PAYMENT

re·mu·ner·a·tive \ri-'myü-nə-rət-iv, -,rāt-\ *adj* : serving to remunerate : GAINFUL

re·nais·sance \,ren-ə-'säns, -'zäns\ *n* 1 *cap* : the revival of classical influences in art and literature and the beginnings of modern science in Europe in the 14th-17th centuries; *also* : the period of the Renaissance 2 *often cap* : a movement or period of vigorous artistic and intellectual activity 3 : REBIRTH, REVIVAL

re·nal \'rēn-²l\ *adj* : of, relating to, or located in or near the kidneys

re·na·scence \ri-'nas-²ns, -'näs-\ *n*, *often cap* : RENAISSANCE

rend \'rend\ *vb* **rent** \'rent\ : **rend·ing** 1 : to remove by violence : WREST 2 : to tear forcibly apart : SPLIT

ren·der \'ren-dər\ *vb* **ren·dered; ren·der·ing** \-d(ə-)riŋ\ 1 : to extract (as lard) by heating 2 : to give to another; *also* : YIELD 3 : to give in return 4 : to do (a service) for another (~ aid) **5** : to cause to be or become : MAKE **6** : to reproduce or represent by artistic or verbal means **7** : TRANSLATE (~ into English)

¹ren·dez·vous \'rän-di-ˌvü, -dā-\ *n, pl* ren·dez·vous \-ˌvüz\ [MF, fr. *rendez vous* present yourselves] **1** : a place appointed for a meeting; *also* : a meeting at an appointed place **2** : a place of popular resort **3** : the process of bringing two spacecraft together syn tryst, engagement, appointment

²rendezvous *vb* -voused \-ˌvüd\ ; -vous·ing \-ˌvü-iŋ\ ; -vouses \-ˌvüz\ : to come or bring together at a rendezvous

ren·di·tion \ren-'dish-ən\ *n* : an act or a result of rendering (first ~ of the work into English)

ren·e·gade \'ren-i-ˌgād\ *n* [Sp *renegado*, fr. ML *renegatus*, fr. pp. of *renegare* to deny, fr. L *re-* re- + *negare* to deny] : one who deserts a faith, cause, principle, or party for another

re·nege \ri-'nig, -'neg, -'nēg, -'nāg\ *vb* re·neged; re·neg·ing **1** : to fail to follow suit when able in a card game in violation of the rules **2** : to go back on a promise or commitment — re·neg·er *n*

re·new \ri-'n(y)ü\ *vb* **1** : to make or become new, fresh, or strong again **2** : to restore to existence : RECREATE, REVIVE **3** : to make or do again : REPEAT (~ a complaint) **4** : to begin again : RESUME (~ed his efforts) **5** : REPLACE (~ the lining of a coat) **6** : to grant or obtain an extension of or on (~ a lease) (~ a subscription) — re·new·er *n*

re·new·able \ri-'n(y)ü-ə-bəl\ *adj* **1** : capable of being renewed **2** : capable of being replaced by natural ecological cycles or sound management procedures (water, wildlife, and forests are ~ resources)

re·new·al \ri-'n(y)ü-əl\ *n* **1** : the act of renewing : the state of being renewed **2** : something renewed

ren·net \'ren-ət\ *n* **1** : the contents of the stomach of an unweaned animal (as a calf) or the lining membrane of the stomach used for curdling milk **2** : rennin or a substitute used to curdle milk

ren·nin \'ren-ən\ *n* : a stomach enzyme that coagulates casein and is used commercially to curdle milk in the making of cheese

re·nounce \ri-'nauns\ *vb* re·nounced; re·nounc·ing **1** : to give up, refuse, or resign usu. by formal declaration **2** : to refuse further to follow, obey, or recognize : REPUDIATE syn abdicate, resign — re·nounce·ment *n*

ren·o·vate \'ren-ə-ˌvāt\ *vb* -vat·ed; -vat·ing **1** : to make like new again : put in good condition : REPAIR **2** : to restore to vigor or activity — ren·o·va·tion

\-ˌren-ə-ˌvā-shən\ *n* — ren·o·va·tor \'ren-ə-ˌvāt-ər\ *n*

re·nown \ri-'naun\ *n* : a state of being widely acclaimed and honored : FAME, CELEBRITY syn honor, glory, reputation, repute — re·nowned \-'naund\ *adj*

¹rent \'rent\ *n* **1** : money or the amount of money paid or due (as monthly) for the use of another's property **2** : property rented or for rent

²rent *vb* **1** : to take and hold under an agreement to pay rent **2** : to give possession and use of in return for rent **3** : to be for rent (~s for $100 a month) — rent·er *n*

³rent *n* **1** : a tear in cloth **2** : a split in a party or organized group : SCHISM

¹rent·al \'rent-°l\ *n* **1** : an amount paid or collected as rent **2** : a property rented **3** : an act of renting

²rental *adj* : of or relating to rent

re·nun·ci·a·tion \ri-ˌnən-sē-'ā-shən\ *n* : the act of renouncing : REPUDIATION

rep *abbr* **1** repair **2** report; reporter **3** representative **4** republic

Rep *abbr* Republican

re·pack·age \(')rē-'pak-ij\ *vb* : to package again or anew; *esp* : to put into a more attractive form

¹re·pair \ri-'paər\ *vb* [ME *repairen*, fr. MF *repairier* to go back to one's country, fr. LL *repatriare*, fr. L *re-* re- + *patria* native country] : to make one's way : GO (~ed to his den)

²repair *vb* [ME *repairen*, fr. MF *reparer*, fr. L *reparare*, fr. re- re- + *parare* to prepare] **1** : to restore to good condition **2** : to restore to a healthy state **3** : REMEDY (~ a wrong) — re·pair·er *n* — re·pair·man \-ˌman\ *n*

³repair *n* **1** : an act of repairing **2** : a result of repairing **3** : condition with respect to need of repairing (in bad ~)

rep·a·ra·tion \ˌrep-ə-'rā-shən\ *n* **1** : the act of making amends for a wrong **2** : amends made for a wrong; *esp* : money paid by a defeated nation in compensation for damages caused during hostilities — usu. used in pl. syn redress, restitution, indemnity

re·par·a·tive \ri-'par-ət-iv\ *adj* **1** : of, relating to, or effecting repairs **2** : serving to make amends

rep·ar·tee \ˌrep-ər-'tē\ *n* **1** : a witty reply **2** : a succession of clever replies; *also* : skill in making such replies

re·past \ri-'past, 'rē-ˌpast\ *n* : a supply of food and drink served as a meal

re·pa·tri·ate \rē-'pā-trē-ˌāt\ *vb* -at·ed; -at·ing : to send or bring back to the country of origin or citizenship (~ profits) (~ prisoners of war) — re·pa·tri·ate \-trē-ət, -trē-ˌāt\ *n* — re·pa·tri·a·tion \-ˌpā-trē-'ā-shən\ *n*

re·pay \rē-'pā\ *vb* -paid \-'pād\ ; -pay·ing **1** : to pay back : REFUND **2** : to give or do in return or requital **3** : to make a return payment to : RECOMPENSE, REQUITE syn remunerate, compensate, reimburse, indemnify — **re-pay·able** *adj* — **re·pay·ment** *n*

re·peal \ri-ˈpēl\ *vb* : to annul by authoritative and esp. legislative action — **repeal** *n* — **re·peal·er** *n*

¹**re·peat** \ri-ˈpēt\ *vb* 1 : to say again 2 : to do again 3 : to say over from memory *syn* iterate, reiterate, reprise — **re·peat·able** *adj* — **re·peat·er** *n*

²**re·peat** \ri-ˈpēt, ˈrē-ˌpēt\ *n* 1 : the act of repeating 2 : something repeated or to be repeated (as a radio or television program)

re·peat·ed \ri-ˈpēt-əd\ *adj* : done or recurring again and again : FREQUENT — **re·peat·ed·ly** *adv*

repeating decimal *n* : a decimal in which a particular digit or sequence of digits repeats itself indefinitely

re·pel \ri-ˈpel\ *vb* **re·pelled; re·pel·ling** 1 : to drive away : REPULSE 2 : to fight against : RESIST 3 : to turn away : REJECT 4 : to cause aversion in : DISGUST

¹**re·pel·lent** *also* **re·pel·lant** \ri-ˈpel-ənt\ *adj* 1 : tending to drive away (a mosquito-*repellent* spray) 2 : causing disgust

²**repellent** *also* **repellant** *n* : something that repels: *esp* : a substance used to prevent insect attacks

re·pent \ri-ˈpent\ *vb* 1 : to turn from sin and resolve to reform one's life 2 : to feel sorry for (something done) : REGRET — **re·pen·tance** \-ˈpent-ᵊns\ *n* — **re·pen·tant** \-ᵊnt\ *adj*

re·per·cus·sion \ˌrē-pər-ˈkəsh-ən, ˌrep-ər-\ *n* 1 : REVERBERATION 2 : a reciprocal action or effect 3 : a widespread, indirect, or unforeseen effect of something done or said

rep·er·toire \ˈrep-ə(r)-ˌtwär\ *n* [F] 1 : a list of plays, operas, pieces, or parts which a company or performer is prepared to present 2 : a list of the skills or devices possessed by a person or needed in his occupation

rep·er·to·ry \ˈrep-ə(r)-ˌtōr-ē\ *n. pl* **-ries** 1 : REPOSITORY 2 : REPERTOIRE 3 : a company that presents its repertoire in the course of one season at one theater

rep·e·ti·tion \ˌrep-ə-ˈtish-ən\ *n* 1 : the act or an instance of repeating 2 : the fact of being repeated

rep·e·ti·tious \-ˈtish-əs\ *adj* : marked by repetition: *esp* : tediously repeating — **rep·e·ti·tious·ly** *adv* — **rep·e·ti·tious·ness** *n*

re·pet·i·tive \ri-ˈpet-ət-iv\ *adj* : REPETITIOUS — **re·pet·i·tive·ly** *adv* — **re·pet·i·tive·ness** *n*

re·pine \ri-ˈpīn\ *vb* **re·pined; re·pin·ing** 1 : to feel or express discontent or dejection 2 : to long for something

repl *abbr* replace; replacement

re·place \ri-ˈplās\ *vb* 1 : to restore to a former place or position 2 : to take the place of : SUPPLANT 3 : to put something new in the place of — **re·place·able** *adj* — **re·plac·er** *n*

re·place·ment \ri-ˈplās-mənt\ *n* 1 : the act of replacing : the state of being replaced : SUBSTITUTION 2 : one that replaces; *esp* : one assigned to a military unit to replace a loss or fill a quota

¹**re·play** \ˈrē-ˈplā\ *vb* : to play again or over

²**re·play** \ˈrē-ˌplā\ *n* 1 : an act or instance of replaying 2 : the playing of a tape (as a videotape)

re·plen·ish \ri-ˈplen-ish\ *vb* : to fill or build up again : stock or supply anew — **re·plen·ish·ment** *n*

re·plete \ri-ˈplēt\ *adj* 1 : fully provided 2 : FULL; *esp* : full of food — **re·plete·ness** *n*

re·ple·tion \ri-ˈplē-shən\ *n* : the state of being replete

rep·li·ca \ˈrep-li-kə\ *n* [It, repetition, fr. *replicare* to repeat, fr. LL, fr. L, to fold back, fr. *re-* back + *plicare* to fold] 1 : a close reproduction or facsimile (as of a painting or statue) esp. by the maker of the original 2 : COPY, DUPLICATE

¹**rep·li·cate** \ˈrep-lə-ˌkāt\ *vb* **-cat·ed; -cat·ing** : DUPLICATE, REPEAT

²**rep·li·cate** \-li-kət\ *n* : one of several identical experiments or procedures

rep·li·ca·tion \ˌrep-lə-ˈkā-shən\ *n* 1 : ANSWER, REPLY 2 : precise copying or reproduction; *also* : an act or process of this

¹**re·ply** \ri-ˈplī\ *vb* **re·plied; re·ply·ing** : to say or do in answer : RESPOND

²**reply** *n, pl* **replies** : ANSWER, RESPONSE

¹**re·port** \ri-ˈpōrt\ *n* [ME, fr. MF, fr. OF, fr. *reporter* to report, fr. L *reportare*, fr. *re-* back + *portare* to carry] 1 : common talk : RUMOR 2 : FAME, REPUTATION 3 : a usu. detailed account or statement 4 : an explosive noise

²**report** *vb* 1 : to give an account of : RELATE, TELL 2 : to serve as carrier of (a message) 3 : to prepare or present (as an account of an event) for a newspaper or a broadcast 4 : to make a charge of misconduct against 5 : to present oneself (as for work) 6 : to make known to the authorities (⟨~ a fire) 7 : to return or present (as a matter referred to a committee) with conclusions and recommendations — **re·port·able** *adj*

re·port·age \ri-ˈpōrt-ij, *esp for 2* ˌrep-ər-ˈtäzh, ˌrep-ȯr-ˈ\ *n* [F] 1 : the act or process of reporting news 2 : writing intended to give an account of observed or documented events

report card *n* : a periodic report on a student's grades

re·port·ed·ly \ri-ˈpōrt-əd-lē\ *adv* : according to report

re·port·er \ri-ˈpōrt-ər\ *n* : one that reports: *esp* : a person who gathers and reports news for a news medium — **re·por·to·ri·al** \ˌrep-ə(r)-ˈtōr-ē-əl\ *adj*

¹**re·pose** \ri-ˈpōz\ *vb* **re·posed; re·pos·ing** 1 : to lay at rest 2 : to be at rest 3 : to lie dead 4 : to take a rest 5 : to rest for support : LIE

²**repose** n 1 : a state of resting (as after exertion); *esp* : SLEEP 2 : CALM, PEACE 3 : cessation or absence of activity, movement, or animation 4 : composure of manner : POISE — **re·pose·ful** *adj*

³**repose** *vb* **re·posed; re·pos·ing** 1 : to place (as trust) in someone or something 2 : to place for control, management, or use

re·pos·i·to·ry \ri-ˈpäz-ə-ˌtōr-ē\ *n, pl* **-ries** 1 : a place where something is deposited or stored 2 : a person to whom something is entrusted

re·pos·sess \ˌrē-pə-ˈzes\ *vb* 1 : to regain possession of 2 : to resume possession of in default of the payment of installments due — **re·pos·ses·sion** \-ˈzesh-ən\ *n*

rep·re·hend \ˌrep-ri-ˈhend\ *vb* : to express disapproval of : CENSURE **syn** criticize, condemn, denounce, blame, pan — **rep·re·hen·sion** \-ˈhen-chən\ *n*

rep·re·hen·si·ble \-ˈhen-sə-bəl\ *adj* : deserving blame or censure : CULPABLE — **rep·re·hen·si·bly** \-blē\ *adv*

rep·re·sent \ˌrep-ri-ˈzent\ *vb* 1 : to present a picture or a likeness of : PORTRAY, DEPICT 2 : to serve as a sign or symbol of 3 : to act the role of 4 : to stand in the place of : act or speak for 5 : to be a member or example of : TYPIFY 6 : to serve as an elected representative of 7 : to describe as having a specified quality or character 8 : to state with the purpose of affecting judgment or action

rep·re·sen·ta·tion \ˌrep-ri-ˌzen-ˈtā-shən\ *n* 1 : the act of representing 2 : one (as a picture or image) that represents something else 3 : the state of being represented in a legislative body; *also* : the body of persons representing a constituency 4 : a usu. formal statement made to effect a change

¹**rep·re·sen·ta·tive** \ˌrep-ri-ˈzent-ət-iv\ *adj* 1 : serving to represent 2 : standing or acting for another 3 : founded on the principle of representation : carried on by elected representatives (~ government) — **rep·re·sen·ta·tive·ly** *adv* — **rep·re·sen·ta·tive·ness** *n*

²**representative** *n* 1 : a typical example of a group, class, or quality 2 : one that represents another; *esp* : one representing a district in a legislative body usu. as a member of a lower house

re·press \ri-ˈpres\ *vb* 1 : CURB, SUBDUE 2 : RESTRAIN, SUPPRESS; *esp* : to exclude from consciousness — **re·pres·sion** \-ˈpresh-ən\ *n* — **re·pres·sive** \-ˈpres-iv\ *adj*

¹**re·prieve** \ri-ˈprēv\ *vb* **re·prieved; re·priev·ing** 1 : to delay the punishment or execution of 2 : to give temporary relief to

²**reprieve** *n* 1 : the act of reprieving : the state of being reprieved 2 : a formal temporary suspension of a sentence

esp. of death 3 : a temporary respite

¹**rep·ri·mand** \ˈrep-rə-ˌmand\ *n* : a severe or formal reproof

²**reprimand** *vb* : to reprove severely or formally

¹**re·print** \ˈrē-ˈprint\ *vb* : to print again

²**re·print** \ˈrē-ˌprint\ *n* : a reproduction of printed matter

re·pri·sal \ri-ˈprī-zəl\ *n* : an act in retaliation for something done by another

re·prise \ri-ˈprēz\ *n* : a recurrence, renewal, or resumption of an action; *also* : a musical repetition

¹**re·proach** \ri-ˈprōch\ *n* 1 : a cause or occasion of blame or disgrace 2 : DISGRACE, DISCREDIT 3 : the act of reproaching : REBUKE — **re·proach·ful** \-fəl\ *adj* — **re·proach·ful·ly** \-ē\ *adv* — **re·proach·ful·ness** *n*

²**reproach** *vb* 1 : CENSURE, REBUKE 2 : to cast discredit on **syn** chide, admonish, reprove, reprimand — **re·proach·able** *adj*

rep·ro·bate \ˈrep-rə-ˌbāt\ *n* 1 : a person foreordained to damnation 2 : a thoroughly bad person : SCOUNDREL — **reprobate** *adj*

rep·ro·ba·tion \ˌrep-rə-ˈbā-shən\ *n* : strong disapproval : CONDEMNATION

re·pro·duce \ˌrē-prə-ˈd(y)üs\ *vb* 1 : to produce again or anew 2 : to bear offspring — **re·pro·duc·ible** \-ˈd(y)ü-sə-bəl\ *adj* — **re·pro·duc·tion** \-ˈdək-shən\ *n* — **re·pro·duc·tive** \-ˈdək-tiv\ *adj*

re·proof \ri-ˈprüf\ *n* : blame or censure for a fault

re·prove \ri-ˈprüv\ *vb* **re·proved; re·prov·ing** 1 : to administer a rebuke to 2 : to express disapproval of **syn** reprimand, admonish, reproach, chide — **re·prov·er** *n*

rept *abbr* report

rep·tile \ˈrep-tᵊl, -ˌtīl\ *n* [ME *reptil*, fr. MF or LL; MF *reptile*, fr. LL *reptile*, fr. L *repere* to creep] : any of a large class of air-breathing scaly vertebrates including snakes, lizards, alligators, and turtles — **rep·til·i·an** \rep-ˈtil-ē-ən\ *adj or n*

re·pub·lic \ri-ˈpəb-lik\ *n* [F *république*, fr. MF *republique*, fr. L *respublica*, fr. *res* thing, wealth + *publica*, fem. of *publicus* public] 1 : a government having a chief of state who is not a monarch and is usu. a president; *also* : a nation or other political unit having such a government 2 : a government in which supreme power is held by the citizens entitled to vote and is exercised by elected officers and representatives governing according to law; *also* : a nation or other political unit having such a form of government

¹**re·pub·li·can** \-li-kən\ *adj* 1 : of, relating to, or resembling a republic 2 : favoring or supporting a republic 3 *cap* : of, relating to, or constituting one of the two major political parties in the

U.S. evolving in the mid-19th century — **re·pub·li·can·ism** *n, often cap*

²**republican** *n* **1** : one that favors or supports a republican form of government **2** *cap* : a member of a republican party and esp. of the Republican party of the U.S.

re·pu·di·ate \ri-'pyüd-ē-ˌāt\ *vb* **-at·ed; -at·ing** [L *repudiare* to cast off, divorce, fr. *repudium* divorce] **1** : to cast off : DISOWN **2** : to refuse to have anything to do with : refuse to acknowledge, accept, or pay (~ a charge) (~ a debt) *syn* spurn, reject, decline — **re·pu·di·a·tion** \-ˌpyüd-ē-'ā-shən\ *n* — **re·pu·di·a·tor** \-'pyüd-ē-ˌāt-ər\ *n*

re·pug·nance \ri-'pəg-nəns\ *n* **1** : the quality or fact of being contradictory or inconsistent **2** : strong dislike, distaste, or antagonism

re·pug·nant \-nənt\ *adj* **1** : marked by repugnance **2** : contrary to a person's tastes or principles : exciting distaste or aversion *syn* repellent, abhorrent, distasteful, obnoxious, revolting, loathsome — **re·pug·nant·ly** *adv*

¹**re·pulse** \ri-'pəls\ *vb* **re·pulsed; re·puls·ing** **1** : to drive or beat back : REPEL **2** : to repel by discourtesy or denial : REBUFF **3** : to cause a feeling of repulsion in : DISGUST

²**repulse** *n* **1** : REBUFF, REJECTION **2** : a repelling or being repelled in hostile encounter

re·pul·sion \ri-'pəl-shən\ *n* **1** : the action of repulsing : the state of being repulsed **2** : the force with which bodies, particles, or like forces repel one another **3** : a feeling of aversion

re·pul·sive \-siv\ *adj* **1** : serving or tending to repel or reject **2** : arousing aversion or disgust *syn* repugnant, revolting, loathsome, noisome — **re·pul·sive·ly** *adv* — **re·pul·sive·ness** *n*

rep·u·ta·ble \'rep-yət-ə-bəl\ *adj* : having a good reputation : ESTIMABLE — **rep·u·ta·bly** \-blē\ *adv*

rep·u·ta·tion \ˌrep-yə-'tā-shən\ *n* **1** : overall quality or character as seen or judged by people in general **2** : place in public esteem or regard

¹**re·pute** \ri-'pyüt\ *vb* **re·put·ed; re·put·ing** : CONSIDER, ACCOUNT

²**repute** *n* **1** : REPUTATION **2** : the state of being favorably known or spoken of

re·put·ed \ri-'pyüt-əd\ *adj* **1** : REPUTABLE **2** : according to reputation : SUPPOSED — **re·put·ed·ly** *adv*

req *abbr* **1** request **2** require; required **3** requisition

¹**re·quest** \ri-'kwest\ *n* **1** : an act or instance of asking for something **2** : a thing asked for **3** : the fact or condition of being asked for (available on ~)

²**request** *vb* **1** : to make a request to or of **2** : to ask for — **re·quest·er** *n*

re·qui·em \'rek-wē-əm, 'rāk-\ *n* [ME, fr. L (first word of the requiem mass), acc. of *requies* rest, fr. *quies* quiet,

rest] **1** : a mass for a dead person: *also* : a musical setting for this **2** : a musical service or hymn in honor of the dead

re·quire \ri-'kwī(ə)r\ *vb* **re·quired; re·quir·ing** **1** : to demand as necessary or essential **2** : COMMAND, ORDER

re·quire·ment \-mənt\ *n* **1** : something (as a condition or quality) required (entrance ~) **2** : NECESSITY

req·ui·site \'rek-wə-zət\ *adj* : REQUIRED, NECESSARY

req·ui·si·tion \ˌrek-wə-'zish-ən\ *n* **1** : formal application or demand (as for supplies) **2** : the state of being in demand or use — **requisition** *vb*

re·quite \ri-'kwīt\ *vb* **re·quit·ed; re·quit·ing** **1** : to make return for : REPAY **2** : to make retaliation for : AVENGE **3** : to make return to for a benefit or service or for an injury — **re·quit·al** \-'kwīt-ᵊl\ *n*

re·re·dos \'rer-ə-ˌdäs\ *n* : a usu. ornamental wood or stone screen or partition wall behind an altar

re·run \'rē-ˌrən, 'rē-'rən\ *n* : the act or an instance of running again or anew; *esp* : a showing of a motion picture or television program after its first run — **re·run** \'rē-'rən\ *vb*

res *abbr* **1** research **2** reservation; reserve **3** residence **4** resolution

re·sale \'rē-ˌsāl, -'sāl\ *n* : the act of selling again usu. to a new party — **re·sal·able** \'rē-'sā-lə-bəl\ *adj*

re·scind \ri-'sind\ *vb* : REPEAL, CANCEL, ANNUL — **re·scind·er** *n* — **re·scis·sion** \-'sizh-ən\ *n*

re·script \'rē-ˌskript\ *n* : an official or authoritative order or decree

res·cue \'res-kyü\ *vb* **res·cued; res·cu·ing** [ME *rescuen*, fr. MF *rescourre*, fr. OF, fr. *re-* re- + *escourre* to shake out, fr. L *excutere*] : to free from danger, harm, or confinement *syn* deliver, save — **rescue** *n* — **res·cu·er** *n*

re·search \ri-'sərch, 'rē-ˌsərch\ *n* **1** : careful or diligent search **2** : studious and critical inquiry and examination aimed at the discovery and interpretation of new knowledge **3** : the collecting of information about a particular subject — **research** *vb* — **re·search·er** *n*

re·sec·tion \ri-'sek-shən\ *n* : the surgical removal of part of an organ or structure

re·sem·blance \ri-'zem-bləns\ *n* : the quality or state of resembling

re·sem·ble \ri-'zem-bəl\ *vb* **-bled; -bling** \-b(ə-)liŋ\ : to be like or similar to

re·sent \ri-'zent\ *vb* : to feel or exhibit annoyance or indignation at — **re·sent·ful** \-fəl\ *adj* — **re·sent·ful·ly** \-ē\ *adv* — **re·sent·ment** *n*

re·ser·pine \ri-'sər-ˌpēn, -pən\ *n* : a drug obtained from rauwolfia and used in treating high blood pressure and nervous tension

res·er·va·tion \ˌrez-ər-'vā-shən\ *n* **1** : an act of reserving **2** : something (as a room in a hotel) arranged for in advance **3** : something reserved: *esp* : a tract of public land set aside for a special use **4** : a limiting condition

¹re·serve \ri-'zərv\ *vb* re·served; re·serv·ing **1** : to store for future or special use **2** : to hold back for oneself **3** : to set aside or arrange to have set aside or held for special use

²reserve *n* **1** : something reserved : STOCK, STORE **2** : a military force withheld from action for later use — usu. used in pl. **3** : the military forces of a country not part of the regular services; *also* : RESERVIST **4** : a tract set apart : RESERVATION **5** : an act of reserving **6** : restraint or caution in one's words or bearing **7** : money or its equivalent kept in hand or set apart to meet liabilities

re·served \ri-'zərvd\ *adj* **1** : restrained in words and actions **2** : set aside for future or special use — re·serv·ed·ly \-'zər-vəd-lē\ *adv* — re·serv·ed·ness \-vəd-nəs\ *n*

re·serv·ist \ri-'zər-vəst\ *n* : a member of a military reserve

res·er·voir \'rez-ə(r)v-,wär, -ə(r)v-,(w)òr\ *n* [F] : a place where something is kept in store; *esp* : an artificial lake where water is collected as a water supply

re·shuf·fle \rē-'shəf-əl\ *vb* **1** : to shuffle again **2** : to reorganize usu. by redistribution of existing elements — reshuffle *n*

re·side \ri-'zīd\ *vb* re·sid·ed; re·sid·ing **1** : to make one's home : DWELL **2** : to be present as a quality or vested as a right

res·i·dence \'rez-əd-əns\ *n* **1** : the act or fact of residing in a place as a dweller or in discharge of a duty or an obligation **2** : the place where one actually lives **3** : a building used as a home : DWELLING **4** : the period of living in a place

res·i·den·cy \'rez-əd-ən-sē\ *n, pl* -cies **1** : the residence of or the territory under a diplomatic resident **2** : a period of advanced training in a medical specialty

¹res·i·dent \-ənt\ *adj* **1** : RESIDING **2** : being in residence **3** : not migratory

²resident *n* **1** : one who resides in a place **2** : a diplomatic representative with governing powers (as in a protectorate) **3** : a physician serving a residency

res·i·den·tial \,rez-ə-'den-chəl\ *adj* **1** : used as a residence or by residents **2** : occupied by or restricted to residences — res·i·den·tial·ly \-ē\ *adv*

¹re·sid·u·al \ri-'zij-(ə-w)əl\ *adj* : being a residue or remainder

²residual *n* **1** : a residual product or substance **2** : a payment (as to an actor or writer) for each rerun after an initial showing (as of a taped TV show)

re·sid·u·ary \ri-'zij-ə-,wer-ē\ *adj* : of,

relating to, or constituting a residue esp. of an estate

res·i·due \'rez-ə-,d(y)ü\ *n* : a part remaining after another part has been taken away : REMAINDER

re·sid·u·um \ri-'zij-ə-wəm\ *n, pl* re·sid·ua \-ə-wə\ [L] **1** : something remaining or residual after certain deductions are made **2** : a residual product syn remainder, rest, balance, remnant

re·sign \ri-'zīn\ *vb* [ME *resignen*, fr. MF *resigner*, fr. L *resignare*, lit., to unseal, cancel, fr. *signare* to sign, seal] **1** : to give up deliberately (as one's position) esp. by a formal act **2** : to give (oneself) over (as to grief or despair) without resistance — re·sign·ed·ly \-'zī-nəd-lē\ *adv*

re·sign \rē-'sīn\ *vb* : to sign again

res·ig·na·tion \,rez-ig-'nā-shən\ *n* **1** : an act or instance of resigning; *also* : a formal notification of such an act **2** : the quality or state of being resigned

re·sil·ience \ri-'zil-yəns\ *n* **1** : the ability of a body to regain its original size and shape after being compressed, bent, or stretched **2** : an ability to recover from or adjust easily to change or misfortune

re·sil·ien·cy \-yən-sē\ *n* : RESILIENCE

re·sil·ient \-yənt\ *adj* : marked by resilience syn flexible, supple

res·in \'rez-ᵊn\ *n* : a substance obtained from the gum or sap of some trees and used esp. in varnishes, plastics, and medicine; *also* : a comparable synthetic product — res·in·ous *adj*

¹re·sist \ri-'zist\ *vb* **1** : to fight against : OPPOSE ⟨∼ aggression⟩ **2** : to withstand the force or effect of ⟨∼ disease⟩ syn combat, withstand, repel — re·sist·ible \-'zis-tə-bəl\ *adj* — re·sist·less *adj*

²resist *n* : something (as a coating) that resists or prevents a particular action

re·sis·tance \ri-'zis-təns\ *n* **1** : the act or an instance of resisting : OPPOSITION **2** : the opposition offered by a body to the passage through it of a steady electric current

re·sis·tant \-tənt\ *adj* : giving or capable of resistance

re·sis·tiv·i·ty \ri-,zis-'tiv-ət-ē, ,rē-\ *n, pl* -ties : capacity for resisting

re·sis·tor \ri-'zis-tər\ *n* : a device used to provide resistance to the flow of an electric current

res·o·lute \'rez-ə-,lüt\ *adj* : firmly determined in purpose : RESOLVED syn steadfast, staunch, faithful, true, loyal — res·o·lute·ly *adv* — res·o·lute·ness *n*

res·o·lu·tion \,rez-ə-'lü-shən\ *n* **1** : the act or process of resolving **2** : the action of solving; *also* : SOLUTION **3** : the quality of being resolute : FIRMNESS, DETERMINATION **4** : a formal statement expressing the opinion, will, or intent of a body of persons

¹re·solve \ri-'zälv\ *vb* re·solved; re·solv·ing **1** : to break up into constituent

parts : ANALYZE **2** : to find an answer to : SOLVE **3** : DETERMINE, DECIDE **4** : to make or pass a formal resolution — **re·solv·able** adj

²resolve n **1** : something resolved **2** : fixity of purpose

res·o·nance \\'rez-ᵊn-əns\\ n **1** : the quality or state of being resonant **2** : a reinforcement of sound in a vibrating body caused by waves from another body vibrating at nearly the same rate

res·o·nant \\'rez-ᵊn-ənt\\ adj **1** : continuing to sound : RESOUNDING **2** : relating to or exhibiting resonance **3** : intensified and enriched by or as if by resonance — **res·o·nant·ly** adv

res·o·nate \\'rez-ᵊn-ˌāt\\ vb **-nat·ed; -nat·ing 1** : to produce or exhibit resonance **2** : REVERBERATE, RESOUND

res·o·na·tor \\-ᵊn-ˌāt-ər\\ n : something that resounds or exhibits resonance

re·sorp·tion \\rē-'sȯrp-shən, -'zȯrp-\\ n : the action or process of breaking down and assimilating something (as a tooth or an embryo)

¹re·sort \\ri-'zȯrt\\ n [ME, fr. MF, resource, recourse, fr. resortir to rebound, resort, fr. OF, fr. sortir to escape, sally] **1** : one looked to for help : REFUGE **2** : RECOURSE **3** : frequent or general visiting (place of ∼) **4** : a frequently visited place : HAUNT **5** : a place providing recreation esp. to vacationers

²resort vb **1** : to go often or habitually **2** : to have recourse (as for aid)

re·sound \\ri-'zaúnd\\ vb **1** : to become filled with sound : REVERBERATE, RING **2** : to sound loudly

re·sound·ing \\-iŋ\\ adj **1** : RESONATING, RESONANT **2** : impressively sonorous (∼ name) **3** : EMPHATIC, UNEQUIVOCAL (a ∼ success) — **re·sound·ing·ly** adv

re·source \\'rē-ˌsȯrs, ri-'sȯrs\\ n [F ressource, fr. OF ressourse relief, resource, fr. resourdre to relieve, lit., to rise again, fr. L resurgere, fr. re- again + surgere to rise] **1** : a source of supply or support — usu. used in pl. **2** pl : available funds **3** : a possibility of relief or recovery **4** : a means of spending leisure time **5** : ability to meet and handle situations — **re·source·ful** \\ri-'sȯrs-fəl\\ adj — **re·source·ful·ness** n

resp abbr respective; respectively

¹re·spect \\ri-'spekt\\ n **1** : relation to something usu. specified : REFERENCE, REGARD **2** : high or special regard : ESTEEM **3** pl : an expression of respect or deference **4** : DETAIL, PARTICULAR — **re·spect·ful** \\-fəl\\ adj — **re·spect·ful·ly** \\-ē\\ adv — **re·spect·ful·ness** n

²respect vb **1** : to consider deserving of high regard : ESTEEM **2** : to refrain from interfering with (∼ another's privacy) **3** : to have reference to : CONCERN — **re·spect·er** n

re·spect·able \\ri-'spek-tə-bəl\\ adj **1** : worthy of respect : ESTIMABLE **2** : decent or correct in conduct : PROPER **3**

: fair in size, quantity, or quality : MODERATE, TOLERABLE **4** : fit to be seen : PRESENTABLE — **re·spect·a·bil·i·ty** \\-ˌspek-tə-'bil-ət-ē\\ n — **re·spect·ably** \\-'spek-tə-blē\\ adv

re·spect·ing \\-tiŋ\\ prep : with regard to

re·spec·tive \\-tiv\\ adj : PARTICULAR, SEPARATE (returned to their ∼ homes)

re·spec·tive·ly \\-lē\\ adv **1** : as relating to each **2** : each in the order given

res·pi·ra·tion \\ˌres-pə-'rā-shən\\ n **1** : an act or the process of breathing **2** : the physical and chemical processes (as breathing and oxidation) by which a living thing obtains the oxygen and eliminates waste gases (as carbon dioxide) — **re·spi·ra·to·ry** \\'res-p(ə-)rə-ˌtōr-ē, ri-'spī-rə-\\ adj — **re·spire** \\ri-'spī(ə)r\\ vb

res·pi·ra·tor \\'res-pə-ˌrāt-ər\\ n : a device covering the mouth or nose esp. to prevent inhaling harmful vapors **2** : a device for artificial respiration

re·spite \\'res-pət\\ n **1** : a temporary delay **2** : an interval of rest or relief

re·splen·dent \\ri-'splen-dənt\\ adj : shining brilliantly : gloriously bright : SPLENDID — **re·splen·dence** \\-dəns\\ n — **re·splen·dent·ly** adv

re·spond \\ri-'spänd\\ vb **1** : ANSWER, REPLY **2** : REACT (∼ to a stimulus) **3** : to show favorable reaction (∼ to medication) — **re·spond·er** n

re·spon·dent \\ri-'spän-dənt\\ n : one who responds; esp : one who answers in various legal proceedings — **respondent** adj

re·sponse \\ri-'späns\\ n **1** : an act of responding **2** : something constituting a reply or a reaction

re·spon·si·bil·i·ty \\ri-ˌspän-sə-'bil-ət-ē\\ n, pl **-ties 1** : the quality or state of being responsible **2** : something for which one is responsible

re·spon·si·ble \\ri-'spän-sə-bəl\\ adj **1** : liable to be called upon to answer for one's acts or decisions : ANSWERABLE **2** : able to fulfull one's obligations : RELIABLE, TRUSTWORTHY **3** : able to choose for oneself between right and wrong **4** : involving accountability or important duties (∼ position) — **re·spon·si·ble·ness** n — **re·spon·si·bly** \\-blē\\ adv

re·spon·sive \\-siv\\ adj **1** : RESPONDING **2** : quick to respond : SENSITIVE **3** : using responses (∼ readings) — **re·spon·sive·ly** adv — **re·spon·sive·ness** n

¹rest \\'rest\\ n **1** : REPOSE, SLEEP **2** : freedom from work or activity **3** : a state of motionlessness or inactivity **4** : a place of shelter or lodging **5** : a silence in music equivalent in duration to a note of the same value; also : a character indicating this **6** : something used as a support — **rest·ful** \\-fəl\\ adj — **rest·ful·ly** \\-ē\\ adv

²rest vb **1** : to get rest by lying down; esp : SLEEP **2** : to cease from action or motion **3** : to give rest to : set at rest **4** : to sit or lie fixed or supported **5** : to place on or against a support **6** : to remain based or founded **7** : to cause to be firmly fixed : GROUND **8** : to remain for action : DEPEND

³**rest** *n* : something that remains over

res·tau·rant \'res-t(ə-)rənt, -tə-ˌränt\ *n* [F, fr. prp. of *restaurer* to restore, fr. L *restaurare*] : a public eating place

res·tau·ra·teur \ˌres-tə-rə-'tər\ *also* **res·tau·ran·teur** \-ˌrän-\ *n* : the operator or proprietor of a restaurant

rest home *n* : an establishment that gives care for the aged or convalescent

res·ti·tu·tion \ˌres-tə-'t(y)ü-shən\ *n* : the act of restoring : the state of being restored; *esp* : restoration of something to its rightful owner **syn** amends, redress, reparation, indemnity, compensation

res·tive \'res-tiv\ *adj* [ME, fr. MF *restif*, fr. *rester* to stop behind, remain, fr. L *restare*, fr. *re-* back + *stare* to stand] **1** : BALKY **2** : UNEASY, FIDGETY **syn** restless, impatient, nervous — **res·tive·ly** *adv* — **res·tive·ness** *n*

rest·less \'rest-ləs\ *adj* **1** : lacking or denying rest **2** : never resting or ceasing : UNQUIET (the ~ sea) **3** : marked by or showing unrest esp. of mind : DISCONTENTED **syn** restive, impatient, nervous, fidgety — **rest·less·ly** *adv* — **rest·less·ness** *n*

re·stor·able \ri-'stōr-ə-bəl\ *adj* : fit for restoring or reclaiming

res·to·ra·tion \ˌres-tə-'rā-shən\ *n* **1** : an act of restoring : the state of being restored **2** : something that is restored; *esp* : a reconstruction or representation of an original form (as of a building)

re·stor·ative \ri-'stōr-ət-iv\ *n* : something that restores esp. to consciousness or health — **restorative** *adj*

re·store \ri-'stōr\ *vb* **re·stored; re·stor·ing 1** : to give back : RETURN **2** : to put back into use or service **3** : to put or bring back into a former or original state : REPAIR, RENEW **4** : to put again in possession of something — **re·stor·er** *n*

re·strain \ri-'strān\ *vb* **1** : to prevent from doing something **2** : to limit, restrict, or keep under control : CURB **3** : to place under restraint or arrest — **re·strain·able** *adj* — **re·strain·er** *n*

re·strained \ri-'strānd\ *adj* : marked by restraint : DISCIPLINED — **re·strain·ed·ly** \-'strā-nəd-lē\ *adv*

re·straint \ri-'strānt\ *n* **1** : an act of restraining : the state of being restrained **2** : a restraining force, agency, or device **3** : deprivation or limitation of liberty : CONFINEMENT **4** : control over one's feelings : RESERVE

re·strict \ri-'strikt\ *vb* **1** : to confine within bounds : LIMIT **2** : to place under restriction as to use — **re·stric·tive** *adj* — **re·stric·tive·ly** *adv*

re·stric·tion \ri-'strik-shən\ *n* **1** : something (as a law or rule) that restricts **2**

: an act of restricting : the state of being restricted

rest room *n* : a room or suite of rooms providing personal facilities (as toilets)

¹**re·sult** \ri-'zəlt\ *vb* [ME *resulten*, fr. ML *resultare*, fr. L, to rebound, fr. *re-* + *saltare* to leap] : to proceed or come about as an effect or consequence — **re·sul·tant** \-'zəlt-ᵊnt\ *adj or n*

²**result** *n* **1** : something that results : EFFECT, CONSEQUENCE **2** : beneficial or discernible effect **3** : something obtained by calculation or investigation

re·sume \ri-'züm\ *vb* **re·sumed; re·sum·ing 1** : to take or assume again **2** : to return to or begin again after interruption **3** : to take back to oneself — **re·sump·tion** \-'zəmp-shən\ *n*

ré·su·mé *or* **re·su·me** *or* **re·su·mé** \'rez-ə-ˌmā, ˌrez-ə-'mā\ *n* [F *résumé*] : SUMMARY; *esp* : a short account of one's career and qualifications usu. prepared by a job applicant

re·sur·gence \ri-'sər-jəns\ *n* : a rising again into life, activity, or prominence — **re·sur·gent** \-jənt\ *adj*

res·ur·rect \ˌrez-ə-'rekt\ *vb* **1** : to raise from the dead **2** : to bring to attention or use again

res·ur·rec·tion \ˌrez-ə-'rek-shən\ *n* **1** *cap* : the rising of Christ from the dead **2** *often cap* : the rising to life of all human dead before the final judgment **3** : REVIVAL

re·sus·ci·tate \ri-'səs-ə-ˌtāt\ *vb* **-tat·ed; -tat·ing** : to revive from a condition resembling death — **re·sus·ci·ta·tion** \ri-ˌsəs-ə-'tā-shən, ˌrē-\ *n* — **re·sus·ci·ta·tor** \-ˌtāt-ər\ *n*

ret *abbr* **1** retain **2** retired **3** return

¹**re·tail** \'rē-ˌtāl, *esp for 2 also* ri-'tāl\ *vb* **1** : to sell in small quantities directly to the ultimate consumer **2** : to tell in detail or to one person after another — **re·tail·er** *n*

²**re·tail** \'rē-ˌtāl\ *n* : the sale of goods in small amounts to ultimate consumers — **retail** *adj or adv*

re·tain \ri-'tān\ *vb* **1** : to hold in possession or use **2** : to engage (as a lawyer) by paying a fee in advance **3** : to keep in a fixed place or position **syn** detain, withhold, reserve

¹**re·tain·er** \-ər\ *n* **1** : one that retains **2** : a servant in a wealthy household; *also* : EMPLOYEE

²**retainer** *n* : a fee paid to secure services (as of a lawyer)

¹**re·take** \'rē-'tāk\ *vb* **-took** \-'tùk\, **-tak·en** \-'tā-kən\, **-tak·ing 1** : to take or seize again **2** : to photograph again

²**re·take** \'rē-ˌtāk\ *n* : a second photographing of a motion-picture scene

re·tal·i·ate \ri-'tal-ē-ˌāt\ *vb* **-at·ed; -at·ing** : to return like for like: *esp* : to get revenge — **re·tal·i·a·tion** \-ˌtal-ē-'ā-shən\ *n* — **re·tal·i·a·to·ry** \-'tal-yə-ˌtōr-ē\ *adj*

re·tard \ri-ˈtärd\ vb : to hold back : delay the progress of syn slow, slacken, detain — **re·tar·da·tion** \ˌrē-ˌtär-ˈdā-shən, ri-\ n — **re·tard·er** n

re·tar·date \-ˈtärd-ˌāt, -ət\ n : a mentally retarded person

re·tard·ed \ri-ˈtärd-əd\ adj : slow or limited in intellectual, emotional, or academic development (a ~ child)

retch \ˈrech, ˈrēch\ vb : to try to vomit

re·ten·tion \ri-ˈten-chən\ n 1 : the act of retaining : the state of being retained 2 : the power of retaining esp. in the mind : RETENTIVENESS

re·ten·tive \-ˈtent-iv\ adj : having the power of retaining; esp : retaining knowledge easily — **re·ten·tive·ness** n

ret·i·cent \ˈret-ə-sənt\ adj : inclined to be silent or secretive : UNCOMMUNICATIVE syn reserved, taciturn, closemouthed — **ret·i·cence** \-səns\ n — **ret·i·cent·ly** adv

ret·i·na \ˈret-ᵊn-ə\ n, pl retinas or reti·nae \-ᵊn-ˌē\ : the sensory membrane lining the eye and receiving the image formed by the lens — **ret·i·nal** \ˈret-ᵊn-əl\ adj

ret·i·nue \ˈret-ᵊn-ˌ(y)ü\ n : the body of attendants or followers of a distinguished person

re·tire \ri-ˈtī(ə)r\ vb re·tired; re·tir·ing 1 : RETREAT 2 : to withdraw esp. for privacy 3 : to withdraw from one's occupation or position 4 : to go to bed 5 : to withdraw from circulation or from the market or from usual use or service 6 : to cause to be out in baseball — **re·tire·ment** n

re·tired \ri-ˈtī(ə)rd\ adj 1 : SECLUDED, QUIET 2 : withdrawn from active duty or from one's occupation 3 : received by or due to one who has retired

re·tir·ee \ri-ˌtī-ˈrē\ n : a person who has retired from an occupation

re·tir·ing \ri-ˈtīr-iŋ\ adj : SHY, RESERVED

¹**re·tort** \ri-ˈtȯrt\ vb [L retortus, pp. of retorquēre, lit., to twist back, hurl back, fr. re- back + torquēre to twist] 1 : to say in reply : answer back usu. sharply 2 : to answer (an argument) by a counter argument 3 : RETALIATE

²**retort** n : a quick, witty, or cutting reply

³**re·tort** \ri-ˈtȯrt, ˈrē-ˌtȯrt\ n [MF retorte, fr. ML retorta, fr. L, fem. of retortus, pp. of retorquēre to twist back; fr. its shape] : a vessel in which substances are distilled or broken up by heat

re·touch \ˈrē-ˈtəch\ vb : TOUCH UP; esp : to change (as a photographic negative) in order to produce a more desirable appearance

re·trace \(ˈ)rē-ˈtrās\ vb : to trace again or in a reverse direction (retraced his steps)

re·tract \ri-ˈtrakt\ vb 1 : to draw back or in 2 : to withdraw (as a charge or promise) : DISAVOW — **re·tract·able** adj — **re·trac·tion** \-ˈtrak-shən\ n

re·trac·tile \ri-ˈtrak-tᵊl, -ˌtīl\ adj : capable of being drawn back or in (~ claws)

¹**re·tread** \ˈrē-ˈtred\ vb re·tread·ed; re·tread·ing : to put a new tread on (a worn tire)

²**re·tread** \ˈrē-ˌtred\ n 1 : a new tread on a tire 2 : a retreaded tire 3 : one pressed into service again; also : REMAKE

¹**re·treat** \ri-ˈtrēt\ n 1 : an act of withdrawing esp. from something dangerous, difficult, or disagreeable 2 : a military signal for withdrawal; also : a military flag-lowering ceremony 3 : a place of privacy or safety : REFUGE 4 : a period of group withdrawal for prayer, meditation, and study

²**retreat** vb 1 : to make a retreat : WITHDRAW 2 : to slope backward

re·trench \ri-ˈtrench\ vb [obs. F retrencher (now retrancher), fr. MF retrenchier, fr. re- + trenchier to cut] 1 : to cut down or pare away : REDUCE, CURTAIL 2 : to cut down expenses : ECONOMIZE — **re·trench·ment** n

ret·ri·bu·tion \ˌre-trə-ˈbyü-shən\ n : something administered or exacted in recompense; esp : PUNISHMENT syn reprisal, vengeance, revenge, retaliation — **re·trib·u·tive** \ri-ˈtrib-yət-iv\ adj — **re·trib·u·to·ry** \-yə-ˌtȯr-ē\ adj

re·trieve \ri-ˈtrēv\ vb re·trieved; re·triev·ing 1 : to search about for and bring in (killed or wounded game) 2 : RECOVER, RESTORE — **re·triev·able** adj — **re·triev·al** \-ˈtrē-vəl\ n

re·triev·er \ri-ˈtrē-vər\ n : one that retrieves; esp : a dog of any of several breeds used esp. for retrieving game

ret·ro·ac·tive \ˌre-trō-ˈak-tiv\ adj : made effective as of a date prior to enactment (a ~ pay raise) — **ret·ro·ac·tive·ly** adv

ret·ro·fire \ˈre-trō-ˌfī(ə)r\ vb : to ignite a retro-rocket — **retrofire** n

ret·ro·fit \ˌre-trō-ˈfit\ vb : to furnish (as an aircraft) with newly available equipment

¹**ret·ro·grade** \ˈre-trə-ˌgrād\ adj 1 : moving or tending backward 2 : tending toward or resulting in a worse condition

²**retrograde** vb 1 : RETREAT 2 : DETERIORATE, DEGENERATE

ret·ro·gres·sion \ˌre-trə-ˈgresh-ən\ n : return to a former and less complex level of development or organization — **ret·ro·gress** \ˌre-trə-ˈgres\ vb — **ret·ro·gres·sive** \ˌre-trə-ˈgres-iv\ adj

ret·ro·rock·et \ˈre-trō-ˌräk-ət\ n : an auxiliary rocket (as on a spacecraft) used to slow forward motion

ret·ro·spect \ˈre-trə-ˌspekt\ n : a review of past events — **ret·ro·spec·tion** \ˌre-trə-ˈspek-shən\ n — **ret·ro·spec·tive** \-ˈspek-tiv\ adj — **ret·ro·spec·tive·ly** adv

ret·ro·vi·rus \ˈre-trō-ˌvī-rəs\ n : any of a group of RNA-containing viruses (as the AIDS virus) that make DNA using RNA instead of the reverse and include numerous viruses causing tumors in animals including man

¹re·turn \ri-ˈtərn\ vb 1 : to go or come back 2 : to pass, give, or send back to an earlier possessor 3 : to put back to or in a former place or state 4 : REPLY, ANSWER 5 : to report esp. officially 6 : to elect to office 7 : to bring in (as profit) : YIELD 8 : to give or perform in return — re·turn·er n

²return n 1 : an act of coming or going back to or from a former place or state 2 : RECURRENCE 3 : a report of the results of balloting 4 : a formal statement of taxable income 5 : the profit from labor, investment, or business : YIELD 6 : the act of returning something 7 : something that returns or is returned; also : a means (as a pipe) of returning 8 : something given in repayment or reciprocation; also : ANSWER, RETORT 9 : an answering play — return adj

¹re·turn·able \ri-ˈtərn-ə-bəl\ adj : capable of being returned (as for reuse or recycling); also : permitted to be returned

²returnable n : a returnable beverage container

re·turn·ee \ri-ˌtər-ˈnē\ n : one who returns

re·union \rē-ˈyü-nyən\ n 1 : an act of reuniting : the state of being reunited 2 : a meeting again of persons who have been separated

¹rev \ˈrev\ n : a revolution of a motor

²rev vb revved; rev·ving : to increase the revolutions per minute of (a motor)

³rev abbr 1 revenue 2 reverse 3 review; reviewed 4 revised; revision 5 revolution

Rev abbr 1 Revelation 2 Reverend

re·vamp \(ˈ)rē-ˈvamp\ vb : RECONSTRUCT, REVISE; esp : to give a new form to old materials

re·vanche \rə-ˈvä^nsh\ n [F] : REVENGE; esp : a usu. political policy designed to recover lost territory or status

re·veal \ri-ˈvēl\ vb 1 : to make known 2 : to show plainly : open up to view

re·veil·le \ˈrev-ə-lē\ n [modif. of F réveillez, imper. pl. of réveiller to awaken, fr. réveiller to awaken, fr. (assumed) VL exvigilare, fr. L vigilare to keep watch, stay awake] : a military signal sounded at about sunrise

¹rev·el \ˈrev-əl\ vb -eled or -elled; -el·ing or -el·ling \-(ə-)liŋ\ 1 : to take part in a revel 2 : to take great delight — rev·el·er or rev·el·ler \-ər\ n — rev·el·ry \-əl-rē\ n

²revel n : a usu. wild party or celebration

rev·e·la·tion \ˌrev-ə-ˈlā-shən\ n 1 : an act of revealing 2 : something revealed; esp : an enlightening or astonishing disclosure

Rev·e·la·tion \ˌrev-ə-ˈlā-shən\ n — see BIBLE table

¹re·venge \ri-ˈvenj\ vb re·venged; re·veng·ing : to inflict harm or injury in return for (a wrong) : AVENGE — re·veng·er n

²revenge n 1 : the act of revenging 2 : a desire to return evil for evil 3 : an opportunity for getting satisfaction syn vengeance, retaliation, retribution, reprisal — re·venge·ful adj

rev·e·nue \ˈrev-ə-ˌn(y)ü\ n [ME, fr. MF, fr. revenir to return, fr. L revenire, fr. re- back + venire to come] 1 : investment income 2 : money collected by a government (as through taxes)

rev·e·nu·er \ˈrev-ə-ˌn(y)ü-ər\ n : a revenue officer or boat

re·verb \ri-ˈvərb, ˈrē-ˌvərb\ n : an electronically produced echo effect in recorded music; also : a device for producing reverb

re·ver·ber·ate \ri-ˈvər-bə-ˌrāt\ vb -at·ed; -at·ing 1 : REFLECT ⟨~ light or heat⟩ 2 : to resound in or as if in a series of echoes — re·ver·ber·a·tion \-ˌvər-bə-ˈrā-shən\ n

re·vere \ri-ˈviər\ vb re·vered; re·ver·ing : to show honor and devotion to : VENERATE syn reverence, worship, adore

²revere n : REVERS

¹rev·er·ence \ˈrev-(ə-)rəns\ n 1 : honor and respect mixed with love and awe 2 : a sign (as a bow or curtsy) of respect

²reverence vb -enced; -enc·ing : to regard or treat with reverence

¹rev·er·end \-rənd\ adj 1 : worthy of reverence : REVERED 2 : being a member of the clergy — used as a title

²reverend n : a member of the clergy

rev·er·ent \-rənt\ adj : expressing reverence — rev·er·ent·ly adv

rev·er·en·tial \ˌrev-ə-ˈren-chəl\ adj : REVERENT

rev·er·ie also rev·ery \ˈrev-(ə-)rē\ n, pl -er·ies 1 : DAYDREAM 2 : the state of being lost in thought

re·vers \ri-ˈviər, -ˈveər\ n, pl re·vers \-ˈviərz, -ˈveərz\ [F] : a lapel esp. on a woman's garment

re·ver·sal \ri-ˈvər-səl\ n : an act or process of reversing

¹re·verse \ri-ˈvərs\ adj 1 : opposite to a previous or normal condition 2 : acting or operating in a manner opposite or contrary 3 : effecting reverse movement — re·verse·ly adv

²reverse vb re·versed; re·vers·ing 1 : to turn upside down or completely about in position or direction 2 : to set aside or change (as a legal decision) 3 : to change to the contrary ⟨~ a policy⟩ 4 : to go or cause to go in the opposite direction 5 : to put (as a car) in reverse — re·vers·ible \-ˈvər-sə-bəl\ adj

³reverse n 1 : something contrary to something else : OPPOSITE 2 : an act or instance of reversing; esp : a change for the worse 3 : the back of something 4 : a gear that reverses something

re·ver·sion \ri-ˈvər-zhən\ n 1 : the right

of succession or future possession (as to a title or property) **2** : return toward some former or ancestral condition; *also* : a product of this — **re·ver·sion·ary** \-zhə-‚ner-ē\ *adj*

re·vert \ri-'vərt\ *vb* **1** : to come or go back ‹∼*ed* to savagery› **2** : to return to a proprietor or his or her heirs **3** : to return to an ancestral type

¹**re·view** \ri-'vyü\ *n* **1** : an act of revising **2** : a formal military inspection **3** : a general survey **4** : INSPECTION, EXAMINATION; *esp* : REEXAMINATION **5** : a critical evaluation (as of a book) **6** : a magazine devoted to reviews and essays **7** : a renewed study of previously studied material **8** : REVUE

²**re·view** \ri-'vyü, *1 also* 'rē-\ *vb* **1** : to examine or study again; *esp* : to reexamine judicially **2** : to hold a review of ‹∼ troops› **3** : to write a critical examination of ‹∼ a novel› **4** : to view retrospectively ‹look back over ‹∼*ed* his life› **5** : to study material again

re·view·er \ri-'vyü-ər\ *n* : one that reviews; *esp* : a writer of critical reviews

re·vile \ri-'vīl\ *vb* **re·viled**; **re·vil·ing** : to abuse verbally : rail at **syn** vituperate, berate, rate, upbraid, scold — **re·vile·ment** *n* — **re·vil·er** *n*

re·vise \ri-'vīz\ *vb* **re·vised**; **re·vis·ing 1** : to look over something written in order to correct or improve **2** : to make a new version of — **re·vis·able** *adj* — **re·vise** *n* — **re·vis·er** *or* **re·vi·sor** \-'vī-zər\ *n* — **re·vi·sion** \-'vizh-ən\ *n*

re·vi·tal·ize \'rē-'vīt-əl-‚īz\ *vb* **-ized**; **-iz·ing** : to give new life or vigor to — **re·vi·tal·iza·tion** \‚rē-‚vīt-əl-ə-'zā-shən\ *n*

re·viv·al \ri-'vī-vəl\ *n* **1** : an act of reviving : the state of being revived **2** : a new publication or presentation (as of a book or play) **3** : an evangelistic meeting or series of meetings

re·vive \ri-'vīv\ *vb* **re·vived**; **re·viv·ing 1** : to return or restore to consciousness or life : become or make active or flourishing again **2** : to bring back into use **3** : to renew mentally — **re·viv·er** *n*

re·viv·i·fy \rē-'viv-ə-‚fī\ *vb* : REVIVE — **re·viv·i·fi·ca·tion** \-‚viv-ə-fə-'kā-shən\ *n*

re·vo·ca·ble \'rev-ə-kə-bəl *also* ri-'vō-kə-bəl\ *adj* : capable of being revoked

re·vo·ca·tion \‚rev-ə-'kā-shən\ *n* : an act or instance of revoking

re·voke \ri-'vōk\ *vb* **re·voked**; **re·vok·ing 1** : to annul by recalling or taking back : REPEAL, RESCIND **2** : RENEGE 1 — **re·vok·er** *n*

¹**re·volt** \ri-'vōlt\ *vb* **1** : to throw off allegiance to a ruler or government : REBEL **2** : to experience disgust or shock **3** : to turn or cause to turn away with disgust or abhorrence — **re·volt·er** *n*

²**revolt** *n* : REBELLION, INSURRECTION

re·volt·ing \-iŋ\ *adj* : extremely offensive — **re·volt·ing·ly** *adv*

re·vo·lu·tion \‚rev-ə-'lü-shən\ *n* **1** : the action by a heavenly body of going round in an orbit **2** : ROTATION **3** : a sudden, radical, or complete change; *esp* : the overthrow or renunciation of one ruler or government and substitution of another by the governed

¹**rev·o·lu·tion·ary** \-shə-‚ner-ē\ *adj* **1** : of or relating to revolution **2** : tending to or promoting revolution **3** : constituting or bringing about a major change

²**revolutionary** *n*, *pl* **-ar·ies** : one who takes part in a revolution or who advocates revolutionary doctrines

rev·o·lu·tion·ist \‚rev-ə-'lü-sh(ə-)nəst\ *n* : REVOLUTIONARY — **revolutionist** *adj*

rev·o·lu·tion·ize \-shə-‚nīz\ *vb* **-ized**; **-iz·ing** : to change fundamentally or completely : make revolutionary — **rev·o·lu·tion·iz·er** *n*

re·volve \ri-'välv\ *vb* **re·volved**; **re·volv·ing 1** : to turn over in the mind : reflect upon : PONDER **2** : to move in an orbit; *also* : ROTATE — **re·volv·able** *adj*

re·volv·er \ri-'väl-vər\ *n* : a pistol with a revolving cylinder of several chambers

re·vue \ri-'vyü\ *n* : a theatrical production consisting typically of brief often satirical sketches and songs

re·vul·sion \ri-'vəl-shən\ *n* **1** : a strong sudden reaction or change of feeling **2** : a feeling of complete distaste or repugnance

revved *past and past part of* REV

revving *pres part of* REV

¹**re·ward** \ri-'wórd\ *vb* **1** : to give a reward to or for **2** : RECOMPENSE

²**reward** *n* **1** : something given in return for good or evil done or received; *esp* : something given or offered for some service or attainment **2** : a stimulus that is administered to an organism after a response and that increases the probability of occurrence of the response **syn** premium, prize, award

re·work \(')rē-'wərk\ *vb* **1** : REVISE **2** : to reprocess for further use

RF *abbr* radio frequency

RFD *abbr* rural free delivery

Rh *symbol* rhodium

RH *abbr* right hand

rhap·so·dy \'rap-səd-ē\ *n*, *pl* **-dies** [L *rhapsodia* portion of an epic poem adapted for recitation, fr. Gk *rhapsōidia* recitation of selections from epic poetry, rhapsody, fr. *rhaptein* to sew, stitch together + *aidein* to sing] **1** : an expression of extravagant praise or ecstasy **2** : an instrumental composition of irregular form — **rhap·sod·ic** \rap-'säd-ik\ *adj* — **rhap·sod·i·cal·ly** \-i-k(ə-)lē\ *adv* — **rhap·so·dize** \'rap-sə-‚dīz\ *vb*

rhea \'rē-ə\ *n* : any of several large flightless 3-toed So. American birds that resemble but are smaller than the African ostrich

rhe·ni·um \'rē-nē-əm\ *n* : a rare heavy hard metallic chemical element

rheo·stat \'rē-ə-‚stat\ *n* : a resistor for

regulating an electric current by means of variable resistances — **rheo·stat·ic** \ˌrē-ə-'stat-ik\ adj

rhe·sus monkey \ˈrē-səs-\ n : a pale brown Indian monkey often used in medical research

rhet·o·ric \ˈret-ə-rik\ n [ME rethorik, fr. MF rethorique, fr. L rhetorica, fr. Gk rhētorikē, lit., art of oratory] : the art of speaking or writing effectively — **rhe·tor·i·cal** \ri-'tōr-i-kəl\ adj — **rhet·o·ri·cian** \ˌret-ə-'rish-ən\ n

rheum \ˈrüm\ n : a watery discharge from the mucous membranes esp. of the eyes or nose — **rheumy** adj

rheu·mat·ic fever \rü-ˌmat-ik-\ n : an acute disease chiefly of children and young adults that is characterized by fever, by inflammation and pain in and around the joints, and by inflammation of the membranes surrounding the heart and the heart valves

rheu·ma·tism \ˈrü-mə-ˌtiz-əm, ˈrüm-ə-\ n : any of various conditions marked by stiffness, pain, or swelling in muscles or joints — **rheu·mat·ic** \rü-'mat-ik\ adj

rheu·ma·toid arthritis \-ˌtȯid-\ n : a progressive constitutional disease characterized by inflammation and swelling of joint structures

Rh factor \ˈär-ˈāch-\ n [rhesus monkey (in which it was first detected)] : any of one or more inherited substances in red blood cells that may cause dangerous reactions in some infants or in transfusions

rhine·stone \ˈrīn-ˌstōn\ n : a colorless imitation stone of high luster made of glass, paste, or gem quartz

rhi·no \ˈrī-nō\ n, pl rhino or rhinos : RHINOCEROS

rhi·noc·er·os \rī-'näs-(ə-)rəs\ n, pl -noc·er·os·es or -noc·er·os or -noc·eri \-'näs-ə-ˌrī\ [ME rinoceros, fr. L rhinoceros, fr. Gk rhinokerōs, fr. rhin-, rhis nose + keras horn] : a large thick-skinned mammal of Africa and Asia with one or two upright horns of keratin on the snout and three toes on each foot

rhi·zome \ˈrī-ˌzōm\ n : a specialized rootlike plant stem that forms shoots above and roots below — **rhi·zom·a·tous** \rī-'zäm-ət-əs\ adj

Rh–neg·a·tive \ˌär-ˌāch-'neg-ət-iv\ adj : lacking Rh factors in the red blood cells

rho·di·um \ˈrōd-ē-əm\ n : a hard ductile metallic chemical element

rho·do·den·dron \ˌrōd-ə-'den-drən\ n : any of various shrubs or trees of the heath family grown for their clusters of large bright flowers

rhom·boid \ˈräm-ˌbȯid\ n : a parallelogram with unequal adjacent sides and angles that are not right angles

rhom·bus \ˈräm-bəs\ n, pl rhom·bus·es or rhom·bi \-ˌbī\ : a parallelogram having all four sides equal

Rh–pos·i·tive \ˌär-ˌāch-'päz-ət-iv\ adj : containing Rh factors in the red blood cells

rhu·barb \ˈrü-ˌbärb\ n [ME rubarbe, fr. MF reubarbe, fr. ML reubarbarum, alter. of rha barbarum, lit., barbarian rhubarb] : a garden plant related to the buckwheat and having thick juicy edible pink and red stems on the leaves

¹**rhyme** \ˈrīm\ n 1 : a composition in verse that rhymes; also : POETRY 2 : correspondence in terminal sounds (as of two lines of verse)

²**rhyme** vb rhymed; rhym·ing 1 : to make rhymes; also : to write poetry 2 : to have rhymes : be in rhyme

rhy·o·lite \ˈrī-ə-ˌlīt\ n : a very acid volcanic rock

rhythm \ˈrith-əm\ n 1 : regular rise and fall in the flow of sound in speech 2 : a movement or activity in which some action or element recurs regularly — **rhyth·mic** \ˈrith-mik\ or **rhyth·mi·cal** \-mi-kəl\ adj — **rhyth·mi·cal·ly** \-k(ə-)lē\ adv

rhythm and blues n : popular music based on blues and Negro folk music

rhythm method n : a method of birth control in which a couple does not have sexual intercourse during the time when ovulation is most likely to occur

RI abbr Rhode Island

ri·al \rē-'ȯl, -'äl\ n — see MONEY table

¹**rib** \ˈrib\ n 1 : any of the series of curved bones of the chest of most vertebrates that are joined to the backbone in pairs and help to support the body wall and protect the organs inside 2 : something resembling a rib in shape or function 3 : an elongated ridge

²**rib** vb ribbed; rib·bing 1 : to furnish or strengthen with ribs 2 : to mark with ridges in knitting

³**rib** vb ribbed; rib·bing : to poke fun at : TEASE — **rib·ber** n

rib·ald \ˈrib-əld\ adj : coarse or indecent esp. in language (~ jokes) — **rib·ald·ry** \-əl-drē\ n

rib·and \ˈrib-ənd\ n : RIBBON

rib·bon \ˈrib-ən\ n 1 : a narrow fabric typically of silk or velvet used for trimming and for badges 2 : a strip of inked cloth (as in a typewriter) 3 : TATTER (torn to ~s)

ri·bo·fla·vin \ˌrī-bə-'flā-vən, 'rī-bə-ˌflā-vən\ n : a growth-promoting vitamin of the vitamin B complex occurring in milk and liver

ri·bo·nu·cle·ic acid \ˌrī-bō-n(y)ù-ˌklē-ik-, -ˌklā-\ n : RNA

ri·bose \ˈrī-ˌbōs\ n : a sugar with five carbon atoms and five oxygen atoms in each molecule that is part of RNA

ri·bo·some \ˈrī-bə-ˌsōm\ n : any of the RNA-rich cytoplasmic granules in a cell that are sites of protein synthesis — **ri·bo·som·al** \ˌrī-bə-'sō-məl\ adj

rice \ˈrīs\ n : an annual grass grown in

warm wet areas for its edible seed; *also* : this seed

rich \'rich\ *adj* 1 . possessing or controlling great wealth : WEALTHY 2 : COSTLY, VALUABLE 3 : deep and pleasing in color or tone 4 : ABUNDANT 5 : containing much sugar, fat, or seasoning; *also* : high in combustible content 6 : FRUITFUL, FERTILE — **rich・ly** *adv* — **rich・ness** *n*

rich・es \'rich-əz\ *n pl* [ME, sing. or pl., fr. *richesse*, lit., richness, fr. OF, fr. *riche* rich] : things that make one rich : WEALTH

Rich・ter scale \'rik-tər-\ *n* : a scale for expressing the magnitude of a seismic disturbance (as an earthquake) in terms of the energy dissipated in it

rick \'rik\ *n* : a large stack (as of hay) in the open air

rick・ets \'rik-əts\ *n* : a deficiency disease of children marked esp. by soft deformed bones and caused by inadequate sunlight or inadequate vitamin D

rick・ett・sia \ri-'ket-sē-ə\ *n, pl* **-si・as** *or* **-si・ae** \-sē-,ē\ : any of a family of rod-shaped microorganisms that cause various diseases (as typhus)

rick・ety \'rik-ət-ē\ *adj* 1 : affected with rickets 2 : FEEBLE 3 : SHAKY

rick・sha *or* **rick・shaw** \'rik-,shȯ\ *n* : a small covered 2-wheeled vehicle pulled by one person and used orig. in Japan

¹**ri・co・chet** \'rik-ə-,shā, *Brit also* -,shet\ *n* : a glancing rebound or skipping (as of a bullet off a wall)

²**ricochet** vb **-cheted** \-,shād\ *or* **-chet・ted** \-,shet-əd\ ; **-chet・ing** \-,shā-iŋ\ *or* **-chet・ting** \-,shet-iŋ\ : to skip with or as if with glancing rebounds

¹**rid** \'rid\ *vb* **rid** *also* **rid・ded; rid・ding** : to make free : CLEAR, RELIEVE — **rid・dance** \'rid-ⁿs\ *n*

rid・den \'rid-ⁿn\ *adj* 1 : being harassed, oppressed, or obsessed by 〈debt-*ridden*〉 〈conscience-*ridden*〉 2 : excessively full of or supplied with 〈slum-*ridden*〉

¹**rid・dle** \'rid-ⁿl\ *n* : a puzzling question to be solved or answered by guessing

²**riddle** vb **rid・dled; rid・dling** \'rid-(ə-)liŋ\ 1 : EXPLAIN, SOLVE 2 : to speak in riddles

³**riddle** *n* : a coarse sieve

⁴**riddle** vb **rid・dled; rid・dling** \'rid-(ə-)liŋ\ 1 : to sift with a riddle 2 : to fill as full of holes as a sieve 3 : PERMEATE

¹**ride** \'rīd\ vb **rode** \'rōd\ ; **rid・den** \'rid-ⁿn\ ; **rid・ing** \'rīd-iŋ\ 1 : to go on an animal's back or in a conveyance (as a boat, car, or airplane); *also* : to sit on and control so as to be carried along 〈~ a bicycle〉 2 : to float or move on water 〈~ at anchor〉 ; *also* : to move like a floating object 3 : to bear along : CARRY 〈*rode* her on their shoulders〉 4 : to travel over a surface 〈car ~s well〉 5 : to proceed over on horseback 6 : to torment by nagging or teasing

²**ride** *n* 1 : an act of riding; *esp* : a trip on horseback or by vehicle 2 : a way (as a lane) suitable for riding 3 : a mechanical device (as a merry-go-round) for riding on 4 : a means of transportation

rid・er \'rīd-ər\ *n* 1 : one that rides 2 : an addition to a document often attached on a separate piece of paper 3 : a clause dealing with an unrelated matter attached to a legislative bill during passage — **rid・er・less** *adj*

¹**ridge** \'rij\ *n* 1 : a range of hills 2 : a raised line or strip 3 : the line made where two sloping surfaces meet — **ridgy** *adj*

²**ridge** vb **ridged; ridg・ing** 1 : to form into a ridge 2 : to extend in ridges

ridge・pole \'rij-,pōl\ *n* : the highest horizontal timber in a sloping roof to which the upper ends of the rafters are fastened

¹**rid・i・cule** \'rid-ə-,kyül\ *n* : the act of exposing to laughter : DERISION

²**ridicule** vb **-culed; -cul・ing** : to laugh at or make fun of mockingly or contemptuously **syn** deride, taunt, twit, mock

ri・dic・u・lous \rə-'dik-yə-ləs\ *adj* : arousing or deserving ridicule : ABSURD, PREPOSTEROUS **syn** laughable, ludicrous, farcical, risible — **ri・dic・u・lous・ly** *adv* — **ri・dic・u・lous・ness** *n*

ri・el \rē-'el\ *n* — see MONEY table

rife \'rīf\ *adj* : WIDESPREAD, PREVALENT, ABOUNDING — **rife** *adv*

riff \'rif\ *n* : a repeated phrase in jazz typically supporting a solo improvisation; *also* : a piece based on such a phrase — **riff** *vb*

riff・raff \'rif-,raf\ *n* [ME *riffe raffe*, fr. *rif and raf* every single one, fr. MF *rif et raf* completely] 1 : RABBLE 2 : REFUSE, RUBBISH

¹**ri・fle** \'rī-fəl\ vb **ri・fled; ri・fling** \-f(ə-)liŋ\ : to ransack esp. in order to steal — **ri・fler** \-f(ə-)lər\ *n*

²**rifle** vb **ri・fled; ri・fling** \-f(ə-)liŋ\ : to cut spiral grooves into the bore of 〈*rifled* arms〉 — **ri・fling** *n*

³**rifle** *n* 1 : a shoulder weapon with a rifled bore 2 *pl* : a body of soldiers armed with rifles — **ri・fle・man** \-fəl-mən\ *n*

rift \'rift\ *n* 1 : CLEFT, FISSURE 2 : ESTRANGEMENT, SEPARATION — **rift** *vb*

¹**rig** \'rig\ vb **rigged; rig・ging** 1 : to fit out (as a ship) with rigging 2 : CLOTHE, DRESS 3 : EQUIP 4 : to set up esp. as a makeshift 〈~ up a shelter〉

²**rig** *n* 1 : the distinctive shape, number, and arrangement of sails and masts of a ship 2 : a carriage with its horse or horses 3 : CLOTHING, DRESS 4 : EQUIPMENT

³**rig** vb **rigged; rig・ging** 1 : to manipulate or control esp. by deceptive or dishonest means 2 : to fix in advance for a desired result — **rig・ger** \'rig-ər\ *n*

rig・ging \'rig-iŋ, -ən\ *n* 1 : the ropes and chains that hold and move masts, sails, and spars of a ship 2 : a network (as in theater scenery) used for support and manipulation

¹right \'rīt\ *adj* **1** : RIGHTEOUS, UPRIGHT **2** : JUST, PROPER **3** : conforming to truth or fact : CORRECT **4** : APPROPRIATE, SUITABLE **5** : STRAIGHT ⟨a ~ line⟩ **6** : GENUINE, REAL **7** : of, relating to, or being the stronger hand in most persons **8** : located nearer to the right hand; *esp* : being on the right when facing in the same direction as the observer **9** : made to be placed or worn outward ⟨~ side of a rug⟩ **10** : NORMAL, SOUND (not in her ~ mind) **syn** correct, accurate, exact, precise, nice — **right·ness** *n*

²right *n* **1** : qualities that constitute what is correct, just, proper, or honorable **2** : something (as a power or privilege) to which one has a just or lawful claim **3** : just action or decision : the cause of justice **4** : the side or part that is on or toward the right side **5** *cap* : political conservatives **6** *often cap* : a conservative position — **right·ward** \-wərd\ *adj*

³right *adv* **1** : according to what is right ⟨live ~⟩ **2** : EXACTLY, PRECISELY ⟨~ here and now⟩ **3** : DIRECTLY ⟨went ~ home⟩ **4** : according to fact or truth ⟨guess ~⟩ **5** : all the way : COMPLETELY ⟨~ to the end⟩ **6** : IMMEDIATELY ⟨~ after lunch⟩ **7** : QUITE, VERY ⟨~ nice weather⟩ **8** : on or to the right ⟨looked ~ and left⟩

⁴right *vb* **1** : to relieve from wrong **2** : to adjust or restore to a proper state or position **3** : to bring or restore to an upright position **4** : to become upright — **right·er** *n*

right angle *n* : an angle whose measure is 90° : an angle whose sides are perpendicular to each other — **right-angled** \'rīt-'aŋ-gəld\ *or* **right-an·gle** \-gəl\ *adj*

right circular cone *n* : CONE 2

right·teous \'rī-chəs\ *adj* : acting or being in accordance with what is just, honorable, and free from guilt or wrong : UPRIGHT **syn** virtuous, noble, moral, ethical — **right·teous·ly** *adv* — **right·teous·ness** *n*

right·ful \'rīt-fəl\ *adj* **1** : JUST; *also* : FITTING **2** : having or held by a legally just claim — **right·ful·ly** \-ē\ *adv* — **right·ful·ness** *n*

right-hand \'rīt-,hand\ *adj* **1** : situated on the right **2** : RIGHT-HANDED **3** : chiefly relied on ⟨his ~ man⟩

right-hand·ed \-'han-dəd\ *adj* **1** : using the right hand habitually or better than the left **2** : designed for or done with the right hand **3** : CLOCKWISE ⟨a ~ twist⟩ — **right-handed** *adv* — **right-hand·ed·ly** *adv* — **right-hand·ed·ness** *n*

right·ly \'rīt-lē\ *adv* **1** : FAIRLY, JUSTLY **2** : PROPERLY **3** : CORRECTLY, EXACTLY

right-of-way \,rīt-ə(v)-'wā\ *n*, *pl* **rights-of-way 1** : a legal right of passage over another person's ground **2** : the area over which a right-of-way

exists **3** : the land on which a public road is built **4** : the land occupied by a railroad **5** : the land used by a public utility **6** : the right of traffic to take precedence over other traffic

right on *interj* — used to express agreement or give encouragement

right-to-life *adj* : opposed to abortion — **right-to-lif·er** \'rīt-tə-'lī-fər\ *n*

right triangle *n* : a triangle having one right angle

rig·id \'rij-əd\ *adj* **1** : lacking flexibility : STIFF **2** : strictly observed **syn** severe, stern, rigorous, stringent — **ri·gid·i·ty** \rə-'jid-ət-ē\ *n* — **rig·id·ly** *adv*

rig·ma·role \'rig-(ə-)mə-,rōl\ *n* [alter. of obs. *ragman roll* (long list, catalog)] **1** : confused or senseless talk **2** : a complex largely meaningless procedure

rig·or \'rig-ər\ *n* **1** : the quality of being inflexible or unyielding : STRICTNESS **2** : HARSHNESS, SEVERITY **3** : a tremor caused by a chill **4** : strict precision : EXACTNESS **syn** difficulty, hardship, vicissitude — **rig·or·ous** *adj* — **rig·or·ous·ly** *adv*

rig·or mor·tis \,rig-ər-'mȯrt-əs\ *n* [NL, stiffness of death] : temporary rigidity of muscles occurring after death

rile \'rīl\ *vb* **riled**; **ril·ing 1** : to make angry **2** : ROIL 1

rill \'ril\ *n* : a very small brook

²rill \'ril\ *or* **rille** \'ril, 'ril-ə\ *n* : a long narrow valley on the moon

¹rim \'rim\ *n* **1** : the outer part of a wheel **2** : an outer edge esp. of something curved : BORDER, MARGIN

²rim *vb* **rimmed**; **rim·ming 1** : to furnish with a rim **2** : to run around the rim of

¹rime \'rīm\ *n* **1** : FROST 2 **2** : frostlike ice tufts formed from fog or cloud on the windward side of exposed objects — **rimy** \'rī-mē\ *adj*

rime *var of* RHYME

rind \'rīnd\ *n* : a usu. hard or tough outer layer ⟨lemon ~⟩

¹ring \'riŋ\ *n* **1** : a circular band worn as an ornament or token or used for holding or fastening ⟨wedding ~⟩ ⟨key ~⟩ **2** : something circular in shape ⟨smoke ~⟩ **3** : a place for contest or display ⟨boxing ~⟩ ; *also* : PRIZEFIGHTING **4** : a group of people who work together for selfish or dishonest purposes — **ring·like** \'riŋ-,līk\ *adj*

²ring *vb* **ringed**; **ring·ing** \'riŋ-iŋ\ **1** : ENCIRCLE **2** : to move in a ring or spirally **3** : to throw a ring over (a mark) in a game (as quoits)

³ring *vb* **rang** \'raŋ\ ; **rung** \'rəŋ\ ; **ring·ing** \'riŋ-iŋ\ **1** : to sound resonantly when struck; *also* : to feel as if filled with such sound **2** : to cause to make a clear metallic sound by striking **3** : to announce or call by or as if by striking a bell ⟨~ an alarm⟩ **4** : to repeat loudly and persistently **5** : to sound a bell ⟨~ for the butler⟩

⁴ring *n* **1** : a set of bells **2** : the clear resonant sound of vibrating metal **3** : resonant tone : SONORITY **4** : a sound or character expressive of a particular quality **5** : an act or instance of ringing; *esp* : a telephone call

¹ring·er \'riŋ-ər\ *n* **1** : one that sounds by ringing **2** : one that enters a competition under false representations **3** : one that closely resembles another

²ringer *n* : one that encircles or puts a ring around

ring·git \'riŋ-git\ *n* — see MONEY table

ring·lead·er \'riŋ-ₗlēd-ər\ *n* : a leader esp. of a group of troublemakers

ring·let \'riŋ-lət\ *n* : a long curl

ring·mas·ter \'riŋ-ₗmas-tər\ *n* : one in charge of performances in a circus ring

ring up *vb* **1** : to total and record esp. by means of a cash register **2** : ACHIEVE ⟨*rang up* many triumphs⟩

ring·worm \'riŋ-ₗwərm\ *n* : a contagious skin disease caused by fungi and marked by ring-shaped discolored patches

rink \'riŋk\ *n* : a level extent of ice marked off for skating or various games; *also* : a similar surface (as of wood) marked off or enclosed for a sport or game ⟨roller-skating ∼⟩

¹rinse \'rins\ *vb* **rinsed; rins·ing** [ME *rincen*, fr. MF *rincer*, fr. (assumed) VL *recentiare*, fr. L *recent-, recens* fresh, recent] **1** : to wash lightly or in water only **2** : to cleanse (as of soap) with clear water **3** : to treat (hair) with a rinse — **rins·er** *n*

²rinse *n* **1** : an act of rinsing **2** : a liquid used for rinsing **3** : a solution that temporarily tints hair

¹ri·ot \'rī-ət\ *n* **1** *archaic* : disorderly behavior **2** : disturbance of the public peace; *esp* : a violent public disorder **3** : random or disorderly profusion (a ∼ of color) — **riot** *vb* — **ri·ot·er** *n* — **ri·ot·ous** *adj*

¹rip \'rip\ *vb* **ripped; rip·ping 1** : to cut or tear open **2** : to saw or split (wood) with the grain — **rip·per** *n*

²rip *n* : a rent made by ripping

RIP *abbr* [L *requiescat in pace*] may he rest in peace, may she rest in peace; [L *requiescant in pace*] may they rest in peace

ri·par·i·an \rə-'per-ē-ən\ *adj* : of or relating to the bank of a stream, river, or lake

rip cord *n* : a cord that is pulled to release the pilot parachute which lifts a main parachute out of its container

ripe \'rīp\ *adj* **rip·er; rip·est 1** : fully grown and developed : MATURE ⟨∼ fruit⟩ **2** : fully prepared for some use or object : READY — **ripe·ly** *adv* — **ripe·ness** *n*

rip·en \'rī-pən\ *vb* **rip·ened; rip·en·ing** \'rī-p(ə-)niŋ\ **1** : to grow or make ripe **2** : to bring to completeness or perfection; *also* : to age or cure (cheese) to develop characteristic flavor, odor, body, texture, and color

rip-off \'rip-ₗȯf\ *n* **1** : an act of stealing

: THEFT **2** : a cheap imitation — **rip off** \(ˈ)rip-ˈȯf\ *vb*

ri·poste \ri-ˈpōst\ *n* [F, modif. of It *risposta*, lit., answer] **1** : a fencer's return thrust after a parry **2** : a retaliatory maneuver or response; *esp* : a quick retort — **riposte** *vb*

rip·ple \'rip-əl\ *vb* **rip·pled; rip·pling** \-(ə-)liŋ\ **1** : to become lightly ruffled on the surface **2** : to make a sound like that of rippling water — **ripple** *n*

rip·saw \'rip-ₗsȯ\ *n* : a coarse-toothed saw used to cut wood in the direction of the grain

rip·stop \'rip-ₗstäp\ *adj* : being a fabric woven in such a way that small tears do not spread ⟨∼ nylon⟩

¹rise \'rīz\ *vb* **rose** \'rōz\; **ris·en** \'riz-ᵊn\; **ris·ing** \'rī-ziŋ\ **1** : to get up from sitting, kneeling, or lying **2** : to get up from sleep or from one's bed **3** : to return from death **4** : to take up arms : go to war; *also* : REBEL **5** : to end a session : ADJOURN **6** : to appear above the horizon **7** : to move upward : ASCEND **8** : to extend above other objects **9** : to attain a higher level or rank **10** : to increase in quantity or in intensity **11** : to come into being : HAPPEN, BEGIN, ORIGINATE

²rise *n* **1** : an act of rising : a state of being risen **2** : BEGINNING, ORIGIN **3** : the elevation of one point above another **4** : an increase in amount, number, or volume **5** : an upward slope **6** : a spot higher than surrounding ground **7** : an angry reaction

ris·er \'rī-zər\ *n* **1** : one that rises **2** : the upright part between stair treads

ris·i·bil·i·ty \ₗriz-ə-ˈbil-ət-ē\ *n, pl* **-ties** : the ability or inclination to laugh — often used in pl.

ris·i·ble \'riz-ə-bəl\ *adj* **1** : able or inclined to laugh **2** : arousing laughter : FUNNY **3** : of or relating to laughter ⟨∼ muscles⟩

¹risk \'risk\ *n* : exposure to possible loss or injury : DANGER, PERIL — **risk·i·ness** \'ris-kē-nəs\ *n* — **risky** *adj*

²risk *vb* **1** : to expose to danger ⟨∼ed his life⟩ **2** : to incur the danger of

ris·qué \ris-ˈkā\ *adj* [F] : verging on impropriety or indecency

rite \'rīt\ *n* **1** : a set form of conducting a ceremony **2** : the liturgy of a church **3** : a ceremonial act or action

rit·u·al \'rich-(ə-w)əl\ *n* **1** : the established form esp. for a religious ceremony **2** : a system of rites **3** : a ceremonial act or action **4** : a customarily repeated act or series of acts — **ritual** *adj* — **rit·u·al·ism** \-ₗiz-əm\ *n* — **rit·u·al·is·tic** \ₗrich-(ə-w)əl-ˈis-tik\ *adj* — **rit·u·al·is·ti·cal·ly** \-ti-k(ə-)lē\ *adv* — **rit·u·al·ly** \'rich-(ə-w)ə-lē\ *adv*

riv *abbr* river

¹ri·val \'rī-vəl\ *n* [MF or L: MF, fr. L *rivalis* one using the same stream as another, rival in love, fr. *rivalis* of a stream, fr. *rivus* stream] **1** : one of two or more trying to get what only one can have **2** : one striving for competitive advantage **3** : one that equals another esp. in desired qualities : MATCH, PEER

²**rival** *adj* : COMPETING

³**rival** *vb* **-valed** *or* **-valled; -val·ing** *or* **-val·ling** \'rīv-(ə-)liŋ\ **1** : to be in competition with **2** : to try to equal or excel **3** : to have qualities that equal another's : MATCH

ri·val·ry \'rī-vəl-rē\ *n, pl* **-ries** : COMPETITION

rive \'rīv\ *vb* **rived** \'rīvd\; **riv·en** \'riv-ən\ *also* **rived; riv·ing** \'rī-viŋ\ **1** : SPLIT, REND **2** : SHATTER

riv·er \'riv-ər\ *n* : a natural stream larger than a brook

riv·er·bank \-ˌbaŋk\ *n* : the bank of a river

riv·er·bed \-ˌbed\ *n* : the channel occupied by a river

riv·er·boat \-ˌbōt\ *n* : a boat for use on a river

riv·er·front \-ˌfrənt\ *n* : the land or area along a river

riv·er·side \'riv-ər-ˌsīd\ *n* : the side or bank of a river

¹**riv·et** \'riv-ət\ *n* : a metal bolt with a head at one end used to fasten things together by being put through holes in them and then being flattened on the plain end to make another head

²**rivet** *vb* : to fasten with or as if with a rivet — **riv·et·er** *n*

riv·u·let \'riv-(y)ə-lət\ *n* : a small stream

ri·yal \rē-'(y)äl, -'(y)al\ *n* — see MONEY table

rm *abbr* **1** ream **2** room

Rn *symbol* radon

RN *abbr* **1** registered nurse **2** Royal Navy

RNA \ˌär-ˌen-'ā\ *n* : any of various nucleic acids (as messenger RNA) that are found esp. in the cytoplasm of cells, have ribose as the 5-carbon sugar, and are associated with protein synthesis

rnd *abbr* round

¹**roach** \'rōch\ *n, pl* **roach** *also* **roach·es** : any of various fishes related to the carp; *also* : any of several sunfishes

²**roach** *n* **1** : COCKROACH **2** : the butt of a marijuana cigarette

road \'rōd\ *n* **1** : ROADSTEAD — often used in pl. **2** : an open way for vehicles, persons, and animals : HIGHWAY **3** : ROUTE, PATH **4** : a series of scheduled visits (as games or performances) in several locations or the travel necessary to make these visits (the team is on the ∼)

road·abil·i·ty \ˌrōd-ə-'bil-ət-ē\ *n* : the qualities (as steadiness and balance) desirable in an automobile on the road

road·bed \'rōd-ˌbed\ *n* **1** : the foundation of a road or railroad **2** : the part of the surface of a road on which vehicles travel

road·block \-ˌbläk\ *n* **1** : a barricade on

the road (a police ∼) **2** : an obstruction to progress

road·run·ner \-ˌrən-ər\ *n* : a largely terrestrial bird of the southwestern U.S. and Mexico that is a speedy runner

road·side \'rōd-ˌsīd\ *n* : the strip of land along a road — **roadside** *adj*

road·stead \-ˌsted\ *n* : an anchorage for ships usu. less sheltered than a harbor

road·ster \'rōd-stər\ *n* **1** : a driving horse **2** : an open automobile with one cross seat

road·way \'rōd-ˌwā\ *n* : ROAD; *esp* : ROADBED

road·work \-ˌwərk\ *n* : conditioning for an athletic contest (as a boxing match) consisting mainly of long runs

roam \'rōm\ *vb* **1** : WANDER, ROVE **2** : to range or wander over or about

¹**roan** \'rōn\ *adj* : of dark color (as black, red, or brown) sprinkled with white (a ∼ horse)

²**roan** *n* : an animal (as a horse) with a roan coat; *also* : its color

¹**roar** \'rōr\ *vb* **1** : to utter a full loud prolonged sound **2** : to make a loud confused sound (as of wind or waves) — **roar·er** *n*

²**roar** *n* : a sound of roaring

¹**roast** \'rōst\ *vb* **1** : to cook by dry heat (as before a fire or in an oven) **2** : to criticize severely or kiddingly

²**roast** *n* **1** : a piece of meat suitable for roasting **2** : an outing at which food is roasted (corn ∼) **3** : severe criticism or kidding

³**roast** *adj* : ROASTED

roast·er \'rō-stər\ *n* **1** : one that roasts **2** : a device for roasting **3** : something adapted to roasting

rob \'räb\ *vb* **robbed; rob·bing** **1** : to steal from **2** : to commit robbery **3** : to deprive of something due or expected — **rob·ber** *n*

robber fly *n* : any of numerous predaceous flies

rob·bery \'räb-(ə-)rē\ *n, pl* **-ber·ies** : the act or practice of robbing; *esp* : theft of something from a person by use of violence or threat

¹**robe** \'rōb\ *n* **1** : a long flowing outer garment; *esp* : one used for ceremonial occasions **2** : a wrap or covering for the lower body (as for sitting outdoors)

²**robe** *vb* **robed; rob·ing** **1** : to clothe with or as with a robe **2** : DRESS

rob·in \'räb-ən\ *n* **1** : a small European thrush with a yellowish red throat and breast **2** : a large No. American thrush with a grayish back, a streaked throat, and a chiefly dull reddish breast

ro·bot \'rō-ˌbät, -bət\ *n* [Czech, fr. *robota* work] **1** : a machine that looks and acts like a human being **2** : an efficient but insensitive person **3** : an automatic apparatus **4** : something guided by automatic controls

ro·bust \rō-'bəst, 'rō-(ˌ)bəst\ *adj* [L *robustus* oaken, strong, fr. *robur* oak, strength] : strong and vigorously healthy — **ro·bust·ly** *adv* — **ro·bust·ness** *n*

¹**rock** \\'räk\\ *vb* **1** : to move back and forth in or as if in a cradle **2** : to sway or cause to sway back and forth

²**rock** *n* **1** : a rocking movement **2** : popular music usu. played on electric instruments and characterized by a strong beat and much repetition

³**rock** *n* **1** : a mass of stony material; *also* : broken pieces of stone **2** : solid mineral deposits **3** : something like a rock in firmness — **rock** *adj* — **rock·like** *adj* — **rocky** *adj*

rock and roll *n* : ²ROCK 2

rock·bound \\'räk-,baund\\ *adj* : fringed or covered with rocks

rock·er \\'räk-ər\\ *n* **1** : one of the curved pieces on which something (as a chair or cradle) rocks **2** : a chair that rocks on rockers **3** : a device that works with a rocking motion **4** : a rock performer, song, or enthusiast

¹**rock·et** \\'räk-ət\\ *n* [It *rocchetta*, lit., small distaff] **1** : a firework that is propelled through the air by the gases produced by a burning substance **2** : a jet engine that operates on the same principle as a firework rocket but carries the oxygen needed for burning its fuel **3** : a rocket-propelled bomb or missile

²**rocket** *vb* **1** : to convey by means of a rocket **2** : to rise abruptly and rapidly

rock·et·ry \\'räk-ə-trē\\ *n* : the study or use of rockets

rocket ship *n* : a rocket-propelled spacecraft

rock·fall \\'räk-,fol\\ *n* : a mass of falling or fallen rocks

rock·fish \\'räk-,fish\\ *n* : any of various important market fishes that live among rocks or on rocky bottoms

rock 'n' roll \\,räk-ən-¹rōl\\ *n* : ²ROCK 2

rock salt *n* : common salt in rocklike masses or large crystals

rock wool *n* : woollike insulation made from molten rock or slag

Rocky Mountain sheep *n* : BIGHORN

ro·co·co \\rə-¹kō-kō\\ *adj* [F, irreg. fr. *rocaille* rock work] : of or relating to an artistic style esp. of the 18th century marked by fanciful curved forms and elaborate ornamentation — **rococo** *n*

rod \\'räd\\ *n* **1** : a straight slender stick **2** : a stick or bundle of twigs used in punishing a person; *also* : PUNISHMENT **3** : a staff borne to show rank **4** — see WEIGHT table **5** *slang* : PISTOL

rode *past of* RIDE

ro·dent \\'rōd-ᵊnt\\ *n* [fr. L *rodent-*, *rodens*, prp. of *rodere* to gnaw] : any of a large order of relatively small mammals (as mice, squirrels, and beavers) with sharp front teeth used for gnawing

ro·deo \\'rōd-ē-,ō, rə-¹dā-ō\\ *n, pl* **ro·de·os** [Sp, fr. *rodear* to surround, fr. *rueda* wheel, fr. L *rota*] **1** : ROUNDUP 1 **2** : a public performance featuring

cowboy skills (as riding and roping)

¹**roe** \\'rō\\ *n, pl* **roe** *or* **roes** : DOE

²**roe** *n* : the eggs of a fish esp. while bound together in a mass

roe·buck \\'rō-,bək\\ *n, pl* **roebuck** *or* **roebucks** : a male roe deer

roe deer *n* : a small nimble European and Asian deer that is reddish brown in summer and grayish in the winter

roent·gen ray \\,rent-gən-\\ *n, often cap 1st R* : X RAY

rog·er \\'räj-ər\\ *interj* — used esp. in radio and signaling to indicate that a message has been received and understood

rogue \\'rōg\\ *n* **1** : a dishonest person : SCOUNDREL **2** : a mischievous person : SCAMP — **rogu·ery** \\'rō-gə-rē\\ *n* — **rogu·ish** \\'rō-gish\\ *adj* — **rogu·ish·ly** *adv* — **rogu·ish·ness** *n*

roil \\'roil, *for 2 also* 'ril\\ *vb* **1** : to make cloudy or muddy by stirring up **2** : RILE 1

rois·ter \\'roi-stər\\ *vb* **rois·tered; rois·ter·ing** \\-st(ə-)riŋ\\ : to engage in noisy revelry : CAROUSE — **rois·ter·er** \\-stər-ər\\ *n*

role *also* **rôle** \\'rōl\\ *n* **1** : an assigned or assumed character; *also* : a part played (as by an actor) **2** : FUNCTION

role model *n* : a person whose behavior in a particular role is imitated by others

¹**roll** \\'rōl\\ *n* **1** : a document containing an official record **2** : an official list of names **3** : something (as a bun) that is rolled up or rounded as if rolled **4** : something that rolls : ROLLER

²**roll** *vb* **1** : to move by turning over and over **2** : to press with a roller **3** : to move on wheels **4** : to sound with a full reverberating tone **5** : to make a continuous beating sound (as on a drum) **6** : to move onward as if by completing a revolution (years ~ed by) **7** : to flow or seem to flow in a continuous stream or with a rising and falling motion (the river ~ed on) **8** : to swing or sway from side to side **9** : to shape or become shaped in rounded form **10** : to utter with a trill

³**roll** *n* **1** : a sound produced by rapid strokes on a drum **2** : a heavy reverberating sound **3** : a rolling movement or action **4** : a swaying movement (as of a ship) **5** : SOMERSAULT

roll·back \\'rōl-,bak\\ *n* : the act or an instance of rolling back

roll back \\'rōl-¹bak\\ *vb* **1** : to reduce (a commodity price) on a national scale **2** : to cause to withdraw : push back

roll bar *n* : an overhead metal bar in an automobile designed to protect riders in case the automobile overturns

roll call *n* : the act or an instance of calling off a list of names (as of soldiers); *also* : a time for a roll call

roll·er \\'rō-lər\\ *n* **1** : a revolving cylinder used for moving, pressing, shaping, applying, or smoothing something **2** : a rod on which something is

rolled up 3 : a long heavy wave on a coast

roll·er coast·er \'rō-lər-ˌkō-stər\ *n* : an elevated railway (as in an amusement park) constructed with sharp curves and steep slopes

roller skate *n* : a skate with wheels instead of a runner — **roller-skate** *vb* — **roller skater** *n*

rol·lick \'räl-ik\ *vb* : ROMP, FROLIC

rol·lick·ing \-iŋ\ *adj* : full of fun and good spirits

roly-poly \ˌrō-lē-'pō-lē\ *adj* : ROTUND

Rom *abbr* 1 Roman 2 Romance 3 Romania 4 Romans

ROM *abbr* read-only memory

ro·maine \rō-'mān\ *n* [F, lit., Roman] : a lettuce with a tall loose head of long crisp leaves

¹Ro·man \'rō-mən\ *n* 1 : a native or resident of Rome 2 : a citizen of the Roman Empire

²Roman *adj* 1 : of or relating to Rome or the Romans 2 *not cap* : relating to type in which the letters are upright (as in this definition) 3 : of or relating to the Roman Catholic Church

Roman candle *n* : a cylindrical firework that discharges balls of fire

Roman Catholic *adj* : of or relating to the body of Christians in communion with the pope and having a liturgy centered in the Mass — **Roman Catholicism** *n*

¹ro·mance \rō-'mans, 'rō-ˌmans\ *n* [ME *romauns*, fr. OF *romans* French, something written in French, fr. L *romanice* in the Roman manner, fr. *romanicus* Roman, fr. *Romanus*] 1 : a medieval tale of knightly adventure 2 : a prose narrative dealing with heroic or mysterious events set in a remote time or place 3 : a love story 4 : a romantic attachment or episode between lovers — **ro·manc·er** *n*

²romance *vb* **ro·manced; ro·manc·ing** 1 : to exaggerate or invent detail or incident 2 : to have romantic fancies 3 : to carry on a romantic episode with

Ro·mance \rō-'mans, 'rō-ˌmans\ *adj* : of or relating to any of several languages developed from Latin

Ro·ma·nian \ru̇-'mā-nē-ən, rō-, -nyən\ *n* 1 : a native or inhabitant of Romania 2 : RUMANIAN 2

Roman numeral *n* : a numeral in a system of notation that is based on the ancient Roman system

Ro·ma·no \rə-'män-ō, rō-\ *n* : a hard Italian cheese that is sharper than Parmesan

¹ro·man·tic \rō-'mant-ik\ *n* : a romantic person; *esp* : a romantic writer, composer, or artist

²romantic *adj* 1 : IMAGINARY 2 : VISIONARY 3 : having an imaginative or emotional appeal 4 : of, relating to, or having the characteristics of romanticism — **ro·man·ti·cal·ly** \-i-k(ə-)lē\ *adv*

ro·man·ti·cism \rō-'mant-ə-ˌsiz-əm\ *n*, *often cap* : a literary movement (as in

early 19th century England) marked esp. by emphasis on the imagination and the emotions and by the use of autobiographical material — **ro·man·ti·cist** \-səst\ *n*, *often cap*

romp \'rämp\ *vb* 1 : to play actively and noisily 2 : to win a contest easily — **romp** *n*

romp·er \'räm-pər\ *n* 1 : one that romps 2 : a child's one-piece garment with the lower part shaped like bloomers — usu. used in pl.

rood \'rüd\ *n* : CROSS, CRUCIFIX

¹roof \'rüf, 'ru̇f\ *n*, *pl* **roofs** \'rüfs, 'ru̇fs; 'rüvz, 'ru̇vz\ 1 : the upper covering part of a building 2 : something suggesting a roof of a building — **roofed** \'rüft, 'ru̇ft\ *adj* — **roof·ing** *n* — **roof·less** *adj*

²roof *vb* : to cover with a roof

roof·top \-ˌtäp\ *n* : a roof esp. of a house

roof·tree \-ˌtrē\ *n* : RIDGEPOLE

¹rook \'ru̇k\ *n* : a common Old World bird resembling the related crow

²rook *vb* : CHEAT, SWINDLE

³rook *n* : a chess piece that can move parallel to the sides of the board across any number of unoccupied squares

rook·ery \'ru̇k-ə-rē\ *n*, *pl* **-er·ies** : a breeding ground or haunt of gregarious birds or mammals; *also* : a colony of such birds or mammals

rook·ie \'ru̇k-ē\ *n* : BEGINNER, RECRUIT; *esp* : a first-year player in a professional sport

¹room \'rüm, 'ru̇m\ *n* 1 : an extent of space occupied by or sufficient or available for something 2 : a partitioned part of a building : CHAMBER; *also* : the people in a room 3 : OPPORTUNITY, CHANCE (∼ to develop his talents) — **room·ful** *n* — **roomy** *adj*

²room *vb* : to occupy lodgings : LODGE — **room·er** *n*

room·ette \rü-'met, ru̇m-'et\ *n* : a small private room on a railroad sleeping car

room·mate \'rüm-ˌmāt, 'ru̇m-\ *n* : one of two or more persons sharing the same room or dwelling

¹roost \'rüst\ *n* : a support on which or a place where birds perch

²roost *vb* : to settle on or as if on a roost

roost·er \'rüs-tər, 'ru̇s-\ *n* : an adult male domestic fowl : COCK

¹root \'rüt, 'ru̇t\ *n* 1 : the leafless usu. underground part of a seed plant that functions in absorption, aeration, and storage or as a means of anchorage; *also* : an underground plant part esp. when fleshy and edible 2 : something (as the basal part of a tooth or hair) resembling a root 3 : SOURCE, ORIGIN 4 : the essential core : HEART (get to the ∼ of the matter) 5 : a number that when taken as a factor an indicated number of times gives a specified number 6 : the lower part — **root·less** *adj* — **root·like** *adj*

²**root** vb **1** : to form roots **2** : to fix or become fixed by or as if by roots : ESTABLISH **3** : UPROOT

³**root** vb **1** : to turn up or dig with the snout ⟨pigs ∼*ing*⟩ **2** : to poke or dig around (as in search of something)

⁴**root** \'rüt\ vb **1** : to applaud or encourage noisily : CHEER **2** : to wish success or lend support to — **root·er** n

root beer n : a sweetened effervescent beverage flavored with extracts of roots and herbs

root·let \'rüt-lət, 'rùt-\ n : a small root

root·stock \-ˌstäk\ n : an underground part of a plant that resembles a rhizome

¹**rope** \'rōp\ n **1** : a large strong cord made of strands of fiber **2** : a hangman's noose **3** : a thick string (as of pearls) made by twisting or braiding

²**rope** vb **roped; rop·ing 1** : to bind, tie, or fasten together with a rope **2** : to separate or divide off by means of a rope **3** : LASSO

Ror·schach test \'rȯr-ˌshäk-\ n : a personality and intelligence test in which a subject interprets ink-blot designs in terms that reveal intellectual and emotional factors

ro·sa·ry \'rō-zə-rē\ n, pl **-ries 1** often cap : a Roman Catholic devotion consisting of meditation on sacred mysteries during recitation of Hail Marys **2** : a string of beads used in praying

¹**rose** past of RISE

²**rose** \'rōz\ n **1** : any of a genus of usu. prickly climbing shrubs with divided leaves and bright often fragrant flowers; also : one of these flowers **2** : something resembling a rose in form **3** : a moderate purplish red color — **rose** adj

ro·sé \rō-'zā\ n [F] : a light pink wine

ro·se·ate \'rō-zē-ət, -zē-ˌāt\ adj **1** : resembling a rose esp. in color **2** : OPTIMISTIC ⟨a ∼ view of the future⟩

rose·bud \'rōz-ˌbəd\ n : the flower of a rose when it is at most partly open

rose·bush \-ˌbùsh\ n : a shrubby rose

rose·mary \'rōz-ˌmer-ē\ n, pl **-mar·ies** [ME rosmarine, fr. L rosmarinus, fr. ros dew + marinus of the sea, fr. mare sea] : a fragrant shrubby mint with evergreen leaves used in perfumery and cooking

ro·sette \rō-'zet\ n [F] **1** : a usu. small badge or ornament of ribbon gathered in the shape of a rose **2** : a circular ornament filled with representations of leaves

rose·wa·ter \'rōz-ˌwȯt-ər, -ˌwät-\ adj : a watery solution of the fragrant constituents of the rose used as a perfume

rose·wood \-ˌwùd\ n : any of various tropical trees with dark red wood streaked with black; also : this wood

Rosh Ha·sha·nah \ˌrȯsh-(h)ə-'shō-nə\ n [Heb rōsh hashshānāh, lit., beginning of the year] : the Jewish New Year observed as a religious holiday in September or October

ros·in \'räz-ᵊn\ n : a hard brittle resin obtained esp. from pine trees and used in varnishes and on violin bows

ros·ter \'räs-tər\ n : a list of personnel; also : the persons listed on a roster **2** : an itemized list

ros·trum \'räs-trəm\ n, pl **rostrums** or **ros·tra** \-trə\ [L Rostra, pl., a platform for speakers in the Roman Forum decorated with the beaks of captured ships, fr. pl. of rostrum beak, ship's beak, fr. rodere to gnaw] : a stage or platform for public speaking

rosy \'rō-zē\ adj **ros·i·er; -est 1** : of the color rose **2** : HOPEFUL, PROMISING — **ros·i·ly** \'rō-zə-lē\ adv — **ros·i·ness** \-zē-nəs\ n

¹**rot** \'rät\ vb **rot·ted; rot·ting** : to undergo decomposition : DECAY

²**rot** n **1** : DECAY **2** : a disease of plants or animals in which tissue breaks down **3** : NONSENSE

¹**ro·ta·ry** \'rōt-ə-rē\ adj **1** : turning on an axis like a wheel **2** : having a rotating part

²**rotary** n, pl **-ries 1** : a rotary machine **2** : a circular road junction

ro·tate \'rō-ˌtāt\ vb **ro·tat·ed; ro·tat·ing 1** : to turn or cause to turn about an axis or a center : REVOLVE **2** : to alternate in a series syn turn, circle, spin, whirl, twirl — **ro·ta·tion** \rō-'tā-shən\ n — **ro·ta·tor** \'rō-ˌtāt-ər\ n — **ro·ta·to·ry** \'rōt-ə-ˌtōr-ē\ adj

ROTC abbr Reserve Officers' Training Corps

rote \'rōt\ n **1** : repetition from memory often without attention to meaning **2** : fixed routine or repetition — **rote** adj

ro·tis·ser·ie \rō-'tis-(ə-)rē\ n [F] **1** : a restaurant specializing in broiled and barbecued meats **2** : an appliance fitted with a spit on which food is rotated before or over a source of heat

ro·to·gra·vure \ˌrōt-ə-grə-'vyùr\ n : PHOTOGRAVURE

ro·tor \'rōt-ər\ n **1** : a part that rotates **2** : a system of rotating horizontal blades for supporting a helicopter

rot·ten \'rät-ᵊn\ adj **1** : having rotted **2** : CORRUPT **3** : extremely unpleasant or inferior — **rot·ten·ness** \-'n-(n)əs\ n

rot·ten·stone \'rät-ᵊn-ˌstōn\ n : a decomposed siliceous limestone used for polishing

ro·tund \rō-'tənd\ adj : rounded out syn plump, chubby, portly, stout — **ro·tun·di·ty** \-'tən-dət-ē\ n

ro·tun·da \rō-'tən-də\ n **1** : a round building; esp : one covered by a dome **2** : a large round room

rou·ble \'rü-bəl\ var of RUBLE

roué \rü-'ā\ n [F, lit., broken on the wheel, fr. pp. of rouer to break on the wheel, fr. ML rotare, fr. L, to rotate; fr. the feeling that such a person deserves this punishment] : a man devoted to a life of sensual pleasure : RAKE

rouge \'rüzh, 'rüj\ n [F, lit., red] **1** : a cosmetic used to give a red color to cheeks and lips **2** : a red powder used in polishing glass, gems, and metal — **rouge** *vb*

¹**rough** \\'rəf\ *adj* **rough·er; rough·est 1** : uneven in surface : not smooth **2** : SHAGGY **3** : not calm : TURBULENT, TEMPESTUOUS **4** : marked by harshness or violence **5** : DIFFICULT, TRYING **6** : coarse or rugged in character or appearance **7** : marked by lack of refinement **8** : CRUDE, UNFINISHED **9** : done or made hastily or tentatively — **rough·ly** *adv* — **rough·ness** *n*

²**rough** *n* **1** : uneven ground covered with high grass esp. along a golf fairway **2** : a crude, unfinished, or preliminary state; *also* : something in such a state **3** : ROWDY, TOUGH

³**rough** *vb* **1** : ROUGHEN **2** : MANHANDLE **3** : to make or shape roughly esp. in a preliminary way — **rough·er** *n*

rough·age \\'rəf-ij\ *n* : coarse bulky food (as bran) whose bulk stimulates the intestine to move its contents along

rough-and-ready \\,rəf-ən-'red-ē\ *adj* : rude or unpolished in nature, method, or manner but effective in action or use

rough-and-tum·ble \\-'təm-bəl\ *n* : rough unrestrained fighting or struggling — **rough-and-tumble** *adj*

rough·en \\'rəf-ən\ *vb* **rough·ened; rough·en·ing** \\-(ə-)niŋ\ : to make or become rough

rough-hewn \\'rəf-'hyün\ *adj* **1** : being rough and unfinished (~ beams) **2** : lacking smooth manners or social grace

rough·house \\'rəf-,haus\ *vb* **rough·housed; rough·hous·ing** : to participate in rough noisy behavior — **roughhouse** *n*

rough·neck \\'rəf-,nek\ *n* **1** : ROWDY, TOUGH **2** : a worker on a crew drilling oil wells

rough·shod \\'rəf-,shäd\ *adv* : with no consideration for the wishes or feelings of others (rode ~ over the opposition)

rou·lette \\rü-'let\ *n* [F, lit., small wheel] **1** : a gambling game in which a whirling wheel is used **2** : a wheel or disk with teeth around the outside

¹**round** \\'raund\ *adj* **1** : having every part of the surface or circumference the same distance from the center **2** : CYLINDRICAL **3** : COMPLETE, FULL **4** : approximately correct; *esp* : exact only to a specific decimal or place (use the ~ number 1400 for the exact figure 1411) **5** : liberal or ample in size or amount **6** : BLUNT, OUTSPOKEN **7** : moving in or forming a circle **8** : of or relating to handwriting that is predominantly curved rather than angular — **round·ish** *adj* — **round·ness** \\'raun(d)-nəs\ *n*

²**round** *prep or adv* : AROUND

³**round** *n* **1** : something round (as a circle, globe, or ring) **2** : a curved or rounded part (as a rung of a ladder) **3** : a circuitous path or course; *also* : an habitually covered route (as of a watchman) **4** : a series or cycle of recurring actions or events **5** : one shot fired by a soldier or a gun; *also* : ammunition for one shot **6** : a period of time or a unit of play in a game or contest **7** : a cut of beef esp. between the rump and the lower leg — **in the round 1** : FREESTANDING **2** : with a center stage surrounded by an audience on all sides (theater *in the round*)

⁴**round** *vb* **1** : to make or become round **2** : to go or pass around or part way around **3** : COMPLETE, FINISH **4** : to become plump or shapely **5** : to express as a round number **6** : to follow a winding course : BEND

¹**round·about** \\'raun-də-,baut\ *n, Brit* : MERRY-GO-ROUND

²**roundabout** *adj* : INDIRECT, CIRCUITOUS

roun·de·lay \\'raun-də-,lā\ *n* **1** : a simple song with refrain **2** : a poem with a refrain recurring frequently or at fixed intervals

round·house \\'raund-,haus\ *n* : a circular building for housing and repairing locomotives

round-shoul·dered \\'raun(d)-'shōl-dərd\ *adj* : having the shoulders stooping or rounded

round-trip *n* : a trip to a place and back

round·up \\'raund-,əp\ *n* **1** : the gathering together of cattle on the range by riding around them and driving them in; *also* : the men and horses engaged in a roundup **2** : a gathering in of scattered persons or things **3** : SUMMARY (news ~) — **round up** \\'raund-'əp\ *vb*

round·worm \\-,wərm\ *n* : NEMATODE

rouse \\'rauz\ *vb* **roused; rous·ing 1** : to wake from sleep **2** : to excite to activity : stir up

roust·about \\'raus-tə-,baut\ *n* : one who does heavy unskilled labor (as on a dock or in an oil field)

¹**rout** \\'raut\ *n* **1** : MOB 1, 2 **2** : DISTURBANCE **3** : a fashionable gathering

²**rout** *vb* **1** : RUMMAGE **2** : to gouge out **3** : to expel by force

³**rout** *n* **1** : a state of wild confusion or disorderly retreat **2** : a disastrous defeat

⁴**rout** *vb* **1** : to put to flight **2** : to defeat decisively

¹**route** \\'rüt, 'raut\ *n* **1** : a traveled way **2** : CHANNEL **3** : a line of travel

²**route** *vb* **rout·ed; rout·ing 1** : to send by a selected route **2** : to arrange and direct the order of

route·man \\-mən, -,man\ *n* : one who sells and makes deliveries on an assigned route

rou·tine \\rü-'tēn\ *n* [F, fr. MF, fr. *route* traveled way] **1** : a round (as of work or play) regularly followed **2** : any regular course of action — **routine** *adj* — **rou·tine·ly** *adv* — **rou·tin·ize** \\-'tēn-,īz\ *vb*

¹**rove** \\'rōv\ *vb* **roved; rov·ing** : to wan-

der over or through : RAMBLE, ROAM —
rov·er n

²**rove** past and past part of REEVE

¹**row** \'rō\ vb 1 : to propel a boat with
oars 2 : to travel or convey in a rowboat 3 : to match rowing skill against
— **row·er** \'rō(-ə)r\ n

²**row** n : an act or instance of rowing

³**row** n 1 : a number of objects in an
orderly sequence 2 : WAY, STREET

⁴**row** \'raů\ n : a noisy quarrel

⁵**row** \'raů\ vb : to engage in a row

row·boat \'rō-ˌbōt\ n : a small boat designed to be rowed

row·dy \'raůd-ē\ adj **row·di·er; -est**
: coarse or boisterous in behavior
: ROUGH — **row·di·ness** \'raůd-ē-nəs\ n
— **rowdy** n — **row·dy·ish** adj — **row·
dy·ism** n

row·el \'raů(-ə)l\ n : a small pointed
wheel on a spur used to urge on a
horse — **rowel** vb

roy·al \'rȯi-əl\ adj 1 : of or relating to a
king or sovereign 2 : resembling or
befitting a king — **roy·al·ly** \-ē\ adv

roy·al·ist \-ə-ləst\ n : an adherent of a
king or of monarchical government

roy·al·ty \'rȯi-əl-tē\ n, pl **-ties** 1 : the
state of being royal 2 : a royal person
: royal persons 3 : a share of a product or profit (as of a mine or oil well)
claimed by the owner for allowing another person to use the property 4 : a
payment made to an author or composer for each copy of a work sold or
to an inventor for each article sold
under a patent

RP abbr relief pitcher

RPM abbr revolutions per minute

RPS abbr revolutions per second

rpt abbr 1 repeat 2 report

RR abbr 1 railroad 2 rural route

RS abbr 1 recording secretary 2 revised statutes 3 right side 4 Royal Society

RSV abbr Revised Standard Version

RSVP abbr [F répondez s'il vous plaît]
please reply

RSWC abbr right side up with care

rt abbr right

RT abbr radiotelephone

rte abbr route

Ru symbol ruthenium

¹**rub** \'rəb\ vb **rubbed; rub·bing** 1 : to
use pressure and friction on a body or
object 2 : to fret or chafe with friction
3 : to scour, polish, erase, or smear by
pressure and friction

²**rub** n 1 : DIFFICULTY, OBSTRUCTION 2
: something grating to the feelings

¹**rub·ber** \'rəb-ər\ n 1 : one that rubs 2
: ERASER 3 : a flexible waterproof elastic substance made from the juice of
various tropical plants or synthetically; also : something made of this material — **rubber** adj — **rub·ber·ize**
\-ˌīz\ vb — **rub·bery** adj

²**rubber** n 1 : a contest that consists of
an odd number of games and is won
by the side that takes a majority 2 : an
extra game played to decide a tie

rub·ber·neck \-ˌnek\ vb : to look about,
stare, or listen with excessive curiosity

rub·ber·neck·er \-ər\ also **rubberneck** n
1 : an idly or overly inquisitive person
2 : a person on a guided tour

rub·bish \'rəb-ish\ n 1 : useless waste
or rejected matter : TRASH 2 : something worthless or nonsensical

rub·ble \'rəb-əl\ n : broken stones or
bricks used in masonry; also : a mass
of such material

ru·bel·la \rü-'bel-ə\ n : GERMAN MEASLES

ru·bi·cund \'rü-bi-(ˌ)kənd\ adj : RED,
RUDDY

ru·bid·i·um \rü-'bid-ē-əm\ n : a soft silvery metallic chemical element

ru·ble \'rü-bəl\ n — see MONEY table

ru·bric \'rü-brik\ n [ME rubrike red
ocher, heading in red letters of part of
a book, fr. MF rubrique, fr. L rubrica,
fr. ruber red] 1 : HEADING, TITLE; also
: CLASS, CATEGORY 2 : a rule esp. for
the conduct of a religious service

ru·by \'rü-bē\ n, pl **rubies** : a precious
stone of a clear red color

ru·by–throat·ed hummingbird \ˌrü-bē-
ˌthrōt-əd-\ n : a bright green and whitish hummingbird of eastern No.
America with a red throat in the male

ruck·us \'rək-əs\ n : ROW, DISTURBANCE

rud·der \'rəd-ər\ n : a movable flat
piece attached vertically at the rear of
a boat or aircraft for steering

rud·dy \'rəd-ē\ adj **rud·di·er; -est** : RED-
DISH; esp : of a healthy reddish complexion — **rud·di·ness** \'rəd-ē-nəs\ n

rude \'rüd\ adj **rud·er; rud·est** 1
: roughly made : CRUDE 2 : UN-
DEVELOPED, PRIMITIVE 3 : IMPOLITE,
DISCOURTEOUS 4 : UNSKILLED — **rude·ly**
adv — **rude·ness** n

ru·di·ment \'rüd-ə-mənt\ n 1 : an elementary principle or basic skill —
usu. used in pl. 2 : something not fully
developed — usu. used in pl. — **ru·di·
men·ta·ry** \ˌrüd-ə-'men-t(ə-)rē\ adj

¹**rue** \'rü\ vb **rued; ru·ing** : to feel regret,
remorse, or penitence for

²**rue** n : REGRET, SORROW — **rue·ful** \-fəl\
adj — **rue·ful·ly** \-ē\ adv — **rue·ful·ness**
n

³**rue** n : a European strong-scented
woody herb with bitter-tasting leaves

rue anemone n : a delicate herb of the
buttercup family with white flowers

ruff \'rəf\ n 1 : a wheel-shaped frilled
collar worn about 1600 2 : a fringe of
hair or feathers around the neck of an
animal — **ruffed** \'rəft\ adj

ruf·fi·an \'rəf-ē-ən\ n [MF rufian] : a
brutal person — **ruf·fi·an·ly** adj

¹**ruf·fle** \'rəf-əl\ vb **ruf·fled; ruf·fling**
\-(ə-)liŋ\ 1 : to roughen the surface of
2 : IRRITATE, VEX 3 : to erect (as hair
or feathers) in or like a ruff 4 : to draw
into or provide with plaits or folds 5
: to flip through (as pages)

²**ruffle** n 1 : RIPPLE 2 : a strip of fabric
gathered or pleated on one edge 3
: RUFF 2

rug \'rəg\ *n* **1** : a piece of heavy fabric usu. with a nap or pile used as a floor covering **2** : a covering for the legs, lap, and feet

rug·by \'rəg-bē\ *n, often cap* [*Rugby* School, Rugby, England, where it was first played] : a football game in which play is continuous and interference and forward passing are not permitted

rug·ged \'rəg-əd\ *adj* **1** : having a rough uneven surface **2** : TURBULENT, STORMY **3** : HARSH, STERN **4** : ROBUST, STURDY — **rug·ged·ly** *adv* — **rug·ged·ness** *n*

¹**ru·in** \'rü-ən\ *n* **1** : complete collapse or destruction **2** : the remains of something destroyed — usu. used in pl. **3** : a cause of destruction **4** : the action of destroying

²**ruin** *vb* **1** : DESTROY **2** : to damage beyond repair **3** : BANKRUPT

ru·in·ation \,rü-ə-'nā-shən\ *n* : RUIN, DESTRUCTION

ru·in·ous \'rü-ə-nəs\ *adj* **1** : RUINED, DILAPIDATED **2** : causing ruin — **ru·in·ous·ly** *adv*

¹**rule** \'rül\ *n* **1** : a guide or principle for governing action : REGULATION **2** : the usual way of doing something **3** : the exercise of authority or control : GOVERNMENT **4** : RULER **2**

²**rule** *vb* **ruled; rul·ing 1** : CONTROL, GOVERN **2** : to be preeminent in : DOMINATE, PREVAIL **3** : to give or state as a considered decision **4** : to mark on paper with or as if with a ruler

rul·er \'rü-lər\ *n* **1** : SOVEREIGN **2** : a straight strip of material (as wood or metal) marked off in units and used for measuring or as a straightedge

rum \'rəm\ *n* **1** : a liquor distilled from a fermented cane product (as molasses) **2** : alcoholic liquor

Rum *abbr* Rumania; Rumanian

Ru·ma·nian \rù-'mā-nē-ən, -nyən\ *n* **1** : ROMANIAN **1 2** : the language of the Romanians — **Rumanian** *adj*

rum·ba \'rəm-bə, 'rùm-\ *n* : a dance of Cuban origin marked by strong rhythmic movements

¹**rum·ble** \'rəm-bəl\ *vb* **rum·bled; rum·bling** \-b(ə-)liŋ\ : to make a low heavy rolling sound; *also* : to travel or move along with such a sound — **rum·bler** \-b(ə-)lər\ *n*

²**rumble** *n* **1** : a low heavy rolling sound **2** : a street fight esp. among gangs

rumble seat *n* : a folding seat in the back of an automobile that is not covered by the top

rum·bling \'rəm-bliŋ\ *n* **1** : RUMBLE **2** : widespread talk or complaints — usu. used in pl.

¹**ru·mi·nant** \'rü-mə-nənt\ *n* : a ruminant mammal

²**ruminant** *adj* **1** : chewing the cud; *also* : of or relating to a group of hoofed mammals (as cattle, deer, and camels) that chew the cud and have a complex 3- or 4-chambered stomach **2** : given

to or engaged in contemplation : MEDITATIVE

ru·mi·nate \'rü-mə-,nāt\ *vb* **-nat·ed; -nat·ing** [L *ruminari* to chew the cud, muse upon, fr. *rumin-, rumen* gullet] **1** : MEDITATE, MUSE **2** : to chew the cud — **ru·mi·na·tion** \,rü-mə-'nā-shən\ *n*

¹**rum·mage** \'rəm-ij\ *vb* **rum·maged; rum·mag·ing** : to poke around in all corners looking for something — **rum·mag·er** *n*

²**rummage** *n* **1** : a miscellaneous collection **2** : an act of rummaging

rum·my \'rəm-ē\ *n* : any of several card games for two or more players

ru·mor \'rü-mər\ *n* **1** : common talk **2** : a statement or report current but not authenticated — **rumor** *vb*

rump \'rəmp\ *n* **1** : the rear part of an animal; *also* : a cut of beef behind the upper sirloin **2** : a small remaining fragment : REMNANT

rum·ple \'rəm-pəl\ *vb* **rum·pled; rum·pling** \-p(ə-)liŋ\ : TOUSLE, MUSS, WRINKLE — **rumple** *n* — **rum·ply** \'rəm-p(ə-)lē\ *adj*

rum·pus \'rəm-pəs\ *n* : DISTURBANCE, FRACAS

rumpus room *n* : a room usu. in the basement of a home that is used for games, parties, and recreation

¹**run** \'rən\ *vb* **ran** \'ran\ ; **run; run·ning 1** : to go at a pace faster than a walk **2** : to take to flight : FLEE **3** : to go without restraint (lets his children ∼) **4** : to go rapidly or hurriedly : HASTEN, RUSH **5** : to perform or bring about by running **6** : to make a quick or casual trip or visit **7** : to contend in a race; *esp* : to enter an election **8** : to put forward as a candidate for office **9** : to move on or as if on wheels : pass or slide freely **10** : to go back and forth : PLY **11** : to move in schools esp. to a spawning ground (shad are *running*) **12** : FUNCTION, OPERATE ⟨left his car *running*⟩ **13** : to continue in force ⟨two years to ∼⟩ **14** : to flow rapidly or under pressure : MELT, FUSE, DISSOLVE; *also* : DISCHARGE **15** : to tend to produce or to recur ⟨family ∼s to blonds⟩ **16** : to take a certain direction **17** : to be current ⟨rumors *running* wild⟩ **18** : to be worded or written **19** : to cause to run **20** : TRACE ⟨∼ down a rumor⟩ **21** : to cause to pass ⟨∼ a wire from the antenna⟩ **22** : to cause to collide **23** : SMUGGLE **24** : MANAGE, CONDUCT, OPERATE ⟨∼ a business⟩ **25** : INCUR ⟨∼ a risk⟩ **26** : to permit to accumulate before settling ⟨∼ a charge account⟩

²**run** *n* **1** : an act or the action of running **2** : a school of migrating fish **3** : a score in baseball **4** : BROOK, CREEK **5** : a continuous series esp. of similar things **6** : persistent heavy demands from depositors, creditors, or customers **7** : the quantity of work turned out in a continuous operation; *also* : a period of operation (as of a

machine or plant) **8** : the usual or normal kind (the ordinary ~ of students) **9** : the distance covered in continuous travel or sailing **10** : a regular course or route; *also* : TRIP, JOURNEY **11** : freedom of movement in a place or area (has the ~ of the house) **12** : an enclosure for animals **13** : an inclined course (as for skiing) **14** : a lengthwise ravel (as in a stocking) — **run·less** *adj*

run·about \ˈrən-ə-ˌbaùt\ *n* : a light wagon, automobile, or motorboat

run·a·gate \ˈrən-ə-ˌgāt\ *n* **1** : VAGABOND **2** : FUGITIVE

run·around \ˈrən-ə-ˌraùnd\ *n* : evasive or delaying action esp. in reply to a request

¹**run·away** \ˈrən-ə-ˌwā\ *n* **1** : one that runs away : FUGITIVE **2** : the act of running away or out of control; *also* : something (as a horse) that is running out of control

²**runaway** *adj* **1** : FUGITIVE **2** : accomplished by elopement (~ marriage) **3** : won by a long lead **4** : subject to uncontrolled changes (~ inflation) **5** : operating out of control (a ~ locomotive)

run·down \ˈrən-ˌdaùn\ *n* : an item-by-item report : SUMMARY

run-down \ˈrən-ˈdaùn\ *adj* **1** : EXHAUSTED **2** : completely unwound **3** : being in poor repair : DILAPIDATED

run down \ˈrən-ˈdaùn\ *vb* **1** : to collide with and knock down **2** : to chase until exhausted or captured **3** : to find by search. **4** : DISPARAGE **5** : to cease to operate for lack of motive power **6** : to decline in physical condition

rune \ˈrün\ *n* **1** : any of the characters of any of several alphabets formerly used by the Germanic peoples **2** : MYSTERY, MAGIC **3** : a poem esp. in Finnish or Old Norse — **ru·nic** \ˈrü-nik\ *adj*

¹**rung** *past part of* RING

²**rung** \ˈrəŋ\ *n* **1** : a rounded crosspiece between the legs of a chair **2** : one of the crosspieces of a ladder **3** : a spoke of a wheel

run-in \ˈrən-ˌin\ *n* **1** : something run in **2** : ALTERCATION, QUARREL

run in \ˈrən-ˈin\ *vb* **1** : to insert as additional matter **2** : to arrest esp. for a minor offense **3** : to pay a casual visit

run·nel \ˈrən-ᵊl\ *n* : BROOK, STREAMLET

run·ner \ˈrən-ər\ *n* **1** : one that runs **2** : a baseball player on base or attempting to reach base **3** : BALLCARRIER **4** : a thin piece or part on which something (as a sled or an ice skate) slides **5** : the support of a drawer or a sliding door **6** : a horizontal branch from the base of a plant that produces new plants **7** : a plant producing runners **8** : a long narrow carpet **9** : a narrow decorative cloth cover for a table or dresser top

run·ner-up \ˈrən-ər-ˌəp\ *n, pl* **runners-up** *also* **runner-ups** : the competitor in a contest who finishes next to the winner

¹**run·ning** \ˈrən-iŋ\ *adj* **1** : FLOWING **2** : FLUID, RUNNY **3** : CONTINUOUS, INCESSANT **4** : measured in a straight line (cost per ~ foot) **5** : of or relating to an act of running **6** : fitted or trained for running (~ horse)

²**running** *adv* : in succession

running light *n* : one of the lights carried by a vehicle (as a ship) at night

run·ny \ˈrən-ē\ *adj* : having a tendency to run (a ~ nose)

run·off \ˈrən-ˌof\ *n* : a final contest (as an election) to a previous indecisive contest

run-of-the-mill \ˌrən-ə-(v)-thə-ˈmil\ *adj* : not outstanding : AVERAGE

run on \ˈrən-ˈon, -ˈän\ *vb* **1** : to continue (matter in type) without a break or a new paragraph **2** : to place or add (as an entry in a dictionary) at the end of a paragraphed item — **run-on** \-ˌon, -ˌän\ *n*

runt \ˈrənt\ *n* : an unusually small person or animal : DWARF — **runty** *adj*

run·way \ˈrən-ˌwā\ *n* **1** : a beaten path made by animals; *also* : a passage for animals **2** : a paved strip of ground for the landing and takeoff of aircraft **3** : a narrow platform from a stage into an auditorium **4** : a support on which something runs

ru·pee \rü-ˈpē, ˈrü-ˌpē\ *n* — see MONEY table

ru·pi·ah \rü-ˈpē-ə\ *n, pl* **rupiah** *or* **rupiahs** — see MONEY table

¹**rup·ture** \ˈrəp-chər\ *n* **1** : a breaking or tearing apart; *also* : HERNIA

²**rupture** *vb* **rup·tured**; **rup·tur·ing** : to cause or undergo rupture

ru·ral \ˈrùr-əl\ *adj* : of or relating to the country, country people, or agriculture

ruse \ˈrüs, ˈrüz\ *n* : a wily subterfuge : TRICK, ARTIFICE

¹**rush** \ˈrəsh\ *n* : a hollow-stemmed grasslike marsh plant — **rushy** *adj*

²**rush** *vb* [ME *russhen*, fr. MF *ruser* to put to flight, deceive] **1** : to move forward or act with too great haste or eagerness or without preparation **2** : to perform in a short time or at high speed **3** : ATTACK, CHARGE — **rush·er** *n*

³**rush** *n* **1** : a violent forward motion **2** : unusual demand or activity **3** : a crowding of people to one place **4** : a running play in football

⁴**rush** *adj* : requiring or marked by special speed or urgency (~ orders)

rush hour *n* : a time when the amount of traffic or business is at a peak

rusk \ˈrəsk\ *n* : a sweet or plain bread baked, sliced, and baked again until dry and crisp

Russ *abbr* Russia; Russian

rus·set \ˈrəs-ət\ *n* **1** : a coarse reddish brown cloth **2** : a variable reddish brown or yellowish brown color **3** : any of various winter apples with rough russet skins — **russet** *adj*

Rus·sian \'rəsh-ən\ *n* **1** : a native or inhabitant of Russia or the U.S.S.R. **2** : the chief language of the U.S.S.R. — **Russian** *adj*

rust \'rəst\ *n* **1** : a reddish coating formed on iron when it is exposed to esp. moist air **2** : any of various diseases causing reddish spots on plants **3** : a reddish orange color — **rust** *vb* — **rusty** *adj*

¹**rus·tic** \'rəs-tik\ *adj* **1** : RURAL **2** : made of the rough limbs of trees ⟨∼ furniture⟩ **3** : AWKWARD, BOORISH **2** : PLAIN, SIMPLE — **rus·ti·cal·ly** \'rəs-ti-k(ə-)lē\ *adv* — **rus·tic·i·ty** \,rəs-'tis-ət-ē\ *n*

²**rustic** *n* : a rustic person

rus·ti·cate \'rəs-ti-,kāt\ *vb* **-cat·ed; -cat·ing** : to go into or reside in the country — **rus·ti·ca·tion** \,rəs-ti-'kā-shən\ *n*

¹**rus·tle** \'rəs-əl\ *vb* **rus·tled; rus·tling** \'rəs-(ə-)liŋ\ **1** : to make or cause a rustle **2** : to cause to rustle ⟨∼ a newspaper⟩ **3** : to act or move with energy or speed; *also* : to procure in this way **4** : to forage food **5** : to steal cattle from the range — **rus·tler** \-(ə-)lər\ *n*

²**rustle** *n* : a quick succession or confusion of small sounds ⟨∼ of leaves⟩

¹**rut** \'rət\ *n* : state or period of sexual excitement esp. in male deer — **rut** *vb*

²**rut** *n* **1** : a track worn by wheels or by habitual passage of something **2** : a usual or fixed routine

ru·ta·ba·ga \,rüt-ə-'bā-gə, ,rüt-\ *n* : a turnip with a large yellowish root

Ruth \'rüth\ *n* — see BIBLE table

ru·the·ni·um \rü-'thē-nē-əm\ *n* : a hard brittle metallic chemical element

ruth·less \'rüth-ləs\ *adj* [fr. *ruth* compassion, pity, fr. ME *ruthe*, fr. *ruen* to rue, fr. OE *hrēowan*] : having no pity : MERCILESS, CRUEL — **ruth·less·ly** *adv* — **ruth·less·ness** *n*

RV *abbr* recreational vehicle

R–value \'är-,val-yü\ *n* : a measure of the resistance of a substance (as insulation) to heat flow

RW *abbr* **1** right worshipful **2** right worthy

rwy *or* **ry** *abbr* railway

-ry \rē\ *n suffix* : -ERY ⟨bigot**ry**⟩

rye \'rī\ *n* **1** : a hardy cereal grass grown for grain or as a cover crop; *also* : its seed **2** : a whiskey distilled from a rye mash

S

¹**s** \'es\ *n, pl* **s's** *or* **ss** \'es-əz\ *often cap* : the 19th letter of the English alphabet

²**s** *abbr, often cap* **1** saint **2** second **3** senate **4** series **5** shilling **6** singular **7** small **8** son **9** south; southern

¹**-s** \s *after sounds* f, k, k̠, p, t, th; əz *after sounds* ch, j, s, sh, z, zh; z *after other sounds*\ *n pl suffix* — used to form the plural of most nouns that do not end in *s*, *z*, *sh*, *ch*, or postconsonantal *y* ⟨head**s**⟩ ⟨book**s**⟩ ⟨boy**s**⟩ ⟨belief**s**⟩ , to form the plural of proper nouns that end in postconsonantal *y* ⟨Mary**s**⟩ , and with or without a preceding apostrophe to form the plural of abbreviations, numbers, letters, and symbols used as nouns ⟨MC**s**⟩ ⟨4**s**⟩ ⟨#**s**⟩ ⟨B**'s**⟩

²**-s** *adv suffix* — used to form adverbs denoting usual or repeated action or state ⟨works night**s**⟩

³**-s** *vb suffix* — used to form the third person singular present of most verbs that do not end in *s*, *z*, *sh*, *ch*, or postconsonantal *y* ⟨fall**s**⟩ ⟨take**s**⟩ ⟨play**s**⟩

S *symbol* sulfur

SA *abbr* **1** Salvation Army **2** seaman apprentice **3** sex appeal **4** [L *sine anno* without year] without date **5** South Africa **6** South America **7** subject to approval

Sab·bath \'sab-əth\ *n* [ME *sabat*, fr. OF & OE, fr. L *sabbatum*, fr. Gk *sabbaton*, fr. Heb *shabbāth*, lit., rest] **1** : the 7th day of the week observed as a day of worship by Jews and some

Christians **2** : Sunday observed among Christians as a day of worship

sab·bat·i·cal \sə-'bat-i-kəl\ *n* : a leave often with pay granted (as to a college professor) usu. every 7th year for rest, travel, or research

sa·ber *or* **sa·bre** \'sā-bər\ *n* [F *sabre*] : a cavalry sword with a curved blade and thick back

saber saw *n* : a light portable electric saw with a pointed reciprocating blade

sa·ble \'sā-bəl\ *n, pl* **sables** **1** : the color black **2** *pl* : mourning garments **3** : a dark brown mammal of northern Europe and Asia related to the martens and valued for its fur; *also* : this fur

¹**sab·o·tage** \'sab-ə-,täzh\ *n* [F] **1** : deliberate destruction of an employer's property or hindering of production by workers **2** : destructive or hampering action by enemy agents or sympathizers in time of war

²**sabotage** *vb* **-taged; -tag·ing** : to practice sabotage on : WRECK

sab·o·teur \,sab-ə-'tər\ *n* : a person who commits sabotage

sac \'sak\ *n* : a baglike part of an animal or plant

SAC \'sak\ *abbr* Strategic Air Command

sac·cha·rin \'sak-(ə-)rən\ *n* : a white crystalline compound used as an artificial sweetener

sac·cha·rine \'sak-(ə-)rən\ *adj* : nauseatingly sweet ⟨∼ poetry⟩

sac·er·do·tal \ˌsas-ər-ˈdōt-ᵊl, ˌsak-\ *adj*
: PRIESTLY — **sac·er·do·tal·ism** *n*

sa·chem \ˈsā-chəm\ *n* : a No. American Indian chief

sa·chet \sa-ˈshā\ *n* [F, fr. OF, dim. of *sac* bag] : a small bag filled with perfumed powder for scenting clothes

¹**sack** \ˈsak\ *n* **1** : a large coarse bag; *also* : a small container esp. of paper **2** : a loose jacket or short coat

²**sack** *vb* : DISMISS, FIRE

³**sack** *n* [modif. of MF *sec* dry, fr. L *siccus*] : a white wine popular in England in the 16th and 17th centuries

⁴**sack** *vb* : to plunder a captured town

sack·cloth \-ˌklȯth\ *n* : a rough garment worn as a sign of penitence

sac·ra·ment \ˈsak-rə-mənt\ *n* **1** : a formal religious act or rite; *esp* : one (as baptism or the Eucharist) held to have been instituted by Christ **2** : the elements of the Eucharist — **sac·ra·men·tal** \ˌsak-rə-ˈment-ᵊl\ *adj*

sa·cred \ˈsā-krəd\ *adj* **1** : set apart for the service or worship of deity **2** : devoted exclusively to one service or use **3** : worthy of veneration or reverence **4** : of or relating to religion : RELIGIOUS **syn** blessed, divine, hallowed, holy, sanctified — **sa·cred·ly** *adv* — **sa·cred·ness** *n*

sacred cow *n* : one that is often unreasonably immune from criticism

¹**sac·ri·fice** \ˈsak-rə-ˌfīs\ *n* **1** : the offering of something precious to deity **2** : something offered in sacrifice **3** : LOSS, DEPRIVATION **4** : a bunt allowing a base runner to advance while the batter is put out; *also* : a fly ball allowing a runner to score after the catch — **sac·ri·fi·cial** \ˌsak-rə-ˈfish-əl\ *adj* — **sac·ri·fi·cial·ly** \-ē\ *adv*

²**sac·ri·fice** *vb* -ficed; -fic·ing **1** : to offer up or kill as a sacrifice **2** : to accept the loss or destruction of for an end, cause, or ideal **3** : to make a sacrifice in baseball

sac·ri·lege \ˈsak-rə-lij\ *n* [ME, fr. OF, fr. L *sacrilegium*, fr. *sacrilegus* one who steals sacred things, fr. *sacr-, sacer* sacred + *legere* to gather, steal] : violation of something consecrated to God **2** : gross irreverence toward a hallowed person, place, or thing — **sac·ri·le·gious** \ˌsak-rə-ˈlij-əs, -ˈlē-jəs\ *adj* — **sac·ri·le·gious·ly** *adv*

sac·ris·tan \ˈsak-rə-stən\ *n* **1** : a church officer in charge of the sacristy **2** : SEXTON

sac·ris·ty \ˈsak-rə-stē\ *n, pl* -ties : VESTRY

sac·ro·il·i·ac \ˌsak-rō-ˈil-ē-ˌak\ *n* : the joint between the upper part of the hipbone and the sacrum

sac·ro·sanct \ˈsak-rō-ˌsaŋkt\ *adj* : SACRED, INVIOLABLE

sa·crum \ˈsak-rəm, ˈsā-krəm\ *n, pl* **sa·cra** \ˈsak-rə, ˈsā-krə\ : the part of the vertebral column that is directly connected with or forms a part of the

pelvis and in man consists of five fused vertebrae

sad \ˈsad\ *adj* **sad·der; sad·dest 1** : GRIEVING, MOURNFUL, DOWNCAST **2** : causing sorrow **3** : DULL, SOMBER — **sad·ly** *adv* — **sad·ness** *n*

sad·den \ˈsad-ᵊn\ *vb* **sad·dened; sad·den·ing** \ˈsad-(ᵊ-)niŋ\ : to make sad

¹**sad·dle** \ˈsad-ᵊl\ *n* **1** : a usu. padded leather-covered seat (as for a rider on horseback) **2** : the upper back portion of a carcass (as of mutton)

²**sad·dle** *vb* **sad·dled; sad·dling** \ˈsad-(ᵊ-)liŋ\ **1** : to put a saddle on **2** : BURDEN

sad·dle·bow \ˈsad-ᵊl-ˌbō\ *n* : the arch in the front of a saddle

saddle horse *n* : a horse suited for or trained for riding

Sad·du·cee \ˈsaj-ə-ˌsē, ˈsad-yə-\ *n* : a member of an ancient Jewish sect opposed to the Pharisees — **Sad·du·ce·an** \ˌsaj-ə-ˈsē-ən, ˌsad-yə-\ *adj*

sad·iron \ˈsad-ˌī(-ə)rn\ *n* : a flatiron with a removable handle

sa·dism \ˈsā-ˌdiz-əm, ˈsad-ˌiz-\ *n* : a sexual perversion in which gratification is associated with inflicting physical or mental pain on others — **sa·dist** \ˈsād-əst, ˈsad-\ *n* — **sa·dis·tic** \sə-ˈdis-tik\ *adj* — **sa·dis·ti·cal·ly** \-ti-k(ə-)lē\ *adv*

SAE *abbr* **1** self-addressed envelope **2** stamped self-addressed envelope

sa·fa·ri \sə-ˈfär-ē, -ˈfar-\ *n* [Ar *safarīy* of a trip] **1** : a hunting expedition esp. in eastern Africa **2** : JOURNEY, TRIP

¹**safe** \ˈsāf\ *adj* **saf·er; saf·est 1** : freed from injury or risk **2** : affording safety; *also* : secure from danger or loss **3** : RELIABLE, TRUSTWORTHY — **safe·ly** *adv*

²**safe** *n* : a container for keeping articles (as valuables) safe

safe-con·duct \-ˈkän-(ˌ)dəkt\ *n* : a pass permitting a person to go through enemy lines

¹**safe·guard** \-ˌgärd\ *n* : a measure or device for preventing accident or injury

²**safeguard** *vb* : to provide a safeguard for : PROTECT

safe·keep·ing \ˈsāf-ˈkē-piŋ\ *n* : a keeping or being kept in safety

safe·ty \ˈsāf-tē\ *n, pl* **safeties 1** : freedom from danger : SECURITY **2** : a protective device **3** : a football play in which the ball is downed by the offensive team behind its own goal line **4** : a defensive football back in the deepest position — **safety** *adj*

safety glass *n* : shatter-resistant material formed of two sheets of glass with a sheet of clear plastic between them

safety match *n* : a match that ignites only when struck on a special surface

saf·flow·er \ˈsaf-ˌlau̇(-ə)r\ *n* : a widely grown Old World herb related to the daisies that has large orange or red flower heads yielding a dyestuff and seeds rich in edible oil

saf·fron \ˈsaf-rən\ *n* : an aromatic deep

orange powder from the flower of a crocus used to color and flavor foods

sag \'sag\ *vb* **sagged; sag·ging 1** : to bend down at the middle **2** : to become flabby : DROOP — **sag** *n*

sa·ga \'säg-ə\ *n* [ON] : a narrative of heroic deeds; *esp* : one recorded in Iceland in the 12th and 13th centuries

sa·ga·cious \sə-'gā-shəs\ *adj* : of keen mind : SHREWD — **sa·gac·i·ty** \-'gas-ət-ē\ *n*

sag·a·more \'sag-ə-ˌmōr\ *n* : a subordinate No. American Indian chief

¹**sage** \'sāj\ *adj* [ME, fr. OF, fr. (assumed) VL *sapius*, fr. L *sapere* to taste, have good taste, be wise] : WISE, PRUDENT — **sage·ly** *adv*

²**sage** *n* : a wise man : PHILOSOPHER

³**sage** *n* [ME, fr. MF *sauge*, fr. L *salvia*, fr. *salvus* healthy; fr. its use as a medicinal herb] **1** : a shrublike mint with leaves used in flavoring : SAGEBRUSH

sage·brush \'sāj-ˌbrəsh\ *n* : any of several low shrubby No. American plants related to the daisies; *esp* : one of the western U.S. with a sagelike odor

Sag·it·tar·i·us \ˌsaj-ə-'ter-ē-əs\ *n* [L, lit., archer] **1** : a zodiacal constellation between Scorpio and Capricorn usu. pictured as a centaur archer **2** : the 9th sign of the zodiac in astrology; *also* : one born under this sign

sa·go \'sā-gō\ *n, pl* **sagos** : a dry granulated starch esp. from the pith of an East Indian palm (**sago palm**)

sa·gua·ro \sə-'wär-ə\ *n, pl* **-ros** [MexSp] : a desert cactus of the southwestern U.S. and Mexico with a tall columnar simple or sparsely branched trunk of up to 60 feet (20 meters)

said *past and past part of* SAY

¹**sail** \'sāl\ *n* **1** : a piece of fabric by means of which the wind is used to propel a ship **2** : a sailing ship **3** : something resembling a sail **4** : a trip on a sailboat

²**sail** *vb* **1** : to travel on a sailing ship **2** : to pass over in a ship **3** : to manage or direct the course of a ship **4** : to glide through the air

sail·boat \-ˌbōt\ *n* : a boat usu. propelled by sail

sail·cloth \-ˌklöth\ *n* : a heavy canvas used for sails, tents, or upholstery

sail·fish \-ˌfish\ *n* : any of a genus of large sea fishes with a very large dorsal fin that are related to the swordfish

sail·ing \'sā-liŋ\ *n* : the action, fact, or pastime of cruising or racing in a sailboat

sail·or \'sā-lər\ *n* : one that sails; *esp* : a member of a ship's crew

sail·plane \'sāl-ˌplān\ *n* : a glider designed to rise in an upward air current

saint \'sānt, *before a name* (ˌ)sānt *or* sənt\ *n* **1** : one officially recognized as preeminent for holiness **2** : one of the spirits of the departed in heaven **3** : a holy or godly person — **saint·ed** \-əd\ *adj* — **saint·hood** \-ˌhùd\ *n*

Saint Ber·nard \-bər-'närd\ *n* : any of a Swiss alpine breed of tall powerful working dogs used esp. formerly in aiding lost travelers

saint·ly \'sānt-lē\ *adj* : relating to, resembling, or befitting a saint — **saint·li·ness** *n*

Saint Val·en·tine's Day \-'val-ən-ˌtīnz-\ *n* : February 14 observed in honor of St. Valentine and as a time for exchanging valentines

¹**sake** \'sāk\ *n* **1** : MOTIVE, PURPOSE **2** : personal or social welfare, safety, or well-being

²**sa·ke** *or* **sa·ki** \'säk-ē\ *n* : a Japanese alcoholic beverage of fermented rice

sa·laam \sə-'läm\ *n* [Ar *salām*, lit., peace] **1** : a salutation or ceremonial greeting in the East **2** : an obeisance performed by bowing very low and placing the right palm on the forehead — **salaam** *vb*

sa·la·cious \sə-'lā-shəs\ *adj* **1** : arousing sexual desire or imagination **2** : LUSTFUL — **sa·la·cious·ly** *adv* — **sa·la·cious·ness** *n*

sal·ad \'sal-əd\ *n* : a cold dish (as of lettuce, vegetables, fish, eggs, or fruit) served with dressing

sal·a·man·der \'sal-ə-ˌman-dər\ *n* : any of an order of amphibians that look like lizards but have scaleless usu. smooth moist skin

sa·la·mi \sə-'läm-ē\ *n* [It] : a highly seasoned sausage of pork and beef

sal·a·ry \'sal-(ə)-rē\ *n, pl* **-ries** [ME *salarie*, fr. L *salarium* salt money, pension, salary, fr. neut. of *salarius* of salt, fr. *sal* salt] : payment made at regular intervals for services

sale \'sāl\ *n* **1** : transfer of ownership of property from one person to another in return for money **2** : ready market : DEMAND **3** : AUCTION **4** : a selling of goods at bargain prices — **sal·able** *or* **sale·able** \'sā-lə-bəl\ *adj*

sales·girl \'sālz-ˌgərl\ *n* : SALESWOMAN

sales·man \-mən\ *n* : a person who sells in a store or to outside customers — **sales·man·ship** *n*

sales·per·son \-ˌpər-sən\ *n* : a salesman or saleswoman

sales·wom·an \-ˌwùm-ən\ *n* : a woman who sells merchandise

sal·i·cyl·ic acid \ˌsal-ə-ˌsil-ik-\ *n* : a crystalline organic acid used in the form of its salts to relieve pain and fever

¹**sa·lient** \'sāl-yənt\ *adj* : jutting forward beyond a line; *also* : PROMINENT **syn** conspicuous, striking, noticeable

²**salient** *n* : a projecting part in a line of defense

¹**sa·line** \'sā-ˌlēn, -ˌlīn\ *adj* : consisting of or containing salt : SALTY — **sa·lin·i·ty** \sā-'lin-ət-ē, sə-\ *n*

²**saline** *n* **1** : a metallic salt esp. with a purgative action **2** : a saline solution

sa·li·va \sə-'lī-və\ *n* : a liquid secreted into the mouth that helps digestion — **sal·i·vary** \'sal-ə-ˌver-ē\ *adj*

sal·i·vate \'sal-ə-ˌvāt\ *vb* **-vat·ed; -vat·ing** : to produce saliva esp. in excess — **sal·i·va·tion** \ˌsal-ə-'vā-shən\ *n*

Salk vaccine \'so(l)k-\ *n* [after Jonas *Salk* b1914 American physician] : a polio vaccine that contains inactivated virus and is given by injection

sal·low \'sal-ō\ *adj* : of a yellowish sickly color ⟨a ~ liverish skin⟩

sal·ly \'sal-ē\ *n, pl* **sallies** **1** : a rushing attack on besiegers by troops of a besieged place **2** : a witty remark or retort **3** : a brief excursion — **sally** *vb*

salm·on \'sam-ən\ *n, pl* **salmon** *also* **salmons** **1** : any of several food fishes with pinkish flesh related to the trouts **2** : a strong yellowish pink

sa·lon \sə-'län, 'sal-ˌän, sa-'lōⁿ *n* [F] : an elegant drawing room; *also* : a fashionable shop ⟨beauty ~⟩

sa·loon \sə-'lün\ *n* **1** : a large drawing room or ballroom esp. on a passenger ship **2** : a place where liquors are sold and drunk : BARROOM **3** *Brit* : SEDAN 2

sal soda \'sal-ˌsōd-ə\ *n* : SODIUM CARBONATE

¹salt \'sȯlt\ *n* **1** : a white crystalline substance that consists of sodium and chlorine and is used in seasoning foods **2** : a saltlike cathartic substance (as Epsom salts) **3** : a compound formed usu. by action of an acid on metal **4** : SAILOR — **salt·i·ness** \'sȯl-tē-nəs\ *n* — **salty** \'sȯl-tē\ *adj*

²salt *vb* : to preserve, season, or feed with salt

³salt *adj* : preserved or treated with salt; *also* : SALTY

SALT *abbr* Strategic Arms Limitation Talks

salt away *vb* : to lay away safely : SAVE

salt·box \'sȯlt-ˌbäks\ *n* : a frame dwelling with two stories in front and one behind and a long sloping roof

salt·cel·lar \'sȯlt-ˌsel-ər\ *n* : a small vessel for holding salt at the table

sal·tine \sȯl-'tēn\ *n* : a thin crisp cracker sprinkled with salt

salt lick *n* : LICK 5

salt·pe·ter \'sȯlt-'pēt-ər\ *n* [fr. earlier *saltpeter*, fr. ME, fr. MF *saltpetre*, fr. ML *sal petrae*, lit., salt of the rock] **1** : POTASSIUM NITRATE **2** : SODIUM NITRATE

salt·wa·ter \ˌsȯlt-ˌwȯt-ər, -ˌwät-\ *adj* : of, relating to, or living in salt water

sa·lu·bri·ous \sə-'lü-brē-əs\ *adj* : favorable to health

sal·u·tary \'sal-yə-ˌter-ē\ *adj* : health-giving; *also* : BENEFICIAL

sal·u·ta·tion \ˌsal-yə-'tā-shən\ *n* : an expression of greeting, goodwill, or courtesy usu. by word or gesture

sa·lu·ta·to·ri·an \sə-ˌlüt-ə-'tōr-ē-ən\ *n* : the student having the 2nd highest rank in a graduating class who delivers the salutatory address

sa·lu·ta·to·ry \sə-'lüt-ə-ˌtōr-ē\ *adj* : relating to or being the welcoming oration delivered at an academic commencement

¹sa·lute \sə-'lüt\ *vb* **sa·lut·ed; sa·lut·ing** **1** : GREET **2** : to honor by special ceremonies **3** : to show respect to (a superior officer) by a formal position of hand, rifle, or sword

²salute *n* **1** : GREETING **2** : the formal position assumed in saluting a superior

¹sal·vage \'sal-vij\ *n* **1** : money paid for saving a ship, its cargo, or passengers when the ship is wrecked or in danger **2** : the saving of a ship **3** : the saving of possessions in danger of being lost **4** : things saved from loss or destruction (as by a wreck or fire)

²salvage *vb* **sal·vaged; sal·vag·ing** : to rescue from destruction

sal·va·tion \sal-'vā-shən\ *n* **1** : the saving of a person from sin or its consequences esp. in the life after death **2** : the saving from danger, difficulty, or evil **3** : something that saves

¹salve \'sav, 'sàv\ *n* : a medicinal ointment

²salve *vb* **salved; salv·ing** : EASE, SOOTHE

sal·ver \'sal-vər\ *n* [F *salve*, fr. Sp *salva* sampling of food to detect poison, tray, fr. *salvar* to save, sample food to detect poison, fr. LL *salvare* to save, fr. L *salvus* safe] : a small serving tray

sal·vo \'sal-vō\ *n, pl* **salvos** *or* **salvoes** : a simultaneous discharge of guns

Sam *or* **Saml** *abbr* Samuel

SAM \'sam, ˌes-ˌā-'em\ *n* [*surface-to-air missile*] : a guided missile for use against aircraft by ground units

sa·mar·i·um \sə-'mer-ē-əm\ *n* : a pale gray lustrous metallic chemical element

¹same \'sām\ *adj* **1** : being the one referred to : not different **2** : SIMILAR syn identical, equivalent, equal, tantamount — **same·ness** *n*

²same *pron* : the same one or ones

³same *adv* : in the same manner

sam·o·var \'sam-ə-ˌvär\ *n* [Russ. fr. *samo-* self + *varit'* to boil] : an urn with a spigot at the base used esp. in Russia to boil water for tea

sam·pan \'sam-ˌpan\ *n* : a flat-bottomed skiff of the Far East usu. propelled by two short oars

¹sam·ple \'sam-pəl\ *n* : a piece or item that shows the quality of the whole from which it was taken : EXAMPLE, SPECIMEN

²sample *vb* **sam·pled; sam·pling** \-p(ə-)liŋ\ : to judge the quality of by a sample

sam·pler \'sam-plər\ *n* : a piece of needlework; *esp* : one testing skill in embroidering

Sam·u·el \'sam-yə(-wə)l\ *n* — see BIBLE table

sam·u·rai \'sam-(y)ə-ˌrī\ *n, pl* **samurai** : a member of a Japanese feudal warrior class practicing a chivalric code

san·a·to·ri·um \ˌsan-ə-'tōr-ē-əm\ *n, pl* **-riums** *or* **-ria** \-ē-ə\ **1** : a health resort **2** : an establishment for the care esp. of convalescents or the chronically ill

sanc·ti·fy \'saŋk-tə-ˌfī\ *vb* **-fied; -fy·ing**

1 : to make holy : CONSECRATE 2 : to free from sin — **sanc·ti·fi·ca·tion** \ˌsaŋk-tə-fə-ˈkā-shən\ n

sanc·ti·mo·nious \ˌsaŋk-tə-ˈmō-nē-əs\ adj : hypocritically pious — **sanc·ti·mo·nious·ly** adv

¹**sanc·tion** \ˈsaŋk-shən\ n 1 : authoritative approval 2 : a measure (as a threat or fine) designed to enforce a law or standard (economic ~s)

²**sanction** vb **sanc·tioned; sanc·tion·ing** \-sh(ə-)niŋ\ : to give approval to : RATIFY **syn** endorse, accredit, certify, approve

sanc·ti·ty \ˈsaŋk-tət-ē\ n, pl **-ties** 1 : GODLINESS 2 : SACREDNESS

sanc·tu·ary \ˈsaŋk-chə-ˌwer-ē\ n, pl **-ar·ies** 1 : a consecrated place (as the part of a church in which the altar is placed) 2 : a place of refuge (bird ~)

sanc·tum \ˈsaŋk-təm\ n, pl **sanctums** also **sanc·ta** \-tə\ : a private office or study : DEN (an editor's ~)

¹**sand** \ˈsand\ n : loose particles of hard broken rock — **sandy** adj

²**sand** vb 1 : to cover or fill with sand 2 : to scour, smooth, or polish with an abrasive (as sandpaper) — **sand·er** n

san·dal \ˈsan-dᵊl\ n : a shoe consisting of a sole strapped to the foot; also : a low or open slipper or rubber overshoe

san·dal·wood \-ˌwu̇d\ n : the fragrant yellowish heartwood of a parasitic tree of southeastern Asia that is much used in ornamental carving and cabinetwork; also : the tree

sand·bag \ˈsan(d)-ˌbag\ n : a bag filled with sand and used in fortifications, as ballast, or as a weapon

sand·bank \-ˌbaŋk\ n : a deposit of sand (as in a bar or shoal)

sand·bar \-ˌbär\ n : a ridge of sand formed in water by tides or currents

sand·blast \-ˌblast\ n : sand blown (as for cleaning stone) by air or steam — **sandblast** vb — **sand·blast·er** n

sand·hog \ˈsand-ˌhȯg, -ˌhäg\ n : a laborer who builds underwater tunnels

sand·lot \ˈsan(d)-ˌlät\ n : a vacant lot esp. when used for the unorganized sports of children — **sand·lot** adj — **sand·lot·ter** n

sand·man \-ˌman\ n : the genie of folklore who makes children sleepy

sand·pa·per \-ˌpā-pər\ n : paper with abrasive (as sand) glued on one side used in smoothing and polishing surfaces — **sandpaper** vb

sand·pip·er \-ˌpī-pər\ n : any of numerous shorebirds with a soft-tipped bill longer than that of the related plovers

sand·stone \-ˌstōn\ n : rock made of sand held together by a natural cement

sand·storm \-ˌstȯrm\ n : a windstorm that drives clouds of sand

sand trap n : a hazard on a golf course consisting of a hollow containing sand

¹**sand·wich** \ˈsand-(ˌ)wich\ n [after John Montagu, 4th Earl of Sandwich †1792

Eng. diplomat] 1 : two or more slices of bread with a layer (as of meat or cheese) spread between them 2 : something resembling a sandwich

²**sandwich** vb : to squeeze or crowd in

sane \ˈsān\ adj **san·er; san·est** : mentally sound and healthy; also : SENSIBLE, RATIONAL — **sane·ly** adv

sang past of SING

sang·froid \ˈsäⁿ-ˈfrwä\ n [F sang-froid, lit., cold blood] : self-possession or an imperturbable state esp. under strain

san·gui·nary \ˈsaŋ-gwə-ˌner-ē\ adj : BLOODY (~ battle)

san·guine \ˈsaŋ-gwən\ adj 1 : RUDDY 2 : CHEERFUL, HOPEFUL

sanit abbr sanitary: sanitation

san·i·tar·i·an \ˌsan-ə-ˈter-ē-ən\ n : a specialist in sanitation and public health

san·i·tar·i·um \ˌsan-ə-ˈter-ē-əm\ n, pl **-i·ums** or **-ia** \-ē-ə\ : SANATORIUM

san·i·tary \ˈsan-ə-ˌter-ē\ adj 1 : of or relating to health : HYGIENIC 2 : free from filth or infective matter

sanitary napkin n : a disposable absorbent pad used to absorb uterine flow (as during menstruation)

san·i·ta·tion \ˌsan-ə-ˈtā-shən\ n : a making sanitary; also : protection of health by maintenance of sanitary conditions

san·i·tize \ˈsan-ə-ˌtīz\ vb **-tized; -tiz·ing** 1 : to make sanitary 2 : to make more acceptable by removing unpleasant features

san·i·ty \ˈsan-ət-ē\ n : soundness of mind

sank past of SINK

sans \(ˌ)sanz\ prep : WITHOUT

San·skrit \ˈsan-ˌskrit\ n : an ancient language that is the classical language of India and of Hinduism — **Sanskrit** adj

San·ta Ana \ˌsant-ə-ˈan-ə\ n [Santa Ana mountains in southern Calif.] : a hot dry wind from the north, northeast, or east in southern California

¹**sap** \ˈsap\ n : a vital fluid; esp : a watery fluid that circulates through a vascular plant — **sap·less** adj

²**sap** vb **sapped; sap·ping** 1 : UNDERMINE 2 : to weaken gradually

sa·pi·ent \ˈsā-pē-ənt, ˈsap-ē-\ adj : WISE, DISCERNING — **sa·pi·ence** \-əns\ n

sap·ling \ˈsap-liŋ\ n : a young tree

sap·phire \ˈsaf-ˌī(ə)r\ n [ME safir, fr. OF, fr. L sapphirus, fr. Gk sappheiros, fr. Heb sappīr, fr. Skt śanipriya, lit., dear to the planet Saturn, fr. Sani Saturn + priya dear] : a hard transparent bright blue precious stone

sap·py \ˈsap-ē\ adj **sap·pi·er; -est** 1 : full of sap 2 : SILLY, FOOLISH

sap·ro·phyte \ˈsap-rə-ˌfīt\ n : a living thing and esp. a plant living on dead or decaying organic matter — **sap·ro·phyt·ic** \ˌsap-rə-ˈfit-ik\ adj

sap·suck·er \'sap-ˌsek-ər\ *n* : any of several small American woodpeckers

sap·wood \-ˌwud\ *n* : the younger active and usu. lighter and softer outer layer of wood (as of a tree trunk)

sar·casm \'sär-ˌkaz-əm\ *n* 1 : a cutting or contemptuous remark 2 : ironic criticism or reproach — **sar·cas·tic** \sär-ˈkas-tik\ *adj* — **sar·cas·ti·cal·ly** \-ti-k(ə-)lē\ *adv*

sar·coph·a·gus \sär-ˈkäf-ə-gəs\ *n, pl* -**gi** \-ˌgī, -ˌjī\ *also* -**gus·es** [L *sarcophagus* (*lapis*) limestone used for coffins, fr. Gk (*lithos*) *sarkophagos*, lit., flesh-eating stone, fr. *sark-*, *sarx* flesh + *phagein* to eat] : a large stone coffin

sar·dine \sär-ˈdēn\ *n, pl* **sardines** *also* **sardine** : a young or small fish preserved esp. in oil for use as food

sar·don·ic \sär-ˈdän-ik\ *adj* : expressing scorn or mockery : bitterly disdainful **syn** ironic, satiric, sarcastic — **sar·don·i·cal·ly** \-i-k(ə-)lē\ *adv*

sa·ri *also* **sa·ree** \'sär-ē\ *n* [Hindi *sārī*] : a garment of southern Asian women that consists of a long cloth draped around the body and head or shoulder

sa·rong \sə-ˈròŋ, -ˈräŋ\ *n* : a loose skirt wrapped around the body and worn by men and women of the Malay archipelago and the Pacific islands

sar·sa·pa·ril·la \ˌsas-(ə-)pe-ˈril-ə, ˌsärs-\ *n* 1 : the root of a tropical American smilax used esp. for flavoring; *also* : the plant 2 : a sweetened carbonated beverage flavored with sassafras and an oil from a birch

sar·to·ri·al \sär-ˈtōr-ē-əl\ *adj* : of or relating to a tailor or tailored clothes — **sar·to·ri·al·ly** \-ē\ *adv*

SASE *abbr* self-addressed stamped envelope

¹**sash** \'sash\ *n* : a broad band worn around the waist or over the shoulder

²**sash** *n, pl* **sash** *also* **sash·es** : a frame for a pane of glass in a door or window; *also* : the movable part of a window

sa·shay \sa-ˈshā\ *vb* 1 : WALK, GLIDE, GO 2 : to strut or move about in an ostentatious manner 3 : to proceed in a diagonal or sideways manner

Sask *abbr* Saskatchewan

Sas·quatch \'sas-ˌkwach, -ˌkwäch\ *n* [from Salish (an American Indian language) *se'sxac* wild men] : a hairy manlike creature reported to exist in the northwestern U.S. and western Canada and said to be a very tall primate

sas·sa·fras \'sas-ə-ˌfras\ *n* [Sp *sasafrás*] : a No. American tree related to the laurel; *also* : its dried bark now known to have carcinogenic properties

sassy \'sas-ē\ *adj* **sass·i·er; -est** : SAUCY

¹**sat** *past and past part of* SIT

²**sat** *abbr* saturate; saturation

Sat *abbr* Saturday

Sa·tan \'sāt-ᵊn\ *n* : DEVIL

sa·tang \sə-ˈtäŋ\ *n, pl* **satang** *or* **satangs** — see *baht* at MONEY table

sa·tan·ic \sə-ˈtan-ik, sā-\ *adj* 1 : of or resembling Satan 2 : extremely malicious or wicked — **sa·tan·i·cal·ly** \-i-k(ə-)lē\ *adv*

satch·el \'sach-əl\ *n* : TRAVELING BAG

sate \'sāt\ *vb* **sat·ed; sat·ing** : to satisfy to the full; *also* : SURFEIT, GLUT

sa·teen \sa-ˈtēn, sə-\ *n* : a cotton cloth finished to resemble satin

sat·el·lite \'sat-ᵊl-ˌīt\ *n* 1 : an obsequious follower of a prince or distinguished person : TOADY 2 : a celestial body that orbits a larger body 3 : a man-made object that orbits a celestial body

sa·ti·ate \'sā-shē-ˌāt\ *vb* -**at·ed; -at·ing** : to satisfy fully or to excess

sa·ti·ety \sə-ˈtī-ət-ē\ *n* : fullness to the point of excess

sat·in \'sat-ᵊn\ *n* : a fabric (as of silk) with a glossy surface — **sat·iny** *adj*

sat·in·wood \'sat-ᵊn-ˌwud\ *n* : a hard yellowish brown wood of satiny luster; *also* : a tree yielding this wood

sat·ire \'sa-ˌtī(ə)r\ *n* : biting wit, irony, or sarcasm used to expose vice or folly; *also* : a literary work having these qualities — **sa·tir·ic** \sə-ˈtir-ik\ *or* **sa·tir·i·cal** \-i-kəl\ *adj* — **sa·tir·i·cal·ly** \-ē\ *adv* — **sat·i·rist** \'sat-ə-rəst\ *n* — **sat·i·rize** \-ə-ˌrīz\ *vb*

sat·is·fac·tion \ˌsat-əs-ˈfak-shən\ *n* 1 : payment through penance of punishment incurred by sin 2 : CONTENTMENT, GRATIFICATION 3 : reparation for an insult 4 : settlement of a claim

sat·is·fac·to·ry \-ˈfak-t(ə-)rē\ *adj* : giving satisfaction : ADEQUATE — **sat·is·fac·to·ri·ly** \-ˈfak-t(ə-)rə-lē\ *adv*

sat·is·fy \'sat-əs-ˌfī\ *vb* -**fied; -fy·ing** 1 : to make happy : GRATIFY 2 : to pay what is due to 3 : to answer or discharge (a claim) in full 4 : CONVINCE 5 : to meet the requirements of — **sat·is·fy·ing·ly** *adv*

sa·trap \'sā-ˌtrap, 'sa-\ *n* [ME, fr. L *satrapes*, fr. Gk *satrapēs*, fr. OPer *xshathrapāvan*, lit., protector of the dominion] : a petty prince : subordinate ruler

sat·u·rate \'sach-ə-ˌrāt\ *vb* -**rat·ed; -rat·ing** 1 : to soak thoroughly 2 : to treat or charge with something to the point where no more can be absorbed, dissolved, or retained (water *saturated* with salt) — **sat·u·ra·ble** \'sach-(ə-)rə-bəl\ *adj* — **sat·u·ra·tion** \ˌsach-ə-ˈrā-shən\ *n*

Sat·ur·day \'sat-ər-dē, -ˌdā\ *n* : the 7th day of the week

Saturday night special *n* : a cheap easily concealed handgun

Sat·urn \'sat-ərn\ *n* : the planet 6th in order from the sun

sat·ur·nine \'sat-ər-ˌnīn\ *adj* : SULLEN, SARDONIC

sa·tyr \'sāt-ər\ *n* 1 *often cap* : a woodland deity in Greek mythology having certain characteristics of a horse or goat **2** : a lecherous man

1sauce \\'sȯs, *3 usu* 'säs\ *n* **1** : a dressing for salads, meats, or puddings **2** : stewed fruit **3** : IMPUDENCE

2sauce \\'sȯs, *2 usu* 'säs\ *vb* **sauced; saucing 1** : to add zest to **2** : to be impudent to

sauce·pan \\'sȯs-ˌpan\ *n* : a cooking pan with a long handle

sau·cer \\'sȯ-sər\ *n* : a rounded shallow dish for use under a cup

saucy \\'sȯs-ē, 'säs-\ *adj* **sau·ci·er; -est** : IMPUDENT, PERT — **sauc·i·ly** \-ə-lē\ *adv* — **sauc·i·ness** \-ē-nəs\ *n*

sau·er·kraut \\'saú-(ə)r-ˌkraút\ *n* [G, fr. *sauer* sour + *kraut* cabbage] : finely cut cabbage fermented in brine

sau·na \\'saú-nə\ *n* **1** : a Finnish steam bath in which the steam is provided by water thrown on hot stones **2** : a dry heat bath; *also* : a room or cabinet used for such a bath

saun·ter \\'sȯnt-ər, 'sänt-\ *vb* : STROLL

sau·sage \\'sȯ-sij\ *n* [deriv. of LL *salsicia*, fr. L *salsus* salted] : minced and highly seasoned meat (as pork) usu. enclosed in a tubular casing

S Aust *abbr* South Australia

sau·té \sȯ-'tā, sō-\ *vb* **sau·téed** *or* **sau·téd; sau·té·ing** [F] : to fry lightly in a little fat — **sauté** *n*

sau·terne \sō-'tərn, sȯ-\ *n*, *often cap* [F *sauternes*] : a usu. semisweet white wine

1sav·age \\'sav-ij\ *adj* [ME *sauvage*, fr. MF, fr. ML *salvaticus*, fr. L *silvaticus* of the woods, wild, fr. *silva* wood, forest] **1** : WILD, UNTAMED **2** : UNCIVILIZED, BARBAROUS **3** : CRUEL, FIERCE — **sav·age·ly** *adv* — **sav·age·ness** *n* — **sav·age·ry** \-(ə-)rē\ *n*

2savage *n* **1** : a member of a primitive human society **2** : a rude, unmannerly, or brutal person

sa·van·na *or* **sa·van·nah** \sə-'van-ə\ *n* [Sp *zavana*] : grassland containing scattered trees

sa·vant \sa-'vänt, sə-, 'sav-ənt\ *n* : a learned man : SCHOLAR

1save \\'sāv\ *vb* **saved; sav·ing 1** : to redeem from sin **2** : to rescue from danger **3** : to preserve or guard from destruction or loss **4** : to put aside as a store or reserve — **sav·er** *n*

2save *n* : a play that prevents an opponent from scoring or winning

3save \(ˌ)sāv\ *prep* : EXCEPT

4save \(ˌ)sāv\ *conj* : BUT

savings and loan association *n* : a cooperative association that holds savings of members in the form of dividend-bearing shares and that invests chiefly in mortgage loans

savings bank *n* : a bank that holds funds of individual depositors in interest-bearing accounts and makes long-term investments (as in mortgage loans)

savings bond *n* : a registered U.S. bond

issued in denominations of $50 to $10,000

sav·ior *or* **sav·iour** \\'sāv-yər\ *n* **1** : one who saves **2** *cap* : Jesus Christ

sa·voir faire \ˌsav-ˌwär-'far\ *n* [F *savoir-faire*, lit., knowing how to do] : readiness in knowing how to act : TACT

1sa·vor *also* **sa·vour** \\'sā-vər\ *n* **1** : the taste and odor of something **2** : a special flavor or quality — **sa·vory** *adj*

2savor *also* **savour** *vb* **sa·vored; sa·vor·ing** \\'sāv-(ə-)riŋ\ **1** : to have a specified taste, smell, or quality **2** : to taste with pleasure

sa·vo·ry \\'sāv-(ə)-rē\ *n, pl* **-ries** : any of several aromatic mints used in cooking

1sav·vy \\'sav-ē\ *vb* **sav·vied; sav·vy·ing** [modif. of Sp *sabe* he knows] : COMPREHEND, UNDERSTAND

2savvy *n* : practical know-how (political ~)

1saw *past of* SEE

2saw \\'sȯ\ *n* : a cutting tool with a blade having a line of teeth along its edge

3saw *vb* **sawed** \\'sȯd\; **sawed** *or* **sawn** \\'sȯn\; **saw·ing** \\'sȯ-(ⁱ)iŋ\ : to cut or divide with or as if with a saw — **saw·yer** \-yər\ *n*

4saw *n* : a common saying : MAXIM

saw·dust \\'sȯ-(ˌ)dəst\ *n* : fine particles made by a saw in cutting

saw·fly \\'sȯ-ˌflī\ *n* : any of numerous insects belonging to the same order as bees and wasps and including many whose larvae are plant-feeding pests

saw·horse \\'sȯ-ˌhȯrs\ *n* : a rack on which wood is rested while being sawed by hand

saw·mill \-ˌmil\ *n* : a mill for sawing logs

saw palmetto *n* : any of several shrubby palms with spiny-toothed petioles

sax·i·frage \\'sak-sə-frij, -ˌfrāj\ *n* [deriv. of LL *saxifraga*, fr. L, lit., breaking rocks] : any of a genus of plants with showy 5-parted flowers and usu. with leaves growing in tufts close to the ground

sax·o·phone \\'sak-sə-ˌfōn\ *n* : a musical instrument consisting of a conical metal tube with a reed mouthpiece and finger keys — **sax·o·phon·ist** \-əst\ *n*

say \\'sā\ *vb* **said** \\'sed\; **say·ing** \\'sā-iŋ\; **says** \\'sez\ **1** : to express in words (~ what you mean) **2** : to state as opinion or belief **3** : PRONOUNCE; *also* : RECITE, REPEAT (~ your prayers) **4** : INDICATE (the clock ~s noon)

2say *n, pl* **says** \\'sāz\ **1** : an expression of opinion **2** : power of decision

say·ing \\'sā-iŋ\ *n* : a commonly repeated statement

say-so \\'sā-(ˌ)sō\ *n* : an esp. authoritative assertion or decision; *also* : the right to decide

sb *abbr* substantive

Sb *symbol* [L *stibium*] antimony

SB *abbr* [NL *scientiae baccalaureus*] bachelor of science

SBA *abbr* Small Business Administration

sc *abbr* 1 scale 2 scene 3 science

Sc *symbol* scandium

SC *abbr* 1 South Carolina 2 Supreme Court

¹**scab** \'skab\ *n* 1 : scabies of domestic animals 2 : a protective crust over a sore or wound 3 : a worker who replaces a striker or works under conditions not authorized by a union 4 : a plant disease in which crusted spots form on stems or leaves — **scab·by** *adj*

²**scab** *vb* **scabbed; scab·bing** 1 : to become covered with a scab 2 : to work as a scab

scab·bard \'skab-ərd\ *n* : a sheath for the blade of a weapon (as a sword)

sca·bies \'skā-bēz\ *n* [L] : contagious itch or mange caused by mites living as parasites under the skin

sca·brous \'skab-rəs, 'skāb-\ *adj* 1 : DIFFICULT, KNOTTY 2 : rough to the touch : SCALY, SCURFY (a ~ leaf) 3 : dealing with suggestive, indecent, or scandalous themes; *also* : SQUALID

scad \'skad\ *n* 1 : a large number or quantity 2 *pl* : a great abundance

scaf·fold \'skaf-əld, -ˌōld\ *n* 1 : a raised platform for workers to sit or stand on 2 : a platform on which a criminal is executed (as by hanging)

scaf·fold·ing \-iŋ\ *n* : a system of scaffolds; *also* : materials for scaffolds

scal·a·wag \'skal-i-ˌwag\ *n* : RASCAL

¹**scald** \'skȯld\ *vb* 1 : to burn with or as if with hot liquid or steam 2 : to heat to just below the boiling point

²**scald** *n* : a burn caused by scalding

¹**scale** \'skāl\ *n* 1 : either pan of a balance 2 : BALANCE — usu. used in pl. 3 : a weighing instrument

²**scale** *vb* **scaled; scal·ing** : WEIGH

³**scale** *n* 1 : one of the small thin plates that cover the body esp. of a fish or reptile 2 : a thin plate 3 : a thin coating, layer, or incrustation 4 : SCALE INSECT — **scaled** \'skāld\ *adj* — **scale·less** \'skāl-ləs\ *adj* — **scaly** *adj*

⁴**scale** *vb* **scaled; scal·ing** : to strip of scales

⁵**scale** *n* [ME, fr. LL *scala* ladder, staircase, fr. L *scalae*, pl., stairs, rungs, ladder] 1 : something divided into regular spaces as a help in drawing or measuring 2 : a graduated series 3 : the size of a sample (as a model) in proportion to the size of the actual thing 4 : a standard of estimation or judgment 5 : a series of musical tones going up or down in pitch according to a specified scheme

⁶**scale** *vb* **scaled; scal·ing** 1 : to go up by or as if by a ladder 2 : to arrange in a graded series

scale insect *n* : any of numerous small insects that live and are often pests on plants and have wingless scale-covered females

scale·pan \'skāl-ˌpan\ *n* : ¹SCALE 1

scal·lion \'skal-yən\ *n* [deriv. of L *ascalonia* (*caepa*) onion of Ascalon (seaport in Palestine)] : an onion without an enlarged bulb

¹**scal·lop** \'skäl-əp, 'skal-\ *n* 1 : any of a family of marine mollusks with radially ridged shell valves; *also* : a large edible muscle of this mollusk 2 : one of a continuous series of rounded projections forming an edge (as in lace)

²**scallop** *vb* 1 : to edge (as lace) with scallops 2 : to bake in a casserole

¹**scalp** \'skalp\ *n* : the part of the skin and flesh of the head usu. covered with hair

²**scalp** *vb* 1 : to remove the scalp from 2 : to obtain for the sake of reselling at greatly increased prices — **scalp·er** *n*

scal·pel \'skal-pəl\ *n* : a small straight knife with a thin blade used esp. in surgery

scam \'skam\ *n* : a fraudulent or deceptive act or operation

scamp \'skamp\ *n* : RASCAL

scam·per \'skam-pər\ *vb* **scam·pered; scam·per·ing** \-p(ə-)riŋ\ : to run nimbly and playfully — **scamper** *n*

scam·pi \'skam-pē\ *n, pl* **scampi** [It] : SHRIMP; *esp* : large shrimp prepared with a garlic-flavored sauce

¹**scan** \'skan\ *vb* **scanned; scan·ning** 1 : to read (verses) so as to show metrical structure 2 : to examine closely 3 : to move an electromagnetic beam across esp. in a regular pattern 4 : to make a scan of (as the human body) **syn** scrutinize, inspect, examine — **scan·ner** \'skan-ər\ *n*

²**scan** *n* 1 : the act or process of scanning 2 : a picture of the distribution of radioactive material in something; *also* : a picture of part of the body made by combining separate pictures taken from different angles or of different sections

Scand *abbr* Scandinavia; Scandinavian

scan·dal \'skan-dᵊl\ *n* [LL *scandalum* stumbling block, offense, fr. Gk *skandalon*] 1 : DISGRACE, DISHONOR 2 : malicious gossip : SLANDER — **scan·dal·ize** *vb* — **scan·dal·ous** *adj* — **scan·dal·ous·ly** *adv*

scan·dal·mon·ger \-ˌməŋ-gər, -ˌmäŋ-\ *n* : a person who circulates scandal

Scan·di·na·vian \ˌskan-də-'nā-vē-ən\ *n* : a native or inhabitant of Scandinavia — **Scandinavian** *adj*

scan·di·um \'skan-dē-əm\ *n* : a white metallic chemical element

¹**scant** \'skant\ *adj* 1 : barely sufficient 2 : having scarcely enough **syn** scanty, skimpy, meager, sparse, exiguous

²**scant** *vb* 1 : SKIMP 2 : STINT

scant·ling \'skant-liŋ\ *n* : a piece of lumber; *esp* : one used for an upright in building

scanty \'skant-ē\ *adj* **scant·i·er; -est** : barely sufficient : SCANT — **scant·i·ly** \'skant-ə-lē\ *adv* — **scant·i·ness** \-ē-nəs\ *n*

scape·goat \'skāp-ˌgōt\ *n* : one that bears the blame for others

scape·grace \-ˌgrās\ *n* [*scape* (escape)] : an incorrigible rascal

scap·u·la \'skap-yə-lə\ *n, pl* **-lae** \-ˌlē\ *or* **-las** [L] : SHOULDER BLADE

scap·u·lar \-lər\ *adj* : of or relating to the shoulder or shoulder blade

scar \'skär\ *n* : a mark left after injured tissue has healed — **scar** *vb*

scar·ab \'skar-əb\ *n* [MF *scarabee*, fr. L *scarabaeus*] : any of a family of large stout beetles; *also* : an ornament (as a gem) representing such a beetle

scarce \'skears\ *adj* **scarc·er**; **scarc·est** 1 : not plentiful 2 : RARE — **scar·ci·ty** \'sker-sət-ē\ *n*

scarce·ly \'skears-lē\ *adv* 1 : BARELY 2 : almost not 3 : very probably not

¹**scare** \'skear\ *vb* **scared**; **scar·ing** : FRIGHTEN, STARTLE

²**scare** *n* : FRIGHT — **scary** *adj*

scare·crow \'skear-ˌkrō\ *n* : a crude figure set up to scare birds away from crops

¹**scarf** \'skärf\ *n, pl* **scarves** \'skärvz\ *or* **scarfs** 1 : a broad band (as of cloth) worn about the shoulders, around the neck, over the head, or about the waist 2 : a long narrow cloth cover for a table or dresser top

²**scarf** *vb* [alter. of earlier *scoff* eat greedily] : to eat greedily

scar·i·fy \'skar-ə-ˌfī\ *vb* **-fied**; **-fy·ing** 1 : to make scratches or small cuts in : wound superficially (~ skin for vaccination) (~ seeds to help them germinate) 2 : to lacerate the feelings of : FLAY — **scar·i·fi·ca·tion** \ˌskar-ə-fə-'kā-shən\ *n*

scar·la·ti·na \ˌskär-lə-'tē-nə\ *n* : SCARLET FEVER

scar·let \'skär-lət\ *n* : a bright red — **scarlet** *adj*

scarlet fever *n* : an acute contagious disease marked by fever, sore throat, and red rash and caused by certain streptococci

scarp \'skärp\ *n* : a line of cliffs produced by faulting or erosion

scath·ing \'skā-thiŋ\ *adj* : bitterly severe

scat·o·log·i·cal \ˌskat-ᵊl-'äj-i-kəl\ *adj* : concerned with obscene matters

scat·ter \'skat-ər\ *vb* 1 : to distribute or strew about irregularly 2 : DISPERSE

scav·enge \'skav-ənj\ *vb* **scav·enged**; **scav·eng·ing** : to work or function as a scavenger

scav·en·ger \'skav-ən-jər\ *n* [alter. of earlier *scavager*, fr. ME *skawager* collector of a toll on goods sold by nonresident merchants, fr. *skawage* toll on goods sold by nonresident merchants, fr. OF *escauwage* inspection] : a person or animal that collects or disposes of refuse or waste

sce·nar·io \sə-'nar-ē-ˌō\ *n, pl* **-i·os** : the plot or outline of a dramatic work; *also* : an account of a projected action

scene \'sēn\ *n* [MF, stage, fr. L *scena*, *scaena* stage, scene, fr. Gk *skēnē* temporary shelter, tent, building forming the background for a dramatic performance, stage] 1 : a division of one act of a play 2 : a single situation or sequence in a play or motion picture 3 : a stage setting 4 : VIEW, PROSPECT 5 : the place of an occurrence or action 6 : a display of strong feeling and esp. anger 7 : a sphere of activity (the fashion ~) — **sce·nic** \'sēn-ik\ *adj*

scen·ery \'sēn-(ə-)rē\ *n, pl* **-er·ies** 1 : the painted scenes or hangings of a stage and the fittings that go with them 2 : a picturesque view or landscape

¹**scent** \'sent\ *n* 1 : ODOR, SMELL 2 : sense of smell 3 : course of pursuit : TRACK 4 : PERFUME 2 — **scent·less** *adj*

²**scent** *vb* 1 : SMELL 2 : to imbue or fill with odor

scep·ter \'sep-tər\ *n* : a staff borne by a sovereign as an emblem of authority

scep·tic \'skep-tik\ *var of* SKEPTIC

sch *abbr* school

¹**sched·ule** \'skej-ül, *esp Brit* 'shed-yül\ *n* 1 : a list of items or details 2 : TIMETABLE

²**schedule** *vb* **sched·uled**; **sched·ul·ing** : to make a schedule of; *also* : to enter on a schedule

sche·mat·ic \ski-'mat-ik\ *adj* : of or relating to a scheme or diagram : DIAGRAMMATIC — **schematic** *n* — **sche·mat·i·cal·ly** \-i-k(ə-)lē\ *adv*

¹**scheme** \'skēm\ *n* 1 : a plan for doing something; *esp* : a crafty plot 2 : a systematic design

²**scheme** *vb* **schemed**; **schem·ing** : to form a plot : INTRIGUE — **schem·er** *n* — **schem·ing** *adj*

Schick test \'shik-\ *n* : a serological test for susceptibility to diphtheria

schil·ling \'shil-iŋ\ *n* — see MONEY table

schism \'siz-əm, 'skiz-\ *n* 1 : DIVISION, SPLIT; *also* : DISCORD, DISSENSION 2 : a formal division in or separation from a religious body 3 : the offense of promoting schism

schis·mat·ic \siz-'mat-ik, skiz-\ *n* : one who creates or takes part in schism — **schismatic** *adj*

schist \'shist\ *n* : a metamorphic crystalline rock

schizo·phre·nia \ˌskit-sə-'frē-nē-ə\ *n* [NL, fr. Gk *schizein* to split + *phrēn* diaphragm, mind] : a psychotic disorder that is characterized by a twisted view of the real world, by a greatly reduced ability to carry out one's daily tasks, and by abnormal ways of thinking, feeling, and behaving — **schiz·oid** \'skit-ˌsȯid\ *adj or n* — **schizo·phren·ic** \ˌskit-sə-'fren-ik\ *adj or n*

schle·miel \shlə-'mēl\ *n* : an unlucky bungler : CHUMP

schmaltz *also* **schmalz** \'shmȯlts, 'shmälts\ *n* [Yiddish *shmalts*, lit., rendered fat] : sentimental or florid music or art — **schmaltzy** *adj*

schnau·zer \'shnaȯt-sər, 's(h)naȯ-zər\ *n*

[G, fr. *schnauze* snout] : a dog of any of three breeds that are characterized by a long head, small ears, heavy eyebrows, mustache and beard, and a wiry coat

schol·ar \ˈskäl-ər\ *n* 1 : STUDENT, PUPIL 2 : a learned man : SAVANT — **schol·ar·ly** *adj*

schol·ar·ship \-ˌship\ *n* 1 : the qualities or learning of a scholar 2 : money awarded to a student to help pay for further education

scho·las·tic \skə-ˈlas-tik\ *adj* : of or relating to schools, scholars, or scholarship

¹**school** \ˈskül\ *n* 1 : an institution for teaching and learning; *also* : the pupils in attendance 2 : a body of persons of like opinions or beliefs (the radical ∼)

²**school** *vb* : TEACH, TRAIN, DRILL

³**school** *n* : a large number of one kind of water animal swimming and feeding together

school·boy \-ˌbȯi\ *n* : a boy attending school

school·fel·low \-ˌfel-ō\ *n* : SCHOOLMATE

school·girl \-ˌgərl\ *n* : a girl attending school

school·house \-ˌhaus\ *n* : a building used as a school

school·marm \-ˌmä(r)m\ *or* **school·ma'am** \-ˌmäm, -ˌmam\ *n* 1 : a woman schoolteacher 2 : a person who exhibits characteristics popularly attributed to schoolteachers

school·mas·ter \-ˌmas-tər\ *n* : a male schoolteacher

school·mate \-ˌmāt\ *n* : a school companion

school·mis·tress \-ˌmis-trəs\ *n* : a woman schoolteacher

school·room \-ˌrüm, -ˌrum\ *n* : CLASSROOM

school·teach·er \-ˌtē-chər\ *n* : one who teaches in a school

schoo·ner \ˈskü-nər\ *n* : a fore-and-aft rigged sailing ship

schuss \ˈshus, ˈshüs\ *vb* [G] : to ski down a slope at high speed — **schuss** *n*

sci *abbr* science; scientific

sci·at·i·ca \sī-ˈat-i-kə\ *n* : pain in the region of the hips or along the course of the nerve at the back of the thigh

sci·ence \ˈsī-əns\ *n* [ME, fr. MF, fr. L *scientia*, fr. *scient-, sciens* having knowledge, fr. prp. of *scire* to know] 1 : an area of knowledge that is an object of study; *esp* : NATURAL SCIENCE 2 : knowledge covering general truths or the operation of general laws especially as obtained and tested through the scientific method — **sci·en·tif·ic** \ˌsī-ən-ˈtif-ik\ *adj* — **sci·en·tif·i·cal·ly** \-i-k(ə-)lē\ *adv* — **sci·en·tist** \ˈsī-ənt-əst\ *n*

science fiction *n* : fiction dealing principally with the impact of actual or imagined science on society or individuals

scientific method *n* : the rules and methods for the pursuit of knowledge involving the finding and stating of a problem, the collection of facts through observation and experiment, and the making and testing of ideas that need to be proven right or wrong

scim·i·tar \ˈsim-ət-ər\ *n* : a curved sword used chiefly by Arabs and Turks

scin·til·la \sin-ˈtil-ə\ *n* : SPARK, TRACE

scin·til·late \ˈsint-ᵊl-ˌāt\ *vb* **-lat·ed; -lat·ing** : SPARKLE, GLEAM — **scin·til·la·tion** \ˌsint-ᵊl-ˈā-shən\ *n*

sci·on \ˈsī-ən\ *n* 1 : a shoot of a plant joined to a stock in grafting 2 : DESCENDANT

scis·sors \ˈsiz-ərz\ *n pl* : a cutting instrument like shears but usu. smaller

scissors kick *n* : a swimming kick in which the legs move like scissors

scle·ro·sis \sklə-ˈrō-səs\ *n* : a usu. abnormal hardening of tissue (as of an artery) — **scle·rot·ic** \-ˈrät-ik\ *adj*

scoff \ˈskäf\ *vb* : MOCK, JEER — **scoff·er** *n*

scoff·law \-ˌlȯ\ *n* : a contemptuous law violator

¹**scold** \ˈskōld\ *n* : a person who scolds

²**scold** *vb* : to censure severely or angrily

sconce \ˈskäns\ *n* : a candlestick or an electric light fixture bracketed to a wall

scone \ˈskōn, ˈskän\ *n* : a biscuit (as of oatmeal) baked on a griddle

¹**scoop** \ˈsküp\ *n* 1 : a large shovel; *also* : a shovellike utensil (a sugar ∼) 2 : an act of scooping 3 : information of immediate interest

²**scoop** *vb* 1 : to take out or up or empty with or as if with a scoop 2 : to make hollow 3 : to report a news item in advance of

scoot \ˈsküt\ *vb* : to go suddenly and swiftly

scoot·er \ˈsküt-ər\ *n* 1 : a child's vehicle consisting of a narrow board mounted between two wheels tandem with an upright steering handle attached to the front wheel 2 : MOTOR SCOOTER

¹**scope** \ˈskōp\ *n* [It *scopo* purpose, goal, fr. Gk *skopos*, fr. *skeptesthai* to watch, look at] 1 : space or opportunity for action or thought 2 : extent covered : RANGE

²**scope** *n* : an instrument (as a microscope or radarscope) for viewing

scorch \ˈskȯrch\ *vb* : to burn the surface of; *also* : to dry or shrivel with heat (∼ed lawns)

¹**score** \ˈskȯr\ *n, pl* **scores** 1 *or pl* **score** : TWENTY 2 : CUT, SCRATCH, SLASH 3 : a record of points made (as in a game) 4 : DEBT 5 : REASON, GROUND 6 : the music of a composition or arrangement with different parts indicated 7 : success in obtaining something (as drugs) esp. illegally

²**score** *vb* **scored; scor·ing** 1 : RECORD 2 : to keep score in a game 3 : to mark with lines, grooves, scratches, or notches 4 : to gain or tally in or as if in

a game ⟨*scored* a point⟩ **5** : to assign a grade or score to ⟨~ the tests⟩ **6** : to compose a score for **7** : SUCCEED — **score-less** *adj* — **scor-er** *n*

sco-ria \'skōr-ē-ə\ *n, pl* **-ri-ae** \-ē-ˌē, -ˌē\ [L] : a rough cindery lava

¹**scorn** \'skȯrn\ *n* : an emotion involving both anger and disgust : CONTEMPT — **scorn-ful** \-fəl\ *adj* — **scorn-ful-ly** \-ē\ *adv*

²**scorn** *vb* : to hold in contempt : DISDAIN — **scorn-er** *n*

Scor-pio \'skȯr-pē-ˌō\ *n* [L, lit., scorpion] **1** : a zodiacal constellation between Libra and Sagittarius usu. pictured as a scorpion **2** : the 8th sign of the zodiac in astrology; *also* : one born under this sign

scor-pi-on \'skȯr-pē-ən\ *n* : any of an order of arthropods related to the spiders and having a poisonous sting at the tip of a long jointed tail

¹**Scot** \'skät\ *n* : a native or inhabitant of Scotland

²**Scot** *abbr* Scotland; Scottish

Scotch \'skäch\ *n* **1** : SCOTS **2** **Scotch** *pl* : the people of Scotland **3** : a whiskey distilled in Scotland esp. from malted barley — **Scotch** *adj* — **Scotch-man** \-mən\ *n* — **Scotch-wom-an** \-ˌwu̇m-ən\ *n*

Scotch pine *n* : a pine that is naturalized in the U.S. from northern Europe and Asia and is a valuable timber tree

scot-free \'skät-'frē\ *adj* : free from obligation, harm, or penalty

Scots \'skäts\ *n* : the English language of Scotland

Scots-man \'skäts-mən\ *n* : SCOTCHMAN

Scots-wom-an \-ˌwu̇-mən\ *n* : SCOTCHWOMAN

Scot-tish \'skät-ish\ *adj* : SCOTCH

scoun-drel \'skaùn-drəl\ *n* : a mean or wicked person : VILLAIN

¹**scour** \'skaù(ə)r\ *vb* **1** : to move rapidly through : RUSH **2** : to examine thoroughly

²**scour** *vb* **1** : to rub (as with a gritty substance) in order to clean **2** : to cleanse by or as if by rubbing

¹**scourge** \'skərj\ *n* **1** : LASH, WHIP **2** : PUNISHMENT; *also* : a cause of affliction (as a plague)

²**scourge** *vb* **scourged; scourg-ing 1** : LASH, FLOG **2** : to punish severely

¹**scout** \'skaùt\ *vb* [ME *scouten*, fr. MF *escouter* to listen, fr. L *auscultare*] **1** : to look around : RECONNOITER **2** : to inspect or observe to get information

²**scout** *n* **1** : a person sent out to get information; *also* : a soldier, airplane, or ship sent out to reconnoiter **2** : a member of either of two youth organizations (**Boy Scouts, Girl Scouts**) — **scout-mas-ter** \-ˌmas-tər\ *n*

³**scout** *vb* : SCORN, SCOFF

scow \'skaù\ *n* : a large flat-bottomed boat with square ends

scowl \'skaùl\ *vb* : to draw down the forehead and make a face in expression of displeasure — **scowl** *n*

SCPO *abbr* senior chief petty officer

scrab-ble \'skrab-əl\ *vb* **scrab-bled; scrab-bling** \-(ə-)liŋ\ **1** : SCRAPE, SCRATCH **2** : CLAMBER, SCRAMBLE **3** : to work hard and long **4** : SCRIBBLE — **scrabble** *n* — **scrab-bler** \(ə-)lər\ *n*

scrag-gly \'skrag-lē\ *adj* : IRREGULAR; *also* : RAGGED, UNKEMPT

scram \'skram\ *vb* **scrammed; scram-ming** : to go away at once

scram-ble \'skram-bəl\ *vb* **scram-bled; scram-bling** \-b(ə-)liŋ\ **1** : to clamber clumsily around **2** : to struggle for or as if for possession of something **3** : to spread irregularly **4** : to mix together **5** : to prepare (eggs) by stirring during frying — **scramble** *n*

¹**scrap** \'skrap\ *n* **1** : FRAGMENT, PIECE **2** : discarded material : REFUSE

²**scrap** *vb* **scrapped; scrap-ping 1** : to make into scrap ⟨~ a battleship⟩ **2** : to get rid of as useless

³**scrap** *n* : FIGHT

⁴**scrap** *vb* **scrapped; scrap-ping** : FIGHT, QUARREL — **scrap-per** *n*

scrap-book \'skrap-ˌbu̇k\ *n* : a blank book in which mementos are kept

¹**scrape** \'skrāp\ *vb* **scraped; scrap-ing 1** : to remove by drawing a knife over; *also* : to clean or smooth by rubbing off the covering **2** : GRATE; *also* : to damage or injure the surface of by contact with something rough **3** : to scrape something with a grating sound **4** : to get together (money) by strict economy **5** : to get along with difficulty — **scrap-er** *n*

²**scrape** *n* **1** : the act or the effect of scraping **2** : a bow accompanied by a drawing back of the foot **3** : an unpleasant predicament

¹**scrap-py** \'skrap-ē\ *adj* **scrap-pi-er; -est** : DISCONNECTED, FRAGMENTARY

²**scrappy** *adj* **scrap-pi-er; -est 1** : QUARRELSOME **2** : having an aggressive and determined spirit

¹**scratch** \'skrach\ *vb* **1** : to scrape, dig, or rub with or as if with claws or nails (a dog ~*ing* at the door) (~*ed* his arm on thorns) **2** : to cause to move or strike roughly and gratingly (~*ed* his nails across the blackboard) **3** : to scrape (as money) together **4** : to cancel or erase by or as if by drawing a line through — **scratchy** *adj*

²**scratch** *n* **1** : a mark made by or as if by scratching; *also* : a sound so made **2** : the starting line in a race **3** : a point at the beginning of a project at which nothing has been done ahead of time (built from ~)

³**scratch** *adj* **1** : made as or used for a trial attempt (~ paper) **2** : made or done by chance (a ~ hit)

scrawl \'skrȯl\ *vb* : to write hastily and carelessly — **scrawl** *n*

scraw-ny \'skrȯ-nē\ *adj* **scraw-ni-er; -est** : very thin : SKINNY

¹**scream** \'skrēm\ *vb* : to cry out loudly and shrilly

²**scream** *n* : a loud shrill cry

scream·ing \'skrēm-iŋ\ *adj* : so striking as to attract notice as if by screaming ⟨~ headlines⟩

screech \'skrēch\ *vb* : SHRIEK — **screech** *n* — **screech·y** \'skrē-chē\ *adj*

¹screen \'skrēn\ *n* **1** : a device or partition used to hide, restrain, protect, or decorate ⟨a wire-mesh window ~⟩; *also* : something that shelters, protects, or conceals **2** : a sieve or perforated material for separating finer from coarser parts (as of sand) **3** : a surface on which an image is made to appear (as in television) **4** : the motion-picture industry

²screen *vb* **1** : to shield with or as if with a screen **2** : to separate with or as if with a screen **3** : to present (as a motion picture) on the screen *syn* hide, conceal, secrete, cover

screen·ing \-iŋ\ *n* : metal or plastic mesh (as for window screens)

¹screw \'skrü\ *n* [ME, fr. MF *escroe* nut, fr. ML *scrofa*, fr. L, sow] **1** : a simple machine consisting of a solid cylinder with a spiral groove around it and a corresponding hollow cylinder into which it fits **2** : a naillike metal piece with a spiral groove and a head with a slot used to fasten pieces of solid material together **3** : PROPELLER

²screw *vb* **1** : to fasten or close by means of a screw **2** : to operate or adjust by means of a screw **3** : to move or cause to move spirally; *also* : to close or set in position by such an action

screw·ball \'skrü-ˌbȯl\ *n* **1** : a baseball pitch breaking in a direction opposite to a curve **2** : a whimsical, eccentric, or crazy person

screw·driv·er \'skrü-ˌdrī-vər\ *n* **1** : a tool for turning screws **2** : a drink made of vodka and orange juice

screwy \'skrü-ē\ *adj* **screw·i·er; -est** **1** : crazily absurd, eccentric, or unusual **2** : CRAZY, INSANE

scrib·ble \'skrib-əl\ *vb* **scrib·bled; scrib·bling** \-(ə-)liŋ\ : to write hastily or carelessly — **scribble** *n* — **scrib·bler** \-(ə-)lər\ *n*

scribe \'skrīb\ *n* **1** : one of a learned class in ancient Palestine serving as copyists, teachers, and jurists **2** : a person whose business is the copying of writing **3** : AUTHOR; *esp* : JOURNALIST

scrim \'skrim\ *n* : a light loosely woven cotton or linen cloth

scrim·mage \'skrim-ij\ *n* : the play between two football teams beginning with the snap of the ball; *also* : practice play between a team's squads — **scrimmage** *vb*

scrimp \'skrimp\ *vb* : to be niggardly : economize greatly ⟨~ and save⟩

scrim·shaw \'skrim-ˌshȯ\ *n* : carved or engraved articles made esp. by American whalers usu. from whalebone or whale ivory — **scrimshaw** *vb*

scrip \'skrip\ *n* **1** : a certificate showing its holder is entitled to something (as stock or land) **2** : paper money issued for temporary use in an emergency

¹script \'skript\ *n* **1** : written matter (as lines for a play or broadcast) **2** : HANDWRITING

²script *abbr* scripture

scrip·ture \'skrip-chər\ *n* **1** *cap* : the books of the Bible — often used in pl. **2** : the sacred writings of a religion — **scrip·tur·al** \'skrip-chə-rəl\ *adj* — **scrip·tur·al·ly** \-ē\ *adv*

scriv·en·er \'skriv-(ə-)nər\ *n* : SCRIBE, WRITER, AUTHOR

scrod \'skräd\ *n* : a young fish (as a cod or haddock); *esp* : one split and boned for cooking

scrof·u·la \'skrȯf-yə-lə\ *n* : tuberculosis of lymph nodes esp. in the neck

scroll \'skrōl\ *n* : a roll of paper or parchment for writing a document; *also* : a spiral or coiled ornamental form suggesting a loosely or partly rolled scroll

scroll saw *n* : JIGSAW

scro·tum \'skrōt-əm\ *n*, *pl* **scro·ta** \-ə\ or **scrotums** [L] : a pouch that in most mammals contains the testes

scrounge \'skraȯnj\ *vb* **scrounged; scroung·ing** : to collect by or as if by foraging

¹scrub \'skrəb\ *n* **1** : a thick growth of stunted trees or shrubs; *also* : an area of land covered with scrub **2** : an inferior domestic animal **3** : a person of insignificant size or standing; *esp* : a player not on the first team — **scrub** *adj* — **scrub·by** *adj*

²scrub *vb* **scrubbed; scrub·bing** **1** : to rub in washing ⟨~ clothes⟩ **2** : to wash by rubbing ⟨~ out a spot⟩ **3** : CANCEL

³scrub *n* : an act or instance of scrubbing ⟨gave the clothes a good ~⟩

scruff \'skrəf\ *n* : the loose skin of the back of the neck : NAPE

scruffy \'skrəf-ē\ *adj* **scruff·i·er; -est** : UNKEMPT, SLOVENLY

scrump·tious \'skrəm(p)-shəs\ *adj* : DELIGHTFUL, EXCELLENT — **scrump·tious·ly** *adv*

¹scru·ple \'skrü-pəl\ *n* [MF *scrupule*, fr. L *scrupulus* small sharp stone, cause of mental discomfort, scruple, dim. of *scrupus* sharp stone] **1** : a point of conscience or honor **2** : hesitation due to ethical considerations

²scruple *vb* **scru·pled; scru·pling** \-p(ə-)liŋ\ : to be reluctant on grounds of conscience : HESITATE

scru·pu·lous \'skrü-pyə-ləs\ *adj* **1** : having moral integrity **2** : PAINSTAKING — **scru·pu·lous·ly** *adv* — **scru·pu·lous·ness** *n*

scru·ti·nize \'skrüt-ən-ˌīz\ *vb* **-nized; -niz·ing** : to examine closely

scru·ti·ny \'skrüt-ᵊn-ē\ *n*, *pl* **-nies** [L *scrutinium*, fr. *scrutari* to search, examine, fr. *scruta* trash] : a careful looking over *syn* inspection, examination, analysis

scu·ba \'sk(y)ü-bə\ *n* [*self-contained underwater breathing apparatus*] : an apparatus for breathing while swimming under water

scuba diver *n* : one who swims under water with the aid of scuba gear

¹scud \'skəd\ *vb* **scud·ded; scud·ding** : to move speedily

²scud *n* : light clouds driven by the wind

¹scuff \'skəf\ *vb* **1** : to scrape the feet while walking : SHUFFLE **2** : to scratch or become scratched or worn away

²scuff *n* **1** : a mark or injury caused by scuffing **2** : a flat-soled slipper without quarter or heel strap

scuf·fle \'skəf-əl\ *vb* **scuf·fled; scuf·fling** \-(ə-)liŋ\ **1** : to struggle confusedly at close quarters **2** : to shuffle one's feet — **scuffle** *n*

¹scull \'skəl\ *n* **1** : an oar for use in sculling; *also* : one of a pair of short oars for a single oarsman **2** : a racing shell propelled by one or two persons using sculls

²scull *vb* : to propel (a boat) by an oar over the stern

scul·lery \'skəl-(ə-)rē\ *n, pl* **-ler·ies** [ME, department of household in charge of dishes, fr. MF *escuelerie*, fr. *escuelle* bowl, fr. L *scutella* drinking bowl] : a small room near the kitchen used for cleaning dishes, culinary utensils, and vegetables

scul·lion \'skəl-yən\ *n* [ME *sculion*, fr. MF *escouillon* dishcloth, alter. of *escouvillon*, fr. *escouve* broom, fr. L *scopa*, lit., twig] : a kitchen helper

sculpt \'skəlpt\ *vb* : CARVE, SCULPTURE

sculp·tor \'skəlp-tər\ *n* : one who produces works of sculpture

¹sculp·ture \'skəlp-chər\ *n* : the act, process, or art of carving or molding material (as stone, wood, or plastic); *also* : work produced this way — **sculp·tur·al** \'skəlp-chə-rəl\ *adj*

²sculpture *vb* **sculp·tured; sculp·tur·ing** : to form or alter as or as if a work of sculpture

scum \'skəm\ *n* **1** : a foul filmy covering on the surface of a liquid **2** : waste matter **3** : RABBLE

scup·per \'skəp-ər\ *n* : an opening in the side of a ship through which water on deck is drained overboard

scurf \'skərf\ *n* : thin dry scales of skin (as dandruff); *also* : a scaly deposit or covering — **scurfy** \'skər-fē\ *adj*

scur·ri·lous \'skər-ə-ləs\ *adj* : coarsely jesting : OBSCENE, VULGAR

scur·ry \'skər-ē\ *vb* **scur·ried; scur·ry·ing** : SCAMPER

¹scur·vy \'skər-vē\ *n* : a disease marked by spongy gums, loosened teeth, and bleeding into the tissues and caused by lack of vitamin C

²scurvy *adj* : MEAN, CONTEMPTIBLE — **scur·vi·ly** \'skər-və-lē\ *adv*

scutch·eon \'skəch-ən\ *n* : ESCUTCHEON

¹scut·tle \'skət-ᵊl\ *n* : a pail for carrying coal

²scuttle *n* : a small opening with a lid esp. in the deck, side, or bottom of a ship

³scuttle *vb* **scut·tled; scut·tling** \'skət-(ᵊ-)liŋ\ : to cut a hole in the deck, side, or bottom of (a ship) in order to sink

⁴scuttle *vb* **scut·tled; scut·tling** \'skət-(ᵊ-)liŋ\ : SCURRY, SCAMPER

scut·tle·butt \'skət-ᵊl-ˌbət\ *n* : GOSSIP

scythe \'sīth\ *n* : an implement for mowing (as grass or grain) by hand — **scythe** *vb*

SD *abbr* **1** South Dakota **2** special delivery

S Dak *abbr* South Dakota

Se *symbol* selenium

SE *abbr* southeast

sea \'sē\ *n* **1** : a large body of salt water **2** : OCEAN **3** : rough water; *also* : a heavy wave **4** : something likened to the sea esp. in vastness — **sea** *adj* — **at sea** : LOST, BEWILDERED

sea anemone *n* : any of numerous coelenterate polyps whose form, bright and varied colors, and cluster of tentacles superficially resemble a flower

sea·bird \'sē-ˌbərd\ *n* : a bird (as a gull) frequenting the open ocean

sea·board \-ˌbōrd\ *n* : SEACOAST; *also* : the land bordering a coast

sea·coast \-ˌkōst\ *n* : the shore of the sea

sea·far·er \-ˌfar-ər\ *n* : SEAMAN

sea·far·ing \-ˌfar-iŋ\ *n* : a mariner's calling — **seafaring** *adj*

sea·food \-ˌfüd\ *n* : edible marine fish and shellfish

sea·go·ing \-ˌgō-iŋ\ *adj* : OCEANGOING

sea horse *n* : any of numerous small sea fishes with the head and forepart of the body sharply flexed like the head and neck of a horse

¹seal \'sēl\ *n, pl* **seals** *also* **seal 1** : any of various large sea mammals occurring chiefly in cold regions and having limbs adapted for swimming **2** : the pelt of a seal

²seal *vb* : to hunt seals

³seal *n* **1** : something that fastens or secures; *also* : GUARANTEE, PLEDGE **2** : a device having a raised design that can be stamped on clay or wax; *also* : the impression made by stamping with such a device **3** : a mark acceptable as having the legal effect of an official seal

⁴seal *vb* **1** : to affix a seal to; *also* : AUTHENTICATE **2** : to fasten with a seal; *esp* : to enclose securely **3** : to determine irrevocably

sea-lane \'sē-ˌlān\ *n* : an established sea route

seal·ant \'sē-lənt\ *n* : a sealing agent

seal·er \'sē-lər\ *n* : a coat applied to prevent subsequent coats of paint or varnish from sinking in

sea level *n* : the level of the surface of the sea esp. at its mean position midway between mean high and low water

sea lion *n* : any of several large Pacific seals with external ears

seal·skin \'sēl-ˌskin\ *n* **1** : ¹SEAL 2 **2** : a garment of sealskin

¹seam \'sēm\ n 1 : the line of junction of two edges and esp. of edges of fabric sewn together 2 : layer of mineral matter (coal ~s) 3 : WRINKLE — seam-less adj

²seam vb 1 : to join by or as if by sewing 2 : WRINKLE, FURROW

sea-man \'sē-mən\ n 1 : one who assists in the handling of ships : MARINER 2 : an enlisted man in the navy ranking next below a petty officer third class

seaman apprentice n : an enlisted man in the navy ranking next below a seaman

seaman recruit n : an enlisted man of the lowest rank in the navy

sea-man-ship \'sē-mən-ˌship\ n : the art or skill of handling a ship

sea-mount \'sē-ˌmaùnt\ n : an underwater mountain

seam-stress \'sēm-strəs\ n : a woman who does sewing

seamy \'sē-mē\ adj seam-i-er; -est 1 : UNPLEASANT 2 : DEGRADED, SORDID

sé-ance \'sā-ˌäns\ n [F] : a spiritualist meeting to receive communications from spirits

sea-plane \'sē-ˌplān\ n : an airplane that can take off from and land on water

sea-port \-ˌpōrt\ n : a port for oceangoing ships

sear \'siər\ vb 1 : WITHER 2 : to burn or scorch esp. on the surface; also : BRAND

¹search \'sərch\ vb [ME cerchen, fr. MF cerchier to go about, survey, search, fr. LL circare to go about, fr. L circum round about] 1 : to look through in trying to find something 2 : SEEK 3 : PROBE — search-er n

²search n : the act of searching

search-light \-ˌlīt\ n : an apparatus for projecting a beam of light; also : the light projected

sea-scape \'sē-ˌskāp\ n 1 : a view of the sea 2 : a picture representing a scene at sea

sea-shore \-ˌshōr\ n : the shore of a sea : SEACOAST

sea-sick \-ˌsik\ adj : nauseated by or as if by the motion of a ship — sea-sick-ness n

sea-side \'sē-ˌsīd\ n : SEASHORE

¹sea-son \'sēz-ᵊn\ n [ME, fr. OF saison, fr. L sation-, satio action of sowing, fr. satus, pp. of serere to sow] 1 : one of the divisions of the year (as spring or summer) 2 : a special period (the Easter ~) — sea-son-al \'sēz-(ᵊ-)nəl\ adj — sea-son-al-ly \-ē\ adv

²season vb sea-soned; sea-son-ing \'sēz-(ᵊ-)niŋ\ 1 : to make pleasant to the taste by use of salt, pepper, or spices 2 : to make (as by aging or drying) suitable for use 3 : to accustom or habituate to something (as hardship) syn harden, inure, acclimatize, toughen — sea-son-er \'sēz-(ᵊ-)nər\ n

sea-son-able \'sēz-(ᵊ-)nə-bəl\ adj : occurring at a fit time syn timely, propi-

tious, opportune — sea-son-ably \-blē\ adv

sea-son-ing \'sēz-(ᵊ-)niŋ\ n : something that seasons : CONDIMENT

¹seat \'sēt\ n 1 : a chair, bench, or stool for sitting on 2 : a place which serves as a capital or center

²seat vb 1 : to place in or on a seat 2 : to provide seats for

seat belt n : straps designed to hold a person steady in a seat

SEATO \'sē-ˌtō\ abbr Southeast Asia Treaty Organization

seat-of-the-pants adj : employing or based on personal experience, judgment, and effort rather than technological aids (~ navigation)

sea urchin n : any of a class of oblate spiny marine echinoderms having thin brittle shells

sea-wall \'sē-ˌwȯl\ n : an embankment to protect the shore from erosion

¹sea-ward \'sē-wərd\ n : the direction or side away from land and toward the open sea

²seaward adj 1 : directed or situated toward the sea 2 : coming from the sea

³seaward also sea-wards \-wərdz\ adv : toward the sea

sea-wa-ter \-ˌwȯt-ər, -ˌwät-\ n : water in or from the sea

sea-way \-ˌwā\ n : an inland waterway that admits ocean shipping

sea-weed \-ˌwēd\ n : a marine alga (as a kelp); also : a mass of marine algae

sea-wor-thy \'sē-ˌwər-thē\ adj : fit for a sea voyage

se-ba-ceous \si-'bā-shəs\ adj : of, relating to, or secreting fatty material

sec abbr 1 second; secondary 2 secretary 3 section 4 [L secundum] according to

SEC abbr Securities and Exchange Commission

se-cede \si-'sēd\ vb se-ced-ed; se-ced-ing : to withdraw from an organized body and esp. from a political body

se-ces-sion \si-'sesh-ən\ n : the act of seceding — se-ces-sion-ist n

se-clude \si-'klüd\ vb se-clud-ed; se-clud-ing : to keep or shut away from others

se-clu-sion \si-'klü-zhən\ n : the act of secluding : the state of being secluded — se-clu-sive \-siv\ adj

¹sec-ond \'sek-ənd\ adj [ME, fr. OF, fr. L secundus second, following, favorable, fr. sequi to follow] 1 : being number two in a countable series 2 : next after the first 3 : ALTERNATE (every ~ year) — second or sec-ond-ly adv

²second n [ME secunde, fr. ML secunda, fr. L, fem. of secundus second; fr. its being the second division of a unit into 60 parts, as a minute is the first] 1 : the 60th part of a minute of time or angular measure 2 : an instant of time

³second n 1 : one that is second 2 : one who assists another (as in a duel) 3 : an inferior or flawed article (as of

merchandise) **4** : the second forward
gear in a motor vehicle

⁴**second** vb **1** : to encourage or give support to **2** : to act as a second to **3** : to support (a motion) by adding one's voice to that of a proposer

sec·ond·ary \'sek-ən-ˌder-ē\ adj **1** : second in rank, value, or occurrence — IN-FERIOR, LESSER **2** : belonging to a second or later stage of development **3** : coming after the primary or elementary (~ schools) syn subordinate, collateral, dependent

secondary sex characteristic n : a physical characteristic (as the breasts of a female mammal or the showy feathers of a male bird) that appears in members of one sex at puberty or in seasonal breeders at breeding season and is not directly concerned with reproduction

second fiddle n : one that plays a supporting or subservient role

sec·ond-guess \ˌsek-ən-ˈges, -ən-\ vb : to think out other strategies or explanations for after the event

sec·ond·hand \ˌsek-ən-ˈhand\ adj **1** : not original **2** : not new — USED (~ clothes) **3** : dealing in used goods

second lieutenant n : a commissioned officer (as in the army) ranking next below a first lieutenant

sec·ond-rate \ˌsek-ən(d)-ˈrāt\ adj : IN-FERIOR

second-story man n : a burglar who enters by an upstairs window

sec·ond-string \ˌsek-ən-ˈstriŋ, ˌsek-ˈəŋ-\ adj : being a substitute (as on a ball team)

se·cre·cy \'sē-krə-sē\ n, pl **-cies 1** : the habit or practice of being secretive **2** : the quality or state of being secret

¹**se·cret** \'sē-krət\ adj **1** : HIDDEN, CON-CEALED (a ~ panel) **2** : COVERT, STEALTHY; also : engaged in detecting or spying (a ~ agent) **3** : kept from general knowledge — **se·cret·ly** adv

²**secret** n **1** : MYSTERY **2** : something kept from the knowledge of others

sec·re·tar·i·at \ˌsek-rə-ˈter-ē-ət\ n **1** : the office of a secretary **2** : the body of secretaries in an office **3** : the administrative department of a governmental organization (the UN ~)

sec·re·tary \'sek-rə-ˌter-ē\ n, pl **-tar·ies 1** : a person employed to handle records, correspondence, and routine work for another person **2** : an officer of a corporation or business who is in charge of correspondence and records **3** : an official at the head of a department of government **4** : a writing desk — **sec·re·tar·i·al** \ˌsek-rə-ˈter-ē-əl\ adj — **sec·re·tary·ship** \'sek-rə-ˌter-ē-ˌship\ n

¹**se·crete** \si-ˈkrēt\ vb **se·cret·ed; se·cret·ing** : to produce and emit as a secretion

²**se·crete** \si-ˈkrēt, ˈsē-krət\ vb **se·cret·ed; se·cret·ing** : HIDE, CONCEAL

se·cre·tion \si-ˈkrē-shən\ n **1** : an act or

process of secreting **2** : a product of glandular activity; esp : one (as a hormone) useful in the organism — **se·cre·to·ry** \-ˈkrēt-ə-rē\ adj

se·cre·tive \'sē-krət-iv, si-ˈkrēt-\ adj : tending to keep secrets or to act secretly — **se·cre·tive·ly** adv — **se·cre·tive·ness** n

¹**sect** \'sekt\ n **1** : a dissenting religious body **2** : a religious denomination **3** : a group adhering to a distinctive doctrine or to a leader

²**sect** abbr section

¹**sec·tar·i·an** \sek-ˈter-ē-ən\ adj **1** : of or relating to a sect or sectarian **2** : limited in character or scope — **sec·tar·i·an·ism** n

²**sectarian** n **1** : an adherent of a sect **2** : a narrow or bigoted person

sec·ta·ry \'sek-tə-rē\ n, pl **-ries** : a member of a sect

¹**sec·tion** \'sek-shən\ n **1** : a part cut off or separated **2** : a distinct part **3** : the appearance that a thing has or would have if cut straight through

²**section** vb **1** : to separate or become separated into sections **2** : to represent in sections

sec·tion·al \'sek-sh(ə-)nəl\ adj **1** : of, relating to, or characteristic of a section **2** : local or regional rather than general in character **3** : divided into sections — **sec·tion·al·ism** n

sec·tor \'sek-tər\ n **1** : a part of a circle between two radii **2** : an area assigned to a military leader to defend

sec·u·lar \'sek-yə-lər\ adj **1** : not sacred or ecclesiastical **2** : not bound by monastic vows (~ priest)

sec·u·lar·ism \'sek-yə-lə-ˌriz-əm\ n : indifference to or exclusion of religion — **sec·u·lar·ist** \-rəst\ n — **secularist** or **sec·u·lar·is·tic** \ˌsek-yə-lə-ˈris-tik\ adj

sec·u·lar·ize \'sek-yə-lə-ˌrīz\ vb **-ized; -iz·ing 1** : to make secular **2** : to transfer from ecclesiastical to civil or lay use, possession, or control — **sec·u·lar·iza·tion** \ˌsek-yə-lə-rə-ˈzā-shən\ n — **sec·u·lar·iz·er** \'sek-yə-lə-ˌrī-zər\ n

¹**se·cure** \si-ˈkyùr\ adj **se·cur·er; -est** [L securus safe, secure, fr. se without + cura care] **1** : easy in mind : free from fear **2** : free from danger or risk of loss : SAFE **3** : CERTAIN, SURE — **se·cure·ly** adv

²**secure** vb **se·cured; se·cur·ing 1** : to make safe : GUARD **2** : to assure payment of by giving a pledge or collateral **3** : to fasten safely (~ a door) **4** : GET, ACQUIRE

se·cu·ri·ty \si-ˈkyùr-ət-ē\ n, pl **-ties 1** : SAFETY **2** : freedom from worry **3** : something (as collateral) given as pledge of payment **4** pl : bond or stock certificates **5** : PROTECTION

secy abbr secretary

se·dan \si-ˈdan\ n **1** : a covered chair borne on poles by two men **2** : an enclosed automobile usu. with front and back seats and a permanent top

se·date \si-ˈdāt\ adj : quiet and dignified in behavior syn staid, sober, serious, solemn — **se·date·ly** adv

¹**sed·a·tive** \'sed-ət-iv\ adj : serving or tending to relieve tension — **se·da·tion** \si-'dā-shən\ n

²**sedative** n : a sedative drug

sed·en·tary \'sed-ºn-ter-ē\ adj : characterized by or requiring much sitting

sedge \'sej\ n : any of a family of plants that are related to the grasses, grow in marshes, and often have three-sided stems — **sedgy** \'sej-ē\ adj

sed·i·ment \'sed-ə-mənt\ n 1 : the material that settles to the bottom of a liquid : LEES, DREGS 2 : material (as stones and sand) deposited by water, wind, or a glacier — **sed·i·men·ta·ry** \,sed-ə-'men-t(ə-)rē\ adj — **sed·i·men·ta·tion** \-,mən-'tā-shən, -,men-\ n

se·di·tion \si-'dish-ən\ n : the causing of discontent, insurrection, or resistance against a government — **se·di·tious** \-əs\ adj

se·duce \si-'d(y)üs\ vb **se·duced; se·duc·ing** 1 : to persuade to disobedience or disloyalty 2 : to lead astray 3 : to entice to unlawful sexual intercourse without the use of force syn tempt, entice, inveigle, lure — **se·duc·er** n — **se·duc·tion** \-'dək-shən\ n — **se·duc·tive** \-tiv\ adj

sed·u·lous \'sej-ə-ləs\ adj [L sedulus, fr. sedulo sincerely, diligently, fr. se without + dolus guile] : DILIGENT, PAINSTAKING

¹**see** \'sē\ vb **saw** \'so\ ; **seen** \'sēn\ ; **see·ing** \'sē-iŋ\ 1 : to perceive by the eye : have the power of sight 2 : EXPERIENCE 3 : UNDERSTAND 4 : to make sure (~ that order is kept) 5 : to meet with 6 : to keep company with esp. in dating 7 : ACCOMPANY, ESCORT syn behold, descry, espy, view, observe, note, discern

²**see** n : the authority or jurisdiction of a bishop

¹**seed** \'sēd\ n, pl **seed** or **seeds** 1 : the grains of plants used for sowing 2 : a ripened ovule of a plant that may develop into a new plant; also : a plant structure (as a spore or small dry fruit) capable of producing a new plant 3 : DESCENDANTS 4 : SOURCE, ORIGIN — **seed·bed** \-,bed\ n — **seed·less** adj — **go to seed** or **run to seed** 1 : to develop seed 2 : DECAY

²**seed** vb 1 : SOW, PLANT (~ land to grass) 2 : to bear or shed seeds 3 : to remove seeds from — **seed·er** n

seed·ling \'sēd-liŋ\ n 1 : a plant grown from seed 2 : a young plant; esp : a tree smaller than a sapling

seed·time \'sēd-,tīm\ n : the season for sowing

seedy \'sēd-ē\ adj **seed·i·er; -est** 1 : containing or full of seeds 2 : inferior in condition or quality : SHABBY

seek \'sēk\ vb **sought** \'sot\ ; **seek·ing** 1 : to search for 2 : to try to reach or obtain (~ fame) 3 : ATTEMPT — **seek·er** n

seem \'sēm\ vb 1 : to give the impression of being : APPEAR 2 : to appear to the observation or understanding

seem·ing \-iŋ\ adj : outwardly apparent — **seem·ing·ly** adv

seem·ly \'sēm-lē\ adj **seem·li·er; -est** : PROPER, DECENT

seep \'sēp\ vb : to leak through fine pores or cracks : percolate slowly — **seep·age** \'sē-pij\ n

seer \'siər\ n : a person who foresees or predicts events : PROPHET

seer·suck·er \'siər-,sək-ər\ n [Hindi śīrśaker, fr. Per shīr-o-shakar, lit., milk and sugar] : a light fabric of linen, cotton, or rayon usu. striped and slightly puckered

see·saw \'sē-,so\ n 1 : a contest in which now one side now the other has the lead 2 : a children's sport of riding up and down on the ends of a plank supported in the middle; also : the plank so used — **seesaw** vb

seethe \'sēth\ vb **seethed; seeth·ing** [archaic seethe boil] : to become violently agitated

seg·ment \'seg-mənt\ n 1 : a division of a thing : SECTION (~ of an orange) 2 : a part cut off from a geometrical figure (as a circle) by a line — **seg·ment·ed** \-,ment-əd\ adj

seg·re·gate \'seg-ri-,gāt\ vb **-gat·ed; -gat·ing** [L segregare, fr. se- apart + greg-, grex herd, flock] : to cut off from others : ISOLATE — **seg·re·ga·tion** \,seg-ri-'gā-shən\ n

seg·re·ga·tion·ist \,seg-ri-'gā-sh(ə-)nəst\ n : one who believes in or practices the segregation of races

sei·gneur \sān-'yər\ n, often cap [MF, fr. ML senior, fr. L, adj., elder] : a feudal lord

¹**seine** \'sān\ n : a large weighted fishing net

²**seine** vb **seined; sein·ing** : to fish or catch with a seine

seis·mic \'sīz-mik, 'sīs-\ adj : of, relating to, resembling, or caused by an earthquake — **seis·mic·i·ty** \sīz-'mis-ət-ē, sīs-\ n

seis·mo·gram \'sīz-mə-,gram, 'sīs-\ n : the record of an earth tremor made by a seismograph

seis·mo·graph \-,graf\ n : an apparatus for recording earthquake data — **seis·mo·graph·ic** \,sīz-mə-'graf-ik, ,sīs-\ adj — **seis·mog·ra·phy** \sīz-'mäg-rə-fē, sīs-\ n

seis·mol·o·gy \sīz-'mäl-ə-jē, sīs-\ n : a science that deals with earthquakes — **seis·mo·log·i·cal** \,sīz-mə-'läj-i-kəl, ,sīs-\ adj — **seis·mol·o·gist** \sīz-'mäl-ə-jəst, sīs-\ n

seis·mom·e·ter \sīz-'mäm-ət-ər, sīs-\ n : a seismograph measuring the actual movement of the ground

seize \'sēz\ vb **seized; seiz·ing** 1 : to lay hold of or take possession of by force 2 : ARREST 3 : UNDERSTAND 4 : to attack or overwhelm physically : AF-

FLICT **syn** take, grasp, clutch, snatch, grab

sei·zure \'sē-zhər\ *n* **1** : the act of seizing : the state of being seized **2** : a sudden attack (as of disease)

sel *abbr* select; selected; selection

sel·dom \'sel-dəm\ *adv* : not often : RARELY

¹se·lect \sə-'lekt\ *adj* **1** : CHOSEN, PICKED; *also* : CHOICE **2** : judicious or restrictive in choice : DISCRIMINATING

²select *vb* : to take by preference from a number or group : pick out : CHOOSE

se·lec·tion \sə-'lek-shən\ *n* **1** : the act of selecting **2** : something selected : CHOICE **3** : a natural or artificial process that increases the chance of propagation of some organisms and decreases that of others

se·lec·tive \sə-'lek-tiv\ *adj* : of or relating to selection : selecting or tending to select ⟨~ shoppers⟩

selective service *n* : a system for calling men up for military service

se·lect·man \si-'lek(t)-ˌman, -mən\ *n* : one of a board of officials elected in towns of most New England states to administer town affairs

sel·e·nite \'sel-ə-ˌnīt\ *n* [L *selenites*, fr. Gk *selēnitēs (lithos)*, lit., stone of the moon, fr. *selēnē* moon; fr. the belief that it waxed and waned with the moon] : a variety of transparent crystalline gypsum

se·le·ni·um \sə-'lē-nē-əm\ *n* : a nonmetallic chemical element that varies in electrical conductivity with the intensity of its illumination

self \'self\ *n, pl* **selves** \'selvz\ **1** : the essential person distinct from all other persons in identity **2** : a particular side of a person's character **3** : personal interest : SELFISHNESS

self- *comb form* **1** : oneself : itself **2** : of oneself or itself **3** : by oneself; *also* : automatic **4** : to, for, or toward oneself

self-abasement	self-condemned
self-accusation	self-confessed
self-acting	self-confidence
self-addressed	self-confident
self-adjusting	self-congratulation
self-administer	self-congratulatory
self-advancement	self-constituted
self-aggrandizement	self-contradiction
	self-contradictory
self-aggrandizing	self-control
self-analysis	self-correcting
self-appointed	self-created
self-asserting	self-criticism
self-assertion	self-cultivation
self-assertive	self-deceit
self-assurance	self-deceiving
self-assured	self-deception
self-awareness	self-defeating
self-betrayal	self-defense
self-closing	self-delusion
self-command	self-denial
self-complacent	self-denying
self-conceit	self-depreciation
self-concern	self-despair

self-destruction	self-operating
self-destructive	self-perception
self-determination	self-perpetuating
self-discipline	self-pity
self-distrust	self-portrait
self-doubt	self-possessed
self-educated	self-possession
self-employed	self-preservation
self-employment	self-proclaimed
self-esteem	self-propelled
self-evident	self-propelling
self-examination	self-protection
self-explaining	self-realization
self-explanatory	self-regard
self-expression	self-registering
self-forgetful	self-reliance
self-fulfilling	self-reliant
self-giving	self-reproach
self-governing	self-respect
self-government	self-respecting
self-help	self-restraint
self-hypnosis	self-rule
self-identity	self-sacrifice
self-image	self-satisfaction
self-importance	self-satisfied
self-important	self-seeking
self-imposed	self-service
self-improvement	self-serving
self-incrimination	self-starting
self-induced	self-styled
self-indulgence	self-sufficiency
self-inflicted	self-sufficient
self-interest	self-supporting
self-limiting	self-sustaining
self-love	self-taught
self-lubricating	self-torment
self-luminous	self-winding
self-mastery	self-worth

self–cen·tered \'self-'sent-ərd\ *adj* : concerned only with one's own self — **self–cen·tered·ness** *n*

self–com·posed \ˌself-kəm-'pōzd\ *adj* : having control over one's emotions

self–con·scious \'self-'kän-chəs\ *adj* **1** : aware of oneself as an individual **2** : uncomfortably conscious of oneself as an object of observation by others — **self–con·scious·ly** *adv* — **self–con·scious·ness** *n*

self–con·tained \ˌself-kən-'tānd\ *adj* **1** : complete in itself **2** : showing self=command; *also* : reserved in manner

self–de·struct \-di-'strəkt\ *vb* : to destroy itself

self–ef·fac·ing \-ə-'fā-siŋ\ *adj* : RETIRING, SHY

self–fer·til·iza·tion \ˌself-ˌfərt-ᵊl-ə-'zā-shən\ *n* : fertilization of a plant or animal by its own pollen or sperm

self·ish \'sel-fish\ *adj* : taking care of one's own comfort, pleasure, or interest excessively or without regard for others — **self·ish·ly** *adv* — **self·ish·ness** *n*

self·less \'self-ləs\ *adj* : UNSELFISH — **self·less·ness** *n*

self–made \'self-'mād\ *adj* : rising from poverty or obscurity by one's own efforts ⟨~ man⟩

self–pol·li·na·tion \ˌself-ˌpäl-ə-'nā-shən\ *n* : pollination of a flower by its own pollen or sometimes by pollen from another flower on the same plant

self–reg·u·lat·ing \'self-'reg-yə-ˌlāt-iŋ\ *adj* : AUTOMATIC

self–righ·teous \-'rī-chəs\ *adj* : strongly convinced of one's own righteousness — **self–righ·teous·ly** *adv*

self·same \'self-ˌsām\ *adj* : precisely the same : IDENTICAL

self–seal·ing \'self-'sē-liŋ\ *adj* : capable of sealing itself (as after puncture)

self–start·er \-'stärt-ər\ *n* : a person who has initiative

self–will \'self-'wil\ *n* : OBSTINACY

sell \'sel\ *vb* **sold** \'sōld\; **sell·ing 1** : to transfer (property) in return for money or something else of value **2** : to deal in as a business **3** : to be sold ⟨cars are ∼*ing* well⟩ — **sell·er** *n*

selling climax *n* : a sharp decline in stock prices for a short time on very heavy trading volume followed by a rally

sell out \(')sel-'aut\ *vb* **1** : to dispose of entirely by sale; *esp* : to sell one's business **2** : BETRAY — **sell·out** \'sel-ˌaut\ *n*

selt·zer \'selt-sər\ *n* [modif. of G *Selterser (wasser)* water of Selters, fr. Nieder *Selters,* Germany] : an artificially prepared water charged with carbon dioxide

sel·vage *or* **sel·vedge** \'sel-vij\ *n* : the edge of a woven fabric so formed as to prevent raveling

selves *pl of* SELF

sem *abbr* **1** semicolon **2** seminar **3** seminary

se·man·tic \si-'mant-ik\ *also* **se·man·ti·cal** \-i-kəl\ *adj* : of or relating to meaning

se·man·tics \si-'mant-iks\ *n sing or pl* **1** : the study of meanings in language **2** : connotative meaning

sema·phore \'sem-ə-ˌfōr\ *n* **1** : a visual signaling apparatus with movable arms **2** : signaling by hand-held flags

sem·blance \'sem-bləns\ *n* **1** : outward appearance **2** : IMAGE, LIKENESS

se·men \'sē-mən\ *n* [NL, fr. L, seed] : a sticky whitish fluid of the male reproductive tract that contains the sperm

se·mes·ter \sə-'mes-tər\ *n* [G, fr. L *semestris* half-yearly, fr. *sex* six + *mensis* month] : half a year; *esp* : one of the two terms into which many colleges divide the school year

semi \ˌsem-i, 'sem-, -ˌī\ *prefix* **1** : precisely half of **2** : half in quantity or value; *also* : half of or occurring halfway through a specified period **3** : partly : incompletely **4** : partial : incomplete **5** : having some of the characteristics of

semiannual	semiconscious
semiarid	semidarkness
semicentennial	semidivine
semicircle	semiformal
semicircular	semigloss
semicivilized	semi–independent
semiclassical	semiliquid
semiliterate	semireligious
semimonthly	semiretired
semiofficial	semiskilled
semipermanent	semisweet
semipolitical	semitransparent
semiprecious	semiweekly
semiprivate	semiyearly
semiprofessional	

semi·au·to·mat·ic \ˌsem-ē-ˌȯt-ə-'mat-ik\ *adj, of a firearm* : employing recoil or gas pressure to eject an empty cartridge case and to load before firing again

semi·co·lon \'sem-i-ˌkō-lən\ *n* : a punctuation mark ; used esp. to separate major sentence elements

semi·con·duc·tor \ˌsem-i-kən-'dək-tər\ *n* : a substance whose electrical conductivity is between that of a conductor and an insulator — **semi·con·duct·ing** \-'dək-tiŋ\ *adj*

semi·dry·ing \ˌsem-i-'drī-iŋ\ *adj* : that dries imperfectly or slowly ⟨a ∼ oil⟩

¹semi·fi·nal \ˌsem-i-'fīn-ᵊl\ *adj* : being next to the last in an elimination tournament

²semi·fi·nal \'sem-i-ˌfīn-ᵊl\ *n* : a semifinal round or match

semi·flu·id \ˌsem-i-'flü-əd, -ˌī-\ *adj* : SEMISOLID

semi·lu·nar \-'lü-nər\ *adj* : crescent=shaped

semi·nal \'sem-ən-ᵊl\ *adj* **1** : of, relating to, or consisting of seed or semen **2** : containing or contributing the seeds of later development : CREATIVE, ORIGINAL — **sem·i·nal·ly** \-ē\ *adv*

sem·i·nar \'sem-ə-ˌnär\ *n* **1** : a course of study pursued by a group of advanced students doing original research under a professor **2** : CONFERENCE

sem·i·nary \'sem-ə-ˌner-ē\ *n, pl* **-nar·ies** [ME, seedbed, nursery, fr. L *seminarium,* fr. *semen* seed] : an educational institution; *esp* : one that gives theological training — **sem·i·nar·i·an** \ˌsem-ə-'ner-ē-ən\ *n*

Sem·i·nole \'sem-ə-ˌnōl\ *n, pl* **Seminoles** *or* **Seminole** : a member of an American Indian people of Florida

semi·per·me·able \ˌsem-i-'pər-mē-ə-bəl\ *adj* : partially but not freely or wholly permeable; *esp* : permeable to some usu. small molecules but not to other usu. larger particles ⟨a ∼ membrane⟩ — **semi·per·me·abil·i·ty** \-ˌpər-mē-ə-'bil-ət-ē\ *n*

semi·soft \-'sȯft\ *adj* : moderately soft; *esp* : firm but easily cut ⟨∼ cheese⟩

semi·sol·id \-'säl-əd\ *adj* : having the qualities of both a solid and a liquid

Sem·ite \'sem-ˌīt\ *n* : a member of any of a group of peoples (as the Jews or Arabs) of southwestern Asia — **Sem·it·ic** \sə-'mit-ik\ *adj*

semi·trail·er \'sem-i-ˌtrā-lər, 'sem-ˌī-\ *n* : a freight trailer that when attached is supported at its forward end by the truck tractor; *also* : a semitrailer with attached tractor

semi·works \'sem-i-ˌwərks, 'sem-ˌī-\ *n pl* : a manufacturing plant operating on a limited commercial scale to provide final tests of a new product or process

semp·stress \'semp-strəs\ *var of* SEAM-STRESS

¹sen \'sen\ *n, pl* **sen** — see *yen* at MONEY table

²sen *n, pl* **sen** — see *rupiah* at MONEY table

³sen *n, pl* **sen** — see *dollar, riel* at MONEY table

⁴sen *n, pl* **sen** — see *ringgit* at MONEY table

⁵sen *abbr* **1** senate; senator **2** senior

sen·ate \'sen-ət\ *n* [ME *senat*, fr. OF, fr. L *senatus*, lit., council of elders, fr. *senex* old, old man] : the upper branch of a legislature

sen·a·tor \'sen-ət-ər\ *n* : a member of a senate — **sen·a·to·ri·al** \ˌsen-ə-'tōr-ē-əl\ *adj*

send \'send\ *vb* **sent** \'sent\; **send·ing** **1** : to cause to go **2** : EMIT **3** : to propel or drive esp. with force **4** : to put or bring into a certain condition — **send·er** *n*

send-off \'send-ˌȯf\ *n* : a demonstration of goodwill and enthusiasm for the beginning of a new venture (as a trip)

se·ne \'sā-(ˌ)nā\ *n, pl* **sene** — see *tala* at MONEY table

Sen·e·ca \'sen-i-kə\ *n, pl* **Seneca** or **Senecas** : a member of an American Indian people of western New York

Sen·e·ga·lese \ˌsen-i-gə-'lēz, -'lēs\ *n, pl* **Senegalese** : a native or inhabitant of Senegal — **Senegalese** *adj*

se·nes·cence \si-'nes-ᵊns\ *n* : the state of being old; *also* : the process of becoming old — **se·nes·cent** \-ᵊnt\ *adj*

sen·gi \'seŋ-gē\ *n, pl* **sengi** — see *zaire* at MONEY table

se·nile \'sēn-ˌīl, 'sen-\ *adj* : OLD, AGED; *esp* : exhibiting loss of mental ability usu. associated with old age — **se·nil·i·ty** \si-'nil-ət-ē\ *n*

¹se·nior \'sē-nyər\ *n* **1** : a person older or of higher rank than another **2** : a member of the graduating class of a high school or college

²senior *adj* [ME, fr. L, older, elder, compar. of *senex* old] **1** : ELDER **2** : more advanced in dignity or rank **3** : belonging to the final year of a school or college course

senior chief petty officer *n* : a petty officer in the navy ranking next below a master chief petty officer

senior citizen *n* : an elderly person; *esp* : one who has retired

senior high school *n* : a school usu. including grades 10 to 12

se·nior·i·ty \sēn-'yȯr-ət-ē\ *n* **1** : the quality or state of being senior **2** : a privileged status owing to length of continuous service

senior master sergeant *n* : a noncommissioned officer in the air force rank-

ing next below a chief master sergeant

sen·i·ti \'sen-ə-tē\ *n, pl* **seniti** — see *pa'anga* at MONEY table

sen·na \'sen-ə\ *n* **1** : any of various cassias **2** : the dried leaflets or pods of a cassia used as a purgative

sen·sa·tion \sen-'sā-shən\ *n* **1** : awareness (as of noise or heat) or a mental process (as seeing or hearing) due to stimulation of a sense organ; *also* : an indefinite bodily feeling **2** : a condition of excitement; *also* : the thing that causes this condition

sen·sa·tion·al \-sh(ə-)nəl\ *adj* **1** : of or relating to sensation or the senses **2** : arousing an intense and usu. superficial interest or emotional reaction — **sen·sa·tion·al·ly** \-ē\ *adv*

sen·sa·tion·al·ism \-ˌiz-əm\ *n* : the use or effect of sensational subject matter or treatment

sen·sa·tion·al·ize \-ˌīz\ *vb* **-ized; -iz·ing** : to present in a sensational manner

¹sense \'sens\ *n* **1** : semantic content : MEANING **2** : the faculty of perceiving by means of sense organs; *also* : a bodily function or mechanism based on this (the pain ∼) **3** : SENSATION, AWARENESS **4** : INTELLIGENCE, JUDGMENT **5** : OPINION (the ∼ of the meeting) — **sense·less** *adj* — **sense·less·ly** *adv*

²sense *vb* **sensed; sens·ing 1** : to be or become aware of : perceive by the senses **2** : to detect (as radiation) automatically

sense organ *n* : a bodily structure (as an eye or ear) that responds to a stimulus (as heat or light) and sends impulses to the brain where they are interpreted as sensations

sen·si·bil·i·ty \ˌsen-sə-'bil-ət-ē\ *n, pl* **-ties** : delicacy of feeling : SENSITIVITY

sen·si·ble \'sen-sə-bəl\ *adj* **1** : capable of being perceived by the senses or by reason; *also* : capable of receiving sense impressions **2** : AWARE, CONSCIOUS **3** : REASONABLE, INTELLIGENT — **sen·si·bly** \-blē\ *adv*

sen·si·tive \'sen-sət-iv\ *adj* **1** : subject to excitation by or responsive to stimuli **2** : having power of feeling **3** : of such a nature as to be easily affected — **sen·si·tive·ness** *n* — **sen·si·tiv·i·ty** \ˌsen-sə-'tiv-ət-ē\ *n*

sensitive plant *n* : any of several mimosas with leaves that fold or droop when touched

sen·si·tize \'sen-sə-ˌtīz\ *vb* **-tized; -tiz·ing** : to make or become sensitive or hypersensitive — **sen·si·ti·za·tion** \ˌsen-sət-ə-'zā-shən\ *n*

sen·si·tom·e·ter \ˌsen-sə-'täm-ət-ər\ *n* : an instrument for measuring sensitivity of photographic material — **sen·si·to·met·ric** \-sət-ə-'me-trik\ *adj* — **sen·si·tom·e·try** \-sə-'täm-ə-trē\ *n*

sen·sor \'sen-ˌsȯr, -sər\ *n* : a device that responds to a physical stimulus

sen·so·ry \'sens-(ə-)rē\ *adj* : of or relating to sensation or the senses

sen·su·al \'sench-(ə-)wəl\ *adj* **1** : relating to the pleasing of the senses **2** : devoted to the pleasures of the senses — **sen·su·al·ist** *n* — **sen·su·al·i·ty** \ ,sen-chə-'wal-ət-ē\ *n* — **sen·su·al·ly** \'sench-(ə-)wə-lē, 'sen-shə-lē\ *adv*

sen·su·ous \'sench-(ə-)wəs\ *adj* **1** : relating to the senses or to things that can be perceived by the senses **2** : VOLUPTUOUS — **sen·su·ous·ly** *adv* — **sen·su·ous·ness** *n*

sent *past and past part of* SEND

¹**sen·tence** \'sent-ᵊns, -ᵊnz\ *n* [ME, fr. OF, fr. L *sententia*, lit., feeling, opinion, fr. *sentire* to feel] **1** : the punishment set by a court **2** : a grammatically self-contained speech unit that expresses an assertion, a question, a command, a wish, or an exclamation

²**sentence** *vb* **sen·tenced; sen·tenc·ing** : to impose a sentence on *syn* condemn, damn, doom

sen·ten·tious \sen-'ten-chəs\ *adj* : using wise sayings or proverbs; *also* : using pompous language

sen·ti \'sent-ē\ *n, pl* **senti** — see *shilling* at MONEY TABLE

sen·tient \'sen-ch(ē-)ənt\ *adj* : capable of feeling : having perception

sen·ti·ment \'sent-ə-mənt\ *n* **1** : FEELING; *also* : thought and judgment influenced by feeling : emotional attitude **2** : OPINION, NOTION

sen·ti·men·tal \ ,sent-ə-'ment-ᵊl\ *adj* **1** : influenced by tender feelings **2** : affecting the emotions *syn* bathetic, maudlin, mawkish, mushy — **sen·ti·men·tal·ism** *n* — **sen·ti·men·tal·ist** *n* — **sen·ti·men·tal·i·ty** \ ,men-'tal-ət-ē, -mən-\ *n* — **sen·ti·men·tal·ly** \-'ment-ᵊl-ē\ *adv*

sen·ti·men·tal·ize \-'ment-ᵊl-,īz\ *vb* **-ized; -iz·ing 1** : to indulge in sentiment **2** : to look upon or imbue with sentiment — **sen·ti·men·tal·iza·tion** \-,ment-ᵊl-ə-'zā-shən\ *n*

sen·ti·mo \sen-'tē-(,)mō\ *n, pl* **-mos** — see *peso* at MONEY TABLE

sen·ti·nel \'sent-(ᵊ-)nᵊl\ *n* [MF *sentinelle*, fr. It *sentinella*, fr. *sentina* vigilance, fr. *sentire* to perceive, fr. L] : one that watches or guards

sen·try \'sen-trē\ *n, pl* **sentries** : SENTINEL, GUARD

sep *abbr* separate, separated

Sep *abbr* September

se·pal \'sēp-əl, 'sep-\ *n* : one of the modified leaves comprising a flower calyx

sep·a·ra·ble \'sep-(ə-)rə-bəl\ *adj* : capable of being separated

¹**sep·a·rate** \'sep-ə-,rāt\ *vb* **-rat·ed; -rat·ing 1** : to set or keep apart : DISUNITE, DISCONNECT, SEVER **2** : to keep apart by something intervening **3** : to cease to be together : PART

²**sep·a·rate** \'sep-(ə-)rət\ *adj* **1** : not connected **2** : divided from each other **3** : SINGLE, PARTICULAR (the ∼ pieces of the puzzle) — **sep·a·rate·ly** *adv*

³**sep·a·rate** *n* : an article of dress designed to be worn interchangeably with others to form various combinations

sep·a·ra·tion \ ,sep-ə-'rā-shən\ *n* **1** : the act or process of separating : the state of being separated **2** : a point, line, means, or area of division

sep·a·rat·ist \'sep-(ə-)rət-əst, 'sep-ə-,rāt-\ *n* : an advocate of separation (as from a political body) — **sep·a·rat·ism** \-rə-,tiz-əm\ *n*

sep·a·ra·tive \'sep-ə-,rāt-iv, 'sep-(ə-)rət-\ *adj* : tending toward, causing or expressing separation

sep·a·ra·tor \'sep-(ə-)rāt-ər\ *n* : one that separates; *esp* : a device for separating cream from milk

se·pia \'sē-pē-ə\ *n* : a brownish gray to dark brown

sep·sis \'sep-səs\ *n, pl* **sep·ses** \'sep-,sēz\ : a poisoned condition due to spread of bacteria or their products in the body

Sept *abbr* September

Sep·tem·ber \sep-'tem-bər\ *n* : the 9th month of the year having 30 days

sep·tic \'sep-tik\ *adj* **1** : PUTREFACTIVE **2** : relating to or characteristic of sepsis

sep·ti·ce·mia \ ,sep-tə-'sē-mē-ə\ *n* : BLOOD POISONING

septic tank *n* : a tank in which sewage is disintegrated by bacteria

sep·tu·a·ge·nar·i·an \sep-,t(y)ü-ə-jə-'ner-ē-ən\ *n* : a person who is 70 or more but less than 80 years old — **septuagenarian** *adj*

Sep·tu·a·gint \sep-'t(y)ü-ə-jənt, 'sep-tə-wə-,jint\ *n* : a Greek version of the Old Testament used by Greek-speaking Christians

¹**sep·ul·cher** *or* **sep·ul·chre** \'sep-əl-kər\ *n* : burial vault : TOMB

²**sepulcher** *or* **sepulchre** *vb* **-chered** *or* **-chred; -cher·ing** *or* **-chring** \-k(ə-)riŋ\ : BURY, ENTOMB

se·pul·chral \sə-'pəl-krəl\ *adj* **1** : relating to burial or the grave **2** : GLOOMY

sep·ul·ture \'sep-əl-,chùr\ *n* **1** : BURIAL, INTERMENT **2** : SEPULCHER

seq *abbr* [L *sequens, sequentes, sequentia*] the following

seqq *abbr* [L *sequentia*] the following ones

se·quel \'sē-kwəl\ *n* **1** : logical consequence **2** : a literary or cinematic work continuing a story begun in a preceding one

se·quence \'sē-kwəns\ *n* **1** : SERIES **2** : chronological order of events **3** : RESULT, SEQUEL *syn* succession, chain, progression, series, train — **se·quen·tial** \si-'kwen-chəl\ *adj*

se·quent \'sē-kwənt\ *adj* **1** : SUCCEEDING, CONSECUTIVE **2** : RESULTANT

se·ques·ter \si-'kwes-tər\ *vb* : to set apart : SEGREGATE

se·ques·trate \'sēk-wəs-,trāt, si-'kwes-\ *vb* **-trat·ed; -trat·ing** : SEQUESTER — **se·ques·tra·tion** \ ,sēk-wəs-'trā-shən, ,sek-\ *n*

se·quin \'sē-kwən\ *n* **1** : an old gold

coin of Turkey and Italy **2** : a small metal or plastic plate used for ornamentation esp. on clothing

se·quoia \si-ˈkwȯi-ə\ *n* : either of two huge California coniferous trees

ser *abbr* **1** serial **2** series

sera *pl of* SERUM

se·ra·glio \sə-ˈral-yō\ *n, pl* **-glios** [It *serraglio*] : HAREM

se·ra·pe \sə-ˈräp-ē\ *n* : a colorful woolen shawl worn over the shoulders esp. by Mexican men

ser·a·phim \ˈser-ə-ˌfim\ *n, pl* **seraphim** : an angel of a high order of celestial beings — **se·raph·ic** \sə-ˈraf-ik\ *adj*

Serb \ˈsərb\ *n* **1** : a native or inhabitant of Serbia, republic, Yugoslavia **2** : a Slavic language of Serbia

sere \ˈsiər\ *adj* : DRY, WITHERED

¹**ser·e·nade** \ˌser-ə-ˈnād\ *n* [F, fr. It *serenata*, fr. *sereno* clear] : music sung or played as a compliment esp. outdoors at night for a lady

²**serenade** *vb* **-nad·ed; -nad·ing** : to entertain with or perform a serenade

ser·en·dip·i·ty \ˌser-ən-ˈdip-ət-ē\ *n* [fr. its possession by the heroes of the Persian fairy tale *The Three Princes of Serendip*] : the gift of finding valuable or agreeable things not sought for — **ser·en·dip·i·tous** \-əs\ *adj*

se·rene \sə-ˈrēn\ *adj* **1** : QUIET, CALM **2** : CLEAR ⟨∼ skies⟩ **syn** tranquil, peaceful, placid — **se·rene·ly** *adv* — **se·ren·i·ty** \sə-ˈren-ət-ē\ *n*

serf \ˈsərf\ *n* : a peasant bound to the land and subject in some degree to the owner — **serf·dom** \-dəm\ *n*

serg *or* **serge** *abbr* sergeant

serge \ˈsərj\ *n* : a twilled woolen cloth

ser·geant \ˈsär-jənt\ *n* [ME, servant, attendant, officer who keeps order, fr. OF *sergent, serjant*, fr. L *servient-, serviens*, prp. *of servire* to serve] **1** : a noncommissioned officer (as in the army) ranking next below a staff sergeant **2** : an officer in a police force

sergeant first class *n* : a noncommissioned officer in the army ranking next below a master sergeant

sergeant major *n, pl* **sergeants major** *or* **sergeant majors 1** : a noncommissioned officer in the army, air force, or marine corps serving as chief administrative assistant in a headquarters **2** : a noncommissioned officer in the marine corps ranking above a first sergeant

¹**se·ri·al** \ˈsir-ē-əl\ *adj* : appearing in parts that follow regularly ⟨a ∼ story⟩ — **se·ri·al·ly** *adv*

²**serial** *n* : a serial story or other writing — **se·ri·al·ist** \-ə-ləst\ *n*

se·ries \ˈsi(ə)r-ēz\ *n, pl* **series** : a number of things or events arranged in order and connected by being alike in some way **syn** succession, progression, sequence, chain, train, string

seri·graph \ˈser-ə-ˌgraf\ *n* : an original silk-screen print — **se·rig·ra·pher**

\sə-ˈrig-rə-fər\ *n* — **se·rig·ra·phy** \-fē\ *n*

se·ri·ous \ˈsir-ē-əs\ *adj* **1** : thoughtful or subdued in appearance or manner : SOBER **2** : requiring much thought or work **3** : EARNEST, DEVOTED **4** : DANGEROUS, HARMFUL **syn** grave, sedate, sober, staid — **se·ri·ous·ly** *adv* — **se·ri·ous·ness** *n*

ser·mon \ˈsər-mən\ *n* [ME, fr. OF, fr. ML *sermon-, sermo*, fr. L, speech, conversation, fr. *serere* to link together] **1** : a religious discourse esp. as part of a worship service **2** : a lecture on conduct or duty

se·rol·o·gy \sə-ˈräl-ə-jē\ *n* : a science dealing with serums and esp. their reactions and properties — **se·ro·log·i·cal** \ˌsir-ə-ˈläj-i-kəl\ *or* **se·ro·log·ic** \-ik\ *adj*

se·rous \ˈsir-əs\ *adj* : of, relating to, resembling, or producing serum; *esp* : thin and watery

ser·pent \ˈsər-pənt\ *n* : SNAKE

¹**ser·pen·tine** \ˈsər-pən-ˌtēn, -ˌtīn\ *adj* **1** : SLY, CRAFTY **2** : WINDING, TURNING

²**ser·pen·tine** \-ˌtēn\ *n* : a dull-green mineral having a mottled appearance

ser·rate \ˈser-ˌāt\ *adj* : having a saw-toothed edge ⟨a ∼ leaf⟩

ser·ried \ˈser-ēd\ *adj* : DENSE

se·rum \ˈsir-əm\ *n, pl* **serums** *or* **se·ra** \-ə\ [L, whey, serum] : the liquid antibody-containing part that can be separated from blood when it clots; *also* : a preparation of animal serum containing specific antibodies and used to prevent or cure disease

serv *abbr* service

ser·vant \ˈsər-vənt\ *n* : a person employed esp. for domestic work

¹**serve** \ˈsərv\ *vb* **served; serv·ing 1** : to work as a servant **2** : to render obedience and worship to (God) **3** : to comply with the commands or demands of **4** : to work through or perform a term of service (as in the army) **5** : PUT IN ⟨*served* five years in jail⟩ **6** : to be of use : ANSWER ⟨pine boughs *served* for a bed⟩ **7** : BENEFIT **8** : to prove adequate or satisfactory for ⟨a pie that ∼*s* eight people⟩ **9** : to make ready and pass out ⟨∼ drinks⟩ **10** : to furnish or supply with something ⟨one power company *serving* the whole state⟩ **11** : to wait on ⟨∼ a customer⟩ **12** : to treat or act toward in a specified way **13** : to put the ball in play (as in tennis) — **serv·er** *n*

²**serve** *n* : the act of serving a ball (as in tennis)

¹**ser·vice** \ˈsər-vəs\ *n* **1** : the occupation of a servant **2** : HELP, BENEFIT **3** : a meeting for worship; *also* : a form followed in worship or in a ceremony ⟨burial ∼⟩ **4** : the act, fact, or means of serving **5** : performance of official or professional duties **6** : a serving of the ball (as in tennis) **7** : a set of dishes or silverware **8** : a branch of public employment; *also* : the persons in it

⟨civil ∼⟩ 9 : military or naval duty syn
use, advantage, account, avail

²**service** vb **ser•viced; ser•vic•ing** : to do
maintenance or repair work on or for

ser•vice•able \ˈsər-və-sə-bəl\ adj : prepared for service : USEFUL, USABLE

ser•vice•man \ˈsər-vəs-ˌman, -mən\ n 1
: a male member of the armed forces 2
: a man employed to repair or maintain equipment

service station n : a retail station for
servicing motor vehicles

ser•vice•wom•an \ˈsər-vəs-ˌwùm-ən\ n
: a female member of the armed
forces

ser•vile \ˈsər-vəl, -ˌvīl\ adj 1 : befitting
a slave or servant 2 : behaving like a
slave : SUBMISSIVE — **ser•vil•i•ty**
\ˌvil-ət-ē\ n

serv•ing \ˈsər-viŋ\ n : HELPING

ser•vi•tor \ˈsər-vət-ər\ n : a male servant

ser•vi•tude \ˈsər-və-ˌt(y)üd\ n : SLAV-
ERY, BONDAGE

ser•vo \ˈsər-vō\ n, pl **servos** 1 : SER-
VOMOTOR 2 : SERVOMECHANISM

ser•vo•mech•a•nism \ˈsər-vō-
ˌmek-ə-ˌniz-əm\ n : a device for automatically correcting the performance
of a mechanism

ser•vo•mo•tor \ˈsər-vō-ˌmōt-ər\ n : a
motor in a servomechanism that sup-
plements a primary control by correcting position or motion

ses•a•me \ˈses-ə-mē\ n : an East Indian
annual herb; also : its seeds that yield
an edible oil (**sesame oil**) and are used
in flavoring

ses•qui•cen•ten•ni•al \ˌses-kwi-sen-ˈten-
ē-əl\ n [L sesqui- one and a half, half
again] : a 150th anniversary or its celebration — **sesquicentennial** adj

ses•qui•pe•da•lian \ˌses-kwə-
pə-ˈdāl-yən\ adj 1 : having many syllables : LONG 2 : using long words

ses•sile \ˈses-ˌīl, -əl\ adj : attached by
the base ⟨a ∼ leaf⟩

ses•sion \ˈsesh-ən\ n 1 : a meeting or
series of meetings of a body (as a
court or legislature) for the transaction of business 2 : a meeting or period devoted to a particular activity

¹**set** \ˈset\ vb **set; set•ting** 1 : to cause to
sit 2 : PLACE 3 : ARRANGE, ADJUST 4
: to cause to be or do 5 : SETTLE, DE-
CREE 6 : to fix in a frame 7 : ESTIMATE
8 : WAGER, STAKE 9 : to make fast or
rigid 10 : to adapt (as words) to something (as music) 11 : to become fixed
or firm or solid 12 : to be suitable : FIT
13 : BROOD 14 : to have a certain direction 15 : to pass below the horizon
16 : to defeat in bridge — **set about**
: to begin to do — **set forth** : to begin
a trip — **set off** 1 : to start out on a
course or a trip 2 : to cause to explode
— **set out** : to begin a trip or undertaking — **set sail** : to begin a voyage

²**set** n 1 : a setting or a being set 2 : DI-
RECTION, COURSE; also : TENDENCY 3
: FORM, BUILD 4 : the fit of something

(as a coat) 5 : an artificial setting for
the scene of a play or motion picture 6
: a group of tennis games in which one
side wins at least six to an opponent's
four or less 7 : a group of persons or
things of the same kind or having a
common characteristic usu. classed
together 8 : a collection of things and
esp. of mathematical elements (as
numbers or points) 9 : an electronic
apparatus ⟨a television ∼⟩

³**set** adj 1 : fixed by authority or custom
2 : DELIBERATE 3 : RIGID 4 : PERSISTENT

set•back \ˈset-ˌbak\ n : a temporary defeat : REVERSE

set back \ˈset-ˈbak\ vb : HINDER, DELAY;
also : REVERSE

set•screw \ˈset-ˌskrü\ n : a screw
screwed through one part tightly upon
or into another part to prevent relative
movement

set•tee \se-ˈtē\ n : a bench or sofa with
a back and arms

set•ter \ˈset-ər\ n : a large long-coated
hunting dog

set•ting \ˈset-iŋ\ n 1 : the frame in
which a gem is set 2 : BACKGROUND,
ENVIRONMENT; also : SCENERY 3 : music written for a text (as of a poem) 4
: the eggs that a fowl sits on for hatching at one time

set•tle \ˈset-əl\ vb **set•tled; set•tling** \ˈset-
(ə-)liŋ\ [ME settlen to seat, bring to
rest, come to rest, fr. OE setlan, fr.
setl seat] 1 : to put in place 2 : to
locate permanently 3 : to make compact 4 : QUIET, CALM 5 : to establish in
life, business, or a home 6 : to direct
one's efforts 7 : to fix by agreement 8
: to give legally 9 : ADJUST, ARRANGE
10 : DECIDE, DETERMINE 11 : to make a
final disposition of ⟨∼ an account⟩ 12
: to come to rest 13 : to reach an
agreement on 14 : to sink gradually to
a lower level 15 : to become clear by
depositing sediment syn set, fix, establish, place — **set•tler** \-(ə-)lər\ n

set•tle•ment \ˈset-əl-mənt\ n 1 : the act
or process of settling 2 : BESTOWAL ⟨a
marriage ∼⟩ 3 : payment of an account 4 : COLONY 5 : a small village 6
: an institution in a poor district of a
city to give aid to the community 7
: adjustment of doubts and differences

set-to \ˈset-ˌtü\ n, pl **set-tos** : FIGHT

set•up \ˈset-ˌəp\ n 1 : the manner or act
of arranging 2 : glass, ice, and nonalcoholic beverage for mixing served to
patrons who supply their own liquor

set up \ˈset-ˈəp\ vb 1 : to place in position; also : ASSEMBLE 2 : CAUSE 3
: FOUND, ESTABLISH

sev•en \ˈsev-ən\ n 1 : one more than six
2 : the 7th in a set or series 3 : something having seven units — **seven** adj
or pron — **sev•enth** \-ənth\ adj or adv
or n

sev•en•teen \ˌsev-ən-ˈtēn\ n : one more
than 16 — **seventeen** adj or pron —
sev•en•teenth \-ˈtēnth\ adj or n

seventeen–year locust *n* : a cicada of the U.S. that has in the North a life of 17 years and in the South of 13 years of which most is spent underground as a nymph and only a few weeks as a winged adult

sev·en·ty \'sev-ən-tē\ *n, pl* **-ties** : seven times 10 — **sev·en·ti·eth** \-tē-əth\ *adj or n* — **seventy** *adj or pron*

seventy–eight \ˌsev-ən-tē-'āt\ *n* : a phonograph record designed to be played at 78 revolutions per minute

sev·er \'sev-ər\ *vb* **sev·ered; sev·er·ing** \-(ə-)riŋ\ : DIVIDE; *esp* : to separate by force (as by cutting or tearing) — **sev·er·ance** \-(ə-)rəns\ *n*

sev·er·al \'sev-(ə-)rəl\ *adj* [ME, fr. ML *separalis*, fr. L *separ* separate, fr. *separare* to separate] 1 : INDIVIDUAL, DISTINCT (federal union of the ~ states) 2 : consisting of an indefinite number but yet not very many — **sev·er·al·ly** \-ē\ *adv*

severance pay *n* : extra pay given an employee upon leaving a job permanently

se·vere \sə-'viər\ *adj* **se·ver·er; -est** 1 : marked by strictness or sternness : AUSTERE 2 : strict in discipline 3 : causing distress and esp. physical discomfort or pain (~ weather) (a ~ wound) 4 : hard to endure (~ trials) **syn** intense, ascetic, astringent, austere — **se·vere·ly** *adv* — **se·ver·i·ty** \-'ver-ət-ē\ *n*

sew \'sō\ *vb* **sewed; sewn** \'sōn\ *or* **sewed; sew·ing** 1 : to fasten by stitches made with thread and needle 2 : to engage in sewing

sew·age \'sü-ij\ *n* : waste materials carried off by sewers

¹sew·er \'sō-(ə)r\ *n* : one that sews

²sew·er \'sü-ər\ *n* : an artificial pipe or channel to carry off waste matter

sew·er·age \'sü-ə-rij\ *n* 1 : SEWAGE 2 : a system of sewers

sew·ing \'sō-iŋ\ *n* 1 : the activity of one who sews 2 : material that has been or is to be sewed

sex \'seks\ *n* 1 : either of two groups into which many living things are divided according to their roles in reproduction and which are distinguished as male and female; *also* : the qualities by which these sexes are differentiated and which directly or indirectly function in reproduction involving two parents 2 : sexual activity or intercourse — **sexed** \'sekst\ *adj* — **sex·less** *adj*

sex·a·ge·nar·i·an \ˌsek-sə-jə-'ner-ē-ən\ *n* : a person who is 60 or more but less than 70 years old — **sexagenarian** *adj*

sex cell *n* : an egg cell or sperm cell

sex chromosome *n* : one of usu. a pair of chromosomes that are usu. similar in one sex but different in the other sex and are concerned with the inheritance of sex

sex hormone *n* : a hormone (as from the gonads or adrenal cortex) that affects the growth or function of the reproductive organs or the development of secondary sex characteristics

sex·ism \'sek-ˌsiz-əm\ *n* : prejudice or discrimination based on sex; *esp* : discrimination against women — **sex·ist** \'sek-səst\ *adj or n*

sex·pot \'seks-ˌpät\ *n* : a sexually stimulating woman

sex symbol *n* : a usu. renowned person (as an entertainer) noted and admired for conspicuous attractiveness

sex·tant \'sek-stənt\ *n* [NL *sextant-, sextans* sixth part of a circle, fr. L, sixth part, fr. *sextus* sixth] : a navigational instrument for measuring the angle between the horizon and the sun or a star in order to determine latitude

sex·tet \sek-'stet\ *n* 1 : a musical composition for six voices or six instruments; *also* : the six performers of such a composition 2 : a group or set of six

sex·ton \'sek-stən\ *n* : one who takes care of church property

sex·u·al \'sek-sh(ə-w)əl\ *adj* : of, relating to, or involving sex or the sexes (a ~ spore) (~ relations) — **sex·u·al·i·ty** \ˌsek-shə-'wal-ət-ē\ *n* — **sex·u·al·ly** \'sek-shə-(wə-)lē\ *adv*

sexual intercourse *n* 1 : intercourse between a male and a female in which the penis is inserted into the vagina 2 : intercourse between individuals which involves genital contact but in which the penis is not inserted into the vagina

sexually transmitted disease *n* : a disease (as syphilis, gonorrhea, or the genital form of herpes simplex) usu. or often transmitted by direct sexual contact

sexy \'sek-sē\ *adj* **sex·i·er; -est** : sexually suggestive or stimulating : EROTIC

SF *abbr* 1 sacrifice fly 2 science fiction

SFC *abbr* sergeant first class

SG *abbr* 1 senior grade 2 sergeant 3 solicitor general 4 surgeon general

sgd *abbr* signed

Sgt *abbr* sergeant

Sgt Maj *abbr* sergeant major

sh *abbr* share

shab·by \'shab-ē\ *adj* **shab·bi·er; -est** 1 : dressed in worn clothes 2 : threadbare and faded from wear 3 : MEAN (~ treatment) — **shab·bi·ly** \'shab-ə-lē\ *adv* — **shab·bi·ness** \-ē-nəs\ *n*

shack \'shak\ *n* : HUT, SHANTY

¹shack·le \'shak-əl\ *n* 1 : something (as a manacle or fetter) that confines the legs or arms 2 : a check on free action made as if by fetters 3 : a device for making something fast or secure

²shackle *vb* **shack·led; shack·ling** \-(ə-)liŋ\ : to fasten with shackles

shad \'shad\ *n, pl* **shad** : any of several sea fishes related to the herrings that swim up rivers to spawn and are important food fish

¹shade \'shād\ *n* 1 : partial obscurity 2 : space sheltered from the light esp. of the sun **3** : PHANTOM **4** : something that shelters from or intercepts light or heat; *also, pl* : SUNGLASSES **5** : a dark color or a variety of a color **6** : a small difference — **shady** *adj*

²**shade** *vb* **shad·ed; shad·ing 1** : to shelter from light and heat **2** : DARKEN, OBSCURE **3** : to mark with degrees of light or color **4** : to show slight differences esp. in color or meaning

shad·ing \'shād-iŋ\ *n* : the color and lines representing darkness or shadow in a drawing or painting

¹**shad·ow** \'shad-ō\ *n* **1** : partial darkness in a space from which light rays are cut off **2** : SHELTER **3** : shade cast upon a surface by something intercepting rays from a light (the ∼ of a tree) **4** : PHANTOM **5** : a shaded portion of a picture **6** : a small portion or degree : TRACE (a ∼ of doubt) **7** : a source of gloom or unhappiness — **shad·owy** *adj*

²**shadow** *vb* **1** : to cast a shadow on **2** : to represent faintly or vaguely **3** : to follow and watch closely : TRAIL

shad·ow·box \'shad-ō-₁bäks\ *vb* : to box with an imaginary opponent esp. for training

¹**shaft** \'shaft\ *n, pl* **shafts 1** : the long handle of a spear or lance **2** : SPEAR, LANCE **3** *or pl* **shaves** \'shāvz\ : POLE; *esp* : one of two poles between which a horse is hitched to pull a vehicle **4** : something (as a column) long and slender **5** : a bar to support a rotating piece or to transmit power by rotation **6** : an inclined opening in the ground (as for finding or mining ore) **7** : a vertical opening (as for an elevator) through the floors of a building

²**shaft** *vb* : to fit with a shaft

shag \'shag\ *n* **1** : a shaggy tangled mat (as of wool) **2** : tobacco cut into fine shreds

shag·gy \'shag-ē\ *adj* **shag·gi·er; -est 1** : rough with or as if with long hair or wool **2** : tangled or rough in surface

shah \'shä, 'shò\ *n, often cap* : a sovereign of Iran

Shak *abbr* Shakespeare

¹**shake** \'shāk\ *vb* **shook** \'shùk\; **shak·en** \'shā-kən\; **shak·ing 1** : to move or cause to move jerkily or irregularly **2** : BRANDISH, WAVE (*shaking* his fist) **3** : to disturb emotionally (*shaken* by her death) **4** : WEAKEN (*shook* his faith) **5** : to bring or come into a certain position, condition, or arrangement by or as if by moving jerkily **6** : to clasp (hands) in greeting or as a sign of goodwill or agreement **syn** tremble, quake, quaver, shiver, quiver — **shak·able** \'shā-kə-bəl\ *adj*

²**shake** *n* **1** : the act or a result of shaking **2** : DEAL, TREATMENT

shake·down \'shāk-₁daún\ *n* **1** : an improvised bed **2** : EXTORTION **3** : a process or period of adjustment **4** : a test (as of a new ship or airplane) under operating conditions

shake down \(')shāk-'daún\ *vb* **1** : to take up temporary quarters **2** : to occupy a makeshift bed **3** : to become accustomed esp. to new surroundings or duties **4** : to settle down **5** : to give a shakedown test to **6** : to obtain money from in a dishonest or illegal manner **7** : to bring about a reduction of

shak·er \'shā-kər\ *n* **1** : one that shakes (pepper ∼) **2** *cap* : a member of a religious sect founded in England in 1747

shake-up \'shāk-₁əp\ *n* : an extensive often drastic reorganization

shaky \'shā-kē\ *adj* **shak·i·er; -est** : UNSOUND, WEAK — **shak·i·ly** \'shā-kə-lē\ *adv* — **shak·i·ness** \-kē-nəs\ *n*

shale \'shāl\ *n* : a rock made up of fine layers and formed from clay, mud, or silt

shall \shəl, (')shal\ *vb, past* **should** \shəd, (')shúd\; *pres sing & pl* **shall** — used as an auxiliary to express a command, what seems inevitable or likely in the future, simple futurity, or determination

shal·lop \'shal-əp\ *n* : a light open boat

shal·lot \shə-'lät\ *n* [modif. of F *échalote*] **1** : the bulb of a perennial herb that is produced in clusters, resembles an onion, and is used in seasoning; *also* : this herb **2** : GREEN ONION

¹**shal·low** \'shal-ō\ *adj* **1** : not deep **2** : not intellectually profound **syn** superficial, sketchy

²**shallow** *n* : a shallow place in a body of water — usu. used in pl.

¹**sham** \'sham\ *n* **1** : something resembling an article of household linen and used in its place as a decoration (a pillow ∼) **2** : COUNTERFEIT, IMITATION

²**sham** *vb* **shammed; sham·ming** : FEIGN, PRETEND — **sham·mer** *n*

³**sham** *adj* : FALSE (∼ pearls)

sha·man \'shäm-ən, 'shā-mən\ *n* [Russ., fr. Tungusic (a language of Siberia)] : a priest who uses magic to cure the sick, to divine the hidden, and to control events

sham·ble \'sham-bəl\ *vb* **sham·bled; sham·bling** \-b(ə-)liŋ\ : to shuffle along — **shamble** *n*

sham·bles \'sham-bəlz\ *n* [*shamble* (meat market) & obs. E *shamble* (table for exhibition of meat for sale)] **1** : a scene of great slaughter **2** : a scene or state of great destruction or disorder

¹**shame** \'shām\ *n* **1** : a painful sense of having done something wrong, improper, or immodest **2** : DISGRACE, DISHONOR **3** : a cause of feeling shame — **shame·ful** \-fəl\ *adj* — **shame·ful·ly** \-ē\ *adv* — **shame·less** *adj* — **shame·less·ly** *adv*

²**shame** *vb* **shamed; sham·ing 1** : DISGRACE **2** : to make ashamed

shame·faced \'shām-'fāst\ *adj* : ASHAMED, ABASHED — **shame·faced·ly** \-'fā-səd-lē, -'fāst-lē\ *adv*

¹sham·poo \sham-ˈpü\ *vb* [Hindi *cāpo,* imper. of *cāpnā* to press, shampoo] : to wash (as the hair) with soap and water or with a special preparation; *also* : to clean (as a rug) similarly

²shampoo *n, pl* **shampoos 1** : the act or process of shampooing **2** : a preparation for use in shampooing

sham·rock \ˈsham-ˌräk\ *n* [IrGael *seamróg,* dim. of *seamar* clover, honeysuckle] : a plant with three leaflets used as an Irish floral emblem

shang·hai \shaŋ-ˈhī\ *vb* **shang·haied; shang·hai·ing** [*Shanghai,* China] : to force aboard a ship for service as a sailor; *also* : to trick or force into something

Shan·gri-la \ˌshaŋ-gri-ˈlä\ *n* [*Shangri-La,* imaginary land depicted in the novel *Lost Horizon* (1933) by James Hilton] : a remote idyllic hideaway

shank \ˈshaŋk\ *n* **1** : the part of the leg between the knee and ankle in man or a corresponding part of a quadruped **2** : a cut of meat from the leg **3** : the narrow part of the sole of a shoe beneath the instep **4** : the part of a tool or instrument (as a key or anchor) connecting the functioning part with a part by which it is held or moved

shan·tung \ˈshan-ˈtəŋ\ *n* : a fabric in plain weave having a slightly irregular surface

shan·ty \ˈshant-ē\ *n, pl* **shanties** : a small roughly built shelter or dwelling

¹shape \ˈshāp\ *vb* **shaped; shap·ing 1** : to form esp. in a particular shape **2** : DESIGN **3** : ADAPT, ADJUST **4** : REGULATE *syn* make, fashion, fabricate, manufacture, frame, mold

²shape *n* **1** : APPEARANCE **2** : surface configuration : FORM **3** : bodily contour apart from the head and face : FIGURE **4** : PHANTOM **5** : CONDITION

shape·less \ˈshāp-ləs\ *adj* **1** : having no definite shape **2** : not shapely — **shape·less·ly** *adv* — **shape·less·ness** *n*

shape·ly \ˈshāp-lē\ *adj* **shape·li·er; -est** : having a pleasing shape — **shape·li·ness** *n*

shard \ˈshärd\ *also* **sherd** \ˈshərd\ *n* : a broken piece : FRAGMENT

¹share \ˈsheər\ *n* **1** : a portion belonging to one person or group **2** : any of the equal interests into which the capital stock of a corporation is divided

²share *vb* **shared; shar·ing 1** : APPORTION **2** : to use or enjoy with others **3** : PARTICIPATE — **shar·er** *n*

³share *n* : PLOWSHARE

share·crop·per \-ˌkräp-ər\ *n* : a farmer who works another's land in return for a share of the crop — **share·crop** *vb*

share·hold·er \-ˌhōl-dər\ *n* : STOCKHOLDER

¹shark \ˈshärk\ *n* : any of various active, predaceous, and mostly large marine fishes with skeletons of cartilage

²shark *n* : a greedy crafty person

shark·skin \-ˌskin\ *n* **1** : the hide of a shark or leather made from it **2** : a fabric (as of cotton or rayon) woven from strands of many fine threads and having a sleek appearance and silky feel

¹sharp \ˈshärp\ *adj* **1** : having a thin cutting edge or fine point : not dull or blunt **2** : COLD, NIPPING (a ∼ wind) **3** : keen in intellect, perception, or attention **4** : BRISK, ENERGETIC **5** : IRRITABLE (a ∼ temper) **6** : causing intense distress (a ∼ pain) **7** : HARSH, CUTTING (∼ words) **8** : affecting the senses as if cutting or piercing (a ∼ sound) (a ∼ smell) **9** : not smooth or rounded (∼ features) **10** : involving an abrupt or extreme change (a ∼ turn) **11** : CLEAR, DISTINCT (mountains in ∼ relief); *also* : easy to perceive (a ∼ contrast) **12** : higher than the true pitch; *also* : raised by a half step **13** : STYLISH (a ∼ dresser) *syn* keen, acute, quick-witted, penetrative — **sharp·ly** *adv* — **sharp·ness** *n*

²sharp *adv* **1** : in a sharp manner **2** : EXACTLY, PRECISELY (left at 8 ∼)

³sharp *n* **1** : a sharp edge or point **2** : a character ♯ indicating a note a half step higher than the note named **3** : SHARPER

⁴sharp *vb* : to raise in pitch by a half step

sharp·en \ˈshär-pən\ *vb* **sharp·ened; sharp·en·ing** \ˈshärp-(ə-)niŋ\ : to make or become sharp — **sharp·en·er** *n* \ˈshärp-(ə-)nər\

sharp·er \ˈshär-pər\ *n* : SWINDLER; *esp* : a cheating gambler

sharp·ie *or* **sharpy** \ˈshär-pē\ *n, pl* **sharp·ies 1** : SHARPER **2** : a person who is exceptionally keen or alert

sharp·shoot·er \ˈshärp-ˌshüt-ər\ *n* : a good marksman — **sharp·shoot·ing** \-iŋ\ *n*

shat·ter \ˈshat-ər\ *vb* : to dash or burst into fragments — **shat·ter·proof** \ˌshat-ər-ˈprüf\ *adj*

¹shave \ˈshāv\ *vb* **shaved; shaved** *or* **shav·en** \ˈshā-vən\; **shav·ing 1** : to slice in thin pieces **2** : to make bare or smooth by cutting the hair from **3** : to cut or pare off by the sliding movement of a razor **4** : to skim along or near the surface of

²shave *n* **1** : any of various tools for cutting thin slices **2** : an act or process of shaving

shav·er \ˈshā-vər\ *n* : an electric-powered razor

shaves *pl of* SHAFT

shav·ing \ˈshā-viŋ\ *n* **1** : the act of one that shaves **2** : something shaved off

shawl \ˈshȯl\ *n* : a square or oblong piece of fabric used esp. by women as a loose covering for the head or shoulders

Shaw·nee \shȯ-ˈnē, shä-\ *n, pl* **Shawnee** *or* **Shawnees** : a member of an American Indian people orig. of the central Ohio valley; *also* : their language

she \(ˈ)shē\ *pron* : that female one (who is ∼); *also* : that one regarded as feminine (∼'s a fine ship)

sheaf \\'shēf\ *n, pl* **sheaves** \\'shēvz\ **1** : a bundle of stalks and ears of grain **2** : a group of things bound together

¹shear \\'shiər\ *vb* **sheared** *or* **shorn** \\'shōrn\ ; **shear·ing 1** : to cut the hair or wool from : CLIP, TRIM **2** : to deprive by or as if by cutting **3** : to cut or break sharply

²shear *n* **1** : any of various cutting tools that consist of two blades fastened together so that the edges slide one by the other — usu. used in pl. **2** *chiefly Brit* : the act, an instance, or the result of shearing **3** : an action or stress caused by applied forces that causes two parts of a body to slide on each other

sheath \\'shēth\ *n, pl* **sheaths** \\'shēthz, 'shēths\ **1** : a case for a blade (as of a knife); *also* : an anatomical covering suggesting such a case **2** : a close-fitting dress usu. worn without a belt

sheathe \\'shēth\ *also* **sheath** \\'shēth\ *vb* **sheathed; sheath·ing 1** : to put into a sheath **2** : to cover with something that guards or protects

sheath·ing \\'shē-thiŋ, -thin\ *n* : material used to sheathe something; *esp* : the first covering of boards or of waterproof material on the outside wall of a frame house or on a timber roof

sheave \\'shiv, 'shēv\ *n* : a grooved wheel or pulley (as on a pulley block)

she-bang \\shi-'baŋ\ *n* : CONTRIVANCE, AFFAIR, CONCERN (blew up the whole ~)

¹shed \\'shed\ *vb* **shed; shed·ding 1** : to cause to flow from a cut or wound (~ blood) **2** : to pour down in drops (~ tears) **3** : to give out (as light) : DIFFUSE **4** : to throw off (as a natural covering) : DISCARD

²shed *n* : a slight structure built for shelter or storage

sheen \\'shēn\ *n* : a subdued luster

sheep \\'shēp\ *n, pl* **sheep 1** : any of a genus of cud-chewing mammals that are stockier than the related goats and lack a beard in the male; *esp* : one raised for meat or for its wool or skin **2** : a timid or defenseless person **3** : SHEEPSKIN

sheep dog *n* : a dog used to tend, drive, or guard sheep

sheep·fold \\'shēp-,fōld\ *n* : a pen or shelter for sheep

sheep·herd·er \\'shēp-,hərd-ər\ *n* : a worker in charge of sheep esp. on open range — **sheep·herd·ing** \-iŋ\ *n*

sheep·ish \\'shē-pish\ *adj* : BASHFUL, TIMID; *esp* : embarrassed by consciousness of a fault — **sheep·ish·ly** *adv*

sheep·skin \\'shēp-,skin\ *n* **1** : the hide of a sheep or leather prepared from it: *also* : PARCHMENT **2** : DIPLOMA

sheer \\'shiər\ *adj* **1** : very thin or transparent **2** : UNQUALIFIED (~ folly) **3** : very steep *syn* pure, simple, absolute, unadulterated, unmitigated — **sheer** *adv*

²sheer *vb* : to turn from a course

¹sheet \\'shēt\ *n* **1** : a broad piece of plain cloth (as for a bed) **2** : a single piece of paper **3** : a broad flat surface (a ~ of water) **4** : something broad and long and relatively thin

²sheet *n* **1** : a rope that regulates the angle at which a sail is set to catch the wind **2** *pl* : spaces at either end of an open boat

sheet·ing \\'shēt-iŋ\ *n* : material in the form of sheets or suitable for forming into sheets

sheikh *or* **sheik** \\'shēk, 'shāk\ *n* : an Arab chief — **sheikh·dom** *or* **sheik·dom** \-dəm\ *n*

shek·el \\'shek-əl\ *n* — see MONEY table

shelf \\'shelf\ *n, pl* **shelves** \\'shelvz\ **1** : a thin flat usu. long and narrow structure fastened horizontally (as on a wall) above the floor to hold things **2** : something (as a sandbar) that suggests a shelf

shelf life *n* : the period of storage time during which a material will remain useful

shell \\'shel\ *n* **1** : a hard or tough outer covering of an animal (as a beetle, turtle, or mollusk) or of an egg or a seed or fruit (as a nut); *also* : something that resembles a shell (a pastry ~) **2** : a light narrow racing boat propelled by oarsmen **3** : a case holding an explosive and designed to be fired from a cannon; *also* : a case holding the charge of powder and shot or bullet for small arms **4** : a plain usu. sleeveless blouse or sweater — **shelled** \\'sheld\ *adj* — **shelly** \\'shel-ē\ *adj*

²shell *vb* **1** : to remove from a shell or husk **2** : BOMBARD — **shell·er** *n*

shel·lac \\shə-'lak\ *n* **1** : a purified lac used esp. in varnishes **2** : lac dissolved in alcohol and used as a varnish

²shellac *vb* **shel·lacked; shel·lack·ing 1** : to coat or treat with shellac **2** : to defeat decisively

shel·lack·ing \\shə-'lak-iŋ\ *n* : a sound drubbing

shell bean *n* : a bean grown esp. for its edible seeds; *also* : its edible seed

shell·fish \-,fish\ *n* : a water animal (as an oyster or lobster) with a shell

shell out *vb* : PAY

shell shock *n* : any of various nervous disorders appearing in soldiers exposed to modern warfare

¹shel·ter \\'shel-tər\ *n* : something that gives protection : REFUGE

²shelter *vb* **shel·tered; shel·ter·ing** \-t(ə-)riŋ\ : to give protection or refuge to *syn* harbor, lodge, house

shelve \\'shelv\ *vb* **shelved; shelv·ing 1** : to slope gradually **2** : to store on shelves **3** : to dismiss from service or use **4** : to put aside : DEFER (~ a proposal)

shelv·ing \\'shel-viŋ\ *n* : material for shelves

she·nan·i·gan \\shə-'nan-i-gən\ *n* **1** : an

underhand trick **2** : questionable conduct — usu. used in pl. **3** : high-spirited or michievous activity — usu. used in pl.

¹shep·herd \'shep-ərd\ n : one who tends sheep

²shepherd vb : to tend as or in the manner of a shepherd

shep·herd·ess \'shep-ərd-əs\ n : a woman who tends sheep

sher·bet \'shər-bət\ n [Turk *serbet*, fr. Per *sharbat*, fr. Ar *sharbah* drink] **1** : a drink of sweetened diluted fruit juice **2** or **sher·bert** \-bərt\ : a frozen dessert of fruit juices, sugar, milk or water, and egg whites or gelatin

sherd var of SHARD

sher·iff \'sher-əf\ n [ME *shirreve*, fr. OE *scīrgerēfa*, lit., shire reeve (local official)] : a county officer charged with the execution of the law and the preservation of order

sher·ry \'sher-ē\ n, pl **sherries** [alter. of earlier *sherris* (taken as pl.), fr. *Xeres* (now *Jerez*), Spain] : a fortified wine with a nutty flavor

Shet·land pony \'shet-lən(d)-\ n : any of a breed of small stocky shaggy hardy ponies

shew \'shō\ Brit var of SHOW

shi·at·su also **shi·at·zu** \shē-'ät-sü\ n [short for Jp *Shiatsuryōhō*] : a finger massage of those bodily areas used in acupuncture

shib·bo·leth \'shib-ə-ləth\ n [Heb *shibbōleth* stream; fr. the use of this word as a test to distinguish the men of Gilead from members of the tribe of Ephraim, who pronounced it *sibbōleth* (Judges 12:5, 6)] **1** : a pet phrase **2** : language that is a criterion for distinguishing members of a group

shied past and past part of SHY

¹shield \'shēld\ n **1** : a broad piece of defensive armor carried on the arm **2** : something that protects or hides

²shield vb : to protect or hide with a shield syn protect, guard, safeguard

shier comparative of SHY

shiest superlative of SHY

¹shift \'shift\ vb **1** : EXCHANGE, REPLACE **2** : to change place, position, or direction : MOVE; also : to change the arrangement of gears transmitting power in an automobile : GET BY, MANAGE syn remove, ship, transfer

²shift n **1** : SCHEME, TRICK **2** : a woman's slip or loose-fitting dress **3** : a group working together alternating with other groups **4** : TRANSFER **5** : GEARSHIFT

shift·less \'shift(t)-ləs\ adj : LAZY, INEFFICIENT — **shift·less·ness** n

shifty \'shif-tē\ adj **shift·i·er; -est 1** : TRICKY; also : ELUSIVE **2** : indicative of a tricky nature (~ eyes)

Shih Tzu \'shēd-'zü\ n : a small short-legged dog of an ancient Chinese breed that has a short muzzle and a long dense coat

shi·lingi \shil-'iŋ-ē\ n, pl **shi·lingi** : the shilling of Tanzania

shill \'shil\ n : one who acts as a decoy (as for a cheater) — **shill** vb

shil·le·lagh also **shil·la·lah** \shə-'lā-lē\ n [*Shillelagh*, town in Ireland famed for its oaks] : CUDGEL, CLUB

shil·ling \'shil-iŋ\ n — SEE MONEY TABLE

shil·ly-shal·ly \'shil-ē-,shal-ē\ vb **shilly-shall·ied; shil·ly-shal·ly·ing 1** : to show hesitation or lack of decisiveness **2** : to waste time

shim \'shim\ n : a thin often tapered piece of wood, metal, or stone used (as in leveling something) to fill in

shim·mer \'shim-ər\ vb **shim·mered; shim·mer·ing** \-(ə-)riŋ\ : to shine waveringly or tremulously : GLIMMER syn flash, gleam, glint, sparkle, glitter — **shimmer** n — **shim·mery** adj

shim·my \'shim-ē\ n, pl **shimmies** : an abnormal vibration esp. in the front wheels of a motor vehicle — **shimmy** vb

¹shin \'shin\ n : the front part of the leg below the knee

²shin vb **shinned; shin·ning** : to climb (as a pole) by gripping alternately with arms or hands and legs

shin·bone \'shin-,bōn, -,bōn\ n : TIBIA

¹shine \'shin\ vb **shone** \'shōn\ or **shined; shin·ing 1** : to give light **2** : GLEAM, GLITTER **3** : to be eminent **4** : to cause to shed light **5** : POLISH

²shine n **1** : BRIGHTNESS, RADIANCE **2** : LUSTER, BRILLIANCE **3** : SUNSHINE

shin·er \'shī-nər\ n **1** : a small silvery fish; esp : any of numerous small freshwater American fishes related to the carp **2** : a bruised eye

¹shin·gle \'shiŋ-gəl\ n **1** : a small thin piece of building material (as wood or an asbestos composition) used in overlapping rows for covering a roof or outside wall **2** : a small sign

²shingle vb **shin·gled; shin·gling** \-g(ə-)liŋ\ : to cover with shingles

³shingle n : a beach strewn with gravel; also : coarse gravel (as on a beach)

shin·gles \'shiŋ-gəlz\ n pl : acute inflammation of the spinal and cranial nerves caused by the chicken pox virus and associated with eruptions and pain along the course of the affected nerves

shin·ny \'shin-ē\ vb **shin·nied; shin·ny·ing** : SHIN

Shin·to \'shin-,tō\ n : the indigenous religion of Japan consisting esp. in reverence of the spirits of natural forces and imperial ancestors — **Shin·to·ism** n — **Shin·to·ist** n or adj

shiny \'shī-nē\ adj **shin·i·er; -est** : BRIGHT, RADIANT; also : POLISHED

¹ship \'ship\ n **1** : a large oceangoing boat **2** : a ship's officers and crew **3** : AIRSHIP, AIRCRAFT, SPACECRAFT

²ship vb **shipped; ship·ping 1** : to put or receive on board a ship for transportation **2** : to have transported by a carrier **3** : to take or draw into a boat (~ oars) (~ water) **4** : to engage to serve on a ship — **ship·per** n

-ship \ˌship\ *n suffix* **1** : state : condition : quality ⟨friend*ship*⟩ **2** : office : dignity : profession ⟨lord*ship*⟩ ⟨clerk*ship*⟩ **3** : art : skill ⟨horseman*ship*⟩ **4** : something showing, exhibiting, or embodying a quality or state ⟨town*ship*⟩ **5** : one entitled to a (specified) rank, title, or appellation ⟨his Lord*ship*⟩ **6** : the body of persons engaged in a specified activity ⟨reader*ship*⟩

ship-board \ˈship-ˌbōrd\ *n* : SHIP

ship-build-er \ˈship-ˌbil-dər\ *n* : one who designs or builds ships

ship-fit-ter \ˈship-ˌfit-ər\ *n* **1** : one who constructs ships **2** : a naval enlisted man who works as a plumber

ship-mate \-ˌmāt\ *n* : a fellow sailor

ship-ment \-mənt\ *n* : the process of shipping; *also* : the goods shipped

ship-ping \ˈship-iŋ\ *n* **1** : SHIPS; *esp* : ships in one port or belonging to one country **2** : transportation of goods

ship-shape \ˈship-ˌshāp\ *adj* : TRIM, TIDY

ship-worm \-ˌwərm\ *n* : any of various wormlike marine clams that burrow in wood and damage wooden ships and wharves

¹ship-wreck \-ˌrek\ *n* **1** : a wrecked ship **2** : destruction or loss of a ship **3** : total loss or failure : RUIN

²shipwreck *vb* : to cause or meet disaster at sea through destruction or foundering

ship-wright \ˈship-ˌrīt\ *n* : a carpenter skilled in ship construction and repair

ship-yard \-ˌyärd\ *n* : a place where ships are built or repaired

shire \ˈshī(ə)r, *in place-name compounds* ˌshiər, shər\ *n* : a county in Great Britain

shirk \ˈshərk\ *vb* : to avoid performing (duty or work) — **shirk-er** *n*

shirr \ˈshər\ *vb* **1** : to make shirring in **2** : to bake (eggs removed from the shell) until set

shirr-ing \ˈshər-iŋ\ *n* : a decorative gathering in cloth made by drawing up parallel lines of stitches

¹shirt \ˈshərt\ *n* **1** : a loose cloth garment usu. having a collar, sleeves, a front opening, and a tail long enough to be tucked inside trousers or a skirt **2** : UNDERSHIRT — **shirt-less** *adj*

shirt-ing \-iŋ\ *n* : cloth suitable for making shirts

shish ke-bab \ˈshish-kə-ˌbäb\ *n* : kabob cooked on skewers

shiv \ˈshiv\ *n, slang* : KNIFE

¹shiv-er \ˈshiv-ər\ *vb* **shiv-ered; shiv-er-ing** \-(ə-)riŋ\ : TREMBLE, QUIVER *syn* shudder, quaver, shake, quake

²shiver *n* : an instance of shivering — **shiv-ery** *adj*

¹shoal \ˈshōl\ *n* **1** : a shallow place in a sea, lake, or river **2** : a sandbank or bar creating a shallow

²shoal *n* : a large group (as of fish)

shoat \ˈshōt\ *n* : a weaned young pig

¹shock \ˈshäk\ *n* : a pile of sheaves of grain set up in the field

²shock *n* [MF *choc*, fr. *choquer* to strike against] **1** : a sharp impact or violent shake or jar **2** : a sudden violent mental or emotional disturbance **3** : the effect of a charge of electricity passing through the body **4** : a state of bodily collapse caused esp. by crushing wounds, blood loss, or burns **5** : an attack of apoplexy or heart disease **6** : SHOCK ABSORBER — **shock-proof** \-ˈprüf\ *adj*

³shock *vb* **1** : to strike with surprise, horror, or disgust **2** : to subject to the action of an electrical discharge

⁴shock *n* : a thick bushy mass (as of hair)

shock absorber *n* : any of several devices for absorbing the energy of sudden shocks in machinery

shock-er \ˈshäk-ər\ *n* : one that shocks; *esp* : a sensational work of fiction or drama

shock-ing \-iŋ\ *adj* : extremely startling and offensive — **shock-ing-ly** *adv*

shock therapy *n* : the treatment of mental disorder by induction of coma or convulsion through the use of drugs or electricity

¹shod-dy \ˈshäd-ē\ *n* **1** : wool reclaimed from old rags; *also* : a fabric made from it **2** : inferior or imitation material **3** : pretentious vulgarity

²shoddy *adj* **shod-di-er; -est 1** : made of shoddy **2** : cheaply imitative : INFERIOR, SHAM — **shod-di-ly** \ˈshäd-ʰl-ē\ *adv* — **shod-di-ness** \-ē-nəs\ *n*

¹shoe \ˈshü\ *n* **1** : a covering for the human foot **2** : HORSESHOE **3** : the part of a brake that presses on the wheel **4** : the casing of an automobile tire

²shoe *vb* **shod** \ˈshäd\ *also* **shoed** \ˈshüd\; **shoe-ing** \ˈshü-iŋ\ : to put a shoe or shoes on

shoe-lace \-ˌlās\ *n* : a lace or string for fastening a shoe

shoe-mak-er \-ˌmā-kər\ *n* : one who makes or repairs shoes

shoe-string \-ˌstriŋ\ *n* **1** : SHOELACE **2** : a small sum of money

shone *past and past part of* SHINE

shook *past of* SHAKE

shook-up \(ˈ)shùk-ˈəp\ *adj* : nervously upset : AGITATED

¹shoot \ˈshüt\ *vb* **shot** \ˈshät\; **shoot-ing 1** : to drive (as an arrow or bullet) forward quickly or forcibly **2** : to hit, kill, or wound with a missile **3** : to cause a missile to be driven forth or forth from ⟨~ a gun⟩ ⟨~ an arrow⟩ **4** : to send forth (as a ray of light) **5** : to thrust forward or out **6** : to pass rapidly along ⟨~ the rapids⟩ **7** : PHOTOGRAPH, FILM **8** : to drive or rush swiftly : DART **9** : to grow by or as if by sending out shoots; *also* : MATURE, DEVELOP — **shoot-er** *n*

²shoot *n* **1** : the aerial part of a plant; *also* : a plant part (as a branch) developed from one bud **2** : an act of shooting (as with a bow or a firearm) **3** : a shooting match

shooting iron *n* : FIREARM

shooting star *n* : METEOR 2

shoot up *vb* : to inject a narcotic into a vein

¹**shop** \'shäp\ *n* [ME *shoppe,* fr. OE *sceoppa* booth] **1** : a place where things are made or worked on : FACTORY, MILL **2** : a retail store ⟨dress ∼⟩

²**shop** *vb* **shopped; shop·ping** : to visit stores for purchasing or examining goods — **shop·per** *n*

shop·keep·er \'shäp-ˌkē-pər\ *n* : a retail merchant

shop·lift \-ˌlift\ *vb* : to steal goods on display from a store — **shop·lift·er** \-ˌlif-tər\ *n*

shop·worn \-ˌwörn\ *adj* : soiled or frayed from much handling in a store

¹**shore** \'shör\ *n* : land along the edge of a body of water — **shore·less** *adj*

²**shore** *vb* **shored; shor·ing** : to give support to : BRACE, PROP

³**shore** *n* : ¹PROP

shore·bird \-ˌbərd\ *n* : any of a large group of birds (as the plovers and sandpipers) mostly found along the seashore

shore patrol *n* : a branch of a navy that exercises guard and police functions

shor·ing \'shör-iŋ\ *n* : the act of supporting with or as if with a prop

shorn *past part of* SHEAR

¹**short** \'shört\ *adj* **1** : not long or tall **2** : not great in distance **3** : brief in time **4** : not coming up to standard or to an expected amount **5** : CURT, ABRUPT **6** : insufficiently supplied **7** : made with shortening : FLAKY **8** : consisting of or relating to a sale of securities or commodities that the seller does not possess or has not contracted for at the time of the sale ⟨∼ sale⟩ — **short·ness** *n*

²**short** *adv* **1** : ABRUPTLY, CURTLY **2** : at some point before a goal aimed at

³**short** *n* **1** : something shorter than normal or standard **2** *pl* : drawers or trousers of less than knee length **3** : SHORT CIRCUIT

⁴**short** *vb* : SHORT-CIRCUIT

short·age \'shört-ij\ *n* : LACK, DEFICIT

short·cake \'shört-ˌkāk\ *n* : a dessert consisting of short biscuit spread with sweetened fruit

short·change \-'chānj\ *vb* : to cheat esp. by giving less than the correct amount of change

short circuit *n* : a connection made between points in an electric circuit between which current does not normally flow — **short–circuit** *vb*

short·com·ing \'shört-ˌkəm-iŋ\ *n* : FAILING, DEFECT

short·cut \-ˌkət\ *n* **1** : a route more direct than that usu. taken **2** : a quicker way of doing something

short·en \'shört-ᵊn\ *vb* **short·ened, short·en·ing** \'shört-(ᵊ-)niŋ\ : to make or become short syn curtail, abbreviate, abridge, retrench

short·en·ing \'shört-(ᵊ-)niŋ\ *n* : a sub-

stance (as lard or butter) that makes pastry tender and flaky

short·hand \'shört-ˌhand\ *n* : a method of writing rapidly by using symbols and abbreviations for letters, words, or phrases : STENOGRAPHY

short·hand·ed \-'han-dəd\ *adj* : short of the needed number of people

short·horn \-ˌhörn\ *n, often cap* : any of a breed of mostly red cattle of English origin

short hundredweight *n* — see WEIGHT table

short–lived \'shört-'līvd, -ˌlivd\ *adj* : of short life or duration

short·ly \'shört-lē\ *adv* **1** : in a few words **2** : in a short time : SOON

short order *n* : an order for food that can be quickly cooked

short shrift *n* **1** : a brief respite from death **2** : little consideration

short·sight·ed \'shört-'sīt-əd\ *adj* **1** : NEARSIGHTED **2** : lacking foresight — **short·sight·ed·ness** *n*

short·stop \-ˌstäp\ *n* : a baseball player defending the area between second and third base

short story *n* : a short invented prose narrative usu. dealing with a few characters and aiming at unity of effect

short–tem·pered \'shört-'tem-pərd\ *adj* : having a quick temper

short–term \-'tərm\ *adj* **1** : occurring over or involving a relatively short period of time **2** : of or relating to a financial transaction based on a term usu. of less than a year

short ton *n* — see WEIGHT table

short·wave \'shört-'wāv\ *n* : a radio wave with a wavelength between 10 and 100 meters

Sho·sho·ne *or* **Sho·sho·ni** \shə-'shō-nē\ *n, pl* **Shoshones** *or* **Shoshoni** : a member of an American Indian people orig. ranging through California, Colorado, Idaho, Nevada, Utah, and Wyoming

¹**shot** \'shät\ *n* **1** : an act of shooting **2** : a stroke or throw in some games **3** : something that is shot : MISSILE, PROJECTILE; *esp* : small pellets forming a charge for a shotgun **4** : a metal sphere that is thrown for distance in the shot put **5** : RANGE, REACH **6** : MARKSMAN **7** : a single photographic exposure **8** : a single sequence of a motion picture or a television program made by one camera **9** : an injection (as of medicine) into the body **10** : a portion (as of liquor or medicine) taken at one time

²**shot** *past and past part of* SHOOT

shot·gun \'shät-ˌgən\ *n* : a gun with a smooth bore used to fire small shot at short range

shot put *n* : a field event consisting in putting the shot for distance

should \shəd, (ˈ)shu̇d\ *past of* SHALL — used as an auxiliary to express condition, obligation or propriety, probability, or futurity from a point of view in the past

¹shoul·der \'shōl-dər\ n 1 : the part of the body of a person or animal where the arm or foreleg joins the body 2 : a projecting part resembling a human shoulder

²shoulder vb **shoul·dered; shoul·der·ing** \-d(ə-)riŋ\ 1 : to push or thrust with the shoulder 2 : to take upon the shoulder 3 : to take the responsibility of

shoulder belt n : an automobile safety belt worn across the torso and over the shoulder

shoulder blade n : the flat triangular bone at the back of the shoulder

shout \'shaut\ vb : to utter a sudden loud cry — **shout** n

shove \'shəv\ vb **shoved; shov·ing** : to push along, aside, or away — **shove** n

¹shov·el \'shəv-əl\ n 1 : a broad long-handled scoop used to lift and throw loose material 2 : the amount of something held by a shovel

²shovel vb -**eled** or -**elled; -el·ing** or -**el·ling** \-(ə-)liŋ\ 1 : to take up and throw with a shovel 2 : to dig or clean out with a shovel

¹show \'shō\ vb **showed** \'shōd\ ; **shown** \'shōn\ or **showed; show·ing** [ME shewen, showen, fr. OE scēawian to look, look at, see] 1 : to cause or permit to be seen : EXHIBIT ⟨~ anger⟩ 2 : CONFER, BESTOW ⟨~ mercy⟩ 3 : REVEAL, DISCLOSE ⟨~ed courage in battle⟩ 4 : INSTRUCT ⟨~ed me how to do it⟩ 5 : PROVE ⟨~s he was guilty⟩ 6 : APPEAR 7 : to be noticeable 8 : to be third in a horse race

²show n 1 : a demonstrative display 2 : outward appearance ⟨a ~ of resistance⟩ 3 : SPECTACLE 4 : a theatrical presentation 5 : a radio or television program 6 : third place in a horse race

¹show·case \'shō-ˌkās\ n : a cabinet for displaying items (as in a store)

²showcase vb **show-cased; show-cas·ing** : EXHIBIT

show·down \'shō-ˌdaun\ n : the final settlement of a contested issue; also : the test of strength by which a contested issue is resolved

¹show·er \'shau(-ə)r\ n 1 : a brief fall of rain 2 : a bath in which water is showered on the person 3 : a party given by friends who bring gifts — **show·ery** adj

²shower vb 1 : to fall in a shower 2 : to bathe in a shower

show·man \'shō-mən\ n : one having a gift for dramatization and visual effectiveness — **show·man·ship** n

show–off \'shō-ˌof\ n : one that seeks to attract attention by conspicuous behavior

show off \'\ \shō-ˈof\ vb 1 : to display proudly 2 : to act as a show-off

show·piece \'shō-ˌpēs\ n : an outstanding example used for exhibition

show·place \-ˌplās\ n : an estate or building that is a showpiece

show up vb : ARRIVE

showy \'shō-ē\ adj **show·i·er; -est** : superficially impressive or striking — **show·i·ly** \'shō-ə-lē\ adv — **show·i·ness** \-ē-nəs\ n

shpt abbr shipment

shrap·nel \'shrap-nᵊl\ n, pl **shrapnel** [Henry Shrapnel †1842 E artillery officer] 1 : a case filled with shot and having a bursting charge which explodes it in flight 2 : bomb, mine, or shell fragments

¹shred \'shred\ n : a narrow strip cut or torn off : a small fragment

²shred vb **shred·ded; shred·ding** : to cut or tear into shreds

shrew \'shrü\ n 1 : any of numerous very small mammals with velvety fur that are related to the moles 2 : a scolding woman

shrewd \'shrüd\ adj : KEEN, ASTUTE — **shrewd·ly** adv — **shrewd·ness** n

shrew·ish \'shrü-ish\ adj : having an irritable disposition : ILL-TEMPERED

shriek \'shrēk\ n : a shrill cry : SCREAM, YELL — **shriek** vb

shrift \'shrift\ n, archaic : the act of shriving

shrike \'shrīk\ n : a grayish or brownish bird that often impales its usu. insect prey upon thorns before devouring it

shrill \'shril\ vb : to make a high-pitched piercing sound

²shrill adj : high-pitched : PIERCING ⟨~ whistle⟩ — **shril·ly** \'shril-lē\ adv

shrimp \'shrimp\ n, pl **shrimps** or **shrimp** 1 : any of various small marine crustaceans related to the lobsters 2 : a small or puny person

shrine \'shrīn\ n [ME, receptacle for the relics of a saint, fr. OE scrīn, fr. L scrinium case, chest] 1 : the tomb of a saint: also : a place where devotion is paid to a saint or deity 2 : a place or object hallowed by its associations

¹shrink \'shriŋk\ vb **shrank** \'shraŋk\ also **shrunk** \'shrəŋk\ ; **shrunk** or **shrunk·en** \'shrəŋ-kən\ 1 : to draw back or away 2 : to become smaller or more compact 3 : to lessen in value syn contract, constrict, compress, condense — **shrink·able** adj

²shrink n : PSYCHIATRIST

shrink·age \'shriŋ-kij\ n 1 : the act of shrinking 2 : a decrease in value 3 : the amount by which something contracts or lessens in extent

shrive \'shrīv\ vb **shrived** or **shrove** \'shrōv\ ; **shriv·en** \'shriv-ən\ or **shrived** : to minister the sacrament of penance to

shriv·el \'shriv-əl\ vb -**eled** or -**elled; -el·ing** or -**el·ling** \-(ə-)liŋ\ : to shrink and draw together into wrinkles : wither up

¹shroud \'shraud\ n 1 : something that covers or screens 2 : a cloth placed over a dead body 3 : one of the ropes leading usu. in pairs from the masthead of a ship to the side to support the mast

²**shroud** *vb* : to veil or screen from view

shrub \'shrəb\ *n* : a low usu. several=
stemmed woody plant — **shrub·by** *adj*

shrub·bery \'shrəb-(ə-)rē\ *n, pl* **-ber·ies**
: a planting or growth of shrubs

shrug \'shrəg\ *vb* **shrugged; shrug·ging**
: to hunch (the shoulders) up to ex=
press doubt, indifference, or dislike
— **shrug** *n*

shrug off *vb* **1** : to brush aside : MINI=
MIZE **2** : to shake off **3** : to remove (a
garment) by wriggling out

sht *abbr* sheet

shtg *abbr* shortage

¹**shuck** \'shək\ *n* : SHELL, HUSK

²**shuck** *vb* : to strip of shucks

shud·der \'shəd-ər\ *vb* **shud·dered;
shud·der·ing** \-(ə-)riŋ\ : TREMBLE,
QUAKE — **shudder** *n*

shuf·fle \'shəf-əl\ *vb* **shuf·fled; shuf·fling**
\-(ə-)liŋ\ **1** : to mix in a disorderly
mass **2** : to rearrange the order of
(cards in a pack) by mixing two parts
of the pack together **3** : to move with
a sliding or dragging gait **4** : to shift
from place to place **5** : to dance in a
slow lagging manner — **shuffle** *n*

shuf·fle·board \'shəf-əl-ˌbōrd\ *n* : a
game in which players use long-han=
dled cues to shove wooden disks into
scoring areas marked on a smooth
surface

shun \'shən\ *vb* **shunned; shun·ning** : to
avoid deliberately or habitually syn
evade, elude, escape, duck

¹**shunt** \'shənt\ *vb* [ME *shunten* to
flinch] : to turn off to one side; *esp*
: to switch (a train) from one track to
another

²**shunt** *n* **1** : a method or device for turn=
ing or thrusting aside **2** : a conductor
joining two points in an electrical cir=
cuit forming a parallel path through
which a portion of the current may
pass

shut \'shət\ *vb* **shut; shut·ting 1** : CLOSE
2 : to forbid entrance into **3** : to lock
up **4** : to fold together (~ a penknife)
5 : to cease or suspend activity (~
down an assembly line)

shut·down \-ˌdaún\ *n* : a temporary
cessation of activity (as in a factory)

shut–in \'shət-ˌin\ *n* : an invalid con=
fined to his home, room, or bed

shut·out \'shət-ˌaút\ *n* : a game or con=
test in which one side fails to score

shut out \ˌshət-ˈaút\ *vb* **1** : EXCLUDE **2**
: to prevent (an opponent) from scor=
ing in a game or contest

shut·ter \'shət-ər\ *n* **1** : a movable cov=
er for a door or window for privacy or
to keep out light or air : BLIND **2** : the
part of a camera that opens and closes
to expose the film

shut·ter·bug \'shət-ər-ˌbəg\ *n* : a
photography enthusiast

¹**shut·tle** \'shət-ᵊl\ *n* **1** : an instrument
used in weaving for passing the hori=
zontal threads between the vertical
threads **2** : a vehicle traveling back

and forth over a short route (a ~ bus)
3 : SPACE SHUTTLE

²**shuttle** *vb* **shut·tled; shut·tling** \'shət-
(ᵊ-)liŋ\ : to move back and forth rapid=
ly or frequently

shut·tle·cock \'shət-ᵊl-ˌkäk\ *n* : a light
feathered object (as of cork or plastic)
used in badminton

shut up *vb* : to cease or cause to cease
talking

¹**shy** \'shī\ *adj* **shi·er** *or* **shy·er** \'shī-(ə)r\;
shi·est *or* **shy·est** \'shī-əst\ **1** : easily
frightened : TIMID **2** : WARY **3** : BASH=
FUL **4** : DEFICIENT, LACKING — **shy·ly**
adv — **shy·ness** *n*

²**shy** *vb* **shied; shy·ing 1** : to shrink back
: RECOIL **2** : to start suddenly aside
through fright (the horse *shied*)

shy·ster \'shī-stər\ *n* : an unscrupulous
lawyer or politician

Si *symbol* silicon

Si·a·mese \ˌsī-ə-ˈmēz, -ˈmēs\ *n, pl* **Sia·
mese** : THAI — **Siamese** *adj*

Siamese twin *n* [fr. Chang †1874 and
Eng †1874 twins born in Siam with
bodies united] : one of a pair of twins
with bodies joined together at birth

¹**sib·i·lant** \'sib-ə-lənt\ *adj* : having, con=
taining, or producing the sound of or a
sound resembling that of the *s* or the
sh in *sash*

²**sibilant** *n* : a sibilant speech sound (as
English \s\, \z\, \sh\, \zh\, \ch\
(= tsh)\, or \j (= dzh)\)

sib·ling \'sib-liŋ\ *n* : one of two or more
offspring of the same parents

sib·yl \'sib-əl\ *n, often cap* : PROPHETESS
— **sib·yl·line** \-ə-ˌlīn, -ˌlēn\ *adj*

sic \'sik, 'sēk\ *adv* : intentionally so
written — used after a printed word or
passage to indicate that it exactly re=
produces an original (said he seed
[*sic*] it all)

sick \'sik\ *adj* **1** : not in good health
: ILL; *also* : of, relating to, or intended
for the sick (~ pay) **2** : NAUSEATED **3**
: LANGUISHING, PINING **4** : DISGUSTED **5**
: MACABRE, SADISTIC (~ jokes) — **sick·
ly** *adj*

sick·bed \'sik-ˌbed\ *n* : a bed on which
one lies sick

sick·en \'sik-ən\ *vb* **sick·ened; sick·en·
ing** \-(ə-)niŋ\ : to make or become
sick — **sick·en·ing·ly** *adv*

sick·le \'sik-əl\ *n* : a cutting tool con=
sisting of a curved metal blade with a
short handle

sickle–cell anemia *n* : an inherited
anemia in which red blood cells tend
to become crescent-shaped and can=
not carry oxygen properly and which
occurs esp. in blacks

sick·ness \'sik-nəs\ *n* **1** : ill health; *also*
: a specific disease **2** : NAUSEA

¹**side** \'sīd\ *n* **1** : a border of an object;
esp : one of the longer borders as con=
trasted with an end **2** : an outer sur=
face of an object **3** : the right or left
part of the trunk of a body **4** : a place
away from a central point or line **5** : a
position regarded as opposite to an=

other 6 : a body of contestants — **side** *adj*

side·arm \-‚ärm\ *adj* : made with a sideways sweep of the arm — **sidearm** *adv*

side arm *n* : a weapon worn at the side or in the belt

side·bar \'sīd-‚bär\ *n* : a short news story accompanying a major story and presenting related topics or additional details

side·board \-‚bōrd\ *n* : a piece of dining-room furniture for holding articles of table service

side·burns \-‚bərnz\ *n pl* : whiskers on the side of the face in front of the ears

side·car \-‚kär\ *n* : a one-wheeled passenger car attached to the side of a motorcycle

side effect *n* : a secondary and usu. adverse effect (as of a drug)

side·kick \'sīd-‚kik\ *n* : PAL, PARTNER

¹**side·long** \-‚lȯŋ\ *adv* : in the direction of or along the side : OBLIQUELY

²**side·long** \-‚lȯŋ\ *adj* : directed to one side : SLANTING ⟨∼ look⟩

side·man \'sīd-‚man\ *n* : a member of a jazz or swing orchestra

side·piece \-‚pēs\ *n* : a piece forming or contained in the side of something

si·de·re·al \sī-'dir-ē-əl, sə-\ *adj* 1 : of or relating to the stars 2 : measured by the apparent motion of the stars

sid·er·ite \'sid-ə-‚rīt\ *n* : a native carbonate of iron that is a valuable iron ore

side·show \'sīd-‚shō\ *n* 1 : a minor show offered in addition to a main exhibition (as of a circus) 2 : an incidental diversion

side·step \-‚step\ *vb* 1 : to step aside 2 : AVOID, EVADE

side·stroke \-‚strōk\ *n* : a swimming stroke which is executed on the side and in which the arms are swept backward and downward and the legs do a scissors kick

side·swipe \-‚swīp\ *vb* : to strike with a glancing blow along the side — **sideswipe** *n*

¹**side·track** \-‚trak\ *n* : SIDING 1

²**sidetrack** *vb* 1 : to switch from a main railroad line to a siding 2 : to turn aside from a purpose

side·walk \'sīd-‚wȯk\ *n* : a paved walk at the side of a road or street

side·wall \-‚wȯl\ *n* 1 : a wall forming the side of something 2 : the side of an automobile tire

side·ways \-‚wāz\ *adv or adj* 1 : from the side 2 : with one side to the front 3 : to, toward, or at one side

side·wind·er \-‚wīn-dər\ *n* : a small pale-colored desert rattlesnake of the southwestern U.S.

sid·ing \'sīd-iŋ\ *n* 1 : a short railroad track connected with the main track 2 : material (as boards) covering the outside of frame buildings

si·dle \'sīd-³l\ *vb* **si·dled; si·dling** \'sīd-(ə-)liŋ\ : to move sideways or side foremost

SIDS *abbr* sudden infant death syndrome

siege \'sēj\ *n* [ME *sege*, fr. OF, seat, blockade] 1 : the placing of an army around or before a fortified place to force its surrender 2 : a persistent attack (as of illness)

sie·mens \'sē-mənz, 'zē-\ *n* : a unit of conductance equivalent to one ampere per volt

si·er·ra \sē-'er-ə\ *n* [Sp, lit., saw, fr. L *serra*] : a range of mountains esp. with jagged peaks

si·es·ta \sē-'es-tə\ *n* [Sp, fr. L *sexta (hora)* noon, lit., sixth hour] : a midday rest or nap

sieve \'siv\ *n* : a utensil with meshes or holes to separate finer particles from coarser or solids from liquids

sift \'sift\ *vb* 1 : to pass through a sieve 2 : to separate with or as if with a sieve 3 : to examine carefully 4 : to scatter by or as if by passing through a sieve — **sift·er** *n*

sig *abbr* 1 signal 2 signature

sigh \'sī\ *vb* 1 : to let out a deep audible breath (as in weariness or sorrow) 2 : GRIEVE, YEARN — **sigh** *n*

¹**sight** \'sīt\ *n* 1 : something seen or worth seeing 2 : the process or power of seeing; *esp* : the sense of which the eye is the receptor and by which qualities of appearance (as position, shape, and color) are perceived 3 : INSPECTION 4 : a device (as a small bead on a gun barrel) that aids the eye in aiming 5 : VIEW, GLIMPSE 6 : the range of vision — **sight·less** *adj*

²**sight** *vb* 1 : to get sight of 2 : to aim by means of a sight

sight·ed \'sīt-əd\ *adj* : having sight

sight·ly \-lē\ *adj* : pleasing to the sight

sight-see·ing \'sīt-‚sē-iŋ\ *adj* : engaged in or used for seeing sights of interest — **sight·seer** \-‚sē-ər\ *n*

¹**sign** \'sīn\ *n* 1 : SYMBOL 2 : a gesture expressing a command, wish, or thought 3 : a notice publicly displayed for advertising purposes or for giving direction or warning 4 : OMEN, PORTENT 5 : TRACE, VESTIGE

²**sign** *vb* 1 : to mark with a sign 2 : to represent by a sign 3 : to make a sign or signal 4 : to write one's name on in token of assent or obligation 5 : to assign legally 6 : to use sign language — **sign·er** *n*

¹**sig·nal** \'sig-n³l\ *n* 1 : a sign agreed on as the start of some joint action 2 : a sign giving warning or notice of something 3 : the message, sound, or image transmitted in electronic communication (as radio)

²**signal** *vb* **-naled** *or* **-nalled; -nal·ing** *or* **-nal·ling** \-nə-liŋ\ 1 : to communicate by signals 2 : to notify by a signal

³**signal** *adj* 1 : DISTINGUISHED, OUTSTANDING ⟨a ∼ honor⟩ 2 : used in signaling — **sig·nal·ly** \-ē\ *adv*

sig·nal·ize \'sig-nə-‚līz\ *vb* **-ized; -iz·ing** : to point out or make conspicuous —

sig·nal·iza·tion \ˌsig-nə-lə-ˈzā-shən\ *n*

sig·nal·man \ˈsig-nᵊl-mən, -ˌman\ *n* : one who signals or works with signals

sig·na·to·ry \ˈsig-nə-ˌtōr-ē\ *n, pl* **-ries** : a person or government that signs jointly with others — **signatory** *adj*

sig·na·ture \ˈsig-nə-ˌchùr\ *n* **1** : the name of a person written by himself **2** : the sign placed after the clef to indicate the key or the meter of a piece of music

sign·board \ˈsīn-ˌbōrd\ *n* : a board bearing a sign or notice

sig·net \ˈsig-nət\ *n* : a small intaglio seal (as in a ring)

sig·nif·i·cance \sig-ˈnif-i-kəns\ *n* **1** : something signified : MEANING **2** : SUGGESTIVENESS **3** : CONSEQUENCE, IMPORTANCE

sig·nif·i·cant \-kənt\ *adj* **1** : having meaning; *esp* : having a hidden or special meaning **2** : having or likely to have considerable influence or effect : IMPORTANT — **sig·nif·i·cant·ly** *adv*

sig·ni·fy \ˈsig-nə-ˌfī\ *vb* **-fied; -fy·ing 1** : to show by a sign **2** : MEAN, IMPORT **3** : to have significance — **sig·ni·fi·ca·tion** \ˌsig-nə-fə-ˈkā-shən\ *n*

sign in *vb* : to make a record of arrival (as by signing a register)

sign language *n* : a formal system of hand gestures used by the deaf to communicate

sign off *vb* : to announce the end (as of a program or broadcast)

sign of the cross : a gesture of the hand forming a cross (as to invoke divine blessing)

sign on *vb* **1** : ENLIST **2** : to announce the start of broadcasting for the day

sign out *vb* : to indicate departure by signing a register or punching a clock

sign·post \ˈsīn-ˌpōst\ *n* : a post bearing a sign

Sikh \ˈsēk\ *n* : an adherent of a religion of India marked by rejection of caste — **Sikh·ism** *n*

si·lage \ˈsī-lij\ *n* : chopped fodder stored in a silo to ferment for use as a rich moist animal feed

¹si·lence \ˈsī-ləns\ *n* **1** : the state of being silent **2** : STILLNESS **3** : SECRECY

²silence *vb* **si·lenced; si·lenc·ing 1** : to reduce to silence **2** : to cause to cease hostile firing or criticism

si·lenc·er \ˈsī-lən-sər\ *n* : a device for muffling the noise of a gunshot

si·lent \ˈsī-lənt\ *adj* **1** : not speaking : MUTE; *also* : TACITURN **2** : STILL, QUIET **3** : performed or borne without utterance **syn** reticent, reserved, closemouthed, close — **si·lent·ly** *adv*

¹sil·hou·ette \ˌsil-ə-ˈwet\ *n* [F] **1** : a representation of the outlines of an object filled in with black or some other uniform color **2** : OUTLINE (~ of a ship)

²silhouette *vb* **-ett·ed; -ett·ing** : to represent by a silhouette; *also* : to show against a light background

sil·i·ca \ˈsil-i-kə\ *n* : a mineral that consists of silicon and oxygen

sil·i·cate \ˈsil-ə-ˌkāt, ˈsil-i-kət\ *n* : a chemical salt that consists of a ...etal combined with silicon and oxygen

si·li·ceous *or* **si·li·cious** \sə-ˈlish-əs\ *adj* : of, relating to, or containing silica or a silicate

sil·i·con \ˈsil-i-kən, ˈsil-ə-ˌkän\ *n* : a nonmetallic chemical element that occurs in combination as the most abundant element next to oxygen in the earth's crust and is used esp. in electronics

sil·i·cone \ˈsil-ə-ˌkōn\ *n* : an organic silicon compound used esp. for lubricants and varnishes

sil·i·co·sis \ˌsil-ə-ˈkō-səs\ *n* : a lung disease caused by prolonged inhaling of silica dusts

silk \ˈsilk\ *n* **1** : a fine strong lustrous protein fiber produced by insect larvae for their cocoons; *esp* : one from moth larvae (**silk·worms** \-ˌwərmz\) used for cloth **2** : thread or cloth made from silk — **silk·en** \ˈsil-kən\ *adj* — **silky** *adj*

silk screen *n* : a stencil process in which coloring matter is forced through the meshes of a prepared silk or organdy screen; *also* : a print made by this process — **silk–screen** *vb*

sill \ˈsil\ *n* **1** : a heavy crosspiece (as of wood or stone) that forms the bottom member of a window frame or a doorway; *also* : a horizontal supporting piece at the base of a structure **2** : a flat mass of igneous rock injected while molten between other rocks

sil·ly \ˈsil-ē\ *adj* **sil·li·er; -est** [ME *sely, silly* happy, innocent, pitiable, feeble, fr. OE *sǣlig*] FOOLISH, ABSURD, STUPID — **sil·li·ness** *n*

si·lo \ˈsī-lō\ *n, pl* **silos** [Sp] : a trench, pit, or tall cylinder in which silage is stored

¹silt \ˈsilt\ *n* **1** : fine earth; *esp* : particles of such soil floating in rivers, ponds, or lakes **2** : a deposit (as by a river) of silt — **silty** *adj*

²silt *vb* : to obstruct or cover with silt — **silt·ation** \sil-ˈtā-shən\ *n*

Si·lu·ri·an \sī-ˈlùr-ē-ən\ *adj* : of, relating to, or being the period of the Paleozoic era between the Ordovician and the Devonian — **Silurian** *n*

¹sil·ver \ˈsil-vər\ *n* **1** : a white ductile metallic chemical element that takes a high polish and is a better conductor of heat and electricity than any other substance **2** : coin made of silver **3** : FLATWARE **4** : a grayish white color — **sil·very** *adj*

²silver *adj* **1** : relating to, made of, or coated with silver **2** : SILVERY

³silver *vb* **sil·vered; sil·ver·ing** \ˈsilv-(ə-)riŋ\ : to coat with or as if with silver — **sil·ver·er** *n*

silver bromide *n* : a light-sensitive compound used esp. in photography

silver chloride *n* : a light-sensitive compound used esp. in photography

sil·ver·fish \'sil-vər-ˌfish\ *n* : a small wingless insect found in houses and sometimes injurious to sized paper and starched clothes

silver iodide *n* : a light-sensitive compound used in photography, rainmaking, and medicine

silver maple *n* : a No. American maple with deeply cut leaves that are green above and silvery white below

silver nitrate *n* : a soluble compound used in photography and as an antiseptic

sil·ver·ware \'sil-vər-ˌwaər\ *n* : FLATWARE

sim·i·an \'sim-ē-ən\ *n* : MONKEY, APE — **simian** *adj*

sim·i·lar \'sim-ə-lər\ *adj* : marked by correspondence or resemblance **syn** alike, akin, comparable, parallel — **sim·i·lar·i·ty** \ˌsim-ə-'lar-ət-ē\ *n* — **sim·i·lar·ly** \'sim-ə-lər-lē\ *adv*

sim·i·le \'sim-ə-(ˌ)lē\ *n* [L, likeness, comparison, fr. neut. of *similis* like, similar] : a figure of speech in which two dissimilar things are compared by the use of *like* or *as* (as in "cheeks like roses")

si·mil·i·tude \sə-'mil-ə-ˌt(y)üd\ *n* : LIKENESS, RESEMBLANCE **syn** similarity, semblance

sim·mer \'sim-ər\ *vb* **sim·mered; sim·mer·ing** \-(ə-)riŋ\ 1 : to stew at or just below the boiling point 2 : to be on the point of bursting out with violence or emotional disturbance — **simmer** *n*

si·mo·nize \'sī-mə-ˌnīz\ *vb* **-nized; -niz·ing** : to polish with or as if with wax

si·mo·ny \'sī-mə-nē, 'sim-ə-\ *n* [LL *simonia*, fr. *Simon Magus* 1st cent. A.D. sorcerer of Samaria (Acts 8:9–24)] : the buying or selling of a church office

sim·pa·ti·co \sim-'pät-i-ˌkō, -'pat-\ *adj* : CONGENIAL, LIKABLE

sim·per \'sim-pər\ *vb* **sim·pered; sim·per·ing** \-p(ə-)riŋ\ : to smile in a silly manner — **simper** *n*

sim·ple \'sim-pəl\ *adj* **sim·pler** \-p(ə-)lər\; **sim·plest** \-p(ə-)ləst\ [ME, fr. OF, plain, uncomplicated, artless, fr. L *simplus, simplex*, lit., single; L *simplus* fr. *sim-* one + *-plus* multiplied by; L *simplex* fr. *sim-* + *-plex* -fold] 1 : not combined with anything else 2 : not other than : MERE 3 : not complex : PLAIN 4 : ABSOLUTE (land held in fee ∼) 5 : STRAIGHTFORWARD; *also* : ARTLESS 6 : UNADORNED 7 : lacking education, experience, or intelligence 8 : developing from a single ovary (a ∼ fruit) **syn** easy, facile, light, effortless — **sim·ple·ness** *n* — **sim·ply** \-plē\ *adv*

sim·ple·ton \'sim-pəl-tən\ *n* : FOOL

sim·plic·i·ty \sim-'plis-ət-ē\ *n* 1 : lack of complication : CLEARNESS 2 : CANDOR, ARTLESSNESS 3 : plainness in manners

or way of life 4 : IGNORANCE, FOOLISHNESS

sim·pli·fy \'sim-plə-ˌfī\ *vb* **-fied; -fy·ing** : to make simple : make less complex : CLARIFY — **sim·pli·fi·ca·tion** \ˌsim-plə-fə-'kā-shən\ *n*

sim·plis·tic \sim-'plis-tik\ *adj* : excessively simple : tending to overlook complexities (a ∼ solution)

sim·u·late \'sim-yə-ˌlāt\ *vb* **-lat·ed; -lat·ing** : to create the effect or appearance of : FEIGN — **sim·u·la·tion** \ˌsim-yə-'lā-shən\ *n* — **sim·u·la·tor** \'sim-yə-ˌlāt-ər\ *n*

si·mul·ta·ne·ous \ˌsī-məl-'tā-nē-əs, ˌsim-əl-\ *adj* : occurring or operating at the same time — **si·mul·ta·ne·ous·ly** *adv* — **si·mul·ta·ne·ous·ness** *n*

¹**sin** \'sin\ *n* 1 : an offense esp. against God 2 : FAULT 3 : a weakened state of human nature in which the self is estranged from God — **sin·less** *adj*

²**sin** *vb* **sinned; sin·ning** : to commit a sin — **sin·ner** *n*

¹**since** \(')sins\ *adv* 1 : from a past time until now 2 : backward in time : AGO

²**since** *prep* 1 : in the period after (changes made ∼ the war) 2 : continuously from (has been here ∼ 1980)

³**since** *conj* 1 : from the time when 2 : seeing that : BECAUSE

sin·cere \sin-'siər\ *adj* **sin·cer·er; sin·cer·est** 1 : free from hypocrisy : HONEST 2 : GENUINE, REAL — **sin·cere·ly** *adv* — **sin·cer·i·ty** \-'ser-ət-ē\ *n*

si·ne·cure \'sī-ni-ˌkyûər, 'sin-i-\ *n* : a well-paid job that requires little work

si·ne die \ˌsī-ni-'dī-ˌē, ˌsin-ā-'dē-ˌā\ *adv* [L, without day] : INDEFINITELY

si·ne qua non \ˌsin-i-ˌkwä-'nän, -'nōn\ *n* [LL, without which not] : an indispensable or essential thing

sin·ew \'sin-yü\ *n* 1 : TENDON 2 : physical strength — **sin·ewy** *adj*

sin·ful \'sin-fəl\ *adj* : marked by or full of sin : WICKED — **sin·ful·ly** \-ē\ *adv* — **sin·ful·ness** *n*

¹**sing** \'siŋ\ *vb* **sang** \'saŋ\ *or* **sung** \'səŋ\; **sung; sing·ing** \'siŋ-iŋ\ 1 : to produce musical tones with the voice; *also* : to utter with musical tones 2 : to produce harmonious sustained sounds (birds ∼ing) 3 : CHANT, INTONE 4 : to make a prolonged shrill sound (locusts ∼ing) 5 : to write poetry; *also* : to celebrate in song or verse 6 : to give information or evidence — **sing·er** *n*

²**sing** *abbr* singular

singe \'sinj\ *vb* **singed; singe·ing** \'sin-jiŋ\ : to scorch lightly the outside of; *esp* : to remove the hair or down from (a plucked fowl) with flame

¹**sin·gle** \'siŋ-gəl\ *adj* 1 : UNMARRIED 2 : being alone : being the only one 3 : having only one feature or part 4 : made for one person or family **syn** sole, unique, lone, solitary, separate, particular — **sin·gle·ness** *n* — **sin·gly** \-glē\ *adv*

²**single** *vb* **sin·gled; sin·gling** \-g(ə-)liŋ\ 1

: to select (one) from a group **2** : to hit a single

³**single** n **1** : a separate person or thing **2** : a hit in baseball that enables the batter to reach first base **3** pl : a tennis match with one player on each side

single bond n : a chemical bond in which one pair of electrons is shared by two atoms in a molecule

single-lens reflex n : a camera having a single lens that forms an image which is either reflected to the viewfinder or recorded on film

sin·gle·ton \'siŋ-gəl-tən\ n : a card that is the only one of its suit orig. held in a hand

sin·gle·tree \-,trē\ n : WHIFFLETREE

sin·gu·lar \'siŋ-gyə-lər\ adj **1** : of, relating to, or constituting a word form denoting one person, thing, or instance **2** : of unusual quality **3** : OUTSTANDING, EXCEPTIONAL **4** : ODD, STRANGE — **singular** n — **sin·gu·lar·i·ty** \,siŋ-gyə-'lar-ət-ē\ n — **sin·gu·lar·ly** \'siŋ-gyə-lər-lē\ adv

sin·is·ter \'sin-əs-tər\ adj [ME, fr. L on the left side, inauspicious] **1** : threatening or foreboding evil or disaster **2** : indicative of lurking evil syn baleful, malign, malefic, maleficent

¹**sink** \'siŋk\ vb **sank** \'saŋk\ or **sunk** \'səŋk\; **sunk**; **sink·ing 1** : SUBMERGE **2** : to descend lower and lower **3** : to grow less in volume or height **4** : to slope downward **5** : to penetrate downward **6** : to fail in health or strength **7** : LAPSE, DEGENERATE **8** : to cause (a ship) to descend to the bottom **9** : to make (a hole or shaft) by digging, boring, or cutting **10** : INVEST — **sink·able** adj

²**sink** n **1** : DRAIN, SEWER **2** : a basin connected with a drain **3** : an extensive depression in the land surface

sink·er \'siŋ-kər\ n : a weight for sinking a fishing line or net

sink·hole \'siŋk-,hōl\ n : a hollow place in which drainage collects

sin·u·ous \'sin-yə-wəs\ adj : bending in and out : WINDING — **sin·u·os·i·ty** \,sin-yə-'wäs-ət-ē\ n

si·nus \'sī-nəs\ n [NL, fr. L curve, hollow] **1** : any of several cavities in the skull mostly connecting with the nostrils **2** : a space forming a channel (as for the passage of blood)

si·nus·itis \,sī-nə-'sīt-əs\ n : inflammation of a sinus esp. of the skull

Sioux \'sü\ n, pl **Sioux** \'sü(z)\ [F] : DAKOTA

sip \'sip\ vb **sipped**; **sip·ping** : to drink in small quantities — **sip** n

¹**si·phon** \'sī-fən\ n [F] **1** : a bent tube through which a liquid can be transferred by means of air pressure up and over the edge of one container and into another container placed at a lower level **2** usu **sy·phon** : a bottle that ejects soda water through a tube when a valve is opened

²**siphon** vb **si·phoned**; **si·phon·ing** \'sīf-(ə-)niŋ\ : to draw off by means of a siphon

sir \(')sər\ n [ME sire sire, fr. OF, fr. L senior, compar. of senex old, old man] **1** : a man of rank or position — used as a title before the given name of a knight or baronet **2** — used in addressing a man without using his name

¹**sire** \'sī(ə)r\ n **1** : FATHER; also, archaic : FOREFATHER **2** archaic : LORD — used as a title of respect esp. in addressing a sovereign **3** : the male parent of an animal (as a horse or dog)

²**sire** vb **sired**; **sir·ing** : BEGET, PROCREATE

si·ren \'sī-rən\ n **1** : a seductive or alluring woman **2** : an electrically operated device for producing a loud shrill warning signal — **siren** adj

sir·loin \'sər-,loin\ n [alter. of earlier surloin, modif. of MF surlonge, fr. sur over (fr. L super) + longe loin] : a cut of beef taken from the part in front of the round

sirup var of SYRUP

si·sal \'sī-səl, -zəl\ n : a strong cordage fiber from an agave; also : this agave

sis·sy \'sis-ē\ n, pl **sissies** : an effeminate boy or man; also : a timid or cowardly person

sis·ter \'sis-tər\ n **1** : a female having one or both parents in common with another individual **2** : a member of a religious order of women : NUN **3** chiefly Brit : NURSE — **sis·ter·ly** adj

sis·ter·hood \-,hùd\ n **1** : the state of being sisters or a sister **2** : a community or society of sisters

sis·ter-in-law \'sis-t(ə-)rən-,lò\ n, pl **sisters-in-law** \-tər-zən-\ : the sister of one's husband or wife; also : the wife of one's brother

sit \'sit\ vb **sat** \'sat\; **sit·ting 1** : to rest upon the buttocks or haunches **2** : ROOST, PERCH **3** : to occupy a seat **4** : to hold a session **5** : to cover eggs for hatching : BROOD **6** : to pose for a portrait **7** : to remain quiet or inactive **8** : FIT **9** : to cause (oneself) to be seated **10** : to place in position **11** : to keep one's seat on (~ a horse) **12** : BABY-SIT — **sit·ter** n

si·tar \si-'tär\ n [Hindi] : an Indian lute with a long neck and a varying number of strings

site \'sīt\ n : LOCATION

sit-in \'sit-,in\ n : an act of sitting in the seats or on the floor of an establishment as a means of organized protest

sit·u·at·ed \'sich-ə-,wāt-əd\ adj : LOCATED, PLACED

sit·u·a·tion \,sich-ə-'wā-shən\ n **1** : LOCATION, SITE **2** : JOB **3** : CONDITION, CIRCUMSTANCES

sit-up \'sit-,əp\ n : an exercise performed from a supine position by raising the trunk to a sitting position usu. while keeping the legs straight and returning to the original position

six \'siks\ n **1** : one more than five **2** : the 6th in a set or series **3** : something having six units; esp : a 6-cylinder engine or automobile — **six** *adj or pron* — **sixth** \'siksth\ *adj or adv or n*

six-gun \'siks-ˌgən\ *n* : a 6-chambered revolver

six-pack \'siks-ˌpak\ *n* : six bottles or cans (as of beer) packaged and purchased together; *also* : the contents of a six-pack

six-pence \-pəns, *US also* -ˌpens\ *n* : the sum of six pence; *also* : an English silver coin of this value — **six-pen-ny** \-pən-ē, *US also* -ˌpen-ē\ *adj*

six-shoot-er \'sik(s)-ˌshüt-ər\ *n* : SIX-GUN

six-teen \siks-'tēn\ *n* : one more than 15 — **sixteen** *adj or pron* — **six-teenth** \-'tēnth\ *adj or n*

six-ty \'siks-tē\ *n, pl* **sixties** : six times 10 — **six-ti-eth** \'siks-tē-əth\ *adj or n* — **sixty** *adj or pron*

siz-able *or* **size-able** \'sī-zə-bəl\ *adj* : quite large — **siz-ably** \-blē\ *adv*

¹size \'sīz\ *n* : physical extent or bulk : DIMENSIONS; *also* : MAGNITUDE

²size *vb* **sized; siz-ing** : to grade or classify according to size

³size *n* : a gluey material used for filling the pores in paper, plaster, or textiles — **siz-ing** \'sī-ziŋ\ *n*

⁴size *vb* **sized; siz-ing** : to cover, stiffen, or glaze with size

siz-zle \'siz-əl\ *vb* **siz-zled; siz-zling** \-(ə-)liŋ\ : to fry or shrivel up with a hissing sound — **sizzle** *n*

SJ *abbr* Society of Jesus

Sk *abbr* Saskatchewan

¹skate \'skāt\ *n, pl* **skates** *also* **skate** : any of numerous rays with thick broad fins

²skate *n* : a metal runner with a frame fitting on a shoe used for gliding over ice 2 : ROLLER SKATE — **skate** *vb* — **skat-er** *n*

skate-board \'skāt-ˌbȯrd\ *n* : a short board mounted on roller-skate wheels — **skate-board-er** \-ər\ *n* — **skate-board-ing** \-iŋ\ *n*

skeet \'skēt\ *n* : trapshooting in which clay targets are thrown in such a way that their angle of flight simulates that of a flushed game bird

skein \'skān\ *n* : a loosely twisted quantity (as of yarn) as it is taken from the reel

skel-e-ton \'skel-ət-ᵊn\ *n* 1 : the usu. bony supporting framework of an animal body 2 : a bare minimum 3 : FRAMEWORK — **skel-e-tal** \-ət-ᵊl\ *adj*

skep-tic \'skep-tik\ *n* 1 : one who believes in skepticism 2 : one having a critical or doubting attitude 3 : one who doubts or disbelieves in religious tenets — **skep-ti-cal** \-ti-kəl\ *adj*

skep-ti-cism \'skep-tə-ˌsiz-əm\ *n* 1 : a doubting state of mind 2 : a doctrine that certainty of knowledge cannot be attained 3 : unbelief in religion

sketch \'skech\ *n* 1 : a rough drawing or outline 2 : a short or slight literary composition (as a story or essay); *also*

: a vaudeville act — **sketch** *vb* — **sketchy** *adj*

¹skew \'skyü\ *vb* : TWIST, SWERVE

²skew *n* : SLANT

skew-er \'skyü-ər\ *n* : a pin for holding meat in form while roasting — **skewer** *vb*

¹ski \'skē\ *n, pl* **skis** [Norw. fr. ON *skīth* stick of wood, ski] : one of a pair of long strips (as of wood) bound one on each foot for gliding over snow

²ski *vb* **skied** \'skēd\; **ski-ing** : to glide on skis — **ski-er** *n*

¹skid \'skid\ *n* 1 : a plank for supporting something above the ground 2 : a device placed under a wheel to prevent turning 3 : a timber or rail over or on which something is slid or rolled 4 : the action of skidding 5 : a runner on the landing gear of an aircraft 6 : ²PALLET

²skid *vb* **skid-ded; skid-ding** 1 : to slide without rotating ⟨a *skidding* wheel⟩ 2 : to slide sideways on the road ⟨the car *skidded* on ice⟩

skid row *n* : a district of cheap saloons frequented by vagrants and alcoholics

skiff \'skif\ *n* : a small open boat

ski lift *n* : CHAIR LIFT

skill \'skil\ *n* 1 : ability to use one's knowledge effectively in doing something 2 : developed or acquired ability **syn** art, craft, cunning, dexterity, expertise, know-how — **skilled** \'skild\ *adj*

skil-let \'skil-ət\ *n* : a frying pan

skill-ful *or* **skil-ful** \'skil-fəl\ *adj* 1 : having or displaying skill : EXPERT 2 : accomplished with skill — **skill-ful-ly** \-ē\ *adv* — **skill-ful-ness** *n*

¹skim \'skim\ *vb* **skimmed; skim-ming** 1 : to take off from the top of a liquid; *also* : to remove (scum or cream) from ⟨~ milk⟩ 2 : to read rapidly and superficially 3 : to pass swiftly over — **skim-mer** *n*

²skim *adj* 1 : having the cream removed 2 : made of skim milk

skim-ming \'skim-iŋ\ *n* : the practice of concealing gambling profits so as to avoid tax payments

ski-mo-bile \'skē-mō-ˌbēl\ *n* : SNOWMOBILE

skimp \'skimp\ *vb* : to give insufficient attention, effort, or funds; *also* : to save by skimping

skimpy \'skim-pē\ *adj* **skimp-i-er; -est** : deficient in supply or execution

¹skin \'skin\ *n* 1 : the outer limiting layer of an animal body; *also* : the usu. thin tough tissue of which this is made 2 : an outer or surface layer (as a rind or peel) — **skin-less** *adj* — **skinned** *adj*

²skin *vb* **skinned; skin-ning** : to free from skin : remove the skin of

³skin *adj* : devoted to showing nudes ⟨~ magazines⟩

skin-dive \'skin-ˌdīv\ *vb* : to swim below the surface of water with a face mask and portable breathing device — **skin diver** *n* — **skin diving** *n*

skin·flint \'skin-ˌflint\ *n* : a very stingy person

skin graft *n* : skin that is taken from one area to replace skin in another area — **skin grafting**

skin·ny \'skin-ē\ *adj* **skin·ni·er; -est** : resembling skin 2 : very thin

skin·ny–dip·ping \-ˌdip-iŋ\ *n* : swimming in the nude

skin-tight \'skin-'tīt\ *adj* : closely fitted to the figure

¹**skip** \'skip\ *vb* **skipped; skip·ping** 1 : to move with leaps and bounds 2 : to leap lightly over 3 : to pass from point to point (as in reading) disregarding what is in between 4 : to pass over without notice or mention

²**skip** *n* : a light bouncing step; *also* : a gait of alternate hops and steps

skip·jack \'skip-ˌjak\ *n* : a small sailboat with bottom similar to a flat V and sides vertical

skip·per \'skip-ər\ *n* [ME, fr. Middle Dutch *schipper*, fr. *schip* ship] : the master of a ship — **skipper** *vb*

skir·mish \'skər-mish\ *n* : a minor engagement in war; *also* : a minor dispute or contest — **skirmish** *vb*

¹**skirt** \'skərt\ *n* : a free-hanging part of a garment extending from the waist down

²**skirt** *vb* 1 : to pass around the outer edge of 2 : BORDER

skit \'skit\ *n* : a brief dramatic sketch

ski tow *n* : SKI LIFT

skit·ter \'skit-ər\ *vb* : to glide or skip lightly or quickly : skim along a surface

skit·tish \'skit-ish\ *adj* 1 : CAPRICIOUS, IRRESPONSIBLE 2 : easily frightened (a ~ horse)

skiv·vy \'skiv-ē\ *n, pl* **skivvies** : men's underwear; *esp* : a T-shirt and briefs or shorts — usu. used in pl.

ski·wear \'skē-ˌwaər\ *n* : clothing suitable for wear while skiing

skulk \'skəlk\ *vb* : to move furtively : SNEAK, LURK — **skulk·er** *n*

skull \'skəl\ *n* : the bony or cartilaginous case that protects the brain and supports the jaws

skull·cap \'skəl-ˌkap\ *n* : a close-fitting brimless cap

¹**skunk** \'skəŋk\ *n, pl* **skunks** *also* **skunk** 1 : any of various No. American mammals related to the weasels that can forcibly eject an ill-smelling fluid when startled 2 : a contemptible person

²**skunk** *vb* : to defeat decisively; *esp* : to shut out in a game

skunk cabbage *n* : a perennial herb of eastern No. America with an unpleasant-smelling early spring flower; *also* : a related herb of the Pacific coast region

sky \'skī\ *n, pl* **skies** 1 : the upper air 2 : HEAVEN — **sky·ey** \'skī-ē\ *adj*

sky·cap \-ˌkap\ *n* : a person employed to carry luggage at an airport

sky·div·ing \-ˌdī-viŋ\ *n* : the sport of jumping from an airplane and executing various body maneuvers before opening a parachute — **sky diver** *n*

sky·jack \-ˌjak\ *vb* : to take control of an airplane in flight by threat of violence — **sky·jack·er** *n* — **sky·jack·ing** *n*

¹**sky·lark** \-ˌlärk\ *n* : a European lark noted for its song and its steep upward flight

²**skylark** *vb* : to frolic boisterously or recklessly

sky·light \'skī-ˌlīt\ *n* : a window in a roof or ceiling — **sky·light·ed** \-ˌlīt-əd\ *adj*

sky·line \-ˌlīn\ *n* 1 : HORIZON 2 : an outline against the sky

¹**sky·rock·et** \-ˌräk-ət\ *n* : ¹ROCKET 1

²**skyrocket** *vb* : ²ROCKET 2

sky·scrap·er \-ˌskrā-pər\ *n* : a very tall building

sky·walk \-ˌwök\ *n* : a usu. enclosed aerial walkway connecting two buildings

sky·ward \-wərd\ *adv* : toward the sky

sky·writ·ing \-ˌrīt-iŋ\ *n* : writing in the sky formed by smoke emitted from an airplane — **sky·writ·er** \-ər\ *n*

slab \'slab\ *n* : a thick flat piece or slice

¹**slack** \'slak\ *adj* 1 : CARELESS, NEGLIGENT 2 : SLUGGISH, LISTLESS 3 : not taut : LOOSE 4 : not busy or active **syn** lax, remiss, neglectful, delinquent, derelict — **slack·ly** *adv* — **slack·ness** *n*

²**slack** *vb* 1 : to make or become slack : LOOSEN, RELAX 2 : SLAKE 2

³**slack** *n* 1 : cessation of movement or flow : LETUP 2 : a part that hangs loose without strain ⟨~ of a rope⟩ 3 : trousers for casual wear — usu. used in pl.

slack·en \'slak-ən\ *vb* **slack·ened; slack·en·ing** \-(ə-)niŋ\ : to make or become slack

slack·er \'slak-ər\ *n* : one that shirks work or evades military duty

slag \'slag\ *n* : the waste left after the melting of ores and the separation of metal from them

slain *past part of* SLAY

slake \'slāk, *for 2 also* 'slak\ *vb* **slaked; slak·ing** 1 : to cause to subside with or as if with refreshing drink ⟨~ thirst⟩ 2 : to cause (lime) to crumble by mixture with water

sla·lom \'släl-əm\ *n* [Norw, lit., sloping track] : skiing in a zigzag course between obstacles

¹**slam** \'slam\ *n* : the winning of every trick or of all tricks but one in bridge

²**slam** *n* : a heavy jarring impact : BANG

³**slam** *vb* **slammed; slam·ming** 1 : to shut violently and noisily 2 : to throw or strike with a loud impact

¹**slan·der** \'slan-dər\ *n* [ME *sclaundre, slaundre*, fr. OF *esclandre*, fr. LL *scandalum* stumbling block, offense] : a false report maliciously uttered and tending to injure the reputation of a person — **slan·der·ous** *adj*

²**slander** *vb* **slan·dered; slan·der·ing**

\-d(ə-)riŋ\ : to utter slander against : DEFAME — **slan·der·er** n

slang \'slaŋ\ n : an informal nonstandard vocabulary composed typically of invented words, arbitrarily changed words, and extravagant figures of speech — **slangy** adj

¹**slant** \'slant\ n 1 : a sloping direction, line, or plane 2 : a particular or personal viewpoint — **slant** adj — **slantwise** \-,wīz\ adv or adj

²**slant** vb 1 : SLOPE 2 : to interpret or present in accordance with a special viewpoint syn incline, lean, list, tilt, heel — **slant·ing·ly** adv

slap \'slap\ vb **slapped; slap·ping** 1 : to strike sharply with the open hand 2 : REBUFF, INSULT — **slap** n

¹**slash** \'slash\ vb 1 : to cut with sweeping strokes 2 : to cut slits in (a garment) 3 : to reduce sharply

²**slash** n 1 : GASH 2 : an ornamental slit in a garment 3 : a clearing in a forest littered with debris; also : the debris present

slat \'slat\ n : a thin narrow flat strip

¹**slate** \'slāt\ n 1 : a dense fine-grained rock that splits into thin layers 2 : a roofing tile or a writing tablet made from this rock 3 : a list of candidates for election

²**slate** vb **slat·ed; slat·ing** 1 : to cover with slate 2 : to designate for action or appointment

slath·er \'slath-ər\ vb **slath·ered; slath·er·ing** \-(ə-)riŋ\ : to spread with or on thickly or lavishly

slat·tern \'slat-ərn\ n : a slovenly woman — **slat·tern·ly** adj

¹**slaugh·ter** \'slȯt-ər\ n 1 : the butchering of livestock for market 2 : great destruction of lives esp. in battle

²**slaughter** vb 1 : to kill (animals) for food : BUTCHER 2 : to kill in large numbers or in a bloody way : MASSACRE

slaugh·ter·house \-,haùs\ n : an establishment where animals are butchered

Slav \'släv, 'slav\ n : a person speaking a Slavic language

¹**slave** \'slāv\ n [ME sclave, fr. OF or ML; OF esclave, fr. ML Sclavus, fr. Sclavus Slav; fr. the reduction to slavery of many Slavic peoples of central Europe] 1 : a person held in servitude as property 2 : a device (as the typewriter unit of a computer) that is directly responsive to another — **slave** adj

²**slave** vb **slaved; slav·ing** : to work like a slave : DRUDGE

¹**slav·er** \'slav-ər, 'släv-\ n : SLOBBER — **slaver** vb

²**slav·er** \'slā-vər\ n : a ship or a person engaged in transporting slaves

slav·ery \'släv-(ə-)rē\ n 1 : wearisome drudgery : the condition of being a slave 3 : the practice of owning slaves syn servitude, bondage, enslavement

¹**Slav·ic** \'slav-lik, 'släv-\ adj : of or relating to the Slavs or their languages

²**Slavic** n : a branch of the Indo-European language family including various languages (as Russian or Polish) of eastern Europe

slav·ish \'slā-vish\ adj 1 : SERVILE 2 : obeying or imitating with no freedom of judgment or choice — **slav·ish·ly** adv

slaw \'slȯ\ n : COLESLAW

slay \'slā\ vb **slew** \'slü\ ; **slain** \'slān\ ; **slay·ing** : KILL — **slay·er** n

sleaze \'slēz\ n : a sleazy quality or appearance

slea·zy \'slē-zē, 'slā-\ adj **slea·zi·er; -est** 1 : FLIMSY, SHODDY 2 : marked by cheapness of character or quality

¹**sled** \'sled\ n : a vehicle on runners adapted esp. for sliding on snow

²**sled** vb **sled·ded, sled·ding** : to ride or carry on a sled

sledge \'slej\ n : SLEDGEHAMMER

²**sledge** n : a strong heavy sled

sledge·ham·mer \'slej-,ham-ər\ n : a large heavy hammer usu. wielded with both hands — **sledgehammer** adj or vb

¹**sleek** \'slēk\ vb 1 : to make smooth or glossy 2 : to gloss over

²**sleek** adj : having a smooth well-groomed look

¹**sleep** \'slēp\ n 1 : a natural periodic suspension of consciousness 2 : a state (as death or coma) suggesting sleep — **sleep·less** adj — **sleep·less·ness** n

²**sleep** vb **slept** \'slept\ ; **sleep·ing** 1 : to rest or be in a state of sleep; also : to spend in sleep 2 : to have sexual intercourse 3 : to provide sleeping space for

sleep·er \'slē-pər\ n 1 : one that sleeps 2 : a horizontal beam to support something on or near ground level 3 : SLEEPING CAR 4 : someone or something unpromising or unnoticed that suddenly attains prominence or value

sleeping bag n : a warmly lined bag for sleeping esp. outdoors

sleeping car n : a railroad car with berths for sleeping

sleeping pill n : a drug in tablet or capsule form taken to induce sleep

sleeping sickness n : a serious disease that is prevalent in tropical Africa, is marked by fever, lethargy, tremors, and loss of weight, and is caused by protozoans transmitted by the tsetse fly

sleep·walk·er \'slēp-,wȯ-kər\ n : one who walks in his sleep

sleepy \'slē-pē\ adj **sleep·i·er; -est** 1 : ready for sleep 2 : quietly inactive — **sleep·i·ly** \'slē-pə-lē\ adv — **sleep·i·ness** \-pē-nəs\ n

sleet \'slēt\ n : frozen or partly frozen rain — **sleet** vb — **sleety** adj

sleeve \'slēv\ n 1 : a part of a garment covering an arm 2 : a tubular part designed to fit over another part — **sleeve·less** adj

¹**sleigh** \'slā\ n : an open usu. horse-

drawn vehicle on runners for use on snow or ice

²**sleigh** vb : to drive or travel in a sleigh

sleight \'slīt\ n 1 : TRICK 2 : DEXTERITY

sleight of hand : a trick requiring skillful manual manipulation

slen·der \'slen-dər\ adj 1 : SLIM, THIN 2 : WEAK, SLIGHT 3 : MEAGER, INADEQUATE

slen·der·ize \-də-ˌrīz\ vb -ized; -iz·ing : to make slender

sleuth \'slüth\ n [short for sleuthhound bloodhound, fr. ME, fr. sleuth track of an animal or person, fr. ON slōth] : DETECTIVE

¹**slew** \'slü\ past of SLAY

²**slew** vb : TURN, VEER, SKID

¹**slice** \'slīs\ n 1 : a thin flat piece cut from something 2 : a wedge-shaped blade (as for serving fish) 3 : a flight of a ball (as in golf) that curves in the direction of the dominant hand of the player propelling it

²**slice** vb **sliced; slic·ing** 1 : to cut a slice from; also : to cut into slices 2 : to hit (a ball) so that a slice results

¹**slick** \'slik\ vb : to make smooth or sleek

²**slick** adj 1 : very smooth : SLIPPERY 2 : CLEVER, SMART

³**slick** n 1 : a smooth patch of water covered with a film of oil 2 : a popular magazine printed on coated paper

slick·er \'slik-ər\ n 1 : a long loose raincoat 2 : a sly tricky person 3 : a city dweller esp. of natty appearance or sophisticated mannerisms

¹**slide** \'slīd\ vb **slid** \'slid\; **slid·ing** \'slīd-iŋ\ 1 : to move smoothly along a surface 2 : to fall by a loss of support 3 : to slip along quietly

²**slide** n 1 : an act or instance of sliding 2 : something (as a cover or fastener) that operates by sliding 3 : a fall of a mass of earth or snow down a hillside 4 : a surface on which something slides 5 : a glass plate on which a specimen is mounted for examination under a microscope 6 : a small transparent image that can be projected on a screen

slid·er \'slīd-ər\ n 1 : one that slides 2 : a baseball pitch that looks like a fastball but curves slightly

slide rule n : an instrument for calculation consisting of a ruler and a medial slide graduated with logarithmic scales

slier comparative of SLY

sliest superlative of SLY

¹**slight** \'slīt\ adj 1 : SLENDER; also : FRAIL 2 : UNIMPORTANT 3 : SCANTY, MEAGER — **slight·ly** adv

²**slight** vb 1 : to treat as unimportant 2 : to ignore discourteously 3 : to perform or attend to carelessly syn neglect, overlook, disregard

³**slight** n : a humiliating discourtesy

¹**slim** \'slim\ adj **slim·mer; slim·mest** [Dutch, bad, inferior, fr. Middle Dutch slimp crooked, bad] 1 : SLENDER, SLIGHT, THIN 2 : SCANTY, MEAGER

²**slim** vb **slimmed; slim·ming** : to make or become slender

slime \'slīm\ n 1 : sticky mud 2 : a slippery substance (as on the skin of a slug or catfish) — **slimy** adj

slim-jim \'slim-ˈjim, -ˌjim\ adj : notably slender

¹**sling** \'sliŋ\ vb **slung** \'sləŋ\; **sling·ing** \'sliŋ-iŋ\ 1 : to throw forcibly : FLING 2 : to hurl with a sling

²**sling** n 1 : a short strap with strings attached for hurling stones or shot 2 : a strap, rope, or chain for holding securely something being lifted, lowered, or carried

sling·shot \'sliŋ-ˌshät\ n : a forked stick with elastic bands for shooting small stones or shot

slink \'sliŋk\ vb **slunk** \'sləŋk\ also **slinked** \'sliŋkt\; **slink·ing** 1 : to move stealthily or furtively 2 : to move sinuously — **slinky** adj

¹**slip** \'slip\ vb **slipped; slip·ping** 1 : to escape quietly or secretly 2 : to slide along or cause to slide along smoothly 3 : to make a mistake 4 : to pass unnoticed or undone 5 : to fall off from a standard or level

²**slip** n 1 : a ramp for repairing ships 2 : a ship's berth between two piers 3 : secret or hurried departure, escape, or evasion 4 : BLUNDER 5 : a sudden mishap 6 : a woman's one-piece garment worn under a dress 7 : PILLOWCASE

³**slip** n 1 : a shoot or twig from a plant for planting or grafting 2 : a long narrow strip; esp : one of paper used for a record ⟨deposit ~⟩

⁴**slip** vb **slipped; slip·ping** : to take slips from (a plant)

slip·knot \'slip-ˌnät\ n : a knot that slips along the rope around which it is made

slipped disk n : a protrusion of one of the disks of cartilage between vertebrae with pressure on spinal nerves resulting esp. in low back pain

slip·per \'slip-ər\ n : a light low shoe that may be easily slipped on and off

slip·pery \'slip-(ə-)rē\ adj **slip·peri·er; -est** 1 : icy, wet, smooth, or greasy enough to cause one to fall or lose one's hold 2 : TRICKY, UNRELIABLE — **slip·peri·ness** n

slip·shod \'slip-ˈshäd\ adj : SLOVENLY, CARELESS ⟨~ work⟩

slip·stream \'slip-ˌstrēm\ n : the stream of air driven aft by the propeller of an aircraft

slip-up \'slip-ˌəp\ n 1 : MISTAKE 2 : ACCIDENT

¹**slit** \'slit\ vb **slit; slit·ting** 1 : SLASH 2 : to cut off or away

²**slit** n : a long narrow cut or opening

slith·er \'slith-ər\ vb : to slip or glide along like a snake — **slith·ery** adj

sliv·er \'sliv-ər\ n : SPLINTER

slob \'släb\ n : a slovenly or boorish person

slob·ber \'släb-ər\ vb **slob·bered; slob-**

ber·ing \-(ə-)riŋ\ : to dribble saliva — slobber n

sloe \'slō\ n : the fruit of the blackthorn

slog vb **slogged; slog·ging 1** : to hit hard : BEAT **2** : to work hard and steadily

slo·gan \'slō-gən\ n [alter. of earlier *slo·gorn,* fr. ScGael *sluagh-ghairm* army cry] : a word or phrase expressing the spirit or aim of a party, group, or cause

sloop \'slüp\ n : a single-masted sailboat with a jib and a fore-and-aft mainsail

¹**slop** \'släp\ n **1** : thin tasteless drink or liquid food — usu. used in pl. **2** : food waste or gruel for animal feed **3** : body and toilet waste — usu. used in pl.

²**slop** vb **slopped; slop·ping 1** : SPILL **2** : to feed with slop (~ hogs)

¹**slope** \'slōp\ vb **sloped; slop·ing** : SLANT, INCLINE

²**slope** n **1** : upward or downward slant or degree of slant **2** : ground that forms an incline **3** : the part of a landmass draining into a particular ocean

slop·py \'släp-ē\ adj **slop·pi·er; -est 1** : MUDDY, SLUSHY **2** : SLOVENLY, MESSY

slosh \'släsh\ vb **1** : to flounder through or splash about in or with water, mud, or slush **2** : to move with a splashing motion

slot \'slät\ n **1** : a long narrow opening or groove **2** : a position in a sequence

slot car n : an electric toy racing car that runs on a grooved track

sloth \'slōth, 'sloth\ n, pl **sloths** \with ths or thz\ **1** : LAZINESS, INDOLENCE **2** : a slow-moving So. and Central American mammal related to the armadillos — **sloth·ful** adj

slot machine n **1** : a machine whose operation is begun by dropping a coin into a slot **2** : a coin-operated gambling machine that pays off according to the matching of symbols on wheels spun by a handle

¹**slouch** \'slauch\ n **1** : a lazy or incompetent person **2** : a loose or drooping gait or posture

²**slouch** vb : to walk, stand, or sit with a slouch : SLUMP

¹**slough** \'slü, 2 usu 'slau\ n **1** : a wet and marshy or muddy place (as a swamp) **2** : a discouraged state of mind

²**slough** \'sləf\ or **sluff** n : something (as a snake's skin) that may be shed

³**slough** \'sləf\ or **sluff** vb : to cast off

slov·en \'sləv-ən\ n [ME *sloveyn* rascal, perh. fr. Flem *sloovin* woman of low character] : an untidy person

slov·en·ly \'sləv-ən-lē\ adj **1** : untidy in dress or person **2** : lazily or carelessly done : SLIPSHOD

¹**slow** \'slō\ adj **1** : SLUGGISH; also : dull in mind : STUPID **2** : moving, flowing, or proceeding at less than the usual speed **3** : taking more than the correct time **4** : registering behind the correct time **5** : not lively : BORING syn dilatory, laggard, deliberate, leisurely —

slow adv — **slow·ly** adv — **slow·ness** n

²**slow** vb **1** : to make slow : hold back **2** : to go slower

slow motion n : motion-picture action photographed so as to appear much slower than normal — **slow–motion** adj

SLR abbr single-lens reflex

sludge \'sləj\ n : a slushy mass : OOZE; esp : solid matter produced by sewage treatment processes

slue var of ²SLEW

¹**slug** \'sləg\ n **1** : a small mass of metal; esp : BULLET **2** : a metal disk for use (as in a slot machine) in place of a coin **3** : any of numerous slimy wormlike mollusks related to the snails **4** : a quantity of liquor drunk

²**slug** vb **slugged; slug·ging** : to strike forcibly and heavily — **slug·ger** n

slug·gard \'sləg-ərd\ n : a lazy person

slug·gish \'sləg-ish\ adj **1** : SLOTHFUL, LAZY **2** : slow in movement or flow **3** : STAGNANT, DULL — **slug·gish·ly** adv — **slug·gish·ness** n

¹**sluice** \'slüs\ n **1** : an artificial passage for water with a gate for controlling the flow; also : the gate so used **2** : a channel that carries off surplus water **3** : an inclined trough or flume for washing ore or floating logs

²**sluice** vb **sluiced; sluic·ing 1** : to draw off through a sluice **2** : to wash with running water : FLUSH

sluice·way \'slüs-‚wā\ n : an artificial channel into which water is let by a sluice

¹**slum** \'sləm\ n : a thickly populated area marked by poverty and dirty or deteriorated houses

²**slum** vb **slummed; slum·ming** : to visit slums esp. out of curiosity; also : to go somewhere or do something that might be considered beneath one's station

¹**slum·ber** \'sləm-bər\ vb **slum·bered; slum·ber·ing** \-b(ə-)riŋ\ **1** : DOZE; also : SLEEP **2** : to be in a sluggish or torpid state

²**slumber** n : SLEEP

slum·ber·ous or **slum·brous** \'sləm-b(ə-)rəs\ adj **1** : SLUMBERING, SLEEPY **2** : PEACEFUL, INACTIVE

slum·lord \'sləm-‚lórd\ n : a landlord who receives unusually large profits from substandard properties

slump \'sləmp\ vb **1** : to sink down suddenly : COLLAPSE **2** : SLOUCH **3** : to decline sharply — **slump** n

slung past and past part of SLING

slunk past and past part of SLINK

¹**slur** \'slər\ vb **slurred; slur·ring 1** : to slide or slip over without due mention or emphasis **2** : to perform two or more successive notes of different pitch in a smooth or connected way

²**slur** n : a curved line ⌣ or ⌢ connecting notes to be slurred; also : a group of slurred notes

³**slur** n : a slighting remark : ASPERSION

slurp \'slərp\ *vb* : to eat or drink noisily — **slurp** *n*

slur·ry \'slər-ē\ *n, pl* **slur·ries** : a watery mixture of insoluble matter

slush \'sləsh\ *n* 1 : partly melted or watery snow 2 : soft mud — **slushy** *adj*

slut \'slət\ *n* 1 : a slovenly woman 2 : PROSTITUTE — **slut·tish** \'slət-ish\ *adj*

sly \'slī\ *adj* **sli·er** *also* **sly·er** \'slī-(-ə)r\ ; **sli·est** *also* **sly·est** \'slī-əst\ 1 : CRAFTY, CUNNING 2 : SECRETIVE, FURTIVE 3 : ROGUISH **syn** tricky, wily, artful, foxy, guileful — **sly·ly** *adv* — **sly·ness** *n*

sm *abbr* small

Sm *symbol* samarium

SM *abbr* 1 [NL *scientiae magister*] master of science 2 sergeant major

SMA *abbr* sergeant major of the army

¹**smack** \'smak\ *n* : characteristic flavor; *also* : a slight trace

²**smack** *vb* 1 : to have a taste 2 : to have a trace or suggestion

³**smack** *vb* 1 : to move (the lips) so as to make a sharp noise 2 : to kiss or slap with a loud noise

⁴**smack** *n* 1 : a sharp noise made by the lips 2 : a noisy slap

⁵**smack** *adv* : squarely and sharply

⁶**smack** *n* : a sailing ship used in fishing

⁷**smack** *n, slang* : HEROIN

SMaj *abbr* sergeant major

¹**small** \'smȯl\ *adj* 1 : little in size or amount 2 : operating on a limited scale 3 : few in number 4 : made up of little things 5 : TRIFLING, UNIMPORTANT 6 : MEAN, PETTY **syn** diminutive, petite, wee, tiny, minute — **small·ish** *adj* — **small·ness** *n*

²**small** *n* : a small part or product ⟨the ~ of the back⟩

small·pox \'smȯl-ˌpäks\ *n* : a contagious virus disease marked by fever and a skin eruption

small-time \'smȯl-ˈtīm\ *adj* : insignificant in performance and standing : MINOR — **small-tim·er** \-ˈtī-mər\ *n*

¹**smart** \'smärt\ *vb* 1 : to cause or feel a stinging pain 2 : to feel or endure distress — **smart** *n*

²**smart** *adj* 1 : making one smart ⟨a ~ blow⟩ 2 : mentally quick : BRIGHT 3 : WITTY, CLEVER 4 : STYLISH 5 : being a guided missile 6 : containing a microprocessor for limited computing capability ⟨~ terminal⟩ **syn** knowing, quick-witted, intelligent, brainy, sharp — **smart·ly** *adv* — **smart·ness** *n*

smart al·eck \'smärt-ˌal-ik\ *n* : a person given to obnoxious cleverness

¹**smash** \'smash\ *n* 1 : a smashing blow; *esp* : a hard overhand stroke in tennis 2 : the act or sound of smashing 3 : collision of vehicles : CRASH 4 : COLLAPSE, RUIN; *esp* : BANKRUPTCY 5 : a striking success : HIT — **smash** *adj*

²**smash** *vb* 1 : to break or be broken into pieces 2 : to move forward with force and shattering effect 3 : to destroy utterly : WRECK

smat·ter·ing \'smat-ə-riŋ\ *n* 1 : superfi-

cial knowledge 2 : a small scattered number or amount

¹**smear** \'smiər\ *n* : a spot left by an oily or sticky substance

²**smear** *vb* 1 : to overspread with something oily or sticky 2 : SMUDGE, SOIL 3 : to injure by slander or insults

¹**smell** \'smel\ *vb* **smelled** \'smeld\ *or* **smelt** \'smelt\ ; **smell·ing** 1 : to perceive the odor of by sense organs of the nose; *also* : to detect or seek with or as if with these organs 2 : to have or give off an odor

²**smell** *n* 1 : the process or power of perceiving odor; *also* : the special sense by which one perceives odor 2 : ODOR, SCENT 3 : an act of smelling — **smelly** *adj*

smelling salts *n pl* : an aromatic preparation used as a stimulant and restorative (as to relieve faintness)

¹**smelt** \'smelt\ *n, pl* **smelts** *or* **smelt** : any of several small food fishes of coastal or fresh waters that are related to the trouts

²**smelt** *vb* : to melt or fuse (ore) in order to separate the metal; *also* : REFINE

smelt·er \'smel-tər\ *n* 1 : one that smelts 2 : an establishment for smelting

smid·gen *also* **smid·geon** *or* **smid·gin** \'smij-ən\ *n* : a small amount : BIT

smi·lax \'smī-ˌlaks\ *n* 1 : any of various mostly climbing and prickly plants related to the lilies 2 : an ornamental plant related to the asparagus

¹**smile** \'smīl\ *vb* **smiled**; **smil·ing** 1 : to look with a smile 2 : to be favorable 3 : to express by a smile

²**smile** *n* : a change of facial expression to express amusement, pleasure, or affection

smirch \'smərch\ *vb* 1 : to make dirty or stained 2 : to bring disgrace on — **smirch** *n*

smirk \'smərk\ *vb* : to wear a self-conscious or conceited smile : SIMPER — **smirk** *n*

smite \'smīt\ *vb* **smote** \'smōt\ ; **smit·ten** \'smit-ᵊn\ *or* **smote**; **smit·ing** \'smīt-iŋ\ 1 : to strike heavily; *also* : to kill by striking 2 : to affect as if by a heavy blow

smith \'smith\ *n* : a worker in metals; *esp* : BLACKSMITH

smith·er·eens \ˌsmith-ə-ˈrēnz\ *n pl* [Ir-Gael *smidirīn*] : FRAGMENTS, BITS

smithy \'smith-ē\ *n, pl* **smith·ies** : a smith's workshop

¹**smock** \'smäk\ *n* : a loose garment worn over other clothes as a protection

²**smock** *vb* : to gather (cloth) in regularly spaced tucks — **smock·ing** *n*

smog \'smäg, 'smȯg\ *n* [blend of *smoke* and *fog*] : a thick haze caused by the action of sunlight on air polluted by smoke and automobile exhaust fumes — **smog·gy** *adj*

¹**smoke** \'smōk\ *n* 1 : the gas from burning material (as coal, wood, or tobac-

co) in which are suspended particles of soot **2** : a mass or column of smoke **3** : something (as a cigarette) to smoke; *also* : the act of smoking — **smoke·less** *adj* — **smoky** *adj*

²**smoke** *vb* **smoked; smok·ing 1** : to emit smoke **2** : to inhale and exhale the fumes of burning tobacco; *also* : to use in smoking (~ a pipe) **3** : to stupefy or drive away by smoke **4** : to discolor with smoke **5** : to cure (as meat) with smoke — **smok·er** *n*

smoke detector *n* : an alarm that sounds automatically when it detects smoke

smoke jumper *n* : a forest-fire fighter who parachutes to locations otherwise difficult to reach

smoke·stack \'smŏk-ˌstak\ *n* : a pipe or funnel through which smoke and gases are discharged

smol·der *or* **smoul·der** \'smōl-dər\ *vb* **smol·dered** *or* **smoul·dered; smol·der·ing** *or* **smoul·der·ing** \-d(ə-)riŋ\ **1** : to burn and smoke without flame **2** : to burn inwardly — **smolder** *n*

smooch \'smüch\ *vb* : KISS, PET — **smooch** *n*

¹**smooth** \'smüth\ *adj* **1** : not rough or uneven **2** : not jarring or jolting **3** : BLAND, MILD **4** : fluent in speech and agreeable in manner **syn** even, flat, level, plane — **smooth·ly** *adv* — **smooth·ness** *n*

²**smooth** *vb* **1** : to make smooth **2** : to free from trouble or difficulty

smooth muscle *n* : muscle with no cross striations that is typical of visceral organs (as the stomach and bladder) and is not under voluntary control

smor·gas·bord \'smȯr-gəs-ˌbȯrd\ *n* [Sw *smörgåsbord*, fr. *smörgås* open sandwich + *bord* table] : a luncheon or supper buffet consisting of many foods

smote *past and past part of* SMITE

¹**smoth·er** \'sməth-ər\ *n* **1** : thick stifling smoke **2** : dense fog, spray, foam, or dust **3** : a confused multitude of things : WELTER

²**smother** *vb* **smoth·ered; smoth·er·ing** \-(ə-)riŋ\ **1** : to kill by depriving of air **2** : SUPPRESS **3** : to cover thickly

SMSgt *abbr* senior master sergeant

¹**smudge** \'sməj\ *vb* **smudged; smudg·ing** : to soil or blur by rubbing or smearing

²**smudge** *n* : a dirty or blurred spot — **smudgy** *adj*

smug \'sməg\ *adj* **smug·ger; smug·gest** : conscious of one's virtue and importance : SELF-SATISFIED — **smug·ly** *adv* — **smug·ness** *n*

smug·gle \'sməg-əl\ *vb* **smug·gled; smug·gling** \-(ə-)liŋ\ **1** : to import or export secretly, illegally, or without paying the duties required by law **2** : to convey secretly — **smug·gler** \'sməg-lər\ *n*

smut \'smət\ *n* **1** : something (as soot) that smudges; *also* : SMUDGE, SPOT **2** : any of various destructive fungous diseases of plants; *also* : a fungus

causing smut **3** : indecent language or matter — **smut·ty** *adj*

smutch \'sməch\ *n* : SMUDGE

Sn *symbol* [LL *stannum*] tin

snack \'snak\ *n* : a light meal : BITE

snaf·fle \'snaf-əl\ *n* : a simple jointed bit for a horse's bridle

¹**snag** \'snag\ *n* **1** : a stump or piece of a tree esp. when under water **2** : an unexpected difficulty **syn** obstacle, obstruction, impediment, bar

²**snag** *vb* **snagged; snag·ging 1** : to become caught on or as if on a snag **2** : to seize quickly : SNATCH

snail \'snāl\ *n* : a small mollusk with a spiral shell into which it can withdraw

snake \'snāk\ *n* **1** : any of numerous long-bodied limbless crawling reptiles : SERPENT **2** : a treacherous person **3** : something that resembles a snake — **snaky** *adj*

snake·bird \'snāk-ˌbərd\ *n* : any of several fish-eating birds related to the cormorants but having a long slender neck and sharp-pointed bill

snake·bite \-ˌbīt\ *n* : the bite of a snake and esp. a venomous snake

¹**snap** \'snap\ *vb* **snapped; snapping 1** : to grasp or slash at something with the teeth **2** : to get or buy quickly **3** : to utter sharp or angry words **4** : to break suddenly with a sharp sound **5** : to give a sharp cracking noise **6** : to throw with a quick motion **7** : FLASH (her eyes *snapped*) **8** : to put a football into play — **snap·per** *n* — **snap·pish** *adj* — **snap·py** *adj*

²**snap** *n* **1** : the act or sound of snapping **2** : something very easy to do : CINCH **3** : a short period of cold weather **4** : a catch or fastening that closes with a click **5** : a thin brittle cookie **6** : ENERGY, VIM; *also* : smartness of movement **7** : the putting of the ball into play in football

snap bean *n* : a bean grown primarily for its young tender pods that are usu. broken in pieces and cooked as a vegetable

snap·drag·on \'snap-ˌdrag-ən\ *n* : any of several garden plants with long spikes of showy 2-lipped flowers

snapping turtle *n* : either of two large edible American turtles with powerful jaws and a strong musky odor

snap·shot \'snap-ˌshät\ *n* : a photograph taken usu. with an inexpensive hand-held camera

snare \'snaər\ *n* : a trap often consisting of a noose for catching birds or mammals — **snare** *vb*

¹**snarl** \'snärl\ *n* : TANGLE

²**snarl** *vb* : to cause to become knotted and intertwined

³**snarl** *vb* : to growl angrily or threateningly

⁴**snarl** *n* : an angry ill-tempered growl

¹**snatch** \'snach\ *vb* **1** : to try to grasp something suddenly **2** : to seize or take away suddenly **syn** clutch, seize, grab, nab

²**snatch** n 1 : a short period 2 : an act of snatching 3 : something brief or fragmentary ⟨~es of song⟩

¹**sneak** \'snēk\ vb **sneaked** \'snēkt\ or **snuck** \'snək\ ; **sneak·ing** : to move, act, or take in a furtive manner — **sneak·ing·ly** adv

²**sneak** n 1 : one who acts in a furtive or shifty manner 2 : a stealthy or furtive move or escape — **sneaky** adj

sneak·er \'snē-kər\ n : a usu. canvas sports shoe with a pliable rubber sole

sneer \'sniər\ vb : to show scorn or contempt by curling the lip or by a jeering tone — **sneer** n

sneeze \'snēz\ vb **sneezed**; **sneez·ing** : to force the breath out suddenly and violently as a reflex act — **sneeze** n

snick·er \'snik-ər\ n : a partly suppressed laugh — **snicker** vb

snide \'snīd\ adj 1 : MEAN, LOW ⟨a ~ trick⟩ 2 : slyly disparaging ⟨a ~ remark⟩

sniff \'snif\ vb 1 : to draw air audibly up the nose 2 : to show disdain or scorn 3 : to detect by or as if by smelling — **sniff** n

snif·fle \'snif-əl\ n 1 pl : a head cold marked by nasal discharge 2 : SNUFFLE — **sniffle** vb

¹**snip** \'snip\ n 1 : a fragment snipped off 2 : a simple stroke of the scissors or shears

²**snip** vb **snipped**; **snip·ping** : to cut off by bits : CLIP; also : to remove by cutting off

¹**snipe** \'snīp\ n, pl **snipes** or **snipe** : any of several long-billed game birds that occur esp. in marshy areas and resemble the related woodcocks

²**snipe** vb **sniped**; **snip·ing** : to shoot at an exposed enemy from a concealed position usu. at long range — **snip·er** n

snip·py \'snip-ē\ adj **snip·pi·er**; **-est** : CURT, SNAPPISH

snips \'snips\ n pl : hand shears used esp. for cutting sheet metal ⟨tin ~⟩

snitch \'snich\ vb 1 : INFORM, TATTLE 2 : PILFER, SNATCH

sniv·el \'sniv-əl\ vb **-eled** or **-elled**; **-el·ing** or **-el·ling** \-(ə-)liŋ\ 1 : to have a running nose; also : SNUFFLE 2 : to whine in a snuffling manner — **snivel** n

snob \'snäb\ n [obs. snob member of the lower classes, fr. E dial., shoemaker] : one who seeks association with persons of higher social position and looks down on those he considers inferior — **snob·bish** adj — **snob·bish·ly** adv — **snob·bish·ness** n

snob·bery \'snäb-(ə-)rē\ n, pl **-ber·ies** : snobbish conduct

¹**snoop** \'snüp\ vb [D snoepen to buy or eat on the sly] : to pry in a furtive or meddlesome way

²**snoop** n : a prying meddlesome person

snooty \'snüt-ē\ adj **snoot·i·er**; **-est** : DISDAINFUL, SNOBBISH

snooze \'snüz\ vb **snoozed**; **snooz·ing** : to take a nap : DOZE — **snooze** n

snore \'snōr\ vb **snored**; **snor·ing** : to breathe with a rough hoarse noise while sleeping — **snore** n

snor·kel \'snòr-kəl\ n [G schnorchel] : a tube projecting above the water used by swimmers for breathing with the face under water — **snorkel** vb

snort \'snòrt\ vb : to force air violently and noisily through the nose ⟨his horse ~ed⟩ — **snort** n

snout \'snaut\ n 1 : a long projecting muzzle (as of a pig) 2 : a usu. large or grotesque nose

¹**snow** \'snō\ n 1 : crystals of ice formed from the vapor of water in the air 2 : a descent or shower of snow crystals — **snowy** adj

²**snow** vb 1 : to fall or cause to fall in or as snow 2 : to cover or shut in with or as if with snow

snow·ball \'snō-,bòl\ vb : to increase or expand at a rapidly accelerating rate

snow·bank \-,baŋk\ n : a mound or slope of snow

snow·belt \-,belt\ n, often cap : a region that receives an appreciable amount of annual snowfall

snow·blow·er \-,blō-ər\ n : a machine in which a rotating spiral blade picks up and propels snow aside

snow·drift \-,drift\ n : a bank of drifted snow

snow·drop \-,dräp\ n : a plant with narrow leaves and a nodding white flower that blooms early in the spring

snow·fall \-,fòl\ n : a fall of snow

snow fence n : a fence across the path of prevailing winds to protect something (as a road) from drifting snow

snow·field \'snō-,fēld\ n : a mass of perennial snow at the head of a glacier

snow·mo·bile \'snō-mō-,bēl\ n : any of various automotive vehicles for travel on snow — **snow·mo·bil·er** \-,bē-lər\ n — **snow·mo·bil·ing** \-,liŋ\ n

snow pea n : any of a variety of the cultivated pea with edible pods

snow·plow \'snō-,plau\ n : a device for clearing away snow

¹**snow·shoe** \-,shü\ n : a light frame of wood strung with thongs that is attached to a shoe or boot to prevent sinking down into soft snow

²**snowshoe** vb **snow·shoed**; **snow·shoe·ing** : to travel on snowshoes

snow·storm \-,stòrm\ n : a storm of falling snow

snow thrower n : SNOWBLOWER

snowy \'snō-ē\ adj **snow·i·er**; **-est** 1 : marked by snow 2 : white as snow

snub \'snəb\ vb **snubbed**; **snub·bing** : to treat with disdain : SLIGHT — **snub** n

snub-nosed \'snəb-'nōzd\ adj : having a nose slightly turned up at the end

snuck past and past part of SNEAK

¹**snuff** \'snəf\ vb 1 : to pinch off the charred end of (a candle) 2 : to put out (a candle) — **snuff·er** n

²**snuff** vb 1 : to draw forcibly into or through the nose 2 : SMELL

³**snuff** n : SNIFF

⁴**snuff** n : pulverized tobacco

snuf·fle \'snəf-əl\ *vb* **snuf·fled; snuf·fling** \-(ə-)liŋ\ **1** : to snuff or sniff audibly and repeatedly **2** : to breathe with a sniffing sound — **snuf·fle** *n*

snug \'snəg\ *adj* **snug·ger; snug·gest 1** : fitting closely and comfortably **2** : CONCEALED — **snug·ly** *adv* — **snug·ness** *n*

snug·gle \'snəg-əl\ *vb* **snug·gled; snug·gling** \-(ə-)liŋ\ : to curl up or draw close comfortably : NESTLE

¹so \(')sō\ *adv* **1** : in the manner indicated **2** : in the same way **3** : THUS **4** : FINALLY **5** : to the extent indicated **6** : THEREFORE

²so *conj* : for that reason ⟨he wanted it, ~ he took it⟩

³so \sō, 'sō\ *pron* **1** : the same ⟨became chairman and remained ~⟩ **2** : approximately that ⟨I'd like a dozen or ~⟩

⁴so *abbr* south; southern

SO *abbr* strikeout

¹soak \'sōk\ *vb* **1** : to remain in a liquid **2** : WET, SATURATE **3** : to draw in by or as if by absorption *syn* drench, steep, impregnate, saturate

²soak *n* **1** : the act of soaking **2** : the liquid in which something is soaked **3** : DRUNKARD

soap \'sōp\ *n* : a cleansing substance made usu. by action of alkali on fat — **soap** *vb* — **soapy** *adj*

soap opera *n* [fr. its frequently being sponsored by soap manufacturers] : a radio or television daytime serial drama

soap·stone \'sōp-ˌstōn\ *n* : a soft stone having a soapy feel and containing talc

soar \'sōr\ *vb* : to fly upward or at a height on as if on wings

sob \'säb\ *vb* **sobbed; sob·bing** : to weep with convulsive heavings of the chest or contractions of the throat — **sob** *n*

so·ber \'sō-bər\ *adj* **so·ber·er** \-bər-ər\ ; **so·ber·est** \-b(ə-)rəst\ **1** : temperate in the use of liquor **2** : not drunk **3** : serious or grave in mood or disposition **4** : not affected by passion or prejudice *syn* solemn, earnest, staid, sedate — **so·ber·ly** *adv* — **so·ber·ness** *n*

so·bri·ety \sə-'brī-ət-ē, sō-\ *n* : the quality or state of being sober

so·bri·quet \'sō-bri-ˌkā, -ˌket\ *n* [F] : NICKNAME

soc *abbr* social; society

so-called \'sō-'kȯld\ *adj* : commonly or popularly but often inaccurately so termed

soc·cer \'säk-ər\ *n* [by shortening & alter. fr. *association football*] : a football game played on a field by two teams with a round inflated ball

¹so·cia·ble \'sō-shə-bəl\ *adj* **1** : liking companionship : FRIENDLY **2** : characterized by pleasant social relations *syn* gracious, cordial, affable, genial — **so·cia·bil·i·ty** \ˌsō-shə-'bil-ət-ē\ *n* — **so·cia·bly** \'sō-shə-blē\ *adv*

²sociable *n* : an informal social gathering

¹so·cial \'sō-shəl\ *adj* **1** : marked by pleasant companionship with one's friends **2** : naturally living or growing in groups or communities ⟨~ insects⟩ **3** : of or relating to human society, the interaction of the group and its members, and the welfare of these members ⟨~ behavior⟩ **4** : of, relating to, or based on rank in a particular society ⟨~ circles⟩ ; *also* : of or relating to fashionable society — **so·cial·ly** \-ē\ *adv*

²social *n* : a social gathering

social disease *n* : VENEREAL DISEASE

so·cial·ism \'sō-shə-ˌliz-əm\ *n* : a theory of social organization based on government ownership, management, and control of the means of production and the distribution and exchange of goods — **so·cial·ist** \'sō-sh-(ə-)ləst\ *n or adj* — **so·cial·is·tic** \ˌsō-shə-'lis-tik\ *adj*

so·cial·ite \'sō-shə-ˌlīt\ *n* : a person prominent in fashionable society

so·cial·ize \'sō-shə-ˌlīz\ *vb* **-ized; -iz·ing 1** : to regulate according to the theory and practice of socialism **2** : to adapt to social needs or uses **3** : to participate actively in a social gathering — **so·cial·iza·tion** \ˌsōsh-(ə-)lə-'zā-shən\ *n*

socialized medicine *n* : medical and hospital services administered by an organized group (as a state agency) and paid for by funds obtained usu. by assessments, taxation, or philanthropy

social science *n* : a science that deals with human society or its elements (as family, state, or race), institutions, and relationships or with a particular aspect of human society — **social scientist** *n*

social work *n* : services, activities, or methods concerned with aiding the economically underprivileged and socially maladjusted — **social worker** *n*

so·ci·ety \sə-'sī-ət-ē\ *n, pl* **-eties** [MF *societé* fr. L *societat-, societas,* fr. *socius* companion] **1** : COMPANIONSHIP **2** : a voluntary association of persons for common ends **3** : a part of a community bound together by common interests and standards; *esp* : a leisure class indulging in social affairs

sociol *abbr* sociology; sociology

so·ci·ol·o·gy \ˌsō-s(h)ē-'äl-ə-jē\ *n* : the study of the development and structure of society and social relationships — **so·ci·o·log·i·cal** \-ə-'läj-i-kəl\ *adj* — **so·ci·ol·o·gist** \-'äl-ə-jəst\ *n*

so·cio·re·li·gious \ˌsō-s(h)ē-ō-ri-'lij-əs\ *adj* : of, relating to, or involving both social and religious factors

¹sock \'säk\ *n, pl* **socks** *or* **sox** \'säks\ : a stocking with a short leg

²sock *vb* : to hit, strike, or apply forcefully

³sock *n* : a vigorous blow : PUNCH

sock·et \'säk-ət\ *n* : an opening or hollow that receives and holds something

socket wrench *n* : a wrench usu. in the

form of a bar and removable socket made to fit a bolt or nut

sock in *vb* : to close to takeoffs or landings by aircraft

¹sod \'säd\ *n* : the surface layer of the soil filled with roots (as of grass)

²sod *vb* **sod·ded; sod·ding** : to cover with sod or turfs

so·da \'söd-ə\ *n* **1** : SODIUM CARBONATE **2** : SODIUM BICARBONATE **3** : SODIUM **4** : SODA WATER **5** : SODA POP **6** : a sweet drink of soda water, flavoring, and often ice cream

soda pop *n* : a carbonated, sweetened, and flavored soft drink

soda water *n* : a beverage of water charged with carbon dioxide

sod·den \'säd-ᵊn\ *adj* **1** : lacking spirit : DULLED **2** : SOAKED, DRENCHED **3** : heavy or doughy from being improperly cooked ⟨~ biscuits⟩

so·di·um \'söd-ē-əm\ *n* : a soft waxy silver white metallic chemical element occurring in nature in combined form (as in salt)

sodium bicarbonate *n* : a white crystalline salt used in cooking and in medicine

sodium carbonate *n* : a carbonate of sodium used esp. in washing and bleaching textiles

sodium chloride *n* : SALT 1

sodium hydroxide *n* : a white brittle caustic substance used in making soap and rayon and in bleaching

sodium nitrate *n* : a crystalline salt used as a fertilizer and in curing meat

sodium thiosulfate *n* : a hygroscopic crystalline salt used as a photographic fixing agent

sod·omy \'säd-ə-mē\ *n* [ME, fr. OF *sodomie*, fr. LL *Sodoma* Sodom: fr. the homosexual proclivities of the men of the city (Gen 19:1–11)] **1** : copulation with a member of the same sex or with an animal **2** : noncoital and esp. anal or oral copulation with a member of the opposite sex — **sod·om·ize** \'säd-ə-,mīz\ *vb*

so·ev·er \sō-'ev-ər\ *adv* **1** : in any degree or manner ⟨how bad ~⟩ **2** : at all : of any kind ⟨any help ~⟩

so·fa \'sō-fə\ *n* [Ar *ṣuffah* long bench] : a couch usu. with upholstered back and arms

soft \'sȯft\ *adj* **1** : not hard or rough : NONVIOLENT **2** : RESTFUL, GENTLE, SOOTHING **3** : emotionally susceptible **4** : not prepared to endure hardship **5** : not containing certain salts that prevent lathering ⟨~ water⟩ **6** : occurring at such a speed as to avoid destructive impact ⟨~ landing of a spacecraft on the moon⟩ **7** : BIODEGRADABLE ⟨a ~ detergent⟩ **8** : not alcoholic; *also* : less detrimental than a hard narcotic *syn* bland, mild, gentle, balmy — **soft·ly** \'sȯft-lē\ *adv* — **soft·ness** \'sȯf(t)-nəs\ *n*

soft·ball \'sȯf(t)-,bȯl\ *n* : a game similar to baseball played with a ball larger

and softer than a baseball; *also* : the ball used in this game

soft·bound \-,baȯnd\ *adj* : not bound in hard covers ⟨~ books⟩

soft coal *n* : bituminous coal

soft·en \'sȯ-fən\ *vb* **soft·ened; soft·en·ing** \'sȯf-(ə-)niŋ\ : to make or become soft — **soft·en·er** \-(ə-)nər\ *n*

soft palate *n* : the fold at the back of the hard palate that partially separates the mouth and the pharynx

soft·ware \'sȯft-,waər\ *n* : the entire set of programs, procedures, and related documentation associated with a system; *esp* : computer programs

soft·wood \-,wu̇d\ *n* **1** : the wood of a coniferous tree (as a pine or fir) as compared to that of a tree producing enclosed seeds **2** : a tree that yields softwood — **softwood** *adj*

sog·gy \'säg-ē\ *adj* **sog·gi·er; -est** : heavy with moisture : SOAKED, SODDEN — **sog·gi·ly** \'säg-ə-lē\ *adv* — **sog·gi·ness** \-ē-nəs\ *n*

soi·gné *or* **soi·gnée** \swän-'yā\ *adj* : elegantly maintained; *esp* : WELL-GROOMED

¹soil \'sȯil\ *vb* **1** : CORRUPT, POLLUTE **2** : to make or become dirty **3** : STAIN, DISGRACE

²soil *n* **1** : STAIN, DEFILEMENT **2** : EXCREMENT, WASTE

³soil *n* **1** : firm land : EARTH **2** : the loose surface material of the earth in which plants grow **3** : COUNTRY, REGION

soi·ree *or* **soi·rée** \swä-'rā\ *n* [F *soirée* evening period, evening party, fr. MF, fr. *soir* evening, fr. L *sero* at a late hour] : an evening party

so·journ \'sō-,jərn, sō-'jərn\ *vb* : to dwell in a place temporarily — **sojourn** *n* — **so·journ·er** *n*

¹sol \'säl, 'sȯl\ *n* : a fluid colloidal system

²sol *abbr* **1** solicitor **2** soluble **3** solution

Sol \'säl\ *n* : SUN

¹sol·ace \'säl-əs\ *n* : COMFORT

²solace *vb* **so·laced; so·lac·ing** : to give solace to : CONSOLE

so·lar \'sō-lər\ *adj* **1** : of, derived from, or relating to the sun **2** : measured by the earth's course in relation to the sun ⟨the ~ year⟩ **3** : operated by or utilizing the sun's heat ⟨~ house⟩

solar cell *n* : a photoelectric cell that converts sunlight into electrical energy and is used as a power source

solar collector *n* : any of various devices for the absorption of solar radiation for the heating of water or buildings or the production of electricity

solar flare *n* : a sudden temporary outburst of energy from a small area of the sun's surface

so·lar·i·um \sō-'lar-ē-əm, sə-\ *n, pl* **-ia** \-ē-ə\ *also* **-ums** : a room exposed to the sun; *esp* : a room (as in a hospital) for exposure of the body to sunshine

solar plexus \'sō-lər-'plek-səs\ *n* **1** : a network of nerves situated behind the stomach 2 : the general area of the stomach below the sternum

solar system *n* : the sun with the group of celestial bodies that revolve about it

solar wind *n* : the continuous radiation of charged particles from the sun's surface

sold *past and past part of* SELL

¹**sol·der** \'säd-ər, 'sȯd-\ *n* : a metallic alloy used when melted to mend or join metallic surfaces

²**solder** *vb* **sol·dered; sol·der·ing** \-(ə-)riŋ\ **1** : to unite or repair with solder **2** : to join securely : CEMENT

soldering iron *n* : a metal device for applying heat in soldering

¹**sol·dier** \'sōl-jər\ *n* [ME *soudier*, fr. OF, fr. *soulde* pay, fr. LL *solidus* a Roman coin, fr. L, solid] : a person in military service; *esp* : an enlisted man — **sol·dier·ly** *adj or adv*

²**soldier** *vb* **sol·diered; sol·dier·ing** \'sōlj-(ə-)riŋ\ **1** : to serve as a soldier **2** : to pretend to work while actually doing nothing

soldier of fortune : ADVENTURER

sol·diery \'sōlj-(ə-)rē\ *n* **1** : a body of soldiers **2** : the profession of soldiering

¹**sole** \'sōl\ *n* **1** : the undersurface of the foot **2** : the bottom of a shoe

²**sole** *vb* **soled; sol·ing** : to furnish (a shoe) with a sole

³**sole** *n* : any of various mostly small-mouthed flatfishes valued as food

⁴**sole** *adj* : ONLY, SINGLE — **sole·ly** \'sō(l)-lē\ *adv*

so·le·cism \'säl-ə-,siz-əm, 'sōl-ə-\ *n* **1** : a mistake in grammar **2** : a breach of etiquette

sol·emn \'säl-əm\ *adj* **1** : marked by or observed with full religious ceremony **2** : FORMAL, CEREMONIOUS **3** : highly serious : GRAVE **4** : SOMBER, GLOOMY **syn** ceremonial, conventional, stately — **so·lem·ni·ty** \sə-'lem-nət-ē\ *n* — **sol·emn·ly** \'säl-əm-lē\ *adv* — **sol·emn·ness** *n*

sol·em·nize \'säl-əm-,nīz\ *vb* **-nized; -niz·ing 1** : to observe or honor with solemnity **2** : to celebrate (a marriage) with religious rites — **sol·em·ni·za·tion** \,säl-əm-nə-'zā-shən\ *n*

so·le·noid \'sō-lə-,nȯid, 'säl-\ *n* : a coil of wire usu. in cylindrical form that when carrying a current acts like a magnet

so·lic·it \sə-'lis-ət\ *vb* **1** : ENTREAT, BEG **2** : to approach with a request or plea **3** : TEMPT, LURE **syn** ask, request, desire — **so·lic·i·ta·tion** \-,lis-ə-'tā-shən\ *n*

so·lic·i·tor \sə-'lis-ət-ər\ *n* **1** : one that solicits **2** : LAWYER; *esp* : a legal official of a city or state

so·lic·i·tous \sə-'lis-ət-əs\ *adj* **1** : WORRIED, CONCERNED **2** : EAGER, WILLING **syn** avid, impatient, keen, anxious — **so·lic·i·tous·ly** *adv*

so·lic·i·tude \sə-'lis-ə-,t(y)üd\ *n* : CONCERN, ANXIETY

¹**sol·id** \'säl-əd\ *adj* **1** : not hollow; *also* : written as one word without a hyphen ⟨a ~ compound⟩ **2** : having, involving, or dealing with three dimensions or with solids **3** : not loose or spongy : COMPACT ⟨a ~ mass of rock⟩ ; *also* : neither gaseous nor liquid : HARD, RIGID ⟨~ ice⟩ **4** : of good substantial quality or kind ⟨~ comfort⟩ **5** : thoroughly dependable : RELIABLE ⟨a ~ citizen⟩; *also* : serious in purpose or character ⟨~ reading⟩ **6** : UNANIMOUS, UNITED ⟨~ for pay increases⟩ **7** : of one substance or character — **solid** *adv* — **so·lid·i·ty** \sə-'lid-ət-ē\ *n* — **sol·id·ly** \'säl-əd-lē\ *adv* — **sol·id·ness** *n*

²**solid** *n* **1** : a geometrical figure (as a cube or sphere) having three dimensions **2** : a solid substance

sol·i·dar·i·ty \,säl-ə-'dar-ət-ē\ *n* : unity based on shared interests, objectives, or standards

solid geometry *n* : a branch of geometry that deals with figures of three-dimensional space

so·lid·i·fy \sə-'lid-ə-,fī\ *vb* **-fied; -fy·ing** : to make or become solid — **so·lid·i·fi·ca·tion** \-,lid-ə-fə-'kā-shən\ *n*

solid–state *adj* **1** : relating to the structure and properties of solid material **2** : not using vacuum tubes

so·lil·o·quize \sə-'lil-ə-,kwīz\ *vb* **-quized; -quiz·ing** : to talk to oneself : utter a soliloquy

so·lil·o·quy \sə-'lil-ə-kwē\ *n, pl* **-quies** [LL *soliloquium,* fr. L *solus* alone + *loqui* to speak] **1** : the act of talking to oneself **2** : a dramatic monologue that gives the illusion of being a series of unspoken reflections

sol·i·taire \'säl-ə-,taər\ *n* **1** : a single gem (as a diamond) set alone **2** : a card game played by one person alone

sol·i·tary \'säl-ə-,ter-ē\ *adj* **1** : being or living apart from others **2** : LONELY, SECLUDED **3** : SOLE, ONLY

sol·i·tude \'säl-ə-,t(y)üd\ *n* **1** : the state of being alone : SECLUSION **2** : a lonely place **syn** isolation

soln *abbr* solution

¹**so·lo** \'sō-lō\ *n, pl* **solos** [It. fr. *solo* alone, fr. L *solus*] **1** : a piece of music for a single voice or instrument with or without accompaniment **2** : an action in which there is only one performer — **solo** *adj or adv* — **so·lo·ist** *n*

²**solo** *adv* : without a companion : ALONE

so·lon \'sō-lən\ *n* **1** : a wise and skillful lawgiver **2** : a member of a legislative body

sol·stice \'säl-stəs\ *n* [ME, fr. OF, fr. L *solstitium,* fr. *sol* sun + *status,* pp. of *sistere* to come to a stop, cause to stand] : the time of the year when the sun is farthest north of the equator (**summer solstice**) about June 22 or farthest south (**winter solstice**) about Dec. 22 — **sol·sti·tial** \säl-'stish-əl\ *adj*

sol·u·ble \'säl-yə-bəl\ *adj* **1** : capable of being dissolved in or as if in a fluid **2** : capable of being solved or explained — **sol·u·bil·i·ty** \,säl-yə-'bil-ət-ē\ *n*

sol·ute \'säl-,yüt\ *n* : a dissolved substance

so·lu·tion \sə-'lü-shən\ *n* **1** : an action or process of solving a problem; *also* : an answer to a problem **2** : an act or the process by which one substance is homogenously mixed with another usu. liquid substance; *also* : a mixture thus formed

solve \'sälv\ *vb* **solved; solv·ing** : to find the answer to or a solution for — **solv·able** *adj*

sol·ven·cy \'säl-vən-sē\ *n* : the condition of being solvent

¹sol·vent \-vənt\ *adj* **1** : able or sufficient to pay all legal debts **2** : dissolving or able to dissolve

²solvent *n* : a usu. liquid substance capable of dissolving or dispersing one or more other substances

som·ber *or* **som·bre** \'säm-bər\ *adj* **1** : DARK, GLOOMY **2** : GRAVE, MELANCHOLY — **som·ber·ly** *adv*

som·bre·ro \səm-'brer-ō\ *n, pl* **-ros** [Sp, fr. *sombra* shade] : a broad-brimmed felt hat worn esp. in the Southwest and in Mexico

¹some \(')səm\ *adj* **1** : one unspecified ⟨~ man called⟩ **2** : an unspecified or indefinite number of ⟨~ berries are ripe⟩ **3** : at least a few or a little ⟨~ years ago⟩

²some \'səm\ *pron* : a certain number or amount ⟨~ of them are here⟩ ⟨~ of it is missing⟩

¹-some \səm\ *adj suffix* : characterized by a (specified) thing, quality, state, or action ⟨awe*some*⟩ ⟨burden*some*⟩

²-some *n suffix* : a group of (so many) members and esp. persons ⟨four*some*⟩

¹some·body \'səm-,bäd-ē, -,bəd-\ *pron* : some person

²somebody *n* : a person of importance

some·day \'səm-,dā\ *adv* : at some future time

some·how \-,hau̇\ *adv* : by some means

some·one \-(,)wən\ *pron* : some person

som·er·sault \'säm-ər-,sȯlt\ *n* [MF *sombresaut* leap, deriv. of L *super* over + *saltus* leap, fr. *salire* to jump] : a leap or roll in which a person turns the heels over the head — **somersault** *vb*

som·er·set \-,set\ *n or vb* : SOMERSAULT

some·thing \'səm-thiŋ\ *pron* : some undetermined or unspecified thing

some·time \'səm-,tīm\ *adv* **1** : at a future time **2** : at an unknown or unnamed time

some·times \'səm-,tīmz\ *adv* : OCCASIONALLY

¹some·what \-,hwät, -,hwət\ *pron* : SOMETHING

²somewhat *adv* : in some degree

some·where \-,hwe(ə)r\ *adv* : in, at, or to an unknown or unnamed place

som·nam·bu·lism \säm-'nam-byə-,liz-əm\ *n* : activity (as walking about) during sleep — **som·nam·bu·list** \-ləst\ *n*

som·no·lent \'säm-nə-lənt\ *adj* : SLEEPY, DROWSY — **som·no·lence** \-ləns\ *n*

son \'sən\ *n* **1** : a male offspring or descendant **2** *cap* : Jesus Christ **3** : a person deriving from a particular source (as a country, race, or school)

so·nar \'sō-,när\ *n* [*so*und *na*vigation *r*anging] : an apparatus that detects the presence and location of submerged objects (as submarines) by sound waves

so·na·ta \sə-'nät-ə\ *n* [It] : an instrumental composition with three or four movements differing in rhythm and mood but related in key

son·a·ti·na \,sän-ə-'tē-nə\ *n* [It, dim. of *sonata*] : a short usu. simplified sonata

song \'sȯŋ\ *n* **1** : vocal music; *also* : a short composition of words and music **2** : poetic composition **3** : a distinctive or characteristic sound (as of a bird) **4** : a small amount (sold for a ~)

song·bird \'sȯŋ-,bərd\ *n* : a bird that utters a series of musical tones

Song of Sol·o·mon \-'säl-ə-mən\ *n* — see BIBLE table

song·ster \-stər\ *n* : one that sings

song·stress \-strəs\ *n* : a female singer

son·ic \'sän-ik\ *adj* : of or relating to sound waves or the speed of sound

sonic boom *n* : an explosive sound produced by an aircraft traveling at supersonic speed

son-in-law \'sən-ən-,lȯ\ *n, pl* **sons-in-law** : the husband of one's daughter

son·net \'sän-ət\ *n* : a poem of 14 lines usu. in iambic pentameter with a definite rhyme scheme

so·no·rous \sə-'nōr-əs, 'sän-ə-rəs\ *adj* **1** : giving out sound when struck **2** : loud, deep, or rich in sound : RESONANT **3** : high-sounding : IMPRESSIVE — **so·nor·i·ty** \sə-'nȯr-ət-ē\ *n*

soon \'sün\ *adv* **1** : before long **2** : PROMPTLY, QUICKLY **3** *archaic* : EARLY **4** : WILLINGLY, READILY

soot \'sut, 'sət, 'süt\ *n* : a fine black powder consisting chiefly of carbon that is formed when something burns and that colors smoke — **sooty** *adj*

sooth \'süth\ *n, archaic* : TRUTH

soothe \'süth\ *vb* **soothed; sooth·ing** **1** : to please by flattery or attention **2** : to calm down : COMFORT — **sooth·er** *n* — **sooth·ing·ly** *adv*

sooth·say·er \'süth-,sā-ər\ *n* : one that foretells events — **sooth·say·ing** \-iŋ\ *n*

¹sop \'säp\ *n* : a conciliatory bribe, gift, or concession

²sop *vb* **sopped; sop·ping** **1** : to steep or dip in or as if in a liquid **2** : to wet thoroughly : SOAK; *also* : to mop up (a liquid)

SOP *abbr* standard operating procedure: standing operating procedure

soph *abbr* sophomore

soph·ism \'säf-,iz-əm\ *n* **1** : an argument correct in form but embodying a subtle fallacy **2** : SOPHISTRY

soph·ist \'säf-əst\ *n* : PHILOSOPHER; *esp* : a captious or fallacious reasoner

so·phis·tic \sä-'fis-tik, sə-\ *or* **so·phis·ti·cal** \-ti-kəl\ *adj* : of or characteristic of sophists or sophistry **syn** fallacious, illogical, unreasonable, unreasoned

so·phis·ti·cat·ed \-tə-ˌkāt-əd\ *adj* **1** : COMPLEX ⟨~ instruments⟩ **2** : made wise or worldly-wise by experience or disillusionment **3** : intellectually appealing ⟨~ novel⟩ — **so·phis·ti·ca·tion** \-ˌfis-tə-'kā-shən\ *n*

soph·ist·ry \'säf-ə-strē\ *n* : subtly deceptive reasoning or argument

soph·o·more \'säf-(ə-)ˌmȯr\ *n* : a student in his or her second year of college or secondary school

soph·o·mor·ic \ˌsäf-ə-'mȯr-ik\ *adj* **1** : being overconfident of knowledge but poorly informed and immature **2** : of, relating to, or characteristic of a sophomore

So·pho·ni·as \ˌsäf-ə-'nī-əs, ˌsō-fə-\ *n* — see BIBLE table

so·po·rif·ic \ˌsäp-ə-'rif-ik\ *adj* **1** : causing sleep or drowsiness **2** : LETHARGIC

so·pra·no \sə-'pran-ō\ *n, pl* -**nos** [It, fr. *sopra* above, fr. L *supra*] **1** : the highest singing voice: *also* : a part for this voice **2** : a singer with a soprano voice — **soprano** *adj*

sorb \'sȯrb\ *vb* : to take up and hold by adsorption or absorption

sor·bet \'sȯr-bət\ *n* : ice having a fruit flavor and typically served between courses as a palate refresher

sor·cery \'sȯrs-(ə-)rē\ *n* [ME *sorcerie*, fr. OF, fr. *sorcier* sorcerer, fr. (assumed) VL *sortiarius*, fr. L *sort-*, *sors* chance, lot] : the use of magic : WITCHCRAFT — **sor·cer·er** \-ər\ *n* — **sor·cer·ess** \-rəs\ *n*

sor·did \'sȯrd-əd\ *adj* **1** : FILTHY, DIRTY **2** : marked by baseness or grossness : VILE — **sor·did·ly** *adv* — **sor·did·ness** *n*

¹sore \'sōr\ *adj* **sor·er; sor·est** **1** : causing pain or distress ⟨a ~ bruise⟩ **2** : painfully sensitive ⟨~ eyes⟩ **3** : SEVERE, INTENSE **4** : IRRITATED, ANGRY — **sore·ly** *adv* — **sore·ness** *n*

²sore *n* **1** : a sore spot on the body; *esp* : one (as an ulcer) with the tissues broken and usu. infected **2** : a source of pain or vexation

sore·head \'sō(ə)r-ˌhed, 'sȯ(ə)r-\ *n* : a person easily angered or discontented

sore throat *n* : painful throat due to inflammation

sor·ghum \'sȯr-gəm\ *n* : a tall variable Old World tropical grass grown widely for its edible seed, for forage, or for its sweet juice which yields a syrup

so·ror·i·ty \sə-'rȯr-ət-ē\ *n, pl* -**ties** [ML *sororitas* sisterhood, fr. L *soror* sister] : a club of girls or women esp. at a college

sorp·tion \'sȯrp-shən\ *n* : the process of sorbing : the state of being sorbed

sor·rel \'sȯr-əl\ *n* : any of several sour-juiced herbs

sor·row \'sär-ō\ *n* **1** : deep distress and regret **2** : a cause of grief or sadness **3** : a display of grief or sadness — **sor·row** *vb* — **sor·row·ful** \-fəl\ *adj* — **sor·row·ful·ly** \-f(ə-)lē\ *adv*

sor·ry \'sär-ē\ *adj* **sor·ri·er; -est** **1** : feeling sorrow, regret, or penitence **2** : MOURNFUL, SAD **3** : causing sorrow, pity, or scorn : WRETCHED

¹sort \'sȯrt\ *n* **1** : a group of persons or things that have similar characteristics : CLASS **2** : WAY, MANNER **3** : QUALITY, NATURE — **out of sorts** **1** : somewhat ill **2** : GROUCHY, IRRITABLE

²sort *vb* **1** : to put in a certain place according to kind, class, or nature **2** : to be in accord : AGREE

sor·tie \'sȯrt-ē, sȯr-'tē\ *n* **1** : a sudden issuing of troops from a defensive position against the enemy **2** : one mission or attack by one airplane

SOS \ˌes-(ˌ)ō-'es\ *n* : a call or request for help or rescue

so–so \'sō-'sō\ *adv or adj* : PASSABLY

sot \'sät\ *n* : a habitual drunkard — **sot·tish** *adj*

sou·brette \sü-'bret\ *n* [F] : a coquettish maidservant or a frivolous young woman in a comedy

souf·flé \sü-'flā\ *n* [F, fr. *soufflé*, pp. of *souffler* to blow, puff up, fr. L *sufflare*, fr. *sub-* up + *flare* to blow] : a spongy dish made light in baking by stiffly beaten egg whites

sough \'saù, 'səf\ *vb* : to make a moaning or sighing sound — **sough** *n*

sought *past and past part of* SEEK

soul \'sōl\ *n* **1** : the immaterial essence of an individual life **2** : the spiritual principle embodied in human beings or the universe **3** : an active or essential part **4** : man's moral and emotional nature **5** : spiritual or moral force **6** : PERSON ⟨a kindly ~⟩ **7** : a strong, positive feeling (as of intense sensitivity and emotional fervor) conveyed esp. by black American performers; *also* : NEGRITUDE — **souled** \'sōld\ *adj* — **soul·less** \'sōl-ləs\ *adj*

²soul *adj* **1** : of, relating to, or characteristic of black Americans or their culture ⟨~ food⟩ ⟨~ music⟩ **2** : designed for or controlled by blacks ⟨~ radio stations⟩

soul brother *n* : a black male

soul·ful \'sōl-fəl\ *adj* : full of or expressing deep feeling — **soul·ful·ly** \-ē\ *adv*

¹sound \'saùnd\ *adj* **1** : not diseased or sickly **2** : free from flaw or defect **3** : FIRM, STRONG **4** : free from error : RIGHT **5** : LEGAL, VALID **6** : THOROUGH **7** : UNDISTURBED ⟨~ sleep⟩ **8** : showing good judgment — **sound·ly** *adv* — **sound·ness** *n*

²sound *n* **1** : the sensation of hearing; *also* : mechanical energy transmitted by longitudinal pressure waves (as in air) that is the stimulus to hearing **2**

: something heard : NOISE, TONE; *also*
: hearing distance : EARSHOT **3** : a musical style — **sound·less** *adj* — **soundproof** \-ˌprüf\ *adj or vb*

³**sound** *vb* **1** : to make or cause to make
a noise **2** : to order or proclaim by a
sound ⟨∼ the alarm⟩ **3** : to convey a
certain impression : SEEM **4** : to examine the condition of by causing to give
out sounds

⁴**sound** *n* : a long passage of water wider
than a strait often connecting two
larger bodies of water ⟨Long Island
∼⟩

⁵**sound** *vb* **1** : to measure the depth of
(water) esp. by a weighted line
dropped from the surface : FATHOM **2**
: PROBE **3** : to dive down suddenly ⟨the
hooked fish ∼ed⟩ — **sound·ing** *n*

sound·er \ˈsaùn-dər\ *n* : one that
sounds; *esp* : a device for making
soundings

sound·stage \ˈsaùn(d)-ˌstāj\ *n* : the part
of a motion-picture studio in which a
production is filmed

soup \ˈsüp\ *n* **1** : a liquid food with
stock as its base and often containing
pieces of solid food **2** : something
having the consistency of soup **3** : an
unfortunate predicament ⟨in the ∼⟩

soup up *vb* : to increase the power of

soup·çon \süp-ˈsōⁿ\ *n* [F] : a little bit
: TRACE

soupy \ˈsü-pē\ *adj* **soup·i·er; -est 1**
: having the consistency of soup **2**
: densely foggy or cloudy

¹**sour** \ˈsaù(ə)r\ *adj* **1** : having an acid or
tart taste ⟨∼ as vinegar⟩ **2** : SPOILED,
PUTRID ⟨a ∼ odor⟩ **3** : UNPLEASANT,
DISAGREEABLE ⟨∼ disposition⟩ — **sour-
ish** *adj* — **sour·ly** *adv* — **sour·ness** *n*

²**sour** *vb* : to become or make sour

source \ˈsȯrs\ *n* **1** : ORIGIN, BEGINNING **2**
: the beginning of a stream of water **3**
: a supplier of information

¹**souse** \ˈsaùs\ *vb* **soused; sous·ing 1**
: PICKLE **2** : to plunge into a liquid **3**
: DRENCH **4** : to make drunk

²**souse** *n* **1** : something (as pigs' feet)
steeped in pickle **2** : a soaking in liquid **3** : DRUNKARD

¹**south** \ˈsaùth\ *adv* : to or toward the
south

²**south** *adj* **1** : situated toward or at the
south **2** : coming from the south

³**south** *n* **1** : the direction to the right of
one facing west **2** : the compass point
directly opposite to north **3** *cap* : regions or countries south of a specified
or implied point; *esp* : the southeastern part of the U.S. — **south·er·ly**
\ˈsəth-ər-lē\ *adj or adv* — **south·ern**
\ˈsəth-ərn\ *adj* — **South·ern·er** *n* —
south·ern·most \-ˌmōst\ *adj* — **southward** \ˈsaùth-wərd\ *adv or adj* —
south·wards \-wərdz\ *adv*

South African *n* : a native or inhabitant
of the Republic of South Africa —
South African *adj*

south·east \saùth-ˈēst, *naut* saù-ˈēst\ *n*
1 : the general direction between

south and east **2** : the compass point
midway between south and east **3** *cap*
: regions or countries southeast of a
specified or implied point — **southeast**
adj or adv — **south·east·er·ly** *adv or
adj* — **south·east·ern** \-ərn\ *adj*

south·paw \ˈsaùth-ˌpȯ\ *n* : a left-handed
baseball pitcher — **southpaw** *adj*

south pole *n*, *often cap S&P* : the
southernmost point of the earth

south·west \saùth-ˈwest, *naut* saù-
ˈwest\ *n* **1** : the general direction between south and west **2** : the compass
point midway between south and west
3 *cap* : regions or countries southwest
of a specified or implied point —
southwest *adj or adv* — **south·west·er-
ly** *adv or adj* — **south·west·ern** \-ərn\
adj

sou·ve·nir \ˌsü-və-ˈnir\ *n* [F] : something serving as a reminder

sou'·west·er \saù-ˈwes-tər\ *n* : a waterproof hat worn at sea in stormy
weather; *also* : a long waterproof coat

¹**sov·er·eign** \ˈsäv-(ə-)rən\ *n* **1** : one possessing the supreme power and au-
thority in a state **2** : a gold coin of the
United Kingdom

²**sovereign** *adj* **1** : EXCELLENT, FINE **2**
: supreme in power or authority **3**
: CHIEF, HIGHEST **4** : having independent authority **syn** dominant,
predominant, paramount, preponderant

sov·er·eign·ty \-tē\ *n, pl -*ties **1** : supremacy in rule or power **2** : power to govern without external control **3** : the
supreme political power in a state

so·vi·et \ˈsōv-ē-ˌet, ˈsäv-, -ē-ət\ *n* **1** : an
elected governmental council in a
Communist country **2** *pl, cap* : the
people and esp. the leaders of the
U.S.S.R. — **so·vi·et·ism** *n, often cap*
— **so·vi·et·ize** *vb, often cap*

¹**sow** \ˈsaù\ *n* : an adult female swine

²**sow** \ˈsō\ *vb* **sowed; sown** \ˈsōn\ *or*
sowed; sow·ing 1 : to plant seed for
growing esp. by scattering **2** : to
strew with or as if with seed **3** : to
scatter abroad — **sow·er** \ˈsō(-ə)r\ *n*

sow bug \ˈsaù-\ *n* : WOOD LOUSE

sox *pl of* SOCK

soy \ˈsȯi\ *n* : a sauce made from soybeans fermented in brine

soy·bean \ˈsȯi-ˌbēn\ *n* : an Asian
legume widely grown for forage and
for its edible seeds that yield a valuable oil (**soybean oil**); *also* : its seed

sp *abbr* **1** special **2** species **3** specimen
4 spelling **5** spirit

Sp *abbr* Spain

SP *abbr* **1** shore patrol; shore patrol-
man **2** shore police **3** specialist

spa \ˈspä\ *n* [*Spa,* watering place in Bel-
gium] **1** : a mineral spring; *also* : a
resort with mineral springs **2** : a commercial establishment with facilities
for healthful exercise

¹**space** \ˈspās\ *n* **1** : a period of time **2**
: some small measurable part of space
3 : the limitless area in which all

things exist and move **4** : an empty place **5** : the region beyond the earth's atmosphere **6** : a definite place (as a seat or stateroom on a train or ship)

²**space** vb **spaced; spac·ing** : to place at intervals

space-age \'spās-ˌāj\ adj : of, relating to, or befitting the age of space exploration (~ technology)

space-craft \-ˌkraft\ n : a vehicle for travel beyond the earth's atmosphere

space-flight \-ˌflīt\ n : flight beyond the earth's atmosphere

space heater n : a device for heating an enclosed space

space-man \'spās-ˌman, -mən\ n : one who travels outside the earth's atmosphere

space-ship \'spās(h)-ˌship\ n : a spacecraft designed to carry one or more passengers

space shuttle n : a reusable spacecraft designed to transport people and cargo between earth and space

space station n : a manned artificial satellite in a fixed orbit serving as a base (as for scientific observation)

space suit n : a suit equipped to make life in space possible for its wearer

space walk n : a period of movement in space outside a spacecraft by an astronaut — **space walk** vb — **space-walk·er** \'spās-ˌwȯ-kər\ n — **space-walk·ing** \-kiŋ\ n

spa·cious \'spā-shəs\ adj : very large in extent : ROOMY syn commodious, capacious, ample — **spa·cious·ly** adv — **spa·cious·ness** n

¹**spade** \'spād\ n : a shovel with a flat blade — **spade·ful** n

²**spade** vb **spad·ed; spad·ing** : to dig with a spade

³**spade** n : any of a suit of playing cards marked with a black figure resembling an inverted heart with a short stem at the bottom

spa·dix \'spād-iks\ n, pl **spa·di·ces** \'spād-ə-ˌsēz\ : a floral spike with a fleshy or succulent axis usu. enclosed in a spathe

spa·ghet·ti \spə-'get-ē\ n [It, fr. pl. of spaghetto, dim. of spago cord, string] : a dough made chiefly from wheat flour and formed in thin solid strings

¹**span** \'span\ n **1** : an English unit of length equal to nine inches (about 23 centimeters) **2** : a limited portion of time **3** : the spread (as of an arch) from one support to another

²**span** vb **spanned; span·ning 1** : MEASURE **2** : to extend across

³**span** n : a pair of animals (as mules) driven together

Span abbr Spanish

span·dex \'span-ˌdeks\ n : an elastic synthetic textile fiber

span·gle \'spaŋ-gəl\ n : a small disk of shining metal used esp. on a dress for ornament — **spangle** vb

Span·iard \'span-yərd\ n : a native or inhabitant of Spain

span·iel \'span-yəl\ n [ME spaniell, fr. MF espaignol, lit., Spaniard, fr. L Hispania Spain] : any of numerous mostly small and short-legged dogs usu. with long wavy hair and large drooping ears

Span·ish \'span-ish\ n **1** : the chief language of Spain and of many countries colonized by the Spanish **2 Spanish** pl : the people of Spain — **Spanish** adj

Spanish American n : a native or inhabitant of one of the countries of America in which Spanish is the national language; also : a resident of the U.S. whose native language is Spanish — **Spanish-American** adj

Spanish fly n : a dried preparation of green European beetles with diuretic and aphrodisiac effects produced by irritating the urinary tract; also : this beetle

Spanish moss n : a plant related to the pineapple that grows in pendent tufts of grayish green filaments on trees in the southern U.S. and the West Indies

spank \'spaŋk\ vb : to strike the buttocks of with the open hand — **spank** n

spank·ing \'spaŋ-kiŋ\ adj : BRISK, LIVELY (~ breeze)

¹**spar** \'spär\ n : a rounded wood or metal piece (as a mast, yard, boom, or gaff) for supporting sail rigging

²**spar** vb **sparred; spar·ring** : to box for practice without serious hitting; also : SKIRMISH, WRANGLE

SPAR \'spär\ n : a member of the women's reserve of the U.S. Coast Guard

¹**spare** \'spaər\ vb **spared; spar·ing 1** : to refrain from punishing or injuring : show mercy to **2** : to exempt from something **3** : to get along without **4** : to use frugally or rarely

²**spare** adj **spar·er; spar·est 1** : held in reserve **2** : SUPERFLUOUS **3** : not liberal or profuse **4** : LEAN, THIN **5** : SCANTY syn meager, sparse, skimpy, exiguous, scant

³**spare** n **1** : a duplicate kept in reserve; esp : a spare tire **2** : the knocking down of all the bowling pins with the first two balls

spar·ing \'spar-iŋ\ adj : SAVING, FRUGAL syn thrifty, economical, provident — **spar·ing·ly** adv

¹**spark** \'spärk\ n **1** : a small particle of a burning substance or a hot glowing particle struck from a mass (as by steel or flint) **2** : a short bright flash of electricity between two points **3** : SPARKLE **4** : a particle capable of being kindled or developed : GERM

²**spark** vb **1** : to emit or produce sparks **2** : to stir to activity : INCITE

³**spark** vb : WOO, COURT

¹**spar·kle** \'spär-kəl\ vb **spar·kled; spar·kling** \-k(ə-)liŋ\ **1** : FLASH, GLEAM **2** : to perform brilliantly **3** : EFFERVESCE — **spar·kler** \-k(ə-)lər\ n

²**sparkle** n 1 : GLEAM 2 : ANIMATION

spark plug n : a device that produces a spark to ignite the fuel mixture in an engine cylinder

spar·row \'spar-ō\ n : any of several small dull singing birds

sparrow hawk n : any of various small hawks or falcons

sparse \'spärs\ adj **spars·er**; **spars·est** : thinly scattered : SCANTY syn meager, spare, skimpy, exiguous, scant — **sparse·ly** adv

spasm \'spaz-əm\ n 1 : an involuntary and abnormal muscular contraction 2 : a sudden, violent, and temporary effort or feeling — **spas·mod·ic** \spaz-'mäd-ik\ adj — **spas·mod·i·cal·ly** \-i-k(ə-)lē\ adv

spas·tic \'spas-tik\ adj : of, relating to, or marked by muscular spasm (~ paralysis) — **spastic** n

¹**spat** \'spat\ past and past part of SPIT

²**spat** n, pl **spat** or **spats** : a young bivalve mollusk (as an oyster)

³**spat** n : a gaiter covering instep and ankle

⁴**spat** n : a brief petty quarrel : DISPUTE

⁵**spat** vb **spat·ted**; **spat·ting** : to quarrel briefly

spate \'spāt\ n : a sudden outburst

spathe \'spāth\ n : a sheathing bract or pair of bracts enclosing an inflorescence (as of the calla lily) and esp. a spadix on the same axis

spa·tial \'spā-shəl\ adj : of or relating to space — **spa·tial·ly** \-ē\ adv

spat·ter \'spat-ər\ vb 1 : to splash with drops of liquid 2 : to sprinkle around — **spatter** n

spat·u·la \'spach-ə-lə\ n : a flexible knifelike implement for scooping, spreading, or mixing soft substances

spav·in \'spav-ən\ n : a bony enlargement of the hock of a horse — **spav·ined** \-ənd\ adj

¹**spawn** \'spón\ vb [ME spawnen, fr. OF espandre to spread out, expand; fr. L expandere, fr. ex- out + pandere to spread] 1 : to produce eggs or offspring esp. in large numbers : GENERATE

²**spawn** n 1 : the eggs of water animals (as fishes or oysters) that lay many small eggs 2 : offspring esp. when produced in great quantities

spay \'spā\ vb **spayed**; **spay·ing** : to remove the ovaries from (a female animal)

SPCA abbr Society for the Prevention of Cruelty to Animals

SPCC abbr Society for the Prevention of Cruelty to Children

speak \'spēk\ vb **spoke** \'spōk\; **spo·ken** \'spō-kən\; **speak·ing** 1 : to utter words 2 : to express orally 3 : to mention in speech or writing 4 : to address an audience 5 : to use or be able to use (a language) in speech

speak·easy \-ē-kē-zē\ n, pl **-eas·ies** : an illicit drinking place

speak·er \'spē-kər\ n 1 : one that

speaks 2 : the presiding officer of a deliberative assembly 3 : LOUDSPEAKER

¹**spear** \'spiər\ n 1 : a long-shafted weapon with a sharp point for thrusting or throwing 2 : a sharp-pointed instrument with barbs (as for spearing fish) — **spear·man** \-mən\ n

²**spear** vb : to strike or pierce with or as if with a spear

³**spear** n : a young shoot (as of asparagus)

spear·head \-,hed\ n : a leading force, element, or influence — **spearhead** vb

spear·mint \-,mint\ n : a common highly aromatic garden mint

spec abbr 1 special 2 specifically

spe·cial \'spesh-əl\ adj 1 : UNCOMMON, NOTEWORTHY 2 : particularly favored 3 : INDIVIDUAL, UNIQUE 4 : EXTRA, ADDITIONAL 5 : confined to or designed for a definite field of action, purpose, or occasion — **special** n — **spe·cial·ly** \-ē\ adv

special delivery n : delivery of mail by messenger for an extra fee

Special Forces n pl : a branch of the army composed of men specially trained in guerrilla warfare

spe·cial·ist \'spesh-(ə-)ləst\ n 1 : one who devotes himself to some special branch of learning or activity 2 : any of four enlisted ranks in the army corresponding to the grades of corporal through sergeant first class

spe·cial·ize \'spesh-ə-,līz\ vb **-ized**; **-iz·ing** : to concentrate one's efforts in a special activity or field; also : to change in an adaptive manner — **spe·cial·iza·tion** \,spesh-ə-lə-'zā-shən\ n

spe·cial·ty \'spesh-əl-tē\ n, pl **-ties** 1 : a particular quality or detail 2 : a product of a special kind or of special excellence 3 : a branch of knowledge, business, or professional work in which one specializes

spe·cie \'spē-shē, -sē\ n : money in coin

spe·cies \'spē-shēz, -sēz\ n, pl **species** [L, appearance, kind, species, fr. specere to look] 1 : SORT, KIND 2 : a category of biological classification ranking just below the genus or subgenus and comprising closely related organisms potentially able to breed with one another

specif abbr specific; specifically

¹**spe·cif·ic** \spi-'sif-ik\ adj 1 : DEFINITE, EXACT 2 : having a unique relation to something ⟨~ antibodies⟩ ; esp : exerting a distinctive and usu. curative or causative influence 3 : of, relating to, or constituting a species — **spe·cif·i·cal·ly** \-i-k(ə-)lē\ adv

²**specific** n : a specific remedy

spec·i·fi·ca·tion \,spes-ə-fə-'kā-shən\ n 1 : the act or process of specifying 2 : a description of work to be done and materials to be used (as in building) — usu. used in pl.

specific gravity n : the ratio of the density of a substance to the density of some substance (as water) taken as a standard when both densities are obtained by weighing in air

spec·i·fy \\'spes-ə-ˌfī\\ *vb* **-fied; -fy·ing** : to mention or name explicitly

spec·i·men \\'spes-ə-mən\\ *n* : an item or part typical of a group or whole

spe·cious \\'spē-shəs\\ *adj* : seeming to be genuine, correct, or beautiful but not really so (~ reasoning)

speck \\'spek\\ *n* **1** : a small spot or blemish **2** : a small particle : BIT — **speck** *vb*

speck·le \\'spek-əl\\ *n* : a little speck — **speckle** *vb*

spec·ta·cle \\'spek-ti-kəl\\ *n* **1** : something exhibited to view; *esp* : an impressive public display **2** *pl* : GLASSES — **spec·ta·cled** \\-kəld\\ *adj*

¹spec·tac·u·lar \\spek-'tak-yə-lər\\ *adj* : SENSATIONAL, STRIKING, SHOWY

²spectacular *n* : an elaborate spectacle

spec·ta·tor \\'spek-ˌtāt-ər\\ *n* : one who looks on (as at a sports event) **syn** observer, witness, bystander, onlooker, eyewitness

spec·ter *or* **spec·tre** \\'spek-tər\\ *n* : a visible disembodied spirit : GHOST

spec·tral \\'spek-trəl\\ *adj* **1** : of, relating to, or resembling a specter **2** : of, relating to, or made by a spectrum

spec·tro·gram \\'spek-trə-ˌgram\\ *n* : a photograph or diagram of a spectrum

spec·tro·graph \\-ˌgraf\\ *n* : an instrument for dispersing radiation into a spectrum and photographing or mapping the spectrum — **spec·tro·graph·ic** \\ˌspek-trə-'graf-ik\\ *adj* — **spec·tro·graph·i·cal·ly** \\-i-k(ə-)lē\\ *adv*

spec·trom·e·ter \\spek-'träm-ət-ər\\ *n* : a spectroscope fitted for measuring spectra — **spec·tro·met·ric** \\ˌspek-trə-'me-trik\\ *adj*

spec·tro·scope \\'spek-trə-ˌskōp\\ *n* : an optical instrument that produces spectra from or by the use of electromagnetic radiation — **spec·tro·scop·ic** \\ˌspek-trə-'skäp-ik\\ *adj* — **spec·tro·scop·i·cal·ly** \\-i-k(ə-)lē\\ *adv* — **spec·tros·co·pist** \\spek-'träs-kə-pəst\\ *n* — **spec·tros·co·py** \\-pē\\ *n*

spec·trum \\'spek-trəm\\ *n, pl* **spec·tra** \\-trə\\ *or* **spectrums** [NL, fr. L, appearance, specter, fr. *specere* to look] **1** : a series of colors formed when a beam of white light is dispersed (as by a prism) so that its parts are arranged in the order of their wavelengths **2** : a series of radiations arranged in regular order **3** : a continuous sequence or range (a wide ~ of political opinions)

spec·u·late \\'spek-yə-ˌlāt\\ *vb* **-lat·ed; -lat·ing** [L *speculari* to spy out, examine, fr. *specula* watchtower, fr. *specere* to look, look at] **1** : REFLECT, MEDITATE **2** : to engage in a business deal where a good profit may be made at considerable risk **syn** think, deliberate, cogitate — **spec·u·la·tion** \\ˌspek-yə-'lā-shən\\ *n* — **spec·u·la·tive**

\\'spek-yə-ˌlāt-iv\\ *adj* — **spec·u·la·tive·ly** *adv* — **spec·u·la·tor** \\-ˌlāt-ər\\ *n*

speech \\'spēch\\ *n* **1** : the act of speaking **2** : TALK, CONVERSATION **3** : a public discourse **4** : LANGUAGE, DIALECT : an individual manner of speaking **6** : the power of speaking — **speech·less** *adj*

¹speed \\'spēd\\ *n* **1** *archaic* : SUCCESS **2** : SWIFTNESS, RAPIDITY **3** : rate of motion or performance **4** : a transmission gear in an automotive vehicle or bicycle **5** : METHAMPHETAMINE; *also* : a related drug **syn** haste, hurry, dispatch, celerity — **speed·i·ly** \\'spēd-ᵊl-ē\\ *adv* — **speedy** *adj*

²speed *vb* **sped** \\'sped\\ *or* **speed·ed; speed·ing 1** *archaic* : PROSPER; *also* : GET ALONG, FARE **2** : to go fast; *esp* : to go at an excessive or illegal speed **3** : to cause to go faster — **speed·er** *n*

speed·boat \\-ˌbōt\\ *n* : a fast motorboat

speed·om·e·ter \\spi-'däm-ət-ər\\ *n* : an instrument for indicating speed or speed and distance traveled

speed·up \\'spēd-ˌəp\\ *n* **1** : ACCELERATION **2** : an employer's demand for accelerated output without increased pay

speed·way \\'spēd-ˌwā\\ *n* : a racecourse for motor vehicles

speed·well \\-ˌwel\\ *n* : a low creeping plant that bears spikes of small usu. bluish flowers and is related to the snapdragon

¹spell \\'spel\\ *n* [ME, talk, tale, fr. OE] **1** : a magic formula : INCANTATION **2** : a controlling influence

²spell *vb* **spelled** \\'speld\\; **spell·ing** : to take the place of for a time in work or duty : RELIEVE

³spell *vb* **spelled** \\'speld, 'spelt\\; **spelling 1** : to name, write, or print in order the letters of a word **2** : MEAN

⁴spell *n archaic* : the relief of one person by another in any work or duty **2** : one's turn at work or duty **3** : a stretch of a specified kind of weather **4** : a period of bodily or mental distress or disorder : ATTACK

spell·bind·er \\-ˌbīn-dər\\ *n* : a speaker of compelling eloquence

spell·bound \\-ˌbaùnd\\ *adj* : held by or as if by a spell : FASCINATED

spell·er \\'spel-ər\\ *n* **1** : one who spells words **2** : a book with exercises for teaching spelling

spe·lunk·er \\spi-'ləŋ-kər, 'spē-ˌləŋ-kər\\ *n* : one who makes a hobby of exploring caves — **spe·lunk·ing** \\-kiŋ\\ *n*

spend \\'spend\\ *vb* **spent** \\'spent\\; **spend·ing 1** : to pay out : USE UP **2** : WEAR OUT, EXHAUST; *also* : to consume wastefully **3** : to cause or permit to elapse : PASS **4** : to make use of — **spend·er** *n*

spend·thrift \\'spen(d)-ˌthrift\\ *n* : one who spends wastefully or recklessly

spent \\'spent\\ *adj* : drained of energy

sperm \\'spərm\\ *n, pl* **sperm** *or* **sperms 1** : SEMEN **2** : a male gamete

sper·ma·to·zo·on \(,)spər-,mat-ə-¹zō-,än, -¹zō-ən\ *n, pl* **-zoa** \-¹zō-ə\ : a motile male gamete of an animal usu. with a rounded or elongated head and a long posterior flagellum

sperm cell *n* : SPERM 2

sperm whale \¹spərm-\ *n* : a whale with conical teeth, no whalebone, and a large fluid-containing cavity in the head

spew \¹spyü\ *vb* : VOMIT

sp gr *abbr* specific gravity

sphag·num \¹sfag-nəm\ *n* : any of a genus of atypical mosses that grow in wet acid areas where their remains become compacted with other plant debris to form peat; *also* : a mass of these mosses

sphere \¹sfiər\ *n* [ME *spere* globe, celestial sphere, fr. MF *espere*, fr. L *sphaera*, fr. Gk *sphaira*, lit., ball] 1 : a globular body 2 : a celestial body 3 : a solid figure so shaped that every point on its surface is an equal distance from the center 4 : range of action or influence : FIELD — **spher·i·cal** \¹sfir-i-kəl, ¹sfer-\ *adj* — **spher·i·cal·ly** \-i-k(ə-)lē\ *adv*

spher·oid \¹sfi(ə)r-,oid, ¹sfe(ə)r-\ *n* : a figure similar to a sphere but not perfectly round — **sphe·roi·dal** \sfir-¹oid-³l\ *adj*

sphinc·ter \¹sfiŋk-tər\ *n* : a muscular ring that closes a bodily opening

sphinx \¹sfiŋks\ *n, pl* **sphinx·es** *or* **sphin·ges** \¹sfin-,jēz\ 1 : a winged monster in Greek mythology having a woman's head and a lion's body and noted for killing anyone unable to answer its riddle 2 : an enigmatic or mysterious person 3 : an ancient Egyptian image having the body of a lion and the head of man, ram, or hawk

spice \¹spīs\ *n* 1 : any of various aromatic plant products (as pepper or nutmeg) used to season or flavor foods 2 : something that adds interest and relish — **spice** *vb* — **spicy** *adj*

spice·bush \¹spīs-,bush\ *n* : an aromatic shrub related to the laurels that bears dense clusters of small yellow flowers followed by scarlet or yellow berries

spick–and–span *or* **spic–and–span** \,spik-ən-¹span\ *adj* : quite new; *also* : spotlessly clean

spic·ule \¹spik-yül\ *n* : a slender pointed body esp. of calcium or silica (sponge ~s)

spi·der \¹spīd-ər\ *n* 1 : any of numerous arachnids that have a 2-part body, eight legs, and two or more pairs of abdominal organs for spinning threads of silk used esp. in making webs for catching prey 2 : a cast-iron frying pan — **spi·dery** *adj*

spider plant *n* : a houseplant of the lily family having long green leaves usu. striped with white and producing tufts of small plants on long hanging stems

spiderweb *n* : the web spun by a spider

spiel \¹spēl\ *vb* : to talk volubly or extravagantly — **spiel** *n*

spig·ot \¹spig-ət, ¹spik-ət\ *n* : FAUCET

¹**spike** \¹spīk\ *n* 1 : a very large nail 2 : any of various pointed projections (as on the sole of a shoe to prevent slipping) — **spiky** *adj*

²**spike** *vb* **spiked**; **spik·ing** 1 : to fasten with spikes 2 : to put an end to : QUASH ⟨~ a rumor⟩ 3 : to pierce with or impale on a spike 4 : to add alcoholic liquor to (a drink)

³**spike** *n* 1 : an ear of grain 2 : a long cluster of usu. stemless flowers

¹**spill** \¹spil\ *vb* **spilled** \¹spild, ¹spilt\ *also* **spilt** \¹spilt\; **spill·ing** 1 : to cause or allow esp. unintentionally to fall, flow, or run out 2 : to lose or allow to be scattered 3 : to cause (blood) to flow 4 : to run out or over with resulting loss or waste — **spill·able** *adj*

²**spill** *n* 1 : an act of spilling; *also* : a fall from a horse or vehicle or in running 2 : something spilled 3 : SPILLWAY

spill·way \-,wā\ *n* : a passage for surplus water to run over or around an obstruction (as a dam)

¹**spin** \¹spin\ *vb* **spun** \¹spən\; **spin·ning** 1 : to draw out (fiber) and twist into thread; *also* : to form (thread) by such means 2 : to form thread by extruding a sticky quickly hardening fluid; *also* : to construct from such thread ⟨spiders ~ their webs⟩ 3 : to produce slowly and by degrees ⟨~ a story⟩ 4 : TWIRL 5 : WHIRL, REEL ⟨my head is spinning⟩ 6 : to move rapidly along — **spin·ner** *n*

²**spin** *n* 1 : a rapid rotating motion 2 : an excursion in a wheeled vehicle

spin·ach \¹spin-ich\ *n* : a dark green herb grown for its edible leaves

spi·nal \¹spīn-³l\ *adj* : of or relating to the backbone or spinal cord — **spi·nal·ly** \-ē\ *adv*

spinal column *n* : BACKBONE

spinal cord *n* : the thick cord of nervous tissue that extends from the brain along the back in the cavity of the backbone and carries nerve impulses to and from the brain

spinal nerve *n* : any of the paired nerves which arise from the spinal cord and pass to various parts of the body and of which there are normally 31 pairs in human beings

spin·dle \¹spin-d³l\ *n* 1 : a round tapering stick or rod by which fibers are twisted in spinning 2 : a turned part of a piece of furniture ⟨the ~s of a chair⟩ 3 : a slender pin or rod which turns or on which something else turns

spin·dling \¹spin-(d)liŋ\ *adj* : SPINDLY

spin·dly \¹spin-(d)lē\ *adj* : being long or tall and thin and usu. weak

spin·drift \¹spin-,drift\ *n* : spray blown from waves

spine \¹spīn\ *n* 1 : BACKBONE 2 : a stiff sharp process esp. on a plant or animal — **spine·less** *adj* — **spiny** *adj*

spi·nel \spə-¹nel\ *n* : a hard crystalline

mineral of variable color used as a gem

spin·et \'spin-ət\ *n* **1** : an early harpsichord having a single keyboard and only one string for each note **2** : a small upright piano

spin·na·ker \'spin-i-kər\ *n* : a large triangular sail set on a long light pole

spinning jen·ny \-,jen-ē\ *n* : an early multiple-spindle machine for spinning wool or cotton

spinning wheel *n* : a small machine for spinning thread or yarn in which a large wheel drives a single spindle

spin–off \'spin-,óf\ *n* **1** : the distribution by a business to its stockholders of particular assets and esp. of stock of another company **2** : a usu. useful by-product (~s from missile research) — **spin off** *vb*

spin·ster \'spin-stər\ *n* : an unmarried woman past the common age for marrying — **spin·ster·hood** \-,hùd\ *n*

spiny lobster *n* : an edible crustacean differing from the related lobster in lacking the large front claws and in having a very spiny carapace

¹**spi·ral** \'spī-rəl\ *adj* : circling around a center like the thread of a screw **2** : winding or coiling around a center or pole in gradually enlarging circles — **spi·ral·ly** \-ē\ *adv*

²**spiral** *n* **1** : something that has a spiral form; *also* : a single turn in a spiral object **2** : a continuously spreading and accelerating increase or decrease

³**spiral** *vb* **-raled** *or* **-ralled; -ral·ing** *or* **-ral·ling 1** : to move in a spiral course **2** : to form into a spiral

spi·rant \'spī-rənt\ *n* : a consonant (as \f\, \s\, \sh\) uttered with decided friction of the oral breath against some part of the oral passage — **spirant** *adj*

spire \'spī(ə)r\ *n* **1** : a slender tapering stalk (as of grass) **2** : a pointed tip (as of a tree or antler) **3** : STEEPLE — **spiry** *adj*

spi·rea *or* **spi·raea** \spī-'rē-ə\ *n* : any of a genus of shrubs related to the roses with dense clusters of small white or pink flowers

¹**spir·it** \'spir-ət\ *n* [ME, fr. OF or L: OF, fr. L *spiritus*, lit., breath] **1** : a life-giving force; *also* : the animating principle : SOUL **2** *cap* : HOLY SPIRIT **3** : SPECTER, GHOST **4** : PERSON **5** : DISPOSITION, MOOD **6** : VIVACITY, ARDOR **7** : essential or real meaning : INTENT **8** : distilled alcoholic liquor **9** : LOYALTY (school ~) — **spir·it·less** *adj*

²**spirit** *vb* : to carry off secretly or mysteriously

spir·it·ed \'spir-ət-əd\ *adj* **1** : ANIMATED, LIVELY **2** : COURAGEOUS

¹**spir·i·tu·al** \'spir-ich-(ə-w)əl\ *adj* **1** : of, relating to, consisting of, or affecting the spirit : INCORPOREAL **2** : of or relating to sacred matters **3** : ecclesiastical rather than lay or temporal — **spir·i·tu·al·i·ty** \,spir-i-chə-'wal-ət-ē\ *n* —

spir·i·tu·al·ize \'spir-ich-(ə-w)ə-,līz\ *vb* — **spir·i·tu·al·ly** \-lē\ *adv*

²**spiritual** *n* : a religious song originating among blacks of the southern U.S.

spir·i·tu·al·ism \'spir-ich-(ə-w)ə-,liz-əm\ *n* : a belief that spirits of the dead communicate with the living usu. through a medium — **spir·i·tu·al·ist** \-ləst\ *n, often cap* — **spir·i·tu·al·is·tic** \,spir-ich-(ə-w)ə-'lis-tik\ *adj*

spir·i·tu·ous \'spir-ich-(ə-w)əs, 'spir-ət-əs\ *adj* : containing alcohol (~ liquors)

spi·ro·chete *also* **spi·ro·chaete** \'spī-rə-,kēt\ *n* : any of an order of spiral bacteria including one that causes syphilis

spirt *var of* SPURT

¹**spit** \'spit\ *n* **1** : a thin pointed rod for holding meat over a fire **2** : a point of land that runs out into the water

²**spit** *vb* **spit·ted; spit·ting** : to pierce with or as if with a spit

³**spit** *vb* **spit** *or* **spat** \'spat\ **spit·ting 1** : to eject (saliva) from the mouth **2** : to send forth forcefully, defiantly, or disgustedly **3** : to rain or snow lightly

⁴**spit** *n* **1** : SALIVA **2** : perfect likeness (~ and image of his father) **3** : a sprinkle of rain or flurry of snow

spit·ball \'spit-,ból\ *n* **1** : paper chewed and rolled into a ball to be thrown as a missile **2** : a baseball pitch delivered after the ball has been moistened with saliva or sweat

¹**spite** \'spīt\ *n* : ill will with a wish to annoy, anger, or defeat : petty malice *syn* malignity, **spleen**, grudge, malevolence — **spite·ful** \-fəl\ *adj* — **spite·ful·ly** \-ē\ *adv* — **spite·ful·ness** *n* — **in spite of** : in defiance or contempt of : NOTWITHSTANDING

²**spite** *vb* **spit·ed; spit·ing** : to treat maliciously (as by insulting or thwarting)

spit·tle \'spit-ªl\ *n* : SALIVA

spit·tle·bug \-,bəg\ *n* : any of numerous leaping insects with froth-secreting larvae that are related to the aphids

spit·toon \spi-'tün\ *n* : a receptacle for spit

¹**splash** \'splash\ *vb* **1** : to dash a liquid about **2** : to scatter a liquid on : SPATTER **3** : to fall or strike with a splashing noise *syn* sprinkle, bespatter, douse, splatter — **splash** *n*

splash·down \'splash-,daùn\ *n* : the landing of a manned spacecraft in the ocean — **splash down** \(')splash-'daùn\ *vb*

splat·ter \'splat-ər\ *vb* : SPATTER — **splatter** *n*

¹**splay** \'splā\ *vb* **1** : to spread out **2** : to slope or slant outward (~ed doorway) — **splay** *n*

²**splay** *adj* **1** : spread out : turned outward **2** : AWKWARD, CLUMSY

spleen \'splēn\ *n* **1** : a vascular organ located near the stomach in most vertebrates that is concerned esp. with the storage, formation, and destruction of blood cells **2** : SPITE, MAL-

ICE **syn** malignity, grudge, malevolence, ill will, spitefulness

splen·did \'splen-dəd\ *adj* [L *splendidus*, fr. *splendēre* to shine] 1 : SHINING, BRILLIANT 2 : SHOWY, GORGEOUS 3 : ILLUSTRIOUS 4 : EXCELLENT **syn** splendent, glorious, sublime, superb — **splen·did·ly** *adv*

splen·dor \'splen-dər\ *n* 1 : BRILLIANCE 2 : POMP, MAGNIFICENCE

sple·net·ic \spli-'net-ik\ *adj* : marked by bad temper or spite

splen·ic \'splen-ik\ *adj* : of, relating to, or located in the spleen

splice \'splīs\ *vb* **spliced; splic·ing** 1 : to unite (as two ropes) by weaving the strands together 2 : to unite (as two timbers or pieces of film) by connecting the ends together — **splice** *n*

splint \'splint\ *n* 1 : a thin strip of wood interwoven with others to make something (as a basket) 2 : material or a device used to protect and keep in place an injured body part (as a broken arm)

¹**splin·ter** \'splint-ər\ *n* : a thin piece of something split off lengthwise : SLIVER

²**splinter** *vb* : to split into splinters

split \'split\ *vb* **split; split·ting** 1 : to divide lengthwise or along a grain or seam 2 : to burst or break in pieces 3 : to divide into parts or sections 4 : LEAVE **syn** rend, cleave, rip, tear — **split** *n*

split-lev·el \'split-'lev-əl\ *n* : a house divided so that the floor in one part is about halfway between two floors in the other

split personality *n* : SCHIZOPHRENIA; *also* : a mental and emotional disorder which is a neurosis and in which the personality becomes separated into two or more parts each of which controls behavior part of the time

split·ting \'split-iŋ\ *adj* : causing a piercing sensation (∼ headache)

splotch \'spläch\ *n* : BLOTCH

splurge \'splərj\ *n* : a showy display or expense — **splurge** *vb*

splut·ter \'splət-ər\ *n* : SPUTTER — **splutter** *vb*

¹**spoil** \'spȯil\ *n* : PLUNDER, BOOTY

²**spoil** *vb* **spoiled** \'spȯild, 'spȯilt\ *or* **spoilt** \'spȯilt\ ; **spoil·ing** 1 : ROB, PILLAGE 2 : to damage seriously : RUIN 3 : to impair the quality or effect of 4 : to damage the disposition of by pampering; *also* : INDULGE, CODDLE 5 : DECAY, ROT 6 : to have an eager desire (∼ing for a fight) **syn** injure, harm, hurt, mar — **spoil·age** \'spȯi-lij\ *n*

spoil·er \'spȯi-lər\ *n* 1 : one that spoils : a device (as on an airplane or automobile) used to disrupt airflow and decrease lift

spoil·sport \'spȯil-ˌspȯrt\ *n* : one who spoils the sport or pleasure of others

¹**spoke** \'spōk\ *past & archaic past part of* SPEAK

²**spoke** *n* 1 : any of the rods extending from the hub of a wheel to the rim 2 : a rung of a ladder

spo·ken \'spō-kən\ *past part of* SPEAK

spokes·man \'spōks-mən\ *n* : one who speaks as the representative of another or others

spokes·per·son \-ˌpər-sən\ *n* : SPOKESMAN

spokes·wom·an \-ˌwùm-ən\ *n* : a woman who speaks as the representative of another or others

spo·li·a·tion \ˌspō-lē-'ā-shən\ *n* : the act of plundering : the state of being plundered

¹**sponge** \'spənj\ *n* 1 : the elastic porous mass of fibers that forms the skeleton of any of a phylum of primitive sea animals; *also* : one of the animals 2 : the act of washing or wiping with a sponge 3 : a spongelike or porous mass or material (as used for sponging) — **spongy** \'spən-jē\ *adj*

²**sponge** *vb* **sponged; spong·ing** 1 : to gather sponges 2 : to bathe or wipe with a sponge 3 : to live at another's expense — **spong·er** *n*

sponge cake *n* : a cake made without shortening

sponge rubber *n* : a cellular rubber resembling natural sponge

spon·sor \'spän-sər\ *n* [LL, fr. L, guarantor, surety, fr. *sponsus*, pp. of *spondēre* to promise] 1 : one who takes the responsibility for some other person or thing : SURETY 2 : GODPARENT 3 : a business firm that pays the cost of a radio or television program usu. in return for advertising time during its course **syn** patron, guarantor, backer — **sponsor** *vb* — **spon·sor·ship** *n*

spon·ta·ne·ous \spän-'tā-nē-əs\ *adj* [LL *spontaneus*, fr. L *sponte* of one's free will, voluntarily] 1 : done or produced freely or naturally 2 : acting or taking place without external force or cause **syn** impulsive, instinctive, automatic, unpremeditated — **spon·ta·ne·ity** \ˌspänt-ən-'ē-ət-ē\ *n* — **spon·ta·ne·ous·ly** \spän-'tā-nē-əs-lē\ *adv*

spontaneous combustion *n* : a bursting into flame of material through heat produced within itself by chemical action (as oxidation)

spoof \'spüf\ *vb* 1 : DECEIVE, HOAX 2 : to make good-natured fun of — **spoof** *n*

¹**spook** \'spük\ *n* : GHOST, APPARITION — **spooky** *adj*

²**spook** *vb* : FRIGHTEN

spool \'spül\ *n* : a cylinder on which flexible material (as thread) is wound

spoon \'spün\ *n* [ME, fr. OE *spōn* splinter, chip] 1 : an eating or cooking implement consisting of a shallow bowl with a handle 2 : a metal piece used on a fishing line as a lure — **spoon** *vb* — **spoon·ful** *n*

spoon·bill \'spün-ˌbil\ *n* : any of several wading birds related to the ibises that have a bill with a broad flat tip

spoon—feed \'spün-ˌfēd\ *vb* **-fed** \-ˌfed\ ;

-feed·ing 1 : to feed by means of a spoon 2 : to present (information) so completely as to preclude independent thought

spoor \'spu̇r, 'spȯr\ n : a track, a trail, a scent, or droppings esp. of a wild animal

spo·rad·ic \spə-'rad-ik\ adj : occurring in scattered single instances syn occasional, rare, scarce, infrequent, uncommon — **spo·rad·i·cal·ly** \-i-k(ə-)lē\ adv

spore \'spȯr\ n : a primitive usu. one-celled reproductive body produced by plants and some lower animals

¹**sport** \'spȯrt\ vb [ME sporten to divert, disport, short for disporten, fr. MF desporter, fr. des- (fr. L dis- apart) + porter to carry, fr. L portare] 1 : to amuse oneself : FROLIC 2 : to wear or display ostentatiously — **sport·ive** adj

²**sport** n 1 : a source of diversion : PASTIME 2 : physical activity engaged in for pleasure 3 : JEST 4 : MOCKERY 〈make ∼ of his efforts〉 5 : BUTT, LAUGHINGSTOCK 6 : one who accepts results cheerfully whether favoring his interests or not 7 : an individual distinguished by a mutation syn play, frolic, fun, recreation — **sporty** adj

³**sport** or **sports** adj : of, relating to, or suitable for sport or casual wear 〈∼ coats〉

sport fish n : a fish important for the sport it affords anglers

sports·cast \'spȯrts-ˌkast\ n : a broadcast dealing with sports events — **sports·cast·er** \-ˌkas-tər\ n

sports·man \'spȯrts-mən\ n 1 : a person who engages in sports and esp. in hunting and fishing 2 : one who plays fairly and wins or loses gracefully — **sports·man·ship** n

sports·wom·an \-ˌwu̇m-ən\ n : a woman who engages in sports

sports·writ·er \-ˌrīt-ər\ n : one who writes about sports esp. for a newspaper — **sports·writ·ing** \-iŋ\ n

¹**spot** \'spät\ n 1 : STAIN, BLEMISH 2 : a small part different (as in color) from the main part 3 : LOCATION, SITE — **spot·less** adj — **spot·less·ly** adv — **on the spot** : in difficulty or danger

²**spot** vb **spot·ted; spot·ting** 1 : to mark or disfigure with spots 2 : to pick out : RECOGNIZE, IDENTIFY

³**spot** adj : being, done, or originating on the spot 〈a ∼ broadcast〉 2 : paid upon delivery 3 : made at random or at a few key points 〈a ∼ check〉

spot-check \'spät-ˌchek\ vb : to make a spot check of

spot·light \-ˌlīt\ n 1 : a circle of brilliant light projected upon a particular area, person, or object (as on a stage); also : the device that produces this light 2 : public notice — **spotlight** vb

spot·ter \'spät-ər\ n 1 : one that keeps watch : OBSERVER 2 : one that removes spots

spot·ty \'spät-ē\ adj **spot·ti·er; -est** : uneven in quality; also : sparsely distributed 〈∼ attendance〉

spou·sal \'spau̇-zəl, -səl\ n : NUPTIALS — usu. used in pl.

spouse \'spau̇s\ n : one's husband or wife

¹**spout** \'spau̇t\ vb 1 : to eject or issue forth forcibly and freely 〈wells ∼ing oil〉 2 : to speak pompously

²**spout** n 1 : a pipe or hole through which liquid spouts 2 : a jet of liquid; esp : WATERSPOUT 2

spp abbr, pl species

¹**sprain** \'sprān\ n : a sudden or severe twisting of a joint with stretching or tearing of ligaments; also : a sprained condition

²**sprain** vb : to subject to sprain

sprat \'sprat\ n : a small European herring; also : a young herring

sprawl \'sprȯl\ vb 1 : to lie or sit with limbs spread out awkwardly 2 : to spread out irregularly — **sprawl** n

¹**spray** \'sprā\ n : a usu. flowering branch or a decorative arrangement of flowers and foliage

²**spray** n 1 : liquid flying in small drops like water blown from a wave 2 : a jet of fine vapor (as from an atomizer) 3 : an instrument (as an atomizer) for scattering fine liquid

³**spray** vb 1 : to scatter or let fall in a spray 2 : to discharge spray on or into — **spray·er** n

spray can n : a pressurized container from which aerosols are sprayed

spray gun n : a device for spraying liquids (as paint or insecticide)

¹**spread** \'spred\ vb **spread; spread·ing** 1 : to scatter over a surface 2 : to flatten out : open out 3 : to stretch, force, or push apart 4 : to distribute over a period of time or among many persons 5 : to pass on from person to person 6 : to cover with something 〈∼ a floor with rugs〉 7 : to prepare for a meal 〈∼ a table〉 — **spread·er** n

²**spread** n 1 : the act or process of spreading 2 : EXPANSE, EXTENT 3 : a prominent display in a magazine or newspaper 4 : a food to be spread on bread or crackers 5 : a cloth cover for a bed 6 : distance between two points : GAP

spree \'sprē\ n : an unrestrained outburst 〈buying ∼〉 : esp : a drinking bout

sprig \'sprig\ n : a small shoot or twig

spright·ly \'sprīt-lē\ adj **spright·li·er; -est** : LIVELY, SPIRITED syn animated, vivacious, gay — **spright·li·ness** n

¹**spring** \'spriŋ\ vb **sprang** \'spraŋ\ or **sprung** \'sprəŋ\; **sprung; spring·ing** \'spriŋ-iŋ\ 1 : to move suddenly upward or forward 2 : to shoot up 〈weeds ∼ up overnight〉 3 : to move quickly by elastic force 4 : to make lame : STRAIN 5 : WARP 6 : to develop 〈a leak〉 through the seams 7 : to make known suddenly 〈∼ a surprise〉 8 : to cause to close suddenly 〈∼ a trap〉

²**spring** n 1 : a source of supply; esp : an issuing of water from the ground 2 : SOURCE, ORIGIN; also : MOTIVE 3 : the season between winter and summer 4 : an elastic body or device that recovers its original shape when it is released after being distorted 5 : the act or an instance of leaping up or forward 6 : RESILIENCE — **springy** adj

spring·board \'spriŋ-ˌbȯrd\ n : a springy board used in jumping or vaulting or for diving

spring fever n : a lazy or restless feeling often associated with the onset of spring

spring tide n : a tide of greater-than-average range that occurs at each new moon and full moon

spring·time \'spriŋ-ˌtīm\ n : the season of spring

¹**sprin·kle** \'spriŋ-kəl\ vb **sprin·kled; sprin·kling** \-k(ə-)liŋ\ : to scatter in small drops or particles — **sprin·kler** \-k(ə-)lər\ n

²**sprinkle** n : a light rainfall

sprin·kling \'spriŋ-kliŋ\ n : SMATTERING

¹**sprint** \'sprint\ vb : to run at top speed esp. for a short distance — **sprint·er** n

²**sprint** n 1 : a short run at top speed 2 : a short distance race

sprite \'sprīt\ n 1 : GHOST, SPIRIT 2 : ELF, FAIRY

spritz vb : SPRAY

sprock·et \'spräk-ət\ n : a tooth on a wheel (**sprocket wheel**) shaped so as to interlock with a chain

¹**sprout** \'spraút\ vb : to send out new growth esp. rapidly ⟨~ing seeds⟩

²**sprout** n : a usu. young and growing plant shoot

¹**spruce** \'sprüs\ vb **spruced; spruc·ing** : to make or become spruce

²**spruce** adj **spruc·er; spruc·est** : neat and smart in appearance syn stylish, fashionable, modish, dapper, natty

³**spruce** n : any of a genus of evergreen pyramid-shaped trees related to the pines and having soft light wood; also : the wood of a spruce

sprung past and past part of SPRING

spry \'sprī\ adj **spri·er** or **spry·er** \'sprī(-ə)r\; **spri·est** or **spry·est** \'sprī-əst\ : NIMBLE, ACTIVE syn agile, brisk, lively, sprightly

spud \'spəd\ n 1 : a sharp narrow spade 2 : POTATO

spume \'spyüm\ n : frothy matter on liquids : FOAM

spu·mo·ni or **spu·mo·ne** \spù-'mō-nē\ n [It spumone, deriv. of spuma foam] : ice cream in layers of different colors, flavors, and textures often with candied fruits and nuts

spun past and past part of SPIN

spun glass n : FIBERGLASS

spunk \'spəŋk\ n [fr. spunk tinder, fr. ScGael spong sponge, tinder, fr. L spongia sponge] : PLUCK, COURAGE — **spunky** adj

¹**spur** \'spər\ n 1 : a pointed device fastened to a rider's boot and used to urge on a horse 2 : something that urges to action 3 : a stiffly projecting part or process (as on the leg of a cock or on some flowers) 4 : a ridge extending sideways from a mountain 5 : a branch of railroad track extending from the main line syn goad, motive, impulse, incentive, inducement — **spurred** \'spərd\ adj — **on the spur of the moment** : on hasty impulse

²**spur** vb **spurred; spur·ring** 1 : to urge a horse on with spurs 2 : INCITE

spurge \'spərj\ n : any of various herbs and woody plants with bitter milky juice

spu·ri·ous \'spyùr-ē-əs\ adj [LL spurius false, fr. L, of illegitimate birth, fr. spurius, n., bastard] : not genuine : FALSE

spurn \'spərn\ vb 1 : to kick away or trample on 2 : to reject with disdain syn repudiate, refuse, decline

¹**spurt** \'spərt\ vb : to gush out : spout forth

²**spurt** n : a sudden gushing or spouting

³**spurt** n 1 : a sudden brief burst of effort or speed 2 : a sharp increase of activity ⟨~ in sales⟩

⁴**spurt** vb : to make a spurt

sput·ter \'spət-ər\ vb 1 : to spit small scattered particles : SPLUTTER 2 : to utter words hastily or explosively in excitement or confusion 3 : to make small popping sounds — **sputter** n

spu·tum \'spyüt-əm\ n, pl **spu·ta** \-ə\ [L] : material that is spit or coughed up and consists of saliva and mucus

¹**spy** \'spī\ vb **spied; spy·ing** 1 : to watch or search for information secretly : act as a spy 2 : to get a momentary or quick glimpse of : SEE

²**spy** n, pl **spies** 1 : one who secretly watches others 2 : one who secretly tries to obtain information for his own country in the territory of an enemy

spy·glass \'spī-ˌglas\ n : a small telescope

sq abbr 1 squadron 2 square

squab \'skwäb\ n, pl **squabs** or **squab** : a young pigeon

squab·ble \'skwäb-əl\ n : a noisy altercation : WRANGLE syn quarrel, spat, row, tiff — **squabble** vb

squad \'skwäd\ n 1 : a small organized group of military personnel 2 : a small group engaged in a common effort

squad car n : a police car connected by two-way radio with headquarters

squad·ron \'skwäd-rən\ n 1 : a body of men in regular formation 2 : any of several units of military organization

squal·id \'skwäl-əd\ adj 1 : filthy or degraded through neglect or poverty 2 : SORDID, DEBASED syn nasty, foul, dirty, grubby

squall \'skwȯl\ n : a sudden violent gust of wind often with rain or snow — **squally** adj

squa·lor \'skwäl-ər\ n : the quality or state of being squalid

squan·der \'skwän-dər\ vb **squan-**

dered; **squan·der·ing** \-d(ə-)riŋ\ : to spend wastefully or foolishly

¹square \'skwaər\ n 1 : an instrument used to lay out or test right angles 2 : a rectangle with all four sides equal 3 : something square 4 : the product of a number multiplied by itself 5 : an area bounded by four streets 6 : an open area in a city where streets meet 7 : a highly conventional person

²square adj **squar·er**; **squar·est** 1 : having four equal sides and four right angles 2 : forming a right angle (cut a ~ corner) 3 : multiplied by itself : SQUARED (X² is the symbol for X ~) 4 : being a unit of square measure equal to a square each side of which measures one unit (a ~ foot) 5 : being of a specified length in each of two dimensions (an area 10 feet ~) 6 : exactly adjusted 7 : JUST, FAIR (a ~ deal) 8 : leaving no balance (make accounts ~) 9 : SUBSTANTIAL (a ~ meal) 10 : highly conservative or conventional — **square·ly** adv

³square vb **squared**; **squar·ing** 1 : to form with four equal sides and right angles or with flat surfaces (~ a timber) 2 : to multiply a number by itself 3 : CONFORM, AGREE 4 : BALANCE, SETTLE (~ an account)

square dance n : a dance for four couples arranged to form a square

square measure n : a unit or system of units for measuring area — see METRIC SYSTEM table, WEIGHT table

square-rigged \'skwaər-'rigd\ adj : having the chief sails extended on yards that are fastened to the masts horizontally and at their center

square-rig·ger \-'rig-ər\ n : a square-rigged craft

square root n : either of the two numbers whose squares are equal to a given number (either +3 or −3 is the square root of 9)

¹squash \'skwäsh, 'skwȯsh\ vb 1 : to beat or press into a pulp or flat mass 2 : QUASH, SUPPRESS

²squash n 1 : the impact of something soft and heavy; also : the sound of such impact 2 : a crushed mass 3 : SQUASH RACQUETS

³squash n, pl **squash·es** or **squash** : a fruit of any of various plants related to the gourds that is used esp. as a vegetable; also : a plant bearing squashes

squash racquets n : a game played on a 4-wall court with a racket and rubber ball

¹squat \'skwät\ vb **squat·ted**; **squat·ting** 1 : to sit down upon the hams or heels 2 : to settle on land without right or title; also : to settle on public land with a view to acquiring title — **squat·ter** n

²squat n : the act or posture of squatting

³squat adj **squat·ter**; **squat·test** : low to the ground; also : short and thick in stature syn thickset, stocky, heavy-set, stubby

squaw \'skwȯ\ n : an American Indian woman

squawk \'skwȯk\ n : a harsh loud cry; also : a noisy protest — **squawk** vb

squeak \'skwēk\ vb 1 : to utter or speak in a weak shrill tone 2 : to make a thin high-pitched sound — **squeak** n — **squeaky** adj

¹squeal \'skwēl\ vb 1 : to make a shrill sound or cry 2 : COMPLAIN, PROTEST 3 : to betray a secret or turn informer

²squeal n : a shrill sharp somewhat prolonged cry

squea·mish \'skwē-mish\ adj 1 : easily nauseated; also : NAUSEATED 2 : easily disgusted syn fussy, nice, dainty, fastidious, persnickety — **squea·mish·ness** n

squee·gee \'skwē-jē\ n : a blade set crosswise on a handle and used for spreading or wiping liquid on, across, or off a surface — **squeegee** vb

¹squeeze \'skwēz\ vb **squeezed**; **squeez·ing** 1 : to exert pressure on the opposite sides or parts of 2 : to obtain by pressure (~ juice from a lemon) 3 : to force, thrust, or cause to pass by pressure — **squeez·er** n

²squeeze n 1 : an act of squeezing 2 : a quantity squeezed out

squeeze bottle n : a flexible plastic bottle that dispenses its contents by being pressed

squelch \'skwelch\ vb 1 : to suppress completely : CRUSH 2 : to move in soft mud — **squelch** n

squib \'skwib\ n 1 : a small firecracker; esp : one that fizzes instead of exploding 2 : a brief witty writing or speech

squid \'skwid\ n, pl **squid** or **squids** : any of numerous 10-armed long-bodied sea mollusks usu. having a slender internal shell

squint \'skwint\ vb 1 : to look or aim obliquely 2 : to close the eyes partly (the glare made him ~) 3 : to be cross-eyed — **squint** n or adj

¹squire \'skwī(ə)r\ n [ME squier, fr. OF esquier, fr. LL scutarius, fr. L scutum shield] 1 : an armor-bearer of a knight 2 : a man gallantly devoted to a lady 3 : a member of the British gentry ranking below a knight and above a gentleman; also : a prominent landowner 4 : a local magistrate

²squire vb **squired**; **squir·ing** : to attend as a squire or escort

squirm \'skwərm\ vb : to twist about like a worm : WRIGGLE

squir·rel \'skwər(-ə)l\ n, pl **squirrels** also **squirrel** [ME squirel, fr. MF esquireul, fr. VL scurius, alter. of L sciurus, fr. Gk skiouros, fr. skia shadow + oura tail] : any of various rodents usu. with a long bushy tail and strong hind legs; also : the fur of a squirrel

¹squirt \'skwərt\ vb : to eject liquid in a thin spurt

²squirt n 1 : an instrument (as a syringe)

for squirting **2** : a small forcible jet of liquid

¹Sr *abbr* **1** senior **2** sister

²Sr *symbol* strontium

SR *abbr* seaman recruit

SRO *abbr* **1** single-room occupancy **2** standing room only

SS *abbr* **1** saints **2** Social Security **3** steamship **4** sworn statement

SSA *abbr* Social Security Administration

SSE *abbr* south-southeast

SSG or **SSgt** *abbr* staff sergeant

ssp *abbr* subspecies

SSR *abbr* Soviet Socialist Republic

SSS *abbr* Selective Service System

SST \ˌes-ˌes-ˈtē\ *n* [*supersonic transport*] : a supersonic passenger airplane

SSW *abbr* south-southwest

st *abbr* **1** stanza **2** state **3** stitch **4** stone **5** street

St *abbr* saint

ST *abbr* **1** short ton **2** standard time

-st — see -EST

sta *abbr* station; stationary

¹stab \ˈstab\ *n* **1** : a wound given by a pointed weapon **2** : a quick thrust; *also* : a brief attempt

²stab *vb* **stabbed; stab·bing** : to pierce or wound with or as if with a pointed weapon; *also* : THRUST, DRIVE

sta·bile \ˈstā-ˌbēl\ *n* : a stable abstract sculpture or construction typically made of sheet metal, wire, and wood

sta·bi·lize \ˈstā-bə-ˌlīz\ *vb* **-lized; -liz·ing 1** : to make stable **2** : to hold steady (~ prices) **syn** steady — **sta·bi·li·za·tion** \ˌstā-bə-lə-ˈzā-shən\ *n* — **sta·bi·liz·er** \ˈstā-bə-ˌlī-zər\ *n*

¹sta·ble \ˈstā-bəl\ *n* : a building in which livestock is sheltered and fed — **sta·ble·man** \-mən, -ˌman\ *n*

²stable *vb* **sta·bled; sta·bling** \-b(ə-)liŋ\ : to put or keep in a stable

³stable *adj* **sta·bler** \-b(ə-)lər\; **sta·blest** \-b(ə-)ləst\ **1** : firmly established; *also* : mentally healthy and well-balanced **2** : steady in purpose : CONSTANT **3** : DURABLE, ENDURING **4** : resistant to chemical or physical change **syn** lasting, permanent, perpetual, perdurable — **sta·bil·i·ty** \stə-ˈbil-ət-ē\ *n*

stac·ca·to \stə-ˈkät-ō\ *adj* [It] : cut short so as not to sound connected (~ notes)

¹stack \ˈstak\ *n* **1** : a large pile (as of hay) **2** : a large quantity **3** : a vertical pipe : SMOKESTACK **4** : an orderly pile (as of poker chips) **5** : a rack with shelves for storing books

²stack *vb* **1** : to pile up **2** : to arrange (cards) secretly for cheating

stack up *vb* : MEASURE UP

sta·di·um \ˈstād-ē-əm\ *n, pl* **-dia** \-ē-ə\ or **-diums** : a structure with tiers of seats for spectators built around a field for sports events

¹staff \ˈstaf\ *n, pl* **staffs** \ˈstafs, ˈstavz\ *or* **staves** \ˈstāvz, ˈstavz\ **1** : a pole, stick, rod, or bar used for supporting, for measuring, or as a symbol of authority; *also* : CLUB, CUDGEL **2** : something that sustains (bread is the ~ of life) **3** : the five horizontal lines on which music is written **4** : a body of assistants to an executive **5** : a group of officers holding no command but having duties concerned with planning and managing

²staff *vb* : to supply with a staff or with workers

staff·er \ˈstaf-ər\ *n* : a member of a staff (as of a newspaper)

staff sergeant *n* : a noncommissioned officer ranking in the army next below a sergeant first class, in the air force next below a technical sergeant, and in the marine corps next below a gunnery sergeant

¹stag \ˈstag\ *n, pl* **stags** *or* **stag** : an adult male of various large deer

²stag *adj* : restricted to or intended for men (a ~ party) (~ movies)

³stag *adv* : unaccompanied by a date

¹stage \ˈstāj\ *n* **1** : a raised platform on which an orator may speak or a play may be presented **2** : the acting profession : THEATER **3** : the scene of a notable action or event **4** : a station or resting place on a traveled road **5** : STAGECOACH **6** : a degree of advance in an undertaking, process, or development **7** : a propulsion unit in a rocket — **stagy** \ˈstā-jē\ *adj*

²stage *vb* **staged; stag·ing** : to produce or perform on or as if on a stage — **stage·able** *adj*

stage·coach \ˈstāj-ˌkōch\ *n* : a horse-drawn coach that runs regularly between stations

stag·fla·tion \ˌstag-ˈflā-shən\ *n* : inflation with stagnant economic activity and high unemployment

¹stag·ger \ˈstag-ər\ *vb* **stag·gered; stag·ger·ing** \-(ə-)riŋ\ **1** : to reel from side to side : TOTTER **2** : to begin to doubt : WAVER **3** : to cause to reel or waver **4** : to arrange in overlapping or alternating positions or times (~ working hours) **5** : ASTONISH — **stag·ger·ing·ly** *adv*

²stagger *n* **1** *pl* : an abnormal condition of domestic mammals and birds associated with damage to the central nervous system and marked by lack of coordination and a reeling unsteady gait **2** : a reeling or unsteady gait or stance

stag·ing \ˈstā-jiŋ\ *n* **1** : SCAFFOLDING **2** : the assembling of troops and matériel in transit in a particular place

stag·nant \ˈstag-nənt\ *adj* **1** : not flowing : MOTIONLESS (~ water in a pond) **2** : DULL, INACTIVE (~ business)

stag·nate \ˈstag-ˌnāt\ *vb* **stag·nat·ed; stag·nat·ing** : to be or become stagnant — **stag·na·tion** \stag-ˈnā-shən\ *n*

staid \ˈstād\ *adj* : SOBER, SEDATE **syn** grave, serious, earnest

¹stain \ˈstān\ *vb* **1** : DISCOLOR, SOIL **2** : to color (as wood, paper, or cloth) by

processes affecting the material itself
3 : TAINT, CORRUPT **4** : DISGRACE
²**stain** *n* **1** : SPOT, DISCOLORATION **2** : a
taint of guilt : STIGMA **3** : a preparation
(as a dye or pigment) used in staining
— **stain·less** *adj*

stainless steel *n* : steel alloyed with
chromium that is highly resistant to
stain, rust, and corrosion

stair \'staər\ *n* **1** : a series of steps or
flights of steps for passing from one
level to another — often used in pl. **2**
: one step of a stairway

stair·case \-ˌkās\ *n* : a flight of steps
with their supporting framework, casing, and balusters

stair·way \-ˌwā\ *n* : one or more flights
of stairs with connecting landings

stair·well \-ˌwel\ *n* : a vertical shaft in
which stairs are located

¹**stake** \'stāk\ *n* **1** : a pointed piece of
material (as of wood) driven into the
ground as a marker or a support **2** : a
post to which a person is bound for
death by burning; *also* : such a death
3 : something that is staked for gain or
loss **4** : the prize in a contest

²**stake** *vb* **staked; stak·ing 1** : to mark the
limits of with stakes **2** : to tether to a
stake **3** : to support or secure with
stakes **4** : to place as a bet

stake·out \'stāk-ˌaút\ *n* : a surveillance
by police (as of an area)

sta·lac·tite \stə-'lak-ˌtīt\ *n* [NL *stalac-
tites*, fr. Gk *stalaktos* dripping] : an
icicle-shaped deposit hanging from
the roof or sides of a cavern

sta·lag·mite \stə-'lag-ˌmīt\ *n* [NL *sta-
lagmites*, fr. Gk *stalagma* drop or *sta-
lagmos* dripping] : a deposit resembling an inverted stalactite rising from
the floor of a cavern

stale \'stāl\ *adj* **stal·er; stal·est 1** : flat
and tasteless from age ⟨~ beer⟩ **2**
: not freshly made ⟨~ bread⟩ **3** : COM-
MONPLACE, TRITE — **stale** *vb*

stale·mate \'stāl-ˌmāt\ *n* : a drawn contest : DEADLOCK — **stalemate** *vb*

¹**stalk** \'stók\ *vb* **1** : to approach ⟨game⟩
stealthily **2** : to walk stiffly or haughtily

²**stalk** *n* : a plant stem; *also* : any slender
usu. upright supporting or connecting
part — **stalked** \'stókt\ *adj*

¹**stall** \'stól\ *n* **1** : a compartment in a
stable or barn for one animal **2** : a
booth or counter where articles may
be displayed for sale **3** : a seat in a
church choir; *also* : a church pew **4**
Brit : a front orchestra seat in a theater

²**stall** *vb* : to bring or come to a standstill
unintentionally ⟨~ an engine⟩

³**stall** *n* : the condition of an airfoil or
aircraft in which lift is lost and the
airfoil or aircraft tends to drop

stal·lion \'stal-yən\ *n* : a male horse

stal·wart \'stól-wərt\ *adj* : STOUT,
STRONG; *also* : BRAVE, VALIANT

sta·men \'stā-mən\ *n* : an organ of a
flower that produces pollen

sta·mi·na \'stam-ə-nə\ *n* [L, pl. of *stamen* warp, thread of life spun by the
Fates] : VIGOR, ENDURANCE

sta·mi·nate \'stā-mə-nət, 'stam-ə-,
-ˌnāt\ *adj* **1** : having or producing stamens **2** : having stamens but no pistils

stam·mer \'stam-ər\ *vb* **stam·mered;
stam·mer·ing** \-(ə-)riŋ\ : to hesitate or
stumble in speaking — **stammer** *n* —
stam·mer·er *n*

¹**stamp** \'stamp; *for 2 also* 'stámp *or*
'stómp\ *vb* **1** : to pound or crush with
a heavy instrument **2** : to strike or
beat with the bottom of the foot **3** : to
impress or imprint with a mark **4** : to
cut out or indent with a stamp or die **5**
: to attach a postage stamp to

²**stamp** *n* **1** : a device or instrument for
stamping **2** : the mark made by
stamping; *also* : a distinctive mark or
quality **3** : the act of stamping **4** : a
paper or a mark put on a thing to show
that a required charge has been paid

¹**stam·pede** \stam-'pēd\ *n* : a wild headlong rush or flight esp. of frightened
animals

²**stampede** *vb* **stam·ped·ed; stam·ped·ing
1** : to flee or cause to flee in panic **2**
: to act or cause to act together suddenly and heedlessly

stance \'stans\ *n* : a way of standing

stanch \'stónch, 'stänch\ *vb* : to check
the flowing of (as blood); *also* : to
cease flowing or bleeding

²**stanch** *var of* ¹STAUNCH

stan·chion \'stan-chən\ *n* : an upright
bar, post, or support

¹**stand** \'stand\ *vb* **stood** \'stúd\ : **standing 1** : to take or be at rest in an upright or firm position **2** : to assume a
specified position **3** : to remain stationary or unchanged **4** : to be steadfast **5** : to act in resistance ⟨~ against
a foe⟩ **6** : to maintain a relative position or rank **7** : to gather slowly and
remain briefly ⟨tears *stood* in her
eyes⟩ **8** : to set upright **9** : ENDURE,
TOLERATE ⟨I won't ~ for that⟩ **10** : to
submit to ⟨~ trial⟩ — **stand pat** : to
oppose or resist change

²**stand** *n* **1** : an act of standing, staying,
or resisting **2** : a stop made to give a
performance **3** : POSITION, VIEWPOINT
4 : a place taken by a witness to testify
in court **5** *pl* : tiered seats for spectators **6** : a raised platform (as for
speakers) **7** : a structure for a small
retail business **8** : a structure for supporting or holding something upright
⟨music ~⟩ **9** : a group of plants growing in a continuous area

stand–alone \'stand-ə-ˌlón\ *adj* : SELF=
CONTAINED; *esp* : capable of operation
independent of a computer

stan·dard \'stan-dərd\ *n* **1** : a figure
adopted as an emblem by a people **2**
: the personal flag of a ruler; *also*
: FLAG **3** : something set up as a rule
for measuring or as a model to be followed **4** : an upright support ⟨lamp ~⟩
— **standard** *adj*

stan·dard–bear·er \-ˌbar-ər\ n : the leader of a cause

stan·dard·ize \'stan-dərd-ˌīz\ vb -ized; -iz·ing : to make standard or uniform — **stan·dard·iza·tion** \ˌstan-dərd-ə-'zā-shən\ n

standard of living : the necessities, comforts, and luxuries that a person or group is accustomed to

standard time n : the time established by law or by general usage over a region or country

stand·by \'stan(d)-ˌbī\ n, pl **stand·bys** \-ˌbīz\ 1 : one that can be relied on 2 : a substitute in reserve — **on standby** : ready or available for immediate action or use

stand–in \'stan-ˌdin\ n 1 : someone employed to occupy an actor's place while lights and camera are readied 2 : SUBSTITUTE

¹**stand·ing** \'stan-diŋ\ adj 1 : ERECT 2 : not flowing : STAGNANT 3 : remaining at the same level or amount for an indefinite period ⟨∼ offer⟩ 4 : PERMANENT 5 : done from a standing position ⟨a ∼ jump⟩

²**standing** n 1 : length of service; also : relative position in society or in a profession : RANK 2 : DURATION

stand·off \'stand-ˌȯf\ n : TIE, DRAW

stand·out \'stand-ˌaȯt\ n : something conspicuously excellent

stand·pipe \'stan(d)-ˌpīp\ n : a high vertical pipe or reservoir for water used to produce a uniform pressure

stand·point \-ˌpȯint\ n : a position from which objects or principles are judged

stand·still \-ˌstil\ n : a state of rest

stank \'staŋk\ past of STINK

stan·za \'stan-zə\ n [It] : a group of lines forming a division of a poem

sta·pes \'stā-ˌpēz\ n, pl **stapes** or **sta·pe·des** \'stā-pə-ˌdēz\ : the small innermost bone of the ear of mammals

staph·y·lo·coc·cus \staf-ə-lō-'käk-əs\ n, pl **-coc·ci** \-'käk-ˌ(s)ī\ : any of various spherical bacteria including some that cause purulent infections — **staph·y·lo·coc·cal** \-'käk-əl\ adj

¹**sta·ple** \'stā-pəl\ n : a U-shaped piece of metal or wire with sharp points to be driven into or through objects and sometimes bent at the ends to hold or fasten one object to another — **staple** vb — **sta·pler** \-p(ə-)lər\ n

²**staple** n 1 : a chief commodity or product 2 : the main part of a thing : chief item 3 : unmanufactured or raw material 4 : a textile fiber suitable for spinning into yarn

³**staple** adj 1 : regularly produced in large quantities 2 : PRINCIPAL, MAIN

¹**star** \'stär\ n 1 : a celestial body that appears as a fixed point of light; esp : such a body that is gaseous, self-luminous, and of great mass 2 : a planet or configuration of planets that is held in astrology to influence one's fortune — usu. used in pl. 3 obs : DESTINY, FORTUNE 4 : a conventional figure representing a star; esp : ASTERISK 5 : an actor or actress playing the leading role 6 : a brilliant performer — **star·dom** \'stärd-əm\ n — **star·less** adj — **star·like** adj — **star·ry** adj

²**star** vb **starred; star·ring** 1 : to adorn with stars 2 : to mark with an asterisk 3 : to play the leading role

star·board \'stär-bərd\ n [ME sterbord, fr. OE stēorbord, fr. stēor- steering oar + bord ship's side] : the right side of a ship or airplane looking forward — **starboard** adj

¹**starch** \'stärch\ vb : to stiffen with starch

²**starch** n : a complex carbohydrate that is stored in plants, is an important foodstuff, and is used in adhesives and sizes, in laundering, and in pharmacy — **starchy** adj

stare \'staər\ vb **stared; star·ing** : to look fixedly with wide-open eyes — **stare** n — **star·er** n

star·fish \'stär-ˌfish\ n : any of a class of echinoderms usu. having five arms arranged around a central disk and feeding largely on mollusks

stark \'stärk\ adj 1 archaic : STRONG, ROBUST 2 : rigid as if in death; also : STRICT 3 : SHEER, UTTER 4 : BARREN, DESOLATE ⟨∼ landscape⟩ : also : UNADORNED ⟨∼ realism⟩ 5 : sharply delineated — **stark** adv — **stark·ly** adv

star·light \'stär-ˌlīt\ n : the light given by the stars

star·ling \'stär-liŋ\ n : a dark brown or in summer glossy greenish black European bird related to the crows that is naturalized and often a pest in No. America

¹**start** \'stärt\ vb 1 : to give an involuntary twitch or jerk (as from surprise) 2 : BEGIN, COMMENCE 3 : to set going 4 : to enter (as a horse) in a contest 5 : TAP ⟨∼ a cask⟩ — **start·er** n

²**start** n 1 : a sudden involuntary motion : LEAP 2 : a spasmodic and brief effort or action 3 : BEGINNING; also : the place of beginning

star·tle \'stärt-ᵊl\ vb **star·tled; star·tling** \'stärt-(ᵊ-)liŋ\ : to frighten or surprise suddenly : cause to start

star·tling adj : causing sudden fear, surprise, or anxiety

starve \'stärv\ vb **starved; starv·ing** [ME sterven to die, fr. OE steorfan] 1 : to perish from hunger 2 : to suffer extreme hunger 3 : to kill with hunger; also : to distress or subdue by famine — **star·va·tion** \stär-'vā-shən\ n

starve·ling \'stärv-liŋ\ n : one that is thin from lack of nourishment

stash \'stash\ vb : to store in a secret place — **stash** n

stat abbr 1 [L statim] immediately 2 statute

¹**state** \'stāt\ n [ME stat, fr. OF & L; OF estat, fr. L status, fr. stare to stand] 1 : mode or condition of being ⟨gaseous ∼ of water⟩ 2 : condition of mind 3

: social position **4** : a body of people occupying a definite territory and organized under one government; *also* : the government of such a body of people **5** : one of the constituent units of a nation having a federal government — **state·hood** \-ˌhu̇d\ *n*

²state *vb* **stat·ed; stat·ing 1** : FIX ⟨*stated* intervals⟩ **2** : to express in words

state·craft \ˈstāt-ˌkraft\ *n* : state management : STATESMANSHIP

state·house \-ˌhau̇s\ *n* : the building in which a state legislature meets

state·ly \ˈstāt-lē\ *adj* **state·li·er; -est 1** : having lofty dignity : HAUGHTY **2** : IMPRESSIVE, MAJESTIC **syn** magnificent, imposing, august — **state·li·ness** *n*

state·ment \ˈstāt-mənt\ *n* **1** : the act or result of presenting in words **2** : a summary of a financial account

state·room \ˈstāt-ˌrüm, -ˌru̇m\ *n* : a private room on a ship or railroad car

state·side \ˈstāt-ˌsīd\ *adj* : of or relating to the U.S. as regarded from outside its continental limits ⟨∼ mail⟩ — **stateside** *adv*

states·man \ˈstāts-mən\ *n* : one skilled in government and wise in handling public affairs; *also* : one influential in shaping public policy — **states·man·like** *adj* — **states·man·ship** *n*

¹stat·ic \ˈstat-ik\ *adj* **1** : acting by mere weight without motion ⟨∼ pressure⟩ **2** : relating to bodies or forces at rest or in equilibrium **3** : not moving : not active **4** : of or relating to stationary charges of electricity **5** : of, relating to, or caused by radio static

²static *n* : noise produced in a radio or television receiver by atmospheric or other electrical disturbances

¹sta·tion \ˈstā-shən\ *n* **1** : the place where a person or thing stands or is appointed to remain **2** : a regular stopping place on a transportation route ⟨a railroad ∼⟩ ⟨a bus ∼⟩; *also* : DEPOT **3** : a place where a fleet is assigned for duty **4** : a stock farm or ranch in Australia or New Zealand **5** : social standing **6** : a complete assemblage of radio or television equipment for sending or receiving

²station *vb* **sta·tioned; sta·tion·ing** \ˈstā-sh(ə-)niŋ\ : to assign to a station

sta·tion·ary \ˈstā-shə-ˌner-ē\ *adj* **1** : fixed in a certain place or position **2** : not changing condition : neither improving nor getting worse

station break *n* : a pause in a radio or television broadcast for announcement of the identity of the network or station

sta·tio·ner \ˈstā-sh(ə-)nər\ *n* : one that sells stationery

sta·tio·nery \ˈstā-shə-ˌner-ē\ *n* : materials (as paper, pens, or ink) for writing; *esp* : letter paper with envelopes

station wagon *n* : an automobile having an interior longer than a sedan's, one or more folding or removable seats to

make carrying light cargo easier, and no trunk

sta·tis·tic \stə-ˈtis-tik\ *n* **1** : a single term or datum in a collection of statistics **2** : a quantity (as the mean) that is computed from a sample

sta·tis·tics \stə-ˈtis-tiks\ *n pl* [G *statistik* study of political facts and figures, fr. NL *statisticus* of politics, fr. L *status* state] **1** : a branch of mathematics dealing with the analysis and interpretation of masses of numerical data **2** : facts collected and arranged in an orderly way for study — **sta·tis·ti·cal** \-ti-kəl\ *adj* — **sta·tis·ti·cal·ly** \-ti-k(ə-)lē\ *adv* — **stat·is·ti·cian** \ˌstat-ə-ˈstish-ən\ *n*

stat·u·ary \ˈstach-ə-ˌwer-ē\ *n, pl* **-ar·ies 1** : the art of making statues **2** : STATUES

stat·ue \ˈstach-ü\ *n* : a likeness of a living being sculptured in a solid substance

stat·u·esque \ˌstach-ə-ˈwesk\ *adj* : resembling a statue esp. in well-proportioned or massive dignity

stat·u·ette \ˌstach-ə-ˈwet\ *n* : a small statue

stat·ure \ˈstach-ər\ *n* **1** : natural height (as of a person) **2** : quality or status gained (as by achievement)

sta·tus \ˈstāt-əs, ˈstat-\ *n* **1** : the state or condition of a person in the eyes of others **2** : condition of affairs

sta·tus quo \-ˈkwō\ *n* [L, state in which] : the existing state of affairs

stat·ute \ˈstach-üt\ *n* : a law enacted by a legislative body

stat·u·to·ry \ˈstach-ə-ˌtōr-ē\ *adj* : imposed by statute : LAWFUL

¹staunch \ˈstȯnch\ *var of* ¹STANCH

²staunch *adj* **1** : WATERTIGHT ⟨a ∼ ship⟩ **2** : FIRM, STRONG; *also* : STEADFAST, LOYAL **syn** resolute, constant, true, faithful — **staunch·ly** *adv*

¹stave \ˈstāv\ *n* **1** : CUDGEL, STAFF **2** : any of several narrow strips of wood placed edge to edge to make something (as a barrel or bucket) **3** : STANZA

²stave *vb* **staved** *or* **stove** \ˈstōv\ ; **stav·ing 1** : to break in the staves of; *also* : to break a hole in **2** : to drive or thrust away ⟨∼ off trouble⟩

staves *pl of* STAFF

¹stay \ˈstā\ *n* : a strong rope or wire used to support or steady something (as a ship's mast)

²stay *vb* **stayed** \ˈstād\ *also* **staid** \ˈstād\ ; **stay·ing 1** : PAUSE, WAIT **2** : to stand firm **3** : LIVE, DWELL **4** : DELAY, POSTPONE **5** : to last out (as a race) **6** : STOP, CHECK **7** : to satisfy (as hunger) for a time **syn** remain, abide, linger, tarry

³stay *n* **1** : STOP, HALT **2** : a residence or sojourn in a place

⁴stay *n* **1** : PROP, SUPPORT **2** : CORSET — usu. used in pl.

⁵stay *vb* : to hold up : PROP

staying power *n* : STAMINA

stbd *abbr* starboard

std *abbr* standard

STD \ˌes-ˌtē-ˈdē\ *n* : SEXUALLY TRANSMITTED DISEASE

Ste *abbr* [F *sainte*] saint (female)

stead \ˈsted\ *n* **1** : ADVANTAGE, AVAIL (stood him in good ∼) **2** : the place or function ordinarily occupied or carried out by another (her brother served in her ∼)

stead·fast \ˈsted-ˌfast\ *adj* **1** : firmly fixed in place **2** : not subject to change **3** : firm in belief, determination, or adherence : LOYAL *syn* resolute, true, faithful, staunch — **stead·fast·ly** *adv* — **stead·fast·ness** *n*

¹steady \ˈsted-ē\ *adj* **steadi·er; -est** **1** : FIRM, FIXED **2** : not faltering or swerving; *also* : CALM **3** : STABLE **4** : CONSTANT, RESOLUTE **5** : REGULAR **6** : RELIABLE, SOBER *syn* uniform, even, stable, constant — **steadi·ly** \ˈsted-ᵊl-ē\ *adv* — **steadi·ness** \-ē-nəs\ *n* — **steady** *adv*

²steady *vb* **stead·ied; steady·ing** : to make or become steady

steak \ˈstāk\ *n* : a slice of meat cut from a fleshy part esp. of a beef carcass

¹steal \ˈstēl\ *vb* **stole** \ˈstōl\; **sto·len** \ˈstō-lən\; **steal·ing 1** : to come or go secretly or gradually **2** : to take and carry away without right or permission **3** : to get for oneself slyly or secretly **4** : to gain a base in baseball by running without the aid of a hit or an error *syn* pilfer, filch, purloin, swipe

²steal *n* **1** : an act of stealing **2** : BARGAIN

stealth \ˈstelth\ *n* : secret or underhanded procedure : FURTIVENESS

stealthy \ˈstel-thē\ *adj* **stealth·i·er; -est** : done by stealth : FURTIVE, SLY *syn* secret, covert, clandestine, surreptitious, underhanded — **stealth·i·ly** \ˈstel-thə-lē\ *adv*

¹steam \ˈstēm\ *n* **1** : the vapor into which water is changed when heated to the boiling point **2** : water vapor when compressed so that it supplies heat and power **3** : POWER, FORCE, ENERGY — **steamy** *adj*

²steam *vb* **1** : to pass off as vapor **2** : to emit vapor **3** : to move by or as if by the agency of steam — **steam·er** *n*

steam·boat \ˈstēm-ˌbōt\ *n* : a boat driven by steam power

steam engine *n* : a reciprocating engine having a piston driven in a closed cylinder by steam

steam·fit·ter \ˈstēm-ˌfit-ər\ *n* : a workman who puts in or repairs equipment (as steam pipes) for heating, ventilating, or refrigerating systems — **steam fitting** *n*

steam·roll·er \-ˈrō-lər\ *n* : a machine for compacting roads or pavements — **steam·roll·er** *also* **steam·roll** \-ˌrōl\ *vb*

steam·ship \-ˌship\ *n* : a ship driven by steam

steed \ˈstēd\ *n* : HORSE

¹steel \ˈstēl\ *n* **1** : iron treated with intense heat and mixed with carbon to make it hard and tough **2** : an article

made of steel **3** : a quality (as hardness of mind) that suggests steel — **steel** *adj* — **steely** *adj*

²steel *vb* **1** : to sheathe, point, or edge with steel **2** : to make able to resist

steel wool *n* : long fine steel shavings used esp. for scouring and smoothing

steel·yard \ˈstēl-ˌyärd\ *n* : a balance in which the object to be weighed is hung from the shorter arm of a lever and is balanced by a weight that slides along the longer arm

¹steep \ˈstēp\ *adj* **1** : having a very sharp slope : PRECIPITOUS **2** : too great or too high (∼ prices) — **steep·ly** *adv* — **steep·ness** *n*

²steep *n* : a steep slope

³steep *vb* **1** : to soak in a liquid; *esp* : to extract the essence of by steeping (∼ tea) **2** : SATURATE (∼ed in learning)

stee·ple \ˈstē-pəl\ *n* : a tall tapering structure built on top of a church tower; *also* : a church tower

stee·ple·chase \-ˌchās\ *n* [fr. the use of church steeples as landmarks to guide the riders] : a race across country by horsemen; *also* : a race over a course obstructed by hurdles

¹steer \ˈstiər\ *n* : a male bovine animal castrated before sexual maturity and usu. raised for beef

²steer *vb* **1** : to direct the course of (as by a rudder or wheel) **2** : GUIDE, CONTROL **3** : to pursue a course of action **4** : to be subject to guidance or direction — **steers·man** \ˈstiərz-mən\ *n*

steer·age \ˈsti(ə)r-ij\ *n* **1** : DIRECTION, GUIDANCE **2** : a section in a passenger ship for passengers paying the lowest fares

stein \ˈstīn\ *n* : an earthenware mug

stel·lar \ˈstel-ər\ *adj* : of or relating to stars : resembling a star

¹stem \ˈstem\ *n* **1** : the main stalk of a plant; *also* : a part that supports another part (as a leaf or fruit) **2** : the bow of a ship **3** : a line of ancestry : STOCK **4** : that part of an inflected word which remains unchanged throughout a given inflection **5** : something resembling the stem of a plant — **stem·less** *adj*

²stem *vb* **stemmed; stem·ming** : to have a specified source : DERIVE

³stem *vb* **stemmed; stem·ming** : to make headway against (∼ the tide)

⁴stem *vb* **stemmed; stem·ming** : to stop or check by or as if by damming

stemmed \ˈstemd\ *adj* : having a stem

stench \ˈstench\ *n* : STINK

sten·cil \ˈsten-səl\ *n* [ME *stanselen* to ornament with sparkling colors, fr. MF *estanceler*, fr. *estancele* spark, fr. (assumed) VL *stincilla*, fr. L *scintilla*] : a piece of thin impervious material (as metal or paper) that is perforated with lettering or a design through which a substance (as ink or paint) is applied to a surface to be printed — **stencil** *vb*

ste·nog·ra·phy \stə-ˈnäg-rə-fē\ *n* : the

art or process of writing in shorthand — **ste·nog·ra·pher** \-fər\ *n* — **steno·graph·ic** \ˌsten-ə-ˈgraf-ik\ *adj*

sten·to·ri·an \sten-ˈtōr-ē-ən\ *adj* : extremely loud

¹step \ˈstep\ *n* **1** : a rest for the foot in ascending or descending : STAIR **2** : an advance made by raising one foot and putting it down in a different spot **3** : manner of walking **4** : a small space or distance **5** : a degree, rank, or plane in a series **6** : a sequential measure leading to a result

²step *vb* **stepped; step·ping 1** : to advance or recede by steps **2** : to go on foot : WALK **3** : to move along briskly **4** : to press down with the foot **5** : to measure by steps **6** : to construct or arrange in or as if in steps

step·broth·er \ˈstep-ˌbrəth-ər\ *n* : the son of one's stepparent by a former marriage

step·child \-ˌchīld\ *n* : a child of one's husband or wife by a former marriage

step·daugh·ter \-ˌdȯt-ər\ *n* : a daughter of one's wife or husband by a former marriage

step down *vb* **1** : to lower the voltage of (a current) by means of a transformer **2** : RETIRE, RESIGN

step·fa·ther \-ˌfäth-ər\ *n* : the husband of one's mother by a subsequent marriage

step·lad·der \ˈstep-ˌlad-ər\ *n* : a light portable set of steps in a hinged frame

step·moth·er \-ˌməth-ər\ *n* : the wife of one's father by a subsequent marriage

step·par·ent \-ˌpar-ənt\ *n* : the husband or wife of one's mother or father by a subsequent marriage

steppe \ˈstep\ *n* [Russ *step'*] : dry level grass-covered land in regions of wide temperature range esp. in southeastern Europe and Asia

step·sis·ter \ˈstep-ˌsis-tər\ *n* : the daughter of one's stepparent by a former marriage

step·son \-ˌsən\ *n* : a son of one's wife or husband by a former marriage

step up \(ˈ)step-ˈəp\ *vb* **1** : to increase the voltage of (a current) by means of a transformer **2** : INCREASE, ACCELERATE — **step-up** \ˈstep-ˌəp\ *n*

ster *abbr* sterling

ste·reo \ˈster-ē-ˌō, ˈstir-\ *n, pl* **ste·re·os 1** : stereophonic reproduction **2** : a stereophonic sound system — **stereo** *adj*

ste·reo·phon·ic \ˌster-ē-ə-ˈfän-ik, ˌstir-\ *adj* : of or relating to sound reproduction designed to create the effect of listening to the original — **ste·reo·phon·i·cal·ly** \-i-k(ə-)lē\ *adv*

ster·e·o·scope \ˈster-ē-ə-ˌskōp, ˈstir-\ *n* [Gk *stereos* solid + *skopein* to look at] : an optical instrument that blends two slightly different pictures of the same subject to give the effect of depth

ste·reo·scop·ic \ˌster-ē-ə-ˈskäp-ik, ˌstir-\ *adj* **1** : of or relating to the stereoscope **2** : characterized by stereoscopy ⟨∼ vision⟩ — **ste·reo·scop·i·cal·ly** \-i-k(ə-)lē\ *adv*

ste·re·os·co·py \ˌster-ē-ˈäs-kə-pē, ˌstir-\ *n* : the seeing of objects in three dimensions

ste·reo·type \ˈster-ē-ə-ˌtīp, ˈstir-\ *n* **1** : a metal printing plate cast from a mold made from set type **2** : something agreeing with a pattern; *esp* : an idea that many people have about a thing or a group and that may often be untrue or only partly true

ste·reo·typed \-ˌtīpt\ *adj* : repeated without variation : lacking originality or individuality **syn** trite, clichéd, commonplace, hackneyed, stale, threadbare

ster·ile \ˈster-əl\ *adj* **1** : unable to bear fruit, crops, or offspring **2** : free from living things and esp. germs — **ste·ril·i·ty** \stə-ˈril-ət-ē\ *n*

ster·il·ize \ˈster-ə-ˌlīz\ *vb* **-ized; -iz·ing** : to make sterile; *esp* : to free from germs — **ster·il·i·za·tion** \ˌster-ə-lə-ˈzā-shən\ *n* — **ster·il·iz·er** \ˈster-ə-ˌlī-zər\ *n*

¹ster·ling \ˈstər-liŋ\ *n* **1** : British money **2** : sterling silver

²sterling *adj* **1** : of, relating to, or calculated in terms of British sterling **2** : having a fixed standard of purity represented by an alloy of 925 parts of silver with 75 parts of copper **3** : made of sterling silver **4** : EXCELLENT

¹stern \ˈstərn\ *adj* **1** : SEVERE, AUSTERE **2** : STOUT, STURDY ⟨∼ resolve⟩ — **stern·ly** *adv* — **stern·ness** *n*

²stern *n* : the rear end of a boat

ster·num \ˈstər-nəm\ *n, pl* **sternums** *or* **ster·na** \-nə\ : a long flat bone or cartilage at the center front of the chest connecting the ribs of the two sides

ste·roid \ˈstir-ˌȯid\ *n* : any of numerous compounds containing a 17-carbon 4-ring system and including various hormones and sugar derivatives — **steroid** *or* **ste·roi·dal** \stə-ˈrȯid-ᵊl\ *adj*

stetho·scope \ˈsteth-ə-ˌskōp\ *n* : an instrument for listening to sounds produced within the body and esp. in the chest

ste·ve·dore \ˈstē-və-ˌdōr\ *n* [Sp *estibador*, fr. *estibar* to pack, fr. L *stipare* to press together] : one who works at loading and unloading ships

¹stew \ˈst(y)ü\ *n* **1** : a dish of stewed meat and vegetables served in gravy **2** : a state of excitement, worry, or confusion

²stew *vb* **1** : to boil slowly : SIMMER **2** : to become excited or worried

stew·ard \ˈst(y)ü-ərd\ *n* [ME, fr. OE *stīweard*, fr. *stī* hall, sty + *weard* ward] **1** : one employed on a large estate to manage domestic concerns (as keeping accounts and directing servants) **2** : one actively concerned with the direction of the affairs of an organization **3** : one who supervises the provision and distribution of food (as on a ship); *also* : an employee on a ship or airplane who serves passengers — **stew·ard·ship** *n*

stew·ard·ess \-əs\ *n* : a woman who is a steward

stg *abbr* sterling

¹**stick** \'stik\ *n* **1** : a cut or broken branch or twig; *also* : a long slender piece of wood **2** : ROD, STAFF **3** : something resembling a stick **4** : a dull uninteresting person

²**stick** *vb* **stuck** \'stək\; **stick·ing 1** : STAB, PRICK **2** : IMPALE **3** : ATTACH, FASTEN **4** : to thrust or project in some direction or manner **5** : to be unable to proceed or move freely **6** : to hold fast by or as if by gluing : ADHERE **7** : to hold to something firmly or closely : CLING **8** : to become jammed or blocked

stick·er \'stik-ər\ *n* : one that sticks (as a bur) or causes sticking (as glue); *esp* : a gummed label

stick insect *n* : any of various usu. wingless insects (as a walkingstick) with a long round body resembling a stick

stick·ler \'stik-(ə-)lər\ *n* : one who insists on exactness or completeness

stick shift *n* : a manually operated gearshift mounted on the steering-wheel column or floor of an automobile

stick-to-it-ive-ness \stik-'tü-ət-iv-nəs\ *n* : dogged perseverance : TENACITY

stick up \(')stik-'əp\ *vb* : to rob at gunpoint — **stick-up** \'stik-ˌəp\ *n*

sticky \'stik-ē\ *adj* **stick·i·er; -est 1** : ADHESIVE **2** : VISCOUS, GLUEY **3** : tending to stick (~ valve)

¹**stiff** \'stif\ *adj* **1** : not pliant : RIGID **2** : not limber (~ joints); *also* : TENSE, TAUT **3** : not flowing or working easily (~ paste) **4** : not natural and easy : FORMAL **5** : STRONG, FORCEFUL (~ breeze) **6** : HARSH, SEVERE syn inflexible, rigid, inelastic — **stiff·ly** *adv* — **stiff·ness** *n*

²**stiff** *vb* : to refrain from tipping (~ a waiter)

stiff·en \'stif-ən\ *vb* **stiff·ened; stiff·en·ing** \-(ə-)niŋ\ : to make or become stiff — **stiff·en·er** \-(ə-)nər\ *n*

stiff-necked \-'nekt\ *adj* : STUBBORN, HAUGHTY

sti·fle \'stī-fəl\ *vb* **sti·fled; sti·fling** \-f(ə-)liŋ\ **1** : SUFFOCATE **2** : QUENCH, SUPPRESS **3** : SMOTHER, MUFFLE **4** : to die because of obstruction of the breath

stig·ma \'stig-mə\ *n, pl* **stig·ma·ta** \stig-'mät-ə, 'stig-mət-ə\ *or* **stigmas** [L] **1** : a mark of disgrace or discredit **2** *pl* : bodily marks resembling the wounds of the crucified Christ **3** : the upper part of the pistil of a flower that receives the pollen in fertilization — **stig·mat·ic** \stig-'mat-ik\ *adj*

stig·ma·tize \'stig-mə-ˌtīz\ *vb* **-tized; -tiz·ing 1** : to mark with a stigma **2** : to set a mark of disgrace upon

stile \'stīl\ *n* : steps used for crossing a fence or wall

sti·let·to \stə-'let-ō\ *n, pl* **-tos** *or* **-toes** [It, dim. of *stilo* stylus, dagger] : a slender dagger

¹**still** \'stil\ *adj* **1** : MOTIONLESS **2** : making no sound : QUIET, SILENT — **still·ness** *n*

²**still** *vb* : to make or become still : QUIET

³**still** *adv* **1** : without motion (sit ~) **2** : up to and during this or that time **3** : in spite of that : NEVERTHELESS **4** : EVEN (ran ~ faster) **5** : BESIDES, YET

⁴**still** *n* **1** : STILLNESS, SILENCE **2** : a static photograph esp. of an instant in a motion picture

⁵**still** *n* **1** : DISTILLERY **2** : apparatus used in distillation

still·birth \'stil-ˌbərth\ *n* : the birth of a dead fetus

still·born \-'bórn\ *adj* : born dead

still life *n, pl* **still lifes** : a picture of inanimate objects

stilt \'stilt\ *n* : one of a pair of poles for walking with each having a step or loop for the foot; *also* : a polelike support of a structure above ground or water level

stilt·ed \'stil-təd\ *adj* : FORMAL, POMPOUS (~ writing)

Stil·ton \'stilt-ᵊn\ *n* : a blue-veined cheese with wrinkled rind

stim·u·lant \'stim-yə-lənt\ *n* **1** : an agent (as a drug) that temporarily increases the activity of an organism or any of its parts **2** : STIMULUS **3** : an alcoholic beverage — **stimulant** *adj*

stim·u·late \-ˌlāt\ *vb* **-lat·ed; -lat·ing** : to make active or more active : ANIMATE, AROUSE syn excite, provoke, motivate, quicken — **stim·u·la·tion** \ˌstim-yə-'lā-shən\ *n* — **stim·u·la·tive** \'stim-yə-ˌlāt-iv\ *adj*

stim·u·lus \'stim-yə-ləs\ *n, pl* **-li** \-ˌlī\ [L] : something that stimulates : SPUR

¹**sting** \'stiŋ\ *vb* **stung** \'stəŋ\; **sting·ing** \'stiŋ-iŋ\ **1** : to prick painfully esp. with a sharp or poisonous process **2** : to cause to suffer acutely — **sting·er** *n*

²**sting** *n* **1** : an act of stinging; *also* : a resultant sore, pain, or mark **2** : a pointed venom-bearing organ (as of a bee)

stin·gy \'stin-jē\ *adj* **stin·gi·er; -est** : not generous : SPARING, NIGGARDLY — **stin·gi·ness** *n*

stink \'stiŋk\ *vb* **stank** \'staŋk\ *or* **stunk** \'stəŋk\ ; **stunk; stink·ing** : to give forth a strong and offensive smell; *also* : to be extremely bad in quality or repute — **stink** *n* — **stink·er** *n*

stink·bug \'stiŋk-ˌbəg\ *n* : any of various true bugs that emit a disagreeable odor

¹**stint** \'stint\ *vb* **1** : to be sparing or frugal **2** : to restrict to a scant allowance : cut short in amount

²**stint** *n* **1** : RESTRAINT, LIMITATION **2** : an assigned amount of work **3** : a period of time spent at a particular activity

sti·pend \'stī-ˌpend, -pənd\ *n* [alter. of ME *stipendy*, fr. L *stipendium*, fr. *stips* gift + *pendere* to weigh, pay] : a fixed sum of money paid periodically for services or to defray expenses

stip·ple \'stip-əl\ *vb* **stip·pled; stip·pling** \-(ə-)liŋ\ **1** : to engrave by means of dots and light strokes instead of by lines **2** : to apply (as paint or ink) with small short touches that together produce an even and softly graded shadow — **stipple** *n*

stip·u·late \'stip-yə-ˌlāt\ *vb* **-lat·ed; -lat·ing** : to make an agreement; *esp* : to make a special demand for something as a condition in an agreement — **stip·u·la·tion** \ˌstip-yə-'lāsh-ən\ *n*

¹stir \'stər\ *vb* **stirred; stir·ring 1** : to move slightly **2** : AROUSE, EXCITE **3** : to mix, dissolve, or make by continued circular movement (~ eggs into cake batter) **4** : to move to activity (as by pushing, beating, or prodding)

²stir *n* **1** : a state of agitation or activity **2** : an act of stirring

³stir *n, slang* : PRISON

stir-fry \'stər-ˌfrī\ *vb* : to fry quickly over high heat while stirring continuously

stir·ring \'stər-iŋ\ *adj* **1** : ACTIVE, BUSTLING **2** : ROUSING, INSPIRING

stir·rup \'stər-əp\ *n* [OE *stigrāp*, lit., mounting rope] **1** : a light frame hung from a saddle to support the foot of a horseback rider **2** : STAPES

¹stitch \'stich\ *n* **1** : a sudden sharp pain esp. in the side **2** : one of the series of loops formed by or over a needle in sewing *syn* twinge, pang, throe

²stitch *vb* **1** : to fasten or join with stitches **2** : to decorate with stitches **3** : SEW

stk *abbr* stock

stoat \'stōt\ *n, pl* **stoats** *also* **stoat** : the European ermine esp. in its brown summer coat

¹stock \'stäk\ *n* **1** *archaic* : a block of wood **2** : a stupid person **3** : a wooden part of a thing serving as its support, frame, or handle **4** *pl* : a device for publicly punishing offenders consisting of a wooden frame with holes in which the feet and hands can be locked **5** : the original from which others derive; *also* : a group having a common origin : FAMILY **6** : farm animals **7** : the supply of goods kept by a merchant **8** : the proprietorship element in a corporation divided to give the owners an interest and usu. voting power **9** : a company of actors playing at a particular theater and presenting a series of plays **10** : liquid in which meat, fish, or vegetables have been simmered that is used as a basis for soup, gravy, or sauce **11** : raw material

²stock *vb* : to provide with stock

³stock *adj* : kept regularly for sale or use; *also* : used regularly : STANDARD

stock·ade \stä-'kād\ *n* [Sp *estacada*, fr. *estaca* stake, pale] : an enclosure of posts and stakes for defense or confinement

stock·bro·ker \-ˌbrō-kər\ *n* : one who executes orders to buy and sell securities

stock car *n* : a racing car having the basic chassis of a commercially produced regular model

stock exchange *n* **1** : a place where trading in securities is accomplished under an organized system **2** : an association of stockbrokers

stock·hold·er \'stäk-ˌhōl-dər\ *n* : one who owns corporate stock

stock·i·nette *or* **stock·i·net** \ˌstäk-ə-'net\ *n* : an elastic knitted textile fabric used esp. for infants' wear and bandages

stock·ing \'stäk-iŋ\ *n* : a close-fitting knitted covering for the foot and leg

stock market *n* **1** : STOCK EXCHANGE 1 **2** : a market for stocks

stock·pile \'stäk-ˌpīl\ *n* : a reserve supply esp. of something essential — **stockpile** *vb*

stocky \'stäk-ē\ *adj* **stock·i·er; -est** : being short and relatively thick : STURDY *syn* thickset, squat, heavyset, stubby

stock·yard \'stäk-ˌyärd\ *n* : a yard for stock; *esp* : one for livestock about to be slaughtered or shipped

stodgy \'stäj-ē\ *adj* **stodg·i·er; -est** : HEAVY, DULL, UNINSPIRED

¹sto·ic \'stō-ik\ *n* [ME, fr. L *stoicus*, fr. Gk *stōikos*, lit., of the portico, fr. *Stoa* (*Poikilē*) the Painted Portico, portico at Athens where Zeno taught] : one who suffers without complaining

²stoic *or* **sto·i·cal** \-i-kəl\ *adj* : not affected by passion or feeling; *esp* : showing indifference to pain *syn* impassive, phlegmatic, apathetic, stolid — **sto·i·cal·ly** \-i-k(ə-)lē\ *adv* — **sto·icism** \'stō-ə-ˌsiz-əm\ *n*

stoke \'stōk\ *vb* **stoked; stok·ing 1** : to stir up a fire **2** : to tend and supply fuel to a furnace — **stok·er** *n*

STOL *abbr* short takeoff and landing

¹stole \'stōl\ *past of* STEAL

²stole *n* **1** : a long narrow band worn round the neck by some clergymen **2** : a long wide scarf or similar covering worn by women

stolen *past part of* STEAL

stol·id \'stäl-əd\ *adj* : not easily aroused or excited : showing little or no emotion *syn* phlegmatic, apathetic, impassive, stoic — **sto·lid·i·ty** \stä-'lid-ət-ē\ *n* — **stol·id·ly** \'stäl-əd-lē\ *adv*

sto·lon \'stō-lən, -ˌlän\ *n* : RUNNER 6

¹stom·ach \'stəm-ək\ *n* **1** : a saclike digestive organ of a vertebrate into which food goes from the mouth by way of the throat and which opens below into the intestine **2** : a cavity in an invertebrate animal that is analogous to a stomach **3** : ABDOMEN **4** : desire for food caused by hunger : APPETITE **5** : INCLINATION, DESIRE

²stomach *vb* : to bear without overt resentment : BROOK

stom·ach·ache \-ˌāk\ n : pain in or in the region of the stomach

stom·ach·er \ˈstəm-i-kər, -i-chər\ n : the front of a bodice often appearing between the laces of an outer garment (as in 16th century costume)

¹**stomp** \ˈstämp, ˈstȯmp\ vb : STAMP

²**stomp** n 1 : STAMP 3 2 : a jazz dance marked by heavy stamping

¹**stone** \ˈstōn\ n 1 : hardened earth or mineral matter : ROCK 2 : a small piece of rock 3 : a precious stone : GEM 4 : a hard abnormal mass in a bodily cavity or duct 5 : a hard stony seed or one (as of a plum) with a stony covering 6 pl usu **stone** : a British unit of weight equal to 14 pounds — **stony** also **ston·ey** \ˈstō-nē\ adj

²**stone** vb **stoned; ston·ing** 1 : to pelt or kill with stones 2 : to remove the stones of (a fruit)

Stone Age n : the first known period of prehistoric human culture characterized by the use of stone tools

stoned \ˈstōnd\ adj 1 : DRUNK 2 : being under the influence of a drug

stood past and past part of STAND

stooge \ˈstüj\ n 1 : a person who plays a subordinate or compliant role to a principal 2 : STRAIGHT MAN

stool \ˈstül\ n 1 : a seat usu. without back or arms 2 : FOOTSTOOL 3 : a seat used while urinating or defecating 4 : a discharge of fecal matter

stool pigeon n : DECOY, INFORMER

¹**stoop** \ˈstüp\ vb 1 : to bend over 2 : CONDESCEND 3 : to humiliate or lower oneself socially or morally

²**stoop** n 1 : an act of bending over 2 : a bent position of head and shoulders

³**stoop** n : a porch or platform at a house door

¹**stop** \ˈstäp\ vb **stopped; stop·ping** 1 : to close (an opening or hole) by filling or covering closely 2 : BLOCK, HALT 3 : to cease to go on 4 : to cease activity or operation 5 : STAY, TARRY syn quit, discontinue, desist, halt, cease

²**stop** n 1 : END, CESSATION 2 : a set of organ pipes of one tone quality; also : a control knob for such a set 3 : OBSTRUCTION 4 : PLUG, STOPPER 5 : an act of stopping : CHECK 6 : a delay in a journey : STAY 7 : a place for stopping 8 chiefly Brit : any of several punctuation marks

stop·gap \ˈstäp-ˌgap\ n : something that serves as a temporary expedient

stop·light \-ˌlīt\ n : TRAFFIC LIGHT

stop·page \ˈstäp-ij\ n : the act of stopping : the state of being stopped

stop·per \ˈstäp-ər\ n : something (as a cork or plug) for sealing an opening

stop·watch \ˈstäp-ˌwäch\ n : a watch having a component (as a hand) that can be started or stopped at will for exact timing

stor·age \ˈstȯr-ij\ n 1 : space for storing; also : cost of storing 2 : the act of storing; esp : the safekeeping of goods (as in a warehouse)

storage battery n : a group of connected cells that converts chemical energy into electrical energy by reversible chemical reactions and that may be recharged by electrical means

¹**store** \ˈstȯr\ vb **stored; stor·ing** 1 : to provide esp. for a future need 2 : to place or leave in a safe location for preservation or future use

²**store** n 1 : something accumulated and kept for future use 2 : a large or ample quantity 3 : STOREHOUSE 4 : a retail business establishment

store·house \-ˌhaùs\ n : a building for storing goods or supplies; also : an abundant source or supply

store·keep·er \-ˌkē-pər\ n : one who operates a retail store

store·room \-ˌrüm, -ˌrùm\ n : a room for storing goods or supplies

sto·ried \ˈstȯr-ēd\ adj : celebrated in story or history

stork \ˈstȯrk\ n : any of various large stout-billed Old World wading birds related to the herons and ibises

¹**storm** \ˈstȯrm\ n 1 : a heavy fall of rain, snow, or hail with high wind 2 : a violent outbreak or disturbance 3 : a mass attack on a defended position — **storm·i·ly** \ˈstȯr-mə-lē\ adv — **storm·i·ness** \-mē-nəs\ n — **stormy** adj

²**storm** vb 1 : to blow with violence; also : to rain, snow, or hail heavily 2 : to make a mass attack against 3 : to be violently angry : RAGE 4 : to rush along furiously

¹**sto·ry** \ˈstȯr-ē\ n, pl **stories** 1 : NARRATIVE, ACCOUNT 2 : REPORT, STATEMENT 3 : ANECDOTE 4 : LIE, FALSEHOOD syn lie, falsehood, untruth, tale, canard

²**story** also **sto·rey** \ˈstȯr-ē\ n, pl **stories** also **storeys** : a floor of a building or the space between two adjacent floor levels

sto·ry·tell·er \-ˌtel-ər\ n : a teller of stories

sto·tin·ka \stȯ-ˈtiŋ-kə, stə-\ n, pl **-tin·ki** \-kē\ — see lev at MONEY table

¹**stout** \ˈstaùt\ adj 1 : BRAVE 2 : FIRM 3 : STURDY 4 : STAUNCH, ENDURING 5 : SOLID 6 : FORCEFUL 7 : BULKY, THICK-SET syn fleshy, fat, portly, corpulent, obese, plump — **stout·ly** adv — **stout·ness** n

²**stout** n : a dark heavy alcoholic beverage brewed from roasted malt and hops

¹**stove** \ˈstōv\ n : an apparatus that burns fuel or uses electricity to provide heat (as for cooking or room heating)

²**stove** past and past part of STAVE

stow \ˈstō\ vb 1 : HIDE, STORE 2 : to pack in a compact mass

stow·away \ˈstō-ə-ˌwā\ n : one who hides on a vehicle to ride free

¹**STP** \ˌes-ˌtē-ˈpē\ n : a psychotropic drug chemically related to amphetamine

²**STP** abbr standard temperature and pressure

strad·dle \ˈstrad-ᵊl\ vb **strad·dled; strad-**

dling \\'strad-(ə-)liŋ\\ **1** : to stand, sit, or walk with legs spread apart **2** : to favor or seem to favor two apparently opposite sides — **straddle** n

strafe \\'sträf\\ vb **strafed; straf·ing 1** : to fire upon with machine guns from a low-flying airplane

strag·gle \\'strag-əl\\ vb **strag·gled; strag·gling** \\-(ə-)liŋ\\ **1** : to wander from the direct course : ROVE, STRAY **2** : to become separated from others of the same kind — **strag·gler** \\-(ə-)lər\\ n — **strag·gly** \\-(ə-)lē\\ adj

¹**straight** \\'strāt\\ adj **1** : free from curves, bends, angles, or irregularities : DIRECT **2** : not wandering from the main point or proper course (~ thinking) : HONEST, UPRIGHT **4** : not marked by confusion : correctly arranged or ordered **5** : UNMIXED, UNDILUTED (~ whiskey) **6** : CONVENTIONAL, SQUARE; also : HETEROSEXUAL

²**straight** adv : in a straight manner

³**straight** n **1** : a straight line, course, or arrangement **2** : the part of a racetrack between the last turn and the finish **3** : a sequence of five cards in a poker hand

straight-arm \\'strāt-ˌärm\\ vb : to ward off an opponent with the arm held straight — **straight-arm** n

straight·away \\'strāt-ə-ˌwā\\ n : a straight stretch (as at a racetrack)

straight·edge \\'strāt-ˌej\\ n : a piece of material with a straight edge for testing straight lines and surfaces or drawing straight lines

straight·en \\'strāt-ᵊn\\ vb **straight·ened; straight·en·ing** \\'strāt-(ᵊ-)niŋ\\ : to make or become straight

straight·for·ward \\strāt-'fȯr-wərd\\ adj **1** : CANDID, HONEST **2** : proceeding in a straight course or manner

straight man n : an entertainer who feeds lines to a comedian

straight·way \\'strāt-'wā, -ˌwā\\ adv : IMMEDIATELY

¹**strain** \\'strān\\ n [ME streen progeny, lineage, fr. OE strēon gain, acquisition] **1** : LINEAGE, ANCESTRY **2** : a group (as of people or plants) of presumed common ancestry **3** : an inherited or inherent character or quality (a ~ of madness in the family) **4** : STREAK, TRACE **5** : MELODY **6** : the general style or tone

²**strain** vb [ME strainen, fr. MF estraindre, fr. L stringere to bind or draw tight, press together] **1** : to draw taut **2** : to exert to the utmost **3** : to strive violently **4** : to injure by improper or excessive use **5** : to filter or remove by filtering **6** : to stretch beyond a proper limit — **strain·er** n

³**strain** n **1** : excessive tension or exertion (as of body or mind) **2** : bodily injury from excessive tension, effort, or use; esp : one in which muscles or ligaments are unduly stretched usu. from a wrench or twist **3** : deforma-

tion of a material body under the action of applied forces

¹**strait** \\'strāt\\ adj [ME, fr. OF estreit, fr. L strictus strait, strict] **1** archaic : NARROW **2** archaic : CONSTRICTED **3** archaic : STRICT **4** : DIFFICULT, STRAITENED

²**strait** n **1** : a narrow channel connecting two bodies of water **2** pl : DISTRESS

strait·en \\'strāt-ᵊn\\ vb **strait·ened; strait·en·ing** \\'strāt-(ᵊ-)niŋ\\ **1** : to hem in : CONFINE **2** : to make distressing or difficult

strait·jack·et or **straight·jack·et** \\'strāt-ˌjak-ət\\ n : a cover or garment of strong material (as canvas) used to bind the body and esp. the arms closely in restraining a violent prisoner or patient — **straitjacket** or **straightjacket** vb

strait·laced or **straight·laced** \\-'lāst\\ adj : strict in observing moral or religious laws

¹**strand** \\'strand\\ n : SHORE; esp : a shore of a sea or ocean

²**strand** vb **1** : to run, drift, or drive upon the shore (a ~ed ship) **2** : to place or leave in a helpless position

³**strand** n **1** : one of the fibers twisted or plaited together into a cord, rope, or cable; also : a cord, rope, or cable made up of such fibers **2** : a twisted or plaited ropelike mass (a ~ of pearls) — **strand·ed** \\'stran-dəd\\ adj

strange \\'strānj\\ adj **strang·er; strang·est** [ME, fr. OF estrange, fr. L extraneus, lit., external, fr. extra outside] **1** : of external origin, kind, or character **2** : NEW, UNFAMILIAR **3** : SHY **4** : UNACCUSTOMED, INEXPERIENCED syn singular, peculiar, eccentric, erratic, odd, queer, quaint, curious — **strange·ly** adv — **strange·ness** n

strang·er \\'strān-jər\\ n **1** : FOREIGNER **2** : INTRUDER **3** : a person with whom one is unacquainted

stran·gle \\'straŋ-gəl\\ vb **stran·gled; stran·gling** \\-g(ə-)liŋ\\ **1** : to choke to death : THROTTLE **2** : STIFLE, SUFFOCATE — **stran·gler** \\-g(ə-)lər\\ n

stran·gu·late \\'straŋ-gyə-ˌlāt\\ vb **-lat·ed; -lat·ing 1** : STRANGLE, CONSTRICT **2** : to become so constricted as to stop circulation

stran·gu·la·tion \\ˌstraŋ-gyə-'lā-shən\\ n : the act or process of strangling or strangulating : the state of being strangled or strangulated

¹**strap** \\'strap\\ n : a narrow strip of flexible material used esp. for fastening, holding together, or wrapping

²**strap** vb **strapped; strap·ping 1** : to secure with a strap **2** : BIND, CONSTRICT **3** : to flog with a strap **4** : STROP

strap·less \\-ləs\\ adj : having no straps; esp : having no shoulder straps

¹**strap·ping** \\'strap-iŋ\\ adj : LARGE, STRONG, HUSKY

²**strap·ping** n : material for a strap

strat·a·gem \\'strat-ə-jəm, -ˌjem\\ n **1** : a trick in war to deceive or outwit the enemy; *also* : a deceptive scheme 2 : skill in deception

strat•e•gy \'strat-ə-jē\ *n, pl* **-gies** [Gk *stratēgia* generalship, fr. *stratēgos* general, fr. *stratos* army + *agein* to lead] 1 : the science and art of military command aimed at meeting the enemy under conditions advantageous to one's own force 2 : a careful plan or method esp. for achieving an end — **stra•te•gic** \strə-'tē-jik\ *adj* — **strat•e•gist** \'strat-ə-jəst\ *n*

strat•i•fy \'strat-ə-,fī\ *vb* **-fied; -fy•ing** : to form or arrange in layers — **strat•i•fi•ca•tion** \,strat-ə-fə-'kā-shən\ *n*

stra•tig•ra•phy \strə-'tig-rə-fē\ *n* : geology that deals with rock strata — **strati•graph•ic** \,strat-ə-'graf-ik\ *adj*

strato•sphere \'strat-ə-,sfiər\ *n* : the portion of the earth's atmosphere higher than 7 miles (11 kilometers) above the earth — **strato•spher•ic** \,strat-ə-'sfi(ə)r-ik, -'sfer-\ *adj*

stra•tum \'strāt-əm, 'strat-\ *n, pl* **stra•ta** \'strāt-ə, 'strat-\ [NL, fr. L, spread, bed, fr. neut. of *stratus*, pp. of *sternere* to spread out] 1 : a bed, layer, or sheetlike mass (as of one kind of rock lying between layers of other kinds of rock) 2 : a level of culture; *also* : a group of people representing one stage in cultural development

¹**straw** \'strȯ\ *n* 1 : stalks of grain after threshing; *also* : a single coarse dry stem (as of a grass) 2 : a thing of small worth : TRIFLE 3 : a prepared tube for sucking up a beverage

²**straw** *adj* 1 : made of straw 2 : having no real force or validity (a ~ vote)

straw•ber•ry \'strȯ-,ber-ē, -b(ə-)rē\ *n* : an edible juicy fruit borne by a low herb with white flowers and long slender runners; *also* : this plant

straw boss *n* : a foreman of a small gang of workers

straw•flow•er \'strȯ-,flaü(-ə)r\ *n* : any of several plants whose flowers can be dried with little loss of form or color

¹**stray** \'strā\ *n* 1 : a domestic animal wandering at large or lost 2 : WAIF

²**stray** *vb* 1 : ROVE, ROAM 2 : to wander from a course : DEVIATE

³**stray** *adj* 1 : having strayed : separated from the group or the main body 2 : occurring at random ⟨~ remarks⟩

¹**streak** \'strēk\ *n* 1 : a line or mark of a different color or texture from its background 2 : a narrow band of light; *also* : a lightning bolt 3 : a slight admixture : TRACE 4 : a brief run (as of luck); *also* : an unbroken series

²**streak** *vb* 1 : to form streaks in or on 2 : to move very swiftly

¹**stream** \'strēm\ *n* 1 : a body of water (as a river) flowing on the earth; *also* : any body of flowing fluid (as water or gas) 2 : a continuous procession ⟨the ~ of history⟩

²**stream** *vb* 1 : to flow in or as if in a

stream 2 : to pour out streams of liquid 3 : to trail out in length 4 : to move forward in a steady stream

stream•bed \'strēm-,bed\ *n* : the channel occupied or formerly occupied by a stream

stream•er \'strē-mər\ *n* 1 : a long narrow ribbonlike flag 2 : a long ribbon on a dress or hat 3 : a newspaper headline that runs across the entire sheet 4 *pl* : AURORA

stream•let \'strēm-lət\ *n* : a small stream

stream•lined \-,līnd\ *adj* 1 : made with contours to reduce resistance to motion through water or air 2 : SIMPLIFIED 3 : MODERNIZED — **streamline** *vb*

street \'strēt\ *n* [ME *strete*, fr. OE *strǣt*, fr. LL *strata* paved road, fr. L, fem. of *stratus*, pp. of *sternere* to spread out] 1 : a thoroughfare esp. in a city, town, or village 2 : the occupants of the houses on a street

street•car \-,kär\ *n* : a passenger vehicle running on rails on city streets

street railway *n* : a company operating streetcars or buses

street•walk•er \'strēt-,wȯ-kər\ *n* : PROSTITUTE

strength \'strength\ *n* 1 : the quality of being strong : ability to do or endure : POWER 2 : TOUGHNESS, SOLIDITY 3 : power to resist attack 4 : INTENSITY 5 : force as measured in numbers ⟨the ~ of an army⟩

strength•en \'streŋ-thən\ *vb* **strengthened; strength•en•ing** \'streŋ-(ə-)niŋ\ : to make, grow, or become stronger — **strength•en•er** \'streŋ-th-(ə-)nər\ *n*

stren•u•ous \'stren-yə-wəs\ *adj* 1 : VIGOROUS, ENERGETIC 2 : requiring energetic effort or stamina — **stren•u•ous•ly** *adv*

strep throat \'strep-\ *n* : an inflammatory sore throat cause by streptococci and marked by fever, prostration, and toxemia

strep•to•coc•cus \,strep-tə-'käk-əs\ *n, pl* **-coc•ci** \-'käk-,(s)ī, -'käk-(,)(s)ē\ : any of various spherical bacteria that usu. grow in chains and include some causing serious diseases — **strep•to•coc•cal** \-əl\ *adj*

strep•to•my•cin \-'mīs-ᵊn\ *n* : an antibiotic produced by soil bacteria and used esp. in treating tuberculosis

¹**stress** \'stres\ *n* 1 : PRESSURE, STRAIN; *esp* : a force that tends to distort a body 2 : a factor that induces bodily or mental tension; *also* : a state induced by such a stress 3 : URGENCY, EMPHASIS 4 : relative prominence of sound 5 : ACCENT; *also* : any syllable carrying the accent

²**stress** *vb* 1 : to put pressure or strain on 2 : to put emphasis on : ACCENT

¹**stretch** \'strech\ *vb* 1 : to spread or reach out : EXTEND 2 : to draw out in length or breadth : EXPAND 3 : to make tense : STRAIN 4 : EXAGGERATE 5

: to become extended without breaking (rubber ~es easily)

²**stretch** *n* **1** : an act of extending or drawing out beyond ordinary or normal limits **2** : a continuous extent in length, area, or time **3** : the extent to which something may be stretched **4** : either of the straight sides of a racecourse

³**stretch** *adj* : easily stretched (~ pants)

stretch·er \'strech-ər\ *n* **1** : one that stretches **2** : a litter (as of canvas) esp. for carrying a disabled person

stretch·er-bear·er \-ˌbar-ər\ *n* : one who carries one end of a stretcher

strew \'strü\ *vb* **strewed; strewed** *or* **strewn** \'strün\ ; **strew·ing 1** : to spread by scattering **2** : to cover by or as if by scattering something over or on **3** : DISSEMINATE

stria \'strī-ə\ *n, pl* **stri·ae** \'strī-ˌē\ **1** : STRIATION **3 2** : a stripe or line (as in the skin)

stri·at·ed muscle \'strī-ˌāt-əd-\ *n* : muscle tissue made up of long thin cells with many nuclei and alternate light and dark stripes that usually connects to and moves the vertebrate skeleton and is mostly under voluntary control

stri·a·tion \strī-'ā-shən\ *n* **1** : the state of being marked with stripes or lines **2** : arrangement of striations or striae **3** : a minute groove, scratch, or channel esp. when one of a parallel series

strick·en \'strik-ən\ *adj* **1** : WOUNDED **2** : afflicted with disease, misfortune, or sorrow

strict \'strikt\ *adj* **1** : allowing no evasion or escape : RIGOROUS (~ discipline) **2** : ACCURATE, PRECISE **syn** stringent, rigid, rigorous — **strict·ly** \'strik-(t)lē\ *adv* — **strict·ness** \'strik(t)-nəs\ *n*

stric·ture \'strik-chər\ *n* **1** : an abnormal narrowing of a bodily passage; *also* : the narrowed part **2** : hostile criticism : a critical remark

¹**stride** \'strīd\ *vb* **strode** \'strōd\ ; **stridden** \'strid-ᵊn\ ; **strid·ing** \'strīd-iŋ\ : to walk or run with long regular steps — **strid·er** *n*

²**stride** *n* **1** : a long step; *also* : the distance covered by such a step **2** : manner of striding : GAIT

stri·dent \'strīd-ᵊnt\ *adj* : harsh sounding : GRATING, SHRILL

strife \'strīf\ *n* : CONFLICT, FIGHT, STRUGGLE **syn** discord, contention, dissension

strike \'strīk\ *vb* **struck** \'strək\ ; **struck** *also* **strick·en** \'strik-ən\ ; **strik·ing** \'strī-kiŋ\ **1** : to take a course : GO (~ out for home) **2** : to touch or hit sharply; *also* : to deliver a blow **3** : to produce by or as if by a blow (*struck* terror in the foe) **4** : to lower (as a flag or sail) **5** : to collide with; *also* : to injure or destroy by collision **6** : DELETE, CANCEL **7** : to produce by impressing (*struck* a medal); *also* : COIN (~ a new cent) **8** : to cause to sound (~ a bell)

9 : to afflict suddenly : lay low (*stricken* with a high fever) **10** : to appear to; *also* : to appear to as remarkable : IMPRESS **11** : to reach by reckoning (~ an average) **12** : to stop work in order to obtain a change in conditions of employment **13** : to cause (a match) to ignite by rubbing **14** : to come upon (~ a detour from the main road) **15** : TAKE ON, ASSUME (~ a pose) — **strik·er** *n*

²**strike** *n* **1** : an act or instance of striking **2** : a sudden discovery of rich ore or oil deposits **3** : a pitched baseball recorded against a batter **4** : the knocking down of all the bowling pins with the 1st ball **5** : a military attack

strike·break·er \-ˌbrā-kər\ *n* : one hired to replace a striking worker

strike·out \-ˌaut\ *n* : an out in baseball as a result of a batter's being charged with three strikes

strike out \(')strīk-'aut\ *vb* **1** : to enter upon a course of action **2** : to start out vigorously **3** : to make an out in baseball by a strikeout

strike up *vb* **1** : to begin or cause to begin to sing or play **2** : BEGIN

strike zone *n* : the area over home plate through which a pitched baseball must pass to be called a strike

strik·ing \'strī-kiŋ\ *adj* : attracting attention : very noticeable **syn** arresting, salient, conspicuous, outstanding, remarkable, prominent — **strik·ing·ly** *adv*

¹**string** \'striŋ\ *n* **1** : a line usu. composed of twisted threads **2** : a series of things arranged as if strung on a cord **3** : a plant fiber (as a leaf vein) **4** *pl* : the stringed instruments of an orchestra **syn** succession, progression, sequence, chain, train

²**string** *vb* **strung** \'strəŋ\ ; **string·ing** \'striŋ-iŋ\ **1** : to provide with strings (~ a racket) **2** : to thread on or as if on a string (~ pearls) **3** : to take the strings out of (~ beans) **4** : to hang, tie, or fasten by a string **5** : to make taut **6** : to extend like a string

string bean *n* : a bean of one of the older varieties of kidney bean that have stringy fibers on the lines of separation of the pods; *also* : SNAP BEAN

stringed instrument *n* : a musical instrument (as a violin, guitar, or piano) sounded by plucking or striking or by drawing a bow across tense strings

strin·gen·cy \'strin-jən-sē\ *n* **1** : STRICTNESS, SEVERITY **2** : SCARCITY (~ of money) — **strin·gent** \-jənt\ *adj*

string·er \'striŋ-ər\ *n* **1** : a long horizontal member in a framed structure or a bridge **2** : a news correspondent paid by the amount of copy

stringy \'striŋ-ē\ *adj* **string·i·er; -est 1** : resembling string esp. in tough, fibrous, or disordered quality (~ meat) (~ hair) **2** : lean and sinewy in build

¹**strip** \'strip\ *vb* **stripped** \'stript\ *also* **stript; strip·ping 1** : to take the cover-

ing or clothing from **2** : to take off one's clothes **3** : to pull or tear off **4** : to make bare or clear (as by cutting or grazing) **5** : PLUNDER, PILLAGE syn divest, denude, deprive, dismantle — **strip·per** n

²**strip** n **1** : a long narrow flat piece **2** : AIRSTRIP

¹**stripe** \'strīp\ vb **striped** \'strīpt\ : **strip·ing** : to make stripes on

²**stripe** n **1** : a line or long narrow division having a different color from the background **2** : a strip of braid (as on a sleeve) indicating military rank or length of service **3** : TYPE, CHARACTER syn description, nature, kind, sort

striped bass \'strīpt-, 'strī-pəd-\ n : a large marine food and sport fish of the Atlantic and Pacific coasts of the U.S.

strip·ling \'strip-liŋ\ n : YOUTH, LAD

strip mine n : a mine that is worked from the earth's surface by the stripping of the topsoil — **strip-mine** vb

strip-tease \'strip-,tēz\ n : a burlesque act in which a performer removes his or her clothing piece by piece — **teas·er** n

strive \'strīv\ vb **strove** \'strōv\ also **strived** \'strīvd\; **striv·en** \'striv-ən\ or **strived**; **striv·ing** \'strī-viŋ\ **1** : to struggle in opposition : CONTEND **2** : to make effort : labor hard syn endeavor, attempt, try, assay

strobe \'strōb\ n **1** : STROBOSCOPE **2** : a device for high-speed intermittent illumination

stro·bo·scope \'strō-bə-,skōp\ n : an instrument for studying rapid motion by means of a rapidly flashing light

strode past of STRIDE

¹**stroke** \'strōk\ vb **stroked**; **strok·ing 1** : to rub gently **2** : to flatter in a manner designed to persuade

²**stroke** n **1** : the act of striking : BLOW, KNOCK **2** : a sudden action or process producing an impact (~ of lightning) **3** : sudden weakening or loss of consciousness or the power to feel caused by rupture or obstruction of an artery of the brain **4** : a vigorous effort **5** : the sound of striking (as of a clock) **6** : one of a series of movements against air or water to get through or over it (the ~ of a bird's wing) **7** : a single movement with or as if with a tool or implement (as a pen) **8** : a rower who sets the pace for a crew

stroll \'strōl\ vb : to walk in a leisurely or idle manner syn saunter, amble, mosey — **stroll** n — **stroll·er** n

strong \'strȯŋ\ adj **stron·ger** \'strȯŋ-gər\; **stron·gest** \'strȯŋ-gəst\ **1** : POWERFUL, VIGOROUS **2** : HEALTHY, ROBUST **3** : of a specified number (an army 10 thousand ~) **4** : not mild or weak **5** : VIOLENT (~ wind) **6** : ZEALOUS **7** : not easily broken **8** : FIRM, SOLID syn stout, sturdy, stalwart, tough — **strong·ly** adv

strong–arm \'strȯŋ-'ärm\ adj : having or using undue force (~ methods)

strong·hold \'strȯŋ-,hōld\ n : a fortified place : FORTRESS

strong·man \'strȯŋ-,man\ n : one who leads or controls by force of will and character or by military strength

stron·tium \'strän-ch(ē-)əm, 'stränt-ē-əm\ n : a soft malleable metallic chemical element

¹**strop** \'sträp\ n : STRAP; esp : one for sharpening a razor

²**strop** vb **stropped**; **strop·ping** : to sharpen a razor on a strop

stro·phe \'strō-fē\ n [Gk strophē, lit., act of turning] : a division of a poem — **stroph·ic** \'sträf-ik\ adj

strove past of STRIVE

struck past and past part of STRIKE

¹**struc·ture** \'strək-chər\ n [ME, fr. L structura, fr. structus, pp. of struere to heap up, build] **1** : the manner of building : CONSTRUCTION **2** : something built (as a house or a dam): also : something made up of interdependent parts in a definite pattern of organization **3** : arrangement or relationship of elements in a substance, body, or system — **struc·tur·al** adj

²**structure** vb **struc·tured**; **struc·tur·ing** : to make into a structure

stru·del \'s(h)trüd-ᵊl\ n [G] : a pastry made of a thin sheet of dough rolled up with filling and baked (apple ~)

¹**strug·gle** \'strəg-əl\ vb **strug·gled**; **strug·gling** \-(ə-)liŋ\ **1** : to make strenuous efforts against opposition : STRIVE **2** : to proceed with difficulty or with great effort syn endeavor, attempt, try, assay

²**struggle** n **1** : CONTEST, STRIFE **2** : a violent effort or exertion

strum \'strəm\ vb **strummed**; **strum·ming** : to play on a stringed instrument by brushing the strings with the fingers (~ a guitar)

strum·pet \'strəm-pət\ n : PROSTITUTE

strung \'strəŋ\ past and past part of STRING

¹**strut** \'strət\ vb **strut·ted**; **strut·ting** : to walk with an affectedly proud gait syn swagger

²**strut** n **1** : a haughty or pompous gait **2** : a bar or rod for resisting lengthwise pressure

strych·nine \'strik-,nīn, -nən, -,nēn\ n : a bitter poisonous alkaloid from some plants used as a poison (as for rats) and medicinally as a stimulant to the central nervous system

¹**stub** \'stəb\ n **1** : STUMP 2 **2** : a short blunt end **3** : a small part of each leaf (as of a checkbook) kept as a memorandum of the items on the detached part

²**stub** vb **stubbed**; **stub·bing** : to strike (as one's toe) against something

stub·ble \'stəb-əl\ n **1** : the cut stem ends of herbs and esp. grasses left in the soil after harvest **2** : a rough surface or growth resembling stubble — **stub·bly** \-(ə-)lē\ adj

stub·born \'stəb-ərn\ adj **1** : FIRM, DE-

TERMINED 2 : done or continued in a willful, unreasonable, or persistent manner 3 : not easily controlled or remedied ⟨a ~ fever⟩ — **stub·born·ly** *adv* — **stub·born·ness** *n*

stub·by \'stəb-ē\ *adj* : short, blunt, and thick like a stub

¹**stuc·co** \'stək-ō\ *n, pl* **stuccos** *or* **stuccoes** [It] : plaster for coating exterior walls

²**stucco** *vb* : to coat with stucco

stuck *past and past part of* STICK

stuck-up \'stək-'əp\ *adj* : CONCEITED

¹**stud** \'stəd\ *n* : a male animal and esp. a horse (**stud·horse** \-ˌhȯrs\) kept for breeding

²**stud** *n* 1 : one of the smaller uprights in a building to which the wall materials are fastened 2 : a removable device like a button used as a fastener or ornament ⟨shirt ~s⟩ 3 : a projecting nail, pin, or rod

³**stud** *vb* **stud·ded; stud·ding** 1 : to supply with or adorn with studs 2 : DOT

⁴**stud** *abbr* student

stud·book \'stəd-ˌbůk\ *n* : an official record of the pedigree of purebred animals

stud·ding \'stəd-iŋ\ *n* 1 : the studs in a building or wall 2 : material for studs

stu·dent \'st(y)üd-ᵊnt\ *n* : SCHOLAR, PUPIL; *esp* : one who attends a school

stud·ied \'stəd-ēd\ *adj* : INTENTIONAL ⟨a ~ insult⟩ *syn* deliberate, considered, premeditated, designed

stu·dio \'st(y)üd-ē-ˌō\ *n, pl* **-dios** 1 : a place where an artist works; *also* : a place for the study of an art 2 : a place where motion pictures are made 3 : a place equipped for the transmission of radio or television programs

stu·di·ous \'st(y)üd-ē-əs\ *adj* : devoted to study — **stu·di·ous·ly** *adv*

¹**study** \'stəd-ē\ *n, pl* **stud·ies** 1 : the use of the mind to gain knowledge 2 : the act or process of learning about something 3 : careful examination 4 : INTENT, PURPOSE 5 : a branch of learning 6 : a room esp. for reading and writing

²**study** *vb* **stud·ied; study·ing** 1 : to engage in study or the study of 2 : to consider attentively or in detail *syn* consider, contemplate, weigh

¹**stuff** \'stəf\ *n* 1 : personal property 2 : raw material 3 : a finished textile fabric; *esp* : a worsted fabric 4 : writing, talk, or ideas of little or transitory worth 5 : an aggregate of matter; *also* : matter of a particular often unspecified kind 6 : fundamental material 7 : special knowledge or capability

²**stuff** *vb* 1 : to fill by packing something into : CRAM 2 : to eat greedily : GORGE 3 : to prepare (as meat) by filling with seasoned bread crumbs and spices 4 : to stop up : PLUG

stuffed shirt \'stəft-\ *n* : a smug, conceited, and usu. pompous and inflexibly conservative person

stuff·ing \'stəf-iŋ\ *n* : material used to fill tightly; *esp* : a mixture of bread

crumbs and spices used to stuff meat and poultry

stuffy \'stəf-ē\ *adj* **stuff·i·er; -est** 1 : lacking fresh air : CLOSE; *also* : blocked up ⟨a ~ nose⟩ 2 : STODGY

stul·ti·fy \'stəl-tə-ˌfī\ *vb* **-fied; -fy·ing** 1 : to cause to appear foolish or stupid 2 : to make untrustworthy; *also* : to make ineffective 3 : to have a dulling effect on — **stul·ti·fi·ca·tion** \ˌstəl-tə-fə-'kā-shən\ *n*

stum·ble \'stəm-bəl\ *vb* **stum·bled; stum·bling** \-b(ə-)liŋ\ 1 : to trip in walking or running 2 : to walk unsteadily; *also* : to speak or act in a blundering or clumsy manner 3 : to blunder morally; *also* : to come or happen by chance — **stumble** *n*

stumbling block *n* : an obstacle to belief, understanding, or progress

¹**stump** \'stəmp\ *n* 1 : the base of a bodily part (as a leg or tooth) left after the rest is removed 2 : the part of a plant and esp. a tree remaining with the root after the top is cut off 3 : a place or occasion for political public speaking — **stumpy** *adj*

²**stump** *vb* 1 : to clear (land) of stumps 2 : to tour (a region) making political speeches 3 : BAFFLE, PERPLEX 4 : to walk clumsily and heavily

stun \'stən\ *vb* **stunned; stun·ning** 1 : to make senseless or dizzy by or as if by a blow 2 : BEWILDER, STUPEFY

stung *past and past part of* STING

stunk *past and past part of* STINK

stun·ning \'stən-iŋ\ *adj* : strikingly beautiful — **stun·ning·ly** *adv*

¹**stunt** \'stənt\ *vb* : to hinder the normal growth of : DWARF

²**stunt** *n* : an unusual or spectacular feat

stu·pe·fy \'st(y)ü-pə-ˌfī\ *vb* **-fied; -fy·ing** 1 : ASTONISH 2 : to make stupid, groggy, or insensible — **stu·pe·fac·tion** \ˌst(y)ü-pə-'fak-shən\ *n*

stu·pen·dous \st(y)ü-'pen-dəs\ *adj* : causing astonishment esp. because of great size or height *syn* tremendous, prodigious, monumental, monstrous — **stu·pen·dous·ly** *adv*

stu·pid \'st(y)ü-pəd\ *adj* [MF *stupide*, fr. L *stupidus*, fr. *stupēre* to be benumbed, be astonished] 1 : very dull in mind 2 : showing or resulting from dullness of mind — **stu·pid·i·ty** \st(y)ü-'pid-ət-ē\ *n* — **stu·pid·ly** \'st(y)ü-pəd-lē\ *adv*

stu·por \'st(y)ü-pər\ *n* 1 : a condition of greatly dulled or completely suspended sense or feeling 2 : a torpid state often following stress or shock — **stu·por·ous** *adj*

stur·dy \'stərd-ē\ *adj* **stur·di·er; -est** [ME, reckless, brave, fr. OF *estourdi* stunned, fr. pp. of *estourdir* to stun] 1 : RESOLUTE, UNYIELDING 2 : STRONG, ROBUST *syn* stout, stalwart, tough, tenacious — **stur·di·ly** \'stərd-ᵊl-ē\ *adv* — **stur·di·ness** \-ē-nəs\ *n*

stur·geon \'stər-jən\ *n* : any of various

large food fishes whose roe is made into caviar

stut·ter \'stət-ər\ *vb* : to speak with involuntary disruption or blocking of sounds — **stutter** *n*

STV *abbr* subscription television

¹sty \'stī\ *n, pl* **sties** : a pen or housing for swine

²sty *or* **stye** \'stī\ *n, pl* **sties** *or* **styes** : an inflamed swelling of a skin gland on the edge of an eyelid

¹style \'stīl\ *n* **1** : a slender pointed instrument or process; *esp* : STYLUS **2** : a way of speaking or writing; *esp* : one characteristic of an individual, period, school, or nation ⟨ornate ∼⟩ **3** : the custom followed in spelling, capitalization, punctuation, and typography **4** : mode of address : TITLE **5** : manner or method of acting, making, or performing; *also* : a distinctive or characteristic manner **6** : a fashionable manner or mode **7** : overall excellence, skill, or grace in performance, manner, or appearance — **stylis·tic** \stī-'lis-tik\ *adj*

²style *vb* **styled; styl·ing 1** : NAME, DESIGNATE **2** : to make or design in accord with a prevailing mode

styl·ing \'stī-liŋ\ *n* : the way in which something is styled

styl·ish \'stī-lish\ *adj* : conforming to an accepted standard of style : FASHIONABLE **syn** modish, smart, chic — **styl·ish·ly** *adv* — **styl·ish·ness** *n*

styl·ist \'stī-ləst\ *n* **1** : a master of style esp. in writing **2** : a developer or designer of styles

styl·ize \'stīl-ˌīz\ *vb* **styl·ized; styl·iz·ing** : to conform to a style; *esp* : to represent or design according to a pattern or style rather than according to nature

sty·lus \'stī-ləs\ *n, pl* **sty·li** \'stī(ə)l-ˌī\ *also* **sty·lus·es** \'stī-lə-səz\ [modif. of L *stilus* stake, stylus] **1** : a pointed implement used by the ancients for writing on wax **2** : a phonograph needle

sty·mie \'stī-mē\ *vb* **sty·mied; sty·mie·ing** : BLOCK, FRUSTRATE

styp·tic \'stip-tik\ *adj* : tending to check bleeding — **styptic** *n*

suave \'swäv\ *adj* [MF, pleasant, sweet, fr. L *suavis*] : persuasively pleasing : smoothly agreeable **syn** urbane, smooth, bland — **suave·ly** *adv* — **suav·i·ty** \'swäv-ət-ē\ *n*

¹sub \'səb\ *n* : SUBSTITUTE — **sub** *vb*

²sub *n* : SUBMARINE

³sub *abbr* **1** subtract **2** suburb

sub- \ˌsəb, 'səb\ *prefix* **1** : under : beneath **2** : subordinate : secondary **3** : subordinate portion of : subdivision of **4** : with repetition of a process described in a simple verb so as to form, stress, or deal with subordinate parts or relations **5** : somewhat **6** : falling nearly in the category of : bordering on

subacute
subagency
subagent
subaqueous

subarctic
subarea
subatmospheric
subaverage
subbasement
subcategory
subclass
subclassify
subclinical
subcontract
subcontractor
subdeacon
subdean
subdiscipline
subentry
subfamily
subfreezing
subgenus
subgroup
subhead
subheading
subhuman
subindex
subinterval
subkingdom
sublease
sublethal
subliterate
subminimal
subminimum

suboptimal
suborder
subparagraph
subparallel
subphylum
subplot
subpolar
subprincipal
subproblem
subprofessional
subprogram
subregion
subroutine
subsaturated
subsection
subsense
subspecies
substage
subsystem
subteen
subtemperate
subthreshold
subtopic
subtotal
subtreasury
subtype
subunit
subvariety
subvisible
subvocal
subzero

sub·al·pine \ˌsəb-'al-ˌpīn, 'səb-\ *adj* **1** : of or relating to the region about the foot and lower slopes of the Alps **2** *cap* : of, relating to, or growing on high upland slopes

sub·al·tern \sə-'bȯl-tərn\ *n* : SUBORDINATE; *also* : a commissioned officer in the British army below the rank of captain

sub·as·sem·bly \ˌsəb-ə-'sem-blē\ *n* : an assembled unit to be incorporated with other units in a finished product

sub·atom·ic \ˌsəb-ə-'täm-ik\ *adj* : of or relating to the inside of the atom or to particles smaller than atoms

sub·com·mit·tee \'səb-kə-ˌmit-ē, ˌsəb-kə-'mit-ē\ *n* : a subordinate division of a committee

sub·com·pact \'səb-'käm-ˌpakt\ *n* : an automobile smaller than a compact

¹sub·con·scious \ˌsəb-'kän-chəs, 'səb-\ *adj* : existing in the mind and affecting thought and behavior without entering conscious awareness — **sub·con·scious·ly** *adv* — **sub·con·scious·ness** *n*

²subconscious *n* : mental activities just below the threshold of consciousness

sub·con·ti·nent \'səb-'känt-(ə-)nənt\ *n* : a vast subdivision of a continent — **sub·con·ti·nen·tal** \ˌsəb-ˌkänt-ᵊn-'ent-ᵊl\ *adj*

sub·cu·ta·ne·ous \ˌsəb-kyu̇-'tā-nē-əs\ *adj* : located, made, or used under the skin ⟨∼ fat⟩ ⟨∼ needle⟩

sub·di·vide \ˌsəb-də-'vīd, 'səb-də-ˌvīd\ *vb* : to divide into several parts; *esp* : to divide (a tract of land) into building lots — **sub·di·vi·sion** \-'-vizh-ən, -ˌvizh-\ *n*

sub·duc·tion \səb-'dək-shən\ *n* : the descent of the edge of one crustal plate beneath the edge of an adjacent plate

sub·due \səb-ˈd(y)ü\ *vb* **sub·dued; sub·du·ing 1** : to bring into subjection : VANQUISH **2** : to bring under control : CURB **3** : to reduce the intensity of

subj *abbr* **1** subject **2** subjunctive

¹sub·ject \ˈsəb-jikt\ *n* [ME, fr. MF, fr. L *subjectus* one under authority & *subjectum* subject of a proposition, fr. *subicere* to subject, lit., to throw under, fr. *sub-* under + *jacere* to throw] **1** : a person under the authority of another **2** : a person subject to a sovereign **3** : an individual subjected to an operation or process **4** : the person or thing discussed or treated : TOPIC, THEME **5** : a word or word group denoting that of which something is predicated

²subject *adj* **1** : being under the power or rule of another **2** : LIABLE, EXPOSED ⟨~ to floods⟩ **3** : dependent on some act or condition ⟨appointment ~ to senate approval⟩ **syn** subordinate, secondary, tributary, collateral, dependent

³sub·ject \səb-ˈjekt\ *vb* **1** : to bring under control : CONQUER **2** : to make liable **3** : to cause to undergo or submit to — **sub·jec·tion** \-ˈjek-shən\ *n*

sub·jec·tive \(ˌ)səb-ˈjek-tiv\ *adj* **1** : of, relating to, or constituting a subject **2** : of, relating to, or arising within one's self or mind in contrast to what is outside : PERSONAL — **sub·jec·tive·ly** *adv* — **sub·jec·tiv·i·ty** \-ˌjek-ˈtiv-ət-ē\ *n*

subject matter *n* : matter presented for consideration, discussion, or study

sub·join \(ˌ)səb-ˈjȯin\ *vb* : APPEND

sub ju·di·ce \(ˈ)sub-ˈyüd-i-ˌkā, ˈsəb-ˈjüd-ə-(ˌ)sē\ *adv* [L] : before a judge or court : not yet legally decided

sub·ju·gate \ˈsəb-ji-ˌgāt\ *vb* **-gat·ed; -gat·ing** : CONQUER, SUBDUE; *also* : ENSLAVE **syn** reduce, overcome, overthrow, vanquish, defeat, beat — **sub·ju·ga·tion** \ˌsəb-ji-ˈgā-shən\ *n*

sub·junc·tive \səb-ˈjəŋk-tiv\ *adj* : of, relating to, or constituting a verb form that represents an act or state as contingent or possible or viewed emotionally (as with desire) ⟨~ mood⟩ — **subjunctive** *n*

sub·let \ˈsəb-ˈlet\ *vb* **-let·; -let·ting** : to let all or a part of (a leased property) to another; *also* : to rent (a property) from a lessee

sub·li·mate \ˈsəb-lə-ˌmāt\ *vb* **-mat·ed; -mat·ing 1** : SUBLIME **2** : to direct the expression of (as an instinctual desire or impulse) from a primitive to a more socially and culturally acceptable form — **sub·li·ma·tion** \ˌsəb-lə-ˈmā-shən\ *n*

¹sub·lime \sə-ˈblīm\ *vb* **sub·limed; sub·lim·ing** : to pass or cause to pass directly from the solid to the vapor state

²sublime *adj* **1** : EXALTED, NOBLE **2** : having awe-inspiring beauty or grandeur **syn** glorious, splendid, superb, resplendent, gorgeous — **sub·lim·i·ty** \-ˈblim-ət-ē\ *n*

sub·lim·i·nal \(ˌ)səb-ˈlim-ən-ᵊl, ˈsəb-\ *adj* **1** : inadequate to produce a sensation or a perception ⟨~ stimuli⟩ **2** : existing or functioning below the threshold of conscious awareness ⟨the ~ mind⟩ ⟨~ techniques in advertising⟩

sub·ma·chine gun \ˌsəb-mə-ˈshēn-ˌgən\ *n* : an automatic firearm fired from the shoulder or hip

¹sub·ma·rine \ˈsəb-mə-ˌrēn, ˌsəb-mə-ˈrēn\ *adj* : UNDERWATER; *esp* : UNDERSEA

²submarine *n* **1** : a naval vessel designed to operate underwater **2** : a large sandwich made from a long split roll with any of a variety of fillings

sub·merge \səb-ˈmərj\ *vb* **sub·merged; sub·merg·ing 1** : to put or plunge under the surface of water **2** : INUNDATE **syn** immerse, duck, dip, dunk — **sub·mer·gence** \-ˈmər-jəns\ *n*

sub·merse \səb-ˈmərs\ *vb* **sub·mersed; sub·mers·ing** : SUBMERGE — **sub·mer·sion** \-ˈmər-zhən\ *n*

¹sub·mers·ible \səb-ˈmər-sə-bəl\ *adj* : capable of being submersed

²submersible *n* : something that is submersible; *esp* : SUBMARINE 1

sub·mi·cro·sco·pic \ˌsəb-ˌmī-krə-ˈskäp-ik\ *adj* : too small to be seen in an ordinary microscope

sub·min·ia·ture \ˌsəb-ˈmin-ē-ə-ˌchúr, ˈsəb-, -ˈmin-i-ˌchúr, -chər\ *adj* : very small

sub·mit \səb-ˈmit\ *vb* **sub·mit·ted; sub·mit·ting 1** : to commit to the discretion or decision of another or of others **2** : YIELD, SURRENDER **3** : to put forward as an opinion — **sub·mis·sion** \-ˈmish-ən\ *n* — **sub·mis·sive** \-ˈmis-iv\ *adj*

sub·nor·mal \ˌsəb-ˈnȯr-məl\ *adj* : falling below what is normal — **sub·nor·mal·i·ty** \ˌsəb-nȯr-ˈmal-ət-ē\ *n*

sub·or·bit·al \ˌsəb-ˈȯr-bət-ᵊl, ˈsəb-\ *adj* : being at or involving less than one orbit

¹sub·or·di·nate \sə-ˈbȯrd-(ə-)nət\ *adj* **1** : of lower class or rank **2** : INFERIOR **3** : submissive to authority **4** : subordinated to other elements in a sentence : DEPENDENT ⟨~ clause⟩ **syn** secondary, subject, tributary, collateral

²subordinate *n* : one that is subordinate

³sub·or·di·nate \sə-ˈbȯrd-ᵊn-ˌāt\ *vb* **-nat·ed; -nat·ing 1** : to place in a lower rank or class **2** : SUBDUE — **sub·or·di·na·tion** \-ˌbȯrd-ᵊn-ˈā-shən\ *n*

sub·orn \sə-ˈbȯrn\ *vb* **1** : to induce secretly to do an unlawful thing **2** : to induce to commit perjury — **sub·or·na·tion** \ˌsəb-ȯr-ˈnā-shən\ *n*

¹sub·poe·na \sə-ˈpē-nə\ *n* [ME *suppena*, fr. L *sub poena* under penalty] : a writ commanding the person named in it to attend court under penalty for failure to do so

²subpoena *vb* **-naed; -na·ing** : to summon with a subpoena

sub·scribe \səb-ˈskrīb\ *vb* **sub·scribed;**

sub·scrib·ing 1 : to sign one's name to a document 2 : to give consent by or as if by signing one's name 3 : to promise to contribute by signing one's name with the amount promised 4 : to place an order by signing 5 : FAVOR, APPROVE **syn** agree, acquiesce, assent, accede — **sub·scrib·er** *n*

sub·script \'səb-ˌskript\ *n* : a symbol (as a letter or number) immediately below or below and to the right or left of another written character — **subscript** *adj*

sub·scrip·tion \səb-'skrip-shən\ *n* 1 : the act of subscribing : SIGNATURE 2 : a purchase by signed order

sub·se·quent \'səb-si-kwənt, -sə-ˌkwent\ *adj* : following after : SUCCEEDING — **sub·se·quent·ly** \-ˌkwent-lē, -kwənt-\ *adv*

sub·ser·vi·ence \səb-'sər-vē-əns\ *n* 1 : a subordinate place or condition; *also* : willingness to serve in a subordinate capacity 2 : SERVILITY — **sub·ser·vi·en·cy** \-ən-sē\ *n* — **sub·ser·vi·ent** \-ənt\ *adj*

sub·set \'səb-ˌset\ *n* : a set each of whose elements is an element of an inclusive set

sub·side \səb-'sīd\ *vb* **sub·sid·ed; sub·sid·ing** [L *subsidere*, fr. *sub-* under + *sidere* to sit down, sink] 1 : to settle to the bottom of a liquid 2 : to tend downward : DESCEND 3 : SINK, SUBMERGE 4 : to become quiet and tranquil **syn** abate, wane, moderate, slacken — **sub·sid·ence** \səb-'sīd-əns, 'səb-səd-əns\ *n*

¹**sub·sid·iary** \səb-'sid-ē-ˌer-ē\ *adj* 1 : furnishing aid or support; *also* : owned or controlled by some main company 2 : of or relating to a subsidy **syn** auxiliary, contributory, subservient, accessory

²**subsidiary** *n, pl* **-iar·ies** : one that is subsidiary; *esp* : a company controlled by another

sub·si·dize \'səb-sə-ˌdīz\ *vb* **-dized; -diz·ing** : to aid or furnish with a subsidy

sub·si·dy \'səb-səd-ē\ *n, pl* **-dies** [ME, fr. L *subsidium* reserve troops, support, assistance, fr. *sub-* near + *sedēre* to sit] : a gift of public money to a private person or company or to another government **syn** grant, appropriation, subvention

sub·sist \səb-'sist\ *vb* 1 : EXIST, PERSIST 2 : to receive the means (as food and clothing) of maintaining life

sub·sis·tence \səb-'sis-təns\ *n* 1 : EXISTENCE 2 : means of subsisting : the minimum (as of food and clothing) necessary to support life

sub·soil \'səb-ˌsȯil\ *n* : a layer of weathered material just under the surface soil

sub·son·ic \ˌsəb-'sän-ik, 'səb-\ *adj* 1 : being or relating to a speed less than that of sound; *also* : moving at such a speed 2 : INFRASONIC

sub·stance \'səb-stəns\ *n* 1 : essential nature : ESSENCE (divine ∼) ; *also*

: the fundamental or essential part or quality (the ∼ of his speech) 2 : physical material from which something is made or which has discrete existence; *also* : matter of particular or definite chemical constitution 3 : material possessions : PROPERTY, WEALTH

sub·stan·dard \ˌsəb-'stan-dərd, 'səb-\ *adj* : falling short of a standard or norm

sub·stan·tial \səb-'stan-chəl\ *adj* 1 : existing as or in substance : MATERIAL; *also* : not illusory : REAL 2 : IMPORTANT, ESSENTIAL 3 : NOURISHING, SATISFYING (∼ meal) 4 : having means : WELL-TO-DO 5 : CONSIDERABLE (∼ profit) 6 : STRONG, FIRM — **sub·stan·tial·ly** \-ē\ *adv*

sub·stan·ti·ate \səb-'stan-chē-ˌāt\ *vb* **-at·ed; -at·ing** 1 : to give substance or body to 2 : VERIFY, PROVE — **sub·stan·ti·a·tion** \-ˌstan-chē-'ā-shən\ *n*

sub·stan·tive \'səb-stən-tiv\ *n* : NOUN; *also* : a word or phrase used as a noun

sub·sta·tion \'səb-ˌstā-shən\ *n* : a station (as a post-office branch) subordinate to another station

¹**sub·sti·tute** \'səb-stə-ˌt(y)üt\ *n* : a person or thing replacing another — **substitute** *adj*

²**substitute** *vb* **-tut·ed; -tut·ing** 1 : to put or use in the place of another 2 : to serve as a substitute — **sub·sti·tu·tion** \ˌsəb-stə-'t(y)ü-shən\ *n*

sub·stra·tum \'səb-ˌstrāt-əm, -ˌstrat-\ *n, pl* **-stra·ta** \-ə\ : the layer or structure lying underneath

sub·struc·ture \'səb-ˌstrək-chər\ *n* : FOUNDATION, GROUNDWORK

sub·sur·face \'səb-ˌsər-fəs\ *n* : earth material near the surface of the ground — **subsurface** *adj*

sub·ter·fuge \'səb-tər-ˌfyüj\ *n* : a trick or device used in order to conceal, escape, or evade **syn** fraud, deception, trickery

sub·ter·ra·nean \ˌsəb-tə-'rā-nē-ən\ *adj* 1 : lying or being underground 2 : SECRET, HIDDEN

sub·tile \'sət-ᵊl\ *adj* **sub·til·er** \'sət-lər, -ᵊl-ər\ ; **sub·til·est** \'sət-ləst, -ᵊl-əst\ : SUBTLE

sub·ti·tle \'səb-ˌtīt-ᵊl\ *n* 1 : a secondary or explanatory title (as of a book) 2 : printed matter projected on a motion-picture screen during or between the scenes

sub·tle \'sət-ᵊl\ *adj* **sub·tler** \'sət-(ᵊ-)lər\ ; **sub·tlest** \'sət-(ᵊ-)ləst\ 1 : hardly noticeable : DELICATE, REFINED 2 : SHREWD, KEEN 3 : CLEVER, SLY — **sub·tle·ty** \-tē\ *n* — **sub·tly** \'sət-(ᵊ-)lē\ *adv*

sub·tract \səb-'trakt\ *vb* : to take away (as one number from another); *also* : to perform the operation of deducting one number from another — **sub·trac·tion** \-'trak-shən\ *n*

sub·tra·hend \'səb-trə-ˌhend\ *n* : a number that is to be subtracted from another

sub·trop·i·cal \ˌsəb-'träp-i-kəl, 'səb-\

also **sub-trop-ic** \-ik\ *adj* : of, relating to, or being regions bordering on the tropical zone

sub-urb \'səb-ˌərb\ *n* **1** : an outlying part of a city; *also* : a small community adjacent to a city **2** *pl* : a residential area adjacent to a city — **sub-ur-ban** \sə-'bər-bən\ *adj or n*

sub-ur-ban-ite \sə-'bər-bə-ˌnīt\ *n* : one living in a suburb

sub-ur-bia \sə-'bər-bē-ə-\ *n* **1** : SUBURBS **2** : suburban people or customs

sub-ven-tion \səb-'ven-chən\ *n* : SUBSIDY, ENDOWMENT

sub-vert \səb-'vərt\ *vb* **1** : OVERTHROW, RUIN **2** : CORRUPT *syn* sabotage, undermine — **sub-ver-sion** \-'vər-zhən\ *n* — **sub-ver-sive** \-'vər-siv\ *adj*

sub-way \'səb-ˌwā\ *n* : an underground way; *esp* : an underground electric railway

suc-ceed \sək-'sēd\ *vb* **1** : to follow next in order or next after another; *esp* : to inherit sovereignty, rank, title, or property **2** : to attain a desired object or end : to be successful

suc-cess \sək-'ses\ *n* **1** : satisfactory completion of something **2** : the gaining of wealth and fame **3** : one that succeeds — **suc-cess-ful** \-fəl\ *adj* — **suc-cess-ful-ly** \-ē\ *adv*

suc-ces-sion \sək-'sesh-ən\ *n* **1** : the order, act, or right of succeeding to a property, title, or throne **2** : the act or process of following in order **3** : a series of persons or things that follow one after another *syn* progression, sequence, chain, train, string

suc-ces-sive \sək-'ses-iv\ *adj* : following in order : CONSECUTIVE — **suc-ces-sive-ly** *adv*

suc-ces-sor \sək-'ses-ər\ *n* : one that succeeds (as to a throne, estate, or office)

suc-cinct \(ˌ)sək-'siŋkt, sə-'siŋkt\ *adj* : BRIEF, CONCISE *syn* terse, laconic, summary, curt, short — **suc-cinct-ly** *adv* — **suc-cinct-ness** *n*

suc-cor \'sək-ər\ *n* [ME *succur*, fr. earlier *sucurs*, taken as pl., fr. OF *sucors*, fr. ML *succursus*, fr. L *succursus*, pp. of *succurrere* to run up, run to help] : AID, HELP, RELIEF — **succor** *vb*

suc-co-tash \'sək-ə-ˌtash\ *n* [from an American Indian language] : beans and kernels of sweet corn cooked together

¹suc-cu-lent \'sək-yə-lənt\ *adj* : full of juice : JUICY; *also* : having fleshy tissues that conserve moisture — **suc-cu-lence** \-ləns\ *n*

²succulent *n* : a succulent plant (as a cactus)

suc-cumb \sə-'kəm\ *vb* **1** : to give up **2** : DIE *syn* submit, capitulate, relent, defer

¹such \(ˈ)səch, (ˌ)sich\ *adj* **1** : of this or that kind **2** : having a quality just specified or to be specified

²such *pron* **1** : such a one or ones (he's the boss, and had the right to act as ∼)

2 : that or those similar or related thereto ⟨boards and nails and ∼⟩

³such *adv* : to that degree : so

such-like \'səch-ˌlīk\ *adj* : SIMILAR

¹suck \'sək\ *vb* **1** : to draw in liquid and esp. mother's milk with the mouth **2** : to draw liquid from by action of the mouth ⟨∼ an orange⟩ **3** : to take in or up or remove by or as if by suction

²suck *n* : the act of sucking : SUCTION

suck-er \'sək-ər\ *n* **1** : one that sucks **2** : a part of an animal's body used for sucking or for clinging **3** : a fish with thick soft lips for sucking in food **4** : a shoot from the roots or lower part of a plant **5** : a person easily deceived

suck-le \'sək-əl\ *vb* **suck-led; suck-ling** \-(ə-)liŋ\ : to give or draw milk from the breast or udder; *also* : NURTURE, REAR

suck-ling \'sək-liŋ\ *n* : a young unweaned mammal

su-cre \'sü-(ˌ)krā\ *n* — see MONEY table

su-crose \'sü-ˌkrōs, -ˌkrōz\ *n* : a sweet sugar obtained esp. from sugarcane or sugar beets

suc-tion \'sək-shən\ *n* **1** : the act of sucking **2** : the act or process of drawing something (as liquid or dust) into a space (as in a vacuum cleaner or a pump) by partially exhausting the air in the space — **suc-tion-al** \-sh(ə-)nəl\ *adj*

sud-den \'səd-ᵊn\ *adj* [ME *sodain*, fr. MF, fr. L *subitaneus*, fr. *subitus* sudden, fr. pp. of *subire* to come up] **1** : happening or coming quickly or unexpectedly ⟨∼ shower⟩; *also* : changing angle or character all at once ⟨∼ turn in the road⟩ **2** : HASTY, RASH ⟨∼ decision⟩ **3** : made or brought about in a short time : PROMPT ⟨∼ cure⟩ *syn* precipitate, headlong, impetuous, hasty — **sud-den-ly** *adv* — **sud-den-ness** *n*

sudden infant death syndrome *n* : death due to unknown causes of an infant in apparently good health that occurs usu. before one year of age

suds \'sədz\ *n pl* : soapy water esp. when frothy — **sudsy** \'səd-zē\ *adj*

sue \'sü\ *vb* **sued; su-ing 1** : PETITION, SOLICIT **2** : to seek justice or right by bringing legal action *syn* appeal

suede *or* **suède** \'swād\ *n* [F *gants de Suède* Swedish gloves] **1** : leather with a napped surface **2** : a fabric with a suedelike nap

su-et \'sü-ət\ *n* : the hard fat from beef and mutton that yields tallow

suff *abbr* **1** sufficient **2** suffix

suf-fer \'səf-ər\ *vb* **suf-fered; suf-fer-ing** \-(ə-)riŋ\ **1** : to feel or endure pain **2** : EXPERIENCE, UNDERGO **3** : to bear loss, damage, or injury **4** : ALLOW, PERMIT *syn* endure, abide, tolerate, stand, brook, stomach — **suf-fer-er** *n*

suf-fer-ance \'səf-(ə-)rəns\ *n* **1** : consent or approval implied by lack of interference or resistance **2** : ENDURANCE, PATIENCE

suf·fer·ing \-(ə-)riŋ\ *n* : PAIN, MISERY, HARDSHIP

suf·fice \sə-¹fīs\ *vb* **suf·ficed; suf·fic·ing** 1 : to satisfy a need : be sufficient 2 : to be capable or competent

suf·fi·cien·cy \sə-¹fish-ən-sē\ *n* 1 : a sufficient quantity to meet one's needs 2 : ADEQUACY

suf·fi·cient \sə-¹fish-ənt\ *adj* : adequate to accomplish a purpose or meet a need — **suf·fi·cient·ly** *adv*

¹**suf·fix** \¹səf-,iks\ *n* : an affix occurring at the end of a word

²**suf·fix** \¹səf-iks, (,)sə-¹fiks\ *vb* : to attach as a suffix — **suf·fix·a·tion** \,səf-,ik-¹sā-shən\ *n*

suf·fo·cate \¹səf-ə-,kāt\ *vb* **-cat·ed; -cat·ing** : STIFLE, SMOTHER, CHOKE — **suf·fo·cat·ing·ly** *adv* — **suf·fo·ca·tion** \,səf-ə-¹kā-shən\ *n*

suf·fra·gan \¹səf-ri-gən\ *n* : an assistant bishop; *esp* : one not having the right of succession — **suffragan** *adj*

suf·frage \¹səf-rij\ *n* [L *suffragium*] 1 : VOTE 2 : the right to vote : FRANCHISE

suf·frag·ette \,səf-ri-¹jet\ *n* : a woman who advocates suffrage for her sex

suf·frag·ist \¹səf-ri-jəst\ *n* : one who advocates extension of the suffrage esp. to women

suf·fuse \sə-¹fyüz\ *vb* **suf·fused; suf·fus·ing** : to spread over or through in the manner of a fluid or light syn infuse, imbue, ingrain, steep — **suf·fu·sion** \-¹fyü-zhən\ *n*

¹**sug·ar** \¹shu̇g-ər\ *n* 1 : a sweet substance that is colorless or white when pure and is chiefly derived from sugarcane or sugar beets 2 : a water-soluble compound (as glucose) similar to sucrose — **sug·ary** *adj*

²**sugar** *vb* **sug·ared; sug·ar·ing** \-(ə-)riŋ\ 1 : to mix, cover, or sprinkle with sugar 2 : SWEETEN ⟨∼ advice with flattery⟩ 3 : to form sugar ⟨a syrup that ∼s⟩ 4 : GRANULATE

sugar beet *n* : a large beet with a white root from which sugar is made

sug·ar·cane \¹shu̇g-ər-,kān\ *n* : a tall grass widely grown in warm regions for the sugar in its stalks

sugar daddy *n* 1 : a well-to-do usu. older man who supports or spends lavishly on a mistress or girlfriend 2 : a generous benefactor of a cause

sugar maple *n* : a maple with a sweet sap; *esp* : one of eastern No. America with sap that is the chief source of maple syrup and maple sugar

sugar pea *n* : SNOW PEA

sug·ar·plum \¹shu̇g-ər-,pləm\ *n* : a small ball of candy

sug·gest \sə(g)-¹jest\ *vb* 1 : to put (as a thought, plan, or desire) into a person's mind 2 : to remind or evoke by association of ideas syn imply, hint, intimate, insinuate, connote

sug·gest·ible \sə(g)-¹jes-tə-bəl\ *adj* : easily influenced by suggestion

sug·ges·tion \-¹jes-chən\ *n* 1 : an act or instance of suggesting; *also* : some-

thing suggested 2 : a slight indication

sug·ges·tive \-¹jes-tiv\ *adj* : tending to suggest something; *esp* : suggesting something improper or indecent — **sug·ges·tive·ly** *adv* — **sug·ges·tive·ness** *n*

sui·cide \¹sü-ə-,sīd\ *n* 1 : the act of killing oneself purposely 2 : one that commits or attempts suicide — **sui·cid·al** \,sü-ə-¹sīd-ᵊl\ *adj*

sui ge·ner·is \,sü-,ī-¹jen-ə-rəs, ,sü-ē-¹jen-\ *adj* [L, of its own kind] : being in a class by itself : UNIQUE

¹**suit** \¹süt\ *n* 1 : an action in court to recover a right or claim 2 : an act of suing or entreating; *esp* : COURTSHIP 3 : a number of things used together ⟨∼ of clothes⟩ 4 : one of the four sets of playing cards in a pack syn prayer, plea, petition, appeal

²**suit** *vb* 1 : to be appropriate or fitting 2 : to be becoming to 3 : to meet the needs or desires of : PLEASE

suit·able \¹süt-ə-bəl\ *adj* : FITTING, PROPER, APPROPRIATE syn fit, meet, apt, happy — **suit·abil·i·ty** \,süt-ə-¹bil-ət-ē\ *n* — **suit·able·ness** \¹süt-ə-bəl-nəs\ *n* — **suit·ably** \-ə-blē\ *adv*

suit·case \¹süt-,kās\ *n* : a flat rectangular traveling bag

suite \¹swēt, *for 4 also* ¹süt\ *n* 1 : a personal staff attending a dignitary or ruler : RETINUE 2 : a group of rooms occupied as a unit : APARTMENT 3 : a modern instrumental composition free in its character and number of movements; *also* : a long orchestral concert arrangement in suite form of material drawn from a longer work 4 : a set of matched furniture for a room

suit·ing \¹süt-iŋ\ *n* : fabric for suits of clothes

suit·or \¹süt-ər\ *n* 1 : one who sues or petitions 2 : one who seeks to marry a woman

su·ki·ya·ki \,skē-¹(y)äk-ē; ,su̇k-ē-¹(y)äk-ē, ,sük-\ *n* : thin slices of meat, bean curd, and vegetables cooked in soy sauce, sake, and sugar

sul·fa \¹səl-fə\ *adj* 1 : related chemically to sulfanilamide 2 : of, relating to, or using sulfa drugs ⟨∼ therapy⟩

sulfa drug *n* : any of various synthetic organic bacteria-inhibiting drugs that are closely related chemically to sulfanilamide

sul·fa·nil·amide \,səl-fə-¹nil-ə-,mīd\ *n* : a sulfur-containing organic compound that is the parent compound of most sulfa drugs

sul·fate \¹səl-,fāt\ *n* : a salt or ester of sulfuric acid

sul·fide \¹səl-,fīd\ *n* : a compound of sulfur

sul·fur *or* **sul·phur** \¹səl-fər\ *n* : a nonmetallic element that occurs in nature combined or free in vulcanizing rubber and in medicine

sulfur dioxide *n* : a heavy pungent toxic gas that is used esp. in bleaching, as a preservative, and as a refrigerant, and is a major air pollutant

sul·fu·ric _1_ səl-'fyūr-ik\\ *adj* : of, relating to, or containing sulfur

sulfuric acid *n* : a heavy corrosive oily strong acid

sul·fu·rous \\'səl-f(y)ə-rəs, *also esp for 1* _1_ səl-'fyür-əs\\ *adj* 1 : of, relating to, or containing sulfur 2 *or* **sul·phu·rous** : of or relating to brimstone or the fire of hell : INFERNAL 3 *or* **sulphurous** : FIERY, INFLAMED (~ sermons)

¹sulk \\'səlk\\ *vb* : to be or become moodily silent

²sulk *n* : a sulky mood or spell

¹sulky \\'səl-kē\\ *adj* : inclined to sulk : MOROSE, MOODY syn surly, glum, sullen, gloomy — **sulk·i·ly** \\'səl-kə-lē\\ *adv* — **sulk·i·ness** \\-kē-nəs\\ *n*

²sulky *n, pl* **sulkies** : a light 2-wheeled vehicle with a seat for the driver and usu. no body

sul·len \\'səl-ən\\ *adj* 1 : gloomily silent : MOROSE 2 : DISMAL, GLOOMY (a ~ sky) syn glum, surly, dour, saturnine — **sul·len·ly** *adv* — **sul·len·ness** \\'səl-ən-(n)əs\\ *n*

sul·ly \\'səl-ē\\ *vb* **sul·lied; sul·ly·ing** : SOIL, SMIRCH, DEFILE

sul·tan \\'səlt-ºn\\ *n* : a sovereign esp. of a Muslim state — **sul·tan·ate** \\-ͺāt\\ *n*

sul·ta·na \\ͺsəl-'tan-ə\\ *n* 1 : a female member of a sultan's family 2 : a pale seedless grape; *also* : a raisin of this grape

sul·try \\'səl-trē\\ *adj* **sul·tri·er; -est** [obs. E *sulter* to swelter, alter. of E *swelter*] : very hot and moist : SWELTERING; *also* : burning hot : TORRID

¹sum \\'səm\\ *n* [ME *summe*, fr. OF, fr. L *summa*, fr. fem. of *summus* highest] 1 : a quantity of money 2 : the whole amount 3 : GIST 4 : the result obtained by adding numbers 5 : a problem in arithmetic syn aggregate, total, whole

²sum *vb* **summed; sum·ming** : to find the sum of by adding or counting

su·mac *also* **su·mach** \\'s(h)ü-ͺmak\\ *n* : any of a genus of trees, shrubs, and woody vines with pinnate compound leaves and spikes of red or whitish berries

sum·ma·rize \\'səm-ə-ͺrīz\\ *vb* **-rized; -riz·ing** : to tell in a summary

¹sum·ma·ry \\'səm-ə-rē\\ *adj* 1 : covering the main points briefly : CONCISE 2 : done without delay or formality (~ punishment) syn terse, succinct, laconic — **sum·mar·i·ly** \\(ͺ)sə-'mer-ə-lē, 'səm-ə-rə-lē\\ *adv*

²summary *n, pl* **-ries** : a concise statement of the main points

sum·ma·tion \\(ͺ)sə-'mā-shən\\ *n* : a summing up; *esp* : a speech in court summing up the arguments in a case

sum·mer \\'səm-ər\\ *n* : the season of the year in a region in which the sun shines most directly : the warmest period of the year — **sum·mery** *adj*

sum·mer·house \\'səm-ər-ͺhaùs\\ *n* : a

covered structure in a garden or park to provide a shady retreat

summer squash *n* : any of various garden squashes (as zucchini) used as a vegetable while immature

sum·mit \\'səm-ət\\ *n* : the highest point

sum·mon \\'səm-ən\\ *vb* **sum·moned; sum·mon·ing** \\-(ə-)niŋ\\ [ME *somonen*, fr. OF *somondre*, fr. (assumed) VL *summonere*, alter. of L *summonēre* to remind secretly] 1 : to call to a meeting : CONVOKE 2 : to send for; *also* : to order to appear in court 3 : to evoke esp. by an act of the will (~ up courage) — **sum·mon·er** *n*

sum·mons \\'səm-ənz\\ *n, pl* **sum·mons·es** 1 : an authoritative call to appear at a designated place or to attend to a duty 2 : a warning or citation to appear in court at a specified time to answer charges

sump·tu·ous \\'səmp-chə(-wə)s\\ *adj* : LAVISH, LUXURIOUS

sum up *vb* : SUMMARIZE

¹sun \\'sən\\ *n* 1 : the shining celestial body around which the earth and other planets revolve and from which they receive light and heat 2 : a celestial body like the sun 3 : SUNSHINE — **sun·less** *adj* — **sun·ny** *adj*

²sun *vb* **sunned; sun·ning** 1 : to expose to or as if to the rays of the sun 2 : to sun oneself

Sun *abbr* Sunday

sun·bath \\'sən-ͺbath, -ͺbåth\\ *n* : an exposure to sunlight or a sunlamp — **sun·bathe** \\-ͺbāth\\ *vb*

sun·beam \\-ͺbēm\\ *n* : a ray of sunlight

sun·bon·net \\-ͺbän-ət\\ *n* : a bonnet with a wide brim to shield the face and neck from the sun

¹sun·burn \\-ͺbərn\\ *vb* **-burned** \\-ͺbərnd\\ *or* **-burnt** \\-ͺbərnt\\; **-burn·ing** : to burn or discolor by the sun

²sunburn *n* : a skin inflammation caused by overexposure to sunlight

sun·dae \\'sən-dē\\ *n* : ice cream served with topping

Sun·day \\'sən-dē, -ͺdā\\ *n* : the 1st day of the week : the Christian Sabbath

sun·der \\'sən-dər\\ *vb* **sun·dered; sun·der·ing** \\-d(ə-)riŋ\\ : to force apart syn sever, part, disjoin, disunite

sun·di·al \\-ͺdī(-ə)l\\ *n* : a device for showing the time of day from the shadow cast on a plate by an object with a straight edge

sun·down \\-ͺdaùn\\ *n* : SUNSET 2

sun·dries \\'sən-drēz\\ *n pl* : various small articles or items

sun·dry \\'sən-drē\\ *adj* : SEVERAL, DIVERS, VARIOUS syn many, numerous

sun·fish \\-ͺfish\\ *n* 1 : a huge sea fish with a deep flattened body 2 : any of a family of American freshwater fishes that are related to the perches, are often brightly colored, and usu. have the body flattened from side to side

sun·flow·er \\-ͺflaù(-ə)r\\ *n* : any of a genus of tall plants related to the daisies and often grown for the oil-rich seeds of their yellow-petaled dark=centered flower heads

sung *past and past part of* SING

sun-glasses \'sən-ˌglas-əz\ *n pl* : glasses to protect the eyes from the sun

sunk *past and past part of* SINK

sunk-en \'sən-kən\ *adj* 1 : SUBMERGED 2 : fallen in : HOLLOW (~ cheeks) 3 : lying in a depression (~ garden) ; *also* : constructed below the general floor level (~ living room)

sun-lamp \'sən-ˌlamp\ *n* : an electric lamp designed to emit radiation of wavelengths from ultraviolet to infra-red

sun-light \-ˌlīt\ *n* : SUNSHINE

sun-lit \-ˌlit\ *adj* : lighted by or as if by the sun

sun-rise \-ˌrīz\ *n* 1 : the apparent rising of the sun above the horizon 2 : the time at which the sun rises

sun-roof \-ˌrüf, -ˌrůf\ *n* : an automobile roof having a panel that can be opened

sun-screen \-ˌskrēn\ *n* : a substance used in suntan preparations to protect the skin

sun-set \-ˌset\ *n* 1 : the apparent descent of the sun below the horizon 2 : the time at which the sun sets

sun-shade \-ˌshād\ *n* : something (as a parasol or awning) used as a protection from the sun's rays

sun-shine \-ˌshīn\ *n* : the direct light of the sun — **sun-shiny** *adj*

sun-spot \-ˌspät\ *n* : one of the dark spots that appear from time to time on the sun's surface

sun-stroke \-ˌstrōk\ *n* : a bodily condition often marked by high fever and collapse and caused by staying in the sun for too long

sun-tan \-ˌtan\ *n* : a browning of the skin from exposure to the sun's rays

sun-up \-ˌəp\ *n* : SUNRISE 2

¹**sup** \'səp\ *vb* **supped; sup-ping** : to take or drink in swallows or gulps

²**sup** *n* : a mouthful esp. of liquor or broth; *also* : a small quantity of liquid

³**sup** *vb* **supped; sup-ping** 1 : to eat the evening meal 2 : to make one's supper (*supped* on roast beef)

sup *abbr* 1 superior 2 supplement; supplementary 3 supply 4 supra

¹**su-per** \'sü-pər\ *n* : SUPERINTENDENT

²**super** *adj* 1 : very fine : EXCELLENT 2 : EXTREME, EXCESSIVE

super- \ˌsü-pər, 'sü-\ *prefix* 1 : over and above : higher in quantity, quality, or degree than : more than 2 : in addition : extra 3 : exceeding a norm 4 : in excessive degree or intensity 5 : surpassing all or most others of its kind 6 : situated above, on, or at the top of 7 : next above or higher 8 : more inclusive than 9 : superior in status or position

superachiever	supercity
superagency	supereminent
superblock	superfine
superbomb	supergalaxy
supergovernment	supersize
superheat	supersized
superhuman	supersophisticated
superhumanly	superspectacle
superindividual	superspy
superliner	superstar
superman	superstate
supermom	superstratum
supernormal	superstrength
superpatriot	superstrong
superpatriotic	supersubtle
superpatriotism	supersubtlety
superphysical	supersystem
superpower	supertanker
superrich	supertax
supersalesman	superwoman
supersecret	

su-per-abun-dant \ˌsü-pər-ə-'bən-dənt\ *adj* : more than ample — **su-per-abun-dance** \-dəns\ *n*

su-per-an-nu-ate \ˌsü-pər-'an-yə-ˌwāt\ *vb* **-at-ed; -at-ing** : to retire and pension because of age or infirmity — **su-per-an-nu-at-ed** *adj*

su-perb \su̇-'pərb\ *adj* [L *superbus* excellent, proud, fr. *super* above] : marked to the highest degree by grandeur, excellence, brilliance, or competence **syn** resplendent, glorious, gorgeous, sublime — **su-perb-ly** *adv*

su-per-car-go \ˌsü-pər-'kär-gō, 'sü-pər-ˌkär-gō\ *n* : an officer on a merchant ship who manages the business part of the voyage

su-per-charg-er \'sü-pər-ˌchär-jər\ *n* : a device for increasing the amount of air supplied to an internal-combustion engine

su-per-cil-i-ous \ˌsü-pər-'sil-ē-əs\ *adj* [L *superciliosus*, fr. *supercilium* eyebrow, haughtiness] : haughtily contemptuous **syn** disdainful, overbearing, arrogant, lordly, superior

su-per-con-duc-tiv-i-ty \'sü-pər-ˌkän-ˌdək-'tiv-ət-ē\ *n* : a complete disappearance of electrical resistance in a substance at temperatures near absolute zero — **su-per-con-duc-tive** \ˌsü-pər-kən-'dək-tiv\ *adj* — **su-per-con-duc-tor** \-'dək-tər\ *n*

su-per-con-ti-nent \'sü-pər-ˌkänt-ᵊn-ənt\ *n* : a hypothetical former large continent from which other continents broke off and drifted away

su-per-du-per \'sü-pər-'dü-pər\ *adj* : of the greatest excellence, size, effectiveness, or impressiveness

su-per-ego \ˌsü-pər-'ē-gō\ *n* : the one of the three divisions of the psyche in psychoanalytic theory that functions to reward and punish through a system of moral attitudes, conscience, and a sense of guilt

su-per-fi-cial \ˌsü-pər-'fish-əl\ *adj* 1 : of or relating to the surface or appearance only 2 : not thorough : SHALLOW **syn** cursory, sketchy — **su-per-fi-ci-al-i-ty** \-ˌfish-ē-'al-ət-ē\ *n* — **su-per-fi-cial-ly** \-'fish-(ə-)lē\ *adv*

su-per-flu-ous \su̇-'pər-flə-wəs\ *adj*

: exceeding what is sufficient or necessary : SURPLUS syn extra, spare, supernumerary — **su·per·flu·i·ty** \ˌsü-pər-ˈflü-ət-ē\ n

su·per·high·way \ˌsü-pər-ˈhī-ˌwā\ n : a broad highway designed for high-speed traffic

su·per·im·pose \-im-ˈpōz\ vb : to lay (one thing) over and above something else

su·per·in·tend \ˌsü-p(ə-)rin-ˈtend\ vb : to have or exercise the charge and oversight of : DIRECT — **su·per·in·ten·dence** \-ˈten-dəns\ n — **su·per·in·ten·den·cy** \-dən-sē\ n — **su·per·in·ten·dent** \-dənt\ n

¹**su·pe·ri·or** \sù-ˈpir-ē-ər\ adj 1 : situated higher up; also : higher in rank or numbers 2 : of greater value or importance 3 : courageously indifferent (as to pain or misfortune) 4 : better than most others of its kind 5 : ARROGANT, HAUGHTY — **su·pe·ri·or·i·ty** \-ˌpir-ē-ˈór-ət-ē\ n

²**superior** n 1 : one who is above another in rank, office, or station; esp : the head of a religious house or order 2 : one higher in quality or merit

¹**su·per·la·tive** \sù-ˈpər-lət-iv\ adj 1 : of, relating to, or constituting the degree of grammatical comparison that denotes an extreme or unsurpassed level or extent 2 : surpassing others : SUPREME syn peerless, incomparable, superb — **su·per·la·tive·ly** adv

²**superlative** n 1 : the superlative degree or a superlative form in a language 2 : the utmost degree : ACME

su·per·mar·ket \ˈsü-pər-ˌmär-kət\ n : a self-service retail market selling foods and household merchandise

su·per·nal \sù-ˈpərn-əl\ adj 1 : of or from on high : TOWERING 2 : of heavenly or spiritual character : ETHEREAL

su·per·nat·u·ral \ˌsü-pər-ˈnach-(ə-)rəl\ adj : of or relating to phenomena beyond or outside of nature; esp : relating to or attributed to a divinity, ghost, or infernal spirit — **su·per·nat·u·ral·ly** \-ē\ adv

su·per·no·va \ˌsü-pər-ˈnō-və\ n : the explosion of a very large star

¹**su·per·nu·mer·ary** \-ˈn(y)ü-mə-ˌrer-ē\ adj : exceeding the usual or required number : EXTRA syn surplus, superfluous, spare

²**supernumerary** n, pl -**ar·ies** : an extra person or thing; esp : an actor hired for a nonspeaking part

su·per·pose \ˌsü-pər-ˈpōz\ vb -**posed**; -**pos·ing** : SUPERIMPOSE — **su·per·po·si·tion** \-pə-ˈzish-ən\ n

su·per·sat·u·rat·ed \ˌsü-pər-ˈsach-ə-ˌrāt-əd\ adj : containing an amount of a substance greater than that required for saturation

su·per·scribe \ˈsü-pər-ˌskrīb, ˌsü-pər-ˈskrīb\ vb -**scribed**; -**scrib·ing** : to write on the top or outside : ADDRESS — **su·per·scrip·tion** \ˌsü-pər-ˈskrip-shən\ n

su·per·script \ˈsü-pər-ˌskript\ n : a symbol (as a numeral or letter) written immediately above or above and to one side of another character

su·per·sede \ˌsü-pər-ˈsēd\ vb -**sed·ed**; -**sed·ing** [MF superceder to refrain from, fr. L supersedēre to be superior to, refrain from, fr. super- above + sedēre to sit] : to take the place of : REPLACE syn displace, supplant

su·per·son·ic \-ˈsän-ik\ adj 1 : ULTRASONIC 2 : being or relating to speeds from one to five times the speed of sound; also : capable of moving at such a speed (a ∼ airplane)

su·per·son·ics \-ˈsän-iks\ n : the science of supersonic phenomena

su·per·sti·tion \ˌsü-pər-ˈstish-ən\ n 1 : beliefs or practices resulting from ignorance, fear of the unknown, or trust in magic or chance 2 : an irrationally abject attitude of mind toward nature, the unknown, or God resulting from superstition — **su·per·sti·tious** \-əs\ adj

su·per·struc·ture \ˈsü-pər-ˌstrək-chər\ n : something built on a base or as a vertical extension

su·per·vene \ˌsü-pər-ˈvēn\ vb -**vened**; -**ven·ing** : to occur as something additional or unexpected syn follow, succeed, ensue

su·per·vise \ˈsü-pər-ˌvīz\ vb -**vised**; -**vis·ing** : OVERSEE, SUPERINTEND — **su·per·vi·sion** \ˌsü-pər-ˈvizh-ən\ n — **su·per·vi·sor** \ˈsü-pər-ˌvī-zər\ n — **su·per·vi·so·ry** \ˌsü-pər-ˈvīz-(ə-)rē\ adj

su·pine \sù-ˈpīn\ adj 1 : lying on the back with face upward 2 : LETHARGIC, SLUGGISH; also : ABJECT syn inactive, inert, passive, idle

supp or **suppl** abbr supplement; supplementary

sup·per \ˈsəp-ər\ n : the evening meal esp. when dinner is taken at midday — **sup·per·time** \-ˌtīm\ n

sup·plant \sə-ˈplant\ vb 1 : to take the place of (another) esp. by force or trickery 2 : REPLACE syn displace, supersede

sup·ple \ˈsəp-əl\ adj **sup·pler** \-(ə-)lər\; **sup·plest** \-(ə-)ləst\ 1 : COMPLIANT, ADAPTABLE 2 : capable of bending without breaking or creasing : LIMBER syn resilient, elastic, flexible

¹**sup·ple·ment** \ˈsəp-lə-mənt\ n 1 : something that supplies a want or makes an addition 2 : a continuation (as of a book) containing corrections or additional material — **sup·ple·men·tal** \ˌsəp-lə-ˈment-əl\ adj — **sup·ple·men·ta·ry** \-ˈment-t(ə)-rē\ adj

²**sup·ple·ment** \ˈsəp-lə-ˌment\ vb : to fill up the deficiencies of : add to

sup·pli·ant \ˈsəp-lē-ənt\ n : one who supplicates : PETITIONER, PLEADER

sup·pli·cant \ˈsəp-li-kənt\ n : SUPPLIANT

sup·pli·cate \ˈsəp-lə-ˌkāt\ vb -**cat·ed**; -**cat·ing** 1 : to make a humble entreaty; esp : to pray to God 2 : to ask earnestly and humbly : BESEECH syn implore, beg, entreat, plead — **sup·pli·ca·tion** \ˌsəp-lə-ˈkā-shən\ n

¹**sup·ply** \sə-ˈplī\ vb **sup·plied; sup·ply·ing** [ME *supplien*, fr. MF *soupleier*, fr. L *supplēre* to fill up, supplement, supply, fr. *sub-* up + *plēre* to fill] **1** : to add as a supplement **2** : to satisfy the needs of **3** : FURNISH, PROVIDE — **sup·pli·er** \-ˈplī(-ə)r\ n

²**supply** n, pl **supplies 1** : the quantity or amount (as of a commodity) needed or available; *also* : PROVISIONS, STORES — usu. used in pl. **2** : the act or process of filling a want or need : PROVISION **3** : the quantities of goods or services offered for sale at a particular time or at one price

sup·ply-side \sə-ˈplī-ˌsīd\ adj : of, relating to, or being an economic theory that recommends the reduction of tax rates to expand economic activity

¹**sup·port** \sə-ˈpōrt\ vb **1** : BEAR, TOLERATE **2** : to take sides with : BACK, ASSIST **3** : to provide with food, clothing, and shelter **4** : to hold up or serve as a foundation for syn uphold, advocate, champion — **sup·port·able** adj — **sup·port·er** n

²**support** n **1** : the act of supporting : the state of being supported **2** : one that supports : PROP, BASE

sup·pose \sə-ˈpōz\ vb **sup·posed; sup·pos·ing 1** : to assume to be true (as for the sake of argument) **2** : EXPECT (I am *supposed* to go) **3** : to think probable — **sup·pos·al** n

sup·posed \sə-ˈpōz(-ə)d\ adj : BELIEVED; *also* : mistakenly believed — **sup·pos·ed·ly** \-ˈpō-zəd-lē, -ˈpōz-dlē\ adv

sup·pos·ing \sə-ˈpō-ziŋ\ conj : if by way of hypothesis : on the assumption that

sup·po·si·tion \ˌsəp-ə-ˈzish-ən\ n **1** : something that is supposed : HYPOTHESIS **2** : the act of supposing

sup·pos·i·to·ry \sə-ˈpäz-ə-ˌtōr-ē\ n, pl **-ries** [ML *suppositorium*, lit., placed beneath] : a small easily melted mass of usu. medicated material for insertion (as into the rectum)

sup·press \sə-ˈpres\ vb **1** : to put down by authority or force : SUBDUE (~ a revolt) **2** : to keep from being known; *also* : to stop the publication or circulation of **3** : to exclude from consciousness : REPRESS — **sup·press·ible** \-ˈpres-ə-bəl\ adj — **sup·pres·sion** \-ˈpresh-ən\ n

sup·pres·sant \sə-ˈpres-ªnt\ n : an agent (as a drug) that tends to suppress rather than eliminate something (as appetite)

sup·pu·rate \ˈsəp-yə-ˌrāt\ vb **-rat·ed; -rat·ing** : to form or give off pus — **sup·pu·ra·tion** \ˌsəp-yə-ˈrā-shən\ n

su·pra \ˈsü-prə, -ˌprä\ adv : earlier in this writing : ABOVE

su·pra·na·tion·al \ˌsü-prə-ˈnash-(ə-)nəl, -ˌprä-\ adj : transcending national boundaries, authority, or interests (~ organizations)

su·prem·a·cist \sù-ˈprem-ə-səst\ n : an advocate of group supremacy

su·prem·a·cy \sù-ˈprem-ə-sē\ n, pl **-cies** : supreme rank, power, or authority

su·preme \sù-ˈprēm\ adj [L *supremus*, superl. of *superus* upper, fr. *super* over, above] **1** : highest in rank or authority **2** : highest in degree or quality (he is ~ among poets) **3** : ULTIMATE (the ~ sacrifice) syn superlative, surpassing, peerless, incomparable — **su·preme·ly** adv — **su·preme·ness** n

Supreme Being n : GOD 1

supt abbr superintendent

supvr abbr supervisor

sur·cease \ˈsər-ˌsēs\ n : CESSATION, RESPITE

¹**sur·charge** \ˈsər-ˌchärj\ vb **1** : to fill to excess : OVERLOAD **2** : to print or write a surcharge on (postage stamps)

²**surcharge** n **1** : an extra fee or cost **2** : an excessive load or burden **3** : something officially printed on a postage stamp to give it a new value or use

sur·cin·gle \ˈsər-ˌsiŋ-gəl\ n : a band passing around a horse's body to make something (as a saddle or pack) fast

¹**sure** \ˈshùr\ adj **sur·er; sur·est** [ME, fr. MF *sur*, fr. L *securus* secure] **1** : firmly established **2** : TRUSTWORTHY, RELIABLE **3** : CONFIDENT **4** : not to be disputed : UNDOUBTED **5** : bound to happen **6** : careful to remember or attend to something (be ~ to lock the door) syn certain, cocksure, positive — **sure·ly** adv — **sure·ness** n

²**sure** adv : SURELY

sure-fire \ˌshùr-ˈfī(ə)r\ adj : certain to get results : DEPENDABLE

sure·ty \ˈshùr-ət-ē\ n, pl **-ties 1** : SURENESS, CERTAINTY **2** : something that makes sure : GUARANTEE **3** : one who becomes a guarantor for another person syn security, bond, bail

¹**surf** \ˈsərf\ n : waves that break upon the shore; *also* : the sound or foam of breaking waves

²**surf** vb : to ride the surf (as on a surfboard) — **surf·er** n — **surf·ing** n

¹**sur·face** \ˈsər-fəs\ n **1** : the outside of an object or body **2** : outward aspect or appearance

²**surface** vb **sur·faced; sur·fac·ing 1** : to give a surface to : make smooth **2** : to rise to the surface

surf·board \ˈsərf-ˌbōrd\ n : a buoyant board used in riding the crests of waves

¹**sur·feit** \ˈsər-fət\ n **1** : EXCESS, SUPERABUNDANCE **2** : excessive indulgence (as in food or drink) **3** : disgust caused by excess (as in eating and drinking)

²**surfeit** vb : to feed, supply, or indulge to the point of surfeit : CLOY

surg abbr surgeon; surgery; surgical

¹**surge** \ˈsərj\ vb **surged; surg·ing 1** : to rise and fall actively : TOSS **2** : to

move in waves **3** : to rise suddenly to a high value

²**surge** *n* **1** : a sweeping onward like a wave of the sea ⟨a ∼ of emotion⟩ **2** : a large billow **3** : a transient sudden increase of current in an electrical circuit

sur·geon \ˈsər-jən\ *n* : a physician who specializes in surgery

sur·gery \ˈsərj-(ə-)rē\ *n, pl* **-ger·ies** [ME *surgerie,* fr. OF *cirurgie, surgerie,* fr. L *chirurgia,* fr. Gk *cheirourgia,* fr. *cheirourgos* surgeon, fr. *cheirourgos* working with the hand, fr. *cheir* hand + *ergon* work] **1** : a branch of medicine concerned with the correction of physical defects, the repair of injuries, and the treatment of disease esp. by operations **2** : a surgeon's operating room or laboratory **3** : work done by a surgeon

sur·gi·cal \ˈsər-ji-kəl\ *adj* : of, relating to, or associated with surgeons or surgery — **sur·gi·cal·ly** \-k(ə-)lē\ *adv*

sur·ly \ˈsər-lē\ *adj* **sur·li·er; -est** [alter. of ME *sirly* lordly, imperious, fr. *sir*] : ILL-NATURED, CRABBED **syn** morose, glum, sullen, sulky, gloomy — **sur·li·ness** *n*

sur·mise \sər-ˈmīz\ *vb* **sur·mised; sur·mis·ing** : GUESS **syn** conjecture, presume, suppose — **surmise** *n*

sur·mount \sər-ˈmaunt\ *vb* **1** : to rise superior to : OVERCOME **2** : to get to or lie at the top of **syn** conquer, lick, master

sur·name \ˈsər-ˌnām\ *n* **1** : NICKNAME **2** : the name borne in common by members of a family

sur·pass \sər-ˈpas\ *vb* **1** : to be superior to in quality, degree, or performance : EXCEL **2** : to be beyond the reach or powers of **syn** transcend, outdo, outstrip, exceed — **sur·pass·ing·ly** *adv*

sur·plice \ˈsər-pləs\ *n* : a loose white outer ecclesiastical vestment usu. of knee length with large open sleeves

sur·plus \ˈsər-(ˌ)pləs\ *n* **1** : quantity left over : EXCESS **2** : the excess of assets over liabilities **syn** superfluity, overabundance, surfeit

¹**sur·prise** \sə(r)-ˈprīz\ *n* **1** : an attack made without warning **2** : a taking unawares **3** : something that surprises **4** : AMAZEMENT, ASTONISHMENT

²**surprise** *also* **sur·prize** *vb* **sur·prised; sur·pris·ing 1** : to come upon and attack unexpectedly **2** : to take unawares **3** : AMAZE **4** : to effect or accomplish by means of a surprise **syn** astonish, astound, amaze, amaze, dumbfound — **sur·pris·ing** *adj* — **sur·pris·ing·ly** *adv*

sur·re·al·ism \sə-ˈrē-ə-ˌliz-əm\ *n* : art, literature, or theater characterized by fantastic or incongruous imagery or effects produced by unnatural juxtapositions and combinations — **sur·re·al·ist** \-ləst\ *n or adj* — **sur·re·al·is·tic** \sə-ˌrē-ə-ˈlis-tik\ *adj* — **sur·re·al·is·ti·cal·ly** \-ti-k(ə-)lē\ *adv*

¹**sur·ren·der** \sə-ˈren-dər\ *vb* **-dered; -der·ing** \-d(ə-)riŋ\ **1** : to yield to the power of another : give up under compulsion **2** : RELINQUISH

²**surrender** *n* : the act of giving up or yielding oneself or the possession of something to another **syn** submission, capitulation

sur·rep·ti·tious \ˌsər-əp-ˈtish-əs\ *adj* : done, made, or acquired by stealth : CLANDESTINE **syn** underhand, covert, furtive — **sur·rep·ti·tious·ly** *adv*

sur·rey \ˈsər-ē\ *n, pl* **surreys** : a 4-wheeled 2-seated horse-drawn carriage

sur·ro·gate \ˈsər-ə-ˌgāt, -gət\ *n* **1** : DEPUTY, SUBSTITUTE **2** : a law officer in some states with authority in the probate of wills, the settlement of estates, and the appointment of guardians

sur·round \sə-ˈraund\ *vb* **1** : to enclose on all sides : ENCIRCLE **2** : to enclose so as to cut off retreat or escape

sur·round·ings \sə-ˈraun-diŋz\ *n pl* : conditions by which one is surrounded

sur·tax \ˈsər-ˌtaks\ *n* : an additional tax over and above a normal tax

sur·tout \(ˌ)sər-ˈtü\ *n* [F, fr. *sur* over (fr. L *super*) + *tout* all, fr. L *totus* whole] : a man's long close-fitting overcoat

surv *abbr* survey; surveying; surveyor

sur·veil·lance \sər-ˈvā-ləns, -ˈvāl-yəns, -ˈvā-əns\ *n* [F] : close watch; *also* : SUPERVISION

¹**sur·vey** \sər-ˈvā\ *vb* **sur·veyed; sur·vey·ing 1** : to look over and examine closely **2** : to find and represent the contours, measurements, and position of a part of the earth's surface (as a tract of land) **3** : to view or study something as a whole **syn** scrutinize, examine, inspect, study — **sur·vey·or** \-ər\ *n*

²**sur·vey** \ˈsər-ˌvā\ *n, pl* **surveys** : the act or an instance of surveying; *also* : something that is surveyed

sur·vey·ing \sər-ˈvā-iŋ\ *n* : the branch of mathematics that teaches the art of making surveys

sur·vive \sər-ˈvīv\ *vb* **sur·vived; sur·viv·ing 1** : to remain alive or existent **2** : OUTLIVE, OUTLAST — **sur·viv·al** *n* — **sur·vi·vor** \-ˈvī-vər\ *n*

sus·cep·ti·ble \sə-ˈsep-tə-bəl\ *adj* **1** : of such a nature as to permit ⟨words ∼ of being misunderstood⟩ **2** : having little resistance to a stimulus or agency ⟨∼ to colds⟩ **3** : easily affected or emotionally moved : RESPONSIVE **syn** sensitive, subject, exposed, prone, liable, open — **sus·cep·ti·bil·i·ty** \-ˌsep-tə-ˈbil-ət-ē\ *n*

su·shi \ˈsü-shē\ *n* [Jp] : cold rice shaped into small cakes and topped or wrapped with garnishes (as of raw fish)

¹**sus·pect** \ˈsəs-ˌpekt, sə-ˈspekt\ *adj* : regarded with suspicion

²**sus·pect** \ˈsəs-ˌpekt\ *n* : one who is suspected (as of a crime)

³sus·pect \sə-'spekt\ *vb* **1** : to have doubts of : MISTRUST **2** : to imagine to be guilty without proof **3** : SURMISE

sus·pend \sə-'spend\ *vb* **1** : to bar temporarily from a privilege, office, or function **2** : to stop temporarily : make inactive for a time **3** : to withhold (judgment) for a time **4** : HANG; *esp* : to hang so as to be free except at one point; *also* : to keep from falling or sinking by some invisible support *syn* stay, postpone, defer

sus·pend·er \sə-'spen-dər\ *n* **1** : one of two supporting straps which pass over the shoulders and to which the trousers are fastened **2** *Brit* : a fastener attached to a garment or garter to hold up a stocking or sock

sus·pense \sə-'spens\ *n* **1** : SUSPENSION **2** : mental uncertainty : ANXIETY **3** : excitement as to an outcome — **sus·pense·ful** *adj*

sus·pen·sion \sə-'spen-chən\ *n* **1** : the act of suspending : the state or period of being suspended **2** : the state of a substance when its particles are mixed with but undissolved in a fluid or solid; *also* : a substance in this state **3** : something suspended **4** : a device by which something is suspended

sus·pen·so·ry \sə-'spens-(ə-)rē\ *adj* **1** : SUSPENDED; *also* : fitted or serving to suspend something **2** : temporarily leaving undetermined

sus·pi·cion \sə-'spish-ən\ *n* **1** : the act or an instance of suspecting something wrong without proof **2** : a slight trace *syn* mistrust, uncertainty, doubt, skepticism

sus·pi·cious \sə-'spish-əs\ *adj* **1** : open to or arousing suspicion **2** : inclined to suspect **3** : showing suspicion — **sus·pi·cious·ly** *adv*

sus·tain \sə-'stān\ *vb* **1** : to provide with nourishment **2** : to keep going : PROLONG (~ed effort) **3** : to hold up : PROP **4** : to hold up under : ENDURE **5** : SUFFER (~ a broken arm) **6** : to support as true, legal, or valid **7** : PROVE, CORROBORATE

sus·te·nance \'səs-tə-nəns\ *n* **1** : FOOD, NOURISHMENT **2** : a supplying with the necessities of life **3** : something that sustains or supports

su·ture \'sü-chər\ *n* **1** : material or a stitch for sewing a wound together **2** : a seam or line along which two things or parts are joined by or as if by sewing (the ~s of the skull)

su·zer·ain \'süz-(ə-)rən, -ə-₁rān\ *n* [F] **1** : a feudal lord **2** : a nation that has political control over another nation — **su·zer·ain·ty** \-tē\ *n*

svc *or* **svce** *abbr* service

svelte \'sfelt\ *adj* [F, fr. It *svelto*, fr. *svellere* to pluck out, modif. of L *evellere*, fr. *e-* out + *vellere* to pluck] : SLENDER, LITHE

svgs *abbr* savings

SW *abbr* **1** shortwave **2** southwest

¹swab \'swäb\ *n* **1** : MOP **2** : a wad of absorbent material esp. for applying medicine or for cleaning; *also* : a sample taken with a swab **3** : SAILOR

²swab *vb* **swabbed; swab·bing** : to use a swab on : MOP

swad·dle \'swäd-²l\ *vb* **swad·dled; swad·dling** \'swäd-(²-)liŋ\ **1** : to bind (an infant) in bands of cloth **2** : to wrap up : SWATHE

swaddling clothes *n pl* : bands of cloth wrapped around an infant

swag \'swag\ *n* : stolen goods : LOOT

swage \'swāj, 'swej\ *n* : a tool used by metal workers for shaping their work — **swage** *vb*

swag·ger \'swag-ər\ *vb* **swag·gered; swag·ger·ing** \-(ə-)riŋ\ **1** : to walk with a conceited swing or strut **2** : BOAST, BRAG — **swagger** *n*

Swa·hi·li \swä-'hē-lē\ *n, pl* **Swahili** *or* **Swahilis** : a language that is a trade and governmental language over much of East Africa and the Congo region

swain \'swān\ *n* [ME *swein* boy, servant, fr. ON *sveinn*] **1** : RUSTIC; *esp* : SHEPHERD **2** : ADMIRER, SUITOR

¹swal·low \'swäl-ō\ *n* : any of various small long-winged migratory birds that often have a deeply forked tail

²swallow *vb* **1** : to take into the stomach through the throat **2** : to envelop or take in as if by swallowing **3** : to accept or believe without question, protest, or anger

³swallow *n* **1** : an act of swallowing **2** : as much as can be swallowed at one time

swal·low·tail \'swäl-ō-₁tāl\ *n* **1** : a deeply forked and tapering tail like that of a swallow **2** : TAILCOAT **3** : any of various large butterflies with the border of the hind wing drawn out into a process resembling a tail — **swal·low·tailed** \₁swäl-ō-'tāld\ *adj*

swam *past of* SWIM

swa·mi \'swäm-ē\ *n* [Hindi *svāmī*, fr. Skt *svāmin* owner, lord] : a Hindu ascetic or religious teacher

¹swamp \'swämp\ *n* : wet spongy land — **swamp** *adj* — **swampy** *adj*

²swamp *vb* **1** : to fill or become filled with or as if with water **2** : OVERWHELM **3**

swamp·land \-₁land\ *n* : SWAMP

swan \'swän\ *n, pl* **swans** *also* **swan** : any of several heavy-bodied longnecked mostly pure white swimming birds related to the geese

¹swank \'swaŋk\ *or* **swanky** \'swaŋ-kē\ *adj* **swank·er** *or* **swank·i·er; -est** : showily smart and dashing; *also* : fashionably elegant

²swank *n* **1** : PRETENTIOUSNESS **2** : ELEGANCE

swans·down \'swänz-₁daùn\ *n* **1** : the very soft down of a swan used esp. for trimming or powder puffs **2** : a soft thick cotton flannel

swan song *n* : a farewell appearance, act, or pronouncement

swap \'swäp\ *vb* **swapped; swap·ping** : TRADE, EXCHANGE — **swap** *n*

sward \'sword\ *n* : the grassy surface of land

¹**swarm** \'sworm\ *n* **1** : a great number of honeybees leaving together from a hive with a queen to start a new colony; *also* : a hive of bees **2** : a large crowd

²**swarm** *vb* **1** : to form in a swarm and depart from a hive **2** : to throng together : gather in great numbers

swart \'swort\ *adj* : SWARTHY

swar·thy \'swor-thē, -thē\ *adj* **swar·thi·er; -est** : dark in color or complexion : dark-skinned

swash \'swäsh\ *vb* : to move about with a splashing sound — **swash** *n*

swash·buck·ler \-,bək-lər\ *n* : a boasting blustering soldier or daredevil — **swash·buck·ling** \-,bək-(ə-)liŋ\ *adj*

swas·ti·ka \'swäs-ti-kə, swä-'stē-\ *n* [Skt *svastika*, fr. *svasti* welfare, fr. *su-* well + *asti* he is] : a symbol or ornament in the form of a cross with the ends of the arms bent at right angles

swat \'swät\ *vb* **swat·ted; swat·ting** : to hit sharply (~ a fly) (~ a ball) — **swat** *n* — **swat·ter** *n*

SWAT *abbr* Special Weapons and Tactics

swatch \'swäch\ *n* : a sample piece (as of fabric) or a collection of samples

swath \'swäth, 'swoth\ *or* **swathe** \'swäth, 'swoth, 'swäth\ *n* [ME, fr. OE *swæth* footstep, trace] **1** : a row of cut grass or grain **2** : the sweep of a scythe or mowing machine or the path cut in mowing

swathe \'swäth, 'swoth, 'swäth\ *vb* **swathed; swath·ing** : to bind or wrap with or as if with a bandage

¹**sway** \'swä\ *n* **1** : a gentle swinging from side to side **2** : a controlling influence **3** : sovereign power : DOMINION

²**sway** *vb* **1** : to swing gently from side to side **2** : RULE, GOVERN **3** : to cause to swing from side to side **4** : BEND, SWERVE; *also* : INFLUENCE **syn** oscillate, fluctuate, vibrate, waver

sway·back \'swä-'bak, -,bak\ *n* : a sagging of the back found esp. in horses — **sway·backed** \-'bakt\ *adj*

swear \'swaər\ *vb* **swore** \'swōr\ ; **sworn** \'swōrn\ ; **swear·ing 1** : to make a solemn statement or promise under oath : vow **2** : to assert emphatically as true with an appeal to God or one's honor **3** : to administer an oath to : to charge or confirm under oath; *also* : to bind by or as if by an oath **5** : to use profane or obscene language — **swear·er** *n*

swear in *vb* : to induct into office by administration of an oath

¹**sweat** \'swet\ *vb* **sweat** *or* **sweat·ed; sweat·ing 1** : to excrete salty moisture from glands of the skin : PERSPIRE **2**

: to form drops of moisture on the surface **3** : to work so that one sweats : TOIL **4** : to cause to sweat **5** : to draw out or get rid of by perspiring **6** : to make a person overwork

²**sweat** *n* **1** : perceptible liquid exuded through pores from glands (**sweat glands**) of the skin : PERSPIRATION **2** : moisture issuing from or gathering on the surface in drops — **sweaty** *adj*

sweat·er \'swet-ər\ *n* **1** : one that sweats **2** : a knitted or crocheted jacket or pullover

sweat·shop \'swet-,shäp\ *n* : a shop or factory in which workers are employed for long hours at low wages and under unhealthy conditions

Swed *abbr* Sweden; Swedish

swede \'swēd\ *n* **1** *cap* : a native or inhabitant of Sweden **2** : RUTABAGA

Swed·ish \'swēd-ish\ *n* **1** : the language of Sweden **2** *Swedish pl* : the people of Sweden — **Swedish** *adj*

¹**sweep** \'swēp\ *vb* **swept** \'swept\ ; **sweep·ing 1** : to remove or clean by brushing **2** : to remove or destroy by vigorous continuous action **3** : to strip or clear by gusts of wind or rain **4** : to move over with speed and force (the tide *swept* over the shore) **5** : to gather in with a single swift movement **6** : to move or extend in a wide curve — **sweep·er** *n* — **sweep·ing** *adj*

²**sweep** *n* **1** : something (as a long oar) that operates with a sweeping motion **2** : a clearing off or away **3** : a winning of all the contests or prizes in a competition **4** : a sweeping movement (~ of a scythe) **5** : CURVE, BEND **6** : RANGE, SCOPE

sweep·ing *n* **1** : the act or action of one that sweeps **2** *pl* : things collected by sweeping : REFUSE

sweep-sec·ond \'swēp-,sek-ənd\ *n* : a hand marking seconds on a timepiece

sweep·stakes \'swēp-,stāks\ *also* **sweep·stake** \-,stāk\ *n, pl* **sweepstakes 1** : a race or contest in which the entire prize may go to the winner; *esp* : a horse race in which the stakes are contributed at least in part by the owners of the horses **2** : any of various lotteries

¹**sweet** \'swēt\ *adj* **1** : being or causing the one of the four basic taste sensations that is caused esp. by table sugar and is identified esp. by the taste buds at the front of the tongue; *also* : pleasing to the taste **2** : KINDLY, MILD **3** : pleasing to a sense other than taste (a ~ smell) (~ music) **4** : not stale or spoiled : WHOLESOME (~ milk) **5** : not salted (~ butter) — **sweet·ish** *adj* — **sweet·ly** *adv* — **sweet·ness** *n*

²**sweet** *n* **1** : something sweet : CANDY **2** : DARLING

sweet·bread \'swēt-,bred\ *n* : the pancreas or thymus of an animal (as a calf or lamb) used for food

sweet·bri·er *also* **sweet·bri·ar** \-,brī(-ə)r\

n : a thorny European rose with fragrant white to deep pink flowers

sweet clover *n* : any of a genus of erect legumes widely grown for soil improvement or hay

sweet corn *n* : an Indian corn with kernels rich in sugar and cooked as a vegetable while immature

sweet·en \'swēt-²n\ *vb* **sweet·ened; sweet·en·ing** \'swēt-(²-)niŋ\ : to make sweet — **sweet·en·er** \'swēt-(²-)nər\ *n* — **sweet·en·ing** *n*

sweet fern *n* : a small No. American shrub with sweet-scented or aromatic leaves

sweet·heart \'swēt-ˌhärt\ *n* : one who is loved

sweet·meat \'swēt-ˌmēt\ *n* : CANDY

sweet pea *n* : a garden plant of the legume family with climbing stems and fragrant flowers of many colors; *also* : its flower

sweet pepper *n* : a large mild thick-walled fruit of a pepper; *also* : a plant related to the potato that bears sweet peppers

sweet potato *n* : a tropical vine related to the morning glory; *also* : its sweet yellow edible root

sweet–talk \'swēt-ˌtȯk\ *vb* : FLATTER, COAX — **sweet talk** *n*

sweet tooth *n* : a craving or fondness for sweet food

sweet wil·liam \swēt-'wil-yəm\ *n*, *often cap W* : a widely cultivated Eurasian pink with small white to deep red or purple flowers often showily spotted, banded, or mottled

¹**swell** \'swel\ *vb* **swelled; swelled** *or* **swollen** \'swō-lən\ ; **swell·ing 1** : to grow big or make bigger **2** : to expand or distend abnormally or excessively (a *swollen* joint); *also* : BULGE **3** : to fill or be filled with emotion (as pride) *syn* expand, amplify, distend, inflate, dilate — **swell·ing** *n*

²**swell** *n* **1** : a long crestless wave or series of waves in the open sea **2** : sudden or gradual increase in size or value **3** : a person dressed in the height of fashion; *also* : a person of high social position or outstanding competence

³**swell** *adj* **1** : FASHIONABLE, STYLISH; *also* : socially prominent **2** : EXCELLENT, FIRST-RATE

swelled head *n* : an exaggerated opinion of oneself : SELF-CONCEIT

swell·head \'swel-ˌhed\ *n* : one who has a swelled head — **swell·head·ed** \-'hed-əd\ *adj*

swel·ter \'swel-tər\ *vb* **swel·tered; swel·ter·ing** \-t(ə-)riŋ\ [ME *sweltren*, fr. *swelten* to die, be overcome by heat, fr. OE *sweltan* to die] : to be faint or oppressed with the heat

swept *past and past part of* SWEEP

swerve \'swərv\ *vb* **swerved; swerv·ing** : to move abruptly aside from a straight line or course *syn* digress, deviate, diverge — **swerve** *n*

¹**swift** \'swift\ *adj* **1** : moving or capable

of moving with great speed **2** : occurring suddenly **3** : READY, ALERT — **swift·ly** *adv* — **swift·ness** \'swif(t)-nəs\ *n*

²**swift** *n* : any of numerous small insect-eating birds with long narrow wings

swig \'swig\ *vb* **swigged; swig·ging** : to drink in long drafts — **swig** *n*

¹**swill** \'swil\ *vb* **1** : to swallow greedily : GUZZLE **2** : to feed (as hogs) on swill

²**swill** *n* **1** : food for animals composed of edible refuse mixed with liquid **2** : GARBAGE

¹**swim** \'swim\ *vb* **swam** \'swam\ ; **swum** \'swəm\ ; **swim·ming 1** : to propel oneself along in water by natural means (as by hands and legs, by tail, or by fins) **2** : to glide smoothly along **3** : FLOAT **4** : to be covered with or as if with a liquid **5** : to be dizzy (his head *swam*) **6** : to cross or go over by swimming — **swim·mer** *n*

²**swim** *n* **1** : an act of swimming **2** : the main current of activity or fashion (in the social ~)

swim·ming \'swim-iŋ\ *n* : the action, art, or sport of swimming and diving

swimming pool *n* : a tank of concrete or plastic designed for swimming

swim·suit \'swim-ˌsüt\ *n* : a suit for swimming or bathing

swin·dle \'swin-d²l\ *vb* **swin·dled; swin·dling** \-(d²)liŋ, -d²l-iŋ\ [fr. *swindler*, fr. G *schwindler* giddy person, fr. *schwindeln* to be dizzy] : CHEAT, DEFRAUD — **swindle** *n* — **swin·dler** \-d(²-)lər\ *n*

swine \'swīn\ *n*, *pl* **swine 1** : any of a family of stout short-legged hoofed mammals with bristly skin and a long flexible snout; *esp* : one widely raised as a meat animal **2** : a contemptible person — **swin·ish** \'swī-nish\ *adj*

¹**swing** \'swiŋ\ *vb* **swung** \'swəŋ\ ; **swing·ing** \'swiŋ-iŋ\ **1** : to move rapidly in an arc **2** : to sway or cause to sway back and forth **3** : to hang so as to move freely back and forth or in a curve **4** : to be executed by hanging **5** : to move or turn on a hinge or pivot **6** : to manage or handle successfully **7** : to march or walk with free swaying movements **8** : to have a steady pulsing rhythm **9** : to be lively and up-to-date; *also* : to engage freely in sex *syn* wield, manipulate, ply, maneuver — **swing·er** *n* — **swing·ing** *adj*

²**swing** *n* **1** : the act of swinging **2** : a swinging blow, movement, or rhythm **3** : the distance through which something swings : FLUCTUATION **4** : a seat suspended by a rope or chain for swinging back and forth for pleasure **5** : jazz music played esp. by a large band and marked by a steady lively rhythm, simple harmony, and a basic melody often submerged in improvisation — **swing** *adj*

swing–by \'swiŋ-ˌbī\ *n*, *pl* **swing–bys** : an interplanetary mission in which a spacecraft uses the gravitational field of a planet near which it passes for changing course

¹swipe \'swīp\ *vb* **swiped; swip·ing 1 :** to strike or wipe with a sweeping motion **2 :** PILFER, SNATCH

²swipe *n* **:** a strong sweeping blow

swirl \'swərl\ *vb* **:** EDDY — **swirl** *n*

swish \'swish\ *n* **1 :** a prolonged hissing sound **2 :** a light sweeping or brushing sound — **swish** *vb*

Swiss \'swis\ *n* **1** *pl* **Swiss :** a native or inhabitant of Switzerland **2 :** a hard cheese with large holes

Swiss chard *n* **:** CHARD

¹switch \'swich\ *n* **1 :** a slender flexible whip, rod, or twig **2 :** a blow with a switch **3 :** a shift from one thing to another **4 :** a device for adjusting the rails of a track so that a locomotive or train may be turned from one track to another; *also* **:** a railroad siding **5 :** a device for making, breaking, or changing the connections in an electrical circuit **6 :** a heavy strand of hair often used in addition to a person's own hair for some coiffures

²switch *vb* **1 :** to punish or urge on with a switch **2 :** WHISK ⟨a cow ~ing her tail⟩ **3 :** to shift or turn by operating a switch **4 :** CHANGE, EXCHANGE

switch·back \'swich-,bak\ *n* **:** a zig-zag road or arrangement of railroad tracks for climbing a steep grade

switch·blade \-,blād\ *n* **:** a pocket-knife with a spring-operated blade

switch·board \-,bōrd\ *n* **:** a panel on which is mounted a group of electric switches so arranged that a number of circuits may be connected, combined, and controlled

switch·hit·ter \-'hit-ər\ *n* **:** a baseball player who bats either right-handed or left-handed — **switch·hit** \-'hit\ *vb*

switch·man \'swich-mən\ *n* **:** one who attends a railroad switch

Switz *abbr* Switzerland

¹swiv·el \'swiv-əl\ *n* **:** a device joining two parts so that one or both can turn freely

²swivel *vb* **-eled** *or* **-elled; -el·ing** *or* **-el·ling** \-(ə-)liŋ\ **:** to swing or turn on or as if on a swivel

swiz·zle stick \'swiz-əl-\ *n* **:** a stick used to stir mixed drinks

swollen *past part of* SWELL

swoon \'swün\ *vb* **:** FAINT — **swoon** *n*

swoop \'swüp\ *vb* **:** to descend or pounce swiftly like a hawk on its prey — **swoop** *n*

sword \'sōrd\ *n* **1 :** a weapon with a long pointed blade and sharp cutting edges **2 :** the use of force

sword·fish \-,fish\ *n* **:** a very large ocean food fish with the bones of the upper jaw prolonged in a long sword-like beak

sword·play \-,plā\ *n* **:** the art or skill of wielding a sword

swords·man \'sōrdz-mən\ *n* **:** one

skilled in wielding a sword; *esp* **:** FENCER

sword·tail \'sōrd-,tāl\ *n* **:** a small brightly marked Central American fish

swore *past of* SWEAR

sworn *past part of* SWEAR

swum *past part of* SWIM

swung *past and past part of* SWING

syb·a·rite \'sib-ə-,rīt\ *n* **:** a lover of luxury **:** VOLUPTUARY

syc·a·more \'sik-ə-,mōr\ *n* **1 :** a Eurasian maple with yellowish green flowers widely planted as a shade tree **2 :** a large spreading tree of eastern and central No. America that has light brown flaky bark and small round fruits hanging on long stalks

sy·co·phant \'sik-ə-fənt\ *n* **:** a servile flatterer — **syc·o·phan·tic** \,sik-ə-'fant-ik\ *adj*

syl *or* **syll** *abbr* syllable

sy·li \'sē-lē\ *n, pl* **sylis** — see MONEY table

syl·lab·i·ca·tion \sə-,lab-ə-'kā-shən\ *n* **:** the dividing of words into syllables

syl·lab·i·fy \sə-'lab-ə-,fī\ *vb* **-fied; -fy·ing :** to form or divide into syllables — **syl·lab·i·fi·ca·tion** \-,lab-ə-fə-'kā-shən\ *n*

syl·la·ble \'sil-ə-bəl\ *n* [ME, fr. MF *sillabe*, fr. L *syllaba*, fr. Gk *syllabē*, fr. *syllambanein* to gather together, fr. *syn* with + *lambanein* to take] **:** a unit of spoken language consisting of an uninterrupted utterance and forming either a whole word (as *cat*) or a commonly recognized division of a word (as *syl* in *syl-la-ble*); *also* **:** one or more letters representing such a unit — **syl·lab·ic** \sə-'lab-ik\ *adj*

syl·la·bus \'sil-ə-bəs\ *n, pl* **-bi** \-,bī\ *or* **-bus·es :** a summary containing the heads or main topics of a speech, book, or course of study

syl·lo·gism \'sil-ə-,jiz-əm\ *n* **:** a logical scheme of a formal argument consisting of a major and a minor premise and a conclusion which must logically be true if the premises are true — **syl·lo·gis·tic** \,sil-ə-'jis-tik\ *adj*

sylph \'silf\ *n* **1 :** an imaginary being inhabiting the air **2 :** a slender graceful woman

syl·van \'sil-vən\ *adj* **1 :** living or located in a wooded area; *also* **:** of, relating to, or characteristic of forest **2 :** abounding in woods or trees **:** WOODED

sym *abbr* **1** symbol **2** symmetrical

sym·bi·o·sis \,sim-,bī-'ō-səs, -bē-\ *n, pl* **-o·ses** \-,sēz\ **:** the living together in close association of two dissimilar organisms esp. when mutually beneficial — **sym·bi·ot·ic** \-'ät-ik\ *adj*

sym·bol \'sim-bəl\ *n* **1 :** something that stands for something else; *esp* **:** something concrete that represents or suggests another thing that cannot in itself be pictured ⟨the lion is a ~ of bravery⟩ **2 :** a letter, character, or sign used in writing or printing relating to a particular field (as mathematics or music) to represent operations, quantities, elements, sounds, or other ideas — **sym·bol·ic** \sim-'bäl-ik\ *also* **sym·bol·i·cal** \-i-kəl\ *adj* — **sym·bol·i·cal·ly** \-k(ə-)lē\ *adv*

sym·bol·ism \'sim-bə-,liz-əm\ *n* : representation of abstract or intangible things by means of symbols or emblems

sym·bol·ize \'sim-bə-,līz\ *vb* **-ized; -iz·ing** 1 : to serve as a symbol of 2 : to represent by symbols — **sym·bol·iza·tion** \,sim-bə-lə-'zā-shən\ *n*

sym·me·try \'sim-ə-trē\ *n, pl* **-tries** 1 : an arrangement marked by regularity and balanced proportions 2 : correspondence in size, shape, and position of parts that are on opposite sides of a dividing line or center syn proportion, balance, harmony — **sym·met·ri·cal** \sə-'me-tri-kəl\ *or* **sym·met·ric** \sə-'me-trik\ *adj* — **sym·met·ri·cal·ly** \-k(ə-)lē\ *adv*

sympathetic nervous system *n* : the part of the autonomic nervous system that is concerned esp. with preparing the body to react to situations of stress or emergency and that tends to depress secretion, decrease the tone and contractility of muscle not under direct voluntary control, and cause the contraction of blood vessels

sym·pa·thize \'sim-pə-,thīz\ *vb* **-thized; -thiz·ing** : to feel or show sympathy — **sym·pa·thiz·er** *n*

sym·pa·thy \'sim-pə-thē\ *n, pl* **-thies** 1 : a relationship between persons or things wherein whatever affects one similarly affects the others 2 : harmony of interests and aims 3 : FAVOR, SUPPORT 4 : the capacity for entering into and sharing the feelings or interests of another; *also* : COMPASSION, PITY 5 : an expression of sorrow for another's loss, grief, or misfortune — **sym·pa·thet·ic** \,sim-pə-'thet-ik\ *adj* — **sym·pa·thet·i·cal·ly** \-i-k(ə-)lē\ *adv*

sym·pho·ny \'sim-fə-nē\ *n, pl* **-nies** 1 : harmony of sounds 2 : a large and complex composition for a full orchestra 3 : a large orchestra of a kind that plays symphonies — **sym·phon·ic** \sim-'fän-ik\ *adj*

sym·po·sium \sim-'pō-zē-əm\ *n, pl* **-sia** \-zē-ə\ *or* **-siums** [L, fr. Gk *symposion*, fr. *sympinein* to drink together, fr. *syn-* together + *pinein* to drink] : a conference at which a particular topic is discussed by various speakers; *also* : a collection of opinions about a subject

symp·tom \'simp-təm\ *n* 1 : a change in an organism indicative of disease or abnormality; *esp* : one (as a headache) that can be sensed only by the individual affected 2 : SIGN, INDICATION — **symp·tom·at·ic** \,simp-tə-'mat-ik\ *adj*

syn *abbr* synonym; synonymous; synonymy

syn·a·gogue *or* **syn·a·gog** \'sin-ə-,gäg\ *n* [ME *synagoge*, fr. OF, fr. LL *synagoga*, fr. Gk *synagōgē* assembly, synagogue, fr. *synagein* to bring together] 1 : a Jewish congregation 2 : the house of worship of a Jewish congregation

syn·apse \'sin-,aps, sə-'naps\ *n* : the point at which a nervous impulse passes from one neuron to another

¹**sync** *also* **synch** \'siŋk\ *vb* **synced** *also* **synched** \'siŋkt\ ; **sync·ing** *also* **synch·ing** \'siŋ-kiŋ\ : SYNCHRONIZE

²**sync** *also* **synch** *n* : SYNCHRONIZATION, SYNCHRONISM — **sync** *adj*

syn·chro·mesh \'siŋ-krō-,mesh, 'sin-\ *adj* : designed for effecting synchronized shifting of gears — **synchromesh** *n*

syn·chro·nize \'siŋ-krə-,nīz, 'sin-\ *vb* **-nized; -niz·ing** 1 : to occur or cause to occur at the same instant 2 : to represent, arrange, or tabulate according to dates or time 3 : to cause to agree in time 4 : to make synchronous in operation — **syn·chro·nism** \-,niz-əm\ *n* — **syn·chro·ni·za·tion** \,siŋ-krə-nə-'zā-shən, ,sin-\ *n* — **syn·chro·niz·er** \'siŋ-krə-,nī-zər, 'sin-\ *n*

syn·chro·nous \'siŋ-krə-nəs, 'sin-\ *adj* 1 : happening at the same time : CONCURRENT 2 : working, moving, or occurring together at the same rate and at the proper time

syn·co·pa·tion \,siŋ-kə-'pā-shən, ,sin-\ *n* : a shifting of the regular musical accent : occurrence of accented notes on the weak beat — **syn·co·pate** \'siŋ-kə-,pāt, 'sin-\ *vb*

syn·co·pe \'siŋ-kə-(,)pē, 'sin-\ *n* : the loss of one or more sounds or letters in the interior of a word (as in *fo'c'sle* from *forecastle*)

¹**syn·di·cate** \'sin-di-kət\ *n* 1 : a group of persons who combine to carry out a financial or industrial undertaking 2 : a business concern that sells materials for publication in many newspapers and periodicals at the same time

²**syn·di·cate** \-də-,kāt\ *vb* **-cat·ed; -cat·ing** 1 : to combine into or manage as a syndicate 2 : to publish through a syndicate — **syn·di·ca·tion** \,sin-də-'kā-shən\ *n*

syn·drome \'sin-,drōm\ *n* : a group of signs and symptoms that occur together and characterize a particular abnormality

syn·er·gism \'sin-ər-,jiz-əm\ *n* : interaction of discrete agencies (as industrial firms) or agents (as drugs) such that the total effect is greater than the sum of the individual effects — **syn·er·gist** \-jəst\ *n* — **syn·er·gis·tic** \-'jis-tik\ *adj* — **syn·er·gis·ti·cal·ly** \-ti-k(ə-)lē\ *adv*

syn·fuel \'sin-,fyül\ *n* [*synthetic*] : a fuel derived from a fossil fuel or from fermentation (as of grain)

syn·od \'sin-əd\ *n* : COUNCIL, ASSEMBLY; *esp* : a religious governing body — **syn·od·al** \-əd-²l, -,äd-²l\ *adj* **syn·od·ic**

\-ik\ *or* syn·od·i·cal \sə-ˈnäd-i-kəl\ *adj*

syn·onym \ˈsin-ə-ˌnim\ *n* : one of two or more words in the same language which have the same or very nearly the same meaning — syn·on·y·mous \sə-ˈnän-ə-məs\ *adj* — syn·on·y·my \-mē\ *n*

syn·op·sis \sə-ˈnäp-səs\ *n, pl* -op·ses \-ˌsēz\ : a condensed statement or outline (as of a treatise) : ABSTRACT

syn·op·tic \sə-ˈnäp-tik\ *also* syn·op·ti·cal \-ti-kəl\ *adj* : characterized by or affording a comprehensive view

syn·tax\ˈsin-ˌtaks\ *n* : the way in which words are put together to form phrases, clauses, or sentences — syn·tac·tic \sin-ˈtak-tik\ *or* syn·tac·ti·cal \-ti-kəl\ *adj*

syn·the·sis \ˈsin-thə-səs\ *n, pl* -the·ses \-ˌsēz\ : the combination of parts or elements into a whole; *esp* : the production of a substance by union of chemically simpler substances — syn·the·size \-ˌsīz\ *vb* — syn·the·siz·er *n*

syn·thet·ic \sin-ˈthet-ik\ *adj* : produced artificially esp. by chemical means; *also* : not genuine — synthetic *n* — syn·thet·i·cal·ly \-i-k(ə-)lē\ *adv*

syph·i·lis \ˈsif-ə-)ləs\ *n* [NL, fr. poem *Syphilis sive Morbus Gallicus* (*Syphilis or the French disease*) (1530) by Girolamo Fracastoro †1553 Ital. physician] : a destructive contagious venereal disease caused by a spirochete — syph·i·lit·ic \ˌsif-ə-ˈlit-ik\ *adj or n*

sy·phon *var of* SIPHON

¹sy·ringe \sə-ˈrinj, ˈsir-inj\ *n* : a device used esp. for injecting liquids into or withdrawing them from the body

²syringe *vb* sy·ringed; sy·ring·ing : to inject or cleanse with or as if with a syringe

syr·up \ˈsər-əp, ˈsir-əp\ *n* 1 : a thick sticky solution of sugar and water often flavored or medicated 2 : the con-

centrated juice of a fruit or plant — syr·upy *adj*

syst *abbr* system

sys·tem \ˈsis-təm\ *n* 1 : a group of units so combined as to form a whole and to operate in unison 2 : the body as a functioning whole; *also* : a group of bodily organs (as the nervous system) that together carry on some vital function 3 : a definite scheme or method of procedure or classification 4 : regular method or order — sys·tem·at·ic \ˌsis-tə-ˈmat-ik\ *also* sys·tem·at·i·cal \-i-kəl\ *adj* — sys·tem·at·i·cal·ly \-k(ə-)lē\ *adv*

sys·tem·atize \ˈsis-tə-mə-ˌtīz\ *vb* -atized; -atiz·ing : to make into a system : arrange methodically

¹sys·tem·ic \sis-ˈtem-ik\ *adj* 1 : of, relating to, or affecting the whole body (~ disease) 2 : acting through the bodily systems after absorption or ingestion by making the organism toxic to a pest (as a mite or insect)

²systemic *n* : a systemic pesticide

systemic lupus erythematosus *n* : a disease characterized by fever, skin rash, and arthritis, often by anemia, by small hemorrhages of the skin and mucous membranes, and in serious cases by involvement of various internal organs

sys·tem·ize \ˈsis-tə-ˌmīz\ *vb* -ized; -izing : SYSTEMATIZE

systems analyst *n* : a person who studies a procedure or business to determine its goals or purposes and to discover the best ways to accomplish them — systems analysis *n*

sys·to·le \ˈsis-tə-(ˌ)lē\ *n* : a rhythmically recurrent contraction esp. of the heart — sys·tol·ic \sis-ˈtäl-ik\ *adj*

Szech·uan *or* Szech·wan \ˈsech-ˌwän\ *adj* : of, relating to, or being a style of Chinese cooking that is spicy, oily, and esp. peppery

T

¹t \ˈtē\ *n, pl* t's *or* ts \ˈtēz\ *often cap* : the 20th letter of the English alphabet

²t *abbr, often cap* 1 tablespoon 2 teaspoon 3 temperature 4 ton 5 transitive 6 troy 7 true

Ta *symbol* tantalum

TA *abbr* teaching assistant

¹tab \ˈtab\ *n* 1 : a short projecting flap, loop, or tag; *also* : a small insert or addition 2 : close surveillance : WATCH (keep ~s on him) 3 : BILL, CHECK

²tab *vb* tabbed; tab·bing : DESIGNATE

tab·bou·leh \tə-ˈbü-lə\ *n* [Ar] : a salad consisting chiefly of wheat, tomatoes, parsley, mint, onions, lemon juice, and olive oil

tab·by \ˈtab-ē\ *n, pl* tabbies : a usu. striped or mottled domestic cat; *also* : a female domestic cat

tab·er·na·cle \ˈtab-ər-ˌnak-əl\ *n* [deriv. of L *taberna* hut] 1 *often cap* : a tent sanctuary used by the Israelites during the Exodus 2 : a receptacle for the consecrated elements of the Eucharist 3 : a house of worship

¹ta·ble \ˈtā-bəl\ *n* 1 : a flat slab or plaque : TABLET 2 : a piece of furniture consisting of a smooth flat slab fixed on legs 3 : a supply of food : BOARD, FARE 4 : a group of people assembled at or as if at a table 5 : a systematic arrangement of data for ready reference 6 : a condensed enumeration — ta·ble·top \-ˌtäp\ *n*

²table *vb* ta·bled; ta·bling \-b(ə-)liŋ\ 1 *Brit* : to place on the agenda 2 : to remove (a parliamentary motion) from consideration indefinitely

tab·leau \ˈtab-ˌlō\ *n, pl* tab·leaux \-ˌlōz\

also **tableaus** [F] **1** : a graphic description : PICTURE **2** : a striking or artistic grouping **3** : a static depiction of a scene usu. presented on a stage by costumed participants

ta·ble·cloth \'tā-bəl-ˌklȯth\ *n* : a covering spread over a dining table before the table is set

ta·ble d'hôte \ˌtäb-əl-ˈdōt\ *n* [F, lit., host's table] : a complete meal of several courses offered at a fixed price

ta·ble·land \'tā-bəl-ˌ(l)and\ *n* : PLATEAU

ta·ble·spoon \-ˌspün\ *n* **1** : a large spoon used esp. for serving **2** : TABLESPOONFUL

ta·ble·spoon·ful \'tā-bəl-ˌspün-ˌfùl\ *n, pl* **-spoonfuls** \-ˌfùlz\ *also* **-spoons·ful** \-ˌspünz-fùl\ : a unit of measure equal to one half fluidounce

tab·let \'tab-lət\ *n* **1** : a flat slab suited for or bearing an inscription **2** : a collection of sheets of paper glued together at one edge **3** : a compressed or molded block of material; *esp* : a usu. disk-shaped medicated mass

table tennis *n* : a game resembling tennis played on a tabletop with wooden paddles and a small hollow plastic ball

ta·ble·ware \'tā-bəl-ˌwaȯr\ *n* : utensils (as of china or silver) for table use

¹**tab·loid** \'tab-ˌlȯid\ *adj* : condensed into small scope

²**tabloid** *n* : a newspaper marked by small pages, condensation of the news, and usu. many photographs; *esp* : one characterized by sensationalism

¹**ta·boo** *also* **ta·bu** \tə-ˈbü, ta-\ *adj* [fr. Tongan, a Polynesian language] **1** : set apart as charged with a dangerous supernatural power : INVIOLABLE **2** : banned esp. as immoral or dangerous

²**taboo** *also* **tabu** *n, pl* **taboos** *also* **tabus 1** : a prohibition against touching, saying, or doing something for fear of immediate harm from a mysterious superhuman force **2** : a prohibition imposed by social usage or as a protection

ta·bor *also* **ta·bour** \'tā-bər\ *n* : a small drum used to accompany a pipe or fife played by the same person

tab·u·lar \'tab-yə-lər\ *adj* **1** : having a flat surface **2** : arranged in a table; *esp* : set up in rows and columns **3** : computed by means of a table

tab·u·late \-ˌlāt\ *vb* **-lat·ed; -lat·ing** : to put into tabular form — **tab·u·la·tion** \ˌtab-yə-ˈlā-shən\ *n* — **tab·u·la·tor** \'tab-yə-ˌlāt-ər\ *n*

TAC \'tak\ *abbr* Tactical Air Command

tach \'tak\ *n* : TACHOMETER

ta·chom·e·ter \ta-ˈkäm-ət-ər, tə-\ *n* [deriv. of Gk *tachys* rapid] : a device to indicate speed of rotation

tachy·car·dia \ˌtak-i-ˈkärd-ē-ə\ *n* : rapid heart action

tachy·on \'tak-ē-ˌän\ *n* : a hypothetical particle held to travel faster than light

tac·it \'tas-ət\ *adj* [F or L; F *tacite*, fr. L *tacitus* silent, fr. *tacēre* to be silent] **1** : expressed without words or speech **2** : implied or indicated but not actually expressed (~ consent) — **tac·it·ly** *adv* — **tac·it·ness** *n*

tac·i·turn \'tas-ə-ˌtərn\ *adj* : disinclined to talk : habitually silent syn uncommunicative, reserved, reticent, closemouthed — **tac·i·tur·ni·ty** \ˌtas-ə-ˈtər-nət-ē\ *n*

¹**tack** \'tak\ *vb* **1** : to fasten with tacks; *also* : to add on **2** : to change the direction of (a sailing ship) from one tack to another **3** : to follow a zigzag course

²**tack** *n* **1** : a small sharp nail with a broad flat head **2** : the direction a ship is sailing as shown by the way the sails are trimmed; *also* : the run of a ship on one tack **3** : a change of course from one tack to another **4** : a zigzag course **5** : a course of action

³**tack** *n* : gear for harnessing a horse

tack·le \'tak-əl, *naut often* 'tāk-\ *n* **1** : GEAR, APPARATUS, EQUIPMENT **2** : the rigging of a ship **3** : an arrangement of ropes and pulleys for hoisting or pulling heavy objects **4** : the act or an instance of tackling; *also* : a football lineman playing between guard and end

²**tackle** *vb* **tack·led; tack·ling** \-(ə-)liŋ\ **1** : to attach and secure with or as if with tackle **2** : to seize, grapple with, or throw down with the intention of subduing or stopping **3** : to set about dealing with (~ a problem)

¹**tacky** \'tak-ē\ *adj* **tack·i·er; -est** : sticky to the touch

²**tacky** *adj* **tack·i·er; -est 1** : SHABBY, SEEDY **2** : marked by lack of style or good taste; *also* : cheaply showy : GAUDY

ta·co \'täk-ō\ *n, pl* **tacos** \-ōz, -ōs\ [MexSp] : a tortilla rolled up with or folded over a filling

tact \'takt\ *n* [F, sense of touch, fr. L *tactus*, fr. *tactus*, pp. of *tangere* to touch] : a keen sense of what to do or say to keep good relations with others — **tact·ful** \-fəl\ *adj* — **tact·ful·ly** \-ē\ *adv* — **tact·less** *adj* — **tact·less·ly** *adv*

tac·tic \'tak-tik\ *n* : a planned action for accomplishing an end

tac·tics \'tak-tiks\ *n sing or pl* **1** : the science of maneuvering forces in combat **2** : the skill of using available means to reach an end — **tac·ti·cal** \-ti-kəl\ *adj* — **tac·ti·cian** \tak-ˈtish-ən\ *n*

tac·tile \'tak-təl, -ˌtīl\ *adj* : of, relating to, or perceptible through the sense of touch

tad·pole \'tad-ˌpōl\ *n* [ME *taddepol*, fr. *tode* toad + *polle* head] : an aquatic larva of a frog or toad that has a tail and gills

tae kwon do \'tī-ˈkwän-ˈdō\ *n* : a Korean martial art resembling karate

taf·fe·ta \'taf-ət-ə\ *n* : a crisp lustrous fabric (as of silk or rayon)

taff·rail \\'taf-,rāl, -rəl\\ *n* : the rail around a ship's stern

taf·fy \\'taf-ē\\ *n, pl* **taffies** : a candy usu. of molasses or brown sugar stretched until porous and light-colored

¹tag \\'tag\\ *n* **1** : a metal or plastic binding on an end of a shoelace **2** : a piece of hanging or attached material **3** : a hackneyed quotation or saying **4** : a descriptive or identifying epithet

²tag *vb* **tagged; tag·ging 1** : to provide or mark with or as if with a tag; *esp* : IDENTIFY **2** : to attach as an addition **3** : to follow closely and persistently ⟨~s along everywhere we go⟩ **4** : to hold responsible for something

³tag *n* : a game in which one player chases others and tries to touch one of them

⁴tag *vb* **tagged; tag·ging 1** : to touch in or as if in a game of tag **2** : SELECT

TAG *abbr* the adjutant general

tag sale *n* : GARAGE SALE

Ta·hi·tian \\tə-'hē-shən\\ *n* **1** : a native or inhabitant of Tahiti **2** : the Polynesian language of the Tahitians — **Tahitian** *adj*

tai·ga \\'tī-gä\\ *n* [Russ] : swampy coniferous northern forest (as of parts of Canada) beginning where the tundra ends

¹tail \\'tāl\\ *n* **1** : the rear end or a process extending from the rear end of an animal **2** : something resembling an animal's tail **3** *pl* : full evening dress for men **4** : the back, last, lower, or inferior part of something; *esp* : the reverse of a coin **5** : one who follows or keeps watch on someone — **tailed** \\'tāld\\ *adj* — **tail·less** \\'tāl-ləs\\ *adj*

²tail *vb* : FOLLOW; *esp* : to follow for the purpose of surveillance **syn** dog, shadow, trail, tag

tail·coat \\-'kōt\\ *n* : a coat with tails; *esp* : a man's full-dress coat with two long tapering skirts at the back

¹tail·gate \\-,gāt\\ *n* : a board or gate at the back end of a vehicle that can be let down (as for loading)

²tailgate *vb* : relating to or being a picnic set up on the tailgate esp. of a station wagon

³tailgate *vb* **tail·gat·ed; tail·gat·ing** : to drive dangerously close behind another vehicle

tail·light \\-,līt\\ *n* : a usu. red warning light mounted at the rear of a vehicle

¹tai·lor \\'tā-lər\\ *n* [ME *taillour*, fr. OF *tailleur*, fr. *taillier* to cut, fr. LL *taliare*, fr. L *talea* twig, cutting] : one whose occupation is making or altering garments

²tailor *vb* **1** : to make or fashion as the work of a tailor **2** : to make or adapt to suit a special purpose

tail pipe *n* : an outlet by which the exhaust gases are removed from an engine

tail·spin \\'tāl-,spin\\ *n* : a rapid descent or downward spiral

tail wind *n* : a wind blowing in the same general direction as the course of a moving airplane or ship

¹taint \\'tānt\\ *vb* **1** : to affect or become affected with something bad and esp. putrefaction **2** : CORRUPT, CONTAMINATE **syn** pollute, defile, soil

²taint *n* : a contaminating mark or influence

ta·ka \\'täk-ə\\ *n* — see MONEY table

¹take \\'tāk\\ *vb* **took** \\'tùk\\; **tak·en** \\'tā-kən\\; **tak·ing 1** : to get into one's hands or possession : GRASP, SEIZE **2** : CAPTURE; *also* : DEFEAT **3** : to obtain or secure for use **4** : to catch or attack through the effect of a sudden force or influence ⟨*taken* ill⟩ **5** : CAPTIVATE, DELIGHT **6** : to bring into a relation ⟨~ a wife⟩ **7** : REMOVE, SUBTRACT **8** : to pick out : CHOOSE **9** : ASSUME, UNDERTAKE **10** : RECEIVE, ACCEPT **11** : to use for transportation ⟨~ a bus⟩ **12** : to become impregnated with : ABSORB ⟨~s a dye⟩ **13** : to receive into one's body (as by eating) ⟨~ a pill⟩ **14** : ENDURE, UNDERGO **15** : to lead, carry, or cause to go along to another place **16** : NEED, REQUIRE **17** : to obtain as the result of a special procedure ⟨~ a snapshot⟩ **18** : to undertake and do, make, or perform ⟨~ a walk⟩ **19** : to take effect : ACT, OPERATE **syn** grab, clutch, snatch, seize, nab, grapple — **tak·er** *n* — **take advantage of 1** : to profit by **2** : EXPLOIT — **take after** : RESEMBLE — **take care** : to be careful — **take care of** : to care for : attend to — **take effect** : to become operative — **take exception** : OBJECT — **take for** : to suppose to be; *esp* : to mistake for — **take place** : HAPPEN — **take to 1** : to go to **2** : to apply or devote oneself to **3** : to conceive a liking for

²take *n* **1** : the number or quantity taken; *also* : PROCEEDS, RECEIPTS **2** : an act or the action of taking **3** : a television or movie scene filmed or taped at one time; *also* : a sound recording made at one time **4** : mental response

take·off \\-,òf\\ *n* **1** : IMITATION; *esp* : PARODY **2** : an act or instance of taking off

take off \\'tāk-'òf\\ *vb* **1** : REMOVE **2** : DEDUCT **3** : to set out : go away **4** : to leave the surface; *esp* : to begin flight

take on *vb* **1** : to begin to perform or deal with; *also* : to contend with as an opponent **2** : ENGAGE, HIRE **3** : to assume or acquire as or as if one's own **4** : to make an unusual show of one's feelings esp. of grief or anger

take over \\'tāk-'ō-vər\\ *vb* : to assume control or possession of or responsibility for — **take·over** \\-,ō-vər\\ *n*

take up *vb* **1** : PICK UP **2** : to begin to occupy **3** : to absorb or incorporate into itself ⟨plants *taking up* nutrients⟩ **4** : to begin to engage in ⟨*took up* jogging⟩ **5** : to make tighter or shorter ⟨*take up* the slack⟩

tak·ings \\'tā-kiŋz\\ *n pl* : receipts esp. of money

ta·la \'täl-ə\ n, pl tala — see MONEY table

talc \'talk\ n : a soft mineral with a soapy feel used esp. in making toilet powder (tal·cum powder \'tal-kəm-\)

tale \'tāl\ n 1 : a relation of a series of events 2 : a report of a confidential matter 3 : idle talk; esp : harmful gossip 4 : a usu. imaginative narrative 5 : FALSEHOOD 6 : COUNT, TALLY

tal·ent \'tal-ənt\ n 1 : an ancient unit of weight and value 2 : the natural endowments of a person 3 : a special often creative or artistic aptitude 4 : mental power : ABILITY 5 : a person of talent syn genius, gift, faculty, aptitude, knack — tal·ent·ed \-əd\ adj

ta·ler \'täl-ər\ n : any of numerous silver coins issued by German states from the 15th to the 19th centuries

tales·man \'tālz-mən\ n [ME tales talesmen, fr. ML tales de circumstantibus such (persons) of the bystanders; fr. the wording of the writ summoning them] : a person summoned for jury duty

tal·is·man \'tal-əs-mən, -əz-\ n, pl -mans [F talisman or Sp talismán or It talismano, fr. Ar ṭilsam, fr. MGk telesma, fr. Gk, consecration, fr. telein to initiate into the mysteries, complete, fr. telos end] : an object thought to act as a charm

¹talk \'tok\ vb 1 : to express in speech : utter words : SPEAK 2 : DISCUSS ⟨~ business⟩ 3 : to influence or cause by talking ⟨~ed him into agreeing⟩ 4 : to use (a language) for communicating 5 : CONVERSE 6 : to reveal confidential information; also : GOSSIP 7 : to give a talk : LECTURE — talk·er n — talk back : to answer impertinently

²talk n 1 : the act of talking 2 : a way of speaking 3 : a formal discussion 4 : REPORT, RUMOR 5 : the topic of comment or gossip (the ~ of the town) 6 : an informal address or lecture

talk·a·tive \'to-kət-iv\ adj : given to talking syn loquacious, chatty, gabby, garrulous — talk·a·tive·ly adv — talk·a·tive·ness n

talk·ing-to \'to-kiŋ-,tü\ n : REPRIMAND, REPROOF

tall \'tol\ adj 1 : high in stature; also : of a specified height ⟨six feet ~⟩ 2 : LARGE, FORMIDABLE ⟨a ~ order⟩ 3 : UNBELIEVABLE, IMPROBABLE ⟨a ~ story⟩ syn lofty, high — tall·ness n

tal·low \'tal-ō\ n : a hard white fat rendered usu. from cattle or sheep tissues and used esp. in soap and lubricants

¹tal·ly \'tal-ē\ n, pl tallies [ME talye, fr. ML talea, fr. L, twig, cutting] 1 : a device for visibly recording or accounting esp. business transactions 2 : a recorded account 3 : a corresponding part; also : CORRESPONDENCE

²tally vb tal·lied; tal·ly·ing 1 : to mark on or as if on a tally 2 : to make a count of : RECKON; also : SCORE 3 : CORRE-

SPOND, MATCH syn square, accord, harmonize, conform, jibe

tal·ly·ho \,tal-ē-'hō\ n, pl -hos 1 : a call of a huntsman at sight of the fox 2 : a four-in-hand coach

Tal·mud \'täl-,mud, 'tal-,məd, 'tal-məd\ n [Heb talmūdh, lit., instruction] : the authoritative body of Jewish tradition — Tal·mu·dic \tal-'m(y)üd-ik, -'məd-; täl-'mud-\ adj — Tal·mud·ist \'täl-,mud-əst, 'tal-məd-\ n

tal·on \'tal-ən\ n : the claw of an animal and esp. of a bird of prey

ta·lus \'tā-ləs, 'tal-əs\ n : rock debris at the base of a cliff

tam \'tam\ n : TAM-O'-SHANTER

ta·ma·le \tə-'mäl-ē\ n [MexSp tamales, pl. of tamal tamale] : ground meat seasoned with chili, rolled in cornmeal dough, wrapped in corn husks, and steamed

tam·a·rack \'tam-ə-,rak\ n : a larch of the northern U.S. and Canada; also : its hard resinous wood

tam·a·rind \'tam-ə-rənd, -,rind\ n [Sp & Pg tamarindo, fr. Ar tamr hindī, lit., Indian date] : a tropical tree of the legume family with hard yellowish wood and feathery leaves; also : its acid brown fruit

tam·ba·la \täm-'bäl-ə\ n, pl -la or -las — see kwacha at MONEY table

tam·bou·rine \,tam-bə-'rēn\ n : a small shallow drum with loose disks at the sides played by shaking or striking with the hand

¹tame \'tām\ adj tam·er; tam·est 1 : reduced from a state of native wildness esp. so as to be useful to man : DOMESTICATED 2 : made docile : SUBDUED 3 : lacking spirit or interest : INSIPID syn submissive, domestic, domesticated — tame·ly adv — tame·ness n

²tame vb tamed; tam·ing 1 : to make or become tame; also : to subject (land) to cultivation 2 : HUMBLE, SUBDUE — tam·able or tame·able \'tā-mə-bəl\ adj — tame·less adj — tam·er n

tam-o'-shan·ter \'tam-ə-,shant-ər\ n [fr. poem Tam o' Shanter (1790) of Robert Burns †1796 Scot. poet] : a Scottish woolen cap with a wide flat circular crown and usu. a pompon in the center

tamp \'tamp\ vb : to drive down or in by a series of light blows

tam·per \'tam-pər\ vb tam·pered; tam·per·ing \-p(ə-)riŋ\ 1 : to carry on underhand negotiations (as by bribery) ⟨~ with a witness⟩ 2 : to interfere so as to weaken or change for the worse ⟨~ with a document⟩ 3 : to try foolish or dangerous experiments

tam·pon \'tam-,pän\ n : a plug (as of cotton) introduced into a cavity usu. to check bleeding or absorb secretions

¹tan \'tan\ vb tanned; tan·ning 1 : to change (hide) into leather esp. by soaking in a liquid containing tannin 2 : to make or become brown (as by ex-

posure to the sun) **3** : WHIP, THRASH

²**tan** *n* **1** : TANBARK; *also* : a tanning material **2** : a brown skin color induced by sun or weather **3** : a light yellowish brown color

³**tan** *abbr* tangent

tan·a·ger \'tan-i-jər\ *n* : any of numerous American passerine birds with brightly colored males

tan·bark \'tan-,bärk\ *n* : bark (as of oak or sumac) that is rich in tannin and used in tanning

¹**tan·dem** \'tan-dəm\ *n* [L, at last, at length (taken to mean ''lengthwise''), fr. *tam* so] **1** : a 2-seated carriage with horses hitched tandem; *also* : its team **2** : a bicycle for two persons sitting one behind the other — **in tandem** : in a tandem arrangement

²**tandem** *adv* : one behind another

³**tandem** *adj* **1** : consisting of things arranged one behind the other **2** : working in conjunction with each other

tang \'taŋ\ *n* **1** : a part in a tool that connects the blade with the handle **2** : a sharp distinctive flavor; *also* : a pungent odor — **tangy** *adj*

tan·gent \'tan-jənt\ *adj* [L *tangent-*, *tangens*, prp. of *tangere* to touch] : TOUCHING; *esp* : meeting a curve or surface and not cutting it if extended

²**tangent** *n* **1** : a tangent line, curve, or surface **2** : an abrupt change of course — **tan·gen·tial** \tan-'jen-chəl\ *adj*

tan·ger·ine \'tan-jə-,rēn, ,tan-jə-'rēn\ *n* : a deep orange loose-skinned citrus fruit; *also* : a tree that bears tangerines

tan·gi·ble \'tan-jə-bəl\ *adj* **1** : perceptible esp. by the sense of touch : PALPABLE **2** : substantially real : MATERIAL (~ rewards) **3** : capable of being appraised syn appreciable, perceptible, sensible, discernible — **tan·gi·bil·i·ty** \,tan-jə-'bil-ət-ē\ *n*

²**tangible** *n* : something tangible; *esp* : a tangible asset

¹**tan·gle** \'tan-gəl\ *vb* **tan·gled**; **tan·gling** \-g(ə-)liŋ\ **1** : to involve so as to hamper or embarrass; *also* : ENTRAP **2** : to unite or knit together in intricate confusion : ENTANGLE

²**tangle** *n* **1** : a tangled twisted mass (as of vines) **2** : a confusedly complicated state : MUDDLE

tan·go \'tan-gō\ *n*, *pl* **tangos** : a dance of Spanish-American origin — **tango** *vb*

tank \'taŋk\ *n* **1** : a large artificial receptacle for liquids **2** : a heavily armed and armored combat vehicle that moves on beltlike tracks — **tank·ful** *n*

tan·kard \'tan-kərd\ *n* : a tall one-handled drinking vessel

tank·er \'tan-kər\ *n* : a vehicle equipped for transporting a liquid

tank top *n* : a sleeveless collarless pullover shirt with shoulder straps

tank town *n* **1** : a town at which trains stop for water **2** : a small town

tan·ner \'tan-ər\ *n* : one that tans hides

tan·nery \'tan-(ə-)rē\ *n*, *pl* **-ner·ies** : a place where tanning is carried on

tan·nic acid \,tan-ik-\ *n* : TANNIN

tan·nin \'tan-ən\ *n* : any of various substances of plant origin used in tanning and dyeing, in inks, and as astringents

tan·sy \'tan-zē\ *n*, *pl* **tansies** [ME *tanesey*, fr. OF *tanesie*, fr. ML *athanasia*, fr. Gk. immortality, fr. *athanatos* immortal, fr. *a*- not + *thanatos* death] : a common weedy herb related to the daisies with an aromatic odor and very bitter taste

tan·ta·lize \'tant-ᵊl-,īz\ *vb* **-lized**; **-liz·ing** [fr. *Tantalus*, mythical Greek king punished in Hades by having to stand up to his chin in water that receded as he bent to drink] : to tease or torment by presenting something desirable but keeping it out of reach — **tan·ta·liz·er** *n* — **tan·ta·liz·ing·ly** *adv*

tan·ta·lum \'tant-ᵊl-əm\ *n* : a hard ductile acid-resisting chemical element

tan·ta·mount \'tant-ə-,maunt\ *adj* : equivalent in value or meaning syn same, equal, identical

tan·trum \'tan-trəm\ *n* : a fit of bad temper

Tan·za·ni·an \,tan-zə-'nē-ən\ *n* : a native or inhabitant of Tanzania — **Tanzanian** *adj*

Tao·ism \'taù-,iz-əm, 'daú-\ *n* : a religion developed from a Chinese mystic philosophy and Buddhist religion — **Tao·ist** \-əst\ *adj or n*

¹**tap** \'tap\ *n* **1** : FAUCET, COCK **2** : liquor drawn through a tap **3** : the removing of fluid from a container or cavity by tapping **4** : a tool for forming an internal screw thread **5** : a point in an electric circuit where a connection may be made

²**tap** *vb* **tapped**; **tap·ping** **1** : to release or cause to flow by piercing or by drawing a plug from a container or cavity **2** : to pierce so as to let out or draw off a fluid **3** : to draw from (~ resources) **4** : to cut in on (a telephone wire) to get information; *also* : to cut in (an electrical circuit) on another circuit **5** : to form an internal screw thread in by means of a tap **6** : to connect (as a gas or water main) with a local supply — **tap·per** *n*

³**tap** *vb* **tapped**; **tap·ping** **1** : to rap lightly **2** : to make (as a hole) by repeated light blows **3** : to repair by putting a half sole on **4** : SELECT; *esp* : to elect to membership

⁴**tap** *n* **1** : a light blow or stroke; *also* : its sound **2** : a small metal plate for the sole or heel of a shoe

¹**tape** \'tāp\ *n* **1** : a narrow band of woven fabric **2** : a narrow flexible strip; *esp* : MAGNETIC TAPE

²**tape** *vb* **taped**; **tap·ing** **1** : to fasten or support with tape **2** : to measure with a tape measure **3** : to record on magnetic tape

tape deck *n* : a device used to play back and often to record on magnetic tapes that usu. has to be connected to a separate audio system

tape measure *n* : a tape marked off in units (as inches) for measuring

tape player *n* : a self-contained device for the playback of recorded magnetic tapes

¹ta·per \'tā-pər\ *n* **1** : a slender wax candle; *also* : a long waxed wick **2** : a gradual lessening of thickness or width in a long object ⟨the ~ of a steeple⟩

²taper *vb* **ta·pered; ta·per·ing** \'tā-p(ə-)riŋ\ **1** : to make or become gradually smaller toward one end **2** : to diminish gradually

tape-re·cord \ˌtāp-ri-'kȯrd\ *vb* : to make a recording of on magnetic tape — **tape recorder** *n* — **tape recording** *n*

tap·es·try \'tap-ə-strē\ *n, pl* **-tries** : a heavy reversible textile that has designs or pictures woven into it and is used esp. as a wall hanging

tape·worm \'tāp-ˌwərm\ *n* : a long flat segmented worm that lives as a parasite in the intestines

tap·i·o·ca \ˌtap-ē-'ō-kə\ *n* : a usu. granular preparation of cassava starch used esp. in puddings; *also* : a dish (as pudding) that contains tapioca

ta·pir \'tā-pər\ *n, pl* **tapir** *or* **tapirs** : any of several large harmless hoofed mammals of tropical America and southeast Asia related to the horses

tap·pet \'tap-ət\ *n* : a lever or projection moved by some other piece (as a cam) or intended to tap or touch something else to cause a particular motion

tap·room \'tap-ˌrüm, -ˌrum\ *n* : BAR-ROOM

tap·root \-ˌrüt, -ˌrut\ *n* : a large main root growing vertically downward and giving off small lateral roots

taps \'taps\ *n sing or pl* : the last bugle call at night blown as a signal that lights are to be put out; *also* : a similar call blown at military funerals and memorial services

tap·ster \'tap-stər\ *n* : BARTENDER

¹tar \'tär\ *n* **1** : a thick dark sticky liquid distilled from organic material (as wood or coal) **2** : SAILOR, SEAMAN

²tar *vb* **tarred; tar·ring** : to smear with or as if with tar

tar·an·tel·la \ˌtar-ən-'tel-ə\ *n* : a lively folk dance of southern Italy in 6/8 time

ta·ran·tu·la \tə-'ranch-(ə-)lə, -'rant-ᵊl-ə\ *n, pl* **tarantulas** *also* **ta·ran·tu·lae** \-'ran-chə-ˌlē, -'rant-ᵊl-ˌē\ **1** : a large European spider once thought very dangerous **2** : any of a family of large hairy American spiders with a sharp bite that is not very poisonous to human beings

tar·dy \'tärd-ē\ *adj* **tar·di·er; -est 1** : moving slowly : SLUGGISH **2** : LATE; *also* : DILATORY **syn** behindhand, overdue, belated — **tar·di·ness** \-ē-nəs\ *n*

¹tare \'taər\ *n* : a weed of fields where grain is grown

²tare *n* : a deduction from the gross weight of a substance and its container made in allowance for the weight of the container — **tare** *vb*

¹tar·get \'tär-gət\ *n* [ME, fr. MF *targette*, dim. of *targe* light shield, of Gmc origin] **1** : a mark to shoot at **2** : an object of ridicule or criticism **3** : a goal to be achieved

²target *vb* : to make a target of

tar·iff \'tar-əf\ *n* [It *tariffa*, fr. Ar *ta'rīf* notification] **1** : a schedule of duties imposed by a government esp. on imported goods; *also* : a duty or rate of duty imposed in such a schedule **2** : a schedule of rates or charges **syn** duty, toll, tax, levy, assessment

tar·mac \'tär-ˌmak\ *n* : a surface paved with crushed stone covered with tar

tarn \'tärn\ *n* : a small mountain lake

tar·nish \'tär-nish\ *vb* : to make or become dull or discolored — **tarnish** *n*

ta·ro \'tär-ō, 'tar-\ *n, pl* **taros** : a tropical plant grown for its edible starchy fleshy root; *also* : this root

tar·ot \'tar-ō\ *n* : one of a set of 22 pictorial playing cards used esp. for fortune-telling

tar·pau·lin \tär-'pȯ-lən, 'tär-pə-\ *n* : a piece of material (as waterproof canvas) used for protecting exposed objects

tar·pon \'tär-pən\ *n, pl* **tarpon** *or* **tarpons** : a large silvery sport fish common in warm coastal waters of the Atlantic esp. off Florida

tar·ra·gon \'tar-ə-gən\ *n* : a small European perennial wormwood with pungent aromatic foliage used as a flavoring

¹tar·ry \'tar-ē\ *vb* **tar·ried; tar·ry·ing 1** : to be tardy : DELAY; *esp* : to be slow in leaving **2** : to stay in or at a place : SOJOURN **syn** remain, wait, linger, abide

²tar·ry \'tär-ē\ *adj* : of, resembling, or smeared with tar

tar sand *n* : sand or sandstone that is naturally soaked with the heavy sticky portions of petroleum

tar·sus \'tär-səs\ *n, pl* **tar·si** \-ˌsī\ [NL] : the part of the foot of a vertebrate between the metatarsus and the leg; *also* : the small bones that support this part of the limb — **tar·sal** \-səl\ *adj or n*

¹tart \'tärt\ *adj* **1** : agreeably sharp to the taste : PUNGENT **2** : BITING, CAUSTIC **syn** sour, acid, acerb — **tart·ly** *adv* — **tart·ness** *n*

²tart *n* **1** : a small pie or pastry shell containing jelly, custard, or fruit **2** : PROSTITUTE

tar·tan \'tärt-ᵊn\ *n* : a twilled woolen fabric with a plaid design of Scottish origin consisting of stripes of varying width and color against a solid background

tar·tar \'tärt-ər\ *n* **1** : a substance in the

juice of grapes deposited (as in wine casks) as a reddish crust or sediment **2** : a hard crust of saliva, debris, and calcium salts on the teeth

tar·tar sauce *or* **tar·tare sauce** \ˌtärt-ər-\ *n* : mayonnaise with chopped pickles, olives, or capers

¹**task** \ˈtask\ *n* [ME *taske*, fr. OF *tasque*, fr. ML *tasca* tax or service imposed by a feudal superior, fr. *taxare* to tax] : a piece of assigned work **syn** job, duty, chore, stint, assignment

²**task** *vb* : to oppress with great labor

task force *n* : a temporary grouping to accomplish a particular objective

task·mas·ter \ˈtask-ˌmas-tər\ *n* : one that imposes a task or burdens another with labor

¹**tas·sel** \ˈtas-əl, ˈtas-\ *n* **1** : a hanging ornament made of a bunch of cords of even length fastened at one end **2** : something suggesting a tassel; *esp* : a male flower cluster of Indian corn

²**tassel** *vb* **-seled** *or* **-selled**; **-sel·ing** *or* **-sel·ling** \-(ə-)liŋ\ : to adorn with or put forth tassels

¹**taste** \ˈtāst\ *vb* **tast·ed**; **tast·ing 1** : EXPERIENCE, UNDERGO **2** : to try or determine the flavor of by taking a bit into the mouth **3** : to eat or drink esp. in small quantities : SAMPLE **4** : to have a specific flavor

²**taste** *n* **1** : a small amount tasted **2** : BIT; *esp* : a sample of experience **3** : the special sense that identifies sweet, sour, bitter, or salty qualities and is mediated by receptors in the tongue **4** : a quality perceptible to the sense of taste; *also* : a complex sensation involving true taste, smell, and touch **5** : individual preference **6** : critical judgment, discernment, or appreciation; *also* : aesthetic quality **syn** tang, relish, flavor, savor — **taste·ful** \-fəl\ *adj* — **taste·ful·ly** \-ē\ *adv* — **taste·less** *adj* — **taste·less·ly** *adv* — **tast·er** *n*

taste bud *n* : a sense organ mediating the sensation of taste

tasty \ˈtā-stē\ *adj* **tast·i·er**; **-est** : pleasing to the taste : SAVORY **syn** palatable, appetizing, toothsome, flavorsome — **tast·i·ness** \ˈtā-stē-nəs\ *n*

tat \ˈtat\ *vb* **tat·ted**; **tat·ting** : to work at or make by tatting

¹**tat·ter** \ˈtat-ər\ *vb* : to make or become ragged

²**tatter** *n* **1** : a part torn and left hanging **2** *pl* : tattered clothing

tat·ter·de·ma·lion \ˌtat-ərd-i-ˈmāl-yən\ *n* : one that is ragged or disreputable

tat·ter·sall \ˈtat-ər-ˌsȯl, -sol\ *n* : a pattern of colored lines forming squares on solid background; *also* : a fabric in a tattersall pattern

tat·ting \ˈtat-iŋ\ *n* : a delicate handmade lace formed usu. by looping and knotting with a single thread and a small shuttle; *also* : the act or process of making such lace

tat·tle \ˈtat-ᵊl\ *vb* **tat·tled**; **tat·tling** \ˈtat-(ᵊ-)liŋ\ **1** : CHATTER, PRATE **2** : to tell

secrets; *also* : to inform against another — **tat·tler** \ˈtat-(ᵊ-)lər\ *n*

tat·tle·tale \ˈtat-ᵊl-ˌtāl\ *n* : one that tattles : INFORMER

¹**tat·too** \ta-ˈtü\ *n*, *pl* **tattoos** [alter. of earlier *taptoo*, fr. D *taptoe*, fr. the phrase *tap toe!* taps shut!] **1** : a call sounded before taps as notice to go to quarters **2** : a rapid rhythmic rapping

²**tattoo** *vb* : to mark (the skin) with tattoos

³**tattoo** *n*, *pl* **tattoos** [Tahitian *tatau*] : an indelible figure fixed upon the body esp. by insertion of pigment under the skin

taught *past and past part of* TEACH

¹**taunt** \ˈtȯnt\ *n* : a sarcastic challenge or insult

²**taunt** *vb* : to reproach or challenge in a mocking manner : jeer at **syn** mock, deride, ridicule, twit — **taunt·er** *n*

taupe \ˈtōp\ *n* : a brownish gray

Tau·rus \ˈtȯr-əs\ *n* [L, lit., bull] **1** : a zodiacal constellation between Aries and Gemini usu. pictured as a bull **2** : the 2d sign of the zodiac in astrology; *also* : one born under this sign

taut \ˈtȯt\ *adj* **1** : tightly drawn : not slack **2** : extremely nervous : TENSE **3** : TRIM, TIDY (a ~ ship) — **taut·ly** *adv* — **taut·ness** *n*

tau·tol·o·gy \tȯ-ˈtäl-ə-jē\ *n*, *pl* **-gies** : needless repetition of an idea, statement, or word; *also* : an instance of such repetition — **tau·to·log·i·cal** \ˌtȯt-ᵊl-ˈäj-i-kəl\ *adj* — **tau·to·log·i·cal·ly** \-i-k(ə-)lē\ *adv* — **tau·tol·o·gous** \tȯ-ˈtäl-ə-gəs\ *adj* — **tau·tol·o·gous·ly** *adv*

tav·ern \ˈtav-ərn\ *n* [ME *taverne*, fr. OF, fr. L *taberna*, lit., hut, shop] **1** : an establishment where alcoholic liquors are sold to be drunk on the premises **2** : INN

taw \ˈtȯ\ *n* **1** : a marble used as a shooter **2** : the line from which players shoot at marbles

taw·dry \ˈtȯ-drē\ *adj* **taw·dri·er**; **-est** [fr. *tawdry lace* (a tie of lace for the neck), fr. *St. Audrey* (St. Etheldreda) †679 queen of Northumbria] : cheap and gaudy in appearance and quality **syn** garish, flashy, chintzy, meretricious — **taw·dri·ly** *adv*

taw·ny \ˈtȯ-nē\ *adj* **taw·ni·er**; **-est** : of a brownish orange color

¹**tax** \ˈtaks\ *vb* **1** : to levy a tax on **2** : CHARGE, ACCUSE **3** : to put under pressure — **tax·able** \ˈtak-sə-bəl\ *adj* — **tax·a·tion** \tak-ˈsā-shən\ *n*

²**tax** *n* **1** : a charge usu. of money imposed by authority on persons or property for public purposes **2** : a heavy charge : STRAIN **syn** assessment, levy, duty, tariff

¹**taxi** \ˈtak-sē\ *n*, *pl* **tax·is** \-sēz\ *also* **tax·ies** : TAXICAB; *also* : a similarly operated boat or airplane

²**taxi** *vb* **tax·ied**; **taxi·ing** *or* **taxy·ing**; **tax·is** *or* **tax·ies 1** : to move along the ground or on the water under an airplane's

own power when starting or after a landing **2** : to go by taxicab

taxi·cab \'tak-sē-ˌkab\ *n* : an automobile that carries passengers for a fare usu. based on the distance traveled

taxi·der·my \'tak-sə-ˌdər-mē\ *n* : the art of preparing, stuffing, and mounting skins of animals — **taxi·der·mist** \-məst\ *n*

tax·on·o·my \tak-'sän-ə-mē\ *n* : classification esp. of animals or plants according to natural relationships — **tax·o·nom·ic** \ˌtak-sə-'näm-ik\ *adj* — **tax·on·o·mist** \tak-'sän-ə-məst\ *n*

tax·pay·er \'taks-ˌpā-ər\ *n* : one who pays or is liable for a tax — **tax·pay·ing** \-iŋ\ *adj*

Tay–Sachs disease \'tā-'saks-\ *n* : a fatal hereditary disease caused by the absence of an enzyme needed to break down fatty material and characterized by a buildup of lipids in the nervous tissue

tb *abbr* tablespoon; tablespoonful

Tb *symbol* terbium

TB \(')tē-'bē\ *n* : TUBERCULOSIS

TBA *abbr, often not cap* to be announced

T–bar lift \ˌtē-ˌbär-\ *n* : a chair lift with a series of T-shaped bars

tbs *or* **tbsp** *abbr* tablespoon; tablespoonful

Tc *symbol* technetium

TC *abbr* teachers college

T cell *n* : a lymphocyte specialized esp. for promoting immunity (as against viruses) or in the rejection of foreign tissues) or for helping make antibodies

TD *abbr* **1** touchdown **2** Treasury Department

TDY *abbr* temporary duty

Te *symbol* tellurium

tea \'tē\ *n* **1** : the cured leaves and leaf buds of a shrub grown chiefly in China, Japan, India, and Sri Lanka; *also* : this shrub **2** : a drink made by steeping tea in boiling water **3** : refreshments usu. including tea served in late afternoon; *also* : a reception at which tea is served

teach \'tēch\ *vb* **taught** \'tot\; **teach·ing** **1** : to cause to know a subject : act as a teacher **2** : to show how (∼ a child to swim) **3** : to make to know the disagreeable consequences of an action **4** : to guide the studies of **5** : to impart the knowledge of (∼ algebra) — **teach·able** *adj* — **teach·er** *n*

teach·ing \-iŋ\ *n* **1** : the act, practice, or profession of a teacher **2** : something taught; *esp* : DOCTRINE

tea·cup \'tē-ˌkəp\ *n* : a small cup used with a saucer for hot beverages

teak \'tēk\ *n* : a tall East Indian timber tree; *also* : its hard durable yellowish brown wood

tea·ket·tle \'tē-ˌket-ᵊl\ *n* : a covered kettle with a handle and spout for boiling water

teal \'tēl\ *n, pl* **teal** *or* **teals** : any of

several small short-necked wild ducks

¹team \'tēm\ *n* [ME *teme*, fr. OE *tēam* offspring, lineage, group of draft animals] **1** : two or more draft animals harnessed to the same vehicle or implement **2** : a number of persons associated in work or activity; *esp* : a group on one side in a match — **team·mate** \'tēm-ˌmāt\ *n*

²team *vb* **1** : to haul with or drive a team **2** : to form a team : join forces

³team *adj* : of or performed by a team

team·ster \'tēm-stər\ *n* : one that drives a team or truck

team·work \-ˌwərk\ *n* : the work or activity of a number of persons acting in close association as members of a unit

tea·pot \'tē-ˌpät\ *n* : a vessel with a spout for brewing and serving tea

¹tear \'tiər\ *n* : a drop of the salty liquid that moistens the eye and inner side of the eyelids — **tear·ful** \-fəl\ *adj* — **tear·ful·ly** \-ē\ *adv*

²tear \'taər\ *vb* **tore** \'tōr\; **torn** \'tōrn\; **tear·ing** **1** : to separate parts of or pull apart by force : REND **2** : LACERATE **3** : to disrupt by the pull of contrary forces **4** : to remove by force : WRENCH **5** : to move or act with violence, haste, or force syn rip, split, cleave, rend

³tear \'taər\ *n* **1** : the act of tearing **2** : a hole or flaw made by tearing : RENT

tear gas \'tiər-\ *n* : a substance that on dispersion in the atmosphere blinds the eyes with tears — **tear gas** *vb*

tear-jerk·er \'tiər-ˌjər-kər\ *n* : an extravagantly pathetic story, song, play, movie, or broadcast

¹tease \'tēz\ *vb* **teased**; **teas·ing** **1** : to disentangle and lay parallel by combing or carding (∼ wool) **2** : to scratch the surface of (cloth) so as to raise a nap **3** : to annoy persistently esp. in fun by goading, coaxing, or tantalizing **4** : to comb (hair) by taking a strand and pushing the short hairs toward the scalp with the comb syn harass, worry, pester, annoy

²tease *n* **1** : the act of teasing or state of being teased **2** : one that teases

tea·sel *also* **tea·zel** *or* **tea·zle** \'tē-zəl\ *n* : a prickly herb or its flower head covered with stiff bracts and used to raise the nap on cloth; *also* : an artificial device used for this purpose

tea·spoon \'tē-ˌspün\ *n* **1** : a small spoon suitable for stirring beverages **2** : TEASPOONFUL

tea·spoon·ful \-ˌfül\ *n, pl* **-spoonfuls** *also* **-spoons·ful** \-ˌspünz-ˌfül\ : a unit of measure equal to one-sixth fluidounce (about 5 milliliters) or one third of a tablespoonful

teat \'tit, 'tēt\ *n* : the protuberance through which milk is drawn from an udder or breast

tech *abbr* **1** technical; technically; technician **2** technological; technology

tech·ne·tium \tek-'nē-sh(ē-)əm\ *n* : a

metallic chemical element produced in certain nuclear reactions

tech·nic \'tek-nik, tek-'nēk\ *n* : TECHNIQUE 1

tech·ni·cal \'tek-ni-kəl\ *adj* [Gk *technikos* of art, skillful, fr. *technē* art, craft, skill] **1** : having special knowledge esp. of a mechanical or scientific subject ⟨~ experts⟩ **2** : of or relating to a particular great, a practical or scientific subject ⟨~ training⟩ **3** : according to a strict interpretation of the rules **4** : of or relating to technique — **tech·ni·cal·ly** \-k(ə-)lē\ *adv*

tech·ni·cal·i·ty \,tek-nə-'kal-ət-ē\ *n, pl* **-ties 1** : a detail meaningful only to a specialist **2** : the quality or state of being technical

technical sergeant *n* : a noncommissioned officer in the air force ranking next below a master sergeant

tech·ni·cian \tek-'nish-ən\ *n* : a person who has acquired the technique of a specialized skill or subject

tech·nique \tek-'nēk\ *n* [F] **1** : the manner in which technical details are treated or basic physical movements are used **2** : technical methods

tech·noc·ra·cy \tek-'näk-rə-sē\ *n* : management of society by technical experts — **tech·no·crat** \'tek-nə-,krat\ *n* — **tech·no·crat·ic** \,tek-nə-'krat-ik\ *adj*

tech·nol·o·gy \tek-'näl-ə-jē\ *n, pl* **-gies** : applied science; *also* : a technical method of achieving a practical purpose — **tech·no·log·i·cal** \,tek-nə-'läj-i-kəl\ *adj*

tec·ton·ics \tek-'tän-iks\ *n sing or pl* **1** : geological structural features **2** : geology dealing with faulting and folding **3** : DIASTROPHISM — **tec·ton·ic** \-ik\ *adj*

ted·dy bear \'ted-ē-,baər\ *n* [*Teddy* Roosevelt, fr. a cartoon depicting the president sparing the life of a bear cub while hunting] : a stuffed toy bear

te·dious \'tēd-ē-əs, 'tē-jəs\ *adj* : tiresome because of length or dullness *syn* boring, tiring, irksome — **te·dious·ly** *adv* — **te·dious·ness** *n*

te·di·um \'tēd-ē-əm\ *n* : TEDIOUSNESS; *also* : BOREDOM

¹tee \'tē\ *n* : a small mound or peg on which a golf ball is placed to be hit at the beginning of play on a hole; *also* : the area from which the ball is hit to begin play

²tee *vb* **teed; tee·ing** : to place (a ball) on a tee

teem \'tēm\ *vb* : to become filled to overflowing : ABOUND *syn* swarm, crawl, flow

teen *adj* : TEENAGE

teen-age \'tēn-,āj\ *or* **teen-aged** \-,ājd\ *adj* : of, being, or relating to people in their teens — **teen·ag·er** \-,ā-jər\ *n*

teens \'tēnz\ *n pl* : the numbers 13 to 19 inclusive; *esp* : the years 13 to 19 in a person's life

tee·ny \'tē-nē\ *adj* **tee·ni·er; -est** : TINY

tee·pee *var of* TEPEE

tee shirt *var of* T-SHIRT

tee·ter \'tēt-ər\ *vb* **1** : to move unsteadily **2** : SEESAW — **teeter** *n*

teeth *pl of* TOOTH

teethe \'tēth\ *vb* **teethed; teeth·ing** : to grow teeth : cut one's teeth

teeth·ing \'tē-thiŋ\ *n* : the process of growth of the first set of teeth through the gums with its accompanying phenomena

tee·to·tal \'tē-'tōt-əl, -,tōt-\ *adj* : of or relating to the practice of complete abstinence from alcoholic drinks — **tee·to·tal·er** *or* **tee·to·tal·ler** \-'tōt-əl-ər\ *n* — **tee·to·tal·ism** \-əl-,iz-əm\ *n*

TEFL *abbr* teaching English as a foreign language

tek·tite \'tek-,tīt\ *n* : a glassy body of probably meteoric origin

tel *abbr* **1** telegram **2** telegraph **3** telephone

tele·cast \'tel-i-,kast\ *vb* **-cast** *also* **-cast·ed; -cast·ing** : to broadcast by television — **telecast** *n* — **tele·cast·er** *n*

tele·com·mu·ni·ca·tion \,tel-i-kə-,myü-nə-'kā-shən\ *n* : communication at a distance (as by telephone or radio)

tele·con·fer·ence \'tel-i-,kän-f(ə-)rəns\ *n* : a conference among people remote from one another held using telecommunications — **tele·con·fer·enc·ing** *n*

teleg *abbr* telegraphy

tele·gen·ic \,tel-ə-'jen-ik, -'jēn-\ *adj* : markedly attractive to television viewers

tele·gram \'tel-ə-,gram\ *n* : a message sent by telegraph

¹tele·graph \-,graf\ *n* : an electric apparatus or system for sending messages by a code over wires — **tele·graph·ic** \,tel-ə-'graf-ik\ *adj*

²telegraph *vb* : to send or communicate by or as if by telegraph — **te·leg·ra·pher** \tə-'leg-rə-fər\ *n*

te·leg·ra·phy \tə-'leg-rə-fē\ *n* : the use or operation of a telegraph apparatus or system

te·lem·e·try \tə-'lem-ə-trē\ *n* : the transmission esp. by radio of measurements made by automatic instruments to a distant station — **tele·me·ter** \'tel-ə-,mēt-ər\ *n*

te·lep·a·thy \tə-'lep-ə-thē\ *n* : apparent communication from one mind to another by extrasensory means — **tele·path·ic** \,tel-ə-'path-ik\ *adj* — **tele·path·i·cal·ly** \-i-k(ə-)lē\ *adv*

¹tele·phone \'tel-ə-,fōn\ *n* : an instrument for transmitting and receiving sounds over long distances by electricity

²telephone *vb* **-phoned; -phon·ing 1** : to send or communicate by telephone **2** : to speak to (a person) by telephone — **tele·phon·er** *n*

te·le·pho·ny \tə-'lef-ə-nē, 'tel-ə-,fō-\ *n* : use or operation of apparatus for transmission of sounds between distant points — **tele·phon·ic** \,tel-ə-'fän-ik\ *adj*

tele·pho·to \ˌtel-ə-ˈfōt-ō\ *adj* : being a camera lens giving a large image of a distant object — **tele·pho·to·graph·ic** \-ˌfōt-ə-ˈgraf-ik\ *adj* — **tele·pho·tog·ra·phy** \-fə-ˈtäg-rə-fē\ *n*

tele·play \ˈtel-i-ˌplā\ *n* : a play written for television

tele·print·er \ˈtel-ə-ˌprint-ər\ *n* : TELETYPEWRITER

¹**tele·scope** \ˈtel-ə-ˌskōp\ *n* : a cylindrical instrument equipped with lenses or mirrors for viewing distant objects

²**telescope** *vb* **-scoped; -scop·ing 1** : to slide or pass or cause to slide or pass one within another like the sections of a hand telescope **2** : COMPRESS, CONDENSE

tele·scop·ic \ˌtel-ə-ˈskäp-ik\ *adj* **1** : of or relating to a telescope **2** : seen only by a telescope **3** : able to discern objects at a distance **4** : having parts that telescope — **tele·scop·i·cal·ly** \-i-k(ə-)lē\ *adv*

tele·text \ˈtel-ə-ˌtekst\ *n* : an electronic system in which printed matter is broadcast by a television station and displayed on a subscriber's television set having a decoder

tele·thon \ˈtel-ə-ˌthän\ *n* : a long television program usu. to solicit funds for a charity

tele·type·writ·er \ˌtel-ə-ˈtīp-ˌrīt-ər\ *n* : a printing device resembling a typewriter used to send and receive signals over telephone lines

tele·vise \ˈtel-ə-ˌvīz\ *vb* **-vised; -vis·ing** : to pick up and usu. broadcast by television

tele·vi·sion \ˈtel-ə-ˌvizh-ən\ *n* [F *télévision,* fr. Gk *tēle* far, at a distance + F *vision* vision] : transmission and reproduction of images by a device that converts light waves into radio waves and then converts these back into visible light rays

tell \ˈtel\ *vb* **told** \ˈtōld\ ; **tell·ing 1** : COUNT, ENUMERATE **2** : to relate in detail : NARRATE **3** : SAY, UTTER **4** : to make known : REVEAL **5** : to report to : INFORM **6** : ORDER, DIRECT **7** : to ascertain by observing **8** : to have a marked effect **9** : to serve as evidence **syn** reveal, disclose, discover, betray

tell·er \ˈtel-ər\ *n* **1** : one that relates : NARRATOR **2** : one that counts **3** : a bank employee handling money received or paid out

tell·ing \ˈtel-iŋ\ *adj* : producing a marked effect : EFFECTIVE **syn** cogent, convincing, sound

tell off *vb* : REPRIMAND, SCOLD

tell·tale \ˈtel-ˌtāl\ *n* **1** : INFORMER, TATTLETALE **2** : something that serves to disclose : INDICATION — **telltale** *adj*

tel·lu·ri·um \tə-ˈlu̇r-ē-əm\ *n* : a chemical element that resembles sulfur in properties

te·mer·i·ty \tə-ˈmer-ət-ē\ *n, pl* **-ties** : rash or presumptuous daring : BOLDNESS **syn** audacity, effrontery, gall, nerve, cheek

temp *abbr* **1** temperature **2** temporary

¹**tem·per** \ˈtem-pər\ *vb* **tem·pered; tem·per·ing** \-p(ə-)riŋ\ **1** : to dilute or soften by the addition of something else 〈∼ justice with mercy〉 **2** : to bring (as steel) to a desired hardness by reheating and cooling **3** : to toughen (glass) by gradual heating and cooling **4** : TOUGHEN **5** : TUNE

²**temper** *n* **1** : characteristic tone : TENDENCY **2** : the hardness or toughness of a substance 〈∼ of a knife blade〉 **3** : a characteristic frame of mind : DISPOSITION **4** : calmness of mind : COMPOSURE **5** : state of feeling or frame of mind at a particular time **6** : heat of mind or emotion **syn** temperament, character, personality, makeup

tem·pera \ˈtem-pə-rə\ *n* [It] : a painting process using an albuminous or colloidal medium as a vehicle; *also* : a painting done in tempera

tem·per·a·ment \ˈtem-p(ə-)rə-mənt\ *n* **1** : characteristic or habitual inclination or mode of emotional response : DISPOSITION (nervous ∼) **2** : excessive sensitiveness or irritability **syn** character, personality, nature, makeup — **tem·per·a·men·tal** \ˌtem-p(ə-)rə-ˈment-ᵊl\ *adj*

tem·per·ance \ˈtem-p(ə-)rəns\ *n* : habitual moderation in the indulgence of the appetites or passions; *esp* : moderation in or abstinence from the use of intoxicating drink

tem·per·ate \ˈtem-p(ə-)rət\ *adj* **1** : not extreme or excessive : MILD **2** : moderate in indulgence of appetite or desire **3** : moderate in the use of intoxicating liquors **4** : having a moderate climate **syn** sober, continent, abstemious

temperate zone *n, often cap T&Z* : the region between the tropic of Cancer and the arctic circle or between the tropic of Capricorn and the antarctic circle

tem·per·a·ture \ˈtem-pər-ˌchu̇r, -p(ə-)rə-ˌchu̇r, -chər\ *n* **1** : degree of hotness or coldness of something (as air, water, or the body) as shown by a thermometer **2** : FEVER

tem·pest \ˈtem-pəst\ *n* [ME, fr. OF *tempeste,* fr. L *tempestas* season, weather, storm, fr. *tempus* time] : a violent wind esp. with rain, hail, or snow

tem·pes·tu·ous \tem-ˈpes-chə-wəs\ *adj* : of, involving, or resembling a tempest : STORMY — **tem·pes·tu·ous·ly** *adv* — **tem·pes·tu·ous·ness** *n*

tem·plate *also* **tem·plet** \ˈtem-plət\ *n* : a gauge, mold, or pattern used as a guide to the form of a piece being made

¹**tem·ple** \ˈtem-pəl\ *n* **1** : an edifice for the worship of a deity **2** : a place devoted to a special or exalted purpose

²**temple** *n* : the flattened space on each side of the forehead esp. of man

tem·po \ˈtem-pō\ *n, pl* **tem·pi** \-(ˌ)pē\ *or* **tempos** [It, lit., time] **1** : the rate of speed of a musical piece or passage **2** : rate of motion or activity : PACE

¹tem·po·ral \'tem-p(ə-)rəl\ *adj* **1** : of, relating to, or limited by time ⟨∼ and spatial bounds⟩ **2** : of or relating to earthly life or secular concerns ⟨∼ power⟩ **syn** profane, secular, lay

²temporal *adj* : of or relating to the temples or the sides of the skull

¹tem·po·rary \'tem-pə-ˌrer-ē\ *adj* : lasting for a time only : TRANSITORY **syn** transient, ephemeral, momentary, impermanent — **tem·po·rar·i·ly** \ˌtem-pə-'rer-ə-lē\ *adv*

²temporary *n, pl* **-rar·ies** : one serving for a limited time

tem·po·rize \'tem-pə-ˌrīz\ *vb* **-rized; -riz·ing 1** : to adapt one's actions to the time or the dominant opinion : COMPROMISE **2** : to draw out matters so as to gain time — **tem·po·riz·er** *n*

tempt \'tempt\ *vb* **1** : to entice to do wrong by promise of pleasure or gain **2** : PROVOKE **3** : to risk the dangers of **4** : to induce to do something : INCITE **syn** inveigle, decoy, seduce, lure — **tempt·er** *n* — **tempt·ing·ly** *adv*

temp·ta·tion \temp-'tā-shən\ *n* **1** : the act of tempting : the state of being tempted **2** : something that tempts

tempt·ress \'temp-trəs\ *n* : a woman who tempts

ten \'ten\ *n* **1** : one more than nine **2** : the 10th in a set or series **3** : something having 10 units — **ten** *adj or pron* — **tenth** \'tenth\ *adj or adv or n*

ten·a·ble \'ten-ə-bəl\ *adj* : capable of being held, maintained, or defended — **ten·a·bil·i·ty** \ˌten-ə-'bil-ət-ē\ *n*

te·na·cious \tə-'nā-shəs\ *adj* **1** : not easily pulled apart : COHESIVE, TOUGH ⟨steel is a ∼ metal⟩ **2** : holding fast ⟨∼ of his rights⟩ **3** : RETENTIVE ⟨∼ memory⟩ — **te·na·cious·ly** *adv* — **te·nac·i·ty** \tə-'nas-ət-ē\ *n*

ten·an·cy \'ten-ən-sē\ *n, pl* **-cies** : the temporary possession or occupancy of something (as a house) that belongs to another; *also* : the period of a tenant's occupancy

ten·ant \'ten-ənt\ *n* **1** : one who rents or leases (as a house) from a landlord **2** : DWELLER, OCCUPANT — **tenant** *vb* — **ten·ant·less** *adj*

tenant farmer *n* : a farmer who works land owned by another and pays rent either in cash or in shares of produce

ten·ant·ry \'ten-ən-trē\ *n, pl* **-ries** : the body of tenants esp. on a great estate

Ten Commandments *n pl* : the commandments of God given to Moses on Mount Sinai

¹tend \'tend\ *vb* **1** : to apply oneself ⟨∼ to your affairs⟩ **2** : to take care of ⟨∼ a plant⟩ **3** : to manage the operations of ⟨∼ a machine⟩ **syn** mind, watch, attend

²tend *vb* **1** : to move or develop one's course in a particular direction **2** : to show an inclination or tendency

ten·den·cy \'ten-dən-sē\ *n, pl* **-cies 1**

: DRIFT, TREND **2** : a proneness to or readiness for a particular kind of thought or action : PROPENSITY **syn** bent, leaning, disposition, inclination

ten·den·tious \ten-'den-chəs\ *adj* : marked by a tendency in favor of a particular point of view : BIASED — **ten·den·tious·ly** *adv* — **ten·den·tious·ness** *n*

¹ten·der \'ten-dər\ *adj* **1** : having a soft texture : easily broken, chewed, or cut **2** : physically weak : DELICATE; *also* : IMMATURE **3** : expressing or responsive to love or sympathy : LOVING, COMPASSIONATE **4** : SENSITIVE, TOUCHY **syn** sympathetic, warm, warmhearted — **ten·der·ly** *adv* — **ten·der·ness** *n*

²tender *n* **1** : an offer or proposal made for acceptance; *esp* : an offer of a bid for a contract **2** : something (as money) that may be offered in payment

³tender *vb* : to present for acceptance

⁴tend·er \'ten-dər\ *n* **1** : one that tends or takes care **2** : a boat carrying passengers and freight to a larger ship **3** : a car attached to a steam locomotive for carrying fuel and water

ten·der·foot \'ten-dər-ˌfu̇t\ *n, pl* **-feet** \-ˌfēt\ *also* **-foots** \-ˌfu̇ts\ **1** : one not hardened to frontier or rough outdoor life **2** : an inexperienced beginner : NEOPHYTE

ten·der·heart·ed \ˌten-dər-'härt-əd\ *adj* : easily moved to love, pity, or sorrow : COMPASSIONATE

ten·der·ize \'ten-də-ˌrīz\ *vb* **-ized; -iz·ing** : to make (meat) tender — **ten·der·iz·er** \'ten-də-ˌrī-zər\ *n*

ten·der·loin \'ten-dər-ˌlȯin\ *n* **1** : a tender strip of beef or pork from near the backbone **2** : a district of a city largely devoted to vice

ten·di·ni·tis *or* **ten·don·itis** \ˌten-də-'nīt-əs\ *n* : inflammation of a tendon

ten·don \'ten-dən\ *n* : a tough cord of dense tissue uniting a muscle with another part (as a bone) — **ten·di·nous** \-də-nəs\ *adj*

ten·dril \'ten-drəl\ *n* : a slender coiling organ by which some climbing plants attach themselves to a support

ten·e·brous \'ten-ə-brəs\ *adj* : shut off from the light : GLOOMY, OBSCURE

ten·e·ment \'ten-ə-mənt\ *n* **1** : a house used as a dwelling **2** : a building divided into apartments for rent to families; *esp* : one meeting only minimum standards of safety and comfort **3** : APARTMENT, FLAT

te·net \'ten-ət\ *n* [L, he holds, fr. *tenēre* to hold] : one of the principles or doctrines held in common by members of an organized group (as a church or profession) **syn** doctrine, dogma, belief

ten·fold \'ten-ˌfōld, -'fōld\ *adj* : being 10 times as great or as many — **ten·fold** \-'fōld\ *adv*

ten–gallon hat *n* : a wide-brimmed hat with a large soft crown

Tenn *abbr* Tennessee

ten·nis \'ten-əs\ *n* : a game played with a ball and racket on a court divided by a net

ten·on \'ten-ən\ *n* : a projecting part in a piece of material (as wood) for insertion into a mortise to make a joint

ten·or \'ten-ər\ *n* **1** : the general drift of something spoken or written : PURPORT **2** : the highest natural adult male voice **3** : TREND, TENDENCY

ten·pen·ny \,ten-ˌpen-ē\ *adj* : amounting to, worth, or costing 10 pennies

tenpenny nail *n* : a nail three inches (about 7.6 centimeters) long

ten·pin \'ten-ˌpin\ *n* : a bottle-shaped bowling pin set in groups of 10 and bowled at in a game (**tenpins**)

¹tense \'tens\ *n* [ME *tens* time, tense, fr. MF, fr. L *tempus*] : distinction of form of a verb to indicate the time of the action or state

²tense *adj* **tens·er; tens·est** [L *tensus*, fr. pp. of *tendere* to stretch] **1** : stretched tight : TAUT **2** : feeling or marked by nervous tension **syn** stiff, rigid, inflexible — **tense·ly** *adv* — **tense·ness** *n* — **ten·si·ty** \'ten-sət-ē\ *n*

³tense *vb* **tensed; tens·ing** : to make or become tense

ten·sile \'ten-səl, -ˌsīl\ *adj* : of or relating to tension (~ strength)

ten·sion \'ten-chən\ *n* **1** : the act of straining or stretching; *also* : the condition of being strained or stretched **2** : a state of mental unrest often with signs of bodily stress **3** : a state of latent hostility or opposition **4** : VOLTAGE

ten-speed \'ten-ˌspēd\ *n* : a bicycle with 10 possible combinations of gears

¹tent \'tent\ *n* **1** : a collapsible shelter of material stretched and supported by poles **2** : a canopy placed over the head and shoulders to retain vapors or oxygen being medically administered

²tent *vb* **1** : to lodge in tents **2** : to cover with or as if with a tent

ten·ta·cle \'tent-i-kəl\ *n* : any of the long flexible projections about the head or mouth (as of an insect, mollusk, or fish) — **ten·ta·cled** \-kəld\ *adj* — **ten·tac·u·lar** \ten-'tak-yə-lər\ *adj*

ten·ta·tive \'tent-ət-iv\ *adj* **1** : not fully worked out or developed (~ plans) **2** : HESITANT, UNCERTAIN (a ~ smile) — **ten·ta·tive·ly** *adv*

ten·u·ous \'ten-yə-wəs\ *adj* **1** : not dense : RARE (a ~ fluid) **2** : not thick : SLENDER (a ~ rope) **3** : having little substance : FLIMSY, WEAK (~ influences) **syn** thin, slim, slight — **te·nu·i·ty** \te-'n(y)ü-ət-ē, tə-\ *n* — **ten·u·ous·ly** \'ten-yə-wəs-lē\ *adv* — **ten·u·ous·ness** *n*

ten·ure \'ten-yər\ *n* : the act, right, manner, or period of holding something (as a landed property or a position)

ten·ured \'ten-yərd\ *adj* : having tenure (~ faculty members)

te·o·sin·te \ˌtā-ō-'sint-ē\ *n* : a large annual grass of Mexico and Central America closely related to maize

te·pee \'tē-(ˌ)pē\ *n* [Dakota *tipi*, fr. *ti* to dwell + *pi* to use for] : an American Indian conical tent usu. of skins

tep·id \'tep-əd\ *adj* **1** : moderately warm : LUKEWARM **2** : HALFHEARTED

te·qui·la \tə-'kē-lə, tā-\ *n* : a Mexican liquor made from mescal

ter *abbr* **1** terrace **2** territory

ter·bi·um \'tər-bē-əm\ *n* : a metallic chemical element

ter·cen·te·na·ry \ˌtər-ˌsen-'ten-ə-rē, tər-'sent-ᵊn-ˌer-ē\ *n*, *pl* **-ries** : a 300th anniversary; *also* : its celebration — **tercentenary** *adj*

ter·cen·ten·ni·al \ˌtər-ˌsen-'ten-ē-əl\ *adj or n* : TERCENTENARY

te·re·do \tə-'rēd-ō, -'rād-\ *n*, *pl* **teredos** *or* **te·red·i·nes** \-'red-ᵊn-ˌēz\ [L] : SHIPWORM

¹term \'tərm\ *n* **1** : END, TERMINATION **2** : DURATION; *esp* : a period of time fixed esp. by law or custom **3** : a mathematical expression connected with another by a plus or minus sign; *also* : any of the members of a ratio or of a series **4** : a word or expression that has a precise meaning in some uses or is limited to a particular subject or field **5** *pl* : PROVISIONS, CONDITIONS (~s of a contract) **6** *pl* : mutual relationship (on good ~s) **7** : AGREEMENT, CONCORD

²term *vb* : to apply a term to : CALL

ter·ma·gant \'tər-mə-gənt\ *n* : an overbearing or nagging woman : SHREW **syn** virago, vixen, scold

¹ter·mi·nal \'tər-mən-ᵊl\ *adj* : of, relating to, or forming an end, limit, or terminus **syn** final, concluding, last, latest

²terminal *n* **1** : EXTREMITY, END **2** : a device at the end of a wire or on electrical equipment for making a connection **3** : either end of a transportation line (as a railroad) with its offices and freight and passenger stations; *also* : a freight or passenger station **4** : a device connected to a communication network used to enter, receive, and display data

ter·mi·nate \'tər-mə-ˌnāt\ *vb* **-nat·ed; -nat·ing** : to bring or come to an end **syn** conclude, finish, complete — **ter·mi·na·ble** \-nə-bəl\ *adj* — **ter·mi·na·tion** \ˌtər-mə-'nā-shən\ *n* — **ter·mi·na·tor** \'tər-mə-ˌnāt-ər\ *n*

ter·mi·nol·o·gy \ˌtər-mə-'näl-ə-jē\ *n*, *pl* **-gies** : the technical or special terms used in a business, art, science, or special subject

ter·mi·nus \'tər-mə-nəs\ *n*, *pl* **-ni** \-ˌnī\ *or* **-nus·es** [L] **1** : final goal : END **2** : either end of a transportation line, travel route, pipeline, or canal; *also* : the station or city at such a place

ter·mite \'tər-ˌmīt\ *n* : any of a large

group of pale soft-bodied social insects that feed on wood

tern \\'tərn\ *n* : any of numerous small seabirds with narrow wings and often a black cap

ter·na·ry \\'tər-nə-rē\ *adj* 1 : of, relating to, or proceeding by threes 2 : having or consisting of three elements or parts 3 : having a mathematical base of three (a ~ logarithm)

terr *abbr* territory

¹**ter·race** \\'ter-əs\ *n* 1 : a flat roof or open platform 2 : a level area next to a building 3 : an embankment with level top 4 : a bank or ridge on a slope to conserve moisture and soil 5 : a row of houses on raised land; *also* : a street with such a row of houses 6 : a strip of park in the middle of a street

²**terrace** *vb* **ter·raced; ter·rac·ing** : to form into a terrace or supply with terraces

ter·ra-cot·ta \\,ter-ə-'kät-ə\ *n* [It *terra cotta,* lit., baked earth] : a reddish brown earthenware used for vases and small statues

ter·ra fir·ma \-'fər-mə\ *n* [NL] : solid ground

ter·rain \tə-'rān\ *n* : the surface features of an area of land (a rough ~)

ter·ra in·cog·ni·ta \'ter-ə-,in-,käg-'nēt-ə\ *n, pl* **ter·rae in·cog·ni·tae** \'ter-,ī-,in-,käg-'nē-tī\ [L] : an unexplored area or field of knowledge

ter·ra·pin \'ter-ə-pən\ *n* : any of various No. American edible turtles of fresh or brackish water

ter·rar·i·um \tə-'rar-ē-əm\ *n, pl* **-ia** \-ē-ə\ *or* **-i·ums** : a vivarium without standing water

ter·res·tri·al \tə-'res-t(r)ē-əl\ *adj* 1 : of or relating to the earth or its inhabitants 2 : living or growing on land (~ plants) **syn** mundane, earthly, worldly

ter·ri·ble \'ter-ə-bəl\ *adj* 1 : exciting terror : FEARFUL, DREADFUL (~ weapons) 2 : hard to bear : DISTRESSING (a ~ situation) 3 : extreme in degree : INTENSE (~ heat) 4 : of very poor quality : AWFUL (a ~ play) **syn** frightful, horrible, shocking, appalling — **ter·ri·bly** \-blē\ *adv*

ter·ri·er \'ter-ē-ər\ *n* [F (*chien*) *terrier,* lit., earth dog, fr. *terrier* of earth, fr. ML *terrarius,* fr. L *terra* earth] : any of various usu. small dogs orig. used by hunters to drive small game from holes

ter·rif·ic \tə-'rif-ik\ *adj* 1 : exciting terror 2 : EXTRAORDINARY, ASTOUNDING (~ speed) 3 : unusually good (makes ~ chili) **syn** terrible, frightful, dreadful, fearful, horrible, awful

ter·ri·fy \'ter-ə-,fī\ *vb* **-fied; -fy·ing** : to fill with terror : FRIGHTEN **syn** scare, terrorize, startle, alarm — **ter·ri·fy·ing·ly** *adv*

ter·ri·to·ri·al \,ter-ə-'tōr-ē-əl\ *adj* 1 : of or relating to a territory (~ government) 2 : of or relating to an assigned area (~ commanders)

ter·ri·to·ry \'ter-ə-,tōr-ē\ *n, pl* **-ries** 1 : a geographical area belonging to or under the jurisdiction of a governmental authority 2 : a part of the U.S. not included within any state but organized with a separate legislature 3 : REGION, DISTRICT; *also* : a region in which one feels at home 4 : a field of knowledge or interest 5 : an assigned area

ter·ror \'ter-ər\ *n* 1 : a state of intense fear : FRIGHT 2 : one that inspires fear **syn** panic, consternation, dread, alarm, dismay, horror, trepidation

ter·ror·ism \'ter-ər-,iz-əm\ *n* : the systematic use of terror esp. as a means of coercion — **ter·ror·ist** \-əst\ *adj or n*

ter·ror·ize \'ter-ər-,īz\ *vb* **-ized; -iz·ing** 1 : to fill with terror : SCARE 2 : to coerce by threat or violence **syn** terrify, frighten, alarm, startle

ter·ry \'ter-ē\ *n, pl* **terries** : an absorbent fabric with a loose pile of uncut loops

terse \'tərs\ *adj* **ters·er; ters·est** [L *tersus* clean, neat, fr. pp. of *tergēre* to wipe off] : effectively brief : CONCISE — **terse·ly** *adv* — **terse·ness** *n*

ter·tia·ry \'tər-shē-,er-ē\ *adj* 1 : of third rank, importance, or value 2 *cap* : of, relating to, or being the earlier period of the Cenozoic era 3 : occurring in or being the third stage

Tertiary *n* : the Tertiary period

TESL *abbr* teaching English as a second language

tes·sel·late \'tes-ə-,lāt\ *vb* **-lat·ed; -lat·ing** : to form into or adorn with mosaic

¹**test** \'test\ *n* [ME, vessel in which metals were assayed, fr. MF, fr. L *testum* earthen vessel] 1 : a critical examination or evaluation : TRIAL 2 : a means or result of testing

²**test** *vb* 1 : to put to test : TRY, EXAMINE 2 : to undergo or score on tests (an ore that ~s high in gold)

tes·ta·ment \'tes-tə-mənt\ *n* 1 *cap* : either of two main divisions of the Bible 2 : EVIDENCE, WITNESS 3 : CREDO 4 : an act to determine the disposition of one's property after death : WILL — **tes·ta·men·ta·ry** \,tes-tə-'ment-(ə-)rē\ *adj*

tes·tate \'tes-,tāt, -tət\ *adj* : having left a valid will

tes·ta·tor \'tes-,tāt-ər, tes-'tāt-\ *n* : a person who dies leaving a valid will

tes·ta·trix \tes-'tā-triks\ *n* : a female testator

¹**tes·ter** \'tēs-tər, 'tes-\ *n* : a canopy over a bed, pulpit, or altar

²**test·er** \'tes-tər\ *n* : one that tests

tes·ti·cle \'tes-ti-kəl\ *n* : TESTIS

tes·ti·fy \'tes-tə-,fī\ *vb* **-fied; -fy·ing** 1 : to make a statement based on personal knowledge or belief : bear witness 2 : to serve as evidence or proof **syn** attest, affirm

tes·ti·mo·ni·al \,tes-tə-'mō-nē-əl\ *n* 1 : a statement testifying to a person's good character or to the worth of something 2 : an expression of appreciation : TRIBUTE — **testimonial** *adj*

tes·ti·mo·ny \'tes-tə-ˌmō-nē\ *n, pl* **-nies** 1 : a solemn declaration made by a witness under oath esp. in a court 2 : evidence based on observation or knowledge 3 : an outward sign : SYMBOL syn evidence, confirmation, proof, testament

tes·tis \'tes-təs\ *n, pl* **tes·tes** \'tes-ˌtēz\ [L, witness, testis] : an oval-shaped male reproductive organ which is usu. located in the scrotum, which produces and secretes various male hormones and esp. testosterone, and in which sperm are produced

tes·tos·ter·one \te-'stäs-tə-ˌrōn\ *n* : a male sex hormone that causes development of the male reproductive system and secondary sex character

test tube *n* : a glass tube closed at one end and used esp. in chemistry and biology

tes·ty \'tes-tē\ *adj* **tes·ti·er; -est** [ME *testif,* fr. Anglo-French (the French of medieval England), headstrong, fr. OF *teste* head, fr. LL *testa* skull, fr. L, shell] : marked by ill humor : easily annoyed

tet·a·nus \'tet-ᵊn-əs\ *n* : a disease caused by bacterial poisons and marked by stiffness and spasms of the muscles with locking of the jaws — **tet·a·nal** \-ᵊl\ *adj*

tetchy \'tech-ē\ *adj* **tetchi·er; -est** : irritably or peevishly sensitive

¹**tête-à-tête** \ˌtāt-ə-ˌtāt\ *n* [F, lit., head to head] : a private conversation between two persons

²**tête-à-tête** \ˌtāt-ə-'tāt\ *adv* : PRIVATELY, FAMILIARLY

³**tête-à-tête** \ˌtāt-ə-ˌtāt\ *adj* : being face-to-face : PRIVATE

¹**teth·er** \'teth-ər\ *n* 1 : a line by which something (as an animal or balloon) is fastened 2 : the limit of one's strength or resources

²**tether** *vb* : to fasten or restrain by or as if by a tether

tet·ra·eth·yl lead \ˌte-trə-ˌeth-əl-\ *n* : a heavy oily poisonous liquid used as an antiknock agent in gasoline

tet·ra·he·dron \-'hē-drən\ *n, pl* **-drons** or **-dra** \-drə\ : a polyhedron that has four faces — **tet·ra·he·dral** \-drəl\ *adj*

tet·ra·hy·dro·can·nab·i·nol \ˌte-trə-ˌhī-drə-kə-'nab-ə-ˌnōl, -ˌnōl\ *n* : THC

te·tram·e·ter \te-'tram-ət-ər\ *n* : a line consisting of four metrical feet

Teu·ton·ic \t(y)ü-'tän-ik\ *adj* : GERMANIC

Tex *abbr* Texas

text \'tekst\ *n* 1 : the actual words of an author's work 2 : the main body of printed or written matter on a page 3 : a scriptural passage chosen as the subject esp. of a sermon 4 : THEME, TOPIC 5 : TEXTBOOK — **tex·tu·al** \'teks-chə(-wə)l\ *adj*

text·book \'teks(t)-ˌbük\ *n* : a book used in the study of a subject

tex·tile \'tek-ˌstīl, 'teks-tᵊl\ *n* : CLOTH; *esp* : a woven or knit cloth

tex·ture \'teks-chər\ *n* 1 : the visual or tactile surface characteristics and appearance of something (a coarse ~) 2 : essential part 3 : basic scheme or structure : FABRIC 4 : overall structure

TGIF *abbr* thank God it's Friday

¹**Th** *abbr* Thursday

²**Th** *symbol* thorium

¹**-th** — see ¹-ETH

²**-th** *or* **-eth** *adj suffix* — used in forming ordinal numbers ⟨hundred*th*⟩

³**-th** *n suffix* 1 : act or process 2 : state or condition ⟨dear*th*⟩

Thai \'tī\ *n, pl* **Thai** *or* **Thais** : a native or inhabitant of Thailand — **Thai** *adj*

thal·a·mus \'thal-ə-məs\ *n, pl* **-mi** \-ˌmī\ [NL] : a subdivision of the brain that receives nerve impulses and sends them to appropriate parts of the brain cortex

thal·li·um \'thal-ē-əm\ *n* : a poisonous metallic chemical element

¹**than** \thən, (')than\ *conj* 1 — used after a comparative adjective or adverb to introduce the second part of a comparison expressing inequality ⟨older ~ I am⟩ 2 — used after *other* or a word of similar meaning to express a difference of kind, manner, or identity ⟨adults other ~ parents⟩

²**than** *prep* : in comparison with ⟨older ~ me⟩

thane \'thān\ *n* 1 : a free retainer of an Anglo-Saxon lord 2 : a Scottish feudal lord

thank \'thaŋk\ *vb* : to express gratitude to ⟨~ed him for the present⟩

thank·ful \'thaŋk-fəl\ *adj* 1 : conscious of benefit received 2 : expressive of thanks 3 : GLAD — **thank·ful·ly** \-ē\ *adv* — **thank·ful·ness** *n*

thank·less \-ləs\ *adj* 1 : UNGRATEFUL 2 : UNAPPRECIATED

thanks \'thaŋks\ *n pl* : an expression of gratitude

thanks·giv·ing \ˌthaŋks-'giv-iŋ\ *n* 1 : the act of giving thanks 2 : prayer expressing gratitude 3 *cap* : the 4th Thursday in November observed as a legal holiday for giving thanks for divine goodness

¹**that** \(')that\ *pron, pl* **those** \(')thōz\ 1 : the one indicated, mentioned, or understood ⟨~'s my wife⟩ 2 : the one farther away or first mentioned ⟨this is an elm, ~'s a maple⟩ 3 : what has been indicated or mentioned ⟨after ~, we left⟩ 4 : the one or ones : IT, THEY ⟨*those* who wish to leave may do so⟩

²**that** *adj, pl* **those** 1 : being the one mentioned, indicated, or understood ⟨~ boy⟩ ⟨*those* people⟩ 2 : being the one farther away or first mentioned ⟨this chair or ~ one⟩

³**that** \thət, (ˌ)that\ *conj* 1 : the following, namely ⟨he said ~ he would⟩ :

also : which is, namely ⟨there's a chance ~ it may fail⟩ 2 : to this end or purpose ⟨shouted ~ all might hear⟩ 3 : as to result in the following, namely ⟨so heavy ~ it can't be moved⟩ 4 : for this reason, namely : BECAUSE ⟨we're glad ~ you came⟩ 5 : I wish this, or I am surprised or indignant at this, namely ⟨~ it should come to this⟩

⁴**that** \ˈthat, (ˌ)that\ *pron* 1 : WHO, WHOM, WHICH ⟨the man ~ saw you⟩ ⟨the man ~ you saw⟩ ⟨the money ~ was spent⟩ 2 : in, on, or at which ⟨the way ~ he drives⟩ ⟨the day ~ it rained⟩

⁵**that** \ˈthat\ *adv* : to such an extent or degree ⟨I like it, but not ~ much⟩

¹**thatch** \ˈthach\ *vb* : to cover with or as if with thatch

²**thatch** *n* 1 : plant material (as straw) for use as roofing 2 : a mat of grass clippings accumulated next to the soil on a lawn 3 : a covering of or as if of thatch ⟨a ~ of white hair⟩

thaw \ˈthȯ\ *vb* 1 : to melt or cause to melt 2 : to become so warm as to melt ice or snow 3 : to abandon aloofness or hostility **syn** liquefy — **thaw** *n*

THC \ˌtē-ˌāch-ˈsē\ *n* [*tetra*hydro*c*annabinol] : a physiologically active chemical from hemp plant resin that is the chief intoxicant in marijuana

¹**the** \thə, *before vowel sounds usu* thē\ *definite article* 1 : that in particular 2 — used before adjectives functioning as nouns ⟨a word to ~ wise⟩

²**the** *adv* 1 : to what extent ⟨~ sooner, the better⟩ 2 : to that extent ⟨the sooner, ~ better⟩

theat *abbr* theater; theatrical

the-a-ter *or* **the-a-tre** \ˈthē-ə-tər\ *n* 1 : a building for dramatic performances; *also* : a building or area for showing motion pictures 2 : a place of enactment of significant events ⟨~ of war⟩ 3 : a place (as a lecture room) resembling a theater 4 : dramatic literature or performance

theater-in-the-round *n* : a theater with the stage in the center of the auditorium

the-at-ri-cal \thē-ˈa-tri-kəl\ *also* **the-at-ric** \-trik\ *adj* 1 : of or relating to the theater 2 : marked by artificiality of emotion : HISTRIONIC 3 : marked by extravagant display : SHOWY **syn** dramatic, melodramatic

the-at-ri-cals \-kəlz\ *n pl* : the performance of plays

the-at-rics \thē-ˈa-triks\ *n pl* 1 : THEATRICALS 2 : staged or contrived effects

the-be \ˈthä-bä\ *n*, *pl* **thebe** — see *pula* at MONEY table

thee \(ˈ)thē\ *pron*, *objective case of* THOU

theft \ˈtheft\ *n* : the act of stealing

thegn \ˈthān\ *n* : THANE 1

their \thər, (ˌ)theər\ *adj* : of or relating to them or themselves

theirs \ˈtheərz\ *pron* : their one : their ones

the-ism \ˈthē-ˌiz-əm\ *n* : belief in the existence of a god or gods — **the-ist** \-əst\ *n or adj* — **the-is-tic** \thē-ˈis-tik\ *adj*

them \(th)əm, (ˈ)them\ *pron, objective case of* THEY

theme \ˈthēm\ *n* 1 : a subject or topic of discourse or of artistic representation 2 : a written exercise : COMPOSITION 3 : a melodic subject of a musical composition or movement — **the-mat-ic** \thi-ˈmat-ik\ *adj*

them-selves \thəm-ˈselvz, them-\ *pron pl* : THEY, THEM — used reflexively, for emphasis, or in absolute constructions ⟨they govern ~⟩ ⟨they ~ couldn't come⟩ ⟨~ busy, they sent me⟩

¹**then** \(ˈ)then\ *adv* 1 : at that time 2 : soon after that : NEXT 3 : in addition : BESIDES 4 : in that case 5 : CONSEQUENTLY

²**then** \ˈthen\ *n* : that time ⟨since ~⟩

³**then** \ˈthen\ *adj* : existing or acting at that time ⟨the ~ king⟩

thence \ˈthens, thens\ *adv* 1 : from that place 2 *archaic* : THENCEFORTH 3 : from that fact : THEREFROM

thence-forth \-ˌfȯrth\ *adv* : from that time forward : THEREAFTER

thence-for-ward \thens-ˈfȯr-wərd, thens-\ *also* **thence-for-wards** \-wərdz\ *adv* : onward from that place or time : THENCEFORTH

the-oc-ra-cy \thē-ˈäk-rə-sē\ *n*, *pl* **-cies** 1 : government by officials regarded as divinely inspired 2 : a state governed by a theocracy — **the-o-crat-ic** \ˌthē-ə-ˈkrat-ik\ *adj*

theol *abbr* theological; theology

the-ol-o-gy \thē-ˈäl-ə-jē\ *n*, *pl* **-gies** 1 : the study of religion and of religious ideas and beliefs; *esp* : a branch of theology treating of God and his relation to the world 2 : a theory or system of theology — **the-o-lo-gian** \ˌthē-ə-ˈlō-jən\ *n* — **the-o-log-i-cal** \-ˈläj-i-kəl\ *adj*

the-o-rem \ˈthē-ə-rəm, ˈthir-əm\ *n* 1 : a statement in mathematics that has been or is to be proved 2 : an idea accepted or proposed as a demonstrable truth : PROPOSITION

the-o-ret-i-cal \ˌthē-ə-ˈret-i-kəl\ *also* **the-o-ret-ic** \-ik\ *adj* 1 : relating to or having the character of theory 2 : existing only in theory — **the-o-ret-i-cal-ly** \-i-k(ə-)lē\ *adv*

the-o-rize \ˈthē-ə-ˌrīz\ *vb* **-rized; -riz-ing** : to form a theory : SPECULATE — **the-o-rist** \-rəst\ *n*

the-o-ry \ˈthē-ə-rē, ˈthir-ē\ *n*, *pl* **-ries** 1 : abstract thought 2 : the general principles of a subject 3 : a plausible or scientifically acceptable general principle offered to explain observed facts 4 : HYPOTHESIS, GUESS

theory of games : GAME THEORY

the-os-o-phy \thē-ˈäs-ə-fē\ *n* : belief about God and the world held to be based on mystical insight — **theo-**

soph·i·cal \thē-ə-'säf-i-kəl\ *adj* — the·os·o·phist \thē-'äs-ə-fəst\ *n*

ther·a·peu·tic \,ther-ə-'pyüt-ik\ *adj* [Gk *therapeutikos*, fr. *therapeuein* to attend, treat, fr. *theraps* attendant] : of, relating to, or dealing with healing and esp. with remedies for diseases — **ther·a·peu·ti·cal·ly** \-i-k(ə-)lē\ *adv*

ther·a·peu·tics \,ther-ə-'pyüt-iks\ *n* : a branch of medical science dealing with the use of remedies

ther·a·py \'ther-ə-pē\ *n, pl* **-pies** : treatment of bodily or mental disorders or maladjustment — **ther·a·pist** \-pəst\ *n*

¹**there** \'thaər, 'theər\ *adv* 1 : in or at that place — often used interjectionally 2 : to or into that place : THITHER 3 : in that matter or respect

²**there** \(,)thar, (,)ther, thər\ *pron* — used as a function word to introduce a sentence or clause (~'s a man here)

³**there** \'thaər, 'theər\ *n* 1 : that place (get away from ~) 2 : that point (you take it from ~)

there·abouts *or* **there·about** \,thar-ə-'baút(s), 'thar-ə-,baút(s), ,ther-ə-'baút(s), 'ther-ə-,\ *adv* 1 : near that place or time 2 : near that number, degree, or quantity

there·af·ter \thar-'af-tər, ther-\ *adv* : after that : AFTERWARD

there·at \-'at\ *adv* 1 : at that place 2 : at that occurrence : on that account

there·by \thar-'bī, ther-, 'tha(ə)r-,bī, 'the(ə)r-,bī\ *adv* 1 : by that : by that means 2 : connected with or with reference to that

there·for \thar-'fór, ther-\ *adv* : for or in return for that

there·fore \'tha(ə)r-,fōr, 'the(ə)r-\ *adv* : for that reason : CONSEQUENTLY

there·from \thar-'frəm, ther-\ *adv* : from that or it

there·in \thar-'in, ther-\ *adv* 1 : in or into that place, time, or thing 2 : in that respect

there·of \-'əv, -'äv\ *adv* 1 : of that or it 2 : from that : THEREFROM

there·on \-'ón, -'än\ *adv* 1 : on that 2 *archaic* : THEREUPON 3

there·to \thar-'tü, ther-\ *adv* : to that

there·un·to \thar-'ən-(,)tü, ,thar-ən-'tü, ,ther-\ *adv, archaic* : THERETO

there·upon \'thar-ə-,pón, 'ther-, -,pän; ,thar-ə-'pón, -'pän, ,ther-\ *adv* 1 : on that matter : THEREON 2 : THEREFORE 3 : immediately after that : at once

there·with \thar-'with, ther-, -'with\ *adv* 1 : with that 2 *archaic* : THEREUPON, FORTHWITH

there·with·al \'tha(ə)r-with-,ól, 'the(ə)r-, -with-\ *adv* 1 *archaic* : BESIDES 2 : THEREWITH

therm *abbr* thermometer

ther·mal \'thər-məl\ *adj* 1 : of, relating to, or caused by heat 2 : designed to prevent the loss of body heat (~ underwear) — **ther·mal·ly** \-ē\ *adv*

thermal pollution *n* : the discharge of liquid (as waste water from a factory) into a natural body of water at a temperature harmful to the environment

therm·is·tor \'thər-,mis-tər\ *n* : an electrical resistor whose resistance varies sharply with temperature

ther·mo·cline \'thər-mə-,klīn\ *n* : a transition layer in a thermally stratified body of water that separates zones of widely different temperature

ther·mo·dy·nam·ics \,thər-mō-dī-'nam-iks\ *n* : physics that deals with the mechanical action or relations of heat — **ther·mo·dy·nam·ic** \-ik\ *adj* — **ther·mo·dy·nam·i·cal·ly** \-i-k(ə-)lē\ *adv*

ther·mom·e·ter \thə(r)-'mäm-ət-ər\ *n* [F *thermomètre*, fr. Gk *thermē* heat + *metron* measure] : an instrument for measuring temperature commonly by means of the expansion or contraction of mercury or alcohol as indicated by its rise or fall in a thin glass tube — **ther·mo·met·ric** \,thər-mə-'me-trik\ *adj* — **ther·mo·met·ri·cal·ly** \-tri-k(ə-)lē\ *adv*

ther·mo·nu·cle·ar \,thər-mō-'n(y)ü-klē-ər\ *adj* 1 : of or relating to changes in the nucleus of atoms of low atomic weight (as hydrogen) that require a very high temperature (as in the hydrogen bomb) 2 : utilizing or relating to a thermonuclear bomb (~ war)

ther·mo·plas·tic \,thər-mə-'plas-tik\ *adj* : capable of softening when heated and of hardening again when cooled (~ resins) — **thermoplastic** *n*

ther·mo·reg·u·la·tor \,thər-mō-'reg-yə-,lāt-ər\ *n* : a device for the regulation of temperature

ther·mos \'thər-məs\ *n* : VACUUM BOTTLE

ther·mo·sphere \'thər-mə-,sfiər\ *n* : the part of the earth's atmosphere that begins at about 50 miles (about 80 kilometers) above the earth's surface, extends to outer space, and is characterized by steadily increasing temperature with height

ther·mo·stat \'thər-mə-,stat\ *n* : a device that automatically controls temperature — **ther·mo·stat·ic** \,thər-mə-'stat-ik\ *adj* — **ther·mo·stat·i·cal·ly** \-i-k(ə-)lē\ *adv*

the·sau·rus \thi-'sór-əs\ *n, pl* **-sau·ri** \-'sór-,ī\ *or* **-sau·rus·es** \-'sór-ə-səz\ [NL, fr. L, treasure, collection, fr. Gk *thēsauros*] : a book of words and their synonyms — **the·sau·ral** \-'sór-əl\ *adj*

these *pl of* THIS

the·sis \'thē-səs\ *n, pl* **the·ses** \'thē-,sēz\ 1 : a proposition that a person advances and offers to maintain by argument 2 : an essay embodying results of original research; *esp* : one written for an academic degree

¹**thes·pi·an** \'thes-pē-ən\ *adj, often cap* [fr. *Thespis*, 6th cent. B.C. Greek poet and reputed originator of tragedy] : relating to the drama : DRAMATIC

²**thespian** *n* : ACTOR

Thess *abbr* Thessalonians

Thes·sa·lo·nians \ˌthes-ə-ˈlō-nyənz, -nē-ənz\ n — see BIBLE table

thew \ˈth(y)ü\ n : MUSCLE, SINEW — usu. used in pl.

they \(ˈ)thā\ pron 1 : those individuals under discussion : the ones previously mentioned or referred to 2 : unspecified persons : PEOPLE

thi·a·mine \ˈthī-ə-mən, -ˌmēn\ also **thi·a·min** \-mən\ n : a vitamin of the vitamin B complex that is essential to normal metabolism and nerve function

¹thick \ˈthik\ adj 1 : having relatively great depth or extent from one surface to its opposite ⟨a ~ plank⟩ ; also : heavily built : THICKSET 2 : densely massed : CROWDED; also : FREQUENT, NUMEROUS 3 : dense or viscous in consistency ⟨~ syrup⟩ 4 : marked by haze, fog, or mist ⟨~ weather⟩ 5 : measuring in thickness ⟨one meter ~⟩ 6 : imperfectly articulated : INDISTINCT ⟨~ speech⟩ 7 : STUPID, OBTUSE 8 : associated on close terms : INTIMATE 9 : EXCESSIVE syn compact, close, dense, crowded, tight — **thick·ly** adv

²thick n 1 : the most crowded or active part 2 : the part of greatest thickness

thick·en \ˈthik-ən\ vb **thick·ened; thick·en·ing** \-(ə-)niŋ\ : to make or become thick — **thick·en·er** \-(ə-)nər\ n

thick·et \ˈthik-ət\ n : a dense growth of bushes or small trees

thick·ness \-nəs\ n 1 : the quality or state of being thick 2 : the smallest of three dimensions ⟨length, width, and ~⟩ 3 : LAYER, SHEET ⟨a single ~ of canvas⟩

thick·set \ˈthik-ˈset\ adj 1 : closely placed or planted 2 : having a thick body : BURLY

thick–skinned \-ˈskind\ adj 1 : having a thick skin 2 : not easily bothered by criticism or insult

thief \ˈthēf\ n, pl **thieves** \ˈthēvz\ : one that steals esp. secretly

thieve \ˈthēv\ vb **thieved; thiev·ing** : STEAL, ROB syn filch, pilfer, purloin, swipe

thiev·ery \ˈthēv-(ə-)rē\ n, pl **-er·ies** : the act of stealing : THEFT

thigh \ˈthī\ n : the part of the vertebrate hind limb between the knee and the hip

thigh·bone \ˈthī-ˌbōn\ n : FEMUR

thim·ble \ˈthim-bəl\ n : a cap or guard used in sewing to protect the finger when pushing the needle — **thim·ble·ful** n

¹thin \ˈthin\ adj **thin·ner; thin·nest** 1 : having little extent from one surface through to its opposite : not thick : SLENDER 2 : not closely set or placed : SPARSE ⟨~ hair⟩ 3 : not dense or not dense enough : more fluid or rarefied than normal ⟨~ air⟩ ⟨~ syrup⟩ 4 : lacking substance, fullness, or strength ⟨~ broth⟩ 5 : FLIMSY syn slim, slight, tenuous — **thin·ly** adv — **thin·ness** \ˈthin-nəs\ n

²thin vb **thinned; thin·ning** : to make or become thin

thine \ˈthīn\ pron, archaic : one or the ones belonging to thee

thing \ˈthiŋ\ n 1 : a matter of concern : AFFAIR ⟨~s to do⟩ 2 pl : state of affairs ⟨~s are improving⟩ 3 : EVENT, CIRCUMSTANCE ⟨the crime was a terrible ~⟩ 4 : DEED, ACT ⟨expected great ~s of him⟩ 5 : a distinct entity : OBJECT 6 : an inanimate object distinguished from a living being 7 pl : POSSESSIONS, EFFECTS ⟨packed his ~s⟩ 8 : an article of clothing 9 : DETAIL, POINT 10 : IDEA, NOTION 11 : something one likes to do : SPECIALTY ⟨doing his ~⟩

think \ˈthiŋk\ vb **thought** \ˈthȯt\ ; **think·ing** 1 : to form or have in the mind 2 : to have as an opinion : BELIEVE 3 : to reflect on : PONDER 4 : to call to mind : REMEMBER 5 : REASON 6 : to form a mental picture of : IMAGINE 7 : to devise by thinking ⟨thought up a plan to escape⟩ syn conceive, fancy, realize, envisage — **think·er** n

think tank n : an institute, corporation, or group organized for interdisciplinary research (as in technological or social problems)

thin·ner \ˈthin-ər\ n : a volatile liquid (as turpentine) used to thin paint

thin–skinned \ˈthin-ˈskind\ adj 1 : having a thin skin 2 : extremely sensitive to criticism or insult

¹third \ˈthərd\ adj : next after the second — **third** or **third·ly** adv

²third n 1 : one of three equal parts of something 2 : one that is third 3 : the 3d forward gear in an automotive vehicle

third degree n : the subjection of a prisoner to mental or physical torture to force a confession

third dimension n 1 : thickness, depth, or apparent thickness or depth that confers solidity on an object 2 : a quality that confers reality — **third-dimensional** adj

third world n, often cap T&W 1 : a group of nations esp. in Africa and Asia that are not aligned with either the Communist or the non-Communist blocs 2 : an aggregate of minority groups within a larger predominant culture 3 : the aggregate of the underdeveloped nations of the world

¹thirst \ˈthərst\ n 1 : a feeling of dryness in the mouth and throat associated with a wish to drink; also : a bodily condition producing this 2 : an ardent desire : CRAVING ⟨a ~ for knowledge⟩ — **thirsty** adj

²thirst vb 1 : to need drink : suffer thirst 2 : to have a strong desire : CRAVE

thir·teen \ˈthər-ˈtēn, ˈthər-\ n : one more than 12 — **thirteen** adj or pron — **thir·teenth** \-ˈtēnth\ adj or n

thir·ty \ˈthərt-ē\ n, pl **thirties** : three times 10 — **thir·ti·eth** \-ē-əth\ adj or n — **thirty** adj or pron

¹**this** \'(')this\ *pron, pl* **these** \'(')thēz\ 1 : the one close or closest in time or space ⟨~ is your book⟩ 2 : what is in the present or under immediate observation or discussion ⟨~ is a mess⟩ ; *also* : what is happening or being done now (after ~ we'll leave)

²**this** *adj, pl* **these** 1 : being the one near, present, just mentioned, or more immediately under observation ⟨~ book⟩ 2 : constituting the immediate past or future (friends all *these* years)

³**this** \'this\ *adv* : to such an extent or degree (we need a book about ~ big)

this·tle \'this-əl\ *n* : any of several tall prickly herbs

this·tle·down \-,daůn\ *n* : the down from the ripe flower head of a thistle

¹**thith·er** \'thith-ər\ *adv* : to that place

²**thither** *adj* : being on the farther side

thith·er·ward \-wərd\ *adv* : toward that place : THITHER

thole \'thōl\ *n* : a pin set in the gunwale of a boat against which an oar pivots in rowing

thong \'thóŋ\ *n* 1 : a strip esp. of leather or hide 2 : a sandal held on the foot by a thong between the toes

tho·rax \'thōr-,aks\ *n, pl* **tho·rax·es** *or* **tho·ra·ces** \'thōr-ə-,sēz\ 1 : the part of the body of a mammal between the neck and the abdomen; *also* : its cavity 2 : the middle of the three main divisions of the body of an insect — **tho·rac·ic** \thə-'ras-ik\ *adj*

tho·ri·um \'thōr-ē-əm\ *n* : a radioactive metallic chemical element

thorn \'thórn\ *n* 1 : a woody plant bearing sharp processes 2 : a sharp rigid plant process that is usu. a modified leafless branch 3 : something that causes distress — **thorny** *adj*

thor·ough \'thər-ō\ *adj* 1 : COMPLETE, EXHAUSTIVE ⟨a ~ search⟩ 2 : very careful : PAINSTAKING ⟨a ~ scholar⟩ 3 : having full mastery — **thor·ough·ly** *adv* — **thor·ough·ness** *n*

¹**thor·ough·bred** \'thər-ə-,bred\ *adj* 1 : bred from the best blood through a long line 2 *cap* : of or relating to the Thoroughbred breed of horses 3 : marked by high-spirited grace

²**thoroughbred** *n* 1 *cap* : any of an English breed of light speedy horses kept chiefly for racing 2 : one (as a pedigreed animal) of excellent quality

thor·ough·fare \-,faər\ *n* : a public road or street

thor·ough·go·ing \,thər-ə-'gō-iŋ\ *adj* : marked by thoroughness or zeal

thorp \'thórp\ *n, archaic* : village

those *pl of* THAT

¹**thou** \'(')thaů\ *pron, archaic* : the person addressed

²**thou** \'thaů\ *n, pl* **thou** : a thousand of something (as dollars)

¹**though** \'thō\ *adv* : HOWEVER, NEVERTHELESS (not for long, ~)

²**though** \(,)thō\ *conj* 1 : despite the fact that ⟨~ the odds are hopeless, they

fight on⟩ 2 : granting that ⟨~ it may look bad, still, all is not lost⟩

¹**thought** \'thót\ *past and past part of* THINK

²**thought** *n* 1 : the process of thinking 2 : serious consideration : REGARD 3 : reasoning power 4 : the power to imagine : CONCEPTION 5 : IDEA, NOTION 6 : OPINION, BELIEF

thought·ful \'thót-fəl\ *adj* 1 : absorbed in thought 2 : marked by careful thinking ⟨a ~ essay⟩ 3 : considerate of others ⟨a ~ host⟩ — **thought·ful·ly** \-ē\ *adv* — **thought·ful·ness** *n*

thought·less \-ləs\ *adj* 1 : insufficiently alert : CARELESS ⟨a ~ worker⟩ 2 : RECKLESS ⟨a ~ act⟩ 3 : lacking concern for others : INCONSIDERATE ⟨~ remarks⟩ — **thought·less·ly** *adv* — **thought·less·ness** *n*

thou·sand \'thaůz-²nd\ *n, pl* **thousands** *or* **thousand** : 10 times 100 — **thousand** *adj* — **thou·sandth** \-²nth\ *adj or n*

thousands digit *n* : the numeral (as 1 in 1456) occupying the thousands place in a number

thousands place *n* : the place four to the left of the decimal point in an Arabic number

thrall \'thról\ *n* 1 : SLAVE, BONDMAN 2 : THRALLDOM

thrall·dom *or* **thral·dom** \'thról-dəm\ *n* : the condition of a thrall

thrash \'thrash\ *vb* 1 : THRESH 1 2 : BEAT, WHIP; *also* : DEFEAT 3 : to move about violently 4 : to go over again and again ⟨~ over the matter⟩ ; *also* : to hammer out ⟨~ out a plan⟩

¹**thrash·er** \'thrash-ər\ *n* : one that thrashes or threshes

²**thrasher** *n* : a long-tailed bird resembling a thrush

¹**thread** \'thred\ *n* 1 : a thin continuous strand of spun and twisted textile fibers 2 : something resembling a textile thread 3 : the ridge or groove that winds around a screw 4 : a train of thought 5 : a continuing element

²**thread** *vb* 1 : to pass a thread through the eye of (a needle) 2 : to pass (as film) through something 3 : to make one's way through or between 4 : to put together on a thread ⟨~ beads⟩ 5 : to form a screw thread on or in

thread·bare \-,baər\ *adj* 1 : worn so that the thread shows : SHABBY 2 : TRITE

thready \-ē\ *adj* 1 : consisting of or bearing fibers of filaments ⟨a ~ bark⟩ 2 : lacking in fullness, body, or vigor

threat \'thret\ *n* 1 : an expression of intent to do harm 2 : one that threatens

threat·en \'thret-²n\ *vb* **threat·ened**; **threat·en·ing** \'thret-(-²)niŋ\ 1 : to utter threats against 2 : to give signs or warning of : PORTEND 3 : to hang over as a threat : MENACE — **threat·en·ing·ly** *adv*

three \'thrē\ *n* 1 : one more than two 2 : the 3d in a set or series 3 : something

having three units — **three** *adj or pron*
3–D \'thrē-'dē\ *n* : three-dimensional form

three–dimensional *adj* 1 : relating to or having three dimensions 2 : giving the illusion of varying distances ⟨a ∼ picture⟩

three·fold \'thrē-ˌfōld, -'fōld\ *adj* 1 : having three parts : TRIPLE 2 : being three times as great or as many — **three·fold** \-'fōld\ *adv*

three·pence \'threp-əns, 'thrip-, 'thrəp-, *US also* 'thrē-pens\ *n* 1 *pl* **threepence** *or* **three·penc·es** : a coin worth three pennies 2 : the sum of three British pennies

three·score \'thrē-'skōr\ *adj* : being three times twenty : SIXTY

three·some \'thrē-səm\ *n* : a group of three persons or things

thren·o·dy \'thren-əd-ē\ *n, pl* **-dies** : a song of lamentation : ELEGY

thresh \'thrash, 'thresh\ *vb* 1 : to separate (as grain from straw) by beating 2 : THRASH — **thresh·er** *n*

thresh·old \'thresh-ˌōld\ *n* 1 : the sill of a door 2 : a point or place of beginning or entering : OUTSET 3 : a point at which a physiological or psychological effect begins to be produced

threw *past of* THROW

thrice \'thrīs\ *adv* 1 : three times 2 : in a threefold manner or degree

thrift \'thrift\ *n* [ME fr. ON, prosperity, fr. *thrīfask* to thrive] : careful management esp. of money : FRUGALITY — **thrift·i·ly** \'thrif-tə-lē\ *adv* — **thrift·less** *adj* — **thrifty** *adj*

thrill \'thril\ *vb* [ME *thirlen, thrillen* to pierce, fr. OE *thyrlian*, fr. *thyrel* hole, fr. *thurh* through] 1 : to have or cause to have sudden sharp feeling of excitement; *also* : TINGLE, SHIVER 2 : TREMBLE, VIBRATE — **thrill** *n* — **thrill·er** *n* — **thrill·ing·ly** \-iŋ-lē\ *adv*

thrive \'thrīv\ *vb* **throve** \'thrōv\ *or* **thrived**; **thriv·en** \'thriv-ən\ *also* **thrived**; **thriv·ing** \'thrī-viŋ\ 1 : to grow luxuriantly : FLOURISH 2 : to gain in wealth or possessions : PROSPER

throat \'thrōt\ *n* : the part of the neck in front of the spinal column; *also* : the passage through it to the stomach and lungs — **throat·ed** \-əd\ *adj*

throaty \'thrōt-ē\ *adj* **throat·i·er; -est** 1 : uttered or produced from low in the throat ⟨a ∼ voice⟩ 2 : heavy, thick, or deep as if from the throat ⟨∼ notes of a horn⟩ — **throat·i·ly** \'thrōt-ᵊl-ē\ *adv* — **throat·i·ness** \-ē-nəs\ *n*

¹throb \'thräb\ *vb* **throbbed; throb·bing** : to pulsate or pound esp. with abnormal force or rapidity : BEAT, VIBRATE

²throb *n* : BEAT, PULSE

throe \'thrō\ *n* 1 : PANG, SPASM 2 *pl* : a hard or painful struggle

throm·bo·sis \thräm-'bō-səs\ *n, pl* **-bo·ses** \-ˌsēz\ : the formation or presence

of a clot in a blood vessel during life — **throm·bot·ic** \-'bät-ik\ *adj*

throm·bus \'thräm-bəs\ *n, pl* **throm·bi** \-ˌbī\ : a clot of blood formed within a blood vessel and remaining attached to its place of origin

throne \'thrōn\ *n* 1 : the chair of state esp. of a king or bishop 2 : royal power : SOVEREIGNTY

¹throng \'thrȯŋ\ *n* 1 : MULTITUDE 2 : a crowding together of many persons

²throng *vb* **thronged; throng·ing** \'thrȯŋ-iŋ\ : CROWD

¹throt·tle \'thrät-ᵊl\ *vb* **throt·tled; throt·tling** \'thrät-(ə-)liŋ\ [ME *throtlen*, fr. *throte* throat] 1 : CHOKE, STRANGLE 2 : SUPPRESS 3 : to reduce the speed of (an engine) by closing the throttle — **throt·tler** \-(ᵊ-)lər\ *n*

²throttle *n* : a valve regulating the flow of steam or fuel to an engine; *also* : the lever controlling this valve

¹through \(')thrü\ *prep* 1 : into at one side and out at the other side of ⟨go ∼ the door⟩ 2 : by way of ⟨entered ∼ a skylight⟩ 3 : AMONG ⟨a path ∼ the trees⟩ 4 : by means of ⟨succeeded ∼ hard work⟩ 5 : over the whole of ⟨rumors swept ∼ the office⟩ 6 : during the whole of ⟨∼ the night⟩ 7 : to and including ⟨Monday ∼ Friday⟩

²through \'thrü\ *adv* 1 : from one end or side to the other 2 : from beginning to end : to completion ⟨see it ∼⟩ 3 : to the core : THOROUGHLY ⟨he was wet ∼⟩ 4 : into the open : OUT ⟨break ∼⟩

³through \'thrü\ *adj* 1 : permitting free passage ⟨a ∼ street⟩ 2 : going from point of origin to destination without change or transfer ⟨∼ train⟩ 3 : coming from or going to points outside a local area ⟨∼ traffic⟩ 4 : FINISHED ⟨∼ with the job⟩

¹through·out \thrü-'aut\ *adv* 1 : EVERYWHERE 2 : from beginning to end

²throughout *prep* 1 : in or to every part of 2 : during the whole period of

through·put \'thrü-ˌput\ *n* : OUTPUT, PRODUCTION ⟨the ∼ of a computer⟩

through·way *var of* THRUWAY

throve *past of* THRIVE

¹throw \'thrō\ *vb* **threw** \'thrü\ ; **thrown** \'thrōn\ ; **throw·ing** 1 : to propel through the air esp. with a forward motion of the hand and arm ⟨∼ a ball⟩ 2 : to cause to fall or fall off 3 : to put suddenly in a certain position or condition ⟨∼ into panic⟩ 4 : to put on or take off hastily ⟨∼ on a coat⟩ 5 : to move (a lever) so as to connect or disconnect parts of something (as a clutch) 6 : to lose intentionally ⟨∼ a game⟩ 7 : to act as host for ⟨∼ a party⟩ *syn* toss, fling, pitch, sling — **throw·er** \'thrō-(ə)r\ *n*

²throw *n* 1 : an act of throwing, hurling, or flinging; *also* : CAST 2 : the distance a missile may be thrown 3 : a light coverlet 4 : a woman's scarf or light wrap

throw·away \'thrō-ə-ˌwā\ *n* : something that is or is designed to be thrown away esp. after one use

throw·back \'thrō-,bak\ *n* : reversion to an earlier type or phase; *also* : an instance or product of this

throw up *vb* **1** : to build hurriedly **2** : VOMIT

thrum \'thrəm\ *vb* **thrummed; thrum·ming** : to play or pluck a stringed instrument idly : STRUM

thrush \'thrəsh\ *n* : any of a large family of small or medium-sized songbirds that are mostly of a plain color often with spotted underparts

¹thrust \'thrəst\ *vb* **thrust; thrust·ing 1** : to push or drive with force : SHOVE **2** : STAB, PIERCE **3** : INTERJECT **4** : to press the acceptance of upon someone

²thrust *n* **1** : a lunge with a pointed weapon **2** : ATTACK **3** : the pressure of one part of a construction against another (as of an arch against an abutment) **4** : the force produced by a propeller or jet or rocket engine that drives a vehicle (as an aircraft) forward **5** : a violent push : SHOVE

thrust·er *also* **thrust·or** \'thrəs-tər\ *n* : one that thrusts; *esp* : a rocket engine

thru·way \'thrü-,wā\ *n* : EXPRESSWAY

¹thud \'thəd\ *vb* **thud·ded; thud·ding** : to move or strike so as to make a thud

²thud *n* **1** : BLOW **2** : a dull sound

thug \'thəg\ *n* [Hindi *thag,* lit., thief, fr. Skt *sthaga* rogue] : a brutal ruffian or assassin

thu·li·um \'th(y)ü-lē-əm\ *n* : a rare metallic chemical element

¹thumb \'thəm\ *n* **1** : the short thick first digit of the human hand or a corresponding digit of a lower animal **2** : the part of a glove or mitten that covers the thumb

²thumb *vb* **1** : to leaf through (pages) with the thumb **2** : to wear or soil with the thumb by frequent handling **3** : to request or obtain (a ride) in a passing automobile by signaling with the thumb

thumb index *n* : a series of notches cut in the fore edge of a book to facilitate reference

¹thumb·nail \'thəm-,nāl\ *n* : the nail of the thumb

²thumb·nail \,thəm-,nāl\ *adj* : BRIEF, CONCISE ⟨a ~ description⟩

thumb·print \'thəm-,print\ *n* : an impression made by the thumb

thumb·screw \'thəm-,skrü\ *n* **1** : a screw with a head that may be turned by the thumb and forefinger **2** : a device of torture for squeezing the thumb

thumb·tack \-,tak\ *n* : a tack with a broad flat head for pressing with one's thumb into a board or wall

¹thump \'thəmp\ *vb* **1** : to strike with or as if with something thick or heavy so as to cause a dull heavy sound **2** : POUND

²thump *n* : a blow with or as if with something blunt or heavy; *also* : the sound made by such a blow

thun·der \'thən-dər\ *n* **1** : the sound following a flash of lightning; *also* : a noise like such a sound **2** : a loud utterance or threat

²thunder *vb* **thun·dered; thun·der·ing** \-d(ə-)riŋ\ **1** : to produce thunder **2** : ROAR, SHOUT

thun·der·bolt \-,bōlt\ *n* : a flash of lightning with its accompanying thunder

thun·der·clap \-,klap\ *n* : a crash of thunder

thun·der·cloud \-,klaůd\ *n* : a dark storm cloud producing lightning and thunder

thun·der·head \-,hed\ *n* : a large cumulus cloud often appearing before a thunderstorm

thun·der·ous \'thən-d(ə-)rəs\ *adj* : producing thunder; *also* : making a noise like thunder — **thun·der·ous·ly** *adv*

thun·der·show·er \'thən-dər-,shaů(-ə)r\ *n* : a shower accompanied by thunder and lightning

thun·der·storm \-,stórm\ *n* : a storm accompanied by thunder and lightning

thun·der·struck \-,strək\ *adj* : stunned as if struck by a thunderbolt

Thurs *or* **Thu** *abbr* Thursday

Thurs·day \'thərz-dē, -,dā\ *n* [deriv. of ON *thōrsdagr,* lit., day of Thor (Norse god)] : the fifth day of the week

thus \'thəs\ *adv* **1** : in this or that manner **2** : to this degree or extent : so **3** : because of this or that : HENCE

¹thwack \'thwak\ *vb* : to strike with something flat or heavy

²thwack *n* : a heavy blow : WHACK

¹thwart \'thwórt\ *vb* **1** : BAFFLE **2** : BLOCK, DEFEAT **syn** balk, foil, outwit, frustrate

²thwart \'thwórt, *naut often* 'thórt\ *adv* : ATHWART

³thwart *adj* : situated or placed across something else

⁴thwart \'th(w)órt\ *n* : a rower's seat extending across a boat

thy \(,)thī\ *adj, archaic* : of, relating to, or done by or to thee or thyself

thyme \'tīm, 'thīm\ *n* [ME, fr. MF *thym,* fr. L *thymum,* fr. Gk *thymon,* fr. *thyein* to make a burnt offering, sacrifice] : any of several mints with aromatic leaves used esp. in seasoning

thy·mine \'thī-,mēn\ *n* : a pyrimidine base that is one of the four bases coding genetic information in the molecular chain of DNA

thy·mus \'thī-məs\ *n* : a glandular organ of the neck that is composed largely of lymphoid tissue, functions esp. in the development of the body's immune system, and tends to disappear or become rudimentary in the adult

thy·ris·tor \thī-'ris-tər\ *n* : a semiconductor device that acts as a switch, rectifier, or voltage regulator

thy·roid \'thī-ˌröid\ *also* **thy·roi·dal** \thī-'röid-ᵊl\ *adj* [NL *thyroides*, fr. Gk *thyreoeidēs* shield-shaped, thyroid, fr. *thyreos* shield shaped like a door, fr. *thyra* door] : of, relating to, or being a large endocrine gland that lies at the base of the neck and produces several iodine-containing hormones that affect growth, development, and metabolism — **thyroid** *n*

thy·rox·ine *or* **thy·rox·in** \thī-'räk-ˌsēn, -sᵊn\ *n* : an iodine-containing amino acid that is the active principle of the thyroid gland and is used to treat thyroid disorders

thy·self \thī-'self\ *pron, archaic* : YOURSELF

Ti *symbol* titanium

ti·ara \tē-'ar-ə, -'er-, -'är-\ *n* 1 : the pope's triple crown 2 : a decorative headband or semicircle for formal wear by women

Ti·bet·an \tə-'bet-ᵊn\ *n* : a native or inhabitant of Tibet — **Tibetan** *adj*

tib·ia \'tib-ē-ə\ *n, pl* **-i·ae** \-ē-ˌē\ *also* **-i·as** [L] : the inner of the two bones of the vertebrate hind limb between the knee and the ankle

tic \'tik\ *n* : a local and habitual twitching of muscles esp. of the face

ti·cal \ti-'käl, 'tik-əl\ *n, pl* **ticals** *or* **tical** : BAHT

¹tick \'tik\ *n* : any of numerous small 8-legged blood-sucking arachnid arthropods

²tick *n* : the fabric case of a mattress or pillow; *also* : a mattress consisting of a tick and its filling

³tick *n* 1 : a light rhythmic audible tap or beat 2 : a small mark used to draw attention to or check something

⁴tick *vb* 1 : to make the sound of a tick or series of ticks 2 : to mark, count, or announce by or as if by ticking beats 3 : to function as an operating mechanism : RUN 4 : to mark or check with a tick

⁵tick *n* : CREDIT; *also* : a credit account

tick·er \'tik-ər\ *n* 1 : something (as a watch) that ticks 2 : a telegraph instrument that prints information (as stock prices) on paper tape 3 *slang* : HEART

ticker tape *n* : the paper ribbon on which a telegraphic ticker prints

¹tick·et \'tik-ət\ *n* 1 : CERTIFICATE, LICENSE, PERMIT; *esp* : a certificate or token showing that a fare or admission fee has been paid 2 : TAG, LABEL 3 : SLATE 3 4 : a summons issued to a traffic offender

²ticket *vb* 1 : to attach a ticket to 2 : to furnish or serve with a ticket

tick·ing \'tik-iŋ\ *n* : a strong fabric used in upholstering and as a mattress covering

tick·le \'tik-əl\ *vb* **tick·led**; **tick·ling** \-(ə-)liŋ\ 1 : to have a tingling sensation 2 : to excite or stir up agreeably : PLEASE, AMUSE 3 : to touch (as a body part) lightly so as to cause uneasiness,

laughter, or spasmodic movements — **tickle** *n*

tick·lish \'tik-(ə-)lish\ *adj* 1 : OVERSENSITIVE, TOUCHY 2 : UNSTABLE ⟨a ~ foothold⟩ 3 : requiring delicate handling ⟨~ subject⟩ 4 : sensitive to tickling — **tick·lish·ly** *adv* — **tick·lish·ness** *n*

tid·al wave \'tīd-ᵊl-\ *n* 1 : an unusually high sea wave that sometimes follows an earthquake 2 : an unusual rise of water alongshore due to strong winds

tid·bit \'tid-ˌbit\ *n* : a choice morsel

¹tide \'tīd\ *n* [ME, time, fr. OE *tīd*] 1 : the alternate rising and falling of the surface of the ocean 2 : something that fluctuates like the tides of the sea — **tid·al** \'tīd-ᵊl\ *adj*

²tide *vb* **tid·ed**; **tid·ing** : to carry through or help along as if by the tide ⟨a loan to ~ him over⟩

tide·land \'tīd-ˌland, -lənd\ *n* 1 : land overflowed during flood tide 2 : land under the ocean within a nation's territorial waters — often used in pl.

tide·wa·ter \-ˌwȯt-ər, -ˌwät-\ *n* 1 : water overflowing land at flood tide 2 : low-lying coastal land

tid·ings \'tīd-iŋz\ *n pl* : NEWS, MESSAGE

¹ti·dy \'tīd-ē\ *adj* **ti·di·er**; **-est** 1 : well ordered and cared for : NEAT 2 : LARGE, SUBSTANTIAL ⟨a ~ sum⟩ — **ti·di·ness** \'tīd-ē-nəs\ *n*

²tidy *vb* **ti·died**; **ti·dy·ing** 1 : to put in order 2 : to make things tidy

³tidy *n, pl* **tidies** : a piece of decorated cloth or needlework used to protect the back or arms of a chair from wear or soil

¹tie \'tī\ *n* 1 : a line, ribbon, or cord used for fastening, uniting, or closing 2 : a structural element (as a beam or rod) holding two pieces together 3 : one of the cross supports to which railroad rails are fastened 4 : a connecting link : BOND ⟨family ~s⟩ 5 : an equality in number (as of votes or scores); *also* : an undecided or deadlocked contest 6 : NECKTIE

²tie *vb* **tied**; **ty·ing** \'tī-iŋ\ *or* **tie·ing** 1 : to fasten, attach, or close by means of a tie 2 : to bring together firmly : UNITE 3 : to form a knot or bow in ⟨~ a scarf⟩ 4 : to restrain from freedom of action : CONSTRAIN 5 : to make or have an equal score with

tie·back \'tī-ˌbak\ *n* : a decorative strip for draping a curtain to the side of a window

tie-dye·ing \'tī-ˌdī-iŋ\ *n* : a method of producing patterns in textiles by tying parts of the fabric so that they will not absorb the dye — **tie-dyed** \-ˌdīd\ *adj*

tie-in \'tī-ˌin\ *n* : CONNECTION

tier \'tiər\ *n* : ROW, LAYER; *esp* : one of two or more rows arranged one above another

tie-rod \'tī-ˌräd\ *n* : a rod used as a connecting member or brace

tie-up \'tī-ˌəp\ *n* 1 : a slowing or stopping of traffic or business 2 : CONNECTION

tiff \\'tif\\ *n* : a petty quarrel — **tiff** *vb*

tif·fin \\'tif-ən\\ *n, chiefly Brit* : LUNCHEON

ti·ger \\'tī-gər\\ *n* : a large tawny black-striped Asian flesh-eating mammal related to the cat — **ti·ger·ish** \\-g(ə-)rish\\ *adj*

¹tight \\'tīt\\ *adj* **1** : so close in structure as not to permit passage of a liquid or gas **2** : fixed or held very firmly in place **3** : TAUT **4** : fitting usu. too closely ⟨~ shoes⟩ **5** : set close together : COMPACT ⟨a ~ formation⟩ **6** : DIFFICULT, TRYING ⟨get in a ~ spot⟩ **7** : STINGY, MISERLY **8** : evenly contested : CLOSE **9** : INTOXICATED **10** : low in supply : hard to get ⟨money is ~⟩ — **tight·ly** *adv* — **tight·ness** *n*

²tight *adv* **1** : TIGHTLY, FIRMLY **2** : SOUNDLY ⟨sleep ~⟩

tight·en \\'tīt-²n\\ *vb* **tight·ened**; **tight·en·ing** \\'tīt-(²-)niŋ\\ : to make or become tight

tight-fist·ed \\'tīt-'fis-təd\\ *adj* : STINGY

tight·rope \\'tīt-,rōp\\ *n* : a taut rope or wire for acrobats to perform on

tights \\'tīts\\ *n pl* : skintight garments covering the body esp. below the waist

tight·wad \\'tīt-,wäd\\ *n* : a stingy person

ti·gress \\'tī-grəs\\ *n* : a female tiger

til·de \\'til-də\\ *n* [Sp, fr. ML *titulus* tittle] : a mark⁻ placed esp. over the letter *n* (as in Spanish *señor* sir) to denote the sound \\n̄\\ or over vowels (as in Portuguese *irmã* sister) to indicate nasal quality

¹tile \\'tīl\\ *n* **1** : a thin piece of fired clay, stone, or concrete used for roofs, floors, or walls; *also* : a hollow or concave earthenware or concrete piece used for a drain **2** : a thin piece (as of a rubber composition) used for covering walls or floors — **til·ing** \\-iŋ\\ *n*

²tile *vb* **tiled**; **til·ing 1** : to cover with tiles **2** : to install drainage tile in — **til·er** *n*

¹till \\(,)til\\ *prep or conj* : UNTIL

²till \\'til\\ *vb* : to work by plowing, sowing, and raising crops : CULTIVATE — **till·able** *adj* — **till·er** *n*

³till \\'til\\ *n* : DRAWER; *esp* : a money drawer in a store or bank

till·age \\'til-ij\\ *n* **1** : the work of tilling land **2** : cultivated land

¹til·ler \\'til-ər\\ *n* [OE *telgor, telgra* twig, shoot] : a sprout or stalk esp. from the base or lower part of a plant

²til·ler \\'til-ər\\ *n* [ME *tiler* stock of a crossbow, fr. MF *telier*, lit., beam of a loom, fr. ML *telarium*, fr. L *tela* web] : a lever used for turning a boat's rudder from side to side

¹tilt \\'tilt\\ *n* **1** : a military exercise in which two combatants charging usu. with lances try to unhorse each other : JOUST; *also* : a tournament of tilts **2** : a verbal contest : DISPUTE **3** : SLANT, TIP

²tilt *vb* **1** : to move or shift so as to incline : TIP **2** : to engage in or as if in combat with lances : JOUST

tilth \\'tilth\\ *n* **1** : TILLAGE **2 2** : the state of aggregation of the soil esp. in relation to its suitability for crop growth

Tim *abbr* Timothy

¹tim·ber \\'tim-bər\\ *n* [ME, fr. OE, building, wood] **1** : wooded land or growing trees from which timber may be obtained **2** : wood for use in making something **3** : a usu. large squared or dressed piece of wood — **tim·ber·land** \\-bər-,land\\ *n*

²timber *vb* **tim·bered**; **tim·ber·ing** \\-b(ə-)riŋ\\ : to cover, frame, or support with timbers

tim·bered \\'tim-bərd\\ *adj* **1** : having walls framed by exposed timbers **2** : covered with growing timber

tim·ber·ing \\'tim-b(ə-)riŋ\\ *n* : a set or arrangement of timbers

tim·ber·line \\'tim-bər-,līn\\ *n* : the upper limit of tree growth on mountains or in high latitudes

timber rattlesnake *n* : a moderate-sized rattlesnake widely distributed through the eastern half of the U.S.

timber wolf *n* : a large usu. gray No. American wolf

tim·bre *also* **tim·ber** \\'tam-bər, 'tim-\\ *n* [F, fr. MF, bell struck by a hammer, fr. OF, drum, fr. MGk *tymbanon* kettledrum, fr. Gk *tympanon*] : the distinctive quality given to a sound by its overtones

tim·brel \\'tim-brəl\\ *n* : a small hand drum or tambourine

¹time \\'tīm\\ *n* **1** : a period during which an action, process, or condition exists or continues ⟨gone a long ~⟩ **2** : LEISURE ⟨found ~ to read⟩ **3** : a point or period when something occurs : OCCASION ⟨the last ~ we met⟩ **4** : a set or customary moment or hour for something to occur ⟨arrived on ~⟩ **5** : AGE, ERA **6** : state of affairs : CONDITIONS ⟨hard ~s⟩ **7** : a rate of speed : TEMPO **8** : a moment, hour, day, or year as indicated by a clock or calendar ⟨what ~ is it⟩ **9** : a system of reckoning time ⟨solar ~⟩ **10** : one of a series of recurring instances; *also, pl* : added or accumulated quantities or examples ⟨five ~s greater⟩ **11** : a person's experience during a particular period ⟨had a good ~ at the beach⟩

²time *vb* **timed**; **tim·ing 1** : to arrange or set the time of : SCHEDULE ⟨~s his calls conveniently⟩ **2** : to set the tempo or duration of ⟨~ a performance⟩ **3** : to cause to keep time with ⟨~s her steps to the music⟩ **4** : to determine or record the time, duration, or rate of ⟨~ a sprinter⟩ — **tim·er** *n*

time bomb *n* **1** : a bomb so made as to explode at a predetermined time **2** : something having the potential of a dangerous delayed reaction

time clock *n* : a clock that records the times of arrival and departure of workers

time frame *n* : a period of time esp. with respect to some action or project

time-hon·ored \'tīm-,än-ərd\ *adj* : honored because of age or long usage

time-keep·er \'tīm-,kē-pər\ *n* 1 : a clerk who keeps records of the time worked by employees 2 : one appointed to mark and announce the time in an athletic game or contest

time·less \'tīm-ləs\ *adj* 1 : UNENDING 2 : not limited or affected by time ⟨~ works of art⟩ — **time·less·ly** *adv* — **time·less·ness** *n*

time·ly \'tīm-lē\ *adj* **time·li·er; -est** 1 : coming early or at the right time : OP-PORTUNE ⟨a ~ arrival⟩ 2 : appropriate to the time ⟨a ~ book⟩ — **time·li·ness** *n*

time-out \'tīm-'aût\ *n* : a brief suspension of activity esp. in an athletic game

time·piece \'tīm-,pēs\ *n* : a device (as a clock) to show the passage of time

times \,tīmz\ *prep* : multiplied by ⟨2 ~ 2 is 4⟩

time-shar·ing \'tīm-,sheär-iŋ\ *n* : simultaneous access to a computer by many users

times sign *n* : the symbol × used to indicate multiplication

time·ta·ble \'tīm-,tā-bəl\ *n* 1 : a table of the departure and arrival times (as of trains) 2 : a schedule showing a planned order or sequence

time warp *n* : an anomaly, discontinuity, or suspension held to occur in the progress of time

time·worn \-,wôrn\ *adj* 1 : worn by time 2 : HACKNEYED, STALE

tim·id \'tim-əd\ *adj* : lacking in courage or self-confidence : FEARFUL — **ti·mid·i·ty** \tə-'mid-ət-ē\ *n* — **tim·id·ly** \'tim-əd-lē\ *adv*

tim·o·rous \'tim-(ə-)rəs\ *adj* : of a timid disposition : AFRAID — **tim·o·rous·ly** *adv* — **tim·o·rous·ness** *n*

tim·o·thy \'tim-ə-thē\ *n* : a grass with long cylindrical spikes widely grown for hay

Tim·o·thy \'tim-ə-thē\ *n* — see BIBLE table

tim·pa·ni \'tim-pə-nē\ *n pl* [It] : a set of kettledrums played by one performer in an orchestra — **tim·pa·nist** \-nəst\ *n*

¹**tin** \'tin\ *n* 1 : a soft white crystalline metallic element malleable at ordinary temperatures but brittle when heated that is used in solders and alloys 2 : a container (as a can) made of tinplate

²**tin** *vb* **tinned; tin·ning** 1 : to cover or plate with tin 2 *chiefly Brit* : to pack in tins : CAN

tinct \'tiŋkt\ *n* : TINCTURE, TINGE

¹**tinc·ture** \'tiŋk-chər\ *n* 1 : a substance that colors or dyes 2 : a slight admixture : TRACE 3 : an alcoholic solution of a medicinal substance syn touch, suggestion, suspicion, soupçon

²**tincture** *vb* **tinc·tured; tinc·tur·ing** : COLOR, TINGE

tin·der \'tin-dər\ *n* : something that catches fire easily; *esp* : a substance used to kindle a fire from a slight spark

tin·der·box \'tin-dər-,bäks\ *n* 1 : a metal box for holding tinder and usu. flint and steel for striking a spark 2 : a highly flammable object or place

tine \'tīn\ *n* : a slender pointed part (as of a fork or an antler) : PRONG

tin·foil \'tin-,fôil\ *n* : a thin metal sheeting usu. of aluminum or tin-lead alloy

¹**tinge** \'tinj\ *vb* **tinged; tinge·ing** *or* **ting·ing** \'tin-jiŋ\ 1 : to color slightly : TINT 2 : to affect or modify esp. with a slight odor or taste

²**tinge** *n* : a slight coloring, flavor, or quality : TRACE syn touch, suggestion, suspicion, tincture

tin·gle \'tiŋ-gəl\ *vb* **tin·gled; tin·gling** \-g(ə-)liŋ\ 1 : to feel a prickling or thrilling sensation 2 : TINKLE — **tingle** *n*

¹**tin·ker** \'tiŋ-kər\ *n* 1 : a usu. itinerant mender of household utensils 2 : an unskillful mender : BUNGLER

²**tinker** *vb* **tin·kered; tin·ker·ing** \-k(ə-)riŋ\ : to repair or adjust something in an unskillful or experimental manner — **tin·ker·er** *n*

¹**tin·kle** \'tiŋ-kəl\ *vb* **tin·kled; tin·kling** \-k(ə-)liŋ\ : to make or cause to make a tinkle

²**tinkle** *n* : a series of short high ringing or clinking sounds

tin·ny \'tin-ē\ *adj* **tin·ni·er; -est** 1 : abounding in or yielding tin 2 : resembling tin: *also* : LIGHT, CHEAP 3 : thin in tone ⟨a ~ voice⟩ — **tin·ni·ly** \'tin-ʻl-ē\ *adv* — **tin·ni·ness** \-ē-nəs\ *n*

tin·plate \'tin-'plāt\ *n* : thin sheet iron or steel coated with tin — **tin·plate** *vb*

tin·sel \'tin-səl\ *n* [MF *etincelle* spark, glitter] 1 : a thread, strip, or sheet of metal, paper, or plastic used to produce a glittering appearance (as in fabrics) 2 : something superficially attractive but of little worth

tin·smith \'tin-,smith\ *n* : one that works with sheet metal (as tinplate)

¹**tint** \'tint\ *n* 1 : a slight or pale coloration : HUE 2 : any of various shades of a color

²**tint** *vb* : to impart a tint to : COLOR

tin·tin·nab·u·la·tion \,tin-tə-,nab-yə-'lā-shən\ *n* 1 : the ringing of bells 2 : a tingling sound as if of bells

tin·ware \'tin-,waər\ *n* : articles made of tinplate

ti·ny \'tī-nē\ *adj* **ti·ni·er; -est** : very small : MINUTE syn miniature, diminutive, wee, lilliputian

¹**tip** \'tip\ *vb* **tipped; tip·ping** 1 : OVERTURN, UPSET 2 : LEAN, SLANT; *also* : TILT

²**tip** *n* : the act or an instance of tipping

³**tip** *n* 1 : the usu. pointed end of something 2 : a small piece or part serving as an end, cap, or point

⁴**tip** *vb* **tipped; tip·ping** 1 : to furnish with a tip 2 : to cover or adorn the tip of

⁵**tip** *n* : a light touch or blow

⁶**tip** *vb* **tipped; tip·ping** : to strike lightly : TAP

⁷**tip** *n* : a piece of expert of confidential information : HINT

⁸**tip** *vb* **tipped; tip·ping** : to impart a piece of information about or to

⁹**tip** *vb* **tipped; tip·ping** : to give a gratuity to

¹⁰**tip** *n* : a gift or small sum given for a service performed or anticipated

tip-off \'tip-ˌȯf\ *n* : WARNING, TIP

tip·pet \'tip-ət\ *n* : a long scarf or shoulder cape

tip·ple \'tip-əl\ *vb* **tip·pled; tip·pling** \-(ə-)liŋ\ : to drink intoxicating liquor esp. habitually or excessively — **tip·pler** \-(ə-)lər\ *n*

tip·ster \'tip-stər\ *n* : one who gives or sells tips esp. for gambling

tip·sy \'tip-sē\ *adj* **tip·si·er; -est** : unsteady or foolish from the effects of alcohol

¹**tip·toe** \'tip-ˌtō\ *n* : the tip of a toe; *also* : the ends of the toes

²**tiptoe** *adv or adj* : on or as if on tiptoe

³**tiptoe** *vb* **tip·toed; tip·toe·ing** : to walk or proceed on or as if on tiptoe

¹**tip-top** \'tip-'täp\ *n* : the highest point

²**tip-top** *adj* : EXCELLENT, FIRST-RATE

ti·rade \tī-'rād, 'tī-ˌrād\ *n* [F, shot, tirade, fr. MF, fr. It *tirata*, fr. *tirare* to draw, shoot] : a prolonged speech of abuse or condemnation

¹**tire** \'tī(ə)r\ *vb* **tired; tir·ing 1** : to make or become weary : FATIGUE **2** : to wear out the patience of : BORE

²**tire** *n* **1** : a wheel band that forms the tread of a wheel **2** : a rubber cushion usu. containing compressed air that encircles a wheel (as of an automobile)

tired \'tī(ə)rd\ *adj* **1** : WEARY, FATIGUED **2** : HACKNEYED

tire·less \'tī(ə)r-ləs\ *adj* : not tiring : UNTIRING, INDEFATIGABLE — **tire·less·ly** *adv* — **tire·less·ness** *n*

tire·some \'tī(ə)r-səm\ *adj* : tending to bore : WEARISOME, TEDIOUS — **tire·some·ly** *adv* — **tire·some·ness** *n*

tis·sue \'tish-ü\ *n* [ME *tissu*, a rich fabric, fr. OF, fr. *tistre* to weave, fr. L *texere*] **1** : a fine lightweight often sheer fabric **2** : NETWORK, WEB **3** : a soft absorbent paper **4** : a mass or layer of cells forming a basic structural element of an animal or plant body

¹**tit** \'tit\ *n* : TEAT

²**tit** *n* : TITMOUSE

Tit *abbr* Titus

ti·tan \'tīt-ᵊn\ *n* **1** *cap* : one of a family of giants overthrown by the gods of ancient Greece **2** : one gigantic in size or power

ti·tan·ic \tī-'tan-ik, tə-\ *adj* : enormous in size, force, or power *syn* immense, huge, gigantic, giant, colossal, mammoth

ti·ta·ni·um \tī-'tān-ē-əm, tə-\ *n* : a gray light strong metallic chemical element used in alloys

tit·bit \'tit-ˌbit\ *var of* TIDBIT

tithe \'tīth\ *n* : a 10th part paid or given esp. for the support of a church — **tithe** *vb* — **tith·er** *n*

tit·il·late \'tit-ᵊl-ˌāt\ *vb* **-lat·ed; -lat·ing 1** : TICKLE **2** : to excite pleasurably — **tit·il·la·tion** \ˌtit-ᵊl-'ā-shən\ *n*

tit·i·vate *or* **tit·ti·vate** \'tit-ə-ˌvāt\ *vb* **-vat·ed; -vat·ing** : to dress up : spruce up

ti·tle \'tīt-ᵊl\ *n* **1** : CLAIM, RIGHT; *esp* : a legal right to the ownership of property **2** : the distinguishing name esp. of an artistic production (as a book) **3** : an appellation of honor, rank, or office **4** : CHAMPIONSHIP *syn* designation, denomination, appellation

ti·tled \'tīt-ᵊld\ *adj* : having a title esp. of nobility

title page *n* : a page of a book bearing the title and usu. the names of the author and publisher

tit·mouse \'tit-ˌmaus\ *n, pl* **tit·mice** \-ˌmīs\ : any of numerous small long-tailed insect-eating birds

tit·ter \'tit-ər\ *vb* : to laugh in an affected or in a nervous or half-suppressed manner — **titter** *n*

tit·tle \'tit-ᵊl\ *n* : a tiny piece : JOT

tit·tle-tat·tle \'tit-ᵊl-ˌtat-ᵊl\ *n* : idle talk : GOSSIP

tit·u·lar \'tich-(ə-)lər\ *adj* **1** : existing in title only : NOMINAL ⟨~ ruler⟩ **2** : of, relating to, or bearing a title ⟨~ role⟩

Ti·tus \'tīt-əs\ *n* — see BIBLE table

tiz·zy \'tiz-ē\ *n, pl* **tizzies** : a highly excited and distracted state of mind

tk *abbr* **1** tank **2** truck

TKO \ˌtē-ˌkā-'ō\ *n* [*technical knockout*] : the termination of a boxing match when a boxer is declared unable to continue the fight

tkt *abbr* ticket

Tl *symbol* thallium

TLC *abbr* tender loving care

T lymphocyte *n* : T CELL

Tm *symbol* thulium

TM *abbr* trademark

T-man \'tē-ˌman\ *n* : a special agent of the U.S. Treasury Department

tn *abbr* **1** ton **2** town

TN *abbr* Tennessee

tng *abbr* training

tnpk *abbr* turnpike

TNT \ˌtē-ˌen-'tē\ *n* : a flammable toxic compound used as a high explosive

¹**to** \tə, (ˈ)tü\ *prep* **1** : in the direction of and reaching ⟨drove ~ town⟩ **2** : in the direction of : TOWARD ⟨walking ~ school⟩ **3** : ON, AGAINST ⟨apply salve ~ a burn⟩ **4** : as far as ⟨can pay up ~ a dollar⟩ **5** : so as to become or bring about ⟨beaten ~ death⟩ ⟨broken ~ pieces⟩ **6** : BEFORE ⟨it's five minutes ~ six⟩ **7** : UNTIL ⟨from May ~ December⟩ **8** : fitting or being a part of : FOR ⟨key ~ the lock⟩ **9** : with the accompaniment of ⟨sing ~ the music⟩ **10** : in relation or comparison with ⟨similar ~ that one⟩ ⟨won 10 ~ 6⟩ **11** : in accordance with ⟨add salt ~ taste⟩ **12** : within the range of ⟨~ my knowl-

edge⟩ **13** : contained, occurring, or included in ⟨two pints ~ a quart⟩ **14** : as regards ⟨agreeable ~ everyone⟩ **15** : affecting as the receiver or beneficiary ⟨whispered ~ her⟩ ⟨gave it ~ me⟩ **16** : for no one except ⟨a room ~ myself⟩ **17** : into the action of ⟨we got ~ talking⟩ **18** — used for marking the following verb as an infinitive ⟨wants ~ go⟩ ⟨easy ~ like⟩ ⟨the man ~ beat⟩ and often used by itself at the end of a clause in place of an infinitive suggested by the preceding context ⟨goes to town whenever he wants ~⟩ ⟨can leave if you'd like ~⟩

²to \'tü\ *adv* **1** : in a direction toward ⟨run ~ and fro⟩ ⟨wrong side ~⟩ **2** : into contact esp. with the frame of a door ⟨the door slammed ~⟩ **3** : to the matter in hand ⟨fell ~ and ate heartily⟩ **4** : to a state of consciousness or awareness ⟨came ~ hours after the accident⟩

TO *abbr* turn over

toad \'tōd\ *n* : a leaping amphibian differing typically from the related frogs in shorter stockier build, rough dry warty skin, and less aquatic habits

toad·stool \-₁stül\ *n* : MUSHROOM; *esp* : one that is poisonous or inedible

toad·y \'tōd-ē\ *n, pl* **toad·ies** : one who flatters in the hope of gaining favors : SYCOPHANT — **toady** *vb*

to-and-fro \₁tü-ən-'frō\ *adj* : forward and backward

¹toast \'tōst\ *vb* **1** : to warm thoroughly **2** : to make (as bread) crisp, hot, and brown by heat

²toast *n* **1** : sliced toasted bread **2** : someone or something in whose honor persons drink **3** : an act of drinking in honor of a toast

³toast *vb* : to propose or drink to as a toast

toast·er \'tō-stər\ *n* : one that toasts; *esp* : an electrical appliance for toasting

toaster oven *n* : a small electrical appliance that bakes, toasts, and usu. broils

toast·mas·ter \'tōst-₁mas-tər\ *n* : one that presides at a banquet and introduces the after-dinner speakers — **toast·mis·tress** \-₁mis-trəs\ *n*

to·bac·co \tə-'bak-ō\ *n, pl* **-cos** [Sp *tabaco*] **1** : a tall broad-leaved herb related to the potato; *also* : its leaves prepared for smoking or chewing or as snuff **2** : manufactured tobacco products

to·bac·co·nist \tə-'bak-ə-nəst\ *n* : a dealer in tobacco

To·bi·as \tə-'bī-əs\ *n* — see BIBLE table

To·bit \'tō-bət\ *n* — see BIBLE table

¹to·bog·gan \tə-'bäg-ən\ *n* [CanF *toboggan*] : a long flat-bottomed light sled made of thin boards curved up at one end

²toboggan *vb* **1** : to coast on a toboggan **2** : to decline suddenly (as in value)

toc·sin \'täk-sən\ *n* **1** : an alarm bell **2** : a warning signal

¹to·day \tə-'dā\ *adv* **1** : on or for this day **2** : at the present time

²today *n* : the present day, time, or age

tod·dle \'täd-°l\ *vb* **tod·dled; tod·dling** \'täd-(°-)liŋ\ : to walk with short tottering steps in the manner of a young child — **toddle** *n* — **tod·dler** \-(°-)lər\ *n*

tod·dy \'täd-ē\ *n, pl* **toddies** [Hindi *tārī* juice of a palm, fr. *tār* a palm, fr. Skt *tāla*] : a drink made of liquor, sugar, spices, and hot water

to-do \tə-'dü\ *n, pl* **to-dos** \-'düz\ : BUSTLE, STIR

¹toe \'tō\ *n* **1** : one of the jointed parts of the front end of a foot **2** : the front part of a foot or hoof

²toe *vb* **toed; toe·ing** : to touch, reach, or drive with the toes

toea \'toi-ə\ *n* — see *kina* at MONEY table

toe·hold \'tō-₁hōld\ *n* **1** : a place of support for the toes **2** : a slight footing

toe·nail \'tō-₁nāl\ *n* : a nail of a toe

tof·fee *or* **tof·fy** \'tȯ-fē, 'täf-ē\ *n, pl* **toffees** *or* **toffies** : candy of brittle but tender texture made by boiling sugar and butter together

tog \'täg, 'tȯg\ *vb* **togged; tog·ging** : to put togs on : DRESS

to·ga \'tō-gə\ *n* : the loose outer garment worn in public by citizens of ancient Rome — **to·gaed** \-gəd\ *adj*

¹to·geth·er \tə-'geth-ər\ *adv* **1** : in or into one place or group **2** : in or into contact or association ⟨mix ~⟩ **3** : at one time : SIMULTANEOUSLY ⟨talk and work ~⟩ **4** : in succession ⟨for days ~⟩ **5** : in or into harmony or coherence ⟨get ~ on a plan⟩ **6** : as a group : JOINTLY — **to·geth·er·ness** *n*

²together *adj* : composed in mind or manner

tog·gery \'täg-(ə-)rē, 'tȯg-\ *n* : CLOTHING

tog·gle switch \'täg-əl-\ *n* : an electric switch operated by pushing a projecting lever through a small arc

togs \'tägz, 'tȯgz\ *n pl* : CLOTHING; *esp* : clothes for a specified use ⟨riding ~⟩

¹toil \'tȯil\ *n* **1** : laborious effort **2** : long fatiguing labor : DRUDGERY — **toil·some** *adj*

²toil *vb* [ME *toilen* to argue, struggle, fr. OF *toeillier* to stir, disturb, dispute, fr. L *tudiculare* to crush, grind, fr. *tudicula* machine for crushing olives, dim. of *tudes* hammer] **1** : to work hard and long **2** : to proceed with laborious effort : PLOD — **toil·er** *n*

³toil *n* [ME *toile* cloth, net, fr. L *tela* web, fr. *texere* to weave, construct] : NET, TRAP — usu. used in pl.

toi·let \'tȯi-lət\ *n* **1** : the act or process of dressing and grooming oneself **2** : BATHROOM **3** : a fixture used in urinating and defecating; *esp* : one consisting essentially of a water-flushed bowl and seat

toi·let·ry \'tȯi-lə-trē\ *n, pl* **-ries** : an article or preparation used in making one's toilet — usu. used in pl.

toi·lette \twä-ˈlet\ *n* 1 : TOILET 1 2 : formal attire; *also* : a particular costume

toilet training *n* : the process of training a child to control bladder and bowel movements and to use the toilet — **toilet train** *vb*

toil·worn \ˈtȯil-ˌwȯrn\ *adj* : showing the effects of toil

To·kay \tō-ˈkā\ *n* : naturally sweet wine from Hungary

toke \ˈtōk\ *n, slang* : a puff on a marijuana cigarette

¹to·ken \ˈtō-kən\ *n* 1 : an outward sign 2 : SYMBOL, EMBLEM 3 : SOUVENIR, KEEPSAKE 4 : a small part representing the whole 5 : a piece resembling a coin issued as money or for use by a particular group on specified terms

²token *adj* 1 : done or given as a token esp. in partial fulfillment of an obligation 2 : MINIMAL, PERFUNCTORY

to·ken·ism \ˈtō-kə-ˌniz-əm\ *n* : the policy or practice of making only a token effort (as to desegregate)

told *past and past part of* TELL

tole \ˈtōl\ *n* : sheet metal and esp. tinplate for use in domestic and ornamental wares

tol·er·a·ble \ˈtäl-(ə-)rə-bəl\ *adj* 1 : capable of being borne or endured 2 : moderately good : PASSABLE — **tol·er·a·bly** \-blē\ *adv*

tol·er·ance \ˈtäl-(ə-)rəns\ *n* 1 : the act or practice of tolerating; *esp* : sympathy or indulgence for beliefs or practices differing from one's own 2 : the allowable deviation from a standard (as of size) 3 : capacity for enduring or adapting (as to a poor environment) *syn* forbearance, leniency, clemency — **tol·er·ant** *adj* — **tol·er·ant·ly** *adv*

tol·er·ate \ˈtäl-ə-ˌrāt\ *vb* **-at·ed; -at·ing** 1 : to allow to be or to be done without hindrance 2 : to endure or resist the action of (as a drug) *syn* abide, bear, suffer, stand, brook — **tol·er·a·tion** \ˌtäl-ə-ˈrā-shən\ *n*

¹toll \ˈtōl\ *n* 1 : a tax paid for a privilege (as for passing over a bridge) 2 : a charge for a service (as for a long-distance telephone call) 3 : the cost in loss or suffering at which something is achieved *syn* levy, assessment, duty, tariff

²toll *vb* 1 : to give signal of : SOUND 2 : to cause the slow regular sounding of (a bell) esp. by pulling a rope 3 : to sound with slow measured strokes 4 : to announce by tolling

³toll *n* : the sound of a tolling bell

toll·booth \ˈtōl-ˌbüth\ *n* : a booth where tolls are paid

toll·gate \ˈtōl-ˌgāt\ *n* : a point where vehicles stop to pay a toll

toll·house \-ˌhau̇s\ *n* : a house or booth where tolls are paid

tol·u·ene \ˈtäl-yə-ˌwēn\ *n* : a liquid hydrocarbon used as a solvent and as an antiknock agent

tom \ˈtäm\ *n* : the male of various animals; *esp* : TOMCAT

¹tom·a·hawk \ˈtäm-ə-ˌhȯk\ *n* : a light ax used as a missile and as a hand weapon by No. American Indians

²tomahawk *vb* : to strike or kill with a tomahawk

to·ma·to \tə-ˈmāt-ō, -ˈmät-\ *n, pl* **-toes** : a usu. large, rounded, and red or yellow pulpy edible berry of a widely grown tropical herb related to the potato; *also* : this herb

tomb \ˈtüm\ *n* 1 : a place of burial : GRAVE 2 : a house, chamber, or vault for the dead

tom·boy \ˈtäm-ˌbȯi\ *n* : a girl of boyish behavior

tomb·stone \ˈtüm-ˌstōn\ *n* : a stone marking a grave

tom·cat \ˈtäm-ˌkat\ *n* : a male cat

Tom Col·lins \ˈtäm-ˈkäl-ənz\ *n* : a tall iced drink with a base of gin

tome \ˈtōm\ *n* : BOOK; *esp* : a large or weighty one

tom·fool·ery \täm-ˈfül-(ə-)rē\ *n* : foolish trifling : NONSENSE

tom·my gun \ˈtäm-ē-ˌgən\ *n* : SUBMACHINE GUN

to·mog·ra·phy \tō-ˈmäg-rə-fē\ *n* : a diagnostic technique using X-ray photographs in which the shadows of structures before and behind the section under study do not show — **to·mo·graph·ic** \ˌtō-mə-ˈgraf-ik\ *adj*

to·mor·row \tə-ˈmär-ō\ *adv* : on or for the day after today — **tomorrow** *n*

tom·tit \ˈtäm-ˌtit, täm-ˈtit\ *n* : any of several small active birds

tom-tom \ˈtäm-ˌtäm\ *n* : a small-headed drum beaten with the hands

ton \ˈtən\ *n, pl* **tons** *also* **ton** 1 — see WEIGHT table 2 : a unit equal to the volume of a long-ton weight of seawater or 35 cubic feet used in reckoning the displacement of ships

to·nal·i·ty \tō-ˈnal-ət-ē\ *n, pl* **-ties** : tonal quality

¹tone \ˈtōn\ *n* [ME, fr. L *tonus* tension, tone, fr. Gk *tonos*, lit., act of stretching; fr. the dependence of the pitch of a musical string on its tension] 1 : vocal or musical sound; *esp* : sound quality 2 : a sound of definite pitch 3 : WHOLE STEP 4 : accent or inflection expressive of an emotion 5 : the pitch of a word often used to express differences of meaning 6 : style or manner of expression 7 : color quality; *also* : SHADE, TINT 8 : the effect in painting of light and shade together with color 9 : the healthy and vigorous condition of a living body or bodily part 10 : general character, quality, or trend *syn* atmosphere, feeling, mood, vein — **ton·al** \ˈtōn-ᵊl\ *adj*

²tone *vb* **toned; ton·ing** 1 : to give a particular intonation or inflection to 2 : to impart tone to 3 : SOFTEN, MELLOW 4 : to harmonize in color : BLEND

tone·arm *n* : the movable part of a

record player that carries the pickup and the needle

tong \\'täŋ, 'tȯŋ\ *n* : a Chinese secret society in the U.S.

tongs \\'täŋz, 'tȯŋz\ *n pl* : a grasping device consisting of two pieces joined at one end by a pivot or hinged like scissors

¹tongue \\'təŋ\ *n* 1 : a fleshy movable process of the floor of the mouth used in tasting and in taking and swallowing food and in man as a speech organ 2 : the flesh of a tongue (as of the ox) used as food 3 : the power of communication 4 : LANGUAGE 1 5 : manner or quality of utterance; *also* : intended meaning 6 : ecstatic usu. unintelligible utterance accompanying religious excitement — usu. used in pl. 7 : something resembling an animal's tongue in being elongated and fastened at one end only — **tongued** \\'təŋd\ *adj* — **tongue-less** *adj*

²tongue *vb* **tongued; tongu-ing** 1 : to touch or lick with the tongue 2 : to articulate notes on a wind instrument

tongue-in-cheek *adj* : with insincerity, irony, or whimsical exaggeration — **tongue in cheek** *adv*

tongue-lash \\'təŋ-ˌlash\ *vb* : CHIDE, REPROVE — **tongue-lash-ing** \-iŋ\ *n*

tongue-tied \\'təŋ-ˌtīd\ *adj* : unable to speak clearly or freely usu. from shortness of jhe membrane under the tongue or from shyness

tongue twister *n* : an utterance that is difficult to articulate because of a succession of similar consonants

¹ton-ic \\'tän-ik\ *adj* 1 : of, relating to, or producing a healthy physical or mental condition : INVIGORATING 2 : relating to or based on the 1st tone of a scale

²tonic *n* 1 : something (as a drug) that invigorates, restores, or refreshes 2 : the 1st degree of a musical scale

¹to-night \tə-'nīt\ *adv* : on this present night or the night following this present day

²tonight *n* : the present or the coming night

ton-nage \\'tən-ij\ *n* 1 : a duty on ships based on tons carried 2 : ships in terms of the number of tons registered or carried 3 : total weight in tons shipped, carried, or mined

ton-sil \\'tän-səl\ *n* : either of a pair of oval masses of spongy tissue that lie one on each side of the throat at the back of the mouth

ton-sil-lec-to-my \ˌtän-sə-'lek-tə-mē\ *n, pl* **-mies** : the surgical removal of the tonsils

ton-sil-li-tis \-'līt-əs\ *n* : inflammation of the tonsils

ton-so-ri-al \tän-'sōr-ē-əl\ *adj* : of or relating to a barber or his work

ton-sure \\'tän-chər\ *n* [ME, fr. ML *tonsura*, fr. L, act of shearing, fr. *tonsus*, pp. of *tondēre* to shear] 1 : the rite of admission to the clerical state by the

clipping or shaving of the head 2 : the shaven crown or patch worn by clerics (as monks)

too \\'(ˌ)tü\ *adv* 1 : in addition : ALSO 2 : EXCESSIVELY 3 : to such a degree as to be regrettable 4 : VERY

took *past of* TAKE

¹tool \\'tül\ *n* 1 : a hand instrument used to aid in mechanical operations 2 : the cutting or shaping part in a machine; *also* : a machine for shaping metal in any way 3 : something used in doing a job (a scholar's books are his ~s) ; *also* : a means to an end 4 : a person used by another : DUPE

²tool *vb* 1 : to shape, form, or finish with a tool : *esp* : to letter or decorate (as a book cover) by means of hand tools 2 : to equip a plant or industry with machines and tools for production 3 : DRIVE, RIDE (~ing along at 60)

¹toot \\'tüt\ *vb* 1 : to sound or cause to sound esp. in short blasts 2 : to blow a wind instrument (as a horn)

²toot *n* : a short blast (as on a horn)

tooth \\'tüth\ *n, pl* **teeth** \\'tēth\ 1 : one of the hard bony structures borne esp. on the jaws of vertebrates and used for seizing and chewing food and as weapons; *also* : a hard sharp structure esp. around the mouth of an invertebrate 2 : something resembling an animal's tooth 3 : one of the projections on the edge of a wheel that fits into corresponding projections on another wheel — **toothed** \\'tütht\ *adj* — **tooth-less** *adj*

tooth-ache \\'tüth-ˌāk\ *n* : pain in or about a tooth

tooth-brush \-ˌbrəsh\ *n* : a brush for cleaning the teeth

tooth-paste \-ˌpāst\ *n* : a paste for cleaning the teeth

tooth-pick \-ˌpik\ *n* : a pointed instrument for removing substances caught between the teeth

tooth powder *n* : a powder for cleaning the teeth

tooth-some \\'tüth-səm\ *adj* 1 : ATTRACTIVE (a ~ blond) 2 : pleasing to the taste : DELICIOUS **syn** palatable, appetizing, savory, tasty

toothy \\'tü-thē\ *adj* **tooth-i-er; -est** : having or showing prominent teeth

¹top \\'täp\ *n* 1 : the highest part, point, or level of something 2 : the stalks and leaves of a plant with edible roots (beet ~s) 3 : the upper end, edge, or surface (the ~ of a page) 4 : an upper piece, lid, or covering 5 : a platform around the head of the lower mast 6 : the highest degree, pitch, or rank

²top *vb* **topped; top-ping** 1 : to remove or trim the top of : PRUNE (~ a tree) 2 : to cover with a top or on the top : CROWN, CAP 3 : to be superior to : EXCEL, SURPASS 4 : to go over the top of 5 : to strike (a golf ball) above the center 6 : to make an end or conclusion (~ off a meal with coffee)

³**top** *adj* : of, relating to, or being at the top : HIGHEST

⁴**top** *n* : a child's toy that has a tapering point on which it is made to spin

to·paz \'tō-ˌpaz\ *n* : a hard silicate mineral that when occurring as perfect yellow crystals is valued as a gem

top·coat \'täp-ˌkōt\ *n* : a lightweight overcoat

top–dress \'täp-ˌdres\ *vb* : to apply material to (as land) without working it in; *esp* : to scatter fertilizer over

top-dress·ing \-iŋ\ *n* : a material used to top-dress soil

tope \'tōp\ *vb* **toped**; **top·ing** : to drink intoxicating liquor to excess

top·er \'tō-pər\ *n* : one that topes; *esp* : DRUNKARD

top flight *n* : the highest level of excellence or rank — **top-flight** *adj*

top hat *n* : a man's tall-crowned hat usu. of beaver or silk

top–heavy \'täp-ˌhev-ē\ *adj* : having the top part too heavy for the lower part

top·ic \'täp-ik\ *n* 1 : a heading in an outlined argument 2 : the subject of a discourse or a section of it : THEME

top·i·cal \-i-kəl\ *adj* 1 : of, relating to, or arranged by topics (a ~ outline) 2 : relating to current or local events — **top·i·cal·ly** \-k(ə-)lē\ *adv*

top·knot \'täp-ˌnät\ *n* 1 : an ornament (as a knot of ribbons) forming a head-dress 2 : a crest of feathers or hair on the top of the head

top·less \-ləs\ *adj* 1 : wearing no clothing on the upper body 2 : featuring topless waitresses or entertainers

top·mast \'täp-ˌmast, -məst\ *n* : the 2d mast above a ship's deck

top·most \'täp-ˌmōst\ *adj* : highest of all : UPPERMOST

top–notch \-'näch\ *adj* : of the highest quality : FIRST-RATE

topog *abbr* topography

to·pog·ra·phy \tə-'päg-rə-fē\ *n* 1 : the art of showing in detail on a map or chart the physical features of a place or region 2 : the outline of the form of a place showing its relief and the position of features as rivers, roads, or cities) — **to·pog·ra·pher** \-fər\ *n* — **top·o·graph·ic** \ˌtäp-ə-'graf-ik\ *or* **top·o·graph·i·cal** \-i-kəl\ *adj*

top·ping \'täp-iŋ\ *n* : something (as a garnish or sauce) that forms a top

top·ple \'täp-əl\ *vb* **top·pled**; **top·pling** \-(ə-)liŋ\ 1 : to fall from or as if from being top-heavy 2 : to push over : OVERTURN; *also* : OVERTHROW

tops \'täps\ *adj* : topmost in quality or eminence (is considered ~ in his field)

top·sail \'täp-ˌsāl, -səl\ *also* **top·s'l** \-səl\ *n* : the sail next above the lowest sail on a mast in a square-rigged ship

top secret *adj* : demanding inviolate secrecy among those concerned

top·side \'täp-ˌsīd\ *adv or adj* 1 : to or on the top or surface 2 : on deck

top·sides \-'sīdz\ *n pl* : the top portion of the outer surface of a ship on each side above the waterline

top·soil \'täp-ˌsȯil\ *n* : surface soil usu. including the organic layer in which plants have most of their roots

top·sy–tur·vy \ˌtäp-sē-'tər-vē\ *adv* 1 : in utter confusion 2 : UPSIDE DOWN — **topsy-turvy** *adj*

toque \'tōk\ *n* : a woman's small hat without a brim

tor \'tȯr\ *n* : a high craggy hill

To·rah \'tȯr-ə\ *n* 1 : a scroll of the first five books of the Old Testament used in a synagogue; *also* : these five books 2 : the body of divine knowledge and law found in the Jewish scriptures and tradition

torch \'tȯrch\ *n* 1 : a flaming light made of something that burns brightly and usu. carried in the hand 2 : something that resembles a torch in giving light, heat, or guidance 3 *chiefly Brit* : FLASHLIGHT — **torch·bear·er** \-ˌbar-ər\ *n* — **torch·light** \-ˌlīt\ *n*

torch song *n* : a popular sentimental song of unrequited love

tore *past of* TEAR

to·re·ador \'tȯr-ē-ə-ˌdȯr\ *n* : BULLFIGHTER

to·re·ro \tə-'rer-ō\ *n, pl* **-ros** [Sp] : BULLFIGHTER

¹**tor·ment** \'tȯr-ˌment\ *n* 1 : extreme pain or anguish of body or mind 2 : a source of vexation or pain

²**tor·ment** \tȯr-'ment\ *vb* 1 : to cause severe suffering of body or mind to 2 : VEX, HARASS syn rack, afflict, try, torture — **tor·men·tor** \-ər\ *n*

torn *past part of* TEAR

tor·na·do \tȯr-'nād-ō\ *n, pl* **-does** *or* **-dos** [modif of Sp *tronada* thunderstorm, fr. *tronar* to thunder, fr. L *tonare*] : a violent destructive whirling wind accompanied by a funnel-shaped cloud that moves over a narrow path

¹**tor·pe·do** \tȯr-'pēd-ō\ *n, pl* **-does** : a thin cylindrical self-propelled submarine weapon

²**torpedo** *vb* **tor·pe·doed**; **tor·pe·do·ing** \-'pēd-ə-wiŋ\ : to hit or destroy with or as if with a torpedo

torpedo boat *n* : a small very fast boat for firing torpedoes

tor·pid \'tȯr-pəd\ *adj* 1 : having lost motion or the power of exertion 2 : SLUGGISH 3 : lacking vigor : DULL — **tor·pid·i·ty** \tȯr-'pid-ət-ē\ *n*

tor·por \'tȯr-pər\ *n* 1 : DULLNESS, APATHY 2 : extreme sluggishness : STAGNATION syn stupor, lethargy, languor, lassitude

¹**torque** \'tȯrk\ *n* : a force that produces or tends to produce rotation or torsion

²**torque** *vb* **torqued**; **torqu·ing** : to impart torque to : cause to twist (as about an axis)

tor·rent \'tȯr-ənt\ *n* [F, fr. L *torrent-*, *torrens*, fr. *torrent-*, *torrens* burning, seething, rushing, fr. prp. of *torrēre* to parch, burn] **1** : a rushing stream (as of water) **2** : a tumultuous outburst

tor·ren·tial \tȯ-ˈren-chəl, tə-\ *adj* : relating to or resembling a torrent (∼ rains)

tor·rid \ˈtȯr-əd\ *adj* **1** : parched with heat esp. of the sun : HOT **2** : ARDENT

torrid zone *n* : the region of the earth between the tropic of Cancer and the tropic of Capricorn

tor·sion \ˈtȯr-shən\ *n* **1** : a twisting of a bodily organ on its own axis **2** : a wrenching by which one part of a body is under pressure to turn about a longitudinal axis while the other part is held fast or is under pressure to turn in the opposite direction — **tor·sion·al** \ˈtȯr-sh(ə-)nəl\ *adj* — **tor·sion·al·ly** \-ē\ *adv*

tor·so \ˈtȯr-sō\ *n, pl* **torsos** *or* **tor·si** \ˈtȯr-ˌsē\ [It., lit., stalk] : the trunk of the human body

tort \ˈtȯrt\ *n* : a wrongful act which does not involve a breach of contract and for which the injured party can recover damages in a civil action

tor·til·la \tȯr-ˈtē-(y)ə\ *n* : a round flat cake of unleavened cornmeal bread usu. eaten hot with a topping of ground meat or cheese

tor·toise \ˈtȯrt-əs\ *n* : TURTLE; *esp* : a land turtle

¹tor·toise·shell \ˈtȯrt-ə-ˌshel, -əs(h)-ˌshel\ *n* **1** : the mottled horny substance of the shell of some turtles used in inlaying and in making various ornamental articles **2** : any of several showy butterflies

²tortoiseshell *adj* : made of or resembling tortoiseshell esp. in spotted brown and yellow coloring

tor·to·ni \tȯr-ˈtō-nē\ *n* : ice cream made of heavy cream often with minced almonds and chopped cherries and flavored with rum

tor·tu·ous \ˈtȯrch-(ə-)wəs\ *adj* **1** : marked by twists or turns : WINDING **2** : DEVIOUS, TRICKY

¹tor·ture \ˈtȯr-chər\ *n* **1** : anguish of body or mind : AGONY **2** : the infliction of severe pain esp. to punish or coerce

²torture *vb* **tor·tured; tor·tur·ing** \ˈtȯrch-(ə-)riŋ\ **1** : to cause intense suffering to : TORMENT **2** : to punish or coerce by inflicting severe pain **3** : TWIST, DISTORT *syn* rack, harrow, afflict, try — **tor·tur·er** *n*

To·ry \ˈtȯr-ē\ *n, pl* **Tories** [IrGael *tōraidhe* pursued man, robber] **1** : a member of a chiefly 18th century British party upholding the established church and the traditional political structure **2** : an American supporter of the British during the American Revolution **3** *often not cap* : an extreme conservative — **Tory** *adj*

¹toss \ˈtȯs, ˈtäs\ *vb* **1** : to fling to and fro or up and down **2** : to throw with a quick light motion; *also* : BANDY **3** : to fling or lift with a sudden motion (∼ed her head angrily) **4** : to move restlessly or turbulently (∼es on the waves) **5** : to twist and turn repeatedly **6** : FLOUNCE **7** : to accomplish readily (∼ off an article) **8** : to decide an issue by flipping a coin

²toss *n* : an act or instance of tossing; *esp* : TOSS-UP l

toss-up \-ˌəp\ *n* **1** : a deciding by flipping a coin **2** : an even chance **3** : something that offers no clear basis for choice

¹tot \ˈtät\ *n* **1** : a small child **2** : a small drink of alcoholic liquor : SHOT

²tot *vb* **tot·ted; tot·ting** : to add up

³tot *abbr* total

¹to·tal \ˈtōt-əl\ *adj* **1** : making up a whole : ENTIRE (∼ amount) **2** : COMPLETE, UTTER (a ∼ failure) **3** : involving a complete and unified effort esp. to achieve a desired effect — **to·tal·ly** \-ē\ *adv*

²total *n* **1** : SUM **2** : the entire amount *syn* aggregate, whole, gross, totality

³total *vb* **to·taled** *or* **to·talled; to·tal·ing** *or* **to·tal·ling** **1** : to add up : COMPUTE **2** : to amount to : NUMBER **3** : to make a total wreck of (a car)

to·tal·i·tar·i·an \tō-ˌtal-ə-ˈter-ē-ən\ *adj* : of or relating to a political regime based on subordination of the individual to the state and strict control of all aspects of life esp. by coercive measures; *also* : advocating, constituting, or characteristic of such a regime — **totalitarian** *n* — **to·tal·i·tar·i·an·ism** \-ē-ə-ˌniz-əm\ *n*

to·tal·i·ty \tō-ˈtal-ət-ē\ *n, pl* **-ties** **1** : an aggregate amount : SUM, WHOLE **2** : ENTIRETY, WHOLENESS

to·tal·iza·tor *or* **to·tal·isa·tor** \ˈtōt-əl-ə-ˌzāt-ər\ *n* : a machine for registering and indicating the number of bets and the odds on a horse or dog race

¹tote \ˈtōt\ *vb* **tot·ed; tot·ing** : CARRY

²tote *vb* **tot·ed; tot·ing** : ADD, TOTAL — usu. used with *up*

to·tem \ˈtōt-əm\ *n* : an object (as an animal or plant) serving as the emblem of a family or clan and often as a reminder of its ancestry; *also* : something usu. carved or painted to represent such an object

totem pole *n* : a pole that is carved with a series of totems and is erected before the houses of some northwest American Indians

tot·ter \ˈtät-ər\ *vb* **1** : to tremble or rock as if about to fall : SWAY **2** : to move unsteadily : STAGGER

tou·can \ˈtü-ˌkan\ *n* : any of a family of fruit-eating birds of tropical America with brilliant coloring and a very large beak

¹touch \ˈtəch\ *vb* **1** : to bring a bodily part (as the hand) into contact with so as to feel **2** : to be or cause to be in contact **3** : to strike or push lightly esp. with the hand or foot **4** : DISTURB, HARM **5** : to make use of (never ∼es alcohol) **6** : to induce to give or lend **7** : to get to : REACH **8** : to refer to in passing : MENTION **9** : to affect the interest of : CONCERN **10** : to leave a mark on; *also* : BLEMISH **11** : to move to sympathetic feeling **12** : to come close : VERGE **13** : to have a bearing : RELATE **14** : to make a usu. brief or incidental stop in port **syn** affect, influence, impress, strike, sway

²**touch** *n* **1** : a light stroke or tap **2** : the act or fact of touching or being touched **3** : the sense by which pressure or traction on the skin or mucous membrane is perceived; *also* : a particular sensation conveyed by this sense **4** : mental or moral sensitiveness : TACT **5** : a small quantity : HINT **6** : a manner of striking or touching esp. the keys of a keyboard instrument **7** : an improving detail (add a few ~*es* to the painting) **8** : distinctive manner or skill (~ of a master) **9** : the state of being in contact (keep in ~) **syn** suggestion, suspicion, tincture, tinge

touch·down \'tǝch-ˌdau̇n\ *n* : the act of scoring six points in American football by being lawfully in possession of the ball on, above, or behind an opponent's goal line

tou·ché \tü-'shā\ *interj* [F] — used to acknowledge a hit in fencing or the success of an argument, an accusation, or a witty point

touch football *n* : football played informally and chiefly characterized by the substitution of touching for tackling

touch·ing \'tǝch-iŋ\ *adj* : capable of stirring emotions **syn** moving, impressive, poignant, affecting

touch off *vb* **1** : to describe with precision **2** : to cause to explode **3** : to release or initiate with sudden intensity

touch·stone \'tǝch-ˌstōn\ *n* : a test or criterion of genuineness or quality **syn** standard, gauge, benchmark, yardstick

touch up \(ˈ)tǝch-'ǝp\ *vb* : to improve or perfect by small additional strokes or alterations

touchy \'tǝch-ē\ *adj* **touch·i·er; -est 1** : easily offended : PEEVISH **2** : calling for tact in treatment (a ~ subject) **syn** irascible, cranky, cross, tetchy, testy

¹**tough** \'tǝf\ *adj* **1** : strong or firm in texture but flexible and not brittle **2** : not easily chewed **3** : characterized by severity and determination (a ~ policy) **4** : capable of enduring strain or hardship : ROBUST **5** : hard to influence : STUBBORN **6** : difficult to accomplish, resolve, or cope with (a ~ problem) **7** : ROWDYISH **syn** tenacious, stout, sturdy, stalwart — **tough·ly** *adv* — **tough·ness** *n*

²**tough** *n* : a tough person : ROWDY

tough·en \'tǝf-ǝn\ *vb* **tough·ened; tough·en·ing** \-(ǝ-)niŋ\ : to make or become tough

tou·pee \tü-'pā\ *n* [F *toupet* forelock] : a small wig for a bald spot

¹**tour** \'tu̇r, *l is also* 'tau̇(ǝ)r\ *n* **1** : one's turn : SHIFT **2** : a journey in which one returns to the starting point

²**tour** *vb* : to travel over as a tourist

tour de force \ˌtu̇rd-ǝ-'fōrs\ *n*, *pl* **tours de force** *same*\ [F] : a feat of strength, skill, or ingenuity

tour·ist \'tu̇r-ǝst\ *n* : one that makes a tour for pleasure or culture

tourist class *n* : economy accommodation on a ship, airplane, or train

tour·ma·line \'tu̇r-mǝ-lǝn, -ˌlēn\ *n* : a mineral that when transparent is valued as a gem

tour·na·ment \'tu̇r-nǝ-mǝnt, 'tǝr-\ *n* **1** : a medieval sport in which mounted armored knights contended with blunted lances or swords; *also* : the whole series of knightly sports, jousts, and tilts occurring at one time and place **2** : a championship series of games or athletic contests

tour·ney \-nē\ *n*, *pl* **tourneys** : TOURNAMENT

tour·ni·quet \'tu̇r-ni-kǝt, 'tǝr-\ *n* : a device (as a bandage twisted tight with a stick) for stopping bleeding or blood flow

tou·sle \'tau̇-zǝl\ *vb* **tou·sled; tou·sling** \'tau̇z-(ǝ-)liŋ\ : to disorder by rough handling : DISHEVEL, MUSS

¹**tout** \'tau̇t\ *vb* : to give a tip or solicit bets on a racehorse — **tout** *n*

²**tout** \'tau̇t, 'tüt\ *vb* : to praise or publicize loudly

¹**tow** \'tō\ *vb* : to draw or pull along behind **syn** tug, haul, drag, lug

²**tow** *n* **1** : an act of towing or condition of being towed **2** : something (as a barge) that is towed

³**tow** *n* : short or broken fiber (as of flax or hemp) used esp. for yarn, twine, or stuffing

to·ward *or* **to·wards** \(ˈ)tō(-ǝ)rd(z), tǝ-'wȯrd(z)\ *prep* **1** : in the direction of (heading ~ the river) **2** : along a course leading to (efforts ~ reconciliation) **3** : in regard to (tolerance ~ minorities) **4** : FACING (the gun's muzzle was ~ him) **5** : close upon (it was getting along ~ sundown) **6** : for part payment of (paid $100 ~ his tuition)

tow·boat \'tō-ˌbōt\ *n* : TUGBOAT

tow·el \'tau̇(-ǝ)l\ *n* : an absorbent cloth or paper for wiping or drying

tow·el·ing *or* **tow·el·ling** \'tau̇-(ǝ-)liŋ\ *n* : a cotton or linen fabric often used for making towels

¹**tow·er** \'tau̇(-ǝ)r\ *n* **1** : a tall structure either isolated or built upon a larger structure (an observation ~) (a bell ~ of a church) **2** : a towering citadel — **tow·ered** \'tau̇(-ǝ)rd\ *adj*

²**tower** *vb* : to reach or rise to a great height **syn** overlook, dominate

tow·er·ing \-iŋ\ *adj* **1** : LOFTY (~ pines) **2** : reaching high intensity (a ~ rage) **3** : EXCESSIVE (~ ambition)

tow·head \'tō-ˌhed\ *n* : a person having

flaxen hair — **tow·head·ed** \-,hed-əd\ *adj*

to·whee \'tō-,hē, 'tō-(,)ē, tō-'hē\ *n* : a common finch of eastern No. America having the male black, white, and reddish; *also* : any of several related finches

to wit \tə-'wit\ *adv* : NAMELY

town \'taůn\ *n* 1 : a compactly settled area usu. larger than a village but smaller than a city 2 : CITY 3 : the inhabitants of a town 4 : a New England territorial and political unit usu. containing both rural and urban areas; *also* : a New England community in which matters of local government are decided by a general assembly **(town meeting)** of qualified voters

town house *n* 1 : the town residence of a person having a country home 2 : a single-family house of two or sometimes three stories connected to another house by a common wall

town·ie *or* **towny** \'taů-nē\ *n, pl* **townies** : a permanent resident of a town as distinguished from a member of another group

towns·folk \'taůnz-,fōk\ *n pl* : TOWNSPEOPLE

town·ship \'taůn-,ship\ *n* 1 : TOWN 4 2 : a unit of local government in some states 3 : an unorganized subdivision of a county; *also* : an administrative division 4 : a division of territory in surveys of U.S. public land containing 36 square miles

towns·man \'taůnz-mən\ *n* 1 : a native or resident of a town or city 2 : a fellow citizen of a town

towns·peo·ple \-,pē-pəl\ *n pl* 1 : the inhabitants of a town or city 2 : townbred persons

tow·path \'tō-,path, -,páth\ *n* : a path (as along a canal) traveled by men or animals towing boats

tow truck *n* : WRECKER 2

tox·emia \täk-'sē-mē-ə\ *n* : a bodily disorder associated with the presence of toxic matter in the blood

tox·ic \'täk-sik\ *adj* [LL *toxicus,* fr. L *toxicum* poison, fr. Gk *toxikon* arrow poison, fr. neut. of *toxikos* of a bow, fr. *toxon* bow, arrow] : of, relating to, or caused by poison or a toxin : POISONOUS — **tox·ic·i·ty** \täk-'sis-ət-ē\ *n*

tox·i·col·o·gy \,täk-sə-'käl-ə-jē\ *n* : a science that deals with poisons and esp. with problems of their use and control — **tox·i·co·log·i·cal** \-'läj-i-kəl\ *or* **tox·i·co·log·ic** \,täk-si-kə-'läj-ik\ *adj* — **tox·i·col·o·gist** \-'käl-ə-jəst\ *n*

toxic shock syndrome *n* : an acute disease probably of bacterial origin that is characterized by fever, sore throat, and diffuse erythema and occurs esp. in menstruating females using tampons

tox·in \'täk-sən\ *n* : a substance produced by a living organism that is very poisonous when introduced into the tissues but is usu. destroyed by diges-

tive processes when taken by mouth

¹toy \'tȯi\ *n* 1 : something trifling 2 : a small ornament : BAUBLE 3 : something for a child to play with

²toy *vb* 1 : FLIRT 2 : to deal with something lightly : TRIFLE 3 : to amuse oneself as if with a plaything

³toy *adj* 1 : DIMINUTIVE 2 : designed for use as a toy

tp *abbr* 1 title page 2 township

tpk *or* **tpke** *abbr* turnpike

tr *abbr* 1 translated; translation; translator 2 transpose 3 troop

¹trace \'trās\ *n* 1 : a mark (as a footprint or track) left by something that has passed : VESTIGE 2 : a minute or barely detectable amount

²trace *vb* **traced; trac·ing** 1 : to mark out : SKETCH 2 : to form (as letters) carefully 3 : to copy (a drawing) by marking lines on transparent paper laid over the drawing to be copied 4 : to follow the trail of : track down 5 : to study out and follow the development of — **trace·able** *adj* — **trac·er** *n*

³trace *n* : either of two lines of a harness for fastening a draft animal to a vehicle

trac·ery \'trās-(ə)-rē\ *n, pl* **-er·ies** : ornamental work having a design with branching or interlacing lines

tra·chea \'trā-kē-ə\ *n, pl* **-che·ae** \-kē-,ē\ *also* **-che·as** : the main tube by which air enters the lungs : WINDPIPE — **tra·che·al** \-kē-əl\ *adj*

trac·ing \'trā-siŋ\ *n* 1 : the act of one that traces 2 : something that is traced 3 : a graphic record made by an instrument for measuring vibrations or pulsations

¹track \'trak\ *n* 1 : a mark left in passing 2 : PATH, ROUTE, TRAIL 3 : a course laid out for racing; *also* : track-and-field sports 4 : one of a series of paths along which material (as music) is recorded (as on magnetic tape) 5 : the course along which something moves; *esp* : a way made by two parallel lines of metal rails 6 : awareness of a fact or progression (lost ~ of his movements) 7 : either of two endless metal belts on which a vehicle (as a tractor) travels

²track *vb* 1 : to follow the tracks or traces of : TRAIL 2 : to make tracks on 3 : to carry on the feet and deposit (~ed mud on the floor) — **track·er** *n*

track·age \'trak-ij\ *n* : lines of railway track

track-and-field \,trak-ən-'fēld\ *adj* : of or relating to athletic contests held on a running track or on the adjacent field

¹tract \'trakt\ *n* 1 : a stretch of land without precise boundaries (broad ~s of prairie) 2 : a defined area of land (a garden ~) 3 : a system of body parts or organs together serving some special purpose (the digestive ~)

²tract *n* : a pamphlet of political or religious propaganda

trac·ta·ble \'trak-tə-bəl\ *adj* **1** : easily controlled : DOCILE **2** : easily wrought : MALLEABLE **syn** amenable, obedient, biddable

trac·tate \'trak-,tāt\ *n* : TREATISE

tract house *n* : any of many similarly designed houses built on a tract of land

trac·tion \'trak-shən\ *n* **1** : the act of drawing : the state of being drawn **2** : the drawing of a vehicle by motive power; *also* : the particular form of motive power used **3** : the adhesive friction of a body on a surface on which it moves **4** : a pulling force applied to a skeletal structure (as a broken bone) by using a special device; *also* : a state of tension created by such a pulling force ⟨a leg in ∼⟩ — **trac·tion·al** \-sh(ə-)nəl\ *adj* — **trac·tive** \'trak-tiv\ *adj*

trac·tor \'trak-tər\ *n* **1** : an automotive vehicle that is borne on four wheels or beltlike metal tracks and is used esp. for drawing farm equipment **2** : a motortruck with short chassis for hauling a trailer

¹trade \'trād\ *n* **1** : one's regular business or work : OCCUPATION **2** : an occupation requiring manual or mechanical skill **3** : the persons engaged in a business or industry **4** : the business of buying and selling or bartering commodities **5** : an act of trading : TRANSACTION **syn** craft, profession, calling, vocation

²trade *vb* **trad·ed; trad·ing 1** : to give in exchange for another commodity : BARTER **2** : to engage in the exchange, purchase, or sale of goods **3** : to deal regularly as a customer — **trade on** : EXPLOIT ⟨*trades on* his family name⟩

trade-in \'trād-,in\ *n* : an item of merchandise taken as part payment of a purchase

trade in \(')trād-'in\ *vb* : to turn in as part payment for a purchase

¹trade·mark \'trād-,märk\ *n* : a device (as a word or mark) that points distinctly to the origin or ownership of merchandise to which it is applied and that is legally reserved for the exclusive use of the owner

²trademark *vb* : to secure the trademark rights for

trade name *n* : a name that is given by a manufacturer or merchant to a product to distinguish it as made or sold by him and that may be used and protected as a trademark

trad·er \'trād-ər\ *n* **1** : a person whose business is buying or selling **2** : a ship engaged in trade

trades·man \'trādz-mən\ *n* **1** : one who runs a retail store : SHOPKEEPER **2** : CRAFTSMAN

trades·peo·ple \-,pē-pəl\ *n pl* : people engaged in trade

trade wind *n* : a wind blowing almost constantly in one direction

trading stamp *n* : a printed stamp of value given as a premium to a retail customer and when accumulated in numbers redeemed in merchandise

tra·di·tion \trə-'dish-ən\ *n* **1** : an inherited, established, or customary pattern of thought or action **2** : the handing down of beliefs and customs by word of mouth or by example without written instruction; *also* : a belief or custom thus handed down — **tra·di·tion·al** \-,dish(ə-)nəl\ *adj* — **tra·di·tion·al·ly** \-ē\ *adv*

tra·duce \trə-'d(y)üs\ *vb* **tra·duced; tra·duc·ing** : to lower the reputation of : DEFAME, SLANDER **syn** malign, libel, calumniate — **tra·duc·er** *n*

¹traf·fic \'traf-ik\ *n* **1** : the business of bartering or buying and selling **2** : communication or dealings between individuals or groups **3** : the movement (as of vehicles) along a route **4** : the passengers or cargo carried by a transportation system

²traffic *vb* **traf·ficked; traf·fick·ing** : to carry on traffic — **traf·fick·er** *n*

traffic circle *n* : ROTARY 2

traffic light *n* : an electrically operated visual signal for controlling traffic

tra·ge·di·an \trə-'jēd-ē-ən\ *n* **1** : a writer of tragedies **2** : an actor who plays tragic roles

tra·ge·di·enne \trə-,jēd-ē-'en\ *n* [F] : an actress who plays tragic roles

trag·e·dy \'traj-əd-ē\ *n, pl* **-dies** [ME *tragedie*, fr. MF, fr. L *tragoedia*, fr. Gk *tragōidia*, fr. *tragos* goat + *aeidein* to sing] **1** : a serious drama describing a conflict between the protagonist and a superior force (as destiny) and having a sad end that excites pity or terror **2** : a disastrous event : CALAMITY; *also* : MISFORTUNE **3** : tragic quality or element

trag·ic \'traj-ik\ *also* **trag·i·cal** \-i-kəl\ *adj* **1** : of, relating to, or expressive of tragedy **2** : appropriate to tragedy **3** : LAMENTABLE, UNFORTUNATE — **trag·i·cal·ly** \-i-k(ə-)lē\ *adv*

¹trail \'trāl\ *vb* **1** : to hang down so as to drag along or sweep the ground **2** : to draw or drag along behind **3** : to extend over a surface in a straggling manner **4** : to follow slowly : lag behind **5** : to follow upon the track of : PURSUE **6** : DWINDLE ⟨her voice ∼ed off⟩ **syn** tag, tail, dog, shadow

²trail *n* **1** : something that trails or is trailed ⟨a ∼ of smoke⟩ **2** : a trace or mark left by something that has passed or been drawn along : TRACK ⟨a ∼ of blood⟩ **3** : a beaten path; *also* : a marked path through woods **4** : SCENT

trail bike *n* : a small motorcycle for use other than on highways

trail·blaz·er \-,blā-zər\ *n* : PATHFINDER, PIONEER — **trail·blaz·ing** \-ziŋ\ *adj or n*

trail·er \'trā-lər\ *n* **1** : one that trails; *esp* : a creeping plant (as an ivy) **2** : a vehicle that is hauled by another (as a tractor) **3** : a vehicle equipped to serve wherever parked as a dwelling or as a place of business

trailing arbutus *n* : a trailing spring-flowering plant of the heath family with fragrant pink or white flowers; *also* : its flower

¹**train** \'trān\ *n* 1 : a part of a gown that trails behind the wearer 2 : RETINUE 3 : a moving file of persons, vehicles, or animals 4 : a connected series (a ~ of thought) 5 : AFTERMATH 6 : a connected line of railroad cars usu. hauled by a locomotive **syn** succession, sequence, procession, chain

²**train** *vb* 1 : to cause to grow as desired ⟨~ a vine on a trellis⟩ 2 : to form by instruction, discipline, or drill 3 : to make or become prepared (as by exercise) for a test of skill 4 : to aim or point at an object ⟨~ guns on a fort⟩ **syn** discipline, school, educate, instruct — **train·er** *n*

train·ee \trā-'nē\ *n* : one who is being trained for a job

train·ing \'trā-niŋ\ *n* 1 : the act, process, or method of one who trains 2 : the knowledge or experience gained by one who trains

train·load \'trān-'lōd\ *n* : the full freight or passenger capacity of a railroad train

train·man \-mən\ *n* : a member of a train crew

traipse \'trāps\ *vb* **traipsed; traips·ing** : TRAMP, WALK

trait \'trāt\ *n* : a distinguishing quality (as of personality) : CHARACTERISTIC

trai·tor \'trāt-ər\ *n* [ME *traitre*, fr. OF, fr. L *traditor*, fr. *traditus*, pp. of *tradere* to hand over, deliver, betray, fr. *trans-* across + *dare* to give] 1 : one who betrays another's trust or is false to an obligation 2 : one who commits treason — **trai·tor·ous** *adj*

tra·jec·to·ry \trə-'jek-t(ə-)rē\ *n*, *pl* **-ries** : the curve that a body (as a planet in its orbit) describes in space

tram \'tram\ *n* 1 *chiefly Brit* : STREETCAR 2 : a boxlike car running on a railway (**tram·way** \-,wā\) in a mine or a logging camp

¹**tram·mel** \'tram-əl\ *n* [ME *tramayle*, a kind of net, fr. MF *tremail*, fr. LL *tremaculum*, fr. L *tres* three + *macula* mesh, spot] : something impeding activity, progress, or freedom

²**trammel** *vb* **-meled** *or* **-melled; -mel·ing** *or* **-mel·ling** \-(ə-)liŋ\ 1 : to catch and hold in or as if in a net 2 : HAMPER **syn** clog, fetter, shackle, hobble

¹**tramp** \'tramp, *1 & 3 are also* 'trämp, 'trŏmp\ *vb* 1 : to walk, tread, or step heavily 2 : to walk about or through; *also* : HIKE 3 : to tread on forcibly and repeatedly

²**tramp** \'tramp, *5 is also* 'trämp, 'trŏmp\ *n* 1 : a foot traveler 2 : a begging or thieving vagrant 3 : an immoral woman; *esp* : PROSTITUTE 4 : a walking trip : HIKE 5 : the succession of sounds made by the beating of feet on a road

6 : a ship that does not follow a regular course but takes cargo to any port

tram·ple \'tram-pəl\ *vb* **tram·pled; tram·pling** \-p(ə-)liŋ\ 1 : to tread heavily so as to bruise, crush, or injure 2 : to inflict injury or destruction 3 : to press down or crush by or as if by treading : STAMP — **trample** *n* — **tram·pler** \-p(ə-)lər\ *n*

tram·po·line \,tram-pə-'lēn, 'tram-pə-,lēn\ *n* [Sp *trampolín*] : a resilient canvas sheet or web supported by springs in a metal frame used as a springboard in tumbling — **tram·po·lin·ist** \-nəst\ *n*

trance \'trans\ *n* [ME, fr. MF *transe*, fr. *transir* to pass away, swoon, fr. L *transire* to pass, pass away, fr. *trans-* across + *ire* go] 1 : DAZE, STUPOR 2 : a prolonged and profound sleeplike condition (as of deep hypnosis) 3 : a state of mystical absorption

tran·quil \'traŋ-kwəl, 'tran-\ *adj* : free from agitation or disturbance : QUIET **syn** serene, placid, peaceful — **tran·quil·li·ty** *or* **tran·quil·i·ty** \tran-'kwil-ət-ē, traŋ-\ *n* — **tran·quil·ly** \'traŋ-kwə-lē, 'tran-\ *adv*

tran·quil·ize *also* **tran·quil·lize** \'traŋ-kwə-,līz, 'tran-\ *vb* **-ized** *also* **-lized; -iz·ing** *also* **-liz·ing** : to make or become tranquil; *esp* : to relieve of mental tension and anxiety

tran·quil·iz·er *also* **tran·quil·liz·er** \-,lī-zər\ *n* : a drug used to relieve tension and anxiety

trans *abbr* 1 transaction 2 transitive 3 translated; translation; translator 4 transportation 5 transverse

trans·act \trans-'akt, tranz-\ *vb* : CARRY OUT, PERFORM; *also* : CONDUCT

trans·ac·tion \-'ak-shən\ *n* 1 : something transacted; *esp* : a business deal 2 : an act or process of transacting 3 *pl* : the records of the proceedings of a society or organization

trans·at·lan·tic \,trans-ət-'lant-ik, ,tranz-\ *adj* : crossing or extending across or situated beyond the Atlantic ocean

trans·ceiv·er \trans-'ē-vər, tranz-\ *n* : a radio transmitter-receiver that uses many of the same components for transmission and reception

tran·scend \trans-'end\ *vb* 1 : to rise above the limits of 2 : SURPASS **syn** exceed, outdo, outshine, outstrip

tran·scen·dent \-'en-dənt\ *adj* 1 : exceeding usual limits : SURPASSING 2 : transcending material existence **syn** superlative, supreme, peerless, incomparable

tran·scen·den·tal \,trans-,en-'dent-ᵊl, -ən-\ *adj* 1 : TRANSCENDENT 2 : of, relating to, or characteristic of transcendentalism; *also* : ABSTRUSE

tran·scen·den·tal·ism \-ᵊl-,iz-əm\ *n* : a philosophy holding that ultimate reality is unknowable or asserting the primacy of the spiritual over the material and empirical — **tran·scen·den·tal·ist** \-ᵊl-əst\ *adj or n*

trans·con·ti·nen·tal \ˌtrans-ˌkänt-ᵊn-'ent-ᵊl\ *adj* : extending or going across a continent

tran·scribe \trans-'krīb\ *vb* **tran·scribed; tran·scrib·ing 1** : to write a copy of **2** : to make a copy of (dictated or recorded matter) in longhand or on a typewriter **3** : to represent (speech sounds) by means of phonetic symbols; *also* : to make a musical transcription of

tran·script \'trans-ˌkript\ *n* **1** : a written, printed, or typed copy **2** : an official copy esp. of a student's educational record

tran·scrip·tion \trans-'krip-shən\ *n* **1** : an act or process of transcribing **2** : COPY, TRANSCRIPT **3** : an arrangement of a musical composition for some instrument or voice other than the original

trans·duc·er \-'d(y)ü-sər\ *n* : a device that is actuated by power from one system and supplies power usu. in another form to a second system

tran·sept \'trans-ˌept\ *n* : the part of a cruciform church that crosses at right angles to the greatest length; *also* : either of the projecting ends

¹trans·fer \trans-'fər, 'trans-ˌfər\ *vb* **trans·ferred; trans·fer·ring 1** : to pass or cause to pass from one person, place, or situation to another : TRANSPORT, TRANSMIT **2** : to make over the possession of : CONVEY **3** : to print or copy from one surface to another by contact **4** : to change from one vehicle or transportation line to another — **trans·fer·able** \trans-'fər-ə-bəl\ *adj* — **trans·fer·al** \-əl\ *n*

²trans·fer \'trans-ˌfər\ *n* **1** : conveyance of right, title, or interest in property from one person to another **2** : an act or process of transferring **3** : one that transfers or is transferred **4** : a ticket entitling a passenger to continue a journey on another route

trans·fer·ence \trans-'fər-əns\ *n* : an act, process, or instance of transferring

trans·fig·ure \trans-'fig-yər\ *vb* **-ured; -ur·ing 1** : to change the form or appearance of **2** : EXALT, GLORIFY — **trans·fig·u·ra·tion** \ˌtrans-ˌfig-(y)ə-'rā-shən\ *n*

trans·fix \trans-'fiks\ *vb* **1** : to pierce through with or as if with a pointed weapon **2** : to hold motionless by or as if by piercing

trans·form \trans-'fȯrm\ *vb* **1** : to change in structure, appearance, or character **2** : to change (an electric current) in potential or type syn transmute, transfigure, transmogrify — **trans·for·ma·tion** \ˌtrans-fər-'mā-shən\ *n* — **trans·form·er** \trans-'fȯr-mər\ *n*

trans·fuse \trans-'fyüz\ *vb* **trans·fused; trans·fus·ing 1** : to cause to pass from one to another **2** : to diffuse into or through **3** : to transfer (as blood) into

a vein of a person or animal — **trans·fu·sion** \-'fyü-zhən\ *n*

trans·gress \trans-'gres, tranz-\ *vb* [F *transgresser*, fr. L *transgressus*, pp. of *transgredi* to step beyond or across, fr. *trans*- across + *gradi* to step] **1** : to go beyond the limits set by (~ the divine law) **2** : to go beyond : EXCEED **3** : SIN — **trans·gres·sion** \-'gresh-ən\ *n* — **trans·gres·sor** \-'gres-ər\ *n*

¹tran·sient \'tranch-ənt\ *adj* **1** : not lasting long : SHORT-LIVED **2** : passing through a place with only a brief stay syn transitory, passing, momentary, fleeting — **tran·sient·ly** *adv*

²tran·sient *n* : one that is transient; *esp* : a transient guest

tran·sis·tor \tranz-'is-tər, trans-\ *n* [*transfer* + *resistor*; fr. its transferring an electrical signal across a resistor] **1** : a small electronic semiconductor device similar in use to a vacuum tube **2** : a radio having transistors

tran·sis·tor·ize \-tə-ˌrīz\ *vb* **-ized; -iz·ing** : to equip (a device) with transistors

tran·sit \'trans-ət, 'tranz-\ *n* **1** : a passing through, across, or over : PASSAGE **2** : conveyance of persons or things from one place to another **3** : usu. local transportation esp. of people by public conveyance **4** : a surveyor's instrument for measuring angles

tran·si·tion \trans-'ish-ən, tranz-\ *n* : passage from one state, place, stage, or subject to another : CHANGE — **tran·si·tion·al** \-'ish-(ə-)nəl\ *adj*

tran·si·tive \'trans-ət-iv, 'tranz-\ *adj* **1** : having or containing an object required to complete the meaning **2** : TRANSITIONAL — **tran·si·tive·ly** *adv* — **tran·si·tive·ness** *n* — **tran·si·tiv·i·ty** \ˌtrans-ə-'tiv-ət-ē, ˌtranz-\ *n*

tran·si·to·ry \'trans-ə-ˌtōr-ē, 'tranz-\ *adj* : of brief duration : SHORT-LIVED, TEMPORARY syn transient, passing, momentary, fleeting

transl *abbr* translated; translation

trans·late \trans-'lāt, tranz-\ *vb* **trans·lat·ed; trans·lat·ing 1** : to bear or change from one place, state, or form to another **2** : to convey to heaven without death **3** : to transfer (a bishop) from one see to another **4** : to turn into one's own or another language — **trans·lat·able** *adj* — **trans·la·tion** \-'lā-shən\ *n* — **trans·la·tor** \-'lāt-ər\ *n*

trans·lit·er·ate \trans-'lit-ə-ˌrāt, tranz-\ *vb* **-at·ed; -at·ing** : to represent or spell in the characters of another alphabet — **trans·lit·er·a·tion** \ˌtrans-ˌlit-ə-'rā-shən, ˌtranz-\ *n*

trans·lu·cent \trans-'lüs-ᵊnt, tranz-\ *adj* : admitting and diffusing light so that objects beyond cannot be clearly distinguished : partly transparent — **trans·lu·cence** \-ᵊns\ *n* — **trans·lu·cen·cy** \-ᵊn-sē\ *n* — **trans·lu·cent·ly** *adv*

trans·mi·grate \-'mī-ˌgrāt\ *vb* : to pass at death from one body or being to another — **trans·mi·gra·tion** \ˌtransmī-ˈgrā-shən, ˌtranz-\ n — **trans·mi·gra·to·ry** \transˈmī-grə-ˌtōr-ē\ adj

trans·mis·sion \-ˈmish-ən\ n 1 : an act or process of transmitting 2 : the passage of radio waves between transmitting stations and receiving stations 3 : the gears by which power is transmitted from the engine of an automobile to the axle that propels the vehicle 4 : something transmitted

trans·mit \-ˈmit\ vb **trans·mit·ted; trans·mit·ting** 1 : to transfer from one person or place to another : FORWARD 2 : to pass on by or as if by inheritance 3 : to cause or allow to spread abroad or to another (~ a disease) 4 : to cause (as light, electricity, or force) to pass through space or a medium 5 : to send out (radio or television signals) syn convey, communicate, impart — **trans·mis·si·ble** \-ˈmis-ə-bəl\ adj — **trans·mit·ta·ble** \-ˈmit-ə-bəl\ adj — **trans·mit·tal** \-ˈmit-ᵊl\ n

trans·mit·ter \-ˈmit-ər\ n 1 : one that transmits 2 : the part of a telephone into which one speaks 3 : an apparatus for transmitting telegraph, radio, or television signals

trans·mog·ri·fy \trans-ˈmäg-rə-ˌfī, tranz-\ vb **-fied; -fy·ing** : to change or alter often with grotesque or humorous effect — **trans·mog·ri·fi·ca·tion** \-ˌmäg-rə-fə-ˈkā-shən\ n

trans·mute \-ˈmyüt\ vb **trans·mut·ed; trans·mut·ing** : to change or alter in form, appearance, or nature syn transform, convert, transfigure, metamorphose — **trans·mu·ta·tion** \ˌtransmyü-ˈtā-shən, ˌtranz-\ n

trans·na·tion·al \ˈnash-(ə-)nəl\ adj : extending beyond national boundaries

trans·oce·an·ic \ˌtrans-ˌō-shē-ˈan-ik, ˌtranz-\ adj 1 : lying or dwelling beyond the ocean 2 : crossing or extending across the ocean

tran·som \ˈtran-səm\ n 1 : a piece (as a crossbar in the frame of a window or door) that lies crosswise in a structure 2 : a window above an opening (as a door) built on and often hinged to a horizontal crossbar

tran·son·ic also **trans·son·ic** \tran(s)-ˈsän-ik\ adj : being, relating to, or moving at a speed that is about that of sound in air or about 741 miles (1185 kilometers) per hour

transp abbr transportation

trans·pa·cif·ic \ˌtrans-pə-ˈsif-ik\ adj : crossing, extending across, or situated beyond the Pacific ocean

trans·par·ent \trans-ˈpar-ənt\ adj 1 : transmitting light : clear enough to be seen through 2 : SHEER, DIAPHANOUS (a ~ fabric) 3 : readily understood : CLEAR; also : easily detected (a ~ lie) syn lucid, translucent, lucent — **trans·par·en·cy** \-ən-sē\ n — **trans·par·ent·ly** adv

tran·spire \trans-ˈpī(ə)r\ vb **trans·pired;**

trans·pir·ing [MF transpirer, fr. L trans- across + spirare to breathe] 1 : to pass off (as watery vapor) through pores or a membrane 2 : to become known : come to light 3 : to take place : OCCUR — **tran·spi·ra·tion** \ˌtrans-pə-ˈrā-shən\ n

¹**trans·plant** \trans-ˈplant\ vb 1 : to take up and set again in another soil or location 2 : to remove from one place and settle or introduce elsewhere : TRANSPORT 3 : to transfer (an organ or tissue) from one part or individual to another 4 : to tolerate or adapt to being transplanted — **trans·plan·ta·tion** \ˌtrans-ˌplan-ˈtā-shən\ n

²**trans·plant** \ˈtrans-ˌplant\ n 1 : something transplanted 2 : the act or process of transplanting

trans·po·lar \ˌtrans-ˈpō-lər\ adj : going or extending across either of the polar regions

¹**trans·port** \trans-ˈpōrt\ vb 1 : to convey from one place to another : CARRY 2 : to carry away by strong emotion : ENRAPTURE 3 : to send to a penal colony overseas syn bear, carry, convey, ferry — **trans·por·ta·tion** \ˌtrans-pər-ˈtā-shən\ n — **trans·port·er** \trans-ˈpōrt-ər\

²**trans·port** \ˈtrans-ˌpōrt\ n 1 : an act of transporting : TRANSPORTATION 2 : strong or intensely pleasurable emotion : RAPTURE 3 : a ship used in transporting troops or supplies; also : a vehicle (as a truck or plane) used to transport persons or goods

trans·pose \trans-ˈpōz\ vb **trans·posed; trans·pos·ing** 1 : to change the position or sequence of (~ the letters in a word) 2 : to write or perform (a musical composition) in a different key syn reverse, invert — **trans·po·si·tion** \ˌtrans-pə-ˈzish-ən\ n

trans·ship \tran(ch)-ˈship, trans-\ vb : to transfer for further transportation from one ship or conveyance to another — **trans·ship·ment** n

tran·sub·stan·ti·a·tion \ˌtrans-əb-ˌstanchē-ˈā-shən\ n : the change in the eucharistic elements from the substance of bread and wine to the substance of the body of Christ with only the appearances of bread and wine remaining

trans·verse \trans-ˈvərs, tranz-\ adj : lying across : set crosswise — **transverse** \ˈtrans-ˌvərs, ˈtranz-\ n — **trans·verse·ly** adv

trans·ves·tite \trans-ˈves-ˌtīt, tranz-\ n : a person and esp. a male who adopts the dress and often the behavior of the opposite sex — **transvestite** adj — **trans·ves·tism** \-ˌtiz-əm\ n

¹**trap** \ˈtrap\ n 1 : a device for catching animals 2 : something by which one is caught unawares 3 : a machine for throwing objects into the air to be targets for shooters; also : a hazard on a golf course consisting of a depression containing sand 4 : a light one-horse

carriage on springs **5** : a device to allow some one thing to pass through while keeping other things out ⟨a ∼ in a drainpipe⟩ **6** *pl* : a group of percussion instruments used in a jazz or dance orchestra

²**trap** *vb* **trapped; trap·ping 1** : to catch in or as if in a trap; *also* : CONFINE **2** : to provide or set (a place) with traps **3** : to set traps for animals esp. as a business *syn* snare, entrap, ensnare, bag, lure, decoy — **trap·per** *n*

³**trap** *n* : any of various dark fine-grained igneous rocks used esp. in making roads

trap·door \'trap-¦dȯr\ *n* : a lifting or sliding door covering an opening in a floor or roof

tra·peze \tra-¦pēz\ *n* : a gymnastic apparatus consisting of a horizontal bar suspended by two parallel ropes

trap·e·zoid \'trap-ə-¦zȯid\ *n* [NL *trapezoides*, fr. Gk *trapezoeidēs* trapezoid-shaped, fr. *trapeza* table, fr. *tra-* four + *peza* foot] : a plane 4-sided figure with two and only two sides parallel — **trap·e·zoi·dal** \¸trap-ə-¦zȯid-ᵊl\ *adj*

trap·pings \'trap-iŋz\ *n pl* **1** : an ornamental covering esp. for a horse **2** : outward decoration or dress

trap·rock \'trap-¦räk\ *n* : ³TRAP

traps \'traps\ *n pl* : personal belongings : LUGGAGE

trap·shoot·ing \'trap-¦shüt-iŋ\ *n* : shooting at clay pigeons sprung from a trap into the air away from the shooter

trash \'trash\ *n* **1** : something of little worth : RUBBISH **2** : a worthless person; *also* : such persons as a group : RIFFRAFF — **trashy** *adj*

trau·ma \'trau̇-mə, 'trȯ-\ *n, pl* **trau·ma·ta** \-mət-ə\ *or* **traumas** [Gk] : a bodily or mental injury usu. caused by an external agent; *also* : a cause of trauma — **trau·mat·ic** \trə-¦mat-ik, trȯ-, trau̇-\ *adj*

¹**tra·vail** \trə-¦vāl, 'trav-¸āl\ *n* **1** : painful work or exertion : TOIL **2** : AGONY, TORMENT **3** : CHILDBIRTH, LABOR *syn* work, drudgery, grind

²**travail** *vb* : to labor hard : TOIL

¹**trav·el** \'trav-əl\ *vb* **-eled** *or* **-elled; -el·ing** *or* **-el·ling** \-(ə-)liŋ\ **1** : to go on or as if on a trip or tour : JOURNEY **2** : to move as if by traveling : PASS ⟨news ∼s fast⟩ **3** : ASSOCIATE **4** : to go from place to place as a salesman **5** : to move from point to point ⟨light waves ∼ very fast⟩ **6** : to journey over or through ⟨∼ing the highways⟩ — **trav·el·er** *or* **trav·el·ler** *n*

²**travel** *n* **1** : the act of traveling : PASSAGE **2** : JOURNEY, TRIP — often used in pl. **3** : the number traveling : TRAFFIC **4** : the motion of a piece of machinery and esp. when to and fro; *also* : length of motion (as of a piston)

traveling bag *n* : a bag carried by hand

and designed to hold a traveler's clothing and personal articles

trav·el·ogue *or* **trav·el·og** \'trav-ə-¸lȯg, -¸läg\ *n* : a usu. illustrated lecture on travel

¹**tra·verse** \'trav-ərs\ *n* : something (as a crosswise beam) that crosses or lies across

²**tra·verse** \trə-¦vərs, tra-¦vərs *or* 'trav-ərs\ *vb* **tra·versed; tra·vers·ing 1** : to pass through : PENETRATE **2** : to go or travel across or over **3** : to extend over **4** : SWIVEL

³**tra·verse** \'tra-¸vərs\ *adj* : TRANSVERSE

trav·er·tine \'trav-ər-¸tēn, -tən\ *n* : a crystalline mineral formed by deposition from spring waters

¹**trav·es·ty** \'trav-ə-stē\ *vb* **-tied; -ty·ing** : to make a travesty of

²**travesty** *n, pl* **-ties** [obs. E *travesty*, disguised, parodied, fr. F *travesti*, pp. of *travestir* to disguise, fr. It *travestire*, fr. *tra-* across (fr. L *trans-*) + *vestire* to dress] : a burlesque and usu. grotesque translation or imitation

¹**trawl** \'trȯl\ *vb* : to fish or catch with a trawl — **trawl·er** *n*

²**trawl** *n* **1** : a large conical net dragged along the sea bottom in fishing **2** : a long fishing line anchored at both ends and equipped with many hooks

tray \'trā\ *n* : an open receptacle with flat bottom and low rim for holding, carrying, or exhibiting articles

treach·er·ous \'trech-(ə-)rəs\ *adj* **1** : characterized by treachery **2** : UNTRUSTWORTHY, UNRELIABLE **3** : providing insecure footing or support *syn* traitorous, faithless, false, disloyal — **treach·er·ous·ly** *adv*

treach·ery \'trech-(ə-)rē\ *n, pl* **-er·ies** : violation of allegiance or trust

trea·cle \'trē-kəl\ *n* [ME *triacle* a medicinal compound, fr. MF, fr. L *theriaca*, fr. Gk *thēriakē* antidote against a poisonous bite, fr. *thērion* wild animal] **1** *chiefly Brit* : MOLASSES **2** : something heavily sweet and cloying

¹**tread** \'tred\ *vb* **trod** \'träd\ ; **trod·den** \'träd-ᵊn\ *or* **trod; tread·ing 1** : to step or walk on or over **2** : to move on foot : WALK; *also* : DANCE **3** : to beat or press with the feet

²**tread** *n* **1** : a mark made by or as if by treading **2** : the manner or sound of stepping **3** : the part of a wheel that makes contact with a road **4** : the horizontal part of a step

trea·dle \'tred-ᵊl\ *n* : a lever device pressed by the foot to drive a machine

tread·mill \'tred-¸mil\ *n* **1** : a mill worked by persons who tread on steps around the edge of a wheel or by animals that walk on an endless belt **2** : a wearisome routine

treas *abbr* treasurer; treasury

trea·son \'trēz-ᵊn\ *n* : the offense of attempting to overthrow the government of one's country or of assisting its enemies in war — **trea·son·able**

\-(ᵊ)nə-bəl\ *adj* — **trea·son·ous**
\-(ᵊ)nəs\ *adj*

¹**trea·sure** \'trezh-ər, 'trāzh-\ *n* **1**
: wealth stored up or held in reserve **2**
: something of great value

²**treasure** *vb* **trea·sured; trea·sur·ing**
\-(ə-)riŋ\ **1** : HOARD **2** : to keep as precious : CHERISH *syn* prize, value, appreciate, esteem

trea·sur·er \'trezh-rər, 'trezh-ər-ər,
'trāzh-\ *n* : an officer entrusted with
the receipt, care, and disbursement of
funds

treasure trove \-ˌtrōv\ *n* **1** : treasure (as
money in gold) which is found hidden
and whose ownership is unknown **2**
: a valuable discovery

trea·sury \'trezh-(ə-)rē, 'trāzh-\ *n, pl*
-sur·ies 1 : a place in which stores of
wealth are kept **2** : the place of deposit and disbursement of collected
funds; *esp* : one where public revenues are deposited, kept, and disbursed **3** *cap* : a governmental department in charge of finances

¹**treat** \'trēt\ *vb* **1** : NEGOTIATE **2** : to deal
with esp. in writing; *also* : HANDLE **3**
: to pay for the food or entertainment
of **4** : to behave or act toward ⟨∼
them well⟩ **5** : to regard in a specified
manner ⟨∼ as inferiors⟩ **6** : to care for
medically or surgically **7** : to subject
to some action (as of a chemical) ⟨∼
soil with lime⟩

²**treat** *n* **1** : food or entertainment paid
for by another **2** : a source of joy or
amusement

trea·tise \'trēt-əs\ *n* : a systematic written exposition or argument

treat·ment \'trēt-mənt\ *n* : the act or
manner or an instance of treating
someone or something; *also* : a substance or method used in treating

trea·ty \'trēt-ē\ *n, pl* **treaties** : an agreement made by negotiation or diplomacy esp. between two or more states or
governments *syn* contract, bargain,
pact, convention

¹**tre·ble** \'treb-əl\ *n* **1** : the highest of the
four voice parts in vocal music : SOPRANO **2** : a high-pitched or shrill
voice or sound **3** : the upper half of
the musical pitch range

²**treble** *adj* **1** : triple in number or
amount **2** : relating to or having the
range of a musical treble **3** : highpitched : SHRILL — **tre·bly** \'treb-
(ə-)lē\ *adv*

³**treble** *vb* **tre·bled; tre·bling** \'treb-
(ə-)liŋ\ : to make or become three
times the size, amount, or number

¹**tree** \'trē\ *n* **1** : a woody perennial plant
usu. with a single main stem and a
head of branches and leaves at the top
2 : a piece of wood adapted to a particular use ⟨a shoe ∼⟩ **3** : something
resembling a tree ⟨a genealogical ∼⟩
— **tree·less** *adj*

²**tree** *vb* **treed; tree·ing** : to drive to or up
a tree ⟨∼ a raccoon⟩

tree farm *n* : an area of forest land managed to ensure continuous commercial production

tree line *n* : TIMBERLINE

tree of heaven : an Asian ailanthus that
is widely grown as a shade and ornamental tree

tree surgery *n* : operative treatment of
diseased trees esp. for control of decay — **tree surgeon** *n*

tre·foil \'trē-ˌfȯil, 'tref-ˌȯil\ *n* **1** : a clover or related herb with leaves with
three leaflets **2** : a decorative design
with three leaflike parts

¹**trek** \'trek\ *vb* **trekked; trek·king 1** : to
travel or migrate by ox wagon **2** : to
make one's way arduously

²**trek** *n* **1** : a migration esp. of settlers by
ox wagon **2** : TRIP; *esp* : one involving
difficulties or strange experiences

trel·lis \'trel-əs\ *n* [ME *trelis*, fr. MF
treliz fabric of coarse weave, trellis,
fr. (assumed) VL *trilicius* woven with
triple thread, fr. L *tres* three + *liceum*
thread] : a structure of latticework

trellis *vb* : to train (as a vine) on a trellis

trem·a·tode \'trem-ə-ˌtōd\ *n* : any of a
class of parasitic worms

trem·ble \'trem-bəl\ *vb* **trem·bled; trem·bling** \-b(ə-)liŋ\ **1** : to shake involuntarily (as with fear or cold) : SHIVER **2**
: to move, sound, pass, or come to
pass as if shaken or tremulous **3** : to
be affected with fear or doubt

tremble *n* : a spell of shaking or quivering : TREMOR

tre·men·dous \tri-'men-dəs\ *adj* **1**
: such as may excite trembling : TERRIFYING **2** : astonishingly large, powerful, great, or excellent *syn* stupendous, monumental, monstrous —
tre·men·dous·ly *adv*

trem·o·lo \'trem-ə-ˌlō\ *n, pl* **-los** [It] : a
rapid fluttering of a tone or alternating
tones to produce a tremulous effect

trem·or \'trem-ər\ *n* **1** : a trembling or
shaking esp. from weakness or disease **2** : a quivering motion of the
earth (as during an earthquake)

trem·u·lous \'trem-yə-ləs\ *adj* **1**
: marked by trembling or tremors
: QUIVERING **2** : TIMOROUS, TIMID —
trem·u·lous·ly *adv*

¹**trench** \'trench\ *n* [ME *trenche* track
cut through a wood, fr. MF, act of
cutting, fr. *trenchier* to cut] **1** : a long
narrow cut in the ground : DITCH; *esp*
: a ditch protected by banks of earth
and used to shelter soldiers **2** : a long
narrow steep-sided depression in the
ocean floor

²**trench** *vb* **1** : to cut or dig trenches in;
also : to drain by trenches **2** : to protect (troops) with trenches **3** : to
come close : VERGE

tren·chant \'tren-chənt\ *adj* **1** : vigorously effective; *also* : CAUSTIC **2**
: sharply perceptive : KEEN **3**
: CLEAR-CUT, DISTINCT *syn* incisive, biting, crisp

tren·cher \'tren-chər\ *n* : a wooden
platter for serving food

tren·cher·man \'tren-chər-mən\ *n* : a hearty eater

trench foot *n* : a painful foot disorder resembling frostbite and resulting from exposure to cold and wet

trench mouth *n* : a contagious infection of the mouth and adjacent parts that is marked by ulceration and caused by bacteria

¹**trend** \'trend\ *vb* 1 : to have or take a general direction : TEND 2 : to show a tendency : INCLINE

²**trend** *n* 1 : a general direction taken (as by a stream or mountain range) 2 : a prevailing tendency : DRIFT 3 : a current style or preference : VOGUE

tre·pan \tri-'pan\ *vb* **tre·panned; tre·pan·ning** : to remove surgically a disk of bone from (the skull) — **tre·pa·na·tion** \,trep-ə-'nā-shən\ *n*

tre·phine \'trē-,fīn\ *n* : a surgical instrument for cutting out circular sections (as of bone or corneal tissue) — **trephine** *vb*

trep·i·da·tion \,trep-ə-'dā-shən\ *n* : nervous agitation : APPREHENSION **syn** horror, terror, panic, consternation, dread, fright, dismay

¹**tres·pass** \'tres-pəs, -,pas\ *n* 1 : SIN, OFFENSE 2 : wrongful entry on real property **syn** transgression, violation, infraction, infringement

²**trespass** *vb* 1 : to commit an offense : ERR, SIN 2 : INTRUDE, ENCROACH; *esp* : to enter unlawfully upon the land of another — **tres·pass·er** *n*

tress \'tres\ *n* : a long lock of hair — usu. used in pl.

tres·tle *also* **tres·sel** \'tres-əl\ *n* 1 : a supporting framework consisting usu. of a horizontal piece with spreading legs at each end 2 : a braced framework of timbers, piles, or steel for carrying a road or railroad over a depression

trey \'trā\ *n, pl* **treys** : a card or the side of a die with three spots

tri·ad \'trī-,ad, -əd\ *n* : a union or group of three usu. closely related persons or things

tri·age \trē-'äzh, 'trē-,äzh\ *n* [F, sifting] : the sorting of and allocation of treatment to patients and esp. battle and disaster victims according to a system of priorities designed to maximize the number of survivors

¹**tri·al** \'trī-(ə)l\ *n* 1 : the action or process of trying or putting to the proof : TEST 2 : the hearing and judgment of a matter in issue before a competent tribunal 3 : a source of vexation or annoyance 4 : a temporary use or experiment to test quality or usefulness 5 : EFFORT, ATTEMPT **syn** cross, ordeal, tribulation, affliction

²**trial** *adj* 1 : of, relating to, or used in a trial 2 : made or done as a test

tri·an·gle \'trī-,aŋ-gəl\ *n* 1 : a figure that has three sides and three angles : a polygon having three sides 2 : something shaped like a triangle — **tri·an·gu·lar** \trī-'aŋ-gyə-lər\ *adj* — **tri·an·gu·lar·ly** *adv*

tri·an·gu·la·tion \(,)trī-,aŋ-gyə-'lā-shən\ *n* : a trigonometric operation for finding a position using bearings from two fixed points a known distance apart — **tri·an·gu·late** \trī-'aŋ-gyə-,lāt\ *vb*

Tri·as·sic \trī-'as-ik\ *adj* : of, relating to, or being the earliest period of the Mesozoic era — **Triassic** *n*

trib *abbr* tributary

tribe \'trīb\ *n* 1 : a social group comprising numerous families, clans, or generations 2 : a group of persons having a common character, occupation, or interest 3 : a group of related plants or animals (the cat ∼) — **trib·al** \'trī-bəl\ *adj*

tribes·man \'trībz-mən\ *n* : a member of a tribe

trib·u·la·tion \,trib-yə-'lā-shən\ *n* [ME *tribulacion,* fr. OF, fr. L *tribulatio,* fr. *tribulare* to press, oppress, fr. *tribulum* drag used in threshing] : distress or suffering resulting from oppression or persecution; *also* : a trying experience **syn** trial, affliction, cross, ordeal

tri·bu·nal \trī-'byün-əl, trib-'yün-\ *n* 1 : the seat of a judge 2 : a court of justice 3 : something that decides or determines (the ∼ of public opinion)

tri·bune \'trib-,yün, trib-'yün\ *n* 1 : an official in ancient Rome with the function of protecting the interests of plebeian citizens from the patricians 2 : a defender of the people

¹**trib·u·tary** \'trib-yə-,ter-ē\ *adj* 1 : paying tribute : SUBJECT 2 : flowing into a larger stream or a lake **syn** subordinate, secondary, dependent

²**tributary** *n, pl* **-tar·ies** 1 : a ruler or state that pays tribute 2 : a tributary stream

trib·ute \'trib-(,)yüt, -yət\ *n* 1 : a payment by one ruler or nation to another as an act of submission or price of protection 2 : a usu. excessive tax, rental, or levy exacted by a sovereign or superior 3 : a gift or service showing respect, gratitude, or affection; *also* : PRAISE **syn** eulogy, citation, encomium, panegyric

trice \'trīs\ *n* : INSTANT, MOMENT

tri·ceps \'trī-,seps\ *n, pl* **tri·ceps·es** *also* **triceps** : a large muscle along the back of the upper arm that is attached at its upper end by three main parts and acts to extend the arm at the elbow joint

tri·chi·na \trik-'ī-nə\ *n, pl* **-nae** \-(,)nē\ *also* **-nas** : a small slender nematode worm that in the larval state is parasitic in the voluntary muscles of flesh-eating mammals (as the hog and human beings)

trich·i·no·sis \,trik-ə-'nō-səs\ *n* : a disease caused by infestation of muscle tissue by trichinae and marked by pain, fever, and swelling

¹**trick** \'trik\ *n* 1 : a crafty procedure meant to deceive 2 : a mischievous

action : PRANK **3** : a childish action **4** : a deceptive or ingenious feat designed to puzzle or amuse **5** : PECULIARITY, MANNERISM **6** : a quick or artful way of getting a result : KNACK **7** : the cards played in one round of a card game **8** : a tour of duty : SHIFT **syn** ruse, maneuver, artifice, wile, feint

²**trick** *vb* **1** : to deceive by cunning or artifice : CHEAT **2** : to dress ornately

trick·ery \'trik-(ə-)rē\ *n* : deception by tricks and strategems

trick·le \'trik-əl\ *vb* **trick·led**; **trick·ling** \-(ə-)liŋ\ **1** : to run or fall in drops **2** : to flow in a thin gentle stream — **trickle** *n*

trick·ster \'trik-stər\ *n* : one who tricks or cheats

tricky \'trik-ē\ *adj* **trick·i·er**, **-est 1** : inclined to trickery (a ~ person) **2** : requiring skill or caution (a ~ situation to handle) **3** : UNRELIABLE

tri·col·or \'trī-ˌkəl-ər\ *n* : a flag of three colors ⟨the French ~⟩

tri·cy·cle \'trī-ˌ(ˌ)sik-əl\ *n* : a 3-wheeled vehicle usu. propelled by pedals

tri·dent \'trīd-ᵊnt\ *n* [L *trident-*, *tridens*, fr. *tres* three + *dent-*, *dens* tooth] : a 3-pronged spear

tried \'trīd\ *adj* **1** : found trustworthy through testing **2** : subjected to trials **syn** reliable, dependable, trusty

tri·en·ni·al \'trī-'en-ē-əl\ *adj* **1** : lasting for three years **2** : occurring or being done every three years — **triennial** *n*

¹**tri·fle** \'trī-fəl\ *n* : something of little value or importance; *esp* : an insignificant amount (as of money)

²**trifle** *vb* **tri·fled**; **tri·fling** \-f(ə-)liŋ\ **1** : to talk in a jesting or mocking manner **2** : to act frivolously or playfully **3** : DALLY, FLIRT **4** : to handle idly : TOY — **tri·fler** \-f(ə-)lər\ *n*

tri·fling \'trī-fliŋ\ *adj* **1** : FRIVOLOUS **2** : TRIVIAL, INSIGNIFICANT **syn** petty, paltry, measly, inconsequential

tri·fo·cals \'trī-'fō-kəlz\ *n pl* : eyeglasses with lenses having one part for close focus, one for intermediate focus, and one for distant focus

tri·fo·li·ate \trī-'fō-lē-ət\ *adj* : having three leaves or leaflets

¹**trig** \'trig\ *adj* : stylishly trim : SMART **syn** tidy, spruce, shipshape

²**trig** *n* : TRIGONOMETRY

¹**trig·ger** \'trig-ər\ *n* [alter. of earlier *tricker*, fr. Dutch *trekker*, fr. Middle Dutch *trecker* one that pulls, fr. *trecken* to pull] : a movable lever that activates a device when it is squeezed; *esp* : the part of a firearm lock moved by the finger to release the hammer in firing — **trigger** *adj* — **trig·gered** \-ərd\ *adj*

²**trigger** *vb* **1** : to fire by pulling a trigger **2** : to initiate, actuate, or set off as if by a trigger

trig·o·nom·e·try \ˌtrig-ə-'näm-ə-trē\ *n* : the branch of mathematics dealing with the relations of the sides and an-

gles of triangles and of methods of deducing from given parts other required parts — **trig·o·no·met·ric** \-nə-'me-trik\ *also* **trig·o·no·met·ri·cal** \-trik-əl\ *adj*

¹**trill** \'tril\ *n* **1** : the alternation of two musical tones a scale degree apart **2** : WARBLE **3** : the rapid vibration of one speech organ against another (as of the tip of the tongue against the teeth)

²**trill** *vb* : to utter as or with a trill

tril·lion \'tril-yən\ *n* **1** : a thousand billions **2** *Brit* : a million billions — **trillion** *adj* — **tril·lionth** \-yənth\ *adj or n*

tril·li·um \'tril-ē-əm\ *n* : any of a genus of herbs of the lily family with an erect stem bearing a whorl of three leaves and a large solitary flower with three petals

tril·o·gy \'tril-ə-jē\ *n, pl* **-gies** : a series of three dramas or literary or musical compositions that are closely related and develop one theme

¹**trim** \'trim\ *vb* **trimmed; trim·ming** [OE *trymian*, *trymman* to strengthen, arrange, fr. *trum* strong, firm] **1** : to put ornaments on : ADORN **2** : to defeat esp. resoundingly **3** : to make trim, neat, regular, or less bulky by or as if by cutting (a ~ beard) (~ a budget) **4** : to cause (a boat) to assume a desired position in the water by arrangement of ballast, cargo, or passengers; *also* : to adjust (as a submarine or airplane) esp. for horizontal motion **5** : to adjust (a sail) to a desired position **6** : to change one's views for safety or expediency — **trim·ly** *adv* — **trim·mer** *n* — **trim·ness** *n*

²**trim** *adj* **trim·mer; trim·mest** : showing neatness, good order, or compactness ⟨~ figure⟩ **syn** tidy, trig, smart, spruce, shipshape

³**trim** *n* **1** : good condition : FITNESS **2** : material used for ornament or trimming; *esp* : the woodwork in the finish of a house esp. around doors and windows **3** : the position of a ship or boat esp. with reference to the horizontal; *also* : the relation between the plane of a sail and the direction of a ship **4** : the position of an airplane at which it will continue in level flight with no adjustments to the controls **5** : something that is trimmed off

tri·ma·ran \'trī-mə-ˌran, ˌtrī-mə-'ran\ *n* : a fast pleasure sailboat with three hulls side by side

tri·mes·ter \trī-'mes-tər, 'trī-ˌmes-tər\ *n* **1** : a period of three or about three months **2** : one of three terms into which an academic year is sometimes divided

trim·e·ter \'trim-ət-ər\ *n* : a line consisting of three metrical feet

trim·ming \'trim-iŋ\ *n* **1** : DEFEAT **2** : the action of one that trims **3** : something that trims, ornaments, or completes

tri·month·ly \trī-'mənth-lē\ *adj* : occurring every three months

trine \'trīn\ *adj* : THREEFOLD, TRIPLE

Trin·i·da·di·an \ˌtrin-ə-'dād-ē-ən, -'dad-\ *n* : a native or inhabitant of the island of Trinidad — **Trinidadian** *adj*

Trin·i·tar·i·an \ˌtrin-ə-'ter-ē-ən\ *n* : a believer in the doctrine of the Trinity — **Trin·i·tar·i·an·ism** \-ē-ə-ˌniz-əm\ *n*

Trin·i·ty \'trin-ət-ē\ *n* 1 : the unity of Father, Son, and Holy Spirit as three persons in one Godhead 2 *not cap* : TRIAD

trin·ket \'triŋ-kət\ *n* 1 : a small ornament (as a jewel or ring) 2 : TRIFLE

trio \'trē-ō\ *n, pl* **tri·os** 1 : a musical composition for three voices or three instruments 2 : the performers of a musical or dance trio 3 : a group or set of three

tri·ode \'trī-ˌōd\ *n* : a vacuum tube with three electrodes

¹trip \'trip\ *vb* **tripped; trip·ping** 1 : to move with light quick steps 2 : to catch the foot against something so as to stumble or cause to stumble 3 : to make a mistake : SLIP; *also* : to detect in a misstep : EXPOSE 4 : to release (as a spring or switch) by moving a catch; *also* : ACTIVATE 5 : to get high on a psychedelic drug

²trip *n* 1 : JOURNEY, VOYAGE 2 : a quick light step 3 : a false step : STUMBLE; *also* : ERROR 4 : the action of tripping mechanically; *also* : a device for tripping 5 : an intense drug-induced hallucinatory experience 6 : pursuit of an obsessive interest (an ego ∼)

tri·par·tite \trī-'pär-ˌtīt\ *adj* 1 : divided into three parts 2 : having three corresponding parts or copies 3 : made between three parties (a ∼ treaty)

tripe \'trīp\ *n* 1 : stomach tissue of a ruminant and esp. an ox used as food 2 : something poor, worthless, or offensive : TRASH

¹tri·ple \'trip-əl\ *vb* **tri·pled; tri·pling** \-(ə-)liŋ\ 1 : to make or become three times as great or as many 2 : to hit a triple

²triple *n* 1 : a triple quantity 2 : a group of three 3 : a hit in baseball that lets the batter reach third base

³triple *adj* 1 : being three times as great or as many 2 : having three units or members 3 : repeated three times

triple bond *n* : a chemical bond in which three pairs of electrons are shared by two atoms in a molecule

triple point *n* : the condition of temperature and pressure under which the gaseous, liquid, and solid forms of a substance can exist in equilibrium

trip·let \'trip-lət\ *n* 1 : a unit of three lines of verse 2 : a group of three of a kind 3 : one of three offspring born at one birth

tri·plex \'trip-ˌleks, 'trī-ˌpleks\ *adj* : THREEFOLD, TRIPLE

¹trip·li·cate \'trip-li-kət\ *adj* : made in three identical copies

²trip·li·cate \-lə-ˌkāt\ *vb* **-cat·ed; -cat·ing** 1 : TRIPLE 2 : to provide three copies of (∼ a document)

³trip·li·cate \-li-kət\ *n* : three copies all alike — used with *in* (typed in ∼)

tri·ply \'trip-(ə-)lē\ *adv* : in a triple degree, amount, or manner

tri·pod \'trī-ˌpäd\ *n* : something (as a caldron, stool, or camera stand) that rests on three legs — **tripod** *or* **tri·po·dal** \'trip-əd-ᵊl, 'trī-ˌpäd-\ *adj*

trip·tych \'trip-tik\ *n* : a picture or carving (as an altarpiece) in three panels side by side

tri·reme \'trī-ˌrēm\ *n* : an ancient galley having three banks of oars

tri·sect \'trī-ˌsekt, trī-'sekt\ *vb* : to divide into three usu. equal parts — **tri·sec·tion** \'trī-ˌsek-shən\ *n*

trite \'trīt\ *adj* **trit·er; trit·est** [L *tritus*, fr. pp. of *terere* to rub, wear away] : used so commonly that the novelty is worn off : STALE **syn** hackneyed, stereotyped, commonplace, clichéd

tri·ti·um \'trit-ē-əm, 'trish-ē-\ *n* : a radioactive form of hydrogen with atoms of three times the mass of ordinary hydrogen atoms

tri·ton \'trīt-ᵊn\ *n* : any of various large marine mollusks with a heavy elongated conical shell; *also* : the shell of a triton

trit·u·rate \'trich-ə-ˌrāt\ *vb* **-rat·ed; -rat·ing** : to rub or grind to a fine powder

¹tri·umph \'trī-əmf\ *n, pl* **tri·umphs** \-əmfs, -əm(p)s\ 1 : the joy or exultation of victory or success 2 : VICTORY, CONQUEST — **tri·um·phal** \trī-'əm-fəl\ *adj*

²triumph *vb* 1 : to celebrate victory or success exultantly 2 : to obtain victory : PREVAIL — **tri·um·phant** \trī-'əm-fənt\ *adj* — **tri·um·phant·ly** *adv*

tri·um·vir \trī-'əm-vər\ *n, pl* **-virs** *also* **-vi·ri** \-və-ˌrī\ : a member of a triumvirate

tri·um·vi·rate \-və-rət\ *n* : a ruling body of three persons

tri·une \'trī-ˌ(y)ün\ *adj, often cap* : being three in one (the ∼ God)

triv·et \'triv-ət\ *n* 1 : a 3-legged stand : TRIPOD 2 : a metal stand with short feet for use under a hot dish

triv·ia \'triv-ē-ə\ *n sing or pl* : unimportant matters : TRIFLES

triv·i·al \'triv-ē-əl\ *adj* [L *trivialis* found everywhere, commonplace, trivial, fr. *trivium* crossroads, fr. *tres* three + *via* way] : of little importance — **triv·i·al·i·ty** \ˌtriv-ē-'al-ət-ē\ *n*

triv·i·um \'triv-ē-əm\ *n, pl* **triv·ia** \-ē-ə\ : the three liberal arts of grammar, rhetoric, and logic in a medieval university

tri·week·ly \trī-'wē-klē\ *adj* 1 : occurring or appearing three times a week 2 : occurring or appearing every three weeks — **triweekly** *adv*

tro·che \'trō-kē\ *n* : a medicinal lozenge

tro·chee \'trō-(ˌ)kē\ *n* : a metrical foot of one accented syllable followed by one unaccented syllable — **tro·cha·ic** \trō-ˈkā-ik\ *adj*

trod *past and past part of* TREAD

trodden *past part of* TREAD

trol·ka \ˈtroi-kə\ *n* [Russ *troĭka* a vehicle drawn by three horses, fr. *troe* three] : a group of three; *esp* : an administrative or ruling body of three

¹**troll** \ˈtrōl\ *vb* **1** : to sing the parts of (a song) in succession **2** : to angle for with a hook and line drawn through the water **3** : to sing or play jovially

²**troll** *n* : a lure used in trolling; *also* : the line with its lure

³**troll** *n* : a dwarf or giant in Teutonic folklore inhabiting caves or hills

trol·ley *or* **trol·ly** \ˈträl-ē\ *n, pl* **trolleys** *or* **trollies** **1** : a device (as a grooved wheel on the end of a pole) to carry current from a wire to an electrically driven vehicle **2** : TROLLEY CAR **3** : a wheeled carriage running on an overhead rail or track

trol·ley·bus \ˈträl-ē-ˌbəs\ *n* : a bus powered electrically from two overhead wires

trolley car *n* : a streetcar powered electrically through a trolley

trol·lop \ˈträl-əp\ *n* **1** : a slovenly woman **2** : a loose woman : WANTON

trom·bone \träm-ˈbōn, ˈträm-ˌbōn\ *n* [It, lit., big trumpet, fr. *tromba* trumpet] : a brass wind instrument that consists of a long metal tube with two turns and a flaring end and that has a movable slide to vary the pitch — **trom·bon·ist** \-ˈbō-nəst, -ˌbō-\ *n*

tromp \ˈträmp, ˈtrömp\ *vb* **1** : TRAMP, MARCH **2** : to stamp with the foot **3** : DEFEAT

¹**troop** \ˈtrüp\ *n* **1** : a cavalry unit corresponding to an infantry company **2** *pl* : armed forces : SOLDIERS **3** : a collection of people or things **4** : a unit of Girl Scouts or Boy Scouts under an adult leader *syn* band, troupe, party, corps

²**troop** *vb* : to move or gather in crowds

troop·er \ˈtrü-pər\ *n* **1** : an enlisted cavalryman; *also* : a cavalry horse **2** : a mounted or state policeman

troop·ship \ˈtrüp-ˌship\ *n* : a ship for carrying troops

trope \ˈtrōp\ *n* : the use of a word or expression in a figurative sense

tro·phy \ˈtrō-fē\ *n, pl* **trophies** : something gained or given in conquest or victory esp. when preserved or mounted as a memorial

trop·ic \ˈträp-ik\ *n* [ME *tropik*, fr. L *tropicus* of the solstice, fr. Gk *tropikos*, fr. *tropē* turn] **1** : either of the two parallels of latitude one approximately 23½ degrees north of the equator (**tropic of Cancer** \-ˈkan-sər\) and one approximately 23½ degrees south of the equator (**tropic of Capricorn** \-ˈkap-rə-ˌkórn\) where the sun is directly overhead when apparently at its greatest distance north or south of the equator **2** *pl, often cap* : the region

lying between the tropics of Cancer and Capricorn — **trop·i·cal** \-i-kəl\ *or* **tropic** *adj*

tro·pism \ˈtrō-ˌpiz-əm\ *n* : involuntary orientation of an organism in response to a source of stimulation; *also* : a reflex reaction involving this

tro·po·sphere \ˈtrōp-ə-ˌsfiər, ˈträp-\ *n* : the portion of the atmosphere which extends outward about 10 miles (16 kilometers) from the earth's surface and in which most weather occurs — **tro·po·spher·ic** \ˌtröp-ə-ˈsfi(ə)r-ik, ˌträp-, -ˈsfer-\ *adj*

¹**trot** \ˈträt\ *n* **1** : a moderately fast gait of a 4-footed animal (as a horse) in which the legs move in diagonal pairs **2** : a jogging gait of a man between a walk and a run

²**trot** *vb* **trot·ted; trot·ting** **1** : to ride, drive, or go at a trot **2** : to proceed briskly : HURRY — **trot·ter** *n*

troth \ˈträth, ˈtrōth, ˈtröth\ *n* **1** : pledged faithfulness : FIDELITY **2** : one's pledged word; *also* : BETROTHAL

trou·ba·dour \ˈtrü-bə-ˌdōr\ *n* [F, fr. Old Provençal *trobador*] : one of a class of poet-musicians flourishing esp. in southern France and northern Italy during the 11th, 12th, and 13th centuries

¹**trou·ble** \ˈtrab-əl\ *vb* **trou·bled; trou·bling** \ˈtrab-(ə-)liŋ\ **1** : to agitate mentally or spiritually : DISTURB, WORRY **2** : to produce physical disorder in : AFFLICT **3** : to put to inconvenience **4** : RUFFLE (~ the waters) **5** : to make an effort *syn* distress, ail, upset, worry — **trou·ble·some** *adj* — **trou·ble·some·ly** *adv* — **trou·blous** \-(ə-)ləs\ *adj*

²**trouble** *n* **1** : the quality or state of being troubled esp. mentally **2** : an instance of distress or annoyance **3** : DISEASE, AILMENT (heart ~) **4** : EXERTION, PAINS (took the ~ to phone) **5** : a cause of disturbance or distress

trou·ble·mak·er \-ˌmā-kər\ *n* : a person who causes trouble

trou·ble·shoot·er \-ˌshüt-ər\ *n* **1** : a worker employed to locate trouble and make repairs in equipment **2** : an expert in resolving disputes or problems — **trou·ble·shoot** *vb*

trough \ˈtrof, ˈtröth, *by bakers often* ˈtrō\ *n, pl* **troughs** \ˈtrofs, ˈtrövz; ˈtröths, ˈtrö(th)z; ˈtröz\ **1** : a long shallow open boxlike container esp. for water or feed for livestock **2** : a gutter along the eaves of a house **3** : a long channel or depression (as between waves or hills)

trounce \ˈträuns\ *vb* **trounced; trounc·ing** **1** : to thrash or punish severely **2** : to defeat decisively

troupe \ˈtrüp\ *n* : COMPANY; *esp* : a group of performers on the stage — **troup·er** *n*

trou·sers \ˈträu-zərz\ *n pl* [alter. of earlier *trouse*, fr. ScGael *triubhas*] : an outer garment extending from the waist to the ankle or sometimes only to the knee, covering each leg separately, and worn esp. by males — **trouser** *adj*

trous·seau \'trü-sō, trü-'sō\ *n, pl* **trousseaux** \-sōz, -'sōz\ *or* **trous·seaus** [F] : the personal outfit of a bride

trout \'traŭt\ *n, pl* **trout** *also* **trouts** [ME, fr. OE *trūht,* fr. LL *tructa,* a fish with sharp teeth, fr. Gk *trōktēs,* lit., gnawer] : any of various mostly freshwater food and game fishes usu. smaller than the related salmons

trout lily *n* : DOGTOOTH VIOLET

trow \'trō\ *vb, archaic* : THINK, SUPPOSE

trow·el \'traŭ-(ə)l\ *n* **1** : any of various hand implements used for spreading, shaping, or smoothing loose or plastic material (as mortar or plaster) **2** : a small flat or scooplike implement used in gardening — **trowel** *vb*

troy \'troĭ\ *adj* : expressed in troy weight (~ ounce)

troy weight *n* : a system of weights based on a pound of 12 ounces and an ounce of 480 grains and used in the U.S. esp. for precious metals and gems — see WEIGHT table

tru·ant \'trü-ənt\ *n* [ME, vagabond, idler, fr. OF, vagrant] : one who shirks duty; *esp* : one who stays out of school without permission — **truan·cy** \-ən-sē\ *n* — **truant** *adj*

truce \'trüs\ *n* **1** : ARMISTICE **2** : a respite esp. from a disagreeable state or action

¹truck \'trək\ *vb* **1** : EXCHANGE, BARTER **2** : to have dealings : TRAFFIC

²truck *n* **1** : BARTER **2** : small goods or merchandise; *esp* : vegetables grown for market **3** : DEALINGS

³truck *n* **1** : a vehicle (as a strong heavy automobile) designed for carrying heavy articles or hauling a trailer **2** : a swiveling frame with springs and one or more pairs of wheels used to carry and guide one end of a locomotive or of a railroad or electric car — **truckload** \-ˌlōd\ *n*

⁴truck *vb* **1** : to transport on a truck **2** : to be employed in driving a truck — **truck·er** *n*

truck·age \'trək-ij\ *n* : transportation by truck; *also* : the cost of such transportation

truck farm *n* : a farm growing vegetables for market — **truck farmer** *n*

truck garden *n* : a garden where vegetables are raised for market

truck·le \'trək-əl\ *vb* **truck·led; truckling** \-(ə-)liŋ\ : to yield slavishly to the will of another : SUBMIT syn fawn, toady, cringe, cower

truc·u·lent \'trək-yə-lənt\ *adj* **1** : feeling or showing ferocity : SAVAGE **2** : aggressively self-assertive : PUGNACIOUS — **truc·u·lence** \-ləns\ *n* — **truc·u·len·cy** \-lən-sē\ *n* — **truc·u·lent·ly** *adv*

trudge \'trəj\ *vb* **trudged; trudg·ing** : to walk or march steadily and usu. laboriously

¹true \'trü\ *adj* **tru·er; tru·est 1** : STEADFAST, LOYAL **2** : conformable to fact or reality (a ~ description) **3** : CONSISTENT (~ to expectations) **4** : properly so called (the ~ stomach) **5** : RIGHTFUL (~ and lawful king) **6** : conformable to a standard or pattern; *also* : placed or formed accurately syn constant, staunch, resolute, steadfast

²true *adv* **1** : TRUTHFULLY **2** : ACCURATELY (the bullet flew straight and ~) : *also* : without variation from type (breed ~)

³true *n* **1** : TRUTH, REALITY — usu. used with *the* **2** : the state of being accurate (as in alignment) (out of ~)

⁴true *vb* **trued; tru·ing** *also* **tru·ing** : to make level, square, balanced, or concentric

true–blue *adj* : marked by unswerving loyalty

true bug *n* : BUG **1**

true–heart·ed \'trü-'härt-əd\ *adj* : FAITHFUL, LOYAL

truf·fle \'trəf-əl, 'trüf-\ *n* **1** : a European underground fungus; *also* : its dark wrinkled edible fruit **2** : a candy made of chocolate, butter, and sugar shaped into balls and coated with cocoa

tru·ism \'trü-ˌiz-əm\ *n* : an undoubted or self-evident truth syn commonplace, platitude, bromide, cliché

tru·ly \'trü-lē\ *adv* **1** : in all sincerity **2** : in agreement with fact **3** : ACCURATELY **4** : in a proper or suitable manner

¹trump \'trəmp\ *n* : TRUMPET

²trump *n* : a card of a designated suit any of whose cards will win over a card that is not of this suit; *also* : the suit itself — often used in pl.

³trump *vb* : to take with a trump

trumped–up \'trəm(p)t-'əp\ *adj* : fraudulently concocted : SPURIOUS

trum·pery \'trəm-p(ə-)rē\ *n* **1** : NONSENSE **2** : trivial articles : JUNK

¹trum·pet \'trəm-pət\ *n* **1** : a wind instrument consisting of a long curved metal tube flaring at one end and with a cup-shaped mouthpiece at the other **2** : something that resembles a trumpet or its tonal quality **3** : a funnel-shaped instrument for collecting, directing, or intensifying sound

²trumpet *vb* **1** : to blow a trumpet **2** : to proclaim on or as if on a trumpet — **trum·pet·er** *n*

¹trun·cate \'trəŋ-ˌkāt, 'trən-\ *adj* : having the end square or blunt

²truncate *vb* **trun·cat·ed; trun·cat·ing** : to shorten by or as if by cutting : LOP — **trun·ca·tion** \ˌtrəŋ-'kā-shən\ *n*

trun·cheon \'trən-chən\ *n* : a policeman's club

trun·dle \'trən-dᵊl\ *vb* **trun·dled; trundling** : to roll along : WHEEL

trundle bed *n* : a low bed that can be slid under a higher bed when not in use

trunk \'trəŋk\ *n* **1** : the main stem of a tree **2** : the body of a person or animal apart from the head and limbs **3** : the main or basal part of something **4** : a box or chest used to hold usu. clothes or personal effects (as of a traveler); *also* : the enclosed luggage space in the rear of an automobile **5** : the long muscular nose of an elephant **6** *pl* : men's shorts worn chiefly for sports **7** : a usu. major channel or passage **8** : a circuit between telephone exchanges

trunk line *n* : a system handling long-distance through traffic

¹**truss** \'trəs\ *vb* **1** : to secure tightly : BIND **2** : to arrange for cooking by binding close the wings or legs of (a fowl) **3** : to support, strengthen, or stiffen by a truss

²**truss** *n* **1** : a collection of structural parts (as beams) forming a rigid framework (as in bridge or building construction) **2** : a device worn to reduce a hernia by pressure

¹**trust** \'trəst\ *n* **1** : assured reliance on the character, strength, or truth of someone or something **2** : a basis of reliance, faith, or hope **3** : confident hope **4** : financial credit **5** : a property interest held by one person for the benefit of another **6** : a combination of firms formed by a legal agreement; *esp* : one that reduces competition **7** : something entrusted to one to be cared for in the interest of another **8** : CARE, CUSTODY **syn** confidence, dependence, faith, reliance

²**trust** *vb* **1** : to place confidence : DEPEND **2** : to be confident : HOPE **3** : ENTRUST **4** : to permit to stay or go or to do something without fear or misgiving **5** : to rely on or on the truth of : BELIEVE **6** : to extend credit to

trust·ee \ˌtrəs-'tē\ *n* **1** : a person to whom property is legally committed in trust **2** : a country charged with the supervision of a trust territory

trust·ee·ship \ˌtrəs-'tē-ˌship\ *n* **1** : the office or function of a trustee **2** : supervisory control by one or more nations over a trust territory

trust·ful \'trəst-fəl\ *adj* : full of trust : CONFIDING — **trust·ful·ly** \-ē\ *adv* — **trust·ful·ness** *n*

trust territory *n* : a non-self-governing territory placed under a supervisory authority by the Trusteeship Council of the United Nations

trust·wor·thy \-ˌwor-t͟hē\ *adj* : worthy of confidence : DEPENDABLE **syn** trusty, tried, reliable — **trust·wor·thi·ness** *n*

¹**trusty** \'trəs-tē\ *adj* **trust·i·er**; **-est** : TRUSTWORTHY, DEPENDABLE

²**trusty** \'trəs-tē, ˌtrəs-'tē\ *n, pl* **trust·ies** : a trusted person; *esp* : a convict considered trustworthy and allowed special privileges

truth \'trüth\ *n, pl* **truths** \'trüt͟hz, 'trüths\ **1** : TRUTHFULNESS, HONESTY **2** : the real state of things : FACT **3** : the body of real events or facts : ACTUAL-

ITY **4** : a true or accepted statement or proposition (the ∼s of science) **5** : agreement with fact or reality : CORRECTNESS **syn** veracity, verity, truthfulness

truth·ful \'trüth-fəl\ *adj* : telling or disposed to tell the truth — **truth·ful·ly** \-ē\ *adv* — **truth·ful·ness** *n*

truth serum *n* : a drug held to induce a subject under questioning to talk freely

¹**try** \'trī\ *vb* **tried**; **try·ing 1** : to examine or investigate judicially **2** : to conduct the trial of **3** : to put to test or trial **4** : to subject to strain, affliction, or annoyance **5** : to extract or clarify (as lard) by melting **6** : to make an effort to do something : ATTEMPT, ENDEAVOR **syn** essay, assay, strive, struggle

²**try** *n, pl* **tries** : an experimental trial

try·ing \'trī-iŋ\ *adj* : severely straining the powers of endurance

try on *vb* : to put on (a garment) to test the fit and looks

try out \(')trī-'aut\ *vb* : to participate in competition esp. for a position on an athletic team or a part in a play — **try·out** \'trī-ˌaut\ *n*

tryst \'trist, 'trīst\ *n* : an agreement (as between lovers) to meet; *also* : an appointed place of meeting **syn** rendezvous, engagement, assignation

tsar \'zär, 't)sär\ *var of* CZAR

tset·se fly \'t)set-sē-, 't)sēt-sē-\ *n* : any of several flies that occur in Africa south of the Sahara desert and include the vector of sleeping sickness

TSgt *abbr* technical sergeant

T-shirt \'tē-ˌshərt\ *n* : a collarless short-sleeved or sleeveless cotton undershirt for men; *also* : an outer shirt of similar design

tsp *abbr* teaspoon; teaspoonful

T square *n* : a ruler with a crosspiece at one end for making parallel lines

tsu·na·mi \(t)su̇-'näm-ē\ *n* [Jp] : a tidal wave caused by an earthquake or volcanic eruption

TT *abbr* Trust Territories

Tu *abbr* Tuesday

tub \'təb\ *n* **1** : a wide low bucketlike vessel **2** : BATHTUB; *also* : BATH **3** : the amount that a tub will hold

tu·ba \'t(y)ü-bə\ *n* : a large low-pitched brass wind instrument

tube \'t(y)üb\ *n* **1** : a hollow cylinder to convey fluids : CHANNEL, DUCT **2** : any of various usu. cylindrical structures or devices **3** : a round metal container from which a paste is squeezed at a tunnel for vehicular or rail travel **5** : an airtight tube of rubber inside a tire to hold air under pressure **6** : ELECTRON TUBE **7** : TELEVISION — **tubed** \'t(y)übd\ *adj* — **tube·less** *adj*

tu·ber \'t(y)ü-bər\ *n* : a short fleshy usu. underground stem (as of a potato plant) bearing minute scalelike leaves each with a bud at its base

tu·ber·cle \'t(y)ü-bər-kəl\ *n* **1** : a small knobby prominence or outgrowth esp. on an animal or plant **2** : a small abnormal lump in an organ or on the skin; *esp* : one caused by tuberculosis

tubercle bacillus *n* : a bacterium that is the cause of tuberculosis

tu·ber·cu·lar \t(y)ú-'bər-kyə-lər\ *adj* **1** : of, resembling, or being a tubercle : TUBERCULATED **2** : TUBERCULOUS

tu·ber·cu·lat·ed \t(y)ú-'bər-kyə-,lăt-əd\ *also* **tu·ber·cu·late** \-lət\ *adj* : having or covered with tubercles

tu·ber·cu·lin \t(y)ú-'bər-kyə-lən\ *n* : a sterile liquid extracted from the tubercle bacillus and used in the diagnosis of tuberculosis esp. in children and cattle

tu·ber·cu·lo·sis \t(y)ú-,bər-kyə-'lō-səs\ *n, pl* **-lo·ses** \-,sēz\ : a communicable bacterial disease typically marked by wasting, fever, and formation of cheesy tubercles often in the lungs — **tu·ber·cu·lous** \-'bər-kyə-ləs\ *adj*

tube·rose \'t(y)úb-,rōz\ *n* : a bulbous herb related to the amaryllis and often grown for its spike of fragrant waxy= white flowers

tu·ber·ous \'t(y)ú-b(ə-)rəs\ *adj* : of, resembling, or being a plant tuber

tub·ing \'t(y)ü-bin\ *n* **1** : material in the form of a tube; *also* : a length of tube **2** : a series of tubes

tu·bu·lar \'t(y)ü-byə-lər\ *adj* : having the form of or consisting of a tube; *also* : made with tubes

tu·bule \'t(y)ü-byül\ *n* : a small tube

¹tuck \'tək\ *n* : a fold stitched into cloth to shorten, decorate, or control fullness

²tuck *vb* **1** : to pull up into a fold ⟨~ed up her skirt⟩ **2** : to make tucks in **3** : to put into a snug often concealing place ⟨~ a book under the arm⟩ **4** : to secure in place by pushing the edges under ⟨~ in a blanket⟩ **5** : to cover by tucking in bedclothes

tuck·er \'tək-ər\ *vb* **tuck·ered; tuck·er·ing** \'tək-(ə-)riŋ\ : EXHAUST, FATIGUE

Tues *or* **Tue** *abbr* Tuesday

Tues·day \'t(y)üz-dē\ *n* : the 3d day of the week

tu·fa \'t(y)ü-fə\ *n* : a porous rock formed as a deposit from springs or streams

tuff \'təf\ *n* : a rock composed of volcanic detritus

¹tuft \'təft\ *n* **1** : a small cluster of long flexible outgrowths (as hairs); *also* : a bunch of soft fluffy threads cut off short and used as ornament **2** : CLUMP, CLUSTER — **tuft·ed** \'təf-təd\ *adj*

²tuft *vb* **1** : to provide or adorn with a tuft **2** : to make (as a mattress) firm by stitching at intervals and sewing on tufts

¹tug \'təg\ *vb* **tugged; tug·ging 1** : to pull hard **2** : to struggle in opposition : CONTEND **3** : to move by pulling hard : HAUL **4** : to tow with a tugboat

²tug *n* **1** : a harness trace **2** : an act of tugging : PULL **3** : a straining effort **4**

: a struggle between opposing people or forces **5** : TUGBOAT

tug·boat \-,bōt\ *n* : a strongly built boat used for towing or pushing

tug-of-war \,təg-ə(v)-'wòr\ *n, pl* **tugs-of-war 1** : a struggle for supremacy **2** : an athletic contest in which two teams pull against each other at opposite ends of a rope

tu·grik *or* **tu·ghrik** \'tü-grik\ *n* — see MONEY table

tu·ition \t(y)ú-'ish-ən\ *n* **1** : INSTRUCTION **2** : the price of or payment for instruction

tu·la·re·mia \,t(y)ü-lə-'rē-mē-ə\ *n* : an infectious bacterial disease esp. of wild rabbits, rodents, humans, and some domestic animals that in humans is marked by symptoms (as fever) of toxemia

tu·lip \'t(y)ü-ləp\ *n* [NL *tulipa*, fr. Turk *tülbend* turban] : any of a genus of Eurasian bulbous herbs related to the lilies and grown for their large showy erect cup-shaped flowers; *also* : a flower or bulb of a tulip

tulip tree *n* : a tall American timber tree with greenish tulip-shaped flowers and soft white wood

tulle \'tül\ *n* : a sheer silk, rayon, or nylon net (a bridal veil of ~)

¹tum·ble \'təm-bəl\ *vb* **tum·bled; tum·bling** \-b(ə-)liŋ\ [ME *tumblen*, fr. *tumben* to dance, fr. OE *tumbian*] **1** : to perform gymnastic feats of rolling and turning **2** : to fall or cause to fall suddenly and helplessly **3** : to fall into ruin **4** : to roll over and over : TOSS **5** : to issue forth hurriedly and confusedly **6** : to come to understand **7** : to throw together in a confused mass

²tumble *n* **1** : a disorderly state **2** : an act or instance of tumbling

tum·ble·down \,təm-bəl-,daún\ *adj* : DILAPIDATED, RAMSHACKLE

tum·bler \'təm-blər\ *n* **1** : one that tumbles; *esp* : ACROBAT **2** : a drinking glass without foot or stem **3** : a movable obstruction in a lock that must be adjusted to a particular position (as by a key) before the bolt can be thrown

tum·ble·weed \'təm-bəl-,wēd\ *n* : a plant that breaks away from its roots in autumn and is driven about by the wind

tum·bril *also* **tum·brel** \'təm-brəl\ *n* **1** : CART **2** : a vehicle carrying condemned persons (as political prisoners during the French Revolution) to a place of execution

tu·mid \'t(y)ü-məd\ *adj* **1** : SWOLLEN, DISTENDED **2** : BOMBASTIC, TURGID

tum·my \'təm-ē\ *n, pl* **tummies** : BELLY, ABDOMEN, STOMACH

tu·mor \'t(y)ü-mər\ *n* : an abnormal and functionless mass of tissue that is not inflammatory and arises from preexistent tissue — **tu·mor·ous** *adj*

tu·mult \'t(y)ü-,məlt\ *n* **1** : disorderly agitation of a crowd usu. with uproar and confusion of voices **2** : DISTUR-

BANCE, RIOT **3** : a confusion of loud noise and usu. turbulent movement **4** : violent agitation of mind or feelings

tu·mul·tu·ous \t(y)ü-ˈməlch-(ə-)wəs, -ˈməl-chəs\ *adj* **1** : marked by tumult **2** : tending to incite a tumult **3** : marked by violent upheaval

tun \ˈtən\ *n* : a large cask

tu·na \ˈt(y)ü-nə\ *n, pl* **tuna** *or* **tunas** [Sp] : any of several mostly large sea fishes related to the mackerels and important for food and sport

tun·able \ˈt(y)ü-nə-bəl\ *adj* : capable of being tuned — **tun·abil·i·ty** \ˌt(y)ü-nə-ˈbil-ət-ē\ *n*

tun·dra \ˈtən-drə\ *n* : a treeless plain of arctic and subarctic regions

¹**tune** \ˈt(y)ün\ *n* **1** : an easily remembered melody **2** : correct musical pitch **3** : harmonious relationship : AGREEMENT ⟨in ∼ with the times⟩ **4** : general attitude ⟨changed his ∼⟩ **5** : AMOUNT, EXTENT ⟨in debt to the ∼ of millions⟩

²**tune** *vb* **tuned; tun·ing 1** : to adjust in musical pitch **2** : to bring or come into harmony : ATTUNE **3** : to adjust a radio or television receiver so as to receive a broadcast **4** : to put in good working order **5** : to adjust the frequency of the output of (a device) to a chosen frequency — **tun·er** *n*

tune·ful \-fəl\ *adj* : MELODIOUS, MUSICAL — **tune·ful·ly** \-ē\ *adv* — **tune·ful·ness** *n*

tune·less \-ləs\ *adj* **1** : UNMELODIOUS **2** : not producing music — **tune·less·ly** *adv*

tune–up \ˈt(y)ün-ˌəp\ *n* : an adjustment to ensure efficient functioning (of an engine ∼)

tung·sten \ˈtəŋ-stən\ *n* [Sw, fr. *tung* heavy + *sten* stone] : a white hard heavy ductile metallic element used for electrical purposes and in hardening alloys (as steel)

tu·nic \ˈt(y)ü-nik\ *n* **1** : a usu. knee-length belted under or outer garment worn by ancient Greeks and Romans **2** : a hip-length or longer blouse or jacket

tuning fork *n* : a 2-pronged metal implement that gives a fixed tone when struck and is useful for tuning musical instruments

Tu·ni·sian \t(y)ü-ˈnēzh-ən, -ˈnizh-\ *n* : a native or inhabitant of Tunisia — **Tunisian** *adj*

¹**tun·nel** \ˈtən-ᵊl\ *n* : an enclosed passage (as a tube or conduit); *esp* : one underground (as in a mine)

²**tunnel** *vb* **-neled** *or* **-nelled; -nel·ing** *or* **-nel·ling** \ˈtən-(ᵊ-)liŋ\ : to make a tunnel through or under

tun·ny \ˈtən-ē\ *n, pl* **tunnies** *also* **tunny** : TUNA

-tu·ple \ˌtəp-əl, ˌtüp-\ *n comb form* : set of (so many) elements

tuque \ˈt(y)ük\ *n* [CanF] : a warm knitted cone-shaped cap with a tassel or

pom-pom worn esp. for winter sports or play

tur·ban \ˈtər-bən\ *n* **1** : a headdress worn esp. by Muslims and made of a cap around which is wound a long cloth **2** : a headdress resembling a Muslim turban; *esp* : a woman's close-fitting hat without a brim

tur·bid \ˈtər-bəd\ *adj* [L *turbidus* confused, turbid, fr. *turba* confusion, crowd] **1** : thick with roiled sediment ⟨a ∼ stream⟩ **2** : heavy with smoke or mist : DENSE **3** : CONFUSED, MUDDLED — **tur·bid·i·ty** \ˌtər-ˈbid-ət-ē\ *n*

tur·bine \ˈtər-bən, -ˌbīn\ *n* [F, fr. L *turbin-, turbo* top, whirlwind, whirl] : an engine whose central drive shaft is fitted with curved vanes whirled by the pressure of water, steam, or gas

tur·bo·elec·tric \ˌtər-bō-i-ˈlek-trik\ *adj* : involving or depending as a power source on electricity produced by turbine generators

tur·bo·fan \-ˌfan\ *n* **1** : a fan that is directly connected to and driven by a turbine and is used to supply air for cooling, ventilation, or combustion **2** : a jet engine having a turbofan

tur·bo·jet \-ˌjet\ *n* : an airplane powered by a jet engine (**turbojet engine**) having a turbine-driven air compressor supplying compressed air to the combustion chamber

tur·bo·prop \-ˌpräp\ *n* : an airplane powered by a jet engine (**turbo–propeller engine**) having a turbine-driven propeller but usu. obtaining additional thrust from the discharge of a jet of hot gases

tur·bot \ˈtər-bət\ *n, pl* **turbot** *also* **turbots** : a European flatfish that is a popular food fish; *also* : any of several similar flatfishes

tur·bu·lence \ˈtər-byə-ləns\ *n* : the quality or state of being turbulent

tur·bu·lent \-lənt\ *adj* **1** : causing violence or disturbance **2** : marked by agitation or tumult : TEMPESTUOUS — **tur·bu·lent·ly** *adv*

tu·reen \tə-ˈrēn, tyü-\ *n* [F *terrine*, fr. MF, fr. fem. of *terrin* of earth, fr. L *terra* earth] : a deep bowl from which foods (as soup) are served at table

¹**turf** \ˈtərf\ *n, pl* **turfs** \ˈtərfs\ *also* **turves** \ˈtərvz\ **1** : the upper layer of soil bound by grass and roots into a close mat; *also* : a piece of this **2** : an artificial substitute for turf (as on a playing field) **3** : a piece of peat dried for fuel **4** : a track or course for horse racing; *also* : horse racing as a sport or business

²**turf** *vb* : to cover with turf

tur·gid \ˈtər-jəd\ *adj* **1** : marked by distension : SWOLLEN **2** : excessively embellished in style or language : BOMBASTIC — **tur·gid·i·ty** \ˌtər-ˈjid-ət-ē\ *n*

¹**Turk** \ˈtərk\ *n* : a native or inhabitant of Turkey

²**Turk** *abbr* Turkey; Turkish

tur·key \'tər-kē\ *n, pl* **turkeys** [*Turkey*, country in western Asia and south-eastern Europe; fr. confusion with the guinea fowl, supposed to be imported from Turkish territory] : a large American bird related to the domestic chicken and widely raised for food; *also* : its flesh

turkey buzzard *n* : TURKEY VULTURE

turkey vulture *n* : an American vulture common in South and Central America and in the U.S.

Turk·ish \'tər-kish\ *n* : the language of Turkey — **Turkish** *adj*

tur·mer·ic \'tər-mə-rik\ *n* : a spice or dyestuff obtained from the large aromatic deep-yellow rhizome of an East Indian perennial herb; *also* : this herb

tur·moil \'tər-ˌmȯil\ *n* : an extremely confused or agitated condition

¹**turn** \'tərn\ *vb* 1 : to move or cause to move around an axis or center : ROTATE, REVOLVE ⟨~ a wheel⟩ 2 : to twist so as to effect a desired end ⟨~ a key⟩ 3 : WRENCH ⟨~ an ankle⟩ 4 : to change or cause to change position by moving through an arc of a circle ⟨~ed his chair to the fire⟩ 5 : to cause to move around a center so as to show another side of ⟨~ a page⟩ 6 : to revolve mentally : PONDER 7 : to become dizzy : REEL 8 : to reverse the sides or surfaces of ⟨~ a pancake⟩ 9 : UPSET, DISORDER ⟨things ~ed topsy-turvy⟩ ⟨~ed his stomach⟩ 10 : to set in another esp. contrary direction 11 : to change one's course or direction 12 : TRANSFER ⟨~ the task over to him⟩ 13 : to go around ⟨~ a corner⟩ 14 : to reach or pass beyond ⟨~ed twenty-one⟩ 15 : to direct toward or away from something; *also* : DEVOTE, APPLY 16 : to have recourse 17 : to become or make hostile 18 : to cause to become of a specified nature or appearance ⟨~s the leaves yellow⟩ 19 : to make or become spoiled : SOUR 20 : to pass from one state to another ⟨water ~s to ice⟩ 21 : CONVERT, TRANSFORM 22 : TRANSLATE, PARAPHRASE 23 : to give a rounded form to; *esp* : to shape by means of a lathe 24 : to gain by passing in trade ⟨~ a quick profit⟩ — **turn color** 1 : BLUSH 2 : to become pale — **turn loose** : to set free

²**turn** *n* 1 : a turning about a center or axis : REVOLUTION, ROTATION 2 : the action or an act of giving or taking a different direction ⟨make a ~⟩ 3 : a change of course or tendency ⟨a ~ for the better⟩ 4 : a place at which something turns : BEND, CURVE 5 : a short walk or trip round about ⟨take a ~ around the deck⟩ 6 : an act affecting another ⟨did him a good ~⟩ 7 : a place, time, or opportunity accorded in a scheduled order ⟨waited his ~ to be served⟩ 8 : a period of duty : SHIFT 9 : a short act esp. in a variety show 10 : a special purpose or requirement ⟨the job serves his ~⟩ 11 : a skillful

fashioning ⟨neat ~ of phrase⟩ 12 : a single round ⟨as of rope passed around an object⟩ 13 : natural or special aptitude 14 : a usu. sudden and brief disorder of body or spirits; *esp* : a spell of nervous shock or faintness

turn·about \'tər-nə-ˌbaȯt\ *n* 1 : a reversal of direction, trend, or policy 2 : RETALIATION

turn·buck·le \'tərn-ˌbək-əl\ *n* : a link with a screw thread at one or both ends for tightening a rod or stay

turn·coat \-ˌkōt\ *n* : one who forsakes his party or principles : RENEGADE

turn down \ˌtərn-'daȯn, 'tərn-\ *vb* : to decline to accept : REJECT — **turn-down** \'tərn-ˌdaȯn\ *n*

turn·er \'tər-nər\ *n* 1 : one that turns or is used for turning 2 : one that forms articles with a lathe

turn·ery \'tər-nə-rē\ *n, pl* **-er·ies** : the work, products, or shop of a turner

turn in *vb* 1 : to deliver up 2 : to inform on 3 : to acquit oneself of ⟨*turn in* a good job⟩ 4 : to go to bed

turn·ing \'tər-niŋ\ *n* 1 : the act or course of one that turns 2 : a place of a change of direction

tur·nip \'tər-nəp\ *n* 1 : a garden herb related to the cabbage with hairy leaves and an edible usu. white root 2 : RUTABAGA 3 : the root of a turnip

turn·key \'tərn-ˌkē\ *n, pl* **turnkeys** : one who has charge of a prison's keys

turn·off \'tərn-ˌȯf\ *n* : a place for turning off esp. from an expressway

turn off \ˌtərn-'ȯf, 'tərn-\ *vb* 1 : to deviate from a straight course or a main road 2 : to stop the functioning or flow of 3 : to cause to lose interest; *also* : to evoke a negative feeling in

turn on *vb* 1 : to get high or cause to get high as a result of using a drug ⟨as marijuana⟩ 2 : EXCITE, STIMULATE

turn·out \'tərn-ˌaȯt\ *n* 1 : an act of turning out 2 : a gathering of people for a special purpose 3 : a widened place in a highway for vehicles to pass or park 4 : manner of dress 5 : net yield : OUTPUT

turn out \ˌtərn-'aȯt, 'tərn-\ *vb* 1 : EXPEL, EVICT 2 : PRODUCE 3 : to come forth and assemble 4 : to get out of bed 5 : to prove to be in the end

¹**turn·over** \'tərn-ˌō-vər\ *n* 1 : UPSET 2 : SHIFT, REVERSAL 3 : a filled pastry made by turning half of the crust over the other half 4 : the volume of business done 5 : movement ⟨as of goods or people⟩ into, through, and out of a place: *esp* : a cycle of purchase, sale, and replacement of a stock of goods 6 : the number of persons hired within a period to replace those leaving or dropped; *also* : the ratio of this number to that of the average force maintained

²**turn·over** \ˌtərn-ˌō-vər\ *adj* : capable of being turned over

turn·pike \'tərn-ˌpīk\ *n* [ME *turnepike* revolving frame bearing spikes and serving as a barrier, fr. *turnen* to turn + *pike*] **1** : TOLLGATE; *also* : an expressway on which tolls are charged **2** : a main road

turn·spit \-₁spit\ *n* : a device for turning a spit

turn·stile \-₁stīl\ *n* : a post with arms pivoted on the top set in a passageway so that persons can pass through only on foot one by one

turn·ta·ble \-₁tā-bəl\ *n* : a circular platform that revolves (as for turning a locomotive or a phonograph record)

turn to *vb* : to apply oneself to work

turn up *vb* **1** : to come to light or bring to light : DISCOVER, APPEAR **2** : to arrive at an appointed time or place **3** : to happen unexpectedly

tur·pen·tine \'tər-pən-₁tīn\ *n* **1** : a mixture of oil and resin obtained from various cone-bearing trees (as pines) **2** : an oil obtained from various turpentines by distillation and used as a solvent and paint thinner; *also* : a similar oil obtained from distillation of pine wood

tur·pi·tude \'tər-pə-₁t(y)üd\ *n* : inherent baseness : DEPRAVITY

turps \'tərps\ *n* : TURPENTINE

tur·quoise *also* **tur·quois** \'tər-₁k(w)òiz\ *n* [ME *turkeis*, *turcas*, fr. MF *turquoyse*, fr. fem. of *turquoys* Turkish, fr. OF, fr. *Turc* Turk] **1** : a blue, bluish green, or greenish gray mineral that contains a little copper and is valued as a gem **2** : a light greenish blue color

tur·ret \'tər-ət\ *n* **1** : a little tower often at an angle of a larger structure and merely ornamental **2** : a revolvable holder in a machine tool **3** : a low usu. revolving structure (as on a tank, warship, or airplane) in which one or more guns are mounted

¹tur·tle \'tərt-ᵊl\ *n*, *archaic* : TURTLEDOVE

²turtle *n*, *pl* **turtles** *also* **turtle** : any of an order of horny-beaked land, freshwater, or sea reptiles with the trunk enclosed in a bony shell

tur·tle·dove \'tərt-ᵊl-₁dəv\ *n* : any of several small wild pigeons; *esp* : any Old World bird noted for plaintive cooing

tur·tle·neck \-₁nek\ *n* : a high close-fitting turnover collar used esp. for sweaters; *also* : a sweater with a turtleneck

turves *pl of* TURF

Tus·ca·ro·ra \₁təs-kə-'rōr-ə\ *n*, *pl* **Tuscarora** *or* **Tuscaroras** : a member of an American Indian people of No. Carolina and later of New York and Ontario

tusk \'təsk\ *n* **1** : a long enlarged protruding tooth (as of an elephant, walrus, or boar) used to dig up food or as a weapon **2** : a long projecting tooth — **tusked** \'təskt\ *adj*

tusk·er \'təs-kər\ *n* : an animal with

tusks; *esp* : a male elephant with two normally developed tusks

¹tus·sle \'təs-əl\ *n* **1** : a physical struggle : SCUFFLE **2** : an intense argument, controversy, or struggle

²tussle *vb* **tus·sled; tus·sling** \-(ə-)liŋ\ : to struggle roughly

tus·sock \'təs-ək\ *n* : a dense tuft esp. of grass or sedge; *also* : a hummock in marsh bound together by roots — **tus·socky** *adj*

tussock moth *n* : any of numerous dull-colored moths that usu. have wingless females and larvae with long tufts of hair

tu·te·lage \'t(y)üt-ᵊl-ij\ *n* **1** : an act of guarding or protecting **2** : the state of being under a guardian or tutor **3** : instruction esp. of an individual

tu·te·lary \'t(y)üt-ᵊl-₁er-ē\ *adj* : acting as a guardian (⟨~ deity⟩ ⟨a ~ power⟩

¹tu·tor \'t(y)üt-ər\ *n* **1** : a person charged with the instruction and guidance of another **2** : a private teacher

²tutor *vb* **1** : to have the guardianship of **2** : to teach or guide individually : COACH ⟨~*ed* the boy in Latin⟩ **3** : to receive instruction esp. privately

tu·to·ri·al \t(y)ü-'tōr-ē-əl\ *n* : a class conducted by a tutor for one student or a small number of students

tut·ti–frut·ti \₁tüt-i-'früt-ē, ₁tüt-\ *n* [It, lit., all fruits] : a confection or ice cream containing chopped usu. candied fruits

tux·e·do \₁tək-'sēd-ō\ *n*, *pl* **-dos** *or* **-does** [*Tuxedo* Park, N.Y.] **1** : a usu. black or blackish blue jacket **2** : semiformal evening clothes for men

TV \'tē-'vē\ *n* : TELEVISION

TVA *abbr* Tennessee Valley Authority

TV dinner \₁tē-₁vē-\ *n* : a frozen packaged dinner that needs only heating before serving

twad·dle \'twäd-ᵊl\ *n* : silly idle talk : DRIVEL — **twaddle** *vb*

twain \'twān\ *n* **1** : TWO **2** : PAIR

twang \'twaŋ\ *n* **1** : a harsh quick ringing sound like that of a plucked bowstring **2** : nasal speech or resonance **3** : the characteristic speech of a region

²twang *vb* **twanged; twang·ing** \'twaŋ-iŋ\ **1** : to sound or cause to sound with a twang **2** : to speak with a nasal twang

tweak \'twēk\ *vb* : to pinch and pull with a sudden jerk and twitch — **tweak** *n*

tweed \'twēd\ *n* [alter. of Sc *tweel* twill, fr. ME *twyll*] **1** : a rough woolen fabric made usu. in twill weaves **2** *pl* : tweed clothing; *esp* : a tweed suit

tweedy \'twēd-ē\ *adj* **tweed·i·er; -est** **1** : of or resembling tweed **2** : given to wearing tweeds **3** : suggestive of the outdoors in taste or habits

tween \(')twēn\ *prep* : BETWEEN

tweet \'twēt\ *n* : a chirping note — **tweet** *vb*

tweet·er \'twēt-ər\ *n* : a small loudspeaker that reproduces sounds of high pitch

twee·zers \'twē-zərz\ *n pl* [obs. E *tweeze*, n. (case for small implements) short for obs. E *etweese*, fr. pl. of obs. E *etwee*, fr. F *étui*] : a small pincerlike implement held between the thumb and forefinger for grasping something

twelve \'twelv\ *n* 1 : one more than 11 2 : the 12th in a set or series 3 : something having 12 units — **twelfth** \'twelfth\ *adj or n* — **twelve** *adj or pron*

twelve·month \-,mənth\ *n* : YEAR

twen·ty \'twent-ē\ *n, pl* **twenties** : two times 10 — **twen·ti·eth** \-ē-əth\ *adj or n* — **twenty** *adj or pron*

twenty–twenty *or* **20/20** \,twent-ē-'twent-ē\ *adj* : having a visual capacity to see detail that is normal for the human eye (~ vision)

twice \'twīs\ *adv* 1 : on two occasions 2 : two times (~ two is four)

¹**twid·dle** \'twid-ᵊl\ *vb* **twid·dled**; **twid·dling** \'twid-(ᵊ-)liŋ\ 1 : to be busy with trifles; *also* : to play idly with something 2 : to rotate lightly or idly

²**twiddle** *n* : TURN, TWIST

twig \'twig\ *n* : a small branch — **twig·gy** *adj*

twi·light \'twī-,līt\ *n* 1 : the light from the sky between full night and sunrise or between sunset and full night 2 : a state of imperfect clarity; *also* : a period of decline — **twilight** *adj*

twill \'twil\ *n* [ME *twyll*, fr. OE *twilic* having a double thread, modif. of L *bilic-, bilix*, fr. *bi-* two + *licium* thread] 1 : a fabric with a twill weave 2 : a textile weave that gives an appearance of diagonal lines in the fabric

twilled \'twild\ *adj* : made with a twill weave

¹**twin** \'twin\ *adj* 1 : born with one another or as a pair at one birth (~ brother) (~ girls) 2 : made up of two similar or related members or parts 3 : being one of a pair (~ city)

²**twin** *vb* **twinned**; **twin·ning** 1 : to bring forth twins 2 : to be coupled with another

³**twin** *n* 1 : either of two offspring produced at a birth 2 : one of two persons or things closely related to or resembling each other

¹**twine** \'twīn\ *n* 1 : a strong thread of two or three strands twisted together 2 : an act of entwining or interlacing — **twiny** *adj*

²**twine** *vb* **twined**; **twin·ing** 1 : to twist together; *also* : to form by twisting 2 : INTERLACE, WEAVE 3 : to coil about a support 4 : to stretch or move in a sinuous manner — **twin·er** *n*

¹**twinge** \'twinj\ *vb* **twinged**; **twing·ing** \'twin-jiŋ\ *or* **twinge·ing** : to affect with or feel a sharp sudden pain

²**twinge** *n* : a sudden sharp stab (as of pain or distress)

¹**twin·kle** \'twiŋ-kəl\ *vb* **twin·kled**; **twin·kling** \-k(ə-)liŋ\ 1 : to shine or cause to shine with a flickering or sparkling light 2 : to appear bright with merri-

ment 3 : to flutter or flit rapidly — **twin·kler** \-k(ə-)lər\ *n*

²**twinkle** *n* 1 : a wink of the eyelids; *also* : the duration of a wink 2 : an intermittent radiance 3 : a rapid flashing motion

twin·kling \'twiŋ-kliŋ\ *n* : the time occupied by a single wink : INSTANT **syn** instant, moment, minute, second, flash

¹**twirl** \'twərl\ *vb* 1 : to whirl round 2 : to pitch in a baseball game **syn** turn, revolve, rotate, circle, spin, swirl, pirouette — **twirl·er** \'twər-lər\ *n*

²**twirl** *n* 1 : an act of twirling 2 : COIL, WHORL

¹**twist** \'twist\ *vb* 1 : to unite by winding one thread or strand round another 2 : WREATHE, TWINE 3 : to turn so as to hurt (~ed her ankle) 4 : to twirl into spiral shape 5 : to subject (as a shaft) to torsion 6 : to turn from the true form or meaning 7 : to pull off or break by torsion 8 : to follow a winding course 9 : to turn around

²**twist** *n* 1 : something formed by twisting or winding 2 : an act of twisting : the state of being twisted 3 : a spiral turn or curve; *also* : SPIN 4 : a turning aside 5 : ECCENTRICITY 6 : a distortion of meaning 7 : an unexpected turn or development 8 : DEVICE, TRICK 9 : a variant approach or method

twist·er \'twis-tər\ *n* 1 : one that twists; *esp* : a ball with a forward and spinning motion 2 : TORNADO; *also* : WATERSPOUT 2

twit \'twit\ *vb* **twit·ted**; **twit·ting** : to reproach, taunt, or tease esp. by reminding of a fault or defect **syn** ridicule, deride, mock, razz

¹**twitch** \'twich\ *vb* 1 : to move or pull with a sudden motion : JERK 2 : to move jerkily : QUIVER

²**twitch** *n* 1 : an act or movement of twitching 2 : a short sharp contraction of muscle fibers

¹**twit·ter** \'twit-ər\ *vb* 1 : to make a succession of chirping noises 2 : to talk in a chattering fashion; *also* : TITTER 3 : to have a slight trembling of the nerves : FLUTTER

²**twitter** *n* 1 : a slight agitation of the nerves 2 : a small tremulous intermittent noise (as made by a swallow) 3 : a light chattering; *also* : TITTER

twixt \(')twikst\ *prep* : BETWEEN

two \'tü\ *n, pl* **twos** 1 : one more than one 2 : the second in a set or series 3 : something having two units — **two** *adj or pron*

two cents *n* 1 : a sum or object of very small value 2 *or* **two cents worth** : an opinion offered on a topic under discussion

two–faced \'tü-'fāst\ *adj* 1 : DOUBLE-DEALING, FALSE 2 : having two faces

two·fold \'tü-,fōld, -'fōld\ *adj* 1 : having two units or members 2 : being twice as much or as many — **twofold** \-'fōld\ *adv*

2,4–D \ˌtü-ˌfōr-ˈdē\ *n* : a white crystalline compound used as a weed killer

2,4,5–T \-ˌfīv-ˈtē\ *n* : an irritant compound used in brush and weed control

two-pen·ny \ˈtəp-əns, *US also* ˈtü-ˌpens\ *n* : the sum of two pence

two-pen·ny \ˈtəp-(ə-)nē, *US also* ˈtü-ˌpen-ē\ *adj* : of the value of or costing twopence

two-ply \ˈtü-ˈplī\ *adj* **1** : woven as a double cloth **2** : consisting of two strands or thicknesses

two-some \ˈtü-səm\ *n* **1** : a group of two persons or things : COUPLE **2** : a golf match between two players

two-step \ˈtü-ˌstep\ *n* : a ballroom dance performed with a sliding step in march or polka time; *also* : a piece of music for this dance — **two-step** *vb*

two-time \ˈtü-ˌtīm\ *vb* : to betray (a spouse or lover) by secret lovemaking with another — **two-tim·er** *n*

two-way *adj* : involving two elements or allowing movement or use in two directions or manners

two-winged fly \ˌtü-ˌwiŋd-\ *n* : any of a large order of insects mostly with one pair of functional wings and another pair that if present are reduced to balancing organs and often with larvae without a head, eyes, or legs

twp *abbr* township

TWX *abbr* teletypewriter exchange

TX *abbr* Texas

-ty *n suffix* : quality : condition : degree (realt*y*)

ty·coon \tī-ˈkün\ *n* [Jp *taikun*, fr. Chin *ta⁴* great + *chün* ruler] **1** : a masterful leader (as in politics) **2** : a powerful businessman or industrialist

tying *pres part of* TIE

tyke \ˈtīk\ *n* : a small child

tym·pan·ic membrane \tim-ˈpan-ik-\ *n* : EARDRUM

tym·pa·num \ˈtim-pə-nəm\ *n*, *pl* **-na** \-nə\ *also* **-nums** : EARDRUM; *also* : MIDDLE EAR — **tym·pan·ic** \tim-ˈpan-ik\ *adj*

¹type \ˈtīp\ *n* [LL *typus*, fr. L & Gk; L *typus* image, fr. Gk *typos* blow, impression, model, fr. *typtein* to strike, beat] **1** : a person, thing, or event that foreshadows another to come : TOKEN, SYMBOL **2** : MODEL, EXAMPLE **3** : a distinctive stamp, mark, or sign : EMBLEM **4** : rectangular blocks usu. of metal each having a face so shaped as to produce a character when printed **5** : the letters or characters printed from or as if from type **6** : general character or form common to a number of individuals and setting them off as a distinguishable class (horses of draft ∼) **7** : a class, kind, or group set apart by common characteristics (a seedless ∼ of orange) ; *also* : something distinguishable as a variety (reactions of this ∼) **syn** sort, nature, character, description

²type *vb* **typed; typ·ing 1** : to represent beforehand as a type **2** : to produce a

copy of; *also* : REPRESENT, TYPIFY **3** : TYPEWRITE **4** : to identify as belonging to a type **5** : TYPECAST

type-cast \-ˌkast\ *vb* **-cast; -cast·ing 1** : to cast (an actor) in a part calling for characteristics possessed by the actor himself **2** : to cast repeatedly in the same type of role

type-face \-ˌfās\ *n* : all type of a single design

type-found·er \-ˌfaün-dər\ *n* : one engaged in the design and production of metal printing type for hand composition — **type-found·ing** \-diŋ\ *n*

type-script \ˈtīp-ˌskript\ *n* : typewritten matter

type-set \-ˌset\ *vb* **-set; -set·ting** : to set in type : COMPOSE — **type-set·ter** \-ˌset-ər\ *n*

type-write \-ˌrīt\ *vb* **-wrote** \-ˌrōt\ ; **-writ·ten** \-ˌrit-ᵊn\ : to write with a typewriter

type-writ·er \-ˌrīt-ər\ *n* **1** : a machine for writing in characters similar to those produced by printers' types by means of types striking through an inked ribbon **2** : TYPIST

type-writ·ing \-ˌrīt-iŋ\ *n* : the use of a typewriter (teach ∼) ; *also* : the printing done with a typewriter

¹ty·phoid \ˈtī-ˌfȯid, tī-ˈfȯid\ *adj* : of, relating to, or being a communicable bacterial disease **(typhoid fever)** marked by fever, diarrhea, prostration, and intestinal inflammation

²typhoid *n* : TYPHOID FEVER

ty·phoon \tī-ˈfün\ *n* : a tropical cyclone in the region of the Philippines or the China sea

ty·phus \ˈtī-fəs\ *n* : a severe infectious disease transmitted esp. by body lice, caused by a rickettsia, and marked by high fever, stupor and delirium, intense headache, and a dark red rash

typ·i·cal \ˈtip-i-kəl\ *adj* **1** : being or having the nature of a type **2** : exhibiting the essential characteristics of a group **3** : conforming to a type — **typ·i·cal·i·ty** \ˌtip-ə-ˈkal-ət-ē\ *n* — **typ·i·cal·ly** \-ē\ *adv* — **typ·i·cal·ness** *n*

typ·i·fy \ˈtip-ə-ˌfī\ *vb* **-fied; -fy·ing 1** : to represent by an image, form, model, or resemblance **2** : to embody the essential or common characteristics of

typ·ist \ˈtī-pəst\ *n* : one who operates a typewriter

ty·po \ˈtī-pō\ *n*, *pl* **typos** : an error in typing or in setting type

ty·pog·ra·pher \tī-ˈpäg-rə-fər\ *n* : one who designs or arranges printing

ty·pog·ra·phy \tī-ˈpäg-rə-fē\ *n* : the art of printing with type; *also* : the style, arrangement, or appearance of matter printed from type — **ty·po·graph·ic** \ˌtī-pə-ˈgraf-ik\ *or* **ty·po·graph·i·cal** \-i-kəl\ *adj* — **ty·po·graph·i·cal·ly** \-ē\ *adv*

ty·ran·ni·cal \tə-ˈran-i-kəl, tī-\ *also* **ty·ran·nic** \-ik\ *adj* : of or relating to a tyrant : DESPOTIC **syn** arbitrary, abso-

lute, autocratic — **ty·ran·ni·cal·ly**
\-i-k(ə-)lē\ *adv*

tyr·an·nize \'tir-ə-₁nīz\ *vb* **-nized; -niz·ing** : to act as a tyrant : rule with un-just severity — **tyr·an·niz·er** *n*

ty·ran·no·saur \tə-¹ran-ə-₁sȯr\ *n*
: TYRANNOSAURUS

ty·ran·no·sau·rus \tə-₁ran-ə-¹sȯr-əs\ *n*
: a very large American flesh-eating dinosaur of the Cretaceous that had small forelegs and walked on its hind legs

tyr·an·nous \'tir-ə-nəs\ *adj* : TYRANNI-CAL — **tyr·an·nous·ly** *adv*

tyr·an·ny \'tir-ə-nē\ *n, pl* **-nies 1** : op-pressive power **2** : the rule or authori-ty of a tyrant : government in which absolute power is vested in a single ruler **3** : a tyrannical act

ty·rant \'tī-rənt\ *n* **1** : an absolute ruler : DESPOT **2** : a ruler who governs op-pressively or brutally **3** : one who uses authority or power harshly

ty·ro \'tī-rō\ *n, pl* **tyros** [ML, fr. L *tiro* young soldier, tyro] : a beginner in learning : NOVICE

tzar \'zär, ¹(t)sär\ *var of* CZAR

U

¹**u** \'yü\ *n, pl* **u's** *or* **us** \'yüz\ *often cap*
: the 21st letter of the English alpha-bet

²**u** *abbr, often cap* unit

¹**U** \'yü\ *adj* : characteristic of the upper classes

²**U** *abbr* **1** [abbr. of *Union of Orthodox Hebrew Congregations*] kosher certi-fication **2** university

³**U** *symbol* uranium

UAE *abbr* United Arab Emirates

UAR *abbr* United Arab Republic

UAW *abbr* United Automobile Work-ers

ubiq·ui·tous \yü-¹bik-wət-əs\ *adj* : ex-isting or being everywhere at the same time : OMNIPRESENT — **ubiq·ui·tous·ly** *adv* — **ubiq·ui·ty** \-wət-ē\ *n*

U–boat \'yü-₁bōt\ *n* [trans. of G *u-boot*, short for *unterseeboot*, lit., undersea boat] : a German submarine

ud·der \'əd-ər\ *n* : an organ (as of a cow) consisting of two or more milk glands enclosed in a large hanging sac and each provided with a nipple

UFO \₁yü-₁ef-¹ō\ *n, pl* **UFO's** *or* **UFOs** \-¹ōz\ : an unidentified flying object; *esp* : FLYING SAUCER

ug·ly \'əg-lē\ *adj* **ug·li·er; -est** [ME, fr. ON *uggligr*, fr. *uggr* fear] **1** : FRIGHT-FUL, DIRE **2** : offensive to the sight : HIDEOUS **3** : offensive or unpleasing to any sense **4** : morally objectionable : REPULSIVE **5** : likely to cause incon-venience or discomfort **6** : SURLY, QUARRELSOME (an ∼ disposition) — **ug·li·ness** \-lē-nəs\ *n*

UHF *abbr* ultrahigh frequency

UK *abbr* United Kingdom

ukase \yü-¹kās, -¹käz\ *n* [F & Russ; F, fr. Russ *ukaz*, fr. *ukazat'* to show, or-der] : an edict esp. of a Russian em-peror or government

Ukrai·ni·an \yü-¹krā-nē-ən\ *n* : a native or inhabitant of the Ukraine, U.S.S.R. — **Ukrainian** *adj*

uku·le·le \₁yü-kə-¹lā-lē\ *n* [Hawaiian *'ukulele*, fr. *'uku* flea + *lele* jumping] : a small usu. 4-stringed guitar popu-larized in Hawaii

ul·cer \'əl-sər\ *n* **1** : an eroded sore of-

ten discharging pus **2** : something that festers and corrupts like an open sore — **ul·cer·ous** *adj*

ul·cer·ate \'əl-sə-₁rāt\ *vb* **-at·ed; -at·ing**
: to cause or become affected with an ulcer — **ul·cer·ative** \-¹əl-sə-₁rāt-iv\ *adj*

ul·cer·ation \₁əl-sə-¹rā-shən\ *n* **1** : the process of forming or state of having an ulcer **2** : ULCER 1

ul·lage \'əl-ij\ *n* [ME *ulage*, fr. MF *eul-lage* act of filling a cask, fr. *eullier* to fill a cask, fr. OF *ouil* eye, bunghole, fr. L *oculus* eye] : the amount that a container (as a cask) lacks of being full

ul·na \'əl-nə\ *n* : the one of the two bones of the human forearm that is on the little-finger side; *also* : a corre-sponding bone of the forelimb of vertebrates above fishes

ul·ster \'əl-stər\ *n* : a long loose over-coat

ult *abbr* **1** ultimate **2** ultimo

ul·te·ri·or \₁əl-¹tir-ē-ər\ *adj* **1** : lying far-ther away : more remote **2** : situated beyond or on the farther side **3** : going beyond what is openly said or shown : HIDDEN (∼ motives)

¹**ul·ti·mate** \'əl-tə-mət\ *adj* **1** : most re-mote in space or time : FARTHEST **2** : last in a progression : FINAL **3** : EX-TREME, UTMOST **4** : finally reckoned **5** : FUNDAMENTAL, ABSOLUTE, SUPREME (∼ reality) **6** : incapable of further analysis or division : ELEMENTAL **7** : MAXIMUM — **ul·ti·mate·ly** *adv*

²**ultimate** *n* : something ultimate

ul·ti·ma·tum \₁əl-tə-¹māt-əm, -¹mät-\ *n, pl* **-tums** *or* **-ta** \-ə\ : a final condition or demand whose rejection will bring about a resort to forceful action

ul·ti·mo \'əl-tə-₁mō\ *adj* [L *ultimo mense* in the last month] : of or occur-ring the month preceding the present

¹**ul·tra** \'əl-trə\ *adj* : going beyond oth-ers or beyond due limits : EXTREME

²**ultra** *n* : EXTREMIST

ul·tra·cen·tri·fuge \₁əl-trə-¹sen-trə-₁fyüj\ *n* : a high-speed centrifuge able to separate small particles (as from colloidal suspension)

ul·tra·con·ser·va·tive \-kən-'sər-vət-iv\ *adj* : extremely conservative

ul·tra·fash·ion·able \-'fash-(ə-)nə-bəl\ *adj* : extremely fashionable

ul·tra·high \-'hī\ *adj* : very high : exceedingly high (~ vacuum)

ultrahigh frequency *n* : a radio frequency between 300 and 3000 megahertz

ul·tra·ma·rine \ˌəl-trə-mə-'rēn\ *n* 1 : a deep blue pigment 2 : a very bright deep blue color

ul·tra·mi·cro·scop·ic \-ˌmī-krə-'skäp-ik\ *adj* : too small to be seen with an ordinary microscope

ul·tra·mod·ern \-'mäd-ərn\ *adj* : extremely or excessively modern in idea, style, or tendency

ul·tra·mon·tane \-'män-ˌtān, -ˌmän-'tān\ *adj* 1 : of or relating to countries or peoples beyond the mountains (as the Alps) 2 : favoring greater or absolute supremacy of papal over national or diocesan authority in the Roman Catholic Church — **ultramontane** *n, often cap* — **ul·tra·mon·tan·ism** \-'mänt-ᵊn-ˌiz-əm\ *n*

ul·tra·pure \-'pyùr\ *adj* : of the utmost purity

ul·tra·short \-'shòrt\ *adj* 1 : very short in duration 2 : having a wavelength below 10 meters

ul·tra·son·ic \ˌəl-trə-'sän-ik\ *adj* : having a frequency too high to be heard by the human ear — **ul·tra·son·i·cal·ly** \-i-k(ə-)lē\ *adv*

ul·tra·son·ics \-'sän-iks\ *n* 1 : ultrasonic vibrations 2 : the science of ultrasonic phenomena

ul·tra·sound \-ˌsaund\ *n* 1 : ultrasonic vibrations 2 : a diagnostic or therapeutic procedure or technique using ultrasound to form a two-dimensional image of internal body structures

ul·tra·vi·o·let \-'vī-ə-lət\ *adj* : having a wavelength shorter than those of visible light and longer than those of X rays (~ radiation) ; *also* : producing or employing ultraviolet radiation — **ultraviolet** *n*

ul·tra vi·res \ˌəl-trə-'vī-rēz\ *adv or adj* [NL, lit., beyond power] : beyond the scope of legal power or authority

ul·u·late \'əl-yə-ˌlāt\ *vb* -lat·ed; -lat·ing : HOWL, WAIL

um·bel \'əm-bəl\ *n* : a flat-topped or ball-shaped flower cluster in which the individual flower stalks all arise at one point on the main stem

um·ber \'əm-bər\ *n* : a brown earthy substance valued as a pigment either in its raw state or burnt — **umber** *adj*

umbilical cord *n* : a cord arising from the navel that connects the fetus with the placenta

um·bi·li·cus \ˌəm-bə-'lī-kəs, ˌəm-'bil-i-\ *n, pl* **um·bi·li·ci** \ˌəm-bə-'lī-ˌkī, -ˌsī; ˌəm-'bil-ə-ˌkī\ *or* **um·bi·li·cus·es** : NAVEL — **um·bil·i·cal** \ˌəm-'bil-i-kəl\ *adj*

um·bra \'əm-brə\ *n, pl* **umbras** *or* **um·brae** \-(ˌ)brē, -ˌbrī\ 1 : SHADE, SHADOW 2 : the conical part of the shadow of a celestial body from which the sun's light is completely blocked

um·brage \'əm-brij\ *n* 1 : SHADE; *also* : FOLIAGE 2 : RESENTMENT, OFFENSE (take ~ at a remark)

um·brel·la \ˌəm-'brel-ə\ *n* 1 : a collapsible shade for protection against weather consisting of fabric stretched over hinged ribs radiating from a center pole 2 : something that resembles an umbrella in shape or purpose

umi·ak \'ü-mē-ˌak\ *n* : an open Eskimo boat made of a wooden frame covered with skins

um·pire \'əm-ˌpī(ə)r\ *n* [ME *oumpere,* alter. of *noumpere* (the phrase *a noumpere* being understood as *an oumpere*), fr. MF *nomper* not equal, not paired, fr. *non* not + *per* equal, fr. L *par*] 1 : one having authority to decide finally a controversy or question between parties 2 : an official in a sport who rules on plays — **umpire** *vb*

ump·teen \'əmp-'tēn\ *adj* : very many : indefinitely numerous — **ump·teenth** \-'tēnth\ *adj*

UN *abbr* United Nations

un- \ˌən, 'ən\ *prefix* 1 : not : IN-, NON- 2 : opposite of : contrary to

unabashed	unappreciative
unabated	unapproachable
unabsorbed	unappropriated
unabsorbent	unapproved
unacademic	unarmored
unaccented	unartistic
unacceptable	unashamed
unacclimatized	unasked
unaccommodating	unassertive
unaccredited	unassisted
unacknowledged	unathletic
unacquainted	unattainable
unadapted	unattempted
unadjusted	unattended
unadorned	unattested
unadventurous	unattractive
unadvertised	unauthentic
unaesthetic	unauthenticated
unaffiliated	unauthorized
unafraid	unavailable
unaggressive	unavenged
unaided	unavowed
unalike	unawakened
unallied	unbaked
unalterable	unbaptized
unalterably	unbeloved
unaltered	unblamed
unambiguous	unbleached
unambiguously	unblemished
unambitious	unblinking
unanchored	unbound
unanimated	unbranched
unannounced	unbranded
unanswerable	unbreakable
unanswered	unbridgeable
unanticipated	unbrotherly
unapologetic	unbruised
unapparent	unbrushed
unappealing	unbudging
unappeased	unburied
unappetizing	unburned
unappreciated	unburnished

uncanceled	uncrowned	uneconomical	unglazed
uncanonical	uncrystallized	unedifying	ungoverned
uncap	uncultivated	uneducated	ungraceful
uncapitalized	uncultured	unembarrassed	ungraded
uncared-for	uncurbed	unemotional	ungrammatical
uncataloged	uncured	unemphatic	ungrounded
uncaught	uncurious	unenclosed	ungrudging
uncensored	uncurtained	unencumbered	unguided
uncensured	uncustomary	unendorsed	unhackneyed
unchallenged	undamaged	unendurable	unhampered
unchangeable	undamped	unenforceable	unhardened
unchanged	undated	unenforced	unharmed
unchanging	undazzled	unengaged	unharvested
unchaperoned	undecided	unenjoyable	unhatched
uncharacteristic	undecipherable	unenlightened	unhealed
unchecked	undecked	unenterprising	unhealthful
unchivalrous	undeclared	unentertaining	unheeded
unchristened	undecorated	unenthusiastic	unhelpful
unclad	undefeated	unenviable	unheralded
unclaimed	undefended	unequipped	unheroic
unclassified	undefiled	unessential	unhesitating
uncleaned	undefinable	unethical	unhindered
unclear	undefined	unexaggerated	unhonored
uncleared	undemanding	unexcelled	unhoused
unclouded	undemocratic	unexceptional	unhurried
uncluttered	undenominational	unexcited	unhurt
uncoated	undependable	unexciting	unhygienic
uncollected	undeserved	unexperienced	unidentified
uncolored	undeserving	unexpired	unidiomatic
uncombed	undetected	unexplained	unimaginable
uncombined	undetermined	unexploded	unimaginative
uncomely	undeterred	unexplored	unimpaired
unconic	undeveloped	unexposed	unimpassioned
uncommercial	undifferentiated	unexpressed	unimpeded
uncompensated	undigested	unexpurgated	unimportant
uncomplaining	undignified	unextinguished	unimposing
uncompleted	undiluted	unfading	unimpressive
uncomplicated	undiminished	unfaltering	unimproved
uncomplimentary	undimmed	unfashionable	unincorporated
uncompounded	undiplomatic	unfashionably	uninfluenced
uncomprehending	undirected	unfathomable	uninformative
unconcealed	undiscerning	unfeasible	uninformed
unconfined	undisciplined	unfed	uninhabitable
unconfirmed	undisclosed	unfeminine	uninhabited
unconformable	undiscovered	unfenced	uninitiated
uncongenial	undiscriminating	unfermented	uninjured
unconnected	undisguised	unfertilized	uninspired
unconquered	undismayed	unfilled	uninstructed
unconsecrated	undisputed	unfiltered	uninstructive
unconsidered	undissolved	unfitted	uninsured
unconsolidated	undistinguished	unflagging	unintended
unconstrained	undistributed	unflattering	uninteresting
unconsumed	undisturbed	unflavored	uninvested
uncontaminated	undivided	unfocused	uninvited
uncontested	undogmatic	unfolded	uninviting
uncontradicted	undomesticated	unforced	unjointed
uncontrolled	undone	unforeseeable	unjustifiable
unconverted	undoubled	unforeseen	unjustified
unconvincing	undramatic	unforgivable	unkept
uncooked	undraped	unforgiving	unknowable
uncooperative	undrawn	unformulated	unknowledgeable
uncoordinated	undreamed	unfortified	unlabeled
uncordial	undressed	unframed	unladylike
uncorrected	undrinkable	unfree	unlamented
uncorroborated	undulled	unfulfilled	unleavened
uncorrupted	undutiful	unfunded	unlicensed
uncountable	undyed	unfunny	unlighted
uncreative	uneager	unfurnished	unlikable
uncredited	uneatable	ungentle	unlimited
uncropped	uneaten	ungentlemanly	unlined
uncrowded	uneconomic	ungerminated	unlisted

unlit
unliterary
unlivable
unlovable
unloved
unloving
unmade
unmalicious
unmanageable
unmanned
unmanufactured
unmapped
unmarked
unmarketable
unmarred
unmarried
unmasculine
unmatched
unmeant
unmeasured
unmeditated
unmelodious
unmentioned
unmerited
unmilitary
unmilled
unmixed
unmolested
unmounted
unmovable
unmoved
unmusical
unnameable
unnamed
unnecessary
unneighborly
unnewsworthy
unnoticeable
unnoticed
unobjectionable
unobliging
unobservant
unobserved
unobserving
unobstructed
unobtainable
unofficial
unofficially
unopened
unopposed
unoriginal
unorthodox
unostentatious
unowned
unpaged
unpaid
unpainted
unpaired
unpalatable
unpardonable
unpasteurized
unpatriotic
unpaved
unperceived
unperceptive
unperformed
unperturbed
unpitied
unplanned
unplanted

unpleasing
unplowed
unpoetic
unpolished
unpolitical
unpolluted
unposed
unpractical
unpracticed
unpredictable
unprejudiced
unpremeditated
unprepared
unpreparedness
unprepossessing
unpressed
unpretending
unpretty
unprivileged
unprocessed
unproductive
unprofessed
unprofessional
unprogrammed
unprogressive
unpromising
unprompted
unpronounceable
unpropitious
unprotected
unproven
unprovided
unprovoked
unpublished
unpunished
unquenchable
unquestioned
unraised
unratified
unreachable
unreadable
unready
unrealistic
unrealized
unrecognizable
unrecompensed
unrecorded
unrecoverable
unredeemable
unrefined
unreflecting
unreflective
unregistered
unregulated
unrehearsed
unrelated
unreliable
unrelieved
unreluctant
unremarkable
unremembered
unremovable
unrepentant
unreported
unrepresentative
unrepressed
unrequited
unresistant
unresisting
unresolved
unresponsive

unrestful
unrestricted
unreturnable
unreturned
unrewarding
unrhymed
unrhythmic
unripened
unromantic
unromantically
unsafe
unsaid
unsalable
unsalted
unsanitary
unsatisfactory
unsatisfied
unscented
unscheduled
unscholarly
unsealed
unseasoned
unseaworthy
unsegmented
unsensational
unsentimental
unserviceable
unsexual
unshaded
unshakable
unshaken
unshapely
unshaven
unshed
unshorn
unsifted
unsigned
unsinkable
unsmiling
unsociable
unsoiled
unsold
unsoldierly
unsolicited
unsolvable
unsolved
unsorted
unspecified
unspectacular
unspent
unspiritual
unspoiled
unspoken
unsportsmanlike
unstained
unstated
unsterile
unstoppable
unstructured
unstylish
unsubdued
unsubstantiated
unsubtle
unsuccessful
unsuccessfully
unsuitable
unsuited
unsullied
unsupervised
unsupportable
unsupported

unsuppressed
unsure
unsurpassed
unsuspected
unsuspecting
unsuspicious
unsweetened
unsymmetrical
unsympathetic
unsystematic
untactful
untainted
untalented
untamed
untanned
untapped
untarnished
untaxed
unteachable
untenable
untenanted
untested
unthankful
unthoughtful
unthrifty
untidy
untilled
untitled
untouched
untraceable
untrained
untrammeled
untranslatable
untraveled
untraversed
untrimmed
untrod
untroubled
untrustworthy
untruthful
unusable
unvaried
unvarying
unventilated
unverifiable
unverified
unversed
unvisited
unwanted
unwarranted
unwary
unwashed
unwatched
unwavering
unweaned
unwearable
unwearied
unweathered
unwed
unwelcome
unwished
unwitnessed
unwomanly
unworkable
unworn
unworried
unwounded
unwoven
unwrinkled

un·able \,ən-'ā-bəl, 'ən-\ *adj* 1 : not able 2 : UNQUALIFIED, INCOMPETENT

un·a·bridged \,ən-ə-'brijd\ *adj* 1 : not abridged (an ∼ edition of Shakespeare) 2 : complete of its class : not based on one larger (an ∼ dictionary)

un·ac·com·pa·nied \,ən-ə-'kəmp-(ə-)nēd\ *adj* : not accompanied; *esp* : being without instrumental accompaniment

un·ac·count·able \,ən-ə-'kaunt-ə-bəl\ *adj* 1 : not to be accounted for : INEXPLICABLE 2 : not responsible — **un·account·ably** \-blē\ *adv*

un·ac·count·ed \-əd\ *adj* : not accounted (the loss was ∼ for)

un·ac·cus·tomed \,ən-ə-'kəs-təmd\ *adj* 1 : not customary : not usual or common 2 : not accustomed or habituated (∼ to noise)

un·adul·ter·at·ed \,ən-ə-'dəl-tə-,rāt-əd\ *adj* : PURE, UNMIXED

un·ad·vised \,ən-əd-'vīzd\ *adj* 1 : done without due consideration : RASH 2 : not prudent — **un·ad·vis·ed·ly** \-'vī-zəd-lē\ *adv*

un·af·fect·ed \,ən-ə-'fek-təd\ *adj* 1 : not influenced or changed mentally, physically, or chemically 2 : free from affectation : NATURAL, GENUINE — **un·af·fect·ed·ly** *adv*

un·alien·able \-'āl-yə-nə-bəl, -'ā-lē-ə-\ *adj* : INALIENABLE

un·aligned \,ən-əl-'īnd\ *adj* : not associated with any one of competing international blocs (∼ nations)

un·al·loyed \,ən-əl-'oid\ *adj* : UNMIXED, UNQUALIFIED, PURE (∼ metals)

un-Amer·i·can \,ən-ə-'mer-ə-kən\ *adj* : not characteristic of or consistent with American customs, principles, or traditions

unan·i·mous \yu̇-'nan-ə-məs\ *adj* [L *unanimus*, fr. *unus* one + *animus* mind] 1 : being of one mind : AGREEING 2 : formed with or indicating the agreement of all — **una·nim·i·ty** \,yü-nə-'nim-ət-ē\ *n* — **unan·i·mous·ly** \yu̇-'nan-ə-məs-lē\ *adv*

un·arm \,ən-'ärm, 'ən-\ *vb* : DISARM

un·armed \,ən-'ärmd\ *adj* : not armed or armored

un·as·sail·able \,ən-ə-'sā-lə-bəl\ *adj* : not assailable : not liable to doubt, attack, or question

un·as·sum·ing \,ən-ə-'sü-miŋ\ *adj* : MODEST, RETIRING

un·at·tached \,ən-ə-'tacht\ *adj* 1 : not married or engaged 2 : not joined or united

un·avail·ing \,ən-ə-'vā-liŋ\ *adj* : being of no avail — **un·avail·ing·ly** *adv*

un·avoid·able \,ən-ə-'void-ə-bəl\ *adj* : not avoidable : INEVITABLE — **un·avoid·ably** \-blē\ *adv*

¹un·aware \,ən-ə-'waər\ *adv* : UNAWARES

²unaware *adj* : not aware : IGNORANT — **un·aware·ness** *n*

un·awares \-'waərz\ *adv* 1 : without knowing : UNINTENTIONALLY 2 : without warning : by surprise (taken ∼)

un·bal·anced \,ən-'bal-ənst\ *adj* 1 : not equally poised or balanced 2 : mentally disordered 3 : not adjusted so as to make credits equal to debits

un·bar \-'bär\ *vb* : UNBOLT, OPEN

un·bear·able \,ən-'bar-ə-bəl\ *adj* : greater than can be borne (∼ pain) — **un·bear·ably** \-blē\ *adv*

un·beat·able \-'bēt-ə-bəl\ *adj* : not capable of being defeated

un·beat·en \-'bēt-³n\ *adj* 1 : not pounded, beaten, or whipped 2 : UNTROD 3 : UNDEFEATED

un·be·com·ing \,ən-bi-'kəm-iŋ\ *adj* : not becoming : UNSUITABLE, IMPROPER — **un·be·com·ing·ly** *adv*

un·be·knownst \,ən-bi-'nōnst\ *also* **un·be·known** \-'nōn\ *adj* : happening without one's knowledge

un·be·lief \,ən-bə-'lēf\ *n* : the withholding or absence of belief : DOUBT

un·be·liev·ing \-'lē-viŋ\ *adj*

un·be·liev·able \-'lē-və-bəl\ *adj* : too improbable for belief : INCREDIBLE — **un·be·liev·ably** \-blē\ *adv*

un·be·liev·er \-'lē-vər\ *n* 1 : DOUBTER 2 : INFIDEL

un·bend \-'bend\ *vb* **-bent** \-'bent\ **-bend·ing** 1 : to free from being bent : make or become straight 2 : UNTIE 3 : to make or become less stiff or more affable : RELAX

un·bend·ing \-'ben-diŋ\ *adj* : formal and distant in manner : INFLEXIBLE

un·bi·ased \,ən-'bī-əst, 'ən-\ *adj* : free from bias; *esp* : UNPREJUDICED

un·bid·den \-'bid-³n\ *also* **un·bid** \-'bid\ *adj* : not bidden : UNASKED

un·bind \-'bīnd\ *vb* **-bound** \-'baund\ **-bind·ing** 1 : to remove bindings from : UNTIE 2 : RELEASE

un·blessed *also* **un·blest** \,ən-'blest, 'ən-\ *adj* 1 : not blessed 2 : EVIL

un·block \-'bläk\ *vb* : to free from being blocked

un·blush·ing \-'bləsh-iŋ\ *adj* 1 : not blushing 2 : SHAMELESS — **un·blush·ing·ly** *adv*

un·bod·ied \-'bäd-ēd\ *adj* 1 : having no body; *also* : DISEMBODIED 2 : FORMLESS

un·bolt \,ən-'bōlt, 'ən-\ *vb* : to open or unfasten by withdrawing a bolt

un·bolt·ed \-'bōl-təd\ *adj* : not fastened by bolts

un·born \-'born\ *adj* : not yet born

un·bos·om \-'búz-əm, -'büz-\ *vb* 1 : DISCLOSE, REVEAL (∼ed his secrets) 2 : to disclose the thoughts or feelings of oneself

un·bound·ed \-'baun-dəd\ *adj* : having no bounds or limits (∼ enthusiasm)

un·bowed \,ən-'baud, 'ən-\ *adj* 1 : not bowed down 2 : UNSUBDUED

un·bri·dled \-'brīd-³ld\ *adj* 1 : UNRESTRAINED 2 : not confined by a bridle

un·bro·ken \-'brō-kən\ *adj* 1 : not damaged 2 : not subdued or tamed 3 : not interrupted : CONTINUOUS

un·buck·le \-'bək-əl\ *vb* : to loose the buckle of : UNFASTEN (∼ a belt)

un·bur·den \-'bərd-ᵊn\ *vb* **1** : to free or relieve from a burden **2** : to relieve oneself of (as cares or worries) : cast off

un·but·ton \-'bət-ᵊn\ *vb* : to unfasten the buttons of ⟨∼ your coat⟩

un·called-for \,ən-'kȯld-,fȯr\ *adj* : not called for, needed, or wanted

un·can·ny \-'kan-ē\ *adj* **1** : GHOSTLY, MYSTERIOUS, EERIE **2** : suggesting superhuman or supernatural powers — **un·can·ni·ly** \-'kan-ᵊl-ē\ *adv*

un·ceas·ing \-'sē-siŋ\ *adj* : never ceasing — **un·ceas·ing·ly** *adv*

un·cer·e·mo·ni·ous \,ən-,ser-ə-'mō-nē-əs\ *adj* : acting without or lacking ordinary courtesy : ABRUPT — **un·cer·e·mo·ni·ous·ly** *adv*

un·cer·tain \,ən-'sərt-ᵊn, 'ən-\ *adj* **1** : not determined or fixed ⟨an ∼ quantity⟩ **2** : subject to chance or change : not dependable **3** : not definitely known **4** : not sure ⟨∼ of the truth⟩ — **un·cer·tain·ly** *adv*

un·cer·tain·ty \-ᵊn-tē\ *n* **1** : lack of certainty : DOUBT **2** : something that is uncertain

un·chain \,ən-'chān, 'ən-\ *vb* : to free by or as if by removing a chain

un·charged \,ən-'chärjd\ *adj* : having no electrical charge

un·char·i·ta·ble \-'char-ət-ə-bəl\ *adj* : not charitable; *esp* : severe in judging others — **un·char·i·ta·ble·ness** *n* — **un·char·i·ta·bly** \-blē\ *adv*

un·chart·ed \-'chärt-əd\ *adj* **1** : not recorded on a map, chart, or plan **2** : UNKNOWN

un·chaste \-'chāst\ *adj* : not chaste — **un·chaste·ly** *adv* — **un·chaste·ness** \-'chās(t)-nəs\ *n* — **un·chas·ti·ty** \-'chas-tət-ē\ *n*

un·chris·tian \-'kris-chən\ *adj* **1** : not of the Christian faith **2** : contrary to the Christian spirit

un·churched \-'chərcht\ *adj* : not belonging to or connected with a church

un·cial \'ən-shəl, -chəl; 'ən-sē-əl\ *adj* [L *uncialis* inch-high, fr. *uncia* twelfth part, ounce, inch] : relating to or written in a form of script with rounded letters used esp. in early Greek and Latin manuscripts — **uncial** *n*

un·cir·cu·lat·ed \,ən-'sər-kyə-,lāt-əd\ *adj* : issued for use as money but kept out of circulation

un·cir·cum·cised \,ən-'sər-kəm-,sīzd, 'ən-\ *adj* : not circumcised; *also* : HEATHEN

un·civ·il \,ən-'siv-əl, 'ən-\ *adj* **1** : not civilized : BARBAROUS **2** : DISCOURTEOUS, ILL-MANNERED, IMPOLITE

un·civ·i·lized \-'siv-ə-,līzd\ *adj* **1** : not civilized : BARBAROUS **2** : remote from civilization : WILD

un·clasp \-'klasp\ *vb* : to open by or as if by loosing the clasp

un·cle \'əŋ-kəl\ *n* [ME, fr. OF, fr. L *avunculus* mother's brother] : the brother of one's father or mother; *also* : the husband of one's aunt

un·clean \,ən-'klēn, 'ən-\ *adj* **1** : morally or spiritually impure **2** : prohibited by ritual law for use or contact **3** : DIRTY, FILTHY — **un·clean·ness** \-'klēn-nəs\ *n*

un·clean·ly \-'klen-lē\ *adj* : morally or physically unclean — **un·clean·li·ness** \-lē-nəs\ *n*

un·clench \-'klench\ *vb* : to open from a clenched position : RELAX

Uncle Tom \,əŋ-kəl-'täm\ *n* [fr. *Uncle Tom*, faithful Negro slave in Harriet Beecher Stowe's novel *Uncle Tom's Cabin* (1851-52)] : a black who is overeager to win the approval of whites

un·cloak \,ən-'klōk, 'ən-\ *vb* **1** : to remove a cloak or cover from **2** : UNMASK, REVEAL

un·clog \-'kläg\ *vb* : to remove an obstruction from

un·close \-'klōz\ *vb* : OPEN — **un·closed** \-'klōzd\ *adj*

un·clothe \-'klōth\ *vb* : to strip of clothes or a covering — **un·clothed** \-'klōthd\ *adj*

un·coil \,ən-'kȯil, 'ən-\ *vb* : to release or become released from a coiled state

un·com·fort·able \,ən-'kəm(p)f-tə-bəl, 'ən-, -'kəm(p)-fərt-ə-\ *adj* **1** : causing discomfort **2** : feeling discomfort : UNEASY — **un·com·fort·ably** \-blē\ *adv*

un·com·mit·ted \,ən-kə-'mit-əd\ *adj* : not committed; *esp* : not pledged to a particular belief, allegiance, or program

un·com·mon \,ən-'käm-ən, 'ən-\ *adj* **1** : not ordinarily encountered : UNUSUAL, RARE **2** : REMARKABLE, EXCEPTIONAL — **un·com·mon·ly** *adv*

un·com·mu·ni·ca·tive \,ən-kə-'myü-nə-,kāt-iv, -ni-kət-\ *adj* : not inclined to talk or impart information : RESERVED

un·com·pro·mis·ing \'ən-'käm-prə-,mī-ziŋ\ *adj* : not making or accepting a compromise : UNYIELDING

un·con·cern \,ən-kən-'sərn\ *n* **1** : lack of care or interest : INDIFFERENCE **2** : freedom from excessive concern or anxiety

un·con·cerned \-'sərnd\ *adj* **1** : not having any part or interest **2** : not anxious or upset : free of worry — **un·con·cern·ed·ly** \-'sər-nəd-lē\ *adv*

un·con·di·tion·al \,ən-kən-'dish-(ə-)nəl\ *adj* : not limited in any way — **un·con·di·tion·al·ly** \-ē\ *adv*

un·con·di·tioned \-'dish-ənd\ *adj* **1** : not subject to conditions **2** : not acquired or learned : INHERENT, NATURAL **3** : producing an unconditioned response ⟨∼ stimuli⟩

un·con·quer·able \,ən-'käŋ-k(ə-)rə-bəl, 'ən-\ *adj* : incapable of being conquered or overcome : INDOMITABLE

un·con·scio·na·ble \-'känch-(ə-)nə-bəl\ *adj* **1** : not guided or controlled by conscience **2** : not in accordance with what is right or just — un·con·scio·na·bly \-blē\ adv

¹un·con·scious \,ən-'kän-chəs, 'ən-\ adj 1 : deprived of consciousness or awareness 2 : not realized by oneself : not consciously done 3 : of or relating to the unconscious — un·con·scious·ly adv — un·con·scious·ness n

²unconscious n : the part of one's mental life of which one is not ordinarily aware and which is revealed esp. in spontaneous behavior (as slips of the tongue) or in dreams

un·con·sti·tu·tion·al \,ən-,kän-stə-'t(y)üsh-(ə-)nəl\ adj : not according to or consistent with the constitution of a state or society — un·con·sti·tu·tion·al·i·ty \-t(y)ü-shə-'nal-ət-ē\ n — un·con·sti·tu·tion·al·ly \-'t(y)üsh-(ə-)nə-lē\ adv

un·con·trol·la·ble \,ən-kən-'trō-lə-bəl\ adj : incapable of being controlled : UNGOVERNABLE — un·con·trol·la·bly \-blē\ adv

un·con·ven·tion·al \-'vench-(ə-)nəl\ adj : not conventional : being out of the ordinary — un·con·ven·tion·al·i·ty \-,ven-chə-'nal-ət-ē\ n — un·con·ven·tion·al·ly \-'vench-(ə-)nə-lē\ adv

un·cork \-'kȯrk, 'ən-\ vb 1 : to draw a cork from 2 : to release from a sealed or pent-up state; also : to let go

un·count·ed \-'kaůnt-əd\ adj 1 : not counted 2 : INNUMERABLE

un·cou·ple \-'kəp-əl\ vb : DISCONNECT

un·couth \-'küth\ adj [OE uncūth unknown, unfamiliar, fr. un- + cūth known] 1 : strange, awkward, and clumsy in shape or appearance 2 : vulgar in conduct or speech : RUDE

un·cov·er \-'kəv-ər\ vb 1 : to make known : DISCLOSE, REVEAL 2 : to expose to view by removing some covering 3 : to take the cover from 4 : to remove the hat from; also : to take off the hat as a token of respect — un·covered \-ərd\ adj

un·crit·i·cal \,ən-'krit-i-kəl, 'ən-\ adj 1 : not critical : lacking in discrimination 2 : showing lack or improper use of critical standards or procedures

un·cross \-'krȯs\ vb : to change from a crossed position (~ed his legs)

unc·tion \'əŋk-shən\ n 1 : the act of anointing as a rite of consecration or healing 2 : exaggerated, assumed, or superficial earnestness of language or manner

unc·tu·ous \'əŋk-chə(-wə)s\ adj [ME, fr. MF or ML; MF unctueux, fr. ML unctuosus, fr. L unctum ointment, fr. unguere to anoint] 1 : FATTY, OILY 2 : full of unction in speech and manner; esp : insincerely smooth — unc·tu·ous·ly adv

un·curl \,ən-'kərl, 'ən-\ vb : to make or become straightened out from a curled or coiled position

un·cut \,ən-'kət, 'ən-\ adj 1 : not cut down or into 2 : not shaped by cutting (an ~ diamond) 3 : not having the

folds of the leaves slit (an ~ book) 4 : not abridged or curtailed

un·daunt·ed \-'dȯnt-əd\ adj : not daunted : not discouraged or dismayed — un·daunt·ed·ly adv

un·de·ceive \,ən-di-'sēv\ vb : to free from deception, illusion, or error

un·de·mon·stra·tive \,ən-di-'män-strət-iv\ adj : restrained in expression of feeling : RESERVED

un·de·ni·able \,ən-di-'nī-ə-bəl\ adj 1 : plainly true : INCONTESTABLE 2 : unquestionably excellent or genuine — un·de·ni·ably \-blē\ adv

¹un·der \'ən-dər\ adv 1 : in or into a position below or beneath something 2 : below some quantity, level, or norm (\$10 or ~) 3 : in or into a condition of subjection, subordination, or unconsciousness (the ether put him ~)

²un·der \,ən-dər, 'ən-\ prep 1 : lower than and overhung, surmounted, or sheltered by (~ a tree) 2 : subject to the authority or guidance of (served ~ him) (had the man ~ contract) 3 : subject to the action or effect of (~ an anesthetic) 4 : within the division or grouping of (items ~ this head) 5 : less or lower than (as in size, amount, or rank) (makes ~ \$5000)

³under \'ən-dər\ adj 1 : lying below, beneath, or on the ventral side 2 : facing or protruding downward 3 : SUBORDINATE 4 : lower than usual, proper, or desired in amount, quality, or degree

un·der·achiev·er \,ən-dər-ə-'chē-vər\ n : one who performs below an expected level of proficiency

un·der·act \-'akt\ vb : to perform feebly or with restraint

un·der·ac·tive \-'ak-tiv\ adj : characterized by abnormally low activity (~ glands) — un·der·ac·tiv·i·ty \-,ak-'tiv-ət-ē\ n

un·der·age \-'āj\ adj : of less than mature or legal age

un·der·arm \-'ärm\ adj 1 : UNDERHAND 2 (an ~ throw) 2 : placed under or on the underside of the arms (~ seams) — underarm adv or n

un·der·bel·ly \'ən-dər-,bel-ē\ n 1 : the underside of a body or mass 2 : a vulnerable area

un·der·bid \,ən-dər-'bid\ vb -bid; -bid·ding 1 : to bid less than another 2 : to bid too low

un·der·body \'ən-dər-,bäd-ē\ n : the lower parts of the body of a vehicle

un·der·bred \,ən-dər-'bred\ adj : marked by lack of good breeding

un·der·brush \'ən-dər-,brəsh\ n : shrubs and small trees growing beneath large trees

un·der·car·riage \'ən-,kar-ij\ n 1 : a supporting framework (as of an automobile) 2 : the landing gear of an airplane

un·der·charge \,ən-dər-'chärj\ vb : to charge (as a person) too little — undercharge \'ən-dər-,chärj\ n

un·der·class·man \,ən-dər-'klas-mən\ n

: a member of the freshman or sophomore class

un·der·clothes \'ən-dər-ˌklō(th)z\ *n pl* : UNDERWEAR

un·der·cloth·ing \-ˌklō-thiŋ\ *n* : UNDERWEAR

un·der·coat \-ˌkōt\ *n* **1** : a coat worn under another **2** : a growth of short hair or fur partly concealed by a longer growth (a dog's ∼) **3** : a coat of paint under another

un·der·coat·ing \-ˌkōt-iŋ\ *n* : a special waterproof coating applied to the underside of a vehicle

un·der·cov·er \ˌən-dər-ˈkəv-ər\ *adj* : acting or executed in secret; *esp* : employed or engaged in secret investigation (∼ agent)

un·der·croft \'ən-dər-ˌkróft\ *n* [ME, fr. *under* + *crofte* crypt, fr. Middle Dutch, fr. ML *crupta*, fr. L *crypta*] : a vaulted chamber under a church

un·der·cur·rent \-ˌkər-ənt\ *n* **1** : a current below the surface **2** : a hidden tendency of feeling or opinion

un·der·cut \ˌən-dər-ˈkət\ *vb* -cut; -cutting **1** : to cut away the underpart of **2** : to offer to sell or to work at a lower rate than **3** : to strike (the ball) obliquely downward so as to give a backward spin or elevation to the shot — **un·der·cut** \'ən-dər-ˌkət\ *n*

un·der·de·vel·oped \ˌən-dər-di-ˈvel-əpt\ *adj* **1** : not normally or adequately developed (∼ muscles) **2** : having a relatively low level of economic development (the ∼ nations)

un·der·dog \'ən-dər-ˌdóg\ *n* **1** : the loser or predicted loser in a struggle **2** : a victim of injustice or persecution

un·der·done \ˌən-dər-ˈdən\ *adj* : not thoroughly done or cooked : RARE

un·der·draw·ers \'ən-dər-ˌdró(-ə)rz\ *n pl* : UNDERPANTS

un·der·em·pha·size \ˌən-dər-ˈem-fə-ˌsīz\ *vb* : to emphasize inadequately — **un·der·em·pha·sis** \-səs\ *n*

un·der·em·ployed \-im-ˈplóid\ *adj* : having less than full-time or adequate employment

un·der·es·ti·mate \-ˈes-tə-ˌmāt\ *vb* : to set too low a value on

un·der·ex·pose \-ik-ˈspōz\ *vb* : to expose (a photographic plate or film) for less time than is needed — **un·der·ex·po·sure** \-ˈspō-zhər\ *n*

un·der·feed \ˌən-dər-ˈfēd\ *vb* -fed \-ˈfed\ ; -feed·ing : to feed inadequately

un·der·foot \-ˈfüt\ *adv* **1** : under the feet (flowers trampled ∼) **2** : close about one's feet : in the way

un·der·fur \'ən-dər-ˌfər\ *n* : the thick soft undercoat of fur lying beneath the longer and coarser hair of a mammal

un·der·gar·ment \-ˌgär-mənt\ *n* : a garment to be worn under another

un·der·gird \ˌən-dər-ˈgərd\ *vb* **1** : to make secure underneath **2** : to brace up : STRENGTHEN

un·der·go \ˌən-dər-ˈgō\ *vb* -went

\-ˈwent\ ; -gone \-ˈgón, -ˈgän\ ; -go·ing \-ˈgō-iŋ, -ˈgó(-)iŋ\ **1** : to be subjected to : ENDURE **2** : to pass through : EXPERIENCE

un·der·grad·u·ate \ˌən-dər-ˈgraj-(ə-)wət, -ə-ˌwāt\ *n* : a student at a university or college who has not taken a first degree

¹un·der·ground \ˌən-dər-ˈgraúnd\ *adv* **1** : beneath the surface of the earth **2** : in secret

²un·der·ground \'ən-dər-ˌgraúnd\ *n* **1** : a space under the surface of the ground; *esp* : SUBWAY **2** : a secret political movement or group; *esp* : an organized body working in secret to overthrow a government or an occupying power **3** : an avant-garde group or movement that operates outside the establishment

³underground \'ən-dər-ˌgraúnd\ *adj* **1** : being or growing under the surface of the ground (∼ stems) **2** : conducted by secret means **3** : produced or published outside the establishment esp. by the avant-garde (∼ movies) ; *also* : of or relating to the avant-garde underground

un·der·growth \'ən-dər-ˌgróth\ *n* : low growth (as of herbs and shrubs) on the floor of a forest

¹un·der·hand \'ən-dər-ˌhand\ *adv* **1** : in an underhanded or secret manner **2** : with an underhand motion

²underhand *adj* **1** : UNDERHANDED **2** : made with the hand kept below the level of the shoulder

¹un·der·hand·ed \ˌən-dər-ˈhan-dəd\ *adv* : UNDERHAND

²underhanded *adj* : marked by secrecy and deception — **un·der·hand·ed·ly** *adv* — **un·der·hand·ed·ness** *n*

un·der·lie \-ˈlī\ *vb* -lay \-ˈlā\ ; -lain \-ˈlān\ ; -ly·ing \-ˈlī-iŋ\ **1** : to lie or be situated under **2** : to be at the basis of : form the foundation of : SUPPORT

un·der·line \'ən-dər-ˌlīn\ *vb* **1** : to draw a line under **2** : EMPHASIZE, STRESS — **underline** *n*

un·der·ling \'ən-dər-liŋ\ *n* : SUBORDINATE, INFERIOR

un·der·lip \ˌən-dər-ˈlip\ *n* : the lower lip

un·der·ly·ing \ˌən-dər-ˈlī-iŋ\ *adj* **1** : lying under or below **2** : FUNDAMENTAL, BASIC (∼ principles)

un·der·mine \-ˈmīn\ *vb* **1** : to excavate beneath **2** : to weaken or wear away secretly or gradually

un·der·most \'ən-dər-ˌmōst\ *adj* : lowest in relative position — **undermost** *adv*

¹un·der·neath \ˌən-dər-ˈnēth\ *prep* **1** : directly under **2** : under subjection to

²underneath *adv* **1** : below a surface or object : BENEATH **2** : on the lower side

un·der·nour·ished \ˌən-dər-ˈnər-isht\ *adj* : supplied with insufficient nourishment — **un·der·nour·ish·ment** \-ˈnər-ish-mənt\ *n*

un·der·pants \'ən-dər-ˌpants\ n pl : short or long pants worn under an outer garment : DRAWERS

un·der·part \-ˌpärt\ n 1 : a part lying on the lower side esp. of a bird or mammal 2 : a subordinate or auxiliary part or role

un·der·pass \-ˌpas\ n : a passage underneath something ⟨a railroad ∼⟩

un·der·pay \ˌən-dər-'pā\ vb : to pay too little

un·der·pin·ning \'ən-dər-ˌpin-iŋ\ n : the material and construction (as a foundation) used for support of a structure — **un·der·pin** \ˌən-dər-'pin\ vb

un·der·play \ˌən-dər-'plā\ vb : to treat or handle with restraint; esp : to play a role with subdued force

un·der·pop·u·lat·ed \ˌən-dər-'päp-yə-ˌlāt-əd\ adj : having a lower than normal or desirable density of population

un·der·priv·i·leged \-'priv-(ə-)lijd\ adj : having fewer esp. economic and social privileges than others

un·der·pro·duc·tion \ˌən-dər-prə-'dək-shən\ n : the production of less than enough to satisfy the demand or of less than the usual supply

un·der·rate \ˌən-də(r)-'rāt\ vb : to rate or value too low

un·der·rep·re·sent·ed \-ˌrep-ri-'zent-əd\ adj : inadequately represented

un·der·score \ˌən-dər-ˌskōr\ vb 1 : to draw a line under : UNDERLINE 2 : EMPHASIZE — **underscore** n

¹un·der·sea \ˌən-dər-'sē\ adj : being, carried on, or used beneath the surface of the sea

²un·der·sea \ˌən-dər-'sē\ or **un·der·seas** \-'sēz\ adv : beneath the surface of the sea

under secretary n : a secretary immediately subordinate to a principal secretary ⟨∼ of state⟩

un·der·sell \-'sel\ vb -sold \-'sōld\; -sell·ing : to sell articles cheaper than

un·der·sexed \-'sekst\ adj : deficient in sexual desire

un·der·shirt \'ən-dər-ˌshərt\ n : a collarless undergarment with or without sleeves

un·der·shoot \ˌən-dər-'shüt\ vb -shot \-'shät\; -shoot·ing 1 : to shoot short of or below (a target) 2 : to fall short of (a runway) in landing an airplane

un·der·shorts \'ən-dər-ˌshōrts\ n pl : SHORT

un·der·shot \ˌən-dər-ˌshät\ adj 1 : having the lower front teeth projecting beyond the upper when the mouth is closed 2 : moved by water passing beneath ⟨an ∼ waterwheel⟩

un·der·side \'ən-dər-ˌsīd, ˌən-dər-'sīd\ n : the side or surface lying underneath

un·der·signed \'ən-dər-ˌsīnd\ n, pl **undersigned** : one who signs his name at the end of a document

un·der·sized \ˌən-dər-'sīzd\ also **un·**

der·size \-'sīz\ adj : of a size less than is common, proper, or normal

un·der·skirt \'ən-dər-ˌskərt\ n : a skirt worn under an outer skirt; esp : PETTICOAT

un·der·slung \ˌən-dər-'sləŋ\ adj : suspended so as to extend below the axles ⟨an ∼ automobile frame⟩

un·der·stand \ˌən-dər-'stand\ vb -stood \-'stüd\; -stand·ing 1 : to grasp the meaning of : COMPREHEND 2 : to have thorough or technical acquaintance with or expertness in ⟨∼ finance⟩ 3 : GATHER, INFER ⟨I ∼ that you spread this rumor⟩ 4 : INTERPRET ⟨we ∼ this to be a refusal⟩ 5 : to have a sympathetic attitude 6 : to accept as settled ⟨it is *understood* that he will pay the expenses⟩ — **un·der·stand·able** \-'stan-də-bəl\ adj — **un·der·stand·ably** \-blē\ adv

¹un·der·stand·ing \ˌən-dər-'stan-diŋ\ n 1 : knowledge and ability to apply judgment : INTELLIGENCE 2 : ability to comprehend and judge ⟨a man of ∼⟩ 3 : agreement of opinion or feeling 4 : a mutual agreement informally or tacitly entered into

²understanding adj : endowed with understanding : TOLERANT, SYMPATHETIC

un·der·state \ˌən-dər-'stāt\ vb 1 : to represent as less than is the case 2 : to state with restraint esp. for greater effect — **un·der·state·ment** n

un·der·stood \ˌən-dər-'stüd\ adj 1 : agreed upon 2 : IMPLICIT

un·der·sto·ry \'ən-dər-ˌstōr-ē, -ˌstȯr-\ n : the plants of a forest undergrowth

un·der·study \'ən-dər-ˌstəd-ē, ˌən-dər-'stəd-ē\ vb : to study another actor's part in order to be his substitute in an emergency — **understudy** \'ən-dər-ˌstəd-ē\ n

un·der·sur·face \'ən-dər-ˌsər-fəs\ n : UNDERSIDE

un·der·take \ˌən-dər-'tāk\ vb -took \-'tük\; -tak·en \-'tā-kən\; -tak·ing 1 : to take upon oneself as a task : set about 2 : to put oneself under obligation 3 : GUARANTEE, PROMISE

un·der·tak·er \'ən-dər-ˌtā-kər\ n : one whose business is to prepare the dead for burial and to take charge of funerals

un·der·tak·ing \'ən-dər-ˌtā-kiŋ, ˌən-dər-'tā-kiŋ; 2 is 'ən-dər-ˌtā-kiŋ only\ n 1 : the act of one who undertakes or engages in any project 2 : the business of an undertaker 3 : something undertaken 4 : PROMISE, GUARANTEE

under–the–counter adj : UNLAWFUL, ILLICIT ⟨∼ sale of drugs⟩

un·der·tone \'ən-dər-ˌtōn\ n 1 : a low or subdued tone or utterance 2 : a subdued color (as seen through and modifying another color)

un·der·tow \-ˌtō\ n : the current beneath the surface that sets seaward when waves are breaking upon the shore

un·der·trick \-ˌtrik\ n : a trick by which

a declarer in bridge falls short of making his contract

un·der·val·ue \,ən-dər-'val-yü\ *vb* **1** : to value or estimate below the real worth **2** : to esteem lightly

un·der·wa·ter \,ən-dər-'wȯt-ər, -,wät-\ *adj* : lying, growing, worn, or operating below the surface of the water — **un·der·wa·ter** \-'wȯt-, -'wät-\ *adv*

under way \-'wā\ *adv* **1** : into motion from a standstill **2** : in progress

un·der·wear \'ən-dər-,wa(ə)r\ *n* : clothing or a garment worn next to the skin and under other clothing

un·der·weight \,ən-dər-'wāt\ *n* : weight below what is normal, average, or necessary — **underweight** *adj*

un·der·wood \'ən-dər-,wu̇d\ *n* : UNDERBRUSH, UNDERGROWTH

un·der·world \-,wərld\ *n* **1** : the place of departed souls : HADES **2** : a social sphere below the level of ordinary life; *esp* : the world of organized crime

un·der·write \'ən-də(r)-,rīt, ,ən-də(r)-'rīt\ *vb* -**wrote** \-,rōt, -'rōt\ ; -**writ·ten** \-,rit-ᵊn, -'rit-ᵊn\ ; -**writ·ing** \-,rīt-iŋ, -'rīt-\ **1** : to write under or at the end of something else **2** : to set one's name to an insurance policy and thereby become answerable for a designated loss or damage **3** : to subscribe to : agree to **4** : to agree to purchase (as bonds) usu. on a fixed date at a fixed price; *also* : to guarantee financial support of — **un·der·writ·er** *n*

un·de·sign·ing \,ən-di-'zī-niŋ\ *adj* : having no artful, ulterior, or fraudulent purpose : SINCERE

un·de·sir·able \-'zī-rə-bəl\ *adj* : not desirable — **undesirable** *n*

un·de·vi·at·ing \,ən-'dē-vē-,āt-iŋ, -'ən-\ *adj* : keeping a true course

un·dies \'ən-dēz\ *n pl* : UNDERWEAR; *esp* : women's underwear

un·do \,ən-'dü, 'ən-\ *vb* -**did** \-'did\ ; -**done** \-'dən\ ; -**do·ing** \-'dü-iŋ\ **1** : to make or become unfastened or loosened : OPEN **2** : to make null or as if not done : REVERSE **3** : to bring to ruin; *also* : UPSET

un·do·ing \-'dü-iŋ\ *n* **1** : LOOSING, UNFASTENING **2** : RUIN; *also* : a cause of ruin **3** : REVERSAL

un·doubt·ed \-'daut-əd\ *adj* : not doubted or called into question : CERTAIN — **un·doubt·ed·ly** *adv*

¹**un·dress** \,ən-'dres, 'ən-\ *vb* : to remove the clothes or covering of : STRIP, DISROBE

²**undress** *n* **1** : informal dress; *esp* : a loose robe or dressing gown **2** : ordinary dress **3** : NUDITY

un·due \-'d(y)ü\ *adj* **1** : not due **2** : exceeding or violating propriety or fitness

un·du·lant \'ən-jə-lənt, 'ən-d(y)ə-\ *adj* : UNDULATING

undulant fever *n* : a human disease caused by bacteria and marked by in-

termittent fever, pain and swelling in the joints, and great weakness

un·du·late \-,lāt\ *vb* -**lated**; -**lating** [LL *undula* small wave, fr. L *unda* wave] **1** : to have a wavelike motion or appearance **2** : to rise and fall in pitch or volume

un·du·la·tion \,ən-jə-'lā-shən, ,ən-d(y)ə-\ *n* **1** : wavy or wavelike motion **2** : pulsation of sound **3** : a wavy appearance or outline — **un·du·la·to·ry** \'ən-jə-lə-,tōr-ē, 'ən-d(y)ə-\ *adj*

un·du·ly \,ən-'d(y)ü-lē, 'ən-\ *adv* : in an undue manner; *esp* : EXCESSIVELY

un·dy·ing \-'dī-iŋ\ *adj* : not dying : IMMORTAL, PERPETUAL

un·earned \-'ərnd\ *adj* : not earned by labor, service, or skill ⟨∼ income⟩

un·earth \,ən-'ərth, 'ən-\ *vb* **1** : to draw from the earth : dig up ⟨∼ buried treasure⟩ **2** : to bring to light : DISCOVER ⟨∼ a secret⟩

un·earth·ly \-lē\ *adj* **1** : not of or belonging to the earth **2** : SUPERNATURAL, WEIRD, TERRIFYING

un·easy \'ən-'ē-zē\ *adj* **1** : AWKWARD, EMBARRASSED ⟨∼ among strangers⟩ **2** : disturbed by pain or worry; *also* : RESTLESS — **un·eas·i·ly** \-'ē-zə-lē\ *adv* — **un·eas·i·ness** \-'ē-zē-nəs\ *n*

un·em·ployed \,ən-im-'plȯid\ *adj* : not employed; *esp* : not engaged in a gainful occupation

un·em·ploy·ment \-'plȯi-mənt\ *n* : lack of employment

un·end·ing \,ən-'en-diŋ, 'ən-\ *adj* : having no ending : ENDLESS

un·equal \,ən-'ē-kwəl, 'ən-\ *adj* **1** : not alike (as in size, amount, number, or value) **2** : not uniform : VARIABLE **3** : badly balanced or matched **4** : INADEQUATE, INSUFFICIENT — **un·equal·ly** \-ē\ *adv*

un·equaled *or* **un·equalled** \-kwəld\ *adj* : not equaled : UNPARALLELED

un·equiv·o·cal \,ən-i-'kwiv-ə-kəl\ *adj* : leaving no doubt : CLEAR — **un·equiv·o·cal·ly** \-ē\ *adv*

un·err·ing \,ən-'e(ə)r-iŋ, -'ər-\ *adj* : making no errors : CERTAIN, UNFAILING — **un·err·ing·ly** *adv*

UNESCO \yü-'nes-kō\ *abbr* United Nations Educational, Scientific, and Cultural Organization

un·even \,ən-'ē-vən, 'ən-\ *adj* **1** : ODD **3** **2** : not even : not level or smooth : RUGGED, RAGGED **3** : IRREGULAR; *also* : varying in quality — **un·even·ly** *adv* — **un·even·ness** \-vən-nəs\ *n*

un·event·ful \,ən-i-'vent-fəl\ *adj* : not eventful : lacking interesting or noteworthy incidents

un·ex·am·pled \,ən-ig-'zam-pəld\ *adj* : UNPRECEDENTED, UNPARALLELED

un·ex·cep·tion·able \,ən-ik-'sep-sh(ə)nə-bəl\ *adj* : not open to exception or objection : beyond reproach

un·ex·pect·ed \,ən-ik-'spek-təd\ *adj* : not expected : UNFORESEEN — **un·ex·pect·ed·ly** *adv*

un·fail·ing \,ən-'fā-liŋ, 'ən-\ *adj* **1** : not

failing, flagging, or waning : CON-
STANT 2 : INEXHAUSTIBLE 3 : INFALLI-
BLE, SURE — **un·fail·ing·ly** adv

un·fair \-'faər\ adj 1 : marked by injustice, partiality, or deception : UNJUST,
DISHONEST 2 : not equitable in business dealings — **un·fair·ly** adv — **un-
fair·ness** n

un·faith·ful \-ən-'fāth-fəl, 'ən-\ adj 1
: not observant of vows, allegiance, or
duty : DISLOYAL 2 : INACCURATE, UN-
TRUSTWORTHY — **un·faith·ful·ly** \-ē\
adv — **un·faith·ful·ness** n

un·fa·mil·iar \,ən-fə-'mil-yər\ adj 1
: not well-known : STRANGE (an ~
place) 2 : not well acquainted (~ with
the subject) — **un·fa·mil·iar·i·ty** \-,mil-
'yar-ət-ē, -,mil-ē-'(y)ar-\ n

un·fas·ten \,ən-'fas-ªn, 'ən-\ vb : to
make or become loose : UNDO, DE-
TACH

un·fa·vor·able \,ən-'fāv-(ə-)rə-bəl, 'ən-\
adj : not favorable — **un·fa·vor·ably**
\-blē\ adv

un·feel·ing \-'fē-liŋ\ adj 1 : lacking feeling : INSENSATE 2 : HARDHEARTED,
CRUEL — **un·feel·ing·ly** adv

un·feigned \-'fānd\ adj : not feigned
: not hypocritical : GENUINE

un·fet·ter \-'fet-ər\ vb 1 : to free from
fetters 2 : LIBERATE

un·fil·ial \,ən-'fil-ē-əl, 'ən-, -'fil-yəl\ adj
: not observing the obligations of a
child to a parent : UNDUTIFUL

un·fin·ished \,ən-'fin-isht\ adj 1 : not
brought to an end 2 : being in a rough
or unpolished state

¹**un·fit** \-'fit\ adj : not fit or suitable: esp
: physically or mentally unsound —
un·fit·ness n

²**unfit** vb : DISABLE, DISQUALIFY

un·fix \-'fiks\ vb 1 : to loosen from a
fastening : DETACH 2 : UNSETTLE

un·flap·pa·ble \-'flap-ə-bəl\ adj : not
easily upset or panicked — **un·flap·pa-
bly** adv

un·fledged \,ən-'flejd\ adj : not feathered or ready for flight; also : IMMA-
TURE, CALLOW

un·flinch·ing \-'flin-chiŋ\ adj : not
flinching or shrinking : STEADFAST —
un·flinch·ing·ly adv

un·fold \-'fōld\ vb 1 : to open the folds
of : open up 2 : to lay open to view
: DISCLOSE 3 : BLOSSOM, DEVELOP

un·for·get·ta·ble \,ən-fər-'get-ə-bəl\ adj
: not to be forgotten — **un·for·get·ta-
bly** \-blē\ adv

un·formed \-'fȯrmd\ adj : not regularly
formed : SHAPELESS

un·for·tu·nate \-'fȯrch-(ə-)nət\ adj 1
: not fortunate : UNLUCKY 2 : attended with misfortune 3 : UNSUITABLE —
unfortunate n — **un·for·tu·nate·ly** adv

un·found·ed \,ən-'faùn-dəd, 'ən-\ adj
: lacking a sound basis : GROUNDLESS

un·freeze \-'frēz\ vb **-froze** \-'frōz\;
-fro·zen \-'frōz-ªn\; **-freez·ing** 1 : to
cause to thaw 2 : to remove from a
freeze (~ prices)

un·fre·quent·ed \,ən-frē-'kwent-əd;

,ən-'frē-kwənt-, 'ən-\ adj : seldom
visited or traveled over

un·friend·ly \,ən-'fren-(d)lē, 'ən-\ adj 1
: not friendly or kind : HOSTILE 2 : UN-
FAVORABLE — **un·friend·li·ness** \-'fren-
(d)lē-nəs\ n

un·frock \-'fräk\ vb : to deprive (as a
priest) of the right to exercise the
functions of his office

un·fruit·ful \-'früt-fəl\ adj 1 : not producing fruit or offspring : UNPRODUC-
TIVE 2 : yielding no desired or valuable result (~ efforts) —
un·fruit·ful·ness n

un·furl \-'fərl\ vb : to loose from a
furled state : UNFOLD

un·gain·ly \-'gān-lē\ adj [un- + gainly
graceful, fr. gain direct, handy, fr.
ME geyn, fr. OE gēn, fr. ON gegn]
: CLUMSY, AWKWARD — **un·gain·li·ness**
\-lē-nəs\ n

un·gen·er·ous \,ən-'jen-(ə-)rəs, 'ən-\ adj
: not generous or liberal : STINGY

un·gird \-'gərd\ vb : to divest of a restraining band or girdle : UNBIND

un·glued \,ən-'glüd\ adj : UPSET, DIS-
ORDERED

un·god·ly \,ən-'gäd-lē, -'gȯd-; 'ən-\ adj
1 : IMPIOUS, IRRELIGIOUS 2 : SINFUL,
WICKED 3 : OUTRAGEOUS — **un·god·li-
ness** \-lē-nəs\ n

un·gov·ern·able \,ən-'gəv-ər-nə-bəl\
adj : not capable of being governed, guided, or restrained : UNRULY

un·gra·cious \-'grā-shəs\ adj 1 : not
courteous : RUDE 2 : not pleasing
: DISAGREEABLE

un·grate·ful \,ən-'grāt-fəl, 'ən-\ adj 1
: not thankful for favors 2 : not pleasing — **un·grate·ful·ly** \-ē\ adv — **un-
grate·ful·ness** n

un·guard·ed \-'gärd-əd\ adj 1 : UNPRO-
TECTED 2 : DIRECT, INCAUTIOUS

un·guent \'əŋ-gwənt, 'ən-\ n : a soothing or healing salve : OINTMENT

¹**un·gu·late** \'əŋ-gyə-lət, 'ən-, -,lāt\ adj
[LL ungulatus, fr. L ungula hoof, fr.
unguis nail, hoof] : having hoofs

²**ungulate** n : a hoofed mammal (as a
cow, horse, or rhinoceros)

Unh symbol unnilhexium

un·hal·lowed \,ən-'hal-ōd, 'ən-\ adj 1
: not consecrated : UNHOLY 2 : IMPI-
OUS, PROFANE 3 : contrary to accepted
standards : IMMORAL

un·hand \,ən-'hand\ vb : to remove the
hand from : let go

un·hand·some \-'han-səm\ adj 1 : not
beautiful or handsome : HOMELY 2
: UNBECOMING 3 : DISCOURTEOUS, RUDE

un·handy \-'han-dē\ adj : INCONVEN-
IENT; also : AWKWARD

un·hap·py \-'hap-ē\ adj 1 : UNLUCKY,
UNFORTUNATE 2 : SAD, MISERABLE 3
: INAPPROPRIATE — **un·hap·pi·ly** \-'hap-
ə-lē\ adv — **un·hap·pi·ness** \-ē-nəs\ n

un·har·ness \-'här-nəs\ vb : to remove
the harness from (as a horse)

un·healthy \-'hel-thē\ adj 1 : not conducive to health : UNWHOLESOME 2
: SICKLY, DISEASED

un·heard \-ˈhərd\ adj 1 : not heard 2 : not granted a hearing

un·heard-of \-ˌəv, -ˌäv\ adj : previously unknown : UNPRECEDENTED

un·hinge \ˌən-ˈhinj, ˈən-\ vb 1 : to take from the hinges 2 : to make unstable (as one's mind)

un·hitch \-ˈhich\ vb : UNFASTEN, LOOSE

un·ho·ly \-ˈhō-lē\ adj : not holy : PROFANE, WICKED — **un·ho·li·ness** \-lē-nəs\ n

un·hook \-ˈhu̇k\ vb : to loose from a hook

un·horse \-ˈhȯrs\ vb : to dislodge from or as if from a horse : UNSEAT

uni·ax·i·al \ˌyü-nē-ˈak-sē-əl\ adj : having only one axis

uni·cam·er·al \ˌyü-ni-kam-(ə-)rəl\ adj : having a single legislative house or chamber

UNI·CEF \ˈyü-nə-ˌsef\ abbr [United Nations International Children's Emergency Fund, its former name] United Nations Children's Fund

uni·cel·lu·lar \ˌyü-ni-ˈsel-yə-lər\ adj : of or having a single cell

uni·corn \ˈyü-nə-ˌkȯrn\ n [ME unicorne, fr. OF, fr. LL unicornis, fr. L, having one horn, fr. unus one + cornu horn] : a mythical animal with one horn in the middle of the forehead

uni·cy·cle \ˈyü-ni-ˌsī-kəl\ n : a vehicle that has a single wheel and is usu. propelled by pedals

uni·di·rec·tion·al \ˌyü-ni-də-ˈreksh(ə-)nəl, -dī-\ adj : having, moving in, or responsive in a single direction ⟨a ~ current⟩ ⟨a ~ microphone⟩

uni·fi·ca·tion \ˌyü-nə-fə-ˈkā-shən\ n : the act, process, or result of unifying : the state of being unified

¹**uni·form** \ˈyü-nə-ˌfȯrm\ adj 1 : having always the same form, manner, or degree : not varying 2 : of the same form with others : conforming to one rule — **uni·form·ly** adv

²**uniform** vb : to clothe with a uniform

³**uniform** n : distinctive dress worn by members of a particular group (as an army or a police force)

uni·for·mi·ty \ˌyü-nə-ˈfȯr-mət-ē\ n, pl **-ties** : the state of being uniform

uni·fy \ˈyü-nə-ˌfī\ vb **-fied; -fy·ing** : to make into a unit or a coherent whole : UNITE

uni·lat·er·al \ˌyü-nə-ˈlat-(ə-)rəl\ adj : of, having, affecting, or done by one side only — **uni·lat·er·al·ly** \-ē-\ adv

un·im·peach·able \ˌən-im-ˈpē-chə-bəl\ adj : exempt from liability to accusation : BLAMELESS; also : not doubtable ⟨an ~ authority⟩

un·in·hib·it·ed \ˌən-in-ˈhib-ət-əd\ adj : free from inhibition; also : boisterously informal — **un·in·hib·it·ed·ly** adv

un·in·tel·li·gent \-ˈtel-ə-jənt\ adj : lacking intelligence

un·in·tel·li·gi·ble \-jə-bəl\ adj : not intelligible : OBSCURE — **un·in·tel·li·gi·bly** \-blē\ adv

un·in·ten·tion·al \ˌən-in-ˈtench-(ə-)nəl\ adj : not intentional — **un·in·ten·tion·al·ly** \-ē\ adv

un·in·ter·est·ed \ˌən-ˈin-t(ə-)rəs-təd, -tə-ˌres-, ˈən-\ adj : not interested : not having the mind or feelings engaged or aroused

un·in·ter·rupt·ed \ˌən-ˌint-ə-ˈrəp-təd\ adj : not interrupted : CONTINUOUS

union \ˈyü-nyən\ n 1 : an act or instance of uniting two or more things into one : the state of being so united : COMBINATION, JUNCTION 2 : a uniting in marriage 3 : something formed by a combining of parts or members; esp : a confederation of independent individuals (as nations or persons) for some common purpose 4 : an organization of workers (as a labor union or a trade union) formed to advance its members' interests esp. in respect to wages and working conditions 5 : a device emblematic of union used on or as a national flag; also : the upper inner corner of a flag 6 : a device for connecting parts (as of a machine); esp : a coupling for pipes

union·ism \ˈyü-nyə-ˌniz-əm\ n 1 : the principle or policy of forming or adhering to a union; esp, cap : adherence to the policy of a firm federal union prior to or during the U.S. Civil War 2 : the principles or system of trade unions — **union·ist** n

union·ize \ˈyü-nyə-ˌnīz\ vb **-ized; -iz·ing** : to form into or cause to join a labor union — **union·iza·tion** \ˌyü-nyən-ə-ˈzā-shən\ n

union jack n 1 : a flag consisting of the part of a national flag that signifies union 2 cap U&J : the national flag of the United Kingdom

unique \yu̇-ˈnēk\ adj 1 : being the only one of its kind : SINGLE, SOLE 2 : very unusual : NOTABLE — **unique·ly** adv — **unique·ness** n

uni·sex \ˈyü-nə-ˌseks\ adj : not distinguishable as male or female; also : suitable or designed for both males or females — **unisex** n

uni·sex·u·al \ˌyü-nə-ˈsek-sh(ə-w)əl\ adj 1 : having only male or only female sex organs 2 : UNISEX

uni·son \ˈyü-nə-sən, -nə-zən\ n [MF, fr. ML unisonus having the same sound, fr. L unus one + sonus sound] 1 : sameness or identity in musical pitch 2 : the condition of being tuned or sounded at the same pitch or at an octave ⟨sing in ~ rather than in harmony⟩ 3 : harmonious agreement or union : ACCORD

unit \ˈyü-nət\ n 1 : the least whole number : ONE 2 : a definite amount or quantity used as a standard of measurement 3 : a single thing or person or group that is a constituent of a whole; also : a part of a military establishment that has a prescribed organization — **unit** adj

Uni·tar·i·an \ˌyü-nə-ˈter-ē-ən\ n : a member of a religious denomination stressing individual freedom of belief — **Uni·tar·i·an·ism** n

uni·tary \'yü-nə-ˌter-ē\ adj 1 : of or relating to a unit : characterized by unity 2 : not divided — **uni·tar·i·ly** \ˌyü-nə-'ter-ə-lē\ adv

unite \yu̇-'nīt\ vb **unit·ed; unit·ing** 1 : to put or join together so as to make one : COMBINE, COALESCE 2 : to join by a legal or moral bond (as nations by treaty); also : to join in interest or fellowship 3 : AMALGAMATE, CONSOLIDATE 4 : to join in an act

unit·ed \yu̇-'nit-əd\ adj 1 : made one : COMBINED 2 : relating to or produced by joint action 3 : being in agreement : HARMONIOUS

unit·ize \'yü-nət-ˌīz\ vb **-ized; -iz·ing** 1 : to form or convert into a unit 2 : to divide into units

uni·ty \'yü-nət-ē\ n, pl **-ties** 1 : the quality or state of being one : ONENESS, SINGLENESS 2 : a definite quantity or combination of quantities taken as one or for which 1 is made to stand in calculation 3 : CONCORD, ACCORD, HARMONY 4 : continuity without change (∼ of purpose) 5 : reference of all the parts of a literary or artistic composition to a single main idea 6 : totality of related parts **syn** solidarity, union, integrity

univ abbr 1 universal 2 university

uni·va·lent \ˌyü-ni-'vā-lənt\ adj : having a valence of one

uni·valve \'yü-ni-ˌvalv\ n : a mollusk (as a snail or whelk) having a shell with one valve — **univalve** adj

uni·ver·sal \ˌyü-nə-'vər-səl\ adj 1 : including, covering, or affecting the whole without limit or exception : UNLIMITED, GENERAL (a ∼ rule) 2 : present or occurring everywhere 3 : used or for use among all (a ∼ language) — **uni·ver·sal·ly** \-ē\ adv

Uni·ver·sal·ist \ˌyü-nə-'vər-s(ə-)ləst\ n : a member of a religious denomination now united with Unitarians that upholds the belief that all men will be saved

uni·ver·sal·i·ty \-vər-'sal-ət-ē\ n : the quality or state of being universal

uni·ver·sal·ize \-'vər-sə-ˌlīz\ vb **-ized; -iz·ing** : to make universal : GENERALIZE — **uni·ver·sal·iza·tion** \-ˌvər-sə-lə-'zā-shən\ n

universal joint n : a shaft coupling for transmitting rotation from one shaft to another not in a straight line with it

Universal Product Code n : a bar code that identifies a product's type and price for entry into a computer or cash register (as at a supermarket checkout)

uni·verse \'yü-nə-ˌvərs\ n [L universum, fr. neut. of universus entire, whole, fr. unus one + versus turned toward, fr. pp. of vertere to turn] : all created things and phenomena viewed as constituting one system or whole

uni·ver·si·ty \ˌyü-nə-'vər-s(ə-)tē\ n, pl **-ties** : an institution of higher learning authorized to confer degrees in various special fields (as theology, law, and medicine) as well as in the arts and sciences generally

un·just \ˌən-'jəst, 'ən-\ adj : characterized by injustice — **un·just·ly** adv

un·kempt \-'kempt\ adj 1 : ROUGH, UNPOLISHED 2 : not combed : DISHEVELED

un·kind \-'kīnd\ adj : wanting in kindness or sympathy : CRUEL, HARSH — **un·kind·ly** \-'kīn-(d)lē\ adv — **un·kind·ness** \-'kīn(d)-nəs\ n

un·kind·ly \-'kīn-(d)lē\ adj : UNKIND — **un·kind·li·ness** n

un·know·ing \ˌən-'nō-iŋ, 'ən-\ adj : not knowing : IGNORANT — **un·know·ing·ly** adv

un·known \-'nōn\ adj : not known : UNFAMILIAR; also : not ascertained — **unknown** n

un·lace \ˌən-'lās, 'ən-\ vb : to loose by undoing a lace

un·lade \-'lād\ vb **-lad·ed; -lad·ed** or **-lad·en** \-'lād-ᵊn\ ; **-lad·ing** : to take the load or cargo from : UNLOAD

un·latch \-'lach\ vb 1 : to open or loose by lifting the latch 2 : to become loosed or opened

un·law·ful \ˌən-'lȯ-fəl, 'ən-\ adj 1 : not lawful : ILLEGAL 2 : ILLEGITIMATE — **un·law·ful·ly** \-ē\ adv

un·lead·ed \-'led-əd\ adj : not treated or mixed with lead or lead compounds

un·learn \-'lərn\ vb : to put out of one's knowledge or memory

un·learned \-'lər-nəd for 1, 2; -'lərnd for 3\ adj 1 : UNEDUCATED, ILLITERATE 2 : not learned by study : not known for 3 : not learned by previous experience

un·leash \-'lēsh\ vb : to free from or as if from a leash

un·less \ən-ˌles, ˌən-\ conj : except on condition that (won't go ∼ you do)

un·let·tered \ˌən-'let-ərd, 'ən-\ adj : not educated : ILLITERATE

¹**un·like** \-'līk\ adj 1 : not like : DISSIMILAR, DIFFERENT 2 : UNEQUAL — **un·like·ness** n

²**unlike** prep 1 : different from (he's quite ∼ his brother) 2 : unusual for (it's ∼ him to be late) 3 : differently from (behaves ∼ his brother)

un·like·li·hood \ˌən-'lī-klē-ˌhùd, 'ən-\ n : IMPROBABILITY

un·like·ly \-'lī-klē\ adj 1 : not likely : IMPROBABLE 2 : likely to fail

un·lim·ber \ˌən-'lim-bər, 'ən-\ vb : to get ready for action

un·list·ed \ˌən-'lis-təd, 'ən-\ adj 1 : not appearing on a list; esp : not appearing in a telephone book 2 : being or involving a security not listed formally on an organized exchange

un·load \-'lōd\ vb 1 : to take away or off : REMOVE (∼ cargo from a hold); also : to get rid of 2 : to take a load from; also : to relieve or set free : UNBURDEN (∼ one's mind of worries) 3

: to get rid of or be relieved of a burden 4 : to sell in volume

un·lock \-'läk\ *vb* 1 : to unfasten through release of a lock 2 : RELEASE (~ed her emotions) 3 : DISCLOSE, REVEAL

un·looked-for \-'lùkt-fòr\ *adj* : UNEXPECTED

un·loose \,ən-'lüs\ *vb* : to relax the strain of : set free; *also* : UNTIE

un·loos·en \-'lüs-ᵊn\ *vb* : UNLOOSE

un·love·ly \-'ləv-lē\ *adj* : having no charm or appeal : not amiable

un·lucky \-'lək-ē\ *adj* 1 : UNFORTUNATE, ILL-FATED 2 : likely to bring misfortune : INAUSPICIOUS 3 : REGRETTABLE — **un·luck·i·ly** \-'lək-ə-lē\ *adv*

un·man \,ən-'man, 'ən-\ *vb* 1 : to deprive of manly courage 2 : CASTRATE

un·man·ly \-'man-lē\ *adj* : not manly : COWARDLY; *also* : EFFEMINATE

un·man·ner·ly \-'man-ər-lē\ *adj* : RUDE, IMPOLITE — **unmannerly** *adv*

un·mask \,ən-'mask\ *vb* 1 : to strip of a mask or a disguise : EXPOSE 2 : to remove one's own disguise (as at a masquerade)

un·mean·ing \-'mē-niŋ\ *adj* : having no meaning : SENSELESS

un·meet \-'mēt\ *adj* : not meet or fit : UNSUITABLE, IMPROPER

un·men·tion·able \-'mench-(ə-)nə-bəl\ *adj* : not fit or proper to be talked about

un·mer·ci·ful \-'mər-si-fəl\ *adj* : not merciful : CRUEL, MERCILESS — **un·mer·ci·ful·ly** \-ē\ *adv*

un·mind·ful \-'mīnd-fəl\ *adj* : not mindful : CARELESS, UNAWARE

un·mis·tak·able \,ən-mə-'stā-kə-bəl\ *adj* : not capable of being mistaken or misunderstood : CLEAR, OBVIOUS — **un·mis·tak·ably** \-blē\ *adv*

un·mit·i·gat·ed \,ən-'mit-ə-,gāt-əd, '-ən-\ *adj* 1 : not softened or lessened 2 : ABSOLUTE, DOWNRIGHT (an ~ liar)

un·moor \-'mùr\ *vb* 1 : to loose from or as if from moorings 2 : to cast off moorings

un·mor·al \-'mòr-əl\ *adj* : having no moral perception or quality : being neither moral nor immoral — **un·mo·ral·i·ty** \,ən-mə-'ral-ət-ē\ *n*

un·muz·zle \-'məz-əl\ *vb* : to remove a muzzle from

un·nat·u·ral \,ən-'nach-(ə-)rəl, 'ən-\ *adj* : contrary to or acting contrary to nature or natural instincts : ARTIFICIAL, IRREGULAR; *also* : ABNORMAL — **un·nat·u·ral·ly** \-ē\ *adv* — **un·nat·u·ral·ness** *n*

un·nec·es·sar·i·ly \,ən-,nes-ə-'ser-ə-lē\ *adv* 1 : not by necessity (spent more money ~) 2 : to an unnecessary degree (~ harsh)

un·nerve \,ən-'nərv, 'ən-\ *vb* : to deprive of nerve, courage, or self-control

un·nil·hex·i·um \,yün-ᵊl-'hek-sē-əm\ *n* ~ *unnil-* (fr. L *unus* one + *nil* zero) ~·ix + NL -*ium*\ : the

chemical element of atomic number 106

un·nil·pen·ti·um \-'pent-ē-əm\ *n* : the chemical element of atomic number 105

un·nil·qua·di·um \-'kwäd-ē-əm\ *n* : the chemical element of atomic number 104

un·num·bered \-'nəm-bərd\ *adj* : not numbered or counted : INNUMERABLE

un·ob·tru·sive \,ən-əb-'trü-siv\ *adj* : not obtrusive or forward : not bold : INCONSPICUOUS — **un·ob·tru·sive·ly** *adv*

un·oc·cu·pied \,ən-'äk-yə-,pīd, 'ən-\ *adj* 1 : not busy : UNEMPLOYED 2 : not occupied : EMPTY, VACANT

un·or·ga·nized \-'òr-gə-,nīzd\ *adj* 1 : not formed or brought into an integrated or ordered whole 2 : not organized into unions (~ labor)

unp *abbr* unpaged

Unp *symbol* unnilpentium

un·pack \,ən-'pak, 'ən-\ *vb* 1 : to separate and remove things packed 2 : to open and remove the contents of

un·par·al·leled \,ən-'par-ə-,leld\ *adj* : having no parallel; *esp* : having no equal or match

un·par·lia·men·ta·ry \,ən-,pär-lə-'ment-ə-rē, -,pärl-yə-, -'men-trē\ *adj* : contrary to parliamentary practice

un·peg \,ən-'peg, 'ən-\ *vb* : to remove a peg from : UNFASTEN

un·per·son \'ən-,pərs-ᵊn, -,pərs-\ *n* : a person who usu. for political or ideological reasons is removed from recognition, consideration, or memory

un·pile \,ən-'pīl, 'ən-\ *vb* : to take or disentangle from a pile

un·pin \-'pin\ *vb* : to remove a pin from : UNFASTEN

un·pleas·ant \-'plez-ᵊnt\ *adj* : not pleasant : DISAGREEABLE — **un·pleas·ant·ly** *adv* — **un·pleas·ant·ness** *n*

un·plug \,ən-'pləg, 'ən-\ *vb* 1 : UNCLOG 2 : to remove (a plug) from a receptacle; *also* : to disconnect from an electric circuit by removing a plug

un·plumbed \-'pləmd\ *adj* 1 : not tested or measured with a plumb line 2 : not thoroughly explored

un·pop·u·lar \,ən-'päp-yə-lər, 'ən-\ *adj* : not popular : looked upon or received unfavorably — **un·pop·u·lar·i·ty** \,ən-,päp-yə-'lar-ət-ē\ *n*

un·prec·e·dent·ed \,ən-'pres-ə-,dent-əd, 'ən-\ *adj* : having no precedent : NOVEL, NEW

un·pre·ten·tious \,ən-pri-'ten-chəs\ *adj* : not pretentious or pompous : MODEST (~ homes)

un·prin·ci·pled \,ən-'prin-sə-pəld, 'ən-\ *adj* : lacking sound or honorable principles : UNSCRUPULOUS

un·print·able \-'print-ə-bəl\ *adj* : unfit to be printed

un·prof·it·able \,ən-'präf-ət-ə-bəl, 'ən-, -'präf-tə-bəl\ *adj* : not profitable : USELESS, VAIN

Unq *symbol* unnilquadium

un·qual·i·fied \ˌən-ˈkwäl-ə-ˌfīd, ˈən-\ *adj* **1** : not having requisite qualifications **2** : not modified or restricted by reservations — **un·qual·i·fied·ly** \-ˌfī-(ə)d-lē\ *adv*

un·ques·tion·able \-ˈkwes-chə-nə-bəl\ *adj* **1** : acknowledged as beyond doubt **2** : INDISPUTABLE — **un·question·ably** \-blē\ *adv*

un·ques·tion·ing \-chə-niŋ\ *adj* : not questioning : accepting without examination or hesitation — **un·question·ing·ly** *adv*

un·qui·et \-ˈkwī-ət\ *adj* **1** : not quiet : AGITATED, DISTURBED **2** : physically, emotionally, or mentally restless : UNEASY

un·quote \ˈən-ˌkwōt\ *n* — used orally to indicate the end of a direct quotation

un·rav·el \ˌən-ˈrav-əl, ˈən-\ *vb* **1** : to separate the threads of **2** : SOLVE ⟨~ a mystery⟩ **3** : to become unraveled

un·read \-ˈred\ *adj* **1** : not read **2** : not well informed through reading **3** : UNEDUCATED

un·re·al \-ˈrē(-ə)l\ *adj* : lacking in reality, substance, or genuineness — **un·re·al·i·ty** \ˌən-rē-ˈal-ət-ē\ *n*

un·rea·son·able \-ˈrēz-(ə-)nə-bəl\ *adj* **1** : not governed by or acting according to reason; *also* : not conformable to reason : ABSURD **2** : exceeding the bounds of reason or moderation — **un·rea·son·able·ness** *n* — **un·rea·son·ably** *adv*

un·rea·soned \-ˈrēz-ᵊnd\ *adj* : not based on reason or reasoning

un·rea·son·ing \-ˈrēz-(ᵊ-)niŋ\ *adj* : not using or showing the use of reason as a guide or control

un·re·con·struct·ed \ˌən-ˌrē-kən-ˈstrək-təd\ *adj* : not reconciled to some political, economic, or social change; *esp* : holding stubbornly to principles, beliefs, or views that are or are held to be outmoded

un·reel \ˌən-ˈrēl, ˈən-\ *vb* **1** : to unwind from or as if from a reel **2** : perform successfully

un·re·gen·er·ate \ˌən-ri-ˈjen-(ə-)rət\ *adj* : not regenerated or reformed

un·re·lent·ing \-ˈlent-iŋ\ *adj* **1** : not yielding in determination : STERN ⟨~ leader⟩ **2** : not letting up or weakening in vigor or pace : CONSTANT — **un·re·lent·ing·ly** *adv*

un·re·mit·ting \-ˈmit-iŋ\ *adj* : CONTINUOUS, INCESSANT, PERSEVERING — **un·re·mit·ting·ly** *adv*

un·re·served \-ˈzərvd\ *adj* **1** : not limited or partial : ENTIRE, UNQUALIFIED ⟨~ enthusiasm⟩ **2** : not cautious or reticent : FRANK, OPEN **3** : not set aside for special use — **un·re·serv·ed·ly** \-ˈzər-vəd-lē\ *adv*

un·rest \ˌən-ˈrest, ˈən-\ *n* : a disturbed or uneasy state : TURMOIL

un·re·strained \ˌən-ri-ˈstrānd\ *adj* **1** : IMMODERATE, UNCONTROLLED **2** : SPONTANEOUS

un·re·straint \-ri-ˈstrānt\ *n* : lack of restraint

un·rid·dle \ˌən-ˈrid-ᵊl, ˈən-\ *vb* : to read the riddle of : SOLVE

un·righ·teous \-ˈrī-chəs\ *adj* **1** : SINFUL, WICKED **2** : UNJUST — **un·righ·teous·ness** *n*

un·ripe \-ˈrīp\ *adj* : not ripe : IMMATURE

un·ri·valed *or* **un·ri·valled** \ˌən-ˈrī-vəld, ˈən-\ *adj* : having no rival : INCOMPARABLE

un·robe \-ˈrōb\ *vb* : DISROBE, UNDRESS

un·roll \-ˈrōl\ *vb* **1** : to unwind a roll of : open out **2** : DISPLAY, DISCLOSE **3** : to become unrolled or spread out

un·roof \-ˈrüf, -ˈrüf\ *vb* : to strip off the roof or covering of

un·ruf·fled \ˌən-ˈrəf-əld, ˈən-\ *adj* **1** : not agitated or upset **2** : not ruffled : SMOOTH ⟨~ water⟩

un·ruly \-ˈrü-lē\ *adj* [ME *unreuly*, fr. *un-* + *reuly* disciplined, fr. *reule* rule, fr. OF, fr. L *regula* straightedge, rule, fr. *regere* to lead straight] : not submissive to rule or restraint : TURBULENT ⟨~ passions⟩ — **un·rul·i·ness** \-ˈrü-lē-nəs\ *n*

UNRWA *abbr* United Nations Relief and Works Agency

un·sad·dle \ˌən-ˈsad-ᵊl, ˈən-\ *vb* **1** : to remove the saddle from a horse **2** : UNHORSE

un·sat·u·rat·ed \-ˈsach-ə-ˌrāt-əd\ *adj* **1** : capable of absorbing or dissolving more of something **2** : containing double or triple bonds between carbon atoms ⟨~ fats or oils⟩ — **un·sat·u·rate** \-rət\ *n*

un·saved \ˌən-ˈsāvd, ˈən-\ *adj* : not saved; *esp* : not rescued from eternal punishment

un·sa·vory \-ˈsāv-(ə-)rē\ *adj* **1** : TASTELESS **2** : unpleasant to taste or smell **3** : morally offensive

un·say \-ˈsā, vb -said \-ˈsed\ : -say·ing \-ˈsā-iŋ\ : to take back (something said) : RETRACT, WITHDRAW

un·scathed \-ˈskāthd\ *adj* : wholly unharmed : not injured

un·schooled \-ˈsküld\ *adj* : not schooled : UNTAUGHT, UNTRAINED

un·sci·en·tif·ic \ˌən-ˌsī-ən-ˈtif-ik\ *adj* : not scientific : not in accord with the principles and methods of science

un·scram·ble \ˌən-ˈskram-bəl, ˈən-\ *vb* **1** : RESOLVE, CLARIFY **2** : to restore (as a radio message) to intelligible form

un·screw \-ˈskrü\ *vb* **1** : to draw the screws from **2** : to loosen by turning

un·scru·pu·lous \-ˈskrü-pyə-ləs\ *adj* : not scrupulous : UNPRINCIPLED — **un·scru·pu·lous·ly** *adv* — **un·scru·pu·lous·ness** *n*

un·seal \-ˈsēl\ *vb* : to break or remove the seal of : OPEN

un·search·able \-ˈsər-chə-bəl\ *adj* : not capable of being searched or explored

un·sea·son·able \-ˈsēz-(ᵊ-)nə-bəl\ *adj* : not seasonable : happening or coming at the wrong time : UNTIMELY — **un·sea·son·ably** \-blē\ *adv*

un·seat \-'sēt\ vb **1** : to throw from one's seat esp. on horseback **2** : to remove from political office

un·seem·ly \-'sēm-lē\ adj : not according with established standards of good form or taste; also : not suitable — **un·seem·li·ness** n

un·seen \,ən-'sēn, 'ən-\ adj : not seen : INVISIBLE

un·seg·re·gat·ed \-'seg-ri-ˌgāt-əd\ adj : not segregated; esp : free from racial segregation

un·self·ish \-'sel-fish\ adj : not selfish : GENEROUS — **un·self·ish·ly** adv — **un·self·ish·ness** n

un·set·tle \,ən-'set-ᵊl, 'ən-\ vb : to move or loosen from a settled position : DISPLACE, DISTURB

un·set·tled \-'set-ᵊld\ adj **1** : not settled : not fixed (as in position or character) **2** : not calm : DISTURBED **3** : not decided in mind : UNDETERMINED **4** : not paid (~ accounts) **5** : not occupied by settlers

un·shack·le \-'shak-əl\ vb : to free from shackles

un·shaped \-'shāpt\ adj : not shaped : RUDE (~ ideas) (~ timber)

un·sheathe \,ən-'shēth, 'ən-\ vb : to draw from or as if from a sheath

un·ship \-'ship\ vb **1** : to remove from a ship **2** : to remove or become removed from position (~ an oar)

un·shod \,ən-'shäd, 'ən-\ adj : not shod : not wearing shoes

un·sight·ly \,ən-'sīt-lē, 'ən-\ adj : unpleasant to the sight : UGLY

un·skilled \-'skild\ adj **1** : not skilled; esp : not skilled in a specified branch of work **2** : not requiring skill (~ labor)

un·skill·ful \-'skil-fəl\ adj : lacking in skill or proficiency — **un·skill·ful·ly** \-ē\ adv

un·sling \-'sliŋ\ vb **-slung** \-'sləŋ\ ; **-sling·ing** \-'sliŋ-iŋ\ **1** : to remove from being slung **2** : to take off the slings of esp. aboard ship

un·snap \-'snap\ vb : to loosen or free by or as if by undoing a snap

un·snarl \-'snärl\ vb : to remove snarls from : UNTANGLE

un·so·phis·ti·cat·ed \,ən-sə-'fis-tə-ˌkāt-əd\ adj **1** : not worldly-wise : lacking sophistication **2** : SIMPLE

un·sought \,ən-'sot, 'ən-\ adj : not sought : not searched for or asked for : not obtained by effort

un·sound \-'saůnd\ adj **1** : not healthy or whole; also : not mentally normal **2** : not valid **3** : not firmly made or fixed — **un·sound·ly** adv — **un·sound·ness** n

un·spar·ing \-'spa(ə)r-iŋ\ adj **1** : HARD, RUTHLESS **2** : not frugal : LIBERAL, PROFUSE

un·speak·able \-'spē-kə-bəl\ adj **1** : impossible to express in words **2** : extremely bad — **un·speak·ably** \-blē\

...-əd adj : free from

spot or stain; esp : free from moral stain

un·sprung \-'sprəŋ\ adj : not sprung; esp : not equipped with springs

un·sta·ble \-'stā-bəl\ adj **1** : not stable **2** : FICKLE, VACILLATING; also : having defective emotional control **3** : readily changing (as by decomposing) in chemical or physical composition or in biological activity (an ~ atomic nucleus)

un·steady \,ən-'sted-ē\ adj : not steady : UNSTABLE — **un·steadi·ly** \-'sted-ᵊl-ē\ adv — **un·steadi·ness** \-'sted-ē-nəs\ n

un·stint·ing \-'stint-iŋ\ adj : giving or being given freely or generously (~ praise)

un·stop \-'stäp\ vb **1** : UNCLOG **2** : to remove a stopper from

un·strap \-'strap\ vb : to remove or loose a strap from

un·stressed \,ən-'strest, 'ən-\ adj : not stressed; esp : not bearing a stress or accent

un·strung \-'strəŋ\ adj **1** : having the strings loose or detached **2** : nervously tired or anxious

un·stud·ied \-'stəd-ēd\ adj **1** : not acquired by study **2** : NATURAL, UNFORCED

un·sub·stan·tial \,ən-səb-'stan-chəl\ adj : INSUBSTANTIAL

un·sung \,ən-'səŋ, 'ən-\ adj **1** : not sung **2** : not celebrated in song or verse (~ heroes)

un·swerv·ing \,ən-'swer-viŋ, 'ən-\ adj **1** : not swerving or turning aside **2** : STEADY

un·tan·gle \-'taŋ-gəl\ vb **1** : DISENTANGLE **2** : to straighten out : RESOLVE (~ a problem)

un·taught \-'tot\ adj **1** : not instructed or taught : IGNORANT **2** : NATURAL, SPONTANEOUS

un·think·able \-'thiŋ-kə-bəl\ adj : not to be thought of or considered as possible : INCREDIBLE

un·think·ing \,ən-'thiŋ-kiŋ, 'ən-\ adj : not thinking; esp : THOUGHTLESS, HEEDLESS — **un·think·ing·ly** adv

un·thought \'ən-'thot\ adj : not anticipated : UNEXPECTED (unthought-of development)

un·tie \-'tī\ vb **-tied; -ty·ing** or **-tie·ing 1** : to free from something that ties, fastens, or restrains : UNBIND **2** : DISENTANGLE, RESOLVE **3** : to become loosened or unbound

un·til \(ˌ)ən-ˌtil\ prep : up to the time of (worked ~ 5 o'clock)

²until conj **1** : up to the time that (wait ~ he calls) **2** : to the point or degree that (ran ~ he was breathless)

un·time·ly \,ən-'tīm-lē, 'ən-\ adv : at an inopportune time : UNSEASONABLY; also : PREMATURELY

²untimely adj : PREMATURE (~ death) ; also : INOPPORTUNE, UNSEASONABLE

un·tir·ing \,ən-'tī-riŋ\ adj : not becoming tired : INDEFATIGABLE — **un·tir·ing·ly** adv

un·to \ˌən-tə, ˈən-(ˌ)tü\ *prep* : TO

un·told \ˌən-ˈtōld, ˈən-\ *adj* **1** : not counted : VAST, NUMBERLESS **2** : not told : not revealed

¹un·touch·able \ˌən-ˈtəch-ə-bəl, ˈən-\ *adj* : forbidden to the touch

²untouchable *n* : a member of the lowest social class in India having in traditional Hindu belief the quality of defiling by contact a member of a higher caste

un·to·ward \ˈən-ˈtō(-ə)rd\ *adj* **1** : difficult to manage : STUBBORN, WILLFUL ⟨an ～ child⟩ **2** : INCONVENIENT, TROUBLESOME ⟨an ～ encounter⟩

un·tried \ˌən-ˈtrīd, ˈən-\ *adj* : not tested or proved by experience or trial; *also* : not tried in court

un·true \-ˈtrü\ *adj* **1** : not faithful : DISLOYAL **2** : not according with a standard of correctness **3** : FALSE

un·truth \ˌən-ˈtrüth, ˈən-\ *n* **1** : lack of truthfulness **2** : FALSEHOOD

un·tune \-ˈt(y)ün\ *vb* **1** : to put out of tune **2** : DISARRANGE, DISCOMPOSE

un·tu·tored \-ˈt(y)üt-ərd\ *adj* : UNTAUGHT, UNLEARNED, IGNORANT

un·twine \-ˈtwīn\ *vb* : UNWIND, DISENTANGLE

un·twist \ˌən-ˈtwist, ˈən-\ *vb* **1** : to separate the twisted parts of : UNTWINE **2** : to become untwined

un·used \-ˈyüst, ˈyüzd *for 1;* -ˈyüzd *for 2*\ *adj* **1** : UNACCUSTOMED **2** : not used

un·usu·al \-ˈyü-zhə(-wə)l\ *adj* : not usual : UNCOMMON, RARE — **un·usu·al·ly** \-ē\ *adv*

un·ut·ter·able \ˌən-ˈət-ə-rə-bəl, ˈən-\ *adj* : being beyond the powers of description : INEXPRESSIBLE — **un·ut·ter·ably** \-blē\ *adv*

un·var·nished \-ˈvär-nisht\ *adj* **1** : not varnished **2** : not embellished : PLAIN ⟨the ～ truth⟩

un·veil \ˌən-ˈvāl, ˈən-\ *vb* **1** : to remove a veil or covering from : DISCLOSE **2** : to remove a veil : reveal oneself

un·voiced \-ˈvȯist\ *adj* **1** : not verbally expressed : UNSPOKEN **2** : VOICELESS

un·war·rant·able \ˌən-ˈwȯr-ənt-ə-bəl\ *adj* : not justifiable : INEXCUSABLE — **un·war·rant·ably** \-blē\ *adv*

un·weave \-ˈwēv\ *vb* **-wove** \-ˈwōv\; **-wo·ven** \-ˈwō-vən\; **-weav·ing** : DISENTANGLE, RAVEL

un·well \ˌən-ˈwəl, ˈən-\ *adj* **1** : SICK, AILING **2** : MENSTRUATING

un·whole·some \-ˈhōl-səm\ *adj* **1** : harmful to physical, mental, or moral well-being **2** : CORRUPT, UNSOUND; *also* : offensive to the senses : LOATHSOME

un·wieldy \-ˈwēl-dē\ *adj* : not easily managed or handled because of size or weight : AWKWARD ⟨an ～ tool⟩

un·will·ing \-ˈwil-iŋ\ *adj* : not willing — **un·will·ing·ly** *adv* — **un·will·ing·ness** *n*

un·wind \-ˈwīnd\ *vb* **-wound** \-ˈwaůnd\; **-wind·ing 1** : to undo something that is wound : loose from coils **2** : to be-come unwound : be capable of being unwound **3** : RELAX

un·wise \ˌən-ˈwīz, ˈən-\ *adj* : not wise : FOOLISH — **un·wise·ly** *adv*

un·wit·ting \-ˈwit-iŋ\ *adj* **1** : not intended : INADVERTENT ⟨～ mistake⟩ **2** : not knowing : UNAWARE — **un·wit·ting·ly** *adv*

un·wont·ed \-ˈwȯnt-əd, -ˈwōnt-, -ˈwənt-\ *adj* **1** : RARE, UNUSUAL **2** : not accustomed by experience — **un·wont·ed·ly** *adv*

un·world·ly \-ˈwərl-(d)lē\ *adj* **1** : not of this world; *esp* : SPIRITUAL **2** : NAIVE **3** : not swayed by worldly considerations — **un·world·li·ness** \-ˈwərl-(d)lē-nəs\ *n*

un·wor·thy \ˌən-ˈwər-thē, ˈən-\ *adj* **1** : BASE, DISHONORABLE **2** : not meritorious : not worthy : UNDESERVING **3** : not deserved : UNMERITED ⟨～ treatment⟩ — **un·wor·thi·ly** \-thə-lē\ *adv* — **un·wor·thi·ness** \-thē-nəs\ *n*

un·wrap \-ˈrap\ *vb* : to free from wrappings : DISCLOSE

un·writ·ten \-ˈrit-ᵊn\ *adj* **1** : not in writing : ORAL, TRADITIONAL ⟨an ～ law⟩ **2** : containing no writing : BLANK

un·yield·ing \ˌən-ˈyēl-diŋ, ˈən-\ *adj* **1** : characterized by lack of softness or flexibility **2** : characterized by firmness or obduracy

un·yoke \-ˈyōk\ *vb* : to free from a yoke; *also* : SEPARATE, DISCONNECT

un·zip \-ˈzip\ *vb* : to zip open : open by means of a zipper

¹up \ˈəp\ *adv* **1** : in or to a higher position or level; *esp* : away from the center of the earth **2** : from beneath a surface (as ground or water) **3** : from below the horizon **4** : in or into an upright position; *esp* : out of bed **5** : with greater intensity ⟨speak ～⟩ **6** : in or into a better or more advanced state or a state of greater intensity or activity ⟨stir ～ a fire⟩ **7** : into existence, evidence, or knowledge ⟨the missing book turned ～⟩ **8** : into consideration ⟨brought the matter ～⟩ **9** : to or at bat **10** : into possession or custody ⟨gave himself ～⟩ **11** : ENTIRELY, COMPLETELY ⟨eat it ～⟩ **12** — used for emphasis ⟨clean ～ a room⟩ **13** : ASIDE, BY ⟨lay ～ supplies⟩ **14** : so as to arrive or approach ⟨ran ～ the path⟩ **15** : in a direction opposite to down **16** : in or into parts ⟨tear ～ paper⟩ **17** : to a stop ⟨pull ～ at the curb⟩ **18** : for each side ⟨the score was 15 ～⟩

²up *adj* **1** : risen above the horizon ⟨the sun is ～⟩ **2** : being out of bed ⟨～ by 6 o'clock⟩ **3** : relatively high ⟨prices are ～⟩ **4** : RAISED, LIFTED ⟨windows are ～⟩ **5** : BUILT, CONSTRUCTED ⟨the house is ～⟩ **6** : grown above a surface ⟨the corn is ～⟩ **7** : moving, inclining, or directed upward **8** : marked by agitation, excitement, or activity **9** : READY; *esp* : highly prepared **10** : going on : taking place ⟨find out what is ～⟩ **11** : EXPIRED, ENDED ⟨the time is ～⟩

12 : well informed ⟨~ on the news⟩ 13 : being ahead or in advance of an opponent ⟨one hole ~ in a match⟩ 14 : presented for or being under consideration 15 : charged before a court ⟨~ for robbery⟩

³**up** *prep* **1** : to, toward, or at a higher point of ⟨~ a ladder⟩ **2** : to or toward the source of ⟨~ the river⟩ **3** : to or toward the northern part of ⟨~ the coast⟩ **4** : to or toward the interior of ⟨traveling ~ the country⟩ **5** : ALONG ⟨walk ~ the street⟩

⁴**up** *n* **1** : an upward course or slope **2** : a period or state of prosperity or success ⟨he had his ~s and downs⟩

⁵**up** *vb* **upped** *or* in 2 **up**; **upped**; **up·ping**; **ups** *or* in 2 **up** **1** : to rise from a lying or sitting position **2** : to act abruptly or surprisingly ⟨she *upped* and left home⟩ **3** : to move or cause to move upward : ASCEND ⟨*upped* prices⟩

Upa·ni·shad \ü-'pän-i-,shäd\ *n* : one of a set of Vedic philosophical treatises

¹**up·beat** \'əp-,bēt\ *n* : an unaccented beat in a musical measure; *esp* : the last beat of the measure

²**upbeat** *adj* : OPTIMISTIC, CHEERFUL

up·braid \,əp-'brād\ *vb* : to criticize, reproach, or scold severely

up·bring·ing \'əp-,briŋ-iŋ\ *n* : the process of bringing up and training

UPC *abbr* Universal Product Code

up·chuck \'ə-,chək\ *vb* : VOMIT

up·com·ing \,əp-'kəm-iŋ\ *adj* : FORTHCOMING, APPROACHING

up·coun·try \,əp-'kən-trē\ *adj* : of or relating to the interior of a country or a region — **up-country** \'əp-'kən-\ *adv*

up·date \,əp-'dāt\ *vb* : to bring up to date — **update** \'əp-,dāt\ *n*

up·draft \'əp-,draft, -,dräft\ *n* : an upward movement of gas (as air)

up·end \,əp-'end\ *vb* : to set, stand, or rise on end

up·front \'əp-'frənt\ *adj* **1** : HONEST, CANDID **2** : ADVANCE ⟨~ payment⟩

up front *adv* : in advance ⟨paid *up front*⟩

¹**up·grade** \'əp-,grād\ *n* **1** : an upward grade or slope **2** : INCREASE, RISE

²**up·grade** \'əp-,grād, ,əp-'grād\ *vb* : to raise to a higher grade or position; *esp* : to advance to a job requiring a higher level of skill

up·growth \'əp-,grōth\ *n* : the process or result of growing up : upward growth : DEVELOPMENT

up·heav·al \,əp-'hē-vəl\ *n* **1** : the action or an instance of uplifting esp. of part of the earth's crust **2** : a violent agitation or change

¹**up·hill** \'əp-'hil\ *adv* : upward on a hill or incline; *also* : against difficulties

²**up·hill** \-,hil\ *adj* **1** : situated on elevated ground **2** : ASCENDING **3** : DIFFICULT, LABORIOUS

up·hold \,əp-'hōld\ *vb* **-held** \-'held\; **-hold·ing 1** : to give support to **2** : to support against an opponent **3** : to keep elevated — **up·hold·er** *n*

up·hol·ster \,əp-'hōl-stər\ *vb* **-stered; -ster·ing** \-st(ə-)riŋ\ : to furnish with or as if with upholstery — **up·hol·ster·er** *n*

up·hol·stery \-st(ə-)rē\ *n, pl* **-ster·ies** [ME *upholdester* upholsterer, fr. *upholden* to uphold, fr. *up* + *holden* to hold] : materials (as fabrics, padding, and springs) used to make a soft covering esp. for a seat

UPI *abbr* United Press International

up·keep \'əp-,kēp\ *n* : the act or cost of keeping up or maintaining; *also* : the state of being maintained

up·land \'əp-lənd, -,land\ *n* : high land esp. at some distance from the sea — **upland** *adj*

¹**up·lift** \,əp-'lift\ *vb* **1** : to lift or raise up : ELEVATE **2** : to improve the condition of esp. morally, socially, or intellectually

²**up·lift** \'əp-,lift\ *n* **1** : a lifting up; *esp* : an upheaval of the earth's surface **2** : moral or social improvement; *also* : a movement to make such improvement

up·mar·ket \,əp-'mär-kət\ *adj* : appealing to wealthy consumers

up·most \'əp-,mōst\ *adj* : UPPERMOST

up·on \ə-'pon, -'pän\ *prep* : ON

¹**up·per** \'əp-ər\ *adj* **1** : higher in physical position, rank, or order **2** : constituting the smaller and more restricted branch of a bicameral legislature **3** *cap* : being a later part or formation of a specific geological period **4** : being toward the interior ⟨the ~ Amazon⟩ **5** : NORTHERN ⟨~ New York State⟩

²**upper** *n* : one that is upper; *esp* : the parts of a shoe or boot above the sole

up·per·case \,əp-ər-'kās\ *adj* : CAPITAL 5 — **uppercase** *n*

upper class *n* : a social class occupying a position above the middle class and having the highest status in a society — **upper-class** *adj*

up·per·class·man \,əp-ər-'klas-mən\ *n* : a junior or senior in a college or high school

upper crust *n* : the highest social class or group; *esp* : the highest circle of the upper class

up·per·cut \'əp-ər-,kət\ *n* : a short swinging punch delivered (as in boxing) in an upward direction usu. with a bent arm

upper hand *n* : MASTERY, ADVANTAGE

up·per·most \'əp-ər-,mōst\ *adv* : in or into the highest or most prominent position — **uppermost** *adj*

up·pish \'əp-ish\ *adj* : UPPITY

up·pi·ty \'əp-ət-ē\ *adj* : ARROGANT, PRESUMPTUOUS

up·raise \,əp-'rāz\ *vb* : to lift up : ELEVATE

¹**up·right** \'əp-,rīt\ *adj* **1** : PERPENDICULAR, VERTICAL **2** : erect in carriage or posture **3** : morally correct : JUST — **upright** *adv* — **up·right·ly** *adv* — **up·right·ness** *n*

²**upright** *n* **1** : the state of being upright

: a vertical position **2** : something that stands upright

upright piano *n* : a piano whose strings run vertically

up·ris·ing \'əp-₁rī-ziŋ\ *n* : INSURRECTION, REVOLT, REBELLION

up-riv·er \'əp-'riv-ər\ *adv or adj* : toward or at a point nearer the source of a river

up·roar \'əp-₁rōr\ *n* [Dutch *oproer*, fr. Middle Dutch, fr. *op* up + *roer* motion] : a state of commotion, excitement, or violent disturbance

up·roar·i·ous \₁əp-'rōr-ē-əs\ *adj* **1** : marked by uproar **2** : extremely funny — **up·roar·i·ous·ly** *adv*

up·root \₁əp-'rüt, -'rut\ *vb* : to remove by or as if by pulling up by the roots

¹up·set \₁əp-'set\ *vb* **-set; -set·ting 1** : to force or be forced out of the usual upright, level, or proper position **2** : to disturb emotionally : WORRY; *also* : to make somewhat ill **3** : UNSETTLE, DISARRANGE **4** : to defeat unexpectedly

²up·set \'əp-₁set\ *n* **1** : an upsetting or being upset; *esp* : a minor physical disorder **2** : a derangement of plans or ideas

up·shot \'əp-₁shät\ *n* : final result

up·side \'əp-₁sīd\ *n* : the upper side

up·side down \₁əp-₁sīd-'daun\ *adv* **1** : with the upper and the lower parts reversed in position **2** : in or into confusion or disorder — **upside–down** *adj*

up·si·lon particle \'yüp-sə-₁län-, 'əp-\ *n* : any of a group of unstable electrically neutral elementary particles that have a mass about 10 times that of a proton

¹up·stage \'əp-'stāj\ *adv or adj* : toward or at the rear of a theatrical stage

²up·stage \₁əp-'stāj\ *vb* : to steal the show from

¹up·stairs \₁əp-'staərz\ *adv* **1** : up the stairs : to or on a higher floor **2** : to or at a higher position

²up·stairs \₁əp-'staərz\ *adj* : situated above the stairs esp. on an upper floor ⟨~ bedroom⟩

³up·stairs \'əp-'staərz, 'əp-₁staərs\ *n sing or pl* : the part of a building above the ground floor

up·stand·ing \₁əp-'stan-diŋ, 'əp-₁stan-diŋ\ *adj* **1** : ERECT **2** : STRAIGHTFORWARD, HONEST

¹up·start \₁əp-'stärt\ *vb* : to jump up suddenly

²up·start \'əp-₁stärt\ *n* : one that has risen suddenly; *esp* : one that claims more personal importance than he warrants — **up·start** \₁əp-'\ *adj*

up·state \'əp-'stāt\ *adj* : of, relating to, or characteristic of a part of a state away from a large city and esp. to the north — **upstate** *adv* — **upstate** *n*

up·stream \'əp-'strēm\ *adv* : at or toward the source of a stream — **upstream** *adj*

up·stroke \'əp-₁strōk\ *n* : an upward stroke (as of a pen)

up·surge \-₁sərj\ *n* : a rapid or sudden rise

up·swept \'əp-₁swept\ *adj* : swept upward ⟨~ hairdo⟩

up·swing \'əp-₁swiŋ\ *n* : an upward swing; *esp* : a marked increase or rise (as in activity)

up·take \'əp-₁tāk\ *n* **1** : UNDERSTANDING, COMPREHENSION ⟨quick on the ~⟩ **2** : the process of absorbing and incorporating esp. into a living organism ⟨~ of iodine by the thyroid gland⟩

up·thrust \'əp-₁thrəst\ *n* : an upward thrust; *esp* : an uplift of part of the earth's crust — **upthrust** *vb*

up·tight \'əp-'tīt\ *adj* **1** : TENSE, NERVOUS, UNEASY; *also* : ANGRY, INDIGNANT **2** : rigidly conventional

up–to–date *adj* **1** : extending up to the present time **2** : abreast of the times : MODERN — **up–to–date·ness** *n*

up·town \'əp-₁taun\ *n* : the upper part of a town or city; *esp* : the residential district — **up·town** \'əp-'taun\ *adj or adv*

¹up·turn \'əp-₁tərn, ₁əp-'tərn\ *vb* **1** : to turn (as earth) up or over **2** : to turn or direct upward

²up·turn \'əp-₁tərn\ *n* : an upward turn esp. toward better conditions or higher prices

¹up·ward \'əp-wərd\ *or* **up·wards** \-wərdz\ *adv* **1** : in a direction from lower to higher **2** : toward a higher or better condition **3** : toward a greater amount or higher number, degree, or rate

²upward *adj* : directed or moving toward or situated in a higher place or level : ASCENDING

upwards *of also* **upward of** *adv* : more than : in excess of ⟨they cost *upwards of* $25 each⟩

up·well \₁əp-'wel\ *vb* : to move or flow upward

up·well·ing \-'wel-iŋ\ *n* : a rising or an appearance of rising to the surface and flowing outward; *esp* : the movement of deep cold usu. nutrient-rich ocean water to the surface

up·wind \'əp-'wind\ *adv or adj* : in the direction from which the wind is blowing

ura·cil \'yur-ə-₁sil\ *n* : a pyrimidine base that is one of the four bases coding genetic information in the molecular chain of RNA

ura·ni·um \yu̇-'rā-nē-əm\ *n* : a silvery heavy radioactive metallic chemical element used as a source of atomic energy

Ura·nus \'yur-ə-nəs, yu̇-'rā-\ *n* [LL, heaven personified as a god, fr. Gk *Ouranos*, fr. *ouranos* sky, heaven] : the planet 7th in order from the sun

ur·ban \'ər-bən\ *adj* : of, relating to, characteristic of, or constituting a city

ur·bane \₁ər-'bān\ *adj* [L *urbanus* urban, urbane, fr. *urbs* city] : very polite and polished in manner : SUAVE

ur·ban·ite \\'ər-bə-ˌnīt\ *n* : one living in a city

ur·ban·i·ty \ˌər-'ban-ət-ē\ *n, pl* **-ties** : the quality or state of being urbane

ur·ban·ize \'ər-bə-ˌnīz\ *vb* **-ized; -iz·ing** : to cause to take on urban characteristics — **ur·ban·iza·tion** \ˌər-bə-nə-'zā-shən\ *n*

ur·chin \'ər-chən\ *n* [ME, fr. MF *herichon*, fr. L *ericius*] : a pert or mischievous youngster

Ur·du \'ur-dü, 'ər-\ *n* [Hindi *urdū-zabān*, lit., camp language] : a language that is an official literary language of Pakistan and is widely used in India

urea \yu-'rē-ə\ *n* : a soluble nitrogenous compound that is the chief solid constituent of mammalian urine

ure·mia \yu-'rē-mē-ə\ *n* : accumulation in the blood of materials normally passed off in the urine resulting in a poisoned condition — **ure·mic** \-mik\ *adj*

ure·ter \'yur-ət-ər\ *n* : a duct that carries the urine from a kidney to the bladder

ure·thra \yu-'rē-thrə\ *n, pl* **-thras** *or* **-thrae** \-(ˌ)thrē\ : the canal that in most mammals carries off the urine from the bladder and in the male also serves as a genital duct — **ure·thral** \-thrəl\ *adj*

ure·thri·tis \ˌyur-i-'thrīt-əs\ *n* : inflammation of the urethra

¹**urge** \'ərj\ *vb* **urged; urg·ing** 1 : to present, advocate, or demand earnestly 2 : to try to persuade or sway ⟨~ a guest to stay⟩ 3 : to serve as a motive or reason for 4 : to impress or impel to some course or activity ⟨the dog *urged* the sheep onward⟩

²**urge** *n* 1 : the act or process of urging 2 : a force or impulse that urges or drives

ur·gent \'ər-jənt\ *adj* 1 : calling for immediate attention : PRESSING 2 : urging insistently — **ur·gen·cy** \-jən-sē\ *n* — **ur·gent·ly** *adv*

uric \'yur-ik\ *adj* : of, relating to, or found in urine

uric acid *n* : a nearly insoluble acid that is the chief nitrogenous excretory product of birds but is present in only small amounts in mammalian urine

uri·nal \'yur-ən-ᵊl\ *n* 1 : a receptacle for urine 2 : a place for urinating

uri·nal·y·sis \ˌyur-ə-'nal-ə-səs\ *n* : analysis of urine usu. for medical purposes

uri·nary \'yur-ə-ˌner-ē\ *adj* 1 : relating to, occurring in, or being organs for the formation and discharge of urine 2 : of, relating to, or found in urine

urinary bladder *n* : a membranous sac in many vertebrates that serves for the temporary retention of urine and discharges by the urethra

uri·nate \'yur-ə-ˌnāt\ *vb* **-nat·ed; -nat·ing** : to discharge urine — **uri·na·tion** \ˌyur-ə-'nā-shən\ *n*

urine \'yur-ən\ *n* : a waste material from the kidneys that is usu. a yellowish watery liquid in mammals but is highly viscous in birds and reptiles

urn \'ərn\ *n* 1 : a vessel that typically has the form of a vase on a pedestal and often is used to hold the ashes of the dead 2 : a closed vessel usu. with a spout for serving a hot beverage

uro·gen·i·tal \ˌyur-ō-'jen-ə-tᵊl\ *adj* : of, relating to, or being the organs or functions of excretion and reproduction

urol·o·gy \yu-'räl-ə-jē\ *n* : a branch of medical science dealing with the urinary or urogenital tract and its disorders — **uro·log·ic** \ˌyur-ə-'läj-ik\ *also* **uro·log·i·cal** \-i-kəl\ *adj* — **urol·o·gist** \yu-'räl-ə-jəst\ *n*

Ur·sa Ma·jor \ˌər-sə-'mā-jər\ *n* [L, lit., greater bear] : the most conspicuous of the northern constellations that contains the stars which form the Big Dipper

Ursa Mi·nor \-'mī-nər\ *n* [L, lit., lesser bear] : the constellation including the north pole of the heavens and the stars that form the Little Dipper with the North Star at the tip of the handle

ur·sine \'ər-ˌsīn\ *adj* : of, relating to, or resembling a bear

ur·ti·car·ia \ˌərt-ə-'kar-ē-ə\ *n* [NL, fr. L *urtica* nettle] : HIVES

us \(ˈ)əs\ *pron, objective case of* WE

US *abbr* United States

USA *abbr* 1 United States Army 2 United States of America

us·able *also* **use·able** \'yü-zə-bəl\ *adj* : suitable or fit for use — **us·abil·i·ty** \ˌyü-zə-'bil-ət-ē\ *n*

USAF *abbr* United States Air Force

us·age \'yü-sij, -zij\ *n* 1 : habitual or customary practice or procedure 2 : the way in which words and phrases are actually used 3 : the action or mode of using 4 : manner of treating

USCG *abbr* United States Coast Guard

USDA *abbr* United States Department of Agriculture

¹**use** \'yüs\ *n* 1 : the act or practice of using or employing something : EMPLOYMENT, APPLICATION 2 : the fact or state of being used 3 : the way of using 4 : USAGE, CUSTOM 5 : the privilege or benefit of using something 6 : the ability or power to use something (as a limb) 7 : the legal enjoyment of property that consists in its employment, occupation, or exercise; *also* : the benefit or profit esp. from property held in trust 8 : USEFULNESS, UTILITY; *also* : the end served : OBJECT, FUNCTION 9 : the occasion or need to employ ⟨he had no more ~ for it⟩ 10 : ESTEEM, LIKING ⟨had no ~ for modern art⟩

²**use** \'yüz\ *vb* **used** \'yüzd; "used to" usu 'yüs-tə\ ; **us·ing** \'yü-ziŋ\ 1 : to put into action or service : EMPLOY 2 : to consume or take (as drugs) regularly 3 : UTILIZE ⟨~ tact⟩; *also*

: MANIPULATE ⟨*used* his friends to get ahead⟩ 4 : to expend or consume by putting to use 5 : to behave toward : TREAT ⟨*used* the horse cruelly⟩ 6 : to benefit from ⟨house could ~ a coat of paint⟩ 7 — used in the past with *to* to indicate a former practice, fact, or state ⟨we *used* to work harder⟩ — **us·er** *n*

used \'yüzd\ *adj* 1 : having been used by another : SECONDHAND ⟨~ cars⟩ 2 : ACCUSTOMED, HABITUATED ⟨~ to the heat⟩

use·ful \'yüs-fəl\ *adj* : capable of being put to use : ADVANTAGEOUS; *esp* : serviceable for a beneficial end — **use·ful·ly** \-ē\ *adv* — **use·ful·ness** *n*

use·less \'yüs-ləs\ *adj* : having or being of no use : WORTHLESS — **use·less·ly** *adv* — **use·less·ness** *n*

USES *abbr* United States Employment Service

use up *vb* : to consume completely

¹**ush·er** \'əsh-ər\ *n* [ME *ussher*, fr. MF *ussier*, fr. (assumed) VL *ustiarius* doorkeeper, fr. L *ostium, ustium* door, mouth of a river] 1 : an officer who walks before a person of rank 2 : one who escorts people to their seats (as in a church or theater)

²**usher** *vb* 1 : to conduct to a place 2 : to precede as an usher, forerunner, or harbinger 3 : INAUGURATE, INTRODUCE ⟨~ in a new era⟩

ush·er·ette \,əsh-ə-'ret\ *n* : a female usher (as in a theater)

USIA *abbr* United States Information Agency

USM *abbr* United States mail

USMC *abbr* United States Marine Corps

USN *abbr* United States Navy

USO *abbr* United Service Organizations

USP *abbr* United States Pharmacopeia

USPS *abbr* United States Postal Service

USS *abbr* United States ship

USSR *abbr* Union of Soviet Socialist Republics

usu *abbr* usual; usually

usu·al \'yü-zhə-(wə)l\ *adj* 1 : accordant with usage, custom, or habit : NORMAL 2 : commonly or ordinarily used 3 : ORDINARY **syn** customary, habitual, accustomed, routine — **usu·al·ly** \'yüzh-(ə-)wə-lē, 'yüzh-(ə-)lē\ *adv*

usu·fruct \'yü-zə-,frəkt\ *n* [L *ususfructus*, fr. *usus et fructus* use and enjoyment] : the legal right to use and enjoy the benefits and profits of something belonging to another

usu·rer \'yü-zhər-ər\ *n* : one that lends money esp. at an exorbitant rate

usu·ri·ous \yü-'zhùr-ē-əs\ *adj* : practicing, involving, or constituting usury ⟨a ~ rate of interest⟩

usurp \yù-'sərp, -'zərp\ *vb* [ME *usurpen*, fr. MF *usurper*, fr. L *usurpare*, lit., to take possession of by use, fr. *usu* (abl. of *usus* use) + *rapere* to

seize] : to seize and hold by force or without right ⟨~ a throne⟩ — **usur·pa·tion** \,yü-sər-'pā-shən, -zər-\ *n* — **usurp·er** \yù-'sər-pər, -'zər-\ *n*

usu·ry \'yüzh-(ə-)rē\ *n, pl* **-ries** [ME, fr. ML *usuria*, alter. of L *usura*, fr. *usus*, pp. of *uti* to use] 1 : the lending of money with an interest charge for its use 2 : an excessive rate or amount of interest charged; *esp* : interest above an established legal rate

UT *abbr* Utah

Ute \'yüt\ *n, pl* **Ute** *or* **Utes** : a member of an American Indian people orig. ranging through Utah, Colorado, Arizona, and New Mexico

uten·sil \yù-'ten-səl\ *n* [ME, vessels for domestic use, fr. MF *utensile*, fr. L *utensilia*, fr. neut. pl. of *utensilis* useful, fr. *uti* to use] 1 : an instrument or vessel used in a household and esp. a kitchen 2 : an article serving a useful purpose

uter·us \'yüt-ə-rəs\ *n, pl* **uteri** \'yüt-ə-,rī\ *also* **uter·us·es** : the muscular organ of a female mammal in which the young develop before birth — **uter·ine** \-,rīn, -rən\ *adj*

utile \'yüt-ᵊl, 'yü-,tīl\ *adj* : USEFUL

util·i·tar·i·an \yù-,til-ə-'ter-ē-ən\ *n* : a person who believes in utilitarianism

²**utilitarian** *adj* 1 : of or relating to utilitarianism 2 : of or relating to utility : aiming at usefulness rather than beauty; *also* : serving a useful purpose

util·i·tar·i·an·ism \-ē-ə-,niz-əm\ *n* : a theory that the greatest good for the greatest number should be the main consideration in making a choice of actions

¹**util·i·ty** \yù-'til-ət-ē\ *n, pl* **-ties** 1 : USEFULNESS 2 : something useful or designed for use 3 : a business organization performing a public service and subject to special governmental regulation 4 : a public service or a commodity (as electricity or water) provided by a public utility; *also* : equipment to provide such or a similar service

²**utility** *adj* 1 : capable of serving esp. as a substitute in various uses or positions ⟨a ~ outfielder⟩ ⟨a ~ knife⟩ 2 : being of a usable but inferior grade ⟨~ beef⟩

uti·lize \'yüt-ᵊl-,īz\ *vb* **-lized; -liz·ing** : to make use of : turn to profitable account or use — **uti·li·za·tion** \,yüt-ᵊl-ə-'zā-shən\ *n*

¹**ut·most** \'ət-,mōst\ *adj* 1 : situated at the farthest or most distant point : EXTREME 2 : of the greatest or highest degree, quantity, number, or amount — **utmost** *n*

uto·pia \yù-'tō-pē-ə\ *n* [fr. *Utopia*, imaginary island described in Sir Thomas More's *Utopia*, fr. Gk *ou* not, *no* + *topos* place] 1 *often cap* : a place of ideal perfection esp. in laws, government, and social conditions 2

: an impractical scheme for social improvement

¹uto·pi·an \-pē-ən\ *adj, often cap* **1** : of, relating to, or resembling a utopia **2** : proposing ideal social and political schemes that are impractical : VISIONARY

²utopian *n* **1** : a believer in the perfectibility of human society **2** : one that proposes or advocates utopian schemes

¹ut·ter \'ət-ər\ *adj* [ME, remote, fr. OE *ūtera* outer, compar. adj. fr. *ūt* out, adv.] : ABSOLUTE, TOTAL ⟨~ ruin⟩ — **ut·ter·ly** *adv*

²utter *vb* [ME *uttren*, fr. *utter* outside, adv., fr. OE *ūtor*, compar. of *ūt* out] **1** : to send forth as a sound : express in usu. spoken words : PRONOUNCE, SPEAK **2** : to put (as currency) into circulation

ut·ter·ance \'ət-ə-rəns, 'ə-trəns\ *n* **1** : something uttered; *esp* : an oral or written statement **2** : the action of uttering with the voice : SPEECH **3** : power, style, or manner of speaking

ut·ter·most \'ət-ər-ˌmōst\ *adj* : EXTREME, UTMOST ⟨the ~ parts of the earth⟩ — **uttermost** *n*

U-turn \'yü-ˌtərn\ *n* : a turn resembling the letter U; *esp* : a 180-degree turn made by a vehicle in a road

UV *abbr* ultraviolet

U-val·ue \'yü-ˌval-yü\ *n* : a measure of the heat transmission through a building part (as a wall) or a given thickness of insulating material a low value of which indicates high insulating effectiveness

uvu·la \'yü-vyə-lə\ *n, pl* **-las** *or* **-lae** \-ˌlē, -ˌlī\ : the fleshy lobe hanging at the back of the palate — **uvu·lar** \-lər\ *adj*

UW *abbr* underwriter

ux·o·ri·ous \ˌək-'sōr-ē-əs, ˌəg-'zōr-\ *adj* : excessively devoted or submissive to a wife

V

¹v \'vē\ *n, pl* **v's** *or* **vs** \'vēz\ *often cap* : the 22d letter of the English alphabet

²v *abbr, often cap* **1** velocity **2** verb **4** verse **5** versus **6** victory **7** vide **8** voice **9** volt; voltage **10** volume **11** vowel

V *symbol* vanadium

Va *abbr* Virginia

VA *abbr* **1** Veterans Administration **2** vice admiral **3** Virginia

va·can·cy \'vā-kən-sē\ *n, pl* **-cies** **1** : a vacating esp. of an office, position, or piece of property **2** : the state of being vacant **3** : a vacant office, position, or tenancy; *also* : the period during which it stands vacant **4** : empty space : VOID

va·cant \'vā-kənt\ *adj* **1** : not occupied ⟨~ seat⟩ ⟨~ room⟩ **2** : EMPTY ⟨~ space⟩ **3** : free from business or care ⟨a few ~ hours⟩ **4** : devoid of thought, reflection, or expression ⟨a ~ smile⟩ — **va·cant·ly** *adv*

va·cate \'vā-ˌkāt\ *vb* **va·cat·ed; va·cat·ing** **1** : to make void : ANNUL **2** : to make vacant (as an office or house); *also* : to give up the occupancy of

¹va·ca·tion \vā-'kā-shən, və-\ *n* : a period of rest from work : HOLIDAY

²vacation *vb* **-tioned; -tion·ing** \-sh(ə-)niŋ\ : to take or spend a vacation — **va·ca·tion·er** \-sh(ə-)nər\ *n*

va·ca·tion·ist \-sh(ə-)nəst\ *n* : a person taking a vacation

va·ca·tion·land \-shən-ˌland\ *n* : an area with recreational attractions and facilities for vacationists

vac·ci·nate \'vak-sə-ˌnāt\ *vb* **-nat·ed; -nat·ing** : to inoculate with a related harmless virus to produce immunity to smallpox; *also* : to administer a vaccine to usu. by injection

vac·ci·na·tion \ˌvak-sə-'nā-shən\ *n* **1** : the act of vaccinating **2** : the scar left by vaccinating

vac·cine \vak-'sēn, 'vak-ˌsēn\ *n* [L *vaccinus* of or from cows, fr. *vacca* cow; so called from the derivation of smallpox vaccine from cows] : material (as a preparation of killed or weakened virus or bacteria) used in vaccinating to induce immunity to a disease

vac·cin·ia \vak-'sin-ē-ə\ *n* : COWPOX

vac·il·late \'vas-ə-ˌlāt\ *vb* **-lat·ed; -lat·ing** **1** : SWAY, TOTTER; *also* : FLUCTUATE **2** : to incline first to one course or opinion and then to another : WAVER — **vac·il·la·tion** \ˌvas-ə-'lā-shən\ *n*

va·cu·ity \va-'kyü-ət-ē, və-\ *n, pl* **-ities** **1** : an empty space **2** : the state, fact, or quality of being vacuous **3** : something that is vacuous

vac·u·ole \'vak-yə-ˌwōl\ *n* : a usu. fluid-filled cavity in tissues or in the protoplasm of an individual cell — **vac·u·o·lar** \ˌvak-yə-'wō-lər, -ˌlär\ *adj*

vac·u·ous \'vak-yə-wəs\ *adj* **1** : EMPTY, VACANT, BLANK **2** : DULL, STUPID, INANE — **vac·u·ous·ly** *adv* — **vac·u·ous·ness** *n*

¹vac·u·um \'vak-yü-əm, -(ˌ)yüm, -yəm\ *n, pl* **vacuums** *or* **vac·ua** \-yə-wə\ [L, fr. neut. of *vacuus* empty] **1** : a space entirely empty of matter **2** : a space from which most of the air has been removed (as by a pump) **3** : VOID, GAP **4** : VACUUM CLEANER — **vacuum** *adj*

²vacuum *vb* : to use a vacuum device (as a vacuum cleaner) on

vacuum bottle *n* : a cylindrical container with a vacuum between an inner and an outer wall used to keep liquids hot or cold

vacuum cleaner *n* : an electrical appliance for cleaning (as floors or rugs) by suction

vac·u·um-packed \ˌvak-yüm-ˈpakt, -yəm-\ *adj* : having much of the air removed before being hermetically sealed

vacuum tube *n* : an electron tube from which most of the air has been removed

va·de me·cum \ˌvād-ē-ˈmē-kəm\ *n, pl* **vade mecums** [L, go with me] : something (as a handbook or manual) carried as a constant companion

VADM *abbr* vice admiral

¹**vag·a·bond** \ˈvag-ə-ˌbänd\ *adj* **1** : WANDERING, HOMELESS **2** : of, characteristic of, or leading the life of a vagrant or tramp **3** : leading an unsettled or irresponsible life

²**vagabond** *n* : one leading a vagabond life; *esp* : TRAMP

va·gar·i·ous \vā-ˈger-ē-əs, və-\ *adj* : marked by vagaries : CAPRICIOUS — **va·gar·i·ous·ly** *adv*

va·ga·ry \ˈvā-gə-rē, və-ˈger-ē\ *n, pl* **-ries** : an odd or eccentric idea or action : WHIM, CAPRICE

va·gi·na \və-ˈjī-nə\ *n, pl* **-nae** \-(ˌ)nē\ *or* **-nas** [L, lit., sheath] : a canal that leads from the uterus to the external opening of the female sex organs — **vag·i·nal** \ˈvaj-ən-ᵊl\ *adj*

vag·i·ni·tis \ˌvaj-ə-ˈnīt-əs\ *n* : inflammation of the vagina

va·gran·cy \ˈvā-grən(t)-sē\ *n, pl* **-cies 1** : the quality or state of being vagrant; *also* : a vagrant act or notion **2** : the offense of being a vagrant

¹**va·grant** \ˈvā-grənt\ *n* : a person who has no job and wanders from place to place

²**vagrant** *adj* **1** : of, relating to, or characteristic of a vagrant **2** : following no fixed course : RANDOM, CAPRICIOUS (~ thoughts) — **va·grant·ly** *adv*

vague \ˈvāg\ *adj* **vagu·er; vagu·est** [MF, fr. L *vagus*, lit., wandering] **1** : not clear, definite, or distinct **2** : not clearly felt or analyzed (a ~ unrest) **syn** obscure, dark, enigmatic, ambiguous, equivocal — **vague·ly** *adv* — **vague·ness** *n*

vain \ˈvān\ *adj* [ME, fr. OF, fr. L *vanus* empty, vain] **1** : of no real value : IDLE, WORTHLESS **2** : FUTILE, UNSUCCESSFUL **3** : proud of one's looks or abilities **syn** conceited, narcissistic, vainglorious — **vain·ly** *adv*

vain·glo·ri·ous \(ˈ)vān-ˈglōr-ē-əs\ *adj* : marked by vainglory : BOASTFUL

vain·glo·ry \ˈvān-ˌglōr-ē\ *n* **1** : excessive or ostentatious pride esp. in one's own achievements **2** : vain display : VANITY

val *abbr* value; valued

va·lance \ˈval-əns, ˈvāl-\ *n* **1** : drapery hanging from an edge (as of an altar, table, or bed) **2** : a drapery or a

decorative frame across the top of a window

vale \ˈvāl\ *n* : VALLEY, DALE

vale·dic·tion \ˌval-ə-ˈdik-shən\ *n* [L *valedictus*, pp. of *valedicere* to say farewell, fr. *vale* farewell + *dicere* to say] : an act or utterance of leave-taking : FAREWELL

vale·dic·to·ri·an \-ˌdik-ˈtōr-ē-ən\ *n* : the student usu. of the highest rank in a graduating class who pronounces the valedictory oration at commencement

vale·dic·to·ry \-ˈdik-t(ə-)rē\ *adj* : bidding farewell : delivered as a valediction (a ~ address) — **valedictory** *n*

va·lence \ˈvā-ləns\ *n* [LL *valentia* power, capacity, fr. L *valēre* to be strong] : the combining power of an atom as shown by the number of electrons in its outermost energy level that are lost, gained, or shared in the formation of chemical bonds

valence electron *n* : an electron in the outer shell of an atom that determines the atom's chemical properties

Va·len·ci·ennes \və-ˌlen-sē-ˈen(z), ˌval-ən-sē-\ *n* : a fine handmade lace

val·en·tine \ˈval-ən-ˌtīn\ *n* : a sweetheart chosen or complimented on St. Valentine's Day; *also* : a greeting card sent on this day

Valentine Day *or* **Valentine's Day** *n* : SAINT VALENTINE'S DAY

¹**va·let** \ˈval-ət, ˈval-(ˌ)ā, va-ˈlā\ *n* **1** : a male servant who takes care of a man's clothes and performs personal services **2** : an attendant in a hotel who performs personal services for customers

²**valet** *vb* : to serve as a valet

val·e·tu·di·nar·i·an \ˌval-ə-ˌt(y)üd-ᵊn-ˈer-ē-ən\ *n* : a person of a weak or sickly constitution; *esp* : one whose chief concern is his invalidism — **val·e·tu·di·nar·i·an·ism** \-ē-ə-ˌniz-əm\ *n*

val·iant \ˈval-yənt\ *adj* : having or showing valor : BRAVE, HEROIC **syn** valorous, doughty, courageous, bold, audacious, dauntless, undaunted, intrepid — **val·iant·ly** *adv*

val·id \ˈval-əd\ *adj* **1** : having legal force (a ~ contract) **2** : founded on truth or fact : capable of being justified or defended : SOUND (a ~ argument) (~ reasons) — **va·lid·i·ty** \və-ˈlid-ət-ē, va-\ *n* — **val·id·ly** \ˈval-əd-lē\ *adv*

val·i·date \ˈval-ə-ˌdāt\ *vb* **-dat·ed; -dat·ing 1** : to make legally valid **2** : to confirm the validity of **3** : VERIFY — **val·i·da·tion** \ˌval-ə-ˈdā-shən\ *n*

va·lise \və-ˈlēs\ *n* [F] : TRAVELING BAG

val·ley \ˈval-ē\ *n, pl* **valleys** : a long depression between ranges of hills or mountains

val·or \ˈval-ər\ *n* [ME, fr. MF *valour*, fr. ML *valor* value, valor, fr. L *valēre* to be strong] : personal bravery **syn** heroism, prowess, gallantry — **val·or·ous** \ˈval-ə-rəs\ *adj*

val·o·ri·za·tion \ˌval-ə-rə-ˈzā-shən\ *n* : the support of commodity prices by any of various forms of government subsidy — **val·o·rize** \ˈval-ə-ˌrīz\ *vb*

valse \ˈvals\ *n* [F] : WALTZ; *esp* : a concert waltz

¹**valu·able** \ˈval-yə-(wə-)bəl\ *adj* 1 : having money value 2 : having great money value 3 : of great use or service **syn** invaluable, priceless, costly, expensive, dear, precious

²**valuable** *n* : a usu. personal possession of considerable value ⟨their ~s were stolen⟩

val·u·ate \ˈval-yə-ˌwāt\ *vb* **-at·ed; -at·ing** : to place a value on : APPRAISE — **val·u·a·tor** \-ˌwāt-ər\ *n*

val·u·a·tion \ˌval-yə-ˈwā-shən\ *n* 1 : the act or process of valuing; *esp* : appraisal of property 2 : the estimated or determined market value of a thing

¹**val·ue** \ˈval-yü\ *n* 1 : a fair return or equivalent in money, goods, or services for something exchanged 2 : the worth of a thing : market price, purchasing power, or estimated worth 3 : an assigned or computed numerical quantity (the ~ of x in an equation) 4 : precise meaning (~ of a word) 5 : distinctive quality of sound in speech 6 : luminosity of a color : BRILLIANCE; *also* : the relation of one detail in a picture to another with respect to lightness or darkness 7 : the relative length of a tone or note 8 : something (as a principle or ideal) intrinsically valuable or desirable (human rather than material ~s) — **val·ue·less** *adj*

²**value** *vb* **val·ued; val·u·ing** 1 : to estimate the monetary worth of : APPRAISE 2 : to rate in usefulness, importance, or general worth 3 : to consider or rate highly : PRIZE, ESTEEM — **val·u·er** *n*

val·ue-add·ed tax *n* : an incremental excise tax that is levied on the value added at each stage of the processing of a raw material or the production and distribution of a commodity

val·ued \ˈval-yüd\ *adj* : highly esteemed : PRIZED

valve \ˈvalv\ *n* 1 : a structure (as in a vein) that temporarily closes a passage or that permits movement in one direction only 2 : one of the pieces into which a ripe seed capsule or pod separates 3 : a device by which the flow of liquid, gas, or loose material in bulk may be regulated by a movable part; *also* : the movable part of such a device 4 : a device in a brass wind instrument for quickly varying the tube length in order to change the fundamental tone by some definite interval 5 : one of the separable usu. hinged pieces of which the shell of some animals and esp. bivalve mollusks consists — **valved** \ˈvalvd\ *adj* — **valve·less** *adj*

val·vu·lar \ˈval-vyə-lər\ *adj* 1 : resembling or functioning as a valve; *also* : opening by valves 2 : of or relating to a valve esp. of the heart

va·moose \va-ˈmüs, va-\ *vb* **va·moosed; va·moos·ing** [Sp *vamos* let us go] *slang* : to leave or go away quickly

¹**vamp** \ˈvamp\ *vb* 1 : to provide with a new vamp 2 : to patch up with a new part 3 : INVENT, IMPROVISE ⟨~ up an excuse⟩

²**vamp** *n* 1 : the part of a boot or shoe upper covering esp. the front part of the foot 2 : a short introductory musical passage often repeated

³**vamp** *n* : a woman who uses her charm and allurements to seduce and exploit men

⁴**vamp** *vb* : to practice seductive wiles on

vam·pire \ˈvam-ˌpī(ə)r\ *n* 1 : a night-wandering bloodsucking ghost 2 : a person who preys on other people; *esp* : a woman who exploits and ruins her lover 3 : any of various bats of Mexico and Central and South America that feed on the blood of animals including man; *also* : any of several bats believed to suck blood

¹**van** \ˈvan\ *n* : VANGUARD

²**van** *n* : a usu. enclosed wagon or motortruck for moving goods or animals; *also* : a versatile enclosed boxlike motor vehicle with side or rear doors and side panels that often have windows

va·na·di·um \və-ˈnād-ē-əm\ *n* : a soft ductile metallic chemical element used to form alloys

Van Al·len belt \van-ˈal-ən-\ *n* : a belt of intense ionizing radiation in the earth's magnetosphere

van·dal \ˈvan-dᵊl\ *n* 1 *cap* : a member of a Germanic people who sacked Rome in A.D. 455 2 : one who willfully mars or destroys property

van·dal·ism \-ˌiz-əm\ *n* : willful or malicious destruction or defacement of public or private property

van·dal·ize \-ˌīz\ *vb* **-ized; -iz·ing** : to subject to vandalism : DAMAGE

Van·dyke \van-ˈdīk\ *n* : a trim pointed beard

vane \ˈvān\ *n* [ME, fr. OE *fana* banner] 1 : a movable device attached to a high object to show the way the wind blows 2 : a thin flat or curved object that is rotated about an axis by a flow of fluid or that rotates to cause a fluid to flow or that redirects a flow of fluid (the ~s of a windmill)

van·guard \ˈvan-ˌgärd\ *n* 1 : the troops moving at the front of an army : VAN 2 : the forefront of an action or movement

va·nil·la \və-ˈnil-ə\ *n* [NL, genus name, fr. Sp *vainilla* vanilla (plant and fruit), dim. of *vaina* sheath, fr. L *vagina* sheath, vagina] : a tropical American climbing orchid with beanlike pods; *also* : its pods or a flavoring extract made from these

van·ish \'van-ish\ *vb* : to pass from sight or existence : disappear completely — **van·ish·er** *n*

van·i·ty \'van-ət-ē\ *n, pl* **-ties** 1 : something that is vain, empty, or useless 2 : the quality or fact of being useless or futile : FUTILITY 3 : undue pride in oneself or one's appearance : CONCEIT 4 : a small case for cosmetics : COMPACT

vanity plate *n* : an automobile license plate bearing distinctive letters or numbers designated by the owner

van·quish \'vaŋ-kwish, 'van-\ *vb* 1 : to overcome in battle or in a contest 2 : to gain mastery over (as an emotion)

van·tage \'vant-ij\ *n* 1 : superiority in a contest 2 : a position giving a strategic advantage or a commanding perspective

van·ward \'van-wərd\ *adj* : being in or toward the vanguard : ADVANCED — **vanward** *adv*

va·pid \'vap-əd, 'vā-pəd\ *adj* : lacking spirit, liveliness, or zest : FLAT, INSIPID — **va·pid·i·ty** \va-'pid-ət-ē\ *n* — **vap·id·ly** \'vap-əd-lē\ *adv* — **vap·id·ness** *n*

¹**va·por** \'vā-pər\ *n* 1 : fine separated particles (as fog or smoke) floating in the air and clouding it 2 : a substance in the gaseous state; *esp* : one that is liquid under ordinary conditions 3 : something insubstantial or fleeting 4 *pl* : a depressed or hysterical nervous condition

²**vapor** *vb* 1 : to rise or pass off in vapor 2 : to emit vapor

va·por·ing \'vā-p(ə-)riŋ\ *n* : an idle, boastful, or high-flown expression or speech — usu. used in pl.

va·por·ish \'vā-p(ə-)rish\ *adj* 1 : resembling or suggestive of vapor 2 : given to fits of depression or hysteria — **va·por·ish·ness** *n*

va·por·ize \'vā-pə-ˌrīz\ *vb* **-ized; -iz·ing** : to convert into vapor — **va·por·iza·tion** \ˌvā-pə-rə-'zā-shən\ *n*

va·por·iz·er \-ˌrī-zər\ *n* : a device that vaporizes something (as a medicated liquid)

vapor lock *n* : a partial or complete interruption of flow of a fluid (as fuel in an internal-combustion engine) caused by the formation of bubbles of vapor in the feeding system

va·por·ous \'vā-p(ə-)rəs\ *adj* 1 : consisting of or characteristic of vapor 2 : producing vapors : VOLATILE 3 : full of vapors : FOGGY, MISTY — **va·por·ous·ly** *adv* — **va·por·ous·ness** *n*

va·pory \'vā-p(ə-)rē\ *adj* : VAPOROUS, VAGUE

va·que·ro \vä-'ker-ō\ *n, pl* **-ros** [Sp, fr. *vaca* cow, fr. L *vacca*] : a ranch hand : COWBOY

var *abbr* 1 variable 2 variant; variation 3 variety 4 various

¹**vari·able** \'ver-ē-ə-bəl\ *adj* 1 : able or apt to vary : CHANGEABLE 2 : FICKLE 3 : not true to type : ABERRANT (a ∼ wheat) — **vari·abil·i·ty** \ˌver-ē-ə-'bil-ət-ē\ *n* — **vari·able·ness** \'ver-ē-ə-bəl-nəs\ *n* — **vari·ably** \-blē\ *adv*

²**variable** *n* 1 : something that is variable 2 : a quantity that may assume a succession of values; *also* : a symbol standing for any one of a class of things

vari·ance \'ver-ē-əns\ *n* 1 : variation or a degree of variation : DEVIATION 2 : DISAGREEMENT, DISPUTE 3 : a license to do something contrary to the usual rule (a zoning ∼) **syn** discord, contention, dissension, strife, conflict

¹**vari·ant** \'ver-ē-ənt\ *adj* 1 : differing from others of its kind or class 2 : varying usu. slightly from the standard or type

²**variant** *n* 1 : one that exhibits variation from a type or norm 2 : one of two or more different spellings or pronunciations of a word

vari·a·tion \ˌver-ē-'ā-shən\ *n* 1 : an act or instance of varying : a change in form, position, or condition : MODIFICATION, ALTERATION 2 : extent of change or difference 3 : divergence in qualities from those typical or usual to a group; *also* : one exhibiting such variation 4 : repetition of a musical theme with modifications in rhythm, tune, harmony, or key

vari·col·ored \'ver-i-ˌkəl-ərd\ *adj* : having various colors : VARIEGATED

var·i·cose \'var-ə-ˌkōs\ *adj* : abnormally and irregularly swollen (∼ veins)

var·i·cos·i·ty \ˌvar-ə-'käs-ət-ē\ *n, pl* **-ties** 1 : the quality or state of being varicose 2 : a varicose part or lesion (as of a vein)

var·ied \'ver-ēd\ *adj* 1 : having many forms or types : DIVERSE 2 : VARIEGATED — **var·ied·ly** *adv*

var·ie·gate \'ver-ē-ə-ˌgāt, 'ver-i-ˌgāt\ *vb* **-gat·ed; -gat·ing** 1 : to diversify in external appearance esp. with different colors 2 : to introduce variety into : DIVERSIFY — **var·ie·gat·ed** *adj* — **var·ie·ga·tion** \ˌver-ē-ə-'gā-shən, ˌver-i-'gā-\ *n*

va·ri·etal \və-'rī-ət-ᵊl\ *adj* : of or relating to a variety; *also* : being a variety rather than an individual or species

va·ri·ety \və-'rī-ət-ē\ *n, pl* **-et·ies** 1 : the state of being varied or various : DIVERSITY 2 : a collection of different things 3 : something varying from other things of the same general kind 4 : any of various groups of plants or animals within a species distinguished by characteristics not constant enough or too unimportant to separate species 5 : entertainment such as is given in a stage presentation comprising a series of performances (as songs, dances, or acrobatic acts)

var·i·o·rum \ˌver-ē-'ōr-əm\ *n* : an edition or text of a work containing notes by various persons or variant readings of the text

var·i·ous \'ver-ē-əs\ *adj* 1 : VARICOLORED 2 : of differing kinds : MUL-

TIFARIOUS **3** : UNLIKE ⟨animals as ∼ as the jaguar and the sloth⟩ **4** : having a number of different aspects **5** : NUMEROUS, MANY **6** : INDIVIDUAL, SEPARATE **syn** divergent, disparate, different, dissimilar, diverse, unalike — **var·i·ous·ly** adv

va·ris·tor \və-'ris-tər\ n : a voltage-dependent electrical resistor

var·let \'vär-lət\ n [ME, fr. MF vaslet, variet young nobleman, page] **1** : ATTENDANT **2** : SCOUNDREL, KNAVE

var·mint \'vär-mənt\ n [alter. of vermin] **1** : an animal considered a pest; esp : a mammal or bird classed as vermin and unprotected by game law **2** : a contemptible person : RASCAL

¹var·nish \'vär-nish\ n **1** : a liquid preparation that is spread on a surface and dries into a hard glossy coating; also : the glaze of this coating **2** : something suggesting varnish by its gloss **3** : outside show : GLOSS

²varnish vb **1** : to cover with varnish **2** : to cover or conceal with something that gives a fair appearance : gloss over

var·si·ty \'vär-sət-ē, -stē\ n, pl **-ties** [by shortening & alter. fr. university] **1** Brit : UNIVERSITY **2** : the principal team representing a college, school, or club

vary \'ver-ē\ vb **var·ied; vary·ing 1** : ALTER, CHANGE **2** : to make or be of different kinds : introduce or have variety : DIVERSIFY, DIFFER **3** : DEVIATE, SWERVE **4** : to diverge structurally or physiologically from typical members of a group

vas·cu·lar \'vas-kyə-lər\ adj [NL vascularis, fr. L vasculum small vessel, dim. of vas vase, vessel] : of or relating to a channel or system of channels for the conveyance of a body fluid (as blood or sap); also : supplied with or containing such vessels and esp. blood vessels

vascular plant n : a plant having a specialized conducting system that includes xylem and phloem

vase \'vās, 'vāz\ n : a usu. round vessel of greater depth than width used chiefly for ornament or for flowers

va·sec·to·my \va-'sek-tə-mē, vā-'zek-\ n, pl **-mies** : surgical excision of all or part of the sperm-carrying ducts of the testis usu. to induce permanent sterility

va·so·con·stric·tion \ˌvas-ō-kən-'strik-shən, ˌvāz-\ n : narrowing of the interior diameter of blood vessels

va·so·con·stric·tor \-tər\ n : an agent (as a nerve fiber or a drug) that initiates or induces vasoconstriction

vas·sal \'vas-əl\ n **1** : a person under the protection of a feudal lord to whom he owes homage and loyalty : a feudal tenant **2** : one occupying a dependent or subordinate position — **vassal** adj

vas·sal·age \-ə-lij\ n **1** : the state of being a vassal **2** : the homage and loyalty due from a vassal **3** : SERVITUDE, SUBJECTION

¹vast \'vast\ adj : very great in size, amount, degree, intensity, or esp. extent **syn** enormous, huge, gigantic, colossal, mammoth — **vast·ly** adv — **vast·ness** n

²vast n : a great expanse : IMMENSITY

vasty \'vas-tē\ adj : VAST, IMMENSE

vat \'vat\ n : a large vessel (as a tub or barrel) esp. for holding liquids in manufacturing processes

VAT abbr value-added tax

vat·ic \'vat-ik\ adj : PROPHETIC, ORACULAR

Vat·i·can \'vat-i-kən\ n **1** : the papal headquarters in Rome **2** : the papal government

va·tu \'vä-ˌtü\ n, pl **vatu** — see MONEY table

vaude·ville \'vȯd-(ə-)vəl, 'vȯd-, 'vȯd-, -(ə-)ˌvil\ n [F, fr. MF, popular satirical song, alter. of vaudevire, fr. vau-de-Vire valley of Vire, fr. Vire, town in northwest France where such songs were composed] : a stage entertainment consisting of unrelated acts (as of acrobats, comedians, dancers, or singers)

¹vault \'vȯlt\ n **1** : an arched masonry structure usu. forming a ceiling or roof; also : something (as the sky) resembling a vault **2** : a room or space covered by a vault esp. when underground and used for a special purpose (as for storage of valuables or wine supplies) **3** : a burial chamber; also : a usu. metal or concrete case in which a casket is enclosed at burial — **vaulty** adj

²vault vb : to form or cover with a vault

³vault vb : to leap vigorously esp. by aid of the hands or a pole — **vault·er** n

⁴vault n : an act of vaulting : LEAP

vault·ed \'vȯl-təd\ adj **1** : built in the form of a vault : ARCHED **2** : covered with a vault

vault·ing \-tiŋ\ adj : leaping upward : reaching for the heights ⟨∼ ambition⟩

vaunt \'vȯnt\ vb [ME vaunten, fr. MF vanter, fr. LL vanitare, fr. L vanitas vanity] : BRAG, BOAST — **vaunt** n

vb abbr verb

VCR \ˌvē-ˌsē-'är\ n [videocassette recorder] : a videotape recorder that uses videocassettes

VD abbr venereal disease

veal \'vēl\ n : the flesh of a young calf

vec·tor \'vek-tər\ n **1** : a quantity that has magnitude and direction **2** : an organism (as a fly) that transmits disease germs

Ve·da \'vād-ə\ n [Skt, lit., knowledge] : any of a class of Hindu sacred writings — **Ve·dic** \'vād-ik\ adj

Ve·dan·ta \vā-'dänt-ə, və-, -'dant-\ n : an orthodox Hindu philosophy based on the Upanishads

veep \'vēp\ n : VICE PRESIDENT

veer \'viər\ vb : to shift from one direction or course to another syn turn, avert, deflect, divert — **veer** n

vee·ry \'vi(ə)r-ē\ n, pl **veeries** : a tawny brown thrush of the woods of the eastern U.S.

veg·an \'vej-ən, 'vē-gən\ n : a strict vegetarian; esp : one who consumes no animal food or dairy products — **veg·an·ism** \'vej-ə-ˌniz-əm, 'vē-gə-\ n

¹**veg·e·ta·ble** \'vej-(ə-)tə-bəl\ adj [ME, fr. ML vegetabilis vegetative, fr. vegetare to grow, fr. L, to animate, fr. vegetus lively, fr. vegēre to rouse, excite] 1 : of, relating to, or growing like plants 2 : made or obtained from plants ⟨∼ oils⟩ ⟨the ∼ kingdom⟩ 3 : suggesting that of a plant ⟨a ∼ existence⟩

²**vegetable** n 1 : PLANT 1 2 : a usu. herbaceous plant grown for an edible part that is usu. eaten with the principal course of a meal; also : such an edible part

veg·e·tal \'vej-ət-ᵊl\ adj 1 : VEGETABLE 2 : VEGETATIVE

veg·e·tar·i·an \ˌvej-ə-'ter-ē-ən\ n : one that believes in or practices living solely on plant products — **vegetarian** adj — **veg·e·tar·i·an·ism** \-ē-ə-ˌniz-əm\ n

veg·e·tate \'vej-ə-ˌtāt\ vb **-tat·ed; -tat·ing** : to grow in the manner of a plant; esp : to lead a dull inert life

veg·e·ta·tion \ˌvej-ə-'tā-shən\ n 1 : the act or process of vegetating; also : a dull inert existence 2 : plant life or cover (as of an area) — **veg·e·ta·tion·al** \-sh(ə-)nəl\ adj

veg·e·ta·tive \'vej-ə-ˌtāt-iv\ adj 1 : of or relating to nutrition and growth esp. as contrasted with reproduction 2 : of, relating to, or composed of vegetation 3 : leading or marked by a passive, stupid, and dull existence

ve·he·mence \'vē-ə-məns\ n : the quality or state of being vehement : INTENSITY, VIOLENCE

ve·he·ment \-mənt\ adj 1 : marked by great force or energy 2 : marked by strong feeling or expression : PASSIONATE 3 : strong in effect : INTENSE — **ve·he·ment·ly** adv

ve·hi·cle \'vē-ˌ(h)ik-əl, 'vē-ə-kəl\ n 1 : a medium by which a thing is applied or administered ⟨linseed oil is a ∼ for pigments⟩ 2 : a medium through or by means of which something is conveyed or expressed 3 : a means of carrying or transporting something : CONVEYANCE syn means, instrument, agent, agency, organ, channel — **ve·hic·u·lar** \vē-'hik-yə-lər\ adj

¹**veil** \'vāl\ n 1 : a piece of often sheer or diaphanous material used to screen or curtain something or to cover the head or face 2 : the state accepted when a woman becomes a nun ⟨take the ∼⟩ 3 : something that hides or obscures like a veil

²**veil** vb : to cover with or as if with a veil : wear a veil

veil·ing \'vā-liŋ\ n 1 : VEIL 2 : any of various sheer fabrics (as net or chiffon)

vein \'vān\ n 1 : a fissure in rock filled with mineral matter; also : a bed of useful mineral matter 2 : one of the tubular branching vessels that carry blood from the capillaries toward the heart 3 : one of the vascular bundles forming the framework of a leaf 4 : one of the thickened ribs that stiffen the wings of an insect 5 : something (as a wavy variegation in marble) suggesting veins 6 : a distinctive mode of expression : STYLE 7 : something of distinctive character considered as running through something else : STRAIN 8 : MOOD, HUMOR — **veined** \'vānd\ adj

²**vein** vb : to form or mark with or as if with veins — **vein·ing** n

vel abbr velocity

ve·lar \'vē-lər\ adj : of or relating to a velum and esp. that of the soft palate

veld or **veldt** \'velt, 'felt\ n [Afrikaans veld, fr. Middle Dutch, field] : open grassland esp. in Africa usu. with scattered shrubs or trees

vel·lum \'vel-əm\ n [ME velim, fr. MF veelin, fr. veelin, adj., of a calf, fr. veel calf] 1 : a fine-grained lambskin, kidskin, or calfskin prepared for writing on or for binding books 2 : a paper manufactured to resemble vellum — **vellum** adj

ve·loc·i·pede \və-'läs-ə-ˌpēd\ n : an early bicycle

ve·loc·i·ty \və-'läs-(ə-)tē\ n, pl **-ties** : quickness of motion : SPEED ⟨the ∼ of light⟩

ve·lour or **ve·lours** \və-'lür\ n, pl **velours** \-'lürz\ : any of various textile fabrics with pile like that of velvet

ve·lum \'vē-ləm\ n, pl **ve·la** \-lə\ : a membranous partition (as the soft palate) resembling a veil

¹**vel·vet** \'vel-vət\ n [ME veluet, velvet, fr. MF velu shaggy, fr. L villus shaggy hair] 1 : a fabric characterized by a short soft dense warp pile 2 : something resembling or suggesting velvet (as in softness or luster) 3 : soft skin covering the growing antlers of deer 4 : the winnings of a player in a gambling game — **velvety** adj

²**velvet** adj 1 : made of or covered with velvet 2 : resembling or suggesting velvet : SMOOTH, SOFT, SLEEK

vel·ve·teen \ˌvel-və-'tēn\ n 1 : a fabric woven usu. of cotton in imitation of velvet 2 pl : clothes made of velveteen

Ven abbr venerable

ve·nal \'vēn-ᵊl\ adj : capable of being bought esp. by underhanded means : MERCENARY, CORRUPT — **ve·nal·i·ty** \vi-'nal-ət-ē\ n — **ve·nal·ly** \'vēn-ᵊl-ē\ adv

ve·na·tion \ve-'nā-shən, vē-\ n : an arrangement or system of veins ⟨the ∼ of the hand⟩ ⟨leaf ∼⟩

vend \'vend\ *vb* : SELL; *esp* : to sell as a hawker or peddler — **vend·ible** *adj*

vend·ee \ven-'dē\ *n* : one to whom a thing is sold : BUYER

vend·er \'ven-dər\ *n* : VENDOR

ven·det·ta \ven-'det-ə\ *n* : a feud between clans or families

vending machine *n* : a coin-operated machine for vending merchandise

ven·dor \'ven-dər, *for 1 also* ven-'dȯr\ *n* **1** : one that vends : SELLER **2** : VENDING MACHINE

¹ve·neer \və-'niər\ *n* [G *furnier*, fr. *furnieren* to veneer, fr. F *fournir* to furnish] **1** : a thin usu. superficial layer of material (brick ∼) ; *esp* : a thin layer of fine wood glued over a cheaper wood **2** : superficial display : GLOSS

²veneer *vb* : to overlay with a veneer

ven·er·a·ble \'ven-ər-(ə-)bəl, 'ven-rə-bəl\ *adj* **1** : deserving to be venerated — often used as a religious title **2** : made sacred by association

ven·er·ate \'ven-ə-ˌrāt\ *vb* **-at·ed; -at·ing** : to regard with reverential respect **syn** adore, revere, reverence, worship — **ven·er·a·tion** \ˌven-ə-'rā-shən\ *n*

ve·ne·re·al \və-'nir-ē-əl\ *adj* : of or relating to sexual intercourse or to diseases transmitted by it (a ∼ infection)

venereal disease *n* : a contagious disease (as gonorrhea or syphilis) that is usu. acquired by having sexual intercourse with someone who already has it

ve·ne·tian blind \və-ˌnē-shən-\ *n* : a blind having thin horizontal parallel slats that can be adjusted to admit a desired amount of light

Ven·e·zue·lan \ˌven-əz-'wā-lən\ *n* : a native or inhabitant of Venezuela — **Venezuelan** *adj*

ven·geance \'ven-jəns\ *n* : punishment inflicted in retaliation for an injury or offense : RETRIBUTION

venge·ful \'venj-fəl\ *adj* : filled with a desire for revenge : VINDICTIVE — **venge·ful·ly** \-ē\ *adv*

ve·nial \'vē-nē-əl, -nyəl\ *adj* : capable of being forgiven : EXCUSABLE (∼ sin)

ven·i·punc·ture \'vēn-ə-ˌpəŋk-chər, 'ven-ə-\ *n* : surgical puncture of a vein esp. for withdrawal of blood or for intravenous medication

ve·ni·re \və-'nī-rē\ *n* : a panel from which a jury is drawn

ve·ni·re fa·ci·as \-'fā-shē-əs\ *n* [ME, fr. ML, you cause to come] : a writ summoning persons to appear in court to serve as jurors

ve·ni·re·man \və-'nī-rē-mən, -'nir-ē-\ *n* : a member of a venire

ven·i·son \'ven-ə-sən, -ə-zən\ *n, pl* **venisons** *also* **venison** [ME, fr. OF *veneison* hunting, game, fr. L *venatio*, fr. *venari* to hunt, pursue] : the edible flesh of a deer

ven·om \'ven-əm\ *n* [ME *venim, venom*, fr. OF *venim*, deriv. of L *venenum* magic charm, drug, poison] **1** : poisonous material secreted by some animals (as snakes, spiders, or bees) and transmitted usu. by biting or stinging **2** : something that poisons or embitters the mind or spirit : MALIGNITY, MALICE

ven·om·ous \'ven-ə-məs\ *adj* **1** : full of venom : POISONOUS **2** : MALIGNANT, SPITEFUL, MALICIOUS **3** : secreting and using venom (∼ snakes) — **ven·om·ous·ly** *adv*

ve·nous \'vē-nəs\ *adj* **1** : of, relating to, or full of veins **2** : being purplish red oxygen-deficient blood present in most veins

¹vent \'vent\ *vb* **1** : to provide with a vent **2** : to serve as a vent for **3** : EXPEL, DISCHARGE **4** : to give expression to

²vent *n* **1** : an opportunity or way of escape or passage : OUTLET **2** : an opening for passage or escape (as of a fluid, gas, or smoke) or for relieving pressure

³vent *n* : a slit in a garment esp. in the lower part of a seam (as of a jacket or skirt)

ven·ti·late \'vent-ᵊl-ˌāt\ *vb* **-lat·ed; -lat·ing** **1** : to discuss freely and openly (∼ a question) **2** : to give vent to (∼ one's grievances) **3** : to cause fresh air to circulate through (as a room or mine) so as to replace foul air **4** : to provide with a vent or outlet **syn** express, vent, air, utter, voice, broach — **ven·ti·la·tor** \-ᵊl-ˌāt-ər\ *n*

ven·ti·la·tion \ˌvent-ᵊl-'ā-shən\ *n* **1** : the act or process of ventilating **2** : circulation of air (as in a room) **3** : a system or means of providing fresh air

ven·tral \'ven-trəl\ *adj* **1** : of or relating to the belly : ABDOMINAL **2** : of, relating to, or located on or near the surface of the body that in humans is the front but in most other animals is the lower surface — **ven·tral·ly** \-ē\ *adv*

ven·tri·cle \'ven-tri-kəl\ *n* **1** : a chamber of the heart that receives blood from the atrium of the same side and pumps it into the arteries **2** : any of the communicating cavities of the brain that are continuous with the central canal of the spinal cord

ven·tril·o·quism \ven-'tril-ə-ˌkwiz-əm\ *n* [LL *ventriloquus* ventriloquist, fr. L *venter* belly + *loqui* to speak; fr. the belief that the voice is produced from the ventriloquist's stomach] : the production of the voice in such a manner that the sound appears to come from a source other than the speaker — **ven·tril·o·quist** \-kwəst\ *n*

ven·tril·o·quy \-kwē\ *n* : VENTRILOQUISM

¹ven·ture \'ven-chər\ *vb* **ven·tured; ven·tur·ing** \'vench-(ə-)riŋ\ **1** : to expose to hazard : RISK **2** : to undertake the risks of : BRAVE **3** : to advance or put forward or expose to criticism or argument (∼ an opinion) **4** : to make a venture : run a risk **5** : proceed despite danger : DARE

²venture *n* **1** : an undertaking involving

chance or risk; *esp* : a speculative business enterprise **2** : something risked in a speculative venture : STAKE

ven·ture·some \\'ven-chər-səm\\ *adj* **1** : involving risk : DANGEROUS, HAZARDOUS **2** : inclined to venture : BOLD, DARING *syn* adventurous, venturous, rash, reckless, foolhardy — **ven·ture·some·ly** *adv* — **ven·ture·some·ness** *n*

ven·tur·ous \\'vench-(ə-)rəs\\ *adj* : VENTURESOME — **ven·tur·ous·ly** *adv* — **ven·tur·ous·ness** *n*

ven·ue \\'ven-yü\\ *n* : the place in which the alleged events from which a legal action arises took place; *also* : the place from which the jury is taken and where the trial is held

Ve·nus \\'vē-nəs\\ *n* : the planet second in order from the sun

Ve·nu·sian \\vi-'n(y)ü-zhən\\ *adj* : of or relating to the planet Venus

Ve·nus's-fly·trap \\‚vē-nəs-(-əz)-'flī-‚trap\\ *or* **Venus fly·trap** *n* : an insectivorous plant of the Carolina coast that has the leaf tip modified into an insect trap

ve·ra·cious \\və-'rā-shəs\\ *adj* **1** : TRUTHFUL, HONEST **2** : TRUE, ACCURATE — **ve·ra·cious·ly** *adv*

ve·rac·i·ty \\və-'ras-ət-ē\\ *n, pl* **-ties** **1** : devotion to truth : TRUTHFULNESS **2** : conformity with fact : ACCURACY **3** : something true

ve·ran·da *or* **ve·ran·dah** \\və-'ran-də\\ *n* : a long open usu. roofed porch

verb \\'vərb\\ *n* : a word that is the grammatical center of a predicate and expresses an act, occurrence, or mode of being

¹ver·bal \\'vər-bəl\\ *adj* **1** : of, relating to, or consisting of words; *esp* : having to do with words rather than with the ideas to be conveyed **2** : expressed in usu. spoken words : not written : ORAL ⟨a ~ contract⟩ **3** : of, relating to, or formed from a verb **4** : LITERAL, VERBATIM — **ver·bal·ly** \\-ē\\ *adv*

²verbal *n* : a word that combines characteristics of a verb with those of a noun or adjective

verbal auxiliary *n* : an auxiliary verb

ver·bal·ize \\'vər-bə-‚līz\\ *vb* **-ized; -iz·ing** **1** : to speak or write in wordy or empty fashion **2** : to express something in words : describe verbally **3** : to convert into a verb — **ver·bal·iza·tion** \\‚vər-bə-lə-'zā-shən\\ *n*

verbal noun *n* : a noun derived directly from a verb or verb stem and in some uses having the sense and constructions of a verb

ver·ba·tim \\(‚)vər-'bāt-əm\\ *adv or adj* : in the same words : word for word

ver·be·na \\(‚)vər-'bē-nə\\ *n* : VERVAIN; *esp* : any of several garden plants with showy spikes of bright often fragrant flowers

ver·biage \\'vər-bē-ij\\ *n* **1** : superfluity of words or words with little meaning : WORDINESS **2** : DICTION, WORDING

ver·bose \\(‚)vər-'bōs\\ *adj* : using more

words than are needed : WORDY *syn* prolix, diffuse, redundant, windy — **ver·bos·i·ty** \\-'bäs-ət-ē\\ *n*

ver·bo·ten \\vər-'bōt-ᵊn\\ *adj* [G] : forbidden usu. by authority and often unreasonably

ver·dant \\'vərd-ᵊnt\\ *adj* **1** : green with growing plants **2** : unripe in experience : GREEN — **ver·dant·ly** *adv*

ver·dict \\'vər-(‚)dikt\\ *n* [alter. of ME *verdit*, fr. Anglo-French (the French of medieval England), fr. OF *ver* true (fr. L *verus*) + *dit* saying, dictum, fr. L *dictum*, fr. *dicere* to say] **1** : the finding or decision of a jury on the matter submitted to it in trial **2** : DECISION, JUDGMENT

ver·di·gris \\'vərd-ə-‚grēs, -‚gris\\ *n* : a green or bluish deposit that forms on copper, brass, or bronze surfaces when exposed to the weather

ver·dure \\'vər-jər\\ *n* : the greenness of growing vegetation; *also* : green vegetation

¹verge \\'vərj\\ *n* **1** : a staff carried as an emblem of authority or office **2** : something that borders or bounds : EDGE, MARGIN **3** : BRINK, THRESHOLD

²verge *vb* **verged; verg·ing** **1** : to be contiguous **2** : to be on the verge or border

³verge *vb* **verged; verg·ing** **1** : to move or extend in some direction or toward some condition : INCLINE **2** : to be in transition or change

verg·er \\'vər-jər\\ *n* **1** *chiefly Brit* : an attendant who carries a verge (as before a bishop) **2** : SEXTON

ve·rid·i·cal \\və-'rid-i-kəl\\ *adj* **1** : TRUTHFUL **2** : not illusory : GENUINE

ver·i·fy \\'ver-ə-‚fī\\ *vb* **-fied; -fy·ing** **1** : to confirm in law by oath **2** : to establish the truth, accuracy, or reality of *syn* authenticate, confirm, corroborate, substantiate, validate — **ver·i·fi·able** *adj* — **ver·i·fi·ca·tion** \\‚ver-ə-fə-'kā-shən\\ *n*

ver·i·ly \\'ver-ə-lē\\ *adv* **1** : in very truth : CERTAINLY **2** : TRULY, CONFIDENTLY

veri·si·mil·i·tude \\‚ver-ə-sə-'mil-ə-‚t(y)üd\\ *n* : the quality or state of appearing to be true : PROBABILITY; *also* : a statement that is apparently true *syn* plausibility

ver·i·ta·ble \\'ver-ət-ə-bəl\\ *adj* : ACTUAL, GENUINE, TRUE — **ver·i·ta·bly** *adv*

ver·i·ty \\'ver-ət-ē\\ *n, pl* **-ties** **1** : the quality or state of being true or real : TRUTH, REALITY **2** : something (as a statement) that is true **3** : HONESTY, VERACITY

ver·meil *n* [MF] **1** \\'vər-məl, -‚māl\\ : VERMILION **2** \\vər-'mā\\ : gilded silver

ver·mi·cel·li \\‚vər-mə-'chel-ē, -'sel-\\ *n* [It. lit., little worms] : a dough made in long solid strings smaller in diameter than spaghetti

ver·mic·u·lite \\(‚)vər-'mik-yə-‚līt\\ *n* : any of various minerals that result usu. from the expansion of mica granules at high temperatures to give a lightweight highly water-absorbent material

ver·mi·form appendix \\'vər-mə-₁form-\ *n* : APPENDIX 2

ver·mi·fuge \\'vər-mə-₁fyüj\ *n* : a medicine for destroying or expelling intestinal worms

ver·mil·ion *also* **ver·mil·lion** \vər-'mil-yən\ *n* : any of a number of very bright red colors not quite as bright as scarlet; *also* : a pigment yielding one of these colors

ver·min \\'vər-mən\ *n, pl* **vermin** [ME, fr. MF, deriv. of L *vermis* worm] : small common harmful or disgusting animals (as lice or mice) that are difficult to get rid of — **ver·min·ous** *adj*

ver·mouth \vər-'müth\ *n* [F *vermout,* fr. G *wermut* wormwood] : a white wine flavored with herbs and often used in combination with other beverages

¹**ver·nac·u·lar** \və(r)-'nak-yə-lər\ *adj* [L *vernaculus* native, fr. *verna* slave born in his master's house] 1 : of, relating to, or being a language or dialect native to a region or country rather than a literary, cultured, or foreign language 2 : of, relating to, or being the normal spoken form of a language 3 : applied to a plant or animal in common speech as distinguished from biological nomenclature (~ names)

²**vernacular** *n* 1 : a vernacular language 2 : the mode of expression of a group or class 3 : a vernacular name of a plant or animal

ver·nal \\'vərn-ᵊl\ *adj* : of, relating to, or occurring in the spring

ver·nal·iza·tion \₁vərn-ᵊl-ə-'zā-shən\ *n* : the act or process of hastening the flowering and fruiting of plants by treating seeds, bulbs, or seedlings so as to shorten the vegetative period — **ver·nal·ize** \\'vərn-ᵊl-₁īz\ *vb*

ver·ni·er \\'vər-nē-ər\ *n* : a short scale made to slide along the divisions of a graduated instrument to indicate parts of divisions

ve·ron·i·ca \və-'rän-i-kə\ *n* : SPEEDWELL

ver·sa·tile \\'vər-sət-ᵊl\ *adj* : turning with ease from one thing or position to another; *esp* : having many aptitudes — **ver·sa·til·i·ty** \₁vər-sə-'til-ət-ē\ *n*

verse \\'vərs\ *n* 1 : a line of poetry; *also* : STANZA 2 : metrical writing distinguished from poetry esp. by its lower level of intensity 3 : POETRY 4 : POEM 5 : one of the short divisions of a chapter in the Bible

versed \\'vərst\ *adj* : familiar from experience, study, or practice : SKILLED

ver·si·cle \\'vər-si-kəl\ *n* : a verse or sentence said or sung by a clergyman and followed by a response from the people

ver·si·fi·ca·tion \₁vər-sə-fə-'kā-shən\ *n* 1 : the making of verses 2 : metrical structure

ver·si·fy \\'vər-sə-₁fī\ *vb* **-fied; -fy·ing** 1 : to write verse 2 : to turn into verse — **ver·si·fi·er** \-₁fī(-ə)r\ *n*

ver·sion \\'vər-zhən\ *n* 1 : TRANSLATION; *esp* : a translation of the Bible 2 : an account or description from a particular point of view esp. as contrasted with another 3 : a form or variant of a type or original

vers li·bre \₁ver-'lēbrᵊ\ *n, pl* **vers li·bres** *same*\ [F] : FREE VERSE

ver·so \\'vər-sō\ *n, pl* **versos** : a left-hand page

ver·sus \\'vər-səs\ *prep* 1 : AGAINST 2 (the champion ~ the challenger) 2 : in contrast or as an alternative to (free trade ~ protection)

vert *abbr* vertical

ver·te·bra \\'vərt-ə-brə\ *n, pl* **-brae** \-₁brā, -₁(₁)brē\ *or* **-bras** [L] : one of the segments of bone or cartilage making up the backbone

ver·te·bral \(₁)vər-'tē-brəl, 'vərt-ə-\ *adj* : of, relating to, or made up of vertebrae : SPINAL

vertebral column *n* : BACKBONE

¹**ver·te·brate** \\'vərt-ə-brət, -₁brāt\ *adj* 1 : having a backbone 2 : of or relating to the vertebrates

²**vertebrate** *n* : any of a large group of animals (as mammals, birds, reptiles, amphibians, or fishes) that have a backbone or in some primitive forms a flexible rod of cells and that have a tubular nervous system arranged along the back and divided into a brain and spinal cord

ver·tex \\'vər-₁teks\ *n, pl* **ver·ti·ces** \\'vərt-ə-₁sēz\ *also* **ver·tex·es** [L *vertex, vortex* whirl, whirlpool, top of the head, summit, fr. *vertere* to turn] 1 : the point opposite to and farthest from the base of a geometrical figure 2 : the termination or intersection of lines or curves (the ~ of an angle) 3 : ZENITH 1 4 : the highest point : TOP, SUMMIT

ver·ti·cal \\'vərt-i-kəl\ *adj* 1 : of, relating to, or located at the vertex : directly overhead 2 : rising perpendicularly from a level surface : UPRIGHT — **vertical** *n* — **ver·ti·cal·i·ty** \₁vərt-ə-'kal-ət-ē\ *n* — **ver·ti·cal·ly** \-k(ə-)lē\ *adv*

ver·tig·i·nous \(₁)vər-'tij-ə-nəs\ *adj* : marked by, suffering from, or tending to cause dizziness

ver·ti·go \\'vərt-i-₁gō\ *n, pl* **-goes** *or* **-gos** : DIZZINESS, GIDDINESS

ver·vain \\'vər-₁vān\ *n* : any of a genus of herbs or low woody plants with often showy heads or spikes of tubular flowers

verve \\'vərv\ *n* : liveliness of imagination; *also* : VIVACITY

¹**very** \\'ver-ē\ *adj* **veri·er; -est** [ME *ver·ray, verry,* fr. OF *verai,* fr. L *verax* truthful, fr. *verus* true] 1 : EXACT, PRECISE (the ~ heart of the city) 2 : exactly suitable (the ~ tool for the job) 3 : ABSOLUTE, UTTER (the *veriest* nonsense) 4 — used as an intensive esp. to emphasize identity (made the ~ walls shake) 5 : MERE, BARE (the ~ idea

scared him) **6** : SELFSAME, IDENTICAL 〈the ~ man I saw〉

²very *adv* **1** : in actual fact : TRULY **2** : to a high degree : EXTREMELY

very high frequency *n* : a radio frequency of between 30 and 300 megahertz

ves·i·cant \'ves-i-kənt\ *n* : an agent that causes blistering — **vesicant** *adj*

ves·i·cle \'ves-i-kəl\ *n* : a membranous and usu. fluid-filled cavity in a plant or animal; *also* : BLISTER — **ve·sic·u·lar** \və-'sik-yə-lər\ *adj*

¹ves·per \'ves-pər\ *n* **1** *cap* : EVENING STAR **2** : a vesper bell **3** *archaic* : EVENING, EVENTIDE

²vesper *adj* : of or relating to vespers or to the evening

ves·pers \-pərz\ *n pl, often cap* : a late afternoon or evening worship service

ves·per·tine \'ves-pər-ˌtīn\ *adj* **1** : of, relating to, or taking place in the evening **2** : active, flowering, or flourishing in the evening

ves·sel \'ves-əl\ *n* **1** : a hollow or concave utensil (as a barrel, bottle, bowl, or cup) for holding something **2** : a person held to be the recipient of a quality (as grace) **3** : a craft bigger than a rowboat for navigation of the water **4** : a tube in which a body fluid (as blood) is contained and circulated

¹vest \'vest\ *vb* **1** : to place or give into the possession or discretion of some person or authority **2** : to clothe with a particular authority, right, or property **3** : to become legally vested **4** : to clothe with or as if with a garment; *esp* : to garb in ecclesiastical vestments

²vest *n* **1** : a man's sleeveless garment for the upper body usu. worn under a suit coat; *also* : a similar garment for women **2** *chiefly Brit* : a man's sleeveless undershirt **3** : a front piece of a dress resembling the front of a vest

¹ves·tal \'ves-t²l\ *adj* : CHASTE — **ves·tal·ly** \-ē\ *adv*

²vestal *n* : a chaste woman

vestal virgin *n* : a virgin consecrated to the Roman goddess Vesta and to the service of watching the sacred fire perpetually kept burning on her altar

vest·ed \'ves-təd\ *adj* : fully and unconditionally guaranteed as a legal right, benefit, or privilege

vested interest *n* : an interest (as in an existing political, economic, or social arrangement) to which the holder has a strong commitment; *also* : one (as a corporation) having a vested interest

ves·ti·bule \'ves-tə-ˌbyül\ *n* **1** : any of various bodily cavities forming or suggesting an entrance to some other part **2** : a passage or room between the outer door and the interior of a building — **ves·tib·u·lar** \ve-'stib-yə-lər\ *adj*

ves·tige \'ves-tij\ *n* [F, fr. L *vestigium* footprint, track, vestige] : a trace or visible sign left by something lost or vanished; *also* : a minute remaining

amount — **ves·ti·gial** \ve-'stij-(ē-)əl\ *adj* — **ves·ti·gial·ly** \-ē\ *adv*

vest·ing \'ves-tiŋ\ *n* : the conveying to an employee of inalienable rights to share in a pension fund; *also* : the right so conveyed

vest·ment \'ves(t)-mənt\ *n* **1** : an outer garment; *esp* : a ceremonial or official robe **2** *pl* : CLOTHING, GARB **3** : a garment or insignia worn by a clergyman when officiating or assisting at a religious service

vest–pocket *adj* : very small 〈a ~ park〉

ves·try \'ves-trē\ *n, pl* **vestries 1** : a room in a church for vestments, altar linens, and sacred vessels **2** : a room used for church meetings and classes **3** : a body administering the temporal affairs of an Episcopal parish

ves·try·man \-mən\ *n* : a member of a vestry

ves·ture \'ves-chər\ *n* **1** : a covering garment (as a robe) **2** : CLOTHING, APPAREL

¹vet \'vet\ *n* : VETERINARIAN, VETERINARY

²vet *adj or n* : VETERAN

vetch \'vech\ *n* : any of several herbs related to the pea including some valued for fodder

vet·er·an \'vet-(ə-)rən\ *n* [L *veteranus*, fr. *veteranus* old, of long experience, fr. *veter-*, *vetus* old] **1** : an old soldier of long service **2** : a former member of the armed forces **3** : a person of long experience in an occupation or skill — **veteran** *adj*

Veterans Day *n* : November 11 observed as a legal holiday in commemoration of the end of hostilities in 1918 and 1945

vet·er·i·nar·i·an \ˌvet-(ə-)rən-'er-ē-ən, ˌvet-²n-\ *n* : one qualified and authorized to treat injuries and diseases of animals

¹vet·er·i·nary \'vet-(ə-)rən-ˌer-ē, 'vet-²n-\ *adj* : of, relating to, or being the medical care of animals and esp. domestic animals

²veterinary *n, pl* **-nar·ies** : VETERINARIAN

¹ve·to \'vēt-ō\ *n, pl* **vetoes** [L, I forbid] **1** : an authoritative prohibition **2** : a power of one part of a government to forbid the carrying out of projects attempted by another part; *esp* : a power vested in a chief executive to prevent the carrying out of measures adopted by a legislature **3** : the exercise of the power of veto; *also* : a document or message stating the reasons for a specific use of this power

²veto *vb* **1** : FORBID, PROHIBIT **2** : to refuse assent to (a legislative bill) so as to prevent enactment or cause reconsideration — **ve·to·er** *n*

vex \'veks\ *vb* **vexed** *also* **vext**; **vex·ing 1** : to bring trouble, distress, or agitation to **2** : to irritate or annoy by petty provocations **3** : to shake or toss about

vex·a·tion \vek-'sā-shən\ *n* **1** : the act of vexing **2** : the quality or state of being vexed : IRRITATION **3** : a cause of trouble or annoyance

vex·a·tious \-shəs\ *adj* **1** : causing vexation : ANNOYING, DISTRESSING **2** : full of distress or annoyance : TROUBLED — **vex·a·tious·ly** *adv* — **vex·a·tious·ness** *n*

vexed \'vekst\ *adj* : fully debated or discussed ⟨a ∼ question⟩

VF *abbr* **1** video frequency **2** visual field

VFD *abbr* volunteer fire department

VFW *abbr* Veterans of Foreign Wars

VG *abbr* **1** very good **2** vicar-general

VHF *abbr* very high frequency

VI *abbr* Virgin Islands

via \'vī-ə, 'vē-ə\ *prep* : by way of ⟨goods shipped ∼ the Panama Canal⟩

vi·a·ble \'vī-ə-bəl\ *adj* **1** : capable of living; *esp* : capable of surviving outside the mother's womb without artificial support ⟨a ∼ fetus⟩ **2** : capable of being put into practice : WORKABLE **3** : having a reasonable chance of succeeding ⟨a ∼ candidate⟩ — **vi·a·bil·i·ty** \ˌvī-ə-'bil-ət-ē\ *n* — **vi·a·bly** \'vī-ə-blē\ *adv*

via·duct \'vī-ə-ˌdəkt\ *n* : a bridge with high supporting towers or piers for carrying a road or railroad over something (as a valley, river, or road)

vi·al \'vī(-ə)l\ *n* : a small vessel for liquids

vi·and \'vī-ənd\ *n* : an article of food

vi·at·i·cum \vī-'at-i-kəm, vē-\ *n, pl* **-cums** *or* **-ca** \-kə\ **1** : the Christian Eucharist given to a person in danger of death **2** : an allowance esp. in money for traveling needs and expenses

vibes \'vībz\ *n pl* **1** : VIBRAPHONE **2** : VIBRATIONS

vi·brant \'vī-brənt\ *adj* **1** : VIBRATING, PULSATING **2** : pulsating with vigor or activity **3** : readily set in vibration : RESPONSIVE, SENSITIVE **4** : sounding from vibration — **vi·bran·cy** \-brən-sē\ *n*

vi·bra·phone \'vī-brə-ˌfōn\ *n* : a percussion instrument like the xylophone but with metal bars and motor-driven resonators

vi·brate \'vī-ˌbrāt\ *vb* **vi·brat·ed; vi·brat·ing 1** : OSCILLATE **2** : to set in vibration **3** : to be in vibration **4** : to respond sympathetically : THRILL **5** : WAVER, FLUCTUATE

vi·bra·tion \vī-'brā-shən\ *n* **1** : a rapid to-and-fro motion of the particles of an elastic body or medium (as a stretched cord) that produces sound **2** : an act of vibrating : a state of being vibrated : OSCILLATION **3** : a trembling motion **4** : VACILLATION **5** : a distinctive usu. emotional emanation or atmosphere that can be instinctively sensed — usu. used in pl. — **vi·bra·tion·al** \-sh(ə-)nəl\ *adj*

vi·bra·to \vi-'brät-ō\ *n, pl* **-tos** [It] : a slightly tremulous effect imparted to vocal or instrumental music

vi·bra·tor \'vī-ˌbrāt-ər\ *n* : one that vibrates or causes vibration; *esp* : a vibrating electrical device used in massage or for sexual stimulation

vi·bra·to·ry \'vī-brə-ˌtōr-ē\ *adj* : consisting in, capable of, or causing vibration

vi·bur·num \vī-'bər-nəm\ *n* : any of a genus of widely distributed shrubs or trees related to the honeysuckle and bearing small usu. white flowers in broad clusters

vic *abbr* vicinity

Vic *abbr* Victoria

vic·ar \'vik-ər\ *n* **1** : an administrative deputy **2** : an Anglican clergyman in charge of a dependent parish — **vi·car·i·ate** \vī-'ker-ē-ət\ *n*

vic·ar·age \'vik-ə-rij\ *n* : the benefice or house of a vicar

vicar–general *n, pl* **vicars–general** : an administrative deputy (as of a Roman Catholic or Anglican bishop)

vi·car·i·ous \vī-'ker-ē-əs, -'kar-\ *adj* **1** : acting for another **2** : done or suffered by one person on behalf of another or others ⟨a ∼ sacrifice⟩ **3** : realized or experienced by one person through sympathetic sharing in the experience of another — **vi·car·i·ous·ly** *adv* — **vi·car·i·ous·ness** *n*

¹vice \'vīs\ *n* **1** : DEPRAVITY, WICKEDNESS **2** : a moral fault; *esp* : an immoral habit **3** : a physical imperfection : BLEMISH **4** : an undesirable behavior pattern in a domestic animal

²vice *chiefly Brit var of* VISE

³vi·ce \'vī-sē\ *prep* : in the place of : SUCCEEDING

vice admiral *n* : a commissioned officer in the navy or coast guard ranking above a rear admiral

vice-ge·rent \'vīs-'jir-ənt\ *n* : an administrative deputy of a king or magistrate — **vice-ge·ren·cy** \-ən-sē\ *n*

vi·cen·ni·al \vī-'sen-ē-əl\ *adj* : occurring once every 20 years

vice presidency *n* : the office of vice president

vice president *n* **1** : an officer ranking next to a president and usu. empowered to act for the president during an absence or disability **2** : a president's deputy in charge of a particular location or function

vice·re·gal \'vīs-'rē-gəl\ *adj* : of or relating to a viceroy

vice·roy \'vīs-ˌrȯi\ *n* : the governor of a country or province who rules as representative of the sovereign — **vice·roy·al·ty** \-əl-tē\ *n*

vice ver·sa \ˌvī-si-'vər-sə, (')vīs-'vər-\ *adv* : with the order reversed : CONVERSELY

vi·chys·soise \ˌvish-ē-'swäz, ˌvē-shē-\ *n* [F] : a thick soup made esp. from leeks or onions and potatoes, cream, and chicken stock and usu. served cold

Vi·chy water \'vish-ē-\ *n* : carbonated water

vic·i·nage \'vis-ᵊn-ij\ *n* : a neighboring or surrounding district : VICINITY

vi·cin·i·ty \və-'sin-ət-ē\ *n, pl* **-ties** [MF *vicinité,* fr. L *vicinitas,* fr. *vicinus* neighboring, fr. *vicus* row of houses, village] **1** : NEARNESS, PROXIMITY **2** : a surrounding area : NEIGHBORHOOD

vi·cious \'vish-əs\ *adj* **1** : addicted to vice : WICKED, DEPRAVED **2** : DEFECTIVE, FAULTY; *also* : INVALID **3** : IMPURE, FOUL **4** : having a savage disposition **5** : MALICIOUS, SPITEFUL **6** : worsened by internal causes that augment each other ⟨~ wage-price spiral⟩ — **vi·cious·ly** *adv* — **vi·cious·ness** *n*

vi·cis·si·tude \və-'sis-ə-ₜt(y)üd, vī-\ *n* **1** : the quality or state of being changeable **2** : a change or succession from one thing to another; *esp* : an irregular, unexpected, or surprising change

vic·tim \'vik-təm\ *n* **1** : a living being offered as a sacrifice in a religious rite **2** : an individual injured or killed (as by disease or accident) **3** : a person cheated, fooled, or injured ⟨a ~ of circumstances⟩

vic·tim·ize \'vik-tə-ₜmīz\ *vb* **-ized; -iz·ing** : to make a victim of — **vic·tim·iza·tion** \ₜvik-tə-mə-'zā-shən\ *n* — **vic·tim·iz·er** \'vik-tə-ₜmī-zər\ *n*

vic·tim·less *adj* : having no victim ⟨considered gambling to be a ~ crime⟩

vic·tor \'vik-tər\ *n* : WINNER, CONQUEROR

vic·to·ria \vik-'tōr-ē-ə\ *n* : a low 4-wheeled carriage with a folding top and a raised seat in front for the driver

¹Vic·to·ri·an \vik-'tōr-ē-ən\ *adj* **1** : of or relating to the reign of Queen Victoria of England or the art, letters, or tastes of her time **2** : typical of the standards, attitudes, or conduct of the age of Victoria esp. when considered prudish or narrow

²Victorian *n* : a person and esp. an author of the Victorian period

vic·to·ri·ous \vik-'tōr-ē-əs\ *adj* **1** : having won a victory : CONQUERING **2** : of, relating to, or characteristic of victory — **vic·to·ri·ous·ly** *adv*

vic·to·ry \'vik-t(ə-)rē\ *n, pl* **-ries** **1** : the overcoming of an enemy or an antagonist **2** : achievement of mastery or success in a struggle or endeavor against odds

¹vict·ual \'vit-ᵊl\ *n* **1** : food usable by man **2** *pl* : food supplies : PROVISIONS

²victual *vb* **-ualed** *or* **-ualled; -ual·ing** *or* **-ual·ling** **1** : to supply with food **2** : to store up provisions

vict·ual·ler *or* **vict·ual·er** \'vit-ᵊl-ər\ *n* : one that supplies provisions (as to an army or a ship)

vi·cu·ña *or* **vi·cu·na** \vi-'kün-yə, vī-; vī-'k(y)ü-nə\ *n* **1** : a So. American wild mammal related to the llama and alpaca; *also* : its wool **2** : a soft fabric woven from the wool of the vicuña; *also* : a sheep's wool imitation of this

vi·de \'vīd-ē, 'vē-ₜdā\ *vb imper* [L] : SEE

— used to direct a reader to another item

vi·de·li·cet \və-'del-ə-ₜset, vī-; vi-'dā-li-ₜket\ *adv* [ME, fr. L, fr. *vidēre* to see + *licet* it is permitted] : that is to say : NAMELY

¹vid·eo \'vid-ē-ₜō\ *n* **1** : TELEVISION **2** : VIDEOTAPE

²video *adj* **1** : relating to or used in transmission or reception of the television image **2** : relating to or being images on a television screen or computer display ⟨a ~ terminal⟩

vid·eo·cas·sette \'vid-ē-ō-kə-ₜset\ *n* **1** : a case containing videotape for use with a VCR **2** : a recording (as of a movie) on a videocassette

videocassette recorder *n* : VCR

vid·eo·disc *or* **vid·eo·disk** \-ₜdisk\ *n* **1** : a disc similar in appearance and use to a phonograph record on which programs have been recorded for playback on a television set; *also* : OPTICAL DISC **2** : a recording (as of a movie) on a videodisc

video game *n* : an electronic game played on a video screen

vid·eo·phone \'vid-ē-ə-ₜfōn\ *n* : a telephone for transmitting both audio and video signals

¹vid·eo·tape \'vid-ē-ō-ₜtāp\ *n* : a recording of visual images and sound made on magnetic tape; *also* : the magnetic tape used for such a recording

²videotape *vb* : to make a videotape of ⟨~ a show⟩

videotape recorder *n* : a device for recording and playing back videotapes

vid·eo·tex \-ₜteks\ *also* **vid·eo·text** \-ₜtekst\ *n* : an interactive electronic communications system in which data transmitted by a computer appears on a subscriber's video display

vie \'vī\ *vb* **vied; vy·ing** \'vī-iŋ\ : to strive for superiority : CONTEND — **vi·er** \'vī(-ə)r\ *n*

Viet·cong \vē-'et-'käŋ, ₜvē-ət-, -'kóŋ\ *n, pl* **Vietcong** : an adherent of the Vietnamese communist movement

Viet·nam·ese \vē-ₜet-nə-'mēz, ₜvē-ət-, -'mēs\ *n, pl* **Vietnamese** : a native or inhabitant of Vietnam — **Vietnamese** *adj*

¹view \'vyü\ *n* **1** : the act of seeing or examining : INSPECTION; *also* : SURVEY **2** : a way of looking at or regarding something **3** : ESTIMATE, JUDGMENT ⟨stated his ~s⟩ **4** : a sight (as of a landscape) regarded for its pictorial quality **5** : extent or range of vision ⟨within ~⟩ **6** : OBJECT, PURPOSE ⟨done with a ~ to promotion⟩ **7** : a picture of a scene

²view *vb* **1** : to look at attentively : EXAMINE **2** : SEE, BEHOLD **3** : to examine mentally : CONSIDER — **view·er** *n*

view·er·ship \-ₜship\ *n* : a television audience esp. with respect to size or makeup

view·find·er \'vyü-ₜfīn-dər\ *n* : a device

on a camera for showing the view to be included in the picture

view·point \-ˌpȯint\ *n* : a position from which something is considered : POINT OF VIEW, STANDPOINT

vi·ges·i·mal \vī-ˈjes-ə-məl\ *adj* : based on the number 20

vig·il \ˈvij-əl\ *n* 1 : a religious observance formerly held on the night before a religious feast 2 : the day before a religious feast observed as a day of spiritual preparation 3 : evening or nocturnal devotions or prayers — usu. used in pl. 4 : an act or a time of keeping awake when sleep is customary; *esp* : WATCH 1

vig·i·lance \ˈvij-ə-ləns\ *n* : the quality or state of being vigilant

vigilance committee *n* : a committee of vigilantes

vig·i·lant \ˈvij-ə-lənt\ *adj* : alertly watchful esp. to avoid danger — **vig·i·lant·ly** *adv*

vig·i·lan·te \ˌvij-ə-ˈlant-ē\ *n* : a member of a volunteer committee organized to suppress and punish crime summarily (as when the processes of law appear inadequate)

¹vi·gnette \vin-ˈyet\ *n* [F, fr. MF *vignete*, fr. dim. of *vigne* vine] 1 : a small decorative design on or just before the title page of a book or at the beginning or end of a chapter 2 : a picture (as an engraving or a photograph) that shades off gradually into the surrounding ground 3 : a short descriptive literary sketch

²vignette *vb* **vi·gnett·ed; vi·gnett·ing** : to finish (as a photograph) in the manner of a vignette

vig·or \ˈvig-ər\ *n* 1 : active strength or energy of body or mind 2 : INTENSITY, FORCE

vig·or·ous \ˈvig-(ə-)rəs\ *adj* 1 : having vigor : ROBUST 2 : done with vigor : carried out forcefully and energetically — **vig·or·ous·ly** *adv* — **vig·or·ous·ness** *n*

Vi·king \ˈvī-kiŋ\ *n* [ON *vīkingr*] : one of the pirate Norsemen plundering the coasts of Europe in the 8th to 10th centuries

vil *abbr* village

vile \ˈvīl\ *adj* **vil·er; vil·est** 1 : morally despicable 2 : physically repulsive : FOUL 3 : of little worth 4 : DEGRADING, IGNOMINIOUS 5 : utterly bad or inferior ⟨~ weather⟩ — **vile·ly** \ˈvīl-lē\ *adv* — **vile·ness** *n*

vil·i·fy \ˈvil-ə-ˌfī\ *vb* **-fied; -fy·ing** : to blacken the character of with abusive language : DEFAME *syn* malign, calumniate, slander, libel, traduce — **vil·i·fi·ca·tion** \ˌvil-ə-fə-ˈkā-shən\ *n* — **vil·i·fi·er** \ˈvil-ə-ˌfī(-ə)r\ *n*

vil·la \ˈvil-ə\ *n* 1 : a country estate 2 : the rural or suburban residence of a wealthy person

vil·lage \ˈvil-ij\ *n* 1 : a settlement usu. larger than a hamlet and smaller than a town 2 : an incorporated minor

municipality 3 : the people of a village

vil·lag·er \ˈvil-ij-ər\ *n* : an inhabitant of a village

vil·lain \ˈvil-ən\ *n* 1 : VILLEIN 2 : a deliberate scoundrel or criminal

vil·lain·ess \-ə-nəs\ *n* : a woman who is a villain

vil·lain·ous \-ə-nəs\ *adj* 1 : befitting a villain : WICKED, EVIL 2 : highly objectionable : DETESTABLE *syn* vicious, iniquitous, nefarious, infamous, corrupt, degenerate — **vil·lain·ous·ly** *adv* — **vil·lain·ous·ness** *n*

vil·lainy \-ə-nē\ *n, pl* **-lain·ies** 1 : villainous conduct; *also* : a villainous act 2 : villainous character or nature : DEPRAVITY

vil·lein \ˈvil-ən, ˈvil-ˌān\ *n* 1 : a free villager of Anglo-Saxon times 2 : an unfree peasant having the status of a slave to a feudal lord

vil·len·age \ˈvil-ə-nij\ *n* 1 : the holding of land at the will of a feudal lord 2 : the status of a villein

vil·lous \ˈvil-əs\ *adj* : covered with fine hairs or villi

vil·lus \ˈvil-əs\ *n, pl* **vil·li** \ˈvil-ˌī, -(ˌ)ē\ : a slender usu. vascular process; *esp* : one of the tiny projections of the mucous membrane of the small intestine that function in the absorption of food

vim \ˈvim\ *n* : robust energy and enthusiasm : VITALITY

vin·ai·grette \ˌvin-i-ˈgret\ *n* [F] 1 : a sauce made typically of oil and vinegar, onions, parsley, and herbs 2 : a small box or bottle for holding aromatic preparations (as smelling salts)

vin·ci·ble \ˈvin-sə-bəl\ *adj* : capable of being overcome or subdued

vin·di·cate \ˈvin-də-ˌkāt\ *vb* **-cat·ed; -cat·ing** 1 : AVENGE 2 : EXONERATE, ABSOLVE 3 : CONFIRM, SUBSTANTIATE 4 : to provide defense for : JUSTIFY 5 : to maintain a right to : ASSERT — **vin·di·ca·tor** \-ˌkāt-ər\ *n*

vin·di·ca·tion \ˌvin-də-ˈkā-shən\ *n* : a vindicating or being vindicated; *esp* : justification against denial or censure

vin·dic·tive \vin-ˈdik-tiv\ *adj* 1 : disposed to revenge 2 : intended for or involving revenge 3 : VICIOUS, SPITEFUL — **vin·dic·tive·ly** *adv* — **vin·dic·tive·ness** *n*

vine \ˈvīn\ *n* [ME, fr. OF *vigne*, fr. L *vinea* vine, vineyard, fr. fem. of *vineus* of wine, fr. *vinum* wine] 1 : GRAPE 2 : a plant whose stem requires support and which climbs (as by tendrils) or trails along the ground; *also* : the stem of such a plant

vin·e·gar \ˈvin-i-gər\ *n* [ME *vinegre*, fr. OF *vinaigre*, fr. *vin* wine + *aigre* keen, sour] : a sour liquid obtained by fermentation (as of cider, wine, or malt) and used in cookery and pickling

vin·e·gary \ˈvin-i-g(ə-)rē\ *adj* 1 : resembling vinegar : SOUR 2 : disagreeable in manner or disposition : CRABBED

vine·yard \\'vin-yərd\ *n* **1** : a plantation of grapevines **2** : an area of physical or mental occupation

vi·nous \\'vī-nəs\ *adj* **1** : of, relating to, or made with wine ⟨∼ medications⟩ **2** : showing the effects of the use of wine

¹vin·tage \\'vint-ij\ *n* **1** : a season's yield of grapes or wine **2** : WINE; *esp* : a usu. superior wine which comes from a single year **3** : the act or period of gathering grapes or making wine **4** : a period of origin ⟨clothes of 1890 ∼⟩

²vintage *adj* **1** : of, relating to, or produced in a particular vintage **2** : of old, recognized, and enduring interest, importance, or quality : CLASSIC ⟨∼ cars⟩ **3** : of the best and most characteristic — used with a proper noun

vint·ner \\'vint-nər\ *n* : a dealer in wines

vi·nyl \\'vīn-ᵊl\ *n* **1** : a chemical derived from ethylene by the removal of one hydrogen atom **2** : a polymer of a vinyl compound or a product (as a textile fiber) made from one

vinyl chloride *n* : a flammable gaseous carcinogenic compound used esp. to make vinyl resins

vi·ol \\'vī-(ə)l\ *n* : a bowed stringed instrument chiefly of the 16th and 17th centuries having a fretted neck and usu. six strings

¹vi·o·la \\vī-'ō-lə, 'vī-ə-lə\ *n* → VIOLET 1; *esp* : any of various hybrid garden plants with white, yellow, purple, or variously colored flowers that resemble but are smaller than the related pansies

²vi·o·la \\vē-'ō-lə\ *n* : an instrument of the violin family slightly larger and tuned lower than a violin — **vi·o·list** \\-ləst\ *n*

vi·o·la·ble \\'vī-ə-lə-bəl\ *adj* : capable of being violated

vi·o·late \\'vī-ə-₁lāt\ *vb* **-lat·ed; -lat·ing 1** : BREAK, DISREGARD ⟨∼ a law⟩ ⟨∼ a frontier⟩ **2** : RAPE **3** : PROFANE, DESECRATE **4** : INTERRUPT, DISTURB ⟨*violated* his privacy⟩ — **vi·o·la·tor** \\-₁lāt-ər\ *n*

vi·o·la·tion \\₁vī-ə-'lā-shən\ *n* : an act or instance of violating : the state of being violated *syn* breach, infraction, trespass, infringement, transgression

vi·o·lence \\'vī-ə-ləns\ *n* **1** : exertion of physical force so as to injure or abuse **2** : injury by or as if by infringement or profanation **3** : intense or furious often destructive action or force **4** : vehement feeling or expression : INTENSITY **5** : jarring quality : DISCORDANCE *syn* compulsion, coercion, duress, constraint

vi·o·lent \\-lənt\ *adj* **1** : marked by extreme force or sudden intense activity; *esp* : marked by improper use of such force **2** : caused by or showing strong feeling ⟨∼ words⟩ **3** : EXTREME, INTENSE **4** : caused by force : not natural ⟨∼ death⟩ — **vi·o·lent·ly** *adv*

vi·o·let \\'vī-ə-lət\ *n* **1** : any of a genus of herbs or woody-stemmed plants usu. with heart-shaped leaves and both aerial and underground flowers; *esp* : one with small solid-colored flowers **2** : a variable color averaging a reddish blue

vi·o·lin \\₁vī-ə-'lin\ *n* : a bowed stringed instrument with four strings that has a shallower body and a more curved bridge than a viol — **vi·o·lin·ist** \\-əst\ *n*

vi·o·lon·cel·lo \\₁vī-ə-lən-'chel-ō\ *n* [It] : CELLO — **vi·o·lon·cel·list** \\-əst\ *n*

VIP \\₁vē-₁ī-'pē\ *n, pl* **VIPs** \\-'pēz\ [*very important person*] : a person of great influence or prestige; *esp* : a high official with special privileges

vi·per \\'vī-pər\ *n* **1** : any of various sluggish heavy-bodied Old World venomous snakes **2** : PIT VIPER **3** : any venomous or reputedly venomous snake **4** : a vicious or treacherous person — **vi·per·ine** \\-pə-₁rīn\ *adj*

vi·ra·go \\və-'räg-ō, -'rāg-\ *n, pl* **-goes** *or* **-gos** [L, manlike heroic woman, fr. *vir* man] : a scolding, quarrelsome, or loud overbearing woman *syn* amazon, termagant, scold, shrew, vixen

vi·ral \\'vī-rəl\ *adj* : of, relating to, or caused by a virus

vi·reo \\'vir-ē-₁ō\ *n, pl* **-eos** [L, a small bird, fr. *virēre* to be green] : any of various small insect-eating American songbirds mostly olive green and grayish in color

¹vir·gin \\'vər-jən\ *n* **1** : an unmarried woman devoted to religion **2** : an unmarried girl or woman **3** *cap* : the mother of Jesus **4** : a person who has not had sexual intercourse

²virgin *adj* **1** : free from stain : PURE, SPOTLESS **2** : CHASTE **3** : befitting a virgin : MODEST **4** : FRESH, UNSPOILED; *esp* : not altered by human activity ⟨∼ forest⟩ **5** : INITIAL, FIRST

vir·gin·al \\'vər-jən-ᵊl\ *adj* : of, relating to, or characteristic of a virgin or virginity — **vir·gin·al·ly** \\-ē\ *adv*

²virginal *n* : a small rectangular spinet without legs popular in the 16th and 17th centuries

Vir·gin·ia creeper \\vər-₁jin-yə-\ *n* : a No. American vine having leaves with five leaflets and bluish black berries

Virginia reel *n* : an American country-dance

vir·gin·i·ty \\vər-'jin-ət-ē\ *n, pl* **-ties 1** : the quality or state of being virgin; *esp* : MAIDENHOOD **2** : the unmarried life : CELIBACY

Vir·go \\'vər-₁gō\ *n* [L, lit., virgin] **1** : a zodiacal constellation between Leo and Libra usu. pictured as a young woman **2** : the 6th sign of the zodiac in astrology; *also* : one born under this sign

vir·gule \\'vər-gyül\ *n* : a mark / used typically to denote "or" (as in *and/or*) or "per" (as in *feet/second*)

vir·i·des·cent \\₁vir-ə-'des-ᵊnt\ *adj* : slightly green : GREENISH

vir·ile \\'vir-əl\ *adj* **1** : having the nature, powers, or qualities of a man **2** : MASCULINE, MALE **3** : MASTERFUL, FORCEFUL — **vi·ril·i·ty** \və-'ril-ət-ē\ *n*

vi·ri·on \'vī-rē-ˌän, 'vir-ē-\ *n* : a complete virus particle consisting of an RNA or DNA core with a protein coat

vi·rol·o·gy \vī-'räl-ə-jē\ *n* : a branch of science that deals with viruses — **vi·rol·o·gist** \-jəst\ *n*

vir·tu \ˌvər-'tü, vir-\ *n* **1** : a love of or taste for objects of art **2** : objects of art (as curios and antiques)

vir·tu·al \'vər-chə-(wə)l\ *adj* : being in essence or in effect though not formally recognized or admitted (a ~ dictator) — **vir·tu·al·ly** \-ē\ *adv*

vir·tue \'vər-chü\ *n* [ME *virtu*, fr. OF, fr. L *virtus* strength, manliness, virtue, fr. *vir* man] **1** : conformity to a standard of right : MORALITY **2** : a particular moral excellence **3** : manly strength or courage : VALOR **4** : a commendable quality : MERIT **5** : active power to accomplish a given effect : POTENCY, EFFICACY **6** : chastity esp. in a woman

vir·tu·os·i·ty \ˌvər-chə-'wäs-ət-ē\ *n, pl* **-ties** : great technical skill in the practice of a fine art

vir·tu·o·so \ˌvər-chə-'wō-sō, -zō\ *n, pl* **-sos** *or* **-si** \-sē, -zē\ [It] **1** : one skilled in or having a taste for the fine arts **2** : one who excels in the technique of an art; *esp* : a highly skilled musical performer **syn** expert, adept, artist, doyen, master — **virtuoso** *adj*

vir·tu·ous \'vərch-(ə-)wəs\ *adj* **1** : having or showing virtue and esp. moral virtue **2** : CHASTE — **vir·tu·ous·ly** *adv*

vir·u·lent \'vir-(y)ə-lənt\ *adj* **1** : highly infectious (a ~ germ); *also* : marked by a rapid and very severe course (a ~ disease) **2** : extremely poisonous or venomous : NOXIOUS **3** : bitterly hostile : MALIGN — **vir·u·lence** \-ləns\ *n* — **vir·u·lent·ly** *adv*

vi·rus \'vī-rəs\ *n* [L, slimy liquid, poison, stench] **1** : any of a large group of submicroscopic infectious agents that have an outside coat of protein around a core of RNA or DNA, that can grow and multiply only in living cells, and that cause important diseases in human beings, lower animals, and plants; *also* : a disease caused by a virus **2** : something (as a corrupting influence) that poisons the mind or spirit

vis *abbr* **1** visibility **2** visual

¹vi·sa \'vē-zə, -sə\ *n* [F] **1** : an endorsement by the proper authorities on a passport to show that it has been examined and the bearer may proceed **2** : a signature by a superior official signifying approval of a document

²visa *vb* **vi·saed** \-zəd, -səd\; **vi·sa·ing** \-zə-iŋ, -sə-\ : to give a visa to (a passport)

vis·age \'viz-ij\ *n* : the face or countenance of a person or sometimes an animal; *also* : LOOK, APPEARANCE

¹vis-à-vis \ˌvēz-ə-'vē, ˌvēs-\ *prep* [F, lit., face-to-face] **1** : face-to-face with : OPPOSITE **2** : in relation to **3** : as compared with

²vis-à-vis *n, pl* **vis-à-vis** \-ə-'vē(z)\ **1** : one that is face-to-face with another **2** : ESCORT **3** : COUNTERPART **4** : TÊTEà-TÊTE

³vis-à-vis *adv* : in company : TOGETHER

viscera *pl of* VISCUS

vis·cer·al \'vis-ə-rəl\ *adj* **1** : felt in or as if in the viscera **2** : of or relating to the viscera — **vis·cer·al·ly** \-ē\ *adv*

vis·cid \'vis-əd\ *adj* : VISCOUS — **vis·cid·i·ty** \vis-'id-ət-ē\ *n*

vis·cos·i·ty \vis-'käs-ət-ē\ *n, pl* **-ties** : the quality of being viscous; *esp* : the property of a fluid that causes it to resist flow

vis·count \'vī-ˌkaunt\ *n* : a member of the British peerage ranking below an earl and above a baron

vis·count·ess \-ˌkaunt-əs\ *n* **1** : the wife or widow of a viscount **2** : a woman who holds the rank of viscount in her own right

vis·cous \'vis-kəs\ *adj* [ME *viscouse*, fr. LL *viscosus* full of birdlime, viscous, fr. L *viscum* mistletoe, birdlime] **1** : having the sticky consistency of glue **2** : having or characterized by viscosity

vis·cus \'vis-kəs\ *n, pl* **vis·cera** \'vis-ə-rə\ : an internal organ of the body; *esp* : one (as the heart or liver) located in the cavity of the trunk

vise \'vīs\ *n* [MF *vis* something winding, fr. L *vitis* vine] : a tool with two jaws for holding or clamping work that typically close by a screw or lever

vis·i·bil·i·ty \ˌviz-ə-'bil-ət-ē\ *n, pl* **-ties 1** : the quality, condition, or degree of being visible **2** : the degree of clearness of the atmosphere

vis·i·ble \'viz-ə-bəl\ *adj* : capable of being seen (~ stars); *also* : MANIFEST, APPARENT (has no ~ means of support) — **vis·i·bly** *adv*

¹vi·sion \'vizh-ən\ *n* **1** : something seen otherwise than by ordinary sight (as in a dream or trance) **2** : a vivid picture created by the imagination **3** : the act or power of imagination **4** : unusual wisdom in foreseeing what is going to happen **5** : the act or power of seeing : SIGHT **6** : something seen; *esp* : a lovely sight

²vision *vb* **vi·sioned; vi·sion·ing** \'vizh-(ə-)niŋ\ : to see in or as if in a vision : IMAGINE, ENVISION

¹vi·sion·ary \'vizh-ə-ˌner-ē\ *adj* **1** : of the nature of a vision : ILLUSORY, UNREAL **2** : seeing or likely to see visions : given to dreaming or imagining **3** : not practical : UTOPIAN **syn** imaginary, fantastic, chimerical, quixotic

²visionary *n, pl* **-ar·ies 1** : one whose ideas or projects are impractical : DREAMER **2** : one who sees visions

¹vis·it \'viz-ət\ *vb* **1** : to go to see in order to comfort or help **2** : to call upon either as an act of courtesy or in a professional capacity **3** : to dwell with for a time as a guest **4** : to come to or upon as a reward, affliction, or punishment **5** : INFLICT **6** : to make a visit or regular or frequent visits **7** : CHAT, CONVERSE — **vis·it·able** *adj*

²visit *n* **1** : a short stay : CALL **2** : a brief residence as a guest **3** : a journey to and stay at a place **4** : a formal or professional call (as by a doctor)

vis·i·tant \'viz-ət-ənt\ *n* : VISITOR

vis·i·ta·tion \₁viz-ə-'tā-shən\ *n* **1** : VISIT; *esp* : an official visit **2** : a special dispensation of divine favor or wrath; *also* : a severe trial

visiting nurse *n* : a nurse employed to visit sick persons or perform public-health services in a community

vis·i·tor \'viz-ət-ər\ *n* : one that visits

vi·sor \'vī-zər\ *n* **1** : the front piece of a helmet; *esp* : a movable upper piece **2** : VIZARD **3** : a projecting part (as on a cap) to shade the eyes — **vi·sored** \-zərd\ *adj*

vis·ta \'vis-tə\ *n* **1** : a distant view through or along an avenue or opening **2** : an extensive mental view over a series of years or events

VISTA *abbr* Volunteers in Service to America

¹vi·su·al \'vizh-(ə-w)əl\ *adj* **1** : of, relating to, or used in sight (∼ organs) **2** : perceived by vision (a ∼ impression) **3** : VISIBLE **4** : done by sight only (∼ navigation) **5** : of or relating to instruction by means of sight (∼ aids) — **vi·su·al·ly** \-ē\ *adv*

²visual *n* : something (as a picture, chart, or film) that appeals to the sight and is used for illustration, demonstration, or promotion — usu. used in pl.

vi·su·al·ize \'vizh-(ə-)wə-₁līz\ *vb* **-ized; -iz·ing** : to make visible; *esp* : to form a mental image of — **vi·su·al·iza·tion** \₁vizh-ə-(wə-)lə-'zā-shən\ *n* — **vi·su·al·iz·er** \'vizh-ə-(wə-)₁lī-zər\ *n*

vi·ta \'vēt-ə, 'vīt-ə\ *n, pl* **vi·tae** \'vē-₁tī, 'vīt-ē\ [L, lit., life] : a brief autobiographical sketch

vi·tal \'vīt-əl\ *adj* **1** : concerned with or necessary to the maintenance of life **2** : full of life and vigor : ANIMATED **3** : of, relating to, or characteristic of life **4** : FATAL, MORTAL (∼ wound) **5** : FUNDAMENTAL, BASIC, INDISPENSABLE — **vi·tal·ly** \-ē\ *adv*

vi·tal·i·ty \vī-'tal-ət-ē\ *n, pl* **-ties 1** : the peculiarity distinguishing the living from the nonliving; *also* : capacity to live : mental and physical vigor **2** : enduring quality **3** : ANIMATION, LIVELINESS

vi·tal·ize \'vīt-əl-₁īz\ *vb* **-ized; -iz·ing** : to impart life or vigor to : ANIMATE, ENERGIZE — **vi·tal·iza·tion** \₁vīt-əl-ə-'zā-shən\ *n*

vi·tals \'vīt-əlz\ *n pl* **1** : vital organs **2** : essential parts

vital signs *n pl* : the pulse rate, respira-

tory rate, body temperature, and sometimes blood pressure of a person

vital statistics *n pl* : statistics dealing with births, deaths, marriages, health, and disease

vi·ta·min \'vīt-ə-mən\ *n* : any of various organic substances that are essential in tiny amounts to most animals and some plants and are mostly obtained from foods

vitamin A *n* : any of several vitamins (as from egg yolk or fish-liver oils) required for healthy epithelium and sight

vitamin B 1 : VITAMIN B COMPLEX **2** *or* **vitamin B₁** : THIAMINE

vitamin B complex *n* : a group of vitamins that are found widely in foods and are essential for normal function of certain enzymes and for growth

vitamin B₆ \-'bē-₁siks\ *n* : any of several compounds that are considered essential to vertebrate nutrition

vitamin B₁₂ \-'bē-'twelv\ *n* : a complex cobalt-containing compound that occurs esp. in liver and is essential to normal blood formation, neural function, and growth; *also* : any of several compounds of similar action

vitamin C *n* : a vitamin found esp. in fruits and vegetables and needed by the body to prevent scurvy

vitamin D *n* : any or all of several vitamins that are needed for normal bone and tooth structure and are found esp. in fish-liver oils, egg yolk, and milk or are produced in response to ultraviolet light

vitamin E *n* : any of various oily fat-soluble liquid compounds that are found esp. in plants and are necessary in the body to prevent such ailments as infertility, the breakdown of muscles, and vascular problems

vitamin K *n* [Dan *koagulation* coagulation] : any of several vitamins that are needed in order for blood to clot properly

vi·ti·ate \'vish-ē-₁āt\ *vb* **-at·ed; -at·ing 1** : CONTAMINATE, POLLUTE; *also* : DEBASE, PERVERT **2** : to make legally without force : INVALIDATE — **vi·ti·a·tion** \₁vish-ē-'ā-shən\ *n* — **vi·ti·a·tor** \'vish-ē-₁āt-ər\ *n*

vi·ti·cul·ture \'vit-ə-₁kəl-chər\ *n* : the growing of grapes — **vi·ti·cul·tur·al** \₁vit-ə-'kəlch(-ə)-rəl\ *adj* — **vi·ti·cul·tur·ist** \-rəst\ *n*

vit·re·ous \'vi-trē-əs\ *adj* **1** : of, relating to, or resembling glass **2** : GLASSY (∼ rocks) **3** : of, relating to, or being the clear colorless transparent jelly (**vitreous humor**) behind the lens in the eyeball

vit·ri·ol \'vi-trē-əl\ *n* : something resembling acid in being caustic, corrosive, or biting — **vit·ri·ol·ic** \₁vi-trē-'äl-ik\ *adj*

vit·tles \'vit-²lz\ *n pl* : VICTUALS

vi·tu·per·ate \vī-'t(y)ü-pə-₁rāt, və-\ *vb* **-at·ed; -at·ing** : to abuse in words

: SCOLD **syn** revile, berate, rate, up-braid, rail, lash — **vi·tu·per·a·tive** \-ˈt(y)ü-p(ə-)ˌrāt-iv, -pə-ˌrāt-\ *adj* — **vi·tu·per·a·tive·ly** *adv*

vi·tu·per·a·tion \(ˌ)vī-t(y)ü-pə-ˈrā-shən, və-\ *n* : lengthy harsh criticism or abuse

vi·va \ˈvē-və\ *interj* [It, long live, fr. *vivere* to live, fr. L] — used to express goodwill or approval

vi·va·ce \vē-ˈväch-ā\ *adv or adj* [It] : in a brisk spirited manner — used as a direction in music

vi·va·cious \və-ˈvā-shəs, vī-\ *adj* : lively in temper or conduct : ANIMATED, SPRIGHTLY — **vi·va·cious·ly** *adv* — **vi·va·cious·ness** *n*

vi·vac·i·ty \-ˈvas-ət-ē\ *n* : the quality or state of being vivacious

vi·var·i·um \vī-ˈvar-ē-əm, -ˈver-\ *n, pl* **-ia** \-ē-ə\ *or* **-iums** : an enclosure for keeping or raising and observing animals or plants indoors; *esp* : one for terrestrial animals

vi·va vo·ce \ˌvī-və-ˈvō-sē\ *adj* [ML, with the living voice] : expressed or conducted by word of mouth : ORAL ⟨*viva voce* examination⟩ ⟨*viva voce* voting⟩ — **viva voce** *adv*

viv·id \ˈviv-əd\ *adj* **1** : having the appearance of vigorous life or freshness : LIVELY **2** : BRILLIANT, INTENSE ⟨a ~ red⟩ **3** : producing a strong impression on the senses : SHARP **4** : calling forth lifelike mental images — **viv·id·ly** *adv* — **viv·id·ness** *n*

viv·i·fy \ˈviv-ə-ˌfī\ *vb* **-fied; -fy·ing 1** : to endue with life : ANIMATE **2** : to make vivid — **viv·i·fi·ca·tion** \ˌviv-ə-fə-ˈkā-shən\ *n* — **viv·i·fi·er** \ˈviv-ə-ˌfī(-ə)r\ *n*

vi·vip·a·rous \vī-ˈvip-(ə-)rəs, və-\ *adj* : producing living young from within the body rather than from eggs — **vi·var·i·ty** \ˌvī-və-ˈpar-ət-ē, ˌviv-ə-\ *n*

vivi·sec·tion \ˌviv-ə-ˈsek-shən, ˈviv-ə-ˌsek-shən\ *n* : the cutting of or operation on a living animal; *also* : animal experimentation

vix·en \ˈvik-sən\ *n* **1** : a female fox **2** : an ill-tempered scolding woman **syn** shrew, scold, termagant, virago

viz \ˈnäm-lē, ˈviz, və-ˈdel-ə-ˌset\ *abbr* videlicet

viz·ard \ˈviz-ərd\ *n* : a mask for disguise or protection

vi·zier \və-ˈziər\ *n* : a high executive officer of many Muslim countries and esp. of the former Turkish empire

vi·zor *var of* VISOR

VOA *abbr* Voice of America

voc *abbr* **1** vocational **2** vocative

vocab *abbr* vocabulary

vo·ca·ble \ˈvō-kə-bəl\ *n* : TERM, NAME; *esp* : a word composed of various sounds or letters without regard to its meaning

vo·cab·u·lary \vō-ˈkab-yə-ˌler-ē\ *n, pl* **-lar·ies 1** : a list or collection of words usu. alphabetically arranged and defined or explained : LEXICON **2** : a

stock of words used in a language by a class or individual or in relation to a subject

vocabulary entry *n* : a word (as the noun *book*), hyphened or open compound (as the verb *cross-refer* or the noun *boric acid*), word element (as the affix *-an*), abbreviation (as *agt*), verbalized symbol (as *Na*), or term (as *master of ceremonies*) entered alphabetically in a dictionary for the purpose of definition or identification or expressly included as an inflected form (as the noun *mice* or the verb *saw*) or as a derived form (as the noun *godlessness* or the adverb *globally*) or related phrase (as *in spite of*) run on at its base word and usu. set in a type (as boldface) readily distinguishable from that of the lightface running text which defines, explains, or identifies the entry

¹**vo·cal** \ˈvō-kəl\ *adj* **1** : uttered by the voice : ORAL **2** : relating to, composed or arranged for, or sung by the human voice ⟨~ music⟩ **3** : of, relating to, or having the power of producing voice **4** : full of voices : RESOUNDING **5** : given to expressing one's feelings or opinions in speech : TALKATIVE; *also* : OUTSPOKEN **syn** articulate, fluent, eloquent

²**vocal** *n* **1** : a vocal sound **2** : a vocal composition or its performance

vocal cords *n pl* : either of two pairs of elastic folds of mucous membrane that project into the cavity of the larynx and function in the production of vocal sounds

vo·cal·ic \vō-ˈkal-ik\ *adj* : of, relating to, or functioning as a vowel

vo·cal·ist \ˈvō-kə-ləst\ *n* : SINGER

vo·cal·ize \-ˌlīz\ *vb* **-ized; -iz·ing 1** : to give vocal expression to : UTTER; *esp* : SING **2** : to make voiced rather than voiceless — **vo·cal·iz·er** *n*

vo·ca·tion \vō-ˈkā-shən\ *n* **1** : a summons or strong inclination to a particular state or course of action (religious ~) **2** : regular employment : OCCUPATION, PROFESSION — **vo·ca·tion·al** \-sh(ə-)nəl\ *adj*

vo·ca·tion·al·ism \-sh(ə-)nəl-ˌiz-əm\ *n* : emphasis on vocational training in education

voc·a·tive \ˈväk-ət-iv\ *adj* : of, relating to, or constituting a grammatical case marking the one addressed — **vocative** *n*

vo·cif·er·ate \vō-ˈsif-ə-ˌrāt\ *vb* **-at·ed; -at·ing** [L *vociferari*, fr. *voc-, vox* voice + *ferre* to bear] : to cry out loudly : CLAMOR, SHOUT — **vo·cif·er·a·tion** \-ˌsif-ə-ˈrā-shən\ *n*

vo·cif·er·ous \vō-ˈsif-(ə-)rəs\ *adj* : making or given to loud outcry : CLAMOROUS — **vo·cif·er·ous·ly** *adv* — **vo·cif·er·ous·ness** *n*

vod·ka \ˈväd-kə\ *n* [Russ, fr. *voda* water] : a colorless liquor of neutral spirits distilled from a mash (as of rye or wheat)

vogue \'vōg\ n [MF, action of rowing, course, fashion, fr. It *voga*, fr. *vogare* to row] **1** : popular acceptance or favor : POPULARITY **2** : a period of popularity **3** : something or someone in fashion at a particular time *syn* mode, fad, rage, craze, trend, fashion

vogu·ish \'vō-gish\ *adj* **1** : FASHIONABLE, SMART **2** : suddenly or temporarily popular

¹voice \'vȯis\ n **1** : sound produced through the mouth by vertebrates and esp. by human beings in speaking or shouting **2** : musical sound produced by the vocal cords : *also* : the power to produce such sound : *also* : one of the melodic parts in a vocal or instrumental composition **3** : the vocal organs as a means of tone production (train the ~) **4** : sound produced by vibration of the vocal cords as heard in vowels and some consonants **5** : the faculty of speech **6** : a sound suggesting vocal utterance (the ~ of the sea) **7** : an instrument or medium of expression **8** : a choice, opinion, or wish openly expressed; *also* : right of expression **9** : distinction of form of a verb to indicate the relation of the subject to the action expressed by the verb

²voice *vb* **voiced; voic·ing 1** : to give voice or expression to : UTTER; *also* : ANNOUNCE **2** : to regulate the tone of (~ the pipes of an organ) *syn* express, vent, air, ventilate

voice box n : LARYNX

voiced \'vȯist\ *adj* **1** : furnished with a voice (soft-*voiced*) **2** : uttered with voice — **voiced·ness** \'vȯis(t)-nəs, 'vȯi-səd-nəs\ n

voice·less \'vȯis-ləs\ *adj* **1** : having no voice **2** : not pronounced with voice — **voice·less·ly** *adv* — **voice·less·ness** n

voice·print \'vȯis-ˌprint\ n : an individually distinctive pattern of voice characteristics that is spectrographically produced

¹void \'vȯid\ *adj* **1** : containing nothing : EMPTY **2** : UNOCCUPIED, VACANT **3** : LACKING, DEVOID (proposals ~ of sense) **4** : VAIN, USELESS **5** : of no legal force or effect : NULL

²void n **1** : empty space : EMPTINESS, VACUUM **2** : a feeling of want or hollowness

³void *vb* **1** : to make or leave empty; *also* : VACATE, LEAVE **2** : DISCHARGE, EMIT (~ urine) **3** : to render void : ANNUL, NULLIFY — **void·able** *adj* — **void·er** n

voi·là \vwä-'lä\ *interj* [F] — used to call attention or to express satisfaction or approval

voile \'vȯil\ n : a sheer fabric from various fibers used for women's clothing and curtains

vol *abbr* **1** volume **2** volunteer

vol·a·tile \'väl-ət-əl\ *adj* **1** : readily becoming a vapor at a relatively low temperature (a ~ liquid) **2** : LIGHTHEARTED **3** : easily erupting into violent action **4** : CHANGEABLE — **vol·a·til·i·ty** \ˌväl-ə-'til-ət-ē\ n — **vol·a·til·ize** \'väl-ət-əl-ˌīz\ *vb*

vol·ca·nic \väl-'kan-ik\ *adj* **1** : of or relating to a volcano **2** : explosively violent : VOLATILE (~ emotions)

volcanic glass n : natural glass produced by cooling of molten lava

vol·ca·nism \'väl-kə-ˌniz-əm\ n : volcanic power or action

vol·ca·no \väl-'kā-nō\ n, pl **-noes** or **-nos** [It *vulcano*, fr. L *Volcanus, Vulcanus* Roman god of fire and metalworking] : an opening in the earth's crust from which molten rock and steam issue; *also* : a hill or mountain composed of the ejected material

vol·ca·nol·o·gy \ˌväl-kə-'näl-ə-jē\ n : a branch of geology that deals with volcanic phenomena — **vol·ca·nol·o·gist** \-kə-'näl-ə-jəst\ n

vole \'vōl\ n : any of various mouselike or ratlike rodents that are closely related to the lemmings and muskrats

vo·li·tion \vō-'lish-ən\ n **1** : the act or the power of making a choice or decision : WILL **2** : a choice or decision made — **vo·li·tion·al** \-'lish-(ə-)nəl\ *adj*

¹vol·ley \'väl-ē\ n, pl **volleys 1** : a flight of missiles (as arrows or bullets) **2** : simultaneous discharge of a number of missile weapons **3** : a pouring forth of many things at the same instant (a ~ of oaths)

²volley *vb* **vol·leyed; vol·ley·ing 1** : to discharge or become discharged in or as if in a volley **2** : to hit an object of play in the air before it touches the ground

vol·ley·ball \-ˌbȯl\ n : a game played by volleying an inflated ball over a net; *also* : the ball used in this game

volt \'vōlt\ n : the mks unit of potential difference and electromotive force equal to the difference in potential between two points in a conducting wire carrying a constant current of one ampere when the power dissipated between the points is equal to one watt

volt·age \'vōl-tij\ n : potential difference measured in volts

vol·ta·ic \väl-'tā-ik, vōl-\ *adj* : of, relating to, or producing direct electric current by chemical action (~ current)

volte-face \ˌvȯlt-(ə-)'fäs\ n : a reversal in policy : ABOUT-FACE

volt·me·ter \'vōlt-ˌmēt-ər\ n : an instrument for measuring in volts the difference in potential between different points of an electrical circuit

vol·u·ble \'väl-yə-bəl\ *adj* : fluent and smooth in speech : GLIB *syn* garrulous, loquacious, talkative — **vol·u·bil·i·ty** \ˌväl-yə-'bil-ət-ē\ n — **vol·u·bly** \'väl-yə-blē\ *adv*

vol·ume \'väl-yəm\ n [ME, fr. MF, fr. L *volumen* roll, scroll, fr. *volvere* to roll] **1** : a series of printed sheets bound typically in book form; *also* : an arbitrary number of issues of a periodical **2** : space occupied as measured by cubic units ⟨the ~ of a cylinder⟩ **3** : sufficient matter to fill a book ⟨her glance spoke ~s⟩ **4** : AMOUNT ⟨increasing ~ of business⟩ ; *also* : an aggregate forming a body or unit **5** : the degree of loudness of a sound *syn* body, bulk, mass

vo·lu·mi·nous \və-ˈlü-mə-nəs\ *adj* **1** : consisting of many folds or windings **2** : BULKY, LARGE **3** : filling or sufficient to fill a large volume or several volumes — **vo·lu·mi·nous·ly** \-ˈlü-mə-nəs-lē\ *adv* — **vo·lu·mi·nous·ness** *n*

¹vol·un·tary \ˈväl-ən-ˌter-ē\ *adj* **1** : done, made, or given freely and without compulsion ⟨a ~ sacrifice⟩ **2** : not accidental : INTENTIONAL ⟨a ~ slight⟩ **3** : of, relating to, or regulated by the will ⟨~ behavior⟩ **4** : having power of free choice ⟨man is a ~ agent⟩ **5** : provided or supported by voluntary action ⟨a ~ hospital⟩ *syn* deliberate, willful, willing, witting — **vol·un·tari·ly** \ˌväl-ən-ˈter-ə-lē\ *adv*

²voluntary *n, pl* **-tar·ies** : an organ solo played in a religious service

voluntary muscle *n* : muscle (as most striated muscle) under voluntary control

¹vol·un·teer \ˌväl-ən-ˈtiər\ *n* **1** : a person who of his own free will offers himself for a service or duty **2** : a plant growing spontaneously esp. from seeds lost from a previous crop

²volunteer *vb* **1** : to offer or give voluntarily **2** : to offer oneself as a volunteer

vo·lup·tu·ary \və-ˈləp-chə-ˌwer-ē\ *n, pl* **-ar·ies** : one whose chief interest in life is the indulgence of sensual appetites

vo·lup·tu·ous \-chə(-wə)s\ *adj* **1** : giving sensual gratification ⟨~ furnishings⟩ **2** : given to or spent in enjoyment of luxury or pleasure *syn* luxurious, epicurean, sensuous, sensual — **vo·lup·tu·ous·ly** *adv* — **vo·lup·tu·ous·ness** *n*

vo·lute \və-ˈlüt\ *n* : a spiral or scroll-shaped decoration

¹vom·it \ˈväm-ət\ *n* : an act or instance of throwing up the contents of the stomach through the mouth; *also* : the matter discharged

²vomit *vb* **1** : to throw up the contents of the stomach as vomit **2** : to belch forth : GUSH

voo·doo \ˈvüd-ü\ *n, pl* **voodoos** [LaF *voudou*] **1** : VOODOOISM **2** : one who practices voodooism **3** : a charm or a fetish used in voodooism — **voodoo** *adj*

voo·doo·ism \-ˌiz-əm\ *n* **1** : a religion derived from African ancestor worship and consisting largely of sorcery **2** : the practice of sorcery

vo·ra·cious \vȯ-ˈrā-shəs, və-\ *adj* **1** : greedy in eating : RAVENOUS **2** : excessively eager : INSATIABLE ⟨a ~ reader⟩ *syn* gluttonous, ravening, rapacious — **vo·ra·cious·ly** *adv* — **vo·ra·cious·ness** *n* — **vo·rac·i·ty** \-ˈras-ət-ē\ *n*

vor·tex \ˈvȯr-ˌteks\ *n, pl* **vor·ti·ces** \ˈvȯrt-ə-ˌsēz\ *also* **vor·tex·es** \ˈvȯr-ˌtek-səz\ : a mass of whirling liquid forming a cavity in the center toward which things are drawn : WHIRLPOOL

vo·ta·ry \ˈvōt-ə-rē\ *n, pl* **-ries 1** : ENTHUSIAST, DEVOTEE; *also* : a devoted adherent or admirer **2** : a devout or zealous worshiper

¹vote \ˈvōt\ *n* [ME, fr. L *votum* vow, wish, fr. *vovēre* to vow] **1** : a choice or opinion of a person or body of persons expressed usu. by a ballot, spoken word, or raised hand; *also* : the ballot, word, or gesture used to express a choice or opinion **2** : the decision reached by voting **3** : the right of suffrage **4** : a group of voters with some common characteristics ⟨the big city ~⟩ — **vote·less** *adj*

²vote *vb* **vot·ed; vot·ing 1** : to cast a vote **2** : to choose, endorse, authorize, or defeat by vote **3** : to express an opinion **4** : to adjudge by general agreement : DECLARE **5** : to offer as a suggestion : PROPOSE **6** : to cause to vote esp. in a given way — **vot·er** *n*

vo·tive \ˈvōt-iv\ *adj* : offered or performed in fulfillment of a vow or in petition, gratitude, or devotion

vou *abbr* voucher

vouch \ˈvau̇ch\ *vb* **1** : PROVE, SUBSTANTIATE **2** : to verify by examining documentary evidence **3** : to give a guarantee **4** : to supply supporting evidence or testimony; *also* : to give personal assurance

vouch·er \ˈvau̇-chər\ *n* **1** : an act of vouching **2** : one that vouches for another **3** : a documentary record of a business transaction **4** : a written affidavit or authorization **5** : a form indicating a credit against future purchases or expenditures

vouch·safe \vau̇ch-ˈsāf\ *vb* **vouch·safed; vouch·saf·ing 1** : to grant or give often in a condescending manner **2** : to grant as a privilege or as a special favor — **vouch·safe·ment** *n*

¹vow \ˈvau̇\ *n* : a solemn promise or assertion; *esp* : one by which a person binds himself or herself to an act, service, or condition

²vow *vb* **1** : to make a vow or as a vow **2** : to bind or commit by a vow — **vow·er** \ˈvau̇-(ə)r\ *n*

vow·el \ˈvau̇(-ə)l\ *n* **1** : a speech sound produced without obstruction or friction in the mouth **2** : a letter representing such a sound

vox po·pu·li \ˈväks-ˈpäp-yə-ˌlī\ *n* [L, voice of the people] : popular sentiment

¹voy·age \ˈvȯi-ij\ *n* [ME, fr. OF *voiage*, fr. LL *viaticum*, fr. L, traveling money, fr. neut. of *viaticus* of a journey, fr. *via* way] : a journey esp. by water from one place or country to another

²**voyage** *vb* **voy·aged; voy·ag·ing** : to take or make a voyage — **voy·ag·er** *n*

voya·geur \ˌvȯi-ə-ˈzhər, ˌvwä-yä-\ *n* [CanF] : a person employed by a fur company to transport goods and men to and from remote stations esp. in the Canadian Northwest

voy·eur \vwä-ˈyər, vȯi-ˈər\ *n* : one who habitually seeks sexual stimulation by visual means — **voy·eur·ism** \-ˌiz-əm\ *n*

VP *abbr* **1** verb phrase **2** vice president

vs *abbr* **1** verse **2** versus

vss *abbr* **1** verses **2** versions

V/STOL *abbr* vertical short takeoff and landing

Vt *or* **VT** *abbr* Vermont

VTOL *abbr* vertical takeoff and landing

VTR *abbr* videotape recorder

vul·ca·nism \ˈvəl-kə-ˌniz-əm\ *n* : VOL-CANISM

vul·ca·nize \ˈvəl-kə-ˌnīz\ *vb* **-nized; -niz·ing** : to treat rubber or rubberlike material chemically to give useful properties (as elasticity and strength) — **vul·ca·ni·za·tion** \ˌvəl-kə-nə-ˈzā-shən\ *n*

Vulg *abbr* Vulgate

vul·gar \ˈvəl-gər\ *adj* [ME, fr. L *vulgaris* of the mob, vulgar, fr. *vulgus* mob, common people] **1** : VERNACULAR (the ~ tongue) **2** : of or relating to the common people : GENERAL, COMMON **3** : lacking cultivation or refinement : BOORISH; *also* : offensive to good taste or refined feelings syn gross, obscene, ribald, dirty, indecent, profane — **vul·gar·ly** *adv*

vul·gar·i·an \ˌvəl-ˈgar-ē-ən\ *n* : a vulgar person

vul·gar·ism \ˈvəl-gə-ˌriz-əm\ *n* **1** : a word or expression originated or used chiefly by illiterate persons **2** : OBSCENITY **3** : VULGARITY

vul·gar·i·ty \ˌvəl-ˈgar-ət-ē\ *n, pl* **-ties 1** : an instance of coarseness of manners or language **2** : the quality or state of being vulgar

vul·gar·ize \ˈvəl-gə-ˌrīz\ *vb* **-ized; -iz·ing** : to make vulgar — **vul·gar·iza·tion** \ˌvəl-gə-rə-ˈzā-shən\ *n* — **vul·gar·iz·er** \ˈvəl-gə-ˌrī-zər\ *n*

Vul·gate \ˈvəl-ˌgāt\ *n* [ML *vulgata*, fr. LL *vulgata editio* edition in general circulation] : a Latin version of the Bible used by the Roman Catholic Church

vul·ner·a·ble \ˈvəln-(ə-)rə-bəl\ *adj* **1** : capable of being wounded : susceptible to wounds **2** : open to attack **3** : liable to increased penalties in contract bridge — **vul·ner·a·bil·i·ty** \ˌvəln-(ə-)rə-ˈbil-ət-ē\ *n* — **vul·ner·a·bly** \ˈvəln-(ə-)rə-blē\ *adv*

vul·pine \ˈvəl-ˌpīn\ *adj* : of, relating to, or resembling a fox esp. in cunning

vul·ture \ˈvəl-chər\ *n* **1** : any of various large birds (as a turkey vulture) related to hawks and eagles but having weaker claws and the head usu. naked and living chiefly on carrion **2** : a rapacious person

vul·va \ˈvəl-və\ *n, pl* **vul·vae** \-ˌvē\ [L] : the external parts of the female genital organs

vv *abbr* **1** verses **2** vice versa

vying *pres part of* VIE

W

¹**w** \ˈdəb-əl-(ˌ)yü\ *n, pl* **w's** *or* **ws** *often cap* : the 23d letter of the English alphabet

²**w** *abbr, often cap* **1** water **2** watt **3** week **4** weight **5** west **6** western **7** wide; width **8** wife **9** with

W *symbol* [G *Wolfram*] tungsten

WA *abbr* **1** Washington **2** Western Australia

Wac \ˈwak\ *n* [*Women's Army Corps*] : a member of the Women's Army Corps

wacky \ˈwak-ē\ *adj* **wacki·er; -est** : EC-CENTRIC, CRAZY

¹**wad** \ˈwäd\ *n* **1** : a little mass, bundle, or tuft (~s of clay) **2** : a soft mass of usu. light fibrous material **3** : a pliable plug (as of felt) used to retain a powder charge (as in a cartridge) **4** : a considerable amount (as of money) **5** : a roll of paper money

²**wad** *vb* **wad·ded; wad·ding 1** : to push a wad into (~ a gun) **2** : to form into a wad **3** : to hold in by a wad (~ a bullet

in a gun) **4** : to stuff or line with a wad : PAD

wad·ding \ˈwäd-iŋ\ *n* **1** : WADS; *also* : material for making wads **2** : a soft mass or sheet of short loose fibers used for stuffing or padding

wad·dle \ˈwäd-ᵊl\ *vb* **wad·dled; wad·dling** \ˈwäd-(ᵊ-)liŋ\ : to walk with short steps swaying from side to side like a duck — **waddle** *n*

wade \ˈwād\ *vb* **wad·ed; wad·ing 1** : to step in or through a medium (as water) more resistant than air **2** : to move or go with difficulty or labor and often with determined vigor (~ through a dull book) — **wad·able** *or* **wade·able** \ˈwäd-ə-bəl\ *adj* — **wade** *n*

wad·er \ˈwäd-ər\ *n* **1** : one that wades **2** : WADING BIRD **3** *pl* : high waterproof rubber boots or trousers for wading

wa·di \ˈwäd-ē\ *n* [Ar] : a watercourse dry except in the rainy season esp. in southwestern Asia and northern Africa

wading bird *n* : any of many long-legged birds (as sandpipers, cranes, or herons) that wade in water in search of food

Waf \'waf\ *n* [Women in the Air Force] : a member of the women's component of the Air Force

wa·fer \'wā-fər\ *n* 1 : a thin crisp cake or cracker 2 : a thin round piece of unleavened bread used in the Eucharist 3 : something (as a piece of candy or an adhesive seal) that resembles a wafer

waf·fle \'wäf-əl\ *n* : a soft but crisped cake of batter cooked in a special hinged metal utensil (**waffle iron**)

¹**waft** \'wäft, 'waft\ *vb* : to cause to move or go lightly by or as if by the impulse of wind or waves

²**waft** *n* 1 : a slight breeze : PUFF 2 : the act of waving

¹**wag** \'wag\ *vb* **wagged**; **wag·ging** 1 : to sway or swing shortly from side to side or to-and-fro (the dog *wagged* his tail) 2 : to move in chatter or gossip (scandal caused tongues to ~)

²**wag** *n* : an act of wagging : a wagging movement

³**wag** *n* : WIT, JOKER

¹**wage** \'wāj\ *vb* **waged**; **wag·ing** 1 : to engage in : CARRY ON (~ a war) 2 : to be in process of being waged

²**wage** *n* 1 : payment for labor or services usu. according to contract 2 *pl* : RECOMPENSE, REWARD

¹**wa·ger** \'wā-jər\ *n* 1 : BET, STAKE 2 : something on which bets are laid : GAMBLE

²**wager** *vb* : BET — **wa·ger·er** *n*

wag·gery \'wag-ə-rē\ *n, pl* **-ger·ies** 1 : mischievous merriment : PLEASANTRY 2 : JEST, TRICK

wag·gish \'wag-ish\ *adj* 1 : SPORTIVE, HUMOROUS 2 : resembling or characteristic of a wag : MISCHIEVOUS, ROGUISH, FROLICSOME

wag·gle \'wag-əl\ *vb* **wag·gled**; **wag·gling** \-(ə-)liŋ\ : to move backward and forward or from side to side : WAG — **waggle** *n*

wag·on \'wag-ən\ *n* 1 : a 4-wheeled vehicle; *esp* : one drawn by animals and used for freight or merchandise 2 : PATROL WAGON 3 : a child's 4-wheeled cart 4 : STATION WAGON

wag·on·er \'wag-ə-nər\ *n* : the driver of a wagon

wag·on·ette \,wag-ə-'net\ *n* : a light wagon with two facing seats along the sides behind a cross seat in front

wa·gon-lit *or* **wagon-lits** \,vä-gōⁿ-'lē\ *n, pl* **wagons-lits** *or* **wagon-lits** \-gōⁿ-'lē(z)\ [F, fr. *wagon* railroad car + *lit* bed] : a railroad sleeping car

wagon train *n* : a group of wagons traveling overland

wag·tail \'wag-,tāl\ *n* : any of various slender-bodied mostly Old World birds with a long tail that jerks up and down

wa·hi·ne \wä-'hē-nā\ *n* 1 : a Polynesian woman 2 : a female surfer

wa·hoo \'wä-,hü\ *n, pl* **wahoos** : a large vigorous food and sport fish related to the mackerel and found in warm seas

waif \'wāf\ *n* 1 : something found without an owner and esp. by chance 2 : a stray person or animal; *esp* : a homeless child

wail \'wāl\ *vb* 1 : LAMENT, WEEP 2 : to make a sound suggestive of a mournful cry 3 : COMPLAIN — **wail** *n*

wail·ful \-fəl\ *adj* : SORROWFUL, MOURNFUL — **wail·ful·ly** \-ē\ *adv*

wain \'wān\ *n* : a usu. large heavy farm wagon

wain·scot \'wān-skət, -,skōt, -,skät\ *n* 1 : a usu. paneled wooden lining of an interior wall of a room 2 : the lower part of an interior wall when finished differently from the rest — **wainscot** *vb*

wain·scot·ing *or* **wain·scot·ting** \-,skōt-iŋ, -,skät-, -skət-\ *n* : material for a wainscot; *also* : WAINSCOT

wain·wright \'wān-,rīt\ *n* : a builder and repairer of wagons

waist \'wāst\ *n* 1 : the narrowed part of the body between the chest and hips 2 : a part resembling the human waist esp. in narrowness or central position (the ~ of a ship) 3 : a garment or part of a garment (as a blouse or bodice) for the upper part of the body

waist·band \-,band\ *n* : a band (as on trousers or a skirt) that fits around the waist

waist·coat \'wes-kət, 'wās(t)-,kōt\ *n, chiefly Brit* : VEST 1

waist·line \'wāst-,līn\ *n* 1 : a line thought of as surrounding the waist at its narrowest part; *also* : the length of this 2 : the line at which the bodice and skirt of a dress meet

¹**wait** \'wāt\ *vb* 1 : to remain inactive in readiness or expectation : AWAIT (~ for orders) 2 : POSTPONE, DELAY (~ dinner for late guests) 3 : to act as attendant or servant (~ on customers) 4 : to attend as a waiter : SERVE (~ tables) (~ at a banquet) 5 : to be ready

²**wait** *n* 1 : a position of concealment usu. with intent to attack or surprise (lie in ~) 2 : an act or period of waiting

wait·er \'wāt-ər\ *n* 1 : one that waits upon another; *esp* : a man who waits on table 2 : TRAY

waiting game *n* : a strategy in which one or more participants withhold action in the hope of an opportunity for more effective action later

waiting room *n* : a room (as at a doctor's office) for the use of persons waiting

wait·ress \'wā-trəs\ *n* : a girl or woman who waits on table

waive \'wāv\ *vb* **waived**; **waiv·ing** [ME *weiven*, fr. OF *weyver*, fr. *waif* lost, unclaimed] 1 : to give up claim to (*waived* his right to a trial) 2 : POSTPONE

waiv·er \'wā-vər\ *n* : the act of waiving right, claim, or privilege; *also* : a document containing a declaration of such an act

¹**wake** \'wāk\ *vb* **woke** \'wōk\ *also* **waked** \'wākt\ ; **wo·ken** \'wō-kən\ *also* **waked** *or* **woke; wak·ing 1** : to be or remain awake; *esp* : to keep watch (as over a corpse) **2** : AWAKE, AWAKEN ⟨the baby *waked* up early⟩ ⟨the thunder *waked* him up⟩

²**wake** *n* **1** : the state of being awake **2** : a watch held over the body of a dead person prior to burial

³**wake** *n* : the track left by a ship in the water; *also* : a track left behind

wake·ful \'wāk-fəl\ *adj* : not sleeping or able to sleep : SLEEPLESS, ALERT — **wake·ful·ness** *n*

wak·en \'wā-kən\ *vb* **wak·ened; wak·en·ing** \'wāk-(ə-)niŋ\ : WAKE

wake-rob·in \'wāk-ˌräb-ən\ *n* : TRILLIUM

wak·ing \'wā-kiŋ\ *adj* : passed in a conscious or alert state ⟨every ~ hour⟩

wale \'wāl\ *n* : a ridge esp. on cloth; *also* : the texture esp. of a fabric

¹**walk** \'wȯk\ *vb* [partly fr. ME *walken*, fr. OE *wealcan* to roll, toss and partly fr. ME *walkien*, fr. OE *wealcian* to roll up, muffle up] **1** : to move or cause to move on foot usu. at a natural unhurried gait ⟨~ to town⟩ ⟨a ~ horse⟩ **2** : to pass over, through, or along by walking ⟨~ the streets⟩ **3** : to perform or accomplish by walking ⟨~ guard⟩ **4** : to follow a course of action or way of life ⟨~ humbly in the sight of God⟩ **5** : to receive a base on balls; *also* : to give a base on balls to — **walk·er** *n*

²**walk** *n* **1** : a going on foot ⟨go for a ~⟩ **2** : a place, path, or course for walking **3** : distance to be walked ⟨a 10-minute ~ from here⟩ **4** : manner of living : CONDUCT, BEHAVIOR; *also* : social or economic status ⟨various ~*s* of life⟩ **5** : manner of walking : GAIT; *esp* : a slow 4-beat gait of a horse **6** : BASE ON BALLS

walk·away \'wȯk-ə-ˌwā\ *n* : an easily won contest

walk·ie-talk·ie \'wȯ-kē-'tȯ-kē\ *n* : a small portable radio transmitting and receiving set

¹**walk-in** \'wȯk-ˌin\ *adj* : large enough to be walked into ⟨a ~ refrigerator⟩

²**walk-in** \'wȯk-ˌin\ *n* **1** : an easy election victory **2** : one that walks in

walking papers *n pl* : DISMISSAL, DISCHARGE

walking stick *n* **1** : a stick used in walking **2** *usu* **walk·ing·stick** : STICK INSECT; *esp* : one common in parts of the U.S.

walk-on \'wȯk-ˌȯn, -ˌän\ *n* : a small part or brief appearance in a dramatic production

walk·out \-ˌau̇t\ *n* **1** : a labor strike **2** : the action of leaving a meeting or organization as an expression of disapproval

walk·over \-ˌō-vər\ *n* : a one-sided contest : an easy victory

walk-up \'wȯk-ˌəp\ *n* : a building or apartment house without an elevator — **walk-up** *adj*

walk·way \-ˌwā\ *n* : a passage for walking

¹**wall** \'wȯl\ *n* [ME, fr. OE *weall*, fr. L *vallum* rampart, fr. *vallus* stake, palisade] **1** : a structure (as of stone or brick) intended for defense or security or for enclosing something **2** : one of the upright enclosing parts of a building or room **3** : the inside surface of a cavity or vessel ⟨the ~ of a boiler⟩ **4** : something like a wall in appearance or function ⟨a tariff ~⟩ — **walled** \'wȯld\ *adj*

²**wall** *vb* **1** : to provide, separate, or surround with or as if with a wall ⟨~ in a garden⟩ **2** : to close (an opening) with or as if with a wall ⟨~ up a door⟩

wal·la·by \'wäl-ə-bē\ *n, pl* **wallabies** *also* **wallaby** : any of various small or medium-sized kangaroos

wall·board \'wȯl-ˌbȯrd\ *n* : a structural material (as of wood pulp or plaster) made in large sheets and used for sheathing interior walls and ceilings

wal·let \'wäl-ət\ *n* **1** : a bag or sack for carrying things on a journey **2** : a pocketbook with compartments (as for personal papers and usu. unfolded money) : BILLFOLD

wall·eye \'wȯl-ˌī\ *n* **1** : an eye with whitish iris or an opaque white cornea **2** : a large vigorous No. American food and sport fish related to the perches — **wall-eyed** \-ˌīd\ *adj*

wall·flow·er \'wȯl-ˌflau̇(-ə)r\ *n* **1** : any of several Old World plants related to the mustards; *esp* : one with showy fragrant flowers **2** : a person who usu. from shyness or unpopularity remains alone (as at a dance)

Wal·loon \wä-'lün\ *n* : a member of a chiefly Celtic people of southern and southeastern Belgium and adjacent parts of France — **Walloon** *adj*

¹**wal·lop** \'wäl-əp\ *vb* [ME, *gallop*, fr. Old Northern French *waloper* to gallop] **1** : to beat soundly : TROUNCE **2** : to hit hard : SOCK

²**wallop** *n* **1** : a powerful blow or impact **2** : the ability to hit hard **3** : emotional or psychological force : IMPACT

wal·lop·ing \'wäl-ə-piŋ\ *adj* **1** : LARGE, WHOPPING **2** : exceptionally fine or impressive

¹**wal·low** \'wäl-ō\ *vb* **1** : to roll oneself about in or as if in deep mud : FLOUNDER ⟨hogs ~*ing* in the mire⟩ **2** : to live in or be filled with excessive pleasure ⟨~ in luxury⟩

²**wallow** *n* : a muddy or dust-filled area where animals wallow

wall·pa·per \'wȯl-ˌpā-pər\ *n* : decorative paper for the walls of a room — **wallpaper** *vb*

wall-to-wall *adj* **1** : covering the entire floor ⟨*wall-to-wall* carpeting⟩ **2** : covering or filling one entire space or time ⟨crowds of *wall-to-wall* people⟩

wal·nut \'wȯl-(ˌ)nət\ *n* [ME *walnot*, fr. OE *wealhhnutu*, lit., foreign nut, fr. *Wealh* Welshman, foreigner + *hnutu* nut] **1** : an edible nut with a furrowed usu. rough shell and an adherent husk from any of a genus of trees related to the hickories; *esp* : the large edible nut of a Eurasian tree **2** : a tree that bears walnuts **3** : the usu. reddish to dark brown wood of a walnut used esp. in cabinetwork and veneers

wal·rus \'wȯl-rəs, 'wäl-\ *n, pl* **walrus** or **wal·rus·es** : either of two large mammals of northern seas related to the seals and having ivory tusks

¹waltz \'wȯlts\ *vb* [G *walzer*, fr. *walzen* to roll, dance, fr. Old High German *walzan* to turn, roll] **1** : to dance a waltz **2** : to move or advance easily, successfully, or conspicuously ⟨he ~ed through customs⟩

²waltz *n* **1** : a gliding dance done to music having three beats to the measure **2** : music for or suitable for waltzing

wam·ble \'wäm-bəl\ *vb* **wam·bled; wam·bling** \-b(ə-)liŋ\ : to progress unsteadily or with a lurching shambling gait

wam·pum \'wäm-pəm\ *n* [short for *wampumpeag*, fr. Narraganset (a North American Indian language) *wompompeag*, fr. *wampan* white + *api* string + *-ag* pl. suffix] **1** : beads made of shells strung in strands, belts, or sashes and used by No. American Indians as money and ornaments **2** *slang* : MONEY

wan \'wän\ *adj* **wan·ner; wan·nest 1** : SICKLY, PALLID; *also* : FEEBLE **2** : DIM, FAINT **3** : LANGUID ⟨a ~ smile⟩ — **wan·ly** *adv* — **wan·ness** \'wän-nəs\ *n*

wand \'wänd\ *n* **1** : a slender staff carried in a procession **2** : the staff of a fairy, diviner, or magician

wan·der \'wän-dər\ *vb* **wan·dered; wan·der·ing** \-d(ə-)riŋ\ **1** : to move about aimlessly or without a fixed course or goal : RAMBLE **2** : STRAY **3** : to go astray in conduct or thought; *esp* : to become delirious — **wan·der·er** *n*

Wan·der·ing Jew *n* : any of several trailing or creeping plants some of which are often planted in hanging baskets

wan·der·lust \'wän-dər-ˌləst\ *n* : strong longing for or impulse toward wandering

¹wane \'wän\ *vb* **waned; wan·ing 1** : to grow gradually smaller or less ⟨the moon ~s⟩ ⟨his strength *waned*⟩ **2** : to lose power, prosperity, or influence **3** : to draw near an end ⟨summer is *waning*⟩

²wane *n* : a waning (as in size or power); *also* : a period in which something is waning

wan·gle \'waŋ-gəl\ *vb* **wan·gled; wan·gling** \-g(ə-)liŋ\ **1** : to obtain by sly or roundabout means; *also* : to use trick-

ery or questionable means to achieve an end **2** : MANIPULATE; *also* : FINAGLE

Wan·kel engine \'väŋ-kəl-, 'waŋ-\ *n* : an internal-combustion rotary engine with a rounded triangular rotor functioning as a piston

¹want \'wȯnt\ *vb* **1** : to fail to possess : LACK ⟨they ~ the necessities of life⟩ **2** : to fall short by ⟨it ~s three minutes to six⟩ **3** : to feel or suffer the need of **4** : NEED, REQUIRE ⟨the house ~s painting⟩ **5** : to desire earnestly : WISH

²want *n* **1** : a lack of a required or usual amount : SHORTAGE **2** : dire need : DESTITUTION **3** : something wanted : DESIRE **4** : personal defect : FAULT

¹want·ing \-iŋ\ *adj* **1** : not present or in evidence : ABSENT **2** : falling below standards or expectations **3** : lacking in ability or capacity : DEFICIENT ⟨~ in common sense⟩

²wanting *prep* **1** : WITHOUT ⟨a book ~ a cover⟩ **2** : LESS, MINUS ⟨a month ~ two days⟩

¹wan·ton \'wȯnt-ᵊn\ *adj* [ME, undisciplined, fr. *wan-* deficient, wrong + *towen*, pp. of *teen* to draw, train, discipline] **1** : UNCHASTE, LEWD, LUSTFUL; *also* : SENSUAL **2** : having no regard for justice or for other persons' feelings, rights, or safety : MERCILESS, INHUMANE ⟨~ cruelty⟩ **3** : having no just cause ⟨a ~ attack⟩ — **wan·ton·ly** *adv* — **wan·ton·ness** *n*

²wanton *n* : a wanton individual; *esp* : a lewd or immoral person

³wanton *vb* **1** : to be wanton : act wantonly **2** : to pass or waste wantonly

wa·pi·ti \'wäp-ət-ē\ *n, pl* **wapiti** or **wapitis** : ELK 2

¹war \'wȯr\ *n* **1** : a state or period of usu. open and declared armed fighting between states or nations **2** : the art or science of warfare **3** : a state of hostility, conflict, or antagonism **4** : a struggle between opposing forces or for a particular end ⟨~ against disease⟩ — **war·less** \-ləs\ *adj*

²war *vb* **warred; war·ring** : to engage in warfare : be in conflict

³war *abbr* warrant

¹war·ble \'wȯr-bəl\ *n* **1** : a melodious succession of low pleasing sounds **2** : a musical trill

²warble *vb* **war·bled; war·bling** \-b(ə-)liŋ\ **1** : to sing or utter in a trilling manner or with variations **2** : to express by or as if by warbling

³warble *n* : a swelling under the hide esp. of the back of cattle, horses, and wild mammals caused by the maggot of a fly (**warble fly**); *also* : its maggot

war·bler \'wȯr-blər\ *n* **1** : SONGSTER **2** : any of various small slender-billed Old World singing birds related to the thrushes and noted for their song **3** : any of various small bright-colored American insect-eating birds with a usu. weak and unmusical song

war·bon·net \'wȯr-ˌbän-ət\ *n* : a feathered American Indian ceremonial headdress

war cry n 1 : a cry used by fighters in war 2 : a slogan used esp. to rally people to a cause

¹**ward** \'wȯrd\ n 1 : a guarding or being under guard or guardianship; esp : CUSTODY 2 : a body of guards 3 : a division of a prison 4 : a division in a hospital 5 : a division of a city for electoral or administrative purposes 6 : a person (as a child) under the protection of a guardian or a law court 7 : a person or body of persons under the protection or tutelage of a government 8 : a means of defense : PROTECTION

²**ward** vb : to turn aside : DEFLECT — usu. used with off ⟨~ off a blow⟩

¹**-ward** \wərd\ also **-wards** \wərdz\ adj suffix 1 : that moves, tends, faces, or is directed toward ⟨windward⟩ 2 : that occurs or is situated in the direction of ⟨seaward⟩

²**-ward** or **-wards** adv suffix 1 : in a (specified) direction ⟨upwards⟩ ⟨afterward⟩ 2 : toward a (specified) point, position, or area ⟨skyward⟩

war dance n : a dance performed by primitive peoples before going to war or in celebration of victory

war·den \'wȯrd-ⁿn\ n 1 : GUARDIAN, KEEPER 2 : the governor of a town, district, or fortress 3 : an official charged with special supervisory or enforcement duties ⟨game ~⟩ ⟨air raid ~⟩ 4 : an official in charge of the operation of a prison 5 : one of two ranking lay officers of an Episcopal parish 6 : any of various British college officials

ward·er \'wȯrd-ər\ n : WATCHMAN, WARDEN

ward heeler \-ˌhē-lər\ n : a local worker for a political boss

ward·robe \'wȯrd-ˌrōb\ n [ME warderobe, fr. OF, fr. warder to guard + robe robe] 1 : a room or closet where clothes are kept; also : CLOTHESPRESS 2 : a collection of wearing apparel ⟨his summer ~⟩

ward·room \-ˌrüm, -ˌr u̇m\ n : the quarters in a warship allotted to the commissioned officers except the captain; esp : the room allotted to these officers for meals

ward·ship \'wȯrd-ˌship\ n 1 : GUARDIANSHIP 2 : the state of being under care of a guardian

ware \'waər\ n 1 : manufactured articles or products of art or craft : GOODS 2 : an article of merchandise ⟨a peddler hawking his ~s⟩ 3 : items (as dishes) of fired clay : POTTERY

ware·house \-ˌhau̇s\ n : a place for the storage of merchandise or commodities : STOREHOUSE — **warehouse** vb — **ware·house·man** \-mən\ n — **ware·hous·er** \-ˌhau̇-zər, -sər\ n

ware·room \'waər-ˌrüm, -ˌr u̇m\ n : a

room in which goods are exhibited for sale

war·fare \'wȯr-ˌfaər\ n 1 : military operations between enemies : WAR; also : an activity undertaken by one country to weaken or destroy another ⟨economic ~⟩ 2 : STRUGGLE, CONFLICT

war·fa·rin \'wȯr-fə-rən\ n : an anticoagulant used as a rodent poison and in medicine

war·head \-ˌhed\ n : the section of a missile containing the charge

war·horse \-ˌhȯrs\ n 1 : a horse for use in war 2 : a veteran soldier or public person (as a politician)

war·like \-ˌlīk\ adj 1 : fond of war ⟨~ peoples⟩ 2 : of, relating to, or useful in war : MILITARY, MARTIAL ⟨~ supplies⟩ 3 : befitting or characteristic of war or of soldiers ⟨~ attitudes⟩

war·lock \-ˌläk\ n [ME warloghe, fr. OE wǣrloga one that breaks faith, the Devil, fr. wǣr faith, troth + -loga (fr. lēogan to lie)] : SORCERER, WIZARD

war·lord \-ˌlȯrd\ n 1 : a high military leader 2 : a military commander exercising local civil power by force ⟨former Chinese ~s⟩

¹**warm** \'wȯrm\ adj 1 : having or giving out heat to a moderate or adequate degree ⟨~ milk⟩ ⟨a ~ stove⟩ 2 : serving to retain heat ⟨~ clothes⟩ 3 : feeling or inducing sensations of heat ⟨~ from exercise⟩ ⟨a ~ climb⟩ 4 : showing or marked by strong feeling : ARDENT ⟨~ support⟩ 5 : marked by tense excitement or hot anger ⟨a ~ campaign⟩ 6 : giving a pleasant impression of warmth, cheerfulness, or friendliness ⟨~ colors⟩ ⟨a ~ tone of voice⟩ 7 : marked by or tending toward injury, distress, or pain ⟨made things ~ for the enemy⟩ 8 : newly made : FRESH ⟨a ~ scent⟩ 9 : near to a goal ⟨getting ~ in a search⟩ — **warm·ly** adv

²**warm** vb 1 : to make or become warm 2 : to give a feeling of warmth or vitality to 3 : to experience feelings of affection or pleasure ⟨she ~ed to her guest⟩ 4 : to reheat for eating ⟨~ed over the roast⟩ 5 : to make ready for operation or performance by preliminary exercise or operation ⟨~ up the motor⟩ 6 : to become increasingly ardent, interested, or competent ⟨the speaker ~ed to his topic⟩ — **warm·er** n

warm–blood·ed \-ˈbləd-əd\ adj : able to maintain a relatively high and constant body temperature essentially independent of that of the surroundings

warmed–over \ˈwȯrmd-ˈō-vər\ adj 1 : REHEATED ⟨~ cabbage⟩ 2 : not fresh or new ⟨~ ideas⟩

warm–heart·ed \ˈwȯrm-ˈhärt-əd\ adj : marked by warmth of feeling : CORDIAL — **warm·heart·ed·ness** n

warming pan n : a long-handled covered pan filled with live coals and formerly used to warm a bed

war·mon·ger \\'wȯr-ˌməŋ-gər, -ˌmäŋ-\ n
: one who urges or attempts to stir up
war

warmth \\'wȯrmth\ n 1 : the quality or
state of being warm 2 : ZEAL, ARDOR,
FERVOR

warm up \(')wȯrm-'əp\ vb : to engage
in exercise or practice esp. before entering a game or contest — **warm–up**
\\'wȯrm-ˌəp\ n

warn \\'wȯrn\ vb 1 : to put on guard
: CAUTION; also : ADMONISH, COUNSEL
2 : to notify esp. in advance : INFORM
3 : to order to go or keep away

¹**warn·ing** \-iŋ\ n 1 : the act of warning
: the state of being warned 2 : something that warns or serves to warn

²**warning** adj : serving as an alarm, signal, summons, or admonition ⟨~ bell⟩
— **warn·ing·ly** adv

¹**warp** \\'wȯrp\ n 1 : the lengthwise
threads on a loom or in a woven fabric
2 : a twist out of a true plane or
straight line (a ~ in a board)

²**warp** vb [ME warpen, fr. OE weorpan
to throw] 1 : to turn or twist out of
shape; also : to become so twisted 2
: to lead astray : PERVERT; also : FALSI-
FY, DISTORT

war paint n : paint put on the face and
body by American Indians as a sign of
going to war

war·path \\'wȯr-ˌpath, -ˌpȧth\ n : the
course taken by a party of American
Indians going on a hostile expedition
— **on the warpath** : ready to fight or
argue

war·plane \-ˌplān\ n : a military airplane; esp : one armed for combat

¹**war·rant** \\'wȯr-ənt, 'wär-\ n 1 : AUTHO-
RIZATION; also : JUSTIFICATION,
GROUND 2 : evidence (as a document)
of authorization; esp : a legal writ authorizing an officer to take action (as
in making an arrest, seizure, or
search) 3 : a certificate of appointment issued to an officer of lower rank
than a commissioned officer

²**warrant** vb 1 : to guarantee security or
immunity to : SECURE 2 : to declare or
maintain positively ⟨I ~ this is so⟩ 3
: to assure (a person) of the truth of
what is said 4 : to guarantee to be as
it appears or as it is represented ⟨~
goods as of the first quality⟩ 5 : SANC-
TION, AUTHORIZE 6 : to give proof of
: ATTEST; also : GUARANTEE 7 : JUSTIFY
⟨his need ~s the expenditure⟩

warrant officer n 1 : an officer in the
armed forces ranking next below a
commissioned officer 2 : a commissioned officer ranking below an ensign in the navy or coast guard and
below a second lieutenant in the marine corps

war·ran·ty \\'wȯr-ən-tē, 'wär-\ n, pl -ties
: an expressed or implied statement
that some situation or thing is as it
appears to be or is represented to be;
esp : a usu. written guarantee of the
integrity of a product and of the mak-

er's responsibility for the repair or replacement of defective parts

war·ren \\'wȯr-ən, 'wär-\ n 1 : an area
for the keeping of small game and esp.
rabbits; also : an area where rabbits
breed 2 : a crowded tenement or district

war·rior \\'wȯr-yər, 'wȯr-ē-ər; 'wär-ē-,
'wär-yər\ n : a man engaged or experienced in warfare

war·ship \\'wȯr-ˌship\ n : a military ship
armed for combat

wart \\'wȯrt\ n 1 : a small usu. horny
projection on the skin; esp : one
caused by a virus 2 : a protuberance
resembling a wart (as on a plant) —
warty adj

wart·hog \\'wȯrt-ˌhȯg, -ˌhäg\ n : an African wild hog with large tusks and two
pairs of rough warty protuberances
below the eyes

war·time \\'wȯr-ˌtīm\ n : a period during
which a war is in progress

wary \\'wa(ə)r-ē\ adj **war·i·er; -est** : very
cautious; esp : careful in guarding
against danger or deception

was past 1st & 3d sing of BE

¹**wash** \\'wȯsh, 'wäsh\ vb 1 : to cleanse
with or as if with a liquid (as water) 2
: to wet thoroughly with water or other liquid 3 : to flow along the border
of ⟨waves ~ the shore⟩ 4 : to pass (a
gas or gaseous mixture) through or
over a liquid for purifying 5 : to pour
or flow in a stream or current 6 : to
move or remove by or as if by the
action of water 7 : to cover or daub
lightly with a liquid (as whitewash) 8
: to run water over (as gravel or ore) in
order to separate valuable matter
from refuse ⟨~ sand for gold⟩ 9 : to
undergo laundering ⟨a dress that
doesn't ~ well⟩ 10 : to stand a test
⟨that story will not ~⟩ 11 : to be worn
away by water

²**wash** n 1 : the act or process or an instance of washing or being washed 2
: articles to be washed or being
washed 3 : the flow or action of a
mass of water (as a wave) 4 : erosion
by waves (as of the sea) 5 West : the
dry bed of a stream 6 : worthless esp.
liquid waste : REFUSE, SWILL 7 : a thin
coat of paint (as watercolor) 8 : a disturbance in the air caused by the passage of a wing or propeller

³**wash** adj : WASHABLE

Wash abbr Washington

wash·able \-ə-bəl\ adj : capable of being washed without damage

wash–and–wear adj : of, relating to, or
constituting a fabric or garment that
needs little or no ironing after washing

wash·ba·sin \\'wȯsh-ˌbās-ᵊn, 'wäsh-\ n
: WASHBOWL

wash·board \-ˌbȯrd\ n : a grooved
board to scrub clothes on

wash·bowl \-ˌbōl\ n : a large bowl for
water for washing hands and face

wash·cloth \-ˌklȯth\ n : a cloth used for
washing one's face and body

wash drawing n : watercolor painting in or chiefly in washes

washed-out \'wȯsht-'aút, 'wäsht-\ adj 1 : faded in color 2 : EXHAUSTED (felt ~ after working all night)

washed-up \'wȯsht-'əp, 'wäsht-\ adj : no longer successful, popular, or needed

wash·er \'wȯsh-ər, 'wäsh-\ n 1 : a ring or perforated plate used around a bolt or screw to ensure tightness or relieve friction 2 : one that washes; esp : a machine for washing

wash·er·wom·an \-,wùm-ən\ n : a woman who works at washing clothes

wash·house \'wȯsh-,haús, 'wäsh-\ n : a house or building used or equipped for washing and esp. for washing clothes

wash·ing \'wȯsh-iŋ, 'wäsh-\ n 1 : material obtained by washing 2 : a thin covering or coat (a ~ of silver) 3 : articles washed or to be washed

washing soda n : SODIUM CARBONATE

Wash·ing·ton's Birthday \,wȯsh-iŋ-tənz-, ,wäsh-\ n : the 3d Monday in February observed as a legal holiday

wash·out \'wȯsh-,aút, 'wäsh-\ n 1 : the washing away of earth (as from a road); also : a place where earth is washed away 2 : FAILURE; also : one who fails in a course of training or study

wash·room \-,rüm, -,rûm\ n : a room equipped with washing and toilet facilities : LAVATORY

wash·stand \-,stand\ n 1 : a stand holding articles needed for washing face and hands 2 : a washbowl permanently set in place

wash·tub \-,təb\ n : a tub for washing clothes or for soaking them before washing

wash·wom·an \'wȯsh-,wùm-ən, 'wäsh-\ n : WASHERWOMAN

washy \'wȯsh-ē, 'wäsh-\ adj **wash·i·er; -est** 1 : WEAK, WATERY 2 : PALLID 3 : lacking in vigor, individuality, or definiteness

wasp \'wäsp, 'wȯsp\ n : any of numerous social or solitary winged insects related to the bees and ants with biting mouthparts and in females and workers a formidable sting

WASP or Wasp n [white Anglo-Saxon Protestant] : an American of northern European and esp. British stock and of Protestant background

wasp·ish \'wäs-pish, 'wȯs-\ adj 1 : SNAPPISH, IRRITABLE 2 : resembling a wasp in form; esp : slightly built

wasp waist n : a very slender waist

¹**was·sail** \'wäs-əl, wä-'säl\ n [ME wæs hæil, fr. ON ves heill be well] 1 : an early English toast to someone's health 2 : a hot drink made with wine, beer, or cider, spices, sugar, and usu. baked apples and that is traditionally served at Christmas 3 : riotous drinking : REVELRY

²**was·sail** vb 1 : CAROUSE 2 : to drink to

the health or thriving of — **was·sail·er** n

Was·ser·mann test \,wäs-ər-mən-, ,väs-\ n : a blood test for infection with syphilis

wast·age \'wā-stij\ n : loss by use, decay, erosion, or leakage or through wastefulness

¹**waste** \'wāst\ n 1 : a sparsely settled or barren region : DESERT; also : uncultivated land 2 : the act or an instance of wasting : the state of being wasted 3 : gradual loss or decrease by use, wear, or decay 4 : material left over, rejected, or thrown away; also : an unwanted product of a manufacturing or chemical process 5 : refuse (as garbage or rubbish) that accumulates about habitations; also : material (as feces) produced but not used by a living body — **waste·ful** \-fəl\ adj — **waste·ful·ly** \-ē\ adv — **waste·ful·ness** n

²**waste** vb **wast·ed; wast·ing** 1 : DEVASTATE 2 : to wear away or diminish gradually : CONSUME 3 : to spend money or use property carelessly or uselessly : SQUANDER; also : to allow to be used inefficiently or become dissipated 4 : to lose or cause to lose weight, strength, or vitality (wasting away from fever) 5 : to become diminished in bulk or substance : DWINDLE — **wast·er** n

³**waste** adj 1 : being wild and uninhabited : BARREN, DESOLATE; also : UNCULTIVATED 2 : RUINED, DEVASTATED (bombs laid ~ the city) 3 : discarded as worthless after being used (~ water) 4 : excreted from or stored in inert form in a living body as a byproduct of vital activity (~ matter from birds) 5 : serving to conduct or hold refuse material; esp : carrying off superfluous water

waste·bas·ket \'wās(t)-,bas-kət\ n : a receptacle for refuse

waste·land \'wāst-,land, -lənd\ n : land that is barren or unfit for cultivation

waste·pa·per \'wās(t)-'pā-pər\ n : paper discarded as used, superfluous, or not fit for use

waste product n : material resulting from a process (as of metabolism or manufacture) that is of no further use to the system producing it

wast·rel \'wā-strəl\ n : one that wastes : SPENDTHRIFT

¹**watch** \'wäch, 'wȯch\ vb 1 : to be or stay awake intentionally : keep vigil (~ed by the patient's bedside) (~ and pray) 2 : to be on the lookout for danger : be on one's guard 3 : to keep guard (~ outside the door) 4 : OBSERVE (~ a game) 5 : to keep in view so as to prevent harm or warn of danger (~ a brush fire carefully) 6 : to keep oneself informed about (~ his progress) 7 : to lie in wait for esp. so as to take advantage of (~ed his opportunity) — **watch·er** n

²**watch** n 1 : the act of keeping awake to

guard, protect, or attend; *also* : a state of alert and continuous attention **2** : close observation **3** : one that watches : LOOKOUT, WATCHMAN, GUARD **4** : an allotted period for being on nautical duty; *also* : the members of a ship's company operating the vessel during such a period **5** : a portable timepiece carried on the person

watch·band \'wäch-ˌband, 'wóch-\ *n* : the bracelet or strap of a wristwatch

watch·case \-ˌkās\ *n* : the outside metal covering of a watch

watch·dog \-ˌdóg\ *n* **1** : a dog kept to guard property **2** : one that guards or protects

watch·ful \'wäch-fəl, 'wóch-\ *adj* : steadily attentive and alert esp. to danger : VIGILANT — **watch·ful·ly** \-ē\ *adv* — **watch·ful·ness** *n*

watch·mak·er \-ˌmā-kər\ *n* : one that makes or repairs watches — **watch·mak·ing** \-ˌmā-kiŋ\ *n*

watch·man \-mən\ *n* : a person assigned to watch : GUARD

watch night *n* : a devotional service lasting until after midnight esp. on New Year's Eve

watch·tow·er \'wäch-ˌtaù(-ə)r, 'wóch-\ *n* : a tower for a lookout

watch·word \-ˌwərd\ *n* **1** : a secret word used as a signal or sign of recognition **2** : a motto used as a slogan or rallying cry

¹wa·ter \'wót-ər, 'wät-\ *n* **1** : the liquid that descends as rain and forms rivers, lakes, and seas **2** : a natural mineral water — usu. used in pl. **3** *pl* : the water occupying or flowing in a particular bed; *also* : a band of seawater bordering on and under the control of a country 〈sailing Canadian ~s〉 **4** : any of various liquids containing or resembling water; *esp* : a watery fluid (as tears, urine, or sap) formed or circulating in a living body **5** : a specified degree of thoroughness or completeness 〈a scoundrel of the first ~〉 **6** : a wavy lustrous pattern (as of a textile)

²water *vb* **1** : to supply with or get or take water 〈~ horses〉 〈the ship ~ed at each port〉 **2** : to treat (as cloth) so as to give a lustrous appearance in wavy lines **3** : to dilute by or as if by adding water to **4** : to form or secrete water or watery matter 〈his eyes ~ed〉 〈my mouth ~ed〉

water ballet *n* : a synchronized sequence of movements performed by a group of swimmers

water bed *n* : a bed whose mattress is a plastic bag filled with water

wa·ter·borne \-ˌbórn\ *adj* : supported or carried by water

water buffalo *n* : a common oxlike often domesticated Asian bovine

water chestnut *n* : any of several aquatic plants (as a Chinese sedge) with edible underground parts or fruits; *also* : the edible part

water closet *n* : a compartment or room

for defecation and urination into a toilet bowl : BATHROOM; *also* : a toilet bowl along with its accessories

wa·ter·col·or \'wót-ər-ˌkəl-ər, 'wät-\ *n* **1** : a paint whose liquid part is water **2** : the art of painting with watercolors **3** : a picture made with watercolors

wa·ter·course \-ˌkórs\ *n* : a stream of water; *also* : the bed of a stream

wa·ter·craft \-ˌkraft\ *n* : a craft for water transport : SHIP, BOAT

wa·ter·cress \-ˌkres\ *n* : a perennial plant with white flowers related to the cabbage, found chiefly in clear running water, and used esp. in salads

wa·ter·fall \-ˌfòl\ *n* : a very steep descent of the water of a stream

water flea *n* : any of various tiny active freshwater crustaceans

wa·ter·fowl \'wót-ər-ˌfaùl, 'wät-\ *n* **1** : a bird that frequents the water **2 waterfowl** *pl* : wild ducks and geese hunted as game

wa·ter·front \-ˌfrənt\ *n* : land or a section of a town fronting or abutting on a body of water

water gap *n* : a pass in a mountain ridge through which a stream runs

water gas *n* : a poisonous flammable gaseous mixture of chiefly hydrogen and carbon monoxide made by forcing air and steam over red-hot coke or coal that is used as a fuel

water glass *n* : a drinking glass

watering place *n* : a resort that features mineral springs or bathing

water lily *n* : any of a family of aquatic plants with floating roundish leaves and showy solitary flowers

wa·ter·line \'wót-ər-ˌlīn, 'wät-\ *n* : any of several lines that are marked on the outside of a ship and correspond with the surface of the water when the ship is afloat on an even keel

wa·ter·logged \-ˌlógd, -ˌlägd\ *adj* : so filled or soaked with water as to be heavy or unmanageable 〈a ~ boat〉

wa·ter·loo \ˌwót-ər-'lü, ˌwät-\ *n, pl* **-loos** [*Waterloo*, Belgium, scene of Napoleon's defeat in 1815] : a decisive defeat

¹wa·ter·mark \'wót-ər-ˌmärk, 'wät-\ *n* **1** : a mark indicating height to which water has risen **2** : a marking in paper visible when the paper is held up to the light

²watermark *vb* : to mark (paper) with a watermark

wa·ter·mel·on \-ˌmel-ən\ *n* : a large roundish or oblong fruit with sweet juicy usu. red pulp; *also* : an African vine related to the squashes that produces watermelons

water moccasin *n* : a venomous snake of the southern U.S. that is a pit viper related to the copperhead

water ouzel *n* : DIPPER 1

water pipe *n* : a tobacco-smoking device so arranged that the smoke is drawn through water

water polo *n* : a team game played in a

swimming pool with a ball resembling a soccer ball

wa·ter·pow·er \'wȯt-ər-ˌpau̇(-ə)r, 'wät-\ *n* : the power of moving water used to run machinery

¹wa·ter·proof \ˌwȯt-ər-'prüf, ˌwät-\ *adj* : not letting water through; *esp* : covered or treated with a material to prevent permeation by water — **wa·ter·proof·ing** \-iŋ\ *n*

²waterproof \ˌwȯt-ər-'prüf, 'wät-\ *n* **1** : a waterproof fabric **2** *chiefly Brit* : RAINCOAT

³waterproof \ˌwȯt-ər-'prüf, ˌwät-\ *vb* : to make waterproof

wa·ter·re·pel·lent \ˌwȯt-ə(r)-ri-'pel-ənt, ˌwät-\ *adj* : treated with a finish that is resistant to penetration by water

wa·ter·re·sis·tant \-ri-'zis-tant\ *adj* : WATER-REPELLENT

wa·ter·shed \'wȯt-ər-ˌshed, 'wät-\ *n* **1** : a dividing ridge between two drainage areas **2** : the region or area drained by a particular body of water

wa·ter·side \-ˌsīd\ *n* : the land bordering a body of water

water ski *n* : a ski used on water when the wearer is towed — **wa·ter·ski** *vb* — **wa·ter·ski·er** \-ˌskē-ər\ *n*

wa·ter·spout \'wȯt-ər-ˌspaut, 'wät-\ *n* **1** : a pipe for carrying off water from a roof **2** : a funnel-shaped cloud extending from a cumulus cloud down to a cloud of spray torn up by whirling winds from an ocean or lake

water strider *n* : any of various long-legged bugs that move about swiftly on the surface of the water

water table *n* : the upper limit of the portion of the ground wholly saturated with water

wa·ter·tight \'wȯt-ər-'tīt, ˌwät-\ *adj* **1** : constructed so as to keep water out **2** : so worded that its meaning cannot be misunderstood or its purpose defeated ⟨a ~ contract⟩

wa·ter·way \'wȯt-ər-ˌwā, 'wät-\ *n* : a navigable body of water

wa·ter·wheel \-ˌhwēl\ *n* : a wheel rotated by direct action of water flowing against it

water wings *n pl* : an air-filled device to give support to a person's body when he is swimming or learning to swim

wa·ter·works \'wȯt-ər-ˌwərks, 'wät-\ *n pl* : a system of reservoirs, pipes, and machinery for supplying water (as to a city)

wa·tery \'wȯt-ə-rē, 'wät-\ *adj* **1** : containing, full of, or giving out water ⟨~ clouds⟩ **2** : being like water : THIN, WEAK ⟨~ lemonade⟩ ; *also* : being soft and soggy ⟨~ turnips⟩

WATS \'wäts\ *abbr* Wide Area Telephone Service

watt \'wät\ *n* [after James Watt †1819 Scottish engineer and inventor] : the metric unit of power equal to the work done at the rate of one joule per second or to the power produced by a current of one ampere across a potential difference of one volt

watt·age \'wät-ij\ *n* : amount of power expressed in watts

wat·tle \'wät-ᵊl\ *n* **1** : a framework of rods with flexible branches or reeds interlaced used for fencing and esp. formerly in building; *also* : material for this framework **2** : a naked fleshy process hanging usu. from the head or neck (as of a bird) — **wat·tled** \-ᵊld\ *adj*

W Aust *abbr* Western Australia

¹wave \'wāv\ *vb* **waved**; **wav·ing** **1** : FLUTTER ⟨flags *waving* in the breeze⟩ **2** : to motion with the hands or with something held in them in signal or salute **3** : to become moved or brandished to-and-fro; *also* : BRANDISH, FLOURISH ⟨~ a sword⟩ **4** : to move before the wind with a wavelike motion ⟨fields of *waving* grain⟩ **5** : to curve up and down like a wave : UNDULATE

²wave *n* **1** : a moving ridge or swell on the surface of water **2** : a wavelike formation or shape ⟨a ~ in the hair⟩ **3** : the action or process of making wavy or curly **4** : a waving motion; *esp* : a signal made by waving something **5** : FLOW, GUSH ⟨a ~ of color swept her face⟩ **6** : a rapid increase : SURGE ⟨a ~ of buying⟩ ⟨a heat ~⟩ **7** : a disturbance somewhat similar to a wave in water that transfers energy progressively from point to point ⟨a light ~⟩ ⟨a sound ~⟩ — **wave·like** *adj*

Wave \'wāv\ *n* [Women Accepted for Volunteer Emergency Service] : a woman serving in the navy

wave·length \'wāv-ˌleŋth\ *n* **1** : the distance in the line of advance of a wave from any one point (as a crest) to the next corresponding point **2** : a particular line of thought esp. as related to mutual understanding

wave·let \-lət\ *n* : a little wave : RIPPLE

wa·ver \'wā-vər\ *vb* **wa·vered**; **wa·ver·ing** \'wāv-(ə-)riŋ\ **1** : to vacillate between choices : fluctuate in opinion, allegiance, or direction **2** : REEL, TOTTER; *also* : QUIVER, FLICKER ⟨~ing flames⟩ **3** : FALTER **4** : to give an unsteady sound : QUAVER — **waver** *n* — **wa·ver·er** *n* — **wa·ver·ing·ly** *adv*

wavy \'wā-vē\ *adj* **wav·i·er**; **-est** : having waves : moving in waves

¹wax \'waks\ *n* **1** : a yellowish plastic substance secreted by bees for constructing the honeycomb **2** : any of various substances resembling beeswax

²wax *vb* : to treat or rub with wax

³wax *vb* **1** : to increase in size, numbers, strength, volume, or duration **2** : to increase in apparent size ⟨the moon ~es toward the full⟩ **3** : to pass from one state to another : BECOME ⟨~ed indignant⟩ ⟨the party ~ed merry⟩

wax bean *n* : a kidney bean with pods that turn creamy yellow to bright yellow when mature enough to use as a snap bean

wax·en \'wak-sən\ adj 1 : made of or covered with wax 2 : resembling wax (as in color or consistency)

wax myrtle n : any of various shrubs or trees with aromatic leaves; esp : an American evergreen shrub that produces small hard berries with a thick coating of white wax used for candles

wax·wing \'waks-ˌwiŋ\ n : any of a genus of singing birds that are mostly brown with a showy crest and velvety plumage

wax·work \-ˌwərk\ n 1 : an effigy usu. of a person in wax 2 pl : an exhibition of wax figures

waxy \'wak-sē\ adj **wax·i·er; -est** 1 : made of or full of wax 2 : WAXEN 2

way \'wā\ n 1 : a thoroughfare for travel or passage : ROAD, PATH, STREET 2 : ROUTE 3 : a course of action (chose the easy ∼) ; also : opportunity, capability, or fact of doing as one pleases (always had his own ∼) 4 : a possible course : POSSIBILITY (no two ∼s about it) 5 : METHOD, MODE (this ∼ of thinking) (a new ∼ of painting) 6 : FEATURE, RESPECT (a good worker in many ∼s) 7 : the usual or characteristic state of affairs (as is the ∼ with old people) ; also : individual characteristic or peculiarity (used to his ∼s) 8 : DISTANCE (a short ∼ from here) (a long ∼ from success) 9 : progress along a course (working his ∼ through college) 10 : something having direction : LOCALITY (out our ∼) 11 : STATE, CONDITION (that is the ∼ things are) 12 pl : an inclined structure upon which a ship is built or is supported in launching 13 : CATEGORY, KIND (get what you need in the ∼ of supplies) 14 : motion or speed of a boat through the water — **by way of** 1 : for the purpose of (by way of illustration) 2 : by the route through : VIA — **out of the way** 1 : WRONG, IMPROPER 2 : SECLUDED, REMOTE — **under way** 1 : in motion through the water 2 : in progress

way·bill \'wā-ˌbil\ n : a paper that accompanies a freight shipment and gives details of goods, route, and charges

way·far·er \'wā-ˌfar-ər\ n : a traveler esp. on foot — **way·far·ing** \-ˌfar-iŋ\ adj

way·lay \'wā-ˌlā\ vb **-laid** \-ˌlād\ ; **-lay·ing** : to lie in wait for often in order to seize, rob, or kill

way-out \'wā-'aut\ adj : FAR-OUT

-ways \ˌwāz\ adv suffix : in (such) a way, course, direction, or manner (sideways)

ways and means n pl : methods and resources for accomplishing something and esp. for raising revenues needed by a state; also : a legislative committee concerned with this function

way·side \'wā-ˌsīd\ n : the side of or land adjacent to a road or path

way station n : an intermediate station on a line of travel (as a railroad)

way·ward \'wā-wərd\ adj [ME, short for awayward turned away, fr. away, adv. + -ward directed toward] 1 : taking one's own and usu. irregular or improper way : DISOBEDIENT (∼ children) 2 : UNPREDICTABLE, IRREGULAR 3 : opposite to what is desired or expected (∼ fate)

WBC abbr white blood cells

WC abbr 1 water closet 2 without charge

WCTU abbr Women's Christian Temperance Union

we \(ˈ)wē\ pron 1 — used of a group that includes the speaker or writer 2 — used for the singular I by sovereigns and by writers (as of editorials)

weak \'wēk\ adj 1 : lacking strength or vigor : FEEBLE 2 : not able to sustain or resist much weight, pressure, or strain 3 : deficient in vigor of mind or character; also : resulting from or indicative of such deficiency (a ∼ policy) (a ∼ will) (weak-minded) 4 : not supported by truth or logic (a ∼ argument) 5 : not able to function properly 6 : lacking skill or proficiency; also : indicative of a lack of skill or aptitude 7 : wanting in vigor of expression or effect 8 : deficient in the usual or required ingredients : of less than usual strength (∼ tea) 9 : not having or exerting authority (∼ government) ; also : INEFFECTIVE, IMPOTENT 10 : of, relating to, or constituting a verb or verb conjugation that forms the past tense and past participle by adding -ed or -d or -t — **weak·ly** adv

weak·en \'wē-kən\ vb **weak·ened; weak·en·ing** \'wēk-(ə-)niŋ\ : to make or become weak syn enfeeble, debilitate, undermine, sap, cripple, disable

weak·fish \'wēk-ˌfish\ n [obs. Dutch weekvis, fr. D week soft + vis fish; fr. its tender flesh] : a common sport and market fish of the Atlantic coast of the U.S. related to the perches; also : any of several related food fishes

weak-kneed \'wēk-'nēd\ adj : lacking willpower or resolution

weak·ling \-liŋ\ n : a person who is physically, mentally, or morally weak

weak·ly \'wēk-lē\ adj : FEEBLE, WEAK

weak·ness \-nəs\ n 1 : the quality or state of being weak; also : an instance or period of being weak (in a moment of ∼ he agreed to go) 2 : FAULT, DEFECT 3 : an object of special desire or fondness (coffee is her ∼)

¹**weal** \'wēl\ n 1 : WELL-BEING, PROSPERITY

²**weal** n : WELT

weald \'wēld\ n [The Weald, wooded district in England, fr. ME Weeld the Weald, fr. OE weald wood, forest] 1 : FOREST 2 : a wild or uncultivated usu. upland region : WOLD

wealth \'welth\ n [ME welthe, welfare,

prosperity, fr. *wele* weal] **1** : abundance of possessions or resources : AFFLUENCE, RICHES **2** : abundant supply : PROFUSION (a ∼ of detail) **3** : all property that has a money or an exchange value; *also* : all objects or resources that have economic value

wealthy \'wel-thē\ *adj* **wealth·i·er; -est** : having wealth : RICH, AFFLUENT, OPULENT

wean \'wēn\ *vb* **1** : to accustom (a young mammal) to take food otherwise than by nursing **2** : to free from a cause of dependence or preoccupation

weap·on \'wep-ən\ *n* **1** : something (as a gun, knife, or club) that may be used to fight with **2** : a means by which one contends against another

weap·on·less \'wep-ən-ləs\ *adj* : lacking weapons : UNARMED

weap·on·ry \-rē\ *n* **1** : WEAPONS **2** : the science of designing and making weapons

¹**wear** \'waər\ *vb* **wore** \'wōr\ ; **worn** \'wōrn\ ; **wear·ing** **1** : to bear on the person or use habitually for clothing or adornment (∼ a coat) (∼ a wig) ; *also* : to carry on the person (∼ a gun) **2** : to have or show an appearance of (∼ a smile) **3** : to impair, diminish, or decay by use or by scraping or rubbing (clothes *worn* to shreds) (letters on the stone *worn* away by weathering) ; *also* : to produce gradually by friction, rubbing, or wasting away (∼ a hole in the rug) **4** : to exhaust or lessen the strength of : WEARY, FATIGUE (*worn* by care and toil) **5** : to endure use : last under use or the passage of time (this cloth ∼s well) **6** : to diminish or fail with the passage of time (the day ∼s on) (the effect of the drug *wore* off) **7** : to grow or become by attrition, use, or age (the coin was *worn* thin) — **wear·able** \'war-ə-bəl\ *adj* — **wear·er** *n*

²**wear** *n* **1** : the act of wearing : the state of being worn (clothes for everyday ∼) **2** : clothing usu. of a particular kind or for a special occasion or use (children's ∼) **3** : wearing or lasting quality (the coat still has lots of ∼ in it) **4** : the result of wearing or use : impairment resulting from use (her suit shows ∼)

wear and tear \,war-ən-'taər\ *n* : the loss or injury to which something is subjected in the course of use; *esp* : normal depreciation

wear down *vb* : to weary and overcome by persistent resistance or pressure

wea·ri·some \'wir-ē-səm\ *adj* : causing weariness : TIRESOME — **wea·ri·some·ly** *adv* — **wea·ri·some·ness** *n*

wear out *vb* **1** : TIRE **2** : to make or become useless by wear

¹**wea·ry** \'wir-ē\ *adj* **wea·ri·er; -est 1** : worn out in strength, endurance, vigor, or freshness **2** : expressing or characteristic of weariness (a ∼ sigh)

3 : having one's patience, tolerance, or pleasure exhausted (∼ of war) — **wea·ri·ly** \'wir-ə-lē\ *adv* — **wea·ri·ness** \-ē-nəs\ *n*

²**weary** *vb* **wea·ried; wea·ry·ing** : to become or make weary : TIRE

wea·sel \'wē-zəl\ *n, pl* **weasels** : any of various small slender flesh-eating mammals related to the minks

weasel word *n* [fr. the weasel's reputed habit of sucking the contents out of an egg while leaving the shell superficially intact] : a word used in order to evade or retreat from a direct or forthright statement or position

¹**weath·er** \'weth-ər\ *n* **1** : condition of the atmosphere with respect to heat or cold, wetness or dryness, calm or storm, clearness or cloudiness **2** : a particular and esp. a disagreeable atmospheric state : RAIN, STORM

²**weather** *vb* **1** : to expose to or endure the action of weather; *also* : to alter (as in color or texture) by such exposure **2** : to sail or pass to the windward of **3** : to bear up against successfully (∼ a storm) (∼ troubles)

³**weather** *adj* : WINDWARD

weath·er·beat·en \'weth-ər-,bēt-ⁿn\ *adj* : altered by exposure to the weather; *also* : toughened or tanned by the weather (∼ face)

weath·er·board \-,bōrd\ *n* : CLAPBOARD

weath·er·board·ing \-,bōrd-iŋ\ *n* : CLAPBOARDS, SIDING

weath·er-bound \-,baûnd\ *adj* : kept in port or at anchor or from travel or sport by bad weather

weath·er·cock \-,käk\ *n* **1** : a weather vane shaped like a rooster **2** : a fickle person

weath·er·glass \'weth-ər-,glas\ *n* : BAROMETER

weath·er·ing \'weth-(ə-)riŋ\ *n* : the action of the weather in altering the color, texture, composition, or form of exposed objects; *also* : alteration thus effected

weath·er·ize \'weth-ə-,rīz\ *vb* **-ized; -iz·ing** : to make (as a house) better protected against winter weather esp. by adding insulation and by caulking joints — **weath·er·iza·tion** \,weth-ə-rə-'zā-shən\ *n*

weath·er·man \-,man\ *n* : one who reports and forecasts the weather : METEOROLOGIST

weath·er·proof \,weth-ər-'prüf\ *adj* : able to withstand exposure to weather without appreciable harm — **weatherproof** *vb*

weather strip *n* : a strip of material to make a seal where a door or window joins the sill or casing — **weath·er·strip** *vb*

weather vane *n* : VANE 1

weath·er·worn \'weth-ər-,wōrn\ *adj* : worn by exposure to the weather

¹**weave** \'wēv\ *vb* **wove** \'wōv\ *or* **weaved; wo·ven** \'wō-vən\ *or* **weaved; weav·ing 1** : to form by interlacing

strands of material; *esp* : to make on a loom by interlacing warp and filling threads ⟨~ cloth⟩ **2** : to interlace (as threads) into a fabric and esp. cloth **3** : SPIN **2 4** : CONTRIVE **5** : to unite in a coherent whole **6** : to work in ⟨*wove* the episodes into a story⟩ **7** : to direct or move in a winding or zigzag course esp. to avoid obstacles ⟨we *wove* our way through the crowd⟩ — **weav·er** *n*
²**weave** *n* : a pattern or method of weaving ⟨a coarse loose ~⟩

¹**web** \'web\ *n* **1** : a fabric on a loom or coming from a loom **2** : COBWEB; *also* : SNARE, ENTANGLEMENT ⟨caught in a ~ of deceit⟩ **3** : an animal or plant membrane; *esp* : one uniting the toes (as in many birds) **4** : NETWORK ⟨a ~ of highways⟩ **5** : the series of barbs on each side of the shaft of a feather
²**web** *vb* **webbed; web·bing 1** : to cover or provide with webs or a network **2** : ENTANGLE, ENSNARE **3** : to make a web

webbed \'webd\ *adj* : having or being toes or fingers united by a web ⟨the ~ feet of ducks⟩
web·bing \'web-iŋ\ *n* : a strong closely woven tape designed for bearing weight and used esp. for straps, harness, or upholstery
web-foot·ed \'web-'fût-əd\ *adj* : having webbed feet
wed \'wed\ *vb* **wed·ded** *also* **wed; wed·ding 1** : to take, give, or join in marriage : enter into matrimony : MARRY **2** : to unite firmly
Wed *abbr* Wednesday
wed·ding \'wed-iŋ\ *n* **1** : a marriage ceremony usu. with accompanying festivities : NUPTIALS **2** : a joining in close association **3** : a wedding anniversary or its celebration
¹**wedge** \'wej\ *n* **1** : a solid triangular piece of wood or metal that tapers to a thin edge and is used to split logs or rocks or to raise heavy weights **2** : something (as an action or policy) that serves to open up a way for a breach, change, or intrusion **3** : a wedge-shaped object or part ⟨a ~ of pie⟩
²**wedge** *vb* **wedged; wedg·ing 1** : to hold firm by or as if by driving in a wedge **2** : to force (something) into a narrow space **3** : to split apart with or as if with a wedge
wed·lock \'wed-,läk\ *n* [ME *wedlok*, fr. OE *wedlāc* marriage bond, fr. *wedd* pledge + -*lāc,* suffix denoting activity] : the state of being married : MARRIAGE, MATRIMONY
Wednes·day \'wenz-dē\ *n* [ME, fr. OE *wōdnesdæg,* lit., day of Odin (supreme god of Norse mythology)] : the 4th day of the week
wee \'wē\ *adj* [ME *we,* fr. *we,* n., little bit, fr. OE *wǣge* weight] **1** : very small : TINY **2** : very early ⟨~ hours of the morning⟩
¹**weed** \'wēd\ *n* : a plant that is not val-

ued where it is growing and is usu. of rank growth; *esp* : one growing in cultivated ground to the damage of a crop
²**weed** *vb* **1** : to clear of or remove weeds or something harmful, inferior, or superfluous ⟨~ a garden⟩ **2** : to get rid of (unwanted items) ⟨~ out the loafers from the crew⟩ — **weed·er** *n*
³**weed** *n* : GARMENT; *esp* : dress worn (as by a widow) as a sign of mourning — usu. used in pl.
weedy \'wēd-ē\ *adj* **1** : full of weeds **2** : resembling a weed esp. in vigor of growth or spread **3** : noticeably lean and scrawny : LANK
week \'wēk\ *n* **1** : seven successive days; *esp* : a calendar period of seven days beginning with Sunday and ending with Saturday **2** : the working or school days of the calendar week
week·day \'wēk-,dā\ *n* : a day of the week except Sunday or sometimes except Saturday and Sunday
¹**week·end** \-,end\ *n* : the period between the close of one working or business or school week and the beginning of the next
²**weekend** *vb* : to spend the weekend
¹**week·ly** \'wēk-lē\ *adj* **1** : occurring, done, produced, or issued every week **2** : computed in terms of one week — **weekly** *adv*
²**weekly** *n, pl* **weeklies** : a weekly publication
ween \'wēn\ *vb, archaic* : IMAGINE, SUPPOSE
wee·ny \'wē-nē\ *also* **ween·sy** \'wēn(t)-sē\ *adj* : exceptionally small
weep \'wēp\ *vb* **wept** \'wept\; **weep·ing 1** : to express emotion and esp. sorrow by shedding tears : BEWAIL, CRY **2** : to drip or exude (liquid) — **weep·er** *n*
weep·ing \'wē-piŋ\ *adj* **1** : TEARFUL **2** : having slender drooping branches
weeping willow *n* : an Asian willow with weeping branches
weepy \'wē-pē\ *adj* : inclined to weep : TEARFUL
wee·vil \'wē-vəl\ *n* : any of a suborder of mostly small beetles with a long head usu. curved into a snout and larvae that feed esp. in fruits or seeds —**wee·vily** *or* **wee·vil·ly** \'wēv-(ə-)lē\ *adj*
weft \'weft\ *n* **1** : WOOF **2** : WEB, FABRIC; *also* : something woven
¹**weigh** \'wā\ *vb* [ME *weyen,* fr. OE *wegan* to move, carry, weigh] **1** : to ascertain the heaviness of by a balance **2** : to have weight or a specified weight **3** : to consider carefully : PONDER **4** : to merit consideration as important : COUNT ⟨evidence ~*ing* against him⟩ **5** : to heave up (an anchor) **6** : to press down with or as if with a heavy weight
²**weigh** *n* [alter. of *way*] : WAY — used in the phrase *under weigh*
weigh in *vb* : to have something weighed; *esp* : to have oneself weighed preliminary to participation in a sports event

¹**weight** \'wāt\ *n* **1** : the amount that something weighs; *also* : the standard amount that something should weigh **2** : a quantity or portion weighing usu. a certain amount **3** : a unit (as a pound or kilogram) of weight or mass; *also* : a system of such units **4** : a heavy object for holding or pressing something down; *also* : a heavy object for throwing or lifting in an athletic contest **5** : BURDEN (a ~ of grief) **6** : IMPORTANCE, CONSEQUENCE (threw his ~ around) **7** : overpowering force **8** : relative heaviness (as of a textile) *syn* significance, moment, consequence, import, authority, prestige, credit

²**weight** *vb* **1** : to load with or as if with a weight **2** : to oppress with a burden (~ed down with cares)

weight·less \'wāt-ləs\ *adj* : having little weight : lacking apparent gravitational pull — **weight·less·ly** *adv* — **weight·less·ness** *n*

weighty \'wāt-ē\ *adj* **weight·i·er; -est 1** : of much importance or consequence : MOMENTOUS, SERIOUS (~ problems) **2** : SOLEMN (a ~ manner) **3** : HEAVY **4** : exerting force, influence, or authority (~ arguments)

weir \'waər, 'wiər\ *n* **1** : a fence set in a waterway for catching fish **2** : a dam

WEIGHTS AND MEASURES[1]

UNIT	EQUIVALENT IN OTHER U.S. UNITS	METRIC EQUIVALENT
	WEIGHT	
	avoirdupois (ordinary commodities)	
ton		
short ton	200 short hundredweight, 2000 pounds	0.907 metric ton
long ton	200 long hundredweight, 2240 pounds	1.016 metric tons
hundredweight		
short hundredweight	100 pounds, 0.05 short ton	45.359 kilograms
long hundredweight	112 pounds, 0.05 long ton	50.802 kilograms
pound	16 ounces, 7000 grains	0.454 kilograms
ounce	16 drams, 437.5 grains	28.350 grams
dram	27.344 grains, 0.0625 ounce	1.772 grams
grain	0.037 dram, 0.002286 ounce	0.0648 gram
	troy (precious metals, jewels)	
pound	12 ounces, 240 pennyweight, 5760 grains	0.0373 kilogram
ounce	20 pennyweight, 480 grains	31.103 grams
pennyweight	24 grains, 0.05 ounce	1.555 grams
grain	0.042 pennyweight, 0.002083 ounce	0.0648 gram
	apothecaries' (drugs)	
pound	12 ounces, 5760 grains	0.373 kilogram
ounce	8 drams, 480 grains	31.103 grams
dram	0.125 ounce, 60 grains	3.888 grams
grain	0.0166 dram, 0.002083 ounce	0.0648 gram
	comparison of weights	
avoirdupois pound	1.215 apothecaries' pound, 1.215 troy pound	0.454 kilogram
apothecaries' or troy pound	0.822 avoirdupois pound	0.373 kilogram
apothecaries' or troy ounce	1.097 avoirdupois ounce	31.103 grams
avoirdupois ounce	0.911 apothecaries' ounce, 0.911 troy ounce	28.350 grams
avoirdupois grain	1 apothecaries grain, 1 troy grain	0.0648 grain

WEIGHTS AND MEASURES[1]

UNIT	EQUIVALENT IN OTHER U.S. UNITS	METRIC EQUIVALENT
	CAPACITY	
	U.S. liquid measure	
gallon	4 quarts (231 cubic inches)	3.785 liters
quart	2 pints (57.75 cubic inches)	0.946 liter
pint	4 gills (28.875 cubic inches)	0.473 liter
gill	4 fluidounces (7.219 cubic inches)	118.294 milliliters
fluidounce	8 fluidrams (1.805 cubic inches)	29.573 milliliters
fluidram	60 minims (0.226 cubic inch)	3.697 milliliters
minim	1/60 fluidram (0.003760 cubic inch)	0.061610 milliliter
	U.S. dry measure	
bushel	4 pecks (2150.42 cubic inches)	35.239 liters
peck	8 quarts (537.605 cubic inches)	8.10 liters
quart	2 pints (67.201 cubic inches)	1.101 liters
pint	½ quart (33.600 cubic inches)	0.551 liter
	LENGTH	
mile	5280 feet, 320 rods, 1760 yards	1.609 kilometers
rod	5.50 yards, 16.5 feet	5.029 meters
yard	3 feet, 36 inches	0.9144 meter
foot	12 inches, 0.333 yard	30.48 centimeters
inch	0.083 feet, 0.028 yard	2.54 centimeters
	AREA	
square mile	640 acres, 102,400 square rods	2.590 square kilometers
acre	4840 square yards, 43,560 square feet	4047 square meters
square rod	30.25 square yards, 0.00625 acres	25.293 square meters
square yard	1296 square inches, 9 square feet	0.836 square meter
square foot	144 square inches, 0.111 square yard	0.093 square meter
square inch	0.0069 square foot, 0.00077 square yard	6.452 square centimeters
	VOLUME	
cubic yard	27 cubic feet, 46,656 cubic inches	0.765 cubic meter
cubic foot	1728 cubic inches, 0.0370 cubic yard	0.028 cubic meter
cubic inch	0.00058 cubic foot, 0.0370 cubic yard	16.387 cubic centimeters

[1]For U.S. equivalents of metric units see Metric System table

in a river for the purpose of directing water to a mill or making a pond
weird \\'wiərd\\ *adj* [ME *wird, werd* fate, destiny, fr. OE *wyrd*] **1** : MAGICAL **2** : UNEARTHLY, MYSTERIOUS **3** : ODD, UNUSUAL, FANTASTIC **syn** eerie, uncanny, spooky — **weird·ly** *adv* — **weird·ness** *n*
Welch \\'welch\\ *var of* WELSH

¹wel·come \\'wel-kəm\\ *vb* **wel·comed; wel·com·ing 1** : to greet cordially or courteously **2** : to accept, meet, or face with pleasure ⟨he ∼s criticism⟩
²welcome *adj* **1** : received gladly into one's presence ⟨a ∼ visitor⟩ **2** : giving pleasure : PLEASING ⟨∼ news⟩ **3** : willingly permitted or admitted ⟨all are ∼

to use the books) **4** — used in the phrase "You're welcome" as a reply to an expression of thanks

³**welcome** n : a cordial greeting or reception

¹**weld** \'weld\ vb **1** : to unite (metal or plastic parts) either by heating and allowing the parts to flow together or by hammering or pressing together **2** : to unite closely or intimately (~ed together in friendship) — **weld·er** n

²**weld** n **1** : a welded joint **2** : union by welding

wel·fare \'wel-ˌfaər\ n **1** : the state of doing well esp. in respect to happiness, well-being, or prosperity (the ~ of mankind) **2** : organized efforts for the social betterment of a group in society **3** : RELIEF 2

welfare state n : a nation or state that assumes primary responsibility for the individual and social welfare of its citizens

wel·kin \'wel-kən\ n : SKY; also : AIR

¹**well** \'wel\ n **1** : a spring with its pool : FOUNTAIN; also : a source of supply (a ~ of information) **2** : a hole sunk in the earth to obtain a natural deposit (as of water, oil, or gas) **3** : an open space (as for a staircase) extending vertically through floors of a structure **4** : something suggesting a well

²**well** vb : to rise up and flow forth : RUN

³**well** adv **bet·ter** \'bet-ər\ ; **best** \'best\ **1** : in a good or proper manner : RIGHTLY; also : EXCELLENTLY, SKILLFULLY **2** : SATISFACTORILY, FORTUNATELY (the party turned out ~) **3** : ABUNDANTLY (eat ~) **4** : with reason or courtesy : PROPERLY (I cannot ~ refuse) **5** : COMPLETELY, FULLY, QUITE (~ worth the price) (well-hidden) **6** : INTIMATELY, CLOSELY (I know him ~) **7** : CONSIDERABLY, FAR (~ over a million) (~ ahead) **8** : without trouble or difficulty (he could ~ have gone) **9** : EXACTLY, DEFINITELY (remember it ~)

⁴**well** adj **1** : PROSPEROUS; also : being in satisfactory condition or circumstances **2** : SATISFACTORY, PLEASING (all is ~) **3** : ADVISABLE, DESIRABLE (it is not ~ to anger him) **4** : free or recovered from infirmity or disease : HEALTHY **5** : FORTUNATE (it is ~ that this has happened)

well-ad·vised \ˌwel-əd-'vīzd\ adj **1** : PRUDENT **2** : resulting from, based on, or showing careful deliberation or wise counsel (~ plans)

well-ap·point·ed \-ə-'póint-əd\ adj : having good and complete equipment

well-be·ing \'wel-'bē-iŋ\ n : the state of being happy, healthy, or prosperous

well-born \-'bórn\ adj : born of good stock either socially or physically

well-bred \-'bred\ adj : having or indicating good breeding : REFINED

well-con·di·tioned \ˌwel-kən-'dish-ənd\ adj **1** : characterized by proper disposition, morals, or behavior **2** : having

a good physical condition : SOUND (~ animal)

well-de·fined \-di-'fīnd\ adj : having clearly distinguishable limits or boundaries (a ~ scar)

well-dis·posed \-dis-'pōzd\ adj : disposed to be friendly, favorable, or sympathetic

well-done \'wel-'dən\ adj **1** : rightly or properly performed **2** : cooked thoroughly

well-fa·vored \-'fā-vərd\ adj : GOOD-LOOKING, HANDSOME

well-fixed \-'fikst\ adj : financially well-off

well-found·ed \-'faún-dəd\ adj : based on sound information, reasoning, judgment, or grounds (~ rumors)

well-groomed \-'grümd, -'grümd\ adj : well and neatly dressed or cared for (~ men) (a ~ lawn)

well-ground·ed \-'graún-dəd\ adj : having a firm foundation

well-head \-ˌhed\ n **1** : the source of a spring or a stream **2** : principal source **3** : the top of or a structure built over a well

well-heeled \-'hēld\ adj : financially well-off

well-knit \-'nit\ adj : well and firmly formed or framed (a ~ argument)

well-known \-'nōn\ adj : fully or widely known

well-mean·ing \-'mē-niŋ\ adj : having or based on excellent intentions

well-nigh \-'nī\ adv : ALMOST, NEARLY

well-off \-'óf\ adj : being in good condition or circumstances; esp : WELL-TO-DO

well-or·dered \-'órd-ərd\ adj : having an orderly procedure or arrangement

well-read \-'red\ adj : well informed through reading

well-round·ed \-'raún-dəd\ adj **1** : broadly trained, educated, and experienced **2** : COMPREHENSIVE (a ~ program of activities)

well-spo·ken \'wel-'spō-kən\ adj **1** : speaking well and esp. courteously **2** : spoken with propriety (~ words)

well·spring \-ˌspriŋ\ n : FOUNTAINHEAD, SPRING

well-timed \-'tīmd\ adj : coming or happening at an opportune moment : TIMELY

well-to-do \ˌwel-tə-'dü\ adj : having more than adequate material resources : PROSPEROUS

well-turned \'wel-'tərnd\ adj **1** : pleasingly rounded : SHAPELY (a ~ ankle) **2** : pleasingly and appropriately expressed (a ~ phrase)

well-wish·er \'wel-ˌwish-ər, -'wish-\ n : one that wishes well to another — **well-wish·ing** \-iŋ\ adj or n

well-worn \-'wórn\ adj **1** : worn by much use (~ shoes) **2** : TRITE **3** archaic : worn well or properly (~ honors)

welsh \'welsh, 'welch\ vb **1** : to cheat by avoiding payment of bets **2** : to

break one's word (~ed on his promises)

Welsh \'welsh\ *n* **1** Welsh *pl* : the people of Wales **2** : the Celtic language of
Wales — **Welsh** *adj* — **Welsh·man**
\-mən\ *n*

Welsh cor·gi \-'kȯr-gē\ *n* [W *corgi,* fr.
cor dwarf + *ci* dog] : a short-legged
long-backed dog with foxy head of either of two breeds of Welsh origin

Welsh rabbit *n* : melted often seasoned
cheese poured over toast or crackers

Welsh rare·bit \-'raər-bət\ *n* : WELSH
RABBIT

¹welt \'welt\ *n* **1** : the narrow strip of
leather between a shoe upper and sole
to which other parts are stitched **2** : a
doubled edge, strip, insert, or seam
for ornament or reinforcement **3** : a
ridge or lump raised on the skin usu.
by a blow; *also* : a heavy blow

²welt *vb* **1** : to furnish with a welt **2** : to
hit hard

¹wel·ter \'wel-tər\ *vb* **1** : WRITHE, TOSS;
also : WALLOW **2** : to rise and fall or
toss about in or with waves **3** : to become deeply sunk, soaked, or involved **4** : to be in turmoil

²welter *n* **1** : TURMOIL **2** : a chaotic mass
or jumble

wel·ter·weight \'wel-tər-ˌwāt\ *n* : a boxer weighing more than 135 but not
over 147 pounds

wen \'wen\ *n* : a cyst formed by blocking of a skin gland and filled with fatty
material

wench \'wench\ *n* [ME *wenche,* short
for *wenchel* child, fr. OE *wencel*] **1** : a
young woman : GIRL **2** : a female servant

wend \'wend\ *vb* : to direct one's
course : proceed on (one's way)

went *past of* GO

wept *past and past part of* WEEP

were *past 2d sing, past pl, or past subjunctive of* BE

were·wolf \'wer-ˌwu̇lf, 'wir-\ *n, pl* **were-
wolves** \-ˌwu̇lvz\ [ME, fr. OE *wer-
wulf,* fr. *wer* man + *wulf* wolf] : a
person transformed into a wolf or capable of assuming a wolf's form

wes·kit \'wes-kət\ *n* : VEST 1

¹west \'west\ *adv* : to or toward the west

²west *n* **1** : the general direction of sunset **2** : the compass point directly opposite to east **3** *cap* : regions or countries west of a specified or implied
point **4** *cap* : Europe and the Ameri-
cas — **west·er·ly** \'wes-tər-lē\ *adv or
adj* — **west·ward** *adv or adj* — **west-
wards** *adv*

³west *adj* **1** : situated toward or at the
west **2** : coming from the west

¹west·ern \'wes-tərn\ *adj* **1** *cap* : of, relating to, or characteristic of a region
conventionally designated West **2**
: lying toward or coming from the
west **3** *cap* : of or relating to the Roman Catholic or Protestant segment
of Christianity — **West·ern·er** *n*

²western *n* **1** : one that is produced in or

is characteristic of a western region
and esp. the western U.S. **2** *often cap*
: a novel, story, motion picture, or
broadcast dealing with life in the western U.S. during the latter half of the
19th century

west·ern·ize \'wes-tər-ˌnīz\ *vb* -**ized;** -**iz-
ing** : to give western characteristics to

¹wet \'wet\ *adj* **wet·ter; wet·test 1** : consisting of or covered or soaked with
liquid (as water) **2** : RAINY **3** : not dry
(~ paint) **4** : permitting or advocating
the manufacture and sale of intoxicating liquor (a ~ town) (a ~ candidate)
syn damp, dank, moist, humid — **wet-
ly** *adv* — **wet·ness** *n*

²wet *n* **1** : WATER; *also* : WETNESS, MOIS-
TURE **2** : rainy weather : RAIN **3** : an
advocate of a wet liquor policy

³wet *vb* **wet** *or* **wet·ted; wet·ting** : to make
or become wet

wet blanket *n* : one that quenches or
dampens enthusiasm or pleasure

weth·er \'weth-ər\ *n* : a male sheep castrated while immature

wet·land \'wet-ˌland, -lənd\ *n* : land or
areas containing much soil moisture

wet nurse *n* : one who cares for and
suckles young not her own

wet suit *n* : a rubber suit for swimmers
that acts to retain body heat by keeping a layer of water against the body
as insulation

wh *abbr* **1** which **2** white

WHA *abbr* World Hockey Association

¹whack \'hwak\ *vb* **1** : to strike with a
smart or resounding blow **2** : to cut
with or as if with a whack

²whack *n* **1** : a smart or resounding
blow; *also* : the sound of such a blow
2 : PORTION, SHARE **3** : CONDITION,
STATE (the machine is out of ~) **4** : an
opportunity or attempt to do something : CHANCE **5** : a single action or
occasion : TIME (made three pies at a
~)

¹whale \'hwāl\ *n, pl* **whales 1** *or pl* **whale**
: any of an order of marine mammals
that lack hind limbs and have the front
limbs modified into flippers; *esp* : one
of the larger members of the order **2**
: a person or thing impressive in size
or quality (a ~ of a story)

²whale *vb* **whaled; whal·ing** : to fish or
hunt for whales

³whale *vb* **whaled; whal·ing 1** : THRASH **2**
: to strike or hit vigorously

whale·boat \-ˌbōt\ *n* : a long narrow
rowboat made with both ends sharp
and sloping and formerly used by
whalers

whale·bone \-ˌbōn\ *n* : a horny substance attached in plates to the upper
jaw of some large whales (**whalebone
whales**)

whal·er \'hwā-lər\ *n* **1** : a person or ship
that hunts whales **2** : WHALEBOAT

wham·my \'hwam-ē\ *n, pl* **wham·mies**
: JINX, HEX

wharf \'hwȯrf\ *n, pl* **wharves** \'hwȯrvz\

also **wharfs** : a structure alongside which ships lie to load and unload

wharf·age \'hwor-fij\ *n* : the provision or use of a wharf; *also* : the charge for using a wharf

wharf·in·ger \'hwor-fən-jər\ *n* : the operator or manager of a wharf

¹**what** \(')hwät, (')hwət\ *pron* 1 — used to inquire about the identity or nature of a being, an object, or some matter or situation ⟨~ is he, a salesman⟩ ⟨~'s that⟩ ⟨~ happened⟩ 2 : that which ⟨I know ~ you want⟩ 3 : WHATEVER 1 ⟨take ~ you want⟩

²**what** *adv* 1 : in what respect : HOW ⟨~ does he care⟩ 2 — used with *with* to introduce a prepositional phrase that expresses cause ⟨kept busy ~ with school and work⟩

³**what** *adj* 1 — used to inquire about the identity or nature of a person, object, or matter ⟨~ books does he read⟩ 2 : how remarkable or surprising ⟨~ an idea⟩ 3 : WHATEVER

¹**what·ev·er** \hwät-'ev-ər\ *pron* 1 : anything or everything that ⟨does ~ he wants to⟩ 2 : no matter what ⟨~ you do, don't cheat⟩ 3 : WHAT 1 — used as an intensive ⟨~ do you mean⟩

²**whatever** *adj* : of any kind at all ⟨no food ~⟩

¹**what·not** \'hwät-,nät\ *pron* : any of various other things that might also be mentioned ⟨paper clips, pins, and ~⟩

²**whatnot** *n* : a light open set of shelves for small ornaments

what·so·ev·er \,hwät-sə-'wev-ər\ *pron or adj* : WHATEVER

wheal \'hwēl\ *n* : a wale or welt on the skin; *also* : a suddenly-appearing itching or burning raised patch of skin

wheat \'hwēt\ *n* : a cereal grain that yields a fine white flour and is the chief breadstuff of temperate regions; *also* : any of several grasses whose white to dark red grains are wheat — **wheat·en** *adj*

wheat germ *n* : the vitamin-rich wheat embryo separated in milling

whee·dle \'hwēd-ᵊl\ *vb* **whee·dled; whee·dling** \'hwēd-(ᵊ-)liŋ\ 1 : to coax or entice by flattery 2 : to gain or get by wheedling

¹**wheel** \'hwēl\ *n* 1 : a disk or circular frame that turns on a central axis 2 : a device whose main part is a wheel 3 : something resembling a wheel (as in being round or turning) 4 : a curving or circular movement 5 : machinery that imparts motion : moving power ⟨the ~s of government⟩ 6 : a person of importance 7 *pl, slang* : AUTOMOBILE — **wheeled** \'hwēld\ *adj* — **wheel·less** \'hwēl-ləs\ *adj*

²**wheel** *vb* 1 : ROTATE, REVOLVE 2 : to change direction as if turning on a pivot 3 : to convey or move on wheels or in a vehicle

wheel·bar·row \-,bar-ō\ *n* : a vehicle with handles and usu. one wheel for conveying small loads

wheel·base \-,bās\ *n* : the distance in inches between the front and rear axles of an automotive vehicle

wheel·chair \-,cheər\ *n* : a chair mounted on wheels esp. for the use of invalids

wheel·er \'hwē-lər\ *n* 1 : one that wheels 2 : something that has wheels — used in combination ⟨a side-*wheel*er⟩ 3 : WHEELHORSE

wheel·er-deal·er \,hwē-lər-'dē-lər\ *n* : a shrewd operator esp. in business or politics

wheel·horse \'hwēl-,hörs\ *n* 1 : a horse in a position nearest the wheels in a tandem or similar arrangement 2 : a steady and effective worker esp. in a political body

wheel·house \-,haůs\ *n* : PILOTHOUSE

wheel·wright \-,rīt\ *n* : a maker and repairer of wheels and wheeled vehicles

¹**wheeze** \'hwēz\ *vb* **wheezed; wheez·ing** : to breathe with difficulty usu. with a whistling sound

²**wheeze** *n* 1 : a sound of wheezing 2 : an often repeated and well-known joke 3 : a trite saying

wheezy \'hwē-zē\ *adj* **wheez·i·er; -est** 1 : inclined to wheeze 2 : having a wheezing sound

whelk \'hwelk\ *n* : a large sea snail; *esp* : one much used as food in Europe

whelm \'hwelm\ *vb* : to overcome or engulf completely : OVERWHELM

¹**whelp** \'hwelp\ *n* 1 : one of the young of various carnivorous mammals (as a dog) 2 : a low contemptible fellow

²**whelp** *vb* : to give birth to ⟨whelps⟩ : bring forth whelps

¹**when** \(')hwen, hwən\ *adv* 1 : at what time ⟨~ will he return⟩ 2 : at or during which time ⟨a time ~ things were upset⟩

²**when** *conj* 1 : at or during the time that ⟨leave ~ I do⟩ 2 : every time that ⟨they all laughed ~ he sang⟩ 3 : in the event that : IF ⟨disqualified ~ he cheats⟩ 4 : ALTHOUGH ⟨quit politics ~ he might have had a great career in it⟩

³**when** \,hwen\ *pron* : what or which time ⟨since ~ have you been the boss⟩

⁴**when** \'hwen\ *n* : the time of a happening

whence \(')hwens\ *adv* 1 : from what place, source, or cause ⟨asked ~ the gifts came⟩ 2 : from or out of which ⟨the land ~ he came⟩

when·ev·er \hwen-'ev-ər, hwən-\ *conj or adv* : at whatever time

when·so·ev·er \'hwen-sə-,wev-ər\ *conj* : at whatever time

¹**where** \(')hweər\ *adv* 1 : at, in, or to what place ⟨~ is he⟩ ⟨~ did he go⟩ 2 : at, in, or to what situation, position, direction, circumstances, or respect ⟨~ does this road lead⟩

²**where** *conj* 1 : at, in, or to what place ⟨knows ~ the house is⟩ 2 : at, in, or to what situation, position, direction, circumstances, or respect ⟨shows ~ the road leads⟩ 3 : WHEREVER ⟨goes ~

he likes) **4** : at, in, or to which place (the town ∼ she lives) **5** : at, in, or to the place at, in, or to which ⟨stay ∼ you are⟩ **6** : in a case, situation, or respect in which ⟨outstanding ∼ endurance is called for⟩
3where \\'hweər\\ *n* **1** : PLACE, LOCATION ⟨the ∼ and how of the accident⟩ **2** : what place ⟨∼ is he from⟩
1where·abouts \-ə-₁baůts\ *also* **whereabout** \-₁baůt\ *adv* : about where ⟨∼ does he live⟩
2whereabouts *n sing or pl* : the place where a person or thing is ⟨his present ∼ are unknown⟩
where·as \hwer-'az\ *conj* **1** : when in fact : while on the contrary **2** : in view of the fact that : SINCE
where·at \-'at\ *conj* **1** : at or toward which **2** : in consequence of which : WHEREUPON
where·by \-'bī\ *conj* : by, through, or in accordance with which ⟨the means ∼ he achieved his goal⟩
1where·fore \'hweər-₁fōr\ *adv* **1** : for what reason or purpose : WHY **2** : THEREFORE
2wherefore *n* : CAUSE, REASON
1where·in \hwer-'in\ *adv* : in what : in what respect ⟨∼ was he wrong⟩
2wherein *conj* **1** : in which : WHERE ⟨the city ∼ he lives⟩ **2** : during which **3** : in what way : HOW ⟨showed him ∼ he was wrong⟩
where·of \-'əv, -'äv\ *conj* **1** : of what ⟨knows ∼ he speaks⟩ **2** : of which or whom ⟨books ∼ the best are lost⟩
where·on \-'ȯn, -'än\ *conj* : on which ⟨the base ∼ it rests⟩
where·so·ev·er \hwer-sə-₁wev-ər\ *conj* : WHEREVER
where·to \-₁tü\ *conj* : to which
where·up·on \'hwer-ə-₁pȯn, -₁pän\ *conj* **1** : on which **2** : closely following and in consequence of which
1wher·ev·er \hwer-'ev-ər\ *adv* : where in the world ⟨∼ did she get that hat⟩
2wherever *conj* **1** : at, in, or to whatever place **2** : in any circumstance in which
where·with \'hwear-₁with, -₁with\ *conj* : with or by means of which
where·with·al \'hwer-with-₁ȯl, -with-\ *n* : MEANS, RESOURCES; *esp* : MONEY
wher·ry \'hwer-ē\ *n, pl* **wherries** : a light boat; *esp* : a long light rowboat sharp at both ends
whet \'hwet\ *vb* **whet·ted; whet·ting 1** : to sharpen by rubbing against or with a hard substance (as a whetstone) **2** : to make keen : STIMULATE ⟨∼ the appetite⟩
wheth·er \'hweth-ər\ *conj* **1** : if it is or was true that ⟨ask ∼ he is going⟩ **2** : if it is or was better (uncertain ∼ to go or stay) **3** : whichever is or was the case, namely that ⟨∼ we succeed or fail, we must try⟩ **4** : EITHER (turned out well ∼ by accident or design)
whet·stone \'hwet-₁stōn\ *n* : a stone for sharpening blades

whey \'hwā\ *n* : the watery part of milk that separates after the milk sours and thickens
1which \(')hwich\ *adj* **1** : being what one or ones out of a group ⟨∼ tie should I wear⟩ **2** : WHICHEVER
2which *pron* **1** : which one or ones ⟨∼ is yours⟩ ⟨∼ are his⟩ ⟨he's a Swede or a Dane, I don't remember ∼⟩ **2** : WHICHEVER ⟨we have all kinds of them; take ∼ you like⟩ **3** — used to introduce a relative clause and to serve as a substitute therein for the substantive modified by the clause ⟨give me the money ∼ is coming to me⟩
1which·ev·er \hwich-'ev-ər\ *adj* : no matter which ⟨∼ way you go⟩
2whichever *pron* : whatever one or ones
which·so·ev·er \₁hwich-sə-'wev-ər\ *pron or adj* : WHICHEVER
whick·er \'hwik-ər\ *vb* : NEIGH, WHINNY — **whicker** *n*
1whiff \'hwif\ *n* **1** : a quick puff or slight gust esp. of air, gas, smoke, or spray **2** : an inhalation of odor, gas, or smoke **3** : a slight trace : HINT
2whiff *vb* **1** : to expel, puff out, or blow away in or as if in whiffs **2** : to inhale an odor
whif·fle·tree \'hwif-əl-(₁)trē\ *n* [alter. of *whippletree*] : the pivoted swinging bar to which the traces of a harness are fastened
Whig \'hwig\ *n* [short for *Whiggamore* (member of a Scottish group that marched to Edinburgh in 1648 to oppose the court party)] **1** : a member or supporter of a British political group of the 18th and early 19th centuries seeking to limit royal authority and increase parliamentary power **2** : an American favoring independence from Great Britain during the American Revolution **3** : a member or supporter of an American political party formed about 1834 to oppose the Democrats
1while \'hwīl\ *n* **1** : a period of time ⟨stay a ∼⟩ **2** : the time and effort used : TROUBLE ⟨worth your ∼⟩
2while \(₁)hwīl\ *conj* **1** : during the time that ⟨she called ∼ you were out⟩ **2** : AS LONG AS ⟨∼ there's life there's hope⟩ **3** : ALTHOUGH ⟨∼ he's respected, he's not liked⟩
3while \'hwīl\ *vb* **whiled; whil·ing** : to cause to pass esp. pleasantly ⟨∼ away an hour⟩
1whi·lom \'hwī-ləm\ *adv* [ME, lit., at times, fr. OE *hwīlum*, dat. pl. of *hwīl* time, while] *archaic* : FORMERLY
2whilom *adj* : FORMER ⟨his ∼ friends⟩
whilst \'hwīlst\ *conj, chiefly Brit* : WHILE
whim \'hwim\ *n* : a sudden wish, desire, or change of mind : NOTION, FANCY, CAPRICE
whim·per \'hwim-pər\ *vb* **whim·pered; whim·per·ing** \-p(ə-)riŋ\ : to make a

low whining plaintive or broken sound — **whimper** n

whim·si·cal \'hwim-zi-kəl\ adj 1 : full of whims : CAPRICIOUS 2 : resulting from or characterized by whim or caprice : ERRATIC — **whim·si·cal·i·ty** \,hwim-zə-'kal-ət-ē\ n — **whim·si·cal·ly** \'hwim-zi-k(ə-)lē\ adv

whim·sy or **whim·sey** \'hwim-zē\ n, pl **whimsies** or **whimseys** 1 : WHIM, CAPRICE 2 : a fanciful or fantastic device, object, or creation esp. in writing or art

whine \'hwīn\ vb **whined**; **whin·ing** [ME whinen, fr. OE hwīnan to whiz] 1 : to utter a usu. high-pitched plaintive or distressed cry; also : to make a sound similar to such a cry 2 : to utter a complaint with or as if with a whine — **whine** n

¹**whin·ny** \'hwin-ē\ vb **whin·nied**; **whin·ny·ing** : to neigh usu. in a low or gentle manner

²**whinny** n, pl **whinnies** : NEIGH

¹**whip** \'hwip\ vb **whipped**; **whip·ping** 1 : to move, snatch, or jerk quickly or forcefully ⟨~ out a gun⟩ 2 : to strike with a slender lithe implement (as a lash) esp. as a punishment; also : SPANK 3 : to drive or urge on by or as if by using a whip 4 : to bind or wrap (as a rope or rod) with cord in order to protect and strengthen; also : to wind or wrap around something 5 : DEFEAT 6 : to stir up : INCITE ⟨~ up enthusiasm⟩ 7 : to produce in a hurry ⟨~ up a meal⟩ 8 : to beat (as eggs or cream) into a froth 9 : to gather together or hold together for united action 10 : to proceed nimbly or briskly; also : to thrash about like a whiplash — **whip·per** n — **whip into shape** : to bring forcefully to a desired state or condition

²**whip** n 1 : a flexible instrument used for whipping 2 : a stroke or cut with or as if with a whip 3 : a dessert made by whipping a portion of the ingredients ⟨prune ~⟩ 4 : a person who handles a whip; esp : a driver of horses 5 : a member of a legislative body appointed by his party to enforce party discipline and to secure the attendance of party members at important sessions 6 : a whipping or thrashing motion ⟨a ~ of his tail⟩

whip·cord \-,kȯrd\ n 1 : a thin tough cord made of braided or twisted hemp or catgut 2 : a cloth that is made of hard-twisted yarns and has fine diagonal cords or ribs

whip hand n : positive control : ADVANTAGE

whip·lash \'hwip-,lash\ n 1 : the lash of a whip 2 : WHIPLASH INJURY

whiplash injury n : injury resulting from a sudden sharp movement of the neck and head (as of a person in a vehicle that is struck from the front or rear)

whip·per·snap·per \'hwip-ər-,snap-ər\

n : a small, insignificant, or presumptuous person

whip·pet \'hwip-ət\ n : any of a breed of small swift slender dogs that are widely used for racing

whipping boy n : SCAPEGOAT

whip·ple·tree \'hwip-əl-(,)trē\ n : WHIFFLETREE

whip·poor·will \'hwip-ər-,wil\ n : an American bird with dull variegated plumage whose call is heard at nightfall and just before dawn

¹**whip·saw** \'hwip-,sȯ\ n 1 : a narrow tapering saw that has hook teeth 2 : a 2-man crosscut saw

²**whipsaw** vb 1 : to saw with a whipsaw 2 : to worst in two opposite ways at once, by a 2-phase operation, or by the collusive action of two opponents

¹**whir** also **whirr** \'hwər\ vb **whirred**; **whir·ring** : to move, fly, or revolve with a whizzing sound : WHIZ

²**whir** also **whirr** n : a continuous fluttering or vibratory sound made by something in rapid motion

¹**whirl** \'hwərl\ vb 1 : to move or drive in a circle or similar curve esp. with force or speed 2 : to turn or cause to turn on or around an axis : SPIN 3 : to turn abruptly : WHEEL 4 : to pass, move, or go quickly 5 : to become dizzy or giddy : REEL

²**whirl** n 1 : a rapid rotating or circling movement; also : something undergoing such a movement 2 : COMMOTION, BUSTLE ⟨the social ~⟩ 3 : a state of mental confusion

whirl·i·gig \'hwər-li-,gig\ n [ME whirlegigg, fr. whirlen to whirl + gigg top] 1 : a child's toy having a whirling motion 2 : MERRY-GO-ROUND 3 : something that continuously whirls or changes; also : a whirling course (as of events)

whirl·pool \'hwərl-,pül\ n : water moving rapidly in a circle so as to produce a depression in the center into which floating objects may be drawn

whirl·wind \-,wind\ n 1 : a small whirling windstorm 2 : a confused rush : WHIRL

whirly·bird \'hwər-lē-,bərd\ n : HELICOPTER

¹**whish** \'hwish\ vb : to move with a whizzing of swishing sound

²**whish** n : a rushing sound : SWISH

¹**whisk** \'hwisk\ n 1 : a quick light sweeping or brushing motion 2 : a small usu. wire kitchen implement for hand beating of food 3 : a flexible bunch (as of twigs, feathers, or straw) attached to a handle for use as a brush

²**whisk** vb 1 : to move nimbly and quickly 2 : to move or convey briskly ⟨~ out a knife⟩ ⟨~ed the children off to bed⟩ 3 : to beat or whip lightly ⟨~ eggs⟩ 4 : to brush or wipe off lightly ⟨~ a coat⟩

whisk broom n : a small broom with a short handle used esp. as a clothes brush

whis·ker \'hwis-kər\ n 1 pl : the part of the beard that grows on the sides of the face or on the chin 2 : one hair of the beard 3 : one of the long bristles or hairs growing near the mouth of an animal (as a cat or bird) — **whis·kered** \-kərd\ adj

whis·key or **whis·ky** \'hwis-kē\ n, pl **whiskeys** or **whiskies** [IrGael uisce beathadh & ScGael uisge beatha, lit., water of life] : a liquor distilled from the fermented mash of grain (as rye, corn, or barley)

¹**whis·per** \'hwis-pər\ vb **whis·pered**; **whis·per·ing** \-p(ə-)riŋ\ 1 : to speak very low or under the breath; also : to tell or utter by whispering ⟨~ a secret⟩ 2 : to make a low rustling sound ⟨~ing leaves⟩

²**whisper** n 1 : something communicated by or as if by whispering : HINT, RUMOR 2 : an act or instance of whispering; esp : speech without vibration of the vocal cords

whist \'hwist\ n : a card game played by four players in two partnerships with a deck of 52 cards

¹**whis·tle** \'hwis-əl\ n 1 : a device by which a shrill sound is produced ⟨steam ~⟩ ⟨tin ~⟩ 2 : a shrill clear sound made by forcing breath out or air in through the puckered lips 3 : the sound or signal produced by a whistle or as if by whistling 4 : the shrill clear note of an animal (as a bird)

²**whistle** vb **whis·tled**; **whis·tling** \-(ə-)liŋ\ 1 : to utter a shrill clear sound by blowing or drawing air through the puckered lips 2 : to utter a shrill note or call resembling a whistle 3 : to make a shrill clear sound esp. by rapid movements ⟨bullets whistled by him⟩ 4 : to blow or sound a whistle 5 : to signal or call by a whistle 6 : to produce, utter, or express by whistling ⟨~ a tune⟩ — **whis·tler** \-(ə-)lər\ n

whis·tle–blow·er \'hwis-əl-,blō-ər\ n : INFORMER

whis·tle–stop \'hwis-əl-,stäp\ n 1 : a small station at which trains stop only on signal 2 : a small community 3 : a brief personal appearance by a political candidate orig. on the rear platform of a touring train

whit \'hwit\ n [prob. alter. of ME wiht, wight creature, thing, bit, fr. OE wiht] : the smallest part or particle imaginable : BIT

¹**white** \'hwīt\ adj **whit·er**; **whit·est** 1 : free from color 2 : of the color of new snow or milk; esp : of the color white 3 : light or pallid in color ⟨lips ~ with fear⟩ 4 : SILVERY; also : made of silver 5 : of, relating to, or being a member of a group or race characterized by light-colored skin 6 : free from spot or blemish : PURE, INNOCENT 7 : BLANK 3 ⟨~ space in printed matter⟩ 8 : not intended to cause harm ⟨a ~ lie⟩ 9 : wearing white ⟨~ friars⟩ 10 : SNOWY ⟨~ Christmas⟩ 11 : ARDENT,

PASSIONATE ⟨~ fury⟩ 12 : conservative or reactionary in politics

²**white** n 1 : the color of maximal lightness that characterizes objects which both reflect and transmit light : the opposite of black 2 : a white or light-colored part or thing ⟨the ~ of an egg⟩; also, pl : white garments 3 : the light-colored pieces in a 2-player board game; also : the person by whom these are played 4 : one that is or approaches the color white 5 : a member of a light-skinned race 6 : a member of a conservative or reactionary political group

white ant n : TERMITE

white·bait \'hwīt-,bāt\ n : the young of a herring or a similar small fish used for food

white blood cell n : a blood cell that does not contain hemoglobin : LEUKOCYTE

white·cap \'hwīt-,kap\ n : a wave crest breaking into foam

white–col·lar \'hwīt-'käl-ər\ adj : of, relating to, or constituting the class of salaried workers whose duties do not require the wearing of work clothes or protective clothing

white dwarf n : a small very dense whitish star of low luminosity

white elephant n [so called because white elephants were venerated in parts of Asia and maintained without being required to work] 1 : an Indian elephant of a pale color that is sometimes venerated in India, Sri Lanka, Thailand, and Burma 2 : something requiring much care and expense and yielding little profit 3 : an object no longer wanted by its owner though not without value to others

white–faced \'hwīt-'fāst\ adj 1 : having a wan pale face 2 : having the face white in whole or in part ⟨~ cattle⟩

white feather n [fr. the superstition that a white feather in the plumage of a gamecock is a mark of a poor fighter] : a mark or symbol of cowardice

white·fish \'hwīt-,fish\ n : any of various freshwater food fishes related to the salmons and trouts

white flag n : a flag of plain white used as a flag of truce or as a token of surrender

white·fly \'hwīt-,flī\ n : any of numerous small insects that are injurious plant pests related to the scale insects

white gold n : a pale alloy of gold esp. with nickel or palladium resembling platinum in appearance

white goods n pl : white fabrics or articles (as sheets or towels) typically made of cotton or linen

White·hall \'hwīt-,hol\ n : the British government

white·head \-,hed\ n : a small whitish lump in the skin due to retention of secretion in an oil gland duct

white heat n : a temperature higher than red heat at which a body becomes brightly incandescent so as to appear white

white–hot *adj* **1** : being at or radiating white heat **2** : FERVID

White House \-,haùs\ *n* **1** : the executive department of the U.S. government **2** : a residence of the president of the U.S.

white lead *n* : a heavy white poisonous carbonate of lead used as a pigment in exterior paints

white matter *n* : the whitish part of nervous tissue consisting mostly of nerve-cell processes

whit·en \'hwīt-ᵊn\ *vb* **whit·ened**; **whit·en·ing** \'hwīt(ᵊ-)niŋ\ : to make or become white *syn* blanch, bleach — **whit·en·er** \'hwīt-(ᵊ-)nᵊr\ *n*

white·ness \'hwīt-nᵊs\ *n* : the quality or state of being white

white pine *n* : a tall-growing pine of eastern No. America with leaves in clusters of five; *also* : its wood

white–pine blister rust *n* : a destructive disease of white pine caused by a rust fungus that passes part of its complex life cycle on currant or gooseberry bushes; *also* : this fungus

white sale *n* : a sale on white goods

white shark *n* : a large and dangerous shark of warm seas that is light colored below and darker above becoming dirty white in older and larger specimens

white slave *n* : a woman or girl held unwillingly for purposes of prostitution — **white slavery** *n*

white·tail \'hwīt-,tāl\ *n* : WHITE-TAILED DEER

white–tailed deer \,hwīt-,tāl-'dᵊr\ *n* : a No. American deer with a rather long tail white on the underside and with forward-arching antlers

white·wall \'hwīt-,wól\ *n* : an automobile tire having a white band on the sidewall

¹white·wash \-,wósh, -,wäsh\ *vb* **1** : to whiten with whitewash **2** : to clear of a charge of wrongdoing by offering excuses, hiding facts, or conducting a perfunctory investigation **3** : to prevent (an opponent) from scoring in a game or contest

²whitewash *n* **1** : a liquid mixture (as of lime and water) for whitening a surface **2** : a clearing of wrongdoing by whitewashing

white·wood \-,wùd\ *n* : any of various trees and esp. a tulip tree having light-colored wood; *also* : the wood of such a tree

¹whith·er \'hwith-ᵊr\ *adv* **1** : to what place **2** : to what situation, position, degree, or end ⟨~ will this drive him⟩

²whither *conj* **1** : to the place at, in, or to which; *also* : to which place **2** : to whatever place

whith·er·so·ev·er \,hwith-ᵊr-sᵊ-'wev-ᵊr\ *conj* : to whatever place

¹whit·ing \'hwīt-iŋ\ *n* : any of several usu. light or silvery food fishes (as a hake) found mostly near seacoasts

²whiting *n* : calcium carbonate in the form of pulverized chalk or limestone used as a pigment and in putty

whit·ish \'hwīt-ish\ *adj* : somewhat white

whit·low \'hwit-,lō\ *n* : a deep inflammation of a finger or toe with pus formation

Whit·sun·day \'hwit-'sᵊn-dē, -sᵊn-,dā\ *n* [ME *Whitsonday*, fr. OE *hwīta sunnandaeg*, lit., white Sunday, prob. fr. the custom of wearing white robes by those newly baptized at this season] : PENTECOST

whit·tle \'hwit-ᵊl\ *vb* **whit·tled**; **whit·tling** \'hwit-(ᵊ-)liŋ\ **1** : to pare or cut off chips from the surface of (wood) with a knife; *also* : to cut or shape by such paring **2** : to reduce, remove, or destroy gradually as if by paring down : PARE ⟨~ down expenses⟩

¹whiz or whizz \'hwiz\ *vb* **whizzed**; **whiz·zing** : to hum, whir, or hiss like a speeding object (as an arrow or ball) passing through air

²whiz or whizz *n, pl* **whiz·zes** : a hissing, buzzing, or whirring sound

³whiz *n, pl* **whiz·zes** : WIZARD 2

who \(ʰ)hü\ *pron* **1** : what or which person or persons ⟨~ did it⟩ ⟨~ is he⟩ ⟨~ are they⟩ **2** : the person or persons that ⟨knows ~ did it⟩ **3** \(ʰ)hü, ü\ — used to introduce a relative clause and to serve as a substitute therein for the substantive modified by the clause ⟨the man ~ lives there is rich⟩ ⟨the people ~ did it were caught⟩

WHO *abbr* World Health Organization

whoa \'wō, 'hwō, 'hō\ *vb imper* — a command (as to a draft animal) to stand still

who·dun·it *also* **who·dun·nit** \hü-'dᵊn-ᵊt\ *n* : a detective story or mystery story presented as a novel, play, or motion picture

who·ev·er \hü'ev-ᵊr\ *pron* : whatever person : no matter who

¹whole \'hōl\ *adj* [ME *hool* healthy, unhurt, entire, fr. OE *hāl*] **1** : being in healthy or sound condition : free from defect or damage : WELL, INTACT **2** : having all its proper parts or elements ⟨~ milk⟩ **3** : constituting the total sum of : ENTIRE ⟨~ continental landmasses⟩ **4** : each or all of the ⟨the ~ family⟩ **5** : not scattered or divided : CONCENTRATED ⟨gave me his ~ attention⟩ **6** : seemingly complete or total ⟨the ~ idea is to help, not hinder⟩ *syn* entire, perfect, intact, sound — **whole·ness** *n*

²whole *n* **1** : a complete amount or sum : a number, aggregate, or totality lacking no part, member, or element **2** : something constituting a complex unity : a coherent system or organization of parts fitting or working together as one — **on the whole 1** : in view of all the circumstances or conditions 2 : in general

whole·heart·ed \'hōl-'härt-əd\ adj : undivided in purpose, enthusiasm, or will : HEARTY, ZESTFUL, SINCERE

whole note n : a musical note equal to one measure of four beats

whole number n : INTEGER

¹**whole·sale** \'hōl-,sāl\ n : the sale of goods in quantity usu. for resale by a retail merchant

²**wholesale** adj 1 : performed on a large scale without discrimination ⟨~ slaughter⟩ 2 : of, relating to, or engaged in wholesaling — **wholesale** adv

³**wholesale** vb **whole·saled; whole·sal·ing** : to sell at wholesale — **whole·sal·er** n

whole·some \'hōl-səm\ adj 1 : promoting mental, spiritual, or bodily health or well-being ⟨~ advice⟩ ⟨a ~ environment⟩ 2 : sound in body, mind, or morals : HEALTHY 3 : PRUDENT ⟨~ respect for the law⟩ — **whole·some·ness** n

whole step n : a musical interval comprising two half steps (as C–D or F#–G#)

whole wheat adj : made of ground entire wheat kernels

whol·ly \'hōl-(l)ē\ adv 1 : COMPLETELY, TOTALLY 2 : SOLELY, EXCLUSIVELY

whom \(')hüm\ pron, objective case of WHO

whom·ev·er \hüm-'ev-ər\ pron, objective case of WHOEVER

whom·so·ev·er \,hüm-sə-'wev-ər\ pron, objective case of WHOSOEVER

¹**whoop** \'h(w)üp, 'h(w)ùp\ vb 1 : to shout or call loudly and vigorously 2 : to make the sound that follows a fit of coughing in whooping cough 3 : to go or pass with a loud noise 4 : to utter or express with a whoop; also : to urge, drive, or cheer with a whoop

²**whoop** n 1 : a whooping sound or utterance : SHOUT, HOOT 2 : a crowing sound accompanying the intake of breath after a fit of coughing in whooping cough

whooping cough n : an infectious disease esp. of children marked by convulsive coughing fits sometimes followed by a whoop

whooping crane n : a large white nearly extinct No. American crane noted for its loud whooping note

whoop·la \'h(w)üp-,lä, 'h(w)ùp-\ n 1 : a noisy commotion 2 : boisterous merrymaking

whop·per \'hwäp-ər\ n : something unusually large or extreme of its kind; esp : a monstrous lie

whop·ping \'hwäp-iŋ\ adj : extremely large

whore \'hōr\ n : PROSTITUTE

whorl \'hwórl, 'hwərl\ n 1 : a row of parts (as leaves or petals) encircling an axis and esp. a plant stem 2 : something that whirls or coils around a center : COIL, SPIRAL 3 : one of the turns of a snail shell

whorled \'hwórld, 'hwərld\ adj : having or arranged in whorls

¹**whose** \(')hüz\ adj : of or relating to whom or which esp. as possessor or possessors, agent or agents, or object or objects of an action ⟨asked ~ bag it was⟩

²**whose** pron : whose one or ones ⟨~ is this car⟩ ⟨~ are those books⟩

who·so \'hü-,sō\ pron : WHOEVER

who·so·ev·er \,hü-sə-'wev-ər\ pron : WHOEVER

whs or **whse** abbr warehouse

whsle abbr wholesale

¹**why** \(')hwī\ adv : for what reason, cause, or purpose ⟨~ did you do it⟩

²**why** conj 1 : the cause, reason, or purpose for which (that is ~ you did it) 2 : for which : on account of which (knows the reason ~ you did it)

³**why** \'hwī\ n, pl **whys** : REASON, CAUSE (the ~s of racial prejudice)

⁴**why** \(,)wī, (,)hwī\ interj — used to express surprise, hesitation, approval, disapproval, or impatience ⟨~, here's what I was looking for⟩

WI abbr 1 West Indies 2 Wisconsin

WIA abbr wounded in action

wick \'wik\ n : a loosely bound bundle of soft fibers that draws up oil, tallow, or wax to be burned in a candle, oil lamp, or stove

wick·ed \'wik-əd\ adj 1 : morally bad : EVIL, SINFUL 2 : FIERCE, VICIOUS 3 : ROGUISH ⟨a ~ glance⟩ 4 : REPUGNANT, VILE ⟨a ~ odor⟩ 5 : HARMFUL, DANGEROUS ⟨a ~ attack⟩ — **wick·ed·ly** adv — **wick·ed·ness** n

wick·er \'wik-ər\ n 1 : a small pliant branch (as an osier or a withe) 2 : WICKERWORK — **wicker** adj

wick·er·work \-,wərk\ n : work made of osiers, twigs, or rods : BASKETRY

wick·et \'wik-ət\ n 1 : a small gate or door; esp : one forming a part of or placed near a larger one 2 : a window-like opening usu. with a grille or grate (as at a ticket office) 3 : a set of three upright rods topped by two crosspieces bowled at in cricket 4 : an arch through which the ball is driven in croquet

wick·i·up \'wik-ē-,əp\ n : a hut used by nomadic Indians of the western and southwestern U.S. with a usu. oval base and a rough frame covered with reed mats, grass, or brushwood

wid abbr widow, widower

¹**wide** \'wīd\ adj **wid·er; wid·est** 1 : covering a vast area 2 : measured across or at right angles to the length 3 : not narrow : BROAD; also : ROOMY 4 : opened to full width (eyes ~ with wonder) 5 : not limited : EXTENSIVE ⟨~ experience⟩ 6 : far from the goal, mark, or truth (a ~ guess) — **wide·ly** adv

²**wide** adv **wid·er; wid·est** 1 : over a great distance or extent : WIDELY (searched far and ~) 2 : over a specified distance, area, or extent 3 : so as to

leave a wide space between ⟨~ apart⟩ **4** : so as to clear by a considerable distance ⟨ran ~ around left end⟩ **5** : COMPLETELY, FULLY ⟨opened her eyes ~⟩

wide-awake \,wīd-ə-'wāk\ *adj* : fully awake; *also* : KNOWING, ALERT ⟨a group of ~ young men⟩

wide-eyed \'wīd-'īd\ *adj* **1** : having the eyes wide open esp. with wonder or astonishment **2** : NAIVE

wide-mouthed \-'wīd-'mautthd, -'mautht\ *adj* **1** : having one's mouth opened wide (as in awe) **2** : having a wide mouth ⟨~ jars⟩

wid-en \'wīd-³n\ *vb* **wid-ened; wid-en-ing** \'wīd-(³-)niŋ\ : to make or become wide : BROADEN

wide-spread \'wīd-'spred\ *adj* **1** : widely scattered or prevalent ⟨~ fear⟩ **2** : widely extended or spread out ⟨~ wings⟩

¹**wid-ow** \'wid-ō\ *n* : a woman who has lost her husband by death and has not married again — **wid-ow-hood** *n*

²**widow** *vb* : to cause to become a widow

wid-ow-er \'wid-ə-wər\ *n* : a man who has lost his wife by death and has not married again

width \'width\ *n* **1** : a distance from side to side : the measurement taken at right angles to the length : BREADTH **2** : largeness of extent or scope; *also* : FULLNESS **3** : a measured and cut piece of material ⟨a ~ of calico⟩ ⟨a ~ of lumber⟩

wield \'wēld\ *vb* **1** : to use or handle esp. effectively ⟨~ a broom⟩ ⟨~ a pen⟩ **2** : to exert authority by means of : EMPLOY ⟨~ influence⟩ — **wield-er** *n*

wie-ner \'wē-nər\ *n* [short for *wiener-wurst*, fr. G, lit., Vienna sausage] : FRANKFURTER

wife \'wīf\ *n, pl* **wives** \'wīvz\ **1** *dial* : WOMAN **2** : a woman acting in a specified capacity — used in combination **3** : a married woman — **wife-hood** *n* — **wife-less** *adj* — **wife-ly** *adj*

wig \'wig\ *n* [short for *periwig*, fr. MF *perruque*, fr. It *perrucca* hair, wig] : a manufactured covering of natural or synthetic hair for the head; *also* : TOUPEE

wi-geon *or* **wid-geon** \'wij-ən\ *n, pl* **wigeon** *or* **wigeons** *or* **widgeon** *or* **widgeons** : any of several freshwater ducks between the teal and the mallard in size

wig-gle \'wig-əl\ *vb* **wig-gled; wig-gling** \-(ə-)liŋ\ **1** : to move to and fro with quick jerky or shaking movements : JIGGLE **2** : WRIGGLE — **wiggle** *n*

wig-gler \'wig-(ə-)lər\ *n* **1** : a larva or pupa of a mosquito **2** : one that wiggles

wig-gly \-(ə-)lē\ *adj* **1** : tending to wiggle ⟨a ~ worm⟩ **2** : WAVY ⟨~ lines⟩

wight \'wīt\ *n* : a living being : CREATURE

wig-let \'wig-lət\ *n* : a small wig used esp. to enhance a hairstyle

¹**wig-wag** \'wig-,wag\ *vb* **1** : to signal by or as if by a flag or light waved according to a code **2** : to make or cause to make a signal (as with the hand or arm)

²**wigwag** *n* **1** : the art or practice of wigwagging **2** : the act of wigwagging

wig-wam \'wig-,wäm\ *n* : a hut of the Indians of the eastern U.S. having typically an arched framework of poles overlaid with bark, rush mats, or hides

¹**wild** \'wīld\ *adj* **1** : living in a state of nature and not ordinarily tamed ⟨~ ducks⟩ **2** : growing or produced without human aid or care ⟨~ honey⟩ ⟨~ plants⟩ **3** : WASTE, DESOLATE ⟨~ country⟩ **4** : UNCONTROLLED, UNRESTRAINED, UNRULY ⟨~ passions⟩ ⟨a ~ young stallion⟩ **5** : TURBULENT, STORMY ⟨a ~ night⟩ **6** : EXTRAVAGANT, FANTASTIC, CRAZY ⟨~ ideas⟩ **7** : indicative of strong passion, desire, or emotion ⟨a ~ stare⟩ **8** : UNCIVILIZED, SAVAGE **9** : deviating from the natural or expected course : ERRATIC ⟨a ~ throw⟩ **10** : having a denomination determined by the holder ⟨deuces ~⟩ — **wild-ly** *adv* — **wild-ness** \'wīl(d)-nəs\ *n*

²**wild** *adv* **1** : WILDLY **2** : without regulation or control ⟨running ~⟩

³**wild** *n* **1** : WILDERNESS **2** : a natural or undomesticated state or existence

wild boar *n* : an Old World wild hog from which most domestic swine are descended

wild carrot *n* : a widely naturalized Eurasian weed that is probably the original of the cultivated carrot

¹**wild-cat** \'wil(d)-,kat\ *n, pl* **wildcats 1** : any of various small or medium-sized cats (as a lynx or ocelot) **2** : a quick-tempered hard-fighting person

²**wildcat** *adj* **1** : not sound or safe ⟨~ schemes⟩ **2** : initiated by a group of workers without formal union approval ⟨~ strike⟩

³**wildcat** *vb* **wild-cat-ted; wild-cat-ting** : to drill an oil or gas well in a region not known to be productive

wil-de-beest \'wil-də-,bēst\ *n, pl* **wildebeests** *also* **wildebeest** [Afrikaans *wildebees*, fr. *wilde* wild + *bees* ox] : GNU

wil-der-ness \'wil-dər-nəs\ *n* [ME, fr. *wildern* wild, fr. OE *wilddēoren* of wild beasts] : an uncultivated and uninhabited region

wild-fire \'wil(d)-,fī(ə)r\ *n* : an uncontrollable fire — **like wildfire** : very rapidly

wild-fowl \-,faul\ *n* : a bird and esp. a waterfowl (as a wild duck) hunted as game

wild-goose chase *n* : the pursuit of something unattainable

wild-life \'wīl(d)-,līf\ *n* : nonhuman living things and esp. wild animals living in their natural environment

wild oat *n* **1** : any of several wild grasses **2** *pl* : offenses and indiscretions attributed to youthful exuberance (was just sowing his *wild oats*)

wild rice *n* : a No. American aquatic grass; *also* : its edible seed

wild·wood \'wīld-ˌwùd\ *n* : a wild or unfrequented wood

¹**wile** \'wīl\ *n* **1** : a trick or stratagem intended to ensnare or deceive; *also* : a playful trick **2** : TRICKERY, GUILE

²**wile** *vb* **wiled; wil·ing** : LURE, ENTICE

¹**will** \wəl, (ˌ)(ə)l, (ˈ)wil\ *vb, past* **would** \wəd, (ə)d, (ˈ)wùd\ *; pres sing & pl* **will 1** : WISH, DESIRE ⟨call it what you ∼⟩ **2** — used as an auxiliary verb to express (1) desire, willingness, or in negative constructions refusal ⟨∼ you have another⟩, (the *won't* do it), (2) customary or habitual action ⟨∼ get angry over nothing⟩, (3) simple futurity ⟨tomorrow we ∼ go shopping⟩, (4) capability or sufficiency ⟨the back seat ∼ hold three⟩, (5) determination or willfulness ⟨I ∼ go despite them⟩, (6) probability ⟨that ∼ be the mailman⟩, (7) inevitability ⟨accidents ∼ happen⟩, or (8) a command ⟨you ∼ do as I say⟩

²**will** \'wil\ *n* **1** : wish or desire often combined with determination ⟨the ∼ to win⟩ **2** : something desired; *esp* : a choice or determination of one having authority or power **3** : the act, process, or experience of willing : VOLITION **4** : the mental powers manifested as wishing, choosing, desiring, or intending **5** : a disposition to act according to principles or ends **6** : power of controlling one's own actions or emotions ⟨a man of iron ∼⟩ **7** : a legal document in which a person declares to whom his possessions are to go after his death

³**will** \'wil\ *vb* **1** : to dispose of by or as if by a will : BEQUEATH **2** : to determine by an act of choice; *also* : DECREE, ORDAIN **3** : INTEND, PURPOSE; *also* : CHOOSE

will·ful *or* **wil·ful** \'wil-fəl\ *adj* **1** : governed by will without regard to reason : OBSTINATE, STUBBORN **2** : INTENTIONAL ⟨∼ murder⟩ — **will·ful·ly** \-lē\ *adv*

wil·lies \'wil-ēz\ *n pl* : a fit of nervousness : JITTERS

will·ing \'wil-iŋ\ *adj* **1** : inclined or favorably disposed in mind : READY ⟨∼ to go⟩ **2** : prompt to act or respond ⟨∼ workers⟩ **3** : done, borne, or accepted voluntarily or without reluctance : VOLUNTARY **4** : of or relating to the will : VOLITIONAL — **will·ing·ly** *adv* — **will·ing·ness** *n*

wil·li·waw \'wil-ē-ˌwò\ *n* : a sudden violent gust of cold land air common along mountainous coasts of high latitudes

will-o'-the-wisp \ˌwil-ə-thə-'wisp\ *n* **1** : a light that appears at night over marshy grounds **2** : a misleading or elusive goal or hope

wil·low \'wil-ō\ *n* **1** : any of numerous quick-growing shrubs and trees with tough pliable shoots used in basketry **2** : an object made of willow wood

wil·low·ware \-ˌwaər\ *n* : dinnerware that is usu. blue and white and that is decorated with a story-telling design featuring a large willow tree by a little bridge

wil·lowy \'wil-ə-wē\ *adj* : PLIANT; *also* : gracefully tall and slender ⟨a ∼ young woman⟩

will-pow·er \'wil-ˌpaù(-ə)r\ *n* : energetic determination : RESOLUTENESS

wil·ly-nil·ly \ˌwil-ē-'nil-ē\ *adv or adj* [alter. of *will I nill I* or *will ye nill ye* or *will he nill he*; *nill* fr. archaic *nill* to be unwilling, fr. ME *nilen*, fr. OE *nyllan*, fr. *ne* not + *wyllan* to wish] : without regard for one's choice : by compulsion ⟨they rushed us along ∼⟩

¹**wilt** \'wilt\ *vb* **1** : to lose or cause to lose freshness and become limp : DROOP **2** : to grow weak or faint : LANGUISH

²**wilt** *n* : any of various plant disorders marked by wilting and often shriveling

wily \'wī-lē\ *adj* **wil·i·er; -est** : full of guile : TRICKY — **wil·i·ness** \'wī-lē-nəs\ *n*

wimp \'wimp\ *n* : a weak or ineffectual person — **wimpy** \'wim-pē\ *adj*

¹**wim·ple** \'wim-pəl\ *n* : a cloth covering worn over the head and around the neck and chin by women esp. in the late medieval period and by some nuns

²**wimple** *vb* **wim·pled; wim·pling** \-p(ə-)liŋ\ **1** : to cover with or as if with a wimple **2** : to ripple or cause to ripple

¹**win** \'win\ *vb* **won** \'wən\ *;* **win·ning** [ME *winnen*, fr. OE *winnan* to struggle] **1** : to gain the victory in or as if in a contest : SUCCEED **2** : to get possession of esp. by effort : GAIN **3** : to gain in or as if in battle or contest; *also* : to be the victor in ⟨won the war⟩ **4** : to obtain by work : EARN **5** : to solicit and gain the favor of; *esp* : to induce to accept oneself in marriage

²**win** *n* : VICTORY; *esp* : 1st place at the finish (as of a horse race)

wince \'wins\ *vb* **winced; winc·ing** : to shrink back involuntarily (as from pain) : FLINCH — **wince** *n*

winch \'winch\ *n* **1** : a machine that has a drum on which a rope or cable is wound for hauling or hoisting — **winch** *vb*

¹**wind** \'wind\ *n* **1** : a movement of the air **2** : a force or agency that carries along or influences : TENDENCY, TREND **3** : BREATH ⟨he had the ∼ knocked out of him⟩ **4** : gas generated in the stomach or intestines **5** : something insubstantial; *esp* : idle words **6** : air carrying a scent (as of game) **7** : INTIMATION ⟨they got ∼ of our plans⟩

8 : WIND INSTRUMENTS; *also, pl* : players of wind instruments

²**wind** *vb* 1 : to get a scent of ⟨the dogs ~*ed* the game⟩ 2 : to cause to be out of breath ⟨he was ~*ed* from the climb⟩ 3 : to allow ⟨as a horse⟩ to rest so as to recover breath

³**wind** \'wīnd, 'wind\ *vb* **wind·ed** \'wīn-dəd, 'win-\ *or* **wound** \'waùnd\ ; **winding** : to sound by blowing ⟨~ a horn⟩

⁴**wind** \'wīnd\ *vb* **wound** \'waùnd\ *also* **wind·ed; wind·ing** 1 : to have a curving course or shape ⟨a river ~*ing* through the valley⟩ 2 : to move or lie so as to encircle 3 : ENTANGLE, INVOLVE 4 : to introduce stealthily : INSINUATE 5 : to encircle or cover with something pliable : WRAP, COIL, TWINE, TWIST ⟨~ a bobbin⟩ 6 : to hoist or haul by a rope or chain and a winch ⟨~ a ship to the wharf⟩ 7 : to tighten the spring of; *also* : CRANK 8 : to raise to a high level ⟨as of excitement⟩ 9 : to cause to move in a curving line or path 10 : to traverse on a curving course

⁵**wind** \'wīnd\ *n* : COIL, TURN

wind·age \'win-dij\ *n* : the influence of the wind in deflecting the course of a projectile through the air; *also* : the amount of such deflection

wind·bag \'win(d)-ˌbag\ *n* : an idly talkative person

wind-blown \-ˌblōn\ *adj* : blown by the wind; *also* : having the appearance of being blown by the wind

wind·break \-ˌbrāk\ *n* : something ⟨as a growth of trees⟩ serving as a shelter from the wind

wind–bro·ken \-ˌbrō-kən\ *adj, of a horse* : having the power of breathing impaired by disease

wind·burn \-ˌbərn\ *n* : skin irritation caused by wind

wind·chill \'win(d)-ˌchil\ *n* : a still-air temperature that would have the same cooling effect on exposed human flesh as a given combination of temperature and wind speed

windchill factor *n* : WINDCHILL

wind·er \'wīn-dər\ *n* : one that winds

wind·fall \'win(d)-ˌfôl\ *n* 1 : something ⟨as a tree or fruit⟩ blown down by the wind 2 : an unexpected or sudden gift, gain, or advantage

wind-flow·er \-ˌflaü(-ə)r\ *n* : ANEMONE

¹**wind·ing** \'wīn-diŋ\ *n* : material ⟨as wire⟩ wound or coiled about an object

²**winding** *adj* 1 : having a pronounced curve; *esp* : SPIRAL ⟨~ stairs⟩ 2 : having a course that winds ⟨a ~ road⟩

wind·ing-sheet \-ˌshēt\ *n* : SHROUD

wind instrument *n* : a musical instrument ⟨as a flute or horn⟩ sounded by wind and esp. by the breath

wind·jam·mer \'win(d)-ˌjam-ər\ *n* : a sailing ship; *also* : one of its crew

wind·lass \'win-dləs\ *n* [ME *wyndlas*, alter. of *wyndas*, fr. ON *vindāss*, fr. *vinda* to wind + *āss* pole] : a winch used esp. on ships for hoisting or hauling

wind·mill \'win(d)-ˌmil\ *n* : a mill or machine worked by the wind turning sails or vanes that radiate from a central shaft

win·dow \'win-dō\ *n* [ME *windowe*, fr. ON *vindauga*, fr. *vindr* wind + *auga* eye] 1 : an opening in the wall of a building to let in light and air; *also* : the framework with fittings that closes such an opening 2 : WINDOWPANE 3 : an opening resembling or suggesting that of a window in a building — **win·dow·less** *adj*

window dressing *n* 1 : display of merchandise in a store window 2 : a showing made to create a good but sometimes false impression

win·dow·pane \'win-dō-ˌpān\ *n* : a pane in a window

win·dow–shop \-ˌshäp\ *vb* : to look at the displays in store windows without going inside the stores to make purchases — **win·dow–shop·per** *n*

win·dow·sill \-ˌsil\ *n* : the horizontal member at the bottom of a window

wind·pipe \'win(d)-ˌpīp\ *n* : the passage for the breath from the larynx to the lungs

wind–proof \-ˈprüf\ *adj* : impervious to wind ⟨a ~ jacket⟩

wind·row \'win-ˌdrō\ *n* 1 : hay raked up into a row to dry 2 : a row of something ⟨as dry leaves⟩ swept up by or as if by the wind

wind shear *n* : a radical shift in wind speed and direction between slightly different altitudes

wind·shield \'win(d)-ˌshēld\ *n* : a transparent screen in front of the occupants of a vehicle

wind sock *n* : an open-ended truncated cloth cone mounted in an elevated position to indicate the direction of the wind

wind·storm \-ˌstórm\ *n* : a storm with high wind and little or no precipitation

wind·swept \'win(d)-ˌswept\ *adj* : swept by or as if by wind ⟨~ plains⟩

wind tunnel *n* : an enclosed passage through which air is blown to determine the effects of wind pressure on an object

wind–up \'wīn-ˌdəp\ *n* 1 : CONCLUSION, FINISH 2 : a series of regular and distinctive motions made by a pitcher preliminary to delivering a pitch

wind up \(ˈ)wīn-ˈdəp\ *vb* 1 : to bring or come to a conclusion : END 2 : SETTLE 3 : to arrive in a place, situation, or condition at the end or as a result of a course of action ⟨*wound up* as paupers⟩ 4 : to give a preliminary swing to the arm

¹**wind·ward** \'win-(d)wərd\ *n* : the point or side from which the wind is blowing

²**windward** *adj* : being in or facing the direction from which the wind is blowing

windy \'win-dē\ *adj* **wind·i·er; -est** 1 : having wind : exposed to winds ⟨a ~

day⟩ ⟨a ~ prairie⟩ **2** : STORMY **3**
: FLATULENT **4** : indulging in or characterized by useless talk : VERBOSE
¹wine \'wīn\ n **1** : fermented grape juice
used as a beverage **2** : the usu. fermented juice of a plant product (as
fruit) used as a beverage ⟨rice ~⟩
²wine vb **wined; win·ing** : to treat to or
drink wine
wine cellar n : a room for storing wines;
also : a stock of wines
wine-grow·er \-ˌgrō-(ə-)r\ n : one that
cultivates a vineyard and makes wine
wine-press \'wīn-ˌpres\ n : a vat in
which juice is expressed from grapes
by treading or by means of a plunger
¹wing \'wiŋ\ n **1** : one of the movable
feathered or membranous paired appendages by means of which a bird,
bat, or insect is able to fly **2** : something suggesting a wing in position,
appearance, or function **3** : a plant or
animal appendage or part likened to a
wing; esp : one that is flat or broadly
extended **4** : a turned-back or extended edge on an article of clothing **5** : a
means of flight or rapid progress **6**
: the act or manner of flying : FLIGHT **7**
pl : the area at the side of the stage out
of sight **8** : one of the positions or
players on either side of a center position or line **9** : either of two opposing
groups within an organization : FAC-
TION **10** : a unit in military aviation
consisting of two or more squadrons
— **wing·less** adj — **on the wing** : in
flight : FLYING — **under one's wing** : in
one's charge or care
²wing vb **1** : to fit with wings; also : to
enable to fly easily **2** : to pass through
in flight : FLY ⟨~ the air⟩ ⟨swallows
~ing southward⟩ **3** : to achieve or accomplish by flying **4** : to let fly : DIS-
PATCH ⟨~ an arrow through the air⟩ **5**
: to wound in the wing ⟨~ a bird⟩ ;
also : to wound without killing
wing-ding \'wiŋ-ˌdiŋ\ n : a wild, lively,
or lavish party
winged \'wiŋd, also except for "esp."
sense of 1 'wiŋ-əd\ adj **1** : having
wings esp. of a specified character **2**
: soaring with or as if with wings : EL-
EVATED **3** : SWIFT, RAPID
wing-span \'wiŋ-ˌspan\ n : WINGSPREAD;
esp : the distance between the tips of
an airplane's wings
wing-spread \-ˌspred\ n : the spread of
the wings; esp : the distance between
the tips of the fully extended wings of
a winged animal
¹wink \'wiŋk\ vb **1** : to close and open
one eye quickly as a signal or hint **2**
: to close and open the eyes quickly
: BLINK **3** : to avoid seeing or noticing
something ⟨~ at a violation of the
law⟩ **4** : TWINKLE, FLICKER **5** : to affect
or influence by or as if by blinking the
eyes ⟨he ~ed back his tears⟩ — **wink-
er** \'wiŋ-kər\ n
²wink n **1** : a brief period of sleep : NAP
2 : an act of winking; esp : a hint or

sign given by winking **3** : INSTANT
⟨dries in a ~⟩
win·ner \'win-ər\ n : one that wins
win·ning \'win-iŋ\ n **1** : VICTORY **2**
: something won; esp : money won at
gambling ⟨large ~s⟩
²winning adj **1** : successful esp. in competition **2** : ATTRACTIVE, CHARMING
win·now \'win-ō\ vb **1** : to remove (as
chaff from grain) by a current of air;
also : to free (as grain) from waste in
this manner **2** : to get rid of (something unwanted) or to separate, sift, or
sort (something) as if by winnowing
wino \'wī-nō\ n, pl **win·os** : one who is
chronically addicted to drinking wine
win·some \'win-səm\ adj [ME winsum,
fr. OE wynsum, fr. wynn joy] **1**
: generally pleasing and engaging ⟨a ~
lass⟩ **2** : CHEERFUL, GAY — **win·some·ly**
adv — **win·some·ness** n
¹win·ter \'win-tər\ n **1** : the season of the
year in any region in which the noon-
day sun shines most obliquely : the
coldest period of the year **2** : YEAR ⟨a
man of 70 ~s⟩ **3** : a time or season of
inactivity or decay
²winter adj : occurring in or surviving
winter; esp : sown in autumn for har-
vesting in the following spring or summer ⟨~ wheat⟩
³winter vb **win·tered; win·ter·ing** \'win-
t(ə-)riŋ\ **1** : to pass or survive the winter **2** : to keep, feed, or manage
through the winter ⟨~ cattle on silage⟩
win·ter·green \'win-tər-ˌgrēn\ n **1** : a
low evergreen plant of the heath family with white bell-shaped flowers and
spicy red berries **2** : any of several
plants related to the wintergreen **3**
: an aromatic oil from the common
wintergreen or its flavor or something
flavored with it
win·ter·ize \'wint-ə-ˌrīz\ vb **-ized; -iz·ing**
: to make ready for winter
win·ter-kill \'wint-ər-ˌkil\ vb : to kill or
die by exposure to winter weather
winter squash n : any of various
squashes or pumpkins that keep well
in storage
win·ter·tide \-ˌtīd\ n : WINTER
win·ter·time \-ˌtīm\ n : WINTER
win·try \'win-trē\ also **win·tery** \'win-
t(ə-)rē\ adj **win·tri·er; -est 1** : of, relating to, or characteristic of winter
: coming in winter ⟨~ weather⟩ **2**
: CHILLING, CHEERLESS ⟨a ~ welcome⟩
¹wipe \'wīp\ vb **wiped; wip·ing 1** : to
clean or dry by rubbing ⟨~ dishes⟩ **2**
: to remove by or as if by rubbing or
cleaning ⟨~ away tears⟩ **3** : to erase
completely : OBLITERATE **4** : DESTROY,
ANNIHILATE ⟨the platoon was wiped
out⟩ **5** : to pass or draw over a surface
⟨wiped his hand across his face⟩ —
wip·er n
²wipe n **1** : an act or instance of wiping;
also : BLOW, STRIKE, SWIPE **2** : something used for wiping
¹wire \'wī(ə)r\ n **1** : metal in the form of
a thread or slender rod; also : a thread

or rod of metal **2** *usu pl* : hidden or secret influences controlling the action of a person or body of persons ⟨pull ∼s to get a nomination⟩ **3** : a line of wire for conducting electric current **4** : a telegraph or telephone wire or system; *esp* : WIRE SERVICE **5** : TELEGRAM, CABLEGRAM **6** : the finish line of a race

²**wire** *vb* **wired; wir·ing 1** : to provide or equip with wire ⟨∼ a house⟩ **2** : to bind, string, or mount with wire **3** : to telegraph or telegraph to

wire-hair \'wī(ə)r-ˌhaər\ *n* : a wire-haired fox terrier

wire-haired \-ˌhaərd\ *adj* : having a stiff wiry outer coat of hair

¹**wire·less** \-ləs\ *adj* **1** : having no wire or wires **2** *chiefly Brit* : RADIO

²**wireless** *n* **1** : wireless telegraphy **2** *chiefly Brit* : RADIO

wire-pull·er \'wī(ə)r-ˌpul-ər\ *n* : one who uses secret or underhanded means to influence the acts of a person or organization — **wire-pull·ing** \-ˌpul-iŋ\ *n*

wire service *n* : a news agency that sends out syndicated news copy by wire to subscribers

wire-tap \-ˌtap\ *vb* : to tap a telephone or telegraph wire to get information — **wiretap** *n* — **wire-tap·per** \-ˌtap-ər\ *n*

wire-worm \-ˌwərm\ *n* : the slender hard-coated larva of certain beetles that is esp. destructive to plant roots

wir·ing \'wī(ə)r-iŋ\ *n* : a system of wires; *esp* : one for distributing electricity through a building

wiry \'wī(ə)r-ē\ *adj* **wir·i·er** \-ē-ər\, **-est 1** : made of or resembling wire **2** : slender yet strong and sinewy — **wir·i·ness** \'wī-rē-nəs\ *n*

Wis *or* **Wisc** *abbr* Wisconsin

Wisd *abbr* Wisdom

wis·dom \'wiz-dəm\ *n* [ME, fr. OE *wīsdom*, fr. *wīs* wise] **1** : accumulated philosophic or scientific learning : KNOWLEDGE; *also* : INSIGHT **2** : good sense : JUDGMENT **3** : a wise attitude or course of action

Wisdom *n* — see BIBLE table

wisdom tooth *n* : the last tooth of the full set on each half of each jaw in man

¹**wise** \'wīz\ *n* : WAY, MANNER, FASHION ⟨in no ∼⟩ ⟨in this ∼⟩

²**wise** *adj* **wis·er; wis·est 1** : having wisdom : SAGE **2** : having or showing good sense or good judgment : SENSIBLE, SOUND, PRUDENT **3** : aware of what is going on : KNOWING; *also* : CRAFTY, SHREWD **4** : possessing inside information — **wise·ly** *adv*

wise·acre \'wī-ˌzā-kər\ *n* [Middle Dutch *wijssegger* soothsayer, fr. Old High German *wizzago*] : SMART ALECK

¹**wise·crack** \'wīz-ˌkrak\ *n* : a clever, smart, or flippant remark

²**wisecrack** *vb* : to make a wisecrack

¹**wish** \'wish\ *vb* **1** : to have a desire : long for : CRAVE, WANT ⟨∼ you were here⟩ ⟨∼ for a puppy⟩ **2** : to form or

express a wish concerning ⟨∼ed him a happy birthday⟩ **3** : BID ⟨he ∼ed me good morning⟩ **4** : to request by expressing a desire ⟨I ∼ you to go now⟩

²**wish** *n* **1** : an act or instance of wishing or desire : WANT; *also* : GOAL **2** : an expressed will or desire : MANDATE

wish-bone \-ˌbōn\ *n* : a forked bone in front of the breastbone in most birds

wish·ful \'wish-fəl\ *adj* **1** : expressive of a wish : HOPEFUL, LONGING; *also* : DESIROUS **2** : according with wishes rather than fact ⟨∼ thinking⟩

wishy-washy \'wish-ē-, wȯsh-ē-, -ˌwȧsh-\ *adj* : WEAK, INSIPID; *also* : morally feeble

wisp \'wisp\ *n* **1** : a small handful (as of hay or straw) **2** : a thin strand, strip, or fragment ⟨a ∼ of hair⟩ ; *also* : a thready streak ⟨a ∼ of smoke⟩ **3** : something frail, slight, or fleeting ⟨a ∼ of a girl⟩ ⟨a ∼ of a smile⟩ — **wispy** *adj*

wis·te·ria \wis-'tir-ē-ə\ *or* **wis·ter·ia** \-'tir-ē-ə *also* -'ter-\ *n* : any of a genus of chiefly Asian mostly woody vines related to the peas and widely grown for their long showy clusters of blue, white, purple, or rose flowers

wist·ful \'wist-fəl\ *adj* : full of longing and unfulfilled desire : YEARNING ⟨a ∼ expression⟩ — **wist·ful·ly** \-ē\ *adv* — **wist·ful·ness** *n*

wit \'wit\ *n* **1** : reasoning power : INTELLIGENCE **2** : mental soundness : SANITY — usu. used in pl. **3** : RESOURCEFULNESS, INGENUITY; *esp* : quickness and cleverness in handling words and ideas **4** : a talent for making clever remarks; *also* : one noted for making witty remarks — **at one's wit's end** : at a loss for a means of solving a problem

¹**witch** \'wich\ *n* **1** : a person believed to have magic power; *esp* : SORCERESS **2** : an ugly old woman : HAG **3** : a charming or alluring girl or woman

²**witch** *vb* : BEWITCH

witch·craft \'wich-ˌkraft\ *n* : the power or practices of a witch : SORCERY

witch doctor *n* : a practitioner of magic in a primitive society

witch·ery \'wich-(ə-)rē\ *n, pl* **-er·ies 1** : SORCERY **2** : FASCINATION, CHARM

witch-grass \'wich-ˌgras\ *n* : any of several grasses that are weeds in cultivated areas

witch hazel \'wich-ˌhā-zəl\ *n* **1** : a No. American shrub bearing small yellow flowers in the fall **2** : an alcoholic solution of material from witch hazel bark used as a soothing astringent lotion

witch-hunt \'wich-ˌhənt\ *n* **1** : a searching out and persecution of persons accused of witchcraft **2** : the searching out and deliberate harassment of those (as political opponents) with unpopular views

witch·ing \'wich-iŋ\ *adj* : of, relating to,

or suitable for sorcery or supernatural occurrences

wi·te·na·ge·mot *or* **wi·te·na·ge·mote** \'wit-ᵊn-ə-gə-ˌmōt\ *n* [OE *witena gemōt*, fr. *witena* (gen. pl. of *wita* sage, adviser) + *gemōt* assembly] : an Anglo-Saxon council of nobles, prelates, and officials to advise the king on administrative and judicial matters

¹**with** \(')with, (')with\ *prep* **1** : AGAINST ⟨a fight ~ his wife⟩ **2** : FROM ⟨parting ~ friends⟩ **3** : in mutual relation to ⟨talk ~ a friend⟩ **4** : in the company of ⟨a professor ~ her students⟩ **5** : AS REGARDS, TOWARD ⟨is patient ~ the children⟩ **6** : compared to ⟨on equal terms ~ another⟩ **7** : in support of ⟨I'm ~ you all the way⟩ **8** : in the presence of : CONTAINING ⟨tea ~ sugar⟩ **9** : in the opinion of : as judged by ⟨their arguments had weight ~ him⟩ **10** : BECAUSE OF, THROUGH ⟨pale ~ anger⟩ **11** : in a manner indicating ⟨work ~ a will⟩ **12** : GIVEN, GRANTED ⟨~ your permission I'll leave⟩ **13** : HAVING ⟨came ~ good news⟩ ⟨stood there ~ his mouth open⟩ **14** : at the time of : right after ⟨~ that he left⟩ **15** : DESPITE ⟨~ all her cleverness, she failed⟩ **16** : so as not to cross or oppose ⟨swim ~ the tide⟩

with·al \with-'ȯl, with-\ *adv* **1** : together with this : BESIDES **2** *archaic* : THEREWITH **3** : on the other hand : NEVERTHELESS

with·draw \with-'drȯ, with-\ *vb* -**drew** \-'drü\ ; -**drawn** \-'drȯn\ ; -**draw·ing** \-'drȯ(-)iŋ\ **1** : to take back or away : draw away : REMOVE **2** : to call back (as from consideration) : RECALL, RESCIND; *also* : RETRACT ⟨~ an accusation⟩ **3** : to go away : RETREAT, LEAVE **4** : to terminate one's participation in or use of something

with·draw·al \-'drȯ(ə-)l\ *n* **1** : an act or instance of withdrawing **2** : the discontinuance of the use or administration of a drug and esp. a habit-forming drug; *also* : the often painful physiological and psychological symptoms produced by withdrawal **3** : a pathological retreat from the real world (as in some schizophrenic states)

with·drawn \with-'drȯn\ *adj* **1** : ISOLATED, SECLUDED **2** : socially detached and unresponsive

withe \'with\ *n* : a slender flexible twig or branch; *esp* : one used as a band or rope

with·er \'with-ər\ *vb* **with·ered**; **with·er·ing** \-(ə-)riŋ\ **1** : to become dry and shrunken; *esp* : to shrivel from or as if from loss of bodily moisture **2** : to lose or cause to lose vitality, force, or freshness **3** : to cause ⟨to feel shriveled or blighted ⟨~ed him with a glance⟩

with·ers \'with-ərz\ *n pl* : the ridge between the shoulder bones of a horse;

also : the corresponding part in other 4-footed animals

with·hold \with-'hōld, with-\ *vb* -**held** \-'held\ ; -**hold·ing** **1** : to hold back : RESTRAIN; *also* : to refrain from granting, giving, or allowing ⟨~ permission⟩ ⟨~ names⟩

withholding tax *n* : a tax on income withheld at the source

¹**with·in** \with-'in, with-\ *adv* **1** : in or into the interior : INSIDE **2** : inside oneself : INWARDLY ⟨calm without but furious ~⟩

²**within** *prep* **1** : inside the limits or influence of ⟨~ call⟩ **2** : in the limits or compass of ⟨~ a mile⟩ **3** : in or to the inner part of ⟨~ the room⟩

³**within** *n* : an inner place or area ⟨revolt from ~⟩

with-it \'with-ət\ *adj* : socially or culturally up-to-date

¹**with·out** \with-'aut, with-\ *prep* **1** : OUTSIDE **2** : LACKING ⟨she's ~ hope⟩; *also* : not accompanied by or showing ⟨spoke ~ thinking⟩ ⟨took his punishment ~ flinching⟩

²**without** *adv* **1** : on the outside : ETERNALLY **2** : with something lacking or absent ⟨has learned to do ~⟩

with·stand \with-'stand, with-\ *vb* -**stood** \-'stud\ ; -**stand·ing** : to stand against : RESIST; *esp* : to oppose (as an attack) successfully

wit·less \'wit-ləs\ *adj* : lacking wit or understanding : mentally defective : FOOLISH — **wit·less·ly** *adv* — **wit·less·ness** *n*

¹**wit·ness** \'wit-nəs\ *n* [ME *witnesse*, fr. OE *witnes* knowledge, testimony, witness, fr. *wit* mind, intelligence] **1** : TESTIMONY ⟨bear ~ to the fact⟩ **2** : one that gives evidence; *esp* : one who testifies in a cause or before a court **3** : one present at a transaction so as to be able to testify that it has taken place **4** : one who has personal knowledge or experience of something **5** : something serving as evidence or proof : SIGN

²**witness** *vb* **1** : to bear witness : TESTIFY **2** : to act as legal witness of **3** : to furnish proof of : BETOKEN **4** : to be a witness of **5** : to be the scene of ⟨this region has ~ed many wars⟩

wit·ted \'wit-əd\ *adj* : having wit or understanding ⟨dull-*witted*⟩

wit·ti·cism \'wit-ə-ˌsiz-əm\ *n* : a witty saying or phrase

wit·ting \'wit-iŋ\ *adj* : done knowingly : INTENTIONAL — **wit·ting·ly** *adv*

wit·ty \'wit-ē\ *adj* **wit·ti·er**; -**est** : marked by or full of wit : AMUSING ⟨a ~ writer⟩ ⟨a ~ remark⟩ **syn** humorous, facetious, jocular, jocose — **wit·ti·ly** \'wit-ᵊl-ē\ *adv* — **wit·ti·ness** \-ē-nəs\ *n*

wive \'wīv\ *vb* **wived**; **wiv·ing** **1** : to marry a woman **2** : to take for a wife

wives *pl of* WIFE

wiz·ard \'wiz-ərd\ *n* [ME *wysard* wise man, fr. *wys* wise] **1** : MAGICIAN, SOR-

CERER 2 : a very clever or skillful person ⟨a ∼ at chess⟩

wiz·ard·ry \'wiz-ə(r)-drē\ *n, pl* **-ries 1** : magic skill : SORCERY, WITCHCRAFT **2** : great skill or cleverness in an activity

wiz·ened \'wiz-ᵊnd\ *adj* : dried up : SHRIVELED, WITHERED

wk *abbr* **1** week **2** work

WL *abbr* wavelength

wmk *abbr* watermark

WNW *abbr* west-northwest

WO *abbr* warrant officer

w/o *abbr* without

woad \'wōd\ *n* : a European herb related to the mustards; *also* : a blue dyestuff made from its leaves

wob·ble \'wäb-əl\ *vb* **wob·bled; wob·bling** \-(ə-)liŋ\ **1** : to move or cause to move with an irregular rocking or side-to-side motion **2** : TREMBLE, QUAVER **3** : WAVER, VACILLATE — **wobble** *n* — **wob·bly** \'wäb-(ə-)lē\ *adj*

woe \'wō\ *n* **1** : a condition of deep suffering from misfortune, affliction, or grief **2** : CALAMITY, MISFORTUNE ⟨economic ∼s⟩

woe·be·gone \'wō-bi-ˌgȯn\ *adj* : exhibiting woe, sorrow, or misery; *also* : DISMAL, DESOLATE

woe·ful *also* **woful** \'wō-fəl\ *adj* **1** : full of woe : AFFLICTED **2** : involving, bringing, or relating to woe **3** : PALTRY, DEPLORABLE — **woe·ful·ly** \-ē\ *adv*

wok \'wäk\ *n* : a bowl-shaped cooking utensil used esp. in the preparation of Chinese food

woke *past of* WAKE

woken *past part of* WAKE

wold \'wōld\ *n* : an upland plain or stretch of rolling land without woods

¹wolf \'wu̇lf\ *n, pl* **wolves** \'wu̇lvz\ **1** : any of several large erect-eared bushy-tailed doglike predatory mammals that often hunt in packs **2** : a fierce or destructive person **3** : a man forward, direct, and zealous in amatory attentions to women — **wolf·ish** *adj*

²wolf *vb* : to eat greedily : DEVOUR

wolf·hound \-ˌhau̇nd\ *n* : any of several large dogs orig. used in hunting wolves

wol·fram \'wu̇l-frəm\ *n* : TUNGSTEN

wol·ver·ine \ˌwu̇l-və-'rēn\ *n, pl* **wolverines** *also* **wolverine** : a dark shaggy-coated flesh-eating mammal of northern forests and associated tundra that is related to the weasels and sables

wom·an \'wu̇m-ən\ *n, pl* **wom·en** \'wim-ən\ [ME, fr. OE *wīfman*, fr. *wīf* woman, wife + *man* human being, man] **1** : an adult female person **2** : WOMANKIND **3** : feminine nature : WOMANLINESS **4** : a female servant or attendant

wom·an·hood \'wu̇m-ən-ˌhu̇d\ *n* **1** : the state of being a woman : the distinguishing qualities of a woman or of womankind **2** : WOMEN, WOMANKIND

wom·an·ish \'wu̇m-ə-nish\ *adj* **1** : of, relating to, or characteristic of a woman

an **2** : suitable to a woman rather than to a man : EFFEMINATE

wom·an·kind \'wu̇m-ən-ˌkīnd\ *n* : the females of the human race : WOMEN

wom·an·like \-ˌlīk\ *adj* : WOMANLY

wom·an·ly \-lē\ *adj* : having qualities characteristic of a woman — **wom·an·li·ness** \-lē-nəs\ *n*

woman suffrage *n* : possession and exercise of suffrage by women

womb \'wüm\ *n* **1** : UTERUS **2** : a place where something is generated or developed

wom·bat \'wäm-ˌbat\ *n* : any of several stocky burrowing Australian marsupials that resemble small bears

wom·en·folk \'wim-ən-ˌfōk\ *also* **wom·en·folks** \-ˌfōks\ *n pl* : WOMEN

¹won \'wən\ *past and past part of* WIN

²won \'wȯn\ *n, pl* **won** — see MONEY table

¹won·der \'wən-dər\ *n* **1** : a cause of astonishment or surprise : MARVEL; *also* : MIRACLE **2** : the quality of exciting wonder ⟨the charm and ∼ of the scene⟩ **3** : a feeling (as of awed astonishment or uncertainty) aroused by something extraordinary or affecting

²wonder *vb* **won·dered; won·der·ing** \-d(ə-)riŋ\ **1** : to feel surprise or amazement **2** : to feel curiosity or doubt

wonder drug *n* : MIRACLE DRUG

won·der·ful \'wən-dər-fəl\ *adj* **1** : exciting wonder : MARVELOUS, ASTONISHING **2** : unusually good : ADMIRABLE — **won·der·ful·ly** \-f(ə-)lē\ *adv* — **won·der·ful·ness** *n*

won·der·land \-ˌland, -lənd\ *n* **1** : an imaginary place of delicate beauty or magical charm **2** : a place that excites admiration or wonder

won·der·ment \-mənt\ *n* **1** : ASTONISHMENT, SURPRISE **2** : a cause of or occasion for wonder **3** : curiosity about something

won·drous \'wən-drəs\ *adj* : WONDERFUL, MARVELOUS — **wondrous** *adv, archaic* — **won·drous·ly** *adv* — **won·drous·ness** *n*

¹wont \'wȯnt, 'wōnt\ *adj* [ME *woned*, *wont*, fr. pp. of *wonen* to dwell, be used to, fr. OE *wunian*] **1** : ACCUSTOMED, USED ⟨as he was ∼ to do⟩ **2** : INCLINED, APT

²wont *n* : CUSTOM, USAGE, HABIT ⟨according to her ∼⟩

wont·ed \'wȯnt-əd, 'wōnt-\ *adj* : ACCUSTOMED, CUSTOMARY ⟨his ∼ courtesy⟩

woo \'wü\ *vb* **1** : to try to gain the love of and usu. marriage with : COURT **2** : SOLICIT, ENTREAT **3** : to try to gain or bring about ⟨∼ public favor⟩ — **woo·er** *n*

¹wood \'wu̇d\ *n* **1** : a dense growth of trees usu. larger than a grove and smaller than a forest — often used in pl. **2** : a hard fibrous substance that is basically xylem and forms the bulk of trees and shrubs beneath the bark; *also* : this material fit or prepared for some use (as burning or building) **3** : something made of wood

²wood *adj* **1** : WOODEN **2** : suitable for holding, cutting, or working with wood **3** *or* **woods** \'wủdz\ : living or growing in woods

³wood *vb* **1** : to supply or load with wood esp. for fuel **2** : to cover with a growth of trees

wood alcohol *n* : METHANOL

wood·bine \'wủd-ˌbīn\ *n* : any of several climbing vines (as a honeysuckle or Virginia creeper)

wood·block \-ˌbläk\ *n* **1** : a block of wood **2** : WOODCUT

wood·chop·per \-ˌchäp-ər\ *n* : one engaged esp. in chopping down trees

wood·chuck \-ˌchək\ *n* : any of several No. American marmots; *esp* : a thickset grizzled marmot of the northeastern U.S. and Canada

wood·cock \'wủd-ˌkäk\ *n, pl* **woodcocks** : a brown No. American game bird with a short neck and long bill that is related to the snipe; *also* : a related and similar bird widespread in the Old World

wood·craft \-ˌkraft\ *n* **1** : skill and practice in matters relating to the woods esp. in maintaining oneself and making one's way or in hunting or trapping **2** : skill in shaping or constructing articles from wood

wood·cut \-ˌkət\ *n* **1** : a relief printing surface engraved on wood **2** : a print from a woodcut

wood·cut·ter \-ˌkət-ər\ *n* : a person who cuts wood esp. as an occupation

wood·ed \'wủd-əd\ *adj* : covered with woods or trees (⁓ slopes)

wood·en \'wủd-ᵊn\ *adj* **1** : made of wood **2** : lacking resilience : STIFF **3** : AWKWARD, CLUMSY — **wood·en·ly** *adv* — **wood·en·ness** \-ᵊn-(n)əs\ *n*

wood·en·ware \'wủd-ᵊn-ˌwaər\ *n* : articles made of wood for domestic use

wood·land \'wủd-lənd, -ˌland\ *n* : land covered with trees : FOREST

wood·lot \'wủd-ˌlät\ *n* : a relatively small area of trees kept usu. to meet fuel and timber needs (a farm ⁓)

wood louse *n* : a small flat grayish crustacean that lives esp. under stones and bark

wood·man \'wủd-mən\ *n* : WOODSMAN

wood·note \-ˌnōt\ *n* : verbal expression that is natural and artless

wood nymph *n* : a nymph living in the woods

wood·peck·er \'wủd-ˌpek-ər\ *n* : any of various usu. brightly marked climbing birds with stiff spiny tail feathers and a chisellike bill used to drill into trees for insects

wood·pile \-ˌpīl\ *n* : a pile of wood and esp. firewood

wood·shed \-ˌshed\ *n* : a shed for storing wood and esp. firewood

woods·man \'wủdz-mən\ *n* : a person who frequents or works in the woods; *esp* : one skilled in woodcraft

woodsy \'wủd-zē\ *adj* : relating to or suggestive of woods

wood·wind \'wủd-ˌwind\ *n* : one of a group of wind instruments including flutes, clarinets, oboes, bassoons, and sometimes saxophones

wood·work \-ˌwərk\ *n* **1** : work made of wood; *esp* : interior fittings (as moldings or stairways) of wood **2** : a place of hiding or seclusion (came out of the ⁓ to claim the lost money)

woody \'wủd-ē\ *adj* **wood·i·er; -est 1** : abounding or overgrown with woods **2** : of or containing wood or wood fibers **3** : resembling or characteristic of wood — **wood·i·ness** \'wủd-ē-nəs\ *n*

woof \'wủf\ *n* [alter. of ME oof, fr. OE ōwef, fr. ō- (fr. *on* on) + *wefan* to weave] **1** : the threads in a woven fabric that cross the warp **2** : a woven fabric; *also* : its texture

woof·er \'wủf-ər\ *n* : a loudspeaker that reproduces sounds of low pitch

wool \'wủl\ *n* **1** : the soft wavy or curly hair of some mammals and esp. the domestic sheep; *also* : something (as a textile or garment) made of wool **2** : material that resembles a mass of wool — **wooled** \'wủld\ *adj*

¹wool·en *or* **wool·len** \'wủl-ən\ *adj* **1** : made of wool **2** : of or relating to the manufacture or sale of woolen products (⁓ mills)

²woolen *or* **woollen** *n* **1** : a fabric made of wool **2** : garments of woolen fabric — usu. used in pl.

wool·gath·er·ing \-ˌgath-(ə-)riŋ\ *n* : the act of indulging in idle daydreaming

¹wool·ly *also* **wooly** \'wủl-ē\ *adj* **wool·li·er; -est 1** : of, relating to, or bearing wool **2** : consisting of or resembling wool **3** : CONFUSED, BLURRY (⁓ thinking) **4** : marked by a lack of order or restraint (the wild and ⁓ West of frontier times)

²wool·ly *also* **wool·ie** *or* **wooly** \'wủl-ē\ *n, pl* **wool·lies** : a garment made from wool; *esp* : underclothing of knitted wool

woolly aphid *n* : a plant louse covered with a dense coat of white filaments

woolly aphis *n* : WOOLLY APHID

woolly bear *n* : any of numerous very hairy caterpillars

wool·sack \'wủl-ˌsak\ *n* **1** *archaic* : a sack of or for wool **2** : the seat of the Lord Chancellor in the House of Lords

woo·zy \'wü-zē\ *adj* **woo·zi·er; -est 1** : BEFUDDLED **2** : somewhat dizzy, nauseated, or weak — **woo·zi·ness** \'wü-zē-nəs\ *n*

¹word \'wərd\ *n* **1** : something that is said; *esp* : a brief remark **2** : a speech sound or series of speech sounds that communicates a meaning; *also* : a graphic representation of such a sound or series of sounds **3** : ORDER, COMMAND **4** *often cap* : the 2d person of the Trinity; *also* : GOSPEL **5** : NEWS, INFORMATION **6** : PROMISE **7** *pl* : QUAR-

REL, DISPUTE **8** : a verbal signal : PASS-
WORD — **word·less** adj

²**word** vb : to express in words : PHRASE

word·age \'wərd-ij\ n **1** : WORDS **2**
: number of words **3** : WORDING

word·book \'wərd-ˌbùk\ n : VOCABU-
LARY, DICTIONARY

word·ing \'wərd-iŋ\ n : verbal expression : PHRASEOLOGY

word of mouth : oral communication

word·play \'wərd-ˌplā\ n : verbal wit

word processing n : the production of
typewritten documents with automat-
ed and usu. computerized text-editing
equipment

word processor n : a keyboard-oper-
ated terminal with a video display and
a magnetic storage device for use in
word processing; also : software to
perform word processing

wordy \'wərd-ē\ adj **word·i·er; -est** : using many words : VERBOSE syn prolix,
diffuse, redundant — **word·i·ness**
\'wərd-ē-nəs\ n

wore past of WEAR

¹**work** \'wərk\ n **1** : TOIL, LABOR; also
: EMPLOYMENT (out of ∼) **2** : TASK, JOB
⟨have ∼ to do⟩ **3** : the transference of
energy when a force produces movement of a body **4** : DEED, ACHIEVEMENT
5 : a fortified structure of any kind **6** pl
: engineering structures **7** pl : the
buildings, grounds, and machinery of
a factory **8** pl : the moving parts of a
mechanism **9** : something produced
by mental effort or physical labor; esp
: an artistic production (as a book or
needlework) **10** : WORKMANSHIP (careless ∼) **11** : material in the process of
manufacture **12** pl : everything possessed, available, or belonging (the
whole ∼s went overboard) : subjection to drastic treatment (gave
him the ∼s) syn occupation, employ-
ment, business, pursuit, calling — **in
the works** : in process of preparation

²**work** adj : used for work ⟨∼ ele-
phants⟩ **2** : suitable or styled for wear
while working ⟨∼ clothes⟩

³**work** vb **worked** \'wərkt\ or **wrought**
\'rot\; **work·ing 1** : to bring to pass
: EFFECT **2** : to fashion or create a useful or desired product through labor or
exertion **3** : to prepare for use (as by
kneading) **4** : to bring into a desired
form by a process of cutting, hammering, scraping, pressing, or stretching
⟨∼ cold steel⟩ **5** : to set or keep in
operation : OPERATE ⟨a pump ∼ed by
hand⟩ **6** : to solve by reasoning or calculation ⟨∼ a problem⟩ **7** : to cause to
toil or labor ⟨∼ed his men hard⟩ : also
: EXPLOIT **8** : to pay for with labor or
service ⟨∼ off a debt⟩ **9** : to bring into
some (specified) position or condition
by stages ⟨the stream ∼ed itself clear⟩
10 : CONTRIVE, ARRANGE ⟨we'll go if we
can ∼ it⟩ **11** : to practice trickery or
cajolery on for some end ⟨∼ed the
management for a free ticket⟩ **12** : EX-
CITE, PROVOKE ⟨∼ed himself into a

rage⟩ **13** : to exert oneself physically
or mentally; esp : to perform work
regularly for wages **14** : to function
according to plan or design **15** : to
produce a desired effect : SUCCEED **16**
: to make way slowly and with difficulty ⟨he ∼ed forward through the
crowd⟩ **17** : to permit of being worked
⟨this wood ∼s easily⟩ **18** : to be in
restless motion; also : FERMENT 1 **19**
: to move slightly in relation to another part; also : to get into a specified
condition slowly or imperceptibly
⟨the knot ∼ed loose⟩ — **work on 1**
: AFFECT **2** : to try to influence or persuade — **work upon** : to have effect
upon : operate on : PERSUADE, INFLU-
ENCE

work·able \'wər-kə-bəl\ adj **1** : capable
of being worked **2** : PRACTICABLE, FEA-
SIBLE — **work·able·ness** n

work·a·day \'wər-kə-ˌdā\ adj **1** : relating to or suited for working days **2**
: PROSAIC, ORDINARY

work·a·hol·ic \ˌwər-kə-ˈhȯl-ik, -ˈhäl-\ n
: a compulsive worker

work·bag \'wər-ˌbag\ n : a bag for
holding implements or materials for
work; esp : a bag for needlework

work·bas·ket \-ˌbas-kət\ n : a basket for
needlework

work·bench \-ˌbench\ n : a bench on
which work esp. of mechanics, ma-
chinists, and carpenters is performed

work·book \-ˌbùk\ n **1** : a booklet out-
lining a course of study **2** : a worker's
manual **3** : a record of work done **4** : a
student's book of problems to be answered directly on the pages

work·box \-ˌbäks\ n : a box for work
instruments and materials

work·day \'wərk-ˌdā\ n **1** : a day on
which work is done as distinguished
from a day off **2** : the period of time in
a day when work is performed

work·er \'wər-kər\ n **1** : one that
works; esp : a person who works for
wages **2** : one of the sexually undeveloped individuals of a colony of
social insects (as bees, ants, or termites) that perform the work of the
community

work ethic n : belief in work as a moral
good

work farm n : a farm on which persons
guilty of minor law violations are confined

work·horse \'wərk-ˌhȯrs\ n **1** : a horse
used chiefly for labor **2** : a person
who undertakes arduous labor

work·house \-ˌhaùs\ n **1** Brit : POOR-
HOUSE **2** : a house of correction where
persons who have committed minor
offenses are confined

¹**work·ing** \'wər-kiŋ\ adj **1** : adequate to
allow work to be done ⟨a ∼ majority⟩
⟨a ∼ knowledge of French⟩ **2** : adopted or assumed to help further work or
activity ⟨a ∼ draft of a treaty⟩ **3** : engaged in work ⟨a ∼ journalist⟩ **4**
: spent at work ⟨∼ life⟩

²**working** n 1 : manner of functioning : OPERATION 2 pl : an excavation made in mining or tunneling

work·ing·man \'wər-kiŋ-ˌman\ n : one who works for wages usu. at manual labor

work·man \'wərk-mən\ n 1 : WORKING-MAN 2 : ARTISAN, CRAFTSMAN

work·man·like \-ˌlīk\ adj : worthy of a good workman : SKILLFUL

work·man·ship \-ˌship\ n : the art or skill of a workman : CRAFTSMANSHIP; also : the quality imparted to something in the process of making it (a vase of exquisite ~)

work·out \'wərk-ˌaut\ n 1 : a practice or exercise to test or improve one's fitness esp. for athletic competition, ability, or performance 2 : a test or trial to determine ability or capacity or suitability

work out \ˌwərk-'aut, 'wərk-\ vb 1 : bring about esp. by resolving difficulties 2 : DEVELOP, ELABORATE 3 : to prove effective, practicable, or suitable 4 : to amount to a total or calculated figure — used with at 5 : to engage in a workout

work·room \'wərk-ˌrüm, -ˌrüm\ n : a room used esp. for manual work

work·shop \-ˌshäp\ n 1 : a small establishment where manufacturing or handicrafts are carried on 2 : a seminar emphasizing exchange of ideas and practical methods and given mainly for adults already employed in the field

work·sta·tion \-ˌstā-shən\ n : an area with equipment for a single worker; also : a usu. intelligent terminal connected to a computer network

work·ta·ble \-ˌtā-bəl\ n : a table for holding working materials and implements (as for needlework)

world \'wərld\ n [ME, fr. OE woruld human existence, this world, age, fr. a prehistoric compound whose first constituent is represented by OE wer man and whose second constituent is akin to OE eald old] 1 : the earth with its inhabitants and all things upon it 2 : people in general 3 : the affairs of men (withdraw from the ~) 4 : UNIVERSE, CREATION 5 : a state of existence : scene of life and action (the ~ of the future) 6 : a distinctive class of persons or their sphere of interest (the musical ~) 7 : a part or section of the earth or its inhabitants by itself 8 : a great number or quantity (a ~ of troubles) 9 : a celestial body esp. if inhabited

world–beat·er \-ˌbēt-ər\ n : one that excels all others of its kind : CHAMPION

world·ling \-liŋ\ n : a person absorbed in the affairs and pleasures of the present world

world·ly \'wərld-lē\ adj 1 : of, relating to, or devoted to this world and its pursuits rather than to religion or spiritual affairs 2 : WORLDLY-WISE, SOPHISTICATED — **world·li·ness** \-lē-nəs\ n

world·ly–wise \-ˌwīz\ adj : possessing a practical and often shrewd understanding of human affairs

world·wide \'wərld-'wīd\ adj : extended throughout the entire world (~ fame)

¹**worm** \'wərm\ n 1 : any of various small long usu. naked and soft-bodied round or flat invertebrate animals (as an earthworm, nematode, tapeworm, or maggot) 2 : a human being who is an object of contempt, loathing, or pity : WRETCH 3 : something that inwardly torments or devours 4 pl : infestation with or disease caused by parasitic worms 5 : a spiral or wormlike thing (as the thread of a screw) — **wormy** adj

²**worm** vb 1 : to free from worms (~ a dog) 2 : to move or cause to move or proceed slowly and deviously 3 : to obtain or extract by artful or insidious pleading, asking, or persuading (~ed the truth out of him) 4 : to insinuate or introduce (oneself) by devious or subtle means

worm–eat·en \'wərm-ˌēt-ᵊn\ adj 1 : eaten or burrowed by worms 2 : PITTED 3 : WORN-OUT, ANTIQUATED (tried to update the ~ regulations)

worm gear n : a mechanical linkage consisting of a short rotating screw whose threads mesh with the teeth of a gear wheel

worm·hole \'wərm-ˌhōl\ n : a hole or passage burrowed by a worm

worm·wood \'wərm-ˌwud\ n 1 : any of a genus of aromatic woody plants including the sagebrush and related plants; esp : one of Europe used in making absinthe 2 : something bitter or grievous : BITTERNESS

worn past part of WEAR

worn–out \'wōrn-'aut\ adj : exhausted or used up by or as if by wear (an old ~ suit) (a ~ automobile)

wor·ri·some \'wər-ē-səm\ adj 1 : causing distress or worry 2 : inclined to worry or fret

¹**wor·ry** \'wər-ē\ vb **wor·ried; wor·ry·ing** 1 : to shake and mangle with the teeth (a terrier ~ing a rat) 2 : to make anxious or upset (his poor health worries his parents) 3 : to feel or express great care or anxiety : FRET — **wor·ri·er** n

²**worry** n, pl **worries** 1 : ANXIETY 2 : a cause of anxiety : TROUBLE

wor·ry·wart \'wər-ē-ˌwort\ n : one who is inclined to worry unduly

¹**worse** \'wərs\ adj, comparative of BAD or of ILL 1 : bad or evil in a greater degree : less good; esp : more unwell 2 : more unfavorable, unpleasant, or painful

²**worse** n 1 : one that is worse 2 : a greater degree of ill or badness

³**worse** adv, comparative of BAD or of ILL : in a worse manner : to a worse extent or degree

wors·en \'wərs-ᵊn\ *vb* **wors·ened; wors·en·ing** \'wərs-(ᵊ-)niŋ\ : to make or become worse

¹wor·ship \'wər-shəp\ *n* [ME *worship* worthiness, repute, respect, reverence paid to a divine being, fr. OE *weorthscipe* worthiness, repute, respect, fr. *weorth* worthy, worth + *-scipe* -ship, suffix denoting quality or condition] **1** *chiefly Brit* : a person of importance — used as a title for officials (as magistrates and some mayors) **2** : reverence toward a divine being or supernatural power; *also* : the expression of such reverence **3** : extravagant respect or admiration for or devotion to an object of esteem (~ of the dollar)

²worship *vb* **-shiped** *or* **-shipped; -ship·ing** *or* **-ship·ping** **1** : to honor or reverence as a divine being or supernatural power **2** : IDOLIZE **3** : to perform or take part in worship — **wor·ship·er** *or* **wor·ship·per** *n*

wor·ship·ful \'wər-shəp-fəl\ *adj* **1** *archaic* : NOTABLE, DISTINGUISHED **2** *chiefly Brit* — used as a title for various persons or groups of rank or distinction **3** : VENERATING, WORSHIPING

¹worst \'wərst\ *adj, superlative of* BAD *or of* ILL **1** : most bad, evil, ill, or corrupt **2** : most unfavorable, unpleasant, or painful; *also* : most unsuitable, faulty, or unattractive **3** : least skillful or efficient **4** : most wanting in quality, value, or condition

²worst *adv, superlative of* ILL *or of* BAD *or* BADLY : to the extreme degree of badness or inferiority : in the worst manner

³worst *n* : one that is worst

⁴worst *vb* : DEFEAT

wor·sted \'wùs-təd, 'wər-stəd\ *n* [ME, fr. *Worsted* (now *Worstead*), England] : a smooth compact yarn from long wool fibers used esp. for firm napless fabrics, carpeting, or knitting; *also* : a fabric made from such yarn

wort \'wərt, 'wȯrt\ *n* : a solution obtained by infusion from malt and fermented to form beer

¹worth \'wərth\ *prep* **1** : equal in value to; *also* : having possessions or income equal to **2** : deserving of (well ~ the effort)

²worth *n* **1** : monetary value : the equivalent of a specified amount or figure **2** : the value of something measured by its qualities or by the esteem in which it is held **3** : moral or personal value : MERIT, EXCELLENCE **4** : WEALTH, RICHES

worth·less \'wərth-ləs\ *adj* **1** : lacking worth : VALUELESS; *also* : USELESS **2** : LOW, DESPICABLE — **worth·less·ness** *n*

worth·while \'wərth-'hwīl\ *adj* : being worth the time or effort spent

¹wor·thy \'wər-thē\ *adj* **wor·thi·er; -est 1** : having worth or value : ESTIMABLE **2** : HONORABLE, MERITORIOUS **3** : having sufficient worth (a man ~ of the hon-

or) — **wor·thi·ly** \'wər-thə-lē\ *adv* — **wor·thi·ness** \-thē-nəs\ *n*

²worthy *n, pl* **worthies** : a worthy person

would \wəd, əd, d, (')wùd\ *past of* WILL **1** *archaic* : wish for : WANT **2** : strongly desire : WISH (I ~ I were young again) **3** — used as an auxiliary to express (1) preference (~ rather run than fight) , (2) wish, desire, or intent (those who ~ forbid gambling) , (3) habitual action (we ~ meet often for lunch) , (4) a contingency or possibility (if he were coming, he ~ be here by now) , (5) probability (~ have won if he hadn't tripped) , or (6) a request (~ you help us) **4** : COULD **5** : SHOULD

would–be \'wùd-,bē\ *adj* : desiring, professing, or having the potential to be (a ~ artist)

¹wound \'wünd\ *n* **1** : an injury involving cutting or breaking of bodily tissue (as by violence, accident, or surgery) **2** : an injury or hurt to feelings or reputation

²wound *vb* : to inflict a wound to or in

³wound \'waùnd\ *past and past part of* WIND

wove *past of* WEAVE

woven *past part of* WEAVE

¹wow \'waù\ *n* : a striking success : HIT

²wow *vb* : to arouse enthusiastic approval

³wow *n* : a distortion in reproduced sound consisting of a slow rise and fall of pitch caused by speed variation in the reproducing system

WP *abbr* word processing; word processor

WPM *abbr* words per minute

wpn *abbr* weapon

¹wrack \'rak\ *n* **1** : a wrecked ship; *also* : WRECKAGE, WRECK **2** : sea vegetation (as kelp) esp. when cast up on the shore

²wrack *n* [ME, fr. OE *wræc* misery, punishment, something driven by the sea] **1** : RUIN, DESTRUCTION **2** : a remnant of something destroyed

wraith \'rāth\ *n, pl* **wraiths** \'rāths, 'rāthz\ **1** : APPARITION; *also* : GHOST, SPECTER **2** : an insubstantial appearance : SHADOW

¹wran·gle \'raŋ-gəl\ *vb* **wran·gled; wran·gling** \-g(ə-)liŋ\ **1** : to quarrel angrily or peevishly : BICKER **2** : ARGUE **3** : to obtain by persistent arguing **4** : to herd and care for (livestock) on the range — **wran·gler** *n*

²wrangle *n* : an angry, noisy, or prolonged dispute or quarrel; *also* : CONTROVERSY

¹wrap \'rap\ *vb* **wrapped; wrap·ping 1** : to cover esp. by winding or folding **2** : to envelop and secure for transportation or storage : BUNDLE **3** : to enclose wholly : ENFOLD **4** : to coil, fold, draw, or twine about something **5** : SURROUND, ENVELOP; *also* : SUFFUSE **6** : INVOLVE, ENGROSS (*wrapped* up in a hobby) **7** : to conceal as if by enveloping or enfolding : HIDE **8** : to put on clothing : DRESS **9** : to be subject to covering or enclosing ⟨∼s up into a small package⟩

²**wrap** n **1** : WRAPPER, WRAPPING **2** : an article of clothing that may be wrapped around a person; esp : an outer garment (as a coat or shawl) **3** pl : SECRECY (kept under ∼s)

wrap·around \'rap-ə-,raůnd\ n : a garment (as a dress) made with a full-length opening and adjusted to the figure by wrapping around

wrap·per \'rap-ər\ n **1** : that in which something is wrapped **2** : one that wraps **3** : an article of clothing worn wrapped around the body

wrap·ping \'rap-iŋ\ n : something used to wrap an object : WRAPPER

wrap-up \'rap-,əp\ n : a summarizing report

wrap up \(')rap-'əp\ vb **1** : SUMMARIZE, SUM UP **2** : to bring to a usu. successful conclusion

wrasse \'ras\ n : any of various usu. brightly colored sea fishes including many food fishes

wrath \'rath\ n **1** : violent anger : RAGE **2** : retributory punishment for an offense or a crime : divine chastisement syn indignation, ire, fury, anger

wrath·ful \-fəl\ adj **1** : filled with wrath : very angry **2** : showing, marked by, or arising from anger — **wrath·ful·ly** \-ē\ adv — **wrath·ful·ness** n

wreak \'rēk\ vb **1** : to exact as a punishment : INFLICT ⟨∼ vengeance on an enemy⟩ **2** : to give free scope or rein to ⟨∼ed his wrath⟩ **3** : BRING ABOUT, CAUSE ⟨∼ havoc⟩

wreath \'rēth\ n, pl **wreaths** \'rēthz, 'rēths\ : something (as boughs or flowers) intertwined into a circular shape

wreathe \'rēth\ vb **wreathed; wreath·ing** **1** : to shape or take on the shape of a wreath : move or extend in circles or spirals **2** : to twist or become twisted esp. so as to show folds or creases ⟨a face wreathed in smiles⟩ **3** : to fold or coil around : ENTWINE

¹**wreck** \'rek\ n **1** : something (as goods) cast upon the land by the sea after a shipwreck **2** : SHIPWRECK **3** : the action of breaking up or destroying something : WRECKING **4** : broken remains (as of a ship or vehicle after heavy damage) **5** : something disabled or in a state of ruin; also : an individual broken in health or strength

²**wreck** vb **1** : SHIPWRECK **2** : to ruin or damage by breaking up : involve in disaster or ruin

wreck·age \'rek-ij\ n **1** : the act of wrecking : the state of being wrecked : RUIN **2** : the remains of a wreck

wreck·er \'rek-ər\ n **1** : one that searches for or works upon the wrecks of ships **2** : a truck equipped to remove disabled cars **3** : one that salvages junked automobile parts **4**

: one that wrecks; esp : one that razes buildings

wren \'ren\ n : any of various small mostly brown singing birds with short wings and tail

¹**wrench** \'rench\ vb **1** : to move with a violent twist **2** : to pull, strain, or tighten with violent twisting or force **3** : to injure or disable by a violent twisting or straining **4** : to change (as the meaning of a word) violently : DISTORT **5** : to snatch forcibly : WREST **6** : to cause to suffer mental anguish

²**wrench** n **1** : a forcible twisting; also : an injury (as to one's ankle) by twisting **2** : a tool for holding, twisting, or turning an object (as a nut or bolt)

¹**wrest** \'rest\ vb **1** : to pull or move by a forcible twisting movement **2** : to gain with difficulty by or as if by force or violence ⟨∼ a living from the barren land⟩ ⟨∼ control of government from the dictator⟩

²**wrest** n : a forcible twist : WRENCH

¹**wres·tle** \'res-əl, 'ras-\ vb **wres·tled; wres·tling** \-(ə-)liŋ\ **1** : to scuffle with an opponent in an attempt to trip him or throw him down **2** : to contend against in wrestling **3** : to struggle for mastery (as with something difficult) ⟨∼ with a problem⟩ — **wres·tler** \'res-lər, 'ras-\ n

²**wrestle** n : the action or an instance of wrestling : STRUGGLE

wres·tling \'res-liŋ\ n : the sport of hand-to-hand combat between two opponents who seek to throw and pin each other

wretch \'rech\ n [ME wrecche, fr. OE wrecca outcast, exile] **1** : a miserable unhappy person **2** : a base, despicable, or vile person

wretch·ed \'rech-əd\ adj **1** : deeply afflicted, dejected, or distressed : MISERABLE **2** : WOEFUL, GRIEVOUS ⟨a ∼ accident⟩ **3** : DESPICABLE ⟨a ∼ trick⟩ **4** : poor in quality or ability : INFERIOR ⟨∼ workmanship⟩ — **wretch·ed·ness** n

wrig·gle \'rig-əl\ vb **wrig·gled; wrig·gling** \-(ə-)liŋ\ **1** : to twist and turn restlessly : SQUIRM ⟨wriggled in his chair⟩; also : to move or advance by twisting and turning ⟨a snake wriggled along the path⟩ **2** : to extricate oneself or bring into a state or place by maneuvering, twisting, or dodging ⟨∼ out of a difficulty⟩ — **wriggle** n

wrig·gler \'rig-(ə-)lər\ n **1** : one that wriggles **2** : WIGGLER 1

wring \'riŋ\ vb **wrung** \'rəŋ\ ; **wring·ing** \'riŋ-iŋ\ **1** : to squeeze or twist esp. so as to make dry or to extract moisture or liquid ⟨∼ clothes⟩ **2** : to get by or as if by forcible exertion or pressure : EXTORT ⟨∼ the truth out of him⟩ **3** : to twist so as to strain or sprain : CONTORT ⟨∼ his neck⟩ **4** : to twist together as a sign of anguish ⟨wrung her hands⟩ **5** : to affect painfully as if by wringing : TORMENT ⟨her plight wrung my heart⟩

wring•er \'riŋ-ər\ *n* : one that wrings; *esp* : a device for squeezing out liquid or moisture (clothes ∼)

¹**wrin•kle** \'riŋ-kəl\ *n* **1** : a crease or small fold on a surface (as in the skin or in cloth) **2** : METHOD, TECHNIQUE **3** : INNOVATION, NOVELTY (the latest ∼ in hairdos) — **wrin•kly** \-k(ə-)lē\ *adj*

²**wrinkle** *vb* **wrin•kled; wrin•kling** \-k(ə-)liŋ\ : to develop or cause to develop wrinkles

wrist \'rist\ *n* : the joint or region between the hand and the arm; *also* : a corresponding part in a lower animal

wrist-band \'rist(t)-,band\ *n* **1** : the part of a sleeve covering the wrist **2** : a band encircling the wrist

wrist•let \'ris(t)-lət\ *n* : a band encircling the wrist; *esp* : a close-fitting knitted band attached to the top of a glove or the end of a sleeve

wrist-watch \-,wäch\ *n* : a small watch attached to a bracelet or strap to fasten about the wrist

writ \'rit\ *n* **1** : something written **2** : a legal order in writing issued in the name of the sovereign power or in the name of a court or judicial authority commanding the performance or nonperformance of a specified act **3** : a written order constituting a symbol of the power and authority of the issuer

write \'rit\ *vb* **wrote** \'rōt\ ; **writ•ten** \'rit-ᵊn\ *also* **writ** \'rit\ ; **writ•ing** \'rit-iŋ\ [ME *writen*, fr. OE *writan* to scratch, draw, inscribe] **1** : to form characters, letters, or words on a surface (as with a pen) (learn to read and ∼) **2** : to form the letters or the words of (as on paper) : INSCRIBE (*wrote* his name) **3** : to put down on paper : give expression to in writing **4** : to make up and set down for others to read : COMPOSE (∼ music) **5** : to pen, typewrite, or dictate a letter to **6** : to communicate by letter : CORRESPOND **7** : to be fitted for writing (this pen ∼s easily)

write–in \'rit-,in\ *n* : a vote cast by writing in the name of a candidate; *also* : a candidate whose name is written in

write in \(')rit-'in\ *vb* : to insert (a name not listed on a ballot) in an appropriate space; *also* : to cast (a vote) in this manner

write off *vb* **1** : to reduce the estimated value of : DEPRECIATE **2** : CANCEL (*write off* a bad debt)

writ•er \'rit-ər\ *n* : one that writes esp. as a business or occupation : AUTHOR

writer's cramp *n* : a painful spasmodic cramp of muscles of the hand or fingers brought on by excessive writing

write–up \'rit-,əp\ *n* : a written account (as in a newspaper); *esp* : a flattering article

writhe \'rith\ *vb* **writhed; writh•ing** **1** : to move or proceed with twists and turns (∼ in pain) **2** : to suffer with shame or confusion : SQUIRM

writ•ing \'rit-iŋ\ *n* **1** : the act of one that writes; *also* : HANDWRITING **2** : something (as a letter, book, or document) that is written or printed **3** : INSCRIPTION **4** : a style or form of composition **5** : the occupation of a writer

wrnt *abbr* warrant

¹**wrong** \'roŋ\ *n* **1** : an injurious, unfair, or unjust act **2** : a violation of the legal rights of another person **3** : something that is contrary to justice, goodness, equity, or law (know right from ∼) **4** : the state, position, or fact of being or doing wrong; *also* : the state of being guilty (in the ∼)

²**wrong** *adj* **wrong•er** \'roŋ-ər\ ; **wrong•est** \'roŋ-əst\ **1** : SINFUL, IMMORAL **2** : not right according to a standard or code : IMPROPER **3** : INCORRECT (a ∼ solution) **4** : UNSATISFACTORY **5** : UNSUITABLE, INAPPROPRIATE **6** : constituting a surface that is considered the back, bottom, inside, or reverse of something (iron only on the ∼ side of the fabric) *syn* false, erroneous, incorrect, inaccurate, untrue — **wrong•ly** *adv*

³**wrong** *adv* **1** : INCORRECTLY **2** : in a wrong direction, manner, position, or relation

⁴**wrong** *vb* **wronged; wrong•ing** \'roŋ-iŋ\ **1** : to do wrong to : INJURE, HARM **2** : to treat unjustly : DISHONOR, MALIGN *syn* oppress, persecute, aggrieve

wrong-do•er \'roŋ-'dü-ər\ *n* : a person who does wrong and esp. moral wrong — **wrong-do•ing** \-'dü-iŋ\ *n*

wrong•ful \'roŋ-fəl\ *adj* **1** : WRONG, UNJUST **2** : UNLAWFUL — **wrong•ful•ly** \-ē\ *adv* — **wrong•ful•ness** *n*

wrong-head•ed \'roŋ-'hed-əd\ *adj* : obstinately wrong : PERVERSE — **wrong-head•ed•ly** *adv* — **wrong-head•ed•ness** *n*

wrote *past of* WRITE

wroth \'roth, 'rōth\ *adj* : filled with wrath : ANGRY

wrought \'rot\ *adj* [ME, fr. pp. of *work-en* to work] **1** : FASHIONED, FORMED (carefully ∼ essays) **2** : ORNAMENTED **3** : beaten into shape by tools : HAMMERED (∼ silver dishes) **4** : deeply stirred : EXCITED (gets easily ∼ up over nothing)

wrought iron *n* : a commercial form of iron that contains less than 0.3 percent carbon and is tough, malleable, and relatively soft — **wrought–iron** *adj*

wrung *past and past part of* WRING

wry \'rī\ *adj* **wry•er** \'rī-(ə)r\ ; **wry•est** \'rī-əst\ **1** : having a bent or twisted shape (a ∼ smile) ; *esp* : turned abnormally to one side : CONTORTED (a ∼ neck) **2** : cleverly and often ironically humorous — **wry•ly** *adv* — **wry•ness** *n*

wry•neck \'rī-,nek\ *n* **1** : any of several birds related to the woodpeckers that

have a peculiar manner of twisting the head and neck **2** : a disorder marked by a twisting of the neck and head
WSW *abbr* west-southwest
wt *abbr* weight

wurst \'wərst, 'wu̇rst\ *n* : SAUSAGE
WV *or* **W Va** *abbr* West Virginia
WW *abbr* World War
w/w *abbr* wall-to-wall
WY *or* **Wyo** *abbr* Wyoming

X

¹**x** \'eks\ *n, pl* **x's** *or* **xs** \'ek-səz\ *often cap* **1** : the 24th letter of the English alphabet **2** : an unknown quantity
²**x** *vb* **x-ed** *also* **x'd** *or* **xed**; **x-ing** *or* **x'ing** : to cancel or obliterate with a series of *x*'s — usu. used with *out*
³**x** *abbr, often cap* experimental
⁴**x** *symbol* **1** times (3 x 2 is 6) **2** by (a 3 x 5 index card) **3** *often cap* power of magnification
Xan·thip·pe \zan-'t(h)ip-ē\ *or* **Xan·tip·pe** \-'tip-ē\ *n* [Gk *Xanthippē*, shrewish wife of Socrates] : an ill-tempered woman
x-ax·is \'eks-,ak-səs\ *n* : the axis of a graph or a system of coordinates in a plane parallel to which abscissas are measured
X chromosome *n* : a sex chromosome that usually occurs paired in each female cell and single in each male cell in organisms (as human beings) in which the male normally has two unlike sex chromosomes
Xe *symbol* xenon
xe·bec \'zē-,bek\ *n* : a usu. 3-masted Mediterranean sailing ship with long overhanging bow and stern
xe·non \'zē-,nän, 'zen-,än\ *n* [Gk, neut. of *xenos* strange] : a heavy gaseous chemical element occurring in minute quantities in air
xe·no·pho·bia \,zen-ə-'fō-bē-ə, ,zēn-\ *n* : fear and hatred of strangers or foreigners or of what is strange or foreign — **xe·no·phobe** \'zen-ə-,fōb, 'zēn-\ *n*
xe·ric \'zir-ik, 'zer-\ *adj* : low or deficient in moisture for the support of life
xe·rog·ra·phy \zə-'räg-rə-fē, zir-'äg-\ *n* : a process for copying printed matter by the action of light on an electrically charged surface in which the latent image usu. is developed with powders — **xe·ro·graph·ic** \,zir-ə-'graf-ik\ *adj*

xe·ro·phyte \'zir-ə-,fīt\ *n* : a plant adapted for growth with a limited water supply — **xe·ro·phyt·ic** \,zir-ə-'fit-ik\ *adj*
XL *abbr* **1** extra large **2** extra long
Xmas \'kris-məs *also* 'eks-məs\ *n* [*X* (symbol for *Christ*, fr. the Gk letter chi (X), initial of *Christos* Christ) + *-mas* (in *Christmas*)] : CHRISTMAS
Xn *abbr* Christian
Xnty *abbr* Christianity
x-ra·di·a·tion \,eks-,rād-ē-'ā-shən\ *n, often cap* **1** : exposure to X rays **2** : radiation consisting of X rays
x-ray \'eks-,rā\ *vb, often cap* : to examine, treat, or photograph with X rays
X ray \'eks-,rā\ *n* **1** : a radiation of the same nature as light rays but of extremely short wavelength that is generated by the striking of a stream of electrons against a metal surface in a vacuum and that is able to penetrate through various thicknesses of solids **2** : a photograph taken with X rays — **X-ray** *adj*
XS *abbr* extra small
xu \'sü\ *n, pl* **xu** — see *dong* at MONEY table
xy·lem \'zī-ləm, -,lem\ *n* : woody tissue of higher plants that transports water and dissolved materials upward, functions also in support and storage, and lies central to the phloem
xy·lo·phone \'zī-lə-,fōn\ *n* [Gk *xylon* wood + *phōnē* voice, sound] : a musical instrument consisting of a series of wooden bars graduated in length to produce the musical scale, supported on belts of straw or felt, and sounded by striking with two small wooden hammers — **xy·lo·phon·ist** \-,fō-nəst\ *n*

Y

¹**y** \'wī\ *n, pl* **y's** *or* **ys** \'wīz\ *often cap* : the 25th letter of the English alphabet
²**y** *abbr* **1** yard **2** year
¹**Y** \'wī\ *n* : YMCA
²**Y** *symbol* yttrium
¹**-y** *also* **-ey** \ē\ *adj suffix* **1** : characterized by : full of (dirty) (clay*ey*) **2** : having the character of : composed of (icy) **3** : like : like that of (home*y*) (wintry) (stagy) **4** : devoted to : addicted to : enthusiastic over (horsy) **5**

: tending or inclined to (sleepy) (chatty) **6** : giving occasion for (specified) action (teary) **7** : performing (specified) action (curly) **8** : somewhat : rather : -ISH (chilly) **9** : having (such) characteristics to a marked degree or in an affected or superficial way (Frenchy)
²**-y** \ē\ *n suffix, pl* **-ies 1** : state : condition : quality (beggary) **2** : activity, place of business, or goods dealt with

(laundry) **3** : whole body or group (soldiery)

³-y *n suffix, pl* **-ies** : instance of a (specified) action ⟨entreaty⟩ ⟨inquiry⟩

YA *abbr* young adult

¹yacht \'yät\ *n* [obs. D *jacht*, fr. Middle Low German *jacht*, short for *jachtschiff*, lit., hunting ship] : any of various relatively small ships used for pleasure cruising or racing

²yacht *vb* : to race or cruise in a yacht

yacht·ing \-iŋ\ *n* : the action, fact, or pastime of racing or cruising in a yacht

yachts·man \'yäts-mən\ *n* : one who owns or sails a yacht

ya·hoo \'yä-hü, 'yā-\ *n, pl* **yahoos** [fr. *Yahoo* one of a race of brutes having the form of men in Jonathan Swift's *Gulliver's Travels*] : a boorish, crass, or stupid person

Yah·weh \'yä-,wā\ *also* **Yah·veh** \-,vā\ *n* : the God of the Hebrews

¹yak \'yak\ *n, pl* **yaks** *also* **yak** : a large long-haired wild or domesticated ox of Tibet and adjacent Asian uplands

²yak *also* **yack** \'yak\ *n* : persistent or voluble talk — **yak** *also* **yack** *vb*

yam \'yam\ *n* **1** : the edible starchy root of a twining vine that largely replaces the potato as food in the tropics; *also* : a plant distantly related to the lilies that produces yams **2** : a usu. deep orange sweet potato

yam·mer \'yam-ər\ *vb* **yam·mered; yam·mer·ing** \-(ə-)riŋ\ [alter. of ME *yomeren* to murmur, be sad, fr. OE *gēomrian*] **1** : WHIMPER **2** : CHATTER — **yammer** *n*

¹yank \'yaŋk\ *n* : a strong sudden pull : JERK

²yank *vb* : to pull with a quick vigorous movement

Yank \'yaŋk\ *n* : YANKEE

Yan·kee \'yaŋ-kē\ *n* **1** : a native or inhabitant of New England; *also* : a native or inhabitant of the northern U.S. **2** : AMERICAN 2

yan·qui \'yäŋ-kē\ *n, often cap* [Sp] : a citizen of the U.S. as distinguished from a Latin American

¹yap \'yap\ *vb* **yapped; yap·ping 1** : BARK, YELP **2** : GAB

²yap *n* **1** : a quick sharp bark **2** : CHATTER

¹yard \'yärd\ *n* [ME, fr. OE *geard* enclosure, yard] **1** : a small enclosed area open to the sky and adjacent to a building **2** : the grounds of a building **3** : an enclosure for livestock **4** : an area set aside for a particular business or activity **5** : a system of railroad tracks for storing cars and making up trains

²yard *n* [ME *yarde*, fr. OE *gierd* twig, measure, yard] **1** — see WEIGHT table **2** : a long spar tapered toward the ends that supports and spreads the head of a sail

yard·age \-ij\ *n* : an aggregate number of yards; *also* : the length, extent, or volume of something as measured in yards

yard·arm \'yärd-,ärm\ *n* : either end of the yard of a square-rigged ship

yard·man \'yärd-mən, -,man\ *n* : a man employed in or about a yard

yard·mas·ter \-,mas-tər\ *n* : the person in charge of a railroad yard

yard·stick \'yärd-,stik\ *n* **1** : a graduated measuring stick three feet long **2** : a standard for making a critical judgment : CRITERION **syn** gauge, touchstone, benchmark, measure

yarn \'yärn\ *n* **1** : a continuous often plied strand composed of fibers or filaments and used in weaving and knitting to form cloth **2** : STORY; *esp* : a tall tale

yar·row \'yar-ō\ *n* : a strong-scented herb related to the daisies that has white or pink flowers in flat clusters

yaw \'yȯ\ *vb* : to deviate erratically from a course ⟨the ship ∼ed in the heavy seas⟩ — **yaw** *n*

yawl \'yȯl\ *n* : a 2-masted fore-and-aft rigged sailboat with the shorter mast aft of the rudder

¹yawn \'yȯn\ *vb* : to open wide; *esp* : to open the mouth wide usu. as an involuntary reaction to fatigue or boredom — **yawn·er** *n*

²yawn *n* : a deep usu. involuntary intake of breath through the wide-open mouth

yawp *or* **yaup** \'yȯp\ *vb* **1** : to make a raucous noise : SQUAWK **2** : CLAMOR, COMPLAIN — **yawp·er** *n*

yaws \'yȯz\ *n pl* : an infectious tropical disease caused by a spirochete closely resembling the causative agent of syphilis

y–ax·is \'wī-,ak-səs\ *n* : the axis of a graph or a system of coordinates in a plane parallel to which the ordinates are measured

Yb *symbol* ytterbium

YB *abbr* yearbook

Y chromosome *n* : a sex chromosome that is characteristic of male zygotes and cells in species in which the male typically has two unlike sex chromosomes

yd *abbr* yard

¹ye \(')yē\ *pron* YOU 1

²ye \yē, yə, *or like* the\ *definite article, archaic* : THE — used by early printers to represent the manuscript word *þe* (the)

¹yea \'yā\ *adv* **1** : YES — used in oral voting **2** : INDEED, TRULY

²yea *n* : an affirmative vote; *also* : a person casting such a vote

year \'yir\ *n* **1** : the period of about 365¼ solar days required for one revolution of the earth around the sun **2** : a cycle of 365 or 366 days beginning with January 1; *also* : a calendar year specified usu. by a number **3** *pl* : a time of special significance ⟨∼s of plenty⟩ **4** *pl* : AGE ⟨advanced in ∼s⟩ **5**

: a period of time other than a calendar year (the school ~)

year·book \-‚bùk\ *n* **1** : a book published annually esp. as a report **2** : a school publication recording the history and activities of a graduating class

year·ling \'yiər-liṅ, 'yər-lən\ *n* : one that is or is rated as a year old

year·long \'yiər-'lȯṅ\ *adj* : lasting through a year

¹year·ly \'yiər-lē\ *adj* : ANNUAL

²yearly *adv* : every year

yearn \'yərn\ *vb* **1** : to feel a longing or craving **2** : to feel tenderness or compassion **syn** long, pine, hanker, hunger, thirst

yearn·ing \-iṅ\ *n* : a tender or urgent longing

year–round \'yiər-'raȯnd\ *adj* : effective, employed, or operating for the full year : not seasonal ⟨a ~ resort⟩

yeast \'yēst\ *n* **1** : a surface froth or a sediment in sugary liquids (as fruit juices) that consists largely of cells of a tiny fungus and is used in making alcoholic liquors and as a leaven in baking **2** : a commercial product containing yeast plants in a moist or dry medium **3** : any of various usu. one-celled fungi that reproduce by budding and promote alcoholic fermentation **4** : the foam of waves : SPUME **5** : something that causes ferment or activity

yeasty \'yē-stē\ *adj* **yeast·i·er; -est 1** : of, relating to, or resembling yeast **2** : UNSETTLED **3** : full of vitality; *also* : FRIVOLOUS

yegg \'yeg\ *n* : one that breaks open safes to steal; *also* : ROBBER

¹yell \'yel\ *vb* : to utter a loud cry or scream : SHOUT

²yell *n* **1** : SHOUT **2** : a cheer used esp. to encourage an athletic team (as at a college)

¹yel·low \'yel-ō\ *adj* **1** : of the color yellow **2** : having a yellow complexion or skin **3** : SENSATIONAL ⟨~ journalism⟩ **4** : COWARDLY — **yel·low·ish** \'yel-ə-wish\ *adj*

²yellow *n* **1** : a color between green and orange in the spectrum : the color of ripe lemons or sunflowers **2** : something yellow; *esp* : the yolk of an egg **3** *pl* : any of several plant virus diseases marked by stunted growth and yellowing of foliage

³yellow *vb* : to make or turn yellow

yellow birch *n* : a No. American birch with thin lustrous gray or yellow bark; *also* : its strong hard pale wood

yellow fever *n* : an acute destructive virus disease marked by prostration, jaundice, fever, and often hemorrhage and transmitted by a mosquito

yellow jack *n* : YELLOW FEVER

yellow jacket *n* : any of various small social wasps having the body barred with bright yellow

yelp \'yelp\ *vb* [ME *yelpen* to boast, cry out, fr. OE *gielpan* to boast, exult] : to utter a sharp quick shrill cry — **yelp** *n*

yen \'yen\ *n, pl* **yen** — see MONEY table

²yen *n* [obs. E slang *yen-yen* craving for opium, fr. Chin *in-yan,* fr. *in* opium + *yan* craving] : a strong desire : LONGING

yeo·man \'yō-mən\ *n* **1** : an attendant or officer in a royal or noble household **2** : a naval petty officer who performs clerical duties **3** : a small farmer who cultivates his own land; *esp* : one of a class of English freeholders below the gentry

yeo·man·ry \'yō-mən-rē\ *n* : the body of yeomen and esp. of small landed proprietors

-yer — see -ER

yer·ba ma·té \‚yer-bə-'mä-‚tā\ *n* : MATÉ

¹yes \'yes\ *adv* — used as a function word esp. to express assent or agreement or to introduce a more emphatic or explicit phrase

²yes *n* : an affirmative reply

ye·shi·va *or* **ye·shi·vah** \yə-'shē-və\ *n, pl* **yeshivas** *or* **ye·shi·voth** \-‚shē-'vōt(h)\ : a Jewish school esp. for religious instruction

yes–man \'yes-‚man\ *n* : a person who endorses uncritically every opinion or proposal of a superior

¹yes·ter·day \'yes-tərd-ē\ *adv* **1** : on the day preceding today **2** : only a short time ago

²yesterday *n* **1** : the day last past **2** : time not long past

yes·ter·year \'yes-tər-‚yiər\ *n* **1** : last year **2** : the recent past

yet \(')yet\ *adv* **1** : in addition : BESIDES; *also* : EVEN **2** : up to now; *also* : STILL **3** : so soon as now ⟨not time to go ~⟩ **4** : EVENTUALLY **5** : NEVERTHELESS, HOWEVER

²yet *conj* : despite the fact that : BUT

ye·ti \'yet-ē, 'yät-\ *n* [Tibetan] : ABOMINABLE SNOWMAN

yew \'yü\ *n* **1** : any of a genus of evergreen trees or shrubs with dark stiff poisonous needles and fleshy fruits **2** : the fine-grained wood of a yew; *esp* : that of an Old World yew

Yid·dish \'yid-ish\ *n* [Yiddish *yidish,* short for *yidish daytsh,* lit., Jewish German] : a language derived from German and spoken by Jews esp. of eastern Europe — **Yiddish** *adj*

¹yield \'yēld\ *vb* **1** : to give as fitting, owed, or required **2** : GIVE UP; *esp* : to give up possession of on claim or demand **3** : to bear as a natural product **4** : PRODUCE, SUPPLY **5** : to bring in : RETURN **6** : to give way (as to force or influence) **7** : to give place **syn** relinquish, cede, waive, surrender

²yield *n* : something yielded; *esp* : the amount or quantity produced or returned

yield·ing \'yēl-diṅ\ *adj* **1** : not rigid or stiff : FLEXIBLE **2** : SUBMISSIVE, COMPLIANT

YMCA \,wī-,em-(,)sē-'ā\ *n* : Young Men's Christian Association

YMHA \,wī-,em-,ā-'chā\ *n* : Young Men's Hebrew Association

YOB *abbr* year of birth

yo·del \'yōd-∍l\ *vb* **yo·deled** *or* **yo·delled;** **yo·del·ing** *or* **yo·del·ling** \'yōd-(∍-)liŋ\ : to sing by suddenly changing from chest voice to falsetto and the reverse; *also* : to shout or call in this manner — **yodel** *n* — **yo·del·er** \'yōd-(∍-)l∍r\ *n*

yo·ga \'yō-gə\ *n* [Skt., lit., yoking, fr. *yunakti* he yokes] **1** *cap* : a Hindu theistic philosophy teaching the suppression of all activity of body, mind, and will in order that the self may realize its distinction from them and attain liberation **2** : a system of exercises for attaining bodily or mental control and well-being

yo·gi \'yō-gē\ *also* **yo·gin** \-gən, -,gin\ *n* **1** : a person who practices yoga **2** *cap* : an adherent of Yoga philosophy

yo·gurt *also* **yo·ghurt** \'yō-gərt\ *n* [Turk] : a soured slightly acid often flavored semisolid milk food made of skimmed cow's milk and milk solids to which cultures of bacteria have been added

¹yoke \'yōk\ *n, pl* **yokes 1** : a wooden bar or frame by which two draft animals (as oxen) are coupled at the heads or necks for working together; *also* : a frame fitted to a person's shoulders to carry a load in two equal portions **2** : a clamp that embraces two parts to hold or unite them in position **3** *pl usu* **yoke** : two animals yoked together **4** : SERVITUDE, BONDAGE **5** : TIE, LINK (the ~ of matrimony) **6** : a fitted or shaped piece esp. at the shoulder of a garment **syn** couple, pair, brace

²yoke *vb* **yoked; yok·ing 1** : to put a yoke on : couple with a yoke **2** : to attach a draft animal to (~ a plow) **3** : JOIN; *esp* : MARRY

yo·kel \'yō-kəl\ *n* : BUMPKIN

yolk \'yō(l)k\ *n* **1** : the yellow rounded inner mass of the egg of a bird or reptile **2** : the stored food material of an egg consisting chiefly of proteins, lecithin, and cholesterol — **yolked** \'yō(l)kt\ *adj*

Yom Kip·pur \,yōm-ki-'pûr, ,yäm-, -'kip-∍r\ *n* [Heb *yōm kippūr*, fr. *yōm* day + *kippūr* atonement] : a Jewish holiday observed in September or October with fasting and prayer as a day of atonement

¹yon \'yän\ *adj* : YONDER

²yon *adv* **1** : YONDER **2** : THITHER (ran hither and ~)

¹yon·der \'yän-dər\ *adv* : at or to that place

²yonder *adj* **1** : more distant (the ~ side of the river) **2** : being at a distance within view (~ hills)

yore \'yōr\ *n* [ME, fr. *yore,* adv., long ago, fr. OE *geāra,* fr. *gēar* year] : time long past (in days of ~)

you \(')yü, yə\ *pron* **1** : the person or persons addressed (~ are a nice person) (~ are nice people) **2** : ONE 2 (~ turn this knob to open it)

¹young \'yəŋ\ *adj* **youn·ger** \'yəŋ-gər\ ; **youn·gest** \'yəŋ-gəst\ **1** : being in the first or an early stage of life, growth, or development **2** : having little experience **3** : recently come into being **4** : YOUTHFUL **5** *cap* : belonging to or representing a new or revived usu. political group or movement — **young·ish** \'yəŋ-ish\ *adj*

²young *n, pl* **young** : young persons or lower animals

young·ling \'yəŋ-liŋ\ *n* : one that is young — **youngling** *adj*

young·ster \-stər\ *n* **1** : a young person **2** : CHILD

your \yər, (')yûr, (')yōr\ *adj* : of or relating to you or yourself

yours \'yürz, 'yōrz\ *pron* : one or the ones belonging to you

your·self \yər-'self\ *pron, pl* **yourselves** \-'selvz\ : YOU — used reflexively, for emphasis, or in absolute constructions (you'll hurt ~) (do it ~) (~ a man, you should understand)

youth \'yüth\ *n, pl* **youths** \'yüthz, 'yüths\ **1** : the period of life between childhood and maturity **2** : a young man; *also* : young persons **3** : YOUTHFULNESS

youth·ful \'yüth-fəl\ *adj* **1** : of, relating to, or appropriate to youth **2** : being young and not yet mature **3** : FRESH, VIGOROUS — **youth·ful·ly** \-ē\ *adv* — **youth·ful·ness** *n*

youth hostel *n* : HOSTEL 2

yowl \'yaül\ *vb* : to utter a loud long mournful cry : WAIL — **yowl** *n*

yo-yo \'yō-(,)yō\ *n, pl* **yo-yos** : a thick grooved double disk with a string attached to its center which is made to fall and rise to the hand by unwinding and rewinding on the string

yr *abbr* **1** year **2** your

yrbk *abbr* yearbook

YT *abbr* Yukon Territory

yt·ter·bi·um \i-'tər-bē-əm\ *n* : a rare metallic chemical element

yt·tri·um \'i-trē-əm\ *n* : a rare metallic chemical element

yu·an \'yü-ən, yü-'än\ *n, pl* **yuan 1** : see MONEY table **2** : the dollar of the Republic of China (Taiwan)

yuc·ca \'yək-ə\ *n* : any of a genus of plants related to the lilies that grow in dry regions and have white cup-shaped flowers in erect clusters; *also* : the flower of this plant

yuck \'yək\ *interj* — used to express rejection or disgust

Yu·go·slav \,yü-gō-'släv, -'slav\ *n* : a native or inhabitant of Yugoslavia — **Yugoslav** *adj* — **Yu·go·sla·vi·an** \-'släv-ē-ən\ *adj or n*

yule \'yül\ *n, often cap* : CHRISTMAS

Yule log *n* : a large log formerly put on the hearth on Christmas Eve as the foundation of the fire

yule·tide \\'yül-ˌtīd\ *n, often cap* : CHRISTMASTIDE

yum·my \\'yəm-ē\ *adj* **yum·mi·er; -est** : highly attractive or pleasing

yup·pie \\'yəp-ē\ *n* [*young urban professional* + *-ie* (as in hipp*ie*)] : a young college-educated adult employed in a well-paying profession and living and working in or near a large city

yurt \\'yu̇rt\ *n* : a light round tent of skins or felt stretched over a lattice framework used by various nomadic tribes in Siberia, U.S.S.R.

YWCA \ˌwī-ˌdəb-əl-yü-(ˌ)sē-'ā\ *n* : Young Women's Christian Association

YWHA \-ˌā-'chā\ *n* : Young Women's Hebrew Association

Z

¹**z** \\'zē\ *n, pl* **z's** *or* **zs** *often cap* : the 26th letter of the English alphabet

²**z** *abbr* **1** zero **2** zone

Z *symbol* atomic number

Zach *abbr* Zacharias

Zach·a·ri·as \ˌzak-ə-'rī-əs\ *n* — see BIBLE table

zaire \zä-'ir, 'zīr\ *n, pl* **zaires** *or* **zaire** — see MONEY table

Zair·ian \zä-'ir-ē-ən\ *n* : a native or inhabitant of Zaire — **Zairian** *adj*

Zam·bi·an \\'zam-bē-ən\ *n* : a native or inhabitant of Zambia — **Zambian** *adj*

¹**za·ny** \\'zā-nē\ *n, pl* **zanies** [It *zanni*, a traditional masked clown, fr. It (dial.) *Zanni*, nickname for *Giovanni* John] **1** : CLOWN, BUFFOON **2** : a silly or foolish person

²**zany** *adj* **za·ni·er; -est 1** : characteristic of a zany **2** : CRAZY, FOOLISH — **za·ni·ly** \\'zā-nə-lē, 'zān-ᵊl-ē\ *adv* — **za·ni·ness** \\'zā-nē-nəs\ *n*

zap \\'zap\ *vb* **zapped; zap·ping** : DESTROY, KILL

zeal \\'zēl\ *n* : eager and ardent interest in the pursuit of something : FERVOR *syn* enthusiasm, passion, ardor

zeal·ot \\'zel-ət\ *n* : a zealous person; *esp* : a fanatical partisan *syn* enthusiast, bigot, fanatic

zeal·ous \\'zel-əs\ *adj* : filled with, characterized by, or due to zeal — **zeal·ous·ly** *adv* — **zeal·ous·ness** *n*

ze·bra \\'zē-brə\ *n, pl* **zebras** *also* **zebra** : any of several African mammals related to the horse but conspicuously striped with black or brown and white or buff

ze·bu \\'zē-b(y)ü\ *n* : an Asian domesticated ox that differs from European cattle with which it crosses freely by a large fleshy hump over the shoulders and a loose skin with hanging folds

Zech *abbr* Zechariah

Zech·a·ri·ah \ˌzek-ə-'rī-ə\ *n* — see BIBLE table

zed \\'zed\ *n, chiefly Brit* : the letter *z*

zeit·geist \\'tsīt-ˌgīst, 'zīt-\ *n* [G, fr. *zeit* time + *geist* spirit] : the general intellectual, moral, and cultural state of an era

Zen \\'zen\ *n* : a Japanese Buddhist sect that teaches self-discipline, meditation, and attainment of enlightenment through direct intuitive insight

ze·na·na \zə-'nän-ə\ *n* : HAREM, SERAGLIO

ze·nith \\'zē-nəth\ *n* **1** : the point in the heavens directly overhead **2** : the highest point : ACME *syn* culmination, pinnacle, apex

ze·o·lite \\'zē-ə-ˌlīt\ *n* : any of various feldsparlike silicates used as water softeners

Zeph *abbr* Zephaniah

Zeph·a·ni·ah \ˌzef-ə-'nī-ə\ *n* — see BIBLE table

zeph·yr \\'zef-ər\ *n* **1** : a breeze from the west; *also* : a gentle breeze **2** : any of various lightweight fabrics and articles of clothing

zep·pe·lin \\'zep-(ə-)lən\ *n* [after Count Ferdinand von *Zeppelin* †1917 Ger. airship manufacturer] : a rigid airship consisting of a cylindrical trussed and covered frame

¹**ze·ro** \\'zē-rō\ *n, pl* **zeros** *also* **zeroes** [deriv. of Ar *ṣifr*] **1** : the numerical symbol 0 **2** : the number represented by the symbol 0 **3** : the point at which the graduated degrees or measurements on a scale (as of a thermometer) begin **4** : the lowest point

²**zero** *adj* **1** : of, relating to, or being a zero **2** : having no magnitude or quantity **3** : ABSENT, LACKING; *esp* : having no modified inflectional form

³**zero** *vb* : TRAIN ⟨∼ in artillery on the crossroads⟩

zero hour *n* : the time at which an event (as a military operation) is scheduled to begin

zest \\'zest\ *n* **1** : a quality of enhancing enjoyment : PIQUANCY **2** : keen enjoyment : RELISH, GUSTO — **zest·ful** \-fəl\ *adj* — **zest·ful·ly** \-ē-\ *adv* — **zest·ful·ness** *n*

¹**zig·zag** \\'zig-ˌzag\ *n* : one of a series of short sharp turns, angles, or alterations in a course; *also* : something marked by such a series

²**zigzag** *adv* : in or by a zigzag path

³**zigzag** *adj* : having short sharp turns or angles

⁴**zigzag** *vb* **zig·zagged; zig·zag·ging** : to form into or proceed along a zigzag

zil·lion \\'zil-yən\ *n* : a large indeterminate number

Zim·ba·bwe·an \zim-'bäb-wē-ən\ *n* : a

native or inhabitant of Zimbabwe —
Zimbabwean *adj*

zinc \\'ziŋk\\ *n* : a bluish white crystalline metallic chemical element that is
commonly found in minerals and is
used esp. as a protective coating for
iron and steel

zinc ointment *n* : ZINC OXIDE OINTMENT

zinc oxide *n* : a white solid used as a
pigment, in compounding rubber, and
in ointments

zinc oxide ointment *n* : an ointment containing 20 percent of zinc oxide and
used for skin disorders

zing \\'ziŋ\\ *n* **1** : a shrill humming noise
2 : VITALITY — **zing** *vb*

zing·er \\'ziŋ-ər\\ *n* **1** : a pointed witty
remark or retort **2** : something causing or meant to cause interest, surprise, or shock

zin·nia \\'zin-ē-ə, 'zēn-yə\\ *n* : any of a
small genus of tropical American
herbs related to the daisies and widely
grown for their showy long-lasting
flower heads

Zi·on \\'zī-ən\\ *n* **1** : the Jewish people **2**
: the Jewish homeland as a symbol of
Judaism or of Jewish national aspiration **3** : HEAVEN **4** : UTOPIA

Zi·on·ism \\'zī-ə-,niz-əm\\ *n* : an international movement orig. for the establishment of a Jewish national or religious community in Palestine and
later for the support of modern Israel
— **Zi·on·ist** \\-nəst\\ *adj or n*

¹zip \\'zip\\ *vb* **zipped; zip·ping** : to move
or act with speed or vigor

²zip *n* **1** : a sudden sharp hissing sound
2 : ENERGY, VIM

³zip *vb* **zipped; zip·ping** : to close or
open with a zipper

zip code *n, often cap Z&I&P* [zone
improvement plan] : a 5-digit number
that identifies each postal delivery
area in the U.S.

zip·per \\'zip-ər\\ *n* : a fastener consisting of two rows of metal or plastic
teeth on strips of tape and a sliding
piece that closes an opening by drawing the teeth together

zip·py \\'zip-ē\\ *adj* **zip·pi·er; -est** : BRISK,
SNAPPY

zir·con \\'zər-,kän\\ *n* : a zirconium-con-
taining mineral several transparent
varieties of which are used as gems

zir·co·ni·um \\,zər-'kō-nē-əm\\ *n* : a cor-
rosion-resistant metallic element with
a high melting point that occurs widely in combination and is used in alloys
and ceramics

zith·er \\'zith-ər, 'zith-\\ *n* : a musical instrument having 30 to 40 strings
played with plectrum and fingers

zi·ti \\'zēt-ē\\ *n, pl* **ziti** [It] : tubular pasta
of medium size

zlo·ty \\'zlȯt-ē\\ *n, pl* **zlo·tys** \\-ēz\\ *or* **zloty**
— see MONEY table

Zn *symbol* zinc

zo·di·ac \\'zōd-ē-,ak\\ *n* [ME, fr. MF *zo-
diaque*, fr. L *zodiacus*, fr. Gk
zōidiakos, fr. *zōidion* carved figure,

sign of the zodiac, fr. dim. of *zōion*
living being, figure] **1** : an imaginary
belt in the heavens that encompasses
the paths of most of the planets and
that is divided into 12 constellations
or signs **2** : a figure representing the
signs of the zodiac and their symbols
— **zo·di·a·cal** \\zō-'dī-ə-kəl\\ *adj*

zom·bi *also* **zom·bie** \\'zäm-bē\\ *n* **1** : the
voodoo snake deity **2** : the supernatu-
ral power held in voodoo belief to enter into and reanimate a dead body

zon·al \\'zōn-ᵊl\\ *adj* : of, relating to, or
having the form of a zone — **zon·al·ly**
\\-ē\\ *adv*

¹zone \\'zōn\\ *n* [L *zona* belt, zone, fr. Gk
zōnē] **1** : any of five great divisions of
the earth's surface made according to
latitude and temperature and including the torrid zone about the equator,
the two temperate zones lying between the torrid zone and the polar
circles, and the two frigid zones lying
between the polar circles and the
poles **2** *archaic* : GIRDLE, BELT **3** : an
encircling band or girdle ⟨a ∼ of trees⟩
4 : an area or region set off or distinguished in some way from adjoining
parts

²zone *vb* **zoned; zon·ing 1** : ENCIRCLE **2**
: to arrange in or mark off into zones;
esp : to divide (as a city) into sections
reserved for different purposes — **zo-
na·tion** \\zō-'nā-shən\\ *n*

zonked \\'zäŋkt\\ *adj* : being or acting as
if under the influence of alcohol or a
drug : HIGH

zoo \\'zü\\ *n, pl* **zoos** : a zoological garden or collection of living animals
usu. for public display

zoo·ge·og·ra·phy \\,zō-ə-jē-'äg-rə-fē\\ *n*
: a branch of biogeography concerned
with the geographical distribution of
animals — **zoo·ge·og·ra·pher** \\-fər\\ *n*
— **zoo·geo·graph·ic** \\-,jē-ə-'graf-ik\\
also **zoo·geo·graph·i·cal** \\-i-kəl\\ *adj*

zoo·keep·er \\'zü-,kē-pər\\ *n* : a person
who keeps or cares for animals in a
zoo

zool *abbr* zoological; zoology

zoological garden *n* : a garden or park
where wild animals are kept for exhibition

zo·ol·o·gy \\zō-'äl-ə-jē\\ *n* : a branch of
biology that deals with animals and
the animal kingdom — **zo·o·log·i·cal**
\\,zō-ə-'läj-i-kəl\\ *adj* — **zo·ol·o·gist** \\zō-
'äl-ə-jəst\\ *n*

zoom \\'züm\\ *vb* **1** : to move with a loud
hum or buzz **2** : to gain altitude quickly **3** : to focus a camera or microscope
using a special lens that permits the
apparent distance of the object to be
varied — **zoom** *n*

zoom lens *n* : a camera lens in which the
image size can be varied continuously
while the image remains in focus

zoo·mor·phic \\,zō-ə-'mȯr-fik\\ *adj* **1**
: having the form of an animal **2** : of,
relating to, or being the representa-

tion of a deity in the form or with the attributes of an animal

zoo·plank·ton \ˌzō-ə-ˈplaŋk-tən, -ˌtän\ *n* : animal life of the plankton

zoo·spore \ˈzō-ə-ˌspȯr\ *n* : a motile spore

zoot suit \ˈzüt-\ *n* : a flashy suit of extreme cut typically consisting of a thigh-length jacket with wide padded shoulders and trousers that are wide at the top and narrow at the bottom — **zoot-suit·er** \-ˌsüt-ər\ *n*

Zo·ro·as·tri·an·ism \ˌzȯr-ə-ˈwas-trē-ə-ˌniz-əm\ *n* : a religion founded by the Persian prophet Zoroaster — **Zo·ro·as·tri·an** \-trē-ən\ *adj or n*

Zou·ave \zü-ˈäv\ *n* : a member of a French infantry unit orig. composed of Algerians wearing a brilliant uniform and conducting a quick spirited drill; *also* : a member of a military unit modeled on the Zouaves

zounds \ˈzaún(d)z\ *interj* [euphemism for *God's wounds*] — used as a mild oath

zoy·sia \ˈzȯi-shə, -zhə, -sē-ə, -zē-ə\ *n* : any of a genus of creeping perennial grasses having fine wiry leaves and including some used as lawn grasses

ZPG *abbr* zero population growth

Zr *symbol* zirconium

zuc·chet·to \zü-ˈket-ō, tsü-\ *n, pl* -**tos** [It] : a small round skullcap worn by Roman Catholic ecclesiastics

zuc·chi·ni \zü-ˈkē-nē\ *n, pl* -**ni** *or* -**nis** [It] : a summer squash of bushy growth with smooth cylindrical dark green fruits; *also* : its fruit

Zu·lu \ˈzü-ˌlü\ *n, pl* Zulu *or* Zulus : a member of a Bantu-speaking people of South Africa; *also* : a Bantu language of the Zulus

Zu·ni \ˈzü-nē\ *or* **Zu·ñi** \-nyē\ *n, pl* Zuni *or* Zunis *or* Zuñi *or* Zuñis : a member of an American Indian people of northeastern Arizona; *also* : the language of the Zuni people

zwie·back \ˈswē-bak, ˈswī-, ˈzwē-, ˈzwī-\ *n* [G, lit., twice baked, fr. *zwie-* twice + *backen* to bake] : a usu. sweetened bread that is baked and then sliced and toasted until dry and crisp

Zwing·li·an \ˈzwiŋ-(g)lē-ən, ˈswiŋ-\ *adj* : of or relating to the Swiss religious reformer Ulrich Zwingli or his teachings — **Zwinglian** *n*

zy·gote \ˈzī-ˌgōt\ *n* : a cell formed by the union of two sexual cells; *also* : the developing individual produced from such a cell — **zy·got·ic** \zī-ˈgät-ik\ *adj*

Foreign Words and Phrases

ab·eunt stu·dia in mo·res \ˈäb-e-ˌu̇nt-ˈstüd-ē-ˌä-ˌin-ˈmō-ˌrās\ [L] : practices zealously pursued pass into habits

à bien·tôt \à-byaⁿ-tō\ [F] : so long : farewell

ab in·cu·na·bu·lis \ˌäb-ˌiŋ-kə-ˈnäb-ə-ˌlēs\ [L] : from the cradle : from infancy

à bon chat, bon rat \à-bōⁿ-ˈshà-bōⁿ-ˈrá\ [F] : to a good cat, a good rat : retaliation in kind

à bouche ou·verte \à-bü-shü-vert\ [F] : with open mouth : eagerly : uncritically

ab ovo us·que ad ma·la \äb-ˈō-vō-ˌu̇s-kwe-ˌäd-ˈmäl-ä\ [L] : from egg to apples : from soup to nuts : from beginning to end

à bras ou·verts \à-brà-zü-ver\ [F] : with open arms : cordially

ab·sit in·vi·dia \ˈäb-ˌsit-in-ˈwid-ē-ˌä\ [L] : let there be no envy or ill will

ab uno dis·ce om·nes \äb-ˈü-nō-ˌdis-ke-ˈóm-ˌnäs\ [L] : from one learn to know all

ab ur·be con·di·ta \äb-ˈu̇r-be-ˈkòn-də-ˌtä\ [L] : from the founding of the city (Rome, founded 753 B.C.) — used by the Romans in reckoning dates

ab·usus non tol·lit usum \ˈäb-ˌü-səs-ˌnōn-ˌtò-lət-ˈü-səm\ [L] : abuse does not take away use, i.e., is not an argument against proper use

à compte \à-kōⁿt\ [F] : on account

à coup sûr \à-kü-sŒr\ [F] : with sure stroke : surely

acte gra·tuit \àk-tə-grà-twē\ [F] : gratuitous impulsive act

ad ar·bi·tri·um \ˌad-är-ˈbit-rē-əm\ [L] : at will : arbitrarily

ad as·tra per as·pe·ra \ˌad-ˈas-trə-pər-ˈas-pə-rə\ [L] : to the stars by hard ways — motto of Kansas

ad ex·tre·mum \ˌad-ik-ˈstrē-məm\ [L] : to the extreme : at last

ad ka·len·das Grae·cas \ˌäd-kə-ˈlen-dəs-ˈgrī-ˌkäs\ [L] : at the Greek calends : never (since the Greeks had no calends)

ad ma·jo·rem Dei glo·ri·am \äd-mä-ˈyōr-ˌem-ˈde-ˌē-ˈglòr-ē-ˌäm\ [L] : to the greater glory of God — motto of the Society of Jesus

ad pa·tres \äd-ˈpä-ˌträs\ [L] : (gathered) to his fathers : deceased

à droite \à-drwät\ [F] : to or on the right hand

ad un·guem \äd-ˈu̇ŋ-ˌgwem\ [L] : to the fingernail : to a nicety : exactly (from the use of the fingernail to test the smoothness of marble)

ad utrum·que pa·ra·tus \ˌäd-ü-ˈtrüm-**

ad vi·vum \äd-ˈwē-ˌwu̇m\ [L] : to the life

ae·gri som·nia \ˈī-grē-ˈsòm-nē-ˌä\ [L] : a sick man's dreams

ae·quam ser·va·re men·tem \ˈī-ˌkwäm-sər-ˌwä-rē-ˈmen-ˌtem\ [L] : to preserve a calm mind

ae·quo ani·mo \ˈī-ˌkwō-ˈän-ə-ˌmō\ [L] : with even mind : calmly

ae·re per·en·ni·us \ˈī-rā-pə-ˈren-ē-ˌu̇s\ [L] : more lasting than bronze

à gauche \à-gōsh\ [F] : to or on the left hand

age quod agis \ˈäg-e-ˌkwòd-ˈäg-is\ [L] : do what you are doing : to the business at hand

à grands frais \à-gräⁿ-fre\ [F] : at great expense

à huis clos \à-wᵊē-klō\ [F] : with closed doors

aide-toi, le ciel t'ai·dera \ed-twà-là-ˈsyel-te-drá\ [F] : help yourself (and) heaven will help you

ai·né \e-nā\ [F] : elder : senior (masc.)

ai·née \e-nā\ [F] : elder : senior (fem.)

à l'aban·don \à-là-bäⁿ-dōⁿ\ [F] : carelessly : in disorder

à la belle étoile \à-là-bel-ā-twàl\ [F] : under the beautiful star : in the open air at night

à la bonne heure \à-là-bò-nœr\ [F] : at a good time : well and good : all right

à la fran·çaise \à-là-fräⁿ-sez\ [F] : in the French style

à l'an·glaise \à-läⁿ-glez\ [F] : in the English style

alea jac·ta est \ˈäl-ē-ˌä-ˌyäk-tə-ˈest\ [L] : the die is cast

à l'im·pro·viste \à-laⁿ-prò-vēst\ [F] : unexpectedly

ali·quan·do bo·nus dor·mi·tat Ho·me·rus \ˌäl-i-ˌkwän-dō-ˈbò-nəs-dòr-ˈmē-ˌtät-hō-ˈmer-əs\ [L] : sometimes (even) good Homer nods

alis vo·lat pro·pri·is \ˈäl-ˌēs-ˈwò-ˌlät-ˈprō-prē-ˌēs\ [L] : she flies with her own wings — motto of Oregon

al·ki \ˈal-ˌkī\ [Chinook Jargon] : by and by — motto of Washington

alo·ha oe \ä-ˌlō-hä-ˈói, -ˈō-ē\ [Hawaiian] : love to you : greetings : farewell

al·ter idem \ˌòl-tər-ˈī-ˌdem, ˌäl-tər-ˈē-\ [L] : second self

a max·i·mis ad mi·ni·ma \ä-ˈmäk-sə-ˌmēs-ˌäd-ˈmin-ə-ˌmä\ [L] : from the greatest to the least

ami·cus hu·ma·ni ge·ne·ris \ä-ˈmē-kəs-hü-ˌmän-ē-ˈgen-ə-rəs\ [L] : friend of the human race

ami·cus us·que ad aras \-ˌu̇s-kwe-**

-äd-'är-₁äs\ [L] : a friend as far as to the altars, i.e., except in what is contrary to one's religion; *also* : a friend to the last extremity

ami de cour \à-₁mēd-ə-'kùr\ [F] : court friend : insincere friend

amor pa·tri·ae \₁äm-₁ór-'pä-trē-₁ī\ [L] : love of one's country

amor vin·cit om·nia \'ä-₁mór-₁wiŋ-kət-'óm-nē-ə\ [L] : love conquers all things

an·cienne no·blesse \äⁿ-syen-ṇó-bles\ [F] : old-time nobility : the French nobility before the Revolution of 1789

an·guis in her·ba \₁äŋ-gwis-in-'her-₁bä\ [L] : snake in the grass

ani·mal bi·pes im·plu·me \'än-i-₁mäl-₁bip-₁äs-im-'plü-mē\ [L] : two-legged animal without feathers (i.e., man)

ani·mis opi·bus·que pa·ra·ti \'än-ə-₁mēs-₁ó-pi-'bùs-kwe-pə-'rät-ē\ [L] : prepared in mind and resources — one of the mottoes of South Carolina

an·no ae·ta·tis su·ae \'än-ō-ī-₁tät-is-'sü-₁ī\ [L] : in the (specified) year of his (or her) age

an·no mun·di \₁än-ō-'mùn-dē\ [L] : in the year of the world — used in reckoning dates from the supposed period of the creation of the world, esp. as fixed by James Ussher at 4004 B.C. or by the Jews at 3761 B.C.

an·no ur·bis con·di·tae \₁än-ō-₁ùr-bis-'kón-də-₁tī\ [L] : in the year of the founded city (Rome, founded 753 B.C.)

an·nu·it coep·tis \₁än-ə-₁wit-'kóip-₁tēs\ [L] : He (God) has smiled on our undertakings — motto on the reverse of the Great Seal of the United States

à peu près \à-pœ-pre\ [F] : nearly : approximately

à pied \à-pyä\ [F] : on foot

après moi le déluge \à-pre-mwà-lə-dā-lēzh\ [F] : after me the deluge (attributed to Louis XV)

à pro·pos de bottes \à-prə-pōd-ə-bót\ [F] : apropos of boots — used to change the subject

à pro·pos de rien \-ryaⁿ\ [F] : apropos of nothing

aqua et ig·ni in·ter·dic·tus \₁äk-wä-et-'ig-nē-₁int-ər-'dik-təs\ [L] : forbidden to be furnished with water and fire : outlawed

Ar·ca·des am·bo \₁är-kə-₁des-'äm-bō\ [L] : both Arcadians : two persons of like occupations or tastes; *also* : two rascals

ar·rec·tis au·ri·bus \ä-'rek-₁tēs-'aù-ri-₁bùs\ [L] : with ears pricked up : attentively

ar·ri·ve·der·ci \ä-₁rē-ve-'der-chē\ [It] : till we meet again : farewell

ars est ce·la·re ar·tem \₁ärs-₁est-kā-₁lär-ē-'är-₁tem\ [L] : it is (true) art to conceal art

ars lon·ga, vi·ta bre·vis \ärs-'lóŋ-gä-₁wē-₁tä-'bre-wis\ [L] : art is long, life is short

a ter·go \ä-'ter-(₁)gō\ [L] : from behind

à tort et à tra·vers \à-₁tòr-ā-à-trà-ver\ [F] : wrong and crosswise : at random : without rhyme or reason

au bout de son la·tin \ō-büd-(ə-)sōⁿ-là-taⁿ\ [F] : at the end of one's Latin : at the end of one's mental resources

au con·traire \ō-kōⁿ-trer\ [F] : on the contrary

au·de·mus ju·ra nos·tra de·fen·de·re \aù-'dā-məs-₁yúr-ə-'nó-strə-dā-'fen-də-rä\ [L] : we dare defend our rights — motto of Alabama

au·den·tes for·tu·na ju·vat \aù-'den-₁tās-fòr-₁tü-nə-'yü-₁wät\ [L] : fortune favors the bold

au·di al·ter·am par·tem \'aù-₁dē-₁äl-tə-₁räm-'pär-₁tem\ [L] : hear the other side

au fait \ō-'fet, -fe\ [F] : to the point : fully competent : fully informed : socially correct

au fond \ō-fōⁿ\ [F] : at bottom : fundamentally

au grand sé·rieux \ō-gräⁿ-sä-ryœ\ [F] : in all seriousness

au pays des aveugles les borgnes sont rois \ō-pā-ē-dä-zà-vœgl⁹-lā-bòrnʸ-ə-sōⁿ-rwä\ [F] : in the country of the blind the one-eyed men are kings

au pied de la lettre \ō-pyäd-là-letr⁹\ [F] : literally

au·rea me·di·o·cri·tas \'aù-rē-ə-₁med-ē-'ó-krə-₁täs\ [L] : the golden mean

au reste \ō-rest\ [F] : for the rest : besides

aus·si·tôt dit, aus·si·tôt fait \ō-sē-tō-dē ō-sē-tō-fe\ [F] : no sooner said than done

aut Cae·sar aut ni·hil \aùt-'kī-sär-₁aùt-'ni-₁hil\ [L] : either a Caesar or nothing

aut Caesar aut nul·lus \-'nùl-əs\ [L] : either a Caesar or a nobody

au·tres temps, au·tres moeurs \ō-trə-täⁿ ō-trə-mœrs\ [F] : other times, other customs

aut vin·ce·re aut mo·ri \aùt-'wiŋ-kə-rē-₁aùt-'mò-₁rē\ [L] : either to conquer or to die

aux armes \ō-zàrm\ [F] : to arms

ave at·que va·le \'ä-₁wā-₁ät-kwe-'wä-lä\ [L] : hail and farewell

à vo·tre san·té \à-vòt-sⁿ-tā, -vó-trə-\ [F] : to your health — used as a toast

beaux yeux \bō-zyœ\ [F] : beautiful eyes : beauty of face

bien en·ten·du \byaⁿ-näⁿ-täⁿ-dœ\ [F] : well understood : of course

bien-pen·sant \byaⁿ-päⁿ-säⁿ\ [F] : right-minded : one who holds orthodox views

bien·sé·ance \byaⁿ-sä-äⁿs\ [F] : propriety

bis dat qui ci·to dat \₁bis-₁dät-kwē-'ki-tō-₁dät\ [L] : he gives twice who gives promptly

bon ap·pé·tit \bò-nà-pā-tē\ [F] : good appetite : enjoy your meal

bon gré, mal gré \'bōⁿ-₁grā-'mál-₁grā\ [F] : whether with good grace or bad : willy-nilly

bo·nis avi·bus \ˌbȯ-ˌnēs-ˈä-wi-ˌbu̇s\ [L] : under good auspices

bon jour \bōⁿ-zhür\ [F] : good day : good morning

bonne foi \bȯn-fwä\ [F] : good faith

bon soir \bōⁿ-swär\ [F] : good evening

bru·tum ful·men \ˌbrüt-əm-ˈfu̇l-men\ [L] : insensible thunderbolt : a futile threat or display of force

buon gior·no \bwȯn-ˈjȯr-nō\ [It] : good day

ca·dit quae·stio \ˌkäd-ət-ˈkwī-stē-ˌō\ [L] : the question drops : the argument collapses

cau·sa si·ne qua non \ˈkau̇-sä-ˌsin-ē-kwä-ˈnōn\ [L] : an indispensable cause or condition

ca·ve ca·nem \ˌkä-wā-ˈkän-ˌem\ [L] : beware the dog

ce·dant ar·ma to·gae \ˈkā-ˌdänt-ˌär-mə-ˈtō-ˌgī\ [L] : let arms yield to the toga : let military power give way to civil power — motto of Wyoming

ce n'est que le pre·mier pas qui coûte \snek-lə-prə-myä-pä-kē-küt\ [F] : it is only the first step that costs

c'est à dire \se-tä-dēr\ [F] : that is to say : namely

c'est au·tre chose \se-tōt-shōz, -tō-trə-\ [F] : that's a different thing

c'est la guerre \se-lä-ger\ [F] : that's war : it cannot be helped

c'est la vie \se-lä-vē\ [F] : that's life : that's how things happen

c'est plus qu'un crime, c'est une faute \se-plü-kœⁿ-krēm-se-tüen-fōt\ [F] : it is worse than a crime, it is a blunder

ce·te·ra de·sunt \ˌkāt-ə-ˌrä-ˈdā-ˌsu̇nt\ [L] : the rest is missing

cha·cun à son goût \shä-kœⁿ-nä-sōⁿ-gü\ [F] : everyone to his taste

châ·teau en Es·pagne \shä-tō-äⁿ-nes-pänʸ\ [F] : castle in Spain : a visionary project

cher·chez la femme \sher-shä-lä-fàm\ [F] : look for the woman

che sa·rà, sa·rà \ˌkā-sä-ˌrä-sä-ˈrä\ [It] : what will be, will be

che·val de ba·taille \shə-vàl-də-bä-ˈtäⁿ\ [F] : war-horse : argument constantly relied on : favorite subject

co·gi·to, er·go sum \ˈkō-gi-ˌtō-ˌer-gō-ˈsu̇m\ [L] : I think, therefore I exist

co·mé·die hu·maine \kȯ-mā-dē-ü̈-men\ [F] : human comedy : the whole variety of human life

comme ci, comme ça \kȯm-sē-kȯm-sà\ [F] : so-so

com·pa·gnon de voy·age \kōⁿ-pà-nʸōⁿ-də-vwà-yàzh\ [F] : traveling companion

compte ren·du \kōⁿt-räⁿ-dᴟ\ [F] : report (as of proceedings in an investigation)

con·cor·dia dis·cors \kän-ˌkȯrd-ē-ä-ˈdis-ˌkȯrs\ [L] : discordant harmony

cor·rup·tio op·ti·mi pes·si·ma \kə-ˈru̇p-tē-ˌō-ˈäp-tə-ˌmē-ˈpes-ə-ˌmä\ [L] : the corruption of the best is the worst of all

coup de maî·tre \küd-(ə-)metrᵃ\ [F] : masterstroke

coup d'es·sai \kü-dä-se\ [F] : experiment : trial

coûte que coûte \küt-kə-küt\ [F] : cost what it may

cre·do quia ab·sur·dum est \ˌkräd-ō-ˈkwē-ä-äp-ˌsu̇rd-əm-ˈest\ [L] : I believe it because it is absurd

cres·cit eun·do \ˌkres-kət-ˈėu̇n-dō\ [L] : it grows as it goes — motto of New Mexico

crise de nerfs or **crise des nerfs** \krēz-də-ner\ [F] : crisis of nerves : nervous collapse : hysterical fit

crux cri·ti·co·rum \ˈkru̇ks-ˌkrit-ə-ˈkōr-əm\ [L] : crux of critics

cum gra·no sa·lis \ˌku̇m-ˌgrän-ō-ˈsäl-is\ [L] : with a grain of salt

cus·tos mo·rum \ˌku̇s-tōs-ˈmȯr-əm\ [L] : guardian of manners or morals : censor

d'ac·cord \dä-kȯr\ [F] : in accord : agreed

dame d'hon·neur \dàm-dȯ-nœr\ [F] : lady-in-waiting

dam·nant quod non in·tel·li·gunt \ˈdäm-ˌnänt-ˌkwȯd-ˌnōn-in-ˈtel-ə-ˌgu̇nt\ [L] : they condemn what they do not understand

de bonne grâce \də-bȯn-gräs\ [F] : with good grace : willingly

de gus·ti·bus non est dis·pu·tan·dum \dā-ˈgu̇s-tə-ˌbu̇s-ˌnōn-ˌest-ˌdis-pu̇-ˈtän-ˌdu̇m\ [L] : there is no disputing about tastes

Dei gra·tia \ˈde-ˌē-ˈgrät-ē-ˌä\ [L] : by the grace of God

de in·te·gro \dā-ˈint-ə-ˌgrō\ [L] : anew : afresh

de l'au·dace, en·core de l'au·dace, et tou·jours de l'au·dace \də-lō-ˈdàs-äⁿ-ˈkȯr-də-lō-ˈdàs-ā-tü-ˈzhür-də-lō-ˈdàs\ [F] : audacity, more audacity, and ever more audacity

de·len·da est Car·tha·go \dā-ˈlen-dä-ˌest-kär-ˈtäg-ō\ [L] : Carthage must be destroyed

de·li·ne·a·vit \dā-ˌlē-nä-ˈä-wit\ [L] : he (or she) drew it

de mal en pis \də-mà-läⁿ-pē\ [F] : from bad to worse

de mi·ni·mis non cu·rat lex \dā-ˈmin-ə-ˌmēs-ˌnōn-ˌkü-ˌrät-ˈleks\ [L] : the law takes no account of trifles

de mor·tu·is nil ni·si bo·num \dā-ˈmȯrt-ə-ˌwēs-ˌnēl-ˌnis-ē-ˈbȯ-ˌnu̇m\ [L] : of the dead (say) nothing but good

de nos jours \də-nō-zhür\ [F] : of our time : contemporary — used postpositively esp. after a proper name

Deo fa·ven·te \ˌdā-ō-fä-ˈvent-ā\ [L] : with God's favor

Deo gra·ti·as \ˌdā-ō-ˈgrät-ē-ˌäs\ [L] : thanks to God

de pro·fun·dis \ˌdā-prō-ˈfu̇n-dēs\ [L] : out of the depths

der Geist der stets ver·neint \der-ˈgīst-der-ˌshtäts-fer-ˈnīnt\ [G] : the spirit that ever denies — applied originally to Mephistopheles

de·si·pe·re in lo·co \dā-'sip-ə-rē-in-'lō-kō\ [L] : to indulge in trifling at the proper time

Deus vult \'dā-əs-'wùlt\ [L] : God wills it — rallying cry of the First Crusade

di·es fau·stus \'dē-,äs-'faù-stəs\ [L] : lucky day

dies in·fau·stus \-'in-,faù-stəs\ [L] : unlucky day

dies irae \-'ē-,rī\ [L] : day of wrath — used of the Judgment Day

Dieu et mon droit \dyœ̄-ā-mō̃'-drwä\ [F] : God and my right — motto on the British royal arms

Dieu vous garde \dyœ̄-vü-gárd\ [F] : God keep you

di·ri·go \'dē-ri-,gō\ [L] : I direct — motto of Maine

dis ali·ter vi·sum \dēs-,äl-ə-ter-'wē-,sùm\ [L] : the Gods decreed otherwise

di·tat De·us \dē-,tät-'dā-,ùs\ [L] : God enriches — motto of Arizona

di·vi·de et im·pe·ra \'dē-wi-,de-,et-'im-pə-,rä\ [L] : divide and rule

do·cen·do dis·ci·mus \dō-,ken-dō-'dis-ki-,mùs\ [L] : we learn by teaching

Do·mi·ne di·ri·ge nos \'dò-mi-,ne-,dē-ri-ge-'nōs\ [L] : Lord, direct us — motto of the City of London

Do·mi·nus vo·bis·cum \'dò-mi-,nùs-wō-'bēs-,kùm\ [L] : the Lord be with you

dul·ce et de·co·rum est pro pa·tria mo·ri \,dùl-,ket-de-'kōr,-est-prō-,pä-trē-,ä-'mō-,rē\ [L] : it is sweet and seemly to die for one's country

dum spi·ro, spe·ro \dùm-'spē-rō-'spä-rō\ [L] : while I breathe I hope — one of the mottoes of South Carolina

dum vi·vi·mus vi·va·mus \dùm-'wē-wē-mùs-wē-'wäm-ùs\ [L] : while we live, let us live

dux fe·mi·na fac·ti \,dùks-,fā-mi-nä-'fäk-,tē\ [L] : a woman was leader of the exploit

ec·ce sig·num \,ek-ē-'sig-,nùm\ [L] : behold the sign : look at the proof

e con·tra·rio \,ā-kón-'trär-ē-,ō\ [L] : on the contrary

écra·sez l'in·fâme \ā-krä-zā-laⁿ-'fäm\ [F] : crush the infamous thing

eheu fu·ga·ces la·bun·tur an·ni \,ā-,heù-fù-'gä-,käs-lä-,bùn-,tùr-'än-,ē\ [L] : alas! the fleeting years glide on

ein' fes·te Burg ist un·ser Gott \īn-,fes-tə-'bùrk-ist-,ùn-zər-'gòt\ [G] : a mighty fortress is our God

em·bar·ras de ri·chesses \äⁿ-bà-räd-(ə)-rē-shes\ [F] : embarrassing surplus of riches : confusing abundance

em·bar·ras du choix \äⁿ-bà-rä-dᵫ-shwä\ [F] : embarrassing variety of choice

en ami \äⁿ-nà-mē\ [F] : as a friend

en ef·fet \äⁿ-nā-fe\ [F] : in fact : indeed

en fa·mille \äⁿ-fä-mēy\ [F] : in or with one's family : at home : informally

en·fant gâ·té \äⁿ-fäⁿ-gä-tā\ [F] : spoiled child

en·fants per·dus \äⁿ-fäⁿ-per-dᵫ\ [F] : lost children : soldiers sent to a dangerous post

en·fin \äⁿ-faⁿ\ [F] : in conclusion : in a word

en gar·con \äⁿ-gàr-sō̃\ [F] : as or like a bachelor

en pan·tou·fles \äⁿ-päⁿ-tüfl\ [F] : in slippers : at ease : informally

en plein air \äⁿ-plen-er\ [F] : in the open air

en plein jour \äⁿ-plaⁿ-zhür\ [F] : in broad day

en règle \äⁿ-regl\ [F] : in order : in due form

en re·tard \äⁿr-(ə)-tár\ [F] : behind time : late

en re·traite \äⁿ-rə-tret\ [F] : in retreat : in retirement

en re·vanche \äⁿr-(ə)-väⁿsh\ [F] : in return : in compensation

en se·condes noces \äⁿs-(ə)-gō̃d-nòs\ [F] : in a second marriage

en·se pe·tit pla·ci·dam sub li·ber·ta·te qui·e·tem \'en-se-,pet-ət-'pläk-i-,däm-,sùb-,lē-ber-,tä-te-kwē-'ā-,tem\ [L] : with the sword she seeks calm repose under liberty — motto of Massachusetts

épa·ter les bour·geois \ā-pá-tā-lā-bür-zhwä\ [F] : to shock the middle classes

e plu·ri·bus unum \,ē-,plùr-ə-bəs-'(y)ü-nəm, ,ä-,plùr-\ [L] : one out of many — used on the seal of the U.S. and on several U.S. coins

ep·pur si muo·ve \äp-,pür-sē-'mwò-vä\ [It] : and yet it does move — attributed to Galileo after recanting his assertion of the earth's motion

Erin go bragh \,er-ən-gə-'brò, -gō-'brä\ [IrGael *go brāth*, lit., till doomsday] : Ireland forever

er·ra·re hu·ma·num est \e-'rär-e-hü-,män-əm-'est\ [L] : to err is human

es·prit de l'es·ca·lier \es-,prēd-les-kà-lyä\ *or* **es·prit d'es·ca·lier** \-prē-des-\ [F] : staircase wit : repartee thought of only too late

es·se quam vi·de·ri \'es-ē-,kwäm-wi-'dä-rē\ [L] : to be rather than to seem — motto of North Carolina

est mo·dus in re·bus \est-'mò-,dùs-in-'rā-,bùs\ [L] : there is a proper measure in things, i.e., the golden mean should always be observed

es·to per·pe·tua \'es-,tō-pər-'pet-ə-,wä\ [L] : may she endure forever — motto of Idaho

et hoc ge·nus om·ne \et-,hōk-,gen-əs-'ôm-ne\ *or* **et id genus omne** \et-,id-\ [L] : and everything of this kind

et in Ar·ca·dia ego \,et-in-är-,käd-ē-ä-'eg-ō\ [L] : I too (lived) in Arcadia

et sic de si·mi·li·bus \et-,sēk-dā-si-'mil-ə-,bùs\ [L] : and so of like things

et tu Bru·te \et-'tü-,brü-te\ [L] : thou too, Brutus — exclamation attributed to Julius Caesar on seeing his friend Brutus among his assassins

eu·re·ka \yu̇-ˈrē-kə\ [Gk] : I have found it — motto of California

Ewig—Weib·li·che \ˌā-vik-ˈvīp-li-kə\ [G] : eternal feminine

ex an·i·mo \ek-ˈsän-ə-ˌmō\ [L] : from the heart : sincerely

ex·cel·si·or \ik-ˈsel-sē-ər, eks-ˈkel-sē-ˌȯr\ [L] : still higher — motto of New York

ex·cep·tio pro·bat re·gu·lam de re·bus non ex·cep·tis \eks-ˈkep-tē-ˌō-ˌprōˌbät-ˈrā-gə-ˌläm-dā-ˈrā-ˌbu̇s-ˌnōneks-ˈkep-ˌtēs\ [L] : an exception establishes the rule as to things not excepted

ex·cep·tis ex·ci·pi·en·dis \eks-ˈkep-ˌtēseks-ˌkip-ē-ˈen-ˌdēs\ [L] : with the proper or necessary exceptions

ex·i·tus ac·ta pro·bat \ˈek-sə-ˌtu̇s-ˌäktə-ˈprō-ˌbät\ [L] : the event justifies the deed

ex li·bris \eks-ˈlē-bris\ [L] : from the books of — used on bookplates

ex me·ro mo·tu \ˌeks-ˌmer-ō-ˈmō-tü\ [L] : out of mere impulse : of one's own accord

ex ne·ces·si·ta·te rei \ˌeks-ne-ˌkes-i-ˈtä-te-ˈrā (-ˌē)\ [L] : from the necessity of the case

ex ni·hi·lo ni·hil fit \eks-ˈni-hi-ˌlō-ˌnihil-ˈfit\ [L] : from nothing nothing is produced

ex pe·de Her·cu·lem \eks-ˌped-e-ˈherkə-ˌlem\ [L] : from the foot (we may judge of the size of) Hercules : from a part we may judge of the whole

ex·per·to cre·di·te \eks-ˌpert-ō-ˈkrädə-ˌte\ [L] : believe one who has had experience

ex un·gue le·o·nem \eks-ˈu̇ŋ-gwe-le-ˈōnem\ [L] : from the claw (we may judge of) the lion : from a part we may judge of the whole

ex vi ter·mi·ni \eks-ˌwē-ˈter-mə-ˌnē\ [L] : from the force of the term

fa·ci·le prin·ceps \ˌfäk-i-le-ˈpriŋ-ˌkeps\ [L] : easily first

fa·ci·lis de·scen·sus Aver·no \ˈfäk-i-lisdā-ˌskän-ˌsu̇s-ä-ˈwer-nō\ or facilis descensus Aver·ni \-()nē\ [L] : the descent to Avernus is easy : the road to evil is easy

fa·çon de par·ler \fä-sōⁿ-də-pär-lā\ [F] : manner of speaking : figurative or conventional expression

faire suivre \fer-swēvrᵊ\ [F] : have forwarded : please forward

fas est et ab ho·ste do·ce·ri \fäs-ˈest-etäb-ˈhō-ste-dō-ˈkä-()rē\ [L] : it is right to learn even from an enemy

Fa·ta vi·am in·ve·ni·ent \ˌfä-tä-ˈwē-ˌäm-in-ˈwen-ē-ˌent\ [L] : the Fates will find a way

fat·ti mas·chii, pa·ro·le fe·mi·ne \ˌfät-tēˈmäs-ˌkē-pä-ˌrō-lā-ˈfā-mē-ˌnā\ [It] : deeds are males, words are females : deeds are more effective than words — motto of Maryland, where it is generally interpreted as meaning "manly deeds, womanly words"

faux bon·homme \fō-bo-nòm\ [F] : pretended good fellow

faux-naïf \fō-nä-ēf\ [F] : pretending to be childlike

femme de cham·bre \fäm-də-shäⁿbrᵊ\ [F] : chambermaid : lady's maid

fes·ti·na len·te \fe-ˌstē-nə-ˈlen-ˌtā\ [L] : make haste slowly

feux d'ar·ti·fice \fœ-där-tē-fēs\ [F] : fireworks : display of wit

fi·at ex·pe·ri·men·tum in cor·po·re vi·li \ˈfē-ˌät-ek-ˌsper-ē-ˈmen-ˌtùm-inˌkòr-pə-re-ˈwē-lē\ [L] : let experiment be made on a worthless body

fi·at jus·ti·tia, ru·at cae·lum \ˌfē-ät-yu̇sˈtit-ē-ä ˌrü-ˌät-ˈkī-ˌlùm\ [L] : let justice be done though the heavens fall

fi·at lux \ˌfē-ˌät-ˈlùks\ [L] : let there be light

Fi·dei De·fen·sor \ˌfid-e-ˌē-dä-ˈfänˌsòr\ [L] : Defender of the Faith — a title of the sovereigns of England

fi·dus Acha·tes \ˌfēd-əs-ä-ˈkä-ˌtäs\ [L] : faithful Achates : trusty friend

fille de cham·bre \fēy-də-shäⁿbrᵊ\ [F] : lady's maid

fille d'hon·neur \fēy-dò-nœr\ [F] : maid of honor

fils \fēs\ [F] : son — used after French proper names to distinguish a son from his father

fi·nem re·spi·ce \ˌfē-ˌnem-ˈrā-spi-ˌke\ [L] : consider the end

fi·nis co·ro·nat opus \ˌfē-nəs-kə-ˈrōˌnät-ˈō-ˌpu̇s\ [L] : the end crowns the work

fluc·tu·at nec mer·gi·tur \ˈflùk-tə-ˌwätˌnek-ˈmer-gə-ˌtu̇r\ [L] : it is tossed by the waves but does not sink — motto of Paris

fo·lie de gran·deur or fo·lie des gran·deurs \fò-lē-də-grän-dœr\ [F] : delusion of greatness : megalomania

fors·an et haec olim me·mi·nis·se ju·va·bit \ˌfòr-ˌsän-ˌet-ˈhīk-ˌō-limˌmem-ə-ˈnis-e-yü-ˈwä-bit\ [L] : perhaps this too will be a pleasure to look back on one day

for·tes for·tu·na ju·vat \ˈfòr-ˌtäs-fòr-ˌtünə-ˈyu̇-ˌwät\ [L] : fortune favors the brave

fron·ti nul·la fi·des \ˈfròn-ˌtē-ˌnùlə-ˈfid-ˌäs\ [L] : no reliance can be placed on appearance

fu·it Ili·um \ˈfü-ət-ˈil-ē-əm\ [L] : Troy has been (i.e., is no more)

fu·ror lo·quen·di \ˌfür-ˌòr-lō-ˈkwen(ˌ)dē\ [L] : rage for speaking

furor po·e·ti·cus \-pò-ˈät-i-kùs\ [L] : poetic frenzy

furor scri·ben·di \-skrē-ˈben-()dē\ [L] : rage for writing

Gal·li·ce \ˈgäl-ə-ˌke\ [L] : in French : after the French manner

gar·çon d'hon·neur \gär-sōⁿ-dò-nœr\ [F] : bridegroom's attendant

garde du corps \gärd-dᵫ-kòr\ [F] : bodyguard

gar·dez la foi \gär-dä-là-fwä\ [F] : keep faith

gau·de·a·mus igi·tur \\,gaud-ē-'äm-əs-'ig-ə-,tùr\ [L] : let us then be merry

gens d'église \zhän-dā-glēz\ [F] : church people : clergy

gens de guerre \zhän-də-ger\ [F] : military people : soldiery

gens du monde \zhän-due-mōⁿd\ [F] : people of the world : fashionable people

gno·thi se·au·ton \gə-'nō-thē-,se-aù-'tōn\ [Gk] : know thyself

grand monde \grän-mōⁿd\ [F] : great world : high society

guerre à ou·trance \ger-á-ü-träⁿs\ [F] : war to the uttermost

gu·ten Tag \güt-'n-'täk\ [G] : good day

has·ta la vis·ta \,äs-tä-lä-'vēs-tä\ [Sp] : good-bye

haut goût \ō-gü\ [F] : high flavor : slight taint of decay

hic et ubi·que \,hēk-et-ù-'bē-kwe\ [L] : here and everywhere

hic ja·cet \hik-'jä-sət, hēk-'yäk-ət\ [L] : here lies — used preceding a name on a tombstone

hinc il·lae la·cri·mae \,hiŋk-,il-,ī-'läk-ri-,mī\ [L] : hence those tears

hoc age \hōk-'äg-e\ [L] : do this : apply yourself to what you are about

hoc opus, hic la·bor est \hōk-'ō-pùs-,hēk-,lä-,bór-'est\ [L] : this is the hard work, this is the toil

homme d'af·faires \òm-dá-fer\ [F] : man of business : business agent

homme d'es·prit \-des-prē\ [F] : man of wit

homme moyen sen·suel \òm-mwà-yaⁿ-säⁿ-swel\ [F] : the average nonintellectual man

ho·mo sum: hu·ma·ni nil a me ali·e·num pu·to \'hò-mō-,sùm hü-,män-ē-'nēl-ä-,mā-,äl-ē-'ä-nəm-'pù-tō\ [L] : I am a man: I regard nothing that concerns man as foreign to my interests

ho·ni soit qui mal y pense \ò-nē-swà-kē-mál-ē-päⁿs\ [F] : shamed be he who thinks evil of it — motto of the Order of the Garter

hu·ma·num est er·ra·re \hü-,män-əm-est-e-'rär-e\ [L] : to err is human

ich dien \ik-'dēn\ [G] : I serve — motto of the Prince of Wales

ici on parle fran·çais \ē-sē-ōⁿ-pàrl-(-ə)-fräⁿ-se\ [F] : French is spoken here

id est \id-'est\ [L] : that is

ig·no·ran·tia ju·ris ne·mi·nem ex·cu·sat \ig-nə-,ränt-ē-ä-,yùr-əs-'nā-mə-nem-eks-'kü-,sät\ [L] : ignorance of the law excuses no one

ig·no·tum per ig·no·ti·us \ig-'nōt-əm-per-ig-'nōt-ē-,ùs\ [L] : (explaining) the unknown by means of the more unknown

il faut cul·ti·ver no·tre jar·din \ēl-fō-küèl-tē-vā-not-zhàr-daⁿ, -nò-trə-zhàr-\ [F] : we must cultivate our garden : we must tend to our own affairs

in ae·ter·num \,in-ī-'ter-,nùm\ [L] : forever

in du·bio \in-'dùb-ē-,ō\ [L] : in doubt : undetermined

in fu·tu·ro \,in-fə-'tùr-ō\ [L] : in the future

in hoc sig·no vin·ces \in-hōk-'sig-nō-'viŋ-,kās\ [L] : by this sign (the Cross) you will conquer

in li·mi·ne \in-'lē-mə-,ne\ [L] : on the threshold : at the beginning

in om·nia pa·ra·tus \in-'òm-nē-ə-pə-'rä-,tùs\ [L] : ready for all things

in par·ti·bus in·fi·de·li·um \in-'pärt-ə-,bùs,-in-fə-'dä-lē-,ùm\ [L] : in the regions of the infidels — used of a titular bishop having no diocesan jurisdiction, usu. in non-Christian countries

in prae·sen·ti \,in-prī-'sen-,tē\ [L] : at the present time

in sae·cu·la sae·cu·lo·rum \in-'sī-kù-,lä-,sī-kə-'lōr-əm, -'sä-kù-,lä-,sä-\ [L] : for ages of ages : forever and ever

insh·al·lah \,in-shä-'lä\ [Ar] : if Allah wills : God willing

in sta·tu quo an·te bel·lum \in-'stä-,tü-kwō-,änt-ē-'bel-əm\ [L] : in the same state as before the war

in·te·ger vi·tae sce·le·ris·que pu·rus \,in-tə-,ger-'wē-,tī-,skel-ə-'ris-kwe-'pü-rəs\ [L] : upright of life and free from wickedness

in·ter nos \,int-ər-'nōs\ [L] : between ourselves

in·tra mu·ros \,in-trä-'mü-,rōs\ [L] : within the walls

in usum Del·phi·ni \in-'ü-səm-del-'fē-nē\ [L] : for the use of the Dauphin : expurgated

in utrum·que pa·ra·tus \,in-ü-'trùm-kwe-pə-'rä-,tùs\ [L] : prepared for either (event)

in·ve·nit \in-'wā-nit\ [L] : he (or she) devised it

in vi·no ve·ri·tas \in-'wē-nō-'wā-rə-,täs\ [L] : there is truth in wine

in·vi·ta Mi·ner·va \in-,wē-,tä-mi-'ner-wä\ [L] : Minerva being unwilling : without natural talent or inspiration

ip·sis·si·ma ver·ba \ip-,sis-ə-,mä-'wer-,bä\ [L] : the very words

ira fu·ror bre·vis est \,ē-rä-'fùr-,òr-bre-wis-,est\ [L] : anger is a brief madness

j'ac·cuse \zhà-kuēz\ [F] : I accuse

jac·ta alea est \'yäk-,tä-,ä-,lē-,ä-'est\ [L] : the die is cast

j'adoube \zhà-düb\ [F] : I adjust — used in chess when touching a piece without intending to move it

ja·nu·is clau·sis \,yän-ə-,wēs-'klaù-,sēs\ [L] : behind closed doors

je main·tien·drai \zhə-maⁿ-tyaⁿ-drä\ [F] : I will maintain — motto of the Netherlands

jeu de mots \zhœd-(ə)-mō\ [F] : play on words : pun

Jo·an·nes est no·men eius \yō-'än-äs-est-,nō-men-'ā-yùs\ [L] : John is his name — motto of Puerto Rico

jo·lie laide \zhò-lē-led\ [F] : good-looking ugly woman : woman who is attractive though not conventionally pretty

jour·nal in·time \zhür-nál-aⁿ-tēm\ [F] : intimate journal : private diary

jus di·vi·num \yüs-di-'wē-₁nùm\ [L] : divine law

jus·ti·tia om·ni·bus \yús-₁tit-ē-₁ä-'òm-ni-₁bús\ [L] : justice for all — motto of the District of Columbia

j'y suis, j'y reste \zhē-sw^yē-zhē-rest\ [F] : here I am, here I remain

la belle dame sans mer·ci \lä-bel-dám-säⁿ-mer-sē\ [F] : the beautiful lady without mercy

la·bo·ra·re est ora·re \'läb-ō-₁rär-ā-₁est-'ō-₁rär-ä\ [L] : to work is to pray

la·bor om·nia vin·cit \'lä-₁bòr-₁òm-nē-₁ä-'wiŋ-kit\ [L] : labor conquers all things — motto of Oklahoma

la·cri·mae re·rum \₁läk-ri-₁mī-'rä-₁rüm\ [L] : tears for things : pity for misfortune; also : tears in things : tragedy in life

lais·sez–al·ler or **lais·ser–al·ler** \le-sā-á-lā\ [F] : letting go : lack of restraint

lap·sus ca·la·mi \₁läp-sùs-'käl-ə-₁mē\ [L] : slip of the pen

lap·sus lin·guae \-'liŋ-₁gwī\ [L] : slip of the tongue

la reine le veut \lá-ren-lə-vœ\ [F] : the queen wills it

la·scia·te ogni spe·ran·za, voi ch'en·tra·te \läsh-'shä-tā-₁ō-n^yē-spä-'rän-tsä-₁vò-ē-kän-'trä-tā\ [It] : abandon all hope, ye who enter

lau·da·tor tem·po·ris ac·ti \laù-'dä-₁tòr-₁tem-pə-ris-'äk-₁tē\ [L] : one who praises past times

laus Deo \laùs-'dā-ō\ [L] : praise (be) to God

le cœur a ses rai·sons que la rai·son ne con·nait point \lə-kœr-á-sā-re-zōⁿk-lá-re-zōⁿn-(ə)kò-ne-pwaⁿ\ [F] : the heart has its reasons that reason knows nothing of

le roi est mort, vive le roi \lə-rwä-e-mòr vēv-lə-rwä\ [F] : the king is dead, long live the king

le roi le veut \-lə-vœ\ [F] : the king wills it

le roi s'avi·se·ra \-sá-vēz-rá\ [F] : the king will consider

le style, c'est l'homme \lə-stēl-se-lòm\ [F] : the style is the man

l'état, c'est moi \lā-tá-se-mwä\ [F] : the state, it is I

l'étoile du nord \lā-twál-dœ-nòr\ [F] : the star of the north — motto of Minnesota

Lie·der·kranz \'lēd-ər-₁kräns\ [G] : wreath of songs : German singing society

lit·tera scrip·ta ma·net \₁lit-ə-₁rä-₁skrip-tə-'män-et\ [L] : the written letter abides

lo·cus in quo \₁lō-kəs-in-'kwō\ [L] : place in which

l'union fait la force \lœ-nyōⁿ-fe-lä-fòrs\ [F] : union makes strength — motto of Belgium

lu·sus na·tu·rae \₁lü-səs-nə-'tùr-ē, -'tür-₁ī\ [L] : freak of nature

ma foi \má-fwä\ [F] : my faith! : indeed

mag·na est ve·ri·tas et prae·va·le·bit \₁mäg-nä-₁est-'wä-ri-₁täs-et-₁prī-wä-'lā-bit\ [L] : truth is mighty and will prevail

mag·ni no·mi·nis um·bra \₁mäg-nē-₁nò-mə-nis-'ùm-brä\ [L] : the shadow of a great name

mai·son de san·té \mā-zōⁿd-(ə)säⁿ-tā\ [F] : private hospital : asylum

ma·lade ima·gi·naire \má-läd-ē-mà-zhē-ner\ [F] : imaginary invalid : hypochondriac

ma·lis avi·bus \₁mäl-₁ēs-'ä-wi-₁bùs\ [L] : under evil auspices

ma·no a ma·no \₁män-ō-ä-'män-ō\ [Sp] : hand to hand : in direct competition or confrontation

man spricht Deutsch \män-shprikt-'dòich\ [G] : German spoken

ma·riage de con·ve·nance \má-ryäzh-də-kōⁿv-näns\ [F] : marriage of convenience

mau·vaise honte \mò-vez-ōⁿt\ [F] : bad shame : bashfulness

mau·vais quart d'heure \mò-ve-kárdœr\ [F] : bad quarter hour : an uncomfortable though brief experience

me·dio tu·tis·si·mus ibis \'med-ē-₁ō-tü-₁tis-ə-mùs-'ē-bis\ [L] : you will go most safely by the middle course

me ju·di·ce \mā-'yüd-ə-ke\ [L] : I being judge : in my judgment

mens sa·na in cor·po·re sa·no \₁mäns-'sän-ə-in-₁kòr-pə-re-'sän-ō\ [L] : a sound mind in a sound body

me·um et tu·um \₁mē-əm-₁et-'tü-əm, ₁mā-əm-\ [L] : mine and thine : distinction of private property

mi·ra·bi·le vi·su \mi-₁räb-ə-lā-'wē-sü\ [L] : wonderful to behold

mi·ra·bi·lia \₁mir-ə-'bil-ē-ə\ [L] : wonders : miracles

mœurs \mœr(s)\ [F] : mores : attitudes, customs, and manners of a society

mo·le ru·it sua \'mō-le-₁rü-it-'sü-ä\ [L] : it collapses from its own bigness

monde \mōⁿd\ [F] : world : fashionable world : society

mon·ta·ni sem·per li·be·ri \mòn-'tän-ē-₁sem-pər-'lē-bə-₁rē\ [L] : mountaineers are always free men — motto of West Virginia

mo·nu·men·tum ae·re per·en·ni·us \₁mò-nə-'men-tùm-₁ī-re-pə-'ren-ē-ùs\ [L] : a monument more lasting than bronze — used of an immortal work of art or literature

mo·ri·tu·ri te sa·lu·ta·mus \₁mòr-ə-'tùr-ē-₁tā-₁säl-ə-'täm-ùs\ or **mori·turi te sa·lu·tant** \-'säl-ə-₁tänt\ [L] : we (or those) who are about to die salute thee

mul·tum in par·vo \₁mùl-təm-in-'pär-vō\ [L] : much in little

mu·ta·to no·mi·ne de te fa·bu·la nar·ra·tur \mü-₁tät-ō-'nō-mə-ne-dä-'tā-₁fäb-ə-lä-nä-'rä-₁tùr\ [L] : with the name changed the story applies to you

na·tu·ram ex·pel·las fur·ca, ta·men us·que re·cur·ret \nä-ˈtü-ˌräm-ek-ˌspel-äs-ˈfu̇r-ˌkä ˌtä-mən-ˈu̇s-kwe-re-ˈku̇r-et\ [L] : you may drive nature out with a pitchfork, but she will keep coming back

na·tu·ra non fa·cit sal·tum \nä-ˈtü-rä-ˌnōn-ˌfäk-ət-ˈsäl-ˌtu̇m\ [L] : nature makes no leap

ne ce·de ma·lis \nā-ˌkā-de-ˈmäl-ˌēs\ [L] : yield not to misfortunes

ne·mo me im·pu·ne la·ces·sit \ˈnā-mō-ˈmä-im-ˌpü-nä-lä-ˈkes-ət\ [L] : no one attacks me with impunity — motto of Scotland and of the Order of the Thistle

ne quid ni·mis \ˌnä-ˌkwid-ˈnim-əs\ [L] : not anything in excess

n'est-ce pas? \nes-pä\ [F] : isn't it so?

nicht wahr? \nikt-ˈvär\ [G] : isn't true? : isn't it so?

nil ad·mi·ra·ri \ˈnēl-ˌäd-mə-ˈrär-ē\ [L] : to be excited by nothing : equanimity

nil de·spe·ran·dum \ˈnēl-ˌdä-spä-ˈrän-ˌdu̇m\ [L] : never despair

nil si·ne nu·mi·ne \ˈnēl-ˌsin-e-ˈnü-mə-ne\ [L] : nothing without the divine will — motto of Colorado

n'im·porte \naⁿ-ˈpȯrt\ [F] : it's no matter

no·lens vo·lens \ˌnō-ˌlenz-ˈvō-ˌlenz\ [L] : unwilling (or) willing : willy-nilly

non om·nia pos·su·mus om·nes \nōn-ˈȯm-nē-ä-ˌpȯ-sə-mu̇s-ˈȯm-ˌnäs\ [L] : we can't all (do) all things

non om·nis mo·ri·ar \nōn-ˈȯm-nis-ˈmȯr-ē-ˌär\ [L] : I shall not wholly die

non sans droict \nōⁿ-säⁿ-drwä\ [OF] : not without right — motto on Shakespeare's coat of arms

non sum qua·lis eram \ˌnōn-ˌsu̇m-ˌkwäl-əs-ˈer-ˌäm\ [L] : I am not what I used to be

nos·ce te ip·sum \ˌnȯs-ke-ˌtā-ˈip-ˌsu̇m\ [L] : know thyself

nos·tal·gie de la boue \nȯs-tȧl-zhēd-(ə-)lȧ-bü\ [F] : nostalgia for the mud : homesickness for the gutter

nous avons chan·gé tout ce·la \nü-zȧ-vȯⁿ-shäⁿ-zhā-tü-slȧ\ [F] : we have changed all that

nous ver·rons ce que nous ver·rons \nü-ve-rōⁿs-(ə-)kə-nü-ve-rōⁿ\ [F] : we shall see what we shall see

no·vus ho·mo \ˌnō-wəs-ˈhō-mō\ [L] : new man : man newly ennobled : upstart

no·vus or·do se·clo·rum \ˈȯr-dō-sā-ˈklȯr-əm\ [L] : a new cycle of the ages — motto on the reverse of the Great Seal of the United States

nu·gae \ˈnü-ˌgī\ [L] : trifles

nuit blanche \nwēⁿ-blänˈsh\ [F] : white night : a sleepless night

nyet \ˈnyet\ [Russ] : no

ob·iit \ˈȯ-bē-ˌit\ [L] : he (or she) died

ob·scu·rum per ob·scu·ri·us \əb-ˈskyu̇r-əm-ˌper-əb-ˈskyu̇r-ē-əs\ [L] : (explaining) the obscure by means of the more obscure

ode·rint dum me·tu·ant \ˈȯd-ə-ˌrint-ˌdu̇m-ˈmet-ə-ˌwänt\ [L] : let them hate, so long as they fear

odi et amo \ˈȯ-ˌdē-et-ˈäm-(ˌ)ō\ [L] : I hate and I love

om·ne ig·no·tum pro mag·ni·fi·co \ˌȯm-ne-ig-ˈnō-ˌtu̇m-ˌprō-mäg-ˈnif-i-ˌkō\ [L] : everything unknown (is taken) as grand : the unknown tends to be exaggerated in importance or difficulty

om·nia mu·tan·tur, nos et mu·ta·mur in il·lis \ˌȯm-nē-ä-mü-ˈtän-ˌtu̇r ˌnōs-ˌet-mü-ˌtäm-ər-in-ˈil-ˌēs\ [L] : all things are changing, and we are changing with them

om·nia vin·cit amor \ˌȯm-nē-ä-ˈwin-kət-ˈäm-ˌȯr\ [L] : love conquers all

onus pro·ban·di \ˌō-nəs-prō-ˈban-ˌdī, -dē\ [L] : burden of proof

ora pro no·bis \ˌō-rä-prō-ˈnō-ˌbēs\ [L] : pray for us

ore ro·tun·do \ˌōr-ā-rō-ˈtu̇n-dō\ [L] : with round mouth : eloquently

oro y pla·ta \ˌōr-ō-ē-ˈplät-ə\ [Sp] : gold and silver — motto of Montana

o tem·po·ra! o mo·res! \ō-ˈtem-pə-rä-ō-ˈmō-ˌräs\ [L] : oh the times! oh the manners!

oti·um cum dig·ni·ta·te \ˈōt-ē-ˌu̇m-ˌku̇m-ˌdig-nə-ˈtä-te\ [L] : leisure with dignity

où sont les neiges d'an·tan? \ü-sōⁿ-lä-nezh-däⁿ-ˈtäⁿ\ [F] : where are the snows of yesteryear?

pal·li·da Mors \ˌpal-id-ə-ˈmȯrz\ [L] : pale Death

pa·nem et cir·cen·ses \ˈpän-ˌem-et-kir-ˈkän-ˌsäs\ [L] : bread and circuses : provision of the means of life and recreation by government to appease discontent

pan·ta rhei \ˌpän-ˌtä-ˈ(h)rā\ [Gk] : all things are in flux

par avance \pȧr-ä-väⁿs\ [F] : in advance : by anticipation

par avion \pȧr-ä-vyōⁿ\ [F] : by airplane — used on airmail

par ex·em·ple \pȧr-äg-zäⁿplˈ\ [F] : for example

par·tu·ri·unt mon·tes, nas·ce·tur ri·di·cu·lus mus \pär-ˌtu̇r-ē-ˌu̇nt-ˈmȯn-ˌtäs näs-ˈkä-ˌtu̇r-ri-ˌdik-ə-lu̇s-ˈmüs\ [L] : the mountains are in labor, and a ridiculous mouse will be brought forth

pa·ter pa·tri·ae \ˈpä-ˌter-ˈpä-trē-ˌī\ [L] : father of his country

pau·cis ver·bis \ˌpau̇-ˌkēs-ˈwer-ˌbēs\ [L] : in a few words

pax vo·bis·cum \ˌpäks-vō-ˈbēs-ˌku̇m\ [L] : peace (be) with you

peine forte et dure \pen-fȯr-tā-dᵫr\ [F] : strong and hard punishment : torture

per an·gus·ta ad au·gus·ta \per-ˈän-ˌgu̇s-tə-äd-ˈau̇-ˌgu̇s-tə\ [L] : through difficulties to honors

père \per\ [F] : father — used after French proper names to distinguish a father from his son

per·eant qui an·te nos nos·tra dix·e·runt \'per-e-ṛänt-kwē-ṛän-te-'nōs-'nōs-trä-dēk-'sā-ṛrunt\ [L] : may they perish who have expressed our bright ideas before us

per·fide Al·bion \per-fēd-àl-byōⁿ\ [F] : perfidious Albion (England)

peu à peu \pœ-à-pœ\ [F] : little by little

peu de chose \pœd-(ə-)shōz\ [F] : a trifle

pièce d'oc·ca·sion \pyes-dō-kä-zyōⁿ\ [F] : piece for a special occasion

pinx·it \'piŋk-sət\ [L] : he (or she) painted it

place aux dames \plás-ō-dàm\ [F] : (make) room for the ladies

ple·no ju·re \ṛplā-nō-'yùr-e\ [L] : with full right

plus ça change, plus c'est la même chose \plœ-sà-shäⁿzh plœ-se-là-mem-shōz\ [F] : the more that changes, the more it's the same thing

plus roy·a·liste que le roi \plœ-rwà-yà-lēst-kəl-rwà\ [F] : more royalist than the king

po·cas pa·la·bras \ṛpō-käs-pä-'läb-räs\ [Sp] : few words

po·e·ta nas·ci·tur, non fit \ṛpō-ṛä-tä-'näs-kə-ṛtür nōn-'fit\ [L] : a poet is born, not made

pol·li·ce ver·so \ṛpò-li-ke-'ver-sō\ [L] : with thumb turned : with a gesture or expression of condemnation

post hoc, er·go prop·ter hoc \'pōst-ṛhōk ṛer-gō-'prōp-tər-ṛhōk\ [L] : after this, therefore on account of it (a fallacy of argument)

post ob·itum \pōst-'ō-bə-ṛtùm\ [L] : after death

pour ac·quit \pür-à-kē\ [F] : received payment

pour le mé·rite \pür-lə-mā-rēt\ [F] : for merit

pro aris et fo·cis \ṛprō-ṛä-ṛrēs-et-'fō-ṛkēs\ [L] : for altars and firesides

pro bo·no pu·bli·co \ṛprō-ṛbō-nō-'pü-bli-ṛkō\ [L] : for the public good

pro hac vi·ce \ṛprō-ṛhäk-'wik-e\ [L] : for this occasion

pro pa·tria \ṛprō-'pä-trē-ṛä\ [L] : for one's country

pro re·ge, le·ge, et gre·ge \ṛprō-'rä-ge-ṛlä-ge-et-'greg-ṛe\ [L] : for the king, the law, and the people

pro re na·ta \ṛprō-ṛrä-'nät-ə\ [L] : for an occasion that has arisen : as needed — used in medical prescriptions

quand même \käⁿ-'mem\ [L] : even though : whatever may happen

quan·tum mu·ta·tus ab il·lo \ṛkwänt-əm-ṛmü-'tät-əs-äb-'il-ō\ [L] : how changed from what he once was

quan·tum suf·fi·cit \ṛkwänt-əm-'səf-ə-ṛkit\ [L] : as much as suffices : a sufficient quantity — used in medical prescriptions

¿quién sa·be? \kyän-'sä-bä\ [Sp] : who knows?

qui fa·cit per ali·um fa·cit per se \kwē-ṛfäk-it-ṛper-'äl-ē-ṛùm- ṛfäk-it-ṛper-'sā\ [L] : he who does (anything) through another does it through himself

quis cus·to·di·et ip·sos cus·to·des? \ṛkwis-kùs-'tōd-ē-ṛet-ip-ṛsōs-kùs-'tō-ṛdäs\ [L] : who will keep the keepers themselves?

qui s'ex·cuse s'ac·cuse \kē-'sek-ṛskuez-'sä-ṛkuez\ [F] : he who excuses himself accuses himself

quis se·pa·ra·bit? \ṛkwis-ṛsä-pə-'räb-it\ [L] : who shall separate (us)? — motto of the Order of St. Patrick

qui trans·tu·lit sus·ti·net \kwē-'träns-tə-ṛlit-'sùs-tə-ṛnet\ [L] : He who transplanted sustains (us) — motto of Connecticut

qui va là? \kē-và-là\ [F] : who goes there?

quo·ad hoc \ṛkwō-ṛäd-'hōk\ [L] : as far as this : to this extent

quod erat de·mon·stran·dum \ṛkwòd-'er-ṛät-ṛdem-ən-'strän-dəm\ [L] : which was to be proved

quod erat fa·ci·en·dum \-'fäk-ē-'en-ṛdúm\ [L] : which was to be done

quod sem·per, quod ubi·que, quod ab om·ni·bus \ṛkwòd-'sem-perṛkwōd-'ùb-i-ṛkwä ṛkwōd-äb-'òm-ni-ṛbùs\ [L] : what (has been held) always, everywhere, by everybody

quod vi·de \ṛkwòd-'wid-ṛe\ [L] : which see

quo·rum pars mag·na fui \'kwōr-əm-ṛpärs-ṛmäg-nə-'fü-ē\ [L] : in which I played a great part

quos de·us vult per·de·re pri·us de·men·tat \ṛkwōs-'de-ùs-ṛwült-'perd-ə-ṛre-ṛprē-ùs- dä-'men-ṛtät\ [L] : those whom a god wishes to destroy he first drives mad

quot ho·mi·nes, tot sen·ten·ti·ae \ṛkwòt-'hō-mə-ṛnäs-ṛtōt-sen-'ten-tē-ṛī\ [L] : there are as many opinions as there are men

quo va·dis? \ṛkwō-'väd-is, -'wäd-\ [L] : whither are you going?

rai·son d'état \re-zōⁿ-dā-tà\ [F] : reason of state

re·cu·ler pour mieux sau·ter \rə-kue-lā-pür-myœ-sō-tā\ [F] : to draw back in order to make a better jump

reg·nat po·pu·lus \'reg-ṛnät-'pō-pə-lùs\ [L] : the people rule — motto of Arkansas

re in·fec·ta \ṛrä-in-'fek-ṛtä\ [L] : the business being unfinished : without accomplishing one's purpose

re·li·gio lo·ci \re-ṛlig-ē-ṛō-'lō-ṛkē\ [L] : religious sanctity of a place

rem acu te·ti·gis·ti \rem-'ä-kü-ṛtet-ə-'gis-tē\ [L] : you have touched the point with a needle : you have hit the nail on the head

ré·pon·dez s'il vous plaît \rā-pōⁿ-dā-sēl-vü-ple\ [F] : reply, if you please

re·qui·es·cat in pa·ce \ṛrek-wē-'es-ṛkät-in-'päk-ṛe, ṛrä-kwē-'es-ṛkät-in-'päch-ṛä\ [L] : may he (or she) rest in peace — used on tombstones

re·spi·ce fi·nem \ṛrä-spi-ke-'fē-ṛnem\

[L] : look to the end : consider the outcome

re·sur·gam \re-'sùr-,gäm\ [L] : I shall rise again

re·te·nue \rət-nὲ\ [F] : self-restraint : reserve

re·ve·nons à nos mou·tons \rəv-nōⁿ-à-nō-mü-tōⁿ\ [F] : let us return to our sheep : let us get back to the subject

ruse de guerre \rὲz-də-ger\ [F] : war stratagem

rus in ur·be \rüs-in-'ùr-,be\ [L] : country in the city

sae·va in·dig·na·tio \,sī-wä-,in-dig-'nät-ē-ō\ [L] : fierce indignation

sal At·ti·cum \,sal-'at-i-kəm\ [L] : Attic salt : wit

salle à man·ger \sál-á-män-zhā\ [F] : dining room

sa·lus po·pu·li su·pre·ma lex es·to \sál-,üs-'pò-pə-,lē-sù-,prā-mə-,leks-'es-tō\ [L] : let the welfare of the people be the supreme law — motto of Missouri

sans doute \sän-'düt\ [F] : without doubt

sans gêne \sän-zhen\ [F] : without embarrassment or constraint

sans peur et sans re·proche \sän-pœr-ā-sän-rə-'prosh\ [F] : without fear and without reproach

sans sou·ci \sän-sü-sē\ [F] : without worry

sa·yo·na·ra \,sä-yə-'när-ə\ [Jp] : goodbye

sculp·sit \'skùlp-sit\ [L] : he (or she) carved it

scu·to bo·nae vo·lun·ta·tis tu·ae co·ro·nas·ti nos \'skü-,tō-'bò-,nī-,vò-lùn-,tät-əs-'tù-,ī-,kòr-ə-,näs-tē-'nōs\ [L] : Thou hast crowned us with the shield of Thy good will — a motto on the Great Seal of Maryland

se·cun·dum ar·tem \se-,kùn-dəm-'är-,tem\ [L] : according to the art : according to the accepted practice of a profession or trade

secundum na·tu·ram \-nä-'tü-,räm\ [L] : according to nature : naturally

se de·fen·den·do \'sä-,dā-,fen-'den-dō\ [L] : in self-defense

se ha·bla es·pa·ñol \sā-,äb-lä-,äs-pä-'n'ò\ [Sp] : Spanish spoken

sem·per ea·dem \,sem-,per-'e-ä-,dem\ [L] : always the same (fem.) — motto of Queen Elizabeth I

sem·per fi·de·lis \,sem-pər-fi-'dā-lis\ [L] : always faithful — motto of the U.S. Marine Corps

sem·per idem \,sem-,per-'ē-,dem\ [L] : always the same (masc.)

sem·per pa·ra·tus \,sem-pər-pä-'rät-əs\ [L] : always prepared — motto of the U.S. Coast Guard

se non è ve·ro, è ben tro·va·to \sā-,nōn-e-'vā-rō-e-,ben-trō-'vä-tō\ [It] : even if it is not true, it is well conceived

sic itur ad as·tra \sēk-'i-,tùr-,äd-'ás-trə\ [L] : thus one goes to the stars : such is the way to immortality

sic sem·per ty·ran·nis \,sik-,sem-pər-ti-

'ran-is\ [L] : thus ever to tyrants — motto of Virginia

sic trans·it glo·ria mun·di \sēk-'trän-sət-,glòr-ē-ä-'mùn-dē\ [L] : so passes away the glory of the world

si jeu·nesse sa·vait, si vieil·lesse pou·vait! \sē-'zhœ-nes,-'sá-ve sē-'vye-yes-'pü-ve\ [F] : if youth only knew, if age only could!

si·lent le·ges in·ter ar·ma \,sil-ent-'lā-,gäs-,int-ər-'är-mä\ [L] : the laws are silent in the midst of arms

s'il vous plait \sēl-vü-ple\ [F] : if you please

si·mi·lia si·mi·li·bus cu·ran·tur \sim-il-ē-ä-sim-'il-ə-bùs-kü-'rän-,tùr\ [L] : like is cured by like

si·mi·lis si·mi·li gau·det \'sim-ə-lis-'sim-ə-lē-'gaù-,det\ [L] : like takes pleasure in like

si mo·nu·men·tum re·qui·ris, cir·cum·spi·ce \,sē-,mò-nə-,ment-əm-rə-'kwē-rəs kir-'kùm-spi-ke\ [L] : if you seek his monument, look around — epitaph of Sir Christopher Wren in St. Paul's, London, of which he was architect

si quae·ris pen·in·su·lam amoe·nam, cir·cum·spi·ce \,sē-,kwī-rəs-pä-,nin-sə-,läm-ə-'mòi-,näm kir-'kùm-spi-ke\ [L] : if you seek a beautiful peninsula, look around — motto of Michigan

sis·te vi·a·tor \,sis-te-wē-'ä-,tòr\ [L] : stop, traveler — used on Roman roadside tombs

si vis pa·cem, pa·ra bel·lum \sē-,wēs-'pä-,kem pä-rä-'bel-,ùm\ [L] : if you wish peace, prepare for war

sol·vi·tur am·bu·lan·do \'sòl-wi-,tùr-,äm-bə-'län-dō\ [L] : it is solved by walking : the problem is solved by a practical experiment

splen·di·de men·dax \'splen-də-,dā-'men-,däks\ [L] : nobly untruthful

spo·lia opi·ma \'spò-lē-ò-ò-'pē-mə\ [L] : rich spoils : the arms taken by the victorious from the vanquished general

sta·tus in quo \'stät-əs-,in-'kwò\ [L] : state in which : the existing state

status quo an·te bel·lum \-,kwò-,änt-ə-'bel-ùm\ [L] : the state existing before the war

sua·vi·ter in mo·do, for·ti·ter in re \'swä-wə-,ter-in-'mòd-ō 'fòrt-ə-,ter-in-'rā\ [L] : gently in manner, strongly in deed

sub ver·bo \'sùb-'wer-bō\ *or* **sub vo·ce** \sùb-'wò-ke\ [L] : under the word — introducing a cross-reference in a dictionary or index

sunt la·cri·mae re·rum \sùnt-,läk-ri-,mī-'rā-rùm\ [L] : there are tears for things

suo ju·re \,sù-ō-'yùr-e\ [L] : in his (or her) own right

suo lo·co \-'lò-kō\ [L] : in its proper place

suo Mar·te \-'mär-te\ [L] : by one's own exertions

su·um cui·que \ˌsü-əm-ˈkwik-we\ [L] : to each his own

tant mieux \täⁿ-myœ\ [F] : so much the better

tant pis \-pē\ [F] : so much the worse

tem·po·ra mu·tan·tur, nos et mu·ta·mur in il·lis \ˌtem-pə-rä-mü-ˈtän-ˌtür ˌnōs-ˌet-mü-ˌtäm-ər-in-ˈil-ˌēs\ [L] : the times are changing, and we are changing with them

tem·pus edax re·rum \ˈtem-pùs-ˌed-ˌäks-ˈrā-rùm\ [L] : time, that devours all things

tem·pus fu·git \ˌtem-pəs-ˈfyü-jət, -ˈfü-git\ [L] : time flies

ti·meo Da·na·os et do·na fe·ren·tes \ˌtim-ē-ˌō-ˈdän-ä-ˌōs-ˌet-ˌdō-nä-fe-ˈren-ˌtäs\ [L] : I fear the Greeks even when they bring gifts

to·ti·dem ver·bis \ˌtòt-ə-ˌdem-ˈwer-bēs\ [L] : in so many words

to·tis vi·ri·bus \ˌtō-ˌtēs-ˈwē-ri-ˌbùs\ [L] : with all one's might

to·to cae·lo \ˌtō-tō-ˈkī-lō\ or toto coe·lo \-ˈkòi-lō\ [L] : by the whole extent of the heavens : diametrically

tou·jours per·drix \tü-zhür-per-drē\ [F] : always partridge : too much of a good thing

tour d'ho·ri·zon \tür-dò-rē-zōⁿ\ [F] : circuit of the horizon : general survey

tous frais faits \tü-fre-fe\ [F] : all expenses defrayed

tout à fait \tü-tà-fe\ [F] : altogether : quite

tout au con·traire \tü-tō-kōⁿ-trer\ [F] : quite the contrary

tout à vous \tü-tà-vü\ [F] : wholly yours : at your service

tout bien ou rien \tü-ˈbyaⁿ-nü-ˈryaⁿ\ [F] : everything well (done) or nothing (attempted)

tout com·pren·dre c'est tout par·don·ner \ˈtü-kōⁿ-prän-ˌdrə se-ˈtü-pàr-dò-nä\ [F] : to understand all is to forgive all

tout court \tü-kür\ [F] : quite short : simply; also : brusquely

tout de même \tüt-mem\ [F] : all the same : nevertheless

tout de suite \tüt-swēt\ [F] : immediately; also : at once : consecutively

tout en·sem·ble \tü-tän-sänbl\ [F] : all together : general effect

tout est per·du fors l'hon·neur \tü-te-per-dü-fòr-lò-nœr\ or tout est perdu hors l'honneur \-dœ-òr-\ [F] : all is lost save honor

tout le monde \tül-mōⁿd\ [F] : all the world : everybody

tranche de vie \tränsh-də-ˈvē\ [F] : slice of life

trist·esse \trē-stes\ [F] : melancholy

tru·di·tur di·es di·e \ˈtrüd-ə-ˌtùr-ˌdī-ˌäs-ˈdi-ˌä\ [L] : day is pushed forth by day : one day hurries on another

tu·e·bor \tü-ˈā-ˌbòr\ [L] : I will defend — a motto on the Great Seal of Michigan

ua mau ke ea o ka ai·na i ka po·no \ˌü-ä-

ˈmä-ù-ke-ˈe-ä-ō-kä-ˈä-ē-nä-ˌē-kä-ˈpō-nō\ [Hawaiian] : the life of the land is established in righteousness — motto of Hawaii

ue·ber·mensch \ˈǚ-bər-ˌmensh\ [G] : superman

ul·ti·ma ra·tio re·gum \ˈùl-ti-mä-ˌrät-ē-ō-ˈrā-gùm\ [L] : the final argument of kings, war

und so wei·ter \ùnt-zō-ˈvī-tər\ [G] : and so on

uno ani·mo \ˌü-nō-ˈän-ə-ˌmō\ [L] : with one mind : unanimously

ur·bi et or·bi \ˌùr-bē-ˌet-ˈòr-bē\ [L] : to the city (Rome) and the world

uti·le dul·ci \ˌüt-ⁱl-e-ˈdùl-ˌkē\ [L] : the useful with the agreeable

ut in·fra \ùt-ˈin-frä\ [L] : as below

ut su·pra \ùt-ˈsü-prä\ [L] : as above

va·de re·tro me, Sa·ta·na \ˌwä-de-ˈrä-trō-ˌmä-ˈsä-tə-ˌnä\ [L] : get thee behind me, Satan

vae vic·tis \ˌwī-ˈwik-ˌtēs\ [L] : woe to the vanquished

va·ria lec·tio \ˌwär-ē-ä-ˈlek-tē-ˌō\ pl va·ri·ae lec·ti·o·nes \ˈwär-ē-ˌī-ˌlek-tē-ˈō-ˌnäs\ [L] : variant reading

va·ri·um et mu·ta·bi·le sem·per fe·mi·na \ˌwär-ē-ˌet-mü-ˈtä-bə-le-ˌsem-per-ˈfä-mə-nä\ [L] : woman is ever a fickle and changeable thing

ve·di Na·po·li e poi mo·ri \ˌvä-dē-ˈnä-pō-lē-ä-ˌpò-ē-ˈmò-rē\ [It] : see Naples, and then die

ve·ni, vi·di, vi·ci \ˌwä-nē-ˌwēd-ē-ˈwē-kē\ [L] : I came, I saw, I conquered

ven·tre à terre \ˌväⁿ-trä-ter\ [F] : belly to the ground : at very great speed

ver·ba·tim ac lit·te·ra·tim \wer-ˈbä-tim-ˌäk-ˌlit-ə-ˈrä-tim\ [L] : word for word and letter for letter

ver·bum sat sa·pi·en·ti est \ˌwer-bùm-ˈsät-ˌsäp-ē-ˈent-ē-ˌest\ [L] : a word to the wise is sufficient

vin·cit om·nia ve·ri·tas \ˌwiŋ-ket-ˈòm-nē-ä-ˈwär-ə-ˌtäs\ [L] : truth conquers all things

vin·cu·lum ma·tri·mo·nii \ˌwiŋ-kə-lüm-ˌmä-trə-ˈmō-nē-ˌē\ [L] : bond of marriage

vir·gi·ni·bus pu·e·ris·que \ˌwir-ˈgin-ə-bùs-ˌpü-ə-ˈrēs-kwe\ [L] : for girls and boys

vir·tu·te et ar·mis \ˌwir-ˈtü-te-ˌet-ˈär-mēs\ [L] : by valor and arms — motto of Mississippi

vis me·di·ca·trix na·tu·rae \ˈwēs-ˌmed-i-ˈkä-triks-nä-ˈtü-ˌrⁱ\ [L] : the healing power of nature

vive la dif·fé·rence \vēv-(ə)-lä-dē-fä-räⁿs\ [F] : long live the difference (between the sexes)

vive la reine \vēv-lä-ren\ [F] : long live the queen

vive le roi \vēv-lə-rwä\ [F] : long live the king

vix·e·re for·tes an·te Aga·mem·no·na \wik-ˌsä-re-ˈfòr-ˌtäs-ˌänt-ˌäg-ə-ˈmem-nə-ˌnä\ [L] : brave men lived before Agamemnon

vogue la ga·lère \vòg-lä-gà-ler\ [F] : let

the galley be kept rowing : keep on, whatever may happen

voi·là \vwà-là\ [F] : there you are : there you see (it)

voi·là tout \vwà-là-tü\ [F] : that's all

vox et prae·te·rea ni·hil \'wōks-et-prī-,ter-e-ä-'ni-,hil\ [L] : voice and nothing more

vox po·pu·li vox Dei \wōks-'pò-pə-,lē-,wōks-'de-ē\ [L] : the voice of the people is the voice of God

Wan·der·jahr \'vän-dər-,yär\ [G] : year of wandering

wie geht's? \vē-'gāts\ [G] : how goes it?

Nations of the World

name and pronunciation	population
Afghanistan \ˈaf-ˈgan-ə-ˌstan\	13,051,000
Albania \al-ˈbā-nē-ə\	2,841,000
Algeria \al-ˈjir-ē-ə\	16,948,000
Andorra \an-ˈdȯr-ə\	40,000
Angola \aŋ-ˈgō-lə, an-\	6,761,000
Antigua and Barbuda \an-ˈtē-gə-ən-bär-ˈbüd-ə\	77,000
Argentina \ˌär-jen-ˈtē-nə\	27,947,000
Australia \ȯ-ˈstrāl-yə\	14,574,000
Austria \ˈȯs-trē-ə\	7,555,000
Bahamas \bə-ˈhäm-əz\	223,000
Bahrain \bä-ˈrān\	359,000
Bangladesh \ˌbäŋ-glə-ˈdesh, -ˈdäsh\	87,052,000
Barbados \bär-ˈbäd-əs, -(ˌ)ōz, -(ˌ)äs\	249,000
Belgium \ˈbel-jəm\	9,849,000
Belize \bə-ˈlēz\	145,000
Benin \bə-ˈnin\	3,338,000
Bhutan \bü-ˈtan, -ˈtän\	1,333,000
Bolivia \bə-ˈliv-ē-ə\	4,613,000
Botswana \bät-ˈswän-ə\	937,000
Brazil \brə-ˈzil\	118,675,000
Brunei \brü-ˈnī\	193,000
Bulgaria \ˌbəl-ˈgar-ē-ə, bùl-\	8,730,000
Burkina Faso \bùr-ˈkē-nə-ˈfä-sō\	5,638,000
Burma \ˈbər-mə\	35,314,000
Burundi \bù-ˈrün-dē\	3,638,000
Cambodia \kam-ˈbōd-ē-ə\	6,646,000
Cameroon \ˌkam-ə-ˈrün\	7,090,000
Canada \ˈkan-əd-ə\	24,098,000
Cape Verde \-ˈvərd\	303,000
Central African Republic \-ˈaf-ri-kən-\	2,055,000
Chad \ˈchad\	4,681,000
Chile \ˈchil-ē\	11,275,000
China, People's Republic of \-ˈchī-nə\	1,031,882,000
Colombia \kə-ˈləm-bē-ə\	26,929,000
Comoro Islands \ˈkäm-ə-ˌrō-\	421,000
Congo \ˈkäŋ-gō\	1,300,000
Costa Rica \ˌkäs-tə-ˈrē-kə\	2,435,000
Cuba \ˈkyü-bə\	9,706,000
Cyprus \ˈsī-prəs\	613,000
Czechoslovakia \ˌchek-ə-slō-ˈväk-ē-ə\	15,283,000
Denmark \ˈden-ˌmärk\	5,119,000
Djibouti \jə-ˈbüt-ē\	323,000
Dominica \ˌdäm-ə-ˈnē-kə\	74,000
Dominican Republic \də-ˌmin-i-kən-\	5,648,000
East Germany \-ˈjər-mən-ē\	16,706,000
Ecuador \ˈek-wə-ˌdȯr\	6,522,000
Egypt \ˈē-jəpt\	36,626,000
El Salvador \el-ˈsal-və-ˌdȯr\	4,813,000
Equatorial Guinea \-ˈgin-ē\	300,000
Ethiopia \ˌē-thē-ˈō-pē-ə\	32,775,000
Fiji \ˈfē-(ˌ)jē\	588,000
Finland \ˈfin-lənd\	4,718,000
France \ˈfrans\	52,656,000
Gabon \ga-ˈbōn\	1,108,000
Gambia \ˈgam-bē-ə\	696,000
Ghana \ˈgän-ə\	12,244,000
Greece \ˈgrēs\	9,707,000
Grenada \grə-ˈnād-ə\	110,000
Guatemala \ˌgwät-ə-ˈmäl-ə\	6,044,000
Guinea \ˈgin-ē\	5,057,000
Guinea-Bissau \-bis-ˈaù\	768,000
Guyana \gī-ˈan-ə\	900,000
Haiti \ˈhāt-ē\	5,054,000
Honduras \hän-ˈd(y)ùr-əs\	3,955,000
Hungary \ˈhəŋ-g(ə-)rē\	10,709,000
Iceland \ˈīs-lənd, -ˌland\	235,000
India \ˈin-dē-ə\	685,185,000
Indonesia \ˌin-də-ˈnē-zhə, -shə\	147,490,000
Iran \i-ˈran, -ˈrän\	33,592,000
Iraq \i-ˈrak, -ˈräk\	12,000,000
Ireland (Irish Republic) \ˈī(ə)r-lənd\	3,443,000
Israel \ˈiz-rē-əl\	4,112,000
Italy \ˈit-ə-lē\	56,244,000
Ivory Coast \ˈīv-(ə-)rē-\	6,710,000
Jamaica \jə-ˈmā-kə\	2,096,000
Japan \jə-ˈpan\	117,057,000
Jordan \ˈjȯrd-ən\	2,152,000
Kenya \ˈken-yə, ˈkēn-\	15,327,000
Kuwait \kə-ˈwāt\	1,356,000
Laos \ˈlaùs, ˈlä-ōs\	4,104,000
Lebanon \ˈleb-ə-nən\	3,161,000
Lesotho \lə-ˈsü-ˌtü\	1,214,000
Liberia \lī-ˈbir-ē-ə\	1,503,000
Libya \ˈlib-ē-ə\	3,224,000
Liechtenstein \ˈlik-tən-ˌs(h)tīn\	26,000
Luxembourg \ˈlək-səm-ˌbərg, ˈlùk-səm-ˌbùrg\	365,000
Madagascar \ˌmad-ə-ˈgas-kər\	7,604,000
Malawi \mə-ˈlä-wē\	5,547,000
Malaysia \mə-ˈlā-zh(ē-)ə\	13,700,000
Maldives \ˈmȯl-ˌdēvz, -ˌdīvz\	143,000
Mali \ˈmäl-ē\	6,525,000
Malta \ˈmȯl-tə\	366,000
Mauritania \ˌmȯr-ə-ˈtā-nē-ə\	1,420,000
Mauritius \mȯ-ˈrish-(ē-)əs\	993,000
Mexico \ˈmek-si-ˌkō\	67,396,000
Monaco \ˈmän-ə-ˌkō\	27,000
Mongolia \män-ˈgōl-yə\	1,595,000
Morocco \mə-ˈräk-ō\	21,392,000

Nations of the World

872

Mozambique
\ ˌmō-zəm-ˈbēk\ 11.674.000
Nauru \nä-ˈü-(ˌ)rü\ 7.000
Nepal \nə-ˈpȯl\ 15.020.000
Netherlands
\ ˈneth-ər-lən(d)z\ 14.386.000
New Zealand \-ˈzē-lənd\ . 3.176.000
Nicaragua
\ ˌnik-ə-ˈräg-wə\ 2.824.000
Niger \ˈnī-jər\ 5.098.000
Nigeria \nī-ˈjir-ē-ə\ 86.126.000
North Korea \-kə-ˈrē-ə\ .. 18.747.000
Norway \ˈnȯr-ˌwā\ 4.091.000
Oman \ō-ˈmän\ 1.079.000
Pakistan \ ˈpak-i-ˌstan.
ˌpäk-i-ˈstän\ 83.782.000
Panama \ˈpan-ə-ˌmä\ 1.825.000
Papua New Guinea
\ ˈpäp-ə-wə-\ 3.011.000
Paraguay \ ˈpar-ə-ˌgwī.
-ˌgwä\ 3.026.000
Peru \pə-ˈrü\ 17.031.000
Philippines \ˌfil-ə-ˈpēnz.
ˈfil-ə-ˌpēnz\ 48.098.000
Poland \ˈpō-lənd\ 35.061.000
Portugal \ˈpȯr-chi-gəl\ ... 9.784.000
Qatar \ ˈkät-ər\ 270.000
Romania \rù-ˈmā-nē-ə\ ... 21.560.000
Rwanda \rù-ˈän-də\ 4.819.000
St. Christopher-Nevis
\sänt-ˈkris-tə-fər-ˈnē-
vəs\ 44.000
St. Lucia \-ˈlü-shə\ 122.000
St. Vincent and the
Grenadines ....
\-ˈvin-sənt . . .
ˌgren-ə-ˈdēnz\ 124.000
San Marino
\ ˌsan-mə-ˈrē-nō\ 19.000
Sao Tome and Principe
\ ˌsaù-tə-ˈmä-ən-
ˌprin-sə-pə\ 89.000
Saudi Arabia \ˌsaùd-ē-ə-
ˈrä-bē-ə. sä-ˌüd-ē-\ 10.025.000
Senegal \ˌsen-i-ˈgȯl\ 5.811.000
Seychelles \sā-ˈchel(z)\ ... 62.000
Sierra Leone
\sē-ˌer-ə-lē-ˈōn\ 2.735.000
Singapore
\ ˈsiŋ-(g)ə-ˌpōr\ 2.414.000
Solomon Islands
\ ˈsäl-ə-mən-\ 197.000
Somalia \sō-ˈmäl-ē-ə\ 5.085.000
South Africa. Republic of . 26.129.000
South Korea \-kə-ˈrē-ə\ .. 37.436.000
Spain \ˈspān\ 37.746.000
Sri Lanka \(ˈ)srē-ˈläŋ-kə.
(ˈ)shrē\ 14.850.000
Sudan \sü-ˈdan\ 20.564.000

Suriname
\ ˌsùr-ə-ˈnäm-ə\ 352.000
Swaziland
\ ˈswäz-ē-ˌland\ 494.000
Sweden \ˈswēd-ən\ 8.208.000
Switzerland
\ ˈswit-sər-lənd\ 6.366.000
Syria \ ˈsir-ē-ə\ 9.172.000
Taiwan (Republic of China)
\tī-ˈwän\ 14.811.000
Tanzania \ˌtan-zə-ˈnē-ə\ .. 17.528.000
Thailand \ˈtī-ˌland.
-lənd\ 44.278.000
Togo \ˈtō-gō\ 2.703.000
Trinidad and Tobago
\ ˈtrin-ə-ˌdad-ən-
tə-ˈbä-gō\ 1.060.000
Tunisia
\t(y)ü-ˈnē-zh(ē-)ə\ 6.966.000
Turkey \ˈtər-kē\ 44.737.000
Uganda \yü-ˈgan-də\ 12.630.000
Union of Soviet Socialist
Republics (U.S.S.R.) ....
\-ˈsō-vē-ˌet.
(ˌ)yü-ˌes-ˌes-ˈär)\ 262.436.000
United Arab Emirates
\-ˈem-ə-rəts\ 1.043.000
United Kingdom of Great
Britain and Northern
Ireland ....
\-ˈbrit-ən. . .
ˈī(ə)r-lənd\ 55.671.000
England \ˈiŋ-glənd\ ....
Northern Ireland ....
Scotland \ˈskät-lənd\ ...
Wales \ ˈwālz\ ....
United States of America
\-ə-ˈmer-i-kə\ 226.504.825
Uruguay \ˈ(y)ùr-ə-ˌgwī.
ˈyùr-ə-ˌgwä\ 2.788.000
Vanuatu \ˌvan-ə-ˈwät-ü\ .. 112.000
Vatican City State
\ ˌvat-i-kən-\ 700
Venezuela
\ ˌven-əz(-ə)-ˈwā-lə\ ... 14.517.000
Vietnam \vē-ˈet-ˈnäm\ 52.742.000
Western Samoa
\-sə-ˈmō-ə\ 156.000
West Germany
\-ˈjər-mə-nē\ 61.371.000
Yemen. People's Demo-
cratic Republic of
\-ˈyem-ən\ 2.158.000
Yemen Arab Republic 5.238.000
Yugoslavia
\ˌyü-gō-ˈsläv-ē-ə\ 22.839.000
Zaire \zä-ˈi(ə)r\ 30.261.000
Zambia \ˈzam-bē-ə\ 5.680.000
Zimbabwe \zim-ˈbäb-wä\ . 7.550.000

Population of Places in the United States
Having 16,500 or More Inhabitants in 1980

A

Aberdeen, S. Dak.	25,956
Aberdeen, Wash.	18,739
Abilene, Tex.	98,315
Acton, Mass.	17,544
Addison, Ill.	29,759
Adrian, Mich.	21,186
Agawam, Mass.	26,271
Aiea, Hawaii	32,879
Akron, Ohio	237,177
Alameda, Calif.	63,852
Alamogordo, N. Mex.	24,024
Albany, Ga.	74,059
Albany, N.Y.	101,727
Albany, Oreg.	26,546
Albert Lea, Minn.	19,200
Albuquerque, N. Mex.	331,767
Alexandria, La.	51,565
Alexandria, Va.	103,217
Alhambra, Calif.	64,615
Alice, Tex.	20,961
Aliquippa, Pa.	17,094
Allen Park, Mich.	34,196
Allentown, Pa.	103,758
Alliance, Ohio	24,315
Alsip, Ill.	17,134
Altamonte Springs, Fla.	22,028
Alton, Ill.	34,171
Altoona, Pa.	57,078
Altus, Okla.	23,101
Alvin, Tex.	16,515
Amarillo, Tex.	149,230
Ames, Iowa	45,775
Amherst, Mass.	33,229
Amsterdam, N.Y.	21,872
Anaheim, Calif.	221,847
Anchorage, Alaska	174,431
Anderson, Ind.	64,695
Anderson, S.C.	27,313
Andover, Mass.	26,370
Annapolis, Md.	31,740
Ann Arbor, Mich.	107,966
Anniston, Ala.	29,523
Ansonia, Conn.	19,039
Antioch, Calif.	43,559
Appleton, Wis.	59,032
Apple Valley, Minn.	21,818
Arcadia, Calif.	45,994
Ardmore, Okla.	23,689
Arlington, Mass.	48,219
Arlington, Tex.	160,113
Arlington Heights, Ill.	66,116
Arnold, Mo.	19,141
Arvada, Colo.	84,576
Asbury Park, N.J.	17,015
Asheville, N.C.	53,583
Ashland, Ky.	27,064
Ashland, Ohio	20,326
Ashtabula, Ohio	23,449
Athens, Ga.	42,549
Athens, Ohio	19,743
Atlanta, Ga.	425,022
Atlantic City, N.J.	40,199
Attleboro, Mass.	34,196

Atwater, Calif.	17,530
Auburn, Ala.	28,471
Auburn, Me.	23,128
Auburn, N.Y.	32,548
Auburn, Wash.	26,417
Augusta, Ga.	47,532
Augusta, Me.	21,819
Aurora, Colo.	158,588
Aurora, Ill.	81,293
Austin, Minn.	23,020
Austin, Tex.	345,496
Azusa, Calif.	29,380

B

Bakersfield, Calif.	105,611
Baldwin, Pa.	24,598
Baldwin Park, Calif.	50,554
Baltimore, Md.	786,775
Bangor, Me.	31,643
Barberton, Ohio	29,751
Barnstable, Mass.	30,898
Barstow, Calif.	17,690
Bartlesville, Okla.	34,568
Bartlett, Tenn.	17,170
Batavia, N.Y.	16,703
Baton Rouge, La.	219,419
Battle Creek, Mich.	35,724
Bay City, Mich.	41,593
Bay City, Tex.	17,837
Bayonne, N.J.	65,047
Baytown, Tex.	56,923
Bay Village, Ohio	17,846
Beaumont, Tex.	118,102
Beavercreek, Ohio	31,589
Beaverton, Oreg.	30,582
Beckley, W. Va.	20,492
Bedford, Tex.	20,821
Bell, Calif.	25,450
Belle Glade, Fla.	16,535
Belleville, Ill.	41,580
Belleville, N.J.	35,367
Bellevue, Nebr.	21,813
Bellevue, Wash.	73,903
Bellflower, Calif.	53,441
Bell Gardens, Calif.	34,117
Bellingham, Wash.	45,794
Bellwood, Ill.	19,811
Belmont, Calif.	24,505
Belmont, Mass.	26,100
Beloit, Wis.	35,207
Bend, Oreg.	17,263
Benton, Ark.	17,717
Berea, Ohio	19,567
Bergenfield, N.J.	25,568
Berkeley, Calif.	103,328
Berkley, Mich.	18,637
Berwyn, Ill.	46,849
Bessemer, Ala.	31,729
Bethany, Okla.	22,130
Bethel Park, Pa.	34,755
Bethlehem, Pa.	70,419
Bettendorf, Iowa	27,381
Beverly, Mass.	37,655
Beverly Hills, Calif.	32,367
Biddeford, Me.	19,638

Big Spring, Tex.	24.804	Butte, Mont.	36.817
Billerica, Mass.	36.727		
Billings, Mont.	66.798	**C**	
Biloxi, Miss.	49.311	Cahokia, Ill.	18.904
Binghamton, N.Y.	55.860	Caldwell, Idaho	17.699
Birmingham, Ala.	284.413	Calumet City, Ill.	39.697
Birmingham, Mich.	21.689	Camarillo, Calif.	37.732
Bismarck, N. Dak.	44.485	Cambridge, Mass.	95.322
Blacksburg, Va.	30.638	Camden, N.J.	84.910
Blaine, Minn.	28.558	Campbell, Calif.	27.067
Bloomfield, Conn.	18.608	Canton, Mass.	18.182
Bloomfield, N.J.	47.792	Canton, Ohio	94.730
Bloomington, Ill.	44.189	Cape Coral, Fla.	32.103
Bloomington, Ind.	52.044	Cape Girardeau, Mo.	34.361
Bloomington, Minn.	81.831	Carbondale, Ill.	26.287
Blue Island, Ill.	21.853	Carlisle, Pa.	18.314
Blue Springs, Mo.	25.927	Carlsbad, Calif.	35.490
Blytheville, Ark.	23.844	Carlsbad, N. Mex.	25.496
Boca Raton, Fla.	49.505	Carmel, Ind.	18.272
Bogalusa, La.	16.976	Carpentersville, Ill.	23.272
Boise, Idaho	102.451	Carrollton, Tex.	40.595
Bolingbrook, Ill.	37.261	Carson, Calif.	81.221
Bossier City, La.	50.817	Carson City, Nev.	32.022
Boston, Mass.	562.994	Carteret, N.J.	20.598
Boulder, Colo.	76.685	Cary, N.C.	21.763
Bountiful, Utah	32.877	Casper, Wyo.	51.016
Bowie, Md.	33.695	Cedar Falls, Iowa	36.322
Bowling Green, Ky.	40.450	Cedar Rapids, Iowa	110.243
Bowling Green, Ohio	25.728	Centerville, Ohio	18.886
Boynton Beach, Fla.	35.624	Central Falls, R.I.	16.995
Bozeman, Mont.	21.645	Cerritos, Calif.	53.020
Bradenton, Fla.	30.170	Champaign, Ill.	58.133
Braintree, Mass.	36.337	Chandler, Ariz.	29.673
Branford, Conn.	23.363	Chapel Hill, N.C.	32.421
Brea, Calif.	27.913	Charleston, Ill.	19.355
Bremerton, Wash.	36.208	Charleston, S.C.	69.510
Bridgeport, Conn.	142.546	Charleston, W. Va.	63.968
Bridgeton, Mo.	18.445	Charlotte, N.C.	314.447
Bridgeton, N.J.	18.795	Charlottesville, Va.	39.916
Bristol, Conn.	57.370	Chattanooga, Tenn.	169.565
Bristol, R.I.	20.128	Chelmsford, Mass.	31.174
Bristol, Tenn.	23.986	Chelsea, Mass.	25.431
Bristol, Va.	19.042	Chesapeake, Va.	114.486
Brockton, Mass.	95.172	Cheshire, Conn.	21.788
Broken Arrow, Okla.	35.761	Chester, Pa.	45.794
Brookfield, Ill.	19.395	Cheyenne, Wyo.	47.283
Brookfield, Wis.	34.035	Chicago, Ill.	3.005.072
Brookline, Mass.	55.062	Chicago Heights, Ill.	37.026
Brooklyn Center, Minn.	31.230	Chico, Calif.	26.601
Brooklyn Park, Minn.	43.332	Chicopee, Mass.	55.112
Brook Park, Ohio	26.195	Chillicothe, Ohio	23.420
Broomfield, Colo.	20.730	Chino, Calif.	40.165
Brownsville, Tex.	84.997	Chula Vista, Calif.	83.927
Brownwood, Tex.	19.396	Cicero, Ill.	61.232
Brunswick, Ga.	17.605	Cincinnati, Ohio	385.457
Brunswick, Me.	17.366	Claremont, Calif.	30.950
Brunswick, Ohio	28.104	Clarksburg, W. Va.	22.371
Bryan, Tex.	44.337	Clarksdale, Miss.	21.137
Buena Park, Calif.	64.165	Clarksville, Tenn.	54.777
Buffalo, N.Y.	357.870	Clearfield, Utah	17.982
Burbank, Calif.	84.625	Clearwater, Fla.	85.528
Burbank, Ill.	28.462	Cleburne, Tex.	19.218
Burlingame, Calif.	26.173	Cleveland, Ohio	573.822
Burlington, Iowa	29.529	Cleveland, Tenn.	26.415
Burlington, Mass.	23.486	Cleveland Heights, Ohio	56.438
Burlington, N.C.	37.266	Cliffside Park, N.J.	21.464
Burlington, Vt.	37.712	Clifton, N.J.	74.388
Burnsville, Minn.	35.674	Clinton, Iowa	32.828
Burton, Mich.	29.976	Clovis, Calif.	33.021
Butler, Pa.	17.026	Clovis, N. Mex.	31.194

Place	Population
Coeur d'Alene, Idaho	20,054
Cohoes, N.Y.	18,144
College Park, Ga.	24,632
College Park, Md.	23,614
College Station, Tex.	37,272
Collinsville, Ill.	19,613
Colonial Heights, Va.	16,509
Colorado Springs, Colo.	215,150
Colton, Calif.	21,310
Columbia, Mo.	62,061
Columbia, S.C.	99,296
Columbia, Tenn.	26,372
Columbia Heights, Minn.	20,029
Columbus, Ga.	169,441
Columbus, Ind.	30,614
Columbus, Miss.	27,383
Columbus, Nebr.	17,328
Columbus, Ohio	564,871
Compton, Calif.	81,286
Concord, Calif.	103,255
Concord, N.H.	30,400
Concord, N.C.	16,942
Connersville, Ind.	17,023
Conroe, Tex.	18,034
Conway, Ark.	20,375
Cookeville, Tenn.	20,535
Coon Rapids, Minn.	35,826
Copperas Cove, Tex.	19,469
Coral Gables, Fla.	43,241
Coral Springs, Fla.	37,349
Corona, Calif.	37,791
Coronado, Calif.	16,859
Corpus Christi, Tex.	231,999
Corsicana, Tex.	21,712
Cortland, N.Y.	20,138
Corvallis, Oreg.	40,960
Costa Mesa, Calif.	82,562
Cottage Grove, Minn.	18,994
Council Bluffs, Iowa	56,449
Coventry, R.I.	27,065
Covina, Calif.	33,751
Covington, Ky.	49,563
Cranston, R.I.	71,992
Crystal, Minn.	25,543
Crystal Lake, Ill.	18,590
Cudahy, Calif.	17,984
Cudahy, Wis.	19,547
Culver City, Calif.	38,139
Cumberland, Md.	25,933
Cumberland, R.I.	27,069
Cupertino, Calif.	34,015
Cuyahoga Falls, Ohio	43,890
Cypress, Calif.	40,391

D

Place	Population
Dallas, Tex.	904,078
Dalton, Ga.	20,939
Daly City, Calif.	78,519
Danbury, Conn.	60,470
Danvers, Mass.	24,100
Danville, Ill.	38,985
Danville, Va.	45,642
Darien, Conn.	18,892
Dartmouth, Mass.	23,966
Davenport, Iowa	103,264
Davie, Fla.	20,877
Davis, Calif.	36,640
Dayton, Ohio	203,371
Daytona Beach, Fla.	54,176
Dearborn, Mich.	90,660

Place	Population
Dearborn Heights, Mich.	67,706
Decatur, Ala.	42,002
Decatur, Ga.	18,404
Decatur, Ill.	94,081
Dedham, Mass.	25,298
Deerfield, Ill.	17,430
Deerfield Beach, Fla.	39,193
Deer Park, Tex.	22,648
Defiance, Ohio	16,810
De Kalb, Ill.	33,099
Delaware, Ohio	18,780
Del City, Okla.	28,424
Delray Beach, Fla.	34,325
Del Rio, Tex.	30,034
Denison, Tex.	23,884
Denton, Tex.	48,063
Denver, Colo.	492,365
Depew, N.Y.	19,819
Derry, N.H.	18,875
Des Moines, Iowa	191,003
Des Plaines, Ill.	53,568
Detroit, Mich.	1,203,339
Dodge City, Kans.	18,001
Dolton, Ill.	24,766
Dothan, Ala.	48,750
Dover, Del.	23,512
Dover, N.H.	22,377
Downers Grove, Ill.	42,572
Downey, Calif.	82,602
Dracut, Mass.	21,249
Duarte, Calif.	16,766
Dubuque, Iowa	62,321
Duluth, Minn.	92,811
Dumont, N.J.	18,334
Duncan, Okla.	22,517
Duncanville, Tex.	27,781
Dunedin, Fla.	30,203
Dunmore, Pa.	16,781
Durham, N.C.	100,831

E

Place	Population
Eagan, Minn.	20,700
Eagle Pass, Tex.	21,407
East Chicago, Ind.	39,786
East Cleveland, Ohio	36,957
East Detroit, Mich.	38,280
East Hartford, Conn.	52,563
East Haven, Conn.	25,028
Eastlake, Ohio	22,104
East Lansing, Mich.	51,392
East Liverpool, Ohio	16,687
East Moline, Ill.	20,907
Easton, Mass.	16,623
Easton, Pa.	26,027
East Orange, N.J.	77,690
East Peoria, Ill.	22,385
East Point, Ga.	37,486
East Providence, R.I.	50,980
East Ridge, Tenn.	21,236
East St. Louis, Ill.	55,200
Eau Claire, Wis.	51,509
Edina, Minn.	46,073
Edinburg, Tex.	24,075
Edmond, Okla.	34,637
Edmonds, Wash.	27,679
El Cajon, Calif.	73,892
El Centro, Calif.	23,996
El Cerrito, Calif.	22,731
El Dorado, Ark.	25,270
Elgin, Ill.	63,798

Greenville, N.C.	35,740
Greenville, S.C.	58,242
Greenville, Tex.	22,161
Greenwich, Conn.	59,578
Greenwood, Ind.	19,327
Greenwood, Miss.	20,115
Greenwood, S.C.	21,613
Gresham, Oreg.	33,005
Gretna, La.	20,615
Griffin, Ga.	20,728
Griffith, Ind.	17,026
Grosse Pointe Woods, Mich.	18,886
Groton, Conn.	41,062
Grove City, Ohio	16,816
Groves, Tex.	17,090
Guilford, Conn.	17,375
Gulfport, Miss.	39,676

H

Hackensack, N.J.	36,039
Hagerstown, Md.	34,132
Hallandale, Fla.	36,517
Haltom City, Tex.	29,014
Hamden, Conn.	51,071
Hamilton, Ohio	63,189
Hammond, Ind.	93,714
Hampton, Va.	122,617
Hamtramck, Mich.	21,300
Hanford, Calif.	20,958
Hannibal, Mo.	18,811
Hanover Park, Ill.	28,850
Harlingen, Tex.	43,543
Harrisburg, Pa.	53,264
Harrison, N.Y.	23,046
Harrisonburg, Va.	19,671
Hartford, Conn.	136,392
Harvey, Ill.	35,810
Hastings, Nebr.	23,045
Hattiesburg, Miss.	40,829
Havelock, N.C.	17,718
Haverhill, Mass.	46,865
Hawthorne, Calif.	56,447
Hawthorne, N.J.	18,200
Hayward, Calif.	94,167
Hazel Park, Mich.	20,914
Hazleton, Pa.	27,318
Helena, Mont.	23,938
Hemet, Calif.	22,454
Hempstead, N.Y.	40,404
Henderson, Ky.	24,834
Henderson, Nev.	24,363
Hendersonville, Tenn.	26,561
Hermosa Beach, Calif.	18,070
Hialeah, Fla.	145,254
Hibbing, Minn.	21,193
Hickory, N.C.	20,757
Highland, Ind.	25,935
Highland Park, Ill.	30,611
Highland Park, Mich.	27,909
High Point, N.C.	63,380
Hillsboro, Oreg.	27,664
Hilo, Hawaii	35,269
Hingham, Mass.	20,339
Hinsdale, Ill.	16,726
Hobart, Ind.	22,987
Hobbs, N. Mex.	29,153
Hoboken, N.J.	42,460
Hoffman Estates, Ill.	37,272
Holland, Mich.	26,281
Hollywood, Fla.	121,323
Holyoke, Mass.	44,678

Homestead, Fla.	20,668
Homewood, Ala.	21,412
Homewood, Ill.	19,724
Honolulu, Hawaii	365,048
Hoover, Ala.	19,792
Hopewell, Va.	23,397
Hopkinsville, Ky.	27,318
Hot Springs, Ark.	35,781
Houma, La.	32,602
Houston, Tex.	1,595,138
Huber Heights, Ohio	35,480
Huntington, W. Va.	63,684
Huntington Beach, Calif.	170,505
Huntington Park, Calif.	46,223
Huntsville, Ala.	142,513
Huntsville, Tex.	23,936
Hurst, Tex.	31,420
Hutchinson, Kans.	40,284

I

Idaho Falls, Idaho	39,590
Imperial Beach, Calif.	22,689
Independence, Mo.	111,806
Indianapolis, Ind.	700,807
Indio, Calif.	21,611
Inglewood, Calif.	94,245
Inkster, Mich.	35,190
Inver Grove Heights, Minn.	17,171
Iowa City, Iowa	50,508
Irvine, Calif.	62,134
Irving, Tex.	109,943
Irvington, N.J.	61,493
Ithaca, N.Y.	28,732

J

Jackson, Mich.	39,739
Jackson, Miss.	202,895
Jackson, Tenn.	49,131
Jacksonville, Ark.	27,589
Jacksonville, Fla.	540,920
Jacksonville, Ill.	20,284
Jacksonville, N.C.	17,056
Jamestown, N.Y.	35,775
Janesville, Wis.	51,071
Jefferson City, Mo.	33,619
Jeffersonville, Ind.	21,220
Jennings, Mo.	17,026
Jersey City, N.J.	223,532
Johnson City, N.Y.	17,126
Johnson City, Tenn.	39,753
Johnston, R.I.	24,907
Johnstown, Pa.	35,496
Joliet, Ill.	77,956
Jonesboro, Ark.	31,530
Joplin, Mo.	38,893
Junction City, Kans.	19,305
Juneau, Alaska	19,528

K

Kailua, Hawaii	35,812
Kalamazoo, Mich.	79,722
Kaneohe, Hawaii	29,919
Kankakee, Ill.	30,141
Kansas City, Kans.	161,087
Kansas City, Mo.	448,159
Kearney, Nebr.	21,158
Kearny, N.J.	35,735
Keene, N.H.	21,449
Kenmore, N.Y.	18,474
Kenner, La.	66,382
Kennewick, Wash.	34,397

Kenosha, Wis.	77,685		Lexington, Ky.	204,165
Kent, Ohio	26,164		Lexington, Mass.	29,479
Kent, Wash.	23,152		Libertyville, Ill.	16,520
Kentwood, Mich.	30,438		Lima, Ohio	47,381
Kettering, Ohio	61,186		Lincoln, Nebr.	171,932
Key West, Fla.	24,382		Lincoln, R.I.	16,949
Killeen, Tex.	46,296		Lincoln Park, Mich.	45,105
Kingsport, Tenn.	32,027		Linden, N.J.	37,836
Kingston, N.Y.	24,481		Lindenhurst, N.Y.	26,919
Kingsville, Tex.	28,808		Lindenwold, N.J.	18,196
Kinston, N.C.	25,234		Little Rock, Ark.	158,461
Kirkland, Wash.	18,779		Littleton, Colo.	28,631
Kirksville, Mo.	17,167		Livermore, Calif.	48,349
Kirkwood, Mo.	27,987		Livonia, Mich.	104,814
Klamath Falls, Oreg.	16,661		Lockport, N.Y.	24,844
Knoxville, Tenn.	175,030		Lodi, Calif.	35,221
Kokomo, Ind.	47,808		Lodi, N.J.	23,956
			Logan, Utah	26,844
L			Logansport, Ind.	17,899
La Canada Flintridge, Calif.	20,153		Lombard, Ill.	37,295
Lackawanna, N.Y.	22,701		Lomita, Calif.	18,807
La Crosse, Wis.	48,347		Lompoc, Calif.	26,267
Lafayette, Calif.	20,879		Long Beach, Calif.	361,334
Lafayette, Ind.	43,011		Long Beach, N.Y.	34,073
Lafayette, La.	81,961		Long Branch, N.J.	29,819
La Grange, Ga.	24,204		Longmont, Colo.	42,942
Laguna Beach, Calif.	17,901		Longview, Tex.	62,762
La Habra, Calif.	45,232		Longview, Wash.	31,052
Lake Charles, La.	75,226		Lorain, Ohio	75,416
Lake Jackson, Tex.	19,102		Los Altos, Calif.	25,769
Lakeland, Fla.	47,406		Los Angeles, Calif.	2,966,763
Lake Oswego, Oreg.	22,868		Los Gatos, Calif.	26,593
Lakewood, Calif.	74,654		Louisville, Ky.	298,451
Lakewood, Colo.	112,860		Loveland, Colo.	30,244
Lakewood, Ohio	61,963		Lowell, Mass.	92,418
Lake Worth, Fla.	27,048		Lubbock, Tex.	173,979
La Mesa, Calif.	50,308		Ludlow, Mass.	18,150
La Mirada, Calif.	40,986		Lufkin, Tex.	28,562
Lancaster, Calif.	48,027		Lumberton, N.C.	18,241
Lancaster, Ohio	34,953		Lynbrook, N.Y.	20,424
Lancaster, Pa.	54,725		Lynchburg, Va.	66,743
Lansdale, Pa.	16,526		Lyndhurst, Ohio	18,092
Lansing, Ill.	29,039		Lynn, Mass.	78,471
Lansing, Mich.	130,414		Lynnwood, Wash.	22,641
La Porte, Ind.	21,796		Lynwood, Calif.	48,548
La Puente, Calif.	30,882			
Laramie, Wyo.	24,410		**M**	
Laredo, Tex.	91,449		McAlester, Okla.	17,255
Largo, Fla.	58,977		McAllen, Tex.	66,281
Las Cruces, N. Mex.	45,086		McKeesport, Pa.	31,012
Las Vegas, Nev.	164,674		Macomb, Ill.	19,863
Lauderdale Lakes, Fla.	25,426		Macon, Ga.	116,896
Lauderhill, Fla.	37,271		Madera, Calif.	21,732
Laurel, Miss.	21,897		Madison, Wis.	170,616
La Verne, Calif.	23,508		Madison Heights, Mich.	35,375
Lawndale, Calif.	23,460		Madisonville, Ky.	16,979
Lawrence, Ind.	25,591		Malden, Mass.	53,386
Lawrence, Kans.	52,738		Mamaroneck, N.Y.	17,616
Lawrence, Mass.	63,175		Manchester, Conn.	49,761
Lawton, Okla.	80,054		Manchester, N.H.	90,936
Layton, Utah	22,862		Manhattan, Kans.	32,644
League City, Tex.	16,578		Manhattan Beach, Calif.	31,542
Leavenworth, Kans.	33,656		Manitowoc, Wis.	32,547
Lebanon, Pa.	25,711		Mankato, Minn.	28,651
Lee's Summit, Mo.	28,741		Mansfield, Conn.	20,634
Lemon Grove, Calif.	20,780		Mansfield, Ohio	53,927
Lenexa, Kans.	18,639		Manteca, Calif.	24,925
Leominster, Mass.	34,508		Maple Grove, Minn.	20,525
Lewiston, Idaho	27,986		Maple Heights, Ohio	29,735
Lewiston, Me.	40,481		Maplewood, Minn.	26,990
Lewisville, Tex.	24,273		Marblehead, Mass.	20,126

Margate, Fla.	36,044	Monroe, La.	57,597
Marietta, Ga.	30,829	Monroe, Mich.	23,531
Marina, Calif.	20,647	Monroeville, Pa.	30,977
Marion, Ind.	35,874	Monrovia, Calif.	30,531
Marion, Iowa	19,474	Montclair, Calif.	22,628
Marion, Ohio	37,040	Montclair, N.J.	38,321
Marlborough, Mass.	30,617	Montebello, Calif.	52,929
Marquette, Mich.	23,288	Monterey, Calif.	27,558
Marshall, Tex.	24,921	Monterey Park, Calif.	54,338
Marshalltown, Iowa	26,938	Montgomery, Ala.	177,857
Marshfield, Mass.	20,916	Moore, Okla.	35,063
Marshfield, Wis.	18,290	Moorhead, Minn.	29,998
Martinez, Calif.	22,582	Morgan Hill, Calif.	17,060
Martinsville, Va.	18,149	Morgantown, W. Va.	27,605
Maryville, Tenn.	17,480	Morristown, N.J.	16,614
Mason City, Iowa	30,144	Morristown, Tenn.	19,683
Massapequa Park, N.Y.	19,779	Morton Grove, Ill.	23,747
Massillon, Ohio	30,557	Moscow, Idaho	16,513
Mattoon, Ill.	19,055	Moss Point, Miss.	18,998
Mayfield Heights, Ohio	21,550	Mountain Brook, Ala.	19,718
Maywood, Calif.	21,810	Mountain View, Calif.	58,655
Maywood, Ill.	27,998	Mount Clemens, Mich.	18,806
Medford, Mass.	58,076	Mountlake Terrace, Wash.	16,534
Medford, Oreg.	39,603	Mount Pleasant, Mich.	23,746
Melbourne, Fla.	46,536	Mount Prospect, Ill.	52,634
Melrose, Mass.	30,055	Mount Vernon, Ill.	17,193
Melrose Park, Ill.	20,735	Mount Vernon, N.Y.	66,713
Memphis, Tenn.	646,356	Muncie, Ind.	77,216
Menlo Park, Calif.	25,673	Mundelein, Ill.	17,053
Menomonee Falls, Wis.	27,845	Munster, Ind.	20,671
Mentor, Ohio	42,065	Murfreesboro, Tenn.	32,845
Merced, Calif.	36,499	Murray, Utah	25,750
Mercer Island, Wash.	21,522	Muscatine, Iowa	23,467
Meriden, Conn.	57,118	Muskegon, Mich.	40,823
Meridian, Miss.	46,577	Muskogee, Okla.	40,011
Merrillville, Ind.	27,677	Myrtle Beach, S.C.	18,446
Mesa, Ariz.	152,453		
Mesquite, Tex.	67,053	**N**	
Methuen, Mass.	36,701	Nacogdoches, Tex.	27,149
Miami, Fla.	346,865	Nampa, Idaho	25,112
Miami Beach, Fla.	96,298	Napa, Calif.	50,879
Michigan City, Ind.	36,850	Naperville, Ill.	42,330
Middletown, Conn.	39,040	Naples, Fla.	17,581
Middletown, N.Y.	21,454	Nashua, N.H.	67,865
Middletown, Ohio	43,719	Nashville, Tenn.	446,027
Middletown, R.I.	17,216	Natchez, Miss.	22,015
Midland, Mich.	37,250	Natchitoches, La.	16,664
Midland, Tex.	70,525	Natick, Mass.	29,461
Midwest City, Okla.	49,559	National City, Calif.	48,772
Milford, Conn.	50,898	Naugatuck, Conn.	26,456
Milford, Mass.	23,390	Nederland, Tex.	16,855
Mililani, Hawaii	21,365	Needham, Mass.	27,901
Millbrae, Calif.	20,058	Neenah, Wis.	22,432
Millington, Tenn.	20,236	New Albany, Ind.	37,103
Millville, N.J.	24,815	Newark, Calif.	32,126
Milpitas, Calif.	37,820	Newark, Del.	25,247
Milton, Mass.	25,860	Newark, N.J.	329,248
Milwaukee, Wis.	636,212	Newark, Ohio	41,200
Milwaukie, Oreg.	17,931	New Bedford, Mass.	98,478
Mineola, N.Y.	20,757	New Berlin, Wis.	30,529
Minneapolis, Minn.	370,951	New Braunfels, Tex.	22,402
Minnetonka, Minn.	38,683	New Brighton, Minn.	23,269
Minot, N. Dak.	32,843	New Britain, Conn.	73,840
Miramar, Fla.	32,813	New Brunswick, N.J.	41,442
Mishawaka, Ind.	40,201	Newburgh, N.Y.	23,438
Mission, Tex.	22,589	New Canaan, Conn.	17,931
Missoula, Mont.	33,388	New Castle, Ind.	20,056
Missouri City, Tex.	24,533	New Castle, Pa.	33,621
Mobile, Ala.	200,452	New Haven, Conn.	126,109
Modesto, Calif.	106,105	New Hope, Minn.	23,087
Moline, Ill.	45,709	New Iberia, La.	32,766

Phenix City, Ala.	26,928
Philadelphia, Pa.	1,688,210
Phillipsburg, N.J.	16,647
Phoenix, Ariz.	789,704
Pico Rivera, Calif.	53,459
Pine Bluff, Ark.	56,636
Pinellas Park, Fla.	32,811
Piqua, Ohio	20,480
Pittsburg, Calif.	33,034
Pittsburg, Kans.	18,770
Pittsburgh, Pa.	423,938
Pittsfield, Mass.	51,974
Placentia, Calif.	35,041
Plainfield, N.J.	45,555
Plainview, Tex.	22,187
Plano, Tex.	72,331
Plantation, Fla.	48,501
Plant City, Fla.	19,270
Plattsburgh, N.Y.	21,057
Pleasant Hill, Calif.	25,124
Pleasanton, Calif.	35,160
Plum, Pa.	25,390
Plymouth, Mass.	35,913
Plymouth, Minn.	31,615
Pocatello, Idaho	46,340
Point Pleasant, N.J.	17,747
Pomona, Calif.	92,742
Pompano Beach, Fla.	52,618
Ponca City, Okla.	26,238
Pontiac, Mich.	76,715
Poplar Bluff, Mo.	17,139
Portage, Ind.	27,409
Portage, Mich.	38,147
Port Angeles, Wash.	17,311
Port Arthur, Tex.	61,251
Port Chester, N.Y.	23,565
Porterville, Calif.	19,707
Port Hueneme, Calif.	17,803
Port Huron, Mich.	33,981
Portland, Me.	61,572
Portland, Oreg.	366,383
Port Orange, Fla.	18,756
Portsmouth, N.H.	26,254
Portsmouth, Ohio	25,943
Portsmouth, Va.	104,577
Pottstown, Pa.	22,729
Pottsville, Pa.	18,195
Poughkeepsie, N.Y.	29,757
Prairie Village, Kans.	24,657
Prattville, Ala.	18,647
Prescott, Ariz.	20,055
Prichard, Ala.	39,541
Providence, R.I.	156,804
Provo, Utah	73,907
Pueblo, Colo.	101,686
Pullman, Wash.	23,579
Puyallup, Wash.	18,251

Q

Quincy, Ill.	42,554
Quincy, Mass.	84,743

R

Racine, Wis.	85,725
Rahway, N.J.	26,723
Raleigh, N.C.	150,255
Rancho Cucamonga, Calif.	55,250
Rancho Palos Verdes, Calif.	36,577
Randolph, Mass.	28,218
Rantoul, Ill.	20,161
Rapid City, S. Dak.	46,492

Raytown, Mo.	31,759
Reading, Mass.	22,678
Reading, Pa.	78,686
Redding, Calif.	41,995
Redlands, Calif.	43,619
Redmond, Wash.	23,318
Redondo Beach, Calif.	57,102
Redwood City, Calif.	54,951
Reno, Nev.	100,756
Renton, Wash.	30,612
Revere, Mass.	42,423
Reynoldsburg, Ohio	20,661
Rialto, Calif.	37,474
Richardson, Tex.	72,496
Richfield, Minn.	37,851
Richland, Wash.	33,578
Richmond, Calif.	74,676
Richmond, Ind.	41,349
Richmond, Ky.	21,705
Richmond, Va.	219,214
Ridgefield, Conn.	20,120
Ridgewood, N.J.	25,208
Riverside, Calif.	170,876
Riviera Beach, Fla.	26,489
Roanoke, Va.	100,220
Rochester, Minn.	57,890
Rochester, N.H.	21,560
Rochester, N.Y.	241,741
Rockford, Ill.	139,712
Rock Hill, S.C.	35,344
Rock Island, Ill.	47,036
Rock Springs, Wyo.	19,458
Rockville, Md.	43,811
Rockville Centre, N.Y.	25,412
Rocky Mount, N.C.	41,283
Rocky River, Ohio	21,084
Rogers, Ark.	17,429
Rohnert Park, Calif.	22,965
Rolling Meadows, Ill.	20,167
Rome, Ga.	29,654
Rome, N.Y.	43,826
Romulus, Mich.	24,857
Roseburg, Oreg.	16,644
Roselle, Ill.	16,948
Roselle, N.J.	20,641
Rosemead, Calif.	42,604
Rosenberg, Tex.	17,995
Roseville, Calif.	24,347
Roseville, Mich.	54,311
Roseville, Minn.	35,820
Roswell, Ga.	23,337
Roswell, N. Mex.	39,676
Roy, Utah	19,694
Royal Oak, Mich.	70,893
Ruston, La.	20,585
Rutherford, N.J.	19,068
Rutland, Vt.	18,436

S

Sacramento, Calif.	275,741
Saginaw, Mich.	77,508
St. Charles, Ill.	17,492
St. Charles, Mo.	37,379
St. Clair Shores, Mich.	76,210
St. Cloud, Minn.	42,566
St. Joseph, Mo.	76,691
St. Louis, Mo.	453,085
St. Louis Park, Minn.	42,931
St. Paul, Minn.	270,230
St. Petersburg, Fla.	238,647
Salem, Mass.	38,220

Salem, N.H.	24,124	Sidney, Ohio	17,657
Salem, Oreg.	89,233	Sierra Vista, Ariz.	24,937
Salem, Va.	23,958	Sikeston, Mo.	17,431
Salina, Kans.	41,843	Simi Valley, Calif.	77,500
Salinas, Calif.	80,479	Simsbury, Conn.	21,161
Salisbury, N.C.	22,677	Sioux City, Iowa	82,003
Salt Lake City, Utah	163,033	Sioux Falls, S. Dak.	81,343
San Angelo, Tex.	73,240	Skokie, Ill.	60,278
San Antonio, Tex.	785,880	Slidell, La.	26,718
San Benito, Tex.	17,988	Smithfield, R.I.	16,886
San Bernardino, Calif.	117,490	Smyrna, Ga.	20,312
San Bruno, Calif.	35,417	Somerset, Mass.	18,813
San Carlos, Calif.	24,710	Somerville, Mass.	77,372
San Clemente, Calif.	27,325	South Bend, Ind.	109,727
San Diego, Calif.	875,538	Southbridge, Mass.	16,665
San Dimas, Calif.	24,014	South El Monte, Calif.	16,623
Sandusky, Ohio	31,360	South Euclid, Ohio	25,713
Sandy City, Utah	50,546	Southfield, Mich.	75,568
San Fernando, Calif.	17,731	South Gate, Calif.	66,784
Sanford, Fla.	23,176	Southgate, Mich.	32,058
Sanford, Me.	18,020	South Holland, Ill.	24,977
San Francisco, Calif.	678,974	Southington, Conn.	36,879
San Gabriel, Calif.	30,072	South Kingstown, R.I.	20,414
San Jose, Calif.	636,550	South Lake Tahoe, Calif.	20,681
San Juan Capistrano, Calif.	18,959	South Milwaukee, Wis.	21,069
San Leandro, Calif.	63,952	South Pasadena, Calif.	22,681
San Luis Obispo, Calif.	34,252	South Plainfield, N.J.	20,521
San Marcos, Calif.	17,479	South Portland, Me.	22,712
San Marcos, Tex.	23,420	South St. Paul, Minn.	21,235
San Mateo, Calif.	77,561	South San Francisco, Calif.	49,393
San Pablo, Calif.	19,750	South Windsor, Conn.	17,198
San Rafael, Calif.	44,700	Sparks, Nev.	40,780
Santa Ana, Calif.	203,713	Spartanburg, S.C.	43,968
Santa Barbara, Calif.	74,542	Spokane, Wash.	171,300
Santa Clara, Calif.	87,746	Springdale, Ark.	23,458
Santa Cruz, Calif.	41,483	Springfield, Ill.	99,637
Santa Fe, N. Mex.	48,953	Springfield, Mass.	152,319
Santa Maria, Calif.	39,685	Springfield, Mo.	133,116
Santa Monica, Calif.	88,314	Springfield, Ohio	72,563
Santa Paula, Calif.	20,552	Springfield, Oreg.	41,621
Santa Rosa, Calif.	83,205	Spring Valley, N.Y.	20,537
Sarasota, Fla.	48,868	Stamford, Conn.	102,453
Saratoga, Calif.	29,261	Stanton, Calif.	23,723
Saratoga Springs, N.Y.	23,906	State College, Pa.	36,130
Saugus, Mass.	24,746	Statesville, N.C.	18,622
Savannah, Ga.	141,390	Staunton, Va.	21,857
Sayreville, N.J.	29,969	Sterling Heights, Mich.	108,999
Scarsdale, N.Y.	17,650	Steubenville, Ohio	26,400
Schaumburg, Ill.	53,305	Stevens Point, Wis.	22,970
Schenectady, N.Y.	67,972	Stillwater, Okla.	38,268
Schofield Barracks, Hawaii	18,851	Stockton, Calif.	149,779
Scituate, Mass.	17,317	Stoneham, Mass.	21,424
Scottsdale, Ariz.	88,412	Stoughton, Mass.	26,710
Scranton, Pa.	88,117	Stow, Ohio	25,303
Seal Beach, Calif.	25,975	Stratford, Conn.	50,541
Seaside, Calif.	36,567	Streamwood, Ill.	23,456
Seattle, Wash.	493,846	Strongsville, Ohio	28,577
Sedalia, Mo.	20,927	Suffolk, Va.	47,621
Seguin, Tex.	17,854	Sulphur, La.	19,709
Selma, Ala.	26,684	Summit, N.J.	21,071
Shaker Heights, Ohio	32,487	Sumter, S.C.	24,890
Sharon, Pa.	19,057	Sunnyvale, Calif.	106,618
Shawnee, Kans.	29,653	Sunrise, Fla.	39,681
Shawnee, Okla.	26,506	Superior, Wis.	29,571
Sheboygan, Wis.	48,085	Syracuse, N.Y.	170,105
Shelton, Conn.	31,314		
Sherman, Tex.	30,413	**T**	
Shively, Ky.	16,819	Tacoma, Wash.	158,501
Shoreview, Minn.	17,300	Talladega, Ala.	19,128
Shreveport, La.	205,820	Tallahassee, Fla	81,548
Shrewsbury, Mass.	22,674	Tamarac, Fla.	29,376

Tampa, Fla.	271,523	Wahiawa, Hawaii	16,911
Taunton, Mass.	45,001	Waipahu, Hawaii	29,139
Taylor, Mich.	77,568	Wakefield, Mass.	24,895
Tempe, Ariz.	106,743	Walla Walla, Wash.	25,618
Temple, Tex.	42,483	Wallingford, Conn.	37,274
Temple City, Calif.	28,972	Walnut Creek, Calif.	53,643
Terre Haute, Ind.	61,125	Walpole, Mass.	18,859
Tewksbury, Mass.	24,635	Waltham, Mass.	58,200
Texarkana, Ark.	21,459	Wareham, Mass.	18,457
Texarkana, Tex.	31,271	Warner Robins, Ga.	39,893
Texas City, Tex.	41,403	Warren, Mich.	161,134
Thomasville, Ga.	18,463	Warren, Ohio	56,629
Thornton, Colo.	40,343	Warrensville Heights, Ohio	16,565
Thousand Oaks, Calif.	77,072	Warwick, R.I.	87,123
Tiffin, Ohio	19,549	Washington, D.C.	637,651
Tinley Park, Ill.	26,171	Washington, Pa.	18,363
Titusville, Fla.	31,910	Waterbury, Conn.	103,266
Toledo, Ohio	354,635	Waterford, Conn.	17,843
Tonawanda, N.Y.	18,693	Waterloo, Iowa	75,985
Topeka, Kans.	115,266	Watertown, Conn.	19,489
Torrance, Calif.	131,497	Watertown, Mass.	34,384
Torrington, Conn.	30,987	Watertown, N.Y.	27,861
Tracy, Calif.	18,428	Watertown, Wis.	18,113
Trenton, Mich.	22,762	Waterville, Me.	17,779
Trenton, N.J.	92,124	Watsonville, Calif.	23,543
Troy, Mich.	67,102	Waukegan, Ill.	67,653
Troy, N.Y.	56,638	Waukesha, Wis.	50,319
Troy, Ohio	19,086	Wausau, Wis.	32,426
Trumbull, Conn.	32,989	Wauwatosa, Wis.	51,308
Tucson, Ariz.	330,537	Waycross, Ga.	19,371
Tulare, Calif.	22,475	Wayne, Mich.	21,159
Tulsa, Okla.	360,919	Webster Groves, Mo.	23,097
Tupelo, Miss.	23,905	Weirton, W. Va.	24,736
Turlock, Calif.	26,287	Wellesley, Mass.	27,209
Tuscaloosa, Ala.	75,211	Wenatchee, Wash.	17,257
Tustin, Calif.	32,317	Weslaco, Tex.	19,331
Twin Falls, Idaho	26,209	West Allis, Wis.	63,982
Tyler, Tex.	70,508	West Bend, Wis.	21,484
		Westchester, Ill.	17,730
U		West Chester, Pa.	17,435
		West Covina, Calif.	80,291
Union City, Calif.	39,406	West Des Moines, Iowa	21,894
Union City, N.J.	55,593	Westerly, R.I.	18,580
University City, Mo.	42,738	Westerville, Ohio	23,414
University Park, Tex.	22,254	Westfield, Mass.	36,465
Upland, Calif.	47,647	Westfield, N.J.	30,447
Upper Arlington, Ohio	35,648	West Hartford, Conn.	61,301
Urbana, Ill.	35,978	West Haven, Conn.	53,184
Urbandale, Iowa	17,869	West Jordan, Utah	27,192
Utica, N.Y.	75,632	West Lafayette, Ind.	21,247
		Westlake, Ohio	19,483
V		Westland, Mich.	84,603
Vacaville, Calif.	43,367	West Memphis, Ark.	28,138
Valdosta, Ga.	37,596	West Mifflin, Pa.	26,279
Vallejo, Calif.	80,303	Westminster, Calif.	71,133
Valley Stream, N.Y.	35,769	Westminster, Colo.	50,211
Valparaiso, Ind.	22,247	Westmont, Ill.	16,718
Vancouver, Wash.	42,834	West New York, N.J.	39,194
Ventura (San Buenaventura),	74,474	West Orange, N.J.	39,510
Calif.		West Palm Beach, Fla.	63,305
Vernon, Conn.	27,974	Westport, Conn.	25,290
Vicksburg, Miss.	25,434	West St. Paul, Minn.	18,527
Victoria, Tex.	50,695	West Springfield, Mass.	27,042
Villa Park, Ill.	23,185	West Warwick, R.I.	27,026
Vincennes, Ind.	20,857	Wethersfield, Conn.	26,031
Vineland, N.J.	53,753	Weymouth, Mass.	55,601
Virginia Beach, Va.	262,199	Wheaton, Ill.	43,043
Visalia, Calif.	49,729	Wheat Ridge, Colo.	30,293
Vista, Calif.	35,834	Wheeling, Ill.	23,266
		Wheeling, W. Va.	43,070
W		White Bear Lake, Minn.	22,538
Waco, Tex.	101,261		

Whitehall, Ohio	21,299
White Plains, N.Y.	46,999
Whittier, Calif.	69,717
Wichita, Kans.	279,272
Wichita Falls, Tex.	94,201
Wickliffe, Ohio	16,790
Wilkes-Barre, Pa.	51,551
Wilkinsburg, Pa.	23,669
Williamsport, Pa.	33,401
Willoughby, Ohio	19,329
Willowick, Ohio	17,834
Wilmette, Ill.	28,229
Wilmington, Del.	70,195
Wilmington, Mass.	17,471
Wilmington, N.C.	44,000
Wilson, N.C.	34,424
Winchester, Mass.	20,701
Winchester, Va.	20,217
Windham, Conn.	21,062
Windsor, Conn.	25,204
Winona, Minn.	25,075
Winston-Salem, N.C.	131,885
Winter Haven, Fla.	21,119
Winter Park, Fla.	22,339
Winthrop, Mass.	19,294
Wisconsin Rapids, Wis.	17,995
Woburn, Mass.	36,626

Woodland, Calif.	30,235
Woodridge, Ill.	22,322
Woonsocket, R.I.	45,914
Wooster, Ohio	19,289
Worcester, Mass.	161,799
Wyandotte, Mich.	34,006
Wyoming, Mich.	59,616

X

Xenia, Ohio	24,653

Y

Yakima, Wash.	49,826
Yarmouth, Mass.	18,449
Yonkers, N.Y.	195,351
Yorba Linda, Calif.	28,254
York, Pa.	44,619
Youngstown, Ohio	115,436
Ypsilanti, Mich.	24,031
Yuba City, Calif.	18,736
Yukon, Okla.	17,112
Yuma, Ariz.	42,433

Z

Zanesville, Ohio	28,655
Zion, Ill.	17,861

Population of the United States in 1980

SUMMARY BY STATES AND DEPENDENCIES
(Figures in parentheses give rank of states in population)

THE STATES AND THE DISTRICT OF COLUMBIA

State	Rank	Population
Alabama	(22)	3.893.888
Alaska	(50)	586.412
Arizona	(29)	2.718.215
Arkansas	(33)	2.286.435
California	(1)	23.667.902
Colorado	(28)	2.889.964
Connecticut	(25)	3.107.576
Delaware	(47)	594.338
District of Columbia		638.333
Florida	(7)	9.746.324
Georgia	(13)	5.463.105
Hawaii	(39)	964.691
Idaho	(41)	943.935
Illinois	(5)	11.426.518
Indiana	(12)	5.490.224
Iowa	(27)	2.913.808
Kansas	(32)	2.363.679
Kentucky	(23)	3.660.777
Louisiana	(19)	4.205.900
Maine	(38)	1.124.660
Maryland	(18)	4.216.975
Massachusetts	(11)	5.737.037
Michigan	(8)	9.262.078
Minnesota	(21)	4.075.970
Mississippi	(31)	2.520.638
Missouri	(15)	4.916.686
Montana	(44)	786.690
Nebraska	(35)	1.569.825
Nevada	(43)	800.493
New Hampshire	(42)	920.610
New Jersey	(9)	7.364.823
New Mexico	(37)	1.302.894
New York	(2)	17.558.072
North Carolina	(10)	5.881.766
North Dakota	(46)	652.717
Ohio	(6)	10.797.630
Oklahoma	(26)	3.025.290
Oregon	(30)	2.633.105
Pennsylvania	(4)	11.863.895
Rhode Island	(40)	947.154
South Carolina	(24)	3.121.820
South Dakota	(45)	690.768
Tennessee	(17)	4.591.120
Texas	(3)	14.229.191
Utah	(36)	1.461.037
Vermont	(48)	511.456
Virginia	(14)	5.356.818
Washington	(20)	4.132.156
West Virginia	(34)	1.949.644
Wisconsin	(16)	4.705.767
Wyoming	(49)	469.557
TOTAL		226.545.805

DEPENDENCIES

	Population
American Samoa	32.297
Guam	105.979
Puerto Rico	3.196.520
Virgin Islands of the U.S.	96.569
Other (Trust Territory of the Pacific Islands, etc.)	132.929
TOTAL	3.564.294
TOTAL U.S. & Dependencies	230.110.099

Population of Places in Canada
Having 16,500 or More Inhabitants in 1981

Place	Population
Ajax, Ont.	25.475
Alma, Que.	26.322
Anjou, Que.	37.346
Aylmer, Que.	26.695
Barrie, Ont.	38.423
Beaconsfield, Que.	19.613
Beauport, Que.	60.447
Belleville, Ont.	34.881
Beloeil, Que.	17.540
Boucherville, Que.	29.704
Brampton, Ont.	149.030
Brandon, Man.	36.242
Brantford, Ont.	74.315
Brockville, Ont.	19.896
Brossard, Que.	52.232
Burlington, Ont.	114.853
Burnaby, B.C.	136.494
Caledon, Ont.	26.645
Calgary, Alta.	592.743
Cambridge, Ont.	77.183
Cap-de-la-Madeleine, Que.	32.626
Charlesbourg, Que.	68.326
Châteauguay, Que.	36.928
Chatham, Ont.	40.952
Chicoutimi, Que.	60.064
Chilliwack, B.C.	40.642
Corner Brook, Nfld.	24.339
Cornwall, Ont.	46.144
Côte-St-Luc, Que.	27.531

Dartmouth, N.S.	62,277	Oshawa, Ont.	117,519
Delta, B.C.	74,692	Ottawa, Ont.	295,163
Dollard-des-Ormeaux,		Outremont, Que.	24,338
Que.	39,940	Owen Sound, Ont.	19,883
Dorval, Que.	17,722	Penticton, B.C.	23,181
Drummondville, Que.	27,347	Peterborough, Ont.	60,620
Dundas, Ont.	19,586	Pickering, Ont.	37,754
East York, Ont.	101,974	Pierrefonds, Que.	38,390
Edmonton, Alta.	532,246	Pointe-aux-Trembles,	
Elliot Lake, Ont.	16,723	Que.	36,270
Etobicoke, Ont.	298,713	Pointe-Claire, Que.	24,571
Fort Erie, Ont.	24,096	Port Alberni, B.C.	19,892
Fort McMurray, Alta.	31,000	Port Colborne, Ont.	19,225
Fredericton, N.B.	43,723	Port Coquitlam, B.C.	27,535
Gaspé, Que.	17,261	Prince Albert, Sask.	31,380
Gatineau, Que.	74,988	Prince George, B.C.	67,559
Glace Bay, N.S.	21,466	Quebec, Que.	166,474
Gloucester, Ont.	72,859	Red Deer, Alta.	46,393
Granby, Que.	38,069	Regina, Sask.	162,613
Grande Prairie, Alta.	24,263	Repentigny, Que.	34,419
Greenfield Park, Que.	18,527	Richmond Hill, Ont.	37,778
Guelph, Ont.	71,207	Rimouski, Que.	29,120
Haldimand, Ont.	16,866	Rouyn, Que.	17,224
Halifax, N.S.	114,594	St. Albert, Alta.	31,996
Halton Hills, Ont.	35,190	St-Bruno-de-Montarville,	
Hamilton, Ont.	306,434	Que.	22,880
Hull, Que.	56,225	St. Catharines, Ont.	124,018
Joliette, Que.	16,987	Ste-Foy, Que.	68,883
Jonquière, Que.	60,354	Ste-Thérèse, Que.	18,750
Kamloops, B.C.	64,048	St. Eustache, Que.	29,716
Kanata, Ont.	19,728	St-Hubert, Que.	60,573
Kelowna, B.C.	59,196	St-Hyacinthe, Que.	38,246
Kingston, Ont.	52,616	St-Jean, Que.	35,640
Kitchener, Ont.	139,734	St-Jérôme, Que.	25,123
La Baie, Que.	20,935	Saint John, N.B.	80,521
Lachine, Que.	37,521	St. John's, Nfld.	83,770
LaSalle, Que.	76,299	St-Lambert, Que.	20,557
Laval, Que.	268,335	St-Laurent, Que.	65,900
Lethbridge, Alta.	54,072	St-Léonard, Que.	79,429
Lévis, Que.	17,895	St. Thomas, Ont.	28,165
London, Ont.	254,280	Sarnia, Ont.	50,892
Longueuil, Que.	124,320	Saskatoon, Sask.	154,210
Markham, Ont.	77,037	Sault Ste. Marie, Ont.	82,697
Mascouche, Que.	20,345	Scarborough, Ont.	443,353
Medicine Hat, Alta.	40,380	Sept-Iles, Que.	29,262
Milton, Ont.	28,067	Shawinigan, Que.	23,011
Mississauga, Ont.	315,056	Sherbrooke, Que.	74,075
Moncton, N.B.	54,743	Sorel, Que.	20,347
Montreal, Que.	980,354	Stoney Creek, Ont.	36,762
Montreal-Nord, Que.	94,914	Stratford, Ont.	26,262
Mont-Royal, Que.	19,247	Sudbury, Ont.	91,829
Moose Jaw, Sask.	33,941	Sydney, N.S.	29,444
Nanaimo, B.C.	47,069	Thetford Mines, Que.	19,965
Nanticoke, Ont.	19,816	Thunder Bay, Ont.	112,486
Nepean, Ont.	84,361	Timmins, Ont.	46,114
Newcastle, Ont.	32,229	Toronto, Ont.	599,217
Newmarket, Ont.	29,753	Trois-Rivières, Que.	50,466
New Westminster,		Val-d'Or, Que.	21,371
B.C.	38,550	Valley East, Ont.	20,433
Niagara Falls, Ont.	70,960	Valleyfield, Que.	29,574
North Bay, Ont.	51,268	Vancouver, B.C.	414,281
North Vancouver, B.C.	33,952	Vanier, Ont.	18,792
North York, Ont.	559,521	Vaughan, Ont.	29,674
Oakville, Ont.	75,773	Verdun, Que.	61,287
Orillia, Ont.	23,955	Vernon, B.C.	19,987

Victoria, B.C.	64,379	Whitby, Ont.	36,698
Victoriaville, Que.	21,838	Windsor, Ont.	192,083
Waterloo, Ont.	49,428	Winnipeg, Man.	564,473
Welland, Ont.	45,448	Woodstock, Ont.	26,603
Westmount, Que.	20,480	York, Ont.	134,617

Population of Canada in 1981
SUMMARY BY PROVINCES AND TERRITORIES

Alberta	2,237,724	Prince Edward Island	122,506
British Columbia	2,744,467	Quebec	6,438,403
Manitoba	1,026,241	Saskatchewan	948,313
New Brunswick	696,403	Yukon Territory	21,836
Newfoundland	567,681	Northwest Territories	45,741
Nova Scotia	847,442	TOTAL	24,098,473
Ontario	8,625,107		

Signs and Symbols

Astronomy

⊙	the sun; Sunday	⊕, ⊖, or ♁	the earth
◍, ☾, or ☽	the moon; Monday	♂	Mars; Tuesday
●	new moon	♃	Jupiter; Thursday
☽, ◍, ☽, ☽	first quarter	♄ or ♄	Saturn; Saturday
○ or ☺	full moon	♅, ⯧, or ♅	Uranus
☾, ◍, ☾, ☾	last quarter	♆, ♆, or ♆	Neptune
☿	Mercury; Wednesday	♇	Pluto
♀	Venus; Friday	☄	comet
		* or ✳	fixed star

Business

a/c	account ⟨in a/c with⟩	%	percent
@	at; each ⟨4 apples @ 5¢ = 20¢⟩	‰	per thousand
℔	per	$	dollars
c/o	care of	¢	cents
#	number if it precedes a numeral ⟨track #3⟩; pounds if it follows ⟨a 5# sack of sugar⟩	£	pounds
		/	shillings
		©	copyrighted
lb	pound; pounds	®	registered trademark

Mathematics

+   plus; positive ⟨a + b = c⟩—used also to indicate omitted figures or an approximation

−   minus; negative

±   plus of minus ⟨the square root of $4a^2$ is ± 2a⟩

×   multiplied by; times ⟨6 × 4 = 24⟩—also indicated by placing a dot between the factors ⟨6·4 = 24⟩ or by writing factors other than numerals without signs

÷ or :   divided by ⟨24 ÷ 6 = 4⟩—also indicated by writing the divisor under the dividend with a line between ⟨$\frac{24}{6}$ = 4⟩ or by writing the divisor after the dividend with an oblique line between ⟨3/8⟩

=   equals ⟨6 + 2 = 8⟩

≠ or ≠	is not equal to
>	is greater than ⟨6>5⟩
>>	is much greater than
<	is less than ⟨3<4⟩
<<	is much less than
≧ or ≥	is greater than or equal to
≦ or ≤	is less than or equal to
≯	is not greater than
≮	is not less than
≈	is approximately equal to
≡	is identical to
∽	equivalent; similar
≅	is congruent to
∝	varies directly as; is proportional to
:	is to; the ratio of
∴	therefore
∞	infinity
∠	angle; the angle ⟨∠ABC⟩
∟	right angle ⟨∟ABC⟩
⊥	the perpendicular; is perpendicular to ⟨AB⊥CD⟩
∥	parallel; is parallel to ⟨AB∥CD⟩
⊙ or ○	circle
⌒	arc of a circle
△	triangle
□	square
▭	rectangle
√ or √	radical—used without a figure to indicate a square root (as in √4=) or with an index above the sign to indicate the root to be taken (as $\sqrt[n]{x}$) if the root is not a square root
( )	parentheses }
[ ]	brackets } indicate that the quantities enclosed by
{ }	braces } them are to be taken together
π	pi; the number 3.14159265+; the ration of the circumference of a circle to its diameter
°	degree ⟨60°⟩
′	minute; foot ⟨30′⟩
″	second; inch ⟨30″⟩
!	factorial—used to indicate the product of all the whole numbers up to and including a given preceding number
∪	union of two sets
∩	intersection of two sets
⊂	is included in, is a subset of
⊃	contains as a subset
∈ or ε	is an element of
∉	is not an element of
Λ or 0	empty set, null set
or φ or { }	

Medicine

ĀA, Ā, *or* āā	of each
℞	take—used on prescriptions; prescription; treatment
☠	poison

APOTHECARIES' MEASURES

℥	ounce
f℥	fluidounce
fℨ	fluidram
ℳ, ℳ, ℳ *or* min	minim

APOTHECARIES' WEIGHTS

℔	pound
℥	ounce (as ℥ i or ℥ j, one ounce; ℥ ss, half an ounce; ℥ iss *or* ℥ jss, one ounce and a half; ℥ ij, two ounces)
ℨ	dram
℈	scruple

Miscellaneous

&	and
&c	et cetera; and so forth
" *or* "	ditto marks
/	virgule; used to mean "or" (as in *and/or*), "and/or" (as in *dead/wounded*), "per" (as in *feet/second*), indicates end of a line of verse; separates the figures of a date (4/8/74)
☞	index *or* fist
<	derived from
>	whence derived
+	and
*	assumed

used in etymologies

†	died—used esp. in genealogies
✚	cross
✱	monogram from Greek XP signifying Christ
卐	swastika
✡	Judaism
☥	ankh
℣	versicle
℟	response
✳	—used in Roman Catholic and Anglican service books to divide each verse of a psalm, indicating where the response begins
✠ *or* +	—used in some service books to indicate where the sign of the cross is to be made; also used by certain Roman Catholic and Anglican prelates as a sign of the cross preceding their signatures

LXX Septuagint
fl or f: relative aperture of a photographic lens
🜨 civil defense
☮ peace

Reference marks

*	asterisk *or* star	§	section *or* numbered clause
†	dagger	‖	parallels
‡	double dagger	¶ *or* ℙ	paragraph

Stamps and stamp collecting

★	unused	⊞	block of four or more
○	used	⊠	entire cover or card

Weather

	barometer, changes of		
⌃	Rising, then falling	●	cloudy (completely overcast)
⟋	Rising, then steady; or rising, then rising more slowly	+	drifting or blowing snow
		❩	drizzle
⟋	Rising steadily, or unsteadily	≡	fog
		෴	freezing rain
√	Falling or steady, then rising; or rising, then rising more quickly	▲▲▲	cold front
		●●●	warm front
		▬▬	stationary front
—	Steady, same as 3 hours ago	)(	funnel clouds
		∞	haze
V	Falling, then rising, same or lower than 3 hours ago	◕	hurricane
		ϐ	tropical storm
		●	rain
⟍	Falling, then steady; or falling then falling more slowly	⁑	rain and snow
		⟝	frost
⟍	Falling steadily, or unsteadily	⋼	sandstorm or dust storm
⌄	Steady or rising, then falling; or falling, then falling more quickly	▽	shower(s)
		▿̇	shower of rain
		⊕̇	shower of hail
◎	calm	△	sleet
○	clear	*	snow
◑	cloudy (partly)	⟨	thunderstorm
		〰	visibility reduced by smoke